31ST EDITION

THE

DIRECTORY

OF

EXECUTIVE

RECRUITERS

2002

KENNEDY INFORMATION

Compiled and published by Kennedy Information, Inc.
publishers of **Executive Recruiter News, The International Directory of Executive Recruiters, SearchSelect®, The Directory of Outplacement and Career Management Firms, Recruiting Trends, The Gold Book of Venture Capital Firms, Human Resource Management News and The Directory of Temporary Placement Firms.**

One Kennedy Place, Route 12 South, Fitzwilliam, NH 03447
Phone: 603-585-3101 Fax: 603-585-9555
E-mail: bookstore@kennedyinfo.com www.kennedyinfo.com
Library of Congress Catalog Card Number 73-642226
ISBN # 1-885922-77-9   Price $47.95

ISSN 0090-6484
ISBN 1-885922-77-9

Foreword

We are proud to present the 31st annual edition of *The Directory of Executive Recruiters,* the most complete listing of executive recruiters prepared today. The Directory, published since 1971, is continually researched, added to and updated by our full-time staff. It is the most in-depth and comprehensive reference for executive recruiters available.

Whether you're buying this guide in order to manage your career over the long-term or to make an immediate change, you will find listed 8,110 search firm office locations, comprehensively cross-indexed by management function, geography and industry. We also identify 14,269 key recruiters, together with their areas of specialty in many cases. *To the best of our knowledge, none of the firms listed here charge the individual job seeker. Please notify us of any listees who appear to be operating in violation of this restriction.*

Before you dig in to this wealth of information, read the Introduction, which will give you important advice on your search and how best to use this book.

It is our objective to make *The Directory of Executive Recruiters* as complete and as easy to use as possible. Accordingly, we always welcome your comments and suggestions on how we can improve the book.

Wayne E. Cooper
Publisher

Jennifer Shay
Database Department Manager
database@kennedyinfo.com

Note: Every effort has been made to verify the information included in this book. However, we assume no responsibility for any errors or omissions and reserve the right to include or eliminate company listings and otherwise edit the list.

Table of Contents

What You Need to Know about Executive Recruiters

There are entire books on how to use executive recruiting services to your best advantage. In the next few pages we give you a brief overview of the subject. This is followed by a question and answer session with tips on why, when and how to interact with recruiters.

We also highly recommend our companion publication, *Kennedy's Pocket Guide to Working with Executive Recruiters.* It contains 30 short chapters of frank advice, including how and when to contact recruiters and how to respond when a headhunter calls. See the back of this book for more details.

Four Facts You Should Know

1) Individuals do not pay fees to search firms.

Executive search firms are paid by the companies who hire them to fill a position, typically a fee of one-third of the job's first year compensation. Search firms are not working for you, but for their paying clients. Therefore, do not expect firms to be overly responsive when you contact them.

If your resume is impressive, they may add you to their database of executives. They may contact you if they have a position that fits your profile or to ask you to recommend other people who might be interested in the job. In either case, you will be starting the process of building a relationship with the recruiter. Every phone call or meeting will probably be noted in the firm's database.

Some companies advertise career counseling and resume mailing services to executives. These services, which can be expensive, are not offered by any of the executive search firms listed in this directory.

2) The difference between retainer and contingency search firms is important.

There are two types of recruiters: Retainer and Contingency. Both charge the client employer a fee and neither should ever charge the prospective employee.

The distinctions between retainer and contingency firms are:

Retainer Firms:

- Retainer recruiters are hired by a client company for an assignment, typically for 90-120 days, and are paid regardless of the results of the search. They may also be kept on retainer by their clients, to fill whatever assignments they have.
- One retainer firm is hired by a client company for a given job opening.
- They are more often used to fill higher level positions with salaries of $100,000 and above.
- For these assignments they will assemble a short "slate" of candidates. Therefore, if a retainer firm seriously considers you for a position, you will probably be part of a small group of candidates.
- While your file is being used by a retained recruiter for an assignment, no other recruiter at that firm can contact you, even if you would be the perfect candidate. As a result, you are unlikely to be contacted by a firm for more than one or two positions a year, at most.
- If you work for a company that has hired the search firm during the last year or two, you will be "off-limits" for any other position it may have, no matter how well qualified you are. For this reason alone, it is important to be known to multiple search firms.

Contingency Firms:

- Contingency recruiters are more often used for junior and mid-level executives, typically for positions with salaries below $100,000.
- Contingency recruiters receive payment only when their candidate is hired.
- Contingency recruiters do not usually work on an exclusive basis with their clients. Since they are competing with other recruiters to provide candidates for each assignment, they tend to work fast and to submit to the client company as many candidates as they can. This means you may be one of many candidates for a given job.
- Contingency recruiters provide you with a great deal of exposure, since they send many resumes to their clients. This can be useful to you early in your career or if you are unemployed. However, bear in mind that you may not always want your resume widely distributed if you are happy in your current job.

When a headhunter calls you, it can be hard to tell whether they are from a contingency or retainer search firm. This directory helps clarify that information. Even so, contingency firms occasionally work on a retainer basis and some retainer firms do contingency work from time to time. Our advice is to ask explicitly the nature of the assignment before giving your permission to any recruiter to distribute your resume.

3) Some search firms specialize, while others don't. Consider both kinds.

Recruiting firms are often generalists, covering many different management functions (e.g. sales) and industries (e.g. textiles). Quite a few firms and many individual recruiters, however, do specialize. To make your search as effective as possible, consider recruiters who cover your function and specialize in your industry. Generalist firms should not be ignored, especially at the higher executive ranks. The largest multiple-office search firms tend to cover all functions and industries, but will often have practice areas for particular areas of expertise.

4) Most recruiters work nationally, so don't limit your search by geography.

At the lower salary levels, companies may be reluctant to consider out-of-town executives because of the expense of interviewing and relocating them. In these instances, search firms may focus on local candidates. However, for many executive appointments, search firms will look nationally or even internationally. It is in your interest to be known to search firms who fill positions in your industry, function and salary range, no matter where they are. A New York recruiter is as likely to have an assignment in Los Angeles as in Boston.

Question & Answer Session: 14 Valuable Tips

Q: What's the best way to contact an executive recruiter: phone, fax, e-mail or mail?
A: Mail or e-mail your resume with a cover letter, and don't follow up by phone, e-mail or mail. Executive recruiters are interested only in the job seekers that fit their current openings. Don't risk alienating a recruiter who may find an opening for you later by taking up his or her valuable time now. Some firms in the directory list web sites. Most of these give detailed advice on whom to contact. You can also use our new online service www.ExecutiveAgent.com and email your resume and cover letter directly to the right recruiters.

Q: Should I send my resume to retainer firms, contingency firms, or both?
A: It depends. Early in your career and for mid-level positions, contingency firms are more likely to help you. Contingency firms also tend to be strong in industries with high turnover such as retailing, advertising, EDP, publishing and healthcare. Senior positions are more likely to be handled by retainer firms. If you are unemployed, it is fine to contact many firms of both kinds. If you are happy in your current job but want to actively manage your career, be careful not to contact any retainer firms your employer uses.

Q: How many resumes should I send out?

A: Resumes are cheap to send, while *perfect* job openings are scarce. Since different search firms know about different job opportunities, you should send your resume and cover letter widely. It makes sense to cover all of the firms in your industry and function. It's also smart to include leading generalist firms and firms in your area or places you're interested in moving to. Your initial objective is to get into multiple firms' databases so that when they have an assignment that matches your background, your name will come up.

Q: Should I include a cover letter?

A: Absolutely. But keep it brief, direct, and adopt a confident tone.

Q: How can I make sure that my resume gets to the right specialist at a recruiting firm?

A: Use the information in this directory wherever possible. Make sure that your resume clearly communicates your employment history and accomplishments. Many recruiters scan resumes into databases. This means you should use standard typefaces and formats, generally following the reverse-chronology model.

Q: How long should I wait before I can expect a response?

A: You won't get a response unless you fit an opening.

Q: Can I count on a headhunter to get me a job?

A: Working with a recruiter should be part of a multi-faceted job search. Recruiters work most effectively for everyone involved when you have made contact before you want to make a job change. They can also be helpful in keeping you abreast of developments within your industry, in newly important skills and specialties you have already or may want to acquire. You can make a good impression with recruiters if you are knowledgeable and helpful to them, possibly recommending other people for positions. Other important steps to take in your job search:

- Network with family, friends, acquaintances and business contacts.
- Contact target firms directly.
- Reply to position listings in newspapers, association and university publications, on-line services etc.
- Subscribe to services that mail or e-mail you information about job openings.

Q: When is the best time to contact a recruiter?

A: Immediately, and on a continuing basis. We do recommend that executives actively manage their careers whether or not they are looking to change jobs. This includes keeping selected recruiters up-to-date with your career progress and accomplishments. Whenever you do want to make a change, recruiters will already know you and understand what your objectives are.

Q: How do I keep my boss from finding out I'm looking for a job?

A: Tell your boss that you often get calls from headhunters because you have given helpful advice in the past. Be careful not to let any recruiter send your resume to companies unless you give specific approval.

Q: Can I cover a single national or international firm with one resume?

A: Spring for the extra postage or use www.executiveagent.com to cover your bases. Even large firms vary in the way they handle resumes, so it's best to be on the safe side and send a resume to each office: some firms centralize, others don't.

Q: Should I concentrate on headhunters that specialize in my job function, or go by industry?

A: Normally both. Review both the list of management functions and the list of industries carefully. Some people may be primarily a specialist in a function (such as a Chief Financial Officer) while others may have general skills but expertise in a particular industry. For many people, both dimensions are relevant. (See recruiter specialty index).

Q: How long can I use my *Directory of Executive Recruiters* before getting a new issue?

A: One year. Turnover in this business is high; new firms are constantly being formed,

partnerships dissolved, addresses changed. Three-quarters of the listings change in some way. Using a current directory pays for itself in time and postage savings alone. For the most up-to-date listings, consider *SearchSelect® for Windows®*, our electronic version of the directory, which is updated monthly.

Q: I've heard a few horror stories — is there any way to tell whether a headhunting firm is trustworthy?

A: There is only one professional association for search firms: the Association of Executive Search Consultants (AESC). Membership in AESC is indicated in the listings and is indicative of a commitment to professionalism in executive recruiting.

International Association of Corporate and Professional Recruitment (IACPR) is an organization of senior-level HR executives and retained executive search consultants. Membership in IACPR is also indicated in the listings.

Q: What other services does Kennedy Information recommend?

A: 1) This directory may also be purchased in electronic form, enabling you to perform speedy and sophisticated searches on the most up-to-date listings. *SearchSelect® for Windows®* can also execute mail merges for cover letters and maintain records of your contacts with firms. A demo of this full-featured and easy to use program is provided on CD included with this book. Find details on the inside back cover.

2) **Labels, Reports, and PC Disks:** If you wish to send letters to a large number of recruiting firms, we have a mailing label service to speed things up.

3.) **www.ExecutiveAgent.com** quickly e-mails your resume and cover letter to your selected list of recruiters. Visit the web site for more details at www.ExecutiveAgent.com

4) Our companion book, *Kennedy's Pocket Guide to Working with Executive Recruiters,* contains invaluable advice and guidance for your job search. The enclosed CD also provides a sampling of these advice articles.

5) An expanded hardbound **Corporate Edition** of this directory is available to assist client organizations seeking executive search assistance. It includes key data on revenues, number of professionals, fee structures, and international contacts.

How to Use This Directory

The Directory of Executive Recruiters has been designed to be useful in a number of ways:

1. Start by referring to the index of 65 management functions and 65 industries. These indexes enable you to find recruiting firms that specialize in your area(s). They also show whether the firm operates on a retainer or contingency basis. Review generalist firms too, a category that includes many of the largest search firms.
2. In addition, you may search for individual recruiters according to their areas of specialization. Refer to the index of recruiter specialties in this directory.
3. You may want to narrow your search to concentrate on recruiting firms in certain locations. To do this, consult our geographic index. Remember that many firms fill executive positions nationally, so it doesn't pay to limit yourself.

You will build your own list of target executive recruiters by using the various indexes. The directory listings contain a wealth of information about each firm, including contact information, brief descriptions and key individual recruiters.

How to Read A Listing

ABC Recruting, Inc.

10 Any Street
Anytown, State, Zip   ← Recruiting firm's name
(555) 123-4567   and main office
Fax: (555) 644-2477   mailing address
E-Mail: recruit@aol.com
Web: http://www.abc.com

Phone, fax, e-mail →
and web addresses

Description: Executive recruiters to U.S.   ← General description
   and European companies for senior   of the firm
   managers. Special emphasis on banking,
   insurance and management consulting.

Whom to contact and →
individual recruiter
specialties

Key Contact - Specialty:
Mr. Joe Green - *Senior executives*
Ms. Mary Brown - *Financial services,*
   consulting

Specific functional →
and industry areas
covered by the firm

Salary minimum: $100,000   ← Lowest salary for
Functions: Generalist, Directors, CFOs   positions handled
Industries: Generalist, Banking, Mgmt.   by this firm
Consulting, Insurance

Networks: ← Membership in networks of
XYZ Recruiting Associates   independent recruiting firms

Professional Associations: AESC, IACPR   ← Membership in
                                               AESC or IACPR

Branch office →
contact information
and specialties

Branches:
200 New Street
Newton, State, Zip
(666) 987-6543
Key Contact - Specialty:
Mr. John Gray- *CEOs, COOs, CFOs*

Retainer Recruiting Firms, A to Z

Firms in this section are retained by the hiring entity and paid at least a portion of their fee immediately to initiate the search. In this edition, we acknowledge that some executive search firms in this category occasionally accept assignments on a contingency basis. These firms are denoted with the symbol (†).

Full street addresses are listed for all U.S., Canada and Mexico locations, when known.

For firms charging on a contingency basis all or part of the time, please refer to the parallel A to Z listing of Contingency Recruiting firms.

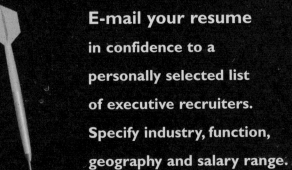

1 to1 Executive Search
(a division of Peppers and Rogers Group)
20 Glover Ave
Norwalk, CT 06850
(203) 642-1400
Fax: (203) 642-1401
Email: kvoghel@1to1.com
Web: www.1to1search.com

Description: We specialize in placing marketing professionals including customer relationship management (CRM), one-to-one marketing, and direct marketing.

Key Contact - Specialty:
Ms. Karen Voghel, Managing Partner - *Sales, direct marketing, CRM, consulting*
Ms. Lynn Sennett, Senior Executive Search Consultant - *Database, direct marketing, CRM, consulting*

Salary minimum: $80,000

Functions: Senior Mgmt., Advertising, Mkt. Research, Mktg. Mgmt., Sales Mgmt., Direct Mktg., Customer Svc., DB Admin., Mgmt. Consultants

Industries: Mfg., Food, Bev., Tobacco, Soap, Perf., Cosmtcs., Drugs Mfg., Motor Vehicles, Computer Equip., Finance, Banking, Services, Pharm Svcs., Mgmt. Consulting, Hospitality, Advertising, Telecoms, Call Centers, Telephony, Digital, Packaging, Software, Database SW, Healthcare

Professional Associations: AIM, AMA, DMA

1EXECStreet[†]
150 Post St Ste 400
San Francisco, CA 94108-4707
(415) 982-0555
Fax: (415) 982-0550
Email: contactus@1execstreet.com
Web: www.1execstreet.com

Description: Our firm meets the needs of two audiences, either high-growth companies and top business professionals by integrating high-speed retained search with a premier career-development website. 1EXECStreet leverages the power of the Internet in the "career marketplace of the future," scaling and enhancing one-to-one interaction to execute successful career and human capital strategies.

Key Contact:
Mr. Todd Greenhalgh, President
Mr. George Veh, Principal

Salary minimum: $75,000

Functions: General Mgmt., Middle Mgmt., Quality, Sales & Mktg., MIS Mgmt., Engineering

Industries: Generalist, Mfg., Chemicals, Plastics, Rubber, Machine, Appliance, Computer Equip., Consumer Elect., Misc. Mfg., Electronic, Elec. Components, Mgmt. Consulting, E-commerce, IT Implementation, Network Infrastructure, Aerospace, Packaging, Mfg. SW, Marketing SW, Networking, Comm. SW

Professional Associations: SHRM

20-20 Foresight Executive Search Inc
1415 W 22nd St Ste 150
Oak Brook, IL 60523
(708) 246-2100
Fax: (708) 246-0677
Email: info@20-20foresight.net
Web: www.20-20foresight.net

Description: We are a premier retained search firm in the real estate, construction, and engineering fields. We hold three basic strengths as the foundation of our firm: expertise, performance, and service.

Key Contact:
Mr. Robert Cavoto, Principal - *Construction (real estate, engineering)*
Mr. Kevin Hayes, Principal - *Construction, engineering, real estate*
Ms. Pilar Aquino, Principal - *Real estate*
Ms. Alissa Cavoto, Principal - *Construction, real estate, engineering*
Mr. Darryl Dougherty, Principal - *Construction, real estate, engineering*
Mr. Nicholas Jerschow, Principal - *Engineering*
Mr. Regis Kenna, Principal - *Construction*
Mr. Jay Walsh, Principal

Salary minimum: $70,000

Functions: Generalist

Industries: Construction, Environmental Svcs., Real Estate

360 Search Advisors Inc
230 Park Ave Ste 1000
New York, NY 10169
(646) 435-5796
Fax: (646) 435-5547
Email: mailbox@360advisors.com
Web: www.360advisors.com

Description: We are a highly specialized retained executive search boutique that focuses on critical assignments for our clients in investment banking and capital markets. The firm was founded by former senior Wall Street executives who understand first hand the tangible and intangible needs of their clients.

Key Contact - Specialty:
Mr. Craig Sanger, President - *Investment banking, capital markets*
Ms. Debbie Ann Gormal, Director - *Investment banking, capital markets*

Salary minimum: $250,000

Functions: Generalist, General Mgmt., Senior Mgmt., Sales Mgmt., HR Mgmt., M&A, Risk Mgmt., IT, MIS Mgmt.

Industries: Banking, Invest. Banking, Brokers, Venture Cap.

A la Carte Int'l Inc
3330 Pacific Ave Ste 500
Virginia Beach, VA 23451-2997
(757) 425-6111
(800) 446-3037
Fax: (757) 425-8507
Email: alacarte@wedofood.com
Web: www.wedofood.com

Description: Our firm is an executive and retainer search firm that functions as a source for "C," "V," and "D" level general, marketing, sales, operations, and technical management personnel for the food industry. We offer compensation and competitive evaluation studies. We also provide web-based comprehensive personality profiles, candidate management and pre-screening software offered through our career assessment subsidiary, www.cppq.com.

Key Contact - Specialty:
Mr. Michael J. Romaniw, President - *General management, sales and marketing management*
Mrs. Kelley P. Nicastro, MS Phyc, Vice President - *Food safety and technology*
Mr. Ron McKeon, Executive Director - *Leadership assessments*
Mrs. Lisa James Gollihur, Director of Research - *Search coordination and fulfillment*
Ms. Cynthia R. Dixon, Systems Administrator - *Search database, office technology*

Salary minimum: $85,000

Functions: Generalist, Mfg., Sales & Mktg., Mkt. Research, Mktg. Mgmt., Sales Mgmt., Personnel, Minorities

Industries: Generalist, Mfg., Food, Bev., Tobacco, Textiles, Apparel, Chemicals, Wholesale, Retail, E-commerce, Hospitality, Restaurants, Advertising, Call Centers, Database SW, Industry Specific SW, Mfg. SW, Marketing SW, Women's

Professional Associations: AMI, IFMA, IFT, MFHA, NAER, NRA, RCA, WFF

A-L Associates Inc[†]
546 5th Ave Fl 6
New York, NY 10036
(212) 878-9000
Fax: (212) 878-9096
Email: general@alassoc.com
Web: www.alassoc.com

Description: Expedient, value added global executive search. Function specializations include most within financial services as well as a broad spectrum of legal and technical disciplines.

Key Contact - Specialty:
Mr. Curt Miller, CEO - *Financial services, technical*
Mr. Edward Orchant, President - *Financial services, capital markets*

Salary minimum: $150,000

Functions: General Mgmt., Product Dev., Finance, IT, MIS Mgmt., Systems Analysis, Systems Dev., Systems Implem., Systems Support, Mgmt. Consultants

Industries: Generalist

Abbott Associates
1025 Highland Dr
St. Maries, ID 83861
(208) 245-9508

Description: Retained executive search and research concentrating on senior-level search, generalists. Industries include: high-technology, finance, telecom, manufacturing, among others.

Key Contact - Specialty:
Ms. Brenda Abbott - *Generalist*

Salary minimum: $60,000

Functions: Generalist

Industries: Energy, Utilities, Mfg., Retail, Finance, Banking, Telecoms, Software, Biotech, Healthcare

Abbott Smith Associates Inc
3290 Franklin Ave
PO Box 318
Millbrook, NY 12545
(845) 677-5300
Fax: (845) 677-3315
Email: abbottsmith@prodigy.net

Description: As specialists in the area of human resources, the major emphasis for thirty five years has been the recruitment of candidates worldwide.

Key Contact - Specialty:
Mr. David W. Brinkerhoff, President - *Human resources*
Ms. Sara P. McWilliams, Vice President - *Human resources*

Salary minimum: $100,000

Functions: HR Mgmt.

Industries: Generalist

Professional Associations: AM, ASTD, HRPS, SHRM

Branches:
2600 Lexington St
Broadview, IL 60153
(708) 649-3318
Fax: (708) 344-2892
Email: abbottsmith@prodigy.net

Key Contact - Specialty:
Mr. David D. Dalenberg, Executive Vice President - *Human resources*
Mr. Frank Calzaretta, Managing Partner - *Human resources*
Ms. Sharon Reese, Managing Partner - *Human resources*
Mr. Justin Hirsch, Managing Partner - *Human resources*
Ms. Christine O'Neill, Managing Partner - *Human resources*

Abécassis Conseil
507 Pl d'Armes Bureau 240
Montreal, QC H2Y 2W8
Canada
(514) 842-8213
Fax: (514) 842-8128
Email: info@abecassis.com
Web: www.abecassis.com

Description: Our firm with each achievement throughout the years, has developed a global vision of a company. Our team is dedicated to the search for competent personnel who best reflect your business image.

Key Contact - Specialty:
Ms. Pauline P. Abécassis, President - *Generalist*

Functions: Generalist, Mfg., Materials, Sales & Mktg., HR Mgmt., Finance, Engineering

Industries: Generalist, Wholesale, Non-profits, Mgmt. Consulting, Telecoms, Insurance

Professional Associations: OAAQ, OCRIQ

Abel Fuller & Zedler LLC
4550 Post Oak Pl Ste 141
Houston, TX 77027
(713) 961-3330
Fax: (713) 961-3337
Email: agarcia@execufirm.com
Web: www.execufirm.com

Description: We are a retained executive search firm conducting searches in senior management. We are a generalist practice versed in bringing the best candidate to our clients.

Key Contact - Specialty:
Mr. Abel R. Garcia, President/CEO - *Generalist*

Salary minimum: $80,000

Functions: Generalist

Industries: Energy, Utilities, Mfg., Transportation, Wholesale, Retail, Finance, Services, Aerospace, Software, Healthcare

Abeln, Magy & Associates
800 E Wayzata Blvd Ste 200
Wayzata, MN 55391
(952) 476-4938
Fax: (952) 404-7470
Email: info@abelnmagy.com
Web: www.abelnmagy.com

Description: Professional retainer search consultants with 100 years of combined experience in a variety of functions.

Key Contact:
Mr. David S. Magy
Ms. Mary Abeln
Mr. Kenneth E. Abeln

Functions: Generalist

Industries: Generalist

Professional Associations: AICPA, SHRM

Networks: EMA Partners Int'l

Accent Personnel Services Inc[†]
(also known as the ACCENT group)
10988 N Harrells Ferry Rd Ste 17
Baton Rouge, LA 70816
(504) 272-1032
Fax: (504) 272-9687
Email: vp@accentpersonnelinc.com
Web: www.accentpersonnelinc.com

Description: Our firm is the executive recruiting division of a 25-year old HR consulting firm. Accent is and has been the prèmier firm for the New Orleans/Baton Rouge industrial region for many years. Our firm, with its international staff, also enjoys a long history of international staffing, with a concentration on Latin America.

Key Contact - Specialty:
Ms. Virginia Pickering, CPC, President - *Executive recruiting*
Ms. Maria Quintero, Director of Latin American Division - *Executive recruiting*

Salary minimum: $75,000

Functions: Directors, Senior Mgmt., Mfg., Sales & Mktg., HR Mgmt., Finance, CFO's, IT, Engineering, Int'l.

Industries: Generalist

Networks: Top Echelon Network

ACCESS Technology[†]
6046 Cornerstone Ct W Ste 134
San Diego, CA 92121-4733
(858) 587-2600
Email: jkennedy@americarecruits.com
Web: www.americarecruits.com

Description: We are an executive search company and consultant to software and hardware technology employers in California and the West. We are primarily a retained firm. We recruit senior-level design and development engineering and middle management candidates. Our specializations include computers, software, peripherals, NAS/SAN, data networks, telephony, ERP/database, Internet/web, fiber optics, semiconductors, wireless, ERP, PLC, and medical instrumentation.

Key Contact - Specialty:
Mr. R. J. Nadel, President - *High technology, semiconductors, storage, software, data communications*

Salary minimum: $85,000

Functions: Senior Mgmt., Middle Mgmt., Product Dev., Automation, Sales Mgmt., Systems Dev., Systems Implem., R&D, Engineering, Architects

Industries: Generalist, Medical Devices, Computer Equip., Test, Measure Equip., Misc. Mfg., Electronic, Elec. Components, E-commerce, IT Implementation, PSA/ASP, New Media, Communications, Telecoms, Telephony, Digital, Wireless, Fiber Optic, Network Infrastructure, Software, Database SW, Development SW, ERP SW, Industry Specific SW, Networking, Comm. SW, Security SW, System SW, Biotech

Professional Associations: AMA, HRCA, SHRM

ADA Executive Search Inc
3716 N Fremont St
Chicago, IL 60613
(773) 883-8978
Fax: (773) 883-8978
Email: adaeziman@adaexecutivesearch.com
Web: www.adaexecutivesearch.com

Description: We are a boutique, generalist firm which conducts management through executive level search assignments for Fortune 500 companies, emerging businesses, for profit, and not-for-profit organizations locally, regionally, and nationally. Our commitment is to develop lasting relationships with diverse and distinguished clients and candidates.

Key Contact:
Ms. Alicia Donn Aeziman, Principal and Founder
Mr. William C. Wheeler, Jr., JD, CAE, Principal and Chief Executive Officer

Salary minimum: $75,000

Functions: Generalist

Industries: Generalist, Construction, Mfg., Retail, Finance, Non-profits, Higher Ed., Mgmt. Consulting, Communications, Government

Professional Associations: ASAE

Adams & Associates Int'l
520 Shorely Dr 201
PO Box 129
Barrington, IL 60011-0129
(847) 304-5300
Email: search@adamsassoc.com
Web: www.adamsassociatesintl.com

Description: We offer senior and mid-level general management recruiting firm that places in manufacturing, technology, and professional services sectors. We are specialists in recruiting for the "Lean Enterprise."

Key Contact - Specialty:
Mr. Adam Zak, President
Ms. Sheila Cunningham, Managing Director - *General management*
Ms. Joan Bennett, Associate Director - *General management*

Salary minimum: $150,000

Functions: Generalist, General Mgmt.

Industries: Generalist, Mfg., Transportation, Venture Cap., Services, Mgmt. Consulting, Communications, Aerospace, Packaging, Software

Professional Associations: AICPA, AME, ASQ, HRMAC, LEI, SAE, SME

Adams Executive Search[†]
3416 Fairfield Trl
Clearwater, FL 33761
(727) 772-1536
(727) 781-3886
Fax: (727) 772-1537
Email: tla@axsearch.com
Web: www.axsearch.com

Description: We offer retained and exclusive search services. Over 78% of our business is repeat business. We specialize in construction and real estate development, which are corporate and multi-site operations. We also service those ancillary functions that support the development process, for example legal, finance, and HR. Our clients include developers, general contractors, and users of commercial, light industrial, residential, hospitality, restaurants, and retail.

Key Contact:
Mr. Thomas Adams, Chairman
Ms. Elizabeth Adams, Vice President

Salary minimum: $80,000

Functions: Generalist

Industries: Construction, Retail, Legal, Accounting, HR Services, Law Enforcement, Hospitality, Real Estate

Professional Associations: NACORE, ULI

G Adams Partners
39 S Lasalle St Ste 714
Chicago, IL 60603
(312) 577-5648
Fax: (312) 577-5651
Email: clientservices@adamspartners.com
Web: www.adamspartners.com

Description: Responsive, client-oriented boutique firm offering tailored services to the nation's leading building, design and real estate firms.

Key Contact:
Mr. Gerald Adams, President - *Construction, architecture, engineering, real estate*
Mr. Adam Chavvaria, Director of Research

Salary minimum: $70,000

Functions: Generalist, Directors, Senior Mgmt., Middle Mgmt., Engineering, Architects, Int'l.

Industries: Generalist, Construction, Real Estate

Professional Associations: AGC, AIA, SMPS

Jerry Adel & Company
3266 Yonge St Ste 1202
Toronto, ON M4N 3P6
Canada
(416) 488-7585
Fax: (416) 481-4065
Email: adelco@netcom.ca

Description: Professional practice providing executive search and related services to medium and large size firms. About 75-80% in manufacturing. Professional technical and administrative positions. $40,000+ salary.

Key Contact - Specialty:
Mr. Jerry Adel, President - *Generalist*

Salary minimum: $40,000

Functions: Generalist, Senior Mgmt., Middle Mgmt., Plant Mgmt., Purchasing, Mktg. Mgmt., Sales Mgmt., CFO's

Industries: Generalist

Adler Management Inc†
(also known as AMI Consulting)
66 Witherspoon St Ste 315
Princeton, NJ 08542
(609) 443-3300
Fax: (609) 443-4439
Email: jadler@amiconsulting.com
Web: www.amiconsulting.com

Description: Our firm specializes in management consulting in the high-technology markets. We recruit, evaluate, and structure management teams for venture backed start-ups, as well as Fortune 500 companies.

Key Contact - Specialty:
Mr. Jack E. Adler, President
Mr. John Sherman, Senior Associate
Mrs. Cheryl Levine, Associate - *Research*

Salary minimum: $100,000

Functions: Generalist, Senior Mgmt., Middle Mgmt., Mktg. Mgmt., Sales Mgmt., IT

Industries: Generalist, Venture Cap., Publishing, New Media, Telecoms, Software

Advance Personnel Resources
6101 W Old Shakopee Rd
PO Box 386002
Bloomington, MN 55438
(763) 546-6779
Fax: (763) 546-2523
Email: ljhapp@aol.com

Description: Retainer based executive search, a generalist firm working in operations, sales and marketing management and financial administration. Salary range $50-200,000. Nationwide.

Key Contact - Specialty:
Mr. Lawrence J. Happe, Owner/Account Manager - *Generalist*

Salary minimum: $50,000

Functions: General Mgmt., Sales & Mktg.

Industries: Generalist, Construction, Food, Bev., Tobacco, Printing, Consumer Elect., Transportation, Wholesale, Finance, Services, HR Services, Media

Branches:
13200 Webster Ave
Savage, MN 55378
(612) 894-8691
Fax: (612) 894-8691
Email: dreblowt@aol.com
Key Contact - Specialty:
Mr. Terry Dreblow - *Generalist*

Advanced Executive Resources
3040 Charlevoix Dr
Grand Rapids, MI 49509-6421
(616) 942-4030
Fax: (616) 942-9950
Email: advexres@aol.com

Description: We provide Michigan organizations their only local source for executive search. Majority of assignments are mid- and high-level technical and/or managerial searches across a variety of industries including die cast, automotive, food, plastics, environmental, oil and retail.

Key Contact:
Mr. Michael D. Harvey, President
Ms. Arlene Toy, Research Manager
Ms. Amber Hill, Account Manager
Mr. Jim Loser, Account Manager
Ms. Annette Anderson, Research Associate

Salary minimum: $50,000

Functions: Generalist, General Mgmt., Mfg., Materials, Sales & Mktg., Engineering, Specialized Svcs.

Industries: Generalist, Mfg., Food, Bev., Tobacco, Lumber, Furniture, Plastics, Rubber, Retail, Software

Advantage Partners Inc
29225 Chagrin Blvd Ste 275
Cleveland, OH 44122
(216) 514-1212
Fax: (216) 514-1213
Email: jimmcpolin@advantagepartnersinc.com
Web: www.advantagepartnersinc.com

Description: Retained search firm specializing in recruiting of senior managers and executive talent for both public and private corporations.

Key Contact:
Ms. Nikki C. Bondi, Managing Partner - *General management, strategy*
Mr. James B. McPolin, Partner - *General management, strategy*
Ms. Pamela Taubert, Principal

Salary minimum: $100,000

Functions: Generalist

Industries: Generalist

Professional Associations: HRPS

Aegis Consulting
633 3rd Ave Fl 27
New York, NY 10017
(212) 687-2200
Fax: (212) 687-0079
Email: info@aegisnet.com
Web: www.aegisnet.com

Description: We are a retained executive search firm specializing in information technology and services, professional services, strategic marketing, and business development across various industries. We are dedicated to excellence and timeliness of our results. We employ a proven, research-based methodology in the execution of searches from top executives to rare functional specialists.

Key Contact - Specialty:
Ms. Nancy Caudill, Managing Director - *Management consulting, professional services, information technology*
Mr. Dante Sucgang, Director - *Information technology, electronic markets, consumer markets, management consulting*
Mr. Jeffrey Zwiff, Director - *Consumer markets, financial services, direct response, media & entertainment*
Mr. Brad W. Hoyda, Principal - *Financial services, information technology, e-business, information services, direct marketing*
Ms. Marci Pepper, Consulting Associate - *Professional services, information technology, media, consumer markets*
Ms. Jill Rothman, Consulting Associate - *Information technology, professional services, management consulting*

Salary minimum: $150,000

Functions: General Mgmt., Senior Mgmt., Sales & Mktg., IT, MIS Mgmt., Mgmt. Consultants

Industries: Energy, Utilities, Mfg., Food, Bev., Tobacco, Transportation, Retail, Finance, Services, Mgmt. Consulting, Media, New Media, Communications

Aegis Group
23875 Novi Rd
Novi, MI 48375-3243
(248) 344-1450
Fax: (248) 347-2231
Email: resume@aegis-group.com
Web: www.aegis-group.com

Description: We are specialists in executive recruiting of senior-level management for hospitals, integrated healthcare systems, managed care/health insurance companies, physician group practices and medical schools through the United States.

Key Contact - Specialty:
Mr. Timothy Ignash, President - *Healthcare*

Salary minimum: $75,000

Functions: Generalist

Industries: Healthcare, Hospitals, Long-term Care, Women's

Professional Associations: ACHE, HFMA

AET Advisors LLC
(formerly known as Taras Associates Inc)
3495 Piedmont Rd NE Bldg 11 Ste 402
Atlanta, GA 30305
(404) 237-8208
Fax: (404) 261-6961
Email: aetadvisors@mindspring.com

Description: A retained executive search and strategic planning consulting practice, focusing exclusively on the real estate industry. Firm functions in every aspect of the industry in organizational/strategic planning.

Key Contact - Specialty:
Mr. Arnold E. Taras, President - *Senior management, real estate, construction*

Salary minimum: $75,000

Functions: General Mgmt., Directors, Senior Mgmt., Middle Mgmt., CFO's, Specialized Svcs., Architects

Industries: Construction, Real Estate

Professional Associations: BOMA, ICSC, MBA, NAHB, NAIOP, NMHC, ULI

Ahern Search Partners
3982 Powell Rd #205
Powell, OH 43065
(740) 363-6946
(614) 436-4126
Fax: (614) 436-4125

Email: emurphy@ahernsearch.com
Web: www.ahernsearch.com

Description: We provide executive search specializing in healthcare technology.

Key Contact - Specialty:
Mrs. Mollie Ahern, Founder - *Healthcare technology*
Ms. Erika Murphy, Senior Consultant - *Internet research, healthcare technology*

Salary minimum: $100,000

Functions: General Mgmt., Health Admin., HR Mgmt., MIS Mgmt., Systems Implem., Mgmt. Consultants

Industries: Generalist, Healthcare, Hospitals

Ahrensdorf & Associates
PO Box 7494
St. Davids, PA 19087-7494
(610) 971-0500
Fax: (610) 971-9530
Email: leeahrensdorf@att.net

Description: Generalist, retainer search firm that stresses service, quality and recruits with the goal of building partnerships with its client base.

Key Contact - Specialty:
Mr. Lee Ahrensdorf, President - *Financial services, healthcare, transportation, pharmaceutical, biotechnology*

Salary minimum: $100,000

Functions: Generalist, General Mgmt., Mfg., Sales & Mktg., HR Mgmt., CFO's, IT, R&D

Industries: Mfg., Chemicals, Drugs Mfg., Medical Devices, Plastics, Rubber, Finance, Banking, Invest. Banking, Non-profits, Pharm Svcs., Telecoms, Wireless, Insurance, Real Estate, Biotech, Healthcare, Hospitals

---

AkamaiSearch
(also known as MRI of Kona)
66-1735 Kawaihae Rd
PO Box 2100
Kamuela, HI 96743
(808) 883-2419
(888) 675-6627
Fax: (808) 776-9939
Email: admin@mrkona.com
Web: www.mrkona.com

Description: We specialize in locating and bringing together today's best technical and sales talent with tomorrow's industry leaders. We pre-qualify both sides of the hiring process to insure that each interview provides mutual benefit, reduces interview burnout and matches the opportunities to your goals.

Key Contact:
Ms. Amy Cody-Quinn, Manager
Mr. Stephanie Gacayan, Office Manager

Functions: Sales & Mktg., Sales Mgmt., IT, Systems Dev., Systems Implem.

Industries: Generalist, Software

AKS Associates Ltd
175 Derby St Ste 27
Hingham, MA 02043-4054
(781) 740-1704
Fax: (781) 740-4383
Email: akssearch@aol.com
Web: www.akssearch.com

Description: Senior-level search focused on general management, financial, information technology and operations functions in the financial services, professional services and not-for-profit industries. Personalized approach using quality standards at competitive fee arrangements.

Key Contact - Specialty:
Mr. Alexander K. Salmela, President - *Finance, information technology, general management*

Salary minimum: $90,000

Functions: General Mgmt., Middle Mgmt., Admin. Svcs., Health Admin., PR, HR Mgmt., CFO's, MIS Mgmt., Mgmt. Consultants

Industries: Generalist, Finance, Non-profits, Higher Ed., Legal, Mgmt. Consulting

---

Cheryl Alexander & Associates
8588 Shadow Creek Dr
Maple Grove, MN 55311
(763) 416-4570
Email: cherylalexander@cherylalexander.com
Web: www.cherylalexander.com

Description: We are a retained executive search firm specializing in senior level positions in technology, manufacturing, marketing, international, finance, human resources, development. Our primary industries include: energy, environmental, telecom and non-profits. We are known as an effective resource for diversity search assignments.

Key Contact:
Ms. Cheryl Alexander, CEO

Salary minimum: $90,000

Functions: Generalist

Industries: Energy, Utilities, Banking, Non-profits, Mgmt. Consulting, E-commerce, IT Implementation, HR SW, Mfg. SW, Marketing SW, Networking, Comm. SW

Networks: US Recruiters.com

Alexander & Company
8308 Barber Oak Dr
Plano, TX 75025
(972) 495-8998
(877) 495-8300
Fax: (214) 495-8999
Email: penny@dhc.net

Description: We offer specialized recruitment of marketing and public relations professionals with a special emphasis on e-Commerce, the Internet, and technology infrastructure.

Key Contact - Specialty:
Ms. Penelope Alexander, Principal - *Marketing, public relations, corporate communications*

Salary minimum: $50,000

Functions: Sales & Mktg., Advertising, Mkt. Research, Mktg. Mgmt., PR

Industries: Energy, Utilities, Mfg., Computer Equip., Consumer Elect., Electronic, Elec. Components, Transportation, Retail, Finance, Services, E-commerce, Hospitality, Media, Advertising, New Media, Communications, Software

---

Alexander Associates
993 Lenox Dr Ste 200
Lawrenceville, NJ 08648
(609) 844-7597
(609) 844-7589
Email: search@alexassociates.com
Web: www.alexassociates.com

Description: We are a leading retainer-based firm performing national searches for clients in the Boston to DC business corridor. The principals of our firm are practicing consultants who increase the effectiveness and competitiveness of our clients' organizations.

Key Contact - Specialty:
Mr. Richard J Alexander, Founding Partner - *Finance & accounting, information technology, sales & marketing, management consultants*

Mr. A Gregory Phinney, Managing Director - *Finance & accounting, information technology, sales & marketing, management consultants*

Salary minimum: $125,000

Functions: General Mgmt., Sales Mgmt., CFO's, IT, MIS Mgmt.

Industries: Generalist

Professional Associations: AESC, AICPA

Alexander Edwards Int'l Inc
501 Madison Ave Fl 4
New York, NY 10022
(212) 593-4300
Fax: (212) 593-4502
Email: info@alexanderedwards.com
Web: www.alexanderedwards.com

Description: Our firm is a global provider of integrated professional services specializing in executive search. AEI delivers solutions that draw on diverse and deep competencies in executive recruitment and human capital development. Most of our work is for leading financial services institutions, science and technology driven businesses, management consulting firms, and Fortune 500 corporations. We have successfully assisted major companies worldwide identify and attract outstanding talent by completing searches for board members, CEOs, CFOs, CIOs, general managers, directors, and functional vice presidents.

Key Contact - Specialty:
Mr. Alexander D. Kolt, President & CEO - *Generalist, financial services, sales & trading, operations, senior management*
Mr. Vincent M. Pizzi, III, Managing Partner, COO/CTO - *Information technology, general management, senior management, middle management, operations*

Salary minimum: $150,000

Functions: Generalist, Directors, Senior Mgmt., Finance, Risk Mgmt., IT, MIS Mgmt., Minorities, Non-profits, Int'l.

Industries: Generalist, Energy, Utilities, Mfg., Finance, Services, Media, Communications, Government, Software, Biotech

Professional Associations: AMA, FMA, GARP, IAFE, RON, SQA, TMA

The Alexander Group
1330 Post Oak Blvd Ste 2800
Four Oaks Pl
Houston, TX 77056
(713) 993-7900
Fax: (713) 993-7979
Email: info@thealexandergroup.com
Web: www.thealexandergroup.com

Description: A national management consulting/retained executive search firm specializing in executive and senior management positions across most functional areas in all major industries including financial services, high-technology, not-for-profit, energy, biotechnology, legal and healthcare. Experience in start-up and high-growth companies.

Key Contact:
Ms. Jane S. Howze, Managing Director
Mr. John C. Lamar, Managing Director

Salary minimum: $80,000

Functions: Generalist, General Mgmt., HR Mgmt., Budgeting, IT, MIS Mgmt., Minorities, Int'l.

Industries: Generalist, Energy, Utilities, Banking, Legal, HR Services, Biotech

Branches:
1902 Wright Pl Ste 200
Carlsbad, CA 92008
(760) 918-5580
Fax: (760) 918-5582

Email: info@thealexandergroup.com
Key Contact:
Ms. Judith S. Hudson, Associate Director

735 Montgomery St Ste 210
San Francisco, CA 94111
(415) 677-8668
Fax: (415) 677-8674
Email: rbrizendine@thealexandergroup.com
Key Contact:
Mr. Raymond E. Brizendine, Director

10 Post Office Sq Ste 600 S
Boston, MA 02109
(617) 988-2827
Email: rmitchell@thealexandergroup.com
Key Contact:
Mr. Robert A. Mitchell, Senior Associate

Alexander Ross & Company
21 E 40th St at Madison Ave
New York, NY 10016
(212) 889-9333
Fax: (212) 481-3565
Email: benrl@alexanderross.com
Web: www.alexanderross.com

Description: Executive search firm dedicated solely
to change management & learning functions
internally and externally (consultants). Known for
in-depth assessment and extensive database of
professionals in these fields.

Key Contact - Specialty:
Mr. Ben Lichtenstein, President - *Management,
learning*

Salary minimum: $110,000

Functions: HR Mgmt., Training, Mgmt.
Consultants

Industries: Generalist

Professional Associations: ASTD, ASTD, HRPS,
ODN

Alexander, Wollman & Stark
1601 Market St Ste 550
Philadelphia, PA 19103
(267) 256-0721
Fax: (267) 256-0725
Email: alexwollstark@aol.com

Description: We are a retainer based search and
consulting firm specializing in physician and
executive search and consulting for academic health
centers, teaching hospitals and managed care
organizations.

Key Contact:
Mr. Raymond Alexander, Principal
Mr. Paul Stark, Principal

Salary minimum: $100,000

Functions: Senior Mgmt., Healthcare, Physicians

Industries: Generalist, Non-profits, Healthcare

Branches:
13 Hathorn Hill
Woodstock, VT 05091
(802) 457-1582
Fax: (802) 457-1688
Email: hwvt@aol.com
Key Contact:
Dr. Harry Wollman, MD, Principal

Allen Associates
4555 Lake Forest Dr 650 Westlake Ctr
Cincinnati, OH 45242
(513) 563-3040
Email: feedback@allensearch.com
Web: www.allensearch.com

Description: Executive search consultants
exclusively focused on critical assignments for
senior decision makers and board members.
Typically, assignments are at the Executive Vice
President - CEO level.

Key Contact - Specialty:
Mr. Michael Allen, President - *Senior level
assignments (EVP-CEO level)*

Salary minimum: $200,000

Functions: Generalist

Industries: Generalist

David Allen Associates[†]
PO Box 56
Haddonfield, NJ 08033-0048
(856) 795-6470
Fax: (856) 795-0175
Email: xsearch@home.com

Description: Boutique serving multinational
companies with whom we have long-term
relationships. With a focus towards finance, the
financial markets, and marketing we serve leaders in
consumer goods, energy, financial services,
multimedia, pharmaceutical and technology
industries. We have affiliates in Atlanta, Chicago,
East Lansing, Los Angeles, New York, and San
Francisco.

Key Contact - Specialty:
Mr. David Ritchings, President - *Finance,
marketing, financial services, multimedia*

Salary minimum: $50,000

Functions: Middle Mgmt., Product Dev., Mkt.
Research, Mktg. Mgmt., HR Mgmt., CFO's,
Budgeting, Cash Mgmt., M&A, Risk Mgmt.

Industries: Energy, Utilities, Mfg., Finance, Pharm
Svcs., HR Services, Hospitality, New Media,
Broadcast, Film, Telecoms, Software, Biotech

Allen Evans Klein Int'l
305 Madison Ave Ste 1650
New York, NY 10165
(212) 983-9300
Fax: (212) 983-4272
Email: info@allenevans.com

Description: We are a retainer-based executive
search and advisory firm for venture-backed and
global 1000 companies. Our vertical markets
include: Internet, more specifically, new media/e-
Commerce/infrastructure; technology; information
services; communications; media; entertainment;
financial services; financial services; publishing;
professional services; and beyond…

Key Contact - Specialty:
Mr. Robert Klein, Managing Partner - *Internet, e-
commerce, new media, technology*

Salary minimum: $100,000

Functions: Generalist, General Mgmt., IT

Industries: Generalist, Venture Cap., Services,
Media, New Media, Software

Kingsley Allen Executive Search
2 Bloor St W Ste 1720
PO Box 37
Toronto, ON M4W 3E2
Canada
(416) 969-9001
Email: gmerovitz@kitsearch.com
Web: www.kitsearch.com

Description: A dynamic downtown bilingual
executive search firm specializing in e-commerce,
direct marketing and general practice.

Key Contact:
Mr. Gerry Merovitz

Salary minimum: $70,000

Functions: Generalist, Sales & Mktg., Finance, IT,
Specialized Svcs.

Industries: Generalist

Allen, Austin, Lowe & Powers
4543 Post Oak Pl Ste 217
Houston, TX 77027
(713) 355-1900
Fax: (713) 355-1901
Email: randrews@aalpsearch.com
Web: www.aalpsearch.com

Description: We combine tremendous resources
with superior search and selection systems in order
to deliver maximum value and "A" players to our
client companies. Our proven track record of
expeditious completion of 100% of all retained
assignments, our unprecedented performance
guarantee and our industry experience make us your
obvious choice for conducting your senior level
searches.

Key Contact - Specialty:
Mr. Robert L. Andrews, Chairman/CEO - *Retail,
food service, manufacturing, sales & marketing,
food industry*
Ms. Suzy Andrews, Director of Research -
Advertising, public relations
Mr. Dick Babcock, Partner/Practice Leader -
Grocery retailing
Mr. Bill Blanford, DDS, Partner/Practice Leader -
Healthcare, medical professionals
Mr. Richard Costin, CPC, Partner/Practice Leader -
Energy, environmental
Mr. Dan Freidman, Partner/Practice Leader -
General
Ms. Judy Hutcheson, Partner/Practice Leader -
Hospitality, real estate
Mr. John Harris, Senior Associate - *General*
Mr. Erik Koestenblatt, Senior Associate -
Insurance, legal
Mr. Morgan McCain, Partner/Practice Leader -
*Manufacturing, sales & marketing, outdoor
recreation*
Mr. Dave Salmons, Partner/Practice Leader -
Beverages
Mr. Mark Spillard, Partner/Practice Leader -
Finance
Mr. Al Sunday, Partner/Practice Leader - *General*
Ms. Lori Weeks, Chief Knowledge Officer -
Research
Mr. King White, Partner/Practice Leader -
Manufacturing, oil & gas, power
Ms. Ylonka Wiggins, CPC, Partner/Practice Leader
- *Information technology*
Ms. Pattie Paddy, Partner/Practice Leader -
Printing & publishing
Mr. Mike Underberg, Partner/Practice Leader -
Pharmaceuticals, automotive
Ms. Andrea Penaloza, Chief Administrator Officer
- *General*

Salary minimum: $90,000

Functions: Generalist

Industries: Energy, Utilities, Construction, Mfg.,
Transportation, Wholesale, Retail, Hospitality,
Media, Telecoms, Real Estate

Branches:
PO Box 1504
Alameda, CA 94501
(510) 521-2992
Fax: (510) 521-2687
Email: msato@aalpsearch.com
Key Contact:
Ms. May Sato, Researcher

4743 Tenbury Ln Ste 100
Rocklin, CA 95677
(877) 547-6401
(916) 791-5533
Fax: (916) 791-5828
Email: jbaker@aalpsearch.com
Key Contact - Specialty:
Mr. Jake Baker, President/COO - *Food
manufacturing, e-commerce, pre-IPO, start-ups*
Mr. Geof Lambert, Partner/Practice Leader -
Hospitality, restaurants

---

21 Old Hickory Ln Ste 100
Branford, CT 06405
(203) 483-1097
Fax: (203) 483-1097
Key Contact - Specialty:
Mr. Clark Wilcox, Partner/Practice Leader -
*International banking, senior level finance,
treasury executives, generalist*

39 Hudson St Ste 202
Hackensack, NJ 07601
(201) 960-5125
Email: ppotluri@aalpsearch.com
Key Contact - Specialty:
Dr. Prakash Potluri, Partner/Practice Leader -
Information technology worldwide

3211 Mockingbird Ln Ste 100
Dallas, TX 75205
(214) 521-9123
Fax: (214) 219-1760
Email: amcclure@aalpsearch.com
Key Contact - Specialty:
Mr. Anthony McClure, P, Partner/Practice Leader -
*Technology, energy, international, banking,
telecommunications*

5921 Copperwood Ln Ste 100
Dallas, TX 75248
(972) 233-1160
Fax: (972) 233-1149
Key Contact - Specialty:
Mr. Wes Jablonski, Partner/Practice Leader - *Food
service, finance & accounting, convenience store,
petroleum retailing*

2203 Timberloch Pl Ste 219
The Woodlands, TX 77380
(281) 681-2617
Fax: (281) 681-2618
Email: mgergen@aalpsearch.com
Key Contact - Specialty:
Mr. Michael Gergen, Parnter/Practice Leader -
Construction, power

1714 S 300 E Ste 100
Salt Lake City, UT 84108
(801) 583-1322
Fax: (801) 583-1222
Key Contact - Specialty:
Ms. Liana Hathaway, Senior Associate - *Food
brokerage*

Allerton, Heneghan & O'Neill
2 Mid America Plz Ste 800
Oak Brook Terrace, IL 60181
(630) 954-2244
Fax: (630) 954-2245
Email: aho@interaccess.com

Description: Retainer-based search firm with long-
standing client relationships with large, multinational companies and smaller, entrepreneurial
organizations. Principal and professional support
person work in tandem on each assignment.

Key Contact - Specialty:
Mr. Donald A. Heneghan, Partner - *Finance &
accounting, information technology, diversity,
marketing*

Salary minimum: $100,000

Functions: Generalist, Senior Mgmt., Plant Mgmt.,
Mktg. Mgmt., Training, CFO's, MIS Mgmt.,
Minorities

Industries: Generalist, Drugs Mfg., Motor Vehicles,
Finance, Mgmt. Consulting, Telecoms, Software

Professional Associations: IACPR, EMA,
HRMAC, HRPS

Networks: Int'l Search Partners (ISPA)

Alliance Enterprises
595 Barbara Pl
Mandeville, LA 70448
(800) 392-5902
Fax: (786) 513-0535

Email: pro_recruiter@techemail.com
Web: www.allsearchusa.com

Description: A boutique retained search firm
specializing in locating senior engineering
management for the transportation and
environmental industries. Our forte is locating
rainmakers - those rare individuals who possesses
both strong technical skills and advanced business
acumen; essential to the leadership of highly
competitive engineering organizations.

Key Contact - Specialty:
S. Olivier, Owner - *Engineering management*

Salary minimum: $100,000

Functions: Senior Mgmt.

Industries: Transportation, Environmental Svcs.,
Haz. Waste

Alliance Search Management Inc
1717 Woodstead Ct Ste 106
The Woodlands, TX 77380
(281) 367-8630
Web: www.alliancesearch.com

Description: This closely held practice, while rich
in diversity of assignments, keeps our "hands off
list" relatively small, assuring our clients the
greatest access to the largest candidate pool.
Seeking to provide optimum service levels, we
accept assignments at all levels of the organization,
setting no minimum fees for our clients. And
finally, we have made a commitment to moving the
search process to more rapid completion.

Key Contact - Specialty:
Ms. Kathy Powell-Florip, President - *Healthcare
management*

Functions: Generalist, Senior Mgmt., Healthcare,
Allied Health, Health Admin., Mktg. Mgmt.,
Finance

Industries: Generalist, Healthcare

Professional Associations: ACHE, HFMA, MGMA

Alper Associates Inc
3949 Old Post Rd Ste 100 B
PO Box 1206
Charlestown, RI 02813
(401) 364-7100
Fax: (401) 364-9933
Email: alperp@aol.com
Web: www.alperassociates.com

Description: Specializing in searches for marketing
executives for healthcare and medical product
companies. Our process is designed to identify and
attract candidates who become significant
contributors to corporate results and culture.

Key Contact:
Mr. Paul Alper, President

Functions: Senior Mgmt.

Industries: Mfg., Medical Devices, Healthcare

Professional Associations: HIDA, NACDS

Alphanumeric Group Inc
555 N First St 200
San Jose, CA 95112
(408) 954-1600
Fax: (408) 954-1674
Email: info@alphanumericgroup.com
Web: www.alphanumericgroup.com

Description: Executive retained search firm
specializing in Sr. level management and
technology specialist for high technology companies
internationally.

Key Contact - Specialty:
Mr. Robert Sanders, CEO/President - *Technology*

Salary minimum: $100,000

Functions: Engineering

Industries: Communications, Telecoms, Digital,
Wireless, Fiber Optic, Network Infrastructure,
Software, Development SW

Ambler Associates
14881 Quorum Dr Ste 450
Dallas, TX 75254
(972) 404-8712
Email: careers@amblerassociates.com
Web: www.amblerassociates.com

Description: Director-level to senior executive-level
positions in a wide range of industries including
high-technology, telecom, new media, chemical,
manufacturing, retail, professional services,
financial services, oil and gas, energy, commercial
banking, and transportation.

Key Contact - Specialty:
Mr. Peter W. Ambler, President - *Generalist*
Mr. Lawrence Hysinger, Principal - *Banking,
finance*

Salary minimum: $60,000

Functions: Generalist

Industries: Energy, Utilities, Mfg., Transportation,
Retail, Finance, Services, Media, Environmental
Svcs., Packaging

American Executive Management Inc
30 Federal St
Salem, MA 01970
(978) 744-5923
Email: execsearch@amexecutive.com
Web: www.amexecutive.com

Description: Leading international search firm.
Extensive experience with major international
corporations including such firms as: ABB, Fluor,
Exxon, G.E. and Raytheon. Excellent performance
and references.

Key Contact - Specialty:
Mr. E. J. Cloutier, Chairman - *General
management (USA, Europe, Middle East, Asia)*
Mr. B. J. Louf, Vice President - *Architectural,
engineering, construction*
Ms. S. Smith, Office Manager
Mr. L. Shelton - *Telecommunications*
Mr. J. Gagola - *Oil, gas, chemical (Europe)*
Mr. P. Pitman - *Hospitality, entertainment*

Salary minimum: $100,000

Functions: Generalist, Senior Mgmt., Middle
Mgmt., Sales & Mktg., HR Mgmt., Finance, IT,
Engineering

Industries: Generalist, Energy, Utilities,
Construction, Equip Svcs., Hospitality, Media,
Telecoms, Defense

Professional Associations: AICHE, IEEE, IMC,
PMI

Branches:
60 State St
Boston, MA 02109
(617) 854-7491
Web: www.aeminfotech.com
Key Contact:
Mr. Patrick R. Stapleton - *Information technology*
Mr. Joshua R. Martin, Information technology

American Express Tax & Business Services
1 S Wacker Dr Ste 800
Chicago, IL 60606
(312) 634-4715
Fax: (312) 634-5527
Email: melissa.s.waggoner@aexp.com
Web: www.axptbschicago.com

Description: The practice recruits senior-level
management positions across all industries and
disciplines. Industry specialties include law firms,
nonprofit organizations, early stage high-tech, and

construction companies. Functional specialties include chief operating and chief financial officers.

Key Contact:
Mr. Thomas Jacob, Senior Consultant
Mrs. Jill Berstein-Iantoni, Senior Consultant
Ms. Monica Wiatr, Senior Consultant

Salary minimum: $90,000

Functions: Generalist, Senior Mgmt.

Industries: Generalist, Construction, Mfg., Non-profits, Legal

American Group Practice Inc
420 Madison Ave Fl 5
New York, NY 10017
(212) 371-3091
Email: agp420@aol.com

Description: Retainer search for practicing physicians, physician executives and senior-level healthcare executives; medical staff planning and medical group practice development, PHOs, MSOs, GPWWs and other physician/hospital relations activities.

Key Contact:
Mr. Ralph Herz, Jr., Medical Director

Salary minimum: $80,000

Functions: Generalist, Healthcare, Physicians, Nurses, Allied Health, Health Admin.

Industries: Healthcare, Hospitals

Professional Associations: ACPE, AHA, MGMA

American Human Resource Associates Ltd (AHRA)
PO Box 18269
Cleveland, OH 44118-0269
(877) 342-5833
(216) 932-6663
Fax: (216) 321-4951
Email: inquiry@ahrasearch.com
Web: www.ahrasearch.com

Description: Our specialties are real estate, which includes land title insurance, residential construction, and mortgage lending; biotechnology, which includes chemistry, genetics, instrumentation, commercialization, production, and general management; leisure and hospitality, which include resort and golf course management.

Key Contact - Specialty:
Mr. Ted Howard, Managing Member - *Real estate, insurance, leisure*
Mrs. Michele Font, Home Office Manager
Ms. Meredith Howard, Staff Consultant - *Biotechnology, chemistry, genetics*

Salary minimum: $95,000

Functions: Generalist

Industries: Hotels, Resorts, Clubs, Recreation, Insurance, Real Estate, Biotech

American Physician Network Inc[†]
1897 Palm Beach Lakes Blvd Ste 213
West Palm Beach, FL 33409
(800) 245-8227
(561) 688-2999
Fax: (888) 699-5512
Email: apn12345@aol.com
Web: www.APN1.com

Description: Specialize in "Connecting Physicians with Their Future." we are dedicated to connecting physicians and physician executives with prime placements nationwide to assure sucessful futures for both the healthcare professional and the medical practice. We also specialize in medical corporate development and practice brokerage services nationwide.

Key Contact - Specialty:
Mr. Bhopindar Singh, MD, Partner - *Physicians, medical corporate development, practice brokerage services*
Mr. Victor Pecaro, BS, Partner - *Physicians, medical corporate development, practice brokerage services*

Salary minimum: $120,000

Functions: Healthcare, Physicians, Health Admin., Mgmt. Consultants

Industries: Healthcare

Professional Associations: ACPE, NAPR

Ames & Ames
PO Box 7404
Menlo Park, CA 94026
(650) 322-4000

Description: We provide key executive search nationwide.

Key Contact:
Mr. A. P. Ames, President

Salary minimum: $150,000

Functions: Generalist

Industries: Medical Devices, Biotech, Healthcare

AmiTech Group[†]
6405 Metcalf Ave Ste 107
Overland Park, KS 66202
(913) 384-9150
(888) CLIENT-1
Fax: (913) 384-9155
Email: amitech@aol.com
Web: www.amitechgroup.com

Description: Professional search and placement firm with specializations in the areas of: Operations Management, Information Technology, Engineering, Sales/Marketing. Thorough and personalized approach with close attention paid to details. Services are retained by client companies for searches locally and nationwide. All searches are directed by a Certified Personnel Consultant (CPC).

Key Contact - Specialty:
Mr. Larry Yoksh, CPC, Managing Director - *Operations management, IT, engineering, sales/marketing*
Ms. Barbara Latenser, Senior Associate - *Operations management, human resources, benefits administration*

Functions: Generalist

Industries: Generalist

Professional Associations: NAPS

Andcor Companies Inc
539 E Lake St
Wayzata, MN 55391
(952) 404-8060
Fax: (952) 404-8089
Email: info@andcor.com
Web: www.andcor.com

Description: We focus exclusively on Minnesota-based emerging growth companies. We offer retained executive search, strategic consulting services and venture capital.

Key Contact - Specialty:
Mr. Dennis D. Anderson, CEO - *Executive*
Ms. Terri Naughtin, Principal - *Executive*
Mr. Jack Hauser, Principal - *Executive, financial*

Salary minimum: $75,000

Functions: Generalist, Directors, Senior Mgmt., Mktg. Mgmt., Sales Mgmt., CFO's, MIS Mgmt.

Industries: Generalist, Mfg., Media, New Media, Software

Anderson & Associates
112 S Tryon St
Charlotte, NC 28284
(704) 347-0090
Fax: (704) 347-0064
Email: info@andersonexecsearch.com
Web: www.andersonexecsearch.com

Description: Retained executive search and related consulting services for a nationwide clientele. Emphasis in financial services, graphic communications, healthcare, manufacturing and non-profit industries. Functional experience: searches for CEO/CFO, directors and senior executives.

Key Contact:
Mr. Douglas K. Anderson, President

Salary minimum: $75,000

Functions: Generalist, General Mgmt., Mfg., Healthcare, Sales & Mktg., HR Mgmt., Finance

Industries: Generalist, Food, Bev., Tobacco, Finance, Hospitality, Packaging, Real Estate, Healthcare

Professional Associations: AESC

Anderson & Schwab Inc
444 Madison Ave
New York, NY 10022-6903
(212) 758-6800
Fax: (212) 755-9576
Email: andersonschwab@aol.com

Description: Specializes in providing a broad variety of consulting services to include business, operations management and personnel work, to the international extractive and processing industries.

Key Contact - Specialty:
Mr. Frank Schwab, Jr., Chief Executive - *Management (upper-level)*
Ms. Ivy S. Wilensky, Vice President - *Senior financial*

Salary minimum: $75,000

Functions: Generalist, General Mgmt., Directors, Senior Mgmt., Middle Mgmt., Admin. Svcs., Legal

Industries: Agri., Forestry, Mining, Energy, Utilities, Chemicals, Metal Products

Professional Associations: AIME, IMC, IPAA, NMA, SME

Branches:
707 17th St Fl 23
Denver, CO 80202
(303) 295-5563
Fax: (303) 382-7455
Email: thomasparker@kpmg.com
Key Contact:
Mr. Thomas Parker, Executive Vice President

Anderson Bradshaw Associates Inc[†]
PO Box 924045
Houston, TX 77292-4045
(713) 869-6789
Email: aba@hal-pc.org
Web: www.hou-tx.com/energyjobs

Description: Domestic and international. Assignments in oil and gas, engineering and construction, environmental and manufacturing for energy and power industry. Additional significant experience with IT positions, Internet companies and telecommunications in general. Also work in commercial construction and aerospace/defense industries.

Key Contact - Specialty:
Mr. Robert W. Anderson, President - *International engineering, construction, oil & gas (on/off shore), process plant operations & maintenance (refineries, chemical, petrochemical plants)*

Salary minimum: $75,000

Functions: Generalist

Industries: Energy, Utilities, Construction, Chemicals, Misc. Mfg., HR Services, E-commerce, Telecoms, Defense, Environmental Svcs., Aerospace

The Andre Group Inc
500 N Gulph Rd Ste 210
King of Prussia, PA 19406
(610) 337-0600
Fax: (610) 337-1333
Email: info@theandregroup.com

Description: We are a recognized leader in recruitment and search of human resource professionals exclusively, representing over 85% of the Fortune 500 clients on nationwide basis. We are the largest in USA.

Key Contact - Specialty:
Mr. Larry Cozzilo, VP/General Manager - *Human resources*

Functions: HR Mgmt., Benefits, Personnel, Training

Industries: Generalist

Professional Associations: IACPR, EMA, HRPS, ODN, SHRM

Branches:
4400 PGA Blvd Ste 700
Palm Beach Gardens, FL 33410
(561) 630-7800
Fax: (561) 630-7872
Email: info@theandregroup.com
Key Contact - Specialty:
Mr. Richard X. Andre, President - *Human resources*

APA Search Inc
721 W Boston Post Rd
Mamaroneck, NY 10543
(914) 698-2800
Fax: (914) 698-8787
Email: info@apasearch.com
Web: www.apasearch.com

Description: Highly resourceful, retained executive-level search - diverse industries. Subspecialties - automotive, retail, hardware. Extremely skilled staff. All searches completed. Our finalist candidates are always the most qualified rather than the most available.

Key Contact:
Mr. Howard Kesten, President

Salary minimum: $75,000

Functions: Generalist

Industries: Paints, Petro. Products, Machine, Appliance, Consumer Elect., Wholesale, Retail, Finance, HR Services, Advertising, Telecoms, Packaging

Professional Associations: AAIA, APAA, ASIA, SEMA, SHRM

Branches:
14000 Military Trl Ste 205
Delray Beach, FL 33484
(561) 637-2408
Fax: (561) 637-2409
Key Contact:
Mr. Lawrence Kesten, General Manager

Argus National Inc
98 Mill Plain Rd Ste 301
Danbury, CT 06811-5148
(203) 790-8420

Description: Management search and recruitment designed for one company...yours.

Key Contact:
Ms. Constance Gruen, Vice President
Mr. Ronald J. Guido, President

Mr. Preston C. Burkart, Vice President

Salary minimum: $50,000

Functions: Generalist

Industries: Generalist

ARI Int'l
1501 Ocean Ave
Seal Beach, CA 90740
(562) 795-5111
Fax: (562) 596-9794
Email: ari.ron@att.net
Web: www.ariinternationalsearch.com

Description: Our firm provides retained domestic and international executive and technical search. We service all functions. We are recognized worldwide for our expertise in consumer products, medical device, cosmetics, aerospace, and technical and executive advanced composite search.

Key Contact - Specialty:
Mr. Ronald L. Curci, President/CEO - *Advanced composites, consumer products*

Salary minimum: $100,000

Functions: Senior Mgmt.

Industries: Chemicals, Medical Devices, Plastics, Rubber, Aerospace

Ariail & Associates
210 Friendly Ave Ste 200
Greensboro, NC 27401
(336) 275-2906
Email: ariailassoc@msn.com
Web: www.ariailassoc.com

Description: A retained search firm specializing in the procurement of senior-level executives in the household furniture and institutional furnishing industry. A 29 year history of successful procurement of CEOs and VPs of sales/marketing, manufacturing, general management and CFOs.

Key Contact - Specialty:
Mr. Randolph C. Ariail, President - *Senior executives, furniture & related industries*

Salary minimum: $100,000

Functions: General Mgmt.

Industries: Lumber, Furniture

Ariel Associates
410 W 53rd St Ste 106
New York, NY 10019-5629
(212) 765-8300
Fax: (212) 765-3450
Email: info@arielassociates.com
Web: www.arielassociates.com

Description: Specialize in placing professionals in publishing and interactive for consumer and trade magazines, journals, newsletters, electronic publishing, and database nationwide. Place publishing, interactive and media professionals in marketing, sales management and human resources positions outside publishing.

Key Contact - Specialty:
Mr. Eugene Fixler, President - *Publishing, media, sales & marketing, interactive*
Ms. Rona Wexler, Executive Vice President - *Publishing, interactive, media, sales & marketing*

Salary minimum: $125,000

Functions: General Mgmt., Senior Mgmt., Sales & Mktg., HR Mgmt., Finance

Industries: Media, Publishing, New Media

Professional Associations: IACPR, AWNY, NEPA, NYNMA

Armitage Associates Ltd
151 Yonge St Ste 1210
Toronto, ON M5C 2W7
Canada
(416) 863-0576
Fax: (416) 863-0092
Email: armitage@interlog.com

Description: Boutique specializing in mid- to senior-level assignments.

Key Contact - Specialty:
Mr. John D. Armitage, Managing Partner - *Financial services, high technology*
Ms. Karen Wood, Director of Research - *Financial services, high technology*

Salary minimum: $80,000

Functions: Generalist, Directors, Senior Mgmt., CFO's, M&A, MIS Mgmt.

Industries: Generalist, Finance, Hospitality, Insurance, Real Estate, Software

J S Armstrong & Associates Inc
3 Embarcadero Ctr Ste 2260
San Francisco, CA 94111
(415) 288-6900
Fax: (415) 288-6905
Email: jarmstrong@jsaa.com
Web: www.jsaa.com

Description: Our firm's success is based on industry exceeding standards for performance, execution and highly personalized service. We achieve results by targeting, aggressively recruiting and thoroughly evaluating the leaders who fit clients' needs.

Key Contact - Specialty:
Ms. Jennifer Sheehan-Armstrong, Managing Director - *High technology*

Salary minimum: $300,000

Functions: Senior Mgmt., Mktg. Mgmt., Sales Mgmt., CFO's, MIS Mgmt., Engineering

Industries: Generalist

William B Arnold Associates Inc
600 S Cherry St Ste 1105
Denver, CO 80246-1716
(303) 393-6662
Web: www.wbaainc.com

Description: We are a generalist search practice that services all industries and functions, including senior and middle management. We are the oldest retained executive search firm in the Rocky Mountain region.

Key Contact - Specialty:
Mr. William B. Arnold, President - *Generalist*
Ms. Sheridan J. Arnold, Vice President - *Generalist*

Salary minimum: $100,000

Functions: Generalist

Industries: Generalist

Artemis Search
2064 Antioch Ct Ste B
Oakland, CA 94611
(510) 339-4191
Fax: (510) 339-4195
Email: williams@artemissearch.com
Web: www.artemissearch.com

Description: Biotechnology, medical device and pharmaceutical industry searches. Retained executive search. CFO, CEO, VP of R&D, public relations managers, directors and VPs. We have worked in virtually every functional area within the Biotech industry. Worked on-site at Genentech, Becton Dickinson and Genenlabs.

Key Contact:
Ms. Shellie Williams

Salary minimum: $100,000

Functions: Senior Mgmt.

Industries: Biotech

Professional Associations: AAPS, ACRP, ACS, AWS, DIA, ISPE, PDA, RAPS

Artgo Inc
2250 SOM Center Rd Ste 120
Willoughby Hills, OH 44094-9655
(440) 585-9226
Fax: (440) 585-9960
Email: adbaldwin@aol.com

Description: Executive search for corporate needs including special capabilities in top and middle management assignments.

Key Contact - Specialty:
Mr. Arthur D. Baldwin, II, President - *Generalist*

Functions: Generalist

Industries: Generalist, Mfg., Electronic, Elec. Components, Non-profits, Higher Ed., Hospitality, Aerospace

J Nicholas Arthur
77 Franklin St Fl 4
Boston, MA 02110
(617) 204-9000
Fax: (617) 482-8005
Email: ncb@tlp-llc.com

Description: Specializes in senior management positions within financial services.

Key Contact - Specialty:
Mr. Nicholas C. Bogard, President - *Senior level financial services*
Mr. Arthur P. Beecher, Managing Director - *Senior level financial services*

Salary minimum: $100,000

Functions: Generalist, Senior Mgmt., Mktg. Mgmt., Sales Mgmt., Direct Mktg., CFO's, Cash Mgmt., M&A

Industries: Generalist, Banking, Invest. Banking, Brokers, Venture Cap., Misc. Financial

Professional Associations: NHRA

The Ascher Group
7 Becker Farm Rd
Roseland, NJ 07068
(973) 597-1900
Fax: (973) 597-1911
Email: sascher@aschergroup.com
Web: www.aschergroup.com

Description: We are the premier provider of contract human resource professionals.

Key Contact - Specialty:
Ms. Susan Ascher, President - *Generalist*

Salary minimum: $50,000

Functions: Generalist, Purchasing, Distribution, Benefits, Training, CFO's, Budgeting

Industries: Generalist, Accounting, Mgmt. Consulting, HR Services

Professional Associations: NATSS, NJASP

Ashford Management Group Inc
2295 Parklake Dr NE Ste 425
Atlanta, GA 30345
(770) 938-6260
Fax: (770) 621-9529
Email: info@ashfordsearch.com
Web: www.ashfordsearch.com

Description: We also provide other services, including management consulting and interview training for the interviewer and the interviewee. Our clients include some of the nation's largest retailers.

Key Contact - Specialty:
Ms. Janis E. Martinez, President - *Retail*

Ms. Sandy Day, Marketing Director - *Retail*
Ms. Karen Cooper, Manager of Special Projects - *Retail*

Functions: Generalist

Industries: Retail

Ashlar-Stone Management Consultants Inc
50 Burnhamthorpe Rd W Ste 401
Mississauga, ON L5B 3C2
Canada
(905) 615-0900
Fax: (905) 615-0917
Web: www.ashlar-stone.com

Description: Small, responsive firm providing high quality executive search services with superior results in all industries. All aspects of an assignment, including research, recruiting, interviewing and shortlist presentation are managed by one consultant only.

Key Contact:
Mr. Stuart K. J. Moore, Principal
Mr. Robert D. Chisholm, Associate
Mr. Robert K. Bonnell, Associate

Salary minimum: $75,000

Functions: Generalist

Industries: Mfg., Transportation, Retail, Mgmt. Consulting, Hospitality, Publishing, Packaging

Ashworth Consultants Inc
53 Fulton St
Boston, MA 02109-1401
(617) 720-0350
Email: ashworthco@aol.com

Description: Provides board level consulting in compensation, management planning & personnel selection for start-ups, threshold companies and established organizations.

Key Contact - Specialty:
Mr. Robert I. Ash, President - *Consulting firms*

Salary minimum: $75,000

Functions: Generalist

Industries: Mgmt. Consulting

ASI
11693 San Vicente Blvd Ste 363
Los Angeles, CA 90049
(310) 277-3456
(415) 331-6789
Email: info@startupsearch.com
Web: www.startupsearch.com

Description: We provide executive search and private capital for early and middle stage technology and Internet companies.

Key Contact - Specialty:
Mr. Beau Buck, Managing Director - *Internet-based start-ups*

Functions: Generalist, Directors, Senior Mgmt., Direct Mktg., Systems Analysis, Systems Dev.

Industries: Generalist, Venture Cap., Hospitality, New Media, Telecoms, Software

Association Executive Resources Group
PO Box 3880
Gaithersburg, MD 20885-3880
(301) 417-7045
Fax: (301) 417-7049
Email: aerggfh@aol.com
Web: www.aerg.org

Description: Dedicated exclusively to searches for CEO and professional staff positions for national trade and professional associations and other not-for-profit organizations. Principals and senior

---

associates total more than 60 years of association management experience.

Key Contact - Specialty:
Mr. Gerard F. Hurley, Chairman/CEO - *National associations, philanthropic groups, fraternal groups*
Mr. Charles D. Rumbarger, Past Chairman - *National associations*

Salary minimum: $100,000

Functions: Generalist, Senior Mgmt., Middle Mgmt.

Industries: Generalist, Non-profits

Association Strategies
1111 N Fairfax St
Alexandria, VA 22314
(703) 683-0580
Email: pakaul@aol.com

Description: Retained executive search firm focused on recruiting for association/nonprofit organizations and the companies that serve the industry.

Key Contact:
Ms. Pamela Kaul

Salary minimum: $85,000

Functions: Generalist, Minorities, Non-profits

Industries: Non-profits, Hospitality, Media

Professional Associations: ASAE, GWSAE, ODN, SHRM

AST/BRYANT
1 Atlantic St
Stamford, CT 06901
(203) 975-7188
Fax: (203) 975-7353
Email: infoeast@astbryant.com
Web: www.astbryant.com

Description: We provide professional services to non-profit institutions in the recruitment of presidents and CEOs and chief development executives.

Key Contact - Specialty:
Mr. Steven T. Ast, Chairman - *Non-profit institutions, CEOs, chief development executives*

Salary minimum: $75,000

Functions: Generalist, Senior Mgmt., Specialized Svcs., Non-profits, Environmentalists

Industries: Generalist, Services, Non-profits, Higher Ed.

Professional Associations: AESC

Branches:
2716 Ocean Park Blvd Ste 3001
Santa Monica, CA 90405
(310) 314-2424
Fax: (310) 399-5774
Email: infowest@astbryant.com
Key Contact - Specialty:
Mr. Christopher P. Bryant, President - *Non-profit institutions, CEOs, chief development executives*

Aster Search Group
555 Madison Ave Ste 2300
New York, NY 10022
(212) 888-6182

Description: We conduct assignments for hospitals, integrated delivery networks, physician practice management companies, managed care companies, long-term care facilities, home care companies and healthcare agencies. Please send only healthcare resumes.

Key Contact - Specialty:
Ms. Eve Cohen, President - *Healthcare*

Salary minimum: $70,000

Functions: Generalist

Industries: Healthcare

Professional Associations: AHHRA, MAHA

Atlanta Executive Partners Inc
PO Box W
Teaticket, MA 02536
(508) 495-4300
Fax: (508) 495-4301
Email: aep@mindspring.com

Description: A systems approach, providing leaders who enhance company performance and competitive standing. Benchmarking to establish clear criteria for acquiring or aligning with executives and companies. Real world solutions from line-management experienced consultants.

Key Contact - Specialty:
Mr. Robert J. Sweet, President - *Technology, telecommunications, manufacturing, communications, aerospace*

Salary minimum: $150,000

Functions: Generalist, General Mgmt., Mfg., Sales & Mktg., Finance, IT, R&D

Industries: Generalist, Computer Equip., Test, Measure Equip., Mgmt. Consulting, Government, Aerospace, Software

Professional Associations: ADPA, AIAA, SAE

Aubin Int'l Inc
30 Rowes Wharf
Boston, MA 02110
(617) 443-9922
Fax: (617) 443-9955
Email: info@aubin.com
Web: www.aubin.com

Description: An international retained management consulting firm offering a partnering philosophy; swift, successful results; leading-edge information systems, and 19 years' experience. Specialists in borderless search, an innovative team-based approach that attracts world-class candidates for every assignment.

Key Contact - Specialty:
Mr. Richard E. Aubin, Chairman/CEO - *High technology*
Mr. J. David Lyons, President - *High technology*

Functions: Generalist, Directors, Senior Mgmt., Mktg. Mgmt., Sales Mgmt., CFO's, MIS Mgmt., Int'l.

Industries: Generalist, New Media, Telecoms, Software

Professional Associations: AESC, IACPR

Audax Corp
3300 Bloor St W Ste 3140 Fl 11
Center Twr
Toronto, ON M8X 2X3
Canada
(416) 231-1819
Email: careerinfo@audaxcorporation.com
Web: www.audaxcorporation.com

Description: We facilitate the recruitment and selection of high performance professionals suited for organizational teams. Thorough research and assessment techniques are our hallmark. We are experienced and equipped to work with a variety of organizations across a broad range of industry in North America.

Key Contact:
Mrs. Trish Langmuir Taylor, President

Salary minimum: $60,000

Functions: Generalist, Directors, Plant Mgmt., Materials Plng., Sales Mgmt., HR Mgmt., CFO's, Mgmt. Consultants

Industries: Generalist, Construction, Chemicals, Test, Measure Equip., Broadcast, Film, Aerospace, Real Estate

Auerbach Associates Inc
65 Franklin St Ste 400
Boston, MA 02110
(617) 451-0095
Fax: (617) 451-5199
Email: info@auerbach-assc.com
Web: www.auerbach-assc.com

Description: Specializes in executive search for colleges and universities, healthcare, not-for-profit institutions, the public sector. Special emphasis on recruitment of women and under-represented groups.

Key Contact - Specialty:
Ms. Judith A. Auerbach, President - *Higher education, healthcare, non-profit institutions*

Functions: Directors, Senior Mgmt., Non-profits

Industries: Non-profits, Higher Ed.

Networks: Associated Consultants in Executive Search Int'l

Auguston and Associates Inc
1010 S Ocean Blvd Ste 601
Pompano Beach, FL 33062
(954) 943-0503
(888) 244-5598
Fax: (954) 784-1660
Email: g.auguston@att.net
Web: www.searchnetint.com

Description: We specialize in medical device manufacturers, all functions: general management, engineering, R&D, operations, manufacturing, regulatory, clinical, quality, sales, marketing, and human resources. With search partners worldwide we help our clients build world class, results-oriented management teams.

Key Contact - Specialty:
Ms. Gail Auguston, President - *Medical manufacturers*

Salary minimum: $100,000

Functions: Generalist, General Mgmt., Mfg., Plant Mgmt., Quality, Sales & Mktg., HR Mgmt., R&D

Industries: Medical Devices

Professional Associations: IPSA, NAPS

Networks: First Interview Network (FIN)

Austin Group Int'l
(a member of Marlar Int'l)
117 Laura Ln Ste 200
Austin, TX 78746
(512) 329-8077
Fax: (512) 327-3997
Email: ray@agisearch.com
Web: www.agisearch.com

Description: We are specialists in recruiting middle and senior-level talent for high-tech companies. We charge hourly search rates that eliminate expensive percentage-based fees. We have extensive in-house research capability. We have offices in over 20 countries through our membership with Marlar Int'l Search Network.

Key Contact - Specialty:
Mr. Ray Holley, CEO - *Senior management*
Ms. Jane O'Neal, President - *Middle and senior-level positions*
Mr. Brian Riley, Partner - *Middle and senior-level positions*
Ms. Suzanne Caraway, Partner - *Middle and senior-level positions (technical management)*
Ms. Katie Smith, Partner - *Middle and senior-level positions*

Salary minimum: $75,000

Functions: Generalist

Industries: Medical Devices, Computer Equip., Communications, Digital, Wireless, Fiber Optic, Software, Security SW, Biotech

Networks: Marlar Int'l

Branches:
335 Bear Wallow Ln
Sedona, AZ 86336
(520) 204-0849
Fax: (520) 204-0829
Email: ray@agisearch.com
Key Contact - Specialty:
Mr. Ray Holley, CEO & Managing Partner - *Senior level searches*

Austin-McGregor Int'l
12005 Ford Rd Ste 540
Dallas, TX 75234
(972) 488-0500
Fax: (972) 488-0535
Email: info@amidallas.com
Web: www.amidallas.com

Description: We've identified and recruited the best talent from around the world, from vice presidents to chief executives to board members. We recruit the kind of people that make a far-reaching impact on an organization, its strategic direction, and its bottom-line.

Key Contact:
Mr. Charles McCreary, President - *High technology, consumer, entertainment, industrial*
Mr. Stephen Sterett, Senior Vice President/Partner
Mr. Jeremy King, Senior Vice President/Partner
Mr. Kirk Durossette, Vice President - *High technology*
Ms. Ardell Archer, Vice President - *High technology, consumer, entertainment, industrial*
Mr. Dru George, Vice President

Salary minimum: $100,000

Functions: Generalist, Senior Mgmt., Mfg., Materials, Sales & Mktg., Finance, IT, R&D

Industries: Mfg., Transportation, Wholesale, Retail, Services, Media

Branches:
4414 Caminito Cuarzo
San Diego, CA 92117
(858) 273-1602
Fax: (858) 273-0943
Email: lynn@san.rr.com
Key Contact - Specialty:
Ms. Lynn Alderete, Senior Vice President/Partner - *High technology, consumer, entertainment, industrial*

105 N 10th
Mattoon, IL 61938
(217) 235-1051
Fax: (217) 235-2053
Email: phicom@ccipost.net
Key Contact - Specialty:
Mr. Paul Bailey, Senior Vice President/Partner - *High technology, consumer, entertainment, industrial*

Automotive Recruiters Int'l Inc
823 Delta Ave Ste 104
Gladstone, MI 49837
(906) 428-9330
Fax: (906) 428-9331
Email: info@automotivestaffing.com
Web: www.automotivestaffing.com

Description: We are an hourly retained executive search firm dedicated to helping automotive suppliers and manufacturers identify and hire the top 20% of talent within the industry.

Key Contact:
Mr. Jeffrey R. Ketchum, Founder

Salary minimum: $75,000

Functions: Generalist

Industries: Mfg., Motor Vehicles, Transportation

Avalon Health Group Inc
PO Box 15969
Savannah, GA 31406
(877) 532-2125
Email: jpufahl@avalonhealth.com
Web: www.avalonexperts.com

Description: Specializing in executive search for senior health care executives.

Key Contact:
Dr. John P. Pufahl, President - *Managed care*
Ms. Linda Tierney, Vice President-Operations

Salary minimum: $100,000

Functions: Generalist, General Mgmt., Senior Mgmt., Healthcare, Sales & Mktg., Finance, CFO's, IT, MIS Mgmt.

Industries: Healthcare, Hospitals

Avery Associates
3 1/2 N Santa Cruz Ave Ste A
Los Gatos, CA 95030
(408) 399-4424
Fax: (408) 399-4423
Email: kimd@averyassoc.net
Web: www.averyassoc.net

Description: Public sector practice is focused on city and county government and agencies throughout Western U.S. Private sector search is focused on administrative positions in technology, communications and financial/general services.

Key Contact - Specialty:
Mr. William Avery, President - *Labor relations executive search*
Mr. Paul Kimura, Principal - *Private sector*
Mr. Gary Brown, Principal - *Executive search*

Salary minimum: $75,000

Functions: Generalist, General Mgmt., Materials, Sales & Mktg., Benefits, Personnel, Training, Finance

Industries: Generalist, Computer Equip., Consumer Elect., Test, Measure Equip., Media, Government, Software

Avery James Inc
6601 Center Dr W Ste 500
Los Angeles, CA 90045
(310) 342-8224
Fax: (310) 342-8212
Email: itsyourmove@averyjames.com
Web: www.averyjames.com

Description: We are a retained executive search firm recruiting executives, senior managers, and highly technical functional specialists. Our practice is primarily technological and industrial based, serving Fortune 100 companies, privately held multi-national firms, and early stage companies.

Key Contact - Specialty:
Ms. Michele James, President - *Engineering, high tech, transportation, diversity search*
Ms. Robin McNeill, Managing Consultant - *Banking*

Salary minimum: $100,000

Functions: General Mgmt., Directors, Mfg., Materials, Distribution, Sales & Mktg., R&D, Engineering, Minorities, Environmentalists

Industries: Generalist, Agri., Forestry, Mining, Construction, Mfg., Computer Equip., Transportation, Defense, Environmental Svcs., Aerospace

Professional Associations: AESC

Avondale Search Int'l Inc
4651 Salisbury Rd Ste 295
Jacksonville, FL 32256
(904) 296-4449
Fax: (904) 296-6478
Email: margot@avondalesearch.com
Web: www.avondalesearch.com

Description: Our firm offers a variety of recruitment solutions that we tailor to each client. Put your most important search assignment in our hands.

Key Contact - Specialty:
Ms. Margot E. Finley, President - *General management, sales & marketing, information technology*

Salary minimum: $50,000

Functions: Generalist, General Mgmt., Sales Mgmt., IT, MIS Mgmt., Systems Analysis, Systems Dev.

Industries: Generalist, Transportation, Software

Professional Associations: AITP, SHRM

The Ayers Group Inc
(a member of Career Partners Int'l)
370 Lexington Ave Fl 25
New York, NY 10017
(212) 599-5656
(212) 889-7788
Fax: (212) 889-6689
Email: bob.deissig@ayers.com
Web: www.ayers.com

Description: Executive search, career transition management, organizational effectiveness consulting, and technical consulting services.

Key Contact - Specialty:
Mr. William L. Ayers, Jr., Chairman/CEO - *Technology, human resources*
Mr. Robert Deissig, President/Recruiting Division - *Technology, human resources*
Mr. George Friedman, Managing Director - *Capital markets, general management*

Salary minimum: $150,000

Functions: General Mgmt., HR Mgmt., MIS Mgmt.

Industries: Generalist, Finance, Banking, Invest. Banking

Professional Associations: IACPR, APCNY, SHRM

Networks: Career Partners Int'l

The Badger Group
4125 Blackhawk Plz Cir Ste 270
Danville, CA 94506
(925) 736-5553
Fax: (925) 736-5554
Email: info@badgergroup.com
Web: www.badgergroup.com

Description: We are committed to bringing an elite level of service, professionalism and ethics to retained executive recruiting. Our work spans the computer industry (all functions) and other industries (IT and finance).

Key Contact - Specialty:
Mr. Fred Badger, President - *Information technology*
Mr. Dick Bruce, Vice President - *Information technology*

Salary minimum: $140,000

Functions: Generalist

Industries: Computer Equip., Consumer Elect., Test, Measure Equip., Telecoms, Defense, Aerospace, Software

Professional Associations: AESC

The Baer Group
3161 Coleridge Rd Ste 300
Cleveland, OH 44118
(440) 371-9982
Email: gherbruck@aol.com

Description: Provides retained search for mid- to senior-level executives in most functions and industries with a specialization in healthcare. Other services include search, industry and market research.

Key Contact - Specialty:
Ms. Gretchen S. Herbruck, President - *Healthcare*

Salary minimum: $70,000

Functions: Generalist, General Mgmt., Mfg., Healthcare, HR Mgmt., Specialized Svcs., Mgmt. Consultants

Industries: Generalist, Mfg., Services, Healthcare

Baines Gwinner NA Inc
(a division of Baines Gwinner Holdings)
70 E 55th St Fl 22
New York, NY 10022
(212) 753-9595
Fax: (212) 753-7150
Email: bainesgwinner@bainesgwinner.com
Web: www.bainesgwinner.com

Description: Global financial services specialty firm with offices in New York City, Hong Kong and London specializing in investment banking, investment management, private equity and private banking.

Key Contact - Specialty:
Ms. Amy Russo, Consultant - *Investment banking, private equity*
Mr. Robert Winter, Consultant - *Investment management*
Mr. John Kim, Consultant - *Investment banking*
Mr. Laurence Ling, Consultant - *Investment management*

Salary minimum: $150,000

Functions: Generalist, CFO's

Industries: Generalist, Finance, Banking, Invest. Banking, Brokers, Venture Cap., Misc. Financial

Baker, Nelms & Montgomery
980 Michigan Ave Ste 930
Chicago, IL 60611
(312) 397-8833
(312) 397-8844
Fax: (312) 397-9631
Email: postoffice@bakernelms.com
Web: www.bakernelms.com

Description: We are a retained search firm focusing on management consulting, professional services, and aligned industry clients. The positions that we place are generally at the managing director/CEO/COO/CTO/CFO levels with senior manager/senior principal work for larger clients. BN&M works on a partnership basis with venture capital and corporate clients in developing management teams for new ventures and in the identification and investigation of new business opportunities.

Key Contact:
Mr. William W. Baker, Partner
Ms. Sharon I. Baker, Partner
Ms. Debra Nelms, Partner
Mr. John O'Donnell, Principal
Ms. Nancy Mora, Principal

Salary minimum: $100,000

Functions: General Mgmt., Senior Mgmt., Sales Mgmt.

Industries: Mgmt. Consulting, E-commerce, IT Implementation, PSA/ASP, Wireless, Accounting SW, Database SW, Development SW, ERP SW, Networking, Comm. SW

Professional Associations: AIP

Baker, Parker & Associates Inc
5 Concourse Pkwy Ste 2440
Atlanta, GA 30328-5347
(770) 804-1996
Fax: (770) 804-1917
Email: confidential@bpasearch.com
Web: www.bpasearch.com

Description: We specialize in value-added senior management searches for most industries and institutions of higher education. Significant experience serving international companies.

Key Contact:
Mr. Jerry H. Baker, Partner
Mr. Daniel F. Parker, Sr., Partner
Mr. Gary L. Daugherty, Senior Vice President
Mr. Stephen Peek, Principal
Ms. Rachel Smith, Principal
Ms. Claudia Parker, Associate
Mrs. Laurie Wilder, Principal

Salary minimum: $100,000

Functions: Generalist

Industries: Generalist

Networks: The Amrop - Hever Group

Baldwin Associates LLC
3 Goose Cove Rd
Bath, ME 04530-4017
(207) 442-7070
Fax: (207) 442-8995
Email: baldwinsearch@aol.com

Description: Our executive search practice is focused on introducing gifted senior executive and general management candidates to our prestigious high-technology clients. For 17 years, we have remained purposefully small and fiercely independent so that our practice members are integrally involved in every phase of all searches.

Key Contact - Specialty:
Mr. Peter Robohm, Partner - *Generalist*

Salary minimum: $150,000

Functions: General Mgmt., Directors, Senior Mgmt., Middle Mgmt., Sales & Mktg., CFO's, IT, Mgmt. Consultants

Industries: Computer Equip., Mgmt. Consulting, Telecoms, Software

The Baldwin Group
PO BOX 158
Arlington Heights, IL 60006-0158
(847) 612-1294
Email: thebaldgrp@aol.com

Description: Our clients receive dependability, thoroughness and professionalism that culminate in attracting outstanding persons which we guarantee for one full year after hire.

Key Contact:
Mr. Keith R. Baldwin, President

Salary minimum: $75,000

Functions: Generalist

Industries: Generalist, Food, Bev., Tobacco, Paints, Petro. Products, Machine, Appliance, Motor Vehicles, Mgmt. Consulting, Defense

Bales Partners Inc
980 N Michigan Ave Ste 1400
Chicago, IL 60611
(312) 214-3998
Fax: (312) 214-3981
Email: pbales@balespartners.com

Description: Our general practice encompasses most functions and industries whose assignments are conducted only by experienced principals.

Key Contact:
Mr. L. Patrick Bales, Partner

Salary minimum: $100,000

Functions: Generalist

Industries: Generalist

Professional Associations: IMESC

Allen Ballach Associates Inc
11 Parkview Blvd Ste 100
Whitby, ON L1N 3M8
Canada
(905) 725-0314
Fax: (905) 725-3418
Email: allen@aballach.com
Web: www.aballach.com

Description: We have twenty years of experience providing senior management and executive-level search and selection solutions to the advanced technology microelectronics and communications market sectors throughout North America and Europe.

Key Contact:
Mr. Allen Ballach, President - *Manufacturing, engineering, advanced technologies*
Ms. Sonya DaCosta, Bsc, Director, Research & Testing

Salary minimum: $100,000

Functions: Generalist

Industries: Generalist

Professional Associations: APPAC

Ballantyne & Associates
PO Box 810
Moss Beach, CA 94038
(650) 728-5730
Email: der@headhunter-usa.com

Description: Specializing in the search for e-commerce (B2B, B2C and B2B2C) professionals; consumer product marketing and advertising management professionals for Fortune 1000, startups and non-profits.

Key Contact - Specialty:
Mr. Tom Ballantyne, President - *Marketing & advertising (consumer products)*

Salary minimum: $100,000

Functions: Generalist, General Mgmt., Mktg. Mgmt., IT

Industries: Generalist, Food, Bev., Tobacco, Computer Equip., Consumer Elect., Invest. Banking, Non-profits, Higher Ed., Mgmt. Consulting, E-commerce, Hospitality, Media, Advertising, New Media, ERP SW, Marketing SW, Biotech

Ballos & Company Inc
45 Fieldstone Dr
Morristown, NJ 07960-2634
(973) 538-4609

Description: Effective, ethical, professional search firm with high percentage repeat business: process, chemical, pharmaceutical, biotechnology, manufacturing and technology driven industries.

Key Contact - Specialty:
Mr. Constantine J. Ballos, President - *Generalist*
Mr. H. P. Ballos, Vice President - *Generalist*

Salary minimum: $100,000

Functions: Generalist, General Mgmt., Mfg., Materials, Sales & Mktg., R&D, Engineering

Industries: Generalist, Paper, Chemicals, Drugs Mfg., Plastics, Rubber, Paints, Petro. Products, Environmental Svcs.

Professional Associations: CDA, DCAT, TAPPI

James Bangert & Associates Inc
15500 Wayzata Blvd Ste 1030 F
Wayzata, MN 55391
(952) 475-3454
Fax: (952) 473-4306
Email: jab@bangertassoc.com

Description: We serve both large corporate clients as well as small start-ups. Successful search assignments range from department/division manager to officer level positions.

Key Contact:
Mr. James Bangert, President

Salary minimum: $75,000

Functions: Senior Mgmt., Mfg., Plant Mgmt., Quality, Sales & Mktg., Mktg. Mgmt., Sales Mgmt., Engineering

Industries: Mfg., Medical Devices, Computer Equip., Test, Measure Equip., Electronic, Elec. Components, Network Infrastructure

Professional Associations: AEA

Banyan Group ESC Ltd
411 Theodore Fremd Ave Fl 2
Rye, NY 10580
(914) 921-1010
Fax: (914) 921-1011
Email: banyan@banyan-group.com
Web: www.banyan-group.com

Description: We perform senior-level searches in the communications and information technology fields. Within that industry group, we work primarily for small and mid-sized technology companies and their venture capital partners.

Key Contact - Specialty:
Mr. David L. Kuhns, Managing Director - *CEO's, executives (technology-based companies)*

Functions: Generalist, Senior Mgmt., Legal, Mktg. Mgmt., CFO's, IT, MIS Mgmt.

Industries: Generalist, Venture Cap., New Media, Broadcast, Film, Telecoms, Software, Healthcare

Professional Associations: NYNMA

The Barack Group Inc
405 Lexington Ave The Chrysler Bldg Fl 50
New York, NY 10174
(212) 867-9700
Fax: (212) 681-9555
Email: rob@barackgroup.com
Web: www.barackgroup.com

Description: A specialized recruiting firm for consumer goods and service, sports and entertainment companies.

Key Contact:
Ms. Brianne Barack, President/CEO
Mr. Robert Strong, COO/Managing Partner

Salary minimum: $100,000

Functions: Advertising, Mktg. Mgmt., Sales Mgmt., PR

Industries: Hospitality, Media, Advertising, New Media, Broadcast, Film, Telecoms

Barger & Sargeant Inc
131 Windermere Rd Ste 600
PO Box 1420
Center Harbor, NH 03226-1420
(603) 253-4700

Description: Founded in 1973. Twice selected in top 50 U.S. search firms by ERN. Noted for thoroughness in consulting, interviewing and board recruiting. A fixed fee is established at commencement of search.

Key Contact - Specialty:
Mr. H. Carter Barger, President - *Senior executives, boards of directors*

Salary minimum: $100,000

Functions: Generalist, Directors, Senior Mgmt., Plant Mgmt., Mktg. Mgmt., Direct Mktg., CFO's

Industries: Generalist, Retail, Banking, Insurance, Healthcare

Professional Associations: AESC

Barleycorn, Renard & Associates
1614 Lancaster Ave
Reynoldsburg, OH 43068
(614) 861-4400
Fax: (614) 861-5558
Email: bcorn@insight.rr.com

Description: Expertise in small and medium size companies in the midwest with concentration in engineering, human resources, legal, sales/marketing, finance and senior-level executives.

Key Contact:
Mr. James W. Barleycorn, President
Ms. Susan Erwin, Vice President
Mr. James A. Renard, Vice President

Salary minimum: $60,000

Functions: Generalist

Industries: Mfg., Food, Bev., Tobacco, Chemicals, Plastics, Rubber, Misc. Mfg., Finance, Non-profits, Accounting, Software, Healthcare

Barnes Development Group LLC
1017 W Glen Oaks Ln Ste 108
Mequon, WI 53092
(262) 241-8468
Fax: (262) 241-8438
Email: resume@barnesdevelopment.com
Web: www.barnesdevelopment.com

Description: Practice dedicated to retained executive search consulting; midwest client base.

Key Contact - Specialty:
Mr. Richard E. Barnes, President - *Manufacturing, service industries*
Ms. Roanne L. Barnes, Executive Vice President - *Long term care, non-profit, service industries*

Salary minimum: $60,000

Functions: Generalist

Industries: Generalist

Professional Associations: AESC, IMC

Fred A Barnette & Associates
5917 Oleander Dr Ste 204
Wilmington, NC 28403
(910) 256-0883
Fax: (910) 256-1183
Email: fbarnette2@aol.com
Web: www.fbarnetteassoc.com

Description: Consultants in executive search. Exclusively healthcare (biotechnology, pharmaceuticals, diagnostics, services, health services, consumer health, CROs, managed care, life sciences). All functions, middle to top management.

Key Contact - Specialty:
Mr. Fred A. Barnette, President - *Generalist, healthcare*

Functions: Generalist, Directors, Senior Mgmt.

Industries: Drugs Mfg., Medical Devices, Pharm Svcs., Biotech, Healthcare

Barone-O'Hara Associates Inc
34 Fackler Rd
Princeton, NJ 08540
(609) 683-5566
Fax: (609) 683-8077
Email: boha4@yahoo.com

Description: We provide executive search exclusively to manufacturers of healthcare devices. We are especially successful with small companies, such as startups, restarts, and fast growth. Our consulting is provided as an adjunct to executive search through CEO resources. International recruiting is also provided through Manfred Marx Associates.

Key Contact - Specialty:
Ms. Marialice Barone, Vice President - *Medical devices*
Mr. James J. O'Hara, President - *Medical devices*

Salary minimum: $90,000

Functions: General Mgmt., Directors, Senior Mgmt., Middle Mgmt., Mfg., Materials, Sales & Mktg., Mkt. Research, Mktg. Mgmt., Sales Mgmt.

Industries: Medical Devices

Bartholdi & Company Inc
2020 Arapahoe St Ste 1110
Denver, CO 80205
(303) 383-2130
Fax: (303) 383-2135
Email: tmalouf@bartholdisearch.com
Web: www.bartholdisearch.com

Description: We are a boutique retained search firm with focus in high technology. The firm recruits senior level executives in all functional levels. Our firm is a member of the Marlar International Search Network.

Key Contact - Specialty:
Ms. Terry Malouf, Partner - *High technology, venture capital (partners, associates)*

Salary minimum: $90,000

Functions: Generalist

Industries: Computer Equip., Invest. Banking, Venture Cap., E-commerce, IT Implementation, Telecoms, Software

Networks: Marlar Int'l

Branches:
10040 E Happy Valley Rd Ste 244
Scottsdale, AZ 85255
(480) 502-2178
Fax: (480) 502-5992
Email: ted@bartholdisearch.com
Key Contact - Specialty:
Mr. Theodore G. Bartholdi, Sr., Managing Partner - *High technology, venture capital (partners, associates)*

12020 Sunrise Valley Dr Ste 160
Reston, VA 20191-3429
(703) 476-5519
Fax: (703) 391-0029
Email: cholt@bartholdisearch.com
Key Contact - Specialty:
Ms. Carol Holt, Partner - *High technology, investment banking*

Barton Associates Inc
4314 Yoakum Blvd
Houston, TX 77006
(713) 961-9111
Fax: (713) 993-9399
Email: gbarton@bartona.com
Web: www.bartona.com

Description: A global retainer practice built on strong client relationships and timely execution of projects. Expertise encompasses most industries and functional areas.

Key Contact - Specialty:
Mr. Gary Barton - *Generalist, consumer marketing, general management, human resources*
Mr. Sean Barton - *Human resources, learning, finance, consulting, energy*

Salary minimum: $75,000

Functions: General Mgmt., HR Mgmt., MIS Mgmt.

Industries: Generalist, Higher Ed., IT Implementation, Hospitality, New Media, Software, ERP SW

Bartram/Taylor Group LLC[†]
60 E 42nd St Ste 3204
New York, NY 10165
(212) 692-9644
Fax: (212) 370-3627
Email: rtaylor@bartramtaylorgroup.com
Web: www.bartramtaylorgroup.com

Description: Our firm over a 15 year track record in placing over 200 analysts, portfolio managers, sales/marketing specialists and traders on both the buy-side and the sell-side. We have over a 95% fulfillment rate for assignments received. Our research methodologies and processes are among the most thorough in our industry.

Key Contact:
Mr. Robert Taylor, Managing Principal
Mr. David Bartram, Managing Principal

Salary minimum: $150,000

Functions: Directors, Senior Mgmt., Middle Mgmt., Cash Mgmt., M&A, Risk Mgmt.

Industries: Finance, Invest. Banking, Brokers, Venture Cap., Misc. Financial

Bason Associates
11311 Cornell Park Dr Ste 200
Cincinnati, OH 45242
(513) 469-9881
Email: execsearch@bason.com
Web: www.bason.com

Description: Generalist firm which recruits upper level executives for most industries. The firms practice is national and international in scope and provides services in executive recruitment, organization development and executive assessment.

Key Contact - Specialty:
Mr. Maurice L. Bason, President - *General management, packaging, capital equipment, plastics*

Salary minimum: $75,000

Functions: Generalist, General Mgmt., Senior Mgmt., Nurses, Sales & Mktg., HR Mgmt., CFO's, Non-profits, Architects

Industries: Construction, Mfg., Wholesale, Finance, Services, Non-profits, Mgmt. Consulting, Advertising, Telecoms, Real Estate, Biotech, Healthcare

Professional Associations: IACPR, SHRM

D V Bateman & Associates
PO Box 2777
Kennebunkport, ME 04046
(207) 967-4976

Description: Generalist executive search practice with experience in most industries and in all functional disciplines. Practice is one of five in full-service HR consulting firm.

Key Contact:
Mr. Don Bateman, Principal
Ms. Cary Morrill, Principal
Mr. James Campbell, Ph.D., Principal
Ms. Kathy Delp, Administrator

Salary minimum: $100,000

Functions: Generalist, General Mgmt., Senior Mgmt., Sales & Mktg., Engineering, Int'l.

Industries: Generalist

Sunny Bates Associates

345 7th Ave Fl 8
New York, NY 10001
(212) 691-5252
Fax: (212) 691-3133
Email: info@sunnybates.com
Web: www.sunnybates.com

Description: We are a retained executive search firm with over a decade of success in placing talent in the new media, publishing and entertainment fields.

Key Contact - Specialty:
Ms. Sunny Bates, President/CEO - *Digital, web-based*
Ms. Marilyn Byrd - *Digital, web-based*
Ms. Jenny Baldwin - *Digital, web-based*

Salary minimum: $100,000

Functions: Generalist, Middle Mgmt., Advertising, Mkt. Research, CFO's, MIS Mgmt., Technicians, Graphic Artists

Industries: Generalist, Advertising, Publishing, New Media

Professional Associations: NYNMA

Battalia Winston Int'l

(a member of The Accord Group)
555 Madison Ave
New York, NY 10022
(212) 308-8080
Fax: (212) 308-1309
Email: information@battaliawinston.com
Web: www.battaliawinston.com

Description: A long-established and highly respected domestic and international executive search firm with expertise in seven practice areas and all functions at the senior-level with emphasis on a professional, responsive and quality service to our clients.

Key Contact:
Ms. Dale Winston, Chairman/CEO

Salary minimum: $150,000

Functions: Generalist

Industries: Generalist

Professional Associations: AESC, AMCF

Networks: Accord Group

Branches:
1888 Century Park E Ste 1150
Los Angeles, CA 90067
(310) 284-8080
Fax: (310) 284-3438
Email: mmcclain@battaliawinston.com
Key Contact:
Mr. M. McClain, Partner

1 Sansome St
Citicorp Ctr
San Francisco, CA 94104
(415) 984-3180
Email: wmason@battaliawinston.com
Key Contact:
Mr. William Mason, Partner

150 S Wacker Dr Ste 1220
Chicago, IL 60606
(312) 704-0050
Fax: (312) 704-0305
Email: jmcsherry@battaliawinston.com
Key Contact:
Mr. James F. McSherry, Managing Director

65 William St
Wellesley, MA 02481
(781) 239-1400
Fax: (781) 239-1415
Email: sgarfinkle@battaliawinston.com
Key Contact:
Mr. Steven M. Garfinkle, Sr Ptnr & Nat'l Tech Practice Leader

379 Thornall St Fl 10
Edison, NJ 08837
(732) 549-8200
Fax: (732) 549-8443
Email: tgallagher@battaliawinston.com
Key Contact:
Mr. Terence M. Gallagher, President/COO

R Gaines Baty Associates Inc

12750 Merit Dr Ste 990
Dallas, TX 75251
(972) 386-7900
Fax: (972) 387-2224
Email: gbaty@rgba.com
Web: www.rgba.com

Description: Full-scale national retained search for specialized mid-to-upper-level management in technology, systems and consulting fields and general and sales/marketing management for technology companies. Personal attention, results-orientation and long-term approach. Twenty-three years in search, doing it right, with extensive repeat and referral clients.

Key Contact - Specialty:
Mr. R. Gaines Baty, President - *Information technology management, consulting management, general management, sales & sales management (for technology companies)*

Salary minimum: $100,000

Functions: Senior Mgmt., Distribution, Sales Mgmt., IT, MIS Mgmt., Mgmt. Consultants

Industries: Generalist, Energy, Utilities, Mfg., Computer Equip., Wholesale, Venture Cap., Services, Equip Svcs., Mgmt. Consulting, New Media, Telecoms, Wireless, Packaging, Software, Healthcare

Professional Associations: IRG, SERC

Branches:
2870 Peachtree Rd Ste 256
Atlanta, GA 30305
(770) 859-9980
Fax: (770) 992-2631
Email: mdickens@rgba.com
Key Contact - Specialty:
Ms. Marcia Dickens - *Financial management, US & international, bilingual candidates*

Martin H Bauman Associates LLC

(a member of TranSearch Int'l)
375 Park Ave Ste 2002
New York, NY 10152
(212) 752-6580
Fax: (212) 755-1096
Email: mhb@baumanassociates.com

Description: Our firm offers a highly personalized service in executive recruitment and assessment, at the core of which is our peerless assessment capability, recognized worldwide.

Key Contact - Specialty:
Mr. Martin H. Bauman, President - *Finance, general management, venture capital, transportation*
Mr. Steven A. Heller, Executive Vice President - *Generalist, insurance*
Ms. Nina Proct, Vice President - *Generalist*

Salary minimum: $165,000

Functions: Generalist, General Mgmt., Directors, Senior Mgmt., Mfg., Purchasing, Distribution, Sales & Mktg., HR Mgmt., Finance

Industries: Generalist

Professional Associations: AESC, ATA

Networks: TranSearch Int'l

Branches:
625 N Michigan Ave Ste 500
Chicago, IL 60611-3108
(312) 751-5407
Fax: (312) 226-6402
Email: ahmhba@mindspring.com
Key Contact - Specialty:
Ms. Audrey Hellinger, Vice President - *Financial services, generalist*

The Bauman Group

220 Main St Ste 200
Los Altos, CA 94022
(650) 941-0800
Fax: (650) 941-1729
Email: baumangrp@aol.com

Description: We are a retained search firm that provides senior-level clinical and regulatory, research, and business development expertise to biotechnology and pharmaceutical.

Key Contact - Specialty:
Ms. Ina Bauman, President - *Biotechnology, pharmaceuticals, MD's, project management*
Ms. Stephanie Greenblatt, Associate - *CRA's, regulatory affairs*

Salary minimum: $100,000

Functions: Healthcare, Physicians, Nurses

Industries: Medical Devices, Biotech, Healthcare

BCA Inc†

3790 Via de la Valle Ste 307
Del Mar, CA 92014
(858) 793-2790
Fax: (858) 793-2793
Email: hr@bcasearch.com
Web: www.hrcareerpage.com

Description: We are one of the few search firms devoted exclusively to human resources. Our functional expertise has allowed us to build a reputation for quick and effective delivery, diversity recruitment expertise, and continued success with difficult and/or extremely focused requirements.

Key Contact - Specialty:
Ms. Cecelia Gonzalez, CEO & Managing Partner - *Human Resources*
Mr. Joe Gonzalez, Managing Partner - *Human Resources*

Salary minimum: $55,000

Functions: HR Mgmt.

Industries: Generalist

Professional Associations: EMA, NAFE, SHRM

BDK Global Search Inc

1115 Sherbrooke St W Ste 2104
Montreal, QC H3A 1H3
Canada
(514) 287-2666
Email: info@bdkglobal.com
Web: www.bdkglobal.com

Description: We are an information systems and technology senior executive search practice, specializing in CIO mandates. Through our managing director, we have accumulated 26 years of experience in satisfying client requirements, serving all industries.

Key Contact - Specialty:
Mr. Brian D. Krecklo, Managing Director - *Information systems & technology*

Salary minimum: $100,000

Functions: IT, MIS Mgmt.

Industries: Generalist

Professional Associations: OCRIQ, OPRHQ

Branches:
2 Bloor St W Ste 700
Toronto, ON M4W 3R1
Canada
(800) 573-2556
Email: info@bdkglobal.com
Key Contact - Specialty:
Mr. Ronald H. Raisman, Senior Recruiter -
*Financial services, venture capital, information
systems, information technology*
Mr. Michael J. Timmons, Senior Consultant -
*Human resources, engineering, information
systems, information technology*
Mr. Wayne Hussey, Senior Recruiter - *Sports,
entertainment, information systems, information
technology*

Beach Executive Search Inc
11324 NW 12th Ct
Coral Springs, FL 33071-6494
(954) 340-7337
Email: wlbeach@bellsouth.net

Description: Generalist retained search firm
specialized in performing a highly personalized
service to client companies located throughout
Central and South Florida that require national
searches.

Key Contact - Specialty:
Mr. William L. Beach, President - *Generalist*

Salary minimum: $75,000

Functions: Generalist

Industries: Generalist

Professional Associations: ACG

The Beam Group
11 Penn Center Plz Ste 502
Philadelphia, PA 19103
(215) 988-2100
Fax: (215) 988-1558
Email: resumes@beamgroup.com
Web: www.beamgroup.com

Description: Generalist search firm with a diverse
group of insurance, financial services, consumer
products and high-tech companies. Particular
expertise in candidate assessment.

Key Contact - Specialty:
Mr. Russell A. Glicksman, President
Ms. Lindsay Bacon, Research Manager -
Generalist
Mr. Chuck Ginsburg - *Generalist*
Ms. Sandi Macan - *Direct marketing, e-commerce,
financial services, marketing, healthcare*
Ms. Suzanne Martin - *Consumer products,
operations research, sales & marketing,
technology*
Mr. Scott McKenna - *Finance, financial services,
human resources, investment management,
marketing*

Salary minimum: $125,000

Functions: General Mgmt., Senior Mgmt.,
Materials, Distribution, Healthcare, Sales &
Mktg., Direct Mktg., HR Mgmt., Finance, MIS
Mgmt.

Industries: Mfg., Food, Bev., Tobacco, Paper,
Soap, Perf., Cosmtcs., Drugs Mfg., Retail,
Finance, Banking, Brokers, Venture Cap.,
Services, HR Services, Publishing, Insurance,
Software, Healthcare

Branches:
600 3rd Ave Fl 16
New York, NY 10016
(212) 476-4100
Fax: (212) 986-7798
Key Contact - Specialty:
Mr. Howard Pines - *Consumer products, financial
services, human resources, investment banking,
manufacturing*

Mr. Richard Coffina - *Asset management, banking,
financial services, human resources*
Ms. Rebecka Lovell - *Finance, human resources,
marketing*
Mr. Jay Santamaria - *Consumer products, logistics,
operations research, pharmaceuticals, sales &
marketing*
Mr. Al Swann - *Consumer products, technology*

J R Bechtle & Company
112 Water St Ste 500
Boston, MA 02109
(617) 722-9980
Fax: (617) 722-4130
Email: jrbech@jrbechtle.com
Web: www.jrbechtle.com

Description: We fill positions requiring extensive
knowledge of European business practices and/or
familiarity with the German language while
covering a broad spectrum of industries. We
concentrate on technical-oriented products,
machinery, high-tech components, and software.

Key Contact:
Mr. Egon L. Lacher, Partner

Salary minimum: $95,000

Functions: Generalist, General Mgmt., Mfg.,
Materials, Sales & Mktg., Finance, IT,
Engineering

Industries: Generalist, Mfg., Transportation,
Finance, Aerospace, Software, Biotech

Branches:
3560 Washington St
San Francisco, CA 94118
(415) 567-2364
Fax: (415) 391-0234
Email: j.bechtle@jrbechtle.com
Key Contact:
Dr. Joachim Bechtle, Partner

1211 W 22nd St Ste 529
Oak Brook, IL 60523
(630) 203-2120
Fax: (603) 527-1379
Email: chicago@jrbechtle.com
Key Contact:
Mr. Herb Haessig, Partner

Becker, Norton & Company
4088 Alpha Dr Alpha Bldg
Allison Park, PA 15101
(412) 486-5553
Fax: (412) 486-4176

Description: A strong regional firm with capability
of conducting national searches. We have extensive
expertise in conducting searches and experience in
marketing, finance, data processing systems and
management disciplines.

Key Contact:
Mr. Robert C. Becker, President

Salary minimum: $60,000

Functions: General Mgmt., Directors, Senior
Mgmt., Middle Mgmt., Sales & Mktg.

Industries: Mfg., Metal Products, Misc. Mfg.,
Retail, Finance, Venture Cap., Services, Media,
Advertising, Real Estate

Professional Associations: APA

The Bedford Consulting Group Inc
(a member of TranSearch Int'l)
60 Bedford Rd
The Bedford House
Toronto, ON M5R 2K2
Canada
(416) 963-9000
Fax: (416) 963-9998
Email: search@bedfordgroup.com
Web: www.bedfordgroup.com

Description: We make the difference for our clients
through our global search capabilities for positions
at the senior management level in diverse industries.
All of our searches are managed by the firm's senior
partners.

Key Contact - Specialty:
Mr. Steven Pezim, Managing Director - *Technology
start-ups to multinationals, retail, consumer
products, pulp & paper*
Mr. Howard J. Pezim, Managing Director -
*Consumer products, manufacturing,
pharmaceuticals, healthcare*
Mr. Russell Buckland, Managing Partner - *Mining,
natural resources*

Salary minimum: $80,000

Functions: Generalist, General Mgmt., Mfg.,
Healthcare, Sales & Mktg., HR Mgmt., Finance,
CFO's, IT, MIS Mgmt.

Industries: Generalist, Mfg., Retail, Finance,
Media, Software, Healthcare

Professional Associations: AESC, IACPR

Networks: TranSearch Int'l

The Bedford Group[†]
154 Quicksand Pond Rd
Little Compton, RI 02837
(401) 635-4646
Fax: (401) 635-8466
Email: bedgroup@meganet.net

Description: Leading specialist in electronics
manufacturing, semiconductor, wireless and
network communications industries. Outstanding
completion record. Off limit recruiting strictly
observed.

Key Contact - Specialty:
Mr. John W. Edwards, Managing Director -
Electronics
Ms. Lillian E. Edwards, Director of Research -
Electronics

Salary minimum: $90,000

Functions: General Mgmt., Senior Mgmt., Middle
Mgmt., Mfg., Product Dev., Quality, Materials,
Sales & Mktg., R&D, Engineering

Industries: Computer Equip., Consumer Elect.,
Telecoms, Wireless, Software

Networks: Top Echelon Network

Behavioral Science Associates Inc[†]
2135 E University Dr Ste 121
Mesa, AZ 85213
(480) 833-2629
Fax: (480) 833-1029
Email: bsa@bsassoc.com
Web: www.bsassoc.com

Description: Retained executive search firm that
blends the best of traditional executive search with
modern psychological assessment and evaluation.
This powerful combination provides well qualified
people that will work effectively within the hiring
company's own corporate environment.

Key Contact - Specialty:
Mr. Robert E. King, President - *Insurance*
Mr. Malcolm S. Morrison, Senior Vice President -
Biotech, legal
Mr. Vincent L. Cavallo, Executive Vice President -
Insurance

Functions: Generalist

Industries: Mfg., Finance, Services, Insurance, Real
Estate, Software, Biotech, Healthcare, Non-
classifiable

Bell Wishingrad Partners Inc
230 Park Ave Ste 1000
New York, NY 10169
(212) 949-6666

Let www.ExecutiveAgent.com e-mail your resume now.

Description: A practice focused upon senior management positions in financial services and affiliated industries. Search activities performed only by partners with limited client base avoiding off-limit conflicts. All resumes should be directed to the Stamford office.

Key Contact - Specialty:
Ms. Vivian Wishingrad, Partner - *Financial services*

Salary minimum: $150,000

Functions: Generalist, Senior Mgmt., Mktg. Mgmt., Sales Mgmt., Cash Mgmt., M&A

Industries: Generalist, Finance, Banking, Invest. Banking, Brokers, Venture Cap., Misc. Financial

Branches:
2701 Summer St
Stamford, CT 06905
(203) 921-2600
Key Contact - Specialty:
Ms. Vivian Wishingrad, Partner - *Financial services*

Belle Isle, Djandji, Brunet
1555 Peel St Ste 1200
Montreal, QC H3A 3L8
Canada
(514) 844-1012
Fax: (514) 844-0539
Email: reception@bidi.com
Web: www.bidi.com

Description: Firm has a broad range of search assignments expertise in the private, public and para-public sectors covering all functional areas and a broad cross-section of industries.

Key Contact:
Mr. Charles Belle Isle, Partner
Mr. Guy Djandji, Partner
Mr. Michel Brunet, Partner

Salary minimum: $75,000

Functions: Senior Mgmt.

Industries: Generalist

Joy Reed Belt Search Consultants Inc
PO Box 18446
Oklahoma City, OK 73154
(405) 842-6336
Fax: (405) 842-6357
Email: drbelt@aol.com
Web: www.joyreedbelt.com

Description: Human resources consulting firm specializing in executive search. Our highly qualified professionals are trained in business and the behavioral sciences and are able to present only those candidates who will fit with your company's philosophy and corporate culture.

Key Contact - Specialty:
Dr. Joy Reed Belt, Ph.D., President - *CEOs, COOs, legal, healthcare, human resources*
Ms. Sharon Wade, Senior Vice President - *Mid level management (generalist)*
Ms. Carolyn Stuart, Vice President - *Accounting & finance, CFOs*
Ms. Robin Nauman, Client Services Coordinator
Ms. Carol Casey, Vice President - Research - *Education, non-profits*

Salary minimum: $60,000

Functions: Senior Mgmt., Middle Mgmt., Healthcare, Health Admin., Benefits, M&A, MIS Mgmt., Attorneys, Paralegals

Industries: Generalist, Energy, Utilities, Services, HR Services, Advertising, Real Estate, Healthcare

Branches:
PO Box 700688
Tulsa, OK 74170-0688
(918) 748-8844
Fax: (405) 842-6357

Email: jrbtulsa@aol.com
Key Contact:
Ms. Brooke Lasiter, Generalist

Bench Int'l Search Inc
116 N Robertson Blvd Ste 800
Los Angeles, CA 90048
(310) 854-9900
Fax: (310) 652-2081
Email: contact@benchinternational.com
Web: www.benchinternational.com

Description: We provide both recruiting and staffing development consulting services to our client base. We are limited to recruiting professionals with advanced degrees for the pharmaceutical, biotechnology and high-technology industries. We serve both the technical and administrative tracks up through executive management.

Key Contact - Specialty:
Ms. Denise DeMan, President/CEO - *Pharmaceutical, biotechnology*

Salary minimum: $100,000

Functions: Generalist, Directors, Senior Mgmt., Middle Mgmt., Mkt. Research, R&D, Minorities

Industries: Generalist, Chemicals, Drugs Mfg., Medical Devices, Pharm Svcs., Biotech, Healthcare

Professional Associations: AACN, AAPS, ACS, AHSR, APUA, AUTM, BIO, DIA, FDLI, LES, RAPS, SCT

Bender Executive Search Management Consulting
45 N Station Plz Ste 315
Great Neck, NY 11021
(516) 773-4300
Fax: (516) 482-5355
Email: benderexec@aol.com
Web: www.marketingexecsearch.com

Description: We provide a tailor-made consultative approach by a former marketing executive with 18 years of experience specializing in marketing search nationwide. We are a multi-resource firm with sophisticated research capability. We are known for quality, thoroughness, fast results, pro-active personalized service, and close collaborative relationships.

Key Contact - Specialty:
Mr. Alan Bender - *Marketing, sales promotion, market research, sales, communications*

Salary minimum: $75,000

Functions: Senior Mgmt., Middle Mgmt., Sales & Mktg., Mgmt. Consultants, Minorities, Int'l.

Industries: Generalist, Mfg., Retail, Banking, Pharm Svcs., Mgmt. Consulting, Hospitality, Media, Telecoms, Healthcare

Professional Associations: IACPR

Bennett Associates
335 Washington St Ste 12
Norwell, MA 02061-1900
(781) 659-9950
Fax: (781) 659-9969
Email: rbennett@bennettsearch.com
Web: www.bennettsearch.com

Description: We serve government and non profit organizations which comprise the civic infrastructure of the country by recruiting experienced leaders into positions that improve the capabilities of these institutions.

Key Contact - Specialty:
Mr. Richard T. Bennett, President - *Civic clients & recruitment's*

Functions: Generalist, Senior Mgmt., Admin. Svcs., Personnel, CFO's, MIS Mgmt., Mgmt. Consultants, Minorities

Industries: Generalist, Transportation, Services, Non-profits, Higher Ed., Law Enforcement, Government

The Bennett Group Inc†
5640 Professional Cir Ste A8
Indianapolis, IN 46241
(317) 247-1240
Fax: (317) 247-6533
Email: benngrp@aol.com

Description: The founder of the firm was trained, during the mid-seventies, by Elmer R. Davis, one of the true pioneers of the search industry. Founded in 1981, the firm consists of professionals whose backgrounds have kept pace with technology in all facets of the electronics and automotive industries.

Key Contact:
Mr. Charles T. Gelatka, President - *Automotive, electronics (engineering, manufacturing mostly)*
Mr. M. D. Bennett, Partner - *Automotive, electronics (engineering, manufacturing mostly)*
Mr. Thomas Fisher, Associate - *Electronics*
Mrs. Diane Gelatka, Partner
Mrs. Roberta Swift, Associate

Salary minimum: $50,000

Functions: Engineering

Industries: Motor Vehicles, Consumer Elect., Test, Measure Equip., Finance, Packaging, Insurance, Software

Professional Associations: ASME, IEEE, ISHM, SAE, SMTA, SPE

Bennett Search & Consulting Company Inc
285-1 W Naomi Dr
Naples, FL 34104
(941) 352-2820
(941) 352-0219
Fax: (941) 353-7719
Email: bbennett@naples.net

Description: Generalist USA - hardware/software, banking, electronics, security, real estate development, golf club staffing, restaurant/hotel management. Senior management, general management, sales, manufacturing, engineering and human resources. Twenty-eight years' quality diversity recruitment and training.

Key Contact - Specialty:
Mr. Robert C. Bennett, Jr., President - *Banks, country clubs, generalist*
Mr. Michael Cottington - *Generalist, legal*
Ms. Kaye Cottington - *Executive assistants, paralegal*
Ms. Colleen Shue - *Computer hardware, software*
Mr. Beirne Brown, Associate - *Restaurants, hotels*
Mr. Michael McFarland - *Research*

Salary minimum: $80,000

Functions: Generalist, Directors, Senior Mgmt., Middle Mgmt., Legal, Nurses, CFO's, IT

Industries: Food, Bev., Tobacco, Finance, Banking, Services, Legal, Accounting, Mgmt. Consulting, Law Enforcement, Hospitality, Environmental Svcs., Real Estate

Bente Hansen Executive Search
12707 High Bluff Dr Fl 2
San Diego, CA 92130
(858) 350-4330
Fax: (760) 634-1533
Email: bente@bentehansen.com
Web: www.bentehansen.com

Description: Our firm is a national retained executive search firm specializing in start-up, mid-sized research, and technology-based companies.

The managing directors are experts at conducting retained searches in the fields of bioscience, telecommunications, software, hardware, e-Commerce, and nonprofit service industries at senior management levels.

Key Contact:
Dr. Bente Hansen, Ph.D., Principal
Ms. Cynthia Hammond, Managing Director, Utah & Northwest
Dr. Mary Colacicco, Ph.D., Managing Director, Not-for-Profit

Functions: Generalist

Industries: Energy, Utilities, Medical Devices, Finance, Services, Hospitality, Media, Communications, Government, Software, Biotech

Branches:
4001 S 700 St 500
Salt Lake City, UT 84107
(435) 658-3360
Email: bente@bentehansen.com
Key Contact:
Ms. Cynthia Hammond, Managing Director, Utah & Northwest

Berardi & Associates
(a division of The Solomon-Page Group LLC)
1140 Ave of the Americas Fl 8
New York, NY 10036
(212) 403-6180
Fax: (212) 764-9690
Email: jmiranda@spges.com
Web: www.spgjobs.com

Description: We provide individual executive search in the magazine publishing, book publishing, educational publishing, and new media industries by media professionals with a total of more than 75 years of experience in the industry.

Key Contact - Specialty:
Ms. Loretta A. Berardi, President - *Educational publishing, new media publishing management*
Ms. Susan Gold, Executive Vice President - *Magazine publishing management*
Mr. James Maurer, Executive Vice President - *New media, e-commerce management*

Functions: Generalist, Senior Mgmt., Middle Mgmt., Advertising, Mktg. Mgmt., Sales Mgmt., Direct Mktg.

Industries: Generalist, Higher Ed., Publishing, New Media

Bergeris & Company Inc
PO Box 341
Larchmont, NY 10538
(914) 833-0519
Fax: (914) 834-6461
Email: bergeris@aol.com

Description: Executive search for sales professionals in commercial and investment banking. Special, but not exclusive, focus on credit and private banking. A truly individualized approach.

Key Contact - Specialty:
Mr. Jim Bergeris - *Investment banking, credit risk management, wealth management*

Salary minimum: $100,000

Functions: Generalist, Cash Mgmt., Credit, M&A, Risk Mgmt.

Industries: Generalist, Finance, Banking, Invest. Banking, Brokers, Venture Cap., Misc. Financial, Mgmt. Consulting

Networks: National Banking Network (NBN)

Berkana Int'l Ltd
18907 Forest Park Dr NE
Seattle, WA 98155
(206) 365-2835
(206) 365-2959
Fax: (206) 547-3843
Email: sonja@headhunters.com
Web: www.headhunters.com

Description: Berkana is a retained, executive and technical search firm specializing in the recruitment of personnel for companies in the high-tech arena.

Key Contact - Specialty:
Ms. Sonja Carson, President/Founder - *Executive, technical*
Mr. Bill Holloman, Operations Manager - *Operations, logistics*

Salary minimum: $50,000

Functions: Generalist

Industries: Computer Equip., Mgmt. Consulting, HR Services, Telecoms, Aerospace, Software, Biotech

Networks: National Consulting Network (NCN)

Berkhemer Clayton Inc
221 S Figueroa St Ste 240
Figueroa Courtyard
Los Angeles, CA 90012
(213) 621-2300
Fax: (213) 621-2309
Email: resume@bcisearch.com
Web: www.berkhemerclayton.com

Description: We are a senior-level firm, handling full range of industries. We have a successful general management track record, strong functional practices in corporate communications, finance, marketing, and technology. We are committed to inclusive process and striving to present a full spectrum of candidates, including men, women, and people of color. Our firm is multi-ethnic owned.

Key Contact - Specialty:
Ms. Betsy Berkhemer-Credaire, President - *Corporate communications, public relations*
Mr. Fred J. Clayton, Executive Vice President - *Finance, human resources, general management*
Ms. Melba Sanders, Vice President - *Diversity*
Ms. Peggy V. Chong, Vice President - *Marketing, technology, general management*
Ms. Julia Justus McGinty - *Non-profit, associations, corporate communications, higher education*

Salary minimum: $100,000

Functions: Generalist, Senior Mgmt., Sales & Mktg., PR, HR Mgmt., Finance, IT, Minorities, Non-profits

Industries: Energy, Utilities, Food, Bev., Tobacco, Wholesale, Retail, Banking, Misc. Financial, Services, Hospitality, Advertising, New Media, Software, Entertainment SW, Biotech, Healthcare

Professional Associations: IABC, PRSA

Best/Coleman and Assoc Inc
1085 Commonwealth Ave Ste 325A1
Boston, MA 02115

Description: Senior management and sales and marketing positions within the retail and wholesale industries. Retained search only.

Key Contact:
Mr. Rob Best, Sr., President
Ms. Claudia A. Coleman, CPC, Associate

Salary minimum: $90,000

Functions: Sales & Mktg., Mktg. Mgmt., Direct Mktg.

Industries: Wholesale, Retail

Bethesda Technologies
(formerly known as Bethesda Pharmaceutical Ltd)
PO Box 30557
Bethesda, MD 20824
(301) 907-8838
Fax: (301) 907-7794
Email: bethesdatech@prodigy.net

Description: Small retained firm with a search practice in the pharmaceutical, biotechnology and information technology industries, focusing on senior-level professionals and executives. Firm based on 20 years of experience in the pharmaceutical industry.

Key Contact:
Ms. Kari Preston, President

Salary minimum: $90,000

Functions: Senior Mgmt., Sales & Mktg., IT, MIS Mgmt., R&D

Industries: Drugs Mfg., Medical Devices, Pharm Svcs., Telecoms, Software, Biotech

BethWise Associates
PO Box 2626
Briarcliff Manor, NY 10510
(914) 762-4077
Email: beth.wise@bwiseassociates.com
Web: www.bwiseassociates.com

Description: We are a retained search boutique specializing in professionals in finance, sales and marketing, and business development. We want to provide our clients with the best people available, as quickly as possible.

Key Contact:
Ms. Beth Wise

Functions: General Mgmt., Sales & Mktg., Finance, Minorities

Industries: Mfg., Food, Bev., Tobacco, Drugs Mfg., Wholesale, Finance, Services, Media, Communications, Insurance, Software, Biotech

Professional Associations: ESRT

BFL Associates Ltd
12 Greenway Plz Ste 1222
Houston, TX 77046-1203
(713) 965-2112
Fax: (713) 965-2114
Email: bjorn@bflassociates.com
Web: www.bflassociates.com

Description: Our firm works to locate and secure the resources clients need to succeed. Clients initially engage our services to locate talent for executive positions. But with capabilities that extend far beyond recruiting, we are frequently able to provide the value-added services of employee retention programs, compensation analysis, and long-term planning for healthy business growth.

Key Contact:
Mr. Bjorn F. Lindgren, President

Salary minimum: $200,000

Functions: Generalist

Industries: Generalist

Bialecki Inc
780 3rd Ave Ste 4203
New York, NY 10017
(212) 755-1090
Web: www.bialecki.com

Description: We place senior level only. We perform highly specialized searches for investment banking talent. We have expertise is in corporate finance sector heads, M&A, all structured products, and risk management. We perform global searches. We have had substantial repeat business.

Key Contact:
Ms. Linda Bialecki, President

Salary minimum: $1,000,000

Functions: Generalist, M&A

Industries: Generalist, Invest. Banking

Professional Associations: AESC

Bialla & Associates Inc
4000 Bridgeway Ste 201
Sausalito, CA 94965
(415) 332-7111
Fax: (415) 332-3964
Email: vito@bialla.com
Web: www.bialla.com

Description: Handle blue chip clients, Internet CEOs, COOs. CFOs, functional heads, i.e. marketing, etc.

Key Contact:
Mr. Vito Bialla, Partner
Mr. H. Scott Thomson, Partner
Mr. W. Jeff Hastings, Partner

Salary minimum: $125,000

Functions: Senior Mgmt., CFO's, Int'l.

Industries: Generalist

Paul J Biestek Associates Inc
800 E NW Hwy Ste 700
PMB 101
Palatine, IL 60074
(847) 825-5131
Web: www.biestek-associates.com

Description: We draw on 30 years of executive search consulting and corporate human resources management experience.

Key Contact - Specialty:
Mr. Paul J. Biestek, President - *Generalist*

Salary minimum: $70,000

Functions: Generalist, Mfg., Materials, Sales Mgmt., Finance, IT, R&D, Engineering

Industries: Generalist, Energy, Utilities, Mfg., Food, Bev., Tobacco, Medical Devices, Machine, Appliance, Defense, Aerospace

Professional Associations: IACPR

Billington & Associates[†]
3250 Wilshire Blvd Ste 900
Los Angeles, CA 90010
(213) 386-7511
Fax: (213) 386-7025

Description: Primary emphasis on middle management recruitment for financial/administrative professionals. Consulting includes finance/organizational areas plus specialty in full range of fundraising activities for non profit organizations.

Key Contact - Specialty:
Mr. Brian J. Billington, President - *Finance, general management, administration*

Salary minimum: $60,000

Functions: Generalist, Middle Mgmt., Health Admin., CFO's, Credit, Non-profits

Industries: Generalist

Biomedical Search Consultants[†]
PO Box 721
Hawleyville, CT 06440-0721
(203) 426-1445
Email: ta4nabio@cs.com

Description: We specialize in pharmaceutical, biopharmaceutical, biological, medical devices, diagnostics, and cosmetic industry specialists.

Key Contact - Specialty:
Mr. Thomas A. Fornabaio, Professional Recruiter
Mr. James T Fornabaio, Professional Recruiter - *Engineering*

Functions: General Mgmt., Middle Mgmt., Mfg., Product Dev., Production, Plant Mgmt., Quality, Packaging, R&D, Engineering

Industries: Chemicals, Soap, Perf., Cosmtcs., Drugs Mfg., Medical Devices, Biotech

---

BioPharmMed[†]
(also known as BPM Resources)
550 N Reo St Ste 300
Tampa, FL 33609
(813) 261-5117
Fax: (813) 805-0502
Email: bpm@ix.netcom.com
Web: www.biopharmmed.com

Description: We offer commitment, knowledge, experience, and results in our retained partnership with clients ranging from start-up ventures to Fortune 500 corporations. We are computer linked to over 695 search firms worldwide. We offer permanent and contract placements. We specialize in biotech, medical device, pharmaceutical, fiber optics, photonics, telecommunications, and opto-electronics.

Key Contact - Specialty:
Ms. Tina Hunter Stewart, President - *Medical device, biotech, pharmaceuticals*

Salary minimum: $80,000

Functions: Generalist, Senior Mgmt.

Industries: Mfg., Drugs Mfg., Medical Devices, Computer Equip., Venture Cap., Telecoms, Fiber Optic, Biotech

Professional Associations: RON

Networks: Recruiters Professional Network (RPN)

BioQuest Inc
100 Spear St Ste 1125
San Francisco, CA 94105
(415) 777-2422
Email: resumes@bioquestinc.com
Web: www.bioquestinc.com

Description: BioQuest is a retained executive search firm that serves emerging and established medical device, biotechnology, pharmaceutical and healthcare services companies. Typical search assignments are for board members, corporate officers, and other key senior managers.

Key Contact:
Mr. Roger J. Anderson, Principal
Dr. H. Jurgen Weber, Ph.D., Principal

Salary minimum: $100,000

Functions: General Mgmt., Directors, Senior Mgmt., Healthcare, CFO's

Industries: Biotech, Healthcare

Branches:
27281 Las Rambles Ste 200
Mission Viejo, CA 92691
(949) 367-4545
Email: hickman@bioquestinc.com
Key Contact - Specialty:
Mr. Dave Mildrew, Consultant - *Healthcare products & services*

Deborah Bishop & Associates
883 Island Dr Ste 212
Alameda, CA 94502
(510) 523-2305

Description: We specialize in high-tech industry. We do retained search only. Integrated circuits, wireless, peripherals, computers.

Key Contact:
Ms. Deborah Bishop, President

Salary minimum: $85,000

Functions: Generalist, Directors, Senior Mgmt., Mfg., Sales & Mktg., Engineering

Industries: Generalist, Computer Equip., New Media, Software

Bishop Partners
708 3rd Ave Ste 2200
New York, NY 10017
(212) 986-3419
Fax: (212) 986-3350
Email: info@bishopnet.com
Web: www.bishoppartners.com

Description: Our firm is dedicated to excellence in providing executive search consulting to the information, communications, and entertainment industries, including both product and service companies in cable, broadcasting, publishing, entertainment, interactive media, and related technology.

Key Contact - Specialty:
Ms. Susan Bishop, President - *Media, entertainment, publishing, telecommunications*
Mr. Bob Saracen, Principal - *Technology, broadband, media, entertainment, publishing*
Ms. Laura Timoney, Vice President - *Media, entertainment, publishing, telecommunications*
Ms. Sheila Yossem, Principal - *Media, entertainment, publishing, telecommunications*
Ms. Pegeen Winston, Vice President - *Media, entertainment, publishing, telecommunications*

Salary minimum: $150,000

Functions: Generalist, General Mgmt., Directors, Senior Mgmt., Sales & Mktg., HR Mgmt., CFO's, MIS Mgmt.

Industries: Hospitality, Media, Advertising, Publishing, New Media, Broadcast, Film, Telecoms

Professional Associations: AESC, CTAM, IRTS, NCTA, WICT

Branches:
11400 W Olympic Blvd Ste 200
Los Angeles, CA 90064
(310) 207-3640
Email: info@bishopnet.com
Key Contact:
Ms. Pegeen Winston, Vice President

The Blackman Kallick Search Division[†]
300 S Riverside Plz Ste 660
Chicago, IL 60606
(312) 207-1040
Fax: (312) 207-1066
Web: www.bkadvice.com/search

Description: Each search assignment custom designed and researched for every client. Unique client mix, dedicated staff, outstanding references. Middle and upper-management specialists. Several clients retained on annual partnership basis.

Key Contact - Specialty:
Mr. Gary M. Wolfson, Managing Partner - *Management, attorneys, accounting, banking & finance, manufacturing*

Salary minimum: $50,000

Functions: Generalist

Industries: Generalist

Professional Associations: HRMAC, IMA

Blackshaw, Olmstead, Lynch & Koenig
3414 Peachtree Rd NE 730 Monarch Plz
Atlanta, GA 30326
(404) 261-7770
Fax: (404) 261-4469
Email: bolandk@mindspring.com
Web: www.transearch.com

Description: We are a retainer only generalist firm, specializing in senior management. Our client base is international.

Key Contact - Specialty:
Mr. Brian Blackshaw, Partner - *Generalist*
Mr. George T. Olmstead, Partner - *Generalist*
Mr. Joel S. Koenig, Partner - *Generalist*
Ms. Lisa Shalet, Vice President-Research - *Generalist*
Ms. Cam Cooper, Senior Vice President - *Hospitality*

Salary minimum: $100,000

Functions: Generalist

Industries: Generalist

Professional Associations: IACPR

Networks: TranSearch Int'l

Branches:
5110 W Goldleaf Cir Ste 115
Los Angeles, CA 90056
(323) 299-2500
Fax: (323) 299-3100
Email: cnewrecru@compuserve.com
Key Contact:
Mr. Chuck Newman, Associate Partner

99 Harbor Rd
Fairfield, CT 06490
(203) 256-3545
Fax: (203) 256-3737
Key Contact:
Mr. John P. Lynch, III, Partner

Blake/Hansen & Schmidt Ltd
5514 Ridgeway Ct
Westlake Village, CA 91362
(805) 879-1192
Email: jeri@blakehansenschmidt.com
Web: www.blakehansenschmidt.com

Description: Blake/Hansen & Schmidt is an alliance partner of the HansenGroup, Ltd. The firm specializes in the packaging & plastics industries and focuses on recruiting middle and senior-level managers, corporate officers and board members.

Key Contact:
Ms. Jeri E. Schmidt, President

Salary minimum: $65,000

Functions: Generalist

Industries: Plastics, Rubber, Packaging

Professional Associations: IOPP, TAPPI, WIP

Blake/Hansen Ltd
(an alliance partner of HansenGroup Ltd)
288 Beach Dr Ste 11-B
St. Petersburg, FL 33701
(727) 417-3777
Web: www.hansengroupltd.com

Description: Board member, officer, senior and middle echelon executive search. Consulting since 1974. Specializing in aviation, aerospace and high-technology industries contracting with DOD and the intelligence community.

Key Contact - Specialty:
Mr. Ty E. Hansen, President - *Aviation, aerospace, defense, high technology*

Salary minimum: $80,000

Functions: Generalist

Industries: Defense, Aerospace

Professional Associations: ADPA, AFCEA, ANA, AOC, NBAA, WC

J: Blakslee Int'l Ltd
645 E Blithedale Ave
Mill Valley, CA 94941
(415) 389-7300
Fax: (415) 389-7302

Email: resumes@jblakslee.com

Description: Senior-level retained executive search to the pharmaceutical, biotechnology and medical device/instrument industry and international capability.

Key Contact - Specialty:
Mr. Jan H. Blakslee, President - *Medical device, pharmaceutical, biotechnology*
Ms. Joyce Mustin, Partner - *Medical device, pharmaceutical, biotechnology*

Salary minimum: $125,000

Functions: Generalist, Directors, Senior Mgmt., Product Dev., Mktg. Mgmt., CFO's, R&D, Engineering

Industries: Generalist, Drugs Mfg., Medical Devices, Biotech, Healthcare

Professional Associations: IACPR, HRPS

Blaney Executive Search
Damonmill Sq
Concord, MA 01742
(978) 371-2192
(978) 371-2193
Email: jblaney@blaneyinc.com
Web: www.blaneyinc.com

Description: Firm specializing in the placement of key individuals in high technology organizations involved in the computer hardware, software and networking/communications fields. We offer our clients a highly professional, customized approach to the search process which results in filling the position with the best possible candidate within a very reasonable time frame.

Key Contact - Specialty:
Mr. John A. Blaney, President - *Marketing & sales vice presidents, engineering vice presidents, CEOs, COOs*

Salary minimum: $150,000

Functions: Senior Mgmt., Sales Mgmt., CFO's, MIS Mgmt., Engineering

Industries: Generalist, Mfg., Software, Biotech

Blau Mancino Associates
12 Roszel Rd Ste C-101
Princeton, NJ 08540
(609) 520-8400
Fax: (609) 520-8993
Email: bma@blaumancino.com
Web: www.blaumancino.com

Description: We provide retained executive search services for the life sciences industry, including pharmaceuticals, biotechnology, medical device, diagnostics and healthcare services. Clients include major and developing corporations in North America.

Key Contact - Specialty:
Mr. Gene Mancino, President - *Bio pharmaceuticals*
Mr. Paul Edgerton, Senior Vice President - *Medical technology*

Salary minimum: $150,000

Functions: General Mgmt., Directors, Senior Mgmt., Materials, Sales & Mktg., Mktg. Mgmt., HR Mgmt., CFO's, M&A, IT

Industries: Drugs Mfg., Medical Devices, Venture Cap., Pharm Svcs., Biotech, Healthcare

Branches:
1303 Rogers Rd Ste 9
Annapolis, MD 21401
(410) 349-1992
Fax: (410) 349-4505
Email: lori@blaumancino.com
Key Contact:
Ms. Lori Berninger, VP

16 N Franklin St Ste 302
Doylestown, PA 18901
(215) 230-8999
Email: paul@blaumancino.com
Key Contact - Specialty:
Mr. Paul Edgerton, Practice Leader - *Medical technology*

Blue Garni & Company
PO Box 2973
Sausalito, CA 94966
(415) 332-1119
Email: pblue@bluegarni.com

Description: Our firm is a retained executive search firm that focuses on general management and senior financial management searches, as well as positions requiring sophisticated analytical, planning, and operational skills. Our client industries include airport planning and consulting, capital equipment lease financing, and equipment management, financial and professional services, management consulting, project and energy finance, manufacturing, and transportation services.

Key Contact:
Mr. Donald Garni, Partner
Ms. Patricia Blue, Partner

Functions: Finance

Industries: Transportation, Finance, Invest. Banking, Misc. Financial, Services, Mgmt. Consulting, New Media

Blum & Company
1412 N Lapham St
Oconomowoc, WI 53066
(262) 569-8853
Fax: (262) 569-8876

Description: A dedicated firm offering flexible, personalized service. Our reputation is built on experience, confidentiality, integrity and professionalism. Our unique fee schedule limits your exposure and assures results.

Key Contact:
Mr. D. L. Buzz Blum, President

Salary minimum: $50,000

Functions: Generalist

Industries: Generalist

Blumenthal-Hart
195 N Harbor Dr Ste 2902
Chicago, IL 60601
(312) 946-1930
Fax: (312) 946-1928
Email: resumes@blumenthal-hart.com
Web: www.blumenthal-hart.com

Description: We are a generalist firm specializing in mid-to-senior-level searches with an emphasis in nonprofit, associations, and higher education. We work closely with our clients to determine the skills, experience, education, style, and other characteristics the ideal candidate needs to be successful.

Key Contact - Specialty:
Ms. Joan H. Blumenthal, Principal - *Generalist*

Salary minimum: $70,000

Functions: Generalist, General Mgmt., Admin. Svcs., Sales & Mktg.

Industries: Generalist, Mfg., Banking, Misc. Financial, Services, Non-profits, Higher Ed., Legal, Accounting, Mgmt. Consulting, HR Services

Professional Associations: IACPR, AFC, AFP, CASE

BMA Int'l†
1115 Sherbrooke W Ste 2405
Montreal, QC H3A 1H3
Canada
(514) 287-9033
Fax: (514) 285-1890

Description: Retained search firm specializing mostly in the placement of highly trained scientists and engineers as well as certain mandates for CEOs and computer personnel.

Key Contact - Specialty:
Ms. Micheline Brunet, President - *General management*
Dr. Jean-Bernard Fabre, Vice President-Research - *Scientists, research development*
Mr. Dean McDougall, Vice President-Research - *Engineering, information technology, scientists*

Salary minimum: $50,000

Functions: Generalist, Senior Mgmt., Advertising, Finance, Systems Analysis, Systems Support, R&D, Engineering

Industries: Generalist, Mfg., Finance, Media, Aerospace, Software

BMF Reynolds Inc
PO Box 157
Somerville, NJ 08876
(908) 371-1760
Fax: (908) 371-1736
Email: inquiry@bmfr.com
Web: www.bmfr.com

Description: The practice focuses on senior management positions, both line and staff, in major industries: utilities, pharmaceutical, medical devices, electronics, diagnostics, chemical and allied manufacturing and services. Professional staff averages 20 years' executive search experience.

Key Contact - Specialty:
Dr. John H. Reynolds - *Pharmaceuticals, nuclear utilities, engineering*
Mr. Bernard J. Ryan - *Finance*

Salary minimum: $120,000

Functions: General Mgmt., Mfg., Sales & Mktg., HR Mgmt., Finance, R&D, Engineering

Industries: Energy, Utilities, Chemicals, Drugs Mfg., Medical Devices, Metal Products, Biotech

Boardroom Consultants
250-38 Thornhill Ave
Little Neck Hills, NY 11362
(212) 328-0440
Fax: (212) 328-0441
Email: info@boardroomconsultants.com
Web: www.boardroomconsultants.com

Description: We are a generalist firm, which recruits senior-level management for all industries. In addition, we specialize in the recruitment of corporate board directors and advisory board members through Boardroom Consultants. Our practice is national in scope and currently includes six executive recruiters based in New York.

Key Contact:
Mr. Roger M. Kenny - *Consumer, high technology, healthcare, heavy manufacturing, board director*
Mr. Peter A. Kindler - *Finance, information technology, board governance*
Mr. William E. Tholke - *High technology, insurance, healthcare, general management, board directors*
Mr. John A. Coleman - *Generalist, financial services*
Mr. Peter W. Eldredge - *Publishing, media, telecommunications*
Ms. Sarah Stewart - *Board director*
Ms. Christine Clark, Consultant
Mr. George Fleck, Consultant
Ms. Jane D. James, Consultant

Ms. Amy S. Lamaker, Consultant

Salary minimum: $175,000

Functions: Generalist, Directors, Senior Mgmt., CFO's, MIS Mgmt., Engineering, Mgmt. Consultants

Industries: Generalist, Motor Vehicles, Finance, Mgmt. Consulting, Media, Healthcare

Professional Associations: AESC, IACPR, NACD

Paul Bodner & Associates Inc
501 S Rancho Dr Ste I-62
Las Vegas, NV 89106
(702) 386-9007
Fax: (702) 386-9016
Email: psbodner@lvcm.com

Description: Our mission is to find that unique person who has the talent and expertise required by our client, but who also matches their values and culture.

Key Contact - Specialty:
Mr. Paul Bodner, President - *Healthcare systems*
Mr. Roy Barraclough, Senior Director - *Practice managers*

Salary minimum: $60,000

Functions: Generalist, Senior Mgmt., Middle Mgmt., Physicians, Sales Mgmt., Training

Industries: Generalist, Healthcare

Professional Associations: NAHHS, NAPR, SNHRA

Branches:
1011 S Valentia St
Denver, CO 80231
(303) 369-0566
Fax: (303) 369-7310
Email: phylblan@aol.com
Key Contact - Specialty:
Ms. Phyllis Vajda, Senior Director - *Physicians, healthcare management, sales & marketing*

Boettcher Associates
120 Bishops Way Ste 126
Brookfield, WI 53005
(262) 782-2205

Description: National generalist executive search firm in all functions in all industries and management consulting in human resource areas including outplacement.

Key Contact - Specialty:
Mr. Jack W. Boettcher, President - *Generalist*

Salary minimum: $50,000

Functions: Generalist, General Mgmt., Mfg., Materials, Sales & Mktg., HR Mgmt., Finance

Industries: Generalist, Metal Products, Machine, Appliance, Transportation, HR Services, Software

Professional Associations: IRRA

Bonell Ryan Inc
630 5th Ave Ste 2607
Rockefeller Center
New York, NY 10111
(212) 332-3340
Fax: (212) 332-3335
Email: info@bonellryan.com
Web: www.bonellryan.com

Description: Executive and middle management search in financial services and ecommerce.

Key Contact:
Ms. Debra Ryan, President

Salary minimum: $150,000

Functions: General Mgmt., Senior Mgmt., Sales & Mktg., Mkt. Research, Mktg. Mgmt., Sales Mgmt., Direct Mktg., Finance, CFO's, Credit

Industries: Banking, Venture Cap., New Media, Telecoms

Bonnell Associates Ltd
2960 Post Rd Ste 200
Southport, CT 06490
(203) 319-7214
Fax: (203) 319-7219
Email: info@bonnellassociates.com
Web: www.bonnellassociates.com

Description: Retained executive search firm offering focus on organizations which are rebuilding/turnaround, startups and dynamic growth environments. Industry experience includes concentration in financial services, healthcare, insurance, telecommunications, airline, banking, hospitality and non-profit. Significant international experience.

Key Contact - Specialty:
Mr. William R. Bonnell, President - *Financial services, media & publishing, managed care, healthcare, finance*
Ms. Linda Buggy, Executive Search Consultant - *Customer service, diversity, healthcare, managed care*

Salary minimum: $100,000

Functions: Generalist

Industries: Finance, Services, Publishing, New Media, Telecoms, Insurance, Software, Biotech, Healthcare

Professional Associations: IACPR, BACC, ESRT, SACIA

Bonner/Menard Int'l
59 E Mill Rd
PO Box 15
Long Valley, NJ 07853
(908) 876-5200
Fax: (908) 876-9275
Email: bonnergroup@worldnet.att.net
Web: www.bonnergroup.com

Description: Retained executive search services for senior-level management, technical, and professional positions in the pharmaceutical and biotechnology industries.

Key Contact:
Mr. Bernard J. Bonner, Partner

Salary minimum: $100,000

Functions: Generalist

Industries: Chemicals, Drugs Mfg., Medical Devices, Biotech

Professional Associations: AAPS, ISPE, PDA, SHRM

Branches:
292 Washington Ave Ext
Albany, NY 12203
(518) 862-9814
Key Contact:
Mr. J. Kirk Menard, Partner

John C Boone & Company
1807 Henley St
Glenview, IL 60025
(847) 998-1905

Description: Over 20 years' executive search experience in multi-disciplines and diverse industries.

Key Contact - Specialty:
Mr. John C. Boone - *Generalist*
Mr. Edward R. Youngman - *Generalist*

Salary minimum: $75,000

Functions: Generalist

Industries: Generalist

The Borton Wallace Company
PO Box 8816
Asheville, NC 28814
(828) 258-1831
Fax: (828) 251-0989
Email: info@bwsearch.com
Web: www.bortonwallace.com

Description: Most functions within pulp & paper, consumer product, polymeric, nonwoven and vertically integrated industries. Executive search, organizational development and staffing consulting services to most manufacturing industries.

Key Contact - Specialty:
Mr. Murray B. Parker, President - *Pulp & paper*

Salary minimum: $60,000

Functions: Generalist

Industries: Energy, Utilities, Mfg., Paper, Printing, Chemicals, Drugs Mfg., Medical Devices, Plastics, Rubber, Haz. Waste, Packaging

Professional Associations: NAER, TAPPI

Bosch & Associates LLC
PO Box 1030
Greens Farms, CT 06436
(203) 255-8700
Fax: (203) 259-4959
Email: ebosch@sprintmail.com
Web: www.boschllc.com

Description: According to client and candidate executive search surveys that we are the best search firm used. Our placement retention rates are some of the best in our industry. We subscribe to a proven executive search methodology, consistently delivering to our clients executives of superior performance. We are extremely well networked in our chosen industries and functional areas.

Key Contact - Specialty:
Mr. Eric E. Bosch, President - *Sales, marketing, finance, general management, human resources*
Mr. Brian Gardner - *Sales, business development, marketing, call center operations, public relations*
Ms. Diane Bosch, Vice President - *General management, sales management, marketing, strategic planning*
Ms. Patricia A. Spodnick - *Human resources, product marketing, finance, sales*
Mr. Kevin Hallock - *Human resources, finance, call center (operations, sales)*
Ms. Amy Matthews - *Marketing communications, advertising, & sales*

Salary minimum: $80,000

Functions: General Mgmt., Product Dev., Sales & Mktg., HR Mgmt., Finance, Mgmt. Consultants, Minorities, Int'l.

Industries: Food, Bev., Tobacco, Drugs Mfg., Computer Equip., Consumer Elect., Pharm Svcs., Equip Svcs., Mgmt. Consulting, HR Services, Advertising, Publishing, New Media, Telecoms, Software, Non-classifiable

Professional Associations: IABC

Bosland Gray Assoc
2001 Rte 46 Ste 310
Waterview Plz
Parsippany, NJ 07054
(973) 402-4964
Email: agray@boslandgray.com

Description: Fee fixed at beginning of search; proven expertise within technical and specialized areas; each assignment commands the direct and personal attention of one of the firm's principals.

Key Contact:
Mr. Andrew Gray, Managing Director
Mr. Richard Bosland, Managing Director

Salary minimum: $80,000

Functions: Generalist

Industries: Generalist, Mfg., Chemicals, Drugs Mfg., Consumer Elect., Retail, Mgmt. Consulting

Boston Search Group Inc[†]
224 Clarendon St Ste 41
Boston, MA 02116-3729
(617) 266-4333
Fax: (781) 735-0562
Email: rprotsik@bsgweb.com
Web: www.bsgweb.com

Description: Our firm is a national leader in retained executive search within the broad fields of Internet content, commerce, community, enabling technologies, solutions, and services. The company specializes in providing leaders for startups, and it does so with a keen appreciation for the unique requirements of pre-IPO companies. Our principals have been engaged to fill more than 100 senior-management searches in the Internet and related fields, since our inception.

Key Contact:
Mr. Ralph Protsik, Co-Founder/Managing Director - *E-learning, e-commerce*
Mr. Clark Waterfall, Co-Founder/Managing Director - *Internet infrastructure, applications, eCommerce*
Mr. Alexander Platt, Vice President, Client Services

Salary minimum: $120,000

Functions: Senior Mgmt.

Industries: Higher Ed., Publishing, New Media, Software

Professional Associations: MECA, MIMC, MITEF, PINNACLE

Boulware & Associates Inc
175 W Jackson Blvd Ste 1841
Chicago, IL 60604
(312) 322-0088
Fax: (312) 322-0092
Email: info@boulwareinc.com
Web: www.boulwareinc.com

Description: A national retained executive search firm doing work in the private, not-for-profit and public sectors. Our work ranges from recruiting senior executives in major corporations to serving executive directors, governors and mayors.

Key Contact:
Ms. Christine Boulware, President - *Public, non-profit, private sector senior management*
Mr. David Erickson-Pearson, Vice President - *Transportation, economic development, human services, non-profit, real estate*
Ms. Marian Alexander deBerry, Vice President - *Human resources, financial services, transportation, senior nonprofit management, inclusion*
Mr. Stephen Sewall, Ph.D., Director of Marketing and Research
Ms. Sia Moody, Research Associate
Mr. Jason Raad, Research Associate
Mr. Marguerite McEnery, Research Associate

Salary minimum: $75,000

Functions: General Mgmt., HR Mgmt., CFO's, Minorities, Non-profits

Industries: Generalist, Transportation, Retail, Finance, Banking, Services, Non-profits, Mgmt. Consulting, Government

Professional Associations: AFP, APTA, ASTD, NCCED, SHRM

Branches:
729 E Phillips Dr S
Littleton, CO 80122
(303) 703-6165
Fax: (303) 703-8144
Email: davidep@boulwareinc.com

Key Contact - Specialty:
Mr. David Erickson-Pearson, Vice President of Sales - *Development (community, economic)*

Bowman & Associates[†]
1660 S Amphlett Blvd Ste 245
San Mateo, CA 94402
(650) 573-0188
Fax: (650) 573-8209
Email: contact@bowmansearch.com
Web: www.bowmansearch.com

Description: Staffed by senior professionals completing middle and senior-level management assignments exclusively for hospitality and leisure industry employers. Primarily retained assignments, both domestic and international.

Key Contact - Specialty:
Mr. Daniel P. Bowman, Managing Partner - *Senior leisure time industry*
Mr. Rion J. Moran, Vice President - *Leisure time industry*

Salary minimum: $50,000

Functions: Generalist

Industries: Hospitality

Bowman & Associates Inc
PO Box 450149
Atlanta, GA 31145
(404) 329-9314
Fax: (404) 320-3114
Email: admin@bowmanassociates.com
Web: www.bowmanassociates.com

Description: Specialize in venture-funded start-up companies in medical devices, diagnostics and biotechnology.

Key Contact - Specialty:
Ms. Mary Bowman, President - *Start-up companies (venture funded), medical devices, diagnostics, biotechnology*
Ms. Diane Westmore, Vice President - *Start-up companies (venture funded), medical devices, diagnostics, biotechnology*
Ms. Louise Sawhill, Partner - *Start-up companies (venture funded), medical devices, diagnostics, biotechnology*

Salary minimum: $90,000

Functions: Senior Mgmt.

Industries: Medical Devices, Biotech, Healthcare

Boyce Cunnane Inc
PO Box 19064
Baltimore, MD 21284-9064
(410) 583-5511
Email: bc@cunnane.com
Web: www.cunnane.com

Description: Our firm specializes exclusively in recruiting mid- and upper-level tax professionals for CPA firms, corporations, and law firms. Our searches have targeted lawyers, accountants, and economists in all tax specialties: compliance, research & planning, IRS audit, employee benefits, personal financial planning, state & local, international, (including transfer pricing, customs, international assignment tax services, and multi-lingual tax consultants).

Key Contact:
Mr. William Cunnane

Salary minimum: $75,000

Functions: Taxes

Industries: Generalist, Construction, Mfg., Finance, Services, Hospitality, Media, Insurance, Software, Healthcare

Professional Associations: AICPA, PICPA

Boyden

364 Elwood Ave
Hawthorne, NY 10532-1217
(914) 747-0093
Fax: (914) 747-0108
Web: www.boyden.com

Description: We have a tradition of providing personalized, high-quality service around the globe, which means you get the benefit of global commitment as well as adaptations by our local offices to your individual needs and requirements.

Key Contact:
Mr. Christopher Clarke, President

Salary minimum: $100,000

Functions: Generalist

Industries: Generalist

Professional Associations: AESC, IACPR

Branches:
2111 E Highland Ave Ste 145
Phoenix, AZ 85016
(602) 224-5500
Email: i-murro@boyden.com
Key Contact:
Ms. Ingrid Murro Botero, Managing Director

275 Battery St Ste 420
Embarcadero Ctr W Twr
San Francisco, CA 94111
(415) 981-7900
Fax: (415) 981-0644
Email: boyden@boydensf.com
Key Contact:
Mr. Frederick J. Greene, Chairman
Mr. Robert Concannon, II, Managing Director
Mr. Putney Westerfield, Managing Director
Mr. Ronald Goerss, Managing Director
Mr. Timothy Jones, Vice President

5201 Blue Lagoon Dr Penthouse
Miami, FL 33126
(305) 476-1200
Fax: (305) 447-9879
Email: alan.griffin@boyden.com
Key Contact:
Mr. Alan Griffin, Managing Partner

3525 Piedmont Rd Ste 202
5 Piedmont Ctr
Atlanta, GA 30305
(404) 995-1700
Email: bill.leslie@boyden.com
Key Contact:
Mr. William Leslie, Partner
Dr. Eike Jordan, Partner
Ms. Marcia Champagne, Partner
Mr. Richard C. Reagan, Partner

180 N Stetson Ave Ste 2500
2 Prudential Plz
Chicago, IL 60601
(312) 565-1300
Fax: (312) 565-2117
Email: alicia@boydenchi.com
Key Contact:
Mr. Richard A. McCallister, Managing Director
Ms. Janet L. Fischer, Partner
Ms. Trina D. Gordon, Partner
Mr. John S. Gude, Partner
Ms. Barbara Byster, Associate
Mr. Steven Jablo, Partner
Ms. Trisha Hutchinson, Research Director
Mr. Nicholaas Van Hevelingen, Partner

217 E Redwood St Ste 1600
Baltimore, MD 21202
(410) 625-3800
Fax: (410) 625-3801
Email: stacy.cook@boyden.com
Key Contact:
Mr. Martin Knott, Principal
Mr. Dale Legal, Managing Director
Mr. Timothy McNamara, Managing Director
Mr. Rayburn Hanzlik, Principal
Mr. Lance Wright, Vice President

300 E Long Lk Ste 375
Bloomfield Hills, MI 48304
(248) 647-4201
Fax: (248) 647-4301
Email: boyden@mich.com
Key Contact:
Mr. John Slosar, Director/Managing Director
Mr. Peter Viall, Senior Vice President
Mr. Scott Cameron, Senior Vice President
Ms. Joan Milligan, Senior Vice President
Mr. Lawrence Pilon, SVP/Managing Director

1390 Timberlake Manor Pkwy Ste 260
Chesterfield, MO 63017
(636) 519-7400
Fax: (636) 519-7410
Email: bjk@boydenstl.com
Key Contact:
Mr. George Zamborsky, Managing Partner
Mr. William Tunney, Jr., Senior Partner
Mr. Howard W. Curtis, Consultant

33 Union Pl Fl 3
Summit, NJ 07901
(973) 267-0980
Fax: (973) 267-6172
Email: gail.daurelio@boyden.com
Key Contact - Specialty:
Mr. Carlyle Newell, Managing Director - *CEO's, general managers, senior management positions*
Mr. Hanson Grant, Associate - *Healthcare, pharmaceuticals, medical, transportant, building products*
Mr. Arthur Perkins, Senior Consultant - *Sales & marketing, R&D, manufacturing management, purchasing, logistics*
Ms. Jennifer Medick-Siler, Director - *Human resource, financial services, services, consumer goods industries*
Ms. Gail D'Aurelio, Director of Research - *Generalist*

3012 Fairmount Blvd
Cleveland, OH 44118
(216) 932-4164
Fax: (216) 932-4164
Email: dan.carney@boyden.com
Key Contact:
Mr. Daniel Carney, Managing Director

221 7th St Ste 302
Pittsburgh, PA 15238-3206
(412) 820-7559
Fax: (412) 820-7572
Email: pittsburgh@boyden.com
Key Contact:
Mr. Thomas T. Flannery, Managing Director - *Generalist, domestic, international*
Mr. E. Wade Close, Jr., Managing Director - *Metals, manufacturing, automotive*
Mr. Thomas Cramer, Managing Director
Mr. Donal Kirwan, Associate
Mr. Cal Douglas, Associate - *Non-profit*
Ms. Stacey M. Holland, Associate

5847 San Felipe Ste 3940
Houston, TX 77057
(713) 655-0123
Fax: (713) 655-0107
Email: info@boydenhou.com
Key Contact:
Mr. Thomas C. Zay, Jr., Managing Director
Mr. James N. J. Hertlein, Partner
Mr. Charlie Rhoads, Partner
Ms. Cheryl Smith, Partner

145, 601 - 10th Ave SW
Calgary, AB T2R 0B2
Canada
(403) 237-6603
Fax: (403) 237-5551
Email: calgary@boyden.ca
Key Contact:
Mr. Robert Travis, Consultant

1250 boul Rene-Levesque Ouest
Bureau 4110
Montreal, QC H3B 4W8
Canada
(514) 935-4560
Fax: (514) 935-4530
Email: montreal@boyden.ca
Key Contact:
Mr. Paul J. Bourbeau, Managing Partner
Mr. Jean-Guy Duchaine, Associate

Boyle & Associates Retained Search Corp

238 Chester St Ste 200
St. Paul, MN 55107
(651) 223-5050
Fax: (651) 297-6286
Email: prboyle@aol.com
Web: www.talenthunt.com

Description: We specialize in finding and securing the best fit for your company's needs through a disciplined retained search process. We provide direct recruiting from an agreed upon list of "source" or "target" companies. We work for our client companies to draw "the best of the doers" to your firm.

Key Contact - Specialty:
Mr. Paul R. Boyle, President - *Management (upper), generalist*

Salary minimum: $65,000

Functions: Generalist, Quality, Materials Plng., Distribution, Mktg. Mgmt., CFO's, Network Admin., Engineering

Industries: Generalist, Agri., Forestry, Mining, Construction, Mfg., Transportation, Services, Media

Professional Associations: MAPS, NAPS

Boyle Ogata Bregman

18301 Von Karman Ave Ste 810
Irvine, CA 92612
(949) 474-0115
Fax: (949) 474-2204
Email: info@bobsearch.com
Web: www.bobsearch.com

Description: We increase employer profits with each executive hire. Our state-of-the-art Performance-Based Search System, identifies top candidates based on ability to produce specific, tangible, measurable results that will impact your bottom line; and, provides the new executive with a business plan containing critical objectives, and an evaluation methodology for the employer.

Key Contact - Specialty:
Mr. Michael Boyle, Principal - *Aerospace, high technology, semiconductor, telecommunications, venture capital (all management functions)*
Mr. Keith Ogata, Principal - *Aerospace, medical devices, pharmaceuticals, manufacturing management, satellites*
Mr. Mark Bregman, Principal - *Executive search (all functions) manufacturing, wholesale, computer equipment, software, e-commerce*

Salary minimum: $80,000

Functions: Generalist

Industries: Generalist, Mfg., Transportation, Wholesale, Services, Media, Communications, Aerospace, Software, Biotech

Professional Associations: ACM, ASQ, BMA, CTIA, ICF, IEEE, IOM, NBAA, RAPS, SAE, SHRM

The Bradbury Management Group Inc

2112 Vizcaya Way
Campbell, CA 95008
(408) 377-5400
Fax: (408) 377-1112

Email: pwbradbury@aol.com

Description: We are known for being very responsive, thorough, and very successful identifying and attracting presidents and "All the president's men" for a variety of high-technology clients. Industries include: microcomputer, peripheral, software,(including Internet), semiconductor and semiconductor equipment, biomedical, telecommunications and environmental.

Key Contact - Specialty:
Mr. Paul W. Bradbury, Jr., Managing Principal - *High technology, upper management*

Salary minimum: $100,000

Functions: General Mgmt., Directors, Int'l.

Industries: Mfg., Computer Equip., Consumer Elect., Test, Measure Equip., Venture Cap., Mgmt. Consulting, HR Services, Telecoms, Haz. Waste, Software, Biotech

Professional Associations: IACPR, EMA, SEMI, SHRM

J T Brady & Associates
10900 Perry Hwy
#12203
Wexford, PA 15090
(412) 934-2228
Fax: (724) 935-8059
Email: jtbrady@nauticom.net
Web: www.jtbrady.net

Description: Created to provide a more cost effective, personalized and timely solution to address clients recruiting needs. We offer a full-service comprehensive process custom tailored for each client.

Key Contact - Specialty:
Mr. Jack Brady, President - *Sales, marketing, operations, client service, human resources*

Salary minimum: $60,000

Functions: Sales & Mktg., Direct Mktg.

Industries: Paper, Printing, Drugs Mfg., Banking, Advertising, Publishing, New Media, Broadcast, Film

Professional Associations: PHRA

Brady Associates Int'l Inc
PO Box 1892
New York, NY 10021
(212) 396-4950

Description: Executive search consultant for the diversified utility and financial services industries.

Key Contact - Specialty:
Ms. Susan E. Harbers, President - *Senior management, middle management, energy, financial services*

Salary minimum: $50,000

Functions: Generalist, General Mgmt., Directors, Senior Mgmt., Middle Mgmt., Sales & Mktg., Finance, IT

Industries: Generalist, Energy, Utilities, Finance

Professional Associations: NYSSA

The Brand Company Inc
181 Shores Dr
Vero Beach, FL 32963
(561) 231-1807
Email: brandinc@earthlink.net
Web: www.home.earthlink.net/~brandinc/

Description: Responsive and personalized client focus on senior-level searches for board directors, general management executives, functional heads and critical technology specialists. Generalist practice with particular experience in manufacturing, distribution and service businesses.

Key Contact - Specialty:
Mr. J. Brand Spangenberg, Chairman - *Senior management, high technology, operations, technical, marketing*

Salary minimum: $75,000

Functions: Generalist, Senior Mgmt., Plant Mgmt., Mktg. Mgmt., Sales Mgmt., HR Mgmt., CFO's, Engineering

Industries: Generalist, Energy, Utilities, Metal Products, Machine, Appliance, Misc. Mfg., Packaging

Brandywine Consulting Group
5 Great Valley Pkwy Ste 322
Malvern, PA 19355
(610) 407-4600
Email: brancon1@aol.com

Description: Broad-based practice with some specialization in chemical process, pulp & paper, packaging, pharmaceuticals and consumer products. Senior-level retained assignments, include behavioral-based interview design and psychological assessment. Minimum compensation cutoff of $70,000.

Key Contact:
Mr. Richard H. Beatty

Salary minimum: $70,000

Functions: Generalist, Directors, Senior Mgmt., Middle Mgmt., Production, Plant Mgmt., Mktg. Mgmt., Sales Mgmt.

Industries: Generalist, Paper, Drugs Mfg., Medical Devices, Pharm Svcs., Healthcare

Professional Associations: EMA, HRPS, SHRM

Brandywine Management Group
8 Drawbridge Rd
Berlin, MD 21811
(410) 208-9791
Fax: (410) 208-9792

Description: Retained search, consulting and outplacement firm engaged in technical, general, senior-level management practices.

Key Contact:
Mr. Jeffrey A. Morse, President - *Pulp & paper, healthcare, technical, senior level executives*
Mr. Stewart Schwartz - *Technical research*
Mr. F. William Gaw - *Pulp & paper, technical*
Ms. Patty Grady

Salary minimum: $55,000

Functions: Generalist, Senior Mgmt., Production, Plant Mgmt., Packaging, Healthcare, Sales & Mktg., HR Mgmt.

Industries: Generalist, Lumber, Furniture, Chemicals, Drugs Mfg., Metal Products, Misc. Mfg., Healthcare

Professional Associations: ASTD, IOPP, PIMA, SHRM, TAPPI

Branches:
203 Morris Ave
Mountain Lakes, NJ 07046
(800) 860-8812
(973) 257-1828
Key Contact - Specialty:
Mrs. Sally Harrison - *Outplacement, senior level*

Branthover Associates
360 Lexington Ave Ste 1300
New York, NY 10017
(212) 949-9400
Fax: (212) 949-5905
Email: search@branassoc.com
Web: www.branthoverassociates.com

Description: A generalist search firm specializing in the placement of executives. Also offer research to clients such as organizational charts, consulting assignment, etc.

Key Contact:
Ms. Jeanne Branthover, CEO
Ms. Lisa Amore, Managing Director
Ms. Judy Brenner, Managing Director

Salary minimum: $100,000

Functions: Generalist

Industries: Generalist

Professional Associations: NAFE

Brault & Associates Ltd
18417 Lanier Island Sq
Leesburg, VA 20176
(703) 771-0200
Fax: (703) 771-0270
Email: jean-pierre@mindspring.com

Description: We are an executive search firm specializing in the high-technology industry and intelligence community, information technology and security, DOD and intelligence systems, systems engineering and integration, Internet, and network security.

Key Contact - Specialty:
Mr. Jean- Pierre Brault, President - *High technology, information technology*

Salary minimum: $125,000

Functions: Senior Mgmt., IT, MIS Mgmt., Int'l.

Industries: Generalist, Non-profits, Mgmt. Consulting, Defense, Software

The Bray Group
354 Brush Hill Rd
Milton, MA 02186
(617) 696-9594
Fax: (617) 696-9594
Email: bobbray@thebraygroup.com
Web: www.thebraygroup.com

Description: An executive search practice that focuses on serving financial services companies and non-profit organizations throughout the United States.

Key Contact:
Mr. Bob Bray, Partner

Salary minimum: $75,000

Functions: Generalist

Industries: Finance, Banking, Invest. Banking, Brokers, Venture Cap., Misc. Financial, Non-profits

The Brazik Group LLC[†]
1444 N Farnsworth Ave Ste 204
Aurora, IL 60505
(630) 820-0785
Fax: (630) 820-1126
Email: chuckbrazik@brazikgroup.com
Web: www.brazikgroup.com

Description: We are a retained executive search and consulting firm. We specialize in retail and wholesale with carefully selected consultants in marketing, operations, and human resources.

Key Contact:
Mr. Charles Brazik, President
Mr. Robert Mayer, Vice President

Salary minimum: $75,000

Functions: Generalist, Directors, Senior Mgmt., Production, Materials Plng., HR Mgmt., CFO's, MIS Mgmt.

Industries: Generalist, Mfg., Metal Products, Misc. Mfg., Wholesale, Retail, HR Services, IT Implementation

Professional Associations: SHRM

[†] occasional contingency assignments

Bredeson Executive Recruitment LLC

100 E Whitestone Blvd Ste 148
PMB 327
Cedar Park, TX 78613-6902
(512) 733-1736
Fax: (512) 733-5727
Email: bredeson@bredesonsearch.com
Web: www.bredesonsearch.com

Description: We are a retained search firm
providing talented and productive professionals to
our clients nationwide. Our expertise includes the
placement of mid to senior level executives
excelling in legal and management consulting
disciplines.

Key Contact - Specialty:
Ms. Sheri Bredeson, President - *Management
consulting, legal*
D. A. Bredeson, Esq. - *Legal*

Salary minimum: $120,000

Functions: Legal, IT, Mgmt. Consultants,
Attorneys

Industries: Generalist

Breitner Clark & Hall Inc

1017 Turnpike St Ste 22A
Canton, MA 02021
(781) 828-6411
Fax: (781) 828-6431
Email: info@breitner.com
Web: www.breitner.com

Description: Healthcare specialists concentrating on
permanent and temporary placement of physicians
and clinical leaders.

Key Contact:
Mr. Owen Breitner, COO

Salary minimum: $80,000

Functions: Physicians, Health Admin.

Industries: Healthcare, Hospitals, Long-term Care,
Dental, Physical Therapy, Occupational Therapy,
Women's

Brenner Executive Resources Inc

1212 Ave of the Americas Fl 3
New York, NY 10036
(212) 391-9119
Email: info@brennerresources.com
Web: www.brennerresources.com

Description: Principal serves clients in media and
entertainment, financial services and manufacturing.
He has extensive experience in handling searches in
information technology for CIOs and CTOs.

Key Contact - Specialty:
Mr. Michael Brenner, Chief Resource - *Consumer,
MIS, communications, media*

Salary minimum: $200,000

Functions: Senior Mgmt., IT, MIS Mgmt.

Industries: Generalist, New Media

Professional Associations: AESC, IACPR,
HRANY, SIM

The Brentwood Group Inc†

170 Kinnelon Rd Ste 7
Kinnelon, NJ 07405
(973) 283-1000
Fax: (973) 283-1220
Email: info@thebrentwoodgroup.com
Web: www.thebrentwoodgroup.com

Description: Our firm of 15 professionals provides
experience, consistency, quality, and results. We are
a cohesive team that understands, executes, and
actually fills your search.

Key Contact - Specialty:
Ms. Doris Banach-Osenni, President - *Management
consulting, direct marketing, financial services,
publishing, senior management*
Ms. Barbara Benkwitt, Vice President - *Chemical
insurance, pharmaceuticals, consulting,
information technology*
Ms. Kathy Sabio, Recruiter - *Management (mid to
senior), pharmaceuticals, communications,
advertising, investment banking*
Ms. Pat Pagana, Recruiter - *Engineering,
consulting, pharmaceuticals, publishing, travel*

Salary minimum: $50,000

Functions: Generalist

Industries: Energy, Utilities, Mfg., Retail, Finance,
Mgmt. Consulting, HR Services, IT
Implementation, Communications, Biotech,
Healthcare

Professional Associations: AAPS, ACS, DMA,
ESRT, IFMA, NSBE, PDA, RAPS, SAE, SHRM,
SLA

The Brentwood Group Ltd

9 Monroe Pkwy Ste 230
Lake Oswego, OR 97035
(503) 697-8136
Fax: (503) 697-8161
Email: contact@brentwoodgroup.com
Web: www.brentwoodgroup.com

Description: We are a results-driven search firm
exclusively dedicated to serving high technology
clients for senior executive requirements.

Key Contact:
Mr. Frank Moscow, President - *High technology,
senior management*
Mr. Lenny White, Director - *High technology,
middle management*
Ms. Ann Akins, Office Manager

Salary minimum: $100,000

Functions: Generalist, Directors, Senior Mgmt.,
Middle Mgmt., Product Dev., Plant Mgmt., Mktg.
Mgmt., CFO's

Industries: Computer Equip., Consumer Elect.,
Test, Measure Equip., Electronic, Elec.
Components, Venture Cap., Telecoms, Network
Infrastructure, Insurance, Software

Professional Associations: AEA, SAO

Networks: Int'l Network Assoc Consultants

Brentwood Int'l

9841 Airport Blvd Ste 420
Los Angeles, CA 90045
(310) 216-0033
Fax: (310) 338-5484
Email: postmaster@brentwoodintl.com

Description: Exclusively executive search
specializing in high-technology, aerospace, financial
services, manufacturing systems, engineering,
marketing and consumer products.

Key Contact - Specialty:
Mr. James Keenan, President - *Generalist*
Ms. Peggy Winston, Senior Consultant - *Human
resources, technology*
Ms. Marilyn Bennett, Senior Associate - *Marketing,
sales*
Ms. Linda Barr, Associate - *High technology*
Mr. Lawrence Broe, Managing Consultant - *High
technology, consumer products*
Ms. Cynthia Whittaker, Managing Consultant -
High technology, aerospace
Ms. Amanda Newhard, Consultant - *High
technology, aerospace*
Dr. Thomas Crooks, Managing Consultant -
Financial services
Mr. Ed Rardin, Consultant - *Manufacturing,
marketing*

Mr. Tom Simpson, Managing Consultant -
Technology marketing

Salary minimum: $75,000

Functions: Generalist, IT

Industries: Services, Mgmt. Consulting, HR
Services, IT Implementation, Digital, Wireless,
Aerospace, Software, Security SW, System SW

Martha Brest

40 Saint Botolph St 48
Boston, MA 02116
(617) 424-1067
Email: mbrest@tiac.net

Description: We specialize in search assignments
for marketing and corporate communications
executives, primarily in financial services, for
example: marketing management, brand
management, product management, product
development, direct marketing, marketing strategy
and consulting, corporate communications,
marketing communications, market research, public
relations, and media relations.

Key Contact:
Ms. Martha Brest, President

Salary minimum: $150,000

Functions: Product Dev., Sales & Mktg.,
Advertising, Mkt. Research, Mktg. Mgmt., Direct
Mktg., PR, Mgmt. Consultants

Industries: Finance, Accounting, Mgmt.
Consulting, Media, Advertising, New Media,
Telecoms, Insurance, Marketing SW

Briant Associates Inc

39 S LaSalle St Ste 714
Chicago, IL 60603
(312) 577-5640
Fax: (312) 577-5651
Email: info@briantassociates.com
Web: www.briantassociates.com

Description: We are a boutique firm specializing in
the consumer products, food, and industrial
manufacturing sectors. Our partners actively lead
each step of the recruitment process. Our specialties
are consultative methodology, emphasizing senior
sales, marketing, supply chain, manufacturing,
engineering, technical, and general management
functional areas

Key Contact - Specialty:
Mr. Rick Bingham, Partner - *Food industry,
industrial manufacturing*
Ms. Larissa Klavins, Partner - *Consumer products
industries (hardware, house wares), packaging,
electronic manufacturing services, miscellaneous
manufacturing*

Salary minimum: $75,000

Functions: Generalist, General Mgmt., Senior
Mgmt., Mfg., Plant Mgmt., Materials,
Distribution, Sales & Mktg., Engineering

Industries: Mfg., Food, Bev., Tobacco, Paints,
Petro. Products, Metal Products, Computer
Equip., Misc. Mfg., Electronic, Elec.
Components, Transportation, Communications,
Packaging

Professional Associations: APICS, ASBE, CLM,
IFT

BridgeGate LLC

18401 Von Karman Ave Ste 440
Irvine, CA 92612
(949) 553-9200
Email: info@bridgegate.com
Web: www.bridgegate.com

Description: We have defined the strategic
discipline of management search and build high
performance teams for emerging and established
companies. By supporting multiple specialties

within a single engagement, we provide a complete recruitment solution.

Key Contact - Specialty:
Mr. Dudley G. Brown, Managing Director - *High technology executive search*
Mr. Kevin Rosenberg, Managing Director - *High technology executive search*
Mr. Joel May, Managing Director - *High technology executive search*

Salary minimum: $100,000

Functions: Generalist, General Mgmt., Directors, Sales & Mktg., HR Mgmt., Finance, IT, Mgmt. Consultants

Industries: Generalist

Branches:
1230 Rosecrans Ste 110
Manhattan Beach, CA 90266
(310) 297-8700
Fax: (310) 297-8706
Email: info@bridgegate.com
Key Contact - Specialty:
Mr. Kevin M. Rosenberg, Managing Director - *Information technology*
Mr. Dudley Brown, Managing Director - *High technology executive search*
Mr. Joel May, Managing Director - *High technology executive search*

Brigham Hill Consultancy
2909 Cole Ave Ste 220
Dallas, TX 75204
(214) 871-8700
Fax: (214) 871-6004
Email: eldredge@brighamhill.com
Web: www.brighamhill.com

Description: Our firm provides retained executive search and related management consulting services by combining the rigorous search protocols of the business world with sensitivity to the unique mission of not-for-profits.

Key Contact - Specialty:
Mr. L. Lincoln Eldredge, President - *Not-for-profits, independent schools, executive directors*
Ms. Deborah Tunnell, Consultant - *Not-for-profits, human service agencies, development*
Ms. Kristina McMillen, Consultant - *Not-for-profits, development*

Salary minimum: $90,000

Functions: Generalist, Non-profits

Industries: Generalist, Non-profits, Higher Ed.

The Brimeyer Group Inc
50 S 9th Ave Ste 101
Hopkins, MN 55343
(952) 945-0246
Email: brimgroup@aol.com
Web: www.brimgroup.com

Description: We provide executive search for local government and non-profit clients. We provide management consulting services to select clients in the Midwest.

Key Contact - Specialty:
Mr. James Brimeyer, President - *Public sector, non-profit, club management*
Ms. Pam Wunderlich, Vice President - *Civil engineering, associations*

Salary minimum: $50,000

Functions: Generalist, Engineering

Industries: Generalist, Hospitality, Government

Professional Associations: MAPS

Brindisi Search
10751 Falls Rd Ste 250
Greenspring Station
Lutherville, MD 21093
(410) 339-7673
(410) 442-5887
Fax: (410) 823-0146
Email: tbrindisi@aol.com
Web: www.brindisisearch.com

Description: We provide innovative, results-focused search capabilities for human resource functions linked to business drivers. We assist cutting-edge corporations of all sizes to enhance their competitiveness by identifying high-impact, human resource and operational leaders.

Key Contact - Specialty:
Mr. Thomas J. Brindisi, President - *Human resources, change management, strategic planning, business development*

Salary minimum: $70,000

Functions: Senior Mgmt., Admin. Svcs., Productivity, PR, HR Mgmt., Benefits, Personnel, Training, M&A, Mgmt. Consultants

Industries: Generalist

Professional Associations: ASQ, ASTD, HRPS, MAPRC, SHRM

The Broadmoor Group LLC
5151 Beltline Rd Ste 715
Dallas, TX 75254
(972) 980-1960
Fax: (972) 980-1689
Email: rneal@thebroadmoorgroup.com
Web: www.thebroadmoorgroup.com

Description: A retained executive search firm specializing in the recruitment of senior management and executive-level professionals.

Key Contact:
Mr. Randall Neal, Sr Vice President/Managing Director
Mr. James Leverette, Senior Vice President
Mr. Donald Tuttle, President
Terry Boles, Senior Vice President

Salary minimum: $100,000

Functions: Generalist

Industries: Energy, Utilities, Mfg., Motor Vehicles, Computer Equip., Test, Measure Equip., Venture Cap., Mgmt. Consulting, Telecoms, Aerospace, Software

Brooke Chase Associates Inc
1800 Ravinia Pl
Orland Park, IL 60462
(708) 873-0033
Fax: (708) 873-9993
Email: brookechase@brookechase.com
Web: www.brookechase.com

Description: We are specialists in the recruitment of sales, marketing, manufacturing, operations, and general management professionals within the hardware, building materials, lawn and garden, automotive, plumbing, kitchen and bath, and packaging industries.

Key Contact - Specialty:
Mr. Joseph J. McElmeel, President - *Sales, marketing, general management*

Salary minimum: $50,000

Functions: Generalist, Senior Mgmt., Middle Mgmt., Plant Mgmt., Quality, Mkt. Research, Mktg. Mgmt., Sales Mgmt.

Industries: Generalist, Lumber, Furniture, Paper, Plastics, Rubber, Paints, Petro. Products, Metal Products, Consumer Elect., Packaging

Professional Associations: ECC, JAS, NAER

Branches:
209 W Second Ave
Gastonia, NC 28052
(704) 852-4050
Fax: (704) 852-9220
Web: www.hsharpe@brookechase.com
Key Contact - Specialty:
Mr. Howard Sharpe, President - *Kitchen & bath, building materials, hardware, lawn & garden, plumbing*

Bernard E Brooks & Associates Inc
PO Box 1861
Spartanburg, SC 29304-1861
(864) 415-0330
Fax: (864) 574-0472
Email: bebrooks2@cs.com

Description: Retained executive search firm with strong record of success recruiting for higher education, healthcare and not-for-profit organizations. Excellent record in diversity recruiting.

Key Contact - Specialty:
Mr. Bernard E. Brooks, President - *Generalist*

Salary minimum: $75,000

Functions: General Mgmt.

Industries: Food, Bev., Tobacco, Computer Equip., Consumer Elect., Finance, Services, Telecoms, Haz. Waste, Software, Healthcare

Brown Venture Associates Inc
3000 Sand Hill Rd Bldg 3 Ste 110
Menlo Park, CA 94025
(650) 233-0205
Fax: (650) 233-1902
Email: info@bva.com
Web: www.bva.com

Description: Retained search firm specializing in CEO and vice president searches for venture backed companies. We also recruit venture capital general partners and consult with v.c. partnerships and boards.

Key Contact - Specialty:
Mr. Jerry Brown, President - *CEO, VC general partners*
Mr. Dan Lankford, Partner - *Board level consulting*

Salary minimum: $200,000

Functions: Senior Mgmt., Mktg. Mgmt., Sales Mgmt., Engineering

Industries: Software

Brownson & Associates Inc
5599 San Felipe Ste 610
Houston, TX 77056
(713) 626-4790
Fax: (713) 877-1745
Email: bbrown3848@aol.com
Web: www.brownson.com

Description: We are a retained executive search firm engaged in a general practice with significant experience in energy, energy services, manufacturing, engineering and construction, chemical, petrochemical, environmental, law, retail, financial services, consumer goods industries and service industries

Key Contact - Specialty:
Mr. Bruce Brownson, Managing Director - *Chemical, energy, environmental, finance, manufacturing*
Ms. Carolyn Cherry Carter, Managing Associate - *Consumer, chemical, generalist*
Ms. Christina Brownson, Senior Associate - *Generalist*
Mr. Steve Mims, Vice President - *Legal, general*

Salary minimum: $75,000

Functions: Generalist

Industries: Energy, Utilities, Construction, Mfg., Wholesale, Retail, Finance, Services, Packaging, Insurance, Software

Brush Creek Partners
521 SE 2nd St Ste C
Lees Summit, MO 64063
(816) 554-2500
Fax: (816) 554-8390
Email: jlunn@brushcreekpartners.com

Description: We conduct senior level searches, serving a wide variety of client needs. Our client base ranges from small privately owned businesses to Fortune 100 multinationals in virtually all major industry sectors. Our approach to strategy development, candidate sourcing, and screening has enabled us to remain client centered versus industry specific.

Key Contact - Specialty:
Mr. Jerry D. Lunn, President/CEO - *Generalist*

Salary minimum: $100,000

Functions: Generalist, Senior Mgmt., Sales & Mktg., HR Mgmt., CFO's, MIS Mgmt., R&D

Industries: Generalist, Chemicals, Computer Equip., Misc. Mfg., Finance, Telecoms, Biotech

BTS Executive Search & Services LLC
6 Landmark Sq Fl 4
Stamford, CT 06901
(203) 855-9212
Email: range@btssearch.com
Web: www.btssearch.com

Description: Dedicated to a highly personalized, quality approach to search. As former practitioners, we understand client requirements at a level that is unparalleled.

Key Contact - Specialty:
Ms. Mary Jane Range, President - *Information technology, e-business*
Mr. Andre Block, Vice President - *Generalist, information technology*
Mr. Joe Donia, Vice President - *Information technology, sales & marketing*

Salary minimum: $150,000

Functions: Senior Mgmt., Middle Mgmt., Mktg. Mgmt., CFO's, MIS Mgmt., Systems Implem., Mgmt. Consultants

Industries: Generalist, Computer Equip., Finance, Banking, Misc. Financial, Mgmt. Consulting, New Media, Telecoms, Software

Professional Associations: SHRM

Charles Buck & Associates Inc
(also known as CareerTeam Partners)
300 E 54th St
PO Box 122
New York, NY 10022
(212) 759-2356

Description: Small quality firm with emphasis on partnering with clients.

Key Contact - Specialty:
Mr. Charles A. Buck, Jr., President - *Senior management, marketing, interior design, luxury goods*

Salary minimum: $85,000

Functions: Generalist, Senior Mgmt., Admin. Svcs., Sales & Mktg., CFO's, Mgmt. Consultants, Non-profits, Architects, Graphic Artists

Industries: Generalist, Non-profits, Legal, Mgmt. Consulting, Hospitality, Advertising, Publishing

Professional Associations: IACMP, SHRM

Buffkin & Associates LLC
424 Church St Ste 2925
Nashville, TN 37219
(615) 742-8491
Fax: (615) 742-8470
Email: info@buffkinassociates.com
Web: www.buffkinassociates.com

Description: Our firm is a retained search firm with the following practices nationally: direct marketing/printing, entertainment/media, technology, and general management. Searches have been completed at the board, executive, and senior levels.

Key Contact - Specialty:
Mr. Craig Buffkin, Managing Partner - *Direct marketing, technology*
Mr. Roland Lundy, Senior Partner - *Entertainment*

Salary minimum: $125,000

Functions: General Mgmt., Sales & Mktg., CFO's

Industries: E-commerce, IT Implementation, Entertainment, Media

Building Industry Associates
774 Mays Blvd 10-369
Incline Village, NV 89451
(800) 831-2510
Email: Biaica@aol.com
Web: www.biaca.com

Description: Executive Search Firm specializing in the Residential Home Construction Industry placing Presidents, CFO's, CEO's, Controllers, Accountants, VPs of Construction, Forward Planning, Land Acquisition, Purchasing Agents, Project Managers, Superintendents, Options Coordinators and Customer Service Personnel.

Key Contact:
Ms. Diane Thurman, President

Salary minimum: $75,000

Functions: Generalist

Industries: Construction

The Burgess Group-Corporate Recruiters Int'l Inc
5 Almargo Dr
New Fairfield, CT 06812
(203) 746-6629
Fax: (203) 746-3777
Email: burgessgrp@worldnet.att.net
Web: www.theburgessgroup.com

Description: Entry to senior-level executive search and diversity recruiting, training and management consulting practice specializing in sales; marketing & strategic planning; accounting, financial services and insurance; purchasing, facilities and security operations; human resources; corporate affairs and media planning; general non-profit management; information technology and corporate boards.

Key Contact - Specialty:
Mr. William H. Burgess, III, President & CEO - *Diversity, corporate board, sales, marketing, facilities*

Salary minimum: $50,000

Functions: Generalist

Industries: Generalist

Professional Associations: AMBAA, BDPA, BMA, FPCUNY, NAACP, NAJA, NBMBAA, NCLR, NHMBAA, NMBC, NMSDC, UNCF

Branches:
1601 3rd Ave Ste 18D
New York, NY 10128
(212) 410-6938
Fax: (212) 410-6939
Email: burgessgrp@worldnet.att.net

Key Contact - Specialty:
Mr. William H. Burgess, III, President & CEO - *Diversity resources planning*

Burke, O'Brien & Bishop Associates Inc
301 N Harrison St Ste 111
Princeton, NJ 08540
(609) 921-3510
Fax: (609) 683-1578
Email: jmsbishop@aol.com

Description: Executive search consulting assignments range from president, CEO, positions with compensation exceeding $1 million to middle management level from a minimum of $100,000. Most functions, with emphasis on general management, finance, marketing and human resources.

Key Contact:
Mr. James F. Bishop, President

Salary minimum: $100,000

Functions: Generalist

Industries: Generalist

J Burkey Associates
900 Laurel Ave
River Edge, NJ 07661
(201) 262-7990
Fax: (201) 262-7955
Email: jburkey@erols.com

Description: We offer executive search services at an hourly-based or fixed fee; it's the clients' choice. Our practice is devoted to pharmaceuticals as an industry category, and to the placement of high-level women in any industry; directorship and up. Our functional expertise has always been and continues to be varied.

Key Contact - Specialty:
Ms. Julie V. Burkey, Principal - *Pharmaceutical (human, animal)*

Salary minimum: $100,000

Functions: Generalist

Industries: Drugs Mfg., Non-classifiable

Professional Associations: AAIV, AVMA, DIA, EWNJ, ICSA, NJAWBO, PDMA, RAPS, SCIP, SHRM

Burkholder Group Inc
(also known as Sales Consultants of Colorado Springs-South)
101 N Cascade Ave Ste 410
Colorado Springs, CO 80903
(719) 867-1222
Fax: (719) 632-6060
Email: info@burkholdergroup.com
Web: www.burkholdergroup.com

Description: We are property and casualty insurance specialists with national practice encompassing all functional disciplines. Our primary focus is on management and executive levels.

Key Contact - Specialty:
Mr. John Burkholder, President - *Insurance, human resources management (all industries)*

Salary minimum: $75,000

Functions: Generalist

Industries: Insurance

The Burling Group Ltd
333 W Wacker Dr Ste 680
Chicago, IL 60606
(312) 346-0888
Email: web@burlinggroup.com
Web: www.burlinggroup.com

Description: We are a generalist firm serving entrepreneurial clients experiencing growth and expansion primarily in the Chicago/Midwest markets.

Key Contact:
Mr. Ronald Deitch, President

Salary minimum: $100,000

Functions: Senior Mgmt., Mfg., Automation, Plant Mgmt., Distribution, HR Mgmt., M&A

Industries: Medical Devices, Metal Products, Machine, Appliance, Consumer Elect., Transportation, Wholesale, Accounting, HR Services, Haz. Waste

Joseph R Burns & Associates Inc
2 Shunpike Rd
Madison, NJ 07940
(973) 377-1350
Fax: (973) 377-9350

Description: Executive search firm with excellent recruitment skills and a demonstrated record of success in servicing our clients with the highest degree of professionalism.

Key Contact - Specialty:
Mr. Joseph R. Burns, President - *Generalist*

Salary minimum: $85,000

Functions: Generalist, General Mgmt., Mfg., Healthcare, Sales & Mktg., HR Mgmt., CFO's, Cash Mgmt., M&A, IT

Industries: Generalist, Food, Bev., Tobacco, Computer Equip., Invest. Banking, Non-profits, New Media, Telecoms, Healthcare

Professional Associations: IACPR

Busch Int'l
(a member of TranSearch Int'l)
One First St Nine
Los Altos, CA 94022-2754
(650) 949-1115
Email: jack@buschint.com
Web: www.buschint.com

Description: Our firm consists of senior consultants specializing in high-technology electronics exclusively. Assignments are with growth companies requiring CEOs, VPs, COOs in marketing, sales, engineering & operations worldwide.

Key Contact:
Mr. Jack Busch, Managing Partner
Mrs. Olga Ocon, Partner
Ms. Olga Ocon, Partner - *Engineering, product management*
Mr. Bertrand Smith, Partner

Salary minimum: $150,000

Functions: Senior Mgmt., Sales & Mktg.

Industries: Computer Equip., Consumer Elect., Test, Measure Equip., Venture Cap., New Media, Telecoms

Networks: TranSearch Int'l

Butterfass, Pepe & MacCallan Inc
PO Box 721
Mahwah, NJ 07430
(201) 512-3330
Fax: (201) 512-0272
Email: staff@bpmi.com
Web: www.bpmi.com

Description: Boutique search firm. Teams are assigned with strengths in areas of assignment, assuring client of consistent, personal attention. Specialties include: fixed income, equities, private placement, M&A, corporate finance, real estate and money management.

Key Contact:
Mr. Stanley W. Butterfass, Principal
Ms. Leonida R. Pepe, Principal
Ms. Deirdre MacCallan, Principal

Salary minimum: $80,000

Functions: Generalist, HR Mgmt., Finance, CFO's, Cash Mgmt., M&A, Risk Mgmt., Minorities

Industries: Generalist, Banking, Invest. Banking, Brokers, Venture Cap., HR Services, Insurance

Professional Associations: IACPR, ACG, HRPS

Byron Leonard Int'l Inc
99 Long Ct Ste 201
Thousand Oaks, CA 91360
(805) 373-7500
Fax: (805) 373-5531
Email: bli@bli-inc.com
Web: www.bli-inc.com

Description: Over 15 years' search experience in growth industries, emphasizing custom fit of candidates to the enterprise, disciplined recruitment methodology, exceptional research. Principals have domestic and international experience. Satisfied clients: start-ups to multinationals.

Key Contact - Specialty:
Mr. Leonard M. Linton, President - *Generalist, Technology, Service*
Mr. Stephen M. Wolf, Principal - *Generalist, Technology, Sales*
Mr. Gary D. Bernard, Principal - *Generalist, service, technology, HR*

Salary minimum: $80,000

Functions: Generalist, Senior Mgmt., Product Dev., Mkt. Research, Mktg. Mgmt., CFO's, MIS Mgmt.

Industries: Generalist, Machine, Appliance, Computer Equip., New Media, Software

C P Consulting
The Hideout
674
Lake Ariel, PA 18436
(570) 698-8321
Fax: (570) 698-8321

Description: Human resource consulting, specializing in the sourcing and screening of executive search candidates. We do not generate names. Unsolicited resumes cannot be responded to.

Key Contact - Specialty:
Ms. Catherine Phillips, Owner - *Financial services*

Salary minimum: $100,000

Functions: Generalist, Directors, Mktg. Mgmt., Benefits, Personnel, Training, CFO's

Industries: Generalist, Banking, Misc. Financial, Legal, Insurance

Professional Associations: AM

Cabot Consultants
1750 Tysons Blvd Ste 400
McLean, VA 22102
(703) 744-1081
Email: craig.stevens@cabotinc.com
Web: www.cabotinc.com

Description: Our firm is a boutique firm with a national client base. The partners are committed to thorough candidate identification and assessment. Our clients are primarily advanced technology and technology-driven companies across a broad spectrum of industries.

Key Contact:
Ms. Laurie Keefe, Principal
Mr. Craig Stevens, Partner
Mr. James Searing, Partner
Ms. Vickie Moore, Partner
Ms. Bonnie Foster, Partner
Mr. Greg Moyer, Partner

Ms. Kathy Epstein, Partner

Salary minimum: $150,000

Functions: Generalist

Industries: Energy, Utilities, Mfg., Finance, Venture Cap., Services, Non-profits, Communications, Defense, Aerospace, Software

The Cadman Consulting Group Inc
500 Park Pl 666 Burrard St
Vancouver, BC V6C 3J8
Canada
(604) 689-4345
Fax: (604) 689-4348
Email: gcadman@cadman.ca
Web: www.cadman.ca

Description: We are a leading provider of IT professionals in both full-time and contract positions.

Key Contact:
Mr. Gary Cadman

Functions: IT

Industries: Generalist

Cadmus Int'l
2900 Wilcrest Dr Ste 105
Houston, TX 77042
(713) 977-1900
Fax: (713) 977-1981
Email: stc@cadmusint.com
Web: www.cadmusint.com

Description: We are a high-tech search and consulting firm that performs retainer/container, on-site/off-site, business unit or client company development and industry intelligence.

Key Contact - Specialty:
Mr. Stephen T. Cadmus, President - *High technology, computer, hardware, software, voice data telecommunication*

Functions: Generalist

Industries: Computer Equip., Consumer Elect., Test, Measure Equip., Venture Cap., Mgmt. Consulting, Telecoms, Software

The Caldwell Partners Int'l
64 Prince Arthur Ave
Toronto, ON M5R 1B4
Canada
(416) 920-7702
Fax: (416) 922-8646
Email: leaders@caldwell.ca
Web: www.caldwellpartners.com

Description: Leading Canadian executive search firm.

Key Contact:
Ms. Kelly A. Blair
Mr. Christopher J. Laubitz
Mr. Marty Parker
Mr. Ronald D. Charles
Mr. Jack Penaligon
Mr. Francis W. H. Brunelle
Mr. C. Douglas Caldwell
Mr. Ralph A. Chauvin
Ms. Anne M. Fawcett

Functions: Generalist

Industries: Generalist

Professional Associations: AESC, IACPR

Branches:
400-3rd Ave SW Ste 3450
Calgary, AB T2P 4H2
Canada
(403) 265-8780
Fax: (403) 263-6508
Key Contact:
Mr. Tim Hamilton, Partner

999 W Hastings St Ste 750
Vancouver, BC V6C 2W2
Canada
(604) 669-3550
Fax: (604) 669-5095
Key Contact:
Ms. Betsy Gibbons, Partner
Mr. Gary Ley

5657 Spring Garden Rd Ste 500
Park Lane Box 247
Halifax, NS B3J 3R4
Canada
(902) 429-5909
Fax: (902) 429-5606
Key Contact:
Ms. Susan Letson, Partner
Ms. Lois Dyer Mann

1840 Sherbrooke St W
Montreal, QC H3H 1E4
Canada
(514) 935-6969
Fax: (514) 935-7402
Email: montreal@caldwellsearch.com
Key Contact:
Mr. Andre Vincent

The Caler Group†

23337 Lago Mar Cir
Boca Raton, FL 33433
(561) 394-8045
Fax: (561) 394-4645
Email: caler@emi.net
Web: www.calergroup.com

Description: Certified minority/women business
enterprise, international retained executive
recruiting company specializing in high-technology,
Internet, data networking, telecommunications,
industries. Functional areas of sales, marketing,
manufacturing, product
development/management/marketing, marketing,
quality, customer service, system engineers, etc.
CEOs to individual contributors.

Key Contact:
Ms. Colleen Perrone, President

Salary minimum: $100,000

Functions: General Mgmt., Senior Mgmt., Mfg.,
Product Dev., Quality, Sales & Mktg., HR Mgmt.,
CFO's, MIS Mgmt., Int'l.

Industries: Generalist, Mfg., Software

Professional Associations: CTIA

Lee Calhoon & Company Inc

1621 Birchrun Rd
PO Box 201
Birchrunville, PA 19421
(610) 469-9000
(800) 469-0896
Fax: (610) 469-0398
Email: lcalhoon@leecalhoon.com
Web: www.leecalhoon.com

Description: We are a retained executive search
firm. Having specialized in healthcare for 30 years,
we are very proud to have earned the recognition of
being one of the leading search firms in the US in
the healthcare sector. Our practice has a focus in
health, information systems and technology, disease
management, and managed care. The corporate
headquarters is based in Pennsylvania with offices
located in Connecticut and Virginia.

Key Contact - Specialty:
Mr. Lee Calhoon, President/CEO - *Healthcare,
managed care, healthcare information systems,
healthcare technology*

Salary minimum: $100,000

Functions: Senior Mgmt., Middle Mgmt.,
Healthcare, Physicians, Nurses, Health Admin.

Industries: Drugs Mfg., Pharm Svcs., Insurance,
Biotech, Healthcare, Hospitals, Women's

Branches:
123 Black Rock
PO Box 504
Redding Ridge, CT 06876-0504
(203) 938-7495
Fax: (801) 640-0630
Email: clake@leecalhoon.com
Key Contact:
Ms. Courtney F. Lake, Managing Director
Mr. Bruce Lake, Managing Director

12728 Stonebriar Ln
Richmond, VA 23233-7053
(804) 360-4415
Email: dfriend1@aol.com
Key Contact:
Mr. Daniel H. Friend, Ph.D., Managing Director

Caliber Associates

125 Strafford Ave Ste 112
Wayne, PA 19087
(610) 971-1880
Fax: (610) 971-1887
Email: steve@caliberassociates.com
Web: www.caliberassociates.com

Description: We specialize in the life sciences, both
emerging organizations and major pharmaceutical
companies, in identifying and selecting key
scientific, technical and general management. Our
focus areas include: general management,
regulatory affairs, quality assurance/quality control,
clinical research/medical affairs, discovery research,
development, operations/manufacturing, project
management, sales/marketing management and
business development.

Key Contact - Specialty:
Mr. Paul S Davit, Vice President - *Life sciences*

Salary minimum: $100,000

Functions: General Mgmt., Product Dev., Plant
Mgmt., Quality, Sales & Mktg., CFO's, R&D

Industries: Drugs Mfg., Medical Devices, Pharm
Svcs., Biotech

Professional Associations: ACP, ASM, BIO,
HRPS, PDA, RAPS

Branches:
5090 Shoreham Pl Ste 201
San Diego, CA 92122
(858) 551-7880
Fax: (858) 551-7887
Email: info@caliberassociates.com
Key Contact - Specialty:
Mr. Steven P Hochberg, President - *Life sciences*
Ms. Lori C. Watson, Principal - *Life sciences*

Callaghan Int'l Inc

119 W 57th St Ste 1220
New York, NY 10019
(212) 265-9200
Fax: (212) 265-0080
Email: KMC@callaghan-international.com
Web: www.callaghan-international.com

Description: We are a full service retained search
firm specializing in diversity placement of senior
level executives. We have a multilingual staff, with
international experience in Europe and Asia. We are
generalists with a background in most industries and
functions. We have exceptional in-house research
capability.

Key Contact:
Ms. Kathryn M. Callaghan, President/CEO

Salary minimum: $150,000

Functions: Senior Mgmt., Mfg., Sales & Mktg., IT,
Engineering, Minorities, Int'l.

Industries: Generalist, Construction, Mfg., Food,
Bev., Tobacco, Soap, Perf., Cosmtcs., Drugs
Mfg., Medical Devices, Computer Equip.,
Consumer Elect., Wholesale, Retail, Finance,
Accounting, Law Enforcement, IT
Implementation, Hospitality, Government,
Insurance, Software, Biotech

Callan Associates Ltd

2021 Spring Rd Ste 175
Oak Brook, IL 60523
(630) 574-9300
Fax: (630) 574-3099
Email: info@callanassociates.com
Web: www.callanassociates.com

Description: We are a leading retained search firm
that provides high quality, personalized senior level
recruiting services to a prestigious group of public
and private manufacturing, industrial, and
professional service organizations in all functions.
Our client base is international in scope, with a
concentration in the Midwest US.

Key Contact - Specialty:
Mr. Robert M. Callan, Managing Partner - *General
management, CEO, COO, board of director
searches*
Ms. Elizabeth C. Beaudin, Partner - *Strategic
procurement, CPO, supply chain/purchasing,
marketing, sales*
Ms. Marianne C. Ray, Partner - *Finance, software,
banking, information technology*
Mr. James R. Stranberg, Partner - *Manufacturing,
logistics, lean manufacturing, quality*
Ms. Caren R. Truhlar, Consultant - *Marketing,
sales, finance*
Mr. Robert M. Ward, CPA, Partner - *Finance,
controller, tax, project management*

Salary minimum: $100,000

Functions: Generalist, Senior Mgmt., Middle
Mgmt., Mfg., Materials, Purchasing, Sales &
Mktg., Finance, IT, Int'l.

Industries: Generalist, Energy, Utilities,
Construction, Mfg., Transportation, Retail,
Finance, Services, Communications, Packaging,
Insurance, Software, Healthcare

Professional Associations: IACPR, HRMAC

Calland & Company

2296 Henderson Mill Rd Ste 222
Atlanta, GA 30345
(770) 270-9100
Fax: (770) 270-9300
Email: calland@mindspring.com

Description: We specialize in board, CEO, COO,
and CFO searches. We have eighteen years of
experience providing proven leadership to emerging
healthcare service companies including: Internet
information technology/services, disease
management, specialty care programs, managed
care, multi-site providers, contract management, and
long-term care.

Key Contact - Specialty:
Mr. Robert H. Calland, President - *Healthcare
service, CEO, COO, CFO, operations*

Salary minimum: $125,000

Functions: Healthcare

Industries: Healthcare

Cambridge Management Planning Inc

2323 Yonge St Ste 203
Toronto, ON M4P 2C9
Canada
(416) 484-8408
Fax: (416) 484-0151
Email: admin@cambridgemgmt.com
Web: www.cambridgemgmt.com

Description: Executive search: middle- to senior-
management searches for a wide range of
corporations in Canada and internationally.

Emphasis placed on highly targeted, in-house market research capabilities.

Key Contact - Specialty:
Mr. Graham Carver, President - *Generalist*

Salary minimum: $85,000

Functions: Generalist

Industries: Generalist

Networks: I-I-C Partners Executive Search Worldwide

Cameron Consulting Group
1112 Austin Ave
Pacific Grove, CA 93950
(831) 646-8415
Fax: (831) 646-8626
Email: jwci@redshift.com

Description: We are an executive recruiting firm specializing in senior line and staff positions and serving all industries with particular emphasis on the biotechnology, pharmaceutical, and semi-conductor business segments.

Key Contact:
Mr. James W. Cameron, President

Salary minimum: $75,000

Functions: Generalist, Sales & Mktg., HR Mgmt., Finance, Network Admin.

Industries: Generalist, Drugs Mfg., Medical Devices, Computer Equip., Consumer Elect., Electronic, Elec. Components, Pharm Svcs., Fiber Optic, Biotech

Professional Associations: CCHRA, SHRM

Campa & Associates
1 Yonge St Ste 2203
Toronto, ON M5E 1E5
Canada
(416) 407-7777
Fax: (416) 214-5764
Email: carl@campasearch.com

Description: We recruit high performance management talent for world-class engineered products manufacturers with a global focus.

Key Contact:
Mr. Carl Campa, President

Salary minimum: $75,000

Functions: Generalist, General Mgmt., Mfg., Plant Mgmt., Materials, Sales & Mktg., Engineering, Mgmt. Consultants

Industries: Generalist, Plastics, Rubber, Metal Products, Machine, Appliance, Motor Vehicles, Misc. Mfg., Aerospace

T M Campbell Company[†]
1111 3rd Ave Ste 2500
Seattle, WA 98101
(206) 583-8355
Fax: (206) 842-7256
Email: lebe@nwlink.com
Web: www.tmcampbell.com

Description: Nationwide executive searches in many industries, including professional services, IT, finance, accounting, and sales/marketing. Flexible pricing and services.

Key Contact - Specialty:
Ms. Leann Ebe, Owner/Consultant - *Sales & marketing*

Salary minimum: $60,000

Functions: Generalist, Sales & Mktg., HR Mgmt., Finance, IT, MIS Mgmt., Systems Implem., Mgmt. Consultants

Industries: Generalist, Finance, Accounting, Government

Campbell/Carlson LLC[†]
831 E Morehead St Ste 750
The Addison Bldg
Charlotte, NC 28202
(704) 373-0234
Fax: (704) 373-0232
Email: recruiting@campbellcarlson.com
Web: www.campbellcarlson.com

Description: Highly focused on recruiting executives who understand the successful application of today's technology to business. Dan Campbell and Cynthia Carlson have more than 50 years of experience recruiting leaders and 25 years running technology companies. The firm's principals are personally involved with every step of each search. We work with clients on both a regional and national basis in a wide range of technology-dependent industries.

Key Contact - Specialty:
Mr. Dan Campbell, Principal - *Technology, distribution, finance, manufacturing*
Ms. Cynthia Carlson, Principal - *Technology, sales, marketing, recruiting, training*

Salary minimum: $100,000

Functions: General Mgmt.

Industries: Generalist

Canadian Career Partners
800-112 4th Ave SW
Calgary, AB T2P 0H3
Canada
(403) 290-0466
(800) 387-8797
Fax: (403) 294-7240
Email: debra.johnstone@career-partners.com
Web: www.career-partners.com

Description: Successfully conduct searches in a broad range of industries and government. Treat every engagement as a partnership with our client, determining the best way to streamline the process without compromising thoroughness.

Key Contact:
Ms. Debra J. Johnstone, Partner
Mr. Clive L. MacRaild, Partner
Mr. Gary R. Agnew, Partner
Mr. Bruce Green, Partner
Mr. Bruce Wade, Partner

Salary minimum: $80,000

Functions: Generalist

Industries: Generalist

Professional Associations: CAMC, CPI, HRIA

Networks: Career Partners Int'l

Canny, Bowen Inc
280 Park Ave Fl 30 W
New York, NY 10017
(212) 949-6611
Fax: (212) 949-5191
Email: main@cannybowen.com
Web: www.cannybowen.com

Description: Specialize in senior executive search. Forty-five years in retainer-based executive search assisting our clients to select and recruit their top management.

Key Contact - Specialty:
Mr. David R. Peasback, President/CEO - *Generalist, senior management, human resources, attorneys, finance*
Mr. Greg Gabel, Managing Director - *Generalist, general management, directors, finance, manufacturing*

Salary minimum: $200,000

Functions: Generalist, Mfg., Sales & Mktg., HR Mgmt., Finance, IT, R&D, Int'l.

Industries: Generalist, Energy, Utilities, Construction, Mfg., Paper, Drugs Mfg., Test, Measure Equip., Transportation, Services, Communications, Packaging

Canpro Executive Search
7321 Victoria Park Ave Ste 302
Markham, ON L3R 2Z8
Canada
(905) 475-3115
Fax: (905) 475-2849
Email: aboyle@canpro.com
Web: www.canpro.com

Description: Executive search to leading Canadian corporations coast to coast.

Key Contact:
Mr. Art Boyle, President

Salary minimum: $50,000

Functions: General Mgmt., Mfg., Materials, Sales & Mktg., HR Mgmt., Finance

Industries: Generalist

The Cantor Concern Inc[†]
315 W 57 St Ste 207
New York, NY 10019
(212) 333-3000
Fax: (212) 245-1012
Email: requests@cantorconcern.com
Web: www.cantorconcern.com

Description: A national search firm with professional staff experienced in business, government, not-for-profit, management consulting search. Company serves all industries and specializes in public affairs, public relations, corporate communications, IR.

Key Contact - Specialty:
Ms. Marie T. Raperto, President - *Public, government, investor relations*

Salary minimum: $50,000

Functions: PR

Industries: Generalist

Professional Associations: IABC, NIRI, PRSA

Branches:
424 Tahmore Dr
Fairfield, CT 06432
(203) 372-2662
Fax: (203) 372-2618
Email: rlferrante@cantorconcern.com
Key Contact:
Mr. Robert Ferrante, Managing Director

5167 Harpers Farm Rd
Columbia, MD 21044
(410) 992-0117
Fax: (410) 992-3096
Email: alwannl@ix.netcom.com
Key Contact:
Mr. Al Wann

Capital Markets Search Int'l
15205 SW 78th Ct Ste E
Miami, FL 33157
(305) 969-0683
(800) 713-0093 x00
Fax: (212) 202-4096
Email: capmkts2000@aol.com
Web: www.capmkts.com

Description: We are a retained search firm with in-depth experience in capital markets consulting and search with more than 14 years' experience.

Key Contact - Specialty:
Ms. Donna Clark, Partner - *Capital markets, e-commerce search, consulting*
Mr. Lawrence Milton, Managing Partner - *Investment management search, asset management search*

Ms. Alison Zenk, Associate Partner - *Capital markets search*
Dr. Meredith Coletti, Associate Partner - *Sophisticated financial products development*

Salary minimum: $100,000

Functions: Generalist

Industries: Finance, Banking, Invest. Banking, Brokers, Venture Cap., Misc. Financial, Legal, Mgmt. Consulting, New Media

Caplan Associates Inc
PO Box 4227
East Hampton, NY 11937
(631) 907-9700
Email: info@caplanassoc.com
Web: www.caplanassoc.com

Description: We are an executive-level search firm servicing only pharmaceuticals, biotechnology, and all disciplines within: general management, business development, marketing, sales, healthcare, clinical regulatory, healthcare publishing, managed care, medical education, and advertising.

Key Contact - Specialty:
Ms. Shellie Caplan, President - *Pharmaceutical, biotechnology, general management, business development, marketing*

Salary minimum: $100,000

Functions: Healthcare

Industries: Pharm Svcs., Advertising, Biotech, Healthcare

Professional Associations: HMC

The Caplan-Taylor Group
897 Oak Park Blvd
PMB 308
Pismo Beach, CA 93449-3293
(805) 481-3000
Fax: (805) 481-2195
Email: jcaplan@caplantaylorgroup.com
Web: www.caplantaylorgroup.com

Description: We specialize in recruiting executives for various healthcare industries. The worldwide emphasis is in the pharmaceutical, biotechnology, medical instrumental/device, diagnostic, e-healthcare and related healthcare areas.

Key Contact - Specialty:
Mr. John Caplan, General Partner - *Senior executives, drugs, pharmaceuticals, healthcare, biotechnology*
Mr. John Taylor, General Partner - *Senior executives, drugs, pharmaceuticals, healthcare, biotechnology*

Salary minimum: $100,000

Functions: Generalist, General Mgmt., Mfg., Sales & Mktg., HR Mgmt., Finance, R&D, Engineering

Industries: Generalist, Drugs Mfg., Medical Devices, Biotech, Healthcare

Capodice & Associates
1243 S Tamiami Trl
Midtown Plz
Sarasota, FL 34239
(941) 906-1990
Fax: (941) 906-1991
Email: picap123@aol.com
Web: www.capodice.com

Description: Retained executive search firm specializing in the restaurant/hospitality, entertainment, franchising and consumer products industries. Senior-level executive placement across all disciplines.

Key Contact - Specialty:
Mr. Peter Capodice, President - *Restaurant, hospitality, franchising, entertainment, consumer products*

Mr. Alan Merry, Vice President - *Restaurant, hospitality, franchising, entertainment, consumer products*
Mr. Chuck Orchowski, Vice President - *Restaurant, hospitality, franchising, entertainment, consumer products*

Salary minimum: $75,000

Functions: Generalist

Industries: Mfg., Food, Bev., Tobacco, Retail, Services, HR Services, Hospitality

Professional Associations: CRFA, IAAPA, IFA, NAFE, NRA, SHRM

Caprio & Associates Inc
2 Mid America Plz Ste 800 S
Oak Brook Terrace, IL 60181
(630) 705-9101
Fax: (630) 705-9102
Email: jcap@acninc.net

Description: We are specialist in recruiting senior-level management for the printing, publishing, packaging, advertising, and graphic arts industries.

Key Contact - Specialty:
Mr. Jerry Caprio, President - *Printing, publishing, packaging, converting*

Salary minimum: $75,000

Functions: Generalist, Senior Mgmt., Plant Mgmt., Packaging, Advertising, Sales Mgmt., Direct Mktg., Graphic Artists

Industries: Generalist, Paper, Printing, Chemicals, Paints, Petro. Products, Advertising, Publishing, Packaging

Professional Associations: AGAC

Capstone Consulting Inc
723 S Dearborn St Printers Row
Chicago, IL 60605
(312) 922-9556
Fax: (312) 922-9558
Email: info@capstoneconsulting.com
Web: www.capstoneconsulting.com

Description: A highly focused search-driven consultancy offering a wide range of strategic business planning services. Committed to the highest level of client partnership; detailed, methodical and personalized attention are our hallmarks.

Key Contact - Specialty:
Mr. Mark R. Ormond, Principal - *Senior executives, tax, sales & marketing, human resources, engineering*
Ms. Lori K. Pedelty, Principal - *Tax, manufacturing, senior executives*

Salary minimum: $75,000

Functions: Generalist, Senior Mgmt., Middle Mgmt., Mfg., Taxes, Systems Implem., Engineering

Industries: Generalist, Mfg., Metal Products, Consumer Elect., Misc. Mfg., Services, Legal, Accounting, Mgmt. Consulting, HR Services

Capstone Inc
1 Global View
Rensselaer Technology Park
Troy, NY 12180
(518) 285-7328
Fax: (518) 285-7467
Email: amy_johnson@mapinfo.com

Description: We offer a turnkey approach to retained search including organizational analysis, position definition, compensation surveys, interview training and final candidate selection as requested.

Key Contact:
Ms. Amy M. Johnson, President

Salary minimum: $70,000

Functions: Generalist, Senior Mgmt., Mfg., Automation, Sales & Mktg., CFO's, Systems Dev., Engineering

Industries: Generalist, Paper, Chemicals, Plastics, Rubber, Software

Cardinal Mark Inc
601 Carlson Pkwy Ste 1050
Minnetonka, MN 55305
(952) 449-3005
Fax: (952) 745-4980
Email: jimz@cardinalmark.com
Web: www.cardinalmark.com

Description: We concentrate our search efforts in the telecommunications and data communications industries. Areas of placement in software have included LANs, WANs, optical networking and storage.

Key Contact:
Mr. Jim Zuehlke

Functions: Mkt. Research

Industries: Media

Cardwell Enterprises Inc
PO Box 59418
Chicago, IL 60659
(773) 273-5774
Fax: (847) 475-6792
Email: cardwellent@aol.com

Description: We recruit quality candidates for positions in corporate communications, investor relations, public relations, government and public affairs on behalf of Fortune 500.

Key Contact - Specialty:
Ms. Jean Cardwell, President - *Communications, public relations, editorial services, speech writing, investor relations*

Salary minimum: $80,000

Functions: Advertising, PR, Minorities

Industries: Generalist

Career Specialists Inc
(also known as Rolfe & Associates)
155 108th Ave NE Ste 200
Pacific Plaza
Bellevue, WA 98004
(425) 455-0582
(425) 455-2508
Fax: (425) 646-9738
Email: prolfe@qwest.net

Description: We work in retained search, and more specifically: CEOs and their direct reports..

Key Contact:
Ms. Pamela Rolfe, President - *CEOs, senior management, generalist*
Ms. Susan Chapman, Vice President

Salary minimum: $100,000

Functions: Generalist, Directors, Senior Mgmt., Mfg., Healthcare, CFO's, IT, Attorneys

Industries: Generalist, Mfg., Textiles, Apparel, Lumber, Furniture, Finance, Banking, Invest. Banking, Legal, E-commerce, Insurance, Mfg. SW, Healthcare

Carlson & Czeswik
740 Mississippi River Blvd Ste 18-G
St. Paul, MN 55116
(651) 698-6400

Description: Executives and senior managers for banking, manufacturing, consumer packaged goods, insurance and financial services. Exceptional quality.

Key Contact - Specialty:
Mr. Frederick R. Czeswik, Partner - *Generalist*

Salary minimum: $75,000

Functions: General Mgmt., Mktg. Mgmt., PR, HR Mgmt., Finance, MIS Mgmt., R&D, Engineering

Industries: Mfg., Food, Bev., Tobacco, Chemicals, Retail, Finance, Banking, Non-profits, Insurance

Branches:
1601 48th St Ste 250
West Des Moines, IA 50266
(515) 225-2525
Key Contact - Specialty:
Mr. Gregory P. Carlson, Partner - *Generalist*

Carlson Research Group
5051 Castello Dr Ste 211
Naples, FL 34103
(941) 649-7576
Fax: (941) 649-8058
Email: bc@carlsonresearch.com
Web: www.carlsonresearch.com

Description: The Carlson Research Group is a nationally recognized recruiting firm offering complete and cost effective recruitment and research solutions to our clients since 1989. We pride ourselves on the accuracy, reliability, and timeliness of our services.

Key Contact:
Mr. Bob Carlson

Salary minimum: $75,000

Functions: General Mgmt., HR Mgmt., Finance, R&D

Industries: Mfg., Medical Devices, Retail, Banking, Pharm Svcs., Hospitality, Insurance, Hospitals

Carlyn Int'l Inc
(also known as MRI of The Woodlands)
1610 Woodstead Ct Ste 495
The Woodlands, TX 77380-3404
(281) 363-9494
Email: carlyn@c-ii.com

Description: All of our searches are focused exclusively in the telecommunications industry and our clients are both vendors and carriers. For the past eight years, we have assisted companies throughout the country to build winning teams by providing talented individuals for senior management and executive positions.

Key Contact:
Ms. Lynette Baker, Managing Partner - *Telecommunications*
Mr. Caren Krochenski, Managing Partner - *Telecommunications*
Ms. Nicole Rollfing, AA
Mr. Frank Tranfa, AE

Salary minimum: $100,000

Functions: Senior Mgmt.

Industries: Telecoms, Telephony, Digital, Wireless, Fiber Optic, Network Infrastructure

Professional Associations: AAFD

The Carnegie Group
PO Box 12506
Charlotte, NC 28220
(704) 845-0521
Email: roninfinger@aol.com

Description: We are a retained executive search firm that assists its clients in recruiting qualified, available individuals from most disciplines and functional areas.

Key Contact:
Mr. Ronald Infinger, Principal
Mr. Robert M. Frazer, Principal

Functions: Generalist

Industries: Generalist, Energy, Utilities, Construction, Mfg., Transportation, Finance, Services, Insurance, Healthcare

Carnegie Partners Inc
1286 Amaranth Dr
Naperville, IL 60564-9331
(630) 236-6336
Fax: (630) 236-6283
Email: kennedy@carnegiepartners.com
Web: www.carnegiepartners.com

Description: Professional executive search and selection systems utilizing scientific processes to identify superior performers. Interviewing and selection training offered at no additional charge to client company with each retained search to improve enterprise wide hiring practices. Behavioral profile reports of 35 to 50 pages provided on each candidate.

Key Contact - Specialty:
Mr. Robert W. Hollis, President/CEO - *Generalist*
Mr. Michael Walters, Chairman - *Metals*
Mr. Michael Morrical, Partner - *Staffing, lighting, electronics*
Mr. Brian D. Wasiele, Partner - *Information technology, metals*
Mr. Robert Powell, Partner - *Metals*
Mr. Michael Williams, Partner - *Sales and marketing*
Mr. Clarke Caldwell, Partner - *Generalist, healthcare, non-profit*
Mrs. Elizabeth Hollis, CFO - *Behavioral profiles, research, marketing*
Mr. Tom Nelson, Board - *Metals*
Mr. Robert Patterson, Board - *Attorneys, legal professionals*
Mr. Dennis Marx, Board - *Finance*
Ms. Terry Recht, Board - *Human resources, healthcare, bio tech*

Salary minimum: $50,000

Functions: Generalist, Sales & Mktg., HR Mgmt.

Industries: Generalist, Mfg., Metal Products, Legal, Mgmt. Consulting, HR Services, E-commerce, Advertising, Software, Biotech, Healthcare

Branches:
18191 Von Karman Ave
Irvine, CA 92612
(949) 474-0129
Fax: (949) 474-0124
Email: jloguidice@carnegiepartners.com
Key Contact - Specialty:
Mr. John Loguidice - *Metals, sales and marketing*

9 Santa Gabriella Ct
Novato, CA 94945
(415) 897-4150
Email: esprotte@carnegiepartners.com
Key Contact - Specialty:
Mr. Erik Sprotte, Partner - *IT, sales and marketing, human resources*

1991 Crocker Rd Ste 600
Westlake, OH 44145
(440) 899-9890
Fax: (440) 892-3376
Email: lrankin@carnegiepartners.com
Key Contact - Specialty:
Mr. Lee Rankin, Partner - *Metals, sales and marketing*

Carpenter Associates Inc
322 S Green St Ste 408
Chicago, IL 60607
(312) 243-1000
Fax: (312) 243-1875
Email: judicarpenter@msn.com

Description: After 20 years' experience with direct marketing industry, I understand clients' needs and consistently make successful matches. This high success rate is a result of a rare blend of experience, personality and intuitive people skills. I develop

long-term relationships with clients based on trust and genuine friendships.

Key Contact - Specialty:
Ms. Judi Carpenter, President - *Direct marketing*

Salary minimum: $70,000

Functions: Direct Mktg.

Industries: Generalist

Professional Associations: CADM, DMA, EDMA, WDMI

Carpenter, Shackleton & Company
58 Foxwood Ln Ste 100
Barrington, IL 60010-1615
(847) 381-2555
Email: m.shackleton@attglobal.net

Description: We are a quality boutique retainer executive search and consulting firm, specializing in recruiting for publicly and privately owned Chicago area clients for all functional areas and many industries.

Key Contact - Specialty:
Mr. George M. Shackleton - *Generalist*
Mr. Michael A. Shackleton - *Generalist*
Mr. Eric G. Carpenter - *Generalist*
Dr. Robert Denker - *Generalist*
Ms. Dora Lee Shackleton - *Sales & marketing*
Ms. Louise Rodriguez, Associate - *Diversity, Minorities*

Functions: Generalist, General Mgmt., Mfg., Healthcare, Sales & Mktg., HR Mgmt., Finance, IT, Engineering, Int'l.

Industries: Generalist, Construction, Mfg., Drugs Mfg., Transportation, Finance, Non-profits, Higher Ed., Aerospace, Healthcare

Professional Associations: IMC

Branches:
253 E Delaware Pl Ste 9F
Chicago, IL 60611-1750
(312) 944-5484
(312) 925-5952
Email: m.shackleton@attglobal.net
Key Contact - Specialty:
Mr. Michael Shackleton - *Generalist*

Carrington & Carrington Ltd
39 S LaSalle St Ste 700
Chicago, IL 60603
(312) 606-0015
Fax: (312) 606-0501
Email: cclltd@cclltd.com
Web: www.cclltd.com

Description: We work across all functional and industry lines with a specific focus on identification of culturally diverse professionals. We are considered specialists in diversity, and we have earned our reputation by successfully placing senior executives in specialized areas.

Key Contact:
Mr. Willie E. Carrington, Principal
Ms. Marian H. Carrington, Principal

Salary minimum: $100,000

Functions: Generalist, Materials, Healthcare, Sales & Mktg., HR Mgmt., Finance, IT, Minorities

Industries: Generalist, Food, Bev., Tobacco, Drugs Mfg., Finance, Telecoms

Professional Associations: AESC

Carris, Jackowitz Associates
201 E 79th St
New York, NY 10021
(212) 879-5482

Description: We are generalists.

Key Contact - Specialty:
Mr. S. Joseph Carris, Partner - *Generalist*

Salary minimum: $75,000

Functions: Generalist, General Mgmt., Directors, Senior Mgmt., Middle Mgmt.

Industries: Generalist

Branches:
PO Box 54
Andover, NJ 07821
(973) 786-5884
Key Contact - Specialty:
Mr. Ronald N. Jackowitz, Partner - *Generalist*

Carson Kolb Healthcare Group Inc
20301 Birch St Ste 101
Newport Beach, CA 92660-1754
(949) 476-2988
Fax: (949) 476-2155
Email: info@carsonkolb.com
Web: www.carsonkolb.com

Description: We strive to provide the most professional and competent representation for healthcare organizations at the greatest value.

Key Contact - Specialty:
Mr. Matthew A. Kolb, President - *Medical, healthcare*
Ms. Sally C. Kolb, Vice President - *Medical, healthcare*

Salary minimum: $80,000

Functions: Physicians

Industries: Healthcare

The Carter Group LLC
305 Royce Woods Ct
Naperville, IL 60565
(888) 560-9877
Fax: (630) 548-5999
Email: mark.bidlake@thecartergroup.com
Web: www.thecartergroup.com

Description: We place senior level, all functions, GM, CEO, and board. We have extensive candidate sourcing, rigorous assessment, presentation, and process management in order to bring searches to a rapid successful conclusion with hires of the highest quality. We are averaging four weeks to source and identify person hired.

Key Contact - Specialty:
Mr. Mark Bidlake, Partner - *Logistics, manufacturing, technology, services*

Salary minimum: $125,000

Functions: General Mgmt., Mfg., Materials, Healthcare, Sales & Mktg., HR Mgmt., Finance, IT, Engineering, Int'l.

Industries: Agri., Forestry, Mining, Energy, Utilities, Construction, Mfg., Food, Bev., Tobacco, Motor Vehicles, Computer Equip., Transportation, Wholesale, Retail, Services, Higher Ed., Hospitality, Media, Communications, Aerospace, Real Estate, Software, Healthcare

Professional Associations: CLM, HRPS, SHRM

Branches:
PO Box 4560
Cary, NC 27519-4560
(919) 816-0999
Email: jack.smith@thecartergroup.com
Key Contact:
Mr. Jack Smith, CCP, Partner

Caruso & Associates Inc
1509 N Military Trl Ste 216
West Palm Beach, FL 33409
(561) 683-2336
Fax: (561) 683-3676
Email: info@carusoassociates.com

Description: Searches are performed by partners of firm and not handed off to other recruiters, a personal hands-on approach to develop a close working relationship with our clients.

Key Contact - Specialty:
Mr. Dennis Caruso, Managing Director - *Real estate*

Salary minimum: $75,000

Functions: Generalist, Senior Mgmt., Mktg. Mgmt., Sales Mgmt., CFO's, MIS Mgmt., Architects

Industries: Generalist, Construction, Finance, Hospitality, Environmental Svcs., Real Estate, Healthcare

Professional Associations: AICPA, NAHB, ULI

Caruthers & Company LLC
1175 Post Rd E
Westport, CT 06880
(203) 221-3234
(203) 454-0414
Fax: (203) 221-7300

Description: National practice focused on senior-level corporate communications, public affairs, marketing services, advertising and marketing assignments. Special expertise in financial services/insurance, consumer and industrial categories.

Key Contact - Specialty:
Mr. Robert D. Caruthers, Principal - *Marketing, public relations, marketing services*

Salary minimum: $75,000

Functions: Advertising, Mkt. Research, Mktg. Mgmt., PR

Industries: Generalist

Cary & Associates
2820 Norris Ave
Winter Park, FL 32803
(407) 647-1145
Email: concary@caryassociates.com
Web: www.caryassociates.com

Description: Our principal was a senior vice president for a $600 million, annual volume, retail chain. He has three years of experience with a recognized search firm and has special knowledge about the convenience store industry.

Key Contact - Specialty:
Mr. Con Cary, Owner - *Generalist, retail, wholesale, manufacturing*

Salary minimum: $50,000

Functions: Generalist, Senior Mgmt., Middle Mgmt., Distribution, Sales Mgmt., CFO's, MIS Mgmt.

Industries: Generalist, Food, Bev., Tobacco, Transportation, Wholesale, Retail, Hospitality

Rosemary Cass Ltd
175 Post Rd W
Westport, CT 06880
(203) 454-2920
Fax: (203) 454-4643
Email: resumes@rosemarycassltd.com
Web: www.rosemarycassltd.com

Description: Specializes in pharmaceutical, biotechnology, medical devices and related healthcare industries. Searches in all disciplines within these industries.

Key Contact:
Ms. Rosemary Cass, President

Salary minimum: $100,000

Functions: Generalist

Industries: Drugs Mfg., Medical Devices

The Cassie Group
26 Main St
Toms River, NJ 08753
(732) 473-1779
Email: cassiegroup@cassie.com
Web: www.cassie.com

Description: We are building management teams for the healthcare industry, more specifically: biotechnology, pharmaceuticals, diagnostics, medical device, and information technology. We have a major focus on emerging technology companies. We have associate locations in US, Europe, and Australia. We work across all functions including, but not limited to: general management, marketing, sales, R&D, operations, HR, QA/QC, and regulatory and information systems.

Key Contact - Specialty:
Mr. Ronald L. Cassie, President - *Medical*
Mr. Lee Morton, Director- Technical Recruiting - *Health information technology*

Salary minimum: $100,000

Functions: Generalist, General Mgmt., Mfg., Sales & Mktg., HR Mgmt., Finance, R&D, Engineering

Industries: Generalist, Medical Devices, Pharm Svcs., Biotech, Healthcare

Professional Associations: AORN, APIC, DCAT, DIA, PAC, PDA, RAPS

Branches:
3120 Governor Dr
San Diego, CA 92122
(858) 452-2101
Fax: (858) 452-2102
Key Contact - Specialty:
Mr. Mike Luecke, Managing Partner - *Biotechnology, pharmaceutical*
Mr. Charles Heiser, Vice President - *Medical device, diagnostics*

12 Running Brook Rd
Bridgewater, NJ 08807
(908) 429-1335
Fax: (908) 218-0213
Email: fredh@cassie.com
Key Contact - Specialty:
Mr. Fred P. Hauck, Ph.D., Vice President - *Biotechnology, pharmaceutical, diagnostic*

PO Box 1674
New Bern, NC 28563-1674
(252) 634-9355
Fax: (252) 634-3090
Email: johns@cassie.com
Key Contact - Specialty:
Mr. John T. Shipherd, Managing Partner - *Biotechnology, pharmaceutical, medical device*

PO Box 521125
Salt Lake City, UT 84152-1125
(801) 272-4668
Email: pingf@cassie.com
Key Contact - Specialty:
Ping Fong, Vice President - *Biotechnology, diagnostic, medical device, pharmaceutical*

Catalyx Group
303 W 42nd St Ste 607
New York, NY 10036
(212) 956-3525
Email: lposter@catalyx.com
Web: www.catalyx.com

Description: Our firm focuses on searches for CEOs and management teams for private-equity buyouts and venture capital portfolio companies. We recruit exceptional CEOs, senior executives, board of director members, and leaders of technology. We also recruit entire management teams for promising startups. Our expertise in biotechnology and information technology, as well as in selected consumer and industrial sectors.

Key Contact - Specialty:
Mr. Lawrence D. Poster, Managing Director - *CEOs, senior management, board of directors, private equity firms, venture capital*

Salary minimum: $100,000

Functions: Directors, Senior Mgmt., Middle Mgmt., Sales & Mktg., Mktg. Mgmt., CFO's, M&A, IT, MIS Mgmt., R&D

Industries: Invest. Banking, Venture Cap., New Media, Software

Branches:
20 Stonepark Ln Ste 100
Nepean, ON K2H 9P4
Canada
(613) 726-7379
Email: pwinter@catalyx.com
Key Contact - Specialty:
Mr. Peter Winter, MS, Director - *Scientists, engineers, MD's, life science (management)*

Michael J Cavanagh & Associates Inc
71 Highbourne Rd
Toronto, ON M5P 2J3
Canada
(416) 324-9661
Email: cavsearch@sympatico.ca

Description: We are one of Canada's most experienced recruiters in aerospace, automotive, electrical and packaged goods industries. Our firm is a generalist operative at the senior-level in Canada. We conduct retainer search activity for a number of multi-billion US-based aerospace companies.

Key Contact:
Mr. Michael Cavanagh, President
Ms. Helena Beran, Research Associate

Salary minimum: $100,000

Functions: Generalist, Senior Mgmt., Plant Mgmt., Purchasing, Mktg. Mgmt., Sales Mgmt., CFO's, MIS Mgmt.

Industries: Generalist, Drugs Mfg., Motor Vehicles, Hospitality, Aerospace, Healthcare

Caywood Partners Ltd
6484 Washington St Ste B
Yountville, CA 94599
(707) 945-1340
(707) 945-1343
Fax: (707) 945-1345
Email: doug@caywood.com
Web: www.caywood.com

Description: We specialize in recruiting executive management teams for early-stage, venture-financed start-up companies in the telecommunications and data communications industry, specifically with companies building next generation Internet infrastructure equipment. The disciplines we specialize in are marketing, sales, business development, operations, customer service/support, and R&D.

Key Contact - Specialty:
Mr. Doug Griffith, Principal/Owner - *LAN, MAN, WAN, telecommunications, data communications*

Salary minimum: $150,000

Functions: Directors, Senior Mgmt., Middle Mgmt., Mfg., Product Dev., Sales & Mktg., Mktg. Mgmt., PR, R&D, Engineering

Industries: Generalist, Communications, Telecoms, Digital, Wireless, Fiber Optic, Network Infrastructure, Networking, Comm. SW

Cejka Search
(a division of Cross Country TravCorps)
222 S Central Ste 400
St. Louis, MO 63105
(314) 727-6650
(800) 678-7858
Fax: (314) 726-1997
Email: gstaub@cejka.com
Web: www.cejka.com

Description: We are a healthcare consulting and search firm offering physician practice opportunities, healthcare employment opportunities, physician and executive search services, and healthcare management consulting. The firm completes more than 600 physician and healthcare executive placements and consulting projects annually for hospitals, groups, managed care organizations, practice management companies, academic medical centers, and health systems.

Key Contact - Specialty:
Ms. Carrie Hackett, Vice President/Principal - *Healthcare*
Ms. Lois Dister, Vice President - *Healthcare*
Ms. Carol Westfall, President - *Healthcare*

Salary minimum: $60,000

Functions: Healthcare

Industries: Healthcare

Professional Associations: AAHP, ACHE, ACPE, ASHHRA, MGMA, NAPR, SHPMAHA

Cendea
13740 Research Blvd Bldg O-1
Austin, TX 78750
(512) 219-6000
Email: info.kd@cendea.com
Web: www.cendea.com

Description: We are a retained firm focused on providing impact leaders who take companies to the next level, by significantly impacting goals, direction, revenue, and profit. We specialize in executive, management, sales, and marketing talent. Our long-term success and excellent reputation are defined by our core values: integrity, service, and results.

Key Contact:
Mr. Wade H. Allen, President
Mr. Steven G. Ledbetter, Senior Partner

Salary minimum: $200,000

Functions: Directors, Senior Mgmt., Sales & Mktg., Mktg. Mgmt., Sales Mgmt., CFO's

Industries: Mfg., Printing, Computer Equip., Banking, Venture Cap., Services, Media, Telecoms, Software

Century City Partners LLC
9200 W Sunset Blvd Ste 715
Los Angeles, CA 90069
(310) 777-0240
Fax: (310) 777-0249
Email: register@ccpllc.net
Web: www.centurycitypartners.com

Description: Track top talent that makes stocks move north! Internet, entertainment, top-tier consulting, consumer products and venture capital industries are the focus.

Key Contact:
Ms. Elizabeth Hamilton, President - *Consumer products, senior management, marketing, finance*
Ms. E. Tjoeng, Associate
Mr. P. Ahdout, Associate
Ms. I. Feldman, Associate
Mr. S. Vahedi, Associate
Mr. A. Ahdoot, Associate
Mr. P. Shabboi, Associate

Salary minimum: $160,000

Functions: Generalist

Industries: Generalist

Professional Associations: IACPR

CEO Resources Inc
200 E State St Ste 101
Media, PA 19063
(610) 565-9767
Fax: (610) 565-9766
Email: info@ceoresources.com
Web: www.ceoresources.com

Description: CEO Resources, Inc. pioneered retained executive search in the mid-Atlantic region's growing high-technology sectors. Since our inception in 1989, we have recruited C and VP level leadership for hundreds of technology companies. The majority of our clients are internet and ecommerce related companies in various stages of development.

Key Contact:
Ms. R. Linda Resnick, President

Salary minimum: $150,000

Functions: Generalist

Industries: Consumer Elect., Electronic, Elec. Components, E-commerce, IT Implementation, New Media, Aerospace, Software

cfoheadhunter.com
21 W 39th St Fl 6
New York, NY 10018
(212) 696-4665
Fax: (212) 382-3480
Email: info@cfoheadhunter.com
Web: www.cfoheadhunter.com

Description: Chief financial officer selection for private equity investors at the portfolio company level.

Key Contact:
Mr. Patrick M. Jennings, President/Managing Partner - *CFO's*
Mr. H. Joe Chin, Partner

Salary minimum: $125,000

Functions: Generalist, CFO's

Industries: Generalist

cFour Partners
100 Wilshire Blvd Ste 1840
Santa Monica, CA 90401
(310) 394-2639
Fax: (310) 394-2669
Email: info@cfour.com
Web: www.cfour.com

Description: We are a specialized executive search firm serving vendors, service providers, and end users involved in the technology, software and semiconductor, networking and telecommunications, digital media and entertainment, and venture capital markets across all functional roles.

Key Contact - Specialty:
Ms. Jennifer Happillon, Director - *Software, digital media, entertainment, e-commerce*
Mr. Robert W. Bellano, Director - *Technology, software, telecommunications, venture capital, e-commerce*
Mr. John Emery, Director - *Information technology, finance, e-commerce*

Salary minimum: $150,000

Functions: Senior Mgmt.

Industries: Energy, Utilities, Computer Equip., Venture Cap., E-commerce, New Media, Broadcast, Film, Telecoms, Wireless, Fiber Optic, Software

Professional Associations: ICSA, SCSC

Networks: ITP Worldwide

Branches:
8880 Rio San Diego Dr Fl 8
San Diego, CA 92108
(619) 209-6106
Fax: (619) 209-6097
Email: info@cfour.com
Key Contact - Specialty:
Mr. Donald Parker, Director - *Biotechnology, software, telecommunications*
Mr. Bradley Little, Director - *Broadband, software, telecommunications, semiconductor, energy/utilities*

Chaloner Associates Inc
36 Milford St
Boston, MA 02118-3612
(617) 451-5170
Fax: (617) 451-8160
Email: chaloner@chaloner.com
Web: www.chaloner.com

Description: We work in the fields of corporate communications, marketing, public relations, advertising, investor relations, internal, orginizational and marketing communications.

Key Contact - Specialty:
Mr. Edward H. Chaloner, President - *Public relations, corporate communications*
Ms. Sally Burke, Senior Associate - *Advertising, marketing*
Mr. Chris McLean, Senior Associate - *Marketing, investor relations*
Ms. Loring Barnes, Associate - *Public relations*
Ms. Michelle Shea, Associate - *Public relations*
Mr. Rich Young, Associate - *Corporate communications, internal communications*
Mr. Tom Lutrzy, Associate - *Communications (Organizational and corporate)*

Salary minimum: $75,000

Functions: Sales & Mktg., Advertising, Mkt. Research, Mktg. Mgmt., Direct Mktg., PR, Graphic Artists

Industries: Generalist

Professional Associations: ACB, AMA, IABC, MPPC, NEHRA, NIRI, PRSA

Chanko-Ward Ltd
2 W 45th St
New York, NY 10036
(212) 869-4040
Fax: (212) 869-0281

Description: In the global marketplace, we have been functional specialists for more than 35 years in the identification and selection of financial, accounting, planning, and information technology professionals in all industries.

Key Contact:
Mr. Jim Chanko, President

Salary minimum: $100,000

Functions: HR Mgmt., Finance, CFO's, Budgeting, Cash Mgmt., M&A, IT

Industries: Generalist

Professional Associations: IACPR

Robert B Channing Consulting
1099 Rebecca St
Oakville, ON L6L 1Y6
Canada
(905) 338-9981
Fax: (905) 338-9982
Email: rbcc@globalserve.net

Description: A small firm working in all sectors and headed by the ex-leader of KPMG's Executive Search Practice. Mr. Channing was also a partner with Korn/Ferry International's Canadian operation.

Key Contact:
Mr. Robert B. Channing, President

Salary minimum: $75,000

Functions: Generalist

Industries: Generalist

The Chase Group Inc
7300 W 110th St Ste 560
Overland Park, KS 66210
(913) 663-3100
Fax: (913) 663-3131
Email: chase@chasegroup.com
Web: www.chasegroup.com

Description: We are an executive search firm specializing in the substantive areas of the pharmaceutical, biotechnology, and diagnostic industries.

Key Contact - Specialty:
Ms. Karen Leathers, President - *Pharmaceutical, biotechnology, diagnostics*
Mr. Ken Allison, COO - *Pharmaceutical, biotechnology, diagnostics*
Mr. Matt Stewart - *Rx (exclusive, contingent searches)*
Mr. Dennis Landis - *Agriculture*
Ms. Angela Garcia - *Advertising, marketing*

Salary minimum: $80,000

Functions: General Mgmt., Senior Mgmt., Mfg., Materials, Sales & Mktg., HR Mgmt., M&A, IT, R&D, Int'l.

Industries: Agri., Forestry, Mining, Drugs Mfg., Medical Devices, Pharm Svcs., Media, Advertising, Biotech, Healthcare

Chase Hunter Group Inc
1143 W North Shore Ave
Chicago, IL 60626
(773) 338-7865
(773) 262-0345
Fax: (773) 338-7869
Email: hunter@enteract.com
Web: www.chase-hunter.com

Description: Our firm is healthcare's partner in superlative search. We place the right people in the right roles in the right institution focusing upon the elusive intangible fit that determines longevity in the workplace. Now celebrating our fifth year, we have a 98% candidate retention rate and a 99% client return rate. We are a boutique firm that is quality and not number driven.

Key Contact - Specialty:
Mr. Bob Douglas, Principal - *Healthcare, middle management, administration, clinical, systems*
Mr. Jim Schneider, Vice President - *Research, systems*

Salary minimum: $50,000

Functions: Generalist, Middle Mgmt., Healthcare, Nurses, Allied Health, Health Admin., MIS Mgmt.

Industries: Generalist, Drugs Mfg., Services, HR Services, Insurance, Healthcare

Professional Associations: ACHE, NAER

ChaseAmerica Inc
11211 Prosperity Farms Rd Ste 210C
Palm Beach Gardens, FL 33410
(561) 622-1120
Fax: (561) 626-4646
Email: chaseamericainc@msn.com
Web: www.chaseamericainc.com

Description: Recruit top talent for companies in leisure, resorts, and sports, builders and developers, real estate investment trusts. Within these specialties, CFO and corporate counsel because that's the business we know better than anyone else.

Key Contact - Specialty:
Mr. David E. Stefan, President - *Sports, golf, apparel, sports products companies*

Salary minimum: $100,000

Functions: Generalist, Senior Mgmt.

Industries: Generalist, Construction, Finance, Hospitality, Real Estate

Networks: Cornerstone Int'l Group

The Cherbonnier Group Inc
(a division of TCG Int'l Inc)
5151 San Felipe Ste 420
Houston, TX 77056
(713) 688-4701
Fax: (713) 960-1168
Email: consult@chergroup.com

Description: Extensive domestic and international experience. Searches have crossed most industry lines and most senior positions both line and staff. Thirty years' executive search experience on worldwide scale. Provide in-depth candidate evaluations.

Key Contact:
Mr. L. Michael Cherbonnier, President

Salary minimum: $100,000

Functions: Generalist

Industries: Generalist, Energy, Utilities, Construction, Mfg., Finance, Services, Communications, Environmental Svcs., Software, Biotech

The Cheyenne Group
60 E 42nd St Ste 2821
New York, NY 10165
(212) 471-5000
Fax: (212) 471-5050
Email: cheyenne1@cheyennegroup.com

Description: We advise and assist management in the recruitment and selection of senior executives and professional personnel in media, entertainment, broadcasting, and publishing industries. We assist management in building businesses, development of corporate structures, and leadership selection.

Key Contact - Specialty:
Ms. Pat Mastandrea, Partner - *Media, entertainment, publishing, new media, communications*
Ms. Anna McCormick Kelch, Partner - *Media, entertainment, publishing, new media, communications*
Ms. Franca Virgili, Partner - *Media, entertainment, publishing, new media, communications*
Ms. Kim Macalister, Partner - *Media, entertainment, publishing, new media, communications*
Ms. Willa Perlman, Partner - *Media, entertainment, publishing, new media, communications*

Salary minimum: $150,000

Functions: Generalist

Industries: Mgmt. Consulting, HR Services, E-commerce, Hospitality, Media, Entertainment SW, HR SW, Marketing SW

Chicago Consulting Partners Ltd
930 4th Ave S
Libertyville, IL 60048
(847) 680-0416
Email: rpugh@ccpltd.com
Web: www.ccpltd.com

Description: Retainer firm specializing in senior positions throughout North America. Principals experienced in industries of specialty.

Key Contact - Specialty:
Mr. Robert Pugh - *Actuaries, employee benefits consulting, financial*
Mr. Brett P. Lichty - *Actuaries, insurance positions, financial*

Salary minimum: $80,000

Functions: Generalist

Industries: Finance, Insurance

Chicago Research Group Inc
PO Box 3757
Chapel Hill, NC 27515
(919) 968-0120
Email: chgoresgrp@mindspring.com

Description: We were founded with one single goal in mind: provide the highest quality business research in the industry... business research that is accurate, thorough and timely.

Key Contact:
Ms. Deborah Marshall
Mr. Robert Ross

Salary minimum: $75,000

Functions: Generalist

Industries: Generalist

Childs & Associates
1862 Independence Sq Ste A
Atlanta, GA 30338
(770) 395-1542
Fax: (770) 395-1090
Email: childsassoc@mindspring.com

Description: Relationship driven generalist executive search firm that emphasizes recruitment of senior and mid-level management in marketing, sales, manufacturing, operations, human resources and finance.

Key Contact:
Ms. Karen H. Childs, President

Salary minimum: $75,000

Functions: Generalist, Senior Mgmt., Mfg., Materials, Sales & Mktg., HR Mgmt., Finance

Industries: Generalist, Agri., Forestry, Mining, Chemicals, Wholesale, HR Services, Publishing, Telecoms

Choi & Burns LLC
590 Madison Ave Fl 26
New York, NY 10022
(212) 755-7051
Fax: (212) 355-2610
Email: search@choiburns.com
Web: www.choiburns.com

Description: Completely client driven, very consultative boutique search firm with exclusive focus on financial services, primarily investment banking and private equity.

Key Contact:
Ms. Julie A. Choi, President/CEO - *Senior positions, investment, banking, venture capital, private equity*
Ms. Bethany E. Burns, Managing Director - *Investment banking, equity research, venture capital*
Ms. Sumi Kang, Principal

Salary minimum: $500,000

Functions: General Mgmt., Directors

Industries: Invest. Banking, Venture Cap.

Professional Associations: AESC

Chowne Beatson Consultants†
1055 W Hastings St Ste 300
Vancouver, BC V6E 2E9
Canada
(604) 609-6161
(604) 689-8016

Description: We offer cost-effective executive search selection services to our corporate clients through our extensive network of senior contacts. Our practice is limited to our local area.

Key Contact - Specialty:
Mr. Godfrey Chowne, Partner - *Manufacturers, distributors, trading companies, financial organizations*
Mr. Grant Beatson, Partner - *Manufacturers, distributors, trading companies, financial organizations*

Functions: Generalist, Senior Mgmt., Middle Mgmt., Benefits, Personnel, CFO's, Mgmt. Consultants, Non-profits

Industries: Generalist, Transportation, Finance, HR Services, Insurance, Real Estate, Biotech

Professional Associations: ACG

Chrisman & Company Inc
350 S Figueroa St Ste 550
Los Angeles, CA 90071
(213) 620-1192
Email: lachrisman@worldnet.att.net

Description: Board member, middle and upper echelon executive searches, nationally.

Key Contact - Specialty:
Mr. Timothy Chrisman, President - *Generalist*

Salary minimum: $90,000

Functions: Generalist, Directors, Senior Mgmt., Middle Mgmt., HR Mgmt., Finance

Industries: Generalist, Banking, Invest. Banking, Brokers, Misc. Financial, Insurance, Real Estate

Christenson, Hutchison, McDowell LLC
466 Southern Blvd
Chatham, NJ 07928-1462
(973) 966-1600
Fax: (973) 966-6933
Email: solutions@chmsearch.com
Web: www.chmsearch.com

Description: Established in 1976. Partner management of all assignments. Nationwide practice, serving large public corporations and small privately held organizations in professional services, biotechnology/pharmaceutical, academia/research centers, and telecommunication industries.

Key Contact - Specialty:
Mr. H. Alan Christenson, Partner
Mr. Robert N. McDowell, Managing Partner
Mr. Paul H. Sartori, Partner - *Biotechnology, pharmaceutical industries*

Salary minimum: $120,000

Functions: Directors, Senior Mgmt., Mktg. Mgmt., Sales Mgmt., HR Mgmt., CFO's, MIS Mgmt., Mgmt. Consultants, Int'l.

Industries: Mfg., Services, Higher Ed., Pharm Svcs., Telecoms, Biotech, Healthcare

Professional Associations: AESC, IACPR

Networks: EMA Partners Int'l

Christian & Timbers
25825 Science Park Dr Ste 400
1 Corporate Exchange
Cleveland, OH 44122
(216) 464-8710
(800) 380-9444
Fax: (216) 464-6160
Email: comments@ctnet.com
Web: www.ctnet.com

Description: Our firm is one of the leading global executive search firms focusing on CEO, board of directors, and senior-level executive assignments.

Key Contact - Specialty:
Mr. Jeffrey E. Christian, Chairman/CEO - *CEO/Board, information technology, networking, telecommunications*

Mr. Mark T. Kesic, Managing Director-Technology & Venture - *Data, telecommunications, enterprise software*
Mr. Adam Kohn, Managing Dir-Prof Svcs & Emerging Tech - *Internet, professional consulting services, telecommunications, utility services, venture capital*
Mr. Michael C. Nieset, Managing Dir-Technology & Board Services - *Software, telecommunications*
Mr. David Nocifora, CFO - *Contract manufacturing, corporate finance & banking, enterprise software, transportation*
Mr. Shawn M. Oglesbee, Managing Dir-Semiconductor & Photonics - *Contract manufacturing, electronics, photonics, semiconductor*
Mr. William "Kip" C. Schmidt, III, Managing Director-Corporate - *Healthcare, medical devices, information technology, manufacturing, automation*
Mr. Gregory Selker, Managing Director-Technology & Venture - *Computer software, data communications, interactive media, online services, internet/e-commerce, telecommunications*

Salary minimum: $150,000

Functions: Senior Mgmt.

Industries: Mfg., Finance, Venture Cap., E-commerce, New Media, Telecoms, Network Infrastructure, Software, Biotech, Non-classifiable

Professional Associations: AESC

Branches:
20833 Stevens Creek Blvd Ste 200
Cupertino, CA 95014
(408) 446-5440
Fax: (408) 446-5445
Key Contact - Specialty:
Mr. David R. Mather, Managing Director - *Communications, computer software, international, internet, e-commerce, professional services*
Ms. Linda Mikula, Managing Director- Technology & Venture - *Communications, enterprise consulting, internet infrastructure, network management*

114 Pacifica Ste 150
Irvine, CA 92618-3326
(949) 727-3400
Fax: (949) 727-1295
Key Contact - Specialty:
Mr. Robert J. Lambert, Managing Director-Technology & Venture - *E-commerce, general consumer retail, software, venture capital*

701 Sutter St Fl 6
San Francisco, CA 94109
(415) 885-8004
Fax: (415) 885-8071
Key Contact - Specialty:
Ms. Vici Wayne, Managing Dir-New Media, Tech & Venture - *Internet, software, e-commerce, new media*

750 Washington Blvd Fl 5
Stamford, CT 06901
(203) 352-6000
Fax: (203) 975-0299
Key Contact - Specialty:
Mr. Mark Esposito, Managing Director-Financial Services - *Asset management, capital markets, financial e-commerce, insurance, investment banking*
Mr. Marc Lewis, Managing Director-Technology & Venture - *Computer hardware, computer software, corporate IT/CIO/CTO, internet, e-commerce, media & communications*

3460 Preston Ridge Rd Ste 175
Alpharetta, GA 30005
(770) 754-1198
Fax: (770) 619-5201
Key Contact - Specialty:
Mr. Russ Gray, Managing Director - *Convergent technologies, telecommunications*

1 S Wacker Dr Ste 1990
Chicago, IL 60606
(312) 281-1160
Fax: (312) 372-6013
Key Contact - Specialty:
Ms. Birgit R. Westphal, Managing Director-
Industrial/Mfg - *Automotive, industrial,
manufacturing*

8840 Stanford Blvd Ste 2900
Columbia, MD 21045
(410) 872-0200
Fax: (410) 872-0208
Key Contact - Specialty:
Mr. William C. Buster Houchins, Managing
Director-Mid Atlantic Ops - *Consulting services,
information technology, internet, new media,
semiconductor & electronics*

24 New England Executive Park
Burlington, MA 01803
(781) 229-9515
Fax: (781) 229-8608
Key Contact - Specialty:
Mr. Stephen P. Mader, President/COO - *Computer
software, data communications, electronic media,
industrial technology, information technology*
Mr. Seth Harris, Managing Director- Technology &
Venture - *Application service providers, data
networking, enterprise software, internet, e-
commerce, RBOC/IXCs/ISPs*
Mr. Len Vairo, Managing Dir- Technology &
Board Svcs - *E-commerce, e-CRM, enterprise
software, managed services outsourcing,
telecommunications*
Mr. Robert Nephew, Managing Director -
*Information technology, systems integration,
systems software, high-tech manufacturing,
insurance*

570 Lexington Ave Fl 19
New York, NY 10022
(212) 588-3500
Fax: (212) 688-5754
Key Contact - Specialty:
Mr. Tom Brennan, Managing Director-Financial
Services - *Asset management, capital markets,
research, sales & trading, structured finance*
Mr. John Daily, Managing Director-Technology -
*E-commerce, computer (software, hardware),
systems integration, IT services, new media*
Ms. Paula Seibel, Managing Director - *E-
commerce, new media, entertainment, travel,
hospitality*

1750 Tysons Blvd Ste 540
McLean, VA 22102
(703) 448-1700
Fax: (703) 447-1740
Key Contact - Specialty:
Mr. Paul Unger, Managing Director- Telecom &
Technology - *Telecommunications, satellite
communications, IT services, communications
(hardware, software), computer (hardware,
software)*
Mr. Gary Roberts, Managing Director-Technology
& Venture - *Computer software, e-commerce,
internet, professional services,
telecommunications*

130 King St W Ste 2130
The Exchange Twr
PO Box 11
Toronto, ON M5X 1A9
Canada
(416) 628-5175
Fax: (416) 628-5015
Key Contact - Specialty:
Mr. David Kinley, Managing Director-Canadian
Operations - *Venture capital, high technology,
telecommunications, financial services, energy*

William J Christopher Associates Inc
307 N Walnut St
West Chester, PA 19380
(610) 696-4397

Email: wjc@wjca.com
Web: www.wjca.com

Description: We have more than 25 years of
successful executive search experience at corporate
and operating levels with companies large, small,
public and private with business in diversified
industries, such as distribution, manufacturing, and
service companies.

Key Contact:
Mr. John Jeffrey Bole, President

Salary minimum: $50,000

Functions: Directors, Senior Mgmt., Middle
Mgmt., Plant Mgmt.

Industries: Mfg., Paper, Printing

Christopher-Westmont & Associates Inc
PO Box 470188
Broadview Heights, OH 44147
(440) 877-0510
Fax: (440) 877-0511
Email: cwestmont@aol.com

Description: Firm is focused on high-technology
including manufacturing, engineering and
operations in automotive and general industry.

Key Contact:
Mr. John R. Donnelly, Consultant - *Automotive
manufacturing, original equipment
manufacturing, suppliers to OEM (Tier 1, Tier 2)*
Mr. Patrick Donnelly, Consultant - *Financial
services, academia*
Mr. Christopher Donnelly, Consultant -
Manufacturing
Mr. Randy Letsch, Partner

Salary minimum: $100,000

Functions: Senior Mgmt., Mfg., Plant Mgmt.,
Quality, Materials, Sales & Mktg., Sales Mgmt.,
HR Mgmt., CFO's, Engineering

Industries: Generalist, Metal Products, Motor
Vehicles, Aerospace, Packaging, Biotech

Churchill & Affiliates Inc
1200 Bustleton Pike Ste 3
Feasterville, PA 19053
(215) 364-8070
Fax: (215) 322-4391
Email: hwasserman@churchillsearch.com
Web: www.churchillsearch.com

Description: Executive search and recruitment for
the telecommunications industry. Specialize in
sales, marketing, engineering and support from
senior management to field sales and support,
domestically and internationally.

Key Contact - Specialty:
Mr. Harvey Wasserman, President -
Telecommunications

Salary minimum: $75,000

Functions: Senior Mgmt.

Industries: Equip Svcs., Advertising, Telecoms,
Telephony, Digital, Fiber Optic, Network
Infrastructure, Software, Networking, Comm. SW

M A Churchill & Associates Inc
1111 Rd Ste 307
Morelyn Plz
Southampton, PA 18966
(215) 953-0300
Email: info@machurchill.com
Web: www.machurchill.com

Description: A highly focused search firm for the
information technology, banking/Wall
Street/financial systems vendors - worldwide.
Recruiting disciplines are sales, marketing,
management, support, pre/post-sales support,

product/marketing management, project
management and senior systems development.

Key Contact:
Mr. Lawrence Sher, Managing Director
Mr. Stuart S. Borden, Vice President
Mr. John H. Spicher, Division Manager
Mr. Brian M. Hochberg, Division Manager
Ms. Pamela A. Wylie, Business Development
Coordinator
Ms. Dolores Garzone, Business Development
Coordinator
Mr. David Caplan, National Accounts Manager
Mr. Jack Warrington, National Accounts Manager

Salary minimum: $50,000

Functions: Generalist, General Mgmt., Sales &
Mktg., Finance, IT, Int'l.

Industries: Generalist, Computer Equip., Finance,
Accounting, Media, Software

Cizek Associates Inc
2390 E Camelback Rd Ste 300
Biltmore Financial Ctr
Phoenix, AZ 85016
(602) 553-1066
Fax: (602) 553-1166
Email: inquiry@cizekassociates.com
Web: www.cizekassociates.com

Description: Generalist firm with strength in
manufacturing, consumer products, technology,
healthcare, non-profit and banking/financial
services. With offices in Phoenix, Chicago, and
Silicon Valley, we serve clients coast to coast and in
Europe.

Key Contact - Specialty:
Ms. Marti J. Cizek, President - *Generalist*
Mr. Edward G. Linskey, Jr., Senior Vice President
- *Generalist*

Salary minimum: $100,000

Functions: Generalist, General Mgmt., Mfg.,
Purchasing, Sales & Mktg., HR Mgmt., Finance,
IT, Int'l.

Industries: Food, Bev., Tobacco, Printing, Medical
Devices, Metal Products, Computer Equip.,
Consumer Elect., Test, Measure Equip., Misc.
Mfg., Venture Cap., Non-profits, Higher Ed.,
Accounting, Equip Svcs., Telecoms

Professional Associations: AMA, APA

Branches:
2021 Midwest Rd Ste 200
Oak Brook, IL 60523
(630) 953-8570
Email: inquiry@cizekassociates.com
Key Contact - Specialty:
Mr. John T. Cizek, Principal - *Generalist*

CJA-The Adler Group Inc
17852 17th St Ste 209
Tustin, CA 92780
(714) 573-1820
Fax: (714) 731-3952
Email: coach@cjapower.com
Web: www.cjapower.com

Description: Creators of Power Hiring, the five-step
recruiting and assessment process now used by
thousands of managers. Also, offer half-day Power
Hiring workshops to all clients. Includes
performance profiles and unique new assessment
tools.

Key Contact - Specialty:
Mr. Louis S. Adler, Chairman - *High technology,
manufacturing, sales & marketing*
Mr. Brad M. Remillard, President - *Distribution,
finance & accounting*

Salary minimum: $80,000

Functions: Generalist, Senior Mgmt., Plant Mgmt., Purchasing, Materials Plng., Mkt. Research, Sales Mgmt., CFO's

Industries: Generalist, Plastics, Rubber, Computer Equip., Hospitality, Telecoms, Software

Professional Associations: NAER

Branches:
5757 Century Blvd Ste 700
Los Angeles, CA 90045
(310) 378-4571
Fax: (310) 791-4434
Email: barryd@cjapower.com
Key Contact:
Mr. Barry A. Deutsch, Managing Director/Senior VP

Arlene Clapp Ltd
4250 Park Glen Rd
Minneapolis, MN 55416
(952) 928-7474
Fax: (952) 928-7475
Email: areneclapp@qwest.net

Description: We specialize in placements in commercial real estate (office, retail, industrial) and construction industries (nationwide).

Key Contact - Specialty:
Ms. Arlene Clapp, President - *Real estate (commercial), construction*

Functions: Generalist

Industries: Construction, Real Estate

Professional Associations: NAIOP

Clarey & Andrews Inc
1200 Shermer Rd Ste 108
Northbrook, IL 60062
(847) 498-2870
Email: ca@clarey-andrews.com

Description: We are a small generalist firm whose assignments are conducted only by experienced principals.

Key Contact - Specialty:
Mr. Jack R. Clarey - *Senior level executives (generalist)*

Salary minimum: $150,000

Functions: Generalist, General Mgmt., Mfg., Sales & Mktg., HR Mgmt., Finance

Industries: Generalist, Mfg.

Professional Associations: AESC

Networks: Penrhyn Int'l

Clarey/Napier Int'l
1221 McKinney Ste 3110
Houston, TX 77010
(713) 238-6705
Fax: (713) 236-4778
Email: cni@cnintl.com

Description: Worldwide executive search specializing in all phases of the energy industry including oil and gas, chemicals, power, refining, petrochemicals, engineering and construction, environmental and management consulting services.

Key Contact:
Mr. William A. Clarey, II, Partner
Ms. Ginger L. Napier, Partner

Salary minimum: $100,000

Functions: Generalist

Industries: Energy, Utilities, Construction, Mfg., Mgmt. Consulting, HR Services

Clarity Partners LLC
94 Edmunds Rd
Wellesley Hills, MA 02481
(781) 431-7719
Fax: (781) 431-0798
Email: claritypartners@mediaone.net

Description: We are a boutique executive search firm focused on senior financial and human resources executives.

Key Contact - Specialty:
Mr. Walter Williams, Managing Partner - *Senior financial executives*

Salary minimum: $150,000

Functions: General Mgmt., Senior Mgmt., HR Mgmt., Finance, CFO's

Industries: Generalist

Professional Associations: AESC, IACPR

Clark Brancato & Associates
45 Brookside Ave
Chester, NY 10918
(845) 469-3074
Fax: (845) 469-3078
Email: info@clarkbrancato.com

Description: Consultants for non-profit executive search and leadership transition, as well as executive coaching, workgroup development, succession planning, and other related services.

Key Contact:
Ms. Leslie Clark Brancato

Salary minimum: $75,000

Functions: General Mgmt., Directors, Senior Mgmt., Middle Mgmt., CFO's, Minorities, Non-profits

Industries: Non-profits

Clark Executive Search Inc
135 N Ferry Rd
PO Box 560
Shelter Island, NY 11964
(631) 749-3540
Fax: (631) 749-3539
Email: mail@clarksearch.com
Web: www.clarksearch.com

Description: A recruiting firm that specializes in finding mid- to senior executives for pharmaceutical, biotechnology and medical device companies. As niche-market specialists, we fully understand the whole drug development process from discovery to finished product.

Key Contact - Specialty:
Ms. Ellen H. Clark, President - *Pharmaceutical, biotech*

Salary minimum: $100,000

Functions: Generalist

Industries: Drugs Mfg., Medical Devices, Pharm Svcs., Biotech

Professional Associations: AAPS, DIA, PDA, TNC

Ken Clark Int'l
2000 Lenox Dr Ste 200
Lawrenceville, NJ 08648
(609) 308-5200
Fax: (609) 308-5250
Email: info@kenclark.com
Web: www.kenclark.com

Description: As a global firm with 11 offices, over 60 consultants, and support staff, we serve only one or two clients in each industry so as to provide virtually unlimited recruiting targets to our select clients. We specialize in biotechnology, pharmaceutical, consumer, industrial, agricultural, medical, scientific, and advanced technology industries.

Key Contact - Specialty:
Mr. Kenneth Clark, Chairman/CEO - *Executive, board level*
Mr. Sundeep Shankwalkar, President-Emerging Markets & Japan - *Emerging markets, Japan*
Mr. William O'Callaghan, Co-President, North America - *Medical devices, pharmaceuticals*

Salary minimum: $120,000

Functions: Generalist, General Mgmt., Mfg., Materials, Sales & Mktg., IT, R&D, Engineering

Industries: Mfg., Chemicals, Soap, Perf., Cosmtcs., Drugs Mfg., Medical Devices, Test, Measure Equip., Pharm Svcs., HR Services, Biotech, Healthcare

Branches:
660 Newport Center Dr Ste 770
Newport Beach, CA 92660
(949) 219-0900
Fax: (949) 219-9800
Email: info-newportbeach@kenclark.com
Key Contact:
Mr. Jeffrey Clark, Co-President, North America

Richard Clarke & Associates Inc
9 W 95th St Ste C
New York, NY 10025
(212) 222-5600
Fax: (212) 222-6204
Email: richardclarkeassociates@msn.com
Web: www.diversityrecruiting.com

Description: Minority recruiting, all skill areas, i.e. accounting, finance, sales, marketing, engineering, IT, law and human resources.

Key Contact:
Mr. Richard Clarke, President

Salary minimum: $70,000

Functions: Generalist, Minorities

Industries: Generalist

Professional Associations: SHRM

Classic Consultants Inc
8051 N Tamiami Trl
Sarasota, FL 34243
(941) 351-3500
(800) 949-6107
Email: cci3513500@aol.com

Description: We are executive search recruiting partnering with special need population providers. We specialize in special education, child and adolescent mental health, mental retardation, and developmental disabilities.

Key Contact:
Ms. Edith Young, CEO

Functions: Generalist

Industries: Long-term Care, Physical Therapy

Clayman & Company
197 Commonwealth Ave Ste 3
Boston, MA 02116
(617) 578-9999
Fax: (617) 578-9929
Email: sclayman@claymaninterests.com

Description: Proud of over 25 years of recruiting of sales and marketing executives for high-technology clients. We rely on our original research plus our database of 40,000+ previously interviewed sales/marketing executives.

Key Contact - Specialty:
Mr. Steven G. Clayman, Managing Partner - *High technology, sales & marketing*
Mr. John H. Crawford, Partner - *High technology, sales & marketing*
Mr. Vincent Brennan, Partner - *High technology, sales & marketing*

Salary minimum: $150,000

Functions: Sales & Mktg.

Industries: Advertising, New Media, Telecoms, Software

CMB Conasa Consulting SC

San Francisco 1838 Ste 303
Col de Valle
ZIP 44185-03100 Mexico City, DF 03100
Mexico
52 5 534 3265
52 5 534 3227
Fax: 52 5 524 0709
Email: conasasc@avantel.net
Web: www.avantel.net/conasasc

Description: The most professional and effective middle-size executive search firm in Mexico, characterized for diversifying its clients in different lines of business, acting without any interference in order to provide the best available candidates, under a strict profile previously agreed upon.

Key Contact - Specialty:
Mr. Fernando Zambrana, Managing Principal - *Management (upper-level), services, commerce*
Ms. Victoria Villareal, Associate Director - *Middle management, industry services, commerce*
Ms. Mariana Martinez, Associate Director - *Middle management, industry and services*

Salary minimum: $75,000

Functions: Generalist, General Mgmt., Mfg., Materials, Sales & Mktg., HR Mgmt., Finance, IT

Industries: Generalist, Mfg., Wholesale, Retail, Finance, Services, Software

Networks: Global Search Partners

Coast Personnel Services Ltd†

Station A
PO Box 2313
Nanaimo, BC V9R 6E8
Canada
(250) 758-1828
Fax: (250) 758-8244
Email: resume@coastpersonnel.com
Web: www.coastpersonnel.com

Description: We have had sixteen years of executive and technical recruiting and consulting experience in Western Canada. Our industry focus is on information technology, forestry, lumber, pulp and paper, and general manufacturing. We specialize in the categories of sales, accounting, management, engineering, technicians, operators, programmers, and designers. We provide personnel consulting to increase productivity and reduce employee turnover.

Key Contact - Specialty:
Mr. Vincent G. B. Willden, President - *Technical sales, engineering, accounting*

Salary minimum: $40,000

Functions: Generalist, General Mgmt., Materials, Sales & Mktg., Finance, IT, Engineering, Specialized Svcs.

Industries: Generalist, Agri., Forestry, Mining, Energy, Utilities, Mfg., Services, Accounting, Communications, Haz. Waste, Software

COBA Executive Search

14947 E Wagon Trail Pl
Aurora, CO 80015
(303) 693-8382
Email: mkiken@qwest.net

Description: We fill positions in a wide range of industries in the US, the Americas, Eastern Europe, and elsewhere. Our candidates are selected not only for skill sets but their ability to blend into the cultural environment of our clients.

Key Contact - Specialty:
Mr. Mark E. Kiken, Ph.D., President - *Manufacturing, software, biotech, high tech, food*

Salary minimum: $85,000

Functions: Generalist

Industries: Agri., Forestry, Mining, Energy, Utilities, Mfg., Food, Bev., Tobacco, Drugs Mfg., Medical Devices, Computer Equip., Communications, Software, Biotech

Professional Associations: RACC

Cochran, Cochran & Yale LLC

955 E Henrietta Rd
Rochester, NY 14623
(716) 424-6060
Fax: (716) 424-6069
Email: roch@ccy.com
Web: www.ccy.com

Description: We provide retained search with specialized divisions, which include: finance, human resources, software, electronics, process manufacturing, and consumer products marketing and sales. The industries that we serve include: pharmaceuticals, plastics, high-tech electronics, aerospace, consumer products, banking, biotechnology, and wine/spirits.

Key Contact - Specialty:
Mr. Gary M. Baker, Partner - *Finance, human resources, marketing executives, manufacturing, supply chain*
Mr. Walter Y. Critchley, President - *CIO, marketing, general management, operations, manufacturing*

Salary minimum: $60,000

Functions: Generalist, General Mgmt., Mfg., Materials, Sales & Mktg., HR Mgmt., Finance, IT

Industries: Energy, Utilities, Food, Bev., Tobacco, Chemicals, Soap, Perf., Cosmtcs., Plastics, Rubber, Machine, Appliance, Banking

Professional Associations: DPMA, IEEE, IMA, SHRM

Branches:
9351 Grant St Ste 250
Denver, CO 80229
(303) 252-4600
Fax: (303) 252-7810
Email: denver@ccy.com
Key Contact - Specialty:
Mr. Chet Marino, Vice President - *Engineering, accounting & finance, information technology, human resources, software*

5900 Main St
Williamsville, NY 14221
(716) 631-1300
Fax: (716) 631-1319
Email: buff@ccy.com
Key Contact - Specialty:
Mr. Walter Critchley, President - *Manufacturing, operations, human resources, finance & accounting, information technology*

Dean M Coe Associates

32 Pine St
Sandwich, MA 02563
(508) 888-8029
Email: dcoe@onemain.com

Description: We are specialists in corporate real estate and non-profit executives.

Key Contact:
Ms. Wendy Borsari, Director of Research

Salary minimum: $100,000

Functions: General Mgmt., Senior Mgmt., Non-profits

Industries: Non-profits, Telecoms, Real Estate

Professional Associations: AESC

The Coelyn Group

1 Park Plz Fl 6
Irvine, CA 92614
(949) 553-8855
Fax: (949) 363-0837
Email: tcg@execsearch.com

Description: Retainer-based executive search firm specializing in senior-level executive positions strictly in life sciences; medical device; pharmaceutical; biotechnology; e-commerce; diagnostics.

Key Contact - Specialty:
Mr. Ronald H. Coelyn, Partner - *Life sciences*
Ms. Carol L. Moson, Partner - *Life sciences*
Ms. Lynn S. Nishimoto, Partner - *Life sciences*
Ms. Kathleen H. Fehling, Partner - *Life sciences*

Salary minimum: $200,000

Functions: Generalist

Industries: Drugs Mfg., Medical Devices, Biotech

Professional Associations: HIMA

Branches:
10151 Deerwood Park Blvd Bldg 200 Ste 250
Jacksonville, FL 32256
(904) 371-3566
Fax: (904) 280-8301
Key Contact - Specialty:
Ms. Kathleen H. Fehling, Partner - *Life sciences*

Coffou Partners Inc

1 IBM Plz 330 N Wabash Ave Ste 2111
Chicago, IL 60611
(312) 464-0896
Fax: (312) 464-0322
Email: info@coffou.com
Web: www.coffou.com

Description: Our firm is a full-service, retainer-based executive search and business consulting firm serving global clients throughout the US and around the world. We conduct mid- and senior-level executive searches for a variety of industries, including healthcare, high technology, consumer products, e-Business, and manufacturing.

Key Contact:
Ms. Sara Coffou, President

Salary minimum: $75,000

Functions: Generalist, General Mgmt., Sales & Mktg., HR Mgmt., IT

Industries: Generalist

Franchot Cohen & Associates Inc

810 Lake St E
Wayzata, MN 55391
(952) 253-0080
Fax: (952) 253-0081
Email: doug@franchotcohen.com
Web: www.franchotcohen.com

Description: We are a general practice firm with particular expertise in small and mid-cap companies and not-for-profits.

Key Contact - Specialty:
Mr. Douglas Franchot, President - *General management*
Ms. Christine Cohen, Vice President - *General management*

Salary minimum: $100,000

Cole, Warren & Long Inc

2 Penn Center Plz Ste 312
Philadelphia, PA 19102
(215) 563-0701
(800) 394-8517
Fax: (215) 563-2907
Email: cwlserch@cwl-inc.com
Web: www.cwl-inc.com

Description: An executive search and general management consulting firm, servicing domestic and int'l clients. Broad range of clients including: financial services, insurance, banking, mfg., information technology, electronics, utilities, healthcare, etc. Unique hourly rate offers many options to clients.

Key Contact - Specialty:
Mr. Ronald Cole, Chairman of the Board - *General management*
Mr. Richard Warren, CMC, President - *General management*
Mr. Richard Lewis, Vice President - *Technical, manufacturing*
Mr. Craig Cole - *Middle management*

Salary minimum: $100,000

Functions: General Mgmt., Senior Mgmt., Mfg., Materials, Sales & Mktg., HR Mgmt., IT, MIS Mgmt., Engineering, Mgmt. Consultants

Industries: Energy, Utilities, Mfg., Finance, Mgmt. Consulting, HR Services, Hospitality, Telecoms, Insurance, Software, Healthcare

Professional Associations: IACPR, AAA, ACG, IMC, SHRM, WTA

Coleman Lew & Associates Inc
326 W 10th St
Charlotte, NC 28202
(704) 377-0362
Fax: (704) 377-0424
Email: mail@colemanlew.com
Web: www.colemanlew.com

Description: Established in 1979, firm is a generalist search firm with national clients. Expertise in the food industry with an extensive database supported by a strong research staff.

Key Contact:
Mr. Charles E. Lew, Principal
Mr. Kenneth D. Carrick, Jr., Principal
Ms. Ann N. Whitlock, Principal
Mr. Thomas M. Brinkley, Principal
Mr. Claude Crocker, Partner

Functions: Generalist

Industries: Generalist

Professional Associations: AESC

Colin Phillips Group Inc
PO Box 4679
Boulder, CO 80306-4679
(303) 604-2116
Fax: (303) 604-2501
Email: cfrager@colinphillips.com
Web: www.colinphillips.com

Description: We are focused on recruiting senior management for technology and defense companies.

Key Contact - Specialty:
Mr. Colin P. Frager, President - *Advanced technology, engineering management, electra-optics*

Salary minimum: $100,000

Functions: Senior Mgmt., Middle Mgmt., Mfg., Sales Mgmt., R&D, Engineering, Int'l.

Industries: Generalist, Computer Equip., Test, Measure Equip., Telecoms, Defense

Professional Associations: IEEE, OSA, SHRM

Colton Bernard Inc
870 Market St Ste 822
San Francisco, CA 94102
(415) 399-8700
Fax: (415) 399-0750
Email: inquiry@coltonbernard.com
Web: www.coltonbernard.com

Description: We provide a full range of marketing, information, organizational, and management recruiting services for the fashion industry exclusively. We also offer, licensing, sales training programs, image development, seminars and workshops, and interactive consumer testing.

Key Contact - Specialty:
Mr. Harry Bernard, Partner/Chief Marketing Officer - *Senior management*
Mr. Roy C. Colton, Partner/Chief Executive Officer - *Senior management*
Mr. Brad Smith, Senior Vice President - *Senior management*

Salary minimum: $100,000

Functions: Generalist, Directors, Senior Mgmt., Mktg. Mgmt., CFO's, MIS Mgmt., Mgmt. Consultants, Int'l.

Industries: Textiles, Apparel, Retail

Professional Associations: AAA, AAMA, NAER, SFFI

The Colton Partnership Inc
39 Broadway Ste 710
New York, NY 10006
(212) 509-1800
Fax: (212) 509-1633
Email: whcolton@aol.com

Description: We are generalists with an expertise in financial services and information technology. We adhere to a dedicated personal service that demands the highest standards of professionalism, honesty and integrity. Our corporate creed is excellence and our quality of work is never compromised in the commitment to our clients' requirements.

Key Contact - Specialty:
Mr. W. Hoyt Colton, Chairman - *Financial services*

Salary minimum: $75,000

Functions: Generalist, HR Mgmt., CFO's, Cash Mgmt., M&A, Risk Mgmt., IT

Industries: Generalist, Finance, New Media, Software

Colucci, Blendow & Johnson
PO Box 10
Half Moon Bay, CA 94019
(650) 712-0103
Email: exsearch@it.netcom.com

Description: Thirty-two years of retained search experience in medical technology including pharmaceuticals, diagnostics, biotechnology, medical devices and instrumentation.

Key Contact:
Mr. Bart A. Colucci, President

Salary minimum: $80,000

Functions: Generalist

Industries: Generalist, Drugs Mfg., Medical Devices, Pharm Svcs., Biotech

Columbia Consulting Group
20 S Charles St Fl 9
Sun Life Bldg
Baltimore, MD 21201
(410) 385-2525
Fax: (410) 385-0044
Email: info@ccgsearch.com
Web: www.ccgsearch.com

Description: Client-retained executive search consultants serving most industries and functions.

Key Contact - Specialty:
Mr. Lawrence J. Holmes, Managing Director - *Generalist*
Mr. Philip H. Grantham, Managing Director - *CEOs, CFOs, CIOs, consulting, COOs*
Ms. Julie Mercer, Managing Director - *Asset management, banking, CEOs, CFOs, COOs*
Mr. Cory T. Holmes, Managing Director - *Banking, brokerage, technology, telecommunications*

Mr. Thomas J. McMahon, Managing Principal - *Generalist*
Ms. Cynthia Bomhardt, Managing Principal - *Generalist*
Ms. Mary S. Grant, Managing Director - *Generalist*

Salary minimum: $120,000

Functions: Generalist

Industries: Energy, Utilities, Mfg., Retail, Finance, Non-profits, Telecoms, Aerospace, Insurance, Software, Healthcare

Professional Associations: AESC, IACPR

Networks: Global Search Partners

Branches:
185 Helios Dr
Jupiter, FL 33477
(561) 748-0232
Fax: (561) 748-0234
Key Contact - Specialty:
Mr. Larry D. Mingle, Managing Director - *Generalist*

767 3rd Ave Fl 29
New York, NY 10017
(212) 832-2525
Fax: (212) 832-7722
Email: info@ccgsearch.com
Key Contact - Specialty:
Ms. Ann Fulgham-MacCarthy, Managing Director - *Direct marketing, house wares, jewelry, new media, merchandising*
Ms. Trish Fillo, Managing Director - *Finance, marketing, healthcare*
Ms. Janet Zipse, Managing Director - *Finance*
Mr. David Vernon, Managing Director - *Generalist*

Combined Resources Inc
25300 Lorain Rd Ste 2C
North Olmsted, OH 44070-2059
(440) 716-8272
(877) 236-9789
Fax: (877) 236-4959
Email: info@cri-search.com
Web: www.cri-search.com

Description: We provide comprehensive recruiting and contract consulting services to meet the unique and demanding requirements of professional service firms and financial institutions. Founded in 1987, we have distinguished our firm by providing excellent, cost-effective service to our clients and confidential, respectful service to our candidates. We guarantee the success of our executive search assignments for one full year.

Key Contact:
Mr. Gilbert Sherman, President

Functions: Legal, Finance, CFO's, IT, MIS Mgmt., Attorneys

Industries: Finance, Legal, Accounting, Mgmt. Consulting, HR Services, Hospitality, Media, Telecoms, Software, Biotech

Professional Associations: RON

Commonwealth Resources Inc[†]
262 Washington St Ste 800
Boston, MA 02108
(617) 250-1100
Fax: (617) 250-1199
Email: mdemore@crijobs.com
Web: www.crijobs.com

Description: We are an executive search firm specializing in construction placement within the engineering, construction management, and general contracting industries. We have over 18 years of experience placing vice presidents, construction managers, project managers, estimators, field engineers, project engineers, schedulers, sales and marketing, and business development individuals in the New England, New York/New Jersey, Florida, and DC Areas.

Key Contact:
Mr. Tim Fraser, Executive Vice President

Functions: Middle Mgmt.

Industries: Construction, Real Estate

Compass Group Ltd
401 S Old Woodward Ste 460
Birmingham, MI 48009-6611
(248) 540-9110
Fax: (248) 647-8288
Email: executivesearch@compassgroup.com
Web: www.compassgroup.com

Description: A leading Midwest-based firm,
working internationally, accepting only retained
engagements. Emphasis in automotive,
manufacturing, high-tech and service industries.
Most disciplines.

Key Contact - Specialty:
Mr. Paul W. Czamanske, President/CEO -
Generalist, CEOs, COOs, board searches
Ms. Christina L. Balian, Vice President - *General
management, strategy, finance, sales &
marketing, automotive*
Mr. James W. Sturtz, Vice President - *General
management, automotive, manufacturing, human
resources*
Ms. Kirsten M. Cook, Consultant - *Generalist*
Ms. Lois Duerk, Research Director - *Generalist*

Salary minimum: $100,000

Functions: General Mgmt., Senior Mgmt., Legal,
Mfg., Materials, Sales & Mktg., HR Mgmt.,
CFO's, Non-profits, Int'l.

Industries: Generalist, Higher Ed., Healthcare

Professional Associations: AESC, ASE, IMC

Networks: The Amrop - Hever Group

Branches:
2021 Spring Rd Ste 750
Commerce Plz Bldg
Oak Brook, IL 60523-1880
(630) 645-9110
Fax: (630) 571-7771
Email: executivesearch@compassgroup.com
Key Contact - Specialty:
Mr. Peter M. Czamanske, Vice President -
*Generalist, manufacturing, information
technology*
Mr. Jerold L. Lipe, Vice President - *Generalist,
general management, manufacturing, purchasing,
human resources*

Comprehensive Search[†]
(a division of Jeffrey W Brown Inc)
316 S Lewis St Cary Bldg
LaGrange, GA 30240
(706) 884-3232
Fax: (706) 884-4106
Email: merritt@comp-search.com
Web: www.comp-search.com

Description: Retainer, contingency, recruitment
research and contract employees provided
nationwide. Synergistically, we also offer contract
employees (we presently have them in most major
U.S. cities), testing, outplacement and spousal
assistance.

Key Contact - Specialty:
Mr. Jeffrey W. Brown, President - *Built
environment*
Ms. Gail W. Standard, Vice President - *Built
environment*
Ms. Merritt S. Shelton, Supervisor/Candidate
Resources - *Building products, interior
furnishings*
Ms. Gail Morin, Vice President - *Building
products, interior furnishings*
Ms. Marilyn McSweeney, Senior Account Manager
- *Contract furnishings*
Mr. Jerry Donahue, Account Manager - *Building
products, interior furnishings*

Mr. Kevin Franks, Operations Manager - *IT*

Salary minimum: $30,000

Functions: Generalist

Industries: Construction, Mfg., Textiles, Apparel,
Lumber, Furniture, Leather, Stone, Glass,
Computer Equip., Hospitality, Advertising,
Government

Professional Associations: ASID, GAPS, ICFIA

Compton Graham Int'l Inc
16680 Partridge Pl 101
Ft. Myers, FL 33908
(941) 433-4660
Fax: (941) 433-5286
Email: comptongraham@mindspring.com

Description: Provides executive search and
recruiting research services, specializing in mid- to
senior-level positions. Key benefits include target
research and e-recruiting resulting in high quality,
cost effective results quickly.

Key Contact - Specialty:
Ms. Jo Ann L. Compton, CMC, President -
Generalist

Salary minimum: $75,000

Functions: Generalist

Industries: Generalist

Professional Associations: CAMC, HRPAO,
HRPS, IMC, SHRM

Branches:
20 Bay St Ste 1205
Toronto, ON M5J 2N8
Canada
(416) 944-2000
Fax: (416) 944-2020
Email: comptongraham@mindspring.com
Key Contact - Specialty:
Ms. Jo Ann Compton, CMC CHRP, President -
Executive search, senior management

Computer Professionals
3601 Algonquin Rd Ste 129
Rolling Meadows, IL 60008
(847) 577-6266
Email: compro@interaccess.com

Description: Single practitioner specialized in
retained executive searches involved in all aspects
of information technology.

Key Contact:
Mr. Kevin B. Hogan, President

Salary minimum: $350,000

Functions: Generalist, Directors, Senior Mgmt.,
Middle Mgmt.

Industries: Generalist, Software

Computer Search Group Ltd
150 N Wacker Dr Ste 2575
Chicago, IL 60606
(312) 269-9950
Email: info@csgforit.com
Web: www.csgforit.com

Description: Professional and executive recruiting
of information technology professionals. Especially
expert in Internet e-commerce technology, ERP,
database and client/server, enterprise networking,
banking technologies, data warehousing/data mining
and distributed computing solutions.

Key Contact - Specialty:
Mr. James Johnston, Managing Director -
Information technology

Salary minimum: $50,000

Functions: Directors, Senior Mgmt., Middle
Mgmt., Product Dev., Sales & Mktg., IT,
Engineering, Mgmt. Consultants

Industries: Generalist

Conard Associates Inc
74 Northeastern Blvd Unit 22A
Nashua, NH 03062
(603) 886-0600
Fax: (603) 886-8886
Email: rod@conard.com
Web: www.conard.com

Description: We provide customer-focused, bottom-
line value process improvement and behavior
change consulting services to companies, and we
help them identify and attract leaders who
demonstrate the core competencies essential to
world-class competition.

Key Contact:
Dr. Rodney J. Conard, President

Salary minimum: $100,000

Functions: Senior Mgmt.

Industries: Generalist

Conboy, Sur & Associates Inc
545 5th Ave Ste 630
New York, NY 10017-3620
(212) 687-4460
Fax: (212) 687-4584
Email: conboysur@aol.com
Web: www.conboysur.com

Description: Generalist, retained executive search
firm that selects, evaluates and recruits senior
management across a broad spectrum of industries
and functional specialties.

Key Contact - Specialty:
Ms. Mary Rose Schiavone, Managing Director -
*High technology, information management,
supply chain, financial management, R&D*
Mr. William K. Sur, Managing Director - *General
management, high technology, consumer goods,
pharmaceuticals, sales & marketing*

Salary minimum: $150,000

Functions: Generalist, Directors, Senior Mgmt.,
Mfg., Materials, Sales & Mktg., Finance, IT

Industries: Generalist, Food, Bev., Tobacco, Paper,
Chemicals, Drugs Mfg., Metal Products,
Telecoms

Concept II Employment Services[†]
236 St. George St Ste 412
Moncton, NB E1C 8M9
Canada
(506) 388-9675
(877) 385-9676
Fax: (506) 388-9674
Email: info@concept2employment.com
Web: www.concept2employment.com

Description: Executive recruitment, temp &
permanent staffing solutions!

Key Contact:
Mr. John Alexander, CEO
Mr. Robert Snider, CD, Manager

Functions: Generalist

Industries: Generalist

CONEX
(a member of InterSearch)
150 E 52nd St Fl 2
New York, NY 10022
(212) 371-3737
Email: info@conex-usa.com
Web: www.conex-usa.com

Description: Generalist firm with broad domestic
and international client base; most industries and
functions.

Key Contact:
Mr. Fred Siegel, President - *Generalist*

Ms. Ann Marie Pizzariello, Executive Vice
President - *Generalist*
Ms. Leslie Siver, Vice President - *Generalist*
Ms. Christina Lopez, Vice President - *Generalist*
Ms. Shiri Levinas, Vice President - *International*
Ms. Jessica Phillips, Researcher

Salary minimum: $120,000

Functions: Generalist

Industries: Generalist

Networks: InterSearch

Robert Connelly & Associates Inc
PO Box 24028
Minneapolis, MN 55424
(952) 925-3039
Fax: (952) 922-5762
Email: robtconn@aol.com
Web: www.robertconnelly.com

Description: A generalist firm with national client
base. Expertise in medium and large corporations at
the middle and upper-management ranks.
Specializing in consumer packaged goods,
agribusiness, architectural/engineering, real estate,
construction and environmental engineering.

Key Contact - Specialty:
Mr. Robert F. Olsen, President - *Real estate,
construction, architecture, agribusiness*

Salary minimum: $50,000

Functions: Generalist

Industries: Generalist, Construction, Legal, Real
Estate, Healthcare

Conroy Partners Ltd
255 5th Ave SW
830 Bow Valley Sq 3
Calgary, AB T2P 3G6
Canada
(403) 261-8080
Fax: (403) 261-8085
Email: mail@conroypartners.com
Web: www.conroypartners.com

Description: Retainer based executive, managerial,
senior professional, executive search firm whose
business is largely focused in Western Canada.
Consulting services are provided to our clients
utilizing our extensive knowledge of domestic and
international recruitment.

Key Contact - Specialty:
Mr. M. J. Conroy, Managing Partner - *Oil & gas,
financial, oil field services, general management*
Mr. Peter G. Edwards, Partner - *Oil & gas, oil field
services, EPCM, Environmental, Transportation,
Food Services*
Mr. S. Scott Doupe, Partner - *Finance, general
management, real estate, utilities, manufacturing*
Mr. Richard W. Lancaster, Partner - *Oil & gas,
financial services, information technology*
Ms. Noranne Dickin, Partner - *Energy, utilities,
financial, high tech, educational/public sector*
Mr. Mark Hopkins, Partner - *Oil & gas, oilfield
services, utilities, professional services, network
technology*

Functions: Generalist, Senior Mgmt., Sales &
Mktg., Mktg. Mgmt., CFO's, MIS Mgmt.,
Specialized Svcs., Non-profits

Industries: Generalist, Energy, Utilities, Mfg.,
Finance, HR Services, Government, Software

Networks: I-I-C Partners Executive Search
Worldwide

Conspectus Inc
222 Purchase St Ste 318
Rye, NY 10580
(914) 925-0600
Email: resume@conspectusinc.com
Web: www.conspectusinc.com

Description: Specializing in security analysts,
portfolio managers and investment bankers.

Key Contact - Specialty:
Mr. Eric Stieglitz, Managing Director - *Wall street,
asset management, brokerage, investment
banking, investor relations*

Salary minimum: $125,000

Functions: Finance, Cash Mgmt.

Industries: Finance, Banking, Invest. Banking,
Venture Cap., Misc. Financial

Professional Associations: NYSSA, SHRM

ConstructionExecutives.com
511 Gravier St Ste 100
New Orleans, LA 70130
(877) 645-2266
Fax: (407) 876-2566
Email: info@constructionexecutives.com
Web: www.constructionexecutives.com

Description: We are providing senior level, retained
executive search for the construction industry. The
positions that we place are CFO, CEO, COO,
president, and other officer level positions.

Key Contact - Specialty:
Mr. Keith Arendt, President - *Construction*

Salary minimum: $100,000

Functions: Senior Mgmt.

Industries: Construction

Consulpro†
(a division of Mel Spotswood Int'l Inc)
470 Somerset St W
Ottawa, ON K1R 5J8
Canada
(613) 236-3417
Fax: (613) 236-7964
Email: conslpro@istar.ca
Web: www.consulpro.yp.ca

Description: Retained search in a variety of
industries - majority high-tech. Owner has 30 years'
business experience.

Key Contact - Specialty:
Mr. Mel Spotswood, President - *Information
technology*

Salary minimum: $50,000

Functions: Generalist

Industries: Generalist

Networks: National Personnel Assoc (NPA)

Consultants' Network†
14851 Jeffrey Rd Ste 171
Irvine, CA 92618-8171
(949) 559-7366
Fax: (949) 559-6538
Email: hitechsearch@earthlink.net
Web: www.hitechsearch.com

Description: We specialize in information
technology. We are a "Preferred Member" of Top
Echelon Network, reputed to be the largest and most
respected network of independent recruiting firms in
the world. We solicit the resumes of world-class
applicants and inquiries of world-class clients or
those determined to become so.

Key Contact:
Mr. Norman R. Card, President

Salary minimum: $80,000

Functions: Senior Mgmt., IT

Industries: Generalist, Mfg., Computer Equip.,
Test, Measure Equip., Electronic, Elec.
Components, Mgmt. Consulting, Telecoms,
Telephony, Digital, Wireless, Fiber Optic,
Software

Networks: Top Echelon Network

The Consulting Group
366 Madison Ave Fl 10
New York, NY 10017
(212) 751-8484
Email: tcgny@aol.com
Web: www.consultinggroupny.com

Description: Specialist in the global securities
markets with a subspecialty in real estate. Clients
include international and domestic banks,
investment banks, insurance companies, pension
managers and other institutional money sources.

Key Contact - Specialty:
Mr. J. Michael Mitchell, Managing Director -
Securities, real estate
Ms. Jessica S. Flagg, Managing Director -
Securities, real estate
Ms. Kate Debold, Director of Research - *Securities,
real estate*
Ms. Jennifer Colasanto, Co-Director
Mr. Tim Christy, Senior Vice President -
Generalist

Salary minimum: $150,000

Functions: Generalist, Senior Mgmt., Middle
Mgmt., Admin. Svcs., CFO's, M&A, Risk Mgmt.,
MIS Mgmt.

Industries: Generalist, Construction, Finance,
Invest. Banking, Brokers, Venture Cap., Misc.
Financial, Real Estate

Professional Associations: ULI

Contract CADD Technologies Inc
1770 King St E
Kitchener, ON N2G 2P1
Canada
(519) 743-4894
Email: people@cctinc.org
Web: www.cctinc.org

Description: We supply engineering personnel to
manufactures across Southwestern Ontario. We
have contract & permanent opportunities for
mechanical, electrical, structural & civil engineers,
technologists and technician with leading
manufacturers.

Key Contact - Specialty:
Mr. Bob Van Slyck, CET, RPR, President -
Engineering
Mr. Rob Van Slyck, BA, CPC, Representative -
Engineering
Mr. Al Hull, BA, RPR, Representative -
Engineering

Functions: Mfg.

Industries: Mfg., Plastics, Rubber, Metal Products,
Motor Vehicles

Professional Associations: ACSESS, APRC

Branches:
3425 Harvester Rd Ste 202
Burlington, ON L5N 3N1
Canada
(905) 632-7617
Fax: (800) 546-4483
Email: people@cctinc.org
Web: www.cctinc.org
Key Contact - Specialty:
Mr. Bob Van Slyck, CET, RPR, Recruiter -
Engineering
Mr. Al Hull, BA, RPR, Representative -
Engineering
Mr. Rob Van Slyck, BA, CPC, Representative -
Engineering

151 York St
London, ON N6A 1A8
Canada
(519) 858-8369
Web: www.cctinc.org
Key Contact:
Mr. Robert Van Slyck, President

119-2550 Argentia Rd
Mississauga, ON L5N 5R1
Canada
(905) 858-1481
Fax: (519) 743-5305
Email: people@cctinc.org
Web: www.cctinc.org
Key Contact - Specialty:
Mr. Bob Van Slyck, Registered Professional
   Recruiter - *Engineering*
Mr. Al Hull, BA, RPR, Representative -
   Engineering
Mr. Rob Van Slyck, BA, CPC, Representative -
   Engineering

Contractor Marketing

7600 Dayton Rd
Fairborn, OH 45324-1904
(937) 864-5854 x11
Fax: (937) 864-7017
Email: walter@contractormarketing.com
Web: www.contractormarketing.com
Description: We are the only national firm that is
committed to help recruit only marketing, sales, and
business development executives with experience
specific to the non-residential construction industry.
Our primary focus is on general building
contractors, occasionally extending beyond that to
contractor-related companies.
Key Contact - Specialty:
Mr. Larry Silver, President - *Marketing, sales,
   business development (contractors)*
Salary minimum: $50,000
Functions: Generalist, Sales & Mktg., Advertising,
   Mkt. Research, Mktg. Mgmt., Sales Mgmt.,
   Direct Mktg., PR
Industries: Generalist, Construction
Professional Associations: ABC, CBDA, CWA

Conway + Associates

1007 Church St Ste 408
Evanston, IL 60201
(847) 866-6832
Fax: (847) 866-6265
Email: conway@sisna.com
Description: Provide industry research, candidate
identification, screening and recommendations to
corporate clients. Services range from research to
full search services with in-depth personal
interviews and reference checks.
Key Contact:
Ms. Maureen Conway, President
Functions: Generalist
Industries: Generalist
Professional Associations: HRMAC, SHRM,
   WAW

Philip Conway Management

320 Hampton Pl
Hinsdale, IL 60521-3823
(630) 655-4566
Description: Specialists in the recruitment of senior
and middle managers. Each assignment handled by
one designated professional from research through
final negotiations and follow up.
Key Contact:
Mr. Philip A. Conway
Salary minimum: $60,000
Functions: Generalist, Senior Mgmt., Middle
   Mgmt., Plant Mgmt., Quality, Sales Mgmt.,
   Personnel, CFO's
Industries: Generalist

Conyngham Partners LLC

75 N Maple Ave Ste 101A
Ridgewood, NJ 07450
(201) 652-3444
Fax: (201) 652-6357
Email: beth@conynghampartners.com
Web: www.conynghampartners.com
Description: A client-focused firm dedicated to
providing high-level consulting service to the
pharmaceutical industry. A boutique firm
specializing in executive search assignments
resulting in the identification of corporate leaders.
Key Contact - Specialty:
Ms. Beth Conyngham, Principal - *Healthcare*
Salary minimum: $100,000
Functions: Generalist, General Mgmt., Mfg., Sales
   & Mktg., HR Mgmt., Finance, IT, R&D
Industries: Generalist, Drugs Mfg., Pharm Svcs.,
   Biotech, Healthcare
Professional Associations: SHRM

Cook & Company

12 Masterton Rd
Bronxville, NY 10708
(914) 779-4838
Email: search@cook-co.com
Web: www.cook-co.com
Description: Our company was formed to assist top
management to create shareholder value by
obtaining competitive advantage in the war for
talent by providing the highest quality executive
search services in the human capital field.
Key Contact - Specialty:
Ms. Patricia S. Cook, Chairman/CEO - *General
   management, consumer, e-business, financial
   services*
Mr. William C. Bush, President/COO - *General
   management, consumer, e-business, financial
   services*
Salary minimum: $200,000
Functions: Directors, Senior Mgmt., Sales &
   Mktg., CFO's
Industries: Retail, Banking, Venture Cap.,
   Hospitality, Publishing, New Media, Healthcare
Professional Associations: AESC, IWF

Cook Associates® Inc

212 W Kinzie St
Chicago, IL 60610
(312) 329-0900
Fax: (312) 329-1528
Email: info@cookassociates.com
Web: www.cookassociates.com
Description: We provide executive search services
to over 50 industries nationally and internationally.
Founded in 1961 we focus on senior-level
assignments across all functional areas. Our long-
term relationships with our clients are built on
integrity, performance and follow-through.
Key Contact - Specialty:
Mr. Jeffrey Posselt, Executive VP, Managing
   Director - *Banking, professional services,
   financial services*
Ms. Mary Kier, Executive VP, Managing Director -
   *Consumer, house wares, hardware, giftware,
   home furnishings*
Mr. John Kins, Chairman - *International*
Mr. Arnie Kins, President - *Mergers & acquisitions*
Mr. John Wynn, Vice President - *Film converting,
   packaging, paper, plastics, thermoforming*
Mr. Frank Whiting, Vice President - *Sporting
   goods, apparel, footwear*
Mr. Art Pawelczyk, Vice President - *Building
   products, cabinetry*
Mr. Walter Rach, Vice President - *Food &
   beverage*

Mr. Martin Walsh, Vice President - *Catalog, direct
   marketing, retail*
Ms. Carolyn Peart, Vice President - *Architects,
   interior design, engineering*
Mr. Joseph Womack, Vice President - *Banking,
   financial services*
Mr. Christian Schiller, Vice President - *Mergers &
   acquisitions*
Mr. Donald Utroska, Vice President - *International*
Mr. Steve Krigbaum, Vice President - *Furniture,
   office products*
Ms. Jane McDowell, Vice President - *Chemical,
   pharmaceuticals*
Ms. Kim Lowden, Vice President - *Office products,
   furniture*
Salary minimum: $100,000
Functions: General Mgmt., Directors, Senior
   Mgmt.
Industries: Generalist
Professional Associations: IACPR
Networks: IMD Int'l Search
Branches:
1620 26 St Water Gardens
South Twr Fl 3
Santa Monica, CA 90404
(310) 255-8281
Fax: (310) 255-8286
Email: info@cookassociates.com
Web: www.cookassociates.com
Key Contact - Specialty:
Ms. Wendy Doulton, Vice President - *Media,
   entertainment and communications*

1539 Pearl St
Boulder, CO 80302
(303) 247-1177
Fax: (303) 544-5806
Email: info@cookassociates.com
Key Contact - Specialty:
Mr. John Olson, Vice President, Managing Director
   - *Industrial*
Ms. Mary Jane Schermer, Vice President,
   Managing Director - *Retail, wholesale, pharmacy,
   ecommerce*
Mr. Charles Travis, Vice President - *Retail,
   wholesale, pharmacy, ecommerce*

5 Concourse Pkwy Ste 2400
Atlanta, GA 30328
(678) 287-5400
Fax: (678) 287-5411
Email: info@cookassociates.com
Key Contact - Specialty:
Mr. Colin Brady, Vice President, Managing
   Director - *Industrial, e-commerce*
Mr. David Reddick, Vice President - *Food &
   beverage, consumer products*
Mr. Donald Gienger, Vice President -
   Telecommunications, technology

230 Park ave Ste 1000
New York, NY 10169
(212) 309-8723
Fax: (212) 808-3020
Email: info@cookassociates.com
Web: www.cookassociates.com
Key Contact - Specialty:
Mr. Gary Klein, Vice President, Manageing
   Director - *Media, entertainment and
   communications*
Ms. Susan Denison, Vice President - *Media,
   entertainment and communications*
Mr. Serguei Zaychenko, Director - *Media,
   entertainment and communications*

The Cooke Group

1001 W Glen Oaks Lane Ste 102
Mequon, WI 53092
(262) 241-9842
(888) 432-7800
Fax: (262) 241-1004
Email: solutions@cookegroup.net
Web: www.cookegroup.net

Description: We are a boutique firm offering executive search, business planning, financial and operations management, and organizational development consulting services to small and medium-sized businesses that have annual revenues of $5 million to over $125 million, and are located in Wisconsin, the Upper Midwest, and Arizona.

Key Contact - Specialty:
Mr. Jeffrey R. Cooke, President - *Strategic planning, organizational development, senior executive recruitment, business turnaround management*
Mr. James T. Lindell, CPA, Executive Vice President - *Financial management, information technology planning, executive recruitment*
Mr. Frederick Luehrs, P.E., Executive Vice President - *Manufacturing operations, strategic alliances, team building, productivity improvement*
Mr. Robert H. Marshall, Consultant - *Executive recruitment, organizational development*

Salary minimum: $75,000

Functions: General Mgmt., Senior Mgmt., Mfg., Plant Mgmt., Productivity, CFO's

Industries: Generalist, Mfg., Metal Products, Misc. Mfg., Wholesale, Finance, Misc. Financial, Accounting, Mgmt. Consulting

Professional Associations: ACG, AICPA, FEI, TEC, WICPA

The Cooper Executive Search Group Inc
PO Box 375
Wales, WI 53183-0375
(262) 968-9049
Fax: (262) 968-9059
Email: cesgroup@aol.com

Description: Full-service firm with particular strengths in transitional and middle market companies. Significant client-side experience provides for unusual sensitivity to client needs.

Key Contact - Specialty:
Mr. Robert M. Cooper, President - *Generalist*

Salary minimum: $90,000

Functions: Generalist

Industries: Food, Bev., Tobacco, Chemicals, Plastics, Rubber, Metal Products, Non-profits, Biotech, Healthcare

The Corim Group
PO Box 191
Dodgeville, WI 53533
(608) 848-3097
Fax: (608) 935-9519

Description: A small aggressive firm that provides targeted, retained search services. The principal has 24 years of senior-level corporate experience and 11 years as a search consultant.

Key Contact - Specialty:
Mr. Donald V. Brown, Senior Partner - *Senior level engineers, management, general managers*

Salary minimum: $60,000

Functions: Generalist, Senior Mgmt., Middle Mgmt., Plant Mgmt., Quality, Materials Plng., Sales Mgmt., Engineering

Industries: Generalist, Chemicals, Medical Devices, Metal Products, Machine, Appliance, Consumer Elect., Misc. Mfg.

Cornell Group Int'l Consulting Inc
1 Corwin Ct Ste 200
Newburgh, NY 12550
(845) 565-8905
(845) 236-3986
Fax: (845) 565-5688

Email: cornell@cornellinternational.com
Web: www.cornellinternational.com

Description: We are a total solutions-oriented search practice with diverse expertise ranging from Fortune 500 to small cap and venture stage companies. We can also offer Internet-based rapid search solutions, through our sister companies, Worldemployment.com and WallstreetJOB.com. This firm is much more than your typical search firm. Our partners hold board seats within several of our client companies including both private and public companies.

Key Contact - Specialty:
Mr. Alan Guarino, CEO - *Financial services, management teams, CEO, COO, CFO*
Ms. Kathleen Guarino, CAO - *Management teams, human resources*
Mr. John Weidner, Senior Managing Partner - *Technology (CIO, CTO), information technology, information systems, new media professional services, human resources*
Ms. Amy Dent, Managing Director - *Technology (CIO, CTO), information technology, information systems, new media professional services, human resources*
Mr. Al Aruza, Senior Managing Partner - *Financial services, brokerage operations, trust services, mid-cap executive management, CEOs*
Mr. Robert Wysocki, Managing Partner - *Investor relations executives, wealth/asset management, CIOs, portfolio managers, buy-side research*
Ms. Lynne Sebastian, Managing Director - *Financial services, brokerage (operations, technology), institutional sales, executive management, CFOs*
Mr. Daniel Gonzalez, Managing Director - *Financial services, brokerage (operations, technology), institutional sales, executive management, CFO*

Salary minimum: $80,000

Functions: Senior Mgmt., Middle Mgmt., Sales & Mktg., Cash Mgmt., M&A

Industries: Finance, Banking, Invest. Banking, Brokers, Venture Cap., Misc. Financial, Mgmt. Consulting, HR Services, New Media, Telecoms, Software, Healthcare

Branches:
1 Washington Ave
PO Box 705
Sandy Hook, CT 06482-0705
(203) 426-8737
Fax: (203) 426-6709
Key Contact:
Ms. Amy Dent, Managing Director
Mr. Robert Wysocki, Partner

The Corporate Advisory Group
16606 Holly Ln
Sugarloaf Key, FL 33042
(305) 745-1652
Email: cagresearch@cswebmail.com
Web: www.cag-fl.com

Description: We provide senior-level executive search across all major business functions within the telecommunications, Internet, and e-Commerce industries.

Key Contact:
Mr. Roy M. Nunn, President

Salary minimum: $150,000

Functions: Senior Mgmt.

Industries: E-commerce, Telecoms, Call Centers, Telephony, Digital, Wireless, Fiber Optic, Network Infrastructure

Corporate Connection Inc†
14444 Beach Blvd Ste 18-245
Jacksonville, FL 32250
(904) 223-3567
(508) 945-1262
Email: cciduggan@aol.com
Web: www.medicalsalesrecruiter.net

Description: We are medical sales recruiters specializing in the placement of B2B, medical, and management professionals.

Key Contact - Specialty:
Ms. Debra Duggan, president - *Medical*

Salary minimum: $30,000

Corporate Direction Inc†
2790 Skypark Dr Ste 106
Torrance, CA 90505
(310) 534-8696
Fax: (310) 534-2721
Email: cordirect@aol.com
Web: www.corporatedirections.com

Description: Our hands on experience in senior management is key to our ability to develop a clear picture of your organization's goals and requirements. We assess your needs and develop accurate, complete descriptions of the positions you are looking to fill.

Key Contact:
Mr. George L. Schmutz, President

Salary minimum: $45,000

Corporate Environment Ltd
PO Box 798
Crystal Lake, IL 60039-0798
(815) 455-6070
Fax: (815) 455-0124
Email: tomsearch@consultant.com

Description: We specialize in environmental-water & wastewater equipment and services. Additionally, specialists in the metal finishing systems and material handling industries. Positions/functions: engineering, operations, sales and marketing, key technical specialist, middle- and senior-level executives $60-250K compensation. Domestic/international clientele.

Key Contact - Specialty:
Mr. Tom McDermott, President - *Technical, industrial products, process capital equipment, environmental, materials handling & metal finishing*

Salary minimum: $60,000

Functions: Generalist, General Mgmt., Senior Mgmt., Middle Mgmt., Mktg. Mgmt., Engineering, Environmentalists

Industries: Generalist, Energy, Utilities, Mfg., Machine, Appliance, Environmental Svcs., Haz. Waste

Corporate Search Int'l†
990 Hammond Dr Ste 825
Atlanta, GA 30328
(770) 399-8477
(770) 399-8499
Fax: (770) 399-8411
Email: laura@corpsearchintl.com
Web: www.corpsearchintl.com

Description: We are consultants in executive search assisting client organizations in identifying, attracting, and recruiting executive talent for opportunities within middle and top management. We have special expertise in consumer products, healthcare, high technology, telecommunications, and services. We have functional expertise in top executive positions, human resources, sales and marketing, and finance. We are known for our follow through and for completing successful searches quickly.

Key Contact:
Mr. William Chambers, III, Exec Vice President
Mr. Keith Collins, Exec Vice President
Mr. Phil Kercher, Managing Director

Salary minimum: $100,000

Functions: Generalist

Industries: Mfg., Paper, Soap, Perf., Cosmtcs.,
Plastics, Rubber, Consumer Elect., Finance,
Hospitality, Packaging, Software, Healthcare

Professional Associations: GHA, GTMA, SHRM

The Corporate Source Group Inc
1 Cranberry Hill
Lexington, MA 02173
(781) 862-1900
Fax: (781) 862-6367
Email: inquiry@csg-search.com
Web: www.csg-search.com

Description: Broad based, professional firm
specializing in targeted search for difficult
assignments. Performance guaranteed,
uncompromising standards.

Key Contact:
Mr. Dana Willis, President

Salary minimum: $100,000

Functions: Generalist, Senior Mgmt., Finance, IT,
Engineering, Int'l.

Industries: Generalist, Finance, Media, Software

Branches:
11601 Wilshire Blvd Ste 500
Los Angeles, CA 90025
(310) 575-4863
Key Contact:
Ms. Karen Hudson

4830 W Kennedy Blvd Ste 495
Tampa, FL 33609
(813) 286-4422
Key Contact:
Mr. Mark Hausherr

625 N Michigan Ave Fl 5
Chicago, IL 60611
(312) 751-4250
Key Contact:
Ms. Barbara McLean

14725 Pommel Dr
Rockville, MD 20850
(301) 217-5868
Key Contact:
Ms. Tara Stotz

90 Park Ave Ste 1600
New York, NY 10016
(212) 984-0738
Key Contact:
Ms. Carolyn Culbreth

301 Grant St Ste 1500
1 Oxford Ctr
Pittsburgh, PA 15219-1417
(412) 577-2962
Key Contact:
Mr. J. Ronald Hagy

Corporate Technologies Executive Search
730 17th St Ste 220
Denver, CO 80202
(303) 571-4800
Fax: (303) 629-0600
Email: tim@ctisearch.com

Description: Mid-level to senior-level management
positions: agribusiness, media and
telecommunications, oil and gas, general US corp.,
cash management, bank cards, investments, private
banking, healthcare.

Key Contact - Specialty:
Mr. Timothy Pendergast, President - *Corporate
finance, capital markets*

Mr. Paul Rubin, President - *Healthcare*
Mr. Greg Hyman, Vice President - *Healthcare*

Salary minimum: $125,000

Functions: Generalist

Industries: Energy, Utilities, Finance, Banking,
Venture Cap., Misc. Financial, Pharm Svcs.,
Mgmt. Consulting, Insurance, Healthcare

Professional Associations: NBN

Branches:
7421 S Brookforest Dr
Evergreen, CO 80439
(303) 670-5593
Fax: (303) 202-3946
Email: pam@ctisearch.com
Key Contact - Specialty:
Ms. Pam Graham - *Banking*

14657 SW Teal Blvd
PMB 222
Beaverton, OR 97007
(503) 590-4169
Fax: (503) 590-7235
Email: corp.tech@gte.net
Key Contact - Specialty:
Mr. William Pendergast, President - *Insurance
(property, casualty), underwriting, claims, loss
control, management*

The Corrigan Group
1482 E Valley Rd SU 221
Santa Barbara, CA 93108
(805) 695-8292

Description: Retained search firm providing highly
professional services to clients in most industries
and the not-for-profit sector. Principal has 20 years'
experience in search profession.

Key Contact - Specialty:
Mr. Gerald F. Corrigan, Managing Partner -
Generalist

Salary minimum: $90,000

Functions: Generalist

Industries: Generalist

Professional Associations: IACPR

Corso, Mizgala + French
(a member of InterSearch)
90 Eglinton Ave E Ste 404
Toronto, ON M4P 2Y3
Canada
(416) 488-4111
Fax: (416) 488-3111
Email: cmf@intersearchcanada.com
Web: www.intersearch-canada.com

Description: Serve private, public sector clients and
non-profit organizations. Broad experience - 50+
combined years of successful middle to senior
recruiting assignments in Canada, Europe and the
United States.

Key Contact:
Mr. John J. Corso, Partner - *Generalist*
Mr. Anthony B. Mizgala, Partner - *Generalist*
Mr. Guy P. French, Partner - *Generalist*
Mr. Ralph G. Hansen, Partner - *Generalist*
Ms. Ana Sekesan, Administrator

Salary minimum: $90,000

Functions: Senior Mgmt.

Industries: Generalist

Professional Associations: CAMC

Courtright & Associates Inc
PO Box 503
Clarks Summit, PA 18411-0503
(570) 586-0735
Fax: (570) 586-0764

Email: rjcx@adelphia.net
Web: www.courtrightassoc.com

Description: We specialize in recruiting for
biotechnology and pharmaceutical firms nationally
and general management positions in Northeast
Pennsylvania.

Key Contact - Specialty:
Mr. Robert J. Courtright, President - *Biotechnology,
management, pharmaceutical*

Salary minimum: $70,000

Functions: Generalist

Industries: Generalist, Drugs Mfg., Biotech

Professional Associations: SHRM

Cowell & Associates Ltd
100 Forest Pl Ste P22
Oak Park, IL 60301
(708) 383-6618
Fax: (708) 383-9012
Email: roycowell@aol.com

Description: Provide specialized highly focused
services in organization development and
evaluation/recruitment of executive talent.
Consultative approach coupled with limited number
of concurrent assignments yields timely quality
results and meaningful relationships.

Key Contact - Specialty:
Mr. Roy A. Cowell, President - *General
management*

Salary minimum: $75,000

Functions: Senior Mgmt., Mktg. Mgmt., CFO's,
Mgmt. Consultants

Industries: Mfg., Services, Telecoms, Software

Cowin Associates[†]
1 Old Country Rd
Carle Place, NY 11514
(516) 741-3020
Fax: (516) 741-4953
Email: cowinone@aol.com

Description: Serving large and small companies in
the aerospace and related high-technology industries
since 1959.

Key Contact - Specialty:
Mr. David M. Cowin, President - *Aerospace
management*

Salary minimum: $60,000

Functions: Generalist

Industries: Mfg., Metal Products, Defense,
Aerospace

The Coxe Group Inc
1218 3rd Ave Ste 1700
Seattle, WA 98101
(206) 467-4040
Fax: (206) 467-4038
Email: consultants@coxegroup.com
Web: www.coxegroup.com

Description: We are a comprehensive firm, which
has exclusively served the design community,
including: architects, engineers, planners, interior
designers, and landscape architects for 34 years. Our
eleven consultants offer a broad base of experience
and a wide range of expertise. Our services include:
general management, marketing, ownership
transition, firm valuation, merger and acquisition,
financial planning, organizational development,
conflict management, and executive search.

Key Contact:
Mr. Hugh Hochberg, Principal
Mr. Peter Piven, Principal
Mr. Bob Mattox, Principal
Mr. Thomas Kvan, Principal
Mr. Sharlene Silverman, Principal

Functions: Engineering, Architects, Graphic Artists
Industries: Construction, Environmental Svcs.

Creative-Leadership Inc
11777 Bernardo Plz Ct Ste 101
San Diego, CA 92128
(858) 592-0506
Fax: (858) 592-0413
Email: resumes@clci.com
Web: www.clci.com

Description: We offer a new paradigm in executive search; the Choosing Winners (TM) System, behavioral assessments and interviewer training.

Key Contact:
Mr. Bob Spence, President/CEO - *Senior management*
Ms. Noni Clayton, Director of Sales & Marketing - *Generalist*
Ms. Susan Collins, Senior Executive Search Coordinator - *Generalist*
Mr. Brian Dobler, Executive Search Coordinator
Ms. Kristen Newman, Executive Search Coordinator
Ms. Christina Sloane, Executive Search Associate
Ms. Adrienne Astengo, Receptionist/Assistant

Salary minimum: $50,000

Functions: Generalist

Industries: Generalist

Crest Associates Inc
366 Crest Ave
Alamo, CA 94507
(925) 945-7374
Fax: (925) 935-9170
Email: bmannas@aol.com

Description: We have conducted retained searches for both companies and search firms for the past 20 years. For search firms, we typically charge on an hourly basis; for companies, the charge is a 25% fee based on annual compensation. We do not specialize but do focused, targeted research and candidate development.

Key Contact:
Ms. Barbara Annas, Principal

Salary minimum: $80,000

Functions: General Mgmt.

Industries: Paper, Computer Equip., Finance, IT Implementation, Telecoms, Software, Development SW, ERP SW, Mfg. SW, Marketing SW

Professional Associations: NAWBO, NCHRA, SHRM

The Cris Group Inc
555 Madison Ave
New York, NY 10022
(212) 752-2838
Fax: (212) 888-3870
Email: jancris@aol.com
Web: www.crisgroup.com

Description: Known for key management assignments, long client relationships and high quality of research and service.

Key Contact:
Ms. Jan Cris, President

Salary minimum: $125,000

Functions: General Mgmt., Finance

Industries: Generalist, Finance, Accounting, Mgmt. Consulting, IT Implementation, Communications, Software, Healthcare

Cristal Partners
333 W Wacker Dr Fl 7
Chicago, IL 60606
(312) 444-9499
Fax: (312) 750-4556
Email: info@cristalpartners.com
Web: www.cristalpartners.com

Description: Clients are start-up to Fortune 100 companies. High integrity; very ethical firm with extremely efficient search process. No unfulfilled promises, hidden fees or agendas. "Clients must prosper first" is basis for successful and lasting partnerships.

Key Contact - Specialty:
Mr. Nelson D. Rodriguez, Managing Director - *Generalist, high technology*

Salary minimum: $75,000

Functions: Generalist

Industries: Generalist

Professional Associations: HRMAC, NHMBAA, TEI

Criterion Search Group Inc
PO Box 466
Wayne, PA 19087
(610) 581-0590
Fax: (610) 581-0594
Email: hare@criterionsg.com
Web: www.criterionsg.com

Description: We are dedicated to high quality retained executive search.

Key Contact - Specialty:
Ms. Beth C. Hare, Principal - *Financial, human resources, generalist*

Salary minimum: $90,000

Functions: General Mgmt., Sales & Mktg., HR Mgmt., Benefits, Training, Finance, IT, MIS Mgmt.

Industries: Mfg., Finance, Services, Media, Software, Healthcare

Professional Associations: ETC, PHRPG, SHRM

Cromwell Partners Inc
441 Lexington Ave Fl 7
New York, NY 10017
(212) 953-3220
Fax: (212) 953-4688
Email: webmaster@cromwell-partners.com
Web: www.cromwell-partners.com

Description: Practice areas include investment banking, commercial banking, private equity, capital markets, sales and trading, equity research, Internet/new media, and information technology.

Key Contact - Specialty:
Mr. Joseph Ziccardi, CEO - *Financial services, information technology*
Mr. Paul Heller, President - *Financial services*

Salary minimum: $100,000

Functions: Generalist

Industries: Finance, Banking, Invest. Banking, Venture Cap., Misc. Financial, Services, Pharm Svcs., New Media, Telecoms, Software

Branches:
200 S Wacker Dr Ste 3100
Chicago, IL 60606
(312) 674-4988
Fax: (312) 674-4501
Email: recruiters@cromwell-partners.com
Web: www.cpinteractive.com

Cross Hill Partners LLC
245 Park Ave Fl 24
New York, NY 10167
(212) 672-1604
Fax: (212) 202-6316
Email: info@crosshillpartners.com
Web: www.crosshillpartners.com

Description: We are a retained search firm founded by career search professionals who together possess over 30 years and over 400 assignments of combined experience.

Key Contact - Specialty:
Mr. Christopher Shea, Managing Partner - *Banking (commercial, investment), capital markets, early stage companies, commercial insurance*
Ms. Diane Shea, Managing Partner - *Corporate finance, reinsurance, private equity, securities analysis, capital markets*

Salary minimum: $150,000

Functions: Senior Mgmt.

Industries: Banking, Invest. Banking, Venture Cap., Misc. Financial, Mgmt. Consulting, E-commerce, IT Implementation, Publishing, New Media, Insurance

Crowder & Company
40950 Woodward Ave Ste 335
Bloomfield Hills, MI 48304
(248) 645-0909
Fax: (248) 645-2366
Email: crowder@crowdercompany.com
Web: www.crowdercompany.com

Description: Results-oriented consulting firm providing multi-disciplinary executive search at the senior management level.

Key Contact:
Mr. Edward W. Crowder, President - *Generalist*
Mr. Mark D. Hokanson, Vice President - *Generalist*
Ms. Kristin C. Schroeder, Director of Operations
Ms. Leticia C. Delos Santos, Database Administrator

Salary minimum: $90,000

Functions: Generalist, General Mgmt., Senior Mgmt., Mfg., Sales & Mktg., HR Mgmt., Finance, Engineering

Industries: Mfg., Chemicals, Plastics, Rubber, Metal Products, Machine, Appliance, Motor Vehicles, Misc. Mfg., Electronic, Elec. Components, Transportation, Packaging

Professional Associations: ACG, ASQ, SAE, SMEI

Timothy D Crowe Jr
26 Higate Rd Ste 101
Chelmsford, MA 01824-4440
(978) 256-2008

Description: Our firm is a small consulting organization dedicated to providing service to only a few companies in the greater Boston area.

Key Contact:
Mr. Timothy D. Crowe, Jr., President

Salary minimum: $50,000

Functions: Generalist

Industries: Mfg., Computer Equip., Test, Measure Equip., Aerospace, Software

Crowe-Innes & Associates LLC
1120 Mar West Ste D
Tiburon, CA 94920
(415) 435-6211
(415) 789-1422
Fax: (415) 435-6867
Email: jenny@croweinnes.com
Web: www.executiverecruit.com

Description: Founded in 1996, our firm conducts senior-level searches within a variety of industries and functional disciplines with a significant emphasis in the Internet, e-commerce and retail/apparel areas. Our clients range in size from newly emerging growth companies to Fortune 500 companies.

Key Contact - Specialty:
Ms. Jenny Crowe-Innes, President & CEO - *Generalist*
Ms. Beth Logan, Vice President - *Generalist*
Ms. Adriene Coffey, Director - *Generalist*

Salary minimum: $150,000

Functions: General Mgmt., Mfg., Materials, Sales & Mktg., HR Mgmt., Finance, CFO's, IT, MIS Mgmt.

Industries: Generalist

Professional Associations: AESC, ACG, FWE, NAWBO, NCHRA, NRF

Crown Advisors Inc
239 Ft. Pitt Blvd
Pittsburgh, PA 15222
(412) 566-1100
Fax: (412) 566-1256
Email: info@crownsearch.com
Web: www.crownsearch.com

Description: Our firm is known for its extensive contacts and knowledge of the real estate, construction, and finance industries. The level of responsiveness, quality, and commitment are unrivaled in this niche market.

Key Contact - Specialty:
Mr. Tom Callahan, Partner - *Construction*
Mr. John Cigna, Partner - *Real estate finance, real estate management, real estate development*
Mr. Philip Canzian, Partner - *Real estate finance, real estate management, real estate development*
Mr. Bert McDermott, Partner - *Real estate finance, real estate management, real estate development*
Mr. Kevin Jones, Partner - *Construction, real estate*

Salary minimum: $60,000

Functions: Generalist

Industries: Energy, Utilities, Construction, Banking, Services, Hospitality, Real Estate

Professional Associations: ABC, AGC, AGC, ICSC, MBAA, MCAA, NAHB, NAIOP, NAREIT, NECA, ULI

Branches:
800 E NW Hwy Ste 700
PMB 920
Palatine, IL 60067
(847) 705-3890
Fax: (847) 963-2114
Email: info@crownsearch.com
Key Contact - Specialty:
Mr. John DiMare, Regional Director - *Real estate, construction, finance*

CSI Consulting†
150 York St Ste 1820
Toronto, ON M5H S35
Canada
(416) 364-6376
Fax: (416) 364-2735
Email: csi@csican.com
Web: www.csican.com

Description: We are a dynamic IT consulting practice, providing customized project resourcing and technology solutions addressing the unique needs of clients across North America.

Key Contact:
Ms. Shylee Holla

Salary minimum: $40,000

Functions: IT

Industries: Generalist

CSI Search
2001 Midwest Rd Ste 310
Oak Brook, IL 60523
(630) 916-1166
Fax: (630) 916-1350
Web: www.csisearch.com

Description: We provide executive search serving clients in health care and health insurance industries.

Key Contact:
Ms. Kathy Ballein, RN, MSHA, Vice President

Salary minimum: $100,000 .

CTR
581 Bellwood Dr Ste 100
Santa Clara, CA 95054
(408) 980-8082
Fax: (408) 727-0651
Email: ctrhr@ix.netcom.com

Description: Mid-level to executive-level recruitment services to corporate clients in high-technology environments.

Key Contact - Specialty:
Mr. Timothy J. Outman, President/Founder - *High technology*

Functions: General Mgmt., Senior Mgmt., Production, Healthcare, Sales & Mktg., Engineering

Industries: Generalist, HR Services, Software, Biotech

Cullen Int'l Executive Search Inc
PO Box 327
Boca Raton, FL 33433
(561) 347-7212
Fax: (561) 347-7213
Email: info@culleninternational.com
Web: www.culleninternational.com

Description: Retained executive search firm specializing in recruitment engagements in the following positions: chairman, board directors, president, CEO, COO, CFO, CIO, vice president human resources, vice president training, vice president sales, vice president marketing. Twenty years' experience in personnel placement business. Guarantee all search engagements and placements to clients.

Key Contact:
Mr. Richard R. Cullen, Chairman/CEO
Ms. Kimberly Cullen, President

Salary minimum: $100,000

Functions: Generalist, Directors, Senior Mgmt., Healthcare, Sales & Mktg., HR Mgmt., Finance, CFO's, IT, Int'l.

Industries: Generalist

M J Curran & Associates Inc
304 Newbury St Ste 509
Boston, MA 02115
(617) 247-7700
Fax: (617) 267-6429
Email: mjcsearch@aol.com

Description: Firm makes use of extensive international & national contacts to provide clients with highest degree of service and professionalism in seeking senior management talent.

Key Contact - Specialty:
Mr. Martin Curran, President - *Generalist*

Salary minimum: $75,000

Functions: Generalist

Industries: Construction, Mfg., Finance, Services, Communications, Aerospace, Real Estate, Software, Healthcare

Professional Associations: DMA

Curran Partners Inc
1 Landmark Sq Fl 18
Stamford, CT 06901
(203) 363-5350
Fax: (203) 363-5353
Email: research@curranpartners.com
Web: www.curranpartners.com

Description: Executive search firm working exclusively on retained assignments.

Key Contact:
Mr. Michael N. Curran, President
Ms. Elizabeth Bailey, Partner
Ms. Whitney Sawyer Dooley, Principal
Mrs. Roslyn Weaving, Office Manager
Mrs. Nancy D. Hintze, Research Associate

Salary minimum: $150,000

Functions: Generalist

Industries: Generalist

Curry Company
25 Eastfield Rd
Mt. Vernon, NY 10552
(914) 667-5735
Email: curryco@telocity.com

Description: A boutique retained executive search firm focusing on domestic and international staffing. The firm specializes in the recruitment of middle- to upper-management executives in most industries and functional areas. We pride ourselves on partnering with our clients.

Key Contact - Specialty:
Ms. Joan Gagan, Managing Director - *Generalist*
Mr. William E. Halpin, Managing Director - *Generalist*

Salary minimum: $100,000

Functions: Generalist, General Mgmt.

Industries: Generalist

The Curtiss Group Int'l
301 Yamato Rd Ste 2112
Northern Trust Plz
Boca Raton, FL 33431
(561) 997-0011
Fax: (561) 997-0087
Email: thecurtiss@aol.com
Web: www.curtissgroup.com

Description: We are the largest retainer-based search firm headquartered in Florida. Our clientele includes a select and limited base of corporations and government agencies requiring national and international expertise.

Key Contact - Specialty:
Mr. William E. Frank, Jr., President - *Senior executives, board of directors*
Mr. Robert L. Beatty, Jr., Executive VP, U.S. Operations - *Senior executives, general management*
Mr. David Miner, Executive VP, International Operations - *Senior executives, general management*
Mr. Lynn H. Bentley, Senior Vice President - *High technology, human resources*
Mr. Joseph M. Bujold, Senior Vice President - *General management*
Mr. John Farrell, Senior Vice President - *Finance, high technology*
Mr. Fernando Gazmuri, Senior Vice President - *General management*
Mr. John M. Rose, Senior Vice President - *General management, manufacturing*

Salary minimum: $150,000

Functions: Generalist

Industries: Generalist

Networks: I-I-C Partners Executive Search Worldwide

Judith Cushman & Associates
1125 12th Ave NW Ste B-1A
Issaquah, WA 98027
(425) 392-8660
Fax: (425) 391-9190
Email: jcushman@jc-a.com
Web: www.jc-a.com

Description: Offering full-spectrum niche recruiting solutions in public relations, corporate communications and investor relations with a strength in high-tech. Judith Cushman & Associates is an on-line business providing in-depth service and results.

Key Contact:
Ms. Judith Cushman, President

Salary minimum: $55,000

Functions: PR

Industries: Media, Advertising

Professional Associations: IACPR, AAUW, FWE, IABC, NIRI, PRSA, WSA

The Custer Group Inc
5115 Maryland Way
PO Box 3372
Brentwood, TN 37024-3372
(615) 843-8767
Fax: (615) 309-0577
Email: research@custergroup.com
Web: www.custergroup.com

Description: We provide intelligent solutions for the identification, recruitment, assessment, and selection of executive talent for corporate clients throughout North America.

Key Contact - Specialty:
Mr. Dwight Custer, President - *All industries, healthcare, technology*
Mr. Bryce W. Custer, Vice President - *All industries, finance, marketing & sales*

Functions: Generalist

Industries: Generalist, Agri., Forestry, Mining, Mfg., Transportation, Finance, Services, Communications, Software, Biotech, Healthcare

Cutler/Krenzke LLC†
350 Bishop's Way Ste 200
Brookfield, WI 53005
(262) 796-6979
Fax: (262) 796-6970
Email: rdcutler@execpc.com
Web: www.ckrecruiting.com

Description: We are a full service executive search firm with a specialization in the power and energy industry. We pride ourselves in experience, proven results, integrity, and quality.

Key Contact:
Mr. Robert Cutler, President - *Nuclear utilities, power industry*
Ms. Vivian Krenzke, SPHR, Vice President

Salary minimum: $75,000

Functions: Generalist

Industries: Energy, Utilities

Cyntal Int'l Ltd
405 Lexington Ave Fl 26
New York, NY 10174
(917) 368-8181
Fax: (917) 368-8180
Email: jobs@cyntal.com

Description: We are a generalist firm for upper middle and senior executive leadership roles.

Key Contact:
Ms. Cynthia D. Vroom, President

Salary minimum: $75,000

Functions: Generalist, Senior Mgmt., Middle Mgmt., Mfg., Mktg. Mgmt., HR Mgmt., Finance, Specialized Svcs.

Industries: Generalist, Mfg., Finance, Services, Media, Communications

Daggett & Kvistad
3015 Hopyard Rd Ste N
Pleasanton, CA 94588
(925) 484-9050
Fax: (925) 484-9054
Email: jdaggett@daggettkvistad.com
Web: www.daggettkvistad.com

Description: We specialize in the semiconductor, semiconductor capital equipment, and robotics industries. Our assignments for our client companies range from sales, marketing, engineering to include electrical, software, analog design, digital design, systems integration, process, and mechanical. Our operations are to include manufacturing, materials, and quality.

Key Contact:
Mr. James W. Daggett, Partner
Mr. Niles K. Kvistad, Partner

Salary minimum: $80,000

Functions: Generalist, Middle Mgmt., Mfg., Product Dev., Automation, Quality, Materials, Sales & Mktg., Engineering

Industries: Computer Equip., Test, Measure Equip., Misc. Mfg., Electronic, Elec. Components, Equip Svcs., Digital, Fiber Optic, Software, Development SW, Industry Specific SW, Marketing SW

Dahl-Morrow Int'l
20 S King St Ste 200
Leesburg, VA 20175
(703) 779-5600
Fax: (703) 779-5678
Email: dmi@dahl-morrowintl.com
Web: www.dahl-morrowintl.com

Description: Founded in January, 1991 to provide seasoned executives for interim and permanent management assignments worldwide. Specialty in communications industry/tele/data/all high-technology.

Key Contact:
Ms. Barbara Steinem, President
Ms. Andy Steinem, CEO
Ms. Mary Brault, Director of Research

Functions: General Mgmt., Sales & Mktg., CFO's, IT, MIS Mgmt., Systems Analysis, Systems Dev., Systems Implem., DB Admin., Int'l.

Industries: Computer Equip., Venture Cap., New Media, Telecoms, Defense, Software

Professional Associations: AFCEA, NVTC, SSPI

DAL Associates Inc
2777 Summer St
Stamford, CT 06905
(203) 961-8777
Fax: (203) 324-2812
Email: dalsearch@aol.com

Description: A generalist executive-management retainer search firm. Experienced in multi-industries and multi-functions.

Key Contact:
Mr. Donald A. Lotufo, Partner
Mr. Michael E. Rush, Managing Partner
Mr. Jack Barwis, Senior Vice President
Mr. James Cunningham, Vice President
Mr. Daniel Ruiz-Diaz, Research Manager
Ms. Linda Reiner, Administrator

Salary minimum: $80,000

Functions: Generalist

Industries: Generalist

Professional Associations: AAPS, HRPS, NEHRA, SHRM

The Dalley Hewitt Company
1401 Peachtree St NE Ste 500
Atlanta, GA 30309
(404) 885-6642
Fax: (404) 870-0288
Email: rives@dalleyhewitt.com
Web: www.dalleyhewitt.com

Description: We are a management recruiting and consulting firm that provides domestic and international clients with a flexible package of executive search services.

Key Contact:
Ms. Rives D. Hewitt, President - *Generalist*
Mr. Werner Boel, Senior Associate
Ms. Debbie Shaw, Associate

Salary minimum: $50,000

Functions: Generalist

Industries: Mfg., Printing, Medical Devices, Computer Equip., Misc. Mfg., Services, Higher Ed., Biotech

Professional Associations: IACPR, EMA, HRPS, SHRM, TIA

Daly & Company Inc
175 Federal St
Boston, MA 02110
(617) 262-2800
Fax: (617) 728-4477
Web: www.dalyco.com

Description: Our industry focus is venture capital financed technology start-ups filling senior requirements, CEO, COO, CFO, VP, and CTO.

Key Contact - Specialty:
Mr. Dan Daly, President - *Rapid growth technology firms, senior positions*

Salary minimum: $125,000

Functions: Generalist, Senior Mgmt., CFO's, MIS Mgmt.

Industries: Generalist, Venture Cap., Software, Biotech, Healthcare

Alfred Daniels & Associates Inc
5795 Waverly Ave
La Jolla, CA 92037
(858) 459-4009
Web: www.alfreddaniels.com

Description: We specialize in worldwide capital markets; debt/equity, including: derivatives, institutional sales, trading, and research; corporate finance; mergers and acquisitions; and asset management. Our clients include commercial and investment banks, money managers, and hedge funds.

Key Contact - Specialty:
Mr. Alfred Daniels, President - *Investment banking*
Ms. Lynn Scullion Reisfeld, Director - *Investment banking*

Salary minimum: $50,000

Functions: General Mgmt., Senior Mgmt., Middle Mgmt., Sales & Mktg., Mktg. Mgmt., Sales Mgmt.

Industries: Finance, Banking, Invest. Banking, Brokers, Venture Cap., Misc. Financial

Dankowski & Associates Inc†
6479 Stoney Ridge Rd NE Ste 200
PO Box 39478
North Ridgeville, OH 44039-0478
(440) 327-8717
Fax: (440) 327-1853

Email: dankowski@aol.com
Web: www.dankowskiassociates.com

Description: Our firm is a local, regional, and national recruiter of human resource professionals from $50,000-$150,000. We have over 30 years of experience in recruiting and 24 years experience as specialists in human resource recruiting.

Key Contact - Specialty:
Mr. Tom Dankowski, President - *Human resources*

Salary minimum: $50,000

Functions: HR Mgmt.

Industries: Generalist

Professional Associations: ACA, ASTD, ASTD, EMA, NOHRPS, SHRM

Networks: National Personnel Assoc (NPA)

Alan Darling Consulting
374 Dover Rd Ste 18
South Newfane, VT 05351
(802) 348-6365

Description: We provide private executive search to an intentionally limited client base, featuring a detailed pre-search survey with written report, and stressing original research as a major source of candidates. Consultants always handle our candidate contact. We work in all industries and functions, but frequently work with high-tech and consumer products clients.

Key Contact - Specialty:
Mr. Alan Darling - *Generalist*

Salary minimum: $100,000

Functions: Generalist, Senior Mgmt., Sales & Mktg., Engineering

Industries: Mfg., Electronic, Elec. Components, Non-profits, Legal, Defense, Aerospace, Healthcare

The Dartmouth Group
(formerly known as Storfer & Assoc)
2500 Johnson Ave Ste 16N
Riverdale Bronx, NY 10463
(718) 884-2411
Fax: (718) 884-3025
Email: hstorf@aol.com

Description: A highly professional, specialized executive search firm offering focused, personalized service and competency-based selection for major companies in the cosmetics, pharmaceutical, healthcare and packaging industries. Established in 1976.

Key Contact - Specialty:
Mr. Herbert F. Storfer, President - *Cosmetics, health & beauty aids, packaging, materials management, purchasing*
Ms. Nancy I. Johnson - *Pharmaceuticals*

Salary minimum: $70,000

Functions: Generalist, Senior Mgmt., Mfg., Materials, Sales & Mktg., HR Mgmt., R&D

Industries: Generalist, Soap, Perf., Cosmtcs., Drugs Mfg., Plastics, Rubber, Pharm Svcs., HR Services, Packaging

Professional Associations: NAER, SHRM

Daubenspeck & Associates Ltd
(a licensee of Foster Partners Inc)
20 N Wacker Dr Ste 1642
Chicago, IL 60606
(312) 453-9410
Fax: (312) 453-9411
Email: information@daubenspeck.com
Web: www.daubenspeck.com

Description: The firm specializes in providing executive search and executive team building, for example, placing entire management teams.

Additionally, the firm trains its clients in building staffing mechanisms.

Key Contact - Specialty:
Mr. Kenneth Daubenspeck, CEO - *Information technology, consulting fields*
Mrs. Rima Daubenspeck - *Information technology, general management, professional services*

Salary minimum: $150,000

Functions: Generalist, Senior Mgmt., Distribution, Personnel, CFO's, IT, Mgmt. Consultants, Minorities

Industries: Generalist, Finance, Hospitality, Media, Insurance, Software, Healthcare

Daudlin, De Beaupre & Company Inc
18530 Mack Ave Ste 315
Grosse Pointe Farms, MI 48236
(313) 771-0029

Description: Search consultants specializing in the recruitment of executives and professionals in the healthcare field throughout the United States.

Key Contact - Specialty:
Mr. Paul T. Daudlin, President - *Healthcare*
Ms. Mary Anne De Beaupre, Executive Vice President - *Healthcare*
Ms. Mary Jane Langlois, Senior Associate - *Healthcare*
Mr. James Delmotte, Ed.D., Vice President - *Healthcare*
Mr. Thomas Dakoske, Ph.D., Senior Associate - *Healthcare*

Salary minimum: $50,000

Functions: Physicians, Nurses, Allied Health, Health Admin.

Industries: Healthcare

Professional Associations: ACHE, ASHHRA

Andre David & Associates Inc
PO Box 700967
Dallas, TX 75370
(972) 250-1986
Fax: (972) 250-2243
Email: ada@gte.net

Description: A management consulting firm engaging in executive search. We perform searches with a high degree of professionalism, a sense of urgency and a commitment to excellence. We bring client and external expertise to search engagements.

Key Contact - Specialty:
Mr. Terry Patch, President - *Human resources*

Salary minimum: $75,000

Functions: Generalist, Production, Plant Mgmt., Mktg. Mgmt., Benefits, Personnel, Budgeting, Mgmt. Consultants, Minorities

Industries: Generalist, Retail, Finance, Mgmt. Consulting, HR Services

Professional Associations: MHRA, NBMBAA

J David Associates Inc
PO Box 1056
Madison, CT 06443
(203) 245-7303
Email: jdaincct@aol.com

Description: Provide executive search expertise, on a retainer basis, working within most functional areas and in many industries. Consumer product clients represent 65% of practice.

Key Contact:
Mr. Joe D. Tuschman, President

Salary minimum: $175,000

Functions: Generalist

Industries: Generalist

David, Warwick, Kennedy & Associates
666 Burrard St Ste 3400
Vancouver, BC V6C 2X8
Canada
(604) 685-9494
Fax: (604) 535-3044
Email: dwksearch@lightspeed.ca
Web: www.biznet.maximizer.com/dwksearch

Description: We are a management consulting firm based in Vancouver, BC. The firm has one main specialty area: executive search. While we are competent in all areas of search, we must admit that we particularity relish assignments which provide even the flimsiest excuse to first startle then ensnare hardworking numerate CPAs or CAs.

Key Contact - Specialty:
Mr. David Kennedy, Principal - *Generalist*

Salary minimum: $50,000

Functions: Finance, CFO's, Taxes, MIS Mgmt., Mgmt. Consultants

Industries: Generalist

Professional Associations: ICMCBC

Davies Park
10235-101 St Oxford Twr Ste 904
Edmonton, AB T5J 3G1
Canada
(780) 420-9900
Fax: (780) 426-2936
Email: search@daviespark.ab.ca
Web: www.daviespark.ab.ca

Description: We provide executive search in Western Canada only. Our principals have over 50 years of experience in business. Our applicants must be eligible to work in Canada and willing to move.

Key Contact - Specialty:
Mr. A. Gerry Davies, Partner - *Healthcare private industry (general)*
Mr. K. Darwin Park, Partner - *Municipal government, education, private industry*
Ms. Elizabeth Hurley, Partner - *Education, government, private industry (general)*

Salary minimum: $70,000

Functions: Generalist, Senior Mgmt., Physicians, Health Admin., HR Mgmt., CFO's, Engineering

Industries: Generalist, Energy, Utilities, Retail, Hospitality, Government, Healthcare

Professional Associations: CCHSE, ICMCA, SMAA

Branches:
300 - 5th Ave SW Ste 2930
Calgary, AB T2P 3C4
Canada
(403) 263-0600
Fax: (403) 269-1080
Email: anelson@daviespark.ab.ca
Key Contact - Specialty:
Mr. Allan C. Nelson, Partner - *Finance & accounting, generalist, oil & gas*

John J Davis & Associates Inc
521 5th Ave Ste 1740
New York, NY 10175
(212) 286-9489
Fax: (973) 467-3706
Email: jdavis1013@aol.com

Description: A highly specialized firm focused exclusively in the senior and middle management areas of information systems and telecommunications. The practice is nationwide.

Key Contact - Specialty:
Mr. John J. Davis, President - *Information systems management*
Mr. Thomas D. Bell, Vice President - *Information systems management*

Mr. Jack P. Long, Vice President - *Information systems management*
Mr. Jack Davis, Vice President - *Information systems management*
Mr. John D. Simon, Managing Director - *Information systems management*

Salary minimum: $150,000

Functions: Generalist, Directors, Admin. Svcs., MIS Mgmt.

Industries: Generalist, Energy, Utilities, Mfg., Drugs Mfg., Transportation, Retail, Finance, Services, Legal, Mgmt. Consulting, E-commerce, IT Implementation, Media, Publishing, Communications, Insurance, Security SW, Healthcare

Professional Associations: SIM

Alan Davis & Associates Inc
538 Main Rd
Hudson Heights, QC J0P 1J0
Canada
(450) 458-3535
Fax: (450) 458-3530
Email: adavis@alandavis.com
Web: www.alandavis.com

Description: We are an executive and professional search firm providing highly innovative solutions for difficult-to-fill positions. We provide a range of professional services to an impressive list of long-standing clients, many of who are world leaders in their respective industries. We specialize in management, engineering, scientific, and information technology specialists.

Key Contact:
Mr. Alan Davis, President
Ms. Diane Bates, Vice President, Operations
Mr. Tom Bursey, Managing Director, Ottawa Office
Ms. Linda Constant, Client Manager & HR Manager

Functions: Directors, Senior Mgmt., Middle Mgmt., Product Dev., HR Mgmt., IT, R&D, Engineering, Technicians, Int'l.

Industries: Generalist, Energy, Utilities, Construction, Mfg., Finance, Pharm Svcs., HR Services, Communications, Aerospace, Software, Biotech

Branches:
155 Queen St Ste 900
Ottawa, ON K1P 6L1
Canada
(613) 224-9950
Fax: (613) 225-6818
Email: tbursey@alandavis.com
Key Contact:
Mr. Tom Bursey, CHRP, Managing Director, Ottawa Office

Davis & Company
3419 Via Lido Ste 615
Newport Beach, CA 92663
(800) 600-4417
(949) 376-6995
Fax: (949) 376-6995
Email: ggdsearch@aol.com

Description: We are a generalist boutique firm serving a limited clientele for maximum effectiveness. We partner with our clients to assure the successful outcome of each assignment.

Key Contact - Specialty:
Mr. G. Gordon Davis, President - *Generalist*
Mr. Troy M. Davis - *Generalist*
Ms. Valerie D. Treaster - *Research*

Salary minimum: $50,000

Functions: Generalist

Industries: Generalist, Metal Products, Motor Vehicles, Test, Measure Equip., Transportation, Aerospace

Branches:
PO Box 953808
Lake Mary, FL 32795-3808
(407) 333-0550
Fax: (407) 333-9185
Email: jgdsearch@hotmail.com
Key Contact - Specialty:
Mr. John Davis, Principal - *Hospitality industry*

Joseph A Davis Consultants Inc
104 E 40th St Ste 203
New York, NY 10016
(212) 682-4006
Fax: (212) 661-0846
Email: jadci@compuserve.com

Description: We are a black-owned firm specializing in recruiting diverse professionals. We work on retained search assignments only.

Key Contact:
Mr. Joseph A. Davis, President
Ms. Winifred R. Davis, Vice President

Salary minimum: $75,000

Functions: Generalist, General Mgmt., Sales & Mktg., HR Mgmt., Finance, IT, Specialized Svcs.

Industries: Generalist, Energy, Utilities, Finance, HR Services, Media

Professional Associations: NAFE, NMBC

Bert Davis Executive Search Inc
425 Madison Ave Ste 14A
New York, NY 10017
(212) 838-4000
Fax: (212) 888-3823
Email: bdavis2289@aol.com

Description: Premier executive search firm specializing in the publishing, communications, multimedia and direct marketing industries. Practice extends nationwide and internationally.

Key Contact:
Mr. Paul F. Gravelle, Executive Vice President
Ms. Lauren Aaron, Vice President
Ms. Tracey Wilmot, Senior Recruiter
Ms. Katharine Berlowe, Senior Recruiter

Salary minimum: $100,000

Functions: Generalist, Middle Mgmt., Product Dev., PR, CFO's, Systems Implem., DB Admin.

Industries: Generalist, Advertising, Publishing, New Media

Professional Associations: BISG, DMA

Day & Associates
577 Airport Bvld Ste 130
Burlingame, CA 94010
(650) 343-2660
Fax: (650) 344-8460
Email: jkday@dayassociates.net

Description: We are consultants in executive search, assisting client organizations in the life science/healthcare, including biotech, pharmaceuticals, device, diagnostic, and medical OTC, and high technology, including software, Internet, and wireless communication. We have high technology segments to identify and attract senior executives, senior management teams and board positions. Our focus is on start-ups, early stage, and mid-size organizations.

Key Contact - Specialty:
Mr. J. Kevin Day, Managing Director - *Healthcare, hightech*

Salary minimum: $150,000

Functions: Directors, Senior Mgmt.

Industries: Drugs Mfg., Medical Devices, Venture Cap., New Media, Communications, Software, Biotech, Healthcare

Professional Associations: AESC

Networks: EMA Partners Int'l

DBL Associates[†]
1334 Park View Ave Ste 100
Manhattan Beach, CA 90266
(310) 546-8121
Email: dlong@dblsearch.com
Web: www.dblsearch.com

Description: We specialize in the placement of CPAs and MBAs in financial, accounting, tax, and information technology positions. Our client base includes financial services, high-tech, healthcare, manufacturing, distribution, entertainment, and Internet companies. We have over eighteen years of experience placing executives in Southern California.

Key Contact - Specialty:
Mr. David B. Long, President - *MBAs, CPAs*

Salary minimum: $75,000

Functions: General Mgmt., Senior Mgmt., Middle Mgmt., Mktg. Mgmt., Finance, IT

Industries: Generalist, Mfg., Retail, Finance, Services, Software, Healthcare

De Funiak & Edwards
1602 Hidden Hills Trl
Long Beach, IN 46360
(219) 878-9790
Fax: (219) 874-5347
Email: bdefuniak@aol.com

Description: High concentration of searches in life and property casualty insurance companies, insurance consulting firms with insurance administration and information systems specialists. Positions from project manager to president.

Key Contact - Specialty:
Mr. William S. De Funiak, Partner - *Insurance, information technology*

Salary minimum: $60,000

Functions: Generalist, MIS Mgmt., Mgmt. Consultants

Industries: Generalist, Mgmt. Consulting, Insurance

Professional Associations: LOMA

Branches:
PO Box 459
Leonardtown, MD 20650
(301) 475-2801
Fax: (301) 475-2802
Email: jacked@deinet.com
Key Contact - Specialty:
Mr. Randolph J. Edwards, Partner - *Insurance, information technology*

Thorndike Deland Associates LLC
275 Madison Ave Ste 1300
New York, NY 10016
(212) 661-6200
Fax: (212) 661-8438
Email: newyork@tdeland.com
Web: www.tdeland.com

Description: Seventy-five years of excellence in executive search. A consumer focused firm specializing in retailing, apparel, packaged goods, financial services, e-commerce, new media and consulting. Solid expertise in all aspects of consumer marketing, operations and corporate finance.

Key Contact - Specialty:
Mr. Joseph J. Carideo, Managing Partner - *Retailing, fashion, apparel*

Mr. William Venable, Partner - *Financial services, investment banking, technology, new media*

Mr. Jeffrey G. Zwiff, Senior Vice President - *Financial services, insurance, new media*

Ms. Carolyn Dursi, Senior Vice President - *Consumer products, telecommunications*

Ms. Ellen Reiser, Principal - *Retail, consumer services, technology, consulting*

Ms. Carol Binen, Vice President/Research - *Generalist*

Ms. Maria Quon, Research Associate - *Retail, consumer goods, telecommunications*

Salary minimum: $150,000

Functions: Generalist, Senior Mgmt., Mkt. Research, Mktg. Mgmt., Sales Mgmt., Direct Mktg., CFO's, IT

Industries: Generalist, Food, Bev., Tobacco, Textiles, Apparel, Wholesale, Retail, Finance, Media, Insurance

Professional Associations: CLM, NRF, NYNMA, SLF

Networks: Greenwich Int'l Group

Edward Dellon Associates Inc
1801 Ave of the Stars Ste 640
Los Angeles, CA 90067
(310) 286-0625
Fax: (310) 277-3069

Description: Especially proficient in the selection and recruitment of development and construction teams for large, complex, high-profile projects around the world.

Key Contact - Specialty:
Mr. Edward Dellon, President - *Real estate, development, construction*

Functions: Generalist, Senior Mgmt., Middle Mgmt., CFO's, Budgeting, Engineering, Architects, Int'l.

Industries: Generalist, Construction, Invest. Banking, Hospitality, Real Estate

Professional Associations: ULI

Branches:
575 Madison Ave
New York, NY 10022
(212) 605-0236
Fax: (212) 308-9834
Key Contact - Specialty:
Mr. Edward Dellon - *Real estate*

Delphi Systems Ltd
6740 Pennsylvania Ave
Kansas City, MO 64113
(816) 333-6944
Fax: (816) 333-6944
Email: dephi@gvi.net
Web: www.eprofiler.com/wings/delphi/primer.html

Description: We conduct a worldwide general practice. Our competitive distinction lies in the use of WingSpread, an Internet mediated, skills-based decision support system to assess, select, acquire, develop and retain executives for our clients.

Key Contact:
Mr. P. Wayne Reagan, CEO

Salary minimum: $200,000

Functions: Generalist

Industries: Generalist

Delta Services
PO Box 1294
Sugar Land, TX 77487-1294
(281) 494-9300
Fax: (281) 494-9394
Email: info@thesearchfirm.com
Web: www.thesearchfirm.com

Description: Executive recruitment to oil and gas, refining, chemical, management consulting and banking industries. We specialize in key operations, engineering, research and financial disciplines ranging from senior staff level to executive management.

Key Contact - Specialty:
Mr. John F. Jansen, President - *Generalist*

Salary minimum: $85,000

Functions: General Mgmt., Plant Mgmt., Sales & Mktg., Finance, R&D, Engineering, Minorities

Industries: Generalist, Plastics, Rubber, Paints, Petro. Products, Banking, Mgmt. Consulting

Denell-Archer Int'l Executive Search
4626 St. Catherine St W
Westmount, QC H3Z 1S3
Canada
(514) 282-9855
Fax: (514) 282-1663
Email: general@denell-archer.com
Web: www.denell-archer.com

Description: Owner operated, detail oriented sharpshooters. Well connected throughout North America and Europe in pharmaceutical, medical, biotech and related suppliers, ie: CROs, marketing and communications firms. Also chemical and plastics related.

Key Contact - Specialty:
Mr. Daniel Ascher, President - *General management, marketing, business development*
Mr. Michael Vice, Senior Associate - *Medical & scientific affairs, governmental affairs, professional affairs*

Salary minimum: $70,000

Functions: General Mgmt., Directors, Senior Mgmt., Middle Mgmt., Sales & Mktg., Advertising, Mkt. Research, Mktg. Mgmt., Sales Mgmt., CFO's

Industries: Mfg., Printing, Chemicals, Drugs Mfg., Medical Devices, Plastics, Rubber, Venture Cap., Pharm Svcs., Media, Advertising, Publishing, New Media, Marketing SW, Biotech, Healthcare, Women's

Professional Associations: OPMA, PMCQ

Denney & Company Inc
Gateway Ctr
PO Box 22156
Pittsburgh, PA 15201
(412) 441-9636

Description: National/European generalist practice. Director, CEO, COO and only senior executive-levels. Clients include financial services, industries, consumer durable/non-durable goods and medical products. Also strategic acquisition search practice.

Key Contact - Specialty:
Mr. Thomas L. Denney, President - *General management*
Mr. Edward B. Denney, Vice President - *General management*

Salary minimum: $300,000

Functions: Generalist, General Mgmt., Directors, Senior Mgmt., Mfg., Sales & Mktg., Int'l.

Industries: Generalist, Agri., Forestry, Mining, Mfg., Finance, Services

Derhak Ireland & Partners Ltd
65 Int'l Blvd Ste 100
Toronto, ON M9W 6L9
Canada
(416) 675-7600
Fax: (416) 675-7833
Email: alderhak@aol.com
Web: www.derhak-ireland.com

Description: We are a firm of senior executive recruitment profesionals, all of whom have extensive management experience in pharmaceuticals, high-tech, automotive, telecommunications and consumer goods.

Key Contact - Specialty:
Mr. Allen R. Derhak, Partner/President - *Generalist*
Mr. Murray W. Clarke, Partner - *Medical, healthcare*
Mr. William M. Derhak, Partner - *Generalist*
Mr. Howard Kleiman, Partner - *Generalist*
Mr. Vincent J. McKnight, Partner - *Engineering*
Mr. David E. Van Schaik, Partner - *Manufacturing*
Mr. Wayne Percy, Partner - *Sales & marketing*

Salary minimum: $75,000

Functions: Generalist, General Mgmt., Mfg., Healthcare, Sales & Mktg., Finance, Engineering

Industries: Generalist, Mfg., Finance, Aerospace, Packaging, Healthcare

Development Resource Group Inc (DRG)
104 E 40th St Ste 304
New York, NY 10016
(212) 983-1600
Fax: (212) 983-1687
Email: search@drgnyc.com
Web: www.drgnyc.com

Description: Specialist in retained search for all not-for-profit CEOs, CFOs, COOs, senior managers and development specialists.

Key Contact:
Mr. David E. Edell, President
Ms. Linda Low, Executive Vice President
Mr. Mary Wheeler, Senior Vice President
Mr. Joyce Lappen, Vice President
Mr. Ellen Bodow, Senior Consultant

Functions: Generalist, Senior Mgmt., Non-profits

Industries: Non-profits, Higher Ed., Government, Development SW, Healthcare

Development Search Specialists
332 Minnesota St
W-1072 1st Nat'l Bank Bldg
St. Paul, MN 55101-1312
(651) 224-3750
Fax: (651) 224-3526
Email: fjl@nonprofitexecs.com

Description: Highly personalized searches for and recruitment of senior-level nonprofit executives for nonprofit organizations and institutions: The majority of searches are for executive directors and senior fundraising personnel.

Key Contact - Specialty:
Mr. Fred J. Lauerman, Owner
Dr. Charles B. Neff, Ph.D., Principal - *College and university presidents*

Salary minimum: $60,000

Functions: Senior Mgmt., Non-profits

Industries: Non-profits

DHR Int'l
10 S Riverside Plz Ste 2220
Chicago, IL 60606
(312) 782-1581
Fax: (312) 782-2096
Web: www.dhrintl.net

Description: We are a generalist firm with specialty practices and national and international coverage. Geographical coverage and lack of client blockage major plus. Two-year placement guarantee.

Key Contact:
Mr. Bob Aylsworth, Senior Vice President - Research
Mr. Steve Campbell, Executive Vice President
Mr. Marty Cerny, Executive Vice President

Mr. Steve Ethington, Executive Vice President
Mr. Warren K. Hendriks, Jr., EVP/Managing Director
Mr. Chuck Hill, Executive Vice President
Mr. David H. Hoffmann, Chairman/CEO
Mr. Michael Loiacano, SVP-Strategic Growth & Operations
Ms. Carolyn Lowe, Executive Vice President
Ms. Mary Lee Montague, EVP/Managing Director
Mr. Steve Murray, Executive Vice President
Mr. Claudio Peca, VP - Strategic Growth & Operations
Mr. Marc Quinlivan, Executive Vice President
Mr. Robert E. Reilly, Jr., President
Ms. Terri Ryan, Executive Vice President
Mr. Bertram Schuster, EVP/Managing Director
Mr. Lynn Small, Senior Vice President
Mr. Lowery Stallings, Executive Vice President
Ms. Marcey Rubin Stamas, Vice Chairman/Managing Director
Mr. Rick Vescio, Executive Vice President
Mr. James Wahle, Executive Vice President
Mr. James Wheary, Managing Director-Global Financial Svcs
Mr. Robert Wittebort, Executive Vice President
Mr. Jack Woods, Executive Vice President

Salary minimum: $75,000

Functions: Generalist

Industries: Generalist

Branches:
11811 N Tatum Ste 3031
Phoenix, AZ 85028
(602) 953-7810
Fax: (602) 953-7811
Key Contact:
Mr. David Bruno, President/Vice Chairman, Retail Division - *Retail operations*
Mr. Gary Hedges, Executive Vice President
Mr. Richard Wilder, Executive Vice President
Mr. Peter Yates, Executive Vice President

18201 Von Karman Ave Ste 1170
Irvine, CA 92612
(949) 852-1700
Fax: (949) 852-1253
Key Contact:
Mr. Larry Cabaldon, Executive Vice President
Mr. Gary Hegenbart, EVP/Managing Director
Mr. Larry King, Executive Vice President
Mr. Ronald E. LaGrow, EVP/Managing Director

2029 Century Park E Ste 1010
Los Angeles, CA 90067-2911
(310) 789-7333
Fax: (310) 789-7350
Key Contact:
Mr. Bill Allison, Executive Vice President
Mr. Richard Crowell, Senior Vice President
Mr. Michael Hagerthy, Executive Vice President

1111 Broadway Ste 2100
Oakland, CA 94607
(510) 273-2305
Fax: (510) 273-2323
Key Contact:
Mr. Tim Russi, Executive Vice President

2818 Congress Rd
Pebble Beach, CA 93953
(831) 658-0700
Fax: (831) 401-2375
Key Contact:
Mr. William Manby, Executive Vice President

4900 Hopyard Rd Ste 100
Pleasanton, CA 94588
(925) 468-4121
Fax: (925) 468-4122
Key Contact:
Mr. David Kurrasch, EVP/Managing Director
Ms. Karen Powell, Executive Vice President

11455 El Camino Real Ste 210
San Diego, CA 92130-2045
(858) 792-7654
Fax: (858) 792-6340

Key Contact:
Mr. Joel T. Grushkin, EVP/Managing Director
Mr. Lee Sharp, Senior Vice President - *Information technology*
Mr. Scott Westover, Executive Vice President

50 California St Ste 1500
San Francisco, CA 94111
(415) 439-5213
Fax: (415) 439-5217
Key Contact:
Mr. Scott Bretschneider, Executive Vice President

5201 Great America Pkwy Ste 320
Santa Clara, CA 95054
(408) 562-6311
Fax: (408) 562-6313
Key Contact:
Mr. Richard Kusiolek, Executive Vice President

1200 17th St Ste 2175
1 Tabor Ctr
Denver, CO 80202
(303) 629-0724
Fax: (303) 629-0724
Key Contact:
Mr. Martin M. Pocs, Vice Chairman
Mr. James Richardson, Executive Vice President
Ms. Joan Van Wyke, Executive Vice President

574 Heritage Rd Ste105A
Heritage Office Park
Southbury, CT 06488
(203) 264-0810
Fax: (203) 262-8742
Key Contact - Specialty:
Mr. Ralph B. DeCristoforo, Executive Vice President - *Healthcare practice*

6 Landmark Sq Fl 4
Stamford, CT 06901
(203) 925-0500
Fax: (203) 925-0515
Key Contact:
Mr. James O'Sullivan, Executive Vice President

1717 Pennsylvania Ave NW Ste 650
Washington, DC 20006
(202) 822-9555
Fax: (202) 822-9525
Key Contact:
Mr. Steve Hayes, Vice Chairman
Mr. James Martin, Executive Vice President
Mr. John Stiner, Executive Vice President

2255 Glades Rd Ste 324 A
Boca Raton, FL 33432
(561) 988-8451
Fax: (561) 988-8452
Key Contact:
Ms. Nancellen Stahl, Senior Vice President - Latin America

6238 Presidential Ct Ste 6
Ft. Myers, FL 33919
(941) 466-9899
Fax: (941) 466-9837
Key Contact:
Mr. Phil Jackson, Executive Vice President

5811 Pelican Bay Blvd Ste 205
Naples, FL 34108-2710
(941) 566-3310
Fax: (941) 566-2098
Key Contact:
Mr. Robert Harloe, Executive Vice President

3201 W Parkland Blvd
Tampa, FL 33609
(813) 348-0931
Fax: (813) 348-9525
Key Contact:
Mr. John Watters, VP/Managing Director

115 Perimeter Ctr Pl Ste 150
Atlanta, GA 30346
(770) 730-5900
Fax: (770) 730-5844
Key Contact:
Mr. Jerry Franzel, EVP/Managing Director
Ms. Margie McRae, Executive Vice President

Mr. Norman Morgan, Executive Vice President
Mr. Billy Max Paul, Executive Vice President
Mr. Ben Spalding, Senior Vice President

2624 Sioux Ct
Rockford, IL 61108
(815) 874-4230
Fax: (815) 874-2274
Key Contact:
Mr. Clay Walker, Executive Vice President

1901 N Roselle Rd Ste 800
Schaumburg, IL 60195
(847) 490-6450
Fax: (847) 490-5892
Key Contact:
Mr. Michael Setze, Executive Vice President

PO Box 6854
Bloomington, IN 47407
(812) 332-2712
Fax: (317) 332-2713
Key Contact:
Mr. James Doan, EVP/Managing Director

1 N Main Ste 619
First National Ctr
Hutchinson, KS 67501
(316) 728-1100
Fax: (316) 728-1110
Key Contact:
Mr. James Wright, EVP/Managing Director

7300 W 110th St Fl 7
Overland Park, KS 66210
(913) 317-1600
Fax: (913) 317-1601
Key Contact:
Mr. Mike Klockenga, Executive Vice President

400 E Pratt Fl 8
Baltimore, MD 21202
(410) 576-8352
Fax: (410) 727-6011
Key Contact:
Mr. Nick Visser, Executive Vice President

100 West Rd Ste 300
Towson, MD 21204
(410) 494-6500
Fax: (410) 821-9327
Key Contact:
Mr. Ken Miller, Executive Vice President

84 State St Fl 6
Boston, MA 02109
(617) 742-5899
Fax: (617) 720-1390
Key Contact:
Mr. Chris Dona, Vice Chairman
Mr. Frank Greaney, Executive Vice President
Ms. Nancy Curtain Murphy, Executive Vice President
Mr. Robert T. Zuzack, Executive Vice President

30 Monument Sq Ste 215 Rm 11
Concord, MA 01742
(978) 369-1350
Fax: (978) 369-9442
Key Contact:
Mr. John L. Alexanderson, Managing Director

11 Laurel Ave
Box 3014 Oak Bluffs
Martha's Vineyard, MA 02557
(508) 693-1933
Fax: (508) 693-5553
Key Contact:
Ms. Jenna Ducas, EVP, Diversity Strategist

6639 Centurion Dr Ste 140
Lansing, MI 48917
(517) 886-9010
Fax: (517) 886-9042
Key Contact:
Mr. Merritt Norvell, President, Education
Mr. Gordon White, Jr., Executive VP/Managing Director

17601 Susan Dr
Minnetonka, MN 55345
(952) 249-0464
Fax: (952) 449-4837
Key Contact:
Mr. Scott Smith, Executive Vice President

601 Carlson Pkwy Ste 1050
Minnetonka, MN 55305
(952) 449-6011
Fax: (952) 449-6009
Key Contact:
Mr. Scott Coleman, Executive Vice President
Mr. Daniel Ellis, Executive Vice President

630 Brockton Ln
Plymouth, MN 55447
(763) 249-0400
Fax: (763) 249-0500
Key Contact:
Mr. Curt Hedeen, EVP/Managing Director

510 Maryville University Dr Ste 220
St. Louis, MO 63141
(314) 205-2115
Fax: (314) 205-2199
Key Contact:
Mr. Mike Burroughs, Executive Vice President
W. Lynton Edwards, Executive Vice President
Mr. Scott Harris, Executive Vice President
Mr. Larry Munson, Executive Vice President

51 JFK Pkwy
Short Hills, NJ 07078
(973) 912-4444
Fax: (973) 912-4454
Key Contact:
Mr. Paul Meringolo, Executive Vice President
Mr. Richard Monastersky, EVP/Managing Director
Mr. Hayes Reilly, EVP/Managing Director
Mr. Booker Rice, Executive Vice President

1001 Franklin Ave Ste 319
Garden City, NY 11530
(516) 739-0010
Fax: (516) 739-2413
Key Contact:
Mr. Michael Carey, Executive Vice President

280 Park Ave Fl 43 W
New York, NY 10017
(212) 883-6800
Fax: (212) 883-9507
Key Contact:
Mr. Robert Anthes, Executive Vice President
Mr. Thomas Cook, Managing Director-Global
  Financial Svcs
Mr. John Cunningham, Executive Vice President
Ms. Deborah DeMaria, Executive Vice President
Mr. Joseph Frohlinger, Executive Vice President
Mr. Simon Gourdine, Executive Vice President
Ms. Debbie Graf, Executive Vice President
Mr. Freddy Kalles, Executive Vice President
Mr. Terence McCarthy, Managing Director, Global
  Financial Svcs
Mr. Declan Maguire, Executive Vice President
Mr. Lars Noble, EVP/Managing Director
Mr. Michael Perry, Executive Vice President
Mr. Carl Simmons, EVP, Education & Sport
  Practice
Mr. Frank T. Spencer, Vice Chairman/Regional
  Managing Director - *Retail*
Mr. John Tarbell, Managing Director, Global
  Financial Svcs

103 Old Orchard Ln
Orchard Park, NY 14127
(716) 648-9260
Fax: (716) 649-2483
Key Contact:
Mr. Patrick Crotty, Executive Vice President

5925 Carnegie Blvd Ste 500
Charlotte, NC 28209
(704) 571-3922
Fax: (704) 571-3921
Key Contact:
Mr. Richard Blumhagen, Executive Vice President
Mr. Gregory O'Brien, Executive Vice President

4819 Emperor Blvd Fl 4
Research Triangle Park
Durham, NC 27703
(919) 313-4770
Fax: (919) 313-4771
Key Contact:
Mr. Art Quinn, Executive Vice President

445 Hutchinson Ave Ste 800
Columbus, OH 43235
(614) 785-6464
Fax: (614) 785-6460
Key Contact:
Mr. Jack Warren, EVP/Managing Director

1500 Market St Centre Sq
E Twr Fl 12
Philadelphia, PA 19102
(215) 665-5683
Fax: (215) 665-5711
Key Contact:
Mr. Michael Volpe, EVP/Managing Director

210 W Rittenhouse Sq Ste 404
Philadelphia, PA 19103
(215) 790-1388
Fax: (215) 790-9880
Key Contact:
Mr. Oliver Tomlin, Executive Vice President

625 Liberty Ave Ste 2800
Dominion Twr
Pittsburgh, PA 15222
(412) 255-3750
Fax: (412) 255-3701
Key Contact:
Mr. Joseph Christman, Executive Vice President
Mr. John Thornburgh, EVP/Managing Director

PO Box 4499
Pittsburgh, PA 15205
(412) 331-4700
Fax: (412) 331-2540
Key Contact:
Mr. Dave Smith, Executive Vice President

2843 S County Trl
East Greenwich, RI 02818
(401) 884-1695
Fax: (401) 884-2394
Key Contact:
Mr. Stephen P. Bartlett, EVP/Managing Director

40 Calhoun St Ste 200
Charleston, SC 29401
(843) 579-2207
Fax: (843) 579-2403
Key Contact:
Mr. Steve Cutter, Executive Vice President

100 Congress Ctr Ste 2100
Austin, TX 78701
(512) 469-6388
Fax: (512) 469-6380
Key Contact:
Mr. Ted Balistreri, EVP/Managing Director

2500 City West Blvd Ste 300
Westchase Ctr
Houston, TX 77042
(713) 267-2266
Fax: (713) 267-2278
Key Contact:
Mr. Boyd Bergen, Executive Vice President
Mr. Phil Gennarelli, Executive Vice President

5215 N O'Connor Blvd Ste1800
Irving, TX 75039
(214) 574-4044
Fax: (214) 574-4048
Key Contact:
Mr. Victor Arias, Jr., EVP/Regional Managing
  Director
Ms. Lynn Cohn, Executive Vice President
Mr. Layne Newman, Executive Vice President
Mr. H. Craig Stoudt, Executive VP/Managing
  Director

201 S Main Ste 900
Salt Lake City, UT 84111
(801) 350-9101
Fax: (801) 350-9102
Key Contact:
Mr. Richard Hill, EVP/Managing Director

22525 SE 64th Pl Ste 201
Issaquah, WA 98027
(425) 557-3681
Fax: (425) 557-3684
Key Contact:
Mr. James Black, EVP/Managing Director

3 Edgewood Dr
Hudson, WI 54016-7115
(715) 386-2308
Fax: (715) 386-2316
Key Contact:
Ms. Lenore Hoolihan, Executive Vice President

Arthur Diamond Associates Inc
4630 Montgomery Ave Ste 200
Bethesda, MD 20814-3436
(301) 657-8866
Fax: (301) 657-8876
Email: bribakow@arthurdiamond.com
Web: www.arthurdiamond.com

Description: Focused on executive, senior and
middle management positions in all major industries
and not for protit associations and foundations. We
firmly believe that an organization's culture,
industry and dynamics often determine the best
candidate criteria.

Key Contact - Specialty:
Mr. Barton R. Ribakow, President - *Real estate,
  technology, energy,*
Ms. Beth Gibbs, Vice President - *Non-profit,
  foundations, associations*

Functions: Directors, Senior Mgmt., Middle Mgmt.

Industries: Generalist

The Dieck Group Inc
102 E Green Bay St Ste 101
Shawano, WI 54166-2444
(715) 524-5000
Fax: (715) 524-5001
Email: dan.dieck@dieckgroup.com
Web: www.dieckgroup.com

Description: Executive search firm focusing on
paper, packaging, chemical, coatings, printing,
machinery, equipment manufacturers.

Key Contact:
Mr. Daniel W. Dieck, President

Salary minimum: $100,000

Functions: General Mgmt., Senior Mgmt., Mfg.,
  Materials, Packaging, Sales & Mktg., HR Mgmt.,
  CFO's

Industries: Food, Bev., Tobacco, Lumber,
  Furniture, Paper, Printing, Chemicals, Plastics,
  Rubber, Packaging

Professional Associations: IACPR, PIMA, SHRM,
  TAPPI

The Diestel Group
2755 E Cottonwood Pkwy Ste 540
Salt Lake City, UT 84111
(801) 365-0400
Fax: (801) 365-0401
Email: brent@diestel.com
Web: www.diestel.com

Description: Skilled consultants utilizing a
collaborative, partnering approach to executive
search and organizational consulting. A focus on
general management positions for leading
companies located in the West.

Key Contact:
Mr. Brent Jespersen, Principal

Ms. Jill Perelson, Principal

Salary minimum: $80,000

Functions: General Mgmt.

Industries: Generalist

DillonGray
2333 San Ramon Valley Blvd Ste 125
San Ramon, CA 94583
(925) 743-4444
Fax: (925) 743-1144
Email: larry@dillongray.com
Web: www.dillongray.com

Description: Our firm developed a unique Internet executive search process, allowing the delivery of candidates to the client through the Internet. We conduct executive searches for technology related companies from startups to fortune five hundred companies across the US. We utilize the advanced candidate assessment technologies of Predictor Systems, which has not experienced a hiring failure after matching candidates to clients in ten years.

Key Contact - Specialty:
Mr. Larry Dillon, CEO - *Technology*
Ms. Helen Schultz, President - *Technology*

Salary minimum: $150,000

Functions: Senior Mgmt., Middle Mgmt., Product Dev., Sales & Mktg., Mktg. Mgmt., CFO's, IT, MIS Mgmt., DB Admin., Engineering

Industries: Electronic, Elec. Components, Venture Cap., Telecoms, Software, Database SW, Marketing SW, Networking, Comm. SW

DiMarchi Partners Inc
7107 LaVista Pl Ste 200
Niwot, CO 80503
(303) 415-9300
Email: mail@dimarchi.com
Web: www.dimarchi.com

Description: A generalist practice, specializing in key contributors; our consultants/partners possess over 70 years of combined experience in successfully evaluating human potential and ability.

Key Contact:
Mr. Paul DiMarchi, President
Mr. Gary Merriman, Partner/Principal
Ms. Kerranne Biley, Research Director

Salary minimum: $150,000

Functions: Senior Mgmt.

Industries: Generalist, Textiles, Apparel, Drugs Mfg., Medical Devices, Machine, Appliance, Computer Equip., Electronic, Elec. Components, Wholesale, Retail, Finance, Venture Cap., Services, Legal, Accounting, Mgmt. Consulting, Advertising, Communications, Telecoms, Fiber Optic, Real Estate, Software, Database SW, ERP SW, Mfg. SW, Marketing SW, Biotech, Healthcare

The Dinerstein Group
45 Rockefeller Plz Ste 2000
New York, NY 10111
(212) 332-3200
Fax: (212) 332-3202
Email: info@dinersteingroup.com
Web: www.dinersteingroup.com

Description: Results-oriented executive search and management consulting firm with focus on emerging growth companies. Client base includes media/new media, information services, telecommunications, consumer products, advertising, public relations, technology, venture capital and private equity companies.

Key Contact:
Ms. Jan Dinerstein, President
Ms. JoAnn Murray, Vice President

Salary minimum: $150,000

Functions: Senior Mgmt., Sales & Mktg., Advertising, Mktg. Mgmt., Direct Mktg., PR, HR Mgmt., CFO's, M&A, IT

Industries: Generalist

Robert W Dingman Company Inc
650 Hampshire Rd Ste 116
Westlake Village, CA 91361
(805) 778-1777
Fax: (805) 778-9288
Email: info@dingman.com
Web: www.dingman.com

Description: Senior management level assignments where need emphasizes a compatible management style, values, personality and goals between the candidates and the client. Ranked as a "Top Fifty" search firm by Executive Recruiter News.

Key Contact - Specialty:
Mr. Robert W. Dingman, Chairman of the Board - *Non-profit, education, board search*
Mr. Bruce Dingman, President - *Hospitality, education, family business, services, non-profit*
Mr. Bret Dalton, Principal - *General management, information technology, service, manufacturing*

Salary minimum: $100,000

Functions: General Mgmt., Senior Mgmt., Middle Mgmt., Mktg. Mgmt., Sales Mgmt., CFO's, Non-profits

Industries: Generalist

Professional Associations: AESC

Dinte Resources Inc
8300 Greensboro Dr Ste 880
McLean, VA 22102
(703) 448-3300
Fax: (703) 448-0215
Email: pdinte@dinte.com
Web: www.dinte.com

Description: High quality retained firm providing executive search and interim executive solutions to corporations and associations thereby assisting them in meeting business objectives.

Key Contact:
Mr. Paul Dinte, President
Mr. Christopher Sunday, Vice President

Salary minimum: $125,000

Functions: Senior Mgmt.

Industries: Energy, Utilities, Finance, Venture Cap., Services, Mgmt. Consulting, Media, Telecoms, Software, Healthcare

The Directorship Search Group Inc
8 Sound Shore Dr Ste 250
Greenwich, CT 06830
(203) 618-7000
Fax: (203) 618-7007
Email: info@directorship.com
Web: www.directorship.com

Description: We are consultants in executive and director search, management succession planning, and corporate governance.

Key Contact - Specialty:
Mr. Russell S. Reynolds, Jr., Chairman/CEO - *Financial services, directors, CEOs*
Mr. Michael P. Kelly, Managing Director - *Healthcare, financial services, information systems, CEOs, COOs*
Mr. Thomas L. McLane, Vice Chairman/Head-Corp. Dir. Practice - *Manufacturing, directors, CEOs, COOs*
Mr. Russell S. Reynolds, III, Managing Director/CFO - *Telecommunications, high technology, CEOs, directors*
Ms. Linda K. Ducruet, Mng Dir/Head-Wealth Mgmt Practice - *Financial services*

Ms. Kathryn Van Cleve Kuhns, Vice President - *Financial services, directors*

Salary minimum: $150,000

Functions: Generalist, General Mgmt., Directors, Senior Mgmt., Healthcare, Physicians, Sales & Mktg., HR Mgmt.

Industries: Generalist, Agri., Forestry, Mining, Mfg., Retail, Finance, Services, Packaging

Professional Associations: AESC, ASCS

Branches:
230 Park Ave Ste 460
New York, NY 10169
(212) 973-9200
Fax: (212) 973-1975
Email: mkelly@directorship.com
Key Contact - Specialty:
Mr. Michael P. Kelly, Managing Director - *Healthcare, financial services, information systems, CEOs, COOs*
Mr. Tom H. Rosenwald, Mng Dir/Head-Mktg & Cons Prods Practice - *Consumer products, marketing, advertising, corporate communications*
Mr. Brian T. Kelley, Jr., Vice President - *Healthcare, technology, manufacturing, CFOs*

Dise & Company Inc
20600 Chagrin Blvd Ste 610
Shaker Heights, OH 44122
(216) 752-1700
Fax: (216) 752-6640
Web: www.diseco.com

Description: Our strength is the rapid identification of the most appropriate candidates given the client's strategic objectives and corporate culture.

Key Contact - Specialty:
Mr. Ralph A. Dise, Jr., President - *Senior executives, board members*
Mr. Brad J. Attewell, Director Executive Search - *Manufacturing, marketing, human resources*
Mr. P. William Marshall, Vice President - *Banking, finance, accounting, investment banking*
Ms. Carolyn Fisher, Administrator - *Client services & support*
Mr. David Tate, Director Executive Search - *Engineering management, sales*

Salary minimum: $75,000

Functions: Generalist

Industries: Mfg., Wholesale, Finance, Services, New Media, Insurance, Real Estate, Software, Biotech

Professional Associations: NOHRPS, SHRM

R J Dishaw & Associates
PO Box 671262
Dallas, TX 75367
(972) 924-5000
Fax: (972) 924-5003
Email: exsearch@msn.com

Description: A generalist firm specializing in quality service. M.S., Ph.D. level in technical, managerial, financial and manufacturing fields.

Key Contact - Specialty:
Mr. Raymond J. Dishaw - *Managerial, scientific, engineering, manufacturing*

Salary minimum: $70,000

Functions: General Mgmt., Directors, Mfg., Automation, Materials Plng., HR Mgmt., IT, R&D, Engineering

Industries: Generalist, Energy, Utilities, Construction, Mfg., Chemicals, Drugs Mfg., Metal Products, Motor Vehicles, Computer Equip., Consumer Elect., Wholesale, Finance, Services, Accounting, Equip Svcs., Media, Telecoms, Defense, Haz. Waste, Aerospace, Packaging, Software, Biotech, Healthcare

Diversified Executive Search

43533 Ridge Park Dr
Temecula, CA 92590
(909) 676-8077
Fax: (909) 699-1581
Email: bhanna@diversifiedjobs.com
Web: www.diversifiedjobs.com

Description: Diversified is your gateway to hidden candidates. With over seventeen years in the staffing industry Diversified has successfully earned a proven reputation. Our agency specializes in mamagement, engineering, fincance, hotel/entertainment, Gaming/Indian Gaming, manfacturing, sales/marketing. Our approach is personal and professional at the same time, which results in matches that are long lasting and effective for both the candidate and the client. Our contract network provides us with quailified referrals which keeps are database updated with recent candidates in the job market.

Key Contact - Specialty:
Ms. Bonnie Hanna, President - *Executive recruiting*

Salary minimum: $15,000

Functions: Generalist

Industries: Drugs Mfg., Medical Devices, Plastics, Rubber, Leather, Stone, Glass, Metal Products, Machine, Appliance, Motor Vehicles, Electronic, Elec. Components, Misc. Financial, Non-profits, Higher Ed., Legal, Accounting, Equip Svcs., Mgmt. Consulting, HR Services, Hotels, Resorts, Clubs, Restaurants, Telecoms, Telephony, Digital, Wireless, Fiber Optic, Network Infrastructure, Accounting SW, Database SW, Development SW, Entertainment SW, HR SW, Industry Specific SW, Mfg. SW, Marketing SW, Networking, Comm. SW

Networks: Int'l Search Group

Diversified Health Search

2005 Market St Ste 3300
One Comerce Sq
Philadelphia, PA 19103
(215) 732-6666
Fax: (215) 568-8399
Email: diversified@divsearch.com
Web: www.diversifiedsearch.com

Description: We are one of the largest health care search firms in the country. Our clients include many faith-based systems, academic institutions, specialty care facilities, for-profit health systems and community hospitals. DHS has been committed to diversity and assisting our clients in evaluating their respective diversity initiatives.

Key Contact - Specialty:
Ms. Cynthia P. Heckscher, Managing Director - *CEO's, healthcare, diversity, CFO's, human resources*
Ms. Judith M. von Seldeneck, President/CEO - *Boards of directors, CEOs, COOs, diversity, healthcare*
Mr. Stephen S. Morreale, Executive Vice President/COO - *CFO, treasurer, controller*
Mr. Ronald Stemphoski, Managing Director - *CEOs, COO, CFOs, VP patient care services, department chairs*
Ms. Cynthia Barth, Managing Director - *Department chair, medical director, nurse executive, CFO, special services*

Salary minimum: $120,000

Functions: General Mgmt., Healthcare, Mktg. Mgmt., Sales Mgmt., HR Mgmt., CFO's, MIS Mgmt., Minorities, Non-profits

Industries: Insurance, Biotech, Healthcare

Professional Associations: AESC, IACPR, AAMC, ACHA, ACHA, AFP, AHA, ARENA, CEOC, CHA, DIA, ESRT, HIMSS, IWF, LES, MGMA, NACD, NAHSE, NAPR, SHRM, WAW

Diversified Management Resources Inc

10 Post Office Sq Ste 600 S
Boston, MA 02109-4603
(617) 338-3040
Fax: (801) 740-2198
Email: search@dmrfinancial.com
Web: www.dmrfinancial.com

Description: We focus exclusively on the financial services business, with an emphasis on sales, marketing and operations management in the mutual funds industry. See www.mutualfundcareersonline.com for review of current searches.

Key Contact:
Mr. Charles A. O'Neill, Principal
Ms. Laura McCoy, Principal

Salary minimum: $100,000

Functions: Generalist, Middle Mgmt., Advertising, Mkt. Research, Mktg. Mgmt., Sales Mgmt., MIS Mgmt.

Industries: Generalist, Invest. Banking

Diversified Search Inc

2005 Market St 1 Commerce Sq Ste 3300
Philadelphia, PA 19103
(215) 732-6666
Fax: (215) 568-8399
Email: diversified@diversifiedsearch.com
Web: www.diversifiedsearch.com

Description: Generalist executive search firm, founded in 1973, serving clients nationwide, and internationally through Global Search Solutions network. Pioneers in partnering executive search with consulting services in coaching and leadership development. Areas of specialty include diversity, financial services, pharmaceuticals, biotechnology, healthcare, consumer products, technology, telecommunications, education, not-for-profit and boards of directors.

Key Contact - Specialty:
Ms. Judith M. von Seldeneck, President/CEO - *Boards of directors, CEOs, COOs, diversity, healthcare*
Mr. Stephen S. Morreale, CPA, Executive Vice President/COO - *Miscellaneous finance, finance*
Mr. B. A. MacLean, Jr., Managing Director - *Banking, investment banking, venture capital, management consulting, e-Commerce*
Mr. Colin Christie, Managing Director - *Pharmaceutical, biotechnology, finance, banking, high technology, manufacturing*
Mr. Bud Locilento, Managing Director - *Banking, miscellaneous financial, services, human resources, healthcare*
Ms. Kim Morrisson, Managing Director - *Non-profits, higher ed, healthcare, women's, diversity*
Ms. Judy Boreham, Managing Director - *Finance, pharmaceutical services, legal, HR services*
Mr. Gerard F. Cattie, Jr., Managing Director - *Miscellaneous financial, non-profits, higher education, IT implementation,*
Ms. Tammy Roberts, Vice President - *Managing consulting, HR services, human resource, healthcare, hospitals*
Ms. Meg Callaghan, Managing Director - *Non-profits, retail, human resource, e-commerce, technology*
Mr. Craig V. Smith, Ph.D., Managing Director - *Higher education, non-profit, technology, miscellaneous financial, endowment management*
Ms. Karen O'Boyle, Chief Sales and Marketing Office - *Management consulting, sales, marketing*

Salary minimum: $120,000

Functions: Generalist, General Mgmt., Mfg., Healthcare, Sales & Mktg., HR Mgmt., CFO's, IT, Minorities, Non-profits

Industries: Generalist, Energy, Utilities, Mfg., Retail, Finance, Services, New Media, Insurance, Software, Biotech, Healthcare

Professional Associations: AESC, IACPR, AAMC, AHA, ARENA, C200, CEOC, CHA, DIA, ESRT, HIMSS, IWF, LES, NACD, NAHSE, NAPR, NYNMA, SHRM, WAW, WMSA

Branches:
260 California St Ste 400
San Francisco, CA 94111
(415) 352-0418
Fax: (415) 956-5642
Email: diversified@divsearch.com
Key Contact - Specialty:
Ms. Judith M. von Seldeneck, President/CEO - *Boards of directors, CEOs, COOs, diversity, healthcare*

3575 Piedmont Rd 15 Piedmont Ctr Ste 300
Atlanta, GA 30305
(404) 262-1049
Fax: (404) 262-1096
Email: diversified@divsearch.com
Key Contact - Specialty:
Ms. Judith M. von Seldeneck, President/CEO - *Boards of directors, CEOs, COOs, diversity, healthcare*

255 State St Fl 5
Boston, MA 02109
(617) 523-6870
Fax: (617) 737-9101
Email: diversified@divsearch.com
Key Contact - Specialty:
Ms. Joan Lucarelli, Managing Director - *New media, telecommunications, high technology, internet, management consulting*
Ms. Susan Hay, Managing Director - *High technology, telecommunications, manufacturing, financial services, energy*

420 Lexington Ave Ste 501
New York, NY 10170
(212) 661-3220
Fax: (212) 661-0240
Email: diversified@divsearch.com
Key Contact - Specialty:
Ms. Rusty Myer, Managing Director - *Financial (management, services), new media, internet, worldwide web, technology*
Ms. Elaine Burfield, Managing Director - *Drugs manufacturing, medical devices, venture capital, pharmaceutical services, biotech*
Mr. Jeffrey Neuberth, Managing Director - *Sales & marketing, finance, CFOs, IT, MIS management*

128 S Tryon St Ste 1570
Charlotte, NC 28202
(704) 331-0006
Fax: (704) 376-5988
Email: diversified@diversifiedsearch.com
Key Contact - Specialty:
Mr. Jeffrey Siegrist, Managing Director - *Natural resources, plastics, paper, textiles, suppliers*

The Diversity Advantage

1 Evertrust Plz Fl 3
Jersey City, NJ 07302
(201) 324-0291
Fax: (201) 324-1485
Email: dmiller@minoritycentral.com
Web: www.thediversityadvantage.com

Description: The convergence of diversity strategy, leading web tools and proactive recruitment enable us to bring new "pipelines" of diverse talent to the corporate marketplace. These tools give us the ability to offer strategic recruitment for experienced hiring needs, conference management as well as university partnerships and sourcing.

Key Contact - Specialty:
Mr. Darryl Miller, Vice President
Dr. Thomas Bachhuber, Vice President - *University resources*

Salary minimum: $75,000

Functions: General Mgmt., Minorities

Industries: Drugs Mfg., Finance, Pharm Svcs., Accounting, Mgmt. Consulting, HR Services, Media, Government

DLB Associates
271 Madison Ave Ste 1406
New York, NY 10016
(212) 953-6460
Fax: (212) 953-6764
Email: only1dlb@aol.com

Description: Boutique firm with a national practice specializing in the recruitment of general management, marketing, advertising, direct response, interactive, corporate communications and new media professionals for consumer and service industries.

Key Contact - Specialty:
Mr. Lawrence E. Brolin, Partner - *Marketing, advertising, direct response, corporate communications, new media*
Ms. Dorothy Goodman-Brolin, President - *Marketing, advertising, direct response, corporate communications, new media*

Salary minimum: $100,000

Functions: Senior Mgmt., Advertising, Mktg. Mgmt., Direct Mktg., PR, Mgmt. Consultants

Industries: Food, Bev., Tobacco, Soap, Perf., Cosmtcs., Banking, Misc. Financial, Mgmt. Consulting, Entertainment, Media

DLG Associates Inc
1515 Mockingbird Ln Ste 560
Charlotte, NC 28209
(704) 522-9993
Fax: (704) 522-7730
Email: info@dlgassociates.com

Description: Specialize in financial services, real estate and MIS/DP custom search; senior officers of the company have combined 70(+) years' executive management experience in banking and/or MIS.

Key Contact - Specialty:
Mr. David J. Guilford, President - *Financial services management, mortgage banking, real estate, corporate lending, capital markets*
Mr. W. Kenneth Goodson, Jr., Executive Vice President - *Mortgage banking, real estate lending, corporate banking, capital markets, information technology*

Salary minimum: $65,000

Functions: Senior Mgmt., Sales & Mktg., Finance, CFO's, Risk Mgmt., IT, MIS Mgmt., Attorneys

Industries: Misc. Financial, Services

Professional Associations: MBAA, NBN

Networks: National Banking Network (NBN)

DMG-Maximus
1800 Century Park E Ste 430
Los Angeles, CA 90067
(310) 475-8001
Fax: (310) 475-8007
Email: searchla@maximus.com
Web: www.dmgmaximus.com

Description: The nation's leading public sector recruiting firm. Specialize in: public sector/not-for-profit, transportation, utilities, engineering, healthcare and education. Recruit in all functional areas within these industries.

Key Contact:
Mr. Norman C. Roberts, Vice President
Ms. Valerie S. Frank, Executive Vice President
Ms. Nicole Seagle, Manager
Ms. Juliet Lee, Manager
Ms. Sherrill Uyeda, Senior Consultant
Ms. Michelle Mevorach, Senior Consultant

Salary minimum: $70,000

Functions: Generalist, Senior Mgmt., Health Admin., HR Mgmt., Finance, IT, Engineering, Non-profits

Industries: Generalist, Energy, Utilities, Transportation, Non-profits, Higher Ed., Telecoms, Government, Healthcare

Branches:
1949 Commonwealth Ln
Tallahassee, FL 32303
(850) 386-1101
Fax: (850) 386-3599
Email: search@dmg.maxinc.com
Key Contact:
Ms. Reneé Narloch, Consultant

630 Dundee Rd Ste 200
Northbrook, IL 60062
(847) 564-9270
Fax: (847) 564-9136
Key Contact:
Mr. Mike Casey, Regional Director

4438 Centerview Dr Ste 302
San Antonio, TX 78228
(210) 735-1400
Fax: (210) 735-1405
Key Contact:
Mr. Lou Fox

DMR Global Inc†
10230 W Sample Rd
Coral Springs, FL 33065
(954) 796-5043
(954) 796-0032
Fax: (954) 796-5044
Email: rondaratany1@msn.com
Web: www.dmrglobal.com

Description: We are a full-service, retained executive search firm that specializes in the financial services, aviation, manufacturing and retail industries. We complete search assignments in all senior and upper-level management positions across all functional areas, including information technology. Long-term business relationships are the foundation of our success!

Key Contact - Specialty:
Mr. Ron Daratany, President - *Financial services, aviation, business development*
Ms. Emily Maynard, Director of Recruiting - *Financial services, aviation recruiting*

Salary minimum: $50,000

Functions: Generalist

Industries: Misc. Mfg., Transportation, Finance, Accounting, Aerospace, Insurance, Accounting SW, Mfg. SW

DNPitchon Associates
60 W Ridgewood Ave
Ridgewood, NJ 07450
(201) 612-8350

Description: Consultancy based executive search practice.

Key Contact - Specialty:
Mr. Daniel N. Pitchon, President - *Generalist*
Ms. Linda A. Belen, Principal - *Generalist*

Salary minimum: $100,000

Functions: Generalist

Industries: Generalist

Professional Associations: APA, SHRM

L J Doherty & Associates
65 Ford Rd
Sudbury, MA 01776
(978) 443-9603
Email: len@ljdassoc.com
Web: www.ljdassoc.com

Description: Computer industry focus: systems, software, telecom/datacom, Internet and information technology services.

Key Contact - Specialty:
Mr. Leonard J. Doherty, Principal - *Computer, communications*

Salary minimum: $90,000

Functions: General Mgmt.

Industries: Mgmt. Consulting, Software

Doherty Int'l Inc
300 W Washington St Ste 704
Chicago, IL 60606
(312) 845-3040
Fax: (312) 845-3969
Email: dohertyint@aol.com

Description: Our success is dramatically reflected in our energized, comprehensive approach to the total transition process. With over 20 years of experience in the transition field, the leadership of the organization feels professionally comfortable and competent in delivering effective programs to a growing list of clients.

Key Contact - Specialty:
Mr. John J. Doherty, President - *Logistics, human resources*

Salary minimum: $100,000

Functions: Generalist, Middle Mgmt., Plant Mgmt., Materials, Mkt. Research, Mktg. Mgmt., HR Mgmt., IT

Industries: Generalist

Doleman Enterprises†
1151 Water Pointe
Reston, VA 20194-1035
(703) 742-5454
Email: doleman@patriot.net
Web: www.patriot.net/users/doleman

Description: Executive search and professional recruitment, logistics management & research analysis, information technology, fiber optics marketing and engineering.

Key Contact - Specialty:
Ms. Linda J. Howard, Principal - *Pharmaceutical, information technology*
Mr. Robert J. Doleman, Principal - *Engineering, research economists, research analysts, fiber optics (marketing, engineering)*
Mr. Howard Miller, Senior Executive - *Generalist*

Salary minimum: $40,000

Functions: Generalist

Industries: Mfg., Chemicals, Computer Equip., Misc. Mfg., Finance, Services, Pharm Svcs., Government, Software, Biotech

The Domann Organization Inc
2455 Bennett Valley Rd Ste B107
Santa Rosa, CA 95404
(800) 923-6626
(707) 527-4114
Fax: (707) 527-0780
Email: info@domannorg.com
Web: www.domannorg.com

Description: We are life science search specialists. Our sectors include: biotechnology, medical devices, diagnostics pharmaceuticals, genomic, bio-informatics. The levels that we place include: CEO, COO, senior vice president, vice president, and director

Key Contact - Specialty:
Mr. William A. Domann,, Jr. - *General management, clinical & medical affairs, regulatory affairs, quality assurance & quality control, research & product development*

Salary minimum: $110,000

Functions: Generalist, General Mgmt., Senior Mgmt.

Industries: Generalist, Drugs Mfg., Medical Devices, Pharm Svcs., Biotech

Professional Associations: AESC, ASQ, DIA, RAPS

Dominguez-Metz & Associates
12 Geary St Ste 604
San Francisco, CA 94108
(415) 765-1505
Fax: (415) 765-1534
Email: nally5@aol.com

Description: Both my partner and I come from retailing, so we have a strong understanding of the retail world.

Key Contact - Specialty:
Ms. Nancy Metz, Partner - *Retailing, manufacturing, e-commerce*
Ms. Connie Dominguez, Partner - *Retailing, manufacturing, e-commerce*

Salary minimum: $50,000

Functions: Generalist, General Mgmt., Product Dev., Distribution, Sales & Mktg., HR Mgmt., Finance, MIS Mgmt.

Industries: Generalist, Textiles, Apparel, Retail, HR Services

Douglas Dorflinger & Associates[†]
9171 Wilshire Blvd Ste 610
Beverly Hills, CA 90210
(310) 276-7091
Fax: (310) 276-7042
Email: dsdassoc@earthlink.net
Web: www.constructionhr.com

Description: We focus on the construction and real estate development industries.

Key Contact - Specialty:
Mr. Doug Dorflinger, President - *Construction, real estate development*

Functions: Generalist

Industries: Construction, Real Estate

Dotson & Associates
412 E 55th St Ste 8A
New York, NY 10022
(212) 593-3651

Description: Specializing in placement of middle- and senior-level marketing, communications, sales and service quality professionals. Expertise in financial services, technology and general communications including direct mail and telemarketing.

Key Contact - Specialty:
Ms. M. Ileen Dotson, Principal - *Marketing & sales*

Salary minimum: $75,000

Functions: Generalist, Health Admin., Advertising, Mkt. Research, Mktg. Mgmt., Sales Mgmt., Direct Mktg., Minorities

Industries: Generalist, Banking, Hospitality, New Media, Broadcast, Film, Telecoms, Healthcare

Professional Associations: NAFE

Steven Douglas Associates Retainer Division
(an alliance with EMA Partners Int'l)
3040 Universal Blvd Ste 180
Weston, FL 33331
(954) 453-8577 x136
(305) 381-8100
Fax: (954) 453-8575
Email: retainerdiv@stevendouglas.com
Web: www.stevendouglas.com

Description: We are a specialty retainer practice led by seasoned professionals committed to providing personal attention to clients' senior executive needs in all functional areas across industry boundaries. Our most recent assignments include logistics, retail, non-profit, healthcare, manufacturing, agriculture, high-tech, and service.

Key Contact:
Mr. Mark E. Young, Managing Director

Salary minimum: $100,000

Functions: Generalist

Industries: Generalist

Douglas Owen Search Consultants
105 Sunnyslopes Crt
Santa Cruz, CA 95060
(831) 425-1351
Fax: (831) 425-1352
Email: doug@owensearch.com
Web: www.owensearch.com

Description: Twenty-six years specializing in retained search for key executives (at the VP level or above) for small - mid sized technology companies. Markets served are broad - communications, computers, software, instrumentation, capital management, engineering, marketing, sales, finance, operations.

Key Contact:
Mr. Doug Owen

Salary minimum: $120,000

Functions: General Mgmt., Sales & Mktg., Finance, Engineering

Industries: PSA/ASP, Communications, Software

Douglas-Allen Inc
1500 Main St Fl 24
PO Box 15368
Springfield, MA 01115
(413) 739-0900
Fax: (413) 734-9109
Email: research@douglas-allen.com
Web: www.douglas-allen.com

Description: Serving the nation's top investment firms in the recruitment of portfolio managers, analysts, and sales & marketing professionals.

Key Contact:
Mr. Robert D. Stevens, CFA, Principal - *Investment management*
Ms. Kimberly A. Leask, Director of Research

Salary minimum: $100,000

Functions: Cash Mgmt.

Industries: Finance

Professional Associations: AIMR

Drake Executive Search[†]
9434 N 134th East Ave Ste 111
Owasso, OK 74055
(918) 272-2608
Fax: (918) 272-2612
Email: DrakeExec@aol.com
Web: www.DrakeExecutiveSearch.com

Description: Nationwide recruiting for the hospitality industry.

Key Contact - Specialty:
Ms. Linda Drake, Ms., President - *Recruiting*

Dressler Associates
624 University Ave
Palo Alto, CA 94301
(650) 323-0456
Fax: (650) 323-2904
Web: www.dresslerassociates.com

Description: A fully retained executive search firm specializing in CEO and vice president positions for early stage technology based, venture funded companies.

Key Contact - Specialty:
Ms. Carol F. Dressler, President - *High technology, CEOs, vice presidents*

Salary minimum: $150,000

Functions: Generalist, Senior Mgmt., Mktg. Mgmt., Engineering

Industries: Generalist, Venture Cap.

Drew Associates Int'l
25 Pompton Ave Ste 305
Verona, NJ 07044
(973) 571-9735

Description: Healthcare industry consultants for physician and executive recruitment and physician practice valuation and acquisition consulting services.

Key Contact - Specialty:
Mr. Robert R. Detore, President - *Healthcare executive*
Mr. Christian Strumolo, Search Consultant - *Physician*
Mr. Richard F. Grady, MD, FAACP Medical Director - *Medical director*

Salary minimum: $80,000

Functions: Generalist, Physicians, Health Admin., Mkt. Research, CFO's, Mgmt. Consultants, Int'l.

Industries: Generalist, Mgmt. Consulting, Healthcare

Professional Associations: NAPR

Robert Drexler Associates Inc[†]
210 River St
Hackensack, NJ 07601
(201) 342-0200
Fax: (201) 342-9062
Email: drexler@engineeringemployment.com
Web: www.engineeringemployment.com

Description: Individual retained and group search terms are available. We are engineering, technical, and executive search consultants. Our clients include pharmaceutical, bio-tech, chemical, petrochemical, petroleum, fuel cell, industrial, commercial, environmental, bridge and highway, engineering construction, transportation, and aerospace.

Key Contact:
Mr. Robert C. Drexler, President

Salary minimum: $65,000

Functions: Generalist, Product Dev., Automation, Plant Mgmt., Sales Mgmt., Engineering, Environmentalists, Architects

Industries: Generalist, Energy, Utilities, Construction, Chemicals, Pharm Svcs., Environmental Svcs., Aerospace, Biotech

Professional Associations: AICHE, ISPE

Drinkwater & Associates
167 West St
Beverly Farms, MA 01915
(978) 922-3676
Email: wdrinkwater@mediaone.net

Description: Our founder is a seasoned search consultant with invaluable experience from Korn/Ferry International. This firm conducts search assignments for premier retained executive search firms, corporations, technology companies, and start-ups. This firm is a strong generalist firm with a team of 12 and a stellar 10-year track record of rapidly delivering qualified candidates at a low cost. Every client is a reference.

Key Contact - Specialty:
Ms. Wendy A. Drinkwater, Principal - *Generalist, technology, consulting, e-business, internet*
Ms. Ashley B. Ullstein, Associate - *Generalist, technology, e-business, internet, tax*
Ms. Patti D. Edington, Associate - *Generalist, consulting, tax/audit, research, financial services*
Mr. Brian McElroy, Associate - *Generalist, technology, financial services, consulting, tax/audit*
Ms. Diane P. Esecson, Associate - *Generalist, retail, technology, internet, e-business*
Ms. Elizabeth Loomis - *Financial services, e-business, internet, consulting*

Salary minimum: $100,000

Functions: Senior Mgmt.

Industries: Generalist, Energy, Utilities, Textiles, Apparel, Brokers, Venture Cap., Services, New Media, Telecoms, Government

---

Du Vall & Associates
10 Emerald Glen
Laguna Niguel, CA 92677-9378
(949) 488-8790
Fax: (949) 488-8793
Email: karen@duvall.com
Web: www.duvall.com

Description: Our firm is a national retained executive search firm with over 20 years experience in the high-tech industry. We are recognized for our success in recruiting top executives, and also known for recruiting entire start-up teams from the executive level to the sales, marketing, and systems engineering teams.

Key Contact - Specialty:
Ms. Karen DuVall, President - *High technology*
Mr. Rick Westcott, Vice President - *High technology*

Functions: General Mgmt., Directors, Senior Mgmt., Middle Mgmt., Sales & Mktg., Mktg. Mgmt., Sales Mgmt., Direct Mktg., CFO's, Mgmt. Consultants

Industries: Services, Mgmt. Consulting, E-commerce, IT Implementation, Communications, Software

---

Ducharme Group Inc
157 Bowood Ave
Toronto, ON M4N 1Y3
Canada
(416) 481-7221
Fax: (416) 481-5641
Email: ducharmegroup@sympatico.ca

Description: We are a boutique firm offering responsive, rigorous, and personalized recruiting services. We can draw on an extensive network of human resources and research professionals, compensation, and career counseling to compliment and enhance process.

Key Contact - Specialty:
Ms. Lynda Ducharme, President - *Executive management, senior management, non-profit, professional services, finance*

Salary minimum: $60,000

Functions: General Mgmt., Senior Mgmt., Middle Mgmt., HR Mgmt., Finance, Non-profits

Industries: Services, Media

J H Dugan & Associates Inc
225 Crossroads Blvd Ste 416
Carmel, CA 93923
(831) 655-5880
Fax: (831) 655-5588
Email: plastic-recruiter@jhdugan.com
Web: www.jhdugan.com

Description: We are a client driven plastics industry talent office search and search research firm. Our founder is plastics experienced, published, speaker, and notable as a leader, director, and past chairperson in both fields. Our clients include world class, as well as, start-up companies. All markets and functions served throughout America, Western Europe, and Hong Kong.

Key Contact - Specialty:
Mr. John H. Dugan, President - *Plastics*

Salary minimum: $50,000

Functions: Generalist, General Mgmt., Mfg., Packaging, Sales & Mktg., M&A, R&D, Engineering

Industries: Generalist, Medical Devices, Plastics, Rubber, Computer Equip., Misc. Mfg., Electronic, Elec. Components, Packaging, Industry Specific SW

Professional Associations: IACPR, AIWF, SPE, SPI

Ronald Dukes Associates LLC
20 N Wacker Dr Ste 2010
Chicago, IL 60606
(312) 357-2895
Fax: (312) 357-2897
Email: ron@rdukesassociates.com
Web: www.rdukesassociates.com

Description: Provide executive search consulting to companies in the general industrial sector to include general management and officer positions in all functional areas with a concentration in the automotive industry.

Key Contact - Specialty:
Mr. Ronald Dukes, President - *General management, senior officers, industrial manufacturers*

Salary minimum: $150,000

Functions: Generalist

Industries: HR SW, Mfg. SW, Marketing SW

Dunlap & Sullivan Associates
29 Pearl St NW Ste 227
Grand Rapids, MI 49503
(616) 458-4142
Fax: (616) 458-4203
Email: dunsul@aol.com

Description: Offer executive search concentrating on senior executive appointments, across a wide spectrum of industries. Building a personal relationship with clients, creating a high precentage of repeat business.

Key Contact:
Mr. John P. Sullivan, Co-Principal
Mr. Stanley R. Dunlap, Co-Principal

Salary minimum: $75,000

Functions: General Mgmt., Senior Mgmt., Middle Mgmt., Quality, Mktg. Mgmt., Sales Mgmt., HR Mgmt., CFO's, MIS Mgmt.

Industries: Lumber, Furniture, Printing, Plastics, Rubber, Metal Products, Machine, Appliance, Motor Vehicles

Branches:
5663 Foxcross Pl
Stuart, FL 34997
(561) 286-3594
Email: dunsul@aol.com
Key Contact:
Mr. Stanley R. Dunlap, Co-Principal

Dunn Associates[†]
229 Limberline Dr
Greensburg, PA 15601
(724) 832-9822
(877) 586-2538
Fax: (724) 832-9836
Email: maddunn@aol.com

Description: Quality recruiting for substantially less. Any industry. Honesty. Integrity. Timeliness. Attention to details. Telephone screening. Full search except face to face interviews. We offer "unbundled" research services as well.

Key Contact - Specialty:
Ms. Margaret A. Dunn, President - *Generalist*
Ms. Jean Pistentis, Research-Recruiting Consultant - *Generalist*

Salary minimum: $60,000

Functions: General Mgmt., Mfg., Materials, Sales & Mktg., HR Mgmt., Finance, CFO's, Risk Mgmt., IT, Engineering

Industries: Generalist, Paper, Chemicals, Paints, Petro. Products, Metal Products, Motor Vehicles, Electronic, Elec. Components, Higher Ed.

Professional Associations: PHTC

Dynamic Synergy Corp
2730 Wilshire Blvd Ste 550
Santa Monica, CA 90403-4747
(310) 586-1000
Fax: (310) 586-1010
Email: info@dynamicsynergy.com
Web: www.dynamicsynergy.com

Description: Our corporation's special talent is to find the best candidate to fulfill the requirements. We provide an extremely high-level of service, quickly generating a short list of qualified candidates. Our short turnaround time results in cost effectiveness. We work with VC-funded pre-IPO start-ups and high-growth companies. Partners with our clients, we offer unique options to exchange equity for our professional search services.

Key Contact - Specialty:
Mr. Mark Landay, Managing Director - *Software industry*

Salary minimum: $100,000

Functions: Senior Mgmt.

Industries: Telecoms, Software

Earley Kielty LLC
2 Penn Plz Ste 1990
New York, NY 10121
(212) 736-5626
Fax: (212) 643-0409
Email: ekainfo@earleykielty.com
Web: www.earleykielty.com

Description: Professional executive search firm conducting retained searches for senior operating and financial executives in all size corporations in a variety of industries including consumer products, entertainment and media, distribution, manufacturing, and financial services.

Key Contact:
Mr. Jay Sterling, Managing Director
Mr. James Dixon, Managing Director
Ms. Conni R. Bullock, Managing Director

Salary minimum: $100,000

Functions: General Mgmt., Sales & Mktg., HR Mgmt., Finance, CFO's, IT, Mgmt. Consultants

Industries: Energy, Utilities, Mfg., Finance, Legal, Media, New Media, Software, Healthcare

Professional Associations: IACPR, AICPA

Branches:
35 Mason St
Greenwich, CT 06830
(203) 661-7420
Fax: (203) 629-4406
Key Contact:
Mr. Chuck Stroble, Managing Director

Early, Cochran & Olson LLC
401 N Michigan Ave Ste 2010
Chicago, IL 60611-4206
(312) 595-4200
Fax: (312) 595-4209
Email: eco94@aol.com
Web: www.ecollc.com

Description: National practice limited to retained searches for lawyers to fill senior corporate and law firm positions. Experienced consultants serve Fortune 500 corporations and major law firms. References furnished.

Key Contact - Specialty:
Ms. Corinne Cochran - *Senior lawyers*
Mr. B. Tucker Olson - *Senior lawyers*
Mr. Bruce R. LeMar - *Senior lawyers*
Mr. Bert H. Early - *Senior lawyers*

Salary minimum: $105,000

Functions: Legal

Industries: Generalist

Eastbourne Associates Inc
330 Motor Pkwy
Hauppauge, NY 11788
(631) 231-2555
Fax: (631) 231-2570
Email: search@eastbourneassociates.com
Web: www.eastbourneassociates.com

Description: Accept only three clients in any one industry. Founding principals personally work on each assignment, providing complete status report and candidate slate in 6-8 weeks. Two-year candidate replacement policy.

Key Contact:
Ms. Rosemary Kissel, President
Mr. Herbert Sokol, Managing Partner

Functions: Generalist

Industries: Mfg., Venture Cap., Services, Pharm Svcs., HR Services, Telecoms, Defense, Aerospace, Software, Biotech

Eastman & Beaudine Inc
5700 W Plano Pkwy Ste 2800
Plano, TX 75093
(972) 267-8891
Fax: (972) 267-8008

Description: Consultants to management in executive selection.

Key Contact:
Mr. Robert E. Beaudine, President/CEO - *Sports, insurance brokerage, real estate, entertainment & media, retail*
Ms. Nancy Berg, CFO/COO

Salary minimum: $100,000

Functions: Generalist, Directors, Senior Mgmt., Mktg. Mgmt., Sales Mgmt., CFO's, MIS Mgmt.

Industries: Generalist, Food, Bev., Tobacco, Venture Cap., HR Services, Hospitality, Insurance, Real Estate

Branches:
1 Ravinia Dr Ste 1110
Atlanta, GA 30346
(770) 390-0801
Fax: (770) 390-0875
Email: frank@beaudine.com
Key Contact - Specialty:
Mr. Frank R. Beaudine, Jr., Senior Vice President - *Human resources, communications, manufacturing, marketing*

eBconnects Inc
740 Monaco Pkwy
Denver, CO 80220
(303) 780-9111
(303) 888-6586
Fax: (303) 321-6391
Email: staff@ebconnects.com
Web: www.ebconnects.com

Description: We are the best suited, most capable executive search professionals to identify, recruit and introduce client companies to the very best of the telecommunications and Internet space management requirements.

Key Contact - Specialty:
Ms. Erika Brown, President - *Marketing, business development, corporate development, telecommunications, consumer packaged goods*

Salary minimum: $80,000

Functions: Generalist, Directors

Industries: Food, Bev., Tobacco, Invest. Banking, Venture Cap., Mgmt. Consulting, HR Services, Media, Advertising, New Media, Telecoms

Professional Associations: AMR, FWE

Ecruiters.net[†]
(an Advanced Marketing Team Inc company)
PO Box 1086
Chanhassen, MN 55317
(952) 233-5750
Email: headhunter@ecruiters.net
Web: www.ecruiters.net

Description: We are a retained executive search firm that specializes in the areas of Internet technology, e-commerce, and specialty and mass market retail executives. We work with the best retail merchants, Internet managers, and technology executives in the country. Our clients range from startup Internet companies to fortune 500 companies and the largest retailers in the world. They all have one thing in common. . . one of them are satisfied with the status quo.

Key Contact - Specialty:
Mr. David Happe, President and CEO - *E-commerce, retail executives*

Functions: Generalist

Industries: Wholesale, Retail

Timothy P Edgar Inc
203 - 1865 Marine Dr
West Vancouver, BC V7V 1J7
Canada
(604) 921-4144
Fax: (604) 921-4184
Email: tpedgar@telus.net

Description: Our firm is a highly successful executive search company that has occupied a unique niche in the Western Canada career market for 21 years enjoying a first-class reputation for putting the right people in the right place. Geography is no barrier to finding that "right person for the right position." With a comprehensive search network in place and extensive use of the Internet, Timothy P. Edgar Inc provides excellent senior management personnel.

Key Contact:
Mr. Tim Edgar, President

Salary minimum: $50,000

Functions: Generalist

Industries: Energy, Utilities, Mfg., Wholesale, Finance, Services, Hospitality, Communications, Environmental Svcs., Software, Biotech

Edgewood Int'l
3018 Edgewood Pkwy
Woodridge, IL 60517-3720
(630) 985-6067
(630) 985-6780
Fax: (630) 985-6069
Email: wocatedgewood@aol.com
Web: www.edgewoodintl.com

Description: We are a small retained executive search firm with a broad area of expertise from highly technical research and development up to general management in a number of industries.

Key Contact - Specialty:
Mr. William O'Connor, Managing Partner - *High technology, electronics, telecommunications, insurance, pension funds*

Salary minimum: $75,000

Functions: General Mgmt., Directors, Senior Mgmt., Middle Mgmt., Healthcare, Mktg. Mgmt., Sales Mgmt., CFO's, IT, MIS Mgmt.

Industries: Drugs Mfg., Medical Devices, Metal Products, Computer Equip., Electronic, Elec. Components, Invest. Banking, Misc. Financial, Pharm Svcs., IT Implementation, Telephony, Fiber Optic, Aerospace, Insurance, Software

Educational Management Network
(a division of Witt/Kieffer)
2015 Spring Rd Ste 510
Oak Brook, IL 60523
(630) 990-1370
Email: info@emnemn.com
Web: www.emnwittkieffer.com

Description: We are the nation's leading executive search firm dedicated to serving education, health care, and not-for-profit communities. We identify outstanding leadership solutions for organizations committed to improving the quality of life. We focus on searches for presidents/chancellors, provosts, vice presidents, deans, and directors of major service/academic units.

Key Contact - Specialty:
Ms. Paula Carabelli, Senior Vice President - *Presidents, vice presidents, deans, directors*
Ms. Nancy Martin, Senior Vice President - *Vice presidents, deans, directors*
Mr. Gary Posner, Vice President and Practice Director - *Vice presidents, deans, directors*
Mr. Emmanuel Berger, Vice President - *Presidents, vice presidents, deans, directors*

Salary minimum: $100,000

Functions: Generalist

Industries: Non-profits, Higher Ed., Mgmt. Consulting

Professional Associations: AAHE, ACE, AHP, CASE, NACUBO

Branches:
2010 Main St
Irvine, CA 92614
(949) 851-5070
Key Contact - Specialty:
Ms. Paula Carabelli, Senior Vice President - *Presidents, vice presidents, deans, directors*

25 Burlington Mall Rd Fl 6
Burlington, MA 01803
(781) 272-8899
Key Contact - Specialty:
Mr. Emanuel D. Berger, Vice President - *Presidents, vice presidents, deans, directors*

98 Old South Rd
Nantucket, MA 02554
(508) 228-6700
Key Contact - Specialty:
Ms. Nancy Martin, Senior Vice President - *Presidents, vice presidents, deans, directors*
Ms. Lucy Leske, Consultant - *Presidents, vice presidents, deans, directors*

3 Park Ave Fl 29
New York, NY 10017
(212) 686-2676
Fax: (212) 686-2527
Key Contact - Specialty:
Ms. Sally-Ann Hard, Consultant - *President, vice presidents, deans, directors*
Ms. Mary Elizabeth Taylor, Consultant - *Presidents, vice presidents, deans, directors*

5143 N Stanford Dr
Nashville, TN 37215
(615) 665-3388
Key Contact - Specialty:
Mr. Gary J. Posner, Senior Vice President - *Presidents, vice presidents, deans, directors*

Bruce Edwards & Associates Inc
PO Box 51206
Durham, NC 27717-1206
(919) 489-5368
Email: bruce@edwardsassoc.com

Description: We are a 100% retained search firm, located in the Research Triangle area of North Carolina. Our clients are primarily headquartered in US senior-level searches for corporations, organizations, and institutions.

Key Contact - Specialty:
Mr. S. Bruce Edwards, President - *Vice presidents, executive vice presidents, COOs, presidents, CEOs*
Mr. George D. Smith, Secretary - *Boards of directors*
Mr. Donald Fish, Senior Recruiter - *Senior management*

Salary minimum: $85,000

Functions: Generalist, Senior Mgmt., Plant Mgmt., Mktg. Mgmt., Sales Mgmt., CFO's, MIS Mgmt., Systems Analysis

Industries: Generalist, Computer Equip., Retail, Venture Cap., Telecoms, Software, Biotech

Effective Search Inc
11718 N Main
Roscoe, IL 61073-9566
(815) 623-7400
Fax: (815) 623-9299
Web: www.esintl.net

Description: Specializing in managers for sales, marketing, accounting, engineering manufacturing and general management, especially those requiring technical degrees (including senior engineer). All searches evaluate candidates working style and interpersonal skills.

Key Contact:
Mr. John A. Cain, Group President
Mr. Bob H. Mullins, Division President
Mr. Christian A. Anderson, Division President

Salary minimum: $60,000

Functions: Generalist, General Mgmt., Mfg., Materials, Sales & Mktg., HR Mgmt., Finance, Engineering

Industries: Generalist, Drugs Mfg., Plastics, Rubber, Metal Products, Machine, Appliance, Computer Equip., Consumer Elect.

Professional Associations: AME, ASM, ASQ

Branches:
5469 Sunbird Dr
Rockford, IL 61111
(815) 654-8535
Fax: (815) 654-0469
Email: esichris@aol.com
Web: www.esintl.com
Key Contact:
Mr. Christian Anderson, Division President

343 W Bagley Rd Ste 402
Berea, OH 44017
(440) 234-2205
Fax: (440) 243-7082
Key Contact:
Mr. Craig B. Toedtman, Division President

925 Harvest Dr Ste 190
Blue Bell, PA 19422
(215) 628-4177
Fax: (215) 628-2780
Key Contact:
Mr. Chris Bilotta, Division President

EFL Associates
7101 College Blvd Ste 550
Overland Park, KS 66210-1891
(913) 451-8866
Fax: (913) 451-3219
Email: eflinfo@eflkc.com
Web: www.eflassociates.com

Description: National/international executive search practice specializing in the most senior-levels of management for a broad base of client companies.

Key Contact:
Mr. Peter K. Lemke, Chairman/CEO
Mr. Jason M. Meschke, President/COO
Ms. Evelyn C. Davis, Senior Vice President
Mr. David A. Wolfram, Senior Vice President
Mr. Jeffrey K. Riley, Exec. Vice President & Managing Partner

Functions: Generalist

Industries: Generalist

Professional Associations: ASTD, SHRM

Networks: TranSearch Int'l

EFL Int'l
8777 E Via De Ventura Ste 300
Scottsdale, AZ 85258-9734
(480) 483-0496
Fax: (480) 483-2832
Email: info@eflinternational.com
Web: www.eflinternational.com

Description: Provide search consulting services to senior management.

Key Contact - Specialty:
Mr. William R. Franquemont, Chairman/CEO - *Generalist*
Mr. Jeffrey D. Franquemont, President - *Generalist, high technology*

Salary minimum: $75,000

Functions: Generalist

Industries: Generalist, Energy, Utilities, Mfg., Wholesale, Retail, Banking, Services, Hospitality, Media, Telecoms

Egan & Associates Inc
128 S 6th Ave
White House Ctr
West Bend, WI 53095
(262) 335-0707
Fax: (262) 335-0625
Email: info@eganassociates.com
Web: www.eganassociates.com

Description: Perform executive searches on a retainer basis only. No contingency work performed. The vast majority of clients are manufacturers with searches being performed for all major disciplines within manufacturing.

Key Contact - Specialty:
Mr. Daniel K. Egan, President - *Generalist*
Ms. Joy V. Massar, Recruiter - *Generalist*

Salary minimum: $70,000

Functions: Mfg.

Industries: Generalist

Eggleston Consulting Int'l
4067 Audubon Dr
Marietta, GA 30068
(770) 579-2344
Fax: (770) 579-1706
Email: dudley@eggcon.com
Web: www.eggcon.com

Description: We specialize in executive search for the real estate industry; retained executive search in all functional areas.

Key Contact - Specialty:
Mr. G. Dudley Eggleston, President - *Real estate*

Salary minimum: $75,000

Functions: Generalist

Industries: Real Estate

Professional Associations: ULI

Richard A Eisner & Company LLP
575 Madison Ave
New York, NY 10022
(212) 355-1700
Fax: (212) 355-2414
Email: david@eisner.rae.com
Web: www.eisnerllp.com

Description: Senior executive searches, compensation and management consulting services for a wide range of companies including mid-sized companies, portfolio companies of venture capital and buyout firms, new USA ventures of non-USA based companies.

Key Contact - Specialty:
Mr. Richard Fisher, Partner - *Financial services, CFOs*

Salary minimum: $80,000

Functions: Generalist, General Mgmt., Mktg. Mgmt., HR Mgmt., Finance, IT, Mgmt. Consultants

Industries: Generalist, Mfg., Finance, Services, Media, Software, Healthcare

Branches:
100 Campus Dr
Florham Park, NJ 07932
(973) 593-7000
Fax: (973) 593-7070
Key Contact:
Mr. Eli Hoffman

Electronic Careers
24955 Pacific Coast Hwy Ste B201
Malibu, CA 90265
(310) 317-6115
Fax: (310) 317-6119
Email: ecareers@electroniccareers.com
Web: www.electroniccareers.com

Description: We provide executive and professional search for sales and engineering in the electronics industry.

Key Contact - Specialty:
Mr. Tom Myers, President - *Engineering, fiber optics, RF*

Functions: Generalist, Senior Mgmt., Sales Mgmt., Engineering

Industries: Generalist, Mfg., Metal Products, Computer Equip., Test, Measure Equip., Telecoms

The Eliot & Carr, Curry Telleri Group
Harmon Cove Twr 3 A/L Lvl Ste 4-A
Secaucus, NJ 07094
(201) 223-1700
Fax: (201) 223-1818
Email: recruit@eliotcarr.com
Web: www.eliotcarr.com

Description: We focus on retainer search engagements for middle- and upper-level management sales, marketing technical positions for all functional areas within the chemical, pharmaceutical plastics, allied industries, and information technology over a broad range of industries.

Key Contact - Specialty:
Dr. Michael J. Curry, Treasurer - *Biotechnology, pharmaceuticals, allied industries*
Mr. Frank C. Telleri, President - *Chemicals, coatings, plastics, allied industries*
Mr. George Sedak, Vice President - *Engineering, information technology*

Salary minimum: $40,000

Functions: Generalist, Mfg., Materials, Sales & Mktg., HR Mgmt., IT, R&D, Engineering

Industries: Generalist, Chemicals, Drugs Mfg., Plastics, Rubber, Paints, Petro. Products, Computer Equip., Software, Biotech

Professional Associations: AICHE, ASQ, CDA, FSCT, IEEE, SACI

Elite Resources Group[†]
71 Baker Blvd Ste 204
Fairlawn, OH 44333
(330) 867-9412
Fax: (330) 867-0468
Email: elite-rg@neo.rr.com

Description: We are a full-service human resource consulting and staffing based business. We focus on conducting executive/management/professional searches in the context of your mission, culture, and direction. We specialize in client requirements and provide very qualified candidates within weeks of accepting an assignment.

Key Contact - Specialty:
Mr. Gary T. Suhay, President - *Transportation, engineering, research & development, quality, technical service & sales*

Salary minimum: $40,000

Functions: Generalist, Production, Materials, Purchasing, Materials Plng., Distribution, R&D, Engineering

Industries: Generalist, Lumber, Furniture, Chemicals, Plastics, Rubber, Machine, Appliance, Misc. Mfg., Transportation, Wholesale, Retail, Finance

Networks: Top Echelon Network

Yves Elkas Inc[†]
485 McGill St # 601
Montreal, QC H2Y 2H4
Canada
(514) 845-0088
Fax: (514) 845-2518
Email: general@elkas.com
Web: www.elkas.com

Description: We provide expertise in executive search and evaluation of prospective candidates. Over the years, we have developed original and sound methodologies in recruitment.

Key Contact - Specialty:
Mr. Yves Elkas, President - *Generalist, senior management, human resources*
Mr. Jacques E. Ouellet, Senior Partner - *Finance, human resources*
Mr. Jean-Pierre Hurtubise, Senior Partner - *Quality, finance, human resources*
Mrs. Sophie Lavoie, Recruiter
Mr. André Robert, Recruiter - *High-tech*
Mr. Pierre D'Aoust, Senior Partner - *Retail, food, distribution*
Mr. Maurizio Cencherle, Recruiter - *Technical, operations, production*

Salary minimum: $50,000

Functions: Generalist, General Mgmt., Mfg., Materials, Sales & Mktg., HR Mgmt., Finance, Engineering

Industries: Generalist, Food, Bev., Tobacco, Misc. Mfg., Transportation, Retail, Venture Cap., Media, Packaging

Professional Associations: CIRA, OCRIQ

Elliot Associates Inc
104 S Broadway
Tarrytown, NY 10591
(914) 631-4904
Fax: (914) 631-6481
Web: www.theelliotgroup.com

Description: We provide nationwide executive search and strategic consulting to the hospitality, foodservice, and manufacturing industries.

Key Contact - Specialty:
Ms. Alice Elliot, CPC, President/CEO - *Hospitality, retail service, foodservice, manufacturing*

Salary minimum: $100,000

Functions: Generalist, General Mgmt., Directors

Industries: Mfg., Food, Bev., Tobacco, Retail, Services, Hospitality

Professional Associations: CHART, CRA, MFHA, NRA, RWF, SFM, SHRM, WFF

Branches:
8501 Wilshire Blvd Ste 165
Beverly Hills, CA 90211
(310) 289-2610
Fax: (310) 289-2613
Email: don@theelliotgroup.com
Key Contact:
Mr. Don Fitzgerald, Regional Vice President

131 Roswell St Ste B2-2
Alpharetta Executive Ctr
Alpharetta, GA 30004
(770) 664-5354
Fax: (770) 664-0233
Email: joan@theelliotgroup.com
Key Contact:
Ms. Joan Ray, Executive Vice President

22 Chase St
Amesbury, MA 01913
(978) 388-1515
Fax: (978) 388-6277
Email: connie@theelliotgroup.com
Key Contact:
Ms. Connie Newkirk, Regional Manager

10901 Reed Hartman Hwy Ste 321
Cincinnati, OH 45242-2835
(513) 792-0113
Fax: (513) 792-0117
Key Contact:
Mr. Rick Badgley, Vice President

3970 Via Siena
Poland, OH 45242
(330) 707-1094
Fax: (330) 707-1096
Email: greg@theelliotgroup.com
Key Contact:
Mr. Greg Palmer, Regional Vice President

5025 Burnet Rd Ste 200
Austin, TX 78756
(512) 454-0477
Fax: (512) 454-0936
Email: troy@theelliotgroup.com
Key Contact:
Mr. Troy Erb, Vice President

The Elliott Company
42 Eighth St - 1412
Charlestown, MA 02129
(617) 241-7648
Email: relliott@elliottco.net
Web: www.elliottco.net

Description: We are an executive resource dedicated to serving companies and supporting clients' profitable growth through retained leadership acquisition, as well as our merchant banking and business development activities. We practice no conflict of interest.

Key Contact - Specialty:
Mr. Roger S. Elliott, President - *Leadership, board members (public companies), executives, multilateral alliances/partnerships*

Salary minimum: $100,000

Functions: General Mgmt., Directors, Senior Mgmt., Mfg., Sales & Mktg., HR Mgmt., CFO's, M&A, Int'l.

Industries: Energy, Utilities, Mfg., Transportation, Finance, Services, Media, Biotech

Professional Associations: AMA, IFEBP, SHRM

David M Ellner Associates
13 Central Dr
Port Washington, NY 11050
(212) 279-0665
Email: elldoda@aol.com

Description: Executive search services tailored to the small and medium-sized organization.

Key Contact - Specialty:
Mr. David M. Ellner, CEO - *Generalist*

Salary minimum: $60,000

Functions: Legal, Sales & Mktg., Finance, IT, R&D

Industries: Finance, Invest. Banking, Media, Publishing, New Media, Software

Elwell & Associates Inc
31920 Nottingwood
Farmington Hills, MI 48334
(734) 662-8775
Fax: (734) 662-2045
Email: selwell@elwellassociates.com
Web: www.elwellassociates.com

Description: Specializing in searches for senior executives, across functions and industries, throughout North America.

Key Contact:
Mr. Richard F. Elwell, Chairman
Mr. Stephen R. Elwell, President

Salary minimum: $90,000

Functions: Generalist, Senior Mgmt., Mfg., Materials, Sales & Mktg., HR Mgmt., Finance, MIS Mgmt., Engineering

Industries: Generalist, Mfg., Venture Cap., Defense, Aerospace, Packaging

Mark Elzweig Company Ltd
183 Madison Ave Ste 1704
New York, NY 10016
(212) 685-7070
Fax: (212) 685-7761
Email: melzweig@elzweig.com
Web: www.elzweig.com

Description: We are specialists in the asset management industry. We handle a variety of searches in the marketing, administration, and investment arenas. Our clients are money management firms and major investment banks.

Key Contact - Specialty:
Mr. Mark Elzweig - *Account marketers (institutional, managed), portfolio managers, client service executives, research analysts*
Ms. Nancy Miller - *Institutional marketers, portfolio managers*

Salary minimum: $200,000

Functions: Senior Mgmt., Middle Mgmt., Product Dev., Sales & Mktg., Cash Mgmt.

Industries: Finance, Banking, Misc. Financial, Services

Emerging Medical Technologies Inc
7784 S Addison Way
Aurora, CO 80016
(303) 699-1990
Fax: (303) 699-7694
Email: tcmemt@aol.com

Description: We serve companies and investors in the fields of medical devices, biotechnology and pharmaceuticals. Specializing in research, product development, marketing, sales, quality and regulatory affairs.

Key Contact - Specialty:
Mr. Thomas C. Miller, President - *Engineering, marketing, regulatory affairs, senior management*
Ms. Susan Osborn, Director - *Sales, regulatory affairs, MIS, product management*

Salary minimum: $75,000

Functions: General Mgmt., Mfg., Sales & Mktg., Specialized Svcs.

Industries: Drugs Mfg., Medical Devices, Pharm Svcs., Biotech, Non-classifiable

Professional Associations: ACP, AIUM, ASMS, CMDA, CVC, PDA, RAPS

Empire Int'l
1147 Lancaster Ave
Berwyn, PA 19312
(610) 647-7976
Fax: (610) 647-8488
Email: info@empire-internl.com
Web: www.empire-internl.com

Description: We are a generalist retained search firm addressing senior-level management engagements throughout the English-speaking world including the United States, Canada, the United Kingdom and the Pacific Rim.

Key Contact:
Mr. Charles V. Combe, II, President
Mr. M. J. Stanford, Vice President
Mr. Paul Lange, Managing Director
Mr. Howard W. Imhof, Senior Consultant
Ms. Jessica E. Bye, Research Manager
Ms. Holly Fitzgerald, Senior Consultant
Mr. Frank Nolan, Jr., Associate
Mr. Kevin O'Keefe, Associate
Ms. Melinda Combe, Vice President
Mr. Thomas MacCarthy, Research Director

Salary minimum: $100,000

Functions: Generalist

Industries: Energy, Utilities, Construction, Mfg., New Media, Broadcast, Film, Aerospace, Packaging, Real Estate, Software, Biotech

Professional Associations: ACS, CMA, IMPS, IPMI, SMTA

The Energists
10260 Westheimer Ste 300
Houston, TX 77042
(713) 781-6881
Fax: (713) 781-2998
Email: search@energists.com
Web: www.energists.com

Description: Specialists (each consultant has a minimum of eighteen years' technical/business energy industry and search experience) in executive search to the upstream and midstream energy industry.

Key Contact - Specialty:
Mr. Alex Preston, President - *Exploration, production*

Salary minimum: $80,000

Functions: Generalist, Senior Mgmt., Middle Mgmt., R&D, Engineering, Int'l.

Industries: Generalist, Energy, Utilities

Professional Associations: AAPG, API, SEG, SPE

The Enfield Company
1605 Juliette Str
Austin, TX 78704
(512) 444-9921

Description: We specialize in facilitating the transition from traditional to new media in educational training. We can also address senior-level searches within the sectors we cut across.

Key Contact - Specialty:
Mr. Herbert E. Smith, Managing Partner - *Higher education publishing, multimedia development, distance learning*
Ms. Kim MacIntosh, Associate - *School publishing (K-12), training*

Salary minimum: $60,000

Functions: Generalist, Senior Mgmt., Advertising, Mkt. Research, Mktg. Mgmt., Direct Mktg., PR, Mgmt. Consultants

Industries: Generalist, Higher Ed., Mgmt. Consulting, Hospitality, Advertising, Publishing, New Media

---

ENI
98 Kellogg Dr
PO Box 073
Wilton, CT 06897
(203) 894-8389
Fax: (203) 894-8395
Email: efnsearch@aol.com

Description: Thirty years of professional search experience servicing a broad range of multinational clients in all functional areas. Strong background in healthcare, consumer products, high-technology and service industries.

Key Contact - Specialty:
Mr. Edgar F. Newman, President - *Generalist*

Salary minimum: $75,000

Functions: Generalist

Industries: Telecoms, Real Estate, Software, Healthcare

Professional Associations: CVG

Branches:
3705 Long Beach Blvd
Holgate, NJ 08008
(609) 207-1376
Email: efnsearch@aol.com
Key Contact:
Mr. Edgatr Newman, President

The Enns Partners
(a division of AmropHever)
100 University Ave Ste 601
South Twr Box 134
Toronto, ON M5J 1V6
Canada
(416) 598-0012
Fax: (416) 598-4328
Web: www.ennshever.com

Description: Experienced consulting firm serving senior executive search requirements across Canada and abroad.

Key Contact - Specialty:
Mr. George Enns, Partner
Mr. Alan Burns, Partner
Ms. Rita Eskudt, Partner
Mr. Jock McGregor, Partner
Mr. Morris Tambor, Partner
Ms. Judi Hutchinson, Partner - *Sales, finance, HR at executive level*

Salary minimum: $100,000

Functions: General Mgmt.

Industries: Generalist

Professional Associations: AESC

Networks: The Amrop - Hever Group

Entelechy Group Inc[†]
13400 Sutton Park Dr S Ste 1504
Jacksonville, FL 32224
(904) 992-2224
Fax: (904) 992-4344
Email: bcebak@medcomsearch.com

Description: We specialize in medical communications. We are dedicated to the development and growth of our customers by providing them with professional executive search consulting services to aid them in the fulfillment of critical personnel needs.

Key Contact:
Mr. William Cebak, CPC, President - *Medical communications*
Ms. Zoe Ann Boyle

Functions: Generalist, Healthcare

Industries: Media, Communications, Healthcare

Professional Associations: AMWA, DIA, HMC

Epsen, Fuller & Associates LLC
460 Bloomfield Ave Ste 211
Montclair, NJ 07042
(973) 233-9500
Fax: (973) 233-9505
Email: tfuller@efasearch.com
Web: www.efasearch.com

Description: We are dedicated to serving the strategic human resource needs of demanding emerging growth and corporate clients. We specialize in acquiring the superior intellectual capital necessary to keep your business dynamic and competitive by deploying our unique and proprietary Human Capital Valuation System (sm).

Key Contact - Specialty:
Mr. Thomas Fuller, President/CEO - *Technology, telecommunications, consumer products, retail*
Ms. Anne Rogers, Senior Consultant - *Technology, telecommunications, consumer products, retail, pharmaceutical*

Salary minimum: $150,000

Functions: Generalist

Industries: Energy, Utilities, Soap, Perf., Cosmtcs., Consumer Elect., Retail, Venture Cap., Pharm Svcs., Advertising, New Media, Telecoms, Biotech

Professional Associations: ASC, CEM, ETC, NJTC, NYNMA, VANJ

Branches:
101 W 6th St
Ground Zero
Austin, TX 78701
(512) 536-7565
Fax: (512) 536-7568
Email: dharap@efasearch.com
Key Contact - Specialty:
Mr. David Harap, Partner - *Technology, telecommunications, pharmaceutical, medical technology, biotech*

11811 N Fwy Ste 500
Houston, TX 77060
(281) 591-4700
Fax: (281) 591-4712
Email: jfuller@efasearch.com
Key Contact - Specialty:
Mr. James Fuller, Managing Director - *Technology, telecommunications, consumer products, retail*
Mr. Richard Ruggiero, Partner - *Energy, exploration, utilities, technology*

Erlanger Associates

2 Soundview Dr
Greenwich, CT 06830
(203) 629-5410
Fax: (203) 629-5444
Email: raerlanger41@aol.com
Web: www.erlanger-associates.com

Description: We focus on searches for operating general partners and line executives in buyouts, turnarounds, and portfolio companies including their parent firms. We also find operating executives in Internet related firms and venture capital groups.

Key Contact - Specialty:
Mr. Richard A. Erlanger, Managing Director - *CEOs, COOs, general managers*
Ms. Carolyn M. Desley, Director of Research - *CEOs, COOs, general managers*

Salary minimum: $175,000

Functions: Generalist, General Mgmt., Senior Mgmt.

Industries: Generalist

Branches:
11300 US Hwy 1 Ste 400
North Palm Beach, FL 33408
(561) 691-6261
Fax: (561) 624-4709
Email: raerlanger41@aol.com
Key Contact - Specialty:
Ms. Lynn Hayden, Manager - *CFOs, operations, marketing*

Ernest, Evans & Koch

5082 E Hampden Ave Ste 214
Denver, CO 80222
(303) 782-9648
Fax: (303) 639-9089
Email: candice@off2work.com
Web: www.off2work.com

Description: We work with CEOs and presidents who are frustrated with their sales team's results. Our services include sales team assessment, skills training and development, and search. Our tools, which are EEOC compliant and are validated up to 96%, reduce the risk of hiring candidates who will not be successful in your environment.

Key Contact - Specialty:
Ms. Candice L. Koch, President - *Sales/sales management, product management*

Salary minimum: $150,000

Functions: Product Dev., Sales Mgmt.

Industries: Finance, Mgmt. Consulting, E-commerce, IT Implementation, New Media, Communications, Call Centers, Telephony, Wireless, Fiber Optic, Network Infrastructure, Software, Networking, Comm. SW, Security SW, Healthcare

Professional Associations: PDMA, RMDMA, SCIP

Networks: Top Echelon Network

ESA

141 Durham Rd Ste 16
Madison, CT 06443
(203) 245-1983
Fax: (203) 245-8428
Email: esa.search@snet.net
Web: www.esa-search.com

Description: Concentration in high-tech industries. Specializing in the full range of functional areas found in most high-technology manufacturing companies.

Key Contact:
Mr. Barry L. Dicker, Managing Partner - *High technology*
Mr. Vincent Bongiovanni, Partner - *High technology*
Mr. Cas Hill, Partner

Mr. Richard Molinelli, Partner

Salary minimum: $60,000

Functions: Generalist, Directors, Senior Mgmt., Mktg. Mgmt., MIS Mgmt., Systems Analysis, Systems Dev., Engineering

Industries: Generalist, Mfg., Aerospace, Software

Networks: National Personnel Assoc (NPA)

ESearch Group

30 Tower Ln
Avon, CT 06001
(860) 677-6770
Web: www.esearchgroup.com

Description: Our functional focus is on senior finance and general management positions. Our industry focus is on technology, professional services, and healthcare.

Key Contact:
Mr. Ronald R. Evans, Managing Director

Salary minimum: $90,000

Functions: Generalist, Senior Mgmt., Mktg. Mgmt., PR, CFO's, M&A, MIS Mgmt.

Industries: Generalist, Invest. Banking, Accounting, Advertising, Software

Branches:
6750 Hillcrest Plaza Dr Ste 308
Dallas, TX 75230
(972) 960-8640
Email: info@esearchgroup.com
Key Contact:
Mr. Ronald R. Evans, Managing Director
Ms. Jennifer Feit

Essex Consulting Group Inc

PO Box 550
Essex, MA 01929
(978) 768-0030
Email: brad@essexsearch.com

Description: We provide management recruitment services to organizations seeking strategically important professionals who will accelerate the realization of specific and time-sensitive business objectives.

Key Contact - Specialty:
Mr. J. Bradley Hildt, Principal - *Financial services, management consulting, technology*

Salary minimum: $125,000

Functions: General Mgmt.

Industries: Finance, Invest. Banking, Venture Cap., Mgmt. Consulting, Media, Software

ET Search Inc

1250 Prospect St Ste 101
La Jolla, CA 92037-3618
(858) 459-3443
Fax: (858) 459-4147
Email: taxpros@etsearch.com
Web: www.etsearch.com

Description: We are the premier retained tax search firm, specializing exclusively in identifying and attracting talented tax executives for major corporations located throughout the United States, Europe, Asia, and Latin America.

Key Contact - Specialty:
Ms. Kathleen Jennings, President - *Tax*
Ms. Diane Stewart, Vice President - *Tax*
Ms. Dawn Miramontes, Corporate Controller - *Tax*
Ms. Elizabeth Posadas, Executive Search Consultant - *Tax*

Salary minimum: $80,000

Functions: Taxes

Industries: Generalist

Ethos Consulting Inc

100 Drakes Landing Rd Ste 100
Greenbrae, CA 94904
(415) 925-0211
Fax: (415) 925-0688
Email: resumes@ethosconsulting.com
Web: www.ethosconsulting.com

Description: Highly personalized, senior-level executive search practice that concentrates on delivering results to clients in a timely and professional manner.

Key Contact:
Mr. Conrad E. Prusak, President - *General management*
Ms. Julie J. Prusak, Vice President - *Consulting, marketing, consumer goods*
Mr. David Bellshaw, Vice President
Mr. Michael R. Truesdell, Vice President - *High technology, CFOs*
Mr. David Newlin, Principal

Salary minimum: $120,000

Functions: Directors, Senior Mgmt., Sales & Mktg., HR Mgmt., CFO's

Industries: Energy, Utilities, Mfg., Retail, Finance, Services, Hospitality, Media, Communications, Software, Biotech

Professional Associations: ACG, HRPS

ETI Search Int'l

990 Hammond Dr Bldg 1 Ste 825
Atlanta, GA 30328
(770) 399-8492
(770) 399-8400
Fax: (770) 399-8487
Email: dbrown@etiatl.com

Description: Retained executive search specializing primarily in telecommunications and high-technology, with significant capabilities in other industries. Senior management to CEO-level searches throughout North America. Some recent assignments have included sourcing internationally experienced candidates for European firms.

Key Contact - Specialty:
Mr. William Chambers, III, President - *Generalist*
Mr. David F. Brown, Exec Vice President/Managing Director - *High technology, telecommunications, international*

Salary minimum: $85,000

Functions: General Mgmt., Directors, Senior Mgmt., Middle Mgmt., Plant Mgmt., HR Mgmt., CFO's, IT, MIS Mgmt., Int'l.

Industries: Generalist, Mfg., Chemicals, Metal Products, Computer Equip., Services, Media, Telecoms, Software, Biotech

The Evenium Group†

15600 Wayzata Blvd Ste 201
Wayzata, MN 55391
(612) 745-0402
Fax: (612) 745-0397
Email: jmcgeady@eveniumgroup.com

Description: We are a retained executive search firm. We function on the belief that success is built on quality people. We are national in scope. We focus on human resources, finance, national sales, and general management roles.

Key Contact - Specialty:
Mr. John McGeady, President - *Consumer goods, human resources, general management*
Mr. Nick DeNicola, COO - *Finance, human resources*

Salary minimum: $70,000

Functions: Generalist

Industries: Mfg., Food, Bev., Tobacco, Paper, Printing, Medical Devices, Finance

Excel Research

PO Box 340066
Columbus, OH 43234-0066
(614) 451-1146
Fax: (614) 451-1147
Email: mendescol@aol.com

Description: Generalist. Executive search
nationwide. Corporations to human resource
departments and retained search firms.

Key Contact - Specialty:
Ms. Norma Mendes, President/Owner - *Generalist*

Functions: Generalist, Directors, Middle Mgmt.,
Mktg. Mgmt., CFO's, Non-profits, Architects

Industries: Generalist, Textiles, Apparel, Retail,
Banking, Accounting, Hospitality, Advertising

ExecuFind Recruiting[†]

360 Brook Ave
Passaic, NJ 07055
(973) 472-4840
(877) 444-3613
Fax: (973) 472-6775
Email: alfarrell@execufind.com
Web: www.execufind.com

Description: We are manufacturing specialist search
firm with clients across the US and Canada. We
distinguish ourselves through in-depth knowledge of
our demanding clients and cutting-edge candidates.
All facets are covered, including: operations,
engineering, finance, sales, and HR. Bilingual
(English-French) are services provided.

Key Contact - Specialty:
Mr. Al Farrell, MBA - *Building materials,*
chemical, metals industry
Ms. Vivian Rabin, MBA - *Generalist*

Salary minimum: $50,000

Functions: Generalist

Industries: Mfg., Food, Bev., Tobacco, Lumber,
Furniture, Paper, Chemicals, Soap, Perf.,
Cosmtcs., Plastics, Rubber, Paints, Petro.
Products, Metal Products, Packaging

ExecuGroup Inc

142 S Main St
PO Box 5040
Grenada, MS 38901
(662) 226-9025
Fax: (662) 226-9090
Email: tray@execugroup.com
Web: www.execugroup.com

Description: We are an executive search firm
specializing in customized recruiting for mid to
senior level management positions across most
industries. Our staff of professionals works with
companies nationwide in the banking, financial
services, manufacturing, and high tech sectors as
business partners to meet staffing, outplacement,
and consulting needs.

Key Contact - Specialty:
Mr. Robert T. Ray, President - *Management (mid,*
senior level)

Salary minimum: $75,000

Functions: Senior Mgmt., Plant Mgmt., Sales &
Mktg., Mktg. Mgmt., HR Mgmt.

Industries: Generalist, Mfg., Finance, Banking,
Brokers, Misc. Financial, Mgmt. Consulting, HR
Services, Insurance, HR SW, Marketing SW

Professional Associations: IACMP, AFSA, SHRM

Branches:
418 Main St
Bethlehem, PA 18018
(610) 954-9977
Fax: (610) 954-9511
Email: jnorwine@execugroup.com

Key Contact - Specialty:
Mr. James O. Norwine, Partner - *Mid to senior*
level management positions (most industries)

ExecuQuest Inc

2050 Breton SE Ste 103
Grand Rapids, MI 49546-5547
(616) 949-1800
Fax: (616) 949-0561
Email: execuquest@aol.com

Description: Midwest executive search firm focused
on mid-level and senior management positions in
manufacturing, banking and financial services
industries. Also handle CFO, controller and
treasurer searches in all industries.

Key Contact:
Mr. William L. Waanders, President - *Generalist*
Ms. Patricia J. Waanders, Research Associate

Salary minimum: $75,000

Functions: General Mgmt., Senior Mgmt., HR
Mgmt., Finance, CFO's

Industries: Generalist, Mfg., Finance, Banking,
Services, Higher Ed.

Professional Associations: ACG, AICPA, FEI, FEI,
IMA, SHRM

ExecuSource Associates Inc[†]

3232 Cobb Pkwy Ste 227
Atlanta, GA 30339
(770) 943-4254
Email: mlarry@execusource.com
Web: www.execusource.com

Description: A retained search firm, dedicated to
providing businesses with a cost effective, efficient
and quality alternative for locating talented
individuals, necessary for long-term organizational
success.

Key Contact - Specialty:
Mr. Melvin P. Larry, President - *Transportation,*
MIS, telecommunications

Salary minimum: $50,000

Functions: Generalist, General Mgmt., Senior
Mgmt.

Industries: Generalist, Mfg., Transportation,
Finance, Accounting, HR Services, Media

Professional Associations: AHRA

ExecuTech

PO Box 707
Kent, OH 44240-0013
(330) 677-0010
Fax: (330) 677-0148
Email: mark@executech.org

Description: Customized search in chemical,
manufacturing, electronics industries with emphasis
in key executives who impact the organization with
favorable significance. Specialty practice groups in
pharmaceutical, polymers, IT, building, finance,
HR, operations, technical and hard-to-find.

Key Contact:
Mr. J. Mark Seaholts, President

Functions: Generalist

Industries: Generalist, Mfg., Finance, Services, HR
Services, Law Enforcement, Hospitality,
Software, Biotech

Executive Careers Ltd

1801 Ave of the Stars Fl 6
Los Angeles, CA 90067
(310) 552-3455
(310) 306-0360
Fax: (310) 578-7524
Email: eclresumes@worldnet.att.net

Description: Generalist practice with strong
specializations in retail, logistics, catalogue, direct
marketing, community-based social services and
museums, middle market, family and emerging
businesses. Managed by industrial psychologist.

Key Contact - Specialty:
Ms. Annette R. Segil - *Generalist, retail, non-*
profit, middle market

Salary minimum: $85,000

Functions: Generalist, General Mgmt.

Industries: Generalist, Mfg., Wholesale, Retail,
Finance, Services, Non-profits, Accounting, HR
Services, Advertising, Broadcast, Film,
Packaging, Entertainment SW, HR SW,
Healthcare, Non-classifiable

Professional Associations: CLM, CNM, DMA,
DMACC, FEI, IABC, IOPP, LADMA, LAHRA,
NAER, NRF, RAMA

Executive Dimensions

5820 Main St Ste 403
Williamsville, NY 14221
(716) 632-9034
Fax: (716) 632-2889
Email: execsearch@executivedimensions.com
Web: www.executivedimensions.com

Description: We are an executive search and
consulting firm that offers a spectrum of services to
an array of industries and organization. Our
searches are innovative, yet approached within a
practical framework to address the ever-changing
needs of your marketplace. Client satisfaction is the
ultimate goal of every executive search we conduct.
We deliver the highest level of expertise and
experience in each executive search engagement.

Key Contact - Specialty:
Ms. Gwen Arcara, President - *Senior-level*
Mr. Scott Patterson, Director - Executive
Placement - *Healthcare*

Salary minimum: $100,000

Functions: Generalist

Industries: Finance, Healthcare

Professional Associations: SHRM

Executive Directions Inc[†]

PO Box 223
Foxboro, MA 02035
(508) 698-3030
Fax: (508) 543-6047
Email: execdir@ici.net
Web: www.executivedirections.com

Description: Over twenty years' experience in
assisting technology and manufacturing companies
with their staffing needs in a wide variety of
functions at senior and executive-level.

Key Contact - Specialty:
Mr. Eric Greenstein, President - *Executives*
Mr. Larry Lencz, Senior Partner - *Executives*

Salary minimum: $90,000

Functions: Generalist

Industries: Mfg., Computer Equip., Test, Measure
Equip., Software

Networks: Top Echelon Network

Branches:
PO Box 893
Hartford, CT 06143-0893
(860) 219-0321
Email: execrep@home.com
Key Contact:
Mr. Rob Pudney, CPC, Director

Executive Directions

(a subsidiary of Pinnacle Int'l)
9701 Cleveland Ave NW
PO Box 3006
North Canton, OH 44720
(330) 499-1001
Fax: (330) 499-2579
Email: execudir@staffing.net
Web: www.executive-directions.com

Description: We provide small, medium, and large corporations with executive search, team building, strategic staffing, interim/contracting, and corporate consulting services while requiring only a minimal initial investment/retainer. Our industry specialization includes: automotive, plastics, resins, compounds, converting, and packaging.

Key Contact - Specialty:
Mr. Paul E. Richards, President/CEO - *Automotive, plastic molding industries*
Mr. R. Glenn Richards, Executive Vice President - *Flexible packaging, resins, compounds, converting*

Salary minimum: $75,000

Functions: Generalist

Industries: Mfg., Packaging

Professional Associations: SBSB, SPE, TAPPI

Networks: Top Echelon Network

Executive Linkage

40960 California Oaks Rd Ste 280
Murrieta, CA 92562
(909) 698-5757
Fax: (909) 698-4010
Email: darren@executivelinkage.com
Web: www.executivelinkage.com

Description: We offer senior-level executive search utilizing Power Hiring and AIRS Techniques to locate top candidates in half the typical retained search time. We have three distinct plans: standard retained, hourly, and performance based (longer searches cost you less). We work in any industry, and we place from director level through president/CEO and board members. The best can cost less, in both time and money.

Key Contact - Specialty:
Mr. Tom Courbat, CEO - *'C'-level & VP searches (all industries)*
Mr. Darren Pacheco, AIRS, CIR, President - *Director-level to CEO searches*
Mrs. Debby Courbat, VP - Finance & Client Satisfaction - *Client service, accounting & finance*

Salary minimum: $75,000

Functions: General Mgmt., Directors, Senior Mgmt., Sales & Mktg., Finance, CFO's

Industries: Mfg., Transportation, Finance, Services, Hospitality, Media, Communications, Software, Biotech, Healthcare

Professional Associations: AEA, AIRS, CFC, SDSIC, SHRM, TEC

Branches:
5355 Mira Sorrento Pl Ste 100
San Diego, CA 92121
(866) 439-3248
Fax: (707) 922-7161
Email: tom@executivelinkage.com
Key Contact - Specialty:
Mr. Tom Courbat, CEO - *'C'-level & VP searches*

The Executive Management Consulting Organization (TEMCO)

PO Box 303
Oconomowoc, WI 53066-0303
(262) 567-2069

Description: We are HR management consultants with a broad range of services including: executive search, personnel management, organization analysis, management training/development, employee/supervisory counseling, team-building workshops and personnel function audits.

Key Contact:
Mr. Thomas E. Masson, President

Salary minimum: $50,000

Functions: Generalist

Industries: Generalist

Executive Manning Corp

3000 NE 30th Pl Ste 405
Ft. Lauderdale, FL 33306
(954) 561-5100
Fax: (954) 564-7483
Email: emc@exmanning.com
Web: www.exmanning.com

Description: We are one of the country's premier executive search and management consulting firms, providing a full spectrum of services relating to human resources.

Key Contact:
Mr. Richard L. Hertan, President/CEO - *Generalist*
Mr. Robert Beaver
Ms. Nancy Mitchell

Salary minimum: $75,000

Functions: Generalist

Industries: Paper, Computer Equip., Pharm Svcs., Mgmt. Consulting

Professional Associations: AMA, SHRM, WAW

The Executive Network Inc

612 View St Fl 2
Victoria, BC V8W 1J5
Canada
(250) 389-2848
Email: executivenetwork@map-xn.com
Web: www.executivenetwork.ca

Description: Our retainer fee search practice includes reasearch and/or selection recruiting based upon advertising response, or a combination of both. Our senior consultant has successfully completed hundreds of assignments. Executive Network Inc. also provides advice on performance linked executive compensation, style, values and 360 degree assessments, and organization reviews.

Key Contact:
Mr. Walter J. Donald, President

Salary minimum: $50,000

Functions: Generalist

Industries: Mfg., Retail, Services, HR Services, Aerospace

Executive Partners Inc

140 Heywood Dr
Glastonbury, CT 06033
(860) 657-1458
(860) 657-9493
Fax: (860) 657-1459
Email: execpart@execpartners.com
Web: www.execpartners.com

Description: Executive search consulting serving technology driven industries worldwide. Special emphasis on the recruitment of Internet technologists, strategic e-commerce consultants, marketing, and business development executives.

Key Contact - Specialty:
Ms. Holly Seymour - *Information technology, strategic management counselor*

Salary minimum: $70,000

Functions: M&A, Systems Analysis, Systems Dev., Systems Implem., Mgmt. Consultants

Industries: Venture Cap., Mgmt. Consulting, New Media, Telecoms

Executive Recruitment Group

2004 Morningside Dr L1
Florence, KY 41042
(859) 384-0718
Fax: (859) 384-0719
Email: resume@erg-retail.com
Web: www.erg-retail.com

Description: We are a national search and recruitment firm dedicated to providing professional staffing solutions to the retail industry. Networking with professionals in executive, merchandise field, multi- and single-unit management, human resources, visual merchandising, loss prevention, and various other roles. We adapt to meet the clients needs.

Key Contact - Specialty:
Ms. Laura Stone, Principal - *Retail industry professions*
Mr. Kenneth Stone, Principal - *retail*

Salary minimum: $35,000

Functions: Sales & Mktg.

Industries: Retail

Executive Resource Group Inc

2470 Windy Hill Rd Ste 300
Marietta, GA 30067
(770) 955-1811
Email: dbalunas@aol.com

Description: Our mission is to provide the highest quality, custom tailored, research based retained executive search services to clients in manufacturing and distribution, consulting, healthcare and retailing for a fixed fee.

Key Contact - Specialty:
Mr. David A. Balunas, President - *Senior level executives, operations, managers*

Salary minimum: $75,000

Functions: Generalist, Senior Mgmt., Mfg., Materials, Sales Mgmt., HR Mgmt., IT, Mgmt. Consultants

Industries: Generalist, Mfg., Plastics, Rubber, Retail, Mgmt. Consulting, Software, Healthcare

Executive Resource Group Inc

29 Oakhurst Rd
Cape Elizabeth, ME 04107
(207) 871-5527
Fax: (207) 799-8624
Email: sibyl@mindspring.com
Web: www.mediahunter.com

Description: We are our client's representative in the marketplace. Qualified women are always included in the final presentation of each search. We represent the character of the client and handle all actions professionally.

Key Contact - Specialty:
Ms. Sibyl Masquelier, President - *Publishing*

Salary minimum: $75,000

Functions: Generalist

Industries: Publishing, New Media, Broadcast, Film

Professional Associations: IACPR, ASTD, EMA, HRPS, IIHR, INMA, MHRA, NAA, NAMME, NENA, NNA, SHRM, WAN, WICI

Executive Resources Int'l LLC

(formerly known as Organization Resources Inc)
63 Atlantic Ave Boston Harbor
Boston, MA 02110
(617) 742-8970
Fax: (617) 523-9093
Email: johncjayeri@aol.com

Description: We are Boston's oldest retained executive search firm, specializing in emerging business and financial services companies and the non-profit sector. 80% of our business is repeat or referral.

Key Contact - Specialty:
Mr. John C. Jay, Managing Director - *Emerging companies*

Salary minimum: $125,000

Functions: General Mgmt., Directors, Senior Mgmt., Middle Mgmt., Sales & Mktg., HR Mgmt., Finance, IT, Specialized Svcs., Int'l.

Industries: Generalist, Mfg., Retail, Finance, Services, Biotech

Professional Associations: IACPR, NEHRA, SBANE

Executive Search Consultants LLC
149 Shortwoods Rd
New Fairfield, CT 06812
(203) 746-0596
Fax: (203) 746-7265
Email: mejesc@mindspring.com

Description: An executive search firm specializing in senior and middle management in management consulting, entertainment and financial services industries.

Key Contact:
Ms. Maryellen James, Owner

Salary minimum: $100,000

Functions: Generalist, Directors, Senior Mgmt., Sales Mgmt., CFO's, MIS Mgmt., Mgmt. Consultants

Industries: Generalist, Retail, Mgmt. Consulting, Hospitality, Software

Professional Associations: SHRM

Executive Search Consultants Int'l Inc
350 5th Ave Ste 5501
Empire State Bldg
New York, NY 10118
(212) 330-1900
Fax: (212) 330-1906
Email: carlcarro@aol.com
Web: www.exsearch.com

Description: Our firm provides executive search and management consulting services on a retainer basis to domestic and international corporations in financial services, consumer packaged goods, technology, media, publishing and direct marketing.

Key Contact:
Mr. Carl R. Carro, Managing Director
Mr. James W. Doyle, Managing Director

Salary minimum: $150,000

Functions: Generalist

Industries: Mfg., Retail, Finance, Mgmt. Consulting, Publishing, New Media, Telecoms, Insurance, Software, Biotech

Professional Associations: IMSA

Networks: IMSA

Executive Search Inc
5401 Gamble Dr Parkdale One Ste 275
Minneapolis, MN 55416
(952) 541-9153

Description: We are dedicated to identifying and tracking high performers in many areas of business. Dedication to results gives us the unique ability to effectively conclude the most demanding assignments.

Key Contact:
Mr. James G. Gresham, President

Salary minimum: $75,000

Functions: Generalist

Industries: Generalist

Executive Search Services (ESS)
2925 4th St Ste 11
Santa Monica, CA 90405
(310) 392-3244
Fax: (310) 581-0432
Email: ess@exec.nu
Web: www.exec.nu

Description: Our firm offers traditional retained search and consulting services at the senior level enhanced by exec.nu, the ess talent pool and other web innovations. ess operates both domestically and internationally for a select client base.

Key Contact - Specialty:
Mr. Matthew M. Susleck, Managing Director - *Engineering, marketing, management, key technical positions*

Salary minimum: $125,000

Functions: General Mgmt., Directors, Senior Mgmt., Middle Mgmt., Sales & Mktg., CFO's, MIS Mgmt., Engineering, Int'l.

Industries: Generalist, Energy, Utilities, Construction, Mfg., Services, Media, Communications, Environmental Svcs., Biotech, Healthcare

Executive Search Solutions LLC
730 Willow Spring Hill Ct
St. Louis, MO 63017
(314) 205-0061
Fax: (314) 514-7503
Email: searchpros@aol.com
Web: www.headhuntersolutionsonline.com

Description: We are a retained search firm specializing in management, engineering, manufacturing, technical, sales, and marketing careers.

Key Contact:
Ms. Janice Lewis, Member

Salary minimum: $50,000

Networks: Top Echelon Network

Executive Search World[†]
66 Queen St Harbor Ct Ste 1802
Honolulu, HI 96813
(808) 526-3812
Fax: (808) 523-9356
Email: jimellis@mail.com
Web: www.executivesearchworld.com

Description: Executive search in Hawaii since 1985 in all industries and all functions. Our consulting advice to companies, integrity and sense of urgency exceeds expectations. We changed our name from Ellis & Associates.

Key Contact - Specialty:
Mr. James P. Ellis, President - *Senior management, information technology, internet, CFO's, high technology*

Salary minimum: $50,000

Functions: Generalist, General Mgmt., Senior Mgmt., Middle Mgmt., Sales & Mktg., Finance, CFO's, IT, MIS Mgmt., Systems Implem.

Industries: Construction, Retail, Finance, E-commerce, Finance, Media, PSA/ASP, Hospitality, New Media, Communications, Software, Biotech, Healthcare

Professional Associations: PATA, PTC, SHRM

Executive Solutions Inc
(also known as Brigade)
PO Box 1974
Cupertino, CA 95015-1974
(408) 871-2210
Email: pobox1974@aol.com

Industries: Generalist

Description: We are a proven retained executive search firm specializing in high technology, entertainment, telecommunications, financial services, and board member searches. You can send your resumes using these guidelines: text only, have the resume in the body of the email (no attachments) and briefly describe in your email your desired position, geographical locations, and compensation history.

Key Contact - Specialty:
Mr. Gary Barnes, President & CEO - *Marketing, sales, finance, corporate communications, public relations*
Ms. Aida Regina, COO - *Finance, engineering*
Dr. R. Bijoux, EVP/Client Services - *Marketing, sales, public relations*

Salary minimum: $150,000

Functions: Generalist

Industries: Generalist

The Executive Source Inc
55 5th Ave Fl 19
New York, NY 10003-4301
(212) 691-5505
Fax: (212) 691-9839
Email: tes5505@aol.com

Description: We focus on providing permanent and interim senior human resources professionals specializing in financial services and management consulting.

Key Contact:
Ms. Sarah J. Marks, Principal
Mr. Richard C. Plazza, Principal

Salary minimum: $125,000

Functions: HR Mgmt.

Industries: Finance, Mgmt. Consulting, HR Services

Professional Associations: IACPR, ASTD, ASTD, FWA, HRANY, HRPS, METRO, NYHRP, ODN, SHRM, WAW

The Executive Source
2201 - 11th Ave Ste 401
Regina, SK S4P 0J8
Canada
(306) 359-2550
Fax: (306) 359-2555
Email: search@theexecutivesource.com
Web: www.theexecutivesource.com

Description: Executive search is our only business. Senior professionals offer independence, consultation, extensive database, documentation, presentation process and guarantee.

Key Contact:
Ms. Holly Hetherington, President

Functions: Generalist, Directors, Senior Mgmt., Plant Mgmt., Finance, CFO's, IT, Engineering

Industries: Generalist, Energy, Utilities, Finance, Higher Ed., Media, Government, Biotech, Non-classifiable

Professional Associations: AESC, CAMC, CPPMA, HRMAR

Branches:
203 - 8th St W
Saskatoon, SK S7M 0B7
Canada
(306) 244-1880
Key Contact:
Ms. Judith Chelsom

The Executive Tree Research Consultants

417 NE 15th Ave
Ft. Lauderdale, FL 33301
(954) 630-2838
(888) 742-8733
Fax: (954) 630-2828
Email: exectree@exectree.com
Web: www.exectree.com

Description: We primarily work with retained firms and corporations to conduct research on an hourly basis. Specifically, we conduct candidate identification, candidate development, marketing/compensation studies and create organzation charts. Our goal is to be the most ethical, client-centered firm you have ever worked with, forming a long standing relationship.

Key Contact - Specialty:
Ms. Carol Purcell, President - *HR, management consulting, retail, transportation, telecom*

Functions: Generalist, Senior Mgmt., Mfg., Sales & Mktg., HR Mgmt., Finance, IT, Engineering

Industries: Generalist, Mfg., Transportation, Finance, Services, Media, Non-classifiable

Professional Associations: APS, IABC, IEEE, SHRM

Branches:
1500 E Broward Blvd
Ft. Lauderdale, FL 33301
(954) 522-7380
Fax: (954) 761-1692
Email: randydenton@exectree.com
Key Contact - Specialty:
Mr. Randall Denton, Director of Research - *Research*
Dr. Johnathon Victor, VP- Recruitment - *Education, medical, tech, web, pharmaceutical*

415 NE 15th Ave
Ft. Lauderdale, FL 33301
(954) 463-9691
Email: lewisjordan@exectree.com
Key Contact - Specialty:
Dr. Lewis James Jordan - *Technologies, software, e-commerce, web*

2636 Maseth Ave
Baltimore, MD 21219
(888) 745-8733
Fax: (954) 761-1692
Email: exectree@exectree.com
Key Contact - Specialty:
Ms. Peggy Antoniak, Office Director - *Government, telecom, education, healthcare, insurance*

ExSearch Latinoamérica†

Seneca 47
Col Polanco
Mexico City, DF 11560
Mexico
52 5 279 2800
52 5279 2818
Fax: 52 5 279 2801
Email: exsearch@exsearch-lat.com
Web: www.exsearch-lat.com

Description: Our strength is in the information technology industry especially with technical and sales executives.

Key Contact - Specialty:
Mr. Salvador Elizaga, General Director - *Sales & marketing, service quality, general management*
Mr. José Sarti, Associate Director - *Information technology*
Mr. Roberto Rochés, Associate Director - *IT*

Salary minimum: $45,000

Functions: Generalist

Industries: Software

Raymond L Extract & Associates

7337 Hyannis Dr
West Hills, CA 91307
(818) 999-2837
Fax: (818) 704-7275
Email: rle50967@csun.edu
Web: www.geocities.com/wallstreet/4042

Description: Broad range of executive search, corporate outplacement and human resources management consulting services. Serves most industries, emphasizing high-tech in early growth stages, from entrepreneurial to managerial, other manufacturing, medical administration.

Key Contact - Specialty:
Mr. Raymond L. Extract, President - *General management, human resources management*

Salary minimum: $80,000

Functions: Generalist

Industries: Mfg., Services, Software, Biotech, Healthcare

Eyler Associates Inc

400 Locust St Ste 170
Des Moines, IA 50309
(515) 245-4244

Description: We have twenty-seven years worth of search experience completing in excess of 425 senior-level assignments and five years of experience managing a $450 million profit center for Deere & Co. We have broad exposure to manufacturing, banking, financial services, insurance, and healthcare.

Key Contact - Specialty:
Mr. Richard N. Eyler, President - *Senior level*

Salary minimum: $75,000

Functions: General Mgmt., Mfg., Sales & Mktg., Finance, IT

Industries: Mfg., Lumber, Furniture, Metal Products, Machine, Appliance, Motor Vehicles, Finance, Banking, Invest. Banking, Venture Cap., Insurance, Healthcare

Fagan & Company

Robb Rd
PO Box 611
Ligonier, PA 15658
(724) 238-9571

Description: Full range domestic and international executive search in industrial areas and financial services. Search and appraisal-related consulting; e.g. organizational development and competitive analysis.

Key Contact - Specialty:
Mr. Charles A. Fagan, III - *Senior management, financial services, administration*
Ms. Stephanie L. Bronder - *Non-profit, institutional advancement, fund-raising, human resources*
Mr. Alfred N. Pilz - *Heavy industry*

Salary minimum: $100,000

Functions: Directors, Senior Mgmt., Int'l.

Industries: Mfg., Finance, Services, Non-profits

Faircastle Technology Group LLC

27 Wells Rd Ste 1117
Monroe, CT 06468-1266
(203) 459-0631
Email: info@faircastle.com
Web: www.faircastle.com

Description: We are established, exclusive specialists in finding the best high-technology executives and bringing them to your table. We have expertise with industry-leading and emerging Internet technology firms. We offer full-service or customized retained search, plus "aggressive interviewing/hiring processes," which are proven, hands-on workshops for hiring managers at startup and large-companies alike. E-mails with attachments are not accepted by our firm.

Key Contact - Specialty:
Ms. Ann Rice Banno, President - *High technology executives, CIO's, e-commerce, internet*

Salary minimum: $150,000

Functions: Directors, Senior Mgmt., Middle Mgmt., CFO's, IT, MIS Mgmt.

Industries: Energy, Utilities, Computer Equip., Retail, Mgmt. Consulting, HR Services, New Media, Software

Professional Associations: ESRT, WIT

Fairfaxx Corp

17 High St
Norwalk, CT 06851
(203) 838-8300
Fax: (203) 851-5844
Email: fairfaxxse@aol.com

Description: Services include executive search worldwide. Two affiliates internationally, four domestic affiliates. Heavy emphasis in the apparel industry.

Key Contact - Specialty:
Mr. Jeffrey Thomas - *Apparel, retail, consumer products*
Mr. Joseph Tucci - *High technology, banking*

Salary minimum: $75,000

Functions: Generalist, General Mgmt.

Industries: Textiles, Apparel, Soap, Perf., Cosmtcs., Wholesale, Retail

Fairfield

721 5th Ave Trump Twr
New York, NY 10022-2523
(212) 838-0220
Email: bbb@fairfield.ch
Web: www.fairfield.ch

Description: This is our twenty-fifth anniversary. We specialize in retail and wholesale apparel manufacturing. Client inquiries invited. E-mailed executive CVs welcome. We don't accept unsolicited hard copy resumes; they will be returned unopened.

Key Contact - Specialty:
Dr. Bruce Barton Buchholtz, MD, Chairman/Managing Director - *Retail, wholesale, apparel manufacturing*

Salary minimum: $75,000

Functions: Generalist

Industries: Textiles, Apparel, Wholesale, Retail

Branches:
9663 Santa Monica Blvd
Beverly Hills, CA 90210-4303
(310) 858-5250
Email: beverlyhills@fairfield.ch
Key Contact:
Dr. Bruce Barton Buchholtz, Chairman of the Board

Paul Falcone Associates

PO Box 115
Mt. Freedom, NJ 07970
(973) 895-5200
Fax: (973) 895-5266
Email: pfasearch@aol.com

Description: Specializing in consumer packaged goods, telecommunications, hospitality and media.

Key Contact:
Mr. Paul S. Falcone, Jr., President

Salary minimum: $75,000

Functions: Generalist

Industries: Drugs Mfg., Consumer Elect.

Leon A Farley Associates
31 Laderman Ln
San Francisco, CA 94111
(415) 989-0989
Email: farleysf@aol.com

Description: I am a single practitioner focusing on general management and CFO searches with over $250,000 compensation in all industries. I also place board positions. I have global reach through my membership in Penrhyn International.

Key Contact - Specialty:
Mr. Leon A. Farley, Managing Partner - *Executives (senior level all industries)*

Salary minimum: $250,000

Functions: Directors, Senior Mgmt., Mktg. Mgmt., CFO's, Int'l.

Industries: Construction, Food, Bev., Tobacco, Finance, Legal, Aerospace

Networks: Penrhyn Int'l

James Farris Associates
909 NW 63rd St
Oklahoma City, OK 73116
(405) 525-5061
Fax: (405) 525-5069
Email: james@jamesfarris.com
Web: www.jamesfarris.com

Description: Retained searches for mid to top level in finance; management; healthcare; insurance; manufacturing; human resources; information systems and technical professions; sales and marketing; along with outplacement and consulting services.

Key Contact - Specialty:
Mr. James W. Farris, President - *Generalist*

Salary minimum: $40,000

Functions: Generalist

Industries: Generalist

The Fawcett Group
39 Ross Rd
Swampscott, MA 01907
(781) 592-9555
Fax: (781) 593-5355
Email: mfawcett@fawcett-group.com
Web: www.fawcett-group.com

Description: Our specialty is in high-technology, small to medium firms. Our strength is in general management, sales and marketing, IS/IT, R&D/engineering and human resources.

Key Contact - Specialty:
Ms. Marcia A. Fawcett, Principal - *Senior management, executive staff*

Salary minimum: $120,000

Functions: Senior Mgmt.

Industries: Mfg., Wholesale, Retail, Services, Media, Software

Ferneborg & Associates Inc
160 Bovet Rd Ste 210
San Mateo, CA 94402
(650) 577-0100
Fax: (650) 577-0122
Email: mailbox@execsearch.com
Web: www.execsearch.com

Description: We are an independently owned retained executive search firm dedicated to identifying and recruiting premier senior-level management executives for its corporate clients.

Key Contact:
Mr. John R. Ferneborg, President
Mr. Jay W. Ferneborg

Mr. John C. Tincu

Salary minimum: $125,000

Functions: Generalist, General Mgmt., Sales & Mktg., Finance

Industries: Generalist, Food, Bev., Tobacco, Finance, Media, Software

Professional Associations: AESC

Ferrari Search Group†
24200 Chagrin Blvd Ste I
Cleveland, OH 44122
(216) 491-1122
Fax: (216) 491-1510
Email: ferrarisearch@hotmail.com

Description: Executive search on a proactive basis serving the financial community on a national basis. We maintain an active computerized database of executives in investment firms, banks, investment banking institutions and corporate financial executives.

Key Contact - Specialty:
Mr. S. Jay Ferrari - *Banking, financial services*
Ms. Kathryn Poole-Ferrari - *Securities industry*

Salary minimum: $60,000

Functions: Generalist

Industries: Finance, Services, Accounting, Mgmt. Consulting, Law Enforcement, Advertising

Networks: National Banking Network (NBN)

FERS Business Services Inc†
401 N Michigan Ave Ste 2800
Chicago, IL 60611
(312) 644-6000
Fax: (312) 644-4423
Email: srodriguez@fers.com
Web: www.fers.com

Description: We represent mostly small to medium-sized privately or closely held businesses in the Chicago area, in a wide variety of industry and service areas. We specialize in financial and accounting, human resources, manufacturing operations and technology related positions.

Key Contact - Specialty:
Ms. Susan Raemer-Rodriguez, Manager-Search and Recruitment Consulti - *Financial*

Salary minimum: $40,000

Functions: Generalist

Industries: Energy, Utilities, Construction, Mfg., Retail, Non-profits, Legal, Accounting, HR Services, Government

Professional Associations: EMA, HRMAC, IMA, SHRM, SHRP

Financial Plus Management Solutions Inc†
372 Bay St Ste 1901
Toronto, ON M5H 2W9
Canada
(416) 594-9232
Email: roman@financialplus.net
Web: www.financialplus.net

Description: We are a firm which has built a reputation of providing high-caliber individuals who bring added value to our clients.

Key Contact - Specialty:
Mr. Roman M. Skrypuch, President/Owner - *Financial services, sales*

Salary minimum: $40,000

Functions: Generalist, General Mgmt., Sales & Mktg., HR Mgmt., Finance, IT

Industries: Generalist, Finance, Accounting, Equip Svcs., HR Services, Software

Financial Search Group Inc†
PO Box 266
North Andover, MA 01845
(978) 682-4123
Fax: (978) 688-0516
Email: finsearch@mediaone.net
Web: www.financialsearchgroupinc.com

Description: Performs mid- and senior-level executive retained searches for corporate finance organizations, equipment lessors and investment banks.

Key Contact - Specialty:
Mr. Paul T. Luther, President - *Equipment leasing, financial services*

Salary minimum: $65,000

Functions: Generalist

Industries: Finance, Banking, Invest. Banking, Misc. Financial, Software

Professional Associations: ELA

Neil Fink Associates
(also known as First Interactive Recruiting)
900 N Point St Ste 210
Ghirardelli Sq
San Francisco, CA 94109-1192
(415) 441-3777
Fax: (415) 775-4925
Email: neil@well.com
Web: www.neilfinkassociates.com

Description: We are an executive search firm servicing the media, entertainment, communications, and technology industries. We are cross functional and successfully completed senior level searches in every discipline, including C-level general management, marketing, sales, finance, engineering, and creative.

Key Contact:
Mr. Neil Fink, Managing Partner

Salary minimum: $150,000

Functions: Generalist, Senior Mgmt., Product Dev., Mktg. Mgmt., Sales Mgmt., MIS Mgmt., Engineering, Int'l.

Industries: Generalist, Computer Equip., Consumer Elect., E-commerce, Media, Communications, Wireless, Software

Professional Associations: SMPTE

Branches:
108 Dole Hill Rd
Holden, ME 04429
(207) 843-4388
Fax: (207) 843-4388
Email: astaub@agate.net
Key Contact:
Ms. Abigail Staub, Senior Search Consultant

Eileen Finn & Associates Inc
237 Park Ave Fl 21
New York, NY 10017
(212) 687-1260
Fax: (212) 551-1473
Email: efinn@sprynet.com
Web: www.eileenfinn.com

Description: We are a Retained Executive Search Firm specializing in the sourcing and placement of Senior Human Resources Professionals for major Corporate, Institutional and Not-For-Profit clients.

Key Contact - Specialty:
Ms. Eileen Finn, President - *Financial services, human resources*

Salary minimum: $100,000

Functions: HR Mgmt.

Industries: Finance, Non-profits, Pharm Svcs., Accounting, Mgmt. Consulting, Hospitality, Publishing, New Media, Insurance, Entertainment SW

Professional Associations: IACPR, FWA, SHRM, WAW, WOWS

The Finnegan Partnerships

PO Box 1183
Palos Verdes Estates, CA 90274-1938
(310) 377-4762
Fax: (240) 414-8108

Description: A national and international management consulting/executive search firm specializing in recruiting CEOs, sales/marketing, financial, operations, development executives and managers. A venture capital fund allows investment in high-growth companies.

Key Contact:
Mr. Richard Finnegan

Salary minimum: $250,000

Functions: Generalist, General Mgmt., Sales & Mktg., CFO's, IT, Mgmt. Consultants

Industries: Generalist, Computer Equip., Consumer Elect., Banking, Mgmt. Consulting, Telecoms, Software

Professional Associations: NASA

First Advisory Services Int'l Inc

(a division of The Systech Organization Inc)
20626 W Liberty Rd
White Hall, MD 21161-9063
(410) 329-2033
(410) 494-6500
Fax: (410) 329-2057
Email: aasoma@aol.com

Description: Full-service consulting corporation, offering global executive search services to new and existing clients.

Key Contact - Specialty:
Mr. Walter J. Sistek, CMC, President - *Generalist*
Mr. George Hankins, Senior Director - *Financial services*
Mr. William M. Fleishman, Director - *High technology, biotechnology*
Mr. Donald Shandler, Director - *Human resource development*
Ms. Catherine E. Meehling, Officer - *University*
Mr. Jack M. Hawkins, Jr., Director - *Global financial, public sector*
Mr. Stephen McSpadden, Director/Legal Advisor - *Legal, healthcare*
Mr. Joseph J. Diblasi, Executive Vice President - *High technology, biotechnology*

Salary minimum: $80,000

Functions: Generalist

Industries: Agri., Forestry, Mining, Mfg., Transportation, Finance, Services, Media, Government, Insurance, Biotech, Healthcare

Professional Associations: IMC

Networks: Computer Search

First Choice Search

PO Box 31324
Seattle, WA 98103-1324
(206) 632-0050
(206) 632-0090
Fax: (206) 632-0060
Email: fcsearch@email.msn.com
Web: firstchoice.8m.com

Description: Partner with select group of clients to act as an extension of their human resource function for the term of a project. Assists in analyzing, researching and recommending organizational changes and needs in relation to the search assignment.

Key Contact:
Ms. Michele J. Sarlat, President

Salary minimum: $50,000

Functions: Mfg., Finance, MIS Mgmt.

Industries: Generalist, Mfg., Paper, Printing, Chemicals, Soap, Perf., Cosmtcs., Plastics, Rubber, Paints, Petro. Products, Leather, Stone, Glass, Software

Professional Associations: TAPPI, TEC

First Union Executive Search

301 S College St Ste 2525
Charlotte, NC 28288-0102
(704) 383-9969
Email: gail.breen@firstunion.com

Description: Multi-disciplined recruiting at mid/senior-levels for super-regional financial institutions.

Key Contact - Specialty:
Mr. Harry W. Wilson, Managing Director - *Financial services*
Ms. Joni Groomes, Director - *Financial services*
Mr. Tom Miller, Director - *Financial services*
Mr. Kevin Parker, Director - *Information technology, financial services*

Salary minimum: $100,000

Functions: Generalist

Industries: Finance, Accounting, HR Services, Advertising, Telecoms, Insurance, Software

Howard Fischer Associates Int'l Inc

1800 JFK Blvd Fl 7
Philadelphia, PA 19103-7401
(215) 568-8363
Fax: (215) 568-4815
Email: howardfischer@hfischer.com
Web: www.hfischer.com

Description: To help our clients improve their lives and their businesses through leadership, recruitment and selection.

Key Contact - Specialty:
Mr. Howard Fischer, CEO - *Directors, CEOs, presidents, COO's, vice presidents*
Mr. Adam Fischer, Partner - *CEOs, COOs, VPs of sales & marketing, CFOs, CIOs*

Salary minimum: $300,000

Functions: Generalist

Industries: Computer Equip., Electronic, Elec. Components, Venture Cap., New Media, Communications, Telecoms, Wireless, Fiber Optic, Network Infrastructure, Software

Networks: ITP Worldwide

Branches:
910 Campisi Way
Campbell, CA 95008
(408) 377-7300

60 State St Ste 700
Boston, MA 02109
(617) 878-2028

5718 Westheimer St Ste 1330
Houston, TX 77057
(713) 974-2300

Fisher & Associates

1063 Lenor Way
San Jose, CA 95128
(408) 554-0156
Fax: (408) 246-7807

Description: We are a retained executive search firm specializing in the placement of high-tech marketing, sales and engineering executives.

Key Contact - Specialty:
Mr. Gary E. Fisher, President - *CEO's, marketing, sales executives*

Salary minimum: $100,000

Functions: Senior Mgmt., Middle Mgmt., Product Dev., Sales & Mktg., Mktg. Mgmt., Sales Mgmt., Engineering

Industries: Computer Equip., Consumer Elect., E-commerce, Communications, Telecoms, Digital, Wireless, Fiber Optic, Network Infrastructure, Software, Industry Specific SW, Networking, Comm. SW, Security SW, System SW

Professional Associations: AESC

Fisher Group[†]

250-6th Ave SW
1500 Bow Valley Sq IV
Calgary, AB T2P 3H7
Canada
(403) 251-3040
Fax: (403) 238-5732
Email: fishergroupexec@aol.com
Web: www.fishergroupexecsearch.com

Description: Administrative and executive search services for major multi national, national and regional companies in the hi-tech, information technology, telecommunication, information systems and oil & gas industries.

Key Contact - Specialty:
Mr. Mel V. Fisher, CMC, Executive Consultant - *Management mid/senior, sales & marketing, finance, information technology, computer*

Salary minimum: $60,000

Functions: General Mgmt., Senior Mgmt., Middle Mgmt., Sales & Mktg., Mktg. Mgmt., Sales Mgmt., CFO's, IT, MIS Mgmt., Network Admin.

Industries: Printing, Drugs Mfg., Medical Devices, Computer Equip., Accounting, Media, Publishing, Telecoms, Software, Biotech

Professional Associations: CAMC, ICMCA

Fisher Personnel Management Services

PO Box 9076
Torrance, CA 90508
(310) 320-6667
Fax: (310) 320-1060
Email: fisherpm@gte.net
Web: www.fisheads.com

Description: Firm works with middle and senior-level management primarily for manufacturing companies. Industries we specialize in are aerospace, aircraft, automotive, consumer products, defense, electronics, high-technology, industrial/manufacturing, packaging, transportation, and truck equipment.

Key Contact - Specialty:
Mr. Neal Fisher, Principal - *Generalist, aircraft, aerospace, agriculture, automotive*
Ms. Judy Gibson, Principal - *Generalist, aircraft, aerospace, agriculture, automotive*

Salary minimum: $80,000

Functions: Generalist, General Mgmt., Mfg., Materials, Sales & Mktg., IT, Engineering

Industries: Generalist, Metal Products, Machine, Appliance, Motor Vehicles, Computer Equip., Consumer Elect., Aerospace

Professional Associations: IACPR, NAER

A G Fishkin & Associates[†]

PO Box 34413
Bethesda, MD 20827
(301) 983-0303
Fax: (301) 983-0415
Email: afishkin@us.net

Description: We recruit medium to senior-level talent for e-Commerce/Internet, wireless/network communications, and information technology. The functions in which we recruit include: senior level sales/marketing management, product management, operations management, management consulting, and program management. We recruit for start-up, pre-IPO, and mid- to large-size companies.

Key Contact - Specialty:
Ms. Anita Fishkin, President - *Information technology, software engineering, telecommunications, communications (wireless, network)*
Mr. Paul Kallfelz, Senior Vice President - *Senior marketing/sales management, senior executive management*

Salary minimum: $50,000

Functions: Generalist

Industries: Mgmt. Consulting, E-commerce, Telecoms, Software

Professional Associations: MAPRC, NAWBO

Fitzgerald Associates
21 Muzzey St
Lexington, MA 02421
(781) 863-1945
Fax: (781) 863-8872
Email: info@fitzsearch.com
Web: www.fitzsearch.com

Description: Extensive, exclusive experience recruiting for the healthcare industry. Clients include MCOs, ASPs, healthcare information management, demand/disease management, e-health, and pharmaceutical marketing services companies, and vendors to those organizations.

Key Contact - Specialty:
Mr. Geoffrey Fitzgerald, Principal - *Managed care, information management, demand management, disease management, internet*
Ms. Diane Fitzgerald, Principal - *Managed care, clinical professionals, medical directors, medical management, call center operations*

Salary minimum: $80,000

Functions: Generalist, Healthcare

Industries: Generalist

Professional Associations: AAHP, AAMCN, AHIMA, AMIA, DIA, DMAA, HBA, HIMSS, NAHDO

Fitzgibbon & Associates
PO Box 1108
Media, PA 19063
(610) 565-7566
Email: fgassocs@aol.com

Description: We are specialists in sensitive searches requiring highest standards of professional representation of the corporation's image in retail and direct response/catalog industries.

Key Contact - Specialty:
Mr. Michael T. Fitzgibbon, Principal - *Direct mail, catalog*

Salary minimum: $80,000

Functions: Generalist, Senior Mgmt., Middle Mgmt., Distribution, Customer Svc., MIS Mgmt.

Industries: Generalist, Communications

The Flagship Group
185 Devonshire St Ste 350
Boston, MA 02110
(617) 728-0220
Email: ac@flagshipboston.com

Description: We are committed to providing our clients with outstanding, customized, quality service that delivers exceptional candidates.

Key Contact - Specialty:
Ms. Anna Coppola, President - *Investment management, financial services*

Salary minimum: $150,000

Functions: Generalist, Mktg. Mgmt., Sales Mgmt., Cash Mgmt., Risk Mgmt.

Industries: Generalist, Invest. Banking, Brokers, Venture Cap.

Professional Associations: IACPR, FWA

Robert M Flanagan & Associates Ltd
Fields Ln JMKB Bldg
North Salem, NY 10560
(914) 277-7210
Fax: (914) 244-8867
Email: rflana8828@aol.com

Description: National practice built on reputation for doing quality search work at the senior-levels of management. Ninety percent of business is with established client base.

Key Contact - Specialty:
Mr. Robert M. Flanagan - *General management, marketing & sales, investment management*
Ms. Amy Normann, Associate - *Marketing, sales*

Salary minimum: $100,000

Functions: Generalist, General Mgmt., Mfg., Materials, Sales & Mktg., HR Mgmt., Finance, IT

Industries: Generalist, Mfg., Wholesale, Finance, Services, Media, Packaging

Flannery, Sarna & Associates
N14 W23777 Stone Ridge Dr Ste 120
Waukesha, WI 53188
(262) 523-1206
Fax: (262) 523-1873
Email: fsasearch@aol.com

Description: We are a Midwestern-based generalist practice with clients nationwide. We have particular expertise in health care and manufacturing. We have completed searches in marketing and sales, operations, finance, human resources, general management, information systems, and regulatory affairs.

Key Contact - Specialty:
Mr. Peter Flannery, President - *Health care, medical products, manufacturing*
Mr. Edmund Sarna, Vice President - *Manufacturing, long term care, automotive*
Ms. Donna Daniels, Executive Recruiter - *Health care, manufacturing*

Salary minimum: $60,000

Functions: Generalist

Industries: Medical Devices, Metal Products, Machine, Appliance, Consumer Elect., Banking, Pharm Svcs., HR Services, Insurance, Biotech, Healthcare

Professional Associations: EMA, SHRM

Flesher & Associates Inc
445 S San Antonio Rd Ste 102
Los Altos, CA 94022
(650) 917-9900
Fax: (650) 917-9903
Email: info@flesher.com
Web: www.flesher.com

Description: We are an executive search firm specializing in building strategic communications teams for high-technology corporations and agencies. Includes middle- and senior-level management searches.

Key Contact - Specialty:
Ms. Susan Flesher, President - *High technology, public relations, corporate communications, marketing communications*

Salary minimum: $90,000

Functions: PR

Industries: Media, Telecoms, Software

Professional Associations: AMA, BMA

Florapersonnel Inc
1740 Lake Markham Rd
Sanford, FL 32771-8964
(407) 320-8177
Fax: (407) 320-8083
Email: hortsearch@aol.com
Web: www.florapersonnel.com

Description: International search firm for the greater horticulture industry. Retained only.

Key Contact:
Mr. Robert F. Zahra, General Manager - *Horticulture*
Mr. Joseph Dalton, Account Executive - *Horticulture*
Mr. Jack Ferrell, Account Executive

Functions: Generalist

Industries: Agri., Forestry, Mining

Professional Associations: NAER

J G Flynn & Associates Inc
885 W Georgia St Ste 1500
Vancouver, BC V6C 3E8
Canada
(604) 689-7205
Fax: (604) 689-2676
Email: recruit@jgflynn.com
Web: www.jgflynn.com

Description: We are an established boutique executive search firm. We enjoy an international reputation as one of the premier direct sourcing firms in North America. Are we generalists? Yes, although we are best known in the areas of engineering, mining, forestry, energy, technology-driven, and information systems organizations. We don't rely on advertising; instead, our research-based approach is thorough, efficient, and discreet.

Key Contact - Specialty:
Mr. Jerry Flynn, President - *Senior management, general management, engineering/technical*
Mr. John English, BA, MBA, Associate - *Generalist, energy, forestry, chemical*
Mr. Wlliam Lee, B.Sc, MBA, Associate - *Information systems, new technology-driven companies, generalist*

Salary minimum: $70,000

Functions: Generalist, General Mgmt., Mfg., HR Mgmt., IT, R&D, Engineering, Int'l.

Industries: Generalist, Agri., Forestry, Mining, Energy, Utilities, Construction, Mfg., Aerospace

FM Industries Inc
10125 Crosstown Cir Ste 300
Eden Prairie, MN 55344
(612) 941-0966
Fax: (612) 941-4462
Email: fmindustries@email.com
Web: www.fmindustries.net

Description: FM Industries is a multi-disciplined human resources consulting and executive search organization representing organizations on a national basis.

Key Contact - Specialty:
Mr. Fred A. Montana, Owner/President - *Generalist*
Ms. Ann Pasch, Sr Vice President - *Generalist*
Mr. Larry Alter, Vice President - *Outplacement*

Fogarty and Associates Inc[†]
6600 France Ave S Ste 210
Edina, MN 55435
(952) 831-2828
Fax: (952) 920-7885
Email: fogarty@fogarty.com
Web: www.fogarty.com

Description: Healthcare consulting and search firm specializing in placement of medical, administrative and clinical personnel. We specialize in executives

Let www.ExecutiveAgent.com e-mail your resume now.

with medical and clinical backgrounds, and medical/clinical personnel with administrative and management experience. Our online services include job posting and searches, and resume posting and searches.

Key Contact - Specialty:
Ms. Colleen Fogarty, President - *Physicians, healthcare*

Salary minimum: $50,000

Functions: Generalist

Industries: Healthcare

Fogec Consultants Inc
PO Box 28806
Milwaukee, WI 53228
(414) 427-0690
Email: tfogec@execpc.com
Web: www.afsc-jobs.com/members/fogecconsultants.htm

Description: Specialize in executive, managerial and professional positions across industry lines. Extensive client-side experience provides for highly personalized service and strong sensitivity to client needs.

Key Contact - Specialty:
Mr. Thomas G. Fogec, President - *Banking, finance & accounting, human resources*

Salary minimum: $50,000

Functions: HR Mgmt., Finance, Cash Mgmt.

Industries: Generalist, Banking, Invest. Banking, Brokers, Accounting

Professional Associations: AFSC, EMA, HRMA, RON, SHRM

Networks: National Banking Network (NBN)

Foley Proctor Yoskowitz
1 Cattano Ave
Morristown, NJ 07960-6820
(973) 605-1000
(800) 238-1123
Fax: (973) 605-1020
Email: fpy@fpysearch.com
Web: www.fpysearch.com

Description: The three partners are trained hospital administrators and seasoned healthcare search executives with long-term client relationships in recruiting CEOs, senior administrators, physician chairmen/executives, product line/department managers, managed care/practice administrators and staff physicians.

Key Contact - Specialty:
Mr. Thomas Foley, FACHE, Senior Partner - *Healthcare executives, senior physician executives (departmental chairs)*
Mr. Richard W. Proctor, CHE, Partner - *Executives, departmental directors, staff physicians*
Mrs. Reggie Yoskowitz, MPH, Partner - *Healthcare executives, senior physician executives (department chairs)*

Salary minimum: $50,000

Functions: Directors, Senior Mgmt., Middle Mgmt., Physicians, Nurses, Health Admin.

Industries: Healthcare

Professional Associations: IACPR, ACHE, AHHRA, AONE, HFMA, MGMA, MHAA, NAHSE, NAWH, NMHA

Branches:
24 E 39th St
New York, NY 10016
(212) 928-1110
(800) 238-1123
Fax: (973) 605-1020
Email: fpy@fpysearch.com

Key Contact - Specialty:
Mr. Thomas J. Foley, FACHE, Senior Partner - *Healthcare executives, senior physician executives, department chairs*
Mr. Richard Proctor, CHE, Partner - *Healthcare executives, department heads, staff physicians*
Mr. Reggie Yoskowitz, MPH, Partner - *Healthcare executives, senior physician executives (departmental chairs)*

L W Foote Company
110-110th Ave NE Ste 603
Bellevue, WA 98004-5840
(425) 451-1660
Fax: (425) 451-1535
Email: email@lwfoote.com
Web: www.lwfoote.com

Description: We have recruited exceptional individuals for clients in a broad range of industries with emphasis in technology (both hardware and software), consumer products and telecommunications.

Key Contact:
Mr. Leland W. Foote, President
Mr. James E. Bloomer, Vice President, General Manager
Ms. Susan Stringer, Senior Associate
Ms. Valerie Rosman, Research Director

Salary minimum: $85,000

Functions: Generalist

Industries: Generalist, Food, Bev., Tobacco, Textiles, Apparel, Computer Equip., Telecoms, Software

Professional Associations: AESC

Forager
1516 Sudeenew Dr
McHenry, IL 60050
(815) 344-0006
Fax: (815) 344-0008
Email: aaforager@imaxx.net

Description: One partner, one search, one client. Partner working exclusively for one client at a time, personalized service.

Key Contact - Specialty:
Ms. Anita Artner, President - *R&D, operations, sales & marketing*

Functions: Generalist, General Mgmt., Materials, HR Mgmt., Finance, R&D, Minorities

Industries: Generalist, Medical Devices, Metal Products, Misc. Mfg., Pharm Svcs., Packaging, Healthcare

Branches:
9124 Hidden Farm Rd
Alta Loma, CA 91737
(909) 980-0120
Email: jmforager@compuserve.com
Key Contact - Specialty:
Ms. Jackie Muhr, Vice President - *Logistics, channel management, e-commerce, sales & marketing*

1623 E Brookside Dr
Littleton, CO 80126
(303) 346-2819
Email: toforager@aol.com
Key Contact - Specialty:
Ms. Tonya Oehler, Account Executive - *R&D, sales & marketing*

34 Lakeside Ln
North Barrington, IL 60010
(847) 842-1010
Email: jcforager@imaxx.net
Key Contact - Specialty:
Ms. Judy Connolly, Vice President - *Sales & marketing, operations, R&D, logistics*

The Ford Group Inc
485 Devon Park Dr Ste 110
Wayne, PA 19087
(610) 975-9007
Fax: (610) 975-9008
Email: info@thefordgroup.com
Web: www.thefordgroup.com

Description: We are a boutique firm specializing in retained executive search for global management consulting firms and selected general management positions for leading corporations.

Key Contact - Specialty:
Ms. Sandra D. Ford, CEO - *Management consulting, finance, human resources, information systems*

Salary minimum: $125,000

Functions: Generalist, Senior Mgmt., HR Mgmt., Finance, CFO's, MIS Mgmt., Systems Implem., Mgmt. Consultants

Industries: Generalist, Drugs Mfg., Finance, Mgmt. Consulting, HR Services, Telecoms, Healthcare

Professional Associations: AICPA, HRPS, IHRIM, IMC, SHRM

Ford Webb Associates Inc
27 Main St
Concord, MA 01742
(978) 371-4900
Email: kbauzte@fordwebb.com

Description: Our search process is distinguished by our attention to the unique structure and needs of each organization we serve. We have recruited Fortune 500 CEOs, over 300 chief executives in the not-for-profit services, advocacy and higher education fields, as well as 60 state and city government cabinet officers.

Key Contact:
Mr. Ted Webb
Ms. Jean Ford

Functions: General Mgmt., Directors, Senior Mgmt.

Industries: Non-profits, Higher Ed., Law Enforcement, Government, Healthcare

Forray Associates Inc
2 Penn Plz Ste 1910
New York, NY 10121
(212) 279-0404
Fax: (212) 279-4223
Email: forray4a@aol.com

Description: Specialize in finance, marketing and sales - all industries - mid- to senior-level management - long standing reputation with Fortune 500 companies and smaller, entrepreneurial environments.

Key Contact:
Ms. Karen Forray, President
Mr. Michael Lutz, Associate

Salary minimum: $80,000

Functions: Senior Mgmt., Sales & Mktg., Mktg. Mgmt., Sales Mgmt., Direct Mktg., PR, Finance, CFO's

Industries: Generalist

Professional Associations: NAWBO

Foster Associates†
209 Cooper Ave
The Livery
Upper Montclair, NJ 07043
(973) 746-2800
Fax: (973) 746-9712
Email: donfoster3@aol.com

Description: Highly personalized comprehensive executive search service. Focused search process helps clients fill critical and urgent staffing needs quickly, saving client resources, time and expense. Recruit hard-to-find top quality senior and mid-level professional and executive talent who can add high value.

Key Contact - Specialty:
Mr. Donald J. Foster, President - *CFO's, controllers, treasury, capital markets, public accounting*

Salary minimum: $80,000

Functions: Finance, CFO's, Cash Mgmt., Taxes, M&A, Risk Mgmt., MIS Mgmt., Mgmt. Consultants, Attorneys

Industries: Generalist, Mfg., Finance, Invest. Banking, Venture Cap., Legal, Accounting, Mgmt. Consulting, Real Estate

Professional Associations: AICPA, NYSCPA

Foster Partners
570 Lexington Ave Fl 14
New York, NY 10022
(212) 893-2300
Fax: (212) 893-2309
Email: recruiting@fosterpartners.com
Web: www.fosterpartners.com

Description: We were formed in January 1990 through a management buyout of KPMG Peat Marwick's executive search practice, which was established in 1962. We conduct senior-level search assignments domestically and internationally and across all industry disciplines, including general management, finance, banking and capital markets and retail.

Key Contact - Specialty:
Mr. Dwight E. Foster, Chairman/ Executive Managing Director - *International*
Ms. Gail Amsterdam, Managing Director - *Retail*
Mr. Gregory Frumess, Managing Director - *Banking, investment services*
Ms. Barbara Kolburne, Managing Director-Int'l Client Services - *International, information, communications, finance/financial control*

Salary minimum: $100,000

Functions: Distribution, CFO's, Budgeting, Cash Mgmt., Credit, Taxes, M&A, Risk Mgmt., IT, MIS Mgmt.

Industries: Mfg., Consumer Elect., Test, Measure Equip., Retail, Finance, Banking, Invest. Banking, Non-profits, Accounting, Equip Svcs., Packaging, Insurance, Software, Marketing SW, Biotech, Healthcare, Non-classifiable

Branches:
2001 M St NW
Washington, DC 20036
(202) 223-9112
Fax: (202) 533-8569
Email: recruiting@fosterpartners.com
Key Contact:
Mr. J. Chris Dowell, Managing Director

200 Crescent Ct Ste 300
Dallas, TX 75201-1885
(214) 880-0432
Fax: (214) 754-2104
Email: recruiting@fosterpartners.com
Key Contact:
Mr. William Rowe, Executive Managing Director - *High technology, financial services*
Mr. William D. Rowe, II, Managing Director

Foy, Schneid & Daniel Inc
555 Madison Ave Fl 12
New York, NY 10022
(212) 980-2525
Email: fsd1brd@aol.com

Description: Professional executive search practice with targeted experience in most industries. The ability and experience of our consultants ensures that clients achieve efficient and quality results.

Key Contact - Specialty:
Ms. Beverly Daniel, Partner - *Management consulting, supply chain management, IT, industry analysis*
Mr. James C. Foy, Partner - *HR marketing, retail*

Salary minimum: $75,000

Functions: Senior Mgmt., Mfg., Materials, Purchasing, Distribution, Sales & Mktg., Mkt. Research, Mgmt. Consultants

Industries: Mfg., Transportation, Retail, Mgmt. Consulting

Professional Associations: CLM, IMC, INFORMS, SIM

Branches:
PO Box 1200
Ridgefield, CT 06877
(203) 438-5115
Fax: (203) 438-0294
Email: fsdsearch@aol.com
Key Contact:
Ms. Beverly R. Daniel

Franchise Recruiters Ltd ®
(a division of Coke & Associates Ltd)
3500 Innsbruck
Lincolnshire Country Club
Crete, IL 60417
(708) 757-5595
Email: franchise@att.net
Web: www.franchiserecruiters.com

Description: We provide our services only for candidates whom are experienced in franchises. Our candidates are guaranteed one year, unconditionally. We have excellent corporate client references. Our specialties include: candidates for sales and marketing, operations, training, real estate, financial, legal, executive, and international development. We have twenty-three years of experience in franchising.

Key Contact - Specialty:
Mr. Jerry C. Wilkerson, President/Founder - *Franchise, executives*

Salary minimum: $50,000

Functions: Directors, Senior Mgmt., Middle Mgmt., Sales Mgmt., IT, Int'l.

Industries: Generalist

Professional Associations: IFA

Branches:
20 Holly St Ste 203
Toronto, ON M4S 3B1
Canada
(416) 322-5730
Email: franchise@att.net
Web: www.franchisecareers.com
Key Contact - Specialty:
Mr. George Kinzie, President - *Franchising management*

Francis & Associates
6923 Vista Dr
West Des Moines, IA 50266
(515) 221-9800
Fax: (515) 221-9806
Email: knovak@francisassociates.com
Web: www.francisassociates.com

Description: We are a very professional firm, known for high quality and timely work. We are generalists working on a national and international basis.

Key Contact:
Mr. Dwaine Francis, Managing Partner
Ms. N. Kay Francis, Managing Partner
Ms. Karen Novak, Executive Vice President

Salary minimum: $100,000

Functions: Generalist

Industries: Generalist

Professional Associations: AESC

Neil Frank & Company
PO Box 3570
Redondo Beach, CA 90277-1570
(310) 937-8950
Fax: (310) 937-9471
Email: neilnick@aol.com
Web: www.neilfrank.com

Description: Functional specialist in public relations, corporate communications, and marketing communications. Retained solo practice.

Key Contact - Specialty:
Mr. Neil Frank, Principal - *Public relations, corporate communications, marketing communications*

Salary minimum: $50,000

Functions: PR

Industries: Advertising

Franklin Allen Consultants Ltd
1205 Franklin Ave Ste 350
Garden City, NY 11530
(516) 248-4511
Fax: (516) 294-6646
Email: fa@franklinallen.com
Web: www.franklinallen.com

Description: We are a generalist firm in business for over 19 years. We recruit for middle management and senior management positions, up to and including president/CEO and board level positions. We specialize in biotechnology, pharmaceutical, health care, hi-tech, merchant banking and consumer and industrial products.

Key Contact - Specialty:
Mr. Howard F. Roher, President - *Senior management, board directors, pharmaceutical industry, fashion industry, furniture industry*
Mr. Allen B. Kupchik, Senior Vice President - *Healthcare, hospitals, pharmaceuticals, medical equipment manufacturers, human resources*

Salary minimum: $75,000

Functions: Generalist

Industries: Mfg., Finance, Pharm Svcs., Accounting, Mgmt. Consulting, Hospitality, New Media, Digital, Software, Biotech, Healthcare

K S Frary & Associates Inc
5 Essex Green Dr Ste 31
Peabody, MA 01960-2923
(978) 573-3233
(978) 573-3234
Fax: (978) 573-3236
Email: kevin@ksfrary.com
Web: www.ksfrary.com

Description: Aggressive, ethical full-service firm with proven assessment skills, strong customer focus and in-depth research capabilities with a record of recruiting leaders who produce results.

Key Contact - Specialty:
Mr. Kevin S. Frary, President - *Manufacturing industries, high technology*
Mr. Ted L. Hubbard - *Manufacturing industries, financial services, publishing*

Salary minimum: $75,000

Functions: Generalist

Industries: Mfg., Banking, Publishing, Telecoms, Biotech

Professional Associations: AVS, HRMG, ISA, SEMI

A W Fraser & Associates

10303 Jasper Ave
2660 Canadian Western Bank Place
Edmonton, AB T5J 3N6
Canada
(780) 428-8578
Fax: (780) 426-2933
Email: edmonton@awfraser.com
Web: www.awfraser.com

Description: Originating from the first national practice of industrial psychology in Canada, A.W. Fraser & Associates has been continuously staffed by Chartered Psychologists and, from the beginning of certification, Certified Management Consultants. Offices are located in Edmonton, Calgary and Vancouver, and the firm has partners across Canada through its association with PSA International.

Key Contact:
Mr. Larry Pelensky

Functions: Generalist

Industries: Generalist

Valerie Frederickson & Company

800 Menlo Ave Ste 220
Menlo Park, CA 94025
(650) 614-0220
Fax: (650) 614-0223
Email: recruiting@vfandco.com
Web: www.vfandco.com

Description: Our firm is a leading Silicon Valley-based full-service human resource management and executive search consulting firm serving both emerging technology companies and large multinational corporations.

Key Contact - Specialty:
Ms. Valerie Frederickson, CMP, CEO/Founder - *Internet, software, hardware, biotechnology*

Salary minimum: $100,000

Functions: Senior Mgmt., Quality, Sales & Mktg., HR Mgmt., Benefits, M&A, IT, MIS Mgmt., Engineering, Int'l.

Industries: Generalist, Mfg., Medical Devices, Computer Equip., Finance, Services, Accounting, Equip Svcs., HR Services, Hospitality, Media, Publishing, New Media, Broadcast, Film, Telecoms, Software, Biotech

Professional Associations: IACMP, NCHRA, SHRM

P N French Associates Inc

126 Noell Farm Rd
Carlisle, MA 01741
(978) 369-4569

Description: Executive search for colleges and universities and related not-for-profit organizations. Conduct searches in a variety of functional areas, but specialize in searches for senior administrators. Excellent reputation for confidentiality.

Key Contact - Specialty:
Mr. Peter N. French, President - *Non-profit*

Salary minimum: $70,000

Functions: Senior Mgmt., Middle Mgmt., Admin. Svcs., Purchasing, Distribution, Finance, IT, Specialized Svcs., Minorities, Non-profits

Industries: Transportation, Non-profits, Higher Ed., New Media, Broadcast, Film

Gerald Frisch Associates Inc

181 E 73rd St
New York, NY 10021
(212) 737-4810

Description: Offering the exclusive GFA planned executive search system.

Key Contact - Specialty:
Mr. Gerald Frisch, President - *General management, MIS*

Salary minimum: $70,000

Functions: Generalist, Senior Mgmt., Mktg. Mgmt., Customer Svc., PR, MIS Mgmt., Mgmt. Consultants

Industries: Generalist, Food, Bev., Tobacco, Drugs Mfg., Banking, Invest. Banking, Pharm Svcs., Mgmt. Consulting, Publishing

Professional Associations: IBRT, IMRT

Frontier Partners Inc

1 Faneuil Hall Market Fl 3
Boston, MA 02109
(617) 570-0740
Fax: (617) 570-0748
Email: mwarter@frontiersearch.com
Web: www.frontiersearch.com

Description: A full service firm dedicated to matching the requirements of its clients with the life goals of its candidates. Focus is on finding top management and entire teams for high-growth, start-up and early-stage companies,and leading municipal and not-for-profit institutions.

Key Contact:
Mr. Mark Warter, President

Salary minimum: $85,000

Functions: Generalist

Industries: Computer Equip., Finance, Venture Cap., Non-profits, Higher Ed., Media, Communications, Government, Software, Healthcare, Non-classifiable

Fulcrum Resource Group Inc

171 Dorset Rd
Waban, MA 02468
(617) 964-1855
Fax: (617) 964-8377
Email: hwigder@fulcrumgroup.com
Web: www.fulcrumgroup.com

Description: Our firm specializes in executive search and team integration. Most of our clients are privately held companies in manufacturing or other traditional industries. They come to us to help them take their organizations to a higher level by finding the right people and building teamwork.

Key Contact - Specialty:
Mr. T. Harvey Wigder, Principal - *Privately held businesses*

Salary minimum: $100,000

Functions: General Mgmt.

Industries: Generalist

Professional Associations: NACD, NESAP, SBANE, SPC, TEC

Furlong Search Inc

550 Tyndall St Ste 11
Los Altos, CA 94022
(650) 856-8484
Fax: (650) 941-7059
Email: furlong5@aol.com

Description: Oldest retained search firm serving the electronic industry exclusively, filling middle managers to CEO positions in all disciplines.

Key Contact:
Mr. James W. Furlong, President

Salary minimum: $150,000

Functions: Generalist

Industries: Generalist, Computer Equip., Consumer Elect., Test, Measure Equip., Software

Branches:
19312 Romar St
Northridge, CA 91324
(818) 885-7044
Fax: (818) 885-7588
Key Contact:
Mr. James W. Furlong, President

634 E Main St
Hillsboro, OR 97123
(503) 640-3221
Key Contact:
Mr. James W. Furlong, President

C F Furr & Company

5917 Oleader Dr Ste 204
Wilmington, NC 28403
(910) 452-2217
Email: cffurrco@mindspring.com

Description: History of achieving excellent results for clients, commitment to successful search completion, principal involvement in every search, exceptional research capabilities, thorough sourcing and screening, comprehensive candidate reports, disciplined communications and follow through, replacement search guarantee.

Key Contact - Specialty:
Mr. C. Franklin Furr, Principal - *Financial services, healthcare*

Salary minimum: $50,000

Functions: General Mgmt., Healthcare, Sales & Mktg., Sales Mgmt., HR Mgmt., Benefits, Finance

Industries: Banking, Invest. Banking, Brokers, Healthcare

The Furst Group Inc

1639 N Alpine Rd
Rockford, IL 61107
(815) 229-7800
Fax: (815) 394-0239
Email: tom@furstsearch.com
Web: www.furstsearch.com

Description: Retained management recruiting and human resources consulting within manufacturing, financial and the service sector. Extensive experience within the call center industry.

Key Contact:
Mr. Thomas C. Furst, President
Dr. Martin E. Pschirrer, Senior Vice President
Ms. Lynn M. Momberger, Vice President
Mr. Kevin Logterman, Vice President
Mr. Robert Pschirrer, Executive Recruiter
Ms. Keri Benhoff, Researcher

Salary minimum: $150,000

Functions: Generalist

Industries: Mfg., Finance, Banking, Invest. Banking, Non-profits, Legal, Accounting, Mgmt. Consulting, HR Services, Telecoms

Furst Group/MPI

555 S Perryville Rd
Rockford, IL 61108-2509
(815) 229-9111
Fax: (815) 229-8926
Web: www.furstgroup.com

Description: Specialists in medical management, cost containment and health insurance markets including HMOs, PPOs, medical group practices, indemnity, hospital, pharmacy, home health and ancillary markets.

Key Contact - Specialty:
Mr. J. Robert Clarke, Principal - *Healthcare*
Mr. Tyler P. Pratt, Principal - *Healthcare*
Ms. Sherrie L. Barch, Principal - *Healthcare*
Mr. Dennis L. Pankratz, Vice President - *Healthcare*

Salary minimum: $100,000

Functions: General Mgmt., Sales & Mktg., HR Mgmt., CFO's, IT, MIS Mgmt., Minorities, Int'l.

Industries: Healthcare

Professional Associations: AAHP, AAMCN, AAPC, AAPPO, ACHE, ACPE, AHA, AHLA, AICPA, ASHHRA, HCCA, HFMA, HIMSS, MGMA, NAHQ, NAHSE

Branches:
80 S 8th St Ste 3430
IDS Ctr
Minneapolis, MN 55402
(612) 339-8500
Fax: (612) 339-8505
Key Contact - Specialty:
Mr. Brad J. Chandler, Vice President - *Healthcare*
Mr. Timothy Frischmon, Vice President - *Healthcare*

1103 Sheppard Ln
Wylie, TX 75098
(972) 429-4610
Fax: (972) 429-4710
Key Contact - Specialty:
Mr. William Fosick, Vice President - *Healthcare*

15401 Weldin Dr
Woodbridge, VA 22193
(703) 580-1737
Fax: (703) 580-0867
Key Contact - Specialty:
Ms. Deanna L. Banks, Vice President - *Healthcare*

Futures Int'l
120 Post Rd W Ste 202
Westport, CT 06880
(203) 221-6488
Email: info@futuresintl.com
Web: www.futuresintl.com

Description: With offices in New York, Connecticut and London, we offer advanced strategic consulting and search services to a select group of clients. We employ a research-driven, creative approach to provide seamless global services to all of our clients and candidates.

Key Contact:
Mr. Richard Stein, Managing Partner

Functions: Generalist

Industries: Finance

Professional Associations: IACPR

Branches:
599 Lexington Ave Fl 23
New York, NY 10022
(212) 836-4762
Email: info@futuresintl.com
Key Contact:
Mr. Richard Stein, Managing Partner

GAAP Inc
1524 Summerhill
Montreal, QC H3H 1B9
Canada
(514) 935-3253
Email: ehughes@gaapsearch.com
Web: www.gaapsearch.com

Description: We are a boutique senior-level retained executive search firm serving a select list of Fortune 500 companies across North America. Visit our website for a more comprehensive overview of our firm.

Key Contact - Specialty:
Mr. Emerson Hughes, Senior Partner - *Senior executives*
Mr. Steve Johnstone, Partner - *Senior executives*
Ms. Shawn Davidson, Partner - *Senior management*
Mr. Mark Halloran, Director Business Development
Ms. Jennifer Young, Partner

Ms. Aggie Wybraniec, Consultant - *Senior executives*
Mr. Frank Connor, Consultant - *Senior executives*
Mr. Kent Fraser, Consultant - *Senior executive*

Salary minimum: $90,000

Functions: Senior Mgmt.

Industries: Mfg., Finance, Pharm Svcs., Accounting, Mgmt. Consulting, HR Services, New Media, Telecoms, Defense

Gaffney Management Consultants Inc
35 N Brandon Dr
Glendale Heights, IL 60139-2024
(630) 307-3380
Fax: (630) 307-3381
Email: info@gaffneyinc.com
Web: www.gaffneyinc.com

Description: Retained executive search firm servicing the needs of major manufacturing and industrial-related organizations both public and private. Effective recruitment in the areas of general management, manufacturing operations, quality, purchasing/materials, finance/accounting, information technology/MIS, product engineering, human resources and sales/marketing.

Key Contact - Specialty:
Mr. Keith Gaffney, Managing Director - *Middle management, directors, vice presidents, generalist (functional)*
Mr. William Gaffney, President/CEO - *Executive level, presidents, CEOs, vice presidents*

Salary minimum: $60,000

Functions: General Mgmt., Mfg., Materials, Sales & Mktg., HR Mgmt., Finance, IT, Int'l.

Industries: Agri., Forestry, Mining, Construction, Mfg., Defense, Environmental Svcs., Aerospace, Software

Branches:
340 E Warm Springs Rd Ste 9-B
Las Vegas, NV 89119
(702) 617-9887
Key Contact:
Mr. David Johnson, Manager - Executive Search

Gahan Associates[†]
11 Ambrose Ave
Malverne, NY 11565
(516) 593-3621
Fax: (516) 593-3625

Description: Over twenty years' successful recruiting experience to corporate and management consulting clients.

Key Contact - Specialty:
Mrs. Ann M. Gahan, Partner - *Management consultants, financial executives, e-commerce*
Mr. Thomas M. Gahan, Partner - *Senior management, middle management, marketing, financial executives*
Ms. Carolyn M. Gahan, Senior Manager - *Non-profit executives, middle management*
Mr. Anthony Cioffoletti, Partner - *Information technology*

Salary minimum: $80,000

Functions: Generalist, Middle Mgmt., Direct Mktg., HR Mgmt., Risk Mgmt., MIS Mgmt., Non-profits

Industries: Generalist, Finance, Services, Pharm Svcs., Mgmt. Consulting, Insurance, Healthcare

Gaines & Associates Int'l Inc
650 N Dearborn St Ste 450
Chicago, IL 60610
(312) 654-2900
Fax: (312) 654-2903
Web: www.gainesintl.com

Description: We are a professional search firm specializing in the design and building industries. We conduct in-depth searches with a level of expertise founded on years of experience. We dedicate ourselves to providing timely effective solutions by assessing needs, finding the right individuals and facilitating communications that benefit both employer and candidate.

Key Contact - Specialty:
Ms. Donna Gaines, President - *Architecture, interior design, construction, real estate, engineering*

Salary minimum: $70,000

Functions: Generalist

Industries: Construction, Real Estate

Professional Associations: AIA, ICSC, IIDA, WTS

Branches:
2000 L St NW Ste 200
Washington, DC 20036
(202) 244-6929
Key Contact:
Ms. Cathie Kempf, Senior Associate

2221 Peachtree Rd Ste P-33
Atlanta, GA 30309
(404) 355-7008
Email: gheath@gainesintl.com
Key Contact:
Mr. Grant Heath, Vice President

11086 Riverview Dr
New Buffalo, MI 49117
(312) 654-2900
Key Contact:
Mr. Charles Roberson, Managing Director
Ms. Donna Gaines, President

Jay Gaines & Company Inc
450 Park Ave Ste 500
New York, NY 10022
(212) 308-9222
Fax: (212) 308-5146
Email: jgandco@jaygaines.com
Web: www.jaygaines.com

Description: Major concentrations of activities are general management, financial services with heavy emphasis on the financial markets, e-commerce, information technology and information based businesses.

Key Contact:
Mr. Jay Gaines, President - *General management, information technology, information industry, financial services*
Ms. Valerie Germain, Managing Director - *Information technology, operations*
Mr. Dick Kurth, Managing Director - *Capital markets, risk management, investment management*
Mr. Tarin Anwar, Managing Director - *Investment banking, capital markets, risk management, investment management, finance*
Mrs. Kathy Fisher, Managing Director - *Financial markets, generalist*
Ms. Marie Rice, Vice President - *Generalist*
Ms. Susan Schaller, Vice President - *Generalist*
Mr. Peter Ellsworth, Vice President - *Financial services, generalist*
Ms. Olga Produvalova

Salary minimum: $250,000

Functions: Generalist

Industries: Generalist, Mfg., Finance, Mgmt. Consulting, Media, Insurance, Software

Professional Associations: AESC

Galloway & Associates Search Consultants Inc

55 St. Clair Ave W Ste 265
Toronto, ON M4V 2Y7
Canada
(416) 969-8989

Description: We have an engineer on staff and MIS experts, excellent business references, professional and thorough approach to searches. Office located in mid-town Toronto.

Key Contact - Specialty:
Mr. Glenn E. Galloway, Principal - *Sales & marketing, administration, manufacturing*

Salary minimum: $50,000

Functions: Materials

Industries: Metal Products, Brokers, Telecoms, Aerospace, Packaging, Software

Gaming Consultants Inc

365 Canal St 1 Canal Pl Ste 2300
New Orleans, LA 70130
(504) 469-0308
Fax: (504) 461-0418
Email: frankhrutherford@aol.com

Description: Executive recruiting consultants. Clients in the major gaming industry, with 26 years of experience. Each search conducted by the partner upon original research.

Key Contact - Specialty:
Mr. Frank H. Rutherford, Owner - *Gaming, casinos, hospitality, hotels, cruise management*
Mr. Charles J. Cox, Jr., Partner - *General & senior executive management*
Mr. Brian T. Murray, Partner - *General, senior, middle management*
Mr. Douglas A. Bolt, Partner - *Middle management*
Mr. Pierre J. Paul, Partner - *Middle management*

Salary minimum: $100,000

Functions: Senior Mgmt., Middle Mgmt., Purchasing, Sales & Mktg., HR Mgmt., Finance, CFO's, Credit, MIS Mgmt., Systems Analysis

Industries: Hospitality

Gans, Gans & Associates Inc

4129 E Fowler Ave
Tampa, FL 33617
(813) 971-6501
Fax: (813) 971-6966
Web: www.gansgans.com

Description: We specialize in diversity search, recruiting individuals of diverse backgrounds, including women and people of various ethnic and racial backgrounds, for executive, management, professional, technical and sales positions.

Key Contact - Specialty:
Ms. Simone Gans Barefield, President/CEO - *Management consultants, minority recruiting, information technology, specialized services*

Salary minimum: $75,000

Functions: Generalist, Senior Mgmt., HR Mgmt., CFO's, IT, MIS Mgmt., Specialized Svcs., Mgmt. Consultants

Industries: Generalist, Energy, Utilities, Mgmt. Consulting, Media, Insurance, Software, Healthcare

Professional Associations: AOCFI, EMA

Branches:
107 N 22nd St
Philadelphia, PA 19103
(215) 751-1724
Fax: (215) 751-1730
Key Contact - Specialty:
Ms. Simone Gans Barefield - *Management consulting, specialized services, general management, information technology*

W N Garbarini & Associates

961 Cherokee Ct
Westfield, NJ 07090
(908) 232-2737
Fax: (908) 232-2326
Email: wngarbarini@home.com

Description: Boutique general search firm with unique personalized service approach.

Key Contact:
Mr. William N. Garbarini, President
Ms. Linda Lauchiere, Vice President-Research

Salary minimum: $100,000

Functions: Generalist, General Mgmt., Healthcare, Sales & Mktg., Mktg. Mgmt., Sales Mgmt., HR Mgmt., Finance, CFO's, IT

Industries: Mfg., Food, Bev., Tobacco, Drugs Mfg., Medical Devices, Computer Equip., Biotech, Healthcare

Gardiner, Townsend & Associates

101 E 52nd St Fl 25
New York, NY 10022
(212) 230-1889
Fax: (212) 838-0424
Email: enpg@gardinertownsend.com
Web: www.gardinertownsend.com

Description: We provide our clients with the best available candidates for top level recruitment regardless of geographic location with a single consultant in charge from start to finish across int'l. barriers using advanced information technology, global industry expertise, cross-cultural judgement.

Key Contact - Specialty:
Mr. E. Nicholas P. Gardiner, President - *Financial services, energy, communications, media*
Mr. John W. Townsend, Partner - *Financial services*

Salary minimum: $180,000

Functions: Generalist, Senior Mgmt., Mkt. Research, CFO's, M&A, MIS Mgmt., Mgmt. Consultants, Int'l.

Industries: Generalist, Energy, Utilities, Banking, Invest. Banking, Mgmt. Consulting, Publishing, Broadcast, Film, Telecoms

Professional Associations: AESC

Gardner-Ross Associates Inc

232 Madison Ave
New York, NY 10016
(212) 689-1133
Fax: (212) 689-4893
Email: gardnrxl@earthlink.net

Description: We are a generalist firm with several sub-specialties such as Venture capital staffing, packaging, P.O.P. displays, magazine publishing, new media and high-technology. Our assignments range from CEO, COO, marketing/sales management, operations and most upper-management positions.

Key Contact - Specialty:
Mr. Marvin Gardner, President - *Venture capital staffing, general manufacturing, POP displays, packaging*
Ms. Elsa Ross, Executive Vice President - *Publishing, service, new media*
Mr. Al Griffin, Vice President - *High technology, packaging, printing*

Salary minimum: $100,000

Functions: Generalist, Middle Mgmt., Plant Mgmt., Health Admin., Direct Mktg., IT, MIS Mgmt., Mgmt. Consultants

Industries: Generalist, Soap, Perf., Cosmtcs., Misc. Mfg., Mgmt. Consulting, Publishing, New Media, Packaging

Dick Garland Consultants

31 E 32nd St
New York, NY 10016
(212) 481-8484
Fax: (212) 481-9582

Description: Clients deal solely with the owner.

Key Contact - Specialty:
Mr. Dick Garland, President - *Credit card*

Functions: Generalist, Sales Mgmt., Budgeting

Industries: Generalist, Misc. Financial, Non-classifiable

Branches:
5 Crest Dr
White Plains, NY 10607
(914) 347-5525
Fax: (914) 347-5280
Email: garland2k@aol.com
Key Contact - Specialty:
Mr. Dick Garland - *Credit cards*

The Garms Group

12 Ferndale Rd
Barrington, IL 60010
(847) 382-7200
Fax: (847) 382-7222
Email: dangarms@garms.com
Web: www.garms.com

Description: We pride ourselves in being a client-driven executive search firm. Our practice is targeted upon a diverse group of start-up and emerging high-technology companies. We specialize in e-commerce, Internet related technologies. (i.e. web-based commerce enablers, CRM, supply chain, B2B, B2C, CRM, CAD, security telecommunications, and optical networks.

Key Contact:
Mr. Daniel S. Garms, President

Salary minimum: $90,000

Functions: General Mgmt., Senior Mgmt., Middle Mgmt., Product Dev., Sales & Mktg., Mktg. Mgmt., Sales Mgmt., IT, Engineering, Mgmt. Consultants

Industries: Energy, Utilities, Construction, Mfg., Computer Equip., Venture Cap., Services, Equip Svcs., Mgmt. Consulting, Media, Publishing, New Media, Broadcast, Film, Telecoms, Government, Aerospace, Software

Professional Associations: ACM, AIIM, AIP, CADS, IPA, URISA

The Garret Group†

(also known as Skurnik, Stecker & Wharton)
342 Parsippany Rd
Parsippany, NJ 07054
(973) 884-0711
Fax: (973) 884-1307
Email: jwharton@staffing.net

Description: Specialists in recruiting engineering, operations, quality assurance and regulatory affairs professionals for the pharmaceutical, medical device and consumer packaged goods industries.

Key Contact - Specialty:
Mr. John P. Wharton, Partner - *Engineering, operations*
Mr. Bernd Stecker - *Engineering, operations*

Salary minimum: $60,000

Functions: Middle Mgmt., Mfg., Product Dev., Quality, Packaging, R&D, Engineering

Industries: Drugs Mfg., Medical Devices, Plastics, Rubber, Consumer Elect., Packaging, Biotech

Professional Associations: ASQ, ISPE, PDA

Branches:
6610 Gasparilla Pines Blvd Unit 235
Englewood, FL 34224
(941) 698-0118
Fax: (941) 698-1158
Key Contact - Specialty:
Mr. James N. Finn - *Engineering*

Garrett Associates Inc
PO Box 53359
Atlanta, GA 30355
(404) 364-0001
Fax: (404) 364-0726
Email: lgarrett@garrettassociatesinc.com
Web: www.garrettassociatesinc.com

Description: We provide coast-to-coast, retained healthcare executive search.

Key Contact - Specialty:
Ms. Linda M. Garrett, Principal - *Healthcare*
Mr. Donald L. Garrett, Principal - *Healthcare*
Ms. Janis Morrison, Vice President - *Healthcare*

Salary minimum: $50,000

Functions: Generalist, General Mgmt.

Industries: Healthcare, Hospitals, Long-term Care

Professional Associations: AAHC, ACHE, AHA, ASCPA, GAHE, GHA, GSHHRA, GSMC

The Garrison Organization†
14225 University Ave Ste 206
Greenview Corporate Bldg
Waukee, IA 50263-8096
(515) 309-4442
Fax: (509) 479-1213
Email: info@garrisonorg.com
Web: www.garrisonorg.com

Description: We are a 15 year-old retained executive search and selection firm exclusive to the financial services industry. Our primary emphasis is life insurance executives and field management

Key Contact - Specialty:
Mr. Ed Garrison, President/CEO - *Chief marketing, sales officers, regional sales officers, regional wholesalers, general agent*
Mr. Cory Garrison, Vice President - *underwriting attorneys & consultants (advanced), field training managers, internal wholesalers, group insurance regional managers*

Salary minimum: $80,000

Functions: Generalist, Senior Mgmt., Middle Mgmt., Legal, Sales & Mktg., Mktg. Mgmt., Sales Mgmt., IT, Mgmt. Consultants, Attorneys

Industries: Generalist, Finance, Insurance

Branches:
400 S Colorado Blvd Ste 600
Denver, CO 80246
(303) 394-9877
Key Contact - Specialty:
Mr. Randall Garrison, CLU, Vice President - *Agency managers, regional sales directors*

Garrison-Randall†
1 Sansome St Fl 21
PMB 190016
San Francisco, CA 94104
(415) 995-8400
Fax: (415) 995-8422
Email: gri@mac.com

Description: We are an executive search firm providing recruitment services to the healthcare industry. We do not work with medical sales, pharmaceuticals, or biotech firms. Please do not submit a resume if you do not have previous experience within the healthcare industry. We will not be able to assist you.

Key Contact - Specialty:
Ms. Rita M. Fornino, Vice President - *Healthcare*

Salary minimum: $70,000

Functions: General Mgmt., Middle Mgmt., Healthcare, HR Mgmt.

Industries: Healthcare

Garthwaite Partners Int'l
13 Arcadia Rd Ste 14
Old Greenwich, CT 06870
(203) 698-0015
(203) 834-1070
Fax: (203) 698-3001
Email: candace@garthwaitepartners.com
Web: www.garthwaitepartners.com

Description: We place senior and middle management positions including finance, HR, sales, marketing, CRM, e-Learning in the following industries: financial services, more specifically capital markets, private equity and private banking, and asset management; healthcare, more specifically managed care, homecare, PBM, and medical devices; and media and entertainment, more specifically new media, entertainment, publishing, and knowledge management. We specialize in producing a diverse slate of candidates.

Key Contact - Specialty:
Dr. Candace Garthwaite, Managing Partner - *Financial services, strategic planning, human resources*
Ms. Linda Buggy, Partner - *Financial services, entertainment/media/communications, managed care, knowledge management, human resources*
Ms. Ida Kowat, Vice President - *Financial services*
Ms. Nina Kayem, Vice President - *Generalist*

Salary minimum: $100,000

Functions: Senior Mgmt., Middle Mgmt., Sales & Mktg., Mktg. Mgmt., HR Mgmt., Training, Finance, Int'l.

Industries: Generalist, Medical Devices, Finance, Banking, Invest. Banking, Venture Cap., Pharm Svcs., Mgmt. Consulting, HR Services, E-commerce, Media, Publishing, New Media, Broadcast, Film, Telecoms, Call Centers, Entertainment SW, Training SW, Healthcare

Professional Associations: APT, FWA, WIM

Peter Gasperini & Associates Inc
42 Crane Rd
Scarsdale, NY 10583
(914) 723-0004

Description: Concentration in financial services industry on a retained basis. Twenty years of search experience on a global basis. Special concentration on investment management and investment banking.

Key Contact - Specialty:
Mr. Peter Gasperini, President - *Financial services*

Salary minimum: $200,000

Functions: Cash Mgmt., M&A

Industries: Banking, Invest. Banking

Gaudette & Company
980 W Paseo del Cilantro
Green Valley, AZ 85614
(520) 648-1963
Fax: (520) 648-5409
Email: azresource@aol.com

Description: IT candidates for software, research, developers and engineering companies. We are your source for potential candidates whose qualifications closely match your requirements.

Key Contact - Specialty:
Mr. Charles L. Gaudette, President - *IT, programmers, engineers, developers*

Salary minimum: $60,000

Functions: Systems Dev.

Industries: Energy, Utilities, Construction, Mfg., Finance, Services, Media, Telecoms, Government, Software, Biotech

Gavin Forbes & Price
3022 Kingsley St Ste A
San Diego, CA 92106
(858) 483-6696

Description: Major international banks, state, regionals, local institutuions in California exclusively, accept search assignments on selective basis, principal conducts search only.

Key Contact - Specialty:
Mr. Daniel Price, Vice President - *Banking*

Salary minimum: $60,000

Functions: Generalist, CFO's, Cash Mgmt., Credit, Taxes, M&A, Risk Mgmt.

Industries: Generalist, Banking

Genesis Consulting Partners
350 S Ardmore Ave
Ardmore, PA 19003
(610) 896-9686
Fax: (610) 896-9687
Email: kelsomjr@aol.com

Description: Ten years' specialization in pharmaceutical and biotechnology industries. Distinct consulting approach with CEO of early stage high-technology ventures on executive recruitment, organization planning, executive assessment, staffing, psychological counseling. Selective partnering with senior-level management in career development strategies & execution.

Key Contact - Specialty:
Mr. Kendall A. Elsom, Jr., President/CEO - *Biotechnology, pharmaceuticals*
Ms. Catrayl Dalyan, Administrative Partner
Ms. Lucy Darlington, Partner - *Human resources, counseling psychotherapist*

Salary minimum: $100,000

Functions: Senior Mgmt.

Industries: Generalist, Drugs Mfg., Biotech

Genesis Corporate Search Ltd
1800, 520 - 5 Ave SW
Calgary, AB T2P 3R7
Canada
(403) 237-8622
Fax: (403) 233-7622
Email: genesis@genesiscorporatesearch.com
Web: www.genesiscorporatesearch.com

Description: Permanent search and placement of oil and gas professionals in Canada, specifically in the areas of engineering, geology, geophysics, accounting/finance and information technology.

Key Contact - Specialty:
Ms. P. F. Hines, President/Managing Partner - *Engineering, geoscience*
Mr. Vernon P. Casey, Partner - *Engineering, geosciences, finance*

Salary minimum: $60,000

Functions: Generalist, Middle Mgmt., CFO's, Cash Mgmt., Engineering

Industries: Energy, Utilities

Geneva Group Int'l Inc
4 Embarcadero Ctr Ste 1400
San Francisco, CA 94111
(415) 433-4646
Fax: (415) 433-6635
Email: isill@aol.com
Web: www.genevagroup.com

Description: Specializes in presidential, board member and officer level searches for Internet, wireless and e-commerce companies. Special emphasis on key officers for venture capital backed, privately held emerging technologies with a focus on ASP, software, Internet, networking and wireless companies.

Key Contact - Specialty:
Mr. Igor M. Sill, Managing Partner - *Software, internet*

Salary minimum: $100,000

Functions: Generalist, Directors, Senior Mgmt.

Industries: Generalist, Venture Cap., New Media, Software

C R Gerald & Associates
158 Baldwin St
Whitby, ON L1M 1C2
Canada
(905) 655-9728
Fax: (905) 655-9729
Email: dgerald@hotmail.com

Description: Relative experiences in country management and software development (product & systems) enhanced by knowledge of our associates when required, have enabled our organization to relate well to client needs, make thoughtful recommendations regarding qualified personnel and fulfill the needs proposed.

Key Contact - Specialty:
Mr. C. Richard Gerald, President - *Information technology, senior executive, sales, technical management*

Salary minimum: $100,000

Functions: Generalist, Senior Mgmt., Mktg. Mgmt., Sales Mgmt., Training, CFO's, MIS Mgmt.

Industries: Generalist, Computer Equip., Mgmt. Consulting, Telecoms, Software

GES Services Inc
630 5th Ave Rockefeller Ctr Fl 20
New York, NY 10111
(212) 332-3260
Fax: (212) 332-3261
Email: ges@gesservices.com

Description: We recruit senior and middle management professionals for personal trust, private banking, financial planning, investment management, and related wealth management disciplines nationwide.

Key Contact - Specialty:
Mr. Mr. Christy Guzzetta, President - *Wealth management*
Ms. Abby J. Norris, Vice President - *Wealth management*

Salary minimum: $100,000

Functions: Generalist

Industries: Finance, Banking, Invest. Banking, Brokers, Misc. Financial, Services, Accounting, Mgmt. Consulting, HR Services

Gibson & Company Inc
250 N Sunnyslope Rd Ste 300
Brookfield, WI 53005
(262) 785-8100
(262) 367-5100

Description: Bruce Gibson has 32 years of experience in officer level executive search, specializing in CEO assignments, as well as direct reports to the CEO: COO, CFO, CIO, CTO, and corporate officers in charge of sales, marketing, operations, human resources. We have field offices in New York, Chicago, Minneapolis, and Monterey, CA.

Key Contact - Specialty:
Mr. Bruce Gibson - *CEOs, COO's, CFOs, CIO's, officer level positions*

Salary minimum: $250,000

Functions: Generalist

Industries: Generalist

Gilbert Tweed Associates Inc
415 Madison Ave
New York, NY 10017
(212) 758-3000
Fax: (212) 832-1040
Email: gtany@aol.com
Web: www.gilberttweed.com

Description: Generalist search practice providing broad range of support services to ensure successful completion of every search. Strong track record recruiting female and minority candidates. Also provides organizational profiling service, seminars-Picking Winners and Keeping Winners.

Key Contact:
Ms. Janet Tweed, CEO
Ms. Stephanie Pinson, President
Ms. Karen DelPrete, Managing Director
Mr. Jack Lusk, Managing Director
Mr. John P. Holmes, Chairman
Mr. Tony Brown
Mr. Richard G. Lipstein
Ms. Kathryn M. Murphy
Ms. Linda Paul, Managing Director - *Energy*
Mr. Robert Fetzer, Managing Director
Ms. Karen N. Pinkman, Managing Director
Ms. Patricia Browne-Zak, Managing Director
Mr. Sabin Danziger, Managing Director
Mr. Theodore Eastwick, Managing Director
Ms. Lucienne de Mestre, Managing Director
Ms. Mai Keklak, Managing Director
Ms. Melissa Harris, Managing Director

Salary minimum: $150,000

Functions: Generalist, General Mgmt., Production, Sales & Mktg., CFO's, MIS Mgmt., R&D, Mgmt. Consultants, Minorities, Int'l.

Industries: Mfg., Invest. Banking, Venture Cap., Misc. Financial, Pharm Svcs., Mgmt. Consulting, HR Services, Broadcast, Film, Telecoms, Haz. Waste

Professional Associations: IACPR, APTA

Branches:
4001 S 700E Ste 500
Salt Lake City, UT 84107
(801) 264-6697
Fax: (801) 264-6696
Email: chammond@translit.com
Key Contact:
Ms. Cindy Hammond, Managing Director

Howard Gilmore & Associates
15 Chelsea Ct
Beachwood, OH 44122
(216) 831-6249

Description: Search and outplacement services in the sales, marketing, management areas, concentration more in the industrial, technical areas domestically.

Key Contact - Specialty:
Mr. Howard A. Gilmore - *Industrial sales & marketing*

Salary minimum: $30,000

Functions: Generalist, Middle Mgmt., Mktg. Mgmt., Sales Mgmt., Training, Mgmt. Consultants

Industries: Energy, Utilities, Metal Products, Misc. Mfg.

James Glavin & Associates Inc
PO Box 7734
Shawnee Mission, KS 66207
(913) 851-1741
Fax: (913) 681-5619
Email: lglavin@kc.rr.com

Description: Executive search firm specializing in client-retained executive recruitment of senior-level information technology professionals. From our Overland Park, KS office we provide services nationally and internationally with the help of associates in Little Rock, Denver and Boston.

Key Contact:
Mr. James E. Glavin, President

Salary minimum: $100,000

Functions: IT, MIS Mgmt.

Industries: Generalist

Glazin/Sisco Executive Search Consultants Inc
95 King St E Ste 500
Toronto, ON M5C 1G4
Canada
(416) 203-3004
Fax: (416) 203-3007
Email: search@glazinsisco.com
Web: www.glazinsisco.com

Description: We are a fully retained executive search firm with an enviable client base, conducting interesting senior-level assignments across Canada. Our industry specialties include real estate, resort, hospitality, retail, and food service.

Key Contact:
Ms. Lynne Glazin, Partner - *Real estate, resort, hospitality, entertainment, sports, tourism*
Ms. Carol Sisco, Partner - *Real estate, resort, hospitality, entertainment, sports*
Ms. Sue Hall, Researcher
Ms. Shelly Silbernagel, Associate

Salary minimum: $80,000

Functions: Generalist, General Mgmt., Mfg., Sales & Mktg., HR Mgmt., Finance, IT

Industries: Generalist, Construction, Retail, Services, Real Estate, Healthcare

Branches:
1066 W Hastings St Ste 2300
Vancouver, BC V6E 3X2
Canada
(604) 687-3828
Fax: (604) 687-3875

J P Gleason Associates Inc
PO Box 33
Cary, IL 60013-0033
(847) 516-8900
Fax: (847) 516-8928
Email: jpgsearch@aol.com
Web: www.jpgleason.com

Description: Higher level search in marketing, sales, finance, HR and operations for clients in transportation, manufacturing, retail and other industries. Personal, consultative approach with limited number of clients.

Key Contact - Specialty:
Mr. James P. Gleason, President - *Human resources, marketing, sales, finance, manufacturing*

Salary minimum: $100,000

Functions: Generalist, General Mgmt., Mfg., Sales & Mktg., HR Mgmt., Finance

Industries: Generalist, Food, Bev., Tobacco, Lumber, Furniture, Metal Products, Computer Equip., Banking, Hospitality

Glines Associates Inc
39 S LaSalle St Ste 714
Chicago, IL 60603
(312) 577-5645
Fax: (312) 577-5651
Email: search@glinesassociates.com
Web: www.glinesassociates.com

Functions: Generalist

Industries: Generalist

Description: Specialist in the healthcare and life sciences industry with nearly twenty years of executive search experience. We function as a knowledgeable partner adding value to the search process and providing an uncommon level of service.

Key Contact - Specialty:
Mr. Larry Glines, President - *Healthcare, life sciences*
Mr. Adam Chavarria, Research Director - *Healthcare, life sciences*

Salary minimum: $90,000

Functions: Generalist

Industries: Drugs Mfg., Medical Devices, Biotech, Healthcare

Professional Associations: AAAS, AACC, BMA

Global Consulting Resources Inc
51 Locust Ave
New Canaan, CT 06840
(203) 966-7780
Fax: (203) 966-8131
Email: atsiropoulos@gloconres.com

Description: Assists the world's largest professional service firms, Fortune 500 companies and technology firms in the areas of executive search, staffing, and consulting.

Key Contact:
Ms. Linda Guinipero, Director, Executive Search Solutions

Functions: Generalist

Industries: Generalist

Global Data Services Inc†
694 Ft Salonga Rd
Northport, NY 11768
(631) 754-0771
Fax: (516) 754-0590
Email: info@globaldatasearch.com
Web: www.globaldatasearch.com

Description: Our firm provides search services to the high-tech industry, including: .COM, B2B, B2C, software, hardware, system integration, fortune 1000 and management consulting companies. Our practice concentrates on searches for executive management, project management, marketing, software development and business development positions. GDS consultants have experience in the high-technology industry.

Key Contact - Specialty:
Mr. Garry Silivanch, CEO/President - *Start-up companies, CEO, president, CFO, venture firms*
Ms. Bernadette Komansky, COO/Vice President Operations - *Research, targeting*
Mr. Bob Walsh, VP- Recruiting - *Database management, recruiting*

Salary minimum: $100,000

Functions: Senior Mgmt., Product Dev., Sales & Mktg., Sales Mgmt., IT, MIS Mgmt., Systems Dev., Systems Implem., Mgmt. Consultants

Industries: Generalist, Chemicals, Drugs Mfg., Computer Equip., Retail, Banking, Invest. Banking, Brokers, Venture Cap., Equip Svcs., Mgmt. Consulting, HR Services, Hospitality, New Media, Broadcast, Film, Telecoms, Software

Global Research
444 E 82nd St Ste 34A
New York, NY 10028
(212) 980-3800
Fax: (212) 650-1732
Email: rrwolfie@aol.com
Web: www.globalresearchnet.com

Description: We provide our clients with both search and unbundled search research to find and place qualified candidates. Our search research

consists of: targeted contact research, organizational breakouts, and third party contacts.

Key Contact - Specialty:
Mr. Richard R. Wolf, President - *Cross industry & functions*

Salary minimum: $30,000

Functions: Generalist

Industries: Banking, Invest. Banking, Brokers, Pharm Svcs., Accounting, HR Services, Advertising, Insurance, Biotech, Healthcare

Global Research Partnership Inc
130 Garth Rd
PMB 114
Scarsdale, NY 10583-3750
(845) 623-8719
(914) 723-4229
Email: gai@grpi.com
Web: www.grpi.com

Description: We unbundle the executive search process offering whatever part of the process the client wishes to outsource. Our experience is global, with over 50% of our business based in the US.

Key Contact:
Ms. Gai Galitzine, Managing Director
Ms. Betty Wong Tomita, Managing Director

Functions: Generalist

Industries: Mfg., Retail, Services, Media, Communications, Packaging, Real Estate, Software, Biotech

Professional Associations: IACPR, ESRT

GlobalNet Partners Inc
(a Global HealthCare Partners company)
401 N Michigan Ave Ste 1200
Chicago, IL 60611
(312) 840-8229
Fax: (773) 665-8682
Email: brad@globalnetpartners.net
Web: www.globalnetpartners.net

Description: We are a retained executive search and consulting firm specializing in e-Business, health care, consulting, and technology. Our partnering approach, lightning-fast fill times, and uncompromising dedication have honored us with executive searches from many of our industry's leading names.

Key Contact - Specialty:
Mr. Brad Newpoff, CPC, Managing Director - *E-business, health care, technology, consulting*
Mr. Mark Gamboa, Vice President - *Health care, consulting, biotechnology, medical device*

Salary minimum: $100,000

Functions: Senior Mgmt., Healthcare, Physicians, Sales & Mktg., HR Mgmt., Benefits, Training, CFO's, IT, Mgmt. Consultants

Industries: Venture Cap., Pharm Svcs., Mgmt. Consulting, HR Services, E-commerce, Telecoms, Telephony, Digital, Wireless, Insurance, Software, Training SW, Biotech, Healthcare, Hospitals, Long-term Care, Dental, Physical Therapy

Professional Associations: AAHP

F Gloss Int'l
1309 Vincent Pl
McLean, VA 22101
(703) 847-0010
Email: fgi@fgloss.com

Description: Our clientele includes both leading and emerging firms and consultancies in the global e-Commerce, information technology, satellite/telecommunications, aerospace, transportation, and travel/hospitality industries. FGI also assists clients in merger and acquisition, joint

venturing, and organizational development activities, as well as in attracting capital and key personnel for promising start-ups.

Key Contact:
Mr. Fred C. Gloss, President

Salary minimum: $100,000

Functions: Generalist, Directors, Senior Mgmt., Mktg. Mgmt., Sales Mgmt., IT, Mgmt. Consultants, Int'l.

Industries: Generalist, Transportation, Mgmt. Consulting, E-commerce, IT Implementation, Hospitality, Communications, Defense, Aerospace, Software

Glou Int'l Inc
687 Highland Ave
Needham, MA 02494
(781) 449-3310
Fax: (781) 449-3358
Email: glou@glou.com
Web: www.glou.com

Description: Retained executive management searches since 1960. Serving both domestic and international firms specializing in the chemistry of the management team. Also consulting providing people audits, cross-cultural and organizational training and networking services.

Key Contact - Specialty:
Mr. Alan Glou, President - *Management, executives, board members, US & international*

Salary minimum: $80,000

Functions: Senior Mgmt.

Industries: Generalist

Professional Associations: ACG, IEEE, NACD

The Tracy Glover Company
14677 Midway Rd Ste 201
Addison, TX 75001
(972) 866-8181
(972) 386-9696
Email: glover@airmail.net

Description: The firm, with offices in New York and Dallas, provides comprehensive retained search services to the financial services industry with unique expertise to deliver diverse candidates.

Key Contact:
Ms. Tracy Glover, Managing Director
Mr. Alan Michlin, Director of Research

Salary minimum: $150,000

Functions: Generalist, Directors, Senior Mgmt., CFO's, Cash Mgmt., M&A, Risk Mgmt., Minorities

Industries: Generalist, Finance, Banking, Invest. Banking, Brokers, Insurance, Real Estate

The Gobbell Company
1601 Dove St Ste 145
Newport Beach, CA 92660
(949) 476-2258
Fax: (949) 955-2980
Email: jgobbell@pacbell.net

Description: Small, high quality retainer firm specializing in California based clients. Emphasize senior management in: entertainment, publishing, telecommunications, engineering, construction, healthcare, food, aerospace, investment, financial services and real estate.

Key Contact - Specialty:
Mr. John J. Gobbell, President - *Senior management*

Salary minimum: $100,000

Functions: Generalist, Senior Mgmt., Admin. Svcs., HR Mgmt., CFO's, R&D, Engineering

---

† occasional contingency assignments

Industries: Generalist, Computer Equip., Consumer Elect., Transportation, Finance, Hospitality, Aerospace

Robert G Godfrey Associates Ltd[†]
137 N Oak Park Ave Ste 208
PO Box 3392
Oak Park, IL 60301-1334
(708) 771-2374
(708) 763-8984
Fax: (708) 763-9488
Email: info@godfreyassociates.com
Web: www.godfreyassociates.com

Description: Highly personalized national executive search practice with an emphasis on efficient, high quality and professional service. Firm has reputation for long-term placements. Also offers recruitment consulting services to include contract recruitment.

Key Contact - Specialty:
Mr. Robert G. Godfrey, President - *Market research, healthcare, information technology, higher education*

Functions: Generalist

Industries: Finance, Services, Non-profits, Higher Ed., Pharm Svcs.

The Gogates Group Inc
630 5th Ave Fl 20
New York, NY 10111
(212) 355-4117
Email: agogates@optonline.net
Web: www2.cybernex.net/~agogates

Description: We have been executive search specialists for the financial services industry for over 25 years. Our emphasis is on quantitatively oriented research analysts, traders, and money managers for investment banks, hedge funds, and private investment firms.

Key Contact - Specialty:
Mr. Andrew Gogates, President - *Financial services, quantitative analysts, risk management*

Salary minimum: $100,000

Functions: Generalist, Risk Mgmt., R&D

Industries: Generalist, Finance, Banking, Invest. Banking, Brokers, Misc. Financial

Professional Associations: IAFE

The Goldman Group Inc[†]
381 Park Ave S Ste 1520
New York, NY 10016
(212) 685-9311
Fax: (212) 532-2740
Email: elaine@thegoldmangroup.com
Web: www.thegoldmangroup.com

Description: Our firm is one of the largest and fastest growing specialized search firms in the country, specializing in public relations, corporate and marketing communications, advertising, sales, marketing, investor relations, and related fields.

Key Contact:
Ms. Elaine Goldman, President
Ms. Anna Mintzer, Director of Research
Ms. Maria Pell, Recruiter
Mr. Barry Piatoff, Recruiter
Mr. Brett Baron, Recruiter
Mr. Rick Kinigson, Senior Recruiter

Salary minimum: $55,000

Functions: Middle Mgmt., Advertising, Mktg. Mgmt., Sales Mgmt., PR

Industries: Generalist

Professional Associations: IABC, NIRI, PRSA, WPO

Fred J Goldsmith Associates
14056 Margate St
Sherman Oaks, CA 91401
(818) 783-3931
Fax: (818) 907-9724

Description: Executive search - transportation, technology, consumer products, distribution, oil and exploration industries, food services and human resource services.

Key Contact - Specialty:
Mr. Fred J. Goldsmith, President - *Technology, distribution, food, consumer packaged goods, natural resources*

Salary minimum: $80,000

Functions: Generalist, Senior Mgmt., Quality, Distribution, Sales Mgmt., Benefits, CFO's, Mgmt. Consultants

Industries: Generalist, Chemicals, Computer Equip., Transportation, Mgmt. Consulting, HR Services, Software

Professional Associations: PIRA, SHRM

David Gomez & Associates Inc[†]
(also known as iHispano.com)
20 N Clark Ste 2900
Chicago, IL 60602
(312) 346-5525
Fax: (312) 346-1438
Web: www.dgai.com

Description: Our firm is a retained executive search company comprised of four core practices: accounting/finance/tax/consulting, advertising/marketing, human resource, and technology each piloted by our diversity practice. In addition, Mr. Gomez has developed an Internet recruiting site called www.iHispano.com, which is an integral tool for introducing Hispanic professionals to corporate hiring managers.

Key Contact - Specialty:
Mr. David P. Gomez, Founder, Chairman & CEO
Mr. Rudy Martinez, Chief Operating Officer - *Diversity practice*

Salary minimum: $70,000

Functions: General Mgmt.

Industries: Generalist

Professional Associations: CMBDC, LBA, NBMBAA, NCLR, NSHMBA

The Goodman Group
PO Box G
San Rafael, CA 94913-3906
(415) 472-6500
Email: kpub@goodmangroup.com
Web: www.goodmangroup.com

Description: Specialists in information systems and technology, healthcare, insurance, ERP, e-commerce, and vertical market software. Extensive experience locating chief executives, VPs, and senior management for start-up companies, software and technology ventures, and consulting firms. Successful track record in recruitment for sales, marketing, consulting, information systems, operations, and software development.

Key Contact - Specialty:
Mr. Lion Goodman, President - *E-commerce, e-business, management consulting, information systems*

Salary minimum: $100,000

Functions: IT

Industries: Healthcare

Professional Associations: HIMSS

Goodwin & Company
1150 Connecticut Ave NW Ste 200
Washington, DC 20036
(202) 785-9292
Fax: (202) 785-9297
Email: mail@goodwinco.com
Web: www.goodwinco.com

Description: A national executive search firm serving corporate and not-for-profit clients in finance, environmental, advocacy, education and philanthropy.

Key Contact:
Mr. Tom Goodwin, President
Mr. James C. Dudney, Senior Associate

Salary minimum: $70,000

Functions: Generalist, Senior Mgmt., PR, CFO's, Minorities, Non-profits, Environmentalists

Industries: Generalist

GordonTyler
2220 Brandywine St
Philadelphia, PA 19130-3109
(215) 569-2344
Email: fpolaski@gordontyler.com
Web: www.gordontyler.com

Description: Specialists in research and development, technical services and engineering for consumer products and services companies.

Key Contact:
Dr. Fern Polaski

Salary minimum: $85,000

Functions: Product Dev., R&D, Engineering

Industries: Food, Bev., Tobacco, Soap, Perf., Cosmtcs., Drugs Mfg., Packaging, Biotech

Gorfinkle & Dane
140 Wood Rd Ste 200
Braintree, MA 02184
(781) 843-8893
Fax: (781) 848-5102
Email: gayleg@gorfinkleanddane.com
Web: www.gorfinkleanddane.com

Description: We are specialists in logistics and supply chain management. Our clients range from multinational companies to small entrepreneurial firms, including: manufacturers, distributors, transportation companies, third party logistics, and consulting firms. Our president and founder has over 16 years of experience in executive search and management consulting.

Key Contact - Specialty:
Ms. Gayle S. Gorfinkle, President - *Logistics & supply chain management*

Salary minimum: $100,000

Professional Associations: ASTL, CLM, WERC

Gossage Sager Associates LLC
590 Wilmot Rd
Deerfield, IL 60015
(312) 961-5536
Fax: (847) 945-5484
Email: gossagesager@altavista.com
Web: www.com/~dsager/gossage.htm

Description: We are exclusively devoted to executive search in academic, public, school, special and state libraries, in addition to organizations (nonprofits and businesses) that serve libraries.

Key Contact - Specialty:
Mr. Wayne Gossage, Chairman - *Libraries (academic, public, special, state)*
Mr. Joseph Garcia, Associate - *Public libraries, cooperative library systems, organizations that serve libraries*

Mr. Donald J. Sager, President - *Libraries (academic, public, school, special, state), cooperative library systems*
Ms. Muriel Regan, Associate - *Libraries (academic, special)*

Salary minimum: $80,000

Functions: Generalist

Industries: Non-profits, Higher Ed., Government, Non-classifiable

Professional Associations: ALA

Branches:
25 W 43rd St Ste 812
New York, NY 10036
(212) 417-9468
Fax: (212) 997-1127
Key Contact:
Mr. Wayne Gossage, Chairman

Gould, McCoy & Chadick Inc
300 Park Ave
New York, NY 10022
(212) 688-8671
Fax: (212) 308-4510
Email: gmc@gmcsearch.com
Web: www.gouldmccoychadick.com

Description: Executive search firm providing comprehensive services to corporations in the identification, assessment and selection of their management personnel. Known for our thoroughness, our assessment ability and quality of our service.

Key Contact:
Mr. William E. Gould, Managing Director - *Generalist (senior level), international*
Ms. Millington F. McCoy, Managing Director - *Generalist (senior level), financial services*
Ms. Susan L. Chadick, Managing Director - *Generalist (senior level), human resources, financial services (all functions)*
Ms. Janice Reals Ellig, Managing Director
Mr. Van G. Young, Managing Director

Salary minimum: $150,000

Functions: Generalist

Industries: Generalist

Professional Associations: AESC, IACPR, HRPS, SHRM

GR Search Inc
(formerly known as Geddes + Rubin Management Inc)
10 Bay St Water Park Pl Ste 1500
Toronto, ON M5J 2R8
Canada
(416) 365-7770
(888)
Fax: (416) 365-7669
Email: gr@grsearch.com
Web: www.grsearch.com

Description: We provide expedient and creative, competency-based, and research-based executive search and selection services for mid to senior level positions in most functional areas and industry sectors.

Key Contact - Specialty:
Mr. Murray Geddes, Partner - *Generalist*
Mr. Ron Rubin, Partner - *Generalist, sales & marketing*

Salary minimum: $50,000

Functions: Generalist

Industries: Generalist

Professional Associations: ASAE, CSAE, HRPAO

Branches:
469 Besserer St
Ottawa, ON K1N 6C2
Canada
(613) 241-2799
Fax: (613) 241-2738
Email: gb@grsearch.com
Key Contact:
Mr. Gerry Bedard, Senior Search Consultant

Graham & Company[†]
10 Saugatuck Ave
Westport, CT 06880
(203) 291-7949
Fax: (203) 341-9704
Email: rachaelsdad@prodigy.net

Description: Client sensitive. Highly focused. Thorough research. Timely and cost conscious results. Attention to detail and subtleties of each assignment. Impeccable integrity and discretion.

Key Contact - Specialty:
Mr. Robert J. Graham, Principal - *Human resources, marketing, financial, communications, corporate attorneys*

Salary minimum: $100,000

Functions: PR, HR Mgmt., Finance

Industries: Generalist

Graham & Company
36 Beach Rd
PO Box 239
Monmouth Beach, NJ 07750
(732) 263-0088
Fax: (732) 222-0804
Email: hscott35@aol.com

Description: Executive search firm with a diversified portfolio of clients in traditional and technology-driven organizations handling executive management assignments in most functional areas.

Key Contact - Specialty:
Mr. Harold Scott, President - *Manufacturing, automotive OE parts (all levels, all positions), specialty chemicals*

Salary minimum: $60,000

Functions: Generalist, Middle Mgmt., Production, Plant Mgmt., Quality, Purchasing, Materials Plng.

Industries: Generalist, Plastics, Rubber, Metal Products, Motor Vehicles

Professional Associations: EMA

Robert Graham Associates
PO Box 1320
Portsmouth, RI 02871-1320
(401) 682-2277
Email: bob51832@aol.com

Description: We are an experienced generalist firm that serves most industries and functions. We place heavy financial/CFOs controllers. We represent Fortune ten firms in area of business development consulting. We also specialize in marketing and human resources/communications and public relations

Key Contact - Specialty:
Mr. Robert W. Graham, Owner - *CFOs, COO's, VP finance, controller, consultants*

Salary minimum: $100,000

Functions: Generalist, Senior Mgmt., Health Admin., Mktg. Mgmt., CFO's

Industries: Generalist, Misc. Mfg., Finance, Banking, HR Services, Healthcare

---

Granger, Counts & Associates
728 Trade Sq W
Troy, OH 45373
(937) 339-1119

Description: Highly responsive search firm for management, professional and technical personnel.

Key Contact:
Mr. Robert L. Counts, President

Salary minimum: $50,000

Functions: Generalist, Senior Mgmt., Plant Mgmt., Materials Plng., Mktg. Mgmt., Personnel, CFO's, Engineering

Industries: Generalist, Food, Bev., Tobacco, Machine, Appliance, Motor Vehicles, Misc. Mfg., Misc. Financial, Accounting

---

A Davis Grant & Company
295 Pierson Ave
Edison, NJ 08837
(732) 494-2266
Fax: (732) 494-3626
Email: info@adg.net
Web: www.adg.net

Description: Executive search firm dedicated exclusively to information systems and technology professionals from project management through chief information officers.

Key Contact - Specialty:
Mr. Allan D. Grossman, Senior Partner - *CIO's, information technology executives*
Ms. Lynn Lewis, Senior Partner - *Senior management, information technology*

Salary minimum: $100,000

Functions: IT, MIS Mgmt., Systems Analysis, Systems Dev., Systems Implem., Systems Support

Industries: Generalist

Professional Associations: IACPR, SIM

Grant Cooper & Associates Inc
9900 Clayton Rd Ste B
St. Louis, MO 63124-1102
(314) 567-4694
Email: mail@grantcooper.com
Web: www.grantcooper.com

Description: Executive search consultants specializing in upper and middle management searches for almost 45 years. Broad experience in most industries including financial services, technology, biotechnology, manufacturing, healthcare, retail and not-for-profit, including most investment banking and capital markets disciplines.

Key Contact:
Ms. Cynthia J. Kohlbry, Managing Principal - *Financial services, e-commerce, technology*
Mr. Kent Rapp, Managing Principal
Mr. James Schmidt, Managing Principal
Mr. Tom M. Horlacher, Principal - *Durable goods manufacturing, technology*
Mr. Stephen Robin, Principal - *E-commerce, media, communications, public relations,*
Mr. John Garavaglia, Principal - *Food, beverage*
Mr. Stephen H. Loeb, Principal - *Generalist, manufacturing*
Mr. J. Dale Meier, Principal - *Generalist*
Ms. Carolyn McCall, Consultant
Ms. Nancy William, Consultant

Salary minimum: $100,000

Functions: Senior Mgmt.

Industries: Mfg., Wholesale, Retail, Finance, Services, Hospitality, Media, Aerospace, Biotech, Healthcare

Professional Associations: IACPR, ACG

Branches:
540 Madison Ave Fl 17
New York, NY 10021
(800) 886-4690
Email: fjirobin@grantcooper.com
Key Contact - Specialty:
Mr. Richard L. Anderson, Principal - *Generalist, retail, distribution*

Grantham, Griffin & Buck Inc
161 Weaver Dairy Rd
Chapel Hill, NC 27514
(919) 932-5650
Fax: (919) 942-1624
Email: info@ggbinc.com
Web: www.integritycareers.com

Description: We are a small, intensive generalist firm, which is highly responsive to client needs, with over 22 years of search experience serving North America. We have strong long-term relationships with our clients.

Key Contact:
Mr. John D. Grantham, President - *COOs, CFOs, general managers, senior vice presidents, vice presidents of marketing*
Mr. Charlie Griffin, Vice President
Mr. John Buck, Vice President

Salary minimum: $95,000

Functions: Generalist, Senior Mgmt., Purchasing, Mkt. Research, Benefits, Personnel, CFO's, R&D

Industries: Generalist, Energy, Utilities, Mfg., Retail, Finance, Aerospace, Packaging

Annie Gray Associates Inc
516 S Hanley
St. Louis, MO 63105
(314) 721-0205
Fax: (314) 721-0948
Email: resume@anniegray.com
Web: www.anniegray.com

Description: We are a boutique firm exclusive to representing the leading corporations and non-profits in the Greater St. Louis area. Our candidate selection is conducted world-wide.

Key Contact:
Ms. Annie Gray, President

Salary minimum: $100,000

Functions: Generalist, Directors, Senior Mgmt., Mfg., CFO's, Non-profits

Industries: Generalist

Graystone Partners LLC
62 Southfield Ave Ste 204
Stamford, CT 06902
(203) 323-0023
Email: contact@graystonepartners.com
Web: www.graystonepartners.com

Description: Nationally known firm specializing in general management, financial officer (CFO, controller, treasury, risk management and internal audit) and consulting/public accounting assignments. Serving all industries including Internet and e-commerce.

Key Contact - Specialty:
Mr. Gregory L. Ohman, Managing Director - *General management, financial officers, consulting*

Salary minimum: $125,000

Functions: Generalist, Senior Mgmt., Mktg. Mgmt., CFO's, Risk Mgmt., Mgmt. Consultants

Industries: Generalist, Transportation, Banking, Venture Cap., Accounting, Mgmt. Consulting, New Media

R Green & Associates Inc
1 S St. Clair St
Toledo, OH 43602
(419) 249-2800
Fax: (419) 249-2803
Email: retain@rgreen.com
Web: www.rgreen.com

Description: Our retained and customized executive search service is appreciated by mostly Fortune 500 manufacturing clients. Our candidate base is very

select and limited to the nation's top performers. We represent growing and profitable clients who are searching for leaders to advance their companies.

Key Contact - Specialty:
Ms. Rita Green, CPC, President - *Generalist*
Ms. Tina Kern, Search Director - *Accounting, human resources*
Mr. Michael Liebenthal, Search Director - *Manufacturing, operations*

Salary minimum: $100,000

Functions: Senior Mgmt.

Industries: Mfg., Plastics, Rubber, Metal Products, Motor Vehicles, Computer Equip., Consumer Elect., Misc. Mfg.

Networks: National Personnel Assoc (NPA)

Greenhaven and Partner Inc
60 E 42nd St Suite 1263
New York, NY 10165
(212) 984-0747
Fax: (212) 972-7036
Email: resumesforGSC@bigfoot.com

Description: Retained search firm nationally placing high technology, publishing professionals and management consultants. $75,000 and up.

Key Contact - Specialty:
Mr. Chris Marshall, Jr. - *Sales & marketing, computers, telecommunications*
Mr. Chester P. Evans, III - *Management consulting*
Mr. Bennett "Andy" Ellis - *Publishing*

Salary minimum: $75,000

Functions: Directors, Finance, MIS Mgmt.

Industries: Mfg., Wholesale, Retail, Finance

A Greenstein & Company
20 Vernon St
Vernon Office Ctr
Norwood, MA 02062
(781) 769-4966

Description: We provide unbundled services, including: research and/or telephone screening, as well as a full-service search. We charge hourly for unbundled services and 30% for full-service. Our clients are primarily in the high-tech, biomedical and financial services industries.

Key Contact - Specialty:
Ms. Arlene Bachant, President - *Engineering, information technology, general management*

Functions: General Mgmt.

Industries: Computer Equip., Banking, Invest. Banking, Brokers

Professional Associations: NEHRA

Greger/Peterson Associates Inc
22208 Skyview Dr
West Linn, OR 97068
(503) 655-4100
Fax: (503) 655-4600
Email: jsp@gregerpeterson.com

Description: Retained only. Culture-sensitive, organizational approach dedicated to quality results and client service. General practice - hospitality/leisure and entertainment/new media specialty.

Key Contact - Specialty:
Mr. Kenneth R. Greger, Founder/Managing Director - *Hospitality, entertainment, new media*
Mr. John S. Peterson, Managing Director - *Hospitality, senior executives*

Salary minimum: $150,000

Functions: Generalist, Senior Mgmt., Mktg. Mgmt., Sales Mgmt., CFO's

Industries: Generalist, Hospitality, New Media

Professional Associations: AHMA

Greywolf Consulting Service Inc
811 Barton Springs Rd Ste 807
Austin, TX 78704
(512) 320-8100
Fax: (512) 320-8220
Email: info@greywolfconsulting.com
Web: www.greywolfconsulting.com

Description: Retained search firm practice specializing in nationwide mid- to senior-level management/executive assignments in leading edge technology industries, including semiconductor, capital equipment, communications and CAE.

Key Contact:
Mr. Kim Butler

C John Grom Executive Search Inc
868 Thelma Dr
Wadsworth, OH 44281
(330) 336-2213
Fax: (330) 336-2035
Email: ribrom@aol.com
Web:
www.commerce.prodigybiz.com/customer/cjohngro mexecutivesearchinc

Description: We recruit at the CEO, COO, CFO, and VP level for a variety of industries. Some of our most recent active clients are private equity firms are looking for leadership for new acquisitions.

Key Contact - Specialty:
Mr. C. John Grom, Principal - *Manufacturing, marketing, finance, human resources*

Salary minimum: $100,000

Functions: Generalist, General Mgmt., Senior Mgmt., Middle Mgmt., Plant Mgmt., Sales & Mktg., HR Mgmt., CFO's

Industries: Generalist, Mfg., Transportation, Finance, Services, Telecoms, Software, Biotech, Healthcare

Grossberg & Associates
1100 Jorie Blvd Ste 221
Oak Brook, IL 60523
(630) 574-0066
Email: bobgsearch@aol.com

Description: Human resource professionals whose sole function is to assist clients in developing a talented management staff.

Key Contact - Specialty:
Mr. Robert M. Grossberg, Managing Partner - *Generalist*
Mr. Bob Williamson, Associate - *Marketing, sales*

Salary minimum: $75,000

Functions: Mfg., Materials, Sales & Mktg., HR Mgmt., Finance, Engineering

Industries: Mfg., Plastics, Rubber, Metal Products, Machine, Appliance, Motor Vehicles, Misc. Mfg., Services, Packaging, Marketing SW

Professional Associations: EMA, SHRM, SHRP

Groton Planning Group
5 Bradford Rd
Wiscasset, ME 04578
(207) 882-6001
Fax: (207) 882-6832
Email: sjk@midcoast.com

Description: Sole practitioner.

Key Contact:
Mr. Stephan J. Kornacki, Principal

Functions: Sales & Mktg.

Industries: Drugs Mfg., Communications, Software, Biotech, Healthcare

Groves & Partners Int'l
1401 Daniel Creek Rd
Mississauga, ON L5V 1V3
Canada
(905) 567-9247
Fax: (905) 567-9469
Email: barry@grovesintl.com
Web: www.grovesintl.com

Description: We recruit for all of the strategic
requirements of today's logistics, distribution and
transportation fields. We recruit for private and
public corporations, third party/distribution
providers and major transportation companies.

Key Contact - Specialty:
Mr. Barry Groves, Partner - *Logistics,
transportation*

Salary minimum: $40,000

Functions: Generalist, General Mgmt., Materials,
Sales & Mktg., HR Mgmt., Finance

Industries: Generalist, Mfg., Transportation, Retail,
Equip Svcs., Mgmt. Consulting, HR Services,
Non-classifiable

Professional Associations: SCL

Growth Consultants of America
PO Box 158544
Nashville, TN 37215
(847) 589-9030
Email: john-haggard@john-haggard.com

Description: We place sales and sales management
executives in the office supplies industry.

Key Contact - Specialty:
Mr. John H. Haggard, Jr., President - *Office supply
industry*

Salary minimum: $60,000

Functions: Middle Mgmt., Sales Mgmt.

Industries: Retail

Growth Strategies Inc†
5448 Estate Oak Cir
Hollywood, FL 33312
(954) 989-2425
Email: steven@vaxainc.com

Description: We have international experience in
working with many segments of the high-
technology industry to provide senior and middle
management leadership with functional expertise in
sales, marketing, corporate development and
management consulting.

Key Contact - Specialty:
Mr. Steve Nathasingh, Managing Director - *High
technology, general management*

Salary minimum: $60,000

Functions: Generalist, Senior Mgmt., Mktg. Mgmt.,
Sales Mgmt., M&A, MIS Mgmt., Mgmt.
Consultants, Int'l.

Industries: Generalist, Computer Equip., Consumer
Elect., Mgmt. Consulting, New Media, Telecoms,
Biotech

GSL Executive Search
1155 University Ave Ste 505
Montreal, QC H3B 3A7
Canada
(514) 878-1199
Fax: (514) 878-1940
Email: gsl@gslexec.com

Description: The three associates in our firm
combine more than 30 years of experience in
executive search. We merged our three separate
practices in early 1997 to become the fastest
growing executive search firm in the province of
Quebec. We recently hired a senior consultant to
handle the IT and financial services sectors. We are

members of The International Recruitment
Consultants (IRC), a dynamic group of independent,
executive search firms active in ten countries.

Key Contact:
Mr. Jean Gaudry, Associate
Mr. Marc Levasseur, Associate
Mr. Gilles Shink, Associate

Salary minimum: $65,000

Functions: Generalist, Mfg., Materials, Sales &
Mktg., HR Mgmt., Finance, Engineering

Industries: Generalist, Agri., Forestry, Mining,
Mfg., Finance, Media, Aerospace, Packaging

GSW Consulting Group Inc
1390 Sioux Trl
Reno, NV 89511-9015
(775) 853-7900
Fax: (775) 853-2221

Description: Provide executive search, executive
compensation and organization planning consulting
services to senior management, primarily in the
U.S., U.K., Europe and Latin America.

Key Contact - Specialty:
Mr. Joel M. Winitz, President - *Executive, senior
management, corporate directors*

Salary minimum: $100,000

Functions: General Mgmt., Directors, Senior
Mgmt., Finance, CFO's

Industries: Generalist, Mfg., Medical Devices,
Computer Equip., Telecoms, Software, Biotech

Wolf Gugler & Associates Ltd
1370 Don Mills Rd Ste 300
Toronto, ON M3B 3N7
Canada
(416) 386-1719
(800) 830-1090
Email: admin@wolfgugler.com
Web: www.wolfgugler.com

Description: We have fifteen years' expertise in
retainer-based executive search and management
appraisals of top performers. We have in-depth
knowledge of home improvement and hardlines,
retailers, and their suppliers. We have also had
significant work also performed in the sales and
marketing disciplines. Candidate self-assessments
are also available on our web site.

Key Contact - Specialty:
Ms. Maria Vieria, Business Manager-Canada
Mr. Wolf Gugler, President - *Sales & marketing,
retailer, supplier, hardware, house wares*

Salary minimum: $55,000

Functions: Senior Mgmt., Middle Mgmt.

Industries: Lumber, Furniture, Paints, Petro.
Products, Machine, Appliance, Consumer Elect.,
Wholesale, Retail, Services, Advertising, HR SW,
Mfg. SW, Marketing SW

Professional Associations: CHHMA, RCC, SMEI

Branches:
1000 W Wilshire
Oklahoma City, OK 73116
(405) 848-3006
(800) 830-1090
Email: admin@wolfgugler.com
Key Contact:
Ms. Linn Henderson, Business Manager

Guidarelli Associates Inc
2933 W John Beers Rd
Stevensville, MI 49127
(616) 429-7001
Fax: (616) 429-7003
Email: shelley@guidarelli.com
Web: www.guidarelli.com

Description: As hiring consultants to the consumer
goods industry, we specialize in mid- and senior-
management marketing talent for $50M companies
to Fortune 100's. This unique niche enables our
consistent involvement with top, classically trained
careers in the industry. We are a cohesive, results
oriented, retained firm. We target mutually valued,
long term client/candidate relationships.

Key Contact - Specialty:
Ms. Shelley Guidarelli, President - *Consumer
products marketing*

Salary minimum: $75,000

Functions: Mktg. Mgmt.

Industries: Food, Bev., Tobacco, Soap, Perf.,
Cosmtcs., Drugs Mfg.

Guidry & East Healthcare Search Consultants†
2018 Island Oak St
Houston, TX 77062
(281) 218-7000
Fax: (281) 218-7977
Email: jim@guidryeast.com
Web: www.guidryeast.com

Description: Client-retained medical and healthcare
searches and related consulting services in
recruiting executives and middle-management.

Key Contact - Specialty:
Mr. Jim Guidry, President - *Administrative,
department directors, healthcare*

Salary minimum: $50,000

Functions: General Mgmt., Directors, Senior
Mgmt., Middle Mgmt.

Industries: Healthcare, Hospitals

Professional Associations: ACHE

Gundersen Partners LLC
30 Irving Pl Fl 2
New York, NY 10003
(212) 677-7660
Fax: (212) 358-0275
Email: lpm@gpllc.com
Web: www.gundersenpartners.com

Description: Specializes in all facets of consumer
marketing. Blue chip client base includes multinational corporations and advertising, direct
marketing, marketing services agencies.

Key Contact - Specialty:
Mr. Steven G. Gundersen, CEO - *Advertising,
general management*
Ms. Tina Moore, Managing Partner - *Creative
services*
Mr. Dennis Troyanos, Principal - *Direct marketing*
Mr. Jeff Gundersen, Principal - *Financial services,
branding*
Ms. Linda Schaler, Principal - *Advertising*
Mr. Peter Fitzpatrick, President - *International,
financial services*
Mr. Norm Sherman, Principal - *Advertising,
general management*

Salary minimum: $100,000

Functions: General Mgmt., Sales & Mktg.

Industries: Generalist, Consumer Elect., Services,
Advertising, New Media

Professional Associations: ACNY, ADC, AIGA,
AWNY, DMA, DMCNY, IAA, IMC, SHRM

Branches:
100 W Long Lake Rd Ste 121
Bloomfield Hills, MI 48304
(248) 258-3800
Fax: (248) 258-9747
Email: edtazzia@mindspring.com
Key Contact - Specialty:
Mr. John Bissell, Managing Partner - *Corporate
marketing*

---

† occasional contingency assignments

Let www.ExecutiveAgent.com e-mail your resume now.

Mr. Ed Tazzia, Managing Director - *Corporate marketing, technology*

Gustin Partners Ltd
2276 Washington St
The Ware Mill
Newton Lower Falls, MA 02462-1452
(617) 332-0800
Fax: (617) 332-0882
Email: info@gustinpartners.com
Web: www.gustinpartners.com

Description: Highly specialized, senior-level expertise in executive and entire management team selection within the information technology industry. All engagements executed by senior partners. Clients range from early-stage to Fortune 500 worldwide.

Key Contact:
Ms. Vivian C. Brocard, Executive Vice President
Mr. Charles Gustin, Chairman and Chief Executive Officer
Mr. Andrew M. Rafey, Vice President
Mr. Paul deGive, Vice President
Mr. Michael Carvey, Vice President

Salary minimum: $150,000

Functions: Generalist, Senior Mgmt., Mktg. Mgmt., Sales Mgmt., CFO's, MIS Mgmt., Systems Implem., Int'l.

Industries: Generalist, Computer Equip., Venture Cap., Mgmt. Consulting, New Media, Telecoms, Software

GWS Partners
PO Box 43046
Chicago, IL 60643
(219) 864-8380
Fax: (219) 864-8364
Email: gsilver123@aol.com
Web: www.gwspartners.com

Description: Practice focuses on conducting senior-level management and board director search engagements for Fortune 500 corporations.

Key Contact - Specialty:
Mr. Gary Silverman, Managing Partner - *Senior management, board of directors*

Salary minimum: $200,000

Functions: Senior Mgmt.

Industries: Generalist

Gynn Associates Inc
100 N Tampa St Ste 3770
Tampa, FL 33602
(813) 221-7410
Fax: (813) 221-7401
Email: gynnsearch@aol.com
Web: www.gynn.com

Description: Proven ability to interpret the operational and organizational needs of clients while attracting, assessing and acquiring the human solution required to attain the business objectives of the client.

Key Contact - Specialty:
Mr. Walter T. Gynn, President - *Real estate, construction, manufacturing*

Salary minimum: $100,000

Functions: Generalist, General Mgmt., Directors, Senior Mgmt., Middle Mgmt., Sales & Mktg., Mktg. Mgmt., Sales Mgmt., HR Mgmt., CFO's

Industries: Construction, Real Estate

Professional Associations: ULI

Haddad Associates
PO Box 462
Tarpon Springs, FL 34688-0462
(727) 939-8078
Fax: (727) 934-4322
Email: rjhaddad@gte.net
Web: www.haddadassociates.com

Description: Small executive search firm providing retained search services for mid- and senior management positions. General practice. Emphasis in consulting industries.

Key Contact:
Mr. Ronald J. Haddad, President

Salary minimum: $100,000

Functions: Generalist

Industries: Generalist, Mgmt. Consulting

Hadley Lockwood Inc
17 State St Fl 38
New York, NY 10004
(212) 785-4405
Fax: (212) 785-4415
Email: info@hadleylockwood.com

Description: Executive search and recruitment for financial and investment companies, with concentration in investment banking, capital markets, securities research and retail regional and branch management. Consulting services regarding entire reorganizations, additional departments and new businesses for the same client.

Key Contact - Specialty:
Mr. Irwin Brandon, President - *Securities (all functions)*
Mr. George McGough, Vice President - *Securities (all functions)*

Salary minimum: $100,000

Functions: Generalist

Industries: Finance, Invest. Banking, Brokers, Venture Cap., Misc. Financial

Haggerman & Associates
3447 S Campbell
Springfield, MO 65807
(417) 881-8639
Fax: (417) 889-6176
Email: hrpeople@aol.com

Description: Human resources consulting firm.

Key Contact:
Ms. Lynne Haggerman, President/Owner

Functions: HR Mgmt.

Industries: Generalist

Professional Associations: SHRM

Halbrecht Lieberman Associates Inc
1200 Summer St Ste 304
Stamford, CT 06905
(203) 327-5630
Fax: (203) 327-0187
Email: admin@hlassoc.com
Web: www.hlassoc.com

Description: We are specialists in information management, telecommunications, advanced technologies, e-Commerce, business process reengineering, and strategic and management consulting. We are a general management executive search for high-tech firms.

Key Contact - Specialty:
Ms. Beverly Lieberman, President - *Information technology, executives*
Mr. David Olsen, Senior Vice President - *Information technology executives*
Mr. Roger Rowell, Vice President/CIO - *Information management, operations*

Salary minimum: $175,000

Functions: IT, MIS Mgmt.

Industries: Generalist

Professional Associations: AESC, SIM, WBDC, WIM

Hale & Estrada LLC
5 Erba Ln D
Scotts Valley, CA 95066
(831) 461-1800
Fax: (831) 461-1801
Email: info@hale-estrada.com
Web: www.hale-estrada.com

Description: Over 25 years of executive recruiting in high-tech and public sector. Search capabilities includes assessment tools and ability to deliver the broadest pool of candidates representing today's diverse marketplace.

Key Contact - Specialty:
Ms. Barbara Estrada, Senior Partner - *Senior management, high technology, biotech, diversity*
Mr. Dick Hale, Senior Partner - *Senior management, high technology, biotech*

Salary minimum: $100,000

Functions: General Mgmt.

Industries: Finance, Digital, Wireless, Government, Software, HR SW, Marketing SW, Networking, Comm. SW, Biotech, Healthcare

Professional Associations: FWE, NCHRA, NHEA

Hale Associates
1816 N Sedgwick St
Chicago, IL 60614
(312) 337-3288
Fax: (312) 337-3451

Description: We service the executive search industry and specialize in research and sourcing services. The firm customizes these services to meet client needs.

Key Contact - Specialty:
Ms. Maureen D. Hale, President - *General management, senior executives*

Salary minimum: $50,000

Functions: Generalist, Senior Mgmt., Mktg. Mgmt., Sales Mgmt., CFO's, Cash Mgmt., Mgmt. Consultants

Industries: Generalist, Metal Products, Banking, Invest. Banking, Brokers, Accounting, Mgmt. Consulting

Professional Associations: RR

K C Hale Inc
PO Box 1215
Avon, CT 06001
(860) 677-7511
Fax: (860) 677-0354

Description: We have extensive search capability and experience in domestic and international asset management, retirement services, and healthcare. We focus on sales, marketing, and operations positions.

Key Contact:
Ms. Kathryn Hale Dumanis, President
Ms. Kathleen M. McCormack, Vice President

Salary minimum: $100,000

Functions: Generalist, Directors, Senior Mgmt., Mkt. Research, Sales Mgmt., Risk Mgmt.

Industries: Generalist, Invest. Banking, Brokers, Misc. Financial, Accounting, HR Services, Insurance, Healthcare

Michael J Hall & Company†
19880 NE 7th Ave Ste D
Poulsbo, WA 98370
(360) 598-3700
Fax: (360) 598-3703
Email: hallco@aejob.com
Web: www.aejob.com

Description: We are a management consulting firm
to the A/E industry. Our recruiting group was added
in 1994 and has become a vital service to many of
our clients.

Key Contact - Specialty:
Ms. Sheila Brown-Alcala, Recruiting Manager -
Architectural, engineering (managers, specialists)
Mr. Michael J. Hall, President - *Architectural,
engineering executives*
Ms. Sandee Watson, Recruiter - *Architects,
planners*
Ms. Krysten Bernard, Recruiter - *Civil engineers,
electrical engineers, structural engineers,
mechanical engineers*

Salary minimum: $24,000

Functions: Generalist, Mktg. Mgmt., Sales Mgmt.,
CFO's, Engineering, Environmentalists,
Architects, Technicians

Industries: Generalist, Energy, Utilities,
Construction, Transportation, Environmental
Svcs., Haz. Waste, Non-classifiable

The Halyburton Company Inc
6201 Fairview Rd Ste 200
Charlotte, NC 28210
(704) 556-9892
Email: halyburton@aol.com
Web: www.halyburtonco.com

Description: We offer search experience in most
industries and disciplines. We strive for excellence
in representing our clients and in evaluating
prospective candidates.

Key Contact - Specialty:
Mr. Robert R. Halyburton, President - *Senior level
management*

Salary minimum: $80,000

Functions: Senior Mgmt., Plant Mgmt., Sales &
Mktg., HR Mgmt., CFO's

Industries: Generalist, Agri., Forestry, Mining,
Mfg., Lumber, Furniture, Plastics, Rubber, Metal
Products, Misc. Mfg.

The Hamilton Group
14406 Seneca Rd
Germantown, MD 20874-3332
(301) 530-9407
Email: boguski@erols.com
Web: www.hamiltongroup.com

Description: Clients consist of Fortune 500, venture
capital funded/emerging companies in the high-
technology industry. Partners, former executives
from industry, serve as advisors to board of
directors, presidents, CEOs and senior management.

Key Contact - Specialty:
Mr. Ronald T. Boguski, Partner - *Senior level
executives, professional services,
telecommunications, network computing, software*

Salary minimum: $125,000

Functions: Generalist, Directors, Senior Mgmt.,
Mfg., Sales & Mktg., CFO's, MIS Mgmt.

Industries: Generalist, Computer Equip., Test,
Measure Equip., Electronic, Elec. Components,
Telecoms, Digital, Wireless, Fiber Optic,
Aerospace, Software, Mfg. SW

Professional Associations: ACG

Hamilton Partners
1 Gorham Island
Westport, CT 06880
(203) 221-9111
Fax: (203) 221-9190
Web: www.hamiltonpartners.cc

Description: We have built our Firm one stone at a
time, ensuring that each new principal shares similar
philosophies and has complementary skills and
experience. Our Firm today has nine principals who
possess a diverse set of experiences and expertise in
executive search, strategy development, human
resources practices, leadership and change
management consulting, as well as broad
operational and human resources line management.

Key Contact:
Mr. Peter Murphy, Principal
Mrs. Dawn Sullivan, Principal
Mr. James Calvan, Principal

Salary minimum: $150,000

Functions: General Mgmt., Senior Mgmt., Mktg.
Mgmt., HR Mgmt., CFO's, IT

Industries: Generalist, Food, Bev., Tobacco, Paper,
Computer Equip., Consumer Elect., Venture Cap.,
IT Implementation, Entertainment, Publishing,
Telecoms, Wireless

Hamilton-Chase & Associates Inc
Seaport Professional Bldg
PO Box 237
Gloucester, MA 01930
(978) 281-1759
Email: jrusso@hamilton-chase.com
Web: www.hamilton-chase.com

Description: Executive and technical search firm
specializing in high-technology. Client
organizations range in size from start-ups to Fortune
500. It employs quantitative interviewing/reference
checking methodology, significantly improving
candidate selection.

Key Contact - Specialty:
Mr. Joseph E. Russo, President - *Generalist*

Salary minimum: $100,000

Functions: Generalist, General Mgmt., Mfg., Sales
& Mktg., HR Mgmt., Finance, IT, Engineering

Industries: Generalist, Mfg., Finance, Media,
Aerospace, Software, Biotech

Branches:
76 Bedford St Custance Pl Ste 18
Lexington, MA 02173
(781) 863-2811
Fax: (508) 281-8023
Key Contact - Specialty:
Mr. Joseph E. Russo, President - *Generalist*

Hamilton-Ryker
698 Perimeter Dr Ste 200
Lexington, KY 40517
(859) 266-5000
Fax: (859) 269-8711
Web: www.hamilton-ryker.com

Description: Firm specializes in search activities for
engineers and manufacturing, data processing,
banking and finance, personnel, all disciplines. Also
outplacement, management consulting and
temporary staffing.

Key Contact:
Mr. Wayne McCreight, Owner
Ms. Shannon Holleran, Regional Vice President

Salary minimum: $40,000

Functions: Generalist, Senior Mgmt., Mfg.,
Purchasing, Mktg. Mgmt., HR Mgmt., Finance

Industries: Generalist, Motor Vehicles, Finance,
Accounting, HR Services, Media, Insurance

Professional Associations: AMA, IMC, SHRM

R C Handel Associates Inc
117 New London Tpke
Glastonbury Common
Glastonbury, CT 06033
(860) 633-3900
Email: rch3900@aol.com

Description: A firm focused upon client service. In
addition to providing professional search and
staffing related consulting, we will tailor our service
to the specific needs of the client.

Key Contact:
Mr. Richard C. Handel, Jr., President

Salary minimum: $70,000

Functions: Generalist

Industries: Mfg., Finance, Banking, Invest.
Banking, Misc. Financial, Insurance

W L Handler & Associates
2255 Cumberland Pkwy NW Bldg 1500
Atlanta, GA 30339
(770) 805-5000
Fax: (770) 805-5020
Email: info@wlhandler.com
Web: www.wlhandler.com

Description: We place middle and senior
management and technical positions. We are noted
for rapid response, unique fee schedule, and high
percent of completion. All of our assignments are
performance guaranteed. Our results are satisfied or
your money back. Unconditional employment is
guaranteed.

Key Contact - Specialty:
Mr. William L. Handler - *Generalist*

Salary minimum: $100,000

Functions: Generalist, General Mgmt., Mfg.,
Materials, Sales & Mktg., HR Mgmt., Finance, IT

Industries: Generalist, Mfg., Finance, Services,
Media

Networks: World Search Group

Handley Group Inc
2370 York Rd
Jamison, PA 18929
(215) 491-4800
Fax: (215) 491-0500
Email: rrodenbaugh@handley.com
Web: www.handley.com

Description: Senior Executive search for the
healthcare industry. Specializing in medical devices,
diagnostics, biotechnology and biopharmaceuticals.

Key Contact - Specialty:
Mr. Robert Rodenbaugh, Managing Partner -
Healthcare

Salary minimum: $100,000

Functions: General Mgmt., Directors, Senior
Mgmt., Sales & Mktg., Mktg. Mgmt.

Industries: Generalist, Drugs Mfg., Medical
Devices, Biotech, Healthcare

Handy Associates Corp
(also known as Handy Partners)
420 Lexington Ave Ste 1644
New York, NY 10017
(212) 697-5600
Fax: (212) 697-8547
Email: pbrennan@handypartners.com
Web: www.handypartners.com

Description: We serve all major industries
including advertising, consumer packaged goods,
publishing, finance/investment banking, insurance,
manufacturing, pharmaceuticals,
telecommunications, e-commerce, the international
maritime and transportation industries and
information technology.

Key Contact - Specialty:
Mr. Patrick J. Brennan, Managing Partner - *Banking, finance*
Mr. Gaffney J. Feskoe, Partner - *International maritime industry, finance*
Mr. Chester A. Hopkins, Partner - *General management, marketing, corporate communications*
Mr. R. Kevin Hughes, Partner - *HR, compensation, finance*

Salary minimum: $100,000

Functions: General Mgmt., Senior Mgmt., Mfg., Production, Advertising, Mktg. Mgmt., CFO's, MIS Mgmt., Network Admin., Minorities

Industries: Generalist

Hanley & Associates
800 Laurel Oak Dr Ste 200
Naples, FL 34108
(941) 643-7474
Email: hainaples@aol.com
Web: www.hanleyassociates.com

Description: Special strengths in placing middle and upper-management, information technology managers in medical/healthcare, financial services and high-technology industries.

Key Contact:
Ms. Dorothy Hanley, President
Mr. Jim Lowrie, Vice President

Salary minimum: $75,000

Functions: Generalist, General Mgmt., Healthcare, Finance, IT, MIS Mgmt.

Industries: Generalist, Banking, Mgmt. Consulting, IT Implementation, Insurance, Software, Healthcare

W Hanley & Associates
230 Park Ave
Box 202
New York, NY 10163-0202
(212) 661-6060
(914) 472-4441

Description: Four-decade-old firm with particular strength in financial recruiting.

Key Contact - Specialty:
Mr. J. Patrick Hanley, Partner - *Generalist*
Mr. Richard T. Hanley, Partner - *Finance*

Salary minimum: $100,000

Functions: Generalist

Industries: Generalist

Hansen Executive Search Inc
1629 S 152nd St
Omaha, NE 68144
(402) 697-7960
Fax: (402) 697-7959

Description: Executive recruitment in consumer packaged goods, specializing in sales/marketing management, MIS, manufacturing and general management.

Key Contact - Specialty:
Mr. James P. Hansen, President - *Consumer packaged goods (sales & marketing, operations, general management)*

Salary minimum: $50,000

Functions: Generalist, General Mgmt., Sales & Mktg., Advertising, Mkt. Research, Mktg. Mgmt., Sales Mgmt.

Industries: Generalist, Food, Bev., Tobacco, Paper, Soap, Perf., Cosmtcs., Drugs Mfg., Finance, Media

Ronald B Hanson Associates†
N9620 Beach Ln
Merrillan, WI 54754
(715) 333-8602
(715) 333-7020
Fax: (715) 333-2811
Email: rbhassoc@aol.com

Description: We are a specialized financial services boutique search firm offering over 99% success rate in retained search completions over the past nine years. Our smaller client list allows us expansive access to candidates.

Key Contact - Specialty:
Mr. Ron Hanson, Owner - *Insurance*

Salary minimum: $60,000

Functions: Generalist

Industries: Insurance

Hanzel & Company Inc
60 E 42nd St Ste 1146
New York, NY 10165
(212) 972-1832

Description: Principal area of practice is in senior management for revenue producing functions of investment banking.

Key Contact:
Mr. Bruce S. Hanzel, Principal
Mr. Robert T. Anderson, Principal

Salary minimum: $80,000

Functions: General Mgmt., M&A

Industries: Invest. Banking, Brokers

Harcor Quest & Associates†
27389 Detroit Rd Ste J-23
Cleveland, OH 44145
(440) 871-5177
Fax: (440) 871-5185
Email: harcorquest@yahoo.com

Description: As generalists, we are a full-service executive search and recruitment firm meeting the wide range of management needs of client companies from both the service and industrial sectors.

Key Contact - Specialty:
Ms. Rachel Taylor, Managing Director - *Senior management*

Salary minimum: $60,000

Functions: General Mgmt., Mfg., Product Dev., Production, Plant Mgmt., Mkt. Research, Finance, IT, R&D, Engineering

Industries: Agri., Forestry, Mining, Mfg., Chemicals, Soap, Perf., Cosmtcs., Drugs Mfg., Medical Devices, Plastics, Rubber, Paints, Petro. Products, Metal Products, Motor Vehicles, Test, Measure Equip., Misc. Mfg., Banking, Accounting, Mgmt. Consulting, HR Services, IT Implementation, Communications, Telecoms, Aerospace, Packaging, Insurance, Software, Development SW, Marketing SW, Networking, Comm. SW, Biotech

Harcourt Group Ltd
2178 Harcourt Dr
Cleveland Heights, OH 44106
(216) 791-6000
Fax: (216) 795-1522
Email: jph@harcourtgroup.com
Web: www.harcourtgroup.com

Description: Together the principals combine the highest level of achievement in research and search methodology. A boutique format has allowed them to deliver the quality and attention which clients deserve.

Key Contact - Specialty:
Mr. James P. Herget, Co-Owner - *Industrial, financial services*
Mrs. Jane K. Herget, Co-Owner - *Industrial, financial services*

Salary minimum: $100,000

Functions: Generalist

Industries: Energy, Utilities, Mfg., Transportation, Wholesale, Finance, Services, Communications, Aerospace, Software, Healthcare

Harris & Associates
4236 Tuller Rd
Dublin, OH 43017
(614) 798-8500
Fax: (614) 798-8588
Email: mail@harrisandassociates.com
Web: www.harrisandassociates.com

Description: We provide retained executive search specializing in the financial services industry. Our clients range from commercial and investment banks to global asset management firms at the local, regional, and national level.

Key Contact:
Mr. Jeffrey G. Harris, President

Salary minimum: $75,000

Functions: Generalist

Industries: Banking, Invest. Banking, Brokers, Venture Cap., Misc. Financial, Accounting, Insurance, Software

The Harris Consulting Corp
444 St. Mary Ave Ste 1400
Winnipeg, MB R3C 3T1
Canada
(204) 942-8735
Fax: (204) 944-8941
Email: resumes@harrisconsult.com
Web: www.harrisconsult.com

Description: We offer proactive and research driven search for management, professional, and executive positions with particular depth of experience, 20 years worth in business, in manufacturing, healthcare, financial services, agribusiness, and not-for-profit sectors.

Key Contact:
Mr. Russell H. May, CMC, CHRP, President
Ms. Lori E. May, BN, RN, Senior Consultant/Project Manager - *Healthcare, not-for-profit*
Mr. Alan Thorlakson, MA, Vice President

Salary minimum: $50,000

Functions: General Mgmt., Senior Mgmt., Mfg., Materials, Healthcare, Sales & Mktg., HR Mgmt., Finance

Industries: Generalist

Professional Associations: CAMC, CIM, HRMAM, LOMA

Harris, Heery & Associates Inc
40 Richards Ave
1 Norwalk W
Norwalk, CT 06854
(203) 857-0808
Fax: (203) 857-0822
Email: bheery@harrisheery.com
Web: www.harrisheery.com

Description: We are a specialized firm for consumer goods and services companies recruiting marketing and sales executives on a domestic and international basis.

Key Contact - Specialty:
Mr. William J. Heery, Senior Vice President - *Consumer marketing*

Mr. Andrew S. Harris, President - *Consumer marketing*
Ms. Linda Leonard, Vice President/Senior Consultant - *Consumer marketing*
Ms. Suzanne Douglass, Senior Consultant - *Consumer marketing*

Salary minimum: $80,000

Functions: General Mgmt., Sales & Mktg., Mktg. Mgmt., Direct Mktg.

Industries: Food, Bev., Tobacco, Textiles, Apparel, Drugs Mfg., Consumer Elect., Banking, Hospitality, Hotels, Resorts, Clubs, Restaurants, Entertainment, New Media, Telecoms, Wireless, Insurance, Healthcare

A E Harrison & Partners Inc
190 Robert Speck Pkwy Ste 209
Mississauga, ON L4Z 3K3
Canada
(905) 615-1577
Fax: (905) 615-0436
Email: mail@aeharrison.com
Web: www.aeharrison.com

Description: A retainer based search company that specializes in the recuitment of sales, marketing and general management executives in most industry sectors.

Key Contact:
Mr. Rick Harrison

Functions: General Mgmt., Sales & Mktg., Sales Mgmt.

Industries: Generalist

Hartman Personnel
4504 Starkey Rd Ste 207
Roanoke, VA 24014
(540) 776-8571
(877) 523-4351
Email: inform@hartman-personnel.com
Web: www.hartman-personnel.com

Description: We are a personnel placement agency that specializes in information systems in the Eastern US.

Key Contact:
Ms. June Hartman, President
Mr. Kevin Hartman, Recruiter
Mr. Forrest Lavinder, Recruiter

Hartsfield Group Inc
PO Box 421217
Atlanta, GA 30342
(770) 901-9711
Fax: (770) 901-9175

Description: Twenty year record of improving clients' competitiveness through leadership selection at the CEO and key functional levels. Clients range from Fortune 1000, mid-size emerging companies to high-technology start-ups.

Key Contact - Specialty:
Mr. Vincent Dee - *General management, those reporting directly to the CEOs*

Salary minimum: $200,000

Functions: Senior Mgmt.

Industries: Mfg., Metal Products, Motor Vehicles, Computer Equip., Venture Cap., Telecoms, Packaging

Professional Associations: ACG, EIA, SLF

Harvard Aimes Group
6 Holcomb St
PO Box 16006
West Haven, CT 06516
(203) 933-1976
Fax: (203) 933-0281

Email: jdg@riskmanagementsearch.com
Web: www.riskmanagementsearch.com

Description: Retained search for risk management (including safety and claims), benefits and insurance professionals in corporate environment only. All consultants have extensive experience working in the field in which they now recruit.

Key Contact - Specialty:
Mr. James J. Gunther, Principal - *Corporate risk management*
Ms. Carole Olderman, Research Associate - *Corporate risk management*

Salary minimum: $50,000

Functions: Risk Mgmt.

Industries: Generalist

Professional Associations: RIMS

Harvard Group Int'l
6000 Lake Forest Dr Ste 400
Atlanta, GA 30328
(404) 459-9045
Fax: (404) 459-9044
Email: executivesearch@harvardgroupintl.com
Web: www.harvardgroupintl.com

Description: Proven track record of prompt professional services from very experienced personnel who assist senior management in improving organizational and market performance in the automotive, communications, aerospace and high-technology industries.

Key Contact - Specialty:
Mr. Thomas Gordy, Senior Partner - *Automotive, communications, aerospace, high technology*

Functions: Generalist, General Mgmt., Mfg., Materials, Sales & Mktg., HR Mgmt., Finance, IT

Industries: Generalist, Energy, Utilities, Motor Vehicles, Telecoms, Aerospace

The Hastings Group
111 Richmond St W Ste 400
Toronto, ON M5H 2G4
Canada
(416) 362-5959
Fax: (416) 214-1632

Description: We have considerable expertise in capital markets, risk management, mergers and acquisitions, valuations, international taxation, CFOs, VPF and controllers and management consultants which includes all areas of business consulting such as: financial services, manufacturing, ERP, information technology, e-commerce and change enablement.

Key Contact - Specialty:
Ms. Gillian Lansdowne, President - *Capital markets, finance, management consultants*

Salary minimum: $100,000

Functions: Generalist, CFO's, Cash Mgmt., Taxes, M&A, Risk Mgmt.

Industries: Generalist, Finance, Accounting

The Hawkins Company
5455 Wilshire Blvd Ste 1406
Los Angeles, CA 90036
(323) 933-3337
Fax: (323) 933-9765
Email: resumebank@thehawkinscompany.com

Description: Retained executive search firm specializing in public and private sector recruitment with strong emphasis on diversity recruitment. Accounting/finance; marketing/sales; human resources; general management.

Key Contact:
Mr. William D. Hawkins, President

Salary minimum: $100,000

Functions: Generalist, Senior Mgmt.

Industries: Consumer Elect., Finance, Non-profits, Higher Ed., Accounting, Law Enforcement, Hospitality, Media, Advertising, Broadcast, Film, Government, Healthcare

William E Hay & Company
20 S Clark St Ste 2305
2 First National Plz
Chicago, IL 60603
(312) 782-6510
Email: wehay20@yahoo.com

Description: A generalist firm representing equal time in the private manufacturing, service and not-for-profit sectors across all functional categories.

Key Contact - Specialty:
Mr. William E. Hay, President - *Senior level executives (all functional areas)*

Salary minimum: $50,000

Functions: Generalist, General Mgmt., Senior Mgmt., Healthcare, Health Admin., Sales & Mktg., HR Mgmt., Finance, CFO's, Mgmt. Consultants

Industries: Construction, Banking, Mgmt. Consulting, Healthcare

Hayden Group Inc
1 Post Office Sq Ste 3830
Boston, MA 02109
(617) 482-2445
Fax: (617) 482-2444

Description: Broad range of senior management, middle management and board search assignments conducted on an exclusive basis for regional, national and international clients with particular emphasis in financial services companies.

Key Contact - Specialty:
Mr. Robert E. Hawley, Partner - *Financial services, senior level*
Mr. Harry B. McCormick, Partner - *Financial services, senior level*

Salary minimum: $150,000

Functions: Generalist

Industries: Finance, Banking, Misc. Financial

Hayman & Company
4311 Oak Lawn Ave Ste 340
Dallas, TX 75219
(214) 953-1900
Fax: (214) 559-2838
Email: hayman@airmail.net

Key Contact:
Mr. Thomas C. Hayman, President

Salary minimum: $80,000

Functions: Generalist

Industries: Generalist

The Haystack Group Inc
15 High St
PO Box 823
Vinalhaven Island, ME 04863-0823
(207) 863-2793
Fax: (207) 863-9916
Email: islandman@islandman.com
Web: www.haystack-group.com

Description: Our areas of expertise are needle in haystack searches within the medical devices, biotechnology, and pharmaceuticals industries. We rely heavily on search research and competitive intelligence to insure our work is exhaustive. We conduct a maximum of three searches at a time, enabling us to complete any project within six weeks.

Let www.ExecutiveAgent.com e-mail your resume now.

Key Contact - Specialty:
Mr. John A. Gasbarre, President - *Medical devices, biotechnology, pharmaceuticals*

Salary minimum: $80,000

Functions: Generalist, Directors, Product Dev., Quality, Sales Mgmt., R&D, Engineering

Industries: Drugs Mfg., Medical Devices, Pharm Svcs., Biotech, Healthcare

Professional Associations: AAPS, ACRP, ASQ, RAPS, SCIP

Networks: Top Echelon Network

Headden Associates
777 108th Ave NE Ste 600
Bellevue, WA 98004
(425) 451-2427
Fax: (425) 646-3015

Description: We conduct mid- to senior-level retained searches over a broad range of disciplines. We have focused on the telecommunications and high-technology industries over the past 15 years. We conduct search work in sales and marketing, finance, operations, engineering and human resources.

Key Contact:
Mr. William P. Headden, Jr., Owner - *Telecommunications, generalist*
Mr. Alex Mott, Partner - *High technology, sales & marketing*
Ms. Carol Reid, Research

Salary minimum: $90,000

Functions: Generalist

Industries: Consumer Elect., Mgmt. Consulting, New Media, Telecoms

HealthCare Recruiters Int'l • Minnesota[†]
18315 Cascade Dr Ste 190
Eden Prairie, MN 55347
(952) 975-4981
Fax: (509) 691-8232
Email: steve.yungner@hcrnetwork.com
Web: www.hcrjobs.com

Description: We specialize in placing top executives in the medical industry. Our clients are medical device, pharmaceutical, biotech and other companies selling a product or service into the healthcare industry. Client size ranges from Fortune 100's to mid-size, small, and start-up organizations.

Key Contact - Specialty:
Mr. Steven J. Yungner, President - *Medical device, pharmaceuticals, biotechnology, healthcare*

Salary minimum: $75,000

Functions: Senior Mgmt.

Industries: Medical Devices, Pharm Svcs., Healthcare

HealthCare Recruiters Int'l • Houston
14015 SW Fwy Bldg 3
Sugar Land, TX 77478
(281) 340-2700
Fax: (281) 340-2720
Email: houston@hcrnetwork.com
Web: www.healthcarerecruiters.com

Description: We are specialists in working with medical manufacturers, managed care organizations, hospitals, and other health care facilities, providing the expertise they need to employee at Executive Levels, Manufacturing, R&D, Information Technology, Finance, Sales & Marketing, as well as other positions.

Key Contact:
Mr. James Tipton, President

Functions: Product Dev., Production, Healthcare

Industries: Drugs Mfg., Medical Devices, Biotech, Healthcare

F P Healy & Company Inc
307 E 44th St Ste E
New York, NY 10017-4404
(212) 661-0366
(800) 374-3259
Fax: (212) 661-0383
Email: fphealy@aol.com

Description: We are an executive search firm that serves all industries, for example: computer, e-Commerce, commercial and industrial technologies, financial services, banking, insurance, aerospace, defense, energy, pharmaceutical, and telemarketing operations.

Key Contact - Specialty:
Mr. Frank P. Healy, President
Mr. Richard P. Healy
Mr. George Saqqal, Managing Director - *Managing director*

Salary minimum: $75,000

Functions: Generalist

Industries: Mfg., Chemicals, Drugs Mfg., Venture Cap., Services, Software

Professional Associations: SHRM

Heath/Norton Associates Inc
545 8th Ave Fl 7
New York, NY 10018-4307
(212) 695-3600

Description: With experience dating back to 1966, we are considered to be one of the more prestigious search firms in the country. The retainer firm specializes in sales, marketing, engineering, manufacturing and general management.

Key Contact - Specialty:
Mr. Richard S. Stoller, Senior Vice President - *Senior level sales & marketing, general management*
Mr. Richard Rosenow, Senior Vice President - *Senior level engineering, manufacturing, general management*

Salary minimum: $75,000

Functions: General Mgmt., Mfg., Materials, Sales & Mktg., Engineering

Industries: Generalist, Mfg.

R W Hebel Associates
4833 Spicewood Springs Rd
Austin, TX 78759
(512) 338-9691
Fax: (512) 338-1308

Description: Retainer search firm specializing in senior healthcare executive recruitment specific to the biotechnology, pharmaceutical; diagnostic and device healthcare sectors.

Key Contact - Specialty:
Mr. Robert W. Hebel, President - *Healthcare, pharmaceutical, device, diagnostic, biotechnology*

Salary minimum: $150,000

Functions: Generalist, Senior Mgmt., Mfg., Product Dev., Mkt. Research, CFO's, R&D

Industries: Generalist, Drugs Mfg., Medical Devices, Venture Cap., Pharm Svcs., Biotech

Hechkoff/Work Executive Search Inc
444 Madison Ave 710
New York, NY 10022
(212) 935-2100
Fax: (212) 935-2199
Email: results@hwsearch.com
Web: www.hwsearch.com

Description: Our extensive network of contacts gives our recruiters a considerable advantage in identifying potential candidates and referrals. Our focused, client centered approach has resulted in hundreds of successful placements.

Key Contact - Specialty:
Mr. Robert B. Hechkoff, President - *Information technology, management consulting, telecommunications*
Mr. Alan J. Work, Executive Vice President - *Information technology, management consulting, financial services*

Salary minimum: $125,000

Functions: IT

Industries: Banking, Mgmt. Consulting, New Media, Telecoms

Hedman & Associates[†]
3312 Woodford Ste 200
Arlington, TX 76013-1139
(817) 277-0888
Email: hedman@onramp.net

Description: Twenty-five years' recruiting experience; strictly confidential; emphasis on identification and assessment of high impact performers, and matching candidates with client needs; special competence identifying profit center management talent.

Key Contact - Specialty:
Mr. Kent R. Hedman, President - *General management*

Salary minimum: $40,000

Functions: Generalist, Int'l.

Industries: Generalist

Professional Associations: SERC

Networks: Recruiters Professional Network (RPN)

Heffelfinger Associates Inc[†]
470 Washington St
Chestnut Green
Norwood, MA 02062
(781) 769-6650
Email: heffone@wn.net

Description: Founded in 1965, specialize in computer/communication industry, both vendor and corporate IS management positions. National and international coverage through NASA-North American Search Alliance partners.

Key Contact - Specialty:
Mr. Thomas V. Heffelfinger, President - *CIO's, CEOs, senior vice presidents, technology oriented companies, CTO's*

Salary minimum: $100,000

Functions: Generalist, General Mgmt., Mfg., Sales & Mktg., Finance, IT, R&D, Int'l.

Industries: Generalist, Computer Equip., Telecoms, Software

Professional Associations: NASA

Heidrick & Struggles Int'l Inc
233 S Wacker Dr Ste 4200
Sears Twr
Chicago, IL 60606-6303
(312) 496-1200
(312) 496-1000
Fax: (312) 496-1290
Web: www.heidrick.com

Description: Consultants in executive search assisting client organizations in identifying, attracting and retaining executive talent for specific opportunities within middle and top management and for boards of directors.

Key Contact:
Mr. Patrick S. Pittard, Chairman/President/CEO

Mr. Gerard R. Roche, Senior Chairman
Mr. Donald M. Kilinski, CFO
Mr. David C. Anderson, President/CEO - *Executive search*
Mr. Piers Marmion, President - Int'l/COO - Executive Search
Dr. Jürgen B. Mülder, Chairman - Executive Search
Mr. Thomas J. Friel, President - Heidrick Ventures
Mr. James Quandt, President/CEO - LeadersOnline

Salary minimum: $150,000

Functions: Generalist

Industries: Generalist

Professional Associations: AESC, IACPR

Branches:
5858 Horton St Ste 170
Emeryville, CA 94608
(510) 420-8650
Fax: (510) 923-1848
Email: emerville@heidrick.com
Key Contact:
Mr. Mark Yowe, Managing Partner

950 Tower Ln Fl 6
Metro Twr Bldg
Foster City, CA 94404
(650) 234-1500
Fax: (650) 350-1000
Email: fostercity@heidrick.com
Key Contact:
Mr. Mark Lonergan, Managing Partner

18101 Von Karman Ave Ste 1050
Irvine, CA 92612
(949) 475-6500
Fax: (949) 475-6525
Email: irvine@h-s.com
Key Contact:
Ms. Judy L. Klein, Managing Partner

10877 Wilshire Blvd Ste 1802
Los Angeles, CA 90024
(310) 209-9600
Fax: (310) 209-9601
Email: losangeles@h-s.com
Key Contact:
Mr. Jeffrey Hodge, Managing Partner

300 S Grand Ave Ste 2400
Los Angeles, CA 90071
(213) 625-8811
Fax: (213) 617-7216
Email: losangeles@heidrick.com
Key Contact:
Ms. Linda Starr, Managing Partner

2740 Sand Hill Rd
Menlo Park, CA 94025-7096
(650) 234-1500
Fax: (650) 854-4191
Email: menlopark@h-s.com
Key Contact:
Mr. Mark Lonergan, Managing Partner

12760 High Bluff Dr Ste 240
San Diego, CA 92130
(858) 794-1970
Fax: (858) 794-9788
Email: sandiego@h-s.com
Key Contact:
Mr. Jeffrey Hodge, Managing Partner

1 California St Ste 2400
San Francisco, CA 94111
(415) 981-2854
Fax: (415) 981-0482
Email: sanfrancisco@h-s.com
Key Contact:
Mr. Laurence O'Neal, Managing Partner

1400 16th St Ste 300 16th Market Sq
Denver, CO 80202
(720) 932-3800
Fax: (720) 932-3858
Email: denver@h-s.com
Key Contact:
Mr. Fred Ley, Principal/Managing Partner

51 Weaver St Greenwich Office Park 3
Greenwich, CT 06831-5150
(203) 862-4600
Fax: (203) 629-1331
Email: greenwich@h-s.com
Key Contact:
Ms. Dona E. Roche-Tarry, Managing Partner

1301 K St NW Ste 500 E
Washington, DC 20005-3317
(202) 289-4450
Fax: (202) 289-4451
Email: washington@h-s.com
Key Contact:
Mr. J. Rucker McCarty, Managing Partner

76 S Laura St Ste 2110
Jacksonville, FL 32202-5448
(904) 355-6674
Fax: (904) 355-6841
Email: jacksonville@h-s.com
Key Contact:
Mr. Charles R. Hoskins, Managing Partner

5301 Blue Lagoon Dr Ste 590
Miami, FL 33126
(305) 262-2606
Fax: (305) 262-6697
Email: miami@h-s.com
Key Contact:
Mr. Bernard Zen Ruffinen, Managing Partner

303 Peachtree St NE Ste 3100
Sun Trust Plz
Atlanta, GA 30308-3201
(404) 577-2410
Fax: (404) 577-4048
Email: atlanta@h-s.com
Key Contact:
Mr. Dale Jones, Managing Partner

233 S Wacker Dr Ste 7000
Sears Twr
Chicago, IL 60606-6402
(312) 496-1000
Fax: (312) 496-1046
Email: chicago@h-s.com
Key Contact:
Ms. Linda Heagy, Managing Partner

150 Federal St Fl 27
Boston, MA 02110
(617) 737-6300
Fax: (617) 737-1888
Email: boston@h-s.com
Key Contact:
Mr. Stuart Sadick, Managing Partner

40 William St
Wellesley, MA 02481
(781) 431-0201
Fax: (781) 431-0375
Email: wellesley@heidrick.com
Key Contact:
Mr. Donald Gordon, Managing Partner

245 Park Ave Ste 4300
New York, NY 10167-0152
(212) 867-9876
Fax: (212) 370-9035
Email: newyork@h-s.com
Key Contact:
Mr. Marvin B. Berenblum, Managing Partner

40 Wall St Fl 48
New York, NY 10005
(212) 699-3000
Fax: (212) 699-3100
Email: wallstreet@h-s.com
Key Contact:
Mr. Barry Bregman, Managing Partner

1001 Winstead Dr Ste 355
Research Triangle Park
Cary, NC 27513
(919) 380-6800
Fax: (919) 573-6052
Email: rtp@heidrick.com
Key Contact:
Mr. Gerry McNamara, Managing Partner

227 W Trade St Ste 1600
Carillon Bldg
Charlotte, NC 28202
(704) 333-1953
Fax: (704) 335-7274
Email: charlotte@h-s.com
Key Contact:
Mr. Gerry McNamara, Managing Partner

600 Superior Ave E Ste 2500
Cleveland, OH 44114-2650
(216) 241-7410
Fax: (216) 241-2217
Email: cleveland@h-s.com
Key Contact:
Ms. Bonnie W. Gwin, Managing Partner

18th & Cherry St Ste 3075
1 Logan Sq
Philadelphia, PA 19103
(215) 988-1000
Fax: (215) 988-9496
Email: philadelphia@h-s.com
Key Contact:
Mr. Kenneth L. Kring, Managing Partner

11921 N Mopac Expwy Ste 360
Austin, TX 78759
(512) 997-1800
Fax: (512) 339-9180
Email: austin@h-s.com
Key Contact:
Mr. Rick Troberman, Managing Partner

5950 Sherry Ln Ste 400
Dallas, TX 75225
(214) 706-7700
Fax: (214) 987-4047
Email: dallas@h-s.com
Key Contact:
Mr. David R. Pasahow, Managing Partner

1221 McKinney St Ste 3050
1 Houston Ctr
Houston, TX 77010
(713) 237-9000
Fax: (713) 751-3018
Email: houston@h-s.com
Key Contact:
Mr. David A. Morris, Managing Partner

1750 Tysons Blvd Ste 300
McLean, VA 22102
(703) 848-2500
Fax: (703) 905-8900
Email: tysonscorner@h-s.com
Key Contact:
Mr. Randall Cochran, Managing Partner

601 Union St Ste 4700
Two Union Sq Bldg
Seattle, WA 98101
(206) 839-8686
Fax: (206) 839-8680
Email: seattle@h-s.com
Key Contact:
Mr. Jason Hancock, Managing Partner

161 Bay St Ste 2310 BCE Pl
PO Box 601
Toronto, ON M5J 2S1
Canada
(416) 361-4700
Fax: (416) 361-4770
Email: toronto@h-s.com
Key Contact:
Mr. Jack H. B. Nederpelt, Managing Partner

1800 McGill College Ste 2112
Place Montreal Trust
Montreal, QC H3A 3J6
Canada
(514) 285-8900
Fax: (514) 285-8812
Email: montreal@h-s.com
Key Contact:
Mr. Jack H. B. Nederpeit, Managing Partner

Ruben Dario No 281 Ofna 1901
Torre Chapultepec
Col Bosque de Chapultepec
Mexico City, MX 11580
Mexico
52 5 280 5200
Fax: 52 5 280 5230
Email: hsmexico@heidrick.com
Key Contact:
Mr. Eduardo Antunovic, Managing Partner

Mexico Torre Dataflux
Batallon de San Patricio # 109, Ofice 404
Colonia Valle Oriente, C P 66269
Garza García, NL
Mexico
52 5 280 5200
Fax: 525 280 5230
Email: monterrey@heidrick.com
Key Contact:
Mr. Eduardo Antunovic, Managing Partner

Heinze & Associates Inc
6125 Blue Cir Dr Ste 218
Minnetonka, MN 55343
(952) 938-2828
Fax: (612) 333-9089

Description: Custom designed search strategy
conducted by experienced professionals. Guaranteed
performance.

Key Contact - Specialty:
Mr. David Heinze, President - *General
management*

Salary minimum: $75,000

Functions: Generalist, Senior Mgmt., Plant Mgmt.,
Mktg. Mgmt., Sales Mgmt., CFO's, MIS Mgmt.

Industries: Generalist, Medical Devices, Machine,
Appliance, Consumer Elect., Misc. Mfg.,
Insurance

Helbling & Associates Inc
117 VIP Dr Northridge Office Plz Ste 320
Wexford, PA 15090
(724) 935-7500
Fax: (724) 935-7531
Email: helbling@helblingsearch.com
Web: www.helblingsearch.com

Description: Leading retained executive search and
management consulting firm specializing
exclusively in the construction and real estate
industries. Our professional staff offers clients more
than 50 years of construction recruiting experience.

Key Contact - Specialty:
Mr. Thomas J. Helbling, President - *Construction,
real estate*

Functions: Generalist

Industries: Construction, Real Estate

Professional Associations: IACPR

Helffrich Int'l
PO Box 1695
Oldsmar, FL 34677-1695
(813) 855-6465
(813) 855-6415
Fax: (813) 855-6625
Email: helffrichintl@mindspring.com
Web: www.higlobalsearch.com

Description: We are an international executive
search firm specializing in mid and senior level
technical and managerial personnel. Only resumes
from candidates with international experience and
foreign language capability are accepted.

Key Contact:
Mr. Alan B. Helffrich, Jr., CPC, President
Mr. Michael D. Helffrich, CPC, Vice President
Ms. Henrietta Helffrich, Office Manager

Salary minimum: $75,000

Functions: General Mgmt., Senior Mgmt., Middle
Mgmt., Mfg., Materials, Sales & Mktg., HR
Mgmt., Finance, IT, Int'l.

Industries: Generalist, Agri., Forestry, Mining,
Energy, Utilities, Construction, Chemicals, Paints,
Petro. Products, Metal Products, Machine,
Appliance, Test, Measure Equip., Environmental
Svcs., Aerospace

Networks: Top Echelon Network

Heller Associates Ltd
200 E Northwest Hwy Ste 200
Palatine, IL 60067
(847) 441-2626
Email: resume@hellerassociates.com
Web: www.hellerassociates.com

Description: Executive search consultants
specializing in mid- to senior sales, marketing and
general management functions within commercial
and consumer industries. We have affiliate
arrangements with other search firms in New York,
Atlanta, Los Angeles, San Francisco, Europe and
Asia.

Key Contact - Specialty:
Mr. Gary A. Heller, President - *Generalist*

Salary minimum: $75,000

Functions: General Mgmt., Directors, Senior
Mgmt., Middle Mgmt., Product Dev.,
Distribution, Sales & Mktg., HR Mgmt., CFO's,
MIS Mgmt.

Industries: Generalist, Computer Equip., Consumer
Elect., Electronic, Elec. Components, Media,
Advertising, New Media, Digital, Wireless,
Software

The Helms Int'l Group[†]
8000 Towers Crescent Dr Ste 1350
Vienna, VA 22182
(703) 760-7881
(302) 226-2389
Email: mhelms@coachwise.com
Web: www.coachwise.com

Description: We place emphasis on senior human
resource positions. We are search consultant with
over 20 years in HR management and know human
resource practices and trends. We work closely with
clients as they select the best person to move the
organizational strategy forward.

Key Contact - Specialty:
Ms. Mary P. Helms, President - *Human resources*

Salary minimum: $80,000

Functions: HR Mgmt.

Industries: Generalist

Professional Associations: GWSAE, ICF, SHRM,
WIT

G W Henn & Company
9420 State Rte 37 E
Sunbury, OH 43074
(740) 965-9912
Fax: (740) 965-1048
Email: gwhenn@aol.com

Description: General recruiting practice focusing on
senior management positions, all industries.
Significant experience in insurance, banking,
manufacturing, information systems and
automotive.

Key Contact - Specialty:
Mr. George W. Henn, Jr., President - *General
management*

Salary minimum: $200,000

Functions: Generalist

Industries: Generalist

The Hennessy Group
1010 Stonyhill Rd Ste 250
Yardley, PA 19067
(215) 497-9950
Fax: (215) 497-9951
Email: edepledge@thehennessygroup.com
Web: www.thehennessygroup.com

Key Contact:
Mr. Robert Hennessy, President - *Pharmaceutical,
chemicals*
Mr. Steven P. DeMorro, COO

Bruce Henry Associates Inc
1975 E Sunrise Blvd Ste 414
Ft. Lauderdale, FL 33304
(954) 763-5966
(888) 935-2424
Fax: (954) 763-5988
Email: bruce@brucehenry.com
Web: www.brucehenry.com

Description: We provide personnel consulting and
executive search for the medical, dental, and non-
profit industries.

Key Contact - Specialty:
Mr. Bruce Henry, President - *Healthcare, dentistry,
non-profit*

Salary minimum: $50,000

Functions: Generalist, General Mgmt., Directors,
Senior Mgmt., Middle Mgmt., Healthcare, Sales
& Mktg., Mktg. Mgmt., Sales Mgmt., Non-profits

Industries: Services, Non-profits, Pharm Svcs.,
Mgmt. Consulting, Healthcare, Dental

The Hensge Company
2100 Manchester Rd Ste 900
Wheaton, IL 60187-4586
(630) 871-1818
Fax: (630) 871-1833
Email: info@hensge.com
Web: www.hensge.com

Description: Our practice is aimed at helping clients
achieve superior strategic results by better
alignment of their organization with their strategic
objectives and culture.

Key Contact - Specialty:
Mr. Bill Hensge, President - *Senior management*

Salary minimum: $100,000

Functions: Generalist

Industries: Mfg., Mgmt. Consulting, HR Services,
Advertising

Professional Associations: TEC, TMA

J Brad Herbeck
3 Hawthorne Pkwy Ste 235
Vernon Hills, IL 60061
(847) 247-1400
Fax: (847) 247-1576
Email: brad@jbradherbeck.com
Web: www.jbradherbeck.com

Description: A generalist firm representing all
major industries.

Key Contact - Specialty:
Mr. J. Brad Herbeck, Principal - *Generalist*

Salary minimum: $150,000

Functions: Generalist

Industries: Generalist

Professional Associations: HRMAC

Herd Freed Hartz
327 NE 58th St
Seattle, WA 98105
(206) 525-9700
Fax: (206) 527-3148

Email: paul@herdfreedhartz.com
Web: www.herdfreedhartz.com

Description: We are a retained search firm serving the technology and venture industry. We place from 'C'-level to director level positions. All of our searches are worked on by partners with over 22 years of search experience. We take on fewer searches to serve you better.

Key Contact - Specialty:
Mr. Paul Freed, Founding Partner - *'C'-level, software, technical, sales/marketing, business development*
Mr. Jim Herd, Founding Partner - *'C'-level, streaming media, biotech, legal, finance*
Mr. Kevin Hartz, Founding Partner - *'C'-level searches, streaming media, sales, marketing, business development*

Salary minimum: $100,000

Functions: Senior Mgmt.

Industries: Venture Cap., Services, Advertising, New Media, Digital, Wireless, Network Infrastructure, Software, Biotech

Professional Associations: SHRM

Networks: Top Echelon Network

Hergenrather & Company
21 Hillside Dr
Rancho Santa Margarita, CA 92688-5554
(949) 635-1200
Fax: (949) 635-1201
Email: rah@hergenrather.com
Web: www.hergenrather.com

Description: We are the first professional executive search organization in the West and was established in Los Angeles. We are engaged in senior-level searches in every functional area and in most industries.

Key Contact - Specialty:
Dr. Richard A. Hergenrather, President/CEO - *Generalist*
Mr. Edmund R. Hergenrather, Founder - *Generalist*

Salary minimum: $75,000

Functions: Generalist, General Mgmt., Mfg., Materials, Sales & Mktg., HR Mgmt., Finance, IT, Engineering, Specialized Svcs.

Industries: Generalist, Mfg., Printing, Computer Equip., Consumer Elect., Electronic, Elec. Components, Transportation, Services, Communications, Aerospace

Heritage Recruiting Group LLC
Lee Farm Corporate Park
PO Box 554
Bethel, CT 06801
(203) 794-1495
Fax: (203) 794-1447
Email: jeffmuth@aol.com
Web: www.heritagerecruiting.com

Description: A boutique retained generalist executive search firm with experience across many industries and disciplines including human resources, marketing, sales, finance, engineering, customer retention, call center management, information technology and others.

Key Contact:
Mr. Jeffry E. Muthersbaugh, President - *Human resources, sales, marketing, information technology, finance*
Mr. Vincent P. Nolan, Vice President
Mr. Michael J. Steinerd, CPC, Vice President

Salary minimum: $65,000

Functions: Generalist

Industries: Generalist

Professional Associations: EMA, SHRM

Hermann & Westmore
9800 D Topanga Canyon Blvd Ste 345
Chatsworth, CA 91311
(818) 717-9000
Fax: (818) 717-9099
Web: www.hermannandwestmore.com

Description: We are a niche firm focused on providing partner level individuals in all disciplines to the CPA and management consulting communities.

Key Contact - Specialty:
Mr. Robert J. Westmore, Partner - *Audit, tax, MAS, big accounting, public accounting*

Salary minimum: $120,000

Functions: Generalist, Finance, CFO's, IT, MIS Mgmt., Mgmt. Consultants

Industries: Generalist, Accounting, Mgmt. Consulting

Branches:
14 N Chatsworth Ave Ste 4D
Larchmont, NY 10538
(914) 833-7723
Fax: (914) 833-7719
Email: geohermann@aol.com
Key Contact - Specialty:
Mr. George A. Hermann - *Audit, tax, MAS, big accounting, public accounting*

Herrerias & Associates[†]
330 Sir Francis Drake Blvd Ste E
San Anselmo, CA 94960
(415) 721-7001
Fax: (415) 721-7003
Email: paul@herrerias.com
Web: www.herrerias.com

Description: We are the premier retained executive search firm for technology companies in the North Bay. We provide recruiting, coaching, and sustaining high-performing teams.

Key Contact - Specialty:
Mr. Paul Herrerias, Executive Director - *Generalist*
Mr. Kurt Weiser - *Sales/marketing*
Mr. Paul Davis - *Finance*
Ms. Mary Richardson - *Human resources*
Ms. Lisa Treshnell - *IT/Tech*

Salary minimum: $75,000

Functions: Generalist, Directors, Sales & Mktg., HR Mgmt., Finance, Mgmt. Consultants

Industries: Accounting, E-commerce, Advertising, New Media, Telecoms, Software, Biotech

Professional Associations: CSCPA, NCHRA

The Herrmann Group Ltd
60 Bloor St W Ste 1100
Toronto, ON M4W 3B8
Canada
(416) 922-4242
Fax: (416) 922-4366
Email: info@herrmanngroup.com
Web: www.herrmanngroup.com

Description: Specialize in building and retaining strong business alliances with our clients. We become an integral part of their organizations and are thereby able to offer valuable support and services. We go beyond supplying people.

Key Contact - Specialty:
Ms. Gerlinde Herrmann, President - *Generalist, mid to senior level*

Salary minimum: $60,000

Functions: Generalist, Senior Mgmt., Mkt. Research, Personnel, Cash Mgmt., Systems Analysis, Mgmt. Consultants

Industries: Generalist

Professional Associations: CCA, HRPAO

Hersher Associates Ltd
3000 Dundee Rd Ste 314
Northbrook, IL 60062-2434
(847) 272-4050
Fax: (847) 272-1998
Email: hersher@hersher.com
Web: www.hersher.com

Description: Healthcare firm nationally known for the recruitment of CIOs and information systems professionals. Clients include integrated delivery networks, academic medical centers, managed care organizations, physician organizations, consulting firms, and IT vendors. Established track record in information systems, executive nursing, finance, administration, and clinical department heads. Nationally recognized as recruitment and retention consulting experts.

Key Contact - Specialty:
Ms. Betsy S. Hersher, President - *Healthcare*
Ms. Linda B. Hodges, Executive Vice President - *Healthcare*

Salary minimum: $75,000

Functions: Directors, Senior Mgmt., Physicians, Nurses, Health Admin., Sales & Mktg., CFO's, IT, MIS Mgmt., Specialized Svcs.

Industries: Higher Ed., Healthcare

Professional Associations: ACHE, AMDIS, CHIM, CHIME, HFMA, HIMSS

Stanley Herz & Company
Mill Pond Office Complex Ste 103
Somers, NY 10589
(914) 277-7500
Fax: (914) 277-7749
Web: www.stanleyherz.com

Description: Retained executive search. Senior management. Operating, financial, sales/marketing. Clients are national. Emphasis on mid-size and emerging companies. Firm profiled in Business Week and Inc. magazine.

Key Contact - Specialty:
Mr. Stanley Herz, Managing Principal - *Senior management*

Salary minimum: $100,000

Functions: General Mgmt., Mfg., Sales & Mktg., Finance

Industries: Generalist

The Hetzel Group Inc
157K Helm Rd
Barrington, IL 60010
(847) 776-7000
Email: htzlgrp@aol.com

Description: Most proud of the long-term client relationships and success of candidates placed. Each search performed by an officer.

Key Contact - Specialty:
Mr. William G. Hetzel, President - *Generalist*
Ms. Karen M. Ross, Vice President - *Generalist*

Salary minimum: $100,000

Functions: Generalist

Industries: Generalist

Heyman Associates Inc
11 Penn Plaza Ste 1105
New York, NY 10001
(212) 784-2717
Fax: (212) 244-9648
Email: info@heymanassociates.com
Web: www.heymanassociates.com

Description: We specialize in senior-level searches in public relations, corporate communications, investor relations, public affairs, and most closely related areas.

Key Contact:
Mr. William C. Heyman, President
Ms. Elisabeth A. Ryan, SVP/Managing Director
Ms. Maryanne B. Rainone, SVP/Director of
Research
Mr. Brian H. Hargrove, Vice President

Salary minimum: $130,000

Functions: PR

Industries: Generalist, Energy, Utilities, Mfg.,
Computer Equip., Finance, Non-profits, Higher
Ed., Aerospace, Biotech, Healthcare

Professional Associations: IABC, NIRI, PRSA,
WICI

HG & Associates
577 Alvin Pl
Highland Park, IL 60035
(847) 459-9516
(847) 433-5494
Email: hgassoc@aol.com

Description: Demonstrated ability to work
successfully for middle market companies
(closely/privately held) to Fortune 500 clients.
Experience both domestic and international in all
functional areas.

Key Contact - Specialty:
Mr. Herb Greenberg, Principal - *Privately held
companies (small to mid-size)*

Salary minimum: $60,000

Functions: Generalist

Industries: Generalist

Higdon Group Inc
230 Park Ave Ste 1455
New York, NY 10169-1499
(212) 986-4662
Fax: (212) 986-5002

Description: A medium-size, high-powered firm
with searches conducted by owners/professionals
with no less than 10 years of experience and
recognized as leaders in the business.

Key Contact - Specialty:
Mr. Henry G. Higdon, Chairman - *Financial
services, investment management, investment
banking, private equity*
Ms. Maryann Bovich, Managing Director -
*Financial services, investment management,
investment banking, private equity*
Ms. Leslie R. Meyers, Managing Director -
*Financial services, investment management,
investment banking, private equity*
Ms. Cynthia S. Strickland, Vice President -
*Financial services, investment management,
investment banking, private equity*
Ms. Nina-Marie Gardner, Director of research -
*Financial services, investment management,
investment banking, private equity*

Salary minimum: $150,000

Functions: General Mgmt., Senior Mgmt., Mktg.
Mgmt., Sales Mgmt., HR Mgmt., CFO's, Int'l.

Industries: Finance, Banking, Invest. Banking,
Brokers, Venture Cap., Misc. Financial

Professional Associations: AESC

Higgins Group Inc
1000 Westlakes Dr Ste 130
Berwyn, PA 19312
(610) 640-2660
Fax: (610) 640-2872
Email: donna@higgins-group.com
Web: www.higgins-group.com

Description: We are a boutique firm focused on
providing exceptional levels of quality and attention
to selected clients. Our process emphasizes urgency,
outstanding fit, and communication. We focus in the

senior levels of pharmaceutical and biotech
companies.

Key Contact:
Ms. Donna Higgins, President

Salary minimum: $150,000

Functions: Generalist

Industries: Drugs Mfg., Pharm Svcs., Biotech

High Desert Executive Search LLC
PO Box 142173
Austin, TX 78714-2173
(512) 821-2299
Email: info@highdesertsearch.com
Web: www.highdesertsearch.com

Description: We are a retained executive search
firm. Our areas of concentration include finance,
human resources, sales, and marketing. We place
directors and above. Not all, but most of our clients
are technology companies in Texas.

Key Contact:
Mr. Jim McCaskill, CPC, President

Salary minimum: $100,000

Functions: Senior Mgmt., Sales Mgmt., HR Mgmt.,
Finance

Industries: Mfg., Services, Communications,
Telecoms, Software

Professional Associations: NAPS, TAPC

Higley, Hall & Company Inc
3 Oak St
Westborough, MA 01581
(508) 836-4292
Fax: (508) 836-4294
Email: higley.hall@verizon.net
Web: www.higleyhall.com

Description: Executive banking background on part
of principal - quality firm.

Key Contact - Specialty:
Mr. Donald L. Hall, President - *Financial, banking*

Salary minimum: $50,000

Functions: Generalist

Industries: Finance, Banking, Misc. Financial

Hill & Associates
(a division of Melfur Int'l Inc Corp)
1370 Trancas St 165
Napa, CA 94558
(707) 258-2000
Email: thill29832@aol.com

Description: Extensive industry knowledge and
contacts. Outstanding ability to build management
teams. I am an ex-Carnation Company sales
manager, with fifteen years' experience in
management consulting and executive search. A
true specialist in the food and beverage industry.

Key Contact:
Mr. Tom Hill, President

Salary minimum: $60,000

Functions: General Mgmt., Directors, Senior
Mgmt., Middle Mgmt., Sales & Mktg., Mktg.
Mgmt., Sales Mgmt., PR, Int'l.

Industries: Food, Bev., Tobacco, Drugs Mfg.,
Advertising, Marketing SW

Networks: First Interview Network (FIN)

Frank P Hill
Rio Guadalquivir 38-701
Col Cuauhtémoc
Mexico City, DF 06500
Mexico
52 5 208 4902
Fax: 52 5 208 8369

Email: fphill@sednmx.com
Web: www.iicpartners-esw.com

Description: Specializing in upper-level executives
search. Particularly strong in sales, marketing,
finance, manufacturing and human resources.

Key Contact:
Mr. Frank P. Hill, General Director - *Generalist*
Ms. Andrea Garcia Sauer, Executive Director -
Generalist
Mr. Roberto E. Tattersfield, Director/VP-Business
Development - *Generalist*
Mr. Anthony Loveman, VP-Business Development

Salary minimum: $50,000

Functions: Generalist, General Mgmt., Mfg., Plant
Mgmt., Materials, Sales & Mktg., HR Mgmt.,
Finance, CFO's

Industries: Generalist, Chemicals, Soap, Perf.,
Cosmtcs., Drugs Mfg., Consumer Elect., Retail

Networks: I-I-C Partners Executive Search
Worldwide

The Himmelfarb Group
1119 Pleasant St
Oak Park, IL 60302
(708) 848-0086
Fax: (708) 848-8001
Email: info@himmelfarbgroup.com
Web: www.himmelfarbgroup.com

Description: We are a small executive search firm
working on a retained basis for not-for-profit
organizations and foundations.

Key Contact - Specialty:
Ms. Susan Himmelfarb, Principal - *Education,
human services, social justice, philanthropy,
community development*
Ms. Jennifer Wheeler, Associate - *Arts and culture,
museums, fund-raising*

Functions: Non-profits

Industries: Non-classifiable

The Hire Net.Work Inc†
5650 Yonge St Ste 1500
Xerox Twr
Willowdale, ON M2M 4G3
Canada
(416) 226-7263
Fax: (416) 512-8304
Email: louis@hire-network.com
Web: www.syntech-employment.com

Description: We provide search, testing, and
consulting services for management and executives,
both permanent and contract. We place across
Canada and have a worldwide database through our
association with AIMS. You can visit their website
at www.aims-network.com.

Key Contact - Specialty:
Mr. Daniel Yolleck, Partner - *Executive*
Mr. Louis Noorden, Partner - *Executive, retail*

Functions: Generalist, General Mgmt., Mfg.,
Healthcare, HR Mgmt., MIS Mgmt., Engineering,
Mgmt. Consultants, Int'l.

Industries: Generalist, Mfg., Retail, Finance, Mgmt.
Consulting, Environmental Svcs., Aerospace,
Healthcare

Professional Associations: ACSESS, AIMS

Branches:
45H Roncesvalles Ave
Toronto, ON M6R 2N5
Canada
(416) 537-4563
Fax: (416) 538-7560
Email: tdr@better.net
Key Contact - Specialty:
Mr. Tim Ryan - *Engineering*

Hitchcock & Associates
2064 Antioch Cr Ste A
Oakland, CA 94611
(510) 339-8675
Fax: (510) 339-8674
Email: nhsearch@best.com
Web: www.hitchcocksearch.com

Description: Research and retained executive search services in the areas of biotechnology, pharmaceutical, high technology, e-commerce and retail. Spanish language and Japanese capabilities and has performed a number of searches in South America. Available to provide on-site consulting and recruiting services.

Key Contact - Specialty:
Ms. Nancy Hitchcock, BA, MA, President -
Biotech, retail, management consulting

Salary minimum: $75,000

Professional Associations: WAW

Hite Executive Search
(a division of W A Hite Int'l Inc)
PO Box 43217
Cleveland, OH 44143-0217
(440) 461-1600
(216) 431-1900
Fax: (440) 461-9177
Email: wahite@hite-mgmt.com
Web: www.hite-mgmt.com

Description: We are director, executive, senior, and general management specialists. We have convenient North central US headquarters. We provide extensive computerized research and database, plus proactive worldwide resource network. We practice quality documentary procedures. We charge a percentage or fixed fee arrangements. We do retainer assignments only.

Key Contact:
Mr. William A. Hite, III, President & CEO -
Management (general, executive)
Mr. Lauren R. Pacini, Vice President - *Information technology*
Ms. Leslie Spieth, Director -Research

Salary minimum: $100,000

Functions: Generalist, General Mgmt., Mfg., Materials, Healthcare, Sales & Mktg., HR Mgmt., Finance, IT, Int'l.

Industries: Generalist

Professional Associations: AMA, APA, RI, SHRM, SME, SMEI

Branches:
3813 Euclid Ave Fl 3
Cleveland, OH 44115-2503
(216) 431-1900
Email: wahite@hite-mgmt.com
Key Contact - Specialty:
Mr. William A. Hite, III, President & CEO -
Director, senior & general management

Hobbs & Towne Inc
PO Box 987
PMB 269
Valley Forge, PA 19482
(610) 783-4600
Fax: (610) 783-4511
Email: hobbstowne@aol.com
Web: www.hobbstwone.com

Description: We are a retained search firm focused in the power technology and emerging technology space. We specialize in working with venture capital and private equity portfolio companies.

Key Contact - Specialty:
Mr. Andrew Towne, President - *Pharmaceutical*
Mr. Robert Hobbs, Managing Partner - *Commercial printing, manufacturing*

Salary minimum: $100,000

Functions: Generalist, General Mgmt., Mfg., Materials, Sales & Mktg., Finance, Engineering

Industries: Generalist, Printing, Drugs Mfg., Misc. Mfg., Venture Cap.

Professional Associations: DIA, RAPS

Hockett Associates Inc
1 First St Ste 9
PO Box 1765
Los Altos, CA 94023
(650) 941-8815
Fax: (650) 941-8817
Email: bill@hockettinc.com
Web: www.hockettinc.com

Description: Senior management search for life science, Internet and e-commerce, technology, and other companies, characterized by comprehensive targeting and networking, personal contact, a limited practice size, high quality and an unusual success rate.

Key Contact - Specialty:
Mr. Bill Hockett, Managing Partner - *Life sciences, technology, education, venture capital*

Salary minimum: $125,000

Functions: General Mgmt., Directors, Senior Mgmt., Mfg., Sales & Mktg., CFO's

Industries: Drugs Mfg., Medical Devices, Venture Cap., New Media, Biotech

Hodge-Cronin & Associates Inc
PO Box 309
Des Plaines, IL 60016-0309
(847) 803-9000
Fax: (847) 803-9106

Description: Worked in most industries and disciplines, international.

Key Contact - Specialty:
Ms. Kathleen A. Cronin, Vice President
Mr. Richard J. Cronin, President - *Generalist*

Salary minimum: $90,000

Functions: Generalist

Industries: Generalist

Professional Associations: IMESC, SHRM

Hoglund & Associates Inc
33 N LaSalle Ste 2600
Chicago, IL 60602
(312) 357-1037
Fax: (312) 732-0990
Email: jhoglund@hoglundassociates.com

Description: Twenty year search firm; results-oriented, takes great pride in providing superior client service and committed to unwavering professional ethics and standards.

Key Contact - Specialty:
Mr. Gerald C. Hoglund, President - *Generalist, marketing, sales, engineering, human resources*

Salary minimum: $70,000

Functions: Generalist

Industries: Generalist

Harvey Hohauser & Associates LLC
5600 New King St Ste 355
Troy, MI 48098
(248) 641-1400
Fax: (248) 641-1929
Email: information@hohauser.com
Web: www.hohauser.com

Description: Management consultants specializing in executive recruitment, management appraisals and organization analysis.

Key Contact:
Mr. Harvey Hohauser, President

Dr. Gerhard Padderatz, Vice President -
International
Ms. Debra Schlutow, Director- Research Services
Mr. Todd Hohauser, Director - Client Services

Salary minimum: $70,000

Functions: General Mgmt., Senior Mgmt., Mfg., Sales & Mktg., HR Mgmt., Finance, IT, Engineering, Int'l.

Industries: Generalist, Mfg., Chemicals, Plastics, Rubber, Paints, Petro. Products, Machine, Appliance, Motor Vehicles, Finance, Non-profits, Government, Insurance, Real Estate

Branches:
3536 Meridian Xing Ste 220-222
Okemos, MI 48864
(517) 349-7007
Fax: (517) 349-7027
Email: glickman@hohauser.com
Key Contact:
Mr. Kenneth S. Glickman, Senior Vice President

200 Allendale Way
Camp Hill, PA 17011
(717) 761-1020
Email: joe@hohauser.com
Key Contact:
Mr. Joseph Schatt, Senior Vice President

Richard D Holbrook Associates
PO Box 43
Marblehead, MA 01945-0043
(781) 639-6200
Email: rholbrook@rdholbrook.com
Web: www.rdholbrook.com

Description: Responsive firm with a quality, solutions-oriented approach to executive search. Our procedure: define the need; understand client's organization, mission, strategic direction, culture; determine the appropriate functional solution; find the right fit.

Key Contact:
Mr. Richard D. Holbrook, President

Functions: Generalist

Industries: Generalist

Holland & Associates Inc
PO Box 488
Chelsea, MI 48118-0488
(734) 475-3701
Fax: (734) 475-7032
Email: general@hollandsearch.com
Web: www.hollandsearch.com

Description: We provide professional and personalized service to clients involved in the design, development, manufacture, marketing and sales of technologically advanced products for consumer and commercial markets.

Key Contact - Specialty:
Mr. Thomas A. Parr, President - *Sales & marketing, manufacturing, operations*
Mr. Paul D. Alman, Vice President - *General management, software*

Salary minimum: $50,000

Functions: Directors, Senior Mgmt., Mfg., Product Dev., Mkt. Research, Mktg. Mgmt., Sales Mgmt., CFO's, Systems Dev., Engineering

Industries: Computer Equip., Finance, Media, Telecoms, Software

Branches:
2700 Porter Rd
Plover, WI 54467
(715) 344-6646
Fax: (715) 344-1674
Key Contact - Specialty:
Mr. Daniel O. Holland, Senior Consultant -
Electrical engineers

Let www.ExecutiveAgent.com e-mail your resume now.

Holland Rusk & Associates

211 E Ontario St Ste 1110
Chicago, IL 60611
(312) 266-9595
Fax: (312) 266-8650
Email: srholland@hollandrusk.com

Description: We provide a highly personalized, customized approach to accurately and professionally serve national and international clients. For 25 years, our owner has developed diverse networks within senior management to offer an array of talented finalists. We are 100% woman-owned.

Key Contact:
Ms. Susan R. Holland, President - *Diversity management roles (women)*
Mr. Kyle R. Holland, Director of Research

Salary minimum: $75,000

Functions: General Mgmt., Directors, Senior Mgmt., Mfg., Sales & Mktg., Finance, Specialized Svcs., Minorities, Int'l.

Industries: Energy, Utilities, Construction, Mfg., Transportation, Environmental Svcs., Packaging

Professional Associations: HRMAC

Hollander Horizon Int'l

1617 Pacific Coast Hwy Ste C
Redondo Beach, CA 90277
(310) 540-3231
Fax: (310) 540-4230
Email: azimmerman@hhisearch.com
Web: www.hhisearch.com

Description: Executive search to the food and consumer products industries. Our practice is limited to and highly accomplished in the areas of research and development, manufacturing, engineering and quality control.

Key Contact - Specialty:
Mr. Arnold Zimmerman, Senior Partner - *Food, consumer products, technical*

Salary minimum: $75,000

Functions: Generalist, Plant Mgmt., Quality, Purchasing, Distribution, Packaging, R&D, Engineering

Industries: Generalist, Food, Bev., Tobacco, Soap, Perf., Cosmtcs., Drugs Mfg.

Professional Associations: AOCS, NAER

Branches:
2668 McNair Dr
Robbinsdale, MN 55422
(763) 521-9568
Key Contact - Specialty:
Mr. Joseph Ayers, Associate - *Food, consumer products (technical)*

16 Wall St
Princeton, NJ 08540
(800) 743-9175
Web: www.wedofood.com
Key Contact - Specialty:
Mr. Michael Hollander, Senior Partner - *Food, consumer products (technical)*

The Hollins Group Inc

225 W Wacker Dr Ste 1575
Chicago, IL 60606-1229
(312) 606-8000
Fax: (312) 606-0213
Email: search@thehollinsgroup.com

Description: Provides senior and board of director-level search services to major corporations, privately held firms, educational institutions and nonprofit organizations across a wide range of industries and functional disciplines. The North American member of Glasford International, a global search alliance that assists multinational organizations in building top management teams.

Key Contact - Specialty:
Mr. Lawrence I. Hollins, President - *Generalist*
Mr. Anthony Leggett, Vice President - *Generalist*
Ms. Lynn Oda, Director - *Generalist*
Mr. Glen Sunahara, Director - *Generalist*
Ms. G. Faye Dant, Consultant - *Generalist*
Mr. Derrick Buckingham, Consultant - *Generalist*
Ms. Courtney A. Jones, Senior Associate - *Generalist*
Ms. Joyce Butts Lewis, Senior Associate - *Generalist*
Ms. Sharon Amos, Associate - *Generalist*
Ms. Tiffany Olson, Manager-Research & Client Services - *Generalist*

Salary minimum: $90,000

Functions: General Mgmt., Mfg., Health Admin., Sales & Mktg., HR Mgmt., Finance, CFO's, MIS Mgmt., Minorities, Non-profits

Industries: Generalist

Professional Associations: HRMAC, SHRM

Branches:
1401 Peachtree St NE Ste 500
Atlanta, GA 30309
(404) 870-8070
Fax: (404) 870-8084
Key Contact - Specialty:
Ms. Nancy M. Hall, VP/Managing Director - *Information technology, academia, financial services*

2 Penn Plz Ste 1500
New York, NY 10121
(212) 292-4929
Fax: (212) 292-4930
Key Contact - Specialty:
Mr. Gregg Smith, Vice President - *Generalist*

Holohan Group Ltd

755 S New Ballas Rd Ste 260
St. Louis, MO 63141-8744
(314) 997-3393
Fax: (314) 997-9103
Email: email@holohangroup.com
Web: www.holohangroup.com

Description: Executive, management, scientific and technical recruitment management consulting firm uniquely composed of a professional staff of Ph.D. senior consultants, serving a core group of technology-driven Fortune 500 companies. The firm concentrates on a persistent focus for each assignment and the development of long-term client relationships.

Key Contact - Specialty:
Mr. Barth A. Holohan, Jr., President - *Medical & regulatory affairs, quality assurance, compliance*
Ms. Gloria J. Luzier, Senior Administrator - *IT*
Ms. Margaret O. Pautler, Senior Consultant - *Business research*
Dr. Gerard A. Dutra, Senior Consultant - *Business development, research & development, marketing and sales, genomics, bioinformatics*
Dr. Alvin M. Janski, Senior Consultant - *Science, technology, research & development, biotechnology*
Dr. Gary H. Brandenburger, Senior Consultant - *Science, technology, pharmaceuticals, medical (imaging, devices), research & development*
Dr. Arnold Hershman, Senior Consultant - *Science, technology, research & development*

Salary minimum: $90,000

Functions: General Mgmt., Legal, Mfg., Product Dev., Quality, Physicians, Sales & Mktg., IT, R&D, Engineering

Industries: Agri., Forestry, Mining, Food, Bev., Tobacco, Chemicals, Drugs Mfg., Medical Devices, Retail, Communications, Biotech

J B Homer Associates Inc

420 Lexington Ave Ste 2328
Graybar Bldg
New York, NY 10170
(212) 697-3300
Fax: (212) 986-5086
Email: jhomer@jbhomer.com
Web: www.jbhomer.com

Description: We are dedicated to the principle that a corporation's executives hold the key to the success of any enterprise. Our total focus is specialized executive recruitment for senior-level information technology executives across all industries both domestic and international.

Key Contact - Specialty:
Ms. Judy B. Homer, President - *Information technology*

Salary minimum: $150,000

Functions: Generalist, IT, MIS Mgmt., Systems Implem., Systems Support

Industries: Generalist, IT Implementation

Professional Associations: AESC, NAFE, WHRM

Hook-Up!†

2866 McKillop Rd
Oakland, CA 94602
(415) 362-3573
Fax: (510) 261-7007
Email: martyp1@pacbell.net
Web: www.hookupjobs.com

Description: We are specialists in interactive media. We pursue a "container" model, charging a modest hourly fee, which is capped by the client and is deducted from eventual placement fees. We have heart, we are fast, and we know interactive.

Key Contact - Specialty:
Mr. Martin Perlmutter, Partner - *Senior management, creative, technical*
Ms. Miki Raver, Partner - *Creative personnel*

Salary minimum: $70,000

Functions: Generalist, Senior Mgmt., Mktg. Mgmt., Sales Mgmt., CFO's, MIS Mgmt., Systems Dev., Graphic Artists

Industries: Generalist, New Media

Hornberger Management Company

1 Commerce Ctr 747
Wilmington, DE 19801-5401
(302) 573-2541
Fax: (302) 573-2507
Email: hmc@hmc.com
Web: www.hmc.com

Description: Board and executive search exclusively for the construction industry (general & specialty contractors, design-build, construction management, real estate developer/owner/builders). Specializing in CEO, COO, CFO & officer-level positions with compensation levels exceeding $100,000. In addition we find outside board directors and excutives for contract positions.

Key Contact - Specialty:
Mr. Frederick C. Hornberger, Jr., President - *Construction*

Salary minimum: $100,000

Functions: Generalist, General Mgmt., Senior Mgmt., Sales & Mktg., HR Mgmt., Finance

Industries: Construction

Branches:
1550 0 de Maisonneuve 801
Montreal, QC H3GIN2
Canada
(514) 931-6408
Fax: (514) 931-6408
Email: hmc@hmc.com

Homero No 1933-1 lo Pisco Polanco
Mexico City, DF 11560
Mexico
52 5 395 1860
Fax: 52 5 395 3702
Email: hmc@hmc.com

Horton Int'l LLC
1801 N Lamar Blvd Ste 222
Austin, TX 78701
(512) 494-9443
Fax: (512) 494-0858
Email: austin@horton-intl.com
Web: www.horton-intl.com

Description: We are a generalist firm that recruits senior-level management for all industries. Our practice is global in scope and currently includes eleven North American recruiters based in five locations, which are: Atlanta, Austin, Chicago, Hartford, and New York. Our international offices number 36 and are located in Eastern and Western Europe, Asia, Australia, and Latin America.

Key Contact - Specialty:
Mr. Michael D. Boxberger, Manager
Mr. Robert Golding, Managing Director - *Advanced technology, biotechnology, healthcare products*

Salary minimum: $120,000

Functions: Generalist, Senior Mgmt., Mfg., Healthcare, Sales & Mktg., HR Mgmt., Finance, IT, Engineering, Int'l.

Industries: Drugs Mfg., Medical Devices, Metal Products, Machine, Appliance, Motor Vehicles, Invest. Banking, Aerospace, Insurance, Software, Biotech

Professional Associations: AESC

Networks: Horton Int'l

Branches:
10 Tower Ln
Avon, CT 06001
(860) 674-8701
Fax: (860) 676-9753
Email: avon@horton-intl.com
Key Contact - Specialty:
Mr. Larry Brown, Managing Director - *Automotive, electronics, manufacturing*
Mr. Robert J. Gilchrist, Managing Director - *Electronics, manufacturing, high technology*
Mr. Robert Savard, Jr., Managing Director - *Financial services, insurance*
Mr. C. Edward Snyder, Managing Director - *Industrial, manufacturing, engineering*
Mr. Peter Borkoski, Principal - *Electronics, manufacturing, high technology, automotive, chemical*
Ms. Christine B. Peterson, Principal - *Financial services, healthcare, advertising, high technology, telecommunications*

5555 Glenridge Connector Ste 200
Atlanta, GA 30342
(404) 459-5950
Fax: (404) 459-5951
Email: atlanta@horton-intl.com
Key Contact:
Ms. Sallie Baker, Director-Administration

70 W Madison Ste 1400
3 First Nat'l Plz
Chicago, IL 60602
(312) 332-3830
Fax: (312) 332-3831
Email: chicago@horton-intl.com
Key Contact - Specialty:
Mr. Dirk A. Himes, Managing Director - *Financial services*

420 Lexington Ave Ste 810
New York, NY 10170
(212) 973-3780
Fax: (212) 973-3798
Email: newyork@horton-intl.com

Key Contact - Specialty:
Mr. Franklin Key Brown, Managing Director - *Financial services*
Mr. David W. Patenge, Managing Director - *Financial services*

Hospitality Executive Search Inc
729 Boylston St
Boston, MA 02116-2639
(617) 266-7000
Fax: (617) 267-2033
Email: jspatt@world.com
Web: www.jspatt.com

Description: Twenty-five plus years of experience and commitment shows in our reputation. We succeed... and we will continue to. We undertake retained hospitality search projects for senior-level and board level. Individual projects commence at $65K. National executive selection and placement since 1976.

Key Contact - Specialty:
Mr. Jonathan M Spatt, President - *Hospitality, food & beverage, human resource, research & development, senior level*

Salary minimum: $65,000

Functions: Generalist, Senior Mgmt., Product Dev., HR Mgmt., CFO's, MIS Mgmt.

Industries: Generalist, Mfg., Food, Bev., Tobacco, Finance, Hospitality, Hotels, Resorts, Clubs, Restaurants, Entertainment, Real Estate, Accounting SW, Development SW, Entertainment SW, HR SW, Training SW

Professional Associations: AHMA, AIWF, CHS, HSMA, IACP, MLA, MRA, NEHRA, NRA, PAII, WCR

Hotard & Associates
5640 Six Forks Rd Ste 202
Raleigh, NC 27609
(919) 866-0792
Fax: (919) 866-0794
Email: jhotard@hotard-assoc.com

Description: We are a retained executive search firm open to assignments in any leadership area but focus on accounting, finance and tax management positions.

Key Contact:
Mr. Joseph Hotard, President

Salary minimum: $100,000

Functions: Generalist, Senior Mgmt., CFO's, Cash Mgmt., Taxes, M&A, IT

Industries: Generalist, Energy, Utilities, Mfg., Finance, Insurance, Software

The Howard-Sloan-Koller Group†
300 E 42nd St Fl 15
New York, NY 10017
(212) 661-5250
Fax: (212) 557-9178
Email: hsk@hsksearch.com
Web: www.hsksearch.com

Description: We are a retained search and consulting for the media industries, primarily publishing, advertising, and digital media. Our specialties are in all forms of print publishing, including magazine, newspapers, newsletters and books, as well as all forms of electronic communications, including online, interactive, internet, and streaming and multimedia. We have strong practices in direct marketing, public relations, advertising (creative and account sides), conferences, and cable.

Key Contact - Specialty:
Mr. Edward R. Koller, Jr., President - *General executive management, sales, sales management, publishing, new media*

Ms. Karen Danziger, Executive Vice President - *Editorial, creative*

Salary minimum: $80,000

Functions: Senior Mgmt., Middle Mgmt., Advertising, Mktg. Mgmt., Sales Mgmt., Direct Mktg., PR, CFO's

Industries: Advertising, Publishing, New Media, Broadcast, Film, Telecoms

Professional Associations: AWNY, BPAA, DMA, NAER, PRSA, SNAP, WNM

Howe & Associates
5 Radnor Corp Ctr Ste 448
Radnor, PA 19087
(610) 975-9124
Fax: (610) 975-0574
Email: execsearch@howe-assoc.com
Web: www.howe-assoc.com

Description: Serves corporations headquartered in the mid-Atlantic region and nationwide. Clients represent a variety of industries, including manufacturing, consumer products, financial services, human resources and telecommunications.

Key Contact - Specialty:
Mr. John R. Fell, III, Principal - *Financial services, generalist, asset management, corporate banking, investment banking*
Mr. I. H. "Chip" Clothier, Principal - *Generalist, consumer products, food & beverage, sales & marketing, information technology*
Mr. Edward F. Walsh, Principal - *Generalist*

Salary minimum: $100,000

Functions: General Mgmt., Mfg., Materials, Sales & Mktg., Mktg. Mgmt., Sales Mgmt., HR Mgmt., Finance, IT, MIS Mgmt.

Industries: Generalist, Mfg., Transportation, Wholesale, Retail, Finance, Services, Hospitality, Media, Telecoms, Software

Professional Associations: IACPR

Robert Howe & Associates†
2296 Henderson Mill Rd Ste 222
Atlanta, GA 30345
(770) 493-8776

Description: Representing small to large manufacturing and service companies, nationally and internationally in recruiting at mid-upper-level management positions.

Key Contact - Specialty:
Mr. Robert W. Hamill, President - *Manufacturing, hospitality (mid-upper management), construction, healthcare*

Salary minimum: $60,000

Functions: Generalist

Industries: Construction, Mfg., Hospitality, Healthcare

HPI Executive Search & HR Consulting
19925 Stevens Creek Blvd
Cupertino, CA 95014
(408) 257-5680
Fax: (408) 366-2088
Email: staff@hpiconsulting.com
Web: www.hpiconsulting.com

Description: We are a full service executive search firm that specializes in human resources and marketing executives.

Key Contact - Specialty:
Mr. James Holley, President - *Human resources Search*

Functions: Mkt. Research, HR Mgmt.

Industries: Transportation, Non-profits, New Media, Telecoms, Digital, Network Infrastructure,

Software, Database SW, Development SW, Biotech

HRCG Inc Executive Search Management Consulting
165 S Union Blvd Ste 456
Lakewood, CO 80228-2211
(303) 987-8888
Fax: (303) 987-8965

Description: A national executive search practice with highly experienced business executives and consultants with backgrounds in consumer goods, high-technology, telecommunications, healthcare, advertising and diversified multinational corporations.

Key Contact - Specialty:
Mr. Joseph L. Zaccaro, President - *Management (upper to mid levels)*
Mr. John F. Kane, Principal - *Management (upper to mid levels)*
Mr. James G. Kennedy - *Management (upper to mid levels)*

Salary minimum: $75,000

Functions: Generalist

Industries: Generalist

Professional Associations: HRPS, ODN, SHRM, WAW

Branches:
10 Universal City Plz Ste 2000
Universal City, CA 91608
(818) 754-3734
Fax: (323) 467-1438
Key Contact - Specialty:
Ms. Megan Barnett, Principal - *Middle to top management*

800 Turnpike St Ste 300
North Andover, MA 01845
(978) 686-5338
Fax: (978) 685-1048
Key Contact - Specialty:
Mr. Al Zink, Principal - *Middle to top management*

8330 Corporate Dr 3
Racine, WI 53406
(262) 884-8674
Fax: (262) 884-8679
Key Contact - Specialty:
Ms. Terri Ladzinski, Principal - *Middle to top management*

HRCS
100 Corporate Pointe Ste 395
Culver City, CA 90230
(310) 348-7799
(800) 660-HRCS
Fax: (310) 348-7750
Email: info@hrcs.com
Web: www.hrcs.com

Description: We are the nation's premier consulting firm specializing in on-site contract recruiting, executive search and recruitment research.

Key Contact:
Mr. Michael Martin, CEO
Mr. Donald A. Lumpkin, President
Mr. Vince Anderson, Vice President-Client Services
Ms. Gail Martin, Vice President

Salary minimum: $60,000

Functions: Generalist, General Mgmt., Mfg., Healthcare, Sales & Mktg., HR Mgmt., Finance, IT

Industries: Generalist, Mfg., Finance, Services, Media, Software, Healthcare

Professional Associations: EMA, ODN, SHRM

HRD Consultants Inc
60 Walnut Ave Ste 100
Clark, NJ 07066
(732) 815-7825
Fax: (732) 815-7810
Email: hrd@aol.com
Web: www.hrdconsultants.com

Description: We offer our clients a long history in human resource recruitment, an extensive network, information regarding trends in human resources and a commitment to excellence.

Key Contact:
Ms. Marcia Glatman, President

Salary minimum: $135,000

Functions: HR Mgmt., Benefits

Industries: Generalist

Professional Associations: AESC, IACPR, HRPS, ODN, WAW

Arnold Huberman Associates Inc†
51 E 25th St Ste 501
New York, NY 10010
(212) 545-9033
Fax: (212) 779-9641
Email: arnie@huberman.com
Web: www.huberman.com

Description: Specialists in management recruiting in the areas of corporate communications and public relations across all industries. Specific expertise in finding public relations agencies for corporations.

Key Contact - Specialty:
Mr. Arnold M. Huberman, President - *Public relations, executive*
Ms. Rachel B. Schwartz, Vice President - *Public relations, executive*

Functions: PR

Industries: Generalist

Hudepohl & Associates Inc
150 W Wilson Bridge Rd Ste 203
Worthington, OH 43085
(614) 854-7300
Email: hudpohl@aol.com

Description: We specialize in, but are not limited to, managing searches for accounting, finance, investment management, and information technology positions. Our experience includes the management of over 200 searches in a wide range of areas, including pension and investment funds, financial services, public education, retail, and public accounting. Our diverse client base includes Fortune 500 companies, public school districts, pension funds, and other not-for-profit entities.

Key Contact - Specialty:
Mr. Gary L. Hudepohl, President - *Finance, accounting, information technology*

Salary minimum: $75,000

Functions: Finance, IT, Non-profits

Industries: Generalist

The Hudson Consulting Group LLC†
(also known as MRI of Colchester)
500 Winding Brook Dr
Glastonbury, CT 06033
(860) 652-8660
Email: mgionta@hudsongrp.com
Web: www.hudsongrp.com

Description: Specialize in computer networking LAN/WAN sales/marketing. Work largely on retained projects from senior-level management through field sales and engineering. Fulfillment time averages 60 to 90 days.

Key Contact - Specialty:
Mr. Michael Gionta, President - *LAN, WAN*

Salary minimum: $75,000

Functions: Sales & Mktg.

Industries: Telecoms

Huey Enterprises Inc†
273 Clarkson Executive Park
Ellisville, MO 63011-2173
(636) 394-9393
Fax: (636) 394-2569
Email: info@huey.com
Web: www.huey.com

Description: Particular strength in direct recruiting of candidates with highly specialized skills. Extensive database of industry talent/contacts in specialization areas supplemented by in-depth knowledge of Internet search and recruiting techniques.

Key Contact:
Mr. Arthur T. Huey, President

Salary minimum: $75,000

Functions: Generalist, General Mgmt., Legal, Sales & Mktg., Finance, R&D, Engineering, Specialized Svcs., Int'l.

Industries: Retail, Finance, Banking, Services, Legal, Accounting, Hospitality, Hotels, Resorts, Clubs, Restaurants, Advertising, Real Estate, Accounting SW, Development SW

Hughes & Company
1626 Belle View Blvd
PO Box 7365
Alexandria, VA 22307-0365
(703) 765-8853
Fax: (703) 765-6828
Email: djh@webbox.com
Web: www.careerresources.com

Description: We are a specialized search firm offering highly personalized, responsive service within the consumer packaged goods and services industry. Our focus is on building management teams. We are known for quality, team-work, and long-term relationships. We concentrate on recruiting exceptional management talent for sales, marketing, financial, legal, and general management positions.

Key Contact - Specialty:
Mr. Donald J. Hughes, Managing Partner - *Natural & organic food products, neutraceuticals, sales, business development, CEO's*
Mr. Martin Smith, Managing Partner - *Marketing, COO's, vice presidents, directors, brand management*
Mr. J. Reid Johnston, Managing Partner - *Finance, CFO's, vice presidents, directors, mergers & acquisitions*
Mr. John Rodgers, Vice President - *Sales, food & non-food products, middle management, consumer goods, division sales managers*
Mr. William B. Casey, Vice President - *Legal, attorneys, paralegals*

Salary minimum: $75,000

Functions: Directors, Senior Mgmt., Middle Mgmt., Advertising, Mktg. Mgmt., Sales Mgmt., Finance, Attorneys, Paralegals, Int'l.

Industries: Mfg., Food, Bev., Tobacco, Paper, Soap, Perf., Cosmtcs., Drugs Mfg., Consumer Elect., Legal

Professional Associations: IPA, RON

E A Hughes & Company Inc
146 E 37th St
New York, NY 10016
(212) 689-4600
Fax: (212) 689-4975
Email: general@eahughes.com
Web: www.eahughes.com

Description: A full-service, generalist search firm with a hands on approach.

Key Contact - Specialty:
Ms. Elaine A. Hughes, President - *Apparel, textile, home fashions, catalog & retail, direct marketing*
Ms. Mary Anne Glynn, Vice President - *Apparel, textile, home fashions, catalog & retail, direct marketing*
Mr. Marvin Lord, Executive Vice President - *Apparel, textile, home fashions, catalog & retail, direct marketing*

Salary minimum: $100,000

Functions: Generalist, Directors, Senior Mgmt., Product Dev., Mkt. Research, Mktg. Mgmt., Sales Mgmt., Direct Mktg.

Industries: Generalist, Textiles, Apparel, Retail

Professional Associations: AESC, DMA, FGI

Human Edge Consulting†
8500 Leslie St Ste 560
Thornhill, ON L3T 7M8
Canada
(905) 771-3905
Fax: (905) 771-3925
Email: humanedge@msn.com

Description: We are a retained search firm servicing assignments in the Greater Toronto area. Positions in sales, marketing, finance, operations, and HR across a diversity of industries.

Key Contact:
Mr. Tony Martin

Salary minimum: $45,000

Functions: Generalist

Industries: Mfg., Lumber, Furniture, Drugs Mfg., Metal Products, Services, Non-profits, Aerospace, Insurance

Professional Associations: APRC, HRPAO, OSTD

The Human Resource Advantage Inc
702 Laurel Ln
Wyckoff, NJ 07481
(201) 848-7333
Fax: (201) 847-9325
Email: pzapka@bellatlantic.net

Description: A retained executive search consulting firm focused on providing exceptional people to our client partners, as well as innovative, just-in-time organizational solutions. Affiliated with JDavid Associates, Inc.

Key Contact:
Mr. Paul Zapka, Principal

Salary minimum: $130,000

Functions: Generalist

Industries: Generalist

The Human Resource Group Inc
8221 Brecksville Rd Ste 103
Cleveland, OH 44141
(440) 838-5818
Email: leaders@hrgroupinc.com
Web: www.hrgroupinc.com

Description: Retained executive search specializing in securing transformational executives with 'World Class' leadership skills.

Key Contact:
Mr. Michael J. Coman, President and CEO
Mr. Ted J. Moore, Vice President

Salary minimum: $100,000

Functions: Generalist

Industries: Mfg., Transportation, Retail, Services, Defense, Aerospace, Packaging, Software, Biotech

Professional Associations: DPMA, EMA, IIE, ODI, SHRM

Human Resource Management Inc
PO Box 361225
Birmingham, AL 35236
(205) 978-7198
(205) 978-7148
Fax: (205) 978-7616
Email: info@hrmasap.com

Description: Generalist human resource management firm noted for its extensive national network of HR professionals. This firm excels at recruiting HR professionals and general management at all leadership levels. Outsourced HR services available as alternative to recruiting services.

Key Contact - Specialty:
Mr. Charles Wilkinson, SPHR, CEO - *Human resource management*
Ms. Paula Garmo, CPC, President - *Human resource management*

Salary minimum: $45,000

Functions: General Mgmt., HR Mgmt.

Industries: Generalist

Professional Associations: SHRM

Human Resource Management Services
5314 S Yale Ave Ste 600
Tulsa, OK 74135
(918) 495-1988
Email: hrmgtservices@mindspring.com

Description: We are a boutique firm specializing in assisting our clients to fill senior financial, human resource, administrative, technical officers, and managerial positions.

Key Contact:
Mr. Richard Messer, SPHR, President

Salary minimum: $80,000

Functions: Generalist, General Mgmt.

Industries: Generalist, Mfg., Retail, Finance, Services, Non-profits, HR Services

Professional Associations: SHRM, SHRMCF

Human Resources Personnel Agency†
916 Garland St
Little Rock, AR 72201
(501) 376-4622
Fax: (501) 376-6416
Email: jobs@employment4u.com
Web: www.employment4u.com

Description: Firm works only with manufacturing related positions. Plant start-ups a specialty. Staff offers over 75 years of hands on manufacturing-experience.

Key Contact:
Mr. M. Ben Traylor, President/CEO - *Manufacturing, materials, purchasing, human resources*
Ms. Mary Lewis, Account Executive
Mr. Lance Click, Account Executive
Mr. Dan Shumate, Account Executive

Functions: Generalist, Automation, Productivity, HR Mgmt., Benefits, Systems Dev., Engineering

Industries: Generalist, Textiles, Apparel, Printing, Plastics, Rubber, Metal Products, Machine, Appliance, Consumer Elect.

HI Hunt & Company Ltd
99 Summer St Ste 1050
Boston, MA 02110
(617) 261-1611
Fax: (617) 443-9444
Email: hihunt@hihunt.net

Description: Worldwide executive search firm specializing in the areas of investment banking, structured finance and fund management businesses.

Key Contact - Specialty:
Mr. Herbert I. Hunt, III, Principal - *Financial services*
Mr. Peter Schibli, Senior Associate - *Financial services*

Salary minimum: $50,000

Functions: Generalist, Finance

Industries: Generalist, Finance

The Hunt Company
(a division of Hunt Management Inc)
35 E 38th St
New York, NY 10016
(212) 889-2020
Email: huntco@optonline.net

Description: Generalist firm. Maintain confidential relationships with clients before, during and after assignments. We will not accept assignments that involve conflicts of interest.

Key Contact:
Mr. Bridgford H. Hunt, President

Salary minimum: $125,000

Functions: Generalist, Directors, Senior Mgmt., CFO's, MIS Mgmt.

Industries: Generalist

The Hunt Group Inc
(also known as J B Hunt Executive Search LLC)
21235 Catawba Ave
Cornelius, NC 28031
(704) 895-2660
Fax: (704) 895-2665
Email: joehunt@jbhunt.net
Web: www.jbhunt.net

Description: Executive search & recruiting firm specializing in the consumer packaged goods and health sciences industries since 1988. We conduct searches for executives and professionals in general management, supply chain/logistics, manufacturing/operations, sales/marketing, scientific affairs and key administrative positions including corporate counsel, finance & human resources.

Key Contact - Specialty:
Mr. Joseph B. Hunt, Senior Partner - *Senior management*

Salary minimum: $100,000

Functions: Generalist

Industries: Mfg., Food, Bev., Tobacco, Chemicals, Soap, Perf., Cosmtcs., Drugs Mfg.

The Hunt Group LLC
800 5th Ave Ste 4100
Seattle, WA 98104
(206) 447-1360
Email: resumes@hunt-group.net
Web: www.hunt-group.net

Description: We are a boutique executive search firm specializing in recruitment of that essential hire for venture-backed communications companies with a focus on hardware, software or services.

Key Contact:
Mr. David Blue, Principal
Mr. Michael Simonitch, Principal

Salary minimum: $250,000

Functions: Senior Mgmt.

Industries: Telecoms

Hunt Howe Partners LLC

1 Dag Hammarskjold Plz Fl 34
New York, NY 10017
(212) 758-2800
Fax: (212) 758-7710
Email: research@hunthowe.com
Web: www.hunthowe.com

Description: Finding leaders who can steer through a turbulent present while creating the future by discovering and skillfully pursuing new routes to success, we think about tomorrow's organization and not just the current structure…longer-term possibilities as well as predictable near-term scenarios…emerging business models as well as today's patterns and practices.

Key Contact - Specialty:
Mr. William S. Howe, Managing Director - *Financial services, health services, industry, pharmaceutical, biotech, media*
Mr. James E. Hunt, Managing Director - *Financial services, high technology, professional services*
Ms. Helga M. Long, Managing Director - *Consumer (retail), pharmaceutical, biotech, transportation, industry/manufacturing*
Mr. Robert B. Whaley, Managing Director - *Financial services, high technology, industry/manufacturing, professional services*
Ms. Carol McCullough, Managing Director - *Consumer/retail, health services, publishing/media*

Salary minimum: $200,000

Functions: Generalist

Industries: Chemicals, Drugs Mfg., Transportation, Finance, Services, Media, Aerospace, Software, Biotech, Healthcare

Professional Associations: AESC

Networks: The Amrop - Hever Group

Hunter Int'l Inc

262 S Britain Rd
Southbury, CT 06488
(203) 264-1000

Description: Results oriented general practice that achieves long-term client relationships. Mostly repeat business in finding mid- and senior management in healthcare, insurance, financial services, consumer and industrial arenas. Research intensive!

Key Contact - Specialty:
Mr. Ron Kelly, President - *Generalist*

Salary minimum: $120,000

Functions: Generalist, Senior Mgmt., Middle Mgmt., Sales & Mktg., HR Mgmt., Finance

Industries: Generalist, Food, Bev., Tobacco, Medical Devices, Finance, Insurance, Real Estate, Biotech, Healthcare

Hunter Search Group

PO Box 27108
West Des Moines, IA 50265
(515) 256-4440
Fax: (515) 287-0707
Email: debra@huntersearchgroup.com
Web: www.huntersearchgroup.com

Description: We specialize in executive management, CFOs, and SVP/sales and marketing for the following industries: services, healthcare, manufacturing, hospitality, and IT. We also offer executive and business coaching and executive assessments.

Key Contact - Specialty:
Ms. Debra S. Habr, President - *Financial services, healthcare, manufacturing, high tech*

Salary minimum: $70,000

Functions: Senior Mgmt., Sales & Mktg., CFO's

Industries: Mfg., Finance, Misc. Financial, Services, IT Implementation, Hospitality, Insurance, Healthcare

Professional Associations: ICF, SHRM

Hunter, Rowan & Crowe[†]

9843 Treasure Cay Ln
Bonita Springs, FL 34135
(941) 495-1389
Fax: (941) 992-7517
Email: crowehrc@infi.net

Description: Management consulting experience provides unique expertise for quick study and understanding of client organization culture to better match candidate styles. Proprietary network and research database.

Key Contact - Specialty:
Mr. Thomas H. Crowe, President - *General management, marketing & sales, manufacturing, finance*

Salary minimum: $70,000

Functions: General Mgmt., Mfg., Sales & Mktg., Finance

Industries: Generalist, Mfg., Transportation, Finance, Hospitality, Media, Packaging

Professional Associations: AMA, AMA

Branches:
PO Box 456
Elkhart Lake, WI 53020-0456
(920) 467-1007
Fax: (920) 467-1244
Email: crowehrc@intella.net
Key Contact:
Ms. Carol Rowan, Research Director

Hunter-Stiles Associates

PO Box 164313
Austin, TX 78716
(512) 347-7708
Email: charles@hunter-stiles.com
Web: www.hunter-stiles.com

Description: We are a high technology focused, executive search firm headquartered in Austin, Texas. Our search work focuses on senior executives, CEOs, COOs, presidents, CFOs, CTOs, and VP level sales and marketing positions. The industries that we serve include: computer, software, telecommunications, e-Business, and Internet related.

Key Contact - Specialty:
Mr. Charles Leadford, CEO/Founder - *Senior management, high-tech*

Salary minimum: $150,000

Functions: Senior Mgmt.

Industries: Computer Equip., Banking, Venture Cap., E-commerce, New Media, Communications, Software, Marketing SW, Networking, Comm. SW, Biotech

Huntington Group

(a wholly owned subsidiary of Hall, Kinion & Associates Inc)
6527 Main St
Trumbull, CT 06611
(888) 390-1166
(203) 261-1166
Fax: (203) 452-9153
Email: emil@hg-ct.com
Web: www.huntington-group.com

Description: Our firm specializes in recruiting director, VP, and C-level talent in the emerging and information technology industries. We are the executive search arm of Hall Kinion, which, through its various divisions, helps companies maximize their investment in human capital.

Key Contact:
Mr. Emil Occhiboi, Managing Director

Salary minimum: $100,000

Functions: Senior Mgmt., Middle Mgmt., Product Dev., Sales & Mktg., CFO's, MIS Mgmt., R&D, Engineering, Mgmt. Consultants

Industries: Generalist, Biotech

Huntress Real Estate Executive Search

PO Box 8667
Kansas City, MO 64114
(816) 383-8180
(520) 625-1233
Fax: (913) 383-8184
Email: info@huntress.net
Web: www.huntress.net

Description: We offer real estate related consulting advisory services. We specialize in management consultants to the real estate, finance and construction industry including organizational planning, compensation studies, and senior executive staffing. We spend major activity on executive search. We also have a southwestern regional office just outside of Tucson, Arizona.

Key Contact - Specialty:
Mr. Stan Stanton, President - *Senior level position (real estate), industrial, construction, finance, retail*
Mr. Glenn Hoffman, Senior Vice President - *Real estate, construction, finance, retail, property management*
Ms. Marilyn Jacob, Senior Vice President - *Real estate, construction, retail*

Salary minimum: $40,000

Functions: Generalist, Directors, Senior Mgmt., Admin. Svcs., Legal, CFO's, M&A, Architects, Attorneys, Int'l.

Industries: Real Estate

Professional Associations: BOMA, ICSC, IREM, NACORE

W Hutt Management Resources Ltd

2349 Fairview St Ste 110
Burlington, ON L7R 2E3
Canada
(905) 637-3800
Fax: (905) 637-3221
Email: whuttmgt@skylinc.net
Web: www.whuttmanagement.com

Description: We are an executive search firm that provides expert, low profile search activity, in the industrial/commercial segments of business; with candidates ranging from design engineers to presidents.

Key Contact - Specialty:
Mr. Wayne Hutt, President - *Generalist*
Ms. Gayle Hutt, Vice President/Secretary - *Administration*

Salary minimum: $40,000

Functions: Generalist

Industries: Mfg.

HVS Executive Search

372 Willis Ave
Mineola, NY 11501
(516) 248-8828
Fax: (516) 742-1905
Email: kkefgen@hvsinternational.com
Web: www.hvsinternational.com

Description: We are a retainer search firm specializing in the recruitment of senior-level executives in the hospitality industry.

Key Contact - Specialty:
Mr. Keith Kefgen, President

Ms. Dena Blum-Rothman, Vice President
Mr. Stephen Rushmore, Secretary/Treasurer
Mr. Dave Mansbach, Vice President - *Restaurants*
Mr. Stephen Goebel, Vice President - *Casinos*
Mr. Michael Kogen, Vice President - *Hotels, cruise lines*

Salary minimum: $75,000

Functions: Generalist

Industries: Hospitality

Professional Associations: AESC, IACPR, AHMA, CHS, HSMAI, ISHC

Hyde, Danforth & Company
5950 Berkshire Ln Ste 1040
Dallas, TX 75225
(214) 691-5966
(713) 871-0990
Fax: (214) 369-7317
Email: resume@hydedanforth.com
Web: www.hydedanforth.com

Description: Over 85% of engagements performed for existing or referred clients. A quality boutique practice serving industry, attorneys, professionals and academia. Also provide H/R career and transition consulting.

Key Contact - Specialty:
Mr. W. Michael Danforth, President - *Generalist*
Mr. W. Jerry Hyde, Executive Vice President - *Generalist*
Mr. Michael R. McGee, SPHR, Vice President - *VPIC human resources consulting*

Salary minimum: $75,000

Functions: Generalist, Mfg., Healthcare, Sales & Mktg., HR Mgmt., Finance, Attorneys

Industries: Generalist, Banking, Legal, Accounting, Hospitality, Insurance, Real Estate

iCom Consultants
350 Steiner St
San Francisco, CA 94117
(415) 863-1045
Fax: (530) 676-9556
Email: info@icomconsultants.com
Web: www.icomconsultants.com

Description: Our firm is focused solely on executive recruiting for emerging technology companies. Within that niche, we focus on marketing, sales, professional services, and business development search. iCOM ties our fee structure to results, aligning our clients and our recruiters interests.

Key Contact:
Ms. Mercedes Chatfield-Taylor, President
Mr. John Flett, Executive Vice President

Salary minimum: $100,000

Identify Inc
99 S Lake Ave Ste 201
Pasadena, CA 91101
(626) 395-0444
Email: info@identifyinc.com
Web: www.identifyinc.com

Description: Performs targeted single position and multiple positions searches utilizing a retained search methodology. Specializes in positions ranging from $50,000-$150,000 in a variety of industries.

Key Contact:
Ms. Christine Teeple, Executive Vice President
Ms. Dianne McGee, Executive Vice President

Salary minimum: $50,000

Functions: Generalist, Directors, Middle Mgmt., Admin. Svcs.

Industries: Finance, Banking, Misc. Financial, Services, Non-profits, Higher Ed., Accounting,

HR Services, Media, Advertising, Telecoms, Software, Marketing SW, Healthcare

IMA Search Inc
106 Peninsula Dr Ste A
PO Box 370
Babylon, NY 11702
(631) 422-3900
Fax: (631) 587-3556
Email: imasearch@aol.com
Web: www.ima-search.com

Description: IMA's experienced business professionals provide a broad range of confidential services to management including: worldwide executive search (retained). As generalists we cover most areas including e-commerce, general consulting, the unique, cost-effective "Talent Reserve Bank" ("TRB" tm), executive assessment, background checks, outplacement. Brochure available including representative client list, fee schedule, bios of principles.

Key Contact - Specialty:
Mr. Paul D. Steinberg, President/CEO - *Generalist, high technology, packaging, retail, travel*
Dr. Steven Martello, Vice President/General Counsel - *Generalist, government, legal*
Ms. Suzanne Welling, Vice President - *Generalist, real estate*

Salary minimum: $85,000

Functions: Generalist

Industries: Generalist

Professional Associations: AESC

John Imber Associates Ltd
3601 Algonquin Rd Ste 129
Rolling Meadows, IL 60008
(847) 506-1700
Fax: (847) 577-1651
Email: rebmi@aol.com

Description: Utilizing a search process designed to attract, select and retain individuals fittingly prepared and motivated to thrive within your unique corporate environment.

Key Contact:
Mr. John Imber, President

Salary minimum: $80,000

Functions: Mfg., Sales & Mktg.

Industries: Mfg.

The IMC Group of Companies
14 E 60th St Ste 1200
New York, NY 10022
(212) 838-9535
Fax: (212) 486-2964
Email: info@imcgroupofcos.com
Web: www.imcgroupofcos.com

Description: Thirty-seven years' experience as senior-level Executive Search Consultants for hospitality/leisure, entertainment industries around the world.

Key Contact:
Mr. Herbert Regehly, President
Ms. Joanna Diamond, Vice President - *Hospitality, gaming, leisure*
Ms. Laurie Raiber, Director-New Media Division

Salary minimum: $95,000

Functions: Generalist, General Mgmt., Senior Mgmt., Int'l.

Industries: Services, Hospitality

Professional Associations: AHMA, HSMA

Branches:
2600 Douglas Rd Penthouse 6
Coral Gables, FL 33134
(305) 444-2211
Fax: (305) 445-5097
Email: susanwong@consultant.com
Key Contact - Specialty:
Ms. Susan Wong, Director - *Hotel, gaming, leisure, cruise line, entertainment*

Impact Search & Strategies
(a division of M-Q Corp)
161 Leverington Ave Ste 102
Philadelphia, PA 19127
(215) 482-8100
Fax: (215) 482-7518
Email: info@impactsearch.com
Web: www.impactsearch.com

Description: Our practice groups include: law; the life sciences, including pharmaceuticals and biotechnology; and emerging technologies. Within our practices, we excel in the following functional areas: senior management, sales, business development, marketing, market research, research & development, and the practice of law.

Key Contact - Specialty:
Ms. Carol Doroba, Vice President - *Information technology*

Salary minimum: $100,000

Functions: Generalist, Senior Mgmt., Admin. Svcs., Mkt. Research, MIS Mgmt., Systems Dev., R&D, Attorneys

Industries: Generalist, Pharm Svcs., Legal, Accounting, HR Services, IT Implementation, Biotech, Healthcare

Infinity Resources LLC
1065 US Hwy 22 W
Bridgewater, NJ 08807
(908) 429-3033
Email: hminfinity@aol.com
Web: www.infinity-resources.com

Description: We are a nationally recognized executive search and human resources consulting firm. We have strong commitment to value added search model. We are also human capital management specialists.

Key Contact:
Ms. Harriet Maphet, President

Salary minimum: $100,000

Functions: Generalist

Industries: Mfg., Food, Bev., Tobacco, Textiles, Apparel, Chemicals, Soap, Perf., Cosmtcs., Drugs Mfg., Medical Devices, Plastics, Rubber, Paints, Petro. Products, Computer Equip., Misc. Mfg., Finance, Banking, Invest. Banking, Venture Cap., Misc. Financial, Services, Non-profits, Pharm Svcs., Mgmt. Consulting, HR Services, E-commerce, IT Implementation, Hospitality, Hotels, Resorts, Clubs, Entertainment, Media, Advertising, Publishing, New Media, Communications, Telecoms, Call Centers, Telephony, Digital, Wireless, Fiber Optic, Network Infrastructure, Insurance, Software, Database SW, Development SW, Doc. Mgmt., Production SW, Entertainment SW, ERP SW, HR SW, Industry Specific SW, Mfg. SW, Marketing SW, Networking, Comm. SW, Biotech, Healthcare

Branches:
2013 Crompond Rd Ste 100
Yorktown Heights, NY 10598
(914) 245-0800
Fax: (914) 245-7795
Email: infinity914@aol.com
Web: www.infinity-resources.com
Key Contact:
Mr. Marc Roberts, Senior Vice President

Ingram Aydelotte & Zeigler

1350 Ave of the Americas Ste 2025
New York, NY 10019
(212) 319-7777
Fax: (212) 319-1632
Web: www.iazsearch.com

Description: Experienced consultants working in most industries and functions on senior management and board of director searches. Dedicated partner attention to each search. Extensive research. Retainer only.

Key Contact:
Mr. D. John Ingram, Partner - *Generalist*
Mr. G. Thomas Aydelotte, Partner - *Generalist*
Mr. Kenneth B. Zeigler, Partner

Salary minimum: $175,000

Functions: Generalist, Health Admin., Sales & Mktg., HR Mgmt., Finance, IT, Non-profits

Industries: Generalist

Networks: I-I-C Partners Executive Search Worldwide

Innovative Partnerships Executive Search

10965 Autillo Way
San Diego, CA 92127
(858) 676-1999
Fax: (858) 676-1911
Email: info@ipexecutivesearch.com
Web: www.ipexecutivesearch.com

Description: We are a national executive search firm specializing in senior-level positions in high-tech, financial services and telecommunications. We also recruit in the areas of health care and higher education. We are a retained search firm. Please visit our web site at www.ipexecutivesearch.com. We also offer additional personalized services on our web page. We look forward to working with you.

Key Contact - Specialty:
Ms. Catherine C. Burton, President - *High technology, telecommunications, financial services, healthcare, higher education*

Salary minimum: $75,000

Functions: Senior Mgmt.

Industries: Banking, Non-profits, Higher Ed., Advertising, Telecoms, Healthcare

Professional Associations: ACSD, AFP, AFP, DSDP, PRSA, SDWP

InSearch Worldwide Corp

1 Landmark Sq
Stamford, CT 06901
(203) 355-3000
Fax: (203) 355-3100
Email: gulian@insearchworldwide.com
Web: www.insearchworldwide.com

Description: We provide strategic recruitment solutions delivered either on-site, on client premises, where our recruitment teams interact on a real-time basis with clients or, off-site, via traditional retained search where dedicated recruitment professionals are deployed from our office locations.

Key Contact:
Mr. Randolph Gulian, President/Managing Director

Salary minimum: $80,000

Functions: General Mgmt., Mktg. Mgmt., Direct Mktg., IT, MIS Mgmt., Systems Implem., Systems Support, Network Admin., DB Admin., Int'l.

Industries: Generalist, Energy, Utilities, Mfg., Food, Bev., Tobacco, Chemicals, Computer Equip., Retail, Finance, Invest. Banking, Brokers, Accounting, Media, Publishing, New Media,

Telecoms, Aerospace, Packaging, Insurance, Real Estate, Software, Biotech, Healthcare

Professional Associations: AMA, NAER, SLF

Branches:
19925 Stevens Creek Blvd
Cupertino, CA 95014-2358
(408) 735-7140
Fax: (408) 725-8885
Email: thawley@insearchworldwide.com
Key Contact:
Mr. Philip Thawley, Senior Vice President/Managing Director

980 N Michigan Ave Ste 1400
Chicago, IL 60611
(312) 988-4821
Fax: (312) 214-3510
Email: halper@insearchworldwide.com
Key Contact:
Mr. Harlan Halper, Senior Vice President/Managing Director

919 3rd Ave Fl 27
New York, NY 10022
(212) 836-4373
Fax: (212) 836-4840
Email: smith@insearchworldwide.com
Key Contact:
Mr. Gil Smith, Senior Vice President/Managing Director

Int'l Management Advisors Inc

PO Box 174
FDR Station
New York, NY 10150-0174
(212) 758-7770

Description: Quality, medium size generalist firm serving multinational and national organizations. We conduct searches in most functional areas. Results through teamwork.

Key Contact:
Ms. Constance W. Klages, President - *Information systems, human resources, generalist*
Mr. Paul J. Harbaugh, Jr., Executive Vice President - *Chemical, retail, marketing*
Mr. Henri J. P. Manassero, Partner - *Hospitality*
Mr. George N. Lumsby, Senior Consultant

Salary minimum: $75,000

Functions: Generalist, Senior Mgmt., Mktg. Mgmt., HR Mgmt., IT, Engineering, Minorities

Industries: Generalist, Energy, Utilities, Non-profits, Mgmt. Consulting, HR Services, Biotech

Int'l Research Group

(a subsidiary of Wilkins & Wilkins Int'l Inc)
345 Manzanita Ave Ste 103
Palo Alto, CA 94306-1023
(650) 833-1040
(650) 833-1050
Fax: (650) 833-1047
Email: swilkins@pacbell.com

Description: All principals have held key positions in science and technology organizations and have recruited for technical, managerial and executive positions in medical technology and biotechnology industries.

Key Contact:
Ms. Sherrie Wilkins, Ph.D., President - *Medical technology, biotechnology*
Mr. Sid Wilkins, Ph.D., Chairman - *Medical technology*
Ms. A. M. Wilkins, Director-Technology Research - *Medical, biotechnology*
Ms. Mary Lou Fasola, Director-Finance/Admin

Salary minimum: $60,000

Functions: Generalist

Industries: Medical Devices

Professional Associations: AAAS, ISPE

Branches:
44817 E Foxtail Rd
PO Box 1495
Coarsegold, CA 93614
(559) 683-5719
Key Contact - Specialty:
Dr. Mark Wilder, Senior Recruiter - *Medical technology*

Intech Summit Group Inc

5075 Shoreham Pl Ste 280
San Diego, CA 92122
(858) 452-2100
Fax: (858) 452-8500
Email: isg@isgsearch.com
Web: www.isgsearch.com

Description: Principals have over 40 years of combined professional search experience at all levels of executive recruitment in healthcare, hi-tech, government, human resources, network communications, finance, educational services, information technology and consulting services industry.

Key Contact - Specialty:
Mr. Michael R. Cohen, Chief Executive Officer - *Healthcare administration, consulting, information technology, human resources, engineering*

Salary minimum: $80,000

Functions: Directors, Finance, Taxes, M&A, Mgmt. Consultants

Industries: Generalist, Drugs Mfg., Misc. Mfg., Finance, Invest. Banking, Brokers, Venture Cap., Misc. Financial, Services, Pharm Svcs., Accounting, Mgmt. Consulting, Telecoms, Government, Insurance, Biotech, Healthcare

Professional Associations: HIMSS, IEEE

Branches:
3150 Pio Pico Dr Ste 100A
Carlsbad, CA 92008
(760) 720-2120
Fax: (760) 720-2121
Key Contact - Specialty:
Ms. Kathy Kinley, Senior Vice President - *Human resources*

Integrated Search Solutions Group LLC (ISSG)

33 Main St
Port Washington, NY 11050
(516) 767-3030
Email: janis@issg.net
Web: www.issg.net

Description: Our focus is information technology, with specialization in conducting senior-level executive searches in the industry segments of outsourcing, e-business, Internet, start-ups, consulting, and CIO/CTO. Our practice is national and includes large established clients to small, pre-IPO companies.

Key Contact - Specialty:
Mr. Laurence Janis, Managing Partner - *Information technology*
Mr. Vincent J. Sessa, Partner - *Information technology*

Salary minimum: $100,000

Functions: IT

Industries: Food, Bev., Tobacco, Consumer Elect., Banking, Invest. Banking, Brokers, Venture Cap., Mgmt. Consulting, Telecoms, Software

Professional Associations: LISTNET

Integrity Network Inc

400 Inverness Dr S 200
Englewood, CO 80112
(303) 220-9752
Fax: (303) 302-5679

Email: judy@integritynetworkinc.com
Web: www.integritynetworkinc.com

Description: We are an executive search firm that specializes in the high-tech industry placing sales and marketing executives in Colorado. Our typical search is with a Colorado based software/Internet company where we are placing a VP of sales, VP of marketing, or VP of business development candidate.

Key Contact - Specialty:
Mrs. Judy Kennelley, President - *VP sales, VP marketing*
Mr. Tom Hickey, Vice President - *VP sales, VP marketing*

Salary minimum: $150,000

Functions: Mktg. Mgmt., Sales Mgmt.

Industries: Software

Integrity Search Inc

1489 Baltimore Pike Ste 104
Mills of Victoria
Springfield, PA 19064
(610) 543-8590
Email: jlong@integritysearchinc.com
Web: www.integritysearchinc.com

Description: Offering a consultive, strategic approach to executive search and management coaching on interviewing and hiring process, plus an unrivaled reputation for treating both candidates and clients with respect and integrity.

Key Contact - Specialty:
Ms. Janet R. Long, President - *Communications, marketing, management consulting*

Salary minimum: $75,000

Functions: Senior Mgmt., Middle Mgmt., Sales & Mktg., HR Mgmt.

Industries: Media

Professional Associations: ASTD, CCM, IABC, PRSA

Intelcap de Mexico SC

(also known as Amrop Int'l)
Calzada del Desierto de los Leones No 46
Col San Angel Inn
Mexico City, DF 01000
Mexico
52 5 616 44 98
52 5 616 38 04
Fax: 52 5 550 81 73
Email: newman@ai.com.mx
Web: www.amrop.com

Description: Our firm is committed to helping private and public sector client organizations achieve greater profitability, performance and efficiency through the engagement of outstanding chief executives and senior managers.

Key Contact:
Mr. Carlos A. Rojas, Managing Partner

Salary minimum: $80,000

Functions: Generalist

Industries: Generalist

Networks: The Amrop - Hever Group

Branches:
Av Lazaro Cardenas 2400 Pte
Edif Los Soles C-13
Garza García, NL 66270
Mexico
52 8 363 2529
52 8 363 29 69
Fax: 52 8 363 2301
Email: monterrey@amrop.com
Key Contact:
Mr. Jose Carrillo, Managing Partner

InteliSearch Inc†

350 Bedford St Ste 304
Stamford, CT 06901
(203) 325-1389
Fax: (203) 325-1678
Email: executivesolutions@intelisearch-inc.com
Web: www.intelisearch-inc.com

Description: This award-winning, best-practices firm specializes in the top 10%, high-impact leadership talent. Our unique team-based approach, alliance-intensive network, and performance metrics accountability drive an industry-leading 85% completion rate within 6 weeks. Our firm's principal, a former global 25 Senior HR executive, is prominent in the minority executive community and maintains the industry's most exhaustive executive diversity database.

Key Contact - Specialty:
Mr. George L. Rodriguez, Managing Principal - *Finance, sales & marketing, human resources, insurance, reinsurance and operations leadership*

Salary minimum: $80,000

Functions: Middle Mgmt.

Industries: Generalist

InternetionalExpertise

121 Baltimore Ave
Larkspur, CA 94939
(415) 927-1985
(415) 927-1980
Fax: (415) 927-2226
Email: kathy@ie1.com
Web: www.ie1.com

Description: We are a venture catalyst firm specializing in executive recruitment in sales, marketing and business development and overall operations. We specialize in next generation technology companies, media companies, established and proven start-ups. For contact information and details, see our website.

Key Contact:
Mr. Robert Montgomery, CEO/President
Ms. Kathy Ryan, Vice President

Functions: Directors, Senior Mgmt., Middle Mgmt., Sales & Mktg., Advertising, Mktg. Mgmt., PR, Finance, Mgmt. Consultants, Int'l.

Industries: Venture Cap., Services, Media, Advertising, Publishing, New Media, Software

---

Interquest Inc

599 Lexington Ave Ste 2300
New York, NY 10022
(212) 319-0790
Fax: (212) 753-0596

Description: We provide recruitment of senior lawyers for corporations and law firms both domestically and internationally. We cover all industries and all legal disciplines. Our specialization in general counsel and partner searches plus law firm mergers.

Key Contact - Specialty:
Mr. Meyer Haberman, President - *General counsel, lateral partner*

Salary minimum: $125,000

Functions: Attorneys

Industries: Generalist

Branches:
98 Cutter Mill Rd Ste 337 S
Great Neck, NY 11021
(516) 482-2330
Fax: (516) 482-2114
Key Contact:
Ms. Milca Garcia

Intersource Ltd†

1509A W 6th St
Austin, TX 78703
(512) 457-0883
Fax: (512) 457-0889
Email: ph@intersourceaustin.com
Web: www.intersourcesearch.com

Description: We are an executive search firm specializing in human resources, accounting/finance, retail sales and marketing/advertising personnel. We place both contract and permanent positions. We are positioned to handle national and international opportunities, and our clients range from entrepreneurial to Fortune 500 companies. We work as a team, committed to getting results.

Key Contact - Specialty:
Ms. Patti Halladay, Principal - *Accounting, finance, human resources, high technology*
Ms. Vikki Loving, CEO - *Accounting, finance, human resources, high technology*

Salary minimum: $75,000

Functions: Directors, Senior Mgmt., Mktg. Mgmt., Sales Mgmt., HR Mgmt., Finance, CFO's, IT, MIS Mgmt., Int'l.

Industries: Retail, Finance, Services, Software

Networks: National Personnel Assoc (NPA)

Branches:
1675 Friendship Church Rd
Murphy, NC 28906
(828) 644-9558
Fax: (828) 644-0296
Email: waggoner@intersourcesearch.com
Web: www.intersourcesearch.com
Key Contact - Specialty:
Ms. Lisa Waggoner, Principal - *Human resources, accounting/finance, high technology*

1523 Pecan Trace Ct
Houston, TX 77479
(281) 343-7851
Fax: (281) 545-8794
Email: isource@compassnet.com
Web: www.intersourcesearch.com
Key Contact - Specialty:
Mr. Thom Besso, President - *Accounting/finance, human resources, high technology, sales & marketing, retail*

IPS Search Inc

980 N Michigan Ave Ste 1400
Chicago, IL 60611
(312) 214-4983
Fax: (312) 214-4949
Email: info@ipssearch.com
Web: www.ipssearch.com

Description: We have specialized in delivering swift and effective client-driven search solutions to the insurance industry globally for over 20 years.

Key Contact - Specialty:
Mr. James W. Evan-Cook, President - *Insurance*
Mr. Edward Snell, Vice President - *Insurance*

Salary minimum: $100,000

Functions: Generalist, Senior Mgmt., CFO's, Risk Mgmt., MIS Mgmt., Int'l.

Industries: Generalist, Insurance

Branches:
300 Park Ave
New York, NY 10022
(212) 572-4871
Email: info@ipssearch.com
Key Contact - Specialty:
Mr. James Evan-Cook - *Insurance*

IR Search

7777 Greenback Ln Ste 201
Citrus Heights, CA 95610
(916) 721-5511
Fax: (916) 721-5007
Email: info@irgroupco.com
Web: www.irgroupco.com

Description: A strategic consulting, M&A and executive search firm specializing in services to the insurance industry.

Key Contact - Specialty:
Mr. Richard Shoemaker, President - *Board members, CEOs, COOs, CFOs*
Ms. Sandra Simmons, CPC, Managing Director - *Life, HMOs, PPOs, annuities*
Mr. Gene Boscacci, Managing Director - *E&S, construction, workers compensation*
Mr. Chuck Winter, Director - *TPAs, outsourced admin services, retail brokerage*

Salary minimum: $65,000

Functions: Senior Mgmt.

Industries: Insurance, Healthcare

Professional Associations: IBA, INS

Isaacson, Miller

334 Boylston St Ste 500
Boston, MA 02116
(617) 262-6500
Fax: (617) 262-6509
Email: info@imsearch.com
Web: www.imsearch.com

Description: We are a national retained firm serving mission-driven organizations in senior-level searches. Fields of expertise include education (both K-12 and higher education), research institutes, healthcare (both community care and academic medical centers), foundations, human and social services, community and economic development, advocacy, conservation and environment, and public management.

Key Contact:
Mr. John Isaacson, Managing Director
Mr. Arnie Miller, Managing Director

Salary minimum: $120,000

Functions: Senior Mgmt., Healthcare, CFO's, Minorities, Non-profits

Industries: Non-profits, Higher Ed., Government, Healthcare

Jackson Resources

101 W 6th St Ste 506
Austin, TX 78701
(512) 236-1227

Description: Our searches are fast, efficient and economical. By canvassing the competition, our clients get a market analysis of their hiring prospects, not just a stack of resumes.

Key Contact - Specialty:
Ms. Jennifer Jackson, President - *Sales & marketing, computers*
Mr. Tim Scoggins, Director of Client Services - *Sales, marketing*

Functions: Sales Mgmt., IT

Industries: Computer Equip., Equip Svcs., Mgmt. Consulting, E-commerce, IT Implementation, Wireless, Fiber Optic, Network Infrastructure, ERP SW, Networking, Comm. SW

Professional Associations: CTIA, WITI

Jacobson Executive Search

120 S LaSalle St Ste 1410
Chicago, IL 60603
(312) 726-1580
Fax: (312) 726-2295

Email: chicago@jacobsonexec.com
Web: www.jacobsonexec.com

Description: Our firm serves the insurance and related industries exclusively. Since our inception, we have been able to offer incomparable industry knowledge, unparalleled candidate selection skills, and unmatched insight into the insurance community.

Key Contact - Specialty:
Mr. Gregory Jacobson, Principal - *Insurance*
Ms. Margaret Resce Milkint, Executive Vice President - *Insurance*

Salary minimum: $50,000

Functions: Generalist, Senior Mgmt., Mktg. Mgmt., Benefits, CFO's, Risk Mgmt.

Industries: Generalist, Insurance

Professional Associations: ASA, CPCU

Branches:
1775 The Exchange Ste 240
Atlanta, GA 30339
(770) 952-3877
Fax: (770) 952-0061
Email: atlanta@jacobsonexec.com
Key Contact - Specialty:
Mr. Gregory P. Jacobson, Principal - *Insurance*

5 Neshaminy Interplex Ste 113
Trevose, PA 19053
(215) 639-5860
Fax: (215) 639-8096
Email: philadelphia@jacobson-associates.com
Key Contact - Specialty:
Mr. Nate Bass, President - *Insurance*

Jade Group LLC

435 6th Ave
Pittsburgh, PA 15219
(412) 288-3037
Fax: (412) 281-6867
Web: www.jadegroup.net

Description: Our primary services include a broad range of industrial relations/human resource management consulting, as well as executive search and placement for short-term and permanent needs.

Key Contact:
Mr. Robert L. Kirkpatrick, Member
Mr. David W. Christopher, Member
Mr. Donald T. Menovich, Member
Mr. Aaron A. Herbick, Member
Mr. Earl W. Schick, Consultant

Salary minimum: $75,000

Functions: Generalist, Middle Mgmt., Plant Mgmt., Mktg. Mgmt., CFO's, Engineering, Attorneys

Industries: Generalist, Agri., Forestry, Mining, Construction, Mfg., Transportation, Accounting, Environmental Svcs.

JAG Group†

311 Lindbergh Blvd Ste 109
St. Louis, MO 63141
(314) 432-6565
Web: www.jaggroup.com

Description: The firm prides itself in being confidential, thorough, and rapid response without sacrificing quality. We specialize in managed care and hospital administration. We provide rather unique fee arrangements.

Key Contact - Specialty:
Mr. John A. Green, President - *Healthcare administration, general management*
Mr. Ben Goldstein, Project Manager - *Healthcare administration*
Ms. Jean Pompelli, Project Manager - *Healthcare administration*
Ms. Heide Green, Project Manager - *Healthcare administration*

Salary minimum: $50,000

Functions: Senior Mgmt., Middle Mgmt., Healthcare, Health Admin., CFO's, MIS Mgmt.

Industries: Healthcare

JBA Associates

23037 SE 27th Way
Issaquah, WA 98029
(425) 557-8804

Description: A full-service retained firm for retail and food services industries.

Key Contact - Specialty:
Mr. James L. Black, Partner - *Retail*

Salary minimum: $50,000

Functions: Generalist, Personnel

Industries: Generalist, Retail, Hospitality

Professional Associations: SHRM

JC Wallin Executive Search

301 Forest Ave Ste 200
Laguna Beach, CA 92651
(949) 494-4914
Email: john@jcwallin.com
Web: www.jcwallin.com

Description: Founder has more than 20 years of progressive, client-retained, executive recruiting experience combining big firm technique and know-how with the responsiveness and partnership of a sole practitioner. Recent assignments across a wide range of functions and industries include searches for directors, vice presidents, and chief officers.

Key Contact:
Mr. John C. Wallin, Managing Director

Salary minimum: $120,000

Functions: General Mgmt., Mfg., Sales & Mktg., HR Mgmt., Finance, IT, Engineering

Industries: Generalist

JDG y Asociados SA de CV

Blvd Rodriguez 78
Hermosillo, SO 83000
Mexico
52 6 214 8276
52 6 214 2875
Fax: 52 6 214 8276
Email: jdgconsu@rtn.uson.mx

Description: We are the most prestigious generalist search firm, with profound knowledge of the Mexican executive market, and serve a select number of national and multinational companies to assure the competitive advantage of broad search universe, without the limiting restraints of large firms. Our firm emphasizes candidates' career path counseling, to insure long-term executive/company association. We specialize in executives that speak Spanish or that are willing to relocate in Mexico or the Southern boarder of the US.

Key Contact - Specialty:
Mr. Jose D. Gurrola, Principal/General Director - *Mexico executive market, multinationals and maquiladoras operating in Mexico & the USA Southwest*
Ing. Laura G. Ciscomani, Associate - *Most functions in industry, commerce and services*

Salary minimum: $60,000

Functions: Generalist, General Mgmt., Mfg., Materials, Sales & Mktg., HR Mgmt., Finance, IT

Industries: Generalist, Construction, Mfg., Wholesale, Retail, Finance, Services, Media

Professional Associations: CANACO, COPARMEX, EAT, USEM

The Jeremiah Group Inc

5 Greeley St
The Medallion Ctr
Merrimack, NH 03054
(603) 429-1000
Fax: (603) 429-1427
Email: mccoy.daniel@worldnet.att.net

Description: Our success is tied to our ability to evaluate and present candidates who are the best fit to the company and the job. This is based on knowledge of the client's culture, business and work style.

Key Contact:
Mr. Daniel J. McCoy, CEO/Managing Partner
Mr. John Lorden, Partner

Functions: General Mgmt., Production, Direct Mktg., R&D

Industries: Consumer Elect., Higher Ed., Mgmt. Consulting, Publishing, New Media

Branches:
35 Crossneck Rd
Marion, MA 02738
(508) 748-2718
Fax: (508) 748-2718
Key Contact:
Mr. Daniel J. McCoy, CEO/Managing Partner

G M Jerolman & Associates LLC

191 Post Rd W
Westport, CT 06880
(203) 221-2603
(203) 481-7444
Fax: (203) 221-2604
Email: gregg@retailithunter.com
Web: www.retailithunter.com

Description: Boutique executive search firm specializing in senior-level information technology assignments for the retail and apparel trade industries. This specialization allows us to surface larger pools of qualified candidates in shorter periods of time.

Key Contact:
Mr. Gregory M. Jerolman, President - *Information technology, retail trade, wholesale trade*
Ms. Deborah Jerolman
Mr. John Gassler

Salary minimum: $80,000

Functions: Generalist, Systems Analysis, Systems Dev., Systems Implem., Systems Support, Network Admin., DB Admin., Mgmt. Consultants

Industries: Generalist, Food, Bev., Tobacco, Textiles, Apparel, Soap, Perf., Cosmtcs., Wholesale, Retail, Software

Professional Associations: NRF, SHRM

JG Consultants Inc

8150 N Central Expy Ste 220
Dallas, TX 75206
(214) 696-9196
Fax: (214) 696-9205

Description: We are recognized for completing difficult retained searches when others have not produced results. We have performed many multi-location, multi-hire searches, as well as recruiting impossible to find candidates. All of our candidates are pre-interviewed and referenced.

Key Contact:
Ms. Jay Stephenson, President - *High technology*
Ms. Ginnie Bellville, Sr Consultant

Functions: Generalist, Senior Mgmt., Product Dev., Sales & Mktg., Mktg. Mgmt., Sales Mgmt., Systems Support, Int'l.

Industries: Generalist, Computer Equip., Venture Cap., New Media, Telecoms, Software

JK Consultants

1123 - 6th St
Manhattan Beach, CA 90266
(310) 376-5257
Fax: (240) 337-5885
Email: contact@jksuccess.com
Web: www.jksuccess.com

Description: Our firm is committed to helping our clients strengthen their leadership capabilities through unsurpassed executive sourcing and business solutions. Our services include executive coaching, corporate relocation services, and much more.

Key Contact:
Mr. Fred Khachi, President

Salary minimum: $80,000

Functions: Generalist

Industries: Generalist

JLI-Boston

230 Commercial St
Boston, MA 02109-1305
(617) 227-4030
Fax: (617) 227-6008
Email: contact@jli-boston.com
Web: www.jli-boston.com

Description: Exclusively in the plastics, packaging and medical device industries. Conducts critical searches for Best-in-Class executives, managers and technical specialists who can significantly impact its clients' capabilities, profits and market position.

Key Contact:
Mr. N. G. Fountas, Managing Director - *Plastics*
Mr. J. Morton, Research Manager

Salary minimum: $60,000

Functions: General Mgmt., Mfg., Packaging, Sales & Mktg., R&D, Engineering, Mgmt. Consultants

Industries: Chemicals, Medical Devices, Plastics, Rubber, Paints, Petro. Products, Mgmt. Consulting, Packaging

Professional Associations: SPI

JLM Consulting Inc

137 N Oak Park Ave Ste 309
Oak Park, IL 60301-1339
(708) 763-9800
Fax: (708) 763-9850
Email: jlm@jlmhrconsulting.com

Description: We specialize in targeted recruitment research designed to provide clients unique and cost effective means to fill current mid- to upper-level management needs in almost every industry.

Key Contact - Specialty:
Mr. James L. Morris, Principal - *Generalist*
Mr. Greg Goldberg, Vice President/Operations - *Finance & accounting, generalist*

Salary minimum: $40,000

Functions: Generalist, General Mgmt., Mfg., Sales & Mktg., HR Mgmt., Finance, R&D, Engineering

Industries: Generalist, Mfg., Finance, Accounting, Mgmt. Consulting, HR Services

Professional Associations: EMA, HRAMM, NBMBAA, SHRM

Branches:
2127 University Park Dr Ste 320
Okemos, MI 48864
(517) 349-5316
Fax: (517) 349-5348
Email: jlmmich@iserv.net
Key Contact - Specialty:
Ms. Shelly M. Madden, Branch Manager - *Human resources, sales & marketing, plastics manufacturing, automotive manufacturing*

PO Box 46244
Minneapolis, MN 55446
(612) 553-7878
Fax: (612) 553-7979
Email: philpeikes@aol.com
Key Contact - Specialty:
Mr. Phil Peikes, Vice President-Sales/Marketing - *Generalist, high technology*

PO Box 6652
Portsmouth, VA 27703
(888) 426-9696
Fax: (757) 686-3567
Email: ssshep@compuserve.com
Key Contact - Specialty:
Mr. Steven Sheppard, Business Development Manager - *Business development*

JM & Company

PO Box 285
Wayne, PA 19087
(610) 964-0200
Fax: (610) 964-8596
Email: jmcompany@jmsearch.com
Web: www.jmsearch.com

Description: Our firm works on a retained basis with companies that require very detailed recruiting, confidentiality, and a thorough knowledge of the industries that we specialize in.

Key Contact - Specialty:
Mr. John C. Marshall, President - *Packaging*
Mr. John D. Hildebrand, Partner - *Plastics*
Mr. Robert A. Sargent, Partner - *Technology, e-commerce*

Salary minimum: $100,000

Functions: Senior Mgmt., Product Dev., Production, Plant Mgmt., Materials, Purchasing, Mktg. Mgmt., Sales Mgmt., HR Mgmt., CFO's

Industries: Generalist, Mfg., Finance, E-commerce, PSA/ASP, Telecoms, Packaging, Software

John & Powers Inc

12935 N Forty Dr Ste 214
St. Louis, MO 63141
(314) 453-0080

Description: Consulting firm which exclusively specializes in executive search to all industries. Clients represented include Fortune 500 companies, medium size organizations and turnaround situations.

Key Contact - Specialty:
Mr. Harold A. John, President - *Generalist*

Salary minimum: $100,000

Functions: Generalist

Industries: Generalist

Johnson & Associates Inc

101 1st St Ste 282
Los Altos, CA 94022
(650) 941-4244
Fax: (650) 941-9093
Email: cheri@jasearch.net
Web: www.jasearch.net

Description: Personnel search specialists primarily in hi-tech, bio-medical, medical instrumentation, medical devices, computer telephony (CTI), telecommunications, computers and peripherals industry. Other assignments have included viticulture and enology (vineyard and winery industries) and segments of commercial property development.

Key Contact - Specialty:
Ms. Cheri Johnson, President - *High technology, technical, management*

Salary minimum: $50,000

Functions: Generalist, Senior Mgmt., Middle Mgmt., Mkt. Research, Sales Mgmt., Systems Dev., R&D, Engineering

Industries: Generalist, Agri., Forestry, Mining, Medical Devices, Computer Equip., New Media, Telecoms, Software

Professional Associations: CSP, NAER, NCHRC

Branches:
313 N Main St Ste Ste B
Sebastopol, CA 95472
(707) 824-9098
Key Contact:
Mr. Bruce Brashares, Senior Recruiter
Mr. Kane Lack, Senior Recruiter

John H Johnson & Associates Inc
310 S Michigan Ave Ste 2600
Chicago, IL 60604
(312) 663-4257
Fax: (312) 663-9761
Email: search@recruitersintl.com
Web: www.recruitersintl.com

Description: Professional retainer-based executive search firm for all industries/ functional areas.

Key Contact:
Mr. John H. Johnson, CEO

Salary minimum: $75,000

Functions: General Mgmt., Mfg., Sales & Mktg., HR Mgmt., Finance, Engineering

Industries: Generalist

Johnson & Company
184 Old Ridgefield Rd
Wilton, CT 06897
(203) 761-1212
Fax: (203) 762-0747
Email: johnson.co@att.net

Description: Quality reputation for recruiting functional heads and general managers.

Key Contact - Specialty:
Mr. Stanley C. Johnson, President - *Functional heads, general managers*

Salary minimum: $100,000

Functions: General Mgmt., Senior Mgmt., Mfg., Sales & Mktg., HR Mgmt., Finance, CFO's, MIS Mgmt.

Industries: Generalist, Food, Bev., Tobacco, Textiles, Apparel, Paper, Printing, Soap, Perf., Cosmtcs., Drugs Mfg., Paints, Petro. Products, Motor Vehicles, Computer Equip., Consumer Elect.

Professional Associations: IACPR

C P Johnson & Company
(a licensee of Foster Partners Inc)
332 Minnestota St Ste W-1372
St. Paul, MN 55101
(651) 222-4420
Fax: (651) 222-7260
Email: cpjohnson@cpjohnson.com
Web: www.cpjohnson.com

Description: We conduct assignments in a broad variety of industries. The firm's principals have helped clients identify and recruit executive and management talent in all major functional areas.

Key Contact:
Mr. Christopher P. Johnson, Managing Director
Mr. Jerry M. Friedmann
Ms. Cynthia A. Stokvis, Director
Mr. Stephen T. Matthews, Managing Associate
Mr. Benjamin C. Johnson, Consulting Associate

Salary minimum: $75,000

Functions: Generalist

Industries: Generalist

L J Johnson & Company†
815 Newport Rd
Ann Arbor, MI 48103
(734) 663-5113
Fax: (509) 355-6168
Email: jobs@jobsbyjohnson.com
Web: www.jobsbyjohnson.com

Description: Retained searches for management, logistics, technical and administrative personnel. Financial and management consultants. Strong emphasis on manufacturing, engineering, automotive Tier 1.

Key Contact - Specialty:
Mr. L. J. Johnson, President - *Manufacturing (all)*

Salary minimum: $40,000

Functions: Generalist

Industries: Generalist

Professional Associations: FEI

Networks: Top Echelon Network

Ronald S Johnson Associates Inc
11661 San Vicente Blvd Ste 400
Los Angeles, CA 90049
(310) 820-5855
Fax: (310) 207-1815
Email: searchrsj@aol.com

Description: Retainer search firm specializing in senior management for medium to high-technology, venture backed companies in hardware, software, network/telecommunications and transportation.

Key Contact:
Mr. Ronald S. Johnson, President
Ms. Pat Kriste, Executive Assistant

Salary minimum: $125,000

Functions: Generalist

Industries: Computer Equip., Venture Cap., Telecoms, Software

Roye Johnston Associates Inc†
2680 Mary Ln Pl
Escondido, CA 92025
(760) 487-5200
(800) 886-6619
Fax: (858) 487-5296

Description: Specialists in occupational medicine, physicians, nurses, nationally and internationally.

Key Contact:
Ms. Roye Johnston, President - *Occupational medicine, physicians, nurses*
Mr. Brian Johnston, Secretary

Salary minimum: $100,000

Functions: Generalist, Physicians

Industries: Generalist, Healthcare

Jonas, Walters & Associates Inc
1110 N Old World Third St Ste 510
Milwaukee, WI 53203-1184
(414) 291-2828
Fax: (414) 291-2822
Email: info@jonaswalters.com
Web: www.jonaswalters.com

Description: Wisconsin's oldest and largest retained search firm with strong Midwest presence. Focus is on recruitment of mid/senior executives for major manufacturers. Excellent client retention record. Separate managed care and physician search divisions.

Key Contact - Specialty:
Mr. William F. Walters, President - *Consumer products, electronics, metal working, engineered products, telecommunications*
Mr. Donald Hucko, Sr Vice President - *Metal working, engineer products, consumer products*

Mr. John Kuhn, Executive Vice President - *Mill work, architectural products, fabricated glass, metals, healthcare*
Mr. Mark W. Oswald, Vice President - *Physician search, healthcare, acute care*
Ms. Desiree SanFelipo, Consultant - *Healthcare*

Salary minimum: $75,000

Functions: General Mgmt., Mfg., Healthcare, Sales & Mktg., Cash Mgmt., IT, R&D, Engineering, Specialized Svcs., Minorities

Industries: Generalist, Mfg., Food, Bev., Tobacco, Finance, Non-profits, Aerospace, Biotech

Jones & Egan Inc
521 5th Ave Ste 1700
New York, NY 10175
(212) 292-5070
Fax: (212) 292-5071

Description: Twenty five years of specialty search experience within financial services plus a deliberate effort to work with a limited number of clients in order to provide a more personalized and focused service.

Key Contact - Specialty:
Mr. John Egan, Principal - *Financial services, generalist*
Mr. Jonathan Jones, Principal - *Financial services, generalist*

Salary minimum: $100,000

Functions: Generalist

Industries: Finance, Banking, Invest. Banking, Misc. Financial

Jones and Jones
10250 SW Greenburg Rd Ste 219
Lincoln Ctr
Portland, OR 97223
(503) 452-6116
Fax: (503) 452-6115
Email: info@jones-jones.com
Web: www.jones-jones.com

Description: We are a sixteen-year-old firm serving technology companies exclusively. The firm provides a full range of retained services associated with executive search and organizational development. We are exclusively retained for all search engagements and paid by our client companies.

Key Contact - Specialty:
Ms. Pamela K. Jones, Principal - *High technology companies*

Functions: Generalist

Industries: Software

Professional Associations: SAO

Jones Management Company
1 Dock St Ste 309
Stamford, CT 06902
(203) 353-1140
Email: info@jones-mgt.com
Web: www.jones-mgt.com

Description: We are a quality provider of executive search and professional consulting services. We offer our clients full-service solutions backed by years of experience and proven methodologies. Our professional approach proves that partnering with us is the most time-efficient and cost-effective method of successfully fulfilling staffing requirements.

Key Contact - Specialty:
Mr. Francis E. Jones, CEO - *Generalist*
Ms. Denise Guest, Senior Associate - *Finance*
Mr. William Ceyrnik, Managing Director - *Generalist*

Salary minimum: $75,000

Functions: Generalist, General Mgmt., Finance, Budgeting, Credit, M&A, IT, Mgmt. Consultants

Industries: Generalist, Finance, Media, Environmental Svcs., Packaging, Real Estate, Software, Healthcare

Professional Associations: IACPR

Branches:
555 5th Ave
New York, NY 10017
(212) 697-8647
Email: info@jones-mgt.com
Key Contact - Specialty:
Ms. Bonnie Jones - *Administrative*

Jones-Parker/Starr

207 S Elliott Rd Ste 155
Chapel Hill, NC 27514
(919) 542-5977
(919) 542-1527
Fax: (919) 542-1622
Email: info@jonesparkerstarr.com
Web: www.jonesparkerstarr.com

Description: We provide consulting services to the executive search profession and act as a resource for multi-national corporations setting up in-house search firms and recruiting HR executives. We undertake only assignments that allow us to add value to an organization. This usually involves organizations undergoing change.

Key Contact - Specialty:
Ms. Janet Jones-Parker, Managing Director - *Professional services, executive search firms, in-house search firms*
Mr. Jonathan Starr, Managing Director - *Professional services, executive search firms, in-house search firms*

Salary minimum: $150,000

Functions: Directors, Senior Mgmt., Middle Mgmt., HR Mgmt., Personnel, Mgmt. Consultants, Minorities, Int'l.

Industries: Generalist

Professional Associations: IACPR, C200, SHRM

Branches:
258 Riverside Dr Ste 5A
New York, NY 10025
(212) 280-6464
Email: louise@jonesparkerstarr.com
Key Contact - Specialty:
Ms. Louise M. Young, Senior Vice President - *Professional services, executive search firms, in-house search firms*

Jordan-Sitter Associates

23995 Bat Cave Rd Ste 200
San Antonio, TX 78266
(210) 651-5561
Fax: (210) 651-5562
Email: info@jordansitter.com
Web: www.jordansitter.com

Description: Construction, mining, industrial and agricultural equipment manufacturers, dealers, rental companies and related businesses on an exclusive and retained basis, only. All disciplines, mostly in North America.

Key Contact:
Mr. William P. Sitter, Owner - *Construction, mining, equipment manufacturers, distributors, industrial*
Mr. Christopher W. Sitter, Associate

Salary minimum: $90,000

Functions: Generalist, General Mgmt., Senior Mgmt., Middle Mgmt., Mfg., Sales & Mktg., Engineering, Int'l.

Industries: Generalist, Agri., Forestry, Mining, Construction, Metal Products, Machine, Appliance, Misc. Mfg., Equip Svcs.

Professional Associations: AED, ARA, CIMA, EMI, FCCI, ICPM, MHEDA

JSG Group Management Consultants

178 Main St Ste 400
Unionville, ON L3R 5T6
Canada
(905) 477-3625
(905) 477-4215
Fax: (905) 477-8211
Email: rbirarda@istar.ca
Web: www.jsggroup.com

Description: Retainer-based executive search firm, specializing in the automotive and technology sectors. Clients include vehicle manufacturers, vehicles and parts distributors, software and services companies and professional services firms.

Key Contact - Specialty:
Mr. Richard W. Birarda, Managing Partner - *General management, technology, automotive, sales & marketing, finance*

Salary minimum: $70,000

Functions: General Mgmt., Plant Mgmt., Mkt. Research, Mktg. Mgmt., Sales Mgmt., CFO's, MIS Mgmt., Engineering, Specialized Svcs., Int'l.

Industries: Motor Vehicles, Retail, Accounting, Mgmt. Consulting, Advertising, Aerospace

Judd Associates

85 Greenwood Rd Morganville Farms
Morganville, NJ 07751
(732) 970-0234
Fax: (732) 970-0017
Email: heidi@judd.net
Web: www.juddassociates.com

Description: We never take on more than 2 to 3 assignments at a time - allowing every client to be our #1 priority. The president of our company personally conducts every assignment.

Key Contact:
Ms. Heidi Judd, President

Salary minimum: $80,000

Functions: Generalist

Industries: Generalist, Mfg., Chemicals, Soap, Perf., Cosmtcs., Drugs Mfg., Medical Devices, Computer Equip., Consumer Elect., Mgmt. Consulting, Software

Julian-Soper & Associates Inc

500 N Michigan Ave Ste 300
Chicago, IL 60611-3375
(312) 396-4128
Fax: (312) 396-4129
Email: jsasearch@aol.com

Description: Management consultants specializing in executive search for mid- to senior-level positions on a nationwide basis.

Key Contact - Specialty:
Ms. Gracemarie Soper, President - *Generalist*

Salary minimum: $50,000

Functions: Generalist, Mfg.

Industries: Generalist, Misc. Financial, Non-profits, Accounting, Mgmt. Consulting, HR Services, Publishing, Telecoms, Packaging, Insurance, Mfg. SW, Healthcare

Julius Group LLC

1263 Beggs Rd
Westminster, MD 21157
(410) 840-9690
Email: resumes@juliusgroup.com
Web: www.juliusgroup.com

Description: We provide executive search solutions to companies on the leading edge of the technology revolution. We offer very personalized, high-quality

search services at the senior executive-level, as well as specialty practices in the areas of sales, marketing, business development, and Internet technical talent.

Key Contact - Specialty:
Mr. James Julius, Managing Partner - *Board members, senior executives, senior sales & marketing talent, internet technical talent*
Dr. Gloria Julius, Managing Partner - *Research*

Salary minimum: $100,000

Functions: Generalist

Industries: Venture Cap., Mgmt. Consulting, HR Services, E-commerce, IT Implementation, Media, Communications, Software

K&P Int'l

4343 Commerce Ct Ste 102
Lisle, IL 60532
(630) 577-1560
Fax: (630) 577-1563
Email: holke@konstroffer.com
Web: www.konstroffer.com

Description: International executive search firm serving all industries for middle and upper-management positions.

Key Contact - Specialty:
Mr. Oluf F. Konstroffer, President - *Generalist*
Ms. Christiane Holke, Senior Executive Search Consultant - *Generalist*
Ms. Heidi Rehner, Executive Search Consultant - *Generalist*

Salary minimum: $100,000

Functions: Generalist, Senior Mgmt., Middle Mgmt., Mfg., Purchasing, Sales & Mktg., HR Mgmt., CFO's, Budgeting, Int'l.

Industries: Generalist, Drugs Mfg., Medical Devices, Plastics, Rubber, Metal Products, Misc. Mfg., Aerospace

Kacevich, Lewis & Brown Inc

300 W Main St Bldg B
Northborough, MA 01532
(508) 393-6002
Fax: (508) 393-9527
Email: joek@klbinc.com
Web: www.klbinc.com

Description: We specialize in the search and replacement of Vice President-level executives in marketing and business development in the networking, internetworking and communications industries.

Key Contact - Specialty:
Mr. Joseph B. Kacevich, Jr., President - *Network, internet*

Salary minimum: $120,000

Functions: Mktg. Mgmt.

Industries: Telecoms, Telephony, Wireless, Fiber Optic, Network Infrastructure, Marketing SW, Networking, Comm. SW

Randy S Kahn & Associates

812 Wallberg Ave
Westfield, NJ 07090
(908) 654-1927
Fax: (908) 654-8575

Description: This firm provides high quality, "unbundled" search services. Because of the breadth and depth of his corporate staff, line and external consulting experience, he can offer uncommon insight into the position/candidate matching process.

Key Contact:
Mr. Randy S. Kahn, President

Salary minimum: $60,000

Functions: Generalist

Industries: Food, Bev., Tobacco, Misc. Mfg., Retail, Finance, Services, Mgmt. Consulting, HR Services, Advertising, Healthcare, Hospitals

Professional Associations: IACPR, ESRT

Kalish & Associates Inc
145 E 84th St Ste 5A
New York, NY 10028-2050
(212) 717-8935
Email: kalishinc@aol.com

Description: We are specialists in mid- and senior-level development personnel for colleges, medical centers, Jewish philanthropies, and other not-for-profit organizations.

Key Contact:
Mr. Mark Kalish, President

Salary minimum: $80,000

Functions: Senior Mgmt., Middle Mgmt.

Industries: Non-profits, Higher Ed.

Kanzer Associates Inc
500 N Michigan Ave Ste 500
Chicago, IL 60611
(312) 464-0831
(312) 464-0893
Fax: (312) 464-3719
Email: wkanzer@kanzer.com
Web: www.kanzer.com

Description: Provides clients with quality focus, aggressive timing, technical competence and commitment to communication, follow-through and delivery of a quality product.

Key Contact - Specialty:
Mr. William F. Kanzer, Principal - *Finance, human resources, manufacturing, sales & marketing, public relations*

Salary minimum: $120,000

Functions: Generalist

Industries: Mfg., Retail, Finance, Services, Media, Aerospace, Insurance, Healthcare

Professional Associations: IACPR

Kaplan & Associates Inc
1220 Wyngate Rd
Wynnewood, PA 19096
(610) 642-5644
Web: www.kasearch.com

Description: K&A helps organizations achieve their long-term business objectives by ensuring they can identify and attract the finest executive talent. We are a generalist firm with particular expertise working with early stage/venture-backed firms; technology companies in e-commerce, software, IT services and telecommunications; and financial institutions.

Key Contact - Specialty:
Mr. Alan J. Kaplan, President - *Technology, telecommunications firms, financial services organizations, start-up, venture-backed companies*
Ms. Brenda G. Reis, Principal - *Technology, telecommunications firms, start-up, venture-backed companies,,healthcare services firms*

Salary minimum: $150,000

Functions: Generalist

Industries: Finance, Banking, Venture Cap., Misc. Financial, HR Services, E-commerce, Media, Communications, Software, Biotech

Professional Associations: IACPR, ACG, GPVG

Gary Kaplan & Associates
201 S Lake Ave Ste 600
Pasadena, CA 91101
(626) 796-8100
Fax: (626) 796-1003
Email: resumes@gkasearch.com
Web: www.gkasearch.com

Description: International executive search firm committed to quality of effort, service and timely completion of assignments. Diversified clients include financial services, entertainment, high-technology, consumer products, higher education, hospitality, natural resources.

Key Contact - Specialty:
Mr. Gary Kaplan, President - *Generalist*
Mr. Walter B. McNichols, Senior Vice President - *Generalist*

Salary minimum: $100,000

Functions: Generalist

Industries: Generalist

Professional Associations: ASTD, SHRM, WAW

Karel & Company†
20 Rice's Ln
Westport, CT 06880-1922
(203) 341-9911
Email: position@optonline.net
Web: www.karel-co.com

Description: The industries that we specialize in are architecture, construction, engineering (not MFR), environmental, real estate, property/facility/asset management, utilities, power, energy, retail, e-Retail, and apparel manufacturing positions, including: president, CEO, COO, CFO, legal, OPs, financial, marketing/sales, HR, engineers, scientist, architects, and designers, only senior-level managers.

Key Contact - Specialty:
Mr. Stephen A. Karel, President/CEO - *Environmental engineering, engineering, architectural, construction, real estate*

Salary minimum: $100,000

Functions: Senior Mgmt., Engineering

Industries: Energy, Utilities, Construction, Textiles, Apparel, Retail, Haz. Waste, Real Estate

Branches:
13522 Delano St
Van Nuys, CA 91401
(818) 785-6700
Email: position@optonline.net
Key Contact:
Mr. H. E. Greer, Vice President

2 Herrada Rd
Santa Fe, NM 87505
(505) 466-6631
Email: position@optonline.net
Key Contact:
Mr. Lawrence Heon, Esq., VP/Associate

Karr & Associates Inc
(formerly known as Howard Karr & Assoc Inc)
1777 Borel Pl Ste 408
San Mateo, CA 94402
(650) 574-5277
Fax: (650) 574-0310
Email: search@karr.com
Web: www.karr.com

Description: Specialized retained executive search firm recruiting chief financial officers (CFO), controllers and other senior financial positions such as chief operating officers (COO) and board of directors when financial experience is important. We work in all industries. Most of our client companies are located in the Western states.

Key Contact - Specialty:
Ms. Cynthia Karr - *CFOs, controllers*

Mr. Howard Karr - *CFOs*
Ms. Liz Karr - *CFOs, controllers*

Salary minimum: $125,000

Functions: CFO's

Industries: Generalist

Professional Associations: AESC

Martin Kartin & Company Inc
211 E 70th St
New York, NY 10021
(212) 628-7676
Fax: (212) 628-8838
Email: mkhdhuntr@aol.com

Description: Individualized service, 20 years of retained search expertise emphasizing consumer products. Affordable fees based on proven results.

Key Contact:
Mr. Martin C. Kartin, President

Salary minimum: $50,000

Functions: Generalist, Senior Mgmt., Mfg., Materials, Sales & Mktg., Finance, R&D

Industries: Generalist, Food, Bev., Tobacco, Textiles, Apparel, Soap, Perf., Cosmtcs., Drugs Mfg., Retail, Media

Chris Kauffman & Company
PO Box 53218
Atlanta, GA 30355
(404) 233-3530
Fax: (404) 262-7960
Email: resumes@kauffco.com
Web: www.kauffco.com

Description: We are an executive search firm specializing in the national placement of management at all levels including executive, mid-, and unit levels including culinary.

Key Contact - Specialty:
Mr. Christopher C. Kauffman, President - *Restaurant*

Functions: Generalist, Senior Mgmt.

Industries: Generalist, Hospitality

Kaye/Bassman Int'l Corp
2 Preston Park S Ste 400
4965 Preston Park Blvd
Plano, TX 75093
(972) 931-5242
Fax: (972) 931-9683
Email: webmaster@kbic.com
Web: www.kbic.com

Description: Helping companies in specialized fields identify, recruit and hire those professionals who clearly stand out exceptionally in their profession.

Key Contact - Specialty:
Mr. Bob Bassman, Chairman/CEO
Mr. Jeff Kaye, President/CEO
Ms. Sandy Bassman, Executive Vice President
Ms. Suzanne Clark, Treasurer
Mr. Bill Baker, Vice President - *Insurance*
Mr. Mike Kittelson, Vice President - *Construction*
Ms. Christin Geiger-Flick, Vice President - *Pharmaceuticals, biotech*
Ms. Tiffany Caldwell, Vice President - *Pharmaceutical, biotech*

Salary minimum: $75,000

Functions: Generalist, Healthcare, Sales & Mktg., Finance, IT, R&D, Engineering

Industries: Generalist, Construction, Chemicals, Insurance, Real Estate, Biotech, Healthcare

Professional Associations: AAHP, AAPS, DIA, RAPS

Kazan Int'l Inc
5 Cold Hill Rd S Ste 26
Mendham, NJ 07945
(973) 543-0300
Email: info@kazansearch.com
Web: www.kazansearch.com

Description: We are a retainer-based executive
search firm dedicated to the healthcare industry. Our
specialization includes senior management positions
in medical devices, diagnostics, biotechnology, and
pharmaceuticals.

Key Contact - Specialty:
Mr. J. Neil Kazan, President - *Healthcare,
pharmaceutical, biotechnology, medical devices,
diagnostics*

Salary minimum: $150,000

Functions: Generalist, General Mgmt., Mfg., Sales
& Mktg., Finance, R&D, Int'l.

Industries: Generalist, Drugs Mfg., Medical
Devices, Venture Cap., Pharm Svcs., Biotech

A T Kearney Executive Search
(a division of AT Kearney Inc)
222 W Adams St Ste 2500
Chicago, IL 60606
(312) 648-0111
Fax: (312) 223-6369
Email: executive_search@atkearney.com
Web: www.executivesearch.atkearney.com

Description: We are a broad line firm serving most
industries and all functions. A division of a global
management consulting firm and a wholly owned
subsidiary of an international information services
company. Emphasis is on quality, tangible results
and value-added service.

Key Contact:
Mr. Steve Fisher, VP/Mng Dir
Mr. Frank Smeekes, Vice President
Mr. Paul Schmidt, Vice President
Mr. Charles W. Sweet, Chairman
Ms. Michelle Smead, Vice President
Mr. Gregory A. Klein, Vice President
Mr. Frank Steck, Vice President
Mr. Benjamin DeBerry, Vice President
Mr. Frank Schroeder, VP/Managing Director-
    Global Technology
Ms. Vivian Fabbro, Vice President
Mr. Ken Norris, Vice President
Mr. Roy Hebard, VP/Managing Director-Consumer
    Industries
Mr. Andy Olson, Vice President
Ms. Mary Lou Gorno, Vice President
Mr. Larry Poore, Vice President

Salary minimum: $150,000

Functions: Generalist

Industries: Generalist

Professional Associations: AESC, IACPR

Branches:
600 Anton Blvd Ste 1000
Plaza Twr
Costa Mesa, CA 92626
(714) 445-6800
Fax: (714) 445-6999
Key Contact:
Mr. Matthew Pierce, Vice President

500 S Grand Ave Biltmore Twr Ste 1780
Los Angeles, CA 90071
(213) 689-6800
Fax: (213) 689-6857
Key Contact:
Mr. Jack Groban, VP/Managing Director
Ms. Gloria Gordon, Vice President

3 Lagoon Dr Ste 160
Redwood Shores, CA 94065
(650) 637-6600
Fax: (650) 637-6699

Key Contact:
Ms. Maggie Yen, Director

4370 LaJolla Village Dr Fl 4
San Diego, CA 92122
(858) 646-3066
Fax: (858) 646-3062
Key Contact:
Ms. Susan Major, Vice President
Ms. Stacey Davenport, Vice President

1 Landmark Sq Ste 2001
Stamford, CT 06901
(203) 969-2222
Fax: (203) 326-8600
Key Contact:
Ms. Irene Latino, Vice President
Mr. Mark J. McMahon, VP/Managing Director-
    Industrial
Ms. Marcia P. Pryde, Vice President
Mr. Frank Carr, Vice President
Mr. Clawson Smith, Vice President
Mr. Michael Case, Vice President

200 S Biscayne Blvd Ste 3500
First Union Financial Ctr
Miami, FL 33131
(305) 577-0046
Fax: (305) 577-3837
Key Contact:
Mr. John Mestepey, Vice President
Mr. Robert Moran, Vice President
Mr. Rodrigo Ocampo, VP/Managing Director
Mr. Kenneth Feldman, Vice President

3455 Peachtree Rd Ste 1600
Atlanta, GA 30326
(404) 760-6600
Fax: (404) 760-6880
Key Contact:
Mr. Richard Citarella, VP/Managing Director
Mr. Ernest Taylor, Vice President

8500 Normandale Lake Blvd Ste 1630
Minneapolis, MN 55437
(952) 921-8436
Fax: (952) 921-8465
Key Contact:
Mr. David M. McQuoid, Vice President

153 E 53rd St
New York, NY 10022
(212) 751-7040
Fax: (212) 350-3150
Key Contact:
Ms. Marlene Berne, Vice President
Mr. Robert Holt, Vice President
Mr. Gene Shen, VP/Managing Director-Financial
    Inst.
Mr. Steve McPherson, Vice President
Mr. Russ Gerson, Vice President

600 Superior Ave E Ste 1200
Bank One Ctr
Cleveland, OH 44114-2650
(216) 241-6880
Fax: (216) 241-2763
Key Contact:
Mr. David Lauderback, Vice President

500 N Akard St Ste 4170
Lincoln Plz
Dallas, TX 75201
(214) 969-0010
Fax: (214) 720-5902
Key Contact:
Mr. Rocky Johnson, Vice President
Mr. G. Schuyler Page, Vice President
Mr. David Hart, Vice President
Mr. Don Townsend, Vice President

333 John Carlyle St
Alexandria, VA 22314
(703) 836-6210
Fax: (703) 519-0391
Key Contact:
Ms. Jean Dowdall, Vice President - *Higher
    education*
Ms. Shelly Storbeck, VP/Managing Director-
    Education

Mr. Chuck Bunting, Vice President
Ms. Janet Greenwood, Vice President

130 Adelaide St W Ste 2710
Toronto, ON M5H 3P5
Canada
(416) 947-1990
Fax: (416) 947-0255
Key Contact:
Mr. Gerry Baker, Vice President
Mr. Jack Harris, Vice President
Ms. Virginia Murray, Vice President
Mr. Richard Wajs, Vice President

Rubén Dario 281 Piso 15
Col Bosques de Chapultepec
Mexico City, MX CP 11580
Mexico
52 5 282 0050
Fax: 52 5 282 0631
Key Contact:
Mr. Philip Mondragon, Vice President

The Keenan Organization Ltd
5041 Birkdale Dr
Ann Arbor, MI 48103
(734) 327-0560
Fax: (734) 327-0561
Email: billkeenan@aol.com

Description: High quality, boutique firm that
conducts retained searches on local, regional or
national basis.

Key Contact - Specialty:
Mr. William E. Keenan, Managing Partner - *Real
estate, industrial*

Salary minimum: $100,000

Functions: Generalist

Industries: Generalist

The Keith-Murray Partnership
17 Sword St
Toronto, ON M5A 3N3
Canada
(416) 926-0491
Fax: (416) 924-0688
Email: info@kmpsearch.com

Description: As a research-driven generalist search
firm dedicated to personalized, value-added service,
we work with non-competitive clients to ensure
unhindered search capabilities and the highest
standards of confidentiality and integrity.

Key Contact:
Ms. M. Keith-Murray, CMC, President

Functions: Generalist, Advertising, Mktg. Mgmt.,
Direct Mktg., PR, HR Mgmt., Cash Mgmt., Non-
profits

Industries: Generalist

Professional Associations: CMA, ICMCO, WEC

Thomas A Kelley & Associates
3000 Sand Hill Rd Bldg 2 Ste 120
Menlo Park, CA 94025
(650) 854-3247
Fax: (650) 854-3509
Email: tom@tak.com

Description: Specialize in top management for
high-technology start-up firms. Perform searches at
vice president and CEO levels for Silicon Valley
based companies in telecom, datacom, hardware,
software, Internet and e-commerce industries.

Key Contact:
Mr. Tom A. Kelley, President

Salary minimum: $125,000

Functions: Senior Mgmt.

Industries: Medical Devices, Computer Equip.,
Equip Svcs., Telecoms, Software, Biotech

S D Kelly & Associates Inc
990 Washington St Ste 314S
Dedham, MA 02026-6719
(781) 326-8038
Fax: (781) 326-6123
Email: info@sdkelly.com
Web: www.sdkelly.com

Description: Specialize in retained and exclusive search within the electronics industry. Search assignments are conducted at all levels in the areas of sales, marketing, program management, applications engineering, design engineering, manufacturing, supply chain, operations and general management. Operate on a national and international basis.

Key Contact - Specialty:
Ms. Susan D. Kelly, President - *Electronic, contract manufacturing, electronic, semiconductor*

Salary minimum: $75,000

Functions: General Mgmt., Senior Mgmt., Mfg., Materials, Sales & Mktg., Sales Mgmt., Engineering, Int'l.

Industries: Mfg., Test, Measure Equip., Electronic, Elec. Components

Professional Associations: ICS, IEEE, ISA, MAPS, MPPC

Networks: US Recruiters.com

Kelly & Company
1285 Ave of the Americas Fl 35
New York, NY 10019-6028
(212) 554-4170
Fax: (212) 554-4171
Email: bkelly@kellyandco.com
Web: www.kellyandco.com

Description: We are a retained executive search firm with expertise in the identification, recruitment, selection and retention of senior executives within human resources and communications.

Key Contact - Specialty:
Mr. William Kelly, President - *Corporate human resources, human resources consulting firms*
Ms. Joelle B. Johnson, Principal - *Corporate communications, internal communications, communications consulting*

Salary minimum: $150,000

Functions: Senior Mgmt., HR Mgmt.

Industries: Mgmt. Consulting, HR Services, Advertising, Insurance, Healthcare

Professional Associations: IACPR, ESRT, HRPS, IABC, IHRIM, SHRM

Kelly Associates
4021 B Monona Dr
Madison, WI 53716
(608) 222-5330
(760) 324-2466
Fax: (608) 222-5330
Email: kellyassociates@webtv.net

Description: The company targets existing private golf clubs as well as new golf courses and associated golf clubs that are searching for a club manager, head golf professional or a golf course superintendent.

Key Contact - Specialty:
Mr. Ronald Kelly, President - *Private clubs managers, golf professionals, golf course superintendents*
Ms. Mary K. Kelly, Secretary/Treasurer - *Private clubs managers, golf professionals, golf course superintendents*

Salary minimum: $75,000

Functions: General Mgmt., Senior Mgmt.

Industries: Hospitality, Hotels, Resorts, Clubs, Entertainment, Recreation

Professional Associations: GMCCA, WGA, WSGA

Kenexa[†]
170 S Warner Rd Ste 110
Wayne, PA 19087
(610) 971-9171
Fax: (610) 971-9181
Email: maureen.mccabe@kenexa.com
Web: www.kenexa.com

Description: We are a global leader in human resources and technology consulting and are the fastest growing comprehensive human resources and IT solutions provider in the business services industry. Selected as an Inc. 500 company for the past four years, we have 17 offices throughout the world.

Key Contact:
Mr. Nooruddin S. Karsan, CEO
Mr. Donald Volk, CFO
Mr. Elliot Clark, COO

Functions: Generalist, Senior Mgmt., Production, Sales Mgmt., Benefits, CFO's, MIS Mgmt., Engineering

Industries: Generalist, Chemicals, Drugs Mfg., Pharm Svcs., Insurance, Biotech, Healthcare

Professional Associations: IACPR, ACM, AFSMI, AICPA, AITP, AMA, AMA, ANA, APICS, APIW, ASCS, ASTD, DIA, DMA, ESRT, IMA, MGMA, NEHRA, NFIB, NHRA, NJCPA, NSPST, PICPA, RAPS, SA, SHRM, SIM, SME, WAW

Branches:
283 N Northlake Blvd
Altamonte Springs, FL 32701
(407) 831-2400
Fax: (407) 831-2484
Key Contact - Specialty:
Mr. Grant Parker, Principal - *Financial Services, Healthcare*

6442 NW 42nd Wy
Boca Raton, FL 33496
(561) 981-8875
Fax: (520) 369-1519
Key Contact - Specialty:
Karin Levy-Gellen, Principal - *Healthcare & Managed Healthcare*

3131 Princeton Pike Bldg 2B Ste 200
Lawrenceville, NJ 08648
(609) 896-8404
Fax: (609) 912-0607
Key Contact - Specialty:
Mr. Grant Parker, Principal - *Human resources*
Mr. Elliot Clark, Principal - *Pharmaceutical*

11 Penn Plz Ste 320
New York, NY 10001
(212) 268-7555
Fax: (212) 268-7373
Email: courtney.dittmann@kenexa.com
Key Contact:
Mr. Grant Parker, Principal
Ms. Courtney Dittmann

1835 Market St Fl 20
11 Penn Ctr
Philadelphia, PA 19103
(800) 935-6694
(215) 546-7330
Fax: (215) 546-7331
Key Contact - Specialty:
Mr. elliot Clark, Principal - *Pharmaceutical*

983 Old Eagle School Rd Ste 605
Wayne, PA 19087
(610) 971-6400
Fax: (610) 971-6410
Key Contact - Specialty:
Mr. Grant Parker, Principal - *Financial Services & Healthcare*
Mr. Kevin Hudson, Principal - *Healthcare, IT, Advanced Technologies*

Mr. Kevin Brown, Principal - *IT, Pharmaceutical, Healthcare, Biotech, Publishing, Media*
Mrs. Elba Rivera-Lopez, Principal - *Financial search, insurance, workers compensation, managed care, group life/disability/accident & health insurance*
Mr. George Vollmer, Principal - *Manufactuing, engineering, IT, healthcare, finance*

Kennedy & Company
20 N WackerDr Ste 1745
Chicago, IL 60606
(312) 372-0099
Fax: (312) 372-0629
Web: www.kennedycompanyinc.com

Description: Executive search practice serving clients nationwide in most functions and industries with expertise in finance, technology manufacturing and service industries.

Key Contact:
Mr. Thomas J. Moran, President/Managinig Director
Ms. Diane Dombeck, Sr Vice President
Ms. Sharman McGurn, Vice President
Ms. Mary Ann Bartoli, Vice President
Ms. Lenore Meyer, Vice President Administration
Ms. Theresa Raczak, Director
Ms. Jane Loop, Director
Mr. Edward Carter, Consultant

Salary minimum: $75,000

Functions: Generalist, Directors, Senior Mgmt., CFO's, Cash Mgmt., M&A, MIS Mgmt., Non-profits

Industries: Generalist, Mfg., Finance, Banking, Invest. Banking, Brokers, Misc. Financial, Non-profits, HR Services, Healthcare

Branches:
4190 Belfort Rd Ste 200
Jacksonville, FL 32216
(904) 281-5030
Fax: (904) 279-9229
Email: jloop@kennedycompanyinc.com
Key Contact:
Ms. Jane Loop, Director

Kensington Int'l
1534 Plaza Ln 327
Burlingame, CA 94011
(650) 343-5779
Email: kisearch@pacbell.net

Description: Retained search. Client base includes: high-tech; software, Internet, fiber optics, wireless, consumer package goods, food and beverage, financial services, professionals: technical (engineering, software) operations, marketing/sales, accounting/finance, technical.

Key Contact - Specialty:
Ms. Holland Kensington Routt, President - *Hi-tech, wireless, fiber optics*

Salary minimum: $90,000

Functions: Generalist, Sales & Mktg., HR Mgmt., Finance, IT

Industries: Generalist, Food, Bev., Tobacco, Wireless, Fiber Optic, Network Infrastructure

Professional Associations: HRCA

Kensington Int'l Inc
1415 W 22nd St Ste 500
Oak Brook, IL 60523
(630) 571-0123
Fax: (630) 571-3139
Email: info@kionline.com
Web: www.kionline.com

Description: Our firm has grown to become one of the largest and most successful retained search firms in the Midwest. Kensington has a niche focus on middle market search activity - emerging leaders in publicly held companies. We are senior leaders in privately-held and mid-cap clients.

Key Contact - Specialty:
Mr. Brian G. Clarke, Partner/Director - *Marketing (senior level), sales, corporate finance, human resources, fortune 250*
Mr. Richard George, Partner/Director - *Manufacturing management (senior level), heavy manufacturing, fortune 1000 & equivalent*
Mr. Scott Robinson, Partner/Director - *Manufacturing (senior level), sales & marketing management, mid cap companies $50-500 million sales, human resources*

Salary minimum: $80,000

Functions: Middle Mgmt.

Industries: Generalist

Professional Associations: SWE

Networks: World Search Group

Kenzer Corp
777 3rd Ave
New York, NY 10017
(212) 308-4300
Fax: (212) 308-1842
Email: ny@kenzer.com
Web: www.kenzer.com

Description: We are a full-service executive search firm with nationwide computer integrated offices. We have over 28 years worth of history of operating with a high air of urgency and the highest standard of professionalism.

Key Contact:
Mr. Robert D. Kenzer, Chairman/CEO - *Food & food services, automotive, not-for-profit, telecommunications, direct mail*
Mr. Eric B. Segal, President/COO - *Food & food services, automotive, not-for-profit, telecommunications, venture capital*
Ms. Elaine Erickson, Executive Vice President-Marketing - *Food & food services, automotive, not-for-profit, telecommunications, direct mail*
Mr. Marc Moskowitz, CFO
Ms. Kitty Keane, Vice President/Administration
Mr. Lou Jankovic, VP/Director-IT

Salary minimum: $50,000

Functions: Generalist, General Mgmt., Mfg., Distribution, Advertising, Direct Mktg., HR Mgmt., Finance, IT

Industries: Mfg., Food, Bev., Tobacco, Textiles, Apparel, Lumber, Furniture, Printing, Soap, Perf., Cosmtcs., Drugs Mfg., Motor Vehicles, Computer Equip., Consumer Elect., Misc. Mfg., Transportation, Wholesale, Retail, Finance, Banking, Invest. Banking, Brokers, Venture Cap., Services, Non-profits, Legal, Accounting, Mgmt. Consulting, HR Services, Hospitality, Restaurants, Media, Advertising, Publishing, New Media, Broadcast, Film, Telecoms, Call Centers, Software, HR SW, Marketing SW

Professional Associations: IMRA

Branches:
6033 W Century Blvd Ste 700
Los Angeles, CA 90045
(310) 417-8577
Fax: (310) 417-3083
Email: la@kenzer.com
Key Contact - Specialty:
Mr. Robert Armstrong, Vice President - *Retail, financial services, manufacturing, high tech, hospitality*

1600 Parkwood Cir NW Ste 310
Atlanta, GA 30339
(770) 955-7210
Fax: (770) 955-6504
Email: atlanta@kenzer.com
Key Contact - Specialty:
Ms. Marie Powell, Vice President - *Retail, financial services, manufacturing, high tech, hospitality*

625 N Michigan Ave Ste 1244
Chicago, IL 60611
(312) 266-0976
Fax: (312) 266-0994
Email: chicago@kenzer.com
Key Contact - Specialty:
Ms. Barbara Kauffman, Vice President - *Retail, financial services, manufacturing, high tech, hospitality*

150 S 5th St Ste 1400
Fifth St Twrs
Minneapolis, MN 55402
(612) 332-7770
Fax: (612) 332-7707
Email: minneapolis@kenzer.com
Key Contact - Specialty:
Ms. Mary Jeanne Scott, Vice President - *Professional services, retail, manufacturing, high tech, hospitality*

3030 LBJ Fwy Triwest Plz Ste 1430
Dallas, TX 75234
(972) 620-7776
Fax: (972) 243-7570
Email: dallas@kenzer.com
Key Contact - Specialty:
Mr. Donald Jones, Vice President - *Retail, financial services, manufacturing, high tech, hospitality*

Kershner & Company
PO Box 341181
Bethesda, MD 20827-1181
(301) 258-7475
Fax: (301) 258-9288
Email: bk@kershnerandco.com
Web: www.kershnerandco.com

Description: We are an executive recruiting firm that places financial executives in the financial services industry. We focus on commercial banks and thrifts, commercial and specialty finance companies; regional investment banks and venture capital firms.

Key Contact - Specialty:
Mr. Bruce Kershner, President - *Commercial banking, investment banking, specialty finance, real estate*

Salary minimum: $75,000

Functions: Generalist

Industries: Finance, Banking, Invest. Banking, Brokers, Venture Cap., Misc. Financial, Insurance, Real Estate

Daniel J Kerstein
9332 E Jewell Cir
Denver, CO 80231
(303) 755-0104
(303) 877-1364
Email: djk@dank.com

Description: We use a consultive method to do executive search. We have found that openings are the effect of problems, we address the cause.

Key Contact - Specialty:
Mr. Daniel J. Kerstein, President - *Software engineering, dot com related*

Salary minimum: $60,000

Functions: Generalist, Systems Dev.

Industries: Computer Equip., Misc. Mfg., Telecoms, Software, Non-classifiable

Michael L Ketner & Associates Inc
100 N Braddock Ave Ste 301
Pittsburgh, PA 15208
(412) 731-8100
Fax: (412) 731-9224
Email: ketner@ketner.com
Web: www.ketner.com

Description: With thirty years' experience and more than 4000 successful search assignments under our

belt we are uniquely qualified to fill any construction executive need paying over $80,000 per year.

Key Contact:
Mr. Michael L. Ketner, CPC, President - *Construction*
Mr. Keith A. Maxin, Vice President - *Construction*
Mr. David Woell, Vice President

Salary minimum: $80,000

Functions: Senior Mgmt.

Industries: Construction

Professional Associations: ABC, AGC

Keystone Executive Search
PO Box 229
New York, NY 10028
(646) 221-6666
Email: vc@usa.com

Description: Our specialties are CIOs, chief information officers, chief security officers, software development, software architects, encryption, moletronics, genetics genome, biotechnology, and molecular engineering.

Key Contact - Specialty:
Mr. Victor Chaves, President - *Internet, software development*

Salary minimum: $100,000

Functions: IT

Industries: Computer Equip., IT Implementation, New Media, Wireless, Software, Biotech

Professional Associations: AESC, CAPS, NAPS, NJAPS, NYACMP

Kiley, Owen & McGovern Inc
PO Box 68
Blackwood, NJ 08012
(856) 227-5332
Fax: (856) 227-5530
Email: kilowen@voicenet.com
Web: www.voicenet.com

Description: International retainer search firm specializing in sales and marketing management, software, engineering in the computer, telecommunications and data communications industries.

Key Contact - Specialty:
Ms. Sheila M. McGovern, President - *Data communications, sales & marketing*
Mr. Tom Vandegrift, Secretary/Treasurer - *Data communications, telecommunications engineering, software*
Mr. Ralph Owen, Consultant - *Data communications, sales & marketing*
Mr. Ed Bryant, Consultant - *Data communications, sales support, applications engineering*

Salary minimum: $60,000

Functions: Senior Mgmt., Middle Mgmt., Product Dev., Sales & Mktg., IT

Industries: Computer Equip., Telecoms, Software

Professional Associations: IACPR

The Kilman Advisory Group
406 Farmington Ave
Farmington, CT 06032-1964
(860) 676-7817
Fax: (860) 676-7839
Email: contact@kilman.com
Web: www.kilman.com

Description: Provide search, outplacement and human resource consulting services to law departments of multinational corporations as well as to select law firms. Completed search assignments in the US, Canada, South America and the Pacific Rim.

Key Contact - Specialty:
Mr. Paul H. Kilman, Principal - *Legal*

Functions: Legal, Attorneys

Industries: Generalist

Professional Associations: NALSC

Kincannon & Reed
2106-C Gallows Rd
Vienna, VA 22182
(703) 761-4046
Fax: (703) 790-1533
Email: krcontact@krsearch.net
Web: www.krsearch.com

Description: The firm provides senior executive and board level recruitment services in agribusiness, food and life sciences both in the US and overseas.

Key Contact:
Mr. Kelly Kincannon, CEO
Ms. Diana Braak, Vice President
Mr. James Leslie, Vice President
Ms. Suzanne Cox, Director
Mr. Stewart Baker, Managing Director

Salary minimum: $120,000

Functions: Generalist

Industries: Agri., Forestry, Mining, Food, Bev., Tobacco, Non-profits, Pharm Svcs., Hospitality, Biotech, Healthcare

Professional Associations: AESC, AAAS

The Kingsley Group
44 Montgomery St Ste 3850
San Francisco, CA 94104
(415) 291-9395
Fax: (415) 291-9373
Email: info@kingsley-group.com
Web: www.kingsley-group.com

Description: We are a general management consulting and executive search firm, with over a decade of experience in the transportation, supply chain and marketing industries. Our international expertise extends to Mexico, Latin America, Southeast Asia and Europe.

Key Contact - Specialty:
Mr. Steven Lautsch, President - *Transportation, supply chain, marketing, general management, consulting*

Salary minimum: $60,000

Functions: General Mgmt., Directors, Senior Mgmt., Middle Mgmt., Mktg. Mgmt., Training, CFO's, Mgmt. Consultants, Int'l.

Industries: Transportation, Accounting, Mgmt. Consulting, HR Services

Professional Associations: CLM

Kinkead Partners
703 Hebron Ave
Glastonbury, CT 06033-5000
(860) 659-4664
Fax: (860) 659-4658
Web: www.kinkeadsearch.com

Description: Retained firm specializing in marketing management in consumer durable, industrial and e-business markets.

Key Contact:
Mr. David Kinkead, Owner

Salary minimum: $125,000

Functions: Mktg. Mgmt.

Industries: Non-classifiable

Professional Associations: IACPR

The Kinlin Company Inc
749 Main St
Osterville, MA 02655
(508) 420-1165
Fax: (508) 428-8525
Email: eck@kinlin.com
Web: www.kinlin.com

Description: We are a retained executive search firm specializing in recruitment of senior investment, sales, and marketing executives with compensation exceeding one million dollars. We have satellite offices in Wellesley and Boston, Massachusetts.

Key Contact - Specialty:
Ms. Ellen C. Kinlin, President - *Investment executives (senior)*
Mr. Dickson Smith, Executive Vice President/Consultant - *Senior investment analysts (both buy and sell side), portfolio managers*
Ms. Molly Lee, Consultant - *Researcher and candidate development*
Ms. Elizabeth Manning - *Researcher and candidate development*

Salary minimum: $500,000

Functions: Sales & Mktg., Mktg. Mgmt., Sales Mgmt., Cash Mgmt., M&A

Industries: Generalist, Invest. Banking, Brokers, Misc. Financial

Professional Associations: IACPR, NEHRA

Branches:
60 State St
Boston, MA 02109
(617) 742-7877
Fax: (617)
Email: kac@kinlin.com
Key Contact - Specialty:
Ms. Karen Costa, Office Manager - *Financial services*

Kinser & Baillou LLC
515 Madison Ave Fl 36
New York, NY 10022
(212) 588-8801
Fax: (212) 588-8802
Email: search@kinserbaillou.com
Web: www.kinserbaillou.com

Description: Assignments done by experienced search professionals. Successful search experience with top corporations and new ventures. Extensive candidate source contacts. Board of directors and management searches.

Key Contact - Specialty:
Mr. Richard Kinser, Partner - *Generalist*
Ms. Astrid von Baillou, Partner - *Generalist*

Salary minimum: $100,000

Functions: Directors, Senior Mgmt.

Industries: Generalist

Professional Associations: AESC

Kiradjieff & Goode Inc
70 Walnut St
Wellesley, MA 02481-2199
(781) 239-8244
Fax: (781) 239-8241
Email: cgoode@kg-inc.com
Web: www.kg-inc.com

Description: Board member, upper and middle echelon executive searches. Broad experience with a passionate commitment to personal service, consistent results and developing long-term client relationships.

Key Contact - Specialty:
Mr. Richard W. Goode, Jr., CEO/Managing Director - *Equity, venture capital, real estate, consumer product, information technology*

Ms. Laura K. Goode, Managing Director - *Equity, venture capital, real estate, consumer product, information technology*

Salary minimum: $100,000

Functions: Generalist, General Mgmt., Mfg., Sales & Mktg., HR Mgmt., Finance, IT

Industries: Generalist, Mfg., Finance, Services, Real Estate, Biotech, Healthcare

Professional Associations: ACG, BHRA, NCFB, TEI

Kittleman & Associates LLC
300 S Wacker Dr Ste 1710
Chicago, IL 60606
(312) 986-1166
Fax: (312) 986-0895
Email: search@kittleman.net
Web: www.kittleman.net

Description: Executive search, management consulting and leadership development exclusively for non-profit organizations including professional associations and private foundations nationwide.

Key Contact:
Mr. Richard M. King, President
Ms. Mary Beth Malone, Vice President
Mr. Edward Rivera, Vice President
Ms. Rhyan Zweifler, Vice President

Salary minimum: $75,000

Functions: Senior Mgmt.

Industries: Non-profits

KL Consultants[†]
7855 JFK Blvd E
North Bergen, NJ 07047
(201) 295-0754
Email: klresource@aol.com

Description: Specialist in recruitment and placement of mid- to senior-level HUMAN RESOURCES PROFESSIONALS nationwide.

Key Contact - Specialty:
Ms. Jill Krumholz, Principal/Owner - *Human resources*

Salary minimum: $75,000

Functions: HR Mgmt., Benefits, Personnel, Training

Industries: Generalist

Professional Associations: ASTD, NAFE, SHRM, WAW

Marc Kleckner & Son[†]
9831 Overhill Dr
Santa Ana, CA 92705
(714) 288-0700
Fax: (714) 288-0400
Email: mlkleckner@msn.com

Description: Thirty years of experience. Never refer a candidate that is already talking with my client. Only select "A" players with a track record and 1040 to prove their income.

Key Contact - Specialty:
Mr. Marc Kleckner, President - *Advertising, mortgage*
Ms. Lisa Kleckner, Vice President - *Advertising, mortgage*

Salary minimum: $50,000

Functions: Generalist

Industries: Printing, Finance, Brokers, Misc. Financial, Services, Hospitality, Media

The Kleinstein Group
33 Wood Ave S
Iselin, NJ 08830
(732) 494-7500
Fax: (732) 494-7579
Email: kgi7500@aol.com
Web: www.kleinsteingroup.com

Description: The firm's unique research approach enables us to present candidates within 3-4 weeks from the initiation of assignment. The firm works on a retainer basis with a wide range of clients, from emerging growth-oriented organizations, to specialty industries, to fortune 100 companies.

Key Contact:
Mr. Jonathan Kleinstein, President
Mrs. Connie Bernardo, Managing Director

Salary minimum: $100,000

Functions: Generalist

Industries: Generalist

The Klenin Group
32107 W Lindero Canyon Rd 8
Westlake Village, CA 91361
(818) 597-3434
Fax: (818) 597-3438
Email: kleningroup@kleningroup.com
Web: www.kleningroup.com

Description: We are a consulting firm specializing in staffing. We have developed a collaborative methodology, which aligns us as a strategic partner. We are not a fee based company, rather we become an integral part of your on going staffing strategy.

Key Contact - Specialty:
Mr. Larry Klenin, CEO - *Telecom, networking, internet, e-commerce*
Ms. Sandra Sadikoff, Exec Vice President - *Telecom, networks, e-commerce*

Salary minimum: $75,000

Functions: Generalist

Industries: Telecoms, Telephony, Digital, Wireless, Fiber Optic, Network Infrastructure, Networking, Comm. SW

Knapp Consultants
184 Old Ridgefield Rd
Wilton, CT 06897
(203) 762-0790
Fax: (203) 762-0747
Email: consultantknapp@aol.com

Description: We are a nationwide executive search/management consulting firm specializing in aerospace, electronics, general manufacturing, and gas turbine industries.

Key Contact - Specialty:
Mr. Ronald A. Knapp - *Aerospace, manufacturing*

Salary minimum: $90,000

Functions: General Mgmt., Directors, Senior Mgmt., Mfg.

Industries: Mfg., Metal Products, Aerospace, Mfg. SW

Koehler & Company
700 N Pilgrim Pkwy
Elm Grove, WI 53122
(262) 796-8010
Fax: (262) 796-8788
Email: koehlerj@execpc.com

Description: We are a well-established, broadly experienced, retainer search firm. We focus on recruiting mid- and upper-level executives for a diversified client base and have conducted searches in manufacturing disciplines including operations, management, sales, marketing, engineering, finance, and purchasing. We are committed to finding high

quality, proven management talent for the clients we serve.

Key Contact:
Mr. John Koehler, President

Salary minimum: $100,000

Functions: Directors, Senior Mgmt., Plant Mgmt., Purchasing, Sales Mgmt.

Industries: Mfg.

Lee Koehn Associates Inc
4380 SW Macadam Ave Ste 185
Portland, OR 97201
(503) 224-9067
Fax: (503) 224-8122
Email: koehn@lkassociates.com
Web: www.lkassociates.com

Description: A boutique retained search firm known for quality, timeliness and results, serving its Westcoast clients. Major emphasis in financial services, hi-tech, telecommunications, manufacturing and healthcare.

Key Contact:
Mr. Lee Koehn, President

Salary minimum: $90,000

Functions: Generalist

Industries: Energy, Utilities, Finance, Banking, Media, Telecoms, Software, Healthcare

T J Koellhoffer & Associates
250 Rte 28 Ste 206
Bridgewater, NJ 08807
(908) 526-6880
Fax: (908) 725-2653
Email: tkoell@aol.com

Description: Specializing in technical and executive recruiting of senior management, manufacturing, R&D, business development and engineering talent for the broadcasting, information processing, telecommunications, scientific instrumentation and biotechnology industries.

Key Contact - Specialty:
Mr. Thomas J. Koellhoffer, President - *Engineering, applied research, telecommunications, biomedical*

Salary minimum: $70,000

Functions: General Mgmt., Sales & Mktg., HR Mgmt., CFO's, Risk Mgmt., IT, MIS Mgmt., R&D, Engineering, Mgmt. Consultants

Industries: Generalist, Mfg., Drugs Mfg., Machine, Appliance, Computer Equip., Consumer Elect., Invest. Banking, Venture Cap., New Media, Broadcast, Film, Defense, Software, Biotech

Professional Associations: ASQ, IEEE, SID

Branches:
1527 Chestnut Ridge Rd
Upper Black Edox, PA 18972
(610) 982-5959
Fax: (610) 982-9111
Email: tkoell@aol.com
Key Contact:
Mr. Thomas J. Keollhoffer, President

Fred Koffler Associates
942 Greenfield Rd
Woodmere, NY 11598
(516) 569-6582

Description: Executive search firm specializing in senior management positions. Retained by client companies to recruit key executives in the area of sales, marketing, finance, engineering R&D, manufacturing and general management.

Key Contact:
Mr. Fred Koffler, President

Salary minimum: $80,000

Functions: Generalist, General Mgmt., Directors, Senior Mgmt., Middle Mgmt., Legal, Mfg.

Industries: Generalist, Transportation, Wholesale, Retail, Finance, Services, Hospitality, Media, Aerospace, Software, Biotech

Koltnow & Company
62 W 45th St Fl 4
New York, NY 10036
(212) 921-8885
Fax: (212) 921-1727
Email: recruit@koltnow.com
Web: www.koltnow.com

Description: Specializing in apparel related services including design, sales, production and senior management. Additional expertise in accessories, catalog and specialty retailers. Work closely with clients to identify needs and find candidates who match specific profiles.

Key Contact - Specialty:
Ms. Emily Koltnow, Principal/Owner - *Apparel related industries*

Salary minimum: $75,000

Functions: Mfg.

Industries: Mfg., Textiles, Apparel

Korban Associates
312 W State St
Kennett Square, PA 19348
(610) 444-8611
Fax: (610) 444-8612
Email: rokorban@korban.com

Description: We are a mid-size firm conducting search for the pharmaceutical/biopharmaceutical industry. We also have extensive experience in other aspects of the life sciences, medical products, food, and nutritionals, consumer products, high-tech, e-Commerce, and Internet industries.

Key Contact:
Mr. Richard O. Korban, President - *Pharmaceuticals, biopharmaceuticals, medical, healthcare, technology based manufacturing*
Mr. Thomas G. MacNamara, Senior Vice President

Salary minimum: $100,000

Functions: Generalist

Industries: Mfg., Software, Biotech, Healthcare

Professional Associations: SHRM

Koren, Rogers & Dowd[†]
701 Westchester Ave Ste 212W
White Plains, NY 10604
(914) 686-5800
Fax: (914) 686-4116
Email: mkoren@korenrogers.com
Web: www.korenrogers.com

Description: Provide finance, accounting, marketing and human resource executive recruiting services with emphasis in consumer/pharmaceutical, Internet, entertainment, media and communication industries.

Key Contact - Specialty:
Mr. Michael Koren, President/CEO - *Finance, general management*

Salary minimum: $100,000

Functions: Generalist, Senior Mgmt., CFO's, Cash Mgmt., Taxes, M&A, MIS Mgmt., Minorities

Industries: Generalist, Food, Bev., Tobacco, Drugs Mfg., Computer Equip., Pharm Svcs., Hospitality, Telecoms, Software

Professional Associations: NAER, NASCP, NYNMA

Korn/Ferry Int'l

200 Park Ave Fl 37
New York, NY 10166
(212) 687-1834
Fax: (212) 986-5684
Web: www.kornferry.com

Description: As the world's largest executive search firm, our clients are among the world's most prestigious public and private institutions. Since our founding, we have conducted over 80,000 searches for clients in every industry and in all parts of the world.

Key Contact:
Mr. Richard Ferry, Founder
Mr. Paul Reilly, Chairman/CEO
Mr. Michael D. Bekins, COO
Mr. Peter Dunn, Vice Chairman
Ms. Elizabeth Murray, CFO
Mr. Gary Hourihan, Executive Vice President - *Organizational development*
Mr. L. Parker Harrell, Executive Director-Search Operations
Mr. Dick Buschman, President - *Europe*
Mr. Don Spetner, Chief Marketing Officer
Mr. James E. Boone, President - *Americas*
Mr. Peter Crist, Vice Chairman

Salary minimum: $150,000

Functions: General Mgmt., Healthcare, Sales & Mktg., HR Mgmt., Finance, CFO's, IT, Non-profits, Int'l.

Industries: Energy, Utilities, Consumer Elect., Retail, Finance, Services, E-commerce, Media, Communications, Networking, Comm. SW, Healthcare

Professional Associations: AESC, IACPR

Branches:
2000 Powell St Ste 1260
Emeryville, CA 94608
(510) 601-1834
Fax: (510) 594-8800
Key Contact:
Mr. Jeffrey Hocking, Office Managing Director

2600 Michelson Dr Ste 720
Irvine, CA 92612
(949) 851-1834
Fax: (949) 833-7608
Key Contact - Specialty:
Ms. Caroline Nahas, Office Managing Director
Mr. Elliot Gordon, Office Managing Director - *Advanced technology, private equity, emerging business*

1800 Century Park E Ste 900
Los Angeles, CA 90067
(310) 552-1834
Fax: (310) 553-6452
Key Contact:
Ms. Caroline Nahas, Office Managing Director

3 Lagoon Dr Ste 280
Redwood City, CA 94065
(650) 632-1834
Fax: (650) 632-1835
Key Contact:
Mr. David Nosal, Office Managing Director

1 Embarcadero Ctr Ste 2101
San Francisco, CA 94111
(415) 956-1834
Fax: (415) 956-8265
Key Contact:
Mr. Bill Caldwell, Office Managing Director

1600 Broadway Ste 2400
Denver, CO 80202
(303) 542-1880
Fax: (303) 542-1885
Key Contact:
Mr. Scott Kingdom, Office Managing Director

695 E Main St Financial Ctr
Stamford, CT 06901
(203) 359-3350
Fax: (203) 327-2044
Key Contact:
Mr. Terence P. McGovern, Office Managing Director
Mr. Michael Decosta, Principal

900 19th St NW Ste 800 Presidential Plz
Washington, DC 20006
(202) 822-9444
Fax: (202) 822-8127
Key Contact:
Mr. Michael Kirkman, Office Managing Director

200 S Biscayne Blvd Ste 4450
Miami, FL 33131
(305) 377-4121
Fax: (305) 377-4428
Key Contact:
Ms. Bonnie Crabtree, Office Managing Director

303 Peachtree St NE Ste 1600
Atlanta, GA 30308
(404) 577-7542
Fax: (404) 584-9781
Key Contact:
Mr. Craig Dunlevie, Office Managing Director

233 S Wacker Dr Ste 3300 Sears Twr
Chicago, IL 60606
(312) 466-1834
Fax: (312) 466-0451
Key Contact:
Mr. Scott Kingdom, Office Managing Director

265 Franklin St Fl 17
Boston, MA 02110
(617) 345-0200
Fax: (617) 345-0544
Key Contact:
Mr. Mark L. Smith, Managing Director - *Professional services, private equity*
Mr. Kevin Conley, Regional Managing Director- New England

80 S 8th St 4816 IDS Ctr
Minneapolis, MN 55402
(612) 333-1834
Fax: (612) 333-8971
Key Contact:
Mr. Jeremy Hanson, Office Managing Director

7 Roszel Rd Fl 5 The Commons
Princeton, NJ 08540
(609) 452-8848
Fax: (609) 452-9699
Key Contact - Specialty:
Mr. Richard Arons, Office Managing Director - *Healthcare devices, biotechnology*

1835 Market St Ste 2626 11 Penn Ctr
Philadelphia, PA 19103
(215) 496-6666
Fax: (215) 568-9911
Key Contact - Specialty:
Mr. David Shabot, Office Managing Director - *Healthcare*

111 Congress Ave Ste 2230
Austin, TX 78701
(512) 236-1834
Fax: (512) 236-1835
Key Contact - Specialty:
Mr. Bill Funk, Office Managing Director - *Education, not-for-profit, associations*

2100 McKinney Ave Ste 1800
Dallas, TX 75201
(214) 954-1834
Fax: (214) 954-1849
Key Contact - Specialty:
Mr. Bill Funk, Office Managing Director - *Education, not-for-profit, associations*

1100 Louisiana Ste 2850
Houston, TX 77002
(713) 651-1834
Fax: (713) 651-0848

Key Contact:
Mr. Greg Barnes, Office Managing Director

8270 Greensboro Dr Ste 850
McLean, VA 22102
(703) 761-7020
Fax: (703) 761-7023
Key Contact - Specialty:
Mr. Kerry Moynihan, Managing Director
Mr. Mike Kirkman, Office Managing Director - *Telecommunications, information systems, technology, utilities*

1301 5th Ave Ste 1500
Seattle, WA 98101
(206) 447-1834
Fax: (206) 447-9261
Key Contact:
Mr. Robert Ferguson, Office Managing Director

520 5th Ave SW Ste 2500
Calgary, AB T2P 3R7
Canada
(403) 269-3277
Fax: (403) 262-9347
Key Contact:
Mr. Michael Honey, Office Managing Director
Mr. John McKay, Managing Director

1055 Dunsmuir St Ste 3300
4 Bentall Ctr
PO Box 49206
Vancouver, BC V7X 1B1
Canada
(604) 684-1834
Fax: (604) 684-1884
Key Contact:
Mr. Grant Spitz, Office Managing Director

181 Bay St Bay Wellington Twr Ste 3320
PO Box 763 BCE Plc
Toronto, ON M5J 2T3
Canada
(416) 365-1841
Fax: (416) 365-0851
Key Contact:
Mr. Elan Pratzer, Office Managing Director

420 McGill St Ste 400
Montreal, QC H2Y 2GI
Canada
(514) 397-9655
Fax: (514) 397-0410
Key Contact:
Mr. Jean-Pierre Bourbonnais, Office Manager

Montes Urales 505 Fl 3
Lomas de Chapultepec
Del Miguel Hidalgo
Mexico City, DF 11000
Mexico
52 5 201 5400
Fax: 52 5 202 4469
Key Contact:
Mr. Horacio McCoy, Reg Managing Director-N Latin America

Padre Mier 1675
Col Obispado
Monterrey, NL 64060
Mexico
52 8 348 4355
Fax: 52 8 333 7362
Key Contact:
Mr. Eduardo Taylor, Office Managing Director

Korn/Ferry Int'l SA de CV

505 Col Lomas de Chapultepec Fl 3
Del Miguel Hidalgo
Mexico City, DF 11000
Mexico
52 5 201 5400
Fax: 52 5 202 4469
Email: horacio.mccoy@kornferry.com
Web: www.kornferry.com

Description: By far Mexico's leading and largest executive search firm.

Key Contact - Specialty:
Mr. Horacio McCoy, President - *Consumer products, advanced technology, financial services*
Mr. Manuel Papayanópulos, Vice President - *Pharmaceuticals, advanced technology*
Mr. Thurston R. Hamer, Vice President - *General management, industry, consumer*
Ms. Maria Elena Valdez, Vice President - *Consumer products*

Salary minimum: $75,000

Functions: Generalist

Industries: Services

Kors Montgomery Int'l
14811 St. Mary's Ln Ste 280
Houston, TX 77079
(713) 840-7101
Fax: (713) 840-7260
Email: info@korsmontgomery.com
Web: www.korsmontgomery.com

Description: Many assignments have an international content. Concentrating on energy, high-technology, software, telecomm and computer services. Strategic alliance with leading independent firms in Europe, North America and Japan.

Key Contact - Specialty:
Mr. R. Paul Kors, Partner - *Technology, energy executives*

Salary minimum: $150,000

Functions: Senior Mgmt.

Industries: Energy, Utilities, Telecoms, Software

Kossuth & Associates Inc
4230 95th Ave NE
Bellevue, WA 98004
(425) 450-9050
Email: consultants@jobschannel.net
Web: www.jobschannel.net

Description: We provide retained search in all functional areas above $70,000 including industry specialization in telecommunications, wireless communications, software, e-Commerce, and the Internet.

Key Contact - Specialty:
Mr. David Kossuth, President - *Telecommunications, wireless, software, internet.*

Salary minimum: $75,000

Functions: General Mgmt., Sales & Mktg., Mkt. Research

Industries: Media, Advertising, New Media, Communications, Telecoms, Call Centers, Telephony, Digital, Wireless, Fiber Optic, Network Infrastructure, Software, Marketing SW, Networking, Comm. SW, Security SW, System SW

Kostmayer Associates Inc
111 Hamlet Hill Rd Ste 1410
Baltimore, MD 21210
(410) 435-2288
Email: rogerkos@earthlink.net

Description: We are a three-generation executive search consulting firm, founded by John H. Kostmayer over 25 years ago in Princeton, N.J. The firm specializes in senior financial services positions and has been recognized for its high quality, fast results, effective communications and unusually thorough methodology.

Key Contact - Specialty:
Mr. Roger C. Kostmayer, Principal - *Financial services, retirement services, asset management, mutual funds, annuities*

Salary minimum: $100,000

Functions: Generalist, Senior Mgmt., Middle Mgmt., Advertising, Mktg. Mgmt., Sales Mgmt., CFO's, MIS Mgmt.

Industries: Misc. Financial, Insurance

Professional Associations: NAVA

Branches:
270 Greenwich Ave
Greenwich, CT 06830
(203) 618-1688
Fax: (203) 618-9691
Email: sjkost@erols.com
Key Contact - Specialty:
Mr. John B. Kostmayer, Principal - *Financial services, retirement services, annuities, mutual funds, insurance*

400 East Pratt St Fl 8
Baltimore, MD 21202
(410) 576-8703
Fax: (410) 659-0853
Email: mckostmayer@yahoo.com
Key Contact - Specialty:
Mr. Matthew C. Kostmayer, Principal - *Financial services, asset management, retirement services, annuities, mutual funds*

The J Kovach Group
201 Penn Ctr Blvd Ste 460
Pittsburgh, PA 15235
(412) 825-5168
Web: www.jkovachgroup.com

Description: Twenty-five years' experience in executive search for the real estate and construction industry. Recently added healthcare specialty ('95) doing administrative and physician recruiting.

Key Contact - Specialty:
Mr. Jerry Kovach, Principal - *Real estate, construction, healthcare industries*

Salary minimum: $50,000

Functions: Generalist

Industries: Construction, Real Estate, Healthcare

Professional Associations: ICSC, IREM, NAIOP

Kraemer, Bentley, Wong & Sermone
4 Main St
Los Altos, CA 94022
(650) 941-1552
Web: www.kbwsinc.com

Description: Fifty percent of the business practice is realized in companies ranging from $600M to Fortune 500 high-technology corporations. The remaining 50% of the practice is comprised of assignments in start-up environments. Other client consulting services include assistance in aligning strategic alliances, co-development partnerships and raising capital funding.

Key Contact - Specialty:
Ms. Katherine R. Kraemer, Principal - *Executive level management, high technology, systems, software, components*
Mr. Mark A. Bentley, Principal - *Executive level management, high technology, systems, software, components*
Mr. Walter W. Wong, Principal - *Executive level management, high technology, systems, software, components*
Mr. Ed E. Sermone, Principal - *Executive level management, high technology, systems, software, components*

Salary minimum: $120,000

Functions: Generalist, Directors, Senior Mgmt., Sales & Mktg., CFO's, Engineering, Mgmt. Consultants

Industries: Generalist, Computer Equip., Consumer Elect., Venture Cap., New Media, Broadcast, Film, Telecoms

C R Krafski & Associates Inc
200 Applebee St Ste 213
Barrington, IL 60010
(847) 382-7870
Fax: (847) 382-0035
Email: krafski@prodigy.net

Description: Executive search and management consulting.

Key Contact:
Ms. Charlene Krafski

Salary minimum: $60,000

Functions: Generalist

Industries: Generalist

Krakower Group Inc
3224 Vista Arroyo
Santa Barbara, CA 93109-1066
(805) 898-0447
Email: kgi4@yahoo.com
Web: www.krakowergroup.com

Description: Over thirty years' serving the computer and telecommunications industries in executive search, management audits, organizational planning, financial resources and consulting.

Key Contact - Specialty:
Mr. Bernard H. Krakower, President - *High technology*

Salary minimum: $100,000

Functions: General Mgmt.

Industries: Drugs Mfg., Medical Devices, Computer Equip., Communications, Real Estate, Software, Biotech

Kramer Executive Resources Inc
900 3rd Ave Fl 12
New York, NY 10022-4082
(212) 832-1122
Fax: (212) 832-2881
Email: kramerexecutive@aol.com
Web: www.kramerexec.com

Description: Our firm specializes in the recruitment of accounting, tax, and financial professionals for placement in public or private accounting, controllership, and finance. In addition, our specialties include turnaround and workout specialists and litigation support.

Key Contact - Specialty:
Mr. Alan L. Kramer, CPA, President - *CFOs, controllers, accounting managers, CPAs*
Ms. Chloe Almour, Senior Vice President - *Litigation support directors, MIS directors*
Mr. Bert Ozwald, Vice President - *Assistant controller, accounting manager*

Salary minimum: $50,000

Functions: Finance, CFO's

Industries: Mfg., Textiles, Apparel, Wholesale, Retail, Banking, Services, Legal, Accounting, Advertising, Publishing, Broadcast, Film, Telecoms, Government, Insurance, Real Estate, Software

Professional Associations: AICPA, NYSSCPA, TMA

J Krauss Associates
28091 Winthrop Cir SW
Bonita Springs, FL 34134
(941) 947-8320
Fax: (941) 947-8318
Email: jkaconsultants@aol.com

Description: Domestic/international executive search, assessment, organization planning of mid-upper and top management including chairmanship.

Key Contact - Specialty:
Mr. Jack Krauss, President - *Abrasives, ophthalmic, powder metallurgy, fiber optics*

Salary minimum: $50,000

Functions: Generalist, Directors, Senior Mgmt., Middle Mgmt., Production, Plant Mgmt., Mktg. Mgmt., Sales Mgmt.

Industries: Generalist, Software, Non-classifiable

Krauthamer & Associates

5530 Wisconsin Ave Ste 1202
Chevy Chase, MD 20815
(301) 654-7533
Fax: (301) 654-0136
Email: gkrauthamer@krauthamerinc.com
Web: www.krauthamerinc.com

Description: We are national/international executive search consultants. We are generalists who place senior to executive level management including board of directors and handle a broad range of industries including aerospace, real estate, healthcare, professional services, technology, power/energy, private equity, manufacturing, transportation, and not-for-profit industries.

Key Contact:
Mr. Gary L Krauthamer, Principal
Ms. Ellen S. Dorfman, Principal
Mr. Todd A Dorfman, Principal

Salary minimum: $100,000

Functions: Generalist

Industries: Generalist, Energy, Utilities, Mfg., Transportation, Finance, Services, Aerospace, Real Estate, HR SW, Healthcare

Professional Associations: APTA, NVTC, SHRM, WC

Kremple & Meade Inc

PO Box 426
Pacific Palisades, CA 90272
(310) 459-4221
Email: tomnet@gte.net

Description: National search firm engaged for senior executive searches in various industries. Experience spans venture-backed start-ups to medium-size companies. CEOs, COOs, management teams.

Key Contact:
Mr. Thomas M. Meade, Partner
Ms. Jeannette Clemens, Director of Research

Salary minimum: $125,000

Functions: General Mgmt., Mfg., Materials, Sales & Mktg., Finance, IT

Industries: Mfg., Finance, New Media, Defense, Aerospace, Packaging, Software, Biotech

Kremple Consulting Group

222 Reward St
Nevada City, CA 95959
(530) 265-5688
Fax: (530) 265-4648
Email: jkremple@kcgresearch.com
Web: www.kcgresearch.com

Description: We are a national firm serving our clients with the highest degree of integrity and the optimum amount of personal attention by a partner of the firm. Research and candidate development services are also available.

Key Contact:
Mr. Jeffrey Kremple, Managing Partner
Mr. Robert Kremple, Senior Partner

Salary minimum: $80,000

Functions: Generalist

Industries: Mfg., Retail, Mgmt. Consulting, HR Services, IT Implementation, Hospitality, New

Media, Broadcast, Film, Communications, Software

D A Kreuter Associates Inc

1100 E Hector St Ste 388
Conshohocken, PA 19428
(610) 834-1100
Web: www.dakassociates.com

Description: National executive search and selection consultants for the diversified, financial services sector, IBID. Handle all functions; specialize in investment management, marketing, sales and senior management.

Key Contact:
Mr. Daniel A. Kreuter, President
Mr. Joel Harrison, Managing Partner
Mr. Steven M. Clark, Partner
Ms. Corinne Weston, Director of Research
Ms. Jeanne Zimbehl, Research Associate

Salary minimum: $100,000

Functions: Generalist, Senior Mgmt., Sales & Mktg.

Industries: Generalist, Finance

Professional Associations: NAVA

Kreutz Consulting Group Inc

585 N Bank Ln Ste 2000
Lake Forest, IL 60045
(847) 234-9115
Fax: (847) 234-9175

Description: Fully computerized, hands-on personalized service, extremely wide and thorough market coverage, domestic and international practice with affiliates worldwide, senior/upper middle management and board of director-levels.

Key Contact - Specialty:
Mr. Gary L. Kreutz, President - *High technology, software, telecommunications, consumer products, e-commerce, consumer marketing*

Salary minimum: $75,000

Functions: Generalist, General Mgmt., Mfg., Sales & Mktg., IT, Engineering, Int'l.

Industries: Generalist, Mfg., Transportation, Services, Hospitality, Real Estate

Professional Associations: AESC, IACPR, HRMAC

Networks: TranSearch Int'l

Seiden Krieger Associates Inc

375 Park Ave
New York, NY 10152
(212) 688-8383
Fax: (212) 688-5289
Web: www.seidenkrieger.com

Description: We specialize in CEOs and professionals who report to CEOs. Frequently, such searches are for companies in transition. Particular expertise in recruiting executives with hands-on experience building telecommunications, software and high-technology businesses.

Key Contact - Specialty:
Mr. Steven A. Seiden, President - *CEOs, directors*
Mr. Dennis F. Krieger, Managing Director - *General management, operating management*

Salary minimum: $100,000

Functions: Generalist

Industries: Generalist

Professional Associations: IACPR, AME, ASQ

Kristan Int'l Inc

12 Greenway Plz Ste 1100
Houston, TX 77046
(713) 961-3040
Fax: (713) 961-3626
Email: executivesearch@kristan.com
Web: www.kristan.com

Description: We are an eighteen-year-old retained executive search firm. We conduct both domestic and international retained assignments for global corporations, service organizations, consulting firms, start-ups, and private enterprises.

Key Contact - Specialty:
Mr. Robert P. Kristan, President - *General management*

Salary minimum: $75,000

Functions: Generalist, Senior Mgmt., Middle Mgmt., Mfg., Sales & Mktg., MIS Mgmt., Mgmt. Consultants

Industries: Generalist, Lumber, Furniture, Leather, Stone, Glass, Computer Equip., Mgmt. Consulting, Software

Sharon Krohn Consulting†

100 W Monroe St Ste 312
Chicago, IL 60603
(312) 251-0039
Fax: (312) 251-0036
Email: sharon@realestateexecutivesearch.com

Description: Executive search and human resource consulting specializing in real estate, construction, architecture and related industries.

Key Contact:
Ms. Sharon Krohn, Principal

Functions: Generalist, Senior Mgmt.

Industries: Construction, Real Estate

Professional Associations: IDRC, SHRM, WBE

Kulper & Company LLC

PO Box 1445
Morristown, NJ 07962-1445
(973) 285-3850
Email: resumes@kulpercompany.com
Web: www.kulpercompany.com

Description: We are an ISO 9002 registered retained executive search firm specializing in fulfilling mid- and senior-level search assignments in the telecommunication/high-tech, higher education, financial services, cons package/pharmaceutical, and not-for-profit industries.

Key Contact - Specialty:
Mr. Keith D. Kulper, President - *Telecommunications, financial services, high technology, not-for-profit, senior level*
Dr. Denise M. Kenny-Kulper, Partner
Mr. Sloan Kulper, Technology Manager & Webmaster - *Technology*

Salary minimum: $100,000

Functions: Generalist

Industries: Mfg., Finance, Services, Media, Communications, Insurance, Software, Biotech

Kunzer Associates Ltd

1415 W 22nd St Ste 150
Oak Brook, IL 60523
(630) 574-0010

Description: Serve clients in most industries and in all functional areas of senior and middle management, domestic and international.

Key Contact - Specialty:
Mr. William J. Kunzer, President - *Generalist*
Mrs. Diane S. Kunzer, Vice President - *Generalist*

Salary minimum: $60,000

Functions: Senior Mgmt., Middle Mgmt., Mfg., Sales & Mktg., HR Mgmt., Finance, IT, R&D, Engineering

Industries: Energy, Utilities, Mfg., Chemicals, Medical Devices, Metal Products, Retail, Finance

John Kurosky & Associates

3 Corporate Park Dr Ste 210
Irvine, CA 92606-5111
(949) 851-6370
Fax: (949) 851-8465
Email: jka@icnt.net

Description: We are a generalist firm which recruits middle to senior-level management for the traditional and high-tech driven firms. We place in all disciplinary functions. The firm's practice is national in scope and currently consists of 12 executive recruiters based in Irvine, California.

Key Contact - Specialty:
Mr. John Kurosky, President - *High technology, generalist, middle management, senior management*
Mr. Ted Bavly, Sr Vice President - *Legal*
Mr. Robert Dosier, Vice President - *Manufacturing*
Mr. Richard Payne, Vice President - *Generalist, legal, risk management*
Mr. John Tokaz, Vice President - *Legal*

Salary minimum: $80,000

Functions: Generalist, General Mgmt., Legal, Mfg., Distribution, Risk Mgmt., Engineering, Attorneys

Industries: Generalist, Mfg., Metal Products, Machine, Appliance, Electronic, Elec. Components, Transportation, Legal, Defense

The Kuypers Company

7717 Watson Dr
Plano, TX 75025
(972) 527-9450
Email: akuypers@thekuyperscompany.com
Web: www.thekuyperscompany.com

Description: Our firm assists both private and public provider and payor healthcare clients in the recruitment and selection of senior level executives. The exceptional 20-year experience and track record of our founder assists in search at the CEO and next lower executive level and in working with search committees.

Key Contact:
Mr. Arnold Kuypers, President

Salary minimum: $125,000

Functions: Generalist

Industries: Healthcare

Marvin Laba & Associates

16030 Ventura Blvd Ste 660
Encino, CA 91436
(818) 808-0072
Fax: (818) 808-0057
Email: resumes@mlasearch.com

Description: The company specializes in department, specialty store, and mass retailers and their vendors and suppliers. Wholesale, retail and e-Commerce management positions of all descriptions are worked on.

Key Contact - Specialty:
Mr. Marvin Laba, President - *Retail and their suppliers*

Salary minimum: $75,000

Functions: Directors, Senior Mgmt., Middle Mgmt., Product Dev., Sales & Mktg., Mkt. Research, Sales Mgmt., HR Mgmt., CFO's

Industries: Textiles, Apparel, Wholesale, Retail, HR Services, E-commerce

Laguzza Associates Ltd

11 McGuire Ln
Croton-on-Hudson, NY 10520
(914) 271-4002
Fax: (914) 271-4002

Description: Specializing in financial functions. Recruiting finance, control executives, vice president of finance, controllers and treasurers.

Key Contact - Specialty:
Mr. John Laguzza, Managing Director - *Vice president of finance, controller, treasurer, MIS, tax - financial functions only*

Salary minimum: $75,000

Functions: Generalist, CFO's, MIS Mgmt.

Industries: Generalist, Drugs Mfg., Machine, Appliance, Pharm Svcs., Defense, Insurance, Biotech, Healthcare

Networks: Associated Consultants in Executive Search Int'l

Branches:
633 3rd Ave Ste 1300
New York, NY 10022
(646) 485-3155
Fax: (646) 485-3156
Key Contact - Specialty:
Mr. John Laguzza - *Financial - function only*

Lamay Associates[†]

1465 Post Rd E
Westport, CT 06880
(203) 256-3593
Fax: (203) 256-3594
Email: bbliss@lamayassociates.com
Web: www.lamayassociates.com

Description: Comprehensive management selection and consultation for all disciplines of direct marketing, database and interactive media, particularly adept at building staff and professional teams for new or expanding direct marketing activities.

Key Contact:
Ms. Barbara P. Bliss, Executive Vice President - *Direct marketing, database management, interactive media*
Ms. Donna L. Toner, Resource Director

Salary minimum: $50,000

Functions: General Mgmt., Directors, Senior Mgmt., Middle Mgmt., Sales & Mktg., Advertising, Sales Mgmt., Direct Mktg., Customer Svc., DB Admin.

Industries: Banking, Media, Advertising, Publishing, New Media, Broadcast, Film, Telecoms

Professional Associations: DMA, DMAW, NEMOA

Lamon + Stuart + Michaels Inc

335 Bay St Ste 701
Toronto, ON M5H 2R3
Canada
(416) 361-7033
(800) 866-4766
Fax: (416) 361-0728
Email: info@lsmconsulting.com
Web: www.lsmconsulting.com

Description: Our services are designed to meet the varied needs of our clients for executive, middle management, technical and professional staff as well as large recruitment projects.

Key Contact - Specialty:
Mr. Wayne Lamon, President - *Generalist, information technology*
Mr. Robert Stuart, Partner - *Generalist*
Mr. George Preger, Partner - *Manufacturing, international, sales*

Ms. Jennifer Hill, Senior Principal Recruitment Services - *Generalist, financial institutions*

Functions: Generalist, Mfg., Sales & Mktg., Finance, IT, Engineering, Mgmt. Consultants

Industries: Generalist, Energy, Utilities, Mfg., Finance, Insurance, Software

Professional Associations: HRPAO, OSTD

Branches:
353 St. Nicolas St Ste 310
Montreal, QC M2Y 2P1
Canada
(514) 842-7171
Fax: (514) 842-0200
Email: psagrh@login.net
Key Contact - Specialty:
Mr. Gilles Rouleau - *Generalist*

The Landstone Group

(also known as MRI of Manhattan at Madison Ave)
295 Madison Ave Fl 36
New York, NY 10017
(212) 972-7300
Fax: (212) 972-7309
Email: admin@landstonegroup.com
Web: www.landstonegroup.com

Description: Our Mission is to help build our clients business through the acquisition of talent. After two decades of working with hundreds of companies and dealing in the new and computer technology executive search field, we have gained the experience to see what our clients' challenges are and how to focus on finding the talent that can drive their business through challenging times and on to the next growth plateau.

Key Contact - Specialty:
Mr. Jeffrey A. Heath, President - *Consumer, wireless communication, new technology*
Mr. Mark Bradley, Vice President - *Computers, hardware, software, ERP, e-commerce*
Mr. Dwight Hall, Vice President - *Consumer electronics, internet (B2B,B2C)*

Salary minimum: $90,000

Functions: Generalist, Senior Mgmt.

Industries: Generalist, Computer Equip., Test, Measure Equip., Venture Cap., Services, Hospitality, New Media, Broadcast, Film, Telecoms, Software

Langley & Associates Inc

PO Box 261606
Highlands Ranch, CO 80163-1606
(303) 694-2228
Fax: (303) 694-2216
Email: clangley@mail.com

Description: Specialize in filling senior-level management positions within the utility industry (CEO, COO, president, GM, senior VP, etc.) Work in all areas of the utility industry, i.e. electric, gas, nuclear power, telecommunications, oil, geothermal, with IOUs, RECs, G &Ts, municipal utilities and PPDs.

Key Contact - Specialty:
Ms. Carol M. Langley, President - *Utility, (senior level management, CEOs, general managers, presidents)*

Functions: Generalist, Directors, Senior Mgmt., Middle Mgmt., Legal, Sales & Mktg., Finance, Engineering

Industries: Generalist, Energy, Utilities, Finance, Mgmt. Consulting, Media, Government

Professional Associations: APPA, NRECA

The Lapham Group Inc

80 Park Ave Ste 3K
New York, NY 10016
(212) 599-0644

Email: llapham@thelaphamgroup.com

Description: Specialize in diversified financial services. Also general management for healthcare and high-technology, retail.

Key Contact - Specialty:
Mr. Lawrence L. Lapham - *Diversified financial services, direct marketing, managed health, HMOs, consumer products*
Mr. Craig L. Lapham - *Diversified financial services, direct marketing, managed health, HMOs, consumer products*

Salary minimum: $100,000

Functions: Generalist

Industries: Retail, Finance, Misc. Financial, Insurance

R H Larsen & Associates Inc

(a division of LarMc Inc)
3900 NE 21st Ave
Ft. Lauderdale, FL 33308
(954) 763-9000
Fax: (954) 563-3805
Email: boblarsen@mindspring.com

Description: The firm's search expertise is at the senior executive level with minimum base salaries at $150,000 in both the public and private market place. Our clients generally have minimum revenues of $500mm and looking to position themselves to break through the $1B level. We assist in the organizational development, executive recruiting, and the successful integration of their M&A activity. We are a " botique" firm.

Key Contact - Specialty:
Mr. Robert H. Larsen, President - *Executive level*
Ms. Nora Colburn, Senior Director - *Human resources*
Mr. Joseph Bello, VicePresident - *Senior executives*
Ms. Marie Olson, Vice President - *Mergers & acquisitions*

Functions: General Mgmt., Mfg., Sales & Mktg., HR Mgmt., Finance, IT

Industries: Generalist

Professional Associations: FAPS

Larsen & Lee Inc[†]

4807 Chevy Chase Blvd
Chevy Chase, MD 20815
(301) 718-4280
Fax: (301) 718-9587
Email: info@llisearch.com

Description: We are specialists in fee-only personal financial planning, estate planning, wealth management, investment advisory, and related searches for senior professionals and executives nationwide.

Key Contact - Specialty:
Mr. Joseph J. Lee, Principal - *Tax, estate planning, personal financial planning*

Salary minimum: $80,000

Functions: Taxes, Specialized Svcs., Attorneys

Industries: Generalist, Finance, Banking, Invest. Banking, Brokers, Venture Cap., Misc. Financial, Legal, Accounting

Larsen Consulting Int'l

1682 Sand Lily Dr
Golden, CO 80401
(303) 526-0999
Fax: (303) 526-4005
Email: les@larsens.com
Web: www.larsens.com

Description: Retained search firm specializing in officer and director-level searches. Serving diverse clients in telecommunications, technology, finance,

non-profit, education, food, health care, service industries and others.

Key Contact - Specialty:
Ms. Anna Maria Larsen, Partner
Mr. Lester Larsen, Partner - *Telecommunications, technology*

Salary minimum: $150,000

Functions: Senior Mgmt.

Industries: Generalist

Professional Associations: IMC

Larsen Int'l Inc

660 Preston Forest Ctr Ste 114
Dallas, TX 75230
(214) 987-0026
(800) 338-7475
Fax: (214) 987-4301
Email: larseninternational@prodigy.net
Web: www.larseninternational.com

Description: We have domestic and international experience in professional search. Our specialties are in mid-to-upper-management executives. We accept senior-level assignments, nationwide, with strong expertise in the consulting engineering, architectural, and security alarm industries.

Key Contact:
Mr. Donald J. Larsen, Principal
Ms. Celia Towsey, Associate

Salary minimum: $70,000

Functions: Generalist

Industries: Construction, Test, Measure Equip., Services, Call Centers, Environmental Svcs., Haz. Waste, Security SW

Professional Associations: AIA, ASCE, CSAA, IEEE, NBFAA, SIA, SIA

Larsen, Whitney, Blecksmith & Zilliacus Inc

888 W 6th St Ste 500
Los Angeles, CA 90017
(213) 243-0033
Fax: (213) 243-0030
Email: lwbz1@mindspring.com

Description: Generalist firm, international, retainer based.

Key Contact - Specialty:
Mr. Richard F. Larsen, Principal - *Banking, financial executives*
Mr. William A. Whitney, Principal - *Generalist, leisure, hospitality, entertainment (themed), non-profit*
Mr. Edward L. Blecksmith, Principal - *Generalist, leisure, hospitality, real estate*
Ms. Sandra M. Hogan, Director of Research - *Generalist, publishing, financial*
Mr. Patrick W. Zilliacus, Principal - *CEOs, directors, technical, operations*

Salary minimum: $75,000

Functions: General Mgmt., Mfg., Healthcare, Sales & Mktg., HR Mgmt., Finance, Engineering

Industries: Energy, Utilities, Construction, Drugs Mfg., Medical Devices, Plastics, Rubber, Motor Vehicles, Computer Equip., Transportation, Finance, Banking, Invest. Banking, Brokers, Venture Cap., Misc. Financial, Services, Non-profits, Pharm Svcs., Accounting, Mgmt. Consulting, Hospitality, Media, Wireless, Fiber Optic, Government, Defense, Aerospace, Packaging, Insurance, Real Estate, Software, Biotech, Healthcare

Larson Associates[†]

PO Box 9005
Brea, CA 92821
(714) 529-4121

Email: ray@consultlarson.com
Web: www.consultlarson.com

Description: Executive and professional search for chemical, electronics, high-tech, industrial firms, management, marketing, sales and technical people. Also, management consulting for human resource and organizational development functions.

Key Contact - Specialty:
Mr. Ray Larson, President - *Management, sales, industrial*

Salary minimum: $50,000

Functions: Generalist, Senior Mgmt., Middle Mgmt., Mktg. Mgmt., Sales Mgmt., MIS Mgmt., Mgmt. Consultants

Industries: Generalist, Chemicals, Plastics, Rubber, Metal Products, Computer Equip., Test, Measure Equip., Misc. Mfg.

LarsonAllen Search LLC

(a division of Larson, Allen, Weishair & Co LLP)
220 S 6th St Ste 1000
Minneapolis, MN 55402-4505
(612) 376-4500
Fax: (612) 376-4850
Email: jkruchoski@larsonallen.com
Web: www.larsonallen.com

Description: Two divisions: one recruits senior-level management for a variety of healthcare entities. The second recruits for executive positions/director-level other than healthcare.

Key Contact - Specialty:
Mr. Jerry Clark, Senior Consultant - *Healthcare administration*
Mr. Tim Voller, Executive Search Consultant - *General executive, management*
Ms. Alexis Todd, Executive Search Marketing Consultant - *General executive, management*
Mr. Patty Schmitz, Executive Search Marketing Consultant - *General executive, management*

Salary minimum: $60,000

Functions: General Mgmt.

Industries: Brokers, Services, Non-profits, Accounting, Insurance, Healthcare, Non-classifiable

Branches:
911-18th St N
PO Box 1067
St. Cloud, MN 56302
(320) 253-8616
Fax: (320) 253-7696
Email: lfujan@larsonallen.com
Key Contact - Specialty:
Ms. Lisa Fujan, Search Consultant - *General*

Lasher Associates

1565 N Park Dr Ste 104
Weston, FL 33326
(954) 217-5081
Email: mick@lasherassociates.com
Web: www.lasherassociates.com

Description: Boutique firm, serving the largest corporations to emerging companies in most industries. Committed to the highest level of performance, confidentiality and professionalism. Specialties in technology based companies and early stage companies.

Key Contact:
Mr. Charles M. Lasher - *Generalist*
Mr. Daniel B. Bronson - *Generalist*
Ms. Susan Hawkins

Functions: Generalist

Industries: Generalist

Michael Latas & Associates Inc
1311 Lindbergh Plz Ctr
St. Louis, MO 63132
(314) 993-6500
Fax: (314) 993-0632
Email: latas@latas.com
Web: www.bbuechler@latas.com

Description: We are dedicated exclusively to serving the construction A/E/P and real estate industry nationwide. We are your premier source for senior management, middle management, and difficult-to-fill professional level needs. We are organized into division specialization, which is backed up by our research director, exhaustive research library, and our support staff of research, sourcing, and recruiting specialists. Our work is strictly confidential.

Key Contact - Specialty:
Mr. Michael Latas - *Generalist*
Mr. Richard L. Latas - *Generalist*
Mr. Gary H. Jesberg - *General contractors, CM, design-build, treatment plant builders, facilities management*
Mr. Edward L. Nickels - *Electrical contracting, power transmission, utilities, telecommunications*
Mr. William Ragan - *Electrical contracting, power transmission, utilities, telecommunications*
Mr. Daniel J. Conroy - *General contractors, CM, design-build, owners reps, manufacturers*
Mr. Rodney Robinson - *Paving (concrete, asphalt), bridge, utilities, dirt, materials*
Mr. Kent L. Lawrence - *Architects, consulting engineers, facility engineering, construction management, environmental engineers*
Mr. William C. Leonard - *General contractors, interior finish, CM, design-build, owners reps*
Mrs. Cindi M. Love - *Architects, consulting engineers, facilities engineering, construction management, environmental engineers*
Ms. Nancy Creasy - *Mechanical, plumbing, sheet metal contractors, fire protection, HVAC service*
Ms. Kathie Foster - *General contractors, CM, design/build, owners reps, structural steel fabricators and erectors*
Mr. William R. Rapp - *Architects, consulting engineers, facilities engineering, construction management, environmental engineers*
Mr. John J. Kainady - *Highway, bridge, concrete & asphalt paving, utilities, dirt*
Mr. Gary Stepanek - *Highway, bridge, concrete & asphalt paving, utilities, dirt*
Mr. Ronald J. Gregory - *General contractors, CM, design-build, owners reps, structural steel fabricators and erectors*
Mr. Dan Van Hoose - *Mechanical, contractors (plumbing, sheet metal), fire protection, HVAC service, manufacturing*
Mr. Rick L. Sippel - *Highway, bridge, concrete & asphalt paving, utilities, dirt*
Mr. Gregory Baker - *Architects, consulting engineers, facilities engineering, construction management, environmental engineers*
Mr. Michael B. Klatch - *General contractors, CM, design-build, owners reps, structural steel fabricators and erectors*
Mrs. Sherry Mueller - *Architects, consulting engineers, facility engineering, construction management, environmental engineers*
Mr. James P. Fox - *Real estate development, land acquisition, property management*
Mr. John H. Patterson - *Residential, multi-family*

Salary minimum: $60,000

Functions: Generalist, Senior Mgmt., Middle Mgmt., Materials, Purchasing, CFO's, Engineering, Environmentalists, Architects

Industries: Generalist, Construction, Haz. Waste, Real Estate

Professional Associations: ABC, ACI, AGC, AIA, ASPE, AWCI, CFMA, CISCA, CSI, EMC, MCAA, NAPA, NFPA, NFSA, NRMCA, NSA, NUCA, PCCA, TCA

Branches:
PO Box 4503
Youngstown, OH 44515
(440) 799-9445
Fax: (216) 799-7612
Email: srusnov@latas.com
Web: www.latas.com
Key Contact - Specialty:
Mr. Samuel Rusnov - *Material handling, metal processing, packaging*

Latham Int'l Ltd
2170 Lawrence Way
Wall, NJ 07719
(732) 449-3000
Fax: (732) 449-1818
Email: jmartin@lathamintl.com
Web: www.lathamintl.com

Description: Established in 1979, we specialize in (post-MBA) positions targeting "fast-track/top-tier" MBAs. Areas of expertise include equity research, strategic planning, sales and management consulting. Operating nationwide, our clients are Fortune 500 industry leaders as well as smaller, more entrepreneurial companies.

Key Contact:
Ms. Jennifer Martin, Director of Research
Ms. Audrey Lynn, President

Salary minimum: $100,000

Functions: CFO's

Industries: Generalist

Latin America Search Associates
2810 E Oakland Park Blvd Ste 104
Ft. Lauderdale, FL 33306
(954) 564-6110
Fax: (954) 564-6119
Web: www.latamsearch.com

Description: Mr. Viglino specializes in executive search for Latin America. He has successfully completed over 600 assignments for multinational companies. The positions involved were international in scope, and were based either in the U.S., or in subsidiaries in Mexico, the Caribbean, or Central and South America.

Key Contact - Specialty:
Mr. Victor P. Viglino, President - *Latin America*

Salary minimum: $60,000

Functions: Generalist

Industries: Generalist

Jean J LaTraverse
1100-1200 McGill College Ave
Montreal, QC H3B 4G7
Canada
(514) 390-2345
Fax: (514) 390-2346
Email: tipit@total.net
Web: www.latraverse.net

Description: I am a Canadian chartered accountant with over 35 years of experience in search and selection of mid-level executives in all industries for opportunities in Montreal and the rest of the province of Quebec, as well as in Ottawa and Toronto in Ontario.

Key Contact:
Mr. Jean J. LaTraverse

Salary minimum: $70,000

Functions: HR Mgmt., Finance, Specialized Svcs.

Industries: Generalist, Legal

Lauer, Sbarbaro Associates
(a member of EMA Partners Int'l)
30 N LaSalle St Ste 4030
Chicago, IL 60602-2588
(312) 372-7050
Fax: (312) 704-4393
Email: sbarbs@aol.com
Web: www.lauersbarbaro-ema.com

Description: Medium size generalist firm operating worldwide with principal participation on every assignment. Known for its long-term client relationships and professional approach to clients and candidates alike. Excellent placement success record.

Key Contact - Specialty:
Mr. Richard D. Sbarbaro, Chairman - *Generalist*
Mr. William J. Yacullo, President - *Generalist*

Salary minimum: $80,000

Functions: Generalist

Industries: Generalist

Professional Associations: AESC, IERA

Networks: EMA Partners Int'l

Lawrence Corporate Resources
27372 N Oak Leaf Ct
Mundelein, IL 60060-9580
(847) 275-8934
Fax: (847) 949-8236
Email: edla@edlawrence.com
Web: www.edlawrence.com

Description: Onsite contract recruiter with specialties in IT and accounting/financial. Contract work exclusively. High-volume recruiter best known for achieving outstanding hiring results with inexperienced hiring managers.

Key Contact - Specialty:
Mr. Ed Lawrence, Contract Recruiter - *Technical (IT), accounting, financial*

Functions: IT

Industries: Generalist

Lawrence-Leiter & Company
4400 Shawnee Mission Pkwy Ste 208
Shawnee Mission, KS 66205
(913) 677-5500
Fax: (913) 677-1975
Email: lleiter@sky.net
Web: www.lawrence-leiter.com

Description: Human resources oriented general management consulting firm with long established executive search division.

Key Contact - Specialty:
Mr. William B. Beeson, Vice President - *Management (upper, all industries)*

Salary minimum: $50,000

Functions: Generalist, General Mgmt., Senior Mgmt., Plant Mgmt., Mktg. Mgmt., CFO's, Engineering

Industries: Generalist

Professional Associations: IMC

W R Lawry Inc[†]
10 Station St Ste 15
PO Box 832
Simsbury, CT 06070
(860) 651-0281
Fax: (800) 945-4143
Email: wlawry@aol.com

Description: Technical recruiting firm specializing in locating specific, highly qualified individuals or managers. Our Philadelphia division specializes in high-level healthcare professionals and executives.

Key Contact - Specialty:
Mr. William R. Lawry, President - *Engineering, telecommunications, quality, medical device, plastics*

Salary minimum: $50,000

Functions: Generalist, Mfg., Product Dev., Plant Mgmt., Quality, Healthcare, R&D, Engineering

Industries: Generalist, Energy, Utilities, Chemicals, Drugs Mfg., Medical Devices, Telecoms

Professional Associations: AICHE, ASQ

Branches:
605 Beverly Ste 102
Holland, PA 18966
(215) 357-9398
Fax: (215) 893-1705
Email: paulbhenry@prodigy.net
Key Contact - Specialty:
Mr. Paul B. Henry, Principal - *Healthcare*

Leader Search Inc
44 Barclay Walk SW
Calgary, AB T2P 4V9
Canada
(403) 262-8545
Fax: (403) 262-8549
Email: recruiting@leadersearch.com
Web: www.leadersearch.com

Description: Retainer firm specializing in fitting right character candidates to the right culture of our clients.

Key Contact:
Mr. R. W. Johnson, President
Ms. Kendra Koss, Partner
Ms. Kathy Northcott, Recruiter
Ms. Pat Massitti

Functions: Generalist, General Mgmt., Mfg., Materials, Sales & Mktg., Finance, Engineering, Specialized Svcs.

Industries: Generalist, Energy, Utilities, Mfg., Finance, Hospitality, Non-classifiable

Leaders-Trust Int'l
(also known as Carce y Asociados)
Pico de Verapaz 449-A D 101
Col Jardines en la Montana
Mexico City, MX CP 14210
Mexico
52 5 630 0132
52 5 630 0265
Fax: 52 5 446 5979
Email: carce@prodigy.net.mx
Web: www.leaderstrust.com

Description: We are an executive search firm which provides excellent professional counsel to national and international firms in top executives search. We build a successful management organization that can fully understand top companies culture, needs and goals in order to link them to top performer individuals who will contribute to their goals.

Key Contact - Specialty:
Ms. Elizabeth Falcon, Partner - *Automotive industrial, consumer, retail, finance, manufacturing industrial*
Mr. Jorge Sebovia, Senior Consultant - *Telecommunications, pharmaceuticals*

Salary minimum: $60,000

Functions: Generalist, Directors, Plant Mgmt., Mktg. Mgmt., HR Mgmt., Credit, MIS Mgmt., Mgmt. Consultants

Industries: Generalist, Food, Bev., Tobacco, Printing, Plastics, Rubber, Motor Vehicles, Banking, Brokers, Pharm Svcs., Telecoms

Leadership Capital Group LLC
2025 E Beltline Ave Ste 101
Grand Rapids, MI 49546
(616) 954-2722
(616) 954-2715
Fax: (616) 954-2732
Email: esearch@leadershipcg.com
Web: www.leadershipcg.com

Description: Leadership Capital Group is a professional services organization offering retained corporate psychology, organization development and executive search functions. Our firm works with organizations of all sizes helping them to not only identify, but also develop their Leadership Capital. We are generalist and work across industries.

Key Contact - Specialty:
Mr. R. Jansen, Partner - *Corporate psychology*
Dr. Stephen Kincaid, Partner - *Corporate psychology*
Ms. Marge Larsen, Partner - *Executive search*
Mr. Scott McLean, Partner - *Mergers & acquisitions*

Salary minimum: $110,000

Functions: Generalist

Industries: Energy, Utilities, Construction, Banking, Invest. Banking, Venture Cap., Pharm Svcs., Legal, Accounting, Mgmt. Consulting, HR Services, IT Implementation, Hospitality, Advertising, Publishing, Telecoms, Aerospace, Software, Entertainment SW, ERP SW, HR SW, Mfg. SW, Biotech, Healthcare, Hospitals

Professional Associations: APA

The Leadership Group
7047 E Greenway Pkwy Ste 250
Scottsdale, AZ 85254
(480) 473-9088
Fax: (480) 473-9089
Email: admin@tlgsearch.com
Web: www.tlgsearch.com

Description: Our specific and focused efforts are in recruiting exceptional senior-level management talent on a retained basis.

Key Contact - Specialty:
Mr. Scott T. Love, President/CEO - *CEO, COO, CFO, president, board*

Salary minimum: $100,000

Functions: General Mgmt., Directors, Senior Mgmt., CFO's

Industries: Generalist, Energy, Utilities, Construction, Real Estate

Professional Associations: ASPA, NAPS

The Lear Group Inc
578 Dover Center Rd Ste 2
Cleveland, OH 44140
(440) 892-9828
Fax: (440) 892-9757
Email: leargroup@aol.com
Web: www.learrecruit.com

Description: We offer executive search and recruitment services to a wide variety of industrial, financial and service clients. Areas of concentration include: general management, sales, marketing, engineering and manufacturing.

Key Contact - Specialty:
Mr. Larry Gregg, Managing Director - *Senior management (all disciplines, manufacturing, capital equipment, P/T, controls)*
Mr. Donal Ross, Director - *Accounting, finance, employee benefits, non-profit*
Mr. Michael Ginley, Director - *Technology transfer, business development, higher education, legal, consulting*

Salary minimum: $100,000

Functions: Generalist, General Mgmt., Senior Mgmt., Legal, Mfg.

Industries: Construction, Mfg., Medical Devices, Metal Products, Machine, Appliance, Motor Vehicles, Finance, Services, Non-profits, Legal, Accounting, Equip Svcs., Mgmt. Consulting, Aerospace, Real Estate, Software, Biotech, Dental

LedbetterStevens Inc
101 Park Ave Ste 2507
New York, NY 10178
(212) 687-6600
Email: lsi@ledbetterstevens.com
Web: www.ledbetterstevens.com

Description: Our firm provides management consulting services to the Life Sciences (biotechnology, pharmaceutical, healthcare, DART (Discovery Acceleration & Resource Technology)and related Information Technology industries, specializing in retained engagements for the recruitment of senior executive, scientific and technical management.

Key Contact:
Ms. Charlene Ledbetter, Managing Director
Ms. Jennifer Stevens, Managing Director

Functions: Generalist

Industries: Drugs Mfg., Venture Cap., Pharm Svcs., Biotech, Healthcare

Professional Associations: AAAS, AAPS, ACRP, ACS, ASCO, ASQ, ASTD, CLMA, DIA, HRPS, IAFP, NIRI, RAPS, SCIP

Ledo Executive Search Services
375 S End Ave Fl 18
New York, NY 10280
(212) 321-2882
Email: bzinn@acedsl.com
Web: www.ledosearch.com

Description: We offer financial-services institutions an alternative to traditional retained search: high-quality, customized, unbundled search services, with a flexible fee structure. The client owns the research and controls the search process.

Key Contact:
Dr. Barbara C. Zinn, Managing Principal

Salary minimum: $150,000

Functions: Generalist, CFO's

Industries: Generalist, Finance, Banking, Invest. Banking, Brokers, Misc. Financial

Professional Associations: ESRT

Lee & Burgess Associates of Colorado
7955 E Arapahoe Ct Ste 3000
Englewood, CO 80112
(303) 770-7733
Fax: (303) 770-0080
Email: edryer@leeandburgess.com
Web: www.leeandburgess.com

Description: We have been operating in the Denver area for over 10 years and have an excellent reputation for quality, performance, dependability, and integrity. Broad industry and functional position search experience encompassing both domestic and international searches. We offer a two year unconditional guarantee on all senior-level retained searches.

Key Contact:
Mr. Edward C Ryer
Mr. Lawrence Winslow, Principal

Salary minimum: $75,000

Functions: Generalist

Industries: Generalist

V J Lehman & Associates Inc

4600 S Ulster St Ste 240
Denver, CO 80237
(303) 846-3003
Fax: (303) 220-8705
Email: vlehman@ix.netcom.com

Description: Generalist retained search firm with a diverse client base with experience in most industries and functions.

Key Contact - Specialty:
Mr. Victor J. Lehman, President - *Generalist*

Salary minimum: $75,000

Functions: Generalist

Industries: Generalist

Lehman McLeskey

98 San Jacinto Blvd Ste 615
San Jacinto Office Ctr
Austin, TX 78701
(512) 478-1131
Fax: (512) 478-1985
Email: mail@lmsearch.com
Web: www.lmsearch.com

Description: Customized search services to recruit senior-level talent for executive positions and corporate boards. Our mission is to find leaders who bring strategic direction and motivation to advance your company's future.

Key Contact - Specialty:
Ms. Jan A. Lehman, Partner - *Executive level management*
Ms. Penny McLeskey, Partner - *Executive level management*

Salary minimum: $100,000

Functions: Generalist, Directors, Senior Mgmt., Plant Mgmt., Mktg. Mgmt., Sales Mgmt., CFO's, Attorneys

Industries: Generalist, Mfg., Computer Equip., Legal, New Media, Broadcast, Film, Telecoms, Software

LeMaster & Ware Inc

7820 Ballantyne Commons Pkwy Ste 201
Charlotte, NC 28277
(704) 940-1800
(888) 286-6733
Fax: (704) 940-1820
Email: sales@lemasterandware.com
Web: www.lemasterandware.com

Description: We are uniquely qualified to find those individuals who have the skills and interpersonal assets to provide maximum success and long-term impact on operational efficiency and effectiveness.

Key Contact:
Mr. Charles C. Ware, President
Mr. Ronald L. Couturier, Executive Vice President
Ms. Jeanette T. Doennig, Vice President-Research
Mr. Heath I. Prior, Director of Operational Development

Salary minimum: $125,000

Functions: Generalist, Senior Mgmt., Middle Mgmt., Mktg. Mgmt., M&A, Mgmt. Consultants

Industries: Generalist, Mfg., Finance, Banking, Invest. Banking, Brokers, Venture Cap., Misc. Financial, Mgmt. Consulting, Insurance, Software

LePage Int'l Inc

800 Rene-Levesque Blvd Ste 2450
Montreal, QC H3B 4V7
Canada
(514) 874-1987
(514) 876-9876
Email: info@lepageintl.com
Web: www.lepageintl.com

Description: Top one in Quebec and Ontario; bilingual firm (French & English) national and international search experience, research-based generalist firm; senior and middle management searches across most functions and industries.

Key Contact:
Mr. Jacques LePage, President/Managing Director

Salary minimum: $75,000

Functions: Generalist, General Mgmt., Mfg., Materials, Sales & Mktg., HR Mgmt., Engineering, Int'l.

Industries: Generalist, Agri., Forestry, Mining, Energy, Utilities, Mfg., Media, Aerospace, Software

Professional Associations: HRPAO, IMC, PRHQ

Networks: World Search Group

J E Lessner Associates Inc

2143 E Newark Rd
Lapeer, MI 48446
(810) 667-9335
Fax: (810) 667-3470
Email: lessner@tir.com
Web: www.tir.com/~lessner/

Description: Perform executive searches, organizational development and outplacement activities.

Key Contact - Specialty:
Mr. Jack Lessner, President - *Organizational development, executive search activities*
Ms. Mary Ann Lessner, Vice President-Staff Admin.
Mr. Mark Lessner, Search Consultant - *Manufacturing, sales, engineering*
Ms. Jan Roodvoets, Search Consultant - *Sales, manufacturing, materials*

Salary minimum: $75,000

Functions: Generalist, General Mgmt., Mfg., Materials, Sales & Mktg., Finance, Engineering, Int'l.

Industries: Generalist, Mfg., Plastics, Rubber, Metal Products, Motor Vehicles, Transportation, Aerospace

Professional Associations: SAE

Levin & Company Inc

28 State St Ste 1100
Boston, MA 02109
(617) 573-5258
Fax: (617) 573-5259
Web: www.levinandcompany.com

Description: We look beyond resumes to character and build complementary teams with special emphasis on workplace diversity. We focus on life sciences, pharmaceuticals and biomedical companies.

Key Contact - Specialty:
Ms. Becky Levin, Founder - *Biotechnology, pharmaceuticals, biomedical*

Salary minimum: $150,000

Functions: Generalist, Directors, Senior Mgmt., CFO's, MIS Mgmt.

Industries: Generalist, Drugs Mfg., Medical Devices, Biotech

Branches:
1888 Century Park E Ste 1900
Los Angeles, CA 90067
(310) 284-6850
Fax: (310) 284-6856
Key Contact - Specialty:
Mr. Christos Richards, Executive Director - *Biotech, e-health, high tech*

1301 Page St
San Francisco, CA 94117
(415) 552-9522
Fax: (415) 552-9608
Key Contact - Specialty:
Evan Fishel, Vice President-Research - *Biotech, e-health*

Alan Levine Associates[†]

275 Turnpike St Ste 202
Canton, MA 02021-2357
(617) 821-1133
Fax: (617) 821-0601
Email: alevine3@aol.com

Description: We are a specialized, personalized, quality search firm with over 21 years of service to the retail, wholesale, direct mail, and consumer packaged goods industries.

Key Contact - Specialty:
Mr. Alan C. Levine, Managing Principal - *Retail, manufacturing, consumer packaged goods, direct mail, big 5 consulting*

Salary minimum: $60,000

Functions: Generalist, Senior Mgmt., Mktg. Mgmt., Sales Mgmt.

Industries: Generalist, Construction, Mfg., Textiles, Apparel, Electronic, Elec. Components, Wholesale, Retail, Legal, Mgmt. Consulting, Communications, Telecoms, Call Centers, Telephony, Digital

Michael Levine Search Consultants

11 E 44th St Ste 500
New York, NY 10017
(212) 328-1940
Fax: (212) 328-1950
Email: search@mlsearch.com
Web: www.mlsearch.com

Description: A boutique firm who can guarantee personalized care in every search. Our contacts are wide and we can find people in places not normally covered by a large firm.

Key Contact:
Mr. Michael Levine, President
Mr. Marcus Brauer, Recruiter
Mr. Brent Sudduth, Recruiter
Mr. Steven Spector, Recruiter
Ms. Linda Larin, Recruiter

Salary minimum: $75,000

Functions: Generalist, Senior Mgmt., Middle Mgmt., Advertising, Mkt. Research, PR, Int'l.

Industries: Generalist, Soap, Perf., Cosmtcs., Retail, Hospitality, Advertising, New Media, Broadcast, Film

Levison Search Associates[†]

PO Box 1133
El Dorado, CA 95623
(530) 626-5110
Fax: (530) 626-5604
Email: rlevison@levisonsearch.com
Web: www.levisonsearch.com

Description: Our firm specializes in recruiting physicians, mid-level practitioners, and executives, more specifically department head level and above for hospitals, HMOs, medical groups, and clinics.

Key Contact - Specialty:
Ms. Regina Levison, President - *Healthcare (all)*
Mr. Michael Levison, Executive Vice President - *Healthcare (all)*
Ms. Marge Ramos, Vice President - *Healthcare (all)*

Salary minimum: $50,000

Functions: Generalist, Physicians, Health Admin.

Industries: Generalist, Healthcare

Professional Associations: MGMA, NAPR

The Levton Group Inc
140 Symington Ave
Toronto, ON M6P 3W4
Canada
(416) 532-0161
Fax: (416) 532-5832
Email: nbreaks@levton.com
Web: www.levton.com

Description: The firm offers recruitment and other human resource services on an hourly rated basis. Our strengths include senior clerical, accounting at all levels, computer professionals, and management. Most of our search activities are in the Greater Toronto and Ontario, Canada area.

Key Contact - Specialty:
Mr. Nick Breaks, Principal - *Human resource*

Salary minimum: $25,000

Functions: Generalist

Industries: Generalist

Professional Associations: HRPAO

Lewis & Blank Int'l
520 S El Camino Real Ste 342
San Mateo, CA 94402-1716
(650) 685-6855
Fax: (650) 685-0671
Email: lbint@lewis-blank.com
Web: www.lewis-blank.com

Description: Our firm is a global executive search firm representing emerging and established life science companies in their recruitment of senior management. Our principals have supported the growth of the biotech, pharmaceutical, and medical device industries over the past 20 years.

Key Contact - Specialty:
Ms. Daphne V. Lewis, Principal - *Biomedical, pharmaceutical, venture, device*
Ms. Paula Blank, Principal - *Biomedical, pharmaceutical, venture, device*

Salary minimum: $140,000

Functions: Generalist, Directors, Senior Mgmt., Product Dev., Physicians, Mktg. Mgmt., CFO's, R&D

Industries: Drugs Mfg., Medical Devices, Invest. Banking, Venture Cap., Biotech, Healthcare

Lewis Companies Inc
162 Cumberland St Renaissance Ct Ste 305
Toronto, ON M5R 3N5
Canada
(416) 929-1506
Fax: (416) 929-8470
Email: lewiscos@interlog.com

Description: This practice is client-driven, results-driven and creative. It operates in most industry and functional sectors. All project activity is conducted in an ethical professional manner. Selection capability is exceptional.

Key Contact - Specialty:
Ms. Lorraine Lewis, Managing Partner - *Generalist*
Mr. Stephen Morrison, MBA, Partner - *Generalist*
Ms. Ann Curran, Partner - *Corporate development*
Ms. Amrita Bhalla, MIR, Partner - *Global aerospace, global IT*
Ms. Michelle Hughes, Partner - *Retail*
Ms. Chantal Haas, Partner - *Bilingual services*

Salary minimum: $60,000

Functions: Senior Mgmt.

Industries: Generalist

Professional Associations: AIAC, BTMT, ECC, OAC

Lexington Associates
25 Burlington Mall Rd Ste 300
Burlington, MA 01803
(781) 238-0246
Fax: (781) 238-6726
Email: dshufelt@lexassoc.com
Web: www.lexassoc.com

Description: We specialize in retained executive searches for high-tech firms. We are uniquely positioned to address major issues facing corporations today, such as e-commerce and the convergence of voice, data, and video.

Key Contact - Specialty:
Mr. Cornel J. Faucher, Managing Partner - *Internet, data networking, telecommunications, video conferencing, computer telephony integration*
Mr. Douglas G. Shufelt, Managing Partner - *Telecommunications, internet related technologies, e-commerce, financial services*

Salary minimum: $125,000

Functions: Senior Mgmt.

Industries: Test, Measure Equip., Venture Cap., New Media, Telecoms

Branches:
1177 High Ridge Rd
Stamford, CT 06905
(203) 321-1298
Fax: (203) 321-2122
Email: dshufelt@lexassoc.com
Key Contact:
Mr. Douglas Shufelt, Managing Partner

LGES (Lautz, Grotte, Engler & Swimley LLC)
1 Bush St Ste 550
San Francisco, CA 94104
(415) 834-3101
Fax: (415) 834-3113
Email: info@lges.com
Web: www.lges.com

Description: Provide senior-level executive search and consulting services to Internet/e-commerce, enterprise software, information technologies and telecommunications industries. Specialists in early-stage and high-growth client companies.

Key Contact - Specialty:
Mr. Lindsay A. Lautz, Principal - *Generalist*
Mr. Lawrence C. Grotte, Principal - *Generalist*
Mr. Peter G. Engler, Principal - *Generalist*
Mr. James W. Watkinson, Principal - *Generalist*

Salary minimum: $150,000

Functions: Senior Mgmt., Product Dev., Sales & Mktg., CFO's, IT, MIS Mgmt., Systems Dev., Systems Implem., Engineering

Industries: Computer Equip., Consumer Elect., Venture Cap., E-commerce, IT Implementation, Entertainment, Media, Communications, Software

Liberty Executive Search
(a subsidiary of KJB Enterprises)
7500 San Felipe Ste 525
Houston, TX 77063
(713) 961-7666
Email: info@thelibertygroup.com
Web: www.thelibertygroup.com

Description: Liberty is an executive search firm which has specialized in the real estate industry since 1977.

Key Contact:
Mr. Rick McCain, CPC, Vice President

The Libra Group Ltd†
1101 S Blvd Ste 202
PO Box 32424
Charlotte, NC 28232
(704) 334-0476
Fax: (704) 334-7186
Email: libragp@aol.com

Description: We are an African American search firm that specializes in diversity. We have 100 percent success at placing middle to upper-level managers.

Key Contact - Specialty:
Grazell R. Howard, Esq., President - *Diversity, senior level talent*
Mr. Frank G. Chester, Vice President - *Human resources*

Salary minimum: $70,000

Functions: Generalist, General Mgmt., Senior Mgmt., Mfg., HR Mgmt., Finance, Engineering, Minorities

Industries: Generalist, Mfg., Paints, Petro. Products, Retail, Finance, Services, Legal, Defense

Lois L Lindauer Searches
437 Boylston St
Boston, MA 02116
(617) 262-1102
Fax: (617) 262-1106
Email: llindauer@lllsearches.com
Web: www.lllsearches.com

Description: We are a retained executive search firm that supports the nonprofit sector by filling mid- to executive-level positions. Our specialty is development.

Key Contact:
Ms. Lois L. Lindauer, Director - *Non-profit management, fundraising, management*
Ms. Jill Lasman, Assistant Director
Ms. Nicole Gakidis, Assistant Director

Salary minimum: $50,000

Functions: Middle Mgmt., Non-profits

Industries: Non-profits, Higher Ed.

Professional Associations: AFP, AHP, AWID

Lindsey & Company Inc
484 Boston Post Rd
PO Box 1273
Darien, CT 06820
(203) 655-1590
Fax: (203) 655-3798
Web: www.lindseycompany.com

Description: General search in all industries and functions.

Key Contact - Specialty:
Mr. Lary L. Lindsey, President - *Generalist*
Mr. Thomas K. McInerney, Managing Partner - *Generalist*
Ms. Hillary A. Morgan, Managing Partner - *Generalist*

Salary minimum: $120,000

Functions: Generalist

Industries: Generalist

Branches:
16 S Green Turtle Ln
PO Box 611177
Rosemary Beach, FL 32461
(850) 231-6908
Fax: (850) 231-6905
Key Contact:
Mr. Robert Brand, Managing Partner

TheLinkPartners
5114 Balcones Woods Dr Ste 307
PMB 301
Austin, TX 78759
(512) 794-4554
Fax: (512) 794-4114
Email: rsgates@thelinkpartners.com
Web: www.thelinkpartners.com

Description: We are a retained firm working
exclusively with growing technology and non-
technology companies to locate chief, VP, and
director level executives.

Key Contact - Specialty:
Ms. Becky Gates, Managing Partner - *CEO, COO,
CFO, CIO, CMO*
Mr. Tom Gates, Partner - *VP & director level*

Salary minimum: $100,000

Functions: Generalist, General Mgmt., Directors,
Senior Mgmt., Mfg., Sales & Mktg., CFO's, MIS
Mgmt.

Industries: Computer Equip., New Media,
Telecoms, Software

Professional Associations: FEI, SHRM

Lipsky Group Inc†
220 Nice Ln Ste 112
Newport Beach, CA 92663
(949) 645-4300
Fax: (949) 645-4522
Email: lipsky@ix.netcom.com
Web: www.lipskygroup.com

Description: We are a boutique executive search
and consulting firm. We specialize in start-ups and
turnarounds. Specifically in the computer
communication marketplace. We do everything
from complete executive staff to full departments (ie
sales & marketing).

Key Contact - Specialty:
Ms. Marla J. Lipsky, President - *High technology
start-ups (computer related), upper management,
sales & marketing*

Salary minimum: $75,000

Functions: Generalist, General Mgmt., Senior
Mgmt., Sales & Mktg., Mkt. Research, Sales
Mgmt.

Industries: Generalist, Computer Equip., Venture
Cap., Communications, Telecoms, Software,
Marketing SW, Networking, Comm. SW,
Security SW

Lipson & Co
1900 Ave of the Stars Ste 2810
Los Angeles, CA 90067
(310) 277-4646
Fax: (310) 277-8585
Email: howard@lipsonco.com
Web: www.lipsonco.com

Description: A boutique firm servicing the
executive needs of the entertainment, high-
technology and consumer goods industries.
Headquartered in Los Angeles, but international in
scope. The company's principals - with firsthand
experience in their specialized industries - have
completed senior-level searches (CEO, presidents,
SVP, etc.) throughout the US, as well as in Japan,
Canada, Australia, the UK, Germany and France.

Key Contact - Specialty:
Mr. Howard R. Lipson, President - *Entertainment,
multimedia, consumer goods*
Ms. Harriet L. Lipson, Senior Vice President -
Entertainment, multimedia, consumer goods

Salary minimum: $100,000

Functions: Senior Mgmt.

Industries: Consumer Elect., Non-profits, Media,
Telecoms, Telephony, Digital, Wireless, Network
Infrastructure

Lipton Associates Inc
575 Lexington Ave Fl 4
New York, NY 10022
(212) 838-0900
Email: blipton@regentbc.com

Description: We are a professional services
company dedicated to providing partner level,
retained search services to law firms. We help law
firms fulfill strategic planning objectives through
the acquisition of law partners and practice groups.

Key Contact - Specialty:
Mr. Robert J. Lipton, President - *Legal*

Salary minimum: $350,000

Functions: Attorneys

Industries: Generalist, Legal

Litchfield & Willis Inc
3900 Essex Ln Ste 650
Houston, TX 77027-5111
(713) 439-8200
Fax: (713) 439-8201
Email: lw@litchwillis.com
Web: www.litchwillis.com

Description: A retained search firm, we also
provide consulting services in succession and
organizational management. Special expertise for
clients in: professional services industry, oil &
gas/energy, emerging companies, manufacturing,
public sector organizations and large national
corporations.

Key Contact:
Ms. Barbara H. Litchfield, Principal - *Engineering,
management, public sector, services industries*
Mr. Jack L. Baber, Senior Vice President - *Oil &
gas, energy, real estate*
Mr. Jim Davenport, Vice President - *Healthcare,
engineering, services*
Ms. Tracy Driehs, Associate

Functions: Generalist

Industries: Generalist

Livingston, Robert & Company
209 Bruce Park Ave
Greenwich, CT 06830
(203) 618-8400

Description: Small, research oriented, general
management oriented, clients are both large
corporations and start-ups. Only the principals work
on assignments.

Key Contact - Specialty:
Mr. Peter R. Livingston - *Senior level general
management*
Mr. Eugene Saxe - *Software, technology, pre-ipo
startups*
Ms. Dorothy C. Pickering - *Sports, fashion, non-
profit*

Salary minimum: $100,000

Functions: General Mgmt., Mfg., Materials, Sales
& Mktg., HR Mgmt., Finance, M&A, IT, Non-
profits

Industries: Mfg., Food, Bev., Tobacco, Textiles,
Apparel, Chemicals, Drugs Mfg., Medical
Devices, Computer Equip., Consumer Elect.,
Transportation, Invest. Banking, Brokers, Venture
Cap., Non-profits, Packaging, Software, Biotech

Lloyd Associates†
35 Glenlake Pkwy Ste 164
Atlanta, GA 30328
(770) 390-0001

Description: We are a generalist practice that place
emphasis on commercial banks, including:
community, major regional, money center banks,
and consulting firms serving these banks. Our
specialties are CEO, CFO, senior lending and credit

officers, retail delivery channels, and payment
systems.

Key Contact - Specialty:
Ms. Carolyn T. Lloyd, Principal/Owner - *Banking*

Salary minimum: $50,000

Functions: Generalist, Cash Mgmt., Risk Mgmt.,
Minorities

Industries: Finance, Banking, Mgmt. Consulting

The Lloyd Group
6916 Prestonshire Ln Ste 100
Dallas, TX 75225
(972) 361-7411
Email: glloyd@tlgusa.com
Web: www.tlgusa.com

Description: An executive search and research
consulting group possessing a thorough
understanding of today's technology-driven
candidate sourcing and relationship building. We
believe in the competitive market advantage of
successful team members and seek constantly to
provide our clients with outstanding candidates.

Key Contact:
Ms. Gwyneth Lloyd, President

Salary minimum: $100,000

Functions: Directors, Senior Mgmt., Middle
Mgmt., Sales Mgmt., IT, Systems Dev., Systems
Implem.

Industries: Generalist, Mgmt. Consulting, IT
Implementation, Software

Locke & Associates
1811 Sardis Rd N Ste 207
Charlotte, NC 28270
(704) 372-6600
Email: flocke@mindspring.com

Description: Executive search engagements
conducted exclusively on a retainer basis in a broad
variety of professional disciplines. Extensive
experience serving engineering and construction,
manufacturing, financial and service industries.

Key Contact - Specialty:
Mr. M. Fred Locke, Jr., President - *General
management*

Salary minimum: $70,000

Functions: Generalist, Senior Mgmt., Plant Mgmt.,
Sales Mgmt., Benefits, CFO's, Engineering, Int'l.

Industries: Generalist, Energy, Utilities,
Construction, Textiles, Apparel, Metal Products,
Banking, Accounting

Branches:
4144 Carmichael Rd Ste 20
Montgomery, AL 36106
(334) 272-7400
Key Contact - Specialty:
Mr. Glen O. Pruitt, Vice President - *Engineering,
construction*

Loewenstein & Associates Inc
5847 San Felipe Ste 1250
Houston, TX 77057
(713) 952-1840
Fax: (713) 952-4534
Email: executivesearch@loewenstein.com
Web: www.loewenstein.com

Description: We provide executive search for
companies who provide products and services to the
manufacturing, process, and energy industries.

Key Contact - Specialty:
Mr. Ron Loewenstein, President - *IT, sales &
marketing, business, technology*

Salary minimum: $100,000

Functions: Generalist, Senior Mgmt., Production, Automation, Sales Mgmt., MIS Mgmt., Systems Implem., Mgmt. Consultants

Industries: Generalist, Energy, Utilities, Chemicals, Computer Equip., Mgmt. Consulting, Software

The Logan Group Inc
7710 Carondelet Ste 506
St. Louis, MO 63105
(314) 862-2828
Email: logangroup@primary.net
Web: www.advr.com/logan/

Description: National/international search firm engaged in quality search and surveys. Activity tailored to clients' needs.

Key Contact - Specialty:
Mr. Brian Ryan, President - *Generalist*

Salary minimum: $60,000

Functions: General Mgmt., Directors, Senior Mgmt., Middle Mgmt., Mfg., Healthcare, Sales & Mktg., HR Mgmt., Finance, IT

Industries: Mfg., Services, Media, Government

Logan, Chace LLC
420 Lexington Ave Ste 845
New York, NY 10017
(212) 949-2500
Fax: (212) 949-5212
Email: admin@loganchace.com

Description: Consultants to management in executive selection. Generalist firm specializing in strategically critical assignments.

Key Contact:
Mr. James P. Logan, III
Mr. Heath I. Chace

Salary minimum: $100,000

Functions: Generalist

Industries: Generalist

Logistics Management Resources Inc
PO Box 2204
New City, NY 10956-0588
(845) 638-4224
Fax: (845) 638-4621
Email: mslater@logisticsresources.com
Web: www.logisticsresources.com

Description: We specialize in placing middle and upper level management in all operational areas nationwide. Our core specialties are in logistics and supply chain management.

Key Contact - Specialty:
Ms. Marjorie Slater, President - *Logistics, materials management, purchasing, supply chain management*

Salary minimum: $85,000

Functions: Generalist, Materials, Purchasing, Distribution, Customer Svc., Mgmt. Consultants

Industries: Generalist, Mfg., Transportation, Services, Packaging, Software

Professional Associations: CLM

Cathryn Lohrisch & Company Inc
3266 Yonge St Ste 1201
Toronto, ON M4N 3P6
Canada
(416) 222-3063
Fax: (416) 222-2430
Email: lohrisch@sympatico.ca

Description: We are a search firm that provides personalized service tailored to clients' needs. Our firm conducts searches for senior staff positions in the private, public, and not-for-profit sectors. Most of the positions that we place are located in Canada.

Key Contact:
Ms. Cathryn Lohrisch, President

Salary minimum: $50,000

Functions: Generalist, General Mgmt., PR, HR Mgmt., Finance

Industries: Generalist, Finance, Non-profits, Higher Ed., HR Services, Government, Insurance

Professional Associations: CAMC, CHRPS, HRPAO

The Longfellow Group
PO Box 481
Hingham, MA 02043
(781) 925-5294
Fax: (781) 925-1178
Email: tlgroup@mediaone.net

Description: We are a boutique firm, specializing in finding the best executive high technology and strategy consulting talent for our clients. Our focus is on chief executives, presidents, partners, vice presidents, and directors.

Key Contact:
Mr. Sam Medalie, President/Founder

Salary minimum: $100,000

Functions: Senior Mgmt.

Industries: Venture Cap., Services, Mgmt. Consulting, E-commerce, Communications, Software

Longshore + Simmons
625 Ridge Pike Ste 410
Plymouth Corporate Ctr
Conshohocken, PA 19428
(610) 941-3400
Fax: (610) 941-2424

Description: Healthcare executive search, including managed care; recruitment for physician leadership, hospital and community-based specialists, primary care; healthcare consulting specializing in compensation, hospital-based practice, market studies, hospital/physician strategies, practice valuation and sales.

Key Contact:
Mr. H. J. Simmons, Principal/COO
Dr. George J. Peckham, MD, Vice President & Chief Medical Executive
Ms. Stephaine J. Underwood, Principal
Mr. Richard Carroll, Principal
Mr. Frank Garofolo, Principal

Salary minimum: $75,000

Functions: Generalist, Directors, Senior Mgmt., Physicians, Health Admin., CFO's, MIS Mgmt.

Industries: Generalist, Drugs Mfg., HR Services, Insurance, Healthcare

Professional Associations: ACPE, CHA, MGMA

J S Lord & Company Inc
266 Main St Ste 7B
Olde Medfield Sq
Medfield, MA 02052
(508) 359-5100
Fax: (508) 359-5660
Email: jslandco@aol.com

Description: Firm founded to provide clients with the focus, commitment and communications necessary to complete searches in a timely manner. Original research and candidate development will be undertaken on each assignment with the goal of presenting final candidates within three to five weeks. Founder has over twenty years of recruitment experience.

Key Contact - Specialty:
Mr. J. Scott Lord, President - *Consumer products, pharmaceuticals, biotechnology, high technology*

Salary minimum: $150,000

Functions: Generalist

Industries: Mfg., Food, Bev., Tobacco, Soap, Perf., Cosmtcs., Drugs Mfg., Medical Devices, Non-profits, Pharm Svcs., Biotech, Healthcare

Professional Associations: CLM, DIA, NEHRA, RAPS

Lowell Johnson Associates LLC
(also known as MRI of Grosse Pointe)
15450 E Jefferson Ave Ste 160
Grosse Pointe Park, MI 48230
(313) 822-6770
Fax: (313) 822-6775
Email: recruitco@earthlink.net
Web: www.recruitco.com

Description: We are dedicated to achieving the highest level of client satisfaction and conducting financial, accounting, tax, IS, and M&A retained searches nationwide. We employ the latest information technology while maintaining strict confidentiality, professionalism, and personal integrity.

Key Contact - Specialty:
Mr. Lowell D. Johnson, President - *CFO, CIO, controller, treasurer, financial management*
Mr. Stephen C. Lo Grasso, Senior Associate - *Accounting & finance, mergers & acquisitions, audit, tax*
Mr. Laurie M. Henderson, Associate - *Accounting & finance, audit, tax*

Salary minimum: $100,000

Functions: Finance, CFO's, Budgeting, Cash Mgmt., Taxes, M&A, MIS Mgmt., Attorneys

Industries: Generalist

Lucerne Partners LLC
225 W 34th St Ste 402
New York, NY 10122-0499
(212) 279-8900
Fax: (212) 279-9085
Email: info@lpsearch.com
Web: www.lpsearch.com

Description: Specializing in finance, treasury, risk management, marketing, business development and sales within financial and professional services and high-technology. All staff members are experienced professionals within their disciplines. Over thirty years of experience in executive search.

Key Contact - Specialty:
Mr. Joseph Ambroso, CPA, Principal - *CFOs, controllers, treasurers, financial managers*
Mr. Robert Bilotta, Principal - *Investment banking, risk management, trading, research*
Mr. Joseph Chiulli, Senior Managing Director - *Operations, sales, marketing, venture capital*
Ms. Sheryl Goldstein, Managing Director - *Marketing, business development, sales*

Salary minimum: $150,000

Functions: General Mgmt.

Industries: Invest. Banking, Venture Cap., Accounting, Mgmt. Consulting, New Media, Telecoms

The John Lucht Consultancy Inc
641 5th Ave
The Olympic Tower
New York, NY 10022
(212) 935-4660

Description: We are an outstanding generalist firm. We provide searches by John Lucht, author of "Rites of Passage at $100,000 to $1 Million+." We will recruit CEOs, outside board members, and senior management in every function. We will also assess current staff. We serve all industries and all functions. We are noted for thoroughness of searching, referencing, and documentation.

Key Contact - Specialty:
Mr. John Lucht, President - *Senior management*

Salary minimum: $250,000

Functions: Generalist, Directors, Senior Mgmt., Mktg. Mgmt., HR Mgmt., CFO's, MIS Mgmt.

Industries: Generalist, Drugs Mfg., Publishing, New Media, Broadcast, Film, Insurance

Professional Associations: AESC, IACPR

The Luciani Group†
754 Sir Frances Drake Blvd Ste 8
San Anselmo, CA 94960
(415) 258-2812
Fax: (415) 258-2811
Email: tom@lucianigroup.com
Web: www.lucianigroup.com

Description: We are a search, consulting organization that does retained searches. We specialize in financial executive placement exclusively. Our firm's clients are in the high-technology industry in the San Francisco Bay Area.

Key Contact - Specialty:
Mr. Thomas G. Luciani, Founder/ President - *Finance executives, treasury, high technology*
Ms. Stacey McGurk, Research Consultant - *Finance executives, high technology*

Functions: Generalist, CFO's, Budgeting, Cash Mgmt., Taxes, M&A, Risk Mgmt., Mgmt. Consultants

Industries: Generalist, Computer Equip., Electronic, Elec. Components, New Media, Broadcast, Film, Communications, Telecoms, Software

Fran Luisi Associates
3 Bamboo Ln
Far Hills, NJ 07931
(908) 470-1005
Fax: (908) 470-1007
Email: fluisi@erols.com
Web: www.franluisi.com

Description: Boutique firm that recruits the progressive human resource professional on a global basis.

Key Contact - Specialty:
Mr. Francis J. Luisi, Principal - *Human resources*

Salary minimum: $100,000

Functions: Generalist, Benefits, Personnel, Training, Mgmt. Consultants, Minorities, Int'l.

Industries: Generalist, HR Services

Professional Associations: AHRSP, EMA, HRPS, IFEBP, IIHR, SHRM, WAW

Charles Luntz & Associates Inc
14323 S Outer Forty Ste 400 S
Chesterfield, MO 63017
(314) 275-7992
Email: chuck@charlesluntz.com
Web: www.charlesluntz.com

Description: Generalist firm representing companies in urban and rural locations. Fill positions considered key to employer. Will unbundle search with hourly billing. Guarantee placements. Have a 30% maximum with no minimum and no penalty for cancellation. Excellent record.

Key Contact:
Mr. Charles E. Luntz, President
Ms. Joy P. Brother, EVP
Mr. Michael C. Luntz, Associate

Salary minimum: $50,000

Functions: Generalist, Directors

Industries: Generalist, Energy, Utilities, Mfg., Finance, Services, Media, Government, Defense, Environmental Svcs., Haz. Waste, Aerospace, Software, Mfg. SW, Marketing SW, Healthcare, Hospitals

Professional Associations: AMA, AMA, AUSA, EMA, GHRA, HRMA, NAFE, RCGA, SHRM

P J Lynch Associates
PO Box 967
Ridgefield, CT 06877
(203) 438-8475
Email: patlynch@pjlynch.com
Web: www.pjlynch.com

Description: Quality orientation to matching highly skilled managers to performance driven organizations. Timely and effective utilization of search process. Resource in providing value added service to our clients, through our understanding of their requirement and culture.

Key Contact - Specialty:
Mr. Patrick J. Lynch, Managing Partner - *Publishing, information products*
Mr. Phil Bartlett, Senior Partner - *Manufacturing, information products*
Dr. Arlene McSweeney, Senior Partner - *Organizational development*

Salary minimum: $80,000

Functions: Generalist, General Mgmt., Sales & Mktg.

Industries: Publishing, New Media, Digital, Software, Database SW

Lynrow Associates LLC
18 Tobacco Rd
Weston, CT 06883
(203) 226-4464
Fax: (203) 226-5764
Email: lynrow@mindspring.com

Description: Senior and middle management searches focusing in the consumer products, financial services and electronic commerce industries.

Key Contact:
Ms. Lynn O'Donnell, President

Salary minimum: $75,000

Functions: Senior Mgmt., Middle Mgmt., Product Dev., Advertising, Mkt. Research, Mktg. Mgmt., Direct Mktg., IT

Industries: Mfg., Food, Bev., Tobacco, Textiles, Apparel, Soap, Perf., Cosmtcs., Drugs Mfg., Finance, Media, Communications, Software

Lyons Associates†
PO Box 984
Saratoga Springs, NY 12866
(518) 583-0444
Fax: (518) 583-0421
Email: slyons@clubjobs-online.com
Web: www.clubjobs-online.com

Description: A generalist retained search firm exclusively to the hospitality industry. Emphasizing the recruitment of middle and upper-level management.

Key Contact - Specialty:
Mr. Sean J. Lyons, Managing Director - *Hospitality*

Salary minimum: $40,000

Functions: Generalist, General Mgmt., Middle Mgmt.

Industries: Generalist, Hospitality, Hotels, Resorts, Clubs, Restaurants, Entertainment, Recreation

Professional Associations: NCA, NRA

Lyons Pruitt Int'l
2357 Lehigh Str
Allentown, PA 18103
(610) 791-0100
(800) 827-5776
Fax: (610) 791-0112
Email: search@lyonspruitt.com
Web: www.lyonspruitt.com

Description: We have been providing executive search services of the highest caliber for a combined 34 years. We specialize in identifying exceptional professionals with a verifiable track record of performance and accomplishment.

Key Contact - Specialty:
Mr. Jim Pruitt, President - *Credit card banks*
Mr. Olin Lyons, Senior Associate - *Plastics*
Mr. Rick Slifka, EVP - *Sales, e-commerce, golf club management*

Salary minimum: $75,000

Functions: Generalist, Senior Mgmt., Production, Sales Mgmt., CFO's, Cash Mgmt., Risk Mgmt., MIS Mgmt.

Industries: Generalist, Plastics, Rubber, Banking, Invest. Banking, Venture Cap., New Media, Software

Branches:
40 Wall St Fl 32
New York, NY 10005
(212) 797-8888
Fax: (212) 797-8896
Email: search@lyonspruitt.com
Key Contact - Specialty:
Mr. Scott Lyons, Vice President - *Financial services*

Lysen Anderson Executive Search Inc†
1460 Woodland Trce
Cumming, GA 30041
(678) 455-0691
Fax: (678) 455-9546
Email: tammy@lysenanderson.com
Web: www.lysenanderson.com

Description: We are generalist firm with expertise in telecommunications, broadband, manufacturing, supply chain, logistics, procurement, IT, ERP, ASP, MSP, sales, marketing, product management, marcom, operations, and general management. Clients include Fortune 500 members, VC-funded start-ups, Georgia's "Top 100" public companies, and many hyper growth companies.

Key Contact:
Mrs. Tammy Anderson Dutremble, Managing Partner
Mrs. Cynthia Lysen Walsh, Managing Partner

Salary minimum: $85,000

Functions: Generalist

Industries: Energy, Utilities, Mfg., Finance, Services, Hospitality, Media, Communications, Aerospace, Packaging, Healthcare

Professional Associations: AMA, CLM, IEEE, PDMA, SAMA, SCTE, SHRM, TAG, WERC

Branches:
Marietta
Marietta, GA 30067
(770) 971-6566
Email: cynthia@lysenanderson.com
Key Contact:
Ms. Cynthia Lysen-Walsh, Managing Partner

M B Partners
602 Sheridan Rd
Evanston, IL 60202
(847) 328-1434
Fax: (847) 328-1445
Email: mbpart@aol.com
Web: www.mbpartnersconsult.com

Description: We are human resources consultants specializing in executive search and human resources consulting.

Key Contact - Specialty:
Ms. Lona Maki, Partner - *Human resources (consulting, search)*
Ms. Mary Beth Byrne, Partner - *Compensation (planning, design), search*

Functions: Generalist

Industries: Generalist

M-Pact Inc
PO Box 1592
Brentwood, TN 37024
(615) 376-0154
Fax: (615) 376-0891
Email: mpact@home.com

Description: Retained executive search firm serving manufacturing sector clients with divisions, facilities and subsidiaries throughout the USA and Canada.

Key Contact:
Mr. Bruce MacDonald, Principal

Salary minimum: $100,000

Functions: Generalist

Industries: Mfg.

Professional Associations: HRPAO, SHRM

M/J/A Partners
2 Mid America Plz Ste 800
Oak Brook Terrace, IL 60181
(630) 990-0033
Fax: (630) 971-8631
Email: julesbb2@aol.com

Description: Forging a partnership with every client, we understand their business strategy, corporate culture and management style. Over 60% of our clients are those previously served. Our target search activity is in the upper middle management to top management levels.

Key Contact - Specialty:
Mr. Manuel J. Alves, President - *General management, finance, human resources*
Mr. Joseph G. Stepich, Senior Vice President - *Human resources, general management, marketing*

Salary minimum: $75,000

Functions: Generalist, Senior Mgmt., Materials Plng., Direct Mktg., HR Mgmt., CFO's, MIS Mgmt., Mgmt. Consultants

Industries: Generalist, Misc. Mfg., Banking, Misc. Financial, Higher Ed., Accounting, Mgmt. Consulting

Professional Associations: IACPR, ACG, EMA, IMC

The Macdonald Group Inc
301 Rte 17 Ste 800
Rutherford, NJ 07070
(201) 939-2312
Fax: (201) 939-7754
Email: macdgrp@aol.com

Description: Generalist firm with national practice. Personal service, cost effective, quality results with urgency!

Key Contact:
Mr. G. William Macdonald, President

Salary minimum: $75,000

Functions: Generalist

Industries: Generalist, Drugs Mfg., Machine, Appliance, Misc. Mfg., Pharm Svcs., Healthcare

Machlowitz Consultants Inc
599 Lexington Ave Ste 2300
New York, NY 10022
(212) 213-2435
Fax: (212) 213-3923
Email: machlowitz@aol.com
Web: www.machlowitz.com

Description: Boutique known for resourceful research, diverse slates, creative solutions, speedy client service and success in unique searches.

Key Contact - Specialty:
Dr. Marilyn Machlowitz, President - *Not for profits, investment banks*

Salary minimum: $100,000

Functions: Generalist

Industries: Generalist

MacKenzie Gray Management Inc
304 - 8th Ave SW Ste 910
Calgary, AB T2P 1C2
Canada
(403) 264-8906
Fax: (403) 264-8907
Email: macgray@cadvision.com

Description: We are a retainer-based Canadian executive search firm. Our clients include corporations and organizations varying in size from small, local based companies to large multinationals, encompassing a broad range of industries.

Key Contact:
Mr. Douglas G. MacKenzie, Managing Partner - *Executive*
Mr. Peter Stack, Senior Associate
Ms. Anna Martin, Executive Assistant

Functions: General Mgmt., Senior Mgmt., Middle Mgmt.

Industries: Agri., Forestry, Mining, Energy, Utilities, Construction, Mfg., Food, Bev., Tobacco, Finance, Misc. Financial, Services, Non-profits, Accounting, HR Services, Hospitality, Recreation, Real Estate

MacNaughton Associates
3600 Lime St Ste 323
Riverside, CA 92501
(909) 788-4951
Email: sperrym@pacbell.net

Description: We handle non-profit, higher education searches. We offer full search services and have extensive experience working with academic search committees and senior management.

Key Contact - Specialty:
Mr. Sperry MacNaughton, President - *Higher education, organization development, marketing, development*

Salary minimum: $75,000

Functions: Generalist, Senior Mgmt., Plant Mgmt., Sales Mgmt., Training, CFO's, MIS Mgmt., Non-profits

Industries: Generalist, Finance, Higher Ed., HR Services, Healthcare

Maczkov-Biosciences Inc
126 Harvard Dr
Larkspur, CA 93949
(415) 924-9360
Email: info@maczkov-biosciences.com
Web: www.maczkov-biosciences.com

Description: Offer percentage of first year's compensation. Twenty years of recruiting senior-level executives in life sciences and information technology sectors.

Key Contact - Specialty:
Mr. Nicholas Maczkov, President/CEO - *Healthcare*

Salary minimum: $120,000

Functions: Directors, Senior Mgmt.

Industries: Biotech

Professional Associations: BIO, RAPS

Madden Associates
PO Box 6775
Moraga, CA 94570
(925) 284-3634
Fax: (925) 284-8286
Email: lpmadden@maddenassociates.com
Web: www.maddenassociates.com

Description: We are a retained executive search and management recruiting organization that applies insight, experience and technology to move a client's business plan to reality.

Key Contact - Specialty:
Ms. Linda Patrick Madden, Principal - *Real estate, home building, consulting, engineering*

Salary minimum: $60,000

Functions: Generalist

Industries: Real Estate, Non-classifiable

Bob Maddox Associates[†]
3134 W Roxboro Rd NE Ste 300
Atlanta, GA 30324
(404) 231-0558
Fax: (404) 231-1074
Email: robertmaddox@mindspring.com

Description: We provide executive search in two divisions, and they are regional sales and sales management personnel, and development and senior director/manager for non-profit (501C3) organizations. Our services include candidate profiling, sourcing, evaluation, presentation, and final selection presentation tailored for each board of directors and/or staff client.

Key Contact - Specialty:
Mr. Robert E. Maddox, Partner - *CEO, marketing, development, executive director, field fund raising*

Functions: Generalist, Directors, Senior Mgmt., Middle Mgmt., Sales & Mktg., Mktg. Mgmt., Sales Mgmt., Non-profits

Industries: Generalist, Construction, Medical Devices, Computer Equip., Test, Measure Equip., Electronic, Elec. Components, Services, Non-profits, Higher Ed., Equip Svcs., Mgmt. Consulting, HR Services, Hospitality, Communications, Telecoms, Call Centers, Government, Marketing SW, Healthcare, Hospitals, Long-term Care

Professional Associations: ASAE, SME

The Madeira Group
(a division of HR Unlimited Inc)
924 Old Logger Rd
PO Box 896
Moscow, PA 18444-0896
(570) 842-8959
Fax: (570) 842-9838
Email: rvierra@madeiragroup.com
Web: www.madeiragroup.com

Description: We are committed to providing a quality executive search service to our clients in a cost effective manner. Our success is defined by one factor... client satisfaction. We specialize in the healthcare industry.

Key Contact - Specialty:
Mr. Ronald Vachon-Vierra, President - *Healthcare*
Mr. William Winterburn, Vice President-Business Dev. & Research - *Healthcare*

Salary minimum: $80,000

Functions: Generalist

Industries: Insurance, Biotech, Healthcare

The Madison Group
342 Madison Ave Ste 1060
New York, NY 10173-1060
(212) 599-0032
Email: inquiries@themadisongroup.net
Web: www.themadisongroup.net

Description: Committed to quality service and unblocked access to candidates in each market served. We strive to provide very personal service to a select group of clients.

Key Contact:
Mr. David Soloway, Managing Director
Ms. Lynn Fernandez, Director of Research
Ms. Ruth Gold, Associate Director
Mr. Philip Tesoriero, Associate Director

Salary minimum: $75,000

Functions: General Mgmt., Senior Mgmt., Middle Mgmt., Sales & Mktg., Mktg. Mgmt., Finance, CFO's, Taxes

Industries: Generalist, Mfg., Finance, Venture Cap., Services, Legal, Accounting, Hospitality, Software, Biotech

Madison MacArthur Inc
33 Madison Ave
Toronto, ON M5R 2S2
Canada
(416) 920-0092
Fax: (416) 920-0099
Email: info@mmsearch.com
Web: www.mmsearch.com

Description: Our firm delivers professional services to communications, marketing, financial, e-commerce and retail industries. As one of Canada's most highly respected executive recruiting firms, we work with our clients to strategically enhance their workforce.

Key Contact:
Mr. Ian MacArthur, Director/Owner - *Sales & marketing (all sectors), financial services*
Ms. Sylvia MacArthur, Director/Owner - *Communications, marketing, advertising (all sectors)*
Mr. Ilio Santilli, Director

Salary minimum: $75,000

Functions: Generalist

Industries: Mfg., Retail, Finance, Hospitality, Media, Communications, Insurance, Software, Healthcare

The Magellan Group
707 Alexander Rd
Princeton, NJ
(609) 895-1414
Fax: (609) 895-1749
Email: krice@magellangroupllc.com
Web: www.magellangroupllc.com

Key Contact - Specialty:
Ms. Kimberley Rice, President - *healthcare (pharmaceutical, biotech, peripheral)*

Salary minimum: $130,000

Functions: Senior Mgmt., R&D, Int'l.

Industries: Mfg., Drugs Mfg., Venture Cap., HR SW, Industry Specific SW, Biotech

Maglio & Company Inc
500 Elm Grove Rd Ste 209
Elm Grove, WI 53122
(262) 784-6020
Fax: (262) 784-6046
Email: consulting@maglioandcompany.com

Description: Board and executive search consultants, with a diverse base of clients both domestically and internationally. Extensive experience establishing North American staff for off-shore corporations.

Key Contact:
Mr. Charles J. Maglio, President
Mr. Wayne B. Clark
Kris Springer

Salary minimum: $75,000

Functions: Generalist, General Mgmt., Mfg., Materials, Sales & Mktg., HR Mgmt., Finance, Engineering

Industries: Generalist, Hospitality, Aerospace, Packaging

Professional Associations: APICS

Magna Consulting Ltd†
260 5th Ave Ste 1100
New York, NY 10001
(212) 481-6110
Fax: (212) 481-6111
Email: magnaus@magnaconsulting.com
Web: www.magnaconsulting.com

Description: We manage the life cycle of strategy consultants working primarily with top tier management consulting firms, in addition to Fortune 500, venture capital and high-tech firms seeking top notch consulting talent.

Key Contact - Specialty:
Ms. Florence Magne, President - *Management consulting*

Salary minimum: $120,000

Functions: Mgmt. Consultants

Industries: Generalist

Maiorino & Weston Associates Inc
90 Grove St 205
Ridgefield, CT 06877
(203) 431-0600
Email: bobm@mwasearch.com
Web: www.mwasearch.com

Description: Generalist, servicing the consumer goods, entertainment, sports, communications and hospitality industries both domestic and international. Concentrations in marketing and sales management, finance, human resources and general management.

Key Contact:
Mr. Robert Maiorino, V, President
Mr. Jeffrey Maiorino, Senior Vice President

Salary minimum: $75,000

Functions: Generalist, General Mgmt., Mfg., HR Mgmt., Finance, Minorities, Int'l.

Industries: Generalist, Food, Bev., Tobacco, Soap, Perf., Cosmtcs., Consumer Elect., HR Services, Hospitality, Media

Management & Human Resources
20 Mohegan Rd
Acton, MA 01720-2535
(978) 246-5559
Fax: (978) 246-5559
Email: mgt_and_hr@email.com

Description: Assuring our client organizations' satisfaction and on-going relationships by delivering quality services coupled with extensive experience, outstanding listening, communications and problem-solving skills together with scrupulous attention to detail and, especially, responsiveness and client service.

Key Contact - Specialty:
Mr. John J. Donnelly, Principal - *Healthcare management*

Salary minimum: $100,000

Functions: Generalist

Industries: Generalist, Non-profits, Mgmt. Consulting, HR Services, Broadcast, Film, Healthcare

Management Advice Int'l Ltd
6 Adelaide St E Ste 400
Toronto, ON M5C 1H6
Canada
(416) 916-6800
(877) 574-6800
Email: sprague@madvice.com

Description: We are a firm with a personal touch who specializes in recruiting generalists who will fit our client's firms. We help firms improve their executive team.

Key Contact - Specialty:
Mr. David Sprague, President - *Generalist*
Mr. Peter Crawford, Principal - *Generalist, marketing*

Salary minimum: $90,000

Functions: Generalist, General Mgmt., Mfg., Materials, Sales & Mktg., Finance

Industries: Generalist

Professional Associations: HRPAO

Management Catalysts
PO Box 70
Ship Bottom, NJ 08008
(609) 597-0079
Fax: (609) 597-2860
Email: mgmtcat@aol.com

Description: Specializing for 20 years in filling R&D and other key technical positions in the food, beverage, consumer product, drug and allied industries, where the right science and engineering professionals can truly make a difference.

Key Contact:
Dr. J. R. Stockton, Principal - *Food, beverage, consumer product, drug & allied companies (R&D)*
Ms. N. O. Boyd, Vice President/Treasurer

Salary minimum: $70,000

Functions: Generalist, Product Dev., Quality, Packaging, R&D, Engineering

Industries: Generalist, Food, Bev., Tobacco, Soap, Perf., Cosmtcs., Drugs Mfg., Medical Devices, Biotech

Professional Associations: ACS, ASM, IFT, SCC

Management Executive Services Associates Inc (MESA)
6019 N Belmont Way
Parker, CO 80134-5503
(303) 841-4512

Description: We have a capital goods manufacturing emphasis. Our firm places corporate and general management, and senior executives in all operations and staff functions. Our firm's principals personally execute search engagements and are seasoned former industrial executives. We have superior retention and promotional record among executive and senior management placements.

Key Contact - Specialty:
Mr. Dennis F. Cook, President - *Manufacturing, general industry, high technology*

Salary minimum: $100,000

Functions: Generalist

Industries: Agri., Forestry, Mining, Mfg., Communications, Defense, Aerospace, Packaging

Professional Associations: AFCEA, ASQ, ASTD, SAMPE, SHRM

MRI of Laguna Hills (Orange County)†
23461 S Pointe Dr Ste 390
Laguna Hills, CA 92653
(949) 768-9112
Email: info@mriorangecounty.com
Web: www.mriorangecounty.com

Description: We are national specialists in automotive aftermarket, retail, chemical, finance, telecommunications, CRM, apparel, manufacturing, electronics, architecture, and construction. Through the Sales Consultants franchise, we have access to video conferencing and branch offices in 900 cities.

Key Contact - Specialty:
Mr. Thomas J. Toole, Co-Owner - *Automotive after-market, multi unit retail, general management, executives*

Salary minimum: $50,000

Functions: Generalist, Senior Mgmt., Mfg., Sales & Mktg., HR Mgmt., Finance, IT, Architects

Industries: Generalist, Construction, Textiles, Apparel, Chemicals, Paints, Petro. Products, Telecoms, Software

Professional Associations: AIA, SHRM

MRI of Pasadena
80 S Lake Ave Ste 711
Pasadena, CA 91101-2638
(626) 744-5342
Fax: (626) 744-5347
Email: mrpasadena@mrpasadena.com
Web: www.mrinet.com

Key Contact - Specialty:
Mr. Rick Caldwell, Managing Director - *Banking, accounting, finance*
Mrs. Toni Santillano, Office Manager/Project Recruiter - *Information technology, accounting, finance*
Mr. Jerry Airheart, Account Executive - *Distribution, manufacturing, engineering, purchasing, finance*
Ms. Karen Chiu, Account Executive - *Information technology, finance, accounting*
Mr. Tom Bednar, Account Executive - *Engineering, manufacturing*

Functions: Generalist

Industries: Mfg., Transportation, Finance, Services, Entertainment, Media, Communications, Aerospace, Packaging, Software

MRI of Silicon Valley
4 N Second St Ste 1230
San Jose, CA 95113
(408) 453-9999
Fax: (408) 452-8510
Email: jrosica@mrisanjose.com
Web: www.mrisiliconvalley.com

Description: We are located in the Silicon Valley and specialize in computer and electronic industry, systems engineering, and IS and IT consulting. We also place in the following industries: semiconductor, semiconductor capital equipment, e-Commerce, and Telecommunications/DataCom/Wireless.

Key Contact - Specialty:
Mr. John Rosica, Principal/Manager - *High technology, electronic commerce*

Salary minimum: $75,000

Functions: Generalist

Industries: Venture Cap., Services, Equip Svcs., Mgmt. Consulting, HR Services, Media, Broadcast, Film, Telecoms, Software, Healthcare

Professional Associations: AMA, RON

MRI of Palm Beach†
1700 E Las Olas Blvd Penthouse 5
Ft. Lauderdale, FL 33301
(954) 525-0355
Fax: (954) 525-0353
Email: tjohasky@hotmail.com
Web: www.mrinet.com

Key Contact - Specialty:
Mr. Tom K. Johasky, Manager
Mr. Daniel Breitfeller, Senior Account Executive - *Telecommunications*
Mr. Andrew Brown, Account Executive - *Telecommunication*
Ms. Annette Nocera, Medical Device Recruiter - *Medical device*
Mr. Toby Blank, Medical Device Recruiter - *Medical device*
Mr. Chris Liggio, Executive Recruiter - *Telecommunication*

MRI New Media†
4020 Park St N
St. Petersburg, FL 33709-4034
(727) 345-8811
(800) 466-5148
Email: jobs@mrinewmedia.com
Web: www.mrinewmedia.com

Description: We can help you focus on the business of your business! We have 13 years worth of experience as an executive search firm, specializing in IT, e-Business, senior strategy, business development, CRM, and HR (consulting & corporate). We are part of Management Recruiters International, the world's largest search firm.

Key Contact:
Ms. Jean Hand, Manager

Functions: Senior Mgmt., Sales & Mktg., Sales Mgmt., HR Mgmt., Benefits, IT, Systems Analysis, Engineering

Industries: Generalist, Pharm Svcs., Mgmt. Consulting, HR Services, E-commerce, New Media, Telecoms, Wireless, Network Infrastructure, ERP SW, HR SW, Networking, Comm. SW

MRI of Lincoln
210 Greentree Ct Bldg Ste 434
Lincoln, NE 68505-2438
(402) 467-5534
Web: www.mrilincoln.com

Description: Group of professionals out of industry, with extensive management background. Focus on middle to top level assignments worldwide. Concentration in automotive parts, biotech, insurance, consumer durables MFG.,IT, and pharmaceutical.

Key Contact - Specialty:
Mr. William J. Elam, Jr., Chairman - *Generalist*
Mrs. Kimarra Elam, Executive Vice President - *Financial services*

Salary minimum: $125,000

Functions: Generalist

Industries: Mfg., Finance, Services, Hospitality, Media, Aerospace, Insurance, Software, Biotech, Healthcare

Professional Associations: APAA

MRI of Nassau Inc†
2303 Grand Ave Ste 200
Baldwin, NY 11510
(516) 771-1200
Email: search@mricg.com

Description: We offer staffing consultation services and customized executive search with specialty practices focusing on financial institutions, investment management, the pension industry, finance, information technology, Internet project

management, sales and marketing, and human resources.

Key Contact - Specialty:
Mr. Thomas Wieder, President - *Banking, financial institutions*
Mr. Warren Harvey, Senior Vice President - *Mutual funds, investment management, asset management*
Mr. Adam Roth, Vice President - *Finance, accounting*
Ms. Sue Dropkin, Vice President - *Information technology, networking*
Ms. Corinne Rigante, Vice President - *Investment management*

Functions: General Mgmt., Senior Mgmt., Middle Mgmt., Sales & Mktg., Sales Mgmt., HR Mgmt., Finance, CFO's, Cash Mgmt., IT

Industries: Generalist, Mfg., Finance, Banking, Invest. Banking, Venture Cap., Misc. Financial, Services, Accounting, Mgmt. Consulting, HR Services, E-commerce, Telecoms, Non-classifiable

MRI of Cherry Hill†
(also known as Banister Int'l)
2005 Market St Ste 555
1 Commerce Sq
Philadelphia, PA 19103
(215) 567-1448
Fax: (215) 567-2153
Email: mrch@mriphiladelphia.com
Web: www.mriphiladelphia.com

Key Contact:
Mr. Terri Boyd, Managing Partner

Functions: Generalist, General Mgmt., Materials, Sales & Mktg., HR Mgmt., Finance, IT, Specialized Svcs.

Industries: Generalist, Mfg., Textiles, Apparel, Medical Devices, Transportation, Retail, Finance, Misc. Financial, Mgmt. Consulting, HR Services, Hospitality

Professional Associations: ASTD, CLM, FEI, IFA, IIA, NAPM, NBMBAA, SHRM

Management Resource Group Ltd
2805 Eastern Ave
Davenport, IA 52803
(563) 323-3333
(800) 249-2443
Fax: (563) 326-0682
Email: mrgdavenport@mrgpeople.com
Web: www.mrgpeople.com

Description: We are a multi-office human resource consulting firm dedicated to increasing organizational effectiveness through creative and customized approaches to the identification, selection, development and transition of people.

Key Contact - Specialty:
Mr. Daniel H. Portes, President - *Senior management, finance*
Ms. Lynn Gibson-Larson, Senior Executive Search Consultant - *Finance, senior management*
Ms. Annette Sherbeyn, Executive Search Consultant - *Generalist*
Mr. William Wilke, Executive Search Consultant - *Non-profit, senior management*

Salary minimum: $70,000

Functions: Senior Mgmt., Mfg., Finance, Non-profits

Industries: Generalist, Construction, Banking, Non-profits, Higher Ed., Healthcare

Management Resources Int'l
160 E 88th St Ste 12G
New York, NY 10028
(212) 722-4885

Description: Executive search assignments conducted for Fortune 500, banking, financial and institutions in most functional areas.

Key Contact:
Mr. F. J. Rotundo, President

Salary minimum: $25,000

Functions: Generalist

Industries: Generalist

Management Search & Consulting Inc
1001 Bishop St 1540
Pacific Twr
Honolulu, HI 96813
(808) 533-4423
Fax: (808) 545-2435
Email: mgmtsearch@hawaii.rr.com

Description: Executive search and recruitment focused on upper-middle and senior-level positions mainly in Hawaii and Pacific rim. Retainer required.

Key Contact:
Mr. Peter Glick, President

Functions: Generalist

Industries: Energy, Utilities, Finance, Misc. Financial, Services, Pharm Svcs., Accounting, Mgmt. Consulting, HR Services, Hotels, Resorts, Clubs, Healthcare

Management Search of RI[†]
One State St Ste 501
Providence, RI 02908
(401) 273-5511
(800) 405-1152
Fax: (401) 273-5573
Email: providence@msi1.com
Web: www.msi1.com

Description: One of New England's largest privately held professional search firms - team focused search; multi-disciplined, corporately mandated minimal industry blacklists. Specialists in mid-level ($50-$400K) search.

Key Contact:
Mr. James L. Meyer, CPC, Partner
Mr. Stephen E. Judge, CPC, Partner

Salary minimum: $50,000

Functions: Generalist, Senior Mgmt., Middle Mgmt., Mfg., Sales Mgmt., Finance, IT, Engineering

Industries: Generalist, Mfg., Plastics, Rubber, Consumer Elect., Finance, Software

Professional Associations: NAPS, NEHRA, RISSA

Mannard & Associates Inc
1600 Golf Rd Ste 1200
Rolling Meadows, IL 60008
(847) 981-5170
Fax: (847) 981-5189

Description: Boutique firm focused on manufacturing companies. Principle markets are machinery, metal fabrication and packaging. Metal and plastic materials are typical. Firm characterized by quality, service, flexibility; strong repeat client base.

Key Contact:
Mr. Thomas B. Mannard, President - *Manufacturing, fortune 500, entrepreneurial run*
Mr. James E. Chavoen, Partner - *General management, sales, financial, technical*
Ms. Kathleen Weinrauch, Vice President
Ms. Michelle M. McGowan, Senior Associate
Mr. James Ryan, Associate

Salary minimum: $70,000

Functions: Generalist, Senior Mgmt., Plant Mgmt., Sales & Mktg., HR Mgmt., Finance, Engineering

Industries: Generalist, Food, Bev., Tobacco, Paper, Plastics, Rubber, Metal Products, Machine, Appliance, Packaging

Professional Associations: IACPR, ASME, HRPS, TAPPI

The Manning Group
55 Public Sq Ste 1715
Cleveland, OH 44113
(216) 664-1857
Fax: (216) 664-1855
Email: manning_group@ex100.com

Description: Our firm is a retained executive search firm whose practice is focused on a select group of companies for whom we execute a wide variety of searches. Most of our assignments are in the manufacturing, financial services, and not for profit sectors.

Key Contact:
Ms. Barbara Behn Deeds, President

Salary minimum: $80,000

Functions: Generalist

Industries: Mfg., Finance, Services, Aerospace, Packaging, Biotech, Healthcare

Professional Associations: ACG, COSE, EMA, HRPS

Michael E Marion & Associates Inc
98 Floral Ave
Murray Hill Sq
Murray Hill, NJ 07974
(908) 771-9330
Fax: (908) 665-9380
Email: info@marionsearch.com

Description: We are regularly retained to conduct individual and group searches in healthcare and consumer products worldwide by Fortune 100 firms as well as emerging companies.

Key Contact:
Mr. Michael E. Marion, President

Salary minimum: $75,000

Functions: Generalist

Industries: Generalist, Drugs Mfg., Medical Devices, Pharm Svcs., Biotech, Healthcare

J L Mark Associates LLP
2000 Arapahoe St Ste 505
Denver, CO 80205
(303) 292-0360
Fax: (303) 292-0361
Email: jlmark@jlmark.com

Description: Generalists with over 28 years' retained search experience at senior management levels. Focus on chemistry: selecting candidates complementary to and compatible with client management style. 12 month guarantee.

Key Contact:
Mr. John L. Mark, Principal - *Generalist*
Ms. Lynne B. Mark, Partner - *Generalist*
Ms. Sandy Bushnell, Recruiter - *Generalist*
Ms. Christine Burtt, Recruiter
Ms. Eliza Stoker, Research Specialist
Ms. Tiffany McCarty, Recruiter/Research Specialist

Salary minimum: $100,000

Functions: Senior Mgmt.

Industries: Generalist

Professional Associations: IACPR

The Mark Method
11835 Carmel Mount Rd
San Diego, CA 92128
(619) 234-9494
Fax: (619) 234-5444

Email: tmm@markmethod.com
Web: www.markmethod.com

Description: Specializing in the Contract Furnishings industry, nationally, all positions.

Key Contact:
Mr. Cary Mark, President

Marks & Company Inc
304 Main Ave Ste 364
Norwalk, CT 06851
(203) 849-0888

Description: National practices in EDP audit, data security, risk management and disaster recovery. Founder is a former Fortune 500 executive with above experience. Associates also have directly related industry experience.

Key Contact:
Ms. Sharon Marks, President
Ms. Whitney Reese, Senior Associate

Salary minimum: $60,000

Functions: Risk Mgmt., MIS Mgmt., Specialized Svcs.

Industries: Generalist, Banking, Invest. Banking

Brad Marks Int'l
1888 Century Park E Ste 2010
Los Angeles, CA 90067
(310) 286-0600
Fax: (310) 286-0479
Email: bodysnatcher@bradmarks.com
Web: www.bradmarks.com

Description: A specialist firm which recruits senior-level management for the entertainment and new media industries. The firm's practice is national and international in scope and currently includes 9 recruiters with over 40 years of combined search experience.

Key Contact:
Mr. Brad Marks, Chairman/CEO - *Entertainment*
Ms. Chanda Smith, Director, Recruiting
Mr. Bob Miggins - *Broadcasting, sales & marketing*
Mr. Justin Marks
Mr. Chris Monjoy

Salary minimum: $100,000

Functions: Senior Mgmt.

Industries: Non-profits, Hospitality, Media, Advertising, Publishing, New Media, Broadcast, Film, Telecoms

Professional Associations: AIM, AWRT, BCFMA, IICS, NAB, NATPE, NCTA, NYNMA, WICT

Markt & Markworth Ltd
20600 Chagrin Blvd Ste 620
Cleveland, OH 44122
(216) 491-3120
Fax: (216) 491-3121
Email: jmarkworth@markt-markworth.com
Web: www.markt-markworth.com

Description: The foundation of our search practice is based on the highest level of professionalism while using technology to shorten response times to fill positions and keeping the client apprised of all activity.

Key Contact - Specialty:
Mr. John H. Markt, Principal - *Generalist, manufacturing, supply chain management*
Ms. Jennifer I. Markworth, Principal - *Generalist, attorney, managed care*

Salary minimum: $100,000

Functions: Generalist, General Mgmt., Materials, Sales & Mktg., HR Mgmt., Finance, IT, Attorneys

Industries: Generalist, Mfg., Transportation, Wholesale, Services, Healthcare, Non-classifiable

---

Professional Associations: CLM

The Marlow Group
5 Great Plain Ave
PO Box 812707
Wellesley, MA 02482
(781) 237-7012
Email: marlowgroup@aol.com

Description: Generalist firm serving emerging high-technology companies - sales, marketing, operations and technical.

Key Contact:
Mr. Paul M. Jones, Managing Director

Salary minimum: $75,000

Functions: Senior Mgmt., Sales & Mktg., Mktg. Mgmt., Sales Mgmt., CFO's

Industries: Computer Equip., New Media, Telecoms, Software, Biotech

Marra Peters & Partners
Millburn Esplanade
Millburn, NJ 07041
(973) 376-8999
Email: marrapeters@aol.com
Web: www.marrapeters.com

Description: Clients are assured of their importance as they receive a sophisticated service in a highly personalized and responsive manner. We provide a consultative approach to retain the executive who will impact your business in the most contributory way.

Key Contact - Specialty:
Mr. John Marra, Jr., President - *Finance, general management, marketing, sales executive*
Mr. Charles J. Pelisson, Vice President - *Marketing, human resources, research & development, sales & distribution*

Salary minimum: $100,000

Functions: Generalist, General Mgmt., Mfg., Sales & Mktg., HR Mgmt., Finance, IT, Specialized Svcs.

Industries: Generalist, Construction, Retail, Mgmt. Consulting, Media, Government, Real Estate

Professional Associations: HRPS, NJSCPA, SHRM

Branches:
7040 Palmetto Park Rd Ste 145
Boca Raton, FL 33433
(561) 347-7778
Key Contact:
Mr. John Marra, President

Marshall Consultants Inc†
1133 Broadway Ste 1600
New York, NY 10010
(646) 486-2600
Fax: (646) 486-6472
Email: gjmny@aol.com
Web: www.marshallconsultants.com

Description: We are the first search firm specializing in communications positions exclusively in the industries of public relations, public affairs, investor relations, marketing communications, etc. We have been serving Fortune 500 for more than 30 years.

Key Contact - Specialty:
Mr. Larry Marshall, Chairman - *Corporate & marketing communications, public relations, investor relations, public affairs, advertising & marketing*
Mr. Justin Meyer, President - *Financial services, corporate communications*
Mr. James Wyckoff, Senior Vice President - *Pharmaceuticals, health care*

Functions: Generalist, Mktg. Mgmt., PR

Industries: Generalist

Professional Associations: IACPR, IABC, IPRA, NIRI, PRSA

The Marshall Group†
31 Cambridge Ln
Lincolnshire, IL 60069
(847) 940-0021
Fax: (847) 940-7031
Email: drmarsh510@aol.com

Description: We provide personal retained search designed to locate and provide management and non-management personnel to high-growth clients. Our firm also works on the placement of sales and management personnel experienced in digital imaging, prepress technologies, and fashion photography for catalogs, magazines, and design agencies.

Key Contact - Specialty:
Mr. Don Marshall, President - *Generalist*

Functions: Generalist

Industries: Generalist

J Martin & Associates
10820 Holman Ave Ste 103
Los Angeles, CA 90024
(310) 475-5380
Email: jmexecsrch@aol.com
Web: www.martinexecsearch.com

Description: Specialization computer/high-technology-medical/healthcare venture capital backed start-up, emerging, high-growth, Fortune 500, CEO to senior sales and marketing levels. Quick results, high quality.

Key Contact - Specialty:
Ms. Judy R. Martin, President - *Computer, high technology, healthcare services*

Salary minimum: $75,000

Functions: Generalist

Industries: Services, Hospitality, New Media, Software

Donovan Martin & Associates
1000 Elwell Ct Ste 217
Palo Alto, CA 94303
(650) 969-8235

Description: We provide executive and professional search services for a variety of companies, from large, long-established firms to the newest start-ups.

Key Contact - Specialty:
Mr. Donovan Martin, Principal - *Executives, CEOs, marketing & sales (vice presidents), CFOs*

Salary minimum: $100,000

Functions: Generalist, Directors, Senior Mgmt., Middle Mgmt.

Industries: Computer Equip., Consumer Elect.

Martin Partners LLC
224 S Michigan Ave Ste 620
Chicago, IL 60604
(312) 922-1800
Email: mwatt@martinpartners.com
Web: www.martinpartners.com

Description: Our firm is a leading executive search firm specializing in building senior management teams. The firm's clients range in size from private equity-backed firms to Fortune 500 corporations, from all sectors of technology, biotech, consulting, and financial services. Martin Partners recently concluded its fifth year in business with continued double-digit growth, making it the fastest growing startup retained executive search firm in the US.

Key Contact:
Mr. Theodore B. Martin, Jr., Founder & CEO - *Emerging businesses, financial services, general management, technology, consulting*
Mr. Thomas A. Jagielo, Partner - *Biotech, pharma, medical device, diagnostics*
Mr. William C. Kingore, Mr., Partner - *Financial services*
Ms. Sally Frantz, Partner - *Technology, consulting, general management*
Mr. Michael R. Aldrich, Principal - *General management, financial services, technology*
Ms. Linda Balkin, Principal - *General management, technology, emerging businesses*
Ms. Kathleen Lehman Hajek, Principal - *General management, consulting, technology*
Ms. Adrianne Kalyna, Principal - *General management, industrial, legal*
Ms. Susan Fitzpatrick, Principal - *Private equity communications*
Ms. Lara Gartner, Director of Recruiting Technologies
Mrs. Martha Watt, H, Director of Marketing

Salary minimum: $120,000

Functions: General Mgmt., Mfg., Sales & Mktg., HR Mgmt., Finance, Mgmt. Consultants

Industries: Mfg., Drugs Mfg., Medical Devices, Consumer Elect., Retail, Finance, Venture Cap., Misc. Financial, Services, Pharm Svcs., Mgmt. Consulting, E-commerce, Media, New Media, Communications, Insurance, Real Estate, Software, Biotech

Professional Associations: AESC

Networks: Alliance Partnership Int'l

George R Martin
PO Box 673
Doylestown, PA 18901-0673
(215) 348-8146
Email: exsearch@comcat.com

Description: Concentrate on marketing, sales, technical and operations functions. Twenty seven year completion rate is high, with excellent stick and promotion ratios. Highly qualified research staff.

Key Contact:
Mr. George R. Martin

Salary minimum: $60,000

Functions: Generalist

Industries: Mfg., Paper, Chemicals, Drugs Mfg., Medical Devices, Plastics, Rubber, Test, Measure Equip., Biotech

The Martwick Group Inc
4380 SW Macadam Ave Ste 575
Portland, OR 97201
(503) 223-7060
Fax: (503) 223-1645
Email: gail@martwick.com

Description: Full-service executive search firm. President has 14 years of successful executive recruitment for Pacific NW clients in high-technology, manufacturing, data processing, medical electronics, consumer products, telecommunications.

Key Contact:
Ms. Gail Martwick, President

Salary minimum: $50,000

Functions: Senior Mgmt.

Industries: Generalist

Maschal/Connors Inc
306 S Bay Ave
PO Box 1301
Beach Haven, NJ 08008
(609) 492-3400

Description: A management consulting firm specializing in recruitment of senior-level management (through CEO and board) for manufacturers in specified industries.

Key Contact:
Mr. Chuck Maschal, President - *Generalist*
Ms. Jennifer Mancini, Director of Research

Salary minimum: $100,000

Functions: Generalist, General Mgmt., Product Dev., Minorities

Industries: Generalist, Mfg., Metal Products, Machine, Appliance, Motor Vehicles, Consumer Elect., Misc. Mfg., Electronic, Elec. Components, Security SW, System SW, Non-classifiable

Masserman & Associates Inc

70 W Red Oak Ln
White Plains, NY 10604
(914) 697-4884
Fax: (914) 697-4885
Email: bruce@masserman.com

Description: We are a national search firm specializing exclusively in the technology marketplace. Our focus is the middle to senior-level executive within the financial services industry. Our ability to understand how technology fits within the business structure is a key factor to our success.

Key Contact - Specialty:
Mr. Bruce Masserman, Principal - *Information technology, financial services, publishing, database marketing*

Salary minimum: $85,000

Functions: IT, MIS Mgmt., Systems Analysis, Systems Dev., Systems Implem., Systems Support, Network Admin., DB Admin.

Industries: Finance, Banking, Invest. Banking, Brokers

Louis Thomas Masterson & Company

1422 Euclid Ave Ste 706
Cleveland, OH 44115-2001
(440) 621-2112
Fax: (216) 621-7320
Email: ltmasterson@ltmco.com
Web: www.ltmco.com

Description: We provide high quality, responsive executive recruiting service. Searches cover many industries and multiple disciplines.

Key Contact - Specialty:
Mr. Louis T. Masterson - *General management*

Salary minimum: $70,000

Functions: Generalist, Senior Mgmt., Mfg., Healthcare, Physicians, Health Admin., HR Mgmt.

Industries: Generalist, Mfg., Chemicals, Paints, Petro. Products, Finance, Services, Healthcare

Matté & Company Inc

124 W Putnam Ave
Greenwich, CT 06830
(203) 661-2224
Fax: (203) 661-5927
Email: matteinquiries@aol.com

Description: We provide consulting services in executive search, leadership assessment of first and second Tier management, and best practices benchmarking. We work mostly for fortune 100 companies. All searches are completed within ten weeks of commencement.

Key Contact - Specialty:
Mr. Norman E. Matté, Chairman - *Leadership development, organizational effectiveness, distribution, technology, international*

Salary minimum: $175,000

Functions: Generalist, General Mgmt., Mfg., Distribution, HR Mgmt., Finance, IT, Int'l.

Industries: Generalist, Food, Bev., Tobacco, Drugs Mfg., Computer Equip., Finance, HR Services

Matte Consulting Group Inc

1010 Sherbrooke St W Ste 1200
Montreal, QC H3A 2R7
Canada
(514) 848-1008
Fax: (514) 848-9157
Email: admin@matteiic.com
Web: www.matteiic.com

Description: An affiliate of IIC Partners, we are a highly dynamic Montreal-based executive search firm specializing in senior recruitments on both a national and international scale.

Key Contact - Specialty:
Mr. Richard Matte, Managing Partner - *Manufacturing, information technology, general management*
Mr. Michael St. Louis, Partner - *Finance & accounting, general management*

Salary minimum: $100,000

Functions: Generalist, General Mgmt., Mfg., Healthcare, Sales & Mktg., Finance, IT

Industries: Generalist, Energy, Utilities, Mfg., Finance, Media, Packaging, Healthcare

Professional Associations: OHRP, OPQ

Networks: I-I-C Partners Executive Search Worldwide

Maxecon Executive Search Consultants

9500 S Dadeland Blvd Ste 601
Miami, FL 33156
(305) 670-1933
Email: maxecon@aol.com

Description: Specializing in executives for Latin American divisions of multinational companies: U.S.-based regional headquarter personnel responsible for the area and executives for subsidiary operations in Latin America/Caribbean.

Key Contact - Specialty:
Mr. Ronald Gerstl, Managing Director - *Senior management multinationals (Latin America)*

Salary minimum: $90,000

Functions: Generalist, Senior Mgmt., Middle Mgmt., Mktg. Mgmt., Sales Mgmt., CFO's, Int'l.

Industries: Generalist, Food, Bev., Tobacco, Soap, Perf., Cosmtcs., Drugs Mfg., Computer Equip., Consumer Elect., Advertising

K Maxin & Associates

Allegheny Ctr Bldg 10 Ste 421
Pittsburgh, PA 15212
(412) 322-2595
(800) 867-8447
Fax: (412) 322-7027
Email: kmaxin@usa.net

Description: Executive search in the construction and real estate industries.

Key Contact - Specialty:
Mr. Keith A. Maxin, President - *Construction, real estate*

Salary minimum: $70,000

Functions: General Mgmt., Directors, Senior Mgmt., Middle Mgmt., Mktg. Mgmt., CFO's, M&A, Engineering, Architects

Industries: Construction, Real Estate

The Mayes Group Ltd†

Daisy Point
PO Box 399
St. Peters, PA 19470
(610) 469-6900
Fax: (610) 469-6088
Email: mayesgroup@aol.com
Web: www.mayesgroup.com

Description: We are a retained executive search firm specializing in managed healthcare. Our clients include: HMOs, PPOs, health systems, disease management, pharmaceutical, and information system companies.

Key Contact - Specialty:
Ms. Abby Mayes, President - *Managed care*

Salary minimum: $75,000

Functions: Generalist, Healthcare

Industries: Generalist

Professional Associations: AAHP, WIMC

Branches:
4134 Gulf of Mexico Dr Ste 207A
Longboat Key, FL 34228
(941) 387-1300
Fax: (941) 387-1311
Email: mayesgroup@aol.com
Key Contact - Specialty:
Ms. Autumn Lee Solomon, Managing Director - *Healthcare (general, managed)*

The Mazzitelli Group Ltd

500 Lake St Ste 209
Excelsior, MN 55331
(952) 476-5449
Fax: (952) 475-4932
Email: tm@mazzsearch.com
Web: www.mazzsearch.com

Description: Generalist retainer search firm.

Key Contact - Specialty:
Ms. Teresa Mazzitelli, President - *Generalist*

Functions: Generalist

Industries: Generalist

The McAllister Group†

5651 Silver Ridge Dr
Stone Mountain, GA 30087
(770) 469-3843
Email: mgigroup@mediaone.net

Description: We offer an established base of clients, with whom we have had relationships with for over 20 years. These clients engage us to identify candidates with hardware and home center industry experience throughout the North Americas in sales, marketing, and general management.

Key Contact:
Mr. David McAllister, Managing Partner

Salary minimum: $75,000

Functions: General Mgmt., Directors, Senior Mgmt., Middle Mgmt., Sales & Mktg., Mkt. Research, Mktg. Mgmt., Sales Mgmt., Int'l.

Industries: Generalist, Lumber, Furniture, Plastics, Rubber, Leather, Stone, Glass, Machine, Appliance

The McAulay Firm

100 N Tryon St Ste 5220
Bank of America Corp Ctr
Charlotte, NC 28202
(704) 342-1880
Fax: (704) 342-0825
Web: www.mcaulay.com

Description: Generalist - all functions and industries.

Key Contact - Specialty:
Mr. Albert L. McAulay, Jr., President - *Generalist*

Mr. Charles C. Lucas, III, Principal - *Generalist*
Mr. Steven B. Smith, Principal - *Generalist*
Mr. J. Gilbert Browne, Principal - *Generalist*

Salary minimum: $100,000

Functions: Generalist

Industries: Generalist, Energy, Utilities, Mfg., Textiles, Apparel, Finance, Venture Cap., Insurance, Real Estate

Professional Associations: AESC

Networks: The Amrop - Hever Group

McBride Associates Inc
1742 N St NW
Washington, DC 20036-2907
(202) 452-1150

Description: Discreet, comprehensive, thorough, small; specialize in select high-level assignments; make every effort to represent clients in the same thoughtful and professional manner as they would seek to represent themselves.

Key Contact - Specialty:
Mr. Jonathan E. McBride, President - *Problem-solving*

Salary minimum: $225,000

Functions: Generalist

Industries: Mfg., Finance, Services, Hospitality, Advertising, Telecoms, Insurance, Software, Biotech, Healthcare

Professional Associations: AESC

K E McCarthy & Associates
9800 S Sepulveda Blvd Ste 720
Los Angeles, CA 90045
(310) 568-4070
Email: kemassoc@aol.com

Description: The firm has wide experience serving financial institutions, technology firms, health care, and consulting organizations in general management emphasizing finance, treasury, capital markets, and information technology executives. We have expertise in search and consultation to growth companies in high technology and financial services.

Key Contact:
Mr. Kevin E. McCarthy, Principal

Salary minimum: $75,000

Functions: Systems Implem., Mgmt. Consultants

Industries: Generalist, Finance, Banking, Invest. Banking, Venture Cap., Mgmt. Consulting, Healthcare, Hospitals

McCooe & Associates Inc
615 Franklin Tpke
Ridgewood, NJ 07450-1929
(201) 445-3161
Fax: (201) 445-8958
Email: mccooe@mcsearch.net
Web: www.mcsearch.net

Description: Specializes in executive recruitment of strategic human resources. Exceptional discernment of best candidate fit in an organization. Offers management consulting in compensation planning, job evaluation, organization development, training and career development.

Key Contact - Specialty:
Mr. John J. McCooe, President - *Senior management*
Mr. Sean J. McCooe, Senior Consultant/Vice President - *Senior management, life science, business development*
Ms. Darryl Cooksley, Independent Consultant - *Healthcare*

Salary minimum: $80,000

Functions: Generalist, Senior Mgmt., Plant Mgmt., Distribution, HR Mgmt., R&D, Engineering, Int'l.

Industries: Generalist, Construction, Chemicals, Medical Devices, Plastics, Rubber, Higher Ed., Healthcare

Professional Associations: AIIE, AMDM, APICS, ASHG, ASHMM, ASHPMM, ASQ, ASSE, ASTD, ASTM, CLM, DCAT, IMC, RAPS, SFB, SHRM, SOCMA

McCormack & Associates
5042 Wilshire Blvd Ste 505
Los Angeles, CA 90036
(323) 549-9200
Fax: (323) 549-9222
Email: jmsearch@earthlink.net
Web: www.mccormackassociates.com

Description: Specialty practice in diversity recruiting for corporations, service providers and not-for-profit organizations. Recruit people of color and alternative sexual orientation for boards of directors and senior management. Secondary focus on healthcare, higher education and associations.

Key Contact:
Mr. Joseph A. McCormack, Managing Partner - *Gay & lesbian, minorities, not-for-profit, diversity recruiting*
Mr. Robert Ankerson, Senior Associate

Salary minimum: $80,000

Functions: Senior Mgmt., Minorities

Industries: Drugs Mfg., Non-profits, Higher Ed., HR Services, Advertising, Publishing, Healthcare

Professional Associations: AESC

Branches:
275 Madison Ave Ste 705
New York, NY 10016
(212) 286-4040
Email: rwsearch@earthlink.net
Key Contact:
Mr. Robert Ankerson, Senior Associate

McCormack & Farrow
949 South Coast Dr Ste 420
Costa Mesa, CA 92626
(714) 549-7222
Email: resumes@mfsearch.com
Web: www.mfsearch.com

Description: We are a general practice retained search in most industries nationwide. We place special emphasis on high technology, start-up, and emerging companies in manufacturing of healthcare and healthcare products.

Key Contact:
Mr. Jerry M. Farrow, Managing Partner
Mr. Kenneth L. Thompson, Partner
Ms. Helen E. Friedman, Partner
Mr. Gene Phelps, Partner
Mr. Jim Wade, Partner
Mr. Jeff McDermott, Partner
Mr. Steve Treibel, Partner
Mr. Kenneth Bertok, Partner

Salary minimum: $120,000

Functions: Generalist, General Mgmt., Mfg., Distribution, Sales & Mktg., HR Mgmt., Finance, IT

Industries: Medical Devices, Computer Equip., Retail, Aerospace, Healthcare

McCracken/Labbett Exec Search
145 King St W Ste 1000
Toronto, ON M5H 1J8
Canada
(416) 363-4749
Email: keith@garymccracken.com
Web: www.garymccracken.com

Description: We are a fully retained, real estate and sales/marketing oriented search practice operating within Gary McCracken Executive Search Inc. Please visit our website.

Key Contact:
Mr. Keith J. Labbett, Partner

Salary minimum: $110,000

Functions: Generalist

Industries: Generalist

GaryMcCracken Executive Search Inc
145 King St W Ste 1000
Toronto, ON M5H 1J8
Canada
(416) 363-8900
Email: gary@garymccracken.com
Web: www.garymccracken.com

Description: An independent, retained executive search firm blending broad executive search expertise with senior executive operating experience.

Key Contact:
Mr. Gary McCracken, President

Salary minimum: $100,000

Functions: Generalist

Industries: Generalist

McCray, Shriver, Eckdahl & Associates Inc
10940 Wilshire Blvd Ste 2100
Los Angeles, CA 90024
(310) 479-7667
Fax: (310) 479-8608
Email: principal@mccray-inc.com
Web: www.mccray-inc.com

Description: We place board-level, presidential, and general management solutions in high technology, industrial, and consumer industries. We have had 28 years of proven success.

Key Contact - Specialty:
Mr. Harold C. McCray, President - *Chairman, CEO, presidents*
Mr. William J. Sheweloff, Vice President - *Senior officer, general management, satellite, communications*
Mr. Maurice Mason, Vice President - *High technology, manufacturing, telecommunications*

Salary minimum: $100,000

Functions: Generalist, Directors, Senior Mgmt., Mfg., Sales & Mktg., HR Mgmt., CFO's, IT, Engineering, Int'l.

Industries: Construction, Mfg., Computer Equip., Consumer Elect., Retail, Services, Media, Communications, Aerospace, Software

M W McDonald & Associates Inc
220 S Cook St Ste 210
Barrington, IL 60010
(847) 842-7400
Fax: (847) 842-7410
Email: research@mwmsearch.com
Web: www.mwmsearch.com

Description: Offering full-service executive-level search and information services to high-technology companies worldwide from start-up companies to those with over $25 billion in assets.

Key Contact - Specialty:
Mr. Michael W. McDonald, President - *High technology*

Salary minimum: $50,000

Functions: Mfg., Sales & Mktg., Finance, IT, R&D, Specialized Svcs., Mgmt. Consultants

Industries: Generalist

Branches:
286 El Dorado St Ste B
Monterey, CA 93940
(831) 646-0300
Email: research@mwmsearch.com
Web: www.mwmsearch.com
Key Contact:
Ms. Pamela Niedermeier

McDonald Associates Int'l
1290 N Western Ave Ste 209
Lake Forest, IL 60045-1257
(847) 234-6889
Fax: (847) 234-6889

Description: Retainer executive search; assist clients with special staffing needs below normal salary level. Depends on the client and client need!

Key Contact - Specialty:
Mr. Stanleigh B. McDonald, Partner - *Generalist*

Salary minimum: $70,000

Functions: Generalist

Industries: Mfg., Transportation, Retail, Aerospace, Software, Biotech, Healthcare

Professional Associations: ASTD, CCA, HRMAC, ODN

McDonald-Rackley Consulting Group[†]
6847 Yorkdale Ct
Lithonia, GA 30058
(770) 484-9276
Email: info@mrconsulting.net
Web: www.mrconsulting.net

Description: We help our clients maintain control of the employment process by providing customized, efficient, cost-effective, unbundled executive search and recruitment research services to an industry in need of new solutions!

Key Contact - Specialty:
Ms. Collette M. Rackley, Principal - *General management, high technology, professional services, manufacturing, diversity*

Salary minimum: $50,000

Functions: Generalist

Industries: Generalist

Professional Associations: RR, SHRM

G E McFarland & Company
535 Colonial Park Dr
Roswell, GA 30075
(770) 992-0900
Fax: (770) 640-0067
Email: gemcfarland@mindspring.com
Web: www.mcfarlandpartners.com

Description: We serve a broad cross-section of client organizations representing most industries, with a particular emphasis on basic manufacturing, information and communication systems, electronics, biomedical technology, aerospace, construction/construction materials, and financial services.

Key Contact:
Mr. Charles P. Beall, Chairman
Mr. Carleton "Tony" Palmer, Managing Partner
Mr. Patrick Garrigan, Partner
Ms. Alissa Hawkins, Director of Research

Salary minimum: $100,000

Functions: Generalist

Industries: Generalist, Construction, Mfg., Aerospace, Packaging, Insurance

Professional Associations: ADAPSO

Clarence E McFeely Inc
39 Brinker Rd
Barrington, IL 60010
(847) 381-0475
Fax: (847) 382-8663
Email: aalphie@aol.com

Description: National generalist practice concentrates on CEO, COO, corporate CFO, CIO and senior executive-level positions. Clients include healthcare, financial services, biotechnology, conglomerates, electronic goods, LBO's, entertainment, broadcasting, medical products and new venture start-ups.

Key Contact - Specialty:
Mr. Clarence E. McFeely, Principal - *CEO, president, COO, CFO, corporate CIO*

Salary minimum: $300,000

Functions: Generalist, Directors, Senior Mgmt., Finance, CFO's, IT, Specialized Svcs.

Industries: Generalist

Professional Associations: AESC

McGrath & Associates Inc
993 Lenox Dr Ste 200
Lawrenceville, NJ 08648
(609) 844-7579
Fax: (609) 844-7548
Email: contactus@mcgrathassociates.com
Web: www.mcgrathassociates.com

Description: We are a retainer-based search firm. Our firm is a boutique with a functional specialization. We focus on information technology, financial planning and control, sales and marketing, security, operations, and consulting. The primary industries served are: telecommunications, information technology, pharmaceutical, financial services, and consulting.

Key Contact - Specialty:
Mr. Steven L. McGrath, President - *Sales & marketing, finance, consultants, e-commerce*
Mr. Peter T. Lins, Vice President - *Information technologies, business development*
Mr. Alex Hraur, Senior Manager - *Telecommunications, information technology, insurance*
Mr. Raymond A. Yedman, Executive Search Consultant - *Sales & marketing, information technology, consulting*

Salary minimum: $75,000

Functions: Generalist, General Mgmt., Mfg., Sales & Mktg., HR Mgmt., Finance, IT, Mgmt. Consultants

Industries: Generalist, Mfg., Finance, Pharm Svcs., Telecoms, Software, Healthcare

McIntyre Associates
8 Forest Park Dr Forest Park Office Green
Farmington, CT 06032
(860) 284-1000
Fax: (860) 284-1111
Email: mcassoc@home.com
Web: www.mcassoc.com

Description: Recruitment of key executives involved in breaking ground in and/or financing emerging technology niche markets, with emphasis on the growing telecom/software-centric convergence of wireless and wireline markets on a global basis.

Key Contact - Specialty:
Mr. Jeffrey F. McIntyre, President - *Wireless, telecommunications executives, electronic commerce software, supply chain solutions software*

Salary minimum: $150,000

Functions: Generalist, Directors, Senior Mgmt., Mkt. Research, Sales Mgmt., CFO's, Int'l.

Industries: Generalist, Software

Professional Associations: CTIA, ICSA, IEC, LES, PCIA, SPA

McKinley Arend Int'l
3200 Southwest Fwy Fl 33
The Phoenix Twr
Houston, TX 77027-7526
(713) 623-6400
Email: jmmckinley@mckinleyarend.com
Web: www.mckinleyarend.com

Description: We are an international firm conducting technical, non-technical, and support searches. We have offices worldwide.

Key Contact - Specialty:
Mr. James M. McKinley, Principal - *Generalist*
Mr. Lewis Arend, Principal - *Generalist*

Functions: Generalist

Industries: Generalist

The McLeod Group Inc
4 Whitney St Ext
Northeast Financial Bldg
Westport, CT 06880
(203) 454-1234
Email: mcleod@discovernet.net

Description: Represents only a few clients to avoid conflicts. Carries out assignments with imagination and urgency. Exploits the search process for information and ideas useful to the client. Always exceeds expectations.

Key Contact:
Mr. Anthony N. Schenck, Managing Partner
Mr. Reuel A. Dorman, Partner

Salary minimum: $150,000

Functions: Finance, M&A

Industries: Invest. Banking

McNamara Search Associates Inc[†]
3070 Harrodsburg Rd Ste 240
Corporate Gateway
Lexington, KY 40503
(606) 296-2828
(859) 296-2818
Fax: (606) 296-9986
Email: mcsearch@prodigy.net
Web: www.mcnamarasearch.com

Description: We provide expert executive, professional and technical search and recruitment services. Our exclusive 'Gold Standard Search Process' is streamlined to deliver maximal results while saving you time and money. With over 20 years' experience, MSA partners with companies to hire outstanding professionals in a variety of fields.

Key Contact - Specialty:
Ms. Lynda Hook McNamara, President - *Executive, manufacturing, human resources, marketing & sales*
Ms. Elaine Marple, Recruitment Manager - *Generalist*

Salary minimum: $45,000

Functions: General Mgmt., Senior Mgmt.

Industries: Generalist, Energy, Utilities, Mfg., Transportation, Finance, Non-profits, HR Services, Hospitality, Communications, Environmental Svcs., Insurance

Professional Associations: SHRM

McNichol Associates
54 W Willow Grove Ave
Philadelphia, PA 19118
(215) 922-4142
Fax: (215) 247-0924
Email: jmcnichol@mcnicholassoc.com

[†] occasional contingency assignments

Description: Specialists in recruiting management for architectural, engineering, construction and environmental industries as well as senior facilities (project, environmental, etc.) managers for institutions and industry.

Key Contact - Specialty:
Mr. John McNichol, Jr., President - *Senior management for professional design, construction engineering, construction, environmental firms*

Salary minimum: $100,000

Functions: Generalist, General Mgmt., Senior Mgmt., Middle Mgmt., Engineering, Environmentalists, Architects

Industries: Generalist, Construction, Environmental Svcs., Haz. Waste

Professional Associations: IACPR, ISPE, PMI, PSMA, SAME, SMPS

Jon McRae & Associates Inc
1930 N Druid Hills Rd NE Ste 200
Atlanta, GA 30319-4120
(404) 325-3252
Fax: (404) 325-9610
Email: jma@jonmcrae.com
Web: www.jonmcrae.com

Description: Executive search counsel for governing boards and presidents of not-for-profit institutions with a focus in private education. Excellence-oriented professionalism accentuated with a personal and intuitive style.

Key Contact - Specialty:
Mr. O. Jon McRae, President/Senior Consultant - *Non-profit, presidents, education*
Dr. William W. Kelly, Senior Vice President - *Non-profit, presidents, education*
Mr. Kenneth B. Orr, Senior Vice President - *Non-profit, presidents, education*
Dr. Maureen S. Biggers, Vice President - *Non-profit, presidents, education*

Salary minimum: $90,000

Functions: Mgmt. Consultants

Industries: Non-profits, Higher Ed.

Professional Associations: ACE, CIC, GFIC, NAIS

MCS Associates
18300 Von Karman Ave Ste 710
Irvine, CA 92612
(949) 263-8700
Fax: (949) 263-0770
Email: info@mcsassociates.com
Web: www.mcsassociates.com

Description: Consulting and litigation support firm that specializes in banking, real estate, financial services. Established in 1973, clients are nationwide, including large and small organizations.

Key Contact - Specialty:
Mr. Norman Katz, Managing Partner - *Banking management, finance, lending*
Mr. Thomas J. Haupert, Managing Director - *Banking management, finance, lending, real estate*

Salary minimum: $75,000

Functions: Senior Mgmt., Legal, Finance, CFO's

Industries: Finance, Banking, Invest. Banking, Misc. Financial, Accounting, Insurance, Real Estate

Professional Associations: ACG

MDR Associates Inc†
9485 SW 72nd St Ste A265
Miami, FL 33173-5413
(305) 271-9213
Fax: (305) 274-1053
Email: sschoen@mdrsearch.com
Web: www.mdrsearch.com

Description: A retainer firm specializing in the recruitment of physicians, physician managers and executives for the healthcare industry. Practice emphasis on medical groups, single and multispecialty groups, HMOs and hospitals, nationwide.

Key Contact:
Ms. Judith E. Berger, President
Mr. Stephen G. Schoen, Executive Director

Salary minimum: $80,000

Functions: Generalist, Physicians, Nurses, Health Admin.

Industries: Healthcare

Professional Associations: ACHE, ACPE, AGPA, AMA, MGMA, NAPR, SHPMAHA

Networks: First Choice (FC)

Branches:
12774 Flat Meadow Ln
Herndon, VA 22071
(703) 620-9475
Email: info@mdr-associates.com
Key Contact - Specialty:
Mr. Michael E. Kurtz, President - *Consulting*

James Mead & Company
15 Old Danbury Rd Ste 202
Wilton, CT 06897-2524
(203) 834-6300
Fax: (203) 834-6301
Email: mailbox@jmeadco.com

Description: The vertically integrated source for clients seeking executive solutions in consumer oriented brand building businesses. Each recruiter has extensive packaged goods general management, sales, marketing and organizational development experience with some of the world's best companies, enabling us to provide significant marketplace advantage and an unmatched value-added consultative relationship.

Key Contact - Specialty:
Mr. James D. Mead, President - *Consumer packaged goods & related industries, sales & marketing, general management*
Mr. Arthur S. Brown, EVP/Partner - *Consumer packaged goods & related industries, sales & marketing, general management*
Ms. Kate H. Bradley, Vice President - *Consumer packaged goods & related industries*

Salary minimum: $140,000

Functions: General Mgmt., Senior Mgmt., Middle Mgmt., Sales & Mktg., Advertising, Mkt. Research, Mktg. Mgmt., Sales Mgmt.

Industries: Food, Bev., Tobacco, Textiles, Apparel, Soap, Perf., Cosmtcs., Drugs Mfg., Consumer Elect., Mgmt. Consulting

Meads & Associates
6700 S Florida Ave Ste 4
Lakeland, FL 33813
(863) 644-0411
Fax: (863) 647-3866
Email: chipmeads@meads.net
Web: www.meads.net

Description: We provide executive recruitment for advertising and public relations agencies. We work in all disciplines, including: management, account, creative, media, research, public relations, sales promotion, telephone production, etc., but our specialty is senior account management talent.

Key Contact - Specialty:
Mr. Walter F. Meads - *Advertising agencies, public relations agencies*

Salary minimum: $50,000

Functions: Generalist, Advertising, PR

Industries: Generalist, Advertising

Professional Associations: IACPR

Med Exec Int'l
100 N Brand Blvd Ste 306-8
Glendale, CA 91203
(818) 552-2036
(800) 507-5277
Fax: (818) 552-2475
Email: rosechristopher@sprintmail.com
Web: www.medexecintl.com

Description: We provide customized search services to clients from the medical device and pharmaceutical industries who entrust their searches for regulatory affairs, clinical research and quality professionals to our care.

Key Contact - Specialty:
Ms. Rosemarie Christopher, Principal - *Technical, medical device, pharmaceutical*

Functions: Directors, Senior Mgmt., Middle Mgmt., Quality, Healthcare, Physicians

Industries: Drugs Mfg., Medical Devices, Electronic, Elec. Components, Pharm Svcs., Biotech

Professional Associations: ACRP, ASQ, DIA, OCRA, RAPS

Networks: Top Echelon Network

Meder & Associates Inc
2201 Waukegan Rd Ste E200
Bannockburn, IL 60015
(847) 914-0200
Fax: (847) 914-0253
Email: pmeder@mederassociates.com
Web: www.mederassociates.com

Description: The firm engages in senior and executive-level search for a wide variety of companies and professional service firms. Positions are normally associated with compensation levels above $150,000. The practice is national in scope of clients and search.

Key Contact:
Mr. Peter F. Meder
Ms. Kathleen A. McCarthy
Mr. Jerome B. Herb
Mr. William H. Wright
Mr. Christopher T. Bertchy
Ms. Anne Driscoll
Ms. Jane M. Clifford

Salary minimum: $150,000

Functions: Generalist, Senior Mgmt., Production, Health Admin., Mktg. Mgmt., CFO's, Mgmt. Consultants

Industries: Generalist, Energy, Utilities, Food, Bev., Tobacco, Motor Vehicles, Finance, Mgmt. Consulting, New Media

Networks: Signium Int'l Inc

Branches:
245 Park Ave Fl 40
New York, NY 10167
(212) 557-4663
Fax: (847) 914-0253
Key Contact:
Mr. Peter F. Meder, Managing Partner

Medfall Inc
103-6453 Morrison St
Niagara Falls, ON L2E 7H1
Canada
(905) 357-6644
Fax: (905) 357-2601
Email: medfall@medfall.com
Web: www.medfall.com

Description: All of our consultants are medical professionals with a unique understanding of the goals and requirements of our clients. Our objective, evidence-based search and screening process, ensures quality and compatibility.

Salary minimum: $80,000

Media Management Resources Inc[†]
6464 S Quebec St Garden Lvl
Englewood, CO 80111
(303) 290-9800
Email: info@mediamanagement.com
Web: www.mediamanagement.com

Description: Our firm is a respected international executive search firm specializing in middle and upper-management serving select clients in telecommunications, new media, and technology.

Key Contact - Specialty:
Mr. Michael S. Wein, Principal -
Telecommunications, media, technology

Salary minimum: $50,000

Functions: Generalist, Senior Mgmt., Engineering, Mgmt. Consultants

Industries: Generalist, Venture Cap., E-commerce, Entertainment, New Media, Broadcast, Film, Telecoms, Call Centers, Telephony, Digital, Network Infrastructure

Branches:
31B Gulf Breeze Pkwy
Gulf Breeze, FL 32561
(850) 934-4880
Email: bwein@mediamanagement.com
Key Contact - Specialty:
Mr. William Wein, Principal -
Telecommunications, media, technology

MedSearch Resources Inc
4673 Hammock Cir
Delray Beach, FL 33445
(561) 637-8004
Fax: (561) 637-0880
Email: glickd@att.net

Description: Retainer based search and consulting firm serving the healthcare industry. Our clients include hospitals, long-term care facilities, physician practice management companies, hospital based and private physician group practices, HMOs, managed care organizations, biotech and pharmaceutical companies, medical marketing/research and advertising firms and healthcare suppliers.

Key Contact - Specialty:
Mr. Douglas Glick, President - *Executives, administrators, exec directors, physicians, directors of nursing*

Salary minimum: $50,000

Functions: Healthcare

Industries: Generalist, Drugs Mfg., Medical Devices, Pharm Svcs., Biotech, Healthcare

Martin H Meisel Associates Inc
55 E 87th St
New York, NY 10128
(212) 369-4300

Description: Retainer search assignments limited to select group of clients. Research built search firm - emphasis presently in medical and healthcare fields.

Key Contact:
Mr. Martin H. Meisel, President - *Healthcare*
Mr. Norman Metzger, Senior Consultant -
Healthcare
Mr. Morris D. Kerstein, MD, FACS, Sr Consultant

Salary minimum: $100,000

Functions: Generalist, Physicians, Nurses, Allied Health, Benefits, Personnel

Industries: Generalist, Healthcare

Melancon & Company
PO Box 2383
McKinney, TX 75070-2383
(972) 231-9963
Email: resumes@melanconcompany.com
Web: www.melanconcompany.com

Description: With roots dating back to 1973, We are a retainer-based executive search firm specializing in the identification and recruitment of key executive talent for high-performance organizations on a regional and national basis. The company is one of the oldest and most highly regarded search firms in the southwest.

Key Contact - Specialty:
Mr. Robert M. Melancon, Managing Principal -
Generalist

Salary minimum: $85,000

Functions: Generalist

Industries: Generalist

Professional Associations: ASTD, SHRM, WAW

Meng, Finseth & Associates Inc
3858 Carson St Ste 202
Del Amo Executive Plz
Torrance, CA 90503
(310) 316-0706
Fax: (310) 316-1064
Email: mengfinseth@aol.com

Description: We are a retainer search firm, serving a broad range clientele, both in the public and private sector.

Key Contact:
Ms. Cameron E. Wisowaty, Associate
Mr. Carl L. Finseth, Executive Vice President
Mr. Charles M. Meng, President
Ms. Marlene M. Rafferty, Vice President/Treasurer
Ms. Diane Natvig, Associate

Salary minimum: $100,000

Functions: Generalist, General Mgmt., Senior Mgmt., Sales & Mktg., HR Mgmt., Finance, Engineering, Non-profits

Industries: Generalist, Energy, Utilities, Higher Ed., Hospitality, Media, Government, Aerospace, Healthcare

Professional Associations: IACPR

The Mercer Group Inc
551 W Cordova Rd
PMB 726
Santa Fe, NM 87501
(505) 466-9500
Fax: (505) 466-1274
Email: mercer@mindspring.com
Web: www.mercergroupinc.com

Description: Specialize in public sector. Full-fledged management consulting firm offering services in strategy, market research, organization studies, organization development, executive search, compensation.

Key Contact - Specialty:
Mr. James L. Mercer, CMC, President/CEO -
Government (state, local)
Ms. Karolyn Prince-Mercer, Vice President -
Government (state, local)

Salary minimum: $50,000

Functions: Generalist, Senior Mgmt., Personnel, Mgmt. Consultants

Industries: Generalist, Higher Ed., Mgmt. Consulting, HR Services, Government

Professional Associations: ICMA, IIE, IMC

Branches:
5579B Chamblee Dunwoody Rd
PMB 511
Atlanta, GA 30338
(770) 551-0403
Fax: (770) 399-9749
Email: mercer@mindspring.com
Key Contact - Specialty:
Stephen D. Egan, Jr., Senior Vice President -
Government (state, local)

3036 Lake Lansing Rd Ste 117
East Lansing, MI 48823
(517) 333-1781
Fax: (517) 332-2547
Key Contact - Specialty:
Mr. Thomas Dority, Senior Vice President -
Government (state, local)

Meridian Partners
8875 Hidden River Pkwy Ste 550
Tampa, FL 33637
(813) 866-7600
Fax: (813) 866-8856
Email: info@meridianpartnersonline.com
Web: www.meridianpartnersonline.com

Description: We are a boutique, retained executive search firm with a commitment to provide a select, demanding client base with "A" level talent. This is achieved through a quantitative, disciplined approach that utilizes original research, strong management consulting skills, a team approach, and the application of leading-edge information systems.

Key Contact - Specialty:
Mr. John B. Henard, Managing Partner -
Technology, e-commerce, internet, telecom, consumer products, food
Mr. Walter U. Baker, Managing Partner - *General management, industrial, international, technology*
Ms. Susan Freeman, Vice President - *Non-profit (marketing)*
Mr. David K. Sowerby, Vice President -
Technology
Ms. Claudia Sanow Henderson, Principal/Consultant - *Telecommunications, general management*

Salary minimum: $125,000

Functions: Generalist

Industries: Generalist

Networks: Signium Int'l Inc

Hutton Merrill & Associates
3333 Bowers Ave Ste 130
Santa Clara, CA 95054
(408) 919-2999

Description: We are a high-technology executive search firm with a primary focus on semiconductors, semiconductor equipment, software and networking. We conduct extensive, original research for every assignment.

Key Contact:
Mr. Thomas J. Hutton
Ms. Barbara Merrill
Ms. Vera Wong

Salary minimum: $150,000

Functions: Generalist, General Mgmt., Mfg., Sales & Mktg., Engineering

Industries: Generalist, Computer Equip., Test, Measure Equip., Software

Professional Associations: IEEE, SEMI

Merrill Lynch & Company
800 Scudders Mill Rd
Plainsboro, NJ 08536
(609) 282-2000
Email: r.kishun@hr.com
Web: www.ml.com

Description: Recognized in both the technology and financial services industries as a premier developer of state-of-the-art business technology solutions, Our private client technology (PCT) is dedicated to innovation and exploration in a work environment that fosters continuous learning and ongoing skills development.

Key Contact - Specialty:
Mr. Randy Kishun, Relationship Manager/Technical Recruiter - *Infrastructure, mainframe, client server, web, e-commerce*

Salary minimum: $50,000

Functions: Directors, Senior Mgmt., HR Mgmt., IT, MIS Mgmt., Systems Analysis, Systems Dev., Systems Implem., Systems Support, Network Admin.

Industries: Generalist, Energy, Utilities, Mfg., Computer Equip., Retail, Finance, Services, Hospitality, Media, Telecoms, Environmental Svcs., Aerospace, Insurance, Software, Healthcare

Professional Associations: SHRM

Merritt, Hawkins & Associates
222 W Las Colinas Blvd Fl 19
Millennium Ctr
Irving, TX 75038
(800) 876-0500
Fax: (972) 868-2275
Email: bsheehan@mhagroup.com
Web: www.merritthawkins.com

Description: We are the oldest company within the MHA Group and largest physician search and consulting firm in the US. We conduct over 2,000 permanent physician searches yearly, publish compensation surveys, and conduct educational programs at conferences nationwide.

Key Contact - Specialty:
Mr. Jim Merritt, President - *Physicians*
Mr. Joe Hawkins, CEO - *Physicians*

Functions: Physicians

Industries: Generalist

Professional Associations: MGMA, NAPS

Branches:
1340 Reynolds
Irvine, CA 92714
(949) 757-7750
Fax: (949) 757-7750
Email: sthomas@mhagroup.com
Key Contact - Specialty:
Mr. Steven Thomas - *Physicians*

5901A Peachtree Dunwoody Rd NE Ste 450
Atlanta, GA 30338-7184
(770) 396-4800
Fax: (770) 481-1115
Email: msmith@mhagroup.com
Web: www.merritt-hawkins.com
Key Contact - Specialty:
Mr. Mark Smith - *Physicians*

310 E 4500 S Ste 440
Salt Lake City, UT 84107
(801) 264-0260
(801) 264-0260
Fax: (801) 264-0255
Email: jcaldwell@mhagroup.com
Web: www.staffcare.com
Key Contact - Specialty:
Mr. Joseph Caldwell - *Physicians*

Messett Associates Inc
7700 N Kendall Dr Ste 304
Miami, FL 33156
(305) 275-1000
Fax: (305) 274-4462
Email: messett@messett.com
Web: www.messett.com

Description: We undertake executive searches, acquisitions, mergers, plus joint venture partner

identification on a worldwide basis from our Miami headquarters and affiliate offices in US, Europe, Latin America and Asia. A partner in International Executive Search, Inc. (IES).

Key Contact - Specialty:
Mr. William J. Messett III, President - *Generalist (top level)*
Mr. William J. Messett IV, Partner - *General, international*

Salary minimum: $100,000

Functions: Generalist, Int'l.

Industries: Agri., Forestry, Mining, Energy, Utilities, Mfg., Transportation, Retail, Finance, Pharm Svcs., Hospitality, Insurance, Software

---

META/MAT Ltd
270 Orchard Pl
Ridgewood, NJ 07450
(201) 803-4400
Email: metamat@ix.netcom.com

Description: We offer unusual depth and breadth of knowledge in finance, high-technology and consumer products businesses.

Key Contact:
Mr. Fred Kopff, President

Salary minimum: $100,000

Functions: Generalist, Directors, Senior Mgmt., Purchasing, CFO's, MIS Mgmt., Engineering

Industries: Generalist, Soap, Perf., Cosmtcs., Medical Devices, Paints, Petro. Products, Invest. Banking, Pharm Svcs., HR Services, Telecoms

Professional Associations: ASTD, SHRM

Metzler & Company
161 Bay St Ste 1320
PO Box 529
Toronto, ON M5J 2S1
Canada
(888) 265-1583
Fax: (416) 955-0418
Email: info@metzler-co.com
Web: www.metzler-co.com

Description: Leading Toronto based generalist executive search firm with particular strength in real estate, senior financial executives, financial services, retail and information technology.

Key Contact - Specialty:
Mr. J. Michael Metzler, President - *Real estate, generalist*
Mr. Gary W. McCracken, Consultant - *Financial services, senior financial executives*
Ms. Roz Baker, Consultant - *Retail trade*
Mr. Larry Sartor, Consultant - *Information technology, senior & mid-level executives*
Mr. Keith J. Labbett, Consultant - *Real estate, sales & marketing*
Mr. Tom Holmes, Consultant - *Senior human resources*

Functions: Generalist, Senior Mgmt., Sales & Mktg., CFO's, M&A, MIS Mgmt., Mgmt. Consultants

Industries: Generalist, Construction, Mfg., Retail, Finance, Services, Media

---

Meyer Associates Inc
5079 Riverhill Rd
Marietta, GA 30068
(770) 565-2020

Description: Since our inception, the goal has been straightforward - to give clients real value. We recognize that use of executive recruiting services is an investment that must produce exceptional returns and tangible benefits.

Key Contact - Specialty:
Mr. Rick M. Meyer - *Management consulting, manufacturing, information technology, sales & marketing, finance*

Salary minimum: $75,000

Functions: Generalist, Senior Mgmt., Middle Mgmt., Mfg., Plant Mgmt., Mktg. Mgmt., Sales Mgmt., Mgmt. Consultants

Industries: Generalist, Mfg., Mgmt. Consulting, IT Implementation, Telecoms

---

mfg/Search Inc[†]
203 N LaSalle St Ste 2100
Chicago, IL 60601
(312) 558-1484
(800) 782-7976
Email: mfg@mfgsearch.com
Web: www.mfgsearch.com

Description: We work exclusively with manufacturing companies. With regional search centers in Atlanta, Bloomfield Hills, Chicago, White Plains, and our administrative office in South Bend, we conduct retained fee search assignments throughout North America.

Key Contact - Specialty:
Mr. Howard Mueller, President - *Generalist*

Salary minimum: $75,000

Functions: Generalist

Industries: Mfg.

Professional Associations: ASM, FMA, SAE, SHRM, SPE, WAI

Branches:
1170 Peachtree St NE Ste 1200
Atlanta, GA 30309
(404) 885-6032
(800) 782-7976
Email: amitry@mfgsearch.com
Key Contact - Specialty:
Mr. Alfred Mitry, Regional Manager - *Generalist*

220 W Colfax Ave Ste 300
South Bend, IN 46601
(219) 282-2547
(800) 782-7976
Email: chris@mfgsearch.com
Key Contact - Specialty:
Ms. Chris Cuenca, Research Manager/Search Associate - *Generalist*

7 W Sq Lake Rd
Bloomfield Hills, MI 48302
(248) 452-5658
(800) 782-7976
Email: wpollock@mfgsearch.com
Key Contact - Specialty:
Mr. Walter Pollock, Executive Vice President - *Generalist*

2 Gannett Dr Ste 200
White Plains, NY 10604
(914) 642-9692
(800) 782-7976
Email: hmueller@mfgsearch.com
Key Contact - Specialty:
Mr. Howard Mueller, President - *Generalist*

Anthony Michael & Company
10 Post Office Sq Ste 600
Boston, MA 02109
(800) 565-5578
Fax: (781) 982-9006
Email: mjk@anthonymichaelco.com
Web: www.anthonymichaelco.com

Description: Our assignments span middle to senior management in the following areas: portfolio management and research, sales and marketing, and investment banking.

Key Contact - Specialty:
Mr. Michael Kulesza, Senior Managing Director - *Investment industry*
Mr. Charlie Carr, Managing Director - *Investment industry*

Salary minimum: $100,000

Functions: Generalist, General Mgmt., Directors, Senior Mgmt., Sales & Mktg., Mktg. Mgmt., Sales Mgmt., Attorneys, Int'l.

Industries: Generalist, Finance, Banking, Invest. Banking, Brokers, Misc. Financial

Professional Associations: AESC

Michael Associates
613 Poplar Ave
Elmhurst, IL 60126
(630) 832-2550
Fax: (630) 832-2556

Description: Searches for general management, specializing in manufacturing management, technical and engineering, personnel and engineering management, materials management, information technology.

Key Contact - Specialty:
Mr. Michael S. Golding, Principal - *Manufacturing, management, engineering, MIS, materials management*

Salary minimum: $40,000

Functions: General Mgmt., Senior Mgmt., Middle Mgmt., Mfg., Materials, HR Mgmt., MIS Mgmt., R&D, Engineering

Industries: Generalist, Mfg., Plastics, Rubber, Metal Products, Motor Vehicles, Misc. Mfg., Electronic, Elec. Components, Packaging

---

John Michael Associates[†]
Washington Dulles Int'l Airport
PO Box 17130
Washington, DC 20041
(703) 471-6300
Fax: (703) 471-4064
Email: gf@searchjma.com
Web: www.searchjma.com

Description: A retained search company for law firms and corporations seeking legal talent. Experience includes work with over 100 law firms and corporations in Los Angeles, New York, Washington D.C., Atlanta, and Charlotte.

Key Contact - Specialty:
Mr. Gary J. Fossett, CEO - *Securities, capital markets, technology, intellectual property, healthcare*
Mr. Brad J. Toynbee, Principal - *Intellectual property, securities, corporate technology, tax, energy*

Salary minimum: $100,000

Functions: Generalist, Senior Mgmt.

Industries: Legal, Mgmt. Consulting

Professional Associations: NALSC

Michael Page Int'l Inc[†]
405 Lexington Ave Fl 28
Chrysler Bldg
New York, NY 10174
(212) 661-4800
Fax: (212) 661-6622
Email: mpi.usa@michaelpage.com
Web: www.michaelpage.com

Description: Our mission is to revolutionize the executive search industry. Operating as the market leader for nearly 26 years, we are the #1 Global Recruitment Firm (Economist Intelligence Unit 2000), with over 95 offices in 15 countries. Our consultants have expertise in the following specialty practices: Front Office Banking, Financial Services (Finance, Accounting & Operations), Corporate Enterprise, Sales, Retail & Marketing, Technology and Management Consulting.

Key Contact - Specialty:
Mr. Jack Bragin, CEO of North American Offices
Ms. Rosalind Coffey, Director - *Financial Services (finance, accounting and operations)*
Ms. Karen Wong, Director - *Front Office Banking*
Mr. Alistair Robinson, Director - *Corporate Enterprise (finance and accounting)*
Mr. Martin Pike, Director - *Sales, retail & marketing*
Mr. John Maloney, Director - *Technology & management consulting*

Salary minimum: $50,000

Functions: Generalist

Industries: Generalist

Gregory Michaels & Associates Inc
804 N Dearborn St
Chicago, IL 60610
(312) 377-2100
Fax: (312) 377-2121
Email: wesearch4@aol.com

Description: Boutique executive search firm recruiting upper-level management.

Key Contact:
Mr. Gregory P. Crecos, Managing Partner
Mr. Joseph J. Scodius, Manager
Ms. Kambrea R. Wendler, Manager
Ms. Mary K. Simon, Senior Consultant
Ms. Lorrie A. Hopp, Senior Consultant
Ms. Heather L. Schulte, Consultant
Ms. R. Yuki Tripp, Consultant

Salary minimum: $275,000

Functions: Generalist, Senior Mgmt., Mktg. Mgmt., Finance

Industries: Mfg., Retail, Finance, Services

Michigan Consulting Group
3037 Benjamin
Royal Oak, MI 48073
(248) 549-7178
Fax: (248) 549-7178
Email: mcg@provide.net

Description: Consultants in executive search assisting our clients to identify, attract and retain 21st century management talent. Senior and middle management generalist practice which serves a broad base of corporate clients. Our mission: Commitment to serve our clients with optimum effectiveness and efficiency reflected in consistent delivery of quality services, quantifiable change and substantial shareholder value.

Key Contact - Specialty:
Mr. David E. Southworth, President - *Officers, senior & general management*
Mr. Edward Southworth, Executive Vice President - *Medical (devices, instruments), prosthesis devices, automotive, senior & general management*
Mr. Gary Bussa, Vice President - *Senior management, general management, CFO, finance & accounting, information technology*
Ms. Kathy Palazzolo, Vice President - *Females, minorities, manufacturing management, information technology, engineers, senior & middle management*
Mr. Douglas Kramer, Vice President - *Metal forming, stamping, precision machining*
Mr. Pedro Salinas Gasga, Vice President - *Manufacturing management, engineers, administration, operations, senior & middle management*
Mr. Rich Krezo, Vice President - *Stamping, metal forming management, engineers, manufacturing, sales*

Mr. Steven Gust, Director - *Information technology, MIS, software development, network distraction*

Salary minimum: $65,000

Functions: Generalist, General Mgmt., Senior Mgmt., Middle Mgmt., Mfg., Sales & Mktg., CFO's, IT, MIS Mgmt., Engineering

Industries: Generalist, Mfg., Chemicals, Drugs Mfg., Medical Devices, Plastics, Rubber, Leather, Stone, Glass, Metal Products, Machine, Appliance, Motor Vehicles, Computer Equip., Misc. Mfg., Defense, Aerospace, Software

Professional Associations: ACG, AMA, FMA, SAE, SPI

Millar Walker & Gay
379 Dundas St E Fl 2
Toronto, QN M5A 2A6
Canada
(416) 365-7818
Email: mwgmt@idirect.com

Description: Specialists in accounting and corporate finance including banking, investment banking, merger acquisition, valuation, fixed income and taxation. We have successful searches as far away as Russia, UK, and USA.

Key Contact - Specialty:
Mr. James G. Millar, Partner - *Corporate finance*
Mr. Warren T. Walker, Partner - *Accounting*

Salary minimum: $50,000

Functions: Generalist, CFO's, Budgeting, Cash Mgmt., Credit, Taxes, M&A, Risk Mgmt.

Industries: Generalist, Agri., Forestry, Mining, Banking, Invest. Banking, Brokers, Venture Cap., Real Estate

---

The Millard Group
(also known as Sales Consultants of Middlesex)
213 Court St Ste 601
Middlesex Corp Ctr
Middletown, CT 06457-0891
(860) 638-5391
Fax: (860) 638-5393
Email: info@themillardgroup.com
Web: www.themillardgroup.com

Description: We are dedicated to providing results based recruiting in the high-technology industry. We have two areas of expertise in the application software industry and the networking industry.

Key Contact - Specialty:
Mr. Craig A. Millard, Managing Partner - *Networking, wireless, e-infrastructure*
Mr. Paul R. Millard, Managing Partner - *ERP, SCM, e-business*

Salary minimum: $100,000

Functions: Senior Mgmt., Sales & Mktg.

Industries: Computer Equip., Communications, Software

Professional Associations: CLM

Millennium Search Group Inc
835 5th Ave Ste 202
Bank of Commerce Bldg
San Diego, CA 92101
(619) 542-7777
Web: www.msgiusa.com

Description: Retained executive search firm specializing exclusively in placement of senior-level executives (partners, vice presidents, principals, senior managers) in management consulting, audit and tax.

Key Contact - Specialty:
Mr. David M. Ferrara, President - *Management consulting, audit, tax*

Mr. Stephen J. Abkin, Executive Vice President - *Management consulting, audit, tax*

Salary minimum: $150,000

Functions: Sales Mgmt., Risk Mgmt., IT, Systems Implem., Mgmt. Consultants

Industries: Accounting, Mgmt. Consulting, E-commerce, IT Implementation, Network Infrastructure, Software, ERP SW, Security SW

Craig Miller Associates
1720 E Garry Ave Ste 207
Santa Ana, CA 92705
(949) 261-7247
Fax: (949) 261-9539
Email: cnmiller@pacbell.net
Web: www.cmasearch.com

Description: Retained executive search firm with a concentration in senior management search in all key functional departments. Significant success in attracting high impact executives for leading both high-growth and turnaround situations.

Key Contact - Specialty:
Mr. Craig N. Miller, President - *Organizational development consulting*
Mr. Scott Seabaugh, Vice President
Mr. Richard Pantuliano, Vice President - *Human resource management consulting*

Salary minimum: $100,000

Functions: Generalist, Senior Mgmt., Mfg., Sales & Mktg., HR Mgmt., Finance, IT, Engineering

Industries: Generalist, Mfg., Medical Devices, Computer Equip., Aerospace, Software

C A Miller Corp
2033 SE 10th Ave Ste 604
Ft. Lauderdale, FL 33316
(954) 767-9034
Fax: (954) 767-8934
Email: chris@camillercorp.com
Web: www.camillercorp.com

Description: We are a boutique firm dedicated to excellence in providing executive search consulting to the telecommunications, software, e-Commerce, Internet, and management consulting industries. Our clients are generally venture-backed, high-tech, small to mid-sized startups based domestically or internationally. We recruit chief-level executives and their senior management teams. Our strength is our technology expertise and a customer-driven, performance-based approach.

Key Contact - Specialty:
Mr. Chris Miller, President - *Executive management (general and senior), information technology, telecommunications, sales and marketing, IT*
Ms. Joyce Edwards, Principal - *Management consulting, consumer products, pharmaceutical, industrial products, retail*

Salary minimum: $125,000

Functions: Senior Mgmt., Sales Mgmt., MIS Mgmt.

Industries: Mgmt. Consulting, E-commerce, IT Implementation, PSA/ASP, Communications, Telecoms, Call Centers, Telephony, Digital, Wireless, Fiber Optic, Network Infrastructure, Software

Miller-Hall HRISearch†
23 Vista Toscana
Tuscany Hills, CA 92532-0215
(909) 245-4116
Email: hrisearch@aol.com
Web: www.hrisearch.com

Description: We are the only nationwide search firm exclusively focused on HRIS (human resource information system) mid- to high-level positions.

We will price your HRIS position using industry benchmarks, prepare your job description or job specifications and present pre-screened qualified candidates.

Key Contact - Specialty:
Mr. Larry Hall, Managing Director - *Human resource information systems*
Mr. Marc S. Miller, Founding Partner - *Human resource information systems*

Salary minimum: $75,000

Functions: Personnel, Systems Analysis, Systems Implem., Mgmt. Consultants

Industries: Generalist

Professional Associations: IHRIM

Million & Associates Inc
Carew Twr Ste 1831
Cincinnati, OH 45202
(513) 579-8770

Description: Search and recruitment for executive, managerial, professional and technical talent for all types of industries, banking and financial organizations and hospital and healthcare industries, exclusively for clients.

Key Contact:
Mr. Ken Million, President
Ms. Kim Kramer, Vice President

Salary minimum: $40,000

Functions: Generalist

Industries: Generalist

Paul Millius Associates
3105 NE Broadway St
Portland, OR 97232
(503) 287-6754
Fax: (503) 287-3828
Email: pmillius@aol.com
Web: www.paulmilliusassoc.com

Description: We are a specialized, retained executive search firm, offering unbundled recruiting services and recruitment consulting. We frequently take on hard to complete searches.

Key Contact - Specialty:
Mr. Paul Millius, Principal - *Government (state, local), information technology, traditional manufacturing*

Functions: Generalist, Senior Mgmt., Middle Mgmt., MIS Mgmt., Systems Dev., Network Admin., Engineering

Industries: Generalist, Metal Products, Misc. Mfg., Non-profits, Government, Software

Herbert Mines Associates Inc
375 Park Ave Ste 301
New York, NY 10152
(212) 355-0909
Fax: (212) 223-2186
Email: hma@herbertmines.com
Web: www.herbertmines.com

Description: Retainer search for senior management for retail, direct marketing, e-commerce, textiles, apparel, specialty food, supermarkets, cosmetics, fashion manufacturing and consumer businesses. Clients range from small to multi-billion dollar conglomerates. Over 80% of assignments are from existing clients.

Key Contact:
Mr. Herbert Mines, Chairman
Mr. Harold Reiter, CEO/President
Mr. Howard Gross, Managing Director
Mr. Gene Manheim, Managing Director
Ms. Maxine Martens, Managing Director - *Cosmetics*
Mr. Brian Meany, Managing Director
Mr. Robert Nahas, Managing Director

Ms. Jane Vergari, Senior Vice President
Ms. Kate Benson, Principal
Ms. Patricia Darcy, Principal
Ms. Mary O'Keefe, Vice President
Ms. Kristin Dennehy, Principal
Ms. Coleen Hollywood, Principal
Ms. Emily Shannon, Principal
Ms. Patricia Accarino, Associate
Ms. Lari-Jean Crames, Associate
Ms. Tania Cross, Associate
Ms. Susan Merjos, Associate
Ms. Cheri O'Reilly, Associate
Ms. Tammy Ramalho, Associate

Salary minimum: $150,000

Functions: Generalist, Directors, Senior Mgmt., Admin. Svcs., Product Dev., Advertising, HR Mgmt., Int'l.

Industries: Generalist, Food, Bev., Tobacco, Textiles, Apparel, Soap, Perf., Cosmtcs., Wholesale, Retail, Mgmt. Consulting, HR Services, Hospitality, Media, Real Estate

Professional Associations: AESC, NRF

Networks: Globe Search Group

Mirtz Morice
1 Dock St Fl 3
Stamford, CT 06902
(203) 964-9266
Fax: (203) 324-3925
Email: mirtzmorice@worldnet.att.net
Web: www.mirtzmorice.com

Description: Beyond executive recruiting, certain consulting services are provided that relate to, support and enhance the search practice. Included are assignments related to management organization and succession planning and compensation.

Key Contact - Specialty:
Mr. P. John Mirtz, Partner - *Generalist*
Mr. James L. Morice, Partner - *Generalist*

Salary minimum: $125,000

Functions: Generalist, Senior Mgmt., Mktg. Mgmt., Personnel, CFO's, MIS Mgmt., Mgmt. Consultants

Industries: Generalist, Food, Bev., Tobacco, Drugs Mfg., Mgmt. Consulting, HR Services, Hospitality, Insurance

Laurie Mitchell & Company Inc†
25018 Hazelmere Rd
Cleveland, OH 44122-3241
(216) 292-6001
Fax: (216) 292-9117

Description: Serving corporate, agency and individual needs with discretion and integrity. Retained search services in public relations, marketing communications, financial communications, advertising and sales promotion.

Key Contact - Specialty:
Ms. Laurie Mitchell, CPC - *Advertising, public relations, consumer marketing*

Salary minimum: $35,000

Functions: Advertising, Mkt. Research, Mktg. Mgmt., Direct Mktg., PR

Industries: Generalist

Professional Associations: AAF, AMA, IABC, OSSA, PRSA

Mitchell/Wolfson Associates
600 Central Ave Ste 375
Highland Park, IL 60035
(847) 266-0600
Email: bobw@highlandconcord.com

Description: Within the insurance industry, we work with primary carriers, reinsurers, brokerage firms, consultants and corporate risk management.

Key Contact - Specialty:
Mr. Robert H. Wolfson, President - *Insurance, actuarial, risk management*

Salary minimum: $100,000

Functions: Generalist, Benefits, Risk Mgmt.

Industries: Generalist, Insurance

MIXTEC Group LLC
709 E Colorado Blvd Ste 250
Pasadena, CA 91101
(626) 440-7077
Email: mixtec@mixtec.net
Web: www.mixtec.net

Description: We specialize in searches for senior executives in the produce, food, and food service industries. We base our search efforts on our in-depth knowledge of these industry sectors and on our top management and consulting experience.

Key Contact:
Dr. Ward A. Fredericks, Chairman
Mr. Christopher C. Nelson, President
Mr. Jerry Butt, Principal
Ms. Brooke Kent, Office Manager - *Research direction*
Mrs. Mary Sanburn, Principal
Mr. Joe Stubbs

Salary minimum: $80,000

Functions: Generalist

Industries: Food, Bev., Tobacco

Professional Associations: IFMA, IFPA, IFT, PMA, UFFVA

Modestino Associates Inc
140 Wood Rd Ste 200
Braintree, MA 02184
(781) 849-3450
Fax: (781) 849-3458
Email: bmodestino@beld.net
Web: www.modestino.com

Description: We specialize in high-tech sales and sales management.

Key Contact:
Mr. William M. Modestino, Principal
Mr. James J. O'Neal

Functions: Sales & Mktg.

Industries: Generalist

Moffitt Int'l Inc
3182 Sweeten Creek Rd
Asheville, NC 28803
(828) 651-8550
Fax: (828) 651-8558
Email: resumes@emoffitt.com
Web: www.emoffitt.com

Description: An internationally recognized, research-based generalist firm with strong market niches.

Key Contact:
Ms. Linda I. Roetman, Director of Pharmaceutical
Mr. G. Alan Folger, Director of Architecture/Engineering
Mr. Bo Boling, Director of Construction
Mr. James Schwab, Director of Information Technology
Mr. Craig Robertson, Director of Waste Management

Functions: Generalist, Senior Mgmt., Healthcare, HR Mgmt., CFO's, IT, Engineering

Industries: Generalist, Construction, Drugs Mfg., Finance, Real Estate, Software, Healthcare

Branches:
6 Commerce Dr Ste 2000
Cranford, NJ 07016
(908) 709-1680
Fax: (908) 709-8946
Key Contact - Specialty:
Mr. Joseph W. Mrozek - *Generalist*

Molloy Partners
340 Broadway
Saratoga Springs, NY 12866
(518) 581-2532
Fax: (518) 581-2832
Email: tom@molloypartners.com

Description: We are engaged by both corporate clients and colleges/universities. On the corporate side we specialize in sales, marketing, finance and manufacturing. In higher education we are retained for senior-level assignments in fundraising, information technology, public relations, finance and administration.

Key Contact - Specialty:
Mr. Thomas Molloy, President - *Senior level, higher education, senior level finance, marketing*

Salary minimum: $75,000

Functions: Generalist, Directors, Senior Mgmt., Sales Mgmt., HR Mgmt., CFO's, MIS Mgmt., Non-profits

Industries: Generalist, Higher Ed., HR Services, Software, Healthcare

Monahan & Associates Inc
(formerly known as The Finance Group LLP)
541 E Shore Dr
Canton, GA 30114
(770) 592-1111
Fax: (770) 345-4639
Email: steve@mrifinance.com
Web: www.mrifinance.com

Description: We are an experienced and respected "retained" executive search firm that specializes in financial services recruiting, specifically focusing on the lending and the leasing areas.

Key Contact - Specialty:
Mr. Stephen C. Monahan, Chairman - *Financial services*

Salary minimum: $55,000

Functions: Finance

Industries: Generalist

Professional Associations: CFA, ELA

Oscar Montaño Inc
200 N Glendora Ave Ste J
Glendora, CA 91741
(626) 335-7342
Fax: (626) 335-8683
Email: owm@oscarmontano.com
Web: www.oscarmontano.com

Description: Specializing in consumer and automotive finance, we provide the complete search process plus industry knowledge. We also do salary surveys, organizational consulting and specialized outplacement.

Key Contact - Specialty:
Mr. Oscar W. Montaño, Principal - *Consumer finance, automotive*

Salary minimum: $80,000

Functions: Senior Mgmt.

Industries: Finance, Banking, Venture Cap., Misc. Financial

Professional Associations: AFSA

Montenido Associates
481 Cold Canyon Rd
Calabasas, CA 91302-2204
(818) 222-2744
(805) 373-7500
Email: swolf@bli-inc.com

Description: Perform middle and upper-level searches for the computer hardware/software, financial services and professional services industries. Specialize in nationwide staffing for field marketing, including sales and technical support for high-technology start-ups.

Key Contact - Specialty:
Mr. Stephen M. Wolf - *High technology, information technology*

Salary minimum: $75,000

Functions: Generalist

Industries: Computer Equip., Misc. Financial, Mgmt. Consulting, Software

Moore Research Associates
25 Karena Ln
Lawrenceville, NJ 08648
(609) 844-0020
Fax: (609) 844-0030
Email: sandeemra@aol.com

Description: Full-service search research firm specializing in the placement of high-level professionals for the pharmaceutical and healthcare industries.

Key Contact - Specialty:
Ms. Sandee Moore, President - *Healthcare, pharmaceutical, manufacturing, engineering*

Salary minimum: $50,000

Functions: Generalist

Industries: Drugs Mfg., Medical Devices, Pharm Svcs., Biotech, Healthcare

Morgan Executive Search Group Ltd
35 Kilbarry Rd
Toronto, ON M5P 1K4
Canada
(416) 485-9192
Email: morgansearchgrp@sprint.ca

Description: We have been in business for thirty-one years, undertaking assignments across North America. Our assignment range is intermediate to senior general management but also includes engineers, senior sales reps, and product managers.

Key Contact:
Mr. Ian Morgan, President - *Generalist*
Mr. Geoff Lovegrove, Partner - *Paper, packaging, technical, manufacturing, sales & marketing*
Mr. Michael Kennerley, Senior Consultant - *Advertising agencies, marketing, promotion*
Ms. Maureen Donaldson, Research Manager

Salary minimum: $60,000

Functions: Mfg., Product Dev., Production, Automation, Materials Plng., Distribution, Sales & Mktg., Advertising, Mkt. Research

Industries: Generalist, Paper, Printing, Chemicals, Plastics, Rubber, Paints, Petro. Products, Metal Products, Motor Vehicles, Test, Measure Equip., Electronic, Elec. Components, Advertising

Morgan/Webber Inc
1111 Rte 110 Ste 300
Farmingdale, NY 11735
(631) 799-2650
(212) 829-5726
Fax: (631) 799-5233
Email: mwinc@optonline.net
Web: www.morganwebber.com

Description: Very successful boutique search firm with strong emphasis on service not process! We tailor our searches to the style, needs and culture of our clients. We bring two decades of successful executive search and consulting to facilitate clients needs. You work directly with the principals.

Key Contact - Specialty:
Mr. Steven M. Lavender, President - *Generalist*

Salary minimum: $75,000

Functions: General Mgmt.

Industries: Mfg., Test, Measure Equip., Banking, Invest. Banking, Hospitality, Publishing, New Media, Broadcast, Film, Software, Biotech

MorganMarshall
2507 James St Ste 210
Syracuse, NY 13206
(315) 437-0665
Fax: (315) 437-1239
Email: hrjobs@morganmarshall.org
Web: www.morganmarshall.org

Description: We are a retained executive placement firm specializing solely in the area of human resources professionals. Our sourcing techniques are unique in that we target the passive job seeker, therefore producing high-quality talent.

Key Contact:
Mr. Marc Rideout, President - *HR management, organization development*
Ms. Carolyn Marasco, Recruiter

Salary minimum: $50,000

Functions: HR Mgmt.

Industries: Generalist

Moriarty/Fox Inc
20 N Wacker Dr Ste 2410
Chicago, IL 60606
(312) 332-4600

Description: For over 25 years, our firm has prided itself on establishing long and productive professional relationships with its many and varied client organizations. The firm's partners are well acquainted with many of the country's business and professional leaders.

Key Contact:
Mr. Philip S. J. Moriarty, President/Founder
Mr. J. Thomas Kenny, Partner

Salary minimum: $100,000

Functions: Generalist

Industries: Generalist

Morris & Berger
201 S Lake Ave Ste 700
Pasadena, CA 91101
(626) 795-0522
Fax: (626) 795-6330
Email: mb@morrisberger.com
Web: www.morrisberger.com

Description: Retained, generalist executive search firm with specialty practice in non-profit sector including academic, arts, social services, foundations.

Key Contact - Specialty:
Ms. Kristine A. Morris, Partner - *Non-profit searches*
Mr. Jay V. Berger, Partner - *Non-profit searches*

Salary minimum: $90,000

Functions: Generalist

Industries: Non-profits, Higher Ed., Government, Healthcare

Professional Associations: AAM, ACE, ACE, AFP, AFP, ASOL

Robert T Morton Associates Inc
35 Fields Pond Rd
Weston, MA 02493
(781) 899-4904
Fax: (781) 899-6514
Email: rtmorton@aol.com

Description: Main focus is placement in a multiplicity of high-technology product areas; software and hardware, including all levels of engineering, marketing, sales and manufacturing.

Key Contact - Specialty:
Mr. Robert T. Morton, President - *High technology*
Ms. Nancy J. Morton, Vice President - *High technology*

Functions: Generalist, Mkt. Research, Mktg. Mgmt., Sales Mgmt., Systems Analysis, Systems Dev., Engineering

Industries: Generalist, Medical Devices, Computer Equip., Mgmt. Consulting, Telecoms, Defense, Software

Morton, Doyle Associates[†]
26 Bellevue Rd
Arlington, MA 02476
(781) 641-1100
Fax: (781) 641-1151
Email: jfd@tiac.net

Description: Specializing in high-technology, information technology and manufacturing industries. Functional specialties in engineering and other technical areas as well as sales and marketing and general management.

Key Contact:
Mr. John F. Doyle, Principal

Salary minimum: $100,000

Functions: General Mgmt., IT, Engineering

Industries: Computer Equip., Test, Measure Equip., Software

Morton, McCorkle & Associates Inc
2190 S Mason Rd Ste 309
St. Louis, MO 63131-1637
(314) 984-9494
Fax: (314) 984-9460
Email: mmacnslt@aol.com

Description: We are an upper-level retained search encompassing most all functions and industries. We are international in scope with emphasis on general management, marketing, and other key line positions. We have had twenty-nine years of exceptional performance.

Key Contact:
Mr. Sam B. McCorkle, President
Mr. John F. Truex, Vice President

Salary minimum: $70,000

Functions: Generalist, Senior Mgmt., Plant Mgmt., Materials, R&D, Engineering, Int'l.

Industries: Generalist, Agri., Forestry, Mining, Food, Bev., Tobacco, Chemicals, Machine, Appliance, Packaging, Biotech

Moss & Company
21481 N 78th St
Scottsdale, AZ 85255
(602) 842-4035
(480) 538-0665
Email: bmoss@mossandco.com
Web: www.mossandco.com

Description: We are a retained executive search firm specializing in the real estate development, construction, civil and geotechnical engineering and property management fields.

Key Contact - Specialty:
Ms. Barbara Moss, Owner - *Real estate development, construction, property management, civil engineering, geotechnical engineering*

Salary minimum: $50,000

Functions: Generalist

Industries: Construction, Finance, Real Estate

Professional Associations: BC, BOMA, MBA, NAIOP, NNCREW, PREI

Branches:
456 Eakin Dr NW
Bainbridge Island, WA 98110
(206) 855-8100
Email: ttorseth@mossandco.com
Key Contact:
Ms. Theresa Torseth, Senior Associate

19232 Ridge Rd SW
Vashon, WA 98070
(206) 463-1694
Email: knjennings@mossandco.com
Key Contact:
Ms. Kirsten Jennings, Senior Associate

Moyer, Sherwood Associates Inc
1285 Ave of the Americas Fl 35
New York, NY 10019
(212) 554-4008
Web: www.moyersherwood.com

Description: We offer highly personal service, rooted in the combination of three approaches: traditional, thorough, confidential executive search consulting; modern, computer-based methodology and a commitment to creativity in our search work.

Key Contact - Specialty:
Mr. David S. Moyer - *Corporate communications, public relations*

Salary minimum: $105,000

Functions: PR

Industries: Generalist

Professional Associations: AESC

Branches:
65 High Ridge
Stamford, CT 06905
(203) 656-2220
Key Contact:
Ms. Jennifer Keister

MPA Executive Search Inc
7900 Blvd Taschereau Ouest Bureau A-204
Brossard, QC J4X 1C2
Canada
(514) 875-3996
(450) 465-6998
Fax: (450) 465-9215
Email: courrier@m-p-a.qc.ca
Web: www.m-p-a.qc.ca

Description: We specialize in the search of intermediate and executive-level personnel. Strong experience in engineering and manufacturing.

Key Contact - Specialty:
Mr. Marc Paquet, President - *Generalist*

Salary minimum: $40,000

Functions: Generalist, General Mgmt., Mfg., Materials, Sales & Mktg., HR Mgmt., Finance, Engineering

Industries: Generalist, Agri., Forestry, Mining, Mfg., Packaging, Biotech, Healthcare

Mruk & Partners
(a member of EMA Partners Int'l)
230 Park Ave Ste 1000
New York, NY 10169
(212) 808-3076

Key Contact - Specialty:
Mr. Edwin S. Mruk, Senior Partner - *Board of directors, general management, healthcare*
Ms. Carol Buckner, Partner - *Law firm administration*

Salary minimum: $100,000

Functions: Directors, Senior Mgmt., Mfg., Health Admin., Sales & Mktg., HR Mgmt., Benefits, CFO's, MIS Mgmt., Int'l.

Industries: Mfg., Services, Hospitality, Publishing, Packaging, Insurance, Real Estate, Biotech, Healthcare

Professional Associations: AESC, IMC

Networks: EMA Partners Int'l

MSA Executive Search
4801 Cliff Ave MSA Bldg Ste 300
Independence, MO 64055
(816) 373-9988
Fax: (816) 478-1929
Email: jgroves@mgmtscience.com
Web: www.mgmtscience.com

Description: Firm is largest employee relations/human resource consulting firm in healthcare industry. This division provides executive search for retained clients only. Provides in-depth executive assessment and candidate profiles.

Key Contact - Specialty:
Ms. Jane Groves, Managing Senior Vice President - *Healthcare executives*

Salary minimum: $85,000

Functions: Generalist

Industries: Healthcare

Professional Associations: ACHE, AHSM, AONE, ASHHRA, HCF

MTA Partners
5068 W Plano Pkwy 227
Plano, TX 75093
(972) 380-1988
Email: mtucker@mtapartners.com

Description: Retained firm specializing in the medical device/service profit industries. Unequalled client service based on limited searches at a time. Over 80% of our candidates go to 2nd interviews with our clients.

Key Contact:
Mr. Michael Tucker, Managing Partner - *Healthcare, non-profit*
Ms. Brooke Myers, Associate
Mrs. Carol Reince, Associate
Mrs. Stephanie Franklin, Associate

Salary minimum: $75,000

Functions: Sales & Mktg., Mktg. Mgmt., Sales Mgmt.

Industries: Drugs Mfg., Medical Devices, Pharm Svcs.

Much & Company Inc
237 Park Ave
Park Ave Atrium
New York, NY 10017
(212) 551-3578
(212) 217-0600
Email: muchandco@aol.com

Description: Financial services, worldwide: specializing in investment management, investment research and investment banking in all the major financial capitals and in the emerging markets.

Key Contact - Specialty:
Mr. Isaac Much, President - *Global investment management, investment strategy, investment research, investment banking*

Salary minimum: $200,000

Functions: Finance

Industries: Finance, Banking, Invest. Banking, Brokers, Venture Cap., Telecoms, Biotech, Healthcare

Branches:
25 Broad St
The Exchange
New York, NY 10004
(212) 217-0600
Email: muchandco@aol.com
Key Contact:
Mr. Isaac Much, President

Mullen Associates Inc
300 Hwy 5 S Ste 7
Pinehurst, NC 28374
(910) 295-0077
Fax: (910) 295-4419
Email: jj@jmullen.com

Description: We are a retained, boutique firm only and our highly personalized service never exceeds more than six on-going searches. Our specialties are paint/coatings, ink, and adhesives.

Key Contact - Specialty:
Mr. James J. Mullen, President - *Paint & coatings, specialty chemicals, ink, adhesives*
Mr. Lawrence C. Fisher, Vice President - *Paint & coatings, specialty chemicals, ink, adhesives*

Salary minimum: $85,000

Functions: Generalist, General Mgmt., Mfg., Sales & Mktg., R&D

Industries: Generalist, Printing, Chemicals, Plastics, Rubber, Paints, Petro. Products, Packaging

Professional Associations: NPCA

Pamela L Mulligan Inc
5 Williamsburg Dr
Gilford, NH 03249
(603) 528-0400
Fax: (603) 528-0404
Email: plminc@worldpath.net
Web: www.mulligansearch.com

Description: Recruiting expertise in managed care and insurance (to include direct marketing, TPA, special risk and employee benefits). Functional titles and areas include: sales, marketing, underwriting, claims, systems, human resources, medical directors, CFO, psychiatrists, utilization and care management and operations.

Key Contact - Specialty:
Ms. Pamela L. Mulligan, President - *Managed care, healthcare, insurance*

Salary minimum: $60,000

Functions: Generalist, Senior Mgmt., Nurses, Mktg. Mgmt., Sales Mgmt., CFO's, MIS Mgmt., Systems Implem.

Industries: Generalist, Insurance, Healthcare

Professional Associations: AAHP, AHA, HIMSS, NAHDO, NAHQ, ONS, PDMA

The Mulshine Company Inc
2517 Rte 35 Ste D-201
Manasquan, NJ 08736
(732) 292-0982
Fax: (732) 528-9065

Description: Dedicated to search for general and middle management and senior individual contributors in R&D, engineering, manufacturing, document management, accounting, finance, venture capital and emerging high-tech companies.

Key Contact:
Mr. Michael A. Mulshine, President/Consultant

Salary minimum: $90,000

Functions: Generalist, General Mgmt., Sales & Mktg., Finance, IT, R&D, Engineering, Specialized Svcs.

Industries: Generalist, Chemicals, Computer Equip., Finance, Aerospace, Software

The Mulshine Company Ltd
24 Fox Hollow Ln
Queensbury, NY 12804
(518) 743-9301
Fax: (518) 761-6684
Email: mail@mulshinecompany.com
Web: www.mulshinecompany.com

Description: We hav eighteen years' experience in specialized scientific and R&D; packaging, product and process development; engineering and manufacturing oriented searches to VP levels for the consumer brands, pharmaceutical, biotech and food industries.

Key Contact:
Mr. Michael G. Mulshine, President

Salary minimum: $50,000

Functions: Directors, Middle Mgmt., Product Dev., Automation, Packaging, R&D, Engineering

Industries: Food, Bev., Tobacco, Chemicals, Soap, Perf., Cosmtcs., Drugs Mfg., Plastics, Rubber, Machine, Appliance, Packaging, Biotech

Multi Processing Inc
20 Crown Hill Rd
Atkinson, NH 03811
(603) 362-6300
Email: jvito@multiprocessing.com
Web: www.multiprocessing.com

Description: Recruiting professionals for computer development; hardware and software; sales marketing and end user applications development.

Key Contact - Specialty:
Mr. Joseph Vito, President - *Engineering, sales & marketing, senior level*

Salary minimum: $60,000

Functions: Generalist, Directors, Senior Mgmt., Mktg. Mgmt., Sales Mgmt., MIS Mgmt., Systems Analysis, Engineering

Industries: Generalist, Media, New Media, Broadcast, Film, Telecoms, Software

R F Mulvaney & Associates Inc
11050 Crabapple Rd C108
PO Box 1996
Roswell, GA 30075
(770) 998-9007
Fax: (770) 998-6259
Email: mulvaney@ix.netcom.com

Description: Established in 1974 serving national clients at search for mid- and executive-levels. Specialize in manufacturing, managed healthcare and consulting engineering.

Key Contact - Specialty:
Mr. Ronald F. Mulvaney, President - *Manufacturing, managed healthcare, consulting engineering*

Salary minimum: $60,000

Functions: General Mgmt., Senior Mgmt., Plant Mgmt., Health Admin., Sales Mgmt., CFO's, Network Admin., Engineering, Architects

Industries: Mfg., Accounting

Jennifer Munro & Partners Inc
33 Normandy Rd
Greenville, SC 29615
(864) 268-6482
Fax: (864) 268-7137

Email: jlmunro10@aol.com

Description: Specialize in performance-driven companies; strong emphasis on behavioral as well as functional compatibility.

Key Contact - Specialty:
Ms. Jennifer Munro, President - *Capital management, finance, banking, manufacturing, high technology*

Salary minimum: $100,000

Functions: Generalist, Senior Mgmt., Middle Mgmt., Plant Mgmt., Mktg. Mgmt., Sales Mgmt., Cash Mgmt., MIS Mgmt.

Industries: Generalist, Construction, Invest. Banking, Brokers, Hospitality, Broadcast, Film

Munroe, Curry & Bond Associates
(a division of Associated Business Consultants Inc)
43 N Main St
PO Box 1299
Medford, NJ 08055
(609) 953-8600

Description: Unique and creative approach, hourly billing, 3-year placement guarantee, 98% retention rate over 3-year period. Candidate assessment includes extensive face-to-face interactive testing to skim the top 2%. The process guarantees market share increase when combining sales search with sales force assessment.

Key Contact:
Ms. M. Louise Milnes, Vice President-Finance
Ms. Delores Bond, Corporate Secretary
Mr. David W. Deming, Director of Operations
Mr. Michael P. Harkins, Director of Research
Mr. Gerald Curry, Operations
Mr. Michael Munroe, General Manager

Salary minimum: $65,000

Functions: Generalist

Industries: Mfg., Transportation, Aerospace, Packaging, Insurance, Real Estate, Software, Biotech, Healthcare, Non-classifiable

Professional Associations: AALAS, RAPS

P J Murphy & Associates Inc
735 N Water St
Milwaukee, WI 53202
(414) 277-9777
Fax: (414) 277-7626
Email: pjmurphy@pjmurphy.com
Web: www.pjmurphy.com

Description: Established firm; retainer only; considerable work with boards in selecting senior people; national in scope.

Key Contact - Specialty:
Dr. Patrick J. Murphy, President - *General management*
Mr. Craig S. Zaffrann, Vice President
Mr. James F. Zahradka, Vice President - *Physicians, healthcare executives*

Salary minimum: $80,000

Functions: Generalist

Industries: Generalist

Murphy Partners Int'l
956 Shoreline Rd
Barrington, IL 60010
(847) 304-1599
Fax: (847) 304-1144
Email: murphy@mpivips.com

Description: High-level, high quality search practice with focus on personal service. President was partner with Big 5 accounting firm. He has 25+ years' search experience; been responsible for over 1000 engagements; significant, 200+ international assignments.

Key Contact - Specialty:
Ms. V. Kolacia, Managing Director - *Hospitality, higher education, accounting, entertainment, insurance*
Ms. K. Froelich, Managing Director - *Food, paper, chemicals, drugs, computer equipment*
Ms. C. Liota, Managing Director - *Finance, information technology, management consulting, new media*

Salary minimum: $100,000

Functions: General Mgmt., Senior Mgmt., Mfg., Healthcare, Sales & Mktg., HR Mgmt., Finance, CFO's, IT, Int'l.

Industries: Generalist, Mfg., Retail, Finance, Services, Pharm Svcs., Hospitality, Insurance, Real Estate, Software, Biotech, Healthcare

Professional Associations: IIHR, SHRM, SHRP

MVC Associates Int'l
3001 N Rocky Point Dr E Ste 200
PMB 2034
Tampa, FL 33607
(813) 891-6644
Fax: (811) 855-5847
Email: careers@mvcinternational.com
Web: www.mvcinternational.com

Description: Leading firm in organization design and search in information based marketing, CRM, E-business go to website for current research and register in our confidential candidate database

Key Contact:
Mr. Mark Van Clief, Managing Director
Ms. Carol Gulyas, Partner

Salary minimum: $100,000

Functions: Sales & Mktg.

Industries: Generalist

Branches:
724 Scoville Ave
Oak Park, IL 60304
(708) 660-0948
Email: careers@mvcinternational.com
Web: www.mvcinternational.com
Key Contact:
Mr. Carol Gulyas

36 Toronto St Ste 850
Toronto, ON M5C 2C5
Canada
(416) 489-1917
Email: careers@mvcinternational.com
Web: www.mvcinternational.com
Key Contact:
Mr. Mark Van Clieaf, Managing Director

Mycoff & Associates
26689 Pleasant Park Rd Ste 260
Conifer, CO 80433
(303) 838-7445
Fax: (303) 838-7428
Email: mail@mycoffassociates.com
Web: www.mycoffassociates.com

Description: Specialists in executive search for electric, natural gas, telecommunications and water industries.

Key Contact:
Mr. Carl A. Mycoff, President

Salary minimum: $70,000

Functions: Generalist, Senior Mgmt., Middle Mgmt., Mktg. Mgmt., CFO's, Cash Mgmt., MIS Mgmt., Engineering

Industries: Generalist, Energy, Utilities, Telecoms

Professional Associations: APPA, AWWA, NRECA

Myers & Associates†
PO BOX 430
Allen, TX 75013
(972) 396-8830
(800) 257-0273
Email: info@stepbeyond.com
Web: www.stepbeyond.com

Description: Our firm is the premier search firm for executive, management, and R&D talent in electronics, manufacturing, operations, and high tech R&D including: optics, bio-electronics, and wireless technologies. Myers & Associates was founded on the core principles of outstanding customer service, integrity, and responsiveness to our clients and candidates. We offer creative, personalized solutions to achieve your strategic business objectives.

Key Contact:
Mr. John Myers, Senior Executive Recruiter

Salary minimum: $80,000

Functions: Generalist, General Mgmt.

Industries: Generalist

DDJ Myers Ltd
2303 N 44th St 14-1740
Phoenix, AZ 85008
(602) 840-9595
(800) 574-8877
Fax: (602) 840-6486
Email: resume@ddjmyers.com
Web: www.ddjmyers.com

Description: We provide recruiting, career and succession planning for financial and technology executives. Organizations use our services for internal and external searches, development and execution of career management processes and comprehensive succession plans.

Key Contact - Specialty:
Ms. Deedee Myers, President/CEO - *Treasury management, finance, interest rate risk, asset & liability, securitization*

Functions: Senior Mgmt., CFO's, Cash Mgmt., Risk Mgmt., IT

Industries: Transportation, Banking, Invest. Banking, Brokers, Equip Svcs., Mgmt. Consulting, HR Services

Nadzam, Horgan & Associates
(a member of Signium Int'l)
1101 S Winchester Blvd Ste J210
San Jose, CA 95128
(408) 260-5100
Fax: (408) 260-5109
Email: nh@nhexecutivesearch.com
Web: www.nhexecutivesearch.com

Description: Consultants to corporate management in executive search, primarily for technology companies, i.e., electronics, information technology, manufacturing and aerospace. Clients range from Fortune 50 to start-up new technology companies.

Key Contact:
Mr. Richard J. Nadzam, Partner
Mr. Thomas F. Horgan, Partner

Salary minimum: $150,000

Functions: Generalist, General Mgmt., Mfg., Sales & Mktg., HR Mgmt., IT, Engineering, Int'l.

Industries: Generalist, Mfg., Media, Aerospace, Software, Biotech

Professional Associations: AESC

Networks: Signium Int'l Inc

Nagler, Robins & Poe Inc
65 William St
Wellesley, MA 02481-3802
(781) 431-1330
Fax: (781) 431-7861
Email: jpoe@nrpinc.com
Web: www.nrpinc.com

Description: Serving clients nationally from offices in Wellesley, Massachusetts. A 20+ year record of quickly meeting client needs coupled with one of the highest success rates in the search industry.

Key Contact - Specialty:
Mr. James B. Poe, Managing Director - *Technology*
Ms. Jeri N. Robins, Managing Director - *Technology*
Mr. Leon G. Nagler, Managing Director - *Consulting, financial services, manufacturing*

Salary minimum: $150,000

Functions: Generalist

Industries: Venture Cap., New Media, Telecoms, Software

Jim Nalepa & Associates
180 N Stetson Ste 700
2 Prudential Plz
Chicago, IL 60601
(312) 372-3750
(630) 986-7000
Email: jim@jimnalepa.com
Web: www.jimnalepa.com

Description: One of Chicago's top executive search consultants, we have over 17 years of recruiting experience. We have successfully delivered the key ingredient of executive success, leadership, to our clients. Seeing the search industry decimated with mergers, IPOs, and false technical solutions and believing that the biggest firms in the search industry are now "shareholder focused" rather than "client focused," Jim Nalepa founded this firm to recapture a client centric vision.

Key Contact - Specialty:
Mr. Jim Nalepa, President - *Leadership*

Salary minimum: $125,000

Functions: General Mgmt., Senior Mgmt., Mfg., Materials, Sales & Mktg., HR Mgmt., Finance, CFO's, IT, Engineering

Industries: Generalist

Professional Associations: RR

National Restaurant Search Inc[†]
555 Sun Valley Dr Ste J-1
Roswell, GA 30076
(770) 650-1800
Fax: (770) 650-1801
Email: john@restaurantheadhunter.com
Web: www.restaurantheadhunter.com

Description: Corporate - work exclusively in the restaurant/hospitality industry. Assignments include president, CEO, COO, finance, franchising, real estate and construction, marketing, human resources and operations at the executive-level. Our executives have restaurant/hotel operations experience.

Key Contact - Specialty:
Mr. John W. Chitvanni, President - *Restaurant executives*

Salary minimum: $50,000

Functions: Generalist

Industries: Generalist, Hospitality

Branches:
28 Water St Ste 308
Batavia, IL 60510
(630) 482-2900
Fax: (630) 482-2922
Email: ron@restaurantheadhunter.com

Key Contact:
Mr. Ronald F. Stockman, Vice President
Mr. Dennis Minchella, Division Vice President

Nativesun Inc
3838 N Central Ave Ste 1750
Phoenix, AZ 85012
(602) 636-4110
Fax: (602) 636-4110
Email: trudyware@indiannativesun.org
Web: www.indiannativesun.org

Description: A Native American executive search firm that promotes visibility and employment of American Indian professionals with bachelor degrees and higher in mid- to upper-level positions in management and technology with tribal entities and corporations across the U.S.

Key Contact - Specialty:
Ms. Trudy Jo Ware, President/CEO - *Native American professionals*

Functions: Minorities

Industries: Generalist

NDH Search
1634 19th St
Santa Monica, CA 90404
(310) 234-2944
Fax: (310) 234-0944
Email: ndhsearch@aol.com

Description: Specializing in architecture and design using a unique and proven method for matching the ideal candidate with the client's particular requirements and personality.

Key Contact - Specialty:
Ms. Nancy Horne, President - *Architecture, interior design, administrative*

Functions: Generalist, Middle Mgmt., Admin. Svcs., Architects

Industries: Generalist, Construction

The Neil Michael Group Inc
350 5th Ave Ste 2711
Empire State Bldg
New York, NY 10118
(212) 631-0999
Fax: (212) 631-0011
Email: neilmichaelgroup@worldnet.att.net
Web: www.neilmichaelgroup.com

Description: Retainer search firm exclusively dealing in biotechnology, pharmaceutical and other life sciences. Extensive focus on emerging growth companies. Broad investment banking and venture capital relationships. International capabilities.

Key Contact:
Dr. Neil M. Solomon, President
Mr. Alfred Middleton, Vice President - *Board searches*
Mr. Andrew R. Newcorn, Vice President
Mr. Craig A. Kasper, Consultant

Salary minimum: $150,000

Functions: Generalist

Industries: Drugs Mfg., Medical Devices, Biotech, Healthcare

Professional Associations: BIO, NYBA

New Directions Search Inc
1127 Wheaton Oaks Ct
PO Box 88
Wheaton, IL 60189
(630) 462-1840
Fax: (630) 462-1862
Email: dalefrank@newdir.com
Web: www.newdirectionssearch.com

Description: We specialize in senior leadership searches primarily with Fortune 500 manufacturing

firms. Disciplines include: corporate leadership, manufacturing operations, supply chain management, purchasing, human resources, engineering, sales, marketing, finance, manufacturing engineering, information technology.

Key Contact:
Mr. Dale A. Frank, President
Mr. John M. Morton, Executive Vice President
Mr. Richard L. Santarelli, Senior Vice President
Mr. Richard B. Schlifke, Senior Vice President
Mr. Douglas W. Scott, Vice President
Mr. Tim Sezonov, Vice President
Ms. Carol Nevin, Search Consultant
Mr. James Owens, Search Consultant

Salary minimum: $100,000

Functions: Generalist

Industries: Generalist

Professional Associations: APICS, SHRM

New Media Staffing LLC
64 Arlington N Ste 200
Meriden, CT 06450
(203) 237-3000
Fax: (203) 634-6860
Email: info@nmstaffing.com
Web: www.nmstaffing.com

Description: Full-service executive search firm with specific skills with Internet sourcing, technology based searches, and creative executive staffing campaigns.

Key Contact - Specialty:
Mr. Robert Simon, Managing Director - *Technology based searches*

Salary minimum: $150,000

Functions: Generalist

Industries: Venture Cap., Telecoms, Software

Professional Associations: IEEE, SAE, SHRM

New World Healthcare Solutions Inc
380 Lexington Ave Ste 1700
New York, NY 10168
(212) 551-7867
Fax: (845) 267-0894
Email: irashapiro@newworldhealthcare.com
Web: www.newworldhealthcare.com

Description: An international firm that specializes in healthcare and provides a unique hiring process which will ensure the hiring of the right candidate. Our organization actively participates in the evaluation process and truly understands the healthcare industry.

Key Contact - Specialty:
Mr. Ira E. Shapiro, CEO - *Healthcare (domestic, international)*
Ms. Julia de Peyster, Senior Vice President - *Healthcare (domestic, international)*
Mr. Gary Marx, Managing Director - *Insurance*

Salary minimum: $90,000

Functions: Healthcare

Industries: Generalist, Insurance, Healthcare

Nexus Int'l
(a member of AIMS Int'l Mgmt Search & KMC Int'l Exec Search)
218 Juan Way
Castle Rock, CO 80104
(303) 768-9282
Email: nexussearch@aol.com
Web: www.nexus-resources.com

Description: Serious search firm with guaranteed results. All consultants have held positions at the senior management level. International in scope with many multinational clients.

Key Contact - Specialty:
Ms. Debra McCart, Managing Partner - *Telecommunications, high technology*
Ms. Melissa Helms Buckner - *Telecommunications, high technology*

Salary minimum: $80,000

Functions: IT, Engineering

Industries: Telecoms

Professional Associations: AIMS

Nicholaou & Company
56 W Piers Dr
Westmont, IL 60559-3227
(630) 960-2382

Description: Personalized search service, mid- to upper-management - nationwide.

Key Contact:
Ms. Jean Nicholaou

Salary minimum: $75,000

Functions: Generalist, General Mgmt., Mfg., Sales & Mktg.

Industries: Generalist, Mfg.

Nichols & Company
PO Box 3561
Boulder, CO 80307-3561
(303) 494-3383
Fax: (303) 499-4117
Email: cnichols@lynx.sni.net
Web: www.nicholsandcompany.com

Description: Retained executive search firm working with international network of clients in industrial and technological specialties. Recruiting senior management and board members.

Key Contact:
Mr. Charles H. Nichols, President

Salary minimum: $90,000

Functions: Senior Mgmt.

Industries: Generalist

Nickerson & Schrieber Associates
2421-A Portola Rd
Ventura, CA 93003
(805) 650-8964
Fax: (805) 650-8976
Email: email@executiverecruiters.com
Web: www.survivalsystems.com

Description: We are the world's largest executive search firm dedicated to the analog industry including power supplies, motors, semiconductors, fuel cells, electric vehicle, and photonics with skills from engineers to CEO.

Key Contact - Specialty:
Mr. Dennis Nickerson - *Analog electronics*
Ms. Sandy Schrieber, CPC - *Analog electronics*

Salary minimum: $75,000

Functions: Generalist, Senior Mgmt., Middle Mgmt., Plant Mgmt., Sales Mgmt., CFO's, Engineering

Industries: Generalist, Test, Measure Equip., Electronic, Elec. Components, HR Services, Communications, Telecoms, Digital, Wireless, Fiber Optic, Network Infrastructure, Marketing SW

Professional Associations: IACPR, CSP, NAPS

The Niemond Corp
PO Box 4106
San Marcos, CA 92069
(760) 591-4127

Description: Founder has 20 years of nationwide retained executive search experience, with emphasis

in the communications, electronics, data processing and defense systems industries.

Key Contact:
Ms. Nancy A. Lodice, Partner
Mr. Wesley E. Niemond, Founder

Salary minimum: $100,000

Functions: Generalist, Middle Mgmt., Plant Mgmt., Materials, Mktg. Mgmt., HR Mgmt., Budgeting, MIS Mgmt.

Industries: Generalist, Medical Devices, Computer Equip., Test, Measure Equip., Haz. Waste

Professional Associations: ADPA, AFCEA, AUSA

The Noebel Search Group Inc[†]
15851 Dallas Parkway Ste 600
Addison, TX 75001
(972) 855-7350
Fax: (972) 855-7351
Email: nsgi@noebelsearch.com
Web: www.noebelsearch.com

Description: We are an executive search firm focused solely on the recruitment and retention of biomedical research and development professionals.

Key Contact - Specialty:
Mr. Todd R. Noebel, President - *Research & development, scientists*

Salary minimum: $60,000

Functions: R&D

Industries: Agri., Forestry, Mining, Chemicals, Soap, Perf., Cosmtcs., Drugs Mfg., Medical Devices, Pharm Svcs., Biotech

Professional Associations: AAAS, CRS, EMS, MASOT, SOT, STP

D R Nolan Associates Inc
320 Bay St Ste 1510
PO Box 16
Toronto, ON M5H 4A6
Canada
(416) 868-9991
Fax: (416) 868-9394
Email: drnolan@sympatico.ca

Description: Seven person executive search firm focusing primarily on financial services.

Key Contact:
D. R. Nolan

Salary minimum: $80,000

Functions: Finance

Industries: Finance

W D Nolte & Company
6 Middlesex Rd
Darien, CT 06820
(203) 323-5858
Fax: (203) 323-0164
Email: wdn.global@worldnet.att.net

Description: Over 20 years as a management consultant serving public and private businesses and institutions in the U.S. and abroad. National and international coverage through North American Search Alliance partners.

Key Contact - Specialty:
Mr. William D. Nolte, Jr., Principal - *Generalist*

Salary minimum: $100,000

Functions: General Mgmt., Mfg., Materials, Sales & Mktg., CFO's, MIS Mgmt.

Industries: Mfg., Finance, Accounting, Mgmt. Consulting, Telecoms, Software

Professional Associations: IMC

Nordeman Grimm Inc
717 5th Ave Fl 26
New York, NY 10022
(212) 935-1000
Fax: (212) 980-1443
Email: resume@nordemangrimm.com
Web: www.nordemangrimm.com

Description: We specialize in recruiting exceptional senior executives. We are known for quality, team work and long-term relationships.

Key Contact - Specialty:
Mr. Jacques C. Nordeman, Chairman - *General management, e-Business, investment companies, new media investment banking, finance*
Mr. David Bentley, Vice Chairman - *E-Business, new media, traditional publishing*
Mr. Frank J. Farrell, President - *E-Business, new media, traditional publishing*

Salary minimum: $150,000

Functions: Generalist

Industries: Generalist

Professional Associations: AESC, IACPR

Norman Broadbent Int'l Inc
2859 Paces Ferry Rd Ste 1400
Atlanta, GA 30339
(770) 955-9550
Fax: (770) 980-9367
Email: normanbroadbent@nbi-atlanta.com
Web: www.normanbroadbent.com

Description: We serve clients primarily in the financial services, new media, entertainment and technology sectors, helping them to build outstanding organizations through executive search.

Key Contact - Specialty:
Mr. Thomas Higgins, COO - *Technology, financial services*

Salary minimum: $150,000

Functions: Directors, Senior Mgmt., Sales & Mktg., Finance, IT, DB Admin., Mgmt. Consultants

Industries: Construction, Mfg., Finance, Non-profits, Legal, Accounting, Media, Communications, Government, Biotech

Professional Associations: AESC, IACPR

Branches:
425 Market St Ste 2200
San Francisco, CA 94105
(415) 955-2790
Fax: (415) 397-6309
Email: nbisf@nbisearch.com
Key Contact - Specialty:
Mr. Kelvin Thompson, President/Chairman - *Financial services, new media, entertainment, technology*
Ms. Linda Bagby, Assistant to President - *Technology*

Northeast Consulting Group
237 Ridgefield Rd
Wilton, CT 06897
(203) 834-8700
Fax: (203) 762-8403
Email: necgsearch@cs.com

Description: We are committed to building partnerships with clients who share our drive for excellence and are serious about building their organization's intellectual power and leadership capital.

Key Contact - Specialty:
Mr. G. Charles Roy, Jr., Managing Director - *Generalist, finance, manufacturing, information technology, human resources*
Ms. Candace L. Roy, Principal - *Generalist, finance, manufacturing, information technology, marketing*

Ms. Courtnie Zuckerberg, Principal - *Generalist, marketing; public relations, healthcare, finance*

Salary minimum: $70,000

Functions: Generalist

Industries: Generalist

Northern Consultants Inc

RR1 Box 558
Stratford, NH 03590
(603) 636-9914
Fax: (603) 636-9914
Email: alcjdb@ncia.net

Description: Specialize in search and operational audits: custom injection molding, plastics packaging and machinery. Also career counseling and alternate career path identification.

Key Contact - Specialty:
Dr. Alta L. Chase, President
Mr. James D. Brown - *Plastics*

Salary minimum: $60,000

Functions: Generalist, Senior Mgmt., Plant Mgmt., Mktg. Mgmt., Sales Mgmt., Engineering

Industries: Generalist, Paper, Plastics, Rubber, Machine, Appliance, Mgmt. Consulting, HR Services, Packaging

Professional Associations: IMC

NPF Associates Ltd Inc[†]

1999 University Dr Ste 405
Coral Springs, FL 33071-6032
(954) 753-8560
Fax: (954) 753-8611
Email: npfassociates@aol.com

Description: Executive search firm specializing in human resources, with a client base of Fortune 500 companies.

Key Contact - Specialty:
Mr. Nick P. Fischler, President - *Human resources*

Salary minimum: $70,000

Functions: HR Mgmt.

Industries: Mfg., Retail, Finance, Services, Hospitality, Communications, Aerospace, Insurance

Professional Associations: HRPS, SHRM, WAW

Branches:
575 Lexington Ave Fl 4
New York, NY 10022
(212) 527-7528
Email: bdfischler@aol.com
Key Contact:
Mr. Nick Fischler, President

Nucci Consulting Group

324 Augusta Dr
Blue Bell, PA 19422
(610) 272-7773
Fax: (610) 278-0488
Email: enucci@earthlink.net
Web: www.NucciConsultingGroup.com

Description: NCG is a Wall Street retained consulting and executive search firm that specializes in lift-outs, acquisitions, mergers and the placement of money managers and analysts.

Key Contact - Specialty:
Ms. Ev Nucci, Chairman & CEO
Ms. Lisa Jensen, Consultant - *Money (managers, analysts)*

Salary minimum: $150,000

Nuessle Kurdziel & Weiss Inc

1601 Market St
5 Penn Ctr Plz
Philadelphia, PA 19103
(215) 561-3700
Fax: (215) 561-3745
Email: nkwsearch@aol.com

Description: Executive search assignments in most functional areas with emphasis on general management, finance, human resources and marketing in most industry classifications. Also perform compensation studies.

Key Contact:
Mr. John F. Kurdziel, Partner
Mr. Warren G. Nuessle, Partner
Mr. Gerald E. Weiss, Partner

Salary minimum: $80,000

Functions: Generalist

Industries: Generalist

Professional Associations: ACG, CDA, CLM

Nursing Technomics

(a division of Nat'l Technomics Inc)
814 Sunset Hollow Rd
West Chester, PA 19380
(610) 436-4551
(800) 772-4551
Fax: (610) 436-0255
Email: jimccrea@chesco.com

Description: Specializing in executive search for executive, management and specialty nurses.

Key Contact - Specialty:
Ms. Joan I. McCrea, Principal - *Nurses, administrative & management*

Salary minimum: $50,000

Functions: Generalist, Nurses, Training, Mgmt. Consultants

Industries: Generalist, Healthcare

Professional Associations: NLN

O'Brien & Company Inc

812 Huron Rd Ste 535
Cleveland, OH 44115
(216) 575-1212
Fax: (216) 575-7502
Email: info@obriencompany.com
Web: www.obriencompany.com

Description: We specialize in three segments, and they are: consumer products, industrial manufacturing, and professional and financial services. We concentrate on general management and the level directly below that, for example: the heads of sales and marketing, manufacturing operations, finance, supply chain, and all other disciplines.

Key Contact - Specialty:
Mr. Timothy M. O'Brien, Principal - *General management, manufacturing, industrial, consumer products, professional and financial services*
Mr. Henry Hecker, Vice President - *Manufacturing, consumer products*
Mr. Dylan Davis, Vice President - *Manufacturing*

Salary minimum: $100,000

Functions: Generalist

Industries: Generalist

O'Brien Consulting Services

171 Swanton St Unit 72
Winchester, MA 01890-1965
(781) 721-4404
Email: ocs@mediaone.net
Web: www.ocs-executivesearch.com

Description: Our previous line management experience in both high technology and manufacturing/distribution industries combined with partner positions with two major search firms. We service the senior level retained executive search industry.

Key Contact - Specialty:
Mr. James J. O'Brien, Jr., President - *Senior level executives, all functions*

Salary minimum: $100,000

Functions: Generalist, Directors, Senior Mgmt.

Industries: Generalist, Energy, Utilities, Mfg., Transportation, Wholesale, Services, Communications, Packaging, Software, Biotech

O'Connor, O'Connor, Lordi Ltd

707 Grant St Ste 2727 Gulf Twr
Pittsburgh, PA 15219-1908
(412) 261-4020
Fax: (412) 261-4480
Email: info@oolltd.com
Web: www.oolltd.com

Description: We have a custom tailored executive recruitment program for middle to upper echelon management with emphasis on sales, marketing, R&D, manufacturing, MIS, finance, and general management.

Key Contact - Specialty:
Mr. Thomas F. O'Connor, President - *Fortune 500*
Mr. Richard E. Brown, Executive Vice President & COO - *Fortune 500*

Salary minimum: $120,000

Functions: Mfg.

Industries: Energy, Utilities, Mfg., Food, Bev., Tobacco, Chemicals, Medical Devices, Finance, Invest. Banking, Venture Cap., Services, Biotech

O'Gorman & Company Inc

52 Cheever Pl
Brooklyn, NY 11231
(718) 802-1141
Email: info@ogormanandcompany.com
Web: www.ogormanandcompany.com

Description: O'Gorman & Company, Inc. is an executive search firm specializing in senior- and mid-level Wall Street professionals. Our areas of expertise are investment banking, capital markets, and asset management. Working strictly on behalf of our client, we identify and recruit the right candidates regardless of whether they are actively seeking a job change. We make a difference to clients because of minimal off-limits, outstanding research, years of executive search success and many years of senior financial industry experience.

Key Contact:
Mary O'Gorman, President

Salary minimum: $150,000

Functions: General Mgmt., Senior Mgmt., Middle Mgmt., Product Dev., Sales & Mktg., M&A, Risk Mgmt., Int'l.

Industries: Finance, Banking, Invest. Banking, Brokers

Professional Associations: ESRT

O'Keefe & Associates Inc

PO Box 1092
Southport, CT 06490
(203) 254-2544
Fax: (203) 254-2126
Email: jokeefe@okeefeinc.com
Web: www.okeefeinc.com

Description: We are a retainer-based firm focused on recruiting outstanding talent for consumer products, foodservice, restaurants, pharmaceuticals, medical devices, information technology, telecommunications and management consulting organizations across a variety of functions. We are unique in that our principals take an active role in every search; we build long-term client relationships; and we've been able to maintain continuity within our recruiting staff.

Key Contact:
Ms. Kathy O'Keefe, Principal
Mr. William Sawyer, Director
Mr. John O'Keefe, Chairman/CEO
Mr. Kevin Keating, Vice President
Mr. Tom Wilczynski, Vice President
Ms. Diane Sweeney, Associate
Ms. Susan Moore, Associate
Ms. Kelly Sawyer, Associate
Mr. Athan Crist, Vice President
Mr. Bill Tohill, Vice President
Mr. Paul Sampson, President

Salary minimum: $100,000

Functions: Generalist, General Mgmt., Mfg., Materials, Sales & Mktg., HR Mgmt., Finance, IT

Industries: Generalist, Food, Bev., Tobacco, Soap, Perf., Cosmtcs., Drugs Mfg., Medical Devices, Mgmt. Consulting, Restaurants, Publishing, Wireless, Network Infrastructure, HR SW

Professional Associations: ESRT, FMI, NDMA, NYNMA

Branches:
54-585 Southern Hills
La Quinta, CA 92253
(760) 771-0142
Fax: (760) 771-3717
Email: rwallace@okeefeinc.com
Key Contact:
Mr. Robert Wallace, Principal

O'Neill & Company
40 Richards Ave
1 Norwalk W
Norwalk, CT 06854
(203) 857-0344
Email: oneillco@optonline.net

Description: We provide nationwide recruitment of senior and middle-level financial management, corporate finance, marketing, and consulting professionals.

Key Contact - Specialty:
Mr. Stephen O'Neill, Principal - *Financial management, marketing*

Salary minimum: $100,000

Functions: Generalist, Sales & Mktg., Mkt. Research, CFO's, Budgeting, Cash Mgmt., Risk Mgmt., Mgmt. Consultants

Industries: Generalist, Mfg., Food, Bev., Tobacco, Medical Devices, Finance, Mgmt. Consulting, Hospitality, Media, New Media, Software, Biotech

Professional Associations: IACMP

O'Rourke Companies Inc
4100 Int'l Plz Ste 530
Ft. Worth, TX 76109
(817) 735-8697
Fax: (817) 731-9130
Email: kro@orourke1.com

Description: Executive search/management consulting firm led by senior human resource professionals serving a broad base of industrial clients. Perform full range of human resource services designed to meet needs of the client.

Key Contact:
Ms. Rachel O'Rourke
Ms. Karen Oney

Salary minimum: $60,000

Functions: Generalist, Senior Mgmt., Middle Mgmt., Sales & Mktg., HR Mgmt., Finance, CFO's, Engineering

Industries: Generalist, Energy, Utilities, Paper, Misc. Mfg., Non-profits

O'Shea, Divine & Rivers Inc
(a member of EMA Partners Int'l company)
130 Newport Center Dr Ste 130
Newport Beach, CA 92660
(949) 720-9070
Fax: (949) 720-9628
Email: info@divinesearch.com
Web: www.divinesearch.com

Description: Generalist firm recruiting senior-level management, primarily manufacturing, distribution, healthcare, financial services, telecommunications, not-for-profit. National in scope, with concentration in Southern California. Affiliates in the major industrial nations.

Key Contact - Specialty:
Mr. Robert S. Divine, Partner
Ms. Geri S. Rivers, Partner - *Specialist*

Salary minimum: $100,000

Functions: Generalist

Industries: Generalist

Professional Associations: AESC

Networks: EMA Partners Int'l

Branches:
2805 Club Dr
Los Angeles, CA 90064
(310) 838-1714
Fax: (310) 839-6083
Email: gerivers@pacbell.net
Key Contact - Specialty:
Ms. Geri Rivers, President - *Generalist*

Dennis P O'Toole & Associates Inc
1865 Palmer Ave Ste 210
Larchmont, NY 10538
(914) 833-3712
(914) 833-3713
Fax: (914) 834-8911
Email: dpotooleassoc@aol.com

Description: A select executive search firm known for personalized service and in-depth recruitment of senior management and hard-to-find specialists for resort, hotel, club and entertainment industries.

Key Contact - Specialty:
Mr. Dennis P. O'Toole, President - *Hospitality, entertainment*

Salary minimum: $90,000

Functions: Generalist, Senior Mgmt., Middle Mgmt., Purchasing, Mktg. Mgmt., Sales Mgmt., HR Mgmt., CFO's

Industries: Generalist, Hospitality

Professional Associations: AESC

O'Toole & Company Inc
1047 Forest
Oak Park, IL 60302
(708) 848-6200

Description: Professional and experienced search for senior and middle management.

Key Contact:
Mr. William R. O'Toole, Principal
Ms. Nancy L. O'Toole, Principal

Salary minimum: $65,000

Functions: General Mgmt., Sales & Mktg., Finance, Cash Mgmt., Mgmt. Consultants

Industries: Generalist, Finance, Brokers, Services, Accounting, Mgmt. Consulting

Oak Technology Partners LLC
900 Larkspur Landing Cir Ste 165
Larkspur, CA 94939
(415) 464-4555
Fax: (415) 464-4550
Email: mraggio@oakllc.com

Description: We are a retained executive search firm specializing in the recruitment of key management talent in the technology industry. Areas of focus include general management, sales and marketing in the software industry.

Key Contact:
Mr. Matthew G. Raggio, Principal - *Officer level, software*
Mr. Scott Swimley, Partner

Salary minimum: $150,000

Functions: Senior Mgmt., Mktg. Mgmt., Sales Mgmt.

Industries: Venture Cap., Software

Ober & Company
11777 San Vicente Blvd Ste 620
Los Angeles, CA 90049
(310) 207-1127

Description: Broad based executive search practice with expertise in high-technology, financial services, information technology, logistics, manufacturing, healthcare and consulting.

Key Contact - Specialty:
Ms. Lynn W. Ober, President - *Generalist*

Salary minimum: $100,000

Functions: Generalist, General Mgmt., Mfg., Healthcare, Sales & Mktg., HR Mgmt., Finance, IT

Industries: Generalist, Mfg., Finance, Services, Software, Biotech, Healthcare

Oberlander & Co Inc
223 E State St
PO Box 789
Geneva, IL 60134
(630) 232-2600
Fax: (630) 232-9240
Email: hiosearch@aol.com

Description: Specialize in providing professional, confidential guidance in management selection.

Key Contact:
Mr. Howard I. Oberlander, President

Salary minimum: $100,000

Functions: Generalist

Industries: Generalist

The Ogdon Partnership
(a division of The Ogdon Group Inc)
375 Park Ave Ste 2409
New York, NY 10152-0175
(212) 308-1600
Fax: (212) 755-3819
Email: info@ogdon.com
Web: www.ogdon.com

Description: We provide general recruiting. We place an emphasis on marketing. We specialize in the areas of advertising/PR, publishing/editorial, direct response, legal/partner-to-partner/general counsel, financial services/high net worth, top management and board positions for venture-owned companies, and consumer packaged goods. We also specialize in new media, including general management, marketing, sales, financial management; and club management.

Key Contact - Specialty:
Mr. Thomas H. Ogdon - *Venture portfolios (CEO's, directors), communications, consumer products (general management executives)*

Ms. Cathy N. Hughes - *Communications, publishing (edit & business side), hospitality, direct mail*
Mr. Edward C. Mattes, Jr. - *New media, internet, legal, medical*
Mr. Anthony J. Iodice - *Sales & marketing, human resource management, finance & accounting, information technology, commercial banking*
Ms. Jane P. Wood - *Senior management, CFOs, cash management, finance, commercial banking*

Salary minimum: $100,000

Functions: General Mgmt., Directors, Senior Mgmt., Sales Mgmt., Direct Mktg., CFO's, Attorneys

Industries: Venture Cap., Legal, Hospitality, Advertising, Publishing, New Media

Professional Associations: IACPR

Ogilvie-Smartt Associates LLC
23 Davenport Way
Hillsborough, NJ 08844
(908) 359-8319
(610) 469-0413
Email: rudy.smartt@osasearch.com
Web: www.osasearch.com

Description: We are a retained executive search firm specializing in all areas of the pharmaceutical industry. Our areas of expertise are: all R&D functions, sales, marketing, business development, manufacturing, and supply chain searches.

Key Contact - Specialty:
Mr. Kit Ogilvie, Partner/Search Consultant - *Pharmaceuticals (R&D, sales & marketing, manufacturing, business development)*
Mr. Rudy Smartt, Partner/Search Consultant - *Sales & marketing, R&D, manufacturing, supply chain, business development*

Salary minimum: $120,000

Functions: Generalist

Industries: Drugs Mfg.

Professional Associations: IACPR

Branches:
104 Barton Dr
Spring City, PA 19475
(610) 469-0413
Email: kit.ogilvie@osasearch.com
Key Contact - Specialty:
Mr. Kit Ogilvie, Partner/Executive Search Consultant - *Pharmaceuticals*

The Oldani Group
188 - 106th Ave NE Ste 420
Bellevue, WA 98004
(425) 451-3938
Fax: (425) 453-6786
Email: searches@theoldanigroup.com
Web: www.theoldanigroup.com

Description: Firm has nationally prominent public sector practice and well established regional practice in not-for-profit. Exceptional skills in targeted recruitments, candidate evaluations and background checks.

Key Contact:
Mr. Jerrold Oldani, President
Ms. Andrea Oldani-Nutt, Vice President
Ms. Marcia Isenberg, Pacific Northwest Regional Affiliate
Ms. Teri Black Brann, California/Southwest Regional Affiliate
Ms. Andrea Battle Sims, Eastern Regional Affiliate
Ms. Jan Wiessner, Midwest Regional Affiliate

Salary minimum: $75,000

Functions: Generalist, Directors, Senior Mgmt., Health Admin., Mktg. Mgmt., MIS Mgmt., Minorities

Industries: Generalist, Construction, Transportation, Non-profits, Law Enforcement, Government

Professional Associations: ASAE, ICMA, NFBPA, SHRM

Oliver & Rozner Associates Inc
823 Walton Ave
Mamaroneck, NY 10543
(914) 381-6242

Description: In-depth recruitment expertise in general management, marketing, sales management, manufacturing, engineering, R&D, finance, information systems and other key staff functions. Reputation for thoroughness, penetrating assessment and careful attention to detail, planning and strategy.

Key Contact:
Mr. Burton L. Rozner, President

Salary minimum: $100,000

Functions: Generalist

Industries: Generalist

Professional Associations: AESC

Olschwanger Partners LLC
7522 Campbell Rd Ste 113-196
Dallas, TX 75248
(972) 931-9144
Fax: (972) 931-9194
Email: pfo@osearch.org
Web: www.osearch.com

Description: We offer a unique perspective and approach as an executive search and business consultant focusing exclusively within the money management industry. Fees are charged on a flat and performance-adjusted basis.

Key Contact - Specialty:
Mr. Paul F. Olschwanger, Managing Director - *Investment management, marketing, sales, client service, portfolio management*
Ms. Debra L. Olschwanger, Vice President - *Investment management, research, business consulting*

Functions: Product Dev., Sales & Mktg., Sales Mgmt., Cash Mgmt.

Industries: Finance, Misc. Financial

Professional Associations: AIMR

OnPoint Partners Inc
666 Old Country Rd Ste 207
Garden City, NY 11530
(516) 470-0747
Fax: (516) 470-6030
Email: info@onpointpartners.com
Web: www.onpointpartners.com

Description: Innovative, national executive search practice organized around financial services, insurance, healthcare and technology disciplines. Special focus on venture-backed start-ups in the e-commerce, B2B, and e-consulting market segments.

Key Contact:
Mr. John R. Prufeta, Chairman
Mr. Scott R. Stern, President
Mr. Robert J. Prufeta, Managing Partner
Mr. John R. Schoonmaker, Managing Partner
Mrs. Tara J. Quinn, Managing Partner/Operations
Ms. Michelle Germano, Managing Partner
Miss Claudia Londono, Director of Research & Development
Mrs. JoAnn Porcelli, Director of Finance

Salary minimum: $75,000

Functions: Generalist

Industries: Venture Cap., Misc. Financial, Services, Mgmt. Consulting, HR Services, Insurance, Software, Healthcare

Professional Associations: AAHP, HIMSS

The Onstott Group
60 William St
Wellesley, MA 02481
(781) 235-3050
Fax: (781) 235-8653
Email: info@onstott.com
Web: www.onstott.com

Description: Retained search firm specializing in recruiting executives for most functional disciplines and industries. Concentration in high-technology, telecommunications, manufacturing, consumer goods, financial and other service businesses and growth industries. International capability.

Key Contact:
Mr. Ben Beaver, Managing Director
Ms. Patricia Campbell, Managing Director
Mr. Joe Onstott, Managing Director

Salary minimum: $150,000

Functions: Generalist

Industries: Generalist

Professional Associations: AESC

Networks: World Search Group

Branches:
1 First St Ste 9
Los Altos, CA 94022
(650) 917-8317
Fax: (650) 917-9794
Key Contact:
Ms. Mary S. Dean, Vice President

Oppedisano & Company Inc
370 Lexington Ave Ste 1200
New York, NY 10017
(212) 696-0144
Fax: (212) 686-3006
Email: oppsearch@aol.com

Description: Our firm provides executive search, merger/acquisition and other consultative services exclusively to the investment management industry.

Key Contact - Specialty:
Mr. Edward Oppedisano, Chairman/CEO - *Investment management, sales & marketing of investment management products, investment research*

Functions: Sales & Mktg.

Industries: Misc. Financial

Opportunity Resources Inc
25 W 43rd St Ste 1017
New York, NY 10036
(212) 575-1688
Fax: (212) 575-0297
Email: search@opportunityresources.net

Description: We have the distinction of being a highly specialized and nationally recognized, retained executive search firm for not-for-profit and cultural organizations. We are results-oriented and tailor each search to meet our clients' needs.

Key Contact - Specialty:
Ms. Freda Mindlin, President - *Non-profit organizations, CEO, mid-management*

Salary minimum: $75,000

Functions: Senior Mgmt.

Industries: Non-profits

Professional Associations: AESC

Organization Consulting Ltd
156 Duncan Mill Rd Ste 5
Don Mills, ON M3B 3N2
Canada
(416) 385-9972
(416) 385-9975

Email: resumes@organizationconsulting.ca
Web: www.organizationconsulting.ca

Description: We are a retainer-based firm and have 20 years of Canadian and US experience at the executive and board levels. OCL's mission is to be a distinguished executive search practice. Although we are small in size, we are large in scope. We are noted for service excellence and building long-term relationships with our clients.

Key Contact:
Mr. Robert F. Johnston, CMC, President
Mr. Terry MacGorman, Principal
Mr. Hugh Farrell, Principal
Ms. Julie Aggio, Research Manager

Salary minimum: $100,000

Functions: General Mgmt., Directors, Senior Mgmt.

Industries: Generalist

Professional Associations: CAMC, IMC

Organizational Resources Inc
(see listing for Executive Resources Int'l LLC)

Orion Consulting Inc
115 Rte 46 Bldg B Ste 13/14
Mountain Lakes, NJ 07046
(973) 402-8866
Fax: (973) 402-9258
Email: oci@orionconsultinginc.com
Web: www.orionconsultinginc.com

Description: Management consulting firm providing retained executive search, organizational development, training, general on and off-site human resource services.

Key Contact - Specialty:
Mr. James V. Dromsky, CEO - *Executive search*
Mr. William Mann, Sr Vice President - *Human resources, consulting*

Salary minimum: $60,000

Functions: Generalist

Industries: Mfg., Invest. Banking, Accounting, Mgmt. Consulting, HR Services, Media, Telecoms, Defense, Aerospace, Packaging, Biotech

Professional Associations: SHRM

Ott & Hansen Inc
1150 Foothill Blvd Ste J
La Canada, CA 91011
(818) 790-0971
Fax: (818) 790-0980
Email: otthansen@aol.com

Description: Boutique firm. Two principals have over 30 years each in generalist search experience. Over 60% of clients are privately owned/closely controlled public companies with $30-300 million revenue.

Key Contact - Specialty:
Mr. George W. Ott, Chairman - *Management (upper-level), general, directors*
Mr. David G. Hansen, President - *Management (upper-level), general*

Salary minimum: $80,000

Functions: General Mgmt., Mfg., Sales & Mktg., HR Mgmt., Finance

Industries: Generalist

Ovca Associates Inc
67 Hillsdale Dr
Newport Beach, CA 92660
(949) 640-2603
Fax: (949) 640-1620

Description: National generalist practice delivering high value-added services to clients in a wide range of industries.

Key Contact:
Mr. William J. Ovca, Jr., President

Salary minimum: $75,000

Functions: Generalist

Industries: Generalist

Overton Consulting
10303 N Port Washington Rd
Mequon, WI 53092
(262) 241-0200
Fax: (414) 241-8291
Email: info@overtonconsulting.com
Web: www.overtonconsulting.com

Description: Retained executive search firm offering tailored recruitment services at executive and director-levels. Strength in academics, financial services, country club management and office products. Full in-house research capabilities.

Key Contact - Specialty:
Mr. Justin V. Strom, Managing Partner - *Financial services, outsourcing*
Mr. Raymond N. Thurber, Partner - *Office product manufacturers*
Ms. Nancy R. Noeske, Ph.D., Partner/Practice Manager - *Academic, non-profit*
Mr. Robert Hutchison, Partner - *Financial services, human resources*
Mr. Fred Swider, Partner - *Country club management*

Salary minimum: $70,000

Functions: Generalist, General Mgmt., Senior Mgmt., Middle Mgmt., Plant Mgmt., Sales & Mktg., CFO's, Non-profits

Industries: Construction, Mfg., Food, Bev., Tobacco, Paper, Finance, Services, Non-profits, Higher Ed., Hospitality, Real Estate

Professional Associations: BPIA, EMA, ICSA, NCA, SHOPA, SHRM

Merle W Owens & Associates
301 Commerce St Ste 2876
Ft. Worth, TX 76102
(817) 335-1776
Fax: (817) 335-1576
Email: search@merle-owens.com

Description: We are a true generalist executive search firm. We have a large long-time client base. We have senior consultants with broad industry and search experience. In 1999, we established a new division, Precise; to fill clients' needs for vital support roles, such as executive assistants, staff accountants, marketing/sales support, IT/IS engineers, call center experts, and other para-professionals.

Key Contact - Specialty:
Mr. Merle W. Owens, Principal - *Energy, manufacturing, healthcare, finance, business services*
Mr. Ivan G. Boon, Consultant - *Manufacturing, finance, aerospace, consumer products*
Ms. Jennifer Owens Dowdy, Consultant - *Medical, healthcare, manufacturing, not-for-profit, business service*
Mr. Jesse W. Owens, Consultant - *Manufacturing, communications, high tech, software, business services*

Salary minimum: $50,000

Functions: Generalist

Industries: Generalist

The Owens Group LLC
7720 Wisconsin Ave Ste 208
Bethesda, MD 20814-3577
(301) 229-2700
Email: tgo@owenssearch.com
Web: www.owenssearch.com

Description: We are focused on mid to senior level postings in e-Commerce, energy, engineering, finance, life, sciences, technology, real estate, construction and assocations. We believe the most important decisions organizations make are about people.

Key Contact:
Mr. Thomas Owens, President

Salary minimum: $100,000

Functions: Senior Mgmt., Middle Mgmt., Sales & Mktg., HR Mgmt., CFO's, MIS Mgmt.

Industries: Energy, Utilities, Construction, Finance, Non-profits, Legal, HR Services, Real Estate, Biotech

---

LaMonte Owens Inc†
PO Box 27742
Philadelphia, PA 19118
(215) 248-0500
Fax: (215) 233-3737
Email: lowens@voicenet.com
Web: www.lo-diversityrecruiting.com

Description: Thirty one years in specialized recruiting of minority and female professional, managerial and executive placement. Diversity recruiters.

Key Contact - Specialty:
Mr. LaMonte Owens, President - *Generalist, diversity recruiting*

Salary minimum: $40,000

Functions: Generalist, Admin. Svcs., Production, Distribution, Sales Mgmt., Systems Dev., Minorities

Industries: Generalist, Energy, Utilities, Drugs Mfg., Finance, HR Services, Software

Professional Associations: EMA, MAAPC, SHRM

P A R Associates Inc
23 West Bay Rd
Osterville, MA 02655
(508) 420-2372
(800) 446-5291
Fax: (508) 420-9268
Email: peter@parassoc.com
Web: www.parassoc.com

Description: We provide general business search practice. We place heavy emphasis on most senior corporate positions ($175K on up), in particular pre-IPO healthcare related companies, especially e-Commerce (ASP through ".com"), telemedicine, medical device equipment, and biotech. We have a strong referral base through East/West coast venture capital community.

Key Contact - Specialty:
Mr. Peter A. Rabinowitz, President - *Healthcare, technology, e-commerce, operations, startups*

Salary minimum: $175,000

Functions: General Mgmt., Healthcare, Physicians, Sales & Mktg., Mktg. Mgmt., Finance, CFO's, IT, MIS Mgmt.

Industries: Generalist, Drugs Mfg., Medical Devices, Services, Pharm Svcs., Insurance, Biotech, Healthcare

Networks: Int'l Search Assoc (ISA)

The Pacific Firm†

2501 9th St Ste 102
Berkeley, CA 94710
(510) 647-1000
Fax: (510) 647-1010
Email: david@pacfirm.com
Web: www.pacfirm.com

Description: Ranked as the number one retained search firm by the San Francisco Business Times, we are the leader in "unbundled" staffing services with offices in the Bay Area, and the Midwest. We specialize in identifying and attracting senior-level executives for emerging companies.

Key Contact - Specialty:
Ms. Stacie Blair, CEO - *Emerging industries*
Mr. David Cain, CFO - *E-commerce, telecom, financial services, publishing*

Salary minimum: $75,000

Functions: General Mgmt., Mfg., Materials, Healthcare, Sales & Mktg., HR Mgmt., Finance, MIS Mgmt.

Industries: Generalist

Branches:
338 Main St Ste 2
Waukesha, WI 53186
(262) 524-8200
Fax: (262) 521-2747
Email: debbie@pacfirm.com
Key Contact:
Ms. Debbie Gale, Managing Director

Page-Wheatcroft & Company Ltd

12222 Merit Dr Ste 450
Dallas, TX 75251
(214) 696-4333
Fax: (214) 696-9595
Email: spage@p-wco.com
Web: www.p-wco.com

Description: National general management search practice with expertise in: financial services, government, law firms, strategy, management and information technology consulting firms and technology driven Fortune 500 companies.

Key Contact - Specialty:
Mr. Stephen J. L. Page, Chairman/CEO - *Senior-level partners & senior executives (law firms, consulting firms, technology-driven businesses)*
Mr. Carl L. Blonkvist, President/COO - *Consulting practice*
Mr. Charles P Campbell, Managing Partner - *Consulting practice*
Ms. Patricia D. McNicholas, Managing Partner - *Consulting practice*
Mrs. Julie Bell, Executive Assistant to CEO - *Consulting practice*

Salary minimum: $200,000

Functions: Generalist, Senior Mgmt., Legal, Mktg. Mgmt., MIS Mgmt., Mgmt. Consultants, Attorneys

Industries: Generalist, Finance, Legal, Mgmt. Consulting, Software

Pailin Group Professional Search Consultants

1412 Main St Ste 601
Center City Plz
Dallas, TX 75202-4018
(214) 752-6100
Fax: (214) 752-6101
Email: pailingroupps@compuserve.com
Web: www.pailingroup.com

Description: We are a firm that recruits management professionals in the following disciplines: accounting, finance, sales, marketing, information technology, engineering, human resources, retail, and health care. Our clients are premier Fortune and major non-profit organizations

that refuse to compromise in the selection of their greatest assets, their people.

Key Contact - Specialty:
Mr. David L. Pailin, Sr., Senior Partner - *Accounting & finance, sales & marketing, media relations*
Ms. Cheryl Pailin, Senior Administrative Partner - *Contract administration, manufacturing, engineering*
Ms. Debra Hosey, Senior Consultant - *Human resources, organizational development, organizational design*
Mr. Robert Martin, Sr., Senior Consultant - *Healthcare, legal*
Ms. Roxxanne Miller, Senior Consultant - *Insurance, financial services, banking, sales, marketing*
Ms. Joan Cox, Accounting & Finance Division Manager - *Accounting & finance*
Mr. Paul Simpson, Sr., Senior Consultant - *Information technology, MIS, data services, networks, software development*
Mr. Joseph Pailin, Jr., General Manager - *Insurance, sales, finance, bonds, trust*

Salary minimum: $75,000

Functions: Generalist, Plant Mgmt., Purchasing, Advertising, Personnel, Cash Mgmt., Systems Analysis, Attorneys

Industries: Generalist, Energy, Utilities, Mfg., Finance, Media, Software, Healthcare

Professional Associations: AESC, IACPR, MHRA, SHRM

Palacios & Associates Inc†

PO Box 362437
San Juan, PR 00936-2437
(787) 761-8160
(787) 622-6433
Fax: (787) 761-8180
Email: jpa@jpalacios.com
Web: www.jpalacios.com

Description: Professional executive search with strong emphasis on ethics and confidentiality. Search leader for the pharmaceutical, biotechnology, chemical and medical device industries, serving most positions. Certified Consultants on the Myers Briggs type psychological indicators and its applications. Over 80% repeated business every year.

Key Contact:
Ms. Jeannette C. De Palacios, CPC, President
Ms. Myrgia M. Palacios, CPC, Vice President

Salary minimum: $50,000

Functions: Generalist

Industries: Generalist, Mfg., Retail, Finance, Services, Hospitality, Media, Software, Biotech, Healthcare

Professional Associations: AIIE, NAER, NAPS, PRMA, SHRM, SME

Kirk Palmer & Associates Inc

500 5th Ave Ste 1500
New York, NY 10110
(212) 983-6477
Fax: (212) 599-2597
Email: resume@kirkpalmer.com
Web: www.kirkpalmer.com

Description: Recognized authorities in the retail and apparel industries. Client base includes many of the top retail and apparel companies in America. Proven expertise in senior management searches within all functional areas.

Key Contact:
Mr. Kirk Palmer, President
Ms. Leslie Cook, Senior Vice President

Salary minimum: $100,000

Functions: Senior Mgmt., Product Dev., Sales & Mktg., Mktg. Mgmt., Sales Mgmt., Direct Mktg., HR Mgmt., Finance, CFO's, IT

Industries: Textiles, Apparel, Wholesale, Retail, Finance

Branches:
122 Maumell St
Hinsdale, IL 60521
(630) 321-0535
Fax: (630) 321-0537
Key Contact:
Ms. Anna Worner, Vice President

306 Moulton St
Hamilton, MA 01982
(978) 468-2485
Fax: (978) 468-4663
Key Contact:
Ms. Leslie Cook, Senior Vice President

Palmer & Company Executive Recruitment Inc

69 Bloor St E Ste 310
Toronto, ON M4W 1A9
Canada
(416) 975-9595
Fax: (416) 975-9068
Email: execsearch@palmerco.ca
Web: www.palmerco.ca

Description: Our practice spans most sectors and industries and we conduct searches at the senior or officer level.

Key Contact:
Mr. Mark Palmer, President
Ms. Elaine Sigurdson, Principal

Salary minimum: $90,000

Pamenter, Pamenter, Brezer & Deganis Ltd

4 Eva Rd Ste 400
Etobicoke, ON M9C 2A8
Canada
(416) 620-5980
Fax: (416) 620-5074

Description: Our search work is usually performed in conjunction with reorganization projects. Recently we conducted a major human resources restructuring project for a leading business school using our employment model.

Key Contact - Specialty:
Mr. Fred Pamenter, President - *University administration, senior executive*
Mr. Craig Pamenter, Recruiter - *Mid-level management*

Salary minimum: $50,000

Functions: Generalist, General Mgmt., Senior Mgmt., Middle Mgmt., Mktg. Mgmt., PR, HR Mgmt., CFO's

Industries: Generalist, Food, Bev., Tobacco, Printing, Misc. Mfg., Higher Ed., Publishing, Packaging, Healthcare

Pappas DeLaney LLC

710 N Plankinton Ave Ste 726
Empire Bldg
Milwaukee, WI 53203
(414) 271-1967
Fax: (414) 271-1981
Email: pdl@pappasdelaney.com

Description: Specializes in highly targeted recruiting for employer clients in the Midwest including board directorships and senior management positions.

Key Contact - Specialty:
Mr. Timothy C. Pappas, Principal - *Generalist*
Ms. Patricia DeLaney Lang, Principal - *Generalist*

Salary minimum: $75,000

---

† occasional contingency assignments

Functions: Generalist, General Mgmt., Mfg., Materials, Health Admin., Sales & Mktg., Risk Mgmt.

Industries: Generalist, Construction, Mfg., Food, Bev., Tobacco, Chemicals, Banking, Insurance, Healthcare

Professional Associations: IMC, SHRM

The PAR Group
(also known as Paul A Reaume Ltd)
100 N Waukegan Rd Ste 200
Lake Bluff, IL 60044
(847) 234-0005
Fax: (847) 234-8309
Email: pargroup@interaccess.com

Description: Searches for top management and senior staff in local government and related organizations and not-for-profit associations (i.e. city manager, police chief, public works director; executive director and association managers).

Key Contact - Specialty:
Mr. Paul A. Reaume, President - *Public, non-profit*
Mr. Robert A. Beezat, Vice President - *Public, non-profit*
Mr. Gerald E. Hagman, Vice President - *Public, non-profit*
Mr. Gregory T. Kuhn, Vice President - *Public, non-profit*
Mr. G. Stevens Bernard, Vice President - *Public, non-profit*

Salary minimum: $45,000

Functions: Senior Mgmt., Middle Mgmt., CFO's, Budgeting, Engineering, Minorities, Environmentalists

Industries: Non-profits, Mgmt. Consulting, HR Services, Law Enforcement, Government, Non-classifiable

Paradigm Technologies Inc[†]
4706 Alton
Troy, MI 48098
(248) 524-9762
Fax: (248) 524-0347
Email: jbeyer@paradigmtechweb.com
Web: www.paradigmtechweb.com

Description: We are at the forefront of recruiting automotive executives who are the pioneers at "world class organizations."

Key Contact - Specialty:
Mr. Joe Beyer, President - *Automotive, executive management, engineering, plant management*
Ms. Melissa Beyer, Vice President - *Automotive, marketing, accounting, human resources*
Mr. Dan Beyer, Recruiter - *Automotive, materials, manufacturing, engineering*
Mr. O'Hara Near, Recruiter - *Information technology*
Mr. Joe Heffernan, Recruiter - *Automotive manufacturing, operations*

Salary minimum: $70,000

Functions: Generalist

Industries: Motor Vehicles

Parenica & Company
19250 Stableford Ln
Cornelius, NC 28031
(704) 896-0060
Email: parenica@sprintmail.com

Description: I conduct 8-10 retained executive search assignments per year, focusing on senior-level information technology and telecommunications management assignments.

Key Contact - Specialty:
Mr. Jim Parenica, President - *Information technology, telecommunications*

Salary minimum: $125,000

Functions: General Mgmt., Senior Mgmt., MIS Mgmt.

Industries: Energy, Utilities, Textiles, Apparel, Mgmt. Consulting

Parente Search LLC
204 S Franklin St
Wilkes-Barre, PA 18701
(570) 829-5066
Fax: (570) 820-8293
Email: check204@aol.com

Description: Near 100% completion rate; deep, long-term client commitments; 75% of volume is repeat business; performance-based contracts; competitively favorable fee and expense structures; clients cite our outperformance of major retainer firms previously used.

Key Contact - Specialty:
Mr. Andrew D. Check, President - *Manufacturing*

Salary minimum: $60,000

Functions: Generalist

Industries: Mfg., Accounting, Mgmt. Consulting, HR Services, Advertising, Telecoms, Healthcare

Jim Parham & Associates Inc[†]
6700 S Florida Ave Ste 33
Lakeland, FL 33813-3312
(863) 644-7097
Web: www.jimparham.com

Description: Specialized executive search for the motor freight industry (LTL,T/L, hazardous haulers, flatbed, tank carriers, refrigerated, van, logistics).

Key Contact - Specialty:
Mr. Jim Parham, President - *Transportation*

Salary minimum: $35,000

Functions: Generalist, General Mgmt., Directors, Senior Mgmt., Middle Mgmt., Distribution, CFO's, MIS Mgmt.

Industries: Generalist, Transportation

Frank Parillo & Associates
1801 E Heim Ave Ste 200
Orange, CA 92865
(714) 921-8008
Email: fparillo@pacbell.net
Web: www.frankparillo.qpg.com

Description: We are serving large, middle, and small companies in the biotechnology, pharmaceutical, biopharmaceuticals medical diagnostics (in vivo and invitro), medical device industries, as well as venture capital-based start-ups. We are focused on middle and senior management. We conduct searches for all executive functions, including general management, research and development, manufacturing, marketing, sales, regulatory affairs, quality assurance, quality control, HR, and engineering.

Key Contact:
Mr. Frank Parillo, President

Salary minimum: $50,000

Functions: Generalist, Senior Mgmt., Middle Mgmt., Product Dev., Production, Mktg. Mgmt., Sales Mgmt., R&D

Industries: Generalist, Chemicals, Drugs Mfg., Medical Devices, Biotech

Professional Associations: AAAS, AACC, ACS

D P Parker & Associates Inc
372 Washington St
Wellesley, MA 02481
(781) 237-1220
Fax: (781) 237-4702
Email: info@dpparker.com
Web: www.dpparker.com

Description: Founded by David P. Parker (ScD.,MIT-Metallurgy). Specialize in R&D/marketing/operations and general management in specialty materials and chemicals, biotechnology, aerospace, electronics and other technically based industries.

Key Contact:
Dr. David P. Parker, President

Salary minimum: $100,000

Functions: Senior Mgmt.

Industries: Chemicals, Drugs Mfg., Plastics, Rubber, Metal Products, Aerospace, Biotech

Professional Associations: AESC, ACS, AICHE, CDMA

Parsons Associates Inc
980 N Michigan Ave Ste 1400
Chicago, IL 60611-4501
(312) 475-9660
Fax: (312) 475-9661
Email: sue.parsons@att.net

Description: Small firm that emphasizes a strong degree of communication and close relationships with a select group of client companies in need of highly talented middle and senior management executives.

Key Contact - Specialty:
Ms. Sue N. Parsons, President - *Generalist*

Salary minimum: $75,000

Functions: Directors, Senior Mgmt., Middle Mgmt., Plant Mgmt., Sales Mgmt., CFO's, MIS Mgmt.

Industries: Generalist, Agri., Forestry, Mining, Mfg., Wholesale, Retail, Finance, Services, Hospitality, Communications, Packaging, Insurance

Professional Associations: HRMAC

Partners Executive Search Consultants Inc
163 Glenvale Blvd
Toronto, ON M4G 2W4
Canada
(416) 467-6812
Fax: (416) 467-8892
Email: randyq@ultratech.net

Description: Interactive and emerging industry specialists

Key Contact - Specialty:
Mr. Randy Quarin, Partner - *New media*

Functions: Generalist

Industries: Advertising, Publishing, New Media, Broadcast, Film, Software

The Partnership Group
7 Becker Farm Rd
Roseland, NJ 07068
(973) 535-8566
Fax: (973) 535-6408
Email: schwartz.tpg@att.net
Web: www.partnershipgroup.com

Description: Human resource consultancy specializing in retained executive search with emphasis on strategic client partnerships. We offer sustained size and critical mass to be effective, but are committed to intense personal service.

Key Contact - Specialty:
Mr. Peter T. Maher, President/CEO - *Financial services, service industries, senior management*
Mr. Raymond Schwartz, EVP/Operations - *Pharmaceutical, telecommunications, vice presidents, top management*
Mr. Michael T. Bucci, SVP-Client Development - *Consumer packaged goods, advertising, middle to senior management*

Salary minimum: $75,000

Functions: Generalist, Middle Mgmt., Plant Mgmt., Health Admin., Mktg. Mgmt., Benefits, CFO's, Mgmt. Consultants

Industries: Generalist, Leather, Stone, Glass, Test, Measure Equip., Finance, HR Services, Healthcare

Professional Associations: RAPS, SCIP, TIA

Partnervision Consulting Group Inc
500 Queens Quay W Ste 908W
Toronto, ON M5V 3K8
Canada
(416) 360-6688
(416) 360-0016
Email: info@partnervision.net
Web: www.partnervision.net

Description: We opened our doors in 1991 as an executive search firm. We conduct executive to senior management searches with proven expertise in human resources, corporate services and finance recruiting. Technologically driven, we use a multipronged search strategy to source the best candidates to staff your positions. www.partnervision.net

Key Contact:
Ms. Lynn Lefebvre, President - *Generalist*
Ms. Kelly McGregor, Business/Project Manager
Mr. Chris Ronneseth, Systems Manager

Salary minimum: $60,000

Functions: General Mgmt., Sales & Mktg., HR Mgmt., Finance

Industries: Generalist

Professional Associations: CHRPS, HRPAO, HRPS

Partridge Associates Inc†
1200 Providence Hwy
Sharon, MA 02067
(781) 784-4144
Fax: (781) 784-4780
Email: robert@partridgeassociates.com
Web: www.partridgeassociates.com

Description: Executive search organization specializing in recruitment for corporate and unit level positions in the hospitality industry. Twenty years of industry experience in hotels, restaurants and food service.

Key Contact:
Mr. Robert J. Partridge, President

Salary minimum: $50,000

Functions: Generalist

Industries: Hospitality

Professional Associations: IACPR, SHRM

Paschal•Murray Executive Search
611 W G St Ste 500
San Diego, CA 92101-5956
(619) 702-8881
Fax: (619) 702-8883
Email: info@paschalmurray.com
Web: www.paschalmurray.com

Description: Working on retainer, we are experts in assisting universities, hospitals, corporations, and non-profit organizations in placing senior and mid-level executives in fund raising, public relations and management positions.

Key Contact - Specialty:
Ms. Colette Murray, President/CEO - *Fundraising, public relations, education management, non-profit management*

Salary minimum: $60,000

Functions: General Mgmt., PR, Non-profits

Industries: Generalist, Drugs Mfg., Non-profits, Higher Ed., Pharm Svcs., Advertising, Healthcare

Professional Associations: AFP, AHP, CASE, IABC, NAER, PRSA

L Patrick & Steeple LLP
150 JFK Pkwy Ste 100
Short Hills, NJ 07078
(973) 847-5932
Fax: (973) 847-6012

Description: Full and modified retained search services. Generalist firm serving most industries and functions.

Key Contact:
Mr. Louis P. Giordano, Partner - *Generalist*
Ms. Dianne Eden, Partner

Salary minimum: $75,000

Functions: Generalist, Senior Mgmt., Middle Mgmt., Mfg., Materials, MIS Mgmt., Engineering

Industries: Generalist

Paul-Tittle Associates Inc
1485 Chain Bridge Rd Ste 304
McLean, VA 22101
(703) 442-0500
Fax: (703) 893-3871
Email: pta@paul-tittle.com
Web: www.paul-tittle.com

Description: Executive search and enterprise recruiting projects for information technology, telecommunications, Internet and interactive multi-media industries. Specializes in mid- and senior-level management and individual contributors in sales, marketing and technology components of above industries.

Key Contact - Specialty:
Mr. David M. Tittle, President - *Information technology*
Mr. Ron Cimino, COO - *E-commerce, telecommunications marketing*
Ms. Yvonne Crosier, Director - *Call centers, customer care, marketing, e-commerce*
Ms. Denise Wertheim, Director - *Federal programs, revenue assurance*
Mr. Malcolm Martin, Director - *Telecom engineering, operations & technology*
Ms. Laura Bryant, Director - *IT, engineering, OSS*
Mr. Clayton Witt, VP-Telephony Practice - *Telecommunications sales*
Ms. Becky Nolton, VP-Telecom Practice - *Telecommunications sales, telecommunications marketing*
Mr. Burt Heacock, Executive Vice President - *Engineering, IT*
Mr. Bruce Phinney, VP- Finance & Accounting - *CFO's*
Ms. Elizabeth Fawkes, Director - *E-commerce, internet content, marketing*

Salary minimum: $80,000

Functions: Generalist, Directors, Senior Mgmt., Middle Mgmt., Sales & Mktg., HR Mgmt., CFO's, IT, Mgmt. Consultants

Industries: Finance, Services, New Media, Telecoms, Government, Defense, Software

---

Peachtree Executive Search
10800 Alpharetta Hwy Ste 208
PO Box 481
Roswell, GA 30076
(770) 998-2272

Description: A small firm focusing on quality service to clients, primarily in the Southeast U.S. with a broad client base.

Key Contact - Specialty:
Mr. Mark F. Snoddy, Jr., President - *General practice*

Salary minimum: $70,000

Functions: Generalist, Senior Mgmt., Plant Mgmt., Mktg. Mgmt., Sales Mgmt., MIS Mgmt., R&D, Technicians

Industries: Generalist, Chemicals, Drugs Mfg., Advertising, Packaging, Insurance, Software

---

The Peak Organization
25 W 31st St
New York, NY 10001-4413
(212) 792-7600
Fax: (212) 792-7698
Web: www.peakorg.com

Description: We bring over ten years of experience in the automotive aftermarket, heavy duty and transportation industries to partner with companies that range from Internet startups to established Fortune 500 players. Specializing in the permanent placement of mid- to senior-level executives, we successfully fill searches that require both industry-specific and discipline-specific knowledge.

Key Contact:
Ms. Beth Schramm, Managing Director
Ms. Michelle Persaud, Associate Director

Salary minimum: $50,000

Functions: Generalist

Industries: Motor Vehicles, Transportation

Professional Associations: APAA, ASIA, SEMA

Pearson & Associates Inc
7400 E McDonald Dr Ste 121
Scottsdale, AZ 85250
(480) 368-9100
(800) 541-3384
Fax: (480) 778-1777
Email: chuck@pearson-assoc.com
Web: www.pearson-assoc.com

Description: We recruit key individuals for clients who trust our vast experience, nationwide network of contacts, our imagination, perseverance, speed, and discretion.

Key Contact - Specialty:
Mr. Chuck Pearson, CEO - *Flat panel displays, executive management high tech*
Ms. Diane Bell, Vice President - *Executive management, entertainment, multimedia*
Mr. Jeff L. Heyden, Managing Director Automotive Practice
Mr. Siebe van der Zee, Managing Director
Mr. Jeff Nelson, Director CFO practice - *CFO's*
Mr. Lawrence Liakos, Director Display Practice - *Displays*
Mr. Bill Haugen, Director - *Pulp and paper*

Salary minimum: $125,000

Functions: Generalist, Senior Mgmt., Middle Mgmt.

Industries: Energy, Utilities, Lumber, Furniture, Paper, Chemicals, Motor Vehicles, Computer Equip., Consumer Elect., Finance, Venture Cap., Services, Mgmt. Consulting, Hospitality, Media, Advertising, Telecoms, Fiber Optic, Software, Entertainment SW

Peck & Associates Ltd
250 S Main St
Thiensville, WI 53092
(262) 238-8700
Fax: (262) 238-9525
Email: jdowning@peckltd.com

Description: Our goal is to exceed our client's expectations. We use a project-driven methodology. Each project is custom designed to meet your needs. We help you make informed choices.

Key Contact:
Ms. Judi Downing

---

† occasional contingency assignments

Functions: Generalist, Directors, Senior Mgmt., Mfg., Benefits, Mgmt. Consultants

Industries: Generalist, Finance

Paul S Pelland PC
51 Charlotte St
Charleston, SC 29403-6440
(843) 853-2757
Email: pelland@bellsouth.net

Description: Foundry and secondary machining/forming specialists. Emphasis on executive and senior management, marketing and technological professionals. Most metal working areas. Emphasis on foundry clients industry worldwide.

Key Contact - Specialty:
Mr. Paul S. Pelland, Senior Partner - *Foundry, primary metals, metal working*
Ms. Jane A. Taylor, Research Administrator - *Foundry, primary metals, metal working*

Salary minimum: $60,000

Functions: General Mgmt., Middle Mgmt., Mfg., Production, Automation, Plant Mgmt., Quality, Sales & Mktg., Sales Mgmt., Engineering

Industries: Mfg., Metal Products, Misc. Mfg.

Professional Associations: ADPA, AFS, ASNT, ASQ

Penn Associates
1500 JFK Blvd Ste 200
2 Penn Ctr Plz
Philadelphia, PA 19102
(215) 854-6336
Email: dickersn@concentric.net

Description: Consulting firm specializing in the recruitment of middle and upper-level human resource executives. We handle search assignments worldwide and provide research services. We bring innovative solutions to staffing problems.

Key Contact - Specialty:
Mr. Joseph A. Dickerson, Principal - *Human resources*

Salary minimum: $80,000

Functions: HR Mgmt., Benefits, Personnel, Training, Mgmt. Consultants

Industries: Generalist

Professional Associations: ASTD, IHRIM, ODN, SHRM, WAW

The Penn Partners Inc
230 S Broad St Fl 19
Philadelphia, PA 19102
(215) 568-9285
Fax: (215) 568-1277

Description: Generalist retainer based search practice. Specializing at the senior and middle management level.

Key Contact - Specialty:
Ms. Kathleen M. Shea, President - *Generalist*
Mr. John F. Smith, Vice President - *Generalist*
Ms. Karen M. Swartz, Manager - *Generalist*
Ms. Cheryl L. Littman, Manager - *Generalist*

Salary minimum: $75,000

Functions: Generalist, General Mgmt., Senior Mgmt., Middle Mgmt., Sales & Mktg., HR Mgmt., Finance

Industries: Generalist, Mfg., Food, Bev., Tobacco, Drugs Mfg., Machine, Appliance, Consumer Elect., Finance, Mgmt. Consulting

Professional Associations: IACPR

People Management Mid-South LLC
2021 21st Ave S Ste 304
Nashville, TN 37212
(615) 463-2800
Fax: (615) 463-2944
Email: info@jobfitmatters.com
Web: www.jobfitmatters.com

Description: We specialize in retained executive search, selection and consultation on issues related to job fit.

Key Contact:
Mr. Tommy Thomas, President/CEO - *Generalist*
Mr. Robert Benson, Vice President

Salary minimum: $75,000

Functions: Generalist

Industries: Generalist

People Management Northeast Inc
1 Darling Dr
Avon, CT 06001
(860) 678-8900
Web: www.jobfit-pmi.com

Description: Our focus is on achieving a sound job fit. This objective is enhanced by our SIMA® assessment process which provides an extra dimension of insight into an individual's motivated abilities which are critical to the successful performance in any job.

Key Contact - Specialty:
Mr. Steven Darter, President - *Generalist, insurance, managed care, manufacturing, general management, senior management's*
Mr. James Bond, Vice President - *Generalist, information systems, life insurance, general management, managed care*
Ms. Karla Hammond, Vice President - *Generalist, human resources, public relations, communications, e-commerce*
Mr. Brian Beaudin, Vice President - *Generalist, general manager, manufacturing, human resources*

Salary minimum: $75,000

Functions: Generalist, General Mgmt., Mfg., Sales & Mktg., HR Mgmt., Finance, IT

Industries: Generalist, Mfg., Services, Insurance, Software, Healthcare

The People Network Inc[†]
400 Northridge Rd Ste 950
Atlanta, GA 30350
(770) 558-1700
Fax: (770) 558-1710
Email: admin@peoplenetwork.com
Web: www.peoplenetwork.com

Description: A full-service IT staffing firm servicing Atlanta and the Southeast. Positions range from help desk to CIO. Candidates seeking permanent, contract or contract-to-perm are all welcome.

Key Contact - Specialty:
Mr. Richard Lewis, CPA, President - *Information technology*

Functions: IT

Industries: Generalist

Professional Associations: GAPS

Networks: Top Echelon Network

People Solutions Executive Search
12740 Hillcrest Rd Ste 110
Dallas, TX 75230
(972) 550-9116
Fax: (972) 580-7929
Email: ellen.menking@people-solutions.com
Web: www.people-solutions.com

Description: Our firm has proven and specialized experience in placing mid- to executive-level human resource professionals nationally. Our highly specialized service and strategic solutions combining research, sourcing and technology with an expansive network - focused on results.

Key Contact - Specialty:
Mr. Ed Rankin, SPHR, CEO - *Executives, human resources*

Salary minimum: $60,000

Functions: Generalist, Directors, Senior Mgmt., Middle Mgmt., HR Mgmt., Benefits, Systems Implem., Network Admin.

Industries: Generalist, Mfg., Retail, Finance, Services, Healthcare

Professional Associations: DHRMA, EMA, NTCA, SHRM

Branches:
4412 Spicewood Springs Ste 400
Austin, TX 78759
(512) 615-5700
Fax: (512) 615-5701
Email: linda.haines@people-solutions.com
Key Contact - Specialty:
Ms. Linda Haines, President - *Human resources*

Perez-Arton Consultants Inc
23 Spring St Rm 304
Ossining-on-Hudson, NY 10562
(914) 762-2100
Email: perezart@bestweb.net

Description: Higher education administration at the presidential, VP, dean and director level. Presidential and board evaluations, board development and institutional assessments. All programmatic and operational areas in higher education and non-profit institutions.

Key Contact:
Ms. Maria M. Perez, President

Salary minimum: $75,000

Functions: Senior Mgmt., Middle Mgmt., Admin. Svcs., CFO's, MIS Mgmt., Non-profits

Industries: Non-profits, Higher Ed.

Professional Associations: ACE

Pergal and Company[†]
(also known as Resource Networking Inc)
6802 Madison Ave
Indianapolis, IN 46227
(800) 373-5229
Fax: (317) 786-9199
Email: don_pergal@hotmail.com
Web: www.pergal.com

Description: Wide range of industry experience, generally focused on new product technology, i.e. biometrics, fuel cells. Searches from engineering management to operations, HR, CFO, COO, and CEO.

Key Contact - Specialty:
Mr. Donald Pergal, President - *Technical upper management*

Salary minimum: $70,000

Functions: Senior Mgmt., Product Dev., Sales & Mktg., Personnel, CFO's, IT, R&D, Engineering

Industries: Mfg., Software, Biotech

Professional Associations: IMDMC, SAE, SAE

Networks: Top Echelon Network

The Perkins Group[†]
7621 Little Ave Ste 216
Charlotte, NC 28226
(704) 543-1111
Fax: (704) 543-0945

Email: info@perkinsgroup.com
Web: www.perkinsgroup.com

Description: A successfully proven 15 year national multi-service retained search firm focused primarily in manufacturing and distribution who provides our clients with staffing programs designed to reduce cycle time and lower costs per hire.

Key Contact - Specialty:
Mr. R. Patrick Perkins, CPC, President - *Generalist, manufacturing, distribution*
Mr. Richard Krumel, CPC, Managing Partner - *Manufacturing, distribution*

Salary minimum: $60,000

Functions: Generalist, General Mgmt., Directors, Senior Mgmt., Middle Mgmt., Mfg., Materials, Sales & Mktg., HR Mgmt., Finance

Industries: Generalist

Professional Associations: NAPS, NCASP

Perras Consulting Inc
2200 Yonge St Ste 1210
Toronto, ON M4S C6
Canada
(416) 481-5548
Fax: (416) 440-1957
Email: pperras@perrasconsulting.com
Web: www.perrasconsulting.com

Description: Our firm is an independently owned, Canadian consulting firm specializing in retained executive search. Utilizing our team's executive search, operations, and human resources consulting expertise, we truly subscribe to an overriding commitment to our clients characterized by high quality work, client satisfaction, value for fees, integrity, innovation, and teamwork. Clients tell us that our approach is refreshingly creative and proactive.

Key Contact:
Mr. Paul Perras, President

Salary minimum: $80,000

Functions: Generalist

Industries: Mfg., Pharm Svcs., Legal, Mgmt. Consulting, HR Services, Wireless, Fiber Optic, Mfg. SW, Marketing SW, Healthcare

Professional Associations: CAMC

R H Perry & Associates Inc
(also known as The Registry for College & Univ Presidents)
2607 31st St NW
Washington, DC 20008
(202) 965-6464
Fax: (202) 338-3953
Email: r.h.perry@worldnet.att.net
Web: www.rhperry-registry.com

Description: Search and personnel consulting firm based in Washington, DC.

Key Contact:
Mr. R. H. Perry, President - *College & university presidents*
Mr. Neil A. Stein, Vice President - *Private sector senior level executives, senior level positions in not-for-profit organizations*
Ms. Sandra Ellis, Director of Research

Functions: Generalist, Directors, Senior Mgmt., HR Mgmt., CFO's

Industries: Generalist, Misc. Financial, Higher Ed., Insurance

Professional Associations: ACE, AMBAE, CIC

Branches:
1127 Rosebank Dr
Columbus, OH 43235
(614) 431-1551
Fax: (614) 431-1252
Email: akoenig@worldnet.att.net

Key Contact - Specialty:
Dr. Allen E. Koenig, Senior Consultant - *Higher education*

Perry-Martel Int'l Inc†
451 Daly Ave
Ottawa, ON K1N 6H6
Canada
(613) 236-6995
Fax: (613) 236-8240
Email: dperry@perrymartel.com
Web: www.perrymartel.com

Description: Our three-dimensional value-based search system has been developed exclusively to meet the needs of the high technology sector. We have consistently found that the positions our clients want filled, push the envelope of career titles and job requirements. The fast changing world of high technology is the first place where new roles and new activities are defined. High-tech is the birthing ground of the new knowledge worker.

Key Contact:
Mr. David Perry, Managing Partner - *Senior executives, information technology*
Ms. Anita Martel, Partner

Salary minimum: $100,000

Functions: Generalist, Senior Mgmt., Sales Mgmt., PR, CFO's, MIS Mgmt., Systems Analysis, Systems Dev.

Industries: Generalist, Computer Equip., Electronic, Elec. Components, New Media, Communications, Aerospace, Software, Mfg. SW

Professional Associations: CATA, CTHRB, SHRC

Barry Persky & Company Inc
256 Post Rd E
Westport, CT 06880-3617
(203) 454-4500
Fax: (203) 454-3318
Email: bpersky@perskysearch.com
Web: www.perskysearch.com

Description: The firm specializes in the recruitment of senior executives and managers, serving domestic and international clients in capital equipment, high technology, basic manufacturing, public services, consumer products, and communications industries.

Key Contact:
Mr. Barry Persky, President
Mr. Mark Evens, Director

Salary minimum: $50,000

Functions: Generalist, Senior Mgmt., Mfg., Sales & Mktg., CFO's, Engineering, Int'l.

Industries: Generalist, Energy, Utilities, Construction, Mfg., Transportation, Services, Media, Environmental Svcs., Aerospace

Professional Associations: IACPR, EMA

Personnel Dynamics Inc†
879 Sumac Rd
Highland Park, IL 60035
(847) 831-1259
Fax: (847) 831-3259
Email: kaplan@personneldynamics.com
Web: www.personneldynamics.com

Description: We provide executive search for marketing, sales, accounting, finance and human resource positions. We consult in all facets of human resources including strategic planning, compensation, training, development and compliance.

Key Contact - Specialty:
Mr. Edward A. Kaplan, President - *Human resources, marketing, sales, finance*

Salary minimum: $60,000

Functions: Generalist, Plant Mgmt., Purchasing, Sales Mgmt., Customer Svc., HR Mgmt., CFO's, Credit

Industries: Generalist, Chemicals, Plastics, Rubber, Metal Products, Accounting, Hospitality, Non-classifiable

Professional Associations: SHRM

The Personnel Group Inc
5821 Cedar Lake Rd
Sunset Ridge Business Park
Minneapolis, MN 55416
(952) 525-1557
Fax: (952) 525-1088
Email: tpg@thepersonnelgroup.com

Description: Search practice is enhanced by executives from the Fortune 100. Practice has internal psychological/behavioral assessment capability. Provides customer with a variety of services including retained search, on-site recruiters and strategic recruiting/search consulting.

Key Contact - Specialty:
Mr. David G. Nelson, President - *Manufacturing, finance, sales & marketing*
Mr. Thomas H. Bodin, Vice President - *General management, healthcare, communications, human resources*
Mr. Wayne A. Carter, Vice President/CFO - *General management, engineering, human resources*

Salary minimum: $75,000

Functions: Generalist, General Mgmt., Mfg., Healthcare, Sales & Mktg., HR Mgmt., Finance, Engineering

Industries: Generalist, Mfg., Finance, Services, Media, Aerospace, Healthcare

The Personnel Perspective LLC
575 W College Ave Ste 101
Santa Rosa, CA 95401
(707) 576-7653
Fax: (707) 576-8190
Email: info@personnelperspective.com
Web: www.personnelperspective.com

Description: We are one of the leading providers of complete human resource management and recruitment solutions to North Bay and Napa Valley businesses. Our team of experts in human resource management and recruitment offers a complete range of solutions, centered around human resource consulting, compliance, compensation, recruitment, and training.

Key Contact - Specialty:
Ms. Carolyn Silvestri, President/Partner - *Business development*
Ms. Jeannette Feldman, Partner - *HR consulting, leadership training*
Ms. Catherine Walker, Associate - *Career consulting, outplacement services, executive search advisor*
Ms. Carol Comini, Associate - *Recruitment*
Ms. Carol Orme, Associate - *Recruitment*

Salary minimum: $50,000

Functions: Generalist, Admin. Svcs., Mfg., Sales & Mktg.

Industries: Generalist, Mfg., Wholesale, Finance, Services, Hospitality, Media, Communications, Packaging, Insurance, Real Estate, Software, Biotech, Healthcare

Professional Associations: RON, SHRM

Peters, Dalton & Graham Inc
2 Concourse Pkwy Ste 155
Atlanta, GA 30328
(770) 650-9707
Fax: (770) 650-9710

Email: staffingexperts@mindspring.com
Web: www.staffing-industry.com

Description: Specialty search practices: all senior-levels and specialties for the Staffing Industry and e-commerce.

Key Contact - Specialty:
Mr. Alec Peters, Chairman/CEO - *Staffing industry*
Mr. Thomas Dalton, Executive Vice President - *Staffing industry, e-commerce*
Mr. Jackson Graham, Senior Vice President - *Staffing industry, e-commerce*
Mr. John Egan, Vice President - *Staffing industry, financial services, e-commerce*

Salary minimum: $100,000

Functions: Generalist

Industries: Non-classifiable

Professional Associations: ASA, NTSA

Richard Peterson & Associates Inc
PO Box 76655
Atlanta, GA 30358
(404) 256-1661
Fax: (404) 256-1662
Email: pet0301@inetmail.att.net

Description: Executive search for a variety of industries.

Key Contact:
Mr. Richard A. Peterson, Principal

Salary minimum: $50,000

Functions: Generalist, Senior Mgmt., Middle Mgmt., Mktg. Mgmt., Benefits, Personnel, CFO's, MIS Mgmt.

Industries: Generalist, Mfg., Misc. Mfg., Finance, Banking

Petrie Partners Inc
PO Box 618663
Orlando, FL 32861
(407) 521-7703
Fax: (407) 521-6080

Description: Our firm combines an exceptionally successful track record with highly personalized service. Outstanding references from clients and candidates over the past decade.

Key Contact:
Mr. Christopher J. Petrie, President
Ms. Colleen Gavigan

Salary minimum: $100,000

Functions: Generalist, Senior Mgmt., Middle Mgmt., Distribution, HR Mgmt., Personnel, Training

Industries: Generalist, Drugs Mfg., Medical Devices, HR Services, Hospitality

Peyser Associates Inc
1717 N Bayshore Dr Ste 4051
Miami, FL 33132
(305) 374-9010

Description: President has over 20 years' experience in executive search and handles all his searches personally assuring high-level expertise and accountability.

Key Contact - Specialty:
Mr. Robert E. Peyser, President - *Financial services*

Salary minimum: $50,000

Functions: Generalist, Senior Mgmt., Automation, Mkt. Research, Systems Implem., Engineering, Int'l.

Industries: Generalist, Food, Bev., Tobacco, Finance, Insurance, Software

Pharmaceutical Recruiters Inc
271 Madison Ave Ste 1200
New York, NY 10016
(212) 557-5627
Fax: (212) 557-5866
Email: pharmrec@aol.com
Web: www.pharmrecruit.com

Description: We recruit upper, middle and senior executives for the pharmaceutical industry.

Key Contact - Specialty:
Ms. Linda S. Weiss, President - *Pharmaceuticals*

Salary minimum: $90,000

Functions: Generalist, Directors, Senior Mgmt., Middle Mgmt., Product Dev., Plant Mgmt., Mkt. Research, Mktg. Mgmt.

Industries: Generalist, Drugs Mfg., Pharm Svcs.

Professional Associations: AAPS, CRS, DIA, HMC, PDA, RAPS

Phase II Management
25 Stonybrook Rd
Westport, CT 06880
(203) 226-7252
Fax: (203) 226-3263
Email: rpfphaseii@aol.com
Web: www.phaseiimgmt.com

Description: Significant experience to Internet & e-businesses, packaging, related industries, manufacturing, equipment, electrical/electronics, flavors/fragrances, food/beverage industrial sales, marketing and distribution. Experienced recruiting for nearly all business disciplines.

Key Contact - Specialty:
Mr. Richard P. Fincher, President - *Generalist*

Salary minimum: $70,000

Functions: Generalist

Industries: Food, Bev., Tobacco, Paper, Printing, Soap, Perf., Cosmtcs., Medical Devices, Plastics, Rubber, Metal Products, New Media, Packaging

Professional Associations: IOPP

J R Phillip & Associates Inc
555 Twin Dolphin Dr Ste 120
Redwood City, CA 94065
(650) 631-6700
Fax: (650) 631-6710
Email: info@jrphillip.com
Web: www.jrphillip.com

Description: Over 25 years of search experience. Clients nationwide. Venture capital backed to Fortune 500 clients.

Key Contact - Specialty:
Mr. John R. Phillip - *Senior management, board level*
Mr. Robert E. Reilly - *Senior management, board level*
Mr. Mark J Kussman - *Senior management, board level*

Salary minimum: $150,000

Functions: Generalist

Industries: Drugs Mfg., Medical Devices, Computer Equip., Test, Measure Equip., Venture Cap., Pharm Svcs., Telecoms, Software, Biotech, Healthcare

Branches:
4370 La Jolla Village Dr Ste 400
San Diego, CA 92122
(858) 546-4490
Fax: (858) 546-9227
Key Contact - Specialty:
Mr. Glenn P. Ambra - *Senior management, board level*
Mr. Niall V. Lawlor - *Senior management, board level*

1000 Park Forty Plz Ste 300
Durham, NC 27713
(919) 313-2560
Fax: (919) 313-2569
Key Contact - Specialty:
Mr. Grant W. Underhill - *Senior management, board level*

Phillips & Associates Inc
62 Derby St Unit 1
Hingham, MA 02043-3718
(781) 740-9699
Email: dphillips@phillipsearch.com
Web: www.phillipsearch.com

Description: We are a healthcare and higher education specialized search firm. The benefits to prospective clients include: healthcare and higher education professionals performing the search, a shorter recruiting cycle, an extensive database and national network of healthcare, and higher education professionals..

Key Contact:
Mr. Daniel J. Phillips, Managing Partner
Mr. Ralph DiPisa, Partner

Salary minimum: $80,000

Functions: Directors

Industries: Non-profits, Higher Ed., Healthcare

Professional Associations: ACHE, ASHHRA, HFMA, MGMA, MHHRA

Phoenix Search
Viaducto Miguel Aleman 259-102
Col Roma Sur
Mexico City, DF 06760
Mexico
52 5 564 6583
Email: contact@phoenix-search.com
Web: www.phoenix-search.com

Description: We cover all Latin America from our offices in Mexico and Brazil. We are the region's leading information technology firm. Our practice is well rounded with successful searches in many industries.

Key Contact - Specialty:
Mr. L. Ignacio Garrote, General Director - *Information technology*

Salary minimum: $50,000

Functions: Generalist, Directors, Senior Mgmt., Mktg. Mgmt., Sales Mgmt., CFO's, MIS Mgmt., Int'l.

Industries: Generalist, Energy, Utilities, Mfg., Transportation, Retail, Software

Networks: World Search Group

Physician Executive Management Center
3403 W Fletcher Ave
Tampa, FL 33618-2813
(813) 963-1800
Fax: (813) 264-2207
Email: info@physicianexecutive.com
Web: www.physicianexecutive.com

Description: We are the only national firm specializing in physician executives. Our clients include: hospital systems, group practices, managed care organizations, and insurance companies who ask us to find physician-only CEOs, vice presidents of medical affairs, medical directors, and department chiefs.

Key Contact - Specialty:
Mr. David R. Kirschman, President - *Physician executives*
Ms. Jennifer R. Grebenschikoff, Vice President - *Physician executives*

Salary minimum: $200,000

Functions: Senior Mgmt.

Industries: Healthcare

Professional Associations: AAHC

Picard Int'l Ltd
125 E 38th St
New York, NY 10016
(212) 252-1620
Fax: (212) 252-0973
Email: office@picardintl.com
Web: www.picardintl.com

Description: Senior executive searches in a broad range of functions including general management, corporate strategy, technology, capital markets in financial services, management consulting, healthcare and high-technology industries.

Key Contact - Specialty:
Mr. Daniel A. Picard, Principal - *Financial services, technology, healthcare, management consulting*
Ms. Georgina Lichtenstein, Principal - *Management consulting, healthcare*
Ms. Kathy Fiess, Principal - *Financial services, investment banking*
Ms. Lauren Ross, Principal - *Management consulting, healthcare*

Salary minimum: $150,000

Functions: Generalist, Health Admin., HR Mgmt., CFO's, Cash Mgmt., Risk Mgmt., MIS Mgmt., Mgmt. Consultants

Industries: Generalist, Banking, Invest. Banking, Mgmt. Consulting, HR Services, Software, Healthcare

Professional Associations: IACPR

Pierce & Associates
6 Venture Ste 100
Irvine, CA 92618
(949) 450-0352
Fax: (949) 450-0348
Email: ssp@piercesearch.com
Web: www.piercesearch.com

Description: We are a highly successful, independently owned executive search firm specializing in placing talented financial executives and managers for our corporate clients.

Key Contact - Specialty:
Mr. Matthew J. Pierce, Partner - *CFOs, senior financial executives, sales & marketing*
Mr. Marty Foxman, Partner - *Human resources, finance*

Salary minimum: $75,000

Functions: Senior Mgmt., HR Mgmt., Finance, CFO's

Industries: Software

Pierce & Crow
100 Drakes Landing Rd Ste 300
Greenbrae, CA 94904
(415) 925-1191
Email: pac@piercecrow.com
Web: www.piercecrow.com

Description: We are an award-winning executive search firm specializing in the recruitment of executive management for the emerging technologies industry since 1978. Our clients include venture-backed start-ups and Fortune 500 companies. You will recognize the names of our clients and partners as those revolutionizing the business of technology.

Key Contact:
Mr. Dennis Crow, Managing Director
Mr. Kevin Barry, Consultant
Ms. Kelly Barrington, Consultant

Functions: Senior Mgmt., Sales & Mktg.

Industries: Software

Pinnacle Executive Group Inc
600 NE Seabrook
Lees Summit, MO 64064
(816) 350-1336
Fax: (816) 350-1311
Email: scott@pinnaclexec.com
Web: www.pinnaclexec.com

Description: We utilize progressive recruitment methods to secure candidates that meet the challenges of major transition and accelerating change found in corporate America today. Identifying chemistry, acumen and drive equals success.

Key Contact:
Mr. Scott Eckley, Managing Partner
Ms. Barbara Eckley, Managing Partner

Salary minimum: $70,000

Functions: Generalist, Directors, Senior Mgmt., Legal, M&A, Risk Mgmt., Attorneys

Industries: Energy, Utilities, Transportation, Finance, Invest. Banking, Venture Cap., Media, Communications, Telecoms

Professional Associations: KCAPS, MAPS

Networks: National Consulting Network (NCN)

Pinsker & Company Inc
508 Ojai
Granite Bay, CA 95746
(916) 797-9166
Fax: (916) 797-9168
Email: pinskerandco@rcsis.com

Description: We are executive selection consultants. We have retained search engagements to locate board members, presidents, CEOs, and the reporting management team.

Key Contact - Specialty:
Mr. Richard J. Pinsker, CMC, President - *Board members, key executives*

Salary minimum: $125,000

Functions: Generalist, Directors, Senior Mgmt., Middle Mgmt.

Industries: Generalist, Food, Bev., Tobacco, Computer Equip., Test, Measure Equip., Misc. Mfg.

Professional Associations: IMC

Pinton Forrest & Madden
(a member of EMA Partners Int'l)
1055 W Hastings St Guinness Twr Ste 2020
Vancouver, BC V6E 2E9
Canada
(604) 689-9970
Fax: (604) 689-9943
Email: pfm@pfmsearch.com
Web: www.pfmsearch.com

Description: We build long-term client relationships through the partners' 65 combined years of recruitment and business management experience plus their direct involvement in each search assignment. A thorough, efficient and timely search process delivers quality candidates to our valued private and public sector clients.

Key Contact:
Mr. Garth Pinton, Partner
Mr. Casey Forrest, Partner
Mr. George Madden, Partner

Salary minimum: $70,000

Functions: Senior Mgmt., Middle Mgmt.

Industries: Generalist, Agri., Forestry, Mining, Energy, Utilities, Mfg., Finance, Services, Communications, Government, Aerospace, Software, Healthcare

---

Professional Associations: AESC

Networks: EMA Partners Int'l

Planigestion Andre Choquette Inc
2810 boul Saint-Martin E
Bureau 203
Laval, QC H7E 4Y6
Canada
(514) 664-3804
Fax: (514) 664-3707
Email: plani-ac@dsuper.net
Web: adapt.qc.ca

Description: Active in all fields with the exception of Data Processing. Positions over $60,000. All senior consultants have managed a business and been on the Management Committee. For positions under $60,000. please contact our subsidiary: ADAPT Inc at 450-664-0443.

Key Contact:
Mr. Andre Choquette, President
Mrs. Isabel Lapointe, Senior consultant
Mr. Claude Choquette, President of ADAPT Inc
Mrs. Annie Gravel, Senior consultant

Plante & Moran LLP
27400 Northwestern Hwy
Southfield, MI 48037
(248) 352-2500
Fax: (248) 352-8018
Email: careers@plante-moran.com
Web: www.plante-moran.com

Description: Specialize in recruiting financial, accounting, administrative, human resources and information technology positions with emphasis in the manufacturing, healthcare, not-for-profit and financial industries. We utilize psychological assessment services to assist in matching candidates to a position.

Key Contact:
Mr. William Hermann, Managing Partner
Ms. Karine Stover, Partner

Salary minimum: $50,000

Functions: Generalist, Senior Mgmt., Middle Mgmt., Quality, Mktg. Mgmt., HR Mgmt., Finance, IT

Industries: Generalist, Construction, Mfg., Transportation, Finance, Services, Packaging

Professional Associations: CFMA, MACPA, MASS

Rene Plessner Associates Inc
375 Park Ave
New York, NY 10152
(212) 421-3490
Fax: (212) 421-3999

Description: A boutique executive search firm specializing in cosmetics, accessories, apparel and fashion-related areas, also consumer packaged goods, retail, and high technology, with an emphasis on entrepreneurial companies.

Key Contact:
Mr. Rene Plessner, President

Salary minimum: $75,000

Functions: Generalist, General Mgmt., Mfg., Sales & Mktg., Advertising, Mktg. Mgmt., Sales Mgmt., PR

Industries: Generalist, Textiles, Apparel, Soap, Perf., Cosmtcs., Computer Equip., Advertising, Aerospace

Professional Associations: IACPR

Gerald Plock Associates Inc
7501 Stallion Cir
Flower Mound, TX 75022
(817) 464-4610

Email: geraldplock@gerladplockassoc.com
Web: www.geraldplockassoc.com

Description: Gerald Plock Assoc., Inc. is a management consulting firm providing executive recruitment to public sector and non-profit organizations worldwide. Gerald Plock is one of the most experienced executive search professionals serving local government/not-profit institutions in the country.

Key Contact - Specialty:
Mr. Gerald Plock, President
Ms. Wendy Lewis, Associate
Ms. Sarah Higginbotham, Associate - *Diversity*

Salary minimum: $75,000

Functions: Generalist

Industries: Non-profits, Higher Ed., Mgmt. Consulting, HR Services, Law Enforcement, Government, Environmental Svcs.

Professional Associations: APT, ICMA, IPMA, SHRM

Branches:
134 Green Bay Rd
Winnetka, IL 60093
(847) 441-5626
Email: wendy@geraldplockassoc.com
Web: www.geraldplockassoc.com
Key Contact:
Ms. Wendy Lewis, Associate

Plummer & Associates Inc

65 Rowayton Ave
Rowayton, CT 06853
(203) 899-1233
Fax: (203) 838-0887
Email: resume@plummersearch.com
Web: www.plummersearch.com

Description: We specialize in CEO, COO, senior officer level assignments for the retail industry, wholesale trade, retail services, e-commerce, quick serve/casual dining, catalogs/direct marketing, manufacturers for the retail industry (toys, cosmetics, apparel) and retail consulting firms.

Key Contact:
Mr. John Plummer, Consultant
Ms. Kathy Mackenna, Consultant
Ms. Heidi Plummer, Consultant/Administration
Ms. Dina Lokets, Consultant/Research

Salary minimum: $150,000

Functions: Generalist

Industries: Textiles, Apparel, Wholesale, Retail, Venture Cap., Mgmt. Consulting, Hospitality

Professional Associations: NRF, WFF

Branches:
142 S Park Sq Ste A
Marietta, GA 30060
(770) 429-9007
Fax: (770) 426-6374
Email: sgill@plummersearch.com
Key Contact:
Ms. Susan Gill, Consultant
Ms. Judy Behm, Consultant

PMO Partners Inc

333 N Michigan Ave Ste 317
Chicago, IL 60601
(312) 726-1143
Fax: (312) 726-1145
Email: pashley@pmopartners.com
Web: www.pmopartners.com

Description: We are a retained executive search firm specializing in banking and financial services.

Key Contact:
Ms. Patricia Ashley, President and CEO
Ms. Deanna Drew, Managing Director

Functions: Generalist

Industries: Banking, Misc. Financial

PNR Int'l Research

5357 W Montrose Ave Ste 2
Chicago, IL 60641
(773) 685-4389
Fax: (773) 685-4415
Email: pwnco@worldnet.att.net

Description: We are a retained industry focused firm conducting quality research, recruitment, assessment, and delivery of executive talent in pharmaceutical, healthcare, information technology, and biotechnology worldwide

Key Contact - Specialty:
Mr. Paul W. Norman, President - *Healthcare, information technology, telecommunications*

Salary minimum: $60,000

Functions: Senior Mgmt., Middle Mgmt., Product Dev., MIS Mgmt., Systems Dev.

Industries: Finance, Telecoms, Digital, Wireless, Fiber Optic, Network Infrastructure, Biotech, Healthcare

Poirier, Hoevel & Company

12400 Wilshire Blvd Ste 915
Los Angeles, CA 90025
(310) 207-3427
Fax: (310) 820-7431
Email: info@phandco.com
Web: www.phandco.com

Description: A retained generalist executive search firm. National and international Fortune 1000 base with emphasis on manufacturing, financial institutions, entertainment, public accounting, consumer products, aerospace, service and high-tech.

Key Contact - Specialty:
Mr. Michael J. Hoevel, Partner - *Generalist*
Mr. Roland L. Poirier, Partner - *Generalist*

Salary minimum: $75,000

Functions: Generalist

Industries: Generalist

Branches:
29906 Scenic Dr NE
Poulsbo, WA 98370
(425) 313-0338
Key Contact - Specialty:
Ms. Kristina A. Hoevel, Managing Director - *Generalist*

Ray Polhill Associates

PO Box 470653
Charlotte, NC 28247
(704) 552-8800
Email: info@equipexec.com
Web: www.polhillassociates.com

Description: Principals with strong industry credentials provide searches for CEO, sales, marketing, product support management. Focus: construction equipment, material handling, engine/power generation, forestry and mining equipment - manufacturer and dealer clients. High standards, client satisfaction.

Key Contact:
Mr. Ray L. Polhill, President

Salary minimum: $60,000

Functions: Generalist

Industries: Energy, Utilities, Construction, Mfg., Finance

Professional Associations: AED

Polson & Company Inc

15 S 5th St Ste750
Minneapolis, MN 55402
(612) 332-6607
Fax: (612) 332-6296
Email: polsoncompany@qwest.net

Description: Full service, retainer fee, executive search firm; generalist.

Key Contact:
Mr. Christopher C. Polson - *Generalist, manufacturing, IT, general management, sales*
Mr. Edgar S. McLellan
Mr. Rich Sachse, Partner

Salary minimum: $100,000

Functions: General Mgmt., Mfg., Product Dev., Plant Mgmt., Distribution, Sales Mgmt., HR Mgmt., CFO's, IT, Mgmt. Consultants

Industries: Generalist

The Poole Group

7700 S Glencoe Way
Littleton, CO 80122
(303) 721-6644
Fax: (303) 721-7724
Email: dvpoole@attglobal.net

Description: We are a retained search firm specializing in sales, marketing, and engineering senior executives in high-tech manufacturing nationwide.

Key Contact:
Mr. Don V. Poole, President - *General management, sales & marketing management, finance*
Ms. Page A. Spalding, Vice President

Salary minimum: $100,000

Functions: Generalist, Senior Mgmt., Mktg. Mgmt., Sales Mgmt., HR Mgmt., CFO's, MIS Mgmt.

Industries: Generalist, Mfg., Finance, Media, Software, Healthcare

David Powell Inc

2995 Woodside Rd Ste 150
Woodside, CA 94062
(650) 851-6000
Fax: (650) 851-5514
Email: dpi@davidpowell.com
Web: www.davidpowell.com

Description: Our primary focus is officer-level searches for emerging and established companies in high-technology industries.

Key Contact:
Mr. David Powell, Chairman/CEO
Ms. Jean Bagileo, Managing Partner
Mr. Steve Balogh, Managing Partner
Mr. David Powell, Jr., Managing Partner
Mr. Bill Wraith, Vice President

Salary minimum: $150,000

Functions: Generalist

Industries: Computer Equip., Consumer Elect., Test, Measure Equip., Invest. Banking, Venture Cap., Telecoms, Software, Biotech, Healthcare

Branches:
1999 S Bascom Ste 1050
Campbell, CA 95008
(408) 558-5000
Fax: (408) 558-0555
Email: hrs@davidpowell.com
Key Contact:
Mr. Robb Kundtz, Managing Partner
Mr. Gary Rockow, Partner

111 Congress St Ste 1200
Austin, TX 78701
(512) 481-1520
Key Contact:
Ms. Carolyn Ruppert, Director

Powers Consultants Inc†
2241A S Brentwood Blvd
St. Louis, MO 63144
(314) 961-8787
(314) 961-6437
Fax: (314) 968-0758
Email: np7969@aol.com

Description: We nationally serve many of the largest and smallest professional service firms within the design and construction industries, providing clients with a unique two-year performance guarantee on placements plus an extremely high (87%) retention stick ratio over the past fifteen years.

Key Contact - Specialty:
Mr. William D. Powers, President/CEO - *Architecture, engineering, construction (all disciplines), hospitality*

Salary minimum: $40,000

Functions: Senior Mgmt., Benefits, Engineering, Environmentalists, Architects

Industries: Construction, Hospitality, Environmental Svcs., Biotech

Branches:
22 Oak Bend Ct
Ladue, MO 63124
(314) 961-8792
Fax: (314) 961-8792
Key Contact - Specialty:
Ms. Janet Powers, Vice President - *Banking, food processing, environmental, management information systems*

Prairie Resource Group Inc†
137 N Oak Park Ave Ste 307
Oak Park, IL 60301
(708) 763-9100
Email: search@prgchicago.com
Web: www.prgchicago.com

Description: Specialized to recruit unique talent for high-tech traditional manufacturing industries. Most effective on technically demanding personnel specifications, where in-depth or esoteric systems, functional and/or engineering/scientific knowledge is required, along with solid business and people skills.

Key Contact - Specialty:
Mr. M. Kent Taylor - *High technology, general operations management, consulting, sales & marketing, software implementation*
Mr. Frank Bernard - *Engineering, construction, accounting & finance*

Salary minimum: $50,000

Functions: Generalist, General Mgmt., Mfg., Finance, IT, R&D, Engineering

Industries: Generalist, Mfg., Finance, Mgmt. Consulting, Telecoms, Software

Professional Associations: AVS, IEEE

Predictor Systems Corp
1796 Equestrian Dr
Pleasanton, CA 94588
(925) 846-9396
Email: helen@predictorsystems.com
Web: www.predictorsystems.com

Description: We utilize the first fully validated interactive interview assessment tool presented in a CD-ROM format to clients. This unique software product enables hiring management to view candidates prior to inviting them in for interviews. The process is tailored to the unique needs of each client.

Salary minimum: $150,000

Functions: Senior Mgmt., Middle Mgmt., Sales & Mktg., Mktg. Mgmt., Sales Mgmt., CFO's, IT, MIS Mgmt., Engineering

Industries: Venture Cap., Telecoms, Software

Branches:
39350 Civic Center Dr Ste 440
Fremont, CA 94538
(925) 846-9396
Email: helen@predictorsystems.com
Key Contact:
Ms. Helen Schultz, President

George Preger & Associates Inc
41 MacPherson Ave
Toronto, ON M5R 1W7
Canada
(416) 922-6336
Fax: (416) 922-4902
Email: consult@georgepreger.com
Web: www.georgepreger.com

Description: A leading independent executive search firm in Canada. All industries and functions. Senior management oriented. We are unique in Canada in the emphasis we place on research and direct servicing.

Key Contact:
Mr. G. A. Preger, MS, President

Salary minimum: $70,000

Functions: Generalist, Directors, Senior Mgmt., Plant Mgmt., Sales Mgmt., CFO's, MIS Mgmt., Engineering

Industries: Generalist, Mfg., Textiles, Apparel, Medical Devices, Motor Vehicles, Consumer Elect., Test, Measure Equip., Aerospace

Professional Associations: ICMCO

Preng & Associates Inc
2925 Briarpark Ste 1111
Houston, TX 77042
(713) 266-2600
Fax: (713) 266-3070
Web: www.preng.com

Description: We have worldwide executive search capabilities specializing in oil and gas, chemicals, power, refining, water resources, energy, e-Commerce, manufacturing, natural resources, petrochemicals, engineering, construction and environmental services.

Key Contact - Specialty:
Mr. David E. Preng - *Energy, chemicals, natural resources, power utilities, energy e-commerce*
Mr. William G. French - *Energy, management consulting, international*
Mr. William J. Mathias - *Energy exploration, production, engineering, information systems*
Mr. Ralph W. Stevens - *Energy, management consulting, manufacturing*
Mr. George M. Rickus - *Power utilities, water utilities*
Mr. Charles L. Carpenter - *Oil field (services, equipment)*

Salary minimum: $100,000

Functions: Generalist, Directors, Senior Mgmt., Middle Mgmt., CFO's, MIS Mgmt., Engineering, Mgmt. Consultants

Industries: Generalist, Energy, Utilities, Construction, Chemicals, Mgmt. Consulting, Environmental Svcs.

Professional Associations: AESC

Lloyd Prescott & Churchill Inc
4803 George Rd Ste 360
President's Plz Ctr
Tampa, FL 33634
(800) 486-3463
Fax: (813) 889-8458
Email: headhunt7@lloydprescott.net
Web: www.lloydprescott.com

Description: Generalist firm providing international and national executive and professional search. Offering our clients the best and the brightest candidates in their field and unique retainer driven custom search programs to accomodate their problems and long and short-term goals as it relates to executive management.

Key Contact - Specialty:
Mr. Sheldon M. Ginsberg, Managing Partner - *Senior management*
Mr. Manuel F. Gordon, Business Affairs Partner - *Senior management*

Salary minimum: $100,000

Functions: Senior Mgmt.

Industries: Generalist, Medical Devices, Banking, Mgmt. Consulting, Hospitality, Aerospace, Real Estate, Software, Biotech, Healthcare

Preston & Company
65 Old Hwy 22 Ste 6
Clinton, NJ 08809
(908) 730-7411
Fax: (908) 730-8911
Email: joe@preston-company.com

Description: Specializations encompass financial services in general. Industry specialties include investment management, mutual funds, broker/dealers, banks, etc. The goal is to develop and maintain long-term relationships with select clients.

Key Contact - Specialty:
Mr. Joe Preston, President - *Financial services*

Salary minimum: $100,000

Functions: Cash Mgmt.

Industries: Finance, Banking, Invest. Banking, Brokers, Venture Cap., Misc. Financial

Professional Associations: ICI, IMCA, NICSA

Prestonwood Associates
266 Main St Ste 12A
Olde Medfield Sq
Medfield, MA 02052
(508) 359-7100
Fax: (508) 359-4007
Email: info@prestonwoodassoc.com
Web: www.prestonwoodassociates.com

Description: Our expertise spans from numerous industries including professional and financial services, law firms, high technology, consumer products, and healthcare. We have a history of continuous access to the highest caliber talent in all executive leadership positions, including CEOs, CFOs, CIOs, HR, marketing, sales, and business development executives.

Key Contact:
Ms. Diane Coletti, President/CEO
Mrs. Beth Kelly, Executive Vice President

Salary minimum: $100,000

Functions: Generalist, Directors, Senior Mgmt., Mkt. Research, Sales Mgmt., PR, MIS Mgmt., Mgmt. Consultants

Industries: Generalist, Computer Equip., Mgmt. Consulting, HR Services, Telecoms, Software

Professional Associations: NEHRA

PRH Management Inc
2777 Summer St
Stamford, CT 06905
(203) 327-3900
Email: peter@prhmanagement.com
Web: www.prhmanagement.com

Description: Since 1973, we have offered a personal service giving each professional the attention needed to attain their unique career objectives. 80% of our candidates are promoted in two years.

Key Contact - Specialty:
Mr. Peter R. Hendelman, President - *Telecommunications, high technology*

Salary minimum: $150,000

Functions: Generalist, Senior Mgmt.

Industries: Mfg., Computer Equip., Venture Cap., E-commerce, New Media, Communications, Telecoms, Software, Accounting SW, ERP SW, HR SW, Marketing SW, Networking, Comm. SW, System SW

PricewaterhouseCoopers Executive Search
145 King St W
Toronto, ON M5H 1V8
Canada
(416) 869-1130
Fax: (416) 814-5733
Email: pwctorontoexecsearch@ca.pwcglobal.com
Web: www.pwcglobal.com/executive.ca

Description: Senior-level consultants work with public, private, government and not-for-profit clients on a broad range of middle management and senior executive searches. Fixed fee arrangement ensures complete objectivity throughout the process.

Key Contact - Specialty:
Mr. Paul F. Crath, Senior Vice President - *Generalist, financial services, mining, manufacturing, communications*
Mr. B. Keith McLean, Senior Vice President - *Generalist, education, not-for-profit*
Mr. Tom Sinclair, Senior Vice President - *Generalist, financial services, high technology*
Mr. Charles Lennox, Vice President - *Information technology, consulting, high technology*
Ms. Margaret Pelton, Vice President - *Healthcare, non-profit*
Ms. Barbara Nixon, Vice President - *Healthcare, non-profit*
Ms. Jordene Lyttle, Vice President - *Not-for-profit, education*
Ms. Elizabeth Zucchiatti, Vice President - *Sales & marketing, consumer packaged goods*

Salary minimum: $70,000

Functions: Generalist, Senior Mgmt., Middle Mgmt., Plant Mgmt., Health Admin., Sales & Mktg., Finance, MIS Mgmt.

Industries: Generalist, Energy, Utilities, Mfg., Finance, Media, Healthcare

Professional Associations: AESC, ICMCC

Branches:
425 - 1st St SW Ste 1200
Calgary, AB T2P 3V7
Canada
(403) 509-7500
Fax: (403) 266-1419
Email: rollie.hearn@ca.pwcglobal.com
Key Contact - Specialty:
Mr. Rollie Hearn, Vice President - *Generalist*
Ms. Diane Wilding, Vice President - *Generalist*

10130 103rd St Ste 2100
Edmonton, AB T5J 3N5
Canada
(780) 441-6800
Fax: (780) 421-3052
Email: rose.mary.holland@ca.pwcglobal.com
Key Contact - Specialty:
Ms. Rose Mary Holland, Vice President - *Generalist*
Mr. Enid Bradley, Vice President - *Generalist*

111 W Hastings St
Vancouver, BC V6E 3R2
Canada
(604) 806-7000
Fax: (604) 806-7749
Email: grant.smith@ca.pwcglobal.com
Key Contact - Specialty:
Mr. Grant Smith, Vice President - *Generalist, mining, club management*
Mr. Robert McMillin, Vice President - *Generalist, manufacturing, associations*

1 Lombard Pl Ste 2300
Winnipeg, MB R3B 0X6
Canada
(204) 926-2400
Fax: (204) 944-1020
Email: karen.swystun@ca.pwcglobal.com
Key Contact - Specialty:
Ms. Karen Swystun, Vice President - *Generalist*
Ms. Cindy Stephenson, Vice President - *Generalist*

1250 Rene-Levesque Blvd W Ste 3500
Montreal, QC H3B 2G4
Canada
(514) 205-5000
Fax: (514) 938-5711
Email: claude.daigneault@ca.pwcglobal.com
Key Contact - Specialty:
Mr. Joseph Beaupre, Vice President - *Generalist*
Mr. Claude Daigneault, Vice President - *Generalist*
Ms. June Carol Lalanne, Vice President - *Generalist*
Ms. Marie-Helene Begin, Vice President - *Generalist*

900 Rene Levesque Blvd E Ste 500
Quebec, QC G1R 2B5
Canada
(418) 522-7001
Fax: (418) 522-1214
Email: michel.chalifour@ca.pwcglobal.com
Key Contact - Specialty:
Mr. Michel Chalifour, Vice President - *Generalist*

Prichard Kymen Inc
12204 - 106 Ave Ste 302
Edmonton, AB T5N 3Z1
Canada
(780) 448-0128
Fax: (780) 453-5246
Email: pkymen@telusplanet.net
Web: www.pkymen.cjb.net

Description: We have recruited in the technical, engineering and mid-senior management areas. Our client base includes an increasing number of Canadian and North American organizations.

Key Contact - Specialty:
Mr. Pat McKinney, Principal - *Executive, technical, middle management*

Functions: Generalist, Senior Mgmt., Production, Distribution, Allied Health, Mktg. Mgmt., HR Mgmt., Engineering

Industries: Generalist, Agri., Forestry, Mining, Construction, Lumber, Furniture, Drugs Mfg., Machine, Appliance, Transportation

Professional Associations: HRIA

The Primary Group Inc
PO Box 916160
Longwood, FL 32791-6160
(407) 869-4111
Fax: (407) 682-3321
Email: primarygroup@pgsearch.com
Web: www.theprimarygroup.com

Description: Executive search and consulting for mutual fund companies, insurance companies, broker-dealers, financial institutions, and institutional investment management companies. Expertise in management and sales from senior to regional levels.

Key Contact - Specialty:
Mr. Ken Friedman, President - *Mutual funds, insurance*

Salary minimum: $50,000

Functions: Generalist

Industries: Finance, Banking, Invest. Banking, Brokers, Venture Cap., Misc. Financial, Insurance

Professional Associations: FPA, NAPS, NAVA

Networks: US Recruiters.com

Primus Associates LC
13915 Burnet Rd Ste 440
Austin, TX 78728
(512) 246-2266
Email: info@primusnet.com
Web: www.primusnet.com

Description: Our high-technology sector specialization enables us to identify and contact target candidates faster and more effectively than generalist firms. Our client companies are located throughout the US and range from start-ups to $22B companies.

Key Contact - Specialty:
Mr. Sam Gassett, President - *High technology executives*

Salary minimum: $100,000

Functions: Generalist, Directors, Senior Mgmt., Middle Mgmt., Sales & Mktg., Sales Mgmt., CFO's, MIS Mgmt., Engineering

Industries: Generalist, Software, Marketing SW

PrinceGoldsmith LLC
420 Lexington Ave Ste 2048
New York, NY 10170
(212) 313-9891
Fax: (212) 313-9892
Email: recruit@princegoldsmith.com

Description: We are a highly focused executive search firm devoted to financial services with a speciality in investment management. We have extensive experience in the recruitment of CEOs, COOs, CFOs as well as portfolio managers, research analysts and sales and marketing professionals. Our partners are "hands on" not only in developing client relationships, but more importantly, in executing search assignments.

Key Contact - Specialty:
Ms. Marylin L. Prince, Partner - *Financial services, investment management*
Mr. Joseph B. Goldsmith, Partner - *Financial services, investment management*
Ms. Megan G. Murray, Vice President - *Financial services, investment management*
Mr. Vincent J. Talamo, Associate - *Financial services, investment management*

Salary minimum: $150,000

Functions: Senior Mgmt., Sales & Mktg., Sales Mgmt., Customer Svc., HR Mgmt., Finance, CFO's, Risk Mgmt., Minorities, Int'l.

Industries: Finance

Professional Associations: AESC

Princeton Search Partners Inc
475 Wall St
Princeton, NJ 08540
(609) 430-9600
Fax: (609) 924-8270
Email: psp@latinipartners.com

Description: Generalist boutique executive search firm providing highly personalized and responsive service to prestigious clients.

Key Contact - Specialty:
Mr. Anthony A. Latini, Executive Search Consultant - *Financial services, technology, healthcare*
Dr. M. Katherine Kraft, Executive Search Consultant - *Human resources*
Mr. William J. Bricker, Executive Search Consultant - *Healthcare*

Salary minimum: $75,000

Functions: Senior Mgmt.

Industries: Finance, Banking, Brokers, Misc. Financial, Accounting, Mgmt. Consulting, Insurance, Accounting SW, HR SW, Healthcare

---

Printlink Graphic Arts Placement Service Ltd
183 Midtown Plz Ste 284
Rochester, NY 14604
(800) 867-3463
Fax: (716) 856-8500
Email: printlink@printlink.com
Web: www.printlink.com

Description: We are a graphic arts professional staffing service for senior/middle print management and all digital prepress positions. Our staff are all veterans of the printing and prepress industry with over 20 years experience each. We use custom designed software to assist in screening, sorting, and matching qualified candidates with prospective employers. We have dedicated databases to facilitate the placement of key employees who are actively employed and seeking a change or better opportunity.

Key Contact:
Mr. Arnold N. Kahn, President

Functions: Generalist

Industries: Printing, Packaging, Doc. Mgmt., Production SW

Branches:
49-6A The Donway W Ste 3007
Don Mills, ON M3C 2E8
Canada
(905) 842-2600
Fax: (800) 856-8501
Email: printlink@printlink.com
Key Contact:
Ms. Myrna Penny, Managing Director

The Prior Resource Group Inc
50 Queen St N Ste 660
Kitchener, ON N2H 6P4
Canada
(519) 570-1100
(888) 607-7467
Fax: (519) 570-1144
Email: prior@priorresource.com
Web: www.priorresource.com

Description: Our firm is a full service human resources firm offering professional, executive, and information technology search services and placing administrative and industrial job candidates for permanent, contract, or temporary positions in a broad range of industries.

Key Contact:
Mr. Mark Reno, President

Functions: Generalist

Industries: Generalist, Mfg., Finance, Services, Communications, Software

---

Prior/Martech Associates Inc
16000 Christensen Rd Ste 310
Seattle, WA 98188-2928
(206) 242-1141
Fax: (206) 242-1255
Email: priormar@ix.netcom.com
Web: www.expert-market.com/priormartech

Description: We assist owners, board members or CEOs in meeting their staffing requirements both from inside the organization through management appraisal or from outside through executive recruiting. We help organizations in governance issues.

Key Contact:
Mr. Paul R. Meyer, Vice President/Principal
Mr. Michael E. McGahan, President

Salary minimum: $75,000

Functions: Generalist

Industries: Generalist

Professional Associations: IMC

Pro Forma Search
8401 Patterson Ave Ste 204
Richmond, VA 23229
(804) 754-8330
Fax: (804) 754-8334
Email: mail@proformasearch.com
Web: www.proformasearch.com

Description: We are a leading search research firm, specializing in the sourcing, screening and referral of finance and accounting professionals for Fortune 500 companies. We are not a contingency or retained recruiting firm. Instead, we work as search research consultants and function as an extension of our clients' recruiting efforts to enhance candidate flow. Our success hinges on our strategic integration of proprietary databases and occupational specialization.

Key Contact - Specialty:
Mr. Lee Weisiger, President - *Finance, accounting*

Salary minimum: $60,000

Functions: Finance

Industries: Generalist

Professional Associations: SHRM

Pro2Serve Recruiting Solutions
(a division of Pro2Serve Inc)
13530 Dulles Technology Dr Ste 110
Herndon, VA 20171
(703) 793-7330
Fax: (703) 793-7342
Email: gthomas@iprinc.com
Web: www.iprinc.com

Description: Full-service HR and management consulting firm. Established in Washington D.C. area for 15 plus years. Specialists in retained executive search and project-based recruiting. Active in all areas of human resource consulting.

Key Contact - Specialty:
Mr. Andrew Fetterolf, President/COO - *Information technology, sales, human resources*

Salary minimum: $50,000

Functions: Generalist, Sales Mgmt., HR Mgmt., IT, Engineering, Mgmt. Consultants

Industries: Generalist, Mgmt. Consulting, HR Services, Defense, Environmental Svcs., Software

Professional Associations: EMA, RON, SHRM

Branches:
6501 Park of Commerce Dr Ste 200
Boca Raton, FL 33487
(561) 443-4494
Fax: (561) 443-7122
Key Contact:
Mr. Calvin Briscoe

1007 Commerce Park Dr Ste 500-A
Oak Ridge, TN 37830
(423) 483-2030
Fax: (423) 483-2660
Key Contact:
Ms. Catherine Phillips

ProductManage.com
721 W 1275 N
Farmington, UT 84025
(801) 447-8676
Fax: (801) 447-8677
Email: brian@productmanage.com
Web: www.productmanage.com

Description: Executive search firm that specializes in the search and placement of product management and product marketing executives and professionals in the computer, software, internet, and telco

industries. We work on a retained fee structure. With access to over 10,000 product management professionals and executives in the "High Tech Space", we have the resources to deliver world class quality in a timely manner.

Key Contact:
Mr. Brian Oscarson, Principal

Salary minimum: $100,000

Functions: General Mgmt., Directors, Senior Mgmt., Middle Mgmt., Mfg., Product Dev., Sales & Mktg., Mkt. Research, Mktg. Mgmt.

Industries: Software

Networks: First Interview Network (FIN)

Professional Research Services Inc
715 Ela Rd 2C
Lake Zurich, IL 60047-6300
(847) 550-6100
(800) 777-4488
Fax: (847) 589-2305
Email: prs@intersurfer.com
Web: www.prs1.com

Description: Nationwide firm providing name generation for search unbundled employment research and search. We provide services in most industries and functions. We primarily deal with mid-level positions.

Key Contact:
Mr. Tom DeBourcy, President
Mr. Mike Silber, Senior Consultant

Salary minimum: $40,000

Functions: Generalist, Distribution, Mkt. Research, Mktg. Mgmt., Sales Mgmt., Direct Mktg., M&A, Systems Support, Engineering

Industries: Generalist, Mfg., Chemicals, Drugs Mfg., Medical Devices, Computer Equip., Banking, Invest. Banking, Venture Cap., Misc. Financial, Telecoms, Network Infrastructure, Aerospace, Packaging, Software, Biotech

---

Professional Search†
521 Cambridge Dr
Muskegon, MI 49441
(231) 798-3537
Fax: (231) 798-8062
Email: info@professionalsearch.net
Web: www.professionalsearch.net

Description: Our staff size, team approach and extensive resources enable us to offer recruiting services in a comprehensive range of areas. Our approach enables us to complete the assignment significantly faster than the industry average time.

Key Contact:
Mr. George McKenzie, President
Ms. Ingrid McKenzie, Director of Client Services

Salary minimum: $50,000

Functions: Generalist

Industries: Generalist

Professional Selection Services
4780 Ashford Dunwoody Rd Ste 426
Atlanta, GA 30338
(770) 393-0109
Fax: (770) 512-0211
Email: smcdowell@profselection.com
Web: www.profselection.com

Description: Mid-management search and selection services. We combine Internet research with effective sourcing and screening techniques to identify, screen and present qualified short-list candidates.

Key Contact - Specialty:
Ms. Sally A. McDowell, Managing Director - *Middle management*

Salary minimum: $70,000

Functions: Generalist

Industries: Drugs Mfg., Pharm Svcs., Mgmt. Consulting, Hospitality, New Media, Telecoms, Software, Biotech, Healthcare

Professional Associations: BABG, GWEN, TAG, TIA

Project Search Inc

PO Box 53057
Edmonton, AB T5N 4A8
Canada
(780) 628-5100
Fax: (780) 628-5104
Email: psi@projectsearch.ca
Web: www.projectsearch.ca

Description: We specialize in sales, marketing, and management recruitment projects. As placement and recruitment experts, finding businesses and people who share the same vision is our greatest challenge and our greatest strength.

Key Contact:
Mr. Bill Schell, Managing Director
Ms. Frema Bram, Executive Assistant
Ms. Caren Mueller, Office Manager

Functions: General Mgmt., Senior Mgmt., Middle Mgmt., Sales & Mktg., Mktg. Mgmt., Sales Mgmt.

Industries: Generalist

ProLinks Inc

1626 Belle View Blvd
PO Box 7365
Alexandria, VA 22307-0365
(703) 765-6873
Fax: (703) 765-6828
Email: golf@careerresources.com
Web: www.careerresources.com

Description: A highly regarded specialized recruiting firm that has both a national and international practice. We are small, cohesive and results oriented. This allows us to provide highly personalized service to a limited clientele.

Key Contact - Specialty:
Mr. Don Hughes, President - *Golf professionals, golf course superintendents, sports*
Ms. J. Reilly Hughes, Vice President - *Private club managers*

Salary minimum: $60,000

Functions: Generalist, Mgmt. Consultants, Int'l.

Industries: Generalist, Mgmt. Consulting, Hospitality, Non-classifiable

Providyn LLP

251 N Illinois St Ste 180
Indianapolis, IN 46204
(703) 834-0572
Fax: (317) 639-4116
Email: info@providyn.com
Web: www.providyn.com

Description: Our firm builds customized, scalable recruitment solutions for its clients. These solutions are focused on overcoming the challenges of a complex market while providing a compelling return on investment. These are also solutions that bring our clients the right number of the highest quality candidates available within a predetermined period of time, guaranteed!

Key Contact:
Mr. Richard R. Butz, Partner - *Pharmaceutical, insurance, banking, big 5 consulting, automotive*
Mr. Mark A. Clevenger, Partner
Mr. Glenn J. Krauser, Partner

Salary minimum: $40,000

Functions: Generalist, Senior Mgmt., Middle Mgmt., Automation, Sales Mgmt., CFO's, MIS Mgmt., Engineering

Industries: Generalist, Plastics, Rubber, Paints, Petro. Products, Metal Products, Banking, Invest. Banking, HR Services, Telecoms, Call Centers, Telephony, Digital, Wireless, Fiber Optic, Network Infrastructure

Professional Associations: IACPR, IAPS, NAPS

Pursuant Legal Consultants

PO Box 2347
Seattle, WA 98111
(206) 682-2599
Email: plclawrs@ix.netcom.com

Description: Our firm is a premier legal recruiting firm in Seattle specializing in professional personnel matters. We have a high-end retainer-based clientele with national and international exposure. Our standards for experience and credentials are extremely high and, therefore, we seek to procure stellar candidates for exceptional opportunities.

Key Contact - Specialty:
Mr. Allen G. Norman, President - *Legal*

Salary minimum: $75,000

Functions: Legal, Attorneys

Industries: Legal

The Pyle Group Ltd

6141 Peppergrass Ct
Westerville, OH 43082
(614) 891-1270
Fax: (614) 891-6380
Email: repyle@att.net
Web: www.pylegroup.com

Description: We provide human capital solutions to the financial services industry for general management functions at the executive, senior and middle management level through extensive networking, a comprehensive database, extensive research capabilities and our internal library.

Key Contact - Specialty:
Mr. Ronald E. Pyle, Managing Member - *Financial services*

Salary minimum: $100,000

Functions: General Mgmt.

Industries: Finance, Banking, Invest. Banking, Brokers, Venture Cap., Misc. Financial

Quantum Int'l Ltd

1915 E Bay Dr Ste 2B
Largo, FL 33771
(727) 587-0000
Fax: (727) 587-0015
Email: quantumnet@pipeline.com

Description: Retained search; may include specialties (such as sales, finance, training, etc.) designated by clients.

Key Contact - Specialty:
Mr. Douglas L. Anderson, Senior Principal - *Technical management*
Ms. Carol D. Small, Senior Principal - *Technical management, marketing management, research management*

Salary minimum: $60,000

Functions: Generalist, Senior Mgmt., Middle Mgmt., Product Dev., Mktg. Mgmt., R&D, Engineering, Mgmt. Consultants

Industries: Generalist, Mfg., Textiles, Apparel, Chemicals, Plastics, Rubber, Accounting, Mgmt. Consulting

Professional Associations: FAPS

Quetico Corp

4545 Fuller Dr Ste 200
Irving, TX 75038
(972) 719-9120
Fax: (972) 719-9122
Email: quetico@anational.com

Description: A retained search firm specializing in placement of human resources, finance and general management professionals in all industries.

Key Contact - Specialty:
Mr. C. Robert Morrison, President - *Human resources, retail*
Ms. Susan S. Morrison, Principal - *Finance, healthcare*

Salary minimum: $60,000

Functions: General Mgmt., Middle Mgmt., Benefits, Personnel, Training, Finance

Industries: Generalist

Professional Associations: HRPS, SHRM, WAW

Quigley Associates

2845 Post Rd Ste 106
Warwick, RI 02886-3145
(401) 732-7622

Description: Personalized, high quality firm serving all segments of the healthcare field. Emphasis on senior management and physician search. National practice backed by over twenty years' experience.

Key Contact:
Mr. Jack Quigley, President

Salary minimum: $75,000

Functions: Generalist, Nurses, Allied Health, Health Admin., HR Mgmt., Benefits, Personnel, Training

Industries: Generalist, HR Services, Insurance, Healthcare

L J Quinn & Associates Inc

260 S Los Robles Ave Ste 301
Pasadena, CA 91101
(626) 793-6044
Fax: (626) 793-7183
Email: ljq@pacbell.net

Description: Our firm performs senior-level executive search and management assessment for both large and small corporations. The firm is rather small for a national organization and, as a result, provides clients a very personal and professional service. Most of the firms' clients are growth-oriented and dynamic organizations in need of creative, line, and staff management.

Key Contact:
Mr. Leonard J. Quinn, President

Salary minimum: $60,000

Functions: Directors, Senior Mgmt., Admin. Svcs., Mktg. Mgmt., Personnel, M&A, MIS Mgmt.

Industries: Computer Equip., Misc. Mfg., Finance, Venture Cap., Misc. Financial, Media, Telecoms, Real Estate, Software

Branches:
90 Park Ave Ste 1700
PMB 196
New York, NY 10016
(212) 687-7798
Key Contact:
Mr. L. J. Quinn

Quorum Associates[†]

12 W 57th St Ste 901
New York, NY 10019
(212) 308-6888
Email: jhbarnes@quorumpartners.com
Web: www.quorumpartners.com

Description: The newly established American subsidiary of Asia's largest and most successful executive search firm focusing on the investment banking industry.

Key Contact:
Mr. Francis Goldwyn, Managing Partner

Salary minimum: $100,000

Functions: Generalist, Senior Mgmt., Middle Mgmt., Personnel, CFO's, Cash Mgmt., Systems Analysis, Int'l.

Industries: Generalist, Finance, Invest. Banking, Venture Cap.

QVS Int'l
3005 River Dr - 501
Savannah, GA 31404
(912) 353-7773
Email: qvsconsult@aol.com

Description: We are an international, retained, and generalist firm. We serve US and foreign firms. We have executive search and support staff divisions. Our firm also provides management consulting in marketing, HR, policy and procedure development, flowcharting of operations, mergers/acquisitions, and organizational development. We have two US and four foreign affiliates.

Key Contact - Specialty:
Mr. B. V. Cooper, President - *Generalist, middle management, senior management, foreign-based firms in US*
Mr. Eric W. Robyn, Senior Vice President - *Generalist, middle management, senior management, foreign-based firms in US*

Salary minimum: $50,000

Functions: Generalist

Industries: Generalist, Construction, Mfg., Transportation, Services, Defense, Environmental Svcs., Aerospace, Packaging, Software

R & L Associates Ltd
145 W 67th St Ste 5E
New York, NY 10023
(212) 496-6066
Fax: (212) 496-5807
Email: rlassociate@aol.com

Description: We are specialists in staffing for the executive search industry, worldwide. Partnering with our clients to help grow and expand their businesses, our searches include: strategy partners, managing directors, consultants, and information/research specialists. The "go-getters" of executive search...we go that extra mile!

Key Contact - Specialty:
Ms. Rochelle Schumer, President/CEO - *Executive search firms, professional services, management consulting*
Mr. Leonard Rehner, COO/Senior Executive Vice President - *Financial services, international investment banking, higher education, museums, galleries*
Mr. Marvin Schumer, Sr Vice President - *Information technology, internet, emerging technologies, software, e-commerce*

Functions: General Mgmt., Senior Mgmt.

Industries: Generalist, Finance, Venture Cap., Higher Ed., Mgmt. Consulting, HR Services, New Media

Professional Associations: ESRT

R J Industries
40 W 55th St Ste 3-B
New York, NY 10019
(212) 953-6995
Email: rjindustry@aol.com

Description: We are one of the nation's leading firms specializing in high-level technology management retained search.

Key Contact - Specialty:
Mr. Ronald J. DiCamillo, President - *Technology management*

Salary minimum: $150,000

Functions: Generalist, General Mgmt., Directors, Senior Mgmt., Product Dev., MIS Mgmt., R&D, Engineering

Industries: Generalist, Food, Bev., Tobacco, Paper, Drugs Mfg., Medical Devices, Aerospace, Biotech

Branches:
1754 15th St Ste 6
Santa Monica, CA 90404
(310) 392-4730
Fax: (310) 396-5965
Key Contact - Specialty:
Mr. Gary Richards, Principal - *Technology management*

2703 DeSoto Dr
Austin, TX 78746
(512) 263-1552
Fax: (512) 263-1553
Key Contact - Specialty:
Mr. John C. Elges, Principal - *Technology management*

R M Associates
PO Box 155
Dublin, OH 43017
(740) 549-0606
Fax: (614) 764-3808

Description: Generalist, national scope-manager level and up. Heavy emphasis in manufacturing, engineering and finance. Principal has 15+ years in retained search - major clients.

Key Contact - Specialty:
Mr. Richard A. Marling, President - *Generalist*

Salary minimum: $60,000

Functions: Generalist, Middle Mgmt., Plant Mgmt., Distribution, Sales Mgmt., CFO's, Engineering

Industries: Generalist

R/K Int'l Inc
1720 Post Rd E Ste 222
Post House
Westport, CT 06880
(203) 255-9490
Fax: (203) 255-9633
Email: info@rkinternational.com
Web: www.rkinternational.com

Description: We bring over 45 years of experience to the search process in a collaborative effort with our clients. All assignments are managed from start to finish by the principals. Integrity and performance are the key to our success.

Key Contact - Specialty:
Mr. Kenneth A. Walsh, President - *Generalist*
Mr. Richard M. Dubrow, Executive Vice President - *Technology*

Salary minimum: $75,000

Functions: Generalist

Industries: Generalist

Frank A Rac & Associates
72 Kings Hwy S
Westport, CT 06880
(203) 226-1390
Fax: (203) 226-0667
Email: far53@aol.com
Web: www.racassociates.com

Description: We are a retained executive search firm that has been in business for over 20 years. We

place senior executives in new economy, as well as the traditional Fortune 1000 companies. We publish a free monthly newsletter, the "Rac Report," which appears on line.

Key Contact - Specialty:
Mr. Frank A. Rac, Founder
Ms. Barbara Pearson, Managing Director - *Technology*

Salary minimum: $200,000

Functions: General Mgmt., Senior Mgmt., Middle Mgmt., Sales & Mktg., HR Mgmt., Finance, Minorities

Industries: Generalist, Energy, Utilities, Mfg., Finance, Communications, Government, Aerospace, Insurance, Software, Biotech, Healthcare

Radosevic Associates
12658-88 Carmel Country Rd
San Diego, CA 92130-3186
(858) 350-0050
Email: franjo@adnc.com

Description: Our president has 32 years of worldwide experience in recruiting, hard-to-find and hard-to-attract, professionals and upper-management individuals, particularly for start-up and high-growth oriented firms in the high-technology fields.

Key Contact - Specialty:
Mr. Frank Radosevic, Founder/President - *High technology generalist*
Ms. Tanya C. Radosevic, Director of Research - *High technology generalist*

Salary minimum: $90,000

Functions: Generalist

Industries: Generalist, Medical Devices, Computer Equip., Consumer Elect., Test, Measure Equip., New Media, Biotech

Raines Int'l Inc
250 Park Ave Fl 17
New York, NY 10177
(212) 997-1100
Fax: (212) 997-0196
Web: www.rainesinternational.com

Description: International generalist firm specializing in middle- to upper-management executives. Concentrations include general management, finance and accounting, marketing, information technology (MIS), strategic planning, operations/procurement, investment banking, real estate/finance, human resources and insurance.

Key Contact:
Mr. Bruce R. Raines, President

Salary minimum: $150,000

Functions: Generalist, General Mgmt., Senior Mgmt., Mfg., Sales & Mktg., Finance, CFO's, M&A, IT, Mgmt. Consultants

Industries: Generalist, Mfg., Food, Bev., Tobacco, Drugs Mfg., Finance, Invest. Banking, Venture Cap., Misc. Financial, Media, Software, Healthcare

Professional Associations: AESC, IACPR

Branches:
70 W Madison Fl 14
Chicago, IL 60602
(312) 214-6100
Fax: (312) 214-6102
Web: www.rainesintl.com
Key Contact:
Mr. Michael Enbar

Ramm Search

(a division of Ramm Assoc)
Military Trail Ctr
PO Box 1150
Jupiter, FL 33468
(561) 741-0323
Fax: (561) 741-0363
Email: info@rammassoc.com

Description: We are the executive search division of the oldest human resources outsourcing company in the nation. We have divisions in labor relations, compensation and benefits, training and development, employee relations, etc. We handle a variety of senior level disciplines on both container and retainer basis and do no contingency work.

Key Contact - Specialty:
Mr. Kenneth Migdol, President - *General management*

Salary minimum: $85,000

Functions: Generalist, Sales & Mktg., HR Mgmt., Finance, IT, R&D, Engineering, Int'l.

Industries: Generalist

Professional Associations: AESC, IACPR, AAA, ACA, AMCF, ASTD, CEOC, IMC, NAM, NAPC, SHRM, SHRMCF, YPO

Networks: Glasford Executive Search Consultants

Rand Associates

204 Lafayette Ctr
Kennebunk, ME 04043
(207) 985-7700
Fax: (207) 985-7879
Email: candidatemail@aol.com

Description: Generalist with a concentration within manufacturing and financial services firms.

Key Contact - Specialty:
Mr. Rand W. Gesing, President - *Manufacturing, financial services*

Functions: Generalist, General Mgmt., Materials, Sales & Mktg., Engineering

Industries: Generalist, Mfg., Food, Bev., Tobacco, Textiles, Apparel, Soap, Perf., Cosmtcs., Medical Devices, Plastics, Rubber, Metal Products, Motor Vehicles, Consumer Elect., Test, Measure Equip., Electronic, Elec. Components, Wholesale, Retail, Finance, Biotech

The Rankin Group Ltd

PO Box 1120
Lake Geneva, WI 53147
(262) 279-5005
Fax: (262) 279-6705
Email: info@rankingroup.net
Web: www.rankingroup.net

Description: National search firm specializing in the recruitment of wealth management professionals for institutional and personal trust, private banking, investment and family office positions.

Key Contact:
Mr. Jeffrey A. Rankin, Chairman
Ms. M. J. Rankin, President

Salary minimum: $100,000

Functions: Generalist, Senior Mgmt., Mktg. Mgmt., Sales Mgmt., CFO's, Non-profits

Industries: Generalist, Finance, Invest. Banking, Misc. Financial, Mgmt. Consulting

Professional Associations: ABA

The Ransford Group

808 Travis St Ste 1200
Houston, TX 77002
(713) 722-7281
(800) 711-3080
Fax: (713) 722-0950

Web: www.ransford.com

Description: We are built upon three concepts: in-depth research, methodical search and industry specialty.

Key Contact - Specialty:
Mr. Dean E. McMann, CEO/Co-Chairman - *Management consulting, software, high technology*
Mr. Thomas W. Smith, Co-Chairman - *Management consulting, tax*
Mr. Mark A. Malinski - *COO*
Mr. Douglas H. Dickey, Managing Partner- Cnslt. & M&A Practice - *Management consulting, tax*
Mr. David R. Chyla, Managing Partner- Executive Search - *Management consulting*
Mr. William L. Hayes - *Management consulting*
Ms. Kimberly Turner
Mr. Richard A. Whittier - *Management consulting, change management*

Salary minimum: $200,000

Functions: Generalist, General Mgmt., Directors, Senior Mgmt., Mktg. Mgmt., CFO's, Taxes, Mgmt. Consultants

Industries: Generalist, Accounting, Mgmt. Consulting, Telecoms, Software

Branches:
2550 N 1st St Ste 301
San Jose, CA 95131
(408) 965-5503
Fax: (800) 945-1961
Key Contact:
Ms. Angela Gregory, Manager

885 3rd Ave Ste 2900
New York, NY 10022
(800) 711-3080
Fax: (800) 945-1961
Key Contact:
Mr. Dean McMann, President-CEO

The Ransom Group Inc

6956 E Broad St Ste 250
Columbus, OH 43213
(614) 866-7821
Fax: (614) 866-7541
Email: ransom@theransomgroup.com
Web: www.theransomgroup.com

Description: We are a retained executive search firm specializing in senior-level recruitment within the healthcare and managed care industry.

Key Contact - Specialty:
Mr. David Ransom, President - *Health care, managed care*
Mr. Kevin O'Brien, Partner - *Healthcare, managed care*
Mr. David Reusser, Partner - *Healthcare, managed care*

Salary minimum: $100,000

Functions: Generalist

Industries: Insurance, Healthcare

Edward Rast & Company

1007 Spencer Ave Ste 100
San Jose, CA 95125-1674
(408) 297-2800
Fax: (408) 297-2888
Email: er@edwardrast.com
Web: www.edwardrast.com

Description: Executive search primarily for Logistics / Small Package Distribution / Operations / Supply Chain / Customer Service / Technical Support and the IS systems that support these areas. Additional senior/middle management searches in Accounting/Finance, Board of Directors, Human Resources, Minority /EEOC and Direct Mail.

Key Contact:
Mr. Edward Rast, Managing Director

Salary minimum: $75,000

Functions: Distribution, Direct Mktg., Minorities

Industries: Generalist, Mfg., Computer Equip., Consumer Elect., Electronic, Elec. Components, Retail, Finance, Banking, Services, Pharm Svcs., E-commerce, Hospitality, Communications, Telecoms, Call Centers, Telephony, Packaging, Insurance, Software, Database SW

Branches:
235 Montgomery St Ste 901
San Francisco, CA 94104-3002
(415) 986-1710
Fax: (415) 986-1711
Email: er@edwardrast.com
Web: edwardrast.com
Key Contact:
Mr. Edward Rast, Managing Director

Ratliff, Taylor & Lekan Inc

20220 Center Ridge Rd Ste 310
Rocky River, OH 44116
(440) 895-8000
Fax: (440) 895-8028
Email: rmclaughlin@rtlinc.com
Web: www.rtlinc.com

Description: We are providers of retained executive search for Northeast Ohio and North America. We focus on building partnerships with our client's business and cultural requirements. Continuous communication is emphasized by us to ensure on-going satisfaction.

Key Contact - Specialty:
Mr. F. E. (Rick) Taylor, COO - *General managers, human resources, financial*
Ms. Elaine Ragazzo, Vice President for Executive search - *Financial, staffing services, marketing & sales*
Ms. Lisa Pagel, Vice President of Executive Search - *Legal, financial, service industries*
Mr. Thomas J. Brandt, Director of Executive Search - *Transportation equipment industry, recreation construction*
Mr. Edward R. Miller, Senior Consultant - *Motor vehicle manufacturing, oil & chemical, all functions*
Ms. Rebecca McLaughlin, Director of Research - *Executive search*

Salary minimum: $100,000

Functions: General Mgmt., Senior Mgmt., Mfg., Materials, Sales & Mktg., HR Mgmt., Finance, IT, Engineering

Industries: Generalist, Energy, Utilities, Construction, Mfg., Motor Vehicles, Misc. Mfg., Retail, Banking, Equip Svcs., Telecoms

Professional Associations: EMA, NOHRPS, SAE, SHRM, SME, WAW

Ray & Associates Inc

4403 1st Ave SE Ste 407
Cedar Rapids, IA 52402-3221
(319) 393-3115
Fax: (319) 393-4931
Email: rayassoc@netins.net
Web: www.rayandassociatesonline.com

Description: We are a national firm specializing in school personnel matters. We have been recruiting and placing school superintendents, principals, and municipal administrators for more than 25 years. Our professional search team and our services are unmatched and our fees are very competitive, especially when the quality of service is taken into consideration.

Key Contact:
Mr. Gary L. Ray, President - *Superintendents (school districts)*
Dr. Robert Decker, Director - *Superintendents (school districts)*
Dr. William Newman, Director

Functions: CFO's

Industries: Higher Ed.

Professional Associations: AASA, NSBA

Ray & Berndtson
301 Commerce St Ste 2300
Ft. Worth, TX 76102
(817) 334-0500
Fax: (817) 334-0779
Email: searchinquiry@rayberndtson.com
Web: www.rayberndtson.com

Description: Retained executive search and management consulting firm serving major worldwide companies across all industries and functions.

Key Contact - Specialty:
Mr. Paul R. Ray, Jr., Chairman/CEO
Mr. Michael J. Murray, VP/Chief Financial Officer
Mr. Breck Ray, IL/Managing Partner - *Energy, utilities*
Mr. John N. Hobart, Partner - *Energy, utilities*
Mr. Jay Kizer, IL/Managing Partner - *Healthcare*
Ms. Renee Baker Arrington, Partner - *Technology*
Mr. Tim Bostick, Principal - *Energy, utilities*

Salary minimum: $150,000

Functions: Generalist

Industries: Generalist

Professional Associations: AESC, IACPR

Branches:
2029 Century Park E Ste 1000
Los Angeles, CA 90067
(310) 557-2828
Fax: (310) 277-0674
Email: searchinquiry@rayberndtson.com
Key Contact - Specialty:
Mr. Scott D. Somers, IL/Managing Partner - *Business, professional services*
Mr. John B. Bohle, Partner - *Industrial products, industrial services*
Ms. Shelly F. Fust, Partner - *Consumer (products, services)*
Mr. Walter Ames, Principal - *Industrial products & services*
Mr. Michael Otte, Principal - *Services (business, professional)*

2479 E Bayshore Rd Ste 801
Palo Alto, CA 94303
(650) 494-2500
Fax: (650) 494-3800
Email: searchinquiry@rayberndtson.com
Key Contact - Specialty:
Mr. John A. Holland, Partner - *Technology*
Mr. James A. McFadzean, Partner - *Technology*

191 Peachtree St NE Ste 3800
Atlanta, GA 30303-1757
(404) 215-4600
Fax: (404) 215-4620
Email: searchinquiry@rayberndston.com
Web: www.rayberndston.com
Key Contact - Specialty:
Ms. Kathleen M. Maloney, Partner - *Technology*
Mr. Robert P. Collins, Partner - *Health care*
Mr. Stephen A. Dezember, Partner - *Healthcare*
Mr. Noel A. Follrath, Partner - *Financial services*
Mr. Clarke Collins, Partner - *Technology*
Mr. John P. "Jack" Schreitmueller, Partner - *Industrial (products, services)*
Ms. Deborah Coogan Seltzer, Partner - *Healthcare*
Mr. Dan Srba, Principal - *Financial services*

233 S Wacker Dr Ste 4020
Sears Twr
Chicago, IL 60606-6310
(312) 876-0730
Fax: (312) 876-6850
Email: searchinquiry@rayberndtson.com
Key Contact - Specialty:
Mr. Donald B. Clark, IL/Managing Partner - *Financial services*

Mr. John P. Doyle, Partner - *Financial services*
Ms. Jane C. Beatty, Partner - *Business, professional services*
Mr. Paul E. Came, Partner - *Consumer (products, services)*
Ms. Lynn K. Cherney, Partner - *Financial services*
Mr. Tim Wujcik, Partner - *Services (business, professional)*
Mr. Charles C. Ratigan, IL/Managing Partner - *Industrial (products, services)*
Mr. Alvin H. Spector, Partner - *Financial services*
Mr. Robert H. Tate, Partner - *Consumer (products, services)*
Mr. R. L. "Larry" Taylor, Partner - *Healthcare*
Mr. Peter Sweeney, Partner - *Industrial products & services*

245 Park Ave Fl 33
New York, NY 10167-3398
(212) 370-1316
Fax: (212) 370-1462
Email: searchinquiry@rayberndtson.com
Key Contact - Specialty:
Ms. Lisa C. Hooker, IL/Managing Partner - *Technology*
Mr. Jacques P. André, Partner - *Financial services*
Mr. Abram Claude, Jr., Partner - *Financial services*
Mr. Frederic M. Comins, Jr., Partner - *Consumer (products, services)*
Mr. Ellery Gordon, Principal - *Services (business, professional)*
Mr. Patrick A. Delhougne, Partner - *Technology*
Ms. Mary Hellen Dunn, Partner - *Financial services*
Ms. Pammy Brooks, Partner - *Services (business, professional)*
Mr. Kenneth M. Rich, Partner - *Financial services*
Ms. Penny Simon, Partner - *Financial services*
Ms. Judy K. Weddle, Partner - *Financial services*
Mr. William H. Weed, Partner - *Business services, professional services*
Mr. Kevin Chase, Partner - *Services (business, professional)*
Ms. G. Angela Henry, Principal - *Healthcare*
Ms. Catherine A. "Cathy" McNamara, Principal - *Consumer (products, services)*
Mr. Peter Kaplan, Principal - *Healthcare, life sciences*

2200 Ross Ave Ste 4500W
Chase Twr
Dallas, TX 75201
(214) 969-7620
Fax: (214) 754-0646
Email: searchinquiry@rayberndtson.com
Key Contact - Specialty:
Mr. David M. Love, II, IL/Managing Partner - *Consumer (products, services)*
Mr. Stephen T. Jordan, Partner - *Financial services*
Ms. Jennifer Schaulin, Principal - *Consumer (products, services)*

600 Travis St Ste 6230
Chase Twr
Houston, TX 77002
(713) 309-1400
Fax: (713) 309-1401
Email: searchinquiry@rayberndtson.com
Key Contact - Specialty:
Ms. Kathleen A. Johnson, Partner - *Business and professional services*
Mr. Randy Lowry, Partner - *Energy & utilities*

710-1050 W Pender St
Vancouver, BC V6E 3S7
Canada
(604) 685-0261
Fax: (604) 684-7988
Email: vancouver@raybern.ca
Key Contact - Specialty:
Mr. Kyle Mitchell, Co-Managing Partner - *Generalist*
Mr. John Tanton, Co-Managing Partner - *Generalist*
Mr. Craig Hemer, Partner
Ms. Caroline Jellinck, Partner
Ms. Lisa Kershaw, Partner

Ms. Catherine Van Alstine, Partner
Mr. Alec Wallace, Partner
Ms. Wendy Carter, Principal - *Business & professional services*

1894 Barrington St Fl 10
Barrington Twr
PO Box 2166
Halifax, NS B3J 3C4
Canada
(902) 421-1330
Fax: (902) 425-1108
Email: info@robsur.com
Key Contact:
Mr. Mark Surrette, Managing Partner
Mr. Jamie Baillie
Ms. Lindsey Clark
Mr. Dan Shaw

200 Bay St S Twr Ste 3150
Toronto, ON M5J 2J3
Canada
(416) 366-1990
Fax: (416) 366-7353
Email: managingpartner@raybern.ca
Key Contact:
Ms. Sue Banting, Partner
Mr. Joseph E. Zinner, Partner
Mr. W. Carl Lovas, Managing Partner
Mr. David Murray, Partner
Mr. Chris Pantelidis, Principal
Mr. Larry Ross, Partner
Mr. Paul R. A. Stanley, Senior Partner
Mr. James H. Stonehouse, Principal
Ms. Christine S. Thomas, Partner
Ms. Elizabeth B. Wright, Partner

1250 W Rene Levesque Blvd Ste 3925
Montreal, QC H3B 4W8
Canada
(514) 937-1000
Fax: (514) 937-1264
Email: managingdirector@ray-berndtson.ca
Web: www.rayberndtson.ca
Key Contact - Specialty:
Mr. Bernard F. Labrecque, Managing Partner - *High technology, software, telecommunications, biotechnology*
Mr. Roger Lachance, Partner - *Manufacturing, print media, forestry*
Mr. Jean E. Laurendeau, Partner - *Financial services, energy-utilities, professional services*

Palo Santo No 6
Col Lomas Altas
Mexico City, DF 11950
Mexico
52 5 259 6010
Fax: 52 5259 4000
Email: gguerra@rayberndtson.com
Web: www.rayberndston.com
Key Contact:
Mr. Craig J. Dudley, Managing Partner
Mr. Gabriel Guerra Castellanos, Managing Partner
Mr. Luis Lezama Cohen, Partner
Mr. Ronald W. Nicholas, Partner

Raycor Search†
2533 N Carson St Ste 4715
Carson City, NV 89706
(800) 472-9267
(800) 472-9267
Fax: (310) 791-5089
Email: raycorsearch@raycorsearch.com
Web: www.raycorsearch.com

Description: We are a retained search firm. We are held on a national retainer by some of the most exciting companies in the IT professional services and software arena today. We have senior positions in sales and management.

Key Contact - Specialty:
Ms. R. Rualo, President
Mr. Tyler Tuttle, Executive Recruiter/Manager - *E-commerce, CRM*

Functions: IT

---

† occasional contingency assignments

Industries: Generalist

Raynak Search

PO Box 1566
Soquel, CA 95073-1566
(831) 477-0548
Fax: (831) 479-1799
Email: laura@raynaksearch.com
Web: www.raynaksearch.com

Description: Results focused Retained Executive Search for CXO and those who report into the office of the president. Focus on behavioral interviewing, corporate compatibility and fit. Serving clients from start-ups to Fortune 100. Lead workshops to identify, interview and evaluate candidates to uncover both competancy and chemistry.

Key Contact:
Ms. Laura Raynak, Principal Consultant
Mr. Richard Pinsker, CMC, Principal

Functions: Senior Mgmt.

Industries: Generalist

Professional Associations: ACG, FWE, IMCUSA, NACD, NCHRA, SVASE

RCE Associates

24 Jefferson Plz
Princeton, NJ 08540
(732) 329-1601
(609) 688-0797
Fax: (732) 329-1603
Email: jwg@plasticsearch.com
Web: www.plasticsearch.com

Description: We have completed over 100 technical and hard to find senior and middle-level executive searches for a variety of manufacturing technologies and service industries. Additionally, we have completed domestic and international assignments in many other functional areas and at the most senior-level.

Key Contact - Specialty:
Mr. John W. Guarniere, President - *Manufacturing, tooling, custom injection molding, precision metal stamping*

Salary minimum: $75,000

Functions: Generalist, General Mgmt., Mfg., Plant Mgmt., Sales & Mktg.

Industries: Generalist, Plastics, Rubber, Metal Products, Misc. Mfg., Electronic, Elec. Components, Services, Mgmt. Consulting, HR Services

Professional Associations: SHRM, SPE

Recruiting Options

PO Box 2448
Staunton, VA 24402-2448
(540) 248-2300
Fax: (540) 248-5530
Email: mail@recruitingoptions.net
Web: www.recruitingoptions.net

Description: Recruiting options, is a candidate sourcing firm specializing in human resources. We identify, source, pre-qualify and refer candidates to our client companies. We operate on a consulting basis with none of the after-hire fees associated with traditional search firms. Our services are a more cost effective HR sourcing alternative to contingency and retained search firms.

Key Contact:
Mr. Steve Zimmerman, SPHR, President

Salary minimum: $50,000

Functions: HR Mgmt.

Industries: Generalist

Redden & McGrath Associates Inc

427 Bedford Rd
Pleasantville, NY 10570
(914) 747-3900
Fax: (914) 747-3984
Email: rddnmcg@aol.com

Description: We are a nationwide general practice firm specializing in direct marketing, marketing research, creative services, and Internet among others for the consumer and business-to-business products and service industries. All of our searches are directly managed by a partner with an emphasis on service and quality.

Key Contact - Specialty:
Ms. Mary Redden, Partner - *Marketing research, marketing*
Ms. Laura McGrath Faller, Partner - *Direct marketing, internet, creative services, marketing*

Salary minimum: $75,000

Functions: Generalist, Mkt. Research, Mktg. Mgmt., Direct Mktg.

Industries: Generalist, Food, Bev., Tobacco, Soap, Perf., Cosmtcs., Banking, Misc. Financial, Hospitality, Publishing, Broadcast, Film

Redwood Partners Ltd

152 Madison Ave Fl 16
New York, NY 10016
(212) 843-8585
Fax: (212) 843-9093
Email: speed@redwoodpartners.com
Web: www.redwoodpartners.com

Description: We are the premier executive search firm in the new media and Internet marketplace. Filling senior management positions nationally, we are building the companies that are building the Internet.

Key Contact - Specialty:
Mr. Michael Flannery, Founder/CEO - *New media, internet, interactive services, electronic commerce software*
Mr. Randy Schoenfeld, President - *New media, internet, interactive services*

Salary minimum: $75,000

Functions: Senior Mgmt.

Industries: Generalist, Media

Professional Associations: AAF, ACNY, CIMA, NYNMA, WNM

Reeder & Associates Ltd

1095 Old Roswell Rd Ste F
Roswell, GA 30076-1665
(770) 649-7523
Fax: (770) 649-7543
Email: submit@reederassoc.com
Web: www.reederassoc.com

Description: Nationally known and recognized for expertise in the managed care/health care industry, we have an extensive data bank and research library of company/organization files and information on key executives and industry profiles. Sixty percent of assignments conducted are for the roles of CEO, COO and/or president/CEO

Key Contact - Specialty:
Mr. Michael S. Reeder, President - *Managed care, healthcare*

Salary minimum: $200,000

Functions: Generalist, Senior Mgmt., Physicians, Health Admin., Mktg. Mgmt., HR Mgmt., CFO's, MIS Mgmt.

Industries: Generalist, Healthcare

Professional Associations: AESC

Reffett & Associates

10900 NE 4th St Ste 2300
Bellevue, WA 98004
(425) 637-2993
Fax: (425) 635-7799
Web: www.reffettassociates.com

Key Contact - Specialty:
Mr. William M. Reffett, Managing Partner - *Retail, supermarket, information technology*

Salary minimum: $125,000

Functions: Generalist, General Mgmt., Directors, Senior Mgmt., Product Dev., CFO's, MIS Mgmt., Mgmt. Consultants

Industries: Generalist, Mfg., Textiles, Apparel, Retail, Venture Cap., Mgmt. Consulting, Hospitality

Branches:
1750 Montgomery St Ste 111
San Francisco, CA 94111
(415) 457-6125

350 Park Ave Fl 8
New York, NY 10022
(212) 333-8728

3200 Northline Ave Ste 130
Greensboro, NC 27480
(336) 856-8128

The Regis Group Ltd†

4292 Revere Cir
Marietta, GA 30062
(770) 998-2188
Fax: (770) 998-2188
Email: regisatl@msn.com

Description: Retained firm committed to servicing our client's requirements in most disciplines through professionalism, confidentiality and integrity, while maintaining an attractive fee structure.

Key Contact:
Mr. Stephan W. Kirschner, President
Mr. Kenneth D. Lee, Director of Recruiting

Salary minimum: $40,000

Functions: Generalist

Industries: Mfg., Plastics, Rubber, Services, Accounting, Mgmt. Consulting, HR Services, Telecoms, Packaging

Reifel & Associates

617 Riford Rd
Glen Ellyn, IL 60137-3923
(630) 469-6651
Fax: (630) 469-6659

Description: Search firm specializing in retained recruiting and industry researching. Search work emphasis in manufacturing operations and lean manufacturing management.

Key Contact - Specialty:
Ms. Laurie L. Reifel - *Generalist*

Salary minimum: $75,000

Functions: Generalist, General Mgmt., Production, Plant Mgmt., Quality, Mktg. Mgmt., CFO's, Mgmt. Consultants

Industries: Generalist, Chemicals, Plastics, Rubber, Paints, Petro. Products, Machine, Appliance, Mgmt. Consulting, HR Services

Daniel F Reilly & Associates Inc

1175 Burbee Pond Rd
West Townshend, VT 05359
(802) 874-8201
(802) 874-8202
Fax: (802) 874-9966
Email: dfreilly@mindspring.com

Description: We provide retained search only to software and Internet industries and the technical needs of hedge funds. We place in all positions, including: programmers, statistical analysts, presales, sales, regional sales, national sales managers, management, project leaders, project managers, software architects, CIOs, CEOs, and CFOs.

Key Contact:
Mr. Daniel F. Reilly, Jr., President

Salary minimum: $60,000

Functions: MIS Mgmt., Systems Analysis, Systems Dev., Systems Implem., Network Admin., DB Admin.

Industries: Software

Rein & Company Inc
(a division of Rein Capital)
150 Airport Rd Ste 700
Lakewood, NJ 08701
(732) 367-5555
Fax: (732) 367-8948
Email: info@reincapital.com
Web: www.reincapital.com

Description: Company caters primarily to venture capitalists and major IT corporations, geography covered: continental US, some European and Far Eastern activity. The firm often co-invests with the venture capitalists.

Key Contact:
Mr. David Rein, Chairman
Mr. Steve Rein, Vice Chairman
Mr. Dan Czermak, CEO - *Technology*
Mr. Dave Shimano, Vice President

Salary minimum: $120,000

Functions: General Mgmt., Senior Mgmt.

Industries: Computer Equip., Consumer Elect., Electronic, Elec. Components, Venture Cap., New Media, Communications

The Douglas Reiter Company Inc
PO Box 947
Lake Oswego, OR 97034
(503) 699-6916
Email: reiterco@aol.com
Web: www.reiterco.com

Description: Our firm specializes in the forest products industry world-wide. With 25 years experience, we possess extensive industry expertise, contacts, and demonstrated track record of success.

Key Contact:
Mr. Douglas Reiter, President/CEO

Functions: Generalist, Mfg.

Industries: Agri., Forestry, Mining, Mfg., Lumber, Furniture, Paper, Chemicals, Mgmt. Consulting, Packaging, Mfg. SW

Networks: SearchNet Int'l

The Remington Group
200 Applebee St Ste 213
Barrington, IL 60010
(847) 577-2000
Fax: (847) 577-2066
Email: sweet@theremingtongroup.com

Description: We specialize in the consumer products area concentrating in the houseware and hardware industries. Our expertise covers consumer packaged goods to hard good durables primarily in the marketing and sales executive area, both domestically and internationally.

Key Contact - Specialty:
Ms. Eleanor Anne Sweet, Managing Director - *Consumer marketing, consumer packaged goods, consumer hardlines, consumer sales executives, consumer management*

Salary minimum: $75,000

Functions: Generalist, Directors, Senior Mgmt., Middle Mgmt., Product Dev., Sales & Mktg., Mktg. Mgmt., Sales Mgmt., PR, Minorities

Industries: Generalist, Food, Bev., Tobacco, Textiles, Apparel, Lumber, Furniture, Soap, Perf., Cosmtcs., Plastics, Rubber, Paints, Petro. Products, Machine, Appliance

Professional Associations: CSHA, HCC

Renaissance Resources
9100 Arboretum Pkwy Ste 270
Richmond, VA 23236
(804) 330-3088
Fax: (804) 330-7188
Email: info@rrsearch.com
Web: www.rrsearch.com

Description: We specialize in providing exceptional search consulting across a spectrum of industries and disciplines. We do this by combining the art and science of conducting search. The firm also provides specific guarantees to ensure the 100% completion and satisfaction of searches.

Key Contact:
Mr. Robert L. Bryant, President - *Banking, finance, manufacturing, information systems*
Mr. David L. Ambruster, Managing Partner - *Manufacturing, engineering, quality, power generation, pulp & paper*
Mr. Alfred Hinkle, Senior Consultant - *Banking, finance, information systems, telecommunications*
Mr. Thomas Askew, Senior Consultant - *Manufacturing, engineering, quality, logistics*
Mr. Michael McAnney, Senior Consultant - *Manufacturing, finance, human resources*
Ms. Lori Bryant, Research

Salary minimum: $70,000

Functions: Generalist, General Mgmt., Mfg., Materials, Sales & Mktg., Finance, IT, Engineering

Industries: Generalist, Energy, Utilities, Mfg., Finance, Services, Software

Professional Associations: ASTD, HRPS, SHRM, WAW

Renaud Foster Management Consultants Inc
100 Sparks St Ste 550
Ottawa, ON K1P 5B7
Canada
(613) 231-6666
(800) 513-8117
Fax: (613) 231-6663
Email: documents@renaudfoster.com
Web: www.renaudfoster.com

Description: We are recognized as one of the leading providers of expert advice, offering integrated management services to boards, CEOs and senior management in the fields of executive search, executive coaching and corporate governance.

Key Contact:
Mr. Tom Foster, Managing Director

Salary minimum: $80,000

Functions: Generalist, Directors, Senior Mgmt., Int'l.

Industries: Generalist, Agri., Forestry, Mining, Mfg., Transportation, Finance, Media, Government

The Repovich-Reynolds Group (TRRG Inc)
283 S Lake Ave Fl 2
Pasadena, CA 91101
(626) 585-9455
Fax: (626) 585-1670
Email: behunted@trrg.com
Web: www.trrg.com

Description: We are a highly respected international search & management consulting firm specializing in the core functional areas: corporate communications, investor relations and marketing. We work with corporations ranging from pre-IPO to large-cap multinational organizations in all industries.

Key Contact - Specialty:
Ms. Smooch S. Reynolds, President/CEO - *Communications, investor relations, marketing*
Ms. Monet M. LeMon, S.V.P./Executive Recruiter - *Communications, investor relations, marketing*
Ms. Michelle Monfor, Director/Executive Recruiter - *Communications, investor relations, marketing*

Salary minimum: $75,000

Functions: Generalist, Mktg. Mgmt., PR

Industries: Generalist

Professional Associations: CCM, IABC, NIRI, PRSA

Reserve Technology Institute†
2610A Dunlavy
Houston, TX 77006
(713) 521-7977
Fax: (713) 521-3607
Email: talent@rti-hou.com
Web: www.rti-hou.com

Description: Process (downstream & upstream) and power engineering specialists, senior management, business/project development, engineering management. Refining, chemical, petrochem, power and process control.

Key Contact - Specialty:
Ms. Mary Needham, President - *Engineering, senior management*

Salary minimum: $70,000

Functions: Generalist

Industries: Energy, Utilities, Construction, Environmental Svcs.

Professional Associations: AICHE, ASME

Resolve Associates Int'l
440 SE 13th Ave
Pompano Beach, FL 33060
(954) 942-8344
Fax: (954) 943-6607
Email: resolve@gate.net
Web: www.resolveassociates.com

Description: We are an international executive search firm that specializes in the recruitment of senior-level executives for "in-country" and regional positions throughout Central and Latin America. Our Fortune 500, multi-national clientele are leaders in Internet/multi-media, IT, telecommunications, pharmaceutical, electronics, manufacturing, business services, distribution, and retail.

Key Contact - Specialty:
Mr. John Juanito Finch, President - *Generalist, senior-level executives, central & latin america*

Salary minimum: $75,000

Functions: Generalist, Int'l.

Industries: Generalist

The Resource Group
(a division of The Direct Marketing Resource Group LLC)
705 Boston Post Rd
Guilford, CT 06437
(203) 453-7070
Fax: (203) 453-7580
Email: ralph@eresourcegrp.com
Web: www.eresourcegrp.com

Description: Largest search firm specializing in the direct marketing, catalog, e-commerce and

---

telemarketing arena's. Work nationwide at the manager, director and VP level.

Key Contact - Specialty:
Mr. Ralph P. Peragine, President - *Direct marketing, catalog marketing, telemarketing (database, analytical) ecommerce operations, direct mail*

Salary minimum: $80,000

Functions: Generalist, Directors, Senior Mgmt., Middle Mgmt., Mkt. Research, Mktg. Mgmt., Direct Mktg., Customer Svc.

Industries: Generalist, Non-classifiable

Professional Associations: AIM, ATA, CADM, DMA, DMASL, DMAW, DMCNY, FDMA, LADMA, MDMA, RMDMA

The Resource Group†
PO Box 331
Red Bank, NJ 07701
(732) 842-6555
Fax: (732) 842-6557

Description: We fill key sales and management positions with companies involved in the sales of equipment and services for cogeneration; power generation; resource recovery and the process industry. We have set up business development groups, domestically and internationally for utilities, oil/gas companies and equipment suppliers.

Key Contact - Specialty:
Mr. Timothy L. Howe, Senior Partner - *Business development, power generation, process (equipment, services)*

Salary minimum: $100,000

Functions: Generalist, Senior Mgmt., Middle Mgmt., Mktg. Mgmt., Sales Mgmt., Engineering, Int'l.

Industries: Generalist, Energy, Utilities, Machine, Appliance

Resource Inc
PO Box 420
Marshfield Hills, MA 02051
(781) 837-8113
Fax: (781) 837-8063
Email: tom@tchresource.com
Web: www.tchresource.com

Description: Highly specialized within the consumer products and medical device industry. Clients range from Fortune 200 to small rapidly growing privately held companies. Placement of senior and mid-level management in the disciplines of manufacturing, quality and R&D, sales and marketing, engineering and technical, supply chain/logistics and finance.

Key Contact:
Mr. Thomas C. Healy, President - *Senior management*
Mr. Edward J. Hanafin, Vice President - *Sales & marketing*
Mr. William D. Healy, Director - *Manufacturing/Technical*

Salary minimum: $50,000

Functions: General Mgmt., Mfg., Production, Plant Mgmt., Sales & Mktg., Engineering

Industries: Mfg., Food, Bev., Tobacco, Chemicals, Soap, Perf., Cosmtcs., Drugs Mfg., Medical Devices, Plastics, Rubber, Consumer Elect., Misc. Mfg., Wholesale, Retail, Packaging, Biotech, Healthcare

Branches:
349 Willow Rd
Belle Mead, NJ 08502
(908) 431-1150
Fax: (908) 431-1151

Key Contact - Specialty:
Mr. William Healy, Recruiter - *Consumer, Rx, med device*

Resource Perspectives Inc
26400 La Alameda Ste 106
Mission Viejo, CA 92691
(949) 635-9741
(949) 282-0042
Email: cherneysd@aol.com

Description: We serve the consumer packaged goods and related industries. We are specialists in research and development, safety, regulatory, engineering, manufacturing, operations, sales/marketing, and general management for foods, beverages, paper, household, toiletries, personal care, and related biotech categories.

Key Contact - Specialty:
Dr. Steven D. Cherney, Principal - *Consumer oriented industries (technical, operations, marketing, general management)*
Mr. Donald F. DeLany, Principal - *Consumer packaged goods, technical, operations, sales & marketing*

Salary minimum: $60,000

Functions: General Mgmt., Middle Mgmt., Mfg., Product Dev., Plant Mgmt., Quality, Packaging, Mkt. Research, R&D, Engineering

Industries: Mfg., Food, Bev., Tobacco, Paper, Soap, Perf., Cosmtcs., Biotech

Professional Associations: ACS, AICHE, CLM, IFT, IOPP, RAPS, SCC, SCC, TAPPI

Shirley I Retter Inc
3 Ascot Manor NW
Atlanta, GA 30327-4201
(770) 502-2677
Fax: (770) 933-0115
Email: sretter@bellsouth.net
Web: www.shirleyretter.com

Description: We are a retained executive search firm with over seven years' experience specializing in the placement of senior-level executives in all fields and functions.

Key Contact:
Ms. Shirley I. Retter

Functions: General Mgmt.

Industries: Mfg., Finance, Services, Hospitality, Media, Communications, Aerospace, Packaging, Real Estate, Software

The Revere Associates Inc
1947 Cleveland-Massillon Rd
PO Box 498
Bath, OH 44210-0498
(330) 666-6442
Fax: (330) 666-0586
Email: mike@fremon.com

Description: Search firm specializing in plastics, paper and other process industries. Work with small privately owned companies, as well as Fortune 500's. Adept at high-technology searches.

Key Contact - Specialty:
Mr. Michael W. Fremon, President - *Process, plastics, chemical, pulp & paper, management*

Salary minimum: $60,000

Functions: Generalist, Product Dev., Plant Mgmt., Mkt. Research, Mktg. Mgmt., Sales Mgmt., R&D

Industries: Generalist, Construction, Paper, Printing, Chemicals, Plastics, Rubber, Test, Measure Equip.

Professional Associations: AICHE, IOPP, SPE, TAPPI

Reyman Associates
20 N Michigan Ave Ste 520
Chicago, IL 60602
(312) 580-0808
Fax: (312) 580-1181
Email: sreyman@reymanassoc.com

Description: Each consultant dedicates exclusive efforts to one client's recruitment needs at a time, producing extremely thorough and expeditious results. Our average turnaround time is four to five weeks. Our goal is to meet and exceed our clients' expectations. We believe individual client focus along with our search expertise is what makes that possible.

Key Contact - Specialty:
Ms. Susan Reyman, President - *Generalist*

Salary minimum: $90,000

Functions: General Mgmt., Mfg., Sales & Mktg., HR Mgmt., Finance, IT, Engineering, Mgmt. Consultants, Attorneys, Int'l.

Industries: Generalist, Mfg., Food, Bev., Tobacco, Paper, Chemicals, Drugs Mfg., Plastics, Rubber, Metal Products, Consumer Elect., Misc. Mfg., Transportation, Wholesale, Retail, Finance, Services, Mgmt. Consulting, Packaging, Insurance

Professional Associations: IACPR, AME, HRMA, NAWBO, SHRP

Russell Reynolds Associates Inc
200 Park Ave Ste 2300
New York, NY 10166-0002
(212) 351-2000
Fax: (212) 370-0896
Email: info@russellreynolds.com
Web: www.russellreynolds.com

Description: We are one of the world's leading providers of executive recruiting services. Founded in New York City, we have grown since inception to more than 300 recruiting professionals working in 33 wholly owned offices around the world. Our business is assisting clients in building their human capital through recruiting and assessing executives.

Key Contact - Specialty:
Mr. Hobson Brown, Jr., President/CEO - *Board of directors, CEOs*
Mr. Albert H. Morris, Chief Financial Officer
Mr. Andrew O. Watson, Director of Human Resources
Ms. Barbara Saidel, Chief Information Officer
Ms. Katherine S. Bryant, Director of Corporate Communications
Mr. James M. Bagley, Co-Manager - *Global HR*
Mr. Joseph A. Bailey, III, Co-Manager - *Sports, media & entertainment management*

Salary minimum: $200,000

Functions: Generalist

Industries: Generalist

Professional Associations: AESC, IACPR

Branches:
333 S Grand Ave Ste 3500
Los Angeles, CA 90071-1539
(213) 253-4400
Fax: (213) 253-4444
Email: jwarren@russellreynolds.com
Key Contact - Specialty:
Mr. Jeffrey M. Warren, Executive Director/Area Manager - *Financial services, general industry*

2500 Sand Hill Rd Ste 105
Menlo Park, CA 94025-7015
(650) 233-2400
Fax: (650) 233-2499
Email: bobrand@russellreynolds.com
Key Contact - Specialty:
Mr. Barry Obrand, Managing Director - *Technology*

101 California St Ste 3140
San Francisco, CA 94111-5829
(415) 352-3300
Fax: (415) 781-7690
Email: bobrand@russellreynolds.com
Key Contact - Specialty:
Mr. Barry S. Obrand, Managing Director -
Technology

1701 Pennsylvania Ave NW Ste 400
Washington, DC 20006-5805
(202) 654-7800
Email: evautour@russellreynolds.com
Key Contact - Specialty:
Mr. Eric L. Vautour, Managing Director -
Government affairs, associations

50 Hurt Plz The Hurt Bldg Ste 600
Atlanta, GA 30303-2914
(404) 577-3000
Fax: (404) 577-2832
Email: jspence@russellreynolds.com
Key Contact - Specialty:
Mr. Joseph Spence, Jr., Managing Director -
Financial services

200 S Wacker Dr Ste 2900
Chicago, IL 60606-5802
(312) 993-9696
Fax: (312) 876-1919
Email: aredmond@russellreynolds.com
Key Contact - Specialty:
Ms. Andrea Redmond, Managing Director -
Financial services
Mr. Charles A. Tribbett, III, Managing Director -
Diversity, board services

45 School St
Old City Hall
Boston, MA 02108-3296
(617) 523-1111
Fax: (617) 523-7305
Email: nhurd@russellreynolds.com
Key Contact - Specialty:
Mr. J. Nicholas Hurd, Managing Director -
Financial Services

90 S 7th St
3050 Norwest Ctr
Minneapolis, MN 55402-3900
(612) 332-6966
Fax: (612) 332-2629
Email: bmacdonald@russellreynolds.com
Key Contact - Specialty:
Mr. Robert W. Macdonald, Jr., Managing Director -
Technology

8401 N Central Expy Ste 650
Lincoln Park
Dallas, TX 75225-4404
(214) 220-2033
Fax: (214) 220-3998
Email: dlove@russellreynolds.com
Key Contact - Specialty:
Mr. David M. Love, Managing Director - *Legal*

500 Dallas St Ste 2840
Houston, TX 77002-4708
(713) 658-1776
Fax: (713) 658-9461
Email: sraben@russellreynolds.com
Key Contact - Specialty:
Mr. Steven Raben, Managing Director - *Natural
resources*
Mr. Ron E. Lumbra, Executive Director - *Natural
resources*

40 King St W Scotia Plz Ste 3500
Toronto, ON M5H 3Y2
Canada
(416) 364-3355
Fax: (416) 364-5174
Email: pcantor@russellreynolds.com
Key Contact - Specialty:
Mr. Paul Cantor, Managing Director - *Financial
services*

Arquímedes 130-3
Col Polanco
Mexico City, DF 11560
Mexico
52 5 281 0440
Fax: 52 5 281 3121
Email: ryturbe@russellreynolds.com
Key Contact - Specialty:
Mr. Rafael Yturbe, Managing Director - *Industrial*

Reynolds Partners
590 Madison Ave Fl 21
New York, NY 10022
(212) 697-8682

Description: Small personal service firm.
Specialists: nonprofit leadership, chief executive,
board diversity, genetic engineers, geneticists and
other positions that are an outgrowth of the Genome
Project which includes positions in agriculture and
biotechnology.

Key Contact:
Ms. Sydney Reynolds, President

Salary minimum: $75,000

Functions: Generalist, Healthcare, Mktg. Mgmt.,
HR Mgmt., MIS Mgmt., Mgmt. Consultants,
Minorities, Non-profits

Industries: Generalist, Pharm Svcs., Mgmt.
Consulting, HR Services, Media, Aerospace,
Biotech, Healthcare

Professional Associations: NCNB, PF, TEI

Rhodes Associates
555 5th Ave Fl 6
New York, NY 10017
(212) 983-2000
Fax: (212) 983-8333
Email: rhodes@rhodesassociates.com
Web: www.rhodesassociates.com

[handwritten: Address OK →]
[handwritten: email is slittman@ ←]

Description: We are a general search practice with
specialization in real estate, investment
management, financial services and investment
banking; including corporate finance, global fixed
income, capital markets, trading and sales.

Key Contact - Specialty:
Mr. Steven Littman, Managing Partner - *Real estate*
Mr. Dominic Castriota, Partner - *Financial services*

Salary minimum: $150,000

Functions: Generalist

Industries: Finance, Banking, Invest. Banking,
Venture Cap., Misc. Financial, Real Estate

RIC Corp
900 E Ocean Blvd 232
Stuart, FL 34994
(561) 287-5409
(561) 288-1811
Web: www.workhappy.com

Description: Highly regarded small firm solving
problems for clients in a fair, efficient and cost
effective manner. Expertise in executive,
management, technical and sales for domestic,
international and emerging markets.

Key Contact - Specialty:
Mr. Tom Welch, President - *Generalist*
Ms. Kathleen A. O'Neill, Vice President -
Generalist

Salary minimum: $100,000

Functions: Senior Mgmt.

Industries: Transportation, Retail, Services, Pharm
Svcs., HR Services, Entertainment, Media, Real
Estate, Healthcare

Professional Associations: NSA, NSA

Rice Cohen Int'l
301 Oxford Valley Rd Ste 1506A
Yardley, PA 19067
(215) 321-4100
Fax: (215) 321-6370
Web: www.ricecohen.com

Description: We are the 26 largest retained search
firms in the US. We are the world's largest firm that
specializes in the training, education, on-line
learning, temporary staffing, and outsourcing
industries. What makes us unique is our 25-step
search and selection process and delivery of talent.

Key Contact - Specialty:
Mr. John Austin, President
Mr. Gene Rice, Founder - *Consultants, designers,
senior executives (consulting & training industry),
management consulting, assessment*
Mr. Jeff Cohen, Founder - *Temporary staffing,
outsourcing, IT services, financial/legal
technology*
Ms. Donna Paulaski, VP- of Strategic Alliance
Mr. Doug Cooperson, Managing Partner -
*Consultants, designers, senior executives
(consulting, training industry), management
consulting, assessment*
Mr. Andrew Brenner, Managing Partner -
*Temporary staffing, outsourcing, IT services,
technology (financial, legal)*
Mr. Jeff Bauer, Managing Director
Mr. Brent Gobrecht, Managing Director - *IT
services*
Mrs. Trish McManus, Managing Director - *E-
health, outsourcing*
Mr. Frank Mayr, Managing Director
Mr. Chuck Weiner, Director of Staffing - *Legal,
financial technology*
Ms. Liz DeForrest, Director of Staffing - *Electrical
electronic components, fiber optics*
Mr. Brian Forsthoffer, Director of Staffing -
Building products, automotive
Mr. Steven Krausen, Director of Staffing - *Security
systems*

Salary minimum: $75,000

Functions: Directors, Senior Mgmt., Middle
Mgmt., Mktg. Mgmt., Sales Mgmt., Training,
Finance, IT, Engineering, Mgmt. Consultants

Industries: Banking, Invest. Banking, Brokers,
Venture Cap., Software, Biotech

Professional Associations: ASTD, NAPS, NATSS

Richards Associates Inc[†]
1562 1st Ave Ste 218
New York, NY 10028
(212) 717-2670
Fax: (212) 717-2668
Email: sharon@richardsassociates.com
Web: www.richardsassociates.com

Description: We are servicing the entertainment,
sports, and consumer products industries. We
specialize in identifying marketing, promotion, and
licensing talent. We also work in related ancillary
industries including communications, advertising,
direct response, and affiliate sales and marketing.

Key Contact - Specialty:
Ms. Sharon Richards, President - *Entertainment
marketing, promotions, licensing, interactive,
public relations, direct response*
Ms. Catherine Goodwin, Associate - *Entertainment
licensing, new media*

Salary minimum: $75,000

Functions: Generalist, Sales & Mktg., Advertising,
Mkt. Research, Direct Mktg., PR, Minorities

Industries: Hospitality, Entertainment, Advertising,
Publishing, New Media, Broadcast, Film,
Entertainment SW, Marketing SW

Richardson Search Group Inc
2313 Coit Rd Ste 114
Plano, TX 75075
(972) 867-3323
Fax: (972) 608-0936
Email: rsearchgrp@aol.com

Description: We are a Texas based retainer-only executive search firm that is experienced in handling financial, health care, and information technology positions for a diverse clientele. Our goal is to always be responsive, selective, and productive.

Key Contact - Specialty:
Mr. James P. Richardson, President - *Commercial real estate, finance, high tech, health care*

Salary minimum: $85,000

Functions: Generalist, Senior Mgmt., Middle Mgmt., Mktg. Mgmt., Sales Mgmt., HR Mgmt., CFO's, MIS Mgmt.

Industries: Generalist, Banking, Invest. Banking, Telecoms, Real Estate

W F Richer Associates Inc
52 Deerfield Ln S
Pleasantville, NY 10570-1840
(212) 682-4000
(914) 747-3441

Description: We are specialists in advanced/emerging technologies. Our practice includes, but is not limited to, CIOs, CTOs, system architects, network designers, and program planners/developers.

Key Contact - Specialty:
Mr. William F. Richer, President - *Information technology, distributed computing, client/server technology, global telecommunications, internet development*
Ms. Joyce Eidenberg Richer, Senior Vice President - *Information technology, distributed computing, client/server technology, global telecommunications, internet development*

Salary minimum: $75,000

Functions: Generalist, IT, MIS Mgmt., Systems Analysis, Systems Dev., Systems Implem., Systems Support, Mgmt. Consultants

Industries: Generalist, Finance, Mgmt. Consulting, Media, New Media, Software

Riddle & McGrath LLC
1040 Crown Pointe Pkwy Ste 310
Atlanta, GA 30338
(770) 804-3190
Fax: (770) 804-3194
Email: candidate.resumes@riddle-mcgrath.com
Web: www.riddle-mcgrath.com

Description: We were established by two veterans of the executive search business to provide the highest level of professional service to a select list of clients. We added a fourth experienced search professional in 2000. Client needs outside the US are met through our network of correspondent firms.

Key Contact - Specialty:
Mr. James E. Riddle, Principal - *General management, sales & marketing, manufacturing, engineering*
Mr. Patrick McGrath, Principal - *Transportation, logistics*
Mr. Edmund A. M. Wooller, Partner - *Manufacturing, sales & marketing, finance & accounting, international, non-profit*
Ms. Nancy O'Brien May, Managing Director - *Human resources, accounting, finance, sales, marketing*

Salary minimum: $90,000

Functions: Senior Mgmt., Mfg., Distribution, Sales & Mktg., HR Mgmt., Finance, MIS Mgmt.

Industries: Generalist, Mfg., Transportation, Services, Packaging

Professional Associations: BABG, CLM, SHRM, WAW

Ridenour & Associates
1555 N Sandburg Terr Ste 602
Chicago, IL 60610
(312) 787-8228
Fax: (312) 787-8528
Email: ssridenour@aol.com
Web: www.ridenourassociates.com

Description: Domestic and international executive search specializing in the recruitment of direct marketing and integrated communications professionals.

Key Contact - Specialty:
Ms. Suzanne S. Ridenour, President - *Direct marketing, new media, interactive executives (including all integrated marketing areas)*

Salary minimum: $75,000

Functions: General Mgmt., Sales & Mktg., IT, Specialized Svcs., Mgmt. Consultants, Minorities, Non-profits, Graphic Artists, Int'l.

Industries: Retail, Media, Insurance, Software, Healthcare

Professional Associations: CADM, DMA, NAWBO, WI

Riotto-Jazylo & Company Inc
600 3rd Ave
New York, NY 10016
(212) 697-4575
Fax: (212) 370-9395
Email: rjc@riottojazylo.com
Web: www.riottojazylo.com

Description: We are a retained-search firm that recruits senior-level executives in wealth management, in technology-based businesses, and in leading domestic and multinational corporations. The firm's practice is national and international in scope and currently includes ten executive recruiters based in New York.

Key Contact - Specialty:
Mr. Anthony R. Riotto, Chairman - *Financial services, wealth management*
Mr. John V. Jazylo, President - *Leading corporations*

Salary minimum: $125,000

Functions: Generalist, Senior Mgmt., Middle Mgmt., Mkt. Research, Mktg. Mgmt., Sales Mgmt., Cash Mgmt., Risk Mgmt.

Industries: Generalist, Banking, Invest. Banking, Brokers, Venture Cap., Misc. Financial

Valletta Ritson & Company
PO Box 7429
Endicott, NY 13760
(800) 844-1738
Fax: (607) 786-8301
Email: vallritco@aol.com
Web: www.vallettaritson.com

Description: Retained Executive search focusing on Sr. Leadership and technology professionals.

Key Contact:
Mr. Frank Valletta, Principal
Ms. Stephanie Andacht, Principal

Salary minimum: $50,000

Functions: General Mgmt., Automation, Sales & Mktg., R&D, Engineering

Industries: Drugs Mfg., Medical Devices, Computer Equip., Test, Measure Equip., Electronic, Elec. Components, Banking, Telecoms, Telephony, Digital, Wireless, Fiber Optic, Aerospace, Software, Biotech

Networks: Top Echelon Network

RMA Search
101 Continental Pl Ste 105
Brentwood, TN 37027
(615) 377-9603
Fax: (615) 370-5768
Email: rmaoi@bellsouth.net
Web: www.oiworldwide.com

Description: Consultants specializing in executive search, corporate outplacement, employee appraisal, attitude surveys and operational consulting projects.

Key Contact:
Ms. Angela B. Horn, Principal

Salary minimum: $30,000

Functions: Generalist

Industries: Generalist

Branches:
301 Gallaher View Rd Ste 111
Knoxville, TN 37919
(615) 691-4733
Fax: (615) 691-4787
Key Contact:
Ms. Ellen E. Bowling, Vice President

1355 Lynnfield Rd
Memphis, TN 38119
(901) 763-1818
Key Contact:
Ms. Lynn Jackson, Senior Vice President

The Robert Driver Company
1620 5th Ave Ste 200
San Diego, CA 92101-2797
(619) 699-0511
Fax: (619) 699-0514
Email: pstafford@rfdriver.com
Web: www.rfdriver.com

Description: Primarily represent Southern California firms for their corporate and national/regional expansion needs; and represent nationally oriented firms in their need to hire western regional talent.

Key Contact - Specialty:
Mr. Peter B. Stafford, Principal - *Financial services, land development, service industries*
Ms. Norma Stafford, Principal - *Title insurance, mortgage banking*
Mr. Chris Stafford, Associate - *Mortgage banking (sub-prime), regional managers, branch managers, loan officers*
Mr. Terry Burns, Vice President - *Executive search*

Functions: Generalist, Senior Mgmt., Middle Mgmt., Admin. Svcs., Sales Mgmt., Direct Mktg., CFO's, Attorneys

Industries: Generalist, Finance, Non-profits, Legal, Accounting, E-commerce, IT Implementation, Call Centers, Insurance, Real Estate

Branches:
4041 MacArthur Blvd Ste 300
Newport Beach, CA 92660-2511
(949) 660-8133
Fax: (619) 699-0514
Email: tburns@rfdriver.com
Key Contact - Specialty:
Mr. Terry Burns, Vice President - *Executive search*

Roberts Ryan & Bentley Inc
1107 Kenilworth Dr Ste 208
Towson, MD 21204
(410) 321-6600
Fax: (410) 321-1347
Email: rrb@rrbentley.com
Web: www.rrbentley.com

Description: Research based retained executive search for mid- and upper-management. Operates within most functional areas with emphasis on general management, finance, information services and marketing.

Key Contact:
Mr. Richard R. Cappe, President
Mr. Richard A. Dannenberg, Vice President

Salary minimum: $100,000

Functions: Generalist, General Mgmt., Advertising, Personnel, Taxes, Systems Dev., Mgmt. Consultants, Minorities

Industries: Generalist, Energy, Utilities, Banking, Mgmt. Consulting, Insurance, Software, Healthcare

Branches:
3206 Sandy Ridge Dr
Clearwater, FL 33761
(727) 786-1312
Fax: (727) 786-3349
Email: rrb@rrbentley.com
Key Contact:
Ms. Sue Ann Whitley, Vice President

233 Madison Ave Ste 322
New York, NY 10016
(212) 367-2131
Email: rrb@rrbentley.com
Key Contact:
Mr. Gregory Reynolds, Vice President

J S Robertson - Retained Search
2242 Camden Ave Ste 203
San Jose, CA 95124
(408) 879-8000
Fax: (408) 879-8001
Email: info@jsrobertson.com
Web: www.jsrobertson.com

Description: Full-service search firm with specialized skill in the semiconductor and related capital equipment industries and the Internet and related systems industries. Very strong emphasis on ensuring cultural and organizational fit in addition to skill and competence matching.

Key Contact - Specialty:
Mr. Jim Robertson - *General management, engineering management, marketing management*
Ms. Sydnie Smith - *Human resources management, marketing management*
Mr. Bob Fisch - *Sales management, marketing management*
Ms. Sandy Mrykalo
Mr. Pamela Hart - *Semiconductor industry*

Salary minimum: $160,000

Functions: General Mgmt., Product Dev., Plant Mgmt., Materials, Purchasing, Sales & Mktg., Benefits, Personnel, CFO's, MIS Mgmt.

Industries: Computer Equip., Consumer Elect., Test, Measure Equip., Software

Bruce Robinson Associates
Harmon Cove Twrs Ste 8 A/L Level
Secaucus, NJ 07094
(201) 617-9595
Fax: (201) 617-1434
Email: bra1970@aol.com
Web: www.bra-search.com

Description: Our organization was formed by Bruce Robinson, who recognized the need to recruit top-flight minority and female talent on an executive search basis. We have grown and now work successfully with major Fortune 500 companies in all areas of search.

Key Contact - Specialty:
Mr. Bruce Robinson, President - *Generalist*
Mr. Eric Robinson, Vice President/Partner - *Generalist*
Mr. John Robinson, Senior Consultant - *Generalist*

Salary minimum: $90,000

Functions: Generalist, Mfg., Materials, Sales & Mktg., HR Mgmt., Budgeting, IT, R&D

Industries: Generalist, Mfg., Services, Media, Insurance, Healthcare, Non-classifiable

Professional Associations: AESC

Robinson, Fraser Group Ltd
13 Clarence Sq
Toronto, ON M5V 1H1
Canada
(416) 977-9174
Fax: (416) 977-7600
Email: es@robinsonfraser.com

Key Contact - Specialty:
Mr. Stephen Robinson, President - *Building competent executive teams*

Salary minimum: $100,000

Functions: Directors, Senior Mgmt., HR Mgmt., CFO's, MIS Mgmt.

Industries: Generalist

Robison Humphreys & Associates Inc
43 Fairway Ct
Shanty Bay, ON L0L 2L0
Canada
(416) 372-5958
(705) 835-2453
Fax: (705) 835-6553
Email: b.humphreys@sympatico.ca

Description: Direct sourcing (no advertising) executive search; over 85% of annual fees from repeat clients or referral from clients/candidates. Client base: Canada, United States, United Kingdom.

Key Contact - Specialty:
Mr. William M. Humphreys, Partner - *CEO, COO, marketing, advertising, sales*
Ms. Margaret H. Robison, Partner - *Advertising, printing, publishing*
Mr. Scott W. Humphreys, Partner - *Sales management, marketing, food & beverage, communications, utilities*

Salary minimum: $50,000

Functions: Generalist, Senior Mgmt., Advertising, Mkt. Research, Mktg. Mgmt., Sales Mgmt., PR, Non-profits

Industries: Generalist, Printing, Finance, Venture Cap., Hospitality, Advertising, Publishing, Insurance

Professional Associations: CICA

The Robsham Group
4 S Marketplace Fl 4
Faneuil Hall
Boston, MA 02109
(617) 742-2944
Fax: (617) 523-0464
Email: robsham1@aol.com
Web: www.robshamgroup.com

Description: Generous and complete involvement in each client's search; detailed screening and interviewing - extensive candidate reports. We work with a sense of urgency.

Key Contact - Specialty:
Ms. Beverly H. Robsham, President/Founder - *Finance, marketing*

Salary minimum: $75,000

Functions: Generalist

Industries: Finance, Mgmt. Consulting, HR Services, Advertising, Publishing, New Media, Broadcast, Film

Professional Associations: IACPR, DMA, SBANE

Rodzik & Associates Inc
8601 Six Forks Rd Ste 400
Raleigh, NC 27615
(919) 846-8150
Fax: (919) 846-9130

Description: Full-service firm with optional services and customized pricing to meet client requirements.

Key Contact - Specialty:
Mr. Gerald F. Rodzik, Managing Director - *Generalist*
Ms. C. L. Rodzik, President - *Generalist*
Mr. T. A. Rodzik, Esq., Secretary/General Counsel - *Legal*
S. M. Rodzik, Ph.D., Treasurer - *Biotechnology consultant*

Salary minimum: $75,000

Functions: Generalist

Industries: Energy, Utilities, Mfg., Finance, Services, Software, Biotech, Healthcare

Rogers - McManamon Executive Search
33781 Via Cascada
San Juan Capistrano, CA 92675
(949) 496-1614
Fax: (949) 496-2305
Email: rogers@mcmanamon.com
Web: www.mcmanamon.com

Description: We are ideally suited to place today's Chief Information Officer (CIO) and Chief Technical Officer (CTO), because we understand today's public and private networks, their applications, and today's information systems. Our strength is communications, having helped network industry firms hire their senior managers over the past decade.

Key Contact - Specialty:
Mr. Tim McManamon, Partner - *Communications (marketing, engineering), CIO*
Ms. Gay Rogers, Partner - *Communications (marketing, engineering), CIO*

Salary minimum: $100,000

Functions: Mktg. Mgmt., MIS Mgmt., R&D

Industries: Generalist, Communications

Rogish Associates Inc
615 Copeland Mill Rd Ste 1F
Westerville, OH 43081
(614) 899-2525
Fax: (614) 899-2524
Email: nick@rogish.com
Web: www.rogish.com

Description: Our mission is to establish long-term relationships with our client organizations and candidates by combining the elements necessary to complete the search assignment in the most professional manner.

Key Contact - Specialty:
Mr. Nick Rogish, President - *Healthcare, health insurance sales, life insurance sales*
Ms. Julie Osborne, OTR/L, Senior Consultant - *Healthcare, long term care, clinical (managers, directors)*
Mr. Kathy Ullom, Marketing/Administrative Coordinator - *Healthcare*
Ms. Kasie Alexander, CPC, Senior Consultant - *Information technology, healthcare*

Salary minimum: $45,000

Functions: Healthcare, HR Mgmt., IT

Industries: Generalist, Healthcare

ROI Int'l Inc
16040 Christensen Rd Ste 310
Seattle, WA 98188
(206) 248-5000
Fax: (206) 248-5005
Email: roi@roi-intl.com
Web: www.roi-intl.com

Description: Executive retained search consulting specializing in the telecommunications industry.

Key Contact - Specialty:
Mr. Marc Goyette, President - *Telecommunications, electronic commerce*
Ms. Margo Goyette, Vice President - *Telecommunications*

Salary minimum: $125,000

Functions: Directors, Senior Mgmt., CFO's

Industries: Telecoms

Rojek Marketing Group Inc†
5005 Rockside Rd Ste 600
Crown Ctr
Cleveland, OH 44131
(440) 573-3780
(440) 256-3890
Fax: (440) 573-3783
Email: rcutcher@rojekmarketing.com
Web: www.rojekmarketing.com

Description: Specialized recruitment services offered for executive and management level marketing, advertising and communications professionals. Industry focus - consumer packaged goods companies, retail, finance, healthcare, insurance, manufacturing. Opportunities primarily in Midwest.

Key Contact - Specialty:
Mr. Ralph Cutcher, Executive Vice President - *Senior marketing management, corporate communications, public relations, brand management, product management*
Ms. Lorraine Rojek, President - *Senior marketing, advertising executives*
Ms. Tina Wascovich, Vice President - *Senior marketing communications, public relations, product managers, marketing managers*

Salary minimum: $50,000

Functions: Generalist

Industries: Mfg., Transportation, Wholesale, Retail, Finance, Services, Mgmt. Consulting, Hospitality, Media, Healthcare

Professional Associations: AAAA, AMA, AMA

Rolland Consulting Group Inc
1 Westmount Sq Ste 1405
Westmount, QC H3Z 2P9
Canada
(514) 937-7112
Fax: (514) 937-9738
Email: rgc@videotron.ca

Description: We specialize in executive recruiting for each client, a specific search strategy.

Key Contact:
Ms. Denise Rolland, President
Ms. Jasmine Asselin, Vice President

Functions: Generalist, Directors, Senior Mgmt., Mfg., Sales & Mktg., HR Mgmt., CFO's, MIS Mgmt.

Industries: Generalist, Mfg., Retail, Media, Aerospace, Healthcare

Rolland Ressources Humaines Inc
560 boul Henri-Bourassa O Ste 202
Montreal, QC H3L 1P4
Canada
(514) 333-6619
Email: rolland@rrh.qc.ca

Description: We provide recruiting services mostly specializing in the financial sector.

Key Contact - Specialty:
Mr. Guy Rolland, President - *Financial services, manufacturing, telecommunications*

Salary minimum: $50,000

Functions: Generalist, General Mgmt., Mfg., Materials, Sales & Mktg., HR Mgmt., Finance, Minorities

Industries: Generalist, Mfg., Paper, Chemicals, Drugs Mfg., Invest. Banking, Venture Cap., Telecoms

Rooney Associates Inc
501 Pennsylvania Ave
Glen Ellyn, IL 60137
(630) 469-7102
Fax: (630) 469-0749
Email: jrooney@exec-recruit.com
Web: www.exec-recruit.com

Description: Boutique firm, highly personalized service. Practice adept in aiding cultural changes, or assignments requiring sensitivity, along with creativity.

Key Contact - Specialty:
Mr. Joseph J. Rooney, President - *Vice president (sales & marketing), general management, high technology, telecommunications, consumer electronics*

Salary minimum: $75,000

Functions: General Mgmt., Directors, Senior Mgmt., Middle Mgmt., Mktg. Mgmt., Sales Mgmt., CFO's, IT

Industries: Computer Equip., Consumer Elect., Telecoms, Software

Ropella & Associates
6988 Pine Blossom Rd
Milton, FL 32570
(850) 983-4777
Fax: (850) 983-6677
Email: ropella@ropella.com
Web: www.ropella.com

Description: The chemical industry is our focus everyday. We track business and employment trends and monitor current developments within commodity, specialty, organic and inorganic chemical manufacturers and distributors around the globe.

Key Contact - Specialty:
Mr. Patrick B. Ropella, President & CEO - *Chemical industry*

Salary minimum: $50,000

Functions: General Mgmt., Directors, Senior Mgmt., Middle Mgmt., Mkt. Research, Mktg. Mgmt., Sales Mgmt.

Industries: Chemicals

Professional Associations: NAER, RON

Networks: Top Echelon Network

Ropes Associates Inc
333 N New River Dr E Fl 3
Ft. Lauderdale, FL 33301-2240
(954) 525-6600
Fax: (954) 779-7279
Email: jropes@ropesassociates.com
Web: www.ropesassociates.com

Description: We specialize in real estate industry including developers, builders and operators of residential, resort, commercial and industrial properties.

Key Contact - Specialty:
Mr. John Ropes, President - *Real estate*

Salary minimum: $150,000

Functions: Generalist, Senior Mgmt., Middle Mgmt., Mktg. Mgmt., Sales Mgmt., CFO's

Industries: Generalist, Construction, Hospitality, Real Estate

Professional Associations: AESC, NAIOP, ULI

W R Rosato & Associates Inc
61 Broadway Fl 26
New York, NY 10006
(212) 509-5700
Fax: (212) 968-0855
Email: wrrinc@aol.com
Web: www.wrrosato.com

Description: Over 20 successful years of search experience dedicated to the support of the investment banking, broker dealer community. Expertise in information technology, quantitative research, analytic, sales and trading, and e-commerce technology.

Key Contact - Specialty:
Mr. William R. Rosato, Principal - *Financial services, information technology*
Mr. Frank M. Colasanto, Principal - *Financial services, information technology*
Mr. Jack Federman, Principal - *Financial services, information technology, quantitative research, e-commerce technology*
Ms. Stephanie Osmer, Associate - *Financial services, information technology*

Salary minimum: $150,000

Functions: IT, MIS Mgmt., Systems Analysis, Systems Dev., Systems Implem., Network Admin., DB Admin.

Industries: Services

Rosebud Research Inc
21 Van Ct
Waldwick, NJ 07463
(201) 612-1055
Email: rosebudres@aol.com

Description: We work specifically for corporations and retained executive search firms on difficult searches by providing customized cost-effective candidate ID and development. We are a results-driven firm with a proven track record of success. We utilize creative, concrete sourcing methods, and a strong business network to present on target, interested candidates.

Key Contact - Specialty:
Ms. Corey Rose, Principal - *Generalist, consulting, e-commerce, information technology sectors*

Salary minimum: $85,000

Functions: General Mgmt., Directors, Senior Mgmt., Middle Mgmt., Sales & Mktg., IT, MIS Mgmt., Systems Implem., Mgmt. Consultants, Minorities

Industries: Banking, Mgmt. Consulting, Hospitality, New Media, Real Estate, Software

Professional Associations: ESRT

Rosenthal Associates/Smith Roth & Squires
230 Park Ave Ste 1000
New York, NY 10169
(212) 268-6300
Fax: (908) 389-0511
Email: abbe@raisearch.com
Web: www.raisearch.com

Description: A boutique search firm specializing in diversity and traditional recruitment for middle and senior management positions. We also provide diversity research, organizational research and compensation studies.

Key Contact - Specialty:
Ms. Abbe Rosenthal, Principal - *Diversity, scientific, senior and mid-management*

Salary minimum: $75,000

Functions: Generalist, Minorities

Industries: Generalist

Professional Associations: IACPR, SCIP, SHRM

Branches:
176 N Euclid Ave
Westfield, NJ 07090
(908) 389-0505
(212) 268-6300
Fax: (908) 389-0511
Email: abbe@raisearch.com
Key Contact - Specialty:
Ms. Abbe L. Rosenthal, President - *Female,
  minority, medical devices, pharmaceuticals,
  consumer products, e-commerce*

Ross & Company Inc
35 Old Post Rd
Southport, CT 06490
(203) 254-9800
Fax: (203) 254-9801
Web: www.rosssearch.com

Description: We are one of the leading executive
recruiting firms, specializing in senior management
searches that target various sectors of the healthcare,
information technology, and communications
industries.

Key Contact:
Mr. H. Lawrence Ross, Managing Director
Mr. James Macdonald, Managing Director
Ms. Diane McIntyre, Managing Director
Ms. Celeste Goodhue, Managing Director
Ms. Heather Beliveau, Senior Associate

Salary minimum: $150,000

Functions: Senior Mgmt.

Industries: Drugs Mfg., Medical Devices, Venture
  Cap., Pharm Svcs., Mgmt. Consulting, E-
  commerce, Media, Software, Biotech, Healthcare

The Rottman Group Inc
1 Seven Acres Dr Ste 200
Little Rock, AR 72223
(501) 228-4433
Fax: (501) 228-4466
Email: djrottman@rottmangroup.com
Web: www.rottmangroup.com

Description: Retained healthcare services oriented
firm that seeks to maximize an organization's human
system by strategically understanding and
approaching recruitment.

Key Contact:
Mr. Don Rottman, President

Salary minimum: $60,000

Functions: Generalist, Materials, Nurses, Health
  Admin., Mktg. Mgmt., HR Mgmt., Finance,
  CFO's, MIS Mgmt., Mgmt. Consultants

Industries: Generalist, Healthcare, Hospitals

Rovner & Associates Inc[†]
20 N Wacker Dr Ste 3121
Chicago, IL 60606
(312) 332-9960
Fax: (312) 332-9965
Email: consultant@rovner.com
Web: www.rovner.com

Description: We specialize in information
technology professionals from CIO, CTO, VP, high-
level strategists, and architects, including their
immediate teams and project and program
managers. We also sub-specialize in high-level
human resource professionals. We pride ourselves
in building long-term relationships by providing
quality search services with uncompromising
thoroughness, high integrity, confidentiality and
delivery.

Key Contact - Specialty:
Ms. Bettyann Rovner, President - *Technology*

Salary minimum: $90,000

Functions: Directors, Sales & Mktg., HR Mgmt.,
  IT, MIS Mgmt., Mgmt. Consultants

Industries: Energy, Utilities, Finance, Services,
  Mgmt. Consulting, HR Services, New Media,
  Telecoms, Software

Rowan & Ruggles LLC
11710 Plaza America Dr Ste 2000
Reston, VA 20190
(703) 871-5235
Fax: (703) 871-5111
Email: info@rowrug.com
Web: www.rowrug.com

Description: We are an executive search and
organizational consultancy committed to helping
you achieve a successful future for your enterprise
or career.

Key Contact:
Mr. Larry Dilworth, Managing Director

Salary minimum: $100,000

Functions: General Mgmt., HR Mgmt., Mgmt.
  Consultants

Industries: Generalist, Energy, Utilities, Mgmt.
  Consulting, HR Services

Professional Associations: NVTC

David Rowe & Associates Inc
9047 Monroe Ave
Brookfield, IL 60513
(708) 387-1000

Description: Our firm conducts searches for all
executive and management levels in hospitals,
hospital systems, organized physician group
practices, and managed care companies. We
conduct searches for deeply skilled networking
consultants and engineers, especially those with a
communications service provider background.

Key Contact - Specialty:
Mr. David E. Rowe, President - *Healthcare
  providers*
Ms. Lydia Imler-Diskin, Vice President -
  Healthcare providers
Ms. Tiffany P. Stoner, Associate - *Networking
  consultants, engineers*

Salary minimum: $80,000

Functions: Senior Mgmt., Middle Mgmt., Health
  Admin., Mgmt. Consultants

Industries: Communications, Telecoms, Telephony,
  Wireless, Network Infrastructure, Networking,
  Comm. SW, Healthcare

RSM McGladrey Search Group[†]
(a division of RSM McGladrey Inc)
400 Locust St Ste 675
Des Moines, IA 50309
(515) 281-9248
Fax: (515) 471-5217
Email: dsmsearch@rsmi.com
Web: www.mcgladrey.com

Description: We work for a variety of client
companies in Iowa. They retain us for the purpose
of recruiting qualified candidates for key positions.
Candidates typically have at least 5-10 years'
experience in a given industry.

Key Contact:
Mr. Russell Jensen, Head of Consulting Services
Mr. Terry Lebo, Senior Manager - *Executives,
  manufacturing, marketing, agriculture,*
Mr. Loren V. Jacobson, CPC, Senior Manager -
  Executives, technology, sales & marketing
Ms. Kathy Bemisdarfer, CPC, PHR, Senior
  Consultant - *Banking, administrative management*

Mr. Leland Erwin, Management Recruiter -
  Manufacturing, engineering, construction
Ms. Stephanie Girard, Administrative/Research
  Assistant

Salary minimum: $35,000

Functions: Generalist, General Mgmt., Sales &
  Mktg., Finance, IT

Industries: Generalist, Agri., Forestry, Mining,
  Construction, Mfg., Banking, Government

Professional Associations: NAPS, SHRM

RSMR Global Resources
219 W Chicago Ave Fl 2
Chicago, IL 60610
(312) 957-0337
Fax: (312) 957-0335
Email: mathews@rsmr.com
Web: www.rsmr.com

Description: We are a retained executive search
firm. Our consultative approach, commitment, and
relationships set us apart in the industries that we
serve, which are: power/energy,
engineering/construction, banking/finance,
equipment/software, telecommunication, and other
segments.

Key Contact - Specialty:
Mr. John Ryan, President - *Corporate banking,
  corporate finance, project finance, commercial
  finance*
Mr. Christopher Swan, Chief Executive Officer -
  *Engineering, energy, utilities, construction,
  operations*
Mr. Michael Morrow, Vice President -
  Manufacturing, industrial products, equipment
Mr. Stephen Rotter, Vice President - *Corporate
  finance, telecom, power marketing*
Mr. Mitchell Bassler, Associate - *Construction,
  instrumentation, controls*

Salary minimum: $90,000

Functions: Generalist, General Mgmt., Mfg.,
  Materials, Sales Mgmt., Cash Mgmt., Risk
  Mgmt., Engineering

Industries: Generalist, Energy, Utilities,
  Construction, Machine, Appliance, Finance,
  Telecoms, Environmental Svcs., Real Estate

Rurak & Associates Inc
1776 Massachusetts Ave NW Ste 300
Washington, DC 20036
(202) 293-7603
Fax: (202) 296-2435
Email: resumes@rurakassociates.com

Description: We are a generalist practice serving
senior management in executive search, selection,
and development. Our clients range from venture-
capitalized start-ups to multinational corporations.
Our search and consulting engagements are
conducted worldwide.

Key Contact:
Mr. Zbigniew T. Rurak
Ms. Krissa Johnson

Salary minimum: $100,000

Functions: Generalist

Industries: Mfg., Medical Devices, Mgmt.
  Consulting, HR Services, IT Implementation,
  Communications, Government, Software, Biotech

Professional Associations: AESC, IACPR, IM

Rusher, Loscavio & LoPresto
142 Sansome St Fl 5
San Francisco, CA 94104
(415) 765-6600
Fax: (415) 397-2842
Email: resumes@rll.com
Web: www.rll.com

Description: Retained executive search in financial services, high-technology, biotechnology, venture-backed staffing, manufacturing, non-profit and service industries. Function specialties in general management, manufacturing, distribution, finance, marketing/sales, MIS, HR, engineering & technical management, executive directors and fund development.

Key Contact - Specialty:
Mr. William H. Rusher, Jr., Chairman of the Board/CEO - *Insurance, high technology, generalist*
Mr. J. Michael Loscavio, President - *High technology, not-for-profit, generalist*
Mr. Robert W. Kile, Senior Partner - *Not-for-profits, generalist*
Dr. James G. Andrews, VP, Organizational Development - *Management consulting, not-for-profit, high technology*

Salary minimum: $120,000

Functions: Generalist, General Mgmt., Mfg., Distribution, Sales & Mktg., HR Mgmt., Finance, MIS Mgmt., Engineering, Non-profits

Industries: Mfg., Computer Equip., Finance, Venture Cap., Non-profits, Biotech

Professional Associations: AESC, EMA, NCHRA, SHRM

Networks: Globe Search Group

Branches:
2479 E Bayshore Rd Ste 700
Palo Alto, CA 94303
(650) 494-0883
Fax: (650) 494-7231
Email: dnelms@rll.com
Key Contact - Specialty:
Mr. Robert L. LoPresto, President - *High technology executives*
Mr. John L. McDonald, Vice President - *High technology executives*

Rushmore • Judge Inc
(also known as RJ Professionals Inc)
65 Queen St W Ste 1602
PO Box 94
Toronto, ON M5H 2M5
Canada
(416) 363-4238
Fax: (416) 363-4239
Email: suzannep@rjprofessionals.com

Description: We are specialists in senior succession, search, and leadership coaching and preparation. Our expertise is in the Canadian financial services sector, including the biannual survey of leadership inventory in financial sector. Our supply chain expertise and direct knowledge is of the Canadian government sector-both search and consulting.

Key Contact - Specialty:
Mr. G. Michael Wolkensperg, President & CEO - *Senior management*
Mr. Gordon Walker, Vice President - *Financial services management*
Ms. Glenda McLachlan, Vice President - *Government (sector services)*
Mr. Robert Smith, Vice President - *General management*
Mr. Clayton Appleton, Vice President - *Health sector*

Salary minimum: $85,000

Functions: Senior Mgmt., Plant Mgmt., Distribution, Healthcare, CFO's, Non-profits

Industries: Generalist, Hospitals, Long-term Care, Physical Therapy

Rust & Associates Inc
1009 Ashley Ln
Libertyville, IL 60048-3813
(847) 816-7878
Fax: (847) 816-7905

Email: john@rustassociates.com
Web: www.rustassociates.com

Description: International generalist firm: guarantee search filled or money back; unconditional two-year guarantee on candidate retention; off limits, lifetime candidates, two-year clients; only expenses charged, travel outside metro Chicago.

Key Contact - Specialty:
Mr. John R. Rust, President - *Generalist*

Salary minimum: $60,000

Functions: Generalist, General Mgmt., Senior Mgmt., Mfg., Sales & Mktg., CFO's, IT

Industries: Generalist, Construction, Mfg., Venture Cap., Services, Aerospace, Healthcare

Rutherford Int'l Executive Search Group Inc
2 Sheppard Ave E Ste 1404
PO Box 60
Toronto, ON M2N 5Y7
Canada
(416) 250-6300
Email: rutherford@rutherfordinternational.com
Web: www.rutherfordinternational.com

Description: Our attention to research and contact networks, combined with our ability to quickly grasp market nuances and trends, provides us with the focus of specialists and the ability of generalists. We offer a balanced global perspective and search presence with in-depth local knowledge and focus.

Key Contact - Specialty:
Mr. Forbes Rutherford, President - *Real estate, investment management*

Salary minimum: $80,000

Functions: Generalist, General Mgmt., R&D, Int'l.

Industries: Construction, Drugs Mfg., Medical Devices, Finance, Banking, Invest. Banking, Misc. Financial, Insurance, Real Estate, Biotech, Healthcare

Professional Associations: NAIOP, REIC

W A Rutledge & Associates
51 Sherman Hill Rd Ste A103
Cornerstone Professional Park Bldg A
Woodbury, CT 06798
(203) 266-0200
Fax: (203) 266-0213

Description: Senior/executive management search across most functional areas in technology based consumer and industrial product companies; heavy pharmaceutical, chemicals, electronics, communications.

Key Contact:
Mr. William A. Rutledge, President

Functions: General Mgmt., Senior Mgmt., Middle Mgmt.

Industries: Chemicals, Drugs Mfg., Consumer Elect., Misc. Financial, Aerospace, Biotech

RWS Partners in Search
5549 CR327
Buffalo, TX 75831
(903) 322-2159
Fax: (940) 322-7209
Email: rolands@flash.net

Description: We are a generalist retained executive search firm with over 20 years of successful experience offering our clients a very personalized, responsive, and professional service performed only by a senior partner. Over 80% of our assignments come from repeat clients. Our experience covers most sectors of the economy for both for-profit and not-for-profit organizations at senior management levels.

Key Contact - Specialty:
Mr. Roland W. Stuebner, Jr., Managing Partner - *Generalist*

Salary minimum: $60,000

Functions: Generalist

Industries: Mfg., Metal Products, Computer Equip., Electronic, Elec. Components, Non-profits, Accounting, Real Estate

Sage Search Partners
22 Oakland Rd
Brookline, MA 02445
(617) 232-3113
Email: herzog-sage@juno.com
Web: www.sagesearch.com

Description: Executive Search Firm specializing in non-profits and higher education. Partners conduct each search in its entirety, without relying on junior associates. Before founding Sage, partners were senior managers at national search firm.

Key Contact:
Dr. Patricia Herzog, Partner
Ms. Paula Fazli, Partner

Functions: Generalist

Industries: Non-profits, Higher Ed.

Sager Company
9540 Midwest Ave
Cleveland, OH 44125
(440) 475-9900
Fax: (216) 475-9910
Email: admin@sagercompany.com
Web: www.sagercompany.com

Description: Multi-discipline practice identifying talent for senior and executive-level opportunities in engineering, general management, human resources, sales, marketing, e-commerce, information systems, production, operations and finance.

Key Contact:
Ms. Stephanie Kovarik, Director Administration
Mr. Michael Gerbasi, Consultant

Salary minimum: $75,000

Functions: Generalist

Industries: Generalist

Sales Consultants of Silicon Valley†
4 N Second St Ste 1230
San Jose, CA 95113
(408) 453-9999
Fax: (408) 452-8510
Email: jrosica@mrisanjose.com
Web: www.mrisiliconvalley.com

Description: We specialize in the computer and electronic, systems engineering, IS and IT consulting, semiconductor, semiconductor capital equipment, e-Commerce infrastructure, wireless, broadband, telecommunications/data communications, ERP,MRP software and ASP industries, also Telecom, DataCom, and Wireless

Key Contact - Specialty:
Mr. John Rosica, Principal/Manager - *High technology*

Salary minimum: $50,000

Functions: Generalist

Industries: Mfg., Venture Cap., Equip Svcs., Mgmt. Consulting, HR Services, New Media, Telecoms, Real Estate, Software

Professional Associations: NCHRA

Sales Kingdom of America
2300 Palm Beach Lakes Blvd Ste 309
West Palm Beach, FL 33409
(518) 373-7041
Fax: (518) 373-1982

Email: jodi@saleskingdom.cc
Web: www.saleskingdom.cc

Description: SalesKingdom is dedicated to the advancement of the sales professional. Over the last 8 years our staff has done nothing but coach, motivate and assist sales professionals in the pursuit of their own goals and dreams. We match up professional salespeople in transition with the organizations who have opportunities.

Key Contact:
Mr. Rocky LaGrone, Executive Vice President - *Corporate sales consultant and trainer*
Mr. Kent Malinowski, President

Functions: Sales Mgmt.

Industries: Generalist

Professional Associations: NAPS

Networks: Accord Group

Eric Salmon & Partners
245 Park Ave Fl 24
New York, NY 10167
(212) 372-8800
Fax: (212) 372-8778
Email: info.usa@ericsalmon.com
Web: www.ericsalmon.com

Description: We are a retained executive search firm with offices in Europe and the US specialized in the recruitment of senior level executives.

Key Contact:
Ms. Susan Landon
Fabrizio Panzeri
Mr. William Venable

Salary minimum: $150,000

Functions: Generalist

Industries: Generalist

Salveson Stetson Group Inc
995 Old Eagle School Rd Ste 315
Wayne, PA 19087
(610) 341-9020
Fax: (610) 341-9025
Email: salveson@ssgsearch.com
Web: www.ssgsearch.com

Description: We are highly consultative in our approach to search. We perform an in-depth organization assessment to begin a search and remain after the search to help the new executive assimilate.

Key Contact:
Mr. John Salveson
Ms. Sally Stetson

Salary minimum: $100,000

Functions: Generalist

Industries: Generalist

Salzmann Gay Associates Inc
275 Commerce Dr Ste 236
Ft. Washington, PA 19034
(215) 654-0285

Description: Retained executive search firm serving clients domestically and internationally.

Key Contact - Specialty:
Ms. Martha Gay, President - *Senior management, finance, marketing*

Salary minimum: $125,000

Functions: Senior Mgmt.

Industries: Generalist

Samson Findings†
315 Louella Ave
Wayne, PA 19087
(610) 687-8422

Email: samsonfind@aol.com

Description: An unrivaled resource consultancy in advanced technology search, assessment and placement.

Key Contact - Specialty:
Mr. Francis Kelly, Consultant - *Energy, biotechnology*
Mr. Samuel Shay Gillin, Principal - *Advanced technology sector, generalist*
Mr. Michael Rotondo, Consultant - *Manufacturing, engineering*

Functions: Generalist

Industries: Energy, Utilities, Mfg., Chemicals, Drugs Mfg., Medical Devices, Media, Telecoms, Biotech

Professional Associations: ACS, ASPP, IEEE, OSA

Morgan Samuels Company
(a division of Executive Decision Int'l LLC)
9171 Wilshire Blvd Ste 600
Beverly Hills, CA 90210
(310) 205-2200
Fax: (310) 205-2207
Email: resume@morgansamuels.com
Web: www.morgansamuels.com

Description: We are a specialty firm which recruits senior-level management for the Internet, financial services, heavy construction and information technology industries. Our practice is national and international in scope and currently includes executive recruiters and staff members based in Beverly Hills, California and Stamford, Connecticut.

Key Contact - Specialty:
Mr. Bert C. Hensley, President/CEO - *Generalist*
Mr. Lewis J. Samuels, Founder - *Engineering, construction, oil & gas, energy utilities*
Mr. Richard J. Morgan, Founder - *Engineering, construction, oil & gas, petroleum, energy utilities*
Mr. Will Gates, Principal - *Healthcare, information technology, consumer products, biotech*
Mr. Andrew Riabokin, Principal - *Internet, high technology, information technology*
Ms. Nancy J. Schlect, Principal - *Construction, environmental, energy, utilities, petroleum*
Ms. Jennifer M. De Felice, Senior Associate - *Marketing, finance*
Mr. Hobie Sheeder, Senior Engagement Manager - *Internet, legal, entertainment, financial services*
Mr. Matthew P. Lozinski, Senior Associate - *Generalist*
Mr. Morgan O'Bryant, Senior Engagement Manager - *Generalist*

Salary minimum: $150,000

Functions: Generalist, Senior Mgmt., Sales & Mktg., HR Mgmt., Finance, IT, Engineering, Mgmt. Consultants

Industries: Generalist, Energy, Utilities, Construction, Mfg., Finance, Services, Environmental Svcs.

Professional Associations: AMA, NSPE

Branches:
750 Washington Blvd Fl 6
Stamford, CT 06901
(203) 327-6800
Email: resume@morgansamuels.com
Key Contact - Specialty:
Mr. Peter E. Murphy, Managing Director - *Industrial consumer goods, insurance*
Ms. Katherine H. Cooke, Principal - *Manufacturing, industrial, consumer goods*

Norm Sanders Associates Inc
2 Village Ct
Hazlet, NJ 07730
(732) 264-3700

Email: mail@normsanders.com
Web: www.normsanders.com

Description: We are one of the leading firms recruiting CIOs, senior-level information systems executives, technology leaders and consulting partners. We have in-depth capabilities to assess both business and technical acumen and utilizes a database of senior-level IS talent.

Key Contact - Specialty:
Mr. Norman D. Sanders, Managing Director - *Senior level information systems*
Mr. Louis B. Hughes, Principal - *Senior level information systems, consulting partners*
Mr. Walter J. McGuigan, Principal - *Senior level information systems*
Ms. Karen M. Sanders, Director - *Senior level information systems*
Mr. Burton H. Helgeson, Senior Associate - *Senior level information systems*
Mr. Todd A. Sanders, Senior Associate - *Senior level information systems*
Ms. Lynda Morrison, Consultant - *Information technology*

Salary minimum: $225,000

Functions: Generalist, MIS Mgmt.

Industries: Generalist, Transportation, Retail, Finance, Hospitality, Publishing

Sanders Management Associates Inc†
300 Lanidex Plz
Parsippany, NJ 07054
(973) 887-3232
Fax: (973) 887-0099
Email: smai@sandersinc.com
Web: www.sandersinc.com

Description: We specialize in placing senior-level information technology managers and management consultants. Our credentials include building practices for major consulting firms and also filling individual retained searches for corporate clients in various industries.

Key Contact:
Mr. Roy Sanders, President
Mr. Jason Sanders, Principal
Mr. Mal Lazinsk, Principal
Mr. Mark Green, Principal

Salary minimum: $150,000

Functions: IT, MIS Mgmt., Mgmt. Consultants

Industries: Generalist

Sanford Rose Associates - Pensacola
3 W Garden St Ste 349
Pensacola, FL 32501
(850) 438-8178
Web: www.sra-pensacola.com

Description: We are national executive search consultants specializing in executive and senior management positions to a broad range of functional areas in the banking, financial services, call center services, food processing, and closely aligned support industries.

Key Contact - Specialty:
Mr. David A. Purkerson, President - *Financial services, specialized machinery manufacturing*

Salary minimum: $100,000

Functions: Senior Mgmt.

Industries: Food, Bev., Tobacco, Finance, Banking, Invest. Banking, Brokers, Venture Cap., Misc. Financial, Services, Higher Ed., Call Centers

Sanford Rose Associates - Lake Forest
655 Rockland Rd Ste 105
Lake Bluff, IL 60044
(847) 482-1210
Fax: (847) 482-1213

Email: jduncan@sanfordrose.com

Description: Highly specialized, experienced resource for top management of early/mid-stage entrepreneurial medical ventures. Often assist in developing business plans and the resulting organizational plan. Find, attract and integrate top-notch talent to build a highly effective organization.

Key Contact:
Mr. James W. Duncan, President - *Medical products, devices, services, biotechnology (all levels & functions)*
Mackenzie Lake, Manager Research and Administration

Salary minimum: $75,000

Functions: Generalist

Industries: Drugs Mfg., Medical Devices, Biotech, Healthcare

Sanford Rose Associates - Lake St. Louis
1000 Lake St. Louis Blvd Ste 213
Lake St. Louis, MO 63367
(888) 258-9082
(636) 625-3124
Fax: (636) 625-6034
Email: emitch2611@aol.com
Web: www.sralsl.com

Description: We specialize in executive level retained search.

Key Contact:
Mr. Mitch Ellis, Managing Director - *Marketing & sales executives, telecommunications, wireless*
Mr. James Ellis, Search Consultant - *Marketing & sales executives, telecommunications, wireless*
Ms. Mary Ellis, Office Manager
Mr. Linda Miller, Search Consultant

Salary minimum: $100,000

Functions: Generalist, General Mgmt., Mfg., Materials, Healthcare, Sales & Mktg., Finance, IT, Engineering

Industries: Generalist, Medical Devices, Computer Equip., IT Implementation, New Media, Telecoms, Software, Mfg. SW

Sathe & Associates Inc
5821 Cedar Lake Rd
Minneapolis, MN 55416
(952) 546-2100
(800) 848-4912
Fax: (952) 546-6930
Email: info@sathe.com
Web: www.sathe.com

Description: Our industry specialties include financial services, manufacturing, banking, environment, medical products, healthcare, hospitality and high-tech.

Key Contact - Specialty:
Mr. Mark Sathe, President - *Generalist (mid-level management, upper-level management)*

Salary minimum: $75,000

Functions: Generalist

Industries: Generalist

Professional Associations: MAPS, SHRM, TCHRA

Satterfield & Associates Inc
7875 Annesdale Dr
Cincinnati, OH 45243
(513) 561-3679
Email: info@satterfield3.com
Web: www.satterfield3.com

Description: We are a retained search firm that specializes in telecommunications, technology (including Internet and web-enabled companies), healthcare, and consumer package goods industries.

Our focus is on senior marketing, sales and business development management, or general management with primary functional experience in marketing or sales.

Key Contact - Specialty:
Mr. Richard Satterfield, Jr., Managing Partner - *General management, sales management, telecommunications*

Salary minimum: $125,000

Functions: General Mgmt., Directors, Senior Mgmt., Healthcare, Sales & Mktg., Advertising, Mkt. Research, Mktg. Mgmt., Sales Mgmt., Direct Mktg.

Industries: Generalist, Drugs Mfg., Retail, Invest. Banking, New Media, Telecoms, Call Centers, Wireless, Insurance, Marketing SW, Healthcare

Branches:
14433 Hawthorne Dr
Carmel, IN 46033
(317) 844-8295
Email: info@satterfield3.com
Web: www.satterfield3.com
Key Contact - Specialty:
Mr. John Kuklinski, Senior Partner - *General management, marketing management, healthcare, new media*

7207 Wooster Pike
Cincinnati, OH 45227
(513) 561-1603
Email: info@satterfield3.com
Key Contact - Specialty:
Ms. Anne Badanes, Senior Partner - *General management, marketing management, telecommunications, direct marketing*

Savage Consultants Inc
1066 W Hastings St Ste 2000
Vancouver, BC V6E 3X2
Canada
(604) 601-8222
Fax: (604) 948-1236
Email: jws@savageconsultants.com
Web: www.savageconsultants.com

Description: We provide exclusive search services for mid-level and senior management positions in industrial firms. In addition, a full range of human resources and labor relations consulting services are provided to our clients.

Key Contact:
Mr. John W. Savage

Functions: Generalist

Industries: Agri., Forestry, Mining, Energy, Utilities, Lumber, Furniture, Paper, Chemicals, Metal Products, Transportation, Mgmt. Consulting, HR Services, HR SW

Savoy Partners Ltd
1620 L St NW Ste 801
Washington, DC 20036
(202) 887-0666
Web: www.savoypartners.com

Description: We are an independent, highly regarded, senior-level boutique executive search firm, whose principals each have more than 21 years of retainer executive search experience. All searches are conducted by our partners, never our associates. We are among the top ten firms in Washington with national practice. We commit to completing our assignment, regardless of the difficulty or length of search.

Key Contact - Specialty:
Mr. Robert J. Brudno, Managing Director - *Generalist*
Ms. Elizabeth Clauhsen, Managing Director - *Generalist*

Salary minimum: $125,000

Functions: Generalist

Industries: Energy, Utilities, Mfg., Finance, Services, Telecoms, Defense, Aerospace, Software, Biotech, Healthcare

Professional Associations: IACPR

David Saxner & Associates Inc (DSA Inc)
3 First Nat'l Plz Ste 1400
Chicago, IL 60602
(312) 214-3360

Description: We recruit senior-level and middle management executives in the real estate industry. We work closely with our clients to facilitate and bring continuity to the recruitment process.

Key Contact - Specialty:
Mr. David Saxner, Principal - *Commercial real estate*
Ms. Rikke Vognsen, Principal - *Commercial real estate*

Salary minimum: $100,000

Functions: General Mgmt.

Industries: Hospitality, Real Estate

Professional Associations: ICSC, MBAA

Schaffer Associates Inc†
6425 Idlewild Rd Ste 200
Charlotte, NC 28212
(704) 535-9939
Fax: (704) 535-9699
Email: jtschaffer@schafferassociates.com
Web: www.schafferassociates.com

Description: We are a broad-based search and consulting firm serving all sectors of the home improvement and construction industries. Our executive search practice focuses on middle and senior level management positions.

Key Contact:
Mr. Jim Schaffer, President

Salary minimum: $50,000

Functions: Generalist

Industries: Construction, Mfg., Lumber, Furniture, Paints, Petro. Products, Metal Products, Wholesale, Retail

Schall Executive Search Partners
800 Nicollet Mall Ste 2890
US Bancorp Ctr
Minneapolis, MN 55402-7000
(612) 338-3119
(888) 808-5000
Fax: (612) 336-4509
Email: mdorow@schallpartners.com
Web: www.schallpartners.com

Description: We tailor our search strategy to meet the needs of your company. We limit the number of searches we handle at any one time which allows us to focus our efforts on your assignment and complete it faster.

Key Contact - Specialty:
Mr. David M. Lyman, Partner - *Financial services, consumer products*
Mr. David R. Schall, Managing Partner - *Retail, financial services, human resources*

Salary minimum: $90,000

Functions: Directors, Senior Mgmt., Plant Mgmt., Materials, Sales & Mktg., HR Mgmt., CFO's

Industries: Generalist, Mfg., Wholesale, Retail, Finance, Services, Hospitality, New Media, Communications, Insurance, Software, Biotech

The Schattle Group†
1130 Ten Rod Rd B-207
North Kingstown, RI 02852
(401) 739-0500
Fax: (401) 295-8564
Email: sdexsearch@aol.com

Description: We specialize in manufacturing, finance, engineering and information systems and technology.

Key Contact - Specialty:
Mr. Donald J. Schattle, President - *Finance, banking, senior management*

Salary minimum: $75,000

Functions: Generalist, General Mgmt., Mfg., Sales & Mktg., Finance, IT, Engineering, Mgmt. Consultants

Industries: Generalist, Mfg., Finance, Banking, Venture Cap., New Media, Telecoms

Networks: National Personnel Assoc (NPA)

Scheffel & Associates LLC
612 Howard St Fl 2
San Francisco, CA 94105
(415) 356-7860
Email: info@scheffelassociates.com
Web: www.scheffelassociates.com

Description: We are a retained practice functionally focused in finance, accounting, information technology and human resources. Our clients are pre-public, venture-backed companies in technology, on-line business and media. Prior we were the core of the search practice at PricewaterhouseCoopers in Silicon Valley.

Key Contact:
Mr. Cliff Scheffel
Ms. Gayle Rydinski
Mr. Ty Yun

Salary minimum: $125,000

Functions: HR Mgmt., CFO's, MIS Mgmt.

Industries: New Media, Telecoms, Software

F B Schmidt Int'l
30423 Canwood Pl Ste 239
Agoura Hills, CA 91301
(818) 706-0500
Fax: (818) 707-0784
Email: info@fbschmidt.com
Web: www.fbschmidt.com

Description: Recruitment specialists in senior-level management functions for consumer oriented firms in the consumer packaged goods, financial, healthcare, telecommunications, electronics, leisure, health and beauty aids, retail, food, and quick serve/restaurant industries.

Key Contact - Specialty:
Dr. Elizabeth Mallen, President - *Senior level executives, consumer (products, services) companies*

Salary minimum: $125,000

Functions: Generalist, Directors, Senior Mgmt., Advertising, Mktg. Mgmt., Sales Mgmt., Direct Mktg., CFO's

Industries: Generalist, Mfg., Retail, Finance, Services, Media, Non-classifiable

Professional Associations: AMA

Schneider, Hill & Spangler Inc
Newtown Square Corporate Campus
PO Box 472
Newtown Square, PA 19073-0472
(610) 240-9500
Fax: (610) 240-9700
Email: info@s-h-s.com
Web: www.s-h-s.com

Description: As one of the nation's oldest retained senior executive search firms, our national practice specializes in turnarounds, start-ups, and IPOs from the new venture to the multinationals. Our partners have successfully represented clients in over eighty industry groups in their "quest for the best" C-level and outside members of the board since 1956.

Key Contact - Specialty:
Mr. Steven A. Schneider, President & CEO - *C-level and outside director search (all industries worldwide)*
Mr. Arthur M. Schneider, Chairman Emeritus - *Financial services*
Mr. J. Walter White, Senior Partner - *All disciplines and industries worldwide*

Salary minimum: $125,000

Functions: General Mgmt., Directors, Senior Mgmt., Finance, CFO's, DB Admin.

Industries: Generalist, Energy, Utilities, Mfg., Wholesale, Retail, Finance, Misc. Financial, Services, Hospitality, Media, Telecoms, Insurance, Real Estate, Software, Biotech, Healthcare

Schuyler Associates Ltd
400 Perimeter Center Ter NE Ste 900
Atlanta, GA 30346
(770) 352-9414
Fax: (770) 512-0211
Email: bert@schuyler-associates.com
Web: www.schuyler-associates.com

Description: We are a boutique, retained executive search firm.

Key Contact - Specialty:
Mr. Lambert Schuyler, President - *Senior management*

Salary minimum: $100,000

Functions: General Mgmt., Mfg., Sales & Mktg., Finance, R&D, Mgmt. Consultants

Industries: Higher Ed., Mgmt. Consulting, Fiber Optic, Healthcare

Professional Associations: BABG, TAG

Schweichler Associates Inc
200 Tamal Vista Bldg 200 Ste 100
Corte Madera, CA 94925
(415) 924-7200
Fax: (415) 924-9152
Email: search@schweichler.com
Web: www.schweichler.com

Description: Reputation for locating exceptional individuals for organizations undergoing rapid growth or change. We focus on recruiting president, CEO, COO, vice president and director-levels. Particularly effective in entrepreneurial (high-tech) environments.

Key Contact - Specialty:
Mr. Lee Schweichler, President - *High technology*
Mr. Thomas A. Tucker, Managing Director/Partner - *High technology*
Mr. Andrew Price, Vice President - *High technology*
Ms. Claudia Bluhm, Vice President - *High technology*
Mr. Dave Mullarkey, Consultant - *High technology*

Salary minimum: $125,000

Functions: General Mgmt., Senior Mgmt., Sales & Mktg., IT

Industries: Computer Equip., Telecoms, Software

Networks: ITP Worldwide

The Schwimmer Group Ltd
1673 46th St
Brooklyn, NY 11204
(212) 668-1414
Fax: (718) 633-5891
Email: sschwimmer@sprintmail.com

Description: We serve the information systems analysis of the financial investments industry by focusing on technology and information systems selection and placement. We fulfill client's consulting and full-time needs at senior- and technical-levels.

Key Contact - Specialty:
Mr. Samuel Schwimmer, President - *Information technology professionals*

Salary minimum: $150,000

Functions: Senior Mgmt., MIS Mgmt., Systems Analysis

Industries: Energy, Utilities, Finance, Services, Hospitality, Media, Communications, Government, Software, Biotech, Healthcare

Scott Executive Search Inc
61 Woodbury Pl Ste 200
Rochester, NY 14618
(716) 264-0330
Email: eannscott@worldnet.att.net

Description: Quality retainer-based executive recruiting for management positions. We focus on service and results.

Key Contact - Specialty:
Ms. E. Ann Scott, President - *Food, consumer packaged goods, interactive, e-commerce, high tech*

Salary minimum: $150,000

Functions: General Mgmt., Senior Mgmt., Product Dev.

Industries: Food, Bev., Tobacco, Banking, New Media, Software

Professional Associations: IACPR

Evan Scott Group Int'l
600 W Germantown Pike Ste 400
Plymouth Meeting, PA 19462-1046
(610) 940-1677
Fax: (610) 394-3264
Email: resumes@evanscottgroup.com
Web: www.evanscottgroup.com

Description: We are a retained executive search firm specializing in converging technology. Led by Evan Scott, formerly senior partner at Howard Fischer Associates, the firm was created to deliver a higher degree of service to its clients than its larger competitors can offer.

Key Contact:
Mr. Evan Scott, President
Mr. Jason Matkowski, Consultant
Ms. Karen Shea, Consultant
Mr. Alan Carlson, Consultant
Ms. Dani De Leo, Associate

Salary minimum: $150,000

Functions: Directors, Senior Mgmt.

Industries: Venture Cap., New Media, Software

Professional Associations: ETC, GPVG

J Robert Scott
(a Fidelity Investments company)
255 State St Fl 5
Boston, MA 02109
(617) 563-2770
Fax: (617) 723-1282
Email: info@j-robert-scott.com
Web: www.j-robert-scott.com

---

† occasional contingency assignments

Description: Process-based approach, proven commitment and dedication to clients. Exceptionally strong research capability and performance based billing. Quality of work is guaranteed. A Fidelity Investments company.

Key Contact - Specialty:
Mr. William A. Holodnak, President - *Financial services, biotechnology, healthcare services, venture capital*
Ms. Maureen Alphonse-Charles, SVP-Management and Development
Mr. Todd Jackowitz, Vice President - *Financial services, biotechnology, specialty retailing, cataloging*
Mr. Aaron Lapat, Vice President - *Software*
Mr. Spencer J. Ball, Vice President - *Healthcare*

Salary minimum: $100,000

Functions: Generalist

Industries: Generalist, Finance, Services, Media, Communications, Software, Biotech, Healthcare

Search Advisors Int'l Corp
212 S Magnolia Ave
Tampa, FL 33606
(813) 221-7555
Fax: (813) 221-7557
Email: admin@searchadvisorsintl.com

Description: We are retained executive search consultants who specialize in long-term client relationships, rather than a functional or industry focus. We succeed by maintaining the highest level of professional and ethical standards, combined with the highest level of customer satisfaction. Our motto is "performance not promises."

Key Contact - Specialty:
Mr. Mark N. Strom, President - *Executive management (all areas)*
Mr. Edward Wilson, Vice President - *Executive management (all areas)*
Mr. James C. Wilkson, Vice President - *Information technologies, telecommunications*
Mr. Philip Harrell, Vice President - *Telecommunications, IPO placement*
Mr. Steve McQuinn, Assistant Vice President - *Banking, financial services*
Mr. Richard Kelso, Assistant Vice President - *Utilities, high tech, telecommunications*

Salary minimum: $75,000

Functions: Generalist

Industries: Generalist, Energy, Utilities, Mfg., Retail, Finance, Services, Media, Communications, Aerospace, Biotech

Professional Associations: IACPR

Search Alliance
750 Menlo Ave Ste 100
Menlo Park, CA 94025
(650) 328-6400
Fax: (650) 328-6460
Email: admin@s3execs.com

Description: With over 25 years of experience, we achieve client satisfaction acting as your advocate in the marketplace. We conduct high-quality retained searches and manage the process through negotiation and close.

Key Contact:
Ms. Fran Safier, Principal
Mr. Marty Silver, Principal

Functions: Generalist

Industries: Medical Devices, Biotech, Healthcare

The Search Alliance Inc
301 1/2 Ctr St
Amelia Island, FL 32034
(904) 277-2535
Fax: (904) 277-7924

Web: www.tsainc.net
Description: Worldwide industry specific executive search with an exemplary record of success and repeat business. Extensive experience in executive team evaluation for restructuring, building bench strength and succession planning.

Key Contact:
Mr. Tom Byrnes, Partner

Salary minimum: $100,000

Functions: Generalist, General Mgmt., Sales & Mktg., HR Mgmt., Finance, IT, R&D, Engineering

Industries: Generalist, Finance, Pharm Svcs., Insurance, Software, Healthcare

Professional Associations: IACPR, ESRT

Branches:
998 Farmington Ave Ste 210
West Hartford, CT 06107
(860) 232-2300
Fax: (860) 232-0004
Key Contact:
Mr. Bill Thomas

Search America®
5908 Meadowcreek Dr
Dallas, TX 75248-5451
(972) 233-3302
Fax: (972) 233-1518
Email: schamerica@aol.com

Description: We represent directors, developers, and municipalities seeking management for golf, country, in-town, and yacht clubs, worldwide. Over 600 successful searches have been completed. We have over 8,000 managers in our database, 100% of searches have been completed with a two-year guarantee. We provide overnight interim management. Board consensus building and orientation, operational and incumbent management evaluation services are available. We are discreet.

Key Contact - Specialty:
Mr. Harvey M. Weiner, President - *Private club management*

Salary minimum: $90,000

Functions: General Mgmt., Directors, Senior Mgmt., Int'l.

Industries: Mgmt. Consulting, HR Services, Hospitality, Hotels, Resorts, Clubs, Restaurants, Recreation, Real Estate, Training SW

Professional Associations: IRG, SERC

The Search Company
(a division of Strategic Search Solutions Inc)
8 Oriole Gardens
Toronto, ON M4V IV7
Canada
(416) 972-9400
Fax: (416) 960-3590
Email: thesearchco@iname.com

Description: A full-service agency made up of experienced human resources, business and communications professionals, we focus on the development of effective executive teams with a specialty practice in communications, public affairs and corporate research disciplines.

Key Contact:
Ms. Rosemary Kaczanowski, President

Salary minimum: $60,000

Functions: Generalist, Senior Mgmt., Middle Mgmt., Advertising, Mkt. Research, PR, Risk Mgmt., Int'l.

Industries: Generalist, Energy, Utilities, Mfg., Finance, Media, Government

Professional Associations: IABC

Search Excellence
2060 Ave de Los Arboles 306
Thousand Oaks, CA 91362
(805) 241-8950
Web: www.searchexcellence.com

Description: Our business mission has been to provide the most professional and ethical executive search services. We focus on totally satisfying our corporate clients' strategic staffing needs. We also coach our clients, at no charge, in a uniquely powerful hiring methodology, so they can significantly raise their hiring accuracy and increase retention.

Key Contact:
Mr. Andrew Smith, President

Salary minimum: $90,000

Functions: Generalist

Industries: Generalist

Professional Associations: NAER

Search Innovations Inc
405 Beaumont Cir
West Chester, PA 19380
(610) 692-2000
(610) 692-6066
Email: resumes@searchinnovations.com
Web: www.searchinnovations.com

Description: We provide premium service for hourly rates, significantly lowering costs per hire. We cater to the banking, consumer products, credit card, insurance, management consulting, mortgage banking, mutual fund, non-profit, pharmaceutical and technology industries.

Key Contact - Specialty:
Ms. Vivian Kessler, President - *Generalist*
Mr. Ehud Israel, Executive Vice President - *Generalist*
Ms. Mary Frances Rubano, Vice President - *Generalist*

Salary minimum: $100,000

Functions: Generalist, Middle Mgmt., Mktg. Mgmt., Direct Mktg., Benefits, Personnel, Training, Cash Mgmt.

Industries: Generalist, Banking, Invest. Banking, Misc. Financial, Pharm Svcs., HR Services, Advertising, Insurance

Search Int'l†
PO Box 81
Newburyport, MA 01950
(978) 465-4000
Fax: (978) 465-4069
Email: searchfirm@aol.com
Web: www.searchinternationalinc.com

Description: Boston Business Journal independently ranks us as the 4th largest overall firm in New England and the highest ranking in the hospitality industry for five consecutive years. We have additional offices in California, Connecticut, Framingham, MA, New York, Philadelphia, Israel, Nassau, and the United Kingdom.

Key Contact - Specialty:
Mr. Brian Eagar, CEO - *Hospitality, investment banking, training, culinary, micro brew*
Mr. Michael Schweiger, CHA, Senior Vice President - *General management, consulting, technology*
Ms. Christine Hawthorne, Executive Director - *Household management, estate management, hospitality sales*
Mrs. Maria Johnson, Director - *Information systems*
Mr. Andrew Lowery, Director - *Hospitality, generalist*
Mr. John Stanley, Vice President - *General hospitality, culinary*
Mr. Elliott Wade, Associate Director - *Management, information services, consulting*

Mr. Jack Gasnier, Executive Vice President - *Hotels, resorts, culinary*
Mr. Joseph Laite, Director-Convention & Conference - *Services, sales*

Salary minimum: $70,000

Functions: Generalist, Middle Mgmt., Sales Mgmt., CFO's, MIS Mgmt., Systems Dev., Systems Support, Int'l.

Industries: Generalist, Food, Bev., Tobacco, Computer Equip., Invest. Banking, Services, Hospitality

Professional Associations: ACF, FCSI

Search Masters Int'l

1101 31st St Ste 120
Downers Grove, IL 60515
(630) 663-9140
Fax: (630) 964-0562
Email: info@searchmastersinternational.com
Web: www.searchmasterinternational.com

Description: We are an executive recruitment firm focused on mid to senior level career positions in the life sciences, including biotechnology, medical device, and pharmaceutical industries.

Key Contact - Specialty:
Ms. Eileen Dougherty, Manager - *Biotechnology, pharmaceutical*

Salary minimum: $50,000

Functions: Generalist

Industries: Drugs Mfg., Pharm Svcs., Biotech

Professional Associations: AAAS, AAPS

Search Partners

36 Rodman St
Narragansett, RI 02882
(401) 455-7777
Fax: (401) 854-2305
Email: srchprtnrs@aol.com

Description: Based in Rhode Island, we specialize in executive and management level searches. Our demonstrated success is based upon a superior combination of talent, resources, and experience within the industry. Our clients and candidates enjoy complete privacy during our executive search process.

Key Contact - Specialty:
Ms. Chantel O'Neill, Senior Director - *Generalist*

Salary minimum: $50,000

Search Partners LLC

990 Highland Dr Ste 110-A
Solana Beach, CA 92075
(858) 755-2005
Fax: (858) 755-8944
Email: agnes@searchpartners.net
Web: www.searchpartners.net

Description: We offer our clients quality searches in all areas, especially marketing, advertising, public relations, media and high-technology.

Key Contact - Specialty:
Mr. Nick Lambesis, CEO/Owner - *Marketing, advertising, public relations, media, high technology*

Functions: Generalist, Health Admin., Sales & Mktg., Mkt. Research, Sales Mgmt., Direct Mktg., PR, Graphic Artists

Industries: Generalist, Media, Advertising, Publishing, New Media, Healthcare

Professional Associations: AAAA, AMA

Search Research Associates Inc

85 Tower Office Park
Woburn, MA 01801-2120
(781) 938-0990
Fax: (781) 933-5385
Email: gordon@gilbertscott.com
Web: www.searchresearch.com

Description: 70% retained search salaries 60K to 120K range, 30% research. We work with approx. 5 search firms across the USA. We also have 3 dedicated researches on our staff just for research.

Key Contact - Specialty:
Mr. Gordon S. Scott, President - *Generalist*
Mr. Garry M. Scott, Director of Research - *Generalist*
Mr. Daniel J. Plasse, Ph.D., Director of Search Services - *Generalist*

Salary minimum: $60,000

Functions: Middle Mgmt., Health Admin., Mktg. Mgmt., Personnel, CFO's, M&A, MIS Mgmt.

Industries: Generalist

Search Synergy Inc†

3004 NE 26th Ave
Portland, OR 97212-3547
(503) 288-2400
Email: ross@searchsynergy.com
Web: www.searchsynergy.com

Description: We specialize in the sporting goods, outdoor, and action sports industries. We place middle to senior level positions.

Key Contact:
Mr. Ross Regis, Principal

Functions: Generalist

Industries: Textiles, Apparel

The SearchAmerica Group Inc†

18511 Heritage Trl
Strongsville, OH 44136-7083
(440) 572-0450
Fax: (440) 572-2000
Email: tsnow@searchamerica.cc
Web: www.searchamerica.cc

Description: We service manufacturers' needs for key management executives in mid-level and above in the consumer, home improvement, builder, and industrial marketplaces throughout North, Central, and South America. We specialize in sales, marketing, and general management positions worldwide.

Key Contact - Specialty:
Mr. Thomas J. Snow, President/CEO - *Sales, marketing, general management*
Mr. Eric Sted, Senior Vice President - *Sales, marketing, general management*

Functions: General Mgmt., Product Dev., Advertising, Mkt. Research, Mktg. Mgmt., Direct Mktg., Customer Svc., HR Mgmt., M&A, Int'l.

Industries: Mgmt. Consulting, HR Services

SearchCom Inc

11300 N Central Expy Ste 100
Dallas, TX 75243
(214) 365-0300
Fax: (214) 365-0311
Email: susana1@airmail.net

Description: Executive search for marketing, advertising and public relations talent for corporations and their agencies, across all industries and on a national basis.

Key Contact - Specialty:
Ms. Susan Abrahamson, President - *Marketing, advertising, public relations*

Salary minimum: $50,000

Functions: Sales & Mktg., Advertising, Mkt. Research, Mktg. Mgmt., Direct Mktg., PR, Graphic Artists

Industries: Generalist

Professional Associations: AMA, BMA, NAWBO

Searchforce Inc

1704 Clearwater-Largo Rd
Clearwater, FL 33756
(727) 588-4400
Fax: (727) 588-0116
Email: sfi@searchforce.com
Web: www.searchforce.com

Description: We place entry-level Ph.D.s/MDs to division president. Small focused firm acting as an extension of your company. Represent small number of clients - no ethical problems.

Key Contact:
Mr. Al DiPalo, Vice President
Ms. Vicki Carr, Vice President
Mr. James Kitt, Director-Research

Salary minimum: $75,000

Functions: Generalist, Senior Mgmt., Middle Mgmt., Product Dev., R&D, Mgmt. Consultants

Industries: Generalist, Chemicals, Soap, Perf., Cosmtcs., Drugs Mfg., Medical Devices, Plastics, Rubber, Paints, Petro. Products, Biotech

Professional Associations: AAAS, ADA, DIA, PDA, RAPS

SearchManagement†

3003 Briggs Ct
Pleasanton, CA 94588
(925) 461-7040
Email: lherbst@searchmgmnt.com
Web: www.searchmgmnt.com

Description: We are a leading provider of executive search services to technology companies seeking senior personnel in core disciplines including sales, marketing, engineering, operations, and finance.

Key Contact - Specialty:
Ms. Lisa C. Herbst, CPA, President - *High technology, sales, marketing, engineering, operations, finance*

Salary minimum: $85,000

Functions: Sales & Mktg., Finance

Industries: Computer Equip., Test, Measure Equip., Services, Media, Software, Biotech, Healthcare

SeBA Int'l LLC†

15 W 26th St Fl 12
New York, NY 10010
(212) 609-4400
Email: sebateam@sebasearch.com
Web: www.sebasearch.com

Description: We specialize in the recruitment of senior business executives for positions in strategic management, such as: strategic planning, corporate business development, e-Business, marketing, etc.; strategic finance, such as equity research, private equity, venture capital, and CFOs, and general management, such as CEOs, COOs, business units leaders, etc. Because of this strategic functional focus, the vast majority of our candidates are current and former management consultants from the top strategy consulting firms.

Key Contact - Specialty:
Mr. Paul Bond, Principal - *Strategic corporate management*
Mrs. Kate Bullis, Principal - *Strategic corporate management*
Mr. Robert Iommazzo, Principal - *Strategic corporate management*

Salary minimum: $150,000

Functions: General Mgmt., Directors, Senior Mgmt., Middle Mgmt., Mktg. Mgmt., HR Mgmt., CFO's, M&A, Mgmt. Consultants, Int'l.

Industries: Generalist

Professional Associations: AESC

Secura Burnett Company LLC
555 California St Ste 3950
San Francisco, CA 94104-1704
(415) 398-0700
Fax: (415) 398-2274

Description: We are an international firm specializing in strategy, M&A advisory and consulting on executive search. We are also committed to providing quality search execution for senior executives in financial services and technology.

Key Contact:
Mr. Louis C. Burnett, Managing Partner
Mr. Scott von Stein, Principal
Ms. Kathleen G. Ursin, Principal
Mr. Gerald E. Parsons, Principal

Salary minimum: $200,000

Functions: Generalist

Industries: Wholesale, Retail, Finance, Services, Mgmt. Consulting, HR Services, Insurance, Real Estate, Software, Biotech

Branches:
2410 Executive Dr Ste D
Indianapolis, IN 46241
(317) 241-4500
Fax: (317) 241-5080
Key Contact:
Mr. Lee D. Ashton, Manager, Midwest Region

Sedlar & Miners
1120 Ave of the Americas Fl 4
New York, NY 10036
(212) 628-1616

Description: Senior management searches in management consulting and the consumer products and services categories. Both principals work on each individual assignment.

Key Contact - Specialty:
Mr. Richard A. Miners - *Information technology, consumer goods & services, general management, sales & marketing, management consultants*
Ms. Jeri L. Sedlar - *Non-profit, general management, sales & marketing, management consultants, chief financial officers*

Salary minimum: $125,000

Functions: Senior Mgmt., Sales & Mktg., Advertising, Mkt. Research, Mktg. Mgmt., Sales Mgmt., Direct Mktg., CFO's, Mgmt. Consultants

Industries: Generalist

Professional Associations: IACPR, SHRM

J R Seehusen Associates Inc
1206 Lakeview Dr
Fairfield, IA 52556
(641) 469-2600
Fax: (641) 472-8580
Email: joe@jrseehusen.com
Web: www.jrseehusen.com

Description: High quality custom senior search and consulting work. 285 assignments completed. Clients range from middle market to Fortune 1000.

Key Contact - Specialty:
Mr. Joseph R. Seehusen, President - *Senior management, general managers, manager (division, plant)*

Salary minimum: $75,000

Functions: Directors, Senior Mgmt., Middle Mgmt., Plant Mgmt., Distribution, Sales & Mktg.,

HR Mgmt., Mgmt. Consultants, Non-profits, Environmentalists

Industries: Mfg., Food, Bev., Tobacco, Venture Cap., Services, Non-profits, Higher Ed., Mgmt. Consulting, HR Services, Law Enforcement, Hospitality, Restaurants, Media, Government, Defense, Entertainment SW

Seitchik Corwin & Seitchik Inc
3443 Clay St
San Francisco, CA 94118-2008
(415) 928-5717
(800) 438-0279
Fax: (415) 928-8075
Web: www.seitchikcorwin.com

Description: We specialize in apparel, textile, footwear, handbag, accessories, home fashions, and related industries, both wholesale and retail.

Key Contact - Specialty:
Mr. J. Blade Corwin, Partner - *Apparel, textiles, footwear & related areas, retail*

Salary minimum: $50,000

Functions: Generalist

Industries: Textiles, Apparel, Retail

Professional Associations: AAMA, SFFI

Branches:
330 E 38th St Ste 5P
New York, NY 10016
(212) 370-3592
Fax: (212) 286-0754
Key Contact - Specialty:
Mr. William Seitchik, Partner - *Apparel, textiles, footwear & related areas, retail*

Robert Sellery Associates Ltd
1155 Connecticut Ave NW Ste 500
Washington, DC 20036
(202) 331-0090
Fax: (202) 333-1167
Email: sellery@sellery.com
Web: www.sellery.com

Description: Our practice is in the not-for-profit sector. We find presidents, CEOs, executive directors, deans, chief development, communication, government relations, and financial officers, including corporate social responsibility and investment officers along with the people reporting to these positions.

Key Contact - Specialty:
Mr. Robert A. Sellery, Jr., Managing Director - *Not-for-profit*

Functions: Generalist, General Mgmt.

Industries: Non-profits, Higher Ed., Mgmt. Consulting, Advertising, Government, Non-classifiable

Professional Associations: AFP, CASE

Sensible Solutions Inc
239 W Coolidge Ave
Barrington, IL 60010
(847) 382-0070
Email: pdelaney@sensibleinc.com
Web: www.sensibleinc.com

Description: We are an executive search consultancy. We are noted for information depth and patterns + ability to be of counsel when the search outcome is critical. We deliver client specific results in recruitment of full time, senior-level executives and senior-level, skill specific portfolio workers. (e.g. temporary executives).

Key Contact - Specialty:
Mr. Patrick J. Delaney, Principal - *Senior level core team employees & portfolio workers*

Salary minimum: $150,000

Functions: Generalist, General Mgmt., Directors, Senior Mgmt., Healthcare, Sales & Mktg., HR Mgmt., Finance, IT, Mgmt. Consultants

Industries: Generalist, Mfg., Transportation, Finance, Services, Media, Software, Biotech, Healthcare, Non-classifiable

Setren, Smallberg & Associates
1330 Broadway Ste 1830
Oakland, CA 94612
(510) 208-0316
Fax: (510) 208-0321
Email: larry@setrensmallberg.com
Web: www.setrensmallberg.com

Description: Our firm is a unique, full-service provider of human resource services to biopharmaceutical companies and other dynamic, emerging industries and companies. We provide management consulting, executive search, compensation, training, and organizational development. Our clients include many prominent and emerging biopharmaceutical companies.

Key Contact - Specialty:
Mr. Larry Setren, Partner - *Biopharmaceutical*
Mr. Victor Smallberg, Partner - *Biopharmaceutical*

Salary minimum: $100,000

Functions: Generalist

Industries: Drugs Mfg., Medical Devices, Biotech

Shaffer Consulting Group Inc
290 Maple Ct Ste 108
Ventura, CA 93003-3510
(805) 642-3808
Fax: (805) 642-3847
Email: general@shafferconsultinggroup.com
Web: www.shafferconsultinggroup.com

Description: We perform executive-level searches across major functional units with an emphasis in computers, biotechnology, telecommunications, and numerous of other high-technology industries. Additional emphasis is placed on serving US companies with operations in Asia.

Key Contact:
Mr. Bradford W. Shaffer, President
Mr. Richard Fitch, Partner
Mr. Ken Barry, Vice President

Salary minimum: $120,000

Functions: Generalist, General Mgmt., Mfg., Sales & Mktg., HR Mgmt., Finance, IT, Engineering

Industries: Generalist, Mfg., Transportation, Banking, Services, Communications, Aerospace, Software, Security SW, Biotech, Healthcare

Shannahan & Company Inc
655 Redwood Hwy Ste 133
Mill Valley, CA 94941
(415) 381-3613
Fax: (415) 381-3879
Email: peter@shannahan.com
Web: www.shannahan.com

Description: We specialize in the financial services area. Our specific focus is in the defined contribution, defined benefit, mutual funds, and investment management areas.

Key Contact - Specialty:
Mr. Peter Shannahan, President - *Financial services*

Salary minimum: $90,000

Functions: Sales & Mktg.

Industries: Finance, Banking, Venture Cap., Misc. Financial

Sharp Placement Professionals Inc[†]
734 Walt Whitman Rd Ste 407
Melville, NY 11747
(631) 439-8888
Fax: (631) 439-8895
Email: recruit@sharpsearch.com
Web: www.sharpsearch.com

Description: We specialize in filling those difficult positions that fall between full-service retained search and general contingency search. We will work out a customized program to fill your recruitment needs.

Key Contact - Specialty:
Mr. Donald Levine, CPC, President - *Mid to upper-level management search*

Salary minimum: $60,000

Functions: General Mgmt., Directors, Senior Mgmt., Sales & Mktg., HR Mgmt., IT

Industries: Generalist, Mfg., Medical Devices, Computer Equip., Consumer Elect., Test, Measure Equip., Accounting, Equip Svcs., Mgmt. Consulting, HR Services, Media, Communications, Telecoms, Aerospace, Software, Biotech

Professional Associations: LISTNET

Networks: Top Echelon Network

Shasteen Medical Search[†]
4180 Fairgreen Dr
Marietta, GA 30068-4108
(770) 565-1191

Description: We perform physician searches only. We are a retained (hourly) and contingency firm. The principle of our business is truth and fairness.

Key Contact - Specialty:
Mr. Stephen P. Shasteen, MA, Owner - *Physicians only*
Mrs. Martha F. Shasteen, Co-Owner - *Physicians*

Salary minimum: $110,000

Functions: Physicians

Industries: Healthcare

Professional Associations: NAPR

M B Shattuck & Associates Inc
PO Box 10527
Oakland, CA 94610
(510) 663-8922
Fax: (510) 663-8923
Email: info@mbshattuck.com
Web: www.mbshattuck.com

Description: Nationwide client base in most industries/functions, for senior/upper middle-levels. Special competence in high-technology (computer related), distribution, telecommunications (networking), general manufacturing and health/medical.

Key Contact - Specialty:
Mr. M. B. Shattuck, President - *Senior level executives, high technology, general manufacturing*

Salary minimum: $90,000

Functions: Generalist

Industries: Motor Vehicles, Computer Equip., Consumer Elect., Test, Measure Equip., Misc. Mfg., Telecoms

Shepherd Bueschel & Provus Inc
401 N Michigan Ave Ste 3020
Chicago, IL 60611
(312) 832-3020
Fax: (312) 832-0001
Email: sbp401@aol.com

Description: Our firm includes three principals and one associate with significant and diverse experience whom are responsible as a team, both for conducting assignments and maintaining client relationships. All three principals are included in the "New Career Makers." The firm has been cited for the quality of its work.

Key Contact:
Mr. David A. Bueschel, Principal
Ms. Barbara L. Provus, Principal
Mr. Daniel M. Shepherd, Principal

Salary minimum: $150,000

Functions: Generalist

Industries: Generalist

Professional Associations: AESC

Sheridan Search
(a division of Adams, Nash, Haskell & Sheridan)
401 N Franklin St Fl 2
Chicago, IL 60610
(312) 822-0232
Fax: (312) 822-9840
Email: jburton@anh.com
Web: www.anh.com

Description: We specialize in search assignments for human resources managers, directors, and VPs. We also search for labor and employee relations managers, directors, and VPs.

Key Contact:
Mr. John A. Sheridan, Vice President

Salary minimum: $100,000

Functions: HR Mgmt.

Industries: Generalist

Professional Associations: ASHHRA, SHRM

Branches:
1717 Dixie Hwy
Ft. Wright, KY 41011
(800) 237-3942
Fax: (859) 578-4777
Email: badams@anh.com

Sherwood Lehman Massucco Inc[†]
3455 W Shaw Ave Ste 110
Fresno, CA 93711-3201
(559) 276-8572
Fax: (559) 276-2351
Email: slinc@employmentexpert.com
Web: www.employmentexpert.com

Description: Executive search for client companies on a nation wide basis.

Key Contact - Specialty:
Mr. Robert F. Sherwood, Vice President - *Manufacturing, food processing, human resources, general management*
Mr. Neal G. Lehman, Vice President - *Information systems, general management, financial, agriculture*
Mr. Harry A. Massucco, President - *Banking, general management*

Salary minimum: $60,000

Functions: Generalist

Industries: Agri., Forestry, Mining, Mfg., Food, Bev., Tobacco, Finance, Banking, Misc. Financial, Accounting, Media, Telecoms, Software

Professional Associations: APICS, SHRM

Networks: Top Echelon Network

Shirley Associates
200 N Larchmont Blvd
Los Angeles, CA 90004
(323) 460-6202
Email: info@shirleyassociates.com
Web: www.shirleyassociates.com

Description: Senior-level international executive search practice serving the needs of most industries.

Particular strengths in technology and non-profit sectors.

Key Contact:
Mr. Martin R. Shirley, Managing Partner - *Manufacturing, finance, NFP's (senior level executives)*
Ms. Laura Burris, Principal

Salary minimum: $100,000

Functions: Generalist, Non-profits

Industries: Computer Equip., Non-profits, Higher Ed., New Media, Software

E L Shore & Associates
2 St. Clair Ave E Ste 1201
Toronto, ON M4T 2T5
Canada
(416) 928-9399
Fax: (416) 928-6509
Email: info@elshore.com

Description: We cover most industries with an emphasis on senior management. Typical searches include retail management, financial services, high-tech, manufacturing and IT. In-depth knowledge of the Canadian market. Dedicated to providing personalized, professional service having a track record of superior results.

Key Contact:
Mr. Earl Shore
Mr. Marty Collis
Ms. Roz Baker

Salary minimum: $75,000

Functions: Generalist, General Mgmt., Sales & Mktg., HR Mgmt., Finance, IT

Industries: Generalist, Mfg., Transportation, Retail, Finance, Services, Aerospace, Insurance

Networks: Globe Search Group

Shore Asociados Ejecutivos S A de CV
Av Constituyentes 117-5o Piso
Col San Miguel Chapultepec
Mexico City, DF 11850
Mexico
52 5 277 3004
52 5271 4065
Fax: 52 5 515 3979
Email: lshore@shore.com.mx
Web: www.shore.com.mx

Description: Most complete personnel service in Mexico, a no nonsense operation, executive placement all levels, bicultural and bilingual associates. Turnkey operations in human resources, consulting in HR.

Key Contact - Specialty:
Mr. Fernando Fernandez De Cordova, CEO - *Generalist*
Ms. Linda Shore, General Director - *Generalist*
Ms. Virginia Franco, Director-Executives - *Generalist*
Ms. Susan Shore, Corporate Director - *Generalist*

Salary minimum: $25,000

Functions: Generalist, General Mgmt., Materials, Sales & Mktg., HR Mgmt., Finance, IT

Industries: Generalist, Construction, Food, Bev., Tobacco, Transportation, Finance, Hospitality, Media

Networks: InterSearch

Branches:
Av Lázaro Cárdenas 4145-501 PH
Fraccionamiento Camino Real
Guadalajara, JAL 45040
Mexico
52 3 647 9012
52 3 647 7886
Fax: 52 3 647 7916
Email: jcoello@shore.com.mx

Key Contact - Specialty:
Mr. Jorge Coello, Director - *Generalist*

Av Lázaro Cárdenas Pte 2400
Edif Losoles piso 1 Ofna A-14
Col San Agustin, San Pedro
Garza García, NL 66270
Mexico
52 8 363 2769
52 8 363 27 80
Fax: 52 8 363 2768
Email: fdominguez@shore.com.mx
Key Contact:
Mr. Alfonso Calderon - *Generalist*
Mr. Francisco Dominguez, Director

Shore Paralax Inc
212 Carnegie Ctr Ste 206
Princeton, NJ 08540
(609) 844-7504
(888) 295-9501
Fax: (888) 295-9503
Email: shoreexec@aol.com
Web: www.shoreparalax.com

Description: We offer a unique search process
designed to ensure cultural as well as technical fit.
Our proprietary rules of leadership program aids
candidates in designing a quick entry strategy in
house research.

Key Contact - Specialty:
Mr. Edward J. Hopkins, President - *Sales,
marketing, general management*
Ms. Betty Semel, Partner - *Financial management,
marketing*
Mr. Russell Glover, Partner - *Financial
management, general management*
Mr. Mark Hopkins, Partner - *Knowledge
management, marketing*

Salary minimum: $80,000

Functions: General Mgmt., Materials Plng., Mktg.
Mgmt., Sales Mgmt., CFO's, M&A, MIS Mgmt.

Industries: Generalist, Food, Bev., Tobacco, Drugs
Mfg., Finance, Banking, Venture Cap., Pharm
Svcs., Biotech

Branches:
125 Half Mile Rd Ste 200
Red Bank, NJ 07701
(732) 933-2746
Email: shoreexec@aol.com
Key Contact:
Ms. Agnes Synder, Financial Manager

Stephen D Shore Retained Executive
7320 Woodlawn Ave
Pittsburgh, PA 15218-2447
(412) 351-2201
Fax: (412) 351-2201
Email: sdshore@stargate.net
Web: www.users.stargate.net/~sdshore

Description: Personalized service. Client oriented,
and confidential.

Key Contact:
Mr. Stephen D. Shore, Owner

Functions: Generalist

Industries: Mfg., Aerospace, Packaging, Software,
Biotech

The Shorr Group
500 N Michigan Ave Ste 820
Chicago, IL 60611
(312) 644-5100
Fax: (312) 644-7122
Email: search@theshoregroup.com
Web: www.theshorrgroup.com

Description: On a retained basis, we identify
candidates who will excel in your workplace in
order to help you hire your organization's future and
we guarantee satisfaction on each assignment.

Key Contact:
Ms. Carol Kurz-Shorr, President

Salary minimum: $30,000

Functions: Generalist, General Mgmt., Mfg., HR
Mgmt., Finance, Engineering, Specialized Svcs.

Industries: Generalist, HR Services

The Shotland Group
18401 Burbank Blvd Ste 117
Tarzana, CA 91356
(818) 995-1501
Fax: (818) 776-1430
Email: shotgrp@aol.com

Description: We are a generalist practice
emphasizing recruitment of mid- and upper-level
management. Our primary areas of specialization
include disciplines within manufacturing and
distribution companies.

Key Contact - Specialty:
Mr. David R. Shotland, President - *Manufacturing,
marketing, engineering, generalist*

Salary minimum: $50,000

Functions: Generalist, Senior Mgmt., Middle
Mgmt., Materials Plng., Distribution, Sales
Mgmt., CFO's, Engineering

Industries: Generalist, Soap, Perf., Cosmtcs., Drugs
Mfg., Medical Devices, Plastics, Rubber, Metal
Products, Consumer Elect., Misc. Mfg.

M Shulman Inc
44 Montgomery St Ste 3085
San Francisco, CA 94104-4804
(415) 398-3488
Fax: (415) 398-2208
Email: mel@mshulman.com

Description: National generalist practice
concentrates on CEO, COO and senior executive-
level positions. Clients include high-technology,
biotechnology, conglomerates, electronic goods,
entertainment, broadcasting, new venture start-ups
and retail.

Key Contact - Specialty:
Mr. Mel Shulman, Partner - *Generalist with
emphasis on high technology, computer, medical,
retail, entertainment industries*

Salary minimum: $225,000

Functions: Senior Mgmt.

Industries: Medical Devices, Retail, Pharm Svcs.,
Mgmt. Consulting, HR Services, Telecoms,
Software, Biotech, Healthcare

John Sibbald Associates Inc
7701 Forsyth Blvd
St. Louis, MO 63105-1817
(314) 727-0227
Email: jsibbald@sibbaldassociates.com
Web: www.sibbaldassociates.com

Description: We are small, by design, to provide
highly personalized service to limited clientele with
emphasis on clubs, resorts, hotels, and related
hospitality industry employers. We recruit
worldwide.

Key Contact - Specialty:
Mr. John R. Sibbald, President - *Generalist*
Ms. Kathryn J. Sibbald, President - *Hospitality*
Mr. Scott McNett, Vice President - *Hospitality*
Mr. Randall Martin, Vice President - *Hospitality*
Ms. Teri Finan, Vice President - *Hospitality
communications*
Mr. W. Red Steger, CCM, Senior Vice President -
Hospitality industry
Mr. Daniel Denehy, CCM, Vice President -
Hospitality industry

Salary minimum: $100,000

Functions: Generalist, General Mgmt., Directors,
Senior Mgmt.

Industries: Hospitality, Hotels, Resorts, Clubs,
Restaurants, Entertainment, Recreation

Professional Associations: CAI, IAER, NCA,
NGCOA

Larry Siegel & Associates Inc
1111 3rd Ave Ste 2880
Seattle, WA 98101
(206) 622-4282
Fax: (206) 622-4058
Email: admin@siegel-associates.com
Web: www.siegel-associates.com

Description: We are a highly experienced generalist
firm specializing in recruitment of senior-level
management in most functional disciplines with
expertise in a wide range of manufacturing,
distribution and service industries.

Key Contact:
Mr. Larry Siegel, President

Salary minimum: $100,000

Functions: Generalist, Mfg., Distribution, Sales &
Mktg., Finance

Industries: Generalist, Mfg., Food, Bev., Tobacco,
Electronic, Elec. Components, Transportation,
Media, Aerospace

RitaSue Siegel Resources Inc
20 E 46th St
New York, NY 10017-2417
(212) 682-2100
Fax: (212) 682-2946
Email: ritasues@ritasue.com
Web: www.ritasuesiegelresources.com

Description: We place design managers and senior
design staff. We specialize in industrial/product
design, such as automotive, consumer, medical, toy,
and furniture; graphic design in all forms of visual
and integrated marketing communications including
brand identity, new media; interior design in retail,
hospitality, corporate, labs, healthcare; architecture
in all industries. We recruit strategic marketing
consultants for brand identity and sales specialists
for design companies.nies.

Key Contact - Specialty:
Ms. RitaSue Siegel, President - *Design
management,*

Salary minimum: $40,000

Functions: Specialized Svcs., Architects, Graphic
Artists

Industries: Generalist, New Media, Non-
classifiable

Professional Associations: AIA, AIGA, ASID,
DMI, IDSA, IFDA, IIDA, SEGD

Signature Search
338 W College Ave Ste 203
Appleton, WI 54911
(920) 749-9300
Email: mmueller@signaturesearch.com
Web: www.signaturesearch.com

Description: Spin-off of 17 year, well established
search firm. Geographical reach is North America
with select Ex-pat. projects (Europe, Pacific Rim,
Latin America). Functional expertise includes: sales,
marketing, top leadership, finance, operations, IT,
HR, R&D. Industries include: manufacturing,
financial management, healthcare.

Key Contact:
Mr. Michael S. Mueller, President
Mr. Charles R. Magee, Vice President

Salary minimum: $100,000

Functions: Generalist

Industries: Paper, Printing, Chemicals, Plastics, Rubber, Misc. Mfg., Finance, Services, Packaging, Healthcare

Professional Associations: PIMA, SHRM, TAPPI

Branches:
6200 Falls of Neuse Rd Ste 200
Raleigh, NC 27609
(919) 431-9700
Email: cmagee@signatureresearch.com
Key Contact:
Mr. Charles R. Magee, Vice President

Signium Int'l Inc
360 Memorial Dr Ste 120
Crystal Lake, IL 60014
(815) 479-9415
Email: contact@signium.com
Web: www.signium.com

Description: Our firm is a global network of retained executive search consultancies, operating in 27 offices in 17 countries. Respected for our quality, integrity, and reputation, we re-branded in late 1998 after being known as the Ward Howell International Group for over 50 years. We provide global executive search and consulting services to major national and multi-national companies.

Key Contact:
Dr. Bernd Prasuhn, Chairman of the Board
Ms. Suzanne Speight, Corporate Secretary

Professional Associations: AESC

Networks: Signium Int'l Inc

Silver & Associates
900 N Point St Ste D-200
Ghirardelli Sq
San Francisco, CA 94109
(415) 202-8506
Fax: (415) 202-8505
Email: silversearch@worldnet.att.net
Web: www.silversearch.org

Description: We are a SF-based executive search firm that recruits outstanding individuals for senior positions nationwide. Areas of expertise include: all categories of retail, apparel, e-tail and all marketing and business development for all industries.

Key Contact - Specialty:
Ms. Denise Silver, MBA, President - *Apparel, retail, high technology, investment banking, financial services*

Salary minimum: $100,000

Functions: General Mgmt., Directors, Senior Mgmt., Product Dev., Sales & Mktg., Mktg. Mgmt., Personnel, Training, Finance

Industries: Textiles, Apparel, Retail, Invest. Banking, Non-profits

Branches:
37 Creek View Cir
Larkspur, CA 94939
(415) 927-2818
Fax: (415) 927-2217
Email: silversearch@worldnet.att.net
Key Contact:
Ms. Denise Silver

L A Silver Associates Inc
463 Worcester Rd Ste 205
Framingham, MA 01701
(508) 879-2603
Fax: (508) 879-8425
Email: lasilver@sprynet.com
Web: www.lasilver.com

Description: We have specialized in providing senior management for pre-IPO software companies on a worldwide basis. We work closely with the VC organization and executive management to ramp up the company's results to achieve IPO status. We are limited partners in two separate billion-dollar

venture capital organizations. All of are assignments are handled by principals only! We handle pre and post IPO (ISV) software only!

Key Contact:
Mr. Lee Silver, President
Ms. Lauren Hahn, Vice President

Salary minimum: $100,000

Functions: Senior Mgmt.

Industries: Software

Daniel A Silverstein Associates Inc
5355 Town Center Rd Ste 1001
Boca Raton, FL 33486
(561) 391-0600
Fax: (561) 391-0180
Email: dsilverstein@dassearch.com
Web: www.dassearch.com

Description: Executive search for pharmaceuticals, biotechnology, diagnostics and managed care. Venture capital-presidents for early stage companies. Top management for HMOs, practice management companies and pharmacy benefit managers.

Key Contact - Specialty:
Mr. Daniel A. Silverstein, President - *Healthcare*

Salary minimum: $100,000

Functions: Generalist, Directors, Senior Mgmt., Mktg. Mgmt., Sales Mgmt., IT, R&D, Mgmt. Consultants

Industries: Generalist, Drugs Mfg., Medical Devices, Venture Cap., Pharm Svcs., Mgmt. Consulting, Biotech

D J Simpson Associates Inc
1900 Minnesota Ct Ste 118
Mississauga, ON L5N 3C9
Canada
(905) 821-2727
Fax: (905) 821-3800
Email: info@djsimpson.com

Description: We combine search with one of the most powerful assessment tools available today to ensure our clients outperform their most worthy opponents. And we have the track record to prove it.

Key Contact:
Mr. David Simpson, General Manager

Salary minimum: $80,000

Functions: General Mgmt., Senior Mgmt.

Industries: Mfg.

Sinclair & Company Inc
37 Alice Dr Apt 12
Concord, NH 03301
(603) 225-2581
(386) 679-5814
Email: sncdg@earthlink.net

Description: Executive search for the computer industry with focus on software tools, advanced applications, manufacturing systems (MRP, MES, ERP), supply chain management, telecommunications, finance and insurance industries.

Key Contact - Specialty:
Mr. Douglas L. Sinclair, Managing Director - *Executive management*

Salary minimum: $85,000

Functions: Generalist, Mfg., Sales & Mktg.

Industries: Generalist, Computer Equip., Mgmt. Consulting, Telecoms, Software

Sink, Walker, Boltrus Int'l
180 Linden St
Wellesley Hills, MA 02482
(781) 237-1199
Fax: (781) 431-0085
Email: dwalker@swbi.com
Web: www.swbi.com

Description: Our primary search assignments are for important senior executive leaders in high-technology markets, including, communications for public and private networks, software, professional services, and capital equipment. The semiconductor industry, general manufacturers, consulting firms, financial services, and VC/LBO firms are represented.

Key Contact - Specialty:
Mr. Douglas G. Walker, Managing Director - *High technology, financial services, manufacturing, CEO's, BOD*
Mr. Cliff Sink, Managing Director - *High technology, operations, research, scientists, semiconductors*
Ms. Sushila Desai, Director - *Financial services (banking, regulated investment companies, investment advisors)*
Mr. Ritt Maloney, Director - *B2B, e-business, IT*

Salary minimum: $125,000

Functions: Generalist, General Mgmt., Mfg., Sales & Mktg., Finance, IT, Specialized Svcs., Int'l.

Industries: Generalist, Computer Equip., Test, Measure Equip., Misc. Mfg., Finance, Mgmt. Consulting, Telecoms, Software

Branches:
2055 Gateway Pl Ste 400
San Jose, CA 95110
(408) 451-3977
(781) 370-1025
Fax: (408) 441-9152
Email: dboltrus@swbi.com
Key Contact:
Ms. Sushila Desai

18352 Dallas Pkwy Ste 136
PMB 547
Dallas, TX 75287
(972) 380-8686
Fax: (972) 458-2747
Email: csink@swbi.com
Key Contact - Specialty:
Mr. Clifton W. Sink - *Telecommunications, high technology, capital equipment, semiconductors*

Ruth Sklar Associates Inc (RSA Executive Search)[†]
475 Park Ave S Fl 10
New York, NY 10016-6901
(212) 213-2929
Fax: (212) 779-9617
Email: ruthsklar@earthlink.net
Web: www.rsaexecutivesearch.com

Description: We emphasize on principal involvement in all phases of search. Recruitment of key executives from finance, healthcare, consumer products, services, microwave electronics and aerospace industries. Specializing in entrepreneurial environments.

Key Contact - Specialty:
Ms. Ruth Sklar, President - *Consumer products, services, healthcare, finance, banking*
Mr. Daniel R. Mazziota, Chairman - *High technology, biotechnology, senior financial*

Salary minimum: $80,000

Functions: Generalist

Industries: Mfg., Finance, Pharm Svcs., Accounting, HR Services, Media, Telecoms, Aerospace, Biotech, Healthcare

Professional Associations: APCNY

Skott/Edwards Consultants
1776 On the Green
Morristown, NJ 07960
(973) 644-0900
Fax: (973) 644-0991
Email: burkland@skottedwards.com
Web: www.skottedwards.com

Description: Industry expertise emphasizing emerging life science, medical devices, healthcare, pharmaceuticals, financial services, high-tech. All functions including management, finance, human resource, manufacturing, sales and marketing, legal, procurement and board of directors.

Key Contact - Specialty:
Mr. Skott B. Burkland, President - *Senior level general management, board of directors, life sciences, pharmaceuticals*
Dr. Charles R. Grebenstein, Ph.D., Senior Vice President - *Emerging life sciences, information technology, senior level general management*
Ms. Lee M. Moldock, Vice President - *Life sciences, information technology*
Mr. Franklin Barbosa, Senior Vice President - *High technology, computer systems, communications, information systems, CAD/CAM*

Salary minimum: $100,000

Functions: Healthcare

Industries: Generalist

Networks: Penrhyn Int'l

Slayton Int'l
(a member of IIC Partners)
181 W Madison Ste 4510
Chicago, IL 60602
(312) 456-0080
Fax: (312) 456-0089
Email: slayton@slaytonintl.com
Web: www.slaytonintl.com

Description: Our firm conducts both national and international work on behalf of our Fortune 500 client corporations and organizations. We are one of the preeminent retained executive search firms. Serving the industrial, consumer product, financial services, and automotive industries, we have an impeccable reputation for the quality of our work.

Key Contact:
Mr. Richard C. Slayton, Chairman
Mr. Richard S. Slayton, President
Mr. Thomas M. Hazlett, Vice President

Salary minimum: $150,000

Functions: Generalist

Industries: Generalist, Mfg., Motor Vehicles, Computer Equip., Consumer Elect., Misc. Mfg., Electronic, Elec. Components, Venture Cap., Telecoms, Software

Professional Associations: IACPR, HRMA

Networks: I-I-C Partners Executive Search Worldwide

Slesinger Management Services
5016 Westpath Ter
Bethesda, MD 20816
(301) 320-0680
Email: lslesinger@erols.com
Web: www.slesingermanagement.com

Description: Retained searches for associations, foundations and other nonprofit organizations. Special expertise in COO, EVP, and director of finance and administration positions; especially in the Washington, DC area.

Key Contact:
Mr. Larry H. Slesinger, CEO

Functions: Senior Mgmt.

Industries: Non-profits

Christopher Smallhorn Executive Recruiting Inc
One Boston Pl Fl 16
Boston, MA 02108
(617) 723-8180

Description: Recruiting senior managers, CEO, COO, CFO, primarily for early stage and emerging companies, nationally and internationally.

Key Contact:
Mr. Christopher Smallhorn, President

Salary minimum: $150,000

Functions: Generalist, General Mgmt., Directors, Healthcare, Health Admin., Mktg. Mgmt., CFO's

Industries: Generalist, Food, Bev., Tobacco, Soap, Perf., Cosmtcs., Drugs Mfg., Medical Devices, Venture Cap., Healthcare

Smith & Laue Search
4370 NE Halsey St
Portland, OR 97213
(503) 460-9181
Fax: (503) 460-9182
Email: csmithlaue@aol.com

Description: We specialize in mid- and senior-level professionals in the agri-business, food processing, feed processing, ingredients and the flavor industries, both in the United States and internationally.

Key Contact - Specialty:
Mr. Charles D. Smith, President - *Senior search, food processing, agribusiness, food ingredients*
Ms. Elizabeth Smith, Vice President - *Food processing*

Salary minimum: $150,000

Functions: Directors, Senior Mgmt.

Industries: Agri., Forestry, Mining, Food, Bev., Tobacco, Venture Cap., Pharm Svcs., Packaging

Smith & Partners Inc
1324 Larchmont Dr
Buffalo Grove, IL 60089
(847) 634-2304

Description: We are a recruiting firm, where I am totally responsible for all aspects of every assignment. We have no magical solutions, we simply gets the job done.

Key Contact - Specialty:
Mr. Richard J. Smith, President/Owner - *Generalist*

Salary minimum: $100,000

Functions: Generalist

Industries: Generalist

Smith & Sawyer LLC
634 Ocean Rd
Indian River Shores, FL 32963
(561) 234-0607
Email: pat@smithsawyer.com
Web: www.smithsawyer.com

Description: We place senior general management positions, such as: CEO, president, and COO in information industries, such as: computers, software, telecom, e-commerce, and IT services. We also place CIOs and CTOs for all industries. We can fill partner/practice leader roles in strategy or IT consulting, principal/partner roles for VC firms, and CEO and board advisory in consulting projects

Key Contact:
Ms. Patricia L. Sawyer, Partner
Mr. Robert L. Smith, Partner

Salary minimum: $150,000

Functions: Directors, Senior Mgmt., MIS Mgmt., Mgmt. Consultants

Industries: Mfg., Computer Equip., Consumer Elect., Wholesale, Retail, Finance, Venture Cap., Misc. Financial, Services, Equip Svcs., Mgmt. Consulting, Media, New Media, Telecoms, Insurance, Software, Healthcare

Smith & Syberg Inc
505 Washington St 2A
Columbus, IN 47201
(812) 372-7254
Fax: (812) 372-7275
Email: mail@smithandsyberg.com
Web: www.smithandsyberg.com

Description: Our search expertise is utilized for senior and executive management level positions. Our clients range from small, entrepreneurial growth companies to Fortune 500 corporations and represent a variety of industries, including manufacturing, airlines, service, and distribution.

Key Contact - Specialty:
Mr. Joseph E. Smith, Partner - *Airline, accounting & finance, manufacturing*
Mr. Keith A. Syberg, Partner - *Manufacturing*

Salary minimum: $100,000

Functions: Mfg.

Industries: Mfg., Food, Bev., Tobacco, Medical Devices, Plastics, Rubber, Metal Products, Motor Vehicles, Misc. Mfg., Transportation

Professional Associations: AESC, AME

Networks: National Personnel Assoc (NPA)

Howard W Smith Associates
Old State House Station
PO Box 230877
Hartford, CT 06123-0877
(860) 549-2060
Fax: (860) 246-7871
Email: hwsmith9@aol.com

Description: Mostly repeat clients, financial service related including investment management, real estate, mortgage banking, marketing, finance and general management.

Key Contact:
Mr. Howard W. Smith, President

Salary minimum: $70,000

Functions: Generalist

Industries: Finance, Legal, Insurance, Real Estate, Healthcare

Adam Smith Executive Search Consulting
2434 S Walter Reed Dr Ste D
Arlington, VA 22206
(703) 998-8118
Fax: (703) 998-6006
Email: adamsmith@adamsmithsearch.com
Web: www.adamsmithsearch.com

Description: Client-centered retained executive search firm. Original, comprehensive research and thorough candidate assessment. Specializing in senior-level critical needs.

Key Contact:
Mr. Adam M. Smith, Managing Director

Salary minimum: $100,000

Functions: Generalist

Industries: Generalist

Professional Associations: APA, HRPS, SHRM, WTPF

Smith James Group Inc
11660 Alpharetta Hwy Ste 515
Roswell, GA 30076
(770) 667-0212

Email: resumes@smithjames.com
Web: www.smithjames.com

Description: Expertise in telecommunications, high-technology, banking, service, utilities industry. Concentration is on senior/middle management and key technical positions.

Key Contact - Specialty:
Mr. James Soutouras, Senior Partner - *Generalist*
Mr. Michael Smith, Senior Partner - *Generalist*

Salary minimum: $75,000

Functions: Generalist

Industries: Generalist

Professional Associations: SHRM, TAG

H C Smith Ltd

20600 Chagrin Blvd Ste 200
Shaker Heights, OH 44122
(216) 752-9966
Fax: (216) 752-9970
Email: info@hcsmith.com
Web: www.hcsmith.com

Description: Professionally managed generalist practice with broad range of global resources. Recognized ability to evaluate and recruit talented minorities and women for executive and board positions.

Key Contact:
Dr. Herbert C. Smith, President/CEO
Ms. Rebecca Ruben Smith, Executive Vice President

Salary minimum: $75,000

Functions: Generalist

Industries: Generalist

Herman Smith Search Inc

161 Bay St Ste 3860 BCE Pl Canada Trust Twr
PO Box 629
Toronto, ON M5J 2S1
Canada
(416) 862-8830
Fax: (416) 869-1809
Email: info@hermansmith.com

Description: International specialists in recruitment, as well as recruitment program design.

Key Contact:
Mr. Herman M. Smith, President/Founder - *CEO, board of directors*
Ms. Janice N. Kussner, Partner - *Management (middle to senior level)*
Mr. Terry Szwec, Partner - *Management (middle to senior level)*
Mr. Gordon Wilson, Partner - *Management (middle to senior level) within finance industry*
Ms. Angela Eckford, Consultant

Salary minimum: $75,000

Functions: Generalist, Senior Mgmt., Middle Mgmt., Mfg., Sales & Mktg., HR Mgmt., CFO's, MIS Mgmt.

Industries: Generalist, Mfg., Transportation, Retail, Finance, Government

Networks: EMA Partners Int'l

Smith Search SC

Barranca del Muerto 472°
Col Alpes Del A Obregon
Mexico City, DF CP 01010
Mexico
52 5 593 8766
Fax: 52 5 593 8969
Email: smith@smithsearch.com
Web: www.smithsearch.com

Description: Mexico's leading independent executive recruitment firm, specializing in the cross-cultural, bilingual executive for companies

primarily in Mexico, but also the United States and most Latin American countries.

Key Contact:
Mr. John E. Smith, Jr., President - *Generalist*
Ms. Maria Elena Pardo, Executive Recruiter
Ms. Ana Luz Smith, Executive Recruiter

Salary minimum: $75,000

Functions: Generalist, Directors, Plant Mgmt., Mktg. Mgmt., CFO's, MIS Mgmt.

Industries: Generalist, Food, Bev., Tobacco, Chemicals, Banking, Invest. Banking, Telecoms

Professional Associations: AESC

Smith, Roth & Squires

237 Park Ave Fl 21 Ste 92
New York, NY 10017
(212) 767-9480
(516) 736-2700
Email: rrothsrs@aol.com
Web: www.smithrothsquires.com

Description: We are senior-level boutique firm serving most industries and all functions. We are a hands on, principal directed firm Our multinational scope, and our demonstrated track record of repetitive business is indicative of our high personal commitment and the strong relationships that we have built and maintain.

Key Contact - Specialty:
Mr. Ronald P. Roth, Principal - *Generalist*
Mr. R. James Squires, Principal - *Generalist*
Ms. Abbe Rosenthal, Principal - *Generalist*

Salary minimum: $125,000

Functions: Generalist

Industries: Generalist

Branches:
7090 N Oracle Rd Ste 178
Tucson, AZ 85704
(520) 544-3600
Fax: (520) 544-8172
Email: rjbsrs@aol.com
Key Contact - Specialty:
Mr. Robert J. Butler, CCP, SPHR, Principal - *Generalist*

A William Smyth Inc

PO Box 380
Ross, CA 94957
(415) 457-8383

Description: Our experience includes related categories for example: consumer packaged goods, high technology, and software where sophisticated marketing is required. We specialize in management consulting, M&A, organization planning, salary surveys, and channel planning.

Key Contact:
Mr. William Smyth, President

Salary minimum: $80,000

Functions: Generalist, General Mgmt., Sales & Mktg., Finance, IT, Int'l.

Industries: Generalist, Food, Bev., Tobacco, Soap, Perf., Cosmtcs., Computer Equip., Finance, Hospitality, Software

Snelling Personnel Services

20 E Timonium Rd Ste 111
Timonium, MD 21093-3400
(410) 561-5701
Fax: (410) 561-0542
Email: timonium@jobs4u.com
Web: www.jobs4u.com

Description: Full-service staffing organization with four locations in the Baltimore Metro Area. We focus on temporary and career placement opportunities in the following areas: administrative,

accounting and finance, creative and scientific/lab and tech staffing.

Key Contact - Specialty:
Mr. Robert E. Greene, CEO
Ms. Linda S. Kaestner, CPC, Director of Sales and Operations/Preside - *Marketing, development*

Functions: Generalist, General Mgmt.

Industries: Mfg., Food, Bev., Tobacco, Drugs Mfg., Medical Devices, Services, Pharm Svcs., Hospitality, Media, Environmental Svcs., Packaging, Insurance, Biotech

Professional Associations: ASA, SHRM

Snowden Associates

400 The Hill
Portsmouth, NH 03801-3736
(603) 431-1553
Fax: (603) 431-3809
Email: snowden44@aol.com

Description: We use a very personal and thorough search process to identify, screen, interview, access and recommend highly qualified key impact candidates for critical positions at our client firms.

Key Contact - Specialty:
Mr. Len Rishkofski, President/CEO - *Generalist*

Salary minimum: $65,000

Functions: Generalist

Industries: Energy, Utilities, Mfg., Wholesale, Finance, Services, Media, Insurance, Biotech, Healthcare

Professional Associations: NEHRA, NHRA, SHRA, SHRM

Branches:
116 S River Rd
Bedford, NH 03110-6734
(603) 626-6777
Fax: (603) 623-3135
Email: snowden101@aol.com
Key Contact - Specialty:
Mr. Al Egan, Vice President - *Generalist*
Mr. Tim McDonough, Vice President - *Generalist*

Snyder & Company

35 Old Avon Village Ste 185
Avon, CT 06001-3822
(860) 521-9760
Fax: (860) 521-2495
Email: jamessnyder@compuserve.com

Description: We are characterized by our exhaustive sourcing methodology and in-depth candidate assessment skills.

Key Contact:
Mr. James F. Snyder, President

Salary minimum: $100,000

Functions: Generalist

Industries: Food, Bev., Tobacco, Drugs Mfg., Medical Devices, Finance, Pharm Svcs., HR Services, Insurance, Biotech, Healthcare

Professional Associations: IMC

Sockwell & Associates

(a member of TranSearch Int'l)
227 W Trade St Ste 1930
Charlotte, NC 28202
(704) 372-1865
Fax: (704) 372-8960
Email: email@sockwell.com
Web: www.sockwell.com

Description: Senior-level functional search for North American clients in for-profit and not-for-profit sectors; most assignments at CEO/COO/CFO or division executive-level; client-focus and internal quality initiatives.

Key Contact:
Mr. J. Edgar Sockwell, Managing Partner
Ms. Lyttleton Rich, Partner
Ms. Susan N. Jernigan, Partner
Mr. Robert B. Sherrill, Director

Salary minimum: $150,000

Functions: Senior Mgmt.

Industries: Mfg., Lumber, Furniture, Printing, Drugs Mfg., Finance, Services, Real Estate, Software, Biotech, Healthcare

Professional Associations: AESC

Networks: TranSearch Int'l

Branches:
2530 Meridian Pkwy Fl 3
Research Triangle Park, NC 27709
(919) 806-4450
Fax: (919) 806-4301

Söderlund Associates Inc
105 W 4th St. Ste 1005
Cincinnati, OH 45202-2717
(800) 349-6919
Fax: (800) 730-1516
Email: eric@soderlund.com
Web: www.soderlund.com

Description: We recruit senior executives for the computer industry in product development, marketing and sales and service.

Key Contact - Specialty:
Mr. Eric Soderlund, President - *High technology, directors, VP's, SVP's*
Ms. Terri Ross, Manager Technology - *High technology*
Ms. Paige Sutkamp, Manager Finance - *High technology*
Ms. Natalie Ruppert, Executive Recruiter - *High technology*
Ms. Judi Becker, Director of Research - *High technology*
Ms. Ruth Ullman, Executive Recruiter - *High tech*
Mr. Brit Soderlund-Roberts, Executive Recruiter - *High tech*

Salary minimum: $150,000

Functions: Mfg., Materials, Sales & Mktg., R&D, Engineering, Int'l.

Industries: Generalist

Solomon-Page Healthcare Group
1140 Ave of the Americas Fl 7
New York, NY 10036
(212) 403-6166
Fax: (212) 824-1505
Email: mgouran@spges.com
Web: www.spgjobs.com

Description: We are highly focused, nationwide, retained executive search in most functional areas for managed healthcare, pharmaceutical, e-health, group insurance, employee benefits, HMOs, hospitals and related healthcare companies and institutions.

Key Contact - Specialty:
Mr. Marc S. Gouran, Group President - *Healthcare*

Salary minimum: $75,000

Functions: Senior Mgmt., Middle Mgmt., Physicians, Sales & Mktg., Mktg. Mgmt., Benefits, DB Admin.

Industries: Pharm Svcs., Mgmt. Consulting, Insurance, HR SW, Healthcare

Professional Associations: AAHP, ACPE, NAHQ, NAMCP

Branches:
7676 Hazard Center Dr Ste 1320
San Diego, CA 92108
(619) 291-2300
Email: dbleau@spgeswest.com

Key Contact - Specialty:
Mr. Donn E. Bleau, Managing Director - *Healthcare*

Soltis Management Services
876 Brower Rd
Radnor, PA 19087-2208
(610) 687-4200
Email: soltis@earthlink.net

Description: Management consultants in executive search, executive assessment, organization issues and management development. Since 1971, an inimitable reputation for confidential, results oriented service to corporate clients. Search assignments 98% successful.

Key Contact - Specialty:
Mr. Charles W. Soltis, President - *Generalist*

Salary minimum: $100,000

Functions: Senior Mgmt.

Industries: Generalist

Branches:
500 5th Ave Ste 5120
New York, NY 10110
(212) 354-8850
Email: soltis@earthlink.net
Key Contact - Specialty:
Ms. Natasha Taylor - *Administrator*

Solutions Group - Birmingham
PO Box 360805
Birmingham, AL 35236
(205) 663-1301
Fax: (205) 663-1306
Email: sgsearch@aol.com

Description: We are a generalist firm with experience in manufacturing, healthcare, and service industries.

Key Contact - Specialty:
Mr. Hinky Verchot, Principal - *Generalist*

Salary minimum: $50,000

Functions: General Mgmt., Mfg., Materials, Healthcare, HR Mgmt., Finance

Industries: Generalist, Energy, Utilities, Mfg., Metal Products, Packaging, Healthcare, Hospitals

Stephen M Sonis Associates[†]
275 Turnpike St Ste 202
Canton, MA 02021-2357
(781) 821-0303
(888) 714-7427
Fax: (781) 821-0601
Email: smsonis@aol.com

Description: We specialize in focused, personalized service for both start-ups and major companies. We are totally client-driven. We represent a creative, intelligent, cost and time effective search alternative.

Key Contact:
Mr. Stephen M. Sonis, Principal

Salary minimum: $50,000

Functions: General Mgmt., Materials, Sales & Mktg., HR Mgmt., Finance

Industries: Generalist

Professional Associations: MPPC

Souder & Associates[†]
PO Box 71
Bridgewater, VA 22812
(540) 828-2365
Fax: (540) 828-2851
Email: resumes@souderandassociates.com
Web: www.souderandassociates.com

Description: We are national executive search firm and recruitment services provider with over a

decade of experience in executive search. We provide recruitment services for manufacturing, food and technology oriented industries.

Key Contact - Specialty:
Mr. E. G. Souder, Jr., President - *Human resources, operations, technical, sales, accounting*
Ms. Deana A. Griffin, Vice President - *Human resources, operations, technical, sales, accounting*

Salary minimum: $40,000

Functions: General Mgmt., Mfg., Sales & Mktg., HR Mgmt., Finance, IT, Int'l.

Industries: Generalist, Printing, Chemicals, Drugs Mfg., Medical Devices, Plastics, Rubber, Metal Products, Hotels, Resorts, Clubs, Restaurants, Communications, Healthcare

Professional Associations: AMA, SHRM

Southern Research Services[†]
5121 Enrlich Rd Ste 107-A
Tampa, FL 33624
(813) 269-9595
Fax: (813) 264-6847
Email: tom.bloch@gte.net

Description: Specialize in locating and qualifying technical/engineering management professionals in the battery, medical products, electric utility industry and electronic components.

Key Contact:
Mr. Thomas L. Bloch, Owner

Salary minimum: $50,000

Functions: General Mgmt.

Industries: Generalist

Professional Associations: NAPS

Networks: Top Echelon Network

SPANUSA®
135 Beach Ave
Mamaroneck, NY 10543
(914) 381-5555
Fax: (914) 381-0811
Email: info@spanusa.net
Web: www.spanusa.net

Description: We are completely focused on Spanish-English and Portuguese-English speaking professionals and executives, Hispanic and non-Hispanic, in the US, as well as in Latin America. We work in most industries and functional areas where the language skills are required in addition to the professional or management expertise.

Key Contact - Specialty:
Mr. Manuel S. Boado, Founder, President & CEO - *Generalist, international, spanish-english speaking executives*

Salary minimum: $70,000

Functions: Generalist

Industries: Generalist, Drugs Mfg., Banking, Invest. Banking, E-commerce, Recreation, Advertising, Telecoms, Mfg. SW, Marketing SW

Networks: Top Echelon Network

Special Markets Group Inc
4732 Old Countryside Cir S
Stone Mountain, GA 30083
(770) 508-0834
(888) 245-2150
Fax: (404) 296-7999
Email: kdlsmgucg@aol.com
Web: www.specialmarketsgroup.com

Description: Retained firm dedicated to providing executive search and human resource consulting to both small entrepreneurial organizations as well as large corporate entities. Expertise in diversity/minority positions and general business.

Key Contact - Specialty:
Mr. Kenneth D. Lee, President - *Generalist, minorities*

Salary minimum: $50,000

Functions: Generalist, Senior Mgmt., Mktg. Mgmt., Sales Mgmt., CFO's, MIS Mgmt., Minorities

Industries: Generalist, Food, Bev., Tobacco, Computer Equip., Finance, Hospitality, Media, Insurance

Professional Associations: BDPA, CLM, NBMBAA

Specialty Consultants Inc
2710 Gateway Twrs
Pittsburgh, PA 15222-1189
(412) 355-8200
Fax: (412) 355-0498
Email: info@specon.com
Web: www.specon.com

Description: We specialize in real estate and construction industries.

Key Contact:
Mr. Paul J. Lewis, Managing Director

Salary minimum: $75,000

Functions: Generalist

Industries: Construction, Real Estate

Professional Associations: ABC, AGC, BOMA, CFMA, ICSC, IREM, MCAA, NACORE, NAHB, NAIOP, NAREIT, NECA, NMHC, PREA, RESSI

Spectrum Consultants
12625 High Bluff Dr Ste 215
San Diego, CA 92130-2054
(858) 259-3232
Fax: (858) 792-7064
Email: spectcon@pacbell.net

Description: We specialize in telecommunications, hi-tech, e-business, aerospace, golf industry, engineering, scientists, advanced materials, general management, and marketing.

Key Contact:
Mr. G. W. Christiansen, Partner
Mr. Stanley Bass, Partner

Salary minimum: $75,000

Functions: Senior Mgmt., Middle Mgmt., Product Dev., CFO's, MIS Mgmt., R&D

Industries: Medical Devices, Motor Vehicles, Telecoms, Aerospace, Software, Biotech

The Spelman & Johnson Group
38 Mulberry St
PO Box 304
Leeds, MA 01053
(413) 584-7089
Fax: (413) 584-4850
Email: info@spelmanandjohnson.com
Web: www.spelmanandjohnson.com

Description: We are a retained search and consulting firm serving higher education. The group focuses on providing a full range of search services to institutions of higher education and also assists institutions in assessing, planning, and evaluating administrative programs and services.

Key Contact:
Mr. William Spelman, President
Ms. Katherine Johnson, Vice President
Ms. Ellen Heffernan, Managing Vice President

Functions: Directors, Senior Mgmt.

Industries: Higher Ed.

Spence Associates Int'l Inc
721 Hollow Tree Ridge Rd
Darien, CT 06820
(203) 662-0685
Fax: (203) 662-0685
Email: web@spenceassociates.com
Web: www.spenceassociates.com

Description: Retainer-based search at the board of director, CEO & VP levels in all Industries.

Key Contact - Specialty:
Mr. Gene Spence, Founder/President - *Technology, internet, international*
Mr. Michael Gaida, Consultant - *Internet, e-business*

Salary minimum: $200,000

Functions: Generalist

Industries: Generalist

Professional Associations: AESC, IACPR

Spencer Stuart
401 N Michigan Ave Ste 3400
Chicago, IL 60611
(312) 822-0080
Fax: (312) 822-0116
Web: www.spencerstuart.com

Description: We are the leading privately held, global executive search firm offering a range of human capital solutions, including senior-level executive search, board director appointments, strategic leadership assessment, and through our web-based recruiting division, Spencer Stuart Talent Network (SSTN), and mid-level executive recruitment.

Key Contact - Specialty:
Mr. Kevin M. Connelly, Office Manager - *Financial services, industrial, insurance, consumer financial services, retail banking*
Ms. Toni S. Smith - *Non-profit, healthcare*
Mr. Thomas J. Snyder - *Consumer (goods, services), retail, fast moving consumer goods & durables*
Mr. Karl Aavik - *Technology, communications, internet*
Mr. Gilbert R. Stenholm - *Consumer (goods, services), board services, fast moving consumer goods & durables*
Ms. Gail H. Vergara - *Healthcare*
Mr. Robert G. Shields - *Utilities, energy, industrial*
Mr. Alvan Turner - *Industrial, automotive*
Ms. Virginia Clarke - *Financial services, consumer financial services, retail banking, investment management, real estate*
Mr. Don Render - *High technology*
Mr. Pat Walsh - *Generalist, consumer (goods, services), fast moving consumer goods & durables, healthcare*
Mr. Greg Welch - *Consumer (goods, services), healthcare, fast moving consumer goods & durables*
Ms. Amanda Fox - *Insurance, life sciences, financial services*
Mr. Richard J. Brennen - *High technology*
Mr. Paul W. Earle - *Healthcare, board services*
Mr. J. Curtis Fee - *Financial services, global securities, wholesale banking, real estate, industrial*
Mr. Joseph M. Kopsick - *Generalist, consumer (goods, services), industrial, fast moving consumer goods & durables*
Mr. Christopher C. Nadherny - *Consumer (goods, services), direct marketing, consumer financial services, retail banking, communications*
Mr. John Puisis - *Life sciences, healthcare*
Mr. Robert L. Heidrick - *Industrial*

Salary minimum: $150,000

Functions: Generalist

Industries: Generalist

Professional Associations: AESC

Branches:
2020 Main St Ste 350
Irvine, CA 92614
(949) 930-8000
Fax: (949) 930-8001
Key Contact - Specialty:
Mr. Tim Pirrung - *Agribusiness, consumer (goods, services), internet*
Ms. Charlene Reed - *Life sciences, technology, communications*

10900 Wilshire Blvd Ste 800
Los Angeles, CA 90024-6524
(310) 209-0610
Fax: (310) 209-0912
Key Contact - Specialty:
Mr. Michael C. Bruce, Office Manager - *Financial services, consumer financial services, retail banking, investment management, global securities*
Ms. Stephanie Davis - *Technology, communications, internet*
Ms. Judy Havas - *Communications, media, consumer (goods, services), direct marketing*
Mr. Tim Pirrung - *Agribusiness, consumer (goods, services), internet*
Ms. Charlene Reed - *Healthcare, life sciences*
Mr. William Goodmen - *Energy, natural resources, industrial*
Mr. Jack Schlosser - *Life sciences*

7041 Koll Center Pkwy Ste 200
Pleasanton, CA 94566
(925) 738-4900
Fax: (925) 738-4902
Key Contact - Specialty:
Mr. Phil Johnston, Office Manager - *High technology*
Mr. Robert Currie - *Technology, communications*
Mr. Bruce Goldberg, MD, MPH - *Life sciences*

525 Market St Ste 3700
San Francisco, CA 94105-2161
(415) 495-4141
Fax: (415) 495-7524
Key Contact - Specialty:
Mr. Joseph E. Griesedieck, Jr. - *Consumer (goods, services), boards, aviation*
Mr. Jed Hughes - *Sports management*
Mr. Tom Seclow - *Consumer (goods, services), technology, communications, internet*
Mr. E. C. Grayson - *Energy, industrial, diversity*
Mr. Jonathan O. White, Office Manager - *Technology, communications, internet, aviation*
Mr. T. Christopher Butler - *Financial services, investment management, global securities, wholesale banking, consumer financial services*
Mr. Bob Damon - *Consumer (goods, services), industrial, restaurant, hospitality*
Ms. Amy de Rham - *Consumer (goods, services), diversity, financial services*
Mr. Kevin Gagan - *Financial services, technology, communications*
Mr. Ray Fortney - *Energy, natural resources, logistics, technology, communications*

2988 Campus Dr Fl 3
San Mateo, CA 94403
(650) 356-5500
Fax: (650) 356-5501
Key Contact - Specialty:
Mr. Jonathan Visbal, Office Manager - *High technology*
Mr. John Ware - *High technology, communications*
Mr. Rick Gostyla - *High technology, board services*
Ms. Nayla Rizk - *High technology*
Mr. Scott Gordon - *High technology*
Ms. Cathy Anterasian - *High technology*
Ms. Debbie Soon - *High technology*
Mr. T. Christopher Butler
Mr. Michael Lynch
Mr. Patrick McGill
Mr. James Buckley - *Technology, communications*

695 E Main St
Financial Ctr
Stamford, CT 06901
(203) 324-6333
Fax: (203) 326-3737
Key Contact - Specialty:
Mr. Harry Somerdyk, Office Manager - *Internet, diversity*
Mr. H. James Krauser - *Real estate, mortgage banking, financial services*
Mr. Tony Thompson - *Media, entertainment, communications*
Mr. J. Rick Richardson - *Financial services, consumer (goods, services), direct marketing, consumer financial services, retail banking*
Mr. Thomas W. Wasson - *High technology*
Mr. Dayton Ogden, Co-Chairman - *Agribusiness, aviation, board services, financial services*
Ms. Susan S. Hart - *Consumer (goods, services), apparel, retail*
Ms. Claudia Lacy Kelly - *Financial services, consumer marketing, investment management*
Mr. Daniel P. Romanello - *High technology*
Mr. James M. Citrin - *Board services, consumer (goods, services), technology, communications, internet*
Mr. Richard Routhier - *Consumer (goods, services)*
Ms. Valerie Harper - *Financial services*
Ms. Sandy Gross - *Consumer (goods, services), financial services*
Ms. Tammy Kien Jersey - *Consumer (goods, services), financial services, internet*
Mr. Greg Jackson - *Industrial*
Mr. Tom Scanlan - *Technology, communications, internet*

220 Alhambra Cir Ste 700
Coral Gables, FL 33134
(305) 443-9911
Fax: (305) 443-2180
Key Contact - Specialty:
Mr. Kenneth V. Eckhart, Office Manager - *Consumer (goods, services), industrial, logistics, supply chain*
Mr. Michael Bell - *Aviation, industrial, internet*
Ms. Karine Gill - *Consumer (goods, services)*
Mr. Brendan Curran - *Aviation, industrial*
Mr. Dominique Virchaux - *Industrial*

945 E Paces Ferry Rd
2600 Resurgens Plz
Atlanta, GA 30326-1379
(404) 504-4400
Fax: (404) 504-4401
Key Contact - Specialty:
Mr. William B. Reeves - *Financial services, insurance, consumer financial services, retail banking*
Mr. Samuel H. Pettway - *Board services, consumer (goods, services), diversity, non-profit*
Ms. Sharon Hall, Office Manager - *Consumer goods, consumer financial services, direct marketing, fast moving consumer goods & durables*
Mr. Carl Gilchrist - *High technology*
Mr. John Mitchell - *Life sciences*
Mr. Richard Perkey - *Financial services, consumer financial services, retail banking*
Mr. Ira Isaacson - *Life sciences*
Mr. Rick Smith - *Technology, communications, internet*
Ms. Conchita Robinson - *Consumer (goods, services), diversity, technology, communications, internet*

24 Federal St
Boston, MA 02110
(617) 531-5731
Fax: (617) 531-5732
Key Contact - Specialty:
Mr. Michael Anderson, Office Manager - *Financial services, insurance*
Ms. Kristine Langdon - *Industrial, life sciences, technology, communications*
Mr. Jerry Noonan - *Consumer (goods, services), technology, communications, internet, media*

Mr. Tom Robinson - *Internet, life sciences*
601 2nd Ave S Ste 4141
Minneapolis, MN 55402
(612) 313-2000
Fax: (612) 313-2001
Key Contact - Specialty:
Mr. Matt Christoff, Office Manager - *Agribusiness, consumer (goods, services)*
Ms. Susan Boren - *Board services, consumer (goods, services), direct marketing*
Mr. Tom Pritzker - *Financial services*

277 Park Ave Fl 29
New York, NY 10172-2998
(212) 336-0200
Fax: (212) 336-0296
Key Contact - Specialty:
Mr. William Clemens, Office Manager - *Consumer (goods, services), financial services, industrial*
Ms. Judith Bacher - *Financial services, investment management, strategic planning, human resources, multimedia*
Mr. Nicholas Young - *Agribusiness, industrial, energy, natural resources, board services*
Ms. Robin Soren - *Financial services, investment management*
Mr. John Wood - *Consumer (goods, services), communications, direct marketing, fast moving consumer goods & durables*
Mr. John Keller - *Communications, high technology*
Mr. John Gibbs, Jr. - *Consumer (goods, services), communications, industrial, fast moving goods & durables, restaurant, hospitality*
Mr. E. Peter McLean - *Financial services, communications, global securities, wholesale banking*
Mr. Thomas J. Neff - *Aviation, board services, consumer (goods, services), financial services, industrial*
Mr. Joel von Ranson - *Consumer (goods, services), technology, communications*
Ms. Andrea de Cholnoky - *Financial services, global securities, wholesale banking, investment management, real estate*
Mr. Joseph H. Boccuzi - *Healthcare, pharmaceuticals, biotechnology*
Ms. Julie H. Daum - *Board services, financial services*
Ms. Marnie McBryde - *Consumer financial services, retail banking, consumer (goods, services), direct marketing, retail, apparel*
Mr. David S. Daniel, CEO - *Consumer (goods, services), apparel, retail*
Mr. Peter Gonye - *Financial services*
Ms. Carrie Pryor - *Board services, consumer (goods, services), internet, technology, communications*

2005 Market St Ste 2350
1 Commerce Sq
Philadelphia, PA 19103
(215) 814-1600
Fax: (215) 814-1681
Key Contact - Specialty:
Ms. Connie B. McCann, Office Manager - *Financial services, consumer financial services, retail banking, investment management, global securities*
Mr. Dennis C. Carey - *Board services, technology, communications*
Mr. Franklin D. Marsteller - *Insurance, financial services*
Mr. Jeff Bell - *Financial services, global securities, wholesale banking, investment management*
Mr. Peter Goossens - *Agribusiness, life sciences, industrial*
Ms. Jennifer Herrmann - *Financial services*
Mr. Jeff Wierichs - *Consumer (goods, services), diversity, internet, logistics, supply chain management*

1717 Main St Ste 5600
Dallas, TX 75201-4605
(214) 672-5200
Fax: (214) 672-5299

Key Contact - Specialty:
Mr. Randall D. Kelley - *Technology, communications, internet*
Mr. John W. Schroeder - *Consumer (goods, services), consumer packaged goods, capital goods manufacturing, transportation, direct marketing*
Mr. Ronald J. Zera - *Consumer (goods, services), diversity, industrial, life sciences, logistics*
Mr. David Beuerlein, Office Manager - *Technology, communications*
Mr. Scott Petty - *Technology, communications, internet*
Mr. Terry W. Price - *Technology, communications, internet*
Mr. O. D. Dan Cruse - *Board services, technology, communications, industrial*
Mr. David N. Konker - *Board services, financial services*

1111 Bagby Ste 1616
Houston, TX 77002-2594
(713) 225-1621
Fax: (713) 658-8336
Key Contact - Specialty:
Mr. Jonathan A. Crystal - *Energy, utilities, industrial*
Mr. Thomas M. Simmons, Office Manager - *Energy, natural resources, financial services*
Mr. Richard J. Preng - *Board services, energy, natural resources, internet*
Ms. Mary Bass - *Board services, technology, communications, internet*
Mr. Eric Nielsen - *Agribusiness, energy, internet, financial services*
Mr. Brad Farnsworth - *Consumer (goods, services), technology, communications, energy, natural resources*

1 University Ave Ste 801
Toronto, ON M5J 2P1
Canada
(416) 361-0311
Fax: (416) 361-6118
Key Contact - Specialty:
Mr. Jeffrey M. Hauswirth, Office Manager - *Aviation, technology, communications, internet*
Mr. Jerry Bliley - *Manufacturing, professional services, consumer (goods, services), board services, industrial*
Mr. Andrew J. MacDougall - *Board services, financial services, logistics, supply chain management*
Mr. David MacEachern - *Consumer (goods, services), energy, financial services, industrial, internet*
Mr. Noel Desautels - *Technology, communications, industrial, life sciences*
Mr. Roger Clarkson - *Consumer (goods, services), technology, communications*
Ms. Sharon Rudy - *Technology, communications, internet*

1981 Ave McGill College Ste 1430
Montreal, QC H3A 2Y1
Canada
(514) 288-3377
Fax: (514) 288-4626
Key Contact - Specialty:
Ms. Manon Vennat - *Aviation, board services, technology, communications, non-profit*
Mr. Jérôme Piché - *Technology, communications, internet*
Mr. Robert Nadeau, Office Manager - *Aviation, life sciences*

Edificio Omega
Campos Eliseos 345 Fl 6
Colonia Polanco
Mexico City, DF 11560
Mexico
52 5 281 4050
Fax: 52 5281 4184
Key Contact - Specialty:
Mr. Samuel Podolsky, Managing Director - Mexico - *Technology, communications*
Mr. Javier Valle, Office Manager - *Life sciences*

Mr. Rafael Rojo - *Consumer (goods, services), industrial*

The Spiegel Group Inc
PO Box 9121
Newton, MA 02464
(617) 558-5545
Email: gspiegel@mediaone.net

Description: We offer proven performance in finding local nationals all over the world for both American and European based high-technology companies. We work with start-up and publicly held companies in the US and abroad.

Key Contact - Specialty:
Ms. Gayle Spiegel, President - *High technology, international*

Salary minimum: $100,000

Functions: General Mgmt., Directors, Senior Mgmt., Sales & Mktg., Mktg. Mgmt., Sales Mgmt., Direct Mktg.

Industries: Chemicals, Medical Devices, Computer Equip., Venture Cap., Advertising, New Media, Telecoms, Software, Biotech

Spilman & Associates
5956 Sherry Ln Ste 1000
Dallas, TX 75225
(214) 528-8994
Fax: (214) 528-9011
Email: spilman@airmail.net

Description: Our focus is the distribution and retail arenas and consulting firms that specialize in those arenas.

Key Contact - Specialty:
Ms. Mary P. Spilman, Principal - *Vertically integrated distribution industries, professional services, technology*

Salary minimum: $60,000

Functions: Generalist, HR Mgmt., Finance, IT, Mgmt. Consultants, Minorities

Industries: Generalist, Food, Bev., Tobacco, Drugs Mfg., Consumer Elect., Finance, Packaging, Software

Professional Associations: DMA, NRF

Splaine & Associates Inc
15951 Los Gatos Blvd
Los Gatos, CA 95032
(408) 354-3664
Email: info@exec-search.com
Web: www.exec-search.com

Description: Our firm conducts retained executive search assignments for companies in high-technology industries, for example: storage, SAN, media, software, systems, networking, communications, wireless, video, and optical networks.

Key Contact - Specialty:
Mr. Charles Splaine, Chairman - *High technology*

Salary minimum: $180,000

Functions: General Mgmt.

Industries: Computer Equip., Electronic, Elec. Components, E-commerce, Communications, Wireless, Network Infrastructure, Software, Development SW

Sports Group Int'l
8601 Six Forks Rd Ste 400
Raleigh, NC 27615
(919) 855-0226
Fax: (919) 855-0793
Email: sgisearch@aol.com
Web: www.sgisearch.com

Description: We are specialists in recruiting general management, marketing/sales and international for sporting goods, recreational products, and services organizations. Our firm conducts searches for best practices professionals who consistently demonstrate positive top line results.

Key Contact - Specialty:
Mr. Joseph A. White, CPC, President - *Apparel, footwear, consumer, golf, sporting goods*

Salary minimum: $75,000

Functions: Senior Mgmt., Product Dev., Sales & Mktg.

Industries: Mfg.

Professional Associations: NAPS

Spriggs & Company Inc
1701 Lake Ave Ste 265
Glenview, IL 60025
(847) 657-7181
Fax: (847) 657-7186
Email: robertspriggs@compuserve.com

Key Contact:
Mr. Robert D. Spriggs, Partner
Mr. William H. Billington, Partner
Mr. Tom McGrath, Partner
Mr. John R. Goldrick, Partner

Functions: Generalist

Industries: Generalist

Spring Associates Inc†
10 E 23rd St
New York, NY 10010-4402
(212) 473-0013
Email: info@springassociates.com
Web: www.springassociates.com

Description: A leader in our field for over 20 years, our clients are both communications departments of major corporations and the public relations firms which serve them.

Key Contact - Specialty:
Mr. Dennis Spring, President - *Public relations, marketing communications, corporate communications*

Salary minimum: $75,000

Functions: PR

Industries: Generalist

Professional Associations: IABC, PRSA

Networks: Int'l Executive Search Assoc

Branches:
2685 Marine Way Ste 1220
Mountain View, CA 94043
(650) 428-0707
Email: info@springassociates.com
Key Contact:
Mr. Dennis Spring, President

Springbrook Partners Inc
16 North St
Hingham, MA 02043
(781) 749-7075
Fax: (781) 749-7599
Email: info@springbrookpartners.com
Web: www.springbrookpartners.com

Description: A generalist retainer firm, we conduct searches in all functional areas, with a focus on the high-technology market.

Key Contact - Specialty:
Mr. Neal O. George, President - *High technology*

Functions: Generalist, Senior Mgmt., Middle Mgmt., Mktg. Mgmt., Sales Mgmt., CFO's, Cash Mgmt., MIS Mgmt.

Industries: Generalist, Computer Equip., Finance, New Media, Telecoms, Software

M H Springer & Associates
2393 Townsgate Rd Ste 102
Thousand Oaks, CA 91361
(818) 710-8955
(805) 446-0090
Fax: (805) 446-6490

Description: Small retained firm specializing in financial services, i.e. banks, savings & loans and mortgage banking.

Key Contact - Specialty:
Mr. Mark H. Springer, President - *Financial services*

Salary minimum: $100,000

Functions: Generalist, Senior Mgmt., CFO's, Risk Mgmt.

Industries: Generalist, Finance, Invest. Banking, Misc. Financial

Springer & Associates
180 N Stetson Ave Ste 3050
2 Prudential Plz
Chicago, IL 60601
(312) 803-2600
Email: info@springer-associates.com
Web: www.springer-associates.com

Description: Retained generalist search firm focused on serving our clients in a strategic and consultative manner across a broad range of needs including board of director and senior-level executive search.

Key Contact:
Mr. Neil A. Springer, Managing Director - *Transportation, industrial equipment, automotive*
Mr. Vincent P. Schwartz, Senior Vice President

Salary minimum: $100,000

Functions: Generalist, Senior Mgmt., Plant Mgmt., Mktg. Mgmt., HR Mgmt., CFO's, MIS Mgmt.

Industries: Generalist, Lumber, Furniture, Chemicals, Motor Vehicles, Transportation, Telecoms

SSA Executive Search Int'l
4350 E Camelback Rd Ste B200
Phoenix, AZ 85018
(480) 998-1744
Email: mail@ssaexec.com
Web: www.ssaexec.com

Description: We are a retained search firm completing management, professional, international, board, legal, financial, and technology assignments for clients throughout the US and internationally. We have a division devoted to corporate board recruitment. SSA's president, Susan F. Shultz, has authored "The Board Book (AMACOM 2000)" to help structure, strengthen, and diversify boards of directors, statutory or advisory.

Key Contact - Specialty:
Ms. Susan F. Shultz, President - *Generalist, boards*

Salary minimum: $100,000

Functions: Generalist

Industries: Generalist

Professional Associations: ABLA, NACD, PCFR, PCIP

Staffing Strategists Int'l Inc
5945 Spring Garden Rd
Halifax, NS B3H 1Y4
Canada
(902) 423-1657
Fax: (902) 423-0277
Email: info@staffingstrategists.com
Web: www.staffingstrategists.com

Description: We are a professional service organization dedicated to providing innovative

---

recruitment and retention solutions for client organizations. We build on the over ten years' experience of Wilson Associates, one of Atlantic Canada's leading executive recruitment firms. We are also the parent company of AtlanticCanadaCareers.com, Atlantic Canada's leading Internet-based career site.

Key Contact - Specialty:
Mr. Jim Wilson, President/CEO - *Generalist*
Mr. Chris Schulz, Vice President/COO - *Generalist*

Salary minimum: $80,000

Functions: Generalist

Industries: Generalist

Networks: InterSearch

Stanton Chase Int'l
100 E Pratt St Ste 2530
Baltimore, MD 21202
(410) 528-8400
Fax: (410) 528-8409
Email: baltimore@stantonchase.com
Web: www.stantonchase.com

Description: With world headquarters in Amsterdam, we are a medium-sized firm of 26 offices in 16 countries. We employ over 100 professionals worldwide. International strengths are banking/financial services, high-technology, distribution, mining/natural resources, healthcare and general manufacturing.

Key Contact - Specialty:
Mr. H. Edward Muendel, Chairman/Managing Director - *Generalist*
Mr. James Mickey Matthews, Director - *Information technology, manufacturing, not-for-profit*
Mr. Dan Hobbs, Associate Principal - *Manufacturing*
Mr. Peter Schweizer, Principal - *High tech*

Salary minimum: $70,000

Functions: General Mgmt., Mfg., Healthcare, Sales & Mktg., HR Mgmt., CFO's, IT, R&D, Engineering, Int'l.

Industries: Generalist

Professional Associations: IACPR

Branches:
2010 Jimmy Durante Blvd Ste 230
Del Mar, CA 92014
(858) 793-5259
Fax: (858) 793-5256
Email: sandiego@stantonchase.com
Key Contact:
Mr. James E. Skeen, Chairman-Advisory Board
Ms. Sabrina Houlberg, Managing Associate

10866 Wilshire Blvd Ste 870
Los Angeles, CA 90024-4111
(310) 474-1029
Fax: (310) 474-6747
Email: losangeles@stantonchase.com
Key Contact - Specialty:
Mr. Edward J. Savage, Managing Director - *Generalist*
Mr. Tim Smith, Associate Principal - *Information technology*

1840 Gateway Dr Fl 2
San Mateo, CA 94404
(650) 378-1441
Fax: (650) 378-1447
Email: siliconvalley@stantonchase.com
Key Contact - Specialty:
Mr. Ted Muendel, Managing Director - *Generalist*
Mr. Jack Hartley, Associate Principal - *High tech*

3463 State St
Santa Barbara, CA 93105
(805) 682-9800
Fax: (805) 569-9876
Email: santabarbara@stantonchase.com

Key Contact:
Ms. Elise Wygant, Associate Principal
181 W Madison St Ste 4850
Chicago, IL 60602
(312) 863-6165
Fax: (312) 863-6166
Email: chicago@stantonchase.com
Key Contact - Specialty:
Mr. James R. Piper, Jr., Managing Director - *Financial services, non-profit, information technology*
Mr. Jeff Levitt, Director of Research - *Generalist*
521 5th Ave Fl 19
New York, NY 10175
(212) 808-0040
Fax: (212) 983-7499
Email: newyork@stantonchase.com
Key Contact:
Mr. Charles D. Wright, Managing Director
Mr. Andrew Sherwood, Managing Director

5420 LBJ Fwy Ste 780
Dallas, TX 75240
(972) 404-8411
Fax: (972) 404-8415
Email: dallas@stantonchase.com
Key Contact:
Mr. Ed H. Moerbe, Managing Director - *Generalist*
Mr. Douglas C. Potter, Principal
Ms. Carole Campbell, Principal
Mr. Kevin Anderson, Principal
Mr. Jerry McFarland, Principal

Amsterdam 289°
Col Hipodromo Condesa
Mexico City, DF 06100
Mexico
52 5564 5650
Fax: 52 5564 3084
Email: mexico@stantonchase.com
Key Contact:
Mr. Jose Brogeras Oliva, Managing Director
Dr. Carmen Suarez, Director
Ms. Gabriela Robles, Director
Mr. Carlos Rodriguez, Director

The Stark Wilton Group
PO Box 4924
East Lansing, MI 48826
(517) 332-4100
Fax: (517) 332-2733
Email: starkwiltongroup@worldnet.att.net

Description: We are a highly personalized firm. All hiring companies have the opportunity to meet our professional staff, who have worked in industry, banking or management consulting before joining the firm.

Key Contact - Specialty:
Ms. Mary Stark, Director - *Healthcare, consumer products, services*
Mr. Wilton Smith, Director - *Telecommunications, high technology, manufacturing*

Salary minimum: $85,000

Functions: Generalist, Senior Mgmt., Physicians, Mkt. Research, Mktg. Mgmt., Cash Mgmt., M&A, Mgmt. Consultants

Industries: Generalist, Food, Bev., Tobacco, Drugs Mfg., Medical Devices, Invest. Banking, Mgmt. Consulting, Media

Staub, Warmbold & Associates Inc
575 Madison Ave
New York, NY 10022
(212) 605-0554
Fax: (212) 759-7304
Web: www.staubwarmbold.com

Description: We provide executive search services to corporations and the not-for-profit sector. Functional areas include general management, finance, marketing and manufacturing.

Key Contact:
Mr. Robert A. Staub, President
Mr. Herman P. Warmbold, Executive Vice President

Salary minimum: $100,000

Functions: Generalist

Industries: Generalist

Stephen, Mason & Sterling Search Group
2 Fries Ct
Houston, TX 77055
(713) 461-0982
(713) 927-4494
Fax: (413) 647-0800
Email: heller@catch22.net
Web: www.catch22.net

Description: Our focus is within the technology, software, telecommunications, and biotech industries. We conduct searches for "C" and "V" level executives. Geographically, we are working in the North and South American markets.

Key Contact - Specialty:
Mr. Joseph S. Heller, Managing Partner - *Technology, software, telecommunications*

Salary minimum: $100,000

Functions: Generalist

Industries: Finance, Services, Communications, Software, Biotech, Healthcare

Professional Associations: ACG, MITEF, TN

Stephen-Bradford Search
1140 Ave of the Americas
New York, NY 10036
(212) 221-6333
(800) 720-0922
Fax: (212) 391-7826
Email: info@stephenbradford.com
Web: www.stephenbradford.com

Description: Executive search specialists for marketing, sales, promotion, and information technology professionals in advertising, consumer products, direct marketing, entertainment, financial services, market research, new media, promotions, publishing and sports marketing.

Key Contact:
Mr. Mitchell L. Berger, CEO
Ms. Erika Weinstein, Managing Director

Salary minimum: $75,000

Functions: Sales & Mktg., IT

Industries: Food, Bev., Tobacco, Soap, Perf., Cosmtcs., Finance, Services, Entertainment, Recreation, Media, Communications, Software

Professional Associations: AWNY, PMAA

Stephens Associates Ltd Inc
480 S 3rd St
PO Box 151-114
Columbus, OH 43215
(614) 469-9990
Fax: (614) 469-0177
Email: saltd@stephensassoc.com
Web: www.stephensassoc.com

Description: We are an industry focused, full-service, all functions, retainer-based firm, with a strong concentration in telecommunications, aerospace and defense, industrial manufacturing, chemical and petrochemical, technology, financial services (banking and investment banking), and venture capital.

Key Contact - Specialty:
Mr. Stephen A. Martinez, Managing Director - *Generalist, high technology*
Mr. William Coleman, Vice President - *Manufacturing, generalist*

Ms. Judith Mitchell, Associate - *Generalist*
Ms. Denise Fooce, Director of Research - *Generalist*

Salary minimum: $100,000

Functions: Generalist

Industries: Generalist, Energy, Utilities, Mfg., Finance, Communications, Aerospace, Packaging, Software, Biotech

Sterling Resources Int'l Inc
666 5th Ave Fl 37
New York, NY 10103
(212) 541-3727
Email: sterlingri@aol.com

Description: Small elite extremely productive boutique. Over 90% success rate. Also specialize in strategic planning with clients, forecasting and projecting.

Key Contact - Specialty:
Ms. Laura J. Lofaro, President - *Investment banking*
Ms. Diane L. Herdling, Executive Vice President - *Investment banking*

Salary minimum: $500,000

Functions: Generalist, Finance

Industries: Generalist, Invest. Banking, Misc. Financial

Professional Associations: IACPR, FWA

Michael Stern Associates Inc
(a member of IMD Int'l Search)
370-70 University Ave
Toronto, ON M5J 2M4
Canada
(416) 593-0100
Fax: (416) 593-5716
Email: search@michaelstern.com
Web: www.michaelstern.com

Description: Recruiting corporate leaders since inception, we are committed to providing superior results with personal service.

Key Contact - Specialty:
Mr. Michael Stern, President - *Generalist*
Mr. Bob Sturgess, Vice President - *Generalist*
Mr. Dane MacCarthy, Vice President - *Generalist*
Mr. James Parr, Vice President - *Generalist*

Salary minimum: $75,000

Functions: Generalist, Senior Mgmt., Mfg., Healthcare, Sales & Mktg., HR Mgmt., CFO's, MIS Mgmt.

Industries: Generalist, Mfg., Retail, Services, Media, Real Estate, Healthcare

Professional Associations: IACPR, AMA, ICMCO

The Stevens Group
PO Box 171079
Arlington, TX 76003-1079
(817) 483-2700
Fax: (817) 483-2718
Email: info@thestevensgroup.com
Web: www.thestevensgroup.com

Description: We recruit superior executive and technical management talent for corporations and management worldwide, providing a tailored approach and access to top candidates unequaled by large search firms.

Key Contact - Specialty:
Mr. Ken G. Stevens, Managing Director - *Generalist*
Mr. Brian Stevens, Director, Research Projects - *Organizational intelligence studies*

Functions: Generalist

Industries: Mfg., Finance, Services, Hospitality, Telecoms, Insurance, Real Estate, Software, Biotech, Healthcare

Professional Associations: IACPR

Stevens, Valentine & McKeever
300 Kings Hwy E Ste 008
Haddonfield, NJ 08033
(856) 795-9222
Fax: (856) 795-3351
Email: svmsrch@att.net
Web: www.execusearchresources.com

Description: Responsive, consultative search and assessment for all functions within the services, e-commerce, insurance and diversified financial service industry with organizational design & development capability within a broad spectrum of industries.

Key Contact - Specialty:
Mr. Leonard W. Stevens, Principal - *Insurance, diversified financial services, e-commerce, HR*
Mr. Donald Murphy, Affiliate - *Organizational design & development*
Ms. Mary Ellen Westbay, Vice President - *Generalist*

Salary minimum: $80,000

Functions: Generalist

Industries: Finance, Services, HR Services, Insurance, Software

Professional Associations: HRPS, NJTC, SHRM

The Stevenson Group Inc (NJ)
560 Sylvan Ave
Englewood Cliffs, NJ 07632
(201) 568-1900
Fax: (201) 568-5132
Email: info@stevensongroup.com
Web: www.stevensongroup.com

Description: Broadly based executive search services on a cross-industry basis. Emphasis on general management, sales and marketing management, administrative and research and development positions within pharmaceuticals, healthcare, information technology, e-business, consumer and personal care industries.

Key Contact - Specialty:
Mr. Stephen M. Steinman, President/CEO - *Pharmaceutical, healthcare, chemicals, consumer products, information technology*
Ms. Jennifer Kay, Vice President - *E-business, information technology*
Ms. Elisabeth Ammann, Vice President - *International, operations management*
Ms. Jane Johnson, Director of Research
Mr. Carl Berke, Vice President - *Pharmaceuticals, biotechnology*

Salary minimum: $100,000

Functions: Generalist, Senior Mgmt., Middle Mgmt., Mktg. Mgmt., CFO's, MIS Mgmt., R&D, Int'l.

Industries: Generalist, Textiles, Apparel, Chemicals, Drugs Mfg., Paints, Petro. Products, Software, Healthcare

Professional Associations: IACPR, HRPS, SHRM

Branches:
2010 Crow Canyon Pl Ste 100
San Ramon, CA 94583
(925) 359-3200
Fax: (925) 359-3299
Email: vnksearch@classic.msn.com
Key Contact - Specialty:
Mr. Victor Kleinman, Senior Vice President/Principal - *Pharmaceuticals, biotechnology, information technology*

2255 Glades Rd Ste 200 E
Boca Raton, FL 33431
(561) 989-5445
Fax: (561) 989-5446

Key Contact - Specialty:
Mr. William Schall, Senior Vice President/Principal - *Pharmaceuticals, biotechnology*

Stewart, Stein & Scott Ltd
1000 Shelard Pkwy Ste 606
Minneapolis, MN 55426
(952) 545-8151
Fax: (952) 545-8464
Email: research@stewartstein.net
Web: www.stewartstein.net

Description: Consultants to management in executive recruitment and selection. Generalist practice serving a broad base of clients. Partners have 50 years of diverse corporate management experience, both domestic and international.

Key Contact - Specialty:
Mr. Terry W. Stein, Partner - *Generalist*
Mr. Jeffrey O. Stewart, Partner - *Generalist*
Mr. Robert Riskin, Vice President - *Generalist*

Salary minimum: $100,000

Functions: Generalist, Senior Mgmt., Health Admin., Mktg. Mgmt., HR Mgmt., CFO's, MIS Mgmt.

Industries: Generalist

Professional Associations: IACPR

Stewart/Laurence Associates Inc
Atrium Executive Park
PO Box 1156
Englishtown, NJ 07726
(732) 972-8000
Fax: (732) 972-8003
Email: mel@stewartlaurence.com
Web: www.stewartlaurence.com

Description: We provide professional recruitment, executive search and outplacement for all areas of high technology and biotech professions including executive, marketing, finance, and legal (venture capital/IPOs).

Key Contact - Specialty:
Mr. Mel Stewart Klein, President - *High technology executives, international, domestic*
Mr. Eric Freer, Vice President - *High technology executives*

Salary minimum: $125,000

Functions: Generalist, General Mgmt.

Industries: Generalist, Printing, Computer Equip., Consumer Elect., Venture Cap., Media, Publishing, New Media, Telecoms, Software, Biotech

Charles Stickler Associates
PO Box 5312C
Lancaster, PA 17606
(717) 569-2881
Web: www.charlesstickler.com

Description: Recruiting specialists for the metals and metal distribution industries.

Key Contact - Specialty:
Mr. Charles W. Stickler, III, CPC, Owner - *Metals*
Mr. Charles W. Stickler, IV, Vice President - *Metals*

Salary minimum: $50,000

Functions: Generalist, General Mgmt., Mfg., Materials, Sales & Mktg., Engineering

Industries: Generalist, Metal Products

Linford E Stiles Associates LLC
46 Newport Rd Ste 208
The Gallery
New London, NH 03257
(603) 526-6566
(800) 322-5185
Fax: (603) 526-6185

Email: aspiegel@lesasearch.com
Web: www.lesasearch.com

Description: We specialize in recruiting executives in a variety of functions with experience in the implementation of lean manufacturing and six sigma principles. A principal who is experienced in helping clients build high performance teams manages every assignment of ours.

Key Contact - Specialty:
Mr. Linford E. Stiles, President - *Senior executives*
Mr. Jake Stiles, Principal - *Manufacturing management, consulting*
Ms. Sabine Fischer, Principal - *Generalist*
Mr. Andrew Spiegel, Search Associate - *Generalist*

Salary minimum: $60,000

Functions: General Mgmt., Senior Mgmt., Plant Mgmt., Materials, Mgmt. Consultants

Industries: Mfg., Lumber, Furniture, Medical Devices, Metal Products, Machine, Appliance, Motor Vehicles, Consumer Elect., Test, Measure Equip., Misc. Mfg., Electronic, Elec. Components, Aerospace

Networks: World Search Group

Stillinger & Associates
1148 Patterson Ln
Pacific Grove, CA 93950
(831) 655-2602
Fax: (831) 648-1544
Email: stillinger@aol.com

Description: We create competitive advantage for our clients by understanding their business, culture and values. Finding executives for any organization, who have not only the skills, but also the right temperament and passion for their work is the key to success.

Key Contact - Specialty:
Mr. Scott R. Stillinger, Principal - *Management consulting, information technology, reinvention, process redesign, change management*
Mrs. Regina V. Stillinger, Principal - *Organization development, change management, transformational consulting*
Mrs. Wauneta Stillinger, Principal - *Management consulting, information technology*

Salary minimum: $75,000

Functions: Generalist, General Mgmt., HR Mgmt., IT, Specialized Svcs., Mgmt. Consultants

Industries: Generalist, Services, Mgmt. Consulting, HR Services, Media

Professional Associations: BAODN, ODN

Branches:
7017 8th Ave
PO Box 274
Tahoma, CA 96142
(530) 525-5545
Fax: (530) 525-5544
Email: skylarc@ibm.net
Key Contact - Specialty:
Mr. Skip Stillinger, Principal - *Information technology, management consulting*

STM Associates
320 S 400 E
Salt Lake City, UT 84111
(801) 531-6500
Fax: (801) 531-6062
Email: stm@stmassociates.com
Web: www.stmassociates.com

Description: Specialize in natural resources, including mining, metals, pulp & paper, chemicals, as well as energy companies and utilities, both national and international. Thirty years repeat business record based on extensive database, original research and personal service.

Key Contact - Specialty:
Mr. Gerald W. Cooke, Principal - *Mining, natural resources, energy, utilities*
Mr. Robert L. Roylance, Principal - *Mining, natural resources, energy, utilities*

Salary minimum: $75,000

Functions: General Mgmt., Senior Mgmt., Mfg., Plant Mgmt., Materials, Sales & Mktg., HR Mgmt., Finance, IT, Int'l.

Industries: Agri., Forestry, Mining, Energy, Utilities, Mfg., Printing, Chemicals, Transportation, Environmental Svcs.

Allan Stolee Inc
PO Box 2596
Pompano Beach, FL 33072
(954) 782-0654
Email: stolee@rcrt.com
Web: www.rcrt.com

Description: A professional firm, we provide executive search consulting and recruitment services locally, nationally and internationally. We are business generalists experienced in recruiting for most forms of commercial enterprise.

Key Contact - Specialty:
Mr. Allan J. Stolee, President - *Generalist*

Salary minimum: $100,000

Functions: Generalist

Industries: Generalist

Stone Murphy
5500 Wayzata Blvd Ste 1020
Minneapolis, MN 55416
(763) 591-2300
Fax: (763) 591-2301
Email: sm@stonemurphy.com
Web: www.stonemurphy.com

Description: We are a retained executive search firm engaged in general practice committed to serving the best interest of its clients.

Key Contact:
Ms. Toni Barnum, Partner - *Financial services*
Mr. Gary Murphy, Partner - *Human resources*
Ms. Kathy Mathias, Managing Director - *Marketing, sales*
Mr. Al Giesen, Managing Director
Mr. Kirk Gove, Senior Associate
Ms. Marci Ytterberg, Senior Associate

Salary minimum: $80,000

Functions: Generalist

Industries: Generalist

Professional Associations: AIMR, AMA, ASTD, ASTD, IEEE, SHRM, WAW

Stonybrook
45 Quarterdeck Ln
PO Box 707
New Castle, NH 03854
(603) 433-7322
Email: robdev@ici.net

Description: We specialize in senior-level retained executive search, and board, senior management level strategic and organizational consulting in the healthcare industry.

Key Contact - Specialty:
Mr. Robert W. DeVore, President - *Healthcare, CEO, COO, CFO, CIO*

Salary minimum: $150,000

Functions: Senior Mgmt., MIS Mgmt.

Industries: Healthcare

Stoopen Asociados SC
(a member of EMA Partners Int'l)
Minerva 92-702
Mexico City, DF 01030
Mexico
52 5 661 6862
52 5 661 8119
Fax: 52 5 661 5872
Email: intl@stoopen.com.mx
Web: www.emapartners.com

Description: We are involved in the executive search of all professions. Our company policy stresses quality not volume. We keep the organization at a size that allows the partners to get involved personally in every assignment.

Key Contact - Specialty:
Ms. Josefina Stoopen, President - *Generalist*
Ms. Lucia Trueba, Vice President - *Generalist*

Salary minimum: $60,000

Functions: Generalist, Senior Mgmt., Plant Mgmt., Materials Plng., Sales & Mktg., HR Mgmt., CFO's, IT

Industries: Generalist, Construction, Mfg., Banking, Mgmt. Consulting, Hospitality, Telecoms

Networks: EMA Partners Int'l

Straight & Company
3415 Merganser Ln
Alpharetta, GA 30022
(770) 663-0448
(678) 366-3367
Fax: (770) 442-1001
Email: gary.straight@straightco.com
Web: www.straightco.com

Description: Search specialists for financial services, investment management, insurance and banking. Strengths in general management, finance, marketing and information processing, call center management and Internet based e-commerce.

Key Contact - Specialty:
Mr. Gary R. Straight, President - *Financial services, marketing management, information processing, e-commerce*
Ms. Carla Herron, Vice President - *Research*

Salary minimum: $75,000

Functions: Generalist

Industries: Finance, Banking, Invest. Banking, Misc. Financial, Telecoms, Insurance

Mark Stranberg & Associates Inc
4 Wadsworth Rd
Sudbury, MA 01776
(978) 440-8800
(978) 440-8486
Fax: (978) 440-8354
Email: mstranberg@att.net

Description: Our practice specializes exclusively in the investment industry. We conduct searches for senior management in disciplines, such as portfolio management, retirement services, sales, marketing, operations and trading.

Key Contact - Specialty:
Mr. Mark Stranberg, Managing Partner - *Investment industry, banking, insurance, mutual fund*

Salary minimum: $100,000

Functions: Generalist, General Mgmt.

Industries: Finance, Banking, Invest. Banking

Networks: SearchNet Int'l

STRATA Performance Group Inc
10825 Watson Rd
St. Louis, MO 63127-1031
(314) 821-0101
Email: rwolf@stratagroup.com
Web: www.stratagroup.com

Description: Our firm offers a unique approach in successfully identifying and recruiting the best talent for our client organizations. We have completed challenging senior level search assignments in the manufacturing, healthcare, construction, and service industries. Our experienced professionals each have in-depth industry experience and STRATA utilizes a state-of-the-art assessment tool in the "front-end" of every search assignment.

Key Contact - Specialty:
Mr. Richard J. Wolf, President - *Manufacturing, finance, high-tech,*
Mr. Joe Wiley, Sr Vice President - *Manufacturing, high-tech*
Mr. Roger Franck, Sr Vice President - *Healthcare executive search*
Mr. Kevin Pallardy, Sr Vice President - *Human resources, financial services, insurance*

Salary minimum: $75,000

Functions: Generalist

Industries: Energy, Utilities, Construction, Mfg., Retail, Finance

Branches:
300 St. Peters Centre Blvd Ste 275
St. Peters, MO 63376
(636) 757-0006
Fax: (636) 757-0005
Email: jstrick@strata-cma.com
Key Contact - Specialty:
Mr. Jack Strick, Manager Recruiting Projects - *Engineering, high-tech*

Strategic Advancement Inc
242 Old New Brunswick Rd Ste 100
Piscataway, NJ 08854
(732) 562-1222
Fax: (732) 562-9448
Email: aborkin@sai-hr.com
Web: www.sai-hr.com

Description: We have created a network of contacts that can assist you in finding the right candidate for the position you wish to fill -- in the shortest amount of time.

Key Contact - Specialty:
Mr. Andrew Borkin, President
Ms. Lisa Gold, Vice President - *Banking, insurance*

Salary minimum: $50,000

Functions: Generalist

Industries: Mfg., Finance, Services, Insurance, Software, Biotech

Professional Associations: ASTD, SHRM

Strategic Alternatives†
3 Portola Rd Ste 3B
Portola Valley, CA 94028
(650) 851-2211
Fax: (650) 851-2288
Email: info@strategicalternatives.com
Web: www.strategicalternatives.com

Description: Silicon Valley executive search firm specializing in senior executive searches for venture-backed start-ups to mature companies. Principals have been founders and senior executives in high-tech start-ups through major corporations and have first hand operations experience and knowledge.

Key Contact - Specialty:
Mr. Ira M. Marks, Principal - *High technology*
Ms. Karen Saucier - *High technology*

Salary minimum: $150,000

Functions: Senior Mgmt.

Industries: Finance, Venture Cap., New Media, Telecoms, Software

Strategic Associates Inc†
11044 Research Blvd Ste B-420
Austin, TX 78759
(512) 218-8222
Fax: (512) 218-8102
Email: sai@strategicassociates.com
Web: www.strategicassociates.com

Description: We are an executive search firm, focusing in the national technology, manufacturing, and life science marketplaces, both in industry and consulting, including e-Business/e-Commerce, ERP software solutions, IT and operations leadership, and supply chain management. Our clients served are Fortune 500, start-up firms, Big 5 consulting firms, major privates, and mid-sized privately held organizations.

Key Contact - Specialty:
Mr. Michael L. Goldman, CPC, President - *Manufacturing, consulting*
Mr. Ralph Cyphers, Account Executive - *Executive level consulting*
Mr. Nad Elias, Account Executive - *Manufacturing, supply chain management*
Mr. Bill Fleming, Account Executive - *Consulting, sales management*
Mr. Steven Burton, Account Executive - *Consumer packaged goods, manufacturing*
Mr. Josh D'Agostino, Account Executive - *Life science, biotechnology*

Salary minimum: $75,000

Functions: General Mgmt., Directors, Senior Mgmt., Middle Mgmt.

Industries: Mfg., Services, Pharm Svcs., Mgmt. Consulting, HR Services, E-commerce, IT Implementation, Communications, Software, ERP SW, Mfg. SW, Biotech

Professional Associations: APICS, CLM, EMA, NAPM

Strategic Executives Inc
1 Landmark Sq
Stamford, CT 06901
(203) 355-3030
Fax: (203) 978-1785
Email: perry@strategicexecutives.com
Web: www.strategicexecutives.com

Description: Executive search consultants specializing in recruiting management consultants, technology and marketing executives and corporate development professionals for client companies wishing to enhance their competitive position.

Key Contact - Specialty:
Mr. James Perry, Senior Vice President/Managing Director - *Management consulting, e-technology, telecommunications*

Salary minimum: $100,000

Functions: General Mgmt., Sales & Mktg., Mktg. Mgmt., Mgmt. Consultants

Industries: Generalist, Energy, Utilities, Chemicals, Retail, Finance, Media, Telecoms, Insurance, Software, Biotech, Healthcare

Professional Associations: AMA, PF

Branches:
919 3rd Ave Fl 27
New York, NY 10022
(212) 836-4848
Fax: (212) 836-4840
Email: mashal@strategicexecutives.com

Key Contact - Specialty:
Ms. Millie Mashal, Senior Vice President/Managing Director - *Management consulting, marketing*

Strategic Search Corp
645 N Michigan Ave Ste 800
Chicago, IL 60611
(312) 944-4000
Fax: (773) 348-7117
Email: ssargis@strategicsearch.com
Web: www.strategicsearch.com

Description: Technical and manufacturing specialists from staff to vice president levels including R&D, quality assurance, manufacturing and product development.

Key Contact - Specialty:
Mr. Scott R. Sargis, Managing Director - *Technical, manufacturing*

Salary minimum: $50,000

Functions: Directors, Senior Mgmt., Middle Mgmt., Mfg., Materials, IT, R&D

Industries: Mfg.

Professional Associations: ACS, ASQ, IEEE, SPE, SPI

StrategicHire†
208 Elden St Ste 200
Herndon, VA 20170
(703) 467-9093
Email: jwatson@strategichire.com
Web: www.strategichire.com

Description: We are a leading edge retained executive search firm specializing in working with emerging and fast growth companies. Our focus is on providing end to end organizational support from the CXX to mid-level marketing. We accomplish our goal by being smarter and faster then our competition.

Key Contact - Specialty:
Mr. Joseph Watson, Principal - *Executive level*
Mr. Mark Sucoloski, Principal - *Executive level*

Salary minimum: $90,000

Functions: General Mgmt.

Industries: Computer Equip., Consumer Elect., Venture Cap., Services, Mgmt. Consulting, HR Services, Hospitality, New Media, Telecoms, Software

Networks: PRO/NET

StratfordGroup
6120 Parkland Blvd
Cleveland, OH 44124
(440) 460-3232
(800) 536-4384
Fax: (440) 460-3230
Email: resumes@stratfordgroup.com
Web: www.stratfordgroup.com

Description: Technological resources, experienced professional staff, a commitment to serve our clients and our unconditional guarantee help make us a nationwide leader in executive search.

Key Contact:
Mr. Larry S. Imely, President
Mr. Eric N. Peterson, Managing Director
Ms. Heidi Geiger, Director
Mr. Paul C. Stefunek, Vice President/National Practice Leader - *Internet, e-commerce*
Mr. John Thornton, Director

Salary minimum: $95,000

Functions: Generalist, Senior Mgmt., Plant Mgmt., Sales Mgmt., Benefits, CFO's, MIS Mgmt.

Industries: Generalist, Construction, Food, Bev., Tobacco, Mgmt. Consulting, Broadcast, Film, Healthcare

---

Branches:
6615 N Scottsdale Rd
Scottsdale, AZ 85250
(480) 368-8116
Fax: (480) 368-7503
Email: richardnosky@stratfordgroup.com
Key Contact:
Mr. Richard Nosky, Director

12424 Wilshire Blvd Ste 860
Los Angeles, CA 90025
(310) 826-4466
Fax: (310) 979-7462
Email: stuartfishler@stratfordgroup.com
Key Contact - Specialty:
Mr. J. Stuart Fishler, Western Region VP/Managing
Director
Ms. Lisa Crane, VP/Practice Leader - *Global
media, entertainment*
Dr. Martin Ross, PhD, Director - *Healthcare,
nonprofit*

475 Sansome St Ste 700
San Francisco, CA 94111
(415) 788-7800
Fax: (415) 788-7710
Email: stuartfishler@stratfordgroup.com
Key Contact:
Mr. J. Stuart Fishler, Western Region
VP/Managing Director
Mr. Mehrdad Moaveni, Director
Mr. Howard Nitschke, Vice President

2150 N First St Ste 250
San Jose, CA 95131
(408) 436-2900
Fax: (408) 436-0643
Email: jeffshiverdaker@stratfordgroup.com
Key Contact - Specialty:
Mr. Jeff Shiverdaker, VP/Managing Director
Mr. Michael Rothstein, Vice President -
Engineering

100 Galleria Pkwy Ste 1150
Atlanta, GA 30339
(678) 385-5000
Fax: (678) 385-5019
Email: billrobertson@stratfordgroup.com
Key Contact:
Mr. William Robertson, VP/Managing Director
Mr. Robert Chandler, FACHE, SVP/Global
Practice Leader, - *Healthcare, pharmaceuticals*
Mr. Charles Edwards, Vice President

1515 W 22nd St
Oak Brook, IL 60521
(800) 536-4384
Fax: (440) 460-3230
Email: wendylalonde@stratfordgroup.com
Key Contact:
Ms. Wendy Pancake

350 Park Ave Fl 22
New York, NY 10022
(212) 319-3810
Fax: (212) 753-2086
Email: billtrautman@stratfordgroup.com
Key Contact - Specialty:
Mr. William Trautman, VP/Managing Director
Mr. George Lumsby, VP/Co-Managing Director -
Diversity
Mr. Robert Altieri, Director
Mr. Donald Doele, Director
Mr. Bob Gladden, Director
Mr. Francis J. Luisi, VP/National Practice Leader -
Human resources
Mr. Richard Philips, Vice President - *Financial
services*

5605 Carnegie Blvd Ste 450
Carnegie X
Charlotte, NC 29209
(704) 643-7979
Fax: (704) 553-5425
Email: harrisonturnbull@stratfordgroup.com
Key Contact:
Mr. Harrison Turnbull, Southern Region
VP/Managing Director

Ms. Valerie Cline, Director
Mr. Richard Dean, VP/Practice Leader - *Consumer
durables, manufacturing*
Ms. Nan Herron, Director
Mr. Paul Miller, Director

1760 Manley Rd
Toledo, OH 43537
(419) 897-5919
Fax: (419) 893-2491
Email: joelepstein@stratfordgroup.com
Key Contact:
Mr. Joel Epstein, Northern Region VP/Managing
Director
Ms. Debbie Galbraith, Director
Ms. Emily Hall, Director

5950 Berkshire Ln Ste 580
Dallas, TX 75225
(214) 696-0666
Fax: (214) 696-1686
Email: fredhalstead@stratfordgroup.com
Key Contact:
Mr. Frederick A. Halstead, VP/Managing Director

4265 San Felipe Ste 740
Lincoln Bldg
Houston, TX 77027
(713) 223-7270
Fax: (713) 223-7279
Email: tomwilson@stratfordgroup.com
Key Contact:
Mr. Tom Wilson, Central Region VP/Managing
Director
Mr. Mark Hordes, Director
Mr. Ewing Walker, VP/National Practice Leader -
Energy
Mr. Bob Shaw, Director

1750 Tysons Blvd Ste 260
McLean, VA 22102
(703) 442-5200
Fax: (703) 790-8349
Email: tedbruccoleri@stratfordgroup.com
Key Contact:
Mr. Theodore Bruccoleri, VP/Managing Director
Mr. James Abruzzo, VP/Managing Director -
Nonprofit, education, philanthropy
Ms. Carole Chandler, Director
Ms. Michele Baird-Counter, Director - *Nonprofit,
education, philanthropy*
Ms. Joan Jackson, Director

Straube Associates

855 Turnpike St
North Andover, MA 01845
(978) 687-1993
Fax: (978) 687-1886
Email: sstraube@straubeassociates.com
Web: www.straubeassociates.com

Description: We are a retained executive search
firm with over 15 years of experience in sourcing
and recruiting candidates for executive-level
positions, which includes expanded services in
human resource consulting. Our primary purpose is
to be flexible to the client's needs and provide the
highest quality service in the most cost effective
manner.

Key Contact:
Mr. Stan Straube, President - *Generalist*
Ms. Kathy Kelley, Vice President - *Marketing &
sales*
Mr. Bill Marlow, Vice President - *Engineering,
high technology*
Ms. Lynda Ferren, Internal Research Manager -
Generalist
Mr. Ed O'Brien, Human Resources Consultant

Salary minimum: $100,000

Functions: Generalist

Industries: Generalist

Professional Associations: BHRA, NEERC,
NEHRA

Networks: Top Echelon Network

Strawn Arnold Leech & Ashpitz Inc

11402 Bee Caves Rd W
Austin, TX 78738
(512) 263-1131
Fax: (512) 263-4149
Email: genmail@salainc.com
Web: www.salainc.com

Description: We place senior-level assignments
with pharmaceutical, biotechnology, medical
device, and health care services companies. We
recruit for major corporations and venture capital
start-ups.

Key Contact - Specialty:
Mr. William M. Strawn, President -
Pharmaceutical, biotechnology
Mr. Jerome M. Arnold, Executive Vice President -
Pharmaceutical, biotechnology
Mr. David M. Leech, Executive Vice President -
Pharmaceutical, biotechnology, medical device
Mr. Jeff Ashpitz, Executive Vice President -
Pharmaceutical, biotechnology, medical device
Mr. Richard D'Antoni, Executive Vice President -
Health care services

Salary minimum: $150,000

Functions: Generalist, Senior Mgmt., Product Dev.,
Mktg. Mgmt., Sales Mgmt., CFO's, R&D, Mgmt.
Consultants

Industries: Generalist, Drugs Mfg., Medical
Devices, Pharm Svcs., Biotech

Strelcheck & Associates Inc

1009 Glen Oaks Ln Ste 211
Mequon, WI 53092
(262) 241-9500
Fax: (262) 241-5559

Description: Physician search: occupational health
and most other specialties. National scope practice
consulting.

Key Contact - Specialty:
Mr. Robert R. Strzelczyk, President - *Physician
search, physician executives, VP of medical
affairs, medical directors*

Professional Associations: MGMA, NAPR

J Stroll Associates Inc†

980 Post Rd E Ste 3
Westport, CT 06880
(203) 227-3688
Fax: (203) 222-0180
Email: joe-stroll@mindspring.com

Description: Identifies suitable candidates for
corporate law EEO, general, contracts, patents, civil,
and partnerships.

Key Contact - Specialty:
Mr. Joseph Stroll, President - *Vice presidents,
corporate law*
Mr. Ray Peters, Executive Vice President -
Paralegals, general corporate, of counsel

Salary minimum: $80,000

Functions: Generalist, Senior Mgmt., Health
Admin., Benefits, Taxes, M&A, Attorneys

Industries: Generalist, Mfg., Drugs Mfg., Pharm
Svcs., Legal, Environmental Svcs., Biotech,
Healthcare

Studley/Toland Executive Search†

60 Walnut St
Wellesley Hills, MA 02481-2151
(781) 239-2330
(781) 254-9186
Fax: (781) 237-5679
Email: btoland@studleygroup.com
Web: www.studleygroup.com

Description: We are a full service firm with
national reach. We place special emphasis on

technology, finance, health care, and biotech industry.

Key Contact - Specialty:
Mr. Fred Studley, SPHR, Principal - *Human resources, finance, manufacturing*
Mr. Brian Toland, Partner - *Technology, finance, bio tech*

Salary minimum: $100,000

Functions: Generalist

Industries: Generalist

Professional Associations: AESC

Sullivan & Associates

344 N Old Woodward Ste 304
Birmingham, MI 48009
(248) 258-0616
Fax: (248) 258-2823
Email: dsullivan@sullivanassociates.com
Web: www.sullivanassociates.com

Description: We are widely recognized as one of the most prestigious Michigan-based retainer firm serving growing client base. Diversified practice re: client size and industry, including healthcare, banking, manufacturing, not-for-profit, etc.

Key Contact:
Mr. Dennis B. Sullivan, President
Mr. Jeffrey A. Evans, Vice President
Ms. Dodie C. David, Vice President
Mr. Douglas Allen, Vice President
Mr. Kevin Mahoney, Vice President

Salary minimum: $75,000

Functions: Senior Mgmt.

Industries: Generalist

Professional Associations: AESC

Joe Sullivan & Associates Inc

9 Feather Hill
PO Box 612
Southold, NY 11971
(631) 765-5050
Fax: (631) 765-9047
Email: jsa612@aol.com
Web: www.joesullivanassociates.com

Description: Retained executive search and recruitment in the media and entertainment industries, with expertise in broadcasting, cable, satellite and the Internet.

Key Contact:
Mr. Joseph J. Sullivan, Jr., President - *Media, entertainment*
Mr. Shane P. Sullivan, Vice President
Ms. Barbara McCollum Sullivan, CFO

Salary minimum: $100,000

Functions: Senior Mgmt.

Industries: Media

Professional Associations: IRTS

Sullivan Associates

175 Derby St Ste25
Hingham, MA 02043
(781) 749-2242
Fax: (781) 749-6777
Email: jl@sullivanassoc.com
Web: www.sullivanassoc.com

Description: We were built on the principle of the modified search concept, which delivers outstanding candidates at substantial savings in fees, expenses and turnaround time. Our account managers provide seamless coordination throughout the assignment.

Key Contact - Specialty:
Mr. Michael H. Sullivan, President/Owner - *Generalist*

Salary minimum: $80,000

Functions: Generalist

Industries: Generalist, Finance, Invest. Banking, Misc. Financial, Services, Advertising, Telecoms, Software, Marketing SW

Professional Associations: AMA

Summit Executive Search Consultants Inc

25 SE 2nd Ave Ste 338
Ingraham Bldg
Miami, FL 33131
(305) 379-5008
Fax: (305) 379-5150
Email: summitsearch@compuserve.com

Description: We offer highly personalized retainer-based search assignments in all functions and industries. We have two basic specialties, and they are: manufacturing sector/automotive industry and diversity/minority/targeted searches for all professions and industries. We have heavy strengths in all engineering titles, R&D, plus occupational safety, industrial hygiene, and ergonomics

Key Contact:
Mr. Alfred J. Holzman, President

Salary minimum: $60,000

Functions: Mfg., Production, Quality, Purchasing, Materials Plng., Systems Dev., Engineering, Minorities

Industries: Plastics, Rubber, Metal Products, Machine, Appliance, Motor Vehicles, Misc. Mfg., Government

Professional Associations: IACPR

Summit Group Int'l Inc†

2920 Sylvan Ramble
Atlanta, GA 30345
(770) 696-4261
Email: sgrp@atl.mediaone.net

Description: Quality, service, integrity and professionalism combined with over 20 years of completion of successful recruiting assignments have been the key to our successful reputation and results.

Key Contact:
Mr. Jan Eason, Partner
Mr. Dotson Benefield

Salary minimum: $60,000

Functions: Middle Mgmt., Mfg., Plant Mgmt., Distribution, Sales Mgmt., HR Mgmt., Engineering

Industries: Generalist, Construction, Mfg., Leather, Stone, Glass, Transportation

Sutton Associates

1200 Stephens Rd
Sidney, OH 45365
(937) 497-1700
Fax: (937) 498-4181
Email: tjsutton@bright.net

Description: We are an executive search and management consulting firm dedicated to providing a personal and professional service to our clients. We are committed to presenting candidates for selection who meet the total needs of our clients.

Key Contact - Specialty:
Mr. Tom J. Sutton, President/Owner - *Middle management, upper management, technical, manufacturing*

Salary minimum: $50,000

Functions: Generalist, Middle Mgmt., Mfg., Materials, HR Mgmt., Finance, Engineering

Industries: Generalist, Mfg., Metal Products, Misc. Mfg., Aerospace

Swartz & Associates Inc

PO Box 14167
Scottsdale, AZ 85267-4167
(480) 998-9159
Fax: (480) 596-1960
Email: info@swartz.com
Web: www.swartz.com

Description: We provide retained search with a particular focus on board of directors, CEO, CFO, VPs in all functional categories on behalf of Arizona based high-tech companies.

Key Contact:
Mr. William K. Swartz, President - *Technology industry*
Ms. Pamela L. Swartz, Executive Vice President

Salary minimum: $100,000

Functions: Generalist, Directors, Senior Mgmt., CFO's, Int'l.

Industries: Generalist, Computer Equip., New Media, Software

Sweeney Harbert Mummert and Gallagher

777 S Harbour Island Blvd Ste 130
Tampa, FL 33602
(813) 229-5360
Fax: (813) 223-1969
Email: davidgallagher@attglobal.net

Description: Specialists in senior-level executive search. A generalist firm serving clients on a nationwide basis. Number of clients per industry limited to two, avoiding blocking conflicts.

Key Contact - Specialty:
Mr. David O. Harbert, Partner - *Generalist*
Mr. James W. Sweeney, Partner - *Generalist*
Mr. David A. Gallagher, Partner - *Generalist*

Salary minimum: $100,000

Functions: Generalist

Industries: Generalist

Arnold Sykes & Associates

7950 Anderson Sq Ste 111
Austin, TX 78757-6816
(512) 451-6337
Fax: (512) 451-4653
Email: arnold_sykes@asykes.com
Web: www.asykes.com

Description: A professional retainer-based search firm specializing in electronic manufacturing, human resources, non-profit and banking/financial services.

Key Contact - Specialty:
Mr. Arnold Sykes, Managing Director - *Banking/financial services, human resources, non-profits*

Salary minimum: $100,000

Functions: General Mgmt., Production, Plant Mgmt., Mktg. Mgmt., Sales Mgmt., Personnel, Training, CFO's, Non-profits

Industries: Chemicals, Test, Measure Equip., Banking, Non-profits, HR Services, Aerospace

Professional Associations: HRPS

Synapse Human Resource Consulting Group

7557 Rambler Rd Ste 1425
Dallas, TX 75231
(214) 891-5977
(214) 384-8877
Email: synapsecon@aol.com

Description: Small, high quality retained search firm with experience in multiple industries. Limited size of practice to insure high quality work with no conflicts of interest. Seek to become strategic business partner with clients. Also offer human resource consulting services.

Key Contact - Specialty:
Mr. Michael Schwartz, President - *Senior management, management consultants, senior sales & marketing*

Salary minimum: $65,000

Functions: Generalist, General Mgmt., Senior Mgmt., Middle Mgmt., Sales & Mktg., Finance, CFO's, IT, MIS Mgmt., Int'l.

Industries: Generalist, Retail, Finance, Services, Accounting, Mgmt. Consulting, HR Services, Media, Advertising, New Media, Real Estate, Software, Healthcare

Professional Associations: ASTD, SHRM

Synergistics Associates Ltd
400 N State St Ste 400
Chicago, IL 60610
(312) 467-5450
Fax: (312) 822-0246
Email: ajbsynerg@aol.com

Description: We are specialists in data processing executives. Principals are former directors MIS from Fortune 100 firms. We have placed more MIS executives than any Chicago firm.

Key Contact - Specialty:
Mr. Alvin J. Borenstine, President - *Information technology, CIO's*

Salary minimum: $125,000

Functions: MIS Mgmt.

Industries: Generalist

Professional Associations: AESC, SIM

The Synergy Organization
3070 Bristol Pike Bldg 2 209
Bensalem, PA 19020
(215) 638-9777
Email: synergy@synergyorg.com
Web: www.synergyorg.com

Description: We are an established and proven national healthcare, information technology, biotechnology, and pharmaceutical executive search/selection firm specializing in the use of psychological testing to help progressive organizations maximize productivity and profitability while simultaneously improving their recruitment, selection, management, leadership development, and retention. We conduct independent executive assessments of internal/external candidates to ensure their success.

Key Contact - Specialty:
Dr. Kenneth R. Cohen, Ph.D., President - *Healthcare, information technology, biotechnology, pharmaceuticals*

Salary minimum: $100,000

Functions: Directors, Senior Mgmt., Middle Mgmt., Nurses

Industries: Mfg., Finance, Venture Cap., Non-profits, Pharm Svcs., Accounting, Mgmt. Consulting, HR Services, E-commerce, Software, Development SW, HR SW, Healthcare, Hospitals, Long-term Care

Professional Associations: ACHE, ASHHRA, ETC, GVFHRA, NJTC, SHRM

Tabb & Associates[†]
665 E Dublin-Granville Rd Ste 410
Columbus, OH 43229
(614) 880-0000
Fax: (614) 880-8888
Email: info@tabbandassociates.com
Web: www.tabbandassociates.com

Description: We specialize in senior and middle-level executives in a diverse group of industrial and consumer firms. Our work is quiet...confidential... and on-target.

Key Contact - Specialty:
Mr. Roosevelt Tabb - *General management*

Salary minimum: $85,000

Functions: Generalist, General Mgmt.

Industries: Mfg., Chemicals, Paints, Petro. Products, Metal Products, Computer Equip., Consumer Elect., Finance, Brokers, Services, Mgmt. Consulting, Telecoms, Insurance

Professional Associations: FMA

Networks: Top Echelon Network

Tactical Alternatives
2819 Crow Canyon Rd Ste 210
San Ramon, CA 94583
(925) 831-3800
Fax: (925) 831-3808
Email: alsal@pacbell.net

Description: We conduct searches for senior-level, hardware/software individuals for computer high-tech companies. Expertise in: R&D, process development, marketing, sales and operations. Assignments are performed with the highest degree of professionalism, sense of urgency and integrity.

Key Contact - Specialty:
Mr. Al Salottolo, Principal - *Computer, high technology*

Salary minimum: $65,000

Functions: Generalist, Directors, Production, Mktg. Mgmt., Sales Mgmt., MIS Mgmt., Systems Dev., Engineering

Industries: Generalist, Computer Equip., HR Services, New Media, Telecoms, Software

TalentFusion
3605 Vartan Way Ste 204
Harrisburg, PA 17110
(717) 221-0825
Fax: (717) 901-8725
Email: info@talentfusion.com
Web: www.talentfusion.com

Description: We provide project based recruitment programs designed to improve our clients critical recruiting metrics. Focused approach to improve recruiter productivity, minimize recruiting cycle times and reduce cost per hire.

Key Contact - Specialty:
Mr. John Laporta, President - *Information technology*

Salary minimum: $60,000

Functions: Generalist, Sales Mgmt., MIS Mgmt., Systems Analysis, Systems Dev., Systems Implem., Systems Support, Network Admin.

Industries: Generalist, Software

Branches:
1228 W Barry 1
Chicago, IL 60657
(773) 296-6733
Fax: (773) 388-0287
Email: mhamacher@augustineinc.com
Web: www.augustineinc.com
Key Contact - Specialty:
Mr. Mike Hamacher - *Information technology*

The Talon Group
16801 Addison Rd Ste 300
Addison, TX 75001
(972) 931-8223
Fax: (972) 931-8063
Email: contact@thetalongroup.com
Web: www.thetalongroup.com

Description: We assist home building and real estate clients through quality-driven management consulting and executive search.

Key Contact - Specialty:
Mr. Robert A. Piper, President - *Real estate, home building, multi-family, development*
Mr. Rodney Hall, Senior Partner - *Real estate, home building, multi-family, development*
Mr. Anthony Cleveland, Senior Partner - *Real estate, home building, multi-family, development*

Salary minimum: $60,000

Functions: Generalist

Industries: Construction, Real Estate

Professional Associations: NAHB

Martin Stevens Tamaren & Associates Inc[†]
25255 Cabot Rd Ste 214
Laguna Hills, CA 92653
(949) 465-0220
(800) 527-2509
Email: martystevens@earthlink.net
Web: www.mst-assoc.com

Description: We specialize in retained director-level and up searches in commercial high-tech, including computer, communications, networking, software, hardware, telecommunications, optical systems/components, wireless, computer chips, finance, manufacturing, engineering, sales, marketing, business development, research and development, and professional services.

Key Contact:
Mr. Martin Stevens, President/CEO - *Computer, communication, networking, software, telecommunication*
Mr. Bruce Tamaren, CFO
Mr. Michael Tamaren, Recuriter

Salary minimum: $125,000

Functions: Generalist, Senior Mgmt., Mktg. Mgmt., Sales Mgmt., Cash Mgmt., Systems Analysis, Systems Dev., Engineering

Industries: Generalist, Electronic, Elec. Components, Venture Cap., Communications, Telecoms, Telephony, Digital, Wireless, Fiber Optic, Network Infrastructure, Networking, Comm. SW

Tandy, Morrison & LaTour LLC
1321 Quarry Ln
Lancaster, PA 17603
(717) 299-5900
Fax: (717) 299-2897
Email: ctandy@tmlsearch.com
Web: www.tmlsearch.com

Description: A small, quality firm, by design. We place principals with significant senior management experience and diverse professional backgrounds. A strong commitment to partnership, understanding clients needs and cultures and providing excellent service.

Key Contact - Specialty:
Mr. Charles W. Tandy, Principal - *Senior management, healthcare, nonprofits, finance, HR*
Ms. Catherine J. Morrison, Principal - *Generalist, senior management, foundations, healthcare, HR*
Dr. Stephen A. LaTour, Principal - *Generalist, marketing*

Salary minimum: $85,000

Functions: Senior Mgmt., Middle Mgmt., Materials, Healthcare, HR Mgmt., CFO's, Risk Mgmt., MIS Mgmt., Non-profits

Industries: Generalist, Drugs Mfg., Medical Devices, Services, Non-profits, Higher Ed., HR Services, E-commerce, Biotech, Healthcare, Hospitals

Branches:
2525 Gross Point Rd
Evanston, IL 60201
(847) 864-4200
Fax: (847) 864-9512
Email: slatour@tmlsearch.com
Key Contact - Specialty:
Dr. Stephen A. LaTour, Principal - *Generalist, marketing*

Ned Tannebaum & Partners
9200 S Dadeland Blvd Ste 516
Miami, FL 33156
(305) 670-0100
Fax: (305) 670-3022
Email: ntptnrs@bellsouth.net

Description: We are a high quality, very personalized one-on-one boutique committed to delivering results as specifically defined by the client and the client's timeframe because anything less than results are excuses.

Key Contact - Specialty:
Mr. Ned Tannebaum, President - *Generalist*

Salary minimum: $150,000

Functions: Generalist, General Mgmt., Sales & Mktg., HR Mgmt., Finance, Mgmt. Consultants, Int'l.

Industries: Generalist, Energy, Utilities, Finance, Mgmt. Consulting, HR Services, Media

Tanner & Associates Inc
15851 Dallas Pkwy Ste 600
Addison, TX 75001
(214) 561-8740
Fax: (214) 561-8695
Email: mike@tannerassociates.com
Web: www.tannerassociates.com

Description: We have a genuine interest and concern for clients & candidates welfare. Small & medium size company expertise. Access to all large telecom and high-tech co's.

Key Contact - Specialty:
Mr. Mike Boate, President - *Telecommunications*

Salary minimum: $150,000

Functions: Senior Mgmt.

Industries: Telecoms, Software

Tannura & Associates Inc
9631 W 153rd St Ste 32
Orland Park, IL 60462
(708) 349-7777
Fax: (708) 349-7799
Email: rtannura@tannura.com
Web: www.tannura.com

Description: We specialize in information systems and technology ranging from high-level technical through executive management including leading edge technology, traditional systems, telecommunications, sales and customer support.

Key Contact - Specialty:
Mr. Robert P. Tannura, President - *Information systems & technology*

Salary minimum: $75,000

Functions: Generalist, IT

Industries: Generalist

Tarnow Associates
150 Morris Ave
Springfield, NJ 07081
(973) 376-3900
Fax: (973) 376-0340
Email: info@tarnow.com
Web: www.tarnow.com

Description: We are a generalist firm working at senior-levels with established market niches in a broad range of industries and disciplines.

Key Contact - Specialty:
Mr. Emil Vogel, President - *Senior management*
Mr. William A. Myers, Senior Vice President - *Senior management, human resources executives*
Ms. Karen Knapp, Vice President - *Senior management*

Salary minimum: $100,000

Functions: Generalist, General Mgmt., Mfg., Sales & Mktg., HR Mgmt., Finance, IT

Industries: Generalist

Professional Associations: IACPR

Tarzian Search Consultants Inc
645 N Michigan Ave Ste 800
Chicago, IL 60611
(312) 867-0001
Fax: (312) 867-0004
Email: wendy@tarziansearch.com

Description: Tarzian Search Consultants, Inc. is an executive search and management consulting firm dedicated to helping its clients further advance their market share and build their brand equity by providing them with recruitment and retention solutions that better align their hiring initiatives with their business objectives.

Key Contact - Specialty:
Ms. Wendy Tarzian, President - *Communications, investor relation, financial communications, corporate communications, public relations*

Salary minimum: $85,000

Professional Associations: EMA, MHRA, NIRI, PRSA, SHRM

Tate & Associates Inc
60 Walnut Ave Ste 100
Clark, NJ 07066
(732) 815-7830
Fax: (732) 815-7845

Description: We are a highly successful retained search firm recognized for timeliness, customization and quality service. We are dedicated to results, professional integrity and commitment to success reflected by 90% repeat business. Specialization includes healthcare, consumer and industrial manufacturers.

Key Contact - Specialty:
Mr. Gene M. Tate, President - *Healthcare, manufacturers, consumer, industrial*

Salary minimum: $65,000

Functions: Senior Mgmt., Middle Mgmt., Mfg., Sales & Mktg., Finance

Industries: Mfg., Biotech

TaxSearch Inc[†]
7050 S Yale Ave Ste 310
Tulsa, OK 74136-9577
(918) 252-3100
Fax: (918) 252-3063
Email: taxsearch@taxsearchinc.com
Web: www.taxsearchinc.com

Description: Our mission is to develop a level of trust and respect with our clients that creates a long-term partnership for solving personnel and recruitment needs in the tax field.

Key Contact - Specialty:
Mr. Anthony Santiago, President - *Tax*
Ms. Sam Bynum, Vice President - *Tax*

Salary minimum: $75,000

Functions: Taxes

Industries: Generalist, Energy, Utilities, Mfg., Finance, Services, Media

Branches:
2205 Middle St
Sullivans Island, SC 29482
(843) 883-5100
Fax: (843) 883-5200
Email: tony@taxsearchinc.com
Key Contact - Specialty:
Mr. Tony Santiago, President - *Tax*

Carl J Taylor & Company
11551 Forest Central Dr Ste 329
Dallas, TX 75243
(214) 340-1188
Fax: (214) 340-1175
Email: carltay@airmail.net

Description: We are an executive search practice with a reputation for completing challenging mid- and senior-level position assignments in a timely and professional manner.

Key Contact:
Mr. Carl J. Taylor, President

Salary minimum: $75,000

Functions: Generalist, IT, R&D, Mgmt. Consultants

Industries: Generalist, Mfg., Drugs Mfg., Medical Devices, Services, Mgmt. Consulting, Healthcare

C N Taylor Executive Search[†]
1160 Bedford Hwy Ste 303
Bayswater Place
Halifax, NS B4A 1C1
Canada
(902) 461-1616
Fax: (902) 435-6300
Email: globalsearch@cntaylor.com
Web: www.cntaylor.com

Description: We are an executive and technical search firm in the business of recruiting the best and brightest people for best-in-class clients worldwide. We have a global executive search network with over 400 Partners.

Key Contact:
Mr. Clifford N. Taylor, CHRP, President

Salary minimum: $50,000

Functions: Generalist

Industries: Energy, Utilities, Construction, Mfg., Transportation, Finance, Communications, Aerospace, Software, Healthcare

Networks: National Personnel Assoc (NPA)

Taylor Search Partners
8000 Ravines Edge Ct
Columbus, OH 43235
(614) 436-6650
Fax: (614) 848-8033
Email: recruiter@taylorsearchpartners.com
Web: www.taylorsearchpartners.com

Description: We provide retained search services for professional, management and executive-level employees. We assist our clients in addressing their strategic hiring issues, specifically positions of greatest importance or sensitivity.

Key Contact - Specialty:
Mr. William Taylor, President
Mr. Jon DeWitt, Executive Vice President
Mr. Mick Shimp, Senior Vice President
Mr. James Cain, Vice President
Ms. Bonnie Trail, Search Project Manager - *Healthcare*

Salary minimum: $100,000

Functions: Generalist, Mfg., Materials, Health Admin., Sales & Mktg., Finance, MIS Mgmt., Mgmt. Consultants

Industries: Generalist, Drugs Mfg., Misc. Mfg., Finance, Pharm Svcs., Advertising, Healthcare

---

[†] occasional contingency assignments

Taylor Winfield
8144 Walnut Hill Ln Ste 1010
Dallas, TX 75231
(972) 392-1400
Fax: (972) 392-1455
Email: administrator@taylorwinfield.com
Web: www.taylorwinfield.com

Description: Our clients include technology companies focused in the public network arena specifically optical networks; Internet companies; software companies specifically in the Internet infrastructure arena and computer hardware companies. We have specific knowledge of private, start-up firms with venture capital funding.

Key Contact:
Ms. Nancy L. Albertini, CEO/Chairman - *Directors & officers*
Ms. Connie Adair, President/COO
Ms. Shelley Kelley, Vice President
Ms. Carrie Thomas, Vice President - *Internet, technology*
Ms. Gale Richards, Vice President

Salary minimum: $200,000

Functions: Senior Mgmt.

Industries: Venture Cap., Mgmt. Consulting, Telecoms, Software

Taylor/Rodgers & Associates Inc
62 Southfield Ave 1 Stamford Landing - 124
Stamford, CT 06902
(203) 323-6080
(203) 323-8645
Fax: (203) 978-0341
Email: taylor@taylor-rodgers.com
Web: www.taylor-rodgers.com

Key Contact:
Mr. Richard Taylor, Managing Partner and CEO
Mr. James R. L. Holdsworth, Jr., Director

Salary minimum: $150,000

Technical Skills Consulting Inc†
2 St. Clair Ave E Ste 800
Toronto, ON M4T 2T5
Canada
(416) 586-7971
Fax: (416) 927-8446
Email: tsc@tscinc.on.ca
Web: www.tscinc.on.ca

Description: We specialize in the recruitment of engineering, technology, and manufacturing professionals for industry.

Key Contact - Specialty:
Mr. Paul MacBean, Senior Consultant - *Engineering, technology, science*
Ms. Roxanne Mars, Consultant - *Engineering, technology, science*
Mr. Don Phaneuf, Consultant - *Engineering, technology, science*

Salary minimum: $50,000

Functions: Generalist, General Mgmt., Mfg., Sales & Mktg., HR Mgmt., Finance, R&D, Engineering

Industries: Generalist, Agri., Forestry, Mining, Construction, Mfg., Aerospace, Packaging, Biotech

The Technology Group
11N356 Williamsburg Dr #D
Elgin, IL 60123
(847) 695-7800
Email: jschwan@tec-group.com
Web: www.tec-group.com

Description: We specialize in management personnel and key individual contributors for information technology companies.

Key Contact - Specialty:
Mr. John Schwan, President - *Information technology*
Ms. Susan Burns, Vice President - *Sales & marketing*

Salary minimum: $75,000

Functions: IT

Industries: Software

Professional Associations: ITVA, NAB, SMEI

Networks: First Interview Network (FIN)

Technology Management Partners
153 2nd St Ste 107
Los Altos, CA 94022
(650) 948-2100
Email: larry@tmpartners.net

Description: We specialize in executive and management placement for venture financed startup and emerging growth technology based companies.

Key Contact - Specialty:
Mr. Larry Webster, President - *Executives, communications, new media*

Salary minimum: $90,000

Functions: Generalist, Senior Mgmt., Middle Mgmt., Mkt. Research, Sales Mgmt., Systems Dev., R&D, Engineering

Industries: Generalist, Computer Equip., Consumer Elect., New Media, Telecoms, Software

Telford, Adams & Alexander
650 Town Center Dr Ste 850-A
Costa Mesa, CA 92626
(714) 850-4309
Fax: (714) 850-4488

Description: We will accept only those assignments where we are can be successful. We rely heavily on repeat business from satisfied clients. All of our work is guaranteed.

Key Contact - Specialty:
Mr. John H. Telford, Jr., Managing Principal - *General management, finance, human resources, marketing*
Ms. Debra M. Zaslav, Principal - *Information technology management, distribution*

Salary minimum: $80,000

Functions: Generalist, Senior Mgmt., Middle Mgmt., Materials Plng., Health Admin., Mktg. Mgmt., CFO's, MIS Mgmt.

Industries: Generalist, Soap, Perf., Cosmtcs., Leather, Stone, Glass, Computer Equip., Transportation, Finance, Government, Healthcare

Branches:
402 W Broadway Ste 900
San Diego, CA 92101-3542
(619) 238-5686
Fax: (619) 687-0002
Key Contact:
Mr. John T. Alexander

TERHAM Management Consultants Ltd
2 Bloor St W Ste 1805
Toronto, ON M4W 3E2
Canada
(416) 968-3636
Fax: (416) 968-6617
Email: consultants@terham.com
Web: www.terham.com

Description: We specialize in mid-senior-level searches in Canada in the areas of marketing, advertising (management, account service, creative, media, production), direct marketing (direct mail, database, telemarketing) and new media.

Key Contact - Specialty:
Mr. Terry Hammond, President - *Senior level marketing, advertising, direct marketing*

Salary minimum: $40,000

Functions: Directors, Senior Mgmt., Middle Mgmt., Sales & Mktg., Int'l.

Industries: HR Services, Advertising, Publishing, New Media

Tesar-Reynes Inc
500 N Michigan Ave Ste 1400
Chicago, IL 60611
(312) 661-0700
Fax: (312) 661-1598
Email: tony@tesar-reynes.com
Web: www.tesar-reynes.com

Description: We are one of the largest specialists in advertising, media, sales promotion, direct marketing, interactive marketing, public relations, research, and integrated marketing management. We will fill most searches in 60-90 days.

Key Contact:
Mr. Tony Reynes, Partner
Mr. Bob Tesar, Partner

Salary minimum: $50,000

Functions: Advertising, Mktg. Mgmt., Direct Mktg., PR, Minorities

Industries: Generalist

James E Thomas & Associates
383 Richmond St Ste 1110
London, ON N6A 3C4
Canada
(519) 661-0476
Fax: (519) 661-0478
Email: jethomas@odyssey.on.ca
Web: www.thomas-hrconsultants.com

Description: We are an executive search firm specializing in senior management searches in manufacturing.

Key Contact:
Mr. James Thomas, President

Functions: General Mgmt.

Industries: Mfg., Services

Thomas Resource Group
(formerly known as Montague Enterprises)
1640 Tiburon Blvd Ste 4
Tiburon, CA 94920
(415) 435-5123
Email: tthomas@infoasis.com

Description: I am an executive search consultant who commits an extraordinary amount of time to, personally conducts each assignment, limits self to three concurrent searches, and has a cost effective fee structure and a highly responsive, personalized, expedient, and tailored approach.

Key Contact:
Mr. Terry Thomas, President
Dr. Norm Mitroff, Consultant

Salary minimum: $90,000

Functions: Generalist, Directors, Senior Mgmt., Mktg. Mgmt., Sales Mgmt., Direct Mktg., HR Mgmt., CFO's

Industries: Generalist, Food, Bev., Tobacco, Drugs Mfg., Medical Devices, New Media, Telecoms, Biotech, Healthcare

Richard Thompson Associates Inc
701 4th Ave S Ste 500
Minneapolis, MN 55415
(612) 339-6060
Fax: (612) 337-9099

Email: rpt@rthompassoc.com
Web: www.rthompassoc.com

Description: We are a senior management and board of directors search consulting services for both nonprofit and for profit organizations.

Key Contact:
Mr. Richard P. Thompson, President

Salary minimum: $60,000

Functions: Non-profits

Industries: Non-profits, Higher Ed., Mgmt. Consulting, Advertising

Thorne, Brieger Associates Inc
11 E 44th St
New York, NY 10017
(212) 682-5424
Fax: (212) 557-4926
Email: sbrieger@thornebrieger.com

Description: We are skilled recruiters and assessors bringing a consultant's approach to solving organizational problems. Assignments carried out by principals only, each with more than 25 years of successful generalist experience.

Key Contact - Specialty:
Mr. Steven M. Brieger, Principal
Mr. Jeffrey M. Stark, Principal - *Chemical industry*

Salary minimum: $100,000

Functions: Generalist

Industries: Textiles, Apparel, Chemicals, Soap, Perf., Cosmtcs., Drugs Mfg., Medical Devices, Plastics, Rubber, Paints, Petro. Products, Media, Advertising, Software

Professional Associations: AQP, SHRM

Branches:
377 Chatham Dr
Chapel Hill, NC 27516
(919) 960-8037
Fax: (919) 960-8047
Email: mikejacobs@thornebrieger.com
Key Contact:
Mr. Mike Jacobs, Principal

Tiburon Group Inc†
4753 N Broadway Ste 500
Chicago, IL 60640
(773) 907-8330
Fax: (773) 907-9481
Email: info@tiburongroup.com
Web: www.tiburongroup.com

Description: We are a leading e-Recruiting solutions firm, which assists companies in leveraging the Internet as an integral part of their recruiting strategy. By utilizing their Internet recruiting expertise, Internet research proficiency, and web-centric services, they provide the front-end recruiting strategy, tools, and resources needed to manage multi-hire staffing initiatives.

Key Contact:
Mr. Carl Kutsmode, Founder and President
Ms. Karen Osefsky, Co-Founder

Salary minimum: $60,000

Functions: Middle Mgmt., Sales & Mktg., IT, R&D, Engineering

Industries: Generalist, Finance, Services, Communications, Aerospace, Software, Biotech, Healthcare

Tierney Associates Inc
239 Schuyler Ave Ste 230
PO Box 2089
Kingston, PA 18704
(570) 825-9500
Fax: (570) 825-9568
Email: gtierney@microserve.net

Description: Our client base focuses largely in worldwide aerospace/automotive/telecom markets. Our clients range from job shops to OEMs manufacturing elex components and systems, including connectors, sensors, switches, power elex, SMT assembly, etc. to complex machined, fabricated, stamped, or cast components. We place extensive general managers/presidents, as well as VPs and directors of all disciplines.

Key Contact - Specialty:
Mr. George F. Tierney, President/CEO - *CEO, president, VP, GM, director assignments*
Mr. Paul J. Argenio, Managing Partner - *Food industry, consumer products, paper, elex*
Mr. Robert A. Pace, Managing Partner - *Electronics, SMT, fluid handling, automotive industry*
Mr. Robert R. Faux, Senior Consultant - *CIM/DCS, power supplies, semi-conductors*
Mr. Michael Slacktish, Senior Consultant - *Generalist*
Ms. Jacklyn I. Green, VP- Research & Administration - *MIS, internet research, primary research*

Salary minimum: $80,000

Functions: Generalist

Industries: Mfg., Aerospace

Tirocchi, Wright Inc
2055 Gateway Pl Ste 400
San Jose, CA 95110
(408) 292-6033
Fax: (916) 624-3600
Email: twisearch@aol.com

Description: We are consultants in executive search. Our primary focus is in high-tech: systems, semiconductors and miscellaneous manufacturing with vertical integration.

Key Contact - Specialty:
Mr. Fred Tirocchi, Principal - *High technology (all functions)*

Salary minimum: $100,000

Functions: Generalist, General Mgmt., Mfg., Materials, Sales & Mktg., HR Mgmt., IT, Engineering

Industries: Generalist, Computer Equip., Consumer Elect., Test, Measure Equip., Packaging, Software

Branches:
3017 Douglas Blvd Ste 300
Roseville, CA 95661
(916) 624-1700
Fax: (916) 624-3600
Email: twisearch@earthlink.net
Key Contact - Specialty:
Ms. Paula G. Wright, Principal - *High technology (all functions)*

TMP Worldwide
(formerly known as Montgomery West)
99 Almaden Blvd Ste 600
San Jose, CA 95113
(408) 292-6600
Fax: (408) 298-5714
Email: resume@tmp.com
Web: www.tmp.com

Description: We use a creative approach to identifying and recruiting senior-level executives in multiple industries and functions. Dedicated to client satisfaction, quality and results, with a commitment to diversity.

Key Contact - Specialty:
Mr. Greg Goodere, VP/Managing Director - *High tech, sales, marketing, finance, human resources*
Mr. A.L. "Mike" Paradis, Search Director - *High tech, sales, marketing, human resources, finance*

Salary minimum: $100,000

Functions: General Mgmt., Senior Mgmt., Sales & Mktg., HR Mgmt., Finance, IT, Engineering, Minorities

Industries: Generalist, Mfg., Finance, Media, Software

TMP Worldwide Executive Search
(a TMP Worldwide company)
622 3rd Ave Fl 37
New York, NY 10017
(212) 351-7000
Fax: (646) 658-0552
Email: gerry.cameron@tmp.com
Web: www.tmp.com

Description: We are a world-class retained executive search firm, whose clients seek leadership at the highest levels of their organizations. We specialize in recruiting at the CEO, COO, CIO, CFO and board of director-level, as well as senior-level operations and staff positions.

Key Contact - Specialty:
Mr. Steven Potter, CEO, TMP Worldwide Executive Search - *Financial services, investment banking*
Mr. Gerard Cameron, Managing Partner - *Private banking*
Ms. Janice Abert, Partner - *Financial services, investment management*
Mr. David Barnes, Partner - *Consumer products, ecommerce*
Mr. Joseph Healey, Partner - *Private equity*
Mr. Georges Holzberger, Partner - *Investment banking, capital markets*
Mr. Harold Johnson, Partner - *Human resources*
Ms. Sara Kampmann, Partner - *Financial services, private banking*
Ms. Bonnie Pease Keeler, MD, Partner - *Healthcare*
Ms. C. C. Leslie, Partner - *Capital markets, financial services, banking, insurance*
Ms. Dina Lewisohn, Principal - *Financial services, investment banking, capital markets, investment management*
Mr. Michael Liebowitz, Partner - *Investment banking, capital markets*
Mr. Joel Millonzi, Partner - *Financial services*
Mr. Robert Molnar, Partner - *Financial services, information technology, technology*
Mr. Marty Nass, Partner - *Real estate, financial services practices*
Mr. Catherine Nathan, Esq., Partner - *Legal*
Ms. Jill Niemczyk, Partner - *Investment banking*
Mr. Jim Phillips, Partner - *Investment management, real estate*
Mr. Fred Rijke, Partner - *Consumer products, financial services, healthcare, industrial, technology*
Mr. Terry Scherck, Partner - *Healthcare, private equity*
Mr. Mike Sullivan, Partner - *Financial services, professional services, technology*
Ms. Elisabeth Wachtel, Partner - *Capital markets, financial services, investment banking, investment management*
Ms. Abbe Goldfarb, Principal - *Private banking, investment management, private equity*
Mr. Douglas Mann, Principal - *Financial services, insurance, technology practices*
Ms. Christine McCann, Principal - *Financial services, investment management, real estate*
Mr. Wendy Murphy, Principal - *Human resources*
Ms. Melissa Norris, Principal - *Investment banking, private equity*
Mr. Glenn Stevens, Consultant - *Investment banking, private equity*

Salary minimum: $150,000

Functions: Generalist, Senior Mgmt., Legal, Healthcare, HR Mgmt., Finance, CFO's, M&A, IT, Attorneys

Industries: Generalist, Energy, Utilities, Mfg., Medical Devices, Transportation, Retail, Finance,

Banking, Invest. Banking, Brokers, Venture Cap., Misc. Financial, Services, Pharm Svcs., Legal, HR Services, E-commerce, IT Implementation, PSA/ASP, Hospitality, Hotels, Resorts, Clubs, Media, Communications, Telecoms, Insurance, Real Estate, Software, Healthcare, Hospitals, Long-term Care, Dental

Branches:
16255 Ventura Blvd Ste 400
Encino, CA 91436
(818) 905-6010
Fax: (818) 905-3330
Email: neal.maslan@tmp.com
Key Contact - Specialty:
Mr. Neal Maslan, Managing Partner - *Healthcare, financial services, private equity practices*
Mr. Stephen Bochner, MD, Partner - *E-health*
Mr. Rick Flam, Partner - *Banking*
Mr. Darin Dewitt, Principal - *E-commerce, healthcare, technology*

222 N Sepulveda Blvd Ste 1780
Los Angeles, CA 90245
(310) 321-3220
Fax: (310) 321-0166
Email: robert.rollo@tmp.com
Key Contact - Specialty:
Mr. Robert Rollo, Managing Partner - *Technology*
Mr. Peter Kelly, Managing Partner - *Healthcare sector*
Mr. Tony Pfannkuche, Partner - *Healthcare*
Ms. Kristine Anderson, Principal - *Technology*
Ms. Bethany George, Principal - *Consumer (products, services) sector, human resources practice*

555 Twin Dolphin Dr Ste 350
Redwood City, CA 94065
(650) 598-7619
Fax: (650) 596-9253
Email: brad.stirn@tmp.com
Key Contact - Specialty:
Mr. Bradley Stirn, Managing Partner - *Financial services, technology practices*
Mr. Michael Ballenger, Partner - *Healthcare*
Mr. Stephen Bochner, MD, Partner - *Healthcare, e-commerce, private equity practices*
Mr. Jack Moyer, Principal - *Technology*

49 Stevenson St 1200
San Francisco, CA 94105
(415) 356-3600
Fax: (415) 356-3601
Email: keith.anderson@tmp.com
Key Contact - Specialty:
Mr. Keith Anderson, Managing Partner - *Industrial, supply chain practices*
Ms. Kristin Hebert, Partner - *Legal*
Ms. Sloan Klein, Consultant - *Financial services, investment management, private equity*
Ms. Rohini Mukand, Consultant - *Technology, ecommerce*

Metro Ctr
One Station Pl
Stamford, CT 06902-6800
(203) 324-4445
Fax: (203) 324-4031
Email: michael.castine@tmp.com
Key Contact - Specialty:
Mr. Michael Castine, Managing Partner - *Financial services, investment management, technology*

191 Peachtree St NE Ste 800
Atlanta, GA 30303-1747
(404) 688-0800
Fax: (404) 688-0133
Email: dave.gallagher@tmp.com
Key Contact - Specialty:
Mr. David W. Gallagher, Managing Director - *Consumer products, hospitality, ecommerce, internet*
Mr. Jeffrey Lemming, Partner - *Fashion, retail, consumer products practices*
Mr. Michael Allred, Partner - *Technology*
Ms. Julia Eakes, Partner - *Fashion, retail, consumer products practices*

Mr. Dan Grassi, Partner - *Technology, healthcare, consumer products*
Mr. Rafael Sierra, Partner - *Healthcare, nonprofit, professional services*
Mr. Noah Waldman, Partner - *Healthcare, insurance, private equity practices*
Mr. Bud Wright, Partner - *Fashion, retail practice, supply chain*
Ms. Carol Green, Consultant - *Consumer products, fashion, retail practices*

225 W Wacker Dr Ste 2100
Chicago, IL 60606-1229
(312) 782-3113
Fax: (312) 782-1743
Email: john.rothschild@tmp.com
Key Contact - Specialty:
Mr. John Rothschild, Managing Partner - *Information technology, private equity, technology practices*
Mr. Mike Corey, Partner - *Insurance*
Ms. Pamela Andrews, Partner - *Technology, professional services*
Mr. Patrick Corey, Partner - *Insurance practice*
Mr. Paul L. Hanson, Partner - *Financial services, insurances practices*
Ms. Linda Mack, Partner - *Banking, consumer banking, financial services, investment banking, private banking*
Mr. Brad Marion, Partner - *Automotive, industrial, technology practices*
Mr. Tom Moran, Partner - *Financial services, healthcare, insurance, professional services practices*
Mr. Timothy O'Donnell, Partner - *Automotive, energy, healthcare, industrial practices*
Mr. Tilman Bender, Consultant - *Technology*
Mr. Brian Schnepff, Consultant - *Financial services, insurance practices*
Mr. Liam Lawrence, Consultant - *Financial services, insurance practices*
Mr. Paul David Hanson, Principal - *Financial services, insurance, technology practices*
Mr. Latham Williams, Partner - *Insurance, legal, healthcare*

99 High St Fl 27
Boston, MA 02110-2320
(617) 292-6242
Fax: (617) 292-6247
Email: john.baker@tmp.com
Key Contact - Specialty:
Mr. John Baker, Managing Partner - *Healthcare*
Mr. Deirdre Bilz Allison, Partner - *Healthcare*
Ms. Kathy Epstein, Partner - *Technology, e-commerce, telecommunications*
Ms. Carol Morley, Partner - *Financial services, investment management practice groups*
Ms. Rachel Hamlin, Consultant - *Investment management, financial services*

7 W Sq Lake Rd Ste 134
Bloomfield Hills, MI 48302
(248) 858-9970
Fax: (248) 585-9971
Email: doug.smith@tmp.com
Key Contact:
Mr. John Rothschild, Managing Partner

7825 Washington Ave S Ste 800
Minneapolis, MN 55439
(952) 903-4663
Fax: (952) 903-4680
Email: michael.kelly@tmp.com
Key Contact - Specialty:
Mr. Michael Kelly, Managing Partner - *Healthcare*

127 Public Sq Key Twr Ste 4110
Cleveland, OH 44114-1216
(216) 694-3000
Fax: (216) 694-3052
Email: mark.elliot@tmp.com
Key Contact - Specialty:
Mr. Mark Elliott, Managing Partner - *Healthcare, Industrial*
Mr. Glenn Anderson, Partner - *Financial devices & industrial*

Mr. Bob Crumbaker, Partner - *Automotive, banking, capital markets, financial devices*
Mr. John Johnson, Partner - *Automotive, human resources, industrial*
Ms. Lee Ann Howard, Principal - *Consumer products, ecommerce, internet, human resources, technology*

816 Congress Ave Ste 1400
Frost Bank Plz
Austin, TX 78701-4039
(512) 425-3900
Fax: (512) 425-3905
Email: tara.pettersson@tmp.com
Key Contact - Specialty:
Ms. Tara Pettersson, Managing Partner - *Internet, e-commerce*
Ms. Judi Webster, Partner - *Technology (internet sector), private equity portfolio*
Mr. Marty Wood, Principal - *Automotive, consumer products, industrial, technology*
Mr. Brad Emerson, Consultant - *Consumer products, ecommerce, industrial, technology*

1601 Elm St Ste 4150
Thanksgiving Twr
Dallas, TX 75201-4768
(214) 754-0019
Fax: (214) 754-0615
Email: judy.stubbs@tmp.com
Key Contact - Specialty:
Ms. Judy Stubbs, Managing Partner - *Consumer products, financial services, healthcare, human resources, industrial*
Mr. Bill Fello, Partner - *Industrial, supply chain*
Mr. David Gabriel, Partner - *Technology*
Mr. Jose Oller, Partner - *Transportation, supply chain and industrial*
Mr. Dave Palmlund, Partner - *Consumer products, human resources, industrial, information technology*
Mr. Grant Wicklund, Partner - *Healthcare*
Mr. Scott Williams, Partner - *Professional services*
Mr. Corey McGuire, Consultant - *Consumer products practice*

1021 Main St Ste 1050
1 City Ctr
Houston, TX 77002-6602
(713) 843-8600
Fax: (713) 843-8605
Email: john.griffin@tmp.com
Key Contact - Specialty:
Mr. John Griffin, Managing Partner - *Energy, natural resources, industrial, financial services*
Mr. Kevin Hofner, Partner - *Industrial, energy, natural resources*
Mr. Mark Anderson, Principal - *Energy, natural resources, industrial, technology*
Mr. Jay Rosenfeld, Principal - *Professional services, technology*
Mr. Bill York, Principal - *Technology, financial services*

2600 400 3rd Ave SW
Calgary, AB T2P 4H2
Canada
(403) 232-8833
Fax: (403) 237-0165
Email: tmp.calgary@tmp.com
Web: www.tmpsearch.com
Key Contact - Specialty:
Dr. Karen Coe, Managing Partner - *High technology, biotechnology, telecommunications, oil & gas, consumer services*
Ms. Jill Couillard, Partner - *Oil and gas, information technology, professional services*
Mr. Andy Sharman, Partner - *Finance, insurance, manufacturing, non-profit sector*
Mr. Mark Raichuk, Search Consultant - *Technology, telecommunication, consulting services*

40 King St W Ste 3200 Scotia Plz
Toronto, ON M5H 3Y2
Canada
(416) 862-1273
Fax: (416) 363-5720
Email: research@tmp.com
Key Contact - Specialty:
Mr. Richard C. E. Moore, Head of Canadian Search
  Operations - *Financial services*
Mr. Hugh Illsley, Partner - *Professional services,
  insurance, consumer products, services, financial
  services*
Ms. Eva Kaufman, Partner - *Internet, e-commerce,
  technology, information technology, professional
  services*
Ms. Lisa Knight, Partner - *Technology,
  professional services*
Mr. Marcelo Mackinlay, Partner - *Human
  resources, energy/natural resources, supply
  chain, automotive, industrial*
Mr. Bill Probert, Partner - *Health care, human
  resources, life sciences, pharmaceuticals*
Mr. Derek Roberts, Partner - *Professional services,
  insurance, financial services*
Ms. Sheila Ross, Partner - *Banking, financial
  services, consumer banking, fashion, retail,
  private banking*
Ms. Denise Tobin-McCarthy, Partner - *Internet, e-
  commerce, technology, information technology,
  professional services*
Mr. John Wallace, Partner - *Internet, e-commerce,
  technology, human resources, information
  technology*
Mr. Phil Lefebvre, Consultant - *Consumer
  (products, services), consumer (durables, non-
  durables), hospitality, leisure*
Mr. Gavin Naimer, Consultant - *Professional
  services, banking, insurance, investment banking,
  capital markets*
Ms. Bernadette Testani, Consultant - *Internet, e-
  commerce, technology*
Ms. Tanya van Biesen, Consultant - *Banking,
  fashion, retail, financial services, investment
  banking, capital markets*

TNS Partners Inc
8140 Walnut Hill Ln Ste 301
Dallas, TX 75231
(214) 369-3565
Fax: (214) 369-9865

Description: We are a generalist firm with an
emphasis on senior management positions in high-
technology, telecommunications, consumer and
industrial manufacturing, services and information
technology.

Key Contact:
Mr. John K. Semyan, Partner
Mr. Craig C. Neidhart, Partner
Mr. Alan R. St. Clair, Vice President
Mr. James M. Peters, Vice President
Mr. John Carter, Vice President
Mr. Rod Monahan, Senior Vice President
Mr. Mike Porter, Vice President
Mr. Bob Diers, Vice President

Salary minimum: $100,000

Functions: Generalist, General Mgmt., Mfg.,
  Materials, HR Mgmt., Finance, IT

Industries: Generalist, Energy, Utilities, Mfg.,
  Wholesale, Services, Aerospace

Madeleine Todd Executive Recruiting
1329 Taylor St Ste 114
San Francisco, CA 94108
(415) 441-7010
Fax: (415) 441-7173
Email: mter@madeleinetodd.com

Description: With a high-level of personalized
attention and service, we have a commitment to
recruiting only people who will make a lasting

impact to your company. 100% placement record.
All clients are repeat clients.
Key Contact:
Ms. Madeleine Todd

Salary minimum: $230,000

Functions: General Mgmt., Senior Mgmt.

Industries: Communications

Skip Tolette Executive Search Consulting
577 W Saddle River Rd
Upper Saddle River, NJ 07458
(201) 327-8214
Fax: (201) 818-0970
Email: skip@tolettesearch.com
Web: www.tolettesearch.com

Description: We are a retainer-based firm
specializing in senior level information technology
recruitment. Our specialties are CIO, development,
operations, strategy, telecommunications, and
consulting.

Key Contact - Specialty:
Mr. Skip Tolette - *Information technology*
Mr. Eric Roeloffs, Director - *Information
  technology*

Salary minimum: $100,000

Functions: IT, MIS Mgmt.

Industries: Generalist

Professional Associations: SIM

Torstaff Personnel
67 Yonge St Ste 503
Toronto, ON M5E 1J8
Canada
(416) 866-8855
Email: jobs@torstaff.com
Web: www.torstaff.com

Description: We are specialists in accounting,
financial, and administrative staffing in the Toronto
and border cities.

Key Contact:
Ms. Kathy Reynolds, Partner
Mr. Frank Lubertino, Partner
Ms. Deirdre Arzheimer, Partner

Trac One [†]
239 Rte 22 E
Green Brook, NJ 08812
(732) 968-1600
Fax: (732) 968-9437

Description: We conduct executive searches for
MIS professionals exclusively as a subsidiary of
Team One, Inc. - a family of companies dedicated to
data processing recruitment, search and consulting
services.

Key Contact - Specialty:
Mr. Thomas C. Wood - *Data processing*

Salary minimum: $75,000

Functions: Generalist, MIS Mgmt., Systems
  Analysis, Systems Dev., Systems Implem.,
  Systems Support, Engineering

Industries: Generalist, Mgmt. Consulting, HR
  Services, Telecoms, Software

Networks: National Personnel Assoc (NPA)

Travaille Executive Search [†]
1730 Rhode Island Ave NW Ste 401
Washington, DC 20036
(202) 463-6342
Fax: (202) 331-7922
Email: travaille@lazer.net

Description: We have an in-depth understanding of
corporate communications and marketing

communications, plus national and international
public affairs. Excellent in finding financial
communicators for start-up companies.

Key Contact - Specialty:
Mr. Benjamin H. Long, President -
  Communications

Salary minimum: $45,000

Functions: Generalist, Admin. Svcs., PR, Graphic
  Artists

Industries: Generalist, Advertising, Publishing,
  New Media

Professional Associations: IABC, NPC, PRSA

Travis & Company Inc
325 Boston Post Rd
Sudbury, MA 01776
(978) 443-4000

Description: We offer top quality search for
executive management. Clients in a wide range of
industries; recognized for expertise in medical
devices, pharmaceuticals, biotechnology, financial
services, telecommunications, ecommerce, and
computer hardware and software.

Key Contact - Specialty:
Mr. John A. Travis, President - *Medical devices,
  biotechnology, pharmaceuticals*
Mrs. Mary K. Morse, Vice President -
  *Biotechnology, medical services,
  telecommunications, financial services*
Mr. Michael J. Travis, Vice President - *Computer
  software & hardware, multimedia*

Salary minimum: $100,000

Functions: Generalist, Senior Mgmt., Plant Mgmt.,
  Mktg. Mgmt., Sales Mgmt., CFO's, R&D,
  Engineering

Industries: Generalist, Drugs Mfg., Medical
  Devices, Computer Equip.

TRH Associates Inc
125 E 38th St
New York, NY 10016
(212) 679-0705
Email: talatrh@acedsl.com

Description: Our search recruiting and competitive
research is conducted on an hourly retainer basis.

Key Contact - Specialty:
Ms. Tala R. Hoffman, President - *Finance, banking,
  consulting, strategic planning, operations*

Salary minimum: $100,000

Functions: Generalist, HR Mgmt., Finance, Mgmt.
  Consultants

Industries: Generalist, Mfg., Banking, Invest.
  Banking, Accounting, Mgmt. Consulting, HR
  Services

Tricom Group Inc
6363 Woodway Ste 250
Houston, TX 77057
(713) 334-2227
Fax: (713) 334-4030
Email: kdean@tricom-group.com
Web: www.tricom-group.com

Description: We are a retained executive search
firm specializing in placing VP level and higher
candidates in the IT industry.

Key Contact:
Ms. Carol Limperos, Sr Principal
Ms. Robbie Leaver, Principal
Mrs. Peggy Thompson, Sr Principal
Mr. Mike McMillin, Principal
Ms. Paula Asinof, Principal
Ms. Heather Cohen, Principal

TriTech Management Resources LLC†
2799 Mabry Rd Mabry House Ste 200
Atlanta, GA 30319
(404) 261-3407
Email: info@tritechpeople.com
Web: www.tritechpeople.com

Description: We are a division of The KPG Group of companies who have been providing human resource and staffing solutions, which range from technology to people. We have been providing these services to organizations around the globe for 30 years. Our firm specializes in the information technology industries, including: software, hardware, internet, and e-Business and working with client companies to identify key management professionals to fill strategic and executive-level positions within their organizations.

Key Contact - Specialty:
Mr. David Turnbull, Managing Partner - *Senior executives (high technology)*
Ms. Indra Bazaz, Partner - *Technology research*

Salary minimum: $75,000

Functions: General Mgmt., Directors, Senior Mgmt., Middle Mgmt., Sales & Mktg., IT, Int'l.

Industries: Generalist, Paper, Computer Equip., Equip Svcs., Mgmt. Consulting, HR Services, Advertising, New Media, Telecoms, Software

Triumph Consulting Inc
2550 Middle Rd Ste 600
Bettendorf, IA 52722
(563) 355-3313
Fax: (563) 355-3633
Email: qc@triumphconsulting.com
Web: www.triumphconsulting.com

Description: We are a national practice concentrating in manufacturing, technology, transportation, and healthcare. The principals have extensive prior senior management experience. Each of our assignments is specifically handled by a designated professional through out all phases of the search process.

Key Contact:
Mr. Daniel G. DePuydt, President
Mr. Scott M. White, Executive Vice President

Salary minimum: $75,000

Functions: Senior Mgmt., Plant Mgmt., Health Admin., Mktg. Mgmt., HR Mgmt., CFO's, MIS Mgmt.

Industries: Generalist, Chemicals, Plastics, Rubber, Machine, Appliance, Consumer Elect., Banking, Publishing, Healthcare

Networks: OI Partners Inc

Branches:
4600 S Syracuse St Ste 200
Denver, CO 80237
(720) 489-0100
Fax: (720) 489-1525
Email: denver@triumphconsulting.com
Key Contact:
Mr. James Ruybal, Partner/General Manager
Ms. Collyn DeNio, Partner

2700 Westown Pkwy Ste 200
West Des Moines, IA 50266
(515) 453-9477
Fax: (515) 222-0565
Email: desmoines@triumphconsulting.com
Key Contact:
Mr. Bob Wigger, Partner

Trowbridge & Company Inc
105 Chestnut St Ste 22
Needham, MA 02492
(781) 444-4200
Fax: (781) 444-1931
Email: rlt80@aol.com

Description: Our consultants specialize in executive search and selection assisting. We have a select number of U.S. and international clients that specialize in identifying, attracting and retaining senior-level executives for all disciplines, including general management.

Key Contact - Specialty:
Mr. Robert L. Trowbridge, President - *High technology (products, services)*

Salary minimum: $80,000

Functions: General Mgmt., Directors, Mfg., Sales & Mktg., HR Mgmt., CFO's, Systems Analysis, Network Admin., Engineering, Attorneys

Industries: Energy, Utilities, Chemicals, Computer Equip., Test, Measure Equip., Invest. Banking, Venture Cap., Legal, Mgmt. Consulting, Telecoms, Defense, Aerospace, Software, Biotech

Professional Associations: NEHRA

Tryon & Heideman LLC
8301 State Line Rd Ste 204
Kansas City, MO 64114
(816) 822-1976
Fax: (816) 822-9333
Email: tryonheideman@sprintmail.com
Web: www.tryonheideman.com

Description: Our firm emphasizes consensus building on the criteria for executive positions before initiating a search. We develop an in-depth understanding of the client's organizational culture to ensure the best possible match.

Key Contact - Specialty:
Ms. Katey Tryon, Partner - *Generalist*
Ms. Mary Marren Heideman, Partner - *Generalist*

Salary minimum: $65,000

Functions: General Mgmt., Materials, Sales & Mktg., HR Mgmt., Finance, Engineering, Specialized Svcs., Non-profits, Attorneys, Int'l.

Industries: Generalist

Professional Associations: ASAE, WAW

Tschudin Inc
2125 Center Ave Ste 500
Ft. Lee, NJ 07024
(201) 302-6000
Fax: (201) 302-6062
Email: accessusa@tschudin.com
Web: www.tschudin.com

Description: We specialize in searches for executives who are crucial for company success. We are especially strong in assignments requiring extraordinary care/depth. Examples: niche businesses, searches involving European and American companies.

Key Contact - Specialty:
Dr. Hugo Tschudin, President - *Generalist*
Mr. Richard Danoff, Chief Operations Officer - *Generalist*

Salary minimum: $70,000

Functions: General Mgmt., Mfg., Plant Mgmt., Sales & Mktg., Mktg. Mgmt., Sales Mgmt., HR Mgmt., Finance, CFO's, R&D

Industries: Generalist

Professional Associations: IMC

TSW Associates LLC†
1 Selleck St Ste 570
Norwalk, CT 06855
(203) 866-7300
Email: tswassoc@aol.com

Description: We recruit investment, research, marketing and client service professionals on behalf of domestic and international investment advisors, mutual fund companies and financial service organizations. We also recruit investment professionals for plan sponsor positions with non-financial corporations.

Key Contact - Specialty:
Mr. Frank M. Wilkinson, Partner - *Investment management, marketing investment services, investment research*
Mr. Robert E. Shultz, Partner - *Investment management, plan sponsors, hedge fund investment professionals*
Mr. Spencer L. Timm, Partner - *Investment management, mutual funds*

Salary minimum: $100,000

Functions: General Mgmt., Directors, Senior Mgmt., Middle Mgmt., Mktg. Mgmt., Cash Mgmt., Non-profits, Int'l.

Industries: Generalist, Finance, Invest. Banking, Misc. Financial

Professional Associations: AIMR, FIAS, FPA, IQR, MFA, SQA

TTG Search
(a member of Lincolnshire Int'l)
4727 Wilshire Blvd Ste 400
Los Angeles, CA 90010
(323) 936-6600
Fax: (323) 936-6721
Email: david@ttgconsultants.com
Web: www.ttgconsultants.com

Description: We are a full-service human resource consulting and retained recruitment firm, specializing in healthcare, food & beverage, accounting/finance, information tech, entertainment, general management.

Key Contact - Specialty:
Mr. David J. Bowman, Chairman/CEO - *General management, entertainment*
Mr. John Bridgeman, President - *Healthcare, financial services, technology, information technology, food & beverage*

Functions: Generalist, General Mgmt., Healthcare, Sales Mgmt., HR Mgmt., Finance, IT

Industries: Generalist, Food, Bev., Tobacco, Retail, Accounting, Hospitality, Broadcast, Film, Healthcare

Networks: Lincolnshire Int'l

W G Tucker & Associates Inc
2400 Ardmore Blvd Ste 403
Pittsburgh, PA 15221-5298
(412) 351-9309
Fax: (412) 351-9195
Email: wgtucker@ix.netcom.com

Description: Our firm is a nationwide executive search and human resources consulting firm. We are recognized for our ability to recruit qualified diversified candidates to fill executive level and key management positions. We also have a human resources consulting division.

Key Contact - Specialty:
Ms. Weida G. Tucker, President/CEO - *Generalist, diversity*

Salary minimum: $60,000

Functions: Generalist, General Mgmt., Materials, Health Admin., Sales & Mktg., HR Mgmt., Finance, IT

Industries: Generalist, Energy, Utilities, Chemicals, Drugs Mfg., Non-profits, Accounting, HR Services

Professional Associations: PPA, SHRM

Networks: Top Echelon Network

Tucker Associates
1015 Mercer Rd
Princeton, NJ 08540
(609) 921-0800
Fax: (609) 921-1293
Email: tuckerassociates@att.net

Description: We offer retained executive searches for client companies in financial services: insurance, banking and securities, nationwide and international. Our practice includes all upper and middle management positions.

Key Contact:
Mr. John J. Tucker, President
Ms. Merlene K. Tucker, Vice President

Salary minimum: $100,000

Functions: Generalist

Industries: Generalist, Finance, Media, Insurance, Healthcare

Tuft & Associates Inc
1209 N Astor St
Chicago, IL 60610
(312) 642-8889
Fax: (312) 642-8883
Email: matuft@tuftassoc.com

Description: We are a specialized executive search firm. National in scope, the firm focuses on CEO and key management staff of not-for-profit associations, philanthropic and academic nursing institutions.

Key Contact - Specialty:
Ms. Mary Ann Tuft, CAE, President - *Non-profit associations*
Ms. Cecile Margulies, Director of Research
Dr. LaVerne Gallman, Associate - *Nursing*
Ms. Betty J. Thomas, Associate - *Nursing*
Dr. Patricia Estok, Associate - *Nursing*
Dr. Billye Brown, Associate - *Nursing*
Ms. Carole Badger, JD, Associate - *Not-for-profit*
Dr. Edythe Hough, Associate - *Nursing*

Salary minimum: $50,000

Functions: General Mgmt., Sales & Mktg., HR Mgmt., Finance, IT

Industries: Non-profits

Professional Associations: ASAE

Tully/Woodmansee Int'l Inc
2928 Kenilworth Blvd
Sebring, FL 33870
(863) 382-1020
Fax: (863) 382-1040
Email: twi@ct.net
Web: www.tully-woodmansee.com

Description: Our firm was established on the principles of providing ethical, timely, and cost effective retained executive search services. TWI is recognized as a valued business partner to a diverse register of emerging Fortune 500 and not-for-profit organizations with extensive experience seeking executives and professionals ranging in annual cash compensation from $65,000 to several million dollars. The firm is structured with exceptional talent, proven systems, and processes to guarantee the identification of a successful candidate, an individual who will make a difference in the organization.

Key Contact - Specialty:
Ms. Margo L. Tully, Partner - *Generalist*
Mr. Bruce Woodmansee, Partner - *Generalist*
Ms. Margaret McInerney, Consultant/Regional Director - *Generalist*
Ms. Pat Trimble, Consultant - *Generalist*
Mr. Sean Rego, Consultant - *Generalist*
Ms. Penny Ogborn, Director of Operations/Consultant - *Generalist*
Ms. Maria Cassidy, Consultant - *Generalist*

Salary minimum: $65,000

Functions: Generalist, General Mgmt., Mfg., Materials, Healthcare, Sales & Mktg., HR Mgmt., Finance, MIS Mgmt., Engineering

Industries: Textiles, Apparel, Retail, Banking, Invest. Banking, Accounting, Mgmt. Consulting, HR Services, Advertising, Software, Healthcare

Professional Associations: BPWCUSA, HRPS, SHRM, WAW, WPO

Branches:
13555 Automobile Blvd Bldg 2 Ste 230
Clearwater, FL 33762-3838
(727) 299-9888
Fax: (727) 299-9878
Email: twi@ct.net
Key Contact - Specialty:
Ms. Maggie McInerney, Consultant/Regional Director - *Generalist*

120 W Broadway
Granville, OH 43023
(740) 321-1131
Fax: (740) 321-1136
Email: twi@ct.net
Key Contact - Specialty:
Mr. Bruce Woodmansee, Partner - *Generalist*

Tuttle Venture Group Inc
5151 Beltline Rd Ste 715
Dallas, TX 75240
(972) 980-1688
Fax: (972) 980-1689
Email: dtuttle@tvg.com
Web: www.tvg.com

Description: Our firm specializes in the high technology industries, for example: telecommunications, IT, software, semiconductor, professional services, and Internet from privately held, emerging growth companies to the Fortune 1000, and possesses international experience and an extremely large repeat client base.

Key Contact:
Mr. Donald E. Tuttle, President/CEO
Mr. Robert T. Pike, Senior Vice President
Mr. Daniel C. Meyer, Senior Vice President

Salary minimum: $150,000

Functions: Generalist

Industries: Medical Devices, Transportation, Venture Cap., Services, Mgmt. Consulting, Communications, Defense, Aerospace, Software, Biotech

Twin Oaks Partners LLC
75 Central St
Boston, MA 02109
(617) 314-3900
Fax: (617) 314-3939
Email: info@topsearch.com
Web: www.topsearch.com

Description: We are a retained executive search firm. Our process enables companies to hire qualified candidates for senior-level opportunities. We primarily work in the financial services arena, specializing in private equity, investment banking, venture capital and investment management.

Key Contact - Specialty:
Mr. Christopher Welles, President - *Financial services, private equity, investment management*
Mr. Nicholas Whitman, Senior Associate - *Financial services, private equity, investment management*
Mr. Charles Gantt, Ph.D., Director of Research - *Research*
Mr. Peter Schibli, Managing Director - *Financial services, private equity, investment management*

Functions: General Mgmt., Senior Mgmt., Finance, CFO's

Industries: Generalist

The Ultimate Source
2147 Avy Ave
Menlo Park, CA 94025
(650) 854-1849
Fax: (650) 854-4555
Email: info@e-ultimatesource.com
Web: www.e-ultimatesource.com

Description: We are specialists in high-technology industries, such as: optical communication, fiber optics, software, hardware, wireless communication, networks, lasers, optics, biotechnology, and semiconductor capital equipment.

Key Contact:
Ms. Jean M. Martin, Principal - *Management*
Mr. Ray Osofsky

Salary minimum: $95,000

Functions: Generalist, Senior Mgmt., Product Dev., Mkt. Research, Sales Mgmt., Systems Dev., Engineering, Int'l.

Industries: Generalist, Mfg., Computer Equip., Test, Measure Equip., Telecoms, Telephony, Digital, Wireless, Fiber Optic, Network Infrastructure, Biotech

van Biesen group
505 3rd St SW Ste 950
Calgary, AB T2P 3E6
Canada
(403) 292-0950
Fax: (403) 292-0959
Email: jvb@vanbiesengroup.com
Web: www.vanbiesengroup.com

Description: We specialize in providing worldwide executive search services to clients that seek exceptional staff for executive management and senior specialist positions.

Key Contact - Specialty:
Mr. Jacques A. H. van Biesen, PEng., Managing Partner - *Senior executive management, senior technical staff*
Ms. Coby van Biesen, Treasurer - *Generalist*
Ms. Catherine Bell, Partner - *Senior executive management, senior technical staff*

Salary minimum: $100,000

Functions: General Mgmt., Directors, Senior Mgmt., Mfg., Product Dev., Mktg. Mgmt., CFO's, MIS Mgmt., Engineering, Int'l.

Industries: Energy, Utilities, Construction, Mfg., Transportation, Services, Environmental Svcs., Software, Biotech, Healthcare

Professional Associations: APEGGA, APEGS, CIPS, CSEG, CSPG, SPE, SPIE

Van Dyke Associates
1755 S Naperville Rd Ste 100
Wheaton, IL 60187
(630) 221-0191

Description: We are an owner operated firm providing high quality professional executive search consulting services to christian organizations, manufacturing companies and service companies/organizations.

Key Contact - Specialty:
Mr. Roger Van Dyke, Owner/President - *Generalist, non-profit organization (christian)*

Salary minimum: $75,000

Functions: Generalist, Senior Mgmt., Middle Mgmt., Health Admin., HR Mgmt., CFO's, Non-profits

Industries: Generalist, Mfg., Food, Bev., Tobacco, Healthcare

---

Peter Van Leer & Associates
26546 N Alma School Pkwy Ste 110
Scottsdale, AZ 85255
(800) 473-3793
Email: insurancesearch@aol.com

Description: We are a retainer search firm
specializing in the insurance industry with emphasis
on recruitment of senior executives in the property
and casualty industry.

Key Contact - Specialty:
Mr. Peter Van Leer, Owner - *Insurance (property,
casualty)*

Salary minimum: $60,000

Functions: Generalist, Senior Mgmt., Direct Mktg.,
Risk Mgmt.

Industries: Generalist, Insurance

VanMaldegiam Associates Inc
500 Park Blvd Ste 800
Itasca, IL 60143
(630) 250-8338

Description: We are a small, exclusive, 100%
generalist, retained executive search consulting firm
with thirty years' experience, MBA and CMC,
maximum of three concurrent assignments, five year
no-raid agreement, research driven, and minimal
client restrictions.

Key Contact - Specialty:
Mr. Norman E. VanMaldegiam, CMC, President -
Generalist

Salary minimum: $100,000

Functions: Senior Mgmt., Mktg. Mgmt., Finance

Industries: Generalist

Professional Associations: IMC, IMESC

VanReypen Enterprises Ltd
PO Box 407
Walworth, NY 14568-0407
(315) 986-3042

Description: We are international executive
recruiters with 46 years' personal international
management experience and 18 years executive
recruiting covering all functional disciplines in all
industries.

Key Contact - Specialty:
Mr. Robert D. VanReypen, President/Treasurer -
*Direct selling industry (all functional
management disciplines)*
Ms. Shirley VanReypen, Vice President/Secretary -
*Direct selling industry (all functional
management disciplines)*

Salary minimum: $40,000

Functions: Generalist, Senior Mgmt., Middle
Mgmt., Admin. Svcs., Mktg. Mgmt., Sales
Mgmt., Direct Mktg., CFO's

Industries: Generalist

Professional Associations: DSA

The Vantage Group
60 E 42nd St Fl 4
New York, NY 10165
(212) 973-9300
Email: resume@vantagesearch.com
Web: www.vantagesearch.com

Key Contact:
Mr. Gregg Grossman, Managing Partner

Salary minimum: $150,000

Functions: General Mgmt.

Industries: Venture Cap., Mgmt. Consulting, New
Media, Software

Venture Resources Inc
1125 N Lindero Canyon Rd Ste A8
Westlake Village, CA 91362
(805) 371-3600
Fax: (805) 371-8720
Email: info@vrisearch.com
Web: www.vrisearch.com

Description: We are a highly specialized executive
search firm working with venture capital based and
emerging publicly held, high-technology companies
at chief executive officer and first-line functional
vice president level.

Key Contact - Specialty:
Mr. William C. White, President - *High technology*

Salary minimum: $120,000

Functions: Generalist, Directors, Senior Mgmt.,
Mktg. Mgmt., Sales Mgmt., CFO's

Industries: Generalist, Medical Devices, Computer
Equip., Test, Measure Equip., HR Services,
Broadcast, Film, Biotech

Networks: Marlar Int'l

Verkamp-Joyce Associates Inc
4320 Winfield Rd Ste 200
Warrenville, IL 60555
(630) 836-8030

Description: We are a management consulting firm
specializing in executive selection. We assist clients
in identifying upper and middle executive
management talent for every major industry
throughout the North America and parts of Europe.

Key Contact:
Ms. Sheila M. Joyce, Partner
Mr. J. Frank Verkamp, Partner

Salary minimum: $100,000

Functions: Generalist

Industries: Construction, Mfg., Finance,
Accounting, Mgmt. Consulting, HR Services,
Haz. Waste, Packaging, Healthcare

Professional Associations: IMESC

The Verriez Group Inc
205 John St
London, ON N6A 1N9
Canada
(519) 673-3463
Fax: (519) 673-4748
Email: verriez@verriez.com
Web: www.verriez.com

Description: Experience with our firm is small and
personal, offering a combination of skills and
expertise to any discipline, with strong finance and
accounting skills. When confidentiality is required,
when advertising is unsuccessful. Seventy-five
percent of business is from repeat clients.

Key Contact - Specialty:
Mr. Paul M. Verriez, President - *Accounting &
finance, sales & marketing management*
Ms. Lynn Sveinbjornson, Senior Consultant -
*Accounting & finance, human resources
management*

Salary minimum: $60,000

Functions: Finance

Industries: Mfg., Misc. Financial, Services,
Accounting, Equip Svcs., Mgmt. Consulting,
Insurance, Software, Biotech, Healthcare

Professional Associations: AESC

Branches:
190 Robert Speck Pkwy
Mississauga, ON L4Z 3K3
Canada
(905) 361-1991
Fax: (905) 897-8385
Email: verriez@verriez.com

Key Contact:
Mr. Paul Verriez, President

Vézina Goodman
1100 de la Gauchetiere W Ste 1100
Montreal, QC H3B 2S2
Canada
(514) 849-2333
Fax: (514) 849-5619
Web: www.emapartners.com

Description: We are a leader in Quebec in senior
executive search and members of board of directors.

Key Contact:
Mr. Claude Vezina, Senior Partner - *Finance,
biotechnology, R&D, sales & marketing*
Mr. Michael P. Goodman, Partner - *Real estate,
finance*
Mr. Richard Laniel, Consultant
Mr. Marc Dufour, Consultant

Salary minimum: $80,000

Functions: Generalist

Industries: Energy, Utilities, Mfg., Finance,
Services, Media, Telecoms, Government,
Aerospace, Real Estate, Biotech

Professional Associations: ICMCQ

Networks: EMA Partners Int'l

Vick & Associates
3325 Landershire Ln Ste 1001
Plano, TX 75023
(800) 364-8425
Fax: (888) 752-8425
Email: info@ad-cast.com
Web: www.ad-cast.com

Description: We are a national search firm working
with hi tech companies staffing sales and marketing
positions with focus on mid-level to senior
positions.

Key Contact - Specialty:
Mr. Bill Vick, CEO - *Marketing executives,
software*

Salary minimum: $70,000

Functions: Generalist

Industries: Computer Equip., Services, Media,
Advertising, Publishing, Telecoms, Software

Professional Associations: PINNACLE, RON

Victory & Associates.com Inc
1609 Yellowstone Ave
Lewisville, TX 75077-2461
(972) 966-0251
Fax: (972) 966-0252
Email: victory@victoryandassociates.com
Web: www.victoryandassociates.com

Description: Our firm's unique niche is that we take
your recruiting project on an hourly basis, so that
your cost per hire is dramatically reduced. We sell
our services in 40-hour increments at $175.00 an
hour and deliver 4 to 6 candidates for each project.

Key Contact:
Ms. LuAnn Victory, President

Salary minimum: $40,000

Functions: Technicians

Industries: Energy, Utilities, Medical Devices,
Finance, Services, Hospitality, Media,
Communications, Real Estate, Healthcare,
Women's

Villareal & Associates Inc
427 S Boston Ste 215
Tulsa, OK 74103
(918) 584-0808
Fax: (918) 584-6281

Email: morey@villareal.com
Web: www.villarealassociates.com

Description: We are a human resources consulting firm specializing in compensation, organization analysis and executive search.

Key Contact - Specialty:
Mr. Morey J. Villareal - *General management*

Salary minimum: $40,000

Functions: General Mgmt.

Industries: Generalist

Villeneuve Associates Inc

1420 5th Ave Fl 22
Seattle, WA 98101
(425) 836-8445
Fax: (425) 868-7658
Email: vai@vaisearch.com
Web: www.vaisearch.com

Description: We are a retained officer-level search firm serving retail, e-Commerce, and food industry clients to recruit simultaneously top talent and create favorable cultures. As a search partner, we provide succession planning, placement, and retention strategies.

Key Contact - Specialty:
Ms. Kim Villeneuve, President/CEO - *Retail, e-commerce, food service*

Salary minimum: $150,000

Functions: Generalist, Senior Mgmt., Advertising, Mktg. Mgmt., Direct Mktg., HR Mgmt., CFO's, MIS Mgmt.

Industries: Generalist, Retail, Hospitality

Professional Associations: NRA, NRF

Branches:
100 Park Ave Fl 16
New York, NY 10017
(212) 928-6658
Email: vai@vaisearch.com
Key Contact - Specialty:
Ms. Liz Knight-Etkin, Sr VP, Research & Recruiting - *Retail, e-commerce, food service*

Vincenty & Company Inc

555 Metro Place N Ste 175
Dublin, OH 43017
(614) 792-2100
(888) 745-6689
Fax: (614) 792-1442
Email: lmvco@aol.com
Web: www.vincentyco.com

Description: We are a nationally retained search firm providing search expertise in the financial services industry, utilizing innovative search techniques and ethical methodologies.

Key Contact - Specialty:
Ms. Lorraine Vincenty, President/Recruiter - *Financial services, stockbrokers, branch managers, institutional, analysts*

Salary minimum: $100,000

Functions: Generalist, CFO's, Cash Mgmt.

Industries: Generalist, Finance, Invest. Banking, Brokers, Misc. Financial, Insurance

Vlcek & Company Inc

620 Newport Center Dr Ste 1100
Newport Beach, CA 92660
(949) 752-0661
Fax: (949) 752-5205
Email: mail@vlcekco.com

Description: Our firm has 21 years of experience in executive search consulting, and our clients include many of the largest companies in the nation. Although we are general search consultants, we have strong practice specialties in operations,

human resources, finance, and general management, and we are well known for our work in the food and beverage industry.

Key Contact - Specialty:
Mr. Thomas J. Vlcek, President - *General management, human resources, operations*
Ms. Suzanne M. Galante, Vice President - *Medical, financial services*

Salary minimum: $100,000

Functions: Senior Mgmt., Middle Mgmt., Mfg., HR Mgmt., Finance

Industries: Generalist

Professional Associations: IACPR, SHRM, WAW

Vojta & Associates

102 Hobson St
Stamford, CT 06902
(203) 357-8022
Fax: (203) 357-8262
Email: mvojta@optonline.net
Web: www.vojta-associates.com

Description: We are a small boutique search firm that offers high-level recruiting, personalized service and a closely monitored search process to deliver the most qualified candidates.

Key Contact - Specialty:
Ms. Marilyn B. Vojta, Principal - *Sales & marketing*

Salary minimum: $85,000

Functions: Middle Mgmt., Mktg. Mgmt., Sales Mgmt.

Industries: Food, Bev., Tobacco, Drugs Mfg., Mgmt. Consulting, Advertising, Publishing, New Media, Broadcast, Film, Telecoms, Non-classifiable

Professional Associations: NYNMA

The Volkman Group LLC

8197 S Newport Ct
Englewood, CO 80112-3103
(720) 493-5541
Fax: (720) 493-5542
Email: artv@volkmangroup.com
Web: www.volkmangroup.com

Description: We are specialist to the LOHAS, natural business, industry. Our firm is a strategic business partner dedicated to long-term client relationships. We provide independent and objective consultation that focuses on understanding your organization, corporate culture, and core values from a senior management perspective. High-profile references include CEOs, board members, financiers, and industry analysts.

Key Contact:
Mr. Art Volkman, President

Salary minimum: $100,000

Functions: Generalist

Industries: Food, Bev., Tobacco, Soap, Perf., Cosmtcs., Drugs Mfg., Biotech

Wakefield Talabisco Int'l

342 Madison Ave Ste 1702
New York, NY 10173
(212) 661-8600
Fax: (212) 661-8832
Email: barbara@wtali.com
Web: www.wtali.com

Description: We are a boutique international retained search firm focusing on senior-level positions in marketing, sales, financial management, e-commerce, retail and fashion.

Key Contact - Specialty:
Ms. Barbara Talabisco, President/CEO - *Consumer businesses, marketing, financial services, e-commerce, fashion*

Salary minimum: $125,000

Functions: Generalist, Senior Mgmt., Middle Mgmt., Mktg. Mgmt., Direct Mktg., Personnel, CFO's, Minorities

Industries: Generalist, Soap, Perf., Cosmtcs., Drugs Mfg., Non-profits, HR Services, Hospitality

Professional Associations: DMA, DSA, NBMBAA

Waken & Associates[†]

327 Dahlonega Rd Ste 303-B
Cumming, GA 30040
(770) 889-5570
Email: info@wakenassociates.com
Web: www.wakenassociates.com

Description: Our firm has provided nationwide executive search for industries such as investment/commercial banking, commercial finance, utilities, energy, "Big 5," accounting, insurance, and other diverse industries. Search emphasis has been given to sectors such corporate finance/capital markets, lending, engineering, management, plant operations, etc. Our compensation range is $75,000 and up.

Key Contact:
Mr. Ron Van Weelde, President

Salary minimum: $75,000

Functions: Generalist, Production, Plant Mgmt., Quality, Productivity

Industries: Energy, Utilities, Construction, Mfg., Finance, Banking, Invest. Banking, Venture Cap., Misc. Financial, Insurance

Walker Group Inc

5305 Ximines Ln
Minneapolis, MN 55442
(612) 551-1480
Fax: (612) 553-1371

Description: We specialize in retail and managed healthcare industry searches on a national basis.

Key Contact - Specialty:
Mr. Walter G. Walker, President - *Managed healthcare, retail*

Salary minimum: $75,000

Functions: Generalist, General Mgmt., Directors, Senior Mgmt., Middle Mgmt., Mktg. Mgmt., Sales Mgmt., CFO's

Industries: Generalist, Retail, Healthcare

J D Walsh & Company

456 Lost District Dr
New Canaan, CT 06840
(203) 972-4359
Email: jdwalsh@ceoexpress.com

Description: We specialize in telecommunication and information services (Internet) industries.

Key Contact - Specialty:
Mr. John Walsh - *Telecommunications*

Salary minimum: $75,000

Functions: General Mgmt.

Industries: Mgmt. Consulting, Media, Telecoms, Software

Deborah Snow Walsh Inc

1000 Skokie Blvd Ste 400
Wilmette, IL 60091
(847) 920-0089
Fax: (847) 920-0884
Email: deborah@dswalsh.com
Web: www.dswalsh.com

Description: We are a retained, executive search firm focusing on senior-level candidates covering all functions and industries, with the reputation for presenting a diverse slate of candidates.

Key Contact:
Ms. Deborah Snow Walsh, President
Ms. Hilary Dexter, Executive Vice President
Ms. Lynda Moore McKay, Senior Vice President
Ms. Ava D. Youngblood, Senior Vice President
Ms. Laura A. Smith, Vice President
Ms. Meredith L. Onion, Vice President
Ms. Melissa Harper, Vice President-Research

Salary minimum: $200,000

Functions: General Mgmt., Senior Mgmt., Sales & Mktg., HR Mgmt., IT

Industries: Generalist

Professional Associations: HRPS, SCIP

Lee H Walton & Associates
379 Jeffrey Pl
Valley Cottage, NY 10989
(845) 268-0292
Fax: (845) 268-0293
Email: leehwalton@aol.com

Description: We conduct executive recruiting services for domestic and international clients in a wide range of industries and functions. We have over 25 years of experience and expertise in Fortune 500, including all industries, especially financial services, consumer products, management consulting/strategic planning, private, venture capital backed small companies and e-Commerce.

Key Contact - Specialty:
Ms. Lee H. Walton - *Generalist*

Salary minimum: $125,000

Functions: Generalist, Middle Mgmt., Sales & Mktg., Advertising, Customer Svc., HR Mgmt., Finance, MIS Mgmt., Mgmt. Consultants, Attorneys

Industries: Generalist, Mfg., Finance, Services, Insurance, Healthcare

Professional Associations: IACPR, ESRT

E K Ward & Associates[†]
(an OI Partners Inc company)
950-A Union Rd Ste 232
West Seneca, NY 14224
(716) 677-2088
Fax: (716) 677-2090
Email: email@ekward.com
Web: www.ekward.com

Description: We conduct executive search services. We specialize in locating hard-to-find talent for a variety of functions/industries including finance, consumer services, engineering, manufacturing, healthcare, as well as professional services at mid-to senior executive-levels.

Key Contact - Specialty:
Ms. Eileen K. Ward, Senior Consultant - Executive Search - *General management, manufacturing, engineering, human resources*
Mrs. Susan Jones, Senior Executive Recruiter - *General management, manufacturing, engineering, human resources*

Salary minimum: $50,000

Functions: Generalist

Industries: Leather, Stone, Glass, Consumer Elect., Test, Measure Equip., Misc. Mfg., Banking, Invest. Banking, Misc. Financial, Non-profits, Accounting, HR Services

Professional Associations: AŠTD, HRPS, IMC, SHRM

Networks: OI Partners Inc

Branches:
4455 Transit Rd Ste 3B
Williamsville, NY 14221
(716) 626-1188
Fax: (716) 626-1430
Email: email@ekward.com
Key Contact - Specialty:
Ms. Lateyfa Ali, General Manager - *General management, manufacturing, engineering, human resources*
Ms. Judy Gooch, Executive Recruiter - *Engineering, human resources, general management*

The Ward Group
8 Cedar St Ste 68
Woburn, MA 01801
(781) 938-4000
Fax: (781) 938-4100
Email: info@wardgrp.com
Web: www.wardgrp.com

Description: Our consultative approach to executive search enables us to successfully recruit talented marketing and communications professionals in a timely manner. Our expertise in assessing the professional and personal variables of both clients and candidates has been the cornerstone of our success.

Key Contact:
Mr. James M. Ward, President - *Marketing, communications*
Mr. Jerry Grady, Vice President - *Marketing, communications*
Mr. Lou Nagy, Vice President - *Marketing, communications*
Ms. Lisa Metropolis, Senior Associate - *Marketing, communications*
Mr. Thomas Jago, Senior Associate - *Marketing, communications*
Ms. Patricia Farris, Director of Operations & Research

Functions: Sales & Mktg.

Industries: Media, Advertising, New Media

Ward Liebelt Associates Inc
1175 Post Rd E
Westport, CT 06880
(203) 454-0414
Fax: (203) 221-7300

Description: We specialize in highly specialized consumer packaged goods, general management, senior marketing management, sales management and recruitment of management consultants.

Key Contact:
Mr. Anthony C. Ward, Partner
Mr. Michael Iserson, Executive Vice President
Mr. Rolly Allen, Senior Vice President

Salary minimum: $75,000

Functions: Sales & Mktg., Advertising, Mktg. Mgmt., Sales Mgmt., Direct Mktg., Customer Svc., PR

Industries: Food, Bev., Tobacco, Soap, Perf., Cosmtcs.

Waring & Associates Ltd
10 Windridge Rd 100
South Barrington, IL 60010
(847) 428-5300
Fax: (847) 428-7857
Email: mail@waring.net
Web: www.waring.net

Description: We are a retained search firm with expertise in recruiting technology executives and leaders for technology companies. We also have extensive experience and capabilities in recruiting executives for China, Japan, India, and other Asian countries.

Key Contact:
Mr. David Waring, President

Salary minimum: $125,000

Functions: General Mgmt., Senior Mgmt., Mfg., Automation, Materials, Sales & Mktg., MIS Mgmt., R&D, Engineering, Int'l.

Industries: Generalist, Agri., Forestry, Mining, Energy, Utilities, Construction, Mfg., Equip Svcs., Communications, Environmental Svcs., Packaging, Software, Mfg. SW, Biotech

Warren Consulting Partners inc
115 Perimeter Ctr Pl Ste 625
Atlanta, GA 30346
(770) 913-1380
Fax: (770) 913-1390
Email: warrenco@bellsouth.net
Web: www.warrenconsult.com

Description: Hi-tech executive recruiters.

Key Contact:
Mr. Gregg Warren, Partner

Salary minimum: $100,000

Functions: Generalist

Industries: Telecoms

Warring & Associates
5673 Stetson Ct
Anaheim Hills, CA 92807
(714) 998-8228

Description: Our practice is limited to retained executive search/business strategy assistance to companies in life and casualty insurance and related enterprise. We are extensively engaged in international insurance regulatory and business-operational advisory services.

Key Contact - Specialty:
Mr. J. T. Warring, President - *Financial services*

Salary minimum: $150,000

Functions: Mgmt. Consultants

Industries: Services

The Washington Firm Ltd
2 Nickerson Courtyard St
Seattle, WA 98109
(206) 284-4800
Fax: (206) 284-8844
Email: wafirm@wafirm.com

Description: In addition to retained executive search, we support our clients with highly experienced human resource and organizational consultants.

Key Contact - Specialty:
Mr. A. R. Battson, Principal - *Senior management*
Ms. Kristina Moris, Principal - *Senior management*

Salary minimum: $60,000

Functions: Generalist, General Mgmt., Sales & Mktg., HR Mgmt., IT

Industries: Generalist, Textiles, Apparel, Telecoms, Software, Biotech

R J Watkins & Company Ltd
3104 4th Ave
San Diego, CA 92103
(619) 299-3094
Fax: (619) 725-4950
Email: info@rjwatkins.com
Web: www.rjwatkins.com

Description: Since our inception, we have created value by attracting high-impact candidates for growth-oriented firms. Our practice groups focus on bioscience and technology. Our additional locations include Los Angeles, Orange County, Hong Kong, and London. Our firm also manages the Aztec Venture Network, a regional venture capital fund.

Key Contact:
Mr. Robert J. Watkins, Founder/Chairman - *Senior executives (for technology companies), biomedical, information technology, software, internet*
Mr. Thomas Murphy, Executive Vice President/Partner
Ms. Megan Magee, Director-Technology Practice

Salary minimum: $125,000

Functions: Generalist, Directors, Senior Mgmt., Product Dev., Mkt. Research, CFO's, IT, MIS Mgmt., R&D

Industries: Generalist, Drugs Mfg., Medical Devices, Computer Equip., Finance, Pharm Svcs., Mgmt. Consulting, Biotech

---

Scott Watson & Associates Inc†
204 37th Ave N #305
St. Petersburg, FL 33704
(800) 610-5770
(727) 521-0477
Fax: (727) 521-9597
Email: recruiter@scottwatson.com
Web: www.scottwatson.com

Description: We are executive search consultants specializing in banking, finance and law.

Key Contact - Specialty:
Mr. Scott Watson, President - *Banking, finance, law*

Salary minimum: $70,000

Functions: Generalist

Industries: Finance, Banking, Misc. Financial, Legal

Professional Associations: AFSC

Waveland Int'l LLC
1 E Wacker Dr Ste 3630
Chicago, IL 60601
(312) 739-9600
Fax: (312) 739-0250
Web: www.wavelandsearch.com

Description: Our firm is a relationship driven and preferred provider focused organization dedicated to long-term partnerships with our clients and providing a high-level of customer service.

Key Contact:
Mr. Phillip D. Greenspan, Partner
Mr. Louis A. Freda

Salary minimum: $125,000

Functions: Generalist, General Mgmt., Mfg., Materials, Sales & Mktg., HR Mgmt., Finance

Industries: Mfg., Food, Bev., Tobacco, Retail, Finance, Software, Biotech

Branches:
3800 Centerville Rd
Greenville, DE 19807
(302) 984-0278
Fax: (302) 984-0258
Email: dbarr@wavelandsearch.com
Key Contact:
Mr. Daniel Barr

2700 Westchester Ave
Purchase, NY 10577
(914) 253-0800
Fax: (914) 253-8884
Key Contact:
Mr. Michael J. Koeller
Mr. Thomas J. Bolger, Partner

Webb, Johnson Associates Inc
280 Park Ave
New York, NY 10017
(212) 661-3700
Fax: (212) 986-4765

Key Contact:
Mr. George H. Webb, Jr., Managing Director
Mr. John W. Johnson, Jr., Managing Director
Mr. Russell E. Marks, Jr., Managing Director
Mr. John W. Malcom, Managing Director
Mrs. Sandra O. Norinsky, Managing Director
Ms. Ruth G. Harris, Principal
Ms. Elvira F. Ryder, Principal
Mr. James R. Johnson, Principal

Salary minimum: $125,000

Functions: Generalist, General Mgmt., Mfg., Sales & Mktg., Finance, IT, Specialized Svcs.

Industries: Generalist

Weber & Company
(also known as MRI of Coral Gables)
255 Alhambra Cir Ste 520
PO Box 141597
Coral Gables, FL 33134
(305) 444-1200
Fax: (305) 444-2266
Email: email@weberstaff.com
Web: www.weberstaff.com

Description: We fulfill positions throughout the world in the medical device and food science industries. As a highly specialized firm, we work with start-ups and Fortune 500 companies in need of change. What makes our firm unique, is our proven track record of developing strategic client relationships.

Key Contact:
Mr. James K. Weber, Managing Partner

Salary minimum: $80,000

Functions: General Mgmt., Mfg., Product Dev., Production, Plant Mgmt., Quality, Healthcare, Sales & Mktg.

Industries: Medical Devices, Electronic, Elec. Components, Mfg. SW, Biotech, Healthcare

---

Weber Executive Search
(a division of Weber Management Consultants Inc)
205 E Main St Ste 2-3A
Huntington, NY 11743
(631) 673-4700
(212) 941-0499
Fax: (631) 673-4885
Email: weberexe@optonline.net

Description: We are a general management consulting and executive search firm specializing in consumer products, including restaurant and hospitality industries.

Key Contact - Specialty:
Mr. Ronald R. Weber, President - *Consumer products*

Salary minimum: $85,000

Functions: Generalist

Industries: Food, Bev., Tobacco, Drugs Mfg., Consumer Elect., Wholesale, Pharm Svcs., Hospitality, Advertising, Packaging, Healthcare

---

S B Webster & Associates†
PO Box 1007
Duxbury, MA 02331
(781) 934-7214
(508) 778-9115
Email: websterwilliam@msn.com

Description: Our success is a direct result of our professional competence in search, our commitment to quality client service and our effective client relationships.

Key Contact - Specialty:
Mr. William L. Webster, President - *General management, information systems, consulting*

Salary minimum: $80,000

Functions: Generalist, Middle Mgmt., Quality, Materials Plng., Sales Mgmt., CFO's, Systems Dev., Mgmt. Consultants

Industries: Generalist, Misc. Mfg., Brokers, Mgmt. Consulting

---

Weinstein & Company
One Apple Hill Ste 316
Natick, MA 01760
(508) 655-3838
Email: lewweinstein@yahoo.com

Description: Founder (MIT, Harvard Business School, Bain & Co.) handles all work; we handle few searches at a time, because of our very high service level. National practices include: consulting firms, hi tech and Internet, media/entertainment/convergence, consumer products, financial services.

Key Contact - Specialty:
Mr. Lewis R. Weinstein, President - *Consulting firms, high technology, media, entertainment, convergence*

Salary minimum: $125,000

Functions: Generalist

Industries: Mfg., Retail, Finance, Mgmt. Consulting, Hospitality, Media, Communications, Software, Biotech, Healthcare

---

S E Weinstein Company
1830 2nd Ave Ste 240
Rock Island, IL 61201
(309) 794-1992
(800) 258-1701
Fax: (309) 794-1993
Email: hunter1830@aol.com

Description: We are a client-retained executive search firm. We specialize in "rural America." Our specialties are engineering, CEO, COO, CFO, board of directors, IT, sales/marketing, manufacturing, et al. We offer a highly personalized, detailed approach with experience in the development of long-term client-company working relationships, worldwide.

Key Contact - Specialty:
Mr. Stanley E. Weinstein, President - *Executive, domestic, international*

Salary minimum: $100,000

Functions: Generalist

Industries: Mfg., Wholesale, Retail, Finance, Media, Aerospace, Insurance, Software, Healthcare

---

Weir Executive Search Associates Inc
2200 Yonge St Ste 1210
Toronto, ON M4S 2C6
Canada
(416) 440-1033
Fax: (416) 440-1957
Email: reception@weirassociates.com
Web: www.weirassociates.com

Description: We are among the few firms in Canada specializing in the recruitment of senior management talent for organizations that build, sell or use information technology.

Key Contact - Specialty:
Mr. Douglas Weir, President - *Information technology*

Salary minimum: $75,000

Functions: Generalist, MIS Mgmt., Systems Dev., Systems Implem.

Industries: Generalist, Finance, Telecoms, Software

Professional Associations: CATA, CIPS

D L Weiss & Associates
18201 Von Karman Ave Ste 310
Irvine, CA 92612-1005
(949) 833-5001
(800) 862-7743
Fax: (949) 833-5073
Email: mail@dlweiss.com
Web: www.dlweiss.com

Description: Our firm serves as a strategic partner in senior level executive selection to clients in a wide variety of industries, including automotive, aerospace, electronics, manufacturing, consumer products, high-tech, communications, and service. We place special emphasis on matching candidate/client chemistry and on adhering to a strict code of ethics.

Key Contact - Specialty:
Mr. David L. Weiss, President - *Automotive, aerospace, manufacturing*
Ms. Wendy A. Worrell, Principal Consultant - *Hi-tech, services, consumer products*

Salary minimum: $150,000

Functions: Generalist

Industries: Energy, Utilities, Mfg., Motor Vehicles, Transportation, Finance, Services, Media, Communications, Aerospace, Biotech

Professional Associations: ACG, JAS, SAE

Wellington Management Group
100 S Broad St Ste 1200
Philadelphia, PA 19110
(215) 569-8900
Fax: (215) 569-4902
Email: wellington@wellingtonmg.com

Description: We are a senior and middle echelon executive search firm consulting with concentration in the telecommunications, information services, pharmaceutical, biotechnology and consumer products industries. We provide consultative services to help clients link management selections with strategic goals.

Key Contact - Specialty:
Mr. Walter R. Romanchek, Principal - *Pharmaceutical, biotechnology, healthcare, chemical*
Mr. Robert S. Campbell, Managing Director - *Telecommunications, information services, consumer products, new media*
Mr. Donald H. Janssen, Principal - *Information technology, consulting*
Mr. Matthew J. Simeone, Principal - *Information technology*
Mr. R. Keith Nehring, Principal - *Telecommunications*
Ms. Cecily G. Craighill, Associate - *Healthcare*

Functions: Generalist, Senior Mgmt., Health Admin., Mktg. Mgmt., Sales Mgmt., CFO's, MIS Mgmt., R&D

Industries: Generalist, Drugs Mfg., Medical Devices, Venture Cap., New Media, Telecoms, Software, Healthcare

Professional Associations: IACPR

Wells Inc
4200 Dublin Rd
Columbus, OH 43221-5005
(614) 876-0651
Fax: (614) 876-4038
Email: mwells@wellsinc.com

Description: We are a management consulting firm specializing in the identification and selection of executives and key personnel for client organizations ranging in size from sole proprietorships to billion dollar corporations.

Key Contact - Specialty:
Mr. Mark Wells, President - *Generalist*

Salary minimum: $100,000

Functions: Generalist

Industries: Energy, Utilities, Mfg., Finance, Accounting, Mgmt. Consulting, Telecoms, Healthcare

The Wentworth Company Inc
479 W 6th St
The Arcade Bldg
San Pedro, CA 90732
(310) 732-2306
(800) 995-9678 x306
Email: catherinependleton@wentco.com
Web: www.wentco.com

Description: We specialize in recruiting department management, on-site contract recruiting, and mid-range single position searches. Training for recruiters. We offer consulting regarding employment department operations and hiring manager satisfaction.

Key Contact:
Ms. Catherine Pendleton, Vice President-Client Services
Mr. John Wentworth, President

Salary minimum: $45,000

Functions: Generalist

Industries: Generalist

Professional Associations: EMA, SHRM

Branches:
8033 Bolt Dr SE
Ada, MI 49301
(616) 682-9567
Fax: (616) 682-9573
Key Contact:
Mr. Dennis R. Woolley, Team Manager

Jude M Werra & Associates LLC
205 Bishop's Way Ste 226
Brookfield, WI 53005
(262) 797-9166
Fax: (262) 797-9540
Email: jmwa@execpc.com

Description: We are human resource consultants, working exclusively under retainer in executive search and selection, succession planning, performance management, assessment.

Key Contact - Specialty:
Mr. Jude M. Werra, CMC, President - *Generalist*

Salary minimum: $108,000

Functions: Generalist

Industries: Generalist, Mfg., Food, Bev., Tobacco, Chemicals, Plastics, Rubber, Metal Products, Machine, Appliance, Motor Vehicles, Venture Cap.

Professional Associations: ACG, ASTD, FFI, HRPS, IMC

Wesley, Brown & Bartle Company Inc
152 Madison Ave Fl 21
New York, NY 10016
(212) 684-6900
Fax: (212) 889-8597
Email: wbbartle@aol.com
Web: www.wbbusa.com

Description: We are the nation's oldest diversity and minority search firm with longstanding diversity and military search and consulting practices. Unconditional two year guarantees.

Key Contact - Specialty:
Mr. Wesley Poriotis, CEO - *Telecommunications, generalist*
Ms. Barbara Mendez-Tucker, Senior Partner - *Manufacturing, information technology*

Mr. Kenneth Arroyo Roldan, Partner - *Diversity staffing, leadership succession planning models, strategy diversity sourcing*
Ms. Tina Belvedere, Senior Recruiter - *Telecommunications, IT, IS*

Salary minimum: $50,000

Functions: Generalist, Directors, Middle Mgmt., Plant Mgmt., Mktg. Mgmt., PR, MIS Mgmt., Minorities

Industries: Generalist, Paper, Drugs Mfg., Consumer Elect., Advertising, Telecoms

Professional Associations: APC, IABC, NIRI, NMBC, SMPS

Western Management Consultants
1188 W Georgia St Ste 2000
Vancouver, BC V6E 4A2
Canada
(604) 687-0391
Fax: (604) 687-2315
Email: search@westernmgmt.com

Description: We specialize in executive search, strategic planning, human resources, information technology, and general management consulting. Local, regional, national and international clients.

Key Contact:
Mr. Brian M. Morrison, CMC
Mr. Roger Welch, CMC
Mr. Adrian Palmer, CMC
Ms. Janet David, CMC
Mr. Richard Savage

Salary minimum: $80,000

Functions: General Mgmt., HR Mgmt., IT

Industries: Generalist

Professional Associations: ICMCC

Branches:
333-5th Ave SW Ste 800
Calgary, AB T2P 3B6
Canada
(403) 531-8200
Fax: (403) 531-8218
Key Contact:
Mr. Mauro Meneghetti

10250-101 St Ste 1500
Edmonton, AB T5J 3P4
Canada
(780) 428-1501
Fax: (780) 429-0256
Key Contact:
Mr. Rick Harvey

65 Queen St W Ste 800
Toronto, ON M5H 2M5
Canada
(416) 362-6863
Fax: (416) 362-0761
Key Contact:
Mr. George Toner
Mr. Mike Bell
Mr. Jim Carlisle
Ms. Kathy Dempster

1004 University Dr
Saskatoon, SK S7N 0K3
Canada
(306) 242-6191
Fax: (306) 665-0025
Key Contact:
Mr. Brian Pratt, CMC

The Westminster Group Inc
174 Wickenden St Fl 3
Providence, RI 02903
(401) 273-9300
Fax: (401) 273-6951
Email: westminster@westmin.com

Description: We specialize in experienced executive search consultants working in most industries and functions on senior management and board of directors search. Retained search only.

Key Contact - Specialty:
Mr. James B. King, Managing Partner - *Financial services*
Mr. Carl Burtner, Partner - *Manufacturing*

Salary minimum: $100,000

Functions: Generalist

Industries: Mfg., Transportation, Finance, Services, Media, Insurance, Software, Healthcare

Networks: Global Search Partners

Weston Consultants Inc
PO Box 216
Weston, MA 02493
(781) 890-3750
Fax: (978) 887-2340

Description: We specialize in executive search in all functional disciplines, in high-technology and other industries. Human resource management consulting: organization and succession planning; compensation, incentives, benefits, performance evaluation and professional development.

Key Contact:
Mr. Edmund J. Walsh, President

Salary minimum: $90,000

Functions: Generalist

Industries: Software

Professional Associations: IEEE, IMC, SBANE

S J Wexler Associates Inc
1120 Ave of the Americas Fl 4
New York, NY 10036
(212) 626-6599
Fax: (212) 626-6598
Email: sjwexler@earthlink.net

Description: We specialize in placing human resource executives in the mid-and senior management levels.

Key Contact - Specialty:
Ms. Suzanne Wexler, President - *Human resources*

Salary minimum: $85,000

Functions: General Mgmt., Product Dev., HR Mgmt.

Industries: Generalist, HR SW

Professional Associations: IACPR, HRPS, SHRM, WAW

Wheeler Associates
30 Surf Rd Ste 30A
Westport, CT 06880
(203) 454-3380
Fax: (203) 454-1632
Email: ctara@wheelerassociates.com
Web: www.wheelerassociates.com

Description: We are a focused boutique specializing in leading edge technology executives, consultants and business leaders. Specialty in Internet and e-business development.

Key Contact - Specialty:
Ms. Susan Tracy, Partner - *Information technology, consulting, outsourcing, services, human resources*

Salary minimum: $125,000

Functions: Directors, Product Dev., Sales & Mktg., HR Mgmt., CFO's, IT, Engineering, Mgmt. Consultants

Industries: Software

Professional Associations: IACPR

Wheeler, Moore & Elam Company
701 N Central Expy Bldg 3 Ste 100
Richardson, TX 75080
(972) 386-8806
Fax: (972) 867-8591
Email: drmark@msn.com

Description: We are a comprehensive, retained national search firm with in-depth research capabilities. A general search practice with broad-based expertise in middle and senior management assignments.

Key Contact - Specialty:
Dr. Mark H. Moore, Partner - *Generalist*
Mr. Robert W. Elam, Partner - *Generalist*

Salary minimum: $60,000

Functions: Generalist

Industries: Generalist

Wheelless/Bennett Group Ltd
227 W Monroe St Fl 19
Chicago, IL 60606
(312) 596-8388
Email: nbennett@wheelless.com
Web: www.wheelless.com

Description: Our firm is a retained executive search firm serving all disciplines of the direct marketing and interactive marketing community. Our clients are the companies that retain our services to identify and qualify candidates, in order to fill professional positions.

Key Contact:
Ms. Neysa Bennett, President - *Executive search*
Ms. Colette Lullo, Researcher

Salary minimum: $90,000

Functions: Direct Mktg.

Industries: Retail, Finance, Services, E-commerce, Media, Communications, Telecoms, Call Centers, Digital, Database SW

Professional Associations: AIM, CADM, DMA, WDMI

Whitbeck & Associates
PO Box 873
Stillwater, MN 55082
(612) 337-0887

Description: We are a retained general executive search firm. We conduct retained legal searches serving law firms and corporations, placing partners, associates, and in-house counsel. We work with law firm mergers/acquisitions and involve situation-specific fee agreements. Our management consulting involves hourly fees.

Key Contact - Specialty:
Ms. Elizabeth C. Whitbeck, President - *Legal, generalist*

Salary minimum: $75,000

Functions: Generalist, Attorneys

Industries: Generalist, Legal

White, Roberts & Stratton Inc†
444 N Michigan Ave Ste 2940
Chicago, IL 60611
(312) 644-5554
Fax: (312) 644-4853
Email: wrsinc2975@aol.com
Web: www.wrs.2e.com

Description: We are a retained executive search firm. Functionally, we are generalists. Our geographic scope is national. Our primary objective is to locate, evaluate, and select prospective candidates for director and vice president level searches in accordance with your specifications. We are also very adept at conducting search assignments that address diversity.

Key Contact:
Mr. Marc P. White, Partner
Mr. William F. Stratton, Partner
Mr. Warren H. Roberts, Partner

Salary minimum: $100,000

Functions: Generalist

Industries: Mfg., Retail, Finance, Services, Accounting, Mgmt. Consulting, HR Services, Hospitality, Media

Professional Associations: AMA, NBMBAA, SHRM

Whitehead Mann Inc
(a Whitehead Mann Group company)
280 Park Ave Fl 25
East Tower
New York, NY 10017
(212) 894-8300
Fax: (212) 697-5718
Email: newyork@wmann.com
Web: www.wmann.com

Description: We are a market leader in recruiting, evaluating, and developing world-class executive talent. We provide an integrated range of leadership services including US board and senior executive search, executive assessment, and executive coaching. Our expertise covers the major business sectors and functions. Meeting the need for corporate diversity is a core value and practice.

Key Contact - Specialty:
Mr. E. Pendleton James, Chairman - *Senior general management, corporate boards*
Mr. Durant A. Hunter, President/CEO - *Senior management*

Salary minimum: $250,000

Functions: Generalist, Directors, Senior Mgmt., Mktg. Mgmt., Sales Mgmt., CFO's, Cash Mgmt., MIS Mgmt., Minorities

Industries: Generalist, Mfg., Retail, Finance, Services, Media, Government, Aerospace, Real Estate, Software, Biotech

Professional Associations: AESC

Branches:
11601 Wilshire Blvd Ste 500
Los Angeles, CA 90025
(310) 575-4806
Fax: (310) 575-4876
Email: usa@wmann.com

1 Int'l Pl Ste 1100
Boston, MA 02110-2600
(617) 598-1200
Fax: (617) 261-9697
Email: usa@wmann.com

Whitehouse & Pimms
14785 Preston Rd Ste 460
Dallas, TX 75254
(972) 866-0066
Fax: (972) 866-9595
Email: mrich@whitehousepimms.com
Web: www.whitehousepimms.com

Description: We are a boutique firm focused exclusively on identifying senior-level executives, namely Cs, VPs, and directors for select opportunities with our clients. Our clients include premier management consulting firms, technology-driven (Internet infrastructure, software, telecommunications, and web-based) companies, and traditional industry leaders. We work throughout North America.

Key Contact - Specialty:
Mr. Mark E. Rich, Vice President - *Officers, senior executives, management consulting, technology, industry*
Mr. Ralph P. Stow, Vice President - *Officers, senior executives, management consulting, technology, industry*

Mr. Steven H. Boykin, Vice President - *Senior practitioners, executive management, management consulting, technology, industry*
Mr. David B. Rich, Vice President - *Senior practitioners, executive management, management consulting, technology, industry*
Ms. Cynthia K. Gilmore, Vice President - *Officers, senior executives, technology, industry*
Ms. Shelly R. Roberts, Vice President - *Senior practitioners, executive management, management consulting, technology, industry*
Mr. Chuck L. Quenette, Vice President - *Senior practitioners, executive management, management consulting, technology, industry*
Mr. Neal D. Fuller, Vice President - *Senior practitioners, executive management, management consulting, technology, industry*

Salary minimum: $150,000

Functions: General Mgmt.

Industries: Energy, Utilities, Mfg., Retail, Mgmt. Consulting, E-commerce, Communications, Software

---

Whitfield & Company
9 Thomas Rd
PO Box 5134
Westport, CT 06881-5134
(203) 341-9600
Email: tony@whitfieldllc.com
Web: www.whitfieldllc.com

Description: We are a retained executive search firm. Our mandate is to assist leading edge companies with the identification, assessment, and selection of outstanding executive talent. Whitfield & Co. was founded to fulfill a vision of developing partnerships with leading edge companies. We are boutique-sized by design. This ensures that each client receives personalized and dedicated service. Our firm is not interested in being everything to everybody. We choose to be everything to a select group of clients.

Key Contact:
Mr. Anthony Hwang, Managing Partner
Mr. George Whitfield, Emeritus Founder

Salary minimum: $120,000

Functions: Senior Mgmt.

Industries: Food, Bev., Tobacco, Computer Equip., Services, Media, Communications, Software, HR SW, Biotech, Healthcare

Networks: Global Partners

Whitney Group
(a subsidiary of Headway Corporate Resources)
850 3rd Ave Fl 11
New York, NY 10022
(212) 508-3500
Fax: (212) 508-3589
Email: recruiter@whitneygroup.com
Web: www.whitneygroup.com

Description: We are a specialist firm with core competencies in financial services, real estate, technology, media and telecommunications, consumer, commercial and industrial, professional services, emerging industries, and human capital management.

Key Contact:
Mr. Gary S. Goldstein, CEO/President
Mr. Jeffrey Sussman, COO
Ms. Alicia C. Lazaro, Vice Chairman
Ms. Julia Harris, Managing Director
Ms. Eileen Tierney, Vice Chairman
Ms. Beth A. Rustin, Managing Director

Salary minimum: $100,000

Functions: Generalist, CFO's, Cash Mgmt., M&A, Risk Mgmt., MIS Mgmt., Mgmt. Consultants, Int'l.

Industries: Generalist, Mfg., Banking, Invest. Banking, Brokers, Venture Cap., Misc. Financial, Services, Media, Communications, Real Estate

Professional Associations: AESC

Branches:
625 N Michigan Ave Ste 2100
Chicago, IL 60611
(312) 587-3030
Fax: (312) 587-0491
Email: research@whitneygroup.com
Key Contact - Specialty:
Mr. Max DeZara, Vice Chairman - *Management consulting, corporate, e-business*
Mr. Larry S. Loubet, Managing Partner - *Real estate*
Mr. Ward P. Feste, Managing Partner - *Real estate*
Mr. Jon Schultz, Managing Partner - *Real estate*

101 Federal St Ste 1900
Boston, MA 02110
(617) 342-7332
Fax: (617) 342-7265
Key Contact:
Ms. Ellen Heller, Senior Vice President

Whittlesey & Associates Inc
300 S High St
West Chester, PA 19382
(610) 436-6500
Fax: (610) 344-0018
Email: whittlesey@searchleaders.com
Web: www.searchleaders.com

Description: We posses recruiting and selecting leadership talent that significantly surpasses our client's expectations.

Key Contact:
Mr. James G. Hogg, Jr., President - *General management, sales & marketing, innovation management, strategic human resource leadership*
Ms. Kate Wallace, Consultant - *Communications, travel*
Mrs. Heather Smith, Consultant - Industry Research - *Consumer goods, pulp and paper, non-wovens*
Mrs. MaryLou Knight, Administrative Manager

Salary minimum: $100,000

Functions: Directors, Senior Mgmt., Product Dev., Plant Mgmt., Sales & Mktg., HR Mgmt.

Industries: Mfg., Food, Bev., Tobacco, Textiles, Apparel, Lumber, Furniture, Paper, Soap, Perf., Cosmtcs., Drugs Mfg., Medical Devices, Retail, Hospitality, Media, Communications, Packaging, Biotech

Professional Associations: ASTD, HRPS, PIMA, SHRM, SLF, TAPPI

The Whyte Group Inc[†]
4701 Sangamore Rd Ste S-210
Bethesda, MD 20816
(301) 263-0724
Fax: (301) 263-0725
Email: whytegroup@aol.com
Web: www.thewhytegroup.com

Description: We are a well-established national firm whose principal goal is to assist clients in obtaining and sustaining the competitive edge. Our focus is in marketing, HRD and general management in the hospitality, banking, construction and information technology industries.

Key Contact - Specialty:
Mr. Roger J. Whyte, President - *Hospitality, banking*
Ms. Deborah McCarthy, Senior Vice President - *General management, construction*
Ms. Kathy Brooks, Senior Associate - *General management*
Ms. Doris Ellis, Associate - *Hospitality*

Salary minimum: $45,000

Functions: Senior Mgmt., Middle Mgmt., Healthcare, Advertising, Direct Mktg., Customer Svc., Personnel, CFO's, MIS Mgmt., Mgmt. Consultants

Industries: Construction, Drugs Mfg., Medical Devices, Banking, Services, Pharm Svcs., Accounting, Mgmt. Consulting, HR Services, Hospitality, Advertising, Biotech

---

Daniel Wier & Associates
333 S Grand Ave Ste 3560
Los Angeles, CA 90071
(213) 628-2580
Fax: (213) 628-2581
Email: dancwier@aol.com

Description: We have significant experience in placement of director and senior management in profit and not-for-profit sector. We have over twenty years' successful search experience. Personal attention is given to every assignment. Documented exceptional placement results.

Key Contact - Specialty:
Mr. Daniel C. Wier, President/CEO - *Professional services*

Salary minimum: $100,000

Functions: Generalist, Directors, Senior Mgmt., Mfg., Sales & Mktg., HR Mgmt., Finance, Mgmt. Consultants

Industries: Generalist, Energy, Utilities, Food, Bev., Tobacco, Misc. Mfg., Banking, Invest. Banking, Mgmt. Consulting, HR Services

---

Wilcoxen, Blackwell, Boynton & Associates
1918 Harrison St Ste 104
Hollywood, FL 33020
(954) 922-4569
Fax: (954) 922-4594

Description: We are a retainer-based firm specializing in senior-level and upper-middle-level assignments in travel and hospitality services.

Key Contact:
Mr. C. E. Wilcoxen, Managing Partner
Mr. Richard N. Boynton, Managing Director
Mr. A. Ashley McGinnis, Senior Advisor

Salary minimum: $60,000

Functions: Generalist, Directors, Senior Mgmt., Middle Mgmt., Advertising, Customer Svc., CFO's, Systems Implem.

Industries: Generalist, Transportation, Hospitality, Software

---

The Wilkie Group Int'l
90 Adelaide St W Ste 400
Toronto, ON M5H 3V9
Canada
(416) 214-1979
(416) 214-9821
Fax: (416) 214-1980
Email: careers@wilkiegroup.com
Web: www.wilkiegroup.com

Description: We are a Canadian based mid-size firm who with our United Kingdom based partners, we provide an executive search and selection services in North America and Internationally.

Key Contact - Specialty:
Mr. Glenn A. Wilkie, President/CEO - *CEO, board, COO, CFO*

Salary minimum: $120,000

Functions: Generalist

Industries: Food, Bev., Tobacco, Textiles, Apparel, Printing, Chemicals, Retail, Invest. Banking, Mgmt. Consulting, Entertainment, Publishing, Insurance

Walter K Wilkins & Company

330 Hartford Rd
South Orange, NJ 07079
(973) 378-8877
Fax: (973) 378-8834
Email: walterkwkw@cs.com

Description: We are a medical search boutique firm. We place physicians only. Our firm works on a retainer basis. We have had twenty-nine years' experience recruiting physicians for key management positions worldwide in insurance medicine and occupational medicine. Our clients served include GE, Exxon, John Deere, Ford, Merrell-Lynch, Prudential, New York Life, Transamerica, Canada Life, Aetna, and Phoenix Mutual.

Key Contact - Specialty:
Mr. Walter K. Wilkins, President - *Physicians, occupational medicine, environmental health, insurance medicine, managed care*
Ms. Barbara King, Vice President - *Employee assistance professionals (EAP)*

Salary minimum: $100,000

Functions: Healthcare, Physicians

Industries: Healthcare

Professional Associations: AAIM, ACOEM

Williams Executive Search Inc

90 S 7th St
4200 Wells Fargo Ctr
Minneapolis, MN 55402
(612) 339-2900
Fax: (612) 305-5040
Email: dubbs@williams-exec.com
Web: www.williams-exec.com

Description: We are a highly regarded, Minneapolis-headquartered firm representing clients requiring national searches. We are a member of IACPR. Recent ('99-2000) searches include: President; CFO; CTO; VP of Operations; VP/GM of Integrated Systems Solutions; VP of Consulting; VP of ASP Operations; several senior & director-level sales, marketing, & business development positions; and several corporate controller positions.

Key Contact - Specialty:
Mr. Bill Dubbs, President - *Generalist*
Ms. Christina Borchers, Principal - *Technology*
Ms. Becky Wilcox, Executive Search Consultant - *Healthcare, med tech*

Salary minimum: $100,000

Functions: Generalist, Senior Mgmt., Sales & Mktg., HR Mgmt., Finance, CFO's, IT, MIS Mgmt., Engineering

Industries: Medical Devices, Venture Cap., New Media, Telecoms, Healthcare

Professional Associations: IACPR, HRPS, NACD, SHRM

Williams, Roth & Krueger Inc

911 N Elm St Ste 328
Hinsdale, IL 60521
(630) 887-7771
Fax: (630) 323-4666
Email: wrkinc@aol.com

Description: We specialize in upper-middle and senior-level searches-all industries and functions. We have extensive experience in general management, sales/marketing, operations, engineering, finance, and technical. We have specific expertise in banking/financial services, electronics, plastics, electromechanical, computer hardware/software/services, telecommunications, consumer products.

Key Contact - Specialty:
Mr. Robert J. Roth, Partner - *Generalist*
Mr. Alan P. Hanley, Partner - *Generalist*

Salary minimum: $100,000

Functions: Generalist

Industries: Energy, Utilities, Construction, Mfg., Finance, Legal, Equip Svcs., Law Enforcement, Telecoms, Defense, Software

Williger & Associates

290 Lake Vista Dr Ste 1000
Porter, IN 46304
(219) 926-9898
Fax: (219) 926-5059
Email: dwilliger@home.com
Web: www.willigerassociates.com

Description: We are an executive recruitment firm exclusively focused on serving our clients with the highest levels of professionalism and integrity. Our mission is to partner with our clients in a consultative process resulting in the recruitment, assessment, and selection of managerial and executive level employees.

Key Contact - Specialty:
Mr. David Williger, Managing Partner - *Financial services, manufacturing*
Ms. Carmen Morales, Partner - *Human resources, manufacturing, real estate*

Salary minimum: $90,000

Functions: General Mgmt., Mfg., Plant Mgmt., Sales & Mktg., HR Mgmt., Finance, CFO's, MIS Mgmt.

Industries: Generalist, Energy, Utilities, Construction, Mfg., Transportation, Wholesale, Retail, Finance, Banking, Invest. Banking, Services, Media, Communications, Packaging, Real Estate, Software, Biotech

Professional Associations: CCI, CFA, EMA, SHRM

Willis & Associates

5122 Spencer Rd
Lyndhurst, OH 44124
(440) 461-4233
Fax: (440) 446-9340
Email: resumeandinfo@aol.com

Description: We have spent twenty-one years in the search field! We are experienced in HR, banking, manufacturing, IT, and general search. We work closely with clients and do unbundled search processes. When the search is unbundled, we are skilled at target company generation, sourcing and prospecting calls, and resume generation. Unsolicited resumes are retained for about six months. Unsolicited e-mailed resumes will be deleted; please use fax.

Key Contact:
Ms. Francille Willis, Principal

Salary minimum: $70,000

Functions: Generalist

Industries: Mfg., Retail, Finance, Services, HR Services, IT Implementation, Packaging, Healthcare

Professional Associations: MBA

William Willis Worldwide Inc

PO Box 4444
Greenwich, CT 06831-0408
(203) 532-9292
Fax: (203) 532-1919
Email: wwwinc@aol.com

Description: We are an international practice with hands-on, personalized consultants to manage executive selection.

Key Contact - Specialty:
Mr. William H. Willis, Jr., President/Managing Director - *CEO's, food, financial services, international, research & development*

Salary minimum: $100,000

Functions: Directors, Senior Mgmt., Mktg. Mgmt., HR Mgmt., CFO's, R&D, Int'l.

Industries: Food, Bev., Tobacco, Chemicals, Soap, Perf., Cosmtcs., Drugs Mfg., Invest. Banking, Broadcast, Film, Biotech

Professional Associations: AESC, IACPR

Networks: World Search Group

Wills Consulting Associates Inc

2 Sound View Dr Ste 100
Greenwich, CT 06830
(203) 622-4930
Fax: (203) 622-4931
Email: jwwca@aol.com

Description: We offer more than fifteen years of success in recruiting communications professionals for Fortune 500 corporations, professional services firms, public relations agencies, and associations throughout the US and globally. Wills formed WCA, continuing a search career that began in New York City. He possesses pre-search experience in public relations, corporate communications, and management consulting.

Key Contact - Specialty:
Mr. James C. Wills, President - *Public affairs, corporate communications, investor relations, marketing communications*

Salary minimum: $120,000

Functions: PR

Industries: Energy, Utilities, Drugs Mfg., Finance, Services, Hospitality, Media, Communications, Aerospace, Biotech, Healthcare

Professional Associations: IABC, NIRI, PRSA

Patricia Wilson Associates

1 Sansome St Ste 2100
San Francisco, CA 94104
(415) 984-3112
Fax: (415) 984-3150
Email: patty@patriciawilson.net
Web: www.patriciawilson.net

Description: We are a retainer executive search firm in San Francisco. We specialize in conducting senior-level searches for general managers and their key reports across almost all industries.

Key Contact:
Ms. Patricia Wilson, Managing Partner

Salary minimum: $180,000

Functions: General Mgmt., Senior Mgmt., Legal, Health Admin., Sales & Mktg., PR, HR Mgmt., Finance, IT

Industries: Mfg., Transportation, Finance, Services, Non-profits, Legal

Networks: Penrhyn Int'l

The Windham Group

PO Box 558
Green, OH 44232-0558
(330) 899-9961
Email: rj-windham@msn.com

Description: We are a dynamic and resourceful firm dedicated to pursuing the best executive talent capable of improving the performance of North American clients.

Key Contact - Specialty:
Mr. Rick Jacobson, President - *Information systems, manufacturing, asset management, insurance*

Salary minimum: $75,000

Functions: Generalist

Industries: Mfg., Retail, Finance, Insurance, Software

Professional Associations: SHRM

---

† occasional contingency assignments

Winguth, Grant & Co

505 Montgomery St Fl 11
San Francisco, CA 94111
(415) 283-1970
Email: sgrant@wgdsearch.com
Web: www.wgdsearch.com

Description: We are a generalist practice focusing on emerging growth companies and larger corporations going through rapid change. In practice our clients are private, public and not-for-profit ranging from start-up to a billion in revenues.

Key Contact - Specialty:
Ms. Susan G. Grant, President - *High growth companies*

Salary minimum: $120,000

Functions: Generalist

Industries: Mfg., Transportation, Biotech, Non-classifiable

Professional Associations: TEC

Winston Personnel Group

253 Executive Park Blvd
PO Box 15366
Winston-Salem, NC 27103
(336) 768-4040
Fax: (336) 765-1865
Email: wpgroup@wpgroup.com
Web: www.wpgroup.com

Description: We are professional recruiters with expertise in engineering, accounting, information technology, office support, payroll, clerical temporary, and industrial temporaries.

Key Contact - Specialty:
Ms. Shirley Shouse, President
Ms. Cannon Simpson, Vice President - *Marketing & sales*

Winthrop Partners Inc

108 Corporate Park Dr Ste 220
White Plains, NY 10604
(914) 253-8282
Fax: (914) 253-6440
Email: winthrop@winthroppartners.com

Description: We are a generalist firm with practice leaders in marketing, information systems, human resources, general management and financial functions.

Key Contact - Specialty:
Mr. Steven Goldshore, President - *Marketing, human resources, financial*
Mr. Vincent Battipaglia, Vice President - *Information systems*
Ms. Dominique Molina, Vice President - *Manufacturing*
Ms. Evelyn Sirena, Vice President - *Information systems*

Salary minimum: $100,000

Functions: Generalist, Directors, Senior Mgmt., HR Mgmt., CFO's, IT

Industries: Food, Bev., Tobacco, Drugs Mfg., Medical Devices, Misc. Mfg., Pharm Svcs., IT Implementation, Publishing, Accounting SW, HR SW, Healthcare

Branches:
189 Windsor Rd
Waban, MA 02468
(617) 558-7666
Fax: (617) 558-7667
Key Contact:
Ms. Faith Friedman, Director

Wisnewski & Associates

3089 Alexander Ave
Santa Clara, CA 95051
(408) 260-0621
Fax: (408) 246-9563

Email: ewisnewski@aol.com

Description: We are a national executive search practice with highly experienced business executives with backgrounds in information technology, telecommunications, MIS and sales management.

Key Contact - Specialty:
Mr. Edward J. Wisnewski, Principal - *Information technology, telecommunications, MIS, sales*

Salary minimum: $70,000

Functions: Generalist

Industries: Generalist, Services, HR Services, New Media, Telecoms

Professional Associations: EMA, NCHRC, SHRM

Witt/Kieffer, Ford, Hadelman & Lloyd

2015 Spring Rd Ste 510
Oak Brook, IL 60523
(630) 990-1370
Fax: (630) 990-1382
Web: www.wittkieffer.com

Description: We are a national executive search firm that specializes in health care, education, and insurance. We recruit senior-level management for integrated healthcare systems, hospitals, managed care, health insurance companies, physician group practices, associations, professional societies, colleges, and universities. Our practice is national in scope with increasing business from selected international clients.

Key Contact - Specialty:
Mr. Jordan M. Hadelman, Chairman/CEO - *Healthcare administration*
Mr. John S. Lloyd, Vice Chairman - *Healthcare administration*
Mr. Michael F. Doody, Senior Vice President/Regional Director - *Healthcare administration*
Ms. Anne Zenzer, Senior Vice President - *Healthcare administration*
Ms. Karen Otto, Vice President - *Healthcare administration*
Mr. Michael J. Corey, Senior Vice President/Regional Director - *Healthcare administration*
Ms. Susan Nalepa, Vice President - *Administration*
Mr. Carson Dye, Vice President /Regional Director - *Healthcare administration*

Salary minimum: $90,000

Functions: Senior Mgmt., Healthcare, HR Mgmt., CFO's, MIS Mgmt., Mgmt. Consultants

Industries: Non-profits, Higher Ed., Insurance, Biotech, Healthcare, Hospitals, Long-term Care

Professional Associations: ACHE, CASE, IFD, NACUBO

Branches:
432 N 44th St Ste 360
Phoenix, AZ 85008
(602) 267-1370
Fax: (602) 244-2722
Key Contact - Specialty:
Mr. Michael F. Meyer, Senior Vice President/Practice Leader - *Corporate managed care, health insurance companies*
Mr. J. Daniel Ford, Senior Vice President - *Healthcare administration*

2200 Powell St Ste 890
Emeryville, CA 94608
(510) 420-1370
Fax: (510) 420-0363
Key Contact - Specialty:
Ms. Elaina Spitaels Genser, Senior Vice President/Regional Director - *Healthcare administration*

2010 Main St Ste 320
Irvine, CA 92614
(949) 851-5070
Fax: (949) 851-2412

Key Contact - Specialty:
Mr. James Gauss, Senior Vice President/Regional Director - *Healthcare administration*
Mr. Richard A. Swan, Senior Vice President - *Healthcare administration*
Ms. Paula Carabelli, Senior Vice President - *Education, non-profit*

3414 Peachtree Rd Ste 452
Atlanta, GA 30326
(404) 233-1370
Fax: (404) 261-1371
Key Contact - Specialty:
Ms. Martha Hauser, Vice President - *Healthcare administration*

4550 Montgomery Ave Ste 615N
Bethesda, MD 20814
(301) 654-5070
Fax: (301) 654-1318
Key Contact - Specialty:
Ms. Anna Wharton Phillips, Senior Vice President/Regional Director - *Healthcare administration*
Mr. Howard T. Jessamy, Vice President - *Healthcare administration*

25 Burlington Mall Rd Fl 6
Burlington, MA 01803
(781) 272-8899
Fax: (781) 272-6677
Key Contact - Specialty:
Mr. Emanuel Berger, Vice President - *Education, non-profit*
Dr. Richard A. von Rueden, Vice President - *Physician executives, healthcare administration*

98 Old South Rd
Nantucket, MA 02554-6000
(508) 228-6700
Fax: (508) 228-6484
Key Contact - Specialty:
Ms. Nancy Archer-Martin, Vice President - *Education*

8000 Maryland Ave Ste 1080
St. Louis, MO 63105
(314) 862-1370
Fax: (314) 727-5662
Key Contact - Specialty:
Dr. Mary Frances Lyons, MD, Vice President/Practice Leader - *Physician executives, healthcare administration*

780 3rd Ave Fl 38
New York, NY 10017
(212) 686-2676
Fax: (212) 686-2527
Key Contact - Specialty:
Mr. Alexander H. Williams, Vice President/Practice Leader - *Healthcare administration, physician executives*

5143 N Stanford Dr
Nashville, TN 37215-4229
(615) 665-3388
Fax: (615) 665-3389
Key Contact - Specialty:
Mr. Gary J. Posner, Vice President/Practice Leader - *Education, not-for-profit*

5420 LBJ Fwy 2 Lincoln Ctr Ste 460
Dallas, TX 75240
(972) 490-1370
Fax: (972) 490-3472
Key Contact - Specialty:
Mr. Keith Southerland, Senior Vice President/Regional Director - *Healthcare administration*
Mr. Peter Goodspeed, Vice President - *Healthcare administration*

10375 Richmond Ave Ste 1625
Houston, TX 77042
(713) 266-6779
Fax: (713) 266-8133
Key Contact - Specialty:
Ms. Marvene Eastham, Senior Vice President - *Healthcare administration*

Mr. Ed Fry, Vice President† - *Healthcare administration*

WJM Associates Inc

675 3rd Ave Ste 1610
New York, NY 10017
(212) 972-7400
(800) 929-0871
Fax: (212) 972-0695
Email: jcornehlsen@wjmassoc.com
Web: www.wjmassoc.com

Description: Our unique executive search process ties developmental assessment and coaching into success on the job. Expertise from "virtual firm" use of research and consultants with dedicated specialties. We focus on culture, change and specific performance profiles that match the competencies required for new economy companies and corporations of the future drive the integration of assessment, coaching, and search where human capital is critical and there is no room for a mistake.

Key Contact:
Mr. James H Cornehlsen, Managing Director
Mr. John P. Finnerty, President
Ms. Judith Firth, Managing Director

Salary minimum: $150,000

Functions: General Mgmt., Sales & Mktg., HR Mgmt., Int'l.

Industries: Generalist, Food, Bev., Tobacco, Printing, Finance, Services, Media, New Media, Software

Professional Associations: IACPR, NYNMA, SIIA

Woessner & Associates

222 S 9th St Ste 4050
4050 Piper Jaffray Tower
Minneapolis, MN 55402
(612) 252-9304
Fax: (612) 343-0305
Email: ron@woessner.com

Key Contact - Specialty:
Mr. Bradford Johnson, Vice President - *Generalist*
Mr. Ronald Woessner, CPA, President - *Generalist*
Ms. Marcia Ballinger, Vice President - *Generalist*

Salary minimum: $75,000

Functions: Generalist

Industries: Generalist

Wojdula & Associates Ltd

N7645 E Lakeshore Dr Ste 100
Whitewater, WI 53190-4251
(262) 473-3023
Email: search@wojdula.com
Web: www.wojdula.com

Description: We are a retainer based search firm with specialization in manufacturing and distribution companies. We have expertise in all functions at the middle to upper management of client companies. We concentrate in the upper Midwest Region.

Key Contact:
Ms. Donna Wojdula, Vice President
Mr. Andy Wojdula, President
Ms. Ann Gallagher, Research Director

Salary minimum: $75,000

Functions: Generalist

Industries: Food, Bev., Tobacco, Soap, Perf., Cosmtcs., Machine, Appliance, Wholesale, Retail, Finance, Banking, Venture Cap., Hospitality, Telecoms

Professional Associations: COLM, DMA, SHRM

D S Wolf Associates Inc

330 Madison Ave Fl 20
New York, NY 10017
(212) 692-9400
Fax: (212) 692-9221
Email: lwestrich@dswolf.com

Description: Specialization in senior-level global executive search within investment banking, capital markets, sales & trading, healthcare, pharmaceuticals, biotechnology & life sciences, venture capital, consumer goods & services (entertainment, new media, telecommunications), and legal/general counsel appointments.

Key Contact:
Mr. David A. Wolf, President

Functions: Generalist

Industries: Banking, Invest. Banking, Venture Cap., Legal, Hospitality, New Media, Telecoms, Biotech, Healthcare

S R Wolman Associates Inc

133 E 35th St
New York, NY 10016
(212) 685-2692
Fax: (212) 889-4379
Email: srwolman@aol.com

Description: We are a generalist search firm with strong specialty in luxury products, traditional packaged goods, design consulting and international. Require monthly retainer, but substantial part of fee is earned when we successfully complete assignment.

Key Contact:
Mr. Steve Wolman, President
Ms. Nannette Willner, Senior Vice President
Ms. Ann E. Fonfa, Consultant
Ms. Stacey Mann, Vice President

Salary minimum: $75,000

Functions: Generalist, Senior Mgmt., Plant Mgmt., Purchasing, Mktg. Mgmt., Sales Mgmt., Int'l.

Industries: Generalist, Food, Bev., Tobacco, Textiles, Apparel, Soap, Perf., Cosmtcs., Drugs Mfg., Hotels, Resorts, Clubs, Advertising, Packaging

Professional Associations: AMA, FG

Woltz & Associates Ltd

PO Box 158
West Dundee, IL 60118
(847) 836-9380
Fax: (847) 836-9385
Email: woltz@msn.com

Description: We have over 20 years' experience in executive search and organizational development, specializing in information technology.

Key Contact - Specialty:
Mr. Kenneth A. Woltz, President/CEO - *Information technology*

Salary minimum: $80,000

Functions: IT

Industries: Generalist

Professional Associations: IMC

M Wood Company

10 S LaSalle St Ste 3700
Chicago, IL 60603
(312) 368-0633
Fax: (312) 368-5052
Email: resume@mwoodco.com
Web: www.mwoodco.com

Description: Founded in 1970, we are a generalist firm which employs a unique consultative approach to recruit middle and senior-level management in a wide array of functions and industries.

Key Contact - Specialty:
Mr. John W. Poracky, Partner - *Information systems, generalist*
Mr. Milton M. Wood, President/CEO - *Information systems, generalist*

Salary minimum: $75,000

Functions: Senior Mgmt., HR Mgmt., CFO's, IT, MIS Mgmt.

Industries: Generalist

Professional Associations: AIMS, AIMS, AIMS, ECC, HRMAC, SIM

The Wood Group Inc

1550 Utica Ave S Ste 425
Minneapolis, MN 55416
(952) 546-6997
Fax: (952) 546-6743
Email: info@thewoodgroupinc.com
Web: www.thewoodgroupinc.com

Description: Our partners draw on a broad range of experience, most notably extensive senior line management in both large and small companies. We recognize our most important responsibility is to represent the client company with discretion, insight and professionalism.

Key Contact - Specialty:
Mr. Michael D. Wood, Chairman - *General management, marketing, finance*

Salary minimum: $125,000

Functions: Generalist

Industries: Generalist

Wood-Snodgrass Inc

12980 Metcalf 130
Overland Park, KS 66213
(913) 681-2200
(800) 207-1958
Fax: (913) 647-1201
Email: ssnodgrass@woodsnod.com
Web: www.isclink.com

Description: We specialize in executive search consulting for not-for-profit organizations, associations, and corporations.

Key Contact:
Mr. Stephen E. Snodgrass, Partner
Mr. William M. Wood, Partner

Salary minimum: $75,000

Functions: Senior Mgmt.

Industries: Energy, Utilities, Finance, Non-profits, Mgmt. Consulting, HR Services, Advertising, Publishing, New Media, Telecoms, Healthcare

Professional Associations: ASAE, SHRM

Woodhouse Associates Inc

1371 Oakland Blvd Ste 100
Walnut Creek, CA 94596
(925) 942-0400
Fax: (925) 942-0409
Email: kennedy-inquiry@woodhous.com

Description: We are a retained, process-oriented, full-service search firm. As of June 2001, we have completed more than 1400 projects in over 20 industries and almost 100 disciplines.

Key Contact - Specialty:
Mr. Tony Fuller, Business Development Manager
Mr. Eric Holzheimer, Managing Director - *Generalist*

Functions: Generalist, Senior Mgmt., Materials, Sales & Mktg., Finance, IT, R&D, Engineering

Industries: Generalist, Mfg., Finance, Media, Software, Biotech

Bruce G Woods Executive Search
25 Highland Park Village Ste 100171
Dallas, TX 75205
(214) 522-9888
Email: bgwoods@airmail.net

Description: We are a privately owned firm offering 23 years of personal attention to clientele. We are a North American and international practice. Our specialties include: e-Business, CRM, software, wireless, telecom, Big 5 consulting, startups, hospitality, and healthcare.

Key Contact - Specialty:
Mr. Bruce Gilbert Woods, Principal - *E-business, high technology, telecommunications, healthcare, financial services*

Salary minimum: $100,000

Functions: Senior Mgmt., Distribution, Healthcare, Physicians, Nurses, Risk Mgmt., IT, MIS Mgmt., Mgmt. Consultants

Industries: Generalist, Energy, Utilities, Mfg., Food, Bev., Tobacco, Transportation, Finance, Services, Media, Biotech, Healthcare

Woodworth Int'l Group
620 SW 5th Ave Ste 1225
Portland, OR 97204
(503) 225-5000
Fax: (503) 225-5005
Email: gwoodworth@woodworth.com
Web: www.woodworth.com

Description: We are team oriented consulting in executive search, human resources, mergers and acquistions.

Key Contact:
Ms. Gail L. Woodworth, President/Principal
Mr. Floyd Hunsaker, Principal
Ms. Nancy Davis, Associate - *Information technology*
Mr. Jerry Calavan, Associate
Mr. Ben Hendrix
Ms. Tracy Bresnahan

Salary minimum: $60,000

Functions: General Mgmt., Mfg., Materials, Sales & Mktg., HR Mgmt., Finance, IT

Industries: Generalist

Professional Associations: OEF, SAO

Branches:
2591 White Owl Dr
Encinitas, CA 92024
(760) 634-6893
Fax: (760) 634-6874
Key Contact:
Ms. Alexa Saxon

Woollett Associates
2680 Bishop Dr Ste 204
San Ramon, CA 94583
(925) 275-1443
Fax: (925) 275-0954
Email: jwoolletts@aol.com
Web: www.waexecsearch.com

Description: We offer high quality, personalized search services to technology companies. Over 30 years in Silicon Valley, with top search firms and in human resource management.

Key Contact:
Mr. James S. Woollett, President

Salary minimum: $70,000

Functions: Generalist, General Mgmt., Mfg., Sales & Mktg., HR Mgmt., Finance, IT, Engineering

Industries: Generalist, Computer Equip., Media, Defense, Aerospace, Software

Working Relationships Inc
6468 City West Pkwy
Eden Prairie, MN 55344
(952) 941-9333
Fax: (952) 941-4334
Email: hutch@workingrelationships.com
Web: www.workingrelationships.com

Description: We help companies select, develop, and retain compatible people with unique search services, coaching, training, and human potential products.

Key Contact - Specialty:
Mr. Russ Lilienthal, President - *Generalist*
Mr. Hutch Walch, Director-Recruiting/Managing Partner - *Generalist*

Functions: Generalist, General Mgmt., Specialized Svcs.

Industries: Generalist

Dick Wray & Consultants Inc
3123 Hannan Ln
Soquel, CA 95073
(800) 525-9729
Fax: (800) 525-9697
Email: dick.wray@dickway.com
Web: www.dickwray.com

Description: We conduct retained searches for corporate retail restaurant and retail business.

Key Contact - Specialty:
Mr. Dick Wray, President/CEO - *Corporate restaurant staff*

Salary minimum: $50,000

Functions: Generalist

Industries: HR Services, Hospitality

Branches:
1499 SW 10th St
Boca Raton, FL 33486
(877) 928-9729
Fax: (877) 929-9729
Email: jill.conrad@dickway.com
Web: www.dickway.com
Key Contact - Specialty:
Ms. Jill Conrad, VP Development - *Hotels, resort casinos*

2211 Brighton Bay Trl
Jacksonville, FL 32246
(800) 710-WRAY
Fax: (800) 711-WRAY
Email: jim.osborn@.dickway.com
Key Contact - Specialty:
Mr. Jim Osborn, Vice President - *Restaurant corporation*

93370 Stoney Ridge Ln
Alpharetta, GA 30022
(800) 846-WRAY
Fax: (800) 953-9729
Email: jim.weber@dickway.com
Key Contact - Specialty:
Mr. Jim Weber, President/COO - *Restaurant (corporation)*

2479 Peachtree Rd 1804
Atlanta, GA 30305
(800) 416-WRAY
Fax: (800) 417-WRAY
Key Contact:
Mr. Chris Kauffman

313 Forkwood Trl
Woodstock, GA 30189
(888) 286-WRAY
Fax: (888) 287-9729
Email: tracy.merrill@dickway.com
Key Contact:
Ms. Tracy Merrill

528 5th St
Annapolis, MD 21403
(800) 341-WRAY
Fax: (800) 372-WRAY

Email: charles.newman@.dickwray.com
Key Contact:
Mr. Charles Newman

433 W 68th Ter
Kansas City, MO 64113
(888) 283-WRAY
Fax: (888) 284-9729
Email: jennifer.tierney@.dickwray.com
Key Contact - Specialty:
Ms. Jennifer Tierney - *Restaurants corporate*

250 Pleasant Valley
St. Charles, MO 63303
(866) 246-9729
Fax: (866) 250-9729
Email: rick.miles@dickwray.com
Web: www.dickwray.com
Key Contact:
Mr. Rick Miles, VP Development

135 Lakeview Dr
Harriman, TN 37748
(888) 785-WRAY
Fax: (888) 786-WRAY
Email: rick.mitchell@dickwray.com
Key Contact - Specialty:
Mr. Rick Mitchell - *Hotel, gaming*

1321 Murfreesboro Rd Ste 600
Nashville, TN 37217
(888) 490-9729
Fax: (888) 482-9729
Email: otis.bishop@dickwray.com
Web: www.dickwray.com
Key Contact:
Mr. Otis Bishop, Exec VP
Ms. Tina Bishop, Exec VP

11261 E Big Cotton Wood Hwy
Brighton, UT 84121
(800) 610-WRAY
Fax: (800) 610-5566
Email: dan.murphy@.dickwray.com
Key Contact:
Mr. Dan Murphy, VCOO/Consultant

WSG Search & Consulting LLC[†]
19 W 21st St Ste 1105
New York, NY 10010
(646) 336-8020
Fax: (646) 336-8017
Email: mail@wsgsearch.com
Web: www.wsgsearch.com

Description: We work primarily at a strategic level to place mid-to-senior level executives in the financial services, telecommunications, Internet, e-Commerce, technology, diversity, and board of directors areas. In addition, we have a professional coaching and diversity consulting practice.

Key Contact - Specialty:
Ms. Robin Wilson, Managing Partner - *Senior management, boards, coaching*
Ms. Angel Stewart, Principal - *Diversity consulting, financial services*

Salary minimum: $125,000

Functions: General Mgmt., Directors, Senior Mgmt., Minorities

Industries: Finance, Banking, Invest. Banking, Venture Cap., Services, Non-profits, Mgmt. Consulting, HR Services, Media, New Media, Government, Insurance, Real Estate

WTW Associates Inc
675 3rd Ave Ste 2808
New York, NY 10017
(212) 972-6990
Fax: (212) 297-0546
Web: www.wtwassociates.com

Description: We are a generalist firm with an international orientation. Industry expertise includes media/entertainment, professional services, high-technology and financial services. Functional emphasis is in general management, finance, information technology and marketing.

Key Contact - Specialty:
Mr. Warren T. Wasp, Jr., President - *Entertainment, multimedia, communications*
Ms. Nancy W. Lombardi, Senior Vice President - *Legal, communications, finance, human resources*
Mr. Thomas P. Schneider, Senior Vice President - *Multimedia, information technology, telecommunications*
Mr. Edward C. Kramer, Senior Vice President - *Digital media, information technology*

Salary minimum: $100,000

Functions: Senior Mgmt., Middle Mgmt.

Industries: Legal, Entertainment, Media, Publishing, New Media, Broadcast, Film, Digital, Entertainment SW

Professional Associations: IACPR, NYNMA

Networks: I-I-C Partners Executive Search Worldwide

Wyatt & Jaffe
4999 France Ave S Ste 260
Minneapolis, MN 55410-1759
(612) 285-2858
Fax: (612) 285-2786
Email: info@wyattjaffe.com
Web: www.wyattjaffe.com

Description: We are recognized by Executive Recruiter News as one of the "50 Leading Retained Search Firms in North America," we are also known for engaging high-level management talent that the marketplace perceives as unattainable.

Key Contact - Specialty:
Mr. James R. Wyatt, President - *High technology, communications*
Mr. Mark Jaffe, Partner - *High technology, communications*

Salary minimum: $180,000

Functions: Generalist

Industries: Generalist, Communications, Software

Professional Associations: IACPR

Branches:
20 Trafalgar Sq Fl 3
Nashua, NH 03063-1985
(603) 882-5350
Fax: (603) 882-4945
Email: vsanchez@wyattjaffe.com
Key Contact - Specialty:
Mr. Kenneth Plasz, Jr., Managing Director - *High technology*

The Wylie Group Ltd
345 N Canal St Ste 1605
Chicago, IL 60606
(312) 822-0333
Fax: (312) 454-1375
Email: wrw@wyliegroup.net

Description: We focus on senior sales, sales management, national accounts, marketing, on a national basis across a spectrum of industries.

Key Contact - Specialty:
Mr. William Wylie, President - *National accounts, sales management*
Ms. Patricia McGuinness, Vice President-Research - *National accounts, sales management*

Salary minimum: $75,000

Functions: Generalist, Sales & Mktg., Mktg. Mgmt., Sales Mgmt.

Industries: Lumber, Furniture, Metal Products, Misc. Mfg., Publishing

Wyndham Mills Int'l Inc†
1825 Barrett Lakes Blvd Ste 500
Kennesaw, GA 30144
(770) 792-1962
Fax: (770) 792-1963
Email: info@wyndmill.com
Web: www.wyndmill.com

Description: We are global search consultants providing executive, managerial and professional level search services to client organizations around the world.

Key Contact - Specialty:
Mr. Cabell M. Poindexter, CEO/President
Mr. Brian Lossie, Senior Vice President
Mr. Clay Poindexter, Vice President - *Energy, utilities*
Mr. Mark A. Wright, Vice President - *Energy, IPP, EPC contractors, utilities*

Salary minimum: $100,000

Functions: General Mgmt., Directors, Senior Mgmt., Middle Mgmt., Mfg., Plant Mgmt., Packaging, Finance, CFO's, Engineering

Industries: Energy, Utilities, Construction, Mfg., Food, Bev., Tobacco, Paper, Paints, Petro. Products, Metal Products, Finance, Banking, Invest. Banking, Services, Equip Svcs., Haz. Waste, Packaging

Branches:
1515 W Corwallis Dr Ste G-107
Greensboro, NC 27408
(336) 275-2622
Fax: (336) 275-3811
Key Contact:
Mr. Rich Fisher, Director

Xagas & Associates
1127 Fargo Blvd Ste 1
Geneva, IL 60134
(630) 232-7044

Description: We specialize in the recruitment of individual contributors, middle managers and senior executives in World Class Quality Initiatives.

Key Contact - Specialty:
Mr. Steve Xagas, President/Founder - *Quality, operations, general managers (mid-senior level), automation specialists*

Salary minimum: $65,000

Functions: Senior Mgmt., Middle Mgmt., Automation, Materials Plng., Mktg. Mgmt., Benefits, Finance, MIS Mgmt., Engineering, Mgmt. Consultants

Industries: Food, Bev., Tobacco, Soap, Perf., Cosmtcs., Drugs Mfg., Medical Devices, Plastics, Rubber, Metal Products, Machine, Appliance, Motor Vehicles, Computer Equip., Consumer Elect., Test, Measure Equip., Mgmt. Consulting, HR Services, Defense, Aerospace, Software

Professional Associations: ASQ, IMESC

Networks: Top Echelon Network

Xavier Associates Inc
28 Main St Bldg 7
North Eaton, MA 02356
(508) 230-9699
Fax: (508) 230-9889
Email: mail@xavierassociates.com
Web: www.xavierassociates.com

Description: We recruit for all disciplines in all industries on a retained basis. Our research company can also be engaged to provide customized research to client companies and recruiting firms. Our firm is known for its diversity search capability and are affiliated with Gatti & Associates.

Key Contact:
Mr. Robert D. Gatti, President

Salary minimum: $70,000

Functions: Generalist

Industries: Generalist

Professional Associations: EMA, MPPC, NAPS, NEHRA

Yaekle & Company
PO Box 615
Granville, OH 43023
(740) 587-7366
Fax: (740) 587-7367
Email: gyc@nextek.net

Description: We are a specialized and targeted executive search firm. The focus of our firm is on advertising, marketing, sales, retail operations, and human resources management.

Key Contact:
Mr. Gary Yaekle, Senior Vice President

Salary minimum: $70,000

Functions: General Mgmt., Senior Mgmt., Sales & Mktg., Advertising, Mkt. Research, Mktg. Mgmt., Sales Mgmt., Direct Mktg., PR, Personnel

Industries: Generalist, Food, Bev., Tobacco, Soap, Perf., Cosmtcs., Motor Vehicles, Retail, Services, Hospitality, Restaurants, Advertising, New Media

The Yorkshire Group Ltd†
182 W Central St
Natick, MA 01760
(508) 653-1222
Fax: (508) 653-2631
Email: info@yorkshireltd.com
Web: www.goodjobhunting.net

Description: Insurance recruiting constitutes the majority of the company business. Retained recruitment is joined by Internet recruiting to address the broad needs of clients.

Key Contact:
Mr. Michael P. Tornesello, President

Salary minimum: $75,000

Functions: Generalist

Industries: Finance, Insurance

Youngs, Walker & Company
1605 Colonial Pkwy Ste 200
Inverness, IL 60067
(847) 991-6900
Fax: (847) 934-6607
Email: info@youngswalker.com
Web: www.youngswalker.com

Description: Chicago-based management consulting firm assisting newspaper and broadcast companies of all sizes in the recruitment of corporate executives and all top and middle-level management.

Key Contact - Specialty:
Mr. Carl Youngs, President - *Newspaper, broadcast*
Mr. Mike Walker, Vice President - *Newspaper, broadcast*

Salary minimum: $85,000

Functions: Generalist, Senior Mgmt., Middle Mgmt., Production, Mktg. Mgmt., Sales Mgmt., CFO's, MIS Mgmt.

Industries: Generalist, Publishing, Broadcast, Film

Professional Associations: NAA

Steven Yungerberg Associates Inc
20735 Linwood Rd
Deep Haven, MN 55331-9387
(952) 470-2288
Fax: (952) 470-3940

Description: Management consulting firm specializing in executive selection and recruitment.

Key Contact - Specialty:
Mr. Steven A. Yungerberg, President - *Investment management, financial services*

Salary minimum: $50,000

Functions: Generalist, Senior Mgmt., Mkt. Research, Benefits, CFO's, Cash Mgmt., M&A, Int'l.

Industries: Generalist, Finance

The Zammataro Company

PO Box 339
Hudson, OH 44236
(330) 656-1055

Description: A generalist firm dedicated to high quality, timely, retainer based recruiting. Experience spans 25 years and includes assignments completed in twenty plus industries.

Key Contact:
Mr. Frank Zammataro, President

Salary minimum: $70,000

Functions: Generalist, General Mgmt., Mfg., Distribution, Sales & Mktg., HR Mgmt., Finance, MIS Mgmt.

Industries: Generalist, Chemicals, Medical Devices, Plastics, Rubber, Metal Products, Computer Equip., Misc. Mfg.

ZanExec LLC†

2063 Madrillon Rd
Vienna, VA 22182
(703) 734-7070
Fax: (703) 734-9440
Email: zan@zanexec.com
Web: www.zanexec.com

Description: We are a retained executive search firm with over 24 years of experience specializing in the areas of high technology line management. Our concentration is in information technology, information systems, systems integration, software development, and telecommunications.

Key Contact - Specialty:
Ms. Zan Vourakis, President - *High technology (line management)*
Mr. Peter Johnson, Vice President - *Professional services, management consulting in IT*

Salary minimum: $100,000

Functions: General Mgmt., Senior Mgmt., Mfg., Sales & Mktg., Sales Mgmt., Finance, IT, DB Admin., Engineering, Mgmt. Consultants

Industries: Generalist, Mfg., Transportation, Finance, Media, Publishing, Communications, Defense, Aerospace, Biotech, Healthcare

---

The Zarkin Group Inc

550 Mamaroneck Ave Ste 310
Harrison, NY 10528-1636
(914) 777-0500
(800) 977-0509
Fax: (914) 777-0536
Email: nzarkin@aol.com

Description: We are a national search firm able to recruit on a regional, metro area, or countrywide basis with 26 years worth of experience. Our principals are involved in every search. Quick response and personal attention offering very competitive fee arrangements for all levels of compensation above $65,000 per year.

Key Contact - Specialty:
Mr. Norman Zarkin, President - *Retail, distribution, marketing & sales, real estate, construction*
Ms. Antonella Russo, Research Manager - *Human resources, sales & marketing*

Salary minimum: $65,000

Functions: General Mgmt., Sales & Mktg., Finance

Industries: Generalist, Mfg., Wholesale, Retail

Professional Associations: ICSC

Branches:
275 Turnpike St Ste 202
Canton, MA 02021
(781) 821-1133
Fax: (781) 821-0601
Email: alevine3@aol.com
Key Contact - Specialty:
Mr. Alan Levine, Partner - *Retail, marketing, manufacturing, legal, technology*

Zatkovich & Associates

101 1st St Ste 529
Los Altos, CA 94022
(650) 737-0671
Fax: (408) 737-7030
Email: zakassoc@aol.com
Web: www.zakassoc.com

Description: Thirty plus years in Silicon Valley, specializing in start-ups and emerging technology companies. True search value is the difference between the best candidate and the best person known to be looking.

Key Contact - Specialty:
Mr. Gary A. Zatkovich, Principal/Founder - *Senior marketing, sales, engineering management*
Mr. Ken Marks, Search Consultant/Partner - *Wireless data, telecommunications*
Mr. Jay Latona, Search Consultant/Partner - *IP telephony, S/W applications, internet*

Salary minimum: $100,000

Functions: IT

Industries: Telecoms, Call Centers, Telephony, Digital, Wireless, Fiber Optic, Network Infrastructure, Software

---

Zay & Company Int'l

(a member of IIC Partners company)
1349 W Peachtree St NW Ste 1740
2 Midtown Plz
Atlanta, GA 30309
(404) 876-9986
Fax: (404) 872-5626
Email: zaymail@zaycointl.com
Web: www.zaycointl.com

Description: We were founded in 1982 to conduct a highly consultative executive search practice in which a principal of the firm would work directly with each client on every search engagement. The validity of this concept and philosophy has been proven by the continuity of the firm's client base and the consistently successful performance of the executives placed.

Key Contact - Specialty:
Mr. Thomas C. Zay, Sr., Chairman - *Apparel, home furnishings, textiles, retail, food processing*
Mr. Geary D. Martin, Consultant - *Engineering, construction, heavy equipment*
Mr. Michael W. Kilpatrick, Consultant - *Consumer package goods, beverages, financial services, advertising, marketing, public relations*

Functions: Generalist, Production, Packaging, HR Mgmt., CFO's, MIS Mgmt., Attorneys

Industries: Generalist, Construction, Plastics, Rubber, Invest. Banking, HR Services, Publishing, Aerospace, Packaging

Professional Associations: IACPR

Networks: I-I-C Partners Executive Search Worldwide

Egon Zehnder Int'l Inc

350 Park Ave Fl 8
New York, NY 10022
(212) 519-6000
Fax: (212) 519-6060
Web: www.zehnder.com

Description: We specialize in recruiting exceptional senior executives. We are known for quality, team - work and long-term relationships Professional management consulting in areas of search, management appraisals, and board appointments.

Key Contact - Specialty:
Mr. A. Daniel Meiland, Chairman/CEO
Mr. Russell E. Boyle
Ms. Maureen Brille
Ms. Celeste Rodgers
Mr. Jean-Pierre van der Spuy
Mr. Robert Baird
Ms. Barbara Park
Mr. Robert Sloan
Mr. Carter L. Burgess, Jr.
Mr. Henrik Aagaard
Ms. Kimberley Van Der Zon
Ms. Eva Leighton
Mr. Christian Robertson
Mr. Marc P. Schappell, Office Manager
Ms. Juliana A. Zinger
Mr. Neil Hindle
Mr. Justus J. O'Brien - *Consumer goods, retail*
Mr. Alan D. Hilliker - *Financial services*

Salary minimum: $150,000

Functions: Generalist, General Mgmt., Directors, Senior Mgmt.

Industries: Generalist, Energy, Utilities, Mfg., Retail, Finance, Services, Communications, Insurance, Biotech, Healthcare

Branches:
350 S Grand Ave California Plz II
Los Angeles, CA 90071
(213) 337-1500
Fax: (213) 621-8901
Key Contact:
Mr. George C. Fifield
Ms. Debbie Shon

1290 Page Mill Rd
Palo Alto, CA 94304-1122
(650) 847-3000
Fax: (650) 847-3050
Key Contact:
Mr. S. Ross Brown
Mr. Jon F. Carter
Ms. Lisa Pieper
Mr. Reynold H. Lewke
Ms. Martha Josephson
Mr. David Majtlis

100 Spear St Ste 920
San Francisco, CA 94105
(415) 228-5200
Fax: (415) 904-7801
Key Contact:
Mr. Jon Carter
Ms. Judy Gilbert
Ms. Jennifer McElrath

501 Brickell Key Dr Ste 300
Miami, FL 33131
(305) 329-4600
Fax: (305) 358-4728
Key Contact:
Ms. Angel Gallinal
Mr. Gabriel Sanchez-Zinny
Mr. German Herrera
Ms. Lauren Smith
Mr. Ronald Tracy

3475 Piedmont Rd Ste 1900
Atlanta, GA 30305
(404) 836-2800
Fax: (404) 876-4578
Key Contact:
Mr. Joel M. Koblentz
Mr. Jonathan Stroup
Ms. Mary Buckle
Mr. Graham Galloway
Mr. Lee Esler
Ms. Laura Lee Gentry
Mr. John Takerer
Mr. Gregory Hiebert
Mr. Scott Walker

Mr. Andrew Dietz
Mr. David Lange

30 S Wacker Dr Ste 3400
Chicago, IL 60606
(312) 260-8800
Fax: (312) 782-2846
Key Contact:
Mr. Kai Lindholst - *Life sciences*
Mr. David Kidd
Ms. Lori von Kapff
Mr. Gregory Jones
Ms. Lynne Boehringer
Mr. Jeff Dodson
Mr. H. Ray Bryant
Mr. Ronald O. Tracy
Mr. Kenneth W. Taylor, Managing Partner
Mr. Louis Kacyn
Ms. Karen Latham
Mr. Keith Meyer
Mr. Karl Alleman
Mr. Brian Stading
Mr. Anthony Will

75 Park Plz Fl 4
Boston, MA 02116
(617) 535-3500
Fax: (617) 457-4949
Key Contact:
Mr. George L. Davis, Jr.
Mr. Gilbert Forest
Ms. Jennifer Buras
Ms. Mary Feely
Mr. Josko Silobrcic

13455 Noel Rd Ste 1400
Galleria Twr 2
Dallas, TX 75240
(972) 728-5910
Fax: (972) 728-5915
Key Contact:
Mr. Brian Reinken
Chris Patrick
Mr. Steven Rivard
Ms. Carol Singleton-Slade

181 Bay St Ste 2900
BCE PI
Toronto, ON M5J 2T3
Canada
(416) 364-0222
Fax: (416) 364-0955
Web: www.egon.org/toronto.html
Key Contact:
Ms. Jan J. Stewart, Office Manager
Mr. David P. Harris
Mr. Jon N. G. Martin
Ms. Pamela A. Warren
Ms. Anne Marie Turnball
Mr. Kenneth Purdy
Mr. Rashid Wasti

1 Pl Ville-Marie Ste 3310 Fl 33
Montreal, QC H3B 3N2
Canada
(514) 876-4249
Fax: (514) 866-0853
Key Contact:
Mr. Pierre Payette
Mr. J. Robert Swidler, Managing Partner
Mr. Andre LeComte

Edificio Torre Optima
Paseo de las Palmas No 405 Desp 703
Mexico City, DF 11000
Mexico
52 5 540 7635
Fax: 52 5 520 9108
Key Contact:
Mr. Dario Pastrana, Managing Partner
Mr. Jose Sanchez Padilla
Mr. Antonio Puron
Mr. Ricardo Weihmann

Zingaro & Company

21936 Briarcliff Dr
Briarcliff, TX 78669-2012
(512) 327-7277
Fax: (512) 327-1774
Email: search@zingaro.com
Web: www.zingaro.com

Description: An executive search firm specializing
in the retained search and selection of senior
management for the healthcare industry, including:
pharmaceuticals, devices, diagnostics,
venture/biotechnology, and pharmaceutical services.

Key Contact - Specialty:
Dr. Ronald J Zingaro, Ph.D., President -
  *Pharmaceutical, pharmaceutical services,
  diagnostics, biotechnology, medical devices*
Ms. Mary H Johnson, Vice President -
  *Pharmaceutical, pharmaceutical services,
  diagnostics, biotechnology, medical devices*

Salary minimum: $100,000

Functions: General Mgmt., Mfg., Healthcare, Sales
& Mktg., Finance, IT, R&D, Engineering,
Specialized Svcs., Int'l.

Industries: Drugs Mfg., Medical Devices, Pharm
Svcs., Biotech, Healthcare

Professional Associations: AAAS, ACRP, DIA,
RAPS

Michael D Zinn & Associates Inc

601 Ewing St Ste C-8
Princeton, NJ 08540
(609) 921-8755
Email: newresumesonly@zinnassociates.com
Web: www.zinnassociates.com

Description: We are a retainer based search firm,
distinguished by our strong commitment to client
service.

Key Contact - Specialty:
Mr. Michael D. Zinn, President - *Financial
  services, general management, technology,
  information systems, pharmaceuticals*

Salary minimum: $90,000

Functions: Generalist

Industries: Chemicals, Drugs Mfg., Medical
Devices, Banking, Invest. Banking, Brokers,
Venture Cap., Accounting, Mgmt. Consulting,
Telecoms

Branches:
1120 Ave of the Americas Fl 4
New York, NY 10036
(212) 391-0070
Email: mdzsec@zinnassociates.com
Key Contact:
Mr. Michael D. Zinn, President

Zurick, Davis & Company Inc

10 Tower Office Park Ste 401
Woburn, MA 01801-2120
(781) 938-1975
Fax: (781) 938-0599
Email: jeffzegas@zurickdavis.com
Web: www.zurickdavis.com

Description: Nationwide practice serving healthcare
clients including integrated networks,
teaching/community hospitals, medical groups,
insurance companies, service companies, PHOs,
MSOs, rehab/nursing homes, subacute, home health,
assisted living, managed care companies, academic
medical centers.

Key Contact - Specialty:
Mr. Jeffrey M. Zegas, Managing Principal -
  Healthcare
Mr. Tom Sager, Principal - *Healthcare*
Ms. Myranne Janoff, Principal - *Healthcare*

Salary minimum: $75,000

Functions: Generalist, Healthcare

Industries: Generalist, Healthcare

Branches:
6890 Sunrise Dr 120-133
Tucson, AZ 85750
(520) 577-9800
Fax: (520) 577-4555
Email: peterdavis@zurickdavis.com
Key Contact - Specialty:
Mr. Peter Davis, Managing Principal -
  Construction, real estate, construction products

ZweigWhite (sm)

1 Apple Hill
PO Box 8325
Natick, MA 01760-2085
(508) 651-1559
Fax: (508) 653-6522
Email: jkreiss@zweigwhite.com
Web: www.zweigwhite.com

Description: Executive search consultants for the
design and construction industries.

Key Contact - Specialty:
Mr. John P. Kreiss, Principal - *Design &
  construction*

Salary minimum: $75,000

Functions: Generalist, Architects

Industries: Construction

Branches:
1212 Broadway Ste 1100
Oakland, CA 94612
(510) 451-9400
Fax: (510) 451-9411
Email: jkreiss@zweigwhite.com
Key Contact - Specialty:
Ms. Kathryn Sprankle, Associate - *Architecture,
  engineering, environmental consulting*

1010 Wisconsin Ave NW Ste 350
Washington, DC 20007
(202) 965-3390
Fax: (202) 965-3394
Email: jkreiss@zweigwhite.com
Key Contact:
Mr. Ray Kogan, Associate

2970 Peachtree Rd Ste 875
Atlanta, GA 30305
(404) 233-3829
Fax: (404) 233-9479
Email: jkreiss@zweigwhite.com
Key Contact:
Mr. Mike Kemether, Associate

8500 College Blvd
Overland Park, KS 66210
(913) 338-7132
Fax: (913) 451-1895
Email: jkreiss@zweigwhite.com
Key Contact:
Mr. Jerry Novacek, Associate

400 Old Hwy 183 Ste AZ
Cedar Park, TX 78613
(512) 342-8009
Fax: (512) 342-0039
Email: jkreiss@zweigwhite.com
Key Contact:
Mr. Mike Rinken, Associate

Zwell Int'l

300 S Wacker Dr Ste 650
Chicago, IL 60606
(312) 551-0404
Fax: (312) 551-0574
Email: info@zwell.com
Web: www.zwell.com

Description: Professional and executive recruiting
with a special emphasis on core competency
assessment.

Key Contact:
Dr. Michael Zwell, President/CEO

Salary minimum: $80,000

Functions: Generalist, Directors, Senior Mgmt.,
Middle Mgmt., Plant Mgmt., CFO's, MIS Mgmt.,
Int'l.

Industries: Generalist, Mfg., Motor Vehicles,
Retail, Finance, Accounting, Hospitality

Professional Associations: HRMAC, SHRM

Branches:
35 E Wacker Dr Ste 500
Chicago, IL 60601
(312) 551-0404
Fax: (312) 551-0574
Email: info@zwell.com
Key Contact - Specialty:
Mr. James Lubawski, President - *Healthcare,
biotech, pharmaceutical, technology transfer*

Contingency Recruiting Firms, A to Z

Agencies and other firms in executive recruiting operating all or part of the time on a fee-paid basis payable on placement. Percentages of retainer and contingency work vary; check with individual firms.

1 for hire
8834 Prichett St
Houston, TX 77096-2628
(713) 666-1001
Fax: (713) 666-9993
Email: hire@1forhire.com

Description: We recruit nationwide for high-technology start-up and mature OEMs, who are seeking tomorrow's talent today. These firms offer challenging careers and will empower your net worth. For these client companies, we find talent faster!

Key Contact - Specialty:
Mr. Howard Frankel, Managing Partner - *Engineering managers (software, hardware)*
Ms. Marcia Frankel, Partner - *Engineers (software, hardware)*

Salary minimum: $50,000

Functions: IT

Industries: Mfg., Computer Equip., Test, Measure Equip., Mgmt. Consulting, Telecoms, Software

Professional Associations: IEEE

Networks: Top Echelon Network

1st American Health Staff
220 Ridgeway LN
Millington, TN 38053
(901) 837-3510
Fax: (901) 837-1589
Email: richard@firstamericanhealthstaff.com
Web: www.firstamericanhealthstaff.com

Description: It is our goal at 1st American Health Staff to provide our clients with "tomorrow's healthcare leaders...today." We focus on permanent placement for medical and pharmaceutical sales professionals.

Key Contact - Specialty:
Mr. Richard Conner, Director/Owner - *Medical recruiting*

Networks: Top Echelon Network

The 500 Staffing Services Inc
465 Morden Rd Fl 2
Oakville, ON L6K 3W6
Canada
(905) 845-0045
Fax: (905) 845-2100
Email: fretz@the500.com
Web: www.the500.com

Description: Our Executive Search division offers Canada-wide professional and management search capabilities within the following industry sectors: information technology/ telecommunication, automotive manufacturing and pharmaceutical/biotechnology.

Key Contact - Specialty:
Mr. William Fretz, Director - Executive Search - *Generalist*

Salary minimum: $75,000

Functions: General Mgmt., Middle Mgmt., Mfg., Product Dev., Production, Automation, Plant Mgmt., Sales & Mktg.

Industries: Drugs Mfg., Medical Devices, Motor Vehicles, Telephony, Wireless, ERP SW, Mfg. SW, Biotech

Professional Associations: ACSESS

Networks: First Interview Network (FIN)

Branches:
1940 Oxford St E Unit 7
London, ON N5V 4L8
Canada
(519) 457-0400
Fax: (519) 457-3419
Email: johnson@the500.com

Key Contact - Specialty:
Mr. Mike Johnson - *Automotive manufacturing, information technology, technology*

275 Slater St Ste 203
Ottawa, ON K1P 6L2
Canada
(613) 237-2888
Fax: (613) 237-2070
Email: scanlon@the500.com
Key Contact - Specialty:
Ms. Carol-Anne Scanlon, Director - *Generalist*

615 ouest, boul Rene-Levesque, bureau 600
Montreal, QC H3B 1P6
Canada
(514) 861-8373
Fax: (514) 866-6180
Email: lavoie@the500.com
Key Contact - Specialty:
Mr. Gille Lavoie, Director - *Generalist*

7 Degrees
PO Box 482
Edmonds, WA 98020
(425) 697-5167
Fax: (425) 775-5882
Email: nwrecruiting@home.com
Web: www.7-degrees.com

Description: Our firm specializes in placing professionals in telecommunications wireless, IT, and software development. We recruit nationwide

Key Contact:
Ms. Lori Barry, Principal

Salary minimum: $45,000

Functions: Directors, Senior Mgmt., Middle Mgmt., Product Dev., Sales & Mktg., Mktg. Mgmt., R&D, Engineering, Architects

Industries: Drugs Mfg., Machine, Appliance, Computer Equip., Consumer Elect., Test, Measure Equip., Electronic, Elec. Components, Venture Cap., E-commerce, IT Implementation, PSA/ASP, Communications, Software, Biotech

Professional Associations: ACA, ASTD, FWE, MITEF, MITVT, SHRM, WSA, WSA

Networks: Computer Search

A C Personnel Services Inc
2400 S Mac Arthur Ste 217
PO Box 271052
Oklahoma City, OK 73137
(405) 728-3503
Fax: (405) 681-7070
Email: acemp777@aol.com

Description: Leaders in professional placements. Listed in the National Registry of Who's Who. This edition is registered in the Library of Congress in Washington, D.C.

Key Contact - Specialty:
Ms. Delores Lantz, President - *Information technology, environmental services, hospitals, schools, commercial*

Functions: Generalist, Direct Mktg., MIS Mgmt., Systems Analysis, Systems Dev., Systems Implem., Systems Support, DB Admin.

Industries: Generalist, Food, Bev., Tobacco, Computer Equip., Hospitality, Media, Telecoms, Environmental Svcs.

A D & Associates Executive Search Inc
5589 Woodsong Dr Ste 100
Atlanta, GA 30338-2933
(770) 393-0021
Fax: (770) 393-9060
Email: hawks@mindspring.com

Description: Finding the best! Generalist firm that values human importance and is committed to

excellence. Search practice covers a broad functional and industry base with typical assignments being in telecommunications, information technology, financial services and human resource management. Creative approach leads to getting the right people in the right jobs in a timely and economical manner... strong client representation.

Key Contact - Specialty:
Mr. A. Dwight Hawksworth, President - *Telecommunications, high technology*

Salary minimum: $50,000

Functions: Generalist, Senior Mgmt., Middle Mgmt., Sales & Mktg., HR Mgmt., Finance, IT, Engineering

Industries: Generalist, Finance, Banking, Accounting, Mgmt. Consulting, HR Services, Communications, Telecoms, Aerospace, Software, Accounting SW, Marketing SW

Professional Associations: GAPS, SHRM

Branches:
PO Box 88005
Dunwoody, GA 30356-8005
(770) 393-0021
Fax: (770) 393-9060
Email: hawks@mindspring.com
Key Contact:
Ms. Jane M. Hawksworth, Corporate Secretary

A First Resource
3800 Heathrow Dr
Winston-Salem, NC 27127
(336) 784-5898
Fax: (336) 784-6702
Email: siburt@a1stresource.com

Description: Providing excellence in candidate selection to those companies who expect no less. Specializing in manufacturing management, engineering, safety, etc.

Key Contact - Specialty:
Ms. Karen L. Siburt, CPC, President - *Manufacturing, engineering, textiles, apparel*

Salary minimum: $30,000

Functions: Generalist

Industries: Mfg., Textiles, Apparel, Lumber, Furniture, Paper, Drugs Mfg., Medical Devices, Plastics, Rubber, Metal Products, Misc. Mfg., Accounting

A J & Associates
204 37th Ave N Ste 120
St. Petersburg, FL 33704
(727) 551-0013
Email: ajnassoc@aol.com
Web: www.cpgsearch.com

Description: Expertise in placing sales, trade marketing, category management, space management, marketing research and consumer marketing professionals ONLY in the consumer packaged goods industry.

Key Contact - Specialty:
Mr. Joe Walsh, Managing Partner - *Category management, trade marketing, sales*
Mr. Andrew Rodriguez, Managing Partner - *Consumer marketing*

Salary minimum: $50,000

Functions: Sales & Mktg.

Industries: Food, Bev., Tobacco, Soap, Perf., Cosmtcs., Consumer Elect.

A Permanent Success Nat'l Career/Search Partners

12658 Washington Blvd Ste 104
Los Angeles, CA 90066
(310) 305-7376
Fax: (310) 306-2929
Email: aps@apscareersearch.com
Web: www.apscareersearch.com

Description: Our firm was founded by the author of "Headhunters Revealed! Career Secrets for Choosing and Using Professional Recruiters." Please visit the website www.HeadHuntersRevealed.com. APS recruits in our specialties locally and nationally. We are affiliated with 700 executive search firms, which allows us to source and place candidates throughout the US and the world.

Key Contact - Specialty:
Mr. Darrell W. Gurney, CPC, Owner - *Sales & marketing, accounting & finance, human resources, MIS, computer professionals*

Functions: Generalist, Middle Mgmt., Mfg., Sales & Mktg., HR Mgmt., Finance, IT

Industries: Generalist, Mfg., Finance, Services, Real Estate, Software

Professional Associations: CSP, FIN, NAPS, RON

Networks: First Interview Network (FIN)

A-K-A (Anita Kaufmann Associates)

729 7th Ave Fl 16
New York, NY 10019
(212) 581-8166
Fax: (212) 581-8173
Email: info@akalegalsearch.com
Web: www.akalegalsearch.com

Description: We specialize in the placement of attorneys in legal, quasilegal and nonlegal positions with corporations, both domestically and internationally. Industry expertise includes financial services (investment banks, commercial banks, hedge funds), management consulting, fashion, pharmaceutical and consumer products companies.

Key Contact - Specialty:
Ms. Anita D. Kaufmann, Esq., President - *Lawyers, compliance professionals*

Functions: Generalist, Legal, Attorneys

Industries: Generalist, Legal

A-S-K Associates Inc

2463 Hamilton Mill Pkwy Ste 280-210
Dacula, GA 30019
(678) 546-1546
Fax: (678) 546-8100
Email: find@askai.com

Description: We specialize in manufacturing, engineering, quality, regulatory, scientific and other technical disciplines within the pharmaceutical and medical device industries.

Key Contact - Specialty:
Mr. Gary Lowy, CPC, President - *Pharmaceutical, medical device industries*

Functions: Mfg., Product Dev., Production, Automation, Plant Mgmt., Quality, Packaging, R&D, Engineering

Industries: Drugs Mfg., Medical Devices

Professional Associations: ASQ, GAPS, ISPE, NAPS

Networks: National Personnel Assoc (NPA)

Aapex Consulting & Recruiting Corp

5022 Kinglet
Houston, TX 77035
(713) 283-8695
Fax: (530) 686-9847

Email: info@aapex1.com
Web: www.aapex1.com

Description: Our firm targets and recruits top level executives in three main areas, and they are: Hispanic, bicultural executives that are fluent in Spanish, telecommunications executives, and information technology executives. We work with sales, management, engineering, and operations personnel. Our main focus is to provide a vehicle where top talent and the companies that are in need of this talent can meet and grow "win, win" employee and employer relationships.

Key Contact - Specialty:
Mr. Stan McCann, President - *Telecommunications, hispanic executives*
Ms. Viridiana McCann, Vice President of Operations - *Hispanic executives*

Salary minimum: $50,000

Functions: Generalist

Industries: Computer Equip., Communications, Software, Development SW, ERP SW, Mfg. SW, Networking, Comm. SW

Networks: Top Echelon Network

Aaron Consulting Inc

PO Box 4757
St. Louis, MO 63108
(314) 367-2627
Fax: (314) 367-2919
Email: aaron@aaronlaw.com
Web: www.aaronlaw.com

Description: Our firm exclusively represents, attorney employers and candidates worldwide. 80-100% of our placements have been with corporate law departments. Our opportunities include: Fortune 100 to small companies and general counsel to staff attorney positions.

Key Contact - Specialty:
Mr. Aaron Williams, CPC, President - *Attorneys*

Salary minimum: $85,000

Functions: Legal

Industries: Generalist

Professional Associations: MAPS, NAPS

ABA Staffing Inc

690 Market St Ste 800
San Francisco, CA 94104
(415) 434-4222
(650) 349-9200
Fax: (415) 434-3958
Email: info@abastaff.com
Web: www.abastaff.com

Description: Our firm recruits talent for organizations in the San Francisco Bay Area. Our clients employ workers in a wide range of disciplines in law firms, corporate legal departments, and administration. Visit us at our San Francisco or Peninsula office locations or on the web.

Key Contact:
Mr. Valli Farmaian, President
Ms. Mandy Farmaian, CSP, Vice President

Functions: Admin. Svcs., Legal, HR Mgmt., Paralegals

Industries: Generalist

Branches:
551 Foster City Blvd Ste D
Foster City, CA 94404
(650) 349-9200
Fax: (650) 349-9721
Email: info@abastaff.com
Key Contact:
Mr. Valli F. Farmaian, President
Ms. Mandy Farmaian, CPC, Vice President - *Business development*

Ms. Jeanne Boes, Operations Manager

Abacus Group LLC

225 W 34th St Ste 709
New York, NY 10122
(212) 812-8444
Fax: (212) 812-8448
Email: info@abacusnyc.com
Web: www.abacusnyc.com

Description: We are specialists in the permanent placement of accounting & finance, accounting support, and office support personnel. Our industries include, but are not limited to: brokerage, banking, media, entertainment, consumer products, real estate, insurance, and public accounting.

Key Contact - Specialty:
Mr. Brian Bereck, Principal - *Accounting, finance*
Mr. Len Frankel, CPA, Principal - *Accounting, finance*
Mr. Bart O'Rourke, ACA, Principal - *Accounting, finance*

Salary minimum: $30,000

Functions: Middle Mgmt., Admin. Svcs., Finance, CFO's, Budgeting, Credit, Taxes

Industries: Generalist, Construction, Mfg., Transportation, Finance, Services, Media, Communications, Insurance, Real Estate, Software, Healthcare

Glen Abbey Executive Search Inc

1155 N Service Rd W Ste11
Oakville, ON L6M 3E3
Canada
(905) 847-0560
Fax: (905) 847-9592
Email: art@execuprolink.com
Web: www.execuprolink.com

Description: We provide personalized and comprehensive search services across all industries with a primary focus on technical sales and marketing positions from entry level to senior management. With an impressive track record of success in identifying only the very best and suitable candidates, we will never compromise our extensive screening and selection process.

Key Contact:
Mr. Arthur Rivard, CMC

Salary minimum: $50,000

Functions: Generalist, Sales & Mktg.

Industries: Generalist, Construction, Food, Bev., Tobacco, Paints, Petro. Products, Machine, Appliance, Consumer Elect., Wholesale, Aerospace, Packaging

Ryan Abbott Search Associates Inc

250 W Main St
Branford, CT 06405
(203) 488-7245
Fax: (203) 481-3724
Email: mcgetric@mail2.nai.net
Web: www.ryanabbott.com

Description: We specialize in recruiting for financial services and pharmaceutical clients.

Key Contact:
Mr. Eugene McGetrick

Salary minimum: $50,000

Cathy Abelson Legal Search

1700 Market St Ste 2130
Philadelphia, PA 19103
(215) 561-3010
Fax: (215) 561-3001
Email: info@abelsonlegalsearch.com
Web: www.abelsonlegalsearch.com

Description: An established company whose skilled professional recruiters identify and place experienced attorneys with firms and corporations primarily in the Philadelphia area, Delaware and New Jersey, and also throughout the United States and several foreign countries.

Key Contact:
Ms. Cathy B. Abelson, President - *Law*
Ms. Sandra G. Mannix, Consultant - *Law*
Ms. Elizabeth F. Shapiro, Principal
Ms. Daniella Drapkin, Attorney Search Consultant
Mrs. Vicki Johnson, Consultant

Functions: Legal, Taxes, M&A, Attorneys

Industries: Generalist, Legal

Professional Associations: NALSC

Abraham & London Ltd
7 Old Sherman Tpke Ste 209
Danbury, CT 06810
(203) 730-4000
Fax: (203) 798-1784
Email: stu@abrahamlondon.com
Web: www.abrahamlondon.com

Description: Middle management through executive-level appointments nationwide with emphasis in staffing sales, marketing, and technical support professionals. Specializing in the converging telecommunications, computer and related hi-tech industries.

Key Contact - Specialty:
Mr. Stuart R. Laub, President - *Telecommunications*

Salary minimum: $45,000

Functions: Sales & Mktg., Mktg. Mgmt., Sales Mgmt., Engineering

Industries: Computer Equip., Equip Svcs., Advertising, New Media, Telecoms, Software

Professional Associations: CAPS, NAPS

Networks: First Interview Network (FIN)

B J Abrams & Associates Inc
550 Frontage Rd 3600
Northfield, IL 60093
(847) 446-2966
Fax: (847) 446-2973
Email: babrams@bjabrams.com

Description: Can handle searches in manufacturing, front door to back, healthcare searches also active. Very active in marketing, communications industry with human resources & financial also a strong area of expertise. But a generalist firm, a contingency firm that functions like a retainer firm. Retainer services also offered.

Key Contact:
Mr. Burton J. Abrams, President - *Generalist, human resources, manufacturing, sales, finance & accounting*
Ms. Carolyn Potter, Sr Associate

Salary minimum: $50,000

Functions: Generalist, Mfg., Materials, Healthcare, Sales & Mktg., HR Mgmt., Finance

Industries: Generalist, Mfg., Media, Healthcare

Professional Associations: CCA, NISHRM, SHRM

Abraxas Technologies Inc
450 N Brand Blvd Ste 410
Glendale, CA 91203
(818) 502-9100
Fax: (818) 502-3311
Email: losangeles@abraxas.com
Web: www.abraxas.com

Description: Broad ranging consulting and placement company covering all areas of IT recruiting.

Key Contact - Specialty:
Mr. John Cosgrave - *Telecom, SAP, siebel*

Functions: Generalist, MIS Mgmt., Systems Analysis, Systems Dev., Systems Implem., Systems Support

Industries: Generalist, Telecoms, Software

Branches:
100 Alexandria Pl Ste 8
Oviendo, FL 32765
(407) 359-0020
Fax: (407) 359-9922
Email: orlando@abraxas.com

ACC Consultants Inc
4848 Tramway Rdg NE 230
Albuquerque, NM 87111
(800) 856-6528
(505) 323-1300
Fax: (505) 323-1400
Email: info@accdentemps.com
Web: www.accdentemps.com

Description: Contingent and retained searches in dental field throughout the U.S. Administration, management and clinical dental functions covered temporary and permanent placement of dentists, dental hygienists, dental assistants and front office management and staff.

Key Contact - Specialty:
Mr. Jerry Berger, President - *Dental, dental administration, dental management*
Ms. Virginia Seebinger - *Dental*
Mr. Larry Seebinger - *Dental*
Ms. Gloria Chavez - *Dental*
Ms. Lisa Esparza, General Manager - *Dental*

Functions: Generalist, Allied Health, Health Admin.

Industries: Generalist, Healthcare

Accelerated Data Decision Inc
27 Main St
Sparta, NJ 07871
(973) 726-5060
Fax: (973) 726-5929
Email: add@mindspring.com
Web: www.addsearch.com

Description: A specialized firm working with owners and high-level managers. Searches done on a strictly confidential basis usually recruiting from the competitor.

Key Contact - Specialty:
Mr. Walter M. Sullivan, President
Ms. Linda Price, Director of Research
Mr. Russell M. Sullivan, BS, Search Consultant - *IT, marketing, sales*

Salary minimum: $25,000

Functions: Generalist

Industries: Mfg., Services, Accounting, HR Services, Government, Defense, Aerospace, Software

Professional Associations: NJAPS

Accent On Achievement Inc
3190 Rochester Rd Dept K
Troy, MI 48083
(248) 528-1390
Fax: (248) 528-9335
Email: kennedy@accountingjobs.net
Web: www.accountingjobs.net

Description: We focus on candidate's goals/objectives. Owner is a former Deloitte & Touche CPA. Offer packages range from $45,000 to $110,000+. Recruiting for staff to director-levels in accounting, SEC reporting and audit.

Key Contact - Specialty:
Ms. Charlene N. Brown, CPA, President - *Accounting, finance, auditors, CPA's*

Salary minimum: $35,000

Functions: Finance

Industries: Energy, Utilities, Construction, Mfg., Wholesale, Retail, Finance, Services, New Media, Real Estate, Healthcare

Professional Associations: IIA, MACPA, MAPS

Networks: Top Echelon Network

Access Associates Inc
1107 Kenilworth Dr Ste 307
Towson, MD 21204
(410) 821-7190
Fax: (410) 821-7823
Email: info@access-associates.com
Web: www.access-associates.com

Description: We conduct thorough market research to find the best candidates with strong technical skills or leadership profiles and managerial experience. All assignments are managed by principals of the firm with assistance from our market research team.

Key Contact - Specialty:
Mr. Charles N. Curlett, President - *Human resources, IT, scientific, engineering, sales, marketing*

Salary minimum: $50,000

Functions: Generalist, Product Dev., Automation, Benefits, Systems Analysis, Systems Dev., Engineering

Industries: Generalist, Medical Devices, Motor Vehicles, HR Services, Aerospace, Software

Professional Associations: MAPRC

Access Data Personnel Inc
649 2nd St
Manchester, NH 03102
(603) 641-6300
Fax: (603) 641-8987
Email: accessdata@aol.com
Web: www.accessdatapersonnel.com

Description: Our firm has fifteen years of experience working exclusively in the information technology recruiting field. Our areas of specialization include: systems and application programming, database, network and communications, operations and management. We work on a regional and national basis.

Key Contact - Specialty:
Mr. Glen A. Axne, President - *Information services*

Salary minimum: $20,000

Functions: IT

Industries: Generalist

Access Partners
1625 17th St Fl 3
Denver, CO 80202
(303) 321-7707
Email: ann@yourheadhunter.com
Web: www.yourheadhunter.com

Description: We provide executive search for senior level management consultants and process improvement professionals.

Key Contact - Specialty:
Mr. Mark Spoor, Partner
Ms. Ann Spoor, Partner - *Director, VP*

Salary minimum: $100,000

Functions: Directors, Mfg., IT, Mgmt. Consultants

Industries: Mgmt. Consulting

Professional Associations: SHRM

Access Staffing Inc
10100 W Sample Rd Ste 302
Coral Springs, FL 33065
(954) 345-0210
Fax: (954) 345-9177
Email: accessit@aol.com

Description: Our firm specializes in search,
recruitment, and placement for the information
technology field, primarily for positions in Florida.
All of our searches are personally coordinated by
company president Jim Scimone, who has 20 years
of IT recruiting experience, plus 10 years of
programming, marketing of computer systems, and
management experience.

Key Contact - Specialty:
Mr. James J. Scimone, President - *Information
technology*

Functions: IT, MIS Mgmt., Systems Analysis,
Systems Dev., Systems Implem., Systems
Support, Network Admin., DB Admin.

Industries: Generalist

Access Systems
101 Gibraltar Dr Ste 2F
Morris Plains, NJ 07950
(973) 984-7960
Fax: (973) 984-7963
Email: jpalzer@worldnet.att.net

Description: Twenty years' successful recruiting
experience, 85%+ of candidates are interviewed in
person. High-level of candidates are referrals.
Industries served are information technology
products and services, data and telecommunications.

Key Contact - Specialty:
Ms. Joanne Palzer, President - *Information
technology sales*

Salary minimum: $50,000

Functions: Sales & Mktg., Sales Mgmt.

Industries: Computer Equip., E-commerce, IT
Implementation, Telecoms, Telephony, Wireless,
Network Infrastructure, Software, Accounting
SW, Database SW, Doc. Mgmt., Production SW

Access/Resources Inc
PO Box 194
Osterville, MA 02655-0194
(508) 428-4637
Email: arirecruit@aol.com

Description: Middle and upper-management
recruiting for industrial clients throughout the
Midwest and Northeast with special capabilities in
financial and general management assignments.

Key Contact - Specialty:
Mr. Peter V. Vangel, CPA, Principal - *Financial,
general management*

Salary minimum: $50,000

Functions: Generalist, Purchasing, Mkt. Research,
Benefits, CFO's, Budgeting, Cash Mgmt., M&A

Industries: Generalist, Mfg., Medical Devices,
Plastics, Rubber, Machine, Appliance, Motor
Vehicles, Computer Equip., Accounting

Professional Associations: AICPA, IMA, MACPA

Branches:
37450 Schoolcraft Rd Ste 150
Livonia, MI 48150
(734) 462-3214
Email: arirecruit@aol.com
Key Contact - Specialty:
Ms. Julie Pawlusiak, Associate - *Financial, general
management*

Account Ability Now
333 Bridge St NW
1210 Bridgewater Pl
Grand Rapids, MI 49504
(616) 235-1149
Fax: (616) 235-1148
Email: aan@accountability.com
Web: www.accountability.com

Description: Specialized in superior accounting and
information systems personnel for the West
Michigan marketplace.

Key Contact - Specialty:
Ms. Julie Schalk, President - *Accounting,
information systems*

Salary minimum: $20,000

Functions: Finance, MIS Mgmt., Systems Analysis,
Systems Dev., Systems Implem., Systems
Support, Network Admin.

Industries: Generalist

Professional Associations: AICPA, IMA, ISACA,
MACPA, MAPS, NATSS, NAWBO, SHRM

Accountancies Financial Staffing
(a division of DM Stone Inc)
100 Bush St Ste 650
San Francisco, CA 94104
(415) 433-6900
Fax: (415) 391-5536
Email: mailbox@dmstone.com
Web: www.dmstone.com

Description: We are a CPA-owned and operated
agency for temporary, temp-to-hire and direct hire
placements. Serving clients in a diverse group of
industries, the firm focuses exclusively on
accounting and finance.

Key Contact - Specialty:
Mr. Steve Gallen, Managing Director
Mr. David M. Stone, CPA, President - *Accounting
& finance, direct hire*

Salary minimum: $25,000

Functions: Finance, CFO's, Budgeting, Cash
Mgmt., Credit, Taxes, M&A

Industries: Generalist, Finance, Banking, Invest.
Banking, Brokers, Venture Cap., Misc. Financial

Professional Associations: AICPA, APA, CSCPA,
CSP

Accountant Profile Inc
1700 W Hwy 36 122 Rosedale Twrs
St. Paul, MN 55113
(651) 636-7760
Fax: (651) 636-7728
Email: greathires@accountantprofile.com

Description: Specialized search firm providing
permanent professional level staffing solutions for
the accounting/finance profession. Our consultants
are degreed financial professionals offering an
average of 10 years of experience in the personnel
placement industry. We offer both contingency and
retained search for diversity of customers.

Key Contact - Specialty:
Ms. Suzanne Roberts, CPC, President/Executive
Recruiter - *Accounting/finance*

Salary minimum: $40,000

Functions: Finance

Industries: Generalist

Professional Associations: MAPS

Accountants On Call
(a division of AOC)
Park 80 W Plz II
Garden State Pkwy @I-80 Fl 9
Saddle Brook, NJ 07663
(201) 843-0006
Fax: (201) 712-1033
Email: saddlebrook@aocnet.com
Web: www.aocnet.com

Description: International specialists in the
placement of temporary and permanent accounting,
bookkeeping, data entry, and other financial
personnel.

Key Contact:
Ms. Diane O'Meally, President
Mr. Patrick Lyons, CFO
Mr. Larry Saltzman, Senior Vice President

Functions: Generalist, Finance, IT

Industries: Generalist

Branches:
1201 S Alma School Rd Ste 6750
Mesa, AZ 85210
(480) 644-0500
Fax: (480) 644-9550
Email: mesa@aocnet.com
Key Contact:
Ms. Stacy Boase, Branch Manager

2111 E Highland Ste B-431
Park 1
Phoenix, AZ 85016
(602) 957-1200
Fax: (602) 957-1222
Email: phoenix@aocnet.com
Key Contact:
Ms. Robin Bumgarner, Area Manager

3500 W Olive Ave Ste 550
Burbank, CA 91505
(818) 845-6600
Fax: (818) 845-6330
Email: burbank@aocnet.com
Key Contact:
Mr. William DeMario, Senior Vice President
Ms. Victoria Kaleta, Area Vice President
Ms. Tisha Cuyugan, Branch Manager

17700 Castleton St Ste 558
Puente Hills Business Ctr III
City of Industry, CA 91748
(626) 912-0090
Fax: (626) 912-8292
Email: cityofindustry@aocnet.com
Key Contact:
Ms. Janette Marx, Branch Manager

1289 E Hillsdale Bl Ste 5
Foster City, CA 94404
(650) 574-0710
Fax: (650) 574-0137
Email: fostercity@aocnet.com
Key Contact:
Ms. Tami Ondeck

6 Centerpointe Dr Ste 250
La Palma, CA 90623
(714) 739-1300
Fax: (714) 521-6500
Email: lapalma@aocnet.com
Key Contact:
Ms. Kira Bruno, Area Vice President
Ms. Merry White, Branch Manager

10990 Wilshire Blvd Ste 1400
Los Angeles, CA 90024-3705
(310) 312-3330
Fax: (310) 444-0606
Email: losangeles@aocnet.com
Key Contact:
Ms. Laurie Matthews, VP Sales Training
Ms. Victoria Kaleta, Area Vice President

800 Wilshire Blvd Ste 850
Los Angeles, CA 90017
(213) 689-4606
Fax: (213) 689-5046

Email: losangeles@aocnet.com

4590 McArthur Blvd Ste 350
Newport Beach, CA 92660-2132
(949) 955-0100
Fax: (949) 955-1347
Email: newportbeach@aocnet.com
Key Contact:
Ms. Kathleen Gans, Area Vice President
Ms. Cathy Eldridge, Branch Manager

1 Kaiser Plz Ste 1030
The Ordway Bldg
Oakland, CA 94612
(510) 986-1800
Fax: (510) 986-8760
Email: oakland@aocnet.com
Key Contact:
Mr. Vito LoGrasso, Branch Manager

4141 Inland Empire Blvd Ste 303
Ontario, CA 91764
(909) 466-8880
Fax: (909) 466-5470
Email: toronto@aocnet.com
Key Contact:
Ms. Julie Daignault, Branch Manager

500 Esplande Dr Ste 760
Oxnard, CA 93030
(805) 988-3668
Fax: (805) 988-3628
Email: oxnard@aocnet.com
Key Contact:
Ms. Victoria Kaleta, Area Vice President

285 Hamilton Ave Ste 280
Palo Alto, CA 94301
(650) 328-8400
Fax: (650) 328-8570
Email: paloalto@aocnet.com
Key Contact:
Ms. Lynda Galliano

6140 Stoneridge Mall Rd Ste 360
Pleasanton, CA 94588
(925) 734-8666
Fax: (925) 734-5550
Email: pleasanton@aocnet.com
Key Contact:
Ms. Julia Holian, Branch Manager

1435 River Park Dr Ste 310
Sacramento, CA 95825
(916) 923-5555
Fax: (916) 923-1662
Email: sacramento@aocnet.com
Key Contact:
Mr. Ernesto Uriarto, Branch Manager

4180 La Jolla Village Dr Ste 200
San Diego, CA 92037
(858) 453-0666
Fax: (858) 453-3373
Email: sandiego@aocnet.com
Web: www.aocnet.com
Key Contact:
Ms. Cyndi McDermott, Area Manager

44 Montgomery St Ste 2310
San Francisco, CA 94104
(415) 398-3366
Fax: (415) 398-2618
Email: sanfrancisco@aocnet.com
Key Contact:
Ms. Sara Boyd, Regional Vice President
Ms. Anne Pasquier, Branch Vice President

970 W 190th St Ste 210
Torrance, CA 90502
(310) 527-2777
Fax: (310) 527-0109
Email: torrance@aocnet.com
Key Contact:
Mr. Steve Shapiro, Branch Vice President

2175 N California Blvd Ste 775
Walnut Creek, CA 94596
(925) 937-1000
Fax: (925) 939-3716
Email: walnutcreek@aocnet.com

Key Contact:
Ms. Anne Silveira, Branch Manager

21700 Oxnard St Ste 850
Woodland Hills, CA 91367
(818) 992-7676
Fax: (818) 992-1360
Email: woodlandhills@aocnet.com
Key Contact:
Mr. David Sprinkle

3100 Arapanoe Ste 116
Boulder, CO 80303
(303) 447-2121
Fax: (303) 447-2131
Email: boulder@aocnet.com
Key Contact:
Mr. Randall Truelock, Branch Manager

1099 18th St Ste 2820
Denver, CO 80202
(303) 291-1212
Fax: (303) 291-1055
Email: denver@aocnet.com
Key Contact:
Mr. Monte Merz, Area Vice President
Ms. Kristie Brown, Branch manager

8400 E Prentice Ave Ste 1420
Englewood, CO 80111
(303) 804-5300
Fax: (303) 804-9616
Email: englewood@aocnet.com
Key Contact:
Mr. Monte Merz, Area Vice President

1150 17th ST NW Ste 408
Washington, DC 20036
(202) 452-0002
Fax: (202) 452-0992
Email: washingtondc@aocnet.com
Key Contact:
Ms. Kelly Bergenstock, Branch Manager

5900 N Andrews Ave Ste 627
Ft. Lauderdale, FL 33309
(954) 771-0333
Fax: (954) 492-9699
Email: ftlauderdale@aocnet.com
Key Contact:
Mr. Dave Watson, Area Director
Ms. Sharon Maffei, Branch Manager

2 Alhambra Plz Ste 640
Miami, Fl 33134
(305) 443-9333
Fax: (305) 443-6589
Key Contact:
Ms. Stacy Calderone, Branch Manager

4890 W Kennedy Blvd Ste 810
Tampa, FL 33609
(813) 282-9050
Fax: (813) 282-9130
Email: tampa@aocnet.com
Key Contact:
Ms. Julie Murphy, Branch Manager

2180 Satellite Blvd Ste 320
Duluth/Norcross, GA 30097
(678) 474-9944
Fax: (678) 474-9414
Email: duluth@aocnet.com
Key Contact:
Mr. Mark Gregory, Area Vice President
Mr. Wade Roberts, Branch Manager

200 N LaSalle St Ste 1745 Fl 17
Chicago, IL 60601
(312) 782-7788
Fax: (312) 782-0171
Email: chicago@aocnet.com
Key Contact:
Ms. Bridget O'Connell, Senior Vice President

3400 Dundee Rd Ste 150
Northbrook, IL 60062-2334
(847) 205-0800
Fax: (847) 205-1230
Email: northbrook@aocnet.com

Key Contact:
Ms. Bridget O'Connell, Senior Vice President
Ms. Cheryl Gillespie, Area Vice President
Ms. Colleen Craig, Branch Manager

1 Lincoln Ctr Ste 1108
Oak Brook, IL 60181
(630) 261-1300
Fax: (630) 261-1334
Email: oakbrook@aocnet.com
Key Contact:
Ms. Alison Gentry, Branch Vice President

1750 E Golf Rd Ste 200
Schaumburg, IL 60173
(847) 413-8800
Fax: (847) 413-9066
Email: schaumburg@aocnet.com
Key Contact:
Mr. Carl Barnard, Branch Manager

111 Monument Cir Ste 3510
Bank 1 Ctr/Twr
Indianapolis, IN 46204
(317) 686-0001
Fax: (317) 686-0007
Email: indianapolis@aocnet.com
Key Contact:
Mr. George Lessmeister, Area Vice President
Ms. Crystal Whitacre, Branch Manager

950 Breckenridge Ln Ste 175
The Springs Office Ctr
Louisville, KY 40207
(502) 893-8333
Fax: (502) 893-5599
Email: louisville@aocnet.com
Key Contact:
Ms. Gina Stefanutti, Branch Manager

201 N Charles St Ste 300
Baltimore, MD 21201
(410) 685-5700
Fax: (410) 685-5736
Email: baltimore@aocnet.com
Key Contact:
Mrs. Lisa Witt, Branch Manager

11400 Rockville Pike Ste 109
Rockville, MD 20852
(301) 519-2300
Fax: (301) 519-3637
Email: rockville@aocnet.com
Key Contact:
Mr. John Ryder, Area Manager

121 High St Fl 2
Boston, MA 02110
(617) 345-0440
Fax: (617) 345-0423
Email: boston@aocnet.com
Key Contact:
Ms. Lynn Cogavin, Area Manager

300 Granite St Fl 4 Ste 411
Braintree, MA 02184
(781) 794-5100
Fax: (781) 356-2225
Email: braintree@aocnet.com
Key Contact:
Ms. Lynne Cogavin, Area Manager

161 Worcester Rd Ste 407
Framingham, MA 01701
(508) 872-7800
Fax: (508) 879-9898
Email: framingham@aocnet.com
Key Contact:
Ms. Patricia Couch, Area Vice President
Ms. Ann Hamel, Branch Manager

3840 Peckered Rd Ste 170
Ann Arbor, MI 48108
(734) 434-1900
Fax: (734) 477-9064
Email: annarbor@aocnet.com
Key Contact:
Mr. Scott Manager, Branch Manager

28411 Northwestern Hwy Ste 910
Detroit, MI 48034
(248) 356-0660
Fax: (248) 356-8740
Email: detroit@aocnet.com
Key Contact:
Ms. Lisa Nathanson, Area Director
Ms. Lynn Moyer, Branch Manager

99 Monroe Ste 102
Campau Square Plaza Bldg
Grand Rapids, MI 49503
(616) 454-9090
Fax: (616) 732-5279
Email: grandrapids@aocnet.com
Key Contact:
Mr. Ted Sims, Branch Manager

2301 W Big Beaver Rd Ste 720
Troy, MI 48084
(248) 649-0700
Fax: (248) 649-5110
Email: troy@aocnet.com
Key Contact:
Ms. Lisa Nathanson, Branch Manager
Ms. Erinn O'Connor, Area Director

1600 W 82nd St Ste 130
Bloomington, MN 55431
(952) 884-9900
Fax: (952) 884-2446
Email: bloomington@aocnet.com
Key Contact:
Ms. Betty Abelson, Area Manager

100 S 5th St Ste 420
Minneapolis, MN 55402
(612) 341-9900
Fax: (612) 341-3284
Email: minneapolis@aocnet.com
Key Contact:
Ms. Michele Pitsch, Branch Manager

911 Main St Ste 701
Commerce Twr
Kansas City, MO 64105
(816) 421-7774
Fax: (816) 421-8224
Email: kansascity@aocnet.com
Key Contact:
Mr. Steve Davee, Branch Manager

111 Westport Plz Ste 512
St. Louis, MO 63146
(314) 576-0006
Fax: (314) 576-7345
Key Contact:
Mr. Rich Thompson, Area Vice President
Robin Hoatlin, Branch Manager

515 N 6th St Ste 1340
1 City Ctr
St. Louis, MO 63101
(314) 436-0500
Fax: (314) 436-0833
Email: stlouis@aocnet.com
Key Contact:
Mr. Clark Young, Branch Manager

10805 Sunset Office Dr Ste 208
Sunset Hills, MO 63127
(314) 966-4900
Fax: (314) 966-6663
Email: sunsethills@aocnet.com
Key Contact:
Mr. Stan Carr, Branch Manager

6787 W Tropicana Ave Ste 103
Las Vegas, NV 89103
(702) 284-7112
Fax: (702) 284-7191
Email: lasvegas@aocnet.com
Key Contact:
Ms. Donna Kelly, Licensee

379 Thornall St Fl 10
Edison, NJ 08837
(732) 321-1700
Fax: (732) 494-4386
Email: edison@aocnet.com

Key Contact:
Mr. Ted Fitzgerald, Area Manager

30 Montgomery St Ste 120
Jersey City, NJ 07302
(201) 333-4227
Fax: (201) 333-4248
Email: jerseycity@aoc.net
Key Contact:
Ms. Mary Hutchins, Branch Manager

72 Eagle Rock Ave
Livingston, NJ 07039
(973) 781-0034
Fax: (973) 781-0658
Email: livingston@aocnet.com
Key Contact:
Mr. Rory Sakin, Senior AVP
Mr. Richard Scott, Branch Manager

10000 Lincoln Dr W Ste 1
Marlton, NJ 08053
(856) 596-9200
Fax: (856) 810-8510
Email: marlton@aocnet.com
Key Contact:
Mr. Mark Libes, Licensee

E 80 Rte 4 Ste 230
The Atrium
Paramus, NJ 07652
(201) 843-8882
Fax: (201) 843-8572
Email: paramus@aocnet.com
Key Contact:
Mr. Neil Lebovitits, Senior Vice President
Ms. Donna Mahan, Division Manager

35 Waterview Blvd
Parsippany, NJ 07054
(973) 331-3890
Fax: (973) 331-3891
Email: parsippany@aocnet.com
Key Contact:
Mr. Rory Sakin, Senior Vice President
Mr. Rita Silverstein, Branch Vice President

125 Village Blvd Ste 240
Princeton, NJ 08540
(609) 452-7117
Fax: (609) 987-0681
Email: princeton@aocnet.com
Key Contact:
Ms. Lori Kennedy, Branch Manager

1200 Veterans Memorial Hwy Ste 300 Ste 300
Hauppauge, NY 11788
(631) 273-8552
Fax: (631) 273-8599
Email: hauppauge@aocnet.com
Web: www.aocnet.com

500 N Broadway Ste 237
The Jericho Atrium
Jericho, NY 11753
(516) 935-0050
Fax: (516) 935-1343
Email: jericho@aocnet.com
Key Contact:
Ms. Dawn McGuinness, Area Vice President

14 Wall St Ste 1715
New York, NY 10005
(212) 619-5550
Fax: (212) 619-8265
Email: wallstreet@aocnet.com
Key Contact:
Ms. Stacy Lentz, Branch Manager

535 5th Ave Ste 1200
New York, NY 10017
(212) 953-7400
Fax: (212) 953-8921
Email: newyork@aocnet.com
Key Contact:
Mr. Neil Lebovitz, Senior Vice President
Mr. Jeremy Lichstrahl, Branch Manager

227 W Trade St Ste 1810
The Carillon Bldg
Charlotte, NC 28202
(704) 376-0006
Fax: (704) 376-4787
Email: charlotte@aocnet.com
Web: www.aocnet.com
Key Contact - Specialty:
Ms. Jennifer Stuebbe, Branch Manager -
  Accounting and finance personnel

1801 Stanley Rd Ste 206
Greensboro, NC 27407
(336) 292-3800
Fax: (336) 292-2245
Email: greensboro@aocnet.com
Key Contact:
Mr. Larry Basel, Area Director
Ms. Krista Akins, Branch Manager

150 S Stratford Rd Ste 305
Winston-Salem, NC 27104
(336) 725-5559
Fax: (336) 725-5557
Email: winston-salem@aocnet.com
Key Contact:
Ms. Lynn Foster, Branch Manager

3560 W Market St Ste 120
Akron, OH 44333
(330) 668-0099
Fax: (330) 668-0029
Email: akron@aocnet.com
Key Contact:
Ms. Nancy Ramirez, Branch Manager

1717 E 9th St Ste 975
Cleveland, OH 44114
(216) 696-5440
Fax: (216) 696-6263
Email: clevelanddt@aocnet.com
Key Contact:
Mr. Brad Qua, Area Vice President

700 Ackerman Rd Ste 390
Columbus, OH 43202
(614) 267-7200
Fax: (614) 267-7595
Email: columbus@aocnet.com
Key Contact:
Mr. Russell Sheets, Licensee

4807 Rockside Rd Ste 530
1 Independence Pl
Independence, OH 44131
(216) 328-0888
Fax: (216) 328-1709
Email: cleveland@aocnet.com
Key Contact:
Ms. Michelle Reynolds, Branch Manager

5110 S Yale Ave 412
Tulsa, OK 74135
(918) 481-3332
Fax: (918) 499-2226
Email: tulsa@aocnet.com
Key Contact:
Ms. Jana Rugg, Branch Manager

1260 NW Waterhouse Ave Ste 160
Beaverton, OR 97204
(503) 439-1555
Fax: (503) 533-2385
Email: beaverton@aocnet.com

601 SW 2nd Ave Ste 1620
Portland, OR 97201
(503) 228-0300
Fax: (503) 220-2529
Email: portland@aocnet.com
Key Contact:
Ms. Cathy Presjak, Branch Manager

1150 Allendale Rd Ste 2250
King of Prussia, PA 19406
(610) 337-8500
Fax: (610) 227-7344
Email: kingofprussia@aocnet.com
Key Contact:
Mr. Michael Goldstein, Licensee

437 Grant St Ste 800
The Frick Bldg
Pittsburgh, PA 15219
(412) 391-0900
Fax: (412) 391-8288
Email: pittsburgh@aocnet.com
Key Contact:
Ms. Laura DeRosa, Branch Manager

10 Weybosset St Ste 201
Providence, RI 02903
(401) 277-9944
Fax: (401) 277-0660
Email: providence@aocnet.com
Key Contact:
Mr. Matthew Lightner, Branch Manager

250 Commonwealth Dr Ste 100
Greenville, SC 29615
(864) 987-0123
Fax: (864) 288-3044
Email: greenville@aocnet.com
Key Contact:
Mr. Keith LoCascio, Branch Manager

6075 Poplar Ave Ste 121
Memphis, TN 38119
(901) 761-1416
Fax: (901) 761-5601
Email: memphis@aocnet.com
Key Contact:
Ms. Luanne Hearn, Staffing Consultant -
    Accounting and finance placements
Mr. Buddy Daves, Branch Manager

14131 Midway Rd Ste 100
Addison, TX 75001
(972) 980-4184
Fax: (972) 980-2359
Email: dallasnorth@aocnet.com

8310 Capital of Texas Hwy N Ste 150
Austin, TX 78731
(512) 346-6000
Fax: (512) 346-6683
Email: austin@aocnet.com
Key Contact:
Mr. Dudley Hawkins, Branch Manager

2828 Routh St Ste 690
Quadrangle Bldg
Dallas, TX 75201
(214) 979-9001
Fax: (214) 979-0046

1612 Summit Ave Ste 420
Ft. Worth, TX 76102-3182
(817) 870-1800
Fax: (817) 870-1890
Email: fortworth@aocnet.com

511 E John Carpenter Frwy Ste 160
Irving, TX 75062
(972) 402-0300
Fax: (972) 402-8988
Email: lascolinas-irving@aocnet.com
Key Contact:
Mr. Anthony Caggiano, Area Vice President
Mr. Brandon Humphreys, Branch Manager

170 S Main St Ste 550
Salt Lake City, UT 84101
(801) 328-3338
Fax: (801) 328-3324
Email: saltlakecity@aocnet.com
Key Contact:
Mr. Monte Merz, Area Vice President

1175 Herndon Pkwy
Herndon, VA 20170
(703) 464-4888
Fax: (703) 464-4884
Email: dulles@aocnet.com
Key Contact:
Mr. Darryl Patton, Branch Manager

6800 Paragon Pl Ste 200
Richmond, VA 23230
(804) 288-8883
Fax: (804) 288-5340
Email: richmond@aocnet.com

Key Contact:
Mr. Glenn Dubiel, Branch Manager

8000 Towers Crescent Dr Ste 825
Tysons Corner, VA 22182
(703) 448-7500
Fax: (703) 448-7538
Email: tysonscorner@aocnet.com
Key Contact:
Mr. Michael Parbs, Area Vice President
Ms. Susan Gallagher, Area Manager

600 108th Ave NE Ste 650
Bellevue, WA 98004
(425) 635-0700
Fax: (425) 635-0315
Email: bellevue@aocnet.com
Key Contact:
Ms. Sue Danbom, Branch Manager

601 Union St Ste 2434
2 Union Sq
Seattle, WA 98101
(206) 467-0700
Fax: (206) 467-9986
Email: seattle@aocnet.com
Key Contact:
Mr. David Adams, Area Vice President

1201 Pacific Ave Ste 1450
Tacoma, WA 98402
(253) 838-1111
Fax: (253) 274-9216
Email: tacoma@aocnet.com
Key Contact:
Mr. Anthony Caputo, Branch Manager

3333 N Mayfair Rd Ste 213
Milwaukee, WI 53222
(414) 771-1900
Fax: (414) 771-2586
Email: milwaukee@aocnet.com
Key Contact:
Ms. Dottie Mahnke, Branch Manager

4950 Yonge St Ste 300
North York, ON M2N 6K1
Canada
(416) 483-2121
Fax: (416) 483-9639
Email: northyork@aocnet.com
Key Contact:
Luciana Acquaviva, Branch Manager

20 Eglinton Ave W Ste 1101
Yonge Eglinton Ctr
Toronto, ON M5K 1K2
Canada
(416) 932-1566
Fax: (416) 932-2766
Email: toronto@aocnet.com
Key Contact:
Ms. Katherine Ciccariarella, Area Manager

Accountants On Call

(a division of AOC)
1921 Palomar Oaks Way Ste 314
The Plaza I
Carlsbad, CA 92008
(760) 431-7770
Fax: (760) 431-3709
Email: carlsbad@aocnet.com
Web: www.aocnet.com

Description: Specializing in placement of
accounting professionals.

Key Contact:
Ms. Jeannette Lyons, Branch Manager
Ms. Tina Fox, Staffing Consultant - *Accountants*
Ms. Missie Lauer, Financial Executive Search
    Recruiter

Functions: Generalist, CFO's, Budgeting, Cash
    Mgmt., Credit, Taxes, M&A

Industries: Generalist, Mfg., Finance, Media,
    Software, Biotech

Accountants On Call

(a division of AOC)
1801 Lee Rd Ste 235
Winter Park, FL 32789
(407) 629-2999
Fax: (407) 629-2927
Email: orlando@aocnet.com
Web: www.aocnet.com

Description: Specialized recruiting in accounting
and finance throughout Central Florida.

Key Contact - Specialty:
Mr. Donald F. Phillips, President - *Accounting &
    finance*

Functions: Generalist, CFO's, Budgeting, Cash
    Mgmt., Credit, Taxes, M&A, Risk Mgmt.

Industries: Generalist

Accountants On Call

(a division of AOC)
3424 Peachtree Rd Ste 125
Atlanta, GA 30326
(404) 261-4800
Fax: (404) 233-1853
Email: atlanta@aocnet.com
Web: www.aocnet.com

Description: An international company specializing
in the placement of accounting and financial
professionals on both a temporary and permanent
basis with positions ranging from entry level to
CFO.

Key Contact - Specialty:
Mrs. Sherry Pontious, Branch Vice President -
    Accounting & finance

Professional Associations: IMA, SHRM

Accountants On Call

(a division of AOC)
5565 Centerview Dr Ste 214
Raleigh, NC 27606
(919) 859-5550
Fax: (919) 859-5575
Email: raleigh@aocnet.com
Web: www.aocnet.com

Description: Specialists in direct hire and temporary
placements of accounting and finance professionals.

Key Contact:
Mr. Mark Gregory, CPA, Area Vice President
Ms. Sue Durphy, CPA, Branch Manager -
    Executive recruitment
Ms. Ingrid Sanchez, Division Manager -
    Temporary recruitment
Ms. Julie Clark, Sales Manager

Functions: Finance

Industries: Generalist

Professional Associations: IMA

Accountants On Call

(a division of AOC)
1101 Kermit Dr Ste 600
Nashville, TN 37217
(615) 399-0200
Fax: (615) 399-2285
Email: nashville@aocnet.com
Web: www.aocnet.com

Description: Full-service accounting and finance
placements.

Key Contact - Specialty:
Mr. Milton H. Ellis, President - *Accounting*

Functions: Generalist

Industries: Generalist

Accountants On Call

(a division of AOC/AES Technical Search)
2000 Post Oak Blvd Ste 1970
1 Post Oak Central
Houston, TX 77056
(713) 961-5603
Fax: (713) 961-3256
Email: houston@aocnet.com
Web: www.aocnet.com

Description: We are financial consulting and
recruiting specialists.

Key Contact - Specialty:
Ms. Annette Monks, Area Manager - *Temporary &
   permanent placement of accounting & finance
   personnel*
Mr. Steven Logan, Executive Recruiter -
   *Permanent placement of accounting & finance
   personnel*
Ms. Jody Dennis, Executive Recruiter - *Permanent
   placement of accounting & finance personnel*
Ms. Michele Black, Senior Consultant Support -
   *Temporary placement of accounting & finance
   personnel*

Functions: Finance

Industries: Generalist

Accounting & Computer Personnel

200 Salina Meadows Pkwy Ste 180
Syracuse, NY 13212
(315) 457-8000
Fax: (315) 457-0029
Email: wew@a-c-p.com
Web: www.a-c-p.com

Description: Over thirty years' experience in
recruitment and placement of professionals in:
accounting, financial management, computer
systems, programming and operations, information
systems management, computer hardware/software
sales and banking.

Key Contact:
Mr. William E. Winnewisser, President - *Computer
   (IS), technical & management, accounting &
   financial management, bankers, business
   attorneys*
Ms. Karen A. Salcido, Recruiter

Salary minimum: $20,000

Functions: Generalist

Industries: Finance, Services, Accounting, Software

Professional Associations: ACM, IMA, IPCCNY

Networks: National Personnel Assoc (NPA)

Accounting & Finance Personnel Inc

1702 E Highland Ave Ste 200
Phoenix, AZ 85016
(602) 277-3700
Fax: (602) 277-8212
Web: www.afpersonnel.com

Description: Firm is owned and operated by
accountants. We specialize in placing accountants in
permanent or temporary positions.

Key Contact - Specialty:
Mr. Michael Nolan, President - *Accounting &
   finance*

Salary minimum: $40,000

Functions: Generalist, CFO's, Budgeting, Cash
   Mgmt., Credit, Taxes, M&A, Risk Mgmt.

Industries: Generalist

Professional Associations: AAFA, IMA

Branches:
1811 Alma School Rd 205
Mesa, AZ 85210
(480) 777-0800
Fax: (480) 491-3969
Web: www.aafa.com

Key Contact:
Ms. Vikki West, Manager

4400 E Broadway Ste 600
Tucson, AZ 85711
(602) 323-3600
Fax: (602) 795-4753
Web: www.aafa.com
Key Contact - Specialty:
Mr. Duane Etter, Manager - *Accounting & finance*

Accounting Advantage

11444 W Olympic Blvd 260
Los Angeles, CA 90064
(310) 445-4111
Fax: (310) 312-8722
Web: www.actadv.com

Description: Our firm specializes in placing all
levels of accounting and financial staff, including
investment banking, on a permanent, contract, and
temporary basis.

Functions: Finance

Industries: Generalist

Accounting Career Consultants

(also known as HR Career Consultants)
1001 Craig Rd Ste 391
St. Louis, MO 63146
(314) 569-9898
Fax: (314) 569-9856
Email: info@careeradvancers.com
Web: www.careeradvancers.com

Description: We are a full service firm that works
on accounting, finance, and human resource
positions at all levels from CFOs and HR directors
to accounting clerks and HR assistants. We can
provide staffing services ranging from consulting,
pay-rolling of employees or temporary services to
direct-hire, executive search, or retained search.

Key Contact - Specialty:
Mr. Melvin Weinberg, CPA, Owner -
   Accounting/finance
Mr. Larry Weinberg, CPA, CPC, CTS, Vice
   President - *Accounting/finance*

Functions: HR Mgmt., Finance

Industries: Generalist

Professional Associations: ASA, MAPS, NAPS

Networks: Top Echelon Network

Accounting Personnel of the Triad

4400 Silas Creek Pkwy Ste 200
Winston-Salem, NC 27104
(336) 768-8188
Fax: (336) 768-1768
Email: dawson@accountingpersonnel.com
Web: www.accountingpersonnel.com

Description: We provide permanent and temporary
search and placement of CPAs and accountants,
primarily in the Piedmont Region of North Carolina.

Key Contact - Specialty:
Mr. Dawson Nesbitt, President - *Accounting*

Salary minimum: $50,000

Functions: Middle Mgmt., Finance, CFO's, Taxes

Industries: Generalist, Accounting SW

Professional Associations: AAFA

ACHIEVE Technical Services

4275-29 Rosewood Dr 163
Pleasanton, CA 94588
(925) 803-1080
Fax: (925) 803-9454
Email: resumes@achieve1.com
Web: www.achieve1.com

Description: We specialize in providing staffing
services for talented telecommunications, data

communication, information technology and
computer professionals in the San Francisco Bay
area.

Key Contact - Specialty:
Mr. Lonnie Barish, MBA, Principal - *Data,
   telecommunications*

Salary minimum: $50,000

Functions: General Mgmt., Directors, Senior
   Mgmt., Middle Mgmt., Product Dev., Sales &
   Mktg., Mktg. Mgmt., MIS Mgmt., Systems Dev.

Industries: Telecoms, Telephony, Digital, Wireless,
   Fiber Optic, Network Infrastructure, ERP SW,
   Networking, Comm. SW, System SW

Professional Associations: CSP, NCHRA, SHRM

Ackerman Johnson Inc

333 N Sam Houston Pkwy E Ste 820
Houston, TX 77060
(281) 999-8879
Fax: (281) 999-7570
Email: jobs@aj-inc.net
Web: www.ackermanjohnson.com

Description: We specialize in sales, sales
management, marketing and marketing management
positions in medical, pharmaceutical, voice and data
communications, consulting, computer
hardware/software, business products/services,
industrial, consumer products and energy.

Key Contact:
Mr. Frederick W. Stang, President

Functions: Generalist, Sales & Mktg.

Industries: Energy, Utilities, Mfg., Food, Bev.,
   Tobacco, Services, Media, Communications,
   Packaging, Software, Biotech

Networks: First Interview Network (FIN)

Acquis Associates Inc

PO Box 1288
Wall, NJ 07719
(732) 280-8425
Email: sharkus@acquis.com
Web: www.acquis.com

Description: Technical/executive recruiting for the
chemical and allied industries.

Key Contact:
Dr. Linda Sharkus, PhD, President

ACSYS Resources Inc

1300 Market St Ste 501
Wilmington, DE 19801
(302) 658-6181
Fax: (302) 658-6244
Email: dvacca@acsysrinc.com
Web: www.acsysinc.com

Description: Permanent/temp/contract specialists in
accounting, finance, banking and data processing -
contingency and retainer.

Key Contact - Specialty:
Mr. Domenic L. Vacca, Managing Director -
   *Accounting, finance, financial services, human
   resources*

Salary minimum: $15,000

Functions: Generalist, Senior Mgmt., Mkt.
   Research, Sales Mgmt., HR Mgmt., Finance,
   CFO's, Taxes

Industries: Generalist, Drugs Mfg., Banking,
   Invest. Banking, Brokers, Accounting, Broadcast,
   Film, Telecoms

Professional Associations: AICPA, IMA

Branches:
1820 Chapel Ave W Ste 168
Cherry Hill, NJ 08002
(856) 910-1824
Fax: (856) 910-1939

Email: info@acsysresources.com
Key Contact - Specialty:
Mr. Michael Shedroff - *Accounting, finance, financial services, banking, information technology*

1850 William Penn Way Ste 106
Lancaster, PA 17601
(717) 390-0888
Fax: (717) 390-2012
Email: info@acsysresources.com
Key Contact - Specialty:
Ms. Monica Yasgur, Senior Consultant - *Accounting, finance, financial services, banking*

1700 Market St Ste 3110
Philadelphia, PA 19103
(215) 568-6810
Fax: (215) 977-0362
Email: info@acsysresources.com
Key Contact - Specialty:
Mr. David Laderman, Director - *Accounting, finance, financial services, banking, information technology*

500 E Swedesford Rd Ste 100
Wayne, PA 19087
(610) 687-6107
Fax: (610) 687-9456
Email: info@acsysresources.com
Key Contact - Specialty:
Mr. David Laderman, Manager - *Accounting, finance, financial services, banking*

ACT
25492 Hillsboro Dr
Laguna Niguel, CA 92677
(949) 365-9090
Email: WeACT4U@actsearch.com
Web: www.actsearch.com

Description: We specialize in executive and technical recruitment for pre-IPO and Fortune 500 companies developing technologies for wireless, multimedia and broadband communications.

Key Contact:
Mr. John Kratz, Owner

Functions: Generalist

Industries: Consumer Elect., Telecoms, Digital, Wireless, Fiber Optic, Network Infrastructure

Professional Associations: IEEE

Action Management Corp
915 S Grand Traverse St
Flint, MI 48502-1042
(810) 234-2828
(800) 771-8571
Fax: (810) 234-5159
Email: info@actionmanagement.com
Web: www.actionmanagement.com

Description: Minority-owned firm specializing in recruitment of minorities and women. We'll provide you with a complete and precise analysis of each candidate's skills, expertise, interests, goals and salary requirements.

Key Contact:
Mr. Nick Morgan, Executive Search Coordinator - *Women, minorities*
Mr. Paul Opsommer, Vice President

Salary minimum: $30,000

Functions: Generalist, Senior Mgmt., Middle Mgmt., Plant Mgmt., Sales Mgmt., Personnel, MIS Mgmt., Engineering, Minorities

Industries: Generalist, Machine, Appliance, Motor Vehicles, HR Services, Media, Telecoms, Software

Professional Associations: IACMP, SHRM

Branches:
1655 N Ft. Myer Dr Ste 700
Arlington, VA 22209
(800) 771-8571
(703) 351-5294
Fax: (810) 234-5159
Key Contact - Specialty:
Mr. Claude High, President - *Minorities (women)*

Action Management Services
6055 Rockside Woods Blvd Ste 160
Cleveland, OH 44131
(440) 642-8777
Fax: (216) 642-1294
Email: ams@bright.net
Web: www.actionmgmt.com

Description: We are a permanent placement firm which handles both contingency and retained searches. We serve greater Cleveland's largest companies in manufacturing, banking, healthcare, distribution and service industries.

Key Contact - Specialty:
Mr. Dale C. Chorba, President/Owner - *Accounting, finance, tax, attorneys*
Mr. Dale M. Chorba, Vice President - *Healthcare, physicians, accounting, finance*

Salary minimum: $50,000

Functions: Healthcare, HR Mgmt., Finance, CFO's, Budgeting, Cash Mgmt., Credit, Taxes, IT

Industries: Generalist

Action Recruiters
13777 Lark Ave
Mason City, IA 50401
(641) 423-1683
Fax: (641) 423-3143
Email: beth@actionrecruiters.com
Web: www.actionrecruiters.com

Description: Our firm specializes in Information Technology placements. We have openings in most IT disciplines all across the United States. Our success is proven and solid. We have a full-service IT employment perspective. We have a broad base of clients from FORTUNE 100 companies to start-up pre-IPO firms. Our clients pay for all fees and most will offer relocation assistance. Our goal is to provide you with personal service and effectively help you find the Job of your Dreams.

Key Contact:
Ms. Beth Lynch, Owner
Mr. Mark Nagle, Co-Owner

Networks: Top Echelon Network

Active Search & Placement Inc
2214 Pacific Coast Hwy Fl 3
Huntington Beach, CA 92648
(714) 969-1926
Fax: (714) 969-0226
Email: nada@investmentemployment.com
Web: www.investmentemployment.com

Description: We conduct targeted searches for portfolio managers, business development officers, research analysts, trust and operations administrators for clients who are investment management, mutual funds and trust companies.

Key Contact - Specialty:
Ms. Nada D. Williston, Partner - *Investment management, mutual funds, trust*

Salary minimum: $45,000

Functions: Cash Mgmt.

Industries: Finance, Banking, Invest. Banking, Brokers, Venture Cap., Misc. Financial

Active Wireless Executive Search Group Inc
801 Beville Rd Ste 201
South Daytona, FL 32119
(386) 304-8727
Fax: (386) 304-8927
Email: info@activewireless.com
Web: www.activewireless.com

Description: Our firm provides retained and exclusive container search and placement recruiting services to vendors in wireless telecommunications. We work with venture capital groups, board members, and executive management focusing on recruiting CEO, COO, CFO, CTO, EVP, VP, and director levels in RF design, software development, systems engineering, and sales and marketing. We have successfully placed professionals with infrastructure vendors, PCS carriers, mobile commerce, hand-sets/mobile computing devices, broadband Internet, and Bluetooth technologies.

Key Contact - Specialty:
Mr. Charles Moore, IWE, Vice President - *Wireless, telecom*

Salary minimum: $100,000

Functions: Generalist

Industries: Wireless

Professional Associations: FAPS, IWE, WIWC

Networks: Top Echelon Network

Acuity Medical Recruitment
500 Wright Rd
Goodman, MS 39079
(866) 422-4312
Email: acuitymed@usa.net
Web: www.members.spree.com/acuitymed/

Description: Quality healthcare depends on qualified, dedicated and reliable physicians - providing the best physicians to fulfill your mandate in giving Americans integrity in healthcare, this is our mission.

Key Contact - Specialty:
Ms. Linda Wright, President - *Physicians*

Salary minimum: $18,000

Functions: Healthcare, Physicians, Minorities

Industries: Generalist, Healthcare

Adam-Bryce Inc
77 Maple Ave
New City, NY 10956
(845) 634-1772
Fax: (845) 634-1912
Email: jobs@adambryce.com
Web: www.adambryce.com

Description: We have been involved in staffing and identifying high potential candidates who through the use of technology have moved their IT organizations into the forefront of their industries.

Key Contact - Specialty:
Ms. Nadine Rubin, President - *Information technology, telecommunications*
Ms. Phyllis Reiss, Executive Recruiter - *Information technology, telecommunications*
Ms. Naomi Laks, Executive Recruiter - *Information technology, telecommunications*

Functions: Generalist, IT, MIS Mgmt.

Industries: Telecoms, Call Centers, Network Infrastructure, Security SW

Networks: Top Echelon Network

Adams & Associates
2132 Briarfield
Camarillo, CA 93010
(805) 484-8815
Fax: (805) 484-7345

Description: We specialize in civil engineering. Placing qualified men and women in the fields of transportation, engineering, architecture and management. Covering all levels from design to top management.

Key Contact - Specialty:
Ms. Lynn Adams, Owner - *Civil engineering*

Functions: Directors, Senior Mgmt., Middle Mgmt., Engineering, Architects

Industries: Generalist, Construction, Transportation

Professional Associations: CELSOC, WTS

Adams & Associates
921 E Main St Ste I
Ventura, CA 93001
(805) 653-7900
Fax: (805) 653-7910
Email: bill@adamsrecruiters.com
Web: www.adamsrecruiters.com

Description: High-technology contingency searches for senior management, sales and sales management, marketing, and IT professionals throughout North America and Europe.

Key Contact - Specialty:
Mr. Bill Adams, President - *High technology, management, sales, technical*

Salary minimum: $45,000

Functions: Generalist, General Mgmt., Senior Mgmt., Middle Mgmt., Sales & Mktg., Sales Mgmt., Finance, IT

Industries: Generalist, Mfg., Accounting, Media, Aerospace, Software

Ray Adams & Associates Executive Search Consultants
PO Box 772714
Houston, TX 77215-2714
(713) 952-2999
Fax: (713) 783-2241
Email: ray1@hal-pc.org

Description: We are an executive search firm. We specialize in financial, accounting, audit, tax, information and technology systems, other business management, and executive.

Key Contact - Specialty:
Mr. Ray Adams, Owner/President - *Financial executives, accountants, auditors, tax, information systems*

Salary minimum: $25,000

Functions: Generalist, Middle Mgmt., Automation, Health Admin., Personnel, Credit, MIS Mgmt., Attorneys

Industries: Generalist, Energy, Utilities, Paints, Petro. Products, Wholesale, Finance, Hospitality, Environmental Svcs., Real Estate

Professional Associations: IIA, IMA, ISACA

J N Adams & Associates Inc
301 S Allen St Ste 103A
State College, PA 16801
(814) 234-0670
Email: jnadams@ceinetworks.com
Web: www.jnadams.com

Description: Our firm is an executive placement firm specializing in the nationwide recruitment of top professionals in industries such as: quality, engineering, and manufacturing. We were established by Eric Berg, our president.

Key Contact - Specialty:
Mr. Eric M. Berg, President - *Quality assurance, engineering, manufacturing professionals*

Functions: Middle Mgmt., Mfg., Production, Plant Mgmt., Quality

Industries: Mfg., Plastics, Rubber, Metal Products, Machine, Appliance, Motor Vehicles, Computer Equip.

Networks: Inter-City Personnel Assoc (IPA)

Arthur Adams & Associates
1046 Ravine Ridge Dr Ste 200
Worthington, OH 43085-2907
(614) 846-5075
Fax: (614) 846-5076
Email: info@adamsrecruiting.com
Web: www.adamsrecruiting.com

Description: Contingency/retainer search in the computer networking sales field on a worldwide basis.

Key Contact - Specialty:
Mr. Arthur Adams, President - *Computer networking sales*

Salary minimum: $200,000

Functions: Generalist, Sales Mgmt.

Industries: Generalist, Computer Equip., Software

Professional Associations: RON

Adams & Ryan Inc
305 Madison Ave Ste 465
New York, NY 10165
(212) 697-7087
Fax: (212) 697-7355
Email: sherry@adamsandryan.com
Web: www.adamsandryan.com

Description: Each candidate is met with fully screened and informed of your company prior to their CV being sent out. All levels from CEOs to sales are interviewed for your approval.

Key Contact - Specialty:
Ms. Sherry Koski, President - *Telecommunications, sales, management, operations*
Mr. Chris Anczarki, Partner - *Telecommunications*
Mr. Steve Kaufman, Senior Consultant - *Telecommunications*

Salary minimum: $35,000

Functions: Sales Mgmt.

Industries: Telecoms

Adams - Gardner
1177 W Loop South 1177
Tractebel Bldg
Houston, TX 77027
(281) 556-6890
(281) 250-1668
Fax: (281) 556-0672
Email: conniek@adamsgardner.com
Web: www.adamsgardner.com

Description: We are a search firm that specializes in the tax accounting arena that places primarily applicants in VPs of finance, CFOs, directors of tax, and controller positions. Our advisors are Big 5 CPAs, CFPs, or CPCs. Each candidate is personally screened by a psychotherapist and by CPA advisors. We are serving clients throughout the US. We perform retained and contingent searches.

Key Contact - Specialty:
Ms. Constance Kelley, CEO, CPC, President - *Accounting searches*
Mr. Donald Kelley, CFO, CPA, Vice President - *Accounting searches*
Ms. Heather Adams, MSW, Secretary - *Accounting searches*

Salary minimum: $100,000

Functions: CFO's

Industries: Energy, Utilities, Construction, Mfg., Finance, Services, Recreation, Media, Communications, Software, Healthcare

The Adams Consulting Group Inc
800 Monroe NW Ste 319
Grand Rapids, MI 49503
(616) 356-5580
Fax: (616) 356-5581
Email: scott@adamsconsulting.net
Web: www.adamsconsulting.net

Description: We are a specialized recruiting and consulting firm. Our philosophy is simple: to serve our clients by immediately responding to their professional staffing needs with honesty and integrity.

Key Contact - Specialty:
Mr. Scott C. Laursen, President - *Information systems*

Salary minimum: $30,000

Functions: Healthcare, IT, Engineering

Industries: Generalist, Biotech

Adams Inc
(also known as Adams Select Staffing)
13906 Gold Cir Ste 101
Omaha, NE 68144-2336
(402) 333-3009
Fax: (402) 333-3448
Email: adams_inc@tconl.com
Web: www.adams-inc.com

Description: We specialize in banking, trust, credit card and information technology placements nationwide. We maintain a database of over 60,000 contacts and have 10 recruiters tracking over 1200 job openings nationally.

Key Contact - Specialty:
Mr. Jay Adams, CPC, President/Owner - *Banking, trust, credit card, information technology*
Ms. Roxane Adams, CPC, Executive Vice President - *Banking, trust, credit card, information technology*

Salary minimum: $40,000

Functions: Generalist, Mkt. Research, CFO's, Cash Mgmt., Credit, IT

Industries: Generalist, Finance, Banking, Misc. Financial, Software

Professional Associations: NAPS

The Addison Consulting Group
12 Strafford Cir Rd
Medford, NJ 08055
(609) 953-7650

Description: We are a specialty firm recruiting all management functions for medical device, biotech and related industries, offering extensive industry experience and a broad business perspective to discerning, growth-oriented companies.

Key Contact - Specialty:
Mr. Sandy Korkuch, Managing Director - *Medical devices, management*

Salary minimum: $50,000

Functions: Generalist, General Mgmt., Mfg., Product Dev., Quality, Sales & Mktg., Engineering

Industries: Medical Devices

AddStaff Executive Search
3 Sequoia Ct
Voorhees, NJ 08043
(856) 424-8828
Email: jobs@addstaff.net
Web: www.addstaff.net

Description: Our firm operates on both retainer and contingency bases. We specialize in the areas of: telecommunications, management, human resources, IT, marketing and sales. All fees are paid *by the company. The average salary of placements is more than $50,000.*

Key Contact - Specialty:
Ms. Suzanne Gricius, SPHR, President - *Human resources, management, marketing, sales, telecommunications, IT*

Functions: General Mgmt., Senior Mgmt., Sales & Mktg., Sales Mgmt., HR Mgmt., IT, MIS Mgmt.

Industries: Services, Communications, Software, ERP SW, HR SW, Biotech, Healthcare

Professional Associations: MAAPC, SHRM

Adel-Lawrence Associates Inc
1208 Hwy 34 Ste 18
Aberdeen, NJ 07747
(732) 566-4914
Fax: (732) 566-9326
Email: larryr@alajobs.com
Web: www.adel-lawrence.com

Description: Nationwide placement of engineering/technical personnel. Specializing in electrical/mechanical/software engineers; computers (networking, help desk, system analysts); telecommunications; IT management; biomedical/x-ray service and field service/repair.

Key Contact - Specialty:
Mr. Larry Radzely, President - *Engineering, software, technical*

Salary minimum: $35,000

Functions: Systems Dev.

Industries: Medical Devices, Computer Equip., Consumer Elect., Test, Measure Equip., Telecoms, Software, Biotech

Professional Associations: AFSMI, MAAPC, NJTRA, SHRM

Networks: Top Echelon Network

Adept Tech Recruiting Inc
219 Glendale Rd
Scarsdale, NY 10583
(914) 523-5857

Description: We focus primarily on placement of personnel in all areas of information technology. Secondarily, we work on placement of personnel in all areas of home health care.

Key Contact - Specialty:
Mr. Fredrick R. Press, President - *Information technology, healthcare, advertising*

Functions: Generalist

Industries: Generalist, Computer Equip., Venture Cap., Services, Software, Healthcare

Adirect Recruiting Corp
468 Queen St E Ste 206
PO Box 22
Toronto, ON M5A 1T7
Canada
(416) 365-9889
Fax: (416) 365-3123
Email: resumes@adirectrecruiting.com
Web: www.adirectrecruiting.com

Description: We provide cost and time effective mid- to mid-senior-level managerial/professional/technical search services to major Canadian companies. We offer three to five week turnaround times with fees ranging from $7,200to $18,000. Over 96% of our assignments are completed successfully.

Key Contact - Specialty:
Mr. Robert Copp, President
Ms. Susan Fox, Vice President - *Human resources*

Salary minimum: $50,000

Functions: Middle Mgmt., Sales & Mktg., Mktg. Mgmt., HR Mgmt.

Industries: Generalist, Food, Bev., Tobacco, Drugs Mfg., Retail, Finance, HR Services, Publishing, New Media, Aerospace, Insurance, Biotech, Healthcare

Adkins & Associates Ltd
119 E Lewis St
PO Box 16062
Greensboro, NC 27416
(336) 378-1261
Fax: (336) 274-7433
Email: resumes@adkinsassociates.com
Web: www.adkinassociates.com

Description: We are focused on fashion, retail, apparel, textile, consumer goods, and media, worldwide. We handle senior and middle-level executive positions in all functional areas.

Key Contact:
Mr. Ken Adkins, CEO. and President - *Fashion*
Mrs. Nancy Adkins, Executive Vice President and Treasurer
Mr. Doug Coley, Senior Vice President
Mr. Rick Rush, Vice President
Ms. Pat Turner, Senior Vice President of Operations

Salary minimum: $50,000

Functions: Generalist

Industries: Textiles, Apparel, Wholesale, Retail, E-commerce, Media, Advertising, Publishing, New Media, Broadcast, Film

Professional Associations: PINNACLE

Administrative Source
13895 E Placita Pezuna
Vail, AZ 85641
(520) 647-3426
Fax: (520) 647-7868
Email: aasource@msn.com
Web: www.administrativesource.com

Description: We are an executive recruitment firm specializing in the commercial real estate industry including property management, retail, and construction. Our placements include CFO/controllers, accountants, financial analysts, asset and property managers, lease administrators, and administrative assistants, as well as other support positions.

Key Contact:
Ms. Dee Pfeiffer

Functions: Generalist

Industries: Retail, Misc. Financial, Accounting, Mgmt. Consulting, Advertising, Real Estate, Entertainment SW, Marketing SW

Adolfson & Associates
6860 S Yosemite Ct Ste 200
Englewood, CO 80112
(303) 290-0240
Fax: (303) 721-6399
Email: adolfson@qwest.net

Description: We are a contingency search firm specializing in the areas of sales and sales management in both the medical and software industries. We place in operations management and general management positions in the healthcare service arena, for example: home healthcare services, physical therapy services, and O&P services.

Key Contact - Specialty:
Mr. Edwin Adolfson, Owner - *Medical, management, sales*

Functions: General Mgmt., Sales Mgmt.

Industries: Software, Healthcare

ADOW Professionals
36 E 4th St Ste 1308
Cincinnati, OH 45202
(888) 645-8800
(513) 721-2369
Fax: (513) 721-3724
Email: nationalsearch@adow.com
Web: www.adow.com

Description: We are experts in recruiting and providing the best talent. We use technology and the human touch. Through our specialized divisions, accountables, DataTechs consulting, and worldwide executeam. We provide the US at a glance.

Key Contact - Specialty:
Ms. Kathleen G. Kern, President/Executive Consultant - *International, top management, scientists, research & development, marketing*
Mr. Jerry L. Kern, Vice President/Executive Consultant - *Accounting, finance, midlevel, executive level, sales and marketing, healthcare*
Ms. Suzy M. Treacy, Executive Consultant - *MIS management, human resource (midlevel, senior management), accounting*
Mr. Neal McFarland, Executive Consultant - *Staff, midlevel, senior level engineering, manufacturing, materials*
Ms. Tiffany Spencer, Executive Consultant - *Technical, administrative*

Salary minimum: $65,000

Functions: Generalist, General Mgmt., Mfg., Packaging, Mkt. Research, Mktg. Mgmt., R&D, Minorities, Int'l.

Industries: Generalist

Professional Associations: OSSA

Networks: Inter-City Personnel Assoc (IPA)

ADV Advanced Technical Services Inc
1037 McNicoll Ave Ste 200
Toronto, ON M1W 3W6
Canada
(416) 502-2545
Fax: (416) 502-2544
Email: contact@advtechnical.com
Web: www.advtechnical.com

Description: Hi-tech recruitment firm, specializing in placing electrical and computer engineers (software, hardware, telecom, datacom, defence/aerospace and advanced manufacturing). We build long-term relationships with candidates and client companies.

Key Contact:
Mr. Paul Hill, President
Mr. Brian Small
Mr. John Penturn
Ms. Celia Lee
Ms. Sahin Jivraj
Mr. Cameron Gausby
Mr. Nigel Buck

Salary minimum: $45,000

Functions: Generalist, Mfg., Product Dev., Engineering

Industries: Generalist, Mfg., Computer Equip., Media, Telecoms, Software

Networks: National Personnel Assoc (NPA)

Advance Consulting Services Inc
1495 Rymco Dr Ste 102
Winston-Salem, NC 27103-2947
(336) 774-8778
Fax: (336) 774-8776
Email: ysanborn@aol.com

Description: We are a small business enterprise offering professional recruiting services within the United States. We are committed to conducting our client's search assignments with the highest standard of confidentiality, discretion and integrity.

Key Contact - Specialty:
Ms. Yevonne Sanborn, President - *Sales & marketing, sales promotion, public relations*

Salary minimum: $40,000

Functions: Senior Mgmt., Product Dev., Sales & Mktg., Advertising

Industries: Food, Bev., Tobacco, Leather, Stone, Glass, Consumer Elect., Finance, Services, Pharm Svcs., Mgmt. Consulting, Advertising

Professional Associations: NAPS

Advance Employment Inc
2546 E Jolly Rd Ste 3
Lansing, MI 48910
(517) 887-0377
Fax: (517) 887-9944
Web: www.advanceteam.com

Description: We are a full-service employment firm serving the temporary, contract, leasing and executive recruiting needs of our client-partners.

Key Contact - Specialty:
Mr. Mark Taylor - *Engineering, information technology, information systems, MIS*

Salary minimum: $40,000

Functions: Generalist, Production, Sales Mgmt., Cash Mgmt., Systems Dev., Systems Support, Engineering

Industries: Generalist, Construction, Mfg., Finance, Accounting, HR Services

---

Advanced Career Solutions Inc
10311 Azuaga St
San Diego, CA 92129
(858) 538-2671
Email: acssearch@prodigy.net
Web: acssearch.tripod.com

Description: We are a national recruiting, career, and employment resource center for sales, management, engineers and service in the mechanical HVAC/R and construction industries.

Key Contact:
Ms. Karen Mattonen

Salary minimum: $55,000

Functions: Generalist, Environmentalists

Industries: Energy, Utilities, Construction, Equip Svcs., Environmental Svcs.

Advanced Careers of Kansas City Inc
6528 Raytown Rd Ste I
Kansas City, MO 64133
(816) 358-6098
Fax: (816) 358-3566
Email: hwillis711@aol.com

Description: We specialize in sales, engineering, and manufacturing professional level positions. We do nationwide as well as local assignments on a contingent basis.

Key Contact - Specialty:
Mr. Hal Willis, CPC, Vice President - *Engineering, manufacturing management*
Ms. Marsha Willis, CPC, President - *Sales, sales management*

Functions: Generalist, Plant Mgmt., Sales Mgmt., Engineering

Industries: Generalist

Advanced Corporate Search
2755 Stearns St Apt 14
Simi Valley, CA 93063
(805) 522-1997
Email: acsigtxecs@aol.com

Description: Our specializations are in the satellite, GPS, RF/microwave, wireless/wire-line and

broadband industries. Sales/sales management, engineering/engineering management and systems integration are what we have expertise in. We have a well-established reputation for honesty and integrity and a long-term proven ability to secure the absolute best. We have the skills to analyze, evaluate, and to motivate both company and candidate to a "win-win" conclusion. Our strong business tendencies enable us to ascertain technical abilities and inter-personal characteristics.

Key Contact - Specialty:
Ms. Jan Gibson, President - *RF/microwave, satellite, GPS, broadband wireless/wireline communication systems*

Salary minimum: $80,000

Functions: Sales Mgmt., Systems Implem., Systems Support, R&D, Engineering

Industries: Electronic, Elec. Components, Wireless, Fiber Optic

---

Advanced Recruiting Inc
5408 NW 109
Oklahoma City, OK 73162
(405) 720-9445
Fax: (405) 720-9133
Email: staffing@adrec.com
Web: www.adrec.com

Description: We specialize in information systems, data processing (all levels) and mid- to senior-level executives for all industries.

Key Contact - Specialty:
Mr. Len Branch, Director of Search - *MIS, data processing*

Salary minimum: $40,000

Functions: Generalist, MIS Mgmt., Systems Analysis, Systems Dev., Systems Implem., Systems Support, Network Admin., DB Admin.

Industries: Generalist, New Media, Telecoms, Software

Professional Associations: OAPS, SHRM

Networks: Top Echelon Network

Branches:
1947 Wadsworth Blvd Ste 394
Lakewood, CO 80227
(303) 936-5699
Fax: (303) 935-2204
Email: advrec@icon.net
Key Contact - Specialty:
Ms. Lynn Owens - *MIS, data processing*

Advanced Resources Inc
15 Sunnen Dr Ste 107
St. Louis, MO 63143
(314) 647-5777
Fax: (314) 212-6650
Email: rhoehne@advr.com
Web: www.advr.com

Description: We offer over fifteen years of professional information systems recruiting service.

Key Contact - Specialty:
Ms. Rebecca Hoehne, President/Recruiting Services - *Information systems*

Functions: Generalist, Systems Analysis, Systems Dev., Systems Implem., Systems Support, Network Admin., DB Admin.

Industries: Generalist, Software

Networks: Top Echelon Network

Advanced Search Group Inc
625 Plainfield Rd Ste 426
Willowbrook, IL 60527
(630) 734-1010
Fax: (630) 734-1011

Email: charlie@advancedsearch.com
Web: www.advancedsearch.com

Description: Specializing in chemE, ME, EE, and chemists, operations and material management with the chemical, pharms, petro, and consumer products nationwide.

Key Contact:
Mr. Charles Diana, President

Functions: Engineering

Industries: Mfg., Food, Bev., Tobacco, Printing, Chemicals, Soap, Perf., Cosmtcs., Drugs Mfg., Plastics, Rubber, Paints, Petro. Products

Networks: National Personnel Assoc (NPA)

Advanced Technology Consultants Inc (ATC)
536 Weddell Dr Ste 7
Sunnyvale, CA 94089
(408) 734-0635
Fax: (408) 734-5833
Email: atci@ix.netcom.com
Web: www.atcconsultants.com

Description: Specialize in software technology in the areas of product development, quality assurance, technical support, documentation and training, professional services (consulting), product marketing and business development.

Key Contact - Specialty:
Mr. Reza Vakili, President - *Middle management, software*
Mr. Tony Morshedi, General Manager - *Technical support, training, system administration, network administration*

Salary minimum: $50,000

Functions: Generalist, Middle Mgmt., Mktg. Mgmt., Systems Analysis, Systems Dev., Systems Implem., Network Admin., DB Admin.

Industries: Generalist, Venture Cap., Mgmt. Consulting, Software

Professional Associations: SSQ

Advancement Inc
899 Skokie Blvd Ste 406
Northbrook, IL 60062
(847) 418-3980
Fax: (847) 418-3985
Email: info@advancement.com
Web: www.advancement.com

Description: We are specialists in technical contingency and retained searches for the telecommunications, DataCom wireless, multimedia, and IC markets. Our service is confidential, national, and client fee based.

Key Contact - Specialty:
Mr. Scott Hall, President - *Technical, data communications, telecommunications, computers, multimedia*
Mr. Brry Menary, Sr Business Partner - *IC technology*

Salary minimum: $40,000

Functions: Directors, Product Dev., Mkt. Research, Mktg. Mgmt., Sales Mgmt., R&D, Engineering

Industries: Generalist

Professional Associations: RON

Networks: Top Echelon Network

Advice Personnel Inc
230 Park Ave Ste 903
New York, NY 10169
(212) 682-4400
Fax: (212) 682-3115
Email: slieff@adviceny.com

Description: We are the New York Metropolitan area specialists in financial accounting, public accounting, tax, and internal audit placements across diverse industry lines in the Metropolitan NY tri-state area. We place CFOs, partners, controllers, and chief administrative officers to staff positions. Our confidential recruitment services tailored to each client.

Key Contact - Specialty:
Ms. Shelley Lieff, CPA, Principal - *CFO, CAO, controller searches*
Mr. Alan Schwartz, CPA, Principal - *Financial, real estate, commercial, closely-held businesses*
Mr. Aaron Greenberg, Principal - *Healthcare, e-commerce, apparel, professional service firms entertainment, all financial positions with public companies*

Salary minimum: $40,000

Functions: Finance, CFO's, Budgeting, Cash Mgmt., Credit, Taxes, M&A, Risk Mgmt.

Industries: Generalist

Professional Associations: AICPA, NYSCPA

Advisors' Search Group Inc
PO Box 419
Scotch Plains, NJ 07076-0419
(908) 654-0109
Email: asgmw@aol.com

Description: We place experienced candidates with over 150 of the New York City Metropolitan Area portfolio/money management firms. The positions that we place include portfolio administration, portfolio assistants, marketing associates/assistants, RFP specialists, performance analysts, settlements, compliance, and corporate actions and systems. We have experience with Advent, Axys, Checkfree APL, Portia, Sungard, FMC and big+.

Key Contact - Specialty:
Mr. Michael A. Weinstock, Senior Vice President - *Portfolio, money management firms*

Salary minimum: $30,000

Functions: Generalist, Sales & Mktg., Mktg. Mgmt., Finance, Cash Mgmt., Systems Dev., Systems Support, DB Admin.

Industries: Generalist, Finance, Invest. Banking, Brokers, Venture Cap., Misc. Financial

The Advocates Group Inc
582 Market St Ste 1101
San Francisco, CA 94104
(415) 433-0278
Email: info@advocatesgroup.com
Web: www.advocatesgroup.com

Description: Our firm is one of the nation's top attorney search and consulting firms, representing top law firms and corporations coast to coast. Our candidates consistently possess top professional and academic credentials, and we have been repeatedly recommended by top legal journals as one of California's premier headhunders.

Key Contact - Specialty:
Mr. Jeffrey S. Stillman, Esq., JD, President/CEO - *Partner/general counsel placements, law firm mergers*
Mr. David Popky, Vice President/CFO - *Partner/general counsel placements, law firm mergers*

Salary minimum: $100,000

Professional Associations: NALSC

AES Search
1 Kalisa Way Ste 212
Paramus, NJ 07652
(201) 261-1600
(800) 545-4518
Fax: (201) 261-4343

Email: aesnj@aol.com
Web: www.aesrecruiting.com

Description: We specialize in the recruitment and placement of professionals in Engineering, Information Technology, Accounting & Finance, Insurance, and Education. Nationwide client focus, with concentration in NY/NJ/CT/PA. We also specializes in contract assignments for Engineers and Information Technology professionals. There is never a fee to the candidate!

Key Contact:
Mr. Nicholas Palermo, President
Ms. Christine Vigorito, Office Manager
Mrs. Josephine Palermo, Secretary/Treasurer
Mr. Daniel Weryzynski, Information Technology Associate
Mr. Paul Stevens, GM/Director - *Information technology*
Ms. Michelle Riley, Assistant Manager - *Information technology*
Mr. Angelo Fiore, Manager, Financial Services Division
Ms. Midge Mooney, Mgr.-Medical & Administrative Support
Mr. Ed Kahn, Recruitment Manager

Functions: Generalist, Mfg., Healthcare, Sales & Mktg., Finance, IT, R&D, Engineering

Industries: Generalist, Finance, IT Implementation

Affinity Executive Search
17210 NE 11th Ct
North Miami Beach, FL 33162-2624
(305) 770-1177
Fax: (305) 770-4010
Email: steve@affinitysearch.com
Web: www.affinitysearch.com

Description: We are a full-service, executive recruitment firm serving technical, managerial, and executive candidates through nationwide placements. Our staffing experts are considered indispensable by the following industries: aerospace (California specialists), semiconductor capital equipment, power supplies and systems, electronic test and measurement, electronic components, specialty materials, wireless communication, LAN/WAN and Internet communication, wire and cable, publishing, and direct mail/marketing.

Key Contact - Specialty:
Mr. Steven Kohn - *Sales & marketing, engineering, manufacturing, presidents, CEOs*
Ms. Renee Leavy - *Research & development, operations, software engineers, electronic engineers*

Salary minimum: $65,000

Functions: Generalist

Industries: Mfg., Finance, Accounting, Media, Communications, Government, Environmental Svcs., Aerospace, Packaging, Software

Professional Associations: IEEE, SMPTE

Networks: Top Echelon Network

Affordable Executive Recruiters
5518 Lemona Ave
Sherman Oaks, CA 91411
(818) 782-8554
Fax: (818) 779-0395
Email: fggerson@earthlink.net

Description: Specializing in CFOs, CEOs, CPAs, controllers, accountants, payroll personnel. Also human resources, credit managers.

Key Contact - Specialty:
Mr. Fred Gerson, Owner - *Financial*

Salary minimum: $30,000

Functions: Generalist, General Mgmt., Legal, Mfg., Sales & Mktg., HR Mgmt., Finance, CFO's, Taxes, Attorneys

Industries: Generalist

Professional Associations: IMA

Aggressive Corp
4701 Auvergne Ave Ste 101
Lisle, IL 60532
(630) 852-3400
Fax: (630) 852-5072
Email: resume@aggressivecorp.com
Web: www.aggressivecorp.com

Description: We are dedicated to assisting our clients through the arduous task of searching for key team members. Our North American practice ranges from middle management through the senior executives in companies that manufacture a product.

Key Contact:
Mr. Adam Gaspar, President
Mr. Raymond J. Kagee, Vice President
Mr. Thomas J. Lane, Vice President

Salary minimum: $75,000

Functions: Generalist, General Mgmt., Mfg., Materials, Sales & Mktg., HR Mgmt., Finance, Engineering

Industries: Generalist, Mfg., Lumber, Furniture, Medical Devices, Metal Products, Machine, Appliance, Motor Vehicles, Computer Equip., Misc. Mfg.

Agra Placements Ltd
4949 Pleasant St Ste 1
W 50th Pl III
West Des Moines, IA 50266-5494
(515) 225-6562
Fax: (515) 225-7733
Email: agraia@netins.net
Web: www.agraplacements.com

Description: The nation's leading firm specializing in the recruitment, screening and selection of management, marketing and technical professionals for international, national, regional and local agribusiness, horticultural, food, and commercial firms.

Key Contact:
Ms. Lori Chenoweth

Salary minimum: $25,000

Functions: Generalist, Mfg., Materials, Sales & Mktg., Engineering

Industries: Generalist, Agri., Forestry, Mining, Food, Bev., Tobacco

Branches:
2200 N Kickapoo Ste 2
Lincoln, IL 62656
(217) 735-4373
Fax: (217) 732-2041
Key Contact:
Mr. Gary Little, President/Partner

55 S Wabash St
PO Box 4
Peru, IN 46970
(765) 472-1988
Fax: (765) 472-7568
Key Contact:
Mr. Doug Rice, Treasurer/Partner

AGRI- Associates
2 Brush Creek Blvd Ste 130
Kansas City, MO 64112
(816) 531-7980
Fax: (816) 531-7982
Email: agrikc@msn.com
Web: www.agriassociates.com

Description: Specialist in personnel search and recruiting for agribusiness, including suppliers of agricultural production inputs, agriculture commodity processors and agricultural production enterprises.

Key Contact - Specialty:
Mr. Glenn J. Person - *Agricultural personnel*

Salary minimum: $35,000

Functions: Generalist, General Mgmt., Production, Plant Mgmt., Quality, Purchasing, Sales & Mktg., Finance, R&D, Engineering

Industries: Generalist, Agri., Forestry, Mining

Professional Associations: AFIA, AOM, GEAPS, NGFA, SPEA

Branches:
18915 Nordhoff St Ste 3
Woodstone Office Plz
Northridge, CA 91324
(818) 701-3094
Fax: (818) 701-5190
Email: agrilerla@hotmail.com
Key Contact:
Mr. Les E. Reardanz, Manager

5200 NW 43rd St Ste 102-179
Gainesville, FL 32606-4482
(352) 372-4200
Fax: (352) 371-6607
Email: popewe@aol.com
Key Contact:
Mr. W. E. Gene Pope, Manager

895-B McFarland Rd
Alpharetta, GA 30004
(770) 475-2201
Fax: (770) 475-1136
Email: mtd_agri@bellsouth.net
Key Contact:
Mr. Michael T. Deal, Manager

2550 Middle Rd
300 NW Bank Twr
Bettendorf, IA 52722
(563) 344-6974
Fax: (563) 344-9199
Email: agridav@earthlink.net
Key Contact:
Mr. Michael S. Vinzenz, Manager

7800 Metro Pkwy Ste 300
Bloomington, MN 55425
(952) 851-9196
Fax: (952) 851-9197
Email: dhansen@bisworks.net
Key Contact:
Mr. Dana Hansen, Manager

PO Box 24046
Omaha, NE 68124-0046
(402) 397-4410
Fax: (402) 397-4411
Email: agriomaha@aol.com
Key Contact:
Mr. Richard W. Robertson, Manager

2632 Maplewood Dr
Columbus, OH 43231
(614) 891-3362
Fax: (614) 891-3382
Email: jmcgregor@columbus.rr.com
Key Contact:
Ms. Jill E. McGregor, Manager

1669 Glenn Rd
Lancaster, PA 17601
(717) 392-6692
Fax: (717) 392-6629
Web: www.nvo.com/agriassociates
Key Contact:
Mr. Frank R. Rauba, Manager

7777 Walnut Grove Rd
PO Box 14
Memphis, TN 38120
(901) 757-8787
Fax: (901) 751-1639
Email: agriline@usit.net
Key Contact:
Mr. Richard E. Thompson, Manager

131 Degan Ste 203
Sundance Sq
Lewisville, TX 75057-3664
(972) 221-7568
Fax: (972) 221-1409
Email: agridallas@ev1.net
Key Contact:
Mr. Lawrence W. Pete Keeley, Manager
Ms. Karen Carlson, Assistant

Agri-Business Services Inc

14705 13th Ave N
Plymouth, MN 55447
(952) 469-6767
Fax: (507) 451-9053
Email: info@agribusinessservices.com
Web: www.agribusinessservices.com

Description: Serve food and allied industries with sales, marketing, manufacturing, operations, engineering, technical and general management professionals.

Key Contact - Specialty:
Mr. Michael J. Morrison, President - *Food processing, sales & marketing, technical, manufacturing, engineering*
Ms. Julie A. Morrison, Vice President, Managing Director - *Food manufacturing, food service, retail foods, sales & marketing, operations*

Salary minimum: $35,000

Functions: Generalist, General Mgmt., Mfg., Materials, Sales & Mktg., R&D, Engineering

Industries: Generalist, Agri., Forestry, Mining, Mfg., Food, Bev., Tobacco, Chemicals, Hospitality, Restaurants, Industry Specific SW, Mfg. SW, Marketing SW, Biotech

Professional Associations: AACC, IFT

Networks: National Personnel Assoc (NPA)

Agri-Tech Personnel Inc

3113 NE 69th St
Kansas City, MO 64119
(816) 453-7200
Fax: (816) 453-6001
Email: dalepickering@msn.com
Web: www.agri-techpersonnel.com

Description: International agri-business recruiters for the grain storage and processing, food manufacturing, drug and chemical industries, finding candidates to fill positions in management, manufacturing, engineering, marketing, R&D, Q.C., administration, etc.

Key Contact - Specialty:
Mr. Dale Pickering, President - *Agriculture, food*

Salary minimum: $30,000

Functions: Generalist

Industries: Agri., Forestry, Mining, Food, Bev., Tobacco, Transportation, Accounting, HR Services, Packaging

Professional Associations: AOM

Agriesti & Associates

16291 Country Day Rd
Poway, CA 92064
(858) 451-7766
Fax: (858) 451-7843
Email: salesjob@san.rr.com

Description: We are a nationwide search firm specializing in consumer products, sales and marketing professionals, also medical and pharmaceuticals sales. We are affiliated with partners across the U.S. to facilitate our searches.

Key Contact - Specialty:
Ms. Kay Agriesti, President - *Sales & marketing, consumer products, medical, pharmaceutical*

Ms. Lisa Tumbiolo, Vice President - *Sales & marketing, consumer products*

Functions: Generalist, Middle Mgmt., Mkt. Research, Mktg. Mgmt., Sales Mgmt.

Industries: Generalist, Mfg., Food, Bev., Tobacco, Textiles, Apparel, Soap, Perf., Cosmtcs., Drugs Mfg., Medical Devices, Healthcare

Professional Associations: CSP

Networks: First Interview Network (FIN)

AJC Search Associates Ltd

119 N Park Ave Ste 207
Rockville Centre, NY 11570
(516) 766-1699
Fax: (516) 766-3889
Email: jayajc@aol.com

Description: Boutique search firm servicing the employee benefits community. Product lines include retirement plans, life and health insurance, long-term care, managed care, capital markets and investments. Specialties include legal, actuarial, consulting, underwriting, sales, computer professionals, marketing, accounting, and customer service. Service is our best policy.

Key Contact:
Mr. Jay Cohen

Salary minimum: $60,000

Functions: Generalist

Industries: Legal, Accounting, Insurance, Software, Healthcare

AJM Professional Services

803 W Big Beaver Rd 357
Troy, MI 48084-4734
(248) 244-2222
Fax: (248) 244-2233
Email: ajminfo@ajmps.com
Web: www.ajmps.com

Description: Specialists in contingency and retained search for information systems and software engineering professionals at managerial and staff levels. Access to a national candidate and client base through various networks and affiliations.

Key Contact - Specialty:
Mr. Charles A. Muller, CPC, Principal - *Information technology*
Mr. Jeffrey Jones, Principal - *Information technology*

Salary minimum: $30,000

Functions: IT, MIS Mgmt., Systems Analysis, Systems Dev., Systems Implem., Systems Support, Network Admin., DB Admin.

Industries: Generalist

Professional Associations: MASS, NAPS

Helen Akullian

280 Madison Ave 604
New York, NY 10016
(212) 532-3210
Email: akullian.agency@att.net

Description: We are a highly selective organization with over 30 years' experience and an outstanding reputation. We have gained our reputation by understanding the complexities of varied personnel needs and then carefully applying company criteria to the proper candidates. We specialize in marketing, public relations, advertising and editorial placements.

Key Contact - Specialty:
Ms. Helen Akullian, President - *Corporate communications*

Salary minimum: $50,000

Functions: Senior Mgmt., Middle Mgmt., Healthcare, Sales & Mktg., PR

Industries: Finance, Banking, Invest. Banking, Misc. Financial, Advertising, Publishing

AL Int'l Resources LLC
2 Melissa Dr
Lemont, IL 60439
(630) 257-9007
(630) 665-6220
Fax: (630) 257-0912
Email: alintresources@aol.com

Description: Executive and technical recruiting services specializing in manufacturing industries.

Key Contact - Specialty:
Ms. Alicia Leal, Principal/President - *Human Resource Consulting*
Mr. Laurence Chipman, Principal/Vice President - *Executive and Technical Recruiting*

Functions: General Mgmt., Senior Mgmt., Middle Mgmt., Admin. Svcs., Mfg., Production, Engineering

Industries: Chemicals, Metal Products, Machine, Appliance, Consumer Elect., Misc. Mfg., Electronic, Elec. Components

Alaska Executive Search Inc
821 N St Ste 204
Anchorage, AK 99501-6093
(907) 276-5707
Fax: (907) 279-3731
Email: anne_b@akexec.com
Web: www.akexec.com

Description: Executive search, employment agency, medSearch, temporary services, technical placements. Specializing in the Alaska marketplace.

Key Contact - Specialty:
Mr. Robert E. Bulmer - *Engineering, management*

Salary minimum: $30,000

Functions: Generalist

Industries: Generalist

Professional Associations: SHRM

The Albrecht Group
104 Iowa Ln Ste 204
Cary, NC 27511
(919) 468-8484
Fax: (919) 468-8126
Email: rgalbrecht@agroupnc.com

Description: Specializing in industry specific searches for senior executives, management, sales, marketing and engineering professionals.

Key Contact:
Mr. Robert Albrecht, President
Mr. Richard Duley, Vice President

Salary minimum: $50,000

Functions: General Mgmt., Mfg., Product Dev., Production, Sales & Mktg., Engineering

Industries: Generalist, Mfg., Medical Devices, Plastics, Rubber, Metal Products, Machine, Appliance, Motor Vehicles, Consumer Elect., Test, Measure Equip., Misc. Mfg., Packaging

Alexander & Associates
5625 FM 1960 W Ste 610
Houston, TX 77069
(281) 397-9420
Fax: (281) 397-9498

Description: Specializing in engineering disciplines serving the petro-chemical, manufacturing, plastics and paper industries.

Key Contact - Specialty:
Mr. Tyler Alexander, President - *Engineering*

Functions: Generalist, Product Dev., Plant Mgmt., Quality, Systems Dev., Systems Implem., Systems Support, Engineering

Industries: Generalist, Textiles, Apparel, Paper, Printing, Chemicals, Plastics, Rubber, Metal Products, Machine, Appliance

Professional Associations: HAAPC

Alexander & Collins
1888 Century Park E 1900
Los Angeles, CA 90067
(310) 277-4656
Fax: (310) 277-7098
Email: sc@alexander-collins.com
Web: www.alexander-collins.com

Description: We are a leading global attorney search firm recognized for our exceptional abilities in providing attorney search services to top Fortune companies throughout the US and in specified international markets, including Asia and Europe. We offer particular expertise in the placement of general counsel.

Key Contact - Specialty:
Ms. Sara E. Collins, Principal - *Attorneys*

Salary minimum: $100,000

Functions: Legal, Attorneys

Industries: Venture Cap., Aerospace, Real Estate, Software

Professional Associations: NAPABA, SCCLA

Alexander & Sterling
9200 Old Katy Rd
Houston, TX 77055
(713) 935-3333
(713) 935-3300
Fax: (713) 935-3374
Email: resume@alexanderandsterling.com

Key Contact - Specialty:
Mr. Bill Sonne, CEO - *Geosciences, programmers, MIS professionals, finance & accounting, energy*

Functions: Finance, IT, MIS Mgmt., Engineering, Attorneys

Industries: Generalist, Legal

The Gerard Alexander Consulting Group Inc
600 S Magnolia Ave Ste 200
Tampa, FL 33606
(813) 258-3336
Fax: (813) 251-6256
Email: resumes@gerardalexander.com
Web: www.gerardalexander.com

Description: We are the premier executive search and recruitment firm to call for placement within the advertising industry. Our unique structure of a dedicated team working together producing superior results over that of an independent lone recruiter allows us intensive search focus in both consumer and business-to-business agencies for all departments.

Key Contact:
Mr. James Wagner, President
Mr. Charles Windish, CEO

Salary minimum: $60,000

Functions: Advertising, Direct Mktg.

Industries: Generalist

Alexander Enterprises Inc
1511 Erbs Mill Rd
Blue Bell, PA 19422
(610) 279-0100
Fax: (610) 279-0124
Email: stephyoung@aol.com

Description: We conduct recruitment searches for all types of pharmaceutical professionals (M.D.s, Ph.D.s, quality, regulatory, safety, data management, IT/IS, medical writers, manufacturing, etc.)

Key Contact - Specialty:
Ms. Florence D. Young, President - *Pharmaceutical*
Ms. Stephanie Young, Vice President - *Pharmaceutical*
Mr. W. Michael Young, Vice President-Marketing - *Pharmaceutical*

Salary minimum: $45,000

Functions: Generalist

Industries: Drugs Mfg., Pharm Svcs., Biotech

Professional Associations: DIA, PDA, RAPS

The Alexander Group
PO Box 316
West Berlin, NJ 08091-0316
(856) 661-9155
Email: tag_hldgs@msn.com

Description: As a minority-owned, retained generalist firm, we are committed to sourcing highly qualified individuals from under-represented groups for inclusion in every candidate slate we present for client approval.

Key Contact:
Mr. Preston Beckley, President

Salary minimum: $75,000

Functions: Generalist

Industries: Drugs Mfg., Medical Devices, Computer Equip., Consumer Elect., Pharm Svcs., Mgmt. Consulting, HR Services, Advertising, Publishing, Telecoms

Professional Associations: BDPA, NBMBAA

Alfeld & Associates
309 Oak Creek Dr 12000 Lawndale
League City, TX 77573
(281) 466-9340
(281) 321-4097
Fax: (713) 321-4523
Email: karl.alfeld@lyondell-citgo.com
Web: www.alfeld-associates.com

Description: Technical and management search services offering successful, unique solutions to the staffing process.

Key Contact - Specialty:
Mr. Karl M. Alfeld, President - *Engineering, technical*

Salary minimum: $50,000

Functions: Generalist

Industries: Paper, Chemicals, Drugs Mfg., Plastics, Rubber, Paints, Petro. Products

Professional Associations: AICHE, NAEP, NAPS

Networks: Marlar Int'l

The Alfus Group Inc
353 Lexington Ave Fl 8
New York, NY 10016
(212) 599-1000
Fax: (212) 599-1523
Email: mail@thealfusgroup.com
Web: www.thealfusgroup.com

Description: International executive search specializing in leisure time/hospitality/real estate/entertainment/sports event management and related industries including hotel, time share, gambling, restaurant, cruise line, airline, club, hospitals and managed care facilities.

Key Contact - Specialty:
Mr. Phillip Alfus, President - *Hospitality, hotels, restaurant, leisure, senior management*
Ms. Paula Caracappa, Director - *Gaming, hotels, resorts, casinos, amusement parks*
Ms. Susan Wilner, Director - *Hotels, resorts, conference centers, convention centers*
Mr. Joshua Reich, Director - *Country clubs, culinary, food service, restaurants, hotels*
Mr. Pat Thompson, Associate - *Real estate, time share, acquisition development*
Ms. Danielle Padwa, Associate - *Sports*
Ms. Michelle Hill, Associate - *Food, security, service industry, hospitals, managed care facilities*
Ms. Lisa Vendetti, Associate - *Advertising, marketing*

Salary minimum: $60,000

Functions: Generalist

Industries: Food, Bev., Tobacco, HR Services, Hospitality, Hotels, Resorts, Clubs, Restaurants, Entertainment, Recreation

Professional Associations: AESC, AHMA, HSMAI, JBF, MPI, NRA, SHRM

Alice Groves Company LLC
700 Canal St Harbour Sq
Stamford, CT 06902
(203) 324-3225

Description: Our firm is dedicated to the thoughtful search and selection of retail and fashion executives who positively and dramatically influence our clients' profit pictures.

Key Contact - Specialty:
Mr. Raymond J. Leavee, Chairman - *Retail*
Mr. Kenneth S. Leavee, President - *Retail*

Salary minimum: $55,000

Functions: Generalist

Industries: Generalist, Retail

All Physicians Placement Services
10534 108 St N
Seminole, FL 33778
(727) 320-0529
Fax: (727) 320-8590
Email: apps-10@email.msn.com
Web: www.allphysiciansplacemnetservices.com

Description: We are one of the most reliable physician search firm's in the Southeast. We offer unique flexible solutions to highly qualified professionals and facilities that look to us for their recruitment needs. Whether deciding to expand your practice or relocating in an highly competitive industry that is rapidly changing these could be the most difficult decisions you will have to make. Our staff is dedicated to the success of your future placement and has over 23 years of experience in the medical industry.

Key Contact - Specialty:
Ms. Nancy Paliki, President - *Physician recruitment*

Functions: Physicians

Industries: Healthcare, Hospitals

Professional Associations: NAPR

Don Allan Associates Inc
PO Box 12988
La Jolla, CA 92039-2988
(858) 587-4800 x2
Email: resume@globalstaffing.com
Web: www.globalstaffing.com

Description: We provide executive search to the information systems, interactive/multimedia, e-Learning, and medical/healthcare industries. Our primary focus is on management, marketing, sales,

technical support, and consulting. We have an unbundled approach to the entire search process.

Key Contact - Specialty:
Mr. David Adler, President - *Sales, sales management, marketing, marketing management, technical*

Salary minimum: $60,000

Functions: Generalist, Sales & Mktg., Sales Mgmt., IT

Industries: Mgmt. Consulting, HR Services, Media, Publishing, Communications, Telecoms, Software, HR SW, Security SW, System SW, Training SW, Healthcare

Professional Associations: ASAE, CSP, HIMSS, IHRIM, IICS, RON, SHRM

Networks: Top Echelon Network

Jeffrey Allan Company Inc
2775 Via De La Valle Ste 200
Del Mar, CA 92014
(800) 886-1522
(858) 792-8666
Fax: (858) 792-8991
Email: jeff@jeffreyallan.com
Web: www.jeffreyallan.com

Description: Our firm is a national and international recruiting firm that has built a reputation for integrity and professionalism. Discover why companies across the country select Jeffrey Allan Company as their preferred search firm.

Key Contact - Specialty:
Mr. Jeffrey Conners, President
Ms. Norma Conners, Executive Vice President
Mr. Brian Elfus, Vice President - *Law, technology*

Salary minimum: $50,000

Functions: General Mgmt., Senior Mgmt., Legal, Purchasing, Sales & Mktg., HR Mgmt., CFO's, IT, Engineering, Int'l.

Industries: Generalist, Consumer Elect., Government

Allard Associates Inc
425 Market St Ste 2200
San Francisco, CA 94105
(800) 291-5279
(415) 661-7562
Fax: (800) 526-7791
Email: recruit@allardassociates.com
Web: www.allardassociates.com

Description: We provide executive placements nationally and globally in credit card, financial services, the payments industry, B2C and B2B e-Commerce, direct marketing, brand building, customer value management, credit risk management, data mining, and predictive analytics.

Key Contact - Specialty:
Ms. Susan Allard, CEO/Founder - *Senior executives, credit card, financial services, marketing, risk management*
Ms. Nina Bates, Senior Associate - *Credit card, risk management, credit operations, call center, customer service*
Ms. Mary Dawson, Senior Associate - *Internet, fraud, compliance, diversity recruiting, research*
Ms. Lucie Fox, Senior Associate - *Credit card, marketing, new industries, CFO's*
Ms. Linda Sprowls, Senior Associate - *Credit card, marketing, direct marketing, minorities, sales*
Ms. Sue Daugherty, Senior Associate - *Credit card, technical database, customer value management, data mining*
Mr. Dave Lazas, Strategic Partner - *HR assessment, HR strategy, process consulting, assessment tools, planning tools*
Ms. Loretta Jensen, Senior Associate - *Credit card, marketing, risk management*

Ms. Dara Jwaideh, Senior Associate - *Senior management, senior risk management, mortgage, alumni consulting*
Ms. Lynn Woodford, Senior Associate - *Consumer financial services, marketing, risk management*

Salary minimum: $80,000

Functions: Senior Mgmt., Middle Mgmt., Sales & Mktg., CFO's, Credit, Risk Mgmt., DB Admin., R&D, Mgmt. Consultants, Minorities

Industries: Finance, Banking

Branches:
1200 Abernathy Rd Ste 1700
Atlanta, GA 30328
(800) 291-5279
Fax: (800) 526-7791
Email: recruit@allardassociates.com
Key Contact - Specialty:
Ms. Susan Schaefer, Senior Associate - *Catalogue, marketing, commercial lending, private label, partnership marketing*

111 John St Ste 210
New York, NY 10038
(800) 291-5279
Fax: (800) 526-7791
Email: recruit@allardassociates.com
Key Contact - Specialty:
Mr. Lou Giacalone, Senior Associate - *Data warehouse, data mining, technology*

Frank E Allen & Associates Inc
15 James St
Florham Park, NJ 07932-1346
(973) 966-1606
Fax: (973) 966-9749
Email: hrjobs@att.net
Web: www.frankallen.com

Description: An executive search resource specializing in employee relations and human resources. Domestic and International.

Key Contact - Specialty:
Mr. Frank Allen, President - *Human resources*
Mr. Mark E. Allen, Vice President - *Human resources*
Ms. Catherine Hind, Manager - *Human resources*
Mr. Reyer Rick Swaak, Senior Consultant - *International human resources*

Salary minimum: $85,000

Functions: HR Mgmt.

Industries: Generalist

Allen & Associates Inc
1700 E Desert Inn Rd Ste 118
Las Vegas, NV 89109
(702) 731-2066
Email: ballen@wizard.com
Web: www.allenandassoc.com

Description: Executive search for hospitality, gaming, development, manufacturing, distribution and retail management.

Key Contact:
Ms. Maggie Eaton-Biesiada, Vice President - *Retail, hospitality*
Ms. Marla Allen, Vice President - *Sales & marketing*
Ms. Erin McCaslin

Salary minimum: $80,000

Functions: Generalist, Senior Mgmt., Mktg. Mgmt., Sales Mgmt., CFO's, Cash Mgmt., MIS Mgmt., Systems Dev.

Industries: Generalist, Mfg., Food, Bev., Tobacco, Computer Equip., Misc. Financial, Hospitality, Software

Allen & Speth of Buffalo Inc
3131 Sheridan Dr Ste 11
Amherst, NY 14226
(716) 836-5070
Fax: (716) 836-5812
Email: admin@allenspeth.com
Web: www.allenspeth.com

Description: We outperform our competition. We specialize in engineering, software, hardware, IT, sales and marketing, accounting, HR, and purchasing in Buffalo, Western New York, and nationally. We are affiliated with over 900 recruiters nationally. We have a database of 3 million resumes. Recruiting is our business; we do it fulltime.

Key Contact - Specialty:
Mr. Stuart Silverman, President - *Engineering, sales, marketing, accounting*

Salary minimum: $40,000

Functions: Generalist, Middle Mgmt., Mfg., Plant Mgmt., Mktg. Mgmt., Sales Mgmt., HR Mgmt., IT, MIS Mgmt., Engineering

Industries: Generalist

Networks: Top Echelon Network

D S Allen Associates
1119 Raritan Rd Ste 2
Clark, NJ 07066
(732) 574-1600
Fax: (732) 574-2778
Email: dallen@dsallen.com
Web: www.dsallen.com

Description: Specializing in the information technology, hi-tech and communications industries for corporate and major consulting organizations. Areas of expertise: CEO, president, vice president, partner and manager levels plus leading sales/marketing executives.

Key Contact - Specialty:
Mr. Don Allen, President - *IT, hi-tech, communications*
Ms. Mary Ann Ulrich, Partner - *IT, management consulting, executive coaching*

Salary minimum: $75,000

Functions: General Mgmt., Directors, Senior Mgmt., Middle Mgmt., Sales & Mktg., Mktg. Mgmt., Sales Mgmt., IT, MIS Mgmt., Mgmt. Consultants

Industries: Generalist, Computer Equip., Mgmt. Consulting, HR Services, Telecoms, Software

Branches:
28188 Moulton Pkwy Ste 820
Laguna Niguel, CA 92677
(949) 360-4449
Fax: (949) 360-6543
Key Contact - Specialty:
Ms. Muriel Levitt, Regional Vice President - *IT, hi-tech, communications*

24200 Chagrin Blvd Ste 222
Beachwood, OH 44122
(216) 831-1701
Fax: (216) 831-2071
Key Contact - Specialty:
Mr. John Falk, Regional Vice President - *IT, hi-tech, communications*

Pat Allen Associates Inc
40 Indian Hill Rd
PO Box Q
Goldens Bridge, NY 10526
(914) 232-1545
Email: dennis@patallen.com
Web: www.patallen.com

Description: Twenty years of specialization in only safety, insurance, plant and construction safety.

Key Contact - Specialty:
Ms. Pat Allen, CPC, President - *Safety engineers, loss control engineers*

Allen Consulting Group Inc
10805 Sunset Office Dr Ste 214
St. Louis, MO 63127
(314) 984-9909
Email: toma@allencg.com
Web: www.allencg.com

Description: Owner has 25 years' experience in the information systems industry. He has been programmer, manager and director. He personally works with each client and candidate to determine and match their unique requirements.

Key Contact - Specialty:
Mr. Thomas R. Allen, President - *Information systems, data processing*

Functions: Generalist, MIS Mgmt., Systems Analysis, Systems Dev., Systems Implem., Systems Support, Network Admin., DB Admin.

Industries: Generalist

Professional Associations: SME

Allen Personnel Services Ltd
181 Wellington St
London, ON N6B 2K9
Canada
(519) 672-7040
Fax: (519) 672-7044
Email: allen.jobs@sympatico.ca
Web: www.allenpersonnel.com

Description: Full-service agency offering local, national and international recruitment. Experienced, knowledgeable and professional consultants who are experts in their field.

Key Contact - Specialty:
Ms. Cathy Monchamp, Consultant - *Accounting/finance, human resources, engineering, manufacturing*
Ms. Linda Disik, Supervisor - *Permanent & contract*
Ms. Tamara Dahl, Consultant - *Engineering, manufacturing, technology, human resources*
Ms. Tina Chambers, Consultant - *Information technology*
Ms. Lorry Dawdy, Consultant - *Human resources, finance, accounting*

Salary minimum: $35,000

Functions: Generalist, Mfg., Materials, Sales & Mktg., HR Mgmt., Finance, IT, Engineering

Industries: Generalist, Mfg., Finance, Communications, Software

Networks: National Personnel Assoc (NPA)

Branches:
1425 Bishop St
Cambridge, ON N1R 6J9
Canada
(519) 623-5510
Fax: (519) 623-1513
Email: allen.work@sympatico.ca
Key Contact - Specialty:
Mr. John Sumilas - *Information technology, manufacturing, engineering*

Allen Thomas Associates Inc
518 Prospect Ave
Little Silver, NJ 07739
(732) 219-5353
Fax: (732) 219-5805
Email: recruit@allenthomas.com
Web: www.allenthomas.com

Description: We are an executive search firm specializing in mid- to upper-management positions in the healthcare industry. This includes all management positions in the hospital, home care, managed care and pharmaceutical fields.

Key Contact - Specialty:
Ms. Linda Forrest, Director - *Consumer products, hospitality, ecommerce, internet*
Mr. Thomas Benoit, FACHE, President - *Healthcare*

Functions: Health Admin.

Industries: Pharm Svcs., Healthcare

Allen-Jeffers Associates
23716 Marlin Cv
Laguna Niguel, CA 92677
(949) 495-1096
Fax: (949) 495-5009
Email: bobjeffers@aol.com
Web: www.smart-office.net/5135

Description: We are an executive and technical search firm specializing in the medical and electronics industries. The measure of our search firm is in the quality and suitability of our candidates.

Key Contact - Specialty:
Mr. Robert Jeffers, Owner - *Medical device, pharmaceuticals, executive, senior technical*

Salary minimum: $75,000

Functions: Generalist, Product Dev.

Industries: Drugs Mfg., Medical Devices, Computer Equip., Venture Cap., Pharm Svcs., Digital, Wireless, Software, Database SW, Development SW, Biotech, Healthcare

Allenetics Executive Search
4360 Turner Rd
PO Box 1401
Monument, CO 80132
(719) 481-1419
Fax: (719) 481-1420
Email: allenetics@att.net
Web: www.allenetics.com

Description: AES is a high tech recruitment agency secializing in Software Development, Financial Services, ERP, CRM, Telecommunications, Network Engineering, IT Management/Development, E-Commerce, B to B Solutions as well as many other industries.

Key Contact:
Mr. Tom Allen, President
Ms. Barbara Allen, Owner

Functions: IT

Industries: Services, Mgmt. Consulting, E-commerce, IT Implementation, Media, New Media, Communications, Telecoms, Call Centers, Telephony, Digital, Wireless, Network Infrastructure, Software, Database SW, Development SW, ERP SW, Networking, Comm. SW, System SW

Allhands Placement Consultants
1209 Kossuth St
Lafayette, IN 47905
(765) 742-1985
Fax: (765) 742-8061
Email: kallhands@aol.com

Description: Executive search and placement within healthcare settings across the U.S. Extensive use of database matching and candidate profiling, to send the right candidate to prospective clients. Competitive fees.

Key Contact - Specialty:
Ms. Kelly Allhands, Owner/President - *Physicians*

Functions: Generalist, Physicians, Health Admin.

Industries: Generalist, Healthcare

The Alliance Search Group Inc
1685 NW 122nd St
Clive, IA 50325
(515) 221-3233
Fax: (515) 221-1295
Email: wjesper@aol.com

Description: We are a full service contingency search firm specializing in the recruitment and placement of candidates in the manufacturing industry. We focus on engineering, materials, management, accounting, HR, and MIS. We offer permanent placement or contract placement.

Key Contact:
Mrs. Wendy Jespersen, President - *Manufacturing recruitment*
Ms. Mary Jones, Vice President

Salary minimum: $25,000

Functions: Mfg.

Industries: Agri., Forestry, Mining, Construction, Mfg., Transportation, Aerospace, Packaging, Insurance, Mfg. SW

Networks: Top Echelon Network

Allied Search Inc
2030 Union St Ste 206
San Francisco, CA 94147
(415) 921-2200
(213) 680-4000
Fax: (415) 921-5309
Email: alliedsearchinc@aol.com
Web: www.alliedsearchinc.com

Description: We recruit and place professionals and executives nationwide (all 50 states) in all industries including start-up companies. Our divisions are executive (CEOs, CIOs, CTOs, CFOs, COOs, etc.), consulting (management, IT, ERP, operational, litigation, computer risk, etc.), information technology (IT), financial (accounting, etc.), audit (IS, IT, internal, financial, operational, etc.), tax, and human resources.

Key Contact - Specialty:
Mr. Donald C. May, Managing Director - *Executive, consulting, IT, financial, audit*

Salary minimum: $40,000

Functions: Generalist, General Mgmt., HR Mgmt., Finance, IT, Mgmt. Consultants, Int'l.

Industries: Generalist

Professional Associations: NAPS

Branches:
3699 Wilshire Blvd Ste 850
Los Angeles, CA 90010
(213) 680-4000
(415) 921-2200
Fax: (213) 680-4080
Email: alliedsearchinc@aol.com
Key Contact - Specialty:
Mr. Donald C. May, Managing Director - *Executive, consulting, IT, financial/audit, HR*

Tom Allison Associates
625 Stagecoach Rd SE
Albuquerque, NM 87123
(505) 275-7771
Fax: (505) 275-7771
Email: tallison@spinn.net

Description: We are a successful nationwide experienced executive search company specializing in the food, consumer products and agriculture industries. We specialize in supervisory to executive-level positions in all classifications.

Key Contact - Specialty:
Mr. Tom Allison, Owner/President - *Food, consumer products, agriculture, produce*

Salary minimum: $40,000

Functions: Generalist, Senior Mgmt., Middle Mgmt., Production, Purchasing, Sales Mgmt., Benefits

Industries: Generalist, Agri., Forestry, Mining, Food, Bev., Tobacco, Machine, Appliance, Wholesale, Retail, Hospitality

Allman & Company Inc
PO Box 4573
Wilmington, NC 28406-1573
(910) 395-5219
Email: s.allman@att.net

Description: We have had more than twenty years experience in helping trust companies with staffing requirements. We were the past Agency of the Year by NCAPS, and Steven L. Allman, CPC, was named Consultant of the Year by NCAPS.

Key Contact - Specialty:
Mr. Steven L. Allman, CPC, President - *Trust banking, retirement plan services*

Salary minimum: $60,000

Functions: Finance, Cash Mgmt.

Industries: Banking, Invest. Banking

Professional Associations: NCASP, NCCDA, NCDA

AllStaff
1355 Remington Rd Ste W
Schaumburg, IL 60173
(847) 882-9777
Fax: (847) 882-9779
Email: allstaff@mindspring.com
Web: www.allstaffusa.com

Description: We are a contract and placement company that specializes in the placement of software and hardware engineers, developers, and sales personnel to our high-tech and telephony clients (Fortune 100-500) here in the Chicago land area.

Key Contact - Specialty:
Mr. Joseph R. Frankian, Vice President - *Software, information technology*
Ms. Shelly Cunningham, Senior Technical Recruiter - *Hardware, software, telecommunications*
Mr. Aris Andrews, Senior Sales Recruiter - *Hardware, software, telecommunications*

Functions: Generalist, Mktg. Mgmt., Systems Analysis, Systems Dev., Systems Implem., Systems Support, Network Admin., DB Admin.

Industries: Generalist, Computer Equip., Consumer Elect., Telecoms, Software

Hill Allyn Associates
PO Box 15247
San Francisco, CA 94115-0247
(415) 773-8580
Email: hillallyn@aol.com

Description: Recruits for sales staff and management positions in San Francisco area and North America. Certified employment specialist (CES) with graduate training in organizational consultation.

Key Contact - Specialty:
Ms. Gayle Hill Vignet, Recruiting Partner - *Generalist*

Salary minimum: $25,000

Functions: Sales Mgmt.

Industries: Generalist

Alpert Executive Search Inc
420 Lexington Ave Ste 2024
New York, NY 10170
(212) 297-9009
Fax: (212) 297-0818
Email: ada@alpertsearch.com
Web: www.alpertsearch.com

Description: Our firm specializes in account planning, strategic planning, brand strategy recruitment, and placement for advertising agencies, brand consultancies, and interactive firms.

Key Contact:
Mrs. Ada Alpert, President

Alpha Resource Group Inc
1916 Brabant Dr
Plano, TX 75025
(972) 527-1616
Fax: (972) 527-4244

Description: Through our worldwide recruitment network, we specialize in professional executive search and placement to many of the industry's finest hotels, resorts, clubs and casinos.

Key Contact - Specialty:
Mr. Sewell B. Pappas, Managing Director - *Hotel, resort*

Salary minimum: $35,000

Functions: Generalist

Industries: Hotels, Resorts, Clubs

Professional Associations: THMA

Alpha Resources
1 Tower Ln Ste 1700
Oak Brook Terrace, IL 60181
(630) 573-2913
Fax: (630) 954-0833
Email: alpharesou@aol.com

Description: Specializes in marketing & sales for semiconductor, integrated circuit and electrical industries. Principal has been in recruiting since July 1979. Work national and some international.

Key Contact - Specialty:
Mr. Daniel P. Cook, General Manager - *Sales & marketing, semiconductors*

Salary minimum: $80,000

Functions: Sales & Mktg.

Industries: Electronic, Elec. Components

Alpha Systems Inc
3325 Sweetwater Dr
Cumming, GA 30041-6641
(770) 887-8558
Email: wgriffin@ga.prestige.net
Web: www.jobbs.com/alpha.html

Description: We specialize in design, engineering, automation, controls, instrumentation, manufacturing, software, systems, distribution, logistics, sales and marketing, operations, purchasing, quality, robotics, materials, components, test engineering, operations, general management in high-tech industries, chemical, food, drug, biotech, plastics, metal fabrication, films, packaging, capital equipment, machinery, digital electronics, RF, microwave, optics, photonics, telecommunications, electronic commerce, and Internet automation, browsing and broadband, optical network, and server applications.

Key Contact:
Mr. William W. Griffin, Owner

Salary minimum: $40,000

Functions: General Mgmt., Middle Mgmt., Mfg., Automation, Plant Mgmt., Materials, Purchasing, Distribution, Sales Mgmt., Engineering

Industries: Generalist, Mfg., Test, Measure Equip., Mgmt. Consulting, Communications, Aerospace, Packaging, Software, Database SW, Development SW, Industry Specific SW, Security SW, System SW, Biotech

Networks: Top Echelon Network

ALS Group
104 Mt. Joy Rd
Milford, NJ 08848
(908) 995-9500
Fax: (908) 995-7032
Email: alsgroup@webspan.net
Web: www.alsgroup.com

Description: Specializing in corporate lending, commercial lending, credit administration, small business lending, commercial real estate lending, asset based, loan work-out, investment banking, private banking, trust, retail lending, foreign exchange, indirect lending and finance. Place portfolio, underwriting, originations, and operations positions within each discipline.

Key Contact - Specialty:
Mr. Scott Lysenko, President - *Banking, finance*
Ms. Lisa Lysenko, Executive Vice President - *Banking, finance*

Salary minimum: $35,000

Functions: Senior Mgmt., Middle Mgmt., Sales & Mktg., Finance, Cash Mgmt., Credit, M&A, Int'l.

Industries: Finance, Banking, Invest. Banking, Brokers, Venture Cap., Misc. Financial

Professional Associations: NJSA

Alta Search
7037 Duncan's Glen Dr
Knoxville, TN 37919-8589
(865) 450-9578
Fax: (865) 450-9581
Email: altasearch@mindspring.com

Description: Sole practitioner with emphasis in, but not limited to, sales and marketing in the electrical and HVAC markets. Executive-level assignments accepted in industry specialty.

Key Contact - Specialty:
Mr. Mark Hill, CRM - *Technical (sales and marketing)*

Salary minimum: $70,000

Functions: Sales & Mktg., Mkt. Research, Mktg. Mgmt., Sales Mgmt.

Industries: Misc. Mfg.

The Altco Group
281 Main St
Woodbridge, NJ 07095-1944
(732) 283-2722
Fax: (732) 283-3666
Email: box100@altco.com
Web: www.altco.com

Description: We specialize in technical, scientific and operations positions for consumer packaged goods and pharmaceutical/medical device companies. Our experience, extensive database and industry contacts allow us to quickly identify the best candidates.

Key Contact - Specialty:
Mr. Ken Altreuter, President - *Consumer packaged goods, operation, technical*
Mr. John Shea, Senior Search Consultant - *Consumer packaged goods (operation, technical)*
Mr. Ingo Petersen, Executive Recruiter - *Packaging engineers*

Salary minimum: $60,000

Functions: Production, Automation, Materials, Packaging, Engineering

Industries: Food, Bev., Tobacco, Soap, Perf., Cosmtcs., Drugs Mfg., Medical Devices, Consumer Elect.

Professional Associations: IFT, IOPP, SHRM

Networks: Inter-City Personnel Assoc (IPA)

Altec/HRC
PO Box 276
Bloomfield Hills, MI 48303-0276
(248) 594-6690
Fax: (248) 594-6691

Description: Specialize in the placement of engineers and all types of various management positions found in manufacturing companies. The emphasis is on making good matches and a hard sell is not used on either side. We also recruit in industrial and technical sales.

Key Contact - Specialty:
Mr. Frank A. Cowall, President - *Technical, mid & upper management*

Salary minimum: $30,000

Functions: Generalist, Middle Mgmt., Mfg., Materials, Sales Mgmt., HR Mgmt., Engineering

Industries: Generalist, Plastics, Rubber, Metal Products, Machine, Appliance, Motor Vehicles, Misc. Mfg.

Professional Associations: HRA

Networks: National Personnel Assoc (NPA)

The Alternatives Group Inc
3201 Pinehurst Dr
Plano, TX 75075-1760
(972) 985-8200
(800) 599-2133
Fax: (972) 612-0025
Email: mbenum@mstaff.com

Description: We specialize in the nationwide placement of sales and sales support personnel.

Key Contact:
Ms. Michele S. Benum, CPC, CEO - *Data processing, sales, telecommunications*
Ms. Gina Lawrence, EVP/General Manager

Salary minimum: $30,000

Functions: Sales & Mktg., MIS Mgmt., Systems Analysis, Systems Dev., Systems Implem., Systems Support, Mgmt. Consultants

Industries: Telecoms, Software

Professional Associations: AITP, DPMA

Alynco Inc
10709 Platte Valley Dr
Little Rock, AR 72212-3629
(501) 221-0066
Fax: (501) 221-0068
Email: fausett@swbell.net

Description: Prior to starting my firm, my personal background was in distribution and transportation. As a result, I feel we are uniquely positioned to assist both clients and candidates in this area.

Key Contact - Specialty:
Mr. A. Smith Fausett, President - *Logistics*

Salary minimum: $50,000

Functions: Distribution

Industries: Generalist

Professional Associations: CLM

Amato & Associates Insurance Recruiters
1313 Medford Rd Ste 100
Wynnewood, PA 19096-2418
(610) 642-9696
Fax: (610) 642-9797

Email: amato2000@home.com

Description: Commercial property/casualty/workers compensation, insurance underwriters, account executives, producers, claims, loss control for carriers, agents/brokers, reinsurers, risk management concentrating in mid-Atlantic and East Coast.

Key Contact - Specialty:
Ms. Bobbi Amato, CPC, President/Owner - *Insurance*

Salary minimum: $30,000

Functions: Generalist

Industries: Insurance

Professional Associations: CPCU, MAAPC, NAWBO, PIA, PLUS

Amato & Associates Inc
126 Peralta Ave
Mill Valley, CA 94941
(415) 388-1875

Description: Commercial insurance is our specialty. We place production oriented commercial insurance positions such as sales, underwriting, A/Es, etc. to upper-level management, such as carriers, brokers, and re-insurers.

Key Contact - Specialty:
Mr. Joseph D. Amato, President - *Insurance*

Salary minimum: $80,000

Functions: Senior Mgmt., Middle Mgmt., Sales & Mktg., Mktg. Mgmt., Sales Mgmt., Risk Mgmt., Systems Implem., Systems Support

Industries: Generalist, Insurance

Professional Associations: CPCU, RIMS

Amber Systems Group LLC
104 S Main St 513
Fond du Lac, WI 54935
(920) 322-9011
Fax: (920) 322-9013
Email: amber@powercom.net

Description: Our firm is a leading information technology and telecommunications recruiting firm dedicated to providing you with exceptional people to best meet your staffing needs. We have over 12 years of local and nationwide recruiting experience. We also have over 20 years of direct experience in information technology and telecommunications.

Key Contact - Specialty:
Ms. Celeste Christ, Owner - *IT, telecommunications professionals*
Mr. Fred Christ, RCDD, Owner - *IT/telecommunications (recruiting, consulting)*

Functions: Sales Mgmt., IT, MIS Mgmt.

Industries: Generalist, Telecoms, Call Centers, Telephony, Digital, Wireless, Fiber Optic, Network Infrastructure, ERP SW, Networking, Comm. SW, Security SW

Professional Associations: BICSI, WAPS, WTA

Ambiance Personnel Inc
7990 SW 117th Ave Ste 125
Miami, FL 33183
(305) 274-7419
Fax: (305) 598-8071
Email: e-mail@ambiancepersonnel.com
Web: www.ambiancepersonnel.com

Description: We are a search and staffing firm specializing in international trade, transportation/logistics, and produce. We handle all sales, marketing, accounting, information technology, traffic, materials management, and senior management for companies engaged in international distribution and supply chain management.

Key Contact - Specialty:
Mr. Eric S. Pollack, President - *Logistics, produce management, sales*

Salary minimum: $40,000

Functions: Distribution

Industries: Mfg., Wholesale, Retail, Finance

Ambridge Management Corp
36 Toronto St Ste 850
Toronto, ON M5C 2C5
Canada
(416) 367-3810
Fax: (416) 367-9458
Email: ambridge@caspar.net

Description: We specialize in investment banking, project finance, treasury and trading positions and risk management positions attached to these roles.

Key Contact:
Mr. Gordon K. Sherwin, President - *Banking, financial services*
Ms. Genevieve Habel, Vice President

Salary minimum: $60,000

Functions: Generalist, Finance, Cash Mgmt., Credit, M&A, Risk Mgmt.

Industries: Generalist, Finance, Banking

AMD & Associates
3455 Peachtree Industrial Blvd Ste 305-266
Duluth, GA 30096
(770) 612-1000
Email: amdsearch@mindspring.com

Description: Excellent skills in building lasting client relationships. Experienced in both senior-level and mid-level retained and contingency search in a broad range of industries. Broad exposure to generalist recruiting with heavy concentration in sales/sales management in medical/healthcare and information systems/technology.

Key Contact - Specialty:
Ms. Anna Marie Denman, Search Consultant - *Generalist, sales & marketing*

Functions: Generalist, Mkt. Research, Mktg. Mgmt., Sales Mgmt., IT

Industries: Generalist, Drugs Mfg., Medical Devices, Misc. Mfg., Pharm Svcs.

America at Work
422 Franklin St
Reading, PA 19602
(610) 372-9675
Fax: (610) 372-5090
Email: ameriwork@aol.com
Web: www.americaatwork.com

Description: We provide professional search firm specializing in the recruitment and placement of bilingual (Spanish and Portuguese) professionals for positions in the US, as well as abroad.

Key Contact - Specialty:
Mr. Nelson A. De Leon, Owner - *Bilingual professionals (Spanish, Portuguese)*

America's Professional Recruiting Inc
6501 Park of Commerce Blvd Ste 230
Boca Raton, FL 33487
(561) 999-9060
Fax: (561) 999-0140
Email: wcarr@amrecruit.com
Web: www.amrecruit.com

Description: Our firm has been in the industry for over 20 years. Our recruiters have gained the reputation of treating clients fairly and professionally.

Key Contact:
Mr. Wayne Carr, President

Functions: Generalist

Industries: Generalist

American Heritage Group Inc
32670 Concord
Madison Heights, MI 48071
(248) 577-1170
Fax: (248) 577-1176
Email: admin@americanheritagegroup.com
Web: www.americanheritagegroup.com

Description: We are a triple disciplined, duel faceted executive recruiting, consulting firm. Placing all levels of the computer, automotive engineering, clerical worlds.

Key Contact - Specialty:
Mr. John Holliday, President - *Computer professionals*
Mr. Robert Drohan, Executive Vice President - *Computer professionals*

Functions: Generalist, Admin. Svcs., Sales Mgmt., Direct Mktg., Customer Svc., Personnel, Systems Implem., Mgmt. Consultants

Industries: Generalist, Plastics, Rubber, Metal Products, Computer Equip., Test, Measure Equip., HR Services, Software

American Incite
917 Hillfield Ct
Oceanside, CA 92054-7013
(760) 754-2444
Fax: (760) 754-2453
Email: executivesearch@americanincite.com
Web: www.americanincite.com

Description: We serve manufacturing and service firms that include automation, HVAC/R, and fuel cell industries. Here's what a client says: "While your fees are substantial, I feel that your efforts to locate, qualify, market the position, and interface as a third party in the finalization process brought value to the process well in excess of your monetary charges."

Key Contact - Specialty:
Mr. Brandon Ebeling, CPC, Senior Partner - *Executive leadership for general management, sales, marketing, operation, engineering*

Salary minimum: $75,000

Functions: General Mgmt., Senior Mgmt., Middle Mgmt., Automation, Mktg. Mgmt., Sales Mgmt., Systems Implem., R&D, Engineering, Technicians

Industries: Agri., Forestry, Mining, Energy, Utilities, Construction, Mfg., Chemicals, Machine, Appliance, Computer Equip., Test, Measure Equip., Misc. Mfg., Electronic, Elec. Components, Services, Equip Svcs., Mgmt. Consulting, Environmental Svcs., Software, Database SW, HR SW, Industry Specific SW

Professional Associations: NAPS

American Logistics Consultants Inc
(a division of American Services Group Int'l)
2215 York Rd Ste 203
Oak Brook, IL 60523
(630) 990-1001
Fax: (630) 990-1009
Email: jduzinski@amlogistics.com
Web: www.amlogistics.com

Description: Full-service recruitment of middle management and executives in the transportation, logistics and supply chain industries.

Key Contact:
Mr. Gerald Duzinski, President - *Logistics, transportation, traffic, shipping, supply chain*
Mr. Ray Lilja, Partner

Salary minimum: $40,000

Functions: Mfg., Materials, Purchasing, Distribution, Sales & Mktg., Sales Mgmt.

Industries: Generalist, Mfg., Transportation, Wholesale, Retail

Professional Associations: CLM

Branches:
124 Park Place Dr
Sinking Spring, PA 19608
(610) 927-9499
Fax: (610) 927-0282
Email: ncurrie@amlogistics.com
Key Contact - Specialty:
Mr. Ned Currie, Vice President - *Logistics*

American Medical Consultants Inc
11625 SW 110th Rd
Miami, FL 33176-3152
(305) 271-9225
Fax: (305) 271-8664
Email: amcmo@bellsouth.net
Web: www.ammedcon.com

Description: A nationwide physician and healthcare recruitment organization that assists hospitals, group practices, HMOs and solo practitioners in meeting their physician and personnel needs.

Key Contact - Specialty:
Mr. Martin H. Osinski, Principal - *Physicians, physician executives*

Salary minimum: $100,000

Functions: Physicians

Industries: Healthcare

Professional Associations: ACHE, AMR, NAPR

Branches:
471 Lexington Ave
Ft. Lauderdale, FL 33325
(954) 424-8777
Fax: (954) 370-1341
Email: amcfl@bellsouth.net
Key Contact - Specialty:
Mr. Michael Kirschner, Principal - *Physicians, physician executives*

American Medical Recruiters
325 Krameria St
Denver, CO 80220
(303) 393-0791
Fax: (303) 393-0683
Email: gmberquist@aol.com
Web: www.medrecruit.com

Description: Recruit for hospital systems across the country and for healthcare information system companies.

Key Contact - Specialty:
Ms. Gailmarie Berquist, President - *Healthcare*

Salary minimum: $60,000

Functions: Generalist, Healthcare, Nurses, Health Admin., MIS Mgmt., Systems Analysis

Industries: Generalist, Healthcare, Hospitals

American Medical Recruiting Company Inc
308 Corporate Dr
Ridgeland, MS 39157
(601) 898-7527
(800) 844-6503 x1527
Fax: (601) 898-7577
Email: recruiter@meamedicalclinics.com

Description: We specialize in physician recruitment for family medicine in Mississippi.

Key Contact:
Mrs. Rachel Williamson, Recruiter

Functions: Generalist, Physicians

Industries: Generalist, Healthcare

American Professional Search Inc

6805 Arno Allisona Rd
College Grove, TN 37046-9216
(615) 368-7979
Fax: (615) 368-7981
Email: amprosinc@sprynet.com

Description: My twenty-four years experience as a
manager and engineer plus my11 years of
experience as a recruiter allows me a thorough
understanding of client requirements, resulting in
the ability to select individuals who will have an
immediate positive impact on the hiring
organization.

Key Contact:
Mr. Ray O'Steen, President - *Manufacturing
engineering*
Mrs. Gloria O'Steen, Vice President

Functions: Mfg., Materials, HR Mgmt.,
Engineering

Industries: Machine, Appliance, Motor Vehicles

Professional Associations: TAPS

Networks: Top Echelon Network

American Recruiters Consolidated Inc

800 W Cypress Creek Rd Ste 310
Ft. Lauderdale, FL 33309
(954) 493-9200
Fax: (954) 493-9582
Email: arci@arcimail.com
Web: www.americanrecruiters.com

Description: We provide retained and contingency
searches for recruitment in pharmaceuticals,
pharmacy, nursing, long-term care, sales &
marketing, human resource, engineering,
manufacturing, HVAC, food equipment, and
technical/high-tech positions. Middle and upper-
level positions are our focus. We also offer human
resources training and consulting.

Key Contact - Specialty:
Mr. Carl R. Carieri, Owner - *Food service
equipment, appliance, sales & marketing,
engineering, manufacturing*
Mr. Gino Scialdone, Owner - *Sales professionals*

Salary minimum: $50,000

Functions: General Mgmt., Senior Mgmt., Middle
Mgmt., Mfg., Healthcare, Sales & Mktg., HR
Mgmt., Finance, IT, Engineering

Industries: Mfg., Pharm Svcs., Accounting, Mgmt.
Consulting, HR Services, Hospitality, Wireless,
Packaging, Biotech, Healthcare

Professional Associations: AIMS, ALFA, NAFEM,
NAPS, SHRM

Branches:
6807 Sand Aster Dr
Carlsbad, CA 92009
(888) 813-5980
(888) 813-5980
Fax: (760) 431-5231
Email: ktobias@arcimail.com
Key Contact - Specialty:
Ms. Kim Tobias, Executive Recruiter - *High
technology*

7936 E Arapahoe Crt Ste 2800
Englewood, CO 80111
(720) 346-5000
Fax: (877) 704-5627
Email: rowens@arcimail.com
Key Contact - Specialty:
Ms. Renee Owens, Franchise Owner - *Long term
care, assisted living*

18623 Tiffany Dr
Miami, FL 33157
(305) 232-5284
Email: sapodaca@arcimail.com
Key Contact - Specialty:
Mr. Steve Apodaca - *Nursing*

1451 W Cypress Creek Rd
Pompano, FL 33309
(954) 958-0330
Fax: (954) 958-0331
Email: glantz@arcimail.com
Key Contact:
Ms. Gina Lantz, Franchise Owner

1100 Circle 75 Pkwy Ste 210
Atlanta, GA 30339
(770) 690-9800
Fax: (770) 690-9850
Email: jphillip@arcimail.com
Key Contact - Specialty:
Ms. Ina Phillip-Jolis, Franchise Owner - *Local
sales professionals*

1622 E Algonquin Rd Ste J
Schaumburg, IL 60173
(847) 303-0560
Fax: (847) 303-0559
Email: cwilson@arcimail.com
Key Contact:
Mr. Craig Wilson, Franchise Owner

6 Oriole Ter
Newton, NJ 07860
(973) 300-4886
Fax: (973) 300-5905
Email: gnomer@arcimail.com
Key Contact - Specialty:
Mr. Gary Nomer, Franchise Owner - *Food, food
services, engineering, manufacturing*

8004 Lorain Ave
Cleveland, OH 44102
(216) 961-3300
Fax: (216) 961-6476
Email: tviets@arcimail.com
Key Contact - Specialty:
Ms. Terri Viets, Franchise Owner - *Pharmacists,
long term care*

3666 Knight Dr
White Creek, TN 37189
(615) 299-5551
Fax: (615) 299-8350
Email: lmansfield@arcimail.com
Key Contact - Specialty:
Ms. Laura Mansfield, Franchise Owner - *Long term
care*

American Recruiters Int'l

3900 NW 79th Ave Ste 401
Miami, FL 33166
(305) 342-0550 x101
(800) 592-1455 x239
Email: reneed@ar-intl.com
Web: www.ar-intl.com

Description: We are a national recruiting firm that
employs over 25 full time recruiters. In May 2001,
The Business Journal named us the number one
executive search firm in Southern Florida. We have
two divisions, and they are: high technology and
generalist. We place at all levels including
executive. Our positions consist of both permanent
and contract opportunities.

Key Contact - Specialty:
Ms. Renee Dixon, High Technology Division
Manager - *Information technology,
telecommunications, engineering - technical and
sales*
Mr. Darcy Penichet, President
Ms. Johnna Andersen-Alvarez,
Operations/Division Mgr. - *Generalist*

Functions: Generalist

Industries: Mfg., Wholesale, Retail, Finance,
Services, Media, Communications, Government,
Insurance, Software

American Resources Corp

601 S LaSalle St Ste A523
Chicago, IL 60605
(866) 272-0101
Fax: (312) 587-9160
Email: arc@ameritech.net
Web: www.american-resources.com

Description: Our dedicated consulting specialists
know the most effective recruitment techniques, the
overall professional market and how to attract the
best candidates.

Key Contact - Specialty:
Mr. Osita Oruche, President/Consultant - *Executive
management, information technology, financial
communities*
Dr. Chuck Mojek, Ph.D., VP-Engineering
Communities - *Engineering, plant manufacturing,
operations*
Mr. Larry Stewart, Vice President-Human
Resources - *General management, sales &
marketing*
Mr. Emmett Vaughn, Director - Corporate Affairs -
Human resources (general)
Ms. Sonia Freeman, Office Manager -
Administration

Salary minimum: $35,000

Functions: Generalist

Industries: Generalist

Professional Associations: AMCF

Networks: World Search Group

Branches:
27424 Winchester Ter
Brownstown, MI 48183
(313) 692-1933
Key Contact:
Mr. Raymond Herbert, Vice President

4206 W North Ave
Milwaukee, WI 53208
(262) 587-9000
Key Contact:
Mr. Roy Evans, Vice President

Americas Project Management Services

741 Riversville Rd
Greenwich, CT 06831
(203) 863-9168
Email: acg03@sprynet.com
Web: www.americaspms.com

Description: The expertise of Americas Project
Management Services is to provide project services
to any company in the development of projects
within the Western hemisphere.

Key Contact - Specialty:
Mr. Laurent Martinez, Managing Director
Mr. Bernard Louette, Project Director -
Engineering

Salary minimum: $50,000

Functions: Production, Budgeting, Engineering,
Int'l.

Industries: Energy, Utilities, Construction,
Chemicals, Telecoms, Telephony, Wireless, Fiber
Optic, Aerospace, Industry Specific SW, Mfg.
SW, System SW, Biotech, Healthcare, Hospitals

AmeriPro Search Inc

326 Stutts Rd
Mooresville, NC 28117
(704) 660-0991
Fax: (704) 660-0944
Email: ameripro@bigfoot.com
Web: www.ameriprosearch.com

Description: Full-service contingency search firm
with emphasis on technical (engineering, design,
CAD,controls, manufacturing, & QA/QC/QE.),

sales (industrial), marketing (industrial & int'l.), financial (corporate & plant) and information systems (midrange & mainframe). Heavy emphasis in MIS, SAP and Oracle.

Key Contact - Specialty:
Mrs. Elaine Brauninger, Administrative Director/Senior Recruiter - *General manufacturing, building products*
Mr. John C. Brauninger, General Manager - *Manufacturing, sales, marketing, MIS, SAP*

Salary minimum: $40,000

Functions: Generalist, General Mgmt., Mfg., Materials, Sales & Mktg., Finance, IT, Engineering

Industries: Generalist, Mfg., Medical Devices, Plastics, Rubber, Machine, Appliance, Motor Vehicles, Software

Professional Associations: ASQ, NAFE, SPE

Networks: Top Echelon Network

AmeriResource Group Inc
2525 NW Expwy Ste 532
Oklahoma City, OK 73112
(405) 842-5900
Fax: (405) 843-9879
Email: staffing@ameriresource.com
Web: www.ameriresource.com

Description: We are a fully integrated human resource company. We provide employees (permanent, contract and temporary) to companies nationwide from entry level to executive management.

Key Contact - Specialty:
Mr. Nick Martire, National Account Manager - *MIS, engineering, finance, human resources, executive management*

Salary minimum: $30,000

Functions: Generalist, General Mgmt., Healthcare, HR Mgmt., Finance, IT, Engineering

Industries: Generalist; Energy, Utilities, Construction, Mfg., Finance, Accounting, HR Services, IT Implementation, Communications, Aerospace, Software

Branches:
5840 S Memorial Dr Ste 212
Tulsa, OK 74145
(918) 627-4900
Fax: (918) 627-4984
Key Contact - Specialty:
Mrs. Diane Hewitt, Branch Manager - *Construction*

AmeriSearch Group Inc
227 N Dixie Way Ste 310
South Bend, IN 46637
(219) 271-6040
Fax: (219) 271-6041
Email: hrmgr@amersch.com
Web: www.amersch.com

Description: Specializing in management, technical & professional positions, primarily accounting, information technology, and manufacturing management.

Key Contact - Specialty:
Mr. Chuck Daniels, President - *Information systems, information technology*

Salary minimum: $40,000

Functions: General Mgmt., Mfg., Finance, IT, Engineering

Industries: Generalist

Professional Associations: PARW

Networks: Top Echelon Network

Ames-O'Neill Associates Inc
PO Box 841
Syosset, NY 11791
(516) 921-4488
Fax: (516) 921-5602
Email: ames@frontiernet.net

Description: We specialize in the recruitment of high-technology specialists in electronics, avionics, aerospace, telecommunications, software engineering and related support functions for commercial and military clients.

Key Contact - Specialty:
Mr. George C. Ames, President - *Commercial, military electronics, avionics, software engineering, telecommunications*

Salary minimum: $40,000

Functions: Mfg., Materials, Sales & Mktg., Finance, IT, R&D, Engineering

Industries: Medical Devices, Computer Equip., Consumer Elect., Test, Measure Equip., Media, Aerospace, Software

Networks: Inter-City Personnel Assoc (IPA)

Amherst Human Resource Group Ltd
401 N Michigan Ave Ste 360
Chicago, IL 60611
(312) 245-0050
Fax: (312) 245-0063
Email: amhersthrg@msn.com

Description: Generalists in middle/upper-management arena with selected specialties such as healthcare, manufacturing, consumer products and services, association management; candidate generation through computerized database, networking resources and research staff.

Key Contact - Specialty:
Ms. Sylvia E. Emerick, President - *Association management*
Ms. Stephanie Rubin, Senior Executive Vice President - *Manufacturing*

Salary minimum: $40,000

Functions: Generalist

Industries: Construction, Transportation, Retail, Finance, Services, Hospitality, Packaging, Insurance, Real Estate, Healthcare

Professional Associations: CHEF, SHRM

Amherst Personnel Group Inc
550 W Old Country Rd
Hicksville, NY 11801-4116
(516) 433-7610
Fax: (516) 433-7848
Email: amherstgr@aol.com

Description: Twenty-fifth year specializing in sales and marketing and retailing management.

Key Contact:
Mr. Charles J. Eibeler, CPC, President
Mr. Donald Porter, Vice President

Salary minimum: $20,000

Functions: Generalist, Sales & Mktg., Advertising, Mktg. Mgmt., Sales Mgmt.

Industries: Generalist, Food, Bev., Tobacco, Soap, Perf., Cosmtcs., Drugs Mfg., Medical Devices, Retail, Healthcare

Professional Associations: APCNY, NJAPS

Networks: First Interview Network (FIN)

AMINEX Corp
148 State St Ste 405
Boston, MA 02109
(617) 248-6883
Fax: (617) 248-8650

Email: aminex@thecia.net
Web: www.aminex.com

Description: We have devoted our full resources and capabilites to provide the insurance industry with talented executives. We believe that attracting leadership talent is of paramount importance to a company's success.

Key Contact - Specialty:
Mr. Lucius F. Sinks, Treasurer - *Insurance, technical, management, marketing*
Mr. Rick Tolstrup, President - *Insurance, technical, management, marketing*
Ms. Lisa Lepore Perry, Corporate Clerk - *Insurance, technical, management, marketing, managed care*

Salary minimum: $30,000

Functions: Generalist, Mkt. Research, Mktg. Mgmt., Sales Mgmt., Customer Svc., Benefits, Personnel, Risk Mgmt.

Industries: Generalist, Insurance

Professional Associations: INS, NIRA

Amos & Associates Inc
633-B Chapel Hill Rd
Burlington, NC 27215
(336) 222-0231
Fax: (336) 222-1214
Email: joy@amosassociates.com
Web: www.amosassociates.com

Description: We are the most recognized Hewlett Packard specialized search firm in the nation. Our large broad base of clients range from small, privately-held growth oriented companies to large Fortune 100 corporations.

Key Contact - Specialty:
Ms. Diane Amos, CPC, President - *Information technology*

Functions: Generalist, MIS Mgmt., Systems Analysis, Systems Dev., Systems Implem., Systems Support, Network Admin., DB Admin.

Industries: Generalist, Mfg., Misc. Mfg., Retail, Pharm Svcs., Insurance, Software, Healthcare

Professional Associations: NAPS, NCASP

Networks: Top Echelon Network

Analog Solutions
204 Lakeside Plz Ste 140
Loudon, TN 37774
(865) 458-4421
Email: analog@analogsolutions.com
Web: www.analogsolutions.com

Description: We set ourselves apart from other recruiting firms in the semiconductor industry by offering a specialized service to a select group of growing companies. We focus on analog and mixed signal design and management. We offer our clients the opportunity to work with the industry's very best, low volume, high service organization.

Key Contact - Specialty:
Mr. Gary Fowler, President - *Electrical engineering, hardware, software*

Salary minimum: $80,000

Functions: Generalist, R&D, Engineering

Industries: Generalist, Computer Equip., Consumer Elect., Electronic, Elec. Components, Wireless, Fiber Optic, Software

Analytic Recruiting Inc
12 E 41st St Fl 9
New York, NY 10017
(212) 545-8511
Fax: (212) 545-8520
Email: email@analyticrecruiting.com
Web: www.analyticrecruiting.com

Description: We specialize in recruitment of people with strong analytical skills. Our practice is nationwide and covers all major business areas including finance, marketing, operations, manufacturing, planning, and systems. Our expertise is in staffing positions that emphasize superior analytical talent and the use of advanced quantitative/modeling techniques and technology in business decision-making. We like to work closely with our clients and are very deliberate in matching skills, career goals, and positions.

Key Contact - Specialty:
Mr. Daniel Raz, Principal - *Credit cards, database marketing*
Ms. Rita Raz, Principal - *Investment banking*

Salary minimum: $45,000

Functions: Product Dev., Mkt. Research, Direct Mktg., Credit, Risk Mgmt., IT, R&D, Mgmt. Consultants

Industries: Generalist, Soap, Perf., Cosmtcs., Drugs Mfg., Finance, Banking, Invest. Banking, Brokers, Venture Cap., Misc. Financial, Mgmt. Consulting, E-commerce, Media, Insurance, Mfg. SW, Marketing SW, Biotech, Healthcare

Professional Associations: NASCP, ORSA, TIMS

Anchor Solutions Inc
10800 Alpharetta Hwy St 208 412
Roswell, GA 30075
(770) 569-7720
Email: talent@anchorsolutions.com
Web: www.anchorsolutions.com

Description: Specializing in the marine/boating industry.

Key Contact:
Mr. Brian Allgood, President

Functions: Mfg., Product Dev., Production, Plant Mgmt., Quality, Purchasing, Materials Plng.

Industries: Mfg., Misc. Mfg.

Professional Associations: ABBRA

Ancilla Resource Corp
2443 Warrenville Rd Ste 600
Lisle, IL 60532-3673
(630) 724-0700
Fax: (630) 724-0777
Email: info@ancillaco.com
Web: www.ancillaco.com

Description: We are a national executive search and management consulting firm that specializes in the high/information technology industry. Our core market begins at the help desk or computer operator level up to the CIO.

Key Contact - Specialty:
Mr. Mark P. Conway, Senior Partner National Operations - *Information technology, high technology*

Salary minimum: $30,000

Functions: MIS Mgmt., Systems Analysis, Systems Dev., Systems Implem., Systems Support, Network Admin., DB Admin.

Industries: Generalist

Branches:
7150 E Camelback Rd Ste 300
Scottsdale, AZ 85251
(800) 380-9236
(480) 724-0700
Fax: (253) 390-8243
Email: info@ancillaco.com
Key Contact - Specialty:
Ms. Martha A. Dawson, Partner - *Information technology, high technology*

8310 Bar X Ter
Colorado Springs, CO 80908
(719) 494-1104
Fax: (253) 390-8243
Key Contact:
Mr. Mark P. Conway, Principal

Andera & Associates
2115 W Crescent Ave A
Anaheim, CA 92801
(714) 776-2179
Fax: (714) 520-4109
Email: gandera@idt.net
Web: www.foodfinancejobs.com

Description: We are dedicated to accounting and finance positions in the Southern California area and national financial searches in the food and beverage industry.

Key Contact - Specialty:
Mr. Greg Andera, Executive Recruiter - *Accounting & finance, food & beverage*

Salary minimum: $70,000

Functions: Senior Mgmt., Finance

Industries: Generalist, Food, Bev., Tobacco, Retail, Accounting, Restaurants, Accounting SW

Professional Associations: CSP

Networks: Top Echelon Network

Andersen & Associates
PO Box 1628
Marshalltown, IA 50158-1628
(641) 752-6152
Fax: (641) 752-6287
Email: info@andersenassociates.com
Web: www.andersenassociates.com

Description: Our firm is a family owned and operated professional recruiting and placement group specializing in executive, information technology, and telecommunications positions. We have business relationships with employing companies located across the Midwest. Our objective is to ensure a satisfying match of skills, expertise, and career goals.

Key Contact - Specialty:
Mrs. Lou Ann Andersen, Owner - *Understanding and solving client needs*
Mrs. Leigh Ann Andersen, Executive Recruiter - *Candidate recruitment and development*
Mr. Erik Andersen, Technical Recruiter - *Candidate screening*

Functions: Sales Mgmt., IT, MIS Mgmt., Systems Analysis, Systems Dev., Network Admin., DB Admin., Engineering, Mgmt. Consultants

Industries: Generalist, Agri., Forestry, Mining, Mfg., Plastics, Rubber, Metal Products, Machine, Appliance, Computer Equip., Electronic, Elec. Components, Finance, Services, IT Implementation, Media, Communications, Insurance, Software, Healthcare

Networks: Top Echelon Network

The Anderson Group
40 Pepperidge Trl
Old Saybrook, CT 06475
(860) 399-0365
Fax: (860) 399-0368
Email: andersonj.l@worldnet.att.net

Description: Search services for the medical device industry for marketing, manufacturing, product development, process, regulatory, quality compliance.

Key Contact - Specialty:
Mr. James L. Anderson, President/Owner - *Medical device*

Salary minimum: $50,000

Functions: Generalist, Middle Mgmt., Product Dev., Quality, Packaging, Mktg. Mgmt., R&D, Engineering

Industries: Generalist, Medical Devices

Anderson Industrial Associates Inc
4950 Hyde Ct
Cumming, GA 30040
(770) 844-9027
Fax: (770) 844-9656
Email: aia@mindspring.com

Description: Professional recruiting firm; degreed engineers placement in electrical, electronics, chemicals, plastics, HVAC, metals, telecommunications and instrumentation; all functions permanent/temporary.

Key Contact - Specialty:
Mr. Gregory D. Anderson, President - *Surface mount technology, RF design, electric motor (design, application), mechanical engineering, other engineering*

Salary minimum: $25,000

Functions: Generalist

Industries: Chemicals, Medical Devices, Telecoms, Government, Defense, Environmental Svcs., Aerospace, Biotech

Professional Associations: GAPS, RON

Networks: Top Echelon Network

Anderson Network Group
PO Box 274-WBB
Dayton, OH 45409-0274
(937) 299-7601
Fax: (937) 299-7602
Email: ang@core.com

Description: Executive placement for manufacturing, third-party logistics and distribution clients with needs in financial, manufacturing/distribution operations and human resources areas.

Key Contact - Specialty:
Mr. Wayne F. Anderson, CPC, Principal - *Accounting, human resources, logistics & distribution*

Salary minimum: $50,000

Functions: Directors, Senior Mgmt., Materials, Distribution, HR Mgmt., Finance

Industries: Generalist, Mfg., Transportation, Services, Insurance

Anderson Young Associates
1 Blue Hill Plz
PO Box 1673
Pearl River, NY 10965
(845) 920-1200
Fax: (845) 920-1220
Email: bjg@andersonyoungassoc.com

Description: Executive search firm that recruits on a retained and contingency basis in the areas of financial services and human resources.

Key Contact - Specialty:
Mr. Barry Geister, President - *Financial services*
Mr. Michael McManamon, Sr Search Consultant - *Human resources*

Functions: Generalist, Sales Mgmt., HR Mgmt., Benefits, Personnel, Finance, Cash Mgmt., Credit

Industries: Generalist, Finance, Banking, Venture Cap., Services, Accounting, Equip Svcs.

Professional Associations: AMA, ELA, SHRM, WAW

Andex Technical Search

101 River St
Milford, CT 06460
(203) 783-1616
Fax: (203) 783-3939
Email: jobs@andex.com
Web: www.andex.com

Description: A technical recruiting firm specializing in the computer industry. Salaries typically range from 40,000 to 250,000+. Nationwide positions.

Key Contact - Specialty:
Mr. Harry Anderson, Managing Director -
Information technology

Functions: IT

Industries: Generalist

Professional Associations: CAPS

Andrews & Associates

6100 Fairview Rd Ste 1205
Charlotte, NC 28210
(704) 556-0088
Fax: (704) 556-0350
Email: resumes@andrewssearch.com
Web: www.andrewssearch.com

Description: We have been assisting companies in locating CFOs and senior-level financial managers in the Carolinas for over 20 years.

Key Contact - Specialty:
Mr. Dwight L. Andrews, CPA, Principal -
Accounting, financial
Mr. Robert P. Wilkerson, Jr., CPA, Associate -
Accounting, financial

Functions: Generalist, CFO's, Budgeting, Cash Mgmt., Taxes, M&A

Industries: Generalist, Mfg., Wholesale, Retail, Misc. Financial, Accounting

Professional Associations: AICPA, IMA, NCACPA

Andrews & Wald Group

(also known as A & W Consulting Inc)
6537 Via Vicenza Ste 17
Delray Beach, FL 33446-3741
(561) 496-2931
Fax: (561) 496-3245
Email: asteve7515@aol.com

Description: We do executive search for management in all disciplines, with years of expertise in sales and marketing, on a contingent or fixed reasonable fee basis anywhere in North America.

Key Contact - Specialty:
Mr. E. Steven Wald, General Manager -
Management

Salary minimum: $30,000

Functions: Generalist, Senior Mgmt., Middle Mgmt., Plant Mgmt., Mktg. Mgmt., Sales Mgmt., CFO's, MIS Mgmt.

Industries: Generalist, Medical Devices, Metal Products, Machine, Appliance, Computer Equip., Test, Measure Equip., Non-profits, Hospitality

Ethan Andrews Associates

PO Box 883362
Steamboat Springs, CO 80488
(970) 870-0391
(877) 288-8735
Email: careers@ethanandrews.com
Web: www.ethanandrews.com

Description: We find and place attorneys and other legal professionals with client companies and law firms.

Key Contact - Specialty:
Mr. Lee Cosgrove, JD, Principal - *Attorneys*

Salary minimum: $50,000

Functions: Directors, Admin. Svcs., Legal, HR Mgmt., Attorneys, Paralegals

Industries: Legal

Andrews Sumitt & Allen Management Inc

8033 Sunset Blvd Ste 1024
Los Angeles, CA 90046
(323) 468-8899
Fax: (323) 468-0236
Email: ttortora@asamanagement.com
Web: www.asamanagement.com

Description: Andrews, Sumitt & Allen Management is a full service executive search consulting company specializing in the hi-tech, financial and entertainment industries, offering an alternative to the standard in-house systems. With over 10 years hands-on experience in project staffing, Andrews, Sumitt & Allen's clients are treated to the professional handling of all aspects of candidate acquisition.

Key Contact:
Mr. Tim Tortora, President
Mr. Michael Banson, COO

Salary minimum: $75,000

Functions: Generalist

Industries: Mfg., Printing, Computer Equip., Consumer Elect., Electronic, Elec. Components, Finance, Banking, Invest. Banking, Brokers, Venture Cap., Misc. Financial, Services, Accounting, Hospitality, Entertainment, Media, New Media, Broadcast, Film, Communications, Telecoms, Digital, Wireless, Fiber Optic, Network Infrastructure, Software, Accounting SW, Database SW, Development SW, Doc. Mgmt., Production SW, Entertainment SW, ERP SW, HR SW, Industry Specific SW, Mfg. SW, Marketing SW, Networking, Comm. SW, Security SW, System SW, Training SW

Angel Group Int'l

(also known as MRI & Sales Consultants of Louisville)
4360 Brownsboro Rd Ste 240
Louisville, KY 40207
(502) 897-0333
Fax: (502) 897-0496
Email: info@angel-group.com
Web: www.angel-group.com

Description: When it comes to filling key executive and managerial positions, our firm is the only search firm your business will ever need. We know how to find talented well-trained professionals who will lead your company to greater success and market share. The scope of our service is not limited by industry, trade, or craft. We serve high-profile, global companies from every enterprise.

Key Contact - Specialty:
Mr. Steve Angel, CEO - *Accounting, financial*
Mr. Bruce Thomas, Vice President - *General manufacturing*
Ms. Barbara Beard, Vice President - *MIS*
Ms. Paula Bryan, Sr Vice President - *Human resources*
Ms. Jennifer Dudley, Account Executive - *Accounting, finance*
Ms. Kathleen Kessler, Account Executive - *Sales, marketing*
Mr. Eddie Johnson, Account Executive - *Sales, marketing*
Mr. Scott Goodwin, Account Executive - *Accounting finance banking*

Functions: Generalist, Production, Distribution, Sales Mgmt., Benefits, Cash Mgmt., Systems Dev., Int'l.

Industries: Generalist, Mfg., Transportation, Retail, Banking, Accounting, Media

Professional Associations: AICPA, IMA, SHRM

Tryg R Angell Ltd

354 Shelton Rd
Trumbull, CT 06611
(203) 377-4541
Fax: (203) 377-4545
Email: tryg.r.angell@snet.com
Web: tryg@snet.com

Description: Senior positions in the pulp and paper industries. National and regional sales and marketing positions as well as technical and production positions for paper, chemical and other industrial companies.

Key Contact - Specialty:
Mr. Tryg R. Angell, Principal - *Paper, sales & marketing, technical*

Salary minimum: $30,000

Functions: Generalist, Senior Mgmt., Product Dev., Plant Mgmt., Mkt. Research, Sales Mgmt., Benefits, Engineering

Industries: Generalist, Energy, Utilities, Construction, Paper, Printing, Chemicals, Paints, Petro. Products, Metal Products

Professional Associations: PIMA, TAPPI

Angus Employment Ltd

1100 Burloak Dr Fl 5
Royal Bank Bldg,
Burlington, ON L7L 6B2
Canada
(905) 319-0773
Fax: (905) 336-9445
Email: resumes@angusemployment.com
Web: www.angusemployment.com

Description: We recruit on behalf of many high-profile firms in all industries for professional occupations at every level.

Key Contact - Specialty:
Mr. Evan Stewart, Director of Recruitment -
Generalist

Functions: Generalist, General Mgmt., Mfg., Sales & Mktg., Finance, IT, Engineering

Industries: Generalist, Mfg., Transportation, Finance, IT Implementation, Aerospace, Software

Professional Associations: ACSESS

The Angus Group Ltd

250 W Court St Ste 100E
Cincinnati, OH 45202-1088
(513) 961-5575
Fax: (513) 961-5616
Email: angus@angusgroup.com
Web: www.angusgroup.com

Description: Recruiting services to businesses, most disciplines. Most professionals in office have 10+ years of experience.

Key Contact - Specialty:
Mr. Thomas R. Angus - *Human resources, general management*
Mr. David Hartig, President - *Engineering, general management*
Mr. Pete Nadherny, CEO - *Banking, finance, accounting, general management*
Mr. Ted Plattenburg, Principal - *Marketing & sales*

Salary minimum: $50,000

Functions: Senior Mgmt., Middle Mgmt., Mfg., Materials, Sales & Mktg., HR Mgmt., Finance, IT, Engineering

Industries: Energy, Utilities, Mfg., Transportation, Retail, Finance, Services, Accounting, HR Services, Media, Advertising, Packaging, Biotech

Networks: National Banking Network (NBN)

Annapolis Consulting Group
752 Leister Dr
Timonium, MD 21093-7418
(410) 453-0283
Fax: (410) 453-9270
Email: rob.srnec@acgsearch.com

Description: Our search firm focuses exclusively on the placement of actuaries and investment/capital markets professionals throughout the U.S. and internationally. Each member of our recruitment team has an average of 12 years of search experience. Our consultants know the market and the opportunities. Our approach goes well beyond calling candidates with "hot" job opportunities.

Key Contact:
Mr. S. Robert Srnec, Managing Director

Functions: Generalist

Industries: Finance, Services, Insurance, Software, Healthcare

ANOVA Search Consultants
PO Box 746
Devon, PA 19333
(610) 971-1947
Fax: (800) 220-2115
Email: anovakyle@aol.com

Description: We specialize in recruiting within the statistical sciences, including: bio-statistics, SAS programmers, data mining, data modeling, and database marketing analysis. We recruit for all levels, nationally.

Key Contact:
Mr. Robert Kyle, Partner

Functions: Direct Mktg., R&D

Industries: Drugs Mfg., Banking, Mgmt. Consulting, Database SW, Marketing SW, Biotech, Healthcare

Ansara, Bickford & Fiske
1252 Elm St Ste 23
West Springfield, MA 01089
(413) 733-0791
Fax: (413) 731-1486
Email: pa@ansara.com
Web: www.ansara.com

Description: We are fully automated, state-of-the-art research capability. We have deep and concise databases drawn from all sources. We attract hard to find engineers in specialty niches. We serve the following industries: pharmaceuticals, biotechnology, medical device, manufacturing, electronics, both military and consumer, and all civil/architectural-engineering disciplines.

Key Contact:
Mr. Peter Ansara, President

Salary minimum: $30,000

Functions: Generalist, Production, Automation, Plant Mgmt., Materials Plng., Distribution, Packaging, Engineering

Industries: Generalist, Machine, Appliance, Computer Equip., Test, Measure Equip., Pharm Svcs., Telecoms, Packaging

Professional Associations: IEEE

Networks: Top Echelon Network

Branches:
34 Main St Ste 202
PO Box 6037
Plymouth, MA 02360
(508) 830-0079
Fax: (508) 830-4627
Email: pk@ansara.com
Key Contact:
Mr. Peter Kratimenos, Managing Owner

Fred Anthony Associates
PO Box 372
Lake Geneva, WI 53147
(262) 245-1940
Fax: (262) 592-0006
Email: fanthony@genevaonline.com

Description: Specialty - paint and coatings and the raw materials for that industry (resins, additives)

Key Contact - Specialty:
Mr. Fred Anthony, President - *Chemical sales & marketing*

Salary minimum: $50,000

Functions: Sales & Mktg.

Industries: Chemicals, Paints, Petro. Products

Networks: First Interview Network (FIN)

David Anthony Personnel Associates Inc
64 E Ridgewood Ave
Paramus, NJ 07652
(201) 262-6100
Fax: (201) 262-7744
Email: dferrara@aol.com
Web: www.davidanthony.com

Description: We specialize in mid- to senior-level banking opportunities throughout metro the NJ and NY region. Our firm concentrates on commercial bank recruiting that focuses on credit and lending. The typical positions that we place are senior credit analysts, commercial loan officers, relationship managers, chief credit officer, etc.

Key Contact - Specialty:
Mr. David K. Ferrara, President - *Banking, data processing*

Salary minimum: $40,000

Functions: Generalist

Industries: Banking

AP Associates (APA)
71 E Mountain Rd
Neshanic Station, NJ 08853
(908) 371-0066
Fax: (908) 371-0067
Email: apa@apassociates.com
Web: www.apassociates.com

Description: Our firm is an executive and high-tech placement firm providing the finest possible talent to meet full time, critical staffing requirements especially within the wireless, fiber-optic, telecomm, network, Internet, data, video, voice, IT/IS, semiconductor, biotech, pharmaceutical, and construction industries, and the emergency response and quality control professions.

Key Contact - Specialty:
Mr. Alex Palyo, Director - *Semiconductors (compound, si), IC design, senior executives, marketing*

Salary minimum: $50,000

Functions: Generalist

Industries: Construction, Electronic, Elec. Components, IT Implementation, Telecoms, Digital, Wireless, Fiber Optic, Network Infrastructure, Biotech, Healthcare

Professional Associations: ASQ, IEEE

APA Employment Agency Inc
700 NE Multnomah St Ste 274
Port of Portland Bldg
Portland, OR 97232-4102
(503) 233-1200
(800) 715-4562
Fax: (503) 233-0071
Web: www.apaemployment.com

Description: We have a large client base in the Portland, Oregon and Vancouver, Washington area. We place many new candidates weekly. Our name would be a good lead for someone trying to relocate.

Key Contact - Specialty:
Ms. Felicia Hintzue, Industrial Manager - *Warehouse, production management, industrial, drivers*
Mr. Dave Knox, Administrative Manager - *Office/administrative, human resources, customer service, accounting, management*
Mr. Jeff Voigt, Professional Manager - *Professionals, sales, management*

Salary minimum: $25,000

Functions: Generalist, General Mgmt., Admin. Svcs., Plant Mgmt., Productivity, Customer Svc., Personnel, Training

Industries: Generalist, Mfg., Misc. Mfg., Transportation, Retail, Services, Non-classifiable

Professional Associations: NAPS, NATSS, SSAO

Branches:
10260 SW Greenburg Rd Ste 400
Beaverton, OR 97223
(503) 293-7694
Fax: (503) 293-7695
Key Contact:
Mr. Les Swanson, General Manager

5500 NE 109th Ct Ste C
Vancouver, WA 98662
(360) 253-1200
(888) 715-4563
Fax: (360) 253-4674
Key Contact:
Ms. Darbi Sadlier - *General management, industrial, administrative, professional*
Ms. Rachell Hall, Sales Representative

Apex Search Inc
45 Sheppard Ave E Ste 900
North York, ON M2N 5W9
Canada
(416) 226-2828
Fax: (416) 226-1417
Email: karen@apexsearch.com
Web: www.apexsearch.com

Description: We are in a strong position of being able to spend time to get to know our clients' environments, technical needs as well as the soft skills necessary to make the proper match.

Key Contact - Specialty:
Ms. Karen Agulnik, Owner - *Information technology*
Ms. Joanne Crossman, Senior Consultant - *Information technology*

Functions: IT, MIS Mgmt., Systems Analysis, Systems Dev., Systems Implem., Systems Support, Network Admin., DB Admin., Mgmt. Consultants

Industries: Mfg., Drugs Mfg.

David Aplin & Associates
10235 - 101 St 2300 Oxford Twr
Edmonton, AB T5J 3G1
Canada
(780) 428-6663
Fax: (780) 421-4680
Email: edmonton@aplin.com
Web: www.aplin.com

Description: We are one of Canada's leading professional search organizations offering clients and candidates a full range of recruitment services in IT, accounting/finance, sales/marketing, engineering, HR and office personnel from intermediate to executive-levels.

Key Contact - Specialty:
Mr. David Aplin, President - *Information technology*
Mr. Michael Bacchus, Branch Manager - *IT sales*
Ms. Jennifer Ward, Senior Consultant - *Information technology*

Salary minimum: $40,000

Functions: Generalist, General Mgmt., Mfg., Sales & Mktg., HR Mgmt., Finance, IT, Engineering

Industries: Generalist, Leather, Stone, Glass, Metal Products, Wholesale, HR Services, New Media, Healthcare

Networks: National Personnel Assoc (NPA)

Branches:
777 - 8th Ave SW
1600, First Alberta Pl
Calgary, AB T2P 3R5
Canada
(403) 261-5903
Fax: (403) 266-7195
Email: calgary@aplin.com
Key Contact - Specialty:
Mr. Michael Bacchus, Branch Manager - *Information technology, sales & marketing, sales management*
Mr. Kieran Longworth, VP-Strategic Development - *Supply chain management*

650 W Georgia St Ste 1400
PO Box 11518
Vancouver, BC V6B 4N7
Canada
(604) 648-2799
Fax: (604) 648-2787
Email: vancouver@aplin.com
Key Contact:
Mr. David Aplin, General Manager

602 Richardson Bldg
1 Lombard Pl
Winnipeg, MB R3B 0X3
Canada
(204) 235-0000
Fax: (204) 235-0002
Email: winnipeg@aplin.com
Key Contact:
Mr. David Aplin, President

APOGEE Inc
PO Box 682977
Orlando, FL 32868
(407) 532-9952
Fax: (407) 578-4919
Email: hrconsultant@aol.com
Web: www.apogeerecruiting.com

Description: I am an independent recruiter, hiring consultant, and background investigator. My specialties include accounting and computer professionals. Recruitment is also provided for other disciplines, as well.

Key Contact:
Ms. Karla Villasenor

Functions: Healthcare, Finance, IT

Industries: Finance, Banking, Accounting, E-commerce, IT Implementation, Hospitals, Physical Therapy, Occupational Therapy

R W Apple & Associates
PO Box 200
Manasquan, NJ 08736
(732) 223-4305
Fax: (732) 223-4325
Email: services@rwapple.com

Description: Provide executive search services to primarily the environmental and engineering consulting industries. Concentrations include environmental engineering, hydrogeology, civil engineering, air pollution control, industrial hygiene, process development, sales and marketing.

Key Contact - Specialty:
Ms. Lynda Apple, President - *Executive search/recruiting, management consulting, human resource consulting*
Mr. Richard W. Apple, Consulting President - *Management consulting, human resources, environmental consulting recruitment*

Salary minimum: $30,000

Functions: Generalist

Industries: Energy, Utilities, Construction, Non-profits, Mgmt. Consulting, HR Services, Environmental Svcs., Haz. Waste

Professional Associations: AWG, AWMA, HMCRI, MASOT, NGWA, SMPS

Apple One Employment Services
990 Knox St.
Torrance, CA 90502
(310) 516-1572
Fax: (310) 516-9256
Email: cduque@mail.appleone.com
Web: www.appleone.com

Description: One-stop service that delivers quality Temporary, Temp-To-Hire and Direct Hire staffing via hundreds of branch offices throughout North America.

Key Contact:
Ms. Marc Goldman, Vice President of Sales and Marketing
Ms. Christine Duque, Director of Communications

Functions: Generalist

Industries: Higher Ed., Legal, Accounting, Mgmt. Consulting, HR Services

Applied Resources Inc
7200 Hemlock Ln N Ste 112
Maple Grove Executive Ctr
Maple Grove, MN 55369
(763) 391-6000
(763) 391-6001
Fax: (763) 424-4843
Email: ari@winternet.com
Web: www.winternet.com/~ari/

Description: Specialists in identifying engineering and manufacturing professionals for local Twin City companies. Dedicated to serving technology driven growth companies in Minnesota. Have developed extensive networks in metal fabrication, data communications software, hardware and medical device industries. We do not normally participate in relocations.

Key Contact - Specialty:
Mr. Michael G. Weiss, CPC, CEO - *Engineering, manufacturing, management*

Salary minimum: $40,000

Functions: Generalist, Product Dev., Purchasing, Mkt. Research, Personnel, Systems Implem., R&D, Engineering

Industries: Generalist, Mfg., Medical Devices, Plastics, Rubber, HR Services, Packaging, Software

Professional Associations: ASQ

Applied Search Associates Inc
PO Box 1207
Dawsonville, GA 30534-1207
(706) 265-2530
Email: applied_search@alltel.net

Description: Our specialty is direct recruiting and placement of hard to find personnel with specific backgrounds, talent and education. We produce results through experience, preparation and individualized attention to all project details.

Key Contact - Specialty:
Mr. Richard B. Rockwell, Sr., President - *Process, manufacturing, sales & marketing, engineering*

Salary minimum: $50,000

Functions: Generalist, General Mgmt., Middle Mgmt., Sales & Mktg., Sales Mgmt.

Industries: Energy, Utilities, Construction, Mfg., Equip Svcs., Digital, Fiber Optic, Software, Industry Specific SW, Mfg. SW, Marketing SW

April Int'l Inc
200 North Ave Ste 6
New Rochelle, NY 10801
(914) 632-2333
Fax: (914) 632-3582
Email: ken@aprilinternational.com
Web: www.aprilinternational.com

Description: Jobs recruitment financial services, investment and commercial banks, accounting, information technology, audit and IT audit, market and credit risk, finance, operations, other executive search.

Key Contact - Specialty:
Mr. Kenneth April, President - *Finance & accounting, credit, treasury, audit*
Mr. Kevin Collins, Vice President
Mr. Fred Stang, Vice President
Ms. Valerie Bowser, Vice President
Mr. Michael Roach, Vice President
Mr. Marty Tarnowsky, Vice President
Mr. Al Rooney, Vice President
Ms. Elizabeth Kachnic, Vice President
Mr. Mainak Adhikary, Vice President - *Finance and accounting*
Mr. Roy Cash, Vice President - *Finance & accounting*

Salary minimum: $60,000

Functions: Generalist, General Mgmt.

Industries: Finance, Banking, Invest. Banking, Brokers, Venture Cap., Misc. Financial, Services, Accounting, Mgmt. Consulting, HR Services, IT Implementation, Media, Communications, Accounting SW, HR SW

AQSPEC Executive Search
PO Box 120712
Big Bear Lake, CA 92315
(909) 866-3369
Fax: (909) 866-1917
Email: info@aqspec.com
Web: www.aqspec.com

Description: We are a full-service executive recruitment specializing in biotechnology, pharmaceutical, and medical device companies. We target all positions in the fields of engineering, research, quality control, clinical, validation, and manufacturing.

Key Contact - Specialty:
Ms. Anne Butler, President - *Biotechnology, pharmaceuticals*
Mr. Chuck Lindeen, Vice President - *Medical*

Salary minimum: $35,000

Functions: Directors

Industries: Drugs Mfg., Medical Devices, Biotech, Healthcare

Charles P Aquavella & Associates
1241 Emerald Sound Blvd
Oak Point, TX 75068
(972) 292-2344
Fax: (801) 729-2132
Email: cpaassoc@aol.com

Description: Human resource consulting and executive search in personnel, general management, all management, manufactured housing and manufacturing.

Key Contact - Specialty:
Mr. Charles P. Aquavella - *Manufacturing (housing, all positions, levels), sales, retail sales*

Salary minimum: $30,000

Functions: Generalist

Industries: Non-classifiable

Aran Rock
318 Utah St Ste 210
San Francisco, CA 94103
(415) 255-1717
Email: kennedy@aranrock.com
Web: www.aranrock.com

Description: We are a computer recruiting firm, specializing in IBM AS/400.

Key Contact - Specialty:
Mr. Colm Byrne - *Computers, IBM AS/400*

Functions: Generalist, MIS Mgmt., Systems Analysis, Systems Dev., Systems Implem., Systems Support, Network Admin., DB Admin.

Industries: Generalist, Software

ARC Associates
75 Gilcreast Rd Ste 305
Londonderry, NH 03053
(603) 425-2488
Fax: (603) 432-2533
Email: kim@arc-associates.com
Web: www.arc-associates.com

Description: Specialized in finance and accounting search throughout New England. Selective target search on both contingency and retained basis.

Key Contact:
Mr. Kim C. Scoggins, Senior Partner - *Finance & accounting*
Mr. Michael W. Cameron, Senior Partner

Salary minimum: $40,000

Functions: Finance

Industries: Generalist

Professional Associations: NNEAPS

ARC Partners Inc
6339 E Greenway Ste 102-341
Scottsdale, AZ 85254
(480) 951-6004
Email: cynthia@arcsearch.com
Web: www.arcsearch.com

Description: We offer over 20 years in human resources and healthcare experience. Full-service recruitment firm.

Key Contact - Specialty:
Ms. Cynthia Allen, President - *Healthcare*

Salary minimum: $40,000

Functions: Healthcare, Physicians, Nurses

Industries: Generalist, Healthcare

ARC Staffing Inc
5471 Pocusset St
Pittsburgh, PA 15217
(412) 422-6110
Fax: (412) 422-6112
Email: alan@arcstaffing.net
Web: www.arcstaffing.net

Description: We are specialists in working with small to medium-sized entrepreneurial firms within distribution, healthcare, and wireless. We are the best listeners in the industry.

Key Contact - Specialty:
Mr. Alan Raeburn, President - *Industrial distribution, manufacturing*

Mr. Adam Raeburn, Vice President - *Software development, e-mail architects, security architects, systems integration*

Salary minimum: $50,000

Functions: Generalist

Industries: Wholesale, Software, Healthcare

Archer Resource Solutions Inc
(a division of Wardrop Engineering Inc)
6725 Airport Rd Fl 6
Mississauga, ON L4V 1V2
Canada
(905) 405-8652
Fax: (905) 405-1738
Email: resumes@archer.ca
Web: www.archer.ca

Description: Our firm is a placement agency that specializes in the engineering and information technology sectors.

Key Contact - Specialty:
Ms. Susan Corazolla, General Manager - *Engineers, designers, project managers*

Functions: Generalist, Mfg., Materials, Engineering

Industries: Generalist, Agri., Forestry, Mining, Mfg., Transportation, Environmental Svcs., Aerospace, Packaging, Software

Professional Associations: ACSESS

Architechs
2 Electronics Ave
Danvers, MA 01923
(978) 777-8500
Email: bob@architechs.net
Web: www.architechs.net

Description: Our firm is a dynamic technical search/recruiting firm with an excellent reputation for providing quality service to distinguished clients and candidates. Our clientele consists of many of the top organizations in the Boston Area, from small start-ups to Fortune 500 firms. We have specialized in developing long term, mutually beneficial relationships with some of the best technical professionals in the field.

Key Contact - Specialty:
Mr. Bob Jones, Principal - *Java (developers, architects)*

Salary minimum: $50,000

Functions: IT, Engineering

Industries: E-commerce, IT Implementation

ARG Associates
201 E Main Ave
PO Box 235
Frazee, MN 56544
(218) 334-6142
Fax: (218) 334-6144
Email: brianbigger@argassociatesinc.com
Web: www.argassociatesinc.com

Description: We are a recognized world leader in executive search with a focus in agri-business, agriculture, food processing, energy & power marketing, farm management, bio-mass, and renewable fuels industries.

Key Contact - Specialty:
Mr. Brian B. Bigger, President - *Agribusiness, food, commodity processing, energy & power marketing, farm management*

Salary minimum: $50,000

Functions: Generalist, General Mgmt., Mfg., Materials, Sales & Mktg., HR Mgmt., Finance, Engineering

Industries: Generalist, Agri., Forestry, Mining, Energy, Utilities, Construction, Mfg., Food, Bev.,

Tobacco, Chemicals, Drugs Mfg., Mfg. SW, Marketing SW, Biotech

The Argus Group Corp
249 Roehampton Ave
Toronto, ON M4P 1R4
Canada
(416) 932-9321
Fax: (416) 932-9387
Email: kennedy@argusgroupcorp.com
Web: www.argusgroupcorp.com

Description: Like the multi-eyed monster of mythical fame, we always keep our watchful eyes out for your best interest: selecting appropriately trained people who can immediately benefit your corporation.

Key Contact - Specialty:
Mr. Alec Reed, President - *Sales & marketing*

Functions: Generalist, Senior Mgmt., Advertising, Mkt. Research, Mktg. Mgmt., Sales Mgmt., Direct Mktg., IT

Industries: Generalist

Professional Associations: ACSESS

ARI Summit Search Specialists
14825 St. Mary's Ln 275
Houston, TX 77079
(281) 497-5840
Fax: (281) 497-5841
Email: summit@airmail.net
Web: www.web2.airmail.net/summit

Description: Over 24 years' specializing in the placement of quality insurance professionals. Nationwide in scope and affiliated with two national recruiting organizations.

Key Contact - Specialty:
Mr. David S. Bunce, Senior Partner - *Insurance (property, casualty)*

Salary minimum: $50,000

Functions: Generalist

Industries: Insurance

Professional Associations: INS, NIRA

Aries Search Group
9925 Haynes Bridge Rd Ste 200-146
Alpharetta, GA 30022
(770) 569-4708
Fax: (770) 569-4709
Email: cmcand6089@aol.com

Description: We specialize in search and recruitment nationally and exclusively to the medical industry. We offer 15 years of experience and strive towards a commitment to becoming partners in strategic planning with our client companies. We specialize in placement of sales and sales management professionals strictly in the medical products industry.

Key Contact - Specialty:
Ms. Cindy McAndrew, President - *Medical, sales, sales management, marketing*

Functions: Sales & Mktg., Sales Mgmt.

Industries: Medical Devices

Networks: The Acumen Society

Arlington Resources Inc
5105 Tollview Dr Ste 265
Rolling Meadows, IL 60008
(847) 590-9490
Fax: (847) 590-9498
Email: hr@arlingtonresources.com
Web: www.arlingtonresources.com

Description: Our firm specializes in identifying, locating and evaluating some of the strongest human resource professionals for our client companies. We are dedicated to quality, professionalism and excellent customer service. We assist human resource professionals locate full-time regular hire, contract and temporary positions.

Key Contact - Specialty:
Ms. Patricia Casey, President - *Human resources*

Functions: HR Mgmt.

Industries: Generalist

Professional Associations: HRMAC, NAPS, SHRM

Armor Personnel
(a division of AP Careers Inc)
181 Queen St E
Brampton, ON L6W 2B3
Canada
(905) 459-1617
Fax: (905) 459-1704
Email: info@armorpersonnel.com

Description: Diversified staffing services firm. Contract staff and comprehensive human resources division to complement recruitment.

Key Contact - Specialty:
Mr. Lou Duggan, President - *General management*

Salary minimum: $40,000

Functions: Generalist, Senior Mgmt., Middle Mgmt., Admin. Svcs., Plant Mgmt., Sales Mgmt., Benefits, CFO's

Industries: Generalist

Professional Associations: APPAC, HRPAO

Networks: Canadian Personnel Services Inc (CPSI)

R & J Arnold & Associates Inc
(also known as MRI of Broomfield)
1401 Walnut St Ste 302
PO Box 2279
Boulder, CO 80306
(303) 447-9940
Fax: (303) 447-0062
Email: r-j-arnold-assoc@worldnet.att.net

Description: We have earned a very solid reputation for surfacing qualified professionals who meet our client's clinical/technical, philosophical and personality needs. Over 50% placed remain with the client over 5 years.

Key Contact - Specialty:
Ms. Janet N. Arnold, Partner - *Healthcare*
Mr. Robert W. Arnold, Partner - *Engineering, chemical*

Functions: Generalist, Senior Mgmt., Middle Mgmt., Physicians, Nurses, Health Admin., MIS Mgmt., Engineering

Industries: Generalist, Healthcare

Arnold Associates
Ten Post Office Square Ste 600 S
Boston, MA 02109
(617) 988-0403
Fax: (617) 988-0406
Email: chris.arnold@esearchfirm.com
Web: www.esearchfirm.com

Description: Our firm is a retained executive search firm specializing in the recruitment of senior managers and executives within the mutual fund, investment management, retirement plan, and financial service industries.

Key Contact - Specialty:
Mr. Christopher Arnold, Principal - *Investment management, mutual funds*

Salary minimum: $100,000

Functions: Generalist, General Mgmt., Sales & Mktg., Finance, IT

Industries: Finance

Aronow Associates Inc
6923 Fairway Lakes Dr
Boynton Beach, FL 33437
(561) 732-6008

Description: Management recruiting for the financial services industry specializing in sales, product management, strategic planning and all marketing functions. Global finance and treasury management for the corporate market.

Key Contact - Specialty:
Mr. Lawrence E. Aronow, President - *Financial services*

Salary minimum: $60,000

Functions: Generalist, General Mgmt., Sales & Mktg., Finance

Industries: Generalist, Finance

Artemis Associates
PO Box 424
Newtown, PA 18940
(215) 579-2244
Email: search@artemisassoc.com
Web: www.artemisassoc.com

Description: We are an Executive Search and Information Technology Consulting Firm focused on providing extremely personalized service to a limited clientele. We specialize in locating and recruiting outstanding mid- to senior-level professionals.

Key Contact:
Mr. Peter Lins
Mr. Robert Minschwaner
Ms. Lorraine Henrie

Salary minimum: $60,000

Functions: General Mgmt., Directors, Healthcare, Sales & Mktg., IT, MIS Mgmt., Engineering, Mgmt. Consultants, Minorities

Industries: Generalist, Energy, Utilities, Mfg., Retail, Finance, Services, Communications, Insurance, Software, Biotech, Healthcare

Networks: PRO/NET

Artemis HRC
(a subsidiary of Computer Partners Corp)
230 N Second St
Brighton, MI 48116
(810) 494-0100
Fax: (810) 494-0200
Email: jpantelas@artemishrc.com
Web: www.artemishrc.com

Description: Development and management of custom recruiting solutions to accomodate clients through all stages of growth. Services range from individual searches through corporate acquisition search.

Key Contact - Specialty:
Mr. Jim Pantelas, President - *Management, technology, communications, sales, manufacturing*
Ms. Cheryl Krisniski, Account Manager - *Information technology, insurance, management, communications*
Ms. Nancy Bredeson, Account Manager - *Insurance, business management, information technology, sales*

Salary minimum: $40,000

Functions: Generalist, General Mgmt., Mfg., Sales & Mktg., HR Mgmt., Finance, IT, Mgmt. Consultants

Industries: Generalist, Mfg., Services, Media, Insurance, Software

ASAP Search & Placement
508 N 2nd St Ste 107
Fairfield, IA 52556
(515) 472-3666
(800) 590-2072
Email: art@aatkinson.com
Web: www.asap.globalverde.com

Description: We are an executive search firm serving the software vendor community.

Key Contact - Specialty:
Mr. Arthur Atkinson, President - *Software vendors, professional services, consulting firms*

Salary minimum: $50,000

Functions: Sales & Mktg., R&D, Engineering

Industries: Software

Professional Associations: RON

Networks: National Personnel Assoc (NPA)

ASAP Search & Recruiters
16 Berry Hill Rd Ste 120
Interstate Ctr
Columbia, SC 29210
(803) 772-6751
Fax: (803) 798-0874
Email: work@asapsearch.com
Web: www.asapsearch.com

Description: Our strength is specializing in the metal working areas of automotive, food and beverage manufacturing and power tools in engineering, management and sales professionals.

Key Contact:
Mr. Richard V. Bramblett - *Metalworking, automotive*
Ms. Jackie Manzi
Mr. Greg Royse
Ms. Denise McCoy, Office Manager
Ms. Jeanette Bramblett

Salary minimum: $30,000

Functions: Generalist, Product Dev., Production, Automation, Plant Mgmt., Quality, Purchasing, Engineering

Industries: Generalist, Metal Products, Machine, Appliance, Motor Vehicles, Test, Measure Equip., Misc. Mfg., Aerospace

Professional Associations: SCAPS

Networks: Top Echelon Network

Ash & Associates Executive Search
PO Box 862
Pompano Beach, FL 33061
(954) 946-3395
Fax: (954) 946-3531
Email: ashassoc9@aol.com

Description: We specialize in finance, marketing, human resources, engineering, information systems, management, telecommunications, international telecommunications, pharmaceuticals, and operations in the state of Florida only with salaries of over $60000. We do not work with entry level, non-profit, publishing, advertising, government, or public relations fields. We work with companies only in Florida. Please do not send a resume if you do not want to live in Florida.

Key Contact - Specialty:
Ms. Janis Ash, President - *Finance, information technology, management, operations, engineering*
Mr. J. DeRiso, Vice President - *Finance, information technology, management, operations, engineering*

Functions: General Mgmt., Sales & Mktg., HR Mgmt., Finance, IT, Engineering

Industries: Mfg., Soap, Perf., Cosmtcs., Drugs Mfg., Medical Devices, Computer Equip., Consumer Elect., Pharm Svcs., HR Services,

Communications, Telecoms, Call Centers, Telephony, Wireless, Database SW, Development SW, ERP SW, HR SW, Mfg. SW, Marketing SW, Biotech

Asheville Search & Consulting

29 Spring Cove Ct
PO Box 549
Arden, NC 28704
(828) 687-7722
Fax: (828) 687-2444
Email: vspinc@mindspring.com

Description: We offer client companies a partnered relationship and the expertise of its principal, who has over twenty years of management experience in both entrepreneurial and established business environments.

Key Contact - Specialty:
Mr. Vincent Putiri, President - *Manufacturing, design, plant support staff*

Salary minimum: $25,000

Functions: Middle Mgmt., Product Dev., Production, Automation, Plant Mgmt., Quality, Materials, HR Mgmt., Finance, Engineering

Industries: Metal Products, Machine, Appliance, Motor Vehicles, Test, Measure Equip., Misc. Mfg., Mgmt. Consulting

Networks: Inter-City Personnel Assoc (IPA)

Ashley-Burns Group Inc

900 Old Roswell Lakes Pkwy Ste 240
Roswell, GA 30076
(770) 650-0056
Fax: (770) 650-5960
Email: pjohns@ashleyburns.com
Web: www.ashleyburns.com

Description: We are a full service corporate placement firm. Some industry specifics include construction, manufacturing, automotive, accounting, legal, and information technology.

Key Contact - Specialty:
Ms. Pamela Johns, President - *General*
Ms. Lori Burns, Vice President - *General*

Salary minimum: $65,000

Functions: General Mgmt., Admin. Svcs., Mfg., Production, HR Mgmt., Finance, IT

Industries: Generalist, Printing, Medical Devices, Metal Products, Misc. Mfg., HR SW, Mfg. SW, Biotech

Professional Associations: GAPS

E J Ashton & Associates Ltd

PO Box 1048
Lake Zurich, IL 60047-1048
(847) 842-9727
Fax: (847) 842-9728
Email: ejaltd@aol.com
Web: ins@insurancerecruiters.com

Description: We are executive recruiters exclusively for the insurance industry nationwide.

Key Contact - Specialty:
Mr. Edmund C. Lipinski, President - *Insurance accounting, financial, tax audit*
Mr. Gene Rowls, Controller - *Insurance claims, underwriting, marketing*

Salary minimum: $40,000

Functions: Generalist, Middle Mgmt., CFO's, Budgeting, Cash Mgmt., Taxes

Industries: Generalist, Insurance

Professional Associations: INS, NIRA

Ashton Computer Professionals Inc

C-15 Chesterfield Pl
North Vancouver, BC V7M 3K3
Canada
(604) 904-0304
Fax: (604) 904-0305
Email: info@acprecruit.com
Web: www.acprecruit.com

Description: We work only with advanced computing and telecommunications professionals. Serve the Pacific Northwest, handling all areas of information technology, technical hardware/software development, engineering and management personnel.

Key Contact - Specialty:
Ms. Barbara L. Ashton, President - *Telecommunications, semiconductor, information technology*

Salary minimum: $35,000

Functions: Generalist, MIS Mgmt., Systems Analysis, Systems Dev., Systems Support, Network Admin., DB Admin., Engineering

Industries: Generalist, Computer Equip., Test, Measure Equip., New Media, Telecoms, Software

Ashway Ltd Agency

295 Madison Ave Ste 1101
New York, NY 10017
(212) 679-3300
Fax: (212) 447-0583

Description: Specialize in executive search and contingency placements in science and technology: physics, engineering, chemistry/biology, mathematics and computer science. We also place actuaries and insurance professionals. We also are technology management consultants.

Key Contact - Specialty:
Mr. Steven King, Office of the President - *Science & technology, insurance*
Mr. Arthur S. Harelick, Office of the President - *Science & technology*

Salary minimum: $35,000

Functions: Senior Mgmt., Middle Mgmt., Mfg., Productivity, Packaging, M&A, R&D, Engineering, Specialized Svcs., Mgmt. Consultants

Industries: Energy, Utilities, Mfg., Venture Cap., Pharm Svcs., Haz. Waste, Aerospace, Packaging, Biotech

Asian Diversity Inc

1270 Broadway Ste 703
New York, NY 10001
(212) 465-8777
Fax: (212) 465-8396
Email: resume@asiandiversity.com
Web: www.asiandiversity.com

Description: We are a diversity, recruiting firm with special emphasis on searching Americans with Asian background in various industries such as computers, investment, banking, sales, and apparel.

Key Contact - Specialty:
Mr. Jino Ahn, Executive Director - *Korean-english bilingual professionals*

Salary minimum: $40,000

Functions: Generalist

Industries: HR Services

Ask Guy Tucker Inc

4990 High Point Rd
Atlanta, GA 30342
(404) 303-7177
Fax: (404) 303-0136
Email: guy@askguy.com
Web: www.askguy.com

Description: The recruiting/headhunting firm for really good advertising folks.

Key Contact - Specialty:
Mr. Guy Tucker, President - *Advertising*

Salary minimum: $40,000

Functions: Generalist, Advertising, PR

Industries: Generalist, Advertising, New Media

Professional Associations: CCA, GAPS

The Aspen Group

5353 W Alabama Ste 420
Houston, TX 77056
(713) 622-0968
Fax: (713) 622-1241
Email: kim.cordray@theaspengrp.com
Web: www.theaspengrp.com

Description: The Aspen Group is a full service search firm specializing in Accounting, Financial and Oil and Gas searches.

Key Contact:
Ms. Peggy Kircher, Division Director

Salary minimum: $50,000

Functions: Finance

Industries: Generalist

Professional Associations: TAPC

ASSET Associates Inc

10036 Sawgrass Dr W Ste 4 S
PO Box 858
Ponte Vedra Beach, FL 32004
(904) 273-2999
Fax: (904) 273-3070
Email: assetassoc@jax-inter.net
Web: www.asset-associates.com

Description: Specialize in recruitment and concentrate exclusively in the pharmaceutical and biopharmaceutical Industries.

Key Contact - Specialty:
Mr. Marvin C. Lemons, General Partner - *Pharmaceuticals, biotechnology*
Mr. Al J. Marcel, General Partner - *Pharmaceuticals, biotechnology*
Mr. Fred T. Icken, General Partner - *Pharmaceuticals, marketing*
Ms. Mary J. Soufleris, General Parnter - *Pharmaceuticals*
Mr. Michael S. Robinson, General Partner - *Pharmaceuticals, sales*

Salary minimum: $45,000

Functions: Generalist, Middle Mgmt., Quality, Nurses, Mkt. Research, Budgeting, MIS Mgmt., R&D

Industries: Generalist, Drugs Mfg.

Asset Group Inc

PO Box 211
Verona, NJ 07044
(973) 571-1367
Email: neilepi@home.com
Web: www.pnr1.com

Description: We have the unusual capability of undertaking international searches from bases in the US, Europe and Singapore. Intensely client-focused, we have a uniquely flexible fee structure, offering clients a fixed fee based on the work involved.

Key Contact - Specialty:
Mr. P. Neil Ralley, President - *Specialty chemicals, filtration products, international*

Salary minimum: $80,000

Functions: Generalist

Industries: Mfg., Chemicals, Soap, Perf., Cosmtcs., Plastics, Rubber, Paints, Petro. Products, Consumer Elect., Misc. Mfg.

Asset Resource Group

98 Battery St Penthouse Ste 603
San Francisco, CA 94111-5529
(415) 434-8800
Fax: (415) 434-8833
Web: www.assetresource.net

Description: We are a professional recruiting and
consulting practice catering to the executive staffing
needs of the real estate and financial services
industries throughout the Western states.

Key Contact - Specialty:
Ms. Elizabeth Creger, Principal - *Real estate*

Salary minimum: $75,000

Functions: Generalist, Middle Mgmt.

Industries: Generalist, Finance, Misc. Financial,
Real Estate

Asset Resource Inc

15 Alicante Aisle
Irvine, CA 92614-5926
(949) 756-1600
Fax: (949) 756-1661
Email: fbailin@earthlink.net

Description: Specialization in data communications
and networking industries, software and hardware
development engineering. Working with start-up,
emerging growth and mature companies. History of
repeat business based on ability to fill requirements.

Key Contact - Specialty:
Mr. Fred Bailin, Senior Consultant - *Engineering,
software/hardware development, communications*
Ms. Fran Shulman, Consultant - *Engineering,
software/hardware development, communications*

Salary minimum: $60,000

Functions: IT, Systems Dev., Systems Implem.,
Engineering

Industries: Telecoms, Software

Associated Recruiters

7144 N Park Manor Dr
Milwaukee, WI 53224-4642
(414) 353-1933
Fax: (414) 353-9418
Email: maury@execpc.com
Web: www.associatedrecruiters.com

Description: CPC serving the packaging industry
since 1979. Primary focus is corrugated and folding
cartons.

Key Contact - Specialty:
Mr. Maurice A. Pettengill, CPC, President -
Corrugated packaging, folding cartons

Salary minimum: $30,000

Functions: Generalist

Industries: Packaging

Professional Associations: IOPP, WAPS

Branches:
17803 Port Boca Cir
Ft. Myers, FL 33908
(941) 590-8995
Fax: (941) 437-9425
Email: hf9110@aol.com

151 Kristiansand Dr Ste 115-C
Williamsburg, VA 23188
(757) 259-2020
Fax: (757) 259-2021
Email: gcnorman@aol.com
Key Contact:
Mr. Maurice Pettengill, President

Associates

222 Franklin St
Grand Haven, MI 49417
(616) 842-8596
Fax: (616) 842-6647
Email: associates@novagate.com

Description: We specialize in the automotive
supply industry primarily at the management and
engineering levels in product development and
manufacturing.

Key Contact - Specialty:
Mr. Robert Clark, Owner - *Automotive supply*

Functions: Generalist, Senior Mgmt., Quality,
Materials Plng., Sales Mgmt., Systems Dev.,
R&D, Engineering

Industries: Generalist, Plastics, Rubber, Paints,
Petro. Products, Metal Products, Machine,
Appliance, Motor Vehicles, Test, Measure Equip.

The Associates

222 NW Davis St Ste 400
Portland, OR 97209
(503) 464-9686
Fax: (503) 464-9660
Email: info@theassoc.com
Web: www.theassociatesinc.com

Description: Our firm provides attorney search
services to law firms nationwide for all practice
areas, including intellectual property and for
corporations in the high-tech, communications,
pharmaceutical, and biotech industries. We also
place contract attorneys and legal support staff.

Key Contact:
Mr. Allen Barteld, CEO
Mr. Ian Shearer, COO

Salary minimum: $75,000

Functions: Legal

Industries: Generalist, Energy, Utilities, Mfg.,
Communications, Government, Aerospace,
Software, Biotech

Astro Executive Search Firm

73 Old Dublin Pike
PMB 308
Doylestown, PA 18901
(215) 345-8736
Fax: (215) 345-9083
Email: annemarie@astroexec.com

Description: We will strive to create high quality
applicant and client company relationships through
focused understanding of each party's needs and
goals, effective communication and a professional
level of understanding of the career fields being
addressed.

Key Contact - Specialty:
Ms. Annemarie T. Danielsen, Owner - *Engineering,
computer science*

Salary minimum: $50,000

Functions: Generalist

Industries: Mfg., Food, Bev., Tobacco, Chemicals,
Drugs Mfg., Paints, Petro. Products, Pharm Svcs.,
Software

W R Atchison & Associates Inc

612 Pasteur Dr Freeman Bldg Ste 209
Greensboro, NC 27403
(336) 855-5943
Fax: (336) 855-5945
Email: watch@nr.infi.net
Web: www.wr-atchison.com

Description: A specialized and creative service for
over 20 years in recruiting engineering,
manufacturing professionals and managerial
personnel for growth and major firms in the
Southeast.

Key Contact - Specialty:
Mr. W. R. Atchison, President/Treasurer -
*Engineering, operations, financial, human
resources, materials management (professional &
managerial positions)*
Ms. Ann G. Atchison, Vice President/Secretary -
Administrative

Salary minimum: $30,000

Functions: Mfg., Production, Automation, Plant
Mgmt., Quality, Materials, HR Mgmt., Finance,
R&D, Engineering

Industries: Generalist, Mfg.

Networks: Inter-City Personnel Assoc (IPA)

Atlanta's Finest Staffing

3301 Buckeye Rd Ste 102
Atlanta, GA 30341
(404) 255-4201
Fax: (770) 234-3900
Email: ed@employmentatlanta.com
Web: www.employmentatlanta.com

Description: Placement service for accountants,
bookkeepers and administrative assistants in the
Atlanta, Georgia area. Partners Ed Freeman and
Carol Smith have recruited the Atlanta area since
1987!

Key Contact:
Mr. Ed Freeman, Partner
Ms. Carol Smith, Partner

Salary minimum: $20,000

Functions: Generalist, Admin. Svcs.

Industries: Generalist

Atlantic Management Resources Inc

5 Mountain Blvd Ste 9
Warren, NJ 07059
(908) 791-9000
Fax: (908) 791-9001
Email: support@amrjobs.com
Web: www.amrjobs.com

Description: We are an executive search firm
specializing the recruitment of pharmaceutical and
medical sales professionals. We recruit on a
nationwide basis and cover the entire sales vertical
from entry level positions to vice presidents of sales
& marketing.

Key Contact:
Mr. Lloyd Mandel, President
Mr. David Benadon, Vice President
Ms. Barbara O'Rourke, Researcher
Mr. Tim Connors, Senior Consultant
Ms. Isabel Torres, Office Manager
Mr. Juan Mayor, Senior Consultant
Mr. Clinton Smith, Senior Consultant
Mr. David Moore, Associate Recruiter

Salary minimum: $45,000

Functions: Middle Mgmt., Sales & Mktg., Sales
Mgmt.

Industries: Pharm Svcs., Biotech, Healthcare

Atlantic Pacific Group

PO Box 4563
Laguna Beach, CA 92652
(949) 376-4938
Fax: (949) 376-4855
Email: lblakemore@apgsearch.com
Web: www.apgsearch.com

Description: Executive search for the temporary
staffing industry, human resources consulting firms
and corporate human resources positions. Other
specialties include sales and sales management
professionals. Hourly consulting includes search
and training.

Key Contact - Specialty:
Ms. Linda Blakemore, Owner/Manager - *Staffing industry, human resources*

Salary minimum: $60,000

Functions: Middle Mgmt., Sales Mgmt., HR Mgmt., Personnel

Industries: Invest. Banking, Services, Pharm Svcs., Accounting, Mgmt. Consulting, HR Services, Advertising

Professional Associations: CSP, NATSS, SHRM

Networks: National Personnel Assoc (NPA)

Atlantic Search Group Inc
1 Liberty Sq
Boston, MA 02109-4825
(617) 426-9700
Fax: (617) 426-9013
Email: jobs@atlanticsearch.com
Web: www.atlanticsearch.com

Description: Specializing in accounting, finance, tax, auditing in all industries. All principals are experienced professional accountants and experienced in the personnel/recruiting business. Committed to arranging only quality interviews.

Key Contact:
Mr. John B. Beckvold, Principal
Mr. Daniel F. Jones, Principal
Ms. Gayla K. Hensley, Principal

Functions: Generalist, CFO's, Budgeting, Cash Mgmt., Credit, Taxes

Industries: Generalist

Professional Associations: AAFA

Atlantic Systems Group
1950 Butler Pk
PMB 235
Conshohocken, PA 19428
(610) 825-6660
Fax: (610) 825-6664
Email: careers@asgjobs.com
Web: www.asgjobs.com

Description: Our firm specializes in information technology recruiting with an emphasis on database software and applications. ASG has clients and candidates nationally.

Key Contact:
Mr. Jim Smiarowski, Owner

Networks: Top Echelon Network

Atlantic West Int'l
1289 N Fordham Blvd Ste A-200
Chapel Hill, NC 27514
(919) 942-3080
Fax: (919) 942-0190
Email: rvawi@aol.com

Description: Executive search and recruitment services focused in the medical device industry for multinational corporations to small, privately held domestic firms.

Key Contact:
Mr. Richard W. Valenti

Salary minimum: $60,000

Functions: Generalist

Industries: Drugs Mfg., Medical Devices, Plastics, Rubber, Biotech

Atomic Personnel Inc
PO Box 11244/Z4
Elkins Park, PA 19027-0244
(215) 885-4223
Email: atomic@dca.net

Description: Professional recruitment for all engineering, technical and scientific fields and industries across the U.S. Staffed by experienced graduate technical professionals. Established 1959.

Key Contact - Specialty:
Mr. Arthur L. Krasnow, President - *Engineering, science*

Salary minimum: $35,000

Functions: Mfg., Packaging, R&D, Engineering

Industries: Energy, Utilities, Construction, Mfg., Chemicals, Medical Devices, Leather, Stone, Glass, Metal Products, Test, Measure Equip., Misc. Mfg., Transportation, Equip Svcs., Fiber Optic, Defense, Haz. Waste, Aerospace, Packaging, Industry Specific SW, Biotech

Professional Associations: MAAPC

ATS Applied Technology Solutions Inc
(a division of Sigma Systems Group)
55 York St Ste 1100
Toronto, ON M5J 1R7
Canada
(416) 369-0008
Fax: (416) 369-0199
Email: info@atsglobal.com
Web: www.atsglobal.com

Description: Our firm will deliver the "Best Business Value" information technology services to our customers by providing highly skilled candidates in order to meet our clients' staffing requirements.

Key Contact - Specialty:
Mr. Dave Chanchlani, President
Mr. Ron Hamilton, Vice President - *Business development*

Salary minimum: $30,000

Functions: IT

Industries: Generalist

Professional Associations: ACSESS

ATS Professional Services
9700 Philips Hwy Ste 108
Jacksonville, FL 32256
(904) 224-1375
Email: misrael@consultats.com
Web: www.consultats.com

Description: Our firm partners with top global organizations to deliver the human capital they need to remain leaders. ATS accomplishes this by, first, understanding its client's culture, and secondly, by implementing its proprietary benchmark methodology, and thirdly, by achieving productive and value-added partnerships that prove its performance standards are the industry's highest.

Key Contact:
Mr. Michael Israel, Vice President - Operations
Mr. Ivan Gordon, Vice President - Business Development

Functions: Generalist, General Mgmt., Senior Mgmt., Legal, Sales & Mktg., IT

Industries: Generalist, Finance, Banking, Invest. Banking, Brokers, Misc. Financial, Accounting, E-commerce, IT Implementation, Software, ERP SW, HR SW, Mfg. SW, Marketing SW

ATS Reliance Technical Group
2323 Yonge St Ste 700
Toronto, ON M4P 2C9
Canada
(416) 482-8002
Fax: (416) 482-1210
Email: ats@atsrecruitment.com
Web: www.atsrecruitment.com

Description: Expert executive recruitment in aerospace, railcar, locomotive, automotive, petrochemical, oil and gas, mining, architecture, materials management, software development and information technology.

Key Contact - Specialty:
Mr. David Jackson, Recruitment Manager - *Manufacturing, engineering consulting*
Mr. Graham Gies, Sales Recruitment Consultant - *Electronics, software, information technology*
Mr. Jason Wahl, Sales Recruitment Consultant - *Engineering, manufacturing*
Mr. Jeff Collier, Recruiting Coordinator - *Engineering*
Mr. Brad Austin, Sales Recruitment Consultant - *Manufacturing, engineering*
Mr. Philip McDougall, Sales Consultant - *Engineering, manufacturing*
Mr. Dave Maynard, Sales Consultant - *Architecture, consulting, manufacturing*

Functions: Generalist, Mfg., Materials, HR Mgmt., IT, Engineering, Architects, Technicians

Industries: Generalist, Agri., Forestry, Mining, Mfg., Chemicals, Medical Devices, Plastics, Rubber, Paints, Petro. Products, Metal Products, Machine, Appliance, Motor Vehicles, Test, Measure Equip., Misc. Mfg., Electronic, Elec. Components, Software

Professional Associations: ACSESS

Branches:
250 Mill St Fl 5
Rochester, NY 14614
(716) 777-4090
Fax: (716) 777-4058
Email: atsreliance.roch@worldnet.att.net
Key Contact - Specialty:
Mr. Chris Bell, Vice President - *Manufacturing, aerospace, IT*
Ms. Connie Tramonto, Recruitment Coordinator - *Manufacturing, engineering*
Ms. Carrie Casale, Recruitment Coordinator - *Aerospace, IT*
Mr. Tim Kolb, Branch Manager - *Engineering, manufacturing*

19125 Northcreek Pkwy Ste 120
Bothell, WA 98011
(425) 488-5839
Fax: (716) 325-1399
Email: anthonybell@atsreliance.com
Key Contact - Specialty:
Mr. Anthony Bell, Branch Manager - *Engineering, aerospace, IT*

1305 11th Ave SW Ste 408
Calgary, AB T3C 3P5
Canada
(403) 261-4600
(888) 818-4600
Fax: (403) 265-2909
Email: calgary@atsrecruitment.com
Key Contact - Specialty:
Mr. Phil White, Branch Manager - *Consulting, oil/gas*
Mr. Stephen McCrum, Recruitment Manager - *Oil/gas, IT, engineering*

8711 W 50 Ave Ste 201
Edmonton, AB T6E 5H4
Canada
(780) 462-1815
Fax: (780) 461-9968
Email: edmonton@atsrecruitment.com
Key Contact - Specialty:
Mr. Danny Mikitka, Recruitment Coordinator - *Engineering*
Mr. Tony Dutchak, Branch Manager - *Engineering*

1501 W Broadway Ste 300
Vancouver, BC V6J 4Z6
Canada
(604) 915-9333
Fax: (604) 915-9339
Email: van.bc@atsrecruitment.com
Key Contact - Specialty:
Mr. Paul Dusome, Recruitment Consultant - *Engineering*
Mr. Ian McDougall, Branch Manager - *Engineering*

S Service Rd Ste 307
lington, ON L7N 3M6
nada
05) 333-9632
Fax: (905) 333-9326
Email: burlington@atsrecruitment.com
Key Contact - Specialty:
Ms. Darlene Vitorino, Recruitment Coordinator -
Engineering
Mr. Aaron Carr, Branch Manager - *Engineering*

171 Queens Ave Ste 601
London, ON N6A 5J7
Canada
(519) 679-2886
Fax: (519) 679-1483
Email: jrose@atsrecruitment.com
Key Contact:
Mr. John Rose, Recruitment Manager -
Engineering and people
Ms. Christine Verwegan, Recruitment Consultant -
Engineering (design, project)
Ms. Charlotte Pickersgill, Recruitment Consultant -
Industrial, maintenance
Mr. Dan Spiers, Jnr Recruitment Consultant

J G Auerbach & Associates
665 Third St Ste 525
San Francisco, CA 94107
(415) 975-8636
(510) 562-9907
Fax: (253) 295-3298
Email: joanne@jgauerbach.com

Description: Search & staffing consulting for
emerging technology companies. Specialty is
building marketing, product management, business
development, sales, and related functions at VP,
Director, and Manager level. Also provide
consulting on staffing strategy & growth issues.

Key Contact:
Ms. JoAnne G. Auerbach, Founder

Salary minimum: $120,000

Functions: Directors, Senior Mgmt., Mktg. Mgmt.,
Sales Mgmt.

Industries: Venture Cap., Telecoms, Software

Aureus Executive
(formerly known as ARI Executive Search)
11825 Q St
Omaha, NE 68137-3503
(800) 273-6679
(402) 891-6940
Email: exec@aureusgroup.com
Web: www.aureusexec.com

Description: We are a generalist firm that recruits
mid- to senior-level executives for all industries.
The firm's practice is national in scope. By function,
we place finance/accounting, marketing, sales
leaders, health care management, operations, project
management, attorneys, purchasing, logistics,
customer service, e-Commerce, and other related
executives.

Key Contact:
Ms. Kathy Caruso

Salary minimum: $70,000

Functions: General Mgmt., Healthcare, Mktg.
Mgmt., Sales Mgmt., Finance

Industries: Generalist, Healthcare, Hospitals, Long-
term Care

Networks: National Personnel Assoc (NPA)

Aurora Tech Search
704 5th Ave E Fl 2
Owen Sound, ON N4K 2R6
Canada
(519) 371-6089
(716) 631-7647
Fax: (519) 371-6626

Email: jmols@log.on.ca
Web: www.ipa.com/eoffice/716-631-7647.html
Description: We provide professional search
services for businesses in the information
technology industry and in the aerospace industry.
Our focus area includes Ontario, Canada and New
York State. A full guarantee for our service is
offered; permanent placement searches offered on
contingency and retainer.

Key Contact - Specialty:
Mr. Jeff Mols, General Manager - *Information
technology, aerospace engineering, sales &
marketing*

Salary minimum: $35,000

Functions: Generalist, Middle Mgmt., Automation,
Materials Plng., Mkt. Research, Training, IT,
Engineering

Industries: Generalist, Computer Equip., Banking,
Telecoms, Aerospace, Software

Professional Associations: APPAC, RON

Cami Austin & Associates
3145 NE 26th Ave
Portland, OR 97212
(503) 493-0999
(503) 493-0930
Fax: (503) 493-1011
Email: camihunter@aol.com

Description: We are professional search consultants
for management, engineering and sales/marketing
talent in the electronics industry including: wireless,
radio frequency, microwave, semiconductors, fiber
optics, instrumentation, satellite communications,
and cellular.

Key Contact - Specialty:
Ms. Cami Austin, President - *Radio frequency,
microwave, wireless, telecommunications
engineers (all types), sales & marketing
operations*

Salary minimum: $50,000

Functions: Sales & Mktg., R&D, Engineering,
Specialized Svcs.

Industries: Electronic, Elec. Components,
Telecoms, Wireless, Fiber Optic, Defense

Professional Associations: IEEE, MTTS

Austin - Allen Company
8127 Walnut Grove Rd
Cordova, TN 38018
(901) 756-0900
Fax: (901) 756-0933
Email: jobs@austinallen.com
Web: www.austinallen.com

Description: Since 1973 we have specialized in
engineering, manufacturing and human resources
positions for manufacturing firms throughout the
United States.

Key Contact - Specialty:
Mr. Search Division - *Engineering, human
resources*

Salary minimum: $35,000

Functions: Engineering

Industries: Mfg.

Networks: Inter-City Personnel Assoc (IPA)

Austin Group
(a division of Alexander, Hoyt & Assoc)
10955 Lowell Ave Ste 450
Overland Park, KS 66210
(913) 663-1339
Fax: (913) 663-1403
Email: ron@austingroupinc.com
Web: www.austingroupinc.com

Description: Client companies are both large
corporations and small organizations. Legal, sales
and marketing, finance, operations, manufacturing,
information technology and restaurant management.

Key Contact - Specialty:
Mr. Ronald H. Like - *Executive, management,
professional, international, domestic*

Salary minimum: $30,000

Functions: Generalist, General Mgmt., Mfg., Sales
& Mktg., Finance, IT, Paralegals

Industries: Generalist, Metal Products, Machine,
Appliance, Misc. Mfg., Wholesale, Misc.
Financial, Services, Pharm Svcs., Legal,
Accounting, IT Implementation, Restaurants,
Telecoms, Call Centers, Telephony, Digital,
Wireless, Fiber Optic

Professional Associations: IACMP

Austin Michaels Ltd Inc
8777 E Via de Ventura Ste 375
Scottsdale, AZ 85258-3345
(480) 483-5000
Fax: (480) 483-6068
Email: frank@austinmichaels.com
Web: www.austinmichaels.com

Description: We offer executive-level searches in
the high-tech industry, start-ups, technology leaders,
Internet companies, and systems/applications
developers that are leaders in their fields. We do this
on a national basis by having a small active client
base. We eliminate the possibility of a conflict of
interest. We provide retained search and
contingency. We will help build and staff your
company.

Key Contact - Specialty:
Mr. Frank O'Brien, President - *'C'-level executives,
senior level sales & marketing, business
development, strategic marketing managers,
senior level engineers*
Mr. Robert Hebert, Senior Vice President -
*Manufacturing, engineering, systems
development, software development*

Salary minimum: $90,000

Functions: Generalist, Directors, Senior Mgmt.,
Middle Mgmt., Mfg., Materials, Sales & Mktg.,
Mktg. Mgmt., IT, Engineering

Industries: Mfg., Computer Equip., Consumer
Elect., Test, Measure Equip., Retail, Finance,
Venture Cap., Services, Equip Svcs., Mgmt.
Consulting, HR Services, E-commerce, PSA/ASP,
Media, Communications, Telecoms, Software

Networks: Associated Consultants in Executive
Search Int'l

Austin Park Management Group Inc
40 Eglinton Ave E Ste 207
Toronto, ON M4P 3A2
Canada
(416) 488-9565
Fax: (416) 488-9601
Email: austin@austinpark.com
Web: www.austinpark.com

Description: Our firm conducts searches at a variety
of functional levels: management, executive and
senior staff based on experience in the Unix and
three tier client/server technology sectors.

Key Contact - Specialty:
Mr. Howard Prince, General Manager -
Professional services, Unix
Mr. Earl Gardiner, President - *Professional
services, Unix*

Salary minimum: $60,000

Functions: IT

Industries: Generalist

Professional Associations: ACSESS

Austin, Hill & Associates

5307 Wirestem Ct
Naperville, IL 60564
(630) 922-6740
Fax: (630) 922-6739
Email: austinhillassoc@aol.com

Description: Search firm principal has extensive
personal experience in sales, marketing, human
resources and finance. Working searches nationally,
we seek superior results for our clients.

Key Contact:
Mr. Michael Hill, President

Salary minimum: $50,000

Functions: General Mgmt., Senior Mgmt., Mfg.,
Plant Mgmt., Sales & Mktg., HR Mgmt., Finance,
IT

Industries: Generalist, Energy, Utilities, Mfg.,
Food, Bev., Tobacco, Soap, Perf., Cosmtcs.,
Finance, Misc. Financial, Software

Automation Technology Search

7309 Del Cielo Way
Modesto, CA 95356
(209) 545-4500
Fax: (209) 545-3060
Email: atsearch@pc-intouch.com

Description: Recruiters of managers and engineers
in design and development involving s/w, h/w,
firmware in the food, metals, plastics, medical and
packaging industries. Specialties are mechanical,
electronic, chemical, computer science engineers.

Key Contact - Specialty:
Mr. Ralph L. Becker, President - *Manufacturing,
engineering, software, IPO clients with stock
option*

Salary minimum: $30,000

Functions: Middle Mgmt., Mfg., Materials, HR
Mgmt., Systems Implem., R&D, Engineering,
Technicians

Industries: Agri., Forestry, Mining, Mfg., Food,
Bev., Tobacco, Plastics, Rubber, Metal Products,
Machine, Appliance

Branches:
PO Box 2152
Livermore, CA 94551
(408) 897-3157
Fax: (408) 897-3010
Email: ingerice@att.net
Key Contact:
Ms. Inge Rice, Owner

Automotive Management Search Inc

2135 Burgess Creek Rd
PO Box 774711
Steamboat Springs, CO 80477
(970) 879-4743
Fax: (970) 879-3710
Email: info@autorecruiters.com
Web: www.autorecruiters.com

Description: Executive search firm specializing in
the automotive industry.

Key Contact - Specialty:
Mr. David Miller, President - *Automotive*

Functions: Generalist, General Mgmt.

Industries: Generalist, Transportation, Wholesale,
Retail

Automotive Personnel LLC

14701 Detroit Rd Ste 430
Cleveland, OH 44107
(216) 226-7958
Fax: (216) 226-7987
Email: employap@aol.com
Web: www.industrialpersonnel.com

Description: Specialize in recruiting personnel for
automotive manufacturers and automotive financial
corporations, banks and automotive lending areas
for finance companies.

Key Contact - Specialty:
Mr. Donald Jasensky, President - *Automotive,
financial*

Salary minimum: $50,000

Functions: General Mgmt.

Industries: Motor Vehicles, Transportation, Finance

Professional Associations: RON

Networks: National Banking Network (NBN)

AutoPeople

23 North St
Brattleboro, VT 05301
(802) 257-2719
(972) 788-1988
Email: blaushild@autopeople.com
Web: www.autopeople.com

Description: Founded and managed by a former
automobile dealer, our only specialty is providing
management to automobile dealerships.

Key Contact:
Mr. Robert Hershman, Vice President -
Management (auto dealership)
Ms. Elisabeth Brown Oude Kotte, Recruitment -
Management (auto dealership)
Mr. Eric L. Blaushild, President

Functions: Generalist, Senior Mgmt.

Industries: Motor Vehicles

Branches:
101 N Main St
Sharon, MA 02067
(781) 793-9070
Email: hershman@autopeople.com
Key Contact - Specialty:
Mr. Robert B. Hershman - *Automotive dealership
management*

5050 Quorum Dr Ste 700
Dallas, TX 75240-7564
(972) 788-1988
Email: blaushild@autopeople.com
Key Contact - Specialty:
Mr. Eric Blaushild - *Automotive (dealership
management)*

Autorecruit Inc

390 Steelcase Rd E Unit 2
Markham, ON L3R 1G2
Canada
(905) 946-0777
Fax: (416) 946-1340
Email: info@blconsultants.com
Web: www.autorecruit.com

Description: We are a recruitment firm specializing
in the automotive industry. We are all RPR certified
recruiters with automotive experience.

Key Contact - Specialty:
Mr. Farid Ahmad - *Automotive manufacturers,
automotive aftermarket companies*

Professional Associations: IPM

availABILITY Personnel Consultants

169 S River Rd
Bedford, NH 03110-6936
(603) 669-4440
Email: availability@availability.org
Web: www.availability.org

Description: Contingency search specialists serving
New England in all aspects of professional staffing
for manufacturing and service industries from 5MM
to Fortune 500 firms and their divisions.

Key Contact:
Mr. Walter D. Kilian, CPC, President

Salary minimum: $40,000

Functions: Generalist

Industries: Mfg., Accounting

Networks: Top Echelon Network

Averon

3710 Rawlins 940
Dallas, TX 75219
(214) 965-0777
(888) 828-3766
Fax: (214) 965-0778
Email: mspiek@averon.com
Web: www.averon.com

Description: We specialize in financial, accounting,
and information technology recruiting/placement
services. We offer enterprise-level consulting
services and products.

Key Contact:
Mr. Martin Spiek, Director of Recruiting -
Financial, accounting, information technology
Mr. Jon Williams, Recruiting Specialist

Salary minimum: $50,000

Functions: Directors, Senior Mgmt., Middle
Mgmt., Finance, CFO's, IT

Industries: Generalist, Mfg., Food, Bev., Tobacco,
Computer Equip., Electronic, Elec. Components,
Transportation, Finance, Services, Restaurants,
Communications, Government, Defense, Real
Estate, Software, Healthcare

Avestruz & Associates Inc

23 Japonica
Irvine, CA 92618
(949) 651-8721
Email: avestruzassoc@home.com
Web: www.avestruzinc.com

Description: Specializing in the placement of
personnel in marketing, sales, administration and
biomedical engineering in the radiology, cardiology,
information systems and surgery industries.

Key Contact - Specialty:
Mr. Alner Avestruz, President - *Medical device*

Salary minimum: $80,000

Functions: Generalist

Industries: Medical Devices, Biotech, Healthcare

Branches:
4634 Chicory Ct
Colorado Springs, CO 80917
(719) 550-1717
Email: ox150@yahoo.com
Key Contact:
Mr. Michael Ochsner, Associate

The B & B Group Inc

9 Junction Dr W Ste 5
Glen Carbon, IL 62034
(618) 288-2927
Fax: (618) 288-2950
Email: bandbgroup@aol.com
Web: www.bnbgrp.com

Description: We are financial industry specialists.
We provide superior candidates in a time effective
manner utilizing networking, referrals, a database of
over 20,000 financial professionals, and plain old-
fashioned hard work.

Key Contact - Specialty:
Mr. Daniel J. Baccarini, President - *Wholesalers,
sales managers, investment bankers, institutional
sales, portfolio managers*
Mr. Glenn J. Smith, Senior Vice President -
Wholesalers, sales managers

Ms. Nina Barker, Account Manager - *Wholesalers, sales managers*
Mr. Matthew Huffman, Account Manager - *Investment bankers, institutional sales*
Mr. Chris Andres, Account Manager - *Senior retail brokers*
Mr. Aaron Muskopf, Account Manager - *Analysts, portfolio managers*

Salary minimum: $50,000

Functions: Generalist

Industries: Finance, Banking, Invest. Banking, Brokers, Venture Cap., Misc. Financial, Insurance

The Bachtler Group

(also known as Sales Consultants of Tallahassee)
2937 Kerry Forest Pkwy Ste A2
Tallahassee, FL 32308
(850) 668-8400
Fax: (850) 668-8880
Email: mribachtler@earthlink.net

Description: Our firm specializes in recruiting in the building products, accounting and finance industries. The recruiters in the firm represent a combined 48 years worth of experience in these industries.

Key Contact - Specialty:
Mr. William Bachtler, Managing Partner - *Building products*
Mrs. Jane Bachtler, Managing Partner - *Accounting and finance*

Bader Research Corp

60 E 42nd Ste 565
New York, NY 10165
(212) 682-4750
(212) 872-2277
Fax: (212) 682-4758

Description: Our 32nd year as specialists in the recruitment of highly qualified attorneys for the nation's leading law firms, corporations and financial institutions. We also effect mergers and acquisitions of law firms.

Key Contact - Specialty:
Mr. Sam Bader, President - *Attorneys*

Salary minimum: $100,000

Functions: Attorneys

Industries: Legal

Professional Associations: NALSC

Badon's Employment Inc

5422 Galeria Dr
Baton Rouge, LA 70816
(225) 295-1240
(800) 769-7708
Fax: (225) 295-3972
Email: recruiting@badon.com
Web: www.badon.com

Description: We are a national recruiting firm located in Louisiana. We have jobs for degreed engineers with experience in the chemical, petrochemical and refinery industries in locations all over the country. We need chemical engineers, mechanical engineers, electrical engineers among others with experience in chemicals, specialty chemicals, plastics, polymers, packaging, etc.

Key Contact - Specialty:
Ms. Barbara Badon, President - *Engineering professionals*

Functions: General Mgmt., Mfg., Product Dev., Production, Plant Mgmt., Quality, Productivity, IT

Industries: Generalist, Energy, Utilities, Mfg., Packaging

Networks: National Personnel Assoc (NPA)

Keith Bagg & Associates Inc

85 Richmond St W Ste 700
Toronto, ON M5H 2C9
Canada
(416) 863-1800
Fax: (416) 350-9600
Email: info@bagg.com
Web: www.bagg.com

Description: We are a full-service search firm covering finance/accounting, sales/marketing, engineering/technical, and general management functions.

Key Contact:
Mr. Geoff Bagg, President
Mr. Bruce McAlpine, Vice President

Salary minimum: $45,000

Functions: Generalist

Industries: Generalist

Professional Associations: ACSESS, NAPS

Networks: Canadian Personnel Services Inc (CPSI)

Bailey Employment System Inc

5 W Branch Rd
Westport, CT 06680-1249
(203) 227-8434
Fax: (203) 227-8151
Email: bailey51@aol.com

Description: We have been recruiting since 1960 and in the healthcare field since 1985. We have successfully placed throughout the United States and attribute our longevity and success to our professionalism.

Key Contact - Specialty:
Mr. Sheldon Leighton, Healthcare Placement Manager - *Physicians*

Functions: Generalist, Physicians

Industries: Generalist, Healthcare

Bailey Professional Search

1604 - 21A St NW
Calgary, AB T2N 2M6
Canada
(403) 289-5802
Fax: (403) 282-7912
Email: nairb@baileysearch.com

Description: We provide executive search for clients based primarily in Western Canada. We offer recruitment of sales and management professionals with specialization in industrial products and services, power, electronics, process control, telecommunications, data communications, and instrumentation.

Key Contact - Specialty:
Mr. Nair H. Bailey, General Manager - *Technical sales management, high technology sales management, product management, account management*

Salary minimum: $35,000

Functions: General Mgmt., Automation, Sales Mgmt.

Industries: Mfg., Test, Measure Equip., Misc. Mfg., Electronic, Elec. Components, Telecoms, Telephony, Digital, Wireless, Network Infrastructure, Mfg. SW

W G Baird & Associates

600 Commerce Dr Ste 602
Coraopolis, PA 15108
(412) 262-0842
Fax: (412) 262-0904
Email: bbaird@ccia.com

Description: We are a company whose principals have spent many years in large and medium sized companies, and who will devote the time it takes to help either clients or candidates to obtain the right fit.

Key Contact - Specialty:
Mr. William Baird, President - *Technical, manufacturing, engineering, human resources*
Mr. Frank Mattison, Director - *Technical, manufacturing, engineering*
Mr. Jeffrey Robinson, Director - *All*

Functions: Generalist, Senior Mgmt., Middle Mgmt., Plant Mgmt., Sales & Mktg., HR Mgmt., Engineering

Industries: Generalist, Textiles, Apparel, Metal Products, Machine, Appliance, Misc. Mfg.

Networks: Inter-City Personnel Assoc (IPA)

Baker, Scott & Company

1259 Rte 46
Parsippany, NJ 07054
(973) 263-3355
Fax: (973) 263-9255
Email: exec.search@bakerscott.com
Web: www.bakerscott.com

Description: Full-service executive search firm specializing in nationwide and international assignments in telecommunications, cable, broadcasting and emerging technologies across functional disciplines.

Key Contact:
Ms. Judy Bouer, Principal
Mr. David Allen, Principal

Salary minimum: $65,000

Functions: Generalist, Senior Mgmt., Middle Mgmt., Advertising, HR Mgmt., CFO's, MIS Mgmt., Int'l.

Industries: Generalist, Media, New Media, Broadcast, Film, Telecoms, Software

Professional Associations: NAER, NAMIC, NCTA, SHRM, WICT

Baldwin & Associates

3975 Erie Ave
Cincinnati, OH 45208-1908
(513) 272-2400
Fax: (513) 527-5929
Email: office@baldwin-assoc.com
Web: www.baldwin-assoc.com

Description: Generalists assisting greater-Cincinnati area companies to fill requirements ranging from individual contributor to executive management. We tailor our service to clients' needs with capability for project, search and ongoing retainer relationships.

Key Contact - Specialty:
Mr. W. Keith Baldwin, President - *Technical, management, CEO*
Ms. Janice F. Seymour, Vice President - *Sales, manufacturing*
Mr. William W. Schrepferman, Vice President - *Human resources, management*
Ms. Nancy Foster, Associate - *Finance, human resource recruitment*
Mr. Thomas Pharr, Associate - *Information systems, information technology, MIS*
Mr. Stephen Krentz, Associate - *Information systems, information technology, MIS*
Ms. Sharon Blake, Associate - *Generalist, sales, legal*
Ms. Kathy Phillips, Associate - *Generalist*
Mr. Philip Morris, Associate - *Generalist*
Mr. Andrew MacKay, Associate - *Sales, sales management, pharmaceutical sales, financial/brokerage recruitment*

Salary minimum: $50,000

Functions: Generalist

Industries: Generalist, Mfg., Finance, Services, Media

Networks: National Personnel Assoc (NPA)

The Bales Company

13400 Sutton Park Dr S Ste 1601
Jacksonville, FL 32224
(904) 398-9080
Fax: (904) 398-8121
Email: bbales@balescompany.com
Web: www.balescompany.com

Description: We provide executive search and sales recruiting specializing in clinical, medical, pharmaceutical, telecommunications, and information technology. We are the co-founder of a 350 firm network of sales and marketing recruiting companies in North America. We are the co-founder of SearchNet, a network of 35 retained search firms around the world.

Key Contact - Specialty:
Ms. Sally Bales, President - *Medical device, international*

Salary minimum: $70,000

Functions: General Mgmt., Directors, Senior Mgmt., Healthcare, Sales & Mktg., Mktg. Mgmt., Sales Mgmt., CFO's, Int'l.

Industries: Medical Devices, Venture Cap., Telecoms, Biotech, Healthcare

Networks: First Interview Network (FIN)

Carol Ball & Company

80 Washington Post Dr
Wilton, CT 06897
(203) 762-1752
Fax: (203) 762-1753
Email: cbsearch@mindspring.com

Description: Specialists in communications professionals for PR agencies and corporate communications departments throughout the USA. Recruit middle, senior and top management level personnel.

Key Contact - Specialty:
Ms. Carol Ball, President - *Public relations, corporate communications*

Salary minimum: $35,000

Functions: Generalist, PR

Industries: Generalist, Pharm Svcs., Mgmt. Consulting, Advertising, New Media

Branches:
88 Colgate Ave
Wyckoff, NJ 07481
(201) 670-7142
Fax: (201) 670-6142
Email: elizbrand@aol.com
Key Contact - Specialty:
Ms. Elizabeth Brand, Recruiter - *Public relations, corporate communications executives*

BallResources

PO Box 480391
Kansas City, MO 64148
(816) 322-2727
Email: ronball@swbell.net

Description: A no frills, get-the-job-done search service for all industrial sales and sales management areas. Specializing in power transmission/motion control/factory automation. National (USA) scope.

Key Contact - Specialty:
Mr. Ronald D. Ball, Owner - *Industrial sales, sales management*

Salary minimum: $25,000

Functions: Generalist, Mktg. Mgmt., Sales Mgmt.

Industries: Generalist, Plastics, Rubber, Metal Products, Machine, Appliance, Test, Measure Equip., Misc. Mfg., Packaging

BancSearch Inc

PO Box 700516
Tulsa, OK 74170-0516
(918) 496-9477
Fax: (918) 494-2003
Email: info@bancsearch.com
Web: www.bancsearch.com

Description: We are a premier recruiting firm that specializes in discovering and placing extremely skilled candidates in the banking and financial industries. We provide the management areas of banking, trust-wealth management, commercial banking, marketing, and credit cards. We have completed searches in thirty-nine states and Puerto Rico.

Key Contact - Specialty:
Ms. Maggie Cunningham, CPC, Managing Director - *Trust*
Mr. Don Cunningham, CPC, President - *Banking*

Functions: Generalist

Industries: Finance, Banking, Invest. Banking, Brokers, Venture Cap., Misc. Financial

Professional Associations: NAPS, NBN

Networks: National Banking Network (NBN)

The Bankers Group

(a division of Executive Directions Inc)
300 W Adams Ste 330
Chicago, IL 60606
(312) 346-9456
Fax: (312) 346-9487
Email: pcc@execdirections.com
Web: www.execdirections.com

Description: Recruitment of banking professionals for investment and brokerage firms, foreign exchange, major money centers and regional banks, leasing and mortgage firms and savings and loan institutions.

Key Contact - Specialty:
Mr. Peter Chappell, Managing Director - *Banking*

Salary minimum: $50,000

Functions: Generalist, Senior Mgmt., Middle Mgmt., Admin. Svcs., Mkt. Research, Mktg. Mgmt., Sales Mgmt., Minorities

Industries: Generalist, Banking, Invest. Banking, Brokers, Misc. Financial, Accounting, HR Services, Insurance

The Bankers Register

1140 Ave of the Americas
New York, NY 10036
(212) 840-0800
Fax: (212) 840-7039
Email: bankers@tbrspg.com

Description: Specialists in the recruitment and placement of banking personnel: commercial, corporate, international, thrift, mortgage/real estate.

Key Contact - Specialty:
Mr. Steven Moss, Associate Director - *Savings, thrifts, credit unions, mortgage*
Mr. Cesar Consing, Associate Director - *International banking*
Ms. Sherry Ambos, Associate Director - *Branch, operations, comm'l finance*
Mr. Ira Smith, Associate Director - *Corporate finance, audit, accounting, loan administration*

Functions: Generalist

Industries: Banking

Professional Associations: APCNY

Bankers Search LLC

PO Box 854
Madison, CT 06443
(203) 245-0694
Fax: (203) 245-9567
Email: tloughlin@bankerssearch.com

Description: For over 30 years we have been providing superior executive recruiting services throughout New England. We cater to all disciplines of banking, focusing on the placement of middle and senior management.

Key Contact - Specialty:
Mr. Timothy M. Loughlin, President - *Banking*

Salary minimum: $60,000

Functions: Generalist

Industries: Banking

Professional Associations: CBA, NBN

BankResources

1 Pioneer Ct
Novato, CA 94945
(415) 209-6160
Email: bankres@worldnet.att.net

Description: We were founded exclusively to provide financial institutions with highly qualified executives, managers and professionals from all banking disciplines to fill staffing requirements on a permanent or project basis.

Key Contact - Specialty:
Mr. Patrick J. Duncan, Principal - *Generalist*

Functions: Generalist

Industries: Banking

Paul C Banks Associates

2715 Bridgegate Cv
Marietta, GA 30068-2203
(770) 565-2346
Fax: (770) 977-0436
Email: pb@paulcbanks.com

Description: We are a contingency search firm specializing in the plastics, packaging, and chemical industries.

Key Contact - Specialty:
Mr. Paul C. Banks, Owner - *Plastics, packaging, chemicals*

Salary minimum: $50,000

Functions: Sales & Mktg., Sales Mgmt.

Industries: Chemicals, Plastics, Rubber, Packaging

Barbachano Int'l Inc

660 Bay Blvd Ste 103
Chula Vista, CA 91910
(619) 427-2310
Fax: (619) 427-2312
Email: barbachano@bipsearch.com
Web: www.bipsearch.com

Description: We provide full service international management search, in Mexico and US, for companies with operations in Mexico or requiring bilingual and diversity professionals for domestic assignment. Our emphasis is on recruiting for manufacturing, high technology, telecommunications, and logistics industries. We have over 40 years of collective recruitment experience with many Fortune 1000 companies. We also offer training and development and international outplacement. We have over 40 partner offices in Europe, Asia, and North America.

Key Contact - Specialty:
Mr. Fernando O. Barbachano, CPC, General Manager - *Accounting, finance, human resources*
Ms. Berenice Barbachano, CPC, President - *Upper management, manufacturing operations, plant management*

Ms. Carmina Flores, Training Consultant - *Human resources, training consulting*
Mr. Jorge Roldan, Search Consultant - *Materials, purchasing, logistics, sales*
Mr. Carlos Acosta, Search Consultant - *Engineering, high tech, quality, manufacturing operations, IT*

Salary minimum: $45,000

Functions: General Mgmt., Mfg., Plant Mgmt., Materials, Purchasing, Sales Mgmt., HR Mgmt., Finance, Engineering, Int'l.

Industries: Mfg., Medical Devices, Plastics, Rubber, Metal Products, Motor Vehicles, Consumer Elect.

Professional Associations: AIMS, APICS, CSP, NAPS, SHRM, WMTA

Barclay Consultants Inc
16 Chestnut Ct Ste B
Brielle, NJ 08730
(732) 223-1131
Description: Professional search firm staffed by individuals from the data and information processing industries. Areas of specialization are sales, marketing and technical.

Key Contact - Specialty:
Mr. Jules Silverman, President - *Sales, sales management, technical support, technical management*
Ms. Linda Pappas, Vice President - *Sales, sales management, technical support, technical management*

Salary minimum: $30,000

Functions: Generalist, Senior Mgmt., Middle Mgmt., Sales Mgmt., Systems Dev., Systems Implem., Systems Support, Mgmt. Consultants

Industries: Generalist, Computer Equip., Consumer Elect., Mgmt. Consulting, Software

Professional Associations: NJAPS

Barcus Associates
PO Box 1059
Van Alstyne, TX 75495
(903) 482-1362
Fax: (903) 482-1365
Email: keithl@barcusassociates.com
Web: www.barcusassociates.com

Description: We focus on sales, marketing, and support roles for high-tech vendors to the financial industry. We offer retained and contingency search and related services.

Key Contact - Specialty:
Mr. Keith Larson, Senior Vice President - *Sales and marketing, management*
Ms. Carolyn Barcus, President - *Sales and sales management*

Networks: Top Echelon Network

Cliff W Bard & Associates Inc
(also known as BardSearch Innovations)
PO Box 120914
West Melbourne, FL 32912-0914
(321) 727-1414
Email: cliff@cwbard.com
Web: www.cwbard.com

Description: We are a national executive search firm specializing in mid-level and executive recruitment of banking, brokerage, financial service, and finance candidates. Our focus is on financial consultants (brokers), bank trust, private banking, investment, and lending sales, relationship manager, portfolio manager, and team leader officers.

Key Contact - Specialty:
Mr. Cliff Bard, CPC, CRC, President/Founder - *Banking, brokerage, accounting, finance*

Ms. Ann Bard, Administrative Mgr /Search Project Mgr - *Mortgage banking, accounting*

Salary minimum: $50,000

Functions: Generalist, Senior Mgmt., Sales Mgmt., Cash Mgmt.

Industries: Finance, Banking, Invest. Banking, Brokers, Misc. Financial, Legal, Accounting

Professional Associations: NAPS

Barnes & Associates Executive Search
1101 Dove St Ste 238
Newport Beach, CA 92660
(949) 253-6750
Fax: (949) 253-6753
Email: msbarnes@ix.netcom.com
Web: www.barnesandassociates.com

Description: We have had twenty-two years of executive search experience in the high-tech industry. Our firm works the entire nation placing executives in the software, networking, and pre-IPO companies.

Key Contact - Specialty:
Ms. Meredith Barnes Schwarz, Principal - *IT, sales & marketing, technical support*
Mr. Michael G. Larsen, Executive Recruiter - *VP sales, VP marketing, product, PR*
Ms. Debra Wilkens, Executive Recruiter - *Sales & marketing*

Salary minimum: $60,000

Functions: Sales & Mktg.

Industries: Computer Equip., New Media, Telecoms, Software

Barnes & Cutright
PO Box 17284
Nashville, TN 37217
(615) 360-1149
Fax: (615) 361-3294
Email: dcc@barnesandcutright.com
Web: www.barnesandcutright.com

Description: We provide professional recruiting services in the areas of accounting/finance, administrative/office support, healthcare management, human resources, sales/marketing, as well as many other areas.

Key Contact - Specialty:
Ms. Dana Cutright, President/Owner - *Accounting & finance, sales & marketing, manufacturing, engineering, information systems*

Salary minimum: $30,000

Functions: Generalist, General Mgmt., Mfg., Health Admin., Sales & Mktg., HR Mgmt., Finance, IT

Industries: Generalist, Mfg., Finance, Higher Ed., Accounting, HR Services, Media, Healthcare

Barone Associates
PO Box 706
Allenwood, NJ 08720-0706
(732) 292-0900
Fax: (732) 292-0880
Email: gaildon@monmouth.com

Description: A firm of industry professionals reacting to and positively affecting the human dynamics of the recruitment/search process. Significant engineering, marketing and manufacturing work in healthcare products, chemical process and manufacturing industries.

Key Contact:
Mr. L. Donald Rizzo, President
Mr. Noel Cram, Electronics Specialist
Mr. Robert Horan

Salary minimum: $30,000

Functions: Generalist, Product Dev., Production, Purchasing, Distribution, Mktg. Mgmt., Sales Mgmt., Engineering

Industries: Generalist, Chemicals, Drugs Mfg., Medical Devices, Plastics, Rubber, Metal Products, Computer Equip., Misc. Mfg.

Barr Associates
93 S West End Blvd Ste 105B
Quakertown, PA 18951
(215) 538-9411
Fax: (215) 538-9466
Email: cbarr@enter.net
Web: www.barr-associates.com

Description: Specialized recruiting firm with in-depth knowledge in the semiconductor industry, established in 1987. Custom recruiting focusing on long-term relationships.

Key Contact - Specialty:
Mr. Charly Barr, Director - *Semiconductors*
Mr. Sharon Barr, Director - *Semiconductors*
Mr. Agim Zabeli, Senior Consultant - *Semiconductor industry (all positions)*
Mr. Tom Ozoroski, Senior Consultant - *Semiconductor industry, engineering*
Mr. Tom Belletieri, Senior Consultant - *Semiconductors, high tech electronics*

Functions: Generalist

Industries: Computer Equip., Electronic, Elec. Components, Digital, Wireless, Biotech

Networks: Inter-City Personnel Assoc (IPA)

Barrett & Company Inc
59 Stiles Rd Ste 105
Salem, NH 03079
(603) 890-1111
Fax: (603) 890-1118
Email: barrettcompany@barrettcompany.com
Web: www.barrettcompany.com

Description: Twenty years in business placing sales and marketing personnel at all levels. We deal 95% in the medical industry including international. Deal quite a bit with start-up medical companies. We also deal in telecom, IT and service related outside sales positions.

Key Contact - Specialty:
Mr. Bill Barrett, President - *Medical sales, sales management,*
Mr. Frank Dion, Vice President - *Medical, start-up medical, marketing,*
Ms. LeeAnne Martino, Account Executive - *Medical device, dental, telecom, payroll services, pharmaceutical*

Salary minimum: $40,000

Functions: Directors, Senior Mgmt., Middle Mgmt., Healthcare, Sales & Mktg., Mkt. Research, Mktg. Mgmt., Sales Mgmt.

Industries: Medical Devices, Pharm Svcs., Telecoms, Healthcare, Dental, Non-classifiable

Barrett Partners
100 N LaSalle St Ste 1420
Chicago, IL 60602
(312) 443-8877
Fax: (312) 443-8866
Email: questions@barrettpartners.com
Web: www.barrettpartners.com

Description: Professional search consultants specializing in the placement of accounting/financial, engineering/technical and information technology candidates for permanent and contract/temporary opportunities.

Key Contact - Specialty:
Mr. Joseph Thielman, CPC, President
Mr. John L. Molitor, CPC, Accounting/Financial Manager - *Accounting, financial*

Mr. Jeffrey McNear, CTS, Operations Manager-
Barrettemps - *Accounting & finance, engineering,
technical, information technology*
Mr. Mike Zilka, CPC, Engineering/Technical
Manager - *Engineering, technical*
Mr. Sam Kovacevic, CPC, Manager - *Information
technology*

Salary minimum: $40,000

Functions: Generalist, Finance, IT, Engineering

Industries: Generalist, Mfg., Finance, Services,
Media, Insurance, Biotech

Professional Associations: IATSS, NAPS, NATSS

Barrett Rose & Lee Inc
55 University Ave Ste 1700
Toronto, ON M5J 2H7
Canada
(416) 363-9700
Fax: (416) 363-8999
Email: info@barrettrose.com
Web: www.barrettrose.com

Description: We recruit professional staff, senior
and mid-level executives in sales and marketing,
operations and administration. Our clients are new-
economy companies such as software creators,
hardware manufacturers and vendors.

Key Contact:
Mr. J. Arthur Clark, President
Mr. H. Peter Heinemann, General Manager

Salary minimum: $60,000

Functions: Middle Mgmt., Mfg., Production,
Purchasing, Mktg. Mgmt., Sales Mgmt., HR
Mgmt., Finance

Industries: Computer Equip., Electronic, Elec.
Components

Manny Barrientos
12605 Ashglen Dr N
Jacksonville, FL 32224
(904) 642-2635
Fax: (603) 676-2861
Email: manuelb1@aol.com
Web: www.wolfganggroup.com

Description: We specialize in executive search for
medical device, pharmaceutical, and biotech
companies in the areas of sales, marketing,
engineering, and R&D. We are affiliated with over
300 search firms. Manny ensures national and
international coverage.

Key Contact - Specialty:
Mr. Manny Barrientos, Executive Recruiter -
Medical device, pharmaceutical, biotech

Salary minimum: $85,000

Functions: General Mgmt., Senior Mgmt.,
Automation, Healthcare, Sales & Mktg., Mkt.
Research, Mktg. Mgmt., Sales Mgmt., CFO's

Industries: Drugs Mfg., Medical Devices, Biotech,
Healthcare

Professional Associations: FIN, MMA

Networks: First Interview Network (FIN)

Bartl & Evins
(a division of Fidelity Employment Group Inc)
420 Jericho Tpke 333
Jericho, NY 11753
(516) 433-3333
Fax: (516) 433-2692
Email: mailbox@bartlandevins.com
Web: www.bartlandevins.com

Description: Our twenty-two years worth of
financial recruiting experience means that we know
many CFOs and controllers. These relationships
translate into a superior resource for our clients. We
now also specialize in the placement of public

accounting professionals with audit, tax, valuation,
and forensic backgrounds.

Key Contact - Specialty:
Ms. Susan Evins, President - *CFOs*
Mr. Frank Bartl, Vice President - *Controllers,
accountants*

Salary minimum: $55,000

Functions: Senior Mgmt., Finance, CFO's,
Budgeting, Cash Mgmt., Credit, Taxes, M&A

Industries: Generalist

Professional Associations: NYSCPA

The Barton Group Inc
33050 Five Mile Rd
Livonia, MI 48154
(734) 458-7555
Fax: (734) 458-5176
Email: bfoster@thebartongroup.com
Web: www.thebartongroup.com

Description: Our firm has two divisions to serve
you, a retained search division and contingent
search division. We are a technology recruiting
firm. All of our work evolves around technology,
manufacturing, and industry. We place electronics,
electrical and mechanical engineering,
manufacturing, product, development, sales,
marketing, software design, information technology,
purchasing, and quality control, automotive, and
non-automotive.

Key Contact - Specialty:
Mr. Barton T. Foster, President/CEO/Executive
Recruiter - *Automotive (technical, electronics,
electronical mechanical engineering,
manufacturing, product development & sales
engineering), executive and leadership roles*
Ms. Dianne Hamilton, Executive Recruiter -
*Electronics, engineering (electronical,
mechanical), sales, marketing, program
managers, purchasing*
Mr. Al Mirsky, Executive Recruiter - *Automotive
electronics electronical mechanical engineering,
manufacturing, product (development, sales)*
Mr. Jerry Prutow, Executive Recruiter -
*Engineering (electronics & electronical),
embedded microprocessor, software (design,
development)*
Ms. Lara E Currie, Executive Recruiter -
*Electronics, engineering (electronical,
mechanical), audio, automotive, microwave*
Ms. Carol Koenig, Admin Assistant/Research
Development
Mr. Jeffrey Sharkey, Executive Recruiter - *Energy
(development, process), oil, gas, electric, fuel
cells*

Salary minimum: $40,000

Functions: General Mgmt., Mfg., Purchasing,
Mktg. Mgmt., Sales Mgmt., Engineering,
Minorities, Int'l.

Industries: Mfg., Plastics, Rubber, Metal Products,
Motor Vehicles, Transportation

Professional Associations: MAPS, SAE

Networks: National Personnel Assoc (NPA)

Bartz & Partners
6465 Wayzata Blvd Ste 777
Minneapolis, MN 55426
(952) 417-2500
Fax: (952) 417-2501
Email: career@bartz-partners.com
Web: www.bartz-partners.com

Description: We provide our clients quality and
timely search and consulting services specializing in
information technology recruitment from the
programmer level to the CIO.

Key Contact - Specialty:
Mr. Douglas Bartz, Partner - *Information systems,
executives & professionals*

Salary minimum: $55,000

Functions: IT, MIS Mgmt., Systems Analysis,
Systems Dev., Systems Implem., Systems
Support, Network Admin., DB Admin.

Industries: Generalist

Basilone-Oliver Executive Search
4840 McKnight Rd Ste 101
Pittsburgh, PA 15237
(412) 369-9501
Fax: (412) 369-9502
Email: email@basilone-oliver.com
Web: www.basilone-oliver.com

Description: We have career opportunities
nationwide in accounting, finance, information
systems, engineering, human resources, marketing,
purchasing and office support. Staffed with
professional writers, we also can assist you in
developing your resume.

Key Contact - Specialty:
Mr. Larry Basilone, Shareholder - *Accounting &
finance*
Mr. Floyd Oliver, Shareholder - *Accounting &
finance*
Mr. William Brundage, Shareholder - *Engineering,
information systems, human resources*
Mr. Frank Caliguiri, Shareholder - *Accounting &
finance*

Functions: Generalist, Legal, Productivity, PR,
Training, Risk Mgmt., DB Admin., Engineering

Industries: Generalist, Legal, Accounting

Professional Associations: AITP, IIA, IMA,
ISACA, PHRA, PHTC, SWE

Branches:
1080 Holcomb Bridge Rd Ste 130
Roswell, GA 30076
(770) 649-0553
Fax: (770) 649-0565
Email: boatl@aol.com
Key Contact - Specialty:
Mr. Kevin Mayfield - *Accounting & finance*

201 S Tryon St Ste 925
Charlotte, NC 28202
(704) 373-2240
Fax: (704) 373-2243
Email: lbasilone@basilone-oliver.com
Key Contact:
Mr. Larry Basilone, Partner

Bassett Laudi Partners
2 Bloor St W Ste 2600
Box 4
Toronto, ON M4W 2G7
Canada
(416) 935-0855
Fax: (416) 935-1106
Email: careers@bassettlaudi.com
Web: www.bassettlaudi.com

Description: We bring together the best human
capital with the best corporations in North America.
We provide Fortune 500 and Fortune 1000
companies with the research and representation they
need to stay ahead in the marketplace by using
leading edge technology to find the right job match
quickly.

Key Contact - Specialty:
Mr. Martyn Bassett, Partner/Owner - *Information
technology*
Mr. Mario Laudi, Partner/Owner - *Information
technology*

Salary minimum: $35,000

Functions: Generalist, IT, MIS Mgmt., Systems
Analysis, Systems Dev., Systems Implem.,
Systems Support, DB Admin.

Industries: Generalist, Software

Bast & Associates Inc

11726 San Vicente Blvd Ste 200
Los Angeles, CA 90049
(310) 207-2100
Fax: (310) 207-3003
Email: bastassoc@aol.com

Description: Executive search for
marketing/advertising management positions with
consumer goods/services firms, specializing in
Western United States.

Key Contact:
Mr. Larry C. Bast, President
Ms. Sue E. Bast, Vice President

Salary minimum: $50,000

Functions: Mktg. Mgmt.

Industries: Food, Bev., Tobacco, Soap, Perf.,
Cosmtcs., Consumer Elect., Hospitality,
Publishing, Broadcast, Film, Telecoms

L Battalin & Company

11129 Sandyshell Way
Boca Raton, FL 33498
(561) 477-3441
Fax: (561) 447-5654
Email: lbatco@aol.com
Web: www.lbatco.com

Description: Specialize in national recruitment and
placement of marketing management within the
consumer packaged goods industry while pursuing
the equal opportunity objectives.

Key Contact - Specialty:
Mr. Laurence H. Battalin - *Consumer packaged
goods, marketing*

Salary minimum: $75,000

Functions: Generalist, Mkt. Research, Mktg.
Mgmt., Minorities

Industries: Generalist, Food, Bev., Tobacco,
Textiles, Apparel, Soap, Perf., Cosmtcs.,
Computer Equip., New Media

Networks: First Interview Network (FIN)

Bay Area Anesthesia Inc

617 S State St
PO Box 1547
Ukiah, CA 95482
(707) 468-9301
Fax: (707) 463-0519
Email: jobs@fastgas.com
Web: www.fastgas.com

Description: Nationwide registry of anesthesia,
radiology, primary care, occupational medical and
surgical physicians; anesthesiologists and CRNAs
(nurse anesthetists). Our company provides both
locum tenens (temp) and permanent placement.

Key Contact - Specialty:
Mr. John Paju, CRNA, President - *Anesthesia*

Functions: Senior Mgmt., Admin. Svcs.,
Healthcare, Physicians, Nurses, Allied Health, HR
Mgmt., Int'l.

Industries: Mgmt. Consulting, HR Services,
Government, Healthcare, Non-classifiable

Professional Associations: NAPR

Bayland Associates

4286 Redwood Hwy 342
San Rafael, CA 94903
(415) 499-8111
Fax: (415) 499-8111
Email: baylandtjk@aol.com

Description: Specializes in conducting national and
local executive searches exclusively within medical
manufacturing, sales and services environments.
Medical diagnostic, therapeutic, instrumentation,

equipment, device and service marketplaces are
where we have the greatest expertise.

Key Contact - Specialty:
Mr. Thomas J. Kunkel, Principal - *Medical device,
instrumentation, information management,
pharmaceuticals*

Salary minimum: $75,000

Functions: Generalist, Senior Mgmt., Mfg., Mktg.
Mgmt., Sales Mgmt., IT, R&D, Engineering

Industries: Drugs Mfg., Medical Devices

The Beardsley Group Inc

1681 Barnum Ave
Stratford, CT 06614
(203) 377-3444
Fax: (203) 375-6295
Email: sales@beardsleygroup.com
Web: www.beardsleygroup.com

Description: We are comprised of individuals who
once worked in the data communications field who
best understand the needs of the client based on
personal experience.

Key Contact - Specialty:
Mr. Harry Roscoe, President - *Data
communications, telecommunications, networking*
Ms. Kathy McCormack, Recruiter - *Data
communications, telecommunications, networking*
Ms. Holly Fassbender, Recruiter - *Data
communications, telecommunications, networking*

Functions: Generalist, Sales Mgmt., Systems
Analysis, Systems Implem., Systems Support

Industries: Generalist, Computer Equip., Telecoms

Beck/Eastwood Recruitment Solutions

28170 Ave Crocker Ste Ste 202
Valencia, CA 91355
(661) 295-6666
Fax: (661) 295-5153
Email: info@beckeastwood.com
Web: www.beckeastwood.com

Description: We raise the level of commitment to
satisfy our clients' needs through innovative
strategic partnerships (co-venture program), expert
direct recruiting, and our recruiting network of over
400 offices nationwide. We serve clients in B2B
hw/sw, infrastructure/networks, supply chain,
fulfillment/digital print, call center, and
medical/pharmaceutical markets.

Key Contact - Specialty:
Mr. Steven Beck, Senior Partner - *Sales &
marketing, information technology*
Mr. Gary Eastwood, Partner - *Sales & marketing,
information technology, outsourced professional
services*

Salary minimum: $50,000

Functions: Generalist, Mktg. Mgmt., Sales Mgmt.

Industries: Generalist, Printing, Drugs Mfg.,
Medical Devices, Plastics, Rubber, Computer
Equip., E-commerce, Telecoms, Call Centers,
Network Infrastructure, Software, Networking,
Comm. SW

Professional Associations: RON

Networks: National Personnel Assoc (NPA)

Hans Becker Associates

2110 15 Mile Rd
Sterling Heights, MI 48310
(810) 978-0550
Fax: (810) 978-0572
Email: hansbec@aol.com

Description: Engineering, manufacturing, sales,
quality, industrial, automotive industries. Serving
Michigan on a contingency fee basis.

Key Contact - Specialty:
Mr. B. Hans Becker, Owner - *Engineering,
manufacturing, sales, marketing*
Ms. Launa Tierney, Executive Recruiter -
Engineering, manufacturing, metal, plastics

Salary minimum: $60,000

Functions: Generalist, Middle Mgmt., Quality,
Engineering

Industries: Mfg., Chemicals, Plastics, Rubber,
Metal Products, Motor Vehicles, Misc. Mfg.,
Mgmt. Consulting

Professional Associations: NAPS

Becker Professional Services

2101 W Commercial Blvd Ste 3000
Ft. Lauderdale, FL 33309
(954) 776-5554
Fax: (954) 776-5855
Email: mbecker@beckerpro.com
Web: www.beckerpro.com

Description: We analyze the specific needs of our
clients and execute a customized search. We
consistently seek feedback from our customers in
order to continually improve the placement process.

Key Contact - Specialty:
Mr. Matthew Becker, CEO - *Accounting, finance,
human resources*
Mr. Dean Gross, Senior Vice President-Business
Developmt - *Accounting, finance, human
resources*
Ms. Marjorie Hawke, Senior Vice President -
Accounting, finance, human resources
Ms. Debra McCarthy, Senior Vice President -
Temporary, accounting, finance, human resources

Functions: HR Mgmt., Finance

Industries: Generalist

Becker Staffing Services Inc

1 Bala Plaza Ste LL36
Bala Cynwyd, PA 19004
(610) 667-3010
(610) 785-9000
Fax: (610) 667-4209
Email: jobs@beckerstaffing.com
Web: www.beckerstaffing.com

Description: We were founded twenty-five years
ago with the mission of providing recruitment and
staffing services through long-term client
relationships. We offer candidates a broad spectrum
of consultation services. We provide retained and
contingency search as well as contract and
temporary staffing.

Key Contact:
Mr. Daniel Becker, President
Mr. Andrew Rinaldi, Vice President Recruitment

Functions: Generalist

Industries: Generalist

Branches:
1150 1st Ave
King of Prussia, PA 19406
(610) 265-4844
Fax: (610) 265-8695
Email: jobs@beckerstaffing.com
Key Contact:
Mr. Ed Green, Manager

1617 JFK Blvd
Philadelphia, PA 19103
(215) 567-6148
Fax: (215) 569-9896
Email: jobs@beckerstaffing.com
Key Contact:
Mr. Harvey Becker, Owner

becker.net.inc

2101 W Commercial Blvd Ste 3000
Ft. Lauderdale, FL 33309
(305) 372-2777
Email: szuckerman@becker-net.com
Web: www.becker-net.com

Description: We are an IT executive search provider for the US and Latin American markets.

Key Contact:
Mr. Steve Zuckerman, Vice President

Salary minimum: $40,000

Functions: IT

Industries: Generalist

Beckman & Associates Legal Search

Rivercenter
PO Box 75142
Cincinnati, OH 45275
(513) 651-2992
Fax: (513) 831-2151
Email: beckman@rof.net

Description: Attorneys only. We work with law firms and corporations nationwide to find qualified attorneys at the partner and associate level. We also provide searches for law firm practice groups and potential merger candidates.

Key Contact - Specialty:
Ms. Susan R. Beckman, President - *Attorneys, healthcare law, corporate law, litigation, employment law*

Functions: Generalist, Legal

Industries: Generalist, Legal

Professional Associations: NALSC

Branches:
PO Box 8167
Aspen, CO 81612
(970) 920-3227
Email: beckman@rof.net
Key Contact - Specialty:
Mr. Charles D. Fagin - *Attorneys*

Robert Beech West Inc

490 S Farrell Dr Ste C-201
Palm Canyon, CA 92262
(760) 864-1380
Email: careers@beechinc.com

Description: Over 22 years' placing sales and marketing managers and senior sales personnel nationally in computer hardware and software industry.

Key Contact - Specialty:
Mr. Robert Beech, President - *Computer (sales & marketing)*

Salary minimum: $60,000

Functions: Generalist, General Mgmt., Senior Mgmt., Middle Mgmt., Mktg. Mgmt., Sales Mgmt., IT, Systems Support

Industries: Generalist, Mfg., Computer Equip., Services, Media, Telecoms, Software

Networks: First Interview Network (FIN)

Branches:
2551 State St
Carlsbad, CA 92008
(760) 434-6635
Email: beechinc@aol.com
Key Contact - Specialty:
Mr. Robert Beech - *Computer sales & marketing*

55 A Galli Dr
San Francisco Office
Novato, CA 94949
(415) 884-2600
Key Contact - Specialty:
Ms. Arleen Beech - *Computer sales & marketing*

Behrens & Company

PO Box 831
Lake Stevens, WA 98258
(360) 658-6054
Fax: (240) 220-5651
Email: rick@behrensco.com
Web: www.behrensco.com

Description: Our firm, which is a professional services company, delivers search solutions for executive, senior sales, sales support, and post-sales positions in emerging technology and high growth industries. Convergent communication, telecommunications, software technology, and capital system technology companies are areas of experience and focus for us. We offer interim placement in professional or technical positions for projects of short duration and on site teams to deliver staffing programs for rapidly growing and newly funded technology companies.

Key Contact - Specialty:
Mr. Rick Behrens, President - *Optical networking, capital systems*
Mr. Steve Kyryk, Vice President - *Operations support systems - OSS, enterprise application integration - EAI*

Salary minimum: $80,000

Functions: Generalist

Industries: Generalist

Professional Associations: NWVG, WSA

Networks: National Personnel Assoc (NPA)

Gary S Bell Associates Inc

55 Harristown Rd
Glen Rock, NJ 07452
(201) 670-4900
Fax: (201) 670-4940
Email: gsbassoc@aol.com

Description: We concentrate on laboratory products and services, pharmaceuticals, medical devices, clinical, and research instrumentation.

Key Contact:
Mr. Gary S. Bell, President
Mr. Andrew Bell

Salary minimum: $65,000

Functions: Healthcare

Industries: Medical Devices, Pharm Svcs., Biotech

William Bell Associates Inc

605 Candlewood Commons
Howell, NJ 07731-2173
(732) 901-6000
Fax: (732) 901-2299
Email: wmbell605@aol.com
Web: www.williambellassociates.com

Description: Specialists in placement of cosmetic chemists and management. Additional areas include purchasing, planning, quality control, quality assurance, packaging and manufacturing.

Key Contact:
Mr. Steven Neidenberg, Vice President - *Cosmetics, chemical, personal care*
Ms. Phyllis Kay, Office Manager - *Generalist*
Ms. Denise Otero, Manager, Technical Recruiting

Functions: Mfg., Product Dev., Production, Quality, Purchasing, Materials Plng., Packaging, Sales & Mktg., Customer Svc., R&D

Industries: Soap, Perf., Cosmtcs.

Professional Associations: ACS, ASQ, SCC, SCC

Edward Bell Associates

50 First St Ste 320
San Francisco, CA 94105
(415) 442-0270
Fax: (415) 442-1862

Email: tech@ebajobs.com
Web: www.ebajobs.com

Description: We specialize in placing accounting, finance, and computer professionals in full time and contract positions. As a local recruiting firm, our recruiters have developed strong business relations with our clients. If any questions or concerns arise, our clients have immediate access to our account managers with authority to resolve all issues.

Key Contact - Specialty:
Mr. Edward Bell, Owner - *Accounting, finance, real estate*
Mr. Luigi Favero, Senior Technical Recruiter - *Data processing*
Ms. Sarah Schloenvogt, Senior Recruiter - *Accounting & finance*
Mr. John Postlethwaite, Financial Recruiter - *Accounting, finance, clerical*

Functions: Generalist, Finance, IT

Industries: Generalist, Finance, Accounting, Real Estate, Software

David Bell Executive Search

277 Richmond St W
Toronto, ON M5V 1X1
Canada
(416) 597-0188
Fax: (416) 597-0432
Email: info@davidbellsearch.com

Description: We are the only executive search firm in Canada that specializes exclusively in all facets of public relations. Our head office is in Toronto, with an office in New York, and an affiliate office in Boston. We provide a wide variety of clients with PR professionals at all levels. We collaborate closely with PR associations and schools to help maintain the highest professional standards for the industry.

Key Contact:
Mr. David Bell

Salary minimum: $50,000

Functions: Direct Mktg., PR

Industries: Generalist, Communications

Professional Associations: CPRS

Bell Oaks Company Inc

300 Colonial Park Ste 240
Roswell, GA 30076
(678) 448-0001
Fax: (770) 552-1088
Email: careers@belloaks.com
Web: www.belloaks.com

Description: Performs executive searches on a retained, contingency or contract basis in the fields of finance/accounting, information technology, engineering and manufacturing/operations. Inc. 500 company with more than 7000 completed searches.

Key Contact:
Mr. Price Harding, President

Salary minimum: $50,000

Functions: Generalist, General Mgmt., Mfg., Materials, Sales & Mktg., Finance, IT, Engineering

Industries: Generalist, Mfg., Finance, Media, Government, Software

Professional Associations: GAPS, MAPS

Branches:
10 Glenlake Pkwy Ste 300
Atlanta, GA 30328
(678) 287-2000
Fax: (678) 287-2001
Email: atlantacareers@belloaks.com
Web: www.belloaks.com
Key Contact:
Mr. Randy Hain, Regional Vice President

Bellwether Associates
PO Box 61663
North Charleston, SC 29419
(800) 944-5027
(843) 851-7110
Fax: (843) 873-0089
Email: lcd@carolinahealthcarejobs.com
Web: www.carolinahealthcarejobs.com

Description: We are a physician recruitment firm specializing in the states of SC, GA, and FL.

Key Contact - Specialty:
Mrs. Leta Davenport, Staffing Specialist - *Physician services*

Benamati & Associates
12247 E Iowa Dr
Aurora, CO 80012
(303) 671-5344
Fax: (303) 671-0450
Email: nben@worldnet.att.net
Web: www.benamatirecruiters.com

Description: We are a full-service engineering recruiting firm specializing in A/E consulting, MEP, design/build, oil and gas, refining, and petrochemical industries. Our specialties are engineering, chemical, electrical, mechanical, and metallurgy. We place staff upward to management positions.

Key Contact - Specialty:
Ms. Nancy Benamati, Owner - *Engineering*

Salary minimum: $60,000

Functions: Mfg., Engineering, Architects

Industries: Energy, Utilities, Construction, Mfg., Chemicals, Paints, Petro. Products, Biotech

Networks: Top Echelon Network

BenchMark Resources LLC
2487 Powell Ave Ste 100
Columbus, OH 43209-1748
(614) 231-3133
Email: dkrantz@benchmarkres.com
Web: www.benchmarkres.com

Description: Setting the standard for direct hire and interim professionals in healthcare, managed care and insurance. We provide professional search, research, selection, consulting and interim professional services to clients in healthcare, managed care and health insurance.

Key Contact - Specialty:
Ms. Deborah Krantz, CPC, Principal - *Healthcare, managed care, insurance*

Salary minimum: $50,000

Functions: Generalist

Industries: Insurance, Healthcare

Professional Associations: INS, MOAESP

J P Bencik Associates
1332 E Fairview Ste 200
Rochester Hills, MI 48306
(248) 651-7426

Description: Executive search/recruitment of middle management and engineering professionals for the automotive, automation, general manufacturing, related service industries (sales, engineering and management). Human resource consulting specialists.

Key Contact - Specialty:
Mr. James P. Bencik, President/Owner - *General management, engineering*

Salary minimum: $35,000

Functions: Generalist, Middle Mgmt., Automation, Mktg. Mgmt., Cash Mgmt., IT, Systems Analysis

---

Industries: Generalist, Plastics, Rubber, Machine, Appliance, Misc. Mfg., Transportation, HR Services, Software

Richard L Bencin & Associates
8553 Timber Trl
Brecksville, OH 44141
(440) 526-6726
Fax: (440) 546-1623
Email: rlbencin@netzero.net
Web: www.rlbencin.com

Description: World's first dedicated specialist in call center management/sales recruiting. Firm's president is the author of three industry texts, and he writes for over 100 industry magazines.

Key Contact - Specialty:
Mr. Richard L. Bencin, President - *Call centers, customer service, telesales*

Salary minimum: $40,000

Functions: Direct Mktg., Customer Svc.

Industries: Generalist

Professional Associations: ATSA, DMA, ICSA, SOCAP

Benford & Associates Inc
3000 Town Ctr Ste 1333
Southfield, MI 48075
(248) 351-0250
Fax: (248) 351-8698
Email: ben4jobs@aol.com

Description: We create a plan, detail strategy tailored for individual corporate clients. Research sources and candidates, bringing to the attention only those individuals especially suited to the particular requirements. Minority recruiting specialist.

Key Contact:
Mr. Edward A. Benford, Manager
Ms. Monica Debry, Manager

Functions: Generalist, Mfg., Product Dev., Purchasing, Personnel, Budgeting, Engineering, Minorities

Industries: Generalist, Food, Bev., Tobacco, Motor Vehicles

Networks: Inter-City Personnel Assoc (IPA)

N L Benke & Associates Inc
1422 Euclid Ave Ste 956
Hanna Bldg
Cleveland, OH 44115-1951
(216) 771-6822
Fax: (216) 771-3568
Email: benke@voyager.net

Description: We talk your language! Our recruiters have prior experience as accountants, bankers, financial or computer professionals. We do not waste your time with unqualified candidates because we know who the top performers are and where to find them.

Key Contact - Specialty:
Mr. Norman L. Benke, President - *Banking, accounting, finance, information technology, human resources*

Salary minimum: $50,000

Functions: Directors, Middle Mgmt.

Industries: Banking, Invest. Banking, Brokers, Venture Cap., Accounting, Mgmt. Consulting, HR Services, Telecoms

Bennett & Associates
2732 Palo Verde
Odessa, TX 79762
(915) 550-9096
Fax: (915) 362-3211

Email: mark.bennett@clearsource.net

Description: We have placed thousands of candidates with hundreds of companies. We place professional and executive level candidates in the oil and gas, petrochemical, medical, and information technology industries.

Key Contact - Specialty:
Mr. Mark Bennett, Owner - *Executive & professional level candidates*

Salary minimum: $40,000

Functions: Senior Mgmt., Middle Mgmt., Physicians, HR Mgmt., Engineering

Industries: Energy, Utilities, Chemicals, Plastics, Rubber, Paints, Petro. Products, Misc. Mfg., Biotech, Healthcare, Hospitals

Networks: Top Echelon Network

Bennett & Company Consulting Group
2135 Manzanita Dr 1
Oakland, CA 94611
(510) 339-3175
Fax: (510) 339-2162
Email: lindabennett@earthlink.net

Description: We specialize in all disciplines of human resources executive and HR management search. Primarily clients are located in the San Francisco/Silicon Valley/Tri Valley regions. Salary ranges of typical search projects are from $85,000 to $175,000. Client companies include high-technology, manufacturing, software, consulting firms, legal and start-ups.

Key Contact - Specialty:
Ms. Linda E. Bennett, Principal - *Human resources, HRIS*

Salary minimum: $85,000

Functions: HR Mgmt.

Industries: Generalist

Professional Associations: AAUW, NCHRC, NHRA, SHRM, TVHRA, WIB

Robert Bennett Associates
PO Box 261
Little Neck, NY 11363
(718) 428-5455
Email: robertbennett@nyc.rr.com

Key Contact - Specialty:
Ms. Mary Bloom, President - *Lawyers*

Salary minimum: $50,000

Functions: Generalist, Mgmt. Consultants, Attorneys, Int'l.

Industries: Generalist, Hospitality, Insurance, Real Estate

Benson Associates
280 Madison Ave Ste 703
New York, NY 10016
(212) 683-5962

Description: Firm's principals have focused on executive recruitment for a total of 45 years.

Key Contact - Specialty:
Mr. Irwin Cohen, Partner - *Marketing, finance, human resources*
Mr. Laurence Rutkovsky, Partner - *Public accounting*

Salary minimum: $75,000

Functions: Middle Mgmt., Advertising, Direct Mktg., HR Mgmt., Finance

Industries: Generalist, Advertising

The Bentley Group Inc
2240 Woolbright Rd Ste 353
Boynton Beach, FL 33426
(561) 734-3550
Fax: (561) 734-3449
Email: bennett@bentleygrp.com
Web: www.bentleygrp.com

Description: We are committed. Our success rests on the continued success and prosperity of our clients. The Bentley Group has developed ethical standards reflecting our long-term commitment to the medical, telecom, and healthcare industries. Our firm was founded with a goal to provide high quality cost effective search services. We believe that controlled processes yield predictable results. We focus our attention on best suiting the needs of our clients and candidates with a consistent goal of growing a long-term partnership.

Key Contact:
Ms. Lisa Vivona, CPC, President - *Medical pharmaceutical sales, sales management*
Mr. Bennett S. Vivona, CPC, Director of Business Development

Functions: Generalist

Industries: Generalist

Benton & Associates
25 Babbitt Hill Rd
Pomfret, CT 06259
(860) 974-8712
(860) 212-5621
Fax: (860) 974-8714
Email: kbenton98@yahoo.com

Description: Benton & Associates specializes in the recruitment of Management and R&D professionals for early-stage communications companies across the United States. We partner with Venture Capital and Angel firms to begin searches prior to series A funding then continue to assist young companies through their pre-IPO growth phases.

Key Contact - Specialty:
Mr. Kevin Benton, President - *Early-stage management, architecture teams*

Functions: Generalist

Industries: Communications, Telecoms, Call Centers, Telephony, Digital, Wireless, Fiber Optic, Network Infrastructure, HR SW, Marketing SW

Networks: Recruiters Professional Network (RPN)

Berg Recruiting Naturally Inc
4250 W Lake Sammamish Pkwy NE Ste 1059
Redmond, WA 98052
(425) 556-5175
(425) 830-0922
Fax: (425) 883-7677
Email: info@bergrecruiting.com
Web: www.bergrecruiting.com

Description: Retained and contingency search firm placing CEOs to territory reps in natural products(nutraceutical and botanicals)and IT industries (e-commerce, Java). Rapid, personalized searches also cross over into pharmaceutical, functional foods and specialty chemical areas. We also provide management consulting, professional training and mediation services.

Key Contact - Specialty:
Ms. Heather Berg, President - *Natural products, high technology*
Ms. Carol Berg, CFO - *Medical*
Mrs. Toni Berg, Treasurer - *Financial, environmental*
Ms. Joan Gulbrandson, Board of Directors - *Executive recruiter*

Salary minimum: $50,000

Functions: Generalist, General Mgmt., Directors, Senior Mgmt., Mfg., Quality, Materials, Healthcare, Allied Health, Sales & Mktg.

Industries: Generalist, Mfg., Food, Bev., Tobacco, Chemicals, Soap, Perf., Cosmtcs., Drugs Mfg., Medical Devices, Wholesale, Retail, Finance, Services, Pharm Svcs., Equip Svcs., Hospitality, Media, Telecoms, Environmental Svcs., Packaging, Real Estate, Software, Biotech, Healthcare, Non-classifiable

Professional Associations: AMIGOS, CANI, IFT, NNFA

Berger & Leff
1 Sansome St Ste 2100
San Francisco, CA 94104
(415) 951-4750
Fax: (415) 951-4751
Email: taxjobs@aol.com
Web: www.lisaleff.com

Description: We are an executive search firm, recruiting tax professionals in a variety of industries including high-tech, manufacturing, and professional organizations.

Key Contact - Specialty:
Ms. Lisa A Leff, Owner - *Taxation*

Salary minimum: $75,000

Functions: Generalist, Taxes

Industries: Generalist, Drugs Mfg., Medical Devices, Computer Equip., Accounting, Software, Biotech

Professional Associations: NCHRC

C Berger Group Inc
327 E Gundersen Dr
Carol Stream, IL 60188
(630) 653-1115
(800) 382-4222
Fax: (630) 653-1691
Email: carolb@cberger.com
Web: www.cberger.com

Description: We conduct searches for managerial, marketing and subject specialists in libraries, information centers and related businesses; supply temporaries to libraries and offer library management consulting and project support services.

Key Contact - Specialty:
Ms. Carol A. Berger, President - *Library (records personnel*
Mr. John Strzynski, Manager Business Development - *Library (records, personnel)*
Ms. Carolyn Nelson, Staff Recruitment Consultant - *Library (records personnel)*
Mr. Joel Patrick Berger, COO - *Library (records, personnel)*

Salary minimum: $50,000

Functions: General Mgmt., Sales & Mktg., HR Mgmt., IT, Specialized Svcs., Mgmt. Consultants

Industries: Mfg., Finance, Services, Communications, Government, Software, Healthcare, Non-classifiable

Professional Associations: AALL, ALA, ARMA, ASA, ASA, NAWBO, SCIP, SLA

Berglund Int'l Resources Inc
1914 Greens Blvd
PO Box 5
Richmond, TX 77469-6692
(713) 629-4031
(888) 515-7375
Fax: (877) 804-9212
Email: sharon@berglundintl.com
Web: www.berglundintl.com

Description: Our goal is to provide our client companies with the most qualified and motivated candidates possible. We strive to become an extension of our client companies - to know what they are looking for in their employees. The successful search results in an employee that not only possesses the technical skills needed by the client, but the interpersonal skills that allow the employee to succeed in the company environment.

Key Contact - Specialty:
Ms. Sharon Berglund, President - *Financial, accounting, information technology*

Salary minimum: $50,000

Functions: Finance

Industries: Energy, Utilities, Mfg.

Professional Associations: NAPS, TAPC

Networks: National Personnel Assoc (NPA)

Berke • Durant & Associates
(a member of Lincolnshire Int'l)
2600 N Military Trl Ste 410
Boca Raton, FL 33431
(561) 989-9889
Fax: (561) 989-3638
Email: mberke@berkedurant.com
Web: www.berkedurant.com

Description: U.S. and Latin America - executive recruiting services: management positions specializing in HR, IT, finance, sales, marketing, customer service. Project Recruiting - multiple positions and locations: customer service, call centers, sales; also, outplacement, coaching and HR consulting services.

Key Contact - Specialty:
Mr. Michael P. Berke, President - *Sales & marketing, senior executives*
Ms. Marilyn C. Durant, SPHR, VP/COO - *Human resources*

Salary minimum: $50,000

Functions: Generalist, General Mgmt., Sales & Mktg., Mktg. Mgmt., HR Mgmt., Finance, CFO's, Mgmt. Consultants, Non-profits, Int'l.

Industries: Generalist, Mfg., Retail, Finance, Services, Media

Professional Associations: IACPR, HRABC, HRAPBC, SHRM

Networks: Lincolnshire Int'l

The Berklee Group Inc
8 New England Executive Park Fl 4 W Wing
Burlington, MA 01803
(781) 272-1477
Fax: (781) 272-1985
Email: berklee@berklee.com
Web: www.berklee.com

Description: We are an executive search firm that specializes in information technology and engineering.

Key Contact:
Mr. Christopher J. Cahill

Functions: Systems Analysis, Systems Dev., Systems Implem., Systems Support, Network Admin., DB Admin., Engineering

Industries: Generalist

Branches:
20 William St
Wellesley, MA 02481
(781) 237-6300
Fax: (781) 237-6310
Email: berklee@berklee.com
Key Contact:
Mr. Paul White

61 Spit Brook Rd Ste 120
Nashua, NH 03060
(603) 888-7022
Fax: (603) 888-7032
Email: berklee@berklee.com
Key Contact - Specialty:
Mr. John T. Morganto, President - *Hardware engineering, software engineering, information technology*

Berkshire Search Associates

PO Box 459
Becket, MA 01223-0459
(413) 623-8855
Fax: (413) 623-8858
Email: bsearch@mindspring.com
Web: www.berkshiresearch.com

Description: We specialize in environmental, hazardous waste remediation, water and wastewater, and hydrogeology industries. We place mechanical, electrical, structural, transportation and civil engineers for A/E firms/MEP firms. We also focus on HVAC/R sales and marketing, and manufacturing. We also place mechanical and HVAC contractors, nationally.

Key Contact - Specialty:
Mr. Donald Munger, CPC, President - *Mechanical, electrical, civil, environmental engineering, HVAC design*

Salary minimum: $45,000

Functions: Generalist, Middle Mgmt., Production, Plant Mgmt., Mktg. Mgmt., Sales Mgmt., Engineering

Industries: Generalist, Energy, Utilities, Construction, Paper, Metal Products, Legal, Environmental Svcs.

Professional Associations: ASHRAE, ASPE, AWMA

Networks: Inter-City Personnel Assoc (IPA)

Berman, Larson, Kane

12 Rte 17 N
Paramus, NJ 07652
(800) 640-0126
(201) 909-0906
Fax: (201) 909-0976
Email: ken@jobsbl.com
Web: www.jobsbl.com

Description: With over 50,000 systems professionals on file, we will isolate an information systems professional to meet your needs. Candidates available for both direct hire and contracting. Our Human Resource Division will assist you with finding a great direct hire or contract opportunity.

Key Contact - Specialty:
Mr. Robert Larson, CPC, President - *Information systems*

Salary minimum: $45,000

Functions: HR Mgmt., Benefits, Personnel, IT, Systems Analysis, Systems Dev., Systems Support, DB Admin.

Industries: Generalist

Professional Associations: NAPS, NJSA

Networks: National Personnel Assoc (NPA)

Bernard, Frigon & Associates Inc

1155 W Rene-Levesque Blvd Fl 25
Montreal, QC H3B 2K4
Canada
(514) 393-8145
Fax: (514) 393-1236
Email: bfrigon@globetrotter.net

Description: Our team is well known for efficient interventions based on extensive knowledge acquired through previous practical management responsibilities in the fields of information systems, management consulting as well as sales management for a major computer manufacturer.

Key Contact - Specialty:
Mr. Bernard Frigon, President - *Information technology*

Functions: Automation, Sales Mgmt., MIS Mgmt., Systems Analysis, Systems Dev., Systems Support, Mgmt. Consultants

Industries: Generalist

Professional Associations: CIPS, FIQ

Bernhart Associates

2068 Greenwood Dr 220
Owatonna, MN 55060
(507) 451-4270
Fax: (507) 451-9433
Email: bgb@bernhart.com
Web: www.bernhart.com

Description: Our firm is a nationally recognized search firm focusing exclusively in direct marketing, concentrating in database marketing, telemarketing management, and statistical analysis..

Key Contact - Specialty:
Mr. Jerry Bernhart, President - *Direct marketing*

Salary minimum: $75,000

Functions: Generalist

Industries: Computer Equip., Misc. Financial, Services, Hospitality, Media, Telecoms, Packaging, Insurance, Software, Healthcare

Professional Associations: ATA, CADM, DMA, DMCNY, IPA, MDMA, PG, RMDMA, RON

Networks: The Acumen Society

Jack Bertram Executive Recruiting

1405 Pine Rock Rd
West Chester, PA 19380-6215
(610) 431-3985

Description: Specialize in engineering with emphasis on electric motors and related products. All functions, design through manufacturing and quality.

Key Contact - Specialty:
Mr. John J. Bertram - *Electromechanical (products)*

Salary minimum: $30,000

Functions: Middle Mgmt., Mfg., Product Dev., Production, Plant Mgmt., Quality, Productivity, Materials, Purchasing, Materials Plng.

Industries: Mfg., Plastics, Rubber, Metal Products, Machine, Appliance, Motor Vehicles, Misc. Mfg.

Besen Associates Inc

115 Rte 46 W C-21
Mountain Lakes, NJ 07046
(973) 334-5533
Fax: (973) 334-4810
Email: besenassoc@aol.com
Web: www.besen.com

Description: Research and engineering for the pharmaceutical industry. Physicians, pharmaceutical scientists, internal medicine, infectious disease, cardio/pulmonary respiratory, rheumatology, endocrinology, general and biotechnical engineers, marketing sales and manufacturing support personnel, regulatory and quality assurance control.

Key Contact - Specialty:
Mr. Douglas Besen, President - *Physicians, presidents, vice presidents, diagnostic, OTC companies*

Functions: Generalist

Industries: Drugs Mfg., Biotech, Healthcare

Professional Associations: AAPS, DIA, RAPS, SHRM

Besner EJ Consultant Inc

417 St. Nicolas Ste 300
Montreal, QC H2Y 2P4
Canada
(514) 987-9522
Fax: (514) 844-1841
Email: besnercslt@nettaxi.com

Description: Recruiting specialists for the transportation, distribution and logistics industries.

Key Contact - Specialty:
Mr. Elliott J. Besner, President - *Transportation, distribution*
Mr. Peter Melanson, Consultant - *Transportation, distribution*

Salary minimum: $20,000

Functions: Distribution

Industries: Services

BEST Search Inc

PO Box 596
Geneva, IL 60134
(630) 365-3200
Fax: (630) 365-3201
Email: audry@bestsearchinc.com
Web: www.bestsearchinc.com

Description: Insurance industry contingency recruiter (commercial property/casualty). Clients include Insurance Cos, Brokers, Law Firms, Corp Risk Mgmt Depts. Senior professional through emerging executive positions (typical salary 80K-200K). New York tri-state area, Chicagoland and Bermuda emphasis.

Key Contact - Specialty:
Ms. Audry Buchanan, President - *Commercial insurance (property, casualty)*

Salary minimum: $60,000

Functions: Generalist

Industries: Insurance

Professional Associations: NHRA, TI

James Betts Associates

3975 Oran Gulf Rd #3
Manlius, NY 13104
(315) 682-3289
(888) 237-5200
Fax: (315) 682-1106
Email: jbetts@bettsassociates.com
Web: www.bettsassociates.com

Description: We offer professional recruitment specializing in both permanent placements and consulting assignments within the Cyborg HRIS/PR user community.

Key Contact:
Mr. James Betts, Owner

Functions: Systems Analysis, Systems Dev., Systems Implem., Systems Support

Industries: Generalist, HR SW

Networks: Top Echelon Network

BeyondTech Solutions Inc

3665 Kingsway Ste 300
Vancouver, BC V5R 5W2
Canada
(604) 433-0617
Fax: (604) 433-0627
Email: skuan@beyond-tech.com
Web: www.beyond-tech.com

Description: We are a provider of technical recruitment services to clients across industry sectors. At BeyondTech Solutions, we believe in making recruitment simple for employers and job seekers. With our convenient contract and permanent staffing options, you can exercise knowledge and freedom in choosing your career or personnel solution.

Key Contact - Specialty:
Ms. Stella Kuan, Account Manager - *Technical recruitment*.

BFW Inc
302 Wymberly Rd
St. Simons Island, GA 31522-1708
(912) 638-0025
Fax: (912) 638-2855
Email: rbuf@darientel.net

Description: Recruitment and placement of investment professionals exclusively, including portfolio managers, CIOs, analysts, finance, compliance and marketing disciplines in buy side, sell side and industry positions.

Key Contact - Specialty:
Mr. E. Ralph Bufkin, President - *Investment professionals, analysts, portfolio managers, fund managers*

Salary minimum: $70,000

Functions: Generalist

Industries: Invest. Banking, Misc. Financial

Professional Associations: GAPS

BG & Associates
10112 Langhorne Ct Ste B
Bethesda, MD 20817
(301) 365-4046
Fax: (301) 365-0435
Email: bgajob@erols.com

Description: In addition to regular recruiting and search services, we offer clients contract staffing, payrolling, and staffing research services. We are a preferred member of the Top Echelon Network, the world's largest network of independent recruitment firms.

Key Contact - Specialty:
Mr. Brian A. Gray, SPHR, President - *Information technology, human resources, finance & accounting, management consultants*
Ms. Linda Cooper, Researcher/Recruiter - *Information technology, human resources, finance & accounting, management consultants*
Ms. Phyllis Washington, Researcher/Recruiter - *General management, materials management, minorities*

Salary minimum: $60,000

Functions: General Mgmt., Sales & Mktg., HR Mgmt., Finance, IT, Specialized Svcs., Minorities

Industries: Generalist

Professional Associations: EMA, SHRM, WAW

Networks: Top Echelon Network

Bickerton & Gordon LLC
60 State St Ste 700
Boston, MA 02109
(617) 371-2929
Fax: (617) 371-2999
Email: info@bickertongordon.com
Web: www.bickertongordon.com

Description: Our firm recruits lawyers, contracts/licensing, patent and other legal personnel for corporations and law firms in all practice areas and industries. With offices in Boston and New York, we recruit general counsel and staff attorneys nationally, internationally, and in New England. Our recruiters include lawyers with partner and general counsel level experience.

Key Contact - Specialty:
Mr. Brion Bickerton, Principal - *Lawyers*
Mr. Richards Gordon, Principal - *Lawyers*

Salary minimum: $40,000

Functions: Legal, Attorneys, Paralegals

Industries: Generalist, Legal

Professional Associations: NALSC

Big 6 Search Int'l Inc
1695 Pinellas Bayway S
E-4 Hidden Lagoon
St. Petersburg, FL 33715
(727) 906-0580
Fax: (727) 906-0581
Email: ken@big6jobs.net
Web: www.BIG6jobs.com

Description: Please visit our website. We specialize in Big 5/top tier consulting firms, B2B product vendors, software companies, pre-IPO, and industry opportunities. Our core focuses are: business development, business intelligence, CRM, data warehousing, EAI, ERP, engineering, information technology, networking, SCM, strategy, telecommunications (telephony and wireless), and web.

Key Contact:
Mr. Kenneth Kubicki, CPA, President

Salary minimum: $10,000

Functions: Generalist

Industries: E-commerce, New Media, Telecoms, Telephony, Wireless, Software, Database SW, Development SW, ERP SW, Networking, Comm. SW

Binder Hospitality Group
526 Silverbrook Dr
Danville, KY 40422-1076
(859) 239-0096
Fax: (859) 238-1256
Email: binder@mis.net

Description: Our firm specializes in search/placement of middle and executive level management for hotels, resorts, country clubs, and restaurants. Our recruiters have extensive operations experience in all phases of hospitality management.

Key Contact - Specialty:
Mr. Kenneth K. Binder, President - *Hospitality, executive, middle management*

Salary minimum: $30,000

Functions: Senior Mgmt., Middle Mgmt., Sales & Mktg., HR Mgmt., Finance

Industries: Hospitality

Professional Associations: CHS

Bioleader® LLC
152 Etna Rd
Lebanon, NH 03766
(317) 272-9985
Fax: (603) 448-1956
Email: bioleader@aol.com
Web: www.bioleader.com

Description: We specialize in executive recruitment for biotechnology, genomics and pharmaceuticals. We have a team of experts who come from the biotechnology field. We can and will find your company the best senior management in the industry.

Key Contact:
Ms. Jamie A. Lowry, Co-Founder - *Biopharmaceuticals*
Dr. Karen Moodie, Executive Vice President - *Research & development, genomics, biotechnology*
Mr. Terry Moodie, Executive Vice President - *Engineering, information technology, biotechnology, genomics*
Dr. Hoi Lui, COO

Salary minimum: $80,000

Functions: Generalist, Senior Mgmt., Middle Mgmt., Legal, Production, Quality, Sales Mgmt., Systems Dev.

Industries: Generalist, Biotech

BioTech Solutions
70 W Red Oak Ln
White Plains, NY 10604
(914) 697-4988
Fax: (914) 697-4885
Email: robert@biotechexecutivesearch.com
Web: www.biotechexecutivesearch.com

Description: We are a national placement firm dedicated to information technology within the financial, pharmaceutical, and consulting industries.

Key Contact - Specialty:
Mr. Robert Azzara, Principal - *Financial, pharmaceutical, information technology*

Salary minimum: $60,000

Functions: IT

Industries: Generalist

The Biras Creek Group
(also known as Sales Consultants of Chatham County)
11500 B US Hwy 15-501 N
Chapel Hill, NC 27517
(919) 928-0082
Fax: (919) 928-0160
Email: admin@go2bcg.com

Key Contact - Specialty:
Mr. James Kessler, Managing Partner - *Integration services, aviation, biomedics*
Ms. Betty Myers, Managing Partner - *Information technology, banking*

Birch & Associés
2155 Guy St Ste 740
Montreal, QC H3H 2R9
Canada
(514) 846-1878
Fax: (514) 846-9395
Email: info@birch-protocole.com
Web: www.birch-protocole.com

Description: Specialists in executive recruiting.We carefully investigate each of our client's needs and provide them with qualified candidates who have been rigorously evaluated. An attentive after-hiring follow-up ensures that the needs of our clients and candidates have been met.Protocol,a division of Birch & Associés is involved in high-tech recruiting.

Key Contact:
Mr. Jerry Birch, President
Mr. Stanley Birch, Vice President

Functions: Generalist

Industries: Generalist, Wholesale, Retail, Finance, Software, Biotech

Bising Group
13205 US Hwy 1 Ste 530
Juno Beach, FL 33408
(561) 626-9637
Email: shawn@bisinggroup.com
Web: www.bisinggroup.com

Description: We provide management placement for finance, banking, and technical IT/IS. We are now offering management temps.

Key Contact - Specialty:
Ms. Shawn Bising, President - *Management*

Salary minimum: $35,000

Functions: Generalist, Senior Mgmt., Middle Mgmt., Finance, Taxes, MIS Mgmt., DB Admin., Engineering

Industries: Generalist, Finance, Banking, IT Implementation, Aerospace, Real Estate, Software

Professional Associations: NAPS, SHRM

BJB Associates
3750 Gateshead Dr
Annapolis, MD 21403
(410) 268-0156
Fax: (410) 265-0545
Email: bjbrecruit@earthlink.net

Description: Recruit for clients in consumer products, non-woven consumer disposable market, medical disposables, paper converters, packaging and supporting chemical and engineering firms to these industries.

Key Contact - Specialty:
Ms. Bobbi Bauman, President/Owner - *Manufacturing (high speed), consumer products, paper converting, packaging*

Salary minimum: $30,000

Functions: Mfg.

Industries: Textiles, Apparel, Paper, Medical Devices, Plastics, Rubber, Packaging

Professional Associations: INDA, TAPPI

Networks: Top Echelon Network

BKG Inc
4 Sawgrass Village Ste 150D
Ponte Vedra Beach, FL 32082
(904) 273-5010
Fax: (603) 843-5846
Email: knipperbkg@prodigy.net

Description: Attorneys only. Fast and efficient but very thorough. Twenty years of experience.

Key Contact - Specialty:
Mr. William Knipper, President - *Legal, attorneys*

Functions: Generalist, Legal

Industries: Generalist, Legal

Edward Black Associates Inc
121 Mount Vernon St
Boston, MA 02108
(617) 227-2322
Fax: (617) 227-7151
Email: recruiters@edwardblack.com
Web: www.edwardblack.com

Key Contact:
Mr. Larry Burns, Sales and Marketing Division

Salary minimum: $50,000

Functions: Mfg., Purchasing, Sales & Mktg., Engineering

Industries: Medical Devices

Branches:
PO Box 688
Franconia, NH 03580
(603) 823-9003
Fax: (603) 823-5038
Email: recruiters@edwardblack.com
Web: www.edwardblack.com
Key Contact:
Mr. Gerry Burns, Civil Engineering Division

2 Saint Andrews Ter
Westerly, RI 02891
(401) 348-6616
Fax: (401) 348-0882
Email: recruiters@edwardblack.com
Web: www.edwardblack.com
Key Contact - Specialty:
Mr. Larry Burns, Engineering/Sales & Marketing Division - *Medical devices*

The Black Leopard
79-180 Fox Run
La Quinta, CA 92253
(800) 360-4191
(760) 771-8400
Fax: (760) 771-9300
Email: tbleopard@aol.com
Web: www.blackleopard.com

Description: We are a nationwide executive search to the newspaper publishing, meat, poultry, and food processing industries. We provide staffing for junior to senior-level executives in editorial, operations, engineering/maintenance, quality assurance, R&D, sales/marketing, logistics, finance, and human resources.

Key Contact - Specialty:
Mr. Jerry Kurbatoff, Owner - *Food processing, newspaper publishing*
Ms. Lauren Kurbatoff, Owner - *Food processing*

Salary minimum: $25,000

Functions: Generalist

Industries: Food, Bev., Tobacco, Publishing

Blackhawk Executive Search Inc
PO Box 73005
San Clemente, CA 92673-0100
(949) 940-9000
Email: resume@blackhawkusa.com
Web: www.blackhawkusa.com

Description: Both principals are CPAs with extensive consulting and banking experience.

Key Contact - Specialty:
Mr. Phil Andersen, CPA, Director - *Financial services, bank trust, sales positions, big 5 positions, CFO's & controllers*
Ms. Phyllis Busser-Andersen, CPA, Director - *Bank trust positions*

Salary minimum: $60,000

Functions: Generalist, Sales & Mktg., CFO's

Industries: Generalist, Finance, Misc. Financial, Services

Professional Associations: AICPA, CSCPA, INS, NBN

Networks: National Banking Network (NBN)

Blackwood Associates Inc
883 Main St
PO Box 1131
Torrington, CT 06790
(860) 489-0494
Fax: (860) 489-1534
Email: blackwood.assoc@snet.net

Description: We are an executive contingency search firm with clients throughout the US.

Key Contact:
Mr. Jeffrey B. Blackwood, President

Functions: Generalist, Legal, Mfg., Finance, Engineering, Attorneys, Paralegals

Industries: Generalist, Construction, Mfg., Finance, Insurance, Healthcare

Blair/Tech Recruiters Inc
77 Milltown Rd
East Brunswick, NJ 08816
(732) 390-5550
Fax: (732) 390-1453
Email: rathbornek@aol.com

Description: Exclusively broad based engineering and scientific disciplines for varied clients in the middle Atlantic and northeastern US.

Key Contact - Specialty:
Mr. Kenneth J. Rathborne, President - *Chemists, chemical engineers*

Salary minimum: $40,000

Functions: Mfg., Automation

Industries: Mfg., Food, Bev., Tobacco, Chemicals, Plastics, Rubber, Paints, Petro. Products, Packaging

Professional Associations: MAAPC

Networks: Inter-City Personnel Assoc (IPA)

Blanton & Company
PO Box 43829
Birmingham, AL 35243-0829
(205) 967-9823
Fax: (205) 967-8020
Email: tblanton@blantonco.com

Description: We are specialists in all disciplines in the biotechnology, paper, industrial process control, medical equipment, semiconductors, computers, telecommmunications, and pharmaceutical industries.

Key Contact:
Ms. Julia Blanton, Sales
Mr. Thomas Blanton, President/Operations

Salary minimum: $75,000

Functions: Generalist

Industries: Paper, Chemicals, Drugs Mfg., Medical Devices, Computer Equip., Test, Measure Equip., Electronic, Elec. Components, Pharm Svcs., Telecoms, Software

Networks: First Interview Network (FIN)

BLB Consulting Inc
110 E 42nd St Ste 1309
New York, NY 10017
(212) 808-0577
(212) 808-0578
Fax: (212) 338-9696
Email: hr@blbco.com
Web: www.blbco.com

Description: Specializing in the placement of human resource professionals in the New York metropolitan area. Clients range from startup human resources departments to major corporations.

Key Contact - Specialty:
Ms. Barbara L. Bartell, CPC, President - *Human resources*

Salary minimum: $50,000

Functions: HR Mgmt.

Industries: Finance, Legal, Accounting, Mgmt. Consulting, HR Services, Hospitality, Media, Insurance, Software

Professional Associations: APCNY, SHRM

David Blevins & Associates Inc
1425 4th Ave Ste 824
Seattle, WA 98101
(206) 521-8953
(877) 562-3933
Fax: (206) 521-8963
Email: daveblevins@earthlink.net
Web: www.imminentstrategies.com

Description: Executive search and recruiting firm serving the wine and luxury beverage industries globally since 1995. Targeted search for all positions and disciplines in the industry. Clients include Fortune 500 companies to small emerging entities. Programs for all budgets. Off-sight human resource for small companies. All HR functions and programs offered. Search services on an hourly basis available.

Key Contact - Specialty:
Mr. David C. Blevins, CEO/President - *Beverage industry (wine, luxury)*

Functions: Specialized Svcs.

Industries: Food, Bev., Tobacco

Branches:
2040 Pebble Beach Dr
Palm Springs, CA 92264
(877) 562-3933
(760) 383-1482
Fax: (253) 383-1483
Email: daveblevins@earthlink.net
Web: www.olympicstrategies.com
Key Contact:
Mr. David Blevins

Michael Bloch Associates Inc
70 Lindon Oaks Dr
Rochester, NY 14625
(585) 388-6440
Email: mb@michaelbloch.com
Web: www.michaelbloch.com

Description: We are a retained legal search firm
serving law firms and corporations, recruiting
associates, partners, and in-house counsel. Our
understanding of the intricacies of legal recruiting
makes us uniquely qualified to produce superior
results. Our searches are conducted in an attentive,
ethical, and professional manner. We also facilitate
mergers and acquisitions of law firms.

Key Contact:
Mr. Michael Bloch, President

Salary minimum: $75,000

Functions: Legal, Attorneys

Industries: Generalist, Legal

The Howard C Bloom Company
5000 Quorum Dr Ste 550
Dallas, TX 75254
(972) 385-6455
Fax: (972) 385-1006
Email: hbloom@bloomlegalsearch.com
Web: www.bloomlegalsearch.com

Description: Our firm places partners, senior
associates, practice areas, law firm mergers, and in-
house counsel.

Key Contact - Specialty:
Mr. Howard Bloom, President - *Attorneys*
Ms. Joyce Bloom, Vice President - *Attorneys*

Salary minimum: $50,000

Functions: Generalist, Attorneys

Industries: Generalist, Legal

Professional Associations: IRG, NALSC, SERC

Bloom, Gross & Associates
625 N Michigan Ave Ste 500
Chicago, IL 60611
(312) 751-3490
Email: kbloom@bloomgross.com
Web: www.bloomgross.com

Description: Our firm specializes in mid- to upper-
level searches in three areas: marketing, public
relations and sales promotion and direct marketing.
We work with Fortune 100 companies and dot-com
start-ups. While we work nationwide, the majority
of our clients are in the Chicagoland area.

Key Contact:
Ms. Karen Bloom, Principal

Salary minimum: $40,000

Functions: Advertising, Mktg. Mgmt., Direct
Mktg., PR, Graphic Artists

Industries: Mfg., Food, Bev., Tobacco, Soap, Perf.,
Cosmtcs., Consumer Elect., Misc. Financial,
Pharm Svcs., Hospitality, Restaurants, Media,
Advertising, New Media, Telecoms, Real Estate,
Healthcare

Professional Associations: EMA, SHRM

Blue Rock Consulting
9 Woodmont St
Portland, ME 04102
(207) 780-0960
Email: bluerock@maine.rr.com
Web: www.bluerock-maine.com

Description: Property casualty recruiting by
experienced insurance professionals who match the
performance needs of our clients with tailored
candidate solutions.

Key Contact - Specialty:
Mr. Paul F. Stulgaitis, President - *Property
insurance, casualty insurance*
Mr. Stuart R. Sayre, CPCU, Chief Operating
Officer - *Property insurance, casualty insurance*

Functions: Generalist

Industries: Insurance

The BMW Group Inc
40 Exchange Pl Ste 700
New York, NY 10005
(212) 943-8800
Fax: (212) 943-8852
Email: bmw40x@aol.com
Web: www.careerobject.com

Description: Full-service organization specializing
in the placement of information technology
professionals.

Key Contact - Specialty:
Mr. Alan Burke, Principal - *Technical*
Mr. Michael Mantel, Principal - *Technical*
Mr. Ronald Weiss, Principal - *Technical*

Salary minimum: $45,000

Functions: IT

Industries: Generalist

Professional Associations: APCNY

Bodner Inc
372 5th Ave Ste 9K
New York, NY 10018
(212) 714-0371

Description: Specialize in placement of accounting
and finance professionals.

Key Contact - Specialty:
Ms. Marilyn S. Bodner, President - *Accounting,
finance*

Salary minimum: $60,000

Functions: Middle Mgmt., Finance

Industries: Generalist

Tom Bogle & Associates
1729 E Palm Canyon Dr Ste 206
Palm Springs, CA 92264
(760) 416-1888
Fax: (760) 416-0023
Email: tom@bogleassociates.com
Web: www.bogleassociates.com

Description: Confidential consulting to attract,
recruit and retain outstanding sales and marketing
talent for companies in the medical
technology/medical device industry, leadership,
staffing issues and organizational development to
start-ups and Fortune 500 firms.

Key Contact - Specialty:
Mr. Tom Bogle, Managing Principal - *Medical
imaging, medical technologies management, sales
& marketing*
Mr. Randy Billingsley, Managing Partner
Mr. Tom Tierney, Managing Partner
Mr. Dean Winter, Managing Partner -
*Manufacturers of $200 million + in capital
equipment*
Mr. Dick Humphrey, Managing Partner - *Start-ups*
Mr. Carter Morgan, Associate

Mr. Rob Fronk, Associate - *Engineering/technical*
Mrs. Patricia Bray, Research Associate - *Sales and
marketing talent research*
Mr. Joe Coronel, Admin. - *Operations*
Mr. John O'Brien, Operations - *Web, data,
research, training, operations*

Salary minimum: $100,000

Functions: Middle Mgmt., Product Dev., Mktg.
Mgmt., Sales Mgmt., Personnel, M&A, Mgmt.
Consultants

Industries: Drugs Mfg., Medical Devices,
Electronic, Elec. Components, Mgmt. Consulting,
Biotech, Healthcare

Branches:
19 Via Terracaleta
Coto de Caza, CA 92679
(949) 766-2864
Fax: (949) 766-2865
Email: dean@bogleassociates.com
Key Contact:
Mr. Dean Winter, Managing Partner

8218 S Albion
Littleton, CO 80122
(303) 770-8881
Fax: (303) 770-8883
Email: dick@bogleassociates.com
Key Contact:
Mr. Dick Humphrey, Managing Partner

814 Durham Rd
Madison, CT 06443
(203) 421-8432
Fax: (203) 245-8749
Email: tierney@bogleassociates.com
Key Contact:
Mr. Tom Tierney, Managing Partner

1549 Green Bay Rd
Highland Park, IL 60035
(847) 266-7308
Fax: (847) 266-7936
Email: randy@bogleassociates.com
Key Contact:
Mr. Randy Billingsley, Managing Partner

11257 Champagne Point Rd
Kirkland, WA 98034
(425) 825-0348
Fax: (425) 825-9849
Email: carter@bogleassociates.com
Key Contact:
Mr. Carter Morgan, Associate

Bohan & Bradstreet Inc
34 Park E Dr
Branford, CT 06405
(203) 488-0068
Fax: (203) 483-8338
Email: resumes@bohan-bradstreet.com
Web: www.bohan-bradstreet.com

Description: Specialize in filling management to
executive-level within emerging business to Fortune
1000 corporations.

Key Contact:
Mr. Edward Bradstreet - *Accounting & finance,
engineering, marketing, manufacturing
operations, information technology*
Mr. Peter Cahill - *Accounting & finance,
engineering, marketing, manufacturing
operations, information technology*
Mr. Peter Hugret - *Accounting & finance,
engineering, marketing, manufacturing
operations, information technology*
Ms. Victoria Pallotto - *Accounting & finance,
engineering, marketing, manufacturing
operations, information technology*
Mr. Edward R. Fialkosky, CPC
Mr. Edward J. Kuzma, CPC
Mr. Philip H. Pearlman, CPA
Mr. Christopher L. Curtis, CPC
Mr. Diane M. Fusco
Mr. Diane A. Brecciaroli, CPC

Salary minimum: $60,000

Functions: Generalist, Senior Mgmt., Mfg., Materials, Sales & Mktg., Finance, IT, Engineering

Industries: Generalist, Mfg., Wholesale, Retail, Finance, Services, Insurance

Dan Bolen & Associates LLC
9741 N 90th Pl Ste 200
Scottsdale, AZ 85258-5045
(480) 767-9000
Fax: (480) 767-0100
Email: danbolen@mindspring.com
Web: www.danbolenassoc.com

Description: Our firm specializes in executive search and recruiting for the rotating and industrial equipment industry, ie. pumps, compressors, motors, turbines, etc. We recruit for all disciplines: general management, sales and marketing, engineering and manufacturing.

Key Contact - Specialty:
Mr. Dan Bolen, Owner - *Sales, sales management, general management, technical, manufacturing*
Mr. Dan Marshall, Executive Search Assistant - *Sales, sales management, general management, technical, pump & rotating equipment*

Functions: Generalist, Senior Mgmt., Middle Mgmt., Product Dev., Production, Plant Mgmt., Sales Mgmt., Engineering

Industries: Generalist, Agri., Forestry, Mining, Energy, Utilities, Paper, Chemicals, Plastics, Rubber, Metal Products, Misc. Mfg.

Mark Bolno & Associates Inc
4910 14th St W Ste 307
Bradenton, FL 34207
(941) 751-2276
Fax: (941) 756-2100
Email: bolno@earthlink.net

Description: We recruit upper-management food and beverage manufacturing. We specialize in R&D, quality assurance and quality control, human resources, sales and marketing, and corporate hotel operations.

Key Contact - Specialty:
Mr. Mark Bolno, President - *Food manufacturing, hotel executives*

Salary minimum: $50,000

Functions: Generalist, Senior Mgmt., Middle Mgmt., Product Dev., Production, Plant Mgmt., HR Mgmt., R&D

Industries: Generalist, Food, Bev., Tobacco, Hospitality

Bolton Group
PO Box 278551
Sacramento, CA 95827
(916) 362-5000
(800) 820-9115
Fax: (800) 820-9115
Email: sherryj@boltongrp.com
Web: www.boltongrp.com

Description: We will cold call into companies, looking for the candidate you specify. We also network with other recruiters for a larger selection of candidates.

Key Contact - Specialty:
Ms. Sherry Junker, Senior Recruiter - *Telecommunications, data communications, networking*

Functions: Generalist, Directors, Middle Mgmt., Product Dev., Production, Systems Analysis, Systems Dev., Engineering

Industries: Generalist, New Media, Broadcast, Film, Telecoms

Professional Associations: CSP, RON

Bond & Company
10 Saugatuck Ave
Westport, CT 06880
(203) 221-3233
Fax: (203) 341-7729
Email: richard.bond@snet.net
Web: www.snetyp.com/bondcompany

Description: We are a boutique, recruiting firm doing mostly financial, some marketing and logistics, for firms in the Northeastern US. We specialize in treasury positions and marketing/financial controller slots. We have done a lot of work for companies with sales in the $200 million to $1 billion range.

Key Contact:
Mr. Richard Bond, Principal

Functions: Finance

Industries: Generalist

Ann Bond Associates Inc
3388 Woods Edge Cir Ste 101
Bonita Springs, FL 34134
(941) 947-0123
Fax: (941) 947-7801
Email: annbondassociates@earthlink.net
Web: www.annbondassociates.com

Description: We represent well known food manufacturers (both privately and publicly held) who seek sales and marketing managers whose customers have included: hotels, restaurants, institutions, supermarkets and food manufacturers. Our president has been specializing in this category since 1980.

Key Contact - Specialty:
Ms. Ann F. Bond, President - *Sales & marketing, middle & upper management*
Mr. Robert S. Bond, Vice President - *Sales & marketing, middle & upper management*

Salary minimum: $60,000

Functions: Sales & Mktg.

Industries: Food, Bev., Tobacco

Professional Associations: ASMC, IFMA

Bone Personnel Inc
6424 Lima Rd
Ft. Wayne, IN 46818
(219) 489-3350
(888) 808-1081
Fax: (219) 490-5866
Email: bruce@bonepersonnel.com
Web: www.bonepersonnel.com

Description: Full Service Licensed emplyment agency specializing in Manufacturing, Engineering, Human Resources, Accounting, Sales/Marketing & Information Technology marketplace. Contingency & Retained Search.

Key Contact - Specialty:
Mr. Bruce A. Bone, CPC, Owner - *Executive search*

Functions: Generalist

Industries: Mfg. SW

Professional Associations: IAPS, NAPS

Networks: Top Echelon Network

Bonifield Associates
1 Eves Dr Ste 115
Marlton, NJ 08053
(856) 596-3300
Fax: (856) 596-8866
Email: info@bonifield.com
Web: www.bonifield.com

Description: All of our professional consultants have experience/background in either banking or insurance. We have over 25 years of experience specializing for clients ranging from $90 billion to $2 billion of assets. We have served over 300 clients.

Key Contact - Specialty:
Mr. Richard L. Tyson, CLU, President - *Insurance*

Salary minimum: $40,000

Functions: Generalist

Industries: Pharm Svcs., Accounting, Insurance, Accounting SW, Biotech, Healthcare

Professional Associations: INS, MAAPC, NAPS

Boone-Scaturro Associates Inc
PO Box 2903
Alpharetta, GA 30023
(770) 740-9737
(800) 749-1884
Fax: (770) 475-5055
Email: mes@boone-scaturro.com
Web: www.boone-scaturro.com

Description: Physician and executive search firm serving the US. Hybrid and retained search. Full search or choose from array of services. Guaranteed to exceed expectations.

Key Contact - Specialty:
Ms. Mary Ellen Scaturro, Executive Vice President - *Physicians, executives, physician executives, mid levels, group practice administrators*
Mr. Charles C. Boone, President - *Executives, administrators*
Mr. Leonard Scaturro, Secretary/Treasurer - *Financial*
Mrs. Teresa Owens-Unser, Director - *Physicians, technology*

Salary minimum: $55,000

Functions: General Mgmt., Healthcare, Physicians

Industries: Mgmt. Consulting, HR Services, Healthcare

Professional Associations: MGMA

Networks: Medical Search Consortium (MSC)

Bor-Maq Associates
1200 Golden Key Cir Ste 228
El Paso, TX 79925
(915) 592-2077
Fax: (915) 595-6658
Email: bormaq@swbell.net
Web: wwwbormaq.com

Description: We are an executive search firm exclusively specializing in search and recruitment for primarily manufacturing companies operating on the US/Mexico border, in Mexico, and South America. Our nationwide executive search is for diversified candidates.

Key Contact - Specialty:
Mr. Manny Aldana, President - *Executives, senior management, international*
Mr. Mario Pinedo, CPA, Associate Recruiter - *Finance, accounting, MIS*
Mr. Joseph Torres - *Engineering*
Mr. Fred Jamison - *Manufacturing*

Salary minimum: $50,000

Functions: Generalist, General Mgmt., Mfg., Materials, HR Mgmt., Finance, IT, Int'l.

Industries: Generalist, Mfg., Plastics, Rubber, Consumer Elect., Misc. Mfg., Finance, Misc. Financial

Borchert Associates

17430 Campbell Rd Ste 111
Dallas, TX 75252
(972) 818-2801
(888) 818-2801
Fax: (972) 818-2777
Email: greg@glborchert.com
Web: www.glborchert.com

Description: We have twenty-four years worth of experience in completing mid-management through executive-level assignments in the metal casting field.

Key Contact:
Mr. Gregory L. Borchert, President - *Metal casting, foundry, automotive*
Ms. Linda Borchert, CPA, Business Manager

Salary minimum: $50,000

Functions: Generalist

Industries: Mfg., Metal Products

Professional Associations: AFS, RON

Born & Bicknell Inc

5605 Coral Gate Blvd
Coral Gate Professional Plz
Margate, FL 33063-1531
(954) 956-0000
(800) 376-2676
Fax: (800) 374-2676
Email: info@bornbicknell.com
Web: www.bornbicknell.com

Description: We offer premium physician recruitment services which are personalized, efficient and cost effective for today's growth oriented healthcare provider organizations.

Key Contact - Specialty:
Ms. Jane E. Born, CEO - *Physician*
Mr. Samuel J. Born, COO - *Physician*
Ms. Helen Bicknell, President - *Physician*

Functions: Generalist, Physicians

Industries: Generalist, Healthcare

Professional Associations: MGMA, NAPR

Branches:
128 Marlou Cir
Ruston, LA 71270
(800) 374-2676
(318) 254-8481
Fax: (318) 254-8335
Key Contact - Specialty:
Ms. Helen M. Bicknell, RN, President - *Physician*

Lynn Borne & Company

6934 Canby Ave Ste 109
Reseda, CA 91335
(818) 881-9353
Fax: (818) 881-2796
Email: jobs@gorillajobs.com
Web: www.gorillajobs.com

Description: Our search and placement services are involved in all areas of management consulting and public accounting. Our industry positions are primarily accounting, tax, finance, and information technology related.

Key Contact:
Mr. Lynn H. Borne, Owner

Functions: Generalist, Finance, Taxes, IT, Mgmt. Consultants

Industries: Generalist

Bornholdt Shivas & Friends Executive Recruiters

400 E 87th St
New York, NY 10128-6533
(212) 557-5252
(516) 767-1849
Fax: (212) 557-5704
Email: jbornhol@optonline.net
Web: www.bsandf.com

Description: We are a global executive search firm that concentrates in packaged goods marketing and sales, prescription/OTC pharmaceutical drugs marketing and sales, as well as software development marketing and sales on a national and international basis.

Key Contact - Specialty:
Mr. John Bornholdt, President - *Marketing, international, telecommunications, interactive advertising, software development*
Ms. Elizabeth Bornholdt, Placement Counselor - *Pharmaceutical, prescription drugs, sales and marketing, executive*
Ms. Lauren Grant, Placement Counselor - *E-commerce, advertising agencies*

Salary minimum: $60,000

Functions: Generalist, General Mgmt., Middle Mgmt.

Industries: Mfg., Food, Bev., Tobacco, Soap, Perf., Cosmtcs., Drugs Mfg., Medical Devices, Computer Equip., Services, Non-profits, Pharm Svcs., Mgmt. Consulting, Restaurants, Media, Communications, Telecoms, Digital, Wireless, Fiber Optic, Network Infrastructure, Software, Biotech

Professional Associations: RON

Networks: First Interview Network (FIN)

Branches:
33 Concord Rd
Port Washington, NY 11050
(516) 767-1849
Fax: (516) 767-6727
Email: jbornhol@optonline.net
Key Contact - Specialty:
Mr. John Bornholdt, President - *Prescription drugs (marketing, sales)*

Bos Business Consultants

4211 N Buffalo St
PO Box 533
Orchard Park, NY 14127
(800) 836-4220
(716) 662-0800
Fax: (716) 662-0623
Email: careersbbc@wzrd.com
Web: www.recruitstaff.com

Description: National recruiting firm working with manufacturing companies helping them locate qualified engineering, marketing, finance, quality, manufacturing engineering, R&D, and IT personnel. Industries are medical device, automotive, consumer durables, aerospace, electronics plus others.

Key Contact - Specialty:
Mr. John Bos, Director - *Engineering, manufacturing, marketing*

Salary minimum: $45,000

Functions: Mfg., Product Dev., Production, Plant Mgmt., Quality, Materials, Mkt. Research, Finance, IT, Engineering

Industries: Generalist, Mfg., Aerospace, Packaging, ERP SW, Industry Specific SW, Mfg. SW, Marketing SW

Networks: Top Echelon Network

The Bostic Group

PO Box 157
Simpsonville, SC 29681-0157
(864) 228-9464
Fax: (864) 228-6564
Email: jbostic@bosticgroup.com
Web: www.bosticgroup.com

Description: We specialize in Information Technology placements. We have openings in most IT disciplines all across the United States. Our clients pay for all fees and most will offer relocation assistance. Please fax or email a resume to see if we can help you in your career advancement. We offer services for career seekers, corporate clients, and professional recruiters.

Key Contact - Specialty:
Mr. Jim Bostic, Sr., President - *Information technology*
Mr. Jim Bostic, Jr., Vice President - *Information technology*

Functions: IT

Industries: Mfg., Wholesale, Retail, Finance, Insurance, Software, Healthcare

Networks: Top Echelon Network

Boston Executive Search

720 Washington St Standish Bldg
Hanover, MA 02339
(781) 829-6798
Email: peter@besc.net
Web: www.besc.net

Description: We are a boutique executive search firm specializing in the financial services industry.

Key Contact:
Mr. Peter Plant, President

Salary minimum: $75,000

Functions: Generalist

Industries: Banking, Invest. Banking, Misc. Financial

Boston Professional Search Inc

(a Staffing Now company)
699 Boylston St Fl 8
1 Exeter Plz
Boston, MA 02116
(617) 451-5900
Fax: (617) 451-3825
Email: jsamuels@bpsjobs.com
Web: www.bpsjobs.com

Description: We specialize in permanent, temporary and contract. Our main areas of focus are accounting/finance, information technology, sales & marketing and legal placement. We are experienced recruiters, dedicated to providing confidential and professional searches to our candidates and clients, always striving to exceed expectations.

Key Contact - Specialty:
Mr. Jonathan Samuels, President - *Sales & marketing, accounting*

Salary minimum: $35,000

Functions: Admin. Svcs., Legal, Sales & Mktg., Finance, CFO's, IT, Engineering

Industries: Generalist

Professional Associations: ASA, MAPS

Bosworth Field Associates

111 Richmond St W Ste 404
Toronto, ON M5H 2G4
Canada
(416) 362-2151
Fax: (416) 362-2195

Description: We have considerable expertise in positions within finance, accounting, tax, and risk management in both the financial services and general industry sectors.

Key Contact:
Ms. Gillian Lansdowne, President

Salary minimum: $50,000

Howard Bowen Consulting

283 N N Lake Blvd Ste 111
Altamonte Lakeside Executive Stes
Altamonte Springs, FL 32701
(407) 830-8854
Fax: (407) 298-0784
Email: hbowencon@worldnet.att.net
Web: www.howardbowenconsulting.com

Description: We are serving management consulting firms on the cutting edge of advanced business processes and technologies. Our firm is a provider of high/middle-level professionals experienced with strategic and tactical-business issues, i.e. e-Purchasing, supply chain, reengineering, IT infrastructure, ERP, strategic support systems, I-purchase, B2B, strategic sourcing, transition to web e-Commerce, integrated systems, network applications implementations, warehousing, and CRM.

Key Contact - Specialty:
Mr. Howard Bowen, President - *Automotive, industrial equipment, IT strategy, supply chain, outsourcing*

Salary minimum: $80,000

Functions: Mgmt. Consultants

Industries: Energy, Utilities, Mfg., Computer Equip., Consumer Elect., Misc. Mfg., Transportation, Media, Aerospace, Software, Biotech

Networks: Top Echelon Network

Bower & Associates

1313 Briarhaven Dr
Bedford, TX 76021
(817) 283-2256
Fax: (508) 464-8019
Email: basearch@flash.net
Web: www.richbower.com

Description: Search for sales management, technical support, engineering, electronics assembly capital equipment, semiconductor, PCB, SEM, test, vision, SMT, robots, software tools for factory automation, HW/SW design engineers.

Key Contact - Specialty:
Mr. Richard Bower, President - *Capital equipment (printed circuit board assembly, semiconductor industries), test equipment*

Salary minimum: $50,000

Functions: Generalist, Mfg., Automation, Materials, Sales & Mktg., Technicians, Int'l.

Industries: Mfg., Computer Equip., Test, Measure Equip., Misc. Mfg., Electronic, Elec. Components, Venture Cap., Equip Svcs., Telecoms, Telephony, Digital, Wireless, Fiber Optic, Network Infrastructure, Defense, Aerospace, Software, ERP SW, Biotech

Professional Associations: RON

BowersThomas

11150 W Olympic Blvd Ste 805
Los Angeles, CA 90064-1544
(310) 477-3244
Fax: (310) 444-1885
Email: bowersthomas@earthlink.net

Description: Global attorney search and placement for corporations and law firms. Ethical, qualitative and insightful search services for all levels of attorneys in commercial practice areas. All have JD/LL.B and U.S. Bar.

Key Contact - Specialty:
Ms. Pat Thomas - *Attorneys (corporations, law firms)*

Salary minimum: $80,000

Functions: Generalist, Attorneys

Industries: Generalist, Mfg., Finance, Legal, Media, Real Estate, Biotech

Professional Associations: NALSC

Bowie & Associates Inc

100 N Beechwood Ave Ste 200
Baltimore, MD 21228-4927
(410) 747-1919
Email: abowie@us.net

Description: We provide corporate and middle management recruitment in third party logistics and supply chain management services.

Key Contact:
Mr. Andrew Bowie

Salary minimum: $60,000

Functions: Generalist

Industries: Transportation

Professional Associations: MAPRC

James T Boyce & Associates

2161 Yonge St Ste 200
Toronto, ON M4S 3A6
Canada
(416) 322-0192
Fax: (416) 322-9590
Email: james.boyce@3web.net

Description: Search and placement services for the Canadian marketplace specializing primarily within the life insurance industry and employee benefit fields.

Key Contact:
Mr. James T. Boyce

Functions: Generalist

Industries: Finance, Accounting, Mgmt. Consulting, HR Services, Insurance, Accounting SW, ERP SW, HR SW

Boykin Hospitality's Hotel Recruiting Concepts

45 W Prospect Ave Guildhall Bldg Ste 1515
Cleveland, OH 44115
(440) 430-1272
(216) 241-6375 x1272
Fax: (216) 430-1273
Email: fsotet@recruitingconcepts.com
Web: www.recruitingconcepts.com

Description: We provide hotel management placement service, and are offering opportunities for experienced hotel management professionals seeking to further advance their careers. You can apply online at our web site.

Key Contact - Specialty:
Mr. Frank J. Sotet, III, Corporate Recruiter - *Hotel, hospitality*

Salary minimum: $35,000

Functions: General Mgmt., Directors, Senior Mgmt., Middle Mgmt., Sales & Mktg., Sales Mgmt., Customer Svc., HR Mgmt.

Industries: Services, Hospitality

Professional Associations: AHMA

BPM Int'l

8345 Diver Ln
Spring Hill, FL 34608
(352) 666-3647
Fax: (352) 666-3648
Email: brianmor@tampabay.rr.com

Description: We provide executive search to the health care industry. We specialize in the managed care/HMOs, pharmaceuticals for the human and veterinary, bio-technology, health insurance, hospitals, physician management/clinics, health networks/systems. We recruit for administrative, medical, clinical, IT, MIS, sales, finance, legal, operations, consulting, reengineering. The positions that we place include: boards, CEOs, CFOs, COOs, CIOs, VPs, directors, managers, general counsels, physicians, and allied health professionals.

Key Contact - Specialty:
Mr. Brian P. Moore, President - *Healthcare recruitment*

Salary minimum: $60,000

Functions: Generalist, Healthcare

Industries: Drugs Mfg., Medical Devices, Non-profits, Pharm Svcs., Mgmt. Consulting, IT Implementation, Advertising, Marketing SW, Biotech, Healthcare, Hospitals, Long-term Care

BPM Recruiters

PO Box 3738
Silverdale, WA 98383
(360) 308-0038
Fax: (360) 598-2979
Email: bpm-recruiters@msn.com
Web: www.biorxjobs.com

Description: Our firm is specializing in specialty sales positions, sales force expansion, initial start-up hiring for bio-pharma companies, management positions, managed care, medical liaison, and regulatory positions.

Key Contact - Specialty:
Ms. Joan Maynard, Partner - *Medical, bio-pharma, pharmaceutical*
Ms. Lisa Ward, Partner - *Medical, bio-pharma, pharmaceutical*

Functions: Generalist

Industries: Industry Specific SW

Networks: Top Echelon Network

BPR Associates

2701 NW Vaughn St Ste 450
Portland, OR 97210
(503) 224-8188
(888) 246-6500
Fax: (503) 224-8478
Email: info@bpr.com
Web: www.bpr.com

Description: Our firm provides recruiting services for leading companies seeking to fill sales, marketing, and management positions. We purposefully do not limit our practice to a narrow industry focus, because first and foremost, we are specialists in search. Our work spans a select group of industries including high tech, manufacturing, consumer products, electronics, service industries, software, and distribution. BPR works primarily with Oregon based firms.

Key Contact - Specialty:
Mr. John Becker, CPC, Owner, Senior Associate - *Sales, marketing, general management*
Mr. Bruce Rodway, Associate - *Sales & marketing positions*

Salary minimum: $50,000

Functions: General Mgmt., Senior Mgmt., Sales & Mktg.

Industries: Food, Bev., Tobacco, Computer Equip., Consumer Elect., Wholesale, Retail, Finance, Banking, Equip Svcs., E-commerce, Entertainment, New Media, Software, Entertainment SW, Biotech

Professional Associations: NAPS

Braam & Associates

845 Chardonnay Cir
Petaluma, CA 94954
(707) 765-9090
Fax: (707) 765-9190
Email: braam10@aol.com

Description: We take pride in locating exceptional candidates with specific qualifications to fill the needs of outstanding clients.

Key Contact - Specialty:
Ms. Christine White, General Partner - *Sales, telecommunication, construction (technical, general), engineering, information technology*

Functions: Generalist, Advertising, Mktg. Mgmt., Sales Mgmt., MIS Mgmt., Systems Implem., Engineering

Industries: Generalist, Construction, Media, Telecoms, Software

Professional Associations: CSP

Brackin & Sayers Associates Inc

1000 McKnight Park Dr
Pittsburgh, PA 15237
(412) 367-4644
Fax: (412) 367-3512
Email: bsayers@brackinandsayers.com
Web: www.brackinandsayers.com

Description: Focus exclusively on the recruitment of human resources, finance and accounting professionals on a worldwide basis utilizing our resources and those of 450 affiliate recruiting firms.

Key Contact - Specialty:
Mr. Jim Brackin, Partner - *Human resources*
Mr. Bruce Sayers, Partner - *Finance & accounting*

Salary minimum: $40,000

Functions: Generalist, HR Mgmt., Finance

Industries: Generalist

Professional Associations: AAFA, SHRM

Networks: National Personnel Assoc (NPA)

Bradford & Galt Inc

4 City Place Dr Ste 100
St. Louis, MO 63141
(314) 434-9200
Fax: (314) 434-9266
Email: bcl@bgcs.com
Web: www.bradfordandgalt.com

Description: Founded as search firm in 1984; expanded services to include information systems contracting/consulting temporary staffing in 1990.

Key Contact:
Mr. Bradford Layton, CEO - *Information systems consulting*
Mr. Carlin Bennett, President
Mr. Steve Kidd, Vice President-Finance & Operations

Salary minimum: $30,000

Functions: Generalist, IT, MIS Mgmt., Systems Analysis, Systems Dev., Systems Implem., Systems Support

Industries: Generalist

Branches:
112 State St Ste D
Peoria, IL 61602
(309) 674-2000
Fax: (309) 674-8300
Key Contact - Specialty:
Mr. Kevin Ardvini, Branch Manager - *IT consulting*

9200 Indian Creek Pkwy Ste 570
Overland Park, KS 66210
(913) 663-1264
Fax: (913) 663-1264

Key Contact - Specialty:
Mr. Fred Dimmel, Branch Manager - *IT consulting*

Bradford Consulting Companies

8 Ridgewood Dr
Trophy Club, TX 76262
(817) 490-1644
Email: carlb@bradfordconsulting.com
Web: www.bradfordconsulting.com

Description: We provide national executive search for mid-level to senior management in most industries. We also conduct POWER Hiring workshops for corporate clients. Our firm is a certified POWER Hiring partner.

Key Contact - Specialty:
Mr. Carl Bradford, President - *Management and key technical positions*

Salary minimum: $100,000

Functions: General Mgmt., Mfg., Materials, Sales & Mktg., Finance, IT, Engineering, Specialized Svcs.

Industries: Generalist

Bradley & Associates

858 Riverwatch Dr
Crescent Springs, KY 41017
(859) 344-1965
Fax: (859) 344-1967
Email: bradl@choice.net
Web: www.users.choice.net/~bradl

Description: We are a small, high-quality firm specializing in technology, finance, and engineering positions throughout the US.

Key Contact - Specialty:
Mr. Ken Bradley, Owner - *Information technology, finance, insurance, engineering*

Salary minimum: $50,000

Functions: Generalist

Industries: Generalist

Bradley & Associates

5341 River Bluff Curve Ste 116
Bloomington, MN 55437
(612) 884-2607
Fax: (612) 884-2019

Description: One person responsible for all aspects of your search, which will be handled professionally, according to your instructions. We prefer your toughest assignments.

Key Contact - Specialty:
Mr. T. John Bradley, President - *Engineering*
Ms. Mary X. Bradley, Vice President - *Production, research & development*

Salary minimum: $35,000

Functions: Generalist, Mfg., Engineering

Industries: Generalist, Food, Bev., Tobacco, Chemicals

Bradshaw & Associates

1850 Parkway Pl Ste 420
Marietta, GA 30067
(770) 426-5600
(770) 993-1600
Fax: (770) 993-6777
Email: info@baserver.com
Web: www.baserver.com

Description: Our career development services specialize in the recruitment and placement of entry to upper-level professional talent with industry nationwide. Over half of our applicants possess technical degrees and/or MBAs. The majority of our staff have between three to fifteen years of experience since earning a minimum of a bachelor's degree.

Key Contact - Specialty:
Mr. Rod Bradshaw, CPC, MHRM, Manager of Consulting - *Generalist*
Mr. Orlando Rodriguez, CPC, Recruiting Manager - *Hospitality*

Functions: Generalist

Industries: Generalist

Professional Associations: GAPS, NAPS

Networks: National Personnel Assoc (NPA)

Bradson Technology Professionals

68 Chamberlain Ave Ste 200
Ottawa, ON K1S 1V9
Canada
(613) 238-1700
Fax: (613) 238-6770
Email: ottawa@bradson.com
Web: www.bradsontechnology.com

Description: People drive technology. Find the right people; build a great company. Bradson Technology Professionals is your source for high-tech recruiting. Our recruiting services include placement, contract consulting, and senior search for hardware engineering, embedded software, web B2B, e-Commerce, localization QA/QC testing, as well as traditional IT application development and infrastructure support positions. The best web-based recruiting technology and pro-active recruiters guarantee our clients get results. We work across Canada, the US, and globally.

Key Contact:
Mr. Kevin O'Rourke, Vice President, Ottawa Region

Salary minimum: $40,000

Functions: Sales Mgmt., IT, MIS Mgmt., Systems Dev., Systems Implem., DB Admin.

Industries: Mfg., Retail, Finance, Banking, Legal, E-commerce, IT Implementation, Communications, Telecoms, Telephony, Digital, Wireless, Government, Aerospace, Software, Accounting SW, Database SW, Development SW, ERP SW, Security SW, System SW, Biotech

M F Branch Associates Inc

PO Box 18105
Asheville, NC 28814
(828) 658-0055
Fax: (828) 645-9866
Email: minniebranch@mfbranch.com
Web: www.mfbranch.com

Description: We are specialists in search for clients in the telecommunication and advanced data communication networking industries for over 25 years. The positions represented include executive management, advanced R&D, marketing, product management, and sales.

Key Contact - Specialty:
Ms. Minnie Branch, President - *Advanced communications*

Salary minimum: $60,000

Functions: Generalist, Directors, Senior Mgmt., Middle Mgmt., Mktg. Mgmt., Sales Mgmt., Systems Dev., R&D

Industries: Telecoms, Telephony, Wireless, Fiber Optic, Network Infrastructure, Software, Networking, Comm. SW

Brandjes Associates

PO Box 5971
Baltimore, MD 21282-5971
(410) 484-5423
Fax: (410) 484-6140
Email: brandjes@pcbank.net

Description: A small, very specialized financial services recruiting firm, primarily banking.

Key Contact - Specialty:
Mr. Michael Brandjes, Principal - *Banking*
Ms. Suzanne Frock, Principal - *Banking*

Salary minimum: $50,000

Functions: Generalist

Industries: Finance, Banking, Invest. Banking, Brokers, Venture Cap.

Professional Associations: MAPRC

Brandt Associates
PO Box 189
Dalton, PA 18414
(570) 563-2058
Fax: (570) 563-2058
Email: wb4cape@aol.com

Description: Recruiting for middle and senior-level management positions with a greater than average success rate. Effective and efficient!!

Key Contact - Specialty:
Mr. William E. Brandt, President - *Human resource management, information systems, MIS management*

Salary minimum: $50,000

Functions: Generalist, Mfg., HR Mgmt., Finance, IT, MIS Mgmt., Systems Analysis

Industries: Generalist, Finance, Accounting, HR Services, Telecoms, Environmental Svcs.

Professional Associations: SHRM

Brandywine Technology Partners
2005 Concord Pike Ste 210
Wilmington, DE 19803
(302) 656-6100
Fax: (302) 656-9100
Email: dick@btpartners.net
Web: www.btpartners.net

Description: We recruit and place information technology professionals in contract and career positions with companies that range from "pre-IPO" to Fortune 100. Most of our assignments are in Southeastern Pennsylvania, South/Central New Jersey, Delaware and Maryland areas, however we frequently conduct nationwide searches at the request of our clients.

Key Contact:
Mr. Vince Borrelli, Partner
Mr. Sean Palat, Partner
Mr. Dick Burkhard, Partner
Ms. Anne Keehan, Partner
Mr. Joel Pierson, Partner

Salary minimum: $50,000

Functions: IT

Industries: Generalist

The Brannon Group Inc
PO Box 1677
Alexandria, VA 22313
(703) 461-9320
Fax: (703) 461-9321
Email: info@brannoninc.com
Web: www.brannoninc.com

Description: We have a staff with over 80 years of combined experience in the plastic industry and extrusion/thermoforming. We know the organizations in these industries. We recruit for all levels, from line operators to engineers, to President/CEOs and all levels of management within the plastic, hotel, and IT industry, extrusion/thermoforming, from sheet to film to pipe, profile and tubing, injection molding, resin, and compounding. We look forward to helping you with your next career move. We also have offices in Atlanta and Houston.

Key Contact - Specialty:
Mr. William W. Brannon, President - *Plastic extrusion, thermoforming, film, sheet, pipe*

Salary minimum: $35,000

Functions: Generalist, Middle Mgmt., Mfg., Plant Mgmt., Quality, Packaging, Sales & Mktg., R&D, Engineering

Industries: Mfg., Plastics, Rubber, IT Implementation, Hospitality, Hotels, Resorts, Clubs, Fiber Optic, Software, Industry Specific SW, Mfg. SW, Marketing SW, Biotech, Healthcare

Professional Associations: SPE

Brantley Communications
1112 Goodwin Dr
Plano, TX 75023
(972) 423-6939
Email: larry@brantleycommunications.com
Web: www.brantleycommunications.com

Description: We specialize in the full time placement of professionals in the advertising and communications industries. We are a contingency firm and work with clients and candidates all across the country.

Key Contact:
Mr. Larry Brantley, Principal

Salary minimum: $30,000

Functions: Generalist

Industries: Media, Communications, Wireless, Packaging, Entertainment SW, Marketing SW, Networking, Comm. SW

Bratland & Associates
5424 Brittany Dr Ste D
McHenry, IL 60050
(815) 344-4335
Fax: (815) 344-6424
Email: al@bratlandcareers.com
Web: www.bratlandcareers.com

Description: We are aligned with the largest network of recruiters in the U.S. Through these affiliations we have access to the databases of about 700 recruiting offices worldwide. Whether you are client or candidate we can open doors for you.

Key Contact:
Mr. A. J. Bratland, President - *Fiber optics, telecommunications*
Ms. Dolores Bratland, Vice President
Ms. Mary Zwaan, Research Analyst

Functions: General Mgmt., Mfg., Plant Mgmt., Quality, R&D, Engineering

Industries: Telecoms, Fiber Optic

Networks: Top Echelon Network

Jerold Braun & Associates
Century City Station
PO Box 67523
Los Angeles, CA 90067
(310) 203-0515
Email: braunsearch@prodigy.net

Description: With 33 years of retail and HR experience, firm specializes in retail, e-commerce, apparel manufacturing, telemarketing and allied fields. Also specializes in all areas of HR management.

Key Contact:
Mr. Jerold Braun, Principal
Ms. Joyce Davis, Principal

Salary minimum: $50,000

Functions: Generalist

Industries: Wholesale, Retail, HR Services

Braun-Valley Associates
373D Vidal St S Ste D2
PO Box 2168
Sarnia, ON N7T 7L7
Canada
(519) 336-4590
(519) 336-4591
Fax: (519) 336-8164
Email: mbraun@mnsi.net

Description: Suppliers of temporary and long-term contract personnel to the industrial sector.

Key Contact - Specialty:
Mr. Mark Braun, Contracts Manager - *Information technology*
Ms. Kathy Furlotte, Manager - *Engineering*

Functions: Generalist, Production, Automation, Plant Mgmt., Quality, Sales Mgmt., Systems Support, Engineering

Industries: Generalist, Chemicals, Drugs Mfg., Plastics, Rubber, Paints, Petro. Products, Machine, Appliance, Motor Vehicles, Misc. Mfg.

Professional Associations: ACSESS

The Bren Group
PO Box 2369
Sedona, AZ 86339
(480) 951-2736
Fax: (520) 282-4731
Email: bren@brengroup.com
Web: www.brengroup.com

Description: Our firm specializes in the travel industry, IT, and web based business. There is no fee to the candidate and all information is confidential. Our candidates and clients may go to our website and access their information and search for jobs, and clients can search for candidates.

Key Contact:
Ms. Brenda Rowenhorst, President

Salary minimum: $35,000

Functions: Generalist

Industries: Transportation, Hospitality, Hotels, Resorts, Clubs, Restaurants, Entertainment, Recreation, Aerospace, Entertainment SW

Networks: Top Echelon Network

Brethet, Barnum & Associates Inc
703 Evans Ave Ste 300
Toronto, ON M9C 5E9
Canada
(416) 621-4900
Fax: (416) 621-9818
Email: bshiley@wwonline.com

Description: As specialists in healthcare, we are committed to excellence in both the quality of our service and the superior people we recruit. Our reputation for integrity and responsiveness to our clients' needs is second to none. We get results!

Key Contact - Specialty:
Mr. Bob Shiley, CPC, Associate - *Biotechnology, healthcare, medical devices, medical sales, pharmaceutical*
Ms. Phyllis Chrzan, Associate - *Medical, pharmaceutical, sales & marketing*
Ms. Anne Brethet, General Manager - *Medical, pharmaceutical, sales & marketing*

Salary minimum: $40,000

Functions: Sales & Mktg.

Industries: Drugs Mfg., Medical Devices, Biotech, Healthcare

Professional Associations: ACSESS, IPSA

Brett Personnel Specialists

2184 Morris Ave
Union, NJ 07083
(908) 687-7772

Description: Expertise in the recruitment of engineering, maintenance, manufacturing and scientific personnel within the pharmaceutical, chemical, electro-mechanical and consumer products industries.

Key Contact:
Mr. Gene Reight, Manager

Salary minimum: $25,000

Functions: Generalist, Middle Mgmt., Production, Plant Mgmt., Quality, Productivity, R&D, Engineering

Industries: Generalist, Chemicals, Soap, Perf., Cosmtcs., Drugs Mfg., Medical Devices, Plastics, Rubber, Paints, Petro. Products, Leather, Stone, Glass

Brian Associates Inc

1407 Edinburg Rd
Princeton Junction, NJ 08550
(609) 936-9760
Fax: (609) 936-9730
Email: brianassoc@aol.com
Web: www.brianassociates.com

Description: We provide executive search for general management, project management, system architecture, system development, e-commerce sales and marketing executives in technology, investment banking, e-commerce, and consulting companies.

Key Contact - Specialty:
Mr. Brian D. Wittlin, Manager - *General management, technical, sales & marketing*
Ms. Deborah M. Rizzo, Project Manager - *Information technology*
Mr. Jonathan J. Braxton, Account Executive - *Technical product design (electronic, digital, optical)*
Ms. Jennifer L. Halding, Account Executive - *Information technology*
Ms. Pia Olivia, RA - *IS*

Salary minimum: $65,000

Functions: Generalist, Senior Mgmt., Product Dev., Mktg. Mgmt., Sales Mgmt., Systems Dev., Systems Implem., R&D, Engineering

Industries: Generalist, Medical Devices, Machine, Appliance, Motor Vehicles, Computer Equip., Invest. Banking, Mgmt. Consulting, E-commerce, IT Implementation, PSA/ASP, Digital, Wireless, Software

Professional Associations: AIC, AICHE, JAS, SOCMA

Bridgecreek Personnel Agency

12792 Valley View Ste 202
Garden Grove, CA 92845
(714) 891-1771
Fax: (714) 892-1567
Email: bfoster1@ix.netcom.com

Description: We specialize in manufacturing and distribution, plastics, chemicals, machine tools and related industries. Positions are national and international in management, sales, engineering, related technical fields.

Key Contact - Specialty:
Mr. William A. Foster, President/Owner - *Manufacturing, distribution management, engineering, sales, management information systems*

Functions: General Mgmt.

Industries: Chemicals, Medical Devices, Plastics, Rubber, Metal Products, Misc. Mfg., Environmental Svcs.

Networks: National Personnel Assoc (NPA)

Bridgemount Solutions Inc

21 Antares Dr Unit 113
Ottawa, ON K2E 7T8
Canada
(613) 224-3982
Email: gary@bridgemount.com
Web: www.bridgemount.com

Description: Hi-tech staffing firm specializing in senior and management level permanent and contract staffing in all areas related to IT firms. Our focus is on outstanding client service that is solution based and second to none.

Key Contact:
Mr. Gary Van Donkersgoed, President

Brinkman & Associates

9115 Riggs Ln Ste B
Overland Park, KS 66212
(913) 341-8422
Fax: (913) 381-2046

Description: Serving the diagnostics, biotechnology, food and beverage markets in sales and marketing, R&D, engineering and quality.

Key Contact:
Dr. Max R. Brinkman, Partner
Ms. Ann R. Brinkman, Partner

Salary minimum: $30,000

Functions: Generalist, Mfg., Materials, Mkt. Research, Mktg. Mgmt., Sales Mgmt., R&D, Engineering

Industries: Generalist, Food, Bev., Tobacco, Drugs Mfg., Medical Devices, Pharm Svcs., Packaging, Biotech, Healthcare

R A Briones & Company

11200 Montwood Dr
El Paso, TX 79936
(915) 629-7222
Fax: (915) 629-7223
Email: briones@whc.net
Web: www.brionessearch.com

Description: General manufacturing with emphasis in bilingual (Spanish) professionals, management, accounting, quality, materials, information technology, sales and marketing and maquiladoras.

Key Contact - Specialty:
Mr. Roberto A. Briones, CPC, Owner/Manager - *Manufacturing*
Ms. Hossana Arias, Sr Executive Recruiter - *Manufacturing*
Ms. Martha Ortiz, Sr Executive Recruiter - *Manufacturing*

Salary minimum: $15,000

Functions: Mfg.

Industries: Mfg., Accounting, Software, Biotech, Healthcare

Professional Associations: APICS, BCAPS, EPSHRM, TAPC

Networks: Top Echelon Network

Bristol Associates Inc

5757 W Century Blvd Ste 628
Los Angeles, CA 90045
(310) 670-0525
Fax: (310) 670-4075
Email: jbright@bristolassoc.com
Web: www.bristolassoc.com

Description: Our specialties are hospitality, gaming, food and beverage industry, healthcare, fixed site entertainment, direct and interactive marketing, and senior living. We have depth of experience and professional knowledge. We use sophisticated

sourcing techniques. Our firm uses focused personal service and is results-oriented.

Key Contact - Specialty:
Mr. James J. Bright, Jr., President - *Gaming*
Ms. Lucy Farber, Vice President - *Gaming*
Ms. Roberta Borer, Exec Vice President - *Healthcare*
Mr. Lee Candiotti, Vice President - *Direct marketing*
Mr. Peter Stern, Vice President - *Food & beverage industry*
Mr. Kelly Nelson, Vice President - *Hotel, hospitality, tour, travel*
Ms. Cherise Vallas, Division Director - *Fixed site entertainment, senior living*

Salary minimum: $75,000

Functions: Generalist

Industries: Food, Bev., Tobacco, Hospitality, Hotels, Resorts, Clubs, Restaurants, Entertainment, Recreation, Advertising, Healthcare, Hospitals, Long-term Care

Britt Associates Inc

3533 Lake Shore Dr
Joliet, IL 60431-8820
(815) 436-8300
Fax: (815) 436-9617
Email: brittassoc@aol.com

Description: Recruitment/placement of logistics/distribution and supply chain/materials management professionals on a national scale. Activity is conducted with all of industrial goods and consumer products manufacturers along with wholesale and retail firms.

Key Contact:
Mr. William E. Lichtenauer, CPC, President

Salary minimum: $40,000

Functions: Production, Materials, Purchasing, Materials Plng., Distribution

Industries: Generalist

Professional Associations: APICS, CLM, IAPS

Networks: Top Echelon Network

The Brixton Group Inc

3718 Providence Rd
Charlotte, NC 28211
(704) 365-0766
Fax: (704) 365-4428
Email: asobel@brixton.net
Web: www.brixton.net

Description: We are a permanent technical recruiting company. We work across all technical platforms helping managers initializing computer oriented resources in achieving their scope of activities on or ahead of schedule and within budget.

Key Contact:
Mr. Andrew Sobel, President

Salary minimum: $50,000

Functions: Generalist

Industries: Generalist

Broad, Waverly & Associates

200 Broad St
PO Box 741
Red Bank, NJ 07701
(732) 741-1010
Fax: (732) 219-9644
Email: broadwav@ix.netcom.com

Description: We offer recruitment and placement of middle to upper property and casualty insurance and accounting candidates.

Key Contact - Specialty:
Mr. Bill I. Saloukas, CPC, President - *Insurance (property, casualty)*

Salary minimum: $50,000

Functions: Generalist, Finance

Industries: Generalist, Insurance

Professional Associations: INS, MAAPC, NJAPS, NJSA

Broadband Media Communications Inc

PO Box 639
San Juan Capistrano, CA 92693
(949) 488-8855
Email: broadbandcareers@broadbandcareers.com
Web: www.broadbandcareers.com

Description: Our network offers telecommunication jobs, resumes, Broad Search Telecom Directory of 8000 telecommunication companies, job agents, candidate agents, career resources, telecommunication news and more! Our website is the most comprehensive career site for the telecommunications professional. Browse 8000 linked telecommunication companies. Search career opportunities and post your resume or Secure Candidate Confidential Profile. You can reach the "Eyeballs that Count.""

Key Contact:
Mr. Mark Clancey, Director - *Business Development - Broadband telecommunications, executive, management, engineering, technical*
Ms. Darcie Renee, Director - *Administration & Research*

Functions: Generalist

Industries: Construction, Test, Measure Equip., Electronic, Elec. Components, HR Services, IT Implementation, New Media, Communications, Software

Brock & Brown Associates

964 Garden City Dr
Monroeville, PA 15146
(412) 856-2276
Fax: (412) 856-2826
Email: brown@brockandbrown.com
Web: www.brockandbrown.com

Description: We are a diversity search firm that specializes in the areas of finance, engineering, and human resources.

Key Contact:
Mr. Orlando Brown, Managing Partner

Salary minimum: $50,000

Functions: Generalist, Directors, Senior Mgmt., Middle Mgmt., Benefits, Personnel, Finance, Minorities

Industries: Generalist, Food, Bev., Tobacco, Chemicals, Drugs Mfg., Misc. Financial, Pharm Svcs., Accounting

Professional Associations: NABA, SHRM, WAW

Networks: Alliance Partnership Int'l

Dan B Brockman

PO Box 913
Barrington, IL 60011
(847) 382-6015
Email: danbbrockman@sprintmail.com
Web: www.trainingjob.com

Description: Specialists in degreed safety engineering practitioners, industrial hygienists, ergonomists, compliance managers (OSHA, EPA and MSHA) and environmental affairs managers, training, learning, on-line, instruction, teaching, CBT, OD, educational specialists.

Key Contact - Specialty:
Mr. Dan B. Brockman, Owner - *Safety engineers*
Ms. Trowby Brockman, Partner - *Instructional design, instructional technology*

Salary minimum: $45,000

Functions: Mfg., Training, Engineering, Environmentalists

Industries: Generalist

Professional Associations: AIHA, ASSE, ASTD, HFES, NSC

Networks: Top Echelon Network

Brookman Associates

12 E 41st St Ste 1400
New York, NY 10017
(212) 213-5666
Fax: (212) 683-4672
Email: brookman96@aol.com

Description: Professional search recruitment and placement services. Over 35 years of experience in both client and provider roles. Management consulting includes all HR activities as well as market research, field analysis, etc.

Key Contact - Specialty:
Mr. Geoffrey Brookman, Principal - *Generalist*

Salary minimum: $75,000

Functions: Generalist, Healthcare, Sales & Mktg., HR Mgmt., Finance, IT, R&D

Industries: Generalist, Mfg., Food, Bev., Tobacco, Drugs Mfg., Medical Devices, Finance, Media, Healthcare

Professional Associations: IACPR, BACC, NYPMA, SHRM

Brookside Consulting Group LLC

PO Box 250343
West Bloomfield, MI 48325-0343
(248) 626-4733
Fax: (248) 626-2853
Email: info@brooksideconsulting.com
Web: www.brooksideconsulting.com

Description: We are an international executive search firm specializing in attorney and executive searches for private law firms and corporate in-house legal departments.

Key Contact - Specialty:
Mr. Martin Rosenfeld, Principal - *Attorneys and legal executives*

Salary minimum: $75,000

Functions: Senior Mgmt., Attorneys

Industries: Generalist, Legal

Professional Associations: NALSC

Broward-Dobbs Inc

1532 Dunwoody Village Pkwy Ste 200
Atlanta, GA 30338
(770) 399-0744
Fax: (770) 395-6881
Email: lukegreene@mindspring.com
Web: www.broward-dobbs.qpg.com

Description: We are a client-oriented executive recruiting firm specializing in engineering, environmental, telecommunications, technical sales, manufacturing, and real estate. Our clients are national ranging from Fortune 100 to small local companies. Personal attention is our emphasis.

Key Contact - Specialty:
Mr. W. Luke Greene, Jr., President - *Engineering, technical sales & marketing, manufacturing*
Mr. Milnor Kessler, Executive Vice President - *Manufacturing*

Salary minimum: $35,000

Functions: Mfg., Production, Automation, Quality, Materials, Purchasing, Packaging, Systems Analysis, Engineering, Environmentalists

Industries: Generalist

Networks: National Personnel Assoc (NPA)

D Brown & Associates Inc

610 SW Alder Ste 1111
Portland, OR 97205
(503) 224-6860
Email: dennis@dbrown.net
Web: www.dbrown.net

Description: One of Oregon's largest independent search and recruitment organizations. Thirty year commitment serving national clientele in the information technology, information systems, healthcare, accounting and construction fields.

Key Contact - Specialty:
Mr. Dennis S. Brown, President - *Information systems, information technology, financial, healthcare*

Salary minimum: $50,000

Functions: Generalist, Budgeting, MIS Mgmt., Systems Analysis, Systems Dev., Systems Implem., Network Admin., DB Admin.

Industries: Generalist, Construction, Software, Healthcare

Networks: National Personnel Assoc (NPA)

Pat Brown & Associates

PO Box 6211
Mesa, AZ 85216-6211
(480) 503-4275
Fax: (480) 503-4329
Email: pat.brown@mindspring.com

Description: Over 20 years of actual experience in the insurance industry.

Key Contact - Specialty:
Ms. Pat Brown, President - *Insurance (property, casualty)*

Salary minimum: $30,000

Functions: Generalist

Industries: Insurance

Professional Associations: NIRA

Ken Brown & Company

1036B W Battlefield
Springfield, MO 65807
(417) 883-9444
Email: bbrown@kenbrown.com
Web: www.kenbrown.com

Description: Executive placement of manufacturing personnel in the food, beverage and consumer products industries.

Key Contact:
Mr. Ken Brown, Vice President

Salary minimum: $30,000

Functions: Generalist, General Mgmt., Senior Mgmt., Middle Mgmt., Mfg., Production, Plant Mgmt., Quality, Materials

Industries: Generalist, Mfg., Food, Bev., Tobacco, Soap, Perf., Cosmtcs., Drugs Mfg.

Professional Associations: MAPS

Johnson Brown Associates Inc

55 Monument Cir Ste 1214
Indianapolis, IN 46204
(317) 237-4328
Fax: (317) 237-4335
Email: danbrown@topechelon.com

Description: We are a responsive traditional search firm conducting dedicated searches. Our emphasis is on close working relationships, and we have an in-depth understanding of client's industry and operations. Our specialties include manufacturing management, engineering, accounting, and human resources.

Key Contact - Specialty:
Mr. Daniel P. Brown, Partner - *Automotive systems, transportation equipment, capital equipment*
Mr. John Kimbrough Johnson, Partner - *Human resources, accounting and finance*
Mr. John Chapman, Senior Consultant - *Electronics, aerospace, medical equipment, electrical equipment*

Salary minimum: $60,000

Functions: Mfg., Materials, HR Mgmt., Finance, Engineering

Industries: Generalist, Mfg., Medical Devices, Plastics, Rubber, Metal Products, Machine, Appliance, Motor Vehicles, Consumer Elect., Test, Measure Equip., Electronic, Elec. Components, Aerospace

Networks: Top Echelon Network

Jim Brown Associates
5214-F Diamond Heights Blvd
PMB 527
San Francisco, CA 94131-2118
(415) 206-9111
Fax: (415) 206-9191
Email: jbrown3@pacbell.net

Description: Nationwide middle management through senior-level executive search, all functions, within the pharmaceutical, biotech and medical device industries. Primary concentration is with marketing communications agencies specializing in healthcare.

Key Contact - Specialty:
Mr. Jim Brown, Owner - *Medical, pharmaceutical*

Salary minimum: $90,000

Functions: Advertising, Mkt. Research, Mktg. Mgmt., Graphic Artists

Industries: Drugs Mfg., Medical Devices, Pharm Svcs., Biotech

Polly Brown Associates
342 Madison Ave Ste 1500
New York, NY 10173
(212) 661-7575
Fax: (212) 808-4126
Email: info@pollybrownassociates.com
Web: www.pollybrownassociates.com

Description: Our clients are the leaders in luxury products/consumer goods, in the categories of cosmetics, fragrances, jewelry and accessories. We primarily focus on searches in the fields of marketing, sales, merchandising, public relations, product development, human resources and finance.

Key Contact - Specialty:
Ms. Polly M. Brown, President - *Cosmetics, fragrances, luxury goods, jewelry*
Ms. Pat Durino, Vice President - *Luxury goods, jewelry, accessories*

Salary minimum: $75,000

Functions: Generalist, General Mgmt., Product Dev., Sales & Mktg., HR Mgmt., Finance, Network Admin.

Industries: Generalist, Textiles, Apparel, Soap, Perf., Cosmtcs., Accounting, HR Services, Hospitality, Advertising

Branches:
1055 Parsippany Blvd Ste 106
Parsippany, NJ 07054
(973) 316-9787
Fax: (973) 316-1594
Email: info@pollybrownassociates.com
Key Contact:
Ms. Lisa Smith, Manager-Recruitment & Research Admin.

Brown, Bernardy, Van Remmen Inc
12100 Wilshire Blvd Ste M-40
Los Angeles, CA 90025
(310) 826-5777
Fax: (310) 820-6330
Email: bbvr@gte.net

Description: Specialists in advertising, publishing, marketing, direct marketing and new media.

Key Contact:
Mr. Roger Van Remmen, President - *Advertising, marketing, direct marketing, new media*
Ms. Cathie Kanuit, Partner - *Publishing, new media, advertising*
Mr. Chris Cochran, Account Executive
Mr. Tom Knaphurst, Account Executive

Salary minimum: $30,000

Functions: Generalist, Advertising, Mkt. Research, Mktg. Mgmt., Sales Mgmt., Direct Mktg.

Industries: Generalist, Advertising, Publishing, New Media

Professional Associations: ACLA, AIEF, DMCG, LADMA, TTRA

Networks: First Interview Network (FIN)

Brownstone Sales & Marketing Group Inc
312 S 22nd St Ste C
New York, NY 10010
(212) 254-8700
Fax: (212) 254-8282
Email: team@b-stone.com

Description: We offer a mix of contingency and retained work for sales professionals. We are highly ethical and hard-working on behalf of the corporation and candidate. Over 50% growth in the past four years.

Key Contact:
Mr. James A. Riely, President - *Sales, sales management*
Mr. Christopher K. Doyle, Managing Partner

Salary minimum: $35,000

Functions: Generalist, General Mgmt., Sales & Mktg., Advertising, Sales Mgmt., Direct Mktg., IT, Network Admin., DB Admin.

Industries: Generalist, Computer Equip., IT Implementation, Network Infrastructure, Software

Bryan & Louis Research
6263 Mayfield Rd Ste 226
Cleveland, OH 44124
(440) 442-8744
Fax: (440) 442-8745

Description: We are specialists in our chosen industries with relationships in-depth across the U.S. and Canada.

Key Contact - Specialty:
Mr. Les Snider, Exec Vice President - *Lubricants, chemicals, plastics, electric, refinery*
Mr. R. Louis Terlizzi, President - *Displays, retail environment, POS in-store graphics*

Salary minimum: $25,000

Functions: General Mgmt., Plant Mgmt., Packaging, Sales & Mktg., Advertising, Sales Mgmt., Customer Svc., Engineering, Architects, Graphic Artists

Industries: Generalist, Printing, Chemicals, Paints, Petro. Products, Metal Products, Retail, Advertising, Packaging

Branches:
25820 Hurlingham Rd
Cleveland, OH 44122
(440) 464-6304
Fax: (440) 442-8745

Key Contact - Specialty:
Mr. L. Bryan Snider, Jr., General Manager - *Chemicals, lubricants, electric, plastics, refinery*

35100 Aspenwood Ln
Willoughby, OH 44094
(440) 942-2063
Email: bryanlouis@usa.net
Key Contact - Specialty:
Mr. Robert L. Terlizzi, Sr. - *Displays, POS graphics, fulfillment, point of purchase, fixturing*

Bryan, Jason & Associates Inc
111 Richmond St W Ste 1200
Toronto, ON M5H 2G4
Canada
(416) 867-9295
Fax: (416) 867-3067
Email: careers@bryan-jason.ca
Web: www.bryan-jason.ca

Description: We are a well established search firm that locates and identifies candidates in the accounting/finance sectors of business. Our emphasis is geared towards the real estate, construction, development and property management field. Our consultants also work with clients looking for professionals that have experience on the operational side of real estate.

Key Contact - Specialty:
Ms. Rickie Bryan, President - *Real estate*
Ms. Bonnie Jason, Vice President - *Real estate*

Salary minimum: $25,000

Functions: Generalist, Middle Mgmt., Admin. Svcs., Benefits, Personnel, Training, Cash Mgmt., Credit

Industries: Generalist, Real Estate

Professional Associations: APPAC

Bryant & Company
PO Box 5171
Winston-Salem, NC 27113
(336) 723-7077
Email: info@bryantcompany.com
Web: www.bryantcompany.com

Description: Information Technology Search & Recruitment.

Key Contact:
Mr. David Bryant

Functions: IT

Industries: Generalist

Professional Associations: NCASP

Bryant Bureau Sales Recruiters
2435 Kimberly Rd Ste 110 N
Bettendorf, IA 52722
(563) 355-4411
Fax: (563) 355-3635
Email: bbureau@netexpress.net
Web: www.bbureau.com

Description: Recruiting and placing sales representatives with industrial, medical, office/computer and business services. Fortune 1000 companies. Local, regional, national. Over 300 offices and affiliates.

Key Contact - Specialty:
Mr. Douglas W. Ryan, President - *Sales, sales management*

Salary minimum: $35,000

Functions: Sales Mgmt.

Industries: Generalist

Professional Associations: IAPS, NAPS

Bryant Research
466 Old Hook Rd Ste 32
Emerson, NJ 07630
(201) 599-0590
Fax: (201) 599-2423
Email: resumes@bryantresearch.com

Description: Pharmaceutical industry research and
development executive recruitment. Primary
emphasis on physician and executive-level R&D
personnel. Also biostatistics, regulatory affairs,
clinical, data management and health
economics/outcomes.

Key Contact - Specialty:
Ms. Lisa Billotti, President - *Clinical research,
health outcomes, drug safety*

Salary minimum: $70,000

Functions: Generalist, Physicians, R&D

Industries: Generalist, Drugs Mfg., Pharm Svcs.

BSA Hospitality
7807 E Oak Shore Dr
Scottsdale, AZ 85258
(480) 483-5400
Fax: (480) 483-5401
Email: bsahospitality@home.com
Web: www.bsahospitality.com

Description: Nationwide hospitality executive
recruiters specializing in senior and mid-level
management positions. Retained search and
contingency recruiting. Serving hospitality
management companies, fine hotels, resorts, country
clubs, restaurants and attractions.

Key Contact - Specialty:
Ms. Bonne Smith, Founder/President - *Hospitality
recruiting*

Salary minimum: $80,000

Functions: Generalist

Industries: Hospitality, Hotels, Resorts, Clubs,
Restaurants

Professional Associations: AHMA

BSC Inc
6101 W Whispering Wind Dr
Glendale, AZ 85310-2714
(602) 524-8377
Fax: (623) 869-0198
Email: wesj@bscincorp.com
Web: www.bscincorp.com

Description: Information technology from
management through developers.

Key Contact:
Mr. Wes Johnson, PMP, PMP, President

Salary minimum: $35,000

Professional Associations: PMI

Networks: Top Echelon Network

btsn Inc
15 Samuel St
Kitchener, ON N2H 1N9
Canada
(877) 287-6462
(519) 569-7474
Email: search@btsn.com
Web: www.btsn.com

Description: We are a search and recruitment firm
specializing in biotechnology, telecommunications,
semi-conductor, and network industries.

Key Contact - Specialty:
Ms. Leslie Stallard, President - *Semiconductor*

Salary minimum: $95,000

Functions: General Mgmt., Mfg., Sales & Mktg.,
HR Mgmt., Finance, R&D, Engineering

Industries: Drugs Mfg., Medical Devices, Test,
Measure Equip., Electronic, Elec. Components,
Telecoms, Telephony, Wireless, Fiber Optic,
Networking, Comm. SW, Biotech

Networks: Top Echelon Network

The Buckley Group
7601 N Federal Hwy Ste 140B
Boca Raton, FL 33487
(561) 241-5010
Fax: (561) 241-5019
Email: consultants@buckleygroup.com
Web: www.buckleygroup.com

Description: We are known nationally as a leader in
placing sales & marketing people in the high-tech
fields. Mainly, PCs/mainframes, telecom, datacom
and software companies.

Key Contact - Specialty:
Mr. Daniel Buckley, President - *High tech sales &
marketing*

Salary minimum: $40,000

Functions: Generalist, Directors, Senior Mgmt.,
Middle Mgmt., Mktg. Mgmt., Sales Mgmt.,
Mgmt. Consultants, Int'l.

Industries: Generalist, Computer Equip., Consumer
Elect., Publishing, New Media, Telecoms,
Software

Branches:
140 S Broadway Ste 4
Pitman, NJ 08071
(856) 256-1844
Fax: (856) 256-1855
Key Contact - Specialty:
Mr. Doug Webster, Principal - *High technology,
sales & marketing*

15851 Dallas Pkwy Ste 600
Addison, TX 75001
(972) 490-1722
Fax: (214) 561-8690
Key Contact - Specialty:
Mr. John Kearney - *High tech sales & marketing*

Buckman/Enochs & Associates Inc
590 Enterprise Dr
Lewis Center, OH 43035
(614) 825-6215
Fax: (614) 825-6242
Email: senochs@buckmanenochs.com
Web: www.buckmanenochs.com

Description: We provide corporate search work on
national level. Our firm specializes in medical,
pharmaceutical, and biotech with an emphasis on
sales and marketing.

Key Contact - Specialty:
Mr. Steve Enochs, President - *Medical (sales &
marketing), pharmaceutical, biotech, sales &
marketing*

Salary minimum: $60,000

Functions: Sales & Mktg.

Industries: Drugs Mfg., Medical Devices,
Computer Equip., Consumer Elect., Pharm Svcs.,
Equip Svcs., Biotech, Healthcare

Networks: First Interview Network (FIN)

Buford Sims & Assocoiates Inc
(dba Capital Recruiting)
4445 N A1A Ste 234
Vero Beach, FL 32963
(561) 231-8650
Fax: (561) 231-8652
Email: crcbs@mindspring.com
Web: www.capitolrecruiting.com

Description: We specialize in the consumer
packaged good industry. We are an executive
recruiting firm that specializes in sales and

marketing. Our recruiting capabilities include: sales,
brand management, broker management, category
management, and beverage sales and operations
management.

Key Contact:
Mr. Buford Sims

Salary minimum: $65,000

Functions: Middle Mgmt., Sales & Mktg.,
Advertising, Mkt. Research, Minorities

Industries: Mfg., Food, Bev., Tobacco

Burchard & Associates
12977 N Outer Forty Dr Ste 315
St. Louis, MO 63141
(314) 878-2270
Fax: (314) 878-1337
Email: srb@exechunter.com
Web: www.exechunter.com

Description: Full-service retained search and
contingent practice. Over 20 years. in accounting &
financial recruitment experience. Extensive clientele
base covering all business sectors. St. Louis member
of AAFA.

Key Contact - Specialty:
Mr. Stephen Burchard, President - *Accounting &
finance*

Salary minimum: $60,000

Functions: Finance

Industries: Mfg., Wholesale, Retail, Telecoms, Real
Estate, Healthcare

Burke & Associates
(a division of The Westfield Group)
1010 Washington Blvd
Stamford, CT 06901
(203) 406-2301
Fax: (203) 406-2315
Email: resume@burkeandassociates.com
Web: www.westfieldgroup.com

Description: Our firm deals with high profile
corporate clients and top business school/Big 6/CPA
firm candidates.

Key Contact - Specialty:
Mr. T. Michael Burke, Managing Partner - *Finance,
operations technology*
Ms. Joanne C. Fiala, Managing Partner - *Human
resources*

Salary minimum: $70,000

Functions: Generalist, Senior Mgmt., Mfg.,
Materials, Sales & Mktg., HR Mgmt., Finance,
Mgmt. Consultants

Industries: Generalist, Food, Bev., Tobacco, Drugs
Mfg., Accounting, HR Services, Publishing,
Telecoms, Software

Professional Associations: IACPR

J Burke & Associates Inc
2000 E Lamar Blvd Ste 600
Arlington, TX 76006
(817) 588-3024
Fax: (817) 274-6763
Email: stoney@jburkeassoc.com
Web: www.jburkeassoc.com

Description: We have an excellent reputation and a
solid network of client companies, as well as
candidates; all projects are handled with confidence,
speed and professionalism. References available
upon request.

Key Contact - Specialty:
Mr. Stoney Burke, President - *Packaging, single
service*
Ms. Kaye Burke, Vice President - *Food industry,
packaging*
Ms. Gayle Smith, Associate - *Packaging, chemical*

Salary minimum: $35,000

Functions: Generalist, Senior Mgmt., Middle Mgmt., Production, Plant Mgmt., Mkt. Research, Mktg. Mgmt., Sales Mgmt.

Industries: Generalist, Food, Bev., Tobacco, Paper, Chemicals, Soap, Perf., Cosmtcs., Plastics, Rubber, Machine, Appliance

The Burke Group
63 Church St Ste 204
St. Catharines, ON L2R 3C4
Canada
(905) 641-3070
(888) 896-3618
Fax: (905) 641-0478
Email: tbg@theburkegroup.com
Web: www.theburkegroup.com

Description: We offer extensive HR expertise in executive recruitment, consulting, outplacement and outsourcing. We provide solutions in areas of assessment, training and development, temporary/contract staffing.

Key Contact - Specialty:
Ms. Anne Charette, CHRP, President - *Generalist*
Ms. Sandra Rooney, Executive Recruitment Specialist - *Generalist*

Functions: Generalist, Senior Mgmt., Plant Mgmt., Health Admin., HR Mgmt., Training, Engineering

Industries: Generalist, Energy, Utilities, Mfg., Finance, Services, Hospitality, Media, Communications, Government, Software, Biotech

Professional Associations: ACSESS, APRC, CAAP, HRPAO

David S Burt Associates
991 Dixon Cir
Billings, MT 59105-2209
(406) 245-9500
Fax: (406) 245-9570
Email: dburtsearch@home.com
Web: www.usaheadhunters.com

Description: We have over seventeen years of chemical industry experience nationwide. We have several exclusive agreements with large chemical companies. Our large database of candidates, our comprehensive nationwide network, and our recruiting capabilities maintain and increase our value to employers. While our national affiliations with the top chemical and environmental companies make us invaluable to our candidates.

Key Contact - Specialty:
Mr. David S. Burt, President - *Chemical, sales & marketing*

Salary minimum: $40,000

Functions: Generalist

Industries: Energy, Utilities, Food, Bev., Tobacco, Paper, Chemicals, Soap, Perf., Cosmtcs., Drugs Mfg., Plastics, Rubber, Paints, Petro. Products, Environmental Svcs., Haz. Waste

Networks: US Recruiters.com

Burton & Grove Inc
1600 Golf Rd Ste 1200
Rolling Meadows, IL 60008
(847) 981-7690
Fax: (847) 628-7907
Email: info@burtonandgrove.com
Web: www.burtonandgrove.com

Description: Based in the Chicago area, we complete searches throughout the U.S. and Canada. Primary focus is on sales and marketing positions within high-tech and select business-to-business clients.

Key Contact - Specialty:
Mr. Steve Crothers, Managing Director - *High tech, business to business (sales and marketing)*

Salary minimum: $70,000

Functions: General Mgmt., Senior Mgmt., Middle Mgmt., Sales & Mktg.

Industries: Services, Communications, Software

Business Answers Int'l
4440 PGA Blvd Ste 505
Palm Beach Gardens, FL 33410
(800) 583-4726
(561) 775-6110
Fax: (561) 775-0520
Email: info@plasticlink.com
Web: www.plasticlink.com

Description: Executive and sales recruitment into the plastics and related industries.

Key Contact - Specialty:
Mr. Richard Rappaport, President - *Plastics*
Mr. Walter Schnieder, Vice President - *Plastics*

Salary minimum: $35,000 ·

Functions: General Mgmt., Directors, Senior Mgmt., Middle Mgmt., Plant Mgmt., Mktg. Mgmt., Sales Mgmt.

Industries: Generalist, Chemicals, Plastics, Rubber

Business Partners Inc
1900 Land O'Lakes Blvd Ste 113
Lutz, FL 33549
(813) 948-1440
(877) 948-1440
Fax: (813) 948-1450
Email: bpijobs@aol.com
Web: www.businesspartnersinc.com

Description: Executive, professional and technical staffing specializing in MIS and data processing with particular emphasis on relational database, object oriented, open systems technology. Also, client requirements as requested.

Key Contact - Specialty:
Mr. Joe Johnson - *Information technology (all industries)*

Salary minimum: $30,000

Functions: Generalist, MIS Mgmt., Systems Analysis, Systems Dev., Systems Implem., Systems Support, Network Admin., DB Admin.

Industries: Generalist, New Media, Telecoms, Software

Networks: Top Echelon Network

Business Recruitment Worldwide
6700 France Ave S Ste 150
Edina, MN 55435
(952) 922-3288
Fax: (952) 926-9188
Email: info@brwsearch.com
Web: www.brwsearch.com

Description: We locate middle to senior-level professionals nationally. Focused search assignments are in retailing, e-retailing, merchandising, store line, replenishment, allocations, human resources, marketing, sales managers, training and development, high-tech and e-commerce.

Key Contact - Specialty:
Ms. Jodi B. Shamblott, Recruiter/Director of Research - *Retail, e-commerce*
Mr. Steve Kenady, Vice President - *Retail, human resources*

Salary minimum: $55,000

Functions: Generalist

Industries: Retail

Professional Associations: MAPS, NAPS, RON

Networks: Top Echelon Network

Business Solutions Worldwide Inc
35 Dorland Farm Ct
PO Box 122
Skillman, NJ 08558-0122
(908) 904-9685
Fax: (908) 904-9685
Email: jgonedes@worldnet.att.net

Description: A marketing focused organization, providing solutions to businesses of all sizes, while taking the time to help all candidates.

Key Contact - Specialty:
Ms. Marcy L. Pollack, Executive Vice President - *Human resource management*
Ms. Ellen G. Kusnetz, Vice President - *General, finance*
Mr. James T. Gonedes, President - *Sales & marketing*

Salary minimum: $50,000

Functions: Generalist

Industries: Generalist

Business Systems of America Inc
200 W Adams St Ste 2015
Chicago, IL 60606
(312) 849-9222
Fax: (312) 849-9260
Email: bsantana@bussysam.com
Web: www.bussysam.com

Description: We provide tested information technology professions to Chicago's Fortune 500 companies. We discover, empower and support the career of the best information technology professions in Chicago.

Key Contact - Specialty:
Mr. Bennett Santana, President - *Information technology professionals*
Mr. Lou Costabile, Account Manager/Recruiter - *Information technology professionals*

Salary minimum: $30,000

Functions: Generalist, IT, MIS Mgmt., Systems Analysis, Systems Dev., Systems Implem., Systems Support, Network Admin.

Industries: Generalist, HR Services

Professional Associations: CMBDC, NATSS

The Butlers Company Insurance Recruiters
3021 Egret Ter Ste 2-B
Safety Harbor, FL 34695-5340
(727) 725-1065
Fax: (727) 726-7125
Email: kbutler@topechelon.com
Web: www.butlerscompany.com

Description: Contingency and retained search of insurance technical through executive; actuarial, accounting, financial, underwriting, loss control, marketing, claims, administrative, DP and sales. Kirby Butler, CPC, previous president of Florida Assoc. (FAPS).

Key Contact - Specialty:
Mr. Kirby B. Butler, Jr., CPC, President - *Insurance executives, upper management, safety management, safety engineers*
Ms. Martha Butler, Secretary/Treasurer - *Insurance, technical, administrative*

Salary minimum: $30,000

Functions: Generalist

Industries: Insurance

Professional Associations: FAPS, NIRA

Networks: Top Echelon Network

Butterfield & Company Int'l Inc

608 Rock Cliff Rd
Boone, NC 28607
(828) 265-2890
Fax: (828) 265-0854
Email: resumes@butterfieldinternational.com
Web: www.butterfieldinternational.com

Description: Specialists in medical imaging and information systems industry, including modalities (CT, MRI, x-ray, ultrasound, nuclear medicine), PACS, image-guided surgery, and HIS/RIS systems.

Key Contact - Specialty:
Mr. N. Blair Butterfield, President - *Medical imaging, computing technologies*

Salary minimum: $50,000

Functions: Generalist

Industries: Medical Devices, Healthcare

Professional Associations: RON

Button Group

1608 Emory Cir
Plano, TX 75093
(972) 985-0619
Web: www.buttongroup.com

Description: Facilities design, engineering & construction, strong emphasis on managers & engineers and specialized services categories. Telecom, electronics, pharmaceuticals, bio-tech, foods, chemicals, nationwide

Key Contact - Specialty:
Mr. David R. Button, Principal - *Facility design, engineering, construction*
Ms. Dianne Vann, Principal - *Telecommunications, manufacturing*

Salary minimum: $60,000

Functions: Generalist, Directors, Senior Mgmt., Mktg. Mgmt., MIS Mgmt., Systems Implem., Engineering, Architects

Industries: Generalist, Construction, Drugs Mfg., Medical Devices, Test, Measure Equip., Telecoms, Wireless, Fiber Optic, Network Infrastructure, Software

Professional Associations: AICHE, AIPE, ASPE, CCIA, CTIA, IEEE, ISPE, NACORE, NCARB, NSPE, PCIA, TIA

Buxton & Associates

12501 CR 74
Eaton, CO 80615
(970) 454-2323
Fax: (970) 454-9122
Email: buxtongw@aol.com
Web: www.buxtonandassociates.com

Description: Our specialty is financial institutions in the Rocky Mountain Region. Most of our searches have been for presidents, senior lenders, commercial lenders, cashiers, and trust professionals.

Key Contact:
Mr. Gary Buxton, Principal

Salary minimum: $40,000

Functions: Finance

Industries: Banking

BVM Int'l Inc

PO Box 15073
Bradenton, FL 34280
(941) 792-2247
Fax: (941) 798-9351
Email: consultant@bvm.net
Web: www.bvm.net

Description: We are a national specialty, staffing firm providing retained and contingency searches in the automotive, consumer electronics, and telecommunications industries. We are specialists in quality assurance/continuous improvement, supply chain management, purchasing, supplier development, and materials management.

Key Contact:
Mr. Bill Van Mater, President

Salary minimum: $65,000

Functions: Middle Mgmt.

Industries: Mfg., Machine, Appliance, Motor Vehicles, Computer Equip., Consumer Elect., Telecoms, Fiber Optic

Professional Associations: APICS, ASQ, NAPM, NAPS, SAE

Thomas Byrne Associates

7 Melrose Dr
Farmington, CT 06032
(860) 676-2468
Fax: (800) 676-0272
Email: info@thomasbyrne.com
Web: www.thomasbyrne.com

Description: We are a financial and accounting recruitment firm focused on placement of former Big 5 CPAs and other high potential individuals. The firm has a second specialty focused on staffing high-end rotational programs with CPAs and MBAs talent being groomed for senior management.

Key Contact - Specialty:
Mr. Thomas Byrne, CPC, Principal - *Accounting and finance*
Ms. Carmela Campbell, Recruiter - *Accounting & finance*

Salary minimum: $50,000

Functions: Finance

Industries: Generalist

Professional Associations: CAPS, NAPS

C A I Personnel Search Group

PO Box 962
Brentwood, TN 37024
(615) 373-8263
(615) 373-4009
Fax: (615) 371-8215
Email: jobs@caipersonnel.com
Web: www.jobguide.net

Description: Recruiting for manufacturing and healthcare industries throughout the U.S.

Key Contact - Specialty:
Mr. P. Gene Cook, PHR, Consultant - *Administrative, technical, operations & senior managers (healthcare, manufacturing)*
Mr. Stephen Cook, CPC, Recruiting Manager - *Engineering, manufacturing*
Mrs. Diana Stewart, Recruiter - *Manufacturing, power engineering*
Mrs. Barbara Olsher, Recruiter - *Healthcare*
Mr. Lamar Durr, Recruiter - *Sales*

Salary minimum: $45,000

Functions: Generalist, Mfg., Quality, Healthcare, Sales Mgmt., HR Mgmt., Finance, IT, Engineering

Industries: Generalist, Construction, Mfg., Finance, Biotech, Healthcare

Professional Associations: NAPS, NAPS, TAPS, TAPS

C and P Marketing Ltd

285 Country Pointe Ct Ste 100
Wentzville, MO 63385
(636) 332-8877
Fax: (636) 639-9001
Email: pkrienke@mail.direcpc.com

Description: Eighteen years' exclusive representation of Midwest community banks in all types of lending positions, senior loan officers and chief executives.

Key Contact - Specialty:
Mr. Paul G. Krienke, President - *Community banking*

Salary minimum: $40,000

Functions: Credit

Industries: Agri., Forestry, Mining, Finance, Banking, Misc. Financial

C G & Company

8303 N Mopac Ste B-322
Austin, TX 78759
(512) 343-0848
Fax: (512) 343-5518
Email: cg@cgcompany.com
Web: www.cgcompany.com

Description: Our firm specializes in the placement of top level executives and managers, as well as professionals, in the information technology, engineering, and semi-conductor.

Key Contact:
Ms. Cathy George, President

Salary minimum: $80,000

Functions: Senior Mgmt., Sales & Mktg., CFO's, IT, Engineering

Industries: Energy, Utilities, Mfg., Computer Equip., Consumer Elect., Venture Cap., HR Services, E-commerce, IT Implementation, Communications, Wireless, Fiber Optic, Network Infrastructure, Software, HR SW, Mfg. SW, Networking, Comm. SW

Professional Associations: AESC

Networks: Top Echelon Network

Angeline Cadenhead Associates

48 Independence Blvd
Asheville, NC 28805
(828) 298-6741
Fax: (770) 234-6651
Email: acadenhead@earthlink.net
Web: www.med-jobs-match.com

Description: We offer nation-wide physician recruitment specializing in the southeast. We have an extensive network with other recruiting firms across the country for faster placement.

Key Contact - Specialty:
Mr. Angeline Cadenhead, BSN, President - *Physician recruiting*

Cadillac Associates

100 S Sunrise Way 353
Palm Springs, CA 92262
(760) 327-0920
(800) 619-4326
Fax: (760) 322-5699
Email: cadsearch@aol.com
Web: www.members.aol.com/cadsearch

Description: Impeccable service operating with specialized account executives. Strict confidentiality and prior consent assured. Seasoned veterans as search managers.

Key Contact - Specialty:
Mr. Dwight Hanna, President - *Healthcare, high technology, hospitality*
Mr. Casey Criste, Senior Partner - *Computer sciences*

Salary minimum: $50,000

Functions: Generalist

Industries: Drugs Mfg., Medical Devices, Retail, Finance, Services, Hospitality, Telecoms, Aerospace, Healthcare

Professional Associations: NAER, NALSC

Branches:
8306 Wilshire Blvd
PO Box 7036
Beverly Hills, CA 90211
(310) 327-0920
(800) 619-4326
Fax: (760) 322-5699
Email: cadsearch@aol.com
Key Contact:
Mr. Casey Christe
Mr. Charlie Crawford

Cadre Cache LLC
425 58th St
Brooklyn, NY 11220
(718) 492-2083
Email: cadrecache@cadrecache.com
Web: www.cadrecache.com

Description: We offer executive search for officer
level banking positions using a disciplined search
methodology, which combines the development of a
comprehensive search profile with original research
and regular communication with the hiring manager
to ensure efficient, appropriate results.

Key Contact - Specialty:
Ms. Kathleen Kargoll, Principal - *Financial*

Functions: Generalist

Industries: Finance, Banking, Invest. Banking,
Misc. Financial

Juliette Lang Cahn Executive Search
12 Beekman Pl
New York, NY 10022
(212) 371-0725

Description: Nationwide executive search for the
plastics industry utilizing 20 years of contacts with
high-level executives. Recruitment of technical,
marketing and sales professionals for leading
plastics companies.

Key Contact - Specialty:
Ms. Juliette Lang Cahn, President - *Extrusion,
plastics*

Salary minimum: $50,000

Functions: Generalist

Industries: Plastics, Rubber

Professional Associations: SPE

Caldwell Legal Recruiting Consultants
561 Atlantic Hwy Ste 100
Northport, ME 04849
(207) 338-9500
Fax: (207) 338-9502
Email: iplaw@caldwellrecruiting.com
Web: www.caldwellrecruiting.com

Description: We are a nationwide intellectual
property placement service. Our clients include both
law firms and the corporate sector. We place all
levels of attorneys from associate to chief patent
counsel positions.

Key Contact - Specialty:
Ms. Kate Caldwell, Principal - *Intellectual property
(attorneys & agents), biotech, computer, high tech
industries*

Functions: Generalist, Attorneys

Industries: Generalist, Legal

California Management Search
(a division of R Marsh & Associates Inc)
881 11th St PMB 117
Lakeport, CA 95453
(707) 263-6000
Fax: (707) 263-6800

Email: careers@cmsearch.net
Web: www.cmsearch.net

Description: We pride ourselves on prompt,
courteous service to our clients. Although most of
our placements are within the Western states, we do
offer service throughout the U.S. through the efforts
of our national network.

Key Contact - Specialty:
Mr. Norman R. Marsh, President - *Insurance,
healthcare*

Functions: Generalist

Industries: Finance, Accounting, Insurance,
Healthcare

Professional Associations: NIRA

California Search Agency Inc
2603 Main St Ste 120
Irvine, CA 92614-6232
(949) 475-0790
Fax: (949) 475-0796
Email: dcrane@jobagency.com
Web: www.jobagency.com

Description: Technical recruiting for small, medium
and large manufacturing and R&D (commercial,
industrial, aerospace and military). Firm specializes
in all disciplines of engineering and manufacturing
personnel.

Key Contact - Specialty:
Mr. Don Crane, President - *Engineering,
manufacturing*
Mr. Mike Baine, Manager - *Engineering,
manufacturing*

Salary minimum: $25,000

Functions: Generalist

Industries: Energy, Utilities, Construction, Mfg.,
Transportation, Equip Svcs., HR Services,
Environmental Svcs., Aerospace, Packaging,
Software, Biotech

Professional Associations: CSP

California Search Consultants Corp (CSC)
2103 El Camino Real
Oceanside, CA 92054
(760) 439-5511
Fax: (760) 439-0751
Email: csccorp@att.net

Description: We are a professional management
consulting firm that recruits people who design,
market, manufacture, and sell electronics from
components through complete systems. This
includes people in the semiconductor business,
telecommunications, networking, power electronics,
and some defense related work.

Key Contact - Specialty:
Mr. Marshall Mack, President - *Electronics,
telecommunications, engineers (BSEE, MSEE),
sales & marketing*

Salary minimum: $40,000

Functions: General Mgmt., Product Dev., Plant
Mgmt., Quality, Materials, Packaging, Sales &
Mktg., R&D, Engineering, Architects

Industries: Test, Measure Equip., Electronic, Elec.
Components, Digital, Wireless, Fiber Optic,
Defense, Packaging

Branches:
5 Cambridge Ctr
Cambridge, MA 02142-1493
(617) 520-1561

200 Park Ave Fl 32
New York, NY 10166
(212) 251-6140
Fax: (212) 251-6111
Web: www.cscconsulting.com

Key Contact:
Mr. Dieter Eisinger, Vice President

California Technology Staffing LLC
1048 Irvine Ave Ste 490
Newport Beach, CA 92660
(888) 879-2651
(949) 693-5999
Fax: (858) 391-3390
Email:
clientservices@californiatechnologystaffing.com
Web: www.californiatechnologystaffing.com

Description: Information technology staffing,
direct-hire and contract, database applications,
enterprise applications,(ERP), e-commerce, Oracle,
Java, C++, SQL, developers, DBAs, web
developers, system architects, data warehousing,
software engineers, programmers, Oracle ERP,
SAP, PeopleSoft, project managers, software quality
assurance, system/network administrators,
consultants.

Key Contact - Specialty:
Mr. Jerry Willenbring, Manager - *Information
technologies*

Salary minimum: $40,000

Functions: IT

Industries: Mfg., Wholesale, Finance, Mgmt.
Consulting, Hospitality, Media, Telecoms,
Software, Biotech, Healthcare

Professional Associations: CSP

The Call Center Group
(a division of J B Brown & Assoc)
820 Terminal Twr
Cleveland, OH 44113
(216) 696-2525
Fax: (216) 696-5825
Email: info@thecallcentergroup.com
Web: www.thecallcentergroup.com

Description: We offer management recruiting for
the call center industry.

Key Contact:
Mr. Kevin O'Neil, Vice President/Director

Salary minimum: $40,000

Functions: Generalist, General Mgmt., Directors,
Senior Mgmt., Middle Mgmt., Direct Mktg.,
Customer Svc.

Industries: Generalist

Callos Personnel Services
5083 Market St
Youngstown, OH 44512
(800) 4-CALLOS
(330) 788-4001
Fax: (330) 783-3966
Email: ytown@callos.com
Web: www.callos.com

Description: Ability to access a national pool of
talent and placement expertise to help you select the
best possible candidate, in the right location.
Experienced staff with the technical capability to
perform effectively. Has 350+ offices, computer
linked, covering USA, Canada, Europe and the
Pacific Rim with specialists in nearly every career
field.

Key Contact:
Mr. Eric Sutton, Vice President-Search/Recruiting
Mr. John G. Callos, CEO
Mr. Thomas Walsh, President

Salary minimum: $25,000

Functions: Generalist, General Mgmt., Mfg.,
Materials, Engineering

Industries: Generalist, Mfg.

Networks: National Personnel Assoc (NPA)

Branches:
118 S Arlington Rd
Akron, OH 44306
(330) 773-2200
Fax: (330) 773-4108

150 Springside Dr Ste C-300
Akron, OH 44333
(800) 344-7091
(330) 665-4400
Fax: (330) 665-4474
Email: akron@callos.com
Key Contact:
Mr. Daniel Wismar, Division Manager

4111 Bradley Cir Ste 100 A
Canton, OH 44718
(330) 649-9350
Fax: (330) 649-9343

136 S Broadway Ave
Salem, OH 44460
(330) 332-1991
(800) 865-6876
Fax: (330) 332-1988

1435 State Rt 303 Streetsboro Plz
Streetsboro, OH 44241
(330) 626-9800
Fax: (330) 626-9731

4087 Youngstown Warren Rd
Warren, OH 44484
(330) 369-6800
Fax: (330) 369-6824

Calver Associates Inc
PO Box 238
Nutrioso, AZ 85932
(520) 339-1924
Fax: (520) 339-4546
Email: jon@plasticsonly.com
Web: www.plasticsonly.com

Description: We offer plastics recruitment nationwide. Our specialties Include: injection, blow molding, thermoforming, and extrusion industries. We place in technical and production supervisory position. We have sixteen years of experience. We provide focused Value added services.

Key Contact:
Mr. Jon Calver, Owner

Functions: General Mgmt.

Industries: Plastics, Rubber

Networks: Top Echelon Network

Camacho Group Inc
PO Box 221
Lake Oswego, OR 97034
(503) 981-4969
Fax: (503) 981-4970
Email: camachogrp@aol.com

Description: Our mission is to provide strategic services and superior customer support to the public and private sector by recruiting and placing only the most highly qualified business professionals.

Key Contact - Specialty:
Ms. Lourdes M. Camacho, President/CEO - *High technology*
Ms. Carmen Bland, Senior Recruiter - *Systems, network, engineering*

Salary minimum: $45,000

Functions: Generalist, IT

Industries: Generalist, Energy, Utilities, Transportation, Finance, Aerospace, Software, Healthcare

Professional Associations: SAO

The Cambridge Group Ltd
1175 Post Rd E
Westport, CT 06880
(203) 226-4243
Fax: (203) 226-3856
Email: info@cambridgegroup.com
Web: www.cambridgegroup.com

Description: Our seasoned staff and computerized database affords our clients the most efficient and expedient searches available. Our specialties include physicians, pharmaceutical, finance, information systems, healthcare, and general management.

Key Contact:
Mr. Alfred Judge, President
Mr. Mike Salvagno, Executive Vice President

Salary minimum: $60,000

Functions: Generalist, Senior Mgmt., Physicians, CFO's, MIS Mgmt., Systems Implem., Network Admin., DB Admin.

Industries: Generalist, Drugs Mfg., Misc. Mfg., Accounting, Mgmt. Consulting, Software, Healthcare

Professional Associations: CAPS, DPMA, NAPR, NAPS

Branches:
291 McLaws Cir
Williamsburg, VA 23185
(757) 565-1150
Fax: (757) 565-0391
Email: fdisalvo@widowmaker.com
Key Contact - Specialty:
Mr. Fred DiSalvo, VP/Managing Director - *Search*

M Campbell Associates
PO Box 41022
Philadelphia, PA 19127
(215) 482-1790
(781) 934-7890
Email: mcampbel@bellatlantic.net
Web: www.mcampbell.net

Description: We are the premier executive recruiting firm for the placement of finance professionals nationwide from two offices: Philadelphia and outside Boston. Our particular expertise in the recruitment of treasury and cash management professionals has earned us national recognition from every segment of finance - corporate, banking, and financial services.

Key Contact:
Mr. Martin Campbell
Ms. Donna K. Campbell

Functions: Senior Mgmt., Middle Mgmt., Product Dev., Sales Mgmt., Finance, CFO's, Cash Mgmt., Taxes, M&A, Risk Mgmt.

Industries: Generalist, Banking, Invest. Banking

Professional Associations: NBN, RON, TMA

Networks: National Banking Network (NBN)

Branches:
PO Box 2469
Duxbury, MA 02331
(781) 934-7890
Fax: (781) 934-7893
Email: mcampel@adelphia.net
Key Contact:
Mr. Martin Campbell, Principal

Campbell, Edgar Inc
4388 49th St
Delta, BC V4K 2S7
Canada
(604) 946-8535
(604) 321-8515
Fax: (604) 946-2384
Email: info@retailcareers.com
Web: www.retailcareers.com

Description: We are the largest recruitment firm in Canada committed to the retail industry. Placement of only highest quality personnel throughout the country. Additional services such as mystery shopping, store auditing and staff training available.

Key Contact - Specialty:
Ms. Elaine Hay, President - *Retail executives*
Mr. Mike Reeves, Consultant - *Store operations, buying, store management*
Ms. Karen Arbas, Senior Consultant - *Store operations, outside sales, store management*
Ms. Rosalie Wald, Recruitment Manager - *Store operations, purchasing, store management*

Salary minimum: $20,000

Functions: Generalist

Industries: Generalist

Professional Associations: ACSESS, RCC, RMABC, WEC

Branches:
1-9059 Shaughnessy St
Vancouver, BC V6P 6R9
Canada
(604) 321-8515
Fax: (604) 321-8541
Email: info@retailcareers.com
Key Contact - Specialty:
Ms. Elaine Hay, President - *Retail store operations, store management*

CanMed Consultants Inc
659 Mississauga Cres
Mississauga, ON L5H 1Z9
Canada
(905) 274-0707
Fax: (905) 274-0067
Email: mraheja@canmed.com
Web: www.canmed.com

Description: Consultants to executives and professionals in the Healthcare sector. Services include executive and professional search, locum/contract employees and an online careers service for the Canadian market.

Key Contact - Specialty:
Dr. Marc C. Raheja, President - *Healthcare sector, senior management*

Salary minimum: $50,000

Functions: Healthcare

Industries: Generalist

Cannibal Central
628 Summer View Cir
Encinitas, CA 92024
(760) 944-9535
Fax: (760) 942-0611
Email: mlittle@cannibalcentral.com
Web: www.cannibalcentral.com

Description: We are a boutique search firm specializing in the building/construction industry. With 14 years of hands on industry experience, we are able to place mid to senior level executive in all positions within the industry.

Key Contact:
Ms. Marcie Little, Executive Recruiter

Salary minimum: $60,000

Functions: Generalist

Industries: Construction

J P Canon Associates
225 Broadway Ste 3602
New York, NY 10007-3001
(212) 233-3131
Fax: (212) 233-0457
Email: jobs@jpcanon.com
Web: www.jpcanon.com

Description: We specialize in the nationwide recruitment of supply chain management, purchasing, e-Commerce, logistics, distribution, collaborative planning forecasting and replenishment [CPFR], customer relationship management [CRM], production planning/inventory management, and user interface systems professionals.

Key Contact - Specialty:
Mr. James Rohan, Partner - *Supply chain management*
Ms. Paula Blumenthal, Partner - *Materials, logistics management*
Mr. Kevin Rohan - *Purchasing*

Salary minimum: $40,000

Functions: Materials, Purchasing, Materials Plng., Distribution, Packaging, Customer Svc., Systems Implem., Mgmt. Consultants

Industries: Generalist

Professional Associations: APICS, CLM, IABF, IIE, IOPP

Networks: Inter-City Personnel Assoc (IPA)

Canyon Consulting Inc
4 Ohio St
New Braunfels, TX 78130
(830) 608-9199
(830) 620-5671
Fax: (830) 608-1639
Email: batwood@canyoncg.com

Description: The recruiters have many years of experience hiring and managing the same type professionals they now recruit. The recruiters are degreed engineers.

Key Contact - Specialty:
Mr. Bob Atwood, President - *Manufacturing*
Mr. Paul Berry, Recruiter - *Quality, regulatory*

Salary minimum: $50,000

Functions: Generalist, Senior Mgmt., Middle Mgmt., Mfg., Materials, Budgeting

Industries: Generalist, Medical Devices, Metal Products, Machine, Appliance, Consumer Elect., Test, Measure Equip., Misc. Mfg.

Professional Associations: ASQ

Capitol Staffing Inc
460 Briarwood Dr Ste 110
Jackson, MS 39206
(601) 957-1755
Fax: (601) 957-3880
Email: capstaffing@earthlink.net
Web: www.capitolstaffing.com

Description: We have built relationships with Jackson area businesses for over 20 years in the telecom- munications, healthcare, legal, financial services, and computer science industries. Accordingly, we attract job applicants with a variety of backgrounds, experience, and skill sets. This enables us to provide you with top-notch candidates from which to select.

Key Contact - Specialty:
Ms. Carolyn Harrison, CPC, President - *Administrative, sales, accounting, IT, engineering*

Sally Caplan & Associates
1420 NW Gilman Blvd Ste 2292
Issaquah, WA 98027
(425) 378-0975
Email: careers@nwlink.com

Description: We are a high technology executive recruiting firm with expertise in enterprise software and e-Commerce. We focus exclusively on sales, marketing, technical sales, professional services, and consultants. Our placements are throughout

North America. We place from senior executives to individual contributors.

Key Contact - Specialty:
Ms. Sally Caplan, President - *High technology*

Salary minimum: $75,000

Functions: Generalist, Directors, Senior Mgmt., Middle Mgmt., Mkt. Research, Mktg. Mgmt., Sales Mgmt., Systems Implem.

Industries: Generalist, Software

Capricorn Search Group LLC
101 West Ave
PO Box 458
Jenkintown, PA 19046
(215) 886-2519
Fax: (610) 896-6958
Email: mindy@capricornsearch.com
Web: www.capricornsearch.com

Description: Our group specializes in the recruitment of accounting and financial professionals. We provide executive search with a personal touch.

Key Contact:
Ms. Mindy Poorman, President

Salary minimum: $60,000

Functions: Senior Mgmt., Finance

Industries: Generalist

The Caradyne Group
752 Blanding Blvd Ste 118
Orange Park, FL 32065
(904) 298-1294
(904) 298-1295
Fax: (904) 298-1296
Email: info@pcsjobs.com
Web: www.pcsjobs.com

Description: Serving the telecommunications industry. We recruit in engineering, sales, marketing, executive-level positions.

Key Contact:
Mr. Tony Martin, Vice President

Salary minimum: $55,000

Functions: Generalist

Industries: Electronic, Elec. Components, E-commerce, Media, Communications, Software, Industry Specific SW, Marketing SW

Networks: Top Echelon Network

Card Resource Group Inc
2155 Second Concession W
Lynden, ON L0R 1T0
Canada
(519) 647-2199
Fax: (519) 647-2099
Email: daina@cardresourcegroup.com
Web: www.cardresourcegroup.com

Description: We are a management and executive search firm servicing the US credit card industry and related industries. We have expertise in marketing, modeling, product management, database management, credit policy, risk management, collections, customer service, operations, and sales.

Key Contact - Specialty:
Ms. Andria Case, Director - *Credit card, marketing, operations, credit, sales*
Ms. Daina Di Veto, Managing Director - *Credit card, marketing, operations, decision management, payment system*

Salary minimum: $65,000

Functions: General Mgmt., Quality, Sales & Mktg., Credit, Risk Mgmt., DB Admin., Mgmt. Consultants

Industries: Banking, Misc. Financial, New Media, Call Centers

Professional Associations: NBN

Networks: National Banking Network (NBN)

Branches:
947 E Johnstown Rd
PMB 247
Columbus, OH 43230
(614) 475-7745
(519) 647-2199
Fax: (519) 647-2099
Email: daina@creditcardrecruiter.com
Web: www.creditcardrecruiter.com
Key Contact - Specialty:
Ms. Daina Di Veto, Managing Director - *Credit card, process improvement, operations, marketing, risk management*

Career & Business Services
142 Rte 306
Monsey, NY 10952
(845) 371-5207
Fax: (845) 425-8053
Email: cbspharma@hotmail.com
Web: www.cbspharma.com

Description: We were founded by a group of pharmaceutical professionals and are committed to fulfilling the challenging demands of corporate recruiting for the pharmaceutical, biotechnology and healthcare industries. Servicing the business and scientific divisions.

Key Contact - Specialty:
Dr. Leonard J. Bradley, Ph.D., President - *Pharmaceutical, biotechnology*
Mr. Yonah Koenig, Account Executive - *Pharmaceutical, biotechnology*
Mr. Ben Miller, Account Executive - *Pharmaceutical, biotechnology*
Ms. Debbra Fisher, Account Executive - *Pharmaceutical, biotechnology*
Ms. Sonia Berman, Account Executive - *Pharmaceutical, biotechnology*

Salary minimum: $100,000

Functions: Generalist, General Mgmt., Mfg., Materials, Healthcare, Sales & Mktg., Finance, R&D

Industries: Generalist, Drugs Mfg., Medical Devices, Wholesale, Biotech

Professional Associations: CRS, HBA

Career Advantage Personnel
1215 E Airport Dr Ste 125
Ontario, CA 91761
(909) 466-9232
Fax: (909) 948-1165
Email: info@careeradvantage.net
Web: www.careeradvantage.net

Description: Executive search, placement and career coaching.

Key Contact:
Ms. Brynda Woods, President

Functions: Generalist

Industries: Generalist

Professional Associations: NAWBO

Career Alternatives Executive Search
1519 N Lakeshore Dr
Harbor Springs, MI 49740
(231) 526-9900
Email: pat@careeralt.com
Web: www.careeralt.com

Description: We are an executive search firm specializing in the sales and marketing areas. Our primary clients are consumer product companies.

We have a second that recruits in the medical and biotech industries.

Key Contact - Specialty:
Mr. Patrick J. Burns, President - *Sales*
Mr. Timothy Sepesy, General Manager - *Medical, bio tech*

Salary minimum: $50,000

Functions: General Mgmt., Sales & Mktg., Mkt. Research, Mktg. Mgmt., Sales Mgmt.

Industries: Generalist, Food, Bev., Tobacco, Textiles, Apparel, Paper, Soap, Perf., Cosmtcs., Drugs Mfg., Medical Devices, Biotech

---

Career Center Inc
194 Passaic St
Hackensack, NJ 07601
(800) 227-3379
Fax: (201) 342-1776
Email: barry@careercenterinc.com
Web: www.careercenterinc.com

Description: We are a multi-office staffing firm.

Key Contact:
Mr. Barry Franzino,Jr., CPC, CTS, President

Functions: General Mgmt., Admin. Svcs., Materials, Nurses, Sales & Mktg., HR Mgmt., Finance, Minorities

Industries: Generalist, Food, Bev., Tobacco, Healthcare, Hospitals, Long-term Care

Professional Associations: EMA, NAPS, NJSA

Career Choice Inc
1 Purlieu Pl Ste 240
Winter Park, FL 32792
(407) 679-5150
Fax: (407) 679-0998
Email: resabase@aol.com

Description: Our success is driven by the research capability to attract top talent for our clients. Our growth is accomplished through innovative strategies, results-oriented associates, quality services and personal attention to detail.

Key Contact - Specialty:
Ms. Colleen Herrick, President/Partner - *Hospitality, marketing, finance, research & development*
Mr. Ray McArdle, Partner - *Hospitality*

Salary minimum: $45,000

Functions: Generalist

Industries: Accounting, HR Services, Hospitality, Hotels, Resorts, Clubs, Restaurants, Entertainment

---

Career Concepts
(also known as MRI of Noblesville)
17677 Cumberland Rd
Noblesville, IN 46060
(317) 773-7590
Fax: (317) 773-7551
Email: arnie@mrnvc.com
Web: www.mrnvc.com

Description: Our firm is an exclusive executive search firm servicing the PEO industry. Our years of experience in staffing for the PEO industry are unparalleled. We take the time to know your needs, and we have the resources to match you with the highest potential candidates. Contact us today to take the first step toward matching the best talent with the best companies!

Key Contact:
Mr. Arnie Eastburn, Managing Director
Mrs. Joann Eastburn, Office Manager
Mrs. Amber Campbell, Account Executive
Mrs. Kim DeVaney, Internal Project Coordinator
Mrs. Keri Burton, Project Coordinator

Professional Associations: NAPEO

Career Consociates Inc
220 Montgomery Penthouse Ste
San Francisco, CA 94104
(415) 398-3894
Email: sharron@ccistaffing.com
Web: www.ccistaffing.com

Description: Our company's secret to success has been our unwavering commitment to learn and care about each of client's and candidate's needs. Successful staffing is our first priority. Doing this and doing it well is what our firm is about because we pride ourselves on our ability to match clients and candidates. We don't just fill jobs; we match people, skills and personalities.

Key Contact:
Ms. Sharron Long, President
Ms. Carol Foster, Recruiter
Ms. Paula Sharpe, Recrutier
Ms. Elaine Halnan, Recruiter
Ms. June Kerschman, Recruiter

Professional Associations: CSP

Career Consulting Group Inc
1100 Summer St
Stamford, CT 06905
(203) 975-8800
Fax: (203) 975-8808
Email: ccg@ccginteractive.com
Web: www.ccginteractive.com

Description: Marketing specialists in market research, decision support, marketing information industry, direct response marketing, database modeling, brand sales analysis, product management, marketing modeling, category management, trade marketing.

Key Contact:
Mr. Gerald Kanovsky, Chairman - *Market research, marketing information, marketing modeling*
Ms. Marlene Kanovsky, President

Salary minimum: $50,000

Functions: Mkt. Research

Industries: Food, Bev., Tobacco, Soap, Perf., Cosmtcs., Drugs Mfg., Retail, Finance, Banking, Advertising, New Media, Communications

Professional Associations: CAPS

Networks: First Interview Network (FIN)

Career Consulting Services Inc (CCS)
PO Box 330
Yellow Jacket, CO 81335
(970) 562-HIRE x21
Fax: (970) 562-3021
Email: kcb@careerconsulting.com
Web: www.careerconsulting.com

Description: Our firm specializes in the employee benefits and retirement services industry placing executive level to entry level candidates coast to coast. We provide both contingency and retained search services. Our relational recruiting philosophy enables us to successfully establish, build and maintain long-term partnerships with our clients and candidates alike.

Key Contact - Specialty:
Ms. Katherine Bredemeier, President - *Employee benefits and retirement services*

Salary minimum: $25,000

Functions: Generalist

Industries: Finance

Career Counseling Inc (CCI)
(also known as CCI Executive Search)
8260 Hwy 81
Owensboro, KY 42301
(270) 785-1100
Fax: (270) 785-1104
Email: headhunter@job4u.com
Web: www.ccisearch.com

Description: We are a privately owned, quality-driven executive search firm that has national and international search capabilities. CCI is an active member of the National Personnel Associates Global Network.

Key Contact - Specialty:
Mr. Steven J. Young, President - *Electromechanical, chemical, mechanical engineering, store fixtures*
Ms. Paula G. Young, CFO - *Plastic, paper & pulp, converting, executive, finance & accounting*

Salary minimum: $35,000

Functions: Generalist, Senior Mgmt., Mfg., Sales & Mktg.

Industries: Mfg., Lumber, Furniture, Plastics, Rubber, Metal Products, Non-classifiable

Networks: National Personnel Assoc (NPA)

Career Development Associates
6330 McLeod Dr Ste 1
Las Vegas, NV 89120
(702) 505-9CDA
(702) 798-0744
Fax: (702) 798-0385
Email: cda1v@cda1v.com
Web: www.cda1v.com

Description: Customized searches and placement in the gaming, hospitality and related industries. Our professionals have excellent contacts and relationships within these fields. Above all confidentiality is guaranteed.

Key Contact:
Mr. Kevin Courtney, CEO
Mr. John Granville, CFO

Salary minimum: $35,000

Functions: Generalist

Industries: Generalist

Career Development Center
(also known as Corporate Connections of Pittsburgh)
5743 Bartlett St
Pittsburgh, PA 15217
(412) 422-2083
Fax: (412) 422-9540
Email: jpdconnect@aol.com

Description: We are consultants in executive search assisting client organizations in identifying and attracting qualified professionals and mid to upper-level managers for specific opportunities.

Key Contact:
Mr. Joe D'Anna, Key Contact

Salary minimum: $50,000

Professional Associations: IPMA, PHRA

Career Enterprises
32125 Solon Rd Ste 160
Solon Marquis Bldg
Solon, OH 44139
(440) 914-1200
Email: info@careerenterprises.com
Web: www.careerenterprises.com

Description: Privately owned contingency and executive search firm. Fully automated national database including access to Internet, capable of management and senior executive-level search as well as staff technical placement.

Key Contact:
Mr. Stuart Taylor, President

Salary minimum: $50,000

Functions: IT

Industries: Generalist

Networks: National Personnel Assoc (NPA)

Career Forum Inc
350 Indiana St Ste 500
Golden, CO 80401
(303) 279-9200
Fax: (303) 279-9296
Email: inquiries@careerforum.com
Web: www.careerforum.com

Description: Executive search consultants specializing in sales, sales management, technical and management positions in high-growth industries including: telecom, software, engineering, IT, e-commerce and direct mail. Other related positions include entry level through Senior VP. We are involved in local, regional and national searches.

Key Contact:
Mr. Stan Grebe, CPC, President
Mr. Kevin Hahn, CPC, National Account Manager - *Sales, sales management, marketing, management, telecommunications*
Ms. Nikki Monnig, Manager of Operations
Mr. David Young, CPC, Senior Account Executive - *Technical sales, technical sales management, construction, telecommunications, contract services*
Ms. Marlene Adzema, Account Manager - *Sales, management, technical*
Ms. Heather Seiden, Account Executive - *Sales, management, technical*
Mrs. Trina Watson, Account Executive
Ms. Heather Albertson, Research Manager

Functions: Generalist

Industries: Food, Bev., Tobacco, Lumber, Furniture, Paper, Medical Devices, Plastics, Rubber, Computer Equip., Consumer Elect., Test, Measure Equip., Electronic, Elec. Components, Telecoms

Professional Associations: JLD, NAPS

Career Image Inc
12784 Panhandle Rd
Hampton, GA 30228
(770) 897-9115
Fax: (770) 897-9533
Email: theheadhunter@prodigy.net

Description: We are a generalist firm specializing in the retail and insurance industries. We also have a research division, in which we bill hourly, and this division is designed to supplement a client's classified advertising program.

Key Contact - Specialty:
Mr. Ellison C. Day, President - *Retail*
Mr. Tony Upchurch, Account Executive - *Retail*
Mr. Ken Leggett, Account Executive - *Retail, grocery*
Ms. Sherri Hunter, Account Executive - *Retail, insurance*
Ms. Betty Rebarick, Account Executive - *Insurance*
Ms. Peggy Mack, Account Executive - *Retail*

Salary minimum: $30,000

Functions: Middle Mgmt.

Industries: Retail, Insurance

Career Images
PO Box 1777
Palm Harbor, FL 34682
(727) 786-9334
Fax: (727) 786-9235
Email: careerimages@tbi.net

Description: We are a national recruiting and search firm specializing in the placement of environmental health, safety and engineering professionals for all major industrial corporations.

Key Contact - Specialty:
Ms. Deborah J. Hunkins, Principal - *Environmental, safety, engineering, ergonomics, health safety*

Salary minimum: $35,000

Functions: Generalist, Quality, Nurses, HR Mgmt., Engineering, Environmentalists

Industries: Generalist, Food, Bev., Tobacco, Paper, Chemicals, Medical Devices, Plastics, Rubber, Metal Products

Networks: Inter-City Personnel Assoc (IPA)

Career Management Group LLC
434 Ridgedale Ave
PMB 11-165
East Hanover, NJ 07936
(973) 428-5239
Fax: (973) 428-5084
Email: careermanage@msn.com
Web: www.careermgtgroup.com

Description: We offer permanent positions in a wide variety of industries. Company offers strong focus in areas of computers, engineering, technical, management, accounting, finance, insurance, legal, sales, marketing, administrative, customer service and human resources.

Key Contact:
Ms. Toni Donofrio, Managing Member

Salary minimum: $30,000

Functions: Generalist

Industries: Finance, Accounting, Telecoms, Telephony, Aerospace, Insurance, Software, Accounting SW, HR SW, Mfg. SW

Career Marketing Associates Inc
7100 E Belleview Ave Ste 102
Greenwood Village, CO 80111-1634
(303) 779-8890
Fax: (303) 779-8139
Email: cma@cmagroup.com
Web: www.cmagroup.com

Description: Since 1968 our only business has been to provide capable personnel to companies nationwide. Each CMA recruiter specializes in a field utilizing his or her background.

Key Contact - Specialty:
Mr. Jan Sather, President
Mr. Terry Leyden - *Toxicology, regulatory affairs*
Mr. Chip Doro, Vice President - *Technical sales, marketing*

Salary minimum: $35,000

Functions: Generalist, Product Dev., Production, MIS Mgmt., Systems Analysis, Systems Dev., Systems Support

Industries: Generalist, Medical Devices, Computer Equip., Test, Measure Equip., Telecoms, Software, Biotech

Networks: National Personnel Assoc (NPA)

Career Profiles
84 Pleasant St
PO Box 4430
Portsmouth, NH 03802
(603) 433-3355
Fax: (603) 433-8678
Email: jobnexus@aol.com

Description: We place individuals with sales, sales management and marketing backgrounds in medical, pharmaceutical, publishing and industrial sales positions. We also place professionals in other disciplines as well.

Key Contact - Specialty:
Ms. Leanne P. Gray, CPC - *Sales*
Mr. Norman G. Gray, RN, CPC - *Sales*

Functions: Sales Mgmt.

Industries: Generalist

Professional Associations: NNEAPS

Career Search Associates
12289 Stratford Dr Ste B
Clive, IA 50325
(515) 440-5600
Fax: (515) 440-0963
Email: kitte@careersearchassoc.com
Web: www.careersearchassoc.com

Description: We are a client-driven, specialized search firm with each recruiter focusing on separate areas of expertise. CSA does recruitment on both a local and national level. Our areas of specialization include: accounting, administrative support, information systems, transportation/logistics, and sales.

Key Contact:
Ms. Kitte Noble, Sales Recruiter
Ms. Traci Shepley, Recruiter - *Information technology*
Ms. Cheryl Campbell, Recruiter - *Transportation, logistics, manufacturing*
Ms. Lorie Quarberg, Recruiter - *Accounting, finance*
Ms. Tami Ruppel, Recruiter - *Administrative*
Ms. Tammy Cline, CPC, President, Owner

Salary minimum: $25,000

Functions: Admin. Svcs., Mfg., Distribution, Sales & Mktg., Sales Mgmt., Finance, IT

Industries: Generalist

Networks: Top Echelon Network

Career Search Consultants llc
955 W Chandler Blvd Ste 11
Chandler, AZ 85225
(480) 814-0855
Fax: (480) 814-0599
Email: paul@cscrecruiters.com
Web: www.cscrecruiters.com

Description: A specialty search firm focused on positions in three main areas: paint, coatings and allied chemicals, the wireless telecommunications, and civil engineering and design. We recruit pro-actively, directly contacting candidates rather than advertising.

Key Contact - Specialty:
Mr. Paul Jentlie, President - *Paint, coatings, allied chemicals*
Mr. Chuck Jentlie, Vice President-Sales - *Wireless telecommunications*

Functions: Generalist, Product Dev., Production, Distribution, Sales Mgmt., R&D, Engineering, Architects

Industries: Energy, Utilities, Construction, Mfg., Chemicals, Paints, Petro. Products, Media, Telecoms, Environmental Svcs., Haz. Waste, Packaging, Real Estate

Professional Associations: ASCE, FSCT, NACE, SSPC

Networks: Top Echelon Network

Career Search Group
1301 Seminole Blvd Ste 128
Largo, FL 33770
(727) 586-2892
Fax: (727) 584-6323
Email: careersearchgroup@hotmail.com

Description: Why us? We offer 20 years of professional recruiting in the medical field on a national basis, specializing in sales, sales management, marketing and product management. We offer the highest degree of professionalism, which is reflected in our closing success rate of over 80%.

Key Contact - Specialty:
Mr. Tony Manatine, President, Medical Recruiter - *Medical sales & marketing, management*
Mr. Brett Searles, Medical Recruiter - *Medical sales, marketing, management*

Functions: General Mgmt., Senior Mgmt., Healthcare, Sales & Mktg., Sales Mgmt.

Industries: Drugs Mfg., Medical Devices, Consumer Elect., Advertising, Telecoms, Biotech, Healthcare

Career Search Inc
PO Box 97007
Raleigh, NC 27624
(919) 789-4866
Fax: (919) 789-4865
Email: careersearch@horizons.net

Description: Our major strength is the integrity of our staff. We have assembled a team of professionals who objectively represent our corporate clients. Each has extensive experience and training and is well equipped to achieve success in the demanding role of a search consultant.

Key Contact - Specialty:
Mr. Ron Burton, President - *Manufacturing, purchasing, materials, quality, engineering*

Salary minimum: $50,000

Functions: Generalist, Production, Plant Mgmt., Quality, Productivity, Purchasing, Materials Plng., Engineering

Industries: Generalist, Plastics, Rubber, Metal Products, Machine, Appliance, Motor Vehicles, Consumer Elect., Test, Measure Equip., Misc. Mfg.

Career Solutions
12749 Red Fox Ct
St. Louis, MO 63043
(314) 576-9700
Fax: (314) 878-0006
Email: foodcareers@aol.com

Description: National food industry specialization. We focus on placements in sales, marketing, R&D, broker management and purchasing. Industries: meat, food ingredients, nutrition, flavors, dairy and beverage.

Key Contact - Specialty:
Mr. Larry Rattner, President - *Food ingredients, sales & marketing, management, R&D, flavors*

Salary minimum: $40,000

Functions: General Mgmt., Directors, Senior Mgmt., Middle Mgmt., Product Dev., Purchasing, Sales & Mktg., Mkt. Research, Mktg. Mgmt., Sales Mgmt.

Industries: Mfg.

Professional Associations: IFT

Career Staffing Int'l Inc
PO Box 0013
Morrison, CO 80465-0013
(303) 697-1982
Fax: (303) 697-3021
Email: career-staff@career-staff.com
Web: www.career-staff.com

Description: Industry: human resources, executive administration, management, finance, operations, sales and marketing, health and medical.

Key Contact - Specialty:
Ms. Judie K. King, CEO - *CFO, generalist, human resources, senior management*

Functions: Generalist, Senior Mgmt., Middle Mgmt., Health Admin., Direct Mktg., CFO's, M&A

Industries: Generalist, Energy, Utilities, Invest. Banking, Misc. Financial, HR Services, Publishing, Telecoms

Professional Associations: CHRA

CareerConnections USA Inc
12827 Westledge Ln
St. Louis, MO 63131
(314) 909-8510
(314) 909-7011
Fax: (314) 909-8513
Email: deb@careerconnectionsusa.com
Web: www.careerconnectionsusa.com

Description: Medical recruitment firm specializing in the placement of sales, management and applications personnel in radiology and information technology.

Key Contact - Specialty:
Mrs. Debra Hill, President
Mr. Brian Hill, Partner - *Medical sales and management*

Functions: Generalist, Sales & Mktg.

Industries: Medical Devices, Software, Biotech, Healthcare

Careers First Inc
(also known as CEO Services Inc)
305 U S Rte 130
Cinnaminson, NJ 08077-3398
(856) 786-0004
(856) 786-3334
Email: info@careersfirst.com
Web: www.careersfirst.com

Description: Outsource your difficult or sensitive technical searches to a reliable, high performance, modest fee resource ready to serve your needs at all levels in information technology, computer and communications specialties.

Key Contact - Specialty:
Ms. Gail Duncan, President - *Computer technologists*

Functions: Generalist

Industries: Generalist

Professional Associations: MAAPC

Careers for Women
80 E 11th St Ste 402
New York, NY 10003
(212) 777-4646
Fax: (212) 777-5949
Email: careers@careersforwomen.com
Web: www.careersforwomen.com

Description: Jobs in New York City Metroplolitan area and California. Executive sales, public relations and marketing. Free seminars for professionals from other industries such as law and education who want to make a career transition into the corporate environment.

Key Contact - Specialty:
Mr. David King, President - *Executive sales*

Functions: Advertising, Mkt. Research, Mktg. Mgmt., Sales Mgmt., Direct Mktg., PR

Industries: Generalist, Finance, Services, Media, Communications, Real Estate

Careers Inc
208 Ponce de Leon Ave Ste 1100
Banco Popular Center
Hato Rey, PR 00918-1036
(787) 764-2298
Fax: (787) 764-2530
Email: careers@careersincpr.com
Web: www.careersincpr.com

Description: We are the largest recruiting firm in the Caribbean area serving all disciplines involved in outplacement and consulting. We offer executive searches for markets in Latin America.

Key Contact - Specialty:
Mr. Rupert R. Amy, President/CEO/Owner - *General senior management*
Ms. Ruth Gonzalez, CPC, General Manager/Partner
Ms. Carla Deyo, CPC, Vice President/Partner - *Sales & marketing*
Ms. Clara Amiama, Senior Consultant/Partner - *Finance, IT*

Salary minimum: $25,000

Functions: Generalist, General Mgmt., Mfg., Healthcare, Sales & Mktg., HR Mgmt., Finance, IT

Industries: Generalist, Construction, Mfg., Finance, Services, Software

Professional Associations: NAPC, PRAHR, PRMA, RISJ, SME

Networks: National Personnel Assoc (NPA)

Careers On Track
150 County Rd
PO Box 222
Tenafly, NJ 07670
(201) 894-0563
Fax: (201) 894-0563
Email: tabortrak@msn.com

Description: Former packaged goods marketing professional provides key general management, marketing, sales, consulting and marketing services people to top product, service and consulting companies within packaged goods industries as well as to other industries where packaged goods marketers have migrated.

Key Contact - Specialty:
Mr. Gary Tabor, President - *Marketing, marketing consulting, marketing services, data based marketing*

Salary minimum: $75,000

Functions: Middle Mgmt., Mktg. Mgmt., Direct Mktg., Mgmt. Consultants

Industries: Food, Bev., Tobacco, Soap, Perf., Cosmtcs., Drugs Mfg., Mgmt. Consulting, Packaging, Insurance, Healthcare

CareersHere.Com
(also known as Cerberus Computing Corp)
1161 Willowhaven Dr
San Jose, CA 95126
(408) 286-2372
Fax: (415) 680-2309
Email: chuck1@cerb.com
Web: www.careershere.com

Description: We are a recruiting firm specializing in the permanent employment of software professionals (programmers, systems administrators, engineers, managers and executives) in the Silicon

Valley area. We work with some of hottest advanced technology companies in the Bay Area.

Key Contact:
Mr. Charles Lamprey, Jr., Director of Recruiting

Salary minimum: $70,000

Functions: IT

Industries: Generalist

Networks: Top Echelon Network

CareerTrac Employment Services Inc
135 W Wells St Ste 518
Milwaukee, WI 53203
(414) 224-8722
Fax: (414) 224-7080
Email: cindy@careertrac.com
Web: www.careertrac.com

Description: Professional search firm specializing in the placement of legal, banking and financial services personnel. Primary focus is attorneys with 3+ years of experience and all administrative personnel employed in a law firm or corporate legal department.

Key Contact - Specialty:
Ms. Cindy Johnson, CPC, President - *Attorneys, paralegals, administrative*
Mr. William L. Lange, Personnel Consultant - *Banking, financial services*
Ms. Connie Kidwell, Personnel Consultant - *Administrative staff*

Functions: Admin. Svcs., Legal, HR Mgmt., Benefits, Personnel, Finance, Attorneys, Paralegals

Industries: Generalist, Finance, Legal, HR Services

Professional Associations: HRMA, NAPS, WAPS

Careerxchange
10689 N Kendall Dr
Penthouse 209
Miami, FL 33176
(305) 595-3800
Fax: (305) 279-8903
Email: jobs@careerxchange.com
Web: www.careerxchange.com

Description: We place full-time and temporary, and temp to hire employees in all industries in the clerical, administrative and professional areas. We service large Fortune 500 companies as well as small to medium size family owned businesses.

Key Contact:
Mr. Sue Romanos, CPC, CTS, President
Ms. Suzanne Hodes, CPC, CTS, Vice President
Mr. Nick Alonso, Jr., Vice President

Salary minimum: $24,900

Professional Associations: ASA, NAPS, NAWBO, SHRM

Branches:
3300 University Dr Ste 302
Coral Springs, FL 33065
(954) 340-7979
Fax: (954) 340-5120
Email: jobs@careerxchange.com
Web: www.careerxchange.com
Key Contact:
Ms. Barbara Cooper, Branch Manager

9050 Pines Blvd Ste 150
Pembroke Pines, FL 33024
(954) 437-0070
Fax: (954) 431-3699
Email: jobs@careerxchange.com
Web: www.careerxchange.com
Key Contact:
Ms. Suzanne Hodes, Vice President

Peter N Carey & Associates Inc
1010 Jorie Blvd Ste 400
Oak Brook, IL 60523
(630) 573-4260
(877) 762-2739
Fax: (630) 573-0529
Email: pncarey1@aol.com

Description: An executive search firm specializing in direct marketing, e-commerce, and the graphic arts industries. The practice is national is scope.

Key Contact - Specialty:
Mr. Peter N. Carey, President - *Direct marketing, e-commerce, graphic arts*

Salary minimum: $60,000

Functions: Generalist

Industries: Paper, Printing, Finance, Non-profits, Mgmt. Consulting, Media, Telecoms, Insurance

Professional Associations: CADM, DMA

The Carey Company
6740 Stony Mountain Rd
Burlington, NC 27217
(336) 421-8009
Fax: (336) 421-9010
Email: careyco@careyco.com
Web: www.careyco.com

Description: Eighteen years' experience in recruitment of information technology executive and technical professionals.

Key Contact - Specialty:
Ms. Brenda Carey, CPC, Owner - *Information technology*

Functions: IT, MIS Mgmt.

Industries: Generalist

Professional Associations: NCASP

Carion Resource Group Inc
6790 Davand Dr Unit 2
Mississauga, ON L5T 2G5
Canada
(905) 795-9187
Email: jobs@carionresource.com
Web: www.carionresource.com

Description: We are executive management and support staff recruiters focused on the Ontario, Canada market. Career transition and outplacement services are offered to companies restructuring or down sizing.

Key Contact - Specialty:
Mr. Harvey Carey, President - *Professional management, manufacturing, distribution*

Salary minimum: $30,000

Functions: Middle Mgmt., Admin. Svcs., Production, Plant Mgmt., Purchasing, Distribution, CFO's, Systems Analysis, Systems Implem., Systems Support

Industries: Generalist

Carlsen Resources Inc
800 Belford Ave Ste 200
Grand Junction, CO 81501
(970) 242-9462
Fax: (970) 242-9074
Email: carlsenres@aol.com
Web: www.carlsenresources.com

Description: Executive-level management positions across all functions in cable TV, telephone, cellular, DBS, wireless, entertainment, multimedia, online and information technology.

Key Contact - Specialty:
Ms. Ann R. Carlsen, Founder/CEO
Ms. Kate Hampford, Executive Vice President

Ms. Anne La Fond, Vice President - *Candidate outreach*
Ms. Jeannine Sommer, Vice President - *Candidate outreach*
Ms. Catherine Hoover, Director - *Candidate outreach*

Salary minimum: $200,000

Functions: Generalist, Mktg. Mgmt., Personnel, CFO's, MIS Mgmt., Minorities, Int'l.

Industries: Generalist, Media, Advertising, New Media, Broadcast, Film, Telecoms

Professional Associations: CTAM, NAMIC, NCTA, SCTE, WICT

Carlson, Bentley Associates
3889 Promontory Ct
Boulder, CO 80304
(303) 443-6500
Fax: (303) 443-3345
Email: cbassoc@bouldernews.infi.net

Description: Specializing in the recruitment of AS/400 data processing professionals.

Key Contact - Specialty:
Mr. Don Miller, Owner - *Data processing, IBM AS/400*

Functions: Generalist, IT, MIS Mgmt., Systems Analysis, Systems Dev., Systems Implem., Systems Support, R&D

Industries: Generalist, Mfg., Wholesale, Retail, Services, Media

---

Carnegie Executive Search Inc
2 Carnegie Rd
Lawrenceville, NJ 08648
(609) 883-8900
Fax: (609) 883-6644
Email: billargust@carnegiesearch.com
Web: www.carnegiesearch.com

Description: We work with integrated marketing communications "production companies." We also work with sales, executive producers, technical directors, creative directors, management executives, and interactive multimedia technicians and designers.

Key Contact:
Mr. William Argust

Functions: Senior Mgmt.

Industries: E-commerce, Entertainment, Advertising, New Media, Broadcast, Film, Non-classifiable

---

Carnegie Resources Inc
1100 S Mint St Ste 102
Charlotte, NC 28203-4034
(704) 375-7701
Fax: (704) 375-7727
Email: jobs2000@bellsouth.net
Web: www.carnegieresources.com

Description: We have over 55 years of experience in recruiting serving the engineering, manufacturing, technical, and purchasing sectors working nationwide.

Key Contact - Specialty:
Mr. Thomas Shearer, President - *Manufacturing, engineering*
Mr. Lee Holland, Vice President - *Product development, product design*
Mr. Rick Linstead, Engineering Manager - *Plastics, metal working, machines*
Mr. Ron McDowell, Engineering Supervisor - *Quality, materials*

Functions: Generalist, Mfg., Product Dev., Engineering

Industries: Mfg., Medical Devices, Plastics, Rubber, Metal Products, Machine, Appliance,

---

Motor Vehicles, Computer Equip., Consumer Elect., Test, Measure Equip., Misc. Mfg.

Professional Associations: APMI, ASQ, NCASP, RON, SAE

Carpenter & Associates

11551 Forest Central Dr Ste 305
Dallas, TX 75243
(972) 691-6585
Fax: (214) 341-4620
Email: efcarpenter@mindspring.com

Description: In business 19 years with a nationwide clientele in retail and direct mail. We work on mid-to senior-level management positions, field and corporate. Contingency search firm.

Key Contact - Specialty:
Ms. Elsie Carpenter, President - *Retail, advertising positions (retail or direct mail) environment*

Salary minimum: $40,000

Functions: Advertising

Industries: Retail

Professional Associations: SERC

Carpenter Legal Search Inc

301 Grant St Ste 3030
1 Oxford Ctr
Pittsburgh, PA 15219-6401
(412) 255-3770
Fax: (412) 255-3780
Email: lcarpenter@carpenterlegalsearch.com
Web: www.carpenterlegalsearch.com

Description: With over fifteen years of legal recruiting experience, we specialize in corporations nationwide and law firms in the Mid-West and Mid-Atlantic. Corporate searches range from general counsel to junior-level positions.

Key Contact - Specialty:
Ms. Lori J. Carpenter, President - *Legal - attorneys only*

Functions: Legal

Industries: Generalist

Professional Associations: NALSC

Carr Management Services Inc

Harvey Rd
Chadds Ford, PA 19317
(610) 358-5630
Fax: (610) 358-5696
Email: carrms@aol.com
Web: www.carrms.com

Description: Offering recruiting services in the areas of biotechnology, biopharmaceuticals, life sciences, research products, diagnostics and healthcare. We have many years of combined experience working in the industries we serve.

Key Contact:
Dr. Denise Carr, President
Dr. James Lowry, Vice President
Ms. Barbara Clos, Vice President

Functions: Middle Mgmt., Mfg., Product Dev., Sales & Mktg., Mkt. Research, Mktg. Mgmt., Sales Mgmt., R&D

Industries: Medical Devices, Biotech

K Carroll & Associates

707 Skokie Blvd Ste 600
Northbrook, IL 60062
(847) 291-4310
Email: kcarroll1@aol.com

Description: Professional and executive search specializing in information systems.

Key Contact - Specialty:
Ms. Kathy Carroll, Owner - *Information systems*

Salary minimum: $50,000

Functions: IT

Industries: Generalist

Cars Group Int'l (CGI)

22540 Manor St Ste 200
St. Clair Shores, MI 48081
(810) 445-0488
Fax: (810) 445-0489
Email: jmartin@carsgroup.com
Web: www.carsgroup.com

Description: We are a worldwide executive search and consulting practice. We accept either retained, contingency, and contract assignments. We provide staffing. Our firm is highly regarded in Detroit, where we are headquartered. We place senior management, sales, business development, sales management, strategic alliances, channels, pre-sales, consultants, engineers, IT, and network professionals primarily for the technology, manufacturing, and medical industries.

Key Contact - Specialty:
Mr. Joseph S. Martin, Senior Partner - *Executive, sales, technology, generalist, automotive*

Salary minimum: $75,000

Functions: Generalist

Industries: Agri., Forestry, Mining, Energy, Utilities, Construction, Mfg., Venture Cap., Services, Telecoms, Defense, Software, Biotech

Professional Associations: ESD, IEEE, MAPS, SAE, SHRM

Carson-Thomas & Associates

315 W 9th St Ste 210
Washington Mutual Bank Bldg
Los Angeles, CA 90015
(213) 489-4480
(213) 489-4482
Fax: (213) 489-7328
Email: carsonthomas@earthlink.net

Description: We have twenty-eight years worth of search/recruitment/placement experience in Greater L.A. and S.C. We have the best reputation for highest quality applicant and client pools (at all levels, including: college graduates with and without experience, administrative support, management through executive, professional, technical).

Key Contact:
Ms. Sandra Carson, Partner - *Management counseling, professional information technology, accounting, human resource management*
Mr. Frank Thomas, Partner - *Support specialist (professional, administrative)*
Ms. Jule Steingrueber, MA, Partner/Office Manager

Functions: Generalist, General Mgmt., Sales & Mktg., HR Mgmt., Finance, IT, Specialized Svcs.

Industries: Generalist

The Carstin Search Group Inc

13601 Preston Rd Ste 313 W
Dallas, TX 75240
(972) 458-7788
Fax: (972) 789-5112
Email: carstin@swbell.net

Description: Strong in property and casualty insurance, call centers and information technology/management information systems. Selective in client base to assure a large candidate pool offering both leadership and technical skills. Confidential collaboration for both client and candidate.

Key Contact - Specialty:
Ms. Jan Noebel, President - *Insurance (property, casualty)*

Mr. Jeff C. Noebel, Vice President - *Call centers, information technology, MIS*

Salary minimum: $60,000

Functions: Generalist, General Mgmt., Directors, Senior Mgmt., Middle Mgmt., Mktg. Mgmt., HR Mgmt., CFO's, Risk Mgmt.

Industries: HR Services, Telecoms, Call Centers, Insurance, Real Estate, Healthcare

Carter McKenzie Inc

200 Executive Dr Ste 210
West Orange, NJ 07052
(973) 736-7100
Fax: (973) 736-9416
Email: recruiter@cartermckenzie.com
Web: www.carter-mckenzie.com

Description: We are an organization whose principal function is the identification and recruitment of professional staff within the field of information systems/technology and human resources.

Key Contact - Specialty:
Mr. Richard Kilcoyne, Chairman - *Information technology, middle & executive management*
Mr. John Capo, President - *Technical management*

Salary minimum: $50,000

Functions: Generalist, Directors, MIS Mgmt., Systems Analysis, Systems Dev., Systems Implem., Systems Support, Mgmt. Consultants

Industries: Generalist, Drugs Mfg., Finance, Brokers, Media, Insurance, Software, Healthcare

Carter, Lavoie Associates

5 Mechanic St
Hope Valley, RI 02832
(401) 539-7600
Fax: (401) 539-6040
Email: search@ids.net
Web: users.ids.net/~search

Description: Placement of professionals in engineering (including chem. engr. automation/process controls), information technology, manufacturing, sales/marketing, finance. Provider of outplacement services and consultations.

Key Contact - Specialty:
Mr. Leo R. Lavoie, Principal - *Generalist*

Salary minimum: $30,000

Functions: Generalist, Production, Materials Plng., Sales Mgmt., Personnel, IT, Engineering

Industries: Generalist, Chemicals, Drugs Mfg., Plastics, Rubber, Software, Healthcare

Carter/MacKay

777 Terrace Ave
Hasbrouck Heights, NJ 07604
(201) 288-5100
Fax: (201) 288-2660
Email: info.nj@cartermackay.com
Web: www.cartermackay.com

Description: A recruiting firm specializing in sales, pre- and post-sales support, sales management, marketing and senior management within the healthcare, information technology and business-to-business sectors. Client companies ranging in size from pre-IPO start-up to Fortune 100.

Key Contact - Specialty:
Mr. Bruce Green, Principal - *Healthcare, sales, sales management, senior management, marketing*
Mr. George Villano, Principal - *Information technology, business to business, sales, sales management, senior management*

Salary minimum: $50,000

Functions: Senior Mgmt., Middle Mgmt., Mktg. Mgmt., Sales Mgmt., Systems Implem., Systems Support

Industries: Drugs Mfg., Medical Devices, Computer Equip., New Media, Software, Biotech, Healthcare

Branches:
300 Congress St Ste 307
Quincy, MA 02169
(617) 689-0029
Fax: (617) 689-0725
Email: info.ma@cartermackay.com
Key Contact - Specialty:
Mr. Michael Rowell, Vice President - *Healthcare, information technology, business to business*

1981 Marcus Ave Ste 201
Lake Success, NY 11042
(516) 616-7700
Fax: (516) 616-4842
Email: info.ny@cartermackay.com
Key Contact - Specialty:
Mr. Larry Orbach, Principal - *Healthcare, information technology, business to business*

2000 Regency Pkwy Ste 460
Cary, NC 27511
(919) 380-1200
Fax: (919) 380-1267
Email: info.nc@cartermackay.com
Key Contact - Specialty:
Mr. Al Hertz, Vice President - *Healthcare, information technology, business to business*

CarterBaldwin
300 Colonial Park Ste 240
Roswell, GA 30076
(678) 448-0000
Fax: (770) 552-1088
Email: careers@carterbaldwin.com
Web: www.carterbaldwin.com

Description: We are a retained executive search firm specializing in senior corporate and divisional management positions where a strong cultural fit is as critical as the right "resume background." Significant expertise in all officer level positions, and culturally critical vice president, and director level roles.

Key Contact:
Ms. Jennifer Poole, Vice President/Managing Partner

Salary minimum: $100,000

Functions: General Mgmt., Directors, Senior Mgmt., Middle Mgmt., Mktg. Mgmt., Sales Mgmt., HR Mgmt., Finance, IT, MIS Mgmt.

Industries: Generalist

Professional Associations: GAPS, NAPS

The CARVIR Group Inc
PO Box 125
Fayetteville, GA 30214
(770) 460-8272
Fax: (770) 460-2216
Web: www.carvir.com

Description: We have worked with a broad spectrum of clients - multinational corporations, as well as start-up companies. We focus on clients in the financial services, technology, manufacturing, consumer products, energy, food and pharmaceutical industries.

Key Contact - Specialty:
Mr. Virgil L. Fludd, President - *Finance, human resources, marketing, sales, general management*
Ms. Carolyn Kelley, Vice President - *Information systems*

Salary minimum: $50,000

Functions: Generalist, Sales & Mktg., HR Mgmt., Finance, IT, Specialized Svcs.

Industries: Generalist, Finance, Services, Media

CAS Comsearch Inc
950 3rd Ave Ste 1701
New York, NY 10022
(212) 593-0861
Fax: (212) 755-4597
Email: comsearch@aol.com

Description: We are an executive search firm founded in 1980 specializing in the telecommunications industry, on-line information industry, as well as new media.

Key Contact - Specialty:
Ms. Gail Kleinberg Koch, President - *Sales & marketing, new media, telecommunications*
Ms. Amy Sherman, Recruiter - *Sales & marketing*

Salary minimum: $40,000

Functions: Sales & Mktg.

Industries: New Media, Telecoms

Casey & Associates Inc
3419 Westminster Ave
PMB 222
Dallas, TX 75205
(214) 522-1010
Fax: (214) 522-8263
Email: techjobs@ccasey.com
Web: www.ccasey.com

Description: Information technology recruiting and consulting services with an emphasis on AS/400 and client server technology. Our placements include CIOs, information systems directors, programmers/analysts, systems programmers, WEB developers, project managers. Recognized for in-depth work with both clients and candidates, resulting in a 90%+ placement rate.

Key Contact - Specialty:
Ms. Carol M. Casey, CPC, President - *Information technology*

Salary minimum: $60,000

Functions: IT, MIS Mgmt., Systems Analysis, Systems Dev.

Industries: Generalist

Professional Associations: IRG, SERC

Casey Accounting & Finance Resources
5150 Tollview Dr Ste 263
Rolling Meadows, IL 60008
(847) 253-9030
Fax: (847) 253-9545
Email: casey@caseyresources.com
Web: www.caseyresources.com

Description: We are specialists in executive placement, contract staffing, and project consulting for accounting and finance professionals.

Key Contact:
Mr. Pete McTague, CPC, Branch Manager

Salary minimum: $45,000

Functions: Finance

Industries: Generalist

Professional Associations: NAPS

Cast Metals Personnel Inc
512 W Burlington Ave
PO Box 2193
La Grange, IL 60525
(708) 354-0085
Fax: (708) 354-2490

Description: An independent full-service placement organization offering the metal casting industry access to management and technical personnel.

Key Contact - Specialty:
Mr. Chuck Lundeen, President - *Management, engineering, technical (casting)*

Salary minimum: $30,000

Functions: Generalist, General Mgmt., Middle Mgmt., Production, Plant Mgmt., Quality, Sales Mgmt., Engineering

Industries: Generalist, Mfg., Metal Products, Motor Vehicles

Professional Associations: AFS

Casten Search Consultants
714 A Southbridge St
Auburn, MA 01501
(508) 832-4442
Fax: (508) 832-2227
Email: hcasten@aol.com

Description: Recruit scientists and engineers from the staff to director-level for the biotech, pharmaceutical and medical device fields.

Key Contact - Specialty:
Mr. Henry Casten, CPC - *Engineering, scientific*

Salary minimum: $40,000

Functions: Product Dev., Production, Quality, R&D

Industries: Medical Devices, Biotech

Castleton Consulting Inc
4199 Campus Dr Ste 550
Irvine, CA 92612
(949) 509-0980
Fax: (949) 509-0504
Email: info@castleton-inc.com
Web: www.castletonconsulting.com

Description: We are an executive search firm specializing in senior management talent for technology-based companies. Our industry expertise includes software, Internet technology, and telecommunications companies, as well as technology consulting services, and "old-economy" industrial sectors. Our functional emphasis is on management, sales, marketing, and business development.

Key Contact:
Ms. Christina Savich, CAC, President

Salary minimum: $80,000

Functions: General Mgmt., Sales & Mktg., IT

Industries: Telecoms, Software

Catalina Medical Recruiters Inc
8686 N Central Ave Ste 166
Phoenix, AZ 85020
(602) 331-1655
(800) 657-0354
Fax: (602) 331-1933
Email: catmedrec@aol.com
Web: www.catalinarecruiters.com

Description: We provide temporary and permanent physician placement to healthcare facilities throughout the Southwest. All specialties.

Key Contact:
Ms. Joan Pearson, CMSR, President - *Physicians (locum tenens)*
Ms. Dee Pones, Vice President

Functions: Generalist, Healthcare, Physicians, Allied Health, Health Admin.

Industries: Generalist, Healthcare

Professional Associations: NAPR

Branches:
7801 N Via Laguna Niguel
Tucson, AZ 85743
(520) 579-2929
Fax: (520) 579-2930

Email: dpones@aol.com
Key Contact - Specialty:
Ms. Dee Pones, CMSR, Vice President - *Locum tenens, physicians*

CBA Companies
PO Box 2132
Alpine, CA 91903
(619) 659-3200
Email: resumes@cbacompanies.com

Description: We are professional recruiters who specialize in software and computer network companies. Our partners have over 30years of experience in the software industry and over ten years experience as professional recruiters.

Key Contact - Specialty:
Mr. Allen F. Joseph, Partner - *Sales, marketing, technical, software*
Ms. Patti D. Joseph, Partner - *Technical software engineers*

Salary minimum: $50,000

Functions: Generalist

Industries: Telecoms, Software

CBC Resources Inc
1300 W Belmont Ste 304
Chicago, IL 60657
(773) 880-1309
Web: www.cbcresources.com

Description: We offer our clients superior customer service in placing candidates with an HRIS, IS, HR, benefits and financial systems background on a nationwide basis.

Key Contact - Specialty:
Ms. Karen Convery, President - *HR systems*

Functions: Generalist, Sales Mgmt., HR Mgmt., IT, Systems Implem., Mgmt. Consultants

Industries: Generalist, Finance, Misc. Financial, Mgmt. Consulting, HR Services, Software

Professional Associations: APA, IHRIM, SHRM

CBI Group Inc
1298 Rockbridge Rd Ste B
Stone Mountain, GA 30087
(770) 925-2915
Fax: (770) 925-2601
Email: cbinc@mindspring.com
Web: www.cbisearch.com

Description: Professional recruiting and search for the architecture, consulting engineering services industry. Specialist in key technical and management positions. National coverage. Member of Professional Services Management Association, National Society of Professional Engineers, American Public Works Association, Water Environment Federation, American Society for Healthcare Engineers, American Institute of Architects.

Key Contact - Specialty:
Mr. Phil Collins, President - *Architects, landscape architects, environmental engineers, transportation engineers, public works engineers*
Mr. Bob Bowers, Vice President - *Mechanical, electrical, structural engineering*

Functions: Generalist

Industries: Construction, Environmental Svcs.

Professional Associations: AIA, APWA, ITE, NSPE, PSMA, WEF

CCL Medical Search
71 Schriever Ln Ste 210
New City, NY 10956-3313
(845) 634-0111
(888) CCL-0021
Fax: (845) 634-0126
Email: cclsearch@aol.com
Web: www.cclmedicalsearch.com

Description: A search firm specializing in healthcare. During the last 15 years we have been instrumental in the growth of many hospitals, nursing homes, health centers and private practices around the US and the Middle East. We are placing administrators, physicians, P.A., P.T., OT nurses, practitioners and other healthcare personnel, to include nursing homes.

Key Contact - Specialty:
Mr. Michael Richter, President - *Healthcare, medical*
Ms. Heidi Hollander, Vice President - *Registered nurses, physical therapists, occupational therapists, physicians assistants, nurse practitioners*
H. Hollander - *Allied health*
Ms. Karen Chafetz, Recruiter - *Physicians, allied health*

Functions: Directors, Healthcare, Physicians, Nurses, Allied Health, Health Admin., Finance, CFO's, Credit, Network Admin.

Industries: Generalist, Healthcare

Professional Associations: AMR, NAPR

Branches:
6590 Via Trento
Delray Beach, FL 33446
(561) 637-3434
Fax: (561) 637-8434
Email: cclsearch@aol.com
Key Contact - Specialty:
Mr. Michael Richter - *Healthcare, medical admin*

2304 Magnolia Ct E Ste 308
Buffalo Grove, IL 60089
(847) 634-3456
Fax: (847) 634-3443
Email: fernrae@aol.com
Key Contact - Specialty:
Ms. Fern Rae - *Physicians, healthcare, allied health*
Ms. Heidi Richter - *Medical, healthcare*

CE Insurance Services
2802 W Azeele St
Tampa, FL 33609
(800) 229-HIRE
Fax: (813) 348-0554
Email: jeff@ceinsurance.com
Web: www.ceinsurance.com

Description: Contingency and retained search of insurance executives, legal, managerial and professional personnel for insurance companies, agencies, brokers and risk managers. Nationally and internationally.

Key Contact - Specialty:
Mr. Jeffrey M. Carter, President/CEO - *Insurance companies*

Salary minimum: $35,000

Functions: Generalist

Industries: Insurance

Professional Associations: FAPS

Cemco Ltd
2 First Nat'l Plz Ste 610
Chicago, IL 60603
(312) 855-1500
Fax: (312) 855-1510
Email: cemco@cemcoltd.com
Web: www.cemcoltd.com

Description: Full-service national executive search firm specializing in accounting and financial services, real estate, professional medical and IT.

Key Contact - Specialty:
Mr. Dillon Hale, President - *Accounting, finance, healthcare, medical, information technology*

Salary minimum: $35,000

Functions: Generalist, Nurses, Health Admin., CFO's, Budgeting, Taxes, MIS Mgmt., Systems Dev.

Industries: Generalist, Misc. Mfg., Accounting, Real Estate, Healthcare

Branches:
2015 Spring Rd Ste 250
Oak Brook, IL 60521
(630) 573-5050
Fax: (630) 573-5060
Email: info@cemcosystems.com
Web: www.cemcosystems.com
Key Contact - Specialty:
Mr. Dave Gordon, General Manager - *MIS, client/server, telecommunication personnel*

11469 Olive Blvd Ste 117
St. Louis, MO 63141
(314) 838-7400
Fax: (314) 838-2228
Key Contact - Specialty:
Mr. Ira Steuer, General Manager - *MIS, client/server, telecommunication personnel*

Center for Executive Opportunities Inc (CEO)
10940 NE 33 Pl Ste 204
Bellevue, WA 98004
(425) 889-2361
Fax: (425) 889-0211
Email: jobline@ceoheadhunters.com
Web: www.ceoheadhunters.com

Description: CEO a search firm specializing in retained and contingent executive searches for managers and executive chief officers in the following industries: law; healthcare; IT; biotech; financial; sales and marketing; engineering; construction; insurance; consulting; and non-profit.

Key Contact:
Mr. Stephen H. Shaw, President
Ms. Vicky McKie, Vice President-Operations

Salary minimum: $75,000

Functions: Generalist

Industries: Generalist

Central Executive Search Inc
6151 Wilson Mills Rd Ste 240
Highland Heights, OH 44143
(440) 461-5400
Fax: (440) 461-8442
Email: staff@centraljobs.com
Web: www.centraljobs.com

Description: Specializing in the paper, printing, packaging, conveting and adhesives industry. Positions range from manufacturing, R&D, engineering, sales/management and marketing. Worldwide searches. Good reputation and very experienced in specialized industries.

Key Contact:
Mr. Gary Giallombardo, President
Ms. Toni Graziano, General Manager
Ms. Stacey Herbert, Marketing Manager
Mr. Kenneth Emser, Account Executive
Mr. Michael Bucci, Account Executive
Ms. Mary Reed, Office Manager

Salary minimum: $50,000

Functions: General Mgmt., Mfg., Sales & Mktg., R&D

Industries: Mfg., Paper, Printing, Chemicals, Plastics, Rubber, Paints, Petro. Products

Centrus Group Inc
1653 Merriman Rd Ste 211
Akron, OH 44313
(330) 864-5800
Fax: (330) 865-9222
Email: hlipton@centrusgroup.com
Web: www.centrusgroup.com

Description: We are a 50% contingent and 50% retained. We specialize in consumer durables, automotive manufacturing, marketing, plant, and division controllers. We place all manufacturing positions. We have 32 years recruiting experience. Our other focus is, crisis management.

Key Contact:
Mr. Harvey Lipton, Director of recruitment

Functions: Generalist

Industries: Mfg., Plastics, Rubber, Motor Vehicles, Misc. Mfg., Venture Cap., Telecoms, Accounting SW, HR SW, Mfg. SW, Marketing SW

Century Associates Inc
1420 Walnut St Ste 1402
Philadelphia, PA 19102
(215) 732-4311
Fax: (215) 735-1804
Email: century@centuryassociates.com
Web: www.centuryassociates.com

Description: We are involved in the nationwide recruitment of sales, technical and marketing professionals in the information technology and medical fields.

Key Contact - Specialty:
Mr. David Allen, President - *Vice presidents, directors of marketing, software*
Mr. Michael Hurley, Vice President - *Sales, sales management, medical, pharmaceutical*

Salary minimum: $60,000

Functions: Generalist, Directors, Senior Mgmt., Sales & Mktg., Mkt. Research, Mktg. Mgmt., Sales Mgmt., PR, Systems Support

Industries: Generalist, Medical Devices, Pharm Svcs., Mgmt. Consulting, Software, Biotech

Professional Associations: MAAPC

Networks: First Interview Network (FIN)

The Century Group
9800 La Cienega Blvd Ste 904
Inglewood, CA 90301
(310) 216-2100
(800) 337-9675
Fax: (310) 216-2116
Email: century@century-group.com
Web: www.century-group.com

Description: One of L.A.'s top search firms according to the "L.A. Business Journal"; specializing in accounting/finance/tax/audit/controllers/CFOs, searches in a broad range of industries in Southern California and has a staff with over 100 years' combined search experience.

Key Contact - Specialty:
Mr. Harry Boxer, CEO - *Accounting, finance, tax & audit, controllers, CFO's*
Mr. Ron Proul, President - *Accounting, finance, tax & audit, controllers, CFO's*
Mr. Don Yaeger, Executive Vice President - *Accounting, finance, tax & audit, controllers, CFO's*

Salary minimum: $30,000

Functions: Finance

Industries: Generalist

Branches:
575 Anton Blvd Fl 6
Costa Mesa, CA 92626
(949) 708-5100
(800) 564-0010
Fax: (714) 708-5111
Email: jeff@century-group.com
Key Contact - Specialty:
Mr. Jeff Lassiter, Recruiting Manager - *Accounting & finance*

550 N Brand Blvd Ste 2150
Glendale, CA 91203
(818) 240-5200
Email: harry@century-group.com
Key Contact:
Mr. Ward Larsen, Recruiting Manager

The Century Group
(a division of SOS Staffing)
8400 W 110th St Ste 310
Overland Park, KS 66211
(913) 451-7666
Fax: (913) 451-2161
Email: nova@censtaffing.com
Web: www.censtaffing.com

Description: We are a large firm with 15 trained consultants. We are twice listed as an INC 500 company and were the winners of the Blue Chip Enterprise Award for KS.

Key Contact:
Ms. JoAnn Wagner, President

Salary minimum: $30,000

Functions: Generalist, Nurses, Health Admin., Sales Mgmt., Credit, Systems Analysis, Systems Dev., R&D, Engineering

Industries: Generalist, Finance, Pharm Svcs., IT Implementation, Healthcare

CFI Resources Inc
7 Clover Dr
Great Neck, NY 11021
(516) 466-1221
Fax: (516) 487-1774
Email: careers@cfires.com
Web: www.cfires.com

Description: Focus on high-technology electronics, semiconductor front- and back-end capital equipment, hardware, software, design automation, robotics, test and measurement, e-commerce, sales, marketing, engineering, applications, field service positions.

Key Contact - Specialty:
Mr. Leo Cohen, Principal - *High technology, sales & marketing, sales (semiconductor equipment), automatic test equipment, electronic design automation*
Mr. Charles Winick, Principal - *High technology, customer support, semiconductor capital equipment sales*

Functions: Generalist

Industries: Computer Equip., Test, Measure Equip., Telecoms, Aerospace, Software

CFOs2GO
3470 Mt. Diablo Blvd Ste 125
Lafayette, CA 94549
(925) 945-7850
Fax: (925) 283-4458
Email: info@cfos2go.com
Web: www.cfos2go.com

Description: Our firm is a full-service senior financial executive placement firm that customizes staffing and consulting solutions to emerging and high-growth companies. The services that we offer include: direct hire, directorships, contract staffing, and consulting. This San Francisco Bay Area-based firm utilizes Internet technologies and a network of

consulting CFOs and CPAs that provide local representation in virtually every venture capital community in the US.

Key Contact - Specialty:
Mr. Robert Weis, President - *Financial management executives*

Functions: Finance

Industries: Generalist

CFR Executive Search Inc
175 W Jackson Blvd Ste 1843
Chicago, IL 60604
(312) 435-0990
(888) 854-4237
Fax: (312) 435-1333
Email: info@cfrsearch.com
Web: www.cfrsearch.com

Description: We assure quality, prescreened accounting, and corporate finance professionals who will meet our clients' specifications. They will possess the appropriate management style and work ethic to fit our clients' culture.

Key Contact - Specialty:
Mr. James Barry, President - *Accounting & finance*
Mr. Joseph Sexton, Vice President - *Accounting & finance*

Salary minimum: $30,000

Functions: Generalist, CFO's, Budgeting, Cash Mgmt., Credit, Taxes, M&A, Risk Mgmt.

Industries: Generalist, Mfg., Transportation, Wholesale, Retail, Misc. Financial, Services, Insurance

Professional Associations: IAPS, NAPS

Chacra, Belliveau & Associates Inc
1550 DeMaisonneuve St W Ste 805
Montreal, QC H3G 1N2
Canada
(514) 931-8801
Fax: (514) 931-1940
Email: stevenc@chacra.com
Web: www.chacra.com

Description: Specializing exclusively in the Information Technology/Systems sector nationally and internationally. Managed and staffed by Information Technology and Human Resource professionals.

Key Contact - Specialty:
Mr. Steven Chacra, President - *Information technology*

Salary minimum: $45,000

Functions: IT, MIS Mgmt., Systems Analysis, Systems Dev., Systems Support, Network Admin., DB Admin.

Industries: Generalist

Professional Associations: ACSESS, CIPS, NAPS

Networks: National Personnel Assoc (NPA)

Chad Management Group
21 St. Clair Ave E Ste 1000
Toronto, ON M4T 1L9
Canada
(416) 968-1000
Fax: (416) 968-7754
Email: jobs@chadman.com
Web: www.chadman.com

Description: A leader in marketing and sales recruitment with long-term success in identifying and delivering the top performers promptly and effectively.

Key Contact:
Mr. Rick A. Chad, President - *Marketing, general management*
Mr. Rick Richter, Consultant - *Sales*

Ms. Laurie Hart, Consultant - *Direct marketing, public relations*
Mr. Gary Rudson, Consultant
Ms. Silvia Butterworth, Consultant

Functions: Generalist, General Mgmt., Product Dev., Materials, Sales & Mktg., Finance, IT, Graphic Artists

Industries: Generalist, Mfg., Food, Bev., Tobacco, Drugs Mfg., Finance, Hospitality, Media, Database SW

Chadwell & Associates Inc
PO Box 1028
Portage, MI 49081-1028
(616) 353-7805
Fax: (616) 353-7802
Email: chadwell@chadwell.com
Web: www.chadwell.com

Description: We follow our recruiter's code of ethics. Within it, we explain how crucial it is to follow the three Rs of recruiting: respect, response and reliability.

Key Contact - Specialty:
Ms. Rebecca A. Chadwell, Engineering Specialist - *Engineering, technical, engineers (quality & sales)*

Functions: Production, Automation, Plant Mgmt., Packaging, Engineering

Industries: Generalist, Mfg., Food, Bev., Tobacco, Machine, Appliance, Packaging

Professional Associations: ASBE, ATBI, B&CMA

Chaitin & Associates Inc
22543 Ventura Blvd Ste 220
Woodland Hills, CA 91364
(818) 225-8655
Fax: (818) 225-8660

Description: We are an executive search firm with over 40 years' experience working for major corporate clients nationwide. We conduct careful searches for all clients from the background of personality, technical background and education for all of our clients.

Key Contact - Specialty:
Mr. Chuck Hayes, Vice President - *Finance, personnel, manufacturing*
Mr. Dick Chaitin, Vice President - *Garment manufacturing, garment sales, retailing*

Salary minimum: $50,000

Functions: Generalist, Senior Mgmt., Middle Mgmt., Plant Mgmt., Productivity, Advertising, Sales Mgmt., Personnel, CFO's

Industries: Generalist, Textiles, Apparel, Drugs Mfg., Consumer Elect., Misc. Mfg., Wholesale, Retail, HR Services

Wayne S Chamberlain & Associates
25835 Narbonne Ave Ste 280-C
Lomita, CA 90717
(310) 534-4840
Fax: (310) 539-9885
Email: wayne@waynechamberlain.com
Web: www.waynechamberlain.com

Description: Our specialization is in the technical placement of professionals in the electronic connector and cable fields. Our typical searches are for sales and marketing managers, design engineers, manufacturing/industrial/quality engineers, and technical management.

Key Contact - Specialty:
Mr. Wayne Chamberlain, Owner - *Electronics, connectors*

Salary minimum: $50,000

Functions: Generalist, Directors, Middle Mgmt., Product Dev., Automation, Plant Mgmt., Quality, Mktg. Mgmt., Sales Mgmt.

Industries: Generalist, Mfg., Plastics, Rubber, Computer Equip., Consumer Elect., Test, Measure Equip., Electronic, Elec. Components, Telecoms, Wireless, Fiber Optic, Mfg. SW, Marketing SW

Professional Associations: CSP, IICIT, OSA

Chamberlain Associates
4244 Riverlook Pkwy
Marietta, GA 30067
(770) 690-0085
(800) 877-9631
Email: chamassoc@aol.com
Web: www.chamberlainassoc.com

Description: We place clinical and management candidates in hospitals and pharmaceutical research companies nationwide.

Key Contact - Specialty:
Ms. Inga Chamberlain, Owner - *Healthcare*

Salary minimum: $50,000

Functions: Generalist, Nurses, Health Admin., IT

Industries: Generalist, Healthcare

Professional Associations: AORN

Vickers Chambless Managed Search
400 Perimeter Center Ter NE Ste 900
Atlanta, GA 30346
(404) 365-0030
Fax: (404) 231-1351
Email: vcms@vcmssearch.com
Web: www.vcmssearch.com

Description: Executive search services exclusively in the healthcare financial and administrative areas. Financial: CFO, controller, assistant controller, reimbursement, auditors. Administrative: medical records, information systems.

Key Contact - Specialty:
Mr. Vickers Chambless, President - *Healthcare administration (especially finance)*

Salary minimum: $40,000

Functions: Generalist, Health Admin., Taxes, M&A, Risk Mgmt., MIS Mgmt.

Industries: Generalist, Healthcare

Professional Associations: HFMA

Chapman & Associates
555 Burrard St 2 Bentall Ctr Ste 1065
PO Box 217
Vancouver, BC V7X 1M8
Canada
(604) 682-7764
Fax: (604) 682-8746
Email: resumes@chapmanassoc.com
Web: www.chapmanassoc.com

Description: With more than 40 years of experience recruiting and selecting mid-level to senior personnel, our firm enjoys a proven track record for professionalism, confidentiality and success.

Key Contact:
Mr. Gary W. Fumano, President - *Sales, marketing, finance, administration, engineering*
Mr. Bruce J. MacKenzie, Managing Parnter - *Sales, marketing, high technology, engineering*
Mr. Bryce A. Stacey, Associate - *Finance, sales, engineering*
Ms. Lynn Armstrong, Associate
Mr. Richard Cameron, Associate

Salary minimum: $50,000

Functions: Generalist, General Mgmt., Mfg., Materials, Sales & Mktg., HR Mgmt., IT, Engineering

Industries: Generalist, Agri., Forestry, Mining, Construction, Mfg., Hospitality, Media

R F Chapman & Company
PO Box 1155
Kihei, HI 96753
(808) 874-8470
Fax: (808) 874-5779
Email: chapman@mauigateway.com
Web: www.hawaiihotelcareers.com

Description: Founded in 1980, we are a Hawaii-based management recruitment firm specializing in the hotel, restaurant and tourism industries. We have had an office in Hawaii since 1988. Our focus is on middle and upper-management and the majority of our work is done on a contingency basis.

Key Contact:
Mr. Bob Chapman

Functions: General Mgmt., Middle Mgmt.

Industries: Hospitality

The Chapman Group Inc
8151 E Evans Rd 4
Scottsdale, AZ 85260
(480) 483-8833
Email: jeffc@thechapmangroup.com
Web: www.thechapmangroup.com

Description: We conduct searches for mission-critical individual contributors, managers and executives for factory automation technology product, software and systems companies throughout North America, Europe and Asia.

Key Contact - Specialty:
Mr. Jeff H. Chapman, Chief Search Consultant - *Factory automation technology*

Salary minimum: $55,000

Functions: Generalist, Senior Mgmt., Middle Mgmt., Automation, Sales Mgmt., Systems Implem., Engineering

Industries: Generalist, Machine, Appliance, Test, Measure Equip., Mgmt. Consulting, Software

Professional Associations: RIA

Charet & Associates
PO Box 435
Cresskill, NJ 07626
(201) 894-5197
Fax: (201) 894-9095
Email: sandy@charet.com
Web: www.charet.com

Description: A well-established firm with a sterling reputation for a high-level of personal attention and one of the most extensive and up to date networks of PR and corporate communications people in the country. Services public relations, corporate communications, public affairs, investor relations and marketing for all industries.

Key Contact:
Ms. Sandra Charet, President
Mr. Gary Epstein, VP- Recruiting Services

Salary minimum: $50,000

Functions: PR

Industries: Generalist

Professional Associations: IABC, NIRI, PRSA

Charles & Associates Inc
816 E 25th St Ste 3
Kearney, NE 68847
(308) 236-8891
Fax: (308) 236-8893
Email: chasassoc@nebi.com

Description: Specialists in the outdoor power/lawn and garden equipment industry covering sales and marketing, engineering, manufacturing, production, quality control and material handling.

Key Contact:
Mr. Charles F. Dummer, CPC, President - *Outdoor power equipment, lawn & garden*
Mrs. Joan Dummer, Vice-President

Functions: Middle Mgmt., Product Dev., Mkt. Research, Mktg. Mgmt., Sales Mgmt., R&D, Engineering

Industries: Generalist

Charter Resources Int'l LC
9396 Charter Xing
Mechanicsville, VA 23116
(804) 550-1395
Fax: (804) 550-9454
Email: msbilodeau@charterresources.com
Web: www.charterresources.com

Description: We are transportation and legal specialists.

Key Contact - Specialty:
Mr. Michael Bilodeau, Principal - *Transportation, legal*

Functions: Generalist

Industries: Transportation, Retail, Services, Legal, Real Estate

Professional Associations: NALSC, SHRM

Chase Partners
181 Bay St BCE Pl Ste 3740
PO Box 798
Toronto, ON M5J 2T3
Canada
(416) 364-6404
Fax: (416) 364-2875

Description: Exclusively executive search for all business sectors. Strengths in recruiting marketing, finance and administration. Broad base of clients in manufacturing, service industries (including financial services) and consumer packaged goods.

Key Contact - Specialty:
Mr. John S. Harrison, President - *Senior executive*

Salary minimum: $100,000

Functions: Generalist, Senior Mgmt.

Industries: Generalist, Mfg., Finance

Chase-Gardner Executive Search Associates Inc
36181 E Lake Rd
Box PMB-A
Palm Harbor, FL 34685
(727) 934-7000
Fax: (727) 934-2390
Email: cgardner@staffing.net
Web: www.chasegardner.com

Description: A full-service executive search and placement agency, servicing our clients and our candidates with a permanent placement division as well as a contract and temporary placement division, including Employer-Of-Record Services.

Key Contact - Specialty:
Mr. Sidney Gardner, President - *Engineering, manufacturing support*

Salary minimum: $45,000

Functions: Generalist, Senior Mgmt., Product Dev., Production, Plant Mgmt., Quality, Personnel, Engineering

Industries: Generalist, Medical Devices, Plastics, Rubber, Metal Products, Machine, Appliance, Motor Vehicles, Environmental Svcs.

Networks: National Personnel Assoc (NPA)

Chatham Search Associates Inc
10 Ridgedale Ave
Florham Park, NJ 07932
(973) 301-0100
Fax: (973) 301-1771
Email: csa@chathamsearch.com
Web: www.chathamsearch.net

Description: Specialize in information system technology placements for both permanent and consulting positions. Placements are made from intermmediate to executive-level technology experts. All searches are conducted with the highest level of professionalism.

Key Contact - Specialty:
Ms. Michelle Pesco, Director/Co-Founder - *Information technology*
Ms. Theresa Ryan-Ulyatt, Director/Co-Founder - *Information technology*

Salary minimum: $50,000

Functions: Generalist, MIS Mgmt., Systems Dev., Systems Support, Network Admin., DB Admin., Engineering, Technicians

Industries: Generalist, Media, Telecoms, Software

Professional Associations: NAFE, NJAWBO

Chaves & Associates
1698 Post Rd E
Westport, CT 06880
(203) 222-2222
Fax: (203) 259-5200
Email: gen@chaves.com
Web: www.in-sitesearch.com

Description: Computer software development and corporate MIS specialties including Internet, object oriented (C++, VB), database (Oracle), technologies and consulting.

Key Contact - Specialty:
Mr. Stephen Ozyck, Senior Partner - *Computer executives*
Mr. Victor Chaves, Chairman of the Board - *Senior computer executives*
Ms. Amanda Fredrick, Senior Director - *Computer professionals*
Mr. Jake Israel, Director - *Computer professionals*

Salary minimum: $30,000

Functions: MIS Mgmt., Systems Analysis, Systems Dev., Systems Implem., Systems Support, Network Admin., DB Admin.

Industries: Venture Cap., Telecoms, Software

Professional Associations: CAPS, NAPS

Branches:
50 Main St Ste 1017
White Plains, NY 10606
(914) 682-6822
Fax: (914) 682-6888
Web: www.chaves.com
Key Contact - Specialty:
Mr. Mike Mitchell - *Computer professionals*

Chelsea Resource Group Inc
10 S Pointe Ct
Bluffton, SC 29910
(843) 706-2336
Fax: (843) 706-2396
Email: crg@topechelon.com
Web: www.chelsearesourcegroup.com

Description: I am a recruiter who has survived the wars with over 21 years of experience in placing high-tech. I am an individual who works across all platforms.

Key Contact:
Ms. Joan Gormley, President

Salary minimum: $60,000

Functions: General Mgmt., Sales & Mktg., IT, Systems Dev., Systems Implem., Network Admin., DB Admin., Architects

Industries: Generalist, Computer Equip., Mgmt. Consulting, E-commerce, Call Centers, Software, Database SW, Development SW, ERP SW, Marketing SW, Security SW, System SW

Networks: Top Echelon Network

Chelsea Resources Inc
18 Oneco St
Norwich, CT 06360
(860) 886-4110
Fax: (860) 886-2210
Email: pat@chelsearesources.com
Web: www.chelsearesources.com

Description: Recognized leaders in medical devices and instrumentation recruiting. Responsive and sucessful. Excel at staffing critical positions quickly. Experienced with venture start-up operations. Clients include Fortune 50 and emerging technology companies.

Key Contact - Specialty:
Mr. Patrick J. Soo Hoo, President - *Medical devices, medical instruments, bio-materials*
Mr. Leo F. Bawza, Vice President - *Medical devices, medical instruments, bio-materials*

Salary minimum: $50,000

Functions: Mfg.

Industries: Drugs Mfg., Medical Devices, Plastics, Rubber, Consumer Elect., Test, Measure Equip.

Networks: Top Echelon Network

Cheney Associates
(a division of Headway Corp Resources)
3190 Whitney Ave 1 Laurel Sq
Hamden, CT 06518
(203) 281-3736
Fax: (203) 281-6881
Email: cheney@nai.net
Web: www.cheney.com

Description: Contingency and retained technical search firm specializing in information technologies, engineering, manufacturing and quality assurance. Services primarily companies in the Northeast region of the USA.

Key Contact:
Mr. Timothy W. Cheney, COO - *Information technology*
Mr. Michael List, President

Functions: Generalist, MIS Mgmt., Systems Analysis, Systems Dev., Systems Implem., Network Admin., DB Admin., Engineering

Industries: Generalist, Mfg., Metal Products, Machine, Appliance, Software, Healthcare

Professional Associations: CAPS, IPA

Networks: Top Echelon Network

Chesapeake Group
4021 Main St
Stratford, CT 06614
(203) 378-5070
Email: jobs@chesgroup.com
Web: www.chesgroup.com

Description: We are an executive search firm placing information technology, sales, and marketing professionals in emerging technology companies across the US.

Key Contact:
Mr. Scott Gardner, Director of Staffing - *Sales & marketing*
Mr. Reed Bocchino, Sales/Marketing Director
Mr. Chris Messina, CFO
Mr. Steve Givens, President

Salary minimum: $75,000

Functions: Middle Mgmt., Sales & Mktg., IT

Industries: Computer Equip., Consumer Elect., E-commerce, IT Implementation, New Media, Fiber Optic, Network Infrastructure, Software, Accounting SW, Database SW, Development SW, ERP SW, Industry Specific SW, Mfg. SW, Networking, Comm. SW

Professional Associations: CAPS, RON

Chester Hill MedEd
1280 Route 46 W
Parsippany, NJ 07054
(973) 402-8400
Fax: (973) 402-8519
Email: ckassor@chme.net
Web: www.chme.net

Description: Our firm specializes in PhDs, PharmDs, and MDs in medical education positions with in pharmaceutical companies, biotech firms, and medical communications companies Please send any questions to chesterhillmeded@rcn.com. Another division of Claire Wright works with executive/administrative support.

Key Contact:
Ms. Cathy Kassor, President
Mr. Tom Buck, Vice President

Functions: Generalist

Industries: Chemicals, Drugs Mfg., Medical Devices, Pharm Svcs., Advertising, Mfg. SW, Women's

Chestnut Partners
5001 W 80th St Ste 960
Southgate Office Plz
Bloomington, MN 55437
(952) 837-2929
Fax: (952) 837-2930
Email: dlloyd@chestnutpartners.com

Description: We are an executive search firm specializing in the recruitment of information technology professionals.

Key Contact - Specialty:
Mr. Richard Lloyd, Managing Partner - *Technology*

Salary minimum: $40,000

Functions: IT

Industries: Generalist

Chicago Financial Search
200 South Wacker Dr
Chicago, IL 60606
(312) 207-0400
Fax: (312) 674-4732
Email: info@chicagofinancial.com
Web: www.chicagofinancial.com

Description: We recruit and place people in the commodities, securities, and banking industries. We specialize in accounting, operations, sales, and IT positions within the financial industry. We now have an office in New York.

Key Contact - Specialty:
Mr. Michael P. Kelly, President
Mr. Richard Wiltgen, Vice President - *Finance, IT*

Salary minimum: $30,000

Functions: General Mgmt.

Industries: Finance

Branches:
245 Park Ave Fl 24
New York, NY 10167
(212) 209-7318
Fax: (212) 372-8798

Chicago Legal Search Ltd
180 N LaSalle St Ste 3350
Chicago, IL 60601
(312) 251-2580
Fax: (312) 251-0223
Email: attorneys@chicagolegalsearch.com
Web: www.chicagolegalsearch.com

Description: Legal recruiting specialists exclusively conducting attorney search and placement for law firms, corporations, financial institutions and not-for-profit foundations primarily in the Chicago metropolitan area.

Key Contact:
Mr. Gary A. D'Alessio, Esq., President - *Legal*
Ms. Chris Percival, Senior Legal Search Consultant - *Legal*
Mr. Alan J. Rubenstein, Esq., Senior Legal Search Consultant - *Legal*
Ms. Shelly Remen Sibul, Esq., Legal Search Consultant - *Legal*
Ms. Eden L. Mandrell, Esq., Legal Search Consultant - *Legal*
Mr. Craig M., Esq. Hoetger, Legal Search Consultant - *Legal*
Ms. Jennifer H., Esq. Seelicke, Legal Search Consultant

Salary minimum: $90,000

Functions: Legal

Industries: Generalist

Professional Associations: NALSC

Joseph Chris Partners
900 Rockmead Dr Ste 101
Kingwood, TX 77339-2116
(281) 359-0060
Fax: (281) 359-0067
Email: joeramirez@josephchris.com
Web: www.josephchris.com

Description: Our clients are real estate and development firms, construction, architectural and engineering companies, and financial institutions that provide funding to the real estate industry. Their portfolios vary and may include raw land, single family, multifamily, commercial, hospitality, senior assisted living, and industrial.

Key Contact - Specialty:
Mr. Joe Ramirez, President - *Real estate, construction industry*

Salary minimum: $75,000

Functions: General Mgmt., Senior Mgmt., Middle Mgmt., Finance, Specialized Svcs., Architects, Int'l.

Industries: Construction, Real Estate

Professional Associations: ICSC, MBA, NAA, NAHB, NAIOP, NAREIT, ULI

Branches:
2265 Roswell Rd Ste 303
Marietta, GA 30062
(770) 579-2836
Fax: (770) 579-3967
Email: ceciliafloyd@josephchris.com
Key Contact:
Ms. Cecilia Floyd

6808 University Ave Ste 105
Middleton, WI 53562
(608) 831-3511
Fax: (608) 831-4641
Email: almarco@josephchris.com
Key Contact:
Mr. Al Marco

Mark Christian & Associates Inc
5844 E Marconi Ave
Scottsdale, AZ 85254
(602) 494-9522
Fax: (602) 953-8991

Email: mchrisassc@aol.com
Web: www.markchristian.com

Description: We offer the information technology (IT) industry a recruiting service to find key people for their organization. Each principal has over 20 years of experience in the information technology industry. Our extensive network of contacts is utilized in all recruiting activity.

Key Contact - Specialty:
Mr. Gary Alexander, Chairman - *Computer industry, management, sales*
Ms. Myra Alexander, President - *Computer industry, sales, technical*
Mr. Phil Batisto, Associate - *Sales*
Mr. Dave Daggett, Associate - *Sales*

Salary minimum: $60,000

Functions: Generalist, Senior Mgmt., Middle Mgmt., Sales Mgmt., Systems Dev., Systems Support

Industries: Computer Equip., Services, Mgmt. Consulting, E-commerce, IT Implementation, Communications, Software

R Christine Associates
Front & Orange Sts
Media, PA 19063
(610) 565-3310
Fax: (610) 565-3313
Email: rcarich@aol.com

Description: We have specialized in personal one-on-one service, recruiting technical and executive professionals in the Philadelphia metropolitan tri-state area. High-tech to smoke stack.

Key Contact - Specialty:
Mr. Rich Christine, CPC, Owner - *Engineering, manufacturing, sales, MIS personnel*

Salary minimum: $40,000

Functions: Mfg., Materials, Sales Mgmt., HR Mgmt., Engineering

Industries: Medical Devices, Metal Products, Machine, Appliance, Test, Measure Equip.

Professional Associations: MAAPC

Networks: Inter-City Personnel Assoc (IPA)

Christopher and Long
15 Worthington
Maryland Heights, MO 63043
(314) 576-6300
(800) 800-5664
Fax: (800) 800-2661
Email: recruit@christopher-and-long.com
Web: www.christopher-and-long.com

Description: For over three decades, our firm has been committed to forming strategic alliances with clients large and small across North America and offshore. Our senior staff, supported by extensive resources, is dedicated to understanding the needs, sharing the urgency, and producing the results needed to solve our clients' staffing challenges.

Key Contact - Specialty:
Mr. Keith A. Long, CEO - *Generalist*
Mr. William Dubuque, General Manager
Ms. Glenda M. Ward, VP-Finance/Administration
Mr. Gary Volz, Senior Consultant of Apparel Division
Mr. Curt Kruse, Senior Consultant of Pharmacy Division - *Pharmacy*
Mr. Cindy Cummings, Senior Consultant of Physicians Division - *Physicians*
Mr. Jeff Baylard, Senior Consultant Food & Beverage Div. - *Food*
Mr. Jim LaChance, Senior Consultant Food & Beverage Div. - *Food*
Mr. Larry Noto, Senior Consultant Tech. & Manuf. Div. - *Generalist*

Functions: Generalist, General Mgmt., Mfg., Materials, Physicians, Sales & Mktg., HR Mgmt., Engineering

Industries: Generalist, Textiles, Apparel, Plastics, Rubber, Metal Products, Machine, Appliance, Motor Vehicles, Retail, Healthcare

Professional Associations: NAPR

Christopher Group Executive Search
8 Sunny Ridge Dr
Asheville, NC 28804
(828) 645-7888
Fax: (828) 645-7833
Email: chrisgroup@charter.net
Web: www.christophergroup.net

Description: Our firm focuses exclusively on the placement of experienced real estate and mortgage professionals, on an international basis. Our clients include: financial institutions, developers, brokerage/property management organizations, corporate real estate entities, REITS/pension funds, and valuation/consulting firms.

Key Contact - Specialty:
Mr. J. Christopher Sprehe, President - *Real estate, mortgage banking, asset management, development, property management*

Salary minimum: $50,000

Functions: Generalist

Industries: Brokers, Real Estate

Professional Associations: AI, BOMA, IREM, MBA, NACORE, NAIOP, NAMB, ULI

Branches:
PO Box 3562
Oakland, CA 94609
(919) 319-3123
Fax: (919) 319-3183
Email: chrisgroup@ibm.net
Key Contact:
Mr. Patrick Sprehe

PO Box 11161
Shawnee Mission, KS 66207-0161
(913) 649-5500
Fax: (919) 319-3183
Email: chrisgroup@ibm.net
Key Contact:
Mr. R. Andrew Sprehe, Vice President

Chrysalis Computer Inc
350 Broadway Ste 415
New York, NY 10013
(212) 431-8750
Fax: (212) 431-8353
Email: chelius@chrysalis-cci.com

Description: Our extensive database and thorough search tactics allow us to find highly qualified candidates and rare skill sets. Then, we go the extra step and screen each candidate for quality through a comprehensive and revealing interview process.

Key Contact:
Ms. Anne Chelius, President

Functions: Generalist, Personnel, IT, Systems Dev., Systems Implem., Network Admin., DB Admin., Mgmt. Consultants

Industries: Generalist, Energy, Utilities, Finance, New Media, Government, Software

Professional Associations: AIIM, FWI, NAWBO

CHS & Associates
9239 Gross Point Rd Ste 302
Skokie, IL 60077
(847) 982-6950
Fax: (847) 655-6116
Email: jobs@chscreativesearch.com

Description: We offer a range of tailored recruitment and search services and fee structures to

meet the needs of our clients. We have experience in a wide range of management functions with an emphasis in, but not limited too, marketing, advertising, creative management, and design.

Key Contact - Specialty:
Mr. Charles Silverstein, Principal - *Generalist*

Salary minimum: $60,000

Functions: Generalist, General Mgmt., Advertising, Mkt. Research, Mktg. Mgmt., Direct Mktg., Personnel, Training, Graphic Artists

Industries: Generalist, Retail, Non-profits, Higher Ed., HR Services, E-commerce, Advertising, Publishing, New Media, Broadcast, Film, Wireless, Fiber Optic, Packaging, Marketing SW

J F Church Associates
PO Box 6128
Bellevue, WA 98008-0128
(425) 644-3278
Email: jfchurch@scn.org

Description: Our services are designed for companies that are manufacturers and/or vendors of computer- based hardware, software or services. Focal areas include sales, sales support and marketing.

Key Contact - Specialty:
Mr. Jim Church, President - *Computer industry (sales & marketing, sales support in computer industry only)*

Salary minimum: $40,000

Functions: Sales & Mktg.

Industries: Mfg., Computer Equip., Services, Software

The Churchill Group
1 Yonge St Ste 1801
Toronto, ON M5E 1W7
Canada
(416) 368-1358
Fax: (416) 369-0515
Email: churchill@bmts.com

Description: Our firm is made up of experienced managers who are familiar with the issues facing organizations today. Each of our consultants has over 20 years of recruitment experience in the manufacturing sector on an international basis.

Key Contact - Specialty:
Mr. Murray Fullerton, President - *Manufacturing*

Salary minimum: $45,000

Functions: Generalist, Mfg.

Industries: Mfg., Printing, Metal Products, Machine, Appliance, Motor Vehicles, Misc. Mfg.

Circlewood Search Group Inc
3307 E Kilgore Rd Ste 2
Kalamazoo, MI 49001-5512
(616) 383-9520
(800) 968-9520
Fax: (616) 383-9530
Email: circlewood@voyager.net
Web: www.circlewood.com

Description: We fill jobs nationwide for physicians, nurses (director, manager, staff, advance practice, CRNA), pharmacists (staff, clinical and director), imaging techs, supervisors, directors (x-ray, ultrasound, nuclear medicine, echo, vascular, CT) and allied health professionals.

Key Contact:
Mr. Peter Militzer, President
Mrs. Amanda Militzer, Vice President

Salary minimum: $40,000

Functions: Directors, Senior Mgmt., Middle Mgmt., Healthcare, Physicians, Nurses, Allied Health, Finance, CFO's, Credit

Industries: Healthcare

Circuit Technology Search Inc
PO Box 44168
Tucson, AZ 85733
(520) 292-9122
Fax: (520) 292-9221
Email: circuit@azstarnet.com
Web: www.circuit-tech-search.com

Description: Practice Limited: Printed Circuit Fabrication: Intimate knowledge of and placement in printed circuit fabrication. In-depth knowledge of technical issues, managerial strata, and suppliers.

Key Contact - Specialty:
Mr. Rick Greenwald - *Printed circuit (fabrication, suppliers)*

Salary minimum: $42,000

Functions: Generalist, Senior Mgmt., Middle Mgmt., Plant Mgmt., Quality, Mktg. Mgmt., Sales Mgmt., Engineering

Industries: Generalist, Mfg., Chemicals, Medical Devices, Machine, Appliance, Computer Equip., Consumer Elect., Test, Measure Equip.

Civilized People
269 E Olive St Ste 205
Long Beach, NY 11561
(516) 897-3025
Fax: (208) 693-2614
Email: civppl@aol.com

Description: We match great people with great opportunities.

Key Contact:
Ms. Ilana Austin, Executive Recruiter

Professional Associations: SHRM

Claimsearch
PO Box 357
Ft. Bragg, CA 95437
(707) 964-1795
(877) 964-1795
Fax: (707) 964-1555
Email: tbayard@mcn.org

Description: We have been recruiting property and casualty claims professionals and risk management personnel and placing them with insurance companies and major corporations for the last 20 years.

Key Contact - Specialty:
Mr. Thomas E. Bayard, CPC, Manager - *Insurance (property, casualty), risk management*
Dr. Apryl Bonham, Consultant - *Insurance (property, casualty), risk management*

Salary minimum: $40,000

Functions: Generalist, Senior Mgmt., Middle Mgmt., Risk Mgmt.

Industries: Insurance

Clanton & Company
1 City Blvd W Ste 820
Orange, CA 92868
(714) 978-7100
Fax: (714) 978-7103
Email: fssearch@aol.com

Description: We were established in 1984 by a trained psychologist to identify personality factors as well as job qualifications in placement of sales managers with food and non-food manufacturers that sell to the food service industry.

Key Contact - Specialty:
Ms. Diane Clanton, President - *Food service sales management*

Salary minimum: $40,000

Functions: Sales Mgmt.

Industries: Food, Bev., Tobacco

Toby Clark Associates Inc
405 E 54th St
New York, NY 10022
(212) 752-5670
Fax: (212) 752-5674
Email: tclarkinc@aol.com

Description: High caliber recruitment for marketing communications, investor relations and public relations for corporations, PR firms and investor relations firms.

Key Contact:
Ms. Toby Clark, President
Ms. Sharon Davis, Executive Vice President

Salary minimum: $75,000

Functions: PR

Industries: Generalist

Howard Clark Associates
PO Box 423
Bellmawr, NJ 08099-0423
(856) 467-3725
Fax: (856) 467-3384
Email: hclark@voicenet.com
Web: www.howardclarkassociates.com

Description: Recruitment of professional candidates for placement with major corporations - nationwide -contingency and search. Also involved in minority/female/disadvantaged recruitment.

Key Contact - Specialty:
Mr. Howard L. Clark, President - *Human resources, sales & marketing, MIS, data processing*
Mr. Jim Anderson, Manager - *Science, business management, engineering, product management, distribution*

Salary minimum: $40,000

Functions: Generalist

Industries: Generalist

R A Clark Consulting Ltd
3355 Lenox Rd Ste 800
Atlanta, GA 30326
(404) 231-0005
(800) 251-0041
Fax: (404) 231-1030
Email: alana@raclark.com
Web: www.raclark.com

Description: Our firm provides executive search and contract services exclusively in the field of human resources. We are committed to providing our clients with unsurpassed service and are recognized as industry experts and the firm of choice when searching for human resource talent.

Key Contact - Specialty:
Mr. Richard Clark, President - *Human resources*
Mr. Chris Daffin, Vice President-National Search - *Human resources, senior level*
Mr. Brian McGonegal, Branch Manager - *Human resources*

Salary minimum: $75,000

Functions: HR Mgmt., Benefits, Personnel, Training

Industries: Generalist

Professional Associations: ESRT, ILRA, SHRM, WAW, WEB

The Clark Group
679 S Lakeshore Dr
Harbor Springs, MI 49740-9117
(231) 526-3210
Fax: (231) 526-3212
Email: larry@theclarkgroup.net

Description: We specialize in recruiting sales, sales support, and marketing executives from around the U.S. in the food, beverage, health and beauty aids, consumer health care, and general merchandise segments of the consumer products industry.

Key Contact - Specialty:
Mr. Larry A. Clark, Owner - *Sales, sales support, marketing executives (food, health & beauty care, general merchandise segments of the consumer product industry)*

Salary minimum: $40,000

Functions: Sales & Mktg.

Industries: Food, Bev., Tobacco, Soap, Perf., Cosmtcs., Drugs Mfg., Consumer Elect.

Professional Associations: FIN

Networks: First Interview Network (FIN)

Clark Personnel Service Inc
4315 Downtowner Loop N
PO Box 991850
Mobile, AL 36691-5501
(334) 342-5511
Fax: (334) 343-5588
Email: webmaster@clarkpersonnel.com
Web: www.clarkpersonnel.com

Description: We are a full-service staffing firm including professional recruiting and temporary staffing.

Key Contact:
Mr. Bob Alston, President

Functions: Generalist, Senior Mgmt., Middle Mgmt., Production, Plant Mgmt., Materials Plng., Sales Mgmt., Engineering

Industries: Generalist, Food, Bev., Tobacco, Textiles, Apparel, Lumber, Furniture, Paper, Chemicals, Metal Products

Professional Associations: NATSS

Networks: Inter-City Personnel Assoc (IPA)

The Clertech Group Inc
7029 Canal Blvd
New Orleans, LA 70124
(504) 288-3971
Fax: (504) 288-3856
Email: gad2@ieee.org

Description: We specialize in often very technical searches for senior engineering, technical and management professionals for utilities and related industries: generation/T&D planning and reliability, automation consulting and marketing support, e.g.

Key Contact - Specialty:
Mr. George A. Dorko, Director - *Electric utility, engineering consultants*

Salary minimum: $50,000

Functions: Generalist, Engineering

Industries: Generalist, Energy, Utilities, Construction, Mfg., Metal Products, Motor Vehicles, Computer Equip., Electronic, Elec. Components, IT Implementation, Database SW, Industry Specific SW, Networking, Comm. SW, System SW

Professional Associations: IEEE

Cleveland Business Consultants
1148 Euclid Ave Ste 416
Cleveland, OH 44115
(216) 781-5300
Fax: (216) 348-6396
Email: cbcsearch@cbc-employment.com
Web: www.cbc-employment.com

Description: We purposely specialize in the NE Ohio region so that all candidates and customers can be met personally. We specialize in employed professionals. Evening interviews are available.

Key Contact - Specialty:
Mr. Don Tillery, Owner/Manager - *Engineering, technical, manufacturing*
Mr. Kurt Bright, Senior Manager - *Engineering, technical, manufacturing*
Mr. Gregory Schmidt, Manager - *Engineering, technical, manufacturing*
Mr. Ted Morris, Manager - *Engineering, technical, manufacturing*
Mr. Tom Williams, Manager - *Information technology, engineering, manufacturing*

Functions: Generalist, Middle Mgmt., Mfg., Materials, IT, Engineering, Architects, Technicians

Industries: Generalist, Mfg., Aerospace

Clin Force Inc
4815 Emperor Blvd Ste 300
Durham, NC 27703
(919) 941-0844
(800) 964-2877
Fax: (919) 941-0071
Email: response@clinforce.com
Web: www.clinforce.com

Description: Our firm has the largest network of qualified professionals in the clinical research industry for contract assignments and direct placement across all disciplines and at all levels including: clinical operations, clinical data sciences, medical review & writing, pharmacoeconomics, regulatory affairs, MDs and PhDs and pre-clinical.

Key Contact - Specialty:
Mr. Tony Sims, President - *Clinical, pharmaceutical*
Mr. Rob Stallings, VP- of Operations - *Pharmaceutical, clinical*
Ms. Ellen Maynard, VP- of Account Development - *Pharmaceutical, clinical*
Mr. Chris Castin, Director of Executive Search - *Pharmaceutical, clinical*

Functions: Generalist

Industries: Drugs Mfg., Medical Devices, Pharm Svcs., Environmental Svcs., Biotech, Healthcare

Clinical Staffing Associates LLC (CSA)
407 Main St Ste 204
Metuchen, NJ 08840
(732) 321-0088
Fax: (732) 321-0394
Email: csa@clinicalstaffing.com
Web: www.clinicalstaffing.com

Description: We are a full-service organization with expertise in both the permanent and contractural staffing arena. We specialize in providing experienced clinical research professionals to the pharmaceutical and biotech industry.

Key Contact - Specialty:
Ms. Carole Ornstein, President - *Pharmaceutical, R&D*
Ms. Susan Lynn Brenner, Vice President - *Pharmaceutical R&D*

Functions: General Mgmt., Healthcare, R&D

Industries: Drugs Mfg., Medical Devices, Pharm Svcs., Biotech

Professional Associations: ACRP, DIA, NJSA

Clinton, Charles, Wise & Company
931 State Rd 434 Ste 1201-319
Altamonte Springs, FL 32714
(407) 682-6790
Fax: (407) 682-1697
Email: ccwc@cfl.rr.com
Web: www.recruitersofccwc.com

Description: We are a firm specializing in recruiting sales, marketing, and management talent in the high technology, financial, and healthcare industries throughout the country (US).

Key Contact - Specialty:
Mr. Craig D. Wise, President - *Sales, computer industry*
Mr. Omari Clinton, Executive Recruiter - *Sales management, computer industry*
Mr. Kamal Charles, Executive Recruiter - *Medical sales, financial sales*
Ms. Annette C Wise, Vice President - *Sales*

Functions: Senior Mgmt., Middle Mgmt., Sales & Mktg., Mkt. Research, Mktg. Mgmt., Sales Mgmt., Systems Implem., Systems Support, Mgmt. Consultants, Minorities

Industries: Drugs Mfg., Medical Devices, Computer Equip., Banking, Software, Healthcare

David E Clutter
5668 S Foresthill St
Littleton, CO 80120
(303) 730-6422
Fax: (303) 730-2028
Email: dclutter@prodigy.net

Description: Specialize in recruiting sales, sales management and product support professionals for manufacturers and their dealers in the construction and mining equipment industries.

Key Contact - Specialty:
Mr. David E. Clutter, Owner - *Construction equipment, mining equipment, sales management, general management, product support management*

Functions: Generalist, Senior Mgmt., Middle Mgmt., Sales & Mktg., Mktg. Mgmt., Sales Mgmt.

Industries: Construction

CMC Consultants Inc
500 N Michigan Ave Ste 1940
Chicago, IL 60611
(312) 670-5300
Fax: (312) 670-5333
Email: carolm@cmcconsult.com
Web: www.cmcconsult.com

Description: Specialists in the professional recruitment of executive-level positions in fields that include accounting, finance, sales, marketing and human resources.

Key Contact - Specialty:
Ms. Carol Marcovich, President - *Generalist*

Salary minimum: $50,000

Functions: Directors, Middle Mgmt., Mfg., Sales & Mktg., HR Mgmt., Finance

Industries: Generalist, Mfg., Retail, Finance, Accounting, HR Services, Insurance

Professional Associations: HRMAC, NAWBO

CMR Executive Search
1835 Savoy Dr Ste 217
Atlanta, GA 30341
(770) 455-9699
Email: msingley@cmresources.com
Web: www.searchexecutive.com

Description: We are an Atlanta-based search firm that handles retained and contingency searches on a national and international basis for mid-level management through top-level executives. Our recruiters are experienced executives who have an average of 25 years experience in management and understand the search process from inception to conclusion.

Key Contact:
Ms. Marjorie Singley-Hall, Practice Director

Functions: General Mgmt.

Industries: Drugs Mfg., Pharm Svcs., Communications, Software, Biotech, Healthcare

Professional Associations: GAPS, TAG

CMS Inc
500 Commercial St
Manchester, NH 03101-1151
(603) 644-7800
Fax: (603) 644-5560
Email: stan@cms-rsi.com
Web: www.cms-rsi.com

Description: We are prominent international specialists in sporting goods, footwear, active-wear, and we place in all specialties and disciplines.

Key Contact - Specialty:
Mr. Stan Clayman, President - *Sporting goods, footwear, apparel*

Salary minimum: $50,000

Functions: Senior Mgmt., Production, Distribution, Health Admin., Mkt. Research, Sales Mgmt., CFO's, MIS Mgmt., Systems Analysis, Graphic Artists

Industries: Textiles, Apparel

CMS Management Services Company
(a division of MSX Int'l & a member of Career Partners Int'l)
401 E Colfax Ste 401
South Bend, IN 46617
(219) 282-3980
Fax: (219) 282-3995
Email: jnoto@msxi.com
Web: www.cmssb.com

Description: Employment service firm specializing in financial and information technology professionals nationwide on a direct hire, temp-to-hire or contract basis.

Key Contact - Specialty:
Mr. Joseph A. Noto, CPA, President - *Accounting, finance*
Mr. Patrick B. Laake, Vice President - *Information technology*

Salary minimum: $30,000

Functions: Finance, IT

Industries: Generalist

Professional Associations: ASA, NAPS

Networks: Career Partners Int'l

Branches:
5920 Castleway W Dr Ste 120
Indianapolis, IN 46250
(317) 842-5777
Fax: (317) 577-3077
Key Contact - Specialty:
Mr. David Reese, Director - Financial Staffing Services - *Accounting & finance*

10420 Old Olive St Rd Ste 205
St. Louis, MO 63141
(314) 989-9823
Fax: (314) 989-1521
Email: dlatka@staffing.net
Key Contact:
Mr. Dan Latka

2717 Ward Cir Ste 102
Brentwood, TN 37027
(615) 377-3700
Fax: (615) 377-8625
Key Contact - Specialty:
Mr. Ron Davis, Manager - *Information technology*

CMW & Associates Inc
PO Box 3004
Springfield, IL 62704
(217) 522-0452
Fax: (217) 241-5974
Email: cmw@topechelon.com
Web: www.cmwassoc.com

Description: We have at least 10 years' experience in our specialty field. Our clients consist of many of the Fortune 500. Our area of expertise is limited to technical placements in the computer, computer sales and degreed engineering fields.

Key Contact - Specialty:
Ms. Charlene Turczyn, Principal - *Information technology*

Salary minimum: $45,000

Functions: Sales & Mktg., IT, MIS Mgmt., Systems Dev., Engineering

Industries: Generalist, Mgmt. Consulting, Software

Professional Associations: AITP, MAPS, SHRM, WIM

Networks: Top Echelon Network

Branches:
711 Old Ballas Rd Ste 110
St. Louis, MO 63141
(800) 618-8706
Fax: (888) RESUME1
Email: tammy@midwest.net
Key Contact:
Ms. Charlene Turczyn

CN Associates
4040 Civic Center Dr Ste 200
San Rafael, CA 94903
(415) 883-1114
Fax: (415) 883-3321
Email: chasn@earthlink.net
Web: www.cnassociates.com

Description: We are a San Francisco area based high-tech executive search firm with a strong focus in sales and marketing. We specialize in software, DataComm, and Internet based applications. CN Associates is also a preferred member of Top Echelon Network, Inc., a major on-line network of executive search firms.

Key Contact - Specialty:
Mr. Charles Nicolosi, Principal - *Software, data communications, telecommunications, sales & marketing, software developers*

Salary minimum: $70,000

Functions: Sales & Mktg., MIS Mgmt., Systems Analysis, Systems Dev., Systems Implem., Systems Support, Network Admin., DB Admin., Mgmt. Consultants

Industries: Mgmt. Consulting, Software

Professional Associations: GGCS, NCHRC, RON

Networks: National Consulting Network (NCN)

CNC Global
350 Albert St Ste 1825
Constitution Sq
Ottawa, ON K1R 1A4
Canada
(613) 786-3220
Fax: (613) 567-2659
Email: ottawa@cncglobal.com
Web: www.cncglobal.com

Description: We are the leading provider of IT and E-commerce staffing and career search services, including permanent placement and contract consulting, recruitment advertising, online career fairs and Internet-based recruitment. Specializing in technology recruitment for two decades. We're ready to help you with your staffing and career search challenges.

Key Contact - Specialty:
Mr. Brennan Senos, Account Manager-Ottawa - *Information technology, telecommunications, engineering*

Functions: Directors, Senior Mgmt., Middle Mgmt., Sales & Mktg., IT, Mgmt. Consultants, Technicians

Industries: Generalist

Professional Associations: ACSESS, OHRPA

Branches:
2501 Blue Ridge Rd Ste 250
Raleigh, NC 27607
(919) 510-9770
Fax: (919) 510-4647
Email: raleigh@cncglobal.com
Key Contact:
Mr. Larry Thompson

16000 Dallas Pkwy Ste 375
Dallas, TX 75248
(972) 725-3315
Email: dallas@cncglobal.com

700 9th Ave SW Ste 2910
South Tower, Western Canada Place
Calgary, AB T2P 3V4
Canada
(403) 263-4501
Fax: (403) 263-4502
Email: calgary@cncglobal.com

10180 101 St Ste 1150
Manulife Pl
Edmonton, AB T5J 3S4
Canada
(780) 497-7750
Fax: (780) 497-7760
Email: edmonton@cncglobal.com

1090 W Georgia St Ste 420
Vancouver, BC V6E 3V7
Canada
(604) 687-5919
Fax: (604) 687-5397
Email: vancouver@cncglobal.com

3 Robert Speck Pkwy Ste 280
Mississauga, ON L4Z 2G5
Canada
(905) 277-9111
Email: mississauga@cncglobal.com

1 West Pierce St Ste 307
Richmond Hill, ON L4B 3K3
Canada
(905) 882-1044
Email: richmondhill@cncglobal.com

60 Bloor St W Fl 14
Toronto, ON M4W 3B8
Canada
(416) 962-4489
Fax: (416) 962-4489
Email: toronto@cncglobal.com

1470 Peel St Ste 720
Montreal, QC H3A 1T1
Canada
(514) 845-5775
Email: montreal@cncglobal.com

CNI
1320 S Dixie Hwy Ste 1105
Gables 1 Twr
Coral Gables, FL 33146
(305) 665-5627
Fax: (305) 665-5633
Email: resumes@cnijoblink.com
Web: www.cnijoblink.com

Description: We specialize in wireless, telecommunications, and financial industries. We have one of the most targeted audiences available on the web. Our visitors are job candidates seeking employment specifically in the telecommunications, wireless, and financial industries.

Key Contact - Specialty:
Ms. Monique Hernandez, President - *Executives*
Mr. Mark Hamdan, Chairman - *Executives*

Functions: General Mgmt., Mfg., Purchasing, Sales & Mktg., HR Mgmt., Training, Finance, IT, Engineering, Technicians

Industries: Invest. Banking, Telecoms

Coast to Coast Executive Search
9769 W 119th Dr Ste 14
Broomfield, CO 80021
(303) 464-1704
Fax: (303) 464-1553
Email: exsrch1@aol.com

Description: Specializing in the hospitality, restaurant, club and food service industry, we offer our clients prompt and efficient closure to their important management openings.

Key Contact - Specialty:
Mr. Dennis Updyke, CPC, Owner - *Hospitality, restaurant, clubs, food service*

Functions: Generalist, Senior Mgmt.

Industries: Hospitality

Cobb & Company
7114 Casa Loma Ave
Dallas, TX 75214
(214) 327-4712
Fax: (214) 327-2813
Email: cobbcoinc@hotmail.com
Web: www.cobbcoinc.com

Description: Our firm is placing scientists, executives and business professionals in the biotech and pharmaceutical industry.

Key Contact:
Mr. Mark Cobb, President
Mr. Mike Cobb

Salary minimum: $80,000

Functions: General Mgmt., Directors, Senior Mgmt., Quality, R&D

Industries: Drugs Mfg., Medical Devices, Pharm Svcs., Legal, Mfg. SW, Marketing SW, Biotech

Professional Associations: AAA, AAAS, AAI, AAPS, ACRP, AIC, AITP, APICS, APS, AS, ASBMB, ACSB, ASNS, ASPET, ASQ, CRS, FASEB, IOPP, ISPE, PDA, PS, RAPS, SCC, SHRM, TTS

Cobb Professional Services Ltd
PO Box 6095
Fishers, IN 46038-6095
(317) 913-0820
Fax: (317) 913-0821
Email: cps@cobb.net
Web: www.cps.cobb.net

Description: We provide services to our clients through retained search, contingency and engagement fee methods. Our guiding principles of integrity, teamwork and honest commitment are applied to each project we undertake.

Key Contact - Specialty:
Mr. Mark A. Cobb, President - *Senior management, executive, marketing, engineering, materials management*
Ms. Lynn A. Cobb, Search Consultant - *Pharmaceutical (manufacturing, QA/QC, R&D, validation, production)*

Salary minimum: $35,000

Functions: Generalist, General Mgmt., Senior Mgmt., Product Dev., Production, Plant Mgmt., Quality, Materials, R&D, Engineering

Industries: Generalist, Construction, Mfg., Drugs Mfg., Medical Devices, Misc. Mfg., Pharm Svcs.

Professional Associations: AAPS, ISPE

Ann Coe & Associates
2033 Sherman Ave Ste 301
Evanston, IL 60201
(847) 864-0668
Email: anncoe@aol.com
Web: www.anncoe.com

Description: We provide professional and executive search specializing in information technology (IT).

Key Contact - Specialty:
Ms. Ann Coe, President/Owner - *Information technology*

Salary minimum: $50,000

Functions: Product Dev., Customer Svc., IT, MIS Mgmt., Systems Analysis, Systems Implem., Systems Support, Network Admin., DB Admin., Technicians

Industries: Generalist

Coleman Legal Staffing
2 Penn Center Ste 1010
Philadelphia, PA 19102
(215) 864-2700
Fax: (215) 864-2709
Email: cls@colemanlegal.com
Web: www.colemanlegal.com

Description: We specialize in recruiting lawyers, partners and associates for law firms and general counsels and staff attorneys for corporations in the Eastern United States. We also assist in law firm mergers and opening of satellite offices. In addition, we provide contract attorneys and paralegals and permanent paralegals to law firms and corporations.

Key Contact - Specialty:
Mr. Michael M. Coleman, Principal - *Legal, paralegal*

Functions: Legal, Attorneys, Paralegals

Industries: Generalist

Professional Associations: NALSC

Branches:
33 Wood Ave S Metropark Office Complex
Iselin, NJ 08830
(732) 603-3896
Email: cls@colemanlegal.com
Key Contact:
Mr. Michael M. Coleman, President

College Executives
(also known as CE Recruiters)
PO Box 1119
Highland City, FL 33846
(863) 534-8548
Email: collegeexecutive@aol.com
Web: www.collegeexecutives.com

Description: A nationwide executive recruiting firm specializing in mid and upper management recruitment & placement in the private/proprietary education sector. CE Recruiters is a nationwide subsidiary of College Executives and specializes in mid and upper management recruitment & placement in the retail industry.

Key Contact:
Dr. Frances Morris

Functions: Generalist, General Mgmt., Directors, Senior Mgmt., Middle Mgmt., Sales & Mktg., Sales Mgmt.

Industries: Retail, Higher Ed., Hospitality, Non-classifiable

Collins & Associates
10188 W
Kalamazoo, MI 49009
(616) 372-3275
Fax: (616) 372-3921
Email: pcollins@collins-associates.com
Web: www.collins-associates.com

Description: Specializing in the western Michigan and northern Indiana area. All areas of computers and computer professionals. Healthcare management, project management and computer professionals. All disciplines in engineering, operations, and management in the manufacturing industries.

Key Contact - Specialty:
Mr. Philip M. Collins, Principal - *Computers*
Mr. Peter A. Collins, CPC, Principal - *Information technologies, healthcare, manufacturing*

Salary minimum: $40,000

Functions: Generalist, Mfg., Health Admin., MIS Mgmt., Systems Analysis, Systems Dev., Systems Implem., Network Admin., DB Admin.

Industries: Generalist, Energy, Utilities, Mfg., Metal Products, Machine, Appliance, Computer Equip., Test, Measure Equip., Misc. Mfg., Electronic, Elec. Components, Retail, Finance, Software, Mfg. SW

Professional Associations: RON

Networks: Inter-City Personnel Assoc (IPA)

Branches:
1550 E Beltline SE Ste 200
Grand Rapids, MI 49506
(616) 977-5726
Fax: (616) 977-5728
Email: petec@collins-associates.com
Key Contact - Specialty:
Mr. Pete Collins - *Manufacturing (automotive, quality)*

S L Collins Associates Inc

PO Box 78945
Charlotte, NC 28277-7044
(704) 321-2400
Fax: (425) 790-3336
Email: collins@slcollins.com
Web: www.slcollins.com

Description: We are well known throughout the pharmaceutical and biotechnology industries for our professionalism, integrity and service to both client companies and candidates. Positions are nationwide and up to the level of senior vice president. Visit our web site for additional information including a listing of available positions.

Key Contact - Specialty:
Mr. Steve L. Collins, President - *Pharmaceutical, biotechnology*
Mr. David Collins, Vice President - *Pharmaceutical, biotech, biological*

Salary minimum: $40,000

Functions: Generalist

Industries: Drugs Mfg., Medical Devices, Pharm Svcs., Biotech, Healthcare

Professional Associations: AAPS, DIA, ISPE, PDA, RAPS

Colorado Corporate Search LLC

283 Columbine St Ste 125
Denver, CO 80206
(303) 333-6464
Fax: (303) 333-2880
Email: amy@coloradosearch.com
Web: www.coloradosearch.com

Description: We know the Colorado accounting & finance community inside out and backwards.

Key Contact - Specialty:
Ms. Amy C. Duclos, President - *Accounting & finance*

Salary minimum: $60,000

Functions: Finance

Industries: Generalist

Columbus Int'l Group

(also known as MRI of Kiawah Island)
180 Meeting St Ste 210
Charleston, SC 29401
(843) 973-3500
Fax: (843) 973-3513
Email: lsc@columbusgroup.net
Web: www.columbusgroup.net

Description: Our firm specializes in delivering customized, on-target searches, both on a retained or a contingency basis. Our interview-to-hire ratio consistently tracks at less than a four-to-one ratio in the information technology, telecommunications, and healthcare industries.

Key Contact:
Mr. L. S. Carper, Manager

Salary minimum: $50,000

Functions: Generalist, Nurses, Sales Mgmt., MIS Mgmt., Systems Dev., Network Admin., Mgmt. Consultants

Industries: Generalist, Services, Mgmt. Consulting, E-commerce, IT Implementation, Communications, Telecoms, Call Centers, Telephony, Fiber Optic, Network Infrastructure, Software, Networking, Comm. SW, Healthcare

Comand Consultants

20 Waterside Plz Ste 600
New York, NY 10010
(212) 481-9381
Fax: (212) 481-9055
Email: mlondon@staffing.net
Web: www.commandconsultants.com

Key Contact:
Mr. Mark London, President

Networks: Top Echelon Network

Commercial Programming Systems Inc

3575 Cahuenga Blvd W Ste 222
Los Angeles, CA 90068
(323) 851-2681
(888) 277-4562
Fax: (323) 851-5681
Email: cps@cpsinc.com
Web: www.cpsinc.com

Description: We are Southern California's contract service of choice for information technology professionals. With offices in Los Angeles, Orange County and Phoenix, AZ, we provide contract, lease to hire and executive placement opportunities.

Key Contact:
Mr. Alan Strong, President

Functions: Generalist, MIS Mgmt., Systems Analysis, Systems Dev., Systems Implem., Systems Support, Network Admin., DB Admin.

Industries: Generalist, Motor Vehicles, Finance, Hospitality, Media, Broadcast, Film, Telecoms, Government

Professional Associations: AITP

Branches:
2425 Camelback Rd Ste 450
Phoenix, AZ 85016
(602) 667-7766
(888) 812-5961
Fax: (602) 912-8514
Email: ted.davenport@cpsinc.com

145 S State College Blvd Ste 290
Brea, CA 92821
(714) 674-0100
(888) 812-5960
Fax: (714) 672-3545
Email: cattman@cpsinc.com

Commonwealth Consultants

5064 Roswell Rd Ste B 101
Atlanta, GA 30342
(404) 256-0000
Fax: (404) 256-3625

Description: Supply computer vendors and consulting firms exceptional candidates with strong computer skills. All levels in the disciplines of programmers, systems analysts, hardware/software engineers, sales, technical support and marketing.

Key Contact:
Mr. David Aiken, Partner
Mr. Tim Panetta, Partner
Mr. Marcus Mouchet, Partner

Salary minimum: $35,000

Functions: Generalist, Sales Mgmt.

Industries: Generalist, Software

Professional Associations: GAPS

Commonwealth Financial Corp

(formerly known as GostaffIT.com)
578 Waterloo Rd Ste 3B
Warrenton, VA 20186
(540) 349-8886
Email: dcraig@gostaffit.com
Web: www.gostaffit.com

Description: We developed a web site and service to assist candidates and companies to better define positions and match qualified candidates. We also built a skill assessment tool and testing capability to help hiring managers identify the best candidate.

Key Contact:
Mr. Michael Atkins, CEO
Mr. Doug Craig, COO

Salary minimum: $60,000

Functions: Generalist

Industries: Mgmt. Consulting, Telecoms, Software

Compensation & Benefits Search

31 Lexington Rd
West Hartford, CT 06119
(860) 236-7422
Fax: (860) 231-8433
Email: warseck@home.com

Description: Specializing in the analytical side of healthcare-stats, survey, epidemiology, outcomes, etc.

Key Contact:
Mr. Bob Warseck

Salary minimum: $80,000

Functions: Generalist

Industries: Healthcare

ComPeople Source Inc

17W070 Burr Oak Ln
Hinsdale, IL 60521
(630) 789-0088
Fax: (630) 789-9950
Email: jack@compeoplesource.com

Description: Our principal, Jack Hillon, has been heading up perm IT search firms since early 1991. Our clients range in size from small IT consulting organizations to multi-billion dollar corporations. We handle any IT-related search, from recruiters, to sales, to technical and management candidates.

Key Contact - Specialty:
Mr. Jack Hillon, President - *Contingency or retained IT search*

Salary minimum: $45,000

The Comperio Group

3617 Betty Dr Ste I
Colorado Springs, CO 80917
(719) 570-1500
Email: resumes@comperiogroup.com
Web: www.comperiogroup.com

Description: Our firm is a retained executive recruiting firm that focuses solely on the computer and communications industries. Through specialization, we have gained a broad and deep understanding of both business sectors. As a result, we recruit quickly and efficiently. This kind of focus is critical in industries where competition for talented managers is fierce and unrelenting.

Key Contact:
Mr. John Taylor, President

Salary minimum: $75,000

Functions: Senior Mgmt., Product Dev., Sales & Mktg.

Industries: Computer Equip., Electronic, Elec. Components, E-commerce, IT Implementation, Communications, Software

CompHealth

4021 S 700 E Ste 300
PO Box 57915
Salt Lake City, UT 84107
(801) 264-6400
(800) 453-3030
Fax: (801) 328-3091
Email: info@comphealth.com
Web: www.comphealth.com

Description: We are the largest, comprehensive healthcare and staffing company in the nation. We provide temporary and permanent placement services for physicians, nurses, allied health professionals, and healthcare executives.

Key Contact:
Mr. Michael Weinholtz, Chief Executive Officer
Mr. Don DeCamp, CPC, Chief Operating Officer
Mr. Sean Dailey, CPA, Chief Financial Officer
Mr. Scott Beck, Chief Marketing Officer
Mr. Brent Blundell, Chief Technical Officer
Mr. Jeff Freeman, EVP - Physician Search Group

Salary minimum: $80,000

Functions: Healthcare, Physicians, Nurses, Allied Health

Industries: Healthcare, Hospitals, Long-term Care, Physical Therapy, Occupational Therapy, Women's

Professional Associations: NAPR

Branches:
25 Van Zant St
Norwalk, CT 06851
(203) 866-1144
(800) 365-8900
Fax: (203) 853-3154
Email: lstewart@comphealth.com
Key Contact:
Mr. Larry Stewart, President - Physician Search Group
Mr. Scott Powell, EVP - Physician Search Group

2000 W Commercial Blvd Ste 117
Ft. Lauderdale, FL 33309
(954) 771-4410
(800) 782-9029
Fax: (954) 771-4558
Email: chagler@comphealth.com
Key Contact:
Mr. Carlos Hagler, Dir Operations - Allied Staffing Group

5352 NW 21st Ter
Ft. Lauderdale, FL 33309
(954) 771-2501
(800) 365-8901
Fax: (954) 771-0046
Email: dbabchick@comphealth.com

Key Contact:
Mr. Don Babchick, EVP - Physician Search Group

1776 Peachtree St NW Ste 330 S
Atlanta, GA 30309
(678) 420-4940
Fax: (404) 724-0889
Email: fscott@comphealth.com
Key Contact:
Fatimah Scott, Branch Mgr - Per Diem Nurse Staffing

3312 Northside Dr Ste D 265
Macon, GA 31210
(478) 757-2277
Fax: (478) 757-8865
Email: sgriffin@comphealth.com
Key Contact:
Ms. Sabrina Griffin, Manager - Per Diem Nurse Staffing

9701 W Higgins Rd Ste 680
Rosemont, IL 60018
(847) 384-9500
(800) 365-8902
Fax: (847) 384-9505
Email: cskarzynski@comphealth.com
Key Contact:
Ms. Carleen Skarzynski, EVP - Physician Search Group

2610 Horizon SE Ste B-2
Grand Rapids, MI 49546-7517
(616) 975-5000
(800) 634-1077
Fax: (616) 975-5030
Email: sandrara@comphealth.com
Key Contact:
Ms. Sandra Raehl, Operations Mgr - Allied Staffing Group

5115 Maryland Way Ste 30
Brentwood, TN 37027
(615) 377-9223
Fax: (615) 377-6904
Email: thart@comphealth.com
Key Contact:
Mr. Tom Hart, President - Per Diem Nurse Staffing

10925 Estate Ln Ste 120
Dallas, TX 75238
(214) 553-4508
(800) 448-9728
Fax: (214) 553-0431
Email: ahall@comphealth.com
Key Contact:
Ms. Anita Hall, Dir Operations - Per Diem Nurse Staffing

1550 W Rosedale Ste 820
Ft. Worth, TX 76104
(817) 332-4437
Fax: (817) 332-4141
Email: ahall@comphealth.com
Key Contact:
Ms. Anita Hall, Dir Operations - Per Diem Nurse Staffing

Compton & Associates

881 Corporate Dr Ste 204
Lexington, KY 40503
(859) 223-0880
Fax: (859) 223-1073
Email: comptonsearch@qx.net
Web: www.comptonsearch.com

Description: We offer placement services throughout the US. Our affiliation with IPA and other networks provides databases of over one million candidates and hundreds of job orders.

Key Contact - Specialty:
Mr. James W. Compton, Principal - *Information technology*
Mr. Tom Reid, Manager Technical Search - *Manufacturing*
Ms. Amy Williams, Recruiting Coordinator - *Manufacturing*

Salary minimum: $50,000

Functions: Generalist

Industries: Generalist

Networks: Inter-City Personnel Assoc (IPA)

CompuPro

29585 N Waukegan Rd Ste 104
Lake Bluff, IL 60044
(847) 549-8603
Email: qmancompupro@attglobal.net

Description: Specialists in the information technology industry and related areas.

Key Contact - Specialty:
Mr. Douglas J. Baniqued, President - *Information technology*

Salary minimum: $50,000

Functions: Generalist, General Mgmt., Finance, IT, MIS Mgmt., Systems Implem., Network Admin., DB Admin.

Industries: Generalist, Mfg., Finance, Services, Media, Software

Networks: Top Echelon Network

Computech Corp

4375 N 75th St
Scottsdale, AZ 85251
(480) 947-7534
Fax: (480) 947-7537
Email: jobs@computech-az.com
Web: www.computech-az.com

Description: Search and consulting firm specializing in Tesseract, PeopleSoft, SAP, Ceridian, ADP CSS Hrizon, Internet, web development, HTML, Java, B2B, e-commerce, client server and other IT positions.

Key Contact:
Mr. Bob Dirickson

Functions: Generalist

Industries: Generalist, Computer Equip., Banking, HR Services, IT Implementation

Computer Career Services

PO Box 655
Waverly, PA 18471
(570) 341-9700
Fax: (570) 383-0029
Email: mike.rescigno@theryangroup.org
Web: www.theryangroup.org

Description: We specialize in recruitment and placement of professionals primarily in Northeastern Pennsylvania (NEPA). We are different from typical "headhunters" whose priority is solely the hiring company. The Ryan Group balances the mutual needs of the hiring company and the professional seeking a new career opportunity.

Key Contact:
Mr. Michael A. Rescigno, Partner
Mr. Donald Ryan, Partner

Salary minimum: $35,000

Functions: Generalist, Middle Mgmt., Production, Finance

Industries: Electronic, Elec. Components, Finance, Misc. Financial, Services, Accounting, Mgmt. Consulting, HR Services, IT Implementation, Defense, Software, Accounting SW, Mfg. SW, Biotech

Computer Careers

110 N Rangeline Rd Ste 207
PO Box 1613
Joplin, MO 64802
(417) 781-2929
Fax: (417) 781-4334
Email: lbaker@computercareers.net
Web: www.computercareers.net

Description: We offer permanent and temporary
information technology staffing, including employer
of record service for part-time and contract
employees.

Key Contact - Specialty:
Mr. Larry Baker, President - *Placement of IT
 professionals*
Mr. Ryan Baker, Recruiter - *Placement of IT
 professionals*
Mr. David Spencer, Recruiter - *Placement of IT
 professionals*

Salary minimum: $30,000

Functions: IT

Industries: Generalist

Networks: Top Echelon Network

Computer Horizons ISG

5045 Orbitor Dr Bldg 7 Ste 200
Mississauga, ON L4W 4Y4
Canada
(905) 602-6085
Fax: (905) 602-6091
Email: toronto@isgjobs.com
Web: www.isgjobs.com

Description: We provide both permanent and
contract information technology personnel to mid
and large-sized companies in various industries
across North America.

Key Contact - Specialty:
Mr. Frank Vrabel, Vice President-Staffing Services
 - *Information technology*
Mr. Taki Giourgas, Vice President, Strategic
 Development - *Information technology*
Mr. Paul Bottero, President - *Information
 technology*

Functions: IT, MIS Mgmt., Systems Analysis,
Systems Dev., Systems Implem., Systems
Support, Network Admin., DB Admin., Graphic
Artists

Industries: Generalist

Branches:
734 7th Ave SW Ste 420
Calgary, AB T2P 3P8
Canada
(403) 265-3380
Fax: (403) 265-3301
Email: calgary@isgjobs.com
Key Contact:
Ms. Andrea Guinn, Vice President-Staffing
 Services

666 Burrard St Ste 1800
Park Pl
Vancouver, BC V6C 3B1
Canada
(604) 484-4810
Fax: (604) 484-4811
Email: vancouver@isgjobs.com
Key Contact:
Ms. Jane Carson, Vice President, Staffing Services

180 Elgin St Ste 801
Ottawa, ON K2P 2K3
Canada
(613) 688-0918
Fax: (613) 688-0917
Email: ottawa@isgjobs.com
Key Contact:
Mr. Mark Cohen, Vice President-Staffing Services

Computer Int'l Consultants Inc

1111 N Westshore Blvd Ste 200B
Tampa, FL 33607-4705
(813) 281-0505
Fax: (813) 281-0913
Email: jobs@cictampa.com
Web: www.cictampa.com

Description: Recruitment experience and
competence by a staff of former Fortune 500
executives that understand corporate structure,
culture and requirements. Staff experience in
information technology.

Key Contact - Specialty:
Ms. Linda M. Mitchell, CEO - *Contract services*
Mr. Michael R. Mitchell, CIO - *Information
 technology*

Salary minimum: $50,000

Functions: Generalist, MIS Mgmt., Systems
Analysis, Systems Dev., Systems Implem.,
Network Admin., DB Admin.

Industries: Generalist, Energy, Utilities,
Transportation, Misc. Financial, IT
Implementation, New Media, Telecoms, Network
Infrastructure, Software, Database SW,
Networking, Comm. SW

Networks: Top Echelon Network

Computer Management Inc

809 Gleneagles Ct Ste 205
Towson, MD 21286
(410) 583-0050
Fax: (410) 494-9410
Email: info@technicaljobs.com
Web: www.technicaljobs.com

Description: We specialize in search and placement
for Information technology professionals, and
software and hardware engineers.

Key Contact:
Ms. Janet Miller, President

Salary minimum: $45,000

Functions: IT, Engineering

Industries: Mfg., Consumer Elect., Test, Measure
Equip., Misc. Mfg., Electronic, Elec.
Components, Finance, Invest. Banking, E-
commerce, IT Implementation, Advertising,
Digital, Wireless, Fiber Optic, Network
Infrastructure, Software

Professional Associations: AITP, MAPRC

Networks: Top Echelon Network

Computer Network Resources Inc

28231 Tinajo
Mission Viejo, CA 92692
(949) 951-5929
Fax: (949) 951-6013
Email: cnrkenmiller@home.com
Web: www.cnrsearch.com

Description: Experienced nationwide firm with
unmatched insurance industry expertise in
information technology. Extensive database of
openings and available candidates. We do not
advertise, we network on a confidential basis.

Key Contact - Specialty:
Mr. Kenneth Miller, President - *High technology,
 insurance, healthcare, financial applications
 (sales, consulting, technical positions)*

Salary minimum: $60,000

Functions: IT

Industries: Services, Mgmt. Consulting, Insurance,
Software

Networks: Computer Search

Computer Personnel Inc

8224 15th Ave NE
Seattle, WA 98115
(206) 985-0282
Fax: (206) 770-1939
Email: ron@cpirecruiting.com
Web: www.cpirecruiting.com

Description: Our practice is focused on information
technology professionals and on those disciplines
related to information technology, for example:
those professionals with expertise in specific
business applications such as SAP, CRS, B2B, e-
Commerce, etc. We have extensive experience with
e-Commerce and business-to-business entities.

Key Contact - Specialty:
Mr. Ron Meints, President - *Information
 technology professionals*

Salary minimum: $30,000

Functions: IT

Industries: Software

Networks: Top Echelon Network

Computer Placement Services

227 5th Ave
Melbourne Beach, FL 32951
(321) 951-0934
(888) 285-9230
Fax: (321) 951-2722
Email: browe@cfl.rr.com
Web: www.careers4u.com

Description: Our firm has been assisting candidates
in meeting their career goals for over seventeen
years. CPS recruiters have direct information
technology industry experience, enabling us to
understand the candidate's current technology and
our client's requirements. Our firm provides out
placement services for major corporations,
contingency, and/or retained searches, contract, and
permanent placements.

Key Contact:
Ms. Bernadette Buda, President

Functions: IT

Industries: Generalist

Networks: Top Echelon Network

Computer Professionals Unlimited

13612 Midway Rd Ste 333
Dallas, TX 75244
(972) 233-1773
Fax: (972) 233-9619
Email: zipzap@cpusearch.com
Web: www.cpusearch.com

Description: We specialize in computer-based
product development, management, key individual
contributors, software/hardware engineering, and
systems architecture. We place information
technologists, client server specialists, graphical
user interface design, network engineering, network
administration, and telecommunication systems,
including voice, data, and cellular. We also recruit
for web-based systems architect/design, e-Business,
and Internet technology specialists.

Key Contact - Specialty:
Mr. V. J. Zapotocky, Owner - *Network
 management, software engineering*
Mr. Mark Allen, Operations Manager -
 Client/server systems, MIS

Salary minimum: $70,000

Functions: Middle Mgmt., Product Dev., IT, MIS
Mgmt., Systems Analysis, Systems Dev., Systems
Implem., Network Admin., DB Admin.,
Engineering

Industries: Generalist, Telecoms, Telephony,
Digital, Wireless, Fiber Optic, Network
Infrastructure, Software

Professional Associations: IRG, SERC

Networks: Top Echelon Network

Computer Recruiters Inc
22276 Buenaventura St
Woodland Hills, CA 91364-5006
(818) 704-7722
Fax: (818) 704-7724
Email: bob@tekjobs.com
Web: www.tekjobs.com

Description: We are specialists for PC (client server), Internet, ERP, data warehouse, midrange, and mainframe. We place in positions, such as database administrators, programmer analysts, network administrators, systems programmers, systems engineers, EDI analysts, EDI coordinators, all managers, etc. We place full time employees and contractors in California. We place no entry-level positions. Over one year IT, paid working experience is required.

Key Contact - Specialty:
Mr. Bob Moore, Manager - *Data processing*

Salary minimum: $50,000

Functions: Generalist, MIS Mgmt., Systems Analysis, Systems Dev., Systems Implem., Systems Support, Network Admin., DB Admin.

Industries: Generalist, Software

Networks: National Consulting Network (NCN)

Computer Strategies Inc
5620 N Kolb Rd Ste 225
Tucson, AZ 85750
(520) 577-7117
(800) 952-9544
Fax: (520) 577-2772
Email: recruiters@computerstrategies.com
Web: www.computerstrategies.com

Description: We are a professional search firm that specializes in the recruitment of information technology professionals for major corporations. We deal with many clients on a nationwide basis including Fortune 500, mid-sized and .com.

Key Contact:
Ms. Debby Brodie, Owner/President - *Information technology*
Mr. Joshua Small, VP- Corporate Recruiting

Salary minimum: $65,000

Functions: Directors, Senior Mgmt., Middle Mgmt., IT, MIS Mgmt., Systems Analysis, Systems Implem., Network Admin., DB Admin.

Industries: Generalist, IT Implementation

Computer Technology Staffing LLC
300 Front St
Lincoln, RI 02865
(401) 726-4800
Fax: (401) 334-2943
Email: positions@ctstaff.com
Web: www.ctstaff.com

Description: We provide retained and contingency technical placement at all levels in system engineering network engineering, software engineering, information systems/information technology, communications, manufacturing, defense, medical device, and financial industries.

Key Contact - Specialty:
Mr. Robert Pencarski, Partner - *Software, hardware, information technology, quality, communications*
Mr. Charles Ostiguy, Partner - *Software, hardware, information technology, quality, communications*

Functions: Generalist

Industries: Mfg., Electronic, Elec. Components, Finance, Communications, Defense, Aerospace,

Software, Networking, Comm. SW, System SW, Biotech

Professional Associations: AAAS, AUTM

Networks: Top Echelon Network

The Comwell Company Inc
227 Rte 206
Flanders, NJ 07836
(973) 927-9400
Fax: (973) 927-0372
Email: mailman@comwellconsultants.com
Web: www.comwellconsultants.com

Description: As we help give people dignity and align their skills, abilities, values and interests with current tasks and future strategies, client organizations become more competitive, productive and profitable.

Key Contact:
Mr. John F. Sobecki, President
Mr. David Gavin, Executive Vice President

Salary minimum: $75,000

Functions: Generalist, Directors, Senior Mgmt., Middle Mgmt., Mkt. Research, Personnel, Training

Industries: Generalist, Chemicals, Misc. Mfg., Finance, HR Services, Media, Healthcare

Professional Associations: SHRM

Concepts in Staffing Inc Executive Search
9 E 37th St Fl 2
New York, NY 10016
(212) 293-4325
Fax: (212) 652-0816
Email: mark@cisnysearch.com
Web: www.cisnysearch.com

Description: We are a global IT executive search and selection services focused on information technology, including New York, Asia, and Latin America.

Key Contact:
Mr. Mark Hermansen, Managing Director

Salary minimum: $100,000

Functions: IT

Industries: Generalist

Concord Search Group
3138 Butler Pike
Plymouth Meeting, PA 19462
(610) 940-0550
Fax: (610) 940-0711
Email: jennifer@concordsearch.com
Web: www.concordsearch.com

Description: Our group specializes in nationwide recruiting and compensation consulting in the fields of sales, management, and executive positions for the telecommunications, Internet, software, e-commerce and new media industries. With over sixty years of combined experience, we have successfully partnered with Fortune 500,the Nasdaq's fastest growing, and the Delaware Valley's fastest growing companies.

Key Contact - Specialty:
Mr. Brian Filippini, Principal
Mrs. Leigh Filippini, Principal - *Telecom, datacom*
Mrs. Phyllis Hilkert, Executive Recruiter - *Software*
Miss Jacqui Gary, Executive Recruiter - *Telecom, internet*
Miss Lynn Wilson, Executive Recruiter - *Telecom*

Salary minimum: $100,000

Functions: Generalist

Industries: Mgmt. Consulting, New Media, Telecoms, Software

Professional Associations: PANMA

Concorde Search Associates
1 N Broadway Ste 400
White Plains, NY 10601
(914) 428-0700
Fax: (914) 428-4865
Email: rgreenwald@concordepersonnel.com

Description: We are a 100% client-driven search firm. Our total thrust is fulfilling and maximizing the corporate staffing goals of our clients. We provide extra commitment and work ethic.

Key Contact - Specialty:
Ms. Anita Greenwald, President - *Banking, finance*

Salary minimum: $25,000

Functions: Generalist, HR Mgmt., Finance

Industries: Generalist, Finance, Banking, Accounting

Professional Associations: APCNY

Confisa Int'l Group
San Juanico No 128
Juriquilla
MEXICO
Queretaro, QRO 76230
Mexico
52 4 234 0411
Fax: 52 4 234 0411
Email: confisaqro@infosel.net.mx

Description: Highly professional executive search firm that performs retained & contingency processes for top leading companies including Fortune 500's. With offices in Mexico City, Queretaro (Mexican Bajio), and Miami FL.

Key Contact - Specialty:
Mr. Juan-Carlos Morones, Partner - *Automotive, manufacturing, food & beverage, information technology*
Mr. Juan Carlos Jaramillo, President - *Various*
Mr. Fernando Morones, Key Account Executive - *Food (ingredients, fragrances), services*
Mr. Salvador Jaramillo, Partner - *Telecomm, food, manufacturing*

Functions: Generalist

Industries: Mfg., Retail, Services, Entertainment, Advertising, Communications, Packaging

ConnectCentral
1817 SR83 Ste 381
Millersburg, OH 44654
(888) 816-1858
(330) 674-9969
Fax: (330) 674-9939
Email: kay@connectcentral.com
Web: www.connectcentral.com

Description: We specialize in high-tech executive, high-tech sales, and technical search throughout the US. Our expertise in energy, utility, CRM, EAM, ERP, HRIS, supply chain software, and consulting. Our technology includes web-based, client-server, Unix, and NT. Our principal has more than 10 years of recruiting experience in entrepreneurial, pre-IPO, and large public companies.

Key Contact:
Ms. Kay Mullins, Principal/Search Consultant

Functions: IT

Industries: Generalist

Networks: Top Echelon Network

Connors, Lovell & Associates Inc
4 Robert Speck Pkwy Ste 280
Mississauga, ON L4Z 1S1
Canada
(905) 566-4051
Fax: (905) 566-1038
Email: mississauga@conlov.com
Web: www.conlov.com

Description: We are committed to performance excellence and are driven by the desire to become one of the most successful search firms in Ontario. As true generalists, we focus on relationship building and long-term partnering.

Key Contact - Specialty:
Ms. Andrée Lovell, CPC, President - *Generalist*
Mr. Barry Connors, Vice President - *Generalist*

Salary minimum: $40,000

Functions: Product Dev., Materials Plng., Allied Health, Cash Mgmt., MIS Mgmt., R&D, Engineering, Graphic Artists

Industries: Mfg., Food, Bev., Tobacco, Textiles, Apparel, Lumber, Furniture, Paper, Printing, Chemicals, Soap, Perf., Cosmtcs., Drugs Mfg., Medical Devices, Metal Products, Retail, Finance, Services, Pharm Svcs., Equip Svcs., Mgmt. Consulting, HR Services, Packaging

Professional Associations: ACSESS

Branches:
22-260 Holiday Inn Dr
Cambridge, ON N3C 4E8
Canada
(519) 651-1004
Fax: (519) 651-2083
Email: careers@conlov.com
Key Contact - Specialty:
Mr. Barry Connors, Vice President - *Generalist*

Construct Management Services
8264 Peony Ln Ste 1
Maple Grove, MN 55311
(612) 420-2696
Fax: (612) 420-2517
Email: rlyngen@aol.com
Web: www.constructionrecruiters.com

Description: Specialists in the construction industry and real estate.

Key Contact - Specialty:
Mr. Robert Lyngen, Managing Director - *Construction, architecture*
Ms. Kim Salzer, Manager - *Construction, real estate, development, architecture*

Salary minimum: $40,000

Functions: Generalist, Senior Mgmt., Architects

Industries: Construction, Printing, Metal Products, Accounting, Real Estate, Software

Professional Associations: AGC

Construction Resources Group Inc
466 94th Ave N
St. Petersburg, FL 33702
(727) 578-1962
Fax: (727) 578-9982
Email: crgharris@aol.com
Web: www.constructionrecruiters.com

Description: Specialize in identifying and recruiting project and staff-level managers and executives exclusively for engineering and construction organizations.

Key Contact - Specialty:
Ms. Cheryl P. Harris, President - *Construction*

Salary minimum: $40,000

Functions: Generalist

Industries: Construction

Professional Associations: ABC, AGC, AGC, AIC, AIC, ASA, NARI

Construction Search Specialists Inc
115 5th Ave S Ste 501
La Crosse, WI 54601
(608) 784-4711
Fax: (608) 784-4904
Email: css@csssearch.com
Web: www.csssearch.com

Description: Executive search and recruiting from mid-management to upper-level exclusively for construction, architecture and engineering industries. Over 25 years of experience. Professional and confidential.

Key Contact - Specialty:
Mr. Duane McClain, President - *Presidents, CEOs, division managers*

Salary minimum: $40,000

Functions: Generalist, Directors, Senior Mgmt., Middle Mgmt., Production, Engineering, Environmentalists, Architects

Industries: Generalist, Construction, Mfg., Transportation, Equip Svcs., Hospitality, Environmental Svcs., Real Estate

Professional Associations: AGC, AIA

Consultant Recruiters
6842 N Park Manor Dr
Milwaukee, WI 53224
(414) 975-5760
Fax: (603) 697-8159
Email: dwcornell@attglobal.net

Description: Management consulting and information technology consulting specialists. Over 15 years' recruiting for highly regarded consulting firms. Principal is former Big 5 consultant.

Key Contact - Specialty:
Mr. Don Cornell, Principal - *Management consulting*

Salary minimum: $75,000

Functions: Mgmt. Consultants

Industries: Generalist

Networks: Top Echelon Network

Consulting & Search Associates Inc
911 Poplar St
Erie, PA 16502
(814) 459-5588
Fax: (814) 459-5582
Email: cnsearch@aol.com

Description: A generalist contingency search firm with an emphasis in the engineering and manufacturing fields. Member of a National Network that exchanges candidates and job orders to facilitate market penetration.

Key Contact - Specialty:
Mr. James P. Lyons, III, CPC, Owner - *Engineering, manufacturing*

Salary minimum: $40,000

Functions: Generalist

Industries: Mfg., Banking, Invest. Banking, Accounting, Equip Svcs., HR Services, Media, Aerospace, Non-classifiable

Networks: National Personnel Assoc (NPA)

The Consulting Group of North America Inc
PO BOX 3714
McLean, VA 22103-3714
(703) 442-8500
(800) 585-5627
Fax: (703) 442-3800

Email: email@tcgna.com
Web: www.tcgna.com

Description: We are a technical search firm placing technical (developers, software engineers, managers) in the high-tech industry. Only those with prior systems experience need apply. Main clients include the Big 6 and private consulting consortiums.

Key Contact - Specialty:
Mr. Roman Mesina, CEO/President - *PeopleSoft, oracle, SAP, BAAN*
Ms. Avery Plavin, Executive Vice President - *Client/server technology, PeopleSoft, SAP, Oracle*

Salary minimum: $50,000

Functions: Generalist, Systems Analysis, Systems Dev., Systems Implem., Systems Support, Network Admin., DB Admin.

Industries: Generalist, Mgmt. Consulting, HR Services, Software

Professional Associations: SHRM

Consulting Resource Group Inc
100 Galleria Pkwy Ste 400
Atlanta, GA 30339
(404) 240-5550
(888) 240-5553
Fax: (941) 403-0989
Email: mailbox@careersinconsulting.com
Web: www.careersinconsulting.com

Description: Specialize in search assignments for boutique, national and international management consulting firms. Focus on a variety of management consulting competency areas, including strategy, process re-engineering, technology consulting, organizational change, and financial advisory services.

Key Contact - Specialty:
Mr. P. Andrew Robinson, Managing Principal - *Management consultants, technology consultants*

Salary minimum: $75,000

Functions: Mgmt. Consultants

Industries: Energy, Utilities, Mfg., Retail, Banking, Mgmt. Consulting, Communications, Insurance, Biotech, Healthcare

Professional Associations: GAPS, NAPS, RON

Networks: Top Echelon Network

Consumer Connection Inc
1200 Whitman Ct NE
Renton, WA 98059
(425) 455-2770
Fax: (425) 454-1702

Description: One-stop shopping for the world of consumer products.

Key Contact - Specialty:
Mr. Gary Chatwin, President - *Sales, consumer products, consumer packaged goods*
Mr. Howard Robboy, President - *Sales, consumer products, consumer packaged goods*
Ms. Susan Eastern, Vice President - *Sales, consumer products, consumer packaged goods*
Ms. Adrien Agoado, Vice President - *Marketing, brand & product management, consumer products*
Ms. Tiffany Burns, Account Executive
Mr. John Webser, Account Executive - *Management*

Salary minimum: $50,000

Functions: Mfg., Sales & Mktg., HR Mgmt.

Industries: Mfg., Food, Bev., Tobacco, Textiles, Apparel, Paper, Soap, Perf., Cosmtcs., Drugs Mfg., Machine, Appliance, Consumer Elect., Mfg. SW

Consumer Search Inc
300 W Main St
Northborough, MA 01532
(508) 393-8506
Fax: (508) 393-7458
Email: conniemcsi@aol.com

Description: Health and beauty care, over-the-counter pharmaceuticals, sales and marketing executives.

Key Contact - Specialty:
Ms. Connie Musso, President - *OTC, HBC, sales & marketing executives*

Salary minimum: $75,000

Functions: Generalist, Directors, Mkt. Research, Mktg. Mgmt., Sales Mgmt.

Industries: Generalist, Pharm Svcs.

Contemporary Services Inc
1701 E Woodfield Rd Ste 1030
Schaumburg, IL 60173
(847) 619-4000
(800) 474-9200
Fax: (847) 619-1077
Email: resumes@contempserv.com
Web: www.mortgagestaff.com

Description: We are a national staffing service providing temporary, temp to hire and direct hire placements in the mortgage and finance industries. We work with all levels of positions from entry level to executive-level.

Key Contact:
Ms. Robyn Lemmer, National Production Manager
Ms. Sadia Sarwar, Executive Search

Functions: Generalist

Industries: Misc. Financial

Professional Associations: MBAA, NAMB, NAPMW, NAPS, NATSS

Networks: National Banking Network (NBN)

Continental Design & Engineering
2710 Enterprise Dr
Anderson, IN 46013
(765) 778-9999
Fax: (765) 778-8590
Email: cdcin@continental-design.com
Web: www.continental-design.com

Description: We are dedicated to providing technical resources to manufacturing firms that enhance and expand their own design and engineering capabilities. Contract and/or permanent employment searches.

Key Contact - Specialty:
Ms. Cathy Mellinger, Director-Recruitment - *Product development, manufacturing engineers*
Ms. Patty Wikle, Senior Executive Recruiter - *Automotive product development, manufacturing engineers*
Mr. Bill Nagengast, Director-Operations - *Automotive (exterior) lighting engineers*
Mr. Tom Epply, President - *Plant managers, industrial engineers, manufacturing*
Mr. Ron Drake, Engineering Manager - *Lean manufacturing, assembly line engineers, plant layout engineers*

Functions: Mfg.

Industries: Motor Vehicles, Mgmt. Consulting

Branches:
550 Stephenson Hwy Ste 203
Troy, MI 48083
(248) 589-1460
Fax: (248) 589-1462
Email: cdcmi@continental-design.com
Key Contact - Specialty:
Ms. Vickey Maisano - *Automotive design engineers*

Continental Search & Outplacement Inc
4134 E Joppa Rd Ste 203
PO Box 43873
Baltimore, MD 21236
(410) 529-7000
(888) 276-6789
Email: dan@consearch.com
Web: www.consearch.com

Description: We are specialists in recruiting AS/400 and Lotus Notes/Domino professionals in direct hire and contract positions across the US.

Key Contact - Specialty:
Mr. Daniel C. Simmons, CPC, President - *Lotus notes/domino*

Salary minimum: $50,000

Functions: IT

Industries: Generalist

Professional Associations: MAPRC

Networks: National Personnel Assoc (NPA)

Continental Search Associates Inc
PO Box 413
Birmingham, MI 48012
(248) 644-4507
Fax: (248) 644-0461
Email: csaresume@aol.com

Description: Midwest's premier search firm specializing exclusively in construction, real estate development and engineering.

Key Contact - Specialty:
Mr. William L. Dewey, President - *Construction, real estate development, engineering*
Mr. William R. Dewey, Executive Vice President - *Construction, real estate development, engineering*

Salary minimum: $30,000

Functions: Senior Mgmt., Engineering

Industries: Generalist, Construction

Professional Associations: MAPS, NAPS

Continental Search Associates
PO Box 14
Pickerington, OH 43147
(614) 837-1300
Fax: (614) 837-4860
Email: jimallen@continentaljobs.com
Web: www.continentaljobs.com

Description: Strong ethics are the guiding principle of our firm. Complete trust is of the utmost importance in relationships between recruiter and client and between recruiter and candidate.

Key Contact - Specialty:
Mr. James R. Allen, Owner - *Manufacturing, scientific*

Salary minimum: $70,000

Functions: Generalist

Industries: Mfg., Metal Products

Networks: Top Echelon Network

Convergence Executive Search
125 Main St Ste A
Newmarket, NH 03857
(603) 659-0900
Fax: (603) 659-0300
Email: becky@convergencesearch.com
Web: www.convergencesearch.com

Description: We are a boutique firm specializing in converging telecommunications. Our clients include both emerging companies and fortune 500 corporations. Our areas of expertise include broadband services, new media, e-Commerce,

telecommunication services, IT, interactive entertainment, advertising sales, and programming networks.

Key Contact - Specialty:
Mr. Corwyn J. Scott, Senior Vice President/Principal - *Cable television*
Mr. Jamie V. Capra, Senior Vice President/Principal - *Cable television*
Ms. Rebecca S. Metschke, Senior Vice President/Principal - *New media only*

Salary minimum: $70,000

Functions: Generalist

Industries: Media, New Media, Telecoms

Professional Associations: AIM, CTAM, NCTA, NYNMA, SCTE

Cook Conway & Associates
9805 NE 116th St Ste 7404
Kirkland, WA 98034
(425) 882-3000
Email: kim@cookconway.com
Web: www.cookconway.com

Description: When you're looking for your next executive level team member, call us. We recognize the needs of your business, whether you're in technology or finance, marketing or manufacturing. We make filling those needs easy for you, and successful for your company.

Key Contact - Specialty:
Ms. Kim Finch Cook, Partner - *Finance*
Mr. Topaz Conway, Partner - *Finance*

Salary minimum: $50,000

Functions: General Mgmt., Directors, Middle Mgmt., Mktg. Mgmt., HR Mgmt., CFO's, MIS Mgmt., R&D, Engineering

Industries: E-commerce, IT Implementation, Communications, Telecoms, Digital, Wireless, Fiber Optic, Network Infrastructure, Software, Biotech

Professional Associations: AAFA

Cooper Management Associates Inc
177 Main St Ste 107
Ft. Lee, NJ 07024
(201) 947-5171
Fax: (201) 947-5306
Email: mcpr@aol.com

Description: Twenty years of national executive recruitment experience for the retail industry. Serving clients in department stores, mass merchandisers, hard and soft goods specialty chains, catalog, home centers and e-commerce.

Key Contact - Specialty:
Mr. Michael Cooper, President - *Retail*

Salary minimum: $60,000

Functions: Generalist

Industries: Retail

Professional Associations: NMRI, NRF

Cooper-Clark & Assoc
6 Chester Dr Ste 200A
Rye, NY 10580
Fax: (914) 698-8857

Key Contact - Specialty:
Ms. Lisa Ann Clark - *Sales & marketing*
Mr. Norman Edward Cooper - *Generalist*

Functions: Senior Mgmt., IT

Industries: Services, Government, Software

COR Management Services Ltd
420 Lexington Ave Ste 3029
New York, NY 10170
(212) 599-2640
Fax: (212) 599-3048
Email: staff@corjobs.com
Web: www.corjobs.com

Description: Permanent placement, supplemental staffing, projects (outsourcing).

Key Contact - Specialty:
Mr. Robert Olman, President - *Information technology, capital markets*

Salary minimum: $50,000

Functions: Generalist, Systems Analysis, Systems Dev., Systems Implem., Systems Support, Network Admin., DB Admin., Mgmt. Consultants

Industries: Generalist, Banking, Invest. Banking, Brokers, Software

Corbin Packaging Professionals
7536-3 Monterey Bay Dr
Mentor Lake, OH 44060-9004
(440) 257-5601

Description: Specialist, packaging & allied industries: process, plastics, conveying, converting. Years of personal experience and contacts within these industries justify specialization. US and Germany.

Key Contact - Specialty:
Mr. Earl Corbin - *Packaging (technical, sales)*

Salary minimum: $40,000

Functions: Generalist, Middle Mgmt., Packaging, Mktg. Mgmt., Sales Mgmt., Engineering

Industries: Generalist, Food, Bev., Tobacco, Paper, Soap, Perf., Cosmtcs., Drugs Mfg., Plastics, Rubber, Machine, Appliance, Packaging

Professional Associations: IOPP

Networks: First Interview Network (FIN)

Core Management Search
5130 Saratoga Ln No Ste 201
Minneapolis, MN 55442
(763) 559-0977
Fax: (763) 559-1664
Email: jlentner@coremanage.com
Web: www.coremanage.com

Description: We are a retained and contingency search firm specializing in identifying and building your organization's core management team. We place mid to senior level management positions. We help you hire the core competencies that you need to take your organization to the next level.

Key Contact:
Ms. Julie Lentner, Principal

Salary minimum: $60,000

Functions: General Mgmt.

Industries: Printing, Medical Devices, Plastics, Rubber, Hotels, Resorts, Clubs, Telecoms, Accounting SW, HR SW, Industry Specific SW, Mfg. SW

Professional Associations: HRP

Cornerstone Executive Management Inc
1820 Lillian Rd
Stow, OH 44224
(330) 686-6727
Fax: (330) 686-6728
Email: cornerstoneexec@neo.rr.com

Description: We are an executive search firm specializing in pharmaceutical and pharmaceutical flexible packaging, and converting.

Key Contact:
Mr. Clifford E. Myers, CPC, President

Salary minimum: $60,000

Functions: General Mgmt., Directors, Senior Mgmt., Middle Mgmt., Mfg., Product Dev., Production, Plant Mgmt., Packaging, R&D

Industries: Chemicals, Drugs Mfg., Medical Devices, Plastics, Rubber, Pharm Svcs., Legal, Accounting, Packaging, Mfg. SW, Biotech

Professional Associations: IOPP, ISPE, NAPS, PDA

Networks: Top Echelon Network

Cornerstone Search Associates Inc
7 Grove St
Belmont, MA 02478
(617) 924-0445
(800) 826-6573
Email: rich@cornerstonesearch.com

Description: We are a nationwide, full-service placement firm specializing in software sales and financial positions. Cornerstone also has recruiters working exclusively in the health care industry, more specifically long-term care, retirement housing, hospitals, etc.

Key Contact - Specialty:
Mr. Richard Rosen, President - *Finance, sales & marketing*

Salary minimum: $75,000

Functions: Generalist, Sales & Mktg.

Industries: Energy, Utilities, Finance, Accounting, HR Services, E-commerce, Telecoms, Software, Accounting SW, Doc. Mgmt., Production SW, ERP SW, Mfg. SW, Biotech, Healthcare

CorpLegal Services
PO Box 1800
Sausalito, CA 94966-1800
(415) 457-8778
Email: connect@corplegal.net
Web: www.corplegal.net

Description: We are a dependable fast-response search firm specializing in finding highly qualified attorneys to work in temporary or permanent positions in corporate legal departments in the San Francisco Bay area.

Key Contact - Specialty:
Mr. Peter Blunt, President - *Corporate attorneys*
Mr. Howard Ash, Business Development Counsel - *Corporate attorneys, corporate paralegals*

Salary minimum: $40,000

Functions: Generalist

Industries: Legal

Professional Associations: ACCA

Corporate Advisors Inc
250 NE 27th St
Miami, FL 33137
(305) 573-7753
Fax: (305) 573-7929
Email: resumes@corporateadvisors.com
Web: www.corporateadvisors.com

Description: Serving south Florida based global multinationals, Latin American gateway headquarters, regional top 200 public/private employers in the e-commerce, consumer, high-technology, telecommunications and financial services industries. Confidential searches in all business functional disciplines at the mid- through senior management levels. Ranked among the top ten executive search firms by The South Florida Business Journal.

Key Contact:
Mr. Jerry Kurtzman, Managing Director

Salary minimum: $75,000

Functions: Senior Mgmt., Middle Mgmt., Sales & Mktg., HR Mgmt., Finance, IT, Int'l.

Industries: Generalist

Professional Associations: SHRM

Networks: Top Echelon Network

Corporate Builders Inc
421 High St Ste 208
Oregon City, OR 97045
(503) 223-4344
Fax: (503) 221-7778
Email: corpbldrs@earthlink.net

Description: Dedicated to research, analysis and consistently better recruiting results. Provide all the hiring companies with a superior recruiting workbook (WIF's) that improves their hiring results.

Key Contact:
Mr. William C. Meysing, President/General Manager
Mr. John Snyder, Senior Associate
Mrs. Joan Johnson, Vice President-Research
Ms. LeAnn Blumenstein, Associate
Ms. Susan Lannis, Systems Improvement Consultant

Salary minimum: $70,000

Functions: Generalist

Industries: Construction

Corporate Careers Inc
7755 Center Ave Fl 11
Huntington Beach, CA 92647
(949) 476-7007
(714) 372-2220
Fax: (949) 476-9019
Email: cci@corporatecareers.com
Web: www.corporatecareers.com

Description: Mid- to senior-level sales and executive placement with special emphasis on staffing temporary help and recruiting industry firms (general, technical, solutions) including branch, regional managers and area vice presidents for national, regional and local firms.

Key Contact - Specialty:
Ms. Dolores Cronin, President - *Staffing industry*

Salary minimum: $50,000

Functions: Senior Mgmt., Sales & Mktg., Sales Mgmt., IT

Industries: HR Services

Professional Associations: ASA, NATSS

The Corporate Connection Ltd
7202 Glen Forest Dr Ste 208
Richmond, VA 23226
(804) 288-8844
Email: thecorporateconnectionltd@msn.com

Description: Full-service recruiting firm with clients and candidate database throughout the Southeast. Over fifty years of combined experience in contingency and search placements in the Southeast and Virginia.

Key Contact - Specialty:
Mr. Marshall W. Rotella, President - *Financial, engineering*

Salary minimum: $25,000

Functions: Generalist

Industries: Generalist

Corporate Consultants

480 Central Ave
Northfield, IL 60093
(847) 446-5627
(815) 877-2024
Fax: (847) 446-3536
Email: irina@corpconsult.net
Web: www.corpconsult.net

Description: We are a national recruiting firm specializing in the high technology industries. For over ten years we have built our reputation on quality and integrity for both companies and candidates we service. Our firm is one of the most successful data/telecommunications recruitment companies in the country and we have experienced rapid growth over last five years, with a continuously growing client base. Our Client base covers the entire US so no matter where you live or want to live, we can find a job for you!

Key Contact:
Mrs. Irina Galper, Recruiter

Functions: Generalist, Sales Mgmt.

Industries: Media, Telecoms

Networks: Top Echelon Network

Corporate Consultants

155 University Ave Ste 1910
Toronto, ON M5H 3B7
Canada
(416) 862-1259
Fax: (416) 862-7926
Email: gordon@corporateconsultants.com
Web: www.corporateconsultants.com

Description: We are a search practice. We place from executive to specialist, operating in: accounting and finance, sales and marketing, operations/manufacturing, supply chain, logistics, and engineering. Our firm is efficient, professional, proven since its founding. Please visit our website.

Key Contact:
Mr. Fred Goldi, President
Mr. Gordon Brown, Vice President

Salary minimum: $60,000

Functions: General Mgmt., Senior Mgmt., Middle Mgmt., Mfg., Materials, Sales & Mktg., Finance, R&D, Engineering

Industries: Generalist

Corporate Consulting Associates Inc

1116 Voorheis Ste 200
Waterford, MI 48328
(248) 706-0006
Fax: (248) 706-0008
Email: bukowicz@corpconsulting.com
Web: www.corpconsulting.com

Description: Our specialties are information technology / systems, engineering, accounting and finance, purchasing/supply chain management, and human resources. Our client base is comprised of Fortune 500 corporations, consulting and public accounting firms, as well as, small to medium size, and privately- held companies. We represent various industries, for example: manufacturing, high tech, service, banking, entertainment, real estate, advertising, consumer products, consulting, retail, etc.

Key Contact - Specialty:
Mr. John Bukowicz, MBA, MSCS, President - *Generalist*
Mr. Gordon Mull, Senior Consultant - *Accounting & finance*
Ms. Kristine Volk, CPA, MST, Senior Consultant - *Accounting & finance*
Ms. Colleen O'Donnell, Senior Consultant - *Information technology & systems*
Ms. Nancy Veliu, Senior Consultant - *Information technology & systems*

Ms. Sharon Bartimay, Senior Consultant - *Engineering*
Ms. Jennifer Martin, Senior Consultant - *Engineering*
Mrs. Susan Bowes, Consultant & Research Analyst - *Human resources*
Mr. Brett Nowak, Senior Consultant - *Engineering*
Mrs. Ellen Letourneau, Senior Consultant - *Human resources*

Functions: General Mgmt., Mfg., Product Dev., Quality, Materials, HR Mgmt., Finance, IT, Minorities

Industries: Generalist

Networks: Associated Consultants in Executive Search Int'l

Corporate Dynamix

6619 N Scottsdale Rd
Scottsdale, AZ 85250
(480) 607-0040
Fax: (480) 607-0054
Email: david@cdynamix.com
Web: www.cdynamix.com

Description: We specialize in the placement of sales, sales management, and pre/post sales support personnel in the high-tech industry.

Key Contact - Specialty:
Ms. Carolyn Stokes, Principal - *Marketing, sales (pre & post)*
Mr. David Sterenfeld, Principal - *Sales, sales management*

Salary minimum: $50,000

Functions: Senior Mgmt., Middle Mgmt., Sales & Mktg., Sales Mgmt.

Industries: Software

Branches:
222 N Sepulveda Blvd Ste 2000
El Segundo, CA 90245
(310) 662-4770
Fax: (310) 662-4771
Email: carolyn@cdynamix.com
Key Contact - Specialty:
Mr. David Sterenfeld, Principal - *Sales, sales management*
Ms. Carolyn Stokes, Principal - *Sales & marketing (pre, post)*

Corporate Image Group

3145 Hickory Hill Ste 204
Memphis, TN 38115
(901) 360-8091
(800) 823-5100
Fax: (901) 360-0813
Email: matthews@corpimg.com
Web: www.corpimg.com

Description: Nationally recognized for placement successes, we are a full-service search firm with clients in Fortune 1000, Big 6 and fast growth firms. Concentration is manufacturing and distribution sectors on a national scale.

Key Contact - Specialty:
Mr. Joseph M. Knose, II, President - *Audit, accounting, finance, senior executives, accounting & finance (international)*
Mr. Barry C. Mathews, Vice President - *Engineering*
Mr. John Wright, Senior Vice President - *Engineering, manufacturing, human resources*
Ms. Judy Presley-Cannon, Vice President - *Engineering, manufacturing, human resources*

Functions: Generalist, Product Dev., Plant Mgmt., Purchasing, Allied Health, Sales Mgmt., Personnel, Finance

Industries: Generalist, Chemicals, Plastics, Rubber, Metal Products, Machine, Appliance, Consumer Elect., Hospitality, Healthcare

Networks: National Personnel Assoc (NPA)

Branches:
PO Box 5765
Pearl, MS 39288
(601) 420-6869
Fax: (601) 420-6870
Email: judy@corpimg.com

Corporate Information Systems Inc

71 Union Ave
Rutherford, NJ 07070
(201) 896-0600
Fax: (201) 896-8009
Email: ksorge@cisrecruiters.com
Web: www.cisrecruiters.com

Description: We specialize in the recruitment of software salespeople, sales managers, and sales support.

Key Contact:
Mr. Carmine Marinaro, President

Salary minimum: $50,000

Functions: Generalist, Sales Mgmt.

Industries: Generalist, Software

Professional Associations: NAPS, NJSA, YEO

Corporate Leads Inc

2009 Mara Park Pl
Williamsburg, VA 23185
(757) 220-8215
Email: careernet@corporateleads.com
Web: www.corporateleads.com

Description: We provide professional search and placement of junior military officers and degreed staff non-commissioned officers in management, engineering, distribution, sales, information technology, and consulting careers.

Key Contact - Specialty:
Mr. Luis Long, President - *Transitioning military placement*

Salary minimum: $40,000

Functions: Generalist, Middle Mgmt., Plant Mgmt., Distribution, Sales Mgmt., IT, Engineering

Industries: Generalist, Telecoms

Professional Associations: SHRM

Branches:
14506 Bladenboro Dr
Cypress, TX 77429
(281) 256-3313
Email: careernet@corporateleads.com
Key Contact:
Mr. Rod Long, Recruiter

Corporate Management Advisors Inc

785 Douglas Ave
Altamonte Springs, FL 32714
(407) 869-1817
Fax: (407) 869-0749
Web: www.cmainc.com

Description: Executive search and consulting for the financial services industry.

Key Contact:
Mr. Brad Hollingsworth
Mr. Thom Hollingsworth
Mr. Gordon Christian

Functions: Personnel

Industries: Finance, Banking, Real Estate

Professional Associations: MBA

Corporate Management Solutions Inc

6527 Constitution Dr
Ft. Wayne, IN 46804-1551
(219) 436-3355
Fax: (219) 436-4080

Email: cmsi@cmsrecruiting.com
Web: www.cmsrecruiting.com

Description: Our firm is a direct hire, company fee paid recruiting firm of technical and professional talent. The disciplines that we have worked in are accounting, engineering, I/S, manufacturing, HR, and sales and marketing. Our specialty areas include sensors, automotive, rubber, plastics, metal fabrication, manufacturing, and operations management.

Key Contact - Specialty:
Mr. Roger Miller, CPC, President - *Accounting, information systems*
Mr. Thomas Havey, CPC, Recruiting Mgr - *Non Electronics - All non electronic industry positions*
Mr. Richard Neff, CPC, Recruiting Mgr - *Electronics Industry - Electronics industry, sensors*

Salary minimum: $50,000

Professional Associations: IAPS, NAPS

Networks: Top Echelon Network

Corporate Moves Inc
PO Box 1638
Williamsville, NY 14231-1638
(716) 633-0234
Fax: (716) 626-9147
Email: corpmoves@aol.com
Web: www.corporatemovesinc.com

Description: Executive search specializing in sales and marketing positions, outside sales to senior-level management opportunities. Providing personal service with expert results. Based in western New York, providing services nationally and internationally. Specialized markets in bio-tech, optics, medical, plastics and start-up teams.

Key Contact:
Ms. Leslie Wilcox Hughes, CRM, President/CEO

Functions: Senior Mgmt., Middle Mgmt., Sales & Mktg., Mktg. Mgmt., Sales Mgmt., R&D, Specialized Svcs., Int'l.

Industries: Generalist, Drugs Mfg., Medical Devices, Plastics, Rubber, Computer Equip., Mgmt. Consulting, Packaging, Software, Biotech, Non-classifiable

Networks: The Acumen Society

Corporate Plus Ltd
3145 Tucker-Norcross Rd Ste 205
Tucker, GA 30084
(770) 934-5101
Fax: (770) 934-5127
Email: w.mcglawn@corporateplusltd.com
Web: www.corporateplusltd.com

Description: Nationwide executive search and management development firm that specializes in the area of diversity staffing. We specialize in sales, human resources, MIS and engineering.

Key Contact - Specialty:
Mr. Walter McGlawn, Principal - *Sales, human resources, MIS, engineering*
Mr. Shawn Menefee, Principal - *Sales, manufacturing, finance*

Salary minimum: $35,000

Functions: Generalist, General Mgmt., Production, Distribution, Sales Mgmt., HR Mgmt., Systems Dev., Minorities

Industries: Generalist, Food, Bev., Tobacco, Transportation, HR Services, Hospitality, Telecoms, Insurance

Professional Associations: AHRA, AHRA, GAPS

Networks: First Interview Network (FIN)

Corporate Recruiters Inc
1107 Bethleham Pike Ste 206
Flourtown, PA 19031
(215) 233-4701
Fax: (215) 233-5603

Description: We have thirty-eight years of experience in successful recruiting for the pharmaceutical, biotech, manufacturing, and distribution industries.

Key Contact:
Mr. Stephen Berlin, President

Salary minimum: $100,000

Functions: Mfg., Physicians, R&D

Industries: Drugs Mfg., Medical Devices, Pharm Svcs., Mfg. SW, Biotech

Professional Associations: NAER

Corporate Recruiters Ltd
1140 W Pender St Ste 490
Vancouver, BC V6E 4G1
Canada
(604) 687-5993
Fax: (604) 687-2427
Email: jobs@corporate.bc.ca
Web: www.corporate.bc.ca

Description: Recruitment firm specializing in the advanced technology industries. This includes: electronic engineering (both hardware and software); information technology; sales and marketing in the high-tech/computer industry.

Key Contact:
Mr. Don Safnuk, President and CEO
Mr. Raymond To
Mr. Bruce Edmond
Ms. Kimberllay Brooks
Ms. Roanne Liew

Salary minimum: $40,000

Functions: Generalist, Product Dev., Sales Mgmt., MIS Mgmt., Systems Analysis, Systems Dev.

Industries: Generalist, Computer Equip., Software

Networks: National Personnel Assoc (NPA)

Corporate Resources, Stevens Inc
110 N Potomac St
Hagerstown, MD 21740
(301) 797-3434
Fax: (301) 797-3331
Email: jgocha1@aol.com

Description: Strong in the HVAC arena.

Key Contact - Specialty:
Ms. Jane Stevens, President/Owner - *Generalist, HVAC, manufacturing, sales, sales management*

Functions: Generalist, Mfg., Healthcare, Sales & Mktg., IT, Engineering

Industries: Generalist, Construction, Mfg., Media, Telecoms, Software, Healthcare

---

Corporate Resources LLC
10999 Reed Hartman Hwy Ste 333
Cincinnati, OH 45242
(513) 793-5807
Fax: (513) 793-5981
Email: ccordell@eos.net
Web: www.corpresources.com/login.asp

Description: Each partner/consultant has 15+ years in recruitment of technical personnel. Corporate Resources on a national network to facilitate clients in areas of IT, engineering, healthcare, accounting, finance and human resources. Both search, contingency and contracting services.

Key Contact - Specialty:
Ms. Cindy Andrew Cordell, Partner/Consultant - *Information systems, finance, human resources*

Salary minimum: $35,000

Functions: Generalist, Materials, Personnel, Finance, IT, Engineering

Industries: Generalist, HR Services, Healthcare

Networks: Top Echelon Network

Corporate Search America Inc
2221 Lee Rd Ste 18
Winter Park, FL 32789
(407) 678-3991
Fax: (407) 678-5887
Email: resume@csasearch.com
Web: www.csasearch.com

Description: Our firm can shortcut your effort in finding the most qualified candidate for your company. We recruited in 96 markets last year. We recruit the nation's best, the candidates that aren't found by running an ad or using Internet search engines.

Key Contact - Specialty:
Mr. James G. Boghos, President/CEO - *Mortgage banking, financial services, relocation*
Mr. Jeff Jackson, Executive Vice President - *Mortgage banking, financial services*
Mr. Mike Schmit, Director of Recruiting - *Architectural, engineering*
Ms. Jacqueline Boghos, Vice President - *Mortgage banking, financial services*
Mr. Nick Armato, Vice President - *Mortgage banking, financial services*
Mr. Joseph Jowdy, Vice President - *Mortgage banking, financial services*

Salary minimum: $25,000

Functions: Generalist, Senior Mgmt., Middle Mgmt., Risk Mgmt.

Industries: Generalist, Finance, Banking, Invest. Banking, Venture Cap., Misc. Financial, Telecoms, Call Centers, Real Estate, HR SW

Professional Associations: MBA, NAMB

Corporate Search Associates
4180 N Mesa Ste 107
El Paso, TX 79902
(915) 534-2583
Fax: (915) 534-2585
Email: csa01@whc.net
Web: www.csajobs.com

Description: Specialists in telecommunication engineers;healthcare,automotive manufacturing. Specialists in Latin America, Spanish speaking and manufacturing professionals.

Key Contact:
Mr. Thomas J. Furnival

Salary minimum: $50,000

Functions: Mfg.

Industries: Mfg., Telecoms, Digital, Wireless, Fiber Optic, Network Infrastructure, Packaging, Hospitals, Physical Therapy

Professional Associations: NAPS, TAPC

Networks: National Personnel Assoc (NPA)

Corporate Search Consultants Inc
509 W Colonial Dr
Orlando, FL 32804
(800) 800-7231
(407) 578-3888
Fax: (407) 578-5153
Email: mail@corpsearch.com
Web: www.corpsearch.com

Description: Our firm specializes in information technology, high-tech sales, financial services, and healthcare.

Key Contact - Specialty:
Mr. Anthony Ciaramitaro, President - *E-commerce, high-tech sales, healthcare*
Mr. Paul Ciaramitaro, Managing Partner - *Information technology, database administration, data security*

Salary minimum: $60,000

Functions: Legal, Healthcare, Allied Health, Finance, IT, Systems Analysis, Systems Support, DB Admin., Attorneys, Paralegals

Industries: Generalist

Professional Associations: ASA, NAPS

Corporate Search Consultants
19 S 6th St Ste 200
Terre Haute, IN 47807
(812) 235-2992
Fax: (812) 235-3029
Email: jobs@csccareers.com
Web: www.csccareers.com

Description: We are connecting talented people with Fortune 500 and emerging growth companies! We are one of the nation's leading search firms in food, beverage, and dairy. We place production, materials, logistics, engineering, maintenance, HR, QA/QC, sanitation, and executive positions.

Key Contact:
Mr. F. Scott Myers, IV, Partner
Mr. Gregg A. Greven, Partner

Salary minimum: $40,000

Functions: Directors, Senior Mgmt., Middle Mgmt., Mfg., Materials, HR Mgmt., Engineering, Minorities

Industries: Food, Bev., Tobacco, Chemicals, Soap, Perf., Cosmtcs., Drugs Mfg.

Networks: National Personnel Assoc (NPA)

Corporate Search Consultants
600 1st Ave Ste 337
Seattle, WA 98104
(206) 332-0233
Fax: (206) 332-0230
Email: mail@cssearch.com

Description: Executive search firm offering flexible, custom designed retained services and established national and international network.

Key Contact - Specialty:
Ms. Mary Beth Barbour - *Generalist*

Salary minimum: $70,000

Functions: Directors, Senior Mgmt., Middle Mgmt., Distribution, Mktg. Mgmt., Sales Mgmt., PR, HR Mgmt., MIS Mgmt., Int'l.

Industries: Construction, Food, Bev., Tobacco, Medical Devices, Retail, Brokers, Non-profits, Biotech, Hospitals

Professional Associations: BPWCUSA, NAFE

Corporate Search Inc
PO Box 5334
Oak Brook, IL 60522
(800) 408-6423
Fax: (800) 735-6394
Email: dyer@interaccess.com

Description: We specialize in executive staffing of sales and finance positions in all industries. We place operations positions in the construction and metals industries.

Key Contact:
Mr. Mark Dyer, General Manager

Salary minimum: $25,000

Functions: General Mgmt., Plant Mgmt., Quality, Materials, Sales Mgmt.

Industries: Construction, Mfg., Metal Products, Transportation, Services, Accounting, Equip Svcs., Media, Telecoms, Packaging, Software

Corporate Search Inc
6800 Jericho Tpke Ste 111
Syosset, NY 11791
(516) 496-3200
Fax: (516) 496-3165
Email: jobs@corporatesearch.com
Web: www.corporatesearch.com

Description: Permanent placement firm involved in the search and recruitment of accounting and finance, office administration, human resources, information technology, sales and marketing, and operations. Location of jobs are in Long Island, New York City and New Jersey.

Key Contact - Specialty:
Ms. Claire Zukerman, CPC, President - *Accounting (public, private), finance, administration, office services, human resources*

Salary minimum: $20,000

Functions: Generalist, Admin. Svcs., Materials, Sales & Mktg., HR Mgmt., Finance, Non-profits, Paralegals

Industries: Generalist, Construction, Mfg., Transportation, Banking, Services, Real Estate, Healthcare

Professional Associations: APCNY

Corporate Search Partners
5950 Sherry Ln Ste 560
Dallas, TX 75225
(214) 361-0082
Fax: (214) 361-5587
Web: www.cspjobs.com

Description: We are a contingency executive search firm specializing in finance, accounting, tax, treasury, investment banking, venture capital, money management, and banking professionals.

Key Contact - Specialty:
Mr. Paxson B. Glenn,, Jr., Principal - *Accounting, finance, banking, technology*
Mr. Mark Falvo, Principal - *Accounting, finance, banking, technology*
Mr. Brian Finch, Principal - *Accounting, finance, banking, technology*
Ms. Kristen Wagner, Principal - *Accounting, finance, banking, technology*

Salary minimum: $45,000

Functions: Generalist, CFO's, Budgeting, Cash Mgmt., Taxes, M&A

Industries: Generalist, Banking, Invest. Banking, Venture Cap.

Branches:
3455 Peachtree Rd NE Ste 500
Atlanta, GA 30326
(404) 467-0002
Fax: (404) 467-0009
Email: resume@cspjobs.com
Key Contact:
Ms. Kristen Wagner, Principal

Corporate Search Technologies
95 Summit Ave
Summit, NJ 07901
(908) 522-0069
Email: newell@cstllc.com
Web: www.cstllc.com

Description: Executive search firm that specializes in diversity and interim placement.

Key Contact - Specialty:
Mr. Wayne A. Newell, Managing Director - *Marketing, sales, biotech*
Mr. Steve Jeffries, Managing Director - *Minorities, research & development*

Ms. Ann Dilailo, Managing Director - *Personnel, human resources*
Mr. Gordon Metsky - *IT consulting*
Mr. Jim McIntosh - *Mergers & acquisitions*

Salary minimum: $60,000

Functions: Generalist, Packaging, Mkt. Research, Mktg. Mgmt., M&A, Network Admin., R&D, Minorities

Industries: Generalist, Soap, Perf., Cosmtcs., Drugs Mfg., Consumer Elect., Venture Cap., Misc. Financial, HR Services, Biotech

Corporate Select Int'l Ltd
401 N Michigan Ave Ste 1200
Chicago, IL 60611
(312) 616-6672
Fax: (312) 616-6678
Email: csiltd@mindspring.com
Web: www.corporateselect.com

Description: We specialize in recruiting professionals and support staff for companies doing business in increasingly international and multicultural environments.

Key Contact:
Ms. Mayumi Cochran, Senior Consultant

Salary minimum: $30,000

Functions: Generalist, Purchasing, Sales & Mktg., HR Mgmt., Finance, IT, Engineering, Int'l.

Industries: Generalist, Chemicals, Medical Devices, Plastics, Rubber, Machine, Appliance, Motor Vehicles, Computer Equip., Misc. Financial

Corporate Software Solutions LLC
108 Barrack Hill Rd
Ridgefield, CT 06877
(203) 431-7631
Email: maiolo@corp-soft.com
Web: www.corp-soft.com

Description: Our firm is a premier IT and financial search/consulting firm which specializes in skilled professionals, marketing the New York Tri-State area. Corporate Software Solutions is organized into three divisions: Corp-Soft Technical Staffing, Corp-Soft Finance, and Corp-Soft Consulting. At Corporate Software Solutions, we realize that it is just as important to find our candidates the positions they want, as it is to find our clients the perfect candidate.

Key Contact - Specialty:
Ms. Dee Dee Lawrence, Principal - *Finance and accounting*
Mr. Rick Maiolo, Principal - *Information technology*

Functions: IT

Industries: Generalist

Corporate Solutions
PO Box 1974
Simpsonville, SC 29681-1974
(864) 228-9508
Email: jwebb@corp-sol.com
Web: www.corp-sol.com

Description: Professional recruiting, search and human resource consulting firm. Specialize in accounting, engineering, information technology and human resources. Affiliated with Top Echelon Network the world's largest computerized independent search firm network.

Key Contact:
Mr. James R. Webb, CPC, President

Salary minimum: $50,000

Functions: Mfg., Materials, HR Mgmt., Finance, IT, Engineering

Industries: Mfg., Finance, Services, Accounting, Equip Svcs., Mgmt. Consulting, Media, Communications, Packaging, Insurance, Software

Professional Associations: SCAPS

Networks: Top Echelon Network

Corporate Staffing Group Inc
3655 Rte 202 Bldg 115
Doylestown, PA 18901
(215) 345-1100
Fax: (215) 345-8177
Email: cbaker@corporatestaffing.com
Web: www.corporatestaffing.com

Description: Representing medium to large firms in the TC industry, private and public switching. Emphasis on general management, marketing and engineering. Significant experience in high-level systems and advance software implementation for AI networks, ATM, packet, wireless PCN/PCS, SONET and Internet. Current in transport and transmission and access markets.

Key Contact - Specialty:
Mr. Charles D. Baker, President - *Telecommunications*
Mrs. Laurie B. Carey, Vice President - *Telecommunications*

Salary minimum: $60,000

Functions: Generalist, Directors, Middle Mgmt., Mktg. Mgmt., Systems Dev., Systems Implem., R&D, Engineering

Industries: Generalist, Computer Equip., Consumer Elect., Test, Measure Equip., Telecoms, Software

Corporate Tracs
600 Peachtree Pkwy Ste 104
Cumming, GA 30041
(770) 886-5880 x24
Fax: (770) 886-7626
Email: chris@ctracs.net
Web: www.ctracs.net

Description: We are recruiting specialists in sales and marketing.

Key Contact:
Mr. Chris Douillard

Functions: Sales & Mktg.

Industries: Mfg., Media, Advertising, Publishing, New Media

Professional Associations: GAPS

Networks: National Personnel Assoc (NPA)

Corrao, Miller, Rush & Wiesenthal
499 Park Ave
New York, NY 10022
(212) 328-6180
Fax: (212) 328-6181
Web: www.cmrw.com

Description: We are a premier search firm specializing exclusively in the placement of exceptional attorneys. Our client roster includes law firms, investment and commercial banking institutions, and corporations worldwide. We conduct contingent and retained partner and associate searches and mergers and acquisitions of groups and firms.

Key Contact:
Ms. Laura S. Corrao, Esq.
Ms. Robin S. Miller, Esq.
Ms. Renee Berliner Rush, Esq.
Ms. Lauren M. Wiesenthal, Esq.

Functions: Generalist, Attorneys

Industries: Generalist, Legal

Leonard Corwen Corporate Recruiting Services
PO Box 350453
New York, NY 11235-0008
(718) 646-7581
Fax: (718) 646-7581
Email: lencor@msn.com

Description: Serving the personnel needs of companies and organizations in the recruitment and placement of corporate communications, public relations, finance, advertising, marketing and publishing personnel at all levels.

Key Contact - Specialty:
Mr. Leonard Corwen, President - *Corporate communications, public relations, publishing, marketing communications, sales & marketing*
Ms. Carol Butler, Vice President - *Financial, non-profit, human resources*

Salary minimum: $40,000

Functions: General Mgmt., Advertising, Mktg. Mgmt., Direct Mktg., PR, Benefits, Training, Graphic Artists

Industries: Printing, Consumer Elect., Banking, Pharm Svcs., Accounting, Mgmt. Consulting, HR Services, Advertising, Publishing, New Media

Professional Associations: ASJA, IABC

Cosier Associates Inc
2300 520-5 Ave SW
Calgary, AB T2P 3R7
Canada
(403) 816-9492
(403) 547-3694
Email: cosierb@home.com

Description: We are technical and professional recruiters to the Western Canadian oil and gas industry. Our practice is limited to Canadian recruiting.

Key Contact - Specialty:
Mr. Brian Cosier, President - *Engineers, geoscientists, oil & gas*

Salary minimum: $70,000

Functions: Generalist, Middle Mgmt., Production, Systems Dev., Engineering

Industries: Generalist, Paints, Petro. Products

J D Cotter Search Inc
2999 E Dublin-Granville Rd Ste 301
Columbus, OH 43231
(614) 895-2065
Fax: (614) 895-3071
Email: jdcot528@aol.com

Description: Contingency or retained. References. Fast, thorough, guaranteed. Client list available. Peak performance and results. Celebrating our 30th anniversary in commitment to excellence in search.

Key Contact:
Mr. Joe Cotter, President
Mr. Dan Cotter, Vice President

Salary minimum: $40,000

Functions: Generalist, Middle Mgmt., Mfg., Materials, HR Mgmt., Finance, IT, Engineering

Industries: Generalist

Coughlin & Associates
PO Box 6902
Monroe, NJ 08831
(609) 409-3380
Fax: (609) 409-3382
Email: jack@jcoughlin.com
Web: www.jcoughlin.com

Description: Our firm specializes in the food, retail, wholesale, manufacturing, and foodservice distributors fields. We have positions ranging from president to assistant, store manager to sales manager.

Key Contact - Specialty:
Mr. Jack Coughlin, President - *Food*

Salary minimum: $50,000

Functions: Senior Mgmt., Middle Mgmt., Specialized Svcs.

Industries: Food, Bev., Tobacco, Paper, Soap, Perf., Cosmtcs., Wholesale, Retail, Restaurants

The Counsel Network
1400, 400 Burnand St
Vancouver, BC V6C 3G2
Canada
(604) 643-1755
(800) COUNSEL
Email: snash@headhunt.com
Web: www.headhunt.com

Description: Established in 1988, We are Canada's oldest and most respected lawyer recruitment firm. We have an unrivalled track record of successful assignments on behalf of blue chip law firms and major corporations. All recruiters are former lawyers, and the firm is endorsed by The Canadian Bar Association (BC, Alberta, Manitoba).

Key Contact:
Mr. Stephen Nash, President/General Counsel - *Legal recruitment, expert opinion*
Ms. Dal Bhathal, Managing Director

Salary minimum: $80,000

Functions: Legal

Industries: Legal

Professional Associations: NALSC

Branches:
888 3rd St W Ste 1500
Calgary, AB T2P 3L8
Canada
(403) 264-3838
Fax: (403) 264-3819
Email: sdunnigan@headhunt.com
Key Contact:
Mr. Sean Dunnigan, QC, Managing Director

CountryHouse Hotels Executive Search
413 Park St
PO Box 2429
Charlottesville, VA 22902
(804) 977-5029
Fax: (804) 977-5431

Description: Major client base - consists of 4 and 5 star hotels and resorts throughout the U.S. Forty years' experience.

Key Contact - Specialty:
Mr. Grant Howlett, President - *Hospitality*
Mr. Steve Samuels, Director of U.S. Recruitment - *Hospitality*

Salary minimum: $25,000

Functions: Generalist, Senior Mgmt., Middle Mgmt., Sales Mgmt., Personnel, CFO's, Mgmt. Consultants

Industries: Generalist, Accounting, HR Services, Advertising, Entertainment SW

Covenant Staffing Inc
3123 Shellbark Dr
Indianapolis, IN 46235
(317) 891-9858
Fax: (317) 981-9863
Email: covenant@indy.net
Web: www.covenantstaffing.com

Description: We are professional IT/IS staffing services including permanent and contract placements. We specialize in web, client server, and AS400 placements.

Key Contact:
Mr. Curtis Cole, CPC, President

Salary minimum: $50,000

Functions: Generalist, Senior Mgmt.

Industries: IT Implementation, Telecoms, Network Infrastructure, Software, Database SW, Development SW, Doc. Mgmt., Production SW

Professional Associations: IAPS

Networks: Top Echelon Network

Coverage Inc
PO Box 341
Cedarhurst, NY 11516-0341
(516) 374-4406
Email: ajs@coveragesearch.com
Web: www.coveragesearch.com

Description: Our firm specializes in the recruitment and selection of logistics and supply chain professionals. Our philosophy, which is based upon expertise and integrity, is to bring a rational and realistic approach to the recruitment process.

Key Contact:
Mr. Arnold Saxe, Director

Salary minimum: $75,000

Functions: Production, Materials, Purchasing, Materials Plng., Distribution, Customer Svc., Mgmt. Consultants

Industries: Generalist

Cowan Search Group
897 S Chiques Rd
Manheim, PA 17545
(717) 892-4646
(717) 892-4647
Fax: (717) 892-4645
Email: csg@success.net

Description: We specialize in recruitment of top quality sales, management and marketing personnel. Other areas of concentration include advertising, telecommunications and computer technology.

Key Contact - Specialty:
Mr. Ken Cowan, President - *Sales & marketing*
Ms. Jenelle Mazzie, Marketing Specialist
Ms. Shanda Teague, Vice President - *Sales, marketing, IT*

Salary minimum: $40,000

Functions: Generalist, Sales & Mktg.

Industries: Equip Svcs., Mgmt. Consulting, Media, Advertising, Publishing, New Media, Communications, Telecoms, Call Centers, Telephony, Wireless, Real Estate, Software, Marketing SW

Professional Associations: PAPS, SME

Cox, Darrow & Owens Inc
6 E Clementon Rd Ste E-4
Gibbsboro, NJ 08026
(856) 782-1300
Fax: (856) 782-7277
Email: cdo@snip.net

Description: Professional recruiting and search service for all business functions. We serve clients in the manufacturing, process and service industries from our suburban Philadelphia location.

Key Contact:
Mr. William R. Cox, President
Mr. Robert J. Darrow, Vice President

Salary minimum: $40,000

Functions: Generalist

Industries: Generalist

Professional Associations: MAAPC, NIRA

Networks: National Personnel Assoc (NPA)

CPI Human Resources Solutions Inc
5203 Maverick Dr
Austin, TX 78727
(512) 873-0966
Email: info@cpipartners.com
Web: www.cpipartners.com

Description: We specialize in providing human resources solutions to pre-IPO companies in the Internet, software and telecommunications industries.

Key Contact - Specialty:
Mr. Erik Chyten, President - *Finance, recruiting*
Mrs. Dawn Chyten, Vice President - *Recruiting, human resources*
Mr. Jan Jensen, Vice President - *Human resources, organizational development*

Functions: Generalist

Industries: Mgmt. Consulting, HR Services, Media, Advertising, New Media, Telecoms, Software

CPS Inc
1 Westbrook Corp Ctr Ste 600
Westchester, IL 60154
(708) 562-0001
Fax: (708) 531-8398
Email: info@cps4jobs.com
Web: www.cps4jobs.com

Description: Dynamic technical firm employing over 60 specialized recruiters. Consistently placing the top 20% of applicants nationwide. Divisionalized into 13 distinct marketplaces: engineering, sales and marketing, production supervision, etc. We do not waste anyone's time.

Key Contact - Specialty:
Mr. H. Douglas Christiansen, President
Ms. Renee Mydlach, Manager - *Engineering*
Mr. Rich Brandeis, Manager - *Chemical, engineering*
Ms. Cheryl Laird, Manager - *Production*
Mr. Dale Graham, Manager - *Technical sales marketing*
Mr. Pat Kilcoyne, Manager - *Actuarial*
Mr. David Schueneman, Manager - *Advertising*
Mr. Dan Tovrog, Manager - *Employee benefits*
Ms. Natalie Sanders, Manager - *Accounting & finance*
Mr. Tom Scalamera, Manager - *Information systems*
Ms. Lee Romano, Manager - *Contract, temporary*

Salary minimum: $25,000

Functions: Generalist, Mfg., Materials, Sales & Mktg., Benefits, IT, R&D, Engineering

Industries: Generalist, Transportation, Misc. Financial, Media, Packaging, Insurance, Software

Branches:
205 N 2nd St
DeKalb, IL 60115
(815) 756-1221
Fax: (815) 756-1350
Key Contact - Specialty:
Mr. Jim Clark, Branch Manager - *Laboratory*

50 Federal St
Boston, MA 02110
(617) 368-3550
Fax: (617) 368-3562
Key Contact:
Ms. Mary O'Connel, Manager

CraigSearch Inc
901 Waterfall Way - 107
Richardson, TX 75080
(972) 644-3264
Fax: (972) 644-4065

Email: craig@craigsearch.com
Web: www.craigsearch.com

Description: Nationwide executive search specializing in placement of middle- and senior-level management within the retail grocery, wholesale grocery and food service distribution industries.

Key Contact - Specialty:
Mr. Edward C. Nemec, Managing Partner - *Retail, wholesale grocery, food services*

Salary minimum: $75,000

Functions: Senior Mgmt.

Industries: Food, Bev., Tobacco, Transportation, Wholesale, Retail, Finance

Crandall Associates Inc
114 E 32nd St Ste 904
New York, NY 10016
(212) 213-1700
Fax: (212) 696-1287
Email: wendy@crandallassociates.com
Web: www.crandallassociates.com

Description: Coast-to-coast searches for all functions in direct marketing, including marketing, management, operations and creative.

Key Contact:
Ms. Wendy Weber, President

Salary minimum: $50,000

Functions: Generalist, General Mgmt., Direct Mktg., Finance, IT, Graphic Artists

Industries: Generalist, Energy, Utilities, Finance, Services, Media, Insurance, Software

Professional Associations: DMA

Networks: National Personnel Assoc (NPA)

The Crawford Group
620 Park Dr NE
Atlanta, GA 30306
(404) 872-8500
Email: tom-crawford@mediaone.net

Description: We cover all areas of advertising agency and corporate marketing placement. No Sales positions

Key Contact - Specialty:
Mr. Tom Crawford, President - *Advertising agencies*

Salary minimum: $35,000

Functions: Advertising

Industries: Media, Advertising, New Media

Creative Financial Staffing
(managed by Crowe, Chizek & Co LLP)
155 Federal St Fl 12
Boston, MA 02110
(617) 753-6012
Fax: (617) 753-6016
Email: amccarthy@cfstaffing.com
Web: www.cfstaffing.com

Description: Temporary, permanent and temp-to-perm accounting & finance and IT placement service affiliated with CPA firms.

Key Contact - Specialty:
Mr. Daniel Casey, President
Mr. Bruce Gobdel, Chairman - *Accounting & finance*

Functions: Generalist, MIS Mgmt., Systems Analysis, Systems Dev., Systems Implem., Systems Support, Network Admin., DB Admin.

Industries: Generalist, Misc. Financial, Accounting, Hospitality

Professional Associations: NATSS

Branches:
2055 E Warner Rd Ste 102
Tempe, AZ 85284
(480) 820-6868
Fax: (480) 831-7136
Email: toni@hhcpa.com

2382 Faraday Ave Ste 130
Carlsbad, CA 92008
(760) 930-1324
Fax: (760) 930-1325
Email: jobs@cfstaffing.com
Key Contact:
Mr. Mike Kinney, Regional Director

1990 S Bundy Dr Ste 370
Los Angeles, CA 90025
(310) 442-5380
Fax: (310) 207-9499
Key Contact:
Mr. Mike Kinney

2744 Sand Hill Rd
Menlo Park, CA 94025-7019
(650) 854-8700
Fax: (650) 854-7666
Email: dcanabou@hoodstrong.com
Key Contact:
Mr. Raul Hernandez

101 California St Ste 1500
San Francisco, CA 94111
(415) 394-9888
Fax: (415) 421-2976
Key Contact:
Mr. Raul Hernandez

1101 W 120th Ave Ste 400
Broomfield, CO 80021
(303) 466-6632
Email: heatherd@cfs-co.com
Key Contact:
Mr. Dan Long, Executive Director

1600 Broadway Ste 1500
Denver, CO 80202
(303) 830-0971
Fax: (303) 861-5261
Email: michellet@cfs-co.com
Key Contact:
Mr. Dan Long

29 S Main St
PO Box 272000
West Hartford, CT 06127-2000
(860) 561-6850
Fax: (860) 521-9241
Email: krb@bshapiro.com
Key Contact:
Ms. Tarah Lelli, Area Manager

899 W Cypress Creek Rd Ste 917
Cambridge Executive Ctr
Ft. Lauderdale, FL 33309
(954) 345-0746
Fax: (954) 557-0547
Email: lsoto@cfstaffing.com
Key Contact:
Ms. Jean Marie Allen

14750 NW 77th Ct Ste 200
Miami Lakes Corporate Ctr
Miami Lakes, FL 33016
(305) 557-1924
Fax: (305) 557-0547
Email: lsoto@cfstaffing.com
Key Contact:
Ms. Jean Marie Allen

480 N Orlando Ave Ste 221
Winter Park, FL 32789-7192
(407) 539-0980
Fax: (407) 539-1828
Email: jhoppe@cfstaffing.com
Key Contact:
Ms. Megan Lynch, Regional Director

5565 Glenridge Highlands 2 Ste 200
Atlanta, GA 30342
(404) 898-7414
Fax: (404) 870-2157

Email: marie.english@hawcpa.com
Key Contact:
Mr. John Gress

1000 Jorie Blvd Ste 250
Oak Brook, IL 60523
(630) 371-1200
Fax: (630) 371-1201
Email: cfs.career@crowechizek.com
Key Contact:
Mr. Gary Gadzinski

3815 River Crossing Pkwy Ste 300
PO Box 40977
Indianapolis, IN 46240-0977
(317) 706-2600
Fax: (317) 706-2660
Email: agreathouse@crowechizek.com
Key Contact:
Ms. Andi Greathouse

8001 Broadway Ste 300
PO Box 10807
Merrillville, IN 46411-0807
(219) 756-4041
Fax: (219) 756-4056
Email: cgreeve@crowechizek.com
Key Contact:
Ms. Toni Foyer

340 Columbia St Ste 105
PO Box 10807
South Bend, IN 46634
(219) 236-7600
Fax: (219) 239-7878
Email: sforrester@crowechizek.com
Key Contact:
Mr. Mike Niedbalski

400 Locust St Ste 675
Des Moines, IA 50309-2372
(515) 558-6648
Fax: (515) 471-5241
Email: russell_jensen@rsmi.com
Key Contact:
Mr. Joe Anzalone, Regional Director

2 N Charles St 210
Baltimore, MD 21201
(410) 347-4955
Fax: (410) 246-0444
Email: michelle_balzer@rsmi.com
Key Contact:
Mr. Ed Barrow

6701 Democracy Blvd Ste 600
Bethesda, MD 20817
(301) 897-4768
Fax: (301) 530-1120
Email: michelle_balzer@rsmi.com
Key Contact:
Mr. Ed Barrow

201 Thomas Johnson Dr
Frederick, MD 21702
(301) 695-9271
Fax: (301) 663-0525
Email: barrow@rsmi.com
Key Contact:
Mr. Ed Barrow

140 Wood Rd Ste 104
Braintree, MA 02184
(781) 356-6775
Fax: (781) 848-8559
Email: maryellen@cfstaffing.com
Key Contact:
Ms. Maryellen Kessinger

28580 Orchard Lake Rd Ste 200
Farmington Hills, MI 48334
(248) 932-1821
Fax: (248) 855-3332
Email: mbartlett@mswplc.com
Key Contact:
Ms. Mary Bartlett

55 Campau Ave NW
300 Riverfront Plz Bldg
Grand Rapids, MI 49503
(616) 752-4280
Fax: (616) 752-4281
Email: djames@crowechizek.com
Key Contact:
Ms. Deena James

7900 Xerxes Ave S Ste 2400
Bloomington, MN 55431-1115
(952) 835-1344
Fax: (952) 835-5845
Email: lhuggett@virchowkrause.com
Key Contact:
Ms. Laura Huggett

707 Broadway NE Ste 400
Albuquerque, NM 87102
(505) 224-2575
Fax: (505) 843-6817
Email: rhamil@cfsnm.com
Web: www.cfstaffingnm.com
Key Contact:
Mr. Ray Hamil

900 Liberty Bldg
Buffalo, NY 14202
(716) 842-0939
Fax: (716) 856-3644
Email: resume@freedmaxick.com
Key Contact:
Mr. Ron Soluri

111 W 40th St Fl 12
New York, NY 10018
(212) 302-4567
Fax: (212) 302-1832
Key Contact:
Mr. Phil Dubinsky

388 S Main Str Ste 403
Akron, OH 44311
(330) 237-0100
Fax: (330) 237-1730
Email: kelly.peters@brunercox.com
Key Contact:
Ms. Tamra Emmett, Search Consultant
Mr. Chris Guest, Searxh Consultant
Ms. Susan Davies, Search Consultant

4690 Munson NW Ste 201
PO Box 35429
Canton, OH 44735-5429
(330) 490-2175
Fax: (330) 497-8383
Email: kelly.peters@brunercox.com
Key Contact:
Ms. Evelyn Hronec

5900 Landerbrook Dr Ste 205
Cleveland, OH 44735-5429
(440) 460-1300
Fax: (440) 460-1302
Email: pthorne@crowechizek.com
Key Contact:
Mr. Tony Rispoli

132 Northwoods Ave
Columbus, OH 43235
(614) 343-7800
Fax: (614) 343-7808
Email: girwin@crowechizek.com
Key Contact:
Mr. Gary Irwin

416 Ponce de Leon Ave Ste 1400
Union Plz Bldg
Hato Rey, PR 00918
(787) 756-7597
Fax: (787) 753-1880
Email: cfs@icepr.com
Key Contact:
Mr. Pedro Rivera

6360 LBJ Fwy Ste 100
Dallas, TX 75240
(214) 969-9355
Fax: (214) 953-0722

Email: jdittrich@bdo.com
Web: www.bdo.com
Key Contact:
Ms. Megan Lynch, Regional Director

700 N Pearl St Ste 2000
Dallas, TX 75201-2867
(214) 969-9355
Fax: (214) 953-0722
Email: jmlinar@bdo.com
Key Contact:
Mr. John Milnar

5718 Westheimer Ste 800
Houston, TX 77057
(713) 260-5238
Fax: (832) 251-8311
Email: tll@fittsroberts.com
Key Contact:
Ms. Megan Lynch, Regional Director

1801 Robert Fulton Dr
Reston, VA 20191
(703) 758-3517
Email: ed.barrow@rsmi.com
Key Contact:
Mr. Ed Barrow

2323 E Capitol Dr
PO Box 2459
Appleton, WI 54912-2459
(920) 739-3304
Fax: (920) 733-5758
Email: ybaumgartner@virchowkrause.com
Key Contact:
Ms. Laura Huggett, Director

4600 American Pkwy
PO Box 7398
Madison, WI 53707-7398
(608) 249-3180
Fax: (608) 249-1411
Email: cfs@virchowkrause.com
Key Contact:
Ms. Laura Braendle

115 S 84th St Ste 400
Milwaukee, WI 53214
(414) 777-5505
Fax: (414) 777-5555
Email: tjames@virchowkrause.com
Key Contact:
Ms. Tonnia James, Executive Recruiter

1000-1190 Hornby St
Vancouver, BC V6C 2T6
Canada
(604) 669-9525
Fax: (604) 687-5617
Email: bcjobs@cfstaffing.com
Key Contact:
Ms. Catharine Dunnett, Branch Manager

201 City Center Dr Ste 900
Mississauga, ON L5B 2T4
Canada
(905) 306-7733
Fax: (905) 306-7716
Email: cfsadmin@hto.com
Key Contact:
Ms. Catharine Dunnett, Branch Manager

45 Sheppard Ave E Ste 900
North York, ON M2N 5W9
Canada
(416) 218-4261
Fax: (416) 218-4262
Email: cfsresume@hto.com
Key Contact:
Ms. Catharine Dunnett, Branch Manager

595 Bay St Ste 303
PO Box 122
Toronto, ON M5G 2C2
Canada
(416) 596-7075
Fax: (416) 596-1456
Email: cfsadmin@hto.com
Key Contact:
Ms. Catharine Dunnett, Manager

Mariano Escobedo No 396-203
Col Nva Anzures
Mexico City, MX CP 11590
Mexico
52 5 203 2761
Fax: 52 5 203 9766
Email: cfsmexic@prodigy.net.mx
Key Contact:
Mr. Enrique Hambleton

Creative HR Solutions

PO Box 1966
Stone Mountain, GA 30083
(678) 938-3770
Email: jgross07@aol.com

Description: We are a multicultural organization providing services in the areas of executive/technical search, human resources management, business development, diversity training and outplacement.

Key Contact - Specialty:
Mr. Jerry Gross, Partner - *Telecommunication, data communication, pre-sales, client server*
Mr. Tim Duckett, Partner - *Financial*
Mr. Solomon Tedla, Principal - *Financial, information technology, lean manufacturing*

Salary minimum: $35,000

Functions: Generalist, Senior Mgmt., Admin. Svcs., Personnel, Training, Systems Analysis, Systems Support, Minorities

Industries: Generalist, Test, Measure Equip., Hospitality, Telecoms, Defense, Software

Professional Associations: ASTD, HAAPC, SHARP, SHRM

Creative Search Affiliates

PO Box 3323
Palm Beach, FL 33480
(561) 659-3747
Fax: (561) 659-3746
Email: resnickcsa@aol.com

Description: We specialize in all phases of brokerage, banking, corporate finance, money management, pension, research analysts and p/mgr local and regional contacts. Twenty-five years in business. Stock brokers - retail and institutional.

Key Contact - Specialty:
Dr. A. Allan Resnick, Partner - *Investment management, stockbrokers, corporate finance executives*
Ms. Mildred Resnick, SVP - *Operations management, investment management, accountants*

Functions: Generalist, M&A

Industries: Generalist, Invest. Banking, Brokers, Venture Cap., Misc. Financial

Cresta Recruiting

PO Box 1741
Horsham, PA 19044
(215) 672-8538
Fax: (215) 672-8539
Email: michelle@crestaltd.com
Web: www.crestaltd.com

Description: Recruitment and placement of information technology specialists including, but not limited to, programmers, developers, networking specialists and upper-management. Engineering and data processing environments.

Key Contact - Specialty:
Ms. Michelle Cresta, President - *Information technology*

Functions: Generalist, MIS Mgmt., Systems Analysis, Systems Dev., Systems Implem., Systems Support, Network Admin., DB Admin.

Industries: Generalist, Misc. Financial, Telecoms, Insurance, Software, Non-classifiable

CRI Professional Search

(formerly known as Consultant Registry Int'l)
1784 Leimert Blvd
Oakland, CA 94602
(510) 531-1681
Fax: (510) 531-9599
Email: chuck@california.com
Web: www.criprosearch.com

Description: Nationwide healthcare professional search specializing in the environments of: patient services, nursing (staff/managers/directors), allied health, imaging/laboratory, information management, MIS and managed care (case managers, managed care contracts, provider relations, risk management, UR/UM, QA).

Key Contact - Specialty:
Mr. Charles W. Acridge, Owner - *Medical*

Salary minimum: $40,000

Functions: Generalist, Directors, Senior Mgmt., Middle Mgmt., Physicians, Nurses, Health Admin., Systems Analysis

Industries: Generalist, Pharm Svcs., Healthcare

Networks: National Personnel Assoc (NPA)

Marlene Critchfield & Company

PO Box 122
Salinas, CA 93902
(831) 753-2466
Fax: (831) 753-2467
Email: marlene@agspecialist.com

Description: The reputation I have gained for commitment to excellence and the highest of ethical standards has opened the door for long-term, repeat business relationships and a National network of colleagues and associates.

Key Contact - Specialty:
Ms. Marlene Critchfield, CPC, Owner - *Food, agriculture processing, manufacturing generalist*

Salary minimum: $40,000

Functions: General Mgmt., Senior Mgmt., Middle Mgmt., Production, Plant Mgmt., Sales & Mktg., HR Mgmt., Finance

Industries: Agri., Forestry, Mining, Mfg., Food, Bev., Tobacco, Chemicals, Consumer Elect., Wholesale, Retail, Accounting, Packaging

Professional Associations: APMA, APMA, GSVA

Criterion Executive Search Inc

5420 Bay Center Dr Ste 101
Tampa, FL 33609-3469
(813) 286-2000
Email: ces@cesfl.com
Web: www.criterionsearch.com

Description: We are a contingency firm consisting of professional recruiters with corporate experience in their fields. Our specialties include: audit, accounting and finance, data processing, information technology, engineering, insurance, legal, manufacturing, medical devices, foundry, and food processing.

Key Contact:
Mr. Richard James, President

Functions: Generalist, General Mgmt., Materials, Purchasing, Packaging, Benefits, Finance, IT, Engineering, Attorneys

Industries: Generalist, Mfg., Medical Devices, Metal Products, Computer Equip., Consumer Elect., Test, Measure Equip., Finance, Banking, Misc. Financial, Legal, Accounting, Mgmt. Consulting, HR Services, Telecoms, Packaging, Insurance

Professional Associations: FAPS, NAPC

Critical Analysis
1563 Solano Ave
PMB 136
Berkeley, CA 94707
(707) 557-5674
Fax: (707) 557-5675
Email: lhopeman@criticalanalysis.com
Web: www.criticalanalysis.com

Description: Our firm specializes in the recruitment of middle to senior-level positions in the biotechnology, medical and healthcare information systems industries.

Key Contact:
Ms. Laura A. Hopeman, Director

Salary minimum: $60,000

Functions: Generalist

Industries: Chemicals, Drugs Mfg., Medical Devices, Pharm Svcs., Software, Biotech, Healthcare

Cromark Int'l Inc
6507D Mississauga Rd
Mississauga, ON L5N 1A6
Canada
(905) 816-9090
Fax: (905) 816-9077
Email: resume@autocontacts.com
Web: www.cromark.com

Description: Automotive industry specialists to manufacturers, dealers, suppliers, finance sources, marketing/advertising firms in recruitment, management consulting, troubleshooting, succession planning and training.

Key Contact - Specialty:
Mr. Ian McEwen, Managing Partner - *Management, automotive industry & related*

Salary minimum: $50,000

Functions: Generalist, Advertising, Mkt. Research, HR Mgmt., Benefits, CFO's, Budgeting, Mgmt. Consultants

Industries: Generalist, Transportation, Wholesale, Retail, Misc. Financial, Equip Svcs., Mgmt. Consulting, Advertising

Branches:
3588 Plymouth Rd 177
Ann Arbor, MI 48105-2603
(800) 580-7575
Email: ccrowe@autocontacts.com
Key Contact - Specialty:
Mr. Clive Crowe, CEO - *Automotive*

Crosby Associates
727 E Bethany Home Rd Ste D125
Phoenix, AZ 85014
(602) 321-7893
Fax: (602) 957-3668
Email: gcrosby@azlink.com

Description: We specialize in recruiting for senior management positions for closely held businesses.

Key Contact - Specialty:
Dr. Georgann Crosby, President - *Family businesses*

Salary minimum: $75,000

Functions: Generalist, Senior Mgmt.

Industries: Generalist

Professional Associations: ACA, FFI

Cross Country Consultants Inc
111 Warren Rd Ste 4B
Hunt Valley, MD 21030
(410) 666-1100
Fax: (410) 666-1119

Email: crosscountrycons@aol.com

Description: Professional recruiters since 1961 specializing in engineering, manufacturing, telecommunications and sales. Engineering disciplines: plastics, electronics, chemical process, consumer products, mechanical engineering

Key Contact - Specialty:
Mr. Sheldon Gottesfeld, President - *Engineering*

Salary minimum: $30,000

Functions: Generalist

Industries: Mfg., Accounting, HR Services, Telecoms, Government, Defense, Packaging, Software

Professional Associations: MAPRC

Networks: National Personnel Assoc (NPA)

Cross-Jordan Corp
5961 Sunlight Garden Way
Las Vegas, NV 89118
(702) 248-1936
Email: crossjordan@lvcm.com

Description: We perform retained executive searches primarily in the technical disciplines (engineering/plant management) and in some cases, contingency recruitment for senior-level contributors. We have 500+ affiliated offices throughout the United States.

Key Contact:
Mr. Norman M. Ferris, President

Salary minimum: $50,000

Functions: Generalist, General Mgmt., Mfg., Materials, Sales & Mktg., HR Mgmt., Finance, IT

Industries: Metal Products

Networks: Top Echelon Network

CrossGate Group
PO Box 3647
Newport Beach, CA 92663
(949) 719-0501
Fax: (949) 673-6143
Email: pam@crossgate.com
Web: www.crossgate.com

Description: We are a national, primarily retained search firm specializing in senior level sales and presales technical support executives. We place field level through senior management, including board level executives for the software, more specifically: e-Commerce, Internet, database, data warehouse, and data mining; storage; and network market spaces.

Key Contact:
Ms. Pam Svalstad

Functions: Generalist

Industries: Computer Equip., Software

Crowe Chizek & Company LLP
330 E Jefferson Blvd
PO Box 7
South Bend, IN 46624
(219) 232-3992
(219) 236-8673
Fax: (219) 239-7878
Email: executivesearch@crowechizek.com
Web: www.crowechizek.com

Description: We offer expertise in searching for accounting and financial professionals, as well as professional, managerial and executive personnel. Specialties include financial institutions, manufacturing, distribution, construction, service, technology and not-for-profit entities.

Key Contact - Specialty:
Ms. Janet G. Racht, Executive - *Banking, finance*
Ms. Lisa M. Malkewicz - *Not-for-profit*
Mr. James G. Miller - *Manufacturing*

Salary minimum: $60,000

Functions: Directors, Senior Mgmt., Middle Mgmt., Mfg., Sales & Mktg., HR Mgmt., Finance, CFO's, IT, Non-profits

Industries: Generalist, Construction, Mfg., Finance, Banking, Non-profits, Accounting, HR Services, Government

Professional Associations: ABA, NAER, NAPS, SHRM

Branches:
899 W Cypress Creek Rd Ste 917
Cambridge Executive Ctr
Ft. Lauderdale, FL 33309
(954) 489-9310
Fax: (954) 489-4741

1 Mid America Plz
PO Box 3697
Oak Brook, IL 60522-3697
(630) 574-7878
Fax: (630) 574-1608

307 S Main St Ste 400
Elkhart, IN 46516
(219) 295-1991
Fax: (219) 522-3032

116 E Berry St Ste 490
Ft. Wayne, IN 46802
(219) 423-1531
Fax: (219) 426-7870

10 W Market St
Indianapolis, IN 46204-2976
(317) 632-1100
Fax: (317) 635-6127

3815 River Crossing Pkwy Ste 300
PO Box 40977
Indianapolis, IN 46240-0977
(317) 569-8989
Fax: (317) 706-2660

8001 Broadway Ste 300
PO Box 10807,
Merrillville, IN 46411-0807
(219) 738-1713
Fax: (219) 756-4056

144 N Broadway
Lexington, KY 40507
(859) 252-6738
Fax: (859) 255-0733

2500 Meidinger Twr
Louisville, KY 40202
(502) 584-2500
Fax: (502) 585-1647

9600 Brownsboro Rd Ste 400
PO Box 22649
Louisville, KY 40252-0649
(502) 326-3996
Fax: (502) 420-4400

55 Campau Ave NW
300 Riverfront Plz Bldg
Grand Rapids, MI 49503
(616) 774-0774
Fax: (616) 752-4226

5900 Landerbrook Dr Ste 205
Landerbrook Corporate Ctr 1
Cleveland, OH 44124
(440) 449-9400
Fax: (440) 460-1320

10 W Broad St Ste 1700
1 Columbus
Columbus, OH 43215
(614) 469-0001
Fax: (614) 365-2222

Crown Int'l Consulting LLC
8097-B Roswell Rd
Atlanta, GA 30350
(888) 917-9264
Fax: (425) 988-8834

Email: mburg@prodigy.net
Web: www.jobs-creditcard.com

Description: A professional recruiting and consulting firm that specializes in the credit card industry, across the US and internationally.

Key Contact:
Mr. Mike Burgess, President

Salary minimum: $35,000

Functions: General Mgmt., Middle Mgmt., Sales & Mktg., Direct Mktg., HR Mgmt., Finance, Credit, Risk Mgmt.

Industries: Finance, Banking, Legal, Accounting, HR Services, Call Centers, Software

Professional Associations: NBN

Networks: National Banking Network (NBN)

Jim Crumpley & Associates
1200 E Woodhurst Dr B-400
Springfield, MO 65804
(417) 882-7555
Fax: (417) 882-8555
Email: recruiter@crumpleyjobs.com
Web: www.crumpleyjobs.com

Description: Retained and contingency search and placement of technical, scientific and engineering personnel for the pharmaceutical and medical device industry.

Key Contact - Specialty:
Mr. Jim Crumpley, Owner - *Pharmaceutical*

Salary minimum: $40,000

Functions: Generalist, Product Dev., Production, Plant Mgmt., Quality, Materials Plng., R&D, Engineering

Industries: Generalist, Drugs Mfg., Medical Devices

Crutchfield Associates Inc
1000 St. Andrews Rd Ste D
Columbia, SC 29210
(803) 772-6152
Fax: (803) 798-4004
Email: laurar@crutchfieldassociates.com
Web: www.crutchfieldassociates.com

Description: We combine old-fashioned proven techniques with today's latest technological tools to find superstars who make an immediate contribution for our clients.

Key Contact:
Mr. Bob Crutchfield, Owner/President - *Management, human resources, executive administration*
Ms. Laura Mims Ruth, Recruiting Manager

Salary minimum: $30,000

Functions: Generalist, Senior Mgmt., Admin. Svcs., Mkt. Research, Sales Mgmt., Customer Svc., Benefits, Training

Industries: Generalist

Professional Associations: SCAPS

CS Associates LLC
PO Box 30926
Tucson, AZ 85751-0926
(520) 327-7999
Email: skconnelly@csassoc.com
Web: www.csassoc.com

Description: We recruit for consulting engineering and architectural firms in the USA. The engineers and architects that we recruit must have PEs, RAs, EIT, or other professional registration in the USA only. We specialize in architects, civil, structural, transportation, traffic, and mechanical, electrical, geo-technical, sanitary, and environmental design engineers. Periodically, we do construction management and other construction specialty areas.

Email your resumes to us using Word .doc attachments only.

Key Contact - Specialty:
Mr. Joseph H. Connelly, III, CPC, Owner - *Consulting engineers, construction, architects*
Ms. Susan D. Connelly, CPC, Owner - *Consulting engineers, construction, architects*

Salary minimum: $60,000

Functions: Engineering, Architects

Industries: Construction

Professional Associations: NAPS

CSG Recruiting & Staffing
8630M Guilford Rd 402
Columbia, MD 21046-2610
(410) 519-1226
Fax: (410) 519-9006
Email: resume@csgrecruiting.com
Web: www.csgrecruiting.com

Description: As a performance driven, results-oriented company, we provide outsourcing solutions for executive recruitment, diversity recruitment, permanent staffing, and pre-employment screening. We are a national firm and fill positions covering sales, marketing, engineering, management, and executive positions.

Key Contact - Specialty:
Mr. Eric F. Womack, Chairman/President/CEO - *Senior management, sales*
Ms. Anita L. Womack, Vice President - *Banking, finance, training*

Salary minimum: $50,000

Functions: Generalist

Industries: Mfg., Services, Hospitality, Media, Defense, Aerospace, Insurance, Software

Professional Associations: RON

CTEW Executive Personnel Services Inc
409 Granville St Ste 1207
United Kingdom Bldg
Vancouver, BC V6C 1T2
Canada
(604) 682-3218
Fax: (604) 683-3211
Email: ctew@imag.net

Description: Full-service search firm servicing clients with executive, managerial and supervisory recruiting assignments across all industry sectors.

Key Contact - Specialty:
Mr. Stan Dahl, Recruiter - *Generalist, environmental, technical*
Ms. Hayley Lau, Group Manager - *Executives*

Salary minimum: $40,000

Functions: Generalist, Senior Mgmt., Production, Sales Mgmt., Cash Mgmt., Systems Implem., Mgmt. Consultants

Industries: Generalist, Mfg., Misc. Financial, Higher Ed., Environmental Svcs., Software

Professional Associations: ACSESS, IPSA

Networks: National Personnel Assoc (NPA)

The Culver Group
6610 Flanders Dr
San Diego, CA 92121
(858) 587-4804 x220
Fax: (858) 587-1185
Email: thill@culvercareers.com
Web: www.culvercareers.com

Description: The Culver Group has over 30 sales offices throughout California, Arizona, & Nevada. We specialize in sales & sales management recruiting throughout the U.S. I specialize in

pharmaceutical sales placement throughout the Western U.S.

Key Contact - Specialty:
Mr. Timothy J. Culver, President
Mr. Mike Hobbs, Executive Vice President
Mr. Ted Hill, Vice President - *Sales, medical, pharmaceutical products*
Mr. John Weaver, Vice President - *Sales, software*
Ms. Tami Sullivan, Vice President - *Retail management, sales, consumer products*

Functions: Sales & Mktg.

Industries: Drugs Mfg., Pharm Svcs., Biotech

Cumberland Group Inc
608 S Washington St Ste 101
Naperville, IL 60540
(630) 416-9494
Fax: (630) 416-3250
Email: jvogus@cumberlandgroup.net
Web: www.cumberlandgroup.net

Description: We provide executive search for sales, management and marketing on a nationwide basis for industrial companies. Strong emphasis on capital equipment and metals industry.

Key Contact - Specialty:
Mr. Jerry Vogus, President - *Capital equipment, metals*

Salary minimum: $45,000

Functions: Automation, Sales & Mktg.

Industries: Mfg., Metal Products, Machine, Appliance

Professional Associations: FMA, RIA

Frank Cuomo & Associates Inc
111 Brook St
Scarsdale, NY 10583
(914) 723-8001
Fax: (914) 472-0507

Description: Broad range of services to include executive search and recruitment for service and manufacturing companies. Particular emphasis on sales, marketing, engineering, general management and manufacturing management.

Key Contact - Specialty:
Mr. Frank Cuomo, President - *Flow control industry, instrumentation industry, environmental industry*

Salary minimum: $30,000

Functions: Generalist

Industries: Energy, Utilities, Construction, Metal Products, Test, Measure Equip., Environmental Svcs., Haz. Waste

Professional Associations: HMCRI, ISA, WEF

Current Resource Group Inc
8351 Roswell Rd 112
Atlanta, GA 30350
(770) 828-0294
Fax: (770) 828-0274
Email: search@currentres.com
Web: www.currentres.com

Description: We provide quality targeted selection of exceptional professionals with technical focus. We work closely with clients and candidates to provide placement retention.

Key Contact - Specialty:
Ms. Stacey Barkan, CPC, President - *Computer, technical*

Salary minimum: $50,000

Functions: Generalist, IT, Systems Analysis, Systems Dev., Systems Implem., Systems Support, Network Admin., DB Admin.

Industries: Generalist, New Media, Software

Professional Associations: GAPS

The Currier-Winn Company Inc

PO Box 902
Cherry Hill, NJ 08003-0902
(856) 429-0710
Fax: (856) 429-8086
Email: currierwinn@mindspring.com

Description: Clients are only Fortune 200 firms in plastics, metal and computer hardware and software industries. We recruit for management, engineering and professional positions on a national basis. We have been members of a national network for the past 12 years.

Key Contact - Specialty:
Mr. E. H. Bauzenberger, III, President - *Hardware, software, plastics, metals*

Salary minimum: $35,000

Functions: Mfg.

Industries: Generalist, Printing, Chemicals, Drugs Mfg., Medical Devices, Plastics, Rubber, Leather, Stone, Glass, Metal Products

Networks: Inter-City Personnel Assoc (IPA)

Tony Curtis & Associates

45 Sheppard Ave E Ste 900
Toronto, ON M5N 5W9
Canada
(416) 224-0500
Fax: (905) 294-3349
Email: tonycurtis@idirect.com
Web: www.jobsinfashion.com

Description: With 20 years' experience, we are the preeminent specialists for recruitment of the top professionals in the needle trade. Our fees are contingency based on 10% of annual salary.

Key Contact - Specialty:
Mr. Tony Curtis, President - *Apparel manufacturing, sales*
Mr. Howard Curtis, Vice President-Sales - *Apparel manufacturing, sales*

Functions: General Mgmt., Middle Mgmt., Admin. Svcs., Mfg., Production, Materials, Sales & Mktg., Finance

Industries: Textiles, Apparel, Leather, Stone, Glass, Wholesale, Retail

The Cutting Edge Group Inc

1201 Broadway Ste 904
New York, NY 10001
(212) 779-3066
Fax: (212) 779-0020
Email: info@cuttingedgejobs.com
Web: www.cuttingedgejobs.com

Description: We specialize in placing sales, marketing, and business development executives at bricks and mortar firms addressing e-Commerce needs, Internet, technology, and biotechnology companies in New York City

Key Contact - Specialty:
Ms. Betsi Rosen, President/CEO - *New media*

Functions: Senior Mgmt., Sales & Mktg., Mkt. Research, Mktg. Mgmt., Sales Mgmt., Direct Mktg., Customer Svc., PR, Finance, Graphic Artists

Industries: Finance, Invest. Banking, Venture Cap., Accounting, Hospitality, Media, Advertising, Publishing, New Media, Software, Healthcare

Professional Associations: NYNMA

CV Associates

85 N Broadway
Nyack, NY 10960
(845) 353-3466
Fax: (845) 353-3405
Email: mail@cvassociates.com
Web: www.cvassociates.com

Description: We provide contingency and retained technical search services, as well as placement assistance to electrical, software, optical, and mechanical engineers within the high technology sector. Our clients develop and manufacture products in telecom/DataCom, computer, instrumentation, and electronic component industries.

Key Contact - Specialty:
Mr. Vince Quiros, CPC, CIR, President - *Telecommunications, data communications, electronics*

Salary minimum: $75,000

Functions: Mfg., Product Dev., R&D, Engineering

Industries: Communications, Telecoms, Telephony, Digital, Wireless, Fiber Optic, Network Infrastructure, Government, Defense, Aerospace

Networks: Top Echelon Network

Cyberna Associates Ltd

999 de Maisonneuve Blvd W Ste 650
Montreal, QC H3A 3L4
Canada
(514) 843-8349
Fax: (514) 843-6993
Email: wbrown@optioncyberna.com

Description: Recruitment and search, executive contracting, outsourcing, consulting. Innovative and customized programs to meet client needs.

Key Contact:
Ms. Wanda Brown, Vice President/General Manager

Salary minimum: $50,000

Functions: General Mgmt., Directors, Middle Mgmt., Materials, Mktg. Mgmt., HR Mgmt., Finance, IT

Industries: Generalist

Cybernautic Associates

30 Valley Rd
San Carlos, CA 94070-2035
(650) 593-5171
Fax: (425) 675-8237
Email: jdz1@cybernautic.com
Web: www.cybernautic.com

Description: We specialize in recruiting information technology and financial executives for national and international positions in the securities trading industry.

Key Contact - Specialty:
Mr. David Zincavage, President - *Information technology, finance*

Salary minimum: $65,000

Functions: Generalist, Finance, IT, R&D, Mgmt. Consultants, Int'l.

Industries: Generalist, Finance, Software, Biotech

Cypress Research Consultants Inc

PO Box 130702
The Woodlands, TX 77393-0702
(281) 367-5427
(281) 367-2699
Email: cysearch@aol.com

Description: Ten years' experience specializing in placement of technical, professional personnel in the polymer and specialty chemical industries.

Key Contact - Specialty:
Ms. Wendy Gentile, Recruiting Consultant - *Plastics, specialty chemicals, R&D*
Mr. Craig Gentile, Recruiting Consultant - *Plastics, specialty chemicals, R&D*
Ms. Lynn Sawyer, Recruiting Consultant - *Plastics, specialty chemicals, R&D*

Functions: Generalist, R&D

Industries: Chemicals, Plastics, Rubber, Paints, Petro. Products, Packaging

Professional Associations: ACS, SPE

Branches:
2515 Acadiana Ln
Seabrook, TX 77586
(281) 326-4033
Email: lea4033@aol.com
Key Contact - Specialty:
Dr. Lea Anderson - *Plastics, specialty chemicals, R&D*

Cyr Associates Inc

177 Worcester St Ste 303
Wellesley Hills, MA 02481
(781) 235-5900
Fax: (781) 239-0140
Email: cyrinc@mindspring.com
Web: www.cyrassociates.com

Description: Our firm recruits for client companies in consumer goods and direct marketing including consumer and business-to-business catalog. We have expertise in footwear, apparel, textiles, food, giftware, arts and crafts, toys, collectibles, home decor, accessories, cosmetics, fragrances, and medical devices.

Key Contact - Specialty:
Mr. Maury N. Cyr, President - *Consumer products, direct marketing*

Salary minimum: $40,000

Functions: Mfg., Materials, Sales & Mktg., Int'l.

Industries: Mfg., Food, Bev., Tobacco, Textiles, Apparel, Lumber, Furniture, Soap, Perf., Cosmtcs., Drugs Mfg., Medical Devices, Plastics, Rubber, Consumer Elect., Misc. Mfg., Wholesale, Services, Advertising, Publishing, Packaging, Development SW, Mfg. SW

Professional Associations: NEDMA

D & M Associates

245 Cedar Blvd Ste 100
Pittsburgh, PA 15228
(412) 343-4892
Fax: (412) 343-4925

Description: Specializing in marketing, advertising, banking, real estate, construction and non-profits.

Key Contact:
Mr. David Stobbe, President
Ms. Mickey Stobbe, Principal

Salary minimum: $40,000

Functions: Generalist, Middle Mgmt., Advertising, Mktg. Mgmt., Minorities, Non-profits, Graphic Artists

Industries: Generalist, Construction, Banking, Media, Advertising, Publishing, Government, Real Estate

Professional Associations: PPA

d.Diversified Services

26211 Central Park Blvd Ste 600
Southfield, MI 48076
(248) 208-0000
Fax: (248) 208-0011
Email: shenes@jobs4you.com
Web: www.jobs4you.com

Description: We are one of Detroit's fastest growing technical staffing companies that does contract and direct placements. Our specialties include the following disciplines: CAD design, engineering, information systems, sales, and technicians.

Key Contact:
Mr. Stephen Henes, President

Charles Dahl Group Inc
77 13th Ave NE Ste 209
Minneapolis, MN 55413
(612) 331-7777
Fax: (612) 331-7778
Email: cdahl@cdassoc.com
Web: www.cdassoc.com

Description: Specialize in legal, research and development, high-technologies and biotech/gene sequencing industries. Concentration in diversity.

Key Contact - Specialty:
Mr. Charles Dahl, President - *CIO's, CEOs, scientists, diversity, international*
Mr. Thomas Dunlap, Vice President - *Engineering, MIS, sales*
Ms. Janice Kuschnov, Vice President - *Engineering, MIS, sales, legal*

Salary minimum: $50,000

Functions: Generalist, Directors, Sales Mgmt., Systems Implem., R&D, Engineering, Minorities

Industries: Generalist, Medical Devices, Computer Equip., Legal, Packaging, Software, Biotech

The DAKO Group
2966 Industrial Row
Troy, MI 48084
(248) 655-0100
Fax: (248) 655-0101
Email: recruiting@dakogroup.com
Web: www.dakogroup.com

Description: We specialize in long-term contractual and permanent placement of technical professionals for the automotive and information technology industries.

Key Contact - Specialty:
Mr. Anthony J. Lioi, Director of Recruiting - *Engineering, information systems*

Functions: Mfg., Product Dev., Production, Quality, Materials, HR Mgmt., IT, Engineering

Industries: Generalist, Chemicals, Plastics, Rubber, Motor Vehicles, Computer Equip., Test, Measure Equip., Mgmt. Consulting, HR Services, Aerospace, Packaging, Software, HR SW

Professional Associations: NTSA

Daley Consulting & Search
1866 Clayton Rd Ste 211
Concord, CA 94520
(925) 798-3866
Fax: (925) 798-4475
Email: mdaley@dpsearch.com
Web: www.dpsearch.com

Description: I specialize in the recruiting and placement of data processing and MIS/IT professionals for clients in the San Francisco Bay area and Northern California. My candidates' expertise includes everything from a two-year programmer level of experience up to, and including, MIS executive-level management.

Key Contact - Specialty:
Mr. Michael F. Daley, Owner/Recruiter - *Information systems, information technology, MIS, data processing*

Salary minimum: $50,000

Functions: IT

Industries: Generalist

Dalton Management Consultants Ltd
189 Berdan Ave
PMB 245
Wayne, NJ 07470
(513) 831-6735
Fax: (513) 831-6735
Email: evonnedalton@aol.com

Key Contact - Specialty:
Ms. Evonne Dalton, President - *Human resources*

Salary minimum: $75,000

Functions: HR Mgmt., Benefits, Training, Mgmt. Consultants

Industries: Generalist

Damon & Associates Inc
333 W Campbell Rd Ste 360
Richardson, TX 75080
(972) 671-6990
Fax: (972) 644-9450
Email: damonofc@aol.com

Description: Sales and sales management: medical, consumer, industrial, software and hardware, contract furniture, office products, information technology, telecommunications and LAN/WAN.

Key Contact - Specialty:
Mr. Richard E. Damon, President - *Sales, sales management*
Mr. H. M. Hailey, Vice President-Operations - *Sales, sales management*

Salary minimum: $30,000

Functions: Generalist, General Mgmt., Mfg., Healthcare, Sales & Mktg., HR Mgmt., Finance, IT

Industries: Generalist

Networks: First Interview Network (FIN)

The Dan Group
300 S Jackson St Ste 100
Denver, CO 80209
(303) 398-7065
Fax: (303) 975-5312
Email: karen@thedangroup.com
Web: www.thedangroup.com

Description: We specialize in the placement of sales and marketing professionals at all levels.

Key Contact - Specialty:
Ms. Karen D. Dandridge, President - *Sales & marketing professionals*

Salary minimum: $40,000

Functions: Sales & Mktg.

Industries: Generalist

Professional Associations: CHRA, NAPS

The Danbrook Group Inc
4100 Spring Valley Rd Ste 700 LB-2
Dallas, TX 75244
(972) 392-0057
Fax: (972) 386-1974
Email: info@danbrook.com

Description: Specialty search firm delivering high-level client service in four major disciplines. Each department consists of a team dedicated to a targeted, professional approach to search.

Key Contact - Specialty:
Mr. Michael Kennedy, Senior Partner - *Insurance*
Ms. Sandra Teter, Partner - *Accounting, finance*

Salary minimum: $30,000

Functions: Generalist, Senior Mgmt., Middle Mgmt., Finance, CFO's, Taxes, IT, Systems Analysis

Industries: Generalist, Finance, Accounting, Insurance

Professional Associations: SERC

Dangerfield, Nadalin & Associates
3701 Kirby Dr Ste 830
Houston, TX 77098
(713) 520-8335
Email: w.dangerfield@thehiringspot.com
Web: www.deaus.com

Description: Retained and contingency based executive search firm specializing in accounting, legal, information technology, retail & restaurant and telecommunications recruiting.

Key Contact:
Mr. William Dangerfield, Partner - *Retail real estate, construction*
Mr. Steven Nadalin, Partner

Salary minimum: $40,000

Functions: Generalist

Industries: Construction, Food, Bev., Tobacco, Textiles, Apparel, Retail, Hospitality, Media, Telecoms, Real Estate, Software

Dangerfield, Nadalin & Associates
3701 Kirby Dr Ste 830
Houston, TX 77098
(800) 278-8966
Fax: (281) 754-4135
Email: w.dangerfield@deaus.com
Web: www.deaus.com

Description: We are a retained and contingency based recruiting firm that places mid to upper level executives in the retail and restaurant industry.

Key Contact:
Mr. Will Dangerfield, Partner
Mr. Stephen Nadalin, Partner

Salary minimum: $35,000

Daniel, Marks Company
6432 E Main St
Reynoldsburg, OH 43068
(614) 863-0818
Fax: (614) 863-0857
Email: dmarks@danielmarks.com
Web: www.danielmarks.com

Description: Retained search and contract professionals servicing manufacturing, telecommunications and healthcare.

Key Contact - Specialty:
Mr. Daniel M. Lowe, CPC, President - *Manufacturing (general management, middle management), telecommunications, healthcare service industries*

Salary minimum: $40,000

Functions: Generalist, Mfg., Materials, Healthcare, Sales & Mktg., Finance, IT, Engineering

Industries: Generalist, Construction, Mfg., Finance, Services, Media, Healthcare

The Danielson Group Inc
PO Box 50692
Denton, TX 76206
(940) 383-0900
Fax: (940) 383-9475
Email: txhdhunter@earthlink.net
Web: www.jobcoach.com

Description: Twenty-five years of executive and technical search/recruitment for both retainer and contingency clients in the rubber, plastics, pharmaceuticals and healthcare industries nationwide; outplacement consulting division and professional on-line job coaching also available.

Key Contact - Specialty:
Mr. Michael A. Pajak, President - *Healthcare, pharmaceuticals, plastics, rubber*

Salary minimum: $45,000

Functions: Middle Mgmt.

Industries: Mfg., Drugs Mfg., Medical Devices, Plastics, Rubber, Healthcare

Professional Associations: PARW

R Dann & Associates LLC
6154 N Hamilton Ste 3N
Chicago, IL 60659
(773) 465-3382
Fax: (773) 465-3402
Email: rdannassoc@aol.com

Description: We recruit qualified professionals uniquely suited for the insurance corporate cultures and business environments. We are professional, aggressive, responsive, and we pride ourselves on our ability to listen to your needs..

Key Contact - Specialty:
Ms. Juanita Dougherty, President - *Insurance, not-for-profit*

Salary minimum: $50,000

Functions: Generalist

Industries: Insurance

Danelle Dann Int'l Inc
237 Park Ave Fl 21
New York, NY 10017
(212) 687-5050
Fax: (212) 687-4645
Email: ddbkng@msn.com

Description: Executive search devoted exclusively to the foreign banking sector with emphasis on treasury and corporate finance.

Key Contact - Specialty:
Ms. Danelle Dann, Managing Director - *Executive search*

Salary minimum: $90,000

Functions: General Mgmt.

Industries: Finance, Banking, Invest. Banking

Dapexs Consultants Inc
5320 W Genesee St
Camillus, NY 13031
(315) 484-9300
Fax: (315) 484-9330
Email: employment@dapexs.com
Web: www.dapexs.com

Description: Search and placement specialists in MIS, information technology, software engineering and finance/accounting. We search, screen, select; present only fully qualified candidates. Our exclusive search plan is tailored to fit specific client needs. Also place professionals on contract basis.

Key Contact - Specialty:
Mr. Peter J. Leofsky, President - *Computer professionals*

Salary minimum: $30,000

Functions: Generalist, Finance, IT, MIS Mgmt., Systems Dev., Systems Implem., Network Admin., DB Admin.

Industries: Generalist

Professional Associations: ACM, IPCCNY, SHRM

Networks: National Personnel Assoc (NPA)

DARE Human Resources Corp
275 Slater St Ste 900
Ottawa, ON K1P 5H9
Canada
(613) 238-4485
Fax: (613) 236-3754
Email: resume@darehr.com
Web: www.darehr.com

Description: Providing leading-edge human resource and technical solutions catered to meet the specific needs of each company we service. Some key strengths include: executive search, technical recruitment, project management, accredited human resource consultants.

Key Contact - Specialty:
Ms. Jocelyne Vitanza, President/CEO - *Executive, information technology, engineering, financial, human resource consulting*
Ms. Alison Shipley, Comptroller - *Financial management, accounting*
Mr. Andrew Ross, Human Resource Consultant & Writer - *Executive, administration, staffing*
Ms. Edith Lèsperance, Human Resource Recruiter - *Administration, operational, government*
Ms. Susan Reilly, Financial Assistant - *Accounts receivable, payroll, finance*
Ms. Nathalie Villeneuve, Customer Service & Support - *Information services, switchboard*
Mr. Jacques Guilini, Account Manager - *Government, IT*
Mr. Stephanie Trudel, HR Coordinator - *Administrative support*

Functions: Generalist

Industries: Finance, Higher Ed., Legal, Mgmt. Consulting, HR Services, IT Implementation, Communications, Government

Professional Associations: APPAC, ESSAC, OBOT, OED

Gail Darling & Associates
25 Butterfield Trl
El Paso, TX 79906
(915) 772-0077
Fax: (915) 772-2440
Email: gdarling@gdarling.com
Web: www.gdarling.com

Description: We offer experienced recruitment and placement services through tenured recruiters worldwide targeting Fortune 500 companies.

Key Contact - Specialty:
Ms. Cynthia Cremeans, Managing Recruiter - *Management, telecommunications*
Mr. Jeff Caruso, Recruiter - *Engineering, manufacturing*

Salary minimum: $30,000

Functions: Generalist, General Mgmt., Mfg., Materials, Sales & Mktg., HR Mgmt., Finance, IT

Industries: Generalist, Mfg., Transportation, Finance, Services, Media, Software

Branches:
4100 Amon Carter Blvd Ste 100
Ft. Worth, TX 76155
(817) 355-9500
Fax: (817) 540-2484
Email: prodesk@gdarling.com
Key Contact - Specialty:
Ms. Val Kolbaba, Recruiter - *Telecommunications, information systems*

Data Bank Corp
927 Avondale Ave
Cincinnati, OH 45229
(513) 559-9300
(800) 733-0020
Fax: (425) 732-9683
Email: jobs@databankcorp.com
Web: www.databankcorp.com

Description: Our mission is to fullfill the career needs of our client, candidates and employees by matching well-qualified, pre-screened information systems executives with rewarding, high-quality career opportunities.

Key Contact - Specialty:
Mr. Wayne Ivey, President - *Executive information systems*

Functions: IT, MIS Mgmt., Systems Analysis, Systems Dev., Systems Implem., Systems Support, Network Admin., DB Admin.

Industries: Generalist

Data Career Center Inc
225 N Michigan Ave Ste 930
Chicago, IL 60601
(312) 565-1060
Fax: (312) 565-0246
Email: datacareercenter@att.net

Description: We are specialist in the placement of information technology and telecommunications personnel.

Key Contact - Specialty:
Mr. Larry Chaplik, President - *Information technology, software programmers, software developers*

Functions: Generalist, Directors, Middle Mgmt., MIS Mgmt., Systems Analysis, Systems Support, Network Admin., DB Admin.

Industries: E-commerce, IT Implementation, Call Centers, Network Infrastructure, Software, Database SW, Development SW

Data Center Personnel
24007 Ventura Blvd Ste 240
Calabasas, CA 91302
(818) 225-2830
Fax: (818) 225-2840
Email: manager@itrecruiting.com
Web: www.itrecruiting.com

Description: We specialize in Informations Systems Staff and Executive search exclusively in Southern California, Los Angeles, Orange County areas.

Key Contact - Specialty:
Mr. Jim Auld, President - *Information systems (staff, executive search)*

Salary minimum: $60,000

Functions: IT

Industries: Generalist

Data Search Network Inc
21218 St. Andrews Blvd Ste 611
Boca Raton, FL 33433
(561) 347-6421
Fax: (561) 347-6429
Email: careers@dsninc.com
Web: www.dsninc.com

Description: Information systems firm serving wide range of clients nationwide. All consultants are principals with direct involvement in the search. Over 20 years' experience in information systems search.

Key Contact - Specialty:
Mr. Ken Gross, Managing Director - *Information systems*

Salary minimum: $75,000

Functions: IT, MIS Mgmt., Systems Analysis, Systems Dev., Systems Implem., Systems Support, Network Admin., DB Admin.

Industries: Generalist

Professional Associations: NAPS

Branches:
PO Box 305
Emerson, NJ 07630
(201) 967-8600
Fax: (201) 265-0207
Key Contact - Specialty:
Ms. JoAnn Skorupski, Managing Director - *Information systems*

The DataFinders Group Inc

25 E Spring Valley Ave
Maywood, NJ 07607
(201) 845-7700
Fax: (201) 845-7365
Email: info@datafinders.net
Web: www.datafinders.net

Description: A nationwide search firm specializing in the data/tele-processing industries in sales, sales management, field support and traditional end-user staff consulting/programming positions on both a permanent and temporary basis.

Key Contact - Specialty:
Mr. Thomas J. Credidio, Vice President - *Line sales, computer industry*
Mr. Peter Warns, President - *Sales management, computer industry*

Salary minimum: $25,000

Functions: Sales & Mktg., Sales Mgmt., IT, Network Admin.

Industries: Computer Equip., Mgmt. Consulting, Software

Datamatics Management Services Inc

330 New Brunswick Ave
Fords, NJ 08863
(732) 738-9600
(732) 738-8500
Fax: (732) 738-9603
Email: nch@datamaticsinc.com
Web: www.datamaticsinc.com

Description: Specialists in service related industries, general management, human resources, data processing, information systems, labor relations, training. Placement concerns center on organization fit within existing management structures, evaluating job requirements and formulation position specifications.

Key Contact - Specialty:
Mr. Norman C. Heinle, Jr., President
Mr. R. Kevin Heinle, Vice President
Mr. William Loss, CPA, Director - *Marketing*

Salary minimum: $50,000

Functions: Generalist

Industries: Generalist

DataPro Personnel Consultants

13355 Noel Rd 1 Galleria Twr Ste 2001
Dallas, TX 75240
(972) 661-8600
Fax: (972) 661-1309
Email: datapro@flash.net
Web: www.dataprorecruiters.com

Description: Since our founding in Dallas/Fort Worth in 1970, we have placed more than 4,000 individuals in information technology positions ranging from programmers to top MIS managers.

Key Contact - Specialty:
Ms. Donna Schuback, Vice President - *Information technology*
Mr. Jeff Davis, Senior Consultant - *Consultants (Big 6), ERP, data warehousing*
Ms. Lynn Kollaritsch, Senior Consultant - *Information technology*

Salary minimum: $40,000

Functions: Generalist, MIS Mgmt., Systems Analysis, Systems Dev., Systems Implem., Systems Support, Network Admin., DB Admin.

Industries: Generalist

Professional Associations: MAPS, TAPS

Networks: Top Echelon Network

Dataware Consulting Inc

423 Bedford Park Ave
Toronto, ON M5M 4M5
Canada
(416) 784-4322
Fax: (416) 784-3333
Email: it@datawareconsulting.com
Web: www.datawareconsulting.com

Description: We provide contract, permanent, and temporary IT personnel ranging from junior programmers to VP level managers, including system administrators, database administrators, network engineers, hardware engineers, business analysts, architects, programmer and system analysts, technical support/help desk analysts, testers, technical writers, and trainers.

Functions: IT, Systems Analysis, Systems Dev., Systems Implem., Systems Support, Network Admin., DB Admin.

Industries: Generalist

Alan N Daum & Associates Inc

6241 Riverside Dr
Dublin, OH 43017
(614) 793-1200
Email: alan@adaum.com
Web: www.adaum.com

Description: Over 25 years' experience recruiting only process control engineers nationally. We have a database of thousands of process control engineers, nationally.

Key Contact - Specialty:
Mr. Alan N. Daum, President - *Process control engineering*

Salary minimum: $55,000

Functions: Automation

Industries: Energy, Utilities, Mfg., Food, Bev., Tobacco, Paper, Chemicals, Soap, Perf., Cosmtcs., Drugs Mfg., Plastics, Rubber, Paints, Petro. Products, Test, Measure Equip.

Networks: Top Echelon Network

The Michael David Group

2595 Hwy I
Saukville, WI 53080
(414) 268-1750
Fax: (414) 268-1753
Email: tmdgpw@aol.com

Description: Conducts retained and contingent searches for general manufacturing, automotive, battery and steel industries for technical, sales and management positions.

Key Contact - Specialty:
Mr. Michael D. Eskra, Director - *Transition management, battery*

Salary minimum: $50,000

Functions: Middle Mgmt., Production

Industries: Mfg., Paper, Chemicals, Metal Products, Consumer Elect., Misc. Mfg., Mgmt. Consulting, HR Services, Aerospace, Packaging

Professional Associations: AICHE

Networks: National Personnel Assoc (NPA)

Davidson, Laird & Associates

29260 Franklin Rd Ste 110
Southfield, MI 48034
(248) 358-2160
Fax: (248) 358-1225
Email: meri@davidson-laird.com

Description: We have an excellent reputation for long-term retention of our candidates with our clients. We attribute that to our team approach to matching and full-service placement with our clients.

Key Contact - Specialty:
Ms. Meri Laird, President - *Automotive, plastics engineering*
Ms. Lori Dow, Managing Partner - *Manufacturing, engineering*

Salary minimum: $35,000

Functions: Generalist, Product Dev., Production, Automation, Plant Mgmt., Quality, Purchasing, Sales & Mktg., Engineering

Industries: Generalist, Food, Bev., Tobacco, Plastics, Rubber, Motor Vehicles

Networks: National Personnel Assoc (NPA)

T A Davis & Associates

604 Green Bay Rd
Kenilworth, IL 60043
(847) 256-8900
Fax: (847) 256-8955
Email: tomd@tadavis.com
Web: www.tadavis.com

Description: Specializing in executive search in the restaurant, hotel, resort and food service industries.

Key Contact:
Mr. Thomas Davis, President

Salary minimum: $60,000

Functions: Generalist

Industries: Hospitality

Anthony Davis & Associates

317 Clarkson Rd Ste 203
Ellisville, MO 63011
(636) 207-7212
Fax: (636) 207-7444
Email: www.bogeykid@aol.com

Description: Thoroughly screen candidates, verify degrees, provide references, discuss salary requirements. Relocation specialist, confidentiality, background information, quality service.

Key Contact - Specialty:
Mr. Kevin Adams, President - *Manufacturing, foundry, diecast, plastics, metalworking*

Functions: Generalist, General Mgmt., Production, Packaging, Sales & Mktg., HR Mgmt., IT, Engineering

Industries: Generalist, Mfg., Mgmt. Consulting, HR Services

Professional Associations: AFS

Carolyn Davis Associates Inc

70 W Red Oak Ln
White Plains, NY 10604
(914) 697-7540
Fax: (914) 697-7566
Email: careers@carolyndavis.net
Web: www.carolyndavis.net

Description: We specialize in the recruitment of property and casualty, life, health and pension professionals. Our commitment to excellence combined with integrity, respect for confidentiality, experience and knowledge of the insurance industry assures a successful search.

Key Contact - Specialty:
Ms. Carolyn Davis, CPC, President - *Insurance*

Functions: Generalist

Industries: Insurance

Donna Davis Associates

2050 Center Ave Ste 550
Ft. Lee, NJ 07024
(201) 592-6000
Fax: (201) 592-5961
Email: dawn@donnadavis.com
Web: www.donnadavisassociates.com

Description: We are a national recruiting firm exclusively dedicated to placing mid- and senior-level human resource professionals.

Key Contact - Specialty:
Ms. Donna Davis, President - *Human resources*

Salary minimum: $50,000

Functions: Generalist, Senior Mgmt., Middle Mgmt., HR Mgmt., Benefits, Personnel, Training

Industries: Generalist, HR Services

Professional Associations: ASTD, EMA, HRPS, NEHRA, SHRM

Bert Davis Publishing Placement Consultants

425 Madison Ave Fl 14
New York, NY 10017
(212) 838-4000
Fax: (212) 935-3291
Email: bdavis@bertdavis.com
Web: www.bertdavis.com

Description: A leading executive placement firm specializing in publishing, publication communication, information and electronic media fields.

Key Contact - Specialty:
Ms. Sally Dougan, Executive Vice President - *Book publishing*
Ms. Wendy Baker, Senior Vice President - *Magazine industry*
Mr. Larry Eidelberg, Vice President - *Technology*
Ms. Linda Rascher, Vice President - *Financial*

Salary minimum: $50,000

Functions: Generalist, General Mgmt., Senior Mgmt., Product Dev., Sales & Mktg., Finance, IT

Industries: Generalist, Advertising, Publishing, New Media, Software

Professional Associations: AWNY, DMA, NAER

Paul Day & Associates (TM)

5020 Celbridge Pl
Raleigh, NC 27613
(919) 845-3307
Fax: (919) 846-8782
Email: donpaul@nc.rr.com
Web: www.paulday-associates.2kweb.net/corpinfo

Description: An executive search and technical recruiting firm, specializing in telecom, aerospace/aircraft, and electric utilities nationwide.

Key Contact - Specialty:
Mr. Paul Gomez, President
Ms. Donna Day, Vice President - *Software, hardware engineering*

Salary minimum: $40,000

Functions: Generalist

Industries: Energy, Utilities, Mfg., Media, Telecoms, Aerospace, Software

DBC Recruiting Network

5672 Peachtree Pkwy Ste E
Norcross, GA 30092
(770) 729-0990
Fax: (770) 729-1183
Email: dbc-jobs@mindspring.com

Description: Executive recruiting in the computer industry, including sales, marketing, sales management and technical support, with a nationwide network of affiliates, including the First Interview Recruiting Network.

Key Contact - Specialty:
Mrs. Debbie Brooks, Owner - *Computer sales, high technology sales*

Functions: Generalist

Industries: Software

Networks: First Interview Network (FIN)

DCA Professional Search

437 Ridge Point Dr
Lewisville, TX 75067
(972) 315-2934
Fax: (972) 315-2334
Email: info@dcaprosearch.com
Web: www.dcaprosearch.com

Description: Specialization in marketing and advertising professionals experienced with Hispanic marketing and advertising. This includes all facets of advertising such as creatives, account service, media, promotions as well as marketing and public relations on the client side. New specialty which started in 2000 includes interactive marketing.

Key Contact - Specialty:
Ms. Doris Aguirre, President - *Hispanic advertising, hispanic marketing*

Salary minimum: $40,000

Functions: Directors, Middle Mgmt., Advertising, Mktg. Mgmt., PR, Minorities

Industries: Advertising, New Media

Professional Associations: AHAA

E W Dean & Associates Inc

(also known as MRI of Pittsburgh - USC)
110 Ft. Couch Rd Fl 3
Upper St. Clair, PA 15241-1030
(412) 833-5833
Fax: (412) 833-6225
Email: eric@ewdean.com
Web: www.ewdean.com

Description: We provide professional search and recruitment services to the technology and manufacturing industries. Our emphasis is on recruitment and placement of operations, technical, professional, and administrative personnel, such as company president/CEOs, general managers, operations managers, manufacturing managers, plant managers, production managers, sales and marketing managers, financial managers, human resources managers, quality managers, engineering managers, mechanical engineers, electrical engineers, SW engineers, industrial engineers, manufacturing/process engineers, plastics/polymer engineers, etc.

Key Contact:
Mr. Eric Dean, Jr., President

Salary minimum: $48,000

Functions: Mfg.

Industries: Mfg., Wireless

Professional Associations: SHRM

Debbon Recruiting Group Inc

PO Box 510323
St. Louis, MO 63151
(314) 846-9101
Fax: (314) 846-8771
Email: jzipfel@earthlink.net

Description: Recruiting specialization since 1978 in technical, staff and line management positions for food and pharmaceutical industries has resulted in industry wide contacts allowing for timely response to individual situations.

Key Contact - Specialty:
Mr. John Zipfel, President - *Food, pharmaceutical (staff, line management, technical positions)*

Salary minimum: $40,000

Functions: Mfg., Plant Mgmt., Quality, Materials, HR Mgmt., Engineering

Industries: Food, Bev., Tobacco, Chemicals, Soap, Perf., Cosmtcs., Drugs Mfg.

DeBellis & Catherine Associates

325 Essjay Rd Ste 300
Williamsville, NY 14221
(716) 632-1500
Fax: (716) 632-8844
Email: mdebellis@dcasearch.com
Web: www.dcasearch.com

Description: We are a search firm covering the professional areas of accounting/finance, banking, insurance, sales/marketing, engineering/manufacturing, food manufacturing, human resources, legal, and IT. We employ 6 recruiters covering the Northeast market, representing companies of every size. Most of our searches are engaged on a partial retained basis.

Key Contact:
Mr. Michael DeBellis, Jr., President

Salary minimum: $25,000

Professional Associations: SHRM

Networks: National Banking Network (NBN)

DeCaster Associates

1346 Wren Ln
Green Bay, WI 54313
(920) 499-6005
Fax: (920) 499-6023
Email: pdecaster@aol.com
Web: www.ipa.com/eoffice/920-499-6005.html

Description: We offer professional search and recruiting services for corporations and law firms. Focused in attorneys (all practice areas) and executive management.

Key Contact - Specialty:
Mr. Paul DeCaster, Principal - *Legal, executive management*

Salary minimum: $75,000

Functions: Legal

Industries: Generalist

Professional Associations: RON

DeCorrevont & Associates

233 S Kenilworth Ave
Oak Park, IL 60302
(708) 445-1199
Fax: (708) 445-0248
Email: jdecor@mediaone.net

Description: Recruiting and search for the healthcare: sales/marketing and tech professions.

Key Contact - Specialty:
Mr. James DeCorrevont, President - *High technology, software, healthcare*

Salary minimum: $40,000

Functions: Generalist, Health Admin., Sales Mgmt., Non-profits

Industries: Generalist, Non-profits, Insurance, Software, Healthcare

Dedeke & Associates

7030 S Yale Ste 310
Tulsa, OK 74136
(918) 491-1181
Fax: (918) 491-9989
Email: bdedeke@webzone.net
Web: www.dedekeandassociates.com

Description: We are an executive search firm that offers professional search services carefully targeted to the specific needs of our clients. We specialize in middle to senior management searches but often perform searches in technical disciplines as requested by our clients. We have over 25 years of domestic and international search experience. We specialize in identifying high potential, proactive executives, managers, and practitioners who can bring added value to your organization.

Key Contact - Specialty:
Mr. Bob Dedeke, principal - *Senior management*

Salary minimum: $60,000

Functions: Generalist

Industries: Energy, Utilities, Construction, Mfg., Transportation, Finance, Services, Communications, Environmental Svcs., Packaging, Software

Deeco Int'l
PO Box 57033
Salt Lake City, UT 84157
(801) 261-3326
Fax: (801) 261-3955
Email: deecoinc@att.net

Description: Executive recruiting, specializing in the medical and pharmaceutical industries.

Key Contact - Specialty:
Ms. Dee McBride, President - *Medical*

Functions: Generalist, Senior Mgmt., Middle Mgmt., Product Dev., Mkt. Research, Mktg. Mgmt., Sales Mgmt., R&D

Industries: Generalist, Drugs Mfg., Medical Devices, Computer Equip., Pharm Svcs., Biotech, Healthcare

Networks: First Interview Network (FIN)

DeepSweep
200 N Larchmont Blvd
Los Angeles, CA 90004-3707
(323) 460-6807
Fax: (323) 692-7805
Email: info@deepsweep.com
Web: www.deepsweep.com

Description: Web-based executive search service providing customers with access to thousands of passive job seekers (non-profit executives who wish to be notified of career opportunities.

Key Contact:
Mr. Jay Speakman, Principal

Salary minimum: $50,000

Functions: Generalist, General Mgmt., Healthcare, Sales & Mktg., HR Mgmt., Finance, IT, Non-profits

Industries: Generalist, Non-profits, Higher Ed.

Deffet Group Inc
7801 Marysville Rd
Ostrander, OH 43061
(740) 666-7600
Fax: (740) 666-7610
Email: dgi@midohio.net
Web: www.deffetgroup.com

Description: Specializing in executive search within the long-term care and retirement housing industries.

Key Contact:
Mr. G. Daniel Deffet

Salary minimum: $50,000

Functions: Healthcare

Industries: Non-profits, Mgmt. Consulting, HR Services, Hospitals, Long-term Care

Professional Associations: AAHSA, OHCA

DEL Technical Services Inc
1411 Opus Pl Ste 310
Downers Grove, IL 60515-1100
(630) 852-6300
Fax: (630) 852-6317
Email: coneill@deltech.com
Web: www.deltech.com

Description: Skill match, as proven process used to match the critical success factors of your ideal candidate with over 100,000 personnel that are not in the job market.

Key Contact - Specialty:
Mr. Chris O'Neill, President - *Technical, engineers, technicians, information technology*

Salary minimum: $25,000

Functions: Generalist, Production, IT, Engineering, Specialized Svcs., Technicians

Industries: Generalist, Energy, Utilities, Construction, Mfg., Haz. Waste, Software

Professional Associations: NTSA

Delacore Resources
116 Oak Ln Ste 101
Hutchinson, MN 55350
(320) 587-4420
Fax: (320) 587-7252
Email: delacore@hutchtel.net
Web: www.mnrecruiter.com

Description: Two divisions: 1.) Physician recruiting (most subspecialty areas); 2.) Allied healthcare professions.

Key Contact - Specialty:
Mr. Verne Meyer, Principal - *Physicians, physician's assistants, nurse practitioners*

Salary minimum: $80,000

Functions: Healthcare, Physicians

Industries: Healthcare

DeLalla - Fried Associates
201 E 69th St Ste 4K
New York, NY 10021
(212) 879-9100
Fax: (212) 472-8963

Description: We have over twenty-one years of specialization experience in the consumer packaged goods and service industries. We provide executive talent on a full-time and project consultant basis.

Key Contact - Specialty:
Ms. Barbara DeLalla - *Consumer packaged goods, service industries*
Ms. Ann Fried - *Consumer packaged goods, service industries*

Salary minimum: $50,000

Functions: Generalist, Directors, Middle Mgmt., Advertising, Mkt. Research, Mktg. Mgmt., Minorities

Industries: Generalist, Food, Bev., Tobacco, Soap, Perf., Cosmtcs., Hospitality, Advertising

Professional Associations: NAER, NAFE

S W Delano & Company
General Delivery
Marlborough, CT 06447
(860) 295-0565
Email: swdelano@aol.com

Description: Fifteen years' experience serving financial services/investment companies. Extensive database, thoughtful screening.

Key Contact:
Mr. Steven W. Delano, Principal

Salary minimum: $80,000

Functions: Generalist, Cash Mgmt., Risk Mgmt.

Industries: Generalist, Brokers, Venture Cap., Misc. Financial, Insurance

Delta Medical Search Associates
615 Rome-Hilliard Rd Ste 107
Columbus, OH 43228-9475
(614) 878-0550

Email: associates@deltasearch.com
Web: www.deltasearch.com

Description: Recruitment of physicians, nurses, licensed healthcare professionals and management personnel for hospitals, clinics and private practices. All our account executives have a medical background to better understand and service your needs.

Key Contact:
Ms. Marilyn Wallace, CPC-PRC, President

Salary minimum: $50,000

Functions: Directors, Senior Mgmt., Middle Mgmt., Healthcare, Physicians, Nurses, Allied Health, Health Admin.

Industries: Healthcare, Hospitals

Professional Associations: MOAESP, NAPS

Delta ProSearch
PO Box 267
Delta, PA 17314-0267
(717) 456-7172
(800) 753-6693
Fax: (717) 456-7593
Email: deltapro@gte.net
Web: www.deltaprosearch.com

Description: We are experienced healthcare professionals with a good knowledge of the industry. Our high standards emphasize quality service, choice referrals and client satisfaction. We specialize in pharmacy and other allied healthcare recruiting.

Key Contact - Specialty:
Mr. John Banister, Jr., President - *Pharmacy, allied health*

Salary minimum: $30,000

Functions: Healthcare

Industries: Pharm Svcs., Healthcare

Delta Resource Group Ltd
PO Box 682262
Marietta, GA 30068
(770) 579-8702
Email: theheadhunter@mindspring.com

Description: Practice focuses on recruitment of experienced technical professionals for information technology with emphasis on the Internet, e-commerce, web & wireless software and development. CRM and related consulting around the Internet are also a significant part of our scope. Additionally, we give special attention to human resource professionals who have experience and interest in companies involved in information technology related to e-commerce.

Key Contact - Specialty:
Mr. Jerry Harmon, Managing Director - *IT, e-commerce, internet, web, wireless technology*

Salary minimum: $60,000

Functions: IT

Industries: Generalist

DeMatteo Associates
PO Box 13955
Albany, NY 12212
(800) 477-8158
Fax: (800) 477-8205
Email: rnato@albany.net

Description: Full-service custom executive search firm. Qualified candidates in sales, engineering and management. Specialize in industrial, manufacturing, insurance markets. National, regional and local searches for clients in the United States and Canada.

Key Contact:
Ms. Robena DeMatteo, President - *Sales & marketing, insurance (claims included), loss control & underwriting, information technology*
Mr. Robert Natowitz, Executive Recruiter - *Engineering, manufacturing, design, management, sales*
Mr. Ryan Flatt, Research Manager

Functions: Generalist, Mfg., Materials, Sales & Mktg., IT, Engineering

Industries: Generalist, Mfg., Services, Media, Insurance, Software

Denson & Associates Inc
Sugar Creek Ctr 14090 SW Frwy Ste 300
Sugar Land, TX 77478
(713) 993-9191
(281) 340-2055
Email: jeff@densonsearch.com
Web: www.densonsearch.com

Description: Provide search services primarily to the exploration and production industry - management, operations, geoscience, engineering, R&D.

Key Contact - Specialty:
Mr. Mike Denson, President - *Oil & gas*

Salary minimum: $75,000

Functions: Generalist, Middle Mgmt., Production, Plant Mgmt., R&D, Engineering, Mgmt. Consultants, Int'l.

Industries: Generalist, Energy, Utilities

Professional Associations: ASME, SPE

Deosystems LLC
175 Lancaster St Ste 220-A
Portland, ME 04101
(207) 879-1039
Fax: (207) 879-1045
Email: info@deosystems.com
Web: www.deosystems.com

Description: We help clients achieve their corporate goals by effectively fulfilling their staffing needs on a contingency basis. We concentrate on placing engineers, product marketing & management, quality assurance and technical support professionals in the high-technology markets of New England.

Key Contact:
Mr. Ed de Oliveira
Mr. Dana Costigan

Salary minimum: $50,000

Functions: Generalist, IT, Systems Analysis, Systems Dev., Engineering

Industries: Telecoms, Software, Biotech

Mee Derby & Company
1522 K St NW Ste 704
Washington, DC 20005
(202) 842-8442
(800) MEE-DERB
Fax: (202) 842-1900
Email: robin@meederby.com
Web: www.meederby.com

Description: Our firm specializes in placing recruiters, sales, and management up through COO level in the staffing industry, IT services, and e-Commerce companies.

Key Contact - Specialty:
Ms. Robin Mee, President - *Staffing industry, IT services, e-commerce*

Functions: Senior Mgmt., Middle Mgmt., Sales Mgmt., Personnel

Industries: Mgmt. Consulting, HR Services, E-commerce, HR SW

Professional Associations: ASA, WARN

Derek Associates Inc
PO Box 13
Mendon, MA 01756-0013
(508) 883-2289
Fax: (508) 883-2264
Email: joren@kersur.net

Description: Specialize in recruiting and placing environmental professionals including geologists, hydrogeologists, industrial hygienists, environmental, chemical and air quality engineers, hazardous waste specialists, business development and technical sales professionals.

Key Contact - Specialty:
Mr. Joren Fishback, Senior Consultant - *Environmental*

Salary minimum: $40,000

Functions: Generalist, Systems Dev., Engineering, Environmentalists

Industries: Generalist, Environmental Svcs., Haz. Waste, Software

Professional Associations: AWMA, EBC-NE, LSPA, NAEP

Descheneaux Recruitment Services Ltd
750 W Pender St Ste 1700
Vancouver, BC V6C 2T8
Canada
(604) 669-9787
Fax: (604) 688-2130
Email: info@insuranceheadhunters.com
Web: www.insuranceheadhunters.com

Description: A placement agency catering exclusively to the insurance industry, recruiting and hiring at all levels of executive, technical, sales and support staff. We bring talent and opportunity together.

Key Contact - Specialty:
Ms. Pat Descheneaux, President - *Insurance*
Ms. Allison Young - *Insurance*
Ms. Karen Pitkethly - *Insurance*

Functions: Generalist

Industries: Insurance

Desert Consulting Inc
36687 Crown St
Palm Desert, CA 92211
(760) 200-2347
Email: jfdesert@aol.com

Description: We provide executive search in the credit card industry.

Key Contact:
Ms. Joy M. Porrello, CPC, President

Functions: Generalist

Industries: Misc. Financial

Design Profiles
50 Lincoln St
Exeter, NH 03833
(603) 778-4880
Fax: (603) 778-4881
Email: info@designprofiles.com

Description: We deliver the right people to those companies on the cutting-edge in the apparel, textile and home furnishing industries. Our proven track record is built upon a foundation of experience in the retail, mail-order and wholesale markets.

Key Contact - Specialty:
Ms. Cheryl Burns-Noble, Owner - *Fashion industry, designers*

Salary minimum: $50,000

Functions: Graphic Artists

Industries: Textiles, Apparel, Soap, Perf., Cosmtcs.

+Desktop Staffing Inc
1904 Capri Ste 100
Schaumburg, IL 60193
(847) 352-4340
Fax: (847) 352-6441
Email: info@deskstaff.com

Description: Graphic arts, marketing, public relations and editorial positions for all industries and levels of positions.

Key Contact - Specialty:
Ms. Cindy Caravello, President - *Graphic arts, editorial, marketing, public relations*

Salary minimum: $25,000

Functions: Generalist, Advertising, Mktg. Mgmt., Direct Mktg., PR, Network Admin., DB Admin., Graphic Artists

Industries: Generalist, Misc. Mfg., Advertising, Publishing, Packaging, Software, Healthcare

Despres & Associates Inc
117 S Cook St Ste 304
Barrington, IL 60010
(847) 382-0625
Fax: (847) 382-1705
Email: rdespres@despres.net
Web: www.despres.net

Description: We specialize in sales and sales management people. We place directors and vice presidents, and other executives in any industry and focus on high technology companies.

Key Contact - Specialty:
Mr. Raoul Despres, President - *Sales, sales management, general management*

Salary minimum: $75,000

Functions: Senior Mgmt., Sales & Mktg., Sales Mgmt.

Industries: Generalist, Printing, E-commerce, New Media, Telecoms, Wireless, Software, Doc. Mgmt., Production SW, ERP SW

Professional Associations: RON

Networks: National Personnel Assoc (NPA)

Development Systems Inc (DSI)
402 Highland Ave Ste 7
Cheshire, CT 06410
(203) 271-3705
(203) 272-0758
Fax: (203) 272-0429
Email: developmentsystems@compuserve.com
Web: www.developmentsystems.com

Description: Highly focused specific IT recruiting in the technical and managerial area. Client driven search with sub-specialties in e-business and e-commerce technology. CIO, IT/IS director/manager, network manager/developers, web manager, software developers, web/intranet/extranet developers, database managers, business analysts and consultants.

Key Contact:
Mr. Arnold C. Bernstein, President
Mr. Andrew P. Bernstein, Sr Vice President

Salary minimum: $75,000

Functions: IT, MIS Mgmt., Systems Analysis, Systems Dev., Systems Implem., Systems Support, Network Admin., DB Admin.

Industries: Transportation, Wholesale, Retail, Mgmt. Consulting, Hospitality

The Devlin Search Group Inc (DSG)
451 Andover St Ste 160
North Andover, MA 01845
(978) 725-8000
(203) 562-3648
Fax: (978) 725-8200
Email: devlinsearchgroup@usa.net
Web: www.devlinsearchgroup.com

Description: Our firm provides you rapid implementation of contingency, retained, and contract search/recruitment/placement services. DSG's services and expertise take your search initiative from requirements to hire. One to one hundred, DSG can service your organizations' worldwide. We never send you just paper; we send you someone we would hire!

Key Contact - Specialty:
Mr. Jack Devlin, President - *IT sales, storage sales, marketing, communications, software and related disciplines*

Salary minimum: $85,000

Functions: Generalist, Senior Mgmt., Middle Mgmt., Product Dev., Materials, Sales & Mktg., Mktg. Mgmt., Sales Mgmt., IT, Mgmt. Consultants

Industries: Generalist

Professional Associations: MAPS

Networks: Top Echelon Network

Devoto & Associates Inc
790 Knoll Dr
San Carlos, CA 94070
(650) 593-8205
(650) 593-2170
Fax: (650) 593-8206
Email: andrea@devotoassociates.com
Web: www.devotoassociates.com

Description: We specialize in placing software and marketing professionals in software and Internet related companies.

Key Contact - Specialty:
Ms. Andrea Devoto, CEO - *Software sales*
Mr. Jeffrey Devoto, MBA, President - *Sales and marketing*

Salary minimum: $75,000

Functions: Sales & Mktg., Mktg. Mgmt., Sales Mgmt.

Industries: Software

Professional Associations: FWE

DFG Executive Search
269 Hamilton St 1
Worcester, MA 01604
(508) 754-3451
Fax: (508) 754-1367
Email: deloresg@ma.ultranet.com

Description: Since 1978, through meticulous search efforts, we source the very best possible talent for each specific situation and have filled positions in virtually every discipline. We are experts at our clients desire for speed plus a thorough, thoughtful survey of the market.

Key Contact - Specialty:
Ms. Delores F. George, CPC, Owner - *Engineering, information technology, systems*

Functions: Generalist, IT, MIS Mgmt., Systems Analysis, Systems Dev., Systems Implem., Engineering

Industries: Generalist, Software

Professional Associations: BPWCUSA, MAPS, SMS

DGA Personnel Group Inc
2691 E Oakland Park Blvd Ste 201
Ft. Lauderdale, FL 33306
(954) 561-1771
Fax: (954) 561-1774
Email: dgagroup@aol.com
Web: www.dgagroup.com

Description: A specialty is providing bilingual/multilingual candidates (on any level) able to travel to Latin America for operations based in South Florida. Our normal marketplace is South Florida with concentration in the Miami area (Dade County), Fort Lauderdale area (Broward County) and the Boca Raton-West Palm Beach areas (Palm Beach County). Our client base is comprised mainly of Fortune 500 and large to mid-sized private companies with presence in South Florida.

Key Contact - Specialty:
Mr. David Grant, President - *Finance, accounting, CPA's*
Mr. Paul Brown, Vice President - *Latin American sales & marketing*

Salary minimum: $50,000

Functions: Generalist

Industries: Drugs Mfg., Medical Devices, Finance, Banking, Accounting, HR Services, Telecoms, Software

Dialogue Consulting Group
782 Bayliss Dr Ste C
Marietta, GA 30068
(770) 579-6050
Fax: (240) 536-4072
Email: dcgroup@bellsouth.net
Web: www.softwarerecruiter.com

Description: We are software sales recruiters.

Key Contact - Specialty:
Mr. Bruce Dreyfus, President - *Software sales*

Salary minimum: $75,000

Functions: Sales Mgmt.

Industries: Accounting, Mgmt. Consulting, Software

Dialogue Partners Inc
PO Box 40163
Memphis, TN 38174-0163
(901) 726-9800
(877) 465-7516
Fax: (901) 726-9803
Email: mbruno@dialoguepartners.com
Web: www.dialoguepartners.com

Description: Our firm is a specialized recruiting firm serving the call center/CRM industry. Our firm is a strategic partner in the hiring process. We work seamlessly to reduce our clients' vacancy costs and maximize their recruiting investment.

Key Contact:
Mr. Michael Bruno, Principal/Recruiter

Salary minimum: $75,000

Networks: Top Echelon Network

Diamond Tax Recruiting
2 Penn Plz Ste 1985
New York, NY 10121
(212) 695-4220
Fax: (212) 695-4053
Email: dtrassoc@aol.com

Description: We have over 23 years of contingency and retained search experience with a specialization within the tax profession. We have a strong concentration within the NY Metropolitan area. We have had a demonstrated record of success while maintaining the highest degree of professionalism.

Key Contact - Specialty:
Mr. Steven Hunter, President - *Taxation, attorneys & non-attorneys*

Salary minimum: $50,000

Functions: Taxes

Industries: Generalist

DiBari & Associates
13399 N 102nd Pl
Scottsdale, AZ 85261
(888) 372-8828
Fax: (888) 427-7233
Email: career@dibari.net
Web: www.dibari.net

Description: We are a staffing and consulting firm specializing in the recruiting and placement of healthcare and advanced technology professionals. Established in 1983 we are proven leaders in high-technology executive search. We are an innovative and progressive executive search firm representing high profile companies worldwide. We are a state-of-the-art company utilizing automated databases and an extensive, continually updated candidate database.

Key Contact - Specialty:
Mr. Franc DiBari - *Medical device, executives*

Salary minimum: $50,000

Networks: Top Echelon Network

Dietsch & Associates
10706 107th St Ste 204
Maple Grove, MN 55369
(763) 424-8619
Fax: (763) 424-5187
Email: dietschassoc@att.net

Description: We are a management recruiting firm that specializes in the group insurance, life insurance, reinsurance, managed care and financial services industries. Specialized areas include self-funded, direct response, special risk, HMO reinsurance, individual life insurance, and variable product areas. Principals have extensive experience in the general management, marketing, sales, engineering, finance and manufacturing areas for the OEM and consumer products industries.

Key Contact - Specialty:
Mr. Roger A. Dietsch, Principal - *Insurance (group & individual), managed care, reinsurance, executive, marketing & sales*
Ms. Audrey D. Haugen, Consultant - *Insurance (individual, group), marketing, underwriting, claim, administrative*
Mr. G. A. Crabtree, Consultant - *Consumer products, general management, marketing & sales*
Mr. B. E. Dietsch, Consultant - *General management (OEM, consumer), product (marketing and sales), engineering*

Salary minimum: $60,000

Functions: General Mgmt., Senior Mgmt., Middle Mgmt., Healthcare, Health Admin., Sales & Mktg., Mktg. Mgmt., Sales Mgmt., Direct Mktg., Specialized Svcs.

Industries: Generalist, Mfg., Insurance

DiFronzo Associates
591 North Ave Ste A
Wakefield, MA 01880
(781) 246-2000
Fax: (781) 246-2444
Email: al@difronzoassoc.com

Description: Information systems recruiting firm. We are right in the heart of the Massachusetts MIS marketplace with easy accessibility to Boston and Rtes. 128 and 495.

Key Contact - Specialty:
Mr. Alfred M. DiFronzo, President - *Information systems*

Salary minimum: $30,000

Functions: Generalist, MIS Mgmt., Systems Analysis, Systems Dev., Systems Implem., Systems Support, Network Admin., DB Admin.

Industries: Generalist, IT Implementation

Professional Associations: NAPS

Digital Careers Inc
12361 Lewis St Ste 201
Garden Grove, CA 92840
(714) 705-1555
Fax: (714) 705-1559
Email: itjobs@digcareers.com
Web: www.digcareers.com

Description: A high-tech employment agency specializing in the placement of information technology professionals with companies throughout Southern California.

Key Contact - Specialty:
Mr. Tim Stevens, President
Mr. Edward Billion, Vice President - *Information technology*

Salary minimum: $60,000

Functions: IT

Industries: Generalist

Networks: Top Echelon Network

Branches:
28202 Cabot Rd Ste 105
Laguna Niguel, CA 92677
(949) 347-7722 .
Fax: (949) 347-7728
Email: robinh@digcareers.com
Key Contact - Specialty:
Ms. Robin Huibregtse, Regional Manager -
Information technology

Digital Coast Group
111 Promenade Ave
Irvine, CA 92612
(949) 733-2932
Fax: (949) 733-2936
Email: clientservices@digitalcoastgroup.net
Web: www.digitalcoastgroup.net

Description: Our firm provides specialized executive search solutions for leading technology companies. We assist both start-up and established companies who demonstrate a significant commitment to growing their business through acquiring, rewarding, and retaining the best talent in the market.

Key Contact - Specialty:
Mr. Chris Henshaw, President - *Senior level executive search*

Digital Prospectors Corp
2193 Commonwealth Ave Ste 365
Brighton, MA 02135-3853
(617) 987-8060
Fax: (617) 987-8142
Email: info@digitalprospectors.com
Web: www.dpcit.com

Description: We specialize in the permanent placement of IT professionals. If the position calls for a computer person, we are the agency to use.

Key Contact - Specialty:
Mr. Chris Roos, Accounts Manager - *Hands-on technical programmer, analysts*
Mr. Andy Hagar, Recruiter - *Hands-on technical programmer, analysts*

Salary minimum: $25,000

Functions: Generalist, MIS Mgmt., Systems Analysis, Systems Dev., Systems Implem., Systems Support, Network Admin., DB Admin.

Industries: Generalist, Mfg., Medical Devices, Finance, Banking, Brokers, Software

DigitalHire
4 Greentree Ctr Ste 301
Marlton, NJ 08053
(856) 552-2500
Fax: (856) 552-2510
Email: info@digitalhire.com
Web: www.digitalhire.com

Description: We specialize in national recruiting contracts in sales, sales management, and support services. Our nationwide capability enables clients to enjoy a primary vendor offering sales and sales management recruiting coverage anywhere in the continental US. Additional services that we offer include: sales and sales management consulting, and sales, and sales assessment testing for better candidate selection.

Key Contact - Specialty:
Mr. Rick DeRose, President - *General management directors, middle management, sales and marketing, healthcare, marketing management*

Salary minimum: $40,000

Functions: Generalist, General Mgmt., Directors, Middle Mgmt., Healthcare, Sales & Mktg., Mktg. Mgmt., Sales Mgmt.

Industries: Food, Bev., Tobacco, Medical Devices, Services, Pharm Svcs., Media, Telecoms, Digital, Wireless, Network Infrastructure, Software, Marketing SW, Healthcare

Professional Associations: MAAPC

Branches:
24000 Alicia Pkwy
PO Box 17-449
Mission Viejo, CA 92691
(949) 215-6588
Fax: (949) 472-5628
Email: cheryl@telecomexecutive.com
Web: www.telecomexecutive.com
Key Contact - Specialty:
Ms. Cheryl Kawalec - *Telecommunications, sales management*
Mr. Pete Markese - *Telecommunications, sales management*

3 Bethesda Metro Ctr Ste 700
Bethesda, MD 20814
(301) 961-4886
Fax: (301) 961-1939
Email: katy@telecomexecutive.com
Web: www.telecomexecutive.com
Key Contact - Specialty:
Ms. Katy O'Brien - *Telecommunications, sales management*
Ms. Sarah McCullough - *Telecommunications, sales management*

116 Village Dr Ste 200
Princeton Forrestal Village
Princeton, NJ 08540
(609) 951-2254
Fax: (609) 951-2293
Email: marci@telecomexecutive.com
Web: www.telecomexecutive.com
Key Contact:
Ms. Marci Yacker Nigro

2 Jane Ct
Secaucus, NJ 07094
(212) 271-3276
Fax: (212) 271-3276
Email: denyse@telecomexecutive.com
Web: www.telecomexecutive.com
Key Contact:
Ms. Denyse Antunes

165 EAB Plaza W Twr Fl 6
Uniondale, NY 11556
(516) 522-2507
Fax: (516) 522-2846
Email: jayne@telecomexecutive.com
Web: www.telecomexecutive.com
Key Contact:
Ms. Jane Lynch

42 Manchester Ct
Berwyn, PA 19312
(610) 644-8815
Fax: (610) 240-4883
Email: pam@telecomexecutive.com
Web: www.telecomexecutive.com
Key Contact:
Ms. Pam Cox

Dilworth & Wooldridge
12 E Greenway Plz Ste 1100
Houston, TX 77046
(713) 521-2800
Fax: (713) 521-2865
Email: dwlegal@dilwoo.com
Web: www.dilwoo.com

Description: Placement of attorneys at law firms and corporations throughout Texas.

Key Contact:
Ms. Nancy K. Wooldridge

Functions: Legal, Personnel

Industries: Legal, HR Services

Professional Associations: NALSC

E P Dine Inc
115 E 57th St Ste 1210
New York, NY 10022
(212) 355-6182
Fax: (212) 755-8486
Email: info@epdine.com
Web: www.epdine.com

Description: Specializing in the placement of general counsel, partners and other senior legal professionals as well as merger of law firms and practices. Concentrating in major industries including financial, telecommunications, technology, chemical, advertising and consumer products.

Key Contact:
Ms. Elaine Dine, President - *General counsel, law firm mergers, partner*
Ms. Laurie Becker - *General counsel, law firm mergers, partner*
Ms. Wendy Schoen
Ms. Leslie Rubenfeld
Ms. Melissa Collery
Ms. Rosemary Moukad
Ms. Amy Echelman
Ms. Joanna Davis

Functions: Generalist, Legal, Attorneys

Industries: Generalist, Legal

Direct Hire from Bennett Frost
6465 N Palm Ste 101
Fresno, CA 93720
(559) 449-0444
Fax: (559) 449-0457
Email: info@bfdirecthire.com
Web: www.bfdirecthire.com

Description: We have been matching job seekers with employment opportunities in California's Central Valley for eight years. We have established partnerships with area businesses and industries of all kinds. Our recruiters use a wide variety of resources to attract top-quality candidates to fill the staffing needs of our clients.

Key Contact:
Ms. Cathy Frost

Functions: Generalist

Industries: Finance, Banking

Direct Marketing Resources Inc

2915 Providence Rd Ste 230
PO Box 15353
Charlotte, NC 28211
(704) 365-5890
(704) 365-5891
Fax: (704) 365-5892
Email: dan@dmresources.com
Web: www.dmresources.com

Description: National search firm specializing exclusively in the direct marketing industry. Functional areas include database marketing, research and analysis, account management, product management and creative.

Key Contact - Specialty:
Mr. Dan Sullivan, President - *Direct marketing*
Ms. Dawn Darcy, Associate Partner - *Database marketing*

Salary minimum: $60,000

Functions: Generalist, Advertising, Mkt. Research, Mktg. Mgmt., Direct Mktg., DB Admin.

Industries: Generalist, Energy, Utilities, Retail, Finance, Pharm Svcs., Mgmt. Consulting, Hospitality, Hotels, Resorts, Clubs, Advertising, New Media, Insurance, Database SW, Marketing SW

Professional Associations: DMA

Branches:
6 Hawthorne Ct
Cherry Hill, NJ 08003
(856) 489-3427
Fax: (856) 424-6829
Email: beverly@dmresources.com
Key Contact:
Ms. Beverly Bingham

Direct Marketing Solutions

1972 U S 60E
Salem, KY 42078-9365
(270) 988-4888
Fax: (270) 988-4887
Email: ingala@apex.net

Description: Recruit and place direct marketing sales, sales support and marketing professionals nationally. Specialize in production firms: DP service bureaus, lettershops, full-service firms, direct response advertising agencies and database marketing firms.

Key Contact - Specialty:
Mr. Thomas A. Ingala, President - *Direct marketing, database marketing*

Functions: Advertising, Mkt. Research, Mktg. Mgmt., Sales Mgmt., Direct Mktg.

Industries: Advertising

Professional Associations: CADM, DMAW, LADMA, NEDMA

Direct Recruiters Inc

24100 Chagrin Blvd Ste 450
Cleveland, OH 44122
(440) 464-5570
Fax: (216) 464-7567
Email: shel@directrecruiters.com
Web: www.directrecruiters.com

Description: We are search consultants providing employment solutions to the specialty practices of AIDC, supply chain, labels, printing systems, packaging, and material handling. We successfully match top-qualified professionals in management, sales, marketing, and technical support with available career opportunities.

Key Contact - Specialty:
Mr. Sheldon Myeroff, CPC, President - *Data collection, supply chain, systems integration*
Ms. Gina Petrello-Pray, Vice President - *Data collection, supply chain, labels, printing systems*
Mr. Michael Rossen, Senior Account Executive - *Material handling, packaging, data collection, supply chain*

Salary minimum: $40,000

Functions: Middle Mgmt., Sales & Mktg., Sales Mgmt.

Industries: Mfg., Wholesale, Packaging, Software, ERP SW, Mfg. SW, Marketing SW

Professional Associations: AIM, APICS, APICS, MHIA, NAPS

Discovery Personnel Inc

PO Box 1228
Burnsville, MN 55337-0228
(952) 431-2500
Fax: (952) 431-2512
Email: jim3@discoverypersonnel.com
Web: www.discoverypersonnel.com

Description: We are a technical recruiting firm specializing in the nationwide placement of manufacturing and technical executives, managers, supervisors, scientists, engineers, technicians and salespeople for the plastics industry with special emphasis on injection molding. Our placements include all areas of industry, for example: automotive, medical, custom molding, house-wares, electronics, telecommunications, toys, computers, etc.

Key Contact:
Ms. Lisa Carpenter, Technical Recruiter - *Marketer*
Mr. Jim Heilman, Technical Recruiter

Salary minimum: $30,000

Functions: Generalist

Industries: Generalist, Mfg., Medical Devices, Plastics, Rubber, Machine, Appliance, Computer Equip., Electronic, Elec. Components, Packaging

Professional Associations: SPE

Networks: Top Echelon Network

Branches:
PO Box 4272
Springfield, MO 65808-4272
(417) 864-4645
Fax: (877) 431-2512
Email: jim@discoverypersonnel.com
Key Contact:
Mr. Jim Heilman, Technical Recruiter

Diversified Consulting Services Inc

PO Box 130
Evergreen, CO 80437-0130
(303) 670-5482
Fax: (303) 670-3507
Email: susan_dcsinc@qwest.net

Description: We are a contingency fee based technical recruiting company specializing in sales, marketing, and engineering in high-tech and information technology companies. Several members of our team also focus on high-level positions, such as: President, VP, CFO, CEO, CTO, COO, etc.

Key Contact - Specialty:
Ms. Susan F. Baker, President - *Information technology, sales, recruiters, management*
Mr. Chet Baker, Vice President - *High tech, telecommunications, internet, VAR's, networking*

Salary minimum: $75,000

Functions: Generalist, Senior Mgmt., Mfg., Sales Mgmt., CFO's, IT, MIS Mgmt., Engineering

Industries: Generalist, Medical Devices, Computer Equip., Telecoms, Software, Biotech

Professional Associations: CAPS, NFIB

Diversified Group

1710 Douglas Dr Ste 200
Golden Valley, MN 55422
(763) 546-8255
Fax: (612) 546-4106
Email: dei@4employment.org
Web: www.4employment.org

Description: We are an outsource HR firm that specializes in recruiting, consulting and testing for small to medium-sized businesses in the Twin Cities Metro area.

Key Contact - Specialty:
Mr. Mike Duthoy, President - *Human resource consultant*

Functions: Generalist

Industries: Construction, Mfg., Accounting, HR Services, Advertising, Publishing, Packaging, Software

Professional Associations: MAPS

Diversified Recruiters Company

43155 Main St Ste 2210
Novi, MI 48375-1774
(248) 344-6700
Fax: (248) 344-6704
Email: jobs.drc@prodigy.net
Web: www.drcjobsearch.com

Description: Our firm, a full service resource, has successfully satisfied the personnel requirements in serving clerical, technical, engineering, managerial, and executive nationwide placements. We assist all aspects of staffing. Visit our web site for details on openings, candidates and all our services.

Key Contact:
Mr. Roger Thomas, Owner

Salary minimum: $40,000

Functions: Engineering

Industries: Plastics, Rubber, Metal Products, Motor Vehicles, Electronic, Elec. Components

Professional Associations: MAPS

Networks: Top Echelon Network

Diversified Technical

7721 San Felipe St Ste 204
Houston, TX 77063
(713) 785-1144
Email: jobs@diversified-technical.com
Web: www.diversified-technical.com

Description: We are a nationwide, executive search firm, affiliated with over 300 other recruiters located across the US. We specialize in all industries/professions including HR, engineering, management, quality, IT/computer, finance, chemist/scientist, environmental, automotive, manufacturing, and many more.

Key Contact:
Mr. D. Morgan, Owner

Salary minimum: $40,000

Functions: Generalist

Industries: Mfg., Finance, Accounting, Telecoms, Environmental Svcs., Aerospace, Packaging, Software

Networks: National Personnel Assoc (NPA)

Diversity Central LLC

PO Box 828
Garner, NC 27529-0828
(919) 662-9101
Fax: (919) 779-7020
Email: dcjobs@bellsouth.net
Web: www.diversitycentral.net

Description: We specialize in placing minority professionals into mid-level to executive-level positions. The major focus is black, Hispanic, Native American and women professionals across a variety of skills.

Key Contact - Specialty:
Mr. Barry Green, President - *Diversity professionals*

Salary minimum: $50,000

Functions: Generalist, General Mgmt., Mfg., Sales & Mktg., HR Mgmt., Finance, IT, Engineering

Industries: Generalist, Mfg., Finance, Media, Aerospace, Software

Professional Associations: BDPA, NABA, NBMBAA, NSBE, SHPE

Dixie Search Associates
(a division of The Fill Corp)
670 Village Trace Ste D Bldg 19
Marietta, GA 30067
(770) 850-0250
Fax: (770) 850-9295
Email: dsa@mindspring.com
Web: www.dixiesearch.com

Description: Leading international search firm working exclusively in the food, beverage and hospitality industries. Search services are unique and broad based in all facets of the industries served.

Key Contact - Specialty:
Mr. Clifford G. Fill, CPC, President - *Food*
Ms. Ellyn H. Fill, Senior Vice President - *Food*

Salary minimum: $35,000

Functions: Generalist

Industries: Mfg., Food, Bev., Tobacco, Soap, Perf., Cosmtcs.,Wholesale, Retail, Hospitality, Packaging

Professional Associations: GAPS

DLR Associates
381 Broadway Ste 4F
Dobbs Ferry, NY 10522
(914) 693-9165
Fax: (914) 479-0193
Email: dlr_ny@hotmail.com

Description: We serve the financial services industry, for example: banks, brokerage, and investment advisory in the areas such as compliance, legal, internal audit, and derivatives.

Key Contact - Specialty:
Mr. David L. Reitman, President - *Finance, banking, legal*

Functions: Senior Mgmt., Middle Mgmt., Legal, Risk Mgmt., Attorneys

Industries: Finance, Banking, Invest. Banking, Brokers, Legal

DMN & Associates
PO Box 748
Harrison, TN 37341
(423) 344-8203
Fax: (423) 344-4930
Email: jazzman617@home.com

Description: Search and recruitment for the medical device industry.

Key Contact:
Mr. Denton Neal, Owner

Functions: Sales & Mktg., Engineering

Industries: Medical Devices, Marketing SW

Networks: US Recruiters.com

DNA Search Inc
16133 Ventura Blvd Ste 805
Encino, CA 91436
(818) 986-6300
Fax: (818) 981-1105
Email: dan@dnasrch.com
Web: www.dnasrch.com

Description: The firm specializes in high-tech placement in the computer industry. We place marketing, sales and technical people with Internet, software, and hardware companies. Also, we specialize in the healthcare industry placing administrators, D.O.N, vice presidents, reg. managers in the long-term care marketplace. We also have a division that places pharmacists.

Key Contact - Specialty:
Mr. Daniel Levy, CEO - *Healthcare, information technology, contract staffing, biotechnology, accounting & finance*
Ms. Sandra Smith, President - *LTC, hi-tech*

Salary minimum: $60,000

Functions: Generalist, Nurses, Health Admin., Mkt. Research, Sales Mgmt., CFO's, IT, Network Admin.

Industries: Generalist, Medical Devices, Pharm Svcs., Mgmt. Consulting, HR Services, Hospitality, Healthcare

Professional Associations: IACPR, CSP

Doctors' Corner Personnel Services
3855 Pacific Coast Hwy Ste 8
Torrance, CA 90505
(310) 373-0931
Fax: (310) 373-7914
Email: drscorner@aol.com
Web: www.doctorscornerpersonnel.com

Description: We provide temporary help and permanent staffing to the healthcare industry. We primarily staff medical & dental offices, groups and hospitals.

Key Contact:
Mr. Gregorius Balk, President

Salary minimum: $25,000

Functions: Generalist

Industries: Healthcare

M T Donaldson Associates Inc
4400 Rte 9 Freehold Executive Ctr
Freehold, NJ 07728
(732) 303-7890
Fax: (732) 536-1211
Email: mtdon@aol.com

Description: Specialize in the cosmetic, HBA, household, chemical and pharmaceutical industry primarily.

Key Contact - Specialty:
Mr. Sal Premister, President - *Manufacturing*

Functions: Generalist, Product Dev., Production, Quality, Purchasing, Materials Plng., Packaging, Engineering

Industries: Generalist, Food, Bev., Tobacco, Chemicals, Soap, Perf., Cosmtcs., Drugs Mfg., Misc. Mfg., Packaging

The Donnelly Group-Sales Recruiters Inc
12536 Glenlea Dr
St. Louis, MO 63043
(314) 469-6400
Fax: (314) 469-4880
Email: ddonnelly@primary.net

Description: Specializes in sales and marketing positions. One to five years' experience through national sales management levels. Nationwide

search. Focus industries are pharmaceuticals, biotech, medical, industrial, high-tech. We listen to client needs and only send qualified, pre-screened candidates. Thank you. Please call.

Key Contact - Specialty:
Mr. Dan Donnelly, Recruiter/Owner - *Sales, sales management, industrial, pharmaceutical, medical*
Mr. Kevin Wenger, Industrial High Tech Recruiter - *Medical capital equipment, disposables, home health*

Salary minimum: $35,000

Functions: Generalist, Sales & Mktg., Sales Mgmt.

Industries: Generalist, Drugs Mfg., Medical Devices, Plastics, Rubber, Metal Products, Machine, Appliance, Pharm Svcs., Telecoms, Software, Industry Specific SW

Networks: First Interview Network (FIN)

The Dorfman Group
12005 E Mission Ln
Scottsdale, AZ 85259
(480) 860-8820
Fax: (480) 860-0888
Email: mikef@thedorfmangroup.com
Web: www.thedorfmangroup.com

Description: We have an in-depth knowledge of the materials handling, logistics, and supply chain management industries. We place professionals nationwide. We are both a contingency and retainer firm.

Key Contact - Specialty:
Mr. Michael Flamer, Vice President - *Material handling, logistics, packaging equipment*

Salary minimum: $55,000

Functions: Generalist, Middle Mgmt., Automation, Purchasing, Distribution, Sales Mgmt., Systems Implem., Engineering

Industries: Generalist, Food, Bev., Tobacco, Metal Products, Machine, Appliance, Misc. Mfg., Packaging

Professional Associations: IOPP, MHMS

Dorst Information Services Inc
821 Franklin Ave Ste 309
Garden City, NY 11530
(516) 294-0884
(516) 697-1175
Fax: (516) 747-8873
Email: info@dorstsearch.com
Web: www.dorstsearch.com

Description: Executive search/high-technology, sales/technical, marketing, operations, domestic/international packages 275k to 2mm. Consulting, software, telco, hardware, professional services, Internet. Work closely with Venture Capital Groups for recruiting top management and to raise and distribute capital.

Key Contact - Specialty:
Mr. Martin Dorst, President - *Consulting, software, telecommunications, hardware, professional services*

Salary minimum: $150,000

Functions: Generalist

Industries: Computer Equip., Mgmt. Consulting, Telecoms, Software

John Doucette Management Services
13025 Yonge St Ste 201
Richmond Hill, ON L4E 1A8
Canada
(416) 346-1174
(416) 704-6201
Fax: (905) 773-0395
Email: doucettesan@sprint.ca

Description: IT Recruiting - WEB, UNIX, Desktop and Networks.

Key Contact:
Mr. John Doucette
Mr. Matthew San, Partner

Salary minimum: $50,000

Functions: IT

Industries: Generalist

Doug Perlstadt & Associates

3330 Pierce St Ste 305
San Francisco, CA 94123
(415) 921-0663
Fax: (603) 687-0024
Email: dougexecs@aol.com

Description: We are an executive recruitment firm specializing in the recruitment of mid- to senior-level management positions for high growth companies in technology, services, consumer, and business-to-business markets. Our areas of expertise include marketing, business development, sales, merchandising, operations, financial, and human resources.

Key Contact - Specialty:
Mr. Douglas Perlstadt, President - *E-commerce, interactive marketing*

Salary minimum: $80,000

Functions: General Mgmt.

Industries: Retail, HR Services, Media, Advertising, New Media, Software

Dougherty & Associates Inc

41 Sutter St PMB 1228
San Francisco, CA 94104
(415) 773-8280
Fax: (415) 925-9993
Email: jobs@lawsearch-sf.com
Web: www.lawsearch-sf.com

Description: Placement of attorneys in law firms and corporate law departments with emphasis on high-technology and Silicon Valley specialty areas.

Key Contact - Specialty:
Ms. Deborah J. Dougherty, President - *Attorney*

Functions: Legal

Industries: New Media, Telecoms, Real Estate, Software, Biotech

Dougherty & Associates

2345 Ashford Dr
Chattanooga, TN 37421-1830
(423) 899-1060
Fax: (423) 855-5138
Email: tnbobbydoc@aol.com

Description: Specialized in sales, engineering and product management positions in specialty chemicals with over 25 years in recruiting, sales and as a hiring field manager in the water treatment industry.

Key Contact - Specialty:
Mr. Robert E. Dougherty, Recruiter - *Chemical sales*

Salary minimum: $35,000

Functions: Product Dev., Sales Mgmt., Customer Svc.

Industries: Energy, Utilities, Mfg., Food, Bev., Tobacco, Textiles, Apparel, Paper, Printing, Chemicals, Plastics, Rubber, Paints, Petro. Products, Metal Products, Haz. Waste

Networks: National Personnel Assoc (NPA)

Steven Douglas Associates

3040 Universal Blvd Ste 190
Weston, FL 33331
(954) 385-8595
(305) 381-8100
Fax: (954) 385-1414
Email: sabrina@stevendouglas.com
Web: www.stevendouglas.com

Description: Commitment to proactively search - identify and most importantly, attract - the best qualified individual for the client's positions. National retainer practice.

Key Contact - Specialty:
Mr. Mark Sadovnick, Executive Vice President - *Financial*
Mr. Steve Sadaka, President - *Financial, HR*
Mr. Mark Young
Mr. Steve Kalisher, Senior Vice President - *Information technology*

Salary minimum: $75,000

Functions: Generalist, Senior Mgmt., Mktg. Mgmt., CFO's, Budgeting, Taxes, M&A, MIS Mgmt.

Industries: Generalist, Invest. Banking, Accounting, HR Services, Real Estate, Healthcare

Scott Douglas Inc

16968 Obsidian Dr Ste 101
Ramona, CA 92065-6839
(760) 788-5560
Fax: (760) 788-5506
Email: mmagic@home.com

Description: Boutique firm specializing in actuarial, managed care/financial engineering professionals. We provide research, account management and candidate screening, profiles and other services.

Key Contact - Specialty:
Mr. Michael F. Magic, President - *Actuaries, financial engineers, medical doctors, insurance executives*

Salary minimum: $50,000

Functions: Generalist, Senior Mgmt.

Industries: Finance, Invest. Banking, Venture Cap., Insurance, Software, Biotech, Healthcare

Professional Associations: SA

Douglas Personnel Associates Inc

4444 Riverside Dr Ste 204
Toluca Lake, CA 91505
(818) 842-2477
Fax: (818) 842-3874
Email: dpaiwest1@earthlink.net
Web: www.douglaspersonnel.com

Description: We are a nationwide search firm specializing in retail. We handle positions in merchandising, planning, design, buying, product development/sourcing, human resources, field (store) management, MIS, visual merchandising, marketing/advertising, logistics, and distribution/warehouse.

Key Contact - Specialty:
Ms. Leslie Klein, Owner/President - *Retail*

Salary minimum: $45,000

Functions: Generalist, Middle Mgmt., Product Dev., Purchasing, Distribution, Sales Mgmt., Personnel, MIS Mgmt., Systems Analysis, Systems Dev.

Industries: Generalist, Retail, HR Services, Advertising, HR SW

Dow Consultants Int'l

370 Lexington Ave Ste 1407
New York, NY 10017
(212) 953-4800
Fax: (212) 953-3611
Email: idow@aol.com

Description: A contingency and retainer-based search firm specializing in middle- to senior-level assignments in investment and commercial banking.

Key Contact - Specialty:
Mr. Ian James Dow, President - *Commercial banking, investment banking*

Salary minimum: $75,000

Functions: M&A, Risk Mgmt.

Industries: Banking, Invest. Banking

Dowd Group Inc

60 Grange Ave
Fair Haven, NJ 07704
(732) 747-8100
Fax: (732) 842-0597
Email: recruiters@dowdgroup.com
Web: www.dowdgroup.com

Description: We are executive recruiters for telecommunications, data storage, and software. Our candidates are limited to management professionals, sales executives, and sales engineers in the above fields.

Key Contact - Specialty:
Mr. Charlie Dowd, President - *Telecommunications*

Functions: Senior Mgmt., Sales & Mktg., Sales Mgmt., MIS Mgmt.

Industries: Communications, Telecoms, Telephony, Digital, Wireless, Fiber Optic, Network Infrastructure, Government

Professional Associations: NJSA

Patricia Dowd Inc

5001 Oceanaire St
Oxnard, CA 93035
(805) 985-8243
Fax: (805) 382-0773
Email: pdowd@pdisearch.com
Web: www.pdisearch.com

Description: We are the first recruiters to specialize in database marketing. Our specialty has evolved into CRM, knowledge-based marketing. Our focus is on all disciplines of database marketing, program management, product marketing, pre- and post-sales, consultants, analysts, professional service, and client service providers. As of May 2001, our primary focus is on candidates and clients in the smart card industry where focus is on sales, alliance/channel marketing, project/product management, business consulting in the government, healthcare, educational, and financial services sectors.

Key Contact - Specialty:
Ms. Patricia Dowd, President - *Database marketing, CRM, knowledge-based marketing, direct marketing*

Salary minimum: $80,000

Functions: Generalist

Industries: Energy, Utilities, Finance, Mgmt. Consulting, Advertising, Publishing, New Media, Telecoms, Insurance, Real Estate, Software

Professional Associations: AIM, DMA, IDWA

C S Dowling Executive Services

(also known as Zaccaria Int'l Inc)
1700 Rte 23 N Ste 100
Wayne, NJ 07470
(973) 696-8000
(888) 236-9832
Fax: (973) 696-1964
Email: dow@dow-tech.com
Web: www.dow-tech.com

Description: We provide executive-level search and selection throughout North America. Positions focus on director, vice president, general manager, CEO, COO levels.

Key Contact - Specialty:
Mr. Chris Dowling, President - *HVAC, building automation, energy services, water, waste water equipment*

Salary minimum: $75,000

Functions: General Mgmt., Directors, Senior Mgmt., Mktg. Mgmt., Sales Mgmt., Engineering

Industries: Generalist

Professional Associations: NJSA

Downing & Downing Inc

8800 Tyler Blvd
Mentor, OH 44060
(440) 255-1177
Fax: (440) 255-1877
Email: info@downing-downing.com
Web: www.downing-downing.com

Description: With over forty years of loss prevention and recruiting experience, we offer the most effective network of individuals in the retail loss prevention (security), safety, risk management, and audit industries in the nation.

Key Contact - Specialty:
Mr. Gus Downing, President - *Loss (prevention, audit)*

Salary minimum: $25,000

Functions: Directors, Middle Mgmt., Risk Mgmt.

Industries: Generalist, Retail, Security SW

Professional Associations: NRF

Downing Teal Inc

650 S Cherry St Ste 610
Denver, CO 80246
(303) 321-3844
Fax: (303) 321-3551
Email: info@jacksongrp.com
Web: www.downingteal.com

Description: We are a firm specializing in international and domestic executive, financial, human resources, engineering, environmental and information technology searches for client companies.

Key Contact:
Mr. George E. Jackson, General Manager - *Generalist executive, professional*
Mr. Paul Gaeke, Executive Search Consultant
Mr. Leigh Freeman, Executive Search Consultant

Salary minimum: $50,000

Functions: Senior Mgmt.

Industries: Energy, Utilities, E-commerce

Professional Associations: CIM, SME, SMME

DP Resources

2443 Avalon Ct
Aurora, IL 60504
(630) 585-6731
Fax: (630) 585-0198
Email: dkainpaul@dpresources.net
Web: www.dpresources.net

Description: Our firm is a recruitment consulting firm. We specialize in the placement of consultants and full time employees within the following industries: retail, banking, engineering, information technology consulting, ISP's, software development, manufacturing, healthcare, e-commerce, telecommunications.

Key Contact - Specialty:
Ms. Danielle Kain-Paul, Principal - *Technical recruiting*

Salary minimum: $30,000

Functions: Generalist

Industries: Generalist

DPSI Medical

(a subsidiary of Diversified Placement Services Inc)
5105 Clinton St Ste 2
Erie, PA 16509
(814) 868-0961
Fax: (814) 868-0961
Web: www.onesourcenetwork.net

Description: Primarily a physician recruiting and consulting firm networking with other recruiters throughout the U.S. serving both facilities groups and individual physicians.

Key Contact - Specialty:
Mr. Ron Spero, President/Owner - *Physicians, administrators, top level management, CEO*
Mrs. Gerry Spero, Vice President - *Medical personnel*
Mr. Joseph B. Spero, Esq., Vice President - *Law, communications*
Ms. Ronette Schneider, PT, Vice President - *Physical therapy, rehabilitation areas*
Mr. Ben Schneider, Vice President - *Technical, sales*

Functions: Generalist, General Mgmt., Materials, Healthcare, Sales & Mktg., Finance, IT, Attorneys

Industries: Generalist, Energy, Utilities, Mfg., Services, Media, Software, Healthcare

Drayton & Associates Inc

6957 Murray Ave
Cincinnati, OH 45227-3371
(513) 271-5724
Email: jbdrayton@fuse.net

Description: Mr. Drayton has 18 years of human resource management experience with major national retailers and 14 years of successful consulting and recruiting experience serving the retail industry.

Key Contact - Specialty:
Mr. Bradley Drayton, President - *Retail management*

Salary minimum: $50,000

Functions: Generalist, General Mgmt., Sales & Mktg., HR Mgmt., Finance, IT

Industries: Generalist, Retail

Dreier Consulting Staff

10 S Franklin Tpke
PO Box 356
Ramsey, NJ 07446
(201) 444-5119
Email: support@dreierconsulting.com
Web: www.dreierconsulting.com

Description: Professional and management recruiters for high-tech industries. Clients manufacture and/or distribute medical, telecommunications, instrumentation, controls, process and automation equipment. Friendly, professional staff with 40 years' experience.

Key Contact - Specialty:
Mr. John S. Dreier, President - *Medical (technical, marketing), telecommunications, electronics, data communications*

Salary minimum: $40,000

Functions: Generalist

Industries: Medical Devices, Computer Equip., Telecoms, Software, Healthcare

Professional Associations: NJSA

Ralph C Dressler, CPC

1930 E Marlton Pike Ste T-9
Cherry Hill, NJ 08003
(856) 489-4010
Email: ralphdcpc@aol.com

Description: Our organization provides the level of services of retained search on a contingency basis. The goal is to perpetuate relationships by striving to make mutually successful long-term matches.

Key Contact - Specialty:
Mr. Ralph C. Dressler, Principal - *Information technology, consulting, pharmaceutical, healthcare*

Functions: IT, MIS Mgmt., Systems Analysis, Systems Dev., Systems Support, Network Admin., DB Admin.

Industries: Generalist

The DRM Group

79 Brook Ln
Lindenhurst, IL 60046
(847) 245-8636
Fax: (847) 245-8637
Email: scarter@ameritech.net
Web: www.constructionrecruiters.com/drm.html

Description: We specialize in the nationwide search and placement of construction professionals exclusively.

Key Contact - Specialty:
Mr. Scott C. Carter, President - *Construction*

Salary minimum: $40,000

Functions: Generalist

Industries: Construction

Drum Associates Inc

150 Broadway Fl 23
New York, NY 10038
(212) 233-7550
Email: kdugan@drum2000.com
Web: www.drumassociates.com

Description: We are a full-service recruitment firm addressing diverse human resource requirements of a number of industries, including financial services and other Fortune 1000 companies.

Key Contact - Specialty:
Mr. Brian Drum, President - *Generalist*
Mr. Kenneth Drum, Vice President/Director of Research - *Generalist*
Mr. Harry Drum, Vice President - *Private banking, banking, sales, marketing*
Ms. Cathy Galan, Vice President - *Banking, credit, corporate banking*
Ms. Mary McGlynn, Vice President - *Banking, cash management, portfolio management operations*
Mr. Joe Pinto, Vice President - *Financial services, accounting, financial reporting, financial auditing*

Salary minimum: $75,000

Functions: General Mgmt., Directors, Middle Mgmt., Mktg. Mgmt., Finance, Cash Mgmt., MIS Mgmt.

Industries: Finance, Banking, Invest. Banking, Misc. Financial

Drummond Associates Inc

50 Broadway Ste 1201
New York, NY 10004
(212) 248-1120
Fax: (212) 248-1171
Email: chetdas@aol.com

Description: We serve NYC Wall Street firms, money center banks, and financial consulting firms. Our coverage includes middle upper-level positions in capital markets including: corporate finance, asset management, technology, and related.

Key Contact - Specialty:
Mr. Chester A. Fienberg, President - *Information technology, consulting*
Mr. Donald Mochwart, Vice President - *Capital markets, operations*

Salary minimum: $40,000

Functions: Generalist, Finance

Industries: Finance, Banking, Invest. Banking, Brokers, Venture Cap., Misc. Financial, Services, Accounting, Mgmt. Consulting

Druthers Agency Inc

2665 30th St Ste 103
Santa Monica, CA 90405
(310) 581-9949
(888) 378-8437
Fax: (310) 581-2899
Email: info@druthersagency.com
Web: www.druthersagency.com

Description: Executive Search Services exclusively for long-term care and continuing care environments. Additionally, we provide consultation and training on recruitment and retention practices.

Key Contact:
Mr. Jeffrey Harris, President

Functions: Generalist

Industries: Healthcare

Professional Associations: AHCA, CAHSA

DRZ Medical Recruiters

6426 S Robb Way
Littleton, CO 80127
(303) 933-1921
Fax: (303) 933-1921
Email: drzm@aol.com

Description: National recruitment firm with experience in placement of medical and pharmaceutical sales representatives as well as management positions, with regional focus in the Rocky Mountain area. Experience in all areas of medical.

Key Contact - Specialty:
Ms. Donna Zickerman, President - *Medical*

Functions: Generalist, Middle Mgmt., Sales Mgmt., MIS Mgmt.

Industries: Generalist, Drugs Mfg., Medical Devices, Healthcare

DSR-Search & Recruitment

801 E Campbell Rd Ste 155
Richardson, TX 75081
(972) 680-8282
Fax: (972) 231-9198
Email: dsr@telecomsearch.com
Web: www.telecomsearch.com

Description: Principal has over 25 years in telecommunications industry. Human resources executive with previous experience at major telecommunications design and manufacturers. Expertise in telephony-based areas, engineering, mid- to senior-level management; switching, access, transmission systems.

Key Contact - Specialty:
Mr. David G. Crowley, Managing Director - *Telecommunications*

Salary minimum: $50,000

Functions: Generalist, Directors, Senior Mgmt., Middle Mgmt., R&D, Engineering

Industries: Generalist, Telecoms, Software

Dukas Associates

236 Payson Rd
Belmont, MA 02478
(617) 484-9268
Fax: (617) 484-8607
Email: dukassoc@aol.com

Description: A precise customized recruitment service specializing in senior biotech marketing and technical personnel; bi-coastal knowledge of companies, personnel and industry trends.

Key Contact - Specialty:
Mr. Theodore Dukas, President - *Medical, biotechnology, sales & marketing, manufacturing research & development*

Salary minimum: $50,000

Functions: Generalist, Product Dev., Mkt. Research, Mktg. Mgmt., Sales Mgmt., R&D, Engineering, Int'l.

Industries: Generalist, Chemicals, Drugs Mfg., Medical Devices, Test, Measure Equip., Biotech

Dumont & Associates Retail Recruitment

2309 W 41st Ave Ste 306
Vancouver, BC V6M 2A3
Canada
(604) 733-8133
(604) 924-1753
Fax: (604) 269-2822
Email: info@retailheadhunter.com
Web: www.retailheadhunter.com

Description: Specialized expertise in the area of managerial and executive recruitment services strictly for the retail profession in Western Canada.

Key Contact - Specialty:
Ms. Brenda Dumont, President - *Senior managerial, executive, retail*
Mr. Paul Iannacone, Associate - *Specialty store management, retail*
Ms. Jackie Ross, Associate - *Store management, fashion retail*

Salary minimum: $45,000

Functions: General Mgmt., Senior Mgmt., Middle Mgmt., Purchasing, Distribution, Advertising, Mktg. Mgmt., HR Mgmt., Finance

Industries: Retail

Professional Associations: ACSESS, HRMBC, RCC, RMABC

M Dunbar & Associates

13607 Runney Meade
Sugar Land, TX 77478
(281) 242-9578
(800) 728-9577
Fax: (281) 242-9578
Email: mdunbar77478@msn.com

Description: As an MT (ASCP) with 16 years in medical sales and 8 years in healthcare executive search, I bring a unique qualification to each search. Medical and healthcare sales, clinical lab products and services, sales management, home healthcare sales and management, allied health, specialized nurse management.

Key Contact - Specialty:
Ms. Meg Dunbar, CPC, Owner - *Healthcare, clinical, technical, professional, administrative*

Salary minimum: $40,000

Functions: Generalist, Senior Mgmt., Middle Mgmt., Nurses, Allied Health, Health Admin., Sales Mgmt., CFO's

Industries: Generalist, Healthcare

The Duncan-O'Dell Group Inc

PO Box 1161
La Porte, TX 77571
(281) 470-1881
Fax: (281) 470-1880

Description: Thirty-two years of business experience. A practice that is multi-national. Area of primary focus is within the manufacturing and sales of rotating equipment (compressors, pumps, turbines)and industrial automation equipment.

Key Contact - Specialty:
Mr. James E. Hall, Managing Partner - *Manufacturing, electro-mechanical, metals, off road equipment, industrial automation equipment*

Salary minimum: $50,000

Functions: Mfg.

Industries: Mfg., Metal Products

Networks: National Personnel Assoc (NPA)

Dunhill Staffing Systems Inc

150 Motor Pkwy
Hauppauge, NY 11788-5111
(631) 952-3000
Fax: (631) 952-3500
Email: info@dunhillstaff.com
Web: www.dunhillstaff.com

Description: A nationwide network of executive recruiting offices (more than 180 locations), specializing in many disciplines.

Key Contact:
Mr. Daniel Abramson, President/COO
Mr. Richard W. Kean, Executive Vice President
Mr. Rich DeSantis, CFO
Mr. Robert Stidham, Vice President Franchise Delelopment
Ms. Katherine Hicinbothem, Marketing Director

Salary minimum: $25,000

Functions: Generalist, Mfg., Healthcare, Sales & Mktg., HR Mgmt., Finance, IT, Engineering

Industries: Generalist, Energy, Utilities, Mfg., Transportation, Wholesale, Finance, Services, Media

Professional Associations: NATSS, NTSA, SHRM

Branches:
2080 S Bascam Ave
Campbell, CA 95008-0635
(408) 369-1900
Fax: (408) 369-8709
Email: jobs@dunhillprof.com
Key Contact:
Mr. Gary Yuhara, President

15375 Barranca Pkwy Ste K-104
Irvine, CA 92618
(949) 341-0616
Fax: (949) 341-0619
Email: mlammanna@msn.com
Key Contact:
Mr Michael Lamanna, President

1215 N Nevada Ste 1
Colorado Springs, CO 80903-2455
(719) 473-7273
Fax: (719) 473-7278
Email: dnhlcos@aol.com
Key Contact:
Mr. Marinus Vanden Hul, President

333 E River Dr Ste 403
East Hartford, CT 06108-4209
(860) 282-8800
Fax: (860) 290-4778

Email: dsseasthartford@snet.net
Key Contact:
Ms. Marsha Wetherbee

850 N Main Ext Bldg 1 Ste D-1
Wallingford, CT 06492-2466
(203) 949-2000
Fax: (203) 949-2008
Email: dsswall@aol.com
Key Contact - Specialty:
Ms. Jamie Schoenfeld - *Information technology,*
telecommunications

226 S Tyndall Pkwy Ste B
Panama City, FL 32404
(850) 785-6888
Fax: (850) 785-0555
Email: dunhillpc@worldnet.att.net

5053 Ocean Ave Ste 59
Sarasota, FL 34242
(941) 349-6200
Fax: (941) 349-8866
Email: dunhillsarasota@home.com
Key Contact:
Mr. John Olson, President

303 Gardenia St Ste 6
West Palm Beach, FL 33401
(561) 833-3400
Fax: (561) 833-8200
Email: opportunities@dunhillwestpalm.com
Key Contact:
Ms. Mari-Jean Phillips, President/Consultant -
Financial services- wall street sector
Terri F. Miller, Consultant - *Engineering*
Ms. Amy Wallis, Consultant - *Information*
technology
Mr. Andrew Brownlee, Office Coordinator

1000 Mansell Exchange W 250
Alpharetta, GA 30022-8260
(770) 442-3910
Fax: (770) 442-0447
Email: dunhillalpha@msn.com
Key Contact:
Mr. Mark Zorin, President

3348 Peachtree Rd NE Ste 150
Twr Place 200
Atlanta, GA 30326-1008
(404) 261-7557
Fax: (404) 237-8361
Email: atlantadunhill@hotmail.com
Key Contact:
Mr. Marvin Bearman, President

211 W Wacker Dr Ste 1150
Chicago, IL 60606-1240
(312) 346-0933
Fax: (312) 346-0837
Email: cstitt@dunhillchicago.com
Key Contact:
Ms. Carrie Stitt, Branch Manager
Ms. Heather Bohnsack

100 Hillcrest Dr
Washington, IL 61571-2200
(309) 444-5510
Fax: (309) 444-5512
Email: dunhill@mwonline.net
Web: www.dunhillmw.com
Key Contact:
Mr. Jay Morris
Ms. Karen A. Morris
Mr. Mark S. Elliot
Mr. Mak Meyers
Ms. Judy Morris
Mr. Chris Gerth
Mrs. Pete Louck

916 E Main St Ste 114
Greenwood, IN 46143-1500
(317) 859-8900
Fax: (317) 859-7200
Email: indysouth@dunhillstaffing.net
Key Contact:
Ms. Angela Niederauser, Branch Manager

PO Box 3001
Iowa City, IA 52244-3001
(319) 354-1407
Fax: (319) 354-1715
Email: lwsdunhill@aol.com
Key Contact:
Mr. Lee Stannard, President

5723 Superior Dr Ste B-4
Baton Rouge, LA 70816-8016
(225) 291-0450
(225) 291-3704
Fax: (225) 292-4411
Email: ffalcon@eatel.net
Key Contact:
Mr. Fritz Falcon, President

7939 Honeygo Blvd Ste 225
Baltimore, MD 21236
(410) 931-4960
Fax: (410) 877-3388
Email: mtitch@aol.com
Key Contact:
Mr. Stuart Harper, Vice President

7185 Columbia Gateway Dr Ste G
Columbia, MD 21046-2525
(410) 290-1515
Fax: (410) 290-1199
Email: dunhillcolmd@msn.com
Key Contact:
Ms. Rosa Harper, President
Mr. Russ Harper
Mr. Stuart Harper

414 Hungerford Dr Ste 252
Rockville, MD 20850-4125
(301) 424-0450
Fax: (301) 762-4694
Email: dunhillmd@msn.com
Key Contact:
Ms. Rosa Harper, President
Mr. Stuart Harper

40770 Garfield Rd
Clinton Township, MI 48038-2534
(810) 412-3333
Fax: (810) 412-3377
Key Contact:
Ms. Pamela Murff, President

855 S Pear Orchard Rd Ste 102
Ridgeland, MS 39157-5133
(601) 956-1060
Fax: (601) 956-1635
Key Contact:
Mr. Ronnie Fulton, President

206A Main St
Festus, MO 63028-1907
(636) 931-4477
Fax: (636) 931-3628
Email: dunspro@jcn1.com
Key Contact:
Mr. Robert Bahr, President
Ms. Julie Bahr, Vice President

801 E 20th St
Joplin, MO 64804-8219
(417) 624-6552
Email: lickteig@joplin.com
Key Contact:
Mr. Mark Lickteig, President
Ms. Pamela Lickteig, Research Associate

4706 S 108 St
Omaha, NE 68144-3210
(402) 334-5772
Fax: (402) 334-5744
Email: schmidt@lendingresources.com
Key Contact:
Ms. Kim Schmidt, President

584 Delaware Ave
Buffalo, NY 14202-1299
(716) 885-3576
Fax: (716) 885-3594
Email: dunbuf@aol.com

775 Park Ave Ste 200-1
Huntington, NY 11743-3990
(631) 421-9500
Fax: (631) 421-9700
Email: dunhill@huntington-atrium.com
Key Contact:
Mr. Joseph Lawless, CPC/President

PO Box 528
Pittsford, NY 14534-0528
(716) 377-7880
Fax: (716) 377-7972
Email: search3535@aol.com
Key Contact:
Mr. Jack Tanner, President

200 E Arlington Blvd Ste D
Greenville, NC 27858-5020
(252) 355-3808
Fax: (252) 355-1865
Email: edb@dunhilljobs.com
Web: www.dunhilljobs.com
Key Contact:
Mr. Ed Belcher

7831 Spinnaker Bay Dr
Sherrills Ford, NC 28673
(828) 478-7000
Fax: (828) 478-9083
Key Contact:
Mr. Tom Barbeau, President

PO Box 67048
Cuyahoga Falls, OH 44222-0048
(330) 929-7110
Key Contact:
Mr. Chuck Woodward, President

247 N Broadway Ste 205
Edmond, OK 73034-3702
(405) 341-0990
Fax: (405) 341-0997
Email: degdun@aol.com
Key Contact:
Mr. Dennis Garton, President

7666 E 61st St Ste 120
Tulsa, OK 74133
(918) 252-4434
Fax: (918) 252-4498
Email: dunhilltulsa@aol.com
Key Contact:
Mr. Curtis Reid, President

233 E Lancaster Ave Ste 101
Ardmore, PA 19003-2321
(610) 642-2223
Fax: (610) 642-2347
Email: scotdunhil@aol.com
Key Contact:
Mr. Alan Trager, President

224 Nazareth Pike Unit 16
Bethlehem, PA 18020-9080
(610) 746-5066
Fax: (610) 746-5799
Email: dunjobs@fast.net
Key Contact:
Ms. Mary Jo Stofflet, President
Ms. Erika Roper, Consultant
Toni Ceraul, Consultant

2318 W 8th St Lower Lvl
Erie, PA 16505
(814) 459-1639
Fax: (814) 459-1989
Email: bazimmer@stargate.com

770 E Market St Ste 185
West Chester, PA 19382-3003
(888) 431-2700
Fax: (888) 431-0329
Email: rthanson@bellatlantic.net
Key Contact:
Mr. Richard Hanson, President

96 Villa Rd
Greenville, SC 29615-3052
(864) 242-9870
Fax: (864) 271-7181
Email: dunhill@acsinc.net

Key Contact:
Mr. Ed Belcher, President
Mr. Duke Haynie, President

100 Allentown Pkwy Ste 104
Allen, TX 75002
(214) 495-7900
Fax: (214) 495-7950
Email: opportunities@dunhillallen.com
Web: www.dunhillallen.com
Key Contact:
Ms. Ann Badmus, President

6320 Southwest Blvd Ste 205
Ft. Worth, TX 76109
(817) 731-7301
Fax: (817) 731-7202
Email: pat@dunhilltexas.com
Key Contact:
Pat Boudreaux, President

350 N Sam Houston Pkwy E Ste 121
Houston, TX 77060
(281) 931-6400
Fax: (281) 931-0929
Email: jobs@dunhillhouston.com
Web: www.dunhillhouston.com
Key Contact:
Mr. Jim Walker, President
Mr. Richard Rice, Vice President

9800 Centre Pkwy Ste 150
Houston, TX 77036
(713) 988-4444
Fax: (713) 270-7575
Email: mw@dunhillhsw.com
Key Contact:
Mr. Mike Wilcoxson, President
Mr. Elias Zinn, CEO

8100 Three Chopt Rd Ste 133
Richmond, VA 23229-4833
(804) 282-2216
Fax: (804) 282-5682
Email: dpsricva@email.msn.com
Key Contact:
Mr. Frank Lassiter, President

336 S Jefferson St
Green Bay, WI 54301-4523
(920) 432-2977
Fax: (920) 432-2038
Key Contact:
Mr. Kramer Rock, President

159 Albert St
London, ON N6A 1L9
Canada
(519) 673-6684
Fax: (519) 673-6792
Email: dps@odyssey.on.ca
Key Contact:
Ms. Lynn Lindsay, President

2 Robert Speck Pkwy Ste 750
Mississauga, ON L4Z 1H8
Canada
(905) 306-3439
Fax: (519) 457-5511
Email: asyed.dunhill@on.aibn.com
Key Contact:
Mr. Arshad Syed, President

Dunhill Professional Search of South Birmingham

2738 18th St S
Birmingham, AL 35209-1904
(205) 877-4580
Fax: (205) 877-4590
Email: dunhillpro@aol.com
Web: www.dunhillbirmingham.com

Description: Contingency search firm with specialties in accounting, information technology, healthcare administration, human resource and office support.

Key Contact - Specialty:
Ms. Peggy A. Clarke, President - *Accounting, finance*

Functions: Generalist, HR Mgmt., Benefits, Personnel, Finance, CFO's, IT, MIS Mgmt.

Industries: Generalist, Accounting, HR Services

Dunhill Professional Search of N San Francisco Bay

601 1st St Ste 200
Benicia, CA 94510-3211
(707) 748-3000
Fax: (707) 748-3001
Email: pcacho@dunhilljob.com
Web: www.dunhillvip.com

Description: We specialize in sales and marketing executives, product marketing managers for software industries, biotech professionals, telecommunications professionals, and real estate professionals.

Key Contact:
Mr. Patrick Cacho, CRP, President - *Sales & marketing executives, relocation professionals*
Mr. Mark Gratis, Account Executive
Ms. Kristi Peters, Account Executive
Mr. Joanie Graham, Research Associate

Salary minimum: $50,000

Functions: Generalist, General Mgmt., Directors, Senior Mgmt., Middle Mgmt., Sales & Mktg., Mktg. Mgmt., Sales Mgmt.

Industries: Generalist, Mfg., Medical Devices, Banking, Telecoms, Real Estate, Software

Professional Associations: NAPS

Dunhill Professional Search of Oakland

3732 Mt. Diablo Blvd Ste 375
Lafayette, CA 94549-3605
(925) 283-5300
Fax: (925) 283-5310
Email: dunprosear@aol.com

Description: We work hard to find a custom fit between the position you need to fill and the person to fill it.

Key Contact - Specialty:
Mr. John F. Tierney, President - *High tech*

Salary minimum: $50,000

Functions: Generalist, General Mgmt., Senior Mgmt., Mfg., Materials, Mkt. Research, IT, Engineering

Industries: Generalist, Food, Bev., Tobacco

Dunhill Professional Search of Los Angeles

4727 Wilshire Blvd Ste 410
Los Angeles, CA 90010-3806
(323) 931-1311
Fax: (323) 931-0565
Email: dunhill@dunhill-la.com
Web: www.dunhillstaff.com

Description: We offer you over twenty five years of experience in recruiting worldwide.

Key Contact - Specialty:
Mr. Raymond R. Cech, President - *Environmental (health & safety), real estate, sales & marketing*
Ms. Heather O'Green, Account Manager - *Hi-tech, software, sales, marketing, engineer*
Ms. Grace Tamayo, Account Executive - *Hi-tech, sales, marketing*
Mr. Daniel Prok, Account Executive - *High technology, computer, software, hardware, sales & marketing*
Mr. Jimmy Scarpello, Account Executive - *Software, hi-tech, sales & marketing,*

Ms. Sophia Kim, Account Executive - *Hi-tech, sales, marketing*

Salary minimum: $75,000

Functions: Generalist, Senior Mgmt., Middle Mgmt., Product Dev., Sales & Mktg., Mktg. Mgmt., Sales Mgmt.

Industries: Generalist, E-commerce, Communications, Telephony, Digital, Wireless, Fiber Optic, Software, Database SW, Doc. Mgmt., Production SW, ERP SW

Professional Associations: AIHA, ICSC

Dunhill Professional Search of San Francisco

268 Bush St
PMB 2909
San Francisco, CA 94104-3599
(877) 751-9697
(415) 956-3700
Fax: (877) 751-9638
Email: dunhill@clarkston.com
Web: www.dunhillstaff.com/safca.htm

Description: We take pride in the fact that many of the Technical and Sales personnel we place with our Client companies have progressed into high-level management positions.

Key Contact:
Mr. George R. Curtiss, President - *Generalist*
Mr. Chris N. Curtiss, Director
Mr. Michael R. Curtiss, Vice President

Salary minimum: $60,000

Functions: General Mgmt., Mfg., Production, Automation, Plant Mgmt., Quality, Sales Mgmt., HR Mgmt., Engineering, Environmentalists

Industries: Generalist, Chemicals, Metal Products, Electronic, Elec. Components, Environmental Svcs.

Dunhill Professional Search of Englewood

1941 S Xanadu Way
Aurora, CO 80014-4310
(303) 755-7466
Fax: (303) 755-7081
Email: jlippe@juno.com
Web: www.dunhillstaff.com

Description: Contingency search, primarily for middle management positions such as engineering, production, quality, R&D, and distribution, in process industries such as food, beverage, cosmetics and medical related manufacturing.

Key Contact - Specialty:
Mr. John L. Lippe, President - *Manufacturing, process*

Salary minimum: $40,000

Functions: Mfg.

Industries: Food, Bev., Tobacco, Soap, Perf., Cosmtcs., Drugs Mfg., Medical Devices

Dunhill Professional Search of Ft Collins

2120 S College Ave Ste 3
Ft. Collins, CO 80525-1465
(970) 221-5630
Fax: (970) 221-5692
Email: dfc@frii.com
Web: www.dunhillstaff.com

Description: We are a privately owned and managed office. We provide personal attention by a staff of four whom average 18 years of recruiting experience. Our specialties are insurance actuaries, banking officers, microelectronics industry and wire and cable industry. We have access to national exchange system with a 40-year record of success.

Key Contact - Specialty:
Mr. Jerold Lyons, President - *Wire and cable industry, engineers, manufacturing engineers*
Mr. Jack Donahue, Technical Recruiter - *Semiconductor engineers*
Mr. Phil Palmer, CPC, Actuary Recruiter - *Insurance actuaries*
Mr. Herb McCulla, Banking Recruiter - *Commercial loan officers, trust, credit, auditor*

Salary minimum: $25,000

Functions: Generalist, Production, Purchasing, Credit, Engineering

Industries: Generalist, Mfg., Plastics, Rubber, Metal Products, Computer Equip., Banking, Software

Dunhill Professional Search of Boulder

PO Box 488
Niwot, CO 80544-0488
(303) 652-8370
Fax: (303) 652-8369
Email: dunbldr@aol.com
Web: www.dunhillstaff.com

Description: Our office is an independently owned franchise, part of a large corporation consisting of 130 offices nationwide and international. Ownership of business has 40 years of experience (supervisors to vice presidents of operations) in the recruiting specialty.

Key Contact:
Mr. Fran Boruff, President - *Manufacturing, food, beverage, durable goods*
Mr. Doug Boruff, Vice President - *Manufacturing, food, beverage, durable goods*
Ms. Bettie Boruff, Administrative Assistant

Functions: Generalist, Senior Mgmt., Production, Plant Mgmt., Quality, Productivity, Purchasing, Materials Plng.

Industries: Generalist, Food, Bev., Tobacco, Chemicals, Drugs Mfg., Transportation

Dunhill Professional Search of New Haven

(also known as Int'l Search.com)
59 Elm St Ste 520
New Haven, CT 06510-2031
(203) 562-0511
Fax: (203) 562-2637
Email: info@nhdunhill.com
Web: www.nhdunhill.com

Description: American companies expanding abroad, foreign companies coming to the US or international corporations expanding into new markets find their mid-level managers through VP level people through us. We also place legal staffing in Connecticut, office support staff in New Haven, and sales and marketing and accounting finance in New England.

Key Contact - Specialty:
Mr. Donald J. Kaiser, President - *Consultants, risk management, international*
Mr. James Kaiser, Director-International - *Sales & marketing, business development, human resources, logistics, transportation*
Ms. Gina Langella, CPA, Director - *Accounting, tax, finance, SAP*
Mr. Jack Chatfield, Director - *Information technology, engineering*
Ms. Elaine Kaiser, International/Domestic Vice President - *International, legal, bilingual, office support*
Mrs. Kim Zarra, Director of Legal Placements - *Paralegal, attorney, legal secretary*

Salary minimum: $35,000

Functions: Senior Mgmt., Middle Mgmt., Admin. Svcs., Legal, Plant Mgmt., Sales & Mktg., Finance, CFO's, Taxes, Int'l.

Industries: Generalist, Energy, Utilities, Construction, Mfg., Food, Bev., Tobacco, Medical Devices, Computer Equip., Transportation, Finance, Services, Legal, Mgmt. Consulting, Hospitality, Advertising, Telecoms, Environmental Svcs., Aerospace, Software, Biotech, Healthcare

Professional Associations: ASA, CWTA, NAPS, NATSS

Networks: Int'l Search Group

Dunhill Professional Search of St Petersburg

1915 E Bay Dr Ste B-3
Largo, FL 33771-2203
(727) 585-0000
(800) 585-2580
Fax: (727) 585-3805
Email: dunhillstpete@mindspring.com
Web: www.dunhillstaff.com

Description: Specializing in engineering, design, product development, and other technical positions from the most senior management down.

Key Contact:
Mr. Richard Williams

Functions: Generalist

Industries: Generalist

Professional Associations: FAPS

Dunhill Professional Search of Orlando

670 N Orlando Ave Ste 1002
Maitland, FL 32751-4477
(407) 599-9840
Fax: (407) 599-9845
Email: rgregory@concentric.net
Web: www.dunhillorlando.com

Description: We provide marketing, finance/accounting, and administrative personnel contingency searches conducted locally or nationwide. In marketing, we specialize in direct marketing, e-Commerce, data mining/CRM, and call center management. In finance/accounting, we handle CFOs, controllers, and accountants. In administrative personnel, we handle all office positions, including receptionists, administrative assistants, bookkeepers, etc.

Key Contact:
Ms. Elaine Gregory, President
Mr. Ron Gregory, Vice President

Salary minimum: $25,000

Functions: Admin. Svcs., Advertising, Mktg. Mgmt., Direct Mktg., CFO's, Budgeting, M&A, Mgmt. Consultants, Graphic Artists

Industries: Generalist, Finance, Accounting, Mgmt. Consulting, E-commerce, Advertising, Call Centers

Dunhill Professional Search of Miami

550 Brickell Ave Ste 502
Miami, FL 33131-2508
(305) 372-5757
Email: solutions@dunhillmiami.com
Web: www.dunhillmiami.com

Description: Although we are located in Miami, Florida; we deliver resources throughout the world. Our engagements have been successful throughout the Americas, Europe, and Asia. Additionally, as the "gateway to the Americas," our Miami office and our multi-lingual/cultural teams support the emerging Hispanic markets in the US and critical markets throughout Latin America.

Key Contact - Specialty:
Mr. Paul J. Gregg, President - *Senior management, international, sales & marketing, engineering, financial services*

Salary minimum: $60,000

Functions: Generalist, General Mgmt., Senior Mgmt., Middle Mgmt., Sales & Mktg., HR Mgmt., CFO's, IT, Engineering, Int'l.

Industries: Generalist, Energy, Utilities, Mfg., Transportation, Finance, Services, Communications, Aerospace, Packaging, Software

Professional Associations: EGSA, NAPS

Dunhill Professional Search of Tampa

4350 W Cypress St Ste 225
Tampa, FL 33607-4158
(813) 872-8118
Fax: (813) 872-6398
Email: go@dunhilltampa.com
Web: www.dunhilltampa.com

Description: Our specialties are healthcare, information technology, and accounting/auditing. We recruit nurse management, hospital techs, hospital administration and finance executives and auditors both financial and EDP. We also specialize in MIS, programmers; network specialists, etc.

Key Contact - Specialty:
Mr. Peter Kramer, President - *Audit, EDP audit*

Salary minimum: $40,000

Functions: Generalist, Middle Mgmt., Healthcare, Nurses, Allied Health, Health Admin., Finance, IT

Industries: Generalist

Dunhill Professional Search of W Atlanta

2110 Powers Ferry Rd Ste 110
Atlanta, GA 30339-5015
(770) 952-0007
Fax: (770) 952-9422
Email: dswatlga@mindspring.com
Web: www.dunhillstaff.com/watga.htm

Description: Technical specialist in supply chain management, materials management, engineering, human resources and manufacturing industry. Effectively use team recruiting with closely networked 200 offices for fast response.

Key Contact - Specialty:
Mr. Jon Harvill, CPC, President - *Manufacturing*

Salary minimum: $40,000

Functions: Mfg., Product Dev., Production, Automation, Plant Mgmt., Materials, Purchasing, Materials Plng.

Industries: Mfg., Transportation, Wholesale, Mgmt. Consulting, HR Services, Aerospace, Packaging, Non-classifiable

Professional Associations: APICS, GAPS, NAPM, NAPS

Dunhill Professional Search of Augusta

801 Broad St Ste 411
SunTrust Bank Bldg
Augusta, GA 30901-3121
(706) 722-5741
Fax: (706) 722-5742
Web: www.dunhillstaff.com

Description: Close, individual attention including resume guidance, concerted marketing effort to agreed upon companies in specific geographic locations. Effort can run months to year or more.

Key Contact - Specialty:
Mr. Frederick P. Gehle, President - *Chemical, pulp & paper, engineering (junior to mid level), process control, automation systems engineers*

Salary minimum: $30,000

Functions: Generalist, Production, Automation, Quality, Productivity, Engineering, Environmentalists

Industries: Generalist, Lumber, Furniture, Paper, Chemicals, Plastics, Rubber, Paints, Petro. Products

Dunhill Staffing of Hawaii

1164 Bishop St Ste 124
Honolulu, HI 96813
(808) 524-2550
Fax: (808) 533-2196
Email: jobsrus@aloha.net
Web: www.dunhillstaff.com

Description: Permanent placement, temporary placement and professional contract staffing of experienced and qualified individuals for client companies and associations in engineering, accounting, data processing, audit, construction fields, technical and sales.

Key Contact:
Ms. Nadine Stollenmaier, President - *Accounting, engineering, technical, information systems, insurance*
Mr. James Stollenmaier, Vice President
Mr. Henry Sotelo, Corporate Secretary - *Engineering, technical*
Mr. Randy Muth, Manager

Salary minimum: $22,000

Functions: Generalist, General Mgmt., Production, Sales & Mktg., Finance, IT, Engineering, Int'l.

Industries: Generalist, Computer Equip., Accounting, IT Implementation, Telecoms, Accounting SW

Professional Associations: DPMA

Dunhill Professional Search of Sandpoint

316 N 2nd Ave Ste D
Sandpoint, ID 83864
(208) 265-2651
Fax: (208) 265-3621
Email: kc@dps-sandpoint.com
Web: www.dps-sandpoint.com

Description: We specialize in technology-oriented sales and marketing.

Key Contact:
Mr. Keith Cutter, President

Salary minimum: $60,000

Functions: Generalist

Industries: Computer Equip., Software, Accounting SW, Database SW, Development SW, Doc. Mgmt., Production SW

Dunhill Professional Search of Rolling Meadows

PO Box 1781
Palatine, IL 60078
(847) 991-8127
Fax: (847) 991-8137
Email: russk@wave3online.com
Web: www.dunhillstaff.com

Description: Our president has 12 years experience as a hiring manager. He understands technology, terminology, etc. Through our membership with Dunhill Professional Search, we have a nationwide network of 100 offices. We have ten years of experience in information technology recruiting.

Key Contact - Specialty:
Mr. Russ Kunke, President - *Information technology*

Salary minimum: $50,000

Functions: Generalist, MIS Mgmt., Systems Analysis, Systems Dev., Systems Implem., Systems Support, Network Admin., DB Admin.

Industries: Generalist

Dunhill Professional Search of Fort Wayne

9918 Coldwater Rd
Ft. Wayne, IN 46825-2040
(219) 489-5966
Fax: (219) 489-6120
Email: jobs@dunhillfw.com
Web: www.dunhillfortwayne.com

Description: Twenty-two years' experience in providing salaried individuals for manufacturing plants. Specialize in the food, food packaging industry.

Key Contact - Specialty:
Mr. Charlie Davis, President - *Manufacturing plant, engineers, quality assurance*

Salary minimum: $30,000

Functions: Generalist, Production, Automation, Plant Mgmt., Quality, Productivity, HR Mgmt., Engineering

Industries: Generalist, Food, Bev., Tobacco, Chemicals, Soap, Perf., Cosmtcs., Drugs Mfg.

Dunhill Professional Search of Indianapolis

950 N Meridian St Ste 110
Indianapolis, IN 46204-4013
(317) 237-7860
Fax: (317) 237-7859
Email: bpg@dunhillstaffing.com
Web: www.dunhillstaffing.com

Description: We specialize in the placement of computer information systems professionals on a permanent as well as a contract basis.

Key Contact - Specialty:
Mr. Mark Rowe, Manager - *Information systems, technology*
Mr. Keith Bosell, Technical Consultant - *Information systems, technology*
Mr. Kristaan Kane, Technical Consultant - *Information systems, information technology*

Functions: Generalist, IT, MIS Mgmt., Systems Analysis, Systems Dev., Systems Implem., Systems Support, Network Admin.

Industries: Generalist, Software

Dunhill Executive Search of Brown County

PO Box 1068
Nashville, IN 47448-1068
(812) 988-1944
Fax: (812) 988-1944
Email: geowrogers@earthlink.net
Web: www.dunhillstaff.com

Description: We actively participate with other Dunhill offices in the exchange of both applicants and job opportunities, which gives a greater exposure of the marketable applicant and a greater potential for us to complete a search for the manufacturer.

Key Contact - Specialty:
Mr. George W. Rogers, President - *Engineering, manufacturing*
Ms. S. L. Rogers, Vice President-Administration - *Engineering, manufacturing*

Salary minimum: $30,000

Functions: Mfg., IT, Engineering

Industries: Generalist

Professional Associations: IIE

Dunhill Professional Search of Greater New Orleans

2424 Edenborn Ave Ste 120
Metairie, LA 70001
(888) 901-5627
Fax: (504) 834-8356
Email: 1dunhill@bellsouth.net
Web: www.dunhilltelecom.com

Description: We are a telecommunications/energy recruiting firm specializing in executive, engineering, switching, data transmission, and sales-oriented prescreened candidates at all levels, as well as human resources at all levels

Key Contact - Specialty:
Mr. Jerald W. Bailey, President - *Telecommunications, utilities, human resources, information technology*

Salary minimum: $30,000

Functions: Generalist, General Mgmt., Senior Mgmt., Middle Mgmt., Sales & Mktg., HR Mgmt., Network Admin., Engineering, Technicians

Industries: HR Services, Telecoms

Professional Associations: NAPS, SHRM

Networks: Top Echelon Network

Dunhill Professional Search of Shreveport

2920 Knight St Ste 140
Shreveport, LA 71105-2412
(318) 861-3576
Fax: (318) 868-9872
Email: dunhillsport@aol.com
Web: www.dunhillstaff.com

Key Contact:
Mr. Butch Troquille, President

Dunhill Professional Search of Middlesex

PO Box 4124
Metuchen, NJ 08840
(732) 906-3370
Fax: (732) 906-3373
Email: dunpro@att.net
Web: www.dunhillstaff.com

Description: We specialize in staffing, engineering, information technology, manufacturing, and production professionals, nationally. Our positions include, but are not limited to: plant management, engineering, R&D, reliability, quality assurance, production, management, materials management, environmental health, and safety.

Key Contact:
Mr. Ralph DeMiranda, President

Salary minimum: $40,000

Functions: Mfg., IT, Engineering

Industries: Generalist

Dunhill Professional Search of Ramsey

10 Cheyenne Ct
Oakland, NJ 07436
(201) 337-2200
Fax: (201) 337-3445
Email: dunhillram@aol.com
Web: www.dunhillstaff.com

Description: Since founded, the firm has placed over 400 executives. One specialty is large-scale staffing expansion projects and total outsourcing of clients HR staffing needs.

Key Contact - Specialty:
Mr. Roger Lippincott, President - *Sales, human resources*

Salary minimum: $30,000

Functions: Generalist, Plant Mgmt., Productivity, Sales Mgmt., Personnel, Training

Industries: Generalist, Drugs Mfg., Computer Equip., Telecoms

Professional Associations: ASQ, ASTD, QPMA

Dunhill Professional Search of Teaneck

1415 Queen Anne Rd
Teaneck, NJ 07666-3521
(201) 837-5077
Fax: (201) 837-5088
Email: dunhill@megapathdsl.net
Web: www.dunhillstaff.com/teanj

Description: We offer comprehensive recruitment services in the following industries: finance and accounting, information technology, healthcare, and office personnel. All candidates are screened, pre-qualified, and interviewed prior to being sent to clients.

Key Contact:
Mr. William Miska, President
Mr. Sheldon Miller, Executive Vice President

Functions: Generalist

Industries: Mfg., Finance, Services, Non-profits, Legal, Insurance, Software, Biotech, Healthcare

Professional Associations: ACHE, AHHRA, HFMA

Dunhill Professional Search of Garden City

140 Old Country Rd Ste 110
Mineola, NY 11501
(516) 248-2259
Fax: (516) 248-2477
Email: info@dps-gc.com
Web: www.dunhillstaff.com

Description: We are a professional contingency search firm specializing in the: accounting, information technology, and sales and marketing industries.

Key Contact:
Mr. Robert Sommella, President
Mr. Anthony Marullo, Vice President

Dunhill Professional Search of Rye Brook

41 Mohegan Ln
Rye Brook, NY 10573-1431
(914) 934-0801
Fax: (914) 934-0825
Email: headhunterone@att.net
Web: www.dunhillstaff.com

Description: We deliver in a timely fashion a selection of over quota performers with checkable track records at no cost to you -- unless you hire.

Key Contact - Specialty:
Mr. Robert J. Morris, President - *Information processing (sales talent)*

Salary minimum: $70,000

Functions: Sales Mgmt.

Industries: Computer Equip., IT Implementation, Call Centers, Software, Database SW, Doc. Mgmt., Production SW, ERP SW, Security SW

Dunhill Professional Search of Raleigh

975 Walnut St Ste 260
Cary, NC 27511-4268
(919) 460-9988
(800) 783-9933
Fax: (919) 460-9931
Email: info@dunhillnc.com
Web: www.dunhillnc.com

Description: We have placed more than two million professionals in new and challenging positions. Our national computerized network of specialists can provide you with all the information necessary to make smart career decisions.

Key Contact - Specialty:
Mr. Jay Babson, President - *Information technology*
Ms. Lelia Babson, Executive Director - *Healthcare, managed care*

Functions: Generalist, Nurses, Allied Health, MIS Mgmt., Systems Analysis, Systems Dev., Systems Implem., Network Admin.

Industries: Generalist, Finance, Telecoms, Network Infrastructure, Healthcare, Hospitals

Professional Associations: NAPS

Dunhill Professional Search of South Charlotte

10801 Johnston Rd Ste 223
Charlotte, NC 28226
(704) 544-8556
(888) 407-1275
Fax: (704) 544-8158
Email: hauger@dpscharlotte.com
Web: www.dunhillstaff.com/schnc

Description: We specialize in the real estate, relocation, and mortgage industries. We place all positions, including senior level executives. We place in sales, business development, client relations, and consultants.

Key Contact:
Mr. Harvey Auger, President
Mr. Chip Auger, Account Executive

Functions: Senior Mgmt., Middle Mgmt., Sales & Mktg., Sales Mgmt.

Industries: Transportation, Finance, Banking, Invest. Banking, Brokers, Misc. Financial, Entertainment, Real Estate, Non-classifiable

Dunhill Professional Search of Fargo

827 28th St SW Ste C
Fargo, ND 58103
(701) 235-3719
(800) 473-2512
Fax: (701) 235-7092
Email: dsfargo@fargocity.com
Web: www.dunhillstaff.com

Description: We specialize in healthcare and engineering, information systems and physicians, sales and marketing, and accounting and finance.

Key Contact - Specialty:
Mr. Kent Hochgraber, President - *Technicians, physicians*
Mrs. Karen Solhjem, Senior Engineering Consultant - *Engineering*
Mr. Ken Farnham, Consultant - *Information systems, accounting*

Salary minimum: $25,000

Functions: Generalist, General Mgmt., Physicians, Health Admin., Sales & Mktg., Finance, IT, Engineering

Industries: Generalist, Machine, Appliance, Banking, Pharm Svcs., Accounting, Hospitality, Software

Dunhill Professional Search of Cincinnati

4015 Executive Park Dr Ste 240
Cincinnati, OH 45241-4015
(513) 769-9675
(888) 769-9675
Fax: (513) 956-5165
Email: dunofc@dunhill-usa.com
Web: www.dunhill-usa.com

Description: We are a contingency and retained search firm, but will also handle contracts. We specialize in logistics, material handling, engineering, and insurance. Our fees are always paid by the clients.

Key Contact - Specialty:
Mr. Michael D. Green, CEO - *Logistics and material handling*
Ms. Judith C. Green, President
Mr. Michael Havens, Vice President - *Engineering, logistics, material handling*
Mr. Greg Starr, Consultant - *Insurance (sales, CSR)*

Salary minimum: $30,000

Functions: Generalist

Industries: Construction, Mfg., Food, Bev., Tobacco, Paper, Plastics, Rubber, Misc. Mfg., Transportation, Wholesale, Retail, Insurance

Dunhill Professional Search of Bucks-Mont

801 W Street Rd Ste 7
Feasterville, PA 19053-7335
(215) 357-6591
Fax: (215) 953-1612
Email: dave@dunhillbm.com
Web: www.dunhillbm.com

Description: Specialize in the permanent placement of sales and marketing, as well as accounting and finance professionals nationwide, also temporary clerical and secretarial help in the greater Philadelphia marketplace.

Key Contact - Specialty:
Ms. Mary F. Bontempo, President - *Office services*
Mr. David M. Bontempo, CPC, CPC/Vice President - *Sales & marketing, accounting & finance*

Salary minimum: $50,000

Functions: Sales & Mktg., Finance

Industries: Mfg., Finance, Banking, Pharm Svcs., Accounting, Advertising, Publishing, Telecoms, Packaging, Software

Professional Associations: MAAPC, NAPS

Dunhill Professional Search of Wilkes-Barre/Scranton

15 Public Sq Ste 202
Wilkes-Barre, PA 18701-3100
(570) 826-8953
Fax: (570) 821-8956
Email: dunhillsearch@msn.com
Web: www.dunhillwilkesbarrescranton.com

Description: Senior executive management, engineering and sales management assignments in electronics, automotive, power transmission related industries for domestic and international clients. Additional emphasis on information systems, EDP auditors and insurance.

Key Contact - Specialty:
Mr. Anthony J Desiderio, CPC, President - *General management, CEO, board chairman, technical*
Ms. Michelle McGinty, Consultant - *Insurance, accounting, finance*
Mr. Joseph M. Zrowka, Consultant - *Accounting, finance*

Salary minimum: $50,000

Functions: Generalist, General Mgmt., Mfg., Materials, Mktg. Mgmt., Sales Mgmt., Risk Mgmt., IT, R&D, Paralegals

Industries: Metal Products, Machine, Appliance, Mgmt. Consulting, Telecoms, Defense, Insurance

Professional Associations: NAPS

Dunhill Professional Search of Yardley

46 E Trenton Ave
Yardley, PA 19067-1060
(215) 428-3430
Fax: (215) 428-3919
Email: careers@dps-yarpa.com
Web: www.dunhillstaff.com

Description: Our firm specializes in permanent and contract placement services in information systems and technology. Consider us your source for IT sales, marketing, and technical professionals nationwide with a concentration in the Northeastern US.

Key Contact:
Ms. Karen Russo, President

Functions: Generalist

Industries: Computer Equip., Consumer Elect., Electronic, Elec. Components, Services, Communications, Software

Professional Associations: ASA, NAPS, NTSA

Dunhill Professional Search of Greenwood

231-F Hampton St
Greenwood, SC 29646-2238
(864) 229-5251
(877) 706-5851
Fax: (864) 229-6306
Email: dunhill@greenwood.net
Web: www.dunhillstaff.com

Description: We provide professional recruiting for wire and cable industry. We recruit engineers and all levels of management in manufacturing and administrative environments.

Key Contact - Specialty:
Mr. Hal Freese, President - *Wire, cable, fiber optics, plastics*

Salary minimum: $40,000

Functions: Mfg., Product Dev., Engineering

Industries: Plastics, Rubber, Metal Products, Electronic, Elec. Components, Telecoms, Fiber Optic

Professional Associations: WAI

Dunhill Professional Search of Memphis

5120 Stage Rd Ste 2
Stage Woods Office Park
Memphis, TN 38134-3149
(901) 386-2500
Web: www.dunhillstaff.com

Description: Contingency recruiting of engineering, manufacturing and distribution candidates for $30-$100K positions located within a 50 mile radius of Memphis, TN.

Key Contact:
Mr. Eugene Rhodes, President
Mr. Mike Rhodes, Consultant

Salary minimum: $30,000

Functions: Mfg., Distribution, Engineering

Industries: Generalist, Mfg. SW

Dunhill Professional Search of Arlington

2912 W Park Row
Arlington, TX 76013-6748
(817) 265-2291
Fax: (817) 265-2294
Email: jobs@dunhillsearch.com
Web: www.dunhillsearch.com

Description: We are celebrating 25 yrs in the industry, specializing in audit and information systems audit. We work with Fortune 500 clients as well as small- to medium- sized companies throughout the U.S. We are computer linked with over 125 Dunhill offices and maintain an extensive job and candidate database.

Key Contact - Specialty:
Mr. Jon Molkentine, President - *Information systems, audit*

Salary minimum: $45,000

Functions: Finance, Risk Mgmt., Systems Implem.

Industries: Generalist

Professional Associations: ISACA, NAPS

Dunhill Professional Search of Corpus Christi

4455 S Padre Island Dr Ste 102
Corpus Christi, TX 78411-5101
(361) 225-2580
(800) 277-3690
Fax: (361) 225-3888
Email: dfry@talentscouts.com
Web: www.talentscouts.com

Description: Our president is a certified personnel consultant with 28 years of experience. We specialize in all engineering functions, mostly product development and manufacturing engineering in the HVAC industry.

Key Contact:
Mr. Don Fry, President - *HVAC, engineers (design & development) manufacturing, stress & finite element analysis*
Ms. Kay Garza, Consultant
Ms. Barbara LaSelva, Consultant

Salary minimum: $40,000

Functions: Product Dev.

Industries: Mfg., Misc. Mfg.

Dunhill Professional Search of Dwtn Fort Worth

669 Airport Fwy Ste 310
Hurst, TX 76053-3963
(817) 282-8367
Fax: (817) 282-1142
Email: abarham@flash.net
Web: www.dunhillstaff.com

Key Contact:
Mr. Andrew Barham, President
Ms. Sue Barham, Staffing Consultant
Ms. Denise Babineau, Account Executive

Functions: Legal

Industries: Generalist

Dunhill Professional Search of Mansfield

110 N Main St
Mansfield, TX 76063-1724
(817) 453-4473
Fax: (817) 453-3932
Email: lanamorris@prodigy.net
Web: www.dunhillmansfield.com

Description: We place qualified candidates in salaried positions within all areas of food and beverage manufacturing and logistics industries.

With over 29 years' experience, we feel we have a strong understanding of these industries.

Key Contact - Specialty:
Ms. Lana K. Morris, CPC, President - *Food, beverage manufacturing, logistics*
Mr. Harry G. Morris, CPC, Executive Vice President - *Food & beverage manufacturing, logistics, food R&D*

Salary minimum: $30,000

Functions: Generalist, General Mgmt., Mfg., Product Dev., Production, Plant Mgmt., Quality, Materials, R&D

Industries: Mfg., Food, Bev., Tobacco, Accounting, Packaging, HR SW, Industry Specific SW, Mfg. SW

Professional Associations: NAPS

Dunhill Professional Search of Rockport

PO Box 1119
Rockport, TX 78381-1119
(361) 727-9797
(888) 974-7723
Fax: (361) 727-9494
Email: search@dunhillrockport.com
Web: www.dunhillstaff.com/roctx

Description: We are a contingency search firm specializing in professional positions in the chemical industry and manufacturing, quality, and management positions in the food and beverage manufacturing industry. We are associated with over 125 Dunhill Staffing offices in the US and Canada.

Key Contact - Specialty:
Mr. Jim Gunnin, President/Managing Partner - *Chemical industry professionals*
Ms. Barbara Gurtner, Vice President, Consultant - *Food & beverage manufacturing*
Ms. Gail Brockett, Recruiter - *Chemical industry customer service professionals*

Functions: Product Dev., Production, Plant Mgmt., Quality, Purchasing, Sales & Mktg., Mkt. Research, Mktg. Mgmt., Customer Svc., HR Mgmt.

Industries: Food, Bev., Tobacco, Chemicals, Plastics, Rubber

Professional Associations: ACS, NAPS

Dunhill Professional Search of New Braunfels

14514 Majestic Prince
San Antonio, TX 78248-1133
(210) 492-5435
Fax: (210) 492-5297
Email: angella@connecti.com
Web: www.dunhillstaff.com

Key Contact:
Ms. Angella Woodard, CPC, President

Functions: Engineering

Industries: Energy, Utilities, Mfg., Transportation, HR Services, Haz. Waste

Dunhill Professional Search of Vermont

PO Box 204
Warren, VT 05674-0204
(802) 496-0115
Fax: (802) 496-0116
Email: dunhill@wcvt.com
Web: www.dunhillstaff.com

Description: Contingency and retainer search for accounting/financial/EDP audit professional, 2+ years' experience. Work closely with Big 6 firms for referrals as well as major MBA schools, customized searches as required.

Key Contact - Specialty:
Mr. Herb Hauser, President/Treasurer - *Accounting & finance, EDP audit, auditing*
Ms. Renate Von Recklinghausen, Vice President - *Accounting & finance, auditing*

Salary minimum: $35,000

Functions: Generalist, Middle Mgmt., Budgeting, Taxes, M&A

Industries: Generalist

Dunhill Professional Search of Vancouver

1681 Chestnut St Ste 400
Vancouver, BC V6J 4M6
Canada
(604) 739-0100
Email: dunvan@home.com
Web: www.dunhillstaff.com/vncan

Description: Executive search firm with a pedigree. We specialize in the placement of proven high achievers in sales, engineering, and finance. We cover a broad base of industries with a significant focus on high-tech and telecommunications.

Key Contact:
Mr. Peter Hamilton, President

Salary minimum: $75,000

Functions: General Mgmt., Plant Mgmt., Sales & Mktg., Sales Mgmt., Finance, Engineering

Industries: Generalist, Food, Bev., Tobacco, Paints, Petro. Products, Banking, Misc. Financial, Telecoms, Call Centers, Telephony, Digital, Wireless, Fiber Optic, Network Infrastructure

Professional Associations: NAPS, VEA

Dunhill Personnel Search of North York

5650 Yonge St Ste 1500
North York, ON M2M 4G3
Canada
(905) 771-6241
Web: www.dunhillstaff.com

Description: Offering confidential mid- to senior-level search in accounting, anywhere in Ontario. We have a networking arrangement with other Dunhill offices. For U.S. Companies with Ontario operations or Canadian companies.

Key Contact:
Mr. Peter Pollock, President

Functions: Finance

Industries: Generalist

The William Dunne Agency Inc

825C Merrimon Ave Ste 370
Asheville, NC 28804
(828) 253-0990
Fax: (828) 253-0089
Email: resume@williamdunneagency.com

Description: We specialize in the identification, screening and referral of qualified commercial finance personnel. We place all levels from CEO to middle management, including auditors, and operations personnel at various levels. Companies Served: asset based lenders, mezzanine lenders, commercial banks, healthcare lenders, leasing companies, inventory lenders, factoring lenders.

Key Contact:
Mr. Darin G. Kohler, President

Functions: Generalist

Industries: Finance, Banking

Dussick Management Associates

149 Durham Rd Ste 27A
Madison, CT 06443
(203) 245-9311
Fax: (203) 245-9570
Email: dussick@aol.com

Description: Since 1984, we have specialized in the executive recruitment and placement of middle and senior-level consumer, trade and category marketing professionals as well as senior-level promotion talent (sales/consumer)in the consumer package goods industry. Our Fortune Top 25 client base has continually utilized our services for more than 10 years.

Key Contact - Specialty:
Mr. Vince Dussick - *Marketing, sales, promotion management*
Ms. Gayle Moran - *Marketing, sales, promotion management*
Ms. Carol Kinney - *Marketing, sales, promotion management*
Mr. Mike Piccione - *Marketing, sales, promotion management*

Salary minimum: $60,000

Functions: Generalist, Senior Mgmt., Healthcare, Advertising, Mktg. Mgmt., Sales Mgmt., HR Mgmt., Int'l.

Industries: Generalist, Food, Bev., Tobacco, Textiles, Apparel, Soap, Perf., Cosmtcs., Drugs Mfg., Consumer Elect., Pharm Svcs.

Networks: First Interview Network (FIN)

G L Dykstra Associates Inc

PO Box 8085
Holland, MI 49422-8035
(616) 786-9419
Fax: (616) 786-9427
Email: genedykstra@hotmail.com

Description: Exclusive executive search and staffing for small, expanding companies of 100 to 1,000 employees. Concentrating on all areas, however primarily manufacturing, engineering, finance and sales management.

Key Contact:
Mr. Gene L. Dykstra, President
Ms. Glenda M. Dykstra, Secretary

Salary minimum: $60,000

Functions: Middle Mgmt.

Industries: Mfg., Plastics, Rubber, Paints, Petro. Products, Metal Products, Motor Vehicles, Accounting

Dynamic Choices Inc

36 Four Seasons Ct Ste 330
Chesterfield, MO 63017
(314) 878-8575

Description: Well-connected information technology specialist with 20 years' high-technology industry experience maintains network of contacts nationwide. Provides professional confidential executive search services on contingency basis.

Key Contact - Specialty:
Ms. Nancy J. Riehl, President - *Information technology*

Salary minimum: $35,000

Functions: Generalist, Sales Mgmt., MIS Mgmt., Systems Analysis, Systems Dev., Systems Implem., Network Admin., Mgmt. Consultants

Industries: Generalist, Computer Equip., Finance, Accounting, Telecoms, Software

Dynamic Computer Consultants Inc

3080 N Civic Center Plz Ste 47
PO Box 3150
Scottsdale, AZ 85271-3150
(480) 990-8179
Fax: (602) 296-0259
Email: jobs@dynamiccomputer.com
Web: www.dynamiccomputer.com

Description: We provide a full range of service including: Permanent placement and consulting in programming, analysis, project management, network support, technical writing, Internet/intranet design and operations and technical support.

Key Contact - Specialty:
Mr. Roc Rogers, President - *Information technology, midrange, mainframe, PC, client server personnel*

Functions: IT

Industries: Generalist

Dynamic Executive Search

197 County Court Blvd Ste 101
Brampton, ON L6W 4P6
Canada
(905) 796-3311
Fax: (905) 796-5251
Email: nancyw@dynamicemployment.com
Web: www.dynamicemployment.com

Description: We are a professional team providing services in recruitment and human resources consulting. We are dedicated to targeting your search through understanding your needs and customizing the search to meet them. Our client base includes start-up, large, and Fortune 500 corporations.

Key Contact:
Mrs. Sylvie Hyndman, President
Mrs. Nancy Weisner, Vice President

Salary minimum: $55,000

Functions: Generalist, Distribution, Finance

Industries: Generalist, Mfg., Finance, Pharm Svcs., Digital, Wireless, Fiber Optic, Healthcare

Professional Associations: BOT, HRPAO, TEC

Dynamic Search Systems Inc

3800 N Wilke Rd Ste 485
Arlington Heights, IL 60004
(847) 259-3444
Fax: (847) 259-3480
Email: resumes@dssjobs.com
Web: www.dssjobs.com

Description: We place information technology professionals including applications developers, programmers, programmer/analysts, systems analysts, project leaders/managers, application managers/directors and technical services/systems programmers, and administrators covering operating systems, telecommunications, and database.

Key Contact - Specialty:
Mr. Michael J. Brindise, Principal - *MIS*

Salary minimum: $25,000

Functions: IT

Industries: Generalist

Professional Associations: IAPS, NAPS

Dynamic Staffing Network

1200 Harger Rd Ste 600
Oak Brook, IL 60523
(630) 572-9980
Fax: (630) 572-9892
Email: rich_bradley@dynastaff.com
Web: www.dynastaff.com

Description: We service the greater Chicago metropolitan area with recruiters that average over seven years in the business. We strive to have our clients look forward to working with us again...and they do.

Key Contact - Specialty:
Mr. Richard Bradley, CPC, Vice President - *Information systems*
Mr. George Custer, Secretary/Treasurer - *Manufacturing, accounting*
Mr. James Gilbert, President - *Engineering*

Functions: Generalist, General Mgmt., Mfg., Materials, Finance, IT, Engineering

Industries: Generalist

Professional Associations: IACPR

E Insurance Group
10563 Greencrest Dr
Tampa, FL 33626
(813) 926-0306
Fax: (813) 926-5393
Email: michael@einsgroup.com
Web: www.einsgroup.com

Description: We are a national insurance search firm committed to insurance and technology industries. Our focus is with agencies and brokerage firms, carriers, reinsurance, T.P.A.s, consulting firms, technology, start-ups, mergers and acquisitions, etc. Our placement activity includes, but is not limited to, executive management, risk management services, sales and marketing, underwriting, project management, CIO, practice leader, healthcare, medical malpractice, and employee benefits.

Key Contact:
Mr. Michael S. Evdemon, II, President

Salary minimum: $75,000

Functions: Generalist, Directors, Senior Mgmt., Middle Mgmt., Healthcare, Sales & Mktg., Mktg. Mgmt., Sales Mgmt., Risk Mgmt., Mgmt. Consultants

Industries: Energy, Utilities, Construction, Legal, Hospitality, Hotels, Resorts, Clubs, Environmental Svcs., Insurance, Biotech, Healthcare, Hospitals

E O Technical
57 North St Ste 320
Danbury, CT 06810
(203) 797-2653
Fax: (203) 797-2657
Email: jeanette@employops.com
Web: www.employops.com

Description: We are a female-owned Connecticut operation open for one purpose; to serve our clients and our applicants.

Key Contact:
Ms. Jeanette Petroski, Owner
Mr. Gary Petroski

Functions: Generalist, MIS Mgmt., R&D

Industries: Generalist, Plastics, Rubber, Banking, Pharm Svcs., Legal, HR Services, IT Implementation, Defense, Insurance, Biotech, Healthcare

Professional Associations: NATSS, RON

Branches:
755 Main St
Monroe, CT 06468
(203) 455-8111
Fax: (203) 455-8112
Email: gary@employops.com
Key Contact - Specialty:
Mr. Gary Petroski - *Technical*

E/Search Int'l
2200 Mountain Rd
PO Box 408
West Suffield, CT 06093-0408
(860) 668-5848
(800) 300-0477
Email: esearch@earthlink.net
Web: www.esearchinternational.net

Description: We work for high-tech companies with highly focused executive-level needs. We specialize in targeting and finding top executives with direct competitors of our client companies.

Key Contact - Specialty:
Mr. Bob Rossow, President - *High technology executives*

Salary minimum: $100,000

Functions: Generalist, Senior Mgmt.

Industries: Electronic, Elec. Components, Communications, Telecoms, Telephony, Digital, Wireless, Network Infrastructure, Software, ERP SW, Mfg. SW, Marketing SW, Networking, Comm. SW

Eagle Consulting Group Inc
12300 Ford Rd Ste 150
Dallas, TX 75234
(972) 247-0990
Fax: (972) 247-4306
Email: mail@eaglesearch.net
Web: www.eaglesearch.net

Description: Our mission is to always provide excellence in performance while assuring the highest standards of professionalism and to meld our candidate delivery systems to meet each client's expectations and corporate objectives.

Key Contact - Specialty:
Mr. William G. Mitchell, President/Managing Director - *Biopharmaceutical*

Salary minimum: $60,000

Functions: Generalist, Senior Mgmt., Mfg., Production, Quality, Materials Plng., R&D, Engineering

Industries: Generalist, Mfg., Drugs Mfg., Pharm Svcs., Healthcare

J M Eagle Partners Ltd
11514 N Port Washington Rd Ste 105
Mequon, WI 53092
(262) 241-1400
Fax: (262) 241-4745
Email: jerry12@execpc.com
Web: www.execpc.com/~jerry12/

Description: A vertical approach to medical industry search. Specialization: in-depth knowledge and reputation within diagnostic imaging (radiology manufacturers).

Key Contact - Specialty:
Mr. Jerry Moses, President - *Medical capital equipment*

Salary minimum: $60,000

Functions: Generalist

Industries: Drugs Mfg., Medical Devices, Pharm Svcs., Equip Svcs., Mgmt. Consulting, HR Services, Software, Mfg. SW, Marketing SW, Biotech

Networks: First Interview Network (FIN)

Eagle Research Inc
373 D Rt 46W
Fairfield, NJ 07004
(973) 244-0992
Fax: (973) 244-1239
Email: asbaron@aol.com
Web: www.eagleresearch.net

Description: Specializing in the pharmaceutical and biotechnology industries with an emphasis in clinical research, medical marketing and activities related to drug development.

Key Contact - Specialty:
Ms. Annette S. Baron, President - *Pharmaceutical*

Functions: Healthcare, Physicians, R&D

Industries: Generalist

Professional Associations: DIA

Eagle Rock Consulting Group
13493 Post Rd
St. Louis, MO 63141
(314) 878-0900
Fax: (314) 878-0902
Email: billgeis@swbell.net

Description: We are a retained and contingent search firm with a focus on accounting and finance.

Key Contact - Specialty:
Mr. Bill Geis, Owner - *Accounting & finance*

Salary minimum: $50,000

Functions: Finance

Industries: Mfg.

Eagle Search Associates
336 Bon Air Ctr
PMB 295
Greenbrae, CA 94904-3017
(415) 398-6066
Fax: (415) 924-8996
Email: mark@eaglesearch.com
Web: www.eaglesearch.com

Description: Specializing in the placement of senior executives, sales management, salespeople and marketing professionals for software, hardware, application and e-commerce Internet vendors in either venture-backed startups or established firms. Additionally place IT managers, project directors and CIOs for Fortune 1000 firms.

Key Contact - Specialty:
Mr. Mark Gideon, Executive Director - *High technology, sales, sales support, managers, MIS executives*

Salary minimum: $80,000

Functions: General Mgmt., Directors, Senior Mgmt., Middle Mgmt.

Industries: Computer Equip., Telecoms, Software

Eagle Technology Group Inc
11575 Theo Trecker Way
Milwaukee, WI 53214
(800) 964-9675
Fax: (414) 453-9720
Email: info@eagleinc.net
Web: www.eagleinc.net

Description: We are a recognized "Future 50 Company" and have emerged as a leader in the placement of engineering, manufacturing, and technical professionals.

Key Contact - Specialty:
Mr. Jayson P. Komp, Vice President - National Operations - *Engineering*

Functions: Generalist, Mfg., Automation, Materials, Packaging, IT, R&D, Engineering, Architects, Technicians

Industries: Generalist, Mfg., Finance, Government, Insurance, Software, Healthcare

Professional Associations: HRMA, NTSA

Branches:
PO Box 1874
Appleton, WI 54912
(920) 720-6009
Fax: (920) 720-6027

Email: db@eagleinc.net
Key Contact - Specialty:
Mr. Don Barker - *Engineering, information systems*

Easley Resource Group Inc

333 S State St Ste 298
Lake Oswego, OR 97034
(503) 699-4067
Fax: (503) 635-3016
Email: jill@glassrecruiters.com
Web: www.glassrecruiters.com

Description: Specialize in bringing together
professionals and career opportunities within the
primary and secondary glass/ceramics industry. We
perform retained, contingency and contract
assignments for many of the best companies in the
our industry. Our energies are directed toward
locating and recruiting the finest talent for our client
companies operating throughout North America.
We do this the old fashioned way. We simply know
the glass industry better than anyone.

Key Contact - Specialty:
Ms. Jill Kohler-Easley, Principal/Recruiter - *Glass
industry*

Functions: Generalist

Industries: Mfg., Leather, Stone, Glass

Networks: Recruiters Professional Network (RPN)

Eastern Consulting Associates Inc

21 Woods Brooke Ct Bldg 5
Ossining, NY 10562-2026
(914) 762-5533
Fax: (914) 762-5544
Email: ceo@ecacorp.com
Web: www.ecacorp.com

Description: We are a leading business and
information systems technology consulting firm in
addition to specializing in executive search and
recruiting within the information technology and
financial disciplines.

Key Contact - Specialty:
Mr. Ralph J. Vaccarella, President/CEO -
*Information technology, finance, general
management*

Salary minimum: $60,000

Functions: Senior Mgmt., IT, MIS Mgmt., Mgmt.
Consultants

Industries: Food, Bev., Tobacco, Textiles, Apparel,
Chemicals, Drugs Mfg., Computer Equip.,
Finance, Banking, Invest. Banking, Misc.
Financial, Pharm Svcs., Mgmt. Consulting,
Hospitality, Insurance, Software, Healthcare

Professional Associations: APCNY

The Eastwing Group

1250 S Grove Ave
Barrington, IL 60010
(847) 381-0977
Fax: (847) 381-0955
Email: rjreastwing@aol.com

Key Contact:
Mr. Russ Riendeau

Salary minimum: $50,000

Functions: General Mgmt., Sales Mgmt., Direct
Mktg., PR, Specialized Svcs., Mgmt. Consultants

Industries: Energy, Utilities, Construction, Mfg.,
Banking, Venture Cap., Mgmt. Consulting,
Hospitality, Haz. Waste, Aerospace, Packaging

Professional Associations: IMC

Networks: First Interview Network (FIN)

eAttorneys

(a division of Net Placement Corp)
817 W Peachtree St Ste 700
Atlanta, GA 30308
(404) 962-8500
(800) 378-6101
Fax: (404) 962-8501
Email: recruitingconsultants@eattorney.com
Web: www.eattorney.com

Description: Taking the place of a traditional search
firm, we are a company that links hundreds of legal
employers with thousands of individual attorneys
and students confidentially via a secured website.

Key Contact - Specialty:
Mr. Samuel B. Kellett, Jr., Executive Vice
President - *Law*

Functions: Generalist, Attorneys

Industries: Generalist, Legal

eBizPeople Inc

6600 S 1100 E Ste 520
Salt Lake City, UT 84121-2400
(801) 264-8900
Email: dirk@ebizpeople.com
Web: www.ebizpeople.com

Description: We are industry experts in the niches
we serve. Additionally we emphasize matching
corporate culture with individual personality and
chemistry. We use computer-assisted personality
assessment tools and face-to-face video conference
interviewing to ensure success.

Key Contact - Specialty:
Mr. Dirk A. Cotterell, President - *Information
technology*

Salary minimum: $80,000

Functions: Sales & Mktg., IT, Systems Analysis,
Systems Dev.

Industries: Consumer Elect., New Media,
Telecoms, Software

EBS Northwest Inc

PO Box 459
Bothell, WA 98041-0459
(425) 486-4235
Fax: (603) 719-1207
Email: resume@ebs-northwest.com
Web: www.ebs-northwest.com

Description: Software development, information
systems, high-tech manufacturing and all types of
engineering placements. Newly started medical
placement division for nursing and hospital
placements. Geographic focus is the Pacific
Northwest.

Key Contact - Specialty:
Mrs. Jeanine K. Kern, President - *Software,
information systems, engineering*

Functions: Quality, Materials, MIS Mgmt.,
Systems Analysis, Systems Dev., Systems
Implem., Systems Support, Network Admin., DB
Admin., Engineering

Industries: Generalist, Energy, Utilities, Mfg.,
Computer Equip., Consumer Elect., Test, Measure
Equip., Electronic, Elec. Components,
Environmental Svcs., Software

Professional Associations: RON, SHRM

ECG Resources Inc

215 N Ocean Ave
Patchogue, NY 11772
(516) 447-1118
Fax: (516) 447-1142
Email: daveglaser@ecgresources.com
Web: www.ecgresources.com

Description: Executive financial planning, estates,
trusts, high net worth taxation, concentrating in the

financial services sector. Contacts include CPAs,
attorneys, CFPs and financial planning professionals
from varied backgrounds.

Key Contact - Specialty:
Mr. David Glaser, President - *Executive financial
planning, estates, trust, tax*

Salary minimum: $50,000

Functions: Generalist, Benefits, Taxes, Attorneys

Industries: Generalist

Eckert Recruiting Services

2112 Timberwood Pl
Nashville, TN 37215
(615) 309-0837
Fax: (615) 373-1794
Email: jobs@hiringconnection.com
Web: www.hiringconnection.com

Description: We are a permanent placement firm
specializing in accounting, sales, and technical
placements.

Key Contact:
Mr. John Eckert

Functions: General Mgmt., Middle Mgmt., Mfg.,
Sales Mgmt., Finance, IT

Industries: Generalist

Professional Associations: TSCPA

Eckler Personnel Network

PO Box 549
Woodstock, VT 05091
(802) 457-1605
Fax: (802) 457-1606
Email: epn@sover.net

Description: Regionalized search and contingency
placement firm specializing in all levels of business
software and management information systems
professionals. Servicing clients throughout the
Northeastern U.S.

Key Contact - Specialty:
Mr. Geoffrey N. Eckler, President - *Information
systems, business software*

Salary minimum: $100,000

Functions: Generalist, Sales & Mktg., MIS Mgmt.;
Systems Analysis, Systems Dev., Systems
Implem., Systems Support, Network Admin., DB
Admin.

Industries: Generalist, Mgmt. Consulting, E-
commerce, IT Implementation, PSA/ASP,
Software

Professional Associations: NNEAPS

Eclectic Int'l Executive Search

139 Welsh St Ste 10
San Francisco, CA 94115
(415) 222-6082
Fax: (415) 371-9705
Email: info@eclectic-usa.com
Web: www.eclectic-usa.com

Description: EclectiC USA, Inc. is strategically
placed with offices in Philadelphia, PA (US
headquarters), Atlanta, GA, and San Francisco, CA.
and is ready to provide critical assistance for your
most difficult staffing challenges or serve as the
search engine for your next career opportunity.
Clients: EclectiC works closely with leading
organizations such as the Big 5, international system
integration and software development firms as well
as pre-IPO start-ups. EclectiC finds talent for
leadership, technology, sales and marketing roles
mainly in the areas of eBusiness Solutions, ERP,
Customer Relation

Key Contact:
Mr. Roel Deuss, Practice Manager

Salary minimum: $80,000

Functions: Generalist

Industries: Energy, Utilities, Services, Pharm Svcs., Mgmt. Consulting, E-commerce, IT Implementation, PSA/ASP, Communications, Telecoms, Call Centers, Telephony, Digital, Wireless, Fiber Optic, Network Infrastructure, Software, Accounting SW, Database SW, Development SW, Doc. Mgmt., Production SW, ERP SW, HR SW, Industry Specific SW, Mfg. SW, Marketing SW, Networking, Comm. SW, Biotech, Healthcare

Edelman & Associates
3 Virginia Dr Ste 200
Lakeville, MA 02347
(508) 947-5300
Email: paul@edeltech.com
Web: www.edeltech.com

Description: Our firm is an executive search and technical recruiting firm serving software, Internet, and electronic commerce companies. Most of our clients are based in the Boston area. We assist them in filling key positions in the Boston area and in other high tech centers across the US.

Key Contact:
Mr. Paul Edelman, Sole Proprietor - *Software, internet, e-commerce*
Ms. Paul Lubin, Vice President/Research - *Data mining, data warehousing*
Ms. Michelle Leonard, Executive Search Associate - *Sales, marketing, business development*
Ms. Susan Denison, Executive Search Associate

Salary minimum: $85,000

Functions: Generalist

Industries: E-commerce, IT Implementation, PSA/ASP, Database SW, Development SW

The Edelstein Group
198 Ave of the Americas Ste 1
New York, NY 10013
(212) 925-7078
Fax: (212) 925-7339
Email: sue@edelsteingroup.com
Web: www.edelsteingroup.com

Description: We specialize in mid-level and senior management searches within the advertising, strategic planning and branding, and Internet industries. Our primary focus is on account management, marketing, account planning, project management, branding, and business development.

Key Contact:
Ms. Sue Edelstein

Salary minimum: $75,000

Functions: General Mgmt., Directors, Senior Mgmt., Middle Mgmt., Advertising

Industries: Advertising, New Media, Marketing SW

Eden & Associates Inc
794 N Valley Rd
Paoli, PA 19301
(610) 889-9993
Fax: (610) 889-9660
Email: beden1@aol.com

Description: We are a specialized national executive search and recruiting organization focusing on serving the critical hiring needs of retailers, distributors, manufacturers, brokers, hospitality trades and related consulting organizations.

Key Contact - Specialty:
Mr. Brooks D. Eden, President - *Senior executives*
Mr. Fred A. Nunziata, Executive Vice President - *Financial, distribution, middle management*
Mr. Earl M. Eden, Senior Chairman - *Administration*

Mr. Greg Edwards, Vice President - *Middle management, retail, sales*

Salary minimum: $65,000

Functions: Generalist, Directors, Senior Mgmt., Middle Mgmt., Purchasing, Distribution, CFO's, MIS Mgmt.

Industries: Generalist, Food, Bev., Tobacco, Transportation, Wholesale, Retail, Advertising, Real Estate

Professional Associations: FMI

The Edge Resource Group
PO Box 457
Greensburg, PA 15601
(724) 523-4795
Fax: (724) 523-5840
Email: edgegrp@westol.com
Web: www.westol.com

Description: Executive search specializing in software sales, senior human resources, and MIS positions.

Key Contact - Specialty:
Ms. Diane L. Schoff, President - *Software sales, senior HR (all industries), senior finance (all industries), MIS, senior level information systems positions*

Salary minimum: $50,000

Functions: Sales Mgmt., HR Mgmt.

Industries: Generalist, Media, Telecoms, Software

Professional Associations: RON

Networks: Top Echelon Network

The Edgewater Group Inc
100 Park Ave Ste 1600
New York, NY 10017
(212) 880-6402
Email: info@ewatergroup.com
Web: www.ewatergroup.com

Description: Our firm is an information technology, recruiting firm servicing technology professionals in the financial services, software, consulting, and pharmaceutical industries throughout the NY Metropolitan Area.

Key Contact:
Mr. Mark Dinowitz, President
Mr. Peter Friedman, Vice President

Salary minimum: $60,000

Functions: IT

Industries: Finance, Pharm Svcs., Accounting, Publishing, Communications, Insurance, Software

EDP Staffing Solutions Inc
4 Shackleford Plz Ste 202
Little Rock, AR 72211
(501) 225-3000
Email: itsearch@swbell.net
Web: www.recruitme.com

Description: Technology can take you part of the way....but it takes an information technology staff with vision, talent and technical know-how to get you to the front of the pack. We are information technology specialists with over 40 years' experience. Call us today!

Key Contact:
Ms. Marjean Bean, CPC, President - *Data processing*
Ms. Ellen Howland, Vice President

Salary minimum: $35,000

Functions: IT

Industries: Generalist

Professional Associations: RON

Edwards & Associates
4015 Goshen Lake Dr S
Augusta, GA 30906
(706) 793-3679
Fax: (706) 796-6611
Email: e4015@mindspring.com
Web: www.edwardsassociates.net

Description: Our primary focus is in sales and sales management (generalist as well as pharmaceutical/medical). Our secondary focus is the staffing industry. Ideal candidate profile has a business product or service background, if not industry specific.

Key Contact - Specialty:
Ms. Lisa Edwards, Owner/President - *Sales, sales management, staffing*

Salary minimum: $25,000

Functions: Sales Mgmt.

Industries: Food, Bev., Tobacco, Textiles, Apparel, Drugs Mfg., Medical Devices, Pharm Svcs., Accounting, Telecoms, Wireless, Fiber Optic, HR SW

Networks: First Interview Network (FIN)

Edwards Search Group Inc
1804 Soscol Ave Ste 201
Napa, CA 94559
(707) 253-9200
Fax: (707) 253-9222
Email: kenn@edwardssg.com
Web: www.edwardssg.com

Description: We are the established leaders in the medical/healthcare contingency search and recruiting field. Our leadership position is in filling professional management and sales positions with quality individuals specifically chosen to meet your needs.

Key Contact - Specialty:
Mr. Kenn Edwards, President - *Medical device, pharmaceutical, sales & marketing*
Mr. Russ Cipriani, Vice President - *Medical device, sales & marketing*

Salary minimum: $50,000

Functions: Sales & Mktg.

Industries: Generalist

Professional Associations: FIN

Networks: First Interview Network (FIN)

Edwards-Polk & Associates
220 Bagley Ave Ste 408
Detroit, MI 48226-1412
(313) 964-3106
Fax: (313) 964-3646
Email: eugenesp@aol.com

Description: We offer complete HR services from compliance audit, assessments, background/reference checks and drug screens through interviews, employee relations, training and exit interviews. One stop shopping.

Key Contact:
Ms. Barbara J. Polk, President
Mr. Eugene S. Polk, Sr., Treasurer/Senior Consultant

Salary minimum: $25,000

Professional Associations: HRAD, SHRM

EFCO Consultants Inc
3 The Balsams
Roslyn, NY 11576
(516) 829-9200
Fax: (516) 484-7387
Email: nfells@efconet.com
Web: www.efconet.com

Description: EFCO specializes in the placement of information technology professionals.

Key Contact - Specialty:
Mr. Norman Fells, President - *Information systems (vendor)*

Salary minimum: $60,000

Functions: General Mgmt., Senior Mgmt., Middle Mgmt., Sales & Mktg., Mktg. Mgmt., Sales Mgmt., IT, Systems Implem., Systems Support, Mgmt. Consultants

Industries: Computer Equip., Mgmt. Consulting, Software

Branches:
5121 Varna Ave
Sherman Oaks, CA 91423
(818) 788-1555
Email: fells@efconet.com
Web: www.efcoconsultants.com
Key Contact:
Mr. Jeffrey Fells, Vice President

1 University Pl Ste 10
New York, NY 10003
(212) 979-5777
Fax: (212) 202-6412
Email: fells@efcnet.com
Web: www.efcoconsultants.com
Key Contact:
Mr. Jeff Fells, Vice President

Eggers Consulting Company Inc

11272 Elm St Ste Eggers Plz
Omaha, NE 68144-4788
(402) 333-3480
Fax: (402) 333-9759
Email: admin@eggersconsulting.com
Web: www.eggersconsulting.com

Description: Professional search and executive recruiting firm that works regionally and nationally. Specializing in banking, data processing, insurance, retail and recruiting. Have placed candidates in client companies in all 50 states.

Key Contact - Specialty:
Mr. James W. Eggers, President
Mr. Raymond Hamilius, Manager - *Retail*
Mr. J. W. Eggers, Manager - *Banking*
Ms. Ellen Hembertt, Treasurer/Vice President
Ms. L. D. Miller, Vice President - *Information technology*

Salary minimum: $25,000

Functions: Generalist, Sales Mgmt., Personnel, IT, MIS Mgmt., Network Admin., DB Admin.

Industries: Generalist, Medical Devices, Retail, Banking, Insurance, Database SW

Networks: First Interview Network (FIN)

W Robert Eissler & Associates Inc

26214 Oak Ridge Dr
The Woodlands, TX 77380
(281) 367-1052
Fax: (281) 292-6489
Email: eissler@eissler.com
Web: www.eissler.com

Description: Recruiters for nationwide senior and middle-level sales, marketing and technical positions. We specialize in the valve, instrumentation, automation, manufacturing software, fluid power, chemical, plastics, filtration, and environmental industries.

Key Contact - Specialty:
Mr. W. Robert Eissler - *Valve industry, process equipment*
Mr. David White - *Plastics*
Mr. Larry Patronella - *Distributed control systems, process software, instrumentation*
Ms. Marie Devaney - *Fluid power*

Mr. Gary Wyatt, Executive Recruiter - *Hazardous waste (treatment, disposal), environmental (engineering, consulting)*

Salary minimum: $25,000

Functions: Generalist

Industries: Mfg., Chemicals, Plastics, Rubber, Metal Products, Test, Measure Equip., Environmental Svcs., Haz. Waste

Professional Associations: AWWA, ISA, SPE, TAPPI

---

eJobs Inc

(also known as Global Employers Network)
12222 Merit Dr Ste 450
Dallas, TX 75251-2229
(972) 934-2100
Fax: (972) 788-1893
Email: info@ejobs.com
Web: www.ejobs.com

Description: Staffing consulting firm providing large-scale recruitment outsourcing, executive search, research, Internet services and other staffing related products and services. Functional emphasis in technologically driven organizations.

Key Contact:
Mr. Bob Lund, CEO

Salary minimum: $50,000

Functions: Sales & Mktg., Sales Mgmt., Finance, IT, MIS Mgmt., Systems Analysis, Network Admin., Engineering

Industries: Generalist, Telecoms, Real Estate, Software

Branches:
580 California St Fl 5 Ste 507
San Francisco, CA 94104
(415) 283-3235
Email: fsobrero@ejobs.com
Key Contact:
Mr. Frank Sobrero, COO

Elan Associates

1215 Parkinson Ave
Palo Alto, CA 94301
(650) 446-4963
(650) 828-3076
Email: chardy@got.net
Web: www.elanworld.com

Description: Elan is a leading provider of high quality search services to the technology industry both domestically and internationally. We work with both mature and early companies looking for staffing solutions both on a full-time or contracting basis. We specialize in senior level positions in the software, internet, networking, and biotech industries. We also provide inhouse recruiting services to growing companies wishing to focus on their core business.

Key Contact - Specialty:
Mr. Christopher Hardy, President
Ms. Eileen Landauer, Director of Search and Selection - *Senior management, technical staff*

Salary minimum: $90,000

Functions: Generalist, Senior Mgmt., Sales & Mktg., MIS Mgmt., Int'l.

Industries: Telecoms, Software, Biotech

The Eldridge Group Ltd

810 S Waukegan Rd Ste 102C
Lake Forest, IL 60045
(847) 295-4800
Fax: (847) 295-9981
Email: teg1@earthlink.net
Web: www.eldridgegroup.com

Description: Our firm is a Chicago Area based search firm with an extensive national network. The

company's founder, David Eldridge Archibald, started in the search business in 1983 with the largest placement firm in the world. Dave ranked in the top 5% of over 1200 search consultants and was encouraged by clients and candidates to strike out on his own. We concentrate on sales/management (primarily in consumer products), B2B, and some medical/pharmaceuticals assignments.

Key Contact - Specialty:
Mr. David Eldridge Archibald, President/Owner - *Sales, management, consumer products*

Functions: Generalist, Sales Mgmt.

Industries: Food, Bev., Tobacco, Paper, Soap, Perf., Cosmtcs., Drugs Mfg., Medical Devices, Computer Equip., Consumer Elect., Services, Pharm Svcs., Equip Svcs., Software, Healthcare

---

Electric Systems Personnel (ESP)

PO Box 6
Dade City, FL 33526
(352) 567-3353
(800) 277-1344
Fax: (352) 567-5348
Email: esppower@tingley.net
Web: www.esppower.2e.com

Description: Locating qualified candidates for key positions in the electric utility industry and their consultants. Resumes released to clients only on candidate's approval.

Key Contact - Specialty:
Mr. Joe Botto, Consultant - *Electric, utilities*
Ms. Lynette Gray, Executive Employment Recruiter/Counselor - *Electric, utilities, consultants*

Functions: Generalist

Industries: Energy, Utilities

Networks: Inter-City Personnel Assoc (IPA)

Electronic Search Inc

3601 Algonquin Rd Ste 820
Rolling Meadows, IL 60008
(847) 506-0700
(800) 356-3501
Fax: (847) 506-9999
Email: email@electronicsearch.com
Web: www.electronicsearch.com

Description: Staffing firm specializing in placements in the computer and telecommunications industry. Emphasis on personal relationships and in providing the right personnel match.

Key Contact - Specialty:
Ms. Linda Shepherd, Operations Manager
Mr. Steve Eddington, President - *Information technology*
Mr. Al Born, Vice President - *Telecommunications*
Ms. Cathy Bayer, Manager - *Customized staffing services for outsource recruiting*

Functions: Generalist, IT, MIS Mgmt., Systems Analysis, Systems Dev., Systems Implem., Engineering, Int'l.

Industries: Generalist, Computer Equip., Misc. Financial, Mgmt. Consulting, Telecoms, Software

Professional Associations: CTIA

Networks: Top Echelon Network

Branches:
990 Highland Dr Ste 212-K
Solana Beach, CA 92075
(858) 792-8108
(800) 355-5927
Fax: (858) 792-8121
Email: jmiller@electronicsearch.com
Key Contact - Specialty:
Mr. John Miller - *Telecommunications*

---

100 Lovers Ln Ste 205
Ft. Myers Beach, FL 33931
(941) 765-8500
(800) 361-4102
Fax: (941) 765-8600
Email: tgriffin@electronicsearch.com
Key Contact - Specialty:
Mr. Terry Griffen - *Telecommunications*

69 Main Ave
Ocean Grove, NJ 07756
(732) 775-5017
(800) 361-7740
Fax: (732) 775-5035
Email: tmanni@electronicsearch.com
Key Contact - Specialty:
Mr. Tom Manni - *Telecommunications*

Elinvar
3200 Beechleaf Ct Ste 409
Raleigh, NC 27604
(919) 878-4454
Fax: (919) 878-0634
Email: info@elinvar.com
Web: www.elinvar.com

Description: We are a locally owned recruiting and
consulting firm specializing in recruiting in the
areas of accounting, finance, and human resources
for temp, temp-to-hire and direct hire and consulting
in all areas of human resource and training.

Key Contact:
Ms. Patti Gillenwater, President and CEO -
Accounting & finance, human resources
Mr. Stuart Levine, Vice President, Human
Resource Services

Salary minimum: $25,000

Functions: Generalist, Purchasing, HR Mgmt.,
Finance, Specialized Svcs.

Industries: Generalist, Mfg., Finance, Services,
Insurance, Real Estate

Professional Associations: NCASP, SHRM

Elite Consultants Inc
976 Florida Central Pkwy Ste 112
Longwood, FL 32750
(407) 831-3448
Fax: (407) 260-1347
Email: elite@totcon.com
Web: www.elite-eci.com

Description: We maintain a large network of
engineers and clients located throughout the U.S.
and China; our resources enable us to quickly match
our clients' need with the right expertise.

Key Contact:
Mrs. Janeen Cepull, General Manager

Functions: Generalist, Systems Dev., Systems
Implem., Systems Support, Network Admin.,
Engineering

Industries: Generalist, Telecoms, Software

Elite Medical Search
100 Crescent Centre Pkwy Ste 360
Tucker, GA 30084
(770) 908-2113
(800) 849-5502
Fax: (770) 908-2203
Email: info@elitesearch.com
Web: www.elitesearch.com

Description: We are a priority search firm working
nationally with clients including many of the
Fortune 500, niche firms and healthcare providers.

Key Contact - Specialty:
Mr. David Alexander, President - *Healthcare*
Mr. Ron Washburn, Administrator - *Medical device*

Salary minimum: $40,000

Functions: Generalist, Product Dev., Production,
Nurses, Health Admin., Systems Dev., R&D,
Engineering

Industries: Generalist, Mfg., Medical Devices,
Pharm Svcs., Healthcare

Professional Associations: AHA, GAPS

Elite Placement Service Inc
3100 Timmons Ln Ste 120
Houston, TX 77027
(713) 403-1388
Email: watson@eliteplacement.com
Web: www.eliteplacement.com

Description: Our firm is an executive search firm
that specializes in the placement of experienced
information technology, management, marketing,
HR, and sales professionals. It is our pleasure to
represent some the most prominent companies in
Texas and the US

Key Contact:
Mrs. Michelle Watson, President

Salary minimum: $50,000

Functions: Directors, Senior Mgmt., Middle
Mgmt., Product Dev., Sales Mgmt., HR Mgmt.,
IT, MIS Mgmt., DB Admin.

Industries: Generalist, Mgmt. Consulting, HR
Services, E-commerce, IT Implementation,
Software, Marketing SW, Networking, Comm.
SW, Security SW, Biotech

Networks: Top Echelon Network

Elite Staffing Services Inc
6046 Cornerstone Ct W
San Diego, CA 92121
(858) 455-8300
Fax: (858) 455-8383
Email: lisad@elitestaffingsvc.com
Web: www.elitestaffingsvc.com

Description: We specialize in the placement of
professionals at all levels of: science and
biotechnology management, information technology
and technical, administration and clerical, human
resources, and accounting and finance. Our clients
are mainly biotechnology, pharmaceutical, and high
technology companies.

Key Contact:
Ms. Lisa DeBenedittis, President

Functions: Generalist

Industries: Mfg., Services, Communications,
Aerospace, Real Estate, Software, Biotech,
Healthcare

Professional Associations: CSP

Gene Ellefson & Associates Inc
330 Town Center Dr Ste 304
Dearborn, MI 48126
(313) 982-6000
(313) 982-6000
Email: gellefson@advdata.net

Description: We specialize in recruiting and placing
with the automotive OEM manufacturers and their
Tier I, II, etc suppliers. We work with engineering,
sales, accounting/finance, and purchasing, etc
positions. Most of the positions are located in and
around the Detroit, MI Area.

Key Contact - Specialty:
Mr. Gene Ellefson, President - *Automotive OEM's,
automotive suppliers*

Salary minimum: $60,000

Functions: Generalist

Industries: Motor Vehicles

Professional Associations: MASS, SAE, SME

Phil Ellis Associates Inc
1908 Eastwood Rd Ste 317
Wilmington, NC 28403
(910) 256-9810
Fax: (910) 256-9887
Email: bethsmith@pellis.com
Web: www.pellis.com

Description: Pharmaceutical, biotechnology,
medical device search and recruiting.

Key Contact - Specialty:
Mr. Phil Ellis, President
Mr. Lee Douglas, Principal - *Science & technology*
Mr. John Lee, Principal - *Operations, quality,
engineering*

Salary minimum: $50,000

Functions: Generalist

Industries: Chemicals, Drugs Mfg., Medical
Devices, Biotech

Ellis Career Consultants
1090 Broadway
West Long Branch, NJ 07764
(732) 222-5333
Fax: (732) 222-2332
Email: info@elliscareer.com
Web: www.elliscareer.com

Description: Placing executive, corporate,
merchandising, distribution, financial and senior
field people in the retail community.

Key Contact - Specialty:
Ms. Lisa Shapiro, President - *Retail*

Salary minimum: $60,000

Functions: Directors, Senior Mgmt., Product Dev.,
Purchasing, Distribution, Advertising, Mktg.
Mgmt., Sales Mgmt., HR Mgmt., Finance

Industries: Textiles, Apparel, Wholesale, Retail

Professional Associations: NAFE, NJSA

Steve Ellis
3207 Colorado Ave Ste 3
Santa Monica, CA 90404
(310) 829-0611
Fax: (310) 829-2024
Email: searchellis@aol.com

Description: We provide individualized executive
search for commercial and corporate banking. We
specialize in financial services and place in sales
and marketing professionals. We recruit for both
retainer and exclusive contingency clients.

Key Contact - Specialty:
Mr. Steve Ellis, President - *Commercial banking,
corporate banking*

Salary minimum: $50,000

Functions: Generalist, Senior Mgmt., Middle
Mgmt.

Industries: Generalist, Banking, Misc. Financial,
Hospitality

The Ellsworth Group
225 Brooklyn Bridge Blvd Ste 6H
Brooklyn, NY 11201
(718) 237-4084
Fax: (718) 855-2859
Email: kennedy@ellsworthgroup.com
Web: www.ellsworthgroup.com

Description: We are a national executive search
firm specializing in placing mid- to upper-level
marketing, communications, e-business and sales
professionals.

Key Contact - Specialty:
Mr. Kirk Nicklas, President - *Marketing,
communications, sales, e-business*

Mr. Rory Kelly, Vice President - *Marketing, communications, sales, e-business*

Salary minimum: $60,000

Functions: Sales & Mktg.

Industries: Finance, Services, Pharm Svcs., Aerospace, Insurance, Healthcare

The Elmhurst Group

4120 Douglas Blvd Ste 306-206
Granite Bay, CA 95746
(916) 772-6720
Fax: (916) 786-2981
Email: teg@elmhurstgroup.com

Description: We are a California-based national recruiting firm focusing on IT and the e-commerce. Our client companies include newly venture capital-backed start-ups to Fortune 500 and 1000 companies. We specialize in linking talent and technology for better business.

Key Contact - Specialty:
Ms. Shari Miller, Principal - *Information technology, e-commerce*

Functions: Senior Mgmt., Middle Mgmt., Product Dev., Sales & Mktg., IT, MIS Mgmt., Systems Dev., Systems Implem., DB Admin., Mgmt. Consultants

Industries: Computer Equip., Venture Cap., Mgmt. Consulting, HR Services, Media, Advertising, New Media, Telecoms, Software

Professional Associations: NAFE, RON, SHRM

Networks: National Personnel Assoc (NPA)

The Elsworth Group

12910 Queens Forest Ste B
San Antonio, TX 78230-1539
(210) 493-7211
Fax: (210) 493-6873
Email: elsworth@txdirect.net

Description: We serve the aerospace, high-technology and other manufacturing industries.

Key Contact:
Ms. Beverly W. O'Daniel, Director - *Aerospace, high technology, manufacturing*
Mr. James E. O'Daniel, Director

Salary minimum: $35,000

Functions: Generalist

Industries: Aerospace

Dana Elwess Placements Inc

7790 E Arapahoe Rd Ste 200
Englewood, CO 80112
(303) 773-6962
Fax: (720) 482-0855
Email: danaelwess@aol.com
Web: www.danaelwesplacements.com

Description: The recruiting resource that serves small, medium and large employers. The only company of its kind to offer multi-market placement positions to identify top candidates in all arenas from accounting to top executive officers.

Key Contact - Specialty:
Ms. Dana Elwess, President - *Communications, insurance, manufacturing, real estate*

Salary minimum: $28,000

Functions: Generalist, General Mgmt., Mfg., Materials, Sales & Mktg., HR Mgmt., Finance

Industries: Generalist, Energy, Utilities, Mfg., Finance, Media, Government, Insurance

Professional Associations: CHRA

Emerald Telecommunications Int'l Inc

1054 Welwyn Dr
Mississauga, ON L5J 3J3
Canada
(905) 823-8505
Fax: (905) 823-6971
Email: kcarroll@sympatico.ca

Description: Technical and professional recruiting, consulting and project management for the international telecommunications industry.

Key Contact:
Mr. Kieran Carroll, President

Salary minimum: $50,000

Functions: Generalist

Industries: Mgmt. Consulting, HR Services, Media, Telecoms

Emerging Technology Search Inc

625 W Crossville Rd Ste 204
Roswell, GA 30075
(770) 643-4994
Fax: (770) 643-4991
Email: careers@emergingtech.com
Web: www.emergingtech.com

Description: Our firm services the information technology, manufacturing, and accounting/finance industries. In 2000, EmergingTech placed over 50 software engineers, project managers, systems analysts, and sales and accounting professionals.

Key Contact - Specialty:
Mr. Peter A. Lehrman, CPC, President - *IT, sales*
Ms. Laura M. Lehrman, Vice President/Controller - *Accounting, finance, audit*

Salary minimum: $50,000

Functions: Sales & Mktg., Finance, IT

Industries: Mfg., Drugs Mfg., Computer Equip., Transportation, Wholesale, Retail, Finance, Services, Hospitality, Media, Communications, Software, Accounting SW, Biotech, Healthcare, Non-classifiable

Professional Associations: GAPS, NAPS

Networks: National Personnel Assoc (NPA)

Emerging Technology Services Inc

1600 Arboretum Blvd Ste 209
Minneapolis, MN 55386-0215
(952) 443-4141
(800) 999-9387
Fax: (952) 443-4146
Email: hq@specializedrecruiters.com
Web: www.keepyouroptionsopen.com

Description: We specialize in recruiting for DBA, Data Warehouse, Data Architecture and Data Administration professionals across the U.S. on both direct and contract basis. Fortune 500 clients.

Key Contact - Specialty:
Mr. Kevin Kapaun, President - *Database administrators, data warehouse analysts, data administrators*

Salary minimum: $60,000

Functions: IT, DB Admin.

Industries: Generalist

Professional Associations: MAPS

Networks: Top Echelon Network

The Emeritus Group Inc

17159 W 13 Mile Rd
Southfield, MI 48076
(248) 647-9763
Fax: (248) 647-9778
Email: jmobrien@mediaone.net
Web: www.emeritusinc.com

Description: This is my "retirement company" I am now able to have fun again--at what I like doing best: Headhunting! I am one of the last of the "headhunters". 30+ years of executive recruiting experience in multiple industries but my first choice is healthcare. Trained 9 presidents of search firms. Check my website--then contact me.

Key Contact:
Mr. J. Michael O'Brien

Salary minimum: $65,000

Functions: Senior Mgmt.

Industries: Mfg., Medical Devices, Services, Non-profits, Mgmt. Consulting, HR Services, Software, Accounting SW, Database SW, HR SW, Healthcare, Hospitals, Long-term Care, Physical Therapy, Occupational Therapy, Women's

Professional Associations: AHHRM, CHA, HFMA, NAHSE

Emerson & Company

4485 Hwy 29 NW Ste 208
Lilburn, GA 30047
(770) 564-3215
Fax: (770) 925-9442
Email: hpopham@mindspring.com

Description: Middle to upper-management recruitment primarily in manufacturing.

Key Contact - Specialty:
Mr. Harold C. Popham, Owner - *Generalist, manufacturing*

Salary minimum: $35,000

Functions: Generalist

Industries: Mfg., Printing, Medical Devices, Wholesale

Emerson Personnel Group

1040 Kings Hwy N Ste 400
Cherry Hill, NJ 08034-1986
(856) 667-9180
Fax: (856) 667-0064
Email: wce@emersonpersonnel.com
Web: www.emersonpersonnel.com

Description: We provide permanent and temporary staffing solutions for employers in the South Jersey/Philadelphia area. We specialize in all areas of office placement, sales, technical and finance placement.

Key Contact - Specialty:
Mr. William Emerson, President - *Generalist*
Mr. Andy Dick, Consultant - *Telecommunication sales*
Ms. Jill Kraus, Consultant - *Finance, programmers*
Ms. Angie Lambrou, Consultant - *Office placement*

Functions: Generalist, General Mgmt., Admin. Svcs., Legal, Sales & Mktg., Finance, IT, Attorneys, Paralegals

Industries: Generalist, Wholesale, Retail, Legal, Telecoms

Professional Associations: NAPS

Empire Consulting Group

N5461 N Shore Ln
Fond du Lac, WI 54935
(920) 922-5779
(920) 322-9537
Fax: (920) 322-9537
Email: empire@powercom.net
Web: www.dice.dlinc.com/empire

Description: Tenured recruiters providing a high quality of service and maintaining high ethical standards. We belong to a network of recruiters and offer our personal guaranty.

Key Contact - Specialty:
Ms. Mary Gerlach, President - *Information systems, SAP, peoplesoft, oracle, BAAN*

Functions: Generalist

Industries: Generalist, Mfg., Computer Equip., Mgmt. Consulting, Software

Employ®
PO Box 2032
Media, PA 19063
(610) 565-1573
Fax: (610) 565-1573

Description: We recruit talent. Talent experienced with various industries in the disciplines of accounting, engineering, human resources and computer systems. We locate that difficult to find candidate.

Key Contact - Specialty:
Ms. Sayre Dixon, Owner/Operator - *Management level*

Salary minimum: $45,000

Functions: General Mgmt.

Industries: Drugs Mfg., Medical Devices, Computer Equip., Finance, Legal, Accounting, Insurance, Software, Biotech, Healthcare

Employers Network Inc
6565 S Dayton St Ste 3100
Greenwood Village, CO 80111
(303) 662-0990
Fax: (303) 662-0880
Email: employersnetwork@flashcom.net
Web: www.employersnetwork.com

Description: We are a private executive, IS/IT, engineering and healthcare search firm located in Denver, CO.

Key Contact - Specialty:
Mr. James L. Anderson, President - *Information systems, information technology, engineering, executive*
Mr. Michael A. Schledorn, Executive Vice President - *Information systems, information technology, engineering, executive*

Salary minimum: $60,000

Functions: Generalist, General Mgmt., IT

Industries: Computer Equip., Electronic, Elec. Components, Mgmt. Consulting, Communications, Telecoms, Telephony, Digital, Wireless, Fiber Optic, Network Infrastructure, Defense, Aerospace, Software, Biotech, Healthcare

Employment Solutions Group Inc
9420 Towne Sq Ave Ste 19
Cincinnati, OH 45242
(513) 791-1234
Fax: (513) 791-1614
Email: chris@esgsearch.com
Web: www.esgsearch.com

Description: We specialize in the search of professionals for both "brick," which includes: store and multi-unit management, merchandising, MIS, store planning, design, construction, and visual merchandising and "click," which includes: e-Commerce merchandising, marketing, web design/development, retailers, and those who serve the retail industry.

Key Contact - Specialty:
Mr. Chris Albrecht, President - *Retail*

Salary minimum: $50,000

Functions: Generalist, General Mgmt., Architects, Graphic Artists

Industries: Construction, Retail, Hospitality, New Media

Networks: Top Echelon Network

Employment Solutions Inc
1422 W Main St Ste 101B
Lewisville, TX 75067
(972) 221-5566
Fax: (972) 219-7154
Email: empsol@aol.com

Description: Recruitment and placement of IT-IS professionals in a wide range of industries.

Key Contact - Specialty:
Ms. Lynne Von Villas, Managing Director - *Information technology, information systems*

Functions: Generalist, IT, MIS Mgmt., Systems Dev., Systems Implem., Systems Support, Network Admin., DB Admin.

Industries: Generalist, Mfg., Media, Software

Professional Associations: TAPS

Energy Executives Inc
527 Medearis Dr
Charlotte, NC 28211
(704) 366-7981
Fax: (770) 564-5584
Email: peak@energyexecs.com
Web: www.energyexecs.com

Description: We successfully apply the years of industry and technical experience gained by our founders and employees to effectively recruiting the highest quality talent possible for our clients. All of our recruiters have energy industry experience, averaging over 8 years of experience in senior level sales and marketing roles. We placed over 50 marketing, sales, engineering, and IT professionals with clients across the US in the energy industry.

Key Contact - Specialty:
Mr. Linda Peak, President - *Sales and marketing*
Mr. Kevin Coons, Vice President - *Business development, consulting, pro services*

Salary minimum: $55,000

Functions: General Mgmt., Directors, Senior Mgmt., Middle Mgmt., Sales & Mktg., Mktg. Mgmt., Sales Mgmt., IT, Mgmt. Consultants

Industries: Energy, Utilities, Mfg., Software

Energy Recruiting Specialists Inc
PO Box 339
Chalfont, PA 18914
(215) 529-5894
Fax: (215) 529-9974
Email: energyspecialist@email.msn.com

Description: Hold ethics and confidentiality in high regard. Hardworking with a strong contact base within the industry. Our main goal is to help candidates and clients progress in the marketplace.

Key Contact - Specialty:
Mr. Michael DeFazio, President - *Energy, finance, development, engineering, marketing*

Salary minimum: $75,000

Functions: Generalist

Industries: Energy, Utilities, Finance

The Engineering Connection
7650 Chippewa Rd Ste 310
Brecksville, OH 44141
(440) 838-5008
Fax: (440) 838-5009
Email: konfal@engconn.com
Web: www.engconn.com

Description: We are thorough and comprehensive in examining the references and accomplishments of our candidates and strive for the ideal match between business and candidate. The result is a

placement which exceeds the expectations of the business.

Key Contact:
Mr. Edward W. Nishnic, President - *Generalist*
Mrs. Jean Konfal, Business Manager

Functions: Engineering

Industries: Generalist

Networks: Top Echelon Network

Engineering Profiles
2216 E Olive Rd Ste 204
Pensacola, FL 32514
(850) 969-9991
Fax: (850) 969-9987
Email: bprice@engineeringprofiles.com
Web: www.engineeringprofiles.com

Description: We specialize in technical, engineering and operations professionals within the chemical process industry. Our focus is on operating companies, primarily concentrating in manufacturing operations, with plant/operations management and technical and engineering support positions as our specialty.

Key Contact - Specialty:
Mr. William G. Price, Owner - *Chemical industry (technical, engineering, operations)*

Salary minimum: $40,000

Functions: Generalist, Product Dev., Production, Plant Mgmt., R&D, Engineering

Industries: Generalist, Paper, Chemicals, Paints, Petro. Products

Engineering Resource Group Inc
101 Gibraltar Dr
Powder Mill Plz
Morris Plains, NJ 07950
(973) 490-7000
Fax: (973) 490-1957
Email: bestnjjobs@aol.com
Web: www.engineeringresource.com

Description: Specialize in professional recruiting of electrical engineers, electronic engineers, software engineers, systems engineers, mechanical engineers and aerospace engineers. We recruit for the aerospace, electronics, telecommunications, industrial and defense markets.

Key Contact - Specialty:
Mr. Branko A. Terkovich, Director - *Engineering*
Mr. James Z. Terkovich, Director - *Engineering*

Salary minimum: $40,000

Functions: Generalist, Engineering

Industries: Generalist, Food, Bev., Tobacco, Drugs Mfg., Plastics, Rubber, Computer Equip., Telecoms, Aerospace, Software

Professional Associations: IEEE, NSPE

Engineering Solutions Int'l
(also known as Engineering Geniuses Int'l)
341 S Meadows Ave
Manhattan Beach, CA 90266
(310) 798-8044
Email: info@engineeringsolutions.com
Web: www.engineeringsolutions.com

Description: We specialize in the placement of biotech, bioinfomatic, neural net, optic artificial intelligence, computer and engineering professionals for research and development applications. We also place executives.

Key Contact - Specialty:
Ms. Urania Van Applebaum, President - *Biotech, AI, neural nets, fuzzy logic, fiber optics*
Ms. Lynda DesLandes, Recruiter - *Engineers, management, telecommunications*

Salary minimum: $50,000

Functions: Generalist, Production, Sales Mgmt., Systems Analysis, Systems Dev., Network Admin., R&D, Engineering

Industries: Generalist, Chemicals, Telecoms, Aerospace, Software, Biotech, Healthcare

Professional Associations: IEEE, OSA, RON, SPIE

Enhance Technology Inc
2670 Union Ave Extended Ste 1216
Memphis, TN 38112
(901) 722-9354
Fax: (901) 205-3956
Email: andy@enhancetechnology.com
Web: www.enhancetechnology.com

Description: Our firm is based in Memphis, TN. Our focus is on technology, financial, and executive recruitment services for clients in the TN-MS-AR tri-state area, although we do have clients that have requested our assistance in other functional and geographic areas. We consider both companies and candidates to be our clients, and firmly believe that relationships are built on ethics, discretion, and integrity. There is no cost to candidates who work with us.

Key Contact - Specialty:
Mr. Andy Wainwright, President - *Executive, information technology*
Mr. Mark McCurdy, CPC, Vice President - *Information technology*

Ensearch Management Consultants
921 Transport Way Ste 29
Petaluma, CA 94954
(800) 473-6776
(707) 766-8700
Fax: (707) 778-1555
Email: inquiry@ensearch.com
Web: www.ensearch.com

Description: Dedicated to the ethical recruitment of advanced practice and administrative nurses within a safe and confidential environment. Our specialty niche is neonatal & pediatric nursing.

Key Contact - Specialty:
Mr. Tim Mattis, Principal - *Healthcare*

Salary minimum: $40,000

Functions: Nurses

Industries: Generalist, Mgmt. Consulting, Healthcare

Professional Associations: APON, CSP, NANN, NAPNAP

Enterprise Search Associates
7031 Corporate Way Ste 102
Dayton, OH 45459
(937) 438-8774
(800) 993-5499
Fax: (937) 438-3753
Email: esacareers@aol.com
Web: www.daytonjobs.com

Description: Permanent positions in information systems for the Dayton/Cincinnati, Ohio marketplace.

Key Contact:
Mr. Jeffrey Linck, Owner

Salary minimum: $45,000

Functions: IT, MIS Mgmt., Systems Analysis, Systems Dev., Network Admin., DB Admin.

Industries: Generalist

Environmental, Health & Safety Search Associates Inc (EH&S)
PO Box 1325
Palm Harbor, FL 34682
(727) 787-3225
Fax: (727) 787-5599
Email: ehs@ehssearch.com
Web: www.ehssearch.com

Description: We are an executive search firm that specializes exclusively in recruiting safety, health, and environmental-related professionals for major industrial corporations. We offer retained, contingency, and/or contract staffing services in these fields.

Key Contact - Specialty:
Mr. Randy L. Williams, President - *Safety, environmental, industrial hygiene*

Salary minimum: $50,000

Functions: Risk Mgmt., Engineering, Environmentalists

Industries: Generalist

Professional Associations: ACHMM, AIHA, ASSE, EMA, NAEM

Equate Executive Search Inc
12 W 37th St Fl 7
New York, NY 10018
(212) 736-0606
Fax: (212) 695-5992
Email: equate@att.net
Web: www.equatejobs.com

Description: We are a small firm connected to a wide network of select recruiters, corporations and academic institutions. We have extensive personal experience working in the fields of information systems and finance.

Key Contact:
Mr. Harry Miller, President - *System architects, e-commerce, data mining, data warehousing*
Ms. Caryn Fox, Managing Director - *Product managers, project managers, business analysis, sales & marketing*
Ms. Susan Casner, Vice President

Salary minimum: $75,000

Functions: Generalist, Directors, Senior Mgmt., Mktg. Mgmt., Sales Mgmt., Risk Mgmt., IT, Mgmt. Consultants

Industries: Generalist, Banking, Invest. Banking, IT Implementation, Network Infrastructure, Software, Security SW, System SW, Training SW

Eric Turner & Associates
(formerly known as Christmas, McIvor & Associates)
33 City Centre Dr Ste 551
Mississauga, ON L5B 2N5
Canada
(905) 270-0404
Fax: (905) 270-0406
Email: jobs@xmasmci.com
Web: www.xmasmci.com

Description: Temporary, contract and permanent placement service covering administrative through senior executive.

Key Contact:
Mr. Keith Turner, General Manager

Functions: Generalist, Mfg., Materials, Sales & Mktg., Finance, IT, Graphic Artists

Industries: Generalist, Consumer Elect., Transportation, Finance, Equip Svcs., HR Services, Telecoms

Erickson & Associates Inc
137 Linda Vista
Sedona, AZ 86336
(520) 203-4093
Fax: (520) 203-4095
Email: eerickson@sedona.net
Web: 4829@smart-office.net

Description: We are a national recruiting and placement firm, primarily for the telecommunication/DataCom disciplines. We have a special interest in attracting the best engineering and computer science professionals in systems, software, or hardware design, development, implementation, test, product management, or marketing. Our client base includes established world-class companies and new start-up organizations.

Key Contact - Specialty:
Mr. Elvin Erickson, CPC, President - *Systems, software, hardware*

Functions: Generalist

Industries: Mfg., Communications, Software

Networks: Top Echelon Network

K L Erickson Worldwide Legal Consulting
(also known as Worldwide Technology Consulting/ScienceSearch)
158 NE Greenwood Ave Ste 4
Bend, OR 97701
(541) 385-5405
Fax: (541) 385-5407
Email: law@eworldwide.com
Web: www.eworldwide.com

Description: Specialize in international attorneys, international trade, finance, joint venture and project finance.

Key Contact - Specialty:
Mr. K. L. Erickson, Owner - *Attorneys*

Functions: Generalist, Legal, Attorneys, Int'l.

Industries: Generalist, Legal

Erspamer Associates
4010 W 65th St Ste 100
Edina, MN 55435
(952) 925-3747
Fax: (952) 925-4022
Email: hdhuntre1@aol.com

Description: Based in the heart of Minneapolis/St. Paul, a worldwide hotbed in the development of innovative medical devices, we offer our medical technology clients a focused depth and breadth of premium caliber candidates that few can match. Technical and technical management positions are our specialty; R&D, engineering, clinical and regulatory affairs, quality systems and manufacturing.

Key Contact - Specialty:
Mr. Roy C. Erspamer, Principal - *Medical device, medical technology, technical, technical management*

Functions: Generalist

Industries: Drugs Mfg., Medical Devices, Plastics, Rubber, Biotech

ERx-Executive Recruitment in Healthcare Marketing & Comm
5340 Alla Rd Ste 200
Los Angeles, CA 90066
(310) 578-7373
Fax: (310) 578-5005
Email: healthcare@erx.net
Web: www.erx.net

Description: We serve the recruitment needs of our healthcare marcom clients from middle to senior level management. Our clients include private and public companies, emerging growth companies, nonprofit organizations and PR/marcom firms with national healthcare practices.

Key Contact - Specialty:
Ms. Deborah Kaufman, Principal - *Healthcare, high technology*

Salary minimum: $75,000

Functions: Advertising, Mkt. Research, Mktg. Mgmt., Direct Mktg., PR

Industries: Healthcare

ESC2000
2315 Susquehanna Trl N
York, PA 17404
(717) 767-1729
Fax: (717) 767-6083
Email: esc2000@esc2000.com
Web: www.esc2000.com

Description: We specialize in retail recruiting from the store manager level to corporate vice president/CEO. We provide our client companies with a low-cost alternative with proven results. We provide contingency-based search at a 15% fee.

Key Contact:
Mr. Tom Russell

Functions: General Mgmt., Directors, Senior Mgmt., Middle Mgmt.

Industries: Retail

ESPro Int'l Inc
73 Lawrenceville St Ste 100
McDonough, GA 30253
(770) 898-5550
Fax: (770) 898-4209
Email: espro@bellsouth.net
Web: www.esprosearch.com

Description: We specialize in the e-commerce security industry, including PKI, firewalls, encryption, VPNs, etc. We have extensive experience placing people in technical, sales, marketing and administrative positions within this industry.

Key Contact:
Mr. Bob Marshall, CPC, CIPC, CEO
Ms. Lori Keefe, VP- Project Coordination

Salary minimum: $70,000

Functions: Generalist

Industries: Non-classifiable

Professional Associations: GAPS, NAPS

The Esquire Group
501 Marquette Ave Ste 1800
Minneapolis, MN 55402
(612) 340-9068
(800) 755-7779
Fax: (612) 340-1218
Email: resume@esquiregroup.com
Web: www.esquiregroup.com

Description: We are a legal placement and recruiting firm providing permanent and contract/temporary/project placement of attorneys, paralegal and legal assistants since 1989. Candidates are placed at leading law firms and in-house corporate legal departments nationwide.

Key Contact - Specialty:
Ms. Patricia A. Comeford, Esq., President/Founder - *Legal*
Mr. Timothy P. Mahoney, Esq., Vice President - *Legal*

Functions: Legal

Industries: Generalist, Legal

Professional Associations: ABA, MBA, NALSC

Branches:
600 17th St S Twr Ste 950
Denver, CO 80202
(303) 892-9300
(800) 755-7779
Fax: (303) 573-5977
Email: libbyr@esquiregroup.com
Key Contact - Specialty:
Ms. Elizabeth J. Ruffing, Esq., Vice President - *Legal*

Essential Solutions Inc
2542 S Bascom Ave Ste 100
Campbell, CA 95008
(408) 369-9500
Fax: (408) 369-9595
Email: info@esiweb.com
Web: www.esiweb.com

Description: Specializing in the placement of key contributors in management, engineering, marketing and sales for emerging communications companies. Specializing in: wireless communications, networking, Internet, multi-media and system semiconductors.

Key Contact - Specialty:
Mr. Art Narita, Principal - *Engineering, sales marketing, professional*
Mr. Aaron C. Woo, Principal - *Engineering, sales & marketing executives*

Salary minimum: $70,000

Functions: Generalist, General Mgmt., Mfg., Sales & Mktg., Finance, IT, R&D, Engineering

Industries: Generalist, Computer Equip., Consumer Elect., Test, Measure Equip., Finance, Media, Software

Professional Associations: CSP, IEEE

Estes Consulting Associates Inc
14 Martingale Way
Pawling, NY 12564
(845) 855-0057
Fax: (845) 855-9766
Email: melissa@ecai.com
Web: www.ecai.com

Description: We are providing professional staffing and consulting, exclusively in technology, with an emphasis on ERP, e-Commerce, Internet, and CRM. Permanent and contract services are available for diversified industries.

Key Contact - Specialty:
Mr. Jeffrey Estes, President - *Technology consulting*
Ms. Melissa Katzman, Director - *Information systems staffing*
Mr. George Joseph, Research Administration - *Project support*

Salary minimum: $60,000

Functions: Budgeting, M&A, IT, MIS Mgmt., Systems Analysis, Systems Dev., Systems Implem., Systems Support, Network Admin., DB Admin.

Industries: Generalist

Professional Associations: ICCA, SHRM

Allen Etcovitch Associates Ltd
(also known as PSA Int'l)
1707 - 666 Sherbrooke St W
Montreal, QC H3A 1E7
Canada
(514) 287-9933
Fax: (514) 287-9940
Email: cvs@aetcovitch.com

Description: Industrial psychologists offering English/French services in recruitment, organizational design, psychological assessments, compensation, career management and

---

outplacement. Clientèle: from small family-owned firms to multinationals.

Key Contact - Specialty:
Mr. Allen Etcovitch, President - *Generalist*
Ms. Marie-José Demers, VP/Senior Consultant - *Generalist*

Salary minimum: $50,000

Functions: Generalist

Industries: Mfg., Textiles, Apparel, Printing, Chemicals, Metal Products, Misc. Mfg., Wholesale, Retail, Packaging, Insurance

Professional Associations: IACMP, APA, BPS, CPA, OPA, OPQ, SIOP

Ethical Search Professional Ltd
100 N Etnyre Ave
Oregon, IL 61061-9402
(815) 732-4773
Fax: (815) 732-4493
Email: jim@ethicalsearch.com
Web: www.ethicalsearch.com

Description: Recruiters specializing in finding and placing technical professionals (engineers, production management and maintenance management) at all levels. We provide services to plant, technical and corporate settings. Our clients are mainly in the food, consumer products, pharmaceutical, paper, converting, chemical processing and related industries.

Key Contact:
Mr. Jim Sullivan, President/Senior Account Manager - *Engineering, production management*
Mr. Paul Santschi, Senior Technical Recruiter - *Engineering*
Mr. Jason Sullivan, Sr Technical Recruiter/Account Manager - *Engineering, production management*
Mr. James Sullivan, Jr., Technical Recruiter - *Engineering*
Ms. Gayle Sullivan, Administrative Manager

Salary minimum: $40,000

Functions: Mfg., Production, Automation, Plant Mgmt., Packaging, Engineering, Minorities

Industries: Mfg., Food, Bev., Tobacco, Paper, Printing, Chemicals, Soap, Perf., Cosmtcs., Drugs Mfg., Plastics, Rubber, Paints, Petro. Products, Packaging

Professional Associations: AICHE, IEEE, IIE, IOPP, SHRM

Networks: Inter-City Personnel Assoc (IPA)

Evans & James Executive Search
PO Box 862232
Marietta, GA 30062
(770) 992-4299
Fax: (770) 992-4496
Email: james@evansandjames.com
Web: www.evansandjames.com

Description: We have 15 years of experience specializing in the "Plastic / Packaging / Paper / Adhesives" Industry. We are capable of finding Sales, Management, Engineering, or Manufacturing Professionals throughout the country.

Key Contact:
Mr. James Ingram, CPC

Salary minimum: $55,000

Functions: Mfg.

Industries: Food, Bev., Tobacco, Paper, Chemicals, Medical Devices, Plastics, Rubber, Packaging

Professional Associations: GAPS, IOPP, NAPS, SPE

Evans Transportation Search

16 The Links Rd Ste 312
Willowdale, ON M2P 1T5
Canada
(416) 224-2277
Fax: (416) 229-1973

Description: A tireless group of headhunters totally committed to recruiting the best talent available in air, ocean and road transportation. Logistics, traffic and distribution, our focus is on emerging growth companies.

Key Contact - Specialty:
Mr. Ray Evans, Director - *Transportation*

Salary minimum: $50,000

Functions: Generalist

Industries: Transportation

Everett Career Management Consultants Inc

PO Box 101805
Ft. Worth, TX 76185-1805
(800) 297-1USA
(817) 989-7400
Fax: (817) 989-7401
Email: ea2000@home.com
Web: www.eaplus.com

Description: Generalist search firm specializing in executive, managerial and professional assignments. We will split fees with reciprocal arrangement on most listings. Primary industries include financial services, electronics, micro-electronics, software, aerospace/defense, etc.

Key Contact - Specialty:
Ms. Julia Lockleer, President - *Financial services, aerospace, defense, electronics*
Mr. Jim Everett, CMP, Director of Employment - *Manufacturing, electronics, telecommunications*

Salary minimum: $65,000

Functions: Generalist

Industries: Finance, Accounting, Mgmt. Consulting, HR Services, Media, Advertising, Aerospace, Insurance, Real Estate, Software

Professional Associations: IACMP, EMA, NBN, RON, SHRM

Networks: National Banking Network (NBN)

Evergreen & Company

160 Mouse Mill Rd
Westport, MA 02790
(800) 828-6705
Fax: (508) 636-8633
Email: maukp@staffing.net
Web: www.evergreenconsultants.com

Description: Search firm specializing in software engineering professionals and information technology managers and specialists. Providing recruiting assistance to manufacturing, financial and service industries.

Key Contact - Specialty:
Ms. Patricia Mauk, Partner - *Information technology*
Mr. Gary Mauk, Jr., Partner - *Information technology*

Salary minimum: $45,000

Functions: IT, MIS Mgmt., Systems Dev., Systems Implem., Network Admin., DB Admin.

Industries: Generalist

Networks: Top Echelon Network

The Excel Group Inc

18350 Mt. Langley Ste 201
Fountain Valley, CA 92708
(714) 593-5927
Fax: (714) 593-0917
Email: frank@xlg.com
Web: www.xlg.com

Description: Specialize in sales, marketing and information technology support recruitment across all experience levels for software and Internet firms. Extensive database of screened high-tech professionals to meet your needs.

Key Contact:
Mr. Frank J. Suwalski, President - *Internet start-ups, sales, sales management*
Mr. Ron Bray, Vice President

Salary minimum: $70,000

Functions: Directors, Sales & Mktg., Advertising, IT, MIS Mgmt., Systems Dev.

Industries: Communications, Software

Professional Associations: AIP

Excel Human Resources Inc

102 Bank St Ste 300
Ottawa, ON K1P 5N4
Canada
(613) 230-5393
Fax: (613) 230-1623
Web: www.excelhr.com

Description: We are a full-service recruiting firm specialized in recruiting/staffing of administrative, management, accounting and information technology positions for the private and public sectors, on both a contract and permanent basis.

Key Contact - Specialty:
Ms. Lisa Dickson, Marketing/Placement Specialist - *Information technology, business systems*
Ms. Shelagh Momy, Client Services Coordinator - *Permanent, administration, accounting*
Ms. Branka Anicic, Marketing/Placement Specialist - *Information technology, software engineering*

Functions: Admin. Svcs., Mktg. Mgmt., HR Mgmt., Finance, IT

Industries: Generalist

Professional Associations: ASA

Exclusive Search Consultants

(also known as Erie Group Inc)
406 State St
Erie, PA 16501
(814) 453-5121
(724) 843-8382
Fax: (814) 454-4017
Email: temppro@aol.com
Web: www.theeriegroup.com

Description: Our success depends upon both satisfied applicants and clients. Client firms rely on our ability to screen and place personnel with professionalism and confidentiality.

Key Contact - Specialty:
Mrs. Paula Teck, President - *Engineering*
Mr. Rudy Surovick, Vice President - *IT*

Functions: Generalist, Mfg., Materials, IT, MIS Mgmt., Systems Analysis, Systems Dev., Engineering

Industries: Generalist, Mfg., Software

Professional Associations: ASA, NAPS

Branches:
725 1/2 3rd Ave
New Brighton, PA 15066
(724) 843-8382
Fax: (724) 843-8402
Email: theeriegroup@aol.com

Key Contact - Specialty:
Ms. Carol Reynolds, Manager - *IT, engineering*

Execu-Source Inc

1117 Perimeter Center W Ste 500 E
Atlanta, GA 30338
(770) 604-9030
Fax: (770) 604-9818
Email: info@execu-sourceinc.com
Web: www.execu-sourceinc.com

Description: We offer recruitment of accounting, financial, controller/CFO, tax, and accounting support, such as A/R, payroll, billing, collections, and bookkeeping professionals. We service all industries in the Metro Atlanta Area.

Key Contact:
Mr. David Flax, CPA

Salary minimum: $25,000

Functions: Finance, CFO's, Budgeting, Cash Mgmt., Taxes, M&A

Industries: Generalist

Execu-Tech Search Inc

3500 W 80th St Ste 20
Minneapolis, MN 55431
(952) 893-6915
Fax: (952) 896-3479

Description: Twenty-five years' experience in executive and technical candidates within the following engineering sectors: mechanical product design and the consulting engineering industry.

Key Contact - Specialty:
Mr. Marv Kaiser, President - *Manufacturing, engineering*
Mr. Greg Kaiser, Vice President - *Engineering, computer software*

Functions: Production, Plant Mgmt., Quality, Engineering

Industries: Construction, Mfg., Food, Bev., Tobacco, Chemicals, Drugs Mfg., Metal Products, Machine, Appliance, Packaging

Professional Associations: ASHRAE, ASME

The ExeculSearch Group

675 3rd Ave
New York, NY 10017-5704
(212) 922-1001
Fax: (212) 972-0250
Email: info@execu-search.com
Web: www.execu-search.com

Description: We provide recruitment of accounting, controller/CFO, tax, healthcare, financial services in both back and middle office, graphics, healthcare, human resources, information technology, legal support, and office support. The industries serviced by our firm are brokerage, communications, insurance, new media, law, banking, retail, investment, real estate, Internet, consumer products, and public accounting firms.

Key Contact - Specialty:
Mr. Edward Fleischman
Mr. Robert Fligel
Mr. Gary Grossman
Mr. Mitchell Peskin - *Financial services*
Mr. Glenn Bernstein - *Temporary, consulting division*

Salary minimum: $30,000

Functions: Generalist, Healthcare, HR Mgmt., Finance, CFO's, Cash Mgmt., IT, Graphic Artists

Industries: Generalist, Finance, Brokers, Accounting, HR Services, Media, Real Estate, Healthcare

Execumax.com
3 Palm Dr
Shalimar, FL 32579
(850) 609-0471
Email: jobs@execumax.com
Web: www.execumax.com

Description: We are an executive search firm specializing in manager, director and VP level positions in the consumer packaged goods industry. We specialize in the supply chain, logistics, manufacturing, sales, marketing, human resources and finance disciplines.

Key Contact - Specialty:
Mr. Ron Todd, President - *Supply chain, logistics, purchasing*

Functions: Mfg.

Industries: Food, Bev., Tobacco

Execusearch
21 Mountainwood Dr
Glenville, NY 12302
(518) 384-2036
Fax: (518) 384-1413
Email: esearch1@aol.com

Description: Specializing in placement of sales and marketing professionals with clients throughout the northeastern U.S. Currently placing in telecommunications, medical/pharmaceutical, business products and consumer products industries. Very competitive fees.

Key Contact - Specialty:
Mr. Mark A. Quinn, President - *Sales, sales management*

Salary minimum: $30,000

ExecuSource Consultants Inc
PO Box 680746
Houston, TX 77268
(281) 257-1340
Fax: (281) 655-9685
Email: info@execusourcejobs.com
Web: www.execusourcejobs.com

Description: We are a nationally focused firm, dedicated to building solid client relationships through integrity, service and performance. Our concentration is on both middle and senior-level management positions for telecommunications related clients, with particular emphasis on wireless technologies.

Key Contact - Specialty:
Mr. Chris Trapani, Managing Director - *Telecommunications (sales, marketing, engineering), management (middle, senior level)*
Ms. Delores Trapani, Vice President - *Telecommunications (sales & marketing)*

Salary minimum: $50,000

Functions: Generalist

Industries: Test, Measure Equip., Telecoms, Call Centers, Telephony, Digital, Wireless, Fiber Optic, Network Infrastructure, Industry Specific SW, Networking, Comm. SW

Professional Associations: RON

Executec Search Agency Inc
2860 E Flamingo Rd Ste J
Las Vegas, NV 89121
(702) 892-8010
(702) 892-8008
Fax: (702) 892-0089
Email: chris@mail.executecsearch.com
Web: www.executecsearch.com

Description: We have been the leader for almost 15 years, placing persons in the scientific marketplace. We specialize in the placement of the following job positions worldwide: president/CEO, general manager, service engineer, software engineer, marketing manager, application chemist, product manager, NSM design engineer, sales engineer, and much more. Our scope of industries includes: biotechnology, analytical chemistry, environment, process, semiconductor, health and safety, and more.

Key Contact - Specialty:
Mr. Mark Moyer, President - *Scientific, biotechnology*
Mr. Chris Avron, VP/Key Account Manager - *Scientific, biotechnology*

Salary minimum: $30,000

Functions: Senior Mgmt., Sales & Mktg.

Industries: Biotech

Executech Resource Consultants
5700 Crooks Rd Ste 105
Troy, MI 48098
(248) 828-3000
Fax: (248) 828-3333
Email: info@executechjobs.com
Web: www.executechjobs.com

Description: We are a leading staffing and employment services firm specializing in providing information systems specialists, automotive engineering professionals, secretarial and clerical personnel and customer service associates.

Key Contact - Specialty:
Mr. Dave Palma, President - *Technology executives, sales, engineers, optics, semiconductor, automotive electronics*
Mr. Jeff Bagnasco, Officer - *Engineers, mechanical*

Functions: Sales & Mktg., IT, Engineering

Industries: Generalist, Plastics, Rubber, Motor Vehicles, Computer Equip., Electronic, Elec. Components, IT Implementation, Fiber Optic, Software, Database SW, Development SW, Security SW, System SW

Professional Associations: MAPS, NAPS

Executive & Technical Recruiters
8045-B Antoine Dr Ste 173
Houston, TX 77088
(281) 272-2017
(832) 545-8164
Fax: (281) 272-2017
Email: bhobbs544@cs.com
Web: www.recruiters.web.com

Description: Our firm is a nationwide executive search and professional recruitment firm committed to providing quality service. Our goals are to find and attract high-achieving individuals to your company. We specialize in the technical markets. Our established networks of contacts and sources allow us to expediently identify candidates whose industry expertise and management experience will enhance the quality of your organization. Visit our other website at www.diversityrecruiters.web.com.

Key Contact:
Mr. Booker Hobbs, Owner, President

Salary minimum: $50,000

Functions: Generalist, Engineering, Minorities

Industries: Generalist, Energy, Utilities, Construction, Mfg., Finance, Services, Government, Aerospace, Software, Healthcare

Professional Associations: ASME

Executive Advantage
PO Box 20415
Bradenton, FL 34204
(941) 747-8256
Email: recruiter@execadvantage.com
Web: www.execadvantage.com

Description: Our firm specializes in upper level management positions, broad in scope, but with a general focus on the food-manufacturing sector. Our methodology is strongly rooted in marketing, and that is from presentation through representation. Executive Advantage - the advantage is yours! ©

Key Contact:
Mr. Ken D'Amelio

Salary minimum: $50,000

Functions: General Mgmt.

Industries: Mfg., Food, Bev., Tobacco, Chemicals, Soap, Perf., Cosmtcs., Drugs Mfg., Medical Devices, Paints, Petro. Products, HR SW, Mfg. SW

Executive BioSearch
405 Via Chico Ste 8
Palos Verdes Estates, CA 90274
(310) 378-1217
Fax: (310) 375-7509
Email: mail@executivebiosearch.com

Description: Our firm is an executive search firm specializing in the scientific/biotechnology and diagnostic industries. We combine over 30 years of experience in the industry working for biomedical companies and executive search. Our areas of recruitment specialization are: senior management, corporate development, marketing, sales, and applications support.

Key Contact:
Mr. Matt Takahashi, President - *Management, marketing, sales, biotechnology, scientific*
Ms. Hope Podway, Senior Recruiter - *Operations, procurement, purchasing, logistics, manufacturing*
Ms. Alise Orr, Senior Recruiter - *Sales & marketing, biotechnology, scientific*
Ms. Colleen Kelly, Consultant
Ms. Carrie Roy, Sr Consultant
Ms. Donna Mackay, Research Associate

Functions: Generalist, Senior Mgmt., Middle Mgmt., Purchasing, Materials Plng., Distribution, Mktg. Mgmt., Sales Mgmt.

Industries: Generalist, Soap, Perf., Cosmtcs., Drugs Mfg., Medical Devices, Pharm Svcs., Biotech

Professional Associations: CSP

Networks: National Personnel Assoc (NPA)

Executive Career Search
PO Box 480
Lightfoot, VA 23090-0480
(757) 564-3013
Fax: (801) 640-0819
Email: headhunter@widomaker.com

Description: Recruiting for the construction materials industries, aggregates, asphalt, sand and gravel, concrete block and cement. Industrial textiles, paper machine clothing, forming-press-dryer fabrics.

Key Contact - Specialty:
Mr. Charles H. Sillery, CPC, Owner/President - *Engineering, data processing*

Salary minimum: $35,000

Functions: Mfg.

Industries: Agri., Forestry, Mining, Construction, Textiles, Apparel

Executive Career Strategies Inc
7900 N University Dr Ste 201
Tamarac, FL 33321
(954) 720-9764
(800) 234-1362
Fax: (954) 720-6576
Email: HdhntECS@aol.com

Description: We specialize in the recruitment and placement of talented professionals on a nationwide basis within all areas of the property/casualty insurance industry. We take pride in our quality performance and high ethical standards.

Key Contact:
Ms. Linda Daniel
Ms. Rena Moosa

Salary minimum: $30,000

Functions: Generalist

Industries: Insurance

Executive Connections Inc

PO Box 1853
Lexington, NC 27293
(336) 956-2002
Fax: (336) 956-2012
Email: ace@executiveconnections.net
Web: www.executiveconnections.net

Description: Our firm works with manufacturing customers, primarily in the southeast. We belong to Top Echelon Network, Inc., which is the largest network of independent recruiters in the country. We are, therefore, able to work all over the country. We are also associated with two international consulting companies, which allows us to operate worldwide. Executive Connections is in its 12th year of operation and has been quite successful in placing all levels of management from CEOs to production supervisors. We cover almost all engineering fields, namely ME, EE, IE, CHEM E, etc.

Key Contact:
Mr. Ace Ragan, President

Salary minimum: $45,000

Networks: Top Echelon Network

Executive Connection

8225 Brecksville Rd Ste 2
Brecksville, OH 44141-1362
(440) 838-5657
Fax: (440) 838-5668
Email: econnect@staffing.net
Web: www.executiveconnection.net

Description: Executive/technical search firm specialists in the recruitment and placement of all disciplines in all manufacturing industries.

Key Contact:
Mr. Steven C. Brandvold, President - *Engineering, quality, operations*
Mr. Vincent Kirkwood, Account Executive - *Elevator*
Ms. Ellen Williams, Consultant

Salary minimum: $35,000

Functions: Generalist

Industries: Mfg., Transportation, HR Services, Advertising

Professional Associations: IIE

Networks: Top Echelon Network

The Executive Consulting Group

701 N Post Oak Rd Ste 610
Houston, TX 77024-3829
(713) 686-9500
Fax: (713) 686-9599
Email: david_gandin@alumni.utexas.net

Description: We service all industries desiring a full range of accounting, tax, audit or financial talent. Our candidates are typically CPAs or MBAs with current or prior experience in public accounting, corporate accounting, corporate tax, corporate finance or financial analysis.

Key Contact - Specialty:
Mr. David L. Gandin, CPC, Partner - *Accounting, tax, financial*
Mr. Tim Staton, Partner - *Accounting, tax, financial*

Salary minimum: $40,000

Functions: Finance

Industries: Generalist

Professional Associations: HAAPC, TAPC

Executive Direction Inc

155 Sansome St Ste 400
San Francisco, CA 94104
(415) 394-5500
Fax: (415) 956-5186
Email: edi@exdir.com
Web: www.exdir.com

Description: We specialize in search and placement of professionals in the areas of information technology, software development, and telecommunications for high technology industries.

Key Contact - Specialty:
Mr. Fred Naderi, President/CEO - *Executive level, IT*

Salary minimum: $80,000

Functions: Generalist, General Mgmt., CFO's, IT, MIS Mgmt., Systems Analysis, Systems Dev., Systems Implem., Systems Support, DB Admin.

Industries: Generalist, Software

Branches:
11877 Miro Cir
San Diego, CA 92131
(858) 536-1876
Fax: (858) 536-1876
Email: edi.sandiego@exdir.com
Key Contact:
Mr. Steve Saust, Director

5900 Balcones Dr Ste 230
Austin, TX 78731
(512) 450-0079
Fax: (512) 450-0582
Email: edi.austin@exdir.com
Key Contact:
Ms. Tricia Guerring, Director

4582-E Kingwood Dr Ste 522
Houston, TX 77345
(281) 812-3655
Fax: (281) 852-9486
Email: edi.houston@exdir.com
Key Contact:
Mr. Eric Lambert, Director

Executive Directions Inc

300 W Adams Ste 330
Chicago, IL 60606
(312) 346-3131
Email: pcc@execdirections.com
Web: www.execdirections.com

Description: Our recruiting professionals have been successfully placing top-level talent for an impressive array of clients. We offer our clients an extensive network of contacts and exceptional service throughout a broad scope of industries and job functions.

Key Contact - Specialty:
Mr. Peter Chappell, President - *All*
Mr. Michael Rimmele, Manager - *IT-MIS*
Ms. Nancy Marver-Ilhan, Manager - *Insurance*

Salary minimum: $50,000

Executive Dynamics Inc (EDI)

2 James Brite Cir
Mahwah, NJ 07430
(201) 327-9070
Fax: (201) 327-9071
Email: edi1@iglide.net

Description: Experienced track record of placement of sales and marketing professionals in both consumer and marketing service companies. Confidential professional services.

Key Contact - Specialty:
Ms. Susan J. Wagner, President - *Sales & marketing*

Salary minimum: $45,000

Functions: Sales & Mktg., Advertising, Mktg. Mgmt., Sales Mgmt.

Industries: Food, Bev., Tobacco, Soap, Perf., Cosmtcs., Drugs Mfg., Consumer Elect., Pharm Svcs., Mgmt. Consulting, Hospitality, Media, Advertising, Publishing, New Media, Broadcast, Film

The Executive Exchange Corp

2517 Hwy 35 G-103
Manasquan, NJ 08736
(732) 223-6655
Fax: (732) 223-1162
Email: execexchan@aol.com
Web: www.theexecutiveexchange.com

Description: Professional recruitment in computer-related sales. Specialists in recruiting recruiters for computer services firms.

Key Contact - Specialty:
Ms. Elizabeth B. Glosser, CPC, Managing Director - *Computer sales, recruiters, managers*

Salary minimum: $25,000

The Executive Group

9191 Towne Center Dr Ste 105
San Diego, CA 92122
(858) 457-8100
Fax: (858) 777-3510
Email: exegroup@careerchoices.net
Web: www.careerchoices.net

Description: General industrial search practice; hi-tech, engineering, legal, finance, banking and biotechnology. Emphasis on mid-management & upper-level management. Also provides outplacement services at a corporate level, career management, development, executive coaching.

Key Contact - Specialty:
Mr. Robert Kaplan, CEO - *Generalist, attorneys*

Salary minimum: $60,000

Functions: Generalist

Industries: Generalist

Executive Management Resources

7830 E Gelding Ste 650
Scottsdale, AZ 85251
(480) 348-1870
Fax: (480) 348-1871
Email: johnd@emrdirect.com
Web: www.emrdirect.com

Description: Customize each search in the telecommunications field to maximize the candidate's career and enhance the client's company. We qualify the candidates per position and examine each company to create the best situation for both parties.

Key Contact:
Mr. John DePhillipo, President

Functions: Generalist, Sales Mgmt., MIS Mgmt., Systems Dev.

Industries: Generalist, Telecoms

Professional Associations: AAPS

Executive Medical Search
111 Pacifica St Ste 250
Irvine, CA 92618
(949) 770-9022
Fax: (949) 770-5658
Email: execumedsearch@yahoo.com
Web: www.executivemedicalsearch.com

Description: We primarily specialize in the homecare, long-term care, hospice, assisted living, and acute care positions. We place area COO, regional VP, VP Ops, VP nursing, VP sales and marketing, VP clinical services, PharmD, general managers, nurse managers, sales, controller, and accounting director positions.

Key Contact - Specialty:
Ms. Diana Brewer, CPC, President/CEO - *Medical*

Salary minimum: $50,000

Functions: Generalist, Senior Mgmt., Middle Mgmt., Healthcare, Nurses, Sales & Mktg., Sales Mgmt., Finance, CFO's, IT

Industries: Pharm Svcs., Accounting, HR Services, Biotech, Healthcare, Hospitals, Long-term Care

Professional Associations: CSP

Networks: Top Echelon Network

Executive Network
533 Tartan
Naperville, IL 60563
(630) 305-7196
Fax: (630) 305-0391
Email: mgt@execnet1.com
Web: www.execnet1.com

Description: We specialize in the recruitment and placement of professionals in the investment management and employee benefits fields. We provide search services to a prestigious client base that includes top mutual funds, TPA's, Fortune 500 corporations, employee benefits consulting and big 5 accounting firms nationwide.

Key Contact - Specialty:
Mr. Neil Atkinson, Principal - *Retirement plan consulting, administration*

Salary minimum: $60,000

Functions: General Mgmt., Directors, Senior Mgmt., Middle Mgmt., Admin. Svcs., Finance, Cash Mgmt.

Industries: Finance, Banking, Invest. Banking, Misc. Financial, Mgmt. Consulting, HR Services

Executive Network & Research Associates
1125 Farmington Ave
Farmington, CT 06032
(860) 409-7550
Fax: (860) 409-7552
Email: jim@executivenetwork.cc
Web: www.executivenetwork.cc

Description: We are an executive search firm specializing in the wholesale apparel, retail, and pharmaceutical markets.

Key Contact:
Mr. Jim Schmunk
Ms. Pat O'Connor

Functions: Generalist

Industries: Textiles, Apparel, Wholesale, Retail, Pharm Svcs., HR Services, E-commerce, Software, Biotech, Healthcare

Professional Associations: CAPS, CBIA

Executive Options Ltd
8707 Skokie Blvd Ste 300
Skokie, IL 60077-2281
(847) 933-8760
Fax: (847) 933-8766

Email: info@execoptions.com
Web: www.execoptions.com

Description: Executive recruiter and search firm specializing in the placement of professionals in consulting, interim and project assignments, as well as permanent part-time and full-time positions in all functions of an organization, including human resources, marketing, finance, and accounting, throughout Illinois.

Key Contact:
Mrs. Andrea Y. Meltzer, President

Salary minimum: $40,000

Functions: Generalist

Industries: Mfg., Retail, Finance, Services, Hospitality, Media, Insurance, Real Estate, Software, Healthcare

Executive Placement Services
1117 Perimeter Ctr W Ste E-302
Atlanta, GA 30338
(770) 396-9114
Fax: (770) 393-3040
Email: recruiter@execplacement.com
Web: www.execplacement.com

Description: We are experienced in recruiting and executive search. Our focus is on middle and upper-management in retail and restaurant/hospitality industries on a national basis. We also work in the local Atlanta market on accounting and finance mid-level positions. Ask us about our hourly fees involving research, identification, qualifying, and applicant data mining, and management.

Key Contact - Specialty:
Mr. John J. Weiss, CPC, President - *Middle to upper management, retail, gaming, hospitality*

Salary minimum: $30,000

Functions: Generalist

Industries: Retail, Hospitality, Hotels, Resorts, Clubs, Restaurants

Professional Associations: GAPS, NAPS, RON

Branches:
PO Box 1140
Waldorf, MD 20604-1140
(301) 934-5457
Fax: (301) 609-6087
Key Contact - Specialty:
Mr. John Ehman - *Retail management & executives*

Executive Placement Consultants
2700 River Rd Ste 107
Des Plaines, IL 60018
(847) 298-6445
Fax: (847) 298-8393
Email: epc@wwa.com
Web: www.epc-chicago.com

Description: Over 20 years of experience in finance, accounting, human resources, financial systems and placement of temp professional, finance and accounting temps.

Key Contact - Specialty:
Mr. Michael Colman, President - *Finance, accounting, human resources, financial systems*

Salary minimum: $35,000

Functions: HR Mgmt., Finance

Industries: Generalist

Professional Associations: AAFA

Executive Pro Search Ltd
70 W Madison St Ste 1400
Chicago, IL 60602
(312) 214-3131
Email: srw@execprosearch.com

Description: Corporate finance/capital markets, merchant & investment banking, structured finance, commercial lending, and private equity.

Key Contact:
Mr. Stephen Wetzel, Partner
Mr. Terry Murphy, Partner

Salary minimum: $50,000

Functions: Finance, M&A

Industries: Generalist, Finance, Banking, Invest. Banking, Venture Cap., Misc. Financial, Mgmt. Consulting

Executive Recruiters Agency Inc
14 Office Park Dr Ste 100
PO Box 21810
Little Rock, AR 72221-1810
(501) 224-7000
Fax: (501) 224-8534
Email: gtdowns@execrecruit.com
Web: www.execrecruit.com

Description: We are dedicated to the delivery of staffing services of the highest quality. Our commitment is to provide our clients with extraordinary value, efficiency through the personal caring of our staff and modern technology.

Key Contact:
Mr. Greg Downs, CPC, Vice President - *Mechanical design engineers, safety engineers, managers*
Mr. Aaron Lubin, President

Salary minimum: $45,000

Functions: Generalist

Industries: Generalist, Mfg., Accounting, Telecoms, Environmental Svcs., Packaging, Software

Professional Associations: SHRM

Networks: First Interview Network (FIN)

Executive Recruiters
PO Box 3447
Vero Beach, FL 32964-3447
(561) 234-6266
Fax: (561) 234-0632
Email: miles@execrecruit.org
Web: www.execrecruit.org

Description: Recruit life insurance agency managers, general agents and agents as well as regional sales managers.

Key Contact - Specialty:
Mr. Miles O'Brien, President - *Life insurance*

Salary minimum: $50,000

Functions: Sales Mgmt.

Industries: Insurance

Executive Recruiters Int'l Inc
PO Box 365
Trenton, MI 48183
(734) 671-6200
Fax: (734) 671-8714
Email: eriinc@execrecruiters.com
Web: www.execrecruiters.com

Description: Technical specialists; automotive, sales, international, manufacturing, management, environmental, computer, finance, healthcare and property management specialists on staff.

Key Contact - Specialty:
Ms. Kathleen A. Sinclair - *Automotive manufacturing (international)*

Salary minimum: $30,000

Functions: General Mgmt., Mfg., Materials, Sales & Mktg., HR Mgmt., Finance, IT, Engineering, Int'l.

Industries: Mfg., Transportation, Finance, HR Services, Hospitality, Media, Packaging

Professional Associations: MASS, NAPS

Executive Recruiters

(also known as BMS Inc)
600 108th Ave NE Ste 242
Bellevue, WA 98004
(206) 447-7404
Fax: (425) 451-8424
Email: info@execr.com
Web: www.execr.com

Description: We are committed to developing continuing client relationships by providing excellent service. We approach each of our employer clients with the highest degree of professionalism, integrity, confidentiality, tact and urgency.

Key Contact - Specialty:
Mr. Jerry Taylor, Manager - *Software, sales & marketing, finance & accounting, product management*
Ms. Nancy Kleid, Senior Consultant - *Marketing, public relations*
Ms. Diana McDevitt, Senior Consultant - *Finance, marketing, executive management*
Mr. Ron Butler, CEO
Ms. Sue Sims, Administrative Assistant - *Administrative*

Salary minimum: $80,000

Functions: Senior Mgmt., Middle Mgmt., Product Dev., Mktg. Mgmt., Sales Mgmt., PR, CFO's, Systems Dev.

Industries: Finance, Invest. Banking, Venture Cap., E-commerce, Media, New Media, Communications, Software

Professional Associations: WSA, WSA

Executive Recruiters

135 Albert St
London, ON N6A 1L9
Canada
(519) 679-2950
(800) 317-4473
Fax: (519) 679-3454
Email: execurec@sprint.ca
Web: www.recruitexec.com

Description: We specialize in permanent placement of senior management, sales, marketing and clinical personnel for the pharmaceutical and medical device marketplace.

Key Contact - Specialty:
Ms. Nancy Howett, Consultant - *Management, sales, marketing*
Mr, Michael Bridgman, Consultant - *Management, sales, marketing, information technology*

Functions: Sales & Mktg.

Industries: Drugs Mfg., Medical Devices, Computer Equip., Telecoms, Software, Biotech, Healthcare

Executive Recruiting Associates

750 W Lake Cook Rd Ste 155
Buffalo Grove, IL 60089
(847) 465-1020
Fax: (847) 465-1546
Email: info@e-recruit-usa.com
Web: www.e-recruit-usa.com

Description: Full service contingency firm, recruiting in a variety of industries. 25 years in business with proven track record. Noted for quality, professionalism and work ethic.

Key Contact - Specialty:
Mr. Tom Malloy, CEO - *Sales, management*

Functions: Generalist

Industries: Drugs Mfg., Plastics, Rubber, Metal Products, Machine, Appliance, Computer Equip., Consumer Elect., Misc. Mfg., Misc. Financial, Accounting, Telecoms

Executive Recruitment Services Inc (ERS Inc)

3210 Ennfield Ln
Duluth, GA 30096
(678) 584-9810
Fax: (678) 584-9811
Email: randall.shute@tmp.com
Web: www.eresourcing.tmp.com

Description: We specialize in high-technology job searches (usually requiring a technical degree) in medical, telecommunications, semiconductor and computer industries.

Key Contact - Specialty:
Mr. Randall Shute, President - *High technology engineering*

Salary minimum: $60,000

Functions: Generalist, Product Dev., Automation, Sales Mgmt., Systems Dev., Systems Implem., R&D, Engineering

Industries: Generalist, Mfg., Medical Devices, Computer Equip., Consumer Elect., Telecoms, Software

Professional Associations: GAPS

Executive Recruitment Services Inc

1134 Leicester Crt
Wheaton, IL 60187
(630) 871-8050
Fax: (630) 871-8190
Email: er1gps@msn.com

Key Contact:
Mr. Gayle Stinn, CRM, President

Functions: Sales & Mktg.

Industries: Food, Bev., Tobacco, Soap, Perf., Cosmtcs., HR SW, Marketing SW

Networks: First Interview Network (FIN)

Executive Referral Services Inc

8770 W Bryn Mawr Ste 110
Chicago, IL 60631
(773) 693-6622
Fax: (773) 693-8466
Email: info@ers-online.com
Web: www.ers-online.com

Description: Our national network, impeccable references and complete commitment to our assignments have resulted in our reputation as the source for recruitment within the hotel, restaurant, retail, club, gaming, entertainment, construction and real estate industries.

Key Contact - Specialty:
Mr. Bruce Freier, CPC, President - *Hospitality, retail, executive*
Mr. Mark Gray, CPC, Vice President - *Restaurant, entertainment, construction*
Mr. Garry Chesla, CPC, Account Executive - *Retail, grocery*
Ms. Melissa Sheedy, Account Executive - *Restaurant management*
Mr. Ian Wennerstrom, Account Executive - *Hotels, food service, sales*
Ms. Kimberly Keuter, Account Executive - *Retail, apparel*

Salary minimum: $25,000

Functions: Generalist

Industries: Retail, Services, Accounting, Hospitality, Real Estate

Professional Associations: HMAI, HSMAI, IAPS, IRA, NAPS

Executive Register Inc

34 Mill Plain Rd
Danbury, CT 06811
(203) 743-5542
Fax: (203) 794-1689
Email: swilliams@exec-reg.com
Web: www.exec-reg.com

Description: We have had 23 years of successful recruitment experience throughout CT and NY in the fields of information technology, accounting/finance, and engineering/manufacturing. We believe that today's search is for tomorrow's success.

Key Contact - Specialty:
Mr. J. Scott Williams, CPC, President - *Information technology*
Mr. Larry V. Hirschauer CPC, CPC, Director - *Engineering manufacturing*

Salary minimum: $50,000

Functions: Middle Mgmt., Mfg., Finance, IT, Systems Dev., DB Admin., Engineering

Industries: Generalist

Professional Associations: CAPS, NAPS

Executive Registry

1200 McGill College Ave Ste 1910
Montreal, QC H3B 2L1
Canada
(514) 866-7981
Fax: (514) 866-7093
Email: er@executive-registry.net

Description: We full-service management recruiters who have been servicing the Montreal and Quebec marketplace for over thirty-five years. We work only with French Canadian candidates.

Key Contact - Specialty:
Mr. Harvey Stewart, President - *General management, finance, real estate*

Salary minimum: $50,000

Functions: Generalist, General Mgmt., Mfg., Sales & Mktg., HR Mgmt., Finance, IT, Engineering

Industries: Generalist, Mfg., Retail, Services, Packaging, Real Estate

Professional Associations: OCRIQ

Networks: National Personnel Assoc (NPA)

Executive Resource Associates

1612 Bay Breeze Dr
Virginia Beach, VA 23454
(757) 481-6221
Fax: (757) 481-1944

Description: We belong to Top Echelon, a recruiting network of over 600 offices throughout US and cover most professional disciplines and industries. We are able to find and place qualified candidates for client companies in technical mid-management positions. We offer confidentiality, honesty, and integrity that is necessary to place the right candidate in the right job.

Key Contact - Specialty:
Mr. Dave David, Director - *Chemicals, plastics, agricultural chemicals, manufacturing*

Functions: Middle Mgmt., Mfg.

Industries: Generalist, Mfg., Paper, Chemicals, Drugs Mfg., Plastics, Rubber, Paints, Petro. Products, Environmental Svcs., Software, ERP SW, Marketing SW, Biotech

Professional Associations: ACS

Networks: Top Echelon Network

Executive Resource Group Inc

1330 Cedar Point Ct #201
Amelia, OH 45102
(513) 947-1447
Fax: (513) 752-3026
Web: www.executiveresource.net

Description: Specialize in the search of superior human resource professionals for our client companies, placing candidates from mid-level up to vice presidential status. We fulfill their needs through our knowledge of their company, products and industry.

Key Contact - Specialty:
Mr. John S. Vujcec, President - *Human resource professionals*

Salary minimum: $50,000

Functions: HR Mgmt.

Industries: Mfg.

Executive Resource Inc

553 S Industrial Dr
PO Box 356
Hartland, WI 53029
(262) 369-2540
Fax: (262) 369-2558
Email: duane@erijobs.com
Web: www.erijobs.com

Description: A professional recruiting firm that specializes in identifying and evaluating those professionals that are in the top 20% of their field, based on skill level and academic achievement.

Key Contact - Specialty:
Mr. William H. Mitton, Executive Vice President - *Accounting & finance, human resources*
Mr. Duane Strong, President - *Manufacturing, engineering professionals, operations professionals*
Mr. Peter Lamb - *Banking*

Salary minimum: $40,000

Functions: Generalist, Mfg., Materials, HR Mgmt., Finance, CFO's, Engineering

Industries: Generalist, Mfg., Lumber, Furniture, Paper, Medical Devices, Plastics, Rubber, Machine, Appliance, Finance

Networks: National Personnel Assoc (NPA)

Executive Resource Systems

PO Box 2992
Capistrano Beach, CA 92624
(949) 496-4300
Fax: (509) 272-0695
Email: brody@erscareers.com
Web: www.erscareers.com

Description: Your resource for permanent and contract placements throughout the USA. On-line with the world's largest candidate database. Over 2000 affiliate recruiters in all 50 states. We specialize in the placement of accounting, engineering, finance, and systems professionals. Many exclusive, retained searches. Performance! Professionalism! Results!

Key Contact - Specialty:
Mr. Steve Brody, President - *Accounting, finance, systems, engineering, human resources*

Salary minimum: $40,000

Functions: Directors, Materials, Purchasing, Finance, CFO's, Budgeting, Credit, Taxes, Risk Mgmt., DB Admin.

Industries: Generalist, Energy, Utilities, Food, Bev., Tobacco, Medical Devices, Plastics, Rubber, Computer Equip., Finance, Accounting, HR Services, Biotech, Healthcare

Professional Associations: CSP

Networks: Top Echelon Network

Executive Resources LLC

16341 Gentian Ln
Morrison, CO 80465
(303) 697-6765
Fax: (303) 265-9391
Email: exresources@earthlink.net

Description: We have twenty years of combined recruiting experience and are certified personnel consultants. We are experts in accounting, IT, engineering, and human resource professionals.

Key Contact - Specialty:
Ms. Carolyn Casey-Moll, Owner - *Accounting, information technology, human resources, sales*

Salary minimum: $30,000

Functions: Generalist

Industries: Generalist

Professional Associations: SHRM

Executive Resources

3816 Ingersoll Ave
Des Moines, IA 50312
(515) 287-6880
Email: iaexecres@aol.com
Web: www.executiveresourcesltd.com

Description: No advertising. Pure search.

Key Contact - Specialty:
Ms. Gerry Mullane, President - *Sales, information technology, insurance, manufacturing, accounting*

Functions: Generalist, Admin. Svcs., Product Dev., Production, Advertising, Mkt. Research, Budgeting

Industries: Generalist, Medical Devices, Plastics, Rubber, Paints, Petro. Products, Venture Cap., Accounting, Packaging

Professional Associations: IAPS, NAPS

Networks: First Interview Network (FIN)

Executive Resources Int'l, Inc

7725-A Siple Ave
Fayetteville, NC 28304-0467
(910) 868-9374
Fax: (910) 868-9269
Email: exresi@aol.com

Description: We are a contingency and retained search firm serving manufacturers' needs for executive, professional and technical talent in the compressor, filtration, pump, actuation, valve, automation, material handling, wire and cable, and process industries. We function globally with the highest degree of confidentiality, ethics, professionalism, and reliable service.

Key Contact - Specialty:
Mr. William G. Teater, Sr., CPC, President - *Metal manufacturers, electrical & electronic, plastic products*

Salary minimum: $50,000

Functions: Generalist, General Mgmt., Mfg., Materials, Sales & Mktg., HR Mgmt., Finance, MIS Mgmt., Int'l.

Industries: Mfg., Medical Devices, Plastics, Rubber, Metal Products, Machine, Appliance, Motor Vehicles, Consumer Elect., Test, Measure Equip., Misc. Mfg., Haz. Waste, Packaging

Executive Resources Int'l

BP 632
Succursale Victoria
Westmount, QC H3Z 2Y7
Canada
(514) 935-3695
(800) 667-5928
Fax: (514) 931-2495
Email: eri@istar.ca

Description: We are an executive search organization recruiting management and technical personnel for service in developing areas and North America.

Key Contact - Specialty:
Mr. G. P. Creighton, Principal - *Generalist*
Mr. Michael E. Berger, Associate Emeritus - *Generalist*

Salary minimum: $40,000

Functions: Senior Mgmt., Middle Mgmt., Admin. Svcs., Distribution, Personnel, Finance, Engineering, Environmentalists, Architects

Industries: Agri., Forestry, Mining, Energy, Utilities, Construction, Misc. Financial, Accounting, Haz. Waste, Non-classifiable

Executive Sales Search Inc

1815 Habersham Trace
Cumming, GA 30041
(770) 889-9665
Fax: (770) 889-9350
Email: lindamende@ga.prestige.net

Description: Search and recruitment in medical, pharmaceutical, and healthcare sales and sales management.

Key Contact - Specialty:
Ms. Linda H. Mende, Owner - *Medical sales, sales management, marketing*

Functions: Middle Mgmt., Sales & Mktg., Sales Mgmt.

Industries: Drugs Mfg., Medical Devices, Pharm Svcs., Biotech, Healthcare, Hospitals, Long-term Care, Dental

Professional Associations: FIN

Networks: First Interview Network (FIN)

Executive Sales Search Inc

8232 Ammonett Dr
Richmond, VA 23235
(804) 560-7327
(804) 560-4726
Fax: (804) 560-7564
Email: info@headhunter-sales.com
Web: www.headhunter-sales.com

Description: Sales & marketing recruiters dealing in senior sales executives and up to VP's and directors of sales and marketing.

Key Contact - Specialty:
Mr. David W. Bell, President - *Sales & marketing recruiting*

Functions: Sales & Mktg.

Industries: Generalist

Networks: Top Echelon Network

Executive Search

13807 Penn St
Whittier, CA 90602
(562) 789-1107
Fax: (562) 789-0107
Email: execsearchinc@aol.com

Description: We specialize in engineers, sales and marketing, graphics, director/VP, quality control, and senior management candidates. We use the performance-Based hiring techniques.

Key Contact:
Ms. Cheryl Johnson

Functions: Generalist, Engineering

Industries: Mfg., Food, Bev., Tobacco, Chemicals, Drugs Mfg., Medical Devices, Plastics, Rubber, Metal Products, Consumer Elect., Misc. Mfg., Electronic, Elec. Components, Communications, Aerospace, Packaging, Software, Biotech, Non-classifiable

Executive Search Associates

140 Newburry St Ste 301
Cambridge, MA 02116
(617) 375-6060
Fax: (617) 375-6050
Email: phil@execsearchusa.com
Web: www.execsearchusa.com

Description: National network and contacts in healthcare, managed care and the sub-specialty of medicare risk and medicaid.

Key Contact - Specialty:
Mr. Philip Morimoto, President/Principal - *Managed care*

Functions: Generalist, Physicians, Health Admin., Sales Mgmt., Direct Mktg., Customer Svc., CFO's, MIS Mgmt.

Industries: Generalist, Insurance, Healthcare

Branches:
468 Jewett Holmwood Rd
East Aurora, NY 14052
(716) 655-2102
Fax: (617) 497-5005
Email: sraymond@adelphia.net
Key Contact:
Ms. Sharon Raymond, Vice President

Executive Search Consultants

2108 Appaloosa Cir
Petaluma, CA 94954-4654
(707) 763-0100
Fax: (707) 765-6963
Email: peg@escba.com
Web: www.escba.com

Description: We specialize in senior software product development & marketing positions for Silicon Valley start-ups. We focus on Internet and networking environments for both software and hardware developers and managers. In general, we look for senior designers, architect, management, director, CTO, VP & CEO/COO level.

Key Contact - Specialty:
Ms. Peg Iversen Grubb, President - *Software product development*

Salary minimum: $85,000

Functions: Product Dev.

Industries: Computer Equip., Consumer Elect., Telecoms, Software

Executive Search Consultants Inc

2436 N Federal Hwy Ste 334
Lighthouse Point, FL 33064
(954) 783-1833
Fax: (954) 783-1890
Email: lenkurtz@mindspring.com
Web: www.insurancerecruiters.com

Description: The company works within the property casualty insurance industry with a majority of the searches for actuaries, claims professionals, marketing staff and underwriters with a concentration in professional liability, national accounts, alternative markets and reinsurance.

Key Contact - Specialty:
Mr. Leonard A. Kurtz, Principal - *Insurance (property, casualty), generalist*

Salary minimum: $50,000

Functions: Generalist

Industries: Insurance

Professional Associations: INS

Networks: US Recruiters.com

Executive Search Consultants Corp

8 S Michigan Ave Ste 1205
Chicago, IL 60603
(312) 251-8400

Description: Recruitment without delegation ensures high quality execution tailored to transform the ideal to tangible. Offering counsel in partnership with client, sharing observations and experience, building fidelity through commitment. Firm size affords full time and attention.

Key Contact - Specialty:
Mr. Jack Flynn, Manager - *Insurance*
Mr. William Weatherstone, President - *Insurance*
Ms. Sandy Kinney, Vice President - *Telecommunications*
Mr. Bill Williams, Senior Consultant - *Oil, gas, electrical utilities*
Mr. Joe Marcello, Senior Consultant - *Non-profit*
Mr. Brent O'Brien, Consultant - *Oil, gas, electrical utilities*

Salary minimum: $50,000

Functions: Generalist, Senior Mgmt., Middle Mgmt., CFO's, Cash Mgmt., Risk Mgmt., Mgmt. Consultants, Non-profits

Industries: Generalist, Energy, Utilities, Broadcast, Film, Insurance

Executive Search Group LLC

30101 Town Center Dr Ste 214
Laguna Niguel, CA 92677-2065
(949) 249-2111
(800) 677-8098
Fax: (949) 249-7999
Email: phil@esg.cc
Web: www.esg.cc

Description: We are specialists in the property casualty insurance field and pension funds, both public and private, including Taft - Hartley. The types of positions filled include: underwriting, claims, auditing, legal, marketing, client services, investor relations, sales, marketing, and IT. Our client base range from carrier companies/brokers/pension fund managers to pension fund advisors.

Key Contact - Specialty:
Mr. Phil Stephenson, Principal - *Insurance, property & casualty, MIS consulting, financial services*

Salary minimum: $50,000

Functions: Generalist, Cash Mgmt.

Industries: Finance, Misc. Financial, Services, IT Implementation, Insurance

Professional Associations: CSP

Networks: National Personnel Assoc (NPA)

Executive Search Group Inc

PO Box 221
Colchester, CT 06415
(860) 537-2373
Fax: (860) 537-2374
Email: exec.search.grp@snet.net

Description: Independent contingency search firm specializing in placements to the armored car industry, packaging industry, and aerospace industry.

Key Contact - Specialty:
Mr. Rudy Brann, Owner - *Packaging, mechanical engineering*

Salary minimum: $30,000

Functions: Generalist, Senior Mgmt., Middle Mgmt., Packaging

Industries: Generalist, Services, Aerospace, Packaging, Non-classifiable

Executive Search Group

413 WoodbridgeRd Ste 200
Rockville Centre, NY 11570
(516) 255-5308
Fax: (516) 255-5309

Email: recruit@optonline.net

Description: Our firm specializes in the recruitment and placement of outstanding individuals in information technology, from Helpdesk to CIO/CTO, as well as sales and sales management for high technology firms.

Key Contact:
Mr. Jeff Goldberg, President

Functions: Sales Mgmt., IT

Industries: Generalist

Executive Search Group

1300 Weathervane Ln Ste 216
Akron, OH 44313
(330) 867-7725
Fax: (330) 867-7724
Email: recruitus@mindspring.com

Description: Executive placement firm specializing in the toy and consumer products industries. Client list includes numerous Fortune 500 companies. Expertise in CEO and Vice President level searches. Firm offers personal service, is aggressive, and ethical.

Key Contact - Specialty:
Mr. David E. Fitzgibbons, CPC, Senior Partner - *Sales, Marketing*

Salary minimum: $45,000

Functions: Senior Mgmt., Middle Mgmt., Mktg. Mgmt., Sales Mgmt.

Industries: Misc. Mfg., Non-classifiable

Professional Associations: NAPS

Executive Search Int'l (ESI)

733 N Magnolia Ave
Orlando, FL 32803
(407) 926-6000
Fax: (407) 425-1539
Email: bwosgien@esiglobal.cc
Web: www.esiglobal.cc

Description: We are a US-based executive recruitment company serving the hospitality industry throughout the world.

Key Contact:
Mr. Bernd K. Wosgien, Chairman/CEO

Functions: Generalist, Senior Mgmt., Middle Mgmt.

Industries: Generalist, Food, Bev., Tobacco, Hospitality, Restaurants

Executive Search Int'l

60 Walnut St
Wellesley, MA 02481
(781) 239-0303
Fax: (781) 235-0465
Email: info@execsearchintl.com

Description: We are a premier, generalist boutique firm providing personalized search and recruiting services for client organizations ranging from multinational corporations to small entrepreneurial businesses, to venture capital backed organizations.

Key Contact:
Mr. Les Gore, Managing Partner

Salary minimum: $100,000

Functions: General Mgmt.

Industries: Generalist, Food, Bev., Tobacco, Soap, Perf., Cosmtcs., Misc. Mfg., Wholesale, Retail, Venture Cap., Services, Media, Marketing SW

Networks: TranSearch Int'l

Executive Search Int'l Inc

3033 W Parker Rd Ste 204
Plano, TX 75023-8029
(972) 424-4714
Fax: (972) 424-5314
Email: mail@esihbc.com
Web: www.esihbc.com

Description: We are specialists in consumer packaged goods industry with key focus on OTC pharmaceuticals, HBC, cosmetics, vitamin/nutritional, and GMDSE from president level to key account managers in sales, market research, and marketing worldwide.

Key Contact - Specialty:
Mr. Ed Nalley, CPC, President/Executive Recruiter - *Sales & marketing, consumer products*
Mr. Jeff Nalley, CPC, Executive Recruiter - *Sales & marketing, consumer products*
Ms. Ginger Nalley, CPC, Executive Recruiter - *Category management, consumer products, marketing & sales*
Ms. Linda Rogers, Project Coordinator - *Category management, consumer products*
Ms. Tina Sparkman, Researcher - *Consumer products, sales & marketing*

Salary minimum: $45,000

Functions: General Mgmt., Directors, Senior Mgmt., Product Dev., Sales & Mktg., Mkt. Research, Sales Mgmt.

Industries: Food, Bev., Tobacco, Soap, Perf., Cosmtcs., Drugs Mfg., Medical Devices, Marketing SW

Professional Associations: IRG, MAPS, NACDS, NAPS, NNFA, PLMA, RON, SERC, TAPS

Executive Search Int'l (ESI) Inc

375 NW Gilman Blvd Ste C101
Issaquah, WA 98027
(425) 391-2465
Fax: (425) 557-9925
Email: seattle@esi-search.com
Web: www.esi-search.com

Description: With an emphasis on emerging technologies, our firm provides companies with highly trained professionals in the IT and telecommunications industries. We maintain offices in Seattle, Silicon Valley, Charlotte, and Seoul, Korea

Key Contact - Specialty:
Mr. Dave Johnson, CEO
Mr. James Shellhammer, CPC, EVP/Search Operations - *Telecommunications, IT*
Mr. D. Scott Miles, MBA, Senior Vice President - *Private equity and retained services division*
Mr. Samuel Apgar, MBA, Vice President Business Development - *Asia pacific region, retained services & equity division*
Ms. Tamara Hynson, Vice President Business Development - *Retained services & private equity division*
Mr. James Rubendall, Vice President Business Development - *Information technology*

Salary minimum: $40,000

Functions: Generalist

Industries: Computer Equip., Telecoms, Software

Networks: Top Echelon Network

Executive Search Ltd

8940 Beckett Rd
West Chester, OH 45069
(513) 874-6901
(513) 714-1060
Fax: (513) 870-6348
Email: executivesearch@executivesearch.net
Web: www.executivesearch.net

Description: Seasoned account executives with extensive prior experience in manufacturing, engineering, marketing, human resources and general manufacturing, foundry, automotive, capital equipment, food, pulp/paper, IS/IT and healthcare. Also provide expert witness services.

Key Contact - Specialty:
Mrs. Terry Cimino, CEO - *Technical, operations, metal fab, machining electronics*
Mr. James J. Cimino, President - *COO's, CEO's, mainly manufacturing, expert witness*

Salary minimum: $65,000

Functions: Generalist

Industries: Energy, Utilities, Mfg., Finance, Equip Svcs., HR Services, Packaging, Software, Biotech, Healthcare

Professional Associations: AFS, IMA, NAFE, NSBE, SAE, TAPPI, WIP

Executive Search Management Inc

2111 W Plum St Ste 388
PO Box 2881
Aurora, IL 60506
(630) 859-2200
Fax: (630) 859-2668
Email: executivesearch@esm-aurora.com

Description: We are a growing search firm whose approach is focuses on the specialized needs of our client companies. We have experienced significant growth in 2000 due to our partnership agreements with many of the top companies. We have associates in the financial, IT, industrial, marketing, engineering, and sales. Our unique approach searching the passive candidate marketplace has provided our client companies with the best available candidates. Our time efficient system can generally close the most difficult searches within 30 days.

Key Contact - Specialty:
Ms. Kristina Erdrich, President/Account Executive - *Financial, IT, telecom*
Mr. John Erdrich, Senior Account Manager - *Industrial, engineering, sales*

Salary minimum: $40,000

Functions: General Mgmt.

Industries: Construction, Mfg., Finance, Services, Equip Svcs., Media, Telecoms, Real Estate, Software

Executive Search Network

2920 N 24th Ave Ste 23
Phoenix, AZ 85015-5949
(602) 254-4341
Fax: (602) 254-2319
Email: marysnow@indirect.com
Web: www.executivesearchnetwork.com

Description: Targeting is our business. We specialize in the recruitment of executives in direct marketing and sales promotional advertising. We place database marketing and CRM specialists.

Key Contact:
Ms. Mary E. Snow, Owner/Recruiter

Salary minimum: $35,000

Functions: Direct Mktg.

Industries: Generalist

Executive Search of New England Inc

131 Ocean St
South Portland, ME 04106
(207) 741-4100
Fax: (207) 741-4110
Email: info@jobsesne.com
Web: www.jobsesne.com

Description: We are one of the area's largest and most diverse search and recruiting firms. Recently,

we celebrated our 29th year recruiting top professional talent for our valued clients. Our staff of eight personnel consultants brings a wealth of experience to a select list of local, regional, national, and international clients.

Key Contact - Specialty:
Mr. Robert L. Sloat, CPC, Partner - *Sales & marketing, banking*
Mr. Robert T. Thayer, Partner - *Finance & accounting*

Salary minimum: $30,000

Functions: Generalist

Industries: Mfg., Banking, Misc. Financial, Services, Advertising, Telecoms

Professional Associations: NNEAPS

Networks: National Personnel Assoc (NPA)

Executive Search of America LLC

22700 Shore Center Dr
Cleveland, OH 44123
(216) 261-7400
Fax: (216) 289-1635
Email: jobs@execsearchamerica.com
Web: www.execsearchamerica.com

Description: Executive search $40,000 - $250,000 salary range. Key disciplines: telecommunications, wireless communications; P.C.S., cellular, paging, software/hardware engineering, AMPS, CDMA, TDMA and GSM technologies, RF engineering. Expertise in wireless recruiting.

Key Contact:
Mr. Scott Carpenter, Vice President
Mr. Marko Prpic, Vice President

Salary minimum: $50,000

Functions: Generalist, Senior Mgmt., Sales & Mktg., Sales Mgmt., IT, Systems Dev., Network Admin., Engineering

Industries: Generalist, Consumer Elect., Test, Measure Equip., Banking, New Media, Telecoms, Wireless

Branches:
8333 Foothill Blvd
Rancho Cucamonga, CA 91730
(909) 579-8244
Fax: (909) 483-7858
Email: socha@execsearchamerica.com
Key Contact:
Mr. Jason Socha, VP

137 Midway Is
Clearwater Beach, FL 33767-2314
(727) 447-4295
Key Contact:
Mr. Edward Carpenter

Executive Search Team

30700 Telegraph Rd Ste 3674
Bingham Farms, MI 48025
(248) 433-9770
Fax: (248) 433-8828
Email: phil.levin@cpijobs.com

Description: We are a contingent fee firm specializing in upper-level recruiting in the areas of general management, finance, information technology, sales, marketing and human resources.

Key Contact:
Mr. Phillip Levin, Chairman - *CEO, COO, CIO, CFO, VP-Sales*
Mr. Marv Talan, Consultant - *Finance, marketing, human resources, sales*
Mr. Roger Manning, Consultant - *Information technology, accounting, sales*
Mr. Joal Burtka, Principal - *Technical, engineers, information technology*
Ms. Theresa Zimmerman, Executive Assistant

Salary minimum: $75,000

Functions: Generalist, Senior Mgmt., Plant Mgmt., Mkt. Research, Budgeting, Systems Analysis, Systems Dev., Mgmt. Consultants

Industries: Generalist, Mfg., Finance, Accounting, Mgmt. Consulting, HR Services, Insurance, Real Estate

J K Executive Search
19777 N 76th St Apt 1132
Scottsdale, AZ 85255
(877) 371-0729
(480) 219-1865
Email: jkexecsrch@aol.com

Description: Property & casualty insurance specialists.

Key Contact:
Ms. Jill Kemper, CPCU, Owner

Salary minimum: $20,000

Functions: Generalist

Industries: Insurance

Professional Associations: CPCU

The Executive Search Corp
772 Central Ave
Kinston, NC 28504
(252) 527-5900
Fax: (252) 527-5592
Email: mdaughety@esn.net
Web: www.pulpandpaperjobs.com

Description: We have over twenty-five years of experience in providing human resource and staffing solutions to the pulp and paper industry, globally. We are providers of all staffing solutions to client companies from retained and contingency search, to temporary, and outplacement. Emphasis is placed on retained search and staffing consulting around the world.

Key Contact:
Mr. J. Mac Daughety, President/Owner

Salary minimum: $80,000

Functions: Mfg.

Industries: Paper, Printing

Professional Associations: PIMA, TAPPI

Executive Selections
494 S Seguin
New Braunfels, TX 78130-7938
(830) 629-6291
Fax: (830) 629-6364
Email: execsel@aol.com

Description: Executive search for life insurance companies. Specialty is attorneys in the estate planning discipline

Key Contact:
Mr. Jim K. Rice

Salary minimum: $65,000

Functions: Directors

Industries: Legal, Insurance

Executive Staffers
6360 LBJ FWY Ste 100
Dallas, TX 75240
(972) 448-8730
Fax: (972) 448-8731
Email: info@executivestaffers.com
Web: www.executivestaffers.com

Description: We are an executive search firm that specializes in the placement of mid-to-senior level advertising, marketing, public relations, and sales professionals. We also conduct searches for "C" class executives.

Key Contact:
Mr. Robert Rota, President

Salary minimum: $50,000

Functions: General Mgmt., Directors, Senior Mgmt., Middle Mgmt., Healthcare, Sales & Mktg., Direct Mktg., PR, HR Mgmt.

Industries: Generalist

Professional Associations: EMA, NAPS, SHRM

Executive Staffing Inc
(also known as Sales Consultants of Miami-Coral Gables)
1320 S Dixie Ste 941
Coral Gables, FL 33146
(305) 666-5991
Fax: (305) 666-5994
Email: dm@execstaff.com
Web: www.execstaff.com

Description: Our company is an international executive search firm that specializes in the placement of management, marketing and business development candidates within the international, information technology, telecommunication, medical, consumer, securities, and financial industries.

Key Contact:
Mr. Dennis McCarthy, President

Executive Strategies Inc
701 Macy Dr
Roswell, GA 30076
(770) 552-3085
Fax: (770) 552-1043
Email: esi@esisearch.com
Web: www.esisearch.com

Description: Extensive senior management experience in a multitude of industries. Understanding of internal and external recruiting processes. Work with clients through the entire process: position description, reference checking and follow-up after placement. Principals are former corporate executives.

Key Contact - Specialty:
Mr. Holland R. Earle, Managing Principal - *General management, information technology, nuclear power, software services*

Salary minimum: $85,000

Functions: Senior Mgmt., HR Mgmt., IT

Industries: Energy, Utilities, Mgmt. Consulting, HR Services, Advertising, New Media

Professional Associations: GAPS, JAG, NAPS, SHRM

Executive Transition Group Inc
(a member of Lincolnshire Int'l an IRM Affiliate)
1415 Rte 70 E Ste 403
Cherry Hill Plz
Cherry Hill, NJ 08034
(856) 354-0018
(888) 384-8726
Fax: (856) 354-8358
Email: etg-inc@ix.netcom.com
Web: www.etgtran.com

Description: Mid management to senior level generalist focus. Executive coaching and cultural assessment is conducted through the search to gauge the corporate placement.

Key Contact:
Mr. Michael McGinn, President
Mr. John Kane, VP Business Development
Ms. Susan Heenan, Director of Systems and Administration

Salary minimum: $75,000

Functions: Generalist

Industries: Generalist

Networks: Lincolnshire Int'l

Executive's Silent Partner Ltd
400 Reservoir Ave
The Calart Twr
Providence, RI 02907
(401) 461-5170
Fax: (401) 461-2370
Email: espsearch@aol.com

Description: Well-known as the premier executive recruiter exclusively for the US jewelry manufacturing and jewelry import/export industry. Regarded as confidant for this close-knit, yet large industry. All searches performed confidentially by owner/principal.

Key Contact - Specialty:
Mr. Edward A. Lemire, CPC, President - *Jewelry, accessories*

Salary minimum: $40,000

Functions: Generalist, General Mgmt., Mfg., Purchasing, Materials Plng., Sales & Mktg., CFO's, M&A

Industries: Generalist, Textiles, Apparel

Professional Associations: JSMA, MJSA, WJA

Executive/Retail Placement Associates
6001 Montrose Rd Ste 702
Rockville, MD 20852
(301) 231-8150
Fax: (301) 881-2918
Email: recruiter@executive-placement.com
Web: www.executive-placement.com

Description: Retail industry specialists for: merchandising, operations, management, finance, distribution, loss prevention and management information systems. Personality testing, employee screening. Employee contracting. Advertising industry specialists: account service, media, creative. Human Resource profession specializing in all HR functions including, management, benefits, recruitment, and compensation.

Key Contact - Specialty:
Mr. Mark J. Suss, President - *Retail all areas, advertising (client side), human resources all areas*

Salary minimum: $35,000

Functions: Generalist, Advertising, HR Mgmt.

Industries: Generalist, Retail, HR Services, Advertising

Professional Associations: MAPRC

Networks: Top Echelon Network

Executivefit
202 Strathmore
PO Box 8
Syracuse, NY 13207-0008
(315) 425-9025
Fax: (315) 424-9473
Email: support@executivefit.com
Web: www.executivefit.com

Description: We place emphasis on a skilled professional fit within the following disciplines: data communications, telecommunications, software, hardware and electrical engineering, pharmaceuticals, and Big 5 management consulting. Our functional disciplines include first- and second-level managers, directors, and vice president levels.

Key Contact - Specialty:
Mr. Tim Dermady, Principal - *Telecommunications, software, hardware engineering, electrical engineering, manufacturing*

Salary minimum: $40,000

Functions: Generalist, Product Dev., Production, Plant Mgmt., Mktg. Mgmt., Sales Mgmt., Systems Dev., DB Admin.

Industries: Generalist, Soap, Perf., Cosmtcs., Drugs Mfg., Computer Equip., Consumer Elect., Telecoms, Aerospace, Software

Networks: Top Echelon Network

Executives by Sterling Inc
1880 S Pierce St Ste 16E
Lakewood, CO 80232
(303) 934-7343
Fax: (720) 294-0660
Email: tom@executives.sterling.com
Web: www.executives.sterling.com

Description: We will direct your management-level placement search or enhance your company goals with our consulting expertise. We make sound placements by matching individual capabilities and goals with the specific needs of our client's firms.

Key Contact - Specialty:
Mr. Art Mangual, Principal - *Hospitality, hotel, resort*
Mr. Tom Mulholland, Principal - *Hospitality, hotel, resort*

Salary minimum: $30,000

Functions: Generalist, General Mgmt., Senior Mgmt., Middle Mgmt., Sales Mgmt., CFO's

Industries: Generalist, Services, Hospitality

EXEK Recruiters Ltd
35 Flatt Rd
Rochester, NY 14623
(716) 292-0550
Fax: (716) 292-5645
Email: exek@exek-recruiters.com
Web: www.exek-recruiters.com

Description: We specialize in the placement of engineers, managers, and technical personnel across industries. Our services range from permanent, contracting, and employer of record capabilities through contingency, con-tainer, and retainer arrangements. We partner with employers across the US. We are members of the Better Business Bureau.

Key Contact - Specialty:
Mr. Larry Ploscowe, Vice President - *Engineers, software, hardware, optical personnel*

Salary minimum: $40,000

Professional Associations: ASQ

Networks: Top Echelon Network

EXETER 2100
Computer Park
PO Box 2120
Hampton, NH 03843
(603) 926-6712
Fax: (603) 926-0536
Email: exeter2100@yahoo.com
Web: www.tba.com

Description: The functions that we recruit in include: communications and information technology, applications and software design, and Smart Technology and instrumentation. We serve all industries and organizations, nationwide.

Key Contact - Specialty:
Mr. Bruce A. Montville, Managing Partner - *Information technology*

Salary minimum: $50,000

Functions: Automation, IT, Systems Implem., Network Admin., Engineering, Non-profits

Industries: Generalist

Professional Associations: DPMA, EMA

ExpatRepat Services Inc
401 Cypress St Ste 625
Abilene, TX 79601
(915) 676-2290
Fax: (915) 676-1383
Email: ers@expat-repat.com
Web: www.expat-repat.com

Description: Drawing on experience and expertise gained as cross cultural consultants, we have an in-depth understanding of global business and management issues faced by companies around the world. Multinationals count on us to solve human resources challenges and identify the leadership capital needed to grow and prosper internationally.

Key Contact - Specialty:
Dr. Robert Scott, President - *Senior HR executives*
Prof. Michael Winegeart, Director - *International assignments in Europe*

Salary minimum: $100,000

Functions: Int'l.

Industries: Generalist

Professional Associations: AMA, SIETAR

Expert Company
PO Box 23
Newington, GA 30446
(800) 864-3710
(912) 857-5020
Fax: (912) 857-3408
Email: smithld@expertco.com
Web: www.expertco.com

Description: We specialize in the placement of information systems professionals primarily in health care and health insurance environments. We are particularly involved in programmers and systems analysts in LAN platforms.

Key Contact:
Mr. Larry Smith, Managing Partner - *Information systems*
Mr. Donnie Smith

Salary minimum: $50,000

Functions: Systems Dev.

Industries: Software, Healthcare

Professional Associations: GAPS

Networks: Top Echelon Network

eXsource Inc
2500 W Nash St Ste E
Wilson, NC 27896-1394
(252) 234-6101
Fax: (413) 812-5348
Email: jobs@exsource-inc.com
Web: www.exsource-inc.com

Description: We specialize in recruiting services for the banking, information technology, and healthcare industries. We are a member of the Top Echelon Network, Inc and national association of personnel services.

Key Contact - Specialty:
Mr. Samuel F. Domby, CPC, President - *Banking information systems, healthcare information systems*

Salary minimum: $25,000

Functions: Senior Mgmt., CFO's, IT, MIS Mgmt., Systems Analysis, Systems Dev., Systems Implem., Network Admin., DB Admin., Mgmt. Consultants

Industries: Generalist, Banking, Software, Healthcare

Professional Associations: NAPS

Networks: Top Echelon Network

F L A G
7304 Denly Ct
Wilmington, NC 28411
(910) 681-5002
Email: flag@flagsearch.com
Web: www.flagsearch.com

Description: Our firm specializes exclusively in the lubricant, coolant, grease, and fuel product industries. We have been serving all sized firms nationwide. Our specialty is in any base stocks, additives, and finished products. We recruit for the industrial, retail, commercial, and automotive markets.

Key Contact - Specialty:
Mr. Tom Warren, Owner - *Fuel, lubricant & grease industry*

Salary minimum: $40,000

Functions: Sales & Mktg., R&D

Industries: Chemicals

Professional Associations: SAE, STLE

Fabian Associates Inc
521 5th Ave Fl 17
New York, NY 10017
(212) 697-9460
Fax: (212) 697-9488
Email: jfab@erols.com

Description: President has extensive experience in accounting and finance, having worked for 15 years in Fortune 500 companies. She is also a CPA and MBA and has many contacts in Fortune companies as well as in the financial services industry.

Key Contact - Specialty:
Ms. Jeanne Fabian, President - *Finance & quantitative analysis, direct marketing*

Salary minimum: $50,000

Functions: Plant Mgmt., Distribution, Physicians, Direct Mktg., Finance, Budgeting, Cash Mgmt., M&A, Risk Mgmt., Systems Dev.

Industries: Generalist, Chemicals, Invest. Banking, Entertainment, Telecoms, Entertainment SW, Hospitals

Professional Associations: AICPA, NYSCPA

FAI
PO Box 200248
Denver, CO 80220-0248
(303) 388-8486
Fax: (303) 355-4213
Email: faifranklin@c.s.com

Description: We are a generalist search firm specializing in the CEO, CFO, CIO, and corporation lawyers. We will split fees.

Key Contact - Specialty:
Mr. Gary Franklin, CEO - *Lawyers*

Salary minimum: $55,000

Functions: Generalist, Senior Mgmt., CFO's, MIS Mgmt., Attorneys

Industries: Generalist

Fairfax Group
9800 Shelard Pkwy Ste 110
Plymouth, MN 55441
(763) 541-9898
Fax: (763) 541-9124
Email: careers@fairfaxgroup.com
Web: www.fairfaxgroup.com

Description: We are specialists in senior level information technology executive search. Our sub-specialties include human resource management and senior financial management professionals, for example: CFOs, controllers, and treasurers.

Key Contact:
Mr. Mark Campbell, Managing Partner

Salary minimum: $90,000

Functions: HR Mgmt., CFO's, IT, MIS Mgmt., Systems Analysis, Systems Dev.

Industries: Generalist

Professional Associations: MAPS, NAPS

Fairway Consulting Group
(also known as MRI of Lynbrook)
300 Merrick Rd Ste 404
Lynbrook, NY 11563-2502
(516) 596-2800
Fax: (516) 596-2801
Email: jrw@jobsrecruiting.com
Web: www.jobsrecruiting.com

Description: We are search firm specializing in executive positions for the pharmaceutical, biotech, consumer products, cable, broadband, and IT industries.

Key Contact:
Mr. John Wiener

Functions: Generalist

Industries: Generalist

Fallon & Company
60 E 42nd St Ste 558
New York, NY 10165
(212) 692-0208
Fax: (212) 692-0116
Email: falloncompany@msn.com

Description: We specialize in executive placement within the financial services industry. We personally meet with and thoroughly interview all candidates and are committed to the long view of what is best for the client.

Key Contact:
Mr. Michael E. Fallon, Managing Director - *Investment, trusts, private banking, capital markets*
Ms. Kathryn Jackson, Research Director

Functions: Middle Mgmt.

Industries: Finance, Banking, Invest. Banking, Brokers, Venture Cap., Misc. Financial, Accounting, New Media

Fallstaff Search Inc
111 Warren Rd Ste 4B
Hunt Valley, MD 21030
(410) 666-1100
Fax: (410) 666-1119
Email: fallstaffsearch@aol.com

Description: We specialize in healthcare, Internet, IT, sales, sales management, marketing, operations, technical support, clinicians.

Key Contact - Specialty:
Mr. Robert Chertkof, President - *Generalist*

Salary minimum: $35,000

Functions: General Mgmt., Senior Mgmt., Middle Mgmt., Healthcare, Physicians, Nurses, Sales & Mktg., IT

Industries: Generalist

Networks: First Interview Network (FIN)

Fament Inc
17 Aldrich Rd Ste B
Columbus, OH 43214
(614) 261-0552
Fax: (614) 261-1820
Email: fament@famentinc.com
Web: www.famentinc.com

Description: Midwest's oldest insurance recruiting firm assisting companies, agencies, brokers and banks with mid- to top-management level personnel needs.

Key Contact - Specialty:
Mr. Marty Shuherk - *Insurance*

Salary minimum: $75,000

Functions: Sales Mgmt.

Industries: Insurance

Professional Associations: IIAA, RIMS

Dorothy W Farnath & Associates Inc
104B Ctr Blvd
N Crossing
Marlton, NJ 08053
(856) 810-2200
Email: office@farnath.com
Web: www.farnath.com

Description: Specialize in recruitment for all positions within the clinical and biotech markets. Our skills in identifying qualified candidates are enhanced by our strong technical education and expertise. Exceptional reputation, consistent ethical standards, excellent references.

Key Contact:
Ms. Dorothy W. Farnath, President - *High level sales & marketing*
Ms. Melissa F. Scott, General Manager - *Generalist*
Mr. Frederick R. Clemens, Associate - *Generalist*
Ms. Barbara N. Toren, Associate - *Generalist*
Ms. Jane Meyers, Associate

Functions: Generalist, Senior Mgmt., Middle Mgmt., Production, Automation, Sales & Mktg., Mktg. Mgmt., Sales Mgmt.

Industries: Medical Devices, Biotech, Healthcare

Professional Associations: MAAPC

Faro Consultants Int'l
2740 Chain Bridge Rd Ste 107
The Legal Centre
Vienna, VA 22181
(703) 281-1122
Fax: (703) 281-6514
Email: farosearch@aol.com
Web: www.farosearch.com

Description: We offer specialized recruiting in compensation and employee benefits consulting, consulting actuaries, and attorneys specializing in ERISA and employee benefits law. We are experts at identifying consulting and legal talent inside and outside of consulting and law firms.

Key Contact - Specialty:
Mr. George Amato, President - *Employee benefits, actuaries, attorneys*
Ms. Susan Lee Moe, Vice President - *International benefits consultants*

Salary minimum: $100,000

Functions: Generalist

Industries: Legal, Mgmt. Consulting

Fast Switch Ltd
37 W Bridge St Ste 200
Dublin, OH 43017
(614) 336-3690
Fax: (614) 336-3695
Email: mark_pukita@fastswitch.com

Description: Our principals have an average of 15 years of experience doing the jobs for which we perform searches. Our clients get only highly qualified candidates because of this; this saves them time and expense. We provide retained search services for both our retained and contingency clients.

Key Contact - Specialty:
Mr. Mark Pukita, Managing Director - *High technology, information systems, sales, general management, cash management*
Ms. Kimberly A. Triplett, Principal - *High technology, information technology, sales, telecommunications*
Ms. Barbara A. Russell, Principal - *High technology, information technology, sales, telecommunications*
Mr. Geoffrey L. Barlow, Principal - *High technology, information technology, sales, telecommunications*
Ms. Susan E. Craig, Principal - *High technology, information technology, sales, telecommunications*
Ms. Lin Hutaff, Principal - *Information technology executives, technology sales, sales managers, executive sales searches*
Ms. Allison Spyker, Principal - *High technology, information technology, sales, telecommunications*

Salary minimum: $60,000

Functions: Sales & Mktg., IT, MIS Mgmt., Systems Analysis, Systems Dev., Systems Implem., Systems Support, Network Admin., DB Admin., Mgmt. Consultants

Industries: Generalist, Computer Equip., Mgmt. Consulting, New Media, Telecoms, Software

Professional Associations: RON

Networks: Top Echelon Network

Federal Placement Services
35 Park Ave Ste 6M
Suffern, NY 10901
(845) 357-5945
Email: fepl@aol.com

Description: We perform executive search exclusively for the commercial banking and financial communities. Our extensive client base is throughout the Northeast.

Key Contact - Specialty:
Ms. Joan Bialkin, Executive Director - *Banking*

Salary minimum: $40,000

Functions: Generalist

Industries: Finance, Banking

James Feerst & Associates Inc
6613 N Eagle Ridge Dr Ste 200
Tucson, AZ 85750-0931
(520) 529-1594
Fax: (520) 529-1314
Email: judithemiller@email.msn.com

Description: Executive search firm specializing in the worldwide pharmaceutical, biotechnology, diagnostics and medical device fields. Broad range of functional experience. Expert in recruiting physicians. Active in the U.S., Europe and Japan.

Key Contact - Specialty:
Mr. James E. Feerst, President - *Pharmaceutical*
Ms. Judith E. Miller, Executive Vice President - *Pharmaceutical*

Salary minimum: $80,000

Functions: Product Dev., Physicians, Health Admin., Mktg. Mgmt., R&D, Engineering

Industries: Generalist, Drugs Mfg., Medical Devices, Pharm Svcs., Biotech, Healthcare

A E Feldman Associates Inc
445 Northern Blvd Ste 10
Great Neck, NY 11021
(516) 719-7900
Fax: (516) 719-7910
Email: info@execrecruiter.com
Web: www.execrecruiter.com

Description: We are a recruitment/search firm specializing in telecommunications and information technology industries. We recruit in all areas and functions of these industries including wireline, wireless, RF, microwave, optics, photonics, networking infrastructure, hardware, software, and professional services. We service vendors, manufacturers, defense/military, and Fortune 500. We provide quick response, high-quality candidates, industry experience, and insight into corporate needs account for our success and client loyalty. Our placements are made nationwide and worldwide.

Key Contact - Specialty:
Mr. Mitchell Feldman, President/CEO - *Telecommunications, information technology*
Mr. Abe Feldman, Chairman - *Watches, jewelry, retailing, fashion*
Ms. Carol Schwam, Senior Vice President - *Telecommunications, information technology*

Salary minimum: $50,000

Functions: Generalist

Industries: Telecoms, Software

Professional Associations: TRA

Feldman, Gray & Associates Inc

45 St. Clair Ave W Ste 700
Toronto, ON M4V 1K9
Canada
(416) 515-7600
Email: general@feldman-gray.com
Web: www.feldman-gray.com

Description: One of Canada's largest retainer executive search practices providing services to a broad range of industries for over 18 years.

Key Contact - Specialty:
Mr. Frank Gray, Senior Partner - *Generalist, senior management*
Mr. Ron Meyers, Principal - *Generalist, senior management*
Mr. Corey Daxon, Senior Consultant - *Middle management, senior management, generalist*
Ms. Vickie Kalles, Senior Consultant - *Middle management, senior management, generalist*

Salary minimum: $60,000

Functions: Generalist

Industries: Generalist

Fergus Partnership Consulting Inc

1325 Ave of the Americas Fl 23
New York, NY 10019-6026
(212) 767-1775
Fax: (212) 315-0351
Email: office@ferguslex.com
Web: www.ferguslex.com

Description: We successfully conduct attorney searches at all levels in the US and internationally with a particular specialization in partner and senior level positions for global law firms and corporations. In addition, we assist law firms in the acquisition of practice groups and in expansion of law offices worldwide.

Key Contact - Specialty:
Mr. Colin Fergus, Principal - *General counsel, senior counsel, partners*
Ms. Jean M. H. Fergus, Esq., Principal - *General counsel, senior counsel, partners*

Salary minimum: $100,000

Functions: Generalist, Attorneys, Int'l.

Industries: Generalist, Legal

Professional Associations: ABA

Fernow Associates

191 Presidential Blvd Ste BN13
Bala Cynwyd, PA 19004-1207
(610) 664-2281
(610) 664-2282
Fax: (610) 664-2779
Email: cfernow@qwest.net

Description: Offers search and placement within the electronics, computer, aerospace, high-technology, information technology, pharmaceutical and nuclear fields. Also provides outplacement for firms who are downsizing within those areas. Serves US and international.

Key Contact - Specialty:
Mr. Charles S. Fernow, President - *Computers, information technology, engineers, scientists, electronics*
Mr. S. George Goich, Senior Vice President - *Human resources, labor relations*
Mr. Robert A. Burchell, Vice President - *Engineering, scientific*

Salary minimum: $40,000

Functions: General Mgmt., Mfg., Sales & Mktg., HR Mgmt., IT, R&D, Int'l.

Industries: Drugs Mfg., Pharm Svcs., Equip Svcs., HR Services, Telecoms, Defense, Aerospace, Biotech

Networks: Top Echelon Network

Ferris & Associates LLC

399 N 117th St Ste 313
Omaha, NE 68154
(402) 758-9093
Fax: (402) 758-9093
Email: bob@fa.coxatwork.com

Description: Professional permanent and contracting search services specializing in MIS, sales, management, marketing. Offer 25 years of corporate business management experience. Nationwide search services.

Key Contact - Specialty:
Mr. Robert M. Ferris, Jr., Owner - *MIS management, sales & marketing*

Salary minimum: $40,000

Functions: Generalist, General Mgmt., Sales & Mktg., IT, MIS Mgmt., Systems Analysis, Systems Dev., Network Admin.

Industries: Generalist, Finance, Banking, Services, Mgmt. Consulting, Insurance, Software

Networks: Top Echelon Network

Guild Fetridge Acoustical Search Inc

520 White Plains Rd Ste 500
Tarrytown, NY 10591
(914) 467-7851
Fax: (914) 467-7847
Email: gfacoustic@aol.com

Description: We are specialists in acoustics, vibration noise control, HVAC, audio, and audio-visual for engineering, scientific, sales and marketing, and management functions.

Key Contact - Specialty:
Mr. Guild Fetridge, President - *Acoustics, vibration, noise control, HVAC, audio*

Salary minimum: $60,000

Functions: Generalist

Industries: Generalist, Construction, Mfg., Machine, Appliance, Motor Vehicles, Misc. Mfg., Defense, Environmental Svcs., Aerospace, Non-classifiable

Professional Associations: ASA, ICIA, INCE

Jerry Fields Associates

(a division of Howard-Sloan-Koller Group)
300 E 42nd St
New York, NY 10017
(212) 661-6644
(212) 661-5250
Fax: (212) 557-9178
Email: hsk@hsksearch.com
Web: www.hsksearch.com

Description: We recruit in the creative, account management, and account planning areas. We provide executive search and consulting for advertising, sales promotion, interactive agencies, design firms, direct marketing companies, and corporations..

Key Contact - Specialty:
Mr. Edward R. Koller, Jr., President - *General management, operations*
Mr. Philip Growick, Managing Director - *Creative (copy), art, graphics*
Ms. Sharon Spielman, Managing Director - *Marketing, advertising agencies, corporate advertising, planning*

Salary minimum: $80,000

Functions: Directors, Senior Mgmt., Middle Mgmt., Advertising, Graphic Artists

Industries: Advertising, New Media

Professional Associations: ACNY, ADC

Financial Connections Company

5008 Andrea Ave
Annandale, VA 22003
(703) 425-4240
Fax: (703) 323-6919
Email: m6272@erols.com

Description: The founder of our firm has over 30 years of management experience in the life insurance and securities fields in addition to numerous certifications in the fields, namely a CLU, CHFC, and FLMI.

Key Contact - Specialty:
Mr. David A. Richard, National Director - *Life insurance, securities, financial services*

Salary minimum: $50,000

Functions: Generalist

Industries: Banking, Invest. Banking, Brokers, Legal, Insurance

Professional Associations: AAII, ASCLUCHFC, IAFP

Financial Executive Search

(a division of AOC)
2001 Gateway Pl Ste 200W
San Jose, CA 95110
(408) 437-9779
Fax: (408) 437-0716
Email: sanjose@aocnet.com
Web: www.aocnet.com

Description: International staffing firm specializing in recruitment and placement of accounting and finance professionals. Over 120 offices. Headquartered in Saddlebrook, NJ.

Key Contact:
Ms. Sara Boyd, Regional Vice President

Salary minimum: $40,000

Functions: Finance

Industries: Generalist

Financial Executive Search

(a division of AOC)
2777 Summer St
Stamford, CT 06905
(203) 327-5100
(914) 968-1100
Fax: (203) 327-5567
Email: stamford@aocnet.com
Web: www.aocnet.com

Description: We are a speciality recruiting firm that places finance and accounting personnel.

Key Contact - Specialty:
Mr. Marvin Sternlicht, CPA, President - *Accounting & finance*
Ms. Robin Freedman, CPA, Senior Recruiter - *Accounting/finance*

Salary minimum: $35,000

Functions: Generalist, CFO's, Budgeting, Cash Mgmt., Credit, Taxes

Industries: Generalist, Finance

Professional Associations: AICPA, APCNY, NAPC, SACIA

Financial Executive Search

(a division of AOC)
250 E 5th St Ste 330
Chiquita Ctr
Cincinnati, OH 45202
(513) 381-4545
Fax: (513) 381-4672
Email: cincinnati@aocnet.com
Web: www.aocnet.com

Description: We work with the top companies and candidates in the accounting & finance field. We are a national organization that meets all of its candidates face to face before presenting them to a client.

Key Contact - Specialty:
Mr. Eric Roth, CPA, Executive Recruiter - *Accounting & finance*

Salary minimum: $30,000

Functions: CFO's, Budgeting, Cash Mgmt., Credit, Taxes, M&A, Risk Mgmt.

Industries: Generalist

Financial Executive Search

(a division of AOC)
2005 Market St Ste 1930
1 Commerce Sq
Philadelphia, PA 19103
(215) 568-5600
Fax: (215) 569-2211
Email: philadelphia@aocnet.com
Web: www.aocnet.com

Description: Through professional memberships, long-term relationships and constant recruiting, we maintain regular contact with professionals who have the experience, skills and bottom-line accomplishments employers are seeking.

Key Contact - Specialty:
Mr. Mark S. Libes, President - *Accounting & finance*

Functions: Generalist, Middle Mgmt., CFO's, Budgeting, Cash Mgmt., Credit, Taxes, Specialized Svcs.

Industries: Generalist

Financial Executive Search

(a division of AOC)
1730-505 Burrard St Bentall 1
Vancouver, BC V7X 1M4
Canada
(604) 669-9096
Fax: (604) 669-9196

Email: vancouver@aocnet.com
Web: www.aocnet.com

Description: We are uniquely qualified to help you attract outstanding accounting and finance professionals to your organization. We specialize in recruiting and placing a wide range of high-level accounting and finance personnel including controllers, accounting managers, cost accountants, credit managers, staff accountants and more.

Key Contact - Specialty:
Ms. Paula Hollander, Branch Manager - *Accounting & finance, clerical*

Salary minimum: $25,000

Functions: Generalist, CFO's, Budgeting, Cash Mgmt., Credit, Taxes, M&A, Risk Mgmt.

Industries: Generalist, Energy, Utilities, Mfg., Finance, Services, Media, Packaging

Financial Placements

5115 Roe Blvd 200
Roeland Park, KS 66216
(913) 261-7000
Email: mikewall@banknews.com
Web: www.banknews.com

Description: Executive Recruiting-Banking

Key Contact:
Mr. Ray Makalous
Mr. Mike Wall, Search Manager

Professional Associations: NBN

Financial Recruiters

1125 Barrington Rdg
Richmond, IN 47374
(800) 445-1793
Fax: (931) 707-9225
Email: billkoz@usit.net
Web: www.financialrecruiters.go.coolebiz.com

Description: Please see our web site for information.

Key Contact - Specialty:
Mr. William Kozlowski, President - *Commercial lending*

Functions: Generalist

Industries: Banking

Branches:
51 Calderwood
Fairfield Glade, TN 38558
(931) 484-8760
Fax: (931) 707-9225
Email: billkoz@usit.net
Key Contact - Specialty:
Mr. William Kozlowski, President - *Commercial lending*

Financial Resource Associates Inc

105 W Orange St
Altamonte Springs, FL 32714
(407) 869-7000
Fax: (407) 682-7291
Email: frasearch@frasearch.com
Web: www.banking-financejobs.com

Description: We are a national executive search firm specializing in the recruitment and placement of middle and senior management executives for mortgage companies, banks, savings and loans, real estate industry and other financial institutions throughout the country.

Key Contact - Specialty:
Mr. John Cannavino, President - *Commercial banking*
Mr. Matthew J Cannavino, Senior Associate - *Commercial banking*

Salary minimum: $40,000

Functions: Finance, CFO's, Budgeting, Cash Mgmt., Credit, Taxes, M&A, Risk Mgmt.

Industries: Finance, Banking, Invest. Banking, Brokers, Venture Cap., Misc. Financial

Professional Associations: FAPS, NAER

Networks: National Banking Network (NBN)

FINANCIALjobs.com

(also known as the Scott-Marlow Agency)
481 El Jina Ln
Ojai, CA 93023
(805) 640-1849
Email: muller@financialjobs.com
Web: www.financialjobs.com

Description: We recruit for accounting and finance jobs in the US and California, from accounting staff to financial analysts, auditors, tax, controllers, CFOs, CIOs, CEOs, and COOs. Our firm accepts paid job ads from companies. We were the winner in the "Top 100 Recruiting Sites" from InterBizNet. There is never a fee to job seekers.

Key Contact - Specialty:
Mr. Michael Muller, Executive Recruiter - *Accounting and financial, CPAs, MBAs, finance (all jobs)*

Salary minimum: $40,000

Functions: Directors, Senior Mgmt., Middle Mgmt., Finance, CFO's, Budgeting, Cash Mgmt., Credit, Taxes

Industries: Generalist, Mfg., Services, Accounting, Mgmt. Consulting, Hospitality

Professional Associations: CSP

Networks: Top Echelon Network

FinancialPeople, LLC

1231 Delaware Ave Ste 1
Buffalo, NY 14209
(716) 884-1734
Fax: (716) 883-0776
Email: jdaily@cpstaffing.com
Web: www.cpstaffing.com

Description: Specialize in accounting, banking, finance, human resources, serve upstate NY and Northwest PA directly, and through membership in AAFA cover entire USA, parts of Canada and Europe.

Key Contact:
Mr. John Daily, CMA

Salary minimum: $30,000

Functions: Generalist, Benefits, Personnel, CFO's, Budgeting, Cash Mgmt., Credit, Taxes

Industries: Generalist, Misc. Mfg., Banking, Accounting, Broadcast, Film, Healthcare

Professional Associations: AAFA, IMA

Find

PO Box 3215
Spring, TX 77383
(281) 298-2001
Fax: (281) 364-8801
Email: kjack@find-gis.com
Web: www.find-gis.com

Description: We specialize in the recruitment of software engineers, programmers, analysts, sales and marketing professionals, and executives in geographical information systems (GIS) and related spatial technology applications only.

Key Contact - Specialty:
Mr. Kenneth Jack, President - *GIS professionals*
Mr. Denis Walsh, Senior Consultant - *Sales, marketing, spatial technologies*
Mr. Joe Raulins, Consultant - *GIS technology*

Salary minimum: $50,000

Functions: General Mgmt., Senior Mgmt., Middle Mgmt., Sales & Mktg., Sales Mgmt., Systems Dev., Systems Implem., DB Admin.

Industries: Software

Finders-Seekers Inc
2372 Hwy K
Bay, MO 65041-4742
(800) 636-2999
(573) 943-6326
Fax: (573) 943-6348
Email: fsi@finderseekers.com
Web: www.finderseekers.com

Description: Executive recruiter for sales and marketing positions within consumer packaged goods (food, beverage, drug) manufacturing companies. Special emphasis in category management and strategic partnering.

Key Contact - Specialty:
Mr. Derek W. Thomas, President/Managing Partner - *Food & drug sales, category management, trade partnering*
Ms. Zee Worstell, Vice President/Recruiting Partner - *Beverage manufacturers, convenience store, food service sales*

Salary minimum: $50,000

Functions: Sales & Mktg.

Industries: Food, Bev., Tobacco, Soap, Perf., Cosmtcs., Drugs Mfg.

Finn & Schneider Associates Inc
1100 17th St NW Ste 505
Washington, DC 20036
(202) 822-8400
Fax: (202) 466-2898
Email: fslegal@aol.com
Web: www.finnschneider.com

Description: Place partners and associates in all legal specialty areas. Advise on law firm mergers and opening of branch offices. Firm has a national and international referral network. Retainer and contingency search.

Key Contact - Specialty:
Ms. Susan Schneider, Partner - *Attorneys*
Ms. Jacquelyn Finn, Partner - *Attorneys*

Functions: Legal

Industries: Banking, Invest. Banking, Venture Cap., Legal, Telecoms, Government, Aerospace, Real Estate, Biotech, Healthcare

Professional Associations: NALSC

Finney-Taylor Consulting Group Ltd
900, 706-7 Ave SW
Calgary, AB T2P 0Z1
Canada
(403) 264-4001
Fax: (403) 264-4057
Email: mailbox@finney-taylor.com
Web: www.finney-taylor.com

Description: Technical recruiting both permanent and contract in the areas of IT.

Key Contact - Specialty:
Mr. David Skode, President - *Information systems*

Salary minimum: $40,000

Functions: Generalist, MIS Mgmt., Systems Analysis, Systems Dev., Systems Implem., Systems Support, Network Admin., DB Admin.

Industries: Generalist, Mfg., Transportation, New Media, Telecoms, Software

Professional Associations: ACSESS

R C Fiore
1335 Fleming Ave Ste 170
Ormond Beach, FL 32174
(904) 615-7675

Description: Twenty plus years' experience, confidentiality, personalized service by our account executives, a client base of the top insurance agencies and companies, industry-wide competitive fee structure. Executive search and placement limited to Florida.

Key Contact - Specialty:
Mr. Richard Fiore, President - *Insurance*

Salary minimum: $20,000

Functions: Generalist

Industries: Insurance

Fipp Associates Inc
PO Box 495
Plainsboro, NJ 08536-0495
(609) 799-2488
Fax: (609) 897-0788
Email: fippinc@att.net

Description: We are a boutique contingency recruiting firm that specializes in the placement of marketing, direct marketing, and advertising account service professionals throughout the US. We also focus on these disciplines in the pharmaceutical and medical equipment industries.

Key Contact - Specialty:
Mr. Steve Fippinger, President - *Advertising account (service, marketing), interactive, new media*

Functions: Generalist, Advertising, Mktg. Mgmt.

Industries: Generalist, Media, Advertising

First Attorney Consultants Ltd
3356 W 95th St
Evergreen Park, IL 60805
(708) 425-5515

Description: Founder formerly practiced with Skadden Arps Slate Meagher & Flom and Mayer Brown & Platt.

Key Contact - Specialty:
Mr. Joseph Marovitch, President - *Attorneys*

Salary minimum: $70,000

Functions: Legal

Industries: Generalist

Professional Associations: CBA

First Call Professional Services
6910 Hillsdale Ct
Indianapolis, IN 46250
(317) 596-3254
Fax: (317) 596-3258
Email: jackkolumbus@staffing.net
Web: www.topechelon.com/firstcall/

Description: We provide contingency and retained search services, US, and international searches. Our firm is a member of the Top Echelon Network. Our specialties include: engineering, manufacturing management, human resources, accounting/finance, sales and marketing, and information technology.

Key Contact - Specialty:
Mr. Jack Kolumbus, Senior Recruiter - *Engineering, manufacturing management, sales & marketing*
Mr. Chuck Henzie, SPHR, Senior Recruiter - *Human resources, accounting, finance, information technology*

Functions: Senior Mgmt., Middle Mgmt., Mfg., Sales & Mktg., HR Mgmt., Finance, IT, Engineering, Int'l.

Industries: Generalist, Mfg.

Networks: Top Echelon Network

First Choice Placement Company
560 Cherokee Rdg
Athens, GA 30606
(706) 549-2758
Fax: (706) 549-8556
Email: aokrog@aol.com

Description: We recruit engineers.

Key Contact:
Mr. Roger Kent - *Engineers*
Ms. Janet Newcomb, Vice President

Salary minimum: $40,000

Functions: Senior Mgmt., Middle Mgmt., Production, Healthcare, Engineering, Mgmt. Consultants, Environmentalists, Architects, Attorneys

Industries: Generalist, Legal

First Search America Inc
PO Box 85
Ardmore, TN 38449
(931) 423-8800
Fax: (931) 423-8801
Email: firstsearch@ardmore.net

Description: We recruit and place experienced, degreed individuals in food processing including poultry, pork, and red meat processing industries. We specialize in general management, sales/marketing, production, research and development, technical services, and all salaried positions. We work nationally and there is never a fee charged to the applicant.

Key Contact - Specialty:
Mr. Jim Fowler, President - *Agribusiness*
Mr. Luke Haggard, Vice President-Operations - *Poultry processing*

Salary minimum: $35,000

Functions: Generalist, Senior Mgmt., Middle Mgmt., Admin. Svcs., Mfg., Mktg. Mgmt., Sales Mgmt., R&D

Industries: Agri., Forestry, Mining, Food, Bev., Tobacco, Drugs Mfg.

Branches:
4023 Poole Valley Rd SW
Decatur, AL 35603
(256) 308-0880
Fax: (256) 308-0990
Key Contact - Specialty:
Mr. Ray Johnson - *Poultry*

First Search Inc
5906 N Milwaukee Ave
Chicago, IL 60646
(773) 774-0001
Fax: (773) 774-5571
Email: info@firstsearch.com
Web: www.firstsearch.com

Description: Technical recruiters servicing the telecom, cellular, PCS and wireless industry from senior executive-levels in engineering, operations, sales and marketing and R&D, as well as temp-to-perm, contracting and specialty staffing.

Key Contact:
Mr. Mike Zarnek, Vice President-Contracts

Salary minimum: $35,000

Functions: Generalist, Systems Implem., Engineering

Industries: Communications, Telecoms, Telephony, Digital, Wireless, Fiber Optic, Network Infrastructure

Networks: Top Echelon Network

Fishel HR Associates Inc

5125 N 16th St Ste B-125
Phoenix, AZ 85016
(602) 266-5600
Fax: (602) 266-5656
Email: fbocker@fishelhr.com
Web: www.fishelhr.com

Description: Thirty plus years' a leading, full-service, contingency search firm recruiting nationwide for various industries in the areas of human resources, engineering, management, financial, and other professional and technical disciplines.

Key Contact:
Mr. Fred Bocker, President/CEO

Salary minimum: $45,000

Functions: HR Mgmt.

Industries: Generalist

Professional Associations: EMA, SHRM

Networks: National Personnel Assoc (NPA)

Jack Stuart Fisher Associates

PO Box 835
Lakewood, NJ 08701
(732) 367-4950
Fax: (732) 367-2012

Description: Full-service search for scientists mostly in biotech and pharmaceutical companies. Involved with funding for CEOs with mergers and acquisitions experience who want to buy their companies or start new companies.

Key Contact - Specialty:
Mr. Jack Stuart Fisher - *Pharmaceutical, biotechnology research*

Salary minimum: $60,000

Functions: Generalist, Directors, Senior Mgmt., Middle Mgmt., DB Admin., R&D, Engineering

Industries: Generalist, Drugs Mfg., Pharm Svcs.

Fisher-Todd Associates

(a division of Winston Resources LLC)
535 5th Ave Ste 701
New York, NY 10017
(212) 986-9052
(212) 557-5000
Fax: (212) 682-1742
Email: fishertodd@winstonstaffing.com

Description: We recruit at mid- to senior-levels of management within functional specialties in a wide variety of industries. We build long-term relationships by bringing professionalism and expertise to the recruitment process. National/international assignments. Specialty: product and service, marketing management, human resources, sales, sales management, market research, sales promotion and corporate communicators.

Key Contact - Specialty:
Mr. Ronald Franz, Vice President/Principal - *Brand management, sales management, communications, human resources*

Salary minimum: $50,000

Functions: Product Dev., Sales & Mktg., Mkt. Research, Mktg. Mgmt., Direct Mktg., HR Mgmt., Benefits, Personnel, Training

Industries: Generalist

Professional Associations: DMA

Fisource.com

20 Park Plz Ste 476
Boston, MA 02116
(617) 948-2146
Fax: (617) 948-2145

Email: julie@fisource.com
Web: www.fisource.com

Description: We are a woman-owned management resources firm. As our name suggests, our primary industry focus is financial services and its supporting services in law, accounting and information technology. We are personable, persuasive and thoroughly professional.

Key Contact - Specialty:
Ms. Julie Jones, Executive Vice President - *Financial services, marketing*
Ms. Margaret Charles, Recruiting Specialist - *Information technology*
Ms. Kate Egan, Recruiting Specialist - *Financial services*

Salary minimum: $50,000

Functions: Generalist, CFO's, Budgeting, Taxes, MIS Mgmt., Systems Analysis, Network Admin., Attorneys

Industries: Generalist, Banking, Venture Cap., Legal, Accounting, Insurance, Real Estate

Professional Associations: MSCPA, SHRM

Branches:
1029 Vermont Ave
Washington, DC 20005
(202) 737-2310
Fax: (202) 737-2389
Email: fisourcedc@fisource.com
Key Contact - Specialty:
Mr. Jeff Locker - *Information technology*

Fitzpatrick & Associates

6187 Sorrento Ave NW
Canton, OH 44718
(330) 497-8994
Fax: (330) 497-8993
Email: fitz@sssnet.com
Web: www.fitzpatrickcareers.com

Description: Technical search & recruitment firm specializing in the datacom, telecom & semiconductor industries. We recruit hardware (board level, FPGA/ASIC, full custom, mixed signal & analog/RF IC), software (embedded, real-time, firmware, device driver, protocols, etc.)

Key Contact - Specialty:
Mr. James Fitzpatrick, Principal - *Hardware, software, firmware, engineers, managers*

Salary minimum: $65,000

Functions: Generalist

Industries: Telecoms, Telephony, Digital, Wireless, Fiber Optic, Network Infrastructure, Software, Networking, Comm. SW, System SW

Networks: Top Echelon Network

Five Star Staffing

5404 Hillsborough St
Raleigh, NC 27606
(919) 854-4488
Fax: (919) 854-4477
Email: fss@fivestarstaffing.net
Web: www.accountingrecruiters.net

Description: Specialize in the placement of accounting and administrative/clerical professionals in temporary, temp-to-hire and direct hire job openings. We place all levels of these professions.

Key Contact - Specialty:
Ms. Barbara Kuley, President - *Accounting, administrative, human resources*
Ms. Deborah Justice, Director of Sales and Service - *Accounting, administrative, human resources*

Salary minimum: $20,000

Functions: Admin. Svcs., Customer Svc., HR Mgmt., Finance

Industries: Generalist, Finance, Accounting

Flack Jacket Consultants Inc

4503 Sunny Slope Ter
Cincinnati, OH 45229
(513) 641-5444
Fax: (513) 641-5888
Email: j.flack@att.net

Description: We have had years of demonstrated success in placing women and minorities with Fortune 500 companies. Our company also offers consulting services for limited outplacement.

Key Contact - Specialty:
Mr. Joseph Flack, President - *Women, minorities*

Salary minimum: $30,000

Functions: Generalist, General Mgmt., Mfg., Healthcare, Sales & Mktg., Finance, Engineering, Minorities

Industries: Generalist, Mfg., Transportation, Services, Media, Healthcare, Non-classifiable

Flaming & Associates

120 W 6th St Ste 120
Newton, KS 67114
(316) 283-3851
Fax: (316) 283-3859
Email: dsplace@southwind.net

Description: We are a professional search and placement firm serving a broad range of clients within a manufacturing environment, in a variety of industries and markets. Our focus is on mid- to upper level positions within operations, engineering, manufacturing, and manufacturing support, including supply chain and quality systems.

Key Contact - Specialty:
Mr. Don Stucky, Owner / Manager - *Manufacturing*

Functions: Generalist

Industries: Metal Products, Machine, Appliance, Misc. Mfg.

Networks: Inter-City Personnel Assoc (IPA)

Susan Fletcher Attorney Employment Services

501 Grant St Ste 450
Union Trust Bldg
Pittsburgh, PA 15219
(412) 281-6609
Fax: (412) 281-2949
Email: sufletcher@aol.com
Web: www.sflawjobs.com

Description: Eighteen years' experience as law school placement director and legal search consultant. Will supply references from client employers and candidates placed.

Key Contact - Specialty:
Ms. Susan Fletcher - *Attorneys (for law firms, corporations)*

Functions: Legal

Industries: Generalist, Mfg., Legal, Accounting

Professional Associations: NALSC

Flex Execs Management Solutions

645 Executive Dr
Willowbrook, IL 60521
(630) 655-0563
Fax: (630) 655-0564
Email: info@flexexecs.com
Web: www.flexexecs.com

Description: We provide executive search for senior and middle management experts on a full-time or interim basis in the fields of human resources, finance and accounting, and senior management. We are a certified Women's Business Enterprise.

Key Contact - Specialty:
Ms. Karen Murphy, Managing Partner - *Senior management, middle management, human resources, finance, operations*
Ms. Kris Swanson, Managing Partner - *Senior management, middle management, human resources, finance, operations*

Salary minimum: $75,000

Functions: General Mgmt., Senior Mgmt., HR Mgmt., Finance

Industries: Generalist, Finance, Mgmt. Consulting, Development SW, HR SW

Professional Associations: HRMAC, ICPAS, SHRM, WEB

Flexible Resources Inc
399 E Putnam Ave Ste 1
Cos Cob, CT 06807
(203) 629-3255
Fax: (203) 629-3257
Email: ct@flexibleresources.com
Web: www.flexibleresources.com

Description: Placement of highly qualified professionals in flexible work arrangements, e.g. permanent part-time, job sharing, telecommuting and interim management staffing.

Key Contact:
Ms. Laurie Young, Principal - *Permanent part-time & interim management staffing*
Ms. Nadine Mockler, Principal

Functions: Generalist, General Mgmt., Purchasing, Sales & Mktg., HR Mgmt., Finance, IT, Mgmt. Consultants

Industries: Generalist, Mfg., Finance, Services, Media, Software, Healthcare

Professional Associations: NAFE, NAWBO, SHRM

Branches:
542 Hopmeadow St Ste 222
Simsbury, CT 06070
(860) 651-5299
Fax: (860) 651-5964
Email: glasspiege@aol.com
Key Contact - Specialty:
Ms. Susan Glasspiegel - *Permanent part-time & interim management staffing*
Ms. Susan Rietano-Davey - *Permanent part-time & interim management staffing*

381 Elliot St Ste 140L
Newton Upper Falls, MA 02464
(617) 559-0088
Fax: (617) 559-0511
Email: boston@flexibleresources.com
Key Contact:
Ms. Caren Lindner - *Management, staffing (permanent part-tim, interim)*
Ms. Kim Whelan - *Management, staffing (permanent part-time, interim)*
Ms. Jane Deutsch

15 Glenridge Pkwy
Montclair, NJ 07042
(973) 746-1937
Fax: (973) 746-7112
Email: nj@flexibleresources.com
Key Contact:
Ms. Lisa Culhane
Ms. Tracey Austin

305 Madison Ave Ste 449
New York, NY 10017
(212) 697-3867
Fax: (212) 697-3877
Email: ct@flexibleresources.com
Key Contact:
Ms. Nadine Mockler, Principal

Flores Financial Services
314 Sage St Ste 100
Lake Geneva, WI 53147
(262) 248-2771
Fax: (262) 248-2562
Email: info@rflores.com
Web: www.floresfinancialservices.com

Description: The leader in executive recruiting for international bankers. We provide a full range of executive search consulting services to international financial institutions and corporations.

Key Contact:
Mr. Robert Flores, President
Ms. Mary Herman, Director
Mr. Tom Royce, Director
Ms. Sally Kasper, Administrative Assistant

Functions: Generalist, Admin. Svcs., Credit, M&A, Risk Mgmt., MIS Mgmt., Systems Analysis, Systems Dev.

Industries: Generalist, Energy, Utilities, Retail, Finance, Banking, Invest. Banking, Brokers, Misc. Financial, Non-profits, E-commerce, IT Implementation

Professional Associations: BAFT

Branches:
500 N Washington St
Alexandria, VA 22314
(703) 748-1200
Fax: (703) 768-5586
Key Contact:
Mr. Jeff Horner, Director

Flowers & Associates
2100 W Alexis
Toledo, OH 43613
(419) 472-6900
Fax: (419) 472-6902
Email: hdhunter@aol.com

Description: Over 25 years experience in assisting companies in their hard-to-fill positions. We are experienced in working with all levels of management with enthusiasm.

Key Contact - Specialty:
Mr. William J. Ross, President - *Manufacturing, engineering*
Mr. Eric W. Ross - *Manufacturing*

Salary minimum: $35,000

Functions: Generalist

Industries: Mfg., Medical Devices, Plastics, Rubber, Metal Products, Machine, Appliance, Motor Vehicles, Computer Equip., Test, Measure Equip.

Networks: Inter-City Personnel Assoc (IPA)

FMK Staffing Services LLC
6750 NW 101st Ter
Parkland, FL 33076
(954) 796-8550
Email: resume@fmkstaffing.com
Web: www.fmkstaffing.com

Description: We specialize in the recruitment of mid- to senior-level information technology executives with strong technical vision and capabilities, who bring above average business acumen to the table. Our focus is on distributed systems and emerging technologies for corporate environments, networking companies, and e-Commerce-driven business units.

Key Contact - Specialty:
Mr. Bob Kalinowski, Managing Partner - *Information technology, networking, web technologies, ecommerce, management*
Ms. Roz McKinnon, Managing Partner - *Information technology, client/server, internet, networking*

Ms. Karen Wiegand, Partner - *Information technology, networking, data sales, telecom sales*

Salary minimum: $90,000

Functions: Sales Mgmt., IT, MIS Mgmt., Systems Analysis, Systems Dev., Systems Implem., Systems Support, Network Admin., DB Admin., Engineering

Industries: Generalist, Media, Telecoms, Digital, Network Infrastructure, System SW

David Fockler & Associates Inc
25944 Paseo Estribo
Monterey, CA 93940
(831) 649-6666
Fax: (831) 649-0600
Email: dave@fockler.com
Web: www.fockler.com

Description: Sales and marketing management positions for food, both retail and food service; consumer products, HBC, foodservice equipment and food ingredient manufacturers. Mid-management ($50K) to lower upper-management ($150K).

Key Contact - Specialty:
Mr. David B. Fockler, Principal - *Sales & marketing management for food, consumer products, food ingredients, food equipment & HBC manufacturers*

Salary minimum: $50,000

Functions: Sales & Mktg., Advertising, Mkt. Research, Mktg. Mgmt., Sales Mgmt.

Industries: Food, Bev., Tobacco, Soap, Perf., Cosmtcs., Drugs Mfg., Consumer Elect.

Professional Associations: FMI, NACDS

Branches:
940 S River Rd
Naperville, IL 60540
(630) 428-4112
Fax: (630) 428-3201
Email: steve@fockler.com
Key Contact - Specialty:
Mr. Steve Swan, Partner - *HBC, consumer products, sales and marketing*

Focus Careers
PO Box 584
Blacklick, OH 43004-0584
(614) 575-8446
(614) 367-0748
Fax: (614) 367-0751
Email: mail@focuscareers.com

Description: Executive search firm specializing in the career development of administration, management and accounting professionals throughout central Ohio.

Key Contact - Specialty:
Mrs. Denise Stewart, CPC, SPHR, Owner - *Real estate, development, energy, telecom*

Functions: General Mgmt., Sales & Mktg., HR Mgmt., Finance, Engineering

Industries: Generalist, Energy, Utilities, Construction, Retail, Banking, Services, Legal, Accounting, Mgmt. Consulting, HR Services, Communications, Telecoms, Telephony, Digital, Wireless, Fiber Optic, Network Infrastructure, Environmental Svcs., Insurance, Real Estate

Professional Associations: HRACO, NAPS, OSSA, SHRM

Focus Executive Search
2852 Anthony Ln S
Minneapolis, MN 55418
(612) 706-4444
Fax: (612) 706-0544

Email: focuses@juno.com
Web: www.focusexecutivesearch.com

Description: Excel at partnering with food, packaging, consumer retail and building product industry companies. Offer an understanding of the industries we serve for timely and successful targeted searches. Recruiters all have previous hands on management experience in their industry specialization. Established client base of leading and emerging companies through a consultative partnering recruiting approach that produces top quality candidates.

Key Contact - Specialty:
Mr. Tim McLafferty, President - *Food, food service, bakery, confectionary, dairy*
Mr. Tim Schultz, Vice President - *Food manufacturing equipment industry, beverage, confectionary, produce*
Mr. Tony Misura, Director of Executive Search - *Building products industry, cabinetry, doors, millwork, lumber*
Ms. Frank Bahr, Industry Manager Packaging - *Packaging, graphics, flexographic printing, packaging (food), thermoforming*
Mr. David Warbler, Research Manager - *Generalist*

Salary minimum: $40,000

Functions: Generalist

Industries: Construction, Mfg., Transportation, Wholesale, Retail, Pharm Svcs., HR Services, Hospitality, Packaging

Professional Associations: FPA, IFMA, IFT, IOPP, NAHB, RBA

Focus Tech
3711-C University Dr
Durham, NC 27707
(919) 419-8909
Fax: (919) 419-8897
Email: cheri@focust.com
Web: www.focust.com

Description: We find superstars that will make our client's systems technology company more profitable. Our team consults with our client, to understand their business, to build a long-term relationship and provide top-notch recruiting services that save time, money and add significant value to our client's company.

Key Contact - Specialty:
Ms. Cheri Comstock, CEO - *Sales vice president, professional services*
Ms. Jackie Larson, President - *Sales vice president, professional services*
Ms. Elizabeth Stevens, Partner - *Sales vice president, professional services*

Functions: Generalist, Sales & Mktg., IT

Industries: Generalist, Software

Professional Associations: WIT

Food Management Search
896 Main St
Springfield, MA 01103
(413) 732-2666
Fax: (413) 732-6466
Email: recruiters@foodmanagementsearch.com
Web: www.foodmanagementsearch.com

Description: We are a contingency firm specializing in recruiting food industry career professionals for food production, supermarket and distribution, food service, restaurant, culinary, hotel food, and beverage and sales and marketing positions nationwide. The positions that we place are in the salary range between $40,000 and $175,000.

Key Contact:
Mr. Joseph Cresci, President

Salary minimum: $40,000

Functions: General Mgmt., Senior Mgmt., Plant Mgmt., Purchasing, Mktg. Mgmt., Sales Mgmt., HR Mgmt., Finance, Int'l.

Industries: Mfg., Food, Bev., Tobacco, Wholesale, Retail, Hospitality, Hotels, Resorts, Clubs, Restaurants, Entertainment, Recreation

FOODPRO Recruiters Inc
14526 Jones Maltsberger Ste 210
San Antonio, TX 78247
(210) 494-9272
Fax: (210) 494-9662
Email: msoulek@foodprorecruiters.com
Web: www.foodprorecruiters.com

Description: Our firm specializes in food and related pharmaceutical manufacturing recruitment. Engineers, supervisors, quality control, operations, R&D, logistics, distribution, maintenance, etc. Not involved with sales and marketing positions.

Key Contact - Specialty:
Mr. Michael Soulek, President/General Manager - *Food, pharmaceutical*

Salary minimum: $30,000

Functions: Mfg., Product Dev., Production, Plant Mgmt., Quality, Distribution, Packaging, HR Mgmt., Engineering, Minorities

Industries: Mfg., Food, Bev., Tobacco

Networks: US Recruiters.com

Forbes & Gunn Consultants Ltd
1420 - 5th Ave Ste 2200
Seattle, WA 98101
(206) 523-7480
Fax: (206) 523-7412
Email: jobs@forbes-gunn.com

Description: Our firm specializes in information technology recruiting and contract consulting.

Key Contact - Specialty:
Mr. Lee Brebber, President - *Information technology*

Salary minimum: $25,000

Functions: Generalist

Industries: E-commerce, IT Implementation, Telecoms, Telephony, Digital, Wireless, Network Infrastructure, Software, Database SW, Development SW

Professional Associations: BCHRMA, CIPS, WSA

Branches:
12000 NE 8th St Ste 205
Bellevue, WA 98005
(425) 455-0130
Fax: (425) 455-0312
Email: mail@forbes-gunn.com
Key Contact - Specialty:
Mr. Lee Brebber, President - *information technology*

1166 Alberni St Ste 1650
Vancouver, BC V6E 3Z3
Canada
(604) 688-6461
Fax: (604) 681-6401
Email: mail@forbes-gunn.com
Key Contact:
Mr. Lee Brebber, President

Ford & Associates Inc
808 Greenbay Trl
Myrtle Beach, SC 29577
(843) 497-5350
Fax: (843) 497-5351
Email: fordsearch@msn.com
Web: www.fordsearch.com

Description: We are specialists in confidential recruiting for engineers, line operations

management, and staff professionals within the textile, chemical, plastics, and metal industries.

Key Contact - Specialty:
Mr. Travis Ford, President - *Textile manufacturing (line & staff positions), chemical, plastic, metal fabrication professionals*
Mrs. Merlin B. Ford, Consultant - *Generalist*

Salary minimum: $38,000

Functions: Generalist, Mfg., Materials, HR Mgmt., Finance, Budgeting, IT, Engineering

Industries: Generalist, Textiles, Apparel, Chemicals, Drugs Mfg., Plastics, Rubber, Metal Products, Machine, Appliance, Motor Vehicles

Professional Associations: SCAPS

Networks: National Consulting Network (NCN)

Ford & Ford
105 Chestnut St Ste 34
Needham, MA 02492
(781) 449-8200
Fax: (781) 444-7335
Email: seek@staffing.net
Web: www.logonajob.com

Description: Our corporate specialties include: technical management, IT management, CFOs, CEOs, treasurers, finance, retail, direct marketing, e-Commerce, call center management, telemarketing, distribution and fulfillment, logistics, information technology and networking, web development, graphic design, consulting, corporate management, human resources, marketing communication, advertising, customer service, and technical documentation. Our industry strengths include: energy, retail, supply chain management, call center, and non-profit.

Key Contact - Specialty:
Ms. Eileen F. Ford, Principal - *Retail, distribution, information technology, logistics, direct marketing*

Salary minimum: $75,000

Functions: Distribution, Sales & Mktg., Direct Mktg., Customer Svc., HR Mgmt., CFO's, Minorities

Industries: Generalist

Professional Associations: NARPC, NEMA

Networks: Top Echelon Network

The Forest Group
(also known as MRI of Forest Acres)
2711 Middleburg Dr Ste 313-A
Columbia, SC 29204-2413
(803) 758-5920
Fax: (803) 758-5921
Email: bill@forestgrp.com

Description: Our firm practices in both technical and financial market segments. Our technical recruiters work with the civil and mechanical engineering disciplines. Our financial recruiters focus primarily on commercial lenders, private bankers, and trust officers.

Key Contact - Specialty:
Mr. William F. Duncan, President - *Engineering, consulting engineering*

Salary minimum: $50,000

Functions: Finance, Engineering

Industries: Energy, Utilities, Construction, Mfg., Finance, Banking, Invest. Banking, Brokers, Venture Cap., Misc. Financial

Forest People Int'l Search Ltd

800-1100 Melville St
Vancouver, BC V6E 4A6
Canada
(604) 669-5635
Fax: (604) 684-4972
Email: people@forestpeople.com
Web: www.forestpeople.com

Description: We are Canada's largest forest industry personnel recruiting firm. Serving all sectors of the forest industry, we recruit executive, operational management, professional and technical personnel for a large client group of forest industry companies across Canada and internationally. We are a competent, cost effective recruiting services by knowledgeable forest industry specialists.

Key Contact - Specialty:
Mr. Ronald J. Hogg, President - *Forest industry, senior management*
Mr. Ian McFall, Senior Consultant - *Forest industry, pulp & paper, panel board management*
Mr. Bill Waschuk, Senior Consultant - *Forest industry, sawmills, re-manufacturing management*

Functions: Personnel

Industries: Agri., Forestry, Mining, HR Services

A W Forrester Company

7310 W McNab Rd Ste 207
Tamarac, FL 33321
(954) 722-7554
Fax: (954) 722-8821
Email: ken@awforrester.com
Web: www.awforrester.com

Description: A full-service executive search firm that accept both contingency and retained search assignments. Our areas of specialty includes health care, insurance, actuarial, underwriting, and employee benefits.

Key Contact - Specialty:
Mr. Ken Forrester, Managing Director - *Benefits consulting (health, welfare)*
Mr. Keneth Moore, Recruiter - *Healthcare actuarial, underwriting*
Mr. Scott Fairbrother, Recruiter - *Benefits manager, benefits vice presidents*

Salary minimum: $40,000

Functions: Senior Mgmt., HR Mgmt., Benefits, Mgmt. Consultants

Industries: Mgmt. Consulting, HR Services, Insurance, HR SW, Healthcare

Forsyte Associates Inc

1749 Central St Ste 4
Stoughton, MA 02072
(781) 344-8600
Fax: (781) 344-1896
Email: resumes@forsyte.com
Web: www.forsyte.com

Description: Our firm is a national executive search firm specializing in software sales, sales management, and presales placements within the business applications software industry. We represent clients from a broad spectrum of the software and services industries, for example: CRM, ERP, e-Commerce, unified messaging, supply-chain, HR/payroll, workforce management, financial applications, web-centric applications, e-Recruiting, and virtually all types of B2B solutions. We offer an in depth knowledge of the industry and an extensive network of excellent candidates.

Key Contact - Specialty:
Mr. Mark Wolbarst, Principal Executive Recruiter - *Business application software sales, sales management, presales, business development*
Mr. David Wolbarst, Executive Recruiter - *Software sales, sales management*

Ms. Lynn Reale, AIRS, Website Management/Online Research
Mr. Seth Miller, Executive Recruiter - *Software (sales, sales management)*

Salary minimum: $60,000

Functions: Sales & Mktg., Sales Mgmt.

Industries: HR Services, E-commerce, Telephony, Software, Accounting SW, ERP SW, HR SW

Fortuna Technologies Inc

(also known as Arnit Infotech Inc)
1270A Lawrence Station Rd Ste A
Sunnyvale, CA 94089
(408) 541-0200
(408) 973-1529
Fax: (408) 541-0300
Email: pad@fortuna.com
Web: www.fortuna.com

Description: Delivers on time under budget, with int'l. sourcing, focus on e-commerce, net dynamics, online carts. Oracle financials, SAP, BAAN, PeopleSoft, DBAs, administrators, Windows, HUI, Java, Corba, Y2K, EDA for financial, manufacturing, utilities, retail and e-commerce areas.

Key Contact - Specialty:
Mr. Pad N. Swami, Vice President - *Oracle applications, peoplesoft, CRM, SAP, dba*
Mr. T. C. Ashok, President - *QA*
Mr. William E. Lynch, Vice President - *Netegrity*

Salary minimum: $50,000

Functions: Generalist, MIS Mgmt., Systems Analysis, Systems Dev., Systems Implem., Systems Support, Network Admin., DB Admin.

Industries: Generalist, Mfg., Wholesale, Finance, Services, Media, Software

Branches:
1437 Oak Tree Rd
Iselin, NJ 08830
(732) 404-1033
Fax: (732) 404-1312
Email: fortunanj@aol.com
Key Contact - Specialty:
Mr. Sanjay Nair - *Client server, internet architects, e-commerce, ERP, unix administrators*

Fortune Personnel Consultants (FPC)

1140 Ave of the Americas Fl 5
New York, NY 10036
(212) 302-1141
(800) 886-7839
Email: fpcinfo@fpcnyc.com
Web: www.fpcweb.com

Description: A national executive search firm comprised of 99 independently owned and operated offices serving more than 20 industries. Involved in all phases of recruitment and permanent placement; offering services on either a contingency or retainer basis. Inter-office relationships foster greater oppertunity for both clients and canidates.

Key Contact:
Mr. Rudy Schott, Founder & CEO
Mr. Dennis Inzinna, President
Mr. Ron Herzog, Director of Operations

Salary minimum: $45,000

Professional Associations: IFA

Branches:
42 Corporate Park Ste 220
Irvine, CA 92606
(949) 250-0650
Fax: (949) 250-8535
Web: www.fpcirvine.com
Key Contact:
Mr. Steve Pandolfo, President
Ms. Elaine Cohen, Executive Recruiter

999 Oronoque Ln
Stratford, CT 06614
(203) 385-5022
Fax: (203) 385-5028
Email: plastics@fpc-stratford.com
Web: www.fpc-stratford.com
Key Contact:
Mr. Eric Kniager, President

982 Douglas Ave Ste 104
Altamonte Springs, FL 32714
(407) 875-0833
Fax: (407) 875-1975
Email: consultant@fpcorlando.com
Web: www.fpcorlando.com
Key Contact:
Mr. Jim Laird, President

2175 Tamiami Trl
Osprey, FL 34229
(941) 966-6441
Fax: (941) 966-1912
Email: fpcvenice@packet.net
Key Contact:
Mr. Jim Shirley, President

1501 Johnson Ferry Rd Ste 220
Marietta, GA 30062
(770) 321-1884
Fax: (770) 321-1887
Email: admin@fpcnoga.com
Key Contact:
Ms. Belinda Brock, Owner
Mr. Joe Brock, Owner

850 E Grand Ave
Lake Villa, IL 60046
(847) 265-3412
Fax: (847) 265-3840
Email: resume@fpclakevilla.com
Key Contact:
Ms. Gail Foote
Mr. John Foote

1200 Envoy Cir Ste 1203
Louisville, KY 40299-1817
(502) 493-4113
Fax: (502) 493-4810
Email: dwest@fpclouisville.com
Web: www.fpclouisville.com
Key Contact:
Mr. Dennis West, President

42 Idlewind St Fortune Ctr
Bel Air, MD 21014
(410) 893-0450
Fax: (410) 893-1121
Email: fcbelair@home.com
Web: www.members.home.net/fcbelair
Key Contact:
Mr. Gary G. Hicks, President
Ms. Joanne R. Hicks, Vice President

10 Crossroads Dr 201
Owings Mills, MD 21117
(410) 581-0012
Fax: (410) 581-2280
Email: execsearch@fpcbalt.com
Web: www.fpcbalt.com
Key Contact:
Mr. Walter Drimer, President

180 Denslow Rd Ste 4
East Longmeadow, MA 01028
(413) 525-3800
Fax: (413) 525-2971
Email: resume@fpcspringfield.com
Web: www.fpcspringfield.com
Key Contact:
Ms. Beverly Godleski
Mr. Charlie Godleski

100 Corporate Pl Ste 200
Peabody, MA 01960
(978) 535-9920
Fax: (978) 535-4482
Email: joe@fpcboston.com
Key Contact:
Mr. Joseph Genovese, President

100 Corporate Pl Ste 200
Peabody, MA 01960
(978) 535-9920
Fax: (978) 535-4482
Email: david@fpcboston.com
Key Contact:
Mr. David Mitchell, President

3407 Berrywood Blvd Ste 202
Columbia, MO 65201
(573) 442-2450
Fax: (573) 442-6304
Email: fpccareers@aol.com
Key Contact:
Mr. Steve Weiner, President

571 W Lake Ave Ste 1
Bay Head, NJ 08742
(732) 714-7600
Fax: (732) 714-7607
Email: fpcjshore@msn.com
Key Contact:
Mr. Jim Kenny, President

595 Stewart Ave Ste 700
Garden City, NY 11530
(516) 794-3100
Fax: (516) 228-9609
Email: manigaulte@aol.com
Key Contact:
Mr. Robert Manigaulte

304 Hodges St
PO Box 628
Oriental, NC 28571
(252) 249-3970
Fax: (252) 249-0995
Email: success@fpcchesapeake.com
Key Contact:
Ms. Sandy Hanes, President

725 NW Lava Rd Ste 100
Bend, OR 97701
(541) 330-8847
Fax: (541) 330-5690
Email: fpcbend@coinet.com
Web: www.jobrecruiters.com
Key Contact:
Mr. John Oliveira, President
Ms. Linda Oliveira, Vice President Finance

2321 Huntingdon Pike
PO Box 59
Huntingdon Valley, PA 19006
(215) 914-1000
Fax: (215) 914-1021
Email: johngwille@aol.com
Key Contact:
Mr. John Wille, President

29 N Market St Ste C
Selinsgrove, PA 17870-1924
(570) 374-6744
Fax: (570) 374-8703
Email: fpchar@sunlink.net
Key Contact:
Mr. David A. Lawer, President

210 W 6th St Ste 901
Ft. Worth, TX 76102
(817) 332-5300
Fax: (817) 332-5310
Email: fpcfw@hotmail.com
Key Contact:
Mr. David Strange, President
Mr. Cory Strange, Vice President

1536 N Woodland Park Dr Ste 200
Layton, UT 84041
(801) 775-0444
Fax: (801) 775-0447
Email: fpcslc@uswest.net
Key Contact:
Mr. Ron Hiniker, President

107 W Federal St Ste 9B
PO Box 885
Middleburg, VA 20118
(540) 554-8440
Fax: (540) 554-2935

Email: ncroce@mindspring.com
Key Contact:
Mr. Nicholas Croce, Jr., President

3206 Ironbound Rd Ste D
Williamsburg, VA 23188
(757) 220-0900
Fax: (757) 220-3099
Email: fpcwf@mindspring.com
Key Contact:
Mr. Walter Fowler, President

15300 W Capital Dr Ste 201
Brookfield, WI 53005
(262) 790-6820
Fax: (262) 790-6721
Email: resume@fpcmilwaukee.com
Key Contact:
Mr. Steve Vierling, President
Ms. Bonnie Koch, Vice President

FPC of Decatur

1414 5th Ave SE Ste A/B
Decatur, AL 35601
(256) 341-0400
Fax: (256) 341-0444
Email: fpcdecatur@earthlink.net
Web: www.fpcrecruiting.com

Description: We have over 30 years of experience as human resource professionals, heavily focused on all aspects of hiring and career development. We are especially proud of our reputation for trust and integrity. We specialize in but are not limited to the chemical industry.

Key Contact - Specialty:
Mr. David L. Harris, President - *Chemical engineers, upper management, finance, environmental, sales & marketing*
Mr. Wade Harris, Vice President - *Mechanical engineers, electrical engineers, industrial engineers, purchasing, logistics*
Ms. Marilyn Harris, Administrator
Ms. Leigh Ann Bolan, Administrative Assistant
Mr. Vince Hunter, Professional Recruiter - *Manufacturing*
Ms. Lisa Cherry, Professional Recruiter/Research - *HR, EHS, research*

Salary minimum: $75,000

Functions: Generalist, Mfg.

Industries: Chemicals, Plastics, Rubber, Paints, Petro. Products, HR Services

FPC of Huntsville

3311 Bob Wallace Ave Ste 204
Huntsville, AL 35805
(256) 534-7282
Fax: (256) 534-7334
Email: careers@fpchuntsville.com
Web: www.fpchuntsville.com

Description: Full-service, nationwide. Areas include general management, managers and professionals in the fields of manufacturing, materials, purchasing, quality, engineering, test and software.

Key Contact - Specialty:
Mr. Bob Langford, Owner - *Operations management, manufacturing engineering, management, electronics*
Ms. Lynn Lamb, Executive Recruiter - *Purchasing & materials, P&IC (all industries)*
Mr. Lindy Bell, Executive Recruiter - *Quality, electronics*
Ms. Anneta Simmons, Executive Recruiter - *Test engineering, test engineering management in electronics, electrical engineering, hardware, software*
Mr. Hugh Hanson, Executive Recruiter - *Quality, medical devices, metals, plastics*
Mr. Bill Okonski, Executive Recruiter - *Logistics, distribution*
Ms. Judy Langford, Office Manager

Mr. Andrew Henshaw, Executive Recruiter - *Engineering (mechanical, industrial, optics), electronic packaging (ME)*
Mr. Bob Henshaw, Executive Recruiter - *Operations management, environmental engineering, safety engineering, human resources*
Mr. Joe Petralia, Executive Recruiter - *Plastics industry*
Mr. Matt Langford, Executive Recruiter - *Accounting & finance, manufacturing & process engineers (electronics industries)*
Mr. Mike Messervy, Executive Recruiter - *Quality, medical devices, metals, plastics*

Salary minimum: $30,000

Functions: Generalist, General Mgmt., Mfg., Materials, Sales & Mktg., HR Mgmt., Finance, Engineering

Industries: Generalist, Plastics, Rubber, Motor Vehicles, Computer Equip., Consumer Elect., Test, Measure Equip., Accounting

FPC of The East Bay

3239 Danville Blvd Ste G
Alamo, CA 94507
(800) 291-9229
(925) 837-6060
Fax: (925) 837-2710
Email: fpcebay@ix.netcom.com
Web: www.netcom.com/~fpcebay

Description: We provide professional, confidential searches for professionals that are pre-screened in the computer hardware, software, Internet, and communications areas. We specialize in engineering, sales, and marketing. We have an extensive database. We network and work with other FPC offices.

Key Contact - Specialty:
Mr. Michael Mullery, President - *High technology professionals, sales & marketing, engineering*

Salary minimum: $50,000

Functions: Senior Mgmt., Middle Mgmt., Product Dev., Sales & Mktg., Mkt. Research, Mktg. Mgmt., Sales Mgmt., IT, R&D, Engineering

Industries: Computer Equip., Consumer Elect., Test, Measure Equip., Telecoms, Software

FPC of San Diego

332 Encinitas Blvd Ste 200
Encinitas, CA 92024
(760) 944-8980
Fax: (760) 944-0075
Email: info@fpcsandiego.com
Web: www.fpcsandiego.com

Description: We are a national executive search firm specializing in the placement of professionals in the medical device, pharmaceutical and biotechnology fields.

Key Contact - Specialty:
Mr. Carmine A. Furioso, President - *Regulatory affairs, quality assurance, quality control, clinical research, engineering*
Ms. Donna DeRario, Vice President - *Regulatory affairs, clinical research, data management*

Functions: Generalist, Directors, Senior Mgmt., Middle Mgmt., Product Dev., Quality, IT, Engineering

Industries: Generalist, Drugs Mfg., Medical Devices, Pharm Svcs., Software, Biotech

FPC of Hermosa Beach

2615 Pacific Coast Hwy Ste 330
Hermosa Beach, CA 90254
(310) 376-6964
Fax: (310) 376-7173
Email: mkasten@ix.netcom.com
Web: www.fpcweb.com

Description: Technical positions in medical device, pharmaceutical and biotech industries, including engineering, research and development, manufacturing management, quality assurance, quality control and regulatory.

Key Contact - Specialty:
Mr. Marc Kasten, President - *Medical device, pharmaceutical, biotechnology*

Salary minimum: $50,000

Functions: Directors, Senior Mgmt., Middle Mgmt., Mfg., Materials Plng., Packaging, R&D, Engineering

Industries: Mfg., Drugs Mfg., Medical Devices, Packaging

FPC of Boulder
4450 Arapahoe Ave Ste 100
Boulder, CO 80303
(303) 448-8843
Fax: (303) 543-9444
Email: gkhan@fpcboulder.com
Web: www.fpcboulder.com

Description: We are proud of our reputation for dependability and integrity. Additionally we only introduce you to the most qualified prospects.

Key Contact - Specialty:
Ms. Gale Kahn, President - *High technology, computer workstations, peripherals, software, sales & marketing*
Mr. Ronald J. Kahn, Vice President-Operations - *Senior technical people*

Functions: Systems Analysis, Systems Dev., Systems Implem., Network Admin., DB Admin., Engineering

Industries: Generalist

FPC of Colorado Springs
6165 Lehman Dr Ste 202
Colorado Springs, CO 80918
(719) 599-7353
Fax: (719) 599-7339
Email: david@fpccos.com
Web: www.fpccos.com

Description: Our firm is dedicated to locating superior talent to fill executive, management, and professional openings throughout the country. We specialize in placing candidates in the high-tech, telecommunications, and medical device industries. We work closely with sales, marketing, and engineering candidates in: storage, e-security, B2B, ERP/MRP/CRM document management/imaging/conversion, telcom/wireless, e-Commerce, and medical device sectors nationwide.

Key Contact - Specialty:
Mr. David Zolowicz, President - *Document management (imaging, conversion), wireless/bluetooth, e-commerce, software, sales, engineers*
Ms. Susan Wright, Executive Recruiter - *Storage (software, hardware, sales, engineers), linux*
Mrs. Katie Baxter, Executive Recruiter - *Medical devices (engineering, sales and marketing)*
Ms. Melinda Zolowicz, Executive Recruiter - *Telecom, e-Security*

Salary minimum: $70,000

Functions: Generalist

Industries: Medical Devices, E-commerce, Telecoms, Telephony, Wireless, Defense, Software, Doc. Mgmt., Production SW, ERP SW, Security SW

FPC of Greenwood Village
7400 E Arapahoe Rd Ste 200
Greenwood Village, CO 80112
(303) 773-0047
Fax: (303) 773-0048
Email: resume@fpcgwv.com
Web: www.fpcgwv.com

Description: Our objective is to excel in the placement industry and to deliver results. We will consult with clients and individuals for accomplishments that are mutually beneficial. We are focused on the consumer products industry including food, beverage, pharmaceutical and related industries and work all manufacturing disciplines.

Key Contact:
Mr. Geoff Pike, President - *Food & beverage processing, pharmaceutical, consumer products manufacturing*
Ms. Vicki Pike, Part Owner

Salary minimum: $40,000

Functions: Mfg., Product Dev., Production, Plant Mgmt., Quality, Purchasing, Materials Plng., Distribution, R&D, Engineering

Industries: Food, Bev., Tobacco, Soap, Perf., Cosmtcs., Drugs Mfg., Misc. Mfg., Packaging

FPC of Golden
390 Union Blvd Ste 250
Lakewood, CO 80228
(303) 989-1544
Fax: (303) 989-1506
Email: fpcgolden@uswest.net
Web: www.concentric.net/~fpcgolden

Description: We recruit actively in medical device and pharmaceutical manufacturing. Our firm's focus includes: sales/marketing/business development, engineering, operations, R&D, QA/RA/CA, human resources, finance, and scientists.

Key Contact - Specialty:
Mr. Bob Blum, President - *Research director*
Ms. Mary McCoy, Executive Recruiter - *Medical device (sales/Mkt), QA, RA*
Mr. Don Daubenmeyer, Executive Recruiter - *Pharmaceuticals*
Mr. Tom Epting, Executive Recruiter - *Medical device, engineering, operations*

Salary minimum: $60,000

Functions: General Mgmt., Mfg., Production, Plant Mgmt., Quality, Sales & Mktg., Finance, R&D, Engineering

Industries: Drugs Mfg., Medical Devices, Mfg. SW

FPC of Denver
7800 S Elati St Ste 319
Littleton, CO 80120
(303) 795-9210
Fax: (303) 795-9215
Email: mail@fpcdenver.com
Web: www.fpcdenver.com

Description: Our firm is an independently owned office with more than 50 years of direct industry experience. As a member of one of the oldest and most reputable professional and executive search firms, we provide personalized service coupled with the extensive network of a national organization.

Key Contact - Specialty:
Mr. Jan Dorfman, PE, President - *Engineering, scientific, clinical, quality, regulatory affairs*

Functions: Senior Mgmt., Middle Mgmt., Mfg., Product Dev., Automation, Quality, Materials, Sales & Mktg., R&D, Engineering

Industries: Food, Bev., Tobacco, Drugs Mfg., Medical Devices, Motor Vehicles, Computer Equip., Consumer Elect., Electronic, Elec.

Components, Transportation, Communications, Digital, Fiber Optic, Biotech

FPC of Wilmington
191 S Chapel St
Newark, DE 19711
(302) 453-0404
Email: bioheadhunter@aol.com
Web: www.fpcweb.com

Description: Our firm was the first in the system to specialize in the biotech and pharmaceuticals industries. Now in our 12th year. Principals have advanced degrees and personal experience in their recruiting specialties. One of approximately one hundred Fortune offices nationwide.

Key Contact - Specialty:
Mr. Leonard A. Weston, President - *Biopharmaceutical industries*
Ms. Joan C. Weston, Vice President - *Biopharmaceuticals industries (research & development)*

Salary minimum: $60,000

Functions: Generalist, Directors, Senior Mgmt., Production, Plant Mgmt., Quality, Systems Analysis, R&D

Industries: Generalist, Biotech

FPC of Tampa
28870 US 19 N Ste 300
Clearwater, FL 33761
(727) 797-9577
Fax: (727) 791-8128
Email: ted.brill@fpctampa.com
Web: www.fpcweb.com

Description: Our recruiters have 39 years of senior manufacturing and recruiting experience. We perform the role of hiring manager to screen candidates to bring our clients uncompromising standards of qualifications to spec.

Key Contact - Specialty:
Mr. Ted Brill, President - *Purchasing, operations, manufacturing management*

Salary minimum: $50,000

Functions: Purchasing

Industries: Mfg., Mgmt. Consulting, Telecoms, Aerospace

FPC of Jacksonville
3000-6 Hartley Rd
Jacksonville, FL 32257
(904) 886-2471
Fax: (904) 886-2472
Email: careers@fpcjax.com
Web: www.fpcjax.com

Description: We are a nationwide leader in the recruitment and placement of middle management and executive-level personnel with major corporations throughout the US. This office specializes in engineers, quality, manufacturing, and strategic sourcing and supply professionals.

Key Contact - Specialty:
Mr. Bob Pepple, President - *Engineers, quality disciplines, manufacturing professionals, material handlers*
Mrs. Pat Pepple, COO - *Operations and training*
Mr. Rob Pepple, VP- of Research - *Research*

Salary minimum: $40,000

Functions: Generalist

Industries: Generalist, Mfg., Plastics, Rubber, Motor Vehicles, Electronic, Elec. Components, Transportation, Communications, Fiber Optic, Packaging, Software

FPC of Palm Beach
1224 US Hwy 1 Ste G
North Palm Beach, FL 33408
(561) 624-7550
Fax: (561) 624-7551
Email: resume@fpcpalmbeach.com
Web: www.fpcpalmbeach.com

Description: We specialize in placement of quality, lean manufacturing, and six sigma executives and professionals for all industries, nationwide. Our specialists also recruit and place engineering, as well as procurement, supply chain, logistics, pharmaceuticals and medical device professionals.

Key Contact - Specialty:
Mr. Eric "Rick" Dmytrow, President/Executive Recruiter - *Quality, lean manufacturing (TPS), six sigma, executives, middle management*
Ms. Susan Kronheim, Executive Recruiter - *Quality (engineers, executives, manufacturing), continuous improvement*
Mr. James Smith, Executive Recruiter - *Quality, pharmaceuticals, medical devices*
Mr. Robert Stevenson, Search Assistant - *Quality, lean manufacturing, six sigma*

Salary minimum: $40,000

Functions: General Mgmt., Mfg., Product Dev., Production, Plant Mgmt., Quality, Productivity, Materials, Engineering, Mgmt. Consultants

Industries: Generalist, Food, Bev., Tobacco, Drugs Mfg., Medical Devices, Plastics, Rubber, Motor Vehicles, Misc. Mfg., Electronic, Elec. Components, Services, Aerospace, Packaging

Professional Associations: ASQ, SAE

FPC of Manatee County
923 4th St W
Palmetto, FL 34221
(941) 729-3674
Fax: (941) 729-7927
Email: fpcmanatee@earthlink.net
Web: www.fpcweb.com

Description: Over 20 years' experience as a plant manager and engineering manager in various high-tech electronic manufacturing operations.

Key Contact - Specialty:
Mr. Jeffrey A. Sangster, President - *Electronic manufacturing (executive, management, technical)*
Mr. Brian Blaine, Director of Placement - *IT/IS professionals (all industries)*
Mr. Samuel Longo, Director of Placement - *Development engineering (high tech industries)*

Salary minimum: $40,000

Functions: Senior Mgmt., Middle Mgmt., Mfg., Product Dev., Production

Industries: Mfg., Computer Equip., Consumer Elect., Misc. Mfg., Software

FPC of Ft Lauderdale
8751 W Broward Blvd Ste 406
Plantation, FL 33324
(954) 473-9900
Fax: (954) 473-9952
Email: search@fpclauderdale.com
Web: www.fpcweb.com

Description: We offer nationwide recruiting and placement services for the pharmaceutical and biotech industries.

Key Contact:
Mr. David Skiles, President
Ms. Karen Skiles

Salary minimum: $50,000

Functions: Generalist

Industries: Drugs Mfg., Pharm Svcs., Biotech

FPC of Sarasota
98 Sarasota Center Blvd Ste C
Sarasota, FL 34240-9770
(941) 378-5262
Fax: (941) 379-9233
Email: recruit@fpcsarasota.com
Web: www.fpcsarasota.com

Description: Our firm is providing professionals for manufacturing companies and supply chain up through the executive-level. We have recruiter specialists available in manufacturing operations, materials, purchasing, engineering, and quality. We have access to a national network of recruiters.

Key Contact - Specialty:
Mr. Arthur R. Grindlinger, President - *Manufacturing, materials management*

Salary minimum: $40,000

Functions: Senior Mgmt., Middle Mgmt., Product Dev., Production, Plant Mgmt., Quality, Materials, Purchasing, Materials Plng., Engineering

Industries: Mfg.

Professional Associations: AIIE, APICS, ASQ, NAPM, SME, SMTA

FPC of Atlanta
6525 The Corners Pkwy Ste 216
Norcross, GA 30092
(770) 246-9757
Fax: (770) 246-0526
Email: search@fpccareers.com
Web: www.fpccareers.com

Description: Executive recruitment for manufacturing, engineering, quality, validation, regulatory affairs, R&D, product development, sensory, pharmaceuticals, medical device, food, personal care, cosmetics, home care, chemicals, plastics and electronics.

Key Contact:
Mr. James M. Deavours, President
Ms. Patricia Deavours, Vice President

Salary minimum: $40,000

Functions: Middle Mgmt., Mfg., Product Dev., Production, Automation, Plant Mgmt., Quality, Packaging, R&D, Engineering

Industries: Mfg., Food, Bev., Tobacco, Chemicals, Soap, Perf., Cosmtcs., Drugs Mfg., Medical Devices, Plastics, Rubber, Consumer Elect., Biotech

Professional Associations: ASQ, IEEE, IFT, IOPP, ISPE, RAPS, SCC

FPC of Savannah
7 E Congress St Ste 712
Savannah, GA 31401
(912) 233-4556
Email: execsearch@fpcsav.com
Web: www.fpcweb.com

Description: We place professionals in manufacturing industries focusing on the following disciplines: manufacturing/industrial engineering, quality engineers/managers, purchasing, human resources, materials management, and operations management.

Key Contact - Specialty:
Mr. Clark W. Smith, President - *Manufacturing management, operations management, materials management, logistics*

Functions: Generalist, Senior Mgmt., Production, Plant Mgmt., Quality, Purchasing, HR Mgmt., Finance, Int'l.

Industries: Generalist, Textiles, Apparel, Paper, Metal Products, Machine, Appliance, Motor Vehicles, Computer Equip., Consumer Elect.

Professional Associations: ASQ, IIE, NAPM, SHRM, SME

FPC of Boise
415 E Park Center Blvd Ste 106
Boise, ID 83706-6504
(208) 343-5190
(800) 783-5190
Fax: (208) 343-6067
Email: fpcboise@qwest.net
Web: www.fpcweb.com

Description: Consultants in executive search for middle and top management positions. Firm is composed of former senior executives from Fortune 500 companies.

Key Contact - Specialty:
Ms. Sandra K. Bishop, President - *Credit card, banking, financial services, human resources*
Mr. Garn Christensen, Vice President - *Financial services, high net worth securities sales*
Mr. Russ Thompson, Director - *Pulp and paper*
Mr. J. D. Hess, Director - *R&D scientist, aerospace*
Mr. Joel Santarone, Director - *Financial services, finance*
Mr. Bob Galloway, Director - *Telecommunications, aerospace*
Mr. Chase Hewes, Director - *Securities sales, financial services*

Salary minimum: $75,000

Functions: Generalist, R&D

Industries: Generalist, Paper, Finance, Banking, Invest. Banking, Brokers, Misc. Financial, Accounting, HR Services, Aerospace, Industry Specific SW

Professional Associations: AMA, PIMA, SHRM, TAPPI

FPC of Arlington Heights
825 E Golf Rd Ste 1146
Arlington Heights, IL 60005
(847) 228-7205
Fax: (847) 228-7206
Email: marshall@fpcarlington.com
Web: www.fpcweb.com

Description: We are specialists in the automotive industry, focusing on engineering, and purchasing professionals.

Key Contact - Specialty:
Mr. Marshall Antonio, President - *Automotive, quality, manufacturing (engineers, managers), purchasing, materials*

Salary minimum: $40,000

Functions: Generalist, Directors, Senior Mgmt., Plant Mgmt., Quality, Purchasing, PR, Engineering

Industries: Generalist, Motor Vehicles, Advertising

Professional Associations: ASQ

FPC of Hinsdale
115 East 1st St Ste 2E
Hinsdale, IL 60521
(630) 920-1952
Fax: (630) 920-0793
Email: fpc@fpc-hinsdale.com
Web: www.fpc-hinsdale.com

Description: Principal has over 20 years' experience as financial professional with Fortune 50 manufacturers. Providing finance/accounting, human resources, and supply chain management professionals up through the executive-level for manufacturing and distribution companies.

Key Contact - Specialty:
Mr. Robert J. Kalember, Jr., President - *Finance & accounting management*

Salary minimum: $50,000

Functions: Production, Materials, Purchasing, Distribution, HR Mgmt., Benefits, Training, Finance, CFO's, Budgeting

Industries: Generalist, Mfg., Transportation, Wholesale, Media, Publishing, Aerospace, Packaging

FPC of Ft Wayne
347 W Berry St Ste 319
Ft. Wayne, IN 46802
(219) 424-5159
Fax: (219) 424-4201
Email: andy@fpcfw.com
Web: www.fpcfw.com

Description: Our firm specializes in the automotive, heavy manufacturing, and electronics industries.

Key Contact:
Mr. Andy Gilbert, President
Ms. Kristy Gilbert, Office Manager

Salary minimum: $12,000

Functions: Mfg., Materials

Industries: Generalist, Medical Devices, Plastics, Rubber, Motor Vehicles, Computer Equip., Consumer Elect., Electronic, Elec. Components, Telecoms, Fiber Optic, Defense, Aerospace

FPC of Kokomo
1904 S Elizabeth St
Kokomo, IN 46902
(765) 868-2242
Fax: (765) 868-2282
Email: fpckoko@indy.net
Web: www.fpckokomocareers.com

Description: We are executive recruiters on a contingency basis for sales/marketing, engineering, quality, and materials professionals in the automotive and electronics industries.

Key Contact:
Mr. Larry Weaver, President

Functions: Product Dev., Quality, Sales & Mktg., Sales Mgmt.

Industries: Motor Vehicles, Consumer Elect., Electronic, Elec. Components

FPC of Mt Vernon
424 Southwind Plaza
Mt. Vernon, IN 47620
(812) 838-1607
Fax: (812) 838-1807
Email: fortmtv@earthlink.net
Web: home.earthlink.net/~fortmtv/

Description: We are part of a national executive search firm comprised of approximately 100 independently owned and operated offices. We are involved in all phases of recruitment and permanent placement offering services on either a contingency or retainer basis. Our primary focus is in accounting/finance and supply chain.

Key Contact:
Mr. Al Gmutza, President

Salary minimum: $40,000

Functions: Middle Mgmt., Materials, Purchasing, Materials Plng., Distribution, Finance, CFO's, Budgeting, M&A

Industries: Generalist, Energy, Utilities

FPC of SW Indiana
201 Main St Ste A
Mt. Vernon, IN 47620
(812) 838-6636
Fax: (812) 838-6648
Email: fortswin@aol.com
Web: www.members.aol.com/gbfort/swin.html

Description: The owner has over 17 years of experience in the engineering, manufacturing, and materials management areas in the chemical and plastics industries with four Fortune 50 companies.

Key Contact - Specialty:
Mr. Gary Fox, Owner - *Engineers, chemists, manufacturing operations*

Salary minimum: $35,000

Functions: Generalist

Industries: Paper, Chemicals, Soap, Perf., Cosmtcs., Drugs Mfg., Plastics, Rubber, Paints, Petro. Products, Metal Products, Packaging

Professional Associations: AICHE, SPE

FPC of South Bend
52303 Emmons Rd Ste 27
Georgetown Ctr
South Bend, IN 46637
(219) 273-3188
Fax: (219) 273-3887
Email: mike@fpcsouthbend.com
Web: www.fpcsouthbend.com

Key Contact - Specialty:
Mr. Michael Petras, President - *Automotive engineers, managers, executives*
Mr. Mark Petras, Vice President/Partner - *Automotive purchasing, supply chain*
Mr. Michael Druley, Executive Recruiter - *Food & beverage - logistics, supply chain management*
Mr. Matthew Petras, Executive Recruiter - *Pharmaceutical (quality, regulatory affairs)*

Functions: Directors, Senior Mgmt., Middle Mgmt., Quality, Purchasing

Industries: Food, Bev., Tobacco, Drugs Mfg., Motor Vehicles, Biotech

FPC of Cedar Rapids
208 Collins Rd NE Ste 204
Cedar Rapids, IA 52402
(319) 373-1163
Fax: (319) 373-1696
Email: careers@fpccr.com
Web: www.fpccr.com

Description: We specialize in placement of professionals and executives in the areas of: sales, marketing, engineering, and operations in the electronics industries, such as: telecommunications, DatacCom, aerospace/avionics, electronic component manufacture, test and measurement, and power supplies.

Key Contact - Specialty:
Ms. Elizabeth Buckeridge, President - *Engineering, operations, HR*
Mr. John Buckeridge, President - *Sales, marketing, finance*

Functions: Senior Mgmt., Plant Mgmt., Quality, Materials, Sales & Mktg., Mktg. Mgmt., Sales Mgmt., Engineering

Industries: Computer Equip., Consumer Elect., Test, Measure Equip., Electronic, Elec. Components, Telecoms, Digital, Wireless, Fiber Optic, Aerospace

FPC of Fayette County
841 Corporate Dr Ste 203
Lexington, KY 40503
(859) 296-2996
Fax: (859) 296-2998
Email: fpcfayette@aol.com
Web: www.fpclexington.com

Description: We are consultants to the automotive and related industries. We are specialists in engineering, quality, purchasing, materials, and operations management.

Key Contact:
Mr. Mark Watson, President - *Engineering, engineering management*
Mrs. Nancie Watson, Vice President

Salary minimum: $50,000

Functions: General Mgmt., Mfg., Quality, Materials, HR Mgmt., Engineering

Industries: Mfg., Plastics, Rubber, Motor Vehicles, Aerospace

FPC of Bangor
17 Elm St
Skowhegan, ME 04976
(207) 474-6110
Fax: (207) 474-5091
Email: info@fpcbangor.com
Web: www.fpcbangor.com

Description: We have nationwide specialization in management recruiting for the pulp and paper and packaging and converting industry. Our industry experience and affiliation makes us unique. We can advise on resume preparation, available career opportunities, interview strategies, and career planning.

Key Contact - Specialty:
Ms. Gilly Hitchcock, Owner - *Sales & marketing, pulp & paper*
Ms. Caren Brown, Director-Technical Recruiting - *Engineers, pulp & paper*
Ms. Leisa Baiko, Recruiting Associate - *Pulp & paper*

Functions: Generalist

Industries: Paper, Printing, Packaging

Professional Associations: PIMA, TAPPI

FPC of Severna Park Inc
PO Box 1583
Severna Park, MD 21146-8538
(410) 544-5151
Fax: (410) 544-6788
Email: jobs@fpcspark.com
Web: www.fpcspark.com

Description: Our firm has successfully assisted our client companies meet their recruiting needs with capable, qualified candidates. Our consultants place professionals nationwide on a contingency or retained search basis. Our recruiters specialize in: engineering, process control, human resources, operations management, information systems, materials management/purchasing.

Key Contact:
Ms. Karen Williams, President
Mr. Ray Williams, President

Functions: Generalist

Industries: Paper

FPC of Topsfield
458 Boston Rd Ste 2P
Topsfield, MA 01983
(978) 887-2032
Fax: (978) 887-2336
Email: plastics@topsfpc.com
Web: www.topsfpc.com

Description: Nationwide recruiting for general management, engineering, operations and sales executives exclusively in the plastics industry. Each recruiter has a particular process expertise that allows very focused search capability.

Key Contact - Specialty:
Mr. James E. Slate, President - *Plastics*

Salary minimum: $50,000

Functions: General Mgmt., Mfg., Quality, Sales & Mktg., R&D, Engineering

Industries: Generalist, Chemicals, Medical Devices, Plastics, Rubber, Paints, Petro. Products

Professional Associations: ASQ, SPE, SPI

Networks: National Personnel Assoc (NPA)

FPC of Westford

484 Groton Rd
Unit 3
Westford, MA 01886
(978) 692-9500
Fax: (877) 866-6335
Email: success@fpcworcester.com
Web: www.fpcworcester.com

Description: We specialize in electronic engineers and engineering managers.

Key Contact:
Mr. Robert C. Putala, President

Salary minimum: $50,000

Functions: Product Dev., Engineering

Industries: Computer Equip., Consumer Elect., Test, Measure Equip., Misc. Mfg., Electronic, Elec. Components, Telecoms, Digital, Wireless, Fiber Optic, Network Infrastructure, Software

FPC of Bloomfield Inc

800 W Long Lake Rd Ste 220
Bloomfield Hills, MI 48302
(248) 642-9383
Fax: (248) 642-9575
Email: exec1@ix.netcom.com

Description: As specialists in their industry and discipline, our search consultants possess in-depth knowledge of the business and resources available. Our searches are therefore focused, achieving results quickly and efficiently.

Key Contact - Specialty:
Mr. Karl Zimmermann, President - *Manufacturing, materials management, purchasing, quality*

Salary minimum: $40,000

Functions: General Mgmt., Middle Mgmt., Production, Plant Mgmt., Quality, Purchasing, Materials Plng., Distribution

Industries: Metal Products, Machine, Appliance, Motor Vehicles, Computer Equip., Consumer Elect., Test, Measure Equip., Misc. Mfg.

Professional Associations: MAPS

FPC of Farmington Hills

33045 Hamilton Ct E Ste 105
Farmington Hills, MI 48334-3380
(248) 324-3700
Fax: (248) 324-1602
Email: hernia2@aol.com

Description: Nationally recognized in engineering, finance, manufacturing and MIS placement.

Key Contact - Specialty:
Mr. Gary Snyder, President - *Engineers, finance*

Salary minimum: $45,000

Functions: Production, Quality, Finance, CFO's

Industries: Generalist, Mfg., Motor Vehicles, Finance, Accounting

Professional Associations: MAPS, MASS, NAPS

FPC of Detroit

17515 W Nine Mile Rd Ste 770
Southfield, MI 48075
(248) 557-7250
Fax: (248) 557-7260
Email: info@fpcdet.com
Web: www.fpcdet.com

Description: Firm specializes in offering legal search services for law firms and corporate legal departments nationwide on a contingency and retained search basis.

Key Contact - Specialty:
Mr. Mark L. Schwartz, President - *Attorneys*

Salary minimum: $60,000

Functions: Legal

Industries: Generalist

FPC of Troy

560 Kirts Blvd Ste 102
Troy, MI 48084
(248) 244-9646
Fax: (248) 244-8568
Email: mdubeck@aol.com
Web: www.fpctroy.com

Description: We are a well-respected executive search firm specializing in the placement of automotive and healthcare professionals. The firm was established in 1988 as a specialized health care provider. Our primary focus has been specialized searches in support of manufacturing firms' targeted personnel needs.

Key Contact - Specialty:
Mr. Michael Dubeck, President - *Manufacturing executives (lean manufacturing, operations engineering)*
Mr. Russell Chalmers, Executive Recruiter - *Manufacturing, engineering*
Mr. Lanson Lee, Office Manager - *Materials management, logistics, purchasing*
Ms. Jessica Boone, Executive Recruiter - *Quality, engineering*
Ms. Bina Menon, Executive Recruiter - *Finance, IT*
Ms. Debra Hunter, Executive Recruiter - *Healthcare, manufacturing*
Mr. Jeremy Smith, Executive Recruiter - *Electronics, powertrain*

Salary minimum: $40,000

Functions: Generalist, Mfg., Production, Plant Mgmt., Materials, Finance, Engineering, Specialized Svcs.

Industries: Generalist, Plastics, Rubber, Paints, Petro. Products, Metal Products, Motor Vehicles, Test, Measure Equip., Mgmt. Consulting, Packaging

FPC of St. Louis

14377 Woodlake Dr Ste 101
Chesterfield, MO 63017
(314) 205-1818
Fax: (314) 205-1822
Email: careers@fpcstlouis.com
Web: www.fpcstlouis.com

Description: We have set a distinguished standard for leadership, integrity and quality in recruitment. We provide prompt, efficient, confidential searches and present only qualified professional, management and executive candidates.

Key Contact:
Mr. Craig Schultz, President - *Automotive, metal fabrication, machinery, equipment*
Mrs. Sandy Schultz, Vice President

Functions: Middle Mgmt., Mfg., Production, Plant Mgmt., Quality, Productivity, Materials, Purchasing, HR Mgmt., Engineering

Industries: Mfg., Food, Bev., Tobacco, Lumber, Furniture, Medical Devices, Plastics, Rubber, Metal Products, Machine, Appliance, Motor Vehicles, Computer Equip., Misc. Mfg.

FPC of Southwest Missouri

5309 S Golden Ave
Springfield, MO 65810
(417) 887-6737
Fax: (417) 887-6955

Email: info@fpcswmo.com
Web: www.fpcswmo.com

Description: Providing professionals nationwide for manufacturing firms seeking the best in executive and technical expertise. Our candidates are thoroughly screened and interviewed prior to presentation to our clients.

Key Contact - Specialty:
Mr. Bill Belle Isle, President - *Manufacturing management, engineering*
Ms. Patrice Belle Isle, Vice President - *Manufacturing management, engineering*

Salary minimum: $40,000

Functions: General Mgmt., Product Dev., Production, Plant Mgmt., Quality, Materials, HR Mgmt., Finance, Engineering

Industries: Mfg., Food, Bev., Tobacco, Drugs Mfg., Medical Devices, Plastics, Rubber, Metal Products, Machine, Appliance, Motor Vehicles, Consumer Elect., Test, Measure Equip., Electronic, Elec. Components, Biotech

Professional Associations: MAPS

FPC of Bozeman

104 E Main St Ste 302
Bozeman, MT 59715
(406) 585-1332
Fax: (406) 585-2255
Email: fpcbozeman@mcn.net
Web: www.fpcweb.com

Description: Recruiting firm specializing in all disciplines within the medical device, pharmaceutical and bio-tech industries.

Key Contact - Specialty:
Mr. Ray Regan, President - *Operations management, biomedical*
Ms. Kate Regan Ciari, Vice President/General Manager - *Sales & marketing, engineering, medical device, pharmaceutical*

Salary minimum: $30,000

Functions: Generalist, Senior Mgmt., Product Dev., Quality, Purchasing, Mktg. Mgmt., R&D, Engineering

Industries: Generalist, Drugs Mfg., Medical Devices, Pharm Svcs., Packaging

FPC of Nashua

505 W Hollis St Ste 208
Nashua, NH 03062
(603) 880-4900
Fax: (603) 880-8861
Email: mail@fpcnashua.com
Web: www.fpcnashua.com

Description: Specialists in the bio-tech, pharmaceutical and medical device industries (with special emphasis on regulatory affairs, quality assurance, quality control, clinical affairs, validation, formulations, analytical chemistry and process development).

Key Contact - Specialty:
Mr. Norman J. Oppenheim, President - *Regulatory affairs*

Salary minimum: $45,000

Functions: Product Dev., Production, Quality, DB Admin., Engineering

Industries: Drugs Mfg., Medical Devices, Biotech

Professional Associations: AAPS, ACRP, DIA, ISPE, NNEAPS, PDA

FPC of New Brunswick

PO Box 509
Maplewood, NJ 07040
(973) 399-8791
Fax: (973) 399-7333

Email: ransum@erols.com

Description: We offer an automated spectrum of diverse chemical and pharmaceutical business, technical, and manufacturing professionals that allow us to target the right candidate, to the right position, when you need them.

Key Contact - Specialty:
Mr. Michael Randolph, Senior Consultant - *Process & design engineering research, technical chemistry*
Dr. Robert Jiggits, Consultant - *Sales & marketing, business development*
Mr. Ed Smith, Consultant - *R&D, QA/QC, manufacturing*

Salary minimum: $60,000

Functions: Sales & Mktg., HR Mgmt., R&D, Engineering, Minorities

Industries: Food, Bev., Tobacco, Chemicals, Soap, Perf., Cosmtcs., Drugs Mfg.

Professional Associations: IACPR, AMCF

Networks: Recruiters Professional Network (RPN)

FPC of Menlo Park
16 Bridge St
Metuchen, NJ 08840
(732) 494-6266
Fax: (732) 494-5669
Email: pprovda@castle.net
Web: www.fpcweb.com

Description: Established more than 25 years ago, this firm has been a leader in recruiting middle and upper-level management personnel for growing companies in the cosmetics, pharmaceutical and chemical industries.

Key Contact - Specialty:
Mr. Peter Provda, President - *Materials management (softgoods industry), cosmetics, manufacturing, engineering*

Salary minimum: $35,000

Functions: Generalist

Industries: Mfg., Food, Bev., Tobacco, Chemicals, Soap, Perf., Cosmtcs., Drugs Mfg., Medical Devices, Plastics, Rubber, HR Services, Packaging

FPC of Bergen County
350 W Passaic St
Rochelle Park, NJ 07662
(201) 843-7621
Fax: (201) 843-8189
Email: mail@fpcbergencounty.com
Web: www.fpcbergencounty.com

Description: Specialists in tech, mid- and senior-level in pharmaceutical, biotech and medical device industries. Areas of specialization include QA, quality engineering, engineering, R&D, regulatory affairs, clinical affairs, QC, microbiology, scientific, manufacturing and statistics. Also specialists in mid- and senior management in purchasing materials management and operations across all industries.

Key Contact - Specialty:
Mr. Howard G. Klein, CPC, President - *Medical device, pharmaceutical, biotechnology, materials management, operations (all industries) & purchasing (all industries)*

Salary minimum: $50,000

Functions: Senior Mgmt., Product Dev., Production, Automation, Quality, Materials, Mkt. Research, Mktg. Mgmt., R&D, Engineering

Industries: Generalist, Drugs Mfg., Medical Devices

Professional Associations: ACRP, ACS, AICPA, APICS, ASQ, DIA, PDA, RAPS, SOCRA

FPC of Somerset
1250 Rte 28 Ste 103
Somerville, NJ 08876
(908) 218-0700
Fax: (908) 218-5055
Email: info@fpcsomerset.com
Web: www.fpcsomerset.com

Description: We are a search firm dedicated to recruiting the best candidates for professional, middle management and executive positions in the pharmaceutical, medical device, and biotechnical industries. We find pharmaceutical jobs, biotech jobs, and medical device jobs for qualified candidates. Confidential searches are conducted nationwide.

Key Contact:
Mr. Joe Jiuliano, President - *Research & development, chemists, formulators, scientists*
Ms. Julie Barnes, Executive Recruiting Consultant - *QA, QC, manufacturing ops, plant mgmnt*
Ms. Margaret Jiuliano, Owner

Professional Associations: AAPS, ACS, ASMS, ASQ, CRS, DIA, ISPE, PDA, RAPS

FPC of Passaic County
41 Vreeland Ave
Totowa, NJ 07512
(973) 812-9819
Fax: (973) 812-9821
Email: stan@fpcpassaic.com
Web: www.fpcpassaic.com

Description: This office, part of a nationwide network, specializes in placing professionals in the areas of Quality, Materials Management & Purchasing within FDA regulated environments. Our office works with large and small companies throughout New England and the Tri-State area. We are constantly searching for exceptional talent to fill middle and upper management positions.

Key Contact:
Mr. Stan Goldberg, President

Salary minimum: $40,000

Functions: Quality, Materials, Purchasing

Industries: Mfg.

Professional Associations: APICS, ASQ

Networks: National Personnel Assoc (NPA)

FPC of Rockland County Inc
71 East Eckerson Rd - A
Spring Valley, NY 10977-3014
(845) 426-3200
Fax: (845) 426-3814
Email: fpcofrc@frontiernet.net
Web: www.fpcweb.com

Description: Nationwide search and placement of quality, manufacturing and design engineers and managers in the mechanical and electromechanical industries, especially in automotive and consumer products. Services available on a contingency as well as a retained search basis. All fees are client (company) paid.

Key Contact - Specialty:
Mr. Mark H. Axelrod, President - *Quality, manufacturing & design, engineering, management*
Mr. Eric M. Axelrod, Sr Technical Recruiter - *Quality assurance (manufacturing)*

Salary minimum: $45,000

Functions: Directors, Middle Mgmt., Mfg., Product Dev., Quality, Personnel, Engineering

Industries: Mfg., Metal Products, Machine, Appliance, Motor Vehicles, Consumer Elect., Misc. Mfg.

Professional Associations: ASQ

FPC of Greensboro
3831 W Market St
Greensboro, NC 27407
(336) 852-4455
Fax: (336) 852-3429
Email: info@fpcgboro.com
Web: www.fpcgboro.com

Description: We provide executive and middle management retainer/contingent recruiting in supply chain management, plant management, focus factory managers, purchasing, quality management, six sigma, engineering management, logistics, transportation, distribution, and 3PL professionals.

Key Contact - Specialty:
Mr. Bill Martin, President - *Plant management, operations*
Mr. Bill Markham, Operations Manager - *Human resources, finance*
Mr. Cliff Green, Director of Quality and Engineering - *Quality, engineering*
Mr. Rich Bremer, Director of Supply Chain - *Logistics, supply chain management, 3PL*
Mr. Scott Crowell, Director of Supply Chain - *Purchasing, materials*
Ms. Rhonda Stone, Executive Recruiter - *Manufacturing, logistics*
Mr. Chris Osl, Director of Supply Chain - *Purchasing*

Salary minimum: $30,000

Functions: General Mgmt., Mfg., Plant Mgmt., Quality, Materials, Purchasing, Materials Plng., HR Mgmt., Finance, Engineering

Industries: Generalist, Energy, Utilities, Mfg., Transportation

Professional Associations: AME, APICS, ASQ, CLM, IIE, NAPM, SHRM, WERC

FPC of Charlotte
315 Main St Ste C
PO Box 460
Pineville, NC 28134-0460
(704) 889-1100
Fax: (704) 889-1109
Email: results@fpccharlotte.com
Web: www.fpccharlotte.com

Description: Executive recruiters specializing in the medical device and electro-mechanical manufacturing industries. Our consultants are all degreed at the BS/masters level and have industry work experience.

Key Contact - Specialty:
Mr. David B. Griffith, President - *Medical devices*

Salary minimum: $45,000

Functions: Senior Mgmt., Mfg., Product Dev., Quality, Materials, Mktg. Mgmt., Finance, R&D, Engineering

Industries: Generalist, Drugs Mfg., Medical Devices, Metal Products, Machine, Appliance, Motor Vehicles, Consumer Elect., Test, Measure Equip., Misc. Mfg., Packaging, Biotech

Professional Associations: APICS, ASQ, NCASP

FPC of Raleigh
7521 Mourning Dove Rd Ste 101
Raleigh, NC 27615
(919) 848-9929
Fax: (919) 848-1062
Email: info@fpcraleigh.com
Web: www.fpcraleigh.com

Description: With over 25 consultants specializing in a variety of disciplines, we have demonstrated that we can effectively handle all salaried staffing needs for our client firms.

Key Contact - Specialty:
Mr. Stan Deckelbaum, CEO - *Electronics, software, hardware, ME, test*

Mr. Rick Deckelbaum, President/COO - *Presidents, CEOs, vice presidents (all industries)*
Mr. Randy A. Cagan, CPC, Senior Vice President/Partner - *Manufacturing, engineering, management*
Mr. C. C. "Jay" Brown, Senior Vice President/Partner - *Pulp & paper (all areas), suppliers, packaging, converting*
Mr. David L. Singer, CPC, Senior Vice President/Partner - *Purchasing*
Mr. Richard D. Gorberg, CPC, Senior Vice President/Partner - *Telecommunications, data communications, wireless, marketing, product management*

Salary minimum: $40,000

Functions: General Mgmt., Senior Mgmt., Legal, Mfg., Materials, Healthcare, Sales & Mktg., HR Mgmt., Finance, Engineering

Industries: Generalist, Mfg., Food, Bev., Tobacco, Textiles, Apparel, Paper, Soap, Perf., Cosmtcs., Drugs Mfg., Medical Devices, Finance, Venture Cap., Misc. Financial, Pharm Svcs., Accounting, HR Services, E-commerce, Communications, Aerospace, Packaging, Software, Mfg. SW, Marketing SW, Biotech, Healthcare

Professional Associations: NCASP

FPC of Cincinnati
8170 Corporate Park Dr Ste 304
Cincinnati, OH 45242-3306
(513) 469-0808
Fax: (513) 469-0824
Email: fpccin@one.net
Web: www.fpcweb.com

Description: Our firm focuses on serving companies within manufacturing and heavy industry. We focus on recruiting in engineering, operations, supply chain, quality, finance and accounting, human resources, and sales management positions for our clients.

Key Contact - Specialty:
Mr. James Pilcher, President - *General management, operations management, printing, packaging*
Mr. Mark Kuehling, Director of Packaging and Supply Chain - *Supply chain management, purchasing, materials, packaging, logistics*
Mr. Chris Pilcher, Director of Quality & Process Managment - *Quality, process improvement, safety, human factors, ergonomics*
Mr. Jake Bell, Director of Finance & Accounting - *Manufacturing (finance and accounting)*
Mr. Jamie Behm, Research Associate - *Internet research*

Salary minimum: $45,000

Functions: Generalist

Industries: Generalist, Mfg., Plastics, Rubber, Metal Products, Machine, Appliance, Motor Vehicles, Test, Measure Equip., Electronic, Elec. Components, Packaging

FPC of Portland
12725 SW 66th Ave Ste 10
Portland, OR 97034
(503) 670-9541
Fax: (503) 670-1594
Email: fpcwp@teleport.com
Web: www.fpcwp.com

Description: We specialize in engineering and manufacturing placements in the following industries: plastics and packaging, automotive, and food & beverage.

Key Contact - Specialty:
Mr. Mark Vague, Owner/President - *Packaging, plastic, pulp & paper, automotive, medical devices*

Salary minimum: $50,000

Functions: Mfg.

Industries: Food, Bev., Tobacco, Paper, Medical Devices, Plastics, Rubber, Motor Vehicles, Packaging

Professional Associations: IOPP, SAE, SHRM, TAPPI

FPC of Allentown
21 N Main St Unit 9
Coopersburg, PA 18036
(610) 282-8245
Fax: (610) 282-8249
Email: fpcallen@aol.com
Web: www.fpcweb.com

Description: Executive recruiters of professionals for positions in high-tech/computer manufacturing companies. We handle all disciplines within typical manufacturing, development, headquarters organizations.

Key Contact:
Mr. Robert E. Graham, President - *High technology, computer manufacturing*
Ms. Sara L. Graham, Vice President

Salary minimum: $40,000

Functions: Generalist, Directors, Middle Mgmt., Production, Productivity, Packaging, Personnel, R&D

Industries: Generalist, Printing, Machine, Appliance, Computer Equip., Consumer Elect., Test, Measure Equip., Misc. Mfg., HR Services

Professional Associations: ASQ, SHRM

FPC of Ft Washington
455 Pennsylvania Ave Ste 105
Ft. Washington, PA 19034
(215) 542-9800
Fax: (215) 540-9312
Email: search@fpcftwash.com
Web: www.fpcftwash.com

Description: We provide nationwide placement of attorneys and other professionals for the insurance and investment industries. Our specialties are partnerships, associate placements and mergers in law firms. We also specialize in information technology professionals specializing in sales, marketing, and technical positions.

Key Contact - Specialty:
Ms. Suzanne S. Richards, President - *Legal, insurance investments*

Functions: Generalist, Benefits, Attorneys

Industries: Generalist, Brokers, Insurance

FPC of Abington
1410 W Street Rd
Warminster, PA 18974
(215) 675-3100
Fax: (215) 675-3080
Email: fpcabi@navpoint.com
Web: www.fpcweb.com

Description: We provide senior-level executive search primarily in pharmaceutical, biotechnology, CRO, and medical device industries. We have highly knowledgeable, seasoned consultants that specialize in regulatory, clinical operations, bio-statistics, data management, business development, manufacturing, engineering, project management, molecular biology, genetics, and information systems.

Key Contact - Specialty:
Mr. Michael Strand, President - *CEO, COO, CFO, sales & marketing, engineering (pharmaceuticals)*
Ms. Lauren Adams, Vice President-Pharmaceutical Services - *Clinical operations, medical directors, drug safety*

Ms. Patricia Wells, Vice President-Business Development - *Biostatistics, clinical data management, bioinformatics,genetics,CFO*
Ms. Michele Hess, Vice President-Regulatory Affairs - *Regulatory, quality*
Ms. Carol Caimi, Vice President-Research & Development - *R&D scientists, toxicology, pharmacology*

Salary minimum: $80,000

Functions: Generalist, Senior Mgmt., Physicians, Sales & Mktg., CFO's, IT, R&D, Engineering, Int'l.

Industries: Generalist, Soap, Perf., Cosmtcs., Drugs Mfg., Medical Devices, Consumer Elect., Finance, Misc. Financial, Pharm Svcs., Legal, Mgmt. Consulting, Biotech, Healthcare

Professional Associations: AAPS, ACRP, AICHE, ASQ, DIA, ISPE, NDMA, PDA, RAPS

FPC of Wayne PA
993 Old Eagle School Rd Ste 419
Wayne, PA 19087
(610) 989-9820
Fax: (610) 989-8505
Email: info@fpcwaynepa.com
Web: www.fpcweb.com

Description: We are an executive search firm specializing in the permanent placement of professional, executive, or middle-management personnel.

Key Contact - Specialty:
Mr. Marshall Danien, President - *Quality, engineering*

Salary minimum: $40,000

Functions: Generalist

Industries: Plastics, Rubber

Professional Associations: ASQ, SPE

FPC of Anderson
100 Miracle Mile Ste F
Anderson, SC 29621
(864) 226-5322
Fax: (864) 225-6767
Email: results@fpcsearch.com
Web: www.fpcsearch.com

Description: Focus on R&D through manufacturing including formulations, analytical chemistry, quality/regulatory compliance, engineering operations and sales for pharmaceutical and medical device industries.

Key Contact - Specialty:
Mr. Daryl Kress, President - *Pharmaceutical, medical devices (professionals)*
Mr. Joe Kaiser, Director - *Pharmaceutical, research & development, scientists*

Salary minimum: $50,000

Functions: Generalist

Industries: Chemicals, Soap, Perf., Cosmtcs., Drugs Mfg., Medical Devices, Pharm Svcs., Biotech, Healthcare

Professional Associations: AAPS, ACS, ASQ, ISPE, PDA, RAPS

FPC of Columbia
108 Columbia Northeast Dr Ste H
Columbia, SC 29223
(803) 788-8877
Fax: (803) 788-1509
Email: generalinfo@fpccolumbia.com
Web: www.fpccolumbia.com

Description: Specializing in the placement of middle management and executive positions in the manufacturing and distribution arenas, we can quickly find the technically qualified, state-of-the-art professional needed by your company.

Key Contact - Specialty:
Mr. Robert Thompson, Vice President/General Manager/Owner - *Materials management*
Mr. Lentz Ivey, Vice President/Owner - *Quality control, manufacturing engineering*
Mr. Dan Ladrech, Vice President, Employee Development - *Quality control*

Salary minimum: $60,000

Functions: Mfg.

Industries: Mfg.

Professional Associations: APICS, ASQ, SCAPS

FPC of Greenville
25 Woods Lake Rd Ste 410
Greenville, SC 29607
(864) 241-7700
Fax: (864) 241-7704
Email: fpcgrev@mindspring.com
Web: www.fpcweb.com

Description: We are not a placement company, but an executive search company. We look (search) for the specific requirements the company needs!

Key Contact - Specialty:
Mr. Alvin Dahl, President - *Pharmaceutical (engineering)*
Mr. Todd Huber, Executive Consultant - *Pharmaceutical (quality, validation)*
Ms. Kristie Tennent, Executive Consultant - *Pharmaceutical (quality, validation)*

Salary minimum: $40,000

FPC of Hilton Head
52 New Orleans Rd Ste 201
Jade Bldg
Hilton Head Island, SC 29928
(843) 842-7221
Fax: (843) 842-7205
Email: recruit@fpchh.com
Web: www.fpchh.com

Description: Our firm specializes in the medical device and pharmaceutical industries with our consultants being experts in their particular disciplines. Purchasing and supply chain management recruiting is also done in technology, electronic, computer, automotive and consumer goods industries.

Key Contact - Specialty:
Mr. David J. Ducharme, President - *Medical device, quality assurance, regulatory affairs*
Mr. Lance Beehler, Vice President - *Medical device, research & development, manufacturing*
Ms. Donne G. Paine, RN, Vice President - *Medical device, clinical affairs, marketing, biotechnology, pharmaceutical*
Ms. Sandra Dietrich, CPA, Vice President - *Purchasing, materials management, medical device, pharmaceutical, telecommunication*

Functions: Generalist, Directors, Middle Mgmt., Product Dev., Production, Quality, Purchasing, Mkt. Research

Industries: Generalist, Drugs Mfg., Medical Devices, Motor Vehicles, Computer Equip., Consumer Elect.

Professional Associations: ACRP, ASQ, RAPS, SCT, SOCRA

FPC of Charleston
890 Johnnie Dodds Blvd Ste 202
Bldg 3
P. O. Box 2544
Mt. Pleasant, SC 29465-2544
(843) 884-0505
Fax: (843) 849-9522

Email: recruiting.partners@fpccharleston.com
Web: www.fpccharleston.com

Description: We are offering fourteen plus years of solid expertise in serving automotive OEM and other manufacturers of fabricated metal, plastic, and assembled parts supplying North American automobile domestic and transplant Tier I and Tier II operations. We are also serving the medical device and pharmaceutical industries.

Key Contact:
Mr. Robert Spears, President - *Automotive manufacturing, quality, engineering*
Mr. Ted Dulaney, Career Counselor - *Medical device, pharmaceutical*
Ms. Barbara Spears, Administration

Salary minimum: $50,000

Functions: Generalist, Middle Mgmt., Product Dev., Production, Plant Mgmt., Quality, Productivity, Purchasing

Industries: Generalist, Textiles, Apparel, Drugs Mfg., Medical Devices, Plastics, Rubber, Metal Products, Machine, Appliance, Motor Vehicles

FPC of Chattanooga
5726 Marlin Rd Ste 212
Franklin Bldg
Chattanooga, TN 37411-4095
(423) 855-0444
Fax: (423) 892-0083
Email: fpcchatt@cdc.net
Web: www.fpcweb.com

Description: We can satisfy needs nationwide through 100 other franchise offices - strong, fast-paced office dedicated to filling every job order and placing every applicant.

Key Contact - Specialty:
Mr. David W. Dickson, CEO - *Manufacturing, consumer goods, human resources*
Ms. Brenda Hays, President - *Apparel (textile & related)*

Salary minimum: $25,000

Functions: Generalist, Middle Mgmt., Production, Plant Mgmt., Purchasing, Distribution, Personnel, Engineering

Industries: Generalist, Textiles, Apparel, Plastics, Rubber, Metal Products, Machine, Appliance, Consumer Elect., Transportation, HR Services

FPC of Memphis
52 Timber Creek Dr Ste 250
Cordova, TN 38018
(901) 757-5031
Fax: (901) 757-5048
Email: fpcmem@ionictech.com
Web: www.fpcweb.com

Description: Specializing in management and technical searches within specific industries and disciplines. Commitment to professionalism, qualified consultants, industry/discipline specialization and confidentiality.

Key Contact - Specialty:
Mr. H. Gordon Taylor, President - *Human resources (all industries)*
Mr. Floyd Schriber, Executive Consultant - *Engineering, operations management*

Salary minimum: $40,000

Functions: Mfg., Product Dev., Production, Plant Mgmt., Quality, Purchasing, HR Mgmt., Finance, Engineering

Industries: Generalist, Mfg., Food, Bev., Tobacco, Paper, Soap, Perf., Cosmtcs.

Professional Associations: SHRM

FPC of The Tri-Cities
2700 S Roan St Ste 206
Johnson City, TN 37601
(423) 926-1123
Fax: (423) 926-1124

Description: Cost effective multi-discipline recruiting across most manufacturing industries. Firm is led by a former Fortune 50 plant manager and satisfaction is always guaranteed.

Key Contact - Specialty:
Mr. Walter E. Engel, President/CEO - *Engineering, manufacturing, human resources, finance, accounting*

Salary minimum: $50,000

Functions: General Mgmt., Mfg., Materials, HR Mgmt., Finance, IT, Engineering

Industries: Mfg., Metal Products, Machine, Appliance, Motor Vehicles, Computer Equip., Test, Measure Equip., Misc. Mfg., Finance, HR Services, Software

FPC of Nashville
406 N Main St
Kingston Springs, TN 37082
(615) 952-9310
Fax: (615) 952-9350
Email: fpcnashville@att.net
Web: www.fpcweb.com

Description: We provide recruiting services for manufacturing firms specializing in operational management, human resources, engineering, quality assurance, materials management, and MIS.

Key Contact - Specialty:
Mr. Tom Oglesby, President - *Operations, engineering*
Ms. Peggy Oglesby, Treasurer - *Office manager*

Salary minimum: $40,000

Functions: Generalist

Industries: Plastics, Rubber, Metal Products, Machine, Appliance, Motor Vehicles

FPC of Concord
9827 Cogdill Rd Ste 4
Knoxville, TN 37932
(865) 966-4002
Fax: (865) 966-4004
Email: fpcconcord@aol.com
Web: www.fpcconcord.com

Description: We are a professional recruiting firm specializing in the placement of chemical and mechanical engineers and healthcare professionals.

Key Contact - Specialty:
Mr. Harry DeNardo, President - *Chemical engineers, mechanical engineers, healthcare professionals*

Salary minimum: $40,000

Functions: Mfg., Quality, Physicians, Engineering

Industries: Generalist, Chemicals, Paints, Petro. Products, Leather, Stone, Glass, Metal Products

FPC of North Dallas
1545 W Mockingbird Ln Ste 1020
Dallas, TX 75232
(214) 634-3929
(800) 618-3929
Fax: (214) 634-7741
Email: phil@fpcndallas.com
Web: www.fpcndallas.com

Description: We offer quick response to both client and candidate needs with 66 years' combined industry experience in medical device, pharmaceutical and general manufacturing.

Key Contact - Specialty:
Mr. Philip H. Pritchett, President/Owner - *Medical devices, pharmaceutical, manufacturing technology*
Mr. Norman Spencer, Consultant - *Medical device, pharmaceutical, manufacturing technology*

Salary minimum: $30,000

Functions: Generalist, Product Dev., Quality, Materials Plng., Mktg. Mgmt., Sales Mgmt., R&D, Engineering

Industries: Generalist, Drugs Mfg., Medical Devices, Plastics, Rubber, Misc. Mfg., Biotech

FPC of Houston

2555 Central Pkwy
Houston, TX 77092
(713) 680-9132
Fax: (713) 680-1737
Email: fpc@onramp.net
Web: www.fpchouston.com

Description: Firm specializes in, petro chemical, specialty chemical and plastics industries. A new division, Alternastaff, specializes in professional temporary placement. Assignments range from specialized technical to managerial up to president of small company.

Key Contact:
Mr. Robert M. Shanley, President
Ms. Suzanne M. Shanley, Vice President

Salary minimum: $35,000

Functions: Mfg., Sales & Mktg., HR Mgmt., Finance, R&D, Engineering

Industries: Mfg., Chemicals, Drugs Mfg., Plastics, Rubber, Finance, Accounting, Environmental Svcs., Aerospace, Packaging

Professional Associations: AICHE, ASME, IEEE, SPE

FPC of San Antonio

10924 Vance Jackson Ste 303-K
San Antonio, TX 78230
(210) 690-9797
(800) 886-2608
Fax: (210) 696-6909
Email: fpcsat@fpcsat.com
Web: www.fpcsat.com

Description: Since 1980, our expertise has been assisting manufacturing/engineering professionals build their careers, by recruiting and placing senior management to engineers, primarily in the medical, electronics, automotive, process and consumer products industries.

Key Contact - Specialty:
Mr. Jim Morrisey, CPC, President/CEO - *General management*
Mr. Stan Witt, CPC, Director - General Manufacturing - *Consumer goods, automation equipment, automotive*
Mr. Ken Larsen, CPC, Director-Medical Manufacturing - *Product development, process development*
Mr. Denny Brubaker, CPC, Director-Electronic Manufacturing - *Computer manufacturing, PCB manufacturing*
Mr. Greg Buschmann, CPC, Director-Process Industries and HR - *Engineering, manufacturing, operations, HR*
Mr. Paul Berry, CPC, Director - Electronic Manufacturing - *Aerospace, black belts, reliability, engineering*
Mr. Bufford Watson, Director - Medical Manufacturing - *Quality, reliability, regulatory affairs, medical device*

Salary minimum: $40,000

Functions: General Mgmt., Mfg., Product Dev., Automation, Plant Mgmt., Quality, HR Mgmt.

Industries: Mfg., Chemicals, Medical Devices, Metal Products, Machine, Appliance, Motor Vehicles, Computer Equip., Consumer Elect., Test, Measure Equip., Misc. Mfg., Electronic, Elec. Components

Professional Associations: ASQ, NAPS, SAAPC, SHRM, TAPC

FPC of Fairfax

112 W Main St Ste 1
Berryville, VA 22611
(540) 955-0500
Fax: (540) 955-0518
Email: career@veriomail.com
Web: www.fortunecareers.com

Description: Established and emerging organizations turn to our expertise for executive staffing. With a 40-year history and a network of over 100 offices, we can provide talent from across the country.

Key Contact - Specialty:
Mr. John Abbene, President - *Supply chain, purchasing, distribution, materials, logistics*
Ms. Sandra Abbene, Vice President - *Engineering, human resources*

Salary minimum: $40,000

Functions: Mfg., Materials, Engineering, Minorities

Industries: Food, Bev., Tobacco, Chemicals, Soap, Perf., Cosmtcs., Plastics, Rubber, Paints, Petro. Products, Metal Products, Machine, Appliance, Motor Vehicles, Computer Equip., Test, Measure Equip., Misc. Mfg., Mgmt. Consulting, HR Services, Telecoms, Defense, Haz. Waste

Professional Associations: APICS, CLM, NAPM

FPC of The Virginia Highland

Rte 1 Box 132
Millboro, VA 24460
(540) 925-2430
Fax: (540) 925-2434
Email: fpcvh@fpcvh.com
Web: www.fpcvh.com

Description: We specialize in placement of middle management professionals in purchasing, materials, logistics, supply chain, and supplier quality.

Key Contact - Specialty:
Ms. Jean Howell, President - *Purchasing, materials management*

Salary minimum: $35,000

Functions: Materials

Industries: Mfg.

FPC of E Seattle

11661 SE First St Ste 202
Bellevue, WA 98005
(425) 450-9665
Fax: (425) 450-0357
Email: danc@fpc-eastseattle.com
Web: www.fpc-eastseattle.com

Description: We are an executive search firm specializing in the off-road heavy equipment, mobile hydraulics, lawn & garden equipment, power hand tools, automotive, biotech and medical equipment industries. We work mostly on a contingency basis building relationships with our customer and at the same time providing satisfaction to the candidates we represent. Fostering a 'win-win' situation is our focus.

Key Contact:
Mr. Daniel Chin, President & Recruiter - *Heavy equipment (off-road), mobile hydraulics*
Mr. Zed Chin, Recruiter - *Biotech, pharmaceutical and medical equipment*
Mr. Danny Ventler, Research Associate

Salary minimum: $45,000

Functions: Generalist, Middle Mgmt., Mfg., Materials, Engineering

Industries: Generalist, Construction, Medical Devices, Machine, Appliance

The Fortus Group

(also known as MRI of Mohawk Valley)
181 Genesee St Ste 600
Utica, NY 13501
(315) 768-3322
(888) 38R-ENAL
Fax: (315) 768-4349
Email: mrmv@dreamscape.com
Web: www.mrioffice.com/mohawkvalley

Description: We are the dialysis recruiting specialists and are committed to the highest standard of locating, recruiting and placing renal professionals at all levels of employment both clinically and in business.

Key Contact:
Mr. Michael Maurizio, President - *Dialysis*
Ms. Patricia Maurizio, Secretary

Functions: Healthcare

Industries: Services

Professional Associations: ANNA, NRAA

Forum Personnel Inc

342 Madison Ave Ste 509
New York, NY 10017
(212) 687-4050
Email: info@forumper.com
Web: www.forumpersonnel.com

Description: Management recruitment firm established in 1974. Areas of specialization include accounting, finance, human resources, marketing/sales and information technology. Permanent and temporary consultant placement.

Key Contact:
Mr. Steve Goldstein, Executive Vice President

Salary minimum: $30,000

Functions: Generalist, Advertising, Mkt. Research, Benefits, Personnel, CFO's, Cash Mgmt., MIS Mgmt.

Industries: Generalist, Misc. Mfg., Finance, Accounting, Media, Advertising

Professional Associations: APCNY, NATSS

Foster, McMillan & Company

(a division of Intromation Inc)
800 Enterprise Dr Ste 128
Oak Brook, IL 60523
(630) 574-0301
(800) 942-2378
Email: fostermcm@cs.com
Web: www.fostermcmillan.com

Description: Placement limited exclusively to attorneys with our clients which include 1500+ law firms and 500+ corporations coast to coast.

Key Contact - Specialty:
Mr. Eugene B. Shea, President - *Attorneys*
Mr. Peter E. Shea, Vice President - *Attorneys*
Ms. Patricia A. Sarlas, Vice President - *Attorneys*

Functions: Legal

Industries: Legal

Fought, Jameson Associates

55 W Monroe Ste 1190
Chicago, IL 60603
(312) 422-8260
Fax: (312) 422-8268
Email: foughtjameson@csi.com

Description: We are owned and operated by two principals both having extensive system engineering and management backgrounds. Our in-depth technical knowledge enables us to quickly assess candidates' interests and potential client opportunities.

Key Contact - Specialty:
Mr. Jay D. Fought, Principal - *Technical, management consulting*
Mr. Brad M. Jameson, Principal - *Technical, management consulting*

Functions: IT, MIS Mgmt., Systems Analysis, Systems Dev., Systems Implem., Systems Support, Network Admin., DB Admin.

Industries: Generalist

Networks: Top Echelon Network

The Fourbes Group Inc
1030 St. George Ave Ste 300
Avenel, NJ 07001
(732) 855-7722
Fax: (732) 855-8406
Email: bobj@fourbes.com
Web: www.fourbes.com

Description: We are a minority-owned firm (2 of 3 owners are women). We go to great lengths to ensure that each deal is a good one - both for the client company and the applicant.

Key Contact:
Ms. Kathleen Burke, CPC, Partner
Mr. Robert Jay, Partner

Functions: Generalist, Middle Mgmt., Admin. Svcs., Production, Plant Mgmt., Purchasing, Customer Svc., Credit

Industries: Generalist, Soap, Perf., Cosmtcs., Misc. Mfg., Accounting, Insurance

Professional Associations: MAAPC, NJASP

Fox Interlink Partners
PO Box 587
Pine, CO 80470
(303) 670-5770
Fax: (303) 838-1900
Email: fox@purplemtn.com
Web: www.telecomemploy.com

Description: We offer permanent placement recruitment only. Our specialties are telecommunications to include: wireless, broadband, data, and IP and some high-tech and Internet. We place middle to upper-management in marketing, sales, engineering, finance, human resources, IT, and customer operations.

Key Contact - Specialty:
Ms. Cheryl Fox, President - *Marketing and sales, engineering, finance, customer operations, telecommunications*

Salary minimum: $40,000

Functions: Directors, Product Dev., Sales & Mktg., Advertising, Mktg. Mgmt., Sales Mgmt., Finance, IT, Engineering, Minorities

Industries: Telecoms

J R Fox Recruiters
PO Box 938
New Monmouth, NJ 07748
(732) 671-7540
Fax: (732) 957-0139
Email: jrfoxrecruiters@home.com

Description: We specialize in the recruit for sales, marketing, and operations positions for manufacturers and distributors in the pet product industry exclusively throughout US. We place the positions ranging from sales reps to CEOs.

Key Contact:
Ms. J. R. Fox, President

Functions: Generalist

Industries: Misc. Mfg.

Larry Fox's Managed Care Resources
12736 Ohio Cir
Omaha, NE 68164
(402) 445-2166
Fax: (402) 445-2178
Email: larryfox@lfmcr.com
Web: www.lfmcr.com

Description: Specializing in HMO, managed care executive postions in administration, finance, operations and medical management.

Key Contact - Specialty:
Mr. Larry Fox, President - *Managed care, HMO*

Functions: Generalist, Directors, Senior Mgmt., Middle Mgmt., Physicians, Health Admin., CFO's, MIS Mgmt.

Industries: Generalist, Insurance, Healthcare

Fox-Morris Associates Inc
(a division of M-Q Corp)
1617 JFK Blvd Ste 1850
Philadelphia, PA 19103-1892
(215) 561-6300
Fax: (215) 561-6333
Email: philadelphia@fox-morris.com
Web: www.fox-morris.com

Description: Our specialty areas include: information technology, pharmaceuticals, human resources, employee benefits, and the food and beverage industry.

Key Contact:
Mr. Scott Hood, Account Executive

Salary minimum: $50,000

Functions: Senior Mgmt., Middle Mgmt., Plant Mgmt., Mktg. Mgmt., MIS Mgmt., Systems Implem., Engineering

Industries: Generalist

Branches:
1940 W Orangewood Ave Ste 207
Orange, CA 92868
(714) 634-2600
Fax: (714) 634-1273
Key Contact:
Mr. David Greenstein, Account Executive

1140 Hammond Dr Ste I-9250
Atlanta, GA 30328
(770) 399-4497
Fax: (770) 399-4499
Key Contact:
Ms. Catherine Kunz, Practice Director

105 Forest Ave Unit 4
Portland, ME 04101
(207) 773-1942
Fax: (207) 773-5069

409 Washington Ave Ste 1020
Baltimore, MD 21204
(410) 296-4500
Fax: (410) 296-8972
Key Contact - Specialty:
Mr. George Simmons, Manager - *Human resources*

1050 Wall St Ste 310
Lyndhurst, NJ 07071
(201) 933-8900
Fax: (201) 933-3221
Key Contact:
Mr. Dennis Connors

14045 Ballantyne Corp Pl Ste 160
Brixham Green 2
Charlotte, NC 28277
(704) 540-5101
Fax: (704) 540-8171
Key Contact:
Ms. Jennifer Re

4700 Rockside Rd Ste 640
Cleveland, OH 44131
(440) 524-6565
Fax: (216) 524-4216
Key Contact:
Ms. Jennifer Filicko

1 Gateway Ctr Fl 18 N Wing
Pittsburgh, PA 15222
(412) 232-0410
Fax: (412) 232-3055
Key Contact - Specialty:
Mr. Murray Leety, Manager - *Engineering, manufacturing, human resources, career transition services, advertising*

5400 LBJ Fwy 1 Lincoln Ctr Ste 1445
Dallas, TX 75240
(972) 404-8044
Fax: (972) 404-0615
Key Contact - Specialty:
Mr. Jerry Sewell, Manager - *Human resources, engineering, executive search, technical sales*

FoxWhite & Associates
15 Miramar Rd
Stuart, FL 34996
(561) 781-1844
Email: foxwhite1@earthlink.net
Web: www.foxwhite.com

Description: Executive search concentrating on placing marketing/brand/product managers within the consumer package goods industry. Associate level to VP of Marketing.

Key Contact - Specialty:
Mr. Louis Volpe, CM, Partner - *Marketing management, consumer packaged goods*

Salary minimum: $50,000

Functions: Directors, Senior Mgmt., Product Dev., Mkt. Research, Mktg. Mgmt.

Industries: Food, Bev., Tobacco, Textiles, Apparel, Soap, Perf., Cosmtcs., Drugs Mfg., Consumer Elect.

Professional Associations: RON

Networks: First Interview Network (FIN)

Franchise Search Inc
48 Burd St Ste 101
Nyack, NY 10960
(845) 727-4103
Fax: (845) 727-3918
Email: dkushell@franchise-search.com

Description: We are a search company dedicated exclusively to franchising domestically and internationally. We represent only franchisor clients, and we place only professional franchise management candidates in franchise sales, operations, training, marketing, legal, financial, real estate, construction, and international development.

Key Contact - Specialty:
Mr. Douglas T. Kushell, President - *Franchise, hospitality*

Salary minimum: $50,000

Functions: Generalist, Senior Mgmt., Middle Mgmt., Int'l.

Industries: Generalist, Hospitality, Real Estate, Non-classifiable

Professional Associations: IFA

Franklin Associates Inc
509 Camden Ave
Stuart, FL 34994
(561) 219-0406
Fax: (561) 219-0860
Email: employ01@bellsouth.net

Description: We are a boutique retainer search firm with national client base. Our firm was founded by a former VP HR, highly specialized, and hands-on. Our industry specialties are real estate/development, biotech, and financial services. Our functional specialties are HR, sales, marketing, finance, and Ops.

Key Contact - Specialty:
Mr. Frank Gardner, Managing Partner - *Human resources, hospitality, real estate, finance, e-commerce*
Ms. Linda Brann, Senior Manager - *Hospitality, travel-related services, sales management*

Salary minimum: $75,000

Functions: General Mgmt., Senior Mgmt., Sales & Mktg., Sales Mgmt., HR Mgmt., Finance

Industries: Generalist, Construction, Medical Devices, Transportation, Banking, Mgmt. Consulting, Hospitality, Real Estate, Biotech

Professional Associations: EMA, IOTA, SHRM

Franklin Int'l Search Inc
PO Box 2566
Framingham, MA 01703-2566
(508) 788-1511
Fax: (508) 788-1818
Email: franintl@rcn.com

Description: We provide recruitment of technical/engineering, sales/marketing, manufacturing, and quality control personnel for the optical networking/DWDM systems and components, semiconductor laser devices, optics/thin films, MEMS/MOEMS, data/telecommunications, LAN/WAN, and data storage/recording fields.

Key Contact - Specialty:
Mr. Stanley L. Shindler, President - *Data storage, data communications, inter-networking, wireless, telecommunications*

Salary minimum: $80,000

Functions: Generalist, Senior Mgmt., Product Dev., Mktg. Mgmt., Sales Mgmt., Systems Support, Engineering

Industries: Generalist, Computer Equip., Test, Measure Equip., Telecoms, Software

Franstaff Inc
73 S Palm Ave Ste 219
Sarasota, FL 34236
(941) 952-9555
Fax: (941) 952-9520
Email: mail@franstaff.com
Web: www.franstaff.com

Description: The largest executive search organization specializing in franchising... and the only recruiting firm staffed with experienced franchising professionals. Providing uniquely qualified management, sales, and support staff to franchisors worldwide.

Key Contact:
Mr. James W. Dement, President - *Franchising*
Mr. Michael Coffee, Vice President - *Franchising*
Ms. Nancy Estep, Vice President

Salary minimum: $50,000

Functions: General Mgmt., Senior Mgmt., Sales & Mktg.

Industries: Retail, Hospitality, Real Estate

Professional Associations: IFA

Frazee Recruiting Consultants Inc
2332 Eastgate Dr Ste E
Baton Rouge, LA 70816
(225) 295-1188
Fax: (225) 291-9277
Email: info@frazeerecruit.com
Web: www.frazeerecruit.com

Description: We offer contingency search for accounting, information technology, engineering, management and sales positions. We also offer contract and temporary staffing in a variey of professional job categories.

Key Contact - Specialty:
Ms. Marianne Frazee, Owner - *Accounting, information technology, engineering*

Salary minimum: $22,000

Functions: Generalist, Mfg., Sales & Mktg., Finance, IT, Engineering

Industries: Generalist, Finance

Professional Associations: LSA, LSA, SHRM

Mel Frazer Consultant
20350 Chapter Dr
Woodland Hills, CA 91364-5609
(818) 703-0040
Fax: (818) 703-0049
Email: melsearch@earthlink.net

Description: We provide middle management medical device and instrumentation contingency search.

Key Contact - Specialty:
Mr. Mel Frazer, Owner - *High technology instruments, computers, software*

Salary minimum: $50,000

Functions: Generalist, Middle Mgmt., Sales Mgmt., MIS Mgmt.

Industries: Generalist, Computer Equip., Consumer Elect., Test, Measure Equip.

Professional Associations: IEEE

Fred Stuart Consulting/Personnel Services
5855 E Naples Plz Ste 310
Long Beach, CA 90803-5078
(562) 439-0921
(888) 782-1384
Fax: (562) 439-2750
Email: fredstuart@fredstuart.com
Web: www.fredstuart.com

Description: Our emphasis is in the employment and recruiting of information technology professionals. We have also placed individuals with experience in human resources, finance and accounting, general management, engineering, architecture, and sales/marketing, etc. This may be accomplished by search, contingency, or project hourly. "Improve your staffing costs with 'Position Control' systems."

Key Contact:
Mr. Fredric S. Hershenson, Owner

Salary minimum: $20,000

Functions: Senior Mgmt., IT

Industries: Generalist, Non-profits, Accounting, Mgmt. Consulting, E-commerce, IT Implementation, PSA/ASP, Software, HR SW, Biotech, Healthcare

Frederick William Int'l
4280 Albany Dr Apt J119
San Jose, CA 95129
(408) 248-4789
Email: fmarrazzo@earthlink.net

Description: We are located in Silicon Valley with affiliates in Hong Kong, Tokyo, Malaysia, London, and Mexico. Our focus is on executives, from directors to VPs in a variety of functions such as sales, marketing, business development, finance, manufacturing, and operations, who have international management experience. Our placement include executives who have expatriate

experience or significant international exposure through travel and operations management.

Key Contact:
Mr. Fred Marrazzo, Principal/Founder

Functions: General Mgmt., Int'l.

Industries: Computer Equip., Test, Measure Equip., E-commerce, Telecoms, Telephony, Wireless, Fiber Optic, Network Infrastructure

Freeman Enterprises
748 Newman Springs Rd
Lincroft, NJ 07738
(732) 933-4296
Fax: (732) 933-4295
Email: lwfreeman@aol.com

Description: We specialize in professional liability insurance positions located anywhere in the United States. Claims, underwriting, marketing and risk management are the primary functional areas. Medical malpractice accounts for more than half of all placements. Other product lines: miscellaneous errors and omissions (E&O), directors and officers (D&O), employment practices liability (EPL), dental, lawyers (LPL), real estate, architects and engineers (A&E).

Key Contact:
Ms. Lynne Freeman, Owner

Salary minimum: $40,000

Functions: Generalist

Industries: Insurance

Fresquez & Associates
405 14th St Ste 206
Oakland, CA 94612
(925) 274-9360
Fax: (925) 274-1875
Email: ernesto@fresquez.com
Web: www.fresquez.com

Description: Search firm that specializes in the recruitment of minority/diversity professionals, particularly strong in Hispanic community for bilingual professionals in accounting, auditing, finance, marketing, management, human resources, information systems and engineering for the US and Latin America.

Key Contact:
Mr. Ernesto Fresquez, Principal - *Hispanic, bilingual professionals (spanish)*
Ms. Jeanette Acosta, Vice President

Salary minimum: $50,000

Functions: Sales & Mktg., HR Mgmt., IT, Minorities

Industries: Generalist

Professional Associations: NSHMBA, PMAA

Branches:
San Juan de La Cruz 655
Col Camino Real
Guadalajara, JAL CP 45040
Mexico

Frey & Sher Associates Inc
1800 N Kent St Ste 1006
Arlington, VA 22209-9998
(703) 524-6500
Fax: (703) 524-6578
Email: info@freysher.com
Web: www.freysher.com

Description: Attorney search specialists placing permanent lawyers in law firms, corporations, privately held business and government agencies. Advise law firms on merger and acquisition activity. Placing more attorneys in DC and Virginia than any other legal recruiting firm. Other offices in Charlottesville, VA; Norfolk, VA and Richmond, VA.

Key Contact - Specialty:
Ms. Florence Frey, Owner - *Legal*
Ms. Eileen Sher, Principal - *Legal*

Salary minimum: $120,000

Functions: Legal

Industries: Legal

Professional Associations: NALSC

Fristoe & Carleton Inc
77 Milford Dr
Hudson, OH 44236
(330) 655-3535
Fax: (330) 655-3585
Email: fristcarl@adjob.com
Web: www.adjob.com

Description: Our principals work primarily with ad agencies and have in-depth ad agency experience. We work outside New York, Chicago, Midwest, and South.

Key Contact:
Mr. Jack Fristoe, President - *Advertising*
Mr. Bob Carleton, Vice President
Ms. Jill Grimm, Executive Recruiter

Salary minimum: $25,000

Functions: PR

Industries: Advertising

Peter Froehlich & Company
PO Box 339
Weatherford, TX 76086
(817) 594-9991
Fax: (817) 594-1337
Email: pfsearch@flash.net
Web: www.flash.net/~pfsearch

Description: Specializing in all levels of management positions for all disciplines within the cable television and telecommunications industry. Clientele include operators and manufacturers.

Key Contact - Specialty:
Mr. Peter Froehlich, CEO - *Management (upper), communications (broadband)*
Mr. Mike Pask, Senior Consultant - *Middle management CATV*
Ms. Karen Egeland, Office Manager
Ms. Valerie Howard, Consultant
Mr. Noel Egeland, Senior Consultant - *Manufacturers (communications)*

Functions: Generalist

Industries: Media, Communications, Telecoms, Call Centers, Telephony, Digital, Wireless, Fiber Optic, Network Infrastructure

Professional Associations: SCTE

Front Line Solutions
6165 Lehman Dr Ste 207A
Colorado Springs, CO 80918
(719) 593-8232
(866) 357-5627
Fax: (719) 593-7834
Email: mikemyers@flsolutions.net
Web: www.flsolutions.net

Description: We are a direct placement and contract recruiting firm, specializing in placing prior military, DoD, defense, and high-tech engineers.

Key Contact:
Mr. Mike Myers, Owner
Mr. Edward Jones, Owner
Mr. Richard Harrold, Owner

Salary minimum: $35,000

Functions: Generalist

Industries: Energy, Utilities, Computer Equip., Consumer Elect., Electronic, Elec. Components, Services, Communications, Government, Environmental Svcs., Aerospace, Software

Networks: Top Echelon Network

The Fry Group Inc
369 Lexington Ave
New York, NY 10017
(212) 557-0011
Fax: (212) 557-3449
Email: folks@frygroup.com
Web: www.frygroup.com

Description: Public relations, corporate communications and marketing communications. Executive and middle management recruitment.

Key Contact - Specialty:
Mr. John M. Fry, President - *Public relations, corporate communications*

Salary minimum: $35,000

Functions: PR

Industries: Generalist

Professional Associations: APCNY, IABC, NAPS

Frye/Joure & Associates Inc
4515 Poplar Ave Ste 209
Memphis, TN 38117-7506
(901) 683-7792
Email: fja@accessllc.net
Web: www.fja-inc.com

Description: Full-service human resources consulting firm with emphasis on organizational effectiveness, staffing, selection and senior-level executive search. Highly successful in filling positions that are difficult to locate candidates for. Discreet.

Key Contact - Specialty:
Dr. Sylvia A. Joure, President - *Generalist*

Salary minimum: $40,000

Functions: Generalist, Senior Mgmt., Production, Distribution, Training, Engineering, Mgmt. Consultants

Industries: Generalist, Machine, Appliance, Misc. Mfg., HR Services, Advertising, New Media

Networks: Top Echelon Network

FSA Inc
2886 Observation Pt
Marietta, GA 30064
(770) 427-8813
Fax: (770) 427-8835
Email: ron@fsasearch.com
Web: www.fsasearch.com

Description: Executive search consultants to the property and casualty insurance industry. Specializing in actuaries and product managers.

Key Contact - Specialty:
Mr. Ronald G. Biagini, CPC, President - *Actuarial (property, casualty)*

Functions: Finance

Industries: Insurance

Professional Associations: GAPS, NAPS, NIRA

S L Fults & Associates
9225 Katy Fwy Ste 206
Houston, TX 77024
(713) 935-9797
Email: mail@slfults.com
Web: www.slfults.com

Description: Executive search firm specializing in e-business, information technology and customer relationship management.

Key Contact:
Ms. Sharon Fults

Functions: IT

Industries: Energy, Utilities, Mfg., Venture Cap., Accounting, Mgmt. Consulting, E-commerce, IT Implementation, Software

Future Employment Service Inc
(also known as Sedona Staffing Services)
3392 Hillcrest Rd
Dubuque, IA 52002
(563) 556-3040
Fax: (563) 556-3041
Email: careers@careerpros.com
Web: www.careerpros.com

Description: Client driven, only seek the most highly qualified candidates. Nationwide search and placement as well as local temporary staffing.

Key Contact - Specialty:
Ms. Carol A. Townsend, President - *Operations, human resources, engineering, chemical engineers, embedded software engineers*

Salary minimum: $35,000

Functions: Generalist

Industries: Generalist

Professional Associations: ASA, NAPS, NATSS

Networks: National Personnel Assoc (NPA)

Branches:
3409 Cedar Heights Dr
Cedar Falls, IA 50613
(319) 268-9204
Fax: (319) 268-9208
Email: sedonacf@aol.com
Key Contact:
Ms. Amy Fay, Manager

2337 Blairs Ferry Rd NE
Cedar Rapids, IA 52402
(319) 378-4487
Fax: (319) 378-4489
Email: sedonacr@aol.com
Key Contact - Specialty:
Mr. Donald Bach, Manager - *Accounting, sales, manufacturing, computers*

108 S Main St
Maquoketa, IA 52060
(319) 652-5699
Fax: (319) 652-4206
Email: sedona@caves.net
Key Contact - Specialty:
Ms. Judy Steiner, Manager - *Sales, manufacturing*

330 Junction Rd
Madison, WI 53717
(608) 664-9977
Fax: (608) 664-9978
Email: sedona330@aol.com
Key Contact:
Ms. Ann Deluhery, Manager

Future Executive Personnel Ltd
425 University Ave Ste 800
Toronto, ON M5G 1T6
Canada
(416) 979-7575
(888) 636-4802
Fax: (416) 979-3030
Email: staff@futureexec.com
Web: www.futureexec.com

Description: We remove the pressure involved in hiring quality staff. We handle every aspect of your search with diligence and professionalism. Our services provide your company with a wide range of benefits: elite candidates, strategic advertising, computerized resources, industry-specific networking, time-saving response, candidate resource bulletins and value-added services.

Key Contact - Specialty:
Mr. Mike Mehta, President - *IT, software executives, CEO, VP*

Salary minimum: $40,000

Functions: General Mgmt., Mfg., Materials, Purchasing, Packaging, Sales & Mktg., Finance, IT, Engineering

Industries: Mfg., Transportation, Finance, Banking, Invest. Banking, Venture Cap., Aerospace, Packaging, Software, Biotech

Branches:
4494 Southside Blvd Ste 200
Jacksonville, FL 32216
(904) 998-1900
(877) 557-7842
Fax: (904) 564-9100
Email: staff@futureexec.com
Key Contact:
Mr. David Tyler

300 Int'l Dr Ste 100
Williamsville, NY 14221
(716) 626-3451
Fax: (716) 626-3001
Email: staff@futureexec.com
Key Contact:
Mr. David Tyler

Futures Inc

1 Hampton Rd Ste 301
Exeter, NH 03833
(603) 775-7800
Fax: (603) 775-7900
Web: www.futuressearch.com

Description: We specialize in retail food and supermarket merchandising and operations, food service sales, retail/consumer sales, and marketing in all disciplines.

Key Contact - Specialty:
Mr. Thomas P. Colacchio, President - *Food service, sales & marketing*
Mr. Richard J. Mazzola, Vice President - *Supermarkets, wholesale industry*

Salary minimum: $40,000

Functions: Generalist, Distribution, Mktg. Mgmt., Sales Mgmt., Direct Mktg., Finance, MIS Mgmt., Minorities

Industries: Generalist, Food, Bev., Tobacco, Hospitality

Professional Associations: FFANE, GMRNE, NEDDBA

G H Enterprises

19901 W Kaibab Rd
Buckeye, AZ 85326
(623) 393-0999
Email: ghills45@hotmail.com

Description: For candidates to be considered, the following is needed to accompany the resume: 3 named companies to contact and why that company should consider you for a position with them. Be as specific as possible, it will make my job and the prospective employers options easier. All requests will be held in strict confidence.

Key Contact - Specialty:
Mr. Glen Hills, General Manager - *Engineering, sales & marketing, computers, accounting*

Salary minimum: $50,000

Functions: Senior Mgmt.

Industries: Mfg., Computer Equip., Misc. Mfg., Accounting, Mgmt. Consulting, Aerospace, Software, Non-classifiable

The Gabor Group

70 W Streetsboro St Ste 312
Hudson, OH 44236
(330) 342-3786
Fax: (330) 342-3881
Email: kgi@gwis.com

Description: We conduct executive search on an exclusive contingency or retained basis for technical, management, and executive personnel. We specialize in purchasing, sourcing, commodity management, materials management, supply chain, quality, Six Sigma, and operations management.

Key Contact - Specialty:
Mr. Robert A. Gabor, President - *Purchasing, quality, human resources, materials management*

Salary minimum: $50,000

Functions: Mfg., Quality, Materials, Purchasing

Industries: Mfg., Medical Devices, Plastics, Rubber, Metal Products, Motor Vehicles, Computer Equip., Consumer Elect., Misc. Mfg., Electronic, Elec. Components, Transportation, HR Services, Publishing, Aerospace, Mfg. SW, Biotech

Professional Associations: ASQ, MOAESP

Networks: Top Echelon Network

Gabriel Worldwide Inc

1601 Market St Fl 24
Philadelphia, PA 19103
(215) 496-9990
Fax: (215) 636-0860
Web: www.gabrielgroup.com

Description: Full-service human resources and management consulting firm able to integrate search objectives with business strategies.

Key Contact - Specialty:
Mr. John Turnblacer, JD, President - *Senior management, CFO, human resources*
Dr. Reggie Owens, Ph.D., Executive Vice President - *Generalist, manufacturing, human resources*
Dr. Janice Presser, Ph.D., Executive Vice President - *Mental health, education*

Functions: Generalist, General Mgmt., Mfg., Sales & Mktg., HR Mgmt., CFO's, IT

Industries: Generalist, Mfg., Finance, Services, Media, Insurance

Gabriele & Company

2 Emery Rd
Bedford, MA 01730-1061
(781) 276-7999
Fax: (781) 276-7933
Email: leslie@gabrieleandcompany.com
Web: www.gabrieleandcompany.com

Description: Recruiters for manufacturing and materials for the New England area.

Key Contact - Specialty:
Ms. Leslie Gabriele, President - *Manufacturing, materials*

Salary minimum: $65,000

Functions: Mfg., Production, Quality, Materials, Purchasing, Materials Plng.

Industries: Generalist

Professional Associations: APICS, ASQ

Gage & Associates

5887 Brockton Ave Ste 200
Riverside, CA 92506
(909) 684-4200
Fax: (909) 684-6138
Email: amgage@earthlink.net
Web: www.gageandassociates.com

Description: We serve the executive talent needs of manufacturing companies, primarily in sales and management. With the increasing use of communication technology, our firm now conducts business almost exclusively by phone, fax, and e-mail.il.

Key Contact - Specialty:
Mr. Arthur M. Gage, President - *Sales*

Mr. Randy Nesbitt, Vice President - *Electronics*

Functions: Senior Mgmt., Sales & Mktg.

Industries: Generalist, Mfg. SW

Gajek Group

29 Cervantes
Newport Beach, CA 92660
(949) 263-8988
Fax: (949) 509-0449
Email: vic@gajekgroup.com
Web: www.gajekgroup.com

Description: Retained and contingency searches in the accounting and finance profession. The partners are Certified Public Accountants with a combined total of over 35 years of experience in the recruiting profession.

Key Contact - Specialty:
Mr. Victor J. Gajek, Partner - *Accounting & finance*

Salary minimum: $40,000

Functions: General Mgmt., Finance, CFO's

Industries: Generalist

Gallant Search Group Inc

431 Boler Rd
PO Box 20086
London, ON N6K 2K0
Canada
(519) 663-1070
Fax: (519) 663-1074
Email: gallant@automotivecareers.com
Web: www.automotivecareers.com

Description: Agency works with the automotive parts manufacturing community in North America. No fee charged to applicants. Twenty years of success to offer all clients. Expert recruiter for materials, plant management, engineering, product design and quality. Contingency fees are offered.

Key Contact:
Mr. Andrew Gallant, President

Salary minimum: $50,000

Functions: General Mgmt., Middle Mgmt., Mfg., Product Dev., Production, Quality, Materials, Engineering

Industries: Mfg., Plastics, Rubber, Metal Products, Motor Vehicles, Consumer Elect., Misc. Mfg., Aerospace

Networks: National Personnel Assoc (NPA)

Gallin Associates Inc

PO Box 1065
Safety Harbor, FL 34695-1065
(727) 724-8303
Fax: (727) 724-8503
Email: gallin@gallinassociates.com
Web: www.gallinassociates.com

Description: Specialists in technical and managerial search for the chemical process, electronics, telecommunications, computer equipment semiconductor industries.

Key Contact - Specialty:
Mr. Lawrence Gallin, President - *Management, engineering*
Mr. John Fabriele - *Research & development*

Salary minimum: $50,000

Functions: Generalist, Mfg., Sales & Mktg., IT, R&D, Engineering

Industries: Generalist, Chemicals, Medical Devices, Plastics, Rubber, Paints, Petro. Products, Computer Equip., Consumer Elect., Software

Professional Associations: IEEE, SAE, SAMPE, SEMI

Networks: Top Echelon Network

Branches:
1784 Alamand Dr
Naples, FL 34102
(941) 403-9210
Fax: (941) 403-9209
Key Contact - Specialty:
Mr. Paul Stepler, President - *Computer, data communications, telecommunications, semiconductor, software development*

The Gammill Group Inc

8425 Pulsar Pl Ste 410
Columbus, OH 43240
(614) 848-7726
Fax: (614) 848-7738
Email: gammill@gammillgroup.com
Web: www.gammillgroup.com

Description: This firm is regarded for its service - taking a partnering approach to executive search; quality - consistently locating the best professionals and speed - agility in responding to customer's needs.

Key Contact:
Mr. Robert A. Gammill, President
Mr. Mark Zeigler, Manager of MIS

Salary minimum: $30,000

Functions: Generalist, Senior Mgmt., Healthcare, Health Admin., Mktg. Mgmt., Sales Mgmt., CFO's, Systems Analysis, DB Admin.

Industries: Generalist, IT Implementation, Insurance, Healthcare, Hospitals

Professional Associations: MGMA

Gandin & Associates Inc

5518 Pinewood Springs Dr
Houston, TX 77066-2719
(281) 580-0700
Fax: (281) 580-0740
Email: david_gandin@alumni.utexas.net

Description: We service clients from all industries desiring professionals with accounting, tax, audit or financial experience. Many of our candidates are CPAs or MBAs with current or prior experience in public accounting, corporate accounting, corporate tax, corporate finance or financial analysis.

Key Contact - Specialty:
Mr. David L. Gandin, CPC, President - *Accounting, tax, finance*

Salary minimum: $40,000

Functions: Finance

Industries: Generalist

Professional Associations: HAAPC, TAPC

Garb & Associates, Legal Placement LLC

2001 Wilshire Blvd Ste 510
Santa Monica, CA 90403
(310) 998-3388
Fax: (310) 998-3392
Email: sgarb@aol.com

Description: We specialize in placing attorneys primarily in the Southern California area.

Key Contact - Specialty:
Ms. Sheila Garb, President - *Lawyers*
Ms. Barbara Wellisch, Vice President - *Lawyers*
Ms. Jessica Meyerson - *Lawyers (in house)*

Salary minimum: $50,000

Functions: Legal, Attorneys

Industries: Generalist

Professional Associations: NALSC

Garrison Resources

23 Kanas Datsi Dr
Brevard, NC 28712
(828) 877-6300
Fax: (828) 877-6302
Email: lizgarrison@attglobal.net

Description: We specialize exclusively in the environmental and occupational health and safety fields. Our clients are primarily Fortune 100 companies. We have an extensive network of contacts among industrial EHS professionals.

Key Contact - Specialty:
Ms. Liz Garrison, President - *Environmental, safety management*

Salary minimum: $80,000

Functions: Environmentalists

Industries: Generalist

Garrison, Phillips & Israel Executive Search

1600 Bay Dr Ste 1000
West Atlantic City, NJ 08232-2912
(609) 641-7945
Fax: (609) 641-7947
Email: garyisrael@gpisearch.com
Web: www.gpisearch.com

Description: Our firm's practice is limited to the hospitality Industry. We serve the nation's premiere hotels, resorts, conference centers, casino hotels, spas, and CVBs. Recognized for impeccable ethical standards our award winning team thrives on solving our clients needs in highly competitive and tight markets.

Key Contact - Specialty:
Mr. Gary Israel, Managing Partner - *Hotel sales & marketing recruiting*

Salary minimum: $35,000

Functions: Senior Mgmt., Middle Mgmt., Sales & Mktg.

Industries: Hospitality

Professional Associations: SME

Richard Gast & Associates Ltd

20992 Bake Pkwy Ste 104
Lake Forest, CA 92630
(949) 472-1130
Fax: (949) 472-0403
Email: dick@rgaltd.com
Web: www.rgaltd.com

Description: We are a leader in the recruitment and placement of human resources professionals nationwide. Serve a diversified clientele including many Fortune 500 corporations. Manage human resource database of 25,000+.

Key Contact - Specialty:
Mr. Richard Gast, President - *Human resources*

Salary minimum: $40,000

Functions: Generalist, HR Mgmt., Benefits, Personnel, Training

Industries: Generalist, Energy, Utilities, Mfg., Finance, Services, Insurance, Software

Professional Associations: EMA, SHRM, WAW

GateSource Partners

14150-A Willard Rd Ste 210
Chantilly, VA 20151-2933
(703) 222-4069
Fax: (703) 222-4255
Email: jobs@gatesource.com
Web: www.gatesource.com

Description: We are a leading executive search firm serving a domestic and international clientele ranging from Fortune 500 companies to emerging entrepreneurial businesses. We focus on the following specialties: computer telephony integration (CTI), call center technology, Internet services and software, customer relationship management (CRM), e-Commerce, and document management and imaging.

Key Contact - Specialty:
Mr. Steve Ratliff, Senior Partner - *Senior management, technology, sales*
Mr. Michael McCollum, Senior Partner - *Call center, technologies, CTI, IVR, ACD*

Salary minimum: $40,000

Functions: Generalist

Industries: Mgmt. Consulting, Telecoms, Software, Biotech

Professional Associations: IACMP

Gateway Group Personnel

1770 Kirby Pkwy Ste 216
Memphis, TN 38138-7405
(901) 756-6050
Fax: (901) 756-8445
Email: garen@gatewaypersonnel.com
Web: www.gatewaypersonnel.com

Description: Contingent search with functional specialty in accounting, finance, auditing and banking. Serve Fortune 500 clients through closely held entities.

Key Contact - Specialty:
Mr. Charles G. Haddad, Owner - *Accounting, banking, audit*
Ms. Darlene R. Murphy, President - *Accounting, banking, audit*

Salary minimum: $25,000

Functions: Finance

Industries: Generalist

Professional Associations: NAPS

Gatti & Associates

266 Main St Ste 21
Medfield, MA 02052
(508) 359-4153
Fax: (508) 359-5902
Email: info@gattihr.com
Web: www.gattihr.com

Description: Specialists in the placement of human resources practitioners such as generalists, employment, compensation and benefits, training and development, college relations, EEO/AA, employee/labor relations or HRIS professionals in all industries.

Key Contact - Specialty:
Mr. Robert D. Gatti, President - *Human resource executives*
Ms. Judith Banker, Principal - *Human resource executives*
Mr. Richard Fleming, Vice President - *Human resource executives*
Ms. Mary Bloomfield, Vice President - *Human resource executives*
Ms. Rita Allen, Vice President - *Human resource executives*
Ms. Janet Mullert, Vice President - *Human resource executives*

Salary minimum: $75,000

Functions: HR Mgmt., Benefits, Personnel, Training

Industries: Generalist

Professional Associations: ASTD, EMA, HRMG, HRPS, IHRIM, NEHRA, SHRM, WAW

Branches:
10 Tower Office Park Ste 508
Woburn, MA 01801
(781) 932-0091

Key Contact - Specialty:
Ms. Rita Allen, Vice President - *Human resources, generalist*

Dianne Gauger & Associates
8573 Buena Tierra Pl Ste 200
Buena Park, CA 90621
(714) 522-4300
Fax: (714) 522-4338

Description: Fourteen years of intense specialization focusing on the automation, industrial controls, process control and automation software markets guarantees our clients receive in-depth qualified industry knowledge and services to assure consistent and expedient results.

Key Contact - Specialty:
Ms. Dianne Gauger, Owner/President - *High technology, sales & marketing, management, engineering*

Salary minimum: $60,000

Functions: General Mgmt., Senior Mgmt., Middle Mgmt., Sales & Mktg., Mktg. Mgmt., Sales Mgmt.

Industries: Software

GCB Executive Search
3653 Canton Hwy Ste 106
Marietta, GA 30066-2618
(770) 517-9017
Fax: (770) 517-9016
Email: rcrtr@bellsouth.net
Web: www.jobconnection.com

Description: Eighty-five percent of all placements in the greater Atlanta area, 100% east of the Mississippi River. Real estate and healthcare finance are areas of specialization, both debt and equity. All structured finance, all debt-side analysis and business development.

Key Contact - Specialty:
Mr. G. Craig Baker, Proprietor - *Financial services, products analysis, financial services & products marketing*

Salary minimum: $40,000

Functions: Generalist

Industries: Finance, Banking, Invest. Banking, Venture Cap., Misc. Financial, Real Estate, Healthcare

Professional Associations: GAPS

Geller Braun & White Inc
11846 Ventura Blvd Ste 120
Studio City, CA 91604
(818) 752-8787
Email: hgeller@gbwsearch.com

Description: We are a boutique recruiting firm specializing in executive placements in the high-tech, healthcare consumer products, manufacturing, and hospitality industries.

Key Contact - Specialty:
Mr. Henry Geller
Ms. Susan Braun - *Healthcare*
Mr. Terry White, Sr Director - *Manufacturing*
Ms. Margo Schneider, Sr Director - *Consumer goods, manufacturing*
Ms. Stacey Silveira, Director - *High-tech, human resources*
Mr. Andrew Will, Director - *Hospitality, restaurant industries*
Mr. Gordon Bohn, Researcher/Recruiter - *Healthcare, high technology, bio-technology*

Functions: Generalist

Industries: Mfg., HR Services, E-commerce, IT Implementation, Hospitality, Communications, Biotech, Healthcare

Gelpi & Associates
PO Box 231187
Harahan, LA 70183-1187
(504) 737-6086
Fax: (504) 737-6089
Email: ggelpi@juno.com

Description: We specialize in the recruitment/placement of qualified insurance personnel. We have over twenty-five years of experience in the insurance industry.

Key Contact - Specialty:
Ms. Gerry Gelpi, CPC, CIPC, CISR, Owner/Manager - *Insurance*

Salary minimum: $30,000

Functions: Generalist

Industries: Insurance

Professional Associations: INS, NIRA

Gemini Executive Search Inc
11819 Coral Berry Ct
Ft. Wayne, IN 46814
(219) 672-9785
Fax: (708) 401-1555
Email: afking1@hotmail.com
Web: www.geminies.com

Description: We are a national contingency search firm specializing in the permanent placement of middle to upper-management within the long-term healthcare and retirement living industries. Included is skilled nursing, independent and assisted living, continuing care retirement communities and Alzheimer's.

Key Contact:
Mr. Thomas M King, President
Ms. Adrienne F. King, Vice President

Salary minimum: $45,000

Functions: General Mgmt., Healthcare, Sales & Mktg., HR Mgmt., Finance, IT, MIS Mgmt., Mgmt. Consultants, Architects

Industries: Hospitality, Healthcare

Genel Associates
223 E Thousand Oaks Blvd Ste 220
Thousand Oaks, CA 91360
(805) 374-8737
Fax: (805) 435-1888
Email: genel@genel.com
Web: www.genel.com

Description: We are a professional, ethical firm that understands client needs and are able to perform target searches fast with excellent results. Client servicing is our forte.

Key Contact - Specialty:
Mr. George Genel, President - *Financial services, high technology, legal, biotechnology, entertainment*

Salary minimum: $45,000

Functions: Generalist, Senior Mgmt., Mfg., Sales & Mktg., Finance, IT, Engineering, Specialized Svcs.

Industries: Generalist, Mfg., Finance, Legal, Media, Software, Biotech

General Engineering Tectonics
4118 Coronado Ave
Stockton, CA 95204
(209) 469-9147
Fax: (209) 469-2614
Email: getcareers@gettec.com
Web: www.gettec.com

Description: We are a recruiting and search consulting firm specializing in finding and profiling high-tech industry personnel. We find the right people at the right time.

Key Contact - Specialty:
Mr. Gary Kroll, Staffing Manager - *Research, sourcing*
Mr. Stan Flott, Recruiter - *Semiconductor*
Ms. Linda Kneen, Recruiter - *Wireless communications*
Mr. Brisa Espinoza, Recruiter - *Hardware design*
Mr. James Baskette, Ph.D., Recruiter - *Finance*

Functions: Engineering

Industries: Computer Equip., Consumer Elect., Misc. Mfg., Accounting, HR Services, Telecoms, Software

Professional Associations: ACM, RON

Networks: National Banking Network (NBN)

General Search and Recruitment
209 W Jackson Ste 804
Chicago, IL 60606
(312) 922-6664
Email: donna@gsr4you.com
Web: www.gsr4you.com

Description: GSR is committed to fulfilling the professional and executive staffing needs of our clients.

Key Contact - Specialty:
Mr. Mike McDonough, President - *Insurance*

Functions: Generalist, General Mgmt., Directors, Senior Mgmt., Middle Mgmt., Sales & Mktg., Mktg. Mgmt., Benefits, Finance

Industries: Insurance

The Genesis Group
880 Lee St Ste 212
Des Plaines, IL 60016
(847) 390-9968
Email: ewsiii@earthlink.net

Description: Executive search for the Financial Services industry

Key Contact:
Mr. Edward W. Schnabel, III, President

Salary minimum: $50,000

Functions: Finance

Industries: Banking

Professional Associations: NBN

Genesis Recruiting
PO Box 2388
Granite Bay, CA 95746
(916) 652-8615
(916) 780-1482
Fax: (916) 652-8583
Email: genesisrec@aol.com

Description: Recruiting engineers and scientists: technical service, marketing and sales professionals. For entry level to senior-level management positions, in the electronic coatings and adhesives, UV cure, paints, plastics, and specialty chemical areas.

Key Contact - Specialty:
Mr. Jerry Kleames, President - *Coatings, adhesives, electronic chemicals*

Salary minimum: $40,000

Functions: Generalist, Senior Mgmt., Middle Mgmt., Quality, Mkt. Research, Sales Mgmt., R&D, Engineering

Industries: Generalist, Printing, Chemicals, Plastics, Rubber, Paints, Petro. Products, Packaging

Professional Associations: AICHE

Genesis Research

1520 Whetstone Ct
Wildwood, MO 63038-1356
(636) 273-6797
Fax: (636) 273-6799
Email: genesis211@earthlink.net
Web: www.genesisresearch.com

Description: We are a national, employer fee paid, contingency search/placement firm specializing in engineering, technical sales, marketing, management, technical service, R&D, plant engineering, and management positions in the chemical, refining, pulp and paper, metal finishing, metal working, water treatment, lubrication, and power generation industry.

Key Contact - Specialty:
Mr. Dennis Lasini, Search Specialist - *Chemical, refining, pulp & paper, metal finishing, metal working*

Salary minimum: $40,000

Functions: Middle Mgmt., Product Dev., Production, Distribution, Mkt. Research, Mktg. Mgmt., Sales Mgmt., Training, Engineering

Industries: Energy, Utilities, Paper, Chemicals, Plastics, Rubber, Paints, Petro. Products, Metal Products, Test, Measure Equip.

Networks: National Personnel Assoc (NPA)

GeniusTechs

12354 Jones Rd
PMB 151
Houston, TX 77070
(888) 878-0380
Fax: (832) 237-2907
Email: dsweet@geniustechs.com
Web: www.geniustechs.com

Description: We are a technology resources search firm specializing in technology professionals of all stripes. We are the only firm to provide the risk free hiring guarantee and payment options over one full year!

Key Contact:
Mr. Daniel Sweet, Owner

Salary minimum: $60,000

Functions: IT

Industries: Generalist

Networks: Top Echelon Network

Gent & Associates Inc

885 Oak Grove Ave Ste 102
Menlo Park, CA 94025
(650) 322-3596
Email: hr@gent-jobs.com
Web: www.gent-jobs.com

Description: We are one of the leading high-tech and executive search firms dedicated to providing available and experienced professionals since 1992. Our client base includes small emerging companies, management consulting firms and the largest and fastest growing organizations in today's high-tech industry. If you require a full-time professional, short-term consultant or a management-level opportunity, we can help.

Key Contact - Specialty:
Mr. Gary Daugenti, Partner - *High technology, executives, middle management*

Salary minimum: $100,000

Functions: Directors

Industries: Drugs Mfg., Medical Devices, Computer Equip., Software, Biotech

Gerdes & Associates

1300 Nicollet Mall 3046
Hyatt Merchandise Mart
Minneapolis, MN 55403
(612) 335-3553
Fax: (612) 335-3552
Email: rgerdes@worldnet.att.com

Description: We are recruiters for art directors, copywriters, and designers for advertising agencies and companies, throughout the US.

Key Contact - Specialty:
Mr. Richard Gerdes, President - *Art directors, copywriters*

Salary minimum: $25,000

Functions: Advertising

Industries: Agri., Forestry, Mining, Mfg., Retail, Finance, Media, Advertising

GFI Professional Staffing Services

127 Washington St
Keene, NH 03431
(603) 357-3116
Fax: (603) 357-7818
Email: jlloyd@gfijobs.com
Web: www.gfijobs.com

Description: We place the top 10% of talent - from entry level to the top tier of management - for a select group of corporations and businesses in New Hampshire and Vermont.

Key Contact:
Ms. Susan V. Breen, CPC, CEO - *Office administration, accounting, information technology, manufacturing, banking*
Ms. Jodi Lloyd, CPC, CTS, General Manager

Salary minimum: $18,000

Functions: General Mgmt.

Industries: Accounting, HR Services, Hospitality, Advertising, Publishing, New Media, Broadcast, Film, Insurance, Healthcare

Professional Associations: NATSS, NEAPS, NNEAPS

Networks: National Personnel Assoc (NPA)

GH&I Recruiting LLC

1200 Ashwood Pkwy Ste 300
Atlanta, GA 30338
(770) 352-9374
Email: lgreene@ghi-cpa.com
Web: www.ghi-recruiting.com

Description: We are an affiliate of GH&I, PC. We have access to leading CPAs, lawyers and financial experts in Atlanta who have helped build our network of talented professionals and hiring companies. We specialize in the placement of management level professionals in accounting, finance, tax, sales, marketing, and operations.

Key Contact - Specialty:
Ms. Lori Greene, Director of Recruiting - *Recruiting*
Mr. John Shurley, CPA, President - *Recruiting*
Ms. Sue Groszkiewicz, Vice President - *Recruiting*

Gibson & Associates Inc

999 3rd Ave Ste 3800
Seattle, WA 98104-4023
(206) 224-3782
Fax: (425) 401-1153
Email: info@gibsonasso.com
Web: www.gibsonasso.com

Description: Financial executive recruiting firm specializing in CPA's.

Key Contact:
Ms. Kristy Gibson, President
Ms. Carolyn Johnson, Vice President

Salary minimum: $30,000

Functions: Senior Mgmt., Finance, CFO's, Budgeting, Cash Mgmt.

Industries: Generalist

Professional Associations: AICPA

Tom Gilbert Associates

9 Duarte Ct
Novato, CA 94949-6616
(415) 883-7026
Email: tomgilbert94949@yahoo.com
Web: www.nvo.com/tgilbert

Description: San Francisco Bay Area search firm that specializes in IT, software developer, telecommunications and high-tech HR searches for client companies that range from Pre-IPO start-ups to established firms.

Key Contact:
Mr. Tom Gilbert, Owner

Salary minimum: $50,000

Functions: Quality, HR Mgmt., Benefits, Personnel, IT, Systems Analysis, Systems Implem., Systems Support, Network Admin., DB Admin.

Industries: Generalist, Mfg., Finance, Banking, Invest. Banking, Brokers, Venture Cap., Equip Svcs., Media, Telecoms, Insurance, Software, Biotech

Gilbert-Scott Associates LLC

85 Tower Office Park
Woburn, MA 01801-2113
(781) 939-5959
Fax: (781) 939-5962
Email: harry@gilbertscott.com
Web: www.gilbertscott.com

Description: Specialist in all industrial and functions relevant to the professional management of real estate and related assets. Additionally, we specialize in information technology. 50% of our business is executive search, 50% contingency search.

Key Contact - Specialty:
Mr. H. Harry Gilbert, Jr., CPM, Managing Partner - *Real estate, generalist, search*
Mr. Gordon S. Scott, Managing Partner - *Search*
Mr. Glen P. Merkle, Senior Recruiter - *Information technology, generalist*
Mr. Norman Davis, Senior Recruiter - *Embedded software, engineers*
Mr. Daniel Plasse, Ph.D., Senior Recruiter - *Real estate, information technology*
Ms. Christy Crawford, Senior Recruiter - *Real estate*
Mr. Charles Estram, Senior Recruiter - *Search*

Salary minimum: $50,000

Functions: Generalist, Middle Mgmt.

Industries: Energy, Utilities, Construction, Mfg., Finance, Services, Media, Communications, Telecoms, Insurance, Real Estate, Software, Biotech, Healthcare

Professional Associations: MAPS, NAPS

Joe L Giles & Associates

18105 Parkside St Ste 14
Detroit, MI 48221-2792
(313) 864-0022
Fax: (313) 864-0490
Email: gilesjobs@msn.com
Web: www.joegilesassoc.com

Description: Placement areas: HVAC and FEA engineers, PLCs and controls engineers, software and network engineers, manufacturing and quality engineers, minority and diversity candidates, CAD and unigraphics designers. Automotive industry:

wiring and wire harness, six sigma, powertrain/engine, SQE, buyer/purchasers, skill trades/journeymen, airbags/seatbelts, MBAs,CPAs.

Key Contact - Specialty:
Mr. Joe L. Giles, Owner - *Engineering, IT, IS*
Ms. Valerie Gamache, Recruiter - *Engineering, IT, IS*
Ms. Aurora Williams, Recruiter - *IT, IS*

Salary minimum: $50,000

Functions: Mfg., Automation, Materials, Purchasing, IT, Systems Analysis, Network Admin., DB Admin., Engineering, Minorities

Industries: Generalist

Professional Associations: NAPS, NATSS

Gillard Associates Legal Search
202 Bussey Str
Dedham, MA 02026
(781) 329-4731
Fax: (781) 329-1357
Email: gillardlgl@aol.com

Description: Follow strict ethical guidelines; firm founded in 1980 to serve legal community.

Key Contact - Specialty:
Ms. Elizabeth A. Gillard, President - *Attorneys*
Ms. Cheryl A. Gillard, Vice President - *Attorneys, paralegals*

Functions: Generalist, Attorneys, Paralegals

Industries: Generalist, Legal

D Gillespie & Associates Inc
450 N Sproul Rd
Broomall, PA 19008
(610) 355-2383
Fax: (610) 355-2385
Email: dgillassoc@icdc.com

Description: We are focused on retained and high-level contingency search assignments with concentration in the Mid-Atlantic States. We specialized in information systems and technology, sales, and marketing and finance, with emphasis on small to mid-sized companies in the technology sector. Most of our clients would fall in the Fortune 500-1000 category or start-up/early phase.

Key Contact - Specialty:
Mr. David D. Gillespie, President/Principal - *Information systems, information technology, senior level finance, general management*
Ms. Carol S. Smolens, Principal - *Information systems, information technology*
Mr. Donald Wardwell, Principal - *Sales & marketing*

Salary minimum: $90,000

Functions: Senior Mgmt., Middle Mgmt., Sales & Mktg., IT

Industries: Mfg., Finance, Services, Mgmt. Consulting, E-commerce, IT Implementation, Communications, Network Infrastructure, Insurance, Software, ERP SW, Networking, Comm. SW, Biotech, Healthcare

Gimbel & Associates
201 NE 2nd St
Ft. Lauderdale, FL 33301
(954) 525-7000
Fax: (954) 525-7300
Email: gimbel@gate.net

Description: Low profile, established, respected, successful firm. Excellent ability to recruit and place strong talent. President was a controller with Motorola.

Key Contact - Specialty:
Mr. Mike Gimbel, President - *Accounting, finance, consulting, information technology*

Salary minimum: $45,000

Functions: Generalist, Healthcare, Finance, CFO's, Cash Mgmt., Taxes, M&A, IT, Mgmt. Consultants, Attorneys

Industries: Generalist, Banking, Accounting, Mgmt. Consulting, Hospitality, Telecoms

GK & K Associates
1409 Hunters Branch Rd
Nashville, TN 37013
(615) 333-7782
Fax: (615) 333-6656
Email: rfeldser@cs.com

Description: An experienced and proven recruitment/placement firm that specializes in the healthcare industry. We create a partnership with our clients that enhances the total recruiting efforts.

Key Contact - Specialty:
Mr. Richard J. Feldser, President - *Healthcare*

Functions: Healthcare

Industries: Mgmt. Consulting, HR Services, Healthcare

Gladwyne Search Inc
(also known as MRI of Ardmore)
44 W Lancaster Ave Ste 225
Ardmore, PA 19003
(610) 642-1040
Fax: (610) 642-1034
Email: rhe@gladwynesearch.com
Web: www.gladwynesearch.com

Description: We recognize the importance of the hiring process. The individual chosen must be able to accomplish the short term, as well as the long-term goals of the organization within the confines of the company's resources. It is therefore, critical that the process be handled in an intelligent and expeditious manner in order to create this proper fit the first time.

Key Contact:
Mr. Robert Eichman, Managing Director
Ms. Addie Eichman

Salary minimum: $25,000

Functions: Generalist

Industries: Food, Bev., Tobacco, Paper, Printing, Soap, Perf., Cosmtcs., Drugs Mfg., Medical Devices, Paints, Petro. Products, Consumer Elect., Pharm Svcs., Packaging

Lawrence Glaser Associates Inc
505 S Lenola Rd Ste 202
Moorestown, NJ 08057
(856) 778-9500
Fax: (856) 778-4390
Email: larryg@lgasearch.com
Web: www.lgasearch.com

Description: We offer executive recruitment for sales and marketing managers in grocery, food, consumer, beverage, confectionery, non-food, HBC, consumer durable, and foodservice/institutional products categories including various services that are sold into those industries.

Key Contact - Specialty:
Mr. Larry Glaser, President - *Sales & marketing managers, grocery, perishable, consumer, confectionery*
Ms. Nicole Maglio, Division Director - *Sales & marketing managers, foodservice, institutional food products*
Ms. Christine M. Slusser, Division Director - *Sales and marketing (managers), HBC, non-food, consumer durable products*

Salary minimum: $70,000

Functions: Sales & Mktg., Mkt. Research, Mktg. Mgmt., Sales Mgmt.

Industries: Food, Bev., Tobacco, Textiles, Apparel, Lumber, Furniture, Paper, Mgmt. Consulting, Advertising, Telecoms

Professional Associations: ASMC, ASMC, EPPA

The GlenOaks Group Inc
10607 Taylor Farm Ct Ste 100
Prospect, KY 40059
(502) 412-8774
Fax: (502) 412-1883
Email: jobs@glenoaksgroup.com
Web: www.glenoaksgroup.com

Description: We are executive search consultants specializing in the recruitment of senior level sales and marketing personnel in the telecommunications and IT industry sectors.

Key Contact - Specialty:
Mr. John Siewertsen, President - *Telecommunications*
Mr. Roger Harris, Executive Search Consultant - *Information technology*
Ms. Janice Smith, Executive Vice President - *Internet, e-commerce*

Salary minimum: $75,000

Functions: Generalist

Industries: Medical Devices, Computer Equip., Test, Measure Equip., New Media, Communications, Software, Networking, Comm. SW, Security SW, Biotech

Professional Associations: SHRM

Networks: First Interview Network (FIN)

The Glenwood Group
6428 Joliet Rd Ste 112
Countryside, IL 60525
(708) 482-3750
Fax: (708) 482-0633
Email: glenwood@glenwoodgrp.com
Web: www.glenwoodgrp.com

Description: Searches conducted on specialized basis for engineering/manufacturing & logistics positions in the foods, consumer products, plastics, metals and paper industries. Recruiting professionals since 1974.

Key Contact - Specialty:
Mr. Frank J. Filippelli, President - *Engineering, manufacturing, chemicals, foods, packaging*

Salary minimum: $40,000

Functions: Mfg., Product Dev., Production, Automation, Distribution, Packaging, R&D, Engineering

Industries: Mfg., Food, Bev., Tobacco, Paper, Soap, Perf., Cosmtcs., Drugs Mfg., Medical Devices, Plastics, Rubber, Metal Products, Machine, Appliance, Consumer Elect., Electronic, Elec. Components, Packaging

Professional Associations: IAPS, NAPS

Networks: National Personnel Assoc (NPA)

Global Career Services Inc
555 5th Ave Fl 8
New York, NY 10017-2416
(212) 599-6769
Fax: (212) 599-4684
Email: info@globalcareers.com
Web: www.globalcareers.com

Description: Our firm is one of the oldest targeted recruitment sites on the Internet. We offer several vertical specialties from which to choose, including branding, consulting, finance, and transportation. The benefits of working with us include: targeted recruiting of qualified candidates by specialty, yet without geographic borders; trial memberships for new subscribers; and free, secure and easy resume posting for candidates.

Key Contact - Specialty:
Mr. Frank Jones, Chairman - *Generalist*
Mr. William Cerynik, Managing Director - *Generalist, finance, consulting*
Ms. Bonita Jones, Vice President - *Generalist, administrative*
Mr. Cory Visi, VP - Internet/Technology - *Marketing, branding, sales*

Functions: Materials, Sales & Mktg., Finance, IT, Specialized Svcs., Int'l.

Industries: Generalist

Professional Associations: SHRM

Branches:
1 Dock St
Stamford, CT 06902
(203) 327-5700
Fax: (203) 353-1305
Email: info@globalcareers.com
Key Contact:
Mr. William Cerynik, Managing Director

Global Consulting Group Inc
195 Main St N
Markham, ON L3P 1Y4
Canada
(905) 472-9677
Fax: (905) 472-9671
Email: info@globalrecruit.com
Web: www.globalrecruit.com

Description: We are an IT recruitment firm that operates nationally and internationally with affiliated groups to service the specialized needs of clients in information technology, sales/marketing, engineering, scientific, and executive search requirements.

Key Contact - Specialty:
Ms. Patricia Chambers, President - *Information technology, sales & marketing, executive level*
Mr. Don Mustill, Vice President, Strategic Resourcing - *Information technology, executive, sales*
Mr. Shawn McEwen, Consultant - *Information technology, executive, sales, general*
Ms. Gail Chambers, Consultant, Office Manager - *Information technology, sales & marketing, scientific*
Dr. Sammy Jakubowicz, Consultant - *Information technology, scientific*
Mr. Bill Johnson, Operations - *Information technology*

Functions: Generalist, Directors, Senior Mgmt., Sales & Mktg., IT, MIS Mgmt., Systems Dev., Engineering

Industries: Generalist, Mfg., Finance, Media, Telecoms, Call Centers, Wireless, Insurance, Software, ERP SW, Marketing SW, Networking, Comm. SW, Biotech

Professional Associations: YTA

Networks: National Personnel Assoc (NPA)

Global Network Recruiting LLC (GNR)
1344 University Ave Ste 260
Rochester, NY 14607
(888) 338-9087
Email: mdelaney@globalnetr.com
Web: www.globalnetr.com

Description: "Engineers working with Engineers." We are Engineers, so we understand technology, which means you get presented the right opportunities. GNR services the high-tech areas from wireless to semiconductor products. -

Key Contact - Specialty:
Mr. Mike DeLaney, Owner/Partner
Mr. Kurt Phelps, Owner/Partner - *Engineering*

Salary minimum: $75,000

Functions: Engineering

Industries: Machine, Appliance, Motor Vehicles, Computer Equip., Consumer Elect., Test, Measure Equip., Misc. Mfg., Electronic, Elec. Components, Communications, Telecoms, Telephony, Digital, Wireless, Fiber Optic, Network Infrastructure, Defense, Security SW

Networks: Top Echelon Network

Global Telecommunications Inc
9901 IH 10 W Ste 800
San Antonio, TX 78230
(210) 354-1111
(210) 558-2828
Fax: (210) 558-4477
Email: globaltinc@aol.com

Description: We are an executive search firm serving client companies in the telecommunication industry:(i.e.: CLECs, Internet, wireless, cellular/pcs, long distance, messaging. Specializing in middle to upper-level management opportunities within sales, marketing and customer service/call center management.

Key Contact - Specialty:
Mr. Robert S. Ott, President - *Cellular, paging, cable, long distance, call center management*

Salary minimum: $60,000

Functions: Senior Mgmt., Middle Mgmt., Sales & Mktg.

Industries: Services, Telecoms, Software

Networks: First Interview Network (FIN)

GlobalQuest Group
12 Greenway Plz Ste 1100
Houston, TX 77046
(713) 964-4007
Fax: (713) 964-4006
Email: rjhsearch@aol.com

Description: Confidential, custom-tailored, attention-to-detail professionalism resulting in solutions to complex recruiting problems.

Key Contact - Specialty:
Mr. Ronald J. Hakim, President - *Sales, sales management, marketing*

Salary minimum: $40,000

Functions: Generalist

Industries: Mfg., Pharm Svcs., Mgmt. Consulting, HR Services, Advertising, Publishing, New Media, Broadcast, Film, Telecoms, Defense

Networks: US Recruiters.com

Branches:
5108 Bellefontaine Dr Ste A
Arlington, TX 76017
(817) 563-1444
Fax: (208) 279-4786
Email: lw_globalquest@msn.com
Key Contact:
Mr. Leonard Wachowiak

GMR Associates Inc
(also known as Genesis Healthcare Consultants)
1310 Hwy 80 E
Calhoun, LA 71225
(318) 644-5050
Fax: (318) 644-0303
Email: gmra@bayou.com
Web: www.storkjobs.com

Description: We are a consulting firm specializing in recruitment of women's health care providers. This includes: ob/gyn physicians and sub-specialists, ob nurse practitioners, and certified nurse midwives.

Key Contact - Specialty:
Mr. Dave Burton - *Healthcare, physicians*

Functions: Physicians, Nurses

Industries: Healthcare

Professional Associations: AHA, AMA, MGMA, NAPR, NAPS

Gnodde Associates
128 N Lincoln St
Hinsdale, IL 60521
(630) 887-9510
Fax: (630) 887-9531
Email: gnoddeassc@msn.com
Web: www.gnoddeassociates.com

Description: We conduct contingency searches for banks and financial institutions. Searches are conducted in the Midwest with an emphasis on the Chicago market.

Key Contact - Specialty:
Mr. R. Dirk Gnodde, Owner - *Banking, financial services*

Salary minimum: $40,000

Functions: Generalist

Industries: Banking

Networks: National Banking Network (NBN)

Godfrey Personnel Inc
300 W Adams Ste 612
Chicago, IL 60606-5194
(312) 236-4455
Fax: (312) 580-6292
Email: jim@godfreypersonnel.com
Web: www.godfreypersonnel.com

Description: Our specialty is recruitment/placement of insurance personnel from technical to senior management; i.e. underwriters, actuaries, claims adjusters (all lines), accounting, customer service reps, risk manager and loss control.

Key Contact - Specialty:
Mr. James R. Godfrey, President - *Insurance, technical, professional, executives*

Salary minimum: $25,000

Functions: Generalist

Industries: Insurance

H L Goehring & Associates Inc
3200 Wrenford St
Dayton, OH 45409-1250
(937) 298-1137

Description: We provide personalized professional executive search activities for middle to top management positions in all corporate disciplines in a wide range of industries. Management and human resource consulting.

Key Contact - Specialty:
Mr. Hal Goehring, SPHR, President - *Middle to top management (all disciplines)*

Salary minimum: $40,000

Functions: General Mgmt., Plant Mgmt., Distribution, Mktg. Mgmt., Sales Mgmt., HR Mgmt., Benefits, CFO's, Mgmt. Consultants

Industries: Generalist, Mfg., Printing

Professional Associations: ASTD, IAGAC, SHRM

Barry M Gold & Company
2402 Michelson Dr Ste 225
Irvine, CA 92612-1323
(949) 660-5677
Fax: (949) 660-5611
Email: bmgco@insurancerecruiting.com
Web: www.insurancerecruiting.com

Description: For over 30 years an award winning executive search firm for the business insurance and benefits professional. 15% retained, 85% contingent, insurance brokerage consultants, executive search, selection and appraisal.

Key Contact - Specialty:
Mr. Barry M. Gold, CAC, Owner - *Insurance, managed care, benefits*

Salary minimum: $40,000

Functions: Sales & Mktg.

Industries: Insurance

Professional Associations: NAPS

Goldbeck Recruiting Inc

789 W Pender Ste 855
Vancouver, BC V6C 1H2
Canada
(604) 684-1428
Fax: (604) 684-1429
Email: henry@goldbeck.com
Web: www.goldbeck.com

Description: Small practice with expertise in sales, marketing, production and plant management, software and technology development.

Key Contact - Specialty:
Mr. Henry Goldbeck, President - *Sales & marketing, production, plant management*

Salary minimum: $35,000

Functions: Generalist, Middle Mgmt., Automation, Plant Mgmt., Purchasing, Materials Plng., Mktg. Mgmt., Engineering

Industries: Generalist, Agri., Forestry, Mining, Energy, Utilities, Construction, Food, Bev., Tobacco, Lumber, Furniture, Paper

Barry Goldberg & Associates Inc

2049 Century Park E Ste 1100
Los Angeles, CA 90067
(310) 277-5800
Fax: (310) 277-7944

Description: Placement of partners and associates at the nation's leading law firms.

Key Contact - Specialty:
Mr. Barry Goldberg - *Attorneys*

Salary minimum: $75,000

Functions: Attorneys

Industries: Legal

Professional Associations: NALSC

Golden Opportunities Employment

PO Box 525
Northfield, NJ 08225-0525
(609) 653-2345
Fax: (810) 283-6258
Email: info@goldenopportunitiesonline.com
Web: www.goldenopportunitiesonline.com

Description: I am an independent recruiter helping small and mid-size businesses throughout Southern New Jersey locate qualified professionals for permanent, career-level job openings. We are serving all industries and maintain a keyword-searchable database of professionals available for work in the region. We encourage professionals to submit resumes for files. We are licensed and regulated by the state of NJ.

Key Contact:
Ms. Dale Duffy Goldfarb, Recruiter/Owner

Joseph Goldring & Associates Inc

7434 Glengrove Dr
Bloomfield Hills, MI 48301-3870
(248) 851-3727
Fax: (248) 851-3728
Email: jgoldring@mediaone.net
Web: www.jobprofessionals.com

Description: We are an independent search organization devoted to providing confidential service on a contingency basis, main areas are

accounting/finance, engineering, information services and medical/healthcare.

Key Contact - Specialty:
Mr. Joe Goldring, President - *CEO, COO*

Salary minimum: $30,000

Functions: General Mgmt.

Industries: Generalist

Professional Associations: MAPS

Networks: National Personnel Assoc (NPA)

Goldstein & Company

(a division of TeamSearch Inc)
1700 N Broadway Ste 307
Walnut Creek, CA 94596
(925) 935-6360
Fax: (925) 939-7980
Email: resume@gc1.com
Web: www.gc1.com

Description: We are the largest electronic publishing, graphic arts recruiting firm in the country. High-tech search firm. Sales marketing IT etc.

Key Contact - Specialty:
Mr. Michael Goldstein, Co-CEO - *Electronic publishing, high technology*
Ms. Peggy Goldstein, Co-CEO - *Information technology*

Functions: Generalist, Mfg., Sales & Mktg., Mkt. Research, Mktg. Mgmt., Sales Mgmt., IT, Technicians

Industries: Generalist, Printing, Computer Equip., Publishing, New Media, Packaging, Software

Branches:
22930 Crenshaw Blvd Ste H
Torrance, CA 90503
(310) 784-2000
Fax: (310) 784-0550
Email: laoffice@gc1.com
Web: www.teamsearch.org
Key Contact - Specialty:
Mr. Peter Leimpeter - *High technology, information technology, electronic publishing*

Gomez Fregoso y Asociados

Salto del Agua 2130
Jardines del Country
Guadalajara, JAL CP 44210
Mexico
52 3 826 1289
Email: gomezfre@orbinet.com.mx

Description: Executive search consultants. Serving clients nationwide in most functions and industries.

Key Contact:
Mr. Miguel Gomez, President
Ms. Monica Vazquez, Partner

Salary minimum: $35,000

Functions: Generalist

Industries: Generalist

Professional Associations: AMCHAM, ARIOAC, DESEM

Abel M Gonzalez & Associates

PO Box 681845
San Antonio, TX 78268
(210) 695-5555
Email: abelsearch@aol.com

Description: specialize HR Human Resources specialists who speak Spanish. EEO, AAP, Diversity, Hispanic, bilingual, Latin, Mexico, staffing, employment, labor, union, generalist, compensation, training, OD,

Key Contact - Specialty:
Mr. Abel M. Gonzalez, President - *HR, human resources, spanish*

Salary minimum: $75,000

Functions: HR Mgmt.

Industries: Generalist

L J Gonzer Associates

1225 Raymond Blvd
Newark, NJ 07102
(973) 624-5600
(800) 631-4218
Fax: (973) 624-7170
Email: ljga@gonzer.com
Web: www.gonzer.com

Description: Professional search with concentration on corporations producing technical or engineered products. Although recruiting is done on an individual basis per each associate, the selection process is by consensus.

Key Contact - Specialty:
Mr. Lawrence J. Gonzer, President - *Engineering, technical fields, information technology*
Mr. Daniel J. Muhlfelder, Executive Vice President - *Engineering, technical fields, information technology*

Salary minimum: $25,000

Functions: Generalist, Production, Systems Dev., Systems Support, Engineering, Mgmt. Consultants, Technicians, Graphic Artists

Industries: Generalist, Energy, Utilities, Machine, Appliance, Mgmt. Consulting, Media, Aerospace, Software

Professional Associations: NJSMEA, NTSA

The Goodkind Group Inc

110 E 42nd St 800
New York, NY 10017
(212) 378-0700
(212) 378-8888
Fax: (212) 378-0780
Email: petergoodkind@goodkind.net
Web: www.goodkind.net

Description: We are a middle management search and staffing firm specializing in human resources, information technology, legal, marketing, finance/investment banking, and accounting. All of the managing directors at our firm have corporate experience relevant to their specialty giving them a unique understanding of the goals and requirements of our clients.

Key Contact - Specialty:
Mr. Peter Goodkind, President
Ms. Jeanne Bonomo, Director of Human Resources Practice - *Generalist*
Mr. Stephen Horowitz, Principal - *Information technology, information systems*
Ms. Patricia Amy, Director of Finance - *Equities, fixed income, investment banking*
Ms. Kristin Vickery, Director Legal Search and Staffing - *Corporate attorney*
Ms. Lynn Glick, Director of Marketing Practice - *Business development*

Salary minimum: $50,000

Functions: Legal, Sales & Mktg., HR Mgmt., Finance, CFO's, IT, Attorneys, Paralegals

Industries: Generalist

Professional Associations: ASTD, NYNMA, SHRM, WAW

Branches:
208 LaSalle St
Chicago, IL 60604
(312) 541-9000
Fax: (312) 541-9002
Email: llupia@strategiclegal.com
Key Contact - Specialty:
Ms. Lynette Lupia, Director of Operations - *Legal*

163 Madison Ave Fl 1
Madison, NJ 07960
(973) 285-4299
Fax: (973) 285-4290
Email: kvickery@strategiclegal.com
Key Contact - Specialty:
Ms. Chris Gury, Director - *Legal*

Gordon-Harris Associates Inc
980 N Michigan Ave Ste 1400
Chicago, IL 60611
(312) 943-2800
Fax: (312) 943-8364
Email: contact@gordonharrissearch.com
Web: www.gordonharrissearch.com

Description: We are a retainer based search firm
specializing in both the manufacturing and service
industries for middle management, executive, and
senior executive level positions. Additionally, we
specialize in areas of continuous improvement,
particularly for companies focused on developing or
expanding world class Six Sigma teams.

Key Contact:
Mr. Daniel Gordon

Salary minimum: $100,000

Functions: Senior Mgmt.

Industries: Generalist

Government Contract Solutions Inc
1401 Chain Bridge Rd Ste 300
McLean, VA 22101
(703) 749-2223
Fax: (703) 749-2244
Email: resume@gcsplacement.com
Web: www.gcsinfo.com

Description: Our firm specializes in the temporary
and permanent placement of contracts, procurement,
pricing, and financial personnel. We work with
junior to executive-level candidates.

Key Contact:
Ms. Whitney Priest, Recruiter

Salary minimum: $35,000

Functions: Generalist, Admin. Svcs., Purchasing,
CFO's, Budgeting, Mgmt. Consultants

Industries: Generalist, Misc. Financial, Accounting,
Mgmt. Consulting, Defense, Aerospace, Software

Professional Associations: NAPM, NATSS,
NCMA

Gowdy Consultants
12059 Starcrest Dr
San Antonio, TX 78247
(210) 499-4444
Fax: (210) 499-4676
Email: gowdycts@texas.net

Description: We specialize in sales and sales
management.

Key Contact - Specialty:
Ms. Olga M. Gowdy, Owner - *Administrative*
Ms. Theresa Gunkle, Consultant - *Sales, sales
management*

Functions: Nurses, Health Admin., Sales & Mktg.,
Sales Mgmt., Minorities

Industries: Generalist, Construction, Mfg., Drugs
Mfg., Medical Devices, Transportation, Services,
Pharm Svcs., Legal, E-commerce, Media,
Advertising, Communications, Telecoms,
Government, Software, Marketing SW,
Networking, Comm. SW, Biotech, Healthcare,
Hospitals

Graham Search Group Inc
1205 N 18th St Ste 215
Professional Bldg
Monroe, LA 71201
(318) 361-2090
Fax: (318) 361-9747
Email: bgraham@bayou.com
Web: www.medicjobs.net

Description: We do confidential executive
placements in the healthcare industry. We do all
areas of management for all areas of the hospital.
Our clients include hospitals, clinics and managed
care companies.

Key Contact:
Ms. Beverly Doles Graham, CEO - *Healthcare*
Ms. Sally Windsor, Project Coordinator

Functions: Generalist, Physicians, Nurses, Allied
Health, Health Admin.

Industries: Generalist, Healthcare

Granger-Thompson Consulting LLC
6507 Jester Blvd Bldg 5 Ste 510-I
Austin, TX 78750
(512) 346-8001
Fax: (512) 346-8003
Email: gtc@gtconsult.net
Web: www.gtconsult.net

Description: We are a client focused professional
search firm. Our areas of specialization include our
finance/operations division, which focuses staff
accountants through CFOs, financial analysts
through VPs of finance, purchasing, HR,
compensation, and COOs; our strategic technical
division, which focuses on product marketing,
product management, and engineering; our strategic
non-technical, marketing, and business
development.

Key Contact:
Mrs. Kendra Granger, Owner
Mrs. Shelia Thompson, Owner

Functions: Sales & Mktg., HR Mgmt., Finance,
CFO's, Engineering

Industries: Generalist

Martin Grant Associates Inc
65 Franklin St
Boston, MA 02110
(617) 357-5380
Fax: (617) 482-6581
Email: martingrant@msn.com
Web: www.insurancecareersearch.com

Description: We are New England's oldest leading
insurance placement firm specializing in all levels
of property/casualty, life/health/pension and risk
management placement.

Key Contact - Specialty:
Mr. Barry Davis, CPC, President - *Insurance*
Ms. Diana Gazzolo, CPC, Vice President -
Insurance

Salary minimum: $20,000

Functions: Generalist

Industries: Insurance

Professional Associations: MAPS, NAPS

The Grant Search Group Inc
2275 Lakeshore Blvd W Ste 514
Toronto, ON M8V 3Y3
Canada
(416) 252-5656
Email: info@gsginc.on.ca
Web: www.gsginc.on.ca

Description: We specialize in the recruitment of all
levels of marketing personnel for firms engaged in
consumer or business-to-business marketing. Our
ongoing contact with marketing personnel enables

---

us to provide rapid sourcing of talent and
minimization of downtime. Call us for details.

Key Contact - Specialty:
Mr. David Bodnaryk, President - *Marketing*

Salary minimum: $50,000

Functions: Mktg. Mgmt.

Industries: Food, Bev., Tobacco, Soap, Perf.,
Cosmtcs., Consumer Elect., Telecoms, Call
Centers, Marketing SW

Grant-Franks & Associates
929 N Kings Hwy
Cherry Hill, NJ 08034
(856) 779-8844
Fax: (856) 779-0898

Description: We function as a human resource
department in the areas of recruitment and selection
for small to mid size companies.

Key Contact:
Ms. Lee Grant

Salary minimum: $30,000

Functions: Generalist, Materials, Sales & Mktg.,
HR Mgmt., Finance, IT

Industries: Generalist, Construction,
Transportation, Finance, Packaging, Insurance

Graphic Arts Employment Services Inc
PO Box 176127
Covington, KY 41017-6127
(859) 331-6567
Email: gaes@printemploy.com
Web: www.printemploy.com

Description: We are national specialists in placing
key operations, management and production
professionals in the printing/packaging industries.

Key Contact - Specialty:
Mr. James Carlin, Owner - *Printing (commercial,
packaging)*

Graphic Arts Marketing Associates Inc
3533 Deepwood Dr
Lambertville, MI 48144-8696
(734) 854-5225
(734) 854-5226
Fax: (734) 854-5224
Email: graphicama@aol.com

Description: Placement in advertising,
merchandising, printing, public relations and
marketing covering all functions from general
management, account executives, production,
creative and media.

Key Contact - Specialty:
Mr. Roger Crawford, President - *Advertising,
marketing*
Ms. Jacqueline Crawford, Vice President -
Advertising, creative

Salary minimum: $30,000

Functions: Sales & Mktg., Advertising, Mkt.
Research, Mktg. Mgmt., Direct Mktg., PR, IT,
Graphic Artists

Industries: Generalist, Media, Advertising,
Publishing, New Media, Broadcast, Film,
Communications, Marketing SW, Networking,
Comm. SW

Graphic Resources & Associates Inc
2265 Roswell Rd Ste 100
Marietta, GA 30062-2974
(770) 509-2295
Fax: (770) 509-2296
Email: jgoro@graphicresources.com
Web: www.graphicresources.com

Description: We are a national recruiting firm
specializing in the printing and packaging industry.

We have over 20 years of experience. We are certified personnel recruiters.

Key Contact:
Mr. Jeffrey Goro, CPC, President

Functions: Generalist

Industries: Printing

Professional Associations: GAPS

Graphic Search Associates Inc

PO Box 373
Newtown Square, PA 19073
(610) 359-1234
Fax: (610) 353-8120
Email: info@graphsrch.com
Web: www.graphsrch.com

Description: Recruiters for the graphic arts industry specializing in staff support, manufacturing, sales, marketing and general management opportunities.

Key Contact - Specialty:
Mr. Roger W. Linde, President - *Senior management*

Salary minimum: $35,000

Functions: Generalist

Industries: Mfg., Printing

Professional Associations: NAER, NAPL, PIA

Grauss & Company

55 New Montgomery St Ste 503
San Francisco, CA 94105
(415) 777-5656
Fax: (415) 777-5606
Email: resume@grauss.com
Web: www.grauss.com

Description: We are a niche recruitment firm servicing the San Francisco, CA Bay Area investment community. We specialize in investment banking, investment management, and institutional brokerage. We have direct experience in the industry and service all levels of the industry placing individuals from administrative to managing directors. We also have a concentration with information technology within the investment community. We recruit San Francisco Bay Area talent only, as no relocation is provided.

Key Contact - Specialty:
Mr. Bryan J. Grauss, President - *Financial, technical*
Mrs. Debra M. Grauss, Vice President/CFO - *Financial services, investment banking, investment management*

Salary minimum: $40,000

Functions: Finance

Industries: Finance, Invest. Banking, Misc. Financial

Ben Greco Associates Inc

445 S Figueroa St Ste 2700
Los Angeles, CA 90071
(213) 612-7766
Fax: (213) 612-7767
Email: bengreco@bengreco.com

Description: Focus upon financial executives. Provide a personal, direct, efficient and confidential process to identify and recruit a quality executive with high performance standards who will make an immediate contribution and have long-term potential for the client company.

Key Contact - Specialty:
Mr. Ben Greco, Director - *Finance, accounting, public accounting*

Salary minimum: $75,000

Functions: Finance

Industries: Generalist

Sheila Greco Associates LLC

174 County Hwy
Amsterdam, NY 12010
(518) 843-4611
Fax: (518) 843-5498
Email: sgreco@sheilagreco.com
Web: www.sheilagreco.com

Description: We are a full-service recruiting firm. We specialize in executive search, research, and competitive analysis. We partner with our clients to develop long term relationships. We offer hourly and flat rates. We work within your budget!

Key Contact:
Ms. Sheila Greco, President
Mr. Joseph Morse, Senior Vice President

Salary minimum: $50,000

Functions: Generalist, Senior Mgmt., Mkt. Research, Benefits, CFO's, IT, Mgmt. Consultants

Industries: Generalist, Mfg., Pharm Svcs., Hospitality, Media, Advertising

Professional Associations: AMA, DIA, HMC, NAFE, SCIP, SHRM, WIT

Greene & Company

5 Powderhouse Ln
PO Box 1025
Sherborn, MA 01770-1025
(508) 655-1210
Fax: (508) 655-2139
Email: timgreene6@cs.com
Web: www.greeneandco.com

Description: We are experienced in search services for banking and financial executives in New England. We also work with investment management companies.

Key Contact - Specialty:
Mr. Timothy G. Greene, President - *Banking, investment banking*

Salary minimum: $65,000

Functions: Finance

Industries: Banking, Invest. Banking

Professional Associations: NEERC

The Greene Group

5504 Stonebridge Rd
Pleasant Garden, NC 27313-0625
(336) 674-5345
Fax: (336) 674-5937
Email: billgreene@triad.rr.com
Web: www.thegreenegroupltd.com

Description: We are an executive and management search firm specializing in the furniture and wood products industries. Other services include interim management, outplacement services and contract services.

Key Contact - Specialty:
Mr. William Greene, President/Owner - *Generalist, furniture, wood products*
Mr. John Ibsen, Vice President-Operations - *Generalist, furniture, wood products*
Ms. Ginny Brown, Executive Recruiter - *Front line supervisors, plant supervisors*
Ms. Sharon Greene, Secretary/Treasurer - *Interim management, outplacement, contract services*

Salary minimum: $25,000

Functions: General Mgmt., Mfg., Product Dev., Plant Mgmt., Mkt. Research, PR, CFO's, Credit, Engineering, Graphic Artists

Industries: Lumber, Furniture, Leather, Stone, Glass, Metal Products

Professional Associations: AFMA

Greene-Levin-Snyder LLC

150 E 58th St Fl 16
New York, NY 10155
(212) 752-5200
Fax: (212) 752-8245
Email: search@glslsg.com

Description: We are a full-service legal search firm, placing attorneys at all levels at major corporations, financial institutions, and top-tier law firms worldwide. Twelve search professionals combine nearly eight decades of search expertise to make up our firm. Our assignments include retained qc and partner searches.

Key Contact - Specialty:
Ms. Karin L. Greene - *Legal*
Ms. Alisa F. Levin, Esq. - *Legal*
Ms. Susan Kurz Snyder, Esq. - *Legal*

Functions: Legal, Attorneys

Industries: Generalist, Mfg., Finance, Banking, Invest. Banking, Brokers, Media, Insurance

Professional Associations: NALSC

Greenfields Metallurgical Search

618 Brighton Ct B
Rolla, MO 65401
(573) 364-0020
Fax: (573) 341-9120
Email: mdoyen@rollanet.org
Web: www.greenfieldsmetallurgicalsearch.com

Description: We provide metallurgical engineering and management search for the light metals industry across North America, with auxiliary support for environmental and safety engineers in the same industry.

Key Contact - Specialty:
Mr. Mike Doyen, President - *Engineering, manufacturing*

Salary minimum: $50,000

Functions: Generalist, Mfg., Engineering

Industries: Mfg., Medical Devices, Metal Products, Motor Vehicles, Computer Equip., Misc. Mfg., Environmental Svcs., Aerospace

Professional Associations: ASM

Greenwich Search Partners LLC

55 Old Field Point Rd
Greenwich, CT 06830
(203) 622-8133
Fax: (203) 622-7344
Email: gsp01@attglobal.net

Description: Every individual associated with us has been a senior manager in a computer firm. We perform searches in the manner we preferred when we were hiring managers.

Key Contact - Specialty:
Mr. Robert Frishman, Principal - *Computer industry, sales management, marketing, consulting*
Ms. M. Susan Jones, Principal - *Computer industry, application software sales*

Salary minimum: $75,000

Functions: Middle Mgmt., Mktg. Mgmt., Sales Mgmt., Systems Implem., Mgmt. Consultants, Technicians

Industries: Computer Equip., Mgmt. Consulting, IT Implementation, Software

Professional Associations: EBES

Gregory, Kyle & Associates Inc

PO Box 901
Concord, NC 28026-0901
(704) 786-1231
Fax: (704) 795-3942

Email: 10210@smart-office.net
Web: www.gregorykyleandassociates.com

Description: With our extensive resources, including a national network of specialists with automotive and manufacturing experience, we can locate the professional you are looking for in a timely manner.

Key Contact - Specialty:
Mr. Greg Picarella, President - *Manufacturing*

Salary minimum: $50,000

Functions: General Mgmt., Mfg., Materials, Sales & Mktg., HR Mgmt., Finance, Engineering

Industries: Mfg.

Professional Associations: NCASP, SHRM

Networks: Top Echelon Network

Greyhorse Search Consultants Inc (GSC)

117 Lee Castleberry Rd Ste 100
Dawsonville, GA 30534
(706) 216-3838
Fax: (706) 216-4515
Email: re@g-s.cc
Web: www.g-s.cc

Description: Our firm provides professional search services to the telecommunication industry. Our clients include such industry leaders as Cable & Wireless, Mitsubishi, and Panasonic among others. We have developed an analytical search methodology that identifies and attracts top industry talent to our clients. Our focus is executives, sales, and sales engineers. Our scope is national. If we may be of assistance to you and your organization, please do not hesitate to contact us.

Key Contact:
Mr. Robert Edwards, President

Functions: Directors, Senior Mgmt., Middle Mgmt., Sales & Mktg., Sales Mgmt.

Industries: Electronic, Elec. Components, Communications, Telecoms, Telephony, Digital, Wireless, Fiber Optic, Network Infrastructure, Networking, Comm. SW

Professional Associations: GAPS

GreyLee Professionals Inc

220 St. James Ave
Goose Creek, SC 29445
(843) 764-2500
(877) 473-9533
Email: it@greylee.com
Web: www.greylee.com

Description: We provide executive recruiting with specialization in information technology and telecommunications professionals with concentration in the Southeast. We also provide options for direct hire, contract, and contract to hire.

Key Contact - Specialty:
Ms. Chrys Rogge, Owner/Executive Recruiter - *Technology professionals*

Networks: Top Echelon Network

Griffiths & Associates

PO Box 13854
Akron, OH 44334
(330) 865-9660
Fax: (330) 865-9483
Email: grifsearch@aol.com

Description: We offer personalized services to our clients for the difficult engineering, technical and manufacturing assignments based upon over twenty years of recruiting experience.

Key Contact - Specialty:
Mr. Bob Griffiths, President - *Engineering, manufacturing, purchasing, distribution, human resources*

Salary minimum: $50,000

Functions: Middle Mgmt., Mfg., Product Dev., Production, Automation, Plant Mgmt., Quality, Materials, Sales Mgmt., Engineering

Industries: Mfg., Food, Bev., Tobacco, Chemicals, Medical Devices, Plastics, Rubber, Paints, Petro. Products, Metal Products, Machine, Appliance, Motor Vehicles, Computer Equip., Consumer Elect., Test, Measure Equip., Electronic, Elec. Components, Aerospace, Packaging

Networks: National Personnel Assoc (NPA)

Grobard & Associates Inc

230 Ridge Bluff Ln
Suwanee, GA 30024
(770) 271-1828
Fax: (770) 271-4026
Email: cygrob@charter.net

Description: Our combined staff has over 50 years of experience in the executive recruiting industry. We specialize in sales and marketing in, but not limited to: medical, pharmaceutical, medical equipment, healthcare, printing, packaging, and office furniture.

Key Contact - Specialty:
Mrs. Eileen Grobard, President/Recruiter - *Pharmaceutical, medical sales*

Functions: Generalist

Industries: Printing, Drugs Mfg., Medical Devices, Pharm Svcs., Packaging, Marketing SW, Healthcare

Professional Associations: GAPS

Groenekamp & Associates

PO Box 2308
Beverly Hills, CA 90213-2308
(310) 855-0119
Fax: (310) 855-0110
Email: hrwag@artnet.net
Web: www.hrwag.com

Description: Executive search and professional staffing in broad range of industries. Also offer wide range of management consulting in human resources.

Key Contact - Specialty:
Mr. William A. Groenekamp, President - *Generalist*

Salary minimum: $50,000

Functions: Generalist

Industries: Generalist

Professional Associations: PIHRA, SHRM, WAW

J B Groner Executive Search Inc

PO Box 101
Claymont, DE 19703
(302) 792-9228
Fax: (610) 497-5500
Email: groner@execjobsearch.com
Web: www.execjobsearch.com

Description: Specializing in senior corporate executives, CFOs, senior accountants, trade association and non-profit executives, engineering managers and executives, IT managers and executives, CIOs, CTOs, human resources executives, sales executives and managers.

Key Contact - Specialty:
Mr. James B. Groner, President - *Executive level, technical, administrative*

Salary minimum: $35,000

Functions: Generalist, General Mgmt.

Industries: Energy, Utilities, Mfg., Chemicals, Drugs Mfg., Medical Devices, Computer Equip., Finance, Services, Non-profits, Accounting, Media, Telecoms, Insurance, Software, ERP SW, HR SW, Biotech, Healthcare

Professional Associations: MAAPC, RON

Gros Plastics Recruiters

155 Franklin Rd Ste 181
Brentwood, TN 37027
(800) 283-5643
(615) 661-4568
Fax: (615) 370-8512
Email: careers@plasticsjobs.com
Web: www.plasticsjobs.com

Description: Serving companies and individuals as the marketplace of professional career opportunites in the plastics industry.

Key Contact - Specialty:
Mr. Dennis Gros, CPC, President/CPC - *Plastics*

Salary minimum: $50,000

Functions: Mfg., Materials

Industries: Mfg., Medical Devices, Plastics, Rubber, Machine, Appliance, Motor Vehicles, Computer Equip., Packaging

Professional Associations: NAPS, SPE, SPI

Networks: Top Echelon Network

Groupe Ranger Inc

2045 Stanley St Fl 14
Montreal, QC H3A 2V4
Canada
(514) 844-1746
Fax: (514) 844-6996
Email: info@groupe-ranger.com
Web: www.groupe-ranger.com

Description: Very active in international searches for American companies established in francophone countries, by supplying French speaking outstanding MIS candidate.

Key Contact - Specialty:
Mr. Jean-Jacques Ranger, President - *Information technology, generalist*
Ms. Lise Hebert, Senior Partner - *Information technology*
Mr. Normand Leduc, Senior Partner - *Generalist*
Ms. Maryse Brouillar, Partner - *Information technology*

Salary minimum: $40,000

Functions: Generalist, General Mgmt., Mfg., Materials, HR Mgmt., IT

Industries: Generalist

Professional Associations: CIPS, FIQ

GRS Global Recruitment Solutions

2040 Yonge St Ste 200
Toronto, ON M4S 1Z9
Canada
(416) 515-2921
Fax: (416) 515-2901
Email: admin@grsglobal.com
Web: www.grsglobal.com

Description: A professional recruitment firm specializing in the pharmaceutical, biotechnology and information technology industries. GRS's two senior partners possess more than eighteen years of combined experience in the recruitment industry. Backed by a team of professional, courteous, and knowledgeable recruitment professionals, GRS provides exceptional recruitment services to both clients and candidates.

Key Contact - Specialty:
Mr. Warren Shapiro, Partner - *Pharmaceutical, biotechnology*

Mr. Larry Goldberg, Partner - *Information technology*

Functions: Generalist

Industries: Drugs Mfg., Medical Devices, Computer Equip., Equip Svcs., Software, Biotech

GSP Int'l
90 Woodbridge Center Dr Ste 110
Woodbridge, NJ 07095
(732) 602-0100
Fax: (732) 602-0108
Email: emailus@gspintl.com
Web: www.gspintl.com

Description: An executive search and placement firm specializing in the accounting and finance professions.

Key Contact - Specialty:
Mr. Edward Kaye, Senior Partner - *Accounting & finance*
Mr. Tony Glennon, Managing Partner - *Accounting & finance*
Mr. John Sicilia, Managing Partner - *Accounting & finance*
Mr. Ray Pirre, Managing Partner - *Accounting & finance*

Salary minimum: $30,000

Functions: Finance

Industries: Generalist

Nadine Guber & Associates Inc
575 Lexington Ave Ste 410
New York, NY 10022
(212) 572-9630
Fax: (212) 572-9635
Email: nadineg@aol.com

Description: We specialize in the placement of advertising agency account management and corporate marketing management executives. Our professionals utilize their experience, extensive database and understanding of clients' cultures to identify uniquely qualified candidates.

Key Contact - Specialty:
Ms. Nadine B. Guber, President - *Marketing, advertising*

Salary minimum: $50,000

Functions: Mktg. Mgmt.

Industries: Advertising, New Media

Professional Associations: AWNY, NYWICI

Michael R Guerin Company
16368 Avenida Suavidad
San Diego, CA 92128
(858) 675-0395
Fax: (858) 675-0393
Email: mrgco1192@aol.com

Description: Author, (RIST) recruiting, interviewing, selecting and training - used to develop three national organizations in high-tech, financial service industry at a senior-level. Most recent directed sales and marketing for Forbes 500 company in support of $40 million to $1.6 billion in annual sales.

Key Contact - Specialty:
Mr. Michael R. Guerin, President - *Software, telecommunications*

Salary minimum: $70,000

Functions: Senior Mgmt., Middle Mgmt., Product Dev., Mktg. Mgmt., Sales Mgmt., Engineering

Industries: Computer Equip., Test, Measure Equip., Equip Svcs., Telecoms, Software

The GullGroup executive search
203 Yacht Club Dr
Rockwall, TX 75032
(972) 772-0582
(972) 772-0585
Fax: (972) 772-0587
Email: gullgrp@swbell.net

Description: We are a concise team of seasoned professionals that provide clients with top talent in the competitive landscape. Our areas of concentration are CRM, ERP, LAN/WAN, and data security, as well as data storage. A segment of the firm specializes in Six Sigma.

Key Contact - Specialty:
Mr. James A. Ryan, CEO - *Information technology executives*
Ms. Betty Ryan, COO - *LAN/WAN engineers*

Salary minimum: $40,000

Functions: Generalist

Industries: Mgmt. Consulting, New Media, Telecoms, Software

Professional Associations: SERC

The Gumbinner Company
509 Madison Ave Ste 708
New York, NY 10022
(212) 688-0129

Description: Professional recruitment by advertising people for advertising people. Advertising account management from account executives to presidents. Client side advertising executives as well. We recruit in the United States and worldwide.

Key Contact - Specialty:
Mr. Paul S. Gumbinner - *Advertising agency account managers*

Salary minimum: $50,000

Functions: Generalist, Advertising, Direct Mktg.

Industries: Generalist, Advertising

H & H Consultants Inc
319 Sharon Amity Ste 200G
Charlotte, NC 28211
(704) 442-0737
Fax: (704) 442-0766

Description: Sixteen-year knowledge of the construction industry working with the top negotiated general contractors in the United States. Five years as in-house human resource specialist for ENR Top 10 contractor provides insight into operation of a construction company.

Key Contact - Specialty:
Mr. Robert Honour, Principal - *Construction*

Functions: Generalist

Industries: Construction

H R Solutions Inc
125 N Main St Ste 201
St. Charles, MO 63301
(636) 916-3399
Fax: (636) 916-3058
Email: hrsol@inlink.com

Description: Principals have combined total experience in excess of 35 years' recruiting mid-management and executive-level candidates. Principals have prior work experience in their respective specializations.

Key Contact - Specialty:
Mr. Robert J. Keymer, President - *Hospitality*
Mr. James McDaniel, Division Vice President - *Home health*
Mr. Jason Wagenknecht, Division Vice President - *Hospitality*

Functions: Generalist, Directors, Senior Mgmt., Middle Mgmt., Sales & Mktg., CFO's, IT

Industries: Generalist, Pharm Svcs., Hospitality, Healthcare

The H S Group Inc
2611 Libal St
Green Bay, WI 54301
(920) 432-7444
Fax: (920) 436-2966
Email: info@thehsgroup.com
Web: www.thehsgroup.com

Description: Over 34 years of experience in management and executive recruiting. We recruit in most industries and the following areas: IS/IT, accounting & finance, operations, engineering, human resources, sales & marketing, logistics, purchasing, board members, executives.

Key Contact:
Mr. Jock Seal, Executive Recruiter/Owner
Mr. Chris Cegelski, Executive Recruiter
Mr. Jeff Lasee, Management Recruiter

Salary minimum: $30,000

Functions: Generalist

Industries: Mfg., Transportation, Finance, Accounting, HR Services, IT Implementation, Media, Packaging, Insurance, Software

Networks: Inter-City Personnel Assoc (IPA)

H T Associates
3030 Salt Creek Ln Ste 121
Arlington Heights, IL 60005
(847) 577-0300
(800) HTA-0040
Fax: (847) 577-8131
Email: htassociates@htassociates.com
Web: www.htassociates.com

Description: Our firm is in its 3rd decade of specializing in the placement of information technology professionals. We continue to assist many of Chicago's premier employers seeking to locate qualified technical talent. H.T. Associates, Inc. is the proud recipient of the Malcolm Baldrige Vendor Quality award for outstanding service and ethical practices. We are proficient in recruiting for virtually all technologies and all experience levels.

Key Contact - Specialty:
Mr. Stephen Higgins, President - *Information technology*
Mr. Robert Tabrosky, Jr., Treasurer - *Information technology*

Salary minimum: $40,000

Functions: Directors, IT

Industries: Generalist

Professional Associations: EMA, SHRM

Networks: EMA Partners Int'l

Stephen M Haas Legal Placement
60 E 42nd St
New York, NY 10165
(212) 661-5555
(800) 224-0750
Fax: (212) 972-1279
Email: recru2r@aol.com

Description: We offer attorney placement in the New York metropolitan area. Our experienced recruiters specialize in all of the various areas of law and we take pride in our long-term relationships with excellent law firms of all sizes. We are one of the oldest and most successful legal search firms.

Key Contact - Specialty:
Ms. Marilyn Wallberg, President - *Real estate, corporate*
Ms. Diane Edelman, Vice President - *Litigation, trusts & estates, labor*

Functions: Legal, Attorneys

Industries: Legal

Professional Associations: NALSC

Russ Hadick & Associates Inc

7100 Corporate Way Ste B
Centerville, OH 45459
(937) 439-7700
Fax: (937) 439-7705
Email: rhadick@rharecruiters.com
Web: www.rharecruiters.com

Description: We interview, reference check and verify degrees before our customers ever see our clients. We've been in business over 20 years. All of our people held top management positions before coming into recruiting.

Key Contact - Specialty:
Mr. Russ Hadick, President - *Engineering, management*
Mr. Ron Toke, VP-Technical Sales - *Engineering*
Mr. Dick Westerfield, Vice President-Sales - *Banking*
Mr. Ted O'Neill, VP- Mfr sales - *Manufacturing management*
Mr. Bob Hadick, Executive Vice President - *Information technology, IS software, engineering*
Mrs. Leana Staton, Vice President - *IT, sales*

Salary minimum: $45,000

Functions: Generalist

Industries: Generalist

Hadley Associates Inc

147 Columbia Tpke Ste 104
Florham Park, NJ 07932-2145
(973) 377-9177
Fax: (973) 377-9223
Email: thadleyassoc@aol.com

Description: National and international search capabilities exclusively for the pharmaceutical, biotechnology, medical device and related healthcare industries. Areas of expertise include: regulatory affairs, QA/QC, clinical research.

Key Contact - Specialty:
Mr. Thomas M. Hadley, President - *Healthcare, regulatory, quality assurance, clinical affairs*

Functions: Quality, R&D, Engineering

Industries: Drugs Mfg., Medical Devices, Pharm Svcs., Biotech, Healthcare

Professional Associations: ACP, AMWA, ASQ, DIA, RAPS

Hahn & Associates Inc

PO Box 41009
Dayton, OH 45441-0009
(937) 436-3141
Fax: (937) 436-3252

Description: Search and placement since 1971. Successful placements with over 700 different client employers. Mr. Hahn in private personnel business since 1960.

Key Contact - Specialty:
Mr. Kenneth R. Hahn, President - *Manufacturing professionals*

Functions: Generalist, Mfg., Product Dev., Plant Mgmt., Quality, Materials, Purchasing, Distribution, HR Mgmt., Engineering

Industries: Generalist, Paper, Plastics, Rubber, Metal Products, Machine, Appliance, Motor Vehicles, Electronic, Elec. Components, HR SW, Mfg. SW

Professional Associations: OSSA

Halbrecht & Company

10195 Main St Ste L
Fairfax, VA 22031
(703) 359-2880
Email: tomm@halbrecht.com
Web: www.halbrecht.com

Description: We are proud of our reputation for assisting our clients in identifying and selecting superior business professionals dedicated to excellence rather than the merely qualified technician. Areas of expertise: information technology, quantitative business professionals, management consultants, e-commerce and B2B.

Key Contact - Specialty:
Mr. Thomas J. Maltby, Partner - *Information systems, quantitative analysts*
Mr. Alec Siegel, Associate - *Information systems, network engineers*
Mr. Thomas Kubiak, Partner - *Quantitative professionals*

Salary minimum: $40,000

Functions: IT, Mgmt. Consultants

Industries: Generalist, Wholesale, Retail, Mgmt. Consulting, Telecoms, Software

Professional Associations: AAAI, AIIM, TIMS

Branches:
PO Box 324
Old Greenwich, CT 06870
(203) 356-0278
Email: halbrechtct@discovernet.net
Key Contact - Specialty:
Mr. Paul Calale, Associate - *Transportation, logistics*

Halcyon Consulting

179 Post Rd W
Westport, CT 06880
(203) 226-6540
Fax: (203) 226-6356
Email: susan@halcyonconsulting.com

Description: We are a custom full-service executive recruiting firm focusing on key marketing disciplines, especially brand management and consumer promotions.

Key Contact - Specialty:
Ms. Sue Burrows, President - *Consumer marketing*
Mr. Dan Sullivan, Management Consultant - *Consumer marketing, brand management*
Ms. Jennifer Hulse, Management Consultant - *Consumer marketing, consumer promotions*
Ms. Sheryl Bates, Consultant - *Consumer marketing*
Ms. Kim Forman, Consultant - *Consumer marketing*

Salary minimum: $75,000

Functions: Sales & Mktg., Advertising, Mkt. Research, Mktg. Mgmt.

Industries: Generalist

William Halderson Associates Inc

100 Gold Creek Cir Ste B
Dahlonega, GA 30533
(706) 864-5800
Email: bill@haldersonsearch.com

Description: We specialize in medical devices, biotechnology, and pharmaceuticals. Our searches include managers, directors, VPs, CFOs, COOs, and CEOs. We also specialize in clinical science liaisons.

Key Contact - Specialty:
Mr. William Halderson, President
Ms. Dot Werner, Associate
Mr. Barry Warren, Associate - *Sales and marketing management*

Salary minimum: $60,000

Functions: Directors, Senior Mgmt., Middle Mgmt., Mktg. Mgmt., Sales Mgmt., CFO's, R&D, Int'l.

Industries: Drugs Mfg., Medical Devices, Pharm Svcs., Biotech, Healthcare

Professional Associations: GAPS

Networks: First Interview Network (FIN)

Hale & Associates

PO Box 6941
New Orleans, LA 70174
(504) 394-2956
Fax: (504) 391-3256
Email: lhale@ix.netcom.com
Web: www.hale-assoc.com

Description: Our firm specializes in the recruitment of executive staff for healthcare systems, independent hospitals and health related corporations.

Key Contact - Specialty:
Mr. Leonard Hale, Principal - *Healthcare executives*
Mr. Mike Johnson, Consultant - *Healthcare, allied health*
Ms. Victoria Turner, Consultant - *Healthcare, nursing management*
Mr. Mike Taylor, Consultant - *Healthcare, information systems*
Ms. Jennifer Johnson, Consultant - *Healthcare, administrative*

Salary minimum: $35,000

Functions: General Mgmt., Directors, Senior Mgmt., Physicians, Nurses, Benefits, Personnel, MIS Mgmt., Systems Analysis, Systems Dev.

Industries: Generalist, Healthcare

Professional Associations: SHRM

Don Hall & Associates

617 Catalina Dr
Waco, TX 76712
(254) 772-0420
(800) 999-0420
Fax: (254) 772-1333
Email: dhall@hot.rr.com
Web: www.millworknetwork.com

Description: Our firm provides national executive and management placement services to manufacturers, distributors, and retailers of windows, doors, stairs, moldings, and related building materials. We specialize in consulting and mergers/acquisitions. We also specialize in unique liquid cleaners for removal of pitch, resins, and rust from saw blades, knives, and heads. We provide millwork, woodwork, and related building materials fields placements only.

Key Contact - Specialty:
Mr. Don Hall, Owner - *Millwork, windows, doors, stairs, moldings*
Ms. Joann Hall, Co-Owner - *Millwork*

Salary minimum: $20,000

Functions: Generalist

Industries: Lumber, Furniture

Professional Associations: NSDJA, WMMPA

Branches:
14711 Mimosa Ln
Tustin, CA 92780
(714) 730-0745
Fax: (714) 730-0277
Email: shep@millworkjobs.com
Web: www.millworkjobs.com
Key Contact - Specialty:
Mr. Jerry Sheppard, Associate - *Millwork, home centers, pro-dealers*

3505 Spalding Ter
Norcross, GA 30092
(770) 441-9071
Web: www.millworkjobs.com
Key Contact - Specialty:
Mr. Emile Castanet, Associate - *Millwork (mergers, consulting)*

Susan Hall Executive Search

3713 Branchwood Dr
Plano, TX 75093
(972) 378-9378
Fax: (972) 378-9379
Email: searchsh@aol.com

Description: With over 10 years' experience recruiting for advertising agencies in the Dallas area, the principal and the three executive recruiters have the ability to identify and recruit individuals who add value to your agency or company.

Key Contact:
Ms. Susan Hall, Principal - *Advertising, marketing communications*
Ms. Kristina Fahrlender, Executive Recruiter
Ms. Diana Valline, Executive Recruiter
Ms. Denise Ince, Executive Recruiter

Salary minimum: $40,000

Functions: Generalist

Industries: Advertising, New Media

Hall Kinion & Associates

185 Berry St Ste 4600
China Basin Lndg
San Francisco, CA 94107
(415) 974-1300
(888) 757-4254
Fax: (415) 371-8450
Email: stars@hallkinion.com
Web: www.hallkinion.com

Description: Our firm is a leading provider of specialized information technology professionals on a contract and permanent basis operating in 41 offices in 14 major technology markets throughout the US and in London.

Key Contact:
Ms. Brenda C. Rhodes, CEO
Mr. Martin A. Kropelnicki, Vice President Corporate Services, CFO
Ms. Rita S. Hazel, Senior Vice President Contract Services
Mr. Craig Silverman, Executive VP, Chief Marketing Officer - *Technical, information systems, software*
Mr. Anthony L. Cefalu, Vice President Finance

Salary minimum: $40,000

Functions: Generalist, Product Dev., IT, MIS Mgmt., Systems Dev., Systems Implem., Systems Support, Network Admin., DB Admin., Engineering

Industries: Generalist, Consumer Elect., Test, Measure Equip., E-commerce, IT Implementation, New Media, Network Infrastructure, Software

Branches:
1201S Alma School Rd Ste 4450
Bank of America Bldg
Mesa, AZ 85210
(888) 833-3308
Fax: (480) 833-3877
Email: pxresume@hallkinion.com
Key Contact:
Mr. Jared Taylor, Manager

1350 41st Ave Ste 104
Capitola, CA 95010
(831) 462-9800
Fax: (831) 462-0148
Email: cpresume@hallkinion.com
Key Contact:
Ms. Joyce Collins

4140 Dublin Blvd Ste 110
Dublin, CA 94568
(888) 770-4254
Fax: (925) 479-9000

2020 Main St Ste 250
Irvine, CA 92614
(877) 797-4254
Fax: (949) 756-0600
Email: irresume@hallkinion.com
Key Contact:
Ms. Mary Costantino

1100 Larkspur Landing Cir Ste 300
Larkspur, CA 94939
(877) 654-4254
Fax: (415) 925-2165

1900 McCarthy Blvd Ste 420
Milpitas, CA 95035
(888) 565-4254
Fax: (408) 428-6484
Email: fmresume@hallkinion.com

1804 Shoreline Blvd Ste 120
Mountain View, CA 94043
(888) 560-4254
Fax: (650) 526-1501
Email: mtresume@hallkinion.com

1435 River Park Dr 510
Sacramento, CA 95815
(916) 646-3000
(877) 946-4254
Fax: (916) 646-3202
Email: sacresume@hallkinion.com
Key Contact:
Ms. Kelly Ballew

2055 Gateway Pl Ste 200
San Jose, CA 95110
(800) 603-6602
Fax: (408) 467-0299
Email: sjresume@hallkinion.com

2550 N 1st St Ste 110
San Jose, CA 95131
(408) 453-9100
Fax: (408) 453-9123
Email: tluo@hallkinion.com
Web: www.asia.hallkinion.com
Key Contact:
Mr. Ken Reed, Managing Director
Mr. Qun "Train" Luo, Manager, Greater China - *Greater China focused hi-tech executive search*
Mr. Rod Szasz, Manager, Japan

2570 N First S41t Ste 400 2570 N First St Ste 400
San Jose, CA 95131-1018
(408) 895-5200
(888) 945-4254
Fax: (408) 383-0902

1700 S El Camino Real Ste 108
San Mateo, CA 94402
(888) 682-6400
Fax: (650) 345-8646
Email: smresumes@hallkinion.com

370 Interlocken Blvd 150
Interlocken Business Park
Broomfield, CO 80021
(888) 990-4254
Fax: (303) 404-2322
Email: bldresume@hallkinion.com
Key Contact:
Ms. Tammy Vaughn, Manager

5613 DTC Pkwy Ste 830
Englewood, CO 80111
(800) 425-5764
Fax: (303) 741-9986
Email: coresume@hallkinion.com
Key Contact:
Mr. Aaron Mills

6527 Main St Lower Lvl
Trumbull, CT 06611
(203) 452-3818
Fax: (203) 452-3203

Email: ctresume@hallkinion.com
Web: www.hallkinion.com

3030 N Rocky Point Dr W Ste 400
Tampa, FL 33607
(813) 207-0100
(800) 441-5720
Fax: (813) 207-0488
Key Contact:
Ms. Juli Reynolds

980 Hammond Dr Ste 775
2 Lakeside Commons
Atlanta, GA 30328
(770) 671-1234
(888) 824-4254
Fax: (770) 671-1922
Email: atresume@hallkinion.com
Key Contact:
Ms. Dari Damazo, e-Services Techincal Recruiting Manager
Mr. Mike Brennan, e-Services Marketing and Sales Manager

440 S LaSalle St Ste 3904
1 Financial Pl
Chicago, IL 60605
(312) 913-0111
(888) 913-0111
Fax: (312) 913-1180
Email: chresume@hallkinion.com
Key Contact:
Ms. Melissa Doble

475 N Martingale Rd Ste 450
Schaumburg, IL 60173
(847) 517-9500
(888) 459-4254
Fax: (847) 517-9400
Key Contact:
Mr. Mike Mercurio

54 Mall Rd Ste G-01
Burlington, MA 01803
(800) 955-4254
Fax: (781) 229-7772
Email: boresume@hallkinion.com
Key Contact:
Ms. Maryann Scarangello, Manager

11100 Wayzata Blvd Ste 202
Crescent Ridge Corporate Ctr
Minneapolis, MN 55305-1542
(763) 543-1300
(888) 440-4254
Fax: (763) 543-1308
Email: mnresume@hallkinion.com
Key Contact:
Ms. Tammy Faiola, Manager

100 Wood Ave S Ste 203
Iselin, NJ 08830
(732) 516-0707
(888) 858-4254
Fax: (732) 516-0714
Email: njresume@hallkinion.com
Key Contact:
Ms. Linda Callari, Manager

590 5th Ave Fl 18
New York, NY 10036
(212) 575-1400
(800) 963-8326
Fax: (212) 575-2640
Email: nyresume@hallkinion.com
Key Contact:
Mr. Ron Herbas

2525 Meridian Pkwy Ste 280
Research Triangle Park
Durham, NC 27713
(800) 365-3031
Fax: (919) 572-6550
Email: ncresume@hallkinion.com
Key Contact:
Mr. Guy Garrett

10260 SW Greenburg Rd Ste 810
Portland, OR 97223
(503) 244-2700
(888) 302-2700
Fax: (503) 244-6522
Email: orresume@hallkinion.com
Key Contact:
Mr. Sean McKeehan
Mr. Jeff Miller

121 SW Salmon St Ste 1220
1 World Trade Ctr
Portland, OR 97204
(888) 388-4254
Fax: (503) 721-0900
Email: poresume@hallkinion.com

119221 Mopac E Ste 140
Stone Creek II
Austin, TX 78759-7267
(512) 349-0960
(888) 788-4231
Fax: (512) 349-0983
Email: auresume@hallkinion.com
Key Contact:
Ms. Beth Valcarcel

901 Mopac Expwy S Ste 343
Barton Oaks Plaza 4
Austin, TX 78746
(512) 306-8400
(888) 788-4254
Fax: (512) 306-8060
Email: au2resume@hallkinion.com
Key Contact:
Ms. Sara Schrage

10375 Richmond Ave Ste 1225
Millennium Twr
Houston, TX 77042-4151
(713) 784-2600
(800) 797-4254
Fax: (713) 784-7999
Email: hn2resume@hallkinion.com
Key Contact:
Ms. Kathleen Nordt

3040 Post Oak Blvd Ste 440
Houston, TX 77056
(713) 622-6800
(888) 622-6889
Fax: (713) 622-6920
Email: hnresume@hallkinion.com
Key Contact:
Mr. Rich Hamilton

1600 N Collins Blvd Ste 2300
Richardson, TX 75080
(888) 989-4254
Fax: (972) 783-2740
Email: dfwresume@hallkinion.com
Key Contact:
Ms. Kim Campbell

60 E S Temple 1370
Eagle Gate Plz
Salt Lake City, UT 84111
(801) 322-2225
(888) 665-2225
Fax: (801) 322-2205
Email: utresume@hallkinion.com
Key Contact:
Mr. Brent Packer

7918 Jones Branch Dr Ste 300
McLean, VA 22102
(877) 997-4254
Fax: (703) 821-8827
Email: varesume@hallkinion.com
Key Contact:
Ms. Betta Beasley, Manager

3001 112th Ave NE Ste 101
Bellevue, WA 98004
(800) 234-1136
Fax: (425) 889-5985
Email: waresume@hallkinion.com
Key Contact:
Ms. Maureen Kerber

19125 N Creek Pkwy Ste 204
Bothell, WA 98011-8000
(888) 821-4254
Fax: (425) 424-9898
Email: botresume@hallkinion.com
Key Contact:
Ms. Angela Aronica, Manager

2825 Eastlake Ave E Ste 120
Seattle, WA 98102
(206) 726-8800
(888) 270-6008
Fax: (206) 726-8833
Email: searesume@hallkinion.com
Key Contact:
Mr. Didi Zahariades

Hall Management Group Inc
201 A Forrest Ave NW
Gainesville, GA 30501
(770) 534-5568
Fax: (770) 534-5572
Email: billlennon@mindspring.com
Web: www.lennonsearch.com

Description: We have over 25 years worth of
recruiting experience as a manufacturing and
technology placement specialist in pharmaceuticals,
medical devices, biotech, and telecommunications.
We are Sunbelt and Atlantic states specialists. We
provide extensive networking for specialty needs.

Key Contact - Specialty:
Mr. Bill Lennon, CPC, Owner/President - *Medical
device, manufacturing, pharmaceuticals,
accounting, IT*

Salary minimum: $50,000

Functions: Generalist, General Mgmt., Senior
Mgmt., Mfg., Quality, HR Mgmt., Finance, IT,
Engineering

Industries: Generalist, Mfg., Drugs Mfg., Medical
Devices, Plastics, Rubber, Machine, Appliance,
Motor Vehicles, Accounting, Telecoms,
Telephony, Wireless, Software, Accounting SW,
Mfg. SW, Biotech

Professional Associations: GAPS, NAPS,
PINNACLE, RON

Networks: Top Echelon Network

hallevy.com
275 Madison Ave Fl 18
New York, NY 10016
(212) 686-4444
Fax: (212) 686-7072
Email: hal@hallevy.com
Web: www.hallevy.com

Description: We are an executive search firm
specializing in advertising direct response. We place
people in direct marketing, advertising, and new
media.

Key Contact - Specialty:
Mr. Hal Levy, President - *Advertising direct
response*
Ms. Eve Levy, Partner - *Advertising direct response*

Salary minimum: $25,000

Functions: Generalist, Advertising, Mktg. Mgmt.,
Direct Mktg., Graphic Artists

Industries: Generalist, Advertising, Publishing,
New Media

Hallman Group Inc
4528 West KL Ave
Kalamazoo, MI 49006
(616) 353-6835
Fax: (616) 353-6845
Email: nancy@hallmangroup.com
Web: www.hallmangroup.com

Description: We are a Midwest search firm
specializing in various disciplines such as

information technology, quality assurance, quality
control, and research & development. We focus in
specific industries, such as pharmaceutical, health
care, manufacturing, and banking. We pre-screen
and qualify thoroughly our candidates and
companies. We do not advertise but work off of our
reputation. Executive and contingency search is our
specialty.

Key Contact - Specialty:
Ms. Nancy L. Hall, President - *Quality
assurance/quality control (pharmaceutical
industry), information technology*
Mr. Kenneth Killman, Vice President - *Information
technology*

Salary minimum: $45,000

Functions: Generalist, IT

Industries: Generalist, Drugs Mfg., Medical
Devices

Professional Associations: MAPS

Halo Insurance Service
PO Box 160272
Mobile, AL 36616
(334) 478-1604
Fax: (334) 645-4680
Email: halo_ins@zebra.net

Description: Executive recruiting which specializes
in the recruitment of group underwriting and
actuarial individuals on the carrier side as well as
benefit analysts and consultants in the consulting
arena.

Key Contact - Specialty:
Mr. Thomas J. Blythe, Owner - *Insurance*

Salary minimum: $30,000

Functions: Generalist

Industries: Insurance

Professional Associations: INS

Robert Ham & Associates Inc
129 S 3rd St
Delavan, WI 53115
(414) 728-3797
Fax: (414) 728-7789

Description: Our specialization is in the "labeling
industry."

Key Contact - Specialty:
Mr. Robert Ham, President - *Label, auto
identification*

Salary minimum: $60,000

Hamblin & Associates
31441 Santa Margarita Pkwy 146
Rancho Santa Margarita, CA 92688
(949) 589-7460
Fax: (949) 459-6070
Email: prosearchd@aol.com

Description: We are a full-service recruiting firm
offering excellent opportunities to clients looking to
expand their scope with diversity and excellence.

Key Contact - Specialty:
Ms. Donna S. Hamblin, Executive Recruiter -
*Technical engineers, software, hardware, project
management, administrative*

Functions: General Mgmt., Mfg., Materials, HR
Mgmt., Finance, IT, Engineering

Industries: Generalist, Food, Bev., Tobacco,
Printing, Chemicals

Hamilton & Company
110 Westwood Rd
Columbus, OH 43214
(614) 262-8535
Fax: (614) 262-8536

Email: ljhamco@hotmail.com

Description: Recruiter brings 22 years of account service and corporate agency management experience to search industry. Known for exceptionally high standards, critical talent assessment, reliable follow-through and client-candidate trust.

Key Contact - Specialty:
Ms. Lisa J. Hamilton - *Advertising, public relations, new media, direct marketing agencies*

Functions: Generalist, Senior Mgmt., Middle Mgmt., Advertising, Mkt. Research, Mktg. Mgmt., Direct Mktg., PR

Industries: Generalist, Advertising, New Media

Hamilton Grey Technology Search
2803 ButterfieldRd Ste 340
Oak Brook, IL 60523
(630) 472-5400
Fax: (630) 472-5444
Email: technologysearch@hamiltongrey.com
Web: www.hamiltongrey.com

Description: We are an information technology search firm specializing in permanent and contract placement. We devote our efforts and considerable technical resources to knowing all the players in the IT universe. This enables us to quickly identify the highest quality candidates and opportunities.

Key Contact:
Mr. Frank Baron, President

Functions: Generalist, MIS Mgmt., Systems Analysis, Systems Dev., Systems Implem., Systems Support, Network Admin., DB Admin.

Industries: Generalist, Mfg., Transportation, Finance, Hospitality, Packaging, Insurance, Healthcare

The Hampton Group
(also known as MRI of Southampton)
33 Flying Point Rd
Southampton, NY 11968
(631) 287-3330
Fax: (631) 287-5610
Email: hamptongrp@hamptongrp.com
Web: www.hamptongrp.com

Description: We are an executive search firm specializing in placing middle and senior-level management in the medical, pharmaceutical and biotech industries. Our knowledge of the marketplace and database profiles of candidates and companies enables us to quickly target and identify contacts which closely match specific profiles.

Key Contact - Specialty:
Ms. Belle Lareau, Partner - *Diagnostics, biotechnology, pharmaceutical*
Mr. Gerard A. Lareau, Partner - *Genetics, biotechnology*
Ms. Valerie Remkus, Executive - *Pharmaceutical, research & development*
Ms. Bev Norindr - *Biotechnology, pharmaceutical, business development, marketing*

Functions: Senior Mgmt.

Industries: Pharm Svcs., Biotech

Professional Associations: ASHG, DIA, RAPS

Hands-on Broadcast
124 W 24th St 6B
New York, NY 10011
(212) 924-5036
Fax: (212) 604-9036
Email: bgspeed@aol.com
Web: www.jobopts.com

Description: We place designers in cable, television and post-production--animators in feature film and multimedia in the US and internationally. Animation has become a strong focus.

Key Contact - Specialty:
Ms. Lorraine Bege, President - *Broadcast, cable, television, animation, entertainment*

Salary minimum: $40,000

Functions: Generalist, Directors, Middle Mgmt., Advertising, Mktg. Mgmt., Direct Mktg., Graphic Artists, Int'l.

Industries: Generalist, Hospitality, Media, Advertising, Publishing, New Media, Broadcast, Film

Professional Associations: BDAI, DMA, PROMAX

Hanna & Associates Inc
7710 N Union Blvd 202
Colorado Springs, CO 80920
(719) 266-5575
Fax: (719) 226-1823
Email: hanna@ahanna.com
Web: www.ahanna.com

Description: Our firm specializes in the architectural and engineering fields at senior level positions. You must be PE or AIA registered to be considered an active candidate. We charge no fees to our candidate. All resumes are held in the strictest of confidence.

Key Contact - Specialty:
Mr. Al Hanna, Principal - *Architecture, engineering*

Salary minimum: $50,000

Functions: Engineering, Architects

Industries: Generalist

The Hanna Group
12140 Fowlers Mill Rd
Chardon, OH 44024
(440) 285-2468
Fax: (440) 285-2066
Email: hanna@hannagroup.com
Web: www.hannagroup.com

Description: Mid to upper-level management search in manufacturing, engineering, finance, human resources and sales/marketing. Specific expertise in commercial vehicle, construction, agricultural equipment, heavy capital equipment, automotive and allied industry.

Key Contact:
Mr. M. A. Jack Hanna, Jr., President - *Finance, engineering, sales & marketing*
Ms. U. T. Hanna, Secretary

Salary minimum: $40,000

Functions: General Mgmt., Mfg., Materials, Sales & Mktg., HR Mgmt., Finance, Engineering, Architects, Attorneys, Int'l.

Industries: Construction, Mfg., Transportation, Advertising, Environmental Svcs., Aerospace

Professional Associations: SAE

Networks: Inter-City Personnel Assoc (IPA)

The Hanover Consulting Group
11707 Hunters Run Dr
Hunt Valley, MD 21030
(410) 785-1912
Fax: (410) 785-1913
Email: tgraff@thehanovergroup.net
Web: www.thehanovergroup.net

Description: Our firm specializes in finding and evaluating top talent for the banking and trust industries. We're in the business of enhancing careers, putting people into positions where they can utilize their talents for greater career growth and make a grater impact for the company that employs them. Our service takes into consideration the career goals, likes and dislikes of the individual and

matches them with the future plans of the client company.

Key Contact - Specialty:
Mr. Thomas D. B. Graff, CSAM, President - *Banking, trust, lending*

Salary minimum: $50,000

Functions: Senior Mgmt., Middle Mgmt., Productivity, Sales & Mktg.

Industries: Banking, Invest. Banking

Professional Associations: MAPRC, NBN

Networks: National Banking Network (NBN)

Harbeck Associates Inc
2003 Claremont Commons
Normal, IL 61761
(309) 454-2456
Fax: (309) 454-2332
Email: bill@harbeckassociates.com
Web: www.greatsalesjobs.com

Description: We are a national sales and executive recruiting firm specializing in the pharmaceutical, biotech, medical equipment, and technology industries. We help our clients staff their sales and sales management divisions.

Key Contact - Specialty:
Ms. Lori Harbeck, President - *Pharmaceutical sales, sales management, medical equipment sales, sales management*
Mr. Bill Baracani, Vice President - *Pharmaceutical, medical equipment sales, sales management, technology sales, sales management*

Salary minimum: $40,000

Functions: Generalist

Industries: Drugs Mfg., Medical Devices, Computer Equip., Misc. Mfg.

The Atticus Graham Group
853 Main St A
Safety Harbor, FL 34695
(727) 793-0299
(727) 793-9079
Fax: (727) 793-0399
Email: janet@atticusgraham.com

Description: Partnered with numerous recruitment firms allows us full access to a broad array of opportunities and candidates within advertising, public relations, sales promotion and direct marketing.

Key Contact - Specialty:
Ms. Janet M. Harberth, Senior Partner - *Advertising, Direct Response, Sales Promotion*
Mr. Peter W. Gagliardi, Senior Partner - *Advertising, direct response, sales promotion*
Mr. David T. McHugh, Senior Partner - *Advertising, direct response, sales promotion*

Salary minimum: $25,000

Functions: Generalist, Advertising, Mkt. Research, Mktg. Mgmt., Direct Mktg.

Industries: Generalist

Harbor Consultants Int'l Inc
PO Box 221616
Chantilly, VA 20153-1616
(703) 352-1888
Email: harbor_gkohler@attglobal.net

Description: A well established and highly regarded international executive search firm with experience in most industries and all functions at the senior-level with emphasis on quality and staffing consulting services.

Key Contact:
Mr. Frank Ojeda
Ms. Georgette Kohler

Functions: Generalist, Attorneys

Industries: Generalist, Legal

Professional Associations: WAW

Harbrowe Inc

PO Box 1240
Marion, MT 59925
(877) 964-7301
Fax: (406) 854-2320
Email: j@harbrowe.com
Web: www.harbrowe.com

Description: Recruiting for
biotechnology/pharmaceutical sales and
management.

Key Contact - Specialty:
Ms. Joanne LeBow, President - *Pharmaceutical,
medical sales*

Functions: Sales & Mktg.

Industries: Drugs Mfg.

Harcourt & Associates

520 Manulife Pl
10180-101 St
Edmonton, AB T5J 3S4
Canada
(780) 425-5555
Fax: (780) 990-1891
Email: recruiter@harcourt.ca
Web: www.harcourt.ca

Description: We provide staff and contract
recruiting services for Alberta businesses. Area of
Recruitment: IT, Technical/Engineering, Insurance,
Accounting, Office Support, Sales & Marketing

Key Contact - Specialty:
Ms. Judy Harcourt, CPC, President - *Association
management, retail management, sales/marketing,
commercial banking, HR management*
Ms. Barbara Perkins, CPC, Vice President - *IT
staff, insurance professionals, accounting
professionals*
Mr. Peter Harcourt, CPC, Chairman/Manager
Technical Division - *Manufacturing, engineering,
project management*
Mr. Don Unger, Group Manager - *Technical sales,
sales management*

Functions: Generalist, Senior Mgmt., Mfg.,
Materials, Sales & Mktg., Finance, IT,
Engineering

Industries: Generalist, Agri., Forestry, Mining,
Energy, Utilities, Construction, Chemicals, Metal
Products, Computer Equip.

Networks: National Personnel Assoc (NPA)

Branches:
1600 - 444 5th Ave SW
Calgary, AB T2P 2T8
Canada
(403) 263-5445
(780) 425-5555
Fax: (780) 990-1891
Email: calgary@harcourt.ca
Key Contact - Specialty:
Mr. Peter Harcourt, CPC, Principal - *Technical
management*

Hardage Group

220 N Main Baird-Brewer Bldg Ste 106
PO Box 208
Dyersburg, TN 38025-0208
(731) 285-3120
(800) 929-5970
Fax: (731) 285-3414
Email: hardage@ecsis.net
Web: www.hardagegroup.com

Description: Principals are seasoned human
resources professionals with extensive executive
recruiting experience. Primarily focused on union-
free manufacturing environments in the functional

areas of human resources, finance, engineering and
general management.

Key Contact - Specialty:
Mr. Phillip Hardage, Owner - *Human resources,
finance, engineering, steel*
Ms. Grace Phelps - *Human resources, printing,
retail*
Ms. Patsy Reasons - *Accounting, safety, food,
automotive*

Salary minimum: $40,000

Functions: Mfg., Production, Automation, HR
Mgmt., Finance

Industries: Generalist, Mfg., Food, Bev., Tobacco,
Printing, Plastics, Rubber, Metal Products,
Machine, Appliance, Motor Vehicles, Misc. Mfg.,
HR Services

Networks: Inter-City Personnel Assoc (IPA)

Herb Hardbrod Consulting Group

PO Box 740251
Boynton Beach, FL 33474-0251
(561) 740-1660
Fax: (561) 740-9880
Email: hardbrodgroup@aol.com

Description: We have thirty years of experience in
pharmaceuticals. Healthcare advertising positions
are our specialty.

Key Contact:
Mr. Herbert Hardbrod, President - *Pharmaceutical
(advertising, marketing)*
Ms. Janet Hunter, Vice President

Salary minimum: $50,000

Functions: Senior Mgmt., Middle Mgmt.,
Healthcare, Advertising, Mktg. Mgmt.,
Specialized Svcs.

Industries: Advertising, Healthcare

Harder Livesay

9390 Research Blvd Bldg 1 Ste 230
Austin, TX 78759
(512) 479-0000
Email: jobs@harderlivesay.com
Web: www.harderlivesay.com

Description: Placement firm specializing in finance
and accounting. Other areas include human
resources and public relations. Industries of
specialization include technology, manufacturing,
semiconductor, telecommunications, public
accounting and services.

Key Contact - Specialty:
Ms. Elizabeth Harder, CPA, Vice President -
Accounting, finance
Ms. Staci Livesay, President - *Accounting, finance*

Salary minimum: $35,000

Functions: Finance, Budgeting

Industries: Food, Bev., Tobacco, Computer Equip.,
Test, Measure Equip., Misc. Mfg., Accounting,
Advertising, Software

Professional Associations: AAFA, AAHCPA,
SHRM, TSCPA, WAW

Robert Harkins Associates Inc

PO Box 236
Ephrata, PA 17522
(717) 733-9664
Fax: (717) 733-9668
Email: info@harkinsassoc.com
Web: www.harkinsassoc.com

Description: The firm offers contingency, retained
search and contract professional placement services
in banking, accounting, finance, engineering,
manufacturing and human resources.

Key Contact - Specialty:
Mr. Robert E. Harkins, CPC, President -
Engineering, manufacturing, human resources
Mr. Thomas M. Dabich, CPC, Vice President - *Info
tech, accounting, finance, banking*

Salary minimum: $40,000

Functions: Generalist

Industries: Generalist

Professional Associations: DPMA

Networks: National Personnel Assoc (NPA)

Harper Associates

29870 Middlebelt
Farmington Hills, MI 48334
(248) 932-1170
Fax: (248) 932-1214
Email: resumes@harperjobs.com
Web: www.harperjobs.com

Description: Hospitality management recruitment
specialists for hotels, restaurants, resorts, country
clubs and food service management companies.
Searches are also conducted in healthcare and
information systems.

Key Contact - Specialty:
Mr. Bennett Schwartz, President - *Hospitality*
Ms. Cindy Krainen, Vice President - *Hospitality*

Functions: Generalist, Middle Mgmt., Nurses,
Health Admin., Mktg. Mgmt., Sales Mgmt., IT,
Non-profits

Industries: Generalist, Retail, Non-profits,
Hospitality, Healthcare

Harper Hewes Inc

1473 Calkins Rd
Pittsford, NY 14534
(716) 321-1700
Fax: (716) 321-1707
Email: dharper@harperhewes.com

Description: Particularly successful in filling high
impact positions. Implementation of virtual project
teams allows us to successfully complete searches
of any size.

Key Contact - Specialty:
Ms. Deborah Harper, President -
*Telecommunications, software, information
systems consulting, management consulting,
business intelligence*

Salary minimum: $75,000

Functions: Senior Mgmt., Middle Mgmt., Sales &
Mktg., Mkt. Research, Mktg. Mgmt., Sales
Mgmt., Direct Mktg., IT, Mgmt. Consultants

Industries: Generalist, Computer Equip., Misc.
Financial, Services, Telecoms, Software

Professional Associations: AWC, NAFE, NAWBO

Networks: Top Echelon Network

Harrington - O'Brien - Conway

67 Emerald St Ste. 702
Keene, NH 03431

Description: General management for most
industries with some concentration in the medical
field.

Key Contact:
Mr. Grady K. Conway
Mr. Christopher Patrick Harrington, Ph.D.
Mr. Mike "Joseph" O'Brien

Salary minimum: $40,000

Functions: General Mgmt., Healthcare, Allied
Health

Industries: Drugs Mfg., Medical Devices, Pharm
Svcs., Biotech, Healthcare

Bob Harrington Associates

(also known as Sanford Rose Associates - Greensboro)
3405 H W Wendover Ave
Greensboro, NC 27407
(336) 852-3003
(336) 852-3058
Fax: (336) 852-3039
Email: sragnc@aol.com

Description: Specialists in the printing, prime and bar code label converting, forms manufacturing, pressure sensitive adhesive coating/laminating, office products, packaging, digital printing, direct mail, and automatic identification hardware, software and supplies companies.

Key Contact - Specialty:
Mr. Robert J. Harrington, CPC, President - *Middle manager, executive level*

Salary minimum: $40,000

Functions: Generalist

Industries: Mfg., Paper, Printing, Chemicals, Computer Equip., Telecoms, Packaging

Professional Associations: NAPS

The Harrington Group

(also known as MRI of Spartanburg)
2811 Reidville Rd Ste 16
Spartanburg, SC 29301
(864) 587-1045
Fax: (864) 587-1048
Email: career@hgus.com
Web: www.hgus.com

Description: Our mission is to be a high integrity executive search and recruiting organization, national in scope, who specializes in the placement of executive-level professionals for information technology organizations and consulting firms.

Key Contact - Specialty:
Mr. Chip Harrington, President - *Information technology*

Salary minimum: $75,000

Functions: Generalist, Sales Mgmt., Benefits, Training, Systems Analysis, Systems Implem., Systems Support, Network Admin.

Industries: Generalist, Mgmt. Consulting, HR Services

Susan Harris & Associates

578 Post Rd E Ste 613
Westport, CT 06880
(203) 227-5700
Fax: (203) 227-5688
Email: shresume@optonline.net
Web: www.susanharris.com

Description: We specialize in the placement of marketing, promotion and sales executives with a special emphasis on promotion agency executives in the New York Metro area.

Key Contact:
Ms. Susan Harris, President

Salary minimum: $30,000

Functions: Generalist

Industries: Advertising

Harris McCully Associates Inc

99 Park Ave Fl 18
New York, NY 10016
(212) 983-1400
Fax: (212) 983-1451
Email: info@harrismccully.com
Web: www.harrismccully.com

Description: A contingency and retainer-based search firm specializing in the placement of middle to senior-level professionals. Our forte is in financial services, yet we work with diverse industries and multiple disciplines.

Key Contact:
Mr. Alan Harris, CEO/President
Mr. Ron Hamara, COO/Senior Executive Vice President

Salary minimum: $75,000

Functions: Generalist, General Mgmt., HR Mgmt., Finance, IT, Int'l.

Industries: Generalist, Textiles, Apparel, Banking, Invest. Banking, Brokers, Venture Cap., Misc. Financial, Hospitality

Professional Associations: IACMP

Harrison Consulting Group Inc

2660 Townsgate Rd Ste 520
Westlake Village, CA 91361
(805) 449-7250
Fax: (805) 449-7230
Email: dhgrue@harrisonsearch.com
Web: www.harrisonsearch.com

Description: Professional recruiters creating winning business relationships. SM for permanent and temporary tax professionals.

Key Contact - Specialty:
Mr. Douglas Harrison Grue, President - *Tax - California only*

Salary minimum: $40,000

Functions: Taxes

Industries: Generalist

Professional Associations: CSP

Harrison Group

PO Box 743
Milltown, NJ 08850
(732) 249-6777
Fax: (732) 249-9108
Email: scott@harrisongroup.com
Web: www.harrisongroup.com

Description: We are a technical search firm that focuses our recruiting efforts primarily in the following industries: pharmaceutical, cosmetics/personal care, and chemical. We place candidates in the following areas: chemists, more specifically analytical R&D, QC, product development, and tech services; engineering, more specifically chemicals, packaging, and industrial; regulatory affairs; regulatory compliance; and quality.

Key Contact:
Mr. Scott W. Szur

Functions: Quality, R&D, Engineering

Industries: Chemicals, Soap, Perf., Cosmtcs., Drugs Mfg., Pharm Svcs.

Networks: Inter-City Personnel Assoc (IPA)

Harrison Moore Inc

16009 Orchard Cir
Omaha, NE 68135-1068
(402) 861-0555
Fax: (402) 861-0557
Email: cmcley@home.com

Description: Specialty in the foundry and machining industries: management, production, operations, quality, technical, tooling, sales, metallurgy, plant engineering and maintenance.

Key Contact - Specialty:
Mr. Curt McLey, President - *Foundry, machining industries*

Functions: General Mgmt., Mfg., Product Dev., Production, Plant Mgmt., Quality, Productivity, Materials, Purchasing, Sales & Mktg.

Industries: Metal Products

Professional Associations: AFS

Donald L Hart & Associates

3 Church St Ste 604
Toronto, ON M5E 1M2
Canada
(416) 862-7104
Fax: (416) 862-7139
Email: info@dlhart.com
Web: www.dlhart.com

Description: We conduct professional IT recruiting in the areas of executive management personnel, key line sales personnel, marketing, program and project management, technical specialists, and engineers. Our fields of expertise include: communication, systems and networks, graphics, applications software, professional services, web design, and xml/html.

Key Contact:
Mr. Donald L. Hart

Functions: Generalist

Industries: Computer Equip., Test, Measure Equip., Mgmt. Consulting, IT Implementation, New Media, Telecoms, Network Infrastructure, Software, Database SW, Mfg. SW

Hart & Company

219 E 69th St Ste 7H
New York, NY 10021
(212) 585-4000
Fax: (212) 585-1294
Email: gghart@aol.com

Description: An executive recruiting organization with focus on the consumer advertising agency and corporate communications industries throughout the US and Canada. Agency positions are in all levels of account management, media and research. Clientside includes advertising and marketing specialists.

Key Contact - Specialty:
Mr. Gerry Hart - *Advertising agencies*

Salary minimum: $30,000

Functions: Advertising, Mktg. Mgmt.

Industries: Advertising, New Media, Broadcast, Film

Hartman & Company

915C W Foothill Blvd PMB 380
Claremont, CA 91711
(909) 621-0117
Fax: (909) 596-4442
Email: hartman@uia.net

Description: Area of specialty is the recruitment and placement of middle and senior level executives in the forest products, building materials and hardlines industries.

Key Contact:
Mr. Dan Hartman, President

Hartman Greene & Wells

1827 Jefferson Pl NW
Washington, DC 20036
(202) 223-7644
Fax: (301) 765-2223
Email: zinagreene@hartmangreene.com
Web: www.hartmangreene.com

Description: In business since 1986, our greatest strength is providing qualified candidates both expeditiously and confidentially in the legal community. Our success is due to our personal touch, we only place in the D.C. area so that we know our clients and meet with our candidates.

Key Contact - Specialty:
Ms. Zina L. Greene, President - *Attorneys*

Functions: Legal

Industries: Generalist

Harvco Consulting

21 N Main St Ste 204
Alpharetta, GA 30004
(770) 664-5512
Fax: (770) 664-5046
Email: atlantamri@mindspring.com

Description: We specialize in Internet integration, start-ups, software/high-tech, manufacturing, CRM, and ERP. We have foundations in pulp and paper, building products, packaging, packaging systems, process sterilization for food/beverage, logistics/distribution, and water analysis. Our primary disciplines include strategic business change, new product development, marketing, sales, financial, MIS, R&D, engineering, operations management, and international.

Key Contact - Specialty:
Mr. John K. Harvey, President - *Food & beverage packaging, building products, logistics*

Salary minimum: $75,000

Functions: Generalist, Product Dev., Packaging, Mktg. Mgmt., Finance, Engineering, Int'l.

Industries: Mfg., Food, Bev., Tobacco, Lumber, Furniture, Paper, Printing, Chemicals, Medical Devices, Plastics, Rubber, Metal Products, Test, Measure Equip., Electronic, Elec. Components, Transportation, Finance, Services, Non-profits, HR Services, E-commerce, Communications, Wireless, Packaging, Software, ERP SW, Marketing SW

Hastings & Hastings Inc

1001 Brickell Bay Dr Fl 29
Miami, FL 33131
(305) 374-2255
Fax: (305) 374-6417
Email: info@hastingsonline.com
Web: www.hastingsonline.com

Description: We have grown to become a highly respected industry leader in placement and staffing with a well-known reputation for excellence. We have continued to increase the services offered by adding a state-of-the-art computer system, executive placement, a temporary-to-permanent department, and a temporary division.

Key Contact - Specialty:
Ms. Lee Roberts, Senior Vice President - *Executive, administrative*
Ms. Jill Brinkley, Vice President - *Executive, administrative*
Ms. Tina Rogers, Account Executive - *Finance, marketing*
Ms. Lynn Hunter, Account Executive - *Technical*
Ms. Claudia Perry, Account Executive - *Finance & accounting*

Functions: Generalist, General Mgmt., Sales & Mktg., HR Mgmt., Finance, IT

Industries: Generalist, Mfg., Finance, Services, Media, Software

The Hastings Group

145 Loblolly Dr
Pine Knoll Shores, NC 28512
(252) 727-5111
Fax: (252) 727-5112
Email: hastingsgr@aol.com
Web: www.hastingsgr.com

Description: We are a professional recruiting firm serving the food industry exclusively. We recruit for Product Developers, Quality Assurance, Engineers, Research, Operations, Maintenance, Marketing/Sales, Production Supervisors, Packaging and Management.

Key Contact:
Ms. Nancy Hastings, President

Mr. Rich Doremus, Partner

Salary minimum: $30,000

Functions: General Mgmt., Directors, Mfg., Product Dev., Production, Quality, Packaging, Sales & Mktg., R&D, Engineering

Industries: Mfg., Food, Bev., Tobacco, Soap, Perf., Cosmtcs.

Professional Associations: AACC, AOCS, IFT

Networks: Inter-City Personnel Assoc (IPA)

Frank W Hastings

1034 Ziegler Rd
PO Box 36
Palm, PA 18070-0036
(215) 541-0303
(215) 541-0304
Fax: (215) 541-0305
Email: fhastings@netcarrier.com

Description: We have been in the recruiting business for 47 years. We only get paid for results. We hold membership in a network of several hundred recruiting firms across North America. This is an invaluable service to applicants and employers by assuring success in their search.

Key Contact - Specialty:
Mr. Frank W. Hastings, President/Owner - *Accounting & finance, data processing, manufacturing, administration, sales & marketing*

Salary minimum: $30,000

Functions: Middle Mgmt., Admin. Svcs., Legal, Mfg., Materials, Sales & Mktg., HR Mgmt., Finance, IT, Engineering

Industries: Generalist

Professional Associations: EMA, SHRM

Networks: Inter-City Personnel Assoc (IPA)

Robert W Havener Associates Inc

2408 Chatau Ct
Fallston, MD 21047
(410) 893-0256
Fax: (410) 420-8125
Email: havenerr@home.com

Description: We have been specializing in the printing and packaging industry since inception. We place presidents, vice presidents, production management, sales and production positions.

Key Contact - Specialty:
Mr. Robert W. Havener, President - *Executive, management, printing, packaging*
Mr. Robert E. Hammock, Vice President - *Production, printing, packaging*

Functions: Generalist, Senior Mgmt., Middle Mgmt., Plant Mgmt., Quality, Sales Mgmt., HR Mgmt., Finance

Industries: Generalist, Paper, Printing

Phyllis Hawkins & Associates Inc

105 E Northern Ave
Phoenix, AZ 85020
(602) 263-0248
Fax: (602) 678-1564
Email: phassoc@qwest.net
Web: www.azlawsearch.com

Description: We conduct attorney searches for law firms and corporations in the Southwestern U.S. Our staff has an in-depth knowledge of the legal communities in our area and substantial experience in legal recruitment.

Key Contact - Specialty:
Ms. Phyllis Hawkins, President - *Attorneys*
Ms. Tracy Tabler - *Attorneys*

Salary minimum: $100,000

Functions: Legal, Attorneys

Industries: Generalist, Non-classifiable

Professional Associations: NALSC

Michael J Hawkins Inc

1615 Colonial Pkwy
Inverness, IL 60067-4732
(847) 705-5400
Fax: (847) 705-9065
Email: mikehawkins@mjhawkinsinc.com
Web: www.mjhawkinsinc.com

Description: The nation's leading executive search organization specializing in the supply segment of the food service industry. Search limited to general management, sales, marketing, engineering and manufacturing executives.

Key Contact:
Mr. Michael J. Hawkins, CFSP, President - *Food service, food retail, food, supplies, equipment manufacturers*
Mrs. Joan Hawkins, Partner

Salary minimum: $50,000

Functions: Senior Mgmt., Mfg.

Industries: Mfg., Paper, Chemicals

Professional Associations: FMI, NAFEM, NPTA

Hayden & Associates Inc

(also known as H R Service of Plymouth)
7825 Washington Ave S Ste 120
Bloomington, MN 55439
(952) 941-6300
Fax: (952) 941-9602
Email: info@haydenassoc.com
Web: www.haydenassoc.com

Description: Large progressive firm with a personal database of over 110,000 candidates. Very client service oriented with 80% of our client companies becoming repeat customers. 300 affiliates nationally.

Key Contact:
Mr. Steve Benedict, COO
Mr. Lowell Singerman, President

Salary minimum: $30,000

Functions: General Mgmt., Sales & Mktg., IT

Industries: Generalist

Networks: First Interview Network (FIN)

Haydon Legal Search

1740 Ridge Ave
Evanston, IL 60201-5918
(847) 475-4222
Fax: (847) 475-0939
Email: haydonsrch@aol.com

Description: Specializing in attorney search & placement since 1979, Meredith Haydon is recognized for providing exceptional recruiting services to law firms and corporate legal departments in the greater Chicago area.

Key Contact - Specialty:
Ms. Meredith Haydon, Principal - *Attorneys*

Functions: Generalist, Attorneys

Industries: Generalist, Legal

Professional Associations: NALSC

Hayman Daugherty Associates Inc

5105 Old Ellis Pointe
Roswell, GA 30076
(800) 765-0432
(770) 772-4558
Fax: (800) 782-4999
Email: kim@haymandaugherty.com
Web: www.haymandaugherty.com

Description: We specialize in building relationships. Our consultants are geographically and specialty divided which allows them to enjoy a high-level of expertise. We understand your needs and can help you accomplish your goals.

Key Contact:
Ms. Kimberly J. Daugherty-Hill, CEO - *Physicians, healthcare, MIS, data processing, information technology*
Mr. James Crawford, President

Salary minimum: $100,000

Functions: Physicians

Industries: Non-classifiable

Professional Associations: MGMA, NAPR

Hayward Simone Associates Inc
1 Wall St Ct Ste 610
New York, NY 10005
(212) 785-3550
Fax: (212) 809-8134
Email: hsa@haysim.com
Web: www.haywardsimone.com

Description: Our areas of expertise include emerging technologies, management and IT consulting, systems development and integration; application implementation, deployment, and business process planning.

Key Contact - Specialty:
Mr. Morris Green, Partner / Co-Founder - *IT recruitment*
Ms. Judith Karpel, Partner / Co-Founder - *IT recruitment*

Functions: IT

Industries: Finance, Banking, Misc. Financial, E-commerce, IT Implementation, Network Infrastructure, Government, Software

Lynn Hazan & Associates Inc
55 E Washington Ste 715
Chicago, IL 60602
(312) 863-5400
(312) 863-5401
Fax: (312) 863-5404
Email: lhazan@enteract.com
Web: www.recruit4u.net

Description: Specialties: marketing, communications, consulting. Values relationship marketing with both candidates and clients. Clients include: PR and ad agencies, corporations, consulting firms, and dot-coms. Positions in corporate and marketing communications, interactive, e-commerce, editorial, art direction, graphic design, web content/design, copywriting, product management, account service. Nation-wide with emphasis on Chicago and Midwest.

Key Contact - Specialty:
Ms. Lynn Hazan, President - *Marketing, communications, consulting, PR, advertising*

Functions: Product Dev., Healthcare, Sales & Mktg., Advertising, Mkt. Research, Mktg. Mgmt., Direct Mktg., PR, IT, Graphic Artists

Industries: Food, Bev., Tobacco, Computer Equip., Consumer Elect., Finance, Services, Non-profits, Higher Ed., Pharm Svcs., Legal, Mgmt. Consulting, Hospitality, Media, Advertising, Publishing, New Media, Packaging, Insurance, Real Estate, Software, Biotech, Healthcare

Professional Associations: AIP, BMA, CADM, CAF, IABC, PRSA, TEC, WICI

Hazard, Young, Attea & Associates Ltd
1151 Waukegan Rd Ste 200
Glenview, IL 60025
(847) 724-8465
Email: hya@enteract.com
Web: www.hyasupersearches.com

Description: Executive search services and management consulting with special emphasis on school districts, higher education.

Key Contact - Specialty:
Dr. William Attea, Managing Partner - *Public schools, superintendents, school administrative personnel*

Professional Associations: AASA

The HBC Group Inc
370 Lexington Ave Ste 2200
New York, NY 10017
(212) 661-8300
Fax: (212) 661-8308
Email: norman@hbcgroupinc.com
Web: www.expage.com/page/hbcgroup

Description: We provide executive search for the banking industry. We specialize in corporate credit, capital markets credit, and origination positions.

Key Contact:
Mr. Norman Gershgorn

Salary minimum: $50,000

Functions: Middle Mgmt.

Industries: Banking

HCI Corp
28 S 5th St
Geneva, IL 60134
(630) 208-3100
Fax: (630) 208-3111
Web: www.hci-search.com

Description: What we offer is the ability to locate, screen and recruit the best possible candidates that fit your stringent criteria. This eliminates many of the risks involved in the hiring process along with finding the top candidates who may not be actively looking.

Key Contact - Specialty:
Mr. Frank Cianchetti, President - *Healthcare*
Mr. Kevin Joy - *Bakery*
Ms. Lindsay Porter - *Toy, consumer products, sporting goods*
Mr. Richard Smith - *Actuarial*
Mr. Wade Kawahara - *Chemical*
Ms. Brenda Schinke - *Packaging*

Functions: Generalist, Senior Mgmt., Production, Plant Mgmt., Sales & Mktg., HR Mgmt., Engineering, Int'l.

Industries: Generalist, Medical Devices, Biotech, Healthcare

HDB Inc
PO BOX 1612
Manchester, MO 63011-1612
(636) 391-7799
Fax: (636) 391-1224
Email: kwolfe@hdbinc.com
Web: www.hdbinc.com

Description: Our philosophy is simple: provide quality service to our client companies and candidates by setting standards of excellence through the commitment of our talents, expertise and resources.

Key Contact - Specialty:
Ms. Kathryn Davis Wolfe, CPC, President - *E-business, e-commerce, ERP, management consulting, information technology, logistics*

Functions: Generalist, MIS Mgmt., Systems Analysis, Systems Dev., Systems Implem., Systems Support, DB Admin., Mgmt. Consultants

Industries: Generalist, Mgmt. Consulting, Software

Professional Associations: APC

Headhunter in LA
22287 Mullholland Hwy Ste 214
Calabasas, CA 91302
(818) 347-8484
Email: headhunterinla@aol.com
Web: www.headhunterinla.net

Description: Executive search for the fashion/apparel industry, including retail, manufacturing, and catalog companies. Expert search capabilities for all divisions. Key search firm for marketing and creative executive talent.

Key Contact:
Ms. Reeve Weiner, President

Salary minimum: $75,000

Functions: Directors, Advertising, Mktg. Mgmt., Graphic Artists

Industries: Textiles, Apparel, Retail

Headhunters Executive Search Inc
96 Princeton St
Nutley, NJ 07110
(973) 667-2799
Email: medsalesplus@aol.com

Description: We recruit and place sales representatives and management primarily in medical products and pharmaceuticals. Secondary placement in consumer sales.

Key Contact - Specialty:
Ms. Maria Mosca, President - *Medical sales, marketing, consumer, pharmaceutical sales*
Ms. Elaine Jones, Vice President - *Medical sales, pharmaceutical sales, marketing, consumer*

Functions: Generalist, Sales Mgmt.

Industries: Generalist, Food, Bev., Tobacco, Drugs Mfg., Medical Devices, Pharm Svcs., Biotech, Healthcare

HeadhunterUSA.com
(a division of Yellow Rose Enterprises)
10701 S R 83 Bldg III
Grafton, OH 44044-9440
(440) 748-7501
Fax: (440) 748-4062
Email: headhuntersusa@prodigy.net
Web:
www.hometown.aol.com/headhuntus/myhomepage/news.html

Description: We are national recruiters for international, national, and regional employers specializing in quality, prescreened, and guaranteed personnel. We provide resume review and pre-interview screening at no cost. We area serving industry and commerce since 1969 Yellow Rose Enterprises identified the need to interface standard consultative practices, the Internet, and computer capabilities to better meet client needs.

Key Contact - Specialty:
Dr. Del Martin, Ph.D., CPC, General Manager - *National sales, sales management*
Mr. Pat Green, Senior Recruiter - *Information technology sales, sales management, technical professionals*
Mr. Ron Scott, Senior Recruiter - *Industrial, medical, consumer sales, sales management*
Mr. Clarke Adams, Senior Recruiter - *Marketing, product managers, advertising*
Ms. Rose Martin, Administrative Manager - *Clerical, customer service, administrative, office managers, accountants*
Mr. Gerrard Berry, Recruiter - *Manufacturing (engineering)*

Salary minimum: $40,000

Functions: Generalist

Industries: Generalist

Health Care Dimensions

335 Manitou Ave
Manitou Springs, CO 80829-2537
(800) 373-3401
(719) 685-4750
Fax: (719) 685-4756
Email: info@healthcaredimensions.com
Web: www.healthcaredimensions.com

Description: The Nation's first executive search firm to dedicate its entire team to supporting the senior living industry...with over 15 years of experience.

Key Contact - Specialty:
Mr. David E. Carpenter, President
Ms. Lisa Hazelton, Partner - *Long term care, post-acute, retirement housing, assisted living*
Ms. Jill Howard, Partner - *Long term care, post-acute, retirement housing, assisted living*
Ms. Nancy West, Partner - *Long term care, post-acute, retirement housing, assisted living*

Salary minimum: $50,000

Functions: Generalist

Industries: Long-term Care

Professional Associations: AAHSA, AHCA, ALFA

Health Care Plus Inc

224 Cape St. John Rd
Annapolis, MD 21401
(800) 348-4040
(410) 571-8399
Fax: (410) 571-0182
Email: info@hcpsearch.com
Web: www.hcpsearch.com

Description: The nation's leading executive search firm serving the post-acute care industry. Clients are for profit and not for profit providers of long-term care, sub-acute care, acute rehabilitation, assisted living and other related post-acute services.

Key Contact:
Mr. Michael Hargrave, Vice President
Ms. Linda Moran, Vice President
Ms. Susan Hargrave, President

Salary minimum: $45,000

Functions: Generalist, Allied Health, Health Admin.

Industries: Generalist, Healthcare

Professional Associations: EMA

Health Care Recruiting

61052 Ladera Rd Ste 400
Bend, OR 97702
(541) 382-1732
Email: hcrjim@bendcable.com
Web: www.health-care-recruiting.com

Description: We recruit for healthcare providers, physicians, and midlevels. HCR has recruited physicians and midlevels, worked with over 1700 client hospitals and clinics throughout the US, and worked ethically and confidentially on each and every search.

Key Contact:
Mr. Jim Ransom

Salary minimum: $100,000

Functions: Healthcare, Physicians, Allied Health, Health Admin.

Industries: Healthcare

Professional Associations: NAPR

Health Search

(a Jeffrey Robbins Company)
1240 N Lakeview Ave Ste 280
Anaheim Hills, CA 92807
(714) 779-7800
Fax: (714) 779-7805
Email: jeff@health-search.net
Web: www.health-search.net

Description: Our firm is a national healthcare executive search firm which conducts management level search in the administrative, financial, and nursing areas within the hospital, home health, managed care, and medical group management sectors of the health care industry.

Key Contact - Specialty:
Mr. Jeffrey Robbins, President - *Healthcare*
Mr. Larry Robinow, Senior Vice President - *Healthcare*
Ms. Kellie Brown, Executive Recruiter - *Healthcare*
Mr. Donald Amaral, Advisor - *Healthcare*
Mr. Jerry Schneider, Consultant - *Healthcare*
Dr. Robert Landman, Medical Advisor - *Healthcare*
Ms. Barbara Carol, Director of Research - *Healthcare*
Ms. Nancy Ryan, Research Associate - *Healthcare*

Salary minimum: $75,000

Functions: Generalist, Healthcare

Industries: Healthcare

Professional Associations: AGPAM, HFMA, MGMA

Health Search Inc

600 S Washington St
El Dorado, KS 67042-2854
(316) 322-8077
(800) 800-6580
Fax: (316) 322-8290
Email: vwaller@southwind.net

Description: Our mission is to serve the medical community by bringing qualified employees and employers together. We offer a 6 month guarantee with our services.

Key Contact - Specialty:
Ms. Victoria Waller, CPC, President - *Allied health, respiratory therapy, pharmacy, medical laboratory*

Salary minimum: $30,000

Functions: Generalist, Allied Health

Industries: Healthcare

Professional Associations: KAPS

Networks: Top Echelon Network

Healthcare Concepts

266 S Front St
Memphis, TN 38103
(800) 442-4346
Fax: (901) 529-9101
Email: susan@healthcareconcepts.com
Web: www.healthcareconcepts.com

Description: One of the nation's oldest executive search firms dedicated to serving the home health industry. Other specialty areas include long-term care, rehab, and acute care. A full range of executive search services including interim management and additional consulting are available.

Key Contact:
Ms. Laurel Reisman, President

Functions: Healthcare

Industries: Generalist

Professional Associations: NAHC

Healthcare Executive Recruiters Inc

1119 Colorado Ave Ste 2
Santa Monica, CA 90401
(310) 260-2554
Fax: (310) 260-6463
Email: sfbr17003@aol.com

Description: Healthcare administrators, nursing executives, nurse managers, CFOs, all senior-level managers in the healthcare industry recruited to fit your individual needs.

Key Contact - Specialty:
Ms. Susan Fleischer, CEO - *Nursing administration, hospital executives*
Ms. Bette Rosenbaum, COO - *Nursing, senior management*

Functions: Generalist, Nurses, Health Admin., HR Mgmt., Finance, IT

Industries: Generalist, Healthcare

Healthcare Recruiters Int'l • Dallas

5220 Spring Valley Rd Ste L 20
Dallas, TX 75240
(972) 661-0055
Fax: (972) 687-0039
Email: dallas@hcrnetwork.com
Web: www.healthcarerecruiters.com

Description: Exclusive healthcare executive search firm emphasizing sales, sales management and clinical management opportunities.

Key Contact - Specialty:
Mr. Jim Wimberly, President/Owner - *Lab, diagnostics, biotechnology, healthcare information systems, managed care*

Salary minimum: $75,000

Functions: Generalist, Senior Mgmt., Middle Mgmt., Sales Mgmt.

Industries: Generalist, Medical Devices, Pharm Svcs., Biotech, Healthcare

Branches:
7821 Coral Way Ste 104
Miami, FL 33155
(786) 388-0908
Fax: (786) 388-0380
Email: southflorida@hcrnetwork.com

318 Creekstone Rdg
Woodstock, GA 30188
(678) 494-2003
Fax: (678) 494-0019
Email: atlanta@hcrnetwork.com
Key Contact:
Mr. Jeff Gedhart

4500 Black Rock Rd Ste 102
Hampstead, MD 21074
(410) 239-6464
Fax: (410) 374-5887
Email: midatlantic@hcrnetwork.com
Key Contact:
Mr. Keith Graham

15400 S Outer 40 Ste 100
Chesterfield, MO 63017
(636) 530-1030
Fax: (636) 530-1039
Email: stlouis@hcrnetwork.com

535 Keisler Dr Ste 202
Cary, NC 27511
(919) 858-7017
Fax: (919) 858-7018
Email: carolinas@hcrnetwork.com
Key Contact:
Ms. Suzette Wood

10144 N Port Washington Rd 1C
Mequon, WI 53092
(262) 241-3333
Fax: (262) 569-6749
Email: wisconsin@hcrnetwork.com

Key Contact:
Mr. Perry Van Laanen

HealthCare Recruiters Int'l • Alabama
1945 Hoover Ct Ste 205
Birmingham, AL 35226
(205) 979-9840
Fax: (205) 979-5879
Email: alabama@hcrnetwork.com
Web: www.healthcarerecruiters.com

Description: Recruit healthcare professionals in all areas; sales, marketing, management, physicians, field services, nursing, physical therapy and pharmacy. Primary focus is sales, marketing, sales management, and marketing management. Primary industries are information systems, capitol equipment, medical surgical, and pharmaceutical. All fees are paid by the employer.

Key Contact:
Mr. Frank Y. Johnson, President - *Healthcare sales & marketing, physicians, management*
Mrs. Coleen Johnson, Office Manager
Mr. Sean Johnson, Recruiter/Researcher

Salary minimum: $35,000

Functions: Senior Mgmt., Product Dev., Healthcare, Sales & Mktg., Mktg. Mgmt., Sales Mgmt., IT

Industries: Drugs Mfg., Medical Devices, Computer Equip., Pharm Svcs., Software, Biotech, Healthcare

HealthCare Recruiters Int'l • Phoenix
4545 E Shea Blvd 209
Phoenix, AZ 85028
(602) 494-9468
Email: phoenix@hcrnetwork.com
Web: www.healthcarerecruiters.com

Description: Our firm specializes in the placement of professionals strictly within the healthcare industry.

Key Contact - Specialty:
Mr. Mike Strieker, CEO
Ms. Suzanne Akre, Senior Account Executive - *Pharmaceutical*
Ms. Darlene Hanson, Account Executive - *Medical device*

Salary minimum: $75,000

Functions: Healthcare, Physicians, Nurses, Health Admin., Mktg. Mgmt., Sales Mgmt.

Industries: Generalist, Medical Devices, Pharm Svcs., Biotech, Healthcare

HealthCare Recruiters Int'l • San Diego
701 Palomar Airport Rd Ste 300
Carlsbad, CA 92009
(760) 931-4790
Fax: (760) 931-9979
Email: sandiego@hcrnetwork.com
Web: www.hcrjobs.com

Description: We provide executive-level medical and biotech recruitment. We do not place any entry-level positions.

Key Contact - Specialty:
Ms. Judy Thurmond, Owner/President - *Medical, biotech*

Salary minimum: $50,000

Functions: Generalist

Industries: Drugs Mfg., Medical Devices, Pharm Svcs., Biotech, Healthcare

HealthCare Recruiters Int'l • Orange County
26361 Crown Valley Pkwy Ste 150
Mission Viejo, CA 92691
(949) 367-7888
Fax: (949) 367-7881
Email: orangecounty@hcrnetwork.com
Web: www.healthcarerecruiters.com

Description: National network of sales, marketing, management specializing only in healthcare.

Key Contact - Specialty:
Ms. Carol Raia, President - *Medical marketing*
Mr. Tony Raia, CFO - *Medical management*

Functions: Generalist

Industries: Drugs Mfg., Medical Devices, Healthcare

HealthCare Recruiters Int'l • Bay Area
220 Montgomery St Ste 969
San Francisco, CA 94104
(415) 773-0333
Fax: (415) 773-0331
Email: bayarea@hcrnetwork.com
Web: www.healthcarerecruiters.com

Description: One of the largest healthcare recruiting firms with 34 offices nationwide. All areas of healthcare, executive, information systems, surgery, sales, engineering, pharmaceutical, diagnostic.

Key Contact:
Ms. Melanie Hillebrand
Ms. Linda Rosen

Functions: Generalist

Industries: Biotech, Healthcare

HealthCare Recruiters Int'l • Los Angeles
15300 Ventura Blvd Ste 207
Sherman Oaks, CA 91403
(818) 981-9510
Fax: (818) 981-9523
Email: la@hcrnetwork.com
Web: www.healthcarerecruiters.com

Description: Medical search firm specialized in pharmaceutical/biotechnology/medical products/services. All organizational departments/levels. Fortune 500 to venture capital.

Key Contact:
Ms. Deborah Wilson, Vice President-Operations - *Medical products manufacturing (full scope)*
Ms. Rita Montgomery, Vice President-Business Development - *Home healthcare, pharmaceutical, biotechnology*
Mr. Glen Smith, President/CEO

Functions: Generalist, General Mgmt., Mfg., Materials, Sales & Mktg., IT, R&D, Engineering

Industries: Generalist, Drugs Mfg., Medical Devices, Pharm Svcs., Biotech, Healthcare

HealthCare Recruiters Int'l • Rockies
6860 S Yosemite Ct Ste 200
Englewood, CO 80112
(303) 779-8570
Fax: (303) 779-7974
Email: info@hcrrockies.com
Web: www.hcrrockies.com

Description: We are experts in sourcing candidates for management, sales, marketing, field support, clinical specialists, QA/RA, and clinical research for pharmaceutical, healthcare, medical device, diagnostic, surgical, nutritional, managed care, and healthcare information system industries.

Key Contact - Specialty:
Ms. Vicki L. Faas, RN, Principal/Senior Vice President - *Information systems, ehealthcare, QA/RA, surgical, medical device*

Mr. Richard Moore, President - *Information systems (healthcare), lab, diagnostics*

Salary minimum: $30,000

Functions: Generalist

Industries: Drugs Mfg., Medical Devices, Pharm Svcs., Biotech, Healthcare, Hospitals, Long-term Care, Dental

Professional Associations: AHIMA, HIMSS, MMA, MSHUG

HealthCare Recruiters Int'l • Central FL
215 Lincoln Ave S
Clearwater, FL 33756
(727) 467-9620
Fax: (727) 467-9249
Email: tampa@hcrnetwork.com
Web: www.healthcarerecruiters.com

Description: We recruit exclusively within the medical industry. We work for companies that manufacture and distribute medical supplies and capital equipment, as well as organizations that provide services to the health care market or are providers of health care services. Our searches include all levels of sales, marketing and all levels of management.

Key Contact:
Mr. Thomas Q. Fleury

Functions: Generalist

Industries: Mfg., Pharm Svcs., E-commerce, Call Centers, Software, Industry Specific SW, Biotech, Healthcare

HealthCare Recruiters Int'l • Chicago
850 N Milwaukee Ave Ste 204
Vernon Hills, IL 60061
(847) 549-5885
Fax: (847) 549-1570
Email: chicago@hcrnetwork.com
Web: www.healthcarerecruiters.com

Description: We are a full-service recruiting firm. We specialize in sales force roll-outs and replacements on a nationwide basis within the medical marketplace.

Key Contact - Specialty:
Mr. Joe Scully, President - *Executives, medical, surgery, pharmaceutical, biotechnology*

Salary minimum: $30,000

Functions: Generalist, General Mgmt., Mfg., Healthcare, Sales & Mktg., IT, R&D, Engineering

Industries: Generalist, Mfg., Medical Devices, Pharm Svcs., Mgmt. Consulting, Biotech, Healthcare

HealthCare Recruiters Int'l • Indiana
11550 N Meridian St Ste 210
Carmel, IN 46032
(317) 843-5522
Fax: (317) 843-5490
Email: indiana@hcrnetwork.com
Web: www.healthcarerecruiters.com

Description: We are all healthcare professionals who understand the needs of the industry.

Key Contact:
Mr. John A. Clark, President/CEO
Ms. Michele Lunik, Account Executive

Functions: Healthcare

Industries: Generalist

HealthCare Recruiters Int'l • New Orleans

3500 N Causeway Blvd Ste 1472
Metairie, LA 70002
(504) 838-8875
Fax: (504) 838-9962
Email: neworleans@hcrnetwork.com
Web: www.healthcarerecruiters.com

Description: Specializing in medical sales, sales management and executive-level positions in healthcare.

Key Contact - Specialty:
Mr. Vic Palazola, President - *Healthcare*

Functions: Product Dev., Sales & Mktg., Sales Mgmt., MIS Mgmt.

Industries: Drugs Mfg., Medical Devices

HealthCare Recruiters Int'l • New England

1 Newbury St Fl 3
Peabody, MA 01960
(978) 535-3302
Fax: (978) 535-3677
Email: mel.robbins@hcrnetwork.com
Web: www.healthcarerecruiters.com

Description: Major emphasis sales, sales management, marketing, medical and pharmaceutical.

Key Contact:
Mr. Melvyn Robbins, President - *Pharmaceutical, clinical lab equipment, diagnostics*
Mr. David Garriss, Vice President

Salary minimum: $40,000

Functions: Middle Mgmt., Production, Plant Mgmt., Quality, Nurses, Allied Health, Sales & Mktg.

Industries: Drugs Mfg., Medical Devices, Software, Biotech, Healthcare

HealthCare Recruiters Int'l • Michigan

10291 E Grand River Ste D
Brighton, MI 48116
(810) 227-7055
Fax: (810) 227-7307
Email: michigan@hcrnetwork.com
Web: www.healthcarerecruiters.com

Description: We provide permanent placements focused on healthcare, which an emphasis on sales, sales management, marketing, market research, and product management, clinical support, and research. We have extensive experience and contacts throughout the Midwest in the pharmaceutical and medical products industries.

Key Contact:
Ms. Gayle Amlie

HealthCare Recruiters Int'l • Mid America

10920 Ambassador Dr Ste 320
Kansas City, MO 64153
(816) 891-7778
Fax: (816) 891-7377
Email: midamerica@hcrnetwork.com
Web: www.healthcarerecruiters.com

Description: We are an executive recruiting firm specializing in the health care industry.

Key Contact:
Ms. Karen Wonderly

HealthCare Recruiters Int'l • NY/NJ

55 Harristown Rd
Glen Rock, NJ 07452
(201) 670-9800
Fax: (201) 670-1908

Email: nynj@hcrnetwork.com
Web: www.healthcarerecruiters.com

Description: Our mission is to help companies and medical facilities grow and succeed by providing the best professionals in the healthcare field. We are wholly dedicated to the healthcare industry.

Key Contact - Specialty:
Mr. Harold B. Conant, President - *Senior management, pharmaceutical, medical*
Ms. Ann M. Moore, Vice President - *Home healthcare, managed care*
Mr. Ronald D. Len, Senior Account Executive - *Laboratory, diagnostic, pharmaceutical, sales & marketing, technical*
Ms. Iris L. Fisher, Senior Account Executive - *Sales, marketing, technical*

Functions: General Mgmt., Senior Mgmt., Middle Mgmt., Product Dev., Sales & Mktg., Mkt. Research, Mktg. Mgmt., Sales Mgmt., IT

Industries: Drugs Mfg., Medical Devices, Pharm Svcs., Software, Biotech, Healthcare

HealthCare Recruiters Int'l • Philadelphia

3 Eves Dr Ste 303
Marlton, NJ 08053
(856) 596-7179
Fax: (856) 596-6895
Email: philadelphia@hcrnetwork.com
Web: www.healthcarerecruiters.com

Description: Executive search firm specializing in healthcare positions.

Key Contact - Specialty:
Mr. Frank Rosamilia, President - *High level*

Functions: Generalist, Senior Mgmt., Nurses, Advertising, Sales Mgmt., CFO's, MIS Mgmt., Engineering

Industries: Generalist, Drugs Mfg., Computer Equip., Biotech, Healthcare

HealthCare Recruiters Int'l • New York

455 Electronics Pkwy Ste 208 Bldg 2
Liverpool, NY 13088
(315) 453-4080
Fax: (315) 453-9525
Email: newyork@hcrnetwork.com
Web: www.healthcarerecruiters.com

Description: Executive recruitment for medical, surgical, pharmaceutical, bio tech, and clinical based positions. Executive management, sales, marketing, clinical specialists, and clinical professionals. Executive bio tech retainer positions. High end sales and marketing positions.

Key Contact - Specialty:
Mr. Dean McNitt, President - *Healthcare*

Functions: Healthcare

Industries: Chemicals, Drugs Mfg., Medical Devices, Computer Equip., Services, Pharm Svcs., Equip Svcs., Software, Biotech, Healthcare

HealthCare Recruiters Int'l • Cincinnati Inc

10 N Locust St Ste C-1
Oxford, OH 45056
(513) 523-8004
Fax: (513) 523-9004
Email: ohio@hcrnetwork.com
Web: www.healthcarerecruiters.com

Description: We are specialists in working with medical manufacturers, managed care organizations, hospitals, and other health care facilities, providing the expertise they need to employee at Executive Levels, Manufacturing, R&D, Information Technology, Finance, Sales & Marketing, as well as other positions.

Key Contact - Specialty:
Mr. Steve Darby, CPC, President - *Healthcare*

Functions: Healthcare

Industries: Drugs Mfg., Medical Devices, Pharm Svcs., Accounting, Mgmt. Consulting, HR Services, Biotech, Healthcare

Professional Associations: NAPS, OSSA

HealthCare Recruiters Int'l • Pittsburgh

428 Forbes Ave
600 Lawyers Bldg
Pittsburgh, PA 15219
(412) 261-2244
(800) 875-5339
Fax: (412) 261-3577
Email: pittsburgh@hcrnetwork.com
Web: www.healthcarerecruiters.com

Description: We are part of a national network of over 30 offices across the country serving the healthcare industry. Linked by our client candidate referral system database we help companies and medical facilities find the best professionals in a confidential manner.

Key Contact:
Ms. Helen Lynch, President/Owner

Functions: Generalist, Healthcare, Sales & Mktg., R&D, Engineering, Minorities, Technicians, Int'l.

Industries: Generalist, Drugs Mfg., Medical Devices, Pharm Svcs., Insurance, Biotech, Healthcare

HealthCare Recruiters Int'l • Midsouth

356 New Byhalia Rd Ste 2
Collierville, TN 38017
(901) 853-0900
Fax: (901) 853-6500
Email: midsouth@hcrnetwork.com
Web: www.healthcarerecruiters.com

Description: Specializing in the healthcare industry. Pharmaceutical-sales, marketing, management, regulatory affairs, compliance. Medical-sales, marketing, management. Hospital-administration-medical engineering. All positions pharmacy.

Key Contact - Specialty:
Mr. Jeb Blanchard, Owner - *Healthcare, medical*

Functions: Product Dev., Healthcare, Sales & Mktg., Mkt. Research, Engineering

Industries: Drugs Mfg., Medical Devices, Pharm Svcs., Software, Biotech, Healthcare

Professional Associations: NAPS, TAPS

Networks: National Personnel Assoc (NPA)

HealthCare Recruiters Int'l • Northwest

321 Park Pl Ste G-116
Kirkland, WA 98033
(425) 576-5115
Fax: (425) 576-5225
Email: northwest@hcrnetwork.com
Web: www.hcrintl.com

Description: Provides customized professional and executive recruiting services to match a healthcare company's unique personnel needs with qualified candidates to build a winning team.

Key Contact - Specialty:
Mr. David C. Garland, President/Owner - *Healthcare*

Salary minimum: $30,000

Functions: Generalist, General Mgmt., Middle Mgmt., Sales & Mktg.

Industries: Drugs Mfg., Medical Devices, Pharm Svcs., Software, Biotech, Healthcare, Hospitals, Long-term Care

Professional Associations: MMA, NAPS

Healthcare Resources Group

3945 SE 15th St Ste 101
Del City, OK 73115
(405) 677-7872
Fax: (405) 672-5053
Email: dan.smith@juno.com

Description: Contingency search firm specializing in the medical field for sales representatives of medical equipment, implants, devices and supplies. Other non-medical sales on occasion. We also help sales people transition from non-medical to medical sales. Nationally affiliated with the First Interview Company.

Key Contact - Specialty:
Mr. Dan Smith, Owner - *Sales, healthcare non-sales*

Functions: Healthcare, Sales Mgmt.

Industries: Generalist, Medical Devices, Pharm Svcs.

Networks: First Interview Network (FIN)

Healthcare Search Associates

11565 Laurel Canyon Blvd Ste 208
Mission Hills, CA 91340
(818) 838-1311
Fax: (818) 838-2010
Email: rasksearch@aol.com

Description: We recruit healthcare professionals throughout the country for managed care, hospitals, skilled nursing, home health and all other healthcare facilities. Listed by the Los Angeles Business Journal as one of the largest firms in Los Angeles county specializing in healthcare recruiting.

Key Contact - Specialty:
Mr. Gregorius K. Balk, President - *Healthcare*
Mr. John Raskin, Director of Account Services - *Healthcare*
Mr. Tony Sands, Senior Account Executive - *Healthcare, nursing, home health, skilled nursing*
Mr. John Grace, Senior Account Executive - *Healthcare*

Salary minimum: $40,000

Functions: Generalist

Industries: Healthcare

Branches:
12304 Santa Monica Blvd Ste 220
Los Angeles, CA 90025
(310) 207-0979
Email: drscorner@aol.com
Key Contact:
Mr. Greg Balk, Office Manager

HealthExec Search Consultants Inc

PO Box 2363
Darien, IL 60561
(630) 960-9690
Fax: (630) 960-2368
Email: healthexecjobs@aol.com
Web: www.healthexecjobs.com

Description: Our search expertise for mid- to upper level managers, consultants and clinical professionals crosses all functional areas in healthcare. Our clients include local, regional and national managed care, medical supply, e-commerce, pharmaceutical, biotechnology, and healthcare consulting organizations. We also conduct searches in traditional healthcare delivery systems, hospitals, physician practices, and national healthcare associations.

Key Contact:
Ms. Julie Marshall

Salary minimum: $50,000

Functions: General Mgmt., Healthcare, Physicians, Nurses, Health Admin., Sales & Mktg., Finance

Industries: Healthcare

Professional Associations: AHA

HealthSearch Associates

19632 Club House Rd Ste 525
Gaithersburg, MD 20886
(301) 258-2656
Fax: (301) 963-0250

Description: We offer life cycle recruiting services to most health care providers. Searches are for mid level and senior management positions in operations, clinical, finance, IT, HR, marketing and fund raising. We are adept at working with either not-for-profit or investor owned environments and all size organizations. Management consulting services include staffing long-term specific recruitment areas or projects, advertising/media development and management, recruitment process development or improvement, and locum tenens HR leadership.

Key Contact:
Mr. Ted Schneider, Vice President

Salary minimum: $50,000

Functions: Physicians, Nurses, Allied Health, Health Admin., CFO's, MIS Mgmt., Systems Implem., Mgmt. Consultants

Industries: Insurance, Healthcare

The Healthsearch Group Inc

109 Croton Ave
Ossining, NY 10562
(914) 941-6107
Fax: (914) 941-1748
Email: healthsearch@healthsearchgroup.com
Web: www.healthsearchgroup.com

Description: We are one of the largest recruiting companies in the Northeast with a healthcare specialty. We pride ourselves on the service we provide our clients and the effectiveness of our search process.

Key Contact - Specialty:
Mr. Alan Gordon, President - *Healthcare*
Mr. Jeff Gordon, Vice President - *Healthcare*

Salary minimum: $40,000

Functions: Generalist, General Mgmt., Healthcare, Physicians, Nurses, Allied Health, Health Admin., Finance

Industries: Generalist, Insurance, Healthcare

Professional Associations: AHHRA

Healthsearch USA Inc

5150 N 16th St Ste B232
Phoenix, AZ 85016
(602) 266-4777
Fax: (602) 266-4477
Email: info@healthsearchusa.com
Web: www.healthsearchusa.com

Description: We are a physician executive search firm. We specialize in permanent and locum tenens. We place physicians, physician assistants, and nurse practitioners.

Key Contact:
Mr. Steven Silverstein, MBA, Chief Executive Officer

Functions: Physicians

Industries: Generalist

Professional Associations: NAPR

HeartBeat Medical Inc

9000 Cypress Green Dr Ste 103
Jacksonville, FL 32256
(904) 287-5557
Fax: (904) 731-5578
Email: hbm@heartbeatmedical.com
Web: www.heartbeatmedical.com

Description: Emphasis on west coast for start-up medical device, R&D and manufacturing companies. Specialize in R&D, Mfg., quality, regulatory, clinical and operations. Fundraising available.

Key Contact - Specialty:
Mr. Scott Bailey, President - *Medical device, R&D, manufacturing, operations*
Ms. Evelyn Bailey, Secretary/Treasurer
Mr. Ed Browning, Senior Recruiter - *Medical device, quality, regulatory, clinical*
Mr. Justin Killebrew, Executive Recruiter - *Medical device*

Functions: Generalist, Mfg., Product Dev., Quality, Sales & Mktg., R&D, Engineering

Industries: Medical Devices, Mgmt. Consulting, HR Services

Professional Associations: ASQ, RAPS

Networks: First Interview Network (FIN)

Heartland National Medical Search

3410 Bellwood Ln
Glenview, IL 60025
(847) 832-1716
(888) 832-7594
Fax: (847) 832-1721
Email: hlmedsrch@aol.com

Description: Specializes in recruitment and placement of physicians and BSN+ nurses in clinical, management and administrative positions. Part of 180 member network of recruiters nationwide. All fees are employer-paid. Our services are free to candidates and confidential.

Key Contact - Specialty:
Ms. Karen Winterburn, President - *Physicians, nurse practitioners, allied health*

Salary minimum: $40,000

Functions: Generalist

Industries: Healthcare

Networks: Recruiters Professional Network (RPN)

E M Heath & Company

233 Needham St Paragon Twrs Fl 3
Newton, MA 02464
(617) 527-8839
Fax: (617) 527-0116
Email: mheath@emheath.com
Web: www.emheath.com

Description: Our firm offers a comprehensive service, which includes retained search, contingency search, and contracting for financial, marketing, and engineering positions. Our areas of concentration include MIS management, systems analysis and design, systems development, integration, product development, product engineering, and sales and marketing management.

Key Contact - Specialty:
Ms. Myrna Heath, CPC, Managing Director - *Finance, marketing, engineering*

Salary minimum: $75,000

Functions: Product Dev., Sales & Mktg., CFO's, IT, Engineering

Industries: Mfg., Chemicals, Misc. Financial, Communications, Telecoms, Digital, Fiber Optic, Network Infrastructure, Mfg. SW, Marketing SW, Networking, Comm. SW, System SW, Biotech

Networks: Top Echelon Network

HEC Group

911 Golf Links Rd Ste 207
Ancaster, ON L9K 1H9
Canada
(905) 648-0013
Fax: (905) 648-7016

Email: hec@hec-group.com
Web: www.hec-group.com

Description: International recruiters with affiliates in most major cities in North America. Major areas of expertise include manufacturing, high-tech and IT positions. Present management has been with company since 1976.

Key Contact - Specialty:
Mr. Robert Leek, General Manager - *Technical*
Ms. Karen Clarke, Partner - *Human resources, administration, sales & marketing*

Functions: Generalist, General Mgmt., Mfg., Sales & Mktg., HR Mgmt., Finance, IT, Engineering

Industries: Generalist, Mfg., Plastics, Rubber, Computer Equip., Aerospace, Software

Professional Associations: APPAC, RON

Networks: National Personnel Assoc (NPA)

Thomas E Hedefine Associates
21 Ardagh St
Toronto, ON M6S 1Y2
Canada
(416) 604-9444
Email: hedefine@sprint.ca

Description: We provide national recruitment activities for leasing finance companies' asset based lenders from line marketing, risk management, and senior management positions.

Key Contact - Specialty:
Mr. Thomas E. Hedefine, President - *Equipment finance, equipment leasing, asset based lending*
Dr. Kathleen P. Shea, Vice President - *Corporate banking, finance*

Salary minimum: $40,000

Functions: Generalist, Credit, M&A, Risk Mgmt.

Industries: Generalist, Finance, Banking, Invest. Banking, Venture Cap., Misc. Financial, Equip Svcs.

Hedlund Corp
1 IBM Plz Ste 2618
Chicago, IL 60611
(312) 755-1400
Email: search@hedlundcorp.com
Web: www.hedlundcorp.com

Description: National management search firm specializing in recruiting consultants.

Key Contact:
Mr. David Hedlund, President - *Management consultants*
Ms. Jean Wittner, Senior Recruiter - *Management consultants*
Ms. Peggy Meller, Senior Recruiter - *Management consultants*
Ms. Ingrid Ramos, Senior Recruiter - *Management consultants*
Ms. Marianne Grierson, Senior Recruiter
Ms. Katherine McGown, Research Assistant
Mr. Keith Pabley, Senior Recruiter

Salary minimum: $70,000

Functions: Generalist, Mfg., Materials, Healthcare, Finance, IT, Mgmt. Consultants

Industries: Generalist, Energy, Utilities, Mfg., Transportation, Finance, Media, Software, Healthcare

Jay Heino Company LLC
7 Penn Plz Ste 830
New York, NY 10001-3900
(212) 279-6780
Fax: (212) 279-6784
Email: jayheino@netzero.net

Description: We have been tax placement specialists for over 24 years, servicing retainer, as

well as contingency clientele. We are one out of a dozen executive search firms, who specialize exclusively in the placement of tax professionals. Our market includes all industries within the US and abroad.

Key Contact - Specialty:
Mr. Jay J. Heino, President - *Tax*

Salary minimum: $50,000

Functions: Taxes

Industries: Generalist, Construction, Mfg., Transportation, Retail, Finance, Services, Media, Communications, Insurance

Heller, Kil Associates Inc
2060 S Halifax Dr
Daytona Beach, FL 32118
(904) 761-5100
Fax: (904) 252-1545
Email: pheller@bellsouth.net

Description: Executive search and professional staffing to the automotive and heavy duty truck parts/components industries specializing in sales, marketing, engineering, quality and manufacturing management to the general manager and presidential level.

Key Contact - Specialty:
Mr. Phillip Heller, President - *Sales, marketing, general management*

Salary minimum: $50,000

Functions: Generalist, General Mgmt., Mfg., Plant Mgmt., Quality, Sales & Mktg., M&A, Engineering

Industries: Motor Vehicles

Branches:
306 Robert Dr
Normal, IL 61761
(309) 454-7077
Fax: (309) 454-8227
Email: hklshapiro@aol.com
Key Contact - Specialty:
Mr. Larry Shapiro - *Engineering, manufacturing management*

Hemingway Personnel Inc
1301 Dove St Ste 960
Newport Beach, CA 92660
(949) 851-1228
Fax: (949) 253-3761
Email: lara@hemingwaypersonnel.com
Web: www.hemingwaypersonnel.com

Description: We provide executive search, contract services, and temporaries serving the accounting and finance professions. We also supply comprehensive accounting testing software to search, temporary firms, and internal recruiting departments.

Key Contact - Specialty:
Ms. Dolores Lara, President - *Accounting, finance*
Mr. Arne Beruldsen, CEO - *Software sales, software support*

Salary minimum: $35,000

Functions: CFO's, Budgeting, Credit, M&A, Risk Mgmt., MIS Mgmt., Systems Dev., Systems Support, Network Admin., DB Admin.

Industries: Generalist

Professional Associations: AAHCPA, ASWA, CUIAA, IMA, NAWBO

Kay Henry Inc
1200 Bustleton Pike Ste 5
Feasterville, PA 19053
(215) 355-1600
Fax: (215) 355-4395
Email: esassani@kayhenryinc.com

Description: All areas of consumer and business-to-business advertising, public relations and marketing as they apply to agencies and corporations including direct marketing, pharmaceutical, ag chem and animal health.

Key Contact - Specialty:
Ms. Kay Henry, President - *Advertising, public relations, marketing*
Ms. Shelley Miller, CPC, Vice President - *Advertising, public relations, marketing*
Ms. Marianne Bellina, Consultant - *Advertising, public relations, marketing*

Salary minimum: $30,000

Functions: Generalist

Industries: Advertising, Publishing, New Media

Professional Associations: AMWA, MAAPC, NAMA, PCA

Henson Enterprises Inc
15311 E Redrock Dr
Fountain Hills, AZ 85268-5816
(480) 816-9911
Fax: (480) 816-9966
Email: jeff@hensonenterprises.com
Web: www.hensonenterprises.com

Description: Dedicated to developing lasting relationships with our client companies through performance, integrity, and professionalism. Our specialists generate enhanced results due to their direct experience and extensive knowledge of select industries. Search focus and expertise includes executive-level assignments in a variety of functional areas for the food, consumer products and high-technology industries.

Key Contact - Specialty:
Mr. Jeff Henson, President/General Manager - *Food processing, consumer products, high technology*

Salary minimum: $65,000

Functions: Generalist

Industries: Food, Bev., Tobacco, Computer Equip., Consumer Elect., Software

Heritage Pacific Corp
14172 Klee Dr Ste 500
Irvine, CA 92606
(800) 927-1566
Fax: (800) 927-1501
Email: gdraper@home.com
Web: www.garydraper.com

Description: Twenty-two years' serving the paper industry exclusively.

Key Contact - Specialty:
Mr. Gary Draper, Managing Director - *Paper industry*

Salary minimum: $50,000

Functions: General Mgmt., Middle Mgmt., Mfg., Production, Plant Mgmt., Sales Mgmt., Engineering

Industries: Paper

Professional Associations: CSP, PIMA, TAPPI

Heritage Search Group Inc
7687 Wyldwood Way Ste 100
Port St. Lucie, FL 34986
(561) 489-5300
Fax: (561) 489-5301
Email: heritage@adelphia.net

Description: Specialize in consumer packaged goods marketing and/or related fields both international and domestic. Different and unique positions. Normally small to medium sized companies. Also place high caliber people in consulting firms, small to medium, in all disciplines.

Key Contact - Specialty:
Mr. Philip Tripician, President - *Consumer packaged goods, marketing*

Salary minimum: $65,000

Functions: Generalist, Directors, Middle Mgmt., Advertising, Mkt. Research, Mktg. Mgmt., Sales Mgmt., Minorities

Industries: Generalist, Food, Bev., Tobacco, Paper, Chemicals, Soap, Perf., Cosmtcs., Drugs Mfg., Mgmt. Consulting, Hospitality

Professional Associations: NAER

Branches:
7932 S Cedar St
Littleton, CO 80120
Fax: (303) 795-2143
Key Contact - Specialty:
Mr. Don Harper, Manager - *Consumer packaged goods (marketing)*

J J Herlihy & Associates Inc
9608 Donna Ave
Northridge, CA 91324
(818) 349-8211
Email: jjherlihy@aol.com

Description: Our firm is primarily oriented towards the sales management, marketing, and general management in the high-tech fields. We are also active in the senior technical roles of the greater computer field.

Key Contact - Specialty:
Mr. Jack Herlihy, CEO - *Sales management, marketing (high technology), technical positions (consulting, TCD, systems integration, e-commerce)*

Salary minimum: $75,000

Functions: Generalist, Senior Mgmt., Middle Mgmt., Mktg. Mgmt., Sales Mgmt., MIS Mgmt., Systems Analysis, Systems Implem.

Industries: Generalist, Computer Equip., Mgmt. Consulting, HR Services, New Media, Software

The Herring Group
600 Pine Forest Dr Ste 130
Maumelle, AR 72113
(501) 851-1234
(501) 851-2962
Fax: (501) 851-7753
Email: th@herringgroup.net
Web: www.herringgroup.net

Description: We are a national recruiter search firm, which has extensive experience in the placement of executives and professionals, ranging from key supervisory positions to vice president and president levels.

Key Contact - Specialty:
Mr. Bill Herring, President - *Transportation, distribution, HR, generalist*
Mr. Tony Horne, Sr Vice President, Operations - *Transportation, distribution, HR, generalist*

Functions: Senior Mgmt., Purchasing, Materials Plng., Distribution, Sales Mgmt., HR Mgmt., CFO's

Industries: Generalist

J D Hersey & Associates
1695 Old Henderson Rd
Columbus, OH 43220
(614) 459-4555
Fax: (614) 459-4544
Email: info1@jdhersey.com
Web: www.jdhersey.com

Description: We specialize in the confidential recruitment of professionals within the Internet, retail, computer, and catalog industries. A typical search targets mid-level to senior-level management

in sales, marketing, merchandising, or operations. Our dedication and professionalism has fostered many long-term relationships.

Key Contact - Specialty:
Mr. Jeffrey D. Hersey, President - *Generalist*

Functions: Directors, Senior Mgmt., Middle Mgmt., Purchasing, Distribution, Sales & Mktg., Mkt. Research, HR Mgmt.

Industries: Wholesale, Retail, Services, Mgmt. Consulting, Media, Advertising, Publishing, New Media, Telecoms, Software

H Hertner Associates Inc
6600 Cowpen Rd Ste 220
Lakes Park Plz
Miami, FL 33014
(305) 556-8882
Fax: (305) 556-5650
Email: hhertner@bellsouth.net
Web: www.legalrecruiting.com

Description: President has 30 years of recruiting expertise, together with the other consultants, work as a team to service corporation needs for in-house general counsel positions, law firms for partners, associates, mergers and legal disciplines.

Key Contact - Specialty:
Mr. Herbert H. Hertner, President - *Legal*
Mr. David J. Block, Esq., JD, Consultant - *Legal*
Ms. Patricia A. Ash, Esq., JD, LLM, Consultant - *Legal*
Mrs. Danielle G. Bowser, Esq., JD, Consultant - *Legal*
Mrs. Pamela R. Hertner, Consultant - *Legal*
Mrs. Donna H. Huck, Consultant - *Legal*
Ms. Karah H. Ashleigh, Consultant - *Legal*
Mr. Charles P. Gallopo, Consultant - *Legal*

Salary minimum: $50,000

Functions: Legal

Industries: Generalist

Professional Associations: NALSC

Robert Hess & Associates Inc
470 Lakeview Cir BRR
Silverthorne, CO 80498
(970) 262-9388
Fax: (970) 262-9432
Email: robhess@robhess.com

Description: We are national recruiters specializing in the homebuilding industry.

Key Contact - Specialty:
Mr. Robert W. Hess, President - *Real estate*

Salary minimum: $50,000

Functions: Generalist

Industries: Real Estate

Hessel Associates Inc
70 W Red Oak Ln
White Plains, NY 10604
(914) 697-7522
Fax: (914) 697-7524
Email: haisearch@aol.com
Web: www.haisearch.com

Description: We are an experienced team of personnel consultants specializing in the recruitment of financial, marketing, and operations professionals with particular emphasis on the financial services industries including banking, brokerage, and insurance.

Key Contact:
Mr. Jeffrey J. Hessel, Principal

Salary minimum: $50,000

Functions: Generalist, Finance, CFO's, Budgeting, Cash Mgmt., M&A, Risk Mgmt., Mgmt. Consultants

Industries: Generalist, Mfg., Finance, Banking, Invest. Banking, Brokers, Misc. Financial, Insurance

Heywood Associates LLC
60 E 42nd St Ste 1822
New York, NY 10165
(212) 350-9327
Email: s.gee@heywoodassociates.com
Web: www.heywoodassociates.com

Description: We are the number one global leader in recruitment. With seven offices throughout the UK and New York and with plans to open additional offices in Australia, Hong Kong, the Americas, and Europe, we truly have a global reach and have a strong track record in delivery.

Key Contact - Specialty:
Mr. Simon Gee, CEO
Mr. Randy Kishun, Principal - Technology - *Technology recruitment to recruitment*
Mr. Richard Gee, Principal - *Professional services*
Mr. Jason Salz, Principal - *Technical recruitment to recruitment*
Mr. Keith Poole, Branch Manager
Mrs. Lisa Clegg, Branch Manager
Mr. Alex Gee, Branch Manager
Mr. Jason Pedlow, Branch Manager - Bristol
Mr. Neil Goble, Principal
Mr. Richard Barker, Principal - Technical, UK - *Technical recruitment to recruitment*
Ms. Olga Boylan, Operations Manager - Dublin
Mr. Andrew Mountney, Operations Manager - Sydney
Ms. Jackie Bell, Principal - Clerical, UK - *Clerical*
Mr. John Matheson, Principal - Professional Services - *Professional services*
Ms. Penny Lawrence, Operations Manager
Mr. Dave Stebbings, Principal - Technology - *Technology*

Functions: HR Mgmt.

Industries: Generalist

Professional Associations: ASA

Hidde & Associates
427 S Boston Ave Ste 913
Tulsa, OK 74103
(918) 749-1530
(800) 538-8516
Fax: (918) 587-7007
Email: hidde@aol.com
Web: www.hiddeassociates.qpg.com

Description: Provide contingency recruiting throughout the United States for all levels of management, marketing, sales, information technology and finance. In addition, provide outplacement services and consulting services to a diverse client base.

Key Contact - Specialty:
Mr. Robert Hidde, Senior Partner - *Executive, management, marketing, sales, finance, outplacement*
Ms. Victoria Reynolds-Hidde, Partner - *Information technology, management, marketing, finance, outplacement*

Salary minimum: $45,000

Functions: Generalist

Industries: Generalist

Higbee Associates Inc
112 Rowayton Ave
Rowayton, CT 06853
(203) 853-7600
Fax: (203) 853-2426
Email: rhigbee@higbeeassociates.com
Web: www.higbeeassociates.com

Description: Retained specialist to the consulting industry at senior-level; global reach; financial services, telecommunications, healthcare, insurance, pharmaceutical as it relates to strategy, operations and information technology. ERP systems (PeopleSoft).

Key Contact:
Mr. R. W. Higbee, President - *Management consultants (principal & partner)*
Mr. Robert Lawrence, Sr Vice President

Salary minimum: $75,000

Functions: Mgmt. Consultants

Industries: Medical Devices, Consumer Elect., Finance, Banking, Mgmt. Consulting, Biotech, Healthcare

Professional Associations: IHRIM

B W Higgins Inc
6828 Alnwick Ct
Indianapolis, IN 46220
(317) 842-6346
Fax: (317) 578-1005
Email: bwhinc@aol.com
Web: www.bwhiggins.com

Description: An established and recognized national search firm dedicated to all facets of the commercial insurance industry, e.g., carrier, brokerage, reinsurance, alternative risk, corporate risk management, e-insurance

Key Contact - Specialty:
Mr. Bruce W. Higgins, Principal - *Insurance*

Salary minimum: $90,000

Functions: Generalist

Industries: Insurance

High Tech Opportunities Inc
264B N Broadway Ste 206
Salem, NH 03079
(603) 893-9486
Fax: (603) 893-9492
Email: hightech@mv.mv.com
Web: www.mv.com/hightech/

Description: Our firm specializes in recruiting for electronic design automation, semiconductor, microprocessor design, and computer hardware professionals, nationally.

Key Contact - Specialty:
Mr. Ron Cooper, CPC, President - *Microelectronics, CAD/EDA, sales & marketing, applications, design*
Mr. Michael Buckley - *Microelectronics, integrated circuits, logic & CPU design, CAE software*
Mr. Ross Cooper - *Microelectronics, RFIC, MMIC design, ASIC*

Salary minimum: $50,000

Functions: Sales & Mktg., Engineering

Industries: Generalist, Electronic, Elec. Components, Digital, Wireless, Network Infrastructure

Professional Associations: NNEAPS

Networks: Top Echelon Network

High Tech Professionals Inc
2775 S Main St Ste G
Kennesaw, GA 30144
(770) 420-7440
Fax: (770) 420-7126
Email: info@htprof.com
Web: www.htprof.com

Description: We are an executive and technical search firm specializing in data warehouse and data management positions. We also work with telecommunication placements and have a niche practice working with Israeli companies.

Key Contact - Specialty:
Mr. Todd S. Porter, President - *Information technology*

Salary minimum: $75,000

Functions: Generalist, Sales & Mktg., IT, DB Admin.

Industries: Generalist, Communications, Software, Biotech

High Tech Recruiters
220 2nd St
Langley, WA 98260
(800) 644-9164
(360) 579-1314
Fax: (888) 944-0426
Email: recruiter@hightechrecruiters.com
Web: www.hightechrecruiters.com

Description: We provide executive search and senior management placement. We believe in finding, hiring, and retaining the right employees. We provide employee loyalty building and leadership team building process and services.

Key Contact - Specialty:
Ms. Lynn Launer, Founder/President
Ms. Barbara Launer, Executive Recruiter - *Technical*

Salary minimum: $60,000

Functions: Generalist

Industries: Computer Equip., E-commerce, Software

Professional Associations: WSA

High Tech Staffing Group
630 NW Freemont
Camas, WA 98607
(360) 210-4771
(888) 420-1122
Fax: (503) 905-6039
Email: jobs@htsg.com
Web: www.htsg.com

Description: We are a Portland, OR based recruiting firm that serves the needs of the high-tech industry in Oregon, Washington, Idaho and California. We provide permanent and temporary placement of applicants and retained searches for executive or managerial positions. Our emphasis is on IT, software and hardware engineering personnel and executive and managerial positions.

Key Contact - Specialty:
Mr. Frank Michael Odia, President - *IT, hardware, software, executive & managerial personnel*

Salary minimum: $65,000

Functions: Generalist, MIS Mgmt., Systems Analysis, Systems Dev., Systems Implem., Systems Support, Mgmt. Consultants

Industries: Generalist, Computer Equip., Test, Measure Equip., Software

Professional Associations: RON

Networks: Inter-City Personnel Assoc (IPA)

High Technology Recruiters Inc
PO Box 1905
Rockville, MD 20849-1905
(301) 315-8910
Email: bob@hitechrecruiters.net
Web: www.hitechrecruiters.net

Description: Our firm specializes in network related information technology fields including data communications, Internet~intranet, e-commerce and telecommunications. High-technology recruiters focuses on staffing positions at all levels for sales, technical support, professional services, and marketing positions nationwide. Experience,

expertise and knowledge specialization and background consultative relationship.

Key Contact - Specialty:
Mr. Bob Bryer, President - *Sales, networking, internet related technologies*

Functions: Sales & Mktg.

Industries: Computer Equip., Telecoms, Government, Software

Networks: National Personnel Assoc (NPA)

Highland & Associates
3830 Valley Center Dr Bldg 705 Ste 646
San Diego, CA 92130
(858) 794-1782
Fax: (858) 794-8209
Email: highlandandassoc@aol.com
Web: www.highlandandassociates.com

Description: We have over 15 years' experience in the commercial real estate industry from east to west coast. Specializing in real estate directors, construction, asset and property management, leasing, finance and administration positions.

Key Contact - Specialty:
Ms. Maryjo Highland, Partner - *Real estate*

Salary minimum: $40,000

Functions: Generalist, Senior Mgmt., Admin. Svcs.

Industries: Generalist, Construction, Real Estate

Professional Associations: ICSC

Highland Concord
(a subsidiary of Mitchell/Wolfson Assoc)
600 Central Ave Ste 375
Highland Park, IL 60035
(847) 266-1100
Email: director@highlandconcord.com
Web: www.highlandconcord.com

Description: We are a mid-to-upper-level contingency recruiting firm specializing in insurance, actuarial, and risk management recruiting. The firm is based in the Chicago area with branch offices in Connecticut and Texas.

Key Contact:
Ms. Ronna Cohen, Vice President

Salary minimum: $50,000

Functions: Risk Mgmt.

Industries: Generalist, Insurance

Highlander Search
210 W Friendly Ave Ste 200
Greensboro, NC 27401
(336) 333-9886
Email: jphighlander@mindspring.com

Description: Fifteen years in executive search, technical recruiting and outplacement consulting has yielded wide industry knowledge and understanding of modern business challenges and goals.

Key Contact - Specialty:
Mr. Jeffrey M. Penley, CPC, President - *Furniture manufacturing, furniture retail, automotive manufacturing*

Salary minimum: $50,000

Functions: Generalist, General Mgmt.

Industries: Lumber, Furniture

Hilleren & Associates Inc
3800 W 80th St Ste 880
Minneapolis, MN 55431
(612) 956-9090
Fax: (952) 956-9009
Email: jerry@hilleren.com
Web: www.hilleren.com

Description: We are a Minneapolis search firm specializing in the building of superior sales and marketing teams. Our greatest expertise is with medical and pharmaceutical manufacturers, advanced technology and service industries.

Key Contact:
Mr. Jerry Hilleren, President

Functions: Healthcare, Sales & Mktg.

Industries: Software, Biotech, Healthcare

Professional Associations: MAPS

Networks: First Interview Network (FIN)

The Hindman Group Inc
4135 Blackhawk Plz Cir Ste 100
Danville, CA 94506
(800) 800-9220
(925) 736-9280
Fax: (800) 241-9220
Email: thgsearch@thehindmangroup.com
Web: www.thehindmangroup.com

Description: Executive search consultants to the food distribution, manufacturing and logistics industries specializing in the recruitment of mid- to top level executives. Also IT/e-commerce.

Key Contact - Specialty:
Mr. Jeffrey J. Hindman, CPC, President - *Food manufacturing, distribution & logistics, IT, e-commerce*

Salary minimum: $85,000

Functions: Generalist, General Mgmt., Mfg., Materials, Healthcare, Sales & Mktg., Finance, IT, Minorities, Int'l.

Industries: Agri., Forestry, Mining, Mfg., Food, Bev., Tobacco, Transportation, Wholesale, Retail, Finance, Services, Accounting, Mgmt. Consulting, HR Services, Hospitality, Software, Biotech

Hintz Associates
PO Box 442
Valhalla, NY 10595-1831
(914) 761-4227
Fax: (914) 948-8630
Email: geohintz@aol.com

Description: Our specialties are cost reduction analysts and internal/external consultants. Our assignments include consultants who specialize in supply chain management, methods improvement and short interval scheduling consultants, lean manufacturing techniques, and industrial engineering.

Key Contact:
Mr. George Hintz, President - *Consultants*
Mr. George Jefferies, Vice President - *Sales consultants*
Ms. DeAnne Cerreta, Research Coordinator
Ms. Dorothy DiMaggio, Administration

Salary minimum: $35,000

Functions: Generalist, Quality, Productivity, Materials, Materials Plng., Sales Mgmt., Training, Systems Analysis, Systems Implem., Mgmt. Consultants

Industries: Generalist, Medical Devices, Motor Vehicles, Misc. Mfg., Banking, Mgmt. Consulting, Insurance, Healthcare

Professional Associations: AOPA, ASTD

Hire Impact Inc
17603 E Peakview Ave
Aurora, CO 80016
(303) 400-8958
Fax: (303) 400-4542
Email: jackie@hireimpact.com
Web: www.hireimpact.com

Description: We are an executive search firm delivering key management, sales, and recruiting talent to select information technology clients. Our specialties include: IT, staffing, and the consulting industry.

Key Contact - Specialty:
Ms. Jacqueline R. Nairne, President/CEO - *Management, sales, IT*

Functions: Sales Mgmt.

Industries: Services, Software

HireKnowledge
100 Boylston St 1070
Boston, MA 02116
(617) 350-3033
Fax: (617) 350-3076
Email: boston@hireknowledge.com
Web: www.hireknowledge.com

Description: We are a staffing firm that specializes in the placement of high-end marketing, creative, and technical professionals.

Key Contact - Specialty:
Ms. Carrie Baris, Recruiting Manager - *Graphic design/project manager*

Functions: IT, Systems Support, Graphic Artists

Industries: Generalist

HireLogix Inc
3800 Steels Ave W
Woodbridge, ON L4l4G9
Canada
(416) 927-1010
Fax: (416) 927-1615
Email: info@hirelogix.com
Web: www.hirelogix.com

Description: High-technology electronics, software, hardware engineering and management.

Key Contact:
Mr. Marcello Perry, Director

Salary minimum: $50,000

Functions: Generalist, Directors, Product Dev., Sales Mgmt., MIS Mgmt., Engineering

Industries: Generalist, Computer Equip., Software

HireStrategy
12021 Sunset Hills Rd Ste 550
Reston, VA 20190
(703) 707-1835
Fax: (703) 707-1836
Email: paul@hirestrategy.com
Web: www.hirestrategy.com

Description: Our firm is an executive recruiting firm that supports sales, technology, and finance and accounting businesses and professionals. Our integrated staffing solution focuses on professionals at both the leadership and individual contributor level and from executive management teams to the staff that supports those teams.

Key Contact - Specialty:
Mr. Paul Villella, President & CEO
Mr. Hector Velez, Vice President - *Technology, sales*
Mr. Chris Owen, Vice President - *Accounting & finance*

Functions: Directors, Senior Mgmt., Middle Mgmt., Sales Mgmt., CFO's, Taxes, MIS Mgmt., Systems Dev., Systems Implem.

Industries: Construction, Food, Bev., Tobacco, Finance, Mgmt. Consulting, E-commerce, IT Implementation, Communications, Telecoms, Digital, Wireless, Network Infrastructure, Software, Accounting SW, Database SW, Development SW, Security SW

Professional Associations: NVTC

Ruth Hirsch Associates Inc
201 E 66th St Ste 7C
New York, NY 10021
(212) 396-0200
Fax: (212) 396-0679
Email: info@ruthhirschassociates.com
Web: www.ruthhirschassociates.com

Description: We are a specialty firm limited to the placement of registered architects, facilities and construction managers, owner's representatives, and interior designers in the NY Metropolitan area.

Key Contact - Specialty:
Ms. Ruth Hirsch, President - *Architecture, interior design, construction, facilities management*

Salary minimum: $65,000

Functions: Generalist

Industries: Construction, Non-classifiable

Professional Associations: AIA

HLH Int'l Inc
(also known as MRI of Aptos)
188 Quail Canyon
Larkin Valley, CA 95076
(831) 688-5200
Fax: (831) 722-7999
Email: hendersoncathy@hotmail.com
Web: www.mriconstruction.com

Description: Consistently ranks in top 5% of all recruiters nationwide. Construction/development specialist in both domestic and international markets. Retained and contingency search.

Key Contact - Specialty:
Ms. Cathy Henderson, Certified Senior Account Manager - *Construction, development*

Salary minimum: $75,000

Functions: Generalist

Industries: Construction, Real Estate

HLR Consulting
2 S Beechwood Rd
Bedford Hills, NY 10507-1712
(914) 242-7300
Fax: (914) 242-7300
Email: gharvey@hlrconsulting.com
Web: www.hlrconsulting.com

Description: An executive search firm specializing in the placement of information technology professionals throughout the New York Tri-State marketplace.

Key Contact - Specialty:
Mr. Gene Harvey, Owner - *Information technology*

Salary minimum: $50,000

Functions: IT, MIS Mgmt., Systems Dev., Systems Implem., Systems Support, Network Admin., DB Admin.

Industries: Finance, Services, Media, Insurance, Software, Healthcare

HM Associates
2 Electronics Ave
Danvers, MA 01923
(978) 762-7474
Fax: (978) 739-9071
Email: hmackenzie@hmassc.com
Web: www.hmassc.com

Description: We provide human resource consulting. We offer retained and contingency search, candidate development and contract recruiting services to the software, hardware and telecommunications industries.

Key Contact - Specialty:
Mr. Hugh MacKenzie, CPC, President - *Software, hardware, marketing, telecommunications*

Salary minimum: $50,000

Functions: Generalist

Industries: Consumer Elect., Test, Measure Equip., Misc. Financial, Defense, Software

Professional Associations: MPPC

HMW Inc
2222 W Spring Creek Pkwy Ste 207B
Plano, TX 75023
(972) 769-0707
Fax: (972) 769-0909
Email: gmartin@hmw-inc.com
Web: www.hmw-inc.com

Description: We are an executive search firm that offer contingency and retainer search for placement within the engineering industry on a national level. We place mostly mid to senior level positions. The types of engineers that we place are: ME, EE, environmental, network, software, hardware, etc.

Key Contact:
Mr. George Martin, CEO
Mr. Phil Wood, President

Functions: Generalist

Industries: Generalist

The Hobart West Group
1608 Walnut St Ste 1702
Philadelphia, PA 19103
(215) 735-9450
Fax: (215) 735-9430
Email: pmcdowan@hobartwest.com
Web: www.hobartwest.com

Description: Personalized approach to every search. Specializing in Fortune 500, legal, healthcare, insurance/HMO and electronics industries.

Key Contact:
Ms. Pat McGowan, General Manager

Functions: Generalist, Admin. Svcs., Legal, Nurses, HR Mgmt., Finance, IT, Technicians

Industries: Generalist, Computer Equip., Finance, Legal, Accounting, Media, Insurance, Healthcare

Hobson Associates
PO Box 278
Cheshire, CT 06410
(203) 272-0227
Fax: (203) 272-1237
Email: hobson@hobsonassoc.com
Web: www.hobsonassoc.com

Description: Our owner is world-renowned industry trainer. We have an aggressive, dynamic, client-oriented approach. Our integrated services are for broad exposure in niche areas. Our specific focus is with sales professionals for high-tech IT clients, as well as the architects, developers, and integrators required for successful implementations. Our services include permanent employees, consultants, and offshore development capabilities.

Key Contact - Specialty:
Mr. Danny Cahill, CPC, President - *Engineering*
Mr. Mark Bassett, CPC, Vice President - *Sales & marketing, high technology*
Mr. Vern Chanski, CPC, Senior Partner - *Information technology, informatics, bioinformatics, wireless, architecture*

Functions: Generalist, IT

Industries: Generalist, Medical Devices, Computer Equip., Misc. Mfg., Mgmt. Consulting, New Media, Wireless, Software, Biotech

Professional Associations: FEI, IMA

Networks: First Interview Network (FIN)

Hochman & Associates Inc
1801 Ave of the Stars Ste 420
Los Angeles, CA 90067
(310) 552-0662
Fax: (310) 552-4650
Email: jhochman@earthlink.net
Web: www.hochmanassociates.com

Description: Networking and disciplined search methodology have consistently allowed us to efficiently find and prepare the perfect match candidates to fill client needs. Extensive, hands-on experience has enhanced Ms. Hochman's ability to complete successful job placements.

Key Contact - Specialty:
Ms. Judith L. Hochman, President - *Finance, banking, investment banking, money management companies, insurance companies*

Salary minimum: $50,000

Functions: Senior Mgmt., Sales & Mktg., Finance, CFO's, Cash Mgmt., M&A, MIS Mgmt.

Industries: Banking, Invest. Banking, Venture Cap., Accounting, Insurance

Hoffman Partnership Group Inc
42 Huntington Ct
Williamsville, NY 14221-5310
(716) 632-3379
(716) 632-1306
Fax: (716) 632-1425
Email: bdhathpg@aol.com
Web: www.hpgrecruit.com

Description: We create long-term client partnerships to consistently fill opportunities in consumer packaged goods (beverage, food, and HBA). Specialize in diversity searches (45% of placements). Expertise in customer team leadership, category management, trade marketing, national accounts and general management.

Key Contact - Specialty:
Mr. Bradley D. Hoffman, President - *Sales & marketing, consumer packaged goods*
Ms. Lisa M. Hoffman, CEO - *Sales & marketing, consumer packaged goods*

Salary minimum: $75,000

Functions: Sales Mgmt.

Industries: Food, Bev., Tobacco, Paper, Soap, Perf., Cosmtcs.

Networks: Top Echelon Network

Hoffman Recruiters
115 Broad St Fl 6
Boston, MA 02110-3032
(617) 535-3700
Fax: (617) 535-3799
Email: contact@hrecruiters.com
Web: www.hrecruiters.com

Description: We are a confidential recruiting service that is free for candidates. Our top priority is being able to understand each clients needs in order to recognize the right candidates immediately.

Key Contact:
Mr. Judd A. Hoffman, President
Mr. Danko Fatovic, CEO

Functions: Senior Mgmt., Sales Mgmt., CFO's, MIS Mgmt., Systems Analysis, Systems Implem., DB Admin.

Industries: Generalist

The Hogan Group Inc
PO Box 18073
Cleveland Heights, OH 44118
(216) 371-9705
Email: thehoganp@aol.com
Web: www.thehogangroup.net

Description: We are a full-service recruitment firm conducting both contingency and retained searches. We specialize in placing clinical research and development, project management, regulatory, clinical data management, medical writing, etc. professionals in pharmaceutical, biotech, and CRO industries.

Key Contact - Specialty:
Ms. Ann B. Hogan, President - *Pharmaceutical, biotechnology, CRO companies*

Salary minimum: $40,000

Functions: Generalist, Directors, Middle Mgmt., Physicians, Nurses, Sales & Mktg., R&D, Minorities

Industries: Generalist, Pharm Svcs., Biotech

Professional Associations: ACRP, DIA

Holampco Int'l
(also known as MRI of Pittsburgh-Shadyside)
5825 Ellsworth Ave
Pittsburgh, PA 15232
(412) 954-0000
Fax: (412) 954-0030
Email: hlc@holampco.com

Description: With the new millennium here, our new name, a combination of the principle names Gary F. Holupka and Patti Lampl, is our personal signature to distinguish and passionately pursue excellence in partnering with you to attract the top talent. We are a professional executive search firm specializing in the building materials, glass, and ceramic industries.

Key Contact - Specialty:
Ms. Patti Lampl
Mr. Gary Holupka - *Building materials*

Functions: Generalist, Mfg.

Industries: Generalist, Mfg., Mfg. SW

Holden & Harlan Associates Inc
PO Box 91
Flossmoor, IL 60422
(708) 799-4447
Fax: (708) 799-4461
Email: info@actuarialrecruiting.com
Web: www.actuarialrecruiting.com

Description: We provide executive recruiting, and specialize in property/casualty actuaries. We place nationally and internationally in insurance companies and consulting and brokerage firms.

Key Contact:
Mr. Jerry Hayes, President - *Actuarial, insurance (property, casualty)*
Ms. Mara Hayes, Corporate Secretary

Salary minimum: $45,000

Functions: CFO's

Industries: Insurance

Holland & Associates Ltd
2345 York Rd Ste 300
Harvest Bldg
Timonium, MD 21093
(410) 557-0044
Fax: (410) 557-8749
Email: ray@hollandcpasearch.com
Web: www.hollandcpasearch.com

Description: We are dedicated exclusively to providing financial and accounting search and recruitment services to Big 5 and large local CPA firms through out the USA. We pride ourselves in locating the top talent in public accounting, proven performers with advanced degrees and outstanding credentials.

Key Contact - Specialty:
Mr. Ray Holland, President - *Accounting & finance*

Salary minimum: $50,000

Functions: Finance

Industries: Accounting, Mgmt. Consulting

Professional Associations: AAA

Networks: World Search Group

Holland Search

(a division of Holland Group)
237 W Northfield Blvd Ste 200
Murfreesboro, TN 37129
(800) 840-8367
Fax: (615) 895-4251
Email: hollsch@edge.net
Web: www.hollandgroup.com

Description: We are part of a full-service agency.
We offer temporary employment (Holland
Employment) and training/consulting (Holland
Consulting).

Key Contact - Specialty:
Ms. Cathy Lamb, Manager of Executive Search -
Management, technical

Salary minimum: $30,000

Functions: Generalist, General Mgmt., Mfg.,
Materials, HR Mgmt., Finance, IT, Engineering

Industries: Generalist, Finance

Hollister Associates Inc

24 School St Fl 6
Boston, MA 02108
(617) 742-3020
Fax: (617) 742-3357
Email: asmith@hollisterinc.com
Web: www.hollisterinc.com

Description: We are one of New England's leading
full-service, privately owned recruiting firms. We
have distinguished ourselves in the crowded staffing
business by concentrating on a fundamental
concept, which is to build and maintain respectful,
productive relationships. We offer full-time and
supplemental/contract placement within the areas
of: accounting and finance, administrative, financial
services, and technology.

Key Contact:
Ms. Kip Hollister, President/CEO - *Administrative*
Mr. David Tomer, Vice President
Mr. Christopher Smith, Director - Financial
Services
Ms. Nancy Walter, Director - Administrative
Placement
Ms. Nancy Doyle, Director - Accounting and
Finance
Mr. Mike Gorman, Director - Contract IT
Mr. Tom Finn, Director - Technology

Functions: Generalist, Senior Mgmt., CFO's, Cash
Mgmt., Systems Implem., Systems Support,
Network Admin., DB Admin.

Industries: Generalist, Invest. Banking, Brokers,
Misc. Financial, Accounting, New Media

Professional Associations: FEI, NATSS

Branches:
31 Milk St Fl 6
Boston, MA 02109
(617) 654-0200
Fax: (617) 695-3807
Email: asmith@hollisterinc.com
Key Contact - Specialty:
Mr. Dave Tomer - *Information technology,
information systems*
Mr. Chris Smith - *Investment*

5 Burlington Woods Ste 101
Burlington, MA 01803
(781) 273-2424
Fax: (781) 229-4388
Email: tmckeon@hollisterinc.com
Key Contact:
Ms. Annie Smith, Marketing

Holloway, Schulz & Partners

1188 W Georgia St Ste 1500
Vancouver, BC V6E 4A2
Canada
(604) 688-9595
Fax: (604) 688-3608
Email: info@recruiters.com
Web: www.recruiters.com

Description: Professional recruitment firm and
search firm since 1972 with consultants specializing
in various disciplines. Searches are conducted on
both a contingency and retainer basis.

Key Contact - Specialty:
Mr. Clive Holloway, Partner - *High technology
management*
Mr. Bill Schulz, Partner - *General management*
Mr. Malcolm McGowan, Partner - *Financial
management, accounting management*
Ms. Dawn A. Longshaw, Senior Associate - *Sales
management, marketing management*
Mr. Terry Dusome, Senior Associate - *Technical
sales, technical management, manufacturing,
engineering*
Mr. James Seidel, Senior Associate - *High
technology*
Ms. Anna Shojania, Senior Associate - *High
technology sales, high technology marketing*
Ms. Catherine Jagger, Senior Associate - *Finance
& accounting*

Salary minimum: $40,000

Functions: Generalist, General Mgmt., Mfg.,
Materials, Sales & Mktg., HR Mgmt., Finance, IT

Industries: Generalist, Construction, Mfg.,
Transportation, Finance, Services, Software

Professional Associations: AAFA, ACSESS

Networks: National Personnel Assoc (NPA)

Katherine Holt Enterprises Ltd

27 Broadbridge Dr
Toronto, ON M1C 3K5
Canada
(416) 208-0139
Fax: (416) 208-0141
Email: kholtltd@idirect.com
Web: www.pm-online.com/~holt

Description: Specializing in property management,
administration & general insurance.

Key Contact - Specialty:
Ms. Katherine Holt, Principal - *Property
management, administration, finance*
Ms. Margaret Rooney, Senior Consultant -
Property management, general insurance

Salary minimum: $40,000

Functions: General Mgmt., Middle Mgmt., Admin.
Svcs., Finance

Industries: Construction, Insurance, Real Estate

Home Health & Hospital Recruiters Inc

2858 Johnson Ferry Rd Ste 250
Marietta, GA 30062
(770) 993-2828
Fax: (770) 993-6448
Email: resumes@hhhr.com
Web: www.hhhr.com

Description: We specialize in the recruitment of
home healthcare, hospice, hospital, assisted living,
and long-term care professionals. In addition, we
also do interim management and consulting.

Key Contact - Specialty:
Mr. Barry P. Savransky, President - *Medical*
Mr. Alan Savransky, Vice President - *Medical*

Salary minimum: $35,000

Functions: Generalist, Directors, Senior Mgmt.,
Middle Mgmt., Healthcare, Nurses, Health
Admin., CFO's, M&A

Industries: Generalist, Healthcare, Hospitals, Long-
term Care

Professional Associations: GAPS

Fred Hood & Associates

23801 Calabasas Rd Ste 2037
Calabasas, CA 91302
(818) 222-6222
Fax: (818) 222-4445
Email: fred@fredhood.com
Web: www.fredhood.com

Description: We locate outstanding marketing,
sales, operations, warehouse, and category
management for the beverage and food industries.

Key Contact:
Mr. Fred L. Hood, President - *Sales & marketing,
distribution, transportation*
Ms. Randi Tomlimson, Account Executive
Ms. Taryn Maupin, Account Executive
Ms. Courtney Hood, Account Executive

Salary minimum: $50,000

Functions: Generalist, Senior Mgmt., Middle
Mgmt., Distribution, Sales Mgmt., PR, Cash
Mgmt., MIS Mgmt.

Industries: Generalist, Food, Bev., Tobacco

J G Hood Associates

PO Box 2667
Westport, CT 06880
(203) 226-1126
(203) 866-0763
Fax: (203) 866-0790
Email: jghood@optonline.net

Description: We are a full-service search firm
specializing in technical, engineering,
manufacturing, information technology,
purchasing/planning, human resources, financial,
marketing/sales, and professional. For top Fortune
and private client companies, including high-tech,
software, consumer product, healthcare, and
pharmaceuticals.

Key Contact:
Ms. Joyce G. Hood, Owner/President

Salary minimum: $45,000

Functions: Generalist

Industries: Generalist

Networks: Inter-City Personnel Assoc (IPA)

Hope Resource Partners Inc

(dba Tri-Force IT Recruiting Specialists)
1203 Lake Ave
Ft. Wayne, IN 46805
(219) 422-4417
Fax: (219) 422-4710
Email: triforce@triforce.com
Web: www.triforce.com

Description: IT Recruiting Specialists. We provide
quality service by utilizing structured methods.
Submitted candidates have the required skills, want
the position and they hit the salary target. Both
direct and contract service available.

Key Contact - Specialty:
Mr. John F. Hope, CPC, President - *IT,
engineering, HR*
Ms. Terri Babcock, Recruiter - *IT*

Salary minimum: $35,000

Functions: HR Mgmt., IT, Engineering

Industries: Generalist, Mfg.

Professional Associations: IAPS, NAPS

Networks: Top Echelon Network

Horizon Medical Search of NH
8 Grenada Cir
Nashua, NH 03062-1429
(877) 598-6611
(603) 598-6611
Fax: (603) 598-6622
Email: horizonmed@aol.com

Description: Specializes in assisting healthcare professionals locate practice opportunities throughout contiguous United States and Canada. All fees are employer paid - no cost to candidates. Counselors are available Monday-Saturday 9:00 a.m. to 8:00 p.m. All communications are confidential.

Key Contact - Specialty:
Mr. Joseph W. DuBois, Jr., President - *Physicians, nurse practitioners, dentists, healthcare executives*
Ms. Sabine G. DuBois, Vice President/Operations/Finance - *Physicians, physicians assistants*
Mr. Anthony G. DuBois, Vice President-Marketing - *Physicians assistants, pharmacists, radiological, ultrasound*

Salary minimum: $50,000

Functions: Healthcare, HR Mgmt., IT, MIS Mgmt., Systems Analysis, Systems Dev., Systems Implem., Systems Support, Network Admin., Attorneys

Industries: Healthcare

Networks: Recruiters Professional Network (RPN)

Horizons Unlimited
9385 Tenaya Way
Kelseyville, CA 95451
(800) 748-5269
Fax: (707) 277-9040
Email: hrzunl@pacific.net

Description: We place sales, technical service, licensing, and technical positions in the chemical and petroleum industries, including: catalyst, process additives, additives, water treatment, adsorbents, alumina, surfactants, and process simulation.

Key Contact - Specialty:
Mr. Bruce Van Buskirk, Owner - *Chemical industry*

Functions: Generalist

Industries: Chemicals

Professional Associations: AICHE

Horton Group Inc
204 S Beverly Dr
Beverly Hills, CA 90212
(310) 777-6600
Fax: (310) 777-6606
Email: art@hortongroupinc.com
Web: www.hortongroupinc.com

Description: We are recruiters in the securities industry serving NYSE brokerage member firms. We place stock-brokers, branch managers, portfolio managers, operations, compliance, and administrative support personnel.

Key Contact:
Ms. Elayne Horton, President
Mr. Arthur Horton, CFO

Salary minimum: $70,000

Hospitality Career Services
5035 E Barwick Dr
Cave Creek, AZ 85331
(480) 585-0707
(480) 513-9332
Email: mitch@hotelheadhunter.com
Web: www.hotelheadhunter.com

Description: We represent the candidates that hotel owners and operators want to hire. We have a staff of five full time recruiters that have worked in the hotel industry and a database of thousands of resumes. Your candidate pool is small, and we have access to the entire pool. A note to our candidates, please do not submit resumes unless you have a minimum of three years experience in a US hotel management capacity.

Key Contact - Specialty:
Mr. Mitchell T. Prager, President - *Hotel management*

Salary minimum: $30,000

Functions: Generalist, General Mgmt., Directors, Senior Mgmt., Middle Mgmt., Production, Sales & Mktg., HR Mgmt., Finance

Industries: Hospitality, Hotels, Resorts, Clubs

Professional Associations: AHMA

Hospitality Int'l
23 W 73rd St Ste 100
New York, NY 10023
(212) 769-8800
Fax: (212) 769-2138
Email: jar@hospitalityinternational.com
Web: www.hospitalityinternational.com

Description: We are a twenty five-year old executive search firm providing our clients with mid-level to senior-level management and sales professionals. We have a hospitality industry focus that includes hotels, restaurants, catering, non-commercial foodservice (for business, education and health care), private clubs, hospitality related technology, and support services throughout the US and Canada.

Key Contact - Specialty:
Mr. Joseph A. Radice, President - *Hotels, food service, restaurants, executive level*
Mr. Michael S. Kogen, Vice President - *Hotels, clubs, restaurants, catering*
Ms. Barbara Brewster, Vice President - *Conference centers, meeting planning, sales*
Mr. Joseph P. Francis, Senior Consultant - *Hotels, resorts, clubs*

Salary minimum: $50,000

Functions: Generalist

Industries: Hospitality

Professional Associations: AHMA, AIWF, HSMAI, NRA, SFM, WFF

Branches:
PO Box 5008
Cortland, NY 13045
(607) 749-3090
Fax: (607) 749-2070
Email: hospitalityintl@clarityconnect.com
Key Contact - Specialty:
Ms. Susan P. Stafford, Vice President - *Hotels, casino management, cruise management, convention center management*

Hospitality Resource Group LLC
745 Barclay Cir Ste 340
Rochester Hills, MI 48307
(248) 299-5544
Fax: (248) 299-8784
Email: staff@hospitalityresource.com
Web: www.hospitalityresource.com

Description: Our executive search services benefit organizations by offering a large database of highly qualified candidates, access to individuals confidentially seeking an opportunity to enhance their career, refer only those individuals who will meet the employers requirements.

Key Contact - Specialty:
Mr. Gregory P. Allowe, President - *Hospitality, general management*

Salary minimum: $50,000

Functions: General Mgmt., Sales & Mktg., HR Mgmt., Finance

Industries: Hospitality

Professional Associations: HMRA, MRA

Branches:
11840 Metro Pkwy
Ft. Myers, FL 33912
(941) 590-3844
Fax: (941) 590-3893
Email: staff@hospitalityresource.com

Hotel Executive Search & Consulting
6750 W Loop St Ste 940
Bellaire, TX 77401
(713) 660-0008
Fax: (713) 660-0009
Email: kenherst@ahotelrecruiter.com

Description: We have over 23 years of experience providing middle and upper-management to the lodging industry worldwide from Houston.

Key Contact - Specialty:
Mr. Kenneth L. Herst, MHS, Owner - *Hotels, resorts*

Salary minimum: $36,000

Functions: Senior Mgmt., Sales Mgmt., Finance, MIS Mgmt., Int'l.

Industries: Hospitality

Professional Associations: GHHMA, THMA

Houser Martin Morris
110 110th Ave NE 503
PO Box 90015
Bellevue, WA 98009-9015
(425) 453-2700
Fax: (425) 453-8726
Email: recruitr@houser.com
Web: www.houser.com

Description: Professional recruiting and search consultants based in the Pacific Northwest providing recruiting and search expertise in a variety of key disciplines for your company.

Key Contact - Specialty:
Mr. Robert Holert, President - *Information technology*
Mr. Josef Verner, Senior Vice President - *Information technology*
Mr. Craig Macdonald, Senior Vice President - *Senior executive retained search*
Ms. Victoria Harris, Principal - *Attorney, legal*

Salary minimum: $50,000

Functions: Generalist, Senior Mgmt., Mfg., Sales Mgmt., Finance, IT, Engineering, Attorneys

Industries: Generalist, Mfg., Transportation, Finance, Legal, Software

Professional Associations: AAM, ASAE, NALSC, NAPS, NBN, NCA, SHRM, SIM, WAW, WSA, WSSCPA

Networks: National Personnel Assoc (NPA)

Jan Howard Associates Ltd
Toronto Eaton Ctr Ste 115
PO Box 515
Toronto, ON M5B 2H1
Canada
(416) 598-1775
Fax: (416) 598-0363
Email: janhoward@vif.ca

Description: We are a full-line agency with over 25 years' serving the greater Toronto area. We also recruit for technical and specialized personnel and contract positions.

Key Contact - Specialty:
Ms. Jan Howard, President - *Administrative, bilingual, information technology, accounting*

Salary minimum: $28,000

Functions: Generalist, Middle Mgmt., Admin. Svcs., Legal, Advertising, Mkt. Research, MIS Mgmt., Network Admin.

Industries: Generalist, Misc. Financial, Legal, Advertising, New Media

---

The Howard Group Inc
(also known as MRI of Leawood)
7600 W 110th St Ste 204
Overland Park, KS 66210-2323
(913) 663-2323
Fax: (913) 663-2424
Email: thgi@earthlink.net
Web: www.thehowardgroup.com

Description: We are a national award-winning firm with dedicated practices in insurance (employee benefits, managed care), pension and retirement planning, voice and data communications, and healthcare technology.

Key Contact - Specialty:
Mr. Brian E. Howard, President - *Insurance, employee benefits*

Salary minimum: $40,000

Functions: Sales & Mktg.

Industries: Banking, Telecoms, Insurance

The Howard Group Ltd
522 Hwy 9 N Ste 101
Manalapan, NJ 07726
(732) 536-0345
Fax: (732) 536-4559
Email: info@thg-ltd.com
Web: www.thg-ltd.com

Description: Our firm is a progressive recruiting firm that specializes in three distinct aspects of the job market. We have a technical recruiting team, which specializes in programming, database design, technical support, network management and design, help desk, as well as all other aspects of the information systems field. The second department, which comprises is the accounting and financial team, we handle all aspects of accounting and finance, from entry-level to executive level. The third department deals with sales/marketing.

Key Contact:
Mr. Howard Engel, President

Functions: Sales & Mktg.

Industries: Energy, Utilities, Construction, Mfg., Transportation, Wholesale, Finance, Communications, Insurance, Software

---

Howard, Williams & Rahaim Inc
105 S Narcissus Ave Ste 806
West Palm Beach, FL 33401-5530
(561) 833-4888
Fax: (561) 833-2343
Email: conyard@aol.com
Web: www.legalsearchnetwork.com

Description: Have specialized in the recruitment of lawyers, at all levels, on behalf of law firm and corporation clients within the State of Florida since 1983 (and NYC 1972-1983). Acquired local recruiting firm in 1996 that specializes in legal support e.g. paralegals, legal secretary, etc.

Key Contact - Specialty:
Mr. John Williams, President - *Attorneys*
Mr. Richard D. Rahaim - *Attorneys*
Ms. Susan Martin - *Paralegals, legal secretaries, administrative, clerical, accounting*

Salary minimum: $60,000

Functions: Generalist, Attorneys, Paralegals

Industries: Generalist, Legal, Accounting

Professional Associations: NALSC

Howard-Sloan Search Inc
1140 Ave of the Americas
New York, NY 10036
(212) 704-0444
(800) 221-1326
Fax: (212) 869-7999
Email: info@howardsloan.com
Web: www.howardsloan.com

Description: Now in our fifth decade, we are a leader in the national and international recruitment of attorneys, paralegal, financial, tax, information technology, and engineering professionals.

Key Contact:
Mr. Mitchell L. Berger, CEO

Salary minimum: $75,000

Functions: Legal, Finance, IT, Engineering

Industries: Generalist

Professional Associations: NALSC

Howard/Carter & Associates Inc
2975 Valmont Rd Ste 320
Boulder, CO 80301
(303) 443-6656
Email: groelants@hmateam.com

Description: We are technical recruiters specializing in healthcare IT / medical imaging and data storage personnel.

Key Contact:
Mr. Gale Howard, Partner

Elizabeth Howe & Associates
PO Box 57157
Chicago, IL 60657
(773) 525-1121
Email: betsy@ejhowe.com
Web: www.ejhowe.com

Description: Recruiting for the computer software industry. Job opportunities are: sales, sales engineer, pre-sales, project management, consulting, product development.

Key Contact:
Ms. Elizabeth Howe, Principal

HQ Search Inc
40 Shuman Blvd Ste 160
Naperville, IL 60563
(630) 778-3416
Email: graham@hqsearch.com
Web: www.hqsearch.com

Description: Specializing in all areas of financial services in: corporations, domestic and international banks, investment banks, venture capital, sales and trading, consulting, pension funds, money management and insurance companies.

Key Contact - Specialty:
Mr. Don Graham, Principal - *Financial services field*

Salary minimum: $50,000

Functions: Finance, CFO's, Cash Mgmt., Credit, M&A, Risk Mgmt.

Industries: Finance, Banking, Invest. Banking, Brokers, Venture Cap., Misc. Financial

---

HR Advantage Inc
PO Box 10319
Burke, VA 22009
(703) 978-6028
Fax: (703) 832-8539
Email: 4492@smart-office.net
Web: www.hradvantageinc.com

Description: Placement agency serving primarily the Washington, DC area. Specializes in recruiting telecommunications executives and professionals for big name and start-up telecommunications firms. Recruits in marketing, sales, finance, legal, HR and customer service.

Key Contact - Specialty:
Ms. Julie B. Rana, President - *Telecommunications*

Salary minimum: $50,000

Functions: HR Mgmt.

Industries: Mgmt. Consulting, HR Services, Media

Professional Associations: AMA, EMA, IEEE, PTC, RON, SHRM, WAW

HR Benefits & Compliance Inc
27 E Ridge
Ridgefield, CT 06877
(203) 438-7979
Fax: (203) 438-1879
Email: info@hrben.com
Web: www.hrben.com

Description: We are recognized for our exceptional abilities in providing customized hospitality search services, which are strategically focused upon our client's corporate culture and work environment, to select hotel companies and ownership/management companies throughout the United States. We conduct result-oriented searches for senior-level hospitality executives.

Key Contact - Specialty:
Mr. Robert J. Marcil, President - *Hospitality, hotel executives, committee management, hotel executive management*

Salary minimum: $50,000

Functions: Directors, Senior Mgmt., Middle Mgmt., Mktg. Mgmt., Sales Mgmt., HR Mgmt., CFO's, M&A, MIS Mgmt.

Industries: Hospitality

Professional Associations: AHMA, AMA, ASTD, CBIA, SHRM

HR Consulting Group Inc
3780 Willowmeade Dr
Snellville, GA 30039
(770) 985-8201
Fax: (770) 982-9063
Email: info@hrconsultants.net
Web: www.hrconsultants.net

Description: We are a client driven firm providing value added searches in sales force automation and ERP placements. Other areas of emphasis are healthcare administration and telecommunications consulting. We have over 15 years' experience and strive to do excellent work on a consistent basis.

Key Contact:
Mr. Larry R. Bishop

Salary minimum: $40,000

Functions: Generalist, HR Mgmt., Systems Implem., Network Admin., Mgmt. Consultants

Industries: Generalist, Mgmt. Consulting, Software, Healthcare

Professional Associations: ACHE, IMC, SHRM

HR Functions Inc
4411 Bluebonnett Dr Ste 106
Stafford, TX 77477
(281) 494-9555
Fax: (281) 494-9556
Email: resumes@hrfunctions.com
Web: www.hrfunctions.com

Description: A full-service human resource consulting firm offering high-level services in staffing, h.r. consulting, and outplacement.

Key Contact:
Mr. John Jordan, President

Salary minimum: $60,000

Functions: Sales & Mktg., Mktg. Mgmt., Finance, Mgmt. Consultants, Minorities

Industries: Generalist, Computer Equip., Consumer Elect., Test, Measure Equip., Retail, Finance, Equip Svcs., Mgmt. Consulting, HR Services, Telecoms, Software

HR Management Services
PO Box 6354
Madison, WI 53716-6354
(888) 476-7444
Email: hrms@hrmanagementservices.com
Web: www.hrmanagementservices.com

Description: Recruiting nationally to find top talent in engineering, architecture, information technology and other professional technical disciplines. Serving clients in Wisconsin, Minnesota, Iowa and Northern Illinois.

Key Contact:
Mr. Paul Gard, President
Ms. Marcia Gard, Vice President

Salary minimum: $50,000

Functions: Engineering, Architects

Industries: Generalist, Construction, Environmental Svcs.

Professional Associations: AIA, NSPE

Hreshko Consulting Group
850 US Hwy 1
North Brunswick, NJ 08902
(732) 545-9000
Fax: (732) 545-0080
Email: frankh@hcgusa.com
Web: www.hcgusa.com

Description: Our founder, Frank M. Hreshko (former director of executive search for Ernst & Young) offers same high quality services found in the Big 5 professional environment.

Key Contact - Specialty:
Mr. Frank M. Hreshko, Managing Director - *Accounting, information technology, sales*
Mr. John C. Diefenbach, Director - *Accounting, finance, international, pharm*
Mr. Michael Franklin, Director-Financial Services - *Financial Services*
Mr. Joseph Talarico, Senior Consultant - *Systems integration, networks*
Mr. Dennis Updike, Director- Sales & Marketing - *Sales, marketing, e-business*
Mr. Daniel Butler, Senior Consultant - *Information technology*
Mr. Mina Kelada, Senior Consultant - *Information technology*
Mr. Art DeVre', Senior Consultant - *Financial services*
Ms. Kim LoPresti, Research Analyst - *Financial services*
Mr. Bill Rider, Senior Consultant - *Information technology*
Mr. Jeff Holmes, Consultant - *Information technology*
Ms. Olga Vignuolo, Director-Research - *Generalist*
Mr. Dave Holmes, Senior Consultant - *Accounting, financial services*

Salary minimum: $50,000

Functions: Generalist

Industries: Drugs Mfg., Banking, Invest. Banking, Brokers, Accounting, Mgmt. Consulting, HR Services, Publishing, New Media, Telecoms

HRNI
815 Newport Rd
Ann Arbor, MI 48103
(734) 663-6446
Fax: (509) 355-6168
Email: john@hrnijobs.com
Web: www.rnijobs.com

Description: We offer retainer and contingency placement services to automotive, manufacturing, Tier Is, plastic manufacturers, IT, third party logistics, etc

Key Contact - Specialty:
Mr. John Johnson, President - *Logistics, manufacturing*

Salary minimum: $30,000

Functions: Generalist

Industries: Generalist

Networks: Top Echelon Network

HRQuest
141 First St SW Ste 11
PO Box 742
Carmel, IN 46082
(317) 581-8880
(317) 581-8808
Fax: (317) 581-8856
Email: fortheasking@hrquest.com
Web: www.insuranceheadhunter.com

Description: For our clients - customized, direct recruitment of candidates with a very high-level of client service on both the property & casualty and life & health sides of the insurance industry. For our candidates - a hub of information about professional opportunities in the insurance industry.

Key Contact - Specialty:
Ms. Carol Albright, CPC - *Insurance*

Functions: Generalist

Industries: Insurance

Professional Associations: IAPS

HTSS Executive Search
1119 Hamilton St
Allentown, PA 18101
(610) 432-4161
(888) 711-4877
Fax: (610) 432-5519
Email: shoff@howellsstaffing.com
Web: www.htssexecutive.com

Description: We pay personal attention to your job search. We will advertise, perform custom searches, match personality to recruit the best people for your management team. Call us for all your recruiting needs - top management, professional, information systems, or technical.

Key Contact:
Ms. Pat Howells, President - *Key executives*
Ms. Sarah Hoff, Executive Recruiter - *Management, sales*
Ms. Kristy Howells, Executive Recruiter
Ms. Chrissy Pearson, Executive Recruiter

Salary minimum: $60,000

Functions: Generalist

Industries: Mfg., Retail, Finance, Services, Hospitality, Restaurants, Software, Healthcare

Professional Associations: SHRM

Networks: Top Echelon Network

Hudson Associates Inc
PO Box 2502
Anderson, IN 46018
(765) 649-1133
Fax: (765) 649-1155

Email: hudassoc@aol.com
Web: www.hudsonassociates.net

Description: Small, highly specialized firm handling L&H and P&C insurance positions. Very active in the placement of attorneys within advanced marketing specialty area, as well as sales and marketing individuals.

Key Contact - Specialty:
Mr. George A. Hudson, Managing Director - *Insurance*

Salary minimum: $70,000

Functions: General Mgmt., Directors, Middle Mgmt., Legal, Mktg. Mgmt., Sales Mgmt., Direct Mktg., Training, CFO's, Taxes

Industries: Insurance

The Hudson Group
10 Station St
PO Box 263
Simsbury, CT 06070
(860) 658-0245
Fax: (860) 651-0835
Email: thehudson@aol.com

Description: Specialists in placing degreed engineering, technical, scientific professionals in hi-tech electronics (in any industry), communications, telecommunications, telephony, materials and R&D. Positions cover design, development, quality assurance/verification, R&D and manufacturing.

Key Contact - Specialty:
Mr. Paul E. Hudson, Co-Owner - *Digital signal processing, algorithm development, radio frequency, microwave, electronic packaging*
Ms. Judy K. Hudson, Co-Owner - *Digital design, analog design, mechanical design, software, quality assurance*

Salary minimum: $40,000

Functions: Generalist, Product Dev., Production, Quality, Systems Analysis, Systems Implem., R&D, Engineering

Industries: Generalist, Computer Equip., Consumer Elect., Telecoms, Defense, Aerospace, Software

Professional Associations: IEEE, NARTE

Hughes & Associates Int'l Inc
3737 Government Blvd Ste 304B
Mobile, AL 36693
(251) 661-8888
Fax: (251) 661-6991
Email: timohughes@aol.com
Web: www.hughesandassoc.com

Description: We provide nationwide recruiting of engineers for Fortune 500 companies and companies who serve those companies.

Key Contact - Specialty:
Mr. Tim Hughes, President - *Engineers, refining, petrochemical, chemical, pulp & paper*

Salary minimum: $48,000

Functions: Engineering

Industries: Energy, Utilities, Food, Bev., Tobacco, Textiles, Apparel, Paper, Printing, Chemicals, Plastics, Rubber, Paints, Petro. Products, Consumer Elect.

Professional Associations: AICHE, ASCE, ASME, TAPPI

Networks: Inter-City Personnel Assoc (IPA)

Hughes & Podesla Personnel Inc
281 E Main St
Somerville, NJ 08876
(908) 231-0880
Fax: (908) 707-1055
Email: ehughes@hugh-pod.com
Web: www.hugh-pod.com

Description: We have been recruiting executive and middle management personnel for 25 years. This experience has given the firm the insight necessary to provide excellence in professional recruiting, an excellence which has become our trademark in the field of personnel placement. Working closely with clients on both search and contingency assignments, we utilize our expertise gained from association with many diverse industries to recruit on a national level.

Key Contact:
Mr. Edward Hughes, President

Salary minimum: $50,000

Functions: Quality, Sales & Mktg., HR Mgmt., Finance, R&D

Industries: Generalist, Drugs Mfg., Medical Devices, Pharm Svcs.

Hughes & Sloan Inc
1360 Peachtree St NE Ste 1010
1 Midtown Plz
Atlanta, GA 30309-3214
(404) 873-3421
Fax: (404) 873-3861
Email: inquiry@hughesandsloan.com
Web: www.hughesandsloan.com

Description: We place attorneys in law firms and corporations in the United States and abroad. More than half of our placements are in-house.

Key Contact:
Ms. Melba N. G. Hughes, President
Ms. Linda Sloan-Young, Executive Vice President
Ms. Tanya R. Cunningham, Director
Ms. Joy Nicholson, Senior Manager
Mr. Carter Hoyt, Consultant
Mr. Neil D. Gottenberg, Consultant
Ms. Karla Worley, Consultant
Ms. Jennifer Volk, Consultant
Ms. Donna Jackson, Consultant
Ms. Sara Gilbert, Consultant

Functions: Generalist, Attorneys

Industries: Generalist, Legal

Professional Associations: NALSC

Hughes & Wilden Associates
3935 Old William Penn Hwy
Murrysville, PA 15668
(724) 733-1130
Fax: (724) 733-1136

Description: We have been in business for over 24 years.

Key Contact - Specialty:
Mr. Roger Sulkowski, Partner - *Transportation, distribution, logistics*
Mr. Joseph Orlich, Partner - *Transportation, distribution, logistics*

Salary minimum: $30,000

Functions: Materials, Purchasing, Materials Plng., Distribution

Industries: Generalist

Professional Associations: CLM, ITCC

Human Capital Resources Inc
475 Central Ave Ste 205
St. Petersburg, FL 33701
(727) 898-0212
Fax: (727) 898-0314
Email: hcr@humancap.com
Web: www.humancap.com

Description: We specialize in the need for professionals in the financial services marketplace. Our clients include banks, third-party marketing firm, product manufacturers and broker/dealers.

Key Contact - Specialty:
Mr. Paul A. Werlin, President - *Financial services, financial institutions, investment programs, mutual funds, insurance*
Mr. John Donovan, Vice President - *Financial services*
Mr. Paul Heise, Executive Recruiter - *Financial services*

Functions: Generalist

Industries: Invest. Banking, Brokers, Misc. Financial

Human Resource Bureau
PO Box 19793-403
Irvine, CA 92623-9793
(949) 660-7966
Fax: (949) 660-0562

Description: Nationwide executive search firm dealing with management of all types earning $60K-$450K, attorneys, engineers, etc.

Key Contact - Specialty:
Ms. Joyce Newberry, Vice President
Mr. Pat Brogan, Principal - *Management, legal*

Salary minimum: $60,000

Functions: General Mgmt.

Industries: Generalist

The Human Resource Department Ltd
23240 Chagrin Blvd Ste 845
4 Commerce Park Sq
Cleveland, OH 44122-5403
(216) 292-6996
Fax: (216) 292-6336
Email: ask@thrd.com

Description: We are a human resources project management firm that provides various human resources functional expertise to clients. Because of our human resources focus, we are able to source the most qualified and talented HR professionals for our clients.

Key Contact - Specialty:
Mr. Charles K. Niles, SPHR, President - *Human resource executives, interim*

Functions: HR Mgmt.

Industries: Generalist

Professional Associations: SHRM

The Human Resources Group Ltd
(a BGR company)
1995 Tremainsville Rd
Toledo, OH 43613-4037
(419) 474-0536
Fax: (419) 474-0569
Email: mcraver@bgrcompanies.com
Web: www.bgrcompanies.com

Description: Our firm includes seventeen recruiters in two regional offices offering retained search, contract employment, and direct hire of information technology specialists on a national basis. We place ERP and e-Business professionals.

Key Contact:
Mr. Mark Craver, Managing Partner - *Information technology*
Mr. Jason Bach, Executive Recruiter
Mr. Greg Links, Executive Recruiter - *Information technology*
Mr. Greg Bach, Executive Recruiter - *Information technology*
Mr. Toby Roscoe, Executive Recruiter

Salary minimum: $48,000

Functions: IT

Industries: Generalist

Human Resources Management Hawaii Inc
210 Ward Ave Ste 126
Honolulu, HI 96814
(808) 536-3438
Fax: (808) 536-0352
Email: hrmhelinski@mciworld.com

Description: Our personal careers reflect successful work experience in administration, management, engineering and MIS. We therefore can better understand your staffing needs and save you time to do what you do best.

Key Contact - Specialty:
Mr. Mike Elinski, President - *Information systems, consultants, financial*

Salary minimum: $40,000

Functions: Generalist, Senior Mgmt., HR Mgmt., CFO's, IT, Engineering, Mgmt. Consultants

Industries: Generalist, Mgmt. Consulting, HR Services, Telecoms, Software

Professional Associations: AITP, SHRM

E F Humay Associates
PO Box 173 R
Fairview Village, PA 19409-0173
(610) 275-1559
Fax: (610) 275-3485
Email: efhumay@msn.com

Description: Recruit for manufacturers and distributors of construction and mining equipment (road, bridge, mining, etc.) in positions for sales, marketing, parts, service, engineering and all management positions.

Key Contact - Specialty:
Mr. Gene Humay, Owner - *Sales, marketing, parts, service, manufacturing*
Ms. Jane Humay - *Sales, marketing, parts, service, manufacturing*

Salary minimum: $50,000

Functions: Generalist, General Mgmt., Directors, Mktg. Mgmt.

Industries: Construction, Mfg., Wholesale, Retail

Professional Associations: AED, AED

Hunegnaw Executive Search
(formerly known as Saber Consulting Group)
641 N High St Ste 109
Columbus, OH 43215
(614) 228-6898
Fax: (614) 228-2866
Email: davidh@teamhes.com
Web: www.teamhes.com

Description: We believe the success of a company depends on the quality of its employees. With that in mind, we recruit the very best candidates from the outside to help our clients achieve their goals.

Key Contact:
Mr. David B. Hunegnaw, President
Mr. Michael Spitale, Vice President

Salary minimum: $50,000

Functions: Sales & Mktg.

Industries: Generalist

Leigh Hunt & Associates Inc
14 Maine St Ste 312
Brunswick, ME 04011
(207) 729-3840
Fax: (207) 729-3888
Email: lhunt@leighhunt.com
Web: www.leighhunt.com

Description: We maintain a database of over 4000 companies and 6000+ candidates-an invaluable resource for job search, recruitment and placement.

The right chemistry between candidate and company equals success.

Key Contact - Specialty:
Leigh Hunt, Owner/President - *Polyurethane, paints & coatings*
Mr. Leonard Mulligan, MBA, Recruiter/Marketing - *Industries*
Mr. Peter Asquith, CPC, Executive Recruiter - *Pulp & paper, paints & coatings, injection molding*

Salary minimum: $40,000

Functions: Generalist

Industries: Paper, Plastics, Rubber, Paints, Petro. Products, Non-classifiable

Professional Associations: ISA, NEAPS, NNEAPS, TAPPI

Hunt For Executives
PO Box 93
East Sandwich, MA 02537
(508) 833-4868
Fax: (508) 833-5298
Email: info@huntforexecutives.com
Web: www.huntforexecutives.com

Description: Our firm is a recruiting firm focusing on upper-level management and executive positions. We also serve mid-level professionals in many disciplines who are on career paths leading to upper-level responsibilities.

Key Contact - Specialty:
Ms. Mary Hunt, President - *Executive placement*
Mr. Randy Hunt, CPA, Director of Retained Search Services - *'C'-level executive placements*

Functions: Senior Mgmt.

Industries: Generalist

Hunt Ltd
1050 Wall St W Ste 330
Lyndhurst, NJ 07071
(201) 438-8200
Fax: (201) 438-8372
Email: info@huntltd.com
Web: www.huntltd.com

Description: Staff is made up of former distribution executives. Company specializes primarily in distribution/transportation opportunities nationwide.

Key Contact - Specialty:
Mr. Alex Metz, CPC, President - *Logistics, distribution, materials management*
Mr. Donald Jacobson, CPC, Vice President - *Logistics, distribution, materials management*

Salary minimum: $45,000

Functions: Generalist, Senior Mgmt., Middle Mgmt., Materials, Purchasing, Materials Plng., Distribution

Industries: Generalist, Food, Bev., Tobacco, Paper, Chemicals, Soap, Perf., Cosmtcs., Drugs Mfg., Medical Devices, Retail

Professional Associations: CLM, SHRM, WERC

Hunt, Patton & Brazeal Inc
7170 S Braden Ste 185
Tulsa, OK 74136
(918) 492-6910
Fax: (918) 492-7023
Email: hpb@huntpatton.com
Web: www.huntpatton.com

Description: We are recruiting specialists for executive, professional, technical engineering, environmental, construction, oil and gas, petroleum, chemical, computer, medical and laboratory industries.

Key Contact - Specialty:
Mr. M. Pat Patton, President - *Generalist*
Mr. John Williams, General Manager - *Generalist*

Salary minimum: $25,000

Functions: Generalist, Senior Mgmt., Middle Mgmt., Production, Plant Mgmt., Purchasing, Mktg. Mgmt., Engineering

Industries: Generalist, Energy, Utilities, Construction, Mfg., Drugs Mfg., Plastics, Rubber, Paints, Petro. Products, Metal Products, Machine, Appliance, Equip Svcs., Environmental Svcs.

Professional Associations: SHRM

Branches:
32065 Castle Ct Ste 225
Evergreen, CO 80439
(303) 526-9492
Fax: (303) 526-9495
Email: hpb@huntpatton.com
Key Contact - Specialty:
Mr. Pat Patton, President - *Generalist*

3 Riverway Ste 170
Houston, TX 77056
(713) 355-8350
Fax: (713) 355-8352
Email: hpb@huntpatton.com
Key Contact - Specialty:
Mr. Pat Patton, President - *Generalist*
Ms. Billie Asaf, Principal Associate - *Generalist*

Hunter & Michaels Executive Search
7502 Greenville Ave Ste 500
Dallas, TX 75231
(214) 750-4666
Fax: (214) 750-4476
Email: ray@hunterm.com

Description: We recruit sales and marketing managers in the consumer packaged goods area. We have an extensive database harvested over twenty years of recruiting experience. Our clients range in size from the Fortune 500 company to the smaller region company that has a niche.

Key Contact - Specialty:
Mr. Ray Smuland, President - *Consumer products sales, consumer products marketing*
Mr. Allen Danforth, Vice President - *Consumer product marketing*

Salary minimum: $80,000

Functions: Sales & Mktg., Sales Mgmt.

Industries: Food, Bev., Tobacco, Textiles, Apparel, Paper, Soap, Perf., Cosmtcs., Drugs Mfg., Plastics, Rubber, Paints, Petro. Products, Consumer Elect., Marketing SW

Hunter Adams Search
537 Merwick Cir
Charlotte, NC 28211
(321) 409-0085
Fax: (704) 364-5072
Email: edziegler@hunteradams.com
Web: www.hunteradams.com

Description: We specialize in the data communications, networking solutions, telecommunications, Outsourcing and e-business industries. Our primary focus is sales, technical support (pre- & post-sales), and marketing related positions. We work at all levels except entry level.

Key Contact:
Mr. Edwin Ziegler, Managing Partner

Salary minimum: $75,000

Functions: Sales & Mktg.

Industries: Telecoms

Professional Associations: RON

Hunter Associates
181 Park Ave
West Springfield, MA 01089
(413) 737-6560
Fax: (413) 785-1295

Email: hunter@hunterworldwide.com
Web: www.hunterworldwide.com

Description: Our particular area of search specialization is contract/subcontract, financial and engineering professionals for domestic and expatriate assignments.

Key Contact - Specialty:
Mr. Daniel M. Shooshan, Principal - *Engineering, administration*

Salary minimum: $45,000

Functions: General Mgmt., Mfg., Materials, IT, Int'l.

Industries: Generalist

Professional Associations: MAPS

Networks: Len Nelson & Assoc Network (NAN)

Morgan Hunter Corp
7600 W 110th St
Overland Park, KS 66210
(913) 491-3434
Fax: (913) 409-1232
Email: mail@morganhunter.com
Web: www.morganhunter.com

Description: Specialized contingency/retainer search firm.

Key Contact - Specialty:
Mr. Jerry Hellebusch, CPC, Owner/President - *Accounting, finance*

Salary minimum: $30,000

Functions: Admin. Svcs., Sales & Mktg., Advertising, Mktg. Mgmt., Sales Mgmt., Finance, IT, Graphic Artists

Industries: Generalist, Computer Equip., Accounting, Advertising, New Media, Telecoms, Software

Professional Associations: AAFA, KAPS, KCAPS, NATSS

The Hunter Group Inc
39577 Woodward Ave Ste 211
Bloomfield Hills, MI 48304
(248) 645-1551
Fax: (248) 645-6130
Email: chris@huntergroup.com
Web: www.huntergroup.com

Description: Combining more than 40 years of recruiting expertise, recognized as Michigan's fastest growing executive search firm.

Key Contact:
Mr. James Lionas, Principal - *Senior level executive*
Mr. Steve Klingensmith, Principal - *Financial*
Ms. Sherry Muir Irwin, Principal - *Technical, automotive*
Mr. Robert Thomas, Principal
Ms. Renee Sakmar, Principal

Salary minimum: $75,000

Functions: Generalist, Senior Mgmt., Mfg., Health Admin., HR Mgmt., CFO's, Engineering

Industries: Generalist, Plastics, Rubber, Metal Products, Motor Vehicles, Misc. Mfg., Healthcare

The Hunter Group
600 Grant St Ste 500
Denver, CO 80203
(303) 861-0405
Fax: (303) 861-0377

Description: Our firm is made up of only experienced recruiters with over 50 years of combined recruiting experience specializing in finance, accounting, human resources, sales marketing, and IT.

Key Contact - Specialty:
Ms. Alice Swanson, Vice President - *Marketing, sales, banking*
Ms. Lori Johnson, Executive Search Consultant - *Accounting, finance, sales, technical*
Ms. Lynne Isles, Executive Search Consultant - *Technical, technical sales, finance*
Ms. Sherrie Morgan, Executive Search Consultant - *Finance, human resources*

Salary minimum: $70,000

Functions: Generalist, Cash Mgmt.

Industries: Generalist, Finance, Services, Advertising, Telecoms, Wireless, Fiber Optic, Marketing SW, Networking, Comm. SW

The Hunter Group
1605 Green Pine Ct
Raleigh, NC 27614
(919) 676-5900
Fax: (919) 676-8510
Email: info@hunts4u.com
Web: www.hunts4u.com

Description: Executive and management level recruiters with emphasis on technology related searches. Client-driven and targeted, with special expertise in competitive recruiting, startups, confidential replacements, workforce diversity, and chief or senior executives. National and international. Incentive based/results driven.

Key Contact - Specialty:
Ms. Martha Lempicke, CPC, Principal - *Generalist*
Mr. Todd Lempicke, Principal - *Generalist*

Salary minimum: $75,000

Functions: Generalist

Industries: Generalist, Services

Hunter Sterling LLC
PO Box 3296
Saratoga, CA 95120
(408) 867-7212
(408) 927-7251
Email: john@huntersterling.com
Web: www.huntersterling.com

Description: We are a retained search firm specializing in "C" level searches in information technology, Internet, software, and information systems.

Key Contact - Specialty:
Dr. John Webster, CEO
Ms. Pat Templin, Ph.D., Senior Vice President - *Transition services*
Mr. Paul Thompson, Vice President - *Information technology*
Mr. Jim Omlid, Vice President - *Information technology*

Salary minimum: $120,000

Functions: Generalist

Industries: Computer Equip., Electronic, Elec. Components, Services, Communications, Software, Biotech

---

Huntington Personnel Consultants Inc
PO Box 1077
Huntington, NY 11743-0640
(631) 549-8888
Fax: (631) 549-3012
Email: jahenry@i-2000.com

Description: We provide recruitment and placement of information technology and software engineering professionals in NY City metropolitan area only.

Key Contact - Specialty:
Ms. Jeannette A. Henry, CPC, President - *Information technology, software engineering*

Salary minimum: $30,000

Functions: IT

Industries: Generalist

Professional Associations: APCNY, NAFE

Huntley Associates Inc
PO Box 868144
Plano, TX 75086-8144
(972) 599-0100
Fax: (972) 599-0300
Email: admin@huntley.com
Web: www.huntley.com

Description: International corporate consultants engaged in business consulting, executive recruiting and the provision of contract consulting professionals.

Key Contact - Specialty:
Mr. David E. Huntley, CPC, President/CEO - *ERP, CRM, e-commerce, ASIC/FPGA design*
Mr. John Galka, Major Account Representative - *Engineering (hardware, software), client/server, mainframe, MIS, IT*
Ms. Eilene Byers, Office Administrator
Ms. Donnie Wheat, Research Assistant - *IT, e-commerce, telecom/datacom*

Salary minimum: $50,000

Functions: Generalist

Industries: Generalist

Professional Associations: BACA, IRG, NAPS, RON

Networks: National Consulting Network (NCN)

Cathy L Hurless Executive Recruiting
6101 Fredericksburg Ln
Madison, WI 53718
(608) 222-5300
(312) 444-2053
Email: hurless@globaldialog.com
Web: www.cathyhurless.com

Description: Media recruiter/advertising industry. Advertising agencies, media management firms, client. Media planning/buying executives.

Key Contact - Specialty:
Ms. Cathy Hurless, President/Executive Recruiter - *Media*
Ms. Marie Mednansky, Executive Recruiter - *Media*
Ms. Robin Peterson, Executive Recruiter - *Media*
Ms. Nancy Kromm, Executive Recruiter - *Media*

Functions: Generalist, Advertising

Industries: Advertising, New Media

L M Hurley & Associates
1286 University Ave Ste 318
San Diego, CA 92103
(619) 296-7124
Fax: (619) 296-5375
Email: lauren@lmhurley.com
Web: www.lmhurley.com

Description: We are a nation wide recruiting firm that specializes in recruiting, interviewing, and the placement of all levels of professionals in the following areas: accounting, administration, biotechnology, finance, HR contract recruiting, human resources, information technology, marketing, and sales. Our services are company fee paid.

Key Contact:
Ms. Lauren Hurley, President

Functions: General Mgmt., Directors, Legal, Sales & Mktg., HR Mgmt., Finance, CFO's, IT, R&D, Engineering

Industries: Construction, Mfg., Finance, Services, Hospitality, Media, Communications, Insurance, Real Estate, Software, Biotech

---

Professional Associations: NAFE

Hutchinson Smiley Ltd
890 Yonge St Ste 1002
Toronto, ON M4W 3P4
Canada
(416) 967-6654
Fax: (416) 967-7393
Email: hsl@pathcom.com

Description: We are a management and information systems consulting firm that specializes in contract and permanent placement of skilled systems resources in the Canadian and Ontario marketplace.

Key Contact - Specialty:
Mr. Robert W. Sydia, President - *Senior information technology management*
Mr. Robert A. Sydia, Vice President - *Information technology technical, information technology management*
Mr. John Nakashima, Resource Consulting - *Information technology technical, information technology management*
Mr. Russell Gnyp, Audit/Accounting - *Audit, accounting, CPA's*

Functions: IT

Industries: Generalist

Professional Associations: CIPS

The Hutton Group Inc
815 Live Oak Rd Ste A
Vero Beach, FL 32963
(561) 234-7333
Fax: (561) 234-9009
Email: info@huttongrouphc.com
Web: www.huttongrouphc.com

Description: Nationwide search and placement for healthcare executives and consultants for national consulting firms, integrated health systems/hospitals, managed care organizations and software companies.

Key Contact - Specialty:
Ms. M. Joan Hutton, President/CEO - *Managed care, healthcare reengineering consultants, health executives, healthcare finance professionals, physicians*

Salary minimum: $50,000

Functions: Physicians, Health Admin., Sales Mgmt., Customer Svc., CFO's, Budgeting, Credit, M&A, Risk Mgmt., Mgmt. Consultants

Industries: Generalist, Telecoms, Network Infrastructure, Healthcare, Hospitals

Professional Associations: AHIMA, FAHQ, HFMA, NAHQ

Hyland Bay Executive Search LLC
(a division of Hyland & Company Inc)
4646 E Greenway Rd Ste 112
Phoenix, AZ 85032
(602) 381-1177
(800) 382-1177
Fax: (602) 381-1024
Email: hbes@hylandbay.com
Web: www.hylandbay.com

Description: Search for the real estate industry only. Handle all corporate positions in the home building industry including master planned communities. Able to place both inexperienced and experienced sales and sales management professionals in sales and marketing positions with new home builders nationwide. All placement fees are employer paid.

Key Contact - Specialty:
Mr. Kenneth J. Hyland, President - *Real estate for new home builders*
Ms. Susan L. Hyland, Executive Vice President - *Real estate for new home builders*

Salary minimum: $20,000

Functions: Sales Mgmt.

Industries: Real Estate

Professional Associations: IREM, NAHB, NAR

Hyman & Associates
PO Box 8943
The Woodlands, TX 77387-8943
(281) 292-1969
Fax: (281) 292-1664
Email: dhyman@iwl.net
Web: www.teamhyman.com

Description: We are committed to providing quality solutions to clients' individualized needs. We have established ourselves as a valuable resource in successfully meeting our clients' needs in diversity recruiting.

Key Contact - Specialty:
Mr. Derry Hyman, President - *Human resources, operations, general management, finance*

Salary minimum: $60,000

Functions: Senior Mgmt., Middle Mgmt., Mfg., Distribution, Sales Mgmt., HR Mgmt., Finance, CFO's, Mgmt. Consultants, Minorities

Industries: Generalist

Professional Associations: NBMBAA, NHMBAA

Networks: First Interview Network (FIN)

---

i j & Associates inc
2525 S Wadsworth Blvd Ste 106
Lakewood, CO 80227
(303) 984-2585
Fax: (303) 984-2589
Email: ilarson@ijassoc.com
Web: www.ijassoc.com

Description: We are presently involved in recruiting for a wide range of clients both in software development and IS technology in state-of-the-art and leading edge technology, more specifically client/server and database. We also do some recruiting in hardware design including software engineers that work on the hardware, such as low level-C coding and assembler.

Key Contact - Specialty:
Ms. Ila Larson, President - *Software engineering, information systems*

Salary minimum: $45,000

Functions: Generalist, MIS Mgmt., Systems Analysis, Systems Dev., Systems Implem., Systems Support, Network Admin., DB Admin.

Industries: Generalist, Drugs Mfg., Computer Equip., New Media, Telecoms, Software

Networks: Top Echelon Network

The Icard Group Inc
120 Boardman Ave Ste F
Traverse City, MI 49684
(616) 929-2196
Fax: (616) 929-3336
Email: icardgrp@traverse.net
Web: www.icardgroup.com

Description: Specialists in automotive quality. We build long-term client relationships. 73% of our business is repeat.

Key Contact - Specialty:
Mr. Bob Icard, Sr., President - *Automotive quality*
Mr. Robert Icard, Jr., Operations Manager - *Automotive quality, engineering*
Ms. Cheryl Valencia-Icard, Vice President - *Automotive quality, engineering*

Salary minimum: $30,000

Functions: Generalist, Directors, Middle Mgmt., Product Dev., Production, Plant Mgmt., Quality, Productivity

---

Industries: Generalist, Plastics, Rubber, Metal Products, Motor Vehicles, Test, Measure Equip.

Branches:
517 1/2 Pleasant Ave
St. Joseph, MI 49085
(616) 983-3100
Fax: (616) 983-3177
Key Contact - Specialty:
Mr. Randy Ludlow, Operations Manager - *Plastics*

IDC Executive Search Inc
405 Central Ave Ste 102
St. Petersburg, FL 33701
(727) 898-6900
Fax: (727) 898-6920
Email: info@idcexec.com
Web: www.idcexec.com

Description: We are a full-service executive search firm with over ten years strictly in the power industry. We have the experience and contacts to match your background to the right position.

Key Contact - Specialty:
Mr. Marc Granet, President - *Independent power, power marketing*
Ms. Jennifer Clark, Office Manager - *Independent power, power marketing*

Salary minimum: $75,000

Functions: Generalist

Industries: Energy, Utilities

Imhoff & Associates Inc
900 79th St S
St. Petersburg, FL 33707
(727) 347-3969
Fax: (727) 347-3970
Email: imhoffasoc@aol.com
Web: www.imhoffandassociates.com

Description: We specialize in retail and other service industries. Our search assignments include middle and senior level management. We offer a depth of experience in executive search, career transition, and human resources.

Key Contact:
Mr. Chuck Imhoff, President

Salary minimum: $50,000

Functions: Generalist

Industries: Retail

Impact Executive Placement
5900 Westslope Dr
Austin, TX 78731
(512) 453-4000
(877) 453-4530
Fax: (512) 374-1705
Email: jobs@impact-ep.com
Web: www.impact-ep.com

Description: Our firm is specializing in the battery and fuel cell industries.

Key Contact:
Mr. Arnie Allen, Owner

Impact Personnel Services
PO Box 4081
Brandon, MS 39047-4081
(601) 992-1591
Fax: (601) 992-5037
Email: staffing@att.net
Web: www.impactjobs.com

Description: We are a full service, executive recruitment firm specializing in the placement of engineering, manufacturing, industrial, and information technology personnel. Whether you are a hiring manager seeking to fill employment opportunities or a job seeker looking for a new career, impact personnel services will offer you a

---

customized plan to assist you in achieving your goals.

Key Contact:
Ms. Jan Prystupa, President

Functions: Generalist

Industries: Energy, Utilities, Construction, Mfg., Textiles, Apparel, Lumber, Furniture, Paper, Medical Devices, Plastics, Rubber, Paints, Petro. Products, Leather, Stone, Glass, Metal Products, Machine, Appliance, Motor Vehicles, Computer Equip., Consumer Elect., Test, Measure Equip., Misc. Mfg., Electronic, Elec. Components, Equip Svcs., HR Services, Packaging, HR SW, Mfg. SW

Professional Associations: LSA

Networks: Top Echelon Network

Impact Source Inc
334 E Lake Rd 218
Palm Harbor, FL 34685
(727) 772-6499
Fax: (727) 772-6599
Email: impacts@tampabay.rr.com
Web: www.impactsource.com

Description: Great people for great companies. We help our clients find and hire great people. Industry specialization: building-product and industrial manufacturers and distributors. People specialization: sales, marketing, plant management, and product engineering.

Key Contact - Specialty:
Mr. John E. Sattler, President - *Sales & marketing*

Salary minimum: $45,000

Functions: General Mgmt., Mfg., Product Dev., Plant Mgmt., Sales & Mktg., Engineering, Architects

Industries: Generalist, Energy, Utilities, Construction, Mfg., Lumber, Furniture, Paper, Chemicals, Plastics, Rubber, Paints, Petro. Products, Leather, Stone, Glass, Metal Products, Machine, Appliance

---

Impex Services Inc
89 Tunxis Hill Rd
Fairfield, CT 06432
(203) 335-5627
Email: elie@resumme.com
Web: www.resumme.com

Description: Our firm was founded by sales engineers and in the business of permanent placement of pre-sales, sales, marketing and business development talent with engineering and information technology organizations nationwide.

Key Contact:
Mr. Elie Klachkin,, MS, JCTC, President

Functions: Sales & Mktg.

Industries: Mfg., Transportation, Services, Communications, Aerospace, Packaging, Software

Professional Associations: CMI

Independent Power Consultants
5065 Westheimer Ste 815 E
Galleria Financial Ctr
Houston, TX 77056
(713) 960-1868
Fax: (713) 960-1917
Email: lahjr2001@msn.com
Web: www.ipcsearch.com

Description: Houston-based firm specializing in worldwide independent power industry executive search. Assignments include positions in trading, business development, project development, project management, operations and asset management.

Key Contact - Specialty:
Mr. Luis A. Hernandez, Jr., President - *Power & energy (independent), worldwide*
Ms. Susan Lo, Research Assistant - *Power & energy (independent)*

Salary minimum: $75,000

Functions: Generalist

Industries: Energy, Utilities, Mgmt. Consulting

Professional Associations: CIPCA, HAAPC

Independent Resource Systems
28222 Agoura Rd Ste 201
Agoura Hills, CA 91301
(818) 865-3150
Fax: (818) 865-3155
Email: speth@irsystems.com
Web: www.irsystems.com

Description: Experience in all facets of high-tech industry from development through marketing on a national basis.

Key Contact - Specialty:
Mr. Don Speth, President - *High technology*

Salary minimum: $60,000

Functions: General Mgmt., Directors, Middle Mgmt., Product Dev., Sales & Mktg., Mkt. Research, Systems Dev., Engineering, Architects

Industries: Computer Equip., Venture Cap., Mgmt. Consulting, HR Services, New Media, Broadcast, Film, Telecoms, Software, Biotech

---

Individual Employment Services (IES)
PO Box 917
Dover, NH 03821
(603) 742-5616
Fax: (603) 742-5695
Email: iesjobs@msn.com

Description: We successfully identify/recruit quality people for quality companies. We offer strict confidentiality at all times and strive for long term matches between client accounts and candidates.

Key Contact - Specialty:
Ms. Anita Labell, Principal - *Executive search*
Mr. James Otis, Principal - *Insurance industry, executive search*

Salary minimum: $75,000

Functions: Senior Mgmt., Admin. Svcs., Sales & Mktg., HR Mgmt., Benefits, Finance, CFO's, IT

Industries: Mfg., Chemicals, Medical Devices, Finance, Pharm Svcs., Accounting, HR Services, IT Implementation, PSA/ASP, Insurance, Biotech

---

Industrial Personnel
(a division of Automotive Personnel LLC)
14701 Detroit Rd Ste 430
Cleveland, OH 44107
(216) 226-7958
(800) 206-6964
Fax: (216) 226-7987
Email: employap@aol.com
Web: www.industrialpersonnel.com

Description: Specializing in recruiting engineers and management personnel for manufacturing corporations.

Key Contact - Specialty:
Mr. Donald Jasensky, President - *Senior level management*

Salary minimum: $60,000

Functions: Mfg., Sales & Mktg.

Industries: Mfg., Chemicals, Plastics, Rubber, Metal Products, Machine, Appliance, Motor Vehicles, Transportation, Wholesale, Finance, Accounting

Professional Associations: RON

Industry Consultants Inc
9121 E Tanque Verde Rd Ste 277
Tucson, AZ 85749
(520) 751-9400
Fax: (520) 751-7673
Email: joecorey@azstarnet.com

Description: Engineering and quality control recruiting within the disciplines of food science, chemistry, microbiology, chemical/industrial/mechanical and electrical engineering. Primarily for food, beverage, personal care and healthcare manufacturers. Also cover fields of logistics, materials management and quality engineering.

Key Contact - Specialty:
Mr. Joe Corey, General Manager - *Logistics, materials management, quality engineering, industrial engineering, process engineering*

Salary minimum: $65,000

Functions: Generalist, Product Dev., Quality, Purchasing, Distribution, Systems Analysis, DB Admin., Minorities

Industries: Generalist, Food, Bev., Tobacco, Printing, Chemicals, Soap, Perf., Cosmtcs., Drugs Mfg.

Professional Associations: AIIE

IndustrySalesPros.com
N Lake Anne
1612 Washington Plz
Reston, VA 20190
(703) 481-9761
(800) 557-1674
Fax: (703) 481-5660
Email: ppp11586@erols.com
Web: www.industrysalespros.com

Description: We are a recruiting firm specializing in the placement of industrial sales and marketing professionals specific to the mechanical, electrical, electronic component markets, for example: motors, drives, motion, process, power transmission, HVAC, etc.

Key Contact:
Mr. Walter Brod, President

Salary minimum: $50,000

Functions: Sales & Mktg., Mktg. Mgmt., Sales Mgmt.

Industries: Energy, Utilities, Mfg., Misc. Mfg., Electronic, Elec. Components, Marketing SW

Professional Associations: ASHRAE, ISA

Infinite Source LLC
741 Garden View Ct Ste 208
Encinitas, CA 92024
(760) 944-5700
(888) 222-6210
Email: info@infinitesource-jobs.com
Web: www.infinitesource-jobs.com

Description: We are a high-tech recruiting company, specializing in software engineering, product management, project management, database administration, networking engineering, ERP, and other high-tech areas. We provide contingency, retained, and contract services to our clients through out the west coast. Infinite Source is building relationships that grow companies and careers.

Key Contact:
Ms. Rita J. Scroggin, President
Ms. Patricia Vesalga, Vice President

Salary minimum: $60,000

Functions: Directors, Senior Mgmt., Middle Mgmt., Product Dev., HR Mgmt., IT, Systems Dev., Network Admin., DB Admin.

Industries: Generalist

Networks: National Personnel Assoc (NPA)

Infonet Resources LLC
628 Hebron Ave Bldg 2 Ste 505
Glastonbury, CT 06033
(860) 652-8000
Fax: (860) 633-4203
Email: resources@netstaffer.com
Web: www.neweconomystaffing.com

Description: We provide retained search for information technology executives and technical leaders for capital markets and leading telecommunications companies. We have particular strength in banking, brokerage, and diversified financial sectors.

Key Contact - Specialty:
Mr. Timothy J. McIntyre, President - *Information technology*

Salary minimum: $100,000

Functions: MIS Mgmt.

Industries: Finance, New Media, Telecoms, Aerospace, Insurance, Real Estate, Software, Healthcare

---

Information Technology Search
PO Box 317
Chadds Ford, PA 19317
(610) 388-0587
Email: aitken@400search.com

Description: We are AS/400 niche specialist for PA, NJ, and DE. We perform highly technical regional and national searches for ERP implementation specialists, directors of IT, and the staff that reports to them. The staff that we place may include application programmers, AS/400 technical support pros, and LAN/WAN engineers and/or administrators. Please send information in text format, rather than attachments.

Key Contact - Specialty:
Ms. Carol Aitken, CPC, President - *AS/400 computer professionals*

Salary minimum: $50,000

Functions: IT, MIS Mgmt., Systems Analysis, Systems Dev., Systems Implem., Systems Support, Network Admin., DB Admin.

Industries: Generalist

Professional Associations: DVCUG, TEC

Information Technology Recruiting Ltd
200 Consumers Rd Ste 100
Toronto, ON M2J 4R4
Canada
(416) 502-3400
(888) 414-7324
Fax: (416) 502-9666
Email: resumes@itrlimited.com
Web: www.itrlimited.com

Description: We offer permanent and contract placement in the information technology field servicing fortune 500 and startup companies in the North American Market place. We place programmers, software developers, architects, web designers, project managers, business analysts, CEO, and CFO positions. Visit our site for real time listings. It is updated daily. Confidentiality is assured. We suggest that you don't post your credentials blindly; you never know who gets your information.

Key Contact - Specialty:
Mr. Fernao Ferreira, President/CEO - *Information technology*
Ms. Simone Ferrier, Vice President - *Information technology*
Mr. Dan Ferreira, Vice President, Systems Development - *Information technology*

Salary minimum: $45,000

Functions: Generalist, IT, Systems Analysis, Systems Dev., Systems Implem., Systems Support, Network Admin., DB Admin.

Industries: Generalist, Telecoms, Software

InfoTech Search
8700 King George Dr Ste 102
Dallas, TX 75235
(972) 638-0058
Fax: (214) 638-0060
Email: haroldharrison@earthlink.net

Description: We provide recruitment of IT management, data architects, database administration, data warehouse, web/e-Commerce developers, and senior technical personnel for companies in Dallas and throughout the US.

Key Contact - Specialty:
Mr. Harold M. Harrison, Owner - *MIS management, database administrators (all level technical skills)*

Salary minimum: $75,000

Functions: IT, MIS Mgmt., Systems Analysis, Systems Dev., Systems Implem., Systems Support, DB Admin.

Industries: Generalist

Professional Associations: DAMAI

Meredith Ingram Ltd
55 W Goethe St Apt 1227
Chicago, IL 60610
(312) 640-0002
(312) 640-0005
Fax: (312) 640-1376
Email: ingrammere@aol.com

Description: A retained recruiting firm whose owner has had over 20 years of national executive sales and marketing management experience with national brands and private label in the grocery industry.

Key Contact - Specialty:
Ms. Meredith Ingram, President - *Consumer packaging goods, sales & marketing, grocery, manufacturing*

Salary minimum: $50,000

Functions: Sales & Mktg.

Industries: Mfg., Food, Bev., Tobacco, Paper, Soap, Perf., Cosmtcs., Drugs Mfg., Paints, Petro. Products, Mgmt. Consulting

Professional Associations: FMI, GMA, NACDS, PLMA

Innovative Healthcare Services Inc
3765 Wetherburn Dr
Clarkston, GA 30021
(404) 298-6490
Fax: (404) 298-5768
Email: adickey232@yahoo.com

Description: We specialize in healthcare, medical care, insurance, medical equipment, pharmaceutical and technology.

Key Contact - Specialty:
Ms. Avis D. Dickey, President/CEO - *Healthcare*

Salary minimum: $50,000

Functions: Generalist, General Mgmt., Healthcare, Sales & Mktg., Finance, IT, Specialized Svcs.

Industries: Generalist, Medical Devices, Pharm Svcs., Healthcare

Professional Associations: ACHE, NAFE, NAHSE

Innovative Medical Recruiting LLC
PO Box 432
Meraux, LA 70075-0432
(504) 281-0117
Fax: (504) 281-0118
Email: dale@innomedical.com
Web: www.innomedical.com

Description: We specialize in the nationwide placement of medical, pharmaceutical, biotech sales, marketing representatives, and executives. We are a contingency search firm, never charging a fee to our client until we are successful in placing a candidate.

Key Contact:
Mr. Dale Busbee, Owner

Functions: Sales Mgmt.

Industries: Drugs Mfg., Medical Devices, Pharm Svcs., Biotech, Healthcare

Professional Associations: MMA, RON

innovativestaffsearch
1603 Babcock Rd Ste 272
San Antonio, TX 78229
(210) 342-1626
(800) 799-5339
Fax: (210) 342-1686
Email: iss@texas.net
Web: www.innovativestaffsearch.com

Description: We specialize in the placement of pharmacists.

Key Contact - Specialty:
Mr. Kevin J. Mero, President - *Pharmacy*

Functions: Generalist, Physicians, Nurses, Allied Health, Health Admin.

Industries: Generalist, Healthcare

Professional Associations: APA, ASHP

Branches:
PO Box 711
Madison, WI 53701-0711
(800) 799-5339
Fax: (608) 251-6660
Email: iss@texas.net
Key Contact - Specialty:
Mr. Kevin J. Mero, President - *Pharmacy, physicians assistant, nurse practitioners*

Inrange Global Consulting
11611 N Meridian St Ste 800
Carmel, IN 46032
(317) 569-4400
Fax: (317) 569-4404
Web: www.igs.inrange.com

Description: As a part of Inrange Technologies Corporation, we provide world-class strategy, implementation, and people solutions to regional, national, and global organizations. Providing end-to-end infrastructure, enterprise, and professional search solutions, we enable clients to meet strategic business objectives through technology. Our professional search solutions serve clients with retained and contingent placement assistance.

Key Contact:
Mr. Jeff Fisher

Salary minimum: $50,000

Functions: Generalist

Industries: Finance, E-commerce, Wireless, Network Infrastructure, Software, Database SW, Development SW, Doc. Mgmt., Production SW, ERP SW, Security SW

Branches:
8400 Normandale Lake Blvd Ste 971
Bloomington, MN 55437
(952) 820-4441
Fax: (952) 820-4442

Key Contact:
Mr. Bob Andersen, Senior Director

4555 Lake Forest Dr
650 Westlake Ctr
Cincinnati, OH 45242
(513) 772-9933
Fax: (513) 772-9936
Key Contact:
Ms. Angie Collins, Manager, Professional Search

445 Hutchinson Ave Ste 850
Columbus, OH 43235
(614) 436-8707
Fax: (614) 436-9707
Key Contact:
Mr. Jack Anderson, Senior Director

The Inside Track
504 Hilltop Dr Ste 200
Weatherford, TX 76086-5724
(817) 599-7094
Fax: (817) 596-0807
Email: trak1@airmail.net
Web: www.the-inside-track.com/home

Description: Telecom/Datacom recruiter and well-known specialist in the wireless industry offering 10+ years' full-service staffing to telecom or datacom service providers and OEM's nationwide. Positions from CEO to manager, in sales, marketing, operations, technical etc.

Key Contact - Specialty:
Mr. Matthew B. DiLorenzo, PE, Owner - *High technology engineering, telecommunications, software, I & C*

Salary minimum: $80,000

Functions: Generalist

Industries: Telecoms, Wireless

Professional Associations: RON

Networks: National Consulting Network (NCN)

Insight Personnel Group Inc
PO Box 941629
Houston, TX 77094
(713) 784-4200
Fax: (713) 784-3040
Email: dpr@neosoft.com
Web: www.insightpersonnel.com

Description: National information technology search. Specialize in Microsoft integration and development, data warehouse, and general IT. Software and professional services sales positions. Clients include professional services groups of well-known computer manufacturers and Houston software companies.

Key Contact - Specialty:
Mr. David P. Richards, Owner - *Computer industry, high technology*
Ms. Joni K. Richards, Owner - *Office, administrative*

Salary minimum: $40,000

Functions: IT

Industries: Computer Equip., Services, Mgmt. Consulting, Software

Networks: National Personnel Assoc (NPA)

Insource group
1700 Alma Ste 100
Plano, TX 75075
(972) 881-1313
Web: www.insourcegroup.com

Description: We specialize in staffing the technology professional.

Key Contact:
Mr. Wayne Rampey, Vice-President

Salary minimum: $50,000

Functions: Generalist, IT, MIS Mgmt., Systems Analysis, Systems Dev., Systems Implem., Systems Support

Industries: Generalist, Software

Insurance Career Center Inc
12 N Main St Ste 20
West Hartford, CT 06107
(860) 561-5880
Fax: (860) 561-8970

Description: Recruit and place experienced insurance personnel - countrywide - with a high concentration in New England - handle mainly property and casualty insurance positions.

Key Contact - Specialty:
Ms. Linda Kiner, President - *Insurance*

Salary minimum: $25,000

Functions: Generalist

Industries: Insurance

Professional Associations: CAPS, NIRA

Insurance Headhunters Inc
19029 US Hwy 19 N Bldg Ste 18E
Clearwater, FL 33764
(727) 531-1600
Fax: (727) 531-1609
Email: wsullivan@i-hh.com
Web: www.i-hh.com

Description: There is confidentiality and trust, in what we do. Know and say, form the bond between our clients and our candidates. By headhunting, our team identifies ideal candidates, preserving your time for only key interviews. From the first handshake, we are facilitator and resource, guiding the complex negotiations that transform strangers to prospects and finally to team partners. That is how relationships are built.

Key Contact:
Mr. William Sullivan

Functions: Generalist

Industries: Insurance

Insurance Personnel Resources Inc
8097-B Roswell Rd
Atlanta, GA 30350
(770) 730-0701
Fax: (770) 730-0703
Email: blerch@mindspring.com
Web: www.insurancepersonnel.net/

Description: We offer recruitment and placement of only experienced insurance personnel at all levels and functions country-wide. Our specialties are property, casualty, life, health, and employee benefits.

Key Contact - Specialty:
Mr. Brent Lerch, President/Owner - *Insurance (property, casualty, life, health)*

Salary minimum: $20,000

Functions: Generalist

Industries: Insurance

Professional Associations: ACA, GAPS, INS, NAPS

Networks: National Personnel Assoc (NPA)

Insurance Recruiting Specialists
115 N Center St
Pickerington, OH 43147
(614) 834-3900
Fax: (614) 834-4983
Email: irsohio@aol.com

Description: We specialize in the recruitment of underwriting, marketing, claims, and loss control personnel in the Midwest region of the US. We are a small, specialized firm which tailors the search to meet the client's needs.

Key Contact - Specialty:
Mr. Steve Barker, Owner - *Insurance*

Salary minimum: $25,000

Functions: Generalist

Industries: Generalist, Insurance

Professional Associations: INS, NIRA

Insurance Search
(also known as Rainbow Personnel)
PO Box 7354
The Woodlands, TX 77387
(281) 367-0137
(281) 367-3742
Fax: (281) 367-3842
Email: rainbowjobs@pdq.net
Web: www.rainbowjobs.com

Description: Property and casualty, risk management, life and health insurance positions. All levels.

Key Contact - Specialty:
Mr. Bert Dionne, CPC, President - *Insurance*
Ms. Wanda Hodges, CPC, Consultant - *Insurance*

Salary minimum: $30,000

Functions: Generalist, General Mgmt., Directors, Senior Mgmt., Legal, Risk Mgmt.

Industries: Insurance, Healthcare

Professional Associations: NIRA

Insurance Staffing Consultants
1288 Columbus Ave Ste 280
San Francisco, CA 94133
(415) 351-1811
Email: brucekm@pacbell.net
Web: www.insurancestaffing.net

Description: We are specialists in the property and casualty insurance market in California. Our candidates must have experience in the P&C industry. Employer inquiries are always welcome.

Key Contact:
Mr. Bruce Marx, Principal Consultant

Salary minimum: $60,000

Functions: Generalist, Senior Mgmt., Middle Mgmt., Mkt. Research, Sales Mgmt., Risk Mgmt., Mgmt. Consultants

Industries: Generalist, Insurance

Professional Associations: NIRA

The Insurance Staffing Group
50 Salem St Bldg B
Lynnfield, MA 01940-2663
(800) 601-1113
Fax: (800) 601-1114
Email: jobs@insurancestaffing.com
Web: www.insurancestaffing.com

Description: Our firm credits its success to the fact that every member of the placement staff has considerable experience in all areas of insurance and financial services.

Key Contact - Specialty:
Mr. Thomas F. Goode, President - *Insurance, financial services*

Salary minimum: $30,000

Functions: Generalist

Industries: Insurance, Healthcare

Professional Associations: IIAA

Int'l Business Partners
221 Balliol St Ste 1714
Toronto, ON M4S 1C8
Canada
(416) 322-3324
Fax: (416) 322-3360
Email: intlbus@ican.net

Description: Our experience covers conventional assignments with small companies to major complex, and highly sophisticated projects spanning a cross-section of industries using our unique personalised approach.

Key Contact - Specialty:
Mr. Les Keremelevich, Senior Partner - *Generalist*

Functions: Generalist

Industries: Generalist

Int'l Consulting Services Inc
541 Castlewood Ln
Buffalo Grove, IL 60089
(847) 537-1611
Fax: (847) 541-1899
Email: headhunter@interlync.com

Description: Design, research and development and process professionals. Twenty-five plus years of hands-on selective recruiting. Strong in electronics engineering, applied physics, scientific software, dynamic mechanical systems, systems engineering, candidates range from group leader to VP engineering. Industries served include instrumentation, control, medical, robotics, opto-electronics, semiconductor, laser, telecommunications, X-ray, defense and consumer electronics.

Key Contact - Specialty:
Mr. Peter A. Sendler, President - *Engineers, physicists, computer scientists, applied mathematicians, management*

Salary minimum: $65,000

Functions: General Mgmt., Product Dev., Automation, Healthcare, R&D, Engineering

Industries: Mfg., Medical Devices, Motor Vehicles, Computer Equip., Consumer Elect., Test, Measure Equip., Misc. Mfg., Electronic, Elec. Components, Telecoms, Telephony, Digital, Defense, Aerospace, Software, Biotech, Healthcare

Int'l Market Recruiters
55 W 39th St Fl 9
New York, NY 10018
(212) 819-9100
Fax: (212) 354-9476
Email: imr@imr-recruiters.com
Web: www.imr-recruiters.com

Description: We specialize in both permanent and temporary placements in the international financial service industries. We have earned a reputation for excellence in finding staff that resolve current situations, as well as becoming important decision makers for our clients.

Key Contact - Specialty:
Mr. Joseph M. Sullivan, President - *Financial services*

Functions: Generalist, Cash Mgmt., Risk Mgmt., Systems Support

Industries: Generalist, Banking, Invest. Banking, Brokers, Misc. Financial

Branches:
112 S Tryon St
Charlotte, NC 28202
(704) 334-1044
Fax: (704) 334-1011
Key Contact - Specialty:
Mr. James Marchetti - *Financial services*

1800 John F Kennedy Blvd
Philadelphia, PA 19103
(215) 981-0488
Fax: (215) 981-0988
Email: imr@imr-recruiters.com
Key Contact - Specialty:
Mr. Douglas Wong - *Financial services*

Int'l Pro Sourcing Inc
407 Executive Dr
Langhorne, PA 19047
(215) 968-7666
Fax: (215) 968-7667
Email: admin@prosourcing.com
Web: www.prosourcing.com

Description: We are highly ethical contingency
recruiters specializing in the placement of
thoroughly screened and qualified candidates in
high-technology, pharmaceutical and medical sales
positions for top notch U.S. companies.

Key Contact - Specialty:
Ms. Joan Gallagher, Owner/Vice President - *Sales*
Ms. Kelly Gallagher, Owner/President - *Sales*

Functions: Sales & Mktg., Mkt. Research, Mktg.
Mgmt., Sales Mgmt., Systems Dev., Systems
Implem., Network Admin.

Industries: Generalist, Drugs Mfg., Medical
Devices, Telecoms, Healthcare

Int'l Recruiting Service
PO Drawer 533976
Orlando, FL 32853
(407) 896-9606
(888) 637-6355
Fax: (407) 896-9191
Email: intlrs@aol.com
Web: www.intlrecruitingservice.com

Description: We are worldwide recruiters in the
Green Industry. Although we had our start in 1950,
Mell D. Leonard has been in business for 50 years
and has had experience in all phases of employment,
including, speaking, seminars and is a legal expert
on employment issues.

Key Contact:
Mr. Mell D. Leonard, Owner - *Agriculture,
horticulture, floriculture, all allied industries*
Ms. Lisa Leonard, Recruiter

Salary minimum: $35,000

Functions: Generalist

Industries: Agri., Forestry, Mining, Construction,
Food, Bev., Tobacco, Chemicals, Retail,
Environmental Svcs., Haz. Waste, Packaging

Int'l Search Consultants
1956 E Vinedo Ln
Tempe, AZ 85284
(888) 866-7276
Fax: (888) 866-6625
Email: annr@iscjobs.com
Web: www.iscjobs.com

Description: We are an elite group of seasoned
professionals who specialize in high caliber sales
and sales management people. We have long
standing relationships with a number of clients.

Key Contact - Specialty:
Ms. Ann E. Zaslow-Rethaber, President/CEO -
Sales management (upper-level)

Salary minimum: $50,000

Functions: Generalist

Industries: Printing, Machine, Appliance, Mgmt.
Consulting, HR Services, Hospitality

Int'l Search Consultants
30827 Mainmast Dr
Agoura Hills, CA 91301
(818) 706-2635
Fax: (818) 706-1358
Email: george@isccnc.com
Web: www.isccnc.com

Description: Specializing in the placement of sales,
service and applications people in the CNC machine
tool industry.

Key Contact - Specialty:
Mr. George Schortz - *CNC machine tool industry*

Salary minimum: $40,000

Functions: General Mgmt., Senior Mgmt., Middle
Mgmt., Automation, Sales & Mktg., Sales Mgmt.

Industries: Mfg., Metal Products, Machine,
Appliance, Test, Measure Equip., Misc. Mfg.

Int'l Staffing Consultants Inc
400 Galleria Pkwy Ste 1500
Atlanta, GA 30339-5948
(770) 218-6810
Fax: (770) 234-4138
Email: iscinc@iscworld.com
Web: www.iscworld.com

Description: National and international staffing of
technical and professional people for most
industries since 1979.

Key Contact - Specialty:
Mr. James R. Gettys, President - *Business
development, engineering, professional*
Mr. Michael L. Corner, Vice President - *Human
resources, engineering, construction, process*

Salary minimum: $35,000

Functions: Generalist

Industries: Energy, Utilities, Construction,
Chemicals, Paints, Petro. Products, Test, Measure
Equip., Transportation, Equip Svcs., HR Services,
Telecoms, Environmental Svcs.

Networks: National Personnel Assoc (NPA)

Int'l Technical Resources
725 N A1A Ste D-106
Jupiter, FL 33477
(561) 743-7006
(561) 745-9551
Fax: (561) 743-1972
Email: itr@gdi.net

Description: Two division firm, one dedicated to
mid-upper-level software development
professionals, one division dedicated to sales,
marketing, implementation professionals. Extremely
confidential and thorough.

Key Contact - Specialty:
Mr. Terry L. Funk, President - *Information
technology*

Salary minimum: $75,000

Functions: Generalist, Mkt. Research, Mktg.
Mgmt., Sales Mgmt., Systems Analysis, Systems
Dev., Systems Implem., Network Admin.

Industries: Generalist, Software

Integra IT Partners Inc
40 Eglinton Ave E Ste 601
Toronto, ON M4P 3A2
Canada
(416) 487-3301
Fax: (416) 440-4025
Email: recruiting@integrait.com
Web: www.integrait.com

Description: We are committed to establishing and
maintaining staffing partnerships based on integrity
and trust, specifically in the information technology
area. We strive to be a valued business partner by

consistently presenting career opportunities to our
candidates and providing staffing solutions to our
clients.

Key Contact - Specialty:
Mr. Walter Jakowlew, President - *Information
technology*
Ms. Robyn Merizzi, Director-Business Operations -
Information technology

Functions: IT

Industries: Generalist

Professional Associations: ACSESS, CIPS

Networks: Alliance Partnership Int'l

IntegraNet Corp
PO Box 510241
New Berlin, WI 53151
(262) 797-6464
Fax: (262) 797-6655
Email: joanne@integranetcorp.com
Web: www.integranetcorp.com

Description: We specialize in professional
recruitment of qualified information technology
staff at all levels and offer consulting services which
maximize cost effectiveness and productivity. We
use power hiring techniques and only present
candidates who can do the job.

Key Contact - Specialty:
Ms. Joanne L. Reinhardt, President - *Information
technology, lotus notes*

Functions: Generalist, MIS Mgmt., Systems
Analysis, Systems Dev., Systems Implem.,
Systems Support, Network Admin., DB Admin.

Industries: Generalist

Professional Associations: NAPS

Integrated Management Solutions
39 Broadway Ste 1601
New York, NY 10006-3003
(212) 509-7800
Fax: (646) 349-5947
Email: hspindel@intman.com

Description: Our firm serves the needs of the
financial services community with special emphasis
on operations, accounting, regulatory, finance, sales,
research, and trading areas.

Key Contact - Specialty:
Mr. Howard Spindel, Senior Managing Director -
Financial services
Mr. Michael E. Stupay, Senior Managing Director -
Financial services
Mr. Robert Kramer, Recruiting Manager -
Financial services
Ms. Sharon Listinger, Recruiter - *Financial
services*

Functions: Generalist, General Mgmt., Finance, IT,
Mgmt. Consultants

Industries: Generalist, Banking, Invest. Banking,
Brokers, Venture Cap., Misc. Financial,
Accounting, Mgmt. Consulting

Intelegra Inc
PO Box 505
Far Hills, NJ 07931-0505
(908) 876-5900
Fax: (908) 876-1788
Email: jpalmer111@intelegra.com
Web: www.intelegra.com

Description: Provides technical help for the
information technology marketplace including
technical sales people, system engineers,
programmers, project managers and executive
consultants. All placements are guaranteed.

Key Contact - Specialty:
Mr. John A. Palmer - *Information technology*

Salary minimum: $50,000

Functions: IT

Industries: E-commerce, IT Implementation, PSA/ASP, Communications, Digital, Wireless, Network Infrastructure, Software, ERP SW, Networking, Comm. SW

Professional Associations: NJSA

Inteliant
(a division of SOS Staffing Services Inc)
10220 SW Greenburg Rd 540
Portland, OR 97223
(503) 977-1907
Fax: (503) 977-1928
Email: portland@inteliant.com
Web: www.inteliant.com

Description: A full-service company that provides the Oregon and SW Washington areas with engineering and technician talent for some of the most recognized companies in the world.

Key Contact - Specialty:
Mr. Craig Smith, CIR, National Recruiting Director - *IT, technical*

Functions: IT

Industries: Generalist

Professional Associations: NTSA

Intellenet LLC
(also known as MRI of Hackensack)
15 Warren St Ste 27
Hackensack, NJ 07601
(201) 343-4450
Fax: (201) 343-0067
Email: vb1@bellatlantic.net
Web: www.techheadhunter.com

Key Contact:
Mr. Tom Crahen, Manager

Salary minimum: $70,000

Functions: Sales Mgmt., Engineering

Industries: Communications, Software

Intelligent Marketing Solutions Inc
200 Park Ave S Ste 518
New York, NY 10003
(212) 420-9777
Email: info@marketingmatchmaker.com
Web: www.marketingmatchmaker.com

Description: A former in-house marketing director with 10+ years' experience for leading firms in NY and London, we will find you your best marketing match.

Key Contact - Specialty:
Ms. Linda Sedloff Orton, President - *Marketing, communications, public relations*

Salary minimum: $100,000

Functions: Mktg. Mgmt.

Industries: Services, Non-profits, Legal, Accounting, Advertising, New Media

Professional Associations: LMA

IntelliSearch
17218 Preston Rd Ste 400
Dallas, TX 75252
(972) 735-3199
Fax: (972) 735-3198
Email: bjhsearch@aol.com

Description: We provide executive search services to the mortgage banking, mortgage finance industry and related industries. Mid to senior-level managers, sales, operations, secondary marketing, wholesale, correspondent, retail, regional, branch and national positions. We are experts in the mortgage business.

Key Contact - Specialty:
Mr. Bradford J. Hopson, President - *Mortgage (banking, finance)*
Mr. Joe Collins, Senior Vice President - *Mortgage (banking, finance)*

Salary minimum: $40,000

Functions: General Mgmt.

Industries: Banking

Inter Link Technology Solutions Inc
4606 S Clyde Morris Blvd Ste 2D
Daytona Beach, FL 32129
(386) 322-5440
(800) 713-9207
Fax: (386) 322-9970
Email: cbaker@interlink-inc.net
Web: www.interlink-inc.net

Description: Inter•Link Technology Solutions represents the only employee owned and operated employment service in Florida, comprised of a consortium of specialists who for years were employed in several technical fields and in many capacities. This insight offers us the unique competitive advantage of having worked "on the inside", understanding what motivates the employer, how the employment process really works and foremost, the trials and tribulations of standing in the job seeker's shoes.

Key Contact:
Mr. John Gould, CEO

Professional Associations: NACCB

Inter-Regional Executive Search (IRES)
191 Hamburg Tpke
Pompton Lakes, NJ 07442
(973) 616-8800
Fax: (973) 616-8115
Email: ceo@iresinc.com
Web: www.iresinc.com

Description: We recruit nationwide, specializing in Eastern US. We have been featured on national TV, CNBC, WSJ, and Fordyce. Our firm specializes in retained executive searches in the six figure range in areas of accounting, financial executives, R&D, chemistry, and insurance underwriting management.

Key Contact - Specialty:
Mr. Frank G. Risalvato, President/CEO - *Insurance, accounting*
Mr. Randall Johnson, VP-Technical Recruiting - *Chemistry, scientific*
Ms. Deb Rosen, VP-Sales Recruiting - *Product managers, marketing managers, consumer products*

Salary minimum: $75,000

Functions: Senior Mgmt., Middle Mgmt., Product Dev.

Industries: Chemicals, Consumer Elect., Misc. Mfg., Electronic, Elec. Components, Services, Accounting, Telecoms, Telephony, Digital, Fiber Optic, Network Infrastructure, Insurance

Interactive Legal Search
4900 Hopyard Rd Ste 240
Pleasanton, CA 94588
(925) 468-0397
(800) 211-1513
Fax: (925) 468-0391
Email: gcils@aol.com
Web: www.interactivelegalsearch.com

Description: Recruit attorneys for multinational corporations and law firms throughout the U.S. and foreign locations. Specializing in the field of technology, we conduct domestic and international searches in the areas of IP, new ventures, strategic alliances, joint ventures, marketing and distribution.

Key Contact - Specialty:
Ms. Gay Carter, President - *Intellectual property, mergers & acquisitions, corporate*
Mr. P. Masen, Vice President - *International*

Salary minimum: $80,000

Functions: Generalist, Legal, Attorneys, Paralegals

Industries: Generalist, Legal, Publishing, New Media, Broadcast, Film, Telecoms, Software

Interactive Search Associates
2949 W Germantown Pike
Norristown, PA 19320
(610) 630-3670
Fax: (610) 630-3678
Email: isa@jobswitch.com
Web: www.jobswitch.com

Description: We are an executive search firm that has been in business over 25 years with account executives specializing in sales, financial, administrative, technical, insurance, EDP, chemical, retail, and healthcare areas.

Key Contact:
Mr. John P. Zerkle, Sr., President
Mr. John Zerkle, Jr., Director

Salary minimum: $50,000

Functions: Generalist, Production, Mkt. Research, Mktg. Mgmt., Sales Mgmt., MIS Mgmt., Engineering

Industries: Generalist, Chemicals, Paints, Petro. Products, Machine, Appliance, Test, Measure Equip., Insurance, Healthcare

Interchange Personnel Inc
1403 Jolliet Ave SW
Calgary, AB T2T 1S3
Canada
(403) 216-1520
Fax: (403) 216-1522
Email: interchange@cadvision.com

Description: Our corporate objective is to provide an objective picture of applicants' positive and negative personality and work traits based on comprehensive behavioral based interviewing and an intuitive sense. We focus on placement in Alberta.

Key Contact - Specialty:
Ms. Karen L. Aiken, President - *Oil, gas, CFO's, engineering, middle management*

Salary minimum: $30,000

Functions: Generalist, Senior Mgmt., Middle Mgmt., Admin. Svcs., Training, CFO's, Engineering

Industries: Generalist, Energy, Utilities, Construction, Invest. Banking, Misc. Financial, HR Services, Real Estate

Professional Associations: HRAC

Intercom Recruitment Ltd
47 Colborne St 301
Toronto, ON M5E 1P8
Canada
(416) 364-5338
Fax: (416) 364-5177
Email: intercom@intercomjobs.ca
Web: www.intercomplacement.com

Description: We are an executive search firm specializing in marketing, advertising and direct marketing for full-time and contract needs.

Key Contact - Specialty:
Mr. Harry Teitelbaum, President - *Advertising, marketing*
Mr. Edward Martin, Chairman - *Marketing*

Salary minimum: $30,000

Functions: Generalist, Sales & Mktg., Advertising, Mkt. Research, Mktg. Mgmt., Direct Mktg.

Industries: Generalist, Mfg., Food, Bev., Tobacco, Finance, Banking, Misc. Financial, Media, Advertising

Intercontinental Executive Group
674 Louis Dr
The Vogel Bldg
Warminster, PA 18974
(215) 957-9012
Fax: (215) 957-1753
Email: dgweir@aol.com
Web: www.iegsearch.com

Description: National/international practice exclusively serving the electrical power generation marketplace industries: utilities, developers, owners, operators, environmental services, legal, project finance, equipment suppliers, AE & EPC firms, etc.

Key Contact - Specialty:
Mr. David G. Weir, Senior Managing Partner - *Power*

Salary minimum: $60,000

Functions: Generalist

Industries: Energy, Utilities, Construction, Mfg., HR Services

Professional Associations: MAAPC

Interim Management Resources Inc (IMR Inc)
420 Britannia Rd E Ste 208
Mississauga, ON L4Z 3L5
Canada
(905) 507-4662
Fax: (905) 507-4644
Email: quality1@idirect.com

Description: We are a human resources/career management consulting firm with extensive experience in conducting effective executive recruitment programs. We specialize in the following industries Printing/Publishing, Telecom and Aerospace.

Key Contact:
Dr. R. J. Nicholls, Director-Business Services
Mr. D. C. Crosbie, President
Mr. Nicholas Hogya, Senior Consultant
Ms. Moira Robinson, Senior Management
Ms. Barb Marsh
Ms. Sharon Foster

Salary minimum: $40,000

Functions: Generalist

Industries: Printing, Telecoms, Aerospace

InterSearch Inc
60 E 56th St
New York, NY 10022-3204
(212) 355-2441
Email: intersearch@aol.com

Description: We are an executive search firm specializing in recruiting individuals for positions in financial services.

Key Contact:
Mr. Meredith Anderson, President

Interspace Inc
373 5th Ave
New York, NY 10016
(212) 532-9700
Fax: (212) 532-0186
Email: info@interspaceinc.com
Web: www.interspaceinc.com

Description: Executive search firm specializing in sales, sales management and technology (permanent and temporary) in all industries.

Key Contact:
Mr. William Ellis, President

Salary minimum: $45,000

Functions: Generalist, Sales Mgmt., MIS Mgmt., Systems Analysis, Systems Dev., Network Admin., Minorities

Industries: Generalist, Printing, Drugs Mfg., Medical Devices, Pharm Svcs., Advertising, Telecoms

Professional Associations: APCNY, NATSS, SHRM

Intrepid Executive Search
28896 Mountain View Ln
Trabuco Canyon, CA 92679
(949) 589-7690
(949) 713-4600
Email: ecrane@intrepidsearch.com
Web: www.intrepidsearch.com

Description: We are a highly focused search firm specializing in delivering the leading talent in the technology market. We specialize in placement of high profile sales, business development, marketing, product marketing/management candidates at individual contributor, manager, director, VP, and EVP level. Examples of technologies covered are: computer software/services, wireless, ASPs, and hardware, more specifically data storage.

Key Contact - Specialty:
Mrs. Elaine Crane, Managing Partner - *Research, recruiting*
Mrs. Ruth Ann Walter, Managing Partner - *Sales, recruiting*

Functions: Directors, Senior Mgmt., Middle Mgmt., Product Dev., Sales & Mktg.

Industries: Mgmt. Consulting, E-commerce, IT Implementation, Communications, Digital, Wireless, Network Infrastructure, Software, Database SW, Development SW, Marketing SW, Networking, Comm. SW, Security SW, System SW

Networks: Top Echelon Network

InvestmentPositions.com
828 2nd Ave Ste 510
New York, NY 10017
(212) 286-1711
Fax: (212) 214-0880
Email: info@investmentpositions.com
Web: www.investmentpositions.com

Description: Global recruitment of investment professionals covering the sell side, buy side and venture capital industry.

Key Contact:
Mr. Tarik Sansal, Managing Partner

Functions: Finance

Industries: Invest. Banking, Brokers, Venture Cap., Misc. Financial

IOS-Information Connection Inc
1162 Highway 17 N
Guyton, GA 31312
(888) 290-0885
Fax: (707) 982-2919
Email: ils@ilsglobe.com
Web: www.ilsglobe.com

Description: We specialize in the nationwide recruitment and placement of information technology and insurance professionals. IT positions include programmers through CIO and president, with an emphasis in e-Commerce and client-server technology. Insurance positions include adjusters and underwriters through regional management, VP, and president.

Key Contact - Specialty:
Ms. Lainie Jenkins, Principal - *Information technology*
Ms. Beverly Flanders, Principal - *Insurance*

Functions: Generalist

Industries: Services, E-commerce, IT Implementation, Communications, Insurance, Software, Database SW, Development SW

IQ Services
15090 Briar Ridge Cir
Ft. Myers, FL 33912
(941) 481-8032
Fax: (941) 481-7199
Email: iq-svces@msn.com

Description: National search for professionals in healthcare, environmental, chemical, manufacturing, information technology and construction. Positions include middle to upper-management, sales and marketing, engineering, professional scientists and computer programmers.

Key Contact - Specialty:
Mr. Kevin Mielcarek, Account Executive - *Telecommunications*

Salary minimum: $25,000

Functions: Generalist, Middle Mgmt., Nurses, Sales Mgmt., Systems Dev., R&D, Engineering, Environmentalists

Industries: Generalist, Chemicals, Broadcast, Film, Telecoms, Environmental Svcs., Haz. Waste, Healthcare

Irvine Search Partners
3 PointeDr Ste 207
Brea, CA 92821
(714) 256-2663
Fax: (714) 671-9545
Email: gilriley@earthlink.net

Description: We place information technology professionals in a full range of positions, including: sales, marketing, technical, and consulting. Our clients include some of the major consulting and software organizations in the US.

Key Contact:
Mr. Gil Riley, Partner - *Computers, consulting, networking, software*
Mr. Al Fuller, Partner

Salary minimum: $80,000

Functions: IT

Industries: Generalist

Beth Isabelle & Associates Inc
7061 Bright Springs Ct
Las Vegas, NV 89113-1344
(702) 873-5258
Email: bethisabelle@email.msn.com

Description: International executive search firm specializing in manufacturing operations in Latin America and domestic/international banking.

Key Contact - Specialty:
Ms. Beth Isabelle, MA, CPC, President - *International manufacturing, banking*

Salary minimum: $50,000

Functions: General Mgmt.

Industries: Finance, Banking, Services, Accounting, IT Implementation

Joan Isbister Consultants
350 W 20th St
New York, NY 10011
(212) 243-8733
Fax: (212) 255-3395
Email: j.isbister@att.net

Description: Graphics and printing industries specialists; professional searches in management, marketing and sales.

Key Contact:
Ms. Joan Isbister, President

Salary minimum: $50,000

Functions: Generalist, Senior Mgmt., Middle Mgmt., Plant Mgmt., Sales Mgmt., Customer Svc.

Industries: Printing

Professional Associations: AGC

ISC of Atlanta

(a division of Int'l Career Continuation Inc)
4350 Georgetown Sq Ste 707
Atlanta, GA 30338
(770) 458-4180
(800) 290-0177
Fax: (770) 458-4131
Email: iscatl@mindspring.com
Web: www.iscatl.com

Description: Successfully meeting the challenges of our changing industry while striving to do business in a friendly and fair way, we push towards gaining the respect and confidence of our clients, candidates and colleagues.

Key Contact - Specialty:
Mr. Arthur Kwapisz, President - *Pharmaceuticals, operations, technology, sales*
Mr. William A. Konrad, Vice President - *Accounting & finance*
Ms. Donna Mulder - *Sales, administrative services*

Salary minimum: $35,000

Functions: Generalist, Senior Mgmt., Middle Mgmt., Plant Mgmt., Sales Mgmt., Finance, R&D, Engineering

Industries: Generalist, Energy, Utilities, Chemicals, Drugs Mfg., Medical Devices, Plastics, Rubber, Misc. Mfg.

Professional Associations: GAPS

Networks: National Personnel Assoc (NPA)

ISC of Houston

333 N Sam Houston Pkwy E Ste 400
Houston, TX 77060
(281) 847-0050
Fax: (281) 847-1357
Email: kburke@ischouston.com
Web: www.ischouston.com

Description: We understand and speak the language of the healthcare and home building industry. Through our national network and superior reputation, we can complete assignments in a timely and cost effective manner.

Key Contact - Specialty:
Ms. Karen Burke, President - *Healthcare*
Mr. Bob Bennett, Vice President - *Home building (single family, multi family)*

Salary minimum: $40,000

Functions: Generalist, Directors, Senior Mgmt., Middle Mgmt., Purchasing, Mktg. Mgmt., Sales Mgmt., CFO's

Industries: Generalist, Construction, Misc. Financial, Accounting, Real Estate, Healthcare

Professional Associations: HFMA

Isotec Management Inc

170 University Ave Ste 900
Toronto, ON M5H 3B3
Canada
(416) 868-0100
Fax: (416) 868-6292
Email: info@isotecmgt.com
Web: www.isotecmgt.com

Description: Our firm provides professional, results-oriented staffing solutions to clients with information technology (IT) recruitment needs. Isotec Management Inc. is committed to providing total customer service to our client companies. We work closely with a select number of growth-oriented companies enabling us to concentrate our resources on specific hiring projects. This approach allows us to identify and represent candidates that excel in their field.

Key Contact:
Mr. Michael Riall, President

Salary minimum: $40,000

Functions: Risk Mgmt., IT, MIS Mgmt., Systems Analysis, Systems Dev., Systems Implem., Systems Support, Network Admin., DB Admin., Mgmt. Consultants

Industries: Generalist

Networks: National Personnel Assoc (NPA)

Ann Israel & Associates Inc

730 5th Ave Ste 900
New York, NY 10019
(212) 333-8730
Fax: (212) 765-4462
Email: aisrael@annisrael.com
Web: www.attorneysearch.com

Description: Serving the global legal community with broad range of services to law firms and corporations including lateral placements of partners/associates, mergers/acquisitions of practice groups and management advisory services.

Key Contact - Specialty:
Ms. Ann M. Israel, President - *Attorneys*
Ms. Ann-Marie Neville, Director of Recruiting - *Attorneys*

Salary minimum: $100,000

Functions: Legal

Industries: Legal

Professional Associations: NALSC

IT Intellect Inc

1026 Towne Lake Hills E
Woodstock, GA 30189
(770) 926-1674
(770) 926-7869
Fax: (770) 926-8764
Email: jobs@itintellect.net
Web: www.itintellect.net

Description: Our firm is an international computer consulting staffing company offering positions in the US and throughout the world.

Key Contact - Specialty:
Mr. Gordon Bell, President - *IT consulting*
Mrs. Christine Bell, Vice President - *IT consulting*

Functions: IT

Industries: Generalist

IT Leaders Inc

PO Box 67002
Lincoln, NE 68506
(402) 441-9340
(800) 575-7716
Fax: (402) 441-9341
Email: kinga@leadersusa.com
Web: www.leadersusa.com

Description: We specialize in the recruitment of all types of information technology professionals from entry level to directorship level. Primary area of clients serviced is in Nebraska, although we have helped source candidates for other offices nationwide. We recruit from all states and help with relocation.

Key Contact - Specialty:
Ms. Kinga A. Wilson, President/Owner - *Information technology*

Salary minimum: $20,000

Functions: Generalist, MIS Mgmt., Systems Analysis, Systems Dev., Systems Implem., Systems Support, Network Admin., DB Admin.

Industries: Generalist

Professional Associations: AITP

IT Resources

PO Box 305
Lexington, MA 02420
(781) 863-2661
Email: staffing@it-resources.com
Web: www.it-resources.com

Description: Specializes in managers and implementors of leading edge information technology, MIS and software in business environment - client server architecture, LAN/WAN, web-based applications and e-commerce.

Key Contact - Specialty:
Mr. Ken Loomis, Owner - *MIS, software development, information technology*

Salary minimum: $40,000

Functions: MIS Mgmt., Systems Analysis, Systems Dev., Systems Implem., Systems Support, Network Admin., DB Admin.

Industries: Generalist

IT Resources Ltd

25 Valleywood Dr Ste 10
Markham, ON L3R 5L9
Canada
(905) 415-1800
Fax: (905) 415-8111
Email: resumes@itrgroup.com
Web: www.itrgroup.com

Description: Our firm specializes in supplying quality contract and permanent information technology staff to leading corporations. Our clientele range from growing entrepreneurial firms to major Fortune 500 companies such as banking and financial services, software, consulting companies, and many more. We have an excellent reputation for building long lasting and rewarding relationships with clients and IT professionals alike.

Key Contact:
Ms. Victoria Greco, President - *Information technology*
Mr. John Danells, Controller

Functions: IT

Industries: Generalist

IT Services

100 Corporate Dr Ste 108
Windsor, CT 06095
(860) 683-2790
Email: info@itservicesusa.com
Web: www.itservicesusa.com

Description: Our firm is an executive information technologies search firm primarily focused in the northeast corridor. The firm has offices in both Boston and Hartford specializing in permanent placement of software and hardware engineers, architects, sales, and management of IT departments.

Key Contact - Specialty:
Mr. Larry Rubin, CPC, Executive Recruiter - *IT management*
Mrs. Beth Jordan, Executive Recruiter - *IT management, engineers*
Mr. Joe Krol, Executive Recruiter - *IT telecommunications*

Mr. Jim Lutz, Executive Recruiter - *IT engineering, sales*

Functions: Senior Mgmt., Middle Mgmt., IT, Systems Dev., Systems Implem.

Industries: Generalist, Finance, E-commerce, IT Implementation, Telecoms, Call Centers, Telephony, Digital, Wireless, Fiber Optic, Network Infrastructure, Insurance, ERP SW, HR SW

Professional Associations: CAPS, MAPS

Branches:
315 Main St Ste 202
North Reading, MA 01864
(978) 664-0223
Email: info@itserviceusa.com
Key Contact - Specialty:
Ms. Beth Jordan, Manager - *IT management, engineering*

Ives & Associates Inc
2931 E Dublin Granville Rd
Columbus, OH 43231
(614) 839-0202
Fax: (614) 839-0203
Email: phyllis@ivesearch.com
Web: www.executivesearchusa.com

Description: We endeavor to form a partnership with our clients. By working together we can find that individual who will fit within our clients particular corporate culture.

Key Contact - Specialty:
Ms. Phyllis E. Ives, CEO - *Human resources, marketing*
Mr. Jay Canowitz, President - *Accounting/finance distribution*

Salary minimum: $55,000

Functions: Generalist, Purchasing, Mkt. Research, HR Mgmt., Finance

Industries: Mfg., Food, Bev., Tobacco, Textiles, Apparel, Paper, Soap, Perf., Cosmtcs., Drugs Mfg., Medical Devices, Consumer Elect., Retail, Finance, Banking, Mgmt. Consulting, HR Services, Media, Advertising, New Media, Telephony, Wireless, Healthcare

Networks: National Personnel Assoc (NPA)

J & D Resources Inc
6555 Quince Rd Ste 425
Memphis, TN 38119
(901) 753-0500
Fax: (901) 753-0550
Email: jdrmail@jdresources.com
Web: www.jdresources.com

Description: We present only the most qualified applicants for your review. We ensure that these individuals are interested in the opportunity you have to offer. Our overall commitment is to you - to find the people that will contribute to your success.

Key Contact - Specialty:
Ms. Jill T. Herrin, CPC, President - *Information technology*
Mr. Danny L. McKinney, CPC, Vice President - *Information technology*

Salary minimum: $25,000

Functions: IT

Industries: Banking

Professional Associations: MSMUG, NAPS

J Ryder Search
43 N Main St
PO Box 241
White River Junction, VT 05001
(802) 296-3732
Fax: (802) 296-2206

Email: jpr@jrydersearch.com
Web: www.jrydersearch.com

Description: We place executive-level positions located in the North East.

Key Contact - Specialty:
Mr. Joseph Ryder, Owner - *Technical management*

Salary minimum: $130,000

Functions: General Mgmt.

Industries: Generalist

J&C Nationwide
1150 Hammond Dr Ste A-1200
Atlanta, GA 30328
(770) 522-1890
(800) 272-2707
Fax: (770) 730-2870
Email: connect@jcnationwide.com
Web: www.jcnationwide.com

Description: Placing physicians, allied health professionals in hospitals, group practices, HMOs and other healthcare settings nationwide in both permanent and locum tenens positions.

Key Contact - Specialty:
Mr. William Goldstein, CEO - *Physician, allied health professionals*

Functions: Generalist, Healthcare, Physicians, Allied Health

Industries: Generalist, Healthcare

Professional Associations: AAFP, NAPR

Jackley Search Consultants
14581 Grand Ave S
Ridge Run Office Ctr
Burnsville, MN 55306-5769
(952) 469-4868
Fax: (952) 469-6762
Email: brian@jackley.com
Web: www.jackley.com

Description: We have had 15 years of experience recruiting engineers, scientists, and technical managers for medical device, electronics, and plastics manufacturing firms. Our clients are involved in researching, developing, and manufacturing devices and systems

Key Contact - Specialty:
Mr. Brian D. Jackley, Principal - *Engineering, engineering management*

Salary minimum: $50,000

Functions: Directors, Middle Mgmt., Mfg., Product Dev., Production, Automation, Plant Mgmt., Quality, R&D, Engineering

Industries: Generalist, Mfg., Drugs Mfg., Medical Devices, Plastics, Rubber, Test, Measure Equip., Misc. Mfg., Electronic, Elec. Components

Ron Jackson & Associates
4405 Mall Blvd Shannon Twrs Ste 315
Union City, GA 30291
(770) 969-6300
Fax: (770) 969-4333
Email: rjacksonandassoc@prodigy.net

Description: Our combined 60 years of experience, which includes search and staffing at all levels, gives us the ability to provide superior service to our clients. In addition to our expert handling of a variety of assignments, we are able to provide access to top quality contract technical recruiters. We offer access to a broad range of diversity candidates.

Key Contact - Specialty:
Mr. Ron Jackson, President - *Generalist*

Salary minimum: $50,000

Functions: Generalist

Industries: Generalist, Food, Bev., Tobacco, Soap, Perf., Cosmtcs., Drugs Mfg., Plastics, Rubber, Wholesale, Services, Communications, Software

Professional Associations: GAPS

Networks: Top Echelon Network

Jackson Roth Associates
54813 Hwy 275
Norfolk, NE 68701
(800) 772-8033
Fax: (402) 379-7850
Email: jacksonroth@earthlink.net

Description: We offer information technology contingency search and contracting in all specialties. We have 14 years of IT recruiting experience. We have preferred member status in the Top Echelon Network, the largest, most prestigious placement network of independent recruiting firms. For contract positions, Top Echelon Contracting becomes the legal Employer of Record™ handling all administrative paperwork, payroll, and unemployment liabilities.

Key Contact:
Ms. Nancy Ulbert, CPC, Senior Search Manager & Owner

Functions: IT, MIS Mgmt., Systems Analysis, Systems Dev., Systems Implem., Systems Support, Network Admin., DB Admin.

Industries: Generalist

Professional Associations: NAPS

Networks: Top Echelon Network

Cindy Jackson Search Int'l (CJSI)
3031 Tisch Way Ste 700
San Jose, CA 95128
(408) 247-6767
Fax: (408) 247-6677
Email: cindycjsi@aol.com

Description: Together we have almost 20 years' experience. Interviewing skills taught to candidates.

Key Contact - Specialty:
Ms. Cindy Jackson, Owner - *Sales, marketing, application engineers - electronic design automation industry only*
Mrs. Tracy Marseline, Recruiter - *Software developers, electronic design automation industry & database*

Salary minimum: $50,000

Functions: Generalist, Mktg. Mgmt., Sales Mgmt., Direct Mktg., Customer Svc., Engineering

Industries: Generalist, Software

The Jacob Group
(also known as MRI of Preston Park)
2301 N Central Expwy Ste 250
Plano, TX 75075
(972) 422-3311
Fax: (972) 422-4001
Email: solutions@jacobgroup.com
Web: www.jacobgroup.com

Description: Executive search firm specializing in all functional areas within consumer products and retail/hospitality. Special capability in large multiple hire projects.

Key Contact - Specialty:
Mr. Donald Jacob, Principal - *Human resources, sales, operations, marketing*

Functions: General Mgmt., Plant Mgmt., Materials, Sales & Mktg., HR Mgmt.

Industries: Generalist

S H Jacobs & Associates Inc

204 Jenkintown Commons
Jenkintown, PA 19046
(215) 886-2700
Fax: (215) 887-3134

Description: Executive search firm dedicated to the marketing, marketing communications and advertising sectors of industry, service companies and ad agencies.

Key Contact - Specialty:
Mr. Saul H. Jacobs, President - *Advertising, marketing communications*
Ms. Lois Wild, Human Resources - *Advertising, marketing communications*
Ms. Lisa Daltirus, Executive Recruiter - *Advertising, marketing communications*
Ms. Susan Rosenthal, Executive Recruiter - *Advertising, marketing communications*

Salary minimum: $50,000

Functions: Senior Mgmt., Middle Mgmt., Advertising, Mkt. Research, Mktg. Mgmt., Direct Mktg., PR

Industries: Food, Bev., Tobacco, Textiles, Apparel, Drugs Mfg., Consumer Elect., Pharm Svcs., Hospitality, Advertising, New Media

Jacobson Associates

120 S LaSalle St Ste 1410
Chicago, IL 60603
(312) 726-1578
Fax: (888) 523-0740
Email: chicago@jacobson-associates.com
Web: www.jacobson-associates.com

Description: We are the nation's largest and oldest executive search firm dedicated specifically to the insurance and related industries. We provide organizations with cost-effective resources in all disciplines and at all levels.

Key Contact - Specialty:
Mr. David Jacobson, Chairman - *Insurance*
Mr. Greg Jacobson, Principal - *Insurance*

Salary minimum: $20,000

Functions: Generalist, Risk Mgmt.

Industries: Generalist, Insurance

Professional Associations: ASA, CPCU

Branches:
1775 The Exchange Ste 240
Atlanta, GA 30339
(770) 952-3877
Fax: (770) 952-0061
Email: atlanta@jacobson-associates.com
Key Contact - Specialty:
Mr. Gregory Jacobson, Principal - *Insurance*

5 Neshaminy Interplex Ste 113
Trevose, PA 19053
(215) 639-5860
Fax: (215) 639-8096
Email: philadelphia@jacobson-associates.com
Key Contact - Specialty:
Mr. Nate Bass, President - *Insurance*

3304 S Broadway Ste 205
Tyler, TX 75701
(903) 592-2591
Fax: (903) 592-3562
Email: dallas@jacobson-associates.com
Key Contact - Specialty:
Mr. Jeffrey Jenkins, Vice President - *Insurance*

K Jaeger & Associates

60 Thoreau St Ste 300
Concord, MA 01742-9116
(978) 369-3352
Fax: (978) 369-0757
Email: kjaeger@acunet.net

Description: We offer retained and contingency search with a difference. Our thorough, consultative approach ensures efficient solutions to sales, marketing, engineering line, and staff searches. Our clients are suppliers of mechanical and electro-mechanical products, controls, and capital equipment sold to industrial markets nationwide.

Key Contact - Specialty:
Mr. Karl Schoellkopf, Managing Director - *Industrial (sales & marketing)*

Salary minimum: $50,000

Functions: Generalist

Industries: Energy, Utilities, Construction, Mfg., Chemicals, Plastics, Rubber, Metal Products, Machine, Appliance, Test, Measure Equip., Misc. Mfg., Electronic, Elec. Components

James & Company

515 E Carefree Hwy Ste 482
Phoenix, AZ 85085
(623) 465-5357
Fax: (602) 296-0163
Email: brucej@cybervault.com
Web: www.salesrecruiter.net

Description: We work in a generalist environment with a concentration in, sales, sales management, engineering, manufacturing, distribution, process management, data telecommunications, information systems, accounting, high-tech fields, and human resources.

Key Contact:
Mr. Bruce James, President

Salary minimum: $50,000

Functions: General Mgmt., Plant Mgmt., Quality, Materials, Sales & Mktg., Engineering, Specialized Svcs.

Industries: Generalist, Mfg., Food, Bev., Tobacco, Lumber, Furniture, Paper, Printing, Plastics, Rubber, Paints, Petro. Products, Metal Products, Machine, Appliance, Motor Vehicles, Consumer Elect., Misc. Mfg., Accounting, Equip Svcs.

James & Richards

1017 W Park Dr
Midland, MI 48640
(517) 839-4949
Fax: (517) 839-4023
Email: jw049@aol.com
Web: www.members.aol.com/jwd49/

Description: Experienced chemists an engineers at all levels for chemical and allied industries. Pharmacy, specialty chemistry, plastics, etc.

Key Contact:
Mr. Jim Dreyer
Mr. Dick Lames

Salary minimum: $50,000

Functions: Middle Mgmt., Mfg., Product Dev., Production, Plant Mgmt., Quality, Materials, R&D, Engineering

Industries: Chemicals, Soap, Perf., Cosmtcs., Drugs Mfg., Plastics, Rubber, Paints, Petro. Products

Networks: Recruiters Professional Network (RPN)

Devon James Associates Inc

15600 NE 8th St Ste B1 - 672
Bellevue, WA 98008
(425) 378-1682
Fax: (425) 378-1683
Email: colleen@devonjames.com
Web: www.devonjames.com

Description: We provide onsite recruiting war rooms for high-tech start-ups; this is where small teams go onsite to hire 10-40 new infrastructure employees in 3-4 months' time. We also provide, retained and contingency recruiting for full-time positions with US companies in software, hardware, networks, e-commerce, Internet, telecommunications, and biotech. Our candidates range from senior to mid-level in product development, engineering, sales, ops, support, business development, marketing, and executive positions.

Key Contact - Specialty:
Ms. Colleen Aylward, President/Hall Monitor - *High technology*
Mr. John Bergen, Director-Onsite Recruiting War Rm Teams - *High tech startups*

Salary minimum: $75,000

Functions: HR Mgmt., Personnel

Industries: Venture Cap., Non-profits, Mgmt. Consulting, HR Services, E-commerce, IT Implementation, Telecoms, Network Infrastructure, Database SW, Development SW, ERP SW, HR SW, Networking, Comm. SW, Biotech

Professional Associations: MITEF, NWVG, WSA

Networks: National Personnel Assoc (NPA)

Branches:
325M Sharon Park Dr Ste 113
Menlo Park, CA 94025
(650) 207-6573
Email: devonjames@devonjames.com
Key Contact - Specialty:
Ms. Colleen Aylward, President/Hall Monitor - *VC portfolio companies (retained, onsite)*
Mr. John Bergen, Director-Onsite Recruiting War Rm Teams - *High tech start-ups*

Lawrence James Associates of Florida

8795 W McNab Rd Ste 202
Ft. Lauderdale, FL 33321
(954) 721-6100
Fax: (954) 726-3555
Email: lawrencejames@mindspring.com
Web: www.lawrence-james.com

Description: An executive search firm specializing in the supermarket and retail industry for over 20 years with relationships in the industry enabling us to identify quickly client and candidates that excel.

Key Contact - Specialty:
Mr. Leonard Okyn, President - *Supermarket industry, retail industry*

Functions: General Mgmt., Distribution, Sales & Mktg., HR Mgmt., Finance, IT

Industries: Wholesale, Retail

Professional Associations: FMI

Branches:
1 Executive Dr Ste 160
Somerset, NJ 08873
(732) 748-1188
Fax: (732) 356-4660
Key Contact - Specialty:
Mr. Larry Hebert - *Supermarket industry*

Victoria James Executive Search Inc

1177 Summer St Fl 2
Stamford, CT 06905
(203) 358-0887
Fax: (203) 358-0864
Email: vjames@victoriajames.com
Web: www.victoriajames.com

Description: Provide national mid- to senior-level executive search services to the direct marketing and Internet communities. We are committed to ensuring exceptional search solutions for candidates and client companies.

Key Contact - Specialty:
Ms. Victoria James, President - *Direct marketing, internet*

Salary minimum: $70,000

Functions: Generalist

Industries: Publishing, Telecoms, Marketing SW, Non-classifiable

Professional Associations: AIM, ATA, DMA, WDMI

Branches:
44 Lightfoot Dr
Stafford, VA 22554
(540) 657-8885
Fax: (540) 657-6083
Email: dsmolen@victoriajames.com
Key Contact - Specialty:
Mr. Dan Smolen, Vice President - *Direct marketing, internet*

R I James Inc

325 Riverside Dr Ste 54
New York, NY 10025-4156
(212) 662-0203
Fax: (212) 864-9602
Email: rijames@earthlink.net

Description: Specialists in mid- to senior-level placement in supply chain business logistics and materials management. Our client references reflect the highest standards of excellence. Recognized by the Council of Logistics Management for professional logistics recruitment.

Key Contact - Specialty:
Ms. Rhoda Isaacs, President - *Logistics (domestic, international)*

Salary minimum: $75,000

Functions: General Mgmt., Directors, Senior Mgmt., Middle Mgmt.

Industries: Generalist

Professional Associations: CLM, IIE

The Jameson Group

1900 Ave of the Stars Ste 670
Los Angeles, CA 90067
(310) 286-0220
Fax: (310) 286-0866
Email: tjg@thejamesongroup.com
Web: www.thejamesongroup.com

Description: We specialize in attorney recruiting and placement for law firms and corporations.

Key Contact - Specialty:
Mr. John B. Jameson, President - *Legal (attorneys)*

Salary minimum: $100,000

Functions: Attorneys

Industries: Legal

Professional Associations: NALSC

Jaral Consultants Inc

PO Box 498
Springfield, NJ 07081
(973) 564-9236
Fax: (973) 379-1275

Description: We specialize in placing in the following areas; fashion, including designers, production, sales and all other technical and professional specialties specific to the fashion industry. Presidents and other top executives are our primary placements.

Key Contact - Specialty:
Mr. Joseph Morgan - *Fashion industry*

Salary minimum: $50,000

Functions: Product Dev., Production, Quality, Sales Mgmt., HR Mgmt., CFO's, IT, MIS Mgmt., Engineering, Int'l.

Industries: Mfg., Textiles, Apparel, Electronic, Elec. Components, Wholesale, Retail

Professional Associations: NJAPS

Jatinen & Associates

20422 Beach Blvd Ste 235
Huntington Beach, CA 92648
(714) 960-9082
Fax: (714) 960-1772
Email: djatinen@prodigy.net

Description: Title insurance and escrow industry. Work all levels of management and senior technical positions.

Key Contact - Specialty:
Mr. Dave Jatinen, Owner - *Insurance (title, escrow)*

Salary minimum: $40,000

Functions: Generalist

Industries: Insurance, Real Estate

Professional Associations: CSP

JCL & Associates

PO Box 9541
Panama City Beach, FL 32417
(850) 230-1888
Fax: (850) 230-0888

Description: Over 30 years in private placement, national and international. Highly specialized in mens, womens, childrens knitwear and intimate apparel from sales/marketing, manufacturing/sourcing, financial, product development/design.

Key Contact:
Ms. Judy Lee, CPC, President

Salary minimum: $30,000

Functions: Generalist, Senior Mgmt., Product Dev., Plant Mgmt., Distribution, Mkt. Research, Sales Mgmt., CFO's, MIS Mgmt.

Industries: Generalist, Textiles, Apparel

JDC Associates

300 Wheeler Rd Ste104
Hauppauge, NY 11788
(631) 231-8581
Fax: (631) 231-8011
Email: jdcassoc@optonline.net

Description: Professional recruiting firm committed to identifying and isolating only the top 10% proven documented performers. Their success is due to their creativity, versatility and commitment to excellence in the marketplace.

Key Contact - Specialty:
Ms. Lori Boyle, President - *Sales, accounting, office support*

Functions: Generalist, Nurses, Sales Mgmt., Customer Svc., Credit, Systems Support, Network Admin.

Industries: Generalist, Drugs Mfg., Medical Devices, Accounting, Healthcare

JDG Associates Ltd

1700 Research Blvd
Rockville, MD 20850
(301) 340-2210
Fax: (301) 762-3117
Email: degioia@jdgsearch.com
Web: www.jdgsearch.com

Description: Recruiters serving the disciplines of computer sciences, electronics, telecommunications engineering, management science and association management.

Key Contact - Specialty:
Mr. Joseph DeGioia, President - *Management consultants*

Salary minimum: $65,000

Functions: IT, MIS Mgmt., Systems Analysis, Systems Dev., Systems Implem., Mgmt. Consultants

Industries: Mgmt. Consulting, Software, Biotech

Professional Associations: MAPRC

Networks: National Personnel Assoc (NPA)

Jefferson-Ross Associates Inc

2 Penn Center Plz Ste 312
Philadelphia, PA 19102
(215) 564-5322
Fax: (215) 587-0766
Email: jeffross@cwl-inc.com

Description: Executive search assignments for professional/technical and mid-management individuals in financial services, insurance, healthcare, information systems and computer services industries nationwide. Over 25 years of experience in professional recruitment and search.

Key Contact - Specialty:
Mr. Craig Zander, President - *Generalist*

Salary minimum: $50,000

Functions: Generalist, General Mgmt., Sales & Mktg., Sales Mgmt., HR Mgmt., Finance, IT

Industries: Generalist, Finance, Insurance, Software, Healthcare

Jenex Technology Placement Inc

1260 Hornby St Ste 104
Vancouver, BC V6Z 1W2
Canada
(604) 687-3585
Fax: (604) 687-5432
Email: jobs@jenex.ca
Web: www.jenex.ca

Description: We are a Vancouver-based recruiter of Western Canada's leading advanced technology professionals. Including software development, programmers, database designers, systems architects and other technical specialists in the industry.

Key Contact - Specialty:
Ms. Jennifer Rigal, Consultant - *High technology, software*
Ms. Allison Guld, Consultant - *High technology, software*

Salary minimum: $30,000

Functions: IT

Industries: Software

Professional Associations: ACSESS, HRMA, TIA

JenKim Int'l Ltd Inc

7040 W Palmetto Park Rd 2-250
Boca Raton, FL 33433
(954) 427-6962
Fax: (954) 427-0021
Email: jnkm7@mindspring.com
Web: www.jenkim.com

Description: We are a highly skilled and professional recruiting/search firm providing expert advice and assistance to those professionals seeking to advance their careers in the computer or telecommunications industry.

Key Contact - Specialty:
Mr. Robert W. Norton, President - *Computer, telecommunications*
Mrs. Jennifer Johnson, Associate Recruiter - *Computer, telecommunications*
Ms. Kim Norton, Associate Recruiter - *Telecommunications*

Salary minimum: $50,000

Functions: Directors, Senior Mgmt., Middle Mgmt., Sales & Mktg., Mktg. Mgmt., Sales Mgmt., Engineering

Industries: Computer Equip., Services, Equip Svcs., Mgmt. Consulting, HR Services, Media, Telecoms, Government, Defense

Jerome & Co
211 Culver Blvd Ste R
Playa del Rey, CA 90293
(310) 305-1812
Fax: (310) 305-8678
Email: jerocomp@aol.com

Description: We are West Coast, manufacturing company, recruiting specialists. We recruit CEOs/presidents/general managers, directors of operations, engineering, materials, quality assurance, human resources, and CFOs/controllers.

Key Contact - Specialty:
Mr. Gerald E. Jerome, President - *Presidents, general managers, vice presidents, manufacturing*

Salary minimum: $70,000

Functions: Generalist, Senior Mgmt., Mfg., Plant Mgmt., Quality, Materials, CFO's, Engineering

Industries: Generalist, Mfg., Drugs Mfg., Medical Devices, Plastics, Rubber, Metal Products, Consumer Elect., Aerospace

Professional Associations: APICS, ASQ, PIRA, SME

JFK Search
10 S 5th St Ste 600
Minneapolis, MN 55402
(612) 332-8082
Fax: (612) 305-4387
Email: jfkser@worldnet.att.net
Web: www.jfksearch.com

Description: Specialist in agency account service recruiting, network with many other recruiters, operate on a national basis.

Key Contact - Specialty:
Mr. James Kessler, President - *Advertising, promotion, public relations account service*

Functions: Senior Mgmt., Advertising, PR

Industries: Generalist

Professional Associations: NAMA

JFW Associates LLC
753 Boston Post Rd Ste 102
PO Box 267
Guilford, CT 06437
(203) 453-1415
Fax: (203) 458-1347
Email: jobs@jfw.com
Web: www.jfw.com

Description: Contingency search for professionals in information technology and software engineering.

Key Contact - Specialty:
Mr. John Wilbur, Manager - *Information technology, software engineering*
Mr. Robert Vissers, Partner - *Information technology, software engineering*

Functions: Generalist, IT, MIS Mgmt., Systems Analysis, Systems Dev., Systems Implem., Systems Support, Network Admin.

Industries: Generalist, Software

Jhirad Consulting Inc
16625 Redmond Way Ste M-400
Redmond, WA 98052-4444
(212) 202-7567
(212) 202-7567
Fax: (212) 202-7567
Email: talent@jhirad.com
Web: www.jhirad.com

Description: Our firm is an executive search and recruiting company with offices in New York and Washington State. We specialize in the finance and technology sector and cater to a wide clientele including investment banks, hedge funds,

management consulting companies, Internet/dot-coms, e-Commerce, and technology companies.

Key Contact - Specialty:
Mr. Ephraim Jhirad, President - *Finance, banking, information technology, management consulting*

Functions: Generalist

Industries: Computer Equip., Finance, Accounting, HR Services, Media, Telecoms, Software

J Jireh & Associates Inc
PO Box 7534
Burbank, CA 91510-7534
(818) 361-7188
Fax: (818) 361-2527
Email: frank@j-jireh.com
Web: www.j-jireh.com

Description: J. Jireh & Associates, Inc. (JJA) was founded in 1996 to provide quality technical staffing and consulting services to corporations and organizations in the southern California area. We believe that we play a very crucial role in bringing together employers and the technical professionals they seek to recruit and employ. We understand that we have two clients to serve and to satisfy - the corporations and organizations that utilize and purchase our services, and the technica

Key Contact - Specialty:
Mr. Frank Liggett, President/CEO
Mr. John Andersen, Vice President - *Technical project, resource management and staffing*

Functions: Generalist, IT

Industries: Generalist, E-commerce, IT Implementation, Telecoms, Call Centers, Telephony, Digital, Wireless, Fiber Optic, Network Infrastructure, Database SW, Development SW, Doc. Mgmt., Production SW, ERP SW

Networks: Top Echelon Network

Jivaro Group
5433 S Emporia Crt
Greenwood Village, CO 80111
(303) 740-0022
Email: sue@jivarogroup.com
Web: www.jivarogroup.com

Description: We are an executive search firm that focuses on the telecommunications, Internet, and high tech industries. We work with clients on their critical leadership, senior sales, and marketing requirements.

Key Contact - Specialty:
Ms. Sue Wyman, President - *Leadership, senior sales & marketing, communications, internet, high tech*

Functions: Directors, Senior Mgmt., Sales & Mktg., Mktg. Mgmt., Sales Mgmt.

Industries: Telecoms, Call Centers, Telephony, Digital, Wireless, Fiber Optic, Network Infrastructure, Marketing SW, Networking, Comm. SW, Training SW

JL & Company
3020 Bridgeway Ste 330
Sausalito, CA 94965
(415) 383-9464
Email: jlco@pobox.com

Description: We are a retained executive search for VC funded and high tech startups. VP/SVP and director level marketing, business development, and sales. We have a Northern California geographic focus. Our representative clients include: Rearden Steel, Dialpad Communications, Looksmart, When.com, Billpoint, LinkExchange, Listen.com, and Snapfish.com.

Key Contact - Specialty:
Mr. Jon R. Love, Principal - *Internet marketing, internet business development, e-commerce*

Salary minimum: $100,000

Functions: Sales & Mktg.

Industries: Media, New Media, Telecoms, Software

JNB Associates Inc
990 Washington St Ste 200
Dedham, MA 02026
(781) 407-0401
Fax: (781) 407-0407
Email: jnb@gis.net

Description: Banking and financial specialists - retainer and some contingency depending on circumstances.

Key Contact:
Mr. Joseph N. Baker, Jr., Chairman - *Banking, financial*
Mr. John C. Mechem, President
Mr. Lin Morisson, Vice Chairman
Mr. Richard D. Lund, Vice Chairman

Salary minimum: $70,000

Functions: Generalist

Industries: Finance, Banking, Invest. Banking

Professional Associations: MBA

The Job Dr
95 Enterprise Ste 330
Aliso Viejo, CA 92656
(949) 360-1800
(877) 915-6237
Fax: (949) 360-1808
Email: ken-info@thejobdr.com
Web: www.thejobdr.com

Description: We are the leading computer and software placement firm in Orange County. We were rated number one in Southern California by "Business 2.0" magazine (3/2000). We have had over $100 million in salaries placed, with a personal and caring touch. We specialize in .Net, C#, C++, VB, VB.Net, SQL, and all Microsoft technologies. We also focus on database, network, SAN, LAN/WAN, VPN, Intra-, Inter-, and extranet environments. We place in the software, product, dot.com, and industry fields.

Key Contact:
Mr. Roger Howland, President

Salary minimum: $75,000

Functions: Senior Mgmt., IT, MIS Mgmt., Systems Analysis, Systems Dev., Systems Implem., DB Admin.

Industries: Generalist

Job Link Inc
2604B El Camino Real #363
Carlsbad, CA 92008-1214
(760) 602-9011
Fax: (760) 438-4116
Email: joblink4u@aol.com
Web: www.joblinkexecutivesearch.com

Description: We specialize in executive, senior and general management positions for the manufacturing, high-technology, biotechnology and pharmaceutical industries. We also work heavily with North American Maquiladora operations. Bilingual (Spanish) recruiting staff.

Key Contact - Specialty:
Ms. Mary Rose Gutierrez, President - *Home healthcare, managed care*
Mr. William McCleary, Manager - *Manufacturing operations management, aerospace, directors, senior management, research & development*

Salary minimum: $65,000

Functions: General Mgmt., Senior Mgmt., Automation, Plant Mgmt., HR Mgmt., CFO's, R&D, Engineering, Int'l.

Industries: Mfg., Food, Bev., Tobacco, Drugs Mfg., Medical Devices, Plastics, Rubber, Metal Products, Machine, Appliance, Test, Measure Equip., Misc. Mfg., Communications, Packaging, HR SW, Mfg. SW, Biotech

Job-Born Candidate Selection Bureau

370 Main St E Ste 305
Hamilton, ON L8N 1J6
Canada
(905) 522-7551
(877) 522-7551
Fax: (905) 522-2952
Email: resumes@job-bornrecruiting.com
Web: www.job-bornrecruiting.com

Description: In addition to recruiting top quality personnel, we are a proactive agency, actively marketing exceptional candidates whom we have isolated and evaluated.

Key Contact - Specialty:
Mrs. Mary Ann Vaughn, CPC, President/Owner - *Generalist*

Functions: Generalist

Industries: Generalist

Professional Associations: ACSESS

John Jay & Co

100 Commercial St Ste 205
Portland, ME 04101
(207) 772-6951
Fax: (207) 772-0159
Email: jhotchkss@aol.com

Description: Small, boutique firm with a very personalized approach. Offers particular expertise in human resources search and can provide H.R. consulting services as well.

Key Contact:
Mr. Jay Hotchkiss, CMC, SPHR, President

Salary minimum: $45,000

Functions: Generalist, Senior Mgmt., Plant Mgmt., HR Mgmt., Finance, R&D, Mgmt. Consultants

Industries: Generalist, Misc. Mfg., Finance, HR Services, Hospitality, Biotech, Healthcare

Professional Associations: ASTD, IMC, SHRM

Paul Johnson & Associates Inc

402 Office Park Dr Ste 100
Birmingham, AL 35223
(205) 871-6510

Description: We specialize in recruiting superb leadership talent for information technology industry. Our mission is to turn client's vision into reality by identifying management team members to run the company (start-up, e-commerce, web-based software).

Key Contact - Specialty:
Mr. Paul R. Johnson, President - *Technology management*

Salary minimum: $80,000

Functions: Sales & Mktg., HR Mgmt.

Industries: Generalist

Professional Associations: SHRM

Johnson Associates Inc

114 N Hale St
Wheaton, IL 60187
(630) 690-9200
Fax: (630) 690-9910
Email: foodsearch@aol.com

Description: We provide both broadline and specialty foodservice distributors and food manufacturers with the best possible talent in every functional area, including: senior management, sales, operations, finance, purchasing, and M.I.S. As national specialists, our commitment to our industry is unmatched by our competitors. Only candidates who possess extensive, successful industry history should apply.

Key Contact:
Mr. Scott Johnson, President - *Food service distribution*
Mr. John Carrigg, Manager - *Non-foods*
Ms. Mary Johnson, Vice President

Salary minimum: $60,000

Functions: Generalist

Industries: Food, Bev., Tobacco, Chemicals, Wholesale, Non-classifiable

Clifton Johnson Associates Inc

1 Monroeville Ctr 725
Pittsburgh, PA 15146
(412) 856-8000
Fax: (412) 856-8026
Email: cj@cliftonjohnson.com
Web: www.cliftonjohnson.com

Description: We are now in our 34th year servicing the engineering, technical, IT, and management sectors. Our files are in the excess of 80,000 engineers and technical professionals with access to 1000s more through our national networks. Please visit our web site to view over 7,000 jobs.

Key Contact:
Mr. Cliff Johnson, President

Salary minimum: $45,000

Functions: Generalist

Industries: Energy, Utilities, Construction, Mfg., Electronic, Elec. Components, Communications, Aerospace, Packaging, Software

Networks: Inter-City Personnel Assoc (IPA)

K E Johnson Associates

4213-187th Pl SE
Issaquah, WA 98027
(425) 747-4559

Description: We provide information technology, project management, and engineering placement services specializing in telecommunications, network service providers, high-tech, and computer related industries.

Key Contact - Specialty:
Mr. Karl Johnson, President - *High technology, scientific, research & development*

Salary minimum: $60,000

Functions: Senior Mgmt., Product Dev., Mkt. Research, IT, Systems Dev., R&D, Engineering

Industries: Generalist, Construction, Mfg., Chemicals, Medical Devices, Computer Equip., Test, Measure Equip., Electronic, Elec. Components, Transportation, Finance, IT Implementation, Media, Communications, Government, Aerospace, Software, Biotech, Healthcare

Johnson Enterprises Inc

180 Broadway Ste 300
New York, NY 10038-2506
(212) 602-9980
Fax: (212) 602-9977
Email: search@johnsonenterprises.com
Web: www.johnsonenterprises.com

Description: Specializing in financial institutions and F500 corporations, we offer a wide range of career opportunities at the mid- to upper-management level on a global basis. Our talent bank

is composed of finance, marketing, human resources, operations and IT executives.

Key Contact:
Ms. Priscilla Johnson, CEO - *Generalist*
Mr. Steve Collins, Managing Director - *Financial services, institutions*
Mr. Howard Baker, Senior Managing Partner - *Generalist*
Mr. Howard O. Smith, Vice President - *Financial services*
Mr. Christopher Byrner, Senior Managing Consultant
Ms. Natalie B. Gansop, Manager-Research - *Marketing*
Ms. Theresa Lasbrey, Office Manager
Ms. Wahida Brooks, Research Associate - *Generalist*
Ms. Susan Byrner, Research Associate
Ms. Antonia Gonsalves, Research Associate
Mr. Bill Bell, Research Associate Trainee

Salary minimum: $100,000

Functions: General Mgmt., Senior Mgmt., Sales & Mktg., Mktg. Mgmt., HR Mgmt., Finance, IT, Mgmt. Consultants, Minorities, Int'l.

Industries: Generalist, Retail, Finance, Accounting, Telecoms

Branches:
3233 N Second St
Harrisburg, PA 17110
(717) 221-0675
Fax: (717) 221-8589
Email: search@johnsonenterprises.com

Johnson Search Associates Inc

2711 W 183rd St Ste 208
Homewood, IL 60430
(800) 325-4525
(708) 957-4525
Fax: (708) 957-4529
Email: rmjsearch@aol.com

Description: We specialize in the recruitment of engineers, sales, and management professionals in the electronics field.

Key Contact - Specialty:
Mr. Robert M. Johnson, President - *Electronics engineering, electronics sales*

Salary minimum: $32,000

Functions: Generalist, Middle Mgmt., Production, Sales Mgmt., Engineering, Technicians

Industries: Generalist, Medical Devices, Computer Equip., Media, Healthcare

J Joseph & Associates

3766 Fishcreek Rd
PMB 322
Stow, OH 44224
(330) 676-0522
Fax: (330) 676-9522
Email: wecare@jjosephrecruiter.com
Web: www.jjosephrecruiter.com

Description: Our firm specializes in field sales staffing for USA. Our clients are exclusive to us. Our focus is national.

Key Contact - Specialty:
Mr. Scott Raymont, President - *Sales*
Mr. Joe McGoldrick, Vice President - *Sales*
Ms. Carolyn James, Operations Manager - *Sales*

Salary minimum: $28,000

Functions: Generalist, Production, Advertising, Mkt. Research, MIS Mgmt., Systems Analysis, Engineering

Industries: Generalist, Paper, Printing, Medical Devices, Computer Equip.

Networks: First Interview Network (FIN)

Joseph Associates Inc
229 Main St
Huntington, NY 11743
(631) 351-5805
Fax: (516) 421-4123
Email: inquiries@jaexecutivesearch.com

Description: We place computer professionals, statisticians, and researchers with job titles ranging from programmer to chief technology officer, while matching candidates' skills and goals to our client company's needs. Our areas of expertise include credit card, direct/database marketing, e-Commerce, new media, and statistical analysis and programming.

Key Contact - Specialty:
Mr. Joseph Nakelski, President - *Statisticians, market research, data management, database marketing, e-com*
Ms. Tara Moore, VP Consulting Services - *SAS, statisticians (permanent, consulting)*
Ms. Denise Milano, VP Contingency Search - *Programming, oracle, java, e-commerce, database administration, media*
Ms. Carolyn Sheppard, VP Retained Search - *E-Com, wireless*
Ms. Dee Schloss, Director, Search Services for New Media - *Media, new media*

Salary minimum: $75,000

Functions: Generalist, MIS Mgmt., Systems Analysis, Systems Dev., Systems Implem., Systems Support, Network Admin., DB Admin.

Industries: Generalist, Drugs Mfg., Banking, Invest. Banking, Insurance, Software, Healthcare

Professional Associations: APCNY

Joseph Consulting Inc
216 Park Ave S
Winter Park, FL 32789
(407) 628-7073
Fax: (407) 628-7074
Email: jerry@josephconsulting.com
Web: www.josephconsulting.com

Description: We are a consulting and recruiting firm specializing in providing information technology, sales, finance, management, and executive level solutions on a contract or direct placement basis.

Key Contact - Specialty:
Mr. Jerry McGee, President/CEO - *Consulting & recruiting-information technology, sales, finance, management, executive*

Salary minimum: $50,000

Functions: Generalist

Industries: Energy, Utilities, Finance, Services, Communications, Aerospace, Insurance, Real Estate, Software, Biotech, Healthcare

Professional Associations: FCCI

Joslin & Associates Ltd
291 Deer Trail Ct Ste C-3
Lake Barrington, IL 60010-1773
(847) 304-1100
Fax: (847) 304-1102
Email: joslinltd@hotmail.com

Description: Optimizing opportunities for individuals and organizations with scientific or technical orientation in the pharmaceutical industry, including search and placement, acquisition and licensing. Extensive industry research and executive experience.

Key Contact - Specialty:
Dr. Robert S. Joslin, Consultant - *Pharmaceutical research & development, quality control, production*

Salary minimum: $60,000

Functions: Directors, Senior Mgmt., Middle Mgmt., Mfg., Product Dev., Quality, Healthcare, R&D, Engineering

Industries: Drugs Mfg., Pharm Svcs.

Professional Associations: AAPS, AFPE, AIC, CPDG, CRS, PDA

The Jotorok Group
4 Richmond Sq
Providence, RI 02906
(401) 521-7989
Fax: (401) 521-7993
Email: jobs@jotorok.com
Web: www.jotorok.com

Description: We are a single source provider to the information technology industry by offering both permanent and contract staffing solutions.

Key Contact - Specialty:
Mr. Ron Wnek, Managing Partner - *Information technology*
Mr. Tom Leonard, Managing Partner - *Information technology*
Mr. Joe DiMuccio, Senior Partner - *Information technology*

Salary minimum: $25,000

Functions: MIS Mgmt., Systems Analysis, Systems Dev., Systems Implem., Systems Support, Network Admin., DB Admin.

Industries: Generalist

Professional Associations: NATSS

Albert A Joyner & Associates Inc
2880 Holcomb Bridge Rd Bldg B-9 Ste 566
Alpharetta, GA 30022
(770) 643-8557
Fax: (770) 518-7059
Email: aljoyner@aol.com

Description: Middle and senior-level multidisciplinary healthcare and hospital executive search. Extensive resources and industry network to provide high quality, professional, personalized, results-driven service.

Key Contact - Specialty:
Mr. Albert A. Joyner, President - *Healthcare executives*
Ms. Jayne N. Joyner, Vice President - *Healthcare executives*

Salary minimum: $70,000

Functions: Generalist

Industries: Healthcare

JP Resources
15 Meagan Dr
Beaufort, SC 29902
(843) 322-0329
Fax: (843) 470-1273
Email: skyjones@islc.net

Description: We provide recruitment research for hard to find and mid- to upper-level management. We specialize in manufacturing, engineering, and sales and marketing.

Key Contact:
Ms. Carolyn Jones, Research Consultant

Salary minimum: $60,000

Functions: Generalist

Industries: Mfg., Retail, Services, Media

JPM Int'l
26034 Acero
Mission Viejo, CA 92691
(949) 699-4300
(800) 685-7856
Fax: (949) 699-4333

Email: leslieo@jpmintl.com
Web: www.jpmintl.com

Description: HR consulting firm specializing in the staffing/retention of all permanent employees hired into an organization. Through our program, Shared Vision, a partnership between us and the client, we achieve a full understanding of your company's needs, corporate cultures, goals and objectives.

Key Contact - Specialty:
Ms. Melissa Hannigan, Managing Partner - *Medical, healthcare*
Ms. Lesley Graham, Managing Partner - *Telecommunications*
Ms. Trish Ryan, President - *Senior management, board members*

Salary minimum: $75,000

Functions: Generalist

Industries: Mfg., Invest. Banking, Venture Cap., Services, Telecoms, Software, Biotech, Healthcare

JRL Executive Recruiters
2700 Rockcreek Pkwy Ste 103
North Kansas City, MO 64117-2519
(816) 471-4022
Fax: (816) 471-8634
Email: larryeason@yahoo.com
Web: www.jrlexecutiverecruiters.com

Description: We are a professional search firm that recruits for technical personnel to senior-level management. The firm practice is national in scope and has worked assignments for international clients.

Key Contact - Specialty:
Mr. Larry E. Eason, President - *Engineering, technical, manufacturing*
Mr. Tony Rice, VP- Information Systems - *Information technologies*

Salary minimum: $45,000

Functions: Generalist, General Mgmt., Mfg., Materials, HR Mgmt., IT, Engineering, Specialized Svcs.

Industries: Generalist, Agri., Forestry, Mining, Energy, Utilities, Construction, Mfg., Transportation, Services, Communications, Environmental Svcs., Packaging, Software

Branches:
2187 Hopkins Ter
Duluth, GA 30096
(770) 446-1291
Fax: (770) 446-0402
Key Contact - Specialty:
Mr. James M. Eason, Vice President - *Engineering, manufacturing*

JRW & Associates
PO Box 180111
Tallahassee, FL 32318
(850) 562-5300
Fax: (850) 562-5350
Email: warren@staffing.net
Web: www.jrw-associates.com/

Description: Our company has developed many contacts over the years. This enriches our base and allows us to present the most qualified candidates possible in our disciplines. From engineers to computer, we have the sources.

Key Contact:
Mr. Rick Warren, Owner

Salary minimum: $30,000

Functions: Mfg., Production, Automation, Productivity, IT, Systems Analysis, Systems Dev., Systems Implem., Network Admin.

Industries: Generalist, Mfg., Paper, Chemicals, Plastics, Rubber, Paints, Petro. Products, Software

Networks: Top Echelon Network

JSK Consulting

910 Athens Hwy Ste K 236
Loganville, GA 30052
(678) 344-5727
Fax: (678) 344-5716
Email: jkelly105@mindspring.com

Description: We are an independent recruitment firm specializing in creative sourcing and placement of executives, middle, and front-line management personnel.

Key Contact - Specialty:
Mr. Justina Kelly, Executive Recruitment Strategist/Owner - *Call center, human resource management*

Functions: General Mgmt., Directors, Middle Mgmt., Purchasing, Customer Svc., HR Mgmt., Benefits, Personnel, Training, Architects

Industries: Non-profits, Pharm Svcs., HR Services, IT Implementation, Hotels, Resorts, Clubs, Restaurants, Call Centers

Professional Associations: SHRM

Networks: Top Echelon Network

JT Associates

89 Comstock Hill Rd
New Canaan, CT 06840
(203) 966-6311
Fax: (203) 966-8149
Email: jtassoc@optonline.net

Description: A contingency/retainer search firm specializing in professional, technical and middle mangement for diversified client base.

Key Contact:
Mr. Joe Fazio, Partner
Ms. Mary Ellen Calderone, Partner

Salary minimum: $50,000

Judge Inc

2500 Northwinds Pkwy Ste 300
Alpharetta, GA 30004
(770) 297-0800
(877) 844-9189
Fax: (678) 297-7558
Email: jwickline@inc.judge.com
Web: www.judgeinc.com

Description: Powerhouse of food industry recruiting with nationwide presence and deep contacts in retail, wholesale, manufacturing, sales/marketing and distribution. Wide-area-networked database, real-time in all offices for maximum exposure and total team concept.

Key Contact - Specialty:
Mr. Jason L. Wickline, CPC, Division Vice President - *Distribution, food industry*

Salary minimum: $30,000

Functions: General Mgmt., Senior Mgmt., Plant Mgmt., Purchasing, Distribution, Sales & Mktg., HR Mgmt., Finance, IT

Industries: Generalist, Food, Bev., Tobacco, Soap, Perf., Cosmtcs., Drugs Mfg., Transportation, Wholesale, Retail

Professional Associations: CLM, GAPS, NAPS

Networks: National Personnel Assoc (NPA)

Juno Systems Inc

516 5th Ave Fl 14
New York, NY 10036
(212) 354-5390
Fax: (212) 354-5391
Email: worldnet@junosytems.com
Web: www.junosystems.com

Description: We recruit IT professionals for both domestic and overseas clients. We specialize in understanding cross-cultural issues in addition to technical competencies.

Key Contact - Specialty:
Ms. Mary J. Kuric, President - *Information technology*

Functions: Generalist, MIS Mgmt., Systems Analysis, Systems Dev., Systems Implem., Systems Support, Network Admin., DB Admin.

Industries: Generalist, Finance, Media, Insurance, Software

Jurasek Associates Inc

448 Turnpike St Ste L2A
South Easton, MA 02375
(508) 230-7260
Fax: (508) 238-5753
Email: info@jurasekassociates.com
Web: www.jurasekassociates.com

Description: With more than 25 years in the recruitment industry offers a full line of search, placement and unbundled search services. We work with companies ranging in size from small start-ups to the more established or larger area firms. Many of our positions are listed exclusively with us due to the high degree of confidence our clients have in our abilities to find the right candidates for them.

Key Contact - Specialty:
Mr. Joseph Jurasek, President - *Technical, sales, marketing, business development*
Mr. Scott Jurasek, Vice President - *Technical, sales, marketing, business development*

Salary minimum: $90,000

Functions: Directors, Middle Mgmt., Mktg. Mgmt., Engineering, Minorities

Industries: Generalist, Communications, Defense, Software, Biotech

Professional Associations: NEHRA

Networks: National Personnel Assoc (NPA)

Just Management Services Inc

701 Enterprise Rd E Ste 805
Safety Harbor, FL 34695
(727) 726-4000
Fax: (727) 725-4966
Email: info@justmgt.com
Web: www.justmgt.com

Description: Broad range of consulting services to the apparel, home furnishings and textile industries, plastics, including; manufacturing consulting, '807' consulting, import sourcing, executive search, associated personnel consulting services.

Key Contact - Specialty:
Mr. Jim Just, Chairman
Ms. Susan Just, President - *Textiles, apparel, plastics, machinery, metals*

Functions: Generalist, General Mgmt., Mfg., Materials, Sales & Mktg., R&D, Engineering

Industries: Generalist, Textiles, Apparel, Medical Devices, Plastics, Rubber, Metal Products, Misc. Mfg.

Branches:
1121 Chucky Pike
Jefferson City, TN 37760
(423) 475-1188
Fax: (423) 471-5155
Key Contact - Specialty:
Ms. Debra Just - *Apparel, plastics*

A H Justice Search Consultants

PO Box 1420
Rockport, TX 78381
(361) 727-1582
Fax: (361) 727-1583

Email: jackiv@pyramid3.net

Description: We have had a seven-year history of providing an ethical, professional, effective service to national firms and candidates. Our concentration is in the manufacturing, engineering, telecommunications, petrochemical oil and gas, and information technology/services.

Key Contact - Specialty:
Mr. J. C. King, Consulting Manager - *Manufacturing, engineering, telecommunications, IT/IS*

Salary minimum: $40,000

Functions: Mfg., Materials, IT

Industries: Generalist, Mfg.

Networks: Top Echelon Network

JWC Associates Inc

34 Fackler Rd
Princeton, NJ 08540
(609) 921-9090
Fax: (609) 683-8077
Email: jwchh500@aol.com

Description: We are an executive search firm. Our clients include pharmaceutical, medical device and biotechnology companies. We concentrate our efforts in the following areas: Marketing: product management, market research and business development. Product Development: engineers and scientists. Operations: plant management, production, quality assurance, quality control and regulatory affairs.

Key Contact - Specialty:
Mr. John Colantoni, President - *Product development, marketing, production*

Salary minimum: $60,000

Functions: Product Dev., Production, Plant Mgmt., Quality, Healthcare, Sales & Mktg., HR Mgmt., CFO's, R&D, Engineering

Industries: Generalist, Chemicals, Drugs Mfg., Medical Devices, Pharm Svcs.

Branches:
7 Thoreau Dr
Manalapan, NJ 07726
(732) 792-2933
Fax: (732) 792-2936
Email: jwchh599@aol.com
Key Contact:
Mr. John Colantoni, President

JWR Associates

605 Shady Brook Ct
Southlake, TX 76092
(817) 410-8550
Fax: (817) 410-8551
Email: jwrassociates@attglobal.net

Description: Information technology recruiting specialists.

Key Contact:
Mr. John W. Reinmiller, Principal

Salary minimum: $75,000

Functions: Directors, Senior Mgmt., Middle Mgmt., Mktg. Mgmt., Sales Mgmt., MIS Mgmt., Systems Dev., Systems Support, Network Admin., DB Admin.

Industries: Generalist, Computer Equip., Telecoms, Software

Professional Associations: IRG

K&C Associates

290 A Oakhurst Ln
Arcadia, CA 91007
(626) 446-3087
Fax: (626) 445-1961

Description: Serving middle and top management positions in the machinery industries. Also the construction, building materials, industrial, mining and municipal, concrete, asphalt, sand/gravel, rock and cement industries. Domestic and international.

Key Contact - Specialty:
Mr. R. G. Kuhnmuench, President - *Construction, concrete, aggregates, cement, mining*

Salary minimum: $40,000

Functions: General Mgmt., Mfg., Materials, Sales & Mktg., Personnel, Engineering, Mgmt. Consultants, Environmentalists, Architects, Int'l.

Industries: Agri., Forestry, Mining, Energy, Utilities, Construction, Mfg., Leather, Stone, Glass, Metal Products, Machine, Appliance, Motor Vehicles, Misc. Mfg., Transportation, Accounting, Equip Svcs., Mgmt. Consulting, HR Services, Media, Advertising, Environmental Svcs., Marketing SW

K&M Int'l Inc
1 Park Plz Fl 6
Irvine, CA 92614
(949) 770-1477
Fax: (949) 770-4707
Email: info@kandminternational.com
Web: www.kandminternational.com

Description: Our extensive database search capabilities allow our consultants to target and market our candidate's background and provide our clients with top-notch employees.

Key Contact - Specialty:
Mr. Paul Kuch, Managing Consultant - *Accounting & finance*
Mr. Chris Miller, Managing Consultant - *Business development, strategic planning*

Salary minimum: $30,000

Functions: Generalist, Product Dev., Purchasing, Mktg. Mgmt., Budgeting, Taxes, Systems Support, Mgmt. Consultants

Industries: Generalist, Construction, Mfg., Wholesale, Finance, Media, Aerospace, Biotech

K2 Resources LP
34 E Putnam Ave Ste 100
Greenwich, CT 06830
(203) 622-6779
Fax: (203) 622-6970
Email: mail@k2resources.com
Web: www.k2resources.com

Description: We are a boutique search firm specializing in the Internet and e-Business markets. K2 has formed partnerships with leading companies and professionals who set the industry standard for excellence.

Key Contact - Specialty:
Ms. Kelly Macaluso Coles, Partner - *Internet, e-commerce, interactive media*
Ms. Kelly Gallagher, Partner - *Internet, e-commerce, interactive media*

Salary minimum: $70,000

Functions: Generalist, Product Dev., Sales & Mktg., Advertising, Mktg. Mgmt., Sales Mgmt., Graphic Artists

Industries: New Media, Software

Professional Associations: NYNMA

Kaas Employment Services
425 2nd St SE Ste 610
Cedar Rapids, IA 52401
(319) 366-1731
Fax: (319) 366-1402
Email: jobs@kaas-emp.com

Description: Contingency search and placement specializing in manufacturing and engineering.

Nationwide placement with concentration in Iowa and Midwest.

Key Contact - Specialty:
Ms. Linda M. Kaas, Owner/Manager - *Engineering, manufacturing*

Functions: Admin. Svcs.

Industries: Mfg.

Professional Associations: EIHRA

Networks: Inter-City Personnel Assoc (IPA)

Kabana Corp
49175 W Pontiac Trl
PO Box 930785
Wixom, MI 48393-0785
(248) 926-6427
Email: kabana@mich.com
Web: www.kabana.com

Description: Automotive OEM supplier positions, specialization includes BSME's, B.S.E.E. multilingual, sales engineers, program, project, plant, quality, materials, purchasing, human resources and account managers.

Key Contact - Specialty:
Mr. Steven E. Kabanuk, Executive Recruiter - *Automotive positions (OEM, production, parts, suppliers)*
Ms. Linda Martin-Postiff, MA, Executive Recruiter - *Automotive positions (OEM, production, parts, suppliers)*

Salary minimum: $40,000

Functions: General Mgmt., Mfg., Materials, Purchasing, Sales & Mktg., Sales Mgmt., HR Mgmt., Engineering, Minorities, Int'l.

Industries: Plastics, Rubber, Paints, Petro. Products, Motor Vehicles

Professional Associations: MAPS

KABL Ability Network
(a division of Syntre Corp)
1727 State St
Santa Barbara, CA 93101
(805) 563-2398
Email: 432kabl@msn.com
Web: www.kabl.com

Description: Network of recruiters specializing in top management of small companies, primarily high-technology and telecommunications. Both permanent and temporary.

Key Contact - Specialty:
Mr. Brad Naegle, President - *Senior management of small companies*

Salary minimum: $90,000

Functions: Senior Mgmt.

Industries: Computer Equip., Telecoms, Software

Kaczmar & Associates
329 S Main St
Doylestown, PA 18901
(215) 230-0750
Email: kaczmar@kaczmar.com
Web: www.kaczmar.com

Description: We specialize in placing senior-level sales and pre- and post-sales consulting support professionals with primarily top 500 independent software vendors and IT services firms in the Mid-Atlantic and Northeast markets.

Key Contact - Specialty:
Mr. Michael A. Kaczmar, Principal - *Software sales executives, software consultants*

Functions: Sales Mgmt., IT

Industries: Software

Richard Kader & Associates
7850 Freeway Cir Ste 201
Cleveland, OH 44130
(440) 891-1700
Fax: (440) 891-1443
Email: kader@acclink.com
Web: www.jobsacrossamerica.com

Description: We handle both local and national searches in sales/marketing, medical, industrial, chemical, engineering, telecommunications, accounting and administrative.

Key Contact - Specialty:
Mr. Richard H. Kader, President - *Industrial sales & marketing*
Mr. Vern Sponseller, Vice President - *Financial, accounting*
Ms. Mamie Rudd, Vice President - *Telecommunications sales & marketing*
Mr. Art DeLong, Vice President - *Industrial sales & marketing*
Mr. James Flash - *Medical sales*

Salary minimum: $40,000

Functions: Generalist

Industries: Generalist

Networks: First Interview Network (FIN)

Robert Kaestner & Associates
3047 Flat Rock Pl 3
Land O' Lakes, FL 34639
(813) 996-5664
Fax: (813) 996-5934
Email: robkae@gte.net
Web: www.kaestner.com

Description: This professional contingency and retained search firm is devoted to serving the office furniture and office supply industries at all disciplines. We cater to the search needs of manufacturers as well as dealers and distributors.

Key Contact - Specialty:
Mr. Bob Kaestner, Principal - *Office furniture, office supplies*
Ms. Pat Kaye, Associate - *Interior design*

Salary minimum: $50,000

Functions: Generalist

Industries: Lumber, Furniture, Wholesale

Networks: Top Echelon Network

Kaleidoscope
3828 Karen Lynn Dr
Glendale, CA 91206
(818) 790-9222
(818) 790-9223
Fax: (818) 790-9225
Email: kscope2k@aol.com
Web: www.kscope-search.com

Description: Our mission is to be a provider of highly specialized search techniques, recognized for commitment to our clients and for the delivery of excellent service.

Key Contact:
Mr. Astrid Grey
Ms. Cindy Orozco

Functions: Generalist, Senior Mgmt., Middle Mgmt., Admin. Svcs., Direct Mktg., HR Mgmt., Finance, IT

Industries: Finance, Banking, Invest. Banking, Venture Cap., Misc. Financial, Accounting, HR Services, Advertising, New Media, Non-classifiable

Professional Associations: CSP

Lisa Kalus & Associates Inc

26 Broadway Ste 400
New York, NY 10004
(212) 837-7889

Description: Recruitment firm specializing in construction, engineering and real estate personnel, primarily in the New York City metropolitan area.

Key Contact - Specialty:
Ms. Lisa Kalus, President - *Construction, engineering, real estate personnel*

Salary minimum: $35,000

Functions: Generalist

Industries: Construction, Real Estate

Kalvert Associates

PO Box 1394
Sugar Land, TX 77487-1394
(281) 438-2410
Email: akalvert@kalvertassociates.com
Web: www.kalvertassociates.com

Description: We specialize in management and technical search in the petroleum refining industry. Client engagements range from $65,000 to $500,000 per year in compensation.

Key Contact - Specialty:
Mr. Arthur Kalvert, Recruitment Consultant - *Petroleum refining*

Functions: Generalist

Industries: Energy, Utilities

Kames & Associates Inc

726 - 2nd St Ste 3B
PO Box 3342
Annapolis, MD 21403-3342
(410) 990-0780
Fax: (410) 990-0784
Email: jobs@kames.com
Web: www.kames.com

Description: Our professional recruiting service specializes in high-tech, hardware, software and systems engineering, e-Commerce, information technology, tele/data communications, fiber optics, digital, analog, RF, and manufacturing areas. We place from the working-level to senior-management and executive-management.

Key Contact:
Mr. Robert Kames, President

Salary minimum: $70,000

Functions: Generalist, Mfg., Quality

Industries: Test, Measure Equip., Electronic, Elec. Components, Telecoms, Digital, Fiber Optic, Network Infrastructure, Defense, Software, ERP SW, Mfg. SW, System SW, Biotech

Professional Associations: IEEE, MAPRC, OSA

Kamp & Associates

PO Box 222
Davidson, NC 28036
(704) 892-5922
Fax: (704) 892-3809
Email: dbkstar@aol.com

Description: We offer long-term staffing and organization solutions by forming meaningful business partnerships with our clients and providing personalized services designed to meet the clients' strategic needs.

Key Contact - Specialty:
Mr. Douglas B. Kamp, President - *Engineering, HR, manufacturing, marketing*

Functions: Generalist

Industries: Generalist

Professional Associations: NCASP

Kane & Associates

2825 Wilcrest Ste 675
Houston, TX 77042
(713) 977-3600
Fax: (713) 430-5512
Email: bkane@jobmenu.com
Web: www.jobmenu.com

Description: We perform searches for a variety of functions and industries. We specialize in the financial,energy and power trading areas. Our searches include candidates for domestic and international positions.

Key Contact - Specialty:
Mr. Bernie Kane, President - *Financial*
Mr. Michael Kane, Vice President - *Power, energy trading*
Mr. Guy Davis, Senior Consultant - *Tax*
Mr. Tony Hughes, Senior Consultant - *Financial, human resources*

Salary minimum: $45,000

Functions: Generalist

Industries: Paper, Chemicals, Plastics, Rubber, Paints, Petro. Products, Brokers, Misc. Financial, Accounting, HR Services, Telecoms, Mfg. SW

Professional Associations: TAPC

Kapp & Associates

PO Box 103
Greenville, SC 29602
(864) 250-0123
Fax: (864) 250-0127
Email: dfkapp@mindspring.com

Description: We complete very specialized, hard to fill, or sensitive searches, from the plant level through senior executives, for manufacturing corporations. We utilize classical search techniques both for contingent and retained searches. Our searches are completed throughout US.

Key Contact - Specialty:
Mr. Donald Kapp, President - *Manufacturing searches*

Salary minimum: $40,000

Functions: Generalist

Industries: Mfg.

Karlyn Group

210 Sylvan Ave
Englewood Cliffs, NJ 07632
(201) 871-9800
Fax: (201) 894-1186
Email: rloikits@karlyn.com
Web: www.karlyn.com

Description: Services offered on a retained or contingency basis in all areas of management, legal, logistics, and sales positions. Middle to upper-level executive.

Key Contact - Specialty:
Ms. Lenore Lieberman, Senior Fashion Counselor - *Fashion*
Ms. Cindy Wright, Senior Counselor - *Logistics, Legal*
Ms. Regina Loikits, Owner - *Technology*
Ms. Cathryn Liggio, Director - *Administrative, temp staff*

Salary minimum: $35,000

Functions: Generalist

Industries: Mfg., Finance, Services, Hospitality, Media, Telecoms, Packaging, Insurance, Software, Healthcare

Professional Associations: CLM, NJSA

Karp & Associates

931 S R 434 Ste 1201
PMB 334
Altamonte Springs, FL 32714-7050
(407) 292-4637
Fax: (407) 294-1695
Email: lindakarp2@juno.com

Description: Fourteen plus years' experience in medical/pharmaceutical sales, marketing and management recruiting. The owner personally has a clinical background as a registered nurse and a background in medical sales.

Key Contact - Specialty:
Ms. Linda S. Karp, President/Owner - *Medical sales & marketing, management*

Functions: General Mgmt., Directors, Product Dev., Healthcare, Physicians, Nurses, Sales & Mktg., Sales Mgmt., HR Mgmt., Int'l.

Industries: Drugs Mfg., Medical Devices, Pharm Svcs., Biotech, Healthcare

Karras Personnel Inc

2 Central Ave
Madison, NJ 07940
(973) 966-6800
Fax: (973) 966-6853
Email: karraspersonnel@mindspring.com
Web: karraspersonnel.home.mindspring.com

Description: Human resources recruiting for professionals in functions of: generalist, staffing, training and organization development, succession planning, compensation, benefits, HRIS, employee relations, labor relations, and affirmative action/equal employment opportunity.

Key Contact - Specialty:
Mr. Bill Karras, President - *Human resources*

Salary minimum: $35,000

Functions: Generalist, HR Mgmt.

Industries: Generalist

Professional Associations: NJHRPG

Kass/Abell & Associates

10780 Santa Monica Blvd Ste 200
Los Angeles, CA 90025
(310) 475-4666
(415) 788-5719
Fax: (310) 475-0485
Email: .attyplcmnt@kassabell.com
Web: www.kassabell.com

Description: Since 1981, We have recruited and placed attorneys for corporate law departments and law firms throughout California. We are networked nationwide to assist attorneys wishing to relocate.

Key Contact - Specialty:
Mr. Peter J. Redgrove, Principal - *Attorneys*

Functions: Legal

Industries: Legal

Professional Associations: NALSC

Katelyn Partners

343 Causeway Blvd
Dunedin, FL 34698
(727) 734-0246
Fax: (727) 734-3222
Email: jimw@katelynpartners.com
Web: www.katelynpartners.com

Description: Eleven years' healthcare industry experience. Fixed fee contingent and retained search. Specialize in clinical, technical and executive-level placements.

Key Contact - Specialty:
Mr. James Whitehurst, President - *Healthcare information systems*

Mr. Edward White, VP-Placement Services - *Healthcare finance*

Salary minimum: $60,000

Functions: Healthcare

Industries: Accounting, HR Services, Healthcare

Leslie Kavanagh Associates Inc

36 W 44th St Ste 1101
New York, NY 10036
(212) 661-0670
Fax: (212) 599-8316
Email: corp@lkasearch.com
Web: www.lkasearch.com

Description: We are a talent management firm specializing in human capital, strategic procurement/global logistics, and information technology.

Key Contact - Specialty:
Mr. Will Pleva, President - *Strategic procurement, global logistics, operations*

Salary minimum: $60,000

Functions: Senior Mgmt., Quality, Materials, Purchasing, HR Mgmt., Benefits, Training, IT, Systems Dev., Network Admin.

Industries: Energy, Utilities, Mfg., Transportation, Finance, Services, Media, Communications, Aerospace, Packaging, Insurance, Software, Biotech

Professional Associations: CLM, IHRIM, NAPM, SHRM, WAW

Jim Kay & Associates

132 Ridge Ave C
Bloomingdale, IL 60108
(630) 825-1500
Fax: (630) 825-3919
Email: jimkayassc@ameritech.net

Description: Cost effective, timely recruiting backed by twenty plus years of client satisfaction in both retained and contingency search assignments.

Key Contact - Specialty:
Mr. Jim Kay, President - *Generalist*

Salary minimum: $65,000

Functions: Generalist, Senior Mgmt., Middle Mgmt., Product Dev., CFO's, Systems Dev., R&D, Engineering

Industries: Generalist, Computer Equip., Consumer Elect., Misc. Mfg., Telecoms, Software

Kay Concepts Inc

PO Box 4825
Palm Harbor, FL 34685
(727) 786-3580
(800) 879-5850
Fax: (208) 988-3822
Email: heidi@kayconcepts.com
Web: www.kayconcepts.com

Description: A full-service firm specializing in the high-tech, manufacturing, and development of electronic systems. Clients develop product primarily to point-of-sale and point-of-service industries.

Key Contact - Specialty:
Ms. Heidi Kay, CPC, President - *High technology engineering, manufacturing, marketing, point of sale, electronic systems*

Functions: Quality, Sales & Mktg., Mktg. Mgmt., IT, Systems Dev., Engineering

Industries: Software

Networks: National Personnel Assoc (NPA)

The Kay Group of 5th Ave

350 5th Ave Ste 2205
Empire State Bldg
New York, NY 10118
(212) 947-4646
Fax: (212) 947-3472
Email: kayrecruit@att.net

Description: Every candidate is interviewed in person before any evaluation is made.

Key Contact - Specialty:
Mr. Bernard A. Feinberg, President - *Advertising agency management*
Mr. Joseph H. Kay, Consultant - *Advertising agency management*

Salary minimum: $40,000

Functions: Directors, Senior Mgmt., Middle Mgmt., Advertising, Direct Mktg., Finance, CFO's, Budgeting, M&A, Mgmt. Consultants

Industries: Metal Products, Advertising, Publishing, New Media

Kaye-Stone Partners

311 Chase Ct
Edgewater, NJ 07020
(201) 945-6757
Fax: (201) 945-8753
Email: kayestone1@aol.com

Description: We are an executive search firm specializing in advertising agencies, for example: general, direct marketing, pharmaceutical, and sales promotion in all levels of account management and media, as well as new media, such as Internet and multimedia.

Key Contact - Specialty:
Ms. Shelley Kaye, President/CEO - *Advertising agency, account management, media*
Mr. Michael Stone, EVP/COO - *New media, internet, multimedia*

Salary minimum: $40,000

Functions: Generalist, Advertising

Industries: Generalist, Media, Advertising, New Media

Professional Associations: ACNY

KDK Associates LLC

575 Waterford Dr
Lake Zurich, IL 60047
(847) 726-2902
Fax: (847) 726-2903
Email: kdkassociates@aol.com
Web: www.kdkassociates.com

Description: Service oriented sales and marketing management recruiting firm specializing in the needs of consumer and business-to-business companies. We will take time to understand your company's goals and management needs.

Key Contact - Specialty:
Mr. Michael J. Neises, Management Recruiter - *Sales & marketing management recruitment*

Salary minimum: $50,000

Functions: Sales & Mktg.

Industries: Generalist, Mfg., Wholesale, Retail, Finance, Services, Hospitality, Media, Communications

Keeley Consulting Inc

161 Bay St Ste 2700
Toronto, ON M5J 2S1
Canada
(416) 572-2028
Fax: (416) 572-4195
Email: info@keeleyconsulting.com
Web: www.keeleyconsulting.com

Description: We are a search firm that specializes in the financial services industry.

Key Contact - Specialty:
Mr. Timothy J. Keeley, Principal - *Financial services*

Salary minimum: $40,000

Functions: Generalist, Senior Mgmt., Middle Mgmt., Mkt. Research, Sales Mgmt., Customer Svc., CFO's, Cash Mgmt.

Industries: Generalist, Finance, Banking, Invest. Banking, Brokers, Venture Cap., Misc. Financial

Professional Associations: TSFA

Keena Staffing Services

147 Ridge St
Glens Falls, NY 12801
(518) 793-9825
Fax: (518) 793-0224
Email: staff@keena.com
Web: www.keena.com/keena/index.html

Description: Our Firm is engaged solely in the recruitment and placement of human resources and labor relations specialists, labor and employment attorneys and industrial health, and safety specialists.

Key Contact - Specialty:
Mr. Paul S. Gerarde, President - *Manufacturing, sales, human resources, accounting, information technology*

Salary minimum: $50,000

Functions: Mfg.

Industries: Mfg.

Jack Kelly & Partners LLC

58 W 58th St Ste 32F
New York, NY 10019
(212) 754-2424
Fax: (212) 754-2442
Web: www.jkandp.com

Description: We are Manhattan's premier consulting firm specializing in permanent placement for design and architectural industries. A thorough understanding of the staffing needs of interior design firms, Internet companies, architecture firms, museums, galleries, design centers, and showrooms allows us to serve a broad base of the country's most elite firms.

Key Contact - Specialty:
Mr. Jack Kelly, Owner - *Designers*
Mr. Stephen Davies, Senior Associate - *Architects*
Mr. Stephen James, Administration - *Human resources*
Ms. Janet Roda - *Design centers, public relations, marketing, showrooms*
Mr. Cruger Fowler - *Galleries, museums*

Salary minimum: $100,000

Functions: Directors, Senior Mgmt., Middle Mgmt., Admin. Svcs., Sales & Mktg., Mktg. Mgmt., Sales Mgmt., Customer Svc., PR, Architects

Industries: Lumber, Furniture, Wholesale, Non-classifiable

Professional Associations: FGI, IFDA, IIDA, LMC

Kerry-Ben Kelly Executive Search

6574 153rd Ave SE
Bellevue, WA 98006
(425) 653-0506
Fax: (425) 653-1625
Email: kbksearch@aol.com

Description: My business experience includes over thirty years of experience as an executive for leading retailers with a national presence. As an executive recruiter, I build relationships with clients and candidates. Please call me for further information.

Key Contact - Specialty:
Mr. Kerry-Ben Kelly, Owner - *Retail, wireless communications, business to business, hospitality, wholesale, healthcare*

Salary minimum: $40,000

Functions: General Mgmt., Senior Mgmt., Middle Mgmt., Healthcare, Sales & Mktg., Mktg. Mgmt., Sales Mgmt., HR Mgmt., Finance

Industries: Generalist, Wholesale, Retail, Hospitality, Hotels, Resorts, Clubs, Restaurants, Entertainment, Communications, Call Centers, Wireless, Healthcare, Non-classifiable

Kelly Law Registry

(a Kelly Services company)
43 Woodland St Ste 280
Hartford, CT 06105
(860) 247-7440
(800) 248-4LAW
Fax: (860) 548-7740
Email: klr17w1@kellylawregistry.com
Web: www.kellylawregistry.com

Description: Full-service placement firm engaged in the permanent placement of general counsel, in-house counsel and paralegals and temporary placement of attorneys and paralegals and legal teams for document reviews/due diligence.

Key Contact:
Mr. Mark Davies, Managing Director

Functions: Generalist, Legal, Attorneys, Paralegals

Industries: Generalist, Legal

Kendall & Davis Company Inc

11325 Concord Village Ave
St. Louis, MO 63123
(314) 843-8838
Fax: (314) 843-2262
Email: info@kendallanddavis.com
Web: www.kendallanddavis.com

Description: Physician recruitment for permanent and locum tenens needs.

Key Contact - Specialty:
Mr. James C. Kendall - *Physicians*

Functions: Generalist, Physicians

Industries: Healthcare, Hospitals

Professional Associations: NAPR

Kenmore Executives Inc

1 S Ocean Blvd Ste 306
Boca Raton, FL 33432
(561) 392-0700
Fax: (561) 750-0818
Email: resumes@kenmoreexecutives.com
Web: www.kenmoreexecutives.com

Description: Specializing in the placement of consultants experienced in the implementation of concepts supporting business re-engineering, lean manufacturing, change management, downsizing, supply chain management, management development, total quality management and strategic planning.

Key Contact - Specialty:
Mr. Lawrence D. Loprete, President - *Management consultants*
Ms. Marilyn Orr, Vice President - *Management consultants*
Mr. Steven LoPrete, Vice President - *Management consultants*
Mr. Joseph LoPrete, Vice President - *Management consultants*

Salary minimum: $60,000

Functions: Mfg., Productivity, Materials, Sales Mgmt., Training, Finance, IT, MIS Mgmt., Mgmt. Consultants

Industries: Generalist, Mgmt. Consulting

William W Kenney

9 Powder Horn Rd
Norwalk, CT 06850
(508) 430-5229

Description: Our extensive nationwide network in the bond sector of the insurance industry facilitates timely placements. We match need with talent in every region of the USA.

Key Contact - Specialty:
Mr. William Kenney, President - *Bonds (surety, fidelity, underwriting)*

Salary minimum: $40,000

Functions: Generalist

Industries: Insurance

Professional Associations: CAPS

Kennison & Associates Inc

21 Custom House St
Boston, MA 02110
(617) 478-2888
Email: info@kennisonassociates.com
Web: www.kennisonassociates.com

Description: We earn the fee. Specialized and experienced. No-nonsense approach to filling your sensitive and important positions. Honesty, integrity and professionalism practiced.

Key Contact:
Ms. Jane Kennison, Founder

Salary minimum: $18,000

Functions: Generalist, MIS Mgmt., Systems Analysis, Systems Dev., Systems Implem., Systems Support, Network Admin., DB Admin.

Industries: Generalist

Professional Associations: NATSS

Branches:
65 William St
Wellesley, MA 02481
(781) 431-8980

The Kent Group Inc

(also known as MRI of Northwest Ohio)
3450 W Central Ave Ste 360
Toledo, OH 43606
(419) 537-1100
Fax: (419) 537-8730
Email: gfruchtman@kent-group.com
Web: www.kent-group.com

Description: Full-service, emphasizing technical/engineering, data processing, financial, marketing and sales, primarily for manufacturing clients. Part of 1000 office national network for United States and international clients.

Key Contact - Specialty:
Mr. Gary Fruchtman - *Steel, pipe & tube, steel products, automotive, food plastics*

Salary minimum: $35,000

Functions: Generalist, Production, Direct Mktg., Finance, MIS Mgmt., Systems Dev., Engineering

Industries: Generalist, Leather, Stone, Glass, Metal Products, Motor Vehicles, Misc. Mfg., Accounting, Software

Kerr & Company Executive Search

10455 N Central Expwy
PMB 301 109
Dallas, TX 75231-2213
(214) 373-0008
Fax: (214) 373-4510

Email: hunt4exec@aol.com

Description: We are a generalist firm assisting clients in a broad range of industries. We are extremely client-centered and work primarily on exclusive searches.

Key Contact - Specialty:
Ms. Laura Kerr, President - *Sales, construction, civil engineering, architecture, brokers*

Salary minimum: $65,000

Functions: Senior Mgmt., Sales & Mktg., Customer Svc., Finance, CFO's, Cash Mgmt., IT, Engineering, Specialized Svcs., Architects

Industries: Construction, Transportation, Finance, Brokers, IT Implementation, Hotels, Resorts, Clubs, Telecoms, Call Centers, Wireless, Network Infrastructure, Real Estate, Software, Development SW, Marketing SW

Kerr Executive Recruiting

1439 Fulbright Ave
Redlands, CA 92373
(909) 798-KERR
Fax: (909) 798-5377
Email: john_kerr@eee.org

Description: Offers very personal, confidential, directed searches enhanced by 17 years of specialty plastics recruiting and significant personal major management background experience. Normally retained and contingent searches can be realistically scheduled.

Key Contact - Specialty:
Mr. John B. Kerr, Jr., President/Owner - *Plastics, rubber*

Salary minimum: $70,000

Functions: Generalist, Middle Mgmt., Product Dev., Plant Mgmt., Productivity, Finance, Engineering, Technicians

Industries: Generalist, Mfg., Plastics, Rubber, Packaging

Professional Associations: SPE

Kersey & Associates Inc

PO Box 18164
Spartanburg, SC 29318
(864) 577-9600
Fax: (864) 542-2727
Email: kersey@teleplex.net
Web: www.kersey.com

Description: We are a retained/contingency professional search firm doing consulting, contracting, and direct hire placements.

Key Contact - Specialty:
Mr. David Kersey, President - *Information technology*

Salary minimum: $45,000

Functions: Finance, IT, MIS Mgmt.

Industries: Generalist

Networks: Top Echelon Network

Blair Kershaw Associates Inc

1903 W 8th St
PMB 302
Erie, PA 16505
(814) 454-5872
Fax: (814) 452-4598

Description: We recruit for manufacturing, engineering, financial, medical and management people in our Tri-state area. Most work is in the $40,000-$60,000 range.

Key Contact - Specialty:
Mr. Blair Kershaw, President - *Manufacturing, finance, engineering, management*

Salary minimum: $40,000

Functions: Generalist, Middle Mgmt., Mfg., Product Dev., Production, Quality, CFO's, Engineering

Industries: Generalist, Food, Bev., Tobacco, Plastics, Rubber, Metal Products, Machine, Appliance, Misc. Mfg., Software

Professional Associations: PANP

Networks: National Personnel Assoc (NPA)

Franklin Key Associates
831 Washington St
Franklin, MA 02038-3323
(508) 520-3500
Fax: (508) 520-3535
Email: bob@franklinkey.com
Web: www.franklinkey.com

Description: We are a premier information systems search and placement firm. We provide executive search, professional placement, and staffing consulting. We believe that just meeting our clients' needs is ordinary; we strive to exceed expectations through a strong team approach that aligns the goals of everyone involved. We work with those who aim to be the best at what they do, because our clients ask us to be the best at what we do.

Key Contact:
Mr. Robert Norton, Principal

Salary minimum: $50,000

Functions: Directors, Senior Mgmt., IT, Systems Dev., Network Admin., DB Admin.

Industries: Computer Equip., Misc. Mfg., Transportation, Wholesale, Retail, Finance, Mgmt. Consulting, E-commerce, IT Implementation, Communications, Telecoms, Network Infrastructure, Insurance, Software, Database SW, Development SW, ERP SW, Networking, Comm. SW, Security SW, System SW, Healthcare

Professional Associations: MAPS

Key Employment
1014 Livingston Ave
North Brunswick, NJ 08902
(732) 249-2454
Fax: (732) 249-2521
Email: gsilberger@aol.com

Description: International search and recruiting for engineering, administration, manufacturing, laboratory, technical sales and marketing. Clients include chemical, power engr., cogeneration, plastics, electrical, electro mechanical, petroleum, environmental, pulp and paper industries.

Key Contact - Specialty:
Mr. Gary Silberger, President - *Engineering power, sales & marketing*

Salary minimum: $40,000

Functions: Generalist, Senior Mgmt., Plant Mgmt., Purchasing, Materials Plng., Mkt. Research, Mktg. Mgmt., Engineering

Industries: Generalist, Energy, Utilities, Construction, Food, Bev., Tobacco, Chemicals, Paints, Petro. Products, Consumer Elect., Advertising

Keysearch Int'l
321 N Mall Dr Ste A201
PO Box 910370
St. George, UT 84790
(435) 634-1196
Fax: (435) 634-1195
Email: keysearch@keysearch.net
Web: www.keysearch.net

Description: We are an international executive search firm specializing in the transportation industry, with a merger and acquisition division.

Through our overseas partner, Elmar Hertzog Und Partner, we can now offer our services worldwide.
Key Contact:
Ms. Deborah L. Keys, President
Functions: Senior Mgmt.
Industries: Services

Kforce
120 W Hyde Park Pl Ste 150
Tampa, FL 33605
(813) 251-1700
(888) 663-3626
Web: www.kforce.com

Description: We are a full-service, web-based, specialty staffing firm providing flexible and permanent staffing solutions for organizations and career management for individuals in the specialty skill areas of information technology, finance and accounting, human resources, engineering, pharmaceutical, healthcare, legal, and scientific. Our exchange and ticker are NASDAQ: KFRC.

Key Contact:
Mr. Ken Pierce, Chief Marketing Officer
Mr. David L. Dunkel, CEO
Mr. Larry Stanczak, COO
Mr. Joe Liberatore, Chief Sales Officer
Mr. William Sanders, CFO
Mr. Dusty Williams, CIO

Functions: Generalist, General Mgmt., Healthcare, HR Mgmt., Finance, CFO's, IT, Engineering, Attorneys, Paralegals

Industries: Generalist, Textiles, Apparel, Paper, Drugs Mfg., Medical Devices, Paints, Petro. Products, Retail, Finance, Banking, Invest. Banking, Brokers, Venture Cap., Misc. Financial, Non-profits, Higher Ed., Pharm Svcs., Legal, Accounting, Equip Svcs., Mgmt. Consulting, HR Services, IT Implementation, Hospitality, Call Centers, Network Infrastructure, Insurance, Software, Networking, Comm. SW, Biotech, Healthcare, Hospitals, Long-term Care, Women's

Branches:
5343 N 16th St Ste 270
Phoenix, AZ 85016
(602) 230-0220
Fax: (602) 248-4204
Key Contact - Specialty:
Mr. Trey Rustmann - *Finance, accounting, information technology*

701 Palomar Airport Rd Ste 300
Carlsbad, CA 92009
(760) 603-9291
Fax: (760) 603-9335
Key Contact - Specialty:
Mr. Avi Khilman - *Finance, accounting*

879 W 190th St Ste 300
Gardena, CA 90248
(310) 323-0900
Fax: (310) 323-1101
Key Contact - Specialty:
Ms. Beth German - *Finance, accounting, information technology*

2102 Business Center Dr Ste 213
Irvine, CA 92612
(949) 253-4157
Fax: (949) 253-4159
Key Contact - Specialty:
Mr. Bruce Rockwell - *Healthcare*

2603 Main St Ste 1100
Irvine, CA 92614
(949) 660-1666
Fax: (949) 660-1858
Email: rgennawey@kforce.com
Key Contact - Specialty:
Mr. Tony Sexton - *Information technology, finance and accounting*

2029 Century Park E 1350
Los Angeles, CA 90067
(310) 284-8800
Fax: (310) 277-7601
Key Contact - Specialty:
Mr. Tom Demetrovich - *Information technology, finance and accounting, legal*

3 Lagoon Dr Ste 155
Redwood City, CA 94065
(650) 628-1850
Fax: (650) 628-1855
Key Contact:
Ms. Ingram Losner

1545 River Park Dr Ste 411
Sacramento, CA 95815
(916) 929-6342
Fax: (916) 929-6179
Key Contact - Specialty:
Ms. Ingram Losner - *Finance and accounting*

4510 Executive Dr Ste 325
San Diego, CA 92121
(858) 550-1600
Fax: (858) 452-7011
Key Contact - Specialty:
Mr. Louis Song - *Information technology, finance and accounting, pharmaceutical*

180 Montgomery St Ste 1860
San Francisco, CA 94104
(415) 228-4500
Fax: (415) 249-3781
Key Contact - Specialty:
Mr. Scott Hopkins - *Finance and accounting, pharmaceutical, science, legal*

425 California St Ste 1200
San Francisco, CA 94104
(415) 591-1700
Fax: (415) 956-3876
Key Contact - Specialty:
Mr. Joe Kruszewski, Area Vice President - *Information technology*

1731 Technology Dr Ste 300
San Jose, CA 95110
(408) 487-2800
(408) 501-1600
Fax: (408) 436-1842
Key Contact - Specialty:
Ms. Michelle Pletkin - *Accounting, finance, information technology, legal*

15260 Ventura Blvd 980
Sherman Oaks, CA 91403
(818) 808-1500
Fax: (818) 808-1560
Key Contact - Specialty:
Mr. Paul Ratajczak - *Information technology, finance and accounting*

325 E Hillcrest Dr Ste 220
Thousand Oaks, CA 91360
(805) 418-1010
(805) 418-1000
Fax: (805) 418-1864
Key Contact - Specialty:
Mr. Tom Demetrovich - *Scientific*

1350 Treat Blvd Ste 150
Walnut Creek, CA 94596
(925) 951-1260
Fax: (925) 951-1288
Key Contact - Specialty:
Ms. Michelle Pletkin - *Finance and accounting, information technology*

5085 List Dr Ste 100
Colorado Springs, CO 80919
(719) 268-8000
Fax: (719) 268-9656
Key Contact - Specialty:
Mr. Rick McFadden - *Information technology*

7730 E Bellview Ave Ste 302
Englewood, CO 80111
(303) 773-3700
Fax: (303) 773-8201

Key Contact - Specialty:
Mr. Rick McFadden - *Finance and accounting, information technology*

111 Founders Plz Ste 1501
East Hartford, CT 06108
(860) 528-0300
Fax: (860) 291-9497
Key Contact - Specialty:
Mr. David Rutter - *Finance and accounting, information technology*

1 Corporate Dr Ste 215
Shelton, CT 06484
(203) 944-9001
Fax: (203) 926-1414
Key Contact - Specialty:
Mr. David Uva - *Finance and accounting, information technology*

1420 K St Ste 900
Washington, DC 20005
(202) 354-8600
Fax: (202) 354-8666
Key Contact - Specialty:
Mr. Andy MacLean - *Finance and accounting*

500 W Cypress Creek Rd Ste 100
Ft. Lauderdale, FL 33309
(954) 928-0800
Fax: (954) 489-2605
Key Contact - Specialty:
Mr. Rich Raniere - *Finance and accounting*

15600 NW 67th Ave Ste 201
Miami Lakes, FL 33014
(305) 698-8502
Fax: (305) 819-9544
Key Contact - Specialty:
Mr. Rich Raniere - *Finance and accounting*

111 N Orange Ave Ste 625
Orlando, FL 32835
(407) 835-3100
Fax: (407) 650-4144
Key Contact - Specialty:
Mr. Tom Gresosky - *Finance and accounting, information technology*
Mr. Chris Planeta - *Engineering*

1001 E Palm Ave
Tampa, FL 33605
(813) 552-1700
Key Contact - Specialty:
Mr. Bruce Rockwell - *Healthcare, scientific, pharmaceutical*
Ms. Shannon Brannigan - *Finance and accounting, information technology, engineering*

4401 W Kennedy Blvd Ste 100
Tampa, FL 33609
(813) 307-2121
Fax: (813) 637-1970
Key Contact - Specialty:
Ms. Amy Palmer - *Healthcare*

5840 W Cypress St Ste A
Tampa, FL 33607
(813) 287-8876
(813) 240-1060
Fax: (813) 289-3284
Key Contact - Specialty:
Mr. Carol Pavesi - *Information technology training*

4170 Ashford Dunwoody Rd Ste 285
Atlanta, GA 30319
(770) 351-1050
Fax: (770) 351-1051
Key Contact - Specialty:
Ms. Christy Brooks - *Finance and accounting, information technology*
Mr. Steven Koehler - *Healthcare, scientific*

20 N Wacker Dr Ste 2850
Chicago, IL 60606
(312) 263-0902
Fax: (312) 263-3023
Key Contact - Specialty:
Ms. Crystal Schroeder - *Finance and accounting, information technology*

2211 S York Rd Ste 380
Oak Brook, IL 60521
(630) 218-7700
Fax: (630) 575-0829
Key Contact - Specialty:
Mr. Brandon Lewis - *Information technology*

3701 W Algonquin Rd Ste 380
Rolling Meadows, IL 60008
(847) 438-7000
Fax: (847) 577-7693
Key Contact - Specialty:
Ms. Crystal Schroeder - *Finance and accounting, information technology*

999 Oakmont Plaza Dr Ste 150
Westmont, IL 60559
(630) 218-7760
Fax: (630) 218-7701
Key Contact - Specialty:
Ms. Debra Brady - *Scientific, healthcare*

111 Monument Cir Ste 2130
Indianapolis, IN 46204
(317) 631-2900
Fax: (317) 682-6100
Key Contact - Specialty:
Mr. Greg Bell - *Finance and accounting, information technology*

7321 Shadeland Station Ste 275
Indianapolis, IN 46256
(317) 585-4000
Fax: (317) 585-4007
Key Contact - Specialty:
Mr. Bruce Rockwell - *Healthcare*

8700 Monrovia St Ste 3000
Lenexa, KS 66215
(913) 890-5050
Fax: (913) 438-8954
Key Contact - Specialty:
Ms. Debra Brady - *Scientific*

10300 W 103rd St Ste 101
Overland Park, KS 66214
(913) 890-5003
Fax: (913) 888-9483
Key Contact - Specialty:
Mr. Kyle Tilley - *Finance and accounting, information technology*

101 S 5th St Ste 2850
Nat'l City Twr
Louisville, KY 40202
(502) 779-4646
Fax: (502) 779-4656
Key Contact - Specialty:
Mr. Bruce Rockwell - *Healthcare*
Mr. Sam Smith - *Healthcare*

4965 US Hwy 42 Ste 2900
Louisville, KY 40222
(502) 339-2900
Fax: (502) 339-2888
Key Contact - Specialty:
Mr. Cliff Freeman - *Finance and accounting, information technology*

120 E Baltimore St Ste 1840
Baltimore, MD 21202
(410) 727-4050
Fax: (410) 727-6808
Key Contact - Specialty:
Ms. Michele Kavanagh - *Finance and accounting, information technology*

155 Federal St Fl 10
Boston, MA 02110-1727
(617) 482-8211
Fax: (617) 482-9084
Email: bcuddy@kforce.com
Key Contact - Specialty:
Mr. Sam Webber - *Finance and accounting, information technology, human resources, engineering*

20 Burlington Mall Rd Ste 400
Burlington, MA 01803
(781) 272-5000
(781) 270-4441
Fax: (781) 270-4443
Key Contact - Specialty:
Mr. David Rutter - *Finance and accounting*

2221 Washington St 1 Newton Exec Park
Bldg 1 Ste 304
Newton, MA 02462
(617) 641-2600
Fax: (617) 641-2600
Key Contact:
Mr. Matt Karpacz

1500 W Park Rd Ste 390
Westborough, MA 01581
(508) 616-5300
Fax: (508) 898-0115
Key Contact - Specialty:
Mr. Eric Preusse - *Information technology*

161 Ottawa NW Ste 409D
Grand Rapids, MI 49503
(616) 459-3600
Fax: (616) 459-3670
Key Contact:
Mr. Matt Peal

2000 Town Ctr Ste 1300
Southfield, MI 48075
(248) 352-6520
Fax: (248) 352-7514
Key Contact - Specialty:
Mr. Chris Buchanan - *Finance and accounting, scientific, information technology*

8500 Normandale Lake Blvd Ste 1590
Bloomington, MN 55437
(612) 835-5100
(612) 835-4282
Fax: (612) 835-1548
Email: dvarner@kforce.com
Key Contact - Specialty:
Mr. Dean M. Varner - *Accounting, finance, information technology*

220 S 6th St Ste 810
Pillsbury Ctr S Bldg
Minneapolis, MN 55402
(612) 630-5000
Fax: (612) 630-0083
Key Contact - Specialty:
Mr. Chad Dohlen - *Finance, accounting*

2 City Pl Dr Ste 100
St. Louis, MO 63141
(314) 212-8700
Fax: (314) 995-5311
Key Contact - Specialty:
Mr. Mark Ryan - *Finance, accounting, information technology, scientific*

2 City Pl Dr Ste 180
St. Louis, MO 63141
(314) 989-0200
Fax: (314) 212-8787
Key Contact - Specialty:
Mr. Mike Macrides - *Information technology*

71 Spit Brook Rd Ste 305
Nashua, NH 03060
(603) 888-1700
Fax: (603) 888-7826
Key Contact:
Mr. Mike Macrides

45 Eisenhower Dr Fl 4
Paramus, NJ 07652
(201) 843-2777
(201) 843-2020
Fax: (201) 843-7404
Key Contact - Specialty:
Mr. Michael Runyan - *Finance, accounting*
Mr. Matt Burgay - *Information technology*

1 Gatehall Dr Fl 3
Parsippany, NJ 07054
(973) 267-3222
Fax: (973) 267-2741

Key Contact - Specialty:
Mr. Bridget Murphy - *Finance, accounting, information technology*

3 Independence Way Ste 204
Princeton, NJ 08540
(609) 452-7277
Fax: (609) 520-1742
Key Contact - Specialty:
Ms. Dawn Serpe - *Finance, accounting, information technology*

100 Woodbridge Center Dr Ste 301
Woodbridge, NJ 07095
(732) 283-9510
Fax: (732) 283-0704
Key Contact - Specialty:
Mr. Dawn Serpe - *Finance, accounting, information technology*

60 E 42nd St Fl 27
New York, NY 10165
(212) 883-7300
Fax: (212) 953-3504
Key Contact - Specialty:
Ms. Adele Chodorow - *Finance, accounting, information technology*

3 Gannett Dr Ste 316
White Plains, NY 10604
(914) 251-9500
Fax: (914) 251-9570
Key Contact - Specialty:
Mr. Mark Davison - *Finance, accounting, information technology*

201 N Tryon St Ste 2660
Charlotte, NC 28202
(704) 331-6970
Fax: (704) 334-6006
Key Contact - Specialty:
Mr. Chris Syvertsen - *Finance, accounting, information technology*

5925 Carnegie Blvd Ste 505 & 501
Charlotte, NC 28209
(704) 398-7970
Fax: (704) 398-7903
Key Contact - Specialty:
Mr. Bruce Rockwell - *Healthcare, scientific*

36 E 7th St Ste 2500
Cincinnati, OH 45202
(513) 333-3400
Fax: (513) 651-3512
Key Contact - Specialty:
Mr. Kurt Lang - *Finance and accounting, information technology*

4750 Wesley Ave Ste 0
Cincinnati, OH 45212
(513) 333-3505
(513) 333-3506
Fax: (513) 731-7555
Key Contact - Specialty:
Mr. Bruce Rockwell - *Healthcare*
Mr. Steve Koehler - *Scientific*

1105 Schrock Rd Ste 510
Columbus, OH 43229
(614) 852-6700
Fax: (614) 846-4439
Email: ssccol@kforce.com
Key Contact - Specialty:
Ms. Susan Cornish - *Finance and accounting, information technology*

1 S Main St Ste 1440
Dayton, OH 45402
(937) 461-4660
Fax: (937) 461-5848
Key Contact - Specialty:
Mr. Kurt Lang - *Finance and accounting, information technology*

3085 Woodman Dr Ste 213
Dayton, OH 45420
(937) 296-1601
Fax: (937) 296-1602
Key Contact - Specialty:
Mr. Bruce Rockwell - *Healthcare*

3 Summit Park Dr Ste 550
Independence, OH 44131
(216) 643-8130
Fax: (216) 328-5909
Key Contact - Specialty:
Mr. Kurt Lang - *Finance and accounting, information technology*

1518 N Main St Ste 1
Lima, OH 45801
(419) 225-6374
Fax: (419) 225-5739
Key Contact - Specialty:
Mr. Bruce Rockwell - *Healthcare*

6877 N High St Ste 209
Worthington, OH 43085
(614) 438-0795
Fax: (614) 825-6789
Key Contact - Specialty:
Mr. Bruce Rockwell - *Healthcare*

15 W 6th St Ste 1604
Tulsa, OK 74119
(918) 592-5555
Fax: (918) 592-0120
Key Contact - Specialty:
Ms. Joyce Deffenbaugh - *Finance and accounting, information technology*

10220 SW Greensburg Rd Ste 625
Portland, OR 97223
(503) 768-4546
Fax: (503) 768-4533
Key Contact - Specialty:
Mr. Victor Harten - *Finance and accounting, information technology*

150 S Warner Rd Ste 238
King of Prussia, PA 19406
(610) 341-1960
Fax: (610) 964-0632
Key Contact - Specialty:
Mr. Tom Lipuma - *Information technology, pharmaceutical*

1760 Market St Fl 12
Philadelphia, PA 19103
(215) 665-1717
Fax: (215) 665-2894
Key Contact - Specialty:
Mr. Andy McKinley - *Finance and accounting, scientific*

603 Stanwix St Ste 1799
2 Gateway Ctr
Pittsburgh, PA 15222
(412) 209-2400
Fax: (412) 209-2423
Key Contact - Specialty:
Ms. Debra Kriess - *Finance and accounting*

681 Andersen Dr Foster Plz VI Fl 2
Pittsburgh, PA 15220
(412) 928-8300
Fax: (412) 928-0474
Key Contact - Specialty:
Mr. Bruce Rockwell - *Healthcare, information technology, engineering*

1255 Drummer Ln Ste 103
4 Glenhardie Corporate Ctr
Wayne, PA 19087
(610) 989-3680
Fax: (610) 989-3692
Key Contact - Specialty:
Mr. Philip Schadler - *Finance and accounting*

8701 N Mopac Ste 455
Austin, TX 78746
(512) 345-7473
Fax: (512) 345-7736
Key Contact - Specialty:
Mr. Craig Jackson - *Finance and accounting, information technology, scientific*

1201 Elm St Ste 4930
Dallas, TX 75270
(214) 915-8200
Fax: (214) 915-8266

Key Contact - Specialty:
Mr. Jeff Combs - *Finance and accounting, information technology*

5429 LBJ Freeway Ste 275
Dallas, TX 75240
(972) 387-1600
Fax: (972) 387-0204
Key Contact - Specialty:
Mr. Bruce Rockwell - *Information technology, healthcare*

5429 LBJ Freeway Ste 580
Dallas, TX 75240
(972) 934-2111
Fax: (972) 383-6189
Key Contact - Specialty:
Ms. Marylee Lajoie - *Finance and accounting, scientific*

801 Cherry St Ste 1025
Ft. Worth, TX 76102
(817) 334-2400
Fax: (817) 810-0567
Key Contact - Specialty:
Ms. Bridget McDonald - *Finance and accounting, information technology*

520 Post Oak Blvd Ste 700
Houston, TX 77027
(713) 479-3500
Fax: (713) 622-3778
Key Contact - Specialty:
Ms. Laura Leno - *Finance and accounting, information technology*

1777 NE Loop 410 Ste 603
San Antonio, TX 78217
(210) 820-2624
Fax: (210) 841-5710
Key Contact:
Mr. Steve Flores

505 E 200 S Ste 300
Salt Lake City, UT 84102
(801) 257-6800
Fax: (801) 364-4549
Key Contact - Specialty:
Ms. Cynthia Timon - *Finance and accounting, information technology*

11240 Waples Mill Rd Ste 301
Fairfax, VA 22030
(703) 345-3000
Fax: (703) 293-9715
Key Contact - Specialty:
Ms. Amy Murphy - *Human resources*

8045 Leesburg Pike Ste 200
Vienna, VA 22182
(703) 342-3100
(202) 354-8600
Fax: (703) 790-1331
Email: amaclean@kforce.com
Key Contact - Specialty:
Ms. Michele Kavanagh - *Finance and accounting, information technology*

Two Union Sq Fl 42
Seattle, WA 98101
(206) 652-3595
Fax: (206) 652-3596
Key Contact - Specialty:
Mr. Victor Harten - *Finance and accounting, information technology*

1233 N Mayfair Rd Ste 300
Milwaukee, WI 53226
(414) 475-7200
Fax: (414) 774-8155
Key Contact - Specialty:
Mr. Bob Schwalbach - *Finance and accounting, information technology*

KGA Inc
1320 Greenway Ter Ste 1
Brookfield, WI 53005
(262) 786-5209
Fax: (262) 786-7961

Let www.ExecutiveAgent.com e-mail your resume now.

Email: k.gunkel@usa.net

Description: Twenty-two years' exclusively recruiting and placing human resources professionals. Speacialize in all human resources placement of candidates with three years or more experience, to include compensation, benefits, staffing, training and development, as well as "generalist" positions up to and including vice president level.

Key Contact - Specialty:
Mr. Keith J. Gunkel, President - *Human resources, personnel*

Salary minimum: $50,000

Functions: Generalist, HR Mgmt., Benefits, Personnel, Training

Industries: Generalist

KGA Professional Search
6818 Burke Ct
Chino, CA 91710
(800) 813-5301
Email: pro.search@verizon.net
Web: www.bringingpeopletogether.com

Key Contact - Specialty:
Mr. James Kenneth, President/Owner
Mrs. Danielle Sigman, Consultant - *Accounting and finance*

Functions: Finance

Industries: Generalist

Networks: Top Echelon Network

KGN Associates
(also known as Hire Expectations LLC)
225 N Michigan Ave Fl 11
Chicago, IL 60601
(312) 819-4300
(312) 819-4372
Fax: (312) 819-6200
Email: careers@kgn.com
Web: www.kgn.com

Description: As a member of the KGN Financial Group, our firm offers its clients and non-clients first class service and high caliber individuals in the accounting and finance career fields. Hire Expectations, LLC has grown to become recognized as a professional minority run group.

Key Contact - Specialty:
Ms. Linda Javor, Director - *Accounting & finance*

Salary minimum: $40,000

Functions: Middle Mgmt.

Industries: Generalist

Professional Associations: NAPS

Networks: PRO/NET

Ki Technologies Inc Executive Search Div
955 N 400 W Bldg 10
North Salt Lake, UT 84054
(888) 283-0399
(801) 517-3602
Email: recruiter@ki-tech.com
Web: www.ki-tech.com

Description: Elite small firm specializing in high-technology engineering, marketing and technical sales professionals both management and hands on contributors; software/hardware engineers, product marketing and management. Mid-level to executive placement.

Key Contact - Specialty:
Mr. James S. Mellos, President - *Computers, MBAs, vice president, high technology, presidents*
Dr. Thomas Bakehorn, Vice President - *Sales & marketing, senior management, CIOs, CEOs*

Mr. Bruce Waltz - *Telecommunications, telephony, data communications, networking, defense*
Ms. Donna Vance - *Digital, engineering, electronics, design, software*
Mr. Jim Mellos, CEO - *High tech*

Salary minimum: $75,000

Functions: Generalist, Systems Analysis, Systems Dev., Engineering, Int'l.

Industries: Computer Equip., Test, Measure Equip., Electronic, Elec. Components, Venture Cap., New Media, Telecoms, Telephony, Digital, Wireless, Fiber Optic, Network Infrastructure, Aerospace, Software, Marketing SW, Networking, Comm. SW, Security SW

Professional Associations: RON

Kimball Personnel Sales Recruiters
2 Cross Rd
Hubbardston, MA 01452
(508) 829-8849
Fax: (508) 829-4862
Email: kimballpr01@aol.com

Description: Staffing and recruitment of sales personnel for the telecommunications, office products, copier, medical, industrial, engineering, computer, retail-service, communications and insurance industries.

Key Contact - Specialty:
Mr. John Kimball, CPC, Owner - *Sales*

Functions: Generalist, Healthcare, Sales & Mktg., Sales Mgmt., Customer Svc.

Industries: Generalist, Media, Telecoms, Insurance

Kimmel & Associates Inc
25 Page Ave
Asheville, NC 28801
(828) 251-9900
Fax: (828) 251-9955
Email: kimmelmail@mindspring.com
Web: www.kimmel.com

Description: We are an aggressive, national recruiting firm specializing in construction, real estate development, solid waste, distribution, transportation, and contract employment.

Key Contact - Specialty:
Mr. Joe W. Kimmel, President - *Construction, real estate & development, CFO, financial, solid waste*

Salary minimum: $80,000

Functions: General Mgmt., Senior Mgmt., Distribution, Sales & Mktg., HR Mgmt., Finance, CFO's

Industries: Generalist, Construction, Mfg., Transportation, Finance, Real Estate

Professional Associations: NAPS

Kincaid Group Inc (KGI)
11230 W Ave Ste 1105
San Antonio, TX 78213
(210) 308-9221
Fax: (210) 308-9201
Email: kincaid@kincaidgroup.com
Web: www.kincaidgroup.com

Description: We are a search consulting firm specializing in medical, technical and executive placement. We assist organizations throughout the entire process of personnel activities from recruiting and training to termination and outplacement.

Key Contact - Specialty:
Mr. Raymond W. Kincaid, President - *Physician, executive*
Mr. Trevor Anderson, Senior Consultant - *Physician, nurse, ancillary*
Mr. Lee Johnson, Senior Consultant - *Nurse, ancillary, technical*

Functions: Generalist, Senior Mgmt., Healthcare

Industries: Generalist, Banking, Misc. Financial, Accounting, Mgmt. Consulting, HR Services, Healthcare, Non-classifiable

Branches:
1150 Bluff Forest
San Antonio, TX 78248
(210) 308-9221
Email: kincaid@kincaidgroup.com
Key Contact:
Ms. Lynn Kincaid, Principal

Kinderis & Loercher Group
149 N Virginia Ste 100
Crystal Lake, IL 60014
(815) 459-3700
Fax: (815) 459-6314
Email: info@kandlgroup.com
Web: www.kandlgroup.com

Description: Commitment to service. Effective results through local concentration. Straight forward, no nonsense style. Priority on ethics.

Key Contact - Specialty:
Mr. Paul Kinderis, President - *Insurance, information technology*

Salary minimum: $20,000

Functions: Generalist, Directors, Senior Mgmt., Middle Mgmt., Finance, Risk Mgmt., IT, Attorneys

Industries: Generalist, Misc. Financial, Insurance, Software, Healthcare

Professional Associations: HOGBI

King Associates
116 Strathmore Ln
Rochester, NY 14609
(716) 288-1214
Fax: (716) 288-9008
Email: king223@aol.com

Description: Our firm specializes in executive recruiting for the financial service industry. We place portfolio managers, pension professionals, trust officers, sales executives, and management personnel.

Key Contact - Specialty:
Mr. Michael King, Principal - *Financial services*

Salary minimum: $50,000

Functions: General Mgmt., Sales & Mktg., Cash Mgmt.

Industries: Banking, Invest. Banking, Brokers, Misc. Financial, Insurance, Non-classifiable

Michael King Associates Inc
600 3rd Ave Fl 26
New York, NY 10016
(212) 687-5490
Fax: (212) 599-5323
Email: mka@michaelking.com
Web: www.michaelking.com

Description: Specializes in making matches between significant Wall Street producers and premier financial firms.

Key Contact:
Mr. Michael King, President
Ms. Dolores Bullard, Vice President

King Search Solutions Inc
9101 LBJ Fwy Ste 400 MB 6
Dallas, TX 75243
(972) 238-1021
(800) 738-1021
Fax: (972) 699-9551
Email: post@kingsearch.com
Web: www.kingsearch.com

Description: We provide executive search, technical recruiting, consulting and professional services for technology companies and information technology environments, including engineering and management talent for software, telecommunications, information technology and Internet.

Key Contact - Specialty:
Ms. Sally King, CPC
Mr. David Farmer, Vice President - *Consulting, professional services*

Functions: Generalist, Mkt. Research, Sales Mgmt., MIS Mgmt., Systems Implem., Systems Support, Engineering

Industries: Generalist, New Media, Telecoms, Software

Professional Associations: ASQ, IEEE, NAPS, NTSA, SERC, TAPS

Branches:
9600 Great Hills Trail Ste 150 W
Austin, TX 78759
(512) 231-9600
Fax: (512) 231-8600
Key Contact:
Ms. Sherrie Williams, Branch Manager

The Kirdonn Group
106 W 11th St Ste 1520
Kansas City, MO 64105
(816) 474-0700
Fax: (816) 474-0702
Email: salespros@kirdonn.net
Web: www.kirdonn.com

Description: A regional firm with a national presence placing sales, sales management, marketing pros specializing in high-technology, telecommunications, consumer, industrial, advertising, office products and builder trades.

Key Contact - Specialty:
Mr. Jim Panus, CPC, President - *Sales, sales management, builders trade*
Mr. Kevin Nolan, National Accounts Manager - *Transportation sales, sales management*
Mr. John Stawarz, Sales Consultant - *Sales, sales management, entry level, executive*

Functions: Sales & Mktg.

Industries: Mfg., Transportation, Finance, Services, Media, Packaging, Software, Biotech, Healthcare

Networks: First Interview Network (FIN)

Branches:
14323 S Outer Forty Ste 600 S
Town & Country
St. Louis, MO 63017
(314) 434-0800
Fax: (314) 434-0341
Email: salelspro@kirdonn2.net
Key Contact - Specialty:
Mr. Larry Zielinski - *Sales, sales management*
Ms. Christy Zielinski, Sales Consultant - *Sales, sales management*

Kirkbride Associates Inc
915 118th Ave SE Ste 370
Bellevue, WA 98005
(888) 764-9782
(425) 453-5268
Fax: (425) 453-5257
Email: kirkbrid@isomedia.com
Web: www.kirkbrideassoc.com

Description: Sales and marketing, HVAC, datacom and medical. Engineering: HVAC and medical. Management: HVAC, datacom, medical.

Key Contact:
Mr. Robert Kirkbride, CEO - *Sales, engineering, marketing, HVAC/R, data communications*
Mr. Richard Logie, Senior Recruiter - *Sales, engineering, technical, HVAC/R*

Mr. Paul Roberts, Senior Recruiter - *Sales, engineering, HVAC/R*
Mr. Greg Waters, Vice President - *HVAC/R*
Mr. Hal Bennett, Recruiter - *Telecom, datacom*
Mr. Al Gross, Recruiter - *HVAC/R, sales, engineering*
Mrs. Terri Wilson, Recruiter - *Medical, healthcare*
Ms. Kris Schrieber, Senior Recruiter

Salary minimum: $45,000

Functions: Directors, Healthcare, Sales Mgmt., Engineering

Industries: Energy, Utilities, Construction, Medical Devices, Misc. Mfg., Services, Telecoms, Healthcare, Non-classifiable

Professional Associations: ASHRAE

Networks: Top Echelon Network

Klein, Landau & Romm
1725 K St NW Ste 602
Washington, DC 20006
(202) 728-0100
(212) 822-1448
Fax: (202) 728-0112
Email: info@jurisjob.com
Web: www.jurisjob.com

Description: The company is the largest legal search firm in Washington D.C. with offices in New York City, Orange County, CA., and affiliates in Hong Kong and London. We specialize in placing attorneys in private firms and corporations nationwide. The company also places temporary attorney division in the Washington D.C. Office.

Key Contact:
Mr. Gary Ethan Klein, Partner
Mr. David Landau, Partner
Mr. Barry Romm, Partner

Functions: Legal, Attorneys

Industries: Generalist

KM Associates
30 Colpitts Rd
Weston, MA 02493
(781) 899-6655
Email: kijobs@kmasearch.com
Web: www.kmasearch.com

Description: We are a sales and marketing executive software search firm specializing primarily in Internet/ software pre-IPO stage companies headquartered in the Massachusetts area. We work with our client's in a partnership methodology combining the advantages of both retained and contingency search.

Key Contact:
Mr. Christopher Mason, Partner - *Software executives*
Mr. Kimball Mason, Partner - *Software consultants*
Mr. Simon Dudek, Consultant

Salary minimum: $75,000

Functions: Sales & Mktg., Sales Mgmt.

Industries: Services, Communications, Software

Joyce C Knauff & Associates
PO Box 624
Wilmette, IL 60091
(847) 251-7284
Fax: (847) 251-6945
Email: jck@interaccess.com
Web: www.jckassociates.com

Description: We are a search firm specializing in the information technology function of corporations and consulting firms.

Key Contact - Specialty:
Ms. Joyce C. Knauff, President - *MIS*

Salary minimum: $45,000

Functions: IT, MIS Mgmt., Systems Analysis, Systems Dev., Systems Implem., Systems Support, Specialized Svcs.

Industries: Generalist

Professional Associations: NAWBO, RI

Koerner & Associates Inc
1904 Kingsbury Dr
Nashville, TN 37215
(615) 371-6162
Fax: (615) 371-6172
Email: koerner.assoc@nashville.com
Web: www.koernerassociates.com

Description: We specialize in the search and placement of attorneys. We take pride in our professionalism and ethical manner of doing business. We conduct attorney searches on a local, regional, national, and worldwide basis. Koerner & Associates, Inc. has been placing attorneys for law firms, corporations, and financial institutions.

Key Contact - Specialty:
Ms. Pam L. Koerner, President - *Attorneys*

Salary minimum: $50,000

Functions: Attorneys

Industries: Generalist

Professional Associations: NALSC

Koll-Fairfield LLC
397 Post Rd
Darien, CT 06820
(203) 655-5001
Fax: (203) 656-2667
Email: careers@kfsearch.com
Web: www.kfsearch.com

Description: We are a full-service boutique recruiting firm offering flexible search products to the accounting, finance, and information technology communities. We are a firm dedicated to providing staffing solutions and quick results.

Key Contact - Specialty:
Mr. Richard Champagne, Principal - *Accounting & finance*
Mr. Bruce Stalowicz, Principal - *Accounting & finance*
Mr. Tom Reynolds, Vice President - *Information technology*

Salary minimum: $80,000

Functions: Finance, IT

Industries: Generalist

Kordus Consulting Group
1470 E Standish Pl
Milwaukee, WI 53217-1958
(414) 228-7979
Fax: (414) 228-1080
Email: kcginc@aol.com

Description: Executive search and management consulting nationwide. Recruitment in areas of marketing, marketing services, advertising, promotions, public relations, communications and research. Corporate and agency positions. Retainer and contingency search.

Key Contact:
Ms. Lee Walther Kordus, President
Mr. Benedict N. Kordus, Partner

Salary minimum: $45,000

Functions: General Mgmt., Senior Mgmt., Middle Mgmt., Sales & Mktg., Advertising, Mkt. Research, Mktg. Mgmt., Direct Mktg., PR, Graphic Artists

Industries: Generalist, Mfg., Food, Bev., Tobacco, Lumber, Furniture, Paper, Soap, Perf., Cosmtcs., Drugs Mfg., Machine, Appliance, Advertising, Healthcare

Professional Associations: AAF, NAPS, WAPS

Michael Kosmetos & Associates Inc

333 Babbitt Rd Ste 300
Cleveland, OH 44123
(216) 261-1950
Fax: (216) 261-9796
Email: retailsearch333@aol.com

Description: Our staff is non-commissioned and we approach projects as a search team. With over 35 years of combined experience this team approach allows us to be expeditious and extremely thorough.

Key Contact - Specialty:
Mr. Michael Kosmetos, President - *Retail*

Salary minimum: $35,000

Functions: Senior Mgmt., Middle Mgmt., Distribution, HR Mgmt.

Industries; Retail

Dana Kowen Associates

330 W Diversy Pkwy Ste 2305
Chicago, IL 60657
(773) 665-2584
(773) 818-2584
Fax: (509) 561-7812
Email: ddkowen@aol.com

Description: We are an executive search and recruitment firm specializing in the identification, evaluation, and placement of uniquely talented human resources and sales professionals. We are committed to providing the highest quality and caliber of services. We focus on establishing long-term relationships with both employers and candidates in lieu of quick placements.

Key Contact - Specialty:
Ms. Dana Kowen, President - *Human resources, recruiting*

Salary minimum: $40,000

Functions: Sales Mgmt., HR Mgmt., Benefits, Personnel, Training

Industries: Generalist, Medical Devices, Pharm Svcs., HR Services

Kozlin Associates Inc

PO Box 393
Clarence, NY 14031
(716) 634-5955
Fax: (716) 626-0549
Email: jeffk@kozlin.com
Web: www.kozlin.com

Description: Our Company is based in Buffalo, N.Y. and is a contingency/retained search firm serving the manufacturing industry. Our firm conducts nationwide research for all types of engineers, as well as mid- to upper-level managers.

Key Contact:
Mr. Jeffrey M. Kozlin, President
Mr. Brian Weber, Recruiter

Salary minimum: $40,000

Functions: Mfg.

Industries: Generalist

Networks: National Personnel Assoc (NPA)

KPA Associates Inc

150 Broadway Ste 1900
New York, NY 10038
(212) 964-3640
(800) 226-5836
Fax: (212) 964-6959
Email: ladams@kpastaff.com
Web: www.kpastaff.com

Description: Full range of services including executive search, managerial and technical staffing and consulting for financial services industries.

Wage and salary surveys available as well as providing staff for consulting projects. An emphasis in start-up operations.

Key Contact:
Mr. Len Adams, CPC, Executive Vice President/COO - *Financial services*
Mr. Antonio Vittorioso, President/CEO

Salary minimum: $25,000

Functions: Generalist

Industries: Finance, Services, Accounting, Mgmt. Consulting, HR Services, New Media, Software

Professional Associations: APCNY

Evie Kreisler & Associates Inc

865 S Figueroa St Ste 104
Los Angeles, CA 90017
(213) 622-8994
Fax: (213) 622-9660
Email: lafd@ekjobs.com
Web: www.kreisler-associates.com

Description: Specialists-all disciplines - retail; apparel wholesale/manufacturing and consumer products. Our consultants have related industry background. We take pride in finding the perfect fit.

Key Contact - Specialty:
Ms. Evie Kreisler, President/CEO - *Retail, apparel wholesale, manufacturing*

Salary minimum: $50,000

Functions: Generalist, Directors, Senior Mgmt., Middle Mgmt., Product Dev., Advertising, Sales Mgmt., CFO's

Industries: Generalist, Textiles, Apparel, Wholesale, Retail, Services, Media

Branches:
333 N Michigan 818
Chicago, IL 60601
(312) 251-0077
Fax: (312) 251-0289
Key Contact - Specialty:
Mr. Wayne Tadda, General Manager - *Retail, apparel wholesale, manufacturing*

1 W 34th St Ste 201
New York, NY 10001
(212) 279-8999
Fax: (212) 268-9660
Key Contact - Specialty:
Ms. Kathy Gross, VP/General Manager - *Retail, apparel wholesale, manufacturing*

2720 Stemmons Fwy Ste 812
Dallas, TX 75207
(972) 631-8994
Fax: (214) 630-2343
Key Contact - Specialty:
Mr. Tony Priftis, VP/Regional Manager - *Retail, apparel wholesale, manufacturing*

Kreisler & Associates LLC

2575 Peachtree Rd Ste 300
Atlanta, GA 30305
(404) 262-0599
Fax: (404) 262-0699
Email: kreisler5d@aol.com
Web: www.kreisler-associates.com

Description: Over 30,000 searches, in consumer products, retailing, manufacturing, finance and e-commerce industries. Our success in attributed to long-term relationship and partnership with clients. Providing management to senior executive management teams.

Key Contact - Specialty:
Ms. Debbi Kreisler, President - *Retail, apparel wholesale, manufacturing*

Functions: Generalist

Industries: Transportation, Wholesale, Retail, Finance, E-commerce, IT Implementation, HR

SW, Mfg. SW, Marketing SW, Networking, Comm. SW

Kressenberg Associates

1112 E Copeland Ste 340
Arlington, TX 76012
(817) 226-8990
(800) 551-5361
Fax: (817) 226-8999

Description: We are a boutique executive search firm conducting search assignments throughout the US on an exclusive basis. Our specialties include trucking dealerships, class 6 to 8; automobile dealerships; veterinary medicine; and capital equipment for the semiconductor industry.

Key Contact - Specialty:
Ms. Sammye Jo Kressenberg, President - *Managed care, sales, sales management, semiconductor capital equipment, truck industry (class 6-8)*
Ms. Kay Trammell, Vice President - *Generalist*

Salary minimum: $50,000

Functions: Generalist, Senior Mgmt., Middle Mgmt., Nurses, Health Admin., Sales Mgmt., HR Mgmt., Benefits, CFO's, Engineering

Industries: Generalist, Motor Vehicles, Computer Equip., Accounting, Healthcare

Kreuzberger & Associates

1000 4th St Ste 150
San Rafael, CA 94901
(415) 459-2300
Fax: (415) 459-2471
Email: info@kreuzberger.com
Web: www.kreuzberger.com

Description: Executive search and contract staffing firm serving the accounting and finance functional arenas throughout the greater Bay Area.

Key Contact - Specialty:
Mr. Neil L. Kreuzberger, CPA, President - *Financial services, technology, venture capital, private equity, telecommunications*
Ms. Keri A. Pon, Vice President - *Contract staffing*

Salary minimum: $30,000

Functions: Finance, CFO's, Budgeting, Cash Mgmt., Credit, Taxes, M&A, Risk Mgmt.

Industries: Mfg., Retail, Finance, Venture Cap., Misc. Financial, Services, Hospitality, Insurance, Real Estate, Software, Biotech, Healthcare

Branches:
115 Sansome St Ste 1200
San Francisco, CA 94104
(415) 398-3995
Fax: (415) 398-5714
Key Contact - Specialty:
Mr. David Petroff - *Financial services, technology, VC, telecommunications*

Todd L Krueger & Associates

PO Box 1289
Seattle, WA 98111
(425) 776-9247
Fax: (425) 338-0255

Description: Expertise assisting all size companies in staffing their corporate tax and accounting departments. Additionally, assist public accounting firms in recruiting specialized and experienced audit and tax personnel.

Key Contact - Specialty:
Mr. Todd L. Krueger, President/Owner - *Accounting & finance, tax*

Salary minimum: $25,000

Functions: Generalist, CFO's, Budgeting, Cash Mgmt., Taxes, Mgmt. Consultants

Industries: Generalist, Accounting, Equip Svcs., Mgmt. Consulting, Hospitality

Kuhn Med-Tech Inc
27128-B Paseo Espada Ste 623
San Juan Capistrano, CA 92675
(949) 496-3500
Fax: (949) 496-1716
Email: der@kuhnmed-tech.com
Web: www.kuhnmed-tech.com

Description: Serving medical device and biotechnology industries. Exclusive contingency and retainers; positions secured for engineers, scientists, marketing/sales and senior management professionals for Fortune 500 companies and exciting start-up ventures.

Key Contact - Specialty:
Mr. Larry A. Kuhn, President - *Medical device, biotechnology, start-up companies, all business development*
Mr. Otis Archie, Jr., Vice President - *Executives, medical device, sales, software, electrical*
Mr. Dennis Lawry, Executive Recruiter - *Medical devices*
Mr. Joseph Halstead, Executive Recruiter - *Medical devices, all computer issues*

Salary minimum: $50,000

Functions: Generalist, General Mgmt., Senior Mgmt., Mfg., Product Dev., Healthcare, Sales & Mktg., Personnel, R&D, Engineering

Industries: Generalist, Drugs Mfg., Medical Devices, Plastics, Rubber, Finance, Venture Cap., Misc. Financial, Software, Development SW, Biotech, Healthcare, Dental

Kunin Associates
900 SE 3rd Ave Ste 204
Ft. Lauderdale, FL 33316
(954) 467-9575
(305) 358-7977
Fax: (954) 467-9585
Email: jkunin@kuninassociates.com
Web: www.kuninassociates.com

Description: We are a professional recruiting firm specializing in the placement of accounting, financial and bookkeeping personnel. We provide personalized service to our clients and deal directly with many of the finest public accounting firms and companies in South Florida.

Key Contact - Specialty:
Ms. Jo-Anne Kunin, CPA, President - *Accounting & finance*
Ms. Lisa Luby, Vice President - *Accounting & finance*

Salary minimum: $25,000

Functions: Middle Mgmt., CFO's, Budgeting, Cash Mgmt., Credit, Taxes, M&A, Risk Mgmt.

Industries: Generalist

Professional Associations: AAFA, AICPA, FICPA, IMA, SHRM

D Kunkle & Associates
PO Box 184
Barrington, IL 60011
(847) 540-8651
Fax: (847) 540-8653
Email: denise.kunkle@att.net

Description: The president brings over 18 years of technical and management experience to the search field. The unique perspective she has gained in building organizations within major consumer packaged goods businesses ensures a more knowledgeable approach and superior search results.

Key Contact - Specialty:
Ms. Denise Kunkle, President - *Packaging, product development, process development, quality (assurance, control), purchasing*

Salary minimum: $45,000

Functions: Product Dev., Quality, Purchasing, Packaging, Graphic Artists

Industries: Food, Bev., Tobacco, Soap, Perf., Cosmtcs., Drugs Mfg., Medical Devices, Packaging

Kurtz Pro-Search Inc
PO Box 4263
Warren, NJ 07059-0263
(908) 647-7789

Description: A candidate must have quality sales, support, marketing and/or management experience dedicated to a career in IT, networking, DataCom, telecommunications, software, hardware or services.

Key Contact - Specialty:
Mr. Sheldon I. Kurtz, President - *Emergency information technology, networking, data communications, telecommunications*

Salary minimum: $75,000

Functions: MIS Mgmt., Systems Analysis, Systems Dev., Systems Implem., Systems Support, Mgmt. Consultants

Industries: Computer Equip., Mgmt. Consulting, New Media, Telecoms, Software

Kutcher Tax Careers Inc
37 Saw Mill River Rd Fl 1
Hawthorne, NY 10532
(914) 592-6887
Fax: (914) 592-0441
Email: kutcher@taxcareers.com
Web: www.taxcareers.com

Description: We are a niche-oriented recruiting firm that specializes exclusively in the tax area. Our clients (corporations and CPA firms) are in the NY Meropolitan area. Our detailed web-site allows clients & candidates to submit their confidential information on-line as well as view sampling of placements made, client (testimonials), principal's background and other pertinent items.

Key Contact - Specialty:
Mr. Howard Kutcher, CPA, President - *Taxation*

Salary minimum: $40,000

Functions: Generalist, Taxes

Industries: Generalist

Professional Associations: AAHCPA, AICPA, APA, ASWA, CRA, CSCPA, HRANY, IAAO, IFA, IMA, NABA, NJSCPA, NYSSCPA, SHRM

Kutt Inc
2336 Canyon Blvd Ste 202
Boulder, CO 80302
(303) 440-4100
(303) 440-6111
Fax: (303) 440-9582
Email: info@kuttinc.com
Web: www.kuttinc.com

Description: Executive search and recruiting firm serving the printing industry only; all levels of positions filled.

Key Contact - Specialty:
Mr. David Huff, Part Owner - *Printing*
Mr. Greg Neighbors, Part Owner - *Printing*

Salary minimum: $40,000

Functions: Generalist

Industries: Printing

Kuttnauer Search Group Inc
6363 Worlington Rd
Bloomfield Hills, MI 48301-1547
(248) 539-9682
Fax: (248) 539-9639
Email: curtis@kuttnauer.com
Web: www.kuttnauer.com

Description: Our firm specializes in the placement of full-time sales executives and sales professionals in the information technology industry. Client companies are hardware, software and services organizations.

Key Contact:
Mr. Curtis Kuttnauer, President

Salary minimum: $100,000

Functions: Senior Mgmt., Sales & Mktg., Sales Mgmt., IT

Industries: Computer Equip., Equip Svcs., E-commerce, IT Implementation, PSA/ASP, Software

Professional Associations: NAPS

Networks: Top Echelon Network

Kyle Associates
PO Box 603
Scarsdale, NY 10583
(914) 723-5070
Fax: (914) 723-5070

Description: A small HR firm providing high quality services to client companies in areas of: recruiting and outplacement. As a small firm, we are able to deliver our services on a customized basis.

Key Contact - Specialty:
Mr. Donald Kyle, President - *Human resources*

Salary minimum: $60,000

Functions: Generalist, General Mgmt., HR Mgmt., Finance, IT

Industries: Generalist, Finance, Banking, Invest. Banking, Brokers, HR Services, Insurance

Professional Associations: IACMP

L & L Associates
1015 E Imperial Hwy Ste C-9
PO Box 541
Brea, CA 92822-0541
(714) 990-5525
Fax: (714) 990-3302
Email: agoldst259@aol.com

Description: Contingency search specializing in supporting recruitment efforts to "Hi-Tech" companies located in Southern California.

Key Contact - Specialty:
Mr. Alan Gold, Partner - *Technical*

Salary minimum: $25,000

Functions: Engineering

Industries: Generalist, Mfg., Telecoms, Aerospace, Software

L T S Associates
1112 Elizabeth
Naperville, IL 60540
(630) 961-3331
Fax: (630) 961-9921
Email: mward@ltsasc.com

Description: We focus on technology sales and information systems industries; mid- and senior-level management, financial and legal counsel, leasing, information systems specialists and sales representatives in: capital equipment including rolling stock, auto, medical and computer equipment.

Key Contact - Specialty:
Ms. Madeleine Ward, Partner - *Financial services, leasing*
Mr. Thomas Dato, Partner - *Technology sales*

Salary minimum: $50,000

Functions: Generalist, Senior Mgmt., Middle Mgmt., Mktg. Mgmt., Sales Mgmt., Cash Mgmt., Risk Mgmt., Systems Dev.

Industries: Generalist, Finance, Banking, Invest.
Banking, Misc. Financial, Equip Svcs., IT
Implementation, Software

La Vista Consulting Inc
1000 Abernathy Rd Ste 1000
Atlanta, GA 30328
(770) 481-7300
Fax: (770) 481-7301
Email: jpope@lavistaconsulting.com
Web: www.lavistaconsulting.com

Description: We specialize in professional level
staffing both in contract and direct hire primarily in
three areas, and they are: accounting and finance,
information technology, and human resources.

Key Contact - Specialty:
Mr. John Pope, Vice President - *Executive
recruiting & search*

Functions: Directors, Mfg., HR Mgmt., Finance,
IT, Engineering

Industries: Generalist, Energy, Utilities, Mfg.,
Transportation, Services, IT Implementation,
Media, Communications, Insurance, Real Estate,
Software, Healthcare, Hospitals, Non-classifiable

Professional Associations: GAPS, SHRM, TAG

Laboratory Resource Group
18 Washington St Ste 158
Canton, MA 02021
(781) 575-9653
Fax: (781) 575-9638

Description: Specializing in scientific, technical and
management positions for the biotech,
pharmaceutical, chemical, environmental, food and
beverage industries. Principal has considerable
laboratory management experience and numerous
contacts in related industries.

Key Contact - Specialty:
Mr. Kevin Boyce, President - *Scientific, technical*

Salary minimum: $30,000

Functions: Generalist, Middle Mgmt., Product
Dev., Production, Plant Mgmt., Quality,
Packaging, R&D

Industries: Generalist, Food, Bev., Tobacco,
Chemicals, Soap, Perf., Cosmtcs., Drugs Mfg.,
Medical Devices, Packaging, Biotech

Networks: Inter-City Personnel Assoc (IPA)

The LaBorde Group
PO Box 36162
Los Angeles, CA 90036-0162
(323) 938-9007
(877) 938-2770
Fax: (323) 938-2770
Email: labordegroup@yahoo.com

Description: Broad based executive recruiting firm
since 1971 emphasizing transportation, ranging
from middle management to key executives earning
six figures. Highway, transit, railroad, civil
engineers and construction management. Also
developing a large international department.

Key Contact - Specialty:
Mr. John LaBorde, Owner - *Construction
management, engineers, railroad, highways, civil
engineering*
Mr. Jim Kelly, Associate - *Construction
management, engineers, RR transit, highways*
Mr. Bob Martin, Researcher - *Architects*
Mr. Michael LaBorde, Associate - *Construction
management, architects*

Salary minimum: $70,000

Functions: Architects

Industries: Energy, Utilities, Construction,
Environmental Svcs.

Professional Associations: WTS

LaCosta & Associates Int'l Inc
9750 Miramar Rd Ste 375
San Diego, CA 92126
(858) 860-1222
Fax: (858) 860-1221
Email: topaul@aol.com

Description: We offer a variety of people
development and recruiting services in the
wireless/telecommunications industry specializing
in marketing, engineering, information technology,
customer service, sales management, executive and
general management. Also provided are retained
and retained-contingent searches to find human
resource and finance professionals across all
industries.

Key Contact - Specialty:
Mr. Paul LaCosta, President - *Wireless,
telecommunications*
Mr. Doug Smith, Account Manager - *Wireless
manufacturers*
Mr. Steve Holman, Account Manager - *Wireless
sales executives*
Ms. Leonore Payne, Account Manager -
Telecommunications, wireless, service providers

Salary minimum: $40,000

Functions: Directors, Senior Mgmt., Sales &
Mktg., Customer Svc., HR Mgmt., CFO's,
Engineering, Int'l.

Industries: Telecoms

Professional Associations: CTIA, PCIA

Lahey Consulting LLC
8 Maywood Rd
Delmar, NY 12054-2117
(518) 439-4439
Email: slahey@laheyconsulting.com
Web: www.laheyconsulting.com

Description: Our sole focus is bringing world-class
brand management/marketing professionals and top
consumer marketing companies together. Our
national candidate and client networks within the
consumer-packaged goods marketing world are
particularly substantial. Our firm performs both
contingency and retained searches depending on
level of position

Key Contact - Specialty:
Mr. Stephen H. Lahey, President - *Brand
(management, marketing)*

Functions: Mktg. Mgmt.

Industries: Food, Bev., Tobacco, Soap, Perf.,
Cosmtcs., Consumer Elect., Marketing SW

Gregory Laka & Company
18201 S Morris
Homewood, IL 60430
(708) 206-2000
Fax: (708) 206-2020
Email: info@laka.com
Web: www.laka.com

Description: Search in all areas of information
technology having a retainer and a contingency
division.

Key Contact:
Mr. Gregory Laka, President

Salary minimum: $50,000

Functions: Generalist, MIS Mgmt., Systems
Analysis, Systems Dev., Systems Implem.,
Systems Support

Industries: Generalist, Software

Branches:
11 E Adams Ste 1000
Chicago, IL 60603
(312) 922-7100
Fax: (312) 922-7199
Key Contact:
Mr. Greg David, President-Chicago Operations

H Lake & Company Inc
(also known as Med-Employ.com)
20 Independence Dr Ste 3A
Freeport, ME 04032
(207) 865-9700
Fax: (508) 861-1555
Email: jms@ime.net

Description: Healthcare recruiters specializing in
nursing, physicians, physical therapists, physician
assistants and nurse practitioners. Representing
hospitals, clinics, HMOs and private practice
throughout the USA.

Key Contact:
Mr. Jack M. Schraeter, President - *Medical, nursing*
Ms. Patricia Lilly, Office Manager

Salary minimum: $40,000

Functions: Generalist

Industries: Healthcare

The Lake City Group
(also known as MRI of Warsaw)
102 S Buffalo St Ste D
Nat'l City Bank Bldg
Warsaw, IN 46580
(219) 371-2525
Fax: (219) 371-2535
Email: gb3@lakecitygroup.com
Web: www.lakecitygroup.com

Description: Our firm is a global executive search
firm specializing in staffing solutions for the
medical device, pharmaceutical, biotech, and dental
industries. Our practice focus includes positions at
all levels of research and product development,
clinical, and regulatory affairs, quality,
manufacturing operations, information technology,
marketing, sales, logistics, and distribution.

Key Contact:
Mr. George Brennan, III

Functions: General Mgmt., Directors, Product
Dev., Packaging, Sales & Mktg., Sales Mgmt., IT,
R&D, Engineering, Int'l.

Industries: Mfg., Medical Devices, Plastics,
Rubber, Metal Products, Computer Equip., Test,
Measure Equip., Electronic, Elec. Components, IT
Implementation, Wireless, Packaging, Software,
Development SW, Industry Specific SW, Mfg.
SW, Marketing SW, Biotech, Dental

Lam Associates
444 Hobron Ln Ste 207H
Honolulu, HI 96815
(808) 947-9815
(800) 258-4526
Fax: (808) 943-8859
Email: lamdocs@aol.com
Web: www.gtesupersite.com/lamphysician

Description: Quality executive search for 48
contiguous states. Established 1988. National
network. Manufacturing engineers & process;
computer programmers; analysts; biomed;
healthcare, physicians, construction managers,
electrical & environmental engineers. Mail resume,
desired states and salary info. Confidential search.

Key Contact - Specialty:
Ms. Pat Lambrecht, General Manager - *Medical*

Salary minimum: $40,000

Functions: Healthcare, Physicians,
Environmentalists

Industries: Construction, Medical Devices, Pharm Svcs., Biotech, Healthcare

Professional Associations: NAPR

LaMorte Search Associates Inc

3003 Yamato Rd Ste 1073
Boca Raton, FL 33434
(561) 997-1100
(800) 422-6306
Fax: (561) 997-1103
Email: lamortesearch@aol.com
Web: www.lamortesearch.com

Description: Specializing exclusively in the insurance industry. We are a confidential source for national placements.

Key Contact - Specialty:
Mr. William LaMorte, President - *Insurance*
Ms. Michelle LaMorte, Executive Vice President - *Insurance*

Salary minimum: $50,000

Functions: Generalist

Industries: Insurance

Professional Associations: NAPS

Lancaster Associates Inc

35 W High St
Somerville, NJ 08876
(908) 526-5440
Fax: (908) 526-1992
Email: rfl@eclipse.net

Description: Small professional organization specializing in pre-screened candidates in all levels of applications and software systems and senior-level management. Heavy need for e-commerce/Internet and data warehousing professionals. Provide consultants with the right to hire.

Key Contact - Specialty:
Mr. Raymond F. Lancaster, Jr. - *Information technology*

Salary minimum: $80,000

Functions: IT

Industries: Chemicals, Drugs Mfg., Medical Devices, Mgmt. Consulting, Software, Biotech

Professional Associations: NAPS, NJAPS

E J Lance Management Associates Inc

60 E 42nd St Fl 51
New York, NY 10165
(212) 490-9600
Fax: (212) 490-7282

Description: Experienced professionals, many with MBAs. All candidates are personally screened. Client names are confidential. Average completion time for assignments is three to four weeks.

Key Contact - Specialty:
Ms. Elizabeth Kay, Partner - *Investment banking*
Mr. Elliot Webb, Partner - *Equity (research, sales)*

Salary minimum: $40,000

Functions: Generalist, Cash Mgmt., M&A

Industries: Invest. Banking

Landsman Foodservice Net

7 Old Creek Ct
Owings Mills, MD 21117
(410) 902-7164
Fax: (410) 363-9049
Email: jeff@lfsn.com
Web: www.lfsn.com

Description: We provide consultative recruitment services. We have expertise in all areas within the foodservice industry. We place all functional areas of management with foodservice distributors and

manufacturers alike. We are a retained and contingency recruiting firm. We also provide industry specific management consulting in sales and logistics.

Key Contact - Specialty:
Mr. Jeffrey B. Landsman, President - *Foodservice (distribution and manufacturing) senior level positions*

Salary minimum: $40,000

Functions: Generalist, General Mgmt., Mfg., Materials, Sales & Mktg., Finance, CFO's, IT

Industries: Food, Bev., Tobacco, Wholesale, Hospitality

The Lane Group

735 N Water Ste 1228
Milwaukee, WI 53202
(414) 226-2400
Fax: (414) 226-2421
Email: info@thelanegroup.net
Web: www.thelanegroup.net

Description: One of the fastest growing executive search firms in the country.

Key Contact:
Mr. Douglas Lane, President - *Telecommunications, computer software, hardware-sales marketing, consulting, advertising*
Mr. Steve Tewes, Vice President - *Consumer products, marketing, marketing research, advertising, sales*
Mr. Donald W. Butler, Vice President - *Financial services, banking, advanced information technology*
Mr. Chris Spahn, National Account Manager - *Consumer products, grocery, food service, retail, ad agencies*
Mr. Dale Kumlien, Vice President - *Pharmaceuticals, medical devices, biotech*
Ms. Sally Drezdzon, Director - *Investment management, investments, accounting, finance*
Mr. John M. Sullivan, National Account Manager - *Investments, banking, financial services*
Mr. Alan Vesey, Director of National Accounts - *Management, marketing, financial services, information technology*
Mr. Elizabeth Schenk, Project Manager - *Construction management, human resources, business development, telecommunications*
Mr. David Petrick, Project Manager
Mr. Sean O'Byrne, Project Manager
Ms. Sarah Wheeler, Proejct Manager

Salary minimum: $40,000

Functions: Generalist, Senior Mgmt., Mktg. Mgmt., Sales Mgmt., HR Mgmt., Finance, IT, Mgmt. Consultants

Industries: Generalist, Medical Devices, Retail, Banking, Accounting, Mgmt. Consulting, New Media, Telecoms

Lane, Easton and Nash llc

(also known as MRI of Pepper Pike)
27629 Chagrin Blvd Ste 108
Cleveland, OH 44122
(216) 839-2870
Fax: (216) 839-2880
Email: main@leandn.com

Key Contact:
Mr. Corey Roth

Lang Staffing Inc

2601 44th St N
St. Petersburg, FL 33713
(727) 521-9810
Fax: (413) 702-3419
Email: info@langstaffing.com
Web: www.langstaffing.com

Description: We provide technical staffing and consulting. We offer contract, temp to hire, permanent placements in the areas of engineering, management, CAD, design engineers, environmental, manufacturing professionals, and IS professionals.

Key Contact - Specialty:
Mr. Dave Langstaff, President - *Technical, professional*

Functions: Mfg., Materials, Distribution, Packaging, Sales Mgmt., Network Admin., R&D, Engineering, Architects, Technicians

Industries: Generalist, Construction, Mfg., Chemicals, Medical Devices, Plastics, Rubber, Misc. Mfg., Electronic, Elec. Components, IT Implementation, Communications, Telecoms, Digital, Wireless, Fiber Optic, Environmental Svcs., Aerospace, Packaging, Mfg. SW, Biotech

Professional Associations: IRG

Networks: PRO/NET

Lange & Associates Inc

107 W Market St
Wabash, IN 46992
(219) 563-7402
Fax: (219) 563-3897
Email: langeassoc@ctlnet.com

Description: We are experts in matching people and opportunities. We recruit all disciplines and specialize in rubber, plastics, metals, and electronics. We place a large concentration in the automotive arena.

Key Contact - Specialty:
Mr. Jim Lange, President - *Engineers, manufacturing managers, accountants*
Mr. Jack Lange, Vice President - *Engineers (support professions), general managers*

Salary minimum: $30,000

Functions: General Mgmt., Mfg., Materials, HR Mgmt., R&D, Engineering, Environmentalists

Industries: Mfg., Chemicals, Plastics, Rubber, Metal Products, HR Services, Aerospace

Networks: Top Echelon Network

The Langford Search Inc

2025 3rd Ave N Ste 301
Birmingham, AL 35203-3323
(205) 328-5477
Fax: (205) 328-5483
Email: tlsearch@aol.com

Description: We seek first to understand our client's business, then both the hard and soft skills required of a successful candidate. We present for consideration only those candidates that possess both.

Key Contact - Specialty:
Mr. K. R. Dick Langford, CEO - *Finance & accounting, information technology, general management*
Ms. Ann S. Langford, President - *Information technology*

Functions: Generalist

Industries: Generalist, Accounting, Software

Professional Associations: AITP

Lanken-Saunders Group

3061 Greyfield Pl
Marietta, GA 30067
(770) 952-7530
Fax: (770) 952-6252
Email: jlanken@aol.com
Web: www.lankensaunders.com

Description: Specific expertise in logistics, transportation, warehousing, distribution positions and requirements. Retained by fortune listed transportation companies. Full-service search firm including training and HR projects

Key Contact - Specialty:
Mr. Joel Lanken, President - *Sales & marketing, finance, logistics, operations, human resources*
Mr. Bud Wallen, Director - *Sales, marketing, operations*
Mr. Wayne Saunders, Vice President - *Training, human resources*
Mr. Sam Herman, Vice President - *Transportation*

Salary minimum: $50,000

Functions: Generalist, General Mgmt.

Industries: Generalist

Lannick Associates
20 Queen St W Ste 1500
Toronto, ON M5H 3R3
Canada
(416) 340-1500
Fax: (416) 340-1344
Email: smcintyre@lannick.com
Web: www.lannick.com

Description: Canada's premier search firm in the accounting and finance field. Specialists in the recruitment of chartered accountants, CGAs, CMAs and MBAs for some of the world's biggest and best-respected public companies in Canada and North America, to new dot-com start-ups. In contact with the best.

Key Contact:
Mr. Lance Osborne, President

Salary minimum: $60,000

Functions: Directors, Senior Mgmt., Middle Mgmt., Finance, CFO's, Budgeting, Cash Mgmt., Taxes, M&A, Risk Mgmt.

Industries: Generalist, Finance

LanSo Int'l Inc
3 Davis Dr
Armonk, NY 10504
(914) 273-8259
Fax: (914) 273-6822

Description: We provide a fee-based consultant service to a diverse clientele in order to assist in their business efforts through strategic staff placements and business introductions.

Key Contact - Specialty:
Mr. Edwin Lew, President - *Financial services*

Salary minimum: $50,000

Functions: Generalist, CFO's, Budgeting, Cash Mgmt., Risk Mgmt., Minorities

Industries: Generalist, Banking, Invest. Banking, Brokers, Misc. Financial

Stephen Laramee & Associates Inc
1 Younge St Ste 1801
Toronto, ON M5E 1W7
Canada
(877) 897-1474
Fax: (413) 369-0515
Email: slaramee@on.aibn.com
Web: www.larameeassociates.com

Description: We provide mid management to and including senior executive search for manufacturing and/or distributor-based organizations. Our practice is limited to Canada.

Key Contact:
Mr. Stephen Laramee, President

Salary minimum: $40,000

Functions: Senior Mgmt., Product Dev., Production, Plant Mgmt., Mktg. Mgmt., Sales Mgmt., CFO's

Industries: Food, Bev., Tobacco, Textiles, Apparel, Lumber, Furniture, Paper, Chemicals, Drugs Mfg., Metal Products

Robert Larned Associates Inc
1 Columbus Ctr Ste 600
Virginia Beach, VA 23462
(757) 498-2700
Fax: (757) 498-4090
Email: rlabob@aol.com
Web: www.rlastaffing.com

Description: We recruit nationally for our Fortune 1000 clients to find top talent leaving the military, including junior military officers and technically rated enlisted personnel, as well as engineers, computer specialists and technical sales.

Key Contact - Specialty:
Mr. Robert T. Larned, President - *Engineers, military personnel*
Ms. Tammy Park - *Engineers, sales & marketing, computer professionals*

Salary minimum: $50,000

Functions: Middle Mgmt., Mfg., Production, Sales Mgmt., IT, Technicians

Industries: Energy, Utilities, Mfg., Food, Bev., Tobacco, Printing, Chemicals, Soap, Perf., Cosmtcs., Metal Products, Machine, Appliance, Computer Equip., Telecoms, Defense, Aerospace, Packaging, Software

Networks: Top Echelon Network

Jack B Larsen & Associates Inc
334 W 8th St
Erie, PA 16502
(800) 239-5737
Fax: (800) 239-5736
Email: info@jblhires.com
Web: www.jblhires.com

Description: Full scope recruiting firm handling permanent and/or temporary contract personnel.

Key Contact:
Mr. Jack B. Larsen, CPC, Owner

Salary minimum: $35,000

Functions: Generalist, Production, Distribution, Sales Mgmt., Benefits, Systems Analysis, Engineering

Industries: Generalist, Plastics, Rubber, Metal Products, Machine, Appliance, Misc. Mfg., Telecoms

Larson Allen Physician Search
(a division of Larson Allen Search LLC)
12801 Flushing Meadows Dr Ste 100
St. Louis, MO 63131
(314) 336-3804
Fax: (314) 453-9530
Email: rcornell@larsonallen.com
Web: www.larsonallen.com

Description: Our firm specializes in physician search and recruitment for healthcare centers and physician groups nationwide.

Key Contact:
Mr. Rich Cornell, Vice President
Mr. Robert deRoode, Vice President

Functions: Generalist, Physicians, Allied Health, Health Admin.

Industries: Generalist, Healthcare

Professional Associations: MGMA, NAPR

Larson, Katz & Young Inc
4515 Daly Dr Ste N
Chantilly, VA 20151
(703) 631-3881
Fax: (703) 631-3882

Email: info@lkyi.com
Web: www.lkyi.com

Description: Nationwide search for healthcare systems vendors specializing in installations, support, product marketing, sales and sales management.

Key Contact - Specialty:
Ms. Marcia Hall, President - *Healthcare information systems*

Salary minimum: $50,000

Functions: Generalist, Middle Mgmt., Materials, Healthcare

Industries: Pharm Svcs., IT Implementation, Software, Healthcare, Hospitals

Professional Associations: RON

LAS Management Consulting Group Inc
23 Kilmer Dr Bldg 1 Ste G
Morganville, NJ 07751
(732) 972-8800
Fax: (732) 972-6770
Email: info@lasmanagement.com
Web: www.lasmanagement.com

Description: Executive search firm specializing in the recruitment and placement of professionals at all levels of management within the technology arena. Areas of specialty include: e-commerce, strategy, architecture, IT risk management, IT audit, network security, security architecture, enterprise systems management, ERP Integrity, mergers and acquisitions due diligence.

Key Contact - Specialty:
Mr. Philip A. Salvatore, President - *Information systems audit, e-security, electronic commerce*
Mr. Tom DeAngelo, Director - *Information systems audit, security, enterprise systems management*

Salary minimum: $75,000

Functions: Generalist, General Mgmt., Directors

Industries: Mfg., Computer Equip., Finance, Services, Hospitality, Entertainment, New Media, Broadcast, Film, Communications, Telecoms, Defense, Aerospace, Insurance, Software, ERP SW, Networking, Comm. SW, Security SW, System SW

Professional Associations: ISACA

Lavine & Associates
23151 Moulton Pkwy
Laguna Hills, CA 92653
(949) 458-7322
Fax: (949) 855-1454
Email: aheadhunter@prodigy.net

Description: Principal has over 25 years' telecommunications background, including multiple start-up experiences.

Key Contact - Specialty:
Mr. Edward R. Lavine, President - *Telecommunications, technology*

Functions: Generalist, Senior Mgmt., Middle Mgmt., Sales Mgmt., Customer Svc., MIS Mgmt., Systems Support

Industries: Generalist, New Media, Telecoms

Lawrence Personnel
1000 Valley Forge Cr Ste 110
King of Prussia, PA 19406
(610) 783-5400
Fax: (610) 783-6008
Email: lawpers@staffing.net
Web: www.lawrencepersonnel.com

Description: Our practice is limited to telecommunications and datacommunications' skills and opportunities. We offer retained and contingency searches. We take on domestic and International assignments. We are a preferred member of the Top Echelon Network.

Key Contact:
Mr. Larry Goldberg, CPC, General Manager

Functions: Generalist

Industries: Communications, Telecoms, Call Centers, Telephony, Digital, Wireless, Fiber Optic, Network Infrastructure

Networks: Top Echelon Network

Lawrence-Balakonis & Associates Inc
Dunwoody Village
PO Box 888241
Atlanta, GA 30356-0241
(770) 587-2342
Fax: (770) 587-5002
Email: balakonisnassoc@mindspring.com

Description: Highly regarded executive search consulting firm specializing in the consumer packaged goods industry nationwide, with a primary focus on sales and marketing middle and senior-level management positions in the grocery products industry.

Key Contact - Specialty:
Mr. Charles L. Balakonis, President - *Sales, marketing, category management, trade marketing*
Mr. J. Robert Lawrence, Executive Vice President - *Senior management*

Salary minimum: $50,000

Functions: Generalist, General Mgmt., Senior Mgmt., Middle Mgmt., Plant Mgmt., Sales & Mktg., Sales Mgmt.

Industries: Generalist, Food, Bev., Tobacco, Paper, Soap, Perf., Cosmtcs., Drugs Mfg., Misc. Mfg.

The Lawson Group Inc
14 New Orleans Rd Ste 15
PO Box 7491
Hilton Head Island, SC 29938
(843) 842-4949
Fax: (843) 842-7650
Email: email@lawsongroup.com
Web: www.lawsongroup.com

Description: We believe American industry is past the need for good people, today the best people are needed. Through our methods of locating and screening people, we are dedicated to that end. We understand the importance of making the right fit for both company and individual.

Key Contact - Specialty:
Mr. James W. Lawson, President - *Pulp & paper industry*
Ms. Mary Bjong, Vice President - *Pulp & paper industry*
Mr. Gregory A. Estes, Manager - *Converting operations*
Mr. Chip Porter, Account Executive - *Converting*

Salary minimum: $40,000

Functions: Generalist

Industries: Paper, Printing, Packaging

Professional Associations: PIMA, SCAPS, TAPPI

LCC Companies
7500 E Deer Valley Dr Ste 145
Scottsdale, AZ 85255
(480) 513-2173
Fax: (480) 513-6466
Email: lcccompanies@mindspring.com

Description: We recruit computer/data processing professionals at all levels. For software companies, we look for developers, marketing and sales. For computer users, we look for programmers, project managers, network integrators and MIS directors.

Key Contact - Specialty:
Mr. Ray Weinhold, Ph.D., Partner - *Information technology*
Ms. Jean Weinhold, Partner - *Information technology*

Salary minimum: $40,000

Functions: Generalist, MIS Mgmt., Systems Analysis, Systems Dev., Systems Implem., Systems Support, Engineering, Technicians

Industries: Generalist, Telecoms, Software

Leader Institute Inc
1225 Johnson Ferry Rd Bldg 300
Marietta, GA 30068
(770) 321-1231
Fax: (801) 382-2452
Email: inquiry@peoplestaff.com
Web: www.peoplestaff.com

Description: Information technology specialists applying search techniques to the Peoplesoft, SAP, Oracle and object oriented markets. CIO search in the Peoplesoft, SAP, Oracle markets.

Key Contact - Specialty:
Mr. Richard Zabor, President - *PeopleSoft, systems applications, data processing, oracle, object oriented programming*

Salary minimum: $60,000

Functions: Senior Mgmt., IT, MIS Mgmt., Systems Analysis, Systems Dev., Systems Implem., Systems Support, DB Admin.

Industries: Generalist, E-commerce, IT Implementation, Software, Accounting SW, Database SW, Development SW, ERP SW, HR SW, Industry Specific SW, Mfg. SW

Professional Associations: NAPS

Leader Network
241 Harding Ct
York, PA 17403
(717) 845-6927
Fax: (717) 854-7079

Description: Total experience 16 years. Self employed 6 years. Contingency search- executive, technical, aluminum and steel industries- nationally.

Key Contact - Specialty:
Ms. D. June Leader, Owner - *Executive, technical, aluminum, steel*

Functions: Generalist, Senior Mgmt., Middle Mgmt., Production, Automation, Sales Mgmt., CFO's, Engineering

Industries: Generalist, Metal Products

Leader Resources Group
165 Emerald Dr
McDonough, GA 30253-5514
(770) 954-0684
Fax: (770) 957-5927
Email: kstep165@aol.com

Description: We are a generalist firm specializing in legal, human resources, and financial positions. We are experienced in sensitive search situations. Our recruiters are thoroughly trained personnel professionals.

Key Contact - Specialty:
Mr. Ken Stephens, Co-Owner - *Legal, financial, human resources*
Ms. Teresa Stephens, Co-Owner - *Computer positions*

Salary minimum: $30,000

Functions: Generalist, Legal, HR Mgmt., Finance, Attorneys

Industries: Generalist, Finance, Legal, Insurance

Professional Associations: GAPS

Lear & Associates Inc
505 Park Ave N Ste 201
Winter Park, FL 32789
(407) 645-4611
Fax: (407) 645-5735
Email: roger@learsearch.com
Web: www.learsearch.com

Description: Our clients utilize us as a branch office to identify and place all levels of insurance professionals on a nationwide basis. Combined with traditional recruiting efforts, our insurance career website has become a valuable tool for clients and insurance candidates.

Key Contact - Specialty:
Mr. Roger R. Lear, President - *Actuarial, claims, underwriting*
Mr. Michael Kyle, Sr Recruiting Specialist - *Insurance (underwriting, claims), reinsurance underwriting, HO, executive level positions*
Mr. Mark Svetic, Retainer Coordinator - *Underwriting, claims (managers, vice presidents)*
Mr. Scott Kotroba, Marketing Director - *Website operations, client relationships*
Mr. Ron Pilgrim, Sr Recruiting Specialist - *Loss control, risk management, underwriting*

Salary minimum: $33,000

Functions: Generalist, HR Mgmt., CFO's, Risk Mgmt., MIS Mgmt.

Industries: Generalist, Hospitality, Insurance, Healthcare

Professional Associations: INS

Reynolds Lebus Associates
PO Box 9177
Scottsdale, AZ 85252
(480) 946-6929
Email: lebus@ix.netcom.com
Web: www.rlebus.com

Description: Mechanical engineers for medical device manufacturing companies.

Key Contact:
Mr. Reynolds Lebus, Owner

Salary minimum: $35,000

Functions: Engineering

Industries: Medical Devices

Professional Associations: AAPS

Lechner & Associates Inc
7737 Holiday Dr
Sarasota, FL 34231
(941) 923-3671
Fax: (941) 923-3675
Email: lechner@lechner.net
Web: www.lechner.net

Description: Technical management - primarily retainer (60%), contingency (40%), medical devices, information technology, insurance, environmental consulting, venture capital before IPO.

Key Contact - Specialty:
Dr. David B. Lechner, President
Mr. David Barnhart, Principal/Vice President - *Environmental, engineer, consulting, management*
Mr. Jim Szesny, Principal/Vice President - *Information technology*
Ms. Lisa Bull, Principal/Vice President - *Insurance executives*

Salary minimum: $70,000

Functions: Generalist

Industries: Environmental Svcs., Packaging, Insurance, Software, Biotech, Healthcare

Susan Lee & Associates
6100 Green Valley Dr Ste 150
Bloomington, MN 55438
(952) 897-1170
Fax: (952) 897-1314
Email: susanlee@susanlee.com
Web: www.susanlee.com

Description: We specialize in the printing and graphics arts technology industry. All the recruiters come from the printing industry and understand the technology. We find the very best candidates.

Key Contact:
Ms. Susan Lee, President

Functions: Generalist

Industries: Paper, Printing, Advertising, Publishing, Packaging

Ricci Lee Associates Inc
100 Drakes Landing Rd Ste 120
Greenbrae, CA 94904
(415) 464-5521
Fax: (415) 464-5519
Email: carol@riccilee.com

Description: Executive search for marketing, advertising and communications professionals.

Key Contact - Specialty:
Ms. Carol Ricci Lee, President/CEO - *Marketing, marketing communications, public relations, advertising*

Salary minimum: $50,000

Functions: Generalist, Advertising, Mkt. Research, Mktg. Mgmt., Direct Mktg., PR

Industries: Generalist, Computer Equip., Consumer Elect., Advertising, Publishing, New Media, Telecoms

Albert G Lee Associates
106 Greenwood Ave
Rumford, RI 02916
(401) 434-7614
Email: aglee@aol.com

Description: Practice specializing in technical; engineering, biotech, medical, pharmaceutical, clinical and MIS; marketing: consumer, retail and industrial; finance: banking, real estate, accounting, taxes; and human resources: benefits, compensation and employee relations.

Key Contact - Specialty:
Mr. Albert G. Lee, CEO - *Technical, pharmaceutical, research & development*

Salary minimum: $60,000

Functions: Generalist, Production, Healthcare, Mktg. Mgmt., Budgeting, MIS Mgmt., R&D, Engineering

Industries: Generalist, Drugs Mfg., Computer Equip., Retail, Pharm Svcs., Biotech, Healthcare

Vincent Lee Associates
91 Fallon Ave
Elmont, NY 11003-3605
(516) 775-8551

Description: Emphasis on accounting, banking, finance, marketing, insurance (property/casualty) and human resources professionals executive search through vice president.

Key Contact - Specialty:
Mr. Vincent Lee, President - *Generalist*
Mr. Brian Lee, Vice President - *Generalist*
Ms. Sheryl Baxter, Vice President - *Generalist*
Ms. Kathy Esposito, Vice President - *Generalist*
Ms. Linda Monte, Executive Recruiter - *Generalist*

Salary minimum: $25,000

Functions: Generalist

Industries: Finance, Banking, Services, Accounting, Insurance

Leeds and Leeds
5200 Maryland Way Ste 206
Brentwood, TN 37027
(615) 371-1119
Fax: (615) 371-1225
Email: info@leedsandleeds.com
Web: www.leedsandleeds.com

Description: We provide professional and efficient service to life insurance, health insurance and managed care organizations, assisting with their recruiting needs.

Key Contact - Specialty:
Mr. Gerald I. Leeds, Principal - *Insurance organizations*

Salary minimum: $50,000

Functions: Finance

Industries: Insurance

Legal Network Inc
2151 Michelson Dr Ste 135
Irvine, CA 92715
(949) 752-8800
Fax: (949) 752-9126
Email: cwampole@legalnetwork.cc
Web: www.legalnetwork.cc

Description: Our national network of candidates provides a valuable resource for most law-related search requests.

Key Contact - Specialty:
Ms. Carole Wampole, President - *Legal*
Mr. Daniel Wampole, General Manager - *Legal*

Functions: Generalist, Legal, Customer Svc., Systems Support, Network Admin., Attorneys, Paralegals

Industries: Generalist, Legal, HR Services

Legal Search Associates
6701 W 64th St Ste 302
Overland Park, KS 66202
(913) 722-3500
Fax: (913) 722-0598
Email: lsa@jdhunter.com
Web: www.jdhunter.com

Description: We recruit experienced, qualified, and highly specialized attorneys for law firms and corporations in the US with a focus on the Midwest, more specifically: Kansas City, St. Louis, Wichita, Omaha, Des Moines, Milwaukee, Minneapolis and Chicago. Other cities that we serve are Detroit, Denver, Dallas, Houston, Austin, and Phoenix.

Key Contact - Specialty:
Dr. Terry W. Bashor, President - *Attorneys*

Salary minimum: $40,000

Functions: Directors, Legal

Industries: Generalist, Legal

Professional Associations: MAPS, NALSC

LegalWorks
1875 Century Park E Ste 1200
Los Angeles, CA 90067
(310) 277-8998
Fax: (310) 277-2133
Email: legalworks@excite.com
Web: www.legalworksone.com

Description: We are a Los Angeles based attorney search firm whose clients include Fortune 500, high-tech and start-up companies, prominent international and domestic law firms and small boutique firms.

Key Contact:
Ms. Randi G. Frisch, Esq., President

Functions: Attorneys

Industries: Generalist

Professional Associations: SBC

Ken Leiner Associates
11510 Georgia Ave Ste 105
Wheaton, MD 20902-1958
(301) 933-8800
Fax: (301) 933-8808
Email: ken@itsearch.com
Web: www.itsearch.com

Description: Our firm focuses on recruiting all levels of sales, marketing, and technical talent for the information technology industry throughout North America and Europe. Our clients include software and systems vendors, integrators, and consulting firms. We work on a contingency or retainer basis and have helped small and large companies succeed in the marketplace.

Key Contact - Specialty:
Mr. Ken Leiner, President - *Information technology*

Salary minimum: $60,000

Functions: General Mgmt., Sales & Mktg., IT, R&D, Engineering, Specialized Svcs., Minorities

Industries: Computer Equip., Test, Measure Equip., Mgmt. Consulting, Telecoms, Software

Professional Associations: MAPRC

Networks: First Interview Network (FIN)

Leith & Associates Inc
24500 Center Ridge Rd Ste 250
Westlake, OH 44145
(440) 808-1130
Fax: (440) 808-1140
Email: manager@leithnet.com
Web: www.leithnet.com

Description: The three prongs or cornerstones in our logo are the client (prospective employers), the candidate (potential employees) and the consultant. This is our triangle team. We consider our clients as partners and treat our candidates like the professionals they are. We are the link that secures the partnership.

Key Contact:
Ms. Louisa Szewczuk, CPC, President

Salary minimum: $30,000

Functions: General Mgmt.

Industries: Computer Equip., Advertising, Telecoms

Networks: First Interview Network (FIN)

Leitner Sarch Consultants
34 S Broadway Ste 102
White Plains, NY 10601
(914) 682-4000
Email: danny@leitnersarch.com
Web: www.leitnersarch.com

Description: We work nationally and specialize in sales, sales management, branch management within the financial services industry.

Key Contact - Specialty:
Mr. Daniel Sarch, President - *Financial sales, financial sales management*

Salary minimum: $80,000

Functions: Sales & Mktg.

Industries: Brokers, Misc. Financial

Professional Associations: PINNACLE

Leland Roberts Inc

900 E 79th St Ste 104
Bloomington, MN 55420
(952) 854-0441
Fax: (952) 814-9820
Email: information@lelandroberts.com
Web: www.lelandroberts.com

Description: We are a leading executive search firm specializing in the technical placement field. We usually work with those looking to fill their full-time employment needs. LeLand Roberts helps professionals find the best environment for ensuring satisfaction with their position. Our goal is to create the best working relationship between both the professional and the company. We speak to our hiring managers and HR professionals to find out what kind of environment the candidate would be working in on a daily basis. We then find what our candidates needs are for the best fit.

Key Contact:
Ms. Merredith Donaldson, General Manager
Mr. Dwight Simpson, Principal

Lending Personnel Services

PO Box 16904
Irvine, CA 92623
(949) 250-8133
Fax: (949) 250-7180
Email: carla@lpsjobs.com
Web: www.lpsjobs.com

Description: Specialists in executive, managerial and staffing placements nationally and locally in mortgage, finance, banking, real estate, development, escrow, insurance, title, high-technology, manufacturing, staffing and human resources.

Key Contact - Specialty:
Ms. Carla Bloch, Owner - *Banking (mortgage, savings & loan, title, escrow)*

Salary minimum: $25,000

Functions: Generalist

Industries: Finance, Banking, Invest. Banking, Brokers, Accounting, Mgmt. Consulting, HR Services, Insurance, Real Estate

Professional Associations: CSP

F P Lennon Associates

300 Berwyn Park Ste 202
Berwyn, PA 19312
(610) 407-0300
(888) 536-6667
Fax: (610) 407-0533
Web: www.fplennon.com

Description: We are recognized as the industry leader in software recruiting within the ERP software world.

Key Contact - Specialty:
Mr. Frank P. Lennon, President - *ERP software search sales & consulting*

Salary minimum: $80,000

Functions: Generalist, Directors, Sales Mgmt., IT, MIS Mgmt., Systems Analysis, Systems Dev., Systems Implem.

Industries: Software

Professional Associations: HRSP, MAAPC

Branches:
1701 W Hillsboro Blvd Ste 305
Deerfield Beach, FL 33442
(954) 418-9900
Fax: (954) 418-0556
Key Contact - Specialty:
Mr. Larry Cadwell - *Software, ERP*

Level A Inc

277 George St N Ste 212
Peterborough, ON K9J 3G9
Canada
(705) 749-1919
Fax: (705) 749-5494
Email: levela@cgocable.net
Web: www.levela.net

Description: We are an A-Level agency specializing in recruitment and placement of administrative, financial, technical, and key management personnel. We provide behavioral profiling, team building, skill evaluation, and validation.

Key Contact - Specialty:
Ms. Kathy Pyle, President - *Professional/key management placement*

Functions: Generalist

Industries: Printing, Finance, Services, Advertising, Network Infrastructure, Aerospace, Packaging, HR SW

Grady Levkov & Company

580 Broadway Ste 1100
New York, NY 10012
(212) 925-0900
Fax: (212) 925-0200
Email: lauren@glcompany.com
Web: www.gradylevkov.com

Description: At Grady Levkov & Company, we spend all day, every day, identifying the talented people that move the technology industry forward. When you're deeply ensconced in the details of your most pressing deadline, we're tracking down your next hire. From software development shops to new media agencies to Wall Street--we will meet your needs with the quality that you deserve.

Key Contact:
Mr. Troy Grady, Managing Director
Mr. Joshua Levkov, Managing Director
Ms. Lauren Bell, Senior Recruiter

Functions: Generalist, Product Dev., Sales & Mktg.

Industries: Computer Equip., Venture Cap., New Media, Telecoms, Software

Lewis & Blackmore Inc

1106 Clayton Ln Ste 524W
Austin, TX 78723
(512) 450-0555
Fax: (512) 450-1009
Email: linda@lbsearch.com
Web: www.lbsearch.com

Description: We specialize in senior-level talent in all disciplines within the high-technology sector, life insurance industry, medical equipment, and sales industry. We take the time to learn the client's business and culture and bring a high-level of integrity and thoroughness to the search process.

Key Contact - Specialty:
Ms. Linda C. Lewis, Partner - *High technology*
Ms. Helen E. Blackmore, Partner - *High technology*

Salary minimum: $80,000

Functions: Generalist

Industries: Medical Devices, Electronic, Elec. Components, IT Implementation, Digital, Wireless, Network Infrastructure, Software, Networking, Comm. SW, Security SW, Biotech

Networks: Associated Consultants in Executive Search Int'l

Lewis Consulting Service

690 Ludlow
Elgin, IL 60120
(847) 289-9059
Fax: (847) 289-7814

Email: dlewis1588@aol.com

Description: We specialize in on- and off-site contract recruiting and contingency searches in the information technology, manufacturing, avionics, telecommunications, retail, distribution, administrative, accounting, transportation, human resources, and engineering field.

Key Contact - Specialty:
Mr. Donnie Lewis, Recruitment Manager - *Recruitment*

Salary minimum: $50,000

Functions: Generalist

Industries: Generalist

Professional Associations: RON

Lexington Software Inc

555 5th Ave Fl 17
New York, NY 10017
(212) 376-7386
Fax: (212) 531-3544
Email: staff@lextn.com
Web: www.lextn.com

Description: Our firm is an executive search organization serving the financial services industry for specific financial experience in risk management, derivatives, quantitative disciplines, and technology-driven trading strategies.

Key Contact - Specialty:
Mr. John Rountree, MBA, MS, Principal - *Derivatives technologies, risk management systems, trading desk analytic, quantitative methods, artificial intelligence*
Ms. Jennifer Foster, BA MA EdD, Principal - *Management learning, human development*

Salary minimum: $75,000

Functions: Cash Mgmt., Taxes, Risk Mgmt., IT, MIS Mgmt., Systems Analysis, Systems Dev., Systems Implem., Systems Support, DB Admin.

Industries: Finance, Banking, Invest. Banking, Brokers, Misc. Financial

Leyendecker Executive Search

(also known as Leyendecker & Associates)
701 N Post Oak Rd Ste 204
Houston, TX 77024-3817
(713) 680-1299
Email: inquiry@leyendecker.com
Web: www.leyendecker.com

Description: The primary focus of our firm is the field of Corporate Finance. Clients include Wall Street and regional investment banks, money center and foreign banks, equity investor groups, mezzanine funds, institutional investors, corporate treasury and M&A departments.

Key Contact - Specialty:
Mr. Douglas Leyendecker, Principal - *Corporate finance, investment banking*
Mr. Jeffery Smith, Principal - *Corporate finance, energy*
Mr. James Ford, Principal - *Corporate finance, equity research*

Salary minimum: $75,000

Functions: Generalist, CFO's, M&A

Industries: Energy, Utilities, Chemicals, Finance, Banking, Invest. Banking, Venture Cap.

The Libra Group Inc

115 New Canaan Ave Ste 700
Norwalk, CT 06850
(203) 849-1409
Fax: (203) 849-1409
Email: libragroup@worldnet.att.net
Web: www.bworks.com/libragroup

Description: Over forty years' broadcast experience with radio/TV stations and national TV representatives. Extensive national broadcast contacts for placement ranging from high performance AE to CEOs. Integrity!

Key Contact - Specialty:
Mr. Robert R. Saracen, CEO - *Radio, television broadcast, management, sales*

Salary minimum: $50,000

Functions: Sales & Mktg., Advertising, Sales Mgmt., Customer Svc., PR, HR Mgmt., Training

Industries: Advertising, Broadcast, Film

Professional Associations: IRTS, SHRM

Pat Licata & Associates
511-104 Keisler Dr
Cary, NC 27511
(919) 859-0511
Fax: (919) 859-0830
Email: pat@patlicata.com
Web: www.patlicata.com

Description: We are specialists in medical, pharmaceutical sales, and sales management on a national level. Our firm is a national award winning office - First Interview.

Key Contact - Specialty:
Ms. Pat Licata, President - *Medical, pharmaceutical (sales, management, product, managers)*

Salary minimum: $35,000

Functions: Generalist, Directors, Middle Mgmt., Sales & Mktg., Mkt. Research, Mktg. Mgmt., Sales Mgmt., Training, Minorities

Industries: Generalist, Drugs Mfg., Medical Devices, Pharm Svcs., Biotech, Healthcare, Hospitals, Long-term Care, Dental, Women's

Networks: First Interview Network (FIN)

Lieberman-Nelson Inc
311 1st Ave N Ste 503
Minneapolis, MN 55401
(612) 338-2432
Fax: (612) 332-8860
Email: l-n@lieberman-nelson.com
Web: www.lieberman-nelson.com

Description: We are the only twin cities based full-service national legal search firm, placing full time attorneys exclusively.

Key Contact - Specialty:
Mr. Howard Lieberman - *Attorneys*
Ms. Nancy Nelson - *Attorneys*

Functions: Legal

Industries: Generalist

Liebman & Associates Inc
9 Darby Dr
South Huntington, NY 11746
(631) 423-7334
Fax: (631) 423-2317
Email: smanyc@aol.com

Description: Executive search firm staffing the temporary, permanent, contract technical and home healthcare industries, mid and upper management levels nationally. Places all levels of sales and sales management within service related to business.

Key Contact:
Ms. Linda Liebman, President

Salary minimum: $50,000

Functions: Middle Mgmt., Sales Mgmt.

Industries: Legal, Accounting, Hospitality, Healthcare

J B Linde & Associates
1415 Elbridge Payne Rd Ste 148
Chesterfield, MO 63017
(636) 532-8040
Fax: (636) 532-0320
Email: jblinde@inlink.com

Description: Technical, management and executive recruiting in the manufacturing arena. Metal working industry i.e.; machining, stamping, welding, etc.

Key Contact - Specialty:
Mr. Roy Kessler, Owner - *Manufacturing management, engineering*

Salary minimum: $50,000

Functions: Generalist

Industries: Generalist

J H Lindell & Company
560 1st St E
Sonoma, CA 95476
(707) 935-1771
Fax: (707) 935-9596
Email: jhlindellco@earthlink.net

Description: We specialize in executive and managerial recruitment and selection exclusively within the real estate development, construction and home building industries.

Key Contact:
Mr. John H. Lindell, President - *Real estate, construction management*
Ms. Leslie S. Lindell, Director of Research

Salary minimum: $50,000

Functions: Generalist, General Mgmt., Purchasing, Mkt. Research, Mktg. Mgmt., Sales Mgmt., CFO's, Engineering

Industries: Generalist, Construction, Real Estate

Branches:
2212 Dupont Dr Ste U
Irvine, CA 92612
(949) 252-1771
(818) 766-8648
Fax: (949) 252-1176
Key Contact:
Mr. James D. Stevens, Vice President
Ms. Donna Hoover, Vice President

David Lindemer Associates Inc
1955 Pauline Blvd 300-B
Ann Arbor, MI 48103-5000
(734) 761-3999
Email: david@lindemer.com
Web: www.lindemer.com

Description: Our concentration is at senior and middle management levels where managerial ability is as critical to success as industry experience. Our industry specialization includes: manufacturing, software for healthcare solutions, services, healthcare administration, and life sciences, especially biotechnology. We also have functional specialties in marketing, product management, human resources, and organization development.

Key Contact:
Mr. David Lindemer

Salary minimum: $85,000

Functions: General Mgmt.

Industries: Software, Biotech, Healthcare, Hospitals

Linden Group Inc
6408 Honegger Dr Ste B
Charlotte, NC 28211
(704) 367-0309
Fax: (704) 365-9883
Email: lindengroup@carolina.rr.com

Description: Our specializations include: food processing, automotive, consumer products, and medical devices. Our disciplines include: manufacturing engineers, process and project engineers, industrial engineers, production managers, plant managers, quality managers and engineers, plant engineers, general managers, R&D managers, and vice presidents.

Key Contact - Specialty:
Mr. Bruce G. Lindal, CPC, President - *Automotive industry, food processing, consumer product, medical devices*

Salary minimum: $45,000

Functions: Generalist, Senior Mgmt., Middle Mgmt., Product Dev., Production, Plant Mgmt., Quality, Materials Plng.

Industries: Generalist, Mfg., Food, Bev., Tobacco, Medical Devices, Metal Products, Motor Vehicles, Misc. Mfg.

Networks: Top Echelon Network

Ginger Lindsey & Associates Inc
8600 N MacArthur Blvd Ste 114-180
Irving, TX 75063
(972) 304-1089
Fax: (972) 304-0983
Email: glininc@aol.com
Web: www.glindsey.com

Description: Specialize in mid- to senior-level placements nationwide in market research with an emphasis on the high-tech, telecommunications, financial services and packaged goods industries.

Key Contact - Specialty:
Ms. Ginger Lindsey, President - *Market research, competitive intelligence*

Salary minimum: $45,000

Functions: Mkt. Research

Industries: Food, Bev., Tobacco, Computer Equip., Consumer Elect., Entertainment, Advertising, New Media, Software, Database SW

Professional Associations: SCIP

Lineal Recruiting Services
46 Copper Kettle Rd
Trumbull, CT 06611
(203) 386-1091
Fax: (203) 386-9788
Email: lisalineal@lineal.com
Web: www.lineal.com

Description: Technical placement of sales, service, management and hourlys exclusively in the electrical power and rotating apparatus industry, emphasizing service and repair of motors, controls, switchgear, transformers, drives, etc. Nationwide, company-paid fees.

Key Contact - Specialty:
Ms. Lisa Lineal, Owner - *Electromechanical systems & service personnel*

Functions: Plant Mgmt., Sales Mgmt., Customer Svc., Engineering, Specialized Svcs., Technicians

Industries: Energy, Utilities, Machine, Appliance, Motor Vehicles, Consumer Elect., Test, Measure Equip., Equip Svcs., Non-classifiable

The Littleton Group Inc
136 Main St
Acton, MA 01720-3553
(978) 263-7221
Fax: (413) 669-1858
Email: jobs@littletongroup.com
Web: www.littletongroup.com

Description: We recruit and place professionals in all the functional disciplines of high-technology specializing in manufacturing, technical operations, purchasing and materials. Our clients are primarily located in New England.

Key Contact - Specialty:
Mr. Carl Tomforde, President - *Manufacturing operations*
Mr. Peter DeFlumeri, Office Manager/Sr. Consultant - *Purchasing, materials*

Functions: Generalist

Industries: Medical Devices, Computer Equip., Misc. Mfg., Transportation, Telecoms, Government, Defense, Environmental Svcs., Software, Biotech

Lloyd Staffing
445 Broadhollow Rd
Melville, NY 11747
(631) 777-7600
Fax: (631) 777-7626
Email: work@lloydstaffing.com
Web: www.lloydstaffing.com

Description: We are a national retained search and contingency placement service with 30 years of experience in many specialties, providing access to the highest quality candidates and positions. We are an industry leader in accounting, biotech, sales and marketing, architecture/engineering, and IT/e-Media.

Key Contact - Specialty:
Mr. Merrill Banks, CPC, President - *General management*

Salary minimum: $50,000

Functions: Generalist

Industries: Services, Media, Communications, Software, Marketing SW, Biotech, Healthcare

Professional Associations: ASA, NACCB, NAPS

Networks: National Personnel Assoc (NPA)

LMB Associates
1468 Sunnyside Ave
Highland Park, IL 60035
(847) 831-5990
Email: info@lmbassociates.com
Web: www.lmbassociates.com

Description: Professional and executive search specializing in information systems.

Key Contact - Specialty:
Ms. Lorena M. Blonsky, President - *Information systems*

Salary minimum: $40,000

Functions: IT

Industries: Generalist

LNH & Associates Inc
152 Sandy Hill Ranch Rd
Elgin, TX 78621
(512) 426-1297
Fax: (512) 285-9634
Email: lnh@constructionrecruiters.com
Web: www.constructionrecruiters.com

Description: We recruit for the construction industry, and specialize in highway, airport, bridge, wastewater treatment, and heavy civil construction.

Key Contact:
Ms. Linda Hunt, President

Salary minimum: $40,000

Functions: Generalist

Industries: Construction

Lock & Associates
10 Four Seasons Pl Ste 902
Etobicoke, ON M9B 6H7
Canada
(416) 626-8383
Fax: (416) 626-6609
Web: www.lock-associates.com

Description: We are Canada's premier national sales, marketing, and management search firm.

Key Contact - Specialty:
Mr. Richard Lock, President
Mr. Peter Zukow - *Generalist*

Functions: Middle Mgmt., Production, Plant Mgmt., Purchasing, Distribution, Sales & Mktg., Mktg. Mgmt., Sales Mgmt., HR Mgmt., Engineering

Industries: Generalist

Networks: First Interview Network (FIN)

Branches:
400 3rd Ave SW
1500 Canterra Twr
Calgary, AB T2P 4H2
Canada
(403) 234-8500
Fax: (403) 234-8503
Key Contact - Specialty:
Mr. David McCorkill, Senior Consultant - *Generalist*

10180-101 St Manulife Pl Ste 1810
Edmonton, AB T5J 3S4
Canada
(780) 429-9044
Fax: (780) 424-1806
Key Contact - Specialty:
Mr. Glenn Lesko, Senior Consultant - *Generalist*

1040 W Georgia St Ste 1770
Vancouver, BC V6E 4H1
Canada
(604) 669-8806
Fax: (604) 669-5385
Key Contact - Specialty:
Mr. Bruce MacDonald - *Generalist*

201 Portage Ave Ste 1106
Winnipeg, MB R3B 3K6
Canada
(204) 987-3744
Fax: (204) 987-3745
Key Contact - Specialty:
Mr. Gary Mattocks - *Generalist*

633 Main St Ste 650
Moncton, NB E1C 9X9
Canada
(506) 389-7835
Fax: (506) 389-7801
Key Contact - Specialty:
Mr. Greg O'Brien - *Generalist*

1969 Water St Ste 2200
Halifax, NS B3J 3R7
Canada
(902) 491-4491
Fax: (902) 429-4327
Key Contact - Specialty:
Mr. Greg O'Brien - *Generalist*

155 Queen St Ste 900
Ottawa, ON K1P 6L1
Canada
(613) 751-4450
Fax: (613) 566-7036
Key Contact - Specialty:
Mr. David Mitchell - *Generalist*

1800 McGill College Ave Ste 3020
Montreal, QC H3A 3J6
Canada
(514) 866-2121
Fax: (514) 866-5257
Key Contact - Specialty:
Mr. Denis Nadeau - *Generalist*

410 22nd St E Ste 480
Saskatoon, SK S7K 5T6
Canada
(306) 244-2000
Fax: (306) 244-0087
Key Contact - Specialty:
Mr. Ray Beaudry - *Generalist*

Locus Inc
PO Box 930
New Haven, WV 25265-0930
(304) 882-2483
Fax: (304) 882-2217
Email: doglady@frognet.net
Web: www.locus-inc.com

Description: Recruit to specific openings emphasizing quality over quantity. Like to work directly with engineering managers and personnel to ensure all requirements are considered.

Key Contact - Specialty:
Ms. Nancy Wainwright, President - *Technical, engineers, managers*

Salary minimum: $20,000

Functions: Generalist, Middle Mgmt., Mfg., Engineering

Industries: Generalist, Metal Products, Machine, Appliance, Motor Vehicles, Misc. Mfg., Aerospace

Networks: National Consulting Network (NCN)

Logic Associates Inc
67 Wall St Ste 2411
New York, NY 10005
(212) 227-8000
Fax: (212) 766-0188
Email: bperry@logicassociates.com
Web: www.logicassociates.com

Description: Regarded as the national leader in corporate insurance/risk management recruiting.

Key Contact:
Mr. Bill Perry, President
Mr. Worth Fiers, Vice President-Risk Management
Mr. John Gallo, Vice President

Salary minimum: $50,000

Functions: Directors, Senior Mgmt., Middle Mgmt., Health Admin., Benefits, Budgeting, Risk Mgmt.

Industries: Generalist, Insurance

LogiPros LLC
2 Lake St
Monroe, NY 10950
(800) 300-7609
Email: search@logipros.com
Web: www.logipros.com

Description: We are a boutique firm organization specializing in the placement of executives for logistics and the supply chain on a national basis.

Key Contact:
Mr. Donald Jacobson

Salary minimum: $75,000

Functions: Productivity, Materials, Purchasing, Materials Plng., Distribution

Industries: Generalist

Professional Associations: CLM, IMRA, NRF, WERC

Logix Inc
1601 Trapelo Rd
Waltham, MA 02451
(781) 890-0500
Fax: (781) 890-3535
Email: logix@logixinc.com
Web: www.logixinc.com

Description: Our seasoned consulting staff is highly specialized in the search and selection of computer professionals ensuring maximum results in a quick, effective, professional manner.

Key Contact - Specialty:
Mr. David M. Zell, President - *Computer professionals*

Salary minimum: $80,000

Functions: IT

Industries: Software

Logue & Rice Inc
(a division of Accounting Principals Inc)
8000 Towers Crescent Dr Ste 650
Vienna, VA 22182-2700
(703) 761-4261
Fax: (703) 761-4248
Email: marc.zeid@accountingprincipals.com

Description: Executive and management search in Washington, D.C. area. Provide contingent and retained services for corporate and non-profit clients. Full range from executives to professionals leaving Big Six accounting firms.

Key Contact:
Mr. Kenneth F. Logue, Chairman
Mr. Marc Zeid, Managing Director

Salary minimum: $35,000

Functions: Generalist, General Mgmt., HR Mgmt., Finance, IT, Mgmt. Consultants

Industries: Generalist, Finance, Mgmt. Consulting, Telecoms, Software, Biotech

Al Londino & Associates
621 Shrewsbury Ave
Shrewsbury, NJ 07702
(732) 219-8889
Fax: (732) 219-9117
Email: alondino@bellatlantic.net

Description: We are an executive search firm specializing in the printing and graphic arts industry. We have over 20 years of management experience in the graphic arts industry. We specialize in finding the right people for executive and management positions in sales, production, administration, and manufacturing.

Key Contact:
Mr. Alexander Londino, Jr., President

Salary minimum: $50,000

Functions: General Mgmt., Mfg., Production, Plant Mgmt., Sales & Mktg., Sales Mgmt., Direct Mktg., Customer Svc., CFO's, IT

Industries: Printing

London Executive Consultants Inc
(also known as OEM Search Int'l)
380 Wellington St Ste 1420
London, ON N6A 5B5
Canada
(519) 434-9167
Fax: (519) 434-6318
Email: info@londonexecutive.com
Web: www.londonexecutive.com

Description: We are a well-established retainer/contingency search firm that works with branch/plant manufacturing companies requiring senior manufacturing and engineering personnel in the $50,000-$300,000 base salary range.

Key Contact - Specialty:
Mr. Paul Nelson, President - *Technical, manufacturing management, engineering*

Salary minimum: $40,000

Functions: Generalist, Mfg., Materials, Sales & Mktg., HR Mgmt., Finance, IT, Engineering

Industries: Generalist, Mfg., Transportation, Environmental Svcs., Aerospace, Packaging

Professional Associations: ACSESS, HRPAO

Networks: National Personnel Assoc (NPA)

William K Long Associates Inc
PO Box 754163
Forest Hills, NY 11375
(212) 571-0960
Fax: (212) 732-0540
Email: williamklongassociates@worldnet.att.net

Description: Insurance and reinsurance specialists.

Key Contact - Specialty:
Ms. Maureen E. Cahill, President - *Insurance, reinsurance*

Functions: Generalist

Industries: Insurance, Healthcare

Professional Associations: APIW

Longo Associates
4040 Civic Center Dr Ste 200
San Rafael, CA 94903-4150
(415) 472-1400
Email: rlongo@longo.com
Web: www.longo.com

Description: We are an executive search and technical recruiting firm, with a high tech focus, state-of-the-art computer-based technology, professional approach, and successful track record. See our web page for background.

Key Contact - Specialty:
Mr. Roger Longo, Principal - *Technical positions*

Functions: General Mgmt.

Industries: Computer Equip., Consumer Elect., Test, Measure Equip., Electronic, Elec. Components, New Media, Communications, Security SW, System SW

Lord & Albus Company
10314 Sweetwood Dr
Houston, TX 77070
(281) 955-5673
Email: jpalbus@hypercon.com
Web: www.hypercon.com/albus

Description: Personalized approach to each search assignment, we will assist in defining the client's needs, coordinate all interviewing, reference checks, salary negotiations. Serve as an extension of your company EEO employer.

Key Contact - Specialty:
Mr. John P. Albus, Owner/Principal - *Manufacturing*

Salary minimum: $40,000

Functions: Mfg.

Industries: Energy, Utilities, Construction, Mfg., Transportation, Services, Communications, Environmental Svcs., Packaging, Software, Biotech

Lordan Associates
366 Homeland Southway
Baltimore, MD 21212
(410) 532-3000
(800) 352-5242
Fax: (650) 745-1381
Email: slordan@lordanassociates.com
Web: www.lordanassociates.com

Description: Our firm specializes in the recruitment of professionals in the e-Business, e-Commerce, and EDI sectors, including sales, marketing, support, and development professionals in the US, UK, and Northern Europe.

Key Contact:
Ms. Susan Lordan, Owner

Functions: Directors, Senior Mgmt., Middle Mgmt., Product Dev., Sales & Mktg., Mktg. Mgmt., Sales Mgmt., Training, Systems Dev., Systems Implem.

Industries: E-commerce, IT Implementation, PSA/ASP, Software, Marketing SW

Professional Associations: MAPRC

Networks: Top Echelon Network

Lowderman & Associates
4902 Township Overlook Ste 100
Marietta, GA 30066
(770) 977-3020
Fax: (770) 977-6549
Email: lowderman1@aol.com

Description: Expanded, flexible and creative search arrangements in hospital executive recruiting. Strong emphasis in all areas of operations, nursing management, department heads, human resources and financial management; with expertise in recruiting minorities.

Key Contact:
Mr. William Lowderman, President

Salary minimum: $55,000

Functions: General Mgmt.

Industries: Healthcare

Bruce Lowery & Associates
PO Box 166
Ada, MI 49301-0166
(616) 676-3500
Fax: (616) 676-3516
Email: blowery@iserv.net

Description: Search firm serving Midwestern United States specializing in middle and upper administrative, finance, sales, marketing, engineering, manufacturing and general management positions.

Key Contact - Specialty:
Mr. Bruce N. Lowery, President - *CEOs, COOs, CFOs, sales, manufacturing management*

Salary minimum: $50,000

Functions: Generalist, General Mgmt., Admin. Svcs., Mfg., Materials, Sales & Mktg., HR Mgmt., Finance

Industries: Generalist, Mfg., Services, Government, Environmental Svcs.

Professional Associations: AICPA

Lucas Group
3384 Peachtree Rd Ste 700 & 800
Atlanta, GA 30326
(404) 239-5625
Fax: (404) 239-5694
Email: cdemartino@lucascareers.com
Web: www.lucasgroupcareers.com

Description: Eighty executive recruiters nationally, each an expert in placing top sales, sales management, marketing, high-technology, human resources and manufacturing/operations talent in their specific niche marketplace.

Key Contact - Specialty:
Ms. Cathy deMartino, Vice President/General Manager - *Chemical, consumer, services, medical, high-tech*
Mr. Tom McGee, Managing Partner - *Chemical, consumer, services, medical, high-tech*

Salary minimum: $60,000

Functions: Generalist

Industries: Mfg., Brokers, Venture Cap., Pharm Svcs., Mgmt. Consulting, HR Services, Media, Telecoms, Insurance, HR SW

Professional Associations: GAPS

Branches:
2231 E Camelback Rd Ste 317
Phoenix, AZ 85016
(602) 954-1325

2600 Michelson Dr Ste 1550
Irvine, CA 92612
(949) 660-9450
Fax: (949) 660-0126
Key Contact - Specialty:
Mr. Tony Tommarello, Managing Partner - *Food service, distribution, high technology, insurance, advertising*

1801 Ave of the Stars Fl 6
Los Angeles, CA 90067
Web: www.lucascareers.com

5405 Morehouse Dr Ste 100
San Diego, CA 92121
(858) 792-4810

601 Montgomery St Ste 715
San Francisco, CA 94111
(415) 781-4340

2000 S Colorado Blvd Ste 2-660
Colorado Center Tower Two
Denver, CO 80222
(303) 512-0600

PO Box 1691
Aiea, HI 96701

105 W Adams Ste 2900
Chicago, IL 60603
(312) 357-1160

441 Lexington Ave Fl 18
New York, NY 10017
(212) 599-2200
Fax: (212) 599-2014
Key Contact - Specialty:
Mr. Edward Gerard, Managing Partner - *Partners, mergers, practice groups*

5001 Spring Valley Rd Ste 200
E Twr
Dallas, TX 75243
(972) 980-4943

2 Riverway Ste 400
Houston, TX 77056
(713) 864-7733
Fax: (713) 864-7887
Key Contact - Specialty:
Mr. Larry Austin, Managing Partner - *Packaging, wireless communications, software, services, construction*

585 Grove St Ste 120
Herndon, VA 20170

Lucas, Berger, McGuire & O'Brien
251 E 50th St Ste 1
New York, NY 10022
(212) 888-4195
(212) 832-6060
Fax: (212) 888-4312
Email: lbcob@aol.com

Description: Our organization is small, discreet, conservative, and we recruit marketing professionals for some of the nation's most prominent consumer marketers and advertising agencies.

Key Contact - Specialty:
Mr. William Lucas, Partner - *Advertising*
Mr. Thomas O'Brien, Partner - *Advertising*
Mr. George McGuire, Partner - *Advertising*
Ms. Gina Arrigo, Sr Vice President - *Advertising*

Salary minimum: $40,000

Functions: Sales & Mktg., Advertising, Mktg. Mgmt., Direct Mktg., PR

Industries: Generalist, Advertising, Publishing, New Media, Broadcast, Film, Telecoms

Professional Associations: NYNMA

Ludwig & Associates Inc
1005 Wagner Ct
Harrison City, PA 15636
(724) 744-4949
Fax: (724) 744-2561
Email: bob@ludwig-recruit.com
Web: www.ludwig-recruit.com

Description: The key principal has 14 years of experience as a sales manager in the consumer products industry. The firm specializes in placing sales and marketing professionals with major consumer product companies.

Key Contact - Specialty:
Mr. Bob Ludwig, President - *Sales & marketing, consumer products*

Salary minimum: $50,000

Functions: Sales & Mktg.

Industries: Food, Bev., Tobacco

Luna Tech Inc
19001 Vashon Hwy SW Ste 204
Vashon, WA 98070
(206) 463-7970
Fax: (206) 463-7972
Email: lunatec1@gte.net
Web: www.lunatechinc.com

Description: Direct recruiting and sourcing for the Northwest in the field of high-technology/information technology.

Key Contact - Specialty:
Ms. Tina M. Shattuck, President - *Information technology, high technology*

Functions: Generalist, Systems Analysis, Systems Dev., Systems Implem., Systems Support, Network Admin., DB Admin., Engineering

Industries: Generalist, Services, Media, Telecoms, Software

Professional Associations: WSA

Lutz Associates
9 Stephen St
Manchester, CT 06040
(860) 647-9338
Fax: (860) 647-7918
Email: lutzassociates@home.com

Description: Executive search and placement: engineering, scientists, manufacturing and marketing nationwide. Specializing in consumer products, medical devices, electronics, rotating machinery, office equipment, CAD/CAM, CIM and AI.

Key Contact - Specialty:
Mr. Allen Lutz, Owner - *Engineering*

Salary minimum: $35,000

Functions: Mfg., Materials, Mktg. Mgmt., IT, R&D, Engineering, Architects

Industries: Medical Devices, Metal Products, Machine, Appliance, Misc. Mfg., Software, Biotech

Lybrook Associates Inc
PO Box 572
Newport, RI 02840
(401) 683-6990
Fax: (401) 683-6355
Email: chemistry@lybrook.com
Web: www.lybrook.com

Description: We are chemistry specialists. We recruit chemists and related scientists, engineers, managers and executives for R&D, applied

research, product development, manufacturing, process, engineering, QA/QC, and technical sales/marketing positions. More specifically, we recruiting chemists and life scientists, polymer scientists and engineers and biotechnologists for positions in analytical, R&D, chemicals, biotechnology, polymers, coatings, adhesives, inks, paper, plastics, organic, pharmaceutical, QA/QC, food, physical chemistry, instrumentation, food, environmental, and more.

Key Contact - Specialty:
Ms. Karen Lybrook - *Chemistry, senior positions, scientists, analytical, pharmaceuticals*
Mr. Christian Lybrook - *Sales & marketing, quality control, chemical engineering*
Mr. David Lybrook - *Plastics, coatings, biotechnology, pharmaceuticals, chemical engineering*

Salary minimum: $30,000

Functions: Product Dev., Quality, R&D, Engineering, Environmentalists, Technicians

Industries: Mfg., Environmental Svcs., Packaging, Biotech

Professional Associations: ACS, SPE, TAPPI

Thomas Lyle & Company
16 S Bothwell
Palatine, IL 60067
(847) 991-5050
Fax: (847) 991-5095
Email: lyle@thomaslyle.com
Web: www.thomaslyle.com

Description: Our specialty is salespeople/sales managers in consumer, industrial and health care on a contingency basis. We do assorted industry retained searches.

Key Contact - Specialty:
Mr. Lyle Stenfors, Senior Partner - *Generalist*
Mr. Thomas G. Beamer, Senior Partner - *Medical sales, sales management*

Functions: Sales & Mktg., Advertising, Mkt. Research, Mktg. Mgmt., Sales Mgmt.

Industries: Generalist, Food, Bev., Tobacco, Printing, Chemicals, Medical Devices, Publishing, Packaging, Software, Healthcare

Networks: First Interview Network (FIN)

The LYNN Group Inc (HLF)
PO Box 158793
Nashville, TN 37215
(615) 340-0800
Fax: (615) 340-0974
Email: heather@thelynngroup.com
Web: www.thelynngroup.com

Description: We are a small firm handling clients in the Southeastern United States. Performing both retained and contingency searches for mid-level and upper-management, we pride ourselves on our hard work, reputation and ethical contributions to the industry.

Key Contact - Specialty:
Ms. Heather Lynn Fike, President - *Entertainment, commercial development, commercial construction, architecture*
Ms. Janice G. Marko, Senior Associate - *Construction, engineering, hospitality, architecture*

Functions: Generalist, General Mgmt., Sales & Mktg., Architects

Industries: Generalist, Construction, Hospitality, Real Estate, Healthcare

Lynx Inc
420 Bedford St Ste 200
Lexington, MA 02420
(781) 274-6400
Fax: (781) 274-6300
Email: discover@lynxinc.com
Web: www.lynxinc.com

Description: Specialized high-quality contingency placement. Our concentrations are in software and information technology.

Key Contact - Specialty:
Mr. Philip J. Hurd, President - *Software, information technology*
Ms. Sophia Navickas, Executive Vice President - *Software, information technology*

Functions: IT

Industries: Generalist

Lyons & Associates Inc
7815 Loch Glen Dr
Crystal Lake, IL 60014-3317
(815) 477-9292
Fax: (815) 477-9296

Description: With a staff extensively experienced in the graphics arts industry, we provide detailed, thorough service to the printing and allied industries.

Key Contact - Specialty:
Mr. Kent T. Lyons, President - *Graphic arts, middle & senior management*

Salary minimum: $45,000

Functions: Generalist

Industries: Printing

Professional Associations: PIA

M & M Associates Inc
11765 West Ave
PMB 286
San Antonio, TX 78216
(210) 340-8772
Email: medjobs@md-jobs.com
Web: www.md-jobs.com

Description: Recipient of awards for top search firm in San Antonio for 6 of 7 past consecutive years. Only non-engineer specialists consistently ranked in top performing 5 (of 8000) statewide.

Key Contact - Specialty:
Mr. Leonard N. Marino, President - *Professional, technical, medicine*

Salary minimum: $65,000

Functions: Generalist, Senior Mgmt., Plant Mgmt., Physicians, Health Admin., CFO's, MIS Mgmt., Engineering

Industries: Generalist, Healthcare

Professional Associations: SAAPC, TAPS

Branches:
300 Queen Ann Ave N
PMB 221
Seattle, WA 98109
(206) 286-7858
Fax: (206) 286-7858
Email: lmarino@idworld.net
Key Contact - Specialty:
Mr. Michael Marino - *MIS, architecture, engineering, medical*

M K & Associates
309 E Brady St
Butler, PA 16001
(724) 285-7474
Fax: (724) 285-8339
Email: info@mkandassoc.com
Web: www.mkandassoc.com

Description: From the benchtop to the plant floor to the boardroom, the people of the food industry are our business. Let's work together to design a personalized strategy for your search.

Key Contact - Specialty:
Mr. John G. Mossman, Partner - *Food*
Ms. Maureen Knowlson, Partner - *Food*

Salary minimum: $35,000

Functions: Middle Mgmt., Product Dev., Production, Plant Mgmt., Quality, R&D, Engineering

Industries: Food, Bev., Tobacco

Professional Associations: AACC, IFT

Machine Tool Staffing
(also known as West & Associates)
14205 Falls Church Dr Ste 2019
Orlando, FL 32837
(407) 855-8334
Fax: (407) 855-8335
Email: hunter8334@aol.com
Web: www.machine-tools.com

Description: We have fourteen years of experience serving the machine tool industry. We specialize in field service engineers, controls engineers, electrical engineers, mechanical engineers, application engineers, CNC programmers, design engineers, and management and sales personnel.

Key Contact - Specialty:
Mr. Al West, President - *Manufacturing, machine tools*

Salary minimum: $35,000

Functions: Mfg., Automation, Plant Mgmt., Sales & Mktg., Sales Mgmt., Engineering, Technicians

Industries: Mfg., Metal Products, Machine, Appliance, Motor Vehicles, Misc. Mfg., Mgmt. Consulting

Networks: Top Echelon Network

The Mackenzie Group
317 Clarkson Ste 203
Ellisville, MO 63011
(636) 207-7447
(800) 215-9550
Fax: (636) 207-7444
Email: mackgroup@aol.com
Web: www.mackenziegroup.com

Description: We specialize in foundry, diecast and metalworking. The president of the company has been in the search and recruitment industry since 1991.

Key Contact - Specialty:
Mr. Brian Poucher, President - *Foundry, diecast, metalworking*

Salary minimum: $30,000

Functions: Generalist, Middle Mgmt., Production, Automation, Plant Mgmt., Quality, Productivity, HR Mgmt.

Industries: Generalist, Plastics, Rubber, Paints, Petro. Products, Metal Products, Machine, Appliance

Professional Associations: RON, SME

Macro Resources
68 E Wacker Pl Ste 400
Chicago, IL 60601
(312) 849-9100
Fax: (312) 849-9120
Email: frank@macroresources.com
Web: www.macroresources.com

Description: We specialize in recruiting information technology professionals. Software Engineers, Developers, DBAs, Internet Developers, Network administrators and security engineers to name a few.

Key Contact - Specialty:
Mr. Frank Roti, President - *Information technology*

Salary minimum: $40,000

Functions: IT, MIS Mgmt., Systems Analysis, Systems Dev., Systems Implem., Network Admin., DB Admin.

Industries: Generalist, Brokers, Services, New Media, Telecoms, Software

Networks: Top Echelon Network

Macrosearch Inc
13353 Bel-Red Rd Ste 206
Bellevue, WA 98005
(425) 641-7252
Fax: (425) 641-0969
Email: macro@macrosearch.com
Web: www.macrosearch.com

Description: We have become a primary personnel resource for the Pacific Northwest in high-technology career recruiting and placement.

Key Contact - Specialty:
Mr. Howard Lazzarini, Executive Recruiter - *High technology*
Ms. Sharon Nagy, Executive Recruiter - *High technology*

Functions: Generalist, MIS Mgmt., Systems Analysis, Systems Dev., Systems Implem., Systems Support, Network Admin., DB Admin.

Industries: Generalist, Software

Branches:
621 Woodland Sq Loop SE 6
Lacey, WA 98503
(360) 459-2699
Fax: (360) 459-2109
Email: southsnd@macrosearch.com
Key Contact - Specialty:
Ms. Lynne Durrell - *High technology*

Madeleine Lav & Associates (MLA)
1270 Ellis Ave
Cambria, CA 93428-5956
(805) 927-3098
Fax: (805) 927-4138
Email: mlav333@aol.com

Description: We have placed senior executives both in corporate and in the field at the premier retail and food service companies in the country.

Key Contact - Specialty:
Ms. Madeleine Lav, President - *Retail, food service*

Salary minimum: $35,000

Functions: Senior Mgmt., Middle Mgmt., Materials, Distribution, Finance, CFO's, IT

Industries: Food, Bev., Tobacco, Retail

Carol Maden Group
2019 Cunningham Dr Ste 218
Hampton, VA 23666
(757) 827-9010
Fax: (757) 827-9081
Email: cmaden@exis.net

Description: We offer 26 years' seasoned experience in all aspects of the employment arena. Our staff conducts a customized tailored search with highly skilled professional recruiters leading the way. We are accurate, detailed and thorough in our recruitment endeavors.

Key Contact - Specialty:
Ms. Carol Maden, President
Ms. Patricia Fridley, General Manager - *Information technology*

Functions: Generalist, Product Dev., Production, MIS Mgmt., Systems Analysis, Systems Dev., DB Admin., Engineering

Industries: Generalist, Plastics, Rubber, Motor Vehicles, Misc. Mfg., Software

Madison Executive Search Inc
11530 Covington Rd
Alpharetta, GA 30005
(973) 729-5520
Fax: (973) 729-9920
Email: mcgroup@mindspring.com

Description: Specialization in the search for telecommunication professionals, is our key competitive advantage. Telecommunications is our area of specialization and core area of focus. Positions include: sales, marketing, general administrative management, operational and technical.

Key Contact:
Mr. Bill Kay, Managing Director

Salary minimum: $40,000

Functions: Generalist

Industries: Telecoms

Magellan Int'l LP
24 Greenway Plz Ste 1110
Houston, TX 77046-2401
(713) 439-7485
Fax: (713) 439-7489
Email: magintl@aol.com
Web: www.magellanintl.com

Description: We specialize in enhancing our clients business by providing the highest caliber candidates. We also give equal, if not greater, attention to the individual needs of all of our candidates.

Key Contact:
Mr. Steven M. Tatar, Partner - *Auditing (financial, IT), management consulting*
Mr. Michael C. Craig, Partner - *Management consulting*
Mr. Timothy W. Johnson, Partner - *Management consulting*
Mr. Jonathan H. Phillips, Partner - *Management consulting*
Ms. Belinda Tekyl, Consultant - *Management consulting*
Ms. Trisha Morris, Associate

Salary minimum: $40,000

Functions: Generalist, Budgeting, Risk Mgmt., MIS Mgmt., Systems Implem., Network Admin., Mgmt. Consultants

Industries: Generalist, Chemicals, Invest. Banking, Pharm Svcs., Mgmt. Consulting, IT Implementation

Professional Associations: HAAPC

The Magenta Group
27031 La Paja Ave Ste 500
Mission Viejo, CA 92691
(949) 582-0600
Email: mgnta@aol.com

Description: As professionals in the graphic arts industry, besides helping clients with search and recruitment efforts, we help clients with general business trends, employment trends, comparative salary levels, benefit and relocation package comparisons as well as mergers and acquisitions.

Key Contact - Specialty:
Mr. Wayne Link, General Manager - *Printing, prepress, business forms*

Salary minimum: $40,000

Functions: Generalist, Senior Mgmt., Middle Mgmt., Production, Plant Mgmt., Sales Mgmt., Customer Svc.

Industries: Generalist, Printing, Publishing, New Media

Professional Associations: CSP
Branches:
23161 Mill Creek Rd
Laguna Hills, CA 92653
(949) 457-0123
Key Contact - Specialty:
Ms. Diane Sneathen - *Printing, prepress, business forms*

Magnum Search
1000 E Golfhurst Ave
Mt. Prospect, IL 60056
(847) 577-0007

Description: Over 35 years' HR management level experience with emphasis in search and recruiting for the metal fabrication & electronics industries.

Key Contact:
Mr. Arthur N. Kristufek, President

Salary minimum: $35,000

Functions: Generalist, Mfg., Materials, Sales & Mktg., HR Mgmt., Personnel, Mgmt. Consultants

Industries: Generalist, Paper, Plastics, Rubber, Metal Products, Machine, Appliance, Consumer Elect., Law Enforcement

Professional Associations: SHRM, SHRP

Maiola & Company
12900 Lake Ave Ste PH29
Cleveland, OH 44107
(216) 521-0011
Fax: (216) 521-0064

Description: We are highly specialized industry experts who form a very cohesive, experienced team which is capable of servicing the entire executive search, marketing and management consulting needs of a corporation.

Key Contact - Specialty:
Ms. Diana E. Maiola, CEO - *Printing, graphic arts*
Ms. Carol M. Pulito, Associate - *Printing, graphic arts*

Salary minimum: $30,000

Functions: Generalist

Industries: Printing

Major Consultants Inc
(a division of MC Inc)
500 N Franklin Tpke Ste 17
Ramsey, NJ 07446
(201) 934-9666
(201) 934-1988
Fax: (201) 818-0339
Email: lordini@majorinc.com
Web: www.majorinc.com

Description: Combine professional recruiting with hands on consulting services in all human resource and labor relations areas. Services include: professional recruiting, arbitration, benefit analyses, staffing & compensation plans, contract negotiations, policy development and contract recruiting.

Key Contact - Specialty:
Mr. Lou Ordini, President - *Management, professional, executive*
Mr. Michael Klinger, Executive Consultant - *Management (upper)*
Ms. Sande Foster, Executive Consultant - *Management, professional, executive*

Salary minimum: $70,000

Functions: Senior Mgmt., Production, Mktg. Mgmt.

Industries: Mfg., Drugs Mfg., Consumer Elect., Misc. Mfg., Services, Non-profits, HR Services, Packaging, Software, Biotech

Professional Associations: NJSA, SHRM

Major Legal Services LLC
1111 Chester Ave
510 Park Plz
Cleveland, OH 44114
(216) 579-9782
Fax: (216) 579-1662
Email: dennis@majorlegalservices.com
Web: www.majorlegalservices.com

Description: We are specialists in temporary and permanent recruiting of attorneys, paralegals, medical-legal professionals, managers and administrators, secretaries and other support staff. Our client base is Midwest law firms and corporate legal departments.

Key Contact - Specialty:
Mr. Dennis J. Foster, President - *Legal*
Ms. Deborah L. Peters, Director of Recruiting - *Legal, attorneys, paralegals, support staff*
Ms. Kathryn Lenz, Recruiter - *Legal, attorneys*
Ms. Lesley Shiels, Recruiter - *Legal, paralegals, support staff*

Functions: Legal, Attorneys, Paralegals

Industries: Generalist, Legal, Healthcare

Professional Associations: ARMA, NALSC, NFPA, OSSA

Major, Hagen & Africa
950 Northgate Dr Ste 303
San Rafael, CA 94903
(415) 444-1770
Fax: (415) 444-1782
Web: www.mhaglobal.com

Description: We are a global leader in attorney search. We place partners and associates in top law firms throughout the US, Asia, and the UK, and general counsel and other in-house attorneys with corporations, investment banks, and other entities worldwide. We also provide consulting and other services with respect to law firm mergers, practice group acquisitions, and the opening of new branch offices.

Key Contact:
Mr. Robert A. Major, Jr., Partner - *Attorneys only*
Mr. Charles J. Fanning, Jr., Partner - *Attorneys only*
Ms. Kimberly Fullerton, Partner - *Attorneys only*
Mr. Carter W. Brown, Chief Executive Officer
Mr. Morgan Reis, Chief Financial Officer
Mr. Richard Latman, Vice President - Marketing
Mr. Larry Wolfson, Director - IT

Functions: Generalist, Attorneys

Industries: Generalist, Legal

Professional Associations: NALSC
Branches:
801 S Figueroa Fl 11
Los Angeles, CA 90017
(213) 689-0700
Fax: (213) 689-0701
Key Contact - Specialty:
Ms. Gigi Birchfield, Senior Managing Director - *Attorneys only*
Ms. Peggy-Jean Harari, Managing Director - *Attorneys only*

470 Ramona St
Palo Alto, CA 94301
(650) 853-1010
Fax: (650) 833-6949
Key Contact - Specialty:
Mr. Carl A. Baier, Managing Director - *Attorneys only*
Ms. Malu M. Rydfors, Managing Director - *Attorneys*

550 W
San Diego, CA 92101
(619) 230-0450
Fax: (619) 230-0456

Key Contact - Specialty:
Ms. Catherine Rogers, Managing Director - *Attorneys only*
Ms. Deborah Ben-Canaan, Managing Director - *Attorneys only*

500 Washington St Fl 5
San Francisco, CA 94111
(415) 956-1010
Fax: (415) 398-2425
Email: infosf@mhaglobal.com
Key Contact - Specialty:
Mr. Robert A. Major, Jr., Partner - *Attorneys only*
Mr. Charles J. Fanning, Jr., Partner - *Attorneys only*
Ms. Kimberly Fullerton, Partner - *Attorneys only*
Ms. Martha Fay Africa - *Attorneys only*
Ms. Anna Marie Armstrong, Managing Director - *Attorneys only*
Ms. Nicole S. Lipman, Managing Director - *Attorneys only*
Mr. Andrew E. Burrows, Managing Director - *Attorneys only*
Mr. Michael P. Brown, Managing Director - *Attorneys only*
Ms. Melissa E. Lamfalusi, Managing Director - *Attorneys only*

1355 Peachtree St Ste 1125
Atlanta, GA 30309
(404) 875-1070
Fax: (404) 875-1090
Email: info@mhaatlanta.com
Key Contact - Specialty:
Mr. Wesley Q. Dobbs, Partner - *Attorneys only*
Ms. Catherine P. Butts, Managing Director - *Attorneys only*
Mr. Thomas C. Benedict, Managing Director - *Attorneys only*
Mr. Robert T. Graff, Managing Director - *Attorneys only*
Ms. Desha D. Dardenne, Managing Director - *Attorneys only*

35 E Wacker Dr Ste 2150
Chicago, IL 60601
(312) 372-1010
Fax: (312) 372-1696
Email: info@mhachicago.com
Key Contact - Specialty:
Ms. Laura J. Hagen, Partner - *Attorneys only*
Ms. Miriam J. Frank, Partner - *Attorneys only*
Ms. Lydia S. Marti, Managing Director - *Attorneys only*
Mr. Quentin D. Calkins, Managing Director - *Attorneys only*
Ms. Susan J. Mitchell, Managing Director - *Attorneys only*
Ms. Judith M. Hudson, Managing Director - *Attorneys only*

570 Lexington Ave Fl 26
New York, NY 10022
(212) 421-1011
(888) 642-5628
Fax: (212) 421-1042
Email: info@mhany.com
Key Contact - Specialty:
Mr. Jonathan Lindsey, Managing Partner - *Attorneys only*
Ms. Janet Markoff, Managing Director - *Attorneys only*
Ms. Allison Ross, Managing Director - *Attorneys only*
Ms. Barbara Kerner, Managing Director - *Attorneys only*
Ms. Anna Tsirulik, Managing Director - *Attorneys only*
Ms. Sang Lee, Managing Director - *Attorneys only*
Ms. Marjorie Schaeffer, Managing Director - *Attorneys only*
Mr. Adam Laden, Managing Director - *Attorneys only*
Ms. Carrie Mandel, Managing Director - *Attorneys only*
Ms. Janet Weider Diamond, Managing Director - *Attorneys only*

Mr. Steven B. Horowitz, Managing Director - *Attorneys only*
Mr. Brian T. Davis, Managing Director - *Attorneys only*

1600 Market St Fl 17
Philadelphia, PA 19103
(215) 581-7379
(877) 482-1010
Key Contact - Specialty:
Mr. Frank M. D'Amore, Senior Managing Director - *Attorneys only*

8 N Main St Ste C
Kingwood, TX 77339
(281) 913-1880
(888) 913-0680
Fax: (281) 913-1882
Key Contact - Specialty:
Mr. David E. Sewell, Senior Managing Director - *Attorneys only*
Mr. B. Cory Hawryluk, Managing Director - *Attorneys only*

Debra Malbin Associates
270 W End Ave Apt 7S
New York, NY 10023
(212) 501-9288
Email: dma270@aol.com

Key Contact:
Ms. Debra Malbin, President
Ms. Jill Ehrenberg, Senior Vice President
Ms. Marie Colletta, Vice President

Salary minimum: $85,000

Functions: Senior Mgmt., Middle Mgmt., Product Dev., Sales & Mktg., Graphic Artists

Industries: Wholesale, Retail, Mfg. SW, Marketing SW

Professional Associations: FG

The Mallard Group
3322 Oak Borough
Ft. Wayne, IN 46804
(219) 436-3970
Fax: (219) 436-7012
Email: mallardgroup@csinet.net

Description: Specializing in technical and executive personnel in electronics and electromechanical industries.

Key Contact:
Mr. Robert Hoffman
Ms. Linda Hoffman

Salary minimum: $45,000

Functions: Generalist

Industries: Mfg., Machine, Appliance, Consumer Elect., Misc. Mfg., Software

Managed Care Resources
PO Box 3004
Coppell, TX 75019
(972) 304-7979
Email: mcr2000@gte.net
Web: www.mcr2020.com

Description: We specialize in the recruitment and placement of professionals in the healthcare industry.

Key Contact - Specialty:
Mr. Thomas L. Sheehan, President - *Managed healthcare*
Ms. Shirley Knauf, Consultant - *Managed healthcare*

Salary minimum: $30,000

Functions: Generalist

Industries: Insurance, Healthcare

Management Advisors Int'l Inc
PO Box 3708
Hickory, NC 28603
(828) 324-5772
Fax: (828) 324-4831
Email: tposton@maisearch.com
Web: www.maisearch.com

Description: We are a management consulting firm specializing in executive search/professional placement for the mortgage banking, commercial banking, capital markets, securities, thrift, real estate finance, accounting and information technology

Key Contact - Specialty:
Mr. William J. Castell, Jr., President - *Mortgage banking*
Mr. Ty Poston, Senior Vice President - *Mortgage banking*

Salary minimum: $50,000

Functions: Senior Mgmt.

Industries: Finance, Banking, Brokers, Services, Mgmt. Consulting, Real Estate

Professional Associations: MBAA

Branches:
2101 Rexford Rd Ste 168W
Charlotte, NC 28211
(704) 521-9595
Email: krandolph@maisearch.com
Key Contact - Specialty:
Ms. Karen Randolph, Branch Manager - *Corporate banking*

Management Associates
(a division of The Systech Organization Inc)
20626 W Liberty Rd
White Hall, MD 21161-9063
(410) 329-2033
Email: aasoma@aol.com

Description: Practice concentrates on senior management appointments across wide spectrum of industry including banking, financial services and insurance.

Key Contact - Specialty:
Mr. Walter J. Sistek, President - *Global generalist*
Mr. George Hankins, Director - *Financial services*
Ms. Beverly Hartman, Director - *Human resource director, healthcare*
Ms. Joyce Ralph Herman, Director - *Marketing, advertising*
Mr. Craig Joseph, Director - *High technology, biotechnology*
Mr. William McFaul, Director - *Generalist*
Ms. Catherine E. Meehling, Administrative Consultant - *Education (higher)*

Salary minimum: $50,000

Functions: Generalist

Industries: Agri., Forestry, Mining, Mfg., Transportation, Finance, Services, Media, Government, Insurance, Biotech, Healthcare

Professional Associations: AEDC, AQP, ASTD

Networks: Computer Search

Management Consultants Corporate Recruiters
PO Box 15601
Scottsdale, AZ 85267-5601
(877) 795-1429
Fax: (877) 795-1429
Email: mgmtconsultants@earthlink.net

Description: We are a national company specializing in sales and sales management positions within the printing and telecommunications industry.

Key Contact:
Mr. John Costas, General Manager

Salary minimum: $50,000

Functions: Sales Mgmt., HR Mgmt.

Industries: Generalist, Printing, Communications, Telecoms, Telephony, Digital, Wireless, Fiber Optic, Network Infrastructure

Management Decision Systems Inc (MDSI)
466 Kinderkamack Rd
Oradell, NJ 07649
(201) 986-1200
Fax: (201) 986-1210
Email: amy@mdsisearch.com
Web: www.mdsisearch.com

Description: Data processing sales specialists. Sales, sales management, pre-sales positions within the computer vendor community.

Key Contact - Specialty:
Mr. Brian Mahoney, President - *Computer software, sales, sales management, technical support*
Mr. Angelo Messina, Vice President - *Computer software, sales, sales management, technical support*
Mr. Richard Deakmann, Vice President - *Computer software, sales, sales management, technical support*
Mr. Victor Delray, Vice President - *Computer software, sales, sales management, technical support*

Salary minimum: $50,000

Functions: Generalist, Sales Mgmt.

Industries: Generalist, Software

Management One Consultants
1200 Bay St Ste 501
Toronto, ON M5R 2A5
Canada
(416) 961-6100
Fax: (416) 961-7018

Description: Our strength is developing long-term relationships with top-notch clients and candidates. You always deal with the partners. Our clients are represented by us in the marketplace in the most professional manner.

Key Contact - Specialty:
Mr. Frank Edelberg, President - *Marketing, sales, finance*
Ms. Dana Stewart - *Marketing*

Salary minimum: $60,000

Functions: Generalist, Senior Mgmt., Mkt. Research, Mktg. Mgmt., Sales Mgmt., Direct Mktg., CFO's, Mgmt. Consultants

Industries: Generalist, Food, Bev., Tobacco, Soap, Perf., Cosmtcs., Consumer Elect., Banking, Advertising, Telecoms, Insurance

Management Principals
1600 Parkwood Cir Ste 500
Atlanta, GA 30339
(770) 937-0944
Fax: (770) 937-0942
Email: atlanta@managementprincipals.com
Web: www.managementprincipals.com

Description: Specialize in the placement of permanent and project based consulting accounting and banking professionals primarily in the Southeast.

Key Contact - Specialty:
Ms. Karen Brady, Branch Manager - *Project management*

Salary minimum: $30,000

Functions: Senior Mgmt., Middle Mgmt., CFO's, Budgeting, Cash Mgmt., Taxes

Industries: Generalist, Banking, Invest. Banking, Brokers, Misc. Financial, Telecoms, Insurance, Healthcare

Professional Associations: GAPS

Branches:
260 California St Ste 400
San Francisco, CA 94111
(415) 421-4370
Fax: (415) 421-4372
Email: sanfrancisco@managementprincipals.com
Key Contact - Specialty:
Ms. Robin Greist, Managing Director - *Project management*

55 W Port Plz Ste 250
St. Louis, MO 63146
(314) 514-9999
Fax: (314) 514-9262
Email: stlouis@managementprincipals.com
Key Contact - Specialty:
Mr. Troy Kilbreath, Branch Manager - *Project management*

831 E Morehead St Ste 540
Charlotte, NC 28202
(704) 342-3832
Fax: (704) 342-3833
Email: charlotte@managementprincipals.com
Key Contact - Specialty:
Ms. Katherine Lambert, Branch Manager - *Project management*

13455 Noel Rd Ste 1000
Galleria Twr 2
Dallas, TX 75240
(972) 778-8144
Fax: (972) 778-8143
Email: dallas@managementprincipals.com
Key Contact - Specialty:
Ms. Kim Yenhana, Branch Manager - *Project management*

Management Profiles
21822 Whipporwill Ln
Bauxite, AR 72011
(501) 602-2920
Fax: (501) 602-2924
Email: info@managementprofiles.com
Web: www.managementprofiles.com

Description: Our firm is an executive search firm that specializes in placing top-level candidates nationwide.

Key Contact - Specialty:
Ms. Windy Peel, Executive Recruiter - *Executive management*

Functions: Generalist

Industries: Mfg., Mgmt. Consulting, HR Services, E-commerce, Communications, Software

Professional Associations: RON

Networks: Inter-City Personnel Assoc (IPA)

Management Recruiters Int'l Inc (MRI)
(a subsidiary of CDI Corp)
200 Public Sq Fl 31
Cleveland, OH 44114-2301
(216) 696-1122
Fax: (216) 696-3221
Email: abs@mrinet.com
Web: www.brilliantpeople.com

Description: Search and recruitment - mid- to senior management and professional. Also provides interim staffing, assessment programs and international capability and videoconferencing services. Full range of staffing services.

Key Contact:
Mr. Allen B. Salikof, President/CEO
Mr. William E. Aglinsky, Senior Vice President/CFO
Mr. Robert A. Angell, VP-Franchise Sales

Mr. Donald L. Goldman, VP-General Counsel/Assistant Secretary
Mr. Jerry R. Hill, VP-Training
Mr. Gary P. Williams, SVP-Franchise Development
Mr. Micahel DeMuch, Vice President-Marketing
Mr. Neil Fox, Vice President/CIO
Mr. George Bojalad, VP-Human Resources
Mr. David Campeas, VP-Company Office Operations
Mr. Michael Rode, VP/Associate Counsel

Salary minimum: $45,000

Functions: Generalist

Industries: Generalist

Professional Associations: IFA

Branches:
614 Clinton Ave Ste 263
Huntsville, AL 35804
(256) 533-0400
Fax: (256) 533-0803
Email: mrnalabama@aol.com
Key Contact:
Renate Banks

215 Fidalgo Ave Ste 101
PO Box 2813
Kenai, AK 99611
(907) 260-6433
Fax: (907) 283-6460
Email: mri@alaska.net
Web: www.mrsca.com
Key Contact:
Dr. Aaron Morse, Co-Manager
Ms. Jeannine Morse, Co-Manager

4800 N Scottsdale Rd Ste 2800
Scottsdale, AZ 85251
(480) 941-JOBS
Fax: (480) 941-1430
Email: info@mriscottsdale.com
Web: www.mriscottsdale.com
Key Contact:
Mr. Dick A. Govig, General Manager
Mr. Todd Govig, Manager

1840 E River Rd Ste 120
Tucson, AZ 85718
(520) 529-0750
Fax: (520) 529-0931
Email: brian@mrtucsonnorth.com
Web: www.mrtucsonnorth.com
Key Contact:
Mr. Brian Bee

102 N First St
Rogers, AR 72756-4511
(501) 621-0706
Fax: (501) 621-9753
Email: mrirogers@arkmola.net
Web: www.mrirogers.com
Key Contact:
Mr. Al McEwen, Manager

28720 Roadside Dr Ste 226
Agoura Hills, CA 91301
(818) 991-4410
(800) 632-3012
Fax: (818) 991-4680
Email: consult@mri-la.com
Web: www.mri-la.com
Key Contact:
Mr. Daniel Crisafulli
Ali Zia

15 Williamsburg Ln Ste A
Stonebridge Professional Village
Chico, CA 95926-2225
(530) 892-9898
Fax: (530) 892-8668
Email: execusrch@msn.com
Web: www.members.aol.com/mrichico
Key Contact:
Mr. Barry Barsuglia, Manager

375 Woodworth Ave Ste 104
Clovis, CA 93612
(559) 297-5900
Fax: (559) 297-5919
Email: klemon@mrnorthfresno.com
Key Contact:
Ms. Kay Lemon

100 Corporate Pointe Ste 380
Culver City, CA 90230
(310) 670-3040
Fax: (310) 670-2981
Email: info@mrila.com
Web: www.mrila.com
Key Contact:
Mr. Mike Bryant, Manager

1724 Picasso Ste E
Davis, CA 95616-0547
(530) 297-5400
Fax: (530) 297-5401
Email: david@healthcareis.com
Key Contact:
Mr. Dave Kushan, CSAM, Manager

14736 Caminito Punta Arenas
Del Mar, CA 92014
(858) 350-3784
Fax: (858) 794-7004
Email: recruit@kayajian-morrison.com
Key Contact:
Mr. Robert Kayajian
Ms. Diane Morrison

2222 Francisco Dr Ste 430
El Dorado Hills, CA 95762
(916) 939-9780
Fax: (916) 939-9785
Email: mrijobs@concentric.net
Key Contact:
Mr. Stan Gardner, Manager

10751 Simmerhorn Rd Ste100
Galt, CA 95632
(209) 745-7093
Key Contact:
Mr. Bill Moersch

315 W Arden Ave Ste 12
Glendale, CA 91203-1158
(818) 956-0400
Fax: (818) 956-0431
Email: info@mrofglendale.com
Web: www.mrofglendale.com
Key Contact - Specialty:
Mr. Marcus Mota e Silva, Partner and Director -
  Manufacturing (executive, managerial, technical)
Mr. Sergio Pires, Partner and Director -
  Manufacturing (executive, managerial, technical, sales)

211 S Glendora Ave Ste C
Glendora, CA 91741
(626) 963-4503
Fax: (626) 857-7468
Email: mrglendora@msn.com
Key Contact:
Mr. Matt J. Albanese, Manager

11925 Wilshire Blvd Ste 211
Los Angeles, CA 90025
(310) 979-7874
Fax: (310) 979-7894
Key Contact:
Mr. Richard F. Roberts, Manager

121 Massol Blvd Ste 210
Los Gatos, CA 95030
(831) 688-5452
Fax: (561) 619-2478
Email: kwkeegan@mrlosgatos.com
Key Contact:
Mr. Kenneth W. Keegan, Co-Manager
Ms. Elizabeth A. Dickerson, Co-Manager
Ms. Kira Lee Keegan, Co-Manager

480 Roland Way Ste 103
Oakland, CA 94621-2065
(510) 635-7901
Fax: (510) 562-7237

Email: mrsc@dnai.com
Web: www.scsanfran.com
Key Contact:
Mr. Tom S. Thrower, Manager

575 Price St Ste 313
Pismo Beach, CA 93449-2553
(805) 773-2816
Fax: (805) 773-2819
Email: keith@gcservices.com
Web: www.mrinet.com/headhunter
Key Contact:
Mr. Keith A. Gilbert, Co-Manager
Ms. Mary Gilbert, Co-Manager

5500 Madison Ave Ste A
Sacramento, CA 95841
(916) 334-7800
Fax: (916) 334-5800
Key Contact:
Mr. Tom Kelly

126 W 25th St Ste 200
San Mateo, CA 94403
(650) 548-4800
Fax: (650) 548-4805
Email: admin@mrica.com
Web: www.mrica.com
Key Contact:
Mr. Michael Shaffer
Ms. Crystal Z. S. Parsons, Managing Partner

2700 N Main St Ste 600
Santa Ana, CA 92705
(714) 565-0010
Fax: (714) 565-0020
Email: admin@socalmri.com
Web: www.socalmri.com
Key Contact:
Mr. Ray Burch

208 W Main St Ste 10
Montgomery Sq
Visalia, CA 93291-6262
(559) 741-7900
Fax: (559) 741-7909
Email: recruit@theworks.com
Key Contact:
Mr. Jim Ely, Manager

20300 Ventura Blvd Ste 380
Woodland Hills, CA 91364
(818) 712-9930
Fax: (818) 712-9975
Key Contact:
Mr. Eman Talei
Mr. Kevin Javaheri

10 Boulder Cres Ste 302 B
Colorado Springs, CO 80903
(719) 389-0600
Fax: (303) 265-9422
Email: jobs@mripikespeak.com
Key Contact:
Mr. Bud O. Reynolds, Manager

PO BOx 102576
Denver, CO 80250-2576
(303) 765-4404
Fax: (303) 765-4432
Key Contact:
Mr. Kurt Haynes

PO Box 909
Durango, CO 81302-0909
(970) 385-4600
Fax: (970) 375-7600
Email: bcooksey@mrdurango.com
Key Contact:
Mr. Ben Cooksey

13275 E Fremont Pl Ste 210
Cobblestone Plz
Englewood, CO 80112-3909
(303) 649-9895
Fax: (303) 649-1523
Email: dshaw@thehighlandsgroup.net
Key Contact:
Mr. Darryl C. Shaw, Manager

6950 S Tucson Way Ste I
Englewood, CO 80112
(720) 874-0777
Fax: (720) 874-0888
Key Contact:
Mr. William Jordan
Ms. Diane Jordan

3042 Evergreen Pkwy Ste 200
Evergreen, CO 80439
(303) 679-6079
(800) 933-5250
Fax: (303) 679-6080
Email: jak@mridenver.com
Web: www.mridenver.com
Key Contact:
Mr. John Kirschner

8791 Wolff Ct Ste 200
Westminster, CO 80031
(303) 650-8870
Fax: (303) 650-8871
Email: recruiter@wgpeople.com
Web: www.wgpeople.com
Key Contact:
Ms. Gloria Kellerhals, Manager

PO Box 5936
Woodland Park, CO 80866
(719) 686-1026
Fax: (719) 686-1027
Email: woodprk!manager@mrinet.com
Key Contact:
Mr. Steve Johnson, Manager

PO Box 6337
Woodland Park, CO 80866
(719) 686-1222
Fax: (719) 686-1202
Key Contact:
Mr. Jerry Bjornstad

39 Locust Ave Ste 205
New Canaan, CT 06840
(203) 966-5800
Fax: (203) 966-2562
Email: hr@mricowser.com
Web: www.mricowser.com
Key Contact:
Ms. Stephanie Cowser
Mr. Kevin Cowser

488 Main Ave
Norwalk, CT 06851
(203) 847-2220
Fax: (203) 847-2224
Key Contact:
Mr. Joseph Mullings
Chris McDonnell

574 Heritage Rd Ste 100
Southbury, CT 06488
(203) 267-6556
Fax: (203) 267-6760
Email: bastolopesllc@snet.net
Key Contact:
Mr. Jose Basto
Mrs. Jocelyn Basto

396 Danbury Rd
Wilton, CT 06897-2024
(203) 834-1111
Fax: (203) 834-2686
Email: careers@mrinorwalk.com
Web: www.mrinorwalk.com
Key Contact:
Mr. Robert C. Schmidt, President

6544 N US Hwy 41N Ste 204 B
Apollo Beach, FL 33572-1706
(813) 645-6239
Fax: (813) 645-8678
Email: bill@mriapollo.com
Web: www.mriapollo.com
Key Contact:
Mr. Bill Handley, Manager

3840-1 Williamsburg Park Blvd
Jacksonville, FL 32257-5586
(904) 448-5200
Fax: (904) 448-1418
Email: steel@steelheadhunter.com
Web: www.steelheadhunter.com
Key Contact - Specialty:
Mr. Charles A. Hansen, Manager - *Metals
technology*

500 Lake Ave Ste 165
Lake Worth, FL 33460
(561) 792-4262
Fax: (561) 792-4266
Email: slprn@bellsouth.net
Key Contact:
Mr. Joseph Poach, Co-Manager
Ms. Shauna Poach, Co-Manager

898 Spanish Dr S
Longboat Key, FL 34228
(941) 753-5837
Fax: (941) 383-6877
Email: lmoore@aol.com
Key Contact:
Ms. Lynn W. Moore, Manager

205 Crystal Grove Blvd Ste 102
Lutz, FL 33549-6452
(813) 948-6880
Fax: (813) 948-6881
Email: mrilutz@earthlink.net
Web: www.brmrlutz-mri.com
Key Contact:
Mr. Bill Rainey, Manager

2600 Maitland Center Pkwy Ste 295
Maitland, FL 32751-7227
(407) 660-0089
Fax: (407) 660-2066
Email: tbrown@prioritysearch.com
Web: www.prioritysearch.com
Key Contact:
Mr. Tom Brown, Co-Manager
Ms. Arlene Brown, Co-Manager

1300 3rd St S Ste 301-A
Naples, FL 34102
(941) 261-8800
Fax: (941) 261-7551
Email: recruiter@automotivehead-hunter.com
Web: www.automotivehead-hunter.com
Key Contact:
Mr. Dan R. Ressler, Manager

685 Royal Palm Beach Blvd Ste 105
Royal Palm Beach, FL 33411
(561) 793-8400
Fax: (561) 793-8471
Email: rbizick@telecomjob.net
Web: www.telecomjob.net
Key Contact:
Mr. Ron Bizick, Manager

950 S Tamiami Trl Ste 208
Sarasota, FL 34236-7818
(941) 953-3500
Fax: (941) 953-3544
Email: jobs@mrisarasota.com
Web: www.mrisarasota.com
Key Contact:
Ms. Teresa Fridley
Mr. Charles Fridley

9500 Koger Blvd Ste 203
St. Petersburg, FL 33702
(727) 577-2116
Fax: (727) 576-5594
Email: mristpete@aol.com
Key Contact:
Mr. Philip Petrillo

1406 Hays St Ste 7
Tallahassee, FL 32301-2843
(850) 656-8444
Fax: (850) 942-2793
Email: mri@tlh.fdt.net
Web: www.managementrecruiters.com
Key Contact:
Ms. Kitte H. Carter, Manager

3802 Ehrlich Rd Ste 101
Tampa, FL 33624-2300
(813) 265-8789
Fax: (813) 265-8902
Email: mri@tampabay.rr.com
Key Contact:
Mr. James Carow

500 N Westshore Blvd Ste 530
Tampa, FL 33609
(813) 289-9355
Fax: (813) 261-4612
Email: dsmith@mritampa.com
Key Contact:
Mr. Dan Smith

328 Banyan Blvd Ste J
West Palm Beach, FL 33401
(561) 832-8788
Fax: (561) 832-7252
Email: mriwpb@quik.com
Web: www.mrautomotive.com
Key Contact:
Mr. William Crouse

2645 Executive Park Dr Ste 141
Weston, FL 33331
(954) 385-3122
Fax: (954) 385-5186
Email: suzanne@mriweston.com
Web: www.mriweston.com
Key Contact:
Mr. Ray George
Ms. Sue George

230 S New York Ave Ste 200
Winter Park, FL 32789-4236
(407) 629-2424
Fax: (407) 629-6424
Email: stacy@parkavegrp.com
Web: www.parkavegrp.com
Key Contact:
Ms. Stacy L. Gulden, Manager

3440 Preston Ridge Rd Ste 450
Alpharetta, GA 30005
(678) 879-1005
Fax: (678) 879-1030
Email: mriatlanta@earthlink.net
Key Contact:
Ms. Tammy Owen
Mr. Bart Heres

1776 Peachtree St NW Ste 306 S
Atlanta, GA 30309
(404) 874-3636
Fax: (404) 874-0221
Email: mratl@bellsouth.net
Key Contact:
Mr. Gene Houchins, Jr., Manager

2500 Cumberland Pkwy Ste 550
Atlanta, GA 30339
(770) 433-8330
Fax: (770) 433-1701
Email: officemanager@mriatlv.com
Web: www.mriatlv.com
Key Contact:
Mr. Richard G. Holland, Manager

1814 Lakefield Ct Ste D
Conyers, GA 30013
(770) 483-3888
Fax: (770) 483-8890
Email: careers@mr-ae.com
Web: www.mr-ae.com
Key Contact:
Mr. Kevin Cable, Co-Manager
Mr. John Cable, Co-Manager

1122 Monticello St
PO Box 590
Covington, GA 30015-0590
(770) 787-9056
Fax: (770) 787-7105
Email: rholt@mrcovington.com
Web: www.mrcovington.com
Key Contact:
Mr. Richard Holt

103 Kelly Mill Rd
Cumming, GA 30040
(770) 205-1650
Fax: (770) 205-1638
Email: wgbrownlee@mindspring.com
Key Contact:
Mr. William Brownlee, Owner/Manager

4227 Pleasant Hill Rd Bldg 13 Ste 200
Duluth, GA 30096
(678) 474-9211
Fax: (678) 474-9252
Email: csutton@mriatlanta-duluth.com
Web: www.mriatlanta-duluth.com
Key Contact:
Mr. Christopher Sutton

2470 Windy Hill Rd Ste 461
Marietta, GA 30067
(770) 955-6445
Fax: (770) 955-6446
Email: ronhollis@mindspring.com
Key Contact:
Mr. Ron Hollis, Manager

118 S 2nd Ave
McRae, GA 31055-1539
(912) 868-5001
Fax: (912) 868-6603
Email: gravesbr@altamaha.net
Key Contact:
Mr. Ron Graves, Manager

406 Line Creek Rd Ste B
Peachtree City, GA 30269
(770) 486-0603
Fax: (770) 631-7684
Email: mrias@mindspring.com
Key Contact:
Mr. Ronald L. Wise, Manager

916 Main St Ste 2000
PO Box 1455
Perry, GA 31069
(478) 988-4444
Fax: (478) 988-4445
Email: twentz.mrmg@mindspring.com
Key Contact:
Mr. Terry M. Wentz, Manager

1201 Macy Dr
Roswell, GA 30076
(770) 645-6009
Fax: (770) 645-0988
Key Contact:
Mr. Tilden Martin, Jr.

9570 Nesbit Ferry Ste 203
Roswell, GA 30022
(770) 587-1161
Fax: (770) 587-1162
Key Contact:
Mr. Guillermo Pino

1626 Frederica Rd Ste 203
St. Simons Island, GA 31522-2509
(912) 634-2390
Fax: (912) 634-2391
Email: lorene@darientel.net
Key Contact:
Ms. Lorene M. Ledingham, Manager

208 Creekstone Rdg
Woodstock, GA 30188
(770) 592-9550
Fax: (770) 924-6206
Email: mrwoodstock@mindspring.com
Key Contact:
Mr. Doug O. Ralston, Manager

PO Box 6314
Aurora, IL 60598
(630) 499-8116
Email: pstray@interaccess.com
Key Contact:
Mr. Brad Baird
Mr. Larry Strayhorn
Ms. Patricia Strayhorn

750 Almar Pkwy Ste 204
Bourbonnais, IL 60914
(815) 929-1900
Fax: (815) 929-0900
Email: tom@myersgroupinc.com
Web: www.myersgroupinc.com
Key Contact:
Mr. Tom Myers

606 S Staley Ste B
Champaign, IL 61821
(217) 355-6900
Fax: (217) 355-2773
Email: ron@embeddedrecruiters.com
Web: www.embeddedrecruiters.com
Key Contact:
Mr. Kenneth C. Williams, General Manager
Mr. Gary Campbell, Manager
Mr. Ron Williams

1921 St. Johns Ave Ste 220
Highland Park, IL 60035-3520
(847) 681-2144
Fax: (847) 681-2140
Email: mbz@parkconsultants.com
Key Contact:
Ms. Sally Salzer, Co-Manager
Ms. Gayle Galloway, Co-Manager

2711 W 183rd St Ste 303
Homewood, IL 60430-2951
(708) 922-3397
Fax: (708) 922-3370
Email: dlb@mritalentscout.com
Web: www.mritalentscout.com
Key Contact:
Mr. Darrell L. Bewsey, Manager

2443 Warrensville Rd Ste 600
Lisle, IL 60532
(630) 416-7400
Fax: (630) 416-0605
Key Contact:
Mr. David Baranski

479 Business Center Dr Ste 104
Kensington Ctr
Mt. Prospect, IL 60056-6037
(847) 298-8780
Fax: (847) 298-8781
Email: plastics@plastics-careers.com
Web: www.plastics-careers.com
Key Contact - Specialty:
Mr. Tom A. Diduca, Manager
Ms. Nancy DiDuca, Manager - *Plastics, quality
engineering*

211 Landmark Dr Ste B5
Normal, IL 61761
(309) 452-1844
Fax: (309) 452-0403
Email: mrbloom@mribloomington.com
Web: www.mribloomington.com
Key Contact:
Mr. Alan Snedden, Manager

211 Waukegan Rd Ste 104
Northfield, IL 60093-2745
(847) 501-3881
Fax: (847) 501-3889
Email: manager@glenview.mrinet.com
Key Contact:
Mr. Fred Brooks, Manager

1415 W 22nd St Ste 725
Oak Brook, IL 60523
(630) 990-8233
Fax: (630) 990-2973
Email: glm@scoakbrook.com
Web: www.scoakbrook.com
Key Contact:
Mr. Gary Miller

101 Plz E Blvd Ste 312
Evansville, IN 47715
(812) 477-5886
Fax: (812) 477-5887
Email: tboyle@mrievansville.com
Key Contact:
Mr. Thomas Boyle

4011 W Jefferson Blvd
Ft. Wayne, IN 46804-6853
(219) 459-1123
Fax: (219) 459-1091
Email: aim@mrifortwayne.com
Web: www.mrifortwayne.com
Key Contact:
Mr. Harold Rudin, Co-Manager

6429-B Oakbrook Pkwy Ste 102
Ft. Wayne, IN 46825
(219) 483-5500
Fax: (219) 483-5777
Email: dc@mrisummitcity.com
Key Contact:
Mr. Doug Copley

1915 Crown Plz Blvd
Plainfield, IN 46168-2015
Email: admin@mrplainfield.com

2519 E Main St Ste 101
Forest Park Bldg
Richmond, IN 47374-5864
(765) 935-3356
Fax: (765) 935-3417
Email: martin@infocom.com
Web: www.infocom.com/~martin/
Key Contact:
Mr. Rande L. Martin, Manager

1455 W Oak St Ste B
Zionsville, IN 46077
(317) 733-9644
Fax: (317) 733-9614
Email: jrudy@mrizionsville.com
Web: www.mrizionsville.com
Key Contact:
Mr. Jim D. Rheude, Manager

150 1st Ave NE Ste 400
Wells Fargo Financial Ctr
Cedar Rapids, IA 52401
(319) 366-8441
Fax: (319) 366-1103
Email: info@mricr.com
Web: www.mricr.com
Key Contact:
Ms. Cynthia Lyness

1312 4th St SW Ste 125
West Ct
Mason City, IA 50401
(641) 424-1680
Fax: (641) 424-6868
Email: mrimc@willowtree.com
Key Contact:
Ms. Cheryl L. Plagge, Manager

12345 W 95th St Ste 201
Lenexa, KS 66215
(913) 859-0700
Fax: (913) 859-0707
Email: mrlenexa@planetkc.com
Web: www.mrilenexa.com
Key Contact:
Mr. Richard Wood
Mr. Marvin Johnston

9401 Indian Creek Pkwy Ste 920
Corporate Woods Bldg 40
Overland Park, KS 66210-2098
(913) 661-9300
Fax: (913) 661-9030
Email: ovrland!manager@mrinet.com
Key Contact:
Mr. Danny Buda, Jr., General Manager

100 N Broadway Ste 405
Wichita, KS 67202
(316) 265-2520
Fax: (316) 265-9105
Email: manager@wichita.mrinet.com
Key Contact:
Mr. Marvin Reimer, Manager

12935 W US Hwy 42
Prospect, KY 40059
(502) 292-0010
Fax: (502) 292-0090

Email: prospectmr@earthlink.net
Key Contact:
Mr. David Wallace

1203 Mt. Eden Rd Ste 1
Shelbyville, KY 40065-8822
(502) 633-6100
Fax: (502) 647-3300
Email: mros@ka.net
Web: www.mrishelbyville.com
Key Contact:
Mr. Barney O. Barnett, Manager

3527 Ridgelake Dr
PO Box 6605
Metairie, LA 70009
(504) 831-7333
Fax: (504) 838-9009
Email: pmlno1@aol.com
Key Contact:
Mr. Edward N. Ameen, General Manager
Mr. Paul M. Luce, CSAM, Manager

710 B Apple St
Norco, LA 70079-2424
(504) 725-0290
Fax: (504) 725-0608
Email: careers@mrinow.com
Web: www.mrinow.com
Key Contact:
Mr. Tom McLain

920 Pierremont Ste 515
Shreveport, LA 71106-8794
(318) 865-8411
Fax: (318) 861-3411
Email: twoods@mageeresource.com
Web: www.mageeresource.com
Key Contact:
Ms. Gerri Magee, Co-Manager
Mr. Charles Magee, Co-Manager

202 Village Sq Ste 3
Slidell, LA 70458
(504) 847-1900
Fax: (504) 847-1984
Email: jpecot@jobscenter.com
Web: www.jobscenter.com
Key Contact:
Mr. Jack L. Pecot, Manager

2083 W St Ste 5A
Annapolis, MD 21401-3030
(410) 841-6600
Fax: (410) 841-6600
Key Contact:
Mr. John Czajkowski, Manager

5606 Ridgefield Rd
Bethesda, MD 20816
(301) 320-3744
Fax: (301) 320-1877
Email: csearch@erols.com
Key Contact:
Mr. Michael C. Prentiss, Manager

5044 Dorsey Hall Dr Ste 204
Dorsey Hall Professional Park
Ellicott City, MD 21042-7739
(410) 884-1363
Fax: (410) 884-1369
Email: mriellic@erols.com
Key Contact:
Mr. Paul Beckham

132 E Main St Ste 300
Salisbury, MD 21801-4921
(410) 548-4473
Fax: (410) 548-4487
Key Contact:
Mr. Fred J. Puente, Manager

12520 Prosperity Dr Ste 220
Silver Spring, MD 20904
(301) 625-5600
Fax: (301) 625-3001
Email: sim@mr-twg.com
Web: www.mr-themeyersgroup.com
Key Contact:
Mr. Stuart Meyers

639 Granite St
Braintree, MA 02184
(781) 848-1666
Fax: (781) 843-8916
Email: braintree@mri-boston.com
Web: www.mri-boston.com
Key Contact:
Mr. Calvin Seitler, Manager

1500 Main St Ste 2008
Springfield, MA 01115
(413) 781-1550
Fax: (413) 731-6566
Email: springfield@mri-boston.com
Web: www.mri-boston.com
Key Contact:
Mr. Jack Mohan, Manager

2000 W Park Dr
Westborough Office Park
Westborough, MA 01581-3901
(508) 366-9900
Fax: (508) 898-9982
Email: westboro@mri-boston.com
Web: www.mri-boston.com
Key Contact:
Ms. Irene Garrity, General Manager

3600 Green Ct Ste 100
Ann Arbor, MI 48105
(734) 769-1720
Fax: (734) 769-0035
Email: info@mrannarbor.com
Web: www.mrannarbor.com
Key Contact:
Mr. Sam N. Sarafa, Manager
Mr. David Sarafa

28 E Michigan Ave
Battle Creek, MI 49017
(616) 968-5440
Fax: (616) 968-5443
Email: leah@jamesclayton.com
Web: www.mricc.com
Key Contact:
Mr. Mark Maire, Managing Director

228 1/2 Washington Ave
Grand Haven, MI 49417
(616) 604-0001
Fax: (616) 604-0005
Key Contact:
Mr. Bruce Bradford-Royle
Ms. Sherri Bradford-Royle

1835 RW Berends SW
Grand Rapids, MI 49509
(616) 336-8484
Fax: (616) 336-7680
Email: mri@cegrp.com
Web: www.cegrp.com
Key Contact:
Mr. Ronald Meadley, President

400 N 136th Ave Ste 6
Bldg 200
Holland, MI 49424-1830
(616) 396-2620
Fax: (616) 396-9465
Email: mri@macatawa.com
Key Contact:
Mr. Robert E. Bakker, CSAM, Manager

2491 Cedar Park Dr
Holt, MI 48842-2184
(517) 694-1153
Fax: (517) 694-6502
Email: mri@voyager.net
Web: www.mrilansingmi.com
Key Contact:
Mr. John A. Peterson, Co-Manager
Ms. Priscilla J. Peterson, Co-Manager

7190 W Houghton Lake Dr Ste 109
Houghton Lake, MI 48629
(517) 422-5700
Fax: (517) 422-5738
Key Contact:
Mr. John L. Harris, Co-Manager
Ms. Vicki M. Harris, Co-Manager

1510 Springport Rd Ste A
Jackson, MI 49202
(517) 841-1336
Fax: (517) 841-1345
Email: don@mrjackson.com
Web: www.mrjackson.com
Key Contact:
Mr. Don Bills, Manager

4021 W Main St Ste 200
Briarwood Valley Office Plz
Kalamazoo, MI 49006
(616) 381-1153
Fax: (616) 381-8031
Email: info@mrikazoo.com
Web: www.mrikazoo.com
Key Contact:
Mr. Cy Tessin, President
Mr. Norm Grosse, Operations Manager

302 S Water St
Marine City, MI 48039-1689
(810) 765-3480
Fax: (810) 765-3420
Email: mri@i-is.com
Key Contact:
Mr. Bob Bommarito, Manager

425 W Huron St Ste 220
Milford, MI 48381
(248) 685-1166
Fax: (248) 676-2928
Email: mrwood@ic.net
Web: www.mrwestoaklanddetroit.com
Key Contact:
Ms. Sue Dolato

44450 Pine Tree Dr Ste 202
Plymouth, MI 48170-3869
(734) 451-5300
Fax: (734) 451-5301
Email: mrplymouth@earthlink.net
Key Contact:
Mr. Joseph Boelter

4901 Towne Ctr Ste 115
Saginaw, MI 48604
(517) 792-5899
Fax: (517) 792-5880
Key Contact:
Mr. Mohammed Khan

3622 Veterans Dr Ste 1
Traverse City, MI 49684
(616) 968-5959
Fax: (616) 968-5961
Email: mrtc@traverse.com
Web: www.traverse.com/mri
Key Contact:
Ms. Mary Barker

755 W Big Beaver Ste 101
Top of Troy
Troy, MI 48084
(248) 764-4200
Fax: (248) 764-4242
Email: troygroup@mrtroy2.com
Web: www.mrtroy.com
Key Contact:
Mr. Ed J. Moeller, Manager

12940 Harriet Ave S Ste 115
Burnsville, MN 55337
(952) 736-9540
Fax: (952) 736-9539
Email: dan@mrijobs.net
Web: www.mrijobs.net
Key Contact:
Mr. Daniel Bessinger

4151 Knob Dr Ste 205
Eagan, MN 55122
Key Contact:
Mr. Robert Horn
Mr. Jeff Horn

351 Second St
Excelsior, MN 55331
(612) 401-3372
Fax: (952) 401-3392

Key Contact:
Mr. Timothy Colleran, Manager

7964 University Ave NE
Fridley, MN 55432
(612) 784-4199
Fax: (612) 717-7378
Email: mrifridley@earthlink.net
Key Contact:
Mr. Al Johnson, Manager
Ms. Jolene D. Johnson

PO Box 1197
Camdenton, MO 65020
(573) 346-4833
Fax: (573) 346-1705
Email: careers@usmo.com
Key Contact:
Ms. Judy H. Hodgson, Co-Owner/Manager
Mr. Robert D. Hodgson, Co-Owner/Manager

200 Fabricator Dr
Meramec Valley Ctr
Fenton, MO 63026
(636) 349-4455
Fax: (636) 326-4207
Key Contact:
Mr. Edward Travis, General Manager
Mr. Glenwood Alley, Manager

712 Broadway Ste 500
Soho Office Ctr
Kansas City, MO 64105
(816) 221-2377
Fax: (816) 221-7164
Key Contact:
Mr. Steve Orr, Co-Manager
Ms. Eileen Mason, Co-Manager

14615 Manchester Rd Ste 202
Manchester, MO 63011-3790
(314) 391-3777
Fax: (636) 391-3444
Email: cdt@chstrfld.mrinet.com
Key Contact:
Mr. Carl D. Travis, Manager

1807 E Edgewood Ste B
The Edgewood
Springfield, MO 65804
(417) 882-6220
Fax: (417) 882-7855
Key Contact:
Mr. Rod Panyik, Manager

201 N Main St Ste 215
St. Charles, MO 63301-2828
(636) 940-7444
Fax: (636) 940-7555
Email: mrstcharles@postnet.com
Web: www.mristc.com
Key Contact:
Mr. Martin White, Manager

11701 Borman Dr Ste 250
St. Louis, MO 63146
(314) 991-4355
Fax: (314) 991-9586
Email: mrwestport@bigfoot.com
Key Contact:
Mr. Phil L. Bertsch, General Manager
Mr. Rob Hunter, Manager
Mr. Chris Heinz, Manager

3301 Rider Trl S Ste 100
St. Louis, MO 63045-1309
(314) 344-0959
Fax: (314) 298-7706
Email: phoene@mricorp.mrinet.com
Key Contact:
Mr. Patrick B. Hoene, Manager

16284 Westwood Business Park Dr
Wildwood, MO 63021-4501
(314) 256-2624
Fax: (314) 256-2644
Email: mrrecruiter@mrwildwood.com
Web: www.mrwildwood.com
Key Contact:
Mr. Steve Howes, Manager

4530 S Eastern Copper Point Ste A-12
Las Vegas, NV 89119-6181
(702) 733-1818
Fax: (702) 733-0102
Email: mrlv@mrlasvegas.com
Web: www.mrlasvegas.com
Key Contact:
Mr. Joel Lalonde, Manager

810 S Durango Dr Ste 109
Las Vegas, NV 89128
(702) 243-8189
Fax: (702) 243-8190
Email: mrsummerlin@hotmail.com
Key Contact:
Mr. Raymond P. Nolan, Manager

40B 1st Ave
Atlantic Highlands, NJ 07716
(732) 708-0320
Fax: (732) 708-0323
Email: mrimiddletown@earthlink.net
Key Contact - Specialty:
Mr. Steve Sumner, President - *Insurance (property, casualty)*
Mrs. Vicki Sumner, Vice President - *Insurance (property, casualty)*

110 Lakeside Dr W
Belvedere, NJ 07823
(908) 475-0033
Fax: (908) 475-0175
Email: jupham@wematchjobs.com
Web: www.wematchjobs.com
Key Contact:
Mr. Jim Upham

10 Anderson Rd Ste 7
Bernardsville, NJ 07924-2319
(908) 204-0070
Fax: (908) 204-9716
Email: compusearch@rcn.com
Key Contact:
Ms. Debbie A. Davidson, Co-Manager
Mr. Marlon W. O'Brien, Co-Manager

971 Rte 202N Fl 2
Branchburg, NJ 08876
(908) 541-9222
Fax: (908) 541-9230
Email: kit@mrbedminster.com
Key Contact:
Ms. Kit Welge, Co-Manager
Mr. Al Hauser, Co-Manager

1011 Rte 22 - W Ste 301 Fl 3
Bridgewater, NJ 08807
(908) 725-2595
Fax: (908) 725-0439
Email: mr@mrbridgewater.com
Web: www.mrbridgewater.com
Key Contact:
Mr. Barry S. Smith, President
Ms. Suzanne Politi, Vice President of Sales - *OM5 administrative services, sales consultants*
Mr. Mark Egner, Vice President of Sales

440 County Rd 513 Ste 207
Califon, NJ 07830
(908) 832-6455
Fax: (908) 832-6525
Key Contact:
Ms. Sarah J. Rodgers, Manager

200 Munsonhurst Rd Ste 104
Sterling Plz
Franklin, NJ 07871
(973) 823-1888
Fax: (973) 823-1620
Email: lance@retailplacement.com
Web: www.retailplacement.com
Key Contact:
Mr. Lance M. Incitti, Manager

855 Bloomfield Ave Ste 205
Glen Ridge, NJ 07028
(973) 259-9990
Fax: (973) 259-9988
Key Contact:
Mr. Michael Potters

Ms. Kate Potters
19 Tanner St
Haddonfield, NJ 08033
(856) 428-2233
Fax: (609) 428-7733
Email: haddon!manager@mrinet.com
Key Contact:
Mr. Roy P. Kelly, Manager

2517 Hwy 35 Ste 101 Bldg E
Manasquan Township, NJ 08736
(732) 528-7410
Fax: (732) 528-7420
Email: careers@mriconnection.com
Key Contact:
Mr. Allan Jordan

46 Bayard St Ste 209
New Brunswick, NJ 08901
(732) 246-1212
Fax: (732) 246-1241
Key Contact:
Mr. Randy Jones
Mr. Michael Rose

750 Hamburg Tpke Ste 203
Pompton Lakes, NJ 07442-1418
(201) 831-7778
Fax: (201) 831-0233
Email: zawickid@idt.net
Key Contact:
Mr. David Zawicki, Manager

186 Princeton-Highstown Rd
Princeton Junction, NJ 08550
Email: manager@windsor.mrinet.com

2494 Moore Rd Ste 1B
Toms River, NJ 08753
(732) 255-9565
Fax: (732) 255-9566
Email: jhoepfner@mritomsriver.com
Key Contact - Specialty:
Mr. John Hoepfner, President - *Promotion marketing (point of purchase)*

151 Fries Mills RD Ste 503-B
University Executive Campus
Turnersville, NJ 08012
(856) 228-4200
Fax: (856) 228-3333
Key Contact:
Ms. Karen Lynch
Mr. Joseph Lynch

1 Woodbridge Ctr Ste 605
Woodbridge, NJ 07095
(732) 636-9000
Fax: (732) 636-5000
Email: pratap@mriwoodbridge.com
Web: www.mriwoodbridge.com
Key Contact:
Pratap Jiandani

55 Newton Ave
Woodbury, NJ 08096-4608
(856) 686-3800
Fax: (856) 686-3805
Email: bwolfson@comcastwork.net
Key Contact:
Mr. Brian Wolfson

2500 Louisiana Blvd NE Ste 506
Albuquerque, NM 87110-4319
(505) 346-4700
Fax: (505) 346-4701
Email: mrits@earthlink.net
Key Contact:
Mr. Tom J. Schneider, Manager

1850 Old Pecos Trl Ste H
Santa Fe, NM 87505-4760
(505) 982-5445
Fax: (505) 982-7170
Email: manager@santafe.mrinet.com
Key Contact:
Mr. Bill Miller, Manager

4 Executive Park Dr
Stuyvesant Plz
Albany, NY 12203-3707
(518) 438-7722
Fax: (518) 438-0948
Email: bob@mrialbany.com
Key Contact:
Mr. Bob T. Mulcahey, Manager

6080 Jericho Tpke Ste 201
Commack Station, NY 11725
(631) 462-6688
Fax: (631) 462-6969
Email: brianf@proactivesearch.com
Web: www.proactivesearch.com
Key Contact:
Mr. Brian Feldman
Mr. Scott Bergman

33 Walt Whitman Rd Ste 107
Huntington Station, NY 11746-3627
(516) 385-0633
Fax: (516) 385-0759
Email: salcon@scfarmington.com
Web: www.networker-search.com
Key Contact:
Mr. Bob Levitt, Manager

2 Church St
PO Box 218
Madrid, NY 13660
(315) 322-0222
Fax: (315) 322-0220
Email: stlawrnc!manager@mrinet.com
Key Contact:
Mr. Nicky Scott, Manager

254 S Main St Fl 3
New City, NY 10956
Email: dgantshar@merrainegroup.com
Key Contact:
Mr. David Gantshar
Ms. Meredith Gantshar

928 Broadway Ste 1017
New York, NY 10010
(212) 979-5902
Fax: (212) 979-5903
Email: jjonas@mrmanhattanfi.com
Web: www.mrmanhattanfi.com
Key Contact:
Mr. John Jonas

225 Main St Ste 204
Northport, NY 11768
(631) 261-0400
Fax: (516) 261-8575
Email: mrautomation@unidial.com
Key Contact - Specialty:
Mr. Sebastian F. LiVolsi, General Manager - *Technical, engineering*

21 Perry St
Port Jefferson, NY 11777
(631) 331-7555
Fax: (631) 331-2814
Email: recruiters@portjeff.net
Key Contact:
Mr. Dominick Patti
Ms. Barbara Patti

16 Main St W Ste 225
Powers Bldg
Rochester, NY 14614-1601
(716) 454-2440
Fax: (716) 454-4092
Email: rocmri@yahoo.com
Key Contact:
Mr. Jerry Annesi, Manager

1721 Black River Blvd Ste 205
Executive Bldg
Rome, NY 13440
(315) 339-6342
Fax: (315) 339-6415
Key Contact:
Mr. Carl Tardugno, Manager

2119 Sunset Ave
Utica, NY 13502
(315) 732-4516
Fax: (315) 732-5689
Email: mribob@borg.com
Key Contact:
Mr. Bob Mosca, Manager

117A Victor Heights Pkwy
Victor, NY 14564
(716) 742-1060
Fax: (716) 742-1098
Email: jeffg@mrivictor.com
Web: www.mrivictor.com
Key Contact:
Mr. Jeff Garrison, Manager

19 Limestone Dr Ste 10
Williamsville, NY 14221
(716) 631-3200
Fax: (716) 631-3222
Email: sheryl@straussgroupinc.com
Web: www.straussgroupinc.com
Key Contact:
Mr. Randy Strauss

PO Box 2376
Banner Elk, NC 28604-2376
(828) 898-8080
Fax: (828) 898-8098
Email: info@mraverycty.com
Key Contact:
Ms. Carroll Hickman

104 E College Ave
PO Box 1405
Boiling Springs, NC 28017-1405
(704) 434-0211
Fax: (704) 434-0274
Email: shelby!manager@mrinet.com
Web: www.jobs-unlimited.com
Key Contact:
Mr. Dave G. Holland, Co-Manager
Mr. Lee S. Sherrill, Co-Manager

PO Box 699
Bunn, NC 27508
(919) 269-6612
Fax: (919) 269-6676
Email: mgtrecrecruiters@mindspring.com
Key Contact:
Mr. Dan P. Cone, Manager

5955 Carnegie Blvd Ste 300
Charlotte, NC 28209
(704) 944-9800
Fax: (704) 944-8098
Email: admin@mricharlotte.com
Web: www.mricharlotte.com
Key Contact:
Mr. Thomas Near, General Manager
Mr. Dave Camp, Manager

2310 S Miami Blvd Ste 232
Durham, NC 27703
(919) 806-0990
Fax: (919) 806-0085
Email: loiribb@mrdurham.com
Key Contact:
Ms. Lori Bush
Mr. Jack Bush

5102 Chapel Hill-Durham Blvd Ste 112
Durham, NC 27707
(919) 489-6521
Fax: (919) 493-4611
Email: sknaussmri@aol.com
Key Contact:
Mr. Arthur Deberry, Manager

6011 Fayetteville Rd Ste 203
Pine Ridge Office Park
Durham, NC 27713-8547
(919) 572-2292
Fax: (919) 572-6556
Email: god@tripark.mrinet.com
Key Contact:
Mr. Robert Bradley, Manager

PO Box 5330
Emerald Isle, NC 28594
(252) 354-7600
Fax: (252) 354-7700
Email: jdl@mremerald.com
Web: www.mr-nc.com
Key Contact:
Mr. James Liles, Manager

835 Highland Ave SE
Hickory, NC 28602-1140
(828) 324-2020
Fax: (828) 324-6895
Email: help@mrihky.com
Web: www.mri.com
Key Contact:
Mr. Scott Volz, General Manager
Mr. Bill Gaillard, CSAM, Manager

PO Box 6077
Hickory, NC 28601
(828) 495-8233
Fax: (828) 495-7431
Email: mrbethlehem@mrbethlehem.com
Web: www.mrbethlehem.com
Key Contact:
Mr. Byron L. King, Manager

109-C Millstone Dr
Old Mill Business Park
Hillsborough, NC 27278
(919) 732-6272
Fax: (919) 732-2118
Email: john@mritech.com
Web: www.mritech.com
Key Contact:
Mr. John Wyatt, Manager

PO Box 8
Louisburg, NC 27549-0008
(919) 496-2153
Fax: (919) 496-1417
Email: dperry@ncol.net
Key Contact:
Mr. Darrell L. Perry, Jr., Manager

106 E Decatur St Ste A
Madison, NC 27025-1906
(336) 427-6153
Fax: (336) 427-6154
Email: mrrock@vnet.net
Web: www.htinfo.com/mrimrrockinghamcty.htm
Key Contact:
Mr. Gerald Summerlin, Manager

1502 N Charlotte Ave
Monroe, NC 28110
(704) 291-7731
Fax: (704) 291-9689
Email: pirwin@mrimonroenc.com
Key Contact:
Mr. Phil Irwin, Manager

322 E Center Ave
Mooresville, NC 28115
(704) 664-4997
Fax: (704) 664-0841
Email: hsykesnet@aol.com
Key Contact:
Mr. Hugh L. Sykes, Manager

630 Davis Dr Ste 220
Morrisville, NC 27713
Key Contact:
Mr. Kirk Sears
Mr. Richard Sears
Ms. Anastasia Pucci

200 N Main St Ste 208
Chamber of Commerce Bldg
Mt. Airy, NC 27030
(336) 786-4212
Fax: (336) 786-8415
Email: plastics@tcia.net
Web: www.theplasticsfirm.com
Key Contact:
Mr. Marc Pumerantz

120 N Franklin St Bldg J Ste 101
Rocky Mount, NC 27804-5448
(252) 446-3456
Fax: (252) 446-3556
Email: mri@rockymountnc.com
Key Contact:
Mr. Danny Sewell

PO Box 2464
Shelby, NC 28151
(704) 480-7889
Fax: (704) 480-7890
Email: mangrec@shelby.net
Key Contact:
Mr. Rex Whicker
Mr. Skip Almond

117 N Center St
Statesville, NC 28677
(704) 871-9890
Fax: (704) 873-2143
Email: manager@statsvil.mrinet.com
Key Contact:
Mr. Neil F. Coleman, Manager

1120 Randolph St Bldg 4 Ste 45
Thomasville, NC 27360
(336) 475-8010
Fax: (336) 475-8621
Email: mrtvl@northstate.net
Key Contact:
Mr. Ron Steed

4020 Oleander Dr Ste 1
Wilmington, NC 28403
(910) 794-4044
Fax: (910) 794-4055
Email: tryan@mrcbeach.com
Key Contact:
Mr. Tom Ryan, President/Owner

150 E Firetower Rd Ste D
Winterville, NC 28590
(252) 439-0966
Fax: (252) 439-0977
Key Contact:
Mr. Gene Taylor, Manager

112 N University Dr Ste 300
Fargo, ND 58102
Key Contact:
Mr. Joe Allen

851 Orchard Ln Ste C
Beavercreek, OH 45434
(937) 427-7222
Fax: (937) 427-7227
Key Contact:
Mr. Tim Shelton, Co-Manager
Mr. Jeff Milam, Co-Manager

866 E Franklin St Ste C
Centerville, OH 45459-5608
Email: gap@mrctv.com
Key Contact:
Mr. George Plotner

9700 Rockside Rd Ste 100
Cleveland, OH 44125-6264
(440) 642-5788
Fax: (216) 642-5933
Key Contact:
Mr. Paul F. Montigny, General Manager
Mr. Robert E. Jacobson, Manager

6025 Dixie Hwy Ste 200
Fairfield, OH 45014-4253
(513) 682-4020
Fax: (513) 682-4030
Email: mri@one.net
Key Contact:
Mr. Joseph J. Bierschwal, Manager

45 Milford Dr Ste 12
Hudson, OH 44236-2750
(330) 650-2300
Fax: (330) 342-1606
Email: mrihudsonjobs@alltel.net
Key Contact:
Mr. Jim Gorian

PO Box 31495
Independence, OH 44131-0495
(216) 621-5522
Fax: (216) 621-0491
Email: riomri1@ameritech.net
Key Contact:
Ms. Monica Rio, Manager

2200 Wales Ave NW Ste 211
Massillon, OH 44646
(330) 834-0600
Fax: (330) 834-0601
Key Contact:
Mr. David Reliford

6690 Beta Dr Mt. Vernon Bldg Ste 100
Mayfield Village, OH 44143
(440) 684-6150
Fax: (440) 684-6153
Email: twesley@mrifluidpower.com
Web: www.mrifluidpower.com
Key Contact:
Mr. Terry R. Wesley, Manager

8039 Broadmoor Rd Mentor 306 Bldg Ste 20
Mentor, OH 44060
(440) 946-2355
Fax: (440) 946-5488
Email: mrilake@earthlink.net
Key Contact - Specialty:
Mr. Ronald Sterling, General Manager - *Banking*
Ms. Cheryl Sterling, Manager - *Banking*

34100 Ctr Ridge Rd Ste 110
Liberty Ctr
North Ridgeville, OH 44039-3220
(440) 327-2800
Fax: (440) 327-6991
Email: poejo@ix.netcom.com
Key Contact:
Mr. James P. Spellacy, Manager

10104 Brewster Ln Ste 150
Powell, OH 43065
(614) 336-3637
Fax: (614) 336-3638
Email: contract@mri-usa-search.com
Web: www.mri-usa-search.com
Key Contact:
Mr. Ken Kessler

3942 N Hampton Dr
Powell, OH 43065
(614) 792-8285
Fax: (614) 792-8265
Email: cbw@delcty.mrinet.com
Key Contact:
Mr. Chris Watkins
Mr. Greg Watkins

8972 Darrow Rd Ste 302A
Twinsburg, OH 44087
(330) 405-0400
Fax: (330) 405-0405
Key Contact:
Mr. Phil Slive

8945 Brookside Ste 202
West Chester, OH 45069
(513) 755-4300
Fax: (513) 755-4301
Email: mriwestchester@mindspring.com
Key Contact:
Mr. Chuck Harris

925 N State St Ste Q
Westerville, OH 43082
(614) 865-1500
Fax: (614) 865-1600
Key Contact:
Mr. Timothy Coan

38210 Glenn Ave
Willoughby, OH 44094-1605
(440) 953-9559
Fax: (440) 953-9944
Email: mriwillo@hotmail.com
Key Contact:
Mr. Thomas Christopher, Owner/Account
 Executive

Ms. Paula Christopher

1300 E 9th St Ste 4
Le Cour Office Park
Edmond, OK 73034-5709
(405) 348-5550
Fax: (405) 348-8808
Email: mri@mriedmond.com
Web: www.mriedmond.com
Key Contact:
Mr. Craig S. Lyman, Manager

205 NW 63rd St Ste 390
Oklahoma City, OK 73116
(405) 607-2425
Fax: (405) 607-2428
Email: careers@mriokcnorth.com
Key Contact:
Mr. Steve Kinney, Manager

5801 E 41st St Ste 440
Tulsa, OK 74135-5614
(918) 663-6744
Fax: (918) 663-1783
Email: mritulsa@msn.com
Web: www.mri-tulsa.com
Key Contact:
Mr. Anthony A. Wolters, General Manager
Mr. Bill Wetterman, Manager
Mr. Mark Wolters

2141 Downyflake Ln
Allentown, PA 18103-4774
(610) 797-8863
Fax: (610) 797-8873
Email: recruiter@mriallentown.com
Web: www.mriallentown.com
Key Contact:
Mr. Gary Filko, Manager

PO Box 648
Chinchilla, PA 18410-0648
(570) 587-9909
Fax: (570) 587-9910
Email: inquiries@mros.com
Web: www.mros.com
Key Contact:
Mr. Victor Kochmer, Co-Manager
Ms. Sheila Kochmer, Co-Manager

428 Pennsylvania Ave Fl 2
Ft. Washington, PA 19034-3408
(215) 793-9444
Fax: (215) 793-9451
Email: marc@voicenet.com
Key Contact:
Ms. Sandra Teichman, Co-Manager
Mr. Mark Teichman, Co-Manager

55 Pierce Ln Ste 202
Montoursville, PA 17754
(570) 368-2277
Fax: (570) 368-7586
Key Contact:
Mr. Wally A. Helt, Manager

171 W Lancaster Ave Fl 2
Paoli, PA 19301
(610) 993-9530
Fax: (610) 993-9740
Key Contact:
Mr. Rick Knoll

1818 Market St Ste 1400
Philadelphia, PA 19103
(267) 256-2320
Fax: (267) 330-0333
Web: www.banister.cc
Key Contact:
Mr. Patrick Sylvester

325 Chestnut St Ste 1106
Constitution Pl
Philadelphia, PA 19106
(215) 829-1900
Fax: (215) 829-1919
Email: mail@mriphiladelphia.net
Key Contact:
Mr. Thomas A. Lucas, Manager

2589 Washington Rd Ste 435
Pittsburgh, PA 15241
(412) 831-7290
Fax: (412) 831-7298
Email: resume@gomri.com
Web: www.gomri.com
Key Contact:
Mr. Jim Gallagher, Co-Manager
Ms. Sallie Gallagher, Co-Manager
Mr. Mark M. Wawrzeniak, Co-Manager

300 Weyman Plz Ste 200
Pittsburgh, PA 15236
(412) 885-5222
Fax: (412) 885-2181
Email: mrpitsth@aol.com
Key Contact:
Mr. Paul R. Rossman, Co-Manager
Mr. Andy J. Hallam, Co-Manager

446 N Claude A Lord Blvd Ste 2
Pottsville, PA 17901
(570) 624-7050
Fax: (570) 624-7055
Key Contact:
Mr. John Hoffman

4031B Skippack Pike
PO Box 879
Skippack, PA 19474
(610) 584-8882
Fax: (610) 584-8801
Email: jmkeller@mripower.com
Web: www.mripower.com
Key Contact:
Mr. Bob Eschenbach, Manager

809 N Bethlehem Pike
PO Box 640
Spring House, PA 19477
(215) 283-1800
Fax: (215) 283-2999
Email: mereisner@merwingroup.com
Key Contact:
Mr. Mark Reisner, Managing Director
Miss Nettie Potter, Administrative Associate
Ms. Nicole Freilich, Administrative Associate

1815 Schadt Ave Ste 4
Peachtree Office Plz
Whitehall, PA 18052-3761
(610) 740-9200
Fax: (610) 740-9224
Email: mrlehigh@profcareer.com
Key Contact:
Mr. Denny P. Farkas, Manager

2300 Computer Ave Ste J54
Willow Grove, PA 19090
(215) 830-9211
Fax: (215) 830-9216
Key Contact:
Ms. Fern Klein, Co-Manager
Mr. Robert Klein, Co-Manager

101 Dyer St Ste 5-A
Providence, RI 02903-3904
(401) 274-2810
Fax: (401) 274-6440
Email: providence@mri-boston.com
Key Contact:
Mr. Stephen W. Morse, General Manager

905 W DeKalb St Ste E
PO Box 690
Camden, SC 29020
(803) 424-1778
Fax: (803) 424-1454
Email: mri@camden.net
Key Contact - Specialty:
Mr. Ev Stephen, owner - *Manufacturing,*
 engineering, sales

2800 Bush River Rd Ste 4
Columbia, SC 29210-5698
(803) 772-0300
Fax: (803) 772-4600
Email: mrilex@bellsouth.net
Key Contact:
Mr. Roger Hall, Co-Manager

Ms. Debbie Hall, Co-Manager

1473 Stuart Engals Blvd
Mt. Pleasant, SC 29464
(864) 216-6565
Fax: (843) 216-6566
Key Contact:
Mr. Patrick Warren

266 W Coleman Blvd Ste 102
Mt. Pleasant, SC 29464
(843) 856-0544
Fax: (843) 856-0547
Email: jdooley@theheadhunter.com
Web: www.theheadhunter.com
Key Contact:
Mr. James L. Dooley, CSAM, Manager

113 Court St
Pickens, SC 29671-2372
(864) 878-1113
Fax: (864) 878-1410
Email: mripickens@mindspring.com
Key Contact:
Mr. Ed Parris, Jr., Manager

231 Wilson Pike Cir Ste 204
Brentwood, TN 37027
(615) 507-1717
Fax: (615) 507-1727
Email: admin@advantage-search.com
Web: www.advantage-search.com
Key Contact:
Mr. Larry Vaughn
Ms. Lynn Varela

65 Lawson Ln
Dyersburg, TN 38024
(901) 285-2499
Fax: (901) 285-1159
Email: btucker@onemain.com
Key Contact:
Mr. William Tucker

4808 Hixson Pike
Hixson, TN 37343
(423) 877-4040
Fax: (423) 877-4466
Key Contact:
Mr. Chub Ensminger, Manager

530 Hwy 321 N Ste 303
Lenoir City, TN 37771-8914
(865) 986-3000
Fax: (865) 986-0874
Email: mrilc@aol.com
Key Contact:
Mr. Ray S. Strobo, Manager

5158 Stage Rd Ste 130
Memphis, TN 38134-3164
(901) 888-2580
Fax: (901) 888-2581
Email: manager@bartlett.mrinet.com
Key Contact:
Mr. George A. Harants, Manager

131 Heritage Park Dr Ste 102
Murfreesboro, TN 37133
(615) 890-7623
Fax: (615) 890-9511
Email: tomhyde@mrjapanese.com
Key Contact:
Mr. Tom G. Hyde, Manager
Yukari Ishii

2625 N Josey Ln Ste 302
Carrollton, TX 75007-5546
(972) 446-2254
Fax: (972) 446-6718
Email: mri.addison@cwix.com
Key Contact:
Mr. Dan Finch, Manager

13101 Preston Rd Ste 560
Dallas, TX 75240
(972) 788-1515
Fax: (972) 701-8242
Email: blineback@mridallas.com
Key Contact:
Mr. Robert Lineback, General Manager

Ms. Pam Lineback, Manager

13747 Montfort Dr Ste 337
Dallas, TX 75240-4460
(972) 788-9288
Fax: (972) 788-9298
Web: www.mrdallas.com
Key Contact:
Ms. Judy Daugherty, Co-Manager - *Printing,
commercial, label, packaging, direct mail*
Mr. Hal Daugherty, Co-Manager - *General
manufacturing, engineering, HR, logistics
distribution, finance*
Mr. Adam Outen, Account Executive - *Food and
beverage (industrial sales), R & D*
Mr. Jay Jones, Account Executive - *Food and
beverage (manufacturing)*
Mr. James Warner, Account Executive - *Medical
device sales & marketing*
Mr. Alan Fine, Account Executive - *Food and
beverage (manufacturing)*
Mr. Ira Sullivan, Account Executive - *Finance and
accounting*
Mrs. Patricia Padgett, Project Coordinator -
Medical device, sales & marketing
Ms. Rhonda Tademy, Administrator

3400 Carlisle St Ste 230
Dallas, TX 75204
(214) 969-0300
Fax: (214) 969-6996
Email: don@mrturtlecreek.com
Key Contact:
Mr. Don Leggett

5646 Milton Ste 427
Dallas, TX 75206

1229 E Pleasant Run Rd Ste 204
Desoto, TX 75115
(972) 224-1467
Fax: (972) 224-7477
Key Contact:
Mr. Edmond Graham
Mr. Lee Keller

6006 N Mesa St Ste 408
El Paso, TX 79912-4623
(915) 833-8211
Fax: (915) 833-8254
Email: mgmtrecep@aol.com
Key Contact:
Ms. Victoria A. Lummus, Co-Manager
Ms. Cindy L. Capanna, Co-Manager

5300 Town & Country Blvd Ste 160
Frisco, TX 75034
(972) 668-6070
Fax: (972) 668-6071
Email: fredjwilliams@earthlink.net
Key Contact:
Mr. Fred J. Williams

1172 Country Club Ln
Ft. Worth, TX 76112
(817) 457-9555
Fax: (817) 457-9998
Email: gary@gmmri.com
Web: www.grmmri.com
Key Contact:
Mr. Gary Morris, President

2200 Space Park Dr Ste 420
Houston, TX 77058-3663
(281) 335-0363
Fax: (281) 335-0362
Email: kray@mrclearlake.com
Key Contact:
Mr. Tom Honeywill

1333 Corporate Dr Ste 211
Irving, TX 75038
(972) 550-2424
Fax: (972) 550-3965
Email: broll@onramp.net
Key Contact:
Mr. Bill Roll, Manager

4201 Wingren Dr Ste 200
Irving, TX 75062
(972) 717-4402
Fax: (972) 717-4502
Email: mriworld@onramp.net
Key Contact:
Mr. Bill Easton, Manager

8432 Sterling Ste 103
Irving, TX 75063
Email: ken@naishgroup.com

8445 Freeport Pkwy Ste 330
Irving, TX 75063
(972) 929-2222
Fax: (972) 929-2223
Email: jobs@itts.com
Key Contact:
Mr. Eric K. Jacobson, Manager

1202 Richardson Dr Ste 112
Richardson, TX 75080
(972) 669-3999
Fax: (972) 669-4737
Email: lpm@mrrichardson.com
Key Contact:
Mr. Lawrence McClung

7550 Interstate Hwy 10 W Ste 1230
San Antonio, TX 78229
(210) 525-1800
Fax: (210) 525-9633
Email: mrg@mrgoicoechea.com
Key Contact:
Mr. Sam Goicoechea, Co-Manager
Ms. Lydia Goicoechea, Co-Manager

107 Palo Pinto St
PO Box 1804
Weatherford, TX 76086
(817) 599-6333
Fax: (817) 599-6332
Email: bbaez@thesciantgroup.com
Key Contact:
Ms. Barbara Baez

1762B Prospector Ave
Park City, UT 84060
(435) 647-5670
Fax: (435) 647-3958
Email: mrpc@mrparkcity.com
Key Contact:
Mr. Gregory C. Esty, Co-Manager
Ms. Janet S. Esty, Co-Manager

6600 S 1100 E Ste 520
Salt Lake City, UT 84121-2400
(801) 264-9800
Fax: (801) 264-9807
Email: dirk@mrislc.com
Web: www.mrislc.com
Key Contact:
Mr. Dirk Cotterell

321 N Mall Dr Bldg VW Ste 101
St. George, UT 84790
(435) 688-9900
Fax: (435) 688-9010
Email: msumner@mriutah.com
Key Contact:
Mr. Michael Sumner
Mr. Robert Hawks

187 St. Paul St Ste 4
Burlington, VT 05401-4689
(802) 865-0541
Fax: (802) 865-3664
Email: mri@mri-vt.com
Key Contact:
Mr. Alan Nyhan, Manager

1700 N Moore St Ste 1005
Arlington, VA 22209
(703) 351-1300
Fax: (703) 351-1562
Email: roger.branch@verizon.net
Key Contact:
Mr. Roger Branch

Let www.ExecutiveAgent.com e-mail your resume now.

2114 Angus Rd Ste 235
Charlottesville, VA 22901-2768
(804) 293-0800
Fax: (804) 293-0813
Email: jrm@charvil.mrinet.com
Key Contact:
Mr. Jim Metzgar, Manager

1039 Sterling Rd Ste 202
Herndon, VA 20170
(703) 467-9110
Fax: (703) 467-9115
Email: chris@mri-reston.com
Key Contact:
Mr. Chris Garcia, Co-Manager
Ms. Linda Garcia, Co-Manager

8783 Mathis Ave
Manassas, VA 20110
(703) 331-0855
Fax: (703) 365-9285
Email: resumes@mrparkplace.com
Key Contact:
Mr. Michael Park
Ms. Jana Park

212 Starling Ave Ste 201
Martinsville, VA 24112-3844
(540) 632-2355
Fax: (540) 632-0153
Email: careers@neocom.net
Key Contact:
Mr. Herschel Gurley, Manager

246 N Washington Ave
PO Box 450
Pulaski, VA 24301
(540) 980-3100
Fax: (540) 980-3300
Email: mrnrv@i-plus.net
Web: www.connectorjobs.com
Key Contact - Specialty:
Mr. Ed J. Beckett, Manager
Mr. Chuck Morris, Account Executive - *General manufacturing*
Mr. Gene Stewart, Account Executive - *General manufacturing*

7229 Forest Ave Ste 210
Highland II
Richmond, VA 23226
(804) 285-2071
Fax: (804) 282-4990
Email: info@richgroupusa.com
Web: www.richgroupusa.com
Key Contact:
Mr. Jay S. Schwartz, Manager

4560 S Blvd Ste 250
Virginia Beach, VA 23452-1160
(757) 490-0331
Fax: (757) 490-0129
Email: murphey@series2000.com
Web: www.jobstofill.com
Key Contact:
Mr. James F. Murphey, Manager

1309 Jamestown Rd Ste 204
Ste 204
Williamsburg, VA 23185
Key Contact:
Mr. Al Polson
Ms. Vicki Polson

400 108th Ave NE Ste 405
Bellevue, WA 98004
(425) 467-1323
Fax: (425) 467-1303
Email: infomrb@mrbellevue.com
Web: www.mrbellevue.com
Key Contact - Specialty:
Mr. Fred Novick - *Telecommunications*

1727 E Marine View Dr Ste B
Everett, WA 98201
(425) 303-0335
Fax: (425) 303-0495
Email: john@mreverett.com
Key Contact:
Mr. John McElroy, PE, Manager

2709 Jahn Ave NW Ste H-11
Gig Harbor, WA 98335
(253) 858-9991
Fax: (253) 858-5140
Email: mritacoma@msn.com
Key Contact:
Mr. Dennis R. Johnson, Manager

2633-A Parkmount Ln SW Ste B
Olympia, WA 98502
(360) 357-9996
Fax: (360) 357-9998
Email: dudley.pitchford@gte.net
Key Contact:
Mr. Jim J. Pitchford, Manager

16040 Christensen Rd Bldg 1 Ste 316
Seattle, WA 98188
(206) 242-7484
Fax: (206) 248-5005
Email: seasouth!manager@mrinet.com
Web: www.mritelecom.com
Key Contact:
Mr. Marc Goyette

633 N Mildred Ste F4
Tacoma, WA 98406
(253) 572-7542
Fax: (253) 565-7291
Email: mmtacoma@uswest.net
Key Contact:
Mr. Bill E. Saylor, Manager

117 Judity Dr
Charleston, WV 25312
(304) 344-5632
Fax: (304) 382-0448
Email: mrcharwv@aol.com
Web: www.htinfo.com/mrimrcharleston.htm
Key Contact:
Mr. Anthony P. Oliverio, Manager

2567 University Ave Ste 3021
Grand Ctrl Business Ctr
Morgantown, WV 26505
(304) 296-9800
Fax: (304) 296-2193
Email: mriray@westco.net
Key Contact:
Mr. Ray Wood

1711 Woolsey St Ste D
Delavan, WI 53115-2020
(262) 728-8886
Fax: (262) 728-8894
Email: mridelavan@genevaonline.com
Key Contact:
Mr. Dean Sanderson, Manager

1245 Cheyenne Ave Ste 102
Grafton, WI 53024
(262) 387-7777
Fax: (262) 387-7770
Email: mharris@mrigrafton.com
Web: www.mrigrafton.com
Key Contact:
Ms. Marinie Harris

PO Box 12708
Green Bay, WI 54307-2708
(920) 434-8770
Fax: (920) 434-9155
Email: mrigb@mrijobs.com
Web: www.mrijobs.com
Key Contact:
Mr. Garland E. Ross, Manager

5307 S 92nd St Ste 125
Valley View Ctr
Hales Corners, WI 53130
(414) 529-8020
Fax: (414) 529-8028
Email: careers@mrims.com
Web: www.pasadagroup.com
Key Contact:
Mr. Mark Simpson

772 Main St Ste 6
Lake Geneva, WI 53147
(262) 348-0100
Fax: (262) 348-0200
Email: mrlakegeneva@genevaonline.com
Key Contact:
Mr. Gary Cook

731 N Jackson St Ste 502
Milwaukee, WI 53202
(414) 278-9778
Fax: (414) 270-4520
Email: curranmri@aol.com
Key Contact:
Ms. Lisa Klug
Mr. Nicholas Curran

735 N Water St Ste 1228
Milwaukee, WI 53202
(414) 226-2420
Fax: (414) 226-2421
Email: mrimke@execpc.com
Web: www.mrimilwaukee.com
Key Contact:
Mr. Doug Lane

311 2nd St
PO Box 579
New Glarus, WI 53574-0595
(608) 527-6581
Fax: (608) 527-6582
Email: mrnewglarus@tds.net
Key Contact:
Mr. Gary Hooper

222 E Main St Ste 201
Port Washington, WI 53074
(262) 268-5187
Fax: (262) 268-5192
Key Contact:
Mr. Christopher Fox
Ms. Kathy Fox

PO Box 54
Banner, WY 82832
(307) 683-3096
Fax: (307) 683-3095
Email: resume@mriwyoming.com
Key Contact:
Ms. Teresa Phillips, Co-Manager
Mr. Bob Phillips, Co-Manager

710 Dorval Dr Ste 210
Toronto, ON L6K 3V7
Canada
Email: jody.leavoy@cdicorp.com
Key Contact:
Jody Leavoy

MRI of Birmingham

100 Carnoustie N
PO Box 381626
Birmingham, AL 35238-1626
(205) 991-6504
Fax: (205) 991-9086
Email: cpark@mri-bham.com
Web: www.brilliantpeople.com

Description: Satisfying your critical demand for people...the resource that ultimately determines an organization's profitability.

Key Contact - Specialty:
Mr. Cleve A. Park, President - *Accounting, human resources, manufacturing*

Salary minimum: $40,000

Functions: Mfg.

Industries: Chemicals, Drugs Mfg., Medical Devices, Metal Products, Banking, Brokers, Pharm Svcs., Packaging, Insurance, Healthcare

MRI of Mobile Company

106 N Bayview St
Fairhope, AL 36532
(251) 929-2705
Fax: (251) 929-2706

Email: rcbrock@zebra.net
Web: www.brilliantpeople.com

Description: Our firm is specializing in data processing professionals.

Key Contact:
Mr. Rufus C. Brock, President

Salary minimum: $18,000

Functions: Generalist, Nurses, Health Admin., Systems Dev., Systems Support, Engineering

Industries: Generalist, Chemicals, Misc. Mfg., Healthcare, Non-classifiable

MRI of Flagstaff
1515 N Main Ste A-1
Flagstaff, AZ 86004
(928) 213-1000
Fax: (928) 213-1001
Web: www.mriflagstaff.com

Description: We are a professional staffing firm specializing in IT sales, more specifically software, hardware, and services.

Key Contact:
Mr. Brian Petersen, Owner/President - *IT Sales*
Mr. John Clair, Account Executive - *IT sales*
Ms. Hope DeMello, Administrative Assistant

Functions: Sales Mgmt.

Industries: Higher Ed., E-commerce, IT Implementation, Call Centers, Network Infrastructure, Software

MRI of Tucson
2480 W Ruthrauff Rd Ste 140E
Tucson, AZ 85705
(520) 408-0702
Fax: (520) 408-0706
Email: careers@mroftucson.com
Web: www.mroftucson.com

Description: Our firm is a member of MRI, which is the number one executive search organization in the world. Our specialties are telecommunications, software and manufacturing.

Key Contact - Specialty:
Mr. John DeJong, Managing Member - *Agriculture, pork production*
Mr. Herb Garman, Managing Member - *Agriculture, wire & cable*

Salary minimum: $50,000

Functions: Generalist, Production, Mkt. Research, Mktg. Mgmt., Sales Mgmt., MIS Mgmt., Systems Analysis

Industries: Generalist, Agri., Forestry, Mining, Misc. Mfg., Telecoms

MRI of Tucson-Foothills
5102 N Ft Buchanan Tr
Tucson, AZ 85750
(520) 529-6818
Fax: (520) 529-6877
Email: admin@mrihitech.com
Web: www.mrihitech.com

Description: We provide executive search services throughout the United States to both candidates and businesses, specializing in the semiconductor and optical networking industries.

Key Contact - Specialty:
Ms. Lorian E. Roethlein, President - *Semi conductor manufacturing*
Mr. John Roethlein, General Manager - *Semi conductor manufacturing*

Salary minimum: $60,000

Functions: Mktg. Mgmt., Engineering

Industries: Telecoms, Digital, Wireless, Fiber Optic, Network Infrastructure

MRI of Little Rock
1701 Centerview Dr Ste 314
Redding Bldg
Little Rock, AR 72211-4313
(501) 224-0801
Fax: (501) 224-0798
Email: mri@search-team.com
Web: www.search-team.com

Description: We are a hybrid search firm working with client firms to attract key administrative, managerial, and technical professionals generally earning $50,000 to $120,000 for manufacturing, food processing, healthcare, information systems, or engineering specialties.

Key Contact:
Mr. Noel K. Hall, President

Salary minimum: $40,000

Functions: General Mgmt., Mfg., Product Dev., Production, Quality, Healthcare, Sales & Mktg., Finance, IT, Engineering

Industries: Energy, Utilities, Construction, Mfg., Food, Bev., Tobacco, Textiles, Apparel, Medical Devices, Plastics, Rubber, Metal Products, Machine, Appliance, Motor Vehicles, Computer Equip., Consumer Elect., Test, Measure Equip., Transportation, Wholesale, Retail, Finance, Accounting, Equip Svcs., Mgmt. Consulting, Telecoms, Packaging, Software, Healthcare, Hospitals

MRI of Anaheim
2300 E Katella Ave Ste 420
Anaheim, CA 92806-6046
(714) 978-1011
Fax: (714) 978-2835
Email: russ@mri-anaheim.com
Web: www.mri-anaheim.com

Description: Our technology group is your gateway to IS/IT staffing solutions worldwide. Utilizing the resources of Management Recruiters offices and networks around the world, the professionals at MRI-Anaheim aid clients with permanent, contract or project-related staffing solutions to meet the challenges in the year 2001 and beyond! Because of industry involvement and client relationships, we also provide individuals seeking to re-engineer their careers with challenging opportunities worldwide.

Key Contact - Specialty:
Mr. Russell Muller, President & General Manager - *Technical principles (emerging technologies)*

Salary minimum: $75,000

Functions: Generalist

Industries: Consumer Elect., Test, Measure Equip., Electronic, Elec. Components, Mgmt. Consulting, Telecoms, Wireless, Fiber Optic, Software

Professional Associations: NAPC

MRI of San Luis Obispo
7360 El Camino Real Ste A
Atascadero, CA 93422
(800) 462-8044
Fax: (805) 462-8047
Email: recruiter@healthcare-exec.com
Web: www.healthcare-exec.com

Description: We specialize in the placement of pharmaceutical/biotech industry positions in sales, marketing, market research, business development, and national accounts.

Key Contact:
Mr. Ralph Bunker, President - *Pharmaceutical, biotechnology, research & development, regulatory, compliance*
Ms. Nancy Hutchison

Salary minimum: $50,000

Functions: Generalist, Directors, Senior Mgmt., Middle Mgmt., Mkt. Research, Mktg. Mgmt., Sales Mgmt., R&D

Industries: Generalist, Drugs Mfg., Medical Devices

MRI of Templeton
7350 El Camino Real Ste 204
Atascadero, CA 93422-4655
(805) 460-0800
Fax: (805) 460-0860
Email: info@mrtempleton.com
Web: www.mrtempleton.com

Description: We are a full service search and recruiting firm specializing in mid to senior level positions in semi-conductors, optical components, and optical networking.

Key Contact:
Mr. Wayne Caruthers

Functions: Generalist

Industries: Electronic, Elec. Components, Telecoms, Fiber Optic, Network Infrastructure

MRI of Benicia
560 1st St Ste C-103
Benicia, CA 94510
(707) 747-7000
Fax: (707) 747-7008
Email: jlc@mrbenicia.com
Web: www.mrbenicia.com

Description: We are a full-service executive search and placement firm specializing in the recruitment and placement of low to upper-level management, engineers, sales, logistics, manufacturing, accounting, and finance personnel. Industry specialties include food and beverage, manufacturing, accounting and finance, sales and logistics.

Key Contact - Specialty:
Mr. Jeffery L. Cundick, General Manager - *Food & beverage manufacturing, logistics*
Mr. Sheila R. Linderman, Account Executive - *Finance and accounting (manufacturing)*
Mr. Ron Forbes, Account Executive - *Warehousing, transportation*

Salary minimum: $30,000

Functions: Generalist

Industries: Mfg., Food, Bev., Tobacco, Soap, Perf., Cosmtcs., Wholesale, Retail, Banking, Accounting

Professional Associations: CLM, NWFPA

MRI of Berkeley
2150 Shattuck Ave Ste 407
Berkeley, CA 94704-1306
(510) 486-8100
Fax: (510) 486-8189
Email: rhoward@mrberkeley.com
Web: www.mrberkeley.com

Description: We have been placing top candidates locally and nationally for over a decade. Our account managers are specialists in their industries and work directly with both candidates and clients.

Key Contact - Specialty:
Mr. Richard H. Howard, General Manager - *Banking*

Salary minimum: $60,000

Functions: Generalist

Industries: Construction, Mfg., Food, Bev., Tobacco, Transportation, Finance, Banking, Misc. Financial, Accounting, Healthcare

MRI of Clovis

150 Clovis Ave Ste 205
Clovis, CA 93612-1152
(559) 299-7992
Fax: (559) 299-2167
Email: food2@pacbell.net
Web: www.mrinet.com

Description: We are a member office of
Management Recruiters International, the world's
largest executive search with 1000 offices in 37
countries. MR. Clovis specializes in the successful
search and placement of supervisors, managers and
executives in the food & beverage processing
industry.

Key Contact - Specialty:
Mr. Gary Hendrickson, General Manager - *Food &
beverage processing*

Salary minimum: $35,000

Functions: Mfg.

Industries: Agri., Forestry, Mining, Mfg., Food,
Bev., Tobacco

Professional Associations: IFT

MRI of Dana Point

24681 La Plaza Dr Ste 280
Dana Point, CA 92629
(949) 443-2800
Fax: (949) 443-2806
Email: careers@mridp.com
Web: www.mridp.com

Description: Our firm is a member of MRI's
International President's Gold Club. Our office is a
full-service executive and management search firm
specializing in all skill sets within the
transportation, manufacturing, logistics,
warehousing-distribution, healthcare, food,
packaging, and information technology industries.
We perform contingency and retained searches
nationally with video conferencing and personality
profile capabilities.

Key Contact - Specialty:
Mr. Ed Provost, President/Owner - *Transportation*

Salary minimum: $30,000

Functions: General Mgmt., Mfg., Purchasing,
Packaging, Healthcare, Sales & Mktg., Finance,
IT, Specialized Svcs.

Industries: Generalist, Mfg., Food, Bev., Tobacco,
Transportation, Finance, Accounting

Professional Associations: CLM

MRI of Emeryville

2354 Powell St Ste A
Emeryville, CA 94608
(510) 658-1405
Fax: (510) 658-1428
Email: admin@mriemery.com
Web: www.biotech-jobs.com

Description: Our specialty is in the biotech industry
in the areas of research and development.

Key Contact - Specialty:
Mr. Mark Hoffman, Manager - *Biotechnology,
pharmaceuticals, medical device*

Salary minimum: $50,000

Functions: Generalist, Middle Mgmt., Product
Dev., Automation

Industries: Generalist, Drugs Mfg., Medical
Devices, Pharm Svcs., Biotech

MRI of Fremont

39270 Paseo Padre Pkwy Ste108
Fremont, CA 94538-1616
(510) 505-5125
Email: search@mrifremont.com
Web: www.mrifremont.com

Description: We are San Francisco Bay area
specialists in human resources and finance and
accounting.

Key Contact - Specialty:
Ms. Diane Anderson, E, Account Executive - *HR,
finance*
Mr. Jim L. Anderson, President - *HR, finance*

Salary minimum: $50,000

Functions: Middle Mgmt.

Industries: Computer Equip., Test, Measure Equip.,
Electronic, Elec. Components

Professional Associations: NCHRA

MRI of Fresno

5715 N West Ave Ste 101
Fresno, CA 93711-2366
(209) 432-3700
(800) 881-4139
Fax: (209) 432-9937
Email: ron@mri-fresno.com
Web: www.mri-fresno.com

Description: We were the 1990 MRI office of the
year. We were also in the top 5% of all MRI offices
for total placements in 2000. We were honored as
Presidents Gold Club, which is rated as top 100
offices of 1000 worldwide offices. We have been in
business for 23 years. Our firm specializes in heavy
construction, software sales, engineering,
telecommunications, accounting, plastics, food,
programmers, information systems, electronics,
pharmaceuticals, buyers and retail managers,
insurance, warehousing, and transportation. We
have the top human resources, information systems
programming department. We have two divisions,
MRI and CompuSearch, which is working
Internet/e-Commerce and MIS.

Key Contact - Specialty:
Mr. Ron L. Johnson, General Manager/President -
Sales, managed care, pharmaceuticals
Mr. Roland Tamayo, CSAM, Sales Manager -
*Electrical engineering, MIS, channel sales,
software sales, e-commerce*
Ms. Maureen McCarthy, CSAM, Account
Executive - *IS programmers, insurance, MIS
Mgrs, CTO's*
Mrs. Santina Roth, CSAM, National Account
Manager - *Food, engineering*
Mrs. Donna Johnson, Controller/Treasurer/Vice
President
Mrs. Tracy Sheran, Account Executive -
Management, JS
Ms. Rachel Sinclair, CSAM - *Building products,
branch managers, logistics, coatings*
Mrs. Catherine Olvera, CSAM, Nat'l. Account
Mgr./Acctg.,Controllers - *Plastic, blow molding*
Mrs. Jennifer Elizondo, CSAM, Sales Manager -
*Pharmaceutical sales, finance, insurance sales,
medical sales*

Functions: Purchasing, Distribution, Benefits,
Training, CFO's, MIS Mgmt., Network Admin.

Industries: Generalist

Professional Associations: NAWC, SHRP

MRI of Huntington Beach

18672 Florida St Ste 302-B
Huntington Beach, CA 92648
(714) 843-6433
Fax: (714) 843-6993
Email: resume@hbmri.com
Web: www.hbmri.com

Description: Our firm specializes in IT, financial,
medical, logistics, consumer products, food, and
restaurants/hospitality.

Key Contact:
Ms. Peggy Smith

Functions: Senior Mgmt., Middle Mgmt.,
Distribution, Finance, CFO's, Budgeting, Cash
Mgmt., M&A, IT, MIS Mgmt.

Industries: Generalist, Food, Bev., Tobacco, Drugs
Mfg., Medical Devices, Finance, Services,
Hospitality, Software, Biotech, Healthcare

MRI of Menlo Park

869 El Camino Real
Menlo Park, CA 94025-4807
(650) 617-9440
Email: ktn@mriresources.com
Web: www.mriresources.com

Key Contact:
Mr. Bruce Solomon, Manager

MRI of Northern California

591 Redwood Hwy Ste 2225
Mill Valley, CA 94941
(415) 383-7044
Fax: (415) 383-1426
Email: ecw@mrimvca.com
Web: www.mrimvca.com

Description: Fifteen plus years' experience in high-
tech recruiting. Individual specialists in
functions/industries listed. Nationwide network of
800 offices. Our specialty is fast response to urgent
needs.

Key Contact - Specialty:
Mr. Eric Wheel, General Manager - *Worldwide
web, virtual reality, educational software*

Salary minimum: $75,000

Functions: Generalist

Industries: Mfg., Invest. Banking, Venture Cap.,
Mgmt. Consulting, New Media, Communications

MRI of Monterey

494 Alvarado St Ste F
Monterey, CA 93940-2717
(831) 649-0737
Fax: (831) 649-0253
Email: mrmonterey@redshift.com

Description: A search firm specializing in surgical
and emergency nursing management with clients
nationwide.

Key Contact - Specialty:
Mr. Richard J. Kashinsky, General Manager -
*Healthcare, surgical, emergency services,
directors, managers*

Salary minimum: $60,000

Functions: Generalist, Nurses, Health Admin.

Industries: Generalist, Healthcare

MRI of Nevada City

313 Railroad Ave Ste 203
Nevada City, CA 95959
(530) 478-6478
Fax: (530) 478-6477
Email: recruiters@mrnc.net
Web: www.mrnc.com

Description: We are an executive recruiting firm
focused on the civil engineering and construction
management professions. We assist leading
engineering organizations build their business by
finding talented candidates for management,
professional, and technical positions. We provide
opportunities to qualified candidates to advance
their careers and meet their personal goals. Our
work is done in a confidential manner.

Key Contact:
Pat Havard

Salary minimum: $60,000

MRI of Orange

1 City Blvd W Ste 300
Orange, CA 92868
(714) 978-0500
Web: www.brilliantpeople.com

Description: We are a fifty million dollar corporate group-owned field office specializing in e-Business, high technology, healthcare and biotechnology, industrial and building products sales, sales marketing, sales management, and non-sales management positions.

Key Contact - Specialty:
Mr. David Pahl, General Manager - *E-business*
Mr. Ray Stayer, CSAM, Senior Account Manager - *Building products*
Mr. Bob Ward, Search Consultant - *Industrial specialist*
Mr. Scott Besso, Search Consultant - *IT, software*
Ms. Erin Favilla, Search Consultant - *Information technology*
Ms. Katie Archer, Search Consultant - *Healthcare*
Mr. Ken King, Search Consultant - *Healthcare, biotech*
Mr. Richard DiGioia, Search Consultant - *Insurance, finance*

Functions: Generalist, General Mgmt., Mfg., Healthcare, Sales & Mktg., HR Mgmt., IT, Specialized Svcs.

Industries: Generalist, Construction, Mfg., Wholesale, Services, Packaging, Software

MRI of Palo Alto

2479 E Bayshore Rd Ste 701
Embarcadero Corporate Ctr
Palo Alto, CA 94303
(650) 852-0667
Fax: (650) 852-0618
Email: hanako@careers911.com
Web: www.careers911.com

Description: Our goal is to be recognized, respected and sought out by our clients as a valuable and essential member of and contributor to their staffing team.

Key Contact - Specialty:
Ms. Hanako Yanagi, General Manager - *Software*

Functions: Generalist, Directors, Senior Mgmt., Middle Mgmt., Sales & Mktg., MIS Mgmt., Systems Analysis, Systems Implem.

Industries: Generalist, Computer Equip., E-commerce, Telecoms, Wireless, Software

MRI of Pleasanton

4125 Mohr Ave Ste M
Pleasanton, CA 94566-4740
(925) 462-8579
Fax: (925) 462-0208
Email: confidential@mricareers.com
Web: www.mricareers.com

Description: Presidents club office, established client base, confidential contingency and retained search.

Key Contact - Specialty:
Mr. Michael T. Machi, President - *Plastics, finance & accounting*

Salary minimum: $50,000

Functions: Generalist, Mfg., Production, Plant Mgmt., Distribution, Sales & Mktg., Sales Mgmt., Finance, DB Admin., Engineering

Industries: Generalist, Plastics, Rubber, Metal Products, Transportation, Finance, Accounting, HR Services, Communications, Software, Industry Specific SW, Mfg. SW

Professional Associations: CLM

MRI of Redlands

(also known as Inland Empire Agency)
19 E Citrus Ave Ste 201
Redlands, CA 92373
(909) 335-2055
Fax: (909) 792-4194
Email: maurice@mrredlands.com
Web: www.mrredlands.com

Description: Single source human resource service. Recruiting for permanent positions, executive temporary placement and outplacement. Fast, efficient, cost effective utilization of our 800 office nationwide network.

Key Contact - Specialty:
Mr. Maurice R. Meyers, President - *Construction, engineering*

Salary minimum: $40,000

Functions: Generalist

Industries: Construction, Transportation, Mgmt. Consulting

MRI of Sacramento

2316 Bell Executive Ln Ste 100
Sacramento, CA 95825
(916) 565-2700
Fax: (916) 565-2828
Email: mrwebres@mrsacramento.com
Web: www.mrsacramento.com

Description: Our difference is that we provide our clients and candidates with leveraged value added services. Services that are specifically included are: executive VIP packaging, compatibility assessments, video-conferencing, and access to MRI International network. Please visit our website http://www.brilliantpeople.com.

Key Contact - Specialty:
Mr. Karl Dinse, President - *Energy*
Ms. Elizabeth Dinse, Vice President - *Accounting, energy, building materials*

Salary minimum: $50,000

Functions: Generalist

Industries: Energy, Utilities, Construction, Mfg., Finance, Banking, Services, Accounting, HR Services

Professional Associations: SAHRA, SHRM

MRI of San Diego

9455 Ridgehaven Ct Ste 100
San Diego, CA 92123-1647
(858) 565-6600
Fax: (858) 565-4937
Email: jobopp@mrisandiego.com
Web: www.mrisandiego.com

Description: We are the San Diego division of Management Recruiters and recruit technical and industrial professionals nationally.

Key Contact - Specialty:
Mr. Harvey J. Baron, President - *General management*

Salary minimum: $30,000

Functions: Generalist

Industries: Drugs Mfg., Medical Devices, HR Services, Communications, Packaging, Software, Biotech

MRI of Mission Viejo

30200 Rancho Viejo Rd Ste F
San Juan Capistrano, CA 92675
(949) 481-2637
Fax: (949) 481-2642
Email: mrimissionviejo@mrimv.com
Web: www.mrinet.com

Key Contact - Specialty:
Mrs. Brenda McGorrian, President - *Finance*

MRI of Thousand Oaks

100 E Thousand Oaks Blvd Ste 115
Thousand Oaks, CA 91360-5713
(805) 497-4708
Fax: (805) 497-4718
Email: clientservices@mri-ecommerce.com
Web: www.mri-ecommerce.com

Description: This particular franchise of MRI focuses on new economy business, e-Commerce, m-Commerce, e-Learning, e-Security, e-Finance, and entertainment.

Key Contact - Specialty:
Mr. Doug Arney, Manager
Ms. Mickey Kampsen, Managing Partner - *E-business, e-security, on-line finance, telecommunications*

Salary minimum: $80,000

Functions: Senior Mgmt., Middle Mgmt.

Industries: Finance, Banking, Invest. Banking, Venture Cap., Services, Mgmt. Consulting, E-commerce, Media, Communications, Software

Professional Associations: AHRC

MRI of Boulder

1401 Walnut St Ste 301
PO Box 4657
Boulder, CO 80306-4657
(303) 447-9900
Fax: (303) 447-9536
Email: sharon@mrboulder.com
Web: www.mrboulder.com

Key Contact:
Ms. Sharon W. Hunter, Manager

Functions: Generalist, IT, MIS Mgmt., Engineering

Industries: Generalist, Construction, Wireless, Fiber Optic

MRI of Colorado Springs

13 S Tejon Ste 501
Colorado Springs, CO 80903
(719) 575-0500
Fax: (719) 575-0505
Email: info@mrcosprings.com
Web: www.mrcosprings.com

Description: Contingency search, working both regionally and nationally with an emphasis on technical positions in the following areas: utilities, information technology, telecommunications, manufacturing engineering, plastics, food manufacturing and staffing industry.

Key Contact - Specialty:
Mr. Mark Merriman, General Manager - *Energy*
Mr. Jack Merriman, Owner - *Energy*

Salary minimum: $40,000

Functions: Generalist

Industries: Generalist, Energy, Utilities, Mfg., Food, Bev., Tobacco, Plastics, Rubber, Paints, Petro. Products, Computer Equip., Misc. Mfg., Mgmt. Consulting, HR Services

MRI of Franktown

2195 N Hwy 83 Ste 23
Franktown, CO 80116
(303) 660-0766
Fax: (303) 660-0065
Email: info@jobs-search.com
Web: www.jobs-search.com

Description: Focus areas include enterprise software and systems development companies, technology start-up companies and telecommunication networking/solutions providers for the voice, data, fax, wireless, multimedia industries.

Key Contact:
Mr. David Empey, President - *Information technology, management, technical*
Mr. James Harlan, Director, Client Services - *Telecommunications, sales & marketing*
Ms. Marcie Norman, Account Executive - *Computer (software, hardware), management, technical*
Ms. Margie Cohen, Account Executive - *Telecommunications*
Mr. Todd Taylor, Account Executive
Ms. Wendy Koceski, Account Executive

Salary minimum: $50,000

Functions: Generalist

Industries: Telecoms, Software

MRI of Keystone-Vail
619 Main St Ste 2-A
PO Box 5627
Frisco, CO 80443-5627
(970) 668-4800
Fax: (970) 668-4807
Email: admin@extremerecruiting.com
Web: www.extremerecruiting.com

Key Contact:
Mr. John Paulus

Salary minimum: $50,000

MRI of Grand Junction
2764 Compass Dr Ste 238
Grand Junction, CO 81506
(970) 241-4043
Fax: (970) 241-4278
Email: dave.murphy@coloradomri.com
Web: www.mrinet.com

Key Contact:
Mr. Dave Murphy

Functions: Generalist

Industries: Drugs Mfg., Medical Devices, Pharm Svcs., Biotech

MRI of Colorado
9350 E Arapahoe Rd Ste 480
Greenwood Village, CO 80112
(303) 799-8188
Fax: (303) 799-0711
Email: resume@mricolorado.com
Web: www.mricolorado.com

Description: We have twenty-seven years of executive recruiting experience. Our principals have conducted searches over a vast range of industries and positions. We are presently in all areas of medical, except sales, scientific/technical, energy/oil and gas, food and beverage, and law.

Key Contact:
Mr. Kent Milius, President - *Senior management, healthcare, food & beverage, law, attorneys*
Mrs. Lynne Milius, Administrative Vice President

Salary minimum: $30,000

Functions: Generalist, Mfg., Nurses, Allied Health, Health Admin., Attorneys

Industries: Generalist, Energy, Utilities, Food, Bev., Tobacco, Medical Devices, Legal, Biotech, Healthcare

MRI of Greenwood Village
5600 S Quebec St Ste 110A
Greenwood Village, CO 80111
(303) 796-9933
Fax: (303) 796-9930
Email: info@mrgv.com
Web: www.mrgv.com

Description: We specialize only on information technology sales and sales management. Due to Mr.

Chamberlin's career in this industry and discipline, we have an extraordinary network.

Key Contact - Specialty:
Mr. Ryan Chamberlin, President/Owner - *Information technology*

Salary minimum: $24,000

Functions: Generalist, Sales Mgmt.

Industries: IT Implementation, Software

MRI of Denver-Golden Hill
7114 W Jefferson Ave Ste 213
Lakewood, CO 80215-3736
(303) 233-8600
Fax: (303) 233-8479
Email: rod@mrigold.com

Description: We are specialists in the fields of custom industrial automation. Our search assignments include: management, project management/engineering, design, sales, and application engineering positions.

Key Contact:
Mr. Rodney D. Bonner, General Manager

Salary minimum: $50,000

Functions: Automation

Industries: Mfg., Medical Devices, Plastics, Rubber, Machine, Appliance, Computer Equip., Misc. Mfg., Electronic, Elec. Components, Fiber Optic, Packaging, Mfg. SW

MRI of Middlesex
154 West St Unit C Bldg 3
Cromwell, CT 06416-2425
(860) 635-0612
Fax: (860) 632-5939
Email: mrimiddlesex@aol.com
Web: www.brilliantpeople.com

Description: Individualized recruitment firm, placing and recruiting on a national basis. Mid management level positions and up.

Key Contact - Specialty:
Mr. Leslie C. Cole, CPC, Manager - *Executive sales & marketing, management, management consulting*

Functions: Generalist, Senior Mgmt., Middle Mgmt., Mkt. Research, Mktg. Mgmt., Sales Mgmt., Mgmt. Consultants

Industries: Generalist, Chemicals, Soap, Perf., Cosmtcs., Drugs Mfg., Paints, Petro. Products, Misc. Mfg., Misc. Financial

MRI of Milford
61 Cherry St
Milford, CT 06460-3414
(203) 876-8755
Fax: (203) 877-1281
Email: milford1manager@mrinet.com
Web: www.mrinet.com

Description: We are specialists in executive, R&D, operations management, and technical recruiting for the biotech, medical device and diagnostics, pharmaceutical, and analytical instrumentation industries.

Key Contact - Specialty:
Ms. Sandra L. Stratman, Senior Partner - *Biotechnology, pharmaceutical, diagnostics*
Ms. Sandra Campbell, Senior Partner - *Pharmaceutical, analytical instrumentation, medical equipment*

Salary minimum: $50,000

Functions: Generalist

Industries: Drugs Mfg., Medical Devices, Pharm Svcs., Biotech

Professional Associations: ISPE

MRI of Hartford-South
2139 Silas Deane Hwy Ste 206A
Rocky Hill, CT 06067-2336
(860) 563-1268
Fax: (860) 563-2305
Email: rogermr@att.net
Web: www.mrinet.com

Description: We place audit, IT audit, and financial professionals.

Key Contact:
Mr. Roger C. Schultz, Manager

Functions: Finance

Industries: Generalist

MRI of Stamford
45 Church St Ste 301
Stamford, CT 06906
(203) 356-9999
Fax: (203) 356-9717
Email: mris@internetcrossings.com
Web: www.internetcrossings.com

Description: Our firm specializes in telecommunications and financial positions. Our focus is sales and marketing, operations and engineering, IT, and financial positions. They have significant staffing experience in opto-electronics and networking. They work on retained or contingency basis depending on the specific search requirements. They meet deadlines.

Key Contact:
Mr. Alex Walker, President

Salary minimum: $50,000

Functions: Generalist

Industries: Finance, Communications, Telecoms, Telephony, Digital, Wireless, Fiber Optic, Network Infrastructure, Security SW, Healthcare

MRI of Winsted/Wireless Careers
PO Box 1017
Winsted, CT 06098-1017
(860) 738-5035
Fax: (860) 738-5039
Email: mri@wirelesscareers.com
Web: www.wirelesscareers.com

Description: We are seasoned executive recruiters focused in the wireless and wire-line industries, providing intelligent global staffing solutions in operations, sales and marketing, and engineering within the telecommunications infrastructure integration industry.

Key Contact - Specialty:
Mr. Jack Bourque, President - *Wireless telecommunications (operations, technical, engineering, sales, administration)*
Mr. Jim Poirot, CSAM, Director, Business Development - *Wireless telecommunications, disruptive technologies, start-ups*

Salary minimum: $60,000

Functions: Generalist

Industries: Test, Measure Equip., Media, Communications, Telecoms, Telephony, Wireless, Fiber Optic, Network Infrastructure

Professional Associations: WAI

MRI of Bartow
160 E Summerlin Ste 208
Bartow, FL 33830
(863) 519-5926
Email: dtitus@gte.net
Web: www.home1.gte.net/dtitus/

Description: We recruit in the water, wastewater, and filtration industry including: sewage, storm-water, process, industrial and muni water, ultra-pure, and chemical process equipment market place.

Key Contact:
Mr. Dave Titus

MRI of Boca Raton

370 W Camino Gardens Blvd Ste 300
Boca Raton, FL 33432
(561) 393-3991
Fax: (561) 393-3992
Email: mrboca@att.net
Web: www.mrboca.com

Description: Technical specialists for the chemicals industry. Range of expertise covers sales to production. Key consideration given to the plastics industry.

Key Contact - Specialty:
Mr. Ernie Labadie, President - *Chemicals*

Functions: Generalist

Industries: Energy, Utilities, Mfg., Chemicals, Drugs Mfg., Plastics, Rubber, Paints, Petro. Products

MRI of Bonita Springs

9240 Bonita Beach Rd Ste 3307
Bonita Springs, FL 34135
(941) 495-7885
Fax: (941) 495-7686
Email: career@mriheadhunter.com
Web: www.mriheadhunter.com

Description: While maintaining a level of professionalism and integrity unsurpassed in recruiting, we are dedicated to the successful placement of qualified professionals within the energy/utility industry. Our technical expertise and world-class service ensures the mutual satisfaction of our candidates and clients resulting in a significant number of long-term relationships.

Key Contact - Specialty:
Mr. Gary F. Shearer, President - *Engineering, electric & gas & water utility industries, management consulting, pulp & paper, forest products*

Salary minimum: $75,000

Functions: Generalist, General Mgmt., Directors, Senior Mgmt., Middle Mgmt., Sales & Mktg., Sales Mgmt., Risk Mgmt., Systems Analysis, Engineering

Industries: Energy, Utilities, Construction, Mgmt. Consulting

Professional Associations: ASCE

MRI of Anna Maria Island

3655 Cortez Rd W Ste 90
Bradenton, FL 34210-3147
(941) 756-3001
Fax: (941) 756-0027
Email: mriflorida@aol.com
Web: www.mriflorida.com

Description: We are highly specialized in placement to the technical areas of paper and food ingredient and including product development, R&D, production, and technical sales/marketing.

Key Contact - Specialty:
Mr. R. Rush Oster, President - *Food, pharmaceutical, medical, paper, steel*

Salary minimum: $40,000

Functions: Generalist, Product Dev., Production, Mkt. Research, Sales Mgmt., CFO's, Mgmt. Consultants

Industries: Generalist, Food, Bev., Tobacco, Paper, Printing, Drugs Mfg., Metal Products, Pharm Svcs.

MRI of Ft Lauderdale

1900 W Commercial Blvd Ste 100
Ft. Lauderdale, FL 33309
(954) 776-4477
Fax: (954) 776-4488
Email: om5florida@aol.com

Key Contact:
Mr. Joel Dickstein, Manager

Functions: Healthcare

Industries: Hospitality, Hotels, Resorts, Clubs, Entertainment, Recreation, Healthcare, Physical Therapy

MRI of West Palm Beach

4000 S 57th Ave Ste 203
Greenacres, FL 33463-4307
(561) 433-2323
Fax: (561) 433-2330
Email: bud@mriwpb.com
Web: www.mriwpb.com

Description: Our specialties include: aerospace, IT with a focus on ERP systems, manufacturing and engineering, marketing and sales, and finance. We offer as part of our service: conferview interviews, complete screening, relocation assistance, and testing and personnel profiles. We also provide: resumes and interview coaching, data screening and editing, career strategies, and PARs and FABs creation.

Key Contact - Specialty:
Mr. Bud Jewell, Manager - *Aerospace*
Mrs. Jane Jewell, Office Manager - *Marketing & sales*

Salary minimum: $50,000

Functions: Generalist

Industries: Metal Products, Machine, Appliance, IT Implementation, Aerospace, ERP SW

Professional Associations: AMA, APICS, ASME

MRI of Hollywood

(also known as Answer Quest Executive Search)
4601 Sheridan St Ste 301
Hollywood, FL 33021-3433
(954) 961-1101
Fax: (954) 961-1106
Email: resume@answerquest.net
Web: www.answerquest.net

Description: Our firm is a leader in identifying and delivering top sales and business development talent in e-Business, wireless, software, and consulting. We find world-class sales and business development executives for early stage, as well as powerhouse companies. By utilizing state of the art tools, such as video conferencing, skill assessment surveys, and behavioral based interviewing, we help you make the right decisions about your company's most important asset, which is it's people. By continually exceeding expectations, we develop long term partnerships with clients and the candidates we place.

Key Contact:
Mr. Paul Silitsky, Manager

Salary minimum: $95,000

MRI of Melbourne

134 5th Ave Ste 208
Indialantic, FL 32903
(321) 951-7644
Fax: (321) 951-4235
Email: mr@mrirecruiter.com
Web: www.mrirecruiter.com

Description: Recruiters specialize in following areas: information technology, engineering in mobil equipment, equipment leasing sales and equipment leasing credit and operations, software sales, satellite engineers, broadcast engineers

Key Contact - Specialty:
Mr. Lawrence K. Cinco, President - *Manager*
Ms. Sue K. Cinco, Vice President - *Mobile equipment*

Functions: Generalist, Mfg., Plant Mgmt., Materials, Healthcare, Sales & Mktg., Finance, IT, R&D, Engineering

Industries: Agri., Forestry, Mining, Energy, Utilities, Construction, Mfg., Metal Products, Motor Vehicles, Computer Equip., Misc. Mfg., Transportation, Retail, Finance, Banking, Venture Cap., Hospitality, Media, Broadcast, Film, Communications, Software, Mfg. SW, Marketing SW, Biotech, Healthcare

Professional Associations: ELA, UAEL

MRI of Jacksonville

12708 San Jose Blvd Ste 1A
Jacksonville, FL 32223
(904) 260-4444
Fax: (904) 260-4666
Email: packmann@leading.net
Web: www.mrijax.com

Description: We are contingency search and recruiting firm specializing in sales and technical positions in the capital equipment packaging machinery industry including automation and robotics. We are experts in placement of medium to ultra-high level candidates with machinery backgrounds. Our firm accepts retainer agreements. All positions begin at over a $40,000 base. All fees are company paid. There are no candidate fees and the hiring company always pays relocations. State-of-the-art recruiting software is used to make exacting matches of candidates to our client's specifications.

Key Contact - Specialty:
Mr. Robert Lee, President - *Packaging, railroad supply*
Mrs. Barbara A. Lee, Vice President/General Manager - *General sales, administration, accounting, telecommunications*

Salary minimum: $35,000

Functions: Generalist, General Mgmt., Mfg., Sales & Mktg., Sales Mgmt., Engineering

Industries: Generalist, Machine, Appliance, Transportation, Telecoms, Packaging

Professional Associations: AAR, IOPP, PMMI, RPI

MRI of Julington Creek

3810-1 Williamsburg Park Blvd
Jacksonville, FL 32257-5584
(904) 737-5151
Fax: (904) 737-5152
Email: bob@mrijobs.com
Web: www.mrijobs.com

Key Contact:
Ms. Donna Eicher, Co-Manager
Mr. Bob Eicher, Co-Manager

MRI of Jensen Beach

3332 NE Sugar Hill Ave
Jensen Beach, FL 34957-3723
(561) 334-8633
Fax: (561) 334-4145
Email: dwll@adelphia.net
Web: www.mrjb.n3.net

Description: We recruit and place top quality sales and marketing talent in the telecommunications and information technology industries both domestically and internationally.

Key Contact - Specialty:
Mr. Douglas W. Lane, President/Owner - *Telecommunications, sales*

Salary minimum: $60,000

Functions: Generalist, Sales & Mktg.

Industries: Telecoms, Call Centers, Telephony, Digital, Wireless, Fiber Optic, Network Infrastructure, Software

MRI of Florida Keys
11450 Overseas Hwy Ste 206
Marathon, FL 33050
(305) 289-1600
Fax: (305) 289-1610
Email: mri@terranova.net
Web: www.mrinet.com

Description: We fill executive and staff recruiting needs for manufacturing companies. 30 years of personal professional experience in management and finance functions including over 20 years as a university finance professor.

Key Contact:
Mr. Michael Binder

MRI of Miami-North
815 NW 57th Ave Ste 110
Miami, FL 33126
(305) 264-4212
Fax: (305) 264-4251
Email: deldiaz@mrmiami.com
Web: www.mrmiami.com

Description: Specializing in confidential search and recruiting assignments for executives, managers and professionals in manufacturing, engineering, administration, sales, data processing and international trade.

Key Contact - Specialty:
Mr. Del Diaz, President - *General management, engineering*

Functions: Generalist

Industries: Generalist, Construction, Mfg., Paper, Finance, Services, Accounting, Advertising, Aerospace, Software

Professional Associations: TAPPI

MRI of Santa Rosa
6088 Berryhill Rd
Milton, FL 32570
(850) 626-3303
Fax: (850) 626-3448
Email: srmri@aol.com
Web: www.mrinet.com

Description: Retainer and contingency firm specializing in healthcare, managed care, and pharmaceutical industry

Key Contact - Specialty:
Mr. John E. Brand, CEO
Ms. Karen M. Brand, Vice President - *Pharmacy (clinical, managerial)*
Mr. Ivan Garcia, CFO - *Physicians & CRNA's*

Functions: Generalist

Industries: Drugs Mfg., Medical Devices, Pharm Svcs., Healthcare

MRI of Lake County Inc
1117 N Donnelly St
Mt. Dora, FL 32757-4259
(352) 383-7101
Fax: (352) 383-7103
Email: mrilakeco@lcia.com

Description: We are manufacturing specialists-production, engineering, management, quality control, technical, and sales. We place particular emphasis in plastics, food processing, transportation equipment, medical manufacturing, pharmaceuticals, chemicals, and electronic components.

Key Contact:
Mr. Roger M. Holloway, Owner/Manager - *Plastics*

Ms. Linda Holloway

Salary minimum: $25,000

Functions: Generalist, Middle Mgmt., Product Dev., Production, Plant Mgmt., Quality, Engineering, Technicians

Industries: Generalist, Food, Bev., Tobacco, Chemicals, Soap, Perf., Cosmtcs., Drugs Mfg., Plastics, Rubber, Metal Products, Motor Vehicles, Misc. Mfg., Electronic, Elec. Components, Mfg. SW

MRI of Chicago West and Ocala, FL
1515 E Silver Springs Blvd Ste 149
Ocala, FL 34470
(352) 620-8001
Fax: (352) 620-8041
Email: mrijobs@interaccess.com
Web: www.mrichicagojobs.com

Description: We deliver innovative, as well as state-of-the-art strategies that meet ever-changing technological advances and health care services. We are motivated to accommodate all those who seek our expertise. We continually strive to recognize clients individually in order to meet their specific needs.

Key Contact - Specialty:
Mr. Larry Strayhorn, Co-Owner/Manager - *Information technology*
Ms. Patricia Strayhorn, Co-Owner/Manager - *Information technology*
Mr. Bruce Fox, Senior Account Executive - *Information technologies, sales*

Salary minimum: $30,000

Functions: Healthcare, IT

Industries: Generalist, Pharm Svcs.

MRI of Orange Park
1542 Kingsley Ave Ste 137
Orange Park, FL 32073-4547
(904) 264-5644
(888) 838-4188
Fax: (904) 264-5966
Email: veronica@lageman.com
Web: www.lageman.com

Description: The MRI global network targets, recruits, and delivers high-impact talent for our clients' needs. Management Recruiters of Orange Park specializes in telecommunications.

Key Contact:
Mr. Regis Lageman, Owner/Manager
Ms. Veronica L. West, Administrative Assistant

Functions: Directors, Healthcare, Sales Mgmt.

Industries: Telecoms, Healthcare

MRI of Northern Palm Beaches
8895 N Military Trl Ste 301B
Palm Beach Gardens, FL 33410
(561) 622-8110
Fax: (561) 622-8440
Email: jim@mrimarketing.com
Web: www.mrimarketing.com

Description: Our mission - executive searches in marketing communications (advertising, promotion, public relations) for corporate and agency clients on a nationwide basis.

Key Contact - Specialty:
Mr. James R. Kissel, Managing Director - *Advertising, public relations, sales promotion*
Mrs. Linda Kissel, Vice President-Office Manager
Mr. Brian J. Kissel, Account Executive - *Advertising (creative), public relations*
Mr. Bernie Diaz, Account Executive - *Advertising, creative, production (all in Hispanic markets)*

Salary minimum: $50,000

Functions: Advertising

Industries: Media, Advertising

MRI of Panama City Beach
13215 Oleander Dr
Panama City Beach, FL 32407-3303
(850) 235-3591
Fax: (850) 235-3591
Email: charles@computershooters.com
Web: www.brilliantpeople.com

Description: Maximum professional search through the largest candidate resume computerized database in the world. Hiring authorities who want the best candidate should contact us today. Candidates, you deserve the best job search. Send us your resume today. As a generalist recruiting firm, our office knows your industry.

Key Contact - Specialty:
Mr. Charles E. Martin, Account Executive - *Generalist*
Ms. Patricia Martin, Account Executive - *Generalist*

Salary minimum: $25,000

Functions: Generalist, General Mgmt., Senior Mgmt., Legal, Mfg., Automation, Plant Mgmt., Quality

Industries: Generalist, Agri., Forestry, Mining, Chemicals, Drugs Mfg., Computer Equip., Finance, Banking, Accounting, Telecoms, Software, Healthcare

MRI of The Everglades
9050 Pines Blvd Ste 460
Pembroke Pines, FL 33024-6400
(954) 442-7754
Fax: (954) 442-7824
Web: www.mrieverglades.com

Key Contact:
Mr. Greg Horton
Mr. Eric Cave

Functions: Generalist

Industries: Energy, Utilities, Telecoms, Packaging, Healthcare

MRI of Pensacola
603 E Government St
Pensacola, FL 32501
(850) 434-6500
Fax: (850) 434-9911
Email: pens@mriplastics.com
Web: www.mriplastics.com

Description: We provide upper-level sales, technical, and manufacturing management recruitment in the plastic industry and packaging industry. Our emphasis is in the injection molding segment of the industry.

Key Contact:
Mr. Ken Kirchgessner, Owner - *Plastics, packaging industry*
Mrs. Pat Kirchgessner, President
Mr. Jody Braxton, Manager - *Injection molding, plastics*
Mr. Davey Willhoit, Executive Recruiter - *Plastic industry*
Ms. Mona Welch, Administrative Assistant
Mrs. Sandy Summerlin, Project Coordinator

Salary minimum: $40,000

Functions: General Mgmt., Directors, Middle Mgmt., Product Dev., Production, Plant Mgmt., Quality, Productivity, Sales Mgmt., Engineering

Industries: Mfg., Plastics, Rubber

Professional Associations: SAM, SPE

MRI of Plantation
8030 Peters Rd Ste D104
Plantation, FL 33324-4038
(954) 916-1890
Fax: (954) 916-1891
Email: mrpfl@earthlink.net
Web: www.mrinet.com

Key Contact:
Mr. Miles Sturgis, Manager

Functions: Generalist, Mfg.

Industries: Chemicals, Drugs Mfg., Medical
Devices, Computer Equip., Retail, Finance,
Services, Telecoms, Software, Biotech,
Healthcare

MRI of St. Lucie County
756 SE Port St Lucie Blvd
Port St. Lucie, FL 34984
(561) 871-1100
Fax: (561) 871-0702
Email: admin@mriretail.com
Web: www.mriretail.com

Description: Sales and marketing representatives,
management, executives, technical support,
consultants, CEOs. The leading management, sales
and marketing recruitment organization for the
high-tech retail market. We recruit sales, marketing
and technical support professionals in the ERP,SAP,
POS, CRM , e-retailing and card payment systems
business segments who market their products to the
retail industry.

Key Contact - Specialty:
Mr. Larry J. Breault, Managing Partner - *Retail
technology industry*

Salary minimum: $50,000

Functions: Directors, Senior Mgmt., Middle
Mgmt., Product Dev., Sales & Mktg., Mkt.
Research, Mktg. Mgmt., Sales Mgmt., IT

Industries: Software

MRI of North Pinellas County
531 Main St Ste F
Safety Harbor, FL 34695
(727) 791-3277
Fax: (727) 446-7732
Email: tim@mrnorthpc.com
Web: www.mrnorthpc.com

Description: We specialize in these specific areas:
packaging, (both corrugated manufacturing and
plastic), healthcare, and information technology.

Key Contact - Specialty:
Mr. Tim Tuttle, Owner - *Packaging*
Ms. Cheryle Tuttle, Co-owner - *Insurance, human
resources*

Salary minimum: $40,000

Functions: Generalist

Industries: Packaging, Healthcare

MRI of Tampa-Bayside
400 N Ashley Dr Ste 1725
Tampa, FL 33602-4300
(813) 229-0545
Fax: (813) 229-0785
Email: larry@mrretail.com
Web: www.mrretail.com

Description: We specialize in all areas of the retail
industry mainly at corporate level and regional and
district level.

Key Contact:
Mr. Larry Scofield, President/Owner - *Retail*
Mrs. Nancy Scofield

Salary minimum: $75,000

Functions: Generalist, Middle Mgmt., Distribution,
Mkt. Research, Training, Budgeting, Systems
Dev., Architects

Industries: Generalist, Retail

MRI of Tampa North
4012 Gunn Hwy Ste 140
Tampa, FL 33624-4724
(813) 264-7165
Email: mrtn@mrtampanorth.com
Web: www.mrtampanorth.com

Description: We are a progressive firm known and
respected within the MRI organization for its
integrity and effectiveness. Our search consultants
and associates make the firm a perennial
"President's Club" performer that consistently ranks
among the top producing offices in the Southeast
region of MRI's 1000 office network.

Key Contact - Specialty:
Mr. Gary King, Managing Partner
Mr. Stephen Fox, Senior Vice President of Sales -
Food and beverage sales

Salary minimum: $40,000

Functions: Directors, Senior Mgmt., Healthcare,
Sales & Mktg., Mktg. Mgmt., Sales Mgmt., IT,
Engineering

Industries: Drugs Mfg., Medical Devices, Pharm
Svcs., Mgmt. Consulting, Restaurants, Telecoms,
Fiber Optic, Network Infrastructure, Insurance,
Industry Specific SW, Security SW, Biotech,
Healthcare

MRI of Venice
333 S Tamiami Trl Ste 295
Venice, FL 34285-2427
(941) 484-3900
Fax: (941) 485-5822
Email: mrvenice@gte.net

Description: Provide value added recruiting
services on a nationwide basis for quality minded
corporations and candidates.

Key Contact - Specialty:
Mr. Walter W. Taylor, President - *Information
technology*
Ms. Winifred C. Taylor, Vice President - *General
manufacturing*

Salary minimum: $40,000

Functions: Generalist, Production, Materials Plng.,
Sales Mgmt., MIS Mgmt., Systems Analysis,
R&D, Engineering

Industries: Generalist, Metal Products, Computer
Equip., Telecoms, Software

MRI of Vero Beach
(also known as Peterson Consulting Group)
80 Royal Palm Pointe Ste 300
Vero Beach, FL 32960
(561) 778-4343
(800) 269-7319
Fax: (561) 794-0371
Email: diana@onlinepcg.com
Web: www.onlinepcg.com

Description: We have been the leader in permanent
placement in the building products industry, for
example: roofing, contracting, concrete,
manufacturing, and engineering, more specifically
mechanical, structural, civil, and electrical for over
20 years. We meet our commitment to clients. The
key to our success is service, integrity, and honesty.

Key Contact - Specialty:
Mr. David A. Peterson, President/CEO - *Building
products*
Ms. Diana K. Peterson, Vice President/CFO -
Building products

Salary minimum: $40,000

Functions: Generalist

Industries: Generalist

Professional Associations: ASHRAE, IIAR,
NRCA, SEANC

MRI of Athens
(also known as Graham Group)
375 Club Dr
Athens, GA 30607
(706) 613-8114
Fax: (706) 613-1648
Email: sgraham@grahamgroupusa.com
Web: www.grahamgroupusa.com

Description: Our firm, an affiliate of Management
Recruiters International, specializes in search and
recruitment of many different industries. We offer a
range of services that guarantees success for our
clients. We would like to provide this level of
service for you.

Key Contact:
Mr. Shane Graham, President & Managing Partner
- *Insurance, finance*
Mr. Bobby Graham, VP & Managing Partner

MRI of Atlanta Downtown Inc
230 Peachtree St NW Ste 1985
Atlanta, GA 30303
(404) 221-1021
Fax: (404) 221-0121
Email: jobs@mriatl.com
Web: www.mriatl.com

Description: We are a franchise provider of staffing
solutions specializing in the medical,
pharmaceutical, telecommunications and
information technology professions.

Key Contact - Specialty:
Mr. Thomas A. Jayroe, Manager - *Medical,
pharmaceutical, sales & marketing*
Mr. Rick Blackwell, Account Executive -
Information technology
Mr. Kurt Meyer, Account Executive -
Telecommunications
Mr. Donald L. Saunders, Account Executive -
Medical, pharmaceutical, sales & marketing

Functions: Generalist, Mkt. Research, Mktg.
Mgmt., Sales Mgmt., MIS Mgmt., Systems
Analysis, Systems Implem., Technicians

Industries: Generalist, Media, Telecoms, Software,
Healthcare

MRI of Atlanta Perimeter Center
1536 Dunwoody Village Pkwy Ste 225
Atlanta, GA 30338
(770) 392-4800
Fax: (770) 392-9600
Email: mriapc@mindspring.com
Web: www.mrinet.com

Key Contact - Specialty:
Mr. Thomas Fischgrund, President - *Marketing and
sales*
Mr. Brian Leo, Account Executive - *Industrial
packaging, paper, adhesives*
Mr. Alex Torres, Account Executive -
Manufacturing, hispanic executive recruiting

Functions: General Mgmt., Mfg., Packaging, Sales
& Mktg., Mkt. Research, Mktg. Mgmt.,
Minorities

Industries: Generalist

MRI of Atlanta North
20 Perimeter Park Dr Ste 101
Atlanta, GA 30341
(770) 455-1958
Fax: (770) 455-6529
Email: resume@mrian.com
Web: www.jobs-staffing.com

Description: Over 15 years' executive search. A top 10% office in the largest search and recruiting firm in the world. Particular strength in healthcare, finance, administration and manufacturing, nationally and internationally.

Key Contact - Specialty:
Mr. Arthur Katz, President - *Generalist, healthcare, manufacturing, factory automation, robotics*

Salary minimum: $35,000

Functions: Generalist, Senior Mgmt., Automation, Plant Mgmt., Healthcare, HR Mgmt., Finance, Engineering

Industries: Generalist, Food, Bev., Tobacco, Chemicals, Soap, Perf., Cosmtcs., Drugs Mfg., Leather, Stone, Glass, Healthcare

MRI of Cartersville
16 Collins Dr Ste A
Cartersville, GA 30120
(770) 607-6630
Fax: (770) 607-6638
Email: mrcareers@mrcartersville.com
Web: www.mrcartersville.com

Key Contact:
Mr. Rick Elliot

Functions: Generalist

Industries: Textiles, Apparel, Lumber, Furniture

MRI of Columbus Inc
233 12th St Ste 818-A
Columbus, GA 31901-2449
(706) 571-9611
Fax: (801) 730-5390
Email: michael@mricolumbusga.com
Web: www.mricolumbusga.com

Description: We specialize in all positions for durable consumer manufactured products. We place positions in financial services in both banking and insurance, IT recruiting for mainfrane, midrange, and mini environments including LAN/WAN connectivity.

Key Contact - Specialty:
Mr. Michael L. Silverstein, President - *Information systems, data processing*

Functions: Generalist, Production, MIS Mgmt., Systems Analysis, Systems Dev., Systems Implem., Engineering

Industries: Generalist, Metal Products, Consumer Elect., Banking, Misc. Financial, IT Implementation, Insurance

MRI of Dalton
1716 Cleveland Hwy Ste 600
Dalton, GA 30721
(706) 226-8550
Fax: (706) 226-8353
Email: mriga@alltel.net
Web: www.mrinet.com

Key Contact:
Ms. Verna F. Webb, Co-Manager
Mr. Donald W. Webb, Co-Manager

Salary minimum: $25,000

Functions: Senior Mgmt., Middle Mgmt.

Industries: Textiles, Apparel, Plastics, Rubber

MRI of The Atlanta Area
3700 Crestwood Pkwy Ste 320
Duluth, GA 30096
(770) 925-2266
Fax: (770) 925-1090
Email: driggs@corpga.com
Web: www.corpga.com

Description: Dedicated to improve our clients' bottom line through customized staffing solutions.

Key Contact:
Mr. David Riggs, President

Salary minimum: $60,000

Functions: Directors, Senior Mgmt., CFO's, Credit, M&A, Risk Mgmt.

Industries: Finance, Banking, Invest. Banking, Venture Cap., Services

MRI of Atlanta West
4260 Bankhead Hwy Ste A
Lithia Springs, GA 30122-1752
(770) 948-5560
Fax: (770) 948-5762
Email: mri@writeme.com

Description: We have the largest network of offices and recruiters to provide more job opportunities and quality candidates. We specialize in placing sales, marketing and senior managers who have experience with consumer goods manufacturers or manufacturers of flexible plastic packaging film.

Key Contact - Specialty:
Mr. Gene Brown, General Manager - *Consumer packaged goods (senior mgt, marketing & sales)*
Mr. Rodney Hill, Senior Account Executive - *Flexible plastic packaging materials*

Salary minimum: $75,000

Functions: Generalist, Senior Mgmt., Middle Mgmt., Distribution, Packaging, Mktg. Mgmt., Sales Mgmt.

Industries: Generalist, Food, Bev., Tobacco, Soap, Perf., Cosmtcs., Drugs Mfg., Plastics, Rubber, Consumer Elect., Packaging

MRI of Marietta
274 N Marietta Pkwy NE Ste C
Marietta, GA 30060-1456
(770) 423-1443
Fax: (770) 423-1303
Email: jkirby@mindspring.com

Description: Principals and account executives are former senior executives with direct experience in hiring decisions. Our client companies frequently cite this factor as distinguishing the professionalism of our firm from others in the search industry.

Key Contact - Specialty:
Mr. James E. Kirby, Managing Principal - *Manufacturing (all functions)*
Mrs. Jayne Kirby, Managing Principal - *Manufacturing (general)*
Mr. David D. Farra, Principal - *Manufacturing, distribution, sales & marketing*

Salary minimum: $40,000

Functions: Generalist

Industries: Energy, Utilities, Mfg., Finance, Services, Hospitality, Telecoms, Defense, Aerospace, Packaging

MRI of Atlanta NE
(also known as The Rivard Group (TRG))
6120 Windsor Trace Dr
Norcross, GA 30092
(770) 613-9585
Fax: (770) 613-9586
Email: drivard@mriatlantane.com
Web: www.mriatlantane.com

Description: We specialize exclusively in the property and casualty insurance industry. We place mid to upper-level executive search/recruitment, permanent and interim placement, management consulting, and video conferencing.

Key Contact - Specialty:
Mr. Richard L. Rivard, President/CEO - *Insurance (property, casualty)*
Ms. Cheryl Barry, Account Executive - *Insurance (property, casualty)*

Salary minimum: $50,000

Functions: Generalist

Industries: Insurance

MRI of Roswell-West
920 Holcomb Bridge Rd Ste 450
Roswell, GA 30076-1974
(770) 649-8778
Fax: (770) 649-8197
Email: rnugent@mrirw.com
Web: www.medevicejobs.com

Description: Our firm specializes in placing candidates in the medical device industry only. Our focus is in marketing, sales, regulatory affairs, quality, engineering, manufacturing and operations.

Key Contact - Specialty:
Mr. Randolph L. Nugent, Principal - *Medical device*
Ms. Belinda Young, Principal - *Medical device marketing*
Mr. Dan Shilt, Principal - *Medical device sales*

Salary minimum: $60,000

Functions: Healthcare

Industries: Medical Devices

MRI of Roswell-North
345 Market Pl Ste 114
Roswell, GA 30075
(770) 642-1230
Fax: (770) 642-6247
Email: jvwalsh@mriroswellnorth.com
Web: www.mriroswellnorth.com

Description: The principals of our firm have a combined 40 years of experience in the property/casualty insurance industry in various underwriting, underwriting management, and branch management positions. We specialize in all technical and management positions within the property/casualty insurance field.

Key Contact - Specialty:
Mr. James Walsh, Managing Director - *Insurance industry*
Mr. Tom Varco, ARM, Director of Recruiting - *Insurance industry*

Salary minimum: $50,000

Functions: Generalist

Industries: Insurance

MRI of Savannah
2431 Habersham St Fl 2
PO Box 22548
Savannah, GA 31403-2548
(912) 232-0132
Fax: (912) 232-0136
Email: manager@expertsearches.com
Web: www.expertsearches.com

Description: Our clients give us high praise for our consultative approach and our thorough pre-screening of candidates. Our highest priorities are saving our clients' time and finding the right match for our candidates.

Key Contact:
Mr. Ron McElhaney, Managing Partner - *Chemicals, plastics*
Mr. Ron McElhaney, Jr., Partner - *Chemicals, plastics, general & high-tech manufacturing, human resources*
Ms. Patty Dixon, Project Coordinator

Salary minimum: $60,000

Functions: Generalist

Industries: Food, Bev., Tobacco, Chemicals, Drugs Mfg., Plastics, Rubber, Paints, Petro. Products, Misc. Mfg.

Professional Associations: ACS, AICHE

MRI of Golden Isles

1626 Frederica Rd Ste 203
St. Simons Island, GA 31522
(912) 634-0087
Fax: (912) 634-2391
Email: satlalla@darientel.net
Web: www.mrinet.com

Description: We are a search/placement
organization that seeks to build strategic
partnerships with clients. We work best in this
environment. We terminate relationships with
clients, and candidates also, when partnerships are
not possible. We strive for the best in all.

Key Contact:
Sat Lalla

MRI of Towne Lake

120 N Medical Pkwy Ste 200 Bldg 200
Woodstock, GA 30189-7062
(770) 592-8389
Fax: (770) 592-5557
Email: sbuck@mindspring.com

Description: We are an executive search firm
specializing in the commercial finance industry. We
recruit primarily in the asset based lending, leverage
finance, commercial, and corporate and business
bankers areas. We do retained, engaged, and
contingent searches throughout the US.

Key Contact:
Mr. Steve Buck

Functions: Generalist

Industries: Banking, Misc. Financial

MRI of Boise

345 Bobwhite Ct Ste 215
Boise, ID 83706-3966
(208) 336-6770
Fax: (208) 336-2499
Email: mriboise@mriboise.com
Web: www.mriboise.com

Description: Our firm specializes in Engineering &
Technical Placements. We are specifically focused
in the following industries: Food Processing,
Mining & Minerals, and Petrochemicals &
Refining.

Key Contact:
Mr. Craig R. Alexander, President/General
   Manager - *Food processing*
Mr. Greg Arndt, Vice President - *Mining, industrial
   minerals*
Mr. Chris Walhof, Account Executive - *Petroleum
   refining, petrochemical*
Ms. Jo Stensars, Account Executive - *Information
   technology, data processing*
Ms. Carrie Austin, Project Coordinator

Salary minimum: $45,000

Functions: Generalist, Product Dev., Plant Mgmt.,
   Quality, Mktg. Mgmt., Sales Mgmt., Personnel,
   Engineering

Industries: Generalist, Agri., Forestry, Mining,
   Energy, Utilities, Food, Bev., Tobacco,
   Chemicals, Paints, Petro. Products, Computer
   Equip., Packaging

Professional Associations: AICHE, AIME, SMME

MRI of Arlington Heights

3415 N Arlington Hts Rd
Arlington Heights, IL 60004
(847) 590-8880
Fax: (847) 590-0847
Email: mri@jobwish.com
Web: www.jobwish.com

Description: We provide search for sales, marketing
and product management professionals for
industrial, consumer, and hard and soft good
manufacturing companies on a world wide basis

including packaging, power transmission, food and
beverage, material handling, sporting goods, and
medical device manufacturers.

Key Contact - Specialty:
Mr. Steve Briody, General Manager - *Packaging*
Mr. Mark Gillespie, CSAM, Team Leader-
   Consumer - *Food & beverage*

Functions: Sales & Mktg., Sales Mgmt.

Industries: Construction, Mfg., Plastics, Rubber,
   Consumer Elect., Packaging

MRI of Barrington

417 N Hough St
Barrington, IL 60010
(847) 382-5544
Fax: (847) 382-5591
Email: hvacjobs@mribarrington.com
Web: www.mribarrington.com

Description: Retained and contingency search firm,
focused primarily on professionals in the HVAC,
refrigeration, building automation systems and
energy services industries. Including technical,
sales, upper and middle management.

Key Contact - Specialty:
Mr. Gary T. Polvere, General Manager - *HVAC,
   building automation systems, refrigeration,
   energy services*
Mr. Jon Difatta, Account Executive - *Construction
   & building systems*
Mr. Jim Van Eaton, Account Executive -
   Consulting engineering
Mr. Kevin Tilton, Account Executive -
   Construction & building systems
Mr. Sean Beachem, Account Executive -
   Construction & building systems
Mr. Steve Carr, Account Executive - *IT business
   development*
Mr. Rob Spooner, Account Executive - *Information
   technology*

Salary minimum: $40,000

Functions: Senior Mgmt., Sales Mgmt.,
   Engineering

Industries: Energy, Utilities

MRI of Batavia

28 S Water St Ste 201
Batavia, IL 60510
(630) 406-8003
Fax: (630) 406-8321
Email: techstaff@inil.com

Key Contact:
Mr. Joseph Valente - *Information technology*
Mrs. Sophia Valente

Functions: IT

Industries: Generalist

MRI of Lincolnshire-Buffalo Grove

1110 W Lake Cook Rd Ste 167
Buffalo Grove, IL 60089
(847) 520-0107
Email: lincolnshire@earthlink.net
Web: www.brilliantpeople.com

Description: Our search firm focuses on the
pharmaceutical and medical device industries, with
an emphasis on general management, marketing and
sales management, and R&D managers. We search
for individuals who have current experience within
these industries, as required by our client
companies.

Key Contact - Specialty:
Mr. Ron DeChant, President - *Pharmaceutical,
   medical device industry*

Functions: General Mgmt., Sales & Mktg., Sales
   Mgmt., R&D

Industries: Drugs Mfg., Medical Devices, Pharm
   Svcs., Biotech

Professional Associations: ASHP, ASHP

MRI of Cherry Valley

1463 S Bell School Rd Ste 3
PO Box 590
Cherry Valley, IL 61011
(815) 399-1942
Fax: (815) 399-2750
Email: mcarter@mrcherryvalley.com
Web: www.mrcherryvalley.com

Key Contact:
Mr. D. Michael Carter, Manager

Salary minimum: $65,000

Functions: Generalist

Industries: Plastics, Rubber, Metal Products, Misc.
   Mfg., Electronic, Elec. Components, Banking,
   Packaging, Accounting SW, Mfg. SW

MRI of Michigan Ave

625 N Michigan Ave Ste 430
Chicago, IL 60611
(312) 279-0140
Fax: (312) 279-0141
Email: office@jobsagent.com
Web: www.jobsagent.com

Description: Our firm specializes in staffing
solutions for the plastics, plastic packaging, and IT
industries.

Key Contact - Specialty:
Mr. Dick Post, President - *Plastic, plastic
   packaging*

Functions: Product Dev., Production, Plant Mgmt.,
   Quality, Productivity, Purchasing, Packaging,
   Mktg. Mgmt., Sales Mgmt., HR Mgmt.

Industries: Food, Bev., Tobacco, Chemicals,
   Plastics, Rubber, Packaging

Professional Associations: SPE

MRI of Decatur

101 S Main St 1 Main Pl Ste 301
Decatur, IL 62523
(217) 428-7030
Fax: (217) 428-7066
Email: manager1@jmnsearch.com

Description: Our firm focuses primarily on
manufacturing/engineering. Other industries served
are finance/banking, human resources, IT, and
sales/marketing.

Key Contact:
Ms. Marsha Norman, Manager

Salary minimum: $40,000

Functions: Generalist

Industries: Mfg., Chemicals, Plastics, Rubber,
   Metal Products, Motor Vehicles, Finance,
   Packaging

MRI of Elgin

472 N McLean Blvd Ste 202
Elgin, IL 60123
(847) 697-2201
Fax: (847) 697-0622
Email: mrelgin@mrelgin.com
Web: www.mrelgin.com

Key Contact:
Mr. Ron C. Reeves, Manager

Functions: Plant Mgmt., Materials, Distribution,
   Healthcare, Direct Mktg., Finance, Architects

Industries: Generalist, Lumber, Furniture, Paper,
   Printing, Pharm Svcs., Publishing, Biotech,
   Healthcare

MRI of Lake Forest, IL

191 E Deerpath Rd Ste 302
Lake Forest, IL 60045
(847) 604-9000
Fax: (847) 604-9020
Email: jobs@mrilf.com
Web: www.mrilf.com

Description: Our office has some 30 years worth of experience in the medical device and biotechnology industry. Of the over 800 MRI offices, we are one of the top producing offices in medical device placement. We do placements in regulatory affairs, quality, clinical, R&D, and marketing arenas.

Key Contact - Specialty:
Mr. Harry J. Cunneff, President - *Medical device, biotechnology, regulatory, quality, clinical*
Mr. Charlie Berg, Account Executive - *Medical device, marketing, product management, engineering, R&D*
Ms. Lauren Welch, Account Executive - *Clinical research, clinical affairs, quality*
Ms. Molle Kleeberger, Account Executive - *Regulatory, quality (pharmaceutical, medical)*
Mr. Marc Staege, Project Coordinator - *Medical device, pharmaceutical regulatory, quality*

Salary minimum: $50,000

Functions: Generalist, Directors, Senior Mgmt., Middle Mgmt., Quality, Mkt. Research, Mktg. Mgmt., R&D

Industries: Generalist, Drugs Mfg., Medical Devices, Biotech

Professional Associations: DIA, MMA, RAPS, SCT

MRI of Chicago-Northwest

1st Bank Plaza Ste 300
Lake Zurich, IL 60047-3109
(847) 550-1300
Fax: (847) 550-1314
Email: it@mrchicago.com
Web: www.mrchicago.com

Description: We pride ourselves in evaluating top sales, executive management, and consulting talent in the information technology and printing/graphics industries nationwide.

Key Contact - Specialty:
Mr. Gary L. Bozza, President/Executive Director - *Information technology, printing, graphics*

Functions: Sales & Mktg.

Industries: Paper, Printing, Computer Equip., Mgmt. Consulting, E-commerce, IT Implementation, PSA/ASP, Software

Professional Associations: CSA

MRI of Mattoon

1405 Lafayette Ave
PO Box 461
Mattoon, IL 61938
(217) 235-9393
Fax: (217) 235-9396
Web: www.mrinet.com

Description: We are a globally active search firm that is highly specialized to the flavor and fragrance industry.

Key Contact:
Mr. David W. Tolle, Manager

Functions: R&D

Industries: Food, Bev., Tobacco, Non-classifiable

Professional Associations: BSF, IFT

MRI of Mundelein

383 N Seymour Ave
Mundelein, IL 60060
(847) 970-5949

Email: info@mri-egret.com
Web: www.mri-egret.com

Description: Our president, and founder, has over 20 years of industry experience with over 15 years of experience at a Fortune 100 manufacturer of electrical products. We are in the electrical industry everyday. We know where the top 'A' players are. You don't have the time to find great people; we do!

Key Contact - Specialty:
Mr. Ted Konnerth
Ms. Prudence Thomp, VP-Business Development - *Electrical distributors*

Functions: Sales & Mktg.

Industries: Misc. Mfg.

MRI of Chicago-Far West

564 S Washington St Ste 203
Naperville, IL 60540
(630) 305-0200
Fax: (630) 305-0273
Email: mrchicagofw@ameritech.net
Web: www.mrinet.com

Key Contact:
Ms. Sherri Chaifetz, Co-Manager
Mr. Marc Chaifetz, Co-Manager

Functions: Generalist

Industries: Generalist

MRI of Springfield

1999 Wabash Ave Ste 206
Springfield, IL 62704
(217) 547-2554
Fax: (217) 547-2560
Email: p.howe@aviationrecruiter.com
Web: www.aviationrecruiter.com

Description: We are the largest and most respected search and staffing company in the world. Aviation, airlines and aerospace are our only industries.

Key Contact - Specialty:
Mr. Phillip T. Howe, President - *Aviation, airlines, aerospace*

Salary minimum: $50,000

Functions: Generalist

Industries: Transportation, Aerospace

Professional Associations: NBAA

MRI of St. Charles, IL

318 S 2nd St
St. Charles, IL 60174-2817
(630) 377-6466
Fax: (630) 377-6642
Email: mri@inil.com

Description: Our firm specialty is management positions in the Midwest including human resources, accounting, engineering, information technology, logistics, supply chain, purchasing, quality, and sales.

Key Contact - Specialty:
Mr. Daniel C. Lasse, President - *Human resources, accounting*

Salary minimum: $40,000

Functions: Mfg., Quality, Sales & Mktg., HR Mgmt., Finance, IT

Industries: Agri., Forestry, Mining, Mfg., Food, Bev., Tobacco, Metal Products, Machine, Appliance, Motor Vehicles, Misc. Mfg., Transportation, Wholesale, Services, Accounting, Mgmt. Consulting, HR Services, Call Centers, Environmental Svcs., Haz. Waste, Insurance, Software, Healthcare

Professional Associations: SHRM

MRI of Brownsburg

65 E Garner Rd Ste 100
Brownsburg, IN 46112
(317) 852-8200
Fax: (317) 852-3955
Email: admin@mrindynw.com
Web: www.mrindynw.com

Description: Our firm is a network affiliate of MRI and located just north west of Indianapolis, Indiana. Our firm specializes in working with companies in a variety of industries including, banking, insurance, mortgage, and public accounting. As for specific positions, we have placed individuals in variety of positions within those industries including commercial lenders, branch managers, tax managers, controllers, accountants, loan officers, underwriters, claims reps, business development managers, and senior level banking executives.

Key Contact:
Mr. Stephen Combs, Manager - *Finance/accounting*
Mr. Charles Combs - *Banking*
Ms. Amy Brugh, Account Executive - *Banking industry*
Mr. Mike Eickhoff, Account Executive - *Insurance (property, casualty) division*
Mr. Shane Frazier, Account Executive - *Industrial (instrumentation, automation division)*
Mrs. Dawn Swinford, Project Recruiter - *Banking division*
Ms. Betsy Card, Project Recruiter

Functions: Finance, Cash Mgmt., Engineering

Industries: Finance, Banking, Mfg. SW

MRI of Indianapolis-North

11611 N Meridian St Ste 220
Carmel, IN 46032
(317) 582-0202
Fax: (317) 582-0303
Email: mrindy@mrindianapolis.com
Web: www.mrindianapolis.com

Description: Thirty years of outstanding success meeting corporate America's total staffing needs. This outstanding firm is lead by George Ceryak, 30 years with MRI and winner of the prestigious office of the decade award for the 80s.

Key Contact:
Mr. George V. Ceryak, Co-Owner - *Executive sales*
Mr. David S. Oberting, Co-Owner

Functions: Generalist, Senior Mgmt., Production, Mkt. Research, Sales Mgmt., Cash Mgmt., Systems Analysis, Systems Dev.

Industries: Generalist, Construction, Mfg., Chemicals, Machine, Appliance, Finance, Accounting, IT Implementation, Marketing SW, Healthcare

MRI of Columbus, IN

2070 Doctors Park Dr
PO Box 2234
Columbus, IN 47201
(812) 372-5500
Fax: (812) 372-8292
Email: mrresume@mrcols.com
Web: www.mrcols.com

Description: Executive search firm specializing in banking, financial, MIS and manufacturing.

Key Contact - Specialty:
Mr. J. Michael Percifield, Owner/Manager - *Banking*

Functions: Generalist, Product Dev., Plant Mgmt., Productivity, Health Admin., Systems Implem., Network Admin., Engineering

Industries: Generalist, Misc. Mfg., Banking, Invest. Banking, Brokers, Insurance

MRI of Indianapolis-Central

8200 Haverstick Rd Ste 240
Indianapolis, IN 46240-2472
(317) 257-5411
Fax: (317) 259-6886
Email: brilliantpeople@mriindy.com
Web: www.mriindy.com

Description: Our office has served hundreds of client companies. Collectively possessing several years of recruiting experience, our team of 55 recruiters filled over 800 positions last year alone.

Key Contact:
Mr. William A. Kuntz, General Manager - *Manufacturing, human resources, accounting, information technology, general management*
Mr. Mark Haering, Director of Operations

Salary minimum: $50,000

Functions: Generalist

Industries: Mfg., Finance, Services, Media, Telecoms, Aerospace, Insurance, Software, Biotech, Healthcare

MRI of Newburgh

3775 Haley Dr Ste A
Newburgh, IN 47630
(812) 842-1000
Fax: (812) 842-4000
Email: jobs@managementrecruitersin.com
Web: www.mrinet.com

Description: We specialize in the recruitment of executives and management for banking, finance, engineering, and healthcare. We operate under a contingency or retained search. Our account executives average over 20 years each in their respective industry or the business industry in general.

Key Contact - Specialty:
Mr. M. Lynn Cooper, President - *Banking, finance*
Mr. Dan Oates, VP & Partner - *Engineering*

Functions: Mfg., Healthcare, Finance, Engineering

Industries: Mfg., Electronic, Elec. Components, Finance, Services, Non-profits, Accounting, HR Services, Insurance, HR SW, Marketing SW, Healthcare, Hospitals, Long-term Care, Physical Therapy, Occupational Therapy, Women's

MRI of Noblesville Inc

15209 Herriman Blvd
Noblesville, IN 46060-4230
(317) 773-4323
Fax: (317) 773-9744
Email: mail@mriweb.com
Web: www.mriweb.com

Description: We are a contingency/retained recruiting firm primarily placing engineers, supervisors, managers, sales engineers, sales management, and vice presidents, in general manufacturing and technical sales. Our regional office is based within 500 miles of Indianapolis, Indiana.

Key Contact:
Mr. H. Peter Isenberg, Managing Partner - *Technical sales, engineering*
Ms. Elizabeth Searle, Partner

Salary minimum: $40,000

Functions: Generalist, Product Dev., Production, Plant Mgmt., Quality, Materials Plng., Sales Mgmt., Engineering

Industries: Generalist, Plastics, Rubber, Metal Products, Machine, Appliance, Motor Vehicles, Misc. Mfg., Packaging

MRI of South Bend

(also known as W Shaw & Associates)
1001 Hickory Rd Ste 7A
South Bend, IN 46615-3723
(219) 234-6380
Fax: (219) 234-6377
Email: mrisouthbend@earthlink.net

Key Contact - Specialty:
Mr. R. William Shaw, President - *Manufacturing, engineering, research & development, sales & marketing, information technology*

Salary minimum: $40,000

Functions: Mfg., Healthcare, Sales & Mktg., Finance, IT, R&D, Engineering

Industries: Generalist, Food, Bev., Tobacco, Drugs Mfg., Medical Devices, Plastics, Rubber, Motor Vehicles, Consumer Elect., Wholesale, Healthcare

MRI of Spencer

589 Hwy 71 S
PO Box 840
Arnolds Park, IA 51331
(712) 332-2011
Fax: (712) 332-2051
Email: brad@nationaljobs.net
Web: www.nationaljobs.net

Description: We are an executive recruiting firm specializing in the placement of professionals in the manufacturing market with an emphasis in engineering and accounting. We also specialize in placing professionals in the hospitality market. We offer pre-interview counseling, feed back after the interviews, and help to negotiate offers and acceptances for the new position.

Key Contact - Specialty:
Mr. Brad Dach, Owner - *General manufacturing, agriculture, engineering*

Functions: Generalist, Mfg., Purchasing, Materials Plng., Finance, Engineering

Industries: Generalist, Mfg., Hospitality

MRI of Quad Cities

2435 Kimberly Rd Penthouse
Alpine Ctr S
Bettendorf, IA 52722
(563) 359-3503
Fax: (563) 359-1681
Email: mriqc@aol.com
Web: www.mri.com

Description: We are an executive search firm specializing in mid to upper level management positions in engineering, IS/IT, sales/marketing, HR, technical, finance, and medical fields.

Functions: Generalist

Industries: Generalist

MRI of Fairfield

106 W Lowe
Fairfield, IA 52556
(641) 469-5811
(800) 499-5811
Email: marksoth@mrff.net
Web: www.mrff.net

Description: Experienced, professional staff dedicated to middle and upper-management contingency placement in information technology, manufacturing, engineering and human resources functions.

Key Contact - Specialty:
Mr. Mark Soth, Manager - *Information technology, human resources*
Ms. Maureen Boehm, Account Executive - *Information technology*
Ms. Dawna Burnett, Account Executive - *Manufacturing, engineering*

Mr. Jeff Kapec, Account Executive - *Software sales, pre/post tech sales support*

Salary minimum: $40,000

Functions: Generalist, General Mgmt., Mfg., Sales & Mktg., HR Mgmt., MIS Mgmt., Systems Analysis, Systems Implem., Engineering

Industries: Generalist, Mfg., Food, Bev., Tobacco, Lumber, Furniture, Computer Equip., Transportation, New Media, Broadcast, Film, Telecoms, Software, Database SW, Development SW, ERP SW, System SW

MRI of Siouxland

4617 Morningside Ave
Sioux City, IA 51106-2943
(712) 276-8454
Fax: (712) 276-8453
Email: mrisc@pionet.net

Description: Complete search, reference checks, personality profiles.

Key Contact - Specialty:
Mr. James A. Rupert, President - *Finance, banking*
Mr. Jim Anderson, Vice President - *Banking*
Ms. Patty Grace, Account Executive - *Metal building (manufacturing & construction)*
Mr. Jon Lageschulte, Account Executive - *Food processing, QA, R&D, plant managers*
Mr. Doug Strohbeen, Account Executive - *Computers, IT*
Mr. Todd VanRooyan, Account Executive - *Banking*

Salary minimum: $30,000

Functions: Generalist, Production, Quality, Mktg. Mgmt., Sales Mgmt., HR Mgmt., Engineering

Industries: Generalist, Construction, Food, Bev., Tobacco, Metal Products, Banking

MRI of Williamsburg

600 Court St
PO Box 1136
Williamsburg, IA 52361-1136
(319) 668-2881
Fax: (319) 668-1404
Email: jobs@wburgcareers.com
Web: www.wburgcareers.com

Description: Agricultural specialists with an emphasis on agronomic, vegetable and farm seed industries in all aspects of management, sales and research. Engineering specialists with an emphasis in manufacturing, senior-level positions, production, operation, management, quality, and human resource.

Key Contact - Specialty:
Mr. John J. Lehnst, Owner - *Agriculture*
Ms. Sharon Thomas, Account Executive - *Agriculture*
Ms. Lori Stecker, Account Executive - *Manufacturing*
Ms. Patti Tiernan, Account Executive - *Manufacturing*
Mrs. Tosha Kukuzke, Account Executive - *Construction*

Functions: General Mgmt., Senior Mgmt., Mfg., Production, Plant Mgmt., Packaging, Sales & Mktg., Engineering, Non-profits, Int'l.

Industries: Agri., Forestry, Mining, Construction, Mfg., Chemicals, Drugs Mfg., Medical Devices, Plastics, Rubber, Metal Products, Machine, Appliance, Motor Vehicles, Misc. Mfg., Pharm Svcs., Packaging, Biotech

Professional Associations: NAMA

MRI of Ft. Scott

PO Box 5020
Ft. Scott, KS 66701
(316) 223-3133

Email: jstark@prorecruit.com
Web: www.procrecruit.com

Description: Highly specialized firm serving the printing industry. Our firm places 100-150 printing professionals annually. Integrity is first, fulfillment second. Positions filled: sales representatives, sales managers, plant managers, COOs, etc.

Key Contact:
Mr. James Stark, Manager

Salary minimum: $30,000

Functions: Generalist, Senior Mgmt., Middle Mgmt., Product Dev., Plant Mgmt., Sales Mgmt., Customer Svc.

Industries: Generalist, Paper, Printing, Publishing

MRI of Topeka
2913 SW Plass Ct
Topeka, KS 66611
(785) 267-5430
Fax: (785) 267-0513

Description: We recruit nationally and internationally in the fields of accounting/finance, agriculture, higher education, information technology, insurance/investments and general manufacturing (e.g. engineers).

Key Contact:
Mr. Matthew C. McFarland, President

Salary minimum: $25,000

Functions: Generalist, General Mgmt., Mfg., Sales & Mktg., Finance, IT, Engineering

Industries: Generalist, Agri., Forestry, Mining, Metal Products, Misc. Financial, Higher Ed., Accounting, Insurance

MRI of Sherwood
1100 SW Wanamaker Ste 7
Topeka, KS 66604
(785) 273-6600
Fax: (785) 273-8455
Email: topjobs@mrsherwood.com

Description: With over 30 years of recruiting experience in our office, we are able to search out the top candidates available, pre-qualify, reference check, and present the best of the best. Our desk specialties include food processing, manufacturing/engineering, and healthcare.

Key Contact - Specialty:
Ms. Carole J. Hawkins, President - *Assisted living, long-term care*
Ms. Helen G. Hurley, Manager - *Food processing*

Functions: Mfg., Production, Plant Mgmt., Quality, Healthcare, Health Admin.

Industries: Construction, Mfg., Food, Bev., Tobacco, Lumber, Furniture, Metal Products, Misc. Mfg., Transportation, Accounting, Mgmt. Consulting, HR Services, Environmental Svcs., Mfg. SW, Healthcare, Hospitals, Long-term Care, Physical Therapy, Occupational Therapy

MRI of Warren County, KY
546 Park St Fairview Park Plz Ste 100
Bowling Green, KY 42101
(270) 782-3820
Fax: (270) 782-3985
Email: rdg21366@hotmail.com
Web: www.grimeslegal.com

Description: We recruit and place attorneys only as a legal search and placement agency.

Key Contact:
Mr. G. D. Grimes, President/Manager
Ms. Nancy C. Grimes, Vice President/Secretary
Mr. Richard D. Grimes, Vice President/Manager

Functions: Generalist, Attorneys

Industries: Generalist, Legal

Professional Associations: NALSC

MRI of Danville
105 Citation Dr Ste A
Danville, KY 40422-9200
(859) 236-0505
Fax: (859) 236-0488
Email: mriky@searnet.com
Web: www.mriky.com

Description: Specialize in electrical, mechanical, process and quality engineers and departmental managers in general metalworking.

Key Contact - Specialty:
Mr. Robert P. DiLuca, President - *Generalist*

Salary minimum: $30,000

Functions: Generalist, Product Dev., Production, Automation, Plant Mgmt., Quality, Engineering

Industries: Generalist, Plastics, Rubber, Metal Products, Machine, Appliance, Motor Vehicles, Test, Measure Equip.

MRI of Lexington
1999 Richmond Rd Fl 2 Ste 2B
Lexington, KY 40502
(859) 269-7227
Fax: (859) 269-6400
Email: kts@mrlex.com
Web: www.mrlex.com

Description: Executive search firm specializing primarily in all aspects of manufacturing with an emphasis on the automotive industry, paints & coatings and property & casualty insurance. Positions range from engineers with 3-5 years' experience to president/CEO.

Key Contact:
Mr. Kent T. Simpson, Manager

Salary minimum: $35,000

Functions: Generalist, General Mgmt.

Industries: Mfg., Plastics, Rubber, Paints, Petro. Products, Metal Products, Machine, Appliance, Motor Vehicles, Misc. Mfg., Packaging, Insurance

MRI of Richmond
213 St. George St Ste B
Richmond, KY 40475-2323
(859) 624-3535
Fax: (859) 624-3539
Email: mr@mrky.com
Web: www.mrky.com

Description: Recruiting specialists serving Kentucky and surrounding states.

Key Contact:
Mr. Ron S. Lawson, General Manager

Functions: Generalist, Product Dev., Production, Automation, Plant Mgmt., Quality, Productivity

Industries: Generalist, Plastics, Rubber, Leather, Stone, Glass, Motor Vehicles

MRI of Versailles
(also known as Amberg Consulting Group)
101 High St Ste D
Versailles, KY 40383
(859) 879-3811
Fax: (859) 879-3911
Email: aamberg@exec-recruiters.net
Web: www.exec-recruiters.net

Description: Our firm serves clients in a variety of manufacturing industries including: construction, industrial, and agricultural machinery, as well as automotive, plastics and metal related components. In order to provide the best selection of fully qualified candidates, our research, recruitment and

selection procedures are generally conducted on a national level.

Key Contact - Specialty:
Mr. Arthur Amberg, President - *General manufacturing*
Mr. Jeffery Hardy, Staffing Consultant - *Metal forming industry*
Ms. Katrina Grantham, Research Consultant - *General manufacturing*

Functions: General Mgmt., Mfg., Materials, Engineering

Industries: Mfg., Plastics, Rubber, Metal Products, Machine, Appliance, Motor Vehicles, Test, Measure Equip., Misc. Mfg., Packaging, Industry Specific SW, Mfg. SW, Marketing SW

Professional Associations: ASAE, ASME, NSPE, SAE

MRI of Monroe
3124 Kilpatrick Blvd
Monroe, LA 71201
(318) 322-2200
Fax: (318) 322-4745
Email: mrmonroe@centurytel.net
Web: www.mrmonroe.com

Description: We offer prompt response in slating candidates for key positions, discount moving rates and special mortgage program if relocation is desired/required. Additional services include outplacement, executive temporary placement and personality profiling. We specialize in the building products, food & beverage, general manufacturing and telecommunications industries.

Key Contact - Specialty:
Mr. Bruce Hursey, President - *Building products*

Salary minimum: $30,000

Functions: Generalist, Mfg., Production, Plant Mgmt., Mktg. Mgmt., Sales Mgmt., HR Mgmt., Engineering

Industries: Generalist, Food, Bev., Tobacco, Lumber, Furniture, Paper, Plastics, Rubber, Metal Products, Machine, Appliance, Motor Vehicles

Professional Associations: SFPA, SHRM

MRI of Baltimore City
7500 Harford Rd
Baltimore, MD 21232
(410) 426-8850
Fax: (410) 254-2585
Email: rondangelo@aol.com
Web: www.mrinet.com

Description: Management Recruiters is the largest search and recruitment organization in the world today. Our office is dedicated to conducting comprehensive candidate searches that are customized to meet each client's specific need. Each of our experienced account executives is extremely knowledgeable about the industry in which they specialize and are committed to monitoring current industry trends, which effect companies like yours.

Key Contact:
Mr. Ron E. D'Angelo, Manager

Salary minimum: $50,000

Functions: Generalist, Sales & Mktg., Risk Mgmt., IT

Industries: Generalist, Computer Equip., E-commerce, IT Implementation, Communications, Telecoms, Insurance, Software

MRI of Columbia
8640 Guilford Rd Ste 224
Columbia, MD 21046
(410) 309-6590
(800) 267-1226
Fax: (410) 309-6595

Email: jobs@plasticjobsource.com
Web: www.plasticjobsource.com

Description: We are the leading plastic recruitment firm in the nation. We provide job opportunities for professionals in plastics and packaging manufacturing. We are serving the appliance, automotive, medical, consumer, industrial, high-tech, packaging, cosmetic, and food and beverage industries. The open "Hot Jobs" listing on our website is updated weekly.

Key Contact - Specialty:
Mr. Randolph Reyes, General Manager/Senior Recruiter - *Plastic engineering, product development, mfg & tooling*
Mr. Mark Villee, Director, Plastic Staffing - *Plastic manufacturing, processing, supervisory, technicians, production engineers*
Ms. Renee Reyes, Recruiter - *Packaging, plastic quality assurance*
Mr. William Bryant, Project Coordinator - *Plastic engineering*
Mr. Ed McGill, Project Coordinator - *Plastic manufacturing, production*

Functions: Mfg.

Industries: Mfg., Media, Telecoms, Packaging

Professional Associations: ASQ, MAPRC, SPE

MRI of Frederick
4 N East St
Frederick, MD 21701
(301) 663-0600
(301) 831-4414
Fax: (301) 663-0454
Email: mgmtrec@mrifrederick.com
Web: www.mrifrederick.com

Description: Specialize in working with any company, any level, within the healthcare, pharmaceutical and medical equipment industries, informations systems and administrative areas.

Key Contact:
Mrs. Pat Webb, Manager

Functions: Generalist, Senior Mgmt., Admin. Svcs., Health Admin., Sales Mgmt., MIS Mgmt., Systems Support

Industries: Generalist, Drugs Mfg., Medical Devices, Pharm Svcs., Accounting, Software

---

MRI of Gaithersburg
963-A Russell Ave A
Gaithersburg, MD 20879
(240) 631-7730
(877) 631-7730
Fax: (240) 631-7731
Email: mrgaithersburg@earthlink.net
Web: www.mrigaithersburgh.com

Description: Our firm specializes in the placement of executive management and technical professionals within the information technology and biotech arenas. We recruit and place executive and general managers, sales and marketing professionals, IT, research and development specialists, systems developers and integrators, and human resources, finance and administration professionals. Our expanding client base includes firms engaged with biotech, high-tech, engineering, scientific research, domestic and international package delivery, web-hosting, manufacturing, and manufacturing execution systems.

Key Contact - Specialty:
Mr. Eric Beebe, President - *Executive IT management, sales*

Salary minimum: $70,000

Functions: General Mgmt., Senior Mgmt., Sales & Mktg., IT, MIS Mgmt., Systems Dev., DB Admin., R&D

Industries: Food, Bev., Tobacco, Consumer Elect., Test, Measure Equip., Electronic, Elec.

Components, Services, Non-profits, Accounting, Equip Svcs., Mgmt. Consulting, HR Services, E-commerce, IT Implementation, Call Centers, Wireless, Fiber Optic, Network Infrastructure, Government, Defense, Aerospace, Software, Development SW, Doc. Mgmt., Production SW, ERP SW, Biotech, Healthcare

MRI of The Baltimore Washington Corridor
7240 Pkwy Dr Ste 150
Hanover, MD 21076
(410) 712-0770
Fax: (410) 712-0510
Email: mribwi@erols.com
Web: www.recruitergurus.com

Description: We offer complete search/placement, permanent/interim in telecommunications, engineering, medical device, electronics, security electronics, sales, management, information systems, software, chemical, filtration, plastics, and sales/marketing. We are adjacent to Baltimore/Washington International Airport. We have access to a videoconferencing network to 400 US and international locations.

Key Contact - Specialty:
Mr. Lee Stubberfield, President - *Senior management, medical device manufacturing, healthcare, home healthcare, sales & marketing*
Ms. Jodie Ballou - *Medical device, engineering, quality, R&D, manufacturing*
Ms. Carole Lombard - *Software sales, sales management, GIS sales, CRM sales, ASP sales*
Mr. J. Jay Tinker, CSAM, CPC - *Telecommunications, electronics, security electronics, engineering, management*
Mr. Joe Bezold - *Finance, banking, management, sales & marketing, compliance*
Ms. Lynn Rodens - *Information systems, information technology, software, development, sales*
Mr. Shakir Contractor - *Information systems, information technology, software, development, sales*

Salary minimum: $40,000

Functions: General Mgmt., Mfg., Packaging, Sales & Mktg., Finance, IT, R&D, Engineering

Industries: Medical Devices, Computer Equip., Consumer Elect., Finance, Accounting, Equip Svcs., Mgmt. Consulting, Telecoms, Software, Biotech

Professional Associations: MAPRC

MRI of Hunt Valley
(also known as Hunt Valley Executive Resources)
201 Int'l Cir Ste 180
Hunt Valley, MD 21031-1366
(410) 785-6313
Fax: (410) 785-6314
Email: info@mrihuntvalley.com
Web: www.mrihuntvalley.com

Description: We are a customer focused executive search and staffing firm. As a network affiliate of the nation's largest search and recruitment organization, our office specializes in transportation, distribution, and logistics talent.

Key Contact - Specialty:
Mr. David E. Wise, MBA, President - *Transportation, distribution, logistics*

Salary minimum: $40,000

Functions: Generalist

Industries: Transportation, Wholesale, Services

Professional Associations: CLM

MRI of Rockville
15717 Crabbs Branch Way Ste 202C
Rockville, MD 20855
(301) 948-7470
Fax: (301) 948-7475
Email: mrr@rockvillerecruiter.com
Web: www.rockvillerecruiter.com

Description: We are a small privately owned office offering "first names" service; yet, we are associated with and offer all the services and resources of the world's largest search firm. Because of the unique blend we are able to present qualified candidates with a minimum of time on the part of our clients.

Key Contact - Specialty:
Mr. Robert Moore, Owner - *Retail, food industry, distribution, warehousing, industrial engineering*
Mr. John Yarbrough, Account Executive - *Pharmaceuticals distribution, warehousing, supply chain, 3PL*
Ms. Lisa Schmidt - *Technology*

Functions: Generalist, Middle Mgmt., Plant Mgmt., Distribution, HR Mgmt., IT, Engineering, Minorities

Industries: Generalist, Textiles, Apparel, Retail, HR Services

Professional Associations: CLM, WERC

MRI of Baltimore
9515 Deereco Rd Ste 900
Timonium, MD 21093
(410) 252-6616
Fax: (410) 252-7076
Email: info@mribaltimore.com
Web: www.mribaltimore.com

Description: Our firm is an internationally recognized, award-winning team of professionals with experience, tenure, expertise, and a history of proven success! MRI Worldwide Baltimore/Timonium is undoubtedly one of the most successful offices in the history of MRI. By currently honoring our 25th anniversary of staffing excellence and unparalleled partnerships with world-class employers and talented job seekers, we set the standard of excellence in the industry by consistently outperforming the masses.

Key Contact:
Ms. Linda A. Burton, CEO
Mr. Ken Davis, President

Functions: Senior Mgmt., Admin. Svcs., Mfg., Packaging, Sales & Mktg., IT, Engineering

Industries: Generalist, Mfg., Telecoms, Packaging, Software, Biotech

Professional Associations: MAPRC

MRI of Boston
607 Boylston St Ste 700
Boston, MA 02116
(617) 262-5050
Fax: (617) 421-9630
Email: boston@mri-boston.com
Web: www.mri-boston.com

Description: We have offered retained and contingency search for over 35 years with over 80 recruiters working in varied industries and specialties.

Key Contact:
Mr. Jack J. Nehiley, Manager

Functions: Generalist

Industries: Generalist

MRI of Torch Lake

11812 SE Torch Lake Dr
PO Box 208
Alden, MI 49612
(231) 331-7900
Fax: (231) 331-7901
Email: headhunter@mritorch.com
Web: www.mritorch.com

Description: As leaders in the professional placement industry, we continually strive to be the best in providing superior talent in a timely fashion. By combining integrity, resourcefulness and teamwork into each recruiting assignment, we deliver long-term human resource solutions.

Key Contact - Specialty:
Mr. Matthew R. Allen, President - *Information technology*

Salary minimum: $40,000

Functions: Generalist, MIS Mgmt., Systems Analysis, Systems Dev., Systems Implem., Systems Support, Network Admin., DB Admin.

Industries: Generalist, Soap, Perf., Cosmtcs., Wholesale, Banking, Insurance, Software, Healthcare, Non-classifiable

MRI of Birmingham

30700 Telegraph Rd Ste 3650
Bingham Farms, MI 48025-4527
(248) 647-7766
Fax: (248) 647-9722
Email: adminmri@recruiters-mri.com
Web: www.recruiters-mri.com

Description: We partner with our clients to bring them the finest talent in the nation.

Key Contact - Specialty:
Mr. Brian Binke, President - *Information technology*
Ms. Ellen McCowan-Binke, Executive Vice President - *Automotive engineering, management*

Salary minimum: $40,000

Functions: Mfg., IT, Engineering

Industries: Construction, Motor Vehicles, Software

MRI of Southeastern Michigan

115 N Main St
PO Box 3
Blissfield, MI 49228-0003
(517) 486-2167
Fax: (517) 486-2324
Email: baker@cass.net

Description: Always looking for production and engineering candidates with metal or plastics background. Have positions available throughout the U.S. If you have these qualifications, please send your resume in confidence.

Key Contact - Specialty:
Ms. Mary W. Snellbaker, Owner - *Manufacturing, engineering*

Functions: Generalist, Mfg., Quality, Materials, HR Mgmt., Finance, Engineering

Industries: Generalist, Plastics, Rubber, Metal Products, Motor Vehicles, Packaging

MRI of Dearborn

3 Parklane Blvd Ste 725
Parklane Twrs W
Dearborn, MI 48126
(313) 336-6650
Fax: (313) 336-7436
Email: visitus@mridearborn.com
Web: www.mridearborn.com

Description: Over twenty-five years in the confidential recruitment and placement of middle management and professionals in most functional disciplines. M/R Nat'l. Office of the year-1987;

Compu-Search Division-Nat'l Office of the year-1989.

Key Contact - Specialty:
Mr. Terrence Tripp, President - *Engineering*
Ms. Elaine Kozlowski, CSAM,CPC, Manager - *Automotive (engineers, manufacturing management)*

Salary minimum: $25,000

Functions: Middle Mgmt., Mfg., Materials, Healthcare, Sales Mgmt., Finance, IT, Systems Dev., Engineering

Industries: Generalist, Mfg., Drugs Mfg., Medical Devices, Motor Vehicles, Misc. Mfg., Misc. Financial, Services, Pharm Svcs., Accounting, Packaging, Software, Biotech, Healthcare

Professional Associations: ESD

MRI of E Detroit/Farmington Hills

34405 W 12 Mile Ste115
Farmington Hills, MI 48331
(248) 324-2100
Fax: (248) 324-2101
Email: info@mridetroit.com
Web: www.mridetroit.com

Description: We are the largest permanent placement firm in the world with the best-trained recruiters and largest network/database available. We have been a locally owned franchise for over 17 years.

Key Contact - Specialty:
Ms. Debra Lawson, President/General Manager - *Human resources, administrative, accounting*

Functions: Generalist, Admin. Svcs., Customer Svc., HR Mgmt., Benefits, Personnel, Finance

Industries: Generalist

MRI of Flint

10751 S Saginaw Rd Ste M
Grand Blanc, MI 48439
(810) 695-0120
Fax: (810) 695-0522
Email: mriflint@aol.com

Description: We are one of 850 franchised offices of Management Recruiters and we rely on corporate national advertising: Wall Street Journal and major radio stations along with news releases sent to all local media.

Key Contact - Specialty:
Mr. Dave Reed, Co-Owner - *Technical, metal stamping, machining, plastics, electro-mechanical*
Mr. Rick Reed, Co-Owner - *Automation & robotics, quality, product development, engineering*
Mrs. Lorrie Thams, Senior Account Executive - *MIS, computer support (general)*

Salary minimum: $25,000

Functions: Generalist

Industries: Mfg., Plastics, Rubber, Metal Products, Motor Vehicles, Test, Measure Equip., Aerospace, Software

MRI of Livonia

37677 Professional Center Dr Ste 100C
Livonia, MI 48154-1138
(734) 953-9590
Fax: (734) 953-0566
Email: mrilivonia@mrilivonia.com
Web: www.mrilivonia.com

Description: We find and place professional and technical persons with employers needing permanent or temporary employees with specific skills and qualifications. We also provide outplacement and relocation assistance.

Key Contact - Specialty:
Mr. Don Eden, President - *Financial-CFO's, controllers, auditors, financial analyst*
Ms. Judy Somershoe, Senior Recruiter - *Human resources & administrative management*
Mr. Matthew Tenfelde, Senior Recruiter/Manager - *Plastics engineers & management*

Salary minimum: $30,000

Functions: General Mgmt., Directors, Middle Mgmt., Mfg., Purchasing, Finance

Industries: Energy, Utilities, Mfg., Food, Bev., Tobacco, Paper, Chemicals, Drugs Mfg., Plastics, Rubber, Paints, Petro. Products, Machine, Appliance, Motor Vehicles, Computer Equip., Consumer Elect., Misc. Mfg., Finance, Accounting, Mgmt. Consulting, Packaging, Accounting SW

Professional Associations: SAE, SME, SPE

MRI of Muskegon

919 W Norton Ave Ste 101
Muskegon, MI 49441
(231) 830-8400
Fax: (231) 830-8500
Email: mrmuskegon@i2k.com

Description: Our account executives know your business. We are industry specialists with a combined total of 40 years of recruiting expertise and are qualified to handle the most difficult assignments.

Key Contact - Specialty:
Mr. John R. Mitchell, Jr., Manager - *Generalist*

Functions: Middle Mgmt., Production, Plant Mgmt., Purchasing, Mktg. Mgmt., CFO's, Engineering

Industries: Lumber, Furniture, Printing, Plastics, Rubber, Metal Products, Motor Vehicles, Misc. Mfg., Accounting, HR Services, Law Enforcement

MRI of North Oakland County

2530 S Rochester Rd
Rochester Hills, MI 48307-4441
(248) 299-1900
Email: mrnocmi@mrnoc.com
Web: www.mmoc.com

Description: Dedicated to helping our clients address their professional staffing needs. We are part of the largest contingency search firm in the United States with over 600 offices nationwide conducting searches throughout the United States and Europe.

Key Contact - Specialty:
Mr. Mark Angott, President - *Banking*

Salary minimum: $25,000

Functions: Generalist

Industries: Mfg., Retail, Finance, Non-profits, Accounting, Equip Svcs., HR Services, Advertising, Software

Professional Associations: AITP, ASQ, ESD, HRA, MBA, SAE, SHRM

MRI of Traverse City

3622 Veterans Dr Ste 1
Traverse City, MI 49684
(231) 947-8000
Fax: (231) 922-9481
Email: mrtc@traverse.com
Web: www.traverse.com/mri

Description: We provide a focused industry expertise that enables us to locate, qualify, and present the most qualified candidates in the areas of automotive, information technology, manufacturing, technology sales, telecommunications, and construction. We service corporations seeking qualified individuals or someone considering a career change; contact us for a confidential analysis of your goals or objectives.

Key Contact - Specialty:
Ms. Mary J. Barker, CSAM, Manager
Mr. Doug Barker, Co-Owner & Recruiter - *Construction*
Mr. Doug Grabe, Recruiter - *Engineering, manufacturing, technical*
Mr. Steve Klein, Recruiter - *Automotive*
Ms. Shawna McLeod, Recruiter - *Automotive*
Mr. Robert Banks, Jr., Recruiter - *Information technology*
Mrs. Rita Melotti, Recruiter - *Manufacturing*
Ms. Christine Krzyszton, Recruiter - *Technology, software, solutions sales*
Mr. Rob Cotton, Recruiter - *Telecommunications*
Mr. Mario De Carolis, Recruiter - *Information technology, peoplesoft*

Salary minimum: $35,000

Functions: Generalist, Mfg., Product Dev., Sales Mgmt., IT, Engineering

Industries: Construction, Mfg., Leather, Stone, Glass, Metal Products, Motor Vehicles, Consumer Elect., Electronic, Elec. Components, Finance, Services, E-commerce, IT Implementation, Hospitality, Communications, Packaging, Insurance, Software, Doc. Mgmt., Production SW, ERP SW, Industry Specific SW, Biotech, Healthcare, Non-classifiable

Networks: Accord Group

MRI of Bloomington
4200 W Old Shakopee Rd Ste 200
Bloomington, MN 55437
(952) 948-0280
Email: mr@jobtip.com
Web: www.jobtip.com

Description: Confidential search in telecommunications, information technology and sales; superior personal service.

Key Contact - Specialty:
Mr. Dale Gustafson, Manager - *IT*

Salary minimum: $50,000

Functions: Sales & Mktg., Sales Mgmt., IT, MIS Mgmt., Systems Analysis, Systems Dev., Systems Implem., Systems Support, Network Admin., DB Admin.

Industries: Generalist, Computer Equip., Software

Professional Associations: MAPS

MRI of Park Rapids
21124 High Pine Ln
Park Rapids, MN 56470
(218) 732-0073
Email: mrpr1@unitelc.com
Web: www.mr-pr.com

Description: The principal has twenty years of direct experience at all levels in the industry of automation and its distribution. This gives the firm a great advantage in finding and recruiting highly qualified candidates.

Key Contact - Specialty:
Mr. Mark A. Copperthite, President - *Automation*

Salary minimum: $40,000

Functions: Generalist, Product Dev., Automation, Materials, Sales & Mktg., Sales Mgmt., Customer Svc., Engineering

Industries: Generalist, Mfg., Machine, Appliance, Test, Measure Equip.

MRI of Rochester
1652 Greenview Dr SW Ste 600
Rochester, MN 55902
(507) 282-2400
Fax: (507) 282-1308
Email: mrrocmn@ismidwest.com
Web: www.ismidwest.com

Description: We specialize in information systems including all IS titles and most common technologies and in general manufacturing including all professional titles for most industries in the upper Midwest.

Key Contact:
Mr. Robert Vierkant, President - *Information systems (upper midwest)*
Ms. Nona E. Vierkant, Vice President
Mr. John Harris, Account Executive - *Information systems (upper midwest)*
Ms. Ellen Newman, Account Executive - *Manufacturing*
Ms. Deah Hested, Account Executive - *Information systems*
Ms. Nona Vierkant

Functions: Mfg., IT

Industries: Generalist

MRI of Salem Corner
1530 Greenview Dr Ste 122
Rochester, MN 55902
(507) 536-0350
Fax: (507) 536-0349
Email: recruiters2@woodhunter.com
Web: www.woodhunter.com

Description: Specialized in the wood products industry as a whole and all management and executive positions. Focused in furniture, kitchen cabinets and bath, architectural millwork, lumber, components, trusses, industrial panels, decorative laminates, fixtures and displays, manufactured homes, doors and windows, sawmills, and building products.

Key Contact:
Ms. Shelley S. Risma, Co-Manager
Mr. Bill E. Risma, Co-Manager

Functions: Generalist

Industries: Construction, Mfg., Lumber, Furniture

MRI of Shakopee
206 Scott St
Shakopee, MN 55379
(952) 496-2552
Fax: (952) 445-3446
Email: mikejb@mn.uswest.net
Web: www.mrinet.com

Description: We are a full-service recruiting firm that specializes in the telecommunications industry exclusively.

Key Contact:
Mr. Michael Brown, Manager

MRI of Minnetonka
4000 Shoreline Dr Ste 1
Spring Park, MN 55384
(952) 471-3013
Fax: (952) 471-3014
Email: mrtonka@fishnet.com

Description: Firm focus: telecommunications and IT industries. Identify qualified candidates for positions in senior management to midlevel management. Assist in the hiring process.

Key Contact - Specialty:
Mr. Karel Van Langen, General Manager - *General management, information technology, telecommunications*

Salary minimum: $75,000

Functions: Senior Mgmt., Middle Mgmt., Mktg. Mgmt., Sales Mgmt., CFO's

Industries: Telecoms, Software

MRI of St. Louis Park
5353 Wayzata Blvd Ste 510
St. Louis Park, MN 55416
(952) 253-5500
Fax: (952) 253-5555
Email: sbush@careergarage.com
Web: www.careergarage.com

Description: We recruit only in the e-Commerce and telecommunications industries, with a focus on sales positions.

Key Contact:
Mr. Steven Bush

Functions: Generalist

Industries: E-commerce, PSA/ASP, Telecoms, Call Centers, Telephony, Digital, Wireless, Fiber Optic, Network Infrastructure, Software

MRI of Winona
1600 Gilmore Ave Ste 100
Winona, MN 55987
(507) 452-2700
(877) 452-2700
Fax: (507) 452-2722
Email: mrwinona@telecomcareer.com
Web: www.telecomcareer.com

Description: We provide staffing exclusively for telecommunications companies and are uniquely qualified to select and present candidates of the highest quality because of extensive hands-on experience in the telecommunications industry.

Key Contact - Specialty:
Mr. James Crigler, Vice President/General Manager - *Telecommunications*

Salary minimum: $25,000

Functions: Generalist, General Mgmt., Senior Mgmt., Middle Mgmt., Sales & Mktg., CFO's, Network Admin., Engineering

Industries: Generalist, Telecoms

MRI of Rankin Company
2506 Lakeland Dr Ste 408
Jackson, MS 39208
(601) 936-7900
Fax: (601) 936-9004
Email: mrvanwick@aol.com

Description: We service the food, beverage, pharmaceutical, and consumer goods industries. The positions that we place include all manufacturing, including engineering, production management, QA, logistics, etc. for plant and executive environments. We service from entry to executive.

Key Contact - Specialty:
Mr. Mike Van Wick, President - *Food operations, engineering, technical*

Salary minimum: $70,000

Functions: Mfg.

Industries: Food, Bev., Tobacco, Drugs Mfg., Consumer Elect.

Professional Associations: ASME, IEEE, IFT, PERYON

Networks: Global Partners

MRI of Jackson
1755 Lelia Dr Ste 102
Jackson, MS 39216
(601) 366-4488
Fax: (601) 366-4699
Email: jmmri@worldnet.att.net
Web: www.mrinet.com

Key Contact:
Mr. J. W. Gardner, General Manager

Functions: Directors, Mfg., Product Dev.

Industries: Generalist, Textiles, Apparel, Lumber, Furniture, Paper, Accounting, Aerospace, Software

MRI of Harrison County
102 W 5th St
Long Beach, MS 39560
(228) 863-8606
Fax: (228) 863-8604
Email: lowerymri@msn.com

Description: Over twenty-five years of experience recruiting in the electric utility industry for electrical engineering, mechanical engineering and chemical engineering, human resources, information technology and other professionals for proven distribution, transmission, substation, generation and corporate positions.

Key Contact - Specialty:
Mr. Gene Lowery, President - *Electric utilities*

Salary minimum: $30,000

Functions: Engineering

Industries: Energy, Utilities, Media

MRI of Lake St Louis
1101 Edgewater Pointe Blvd
Lake St. Louis, MO 63367-2906
(636) 625-1780
Fax: (636) 625-1788
Email: mrilsl@inlink.com
Web: www.mrlakestlouis.com

Description: We provide executive search and placement.

Key Contact:
Mr. Terry Bacigalupo, Manager

MRI of Laurie
PO Box 1509
Laurie, MO 65038-1509
(573) 374-9338
Fax: (573) 374-7745
Email: mri@lakeozark.net
Web: www.ozarkgroup.com

Key Contact:
Mr. Mike Cartella, Co-Manager
Ms. Janet Cartella, Co-Manager

Functions: Middle Mgmt., Mfg., Quality, Materials, Engineering

Industries: Computer Equip., Consumer Elect., Misc. Mfg., Electronic, Elec. Components

Professional Associations: SMTA

MRI of Omaha
7171 Mercy Rd Ste 252
Omaha, NE 68106-2696
(402) 397-8320
Fax: (402) 397-6322
Email: mriomaha@novia.net
Web: www.mriomaha.com

Key Contact - Specialty:
Mr. Todd Dawson, CSAM, President - *Group insurance, IT, accounting, engineering, financial svcs*

Salary minimum: $30,000

Functions: Generalist

Industries: Food, Bev., Tobacco, Finance, Banking, Accounting, IT Implementation, Insurance

MRI of North Reno
1350 Stardust St
A-5
Reno, NV 89503-4264
(775) 787-8009
Fax: (775) 787-8066
Email: reno@higherhorizons.com

Description: We provide professional recruiting services, by searching for and recruiting candidates to fill professional and executive positions in the area of manufacturing and engineering; IT and telecom.; sales and marketing; and financial.

Key Contact:
Mrs. Penny Todd, President
Mr. Ken Alkire, Account Executive - *Manufacturing*
Mrs. Brenda Cook, Recruiter

Functions: Generalist, General Mgmt., Senior Mgmt., Sales Mgmt., Finance, IT, MIS Mgmt.

Industries: Generalist, Mfg., Computer Equip., Telecoms, Software, Biotech

MRI of Reno
1025 Ridgeview Dr Ste 120
Reno, NV 89509-6321
(775) 826-5243
Fax: (775) 826-8329

Description: Specialties are general manufacturing, industrial sales. All national desks.

Key Contact - Specialty:
Mr. Ed Trapp, Manager/Owner - *Sales & marketing*

Salary minimum: $30,000

Functions: Plant Mgmt., Quality, Distribution, Sales Mgmt.

Industries: Generalist

MRI of Lake Tahoe, NV
PO Box 4766
Stateline, NV 89449
(775) 588-7388
Fax: (775) 588-7380
Email: jcargill@searchpros.net
Web: www.searchpros.net

Description: Specialists in gaming, construction, transportation and logistics from technical through CEO. Interim and permanent, nationwide, references available. Retained and contingency searches.

Key Contact - Specialty:
Mr. Jim Cargill, Owner/General Manager - *Gaming, construction*
Mr. David C. Bailey, Account Executive - *Transportation, distribution, logistics*

Salary minimum: $50,000

Functions: Generalist, Directors, Senior Mgmt., Middle Mgmt., Distribution, Architects

Industries: Generalist, Construction, Transportation, Hospitality

MRI of Bedford
4 Bedford Farms
Bedford, NH 03110
(603) 669-9800
Email: mbacon@mri-boston.com
Web: www.mri-boston.com

Description: Our firm is part of MRI, the largest search and recruitment organization in the world today. Our office in Bedford is dedicated to providing customized staffing solutions that address the unique challenges facing employers in the areas of finance, MIS, data communications, software, graphic arts, securities printing-publishing, engineering, IT, new media, consumer sales and marketing, commercial and industrial DataCom sales, retail, e-Commerce, and apparel.

Key Contact - Specialty:
Mr. Michael Bacon, Sr Vice President / General Manager - *Datacom commercial/industrial (sales & marketing)*

Salary minimum: $75,000

Functions: Generalist

Industries: Generalist, Mfg., Finance, Services, Media, Communications, Aerospace, Software, Biotech, Healthcare

MRI of Bay Head
106 Bridge Ave
Bay Head Commons
Bay Head, NJ 08742
(732) 714-1300
Fax: (732) 714-1311
Email: recruiter@mrielectrical.com
Web: www.mrielectrical.com

Description: Our firm specializes in all jobs (except clerical) in: electrical, electronics, factory automation, process controls, hardware, software and services. Sales, marketing, engineering, manufacturing, service and management.

Key Contact - Specialty:
Mr. Robert P. Ceresi, General Manager - *Electrical, electronics, computer automation*
Ms. Carole Ceresi, Co-Manager - *Electrical, electronics, computer automation*

Salary minimum: $40,000

Functions: Middle Mgmt., Mfg., Sales & Mktg., Systems Dev., Systems Implem., R&D, Engineering

Industries: Machine, Appliance, Computer Equip., Test, Measure Equip., Misc. Mfg., Equip Svcs.

Professional Associations: IEEE

MRI of Windsor
186 Princeton-Hightstown Rd
Cranbury, NJ 08512-1939
(609) 897-0055
Fax: (609) 897-0099
Email: retailexecmgmt@mripnt.com
Web: www.retailexecmgmtmri.com

Description: We are devoted to the permanent placement of executive-level professionals in the retail, logistics and associated industries.

Key Contact - Specialty:
Mr. Robert Walling, President - *Retail*

Salary minimum: $50,000

Functions: Generalist, Direct Mktg., HR Mgmt.

Industries: Generalist, Transportation, Retail, Real Estate

MRI of Orange County, NY
16 Birch Run Ave
Denville, NJ 07834
(845) 447-9509
(973) 625-4822
Fax: (973) 625-8117
Email: mriny@warwick.net

Description: Confidential, honest professionals. We are committed to the pursuit of excellence with integrity and standards that put us ahead of our competitors.

Key Contact - Specialty:
Ms. Carolyn A. Chermak, President - *Generalist, engineering*

Functions: Sales & Mktg., IT, Engineering, Environmentalists

Industries: Energy, Utilities, Environmental Svcs., Software

MRI of Fairfield

271 Rte 46 W Ste D206
Fairfield, NJ 07004
(973) 575-6660
Fax: (973) 575-9669
Email: mparker@mriscience.com
Web: www.mrinet.com

Description: We serve the pharmaceutical industry primarily in the areas of clinical research, quality assurance, and regulatory affairs.

Key Contact:
Mr. Mario Parker

MRI of Morris County, NJ

17 Hanover Rd Ste 450
Florham Park, NJ 07932
(973) 593-0400
Fax: (973) 593-0150
Email: sue@mrimc.com
Web: www.mrimc.com

Description: Specialty: building national remote sales teams for clients. Sales, technical support and marketing positions. Industry specialists: hardware and software data communications, telecommunications, data systems and converging technologies.

Key Contact - Specialty:
Ms. Susan M. Young, General Manager -
  Marketing, data systems, data communications, converging technologies, business development
Mr. Wayne Young, President - *Data communications sales, technical support, sales management, converging technologies*

Salary minimum: $75,000

Functions: Senior Mgmt., Sales & Mktg., Mktg. Mgmt., Sales Mgmt., Direct Mktg.

Industries: Computer Equip., Test, Measure Equip., New Media, Broadcast, Film, Telecoms, Software

MRI of North Warren

1298 Rte 519 American House Annex
PO Box 244
Hope, NJ 07844-0244
(908) 459-5798
Fax: (908) 459-4672
Email: hankmagn@ptd.net

Description: Specialists in finding mechanical engineers, human resources generalists and compensation and benefits experts.

Key Contact - Specialty:
Mr. Henry F. Magnusen, Manager - *Human resources change agents, mechanical engineers*

Functions: Generalist, Mfg., Product Dev., Plant Mgmt., Quality, HR Mgmt., Benefits, Training, Engineering

Industries: Generalist, Machine, Appliance

MRI of Medford, NJ

30 Jackson Rd Ste C-4
Medford, NJ 08055
(609) 654-9109
Fax: (609) 654-9166
Email: resumes@pharmabiojobs.com
Web: www.pharmabiojobs.com

Description: Nationwide search for engineering, scientific and executive personnel. All disciplines for middle to upper-management. Serving pharmaceutical, chemical, construction and biotechnology industries.

Key Contact - Specialty:
Mr. Norman Talbot, General Manager - *Technical recruitment*

Salary minimum: $50,000

Functions: Generalist, Senior Mgmt., Middle Mgmt., Plant Mgmt., Quality, Sales Mgmt., Engineering

Industries: Generalist, Drugs Mfg., Medical Devices, Biotech

Professional Associations: AICHE, ISPE, MAAPC, PDA

MRI of Edison

276 Main St
Metuchen, NJ 08840
(732) 767-1025
Fax: (732) 767-1218
Email: jobs@mrieng.com
Web: www.mrieng.com

Description: We have over 20 years of direct, hands-on engineering experience and specialize in placing engineers, engineering management, quality, validation and IT people in the chemical, pharmaceutical and biotech industries worldwide.

Key Contact - Specialty:
Mr. Frank Noorani, President - *Engineering for manufacturing*
Ms. Firoz Noorani, Manager - *Engineering for manufacturing*
Ms. Kathleen Gaber, Project Coordinator - *Quality, validation*
Mr. Albert Bull, Account Executive - *Information technology*

Salary minimum: $40,000

Functions: Production, Automation, Plant Mgmt., Quality, Packaging, IT, Engineering

Industries: Chemicals, Drugs Mfg., Medical Devices, Pharm Svcs., Packaging, Software, Biotech

MRI of Short Hills

181 Millburn Ave
Millburn, NJ 07041
(973) 379-4020
(877) 379-4020
Fax: (973) 379-2699
Email: recruiter@mrishorthills.com
Web: www.mrishorthills.com

Description: Management Recruiters of Short Hills is dedicated to executive search for IT sales, sales management, and marketing professionals. Our senior recruiters have over 20 years of IT experience. Ensuring a balance of an individual's career goals with our clients' growth needs, we believe serious candidates will demonstrate their qualifications for the opportunity we help them pursue. We assure you a high-level of service and integrity.

Key Contact:
Mr. Martin Nicoll, President - *Information technology sales*
Mr. Gary Kassin, Account Executive - *Information technology sales*
Mr. Richard Sciacca, Account Executive
Mr. Sharon Nicoll, Internet Recruiter

Salary minimum: $50,000

Functions: Generalist, Sales Mgmt.

Industries: Generalist, Mgmt. Consulting, Telecoms, Software

MRI of Union County

(also known as OfficeMates 5)
1100 Springfield Ave
Mountainside, NJ 07092
(908) 789-9400
Fax: (908) 789-8845
Email: jimmalfetti@mriunion.com
Web: www.mriunion.com

Description: We are a recruiting firm that is doing it right.

Key Contact:
Mr. Ro Malfetti, Managing Partner
Mr. Jim Malfetti, Managing Partner

Functions: Generalist, Admin. Svcs., Sales & Mktg.

Industries: Construction, Mfg., Consumer Elect., Wholesale, Finance, Invest. Banking, Venture Cap., Services, Equip Svcs., HR Services, Hospitality, Media, Communications, Aerospace, Packaging, Insurance, Real Estate, Software, Accounting SW

Professional Associations: SHRM, SHRMCF

Networks: Associated Consultants in Executive Search Int'l

MRI of Bordentown

1200 S Church St Ste 20
Village II
Mt. Laurel, NJ 08054
(856) 727-0005
Fax: (856) 727-3444
Email: rrr.mri@att.net

Description: Search for management consulting firms for utility industry: utilities and energy firms, web enablement; insurance industry-P&C claims and, underwriting & marketing.

Key Contact - Specialty:
Mr. Randy R. Ruschak, Managing Director -
  Management consulting, energy, utilities
Ms. Christine Buchanan, Director - *Insurance - Claims (property, casualty), underwriting, insurance*

Salary minimum: $45,000

Functions: Generalist, Middle Mgmt., Mgmt. Consultants

Industries: Generalist, Energy, Utilities, Insurance

MRI of New Providence

150 Floral Ave
New Providence, NJ 07974-1511
(908) 771-0600
Fax: (908) 771-0779
Email: mrinp@mrinp.com
Web: www.mrinp.com

Description: Part of largest executive search firm in the world. New services include interim executive placement and video conferencing to produce superior results.

Key Contact - Specialty:
Mr. Andrew S. Miller, President - *Consumer products, information technology*

Salary minimum: $40,000

Functions: Generalist, General Mgmt., Sales & Mktg., Credit, Risk Mgmt., IT, R&D, Engineering

Industries: Generalist, Food, Bev., Tobacco, Soap, Perf., Cosmtcs., Drugs Mfg., Hospitality, Software, Biotech

MRI of Pennington

1598 Reed Rd Ste 1
Pennington, NJ 08534
(609) 737-7331
Fax: (609) 737-5109

Key Contact:
Mr. Michael Flanagan

Salary minimum: $30,000

MRI of Montgomery

814 Executive Dr
Princeton, NJ 08540
(609) 497-4550
Fax: (609) 497-4551
Email: mrimontgomery1@earthlink.net
Web: www.plasticspkg.com

Description: We provide search and recruit in the plastics and plastics packaging fields. We specialize in new market development in plastic polymers and all operations, sales/marketing, and engineering positions in plastics packaging with focus on injection molding, film extrusions, thermoforming, and blown bottles. Visit our website.

Key Contact:
Mr. Rich Strenkowski

Functions: Mfg., Product Dev., Packaging, Sales & Mktg., Engineering

Industries: Generalist, Mfg., Chemicals, Plastics, Rubber, Packaging, Mfg. SW

MRI of Northern Monmouth County
1129 Broad St Ste 8
Shrewsbury, NJ 07702-4333
(732) 578-0100
Fax: (732) 578-1800
Email: jobs@mrienergy.com
Web: www.mrienergy.com

Description: We offer executive recruitment for the energy industry and for the communications industry.

Key Contact:
Mr. Robert E. Goehring, Manager

Functions: Engineering

Industries: Energy, Utilities, Construction, Mfg., Telecoms, Digital, Fiber Optic

MRI of Stanhope
4 Waterloo Rd Waterloo Executive Plz
Stanhope, NJ 07874
(973) 691-2020
Fax: (973) 691-0728
Email: janet@ittrade.com
Web: www.ittrade.com

Description: Our focus is to place architects, developers, presenters (pre-sales), implementation teams (on-staff consultants), project managers and sales executives who develop, design, sell, and implement next generation, complex enterprise technologies, which empower fortune 500 companies to compete on a global scale.

Key Contact - Specialty:
Mr. Arthur L. Young, Managing Director - *E-commerce*
Ms. Janet Joyce, Director - *E-commerce*

Salary minimum: $90,000

Functions: Middle Mgmt., Sales & Mktg., IT, Systems Implem.

Industries: Communications, Digital, Wireless, Network Infrastructure, Software, Database SW, Marketing SW, Networking, Comm. SW, Security SW

MRI of The Sandias
10400 Academy NE Ste 204
Albuquerque, NM 87111
(505) 292-9800
Fax: (505) 292-9810
Email: don@mrisandias.com
Web: www.mrisandias.com

Description: Our firm specializes in the placement of information systems and software development professionals.

Key Contact - Specialty:
Mr. Don Ancona, President/Owner - *Information systems, software development*

Salary minimum: $50,000

Functions: IT, Engineering

Industries: Generalist, Construction, Mfg., Electronic, Elec. Components, Biotech

MRI of Broome County
20 Hawley St Fl 6
W Twr
Binghamton, NY 13901
(607) 722-2243
(800) 805-1581
Fax: (607) 722-2456
Email: rhc@therecruiters.com
Web: www.therecruiters.com

Description: We are functional experts in information technology, engineering, and finance, professionally trained in the art of search and recruitment. We are solution oriented and understand the problems, needs, and expectations of your functional executives and organizations.

Key Contact - Specialty:
Mr. Robert H. Clingan, President - *Information technology, engineering, sales & marketing (technical)*
Mr. Mark J. Wallace, Executive Vice President - *Finance*

Salary minimum: $40,000

Functions: General Mgmt., Finance, IT, Engineering

Industries: Generalist, Mfg., Paper, Plastics, Rubber, Misc. Mfg., Services, Non-profits, Higher Ed., Accounting, IT Implementation, Communications, Network Infrastructure, Packaging, Software, Mfg. SW, System SW

MRI of Great Neck
98 Cutter Mill Rd Ste 234 S
Great Neck, NY 11021-3006
(516) 482-4000
Fax: (516) 482-5772
Email: headhunter@mrgreatneck.com

Description: Principal of firm is a former lawyer, investment banker and real estate consultant and developer. Highly selective in client base.

Key Contact - Specialty:
Mr. Stuart Kaufman, Principal - *Real estate, legal, environmental, consulting*

Salary minimum: $50,000

Functions: Generalist, Attorneys

Industries: Generalist, Real Estate

Professional Associations: BOMA, IFMA, NYSBA

MRI of Upper Westchester
118 N Bedford Rd Ste 103
Mt. Kisco, NY 10549-9998
(914) 241-2788
Fax: (914) 241-2783
Email: vnepplemri@aol.com

Description: Our office specializes totally in the food/beverage industry and our expertise is sales, sales management, marketing, and manufacturing. We limit the number of searches we accept so we can offer our clients an uncompromised level of commitment to their needs.

Key Contact - Specialty:
Mr. Vern D. Nepple, President/Managing Partner - *Food, beverage*
Ms. Rosemarie Nepple, Vice President/Managing Partner - *Food, beverage*

Salary minimum: $50,000

Functions: Plant Mgmt., Sales & Mktg.

Industries: Food, Bev., Tobacco

MRI of Manhattan on Broadway
1650 Broadway Ste 410
New York, NY 10019
(212) 974-7676
Fax: (212) 974-8585

Email: info@mrusa.com
Web: www.mrusa.com

Description: Part of the largest and most successful executive search and recruitment organizations offering permanent and interim staffing solutions as well as outplacement and video conferencing services.

Key Contact - Specialty:
Mr. Richard Cohen, President - *Banking, credit card, investment banking, marketing, risk analysts*

Salary minimum: $45,000

Functions: Generalist, Directors, Middle Mgmt., Mktg. Mgmt., Direct Mktg., Credit, Risk Mgmt.

Industries: Generalist, Finance, Banking, Misc. Financial

MRI of Gramercy
200 Park Ave S Ste 1510
New York, NY 10003
(212) 505-5530
Email: admin1@quik.com
Web: www.managementrecruitersny.com

Description: Consummate professionals, committed to the pursuit of excellence with uncompromising integrity. These are the standards which set us apart from the crowd.

Key Contact - Specialty:
Mr. Stephen D. Schwartz, President - *Advertising (agency, corporate), marketing (agency, corporate), PR (marketing), communications, corporate communications*
Mr. James K. Harragan, Account Executive - *Publishing, consumer sales, telemarketing*

Salary minimum: $35,000

Functions: Generalist, Advertising, Mkt. Research, Mktg. Mgmt., Sales Mgmt., Direct Mktg., Customer Svc., PR

Industries: Generalist, Pharm Svcs., Media, Advertising, Publishing, New Media, Telecoms, Healthcare

MRI of Saratoga
444 Broadway Ste 202
Saratoga Springs, NY 12866
(518) 580-0044
Fax: (518) 580-0055
Email: mrsaratoga@earthlink.net

Description: We specialize in executive search and all functions in the following market segments: manufacturing, business consulting, and fuel sales.

Key Contact - Specialty:
Mr. Jim Pabis, President - *General manufacturing, engineering*

Functions: Generalist, Senior Mgmt., Middle Mgmt., Sales Mgmt., Customer Svc., CFO's, MIS Mgmt., Engineering, Mgmt. Consultants

Industries: Generalist, Chemicals, Misc. Mfg., Mgmt. Consulting, Security SW

MRI of Kingston
PO Box 386
Stone Ridge, NY 12484-0386
(845) 339-1300
Fax: (845) 339-1443
Email: bobmrik@attglobal.net

Description: The industries that we specialize in are chemical, plastic, biotech, pharmaceutical raw material, R&D, sales, marketing, and international.

Key Contact:
Mr. Robert A. Mackenzie, CSAM, CPC, President

Functions: Directors, Sales & Mktg., R&D

Industries: Chemicals, Plastics, Rubber, Paints, Petro. Products, Biotech

MRI of Woodbury
100 Crossways Park W Ste 208
Plaza Bldg
Woodbury, NY 11797
(516) 364-9290
Fax: (516) 364-4478
Email: mrcareers@mrcareers.com
Web: www.mrcareers.com

Description: Specialize in placing middle and
senior management personnel in pharmaceutical,
medical device, data processing, banking and
consumer products.

Key Contact - Specialty:
Mr. Bill Jose, General Manager - *Pharmaceutical
consumer products*
Mr. Warren Kornfeld, Vice President - *Information
technology*

Salary minimum: $35,000

Functions: Generalist, Physicians, Mktg. Mgmt.,
Sales Mgmt., MIS Mgmt., Systems Analysis,
Systems Dev., R&D

Industries: Generalist, Drugs Mfg., Medical
Devices, Consumer Elect., Pharm Svcs.,
Insurance, Software

MRI of Asheville
53 Arlington St
Asheville, NC 28801
(828) 258-9646
Fax: (828) 252-0866
Email: paul@mrasheville.com
Web: www.mrasheville.com

Description: Search and recruitment specialists for
upper and middle management professionals.

Key Contact - Specialty:
Mr. Paul M. Rumson, Co-Manager - *Engineering*
Ms. Barbara A. Rumson, Co-Manager -
Engineering

Salary minimum: $35,000

Functions: Generalist, Product Dev., Automation,
Plant Mgmt., Quality, Purchasing, Engineering,
Int'l.

Industries: Generalist, Drugs Mfg., Medical
Devices, Plastics, Rubber, Metal Products,
Machine, Appliance, Motor Vehicles, Computer
Equip.

MRI of Gastonia North
1641 Hephzibah Church Rd
Bessemer City, NC 28016
(704) 435-4300
Fax: (704) 435-3428
Email: search@kissfrog.com
Web: www.kissfrog.com

Description: We are specializing in consulting,
engineering and construction. The positions that we
place are in project management, technical
specialist, engineers, and scientists. We place from
technical level through division managers.

Key Contact:
Ms. Mary Deal
Mr. Chuck Deal

Salary minimum: $50,000

Networks: Top Echelon Network

MRI of Burlington
336 Holly Hill Ln
Burlington, NC 27215
(336) 584-1444
Fax: (336) 584-9754
Email: mgmtrec@netpath.net
Web: www.mriburlington.com

Description: Providing technical, production, sales
and marketing resources to clients in the specialty
materials (i.e. chemicals, plastics, rubber, polymers)

and the web processing (i.e. paper, film, tape, label,
converting) industries.

Key Contact - Specialty:
Mr. Dick Pike, Owner/Manager - *Paper & film
converting, chemicals, plastics*

Salary minimum: $30,000

Functions: Generalist

Industries: Paper, Printing, Chemicals, Plastics,
Rubber

Professional Associations: AICHE, SPE, TAPPI

MRI of Chapel Hill
88 Vilcom Centre Dr Ste 185
Chapel Hill, NC 27514-1660
(919) 928-1101
Fax: (919) 928-1102
Email: rice@mrchapelhill.com
Web: www.mrchapelhill.com

Description: Guaranteed searches, high quality
candidates, cultural matches. Professionals in
sales/manufacturing: hardware, lawn and garden,
building materials; quality/manufacturing: plastics
and automotive industries; marketing/technical:
communications and telecommunications;
sales/presales engineers/implementors: ERP process
systems.

Key Contact - Specialty:
Mr. M. Rice Day, Jr., President/Owner - *Hardware,
lawn & garden, building materials*

Functions: Generalist, Senior Mgmt., Middle
Mgmt., Production, Plant Mgmt., Quality, Mktg.
Mgmt., Sales Mgmt.

Industries: Generalist, Lumber, Furniture, Plastics,
Rubber, Paints, Petro. Products, Wholesale,
Retail, Telecoms

MRI of Charlotte-East
2101 Sardis Rd N Ste 205
Charlotte, NC 28227
(704) 849-9200
Fax: (704) 849-9207
Email: mrce@makegooddecisions.com
Web: www.mricharlotte-east.com

Description: Franchise office of Management
Recruiters Int'l. Nation's largest contingency search
firm, operating for more than 35 years and having
over 500 offices nationwide with a complex referral
system.

Key Contact:
Mr. Frank A. Quinn, CSAM, General Manager
Ms. Peggy Quinn, Manager

Salary minimum: $30,000

MRI of Davidson
710 Northeast Dr Ste 8
Davidson, NC 28036-7434
(704) 896-8890
Fax: (704) 896-8933
Email: chrisalar@mrdavidson.com

Description: We specialize in engineering,
manufacturing, quality, and IT.

Key Contact:
Mr. Chris Alar, Owner

Salary minimum: $45,000

MRI of Enfield
111 NW Railroad St
Enfield, NC 27823-1334
(252) 445-4251
Fax: (252) 445-4253
Email: search2@mindspring.com
Web: www.mrinet.com

Description: Our firm, an MRI affiliate, specializes
in the paper and plastic packaging industry,

covering the areas of film and foam extrusion, as
well as converting, coating, laminating, and
flexographic, and rotogravure printing.

Key Contact:
Mr. Marvin G. Snook, Co-Manager
Ms. Maria P. Snook, Co-Manager

MRI of Fayetteville
951 S McPherson Church Rd Ste 105
Fayetteville, NC 28303
(910) 483-2555
Fax: (910) 483-6524
Email: mrifaync@worldnet.att.net
Web: www.home.att.net/~mrifaync/

Description: We specialize in key account
development in all areas of manufacturing
operations: engineering, quality, design, electrical,
mechanical, financial, human resources,
management--in various industries including
appliances, motors, electronics and automotives.

Key Contact - Specialty:
Mr. John R. Semmes, Owner/Manager - *General
manufacturing*

Salary minimum: $30,000

Functions: Generalist, Mfg., Product Dev.,
Production, Plant Mgmt., Quality, Materials, HR
Mgmt., Finance, Engineering

Industries: Mfg.

MRI of Graham
9 SE Court Sq Ste 200
PO Box 1349
Graham, NC 27253
(336) 229-1233
Fax: (336) 229-1454
Email: mrgraham@mrgraham.com
Web: www.mribiotech.com

Description: We work exclusively with
biotechnology clients. If you are not already in the
biotech industry, please do not contact us.

Key Contact:
Mr. Mac Allen, Manager

Functions: Generalist

Industries: Biotech

MRI of Greensboro
324 W Wendover Ave Ste 230
Greensboro, NC 27408
(336) 378-1818
Fax: (336) 378-0129
Email: mrigso@mrgreensboro.com
Web: www.mrigreensboro.com

Description: Our network targets, recruits and
delivers high-impact talent for our clients' critical
needs. Our mission is to be the world's preferred and
preeminent provider of staffing solutions.

Key Contact:
Mr. C. Mitchell Oakley, Jr., President

Salary minimum: $40,000

Functions: Generalist, General Mgmt., Mfg., Sales
& Mktg., R&D, Engineering, Specialized Svcs.

Industries: Generalist, Textiles, Apparel,
Chemicals, Drugs Mfg., Motor Vehicles, Retail,
Services, Hospitality, Media, Communications,
Biotech, Healthcare

MRI of High Point-North
2376 Hickswood Rd Ste 105
High Point, NC 27265
(336) 841-0123
Fax: (336) 841-0047
Email: greg@mreverhart.com
Web: www.mreverhart.com

Description: Our firm focuses on the pharmaceutical industry, and specializes in the functional areas of research and development, manufacturing and operations, regulatory affairs and compliance, quality assurance, quality control, validation, and engineering.

Key Contact - Specialty:
Mr. Gregory Everhart, Managing Partner - *Manufacturing, research and development*
Mrs. Dianna Langley, Account Executive - *Regulatory affairs and compliance*
Mrs. Joanne Serico, Research Administrator - *Pharmaceutical*

Salary minimum: $50,000

MRI of High Point

110 Scott
High Point, NC 27262-7832
(336) 869-1200
Fax: (336) 869-1566
Email: mrihp@aol.com
Web: www.mrinet.com

Key Contact:
Mr. Stephen Smith, President and General Manager

MRI of Charlotte-North

103 Commerce Center Dr Ste 102
Huntersville, NC 28078
(704) 947-0660
Fax: (704) 947-0705
Email: lduke@mrcn.com
Web: www.mrcn.com

Description: Our firm specializes in human resource and management consulting executive search. Our key functional areas include compensation, human resource systems, human resource strategy, customer relationship management, change management, and IT.

Key Contact - Specialty:
Mr. Lawrence Duke, Owner - *Human resources, management consulting*

Functions: Generalist, HR Mgmt., Benefits, Training, MIS Mgmt., Systems Dev., Systems Support, Mgmt. Consultants

Industries: Generalist

MRI of Kannapolis

1787 Dale Earnhard Blvd
Kannapolis, NC 28083
(704) 938-6144
Fax: (704) 938-3480
Email: mrkannapolis@mrkannapolis.com
Web: www.mrkannapolis.com

Description: Offering a full range of recruiting services for information systems staff. Highly successful in recruiting either an entire development team or one top notch CIO.

Key Contact:
Mr. T. H. Whitley, Manager - *Information systems*
Mr. Mac Swaringen

Functions: Production, Automation, Sales & Mktg., IT

Industries: Generalist, Mfg., Computer Equip., Telecoms, Software

MRI of Kings Mountain

608 W King St Ste B
PO Box 1969
Kings Mountain, NC 28086
(704) 739-4401
Fax: (704) 739-0544
Web: www.mrikingsmountain.com

Description: We are an executive search firm and human resource service organization dedicated to being your preeminent provider of human resource and staffing solutions. We excel at locating,

attracting, screening, and making available the very best candidates for our clients needs. We have professionals who take a personalized approach to recruiting. Our effectiveness is based on over 40 years of extensive industry experience and on knowing as much as possible about the industries and people we serve.

Key Contact:
Mr. Lee Sherrill

MRI of Kinston

2857 Hull Rd
PO Box 219
Kinston, NC 28502-0219
(252) 527-9191
Fax: (252) 527-3625
Email: mrkinston@esn.net
Web: www.mrkinston.com

Description: Our firm has gas eight account executives and a manager with over 40 years of combined experience in recruiting engineering, manufacturing, healthcare professionals, and managers.

Key Contact:
Mr. Al W. Turner, President

Salary minimum: $30,000

Functions: Middle Mgmt.

Industries: Mfg., Textiles, Apparel, Paper, Medical Devices, Metal Products, Machine, Appliance, Motor Vehicles, Computer Equip., Consumer Elect., Test, Measure Equip.

MRI of Lillington

805 S 8th St
PO Box 8
Lillington, NC 27546
(910) 814-1000
Fax: (910) 814-1099
Email: mribuck@earthlink.net
Web: www.mrilillington.com

Description: We specialize in two fields, and they are the electronics industry and the health industry.

Key Contact - Specialty:
Mr. Buck Enquist, Manager
Mrs. Kathy Enquist, Account Executive - *Health*

Functions: Product Dev., Healthcare, Sales & Mktg., Engineering

Industries: Electronic, Elec. Components, Telecoms, Telephony, Digital, Wireless, Fiber Optic, Network Infrastructure, Hospitals, Long-term Care

MRI of Lake Norman

335 S Broad St
PO Box 884
Mooresville, NC 28115-3207
(704) 660-9144
Fax: (704) 660-9149
Email: johnb@mrlakenorman.com
Web: www.mrlakenorman.com

Description: We screen candidates, reference check, verify all degrees, and assist in relocation. We work with client companies and candidate to provide best fit possible for all involved.

Key Contact:
Mr. John E. Bigliardi, Manager

Functions: Generalist, General Mgmt., Middle Mgmt., Mfg., Materials, Purchasing, Healthcare, HR Mgmt., Finance, IT

Industries: Generalist, Printing, Consumer Elect., Misc. Mfg., Broadcast, Film, Telecoms, Aerospace

Professional Associations: ASQ

MRI of Mt. Airy-Mayberry

(also known as The Mayberry Group)
143 Ellis Acres Ln Ste 2
Mt. Airy, NC 27030
(336) 789-3200
Fax: (336) 719-2227
Email: mrmayberry@advi.net
Web: www.mrmayberry.com

Description: In textiles, apparel, retail and information systems, we have successfully completed searches for companies ranging from Fortune 500 to small growth companies in manufacturing, engineering, sourcing, quality, MIS, sales, merchandising and design, both domestic and international.

Key Contact:
Mr. Ron Ellis, Manager

Functions: Generalist, Middle Mgmt., Plant Mgmt., Quality, MIS Mgmt., Systems Implem., Network Admin., DB Admin.

Industries: Generalist, Textiles, Apparel, Retail, Software

Branches:
716 Azalea Dr
Rockville, MD 20850
(301) 251-1919
Fax: (301) 424-9674
Email: pbeyer@mrmayberry.com
Key Contact - Specialty:
Ms. Paige Beyer - *Information technology*

29 JC Long Blvd Ste 205
Isle of Palms, SC 29451
(843) 886-9298
Fax: (843) 886-9299
Email: jnew5250@aol.com
Key Contact - Specialty:
Mr. Jeff Newcomb - *Retail*

MRI of Mt. Airy

231 N Main St
Mt. Airy, NC 27030-3809
(336) 719-2250
Fax: (336) 719-2350
Email: mrmtairy@advi.net

Description: Our search firm specializes in two industries, and they are as follows: banking and manufacturing/electronics. Our desks cover all functions within the bank at the staff and management level with typical salaries beginning at $70,000.00. We are national in scope and our experience of over 25 years in the industry employers, lends to our quick understanding for the subsequent match of qualified candidates for satisfied clients. Within manufacturing/electronics, our desks cover R&D, engineering product, quality, manufacturing, as well as manufacturing support functions in the semi-conductor and electronic passive components industry. We are national in scope.

Key Contact - Specialty:
Mr. Donald F. Hackett, Owner/Manager - *Manufacturing, electronic components*

Salary minimum: $55,000

Functions: Generalist, General Mgmt., Senior Mgmt., Middle Mgmt., Product Dev.

Industries: Mfg., Electronic, Elec. Components, Banking

MRI of New Bern

2807 Nuse Blvd Ste 3
New Bern, NC 28562
(252) 633-1900
Fax: (252) 633-3121
Email: mrinewbern@coastalnet.com
Web: www.mrinewbern.com

Description: Our firm recruits mainly in the manufacturing arena. We place from CFOs, HR professionals, QC, plant managers, all engineering positions, etc.

Key Contact:
Mr. Fred Eatman, Manager

Functions: Generalist, Mfg., HR Mgmt.

Industries: Mfg., Fiber Optic, Accounting SW, ERP SW, HR SW, Industry Specific SW, Mfg. SW

MRI of Pinehurst
180 Westgate Dr 1
PO Box 4834
Pinehurst, NC 28374
(910) 215-9933
Fax: (910) 215-9934
Email: papergirl33@mindspring.com
Web: www.brilliantpeople.com

Description: Our teams of recruiting professionals specialize in placing top-notch candidates in the pulp and paper industry nationwide and in general manufacturing regionally. We seek degreed individuals with solid records of accomplishments for positions at all levels and disciplines with the exception of sales.

Key Contact:
Mr. Doug Wright, General Manager
Ms. Anne B. Wright, Manager

Salary minimum: $40,000

Functions: Generalist

Industries: Mfg., Lumber, Furniture, Paper

Professional Associations: SME, TAPPI

MRI of Chatham
290 East St Ste 210
PO Box 905
Pittsboro, NC 27312
(919) 545-2288
Email: admin@mrchatham.com
Web: www.mrchatham.com

Description: Our firm is part of Management Recruiters International. MRI is the world's largest search and recruitment firm, with over 800 offices and 5000 recruiters covering all facets of industry. Our office specializes in e-Learning/training, medical device sales, and quality assurance professionals.

Key Contact - Specialty:
Mr. Randy Carson, President - *E-learning and training*

Functions: Quality, Sales & Mktg., Sales Mgmt.

Industries: Generalist, Medical Devices

MRI of Raleigh
5171 Glenwood Ave Ste 350
Raleigh, NC 27612
(919) 781-0400
Fax: (919) 881-0117
Email: resumes@mriraleigh.com
Web: www.mriraleigh.com

Description: Our firm is a member of the President's Platinum Club of MRI, which includes only the top 3% of 1,000 MRI offices. We are an established award-winning national executive search firm with specialties by industry, which are accounting/financial, biotech, chemicals, construction, electronics, engineering, healthcare, IT, manufacturing, materials, packaging, pharmaceuticals, R&D, sales/marketing, software, and telecommunications.

Key Contact - Specialty:
Ms. Linda Stanley, Managing Partner - *Manufacturing, engineering, sales, marketing, R&D*

Salary minimum: $50,000

Functions: Generalist

Industries: Generalist

MRI of Rocky Mount-Southwest
120 N Franklin St Bldg J Ste 101
PO Box 4139
Rocky Mount, NC 27803-4139
(252) 442-8000
Fax: (252) 442-9000
Email: rckyeast!manager@mrinet.com
Web: www.mrigreatjobs.com

Description: Food industry and retail sales for consumer goods specialists.

Key Contact - Specialty:
Mr. Bob Manning, President - *Food, manufacturing*
Ms. Jan Manning, Vice President
Mr. Dave Weddell, Account Executive - *Food industry*
Mrs. Sherry Strickland, Account Executive - *HBA, consumer goods sales*
Mrs. Karen Carney, Account Executive - *Food industry*
Mr. Stan Herndon, Account Executive - *Food industry*

Functions: Generalist, Middle Mgmt., Product Dev., Quality, Mkt. Research, Sales Mgmt., R&D, Engineering

Industries: Generalist, Agri., Forestry, Mining, Food, Bev., Tobacco, Hospitality, Aerospace

MRI of Person County
PO Box 1354
Roxboro, NC 27573
(336) 597-4000
Fax: (336) 597-4011
Web: www.mriofpersoncounty.com

Key Contact:
Mr. Don Buckner
Mrs. Angie Craven
Ms. Nichole Perkins

MRI of Boone
3657 Valle Cir
PO Box 691
Valle Crucis, NC 28691
(828) 963-5111
(888) 476-9411
Fax: (828) 963-5161
Email: resume@mriboone.com
Web: www.mriboone.com

Description: Specialize in providing the health information systems and receivables management industries with sales and technical talent. We provide sales, marketing and technical talent for vendors and healthcare providers.

Key Contact - Specialty:
Mr. Donald L. Driscoll, President - *HIS sales*
Mr. Matthew Murray, Account Executive - *MIS, HIS*
Mr. Walt Reis, Account Executive - *Management (receivables)*

Functions: Healthcare

Industries: Generalist

Professional Associations: HIMSS

MRI of Wilmington
4024 Oleander Dr Ste 1-B
Oleander Office Park
Wilmington, NC 28403
(910) 791-2999
Email: harrylb@bellsouth.net

Description: Each account executive is grounded in two fundamentals: professionalism and recruiting within a specific industry group which is his/her desk specialty.

Key Contact - Specialty:
Mr. Harry L. Bargholz, SPHR - *Human resource*

Salary minimum: $30,000

Functions: Generalist, Healthcare, HR Mgmt., Benefits, Personnel, Training

Industries: Generalist, Medical Devices, HR Services

Professional Associations: SHRM

MRI of Winston-Salem
PO Box 17054
Winston-Salem, NC 27116
(336) 723-0484
Fax: (336) 723-0841
Email: search@mriws.com
Web: www.brilliantpeople.com

Description: Providing management, technical and executive recruiting services in manufacturing accounting, logistics/supply chain, food/beverage and chemical/environmental industries.

Key Contact - Specialty:
Mr. Mike Jones, General Manager
Mrs. Judy Jones, Assistant Manager - *Manufacturing, accounting, logistics, supply chain management*
Mr. Ken White, Certified Senior Account Manager - *Chemical, environmental, health & safety*
Mrs. Terri Frank, Recruiter - *Food (processing, manufacturing)*

Salary minimum: $40,000

Functions: General Mgmt., Mfg., Materials, Finance, Int'l.

Industries: Energy, Utilities, Mfg., Food, Bev., Tobacco, Chemicals, Soap, Perf., Cosmtcs., Drugs Mfg., Plastics, Rubber, Paints, Petro. Products, Misc. Mfg., Finance, Accounting, Packaging, Biotech

MRI of Ghent
(also known as Executive Solutions Inc)
843 N Cleveland Massillon Rd Ste UP 12B
Akron, OH 44333-2185
(330) 666-3354
Fax: (330) 666-5655
Email: jchadbourne@mriexecutivesolutions.com
Web: www.mriexecutivesolutions.com

Description: We are specialists in transportation, logistics, and supply chain management. If any part of your organization involves moving a product from one point to another by any mode or combination of modes, whether-it-be by land, sea, or air, we will meet your needs for any position level and any functional discipline. MRI Executive Solutions is a member of the world's largest executive search organization. Through our MRI franchise membership, we have access to more than 1,000 national and international locations supporting over 5,000 recruiters specializing in a variety of industries and disciplines.

Key Contact - Specialty:
Mr. Jim Chadbourne, Managing Partner - *Transportation, logistics, supply chain management*

Salary minimum: $30,000

Functions: Generalist

Industries: Mfg., Motor Vehicles, Computer Equip., Transportation, Wholesale, Retail, Mgmt. Consulting, E-commerce, IT Implementation, Haz. Waste

Professional Associations: ATA, CLM

MRI of Akron
1900 W Market St
Akron, OH 44313-6927
(330) 867-2900
Fax: (330) 867-3830
Email: info@mrakron.com
Web: www.mrakron.com

Description: For 25 years, companies have relied on us to locate, identify and attract top candidates for rubber and plastics professional and executive opportunities.

Key Contact - Specialty:
Mr. Tom Gerst, Owner - *Plastic*
Mr. Art Smucker, Account Executive - *Rubber*
Mr. Mike Gerst, Project Coordinator - *Plastics*
Mr. Jake Dragomire, Account Executive - *Rubber, plastics*
Mr. Robert Dixson, Account Executive - *Plastics*
Mr. Kevin Butler, Account Executive - *Plastics*

Salary minimum: $40,000

Functions: Engineering

Industries: Plastics, Rubber

Professional Associations: ACS, SAE, SPE

MRI of Beachwood-Cleveland
23210 Chagrin Blvd Ste 200
1 Commerce Park Sq
Beachwood, OH 44122-5425
(216) 896-9600
Fax: (216) 896-9601
Email: hire@mribeach.com

Key Contact:
Mr. Jeff Schonberg

Salary minimum: $50,000

Functions: Generalist

Industries: Retail, Finance, Accounting, Telecoms, Software

MRI of Moreland Hills
23215 Commerce Park Dr Ste 210
Beachwood, OH 44122-5843
(216) 591-0600
Fax: (216) 591-0555
Email: info@mriresults.com
Web: www.mriresults.com

Description: We specialize in direct marketing, database marketing, e-CRM, sales, print, and e-Marketing. We recruit for mid to senior level managers, salespersons, marketing professionals, and executives in these industry areas.

Key Contact - Specialty:
Mr. Jeff Rothman, Manager
Mr. Dan Marks, Account Executive - *Direct mail, CRM software*
Ms. Peg Glover, Recruiting Specialist - *Direct mail, CRM software*

Salary minimum: $40,000

Functions: Mgmt. Consultants

Industries: E-commerce, IT Implementation, Media, Database SW, Development SW, Doc. Mgmt., Production SW, Industry Specific SW, Marketing SW, Networking, Comm. SW

MRI of Mayfield Heights
23611 Chagrin Blvd Ste 380
Beachwood, OH 44122
(216) 595-1240
Fax: (216) 595-1245
Email: mrijoe@mindspring.com

Description: High-technology sales/software and hardware. Focus on senior-level sales and sales management. Concentration on key high end technology and leading edge companies.

Key Contact:
Mr. Joe Shepard, President

Functions: Sales Mgmt., Systems Support

Industries: Generalist

MRI of Youngstown
8090 Market St Ste 2
Boardman, OH 44512-6216
(330) 726-6656
Fax: (330) 726-0199
Email: mrcsy@earthlink.net
Web: www.mrnetworking.com

Description: Experienced executive recruiting firm specializing in MIS, LAN/WAN, client server as well as engineering, sales and manufacturing.

Key Contact - Specialty:
Mr. Donald A. Somers, President - *Information systems*

Salary minimum: $25,000

Functions: Generalist, MIS Mgmt., Systems Analysis, Systems Dev., Systems Implem., Systems Support, Network Admin., DB Admin.

Industries: Generalist, Finance, Banking, Telecoms, Software, Healthcare

MRI of Cleveland-SW
3511 Center Rd Ste J
MRI Office Complex
PO Box 178
Brunswick, OH 44212-0178
(330) 273-4300
Fax: (330) 273-2862
Email: contactmri@aol.com
Web: www.mrinet.com

Description: We were the runner-up for MRI's "Best of Class Award" for the 2000 President's Gold Club award winning office. We specialize in photonics, fiber optics, electronics, finance and accounting, primary metals, engineering, and manufacturing management.

Key Contact:
Mr. Robert A. Boal, Manager

Salary minimum: $80,000

Functions: Senior Mgmt., Middle Mgmt., Product Dev., Production, Plant Mgmt., Quality, Finance, Taxes, R&D, Engineering

Industries: Generalist, Mfg., Plastics, Rubber, Metal Products, Consumer Elect., Test, Measure Equip., Misc. Mfg., Finance, Banking, Accounting, Hospitality, Telecoms

MRI of Chagrin Falls, OH
10 N Main St
PO Box 446
Chagrin Falls, OH 44022
(440) 247-7350
Fax: (440) 247-7715
Email: mricleveland@compuserve.com
Web: www.mrihvac.com

Description: Executive recruiters working on retained and contingency searches for sales and technical engineering positions. Specializing in HVAC, mechanical contracting, temperature controls, software sales, hardware sales, e-commerce.

Key Contact - Specialty:
Mr. Gary Gardiner, President - *HVAC, sales engineering, mechanical contracting, electrical contracting, temperature controls*

Salary minimum: $50,000

Functions: Generalist

Industries: Energy, Utilities, Construction, Mfg., Test, Measure Equip., Haz. Waste, Packaging, Software

Professional Associations: AEE, ASHRAE, RSES

MRI of Cincinnati
8 E 4th St
Management Recruiters Corp Ctr
Cincinnati, OH 45202
(513) 651-5500
Fax: (513) 651-3298
Email: careers@mricincy.com
Web: www.mricincy.com

Description: The average tenure of our office is over 12 years. Our account executives have received numerous national awards from corporate.

Key Contact:
Mr. Joseph B. McCullough, President
Ms. Kathy Schiess, Vice President - *Administrative support, clerical*
Mr. Joe Mehl, Operations Manager - *Engineering, general manufacturing*
Ms. Beth Simminger, Director of Marketing
Mr. Anthony D'eramo

Functions: Generalist, Mfg., Sales & Mktg., HR Mgmt., Finance, IT, Engineering

Industries: Generalist, Mfg., Finance, Services

MRI of Cincinnati-Sharonville
(also known as Sales Consultants of Cincinnati-Sharonville)
4050 Executive Park Dr Ste 125
Cincinnati, OH 45241-2020
(513) 769-4747
Fax: (513) 769-0471
Email: resumes@mricinci.com
Web: www.mricinci.com

Description: National retained/contingency executive search firm specializing in general management, manufacturing, engineering, finance/accounting and sales/marketing in paper, packaging, printing, publishing, building products, construction, chemical and plastic industries. Nation's largest search firm with 700 offices. Top 10% ranked office nationally.

Key Contact - Specialty:
Mr. William E. O'Reilly, President/CEO - *Packaging, paper, printing, publishing, plastic*

Salary minimum: $40,000

Functions: General Mgmt., Senior Mgmt., Middle Mgmt., Plant Mgmt., Quality, Packaging, Mktg. Mgmt., Sales Mgmt., Engineering, Graphic Artists

Industries: Generalist

MRI of Cleveland-Airport
7550 Lucerne Dr Islander Park Two Ste 110
Cleveland, OH 44130
(440) 243-5151
Fax: (440) 243-4868
Email: jad@mricleveland.com
Web: www.mricleveland.com

Description: Worlds largest search, recruitment and staffing company, based out of Cleveland, OH with over 700 offices and 4,000 account executives specializing in virtually every industry at every level on an international basis.

Key Contact - Specialty:
Mr. Jeff Dipaolo, General Manager
Mr. Tom McGuire, CSAM, Executive Recruiter - *Sales & marketing, consumer packaged goods*

Salary minimum: $25,000

Functions: Sales & Mktg.

Industries: Food, Bev., Tobacco, Soap, Perf., Cosmtcs.

MRI of Cleveland

20600 Chagrin Blvd Ste 703
Cleveland, OH 44122
(216) 561-6776
Fax: (216) 561-2393
Email: manager@clevecent.mrinet.com
Web: www.careers-recruiters.com

Description: Full-service; contingency and retainer search, temporary executives, national video interviewing network. Heavy experience in multi-opening national projects and team approach to staffing.

Key Contact:
Ms. Mary Hardy

Functions: Generalist, Plant Mgmt., Health Admin., Sales & Mktg., CFO's, IT, Engineering

Industries: Generalist, Food, Bev., Tobacco, Lumber, Furniture, Printing, Finance, Insurance, Healthcare

MRI of Columbus

2300 E Dublin-Granville Rd
Columbus, OH 43229-3374
(614) 794-3200
Fax: (614) 794-3233
Email: mrcmanager@mricolumbus.com
Web: www.mricolumbus.com

Description: We are the #1 contingency firm in central Ohio (per Business First). In our 25-year history more than half of our recruiters have earned the CSAM/CPC designation which shows our experience, tenure, professionalism and value to our clients. Our OM5/Daystar operation provides administrative and operations staffing services.

Key Contact:
Mr. Richard Stoltz, President - *Information systems*
Ms. Barbara Stoltz, Vice President

Salary minimum: $20,000

Functions: Generalist, Admin. Svcs., Distribution

Industries: Generalist, Construction, Mfg., Plastics, Rubber, HR Services

Professional Associations: ASA, MOAESP, NAPS, OSSA, SHRM

MRI of Columbus-Downtown

555 S Front St Ste 100
Columbus, OH 43215
(614) 252-6200
Fax: (614) 252-4744
Email: jrz@mricols.com
Web: www.mrcolumbusdt.com

Description: Executive and mid-management staffing firm that specializes in IT, financial, manufacturing, retail, healthcare, HR marketplaces. We staff sales, technical, and executive-level assignments. We work on a retained, engaged, and contingency basis. We are the largest search firm in central Ohio and one of the five largest offices for MRI.

Key Contact - Specialty:
Mr. John R. Zambito, General Manager - *IT, manufacturing*

Salary minimum: $70,000

Functions: Generalist

Industries: Energy, Utilities, Mfg., Retail, Finance, Pharm Svcs., Mgmt. Consulting, Insurance, Software, Biotech, Healthcare

MRI of Dayton

(also known as Noble Staffing Services & Sales Consultants)
333 W First St Ste 515
Dayton, OH 45402
(937) 228-8271
Fax: (937) 228-2620

Email: info@mridayton.com
Web: www.mridayton.com

Description: We are a franchisee of the largest professional placement service in the world. Dr. Kotler was named Management Recruiters International account executive of the decade for the 80s.

Key Contact - Specialty:
Mr. Jeffrey M. Noble, CEO
Dr. Gerald R. Kotler, President - *Engineering*

Functions: Mfg., Materials, IT, MIS Mgmt., Systems Analysis, Systems Dev., Systems Implem., Systems Support, Network Admin., Engineering

Industries: Generalist

Professional Associations: ASA, OSSA

MRI of North Canton

PO Box 2970
North Canton, OH 44720
(330) 497-0122
Fax: (330) 497-9730
Email: mrnc@raex.com
Web: www.mrnc.com

Description: Our firm is a full service provider of human resource services for IT candidates and client companies. We are a contingency search firm. That is that companies pay a fee only when they hire someone as a result of our efforts. Candidates do not pay for our services. Hiring and career change decisions are some of the most important decisions made by companies and candidates, thus we are committed to the highest standards of openness, integrity, and performance.

Key Contact - Specialty:
Mr. Mike Collins, Account Executive - *General IT positions within Ohio*
Ms. Ginny Collins, Vice President
Mr. Jim Shelton, Account Executive - *Peoplesoft software positions*

Salary minimum: $25,000

Functions: IT, MIS Mgmt., Systems Analysis, Systems Dev., Systems Implem., Systems Support, Network Admin., DB Admin.

Industries: Generalist, Mfg., Motor Vehicles, Wholesale, Retail, Finance, Services, Communications, Aerospace, Healthcare

MRI of Sidney

(also known as Uniacke & Assoc)
113 N Ohio Ave Ste 400
The Ohio Bldg
Sidney, OH 45365-2749
(937) 497-7080
Fax: (937) 497-7061
Email: kuniacke@wesnet.com

Description: Our 25 years' experience in the food industry offers an insider's perspective beneficial to your company by focusing on your total company needs relative to personality, company atmosphere and skill sets.

Key Contact - Specialty:
Mr. Keith J. Uniacke, President - *Food industry*
Ms. Diane Milanese, Account Executive - *Food industry*

Salary minimum: $65,000

Functions: Generalist, General Mgmt., Product Dev., Production, Plant Mgmt., Quality, Sales & Mktg., R&D

Industries: Food, Bev., Tobacco, Consumer Elect.

MRI of Solon

(also known as MRI of Cleveland-SE)
6175 Som Center Rd Ste 120
Solon, OH 44139
(440) 542-2800
Fax: (440) 542-2801
Email: am-ployeez@mrisolon.com
Web: www.mrisolon.com

Description: Our firm was founded on the commitment to make a positive impact on the customers we serve, and on the individuals who trust us to enhance their career. Our specialty is the manufacturing industry, with a focus on automation and motion control, media clarification, fluid handling, power transmission, and instrumentation.

Key Contact:
Mr. Tom Andrews, President

Functions: Mfg., Product Dev., Automation, Mktg. Mgmt., Engineering

Industries: Agri., Forestry, Mining, Construction, Mfg., Transportation, Aerospace, Development SW, ERP SW, Mfg. SW, Marketing SW

MRI of Westerville

480 Olde Worthington Rd Ste 125
Westerville, OH 43082
(614) 794-5570
Fax: (614) 794-5575
Email: vickie@mricareer.com
Web: www.mricareer.com

Key Contact:
Ms. Linda LaCerva, President

MRI of Oklahoma City

3441 W Memorial Rd Ste 4
Memport Office Park
Oklahoma City, OK 73134-7000
(405) 752-8848
Fax: (405) 752-8783
Email: gary@mriokc.com
Web: www.mriokc.com

Description: We were the office of the year for the Franchise, Management Recruiters for 94-96, 98, 99, and 2000. We place in the Southwest region. We have been in the President's Gold Club for 6 years, which is the top 5% in MRI.

Key Contact:
Mr. Gary P. Roy, President

Salary minimum: $30,000

Functions: Generalist, Senior Mgmt., Sales Mgmt.

Industries: Computer Equip., Finance, Invest. Banking, Venture Cap., Misc. Financial, Services, Mgmt. Consulting, Communications, Insurance, Software, Biotech, Healthcare

MRI of Bend

61419 S Hwy 97 Ste V
Bend, OR 97702-2103
(541) 383-8550
Fax: (541) 383-8599
Email: mrbend@bendnet.com

Description: Employer-based executive recruiter firm recruiting engineers through executives for hi-tech, laser, printed circuit boards (PCB), and software companies.

Key Contact:
Mr. Manney C. Lopez, Owner/Manager

Salary minimum: $50,000

Functions: Generalist, Mfg.

Industries: Mfg., Chemicals, Plastics, Rubber, Misc. Mfg., Electronic, Elec. Components, Communications, Telecoms, Fiber Optic, Environmental Svcs., Aerospace, Packaging, Software, Mfg. SW

MRI of Portland

2020 Lloyd Ctr
Portland, OR 97232-1376
(503) 287-8701
Fax: (503) 282-4380
Email: manager@mrportland.com
Web: www.mrportland.com

Description: Our mission is to be the best at identifying, qualifying, and delivering the best talent for our client companies.

Key Contact:
Ms. Elvita B. Engelgau, Co-Manager
Mr. Larry P. Engelgau, Co-Manager

Salary minimum: $50,000

Functions: General Mgmt., Mfg., Physicians, Nurses, Health Admin., Sales & Mktg., HR Mgmt., Finance, R&D, Attorneys

Industries: Generalist, Construction, Mfg., Transportation, Wholesale, Retail, Finance, Pharm Svcs., Legal, Accounting, HR Services, Media, Communications, Accounting SW, HR SW, Biotech, Healthcare, Hospitals

Networks: Int'l Search Assoc (ISA)

MRI of Bethlehem

3895 Adler Pl Ste 150A
Bethlehem, PA 18017-9092
(610) 974-9770
Fax: (610) 974-9775
Email: mribeth@enter.net
Web: www.mribeth.com

Description: Our office specializes in recruiting for all areas of the food industry. We find the best candidates for our clients. We also specialize in logistics, chemicals and insurance. Sales and marketing national and global.

Key Contact - Specialty:
Mr. Fred R. Meyer, President - *Food, chemicals, logistics, marketing*
Ms. Gayle A. McGeehan, Vice President - *Food, chemicals, marketing*

Salary minimum: $40,000

Functions: Packaging, Sales & Mktg., Engineering

Industries: Food, Bev., Tobacco, Chemicals, Drugs Mfg., Telecoms, Packaging, Non-classifiable

MRI of Carlisle

21 State Ave Ste 103
Carlisle, PA 17013
(717) 249-2626
Fax: (717) 249-4843
Email: resume@mritcg.com
Web: www.mritcg.com

Description: Our firm is a full service executive search and recruitment firm serving today's best in class organizations!

Key Contact:
Mr. Bert Wendeln, Owner/President - *Senior level executives*
Ms. Shelly Wendeln, Co-Owner

Salary minimum: $40,000

Functions: Generalist

Industries: Mfg., Retail, Finance, IT Implementation, Call Centers, Insurance, Accounting SW, Mfg. SW, Healthcare

MRI of The Brandywine Valley

120 E Uwchlan Ave Ste 204
Exton, PA 19341
(610) 524-1666
Email: projmgr@mribrandywine.com
Web: www.mribrandywine.com

Description: Diverse office conducting searches in most industries, including energy/utilities, pharmaceuticals, biotech, chemicals, software/computer services, and manufacturing. Specializing in senior and middle management, engineering, supply chain, finance, sales/marketing, IT and HR.

Key Contact:
Mr. Jack Solomon, Principal
Mr. Bill Spillane, Principal

Functions: Generalist

Industries: Energy, Utilities, Mfg., Wholesale, Finance, Services, Aerospace, Packaging, Software, Biotech, Healthcare

MRI of Cranberry

1310 Freedom Crider Rd
Freedom, PA 15042
(724) 775-9030
Fax: (724) 775-9031
Email: sandy-dawson@hotmail.com
Web: www.mrinet.com

Description: Our focus is on corporate finance and accounting executives between the manager and CFO level, as well as Big 5 placements. We also work on international executives, such as VPs international, country heads, etc.

Key Contact:
Mr. Sanford Dawson

Salary minimum: $70,000

MRI of Lancaster

1148 Elizabeth Ave Ste 10
Lancaster, PA 17601
(717) 397-6444
Fax: (717) 397-6793
Email: mroflanc@infi.net
Web: www.mrlancpa.com

Description: Our firm provides total staffing solutions across the US. Our account executives specialize in human resources, human resources consulting, and e-Human resources/e-Business human resources.

Key Contact - Specialty:
Ms. Karen Rodebaugh, Executive Vice President & COO - *Human resources*
Mr. Thomas L. Rodebaugh, Jr., Managing Director - *HR (compensation, benefits, HRIS/HRIM, OD)*

Functions: HR Mgmt.

Industries: Generalist, Mgmt. Consulting, HR Services

MRI of Pittsburgh-A-K Valley

2644 Leechburg Rd Fl 2
Lower Burrell, PA 15068
(724) 334-0400
Fax: (724) 334-0700
Email: fgigler@mripittsburghakv.com
Web: www.mripittsburghakv.com

Description: We specialize in the pharmaceutical, biotech, and healthcare industries.

Key Contact - Specialty:
Mr. Frank Gigler
Mr. Steve Fetterman, Account Executive - *Science*
Mr. Todd McDermott, Account Executive - *Business development*

MRI of McMurray (Pittsburgh SW)

115 Hidden Valley Rd
McMurray, PA 15317
(724) 942-4100
Fax: (724) 942-4111
Email: manager@chemicaljobs.com
Web: www.chemicaljobs.com

Description: One of the top offices within the Management Recruiters system for recruiting technical talent within the chemically related fields. Place BS/MS/PhD level chemists and chemical engineers up to the V.P. level.

Key Contact - Specialty:
Mr. Michael Fosnot, Managing Partner - *Chemicals, technical*

Functions: Generalist

Industries: Chemicals, Plastics, Rubber, Paints, Petro. Products

Professional Associations: ACS, FSCT

MRI of Westmoreland County

3122 Carson Ave
Murrysville, PA 15668-1815
(724) 325-4011
Fax: (724) 325-1760
Email: mriwc@mriwc.com
Web: www.mriwc.com

Description: Chemical industry: sales, marketing, technical support, chemists, production, manufacturing, process engineers, process development engineers and project engineers.

Key Contact - Specialty:
Mr. Frank Williamson, President - *Chemical industry*

Salary minimum: $40,000

Functions: Middle Mgmt., Mfg., Product Dev., Production, Sales Mgmt., Engineering

Industries: Mfg., Textiles, Apparel, Printing, Chemicals, Plastics, Rubber, Paints, Petro. Products

MRI of Newtown Square

3415 W Chester Pike Ste 303
Newtown Square, PA 19073
(610) 353-2705
Fax: (610) 356-8731
Email: sandy@mrns.com

Description: Our focus is the IT software market including, but not limited, to ERP, supply chain, financial and accounting, CRM, data warehousing, and the industrial controls market including electrical controls, PLC, drives, motion controls, machine vision, robotics, process instrument, process controls like DCS, HMI Scada software, advanced control software, and MES and supply chain software segments. We place sales, marketing, and technical service professionals, middle, and upper-level managers.

Key Contact - Specialty:
Mr. Sandy Bishop, Manager - *Factory automation controls hardware & software, machine vision, robotics, sales & marketing, technical support*

Salary minimum: $50,000

Functions: Middle Mgmt., Automation, Sales & Mktg.

Industries: Computer Equip., Software

MRI of Pittsburgh

112 Washington Plc Ste 1400
2 Chatham Ctr
Pittsburgh, PA 15219-3423
(412) 566-2100
Fax: (412) 566-2229
Email: lc@mrpitt.com
Web: www.mrpitt.com

Description: Executive search firm specializing in financial services, information technology, telecommunications and pharmaceutical/medical recruiting.

Key Contact:
Ms. Laura Connelly, General Manager - *Telecommunications*
Ms. Denise Muiter, Practice Manager - *Telecommunications*

Mr. Nick Colinear, Practice Manager - *Information technology*

Mr. Jon Bender, Operations Manager

Functions: Generalist

Industries: Invest. Banking, Pharm Svcs., E-commerce, Telecoms, Call Centers, Digital, Wireless, Network Infrastructure, Software, Biotech

MRI of West View
800 Perry Hwy Ste 2
Pittsburgh, PA 15229
(412) 635-3001
Fax: (412) 635-3002
Email: mary@mrwestview.com
Web: www.mrwestview.com

Description: Over 30 years' experience in the construction industry. Clients are large general contractors, construction managers, architectural firms, engineering firms and design-build firms nationwide. Project managers, estimators, superintendents, architects, civil engineers and upper-management. Resumes remain confidential until candidate authorizes release.

Key Contact:
Mr. Thomas Moore

Salary minimum: $40,000

Functions: Generalist

Industries: Construction

Professional Associations: ASPE, SMPS

MRI of Mt. Lebanon
(also known as Mount Lebanon Group LLC)
393 Vanadium Rd Ste 303
Pittsburgh, PA 15243
(866) 278-1674
(412) 278-1674
Fax: (412) 278-1696
Email: info@mr-mtlebanon.net
Web: www.mr-mtlebanon.net

Description: We are an executive search firm specializing in engineering, human resource, and retail professionals.

Key Contact - Specialty:
Mr. James Moran, President/Managing Director - *Human resources*

Salary minimum: $40,000

MRI of Pittsburgh-North
435 Broad St
PO Box 69
Sewickley, PA 15143
(412) 741-5805
Fax: (412) 741-3801
Email: main@mripitt.com
Web: www.mrpitt.com

Description: Specialties: data processing, medical (DR), medical device sales, medical administration (HMO).

Key Contact - Specialty:
Mr. Richard Lampl, General Manager
Ms. Joni Lampl, Manager - *MIS*

Salary minimum: $30,000

Functions: Generalist, Physicians, Health Admin., MIS Mgmt., Systems Analysis, Systems Dev., Systems Implem., Systems Support

Industries: Generalist, Medical Devices, IT Implementation

MRI of Bucks County
650 Louis Dr Ste 170
Warminster, PA 18974
(215) 675-6440
Fax: (215) 675-1446

Email: careers@mribucks.com
Web: www.mrinet.com

Key Contact:
Mr. Michael Mashack, General Manager

Functions: Generalist

Industries: Construction, Finance, Real Estate

Professional Associations: ELA, IREM

MRI of Reading
(also known as The StoneBridge Group Inc)
4 Park Plz Ste 201
Wyomissing, PA 19610
(610) 375-1500
Fax: (610) 375-1504
Email: mrireading@mrireading.com
Web: www.mrireading.com

Description: Our firm offers staffing solutions in the following: engineering, logistics, supply chain and transportation, retail management, sales and marketing, manufacturing management, medical device and pharmaceutical, finance, accounting, and insurance and risk management.

Key Contact - Specialty:
Mr. Jeff Burridge, President - *Engineering, general manufacturing*

Salary minimum: $35,000

Functions: General Mgmt., Middle Mgmt., Mfg., Materials, Purchasing, Materials Plng., Healthcare, Sales & Mktg., Finance, Engineering

Industries: Generalist, Finance, Banking, Invest. Banking, Insurance

Professional Associations: MAAPC

MRI of Puerto Rico
289 JT Pinero Ave Ste 200
San Juan, PR 00927
(787) 766-4020
Fax: (787) 763-0870
Email: recruiters@jobgallery.com
Web: www.jobgallery.com

Description: Specializing in: 1. Bilingual, bicultural talent for Puerto Rico, the Caribbean and Latin America. 2. Proven performers for both management and staff positions. 3. Motivated candidates who realistically will accept your offer if selected.

Key Contact:
Mr. Carlos R. Rodriguez, President

Salary minimum: $15,000

Functions: Generalist

Industries: Generalist

MRI of Aiken
PO Box 730
Aiken, SC 29802
(803) 648-1361
Fax: (803) 642-5114
Email: manager@aiken.mrinet.com

Description: Fee paid, national specialists in utilities, primary metals, computers, automotive, appliance and electrical components, glass-ceramics, plastics, building materials, brick, tile, refrigeration equipment mfg,electric utilities.

Key Contact - Specialty:
Mr. Michael Hardwick, Managing Partner - *Glass manufacturing*
Mr. Leo Tatarenchik, Partner - *Appliance, HB/AC equipment manufacturing*
Mr. Robert Barnett, Partner - *Power & energy*
Mr. Guy Hill, Partner - *Primary metals*
Mr. David Johnson, Partner - *Automotive & vehicle manufacturing*
Mr. Len Kane, Partner - *Plastics, consumer disposables*

Salary minimum: $40,000

Functions: Generalist, Admin. Svcs., Production, Purchasing, Packaging, Mktg. Mgmt., CFO's, MIS Mgmt.

Industries: Generalist, Energy, Utilities, Plastics, Rubber, Leather, Stone, Glass, Metal Products, Motor Vehicles

MRI of Anderson
PO Box 2874
Anderson, SC 29622
(864) 225-1258
Fax: (864) 225-2332
Email: mrand@charter.net
Web: www.career-hunter.com

Description: Our firm specializes in permanent career placement in information technology, pharmaceutical, bioinfomatics, medical device, construction, and general manufacturing companies on a national basis. We will confidently meet your needs with professional attention and outstanding service that has been our trademark for the past 20 years.

Key Contact - Specialty:
Mr. Rod Pagan, Manager
Ms. Valerie Scott-Wagner, Senior Account Executive - *Bioinfomatics, information technology*

MRI of Spring Valley
129-B S Main St
PO Box 825
Blythewood, SC 29016-8780
(803) 714-1064
Fax: (803) 714-1065
Email: chenry@mrspringvalley.com
Web: www.mrinet.com

Description: We specialize in recruiting for the building materials industry: sales, sales management, product management, etc. Our primary clients are manufacturers and distributors of building materials. We are also recruiters working the healthcare industry: nuclear medicine, ER nurses, etc.

Key Contact:
Mr. Charles Henry, President & General Manager - *Building materials*
Mrs. Ann Henry, Vice-President, Administration

Functions: Product Dev., Purchasing, Sales & Mktg., Sales Mgmt.

Industries: Construction

MRI of Charleston
4 Carriage Ln Ste 301
Charleston, SC 29407
(843) 556-6461
Fax: (843) 556-4803
Email: mr@search-jobs.com
Web: www.search-jobs.com

Key Contact:
Mr. Bob Bean, Manager

Functions: Mfg., Plant Mgmt., Healthcare, IT

Industries: Metal Products, Machine, Appliance, Misc. Mfg., Hospitals, Long-term Care

MRI of Columbia
1512 Laurel St
Columbia, SC 29201
(803) 254-1334
Fax: (803) 254-1527
Email: recruiter@mricolumbia.com
Web: www.brilliantpeople.com

Key Contact - Specialty:
Mr. Robert Keen, Jr., Manager/Owner - *Anesthetist*
Mr. Fred Berry, Senior Account Executive - *Radiology, medical imaging*

Let www.ExecutiveAgent.com e-mail your resume now.

Mr. John W. C. Brandon, Account Executive - *Sales*

Mrs. Elizabeth Millen, Account Executive - *Pharmacy*

Functions: Healthcare, Sales & Mktg.

Industries: Generalist, Medical Devices, Pharm Svcs., Biotech, Hospitals

MRI of Florence

1224 W Evans St
PO Box 5320
Florence, SC 29501-3322
(843) 664-1112
Fax: (843) 673-2701
Email: recruiter@mrflorence.com
Web: www.mrflorence.com

Description: We identify, recruit and deliver manufacturing and manufacturing support managers, executives and technical professionals for clients who are or want to become world class manufacturers.

Key Contact - Specialty:
Mr. Alan Feimster, President - *Manufacturing, (support)*

Salary minimum: $20,000

Functions: Mfg., Production, Materials

Industries: Mfg.

MRI of Greenville

330 Pelham Rd Ste 109-B
Greenville, SC 29615
(864) 370-1341
Fax: (864) 370-9633
Email: mdsgville@aol.com
Web: www.mrigreenvillesc.com

Description: The search and recruiting specialists - 400 offices. This office specializes in industrial sales and marketing in the electrical and mechanical industries.

Key Contact:
Mr. M. D. Scarboro, President - *Industrial, electrical, automation*
Ms. Dee Scarboro

Functions: Sales & Mktg.

Industries: Energy, Utilities, Misc. Mfg.

MRI of North Charleston

4975 Lacross Rd Ste 311
North Charleston, SC 29406-6525
(843) 744-5888
Fax: (843) 744-4666
Email: fbabyak@febrecruiters.com

Description: As part of a network of over 750 offices, we bring together top quality candidates and top flight employers.

Key Contact:
Mr. Fran Babyak, President/Owner

Salary minimum: $40,000

Functions: Generalist, Mfg., Materials, Healthcare, Sales & Mktg., Finance, IT, Engineering

Industries: Generalist, Mfg., Wholesale, Retail, Finance, Media, Software, Healthcare

MRI of Orangeburg

2037 St. Matthews Rd
Orangeburg, SC 29118
(803) 531-4101
Fax: (803) 536-3714
Email: mro@carolinarecruiters.com
Web: www.carolinarecruiters.com

Description: Our firm is an integral part of the world's largest executive search and recruitment franchise.

Key Contact:
Mr. Ed Chewning, Jr., Co-Manager
Mr. Dick B. Crawford, Co-Manager

Salary minimum: $40,000

Professional Associations: SHRM

MRI of Georgetown

PO Box 2715
Pawleys Island, SC 29585
(843) 357-1688
(888) 525-2323
Fax: (843) 357-1708
Email: mrigtown@mail.com

Description: Specializes in middle to senior-level management positions for clients in insurance and managed care, or other industries requiring operations, finance, information systems professionals.

Key Contact - Specialty:
Mr. Scott Knowles, Executive Director - *Insurance, finance, information*

Salary minimum: $40,000

Functions: Generalist, Directors, Senior Mgmt., Middle Mgmt., Healthcare, Sales & Mktg., Finance, IT

Industries: Generalist, Drugs Mfg., Medical Devices, Pharm Svcs., Insurance

MRI of Summerville

1675 N Main St Ste B
Summerville, SC 29483
(800) 807-1977
(843) 821-1119
Fax: (843) 821-1117
Email: mris@mrsummerville.com
Web: www.mrsummerville.com

Description: Our firm is part of Management Recruiters International. Our firm is dedicated to providing customized staffing solutions that address the unique challenges facing employers in the area of healthcare.

Key Contact - Specialty:
Mr. Norm Moran, President - *Healthcare*
Mr. Lewis Lanier, Director of Professional Recruitment - *Healthcare*
Ms. Punky Buckner, Project Manager - *Healthcare*
Miss Melissa Varner, Administrative Assistant - *Healthcare*

Functions: Healthcare, Nurses, Allied Health, Health Admin.

Industries: Healthcare, Hospitals, Dental, Women's

MRI of Myrtle Beach Inc

1500 Hwy 17 N Ste 308
Surfside Beach, SC 29575-6080
(843) 477-8800
Fax: (843) 477-8304
Email: mrimb@sccoast.net
Web: www.jobquestsite.com

Description: We provide a superior recruiting service for corporate clients to aid in their growth and to provide candidates with the most rewarding career opportunities in their pursuit of excellence.

Key Contact - Specialty:
Mr. Mark E. Lewis, President - *Food & beverage operations, manufacturing*

Salary minimum: $40,000

Functions: Generalist, Production, Plant Mgmt., Quality, Materials, Mktg. Mgmt., Engineering

Industries: Generalist, Mfg., Food, Bev., Tobacco, Plastics, Rubber, Machine, Appliance, Motor Vehicles, Consumer Elect., Misc. Mfg., Transportation, Retail

MRI of Travelers Rest

907 N Main St
PO Box 639
Travelers Rest, SC 29690-0639
(864) 834-0643
Fax: (864) 834-0275
Email: gcmrtr@aol.com

Description: One of 1,000 offices that are fully computerized with inter-office referral, executive search profile program, video conferencing centers, and a custom designed information technology program that optimizes information and communication flow within each office, between management recruiters offices, and between individual offices and the business world.

Key Contact:
Mr. Guy W. Carter, President - *General manufacturing, information systems*
Ms. Gail Carter, Manager

Salary minimum: $30,000

Functions: Mfg., IT

Industries: Mfg., Textiles, Apparel, Chemicals, Drugs Mfg., Plastics, Rubber, Metal Products, Misc. Mfg., Electronic, Elec. Components, Transportation, Wholesale, Finance, Services, Hospitality, Packaging, Insurance, Hospitals

MRI of Sioux Falls LLP

116 W 69th St - Ste 200
Sioux Falls, SD 57108
(605) 367-6939
Fax: (605) 367-6940
Email: get@agoodjob.com
Web: www.agoodjob.com

Description: Permanent & interim search and placement; executive, professional, management, technical, sales/marketing.

Key Contact - Specialty:
Mr. David J. Good, Partner - *Intangible*
Mr. Robert B. Good, Partner - *Banking & related*

Salary minimum: $30,000

Functions: Generalist

Industries: Construction, Mfg., Wholesale, Finance, Services, Telecoms, Insurance, Software

MRI of Chattanooga-Brainerd

7010 Lee Hwy Ste 216
Chattanooga, TN 37421
(423) 894-5500
Fax: (423) 894-1177
Email: mrichatt@cdc.net
Web: www.mrichattanooga.com

Description: Full-service recruitment, outplacement and video-conference center both retained and contingency search. Specialties include: technical, management, medical and pharmaceutical sales/marketing and information systems.

Key Contact:
Mr. Bill Cooper, President - *General manufacturing, technical, chemical, medical sales & marketing, pharmaceutical sales & marketing*
Mrs. Barbara Cooper, Secretary/Vice President

Salary minimum: $40,000

Functions: Generalist

Industries: Generalist, Drugs Mfg., Medical Devices, Plastics, Rubber, Motor Vehicles, Consumer Elect., Misc. Mfg.

MRI of Columbia, TN

1117 Trotwood Ave Ste 201
Columbia, TN 38401-3033
(931) 388-5586
Fax: (931) 380-0615
Web: www.mritn.com

Description: Management Recruiters of Columbia, Tennessee, focuses on Management, Administrative and Technical recruiting for automotive and related industries with manufacturing locations in Tennessee, Kentucky and surrounding states.

Key Contact:
Mr. Douglas Holt, Manager - *Automotive manufacturing*
Ms. Marianne Stevick, Account Executive - *Automotive manufacturing*
Mrs. Racheal Taylor, Administrative Assistant

Salary minimum: $25,000

Functions: Generalist

Industries: Mfg., Plastics, Rubber, Metal Products, Motor Vehicles

Professional Associations: ASQ, SAE

MRI of Cordova
1181 Vickery Ln Ste 201
Cordova, TN 38018
(901) 432-1674
Fax: (901) 432-2674
Email: mrecruit@midsouth.rr.com
Web: www.mricordova.com

Description: Our firm is an extremely aggressive search firm. We specialize in a variety of industries. Whether you're looking for entry-level professionals or executive caliber talent, we are the perfect place to spearhead your next search.

Key Contact:
Mr. Eddy Hatcher, President - *Manufacturing*
Mrs. Merrin Cantin, Account Executive - *Accounting, healthcare*
Mr. Jason Martin, Account Executive - *Insurance*
Mr. Dean Proffer, Account Executive - *Information technology*
Mrs. Amy Glenn, Project Coordinator
Mr. Josh Hatcher, Webmaster / Marketing Manager

Functions: Generalist

Industries: Generalist

MRI of Franklin
236 Public Sq Ste 201
Franklin, TN 37064-2520
(615) 791-4391
Fax: (615) 791-4769
Email: rhmarriott@earthlink.net

Description: One of approximately 800 offices of the world's largest contingency search and recruitment organization. This office specializes in the printing industry.

Key Contact - Specialty:
Mr. Roger H. Marriott, President - *Printing industry, sales, sales management, technical*
Ms. Gloria A. Marriott, Secretary/Treasurer - *Printing industry, sales, sales management, technical*

Salary minimum: $35,000

Functions: Generalist

Industries: Generalist, Printing

MRI of Johnson City
904 Sunset Dr Ste 9B
Johnson City, TN 37604-3674
(423) 952-0900
Fax: (423) 952-0999
Email: mri@naxs.net

Key Contact:
Mr. Keith Dawson, Manager

Salary minimum: $35,000

Functions: Mfg., Materials, Engineering

Industries: Mfg., Plastics, Rubber, Metal Products, Machine, Appliance, Motor Vehicles, Consumer Elect., Mgmt. Consulting, Software

MRI of Memphis
(also known as The Delta Group Inc)
5050 Poplar Ave White Station Twr Ste 1103
Memphis, TN 38157
(901) 844-8000
Fax: (901) 844-8001
Email: tdginc@earthlink.net
Web: www.mrinet.com

Description: We specialize in engineering, manufacturing, marketing and sales professionals.

Key Contact - Specialty:
Mr. Raymond F. Wojcik, President - *Consumer products, sales & marketing, management*
Mr. Don Frease, Account Executive - *Engineering, information technology*
Ms. Rani Cochran, Account Executive - *Sales & marketing*

Salary minimum: $60,000

Functions: General Mgmt., Sales & Mktg., Mkt. Research, Sales Mgmt., Engineering

Industries: Mfg., Food, Bev., Tobacco, Textiles, Apparel, Paper, Chemicals, Soap, Perf., Cosmtcs., Drugs Mfg., Consumer Elect.

MRI of Memphis
5495 Winchester Rd Ste 5
Memphis, TN 38115
(901) 794-3130
(901) 794-3137
Fax: (901) 794-5671
Email: mrimemphis@earthlink.net

Description: Search and recruiting specialists. Affiliate of the world's largest search firm---800 offices nationwide.

Key Contact - Specialty:
Mr. Wally Watson, Owner/General Manager - *Logistics, management*

Functions: Generalist

Industries: Generalist

MRI of Stones River
232 Heritage Park Dr Ste 101
Murfreesboro, TN 37129
(615) 494-1333
Fax: (615) 494-1372
Email: info@mristonesriver.com
Web: www.mristonesriver.com

Key Contact:
Mr. Wayne Moore

Functions: General Mgmt., Middle Mgmt., Mfg., Product Dev., Production, Automation, Plant Mgmt., Materials, HR Mgmt., Engineering

Industries: Metal Products, Machine, Appliance, Motor Vehicles, Computer Equip., Consumer Elect., Test, Measure Equip., Misc. Mfg., Electronic, Elec. Components, Telephony, Fiber Optic

MRI of Nashville Inc
4701 Trousdale Dr Ste 208
Nashville, TN 37220-1385
(615) 333-6067
Email: office@mrnashville.com
Web: www.mrnashville.com

Description: Healthcare industry specialists.

Key Contact - Specialty:
Mr. John W. Anderson, President - *Healthcare*

Functions: Healthcare

Industries: Healthcare

MRI of Fort Worth-Arlington
1001 W Randol Mill Rd
Arlington, TX 76012
(817) 469-6161
Fax: (817) 462-9155
Email: adminstrator@topcareers.com
Web: www.topcareers.com

Description: We have been consistent as a leading mid-size MRI office. We are specializing in placing engineering, oil and gas, electronic, energy, transmission, power marketing, process and controls, manufacturing, environmental, chemical, plastics, printing, packaging, telecommunications, and graphic art professionals world wide.

Key Contact - Specialty:
Mr. Robert J. Stoessel, CPC, General Manager - *Manufacturing, energy, oil & gas,*
Mr. Larry Laux, Director - *Power & gas (marketing), transmission planning, risk management, generation, technical/analyst, operations*

Salary minimum: $50,000

Functions: General Mgmt.

Industries: Energy, Utilities, Construction, Food, Bev., Tobacco, Printing, Test, Measure Equip., Misc. Mfg., Electronic, Elec. Components, Digital, Wireless, Mfg. SW

Professional Associations: MAPC, TAPC

MRI of North West Austin
PO Box 27258
Austin, TX 78755-2258
(512) 338-0880
Fax: (512) 338-0481
Email: mraustinnw@aol.com

Description: Our experience as industry managers makes us uniquely qualified to find the individual you are looking for who is not looking for you.

Key Contact - Specialty:
Ms. Lorraine Keller, President - *Technical*

Salary minimum: $45,000

Functions: Mfg., Product Dev., R&D, Engineering

Industries: Mfg., Chemicals, Plastics, Rubber, Paints, Petro. Products, Machine, Appliance, Misc. Mfg., Packaging

MRI of Austin
1250 Capital of Texas Hwy S Ste 390
3 Cielo Ctr
Austin, TX 78746-2605
(512) 327-8292
Fax: (512) 327-3901
Email: admin@mriaustin.com
Web: www.mriaustin.com

Description: Our firm is one of the top offices in the MRI system of 900 offices. Our areas of specialty include IT, healthcare, market research, industrial refrigeration, insurance, and sales.

Key Contact:
Ms. Joyce Dailey, General Manager

Salary minimum: $40,000

Functions: Generalist, Mfg., Healthcare, Sales & Mktg., Advertising, IT, R&D

Industries: Generalist, Mfg., Advertising, Software, Biotech, Healthcare

MRI of Bellaire
4500 Bissonnet Ste 355
Bellaire, TX 77401-2418
(713) 668-8501
Fax: (713) 668-8502
Email: resume@mr-bellaire.com
Web: www.mri-bellaire.com

Description: We perform both retained and contingency searches, focusing on consumer electronics, home automation, lighting, consumer products, printing, and wireless industries. Our focus is in the sales/marketing arenas.

Key Contact - Specialty:
Mr. Tony Marolda, Manager - *Lighting, home automation, consumer products*
Mr. Bruce Crosthwait, Manager - *Consumer electronics, printing, wireless, telecom*

Salary minimum: $50,000

Functions: Product Dev., Sales & Mktg., Mktg. Mgmt., Sales Mgmt., DB Admin.

Industries: Generalist, Printing, Consumer Elect., Hospitality, Publishing, New Media, Communications, Telecoms, Digital, Wireless, Software, Mfg. SW

MRI of Dallas North
15150 Preston Rd Ste 300
Dallas, TX 75248
(972) 991-4500
Fax: (972) 991-6226
Email: gbuntrock@sprynet.com

Description: Our mission is to provide a quality of service that meets or exceeds our client's expectations. We focus our services on the following: quality candidates, timely completion, the matching of the client's opportunity with the candidate's desires, and thorough interactive communication. MRDN has established an expertise in providing individuals, who are professionals in the areas of: distribution/logistics management, high technology, manufacturing management, sales professionals, high-tech, and software

Key Contact - Specialty:
Mr. George Buntrock, President - *Distribution, logistics*

Salary minimum: $50,000

Functions: General Mgmt., Plant Mgmt., Materials, Sales Mgmt., HR Mgmt., IT

Industries: Mfg., Misc. Mfg., Transportation, Wholesale, Retail, IT Implementation, PSA/ASP, Software, Accounting SW, ERP SW, HR SW

MRI of Dallas
5501 LBJ Frwy Ste 120
Dallas, TX 75240
(972) 789-1000
Fax: (972) 789-1025
Email: tim@mriadvantage.com

Description: We offer construction recruiting.

Key Contact - Specialty:
Mr. Tim Matthews, President - *Project managers, estimators, superintendents*
Mr. Dylan Magee, National Accounts Manager - *Project managers, estimators, superintendents*

MRI of Addison
(also known as Burt Moses Associates Inc)
15400 Knoll Trail Ste 230
Dallas, TX 75248-3465
(972) 702-0480
Fax: (972) 702-0482
Email: bmoses@bmasearch.com
Web: www.bmasearch.com

Description: We are an executive search firm for property and casualty insurance professionals. We place technical levels and higher. We have a combined 60 years worth of experience in the insurance industry.

Key Contact - Specialty:
Mr. Burt Moses, CPCU, Owner - *Insurance (property, casualty)*
Mr. Curtis Powell, Account Manager - *Insurance (property, casualty)*

Mr. Fred Wilkinson, Account Manager - *Property and casualty insurance*

Salary minimum: $50,000

Functions: Generalist

Industries: Insurance

Professional Associations: CPCU

MRI of Fort Worth-Southwest
6300 Ridglea Pl Ste 1005
Ft. Worth, TX 76116
(817) 989-9700
Fax: (817) 569-1126
Email: careers@mrifortworth.com
Web: www.mrifortworth.com

Description: We provide executive recruitment focusing on telecommunications, information technology, health care, civil, electrical, mechanical, architectural, software, hardware and embedded engineering, human resources, and banking.

Key Contact:
Mr. Don Neubauer
Mr. Les Siter

Functions: Generalist, IT, Engineering

Industries: Generalist, Energy, Utilities, Construction, Mfg., Finance, Communications, Software, Healthcare

MRI of Ft Worth-Downtown
500 W 7th St Ste 1720 Unit 14
Ft. Worth, TX 76102-4739
(817) 348-8900
Fax: (815) 364-4774
Email: info@mrifw.com
Web: www.mrifw.com

Key Contact:
Mr. Lee Shahwan, Manager

Functions: General Mgmt., Senior Mgmt., Mfg., Engineering

Industries: Mfg., E-commerce, IT Implementation, Communications, Defense, Aerospace, Packaging, Software, Database SW, Mfg. SW, Networking, Comm. SW

MRI of Houston
1360 Post Oak Blvd Ste 2110
Houston, TX 77056
(713) 850-9850
(800) 878-0995
Fax: (713) 850-1429
Email: mrhouston@mrhouston.com
Web: www.mrhouston.com

Description: Retained and contingency search - healthcare, engineering, manufacturing, financial, information services, sales and marketing, middle management and senior management, medical and pharmaceutical sales, retail.

Key Contact:
Mr. Keith Kornfuehrer, Manager - *Sales management, executives*
Mr. James Maranto

Salary minimum: $50,000

Functions: Generalist, Senior Mgmt., Production, Allied Health, Health Admin., CFO's, MIS Mgmt., Engineering

Industries: Generalist, Energy, Utilities, Chemicals, Retail, Invest. Banking, Pharm Svcs., Accounting, Healthcare

MRI of Champions
14614 Falling Creek Dr Ste 214
Houston, TX 77068-2941
(281) 580-6020
Fax: (281) 580-6029

Email: gakin@mrichampions.com
Web: www.mrichampions.com

Description: Providing nationwide permanent placement, interim executive and outplacement services to clients needing candidates in sales engineering, manufacturing, cutting tools, mechanical and electrical engineering design and employee benefits consulting.

Key Contact - Specialty:
Mr. Gary K. Akin, Manager - *General manufacturing*
Ms. Nicola Akin, Co-Manager
Mr. James C. Barkley, Certified Senior Account Manager - *Generalist*
Mr. Joe Slack, Account Executive - *General manufacturing*
Ms. Robin Morris, Account Executive - *Benefit administration outsourcing*

Salary minimum: $35,000

Functions: Mfg., Product Dev., Production, Automation, Packaging, Benefits, Systems Implem., Engineering

Industries: Generalist, Mfg., Medical Devices, Metal Products, Equip Svcs., Packaging

Professional Associations: ASME, ASPA, SME

MRI of Houston-West
(also known as Albrecht & Assoc Executive Search Consultants)
10700 Richmond Ave Ste 217
Houston, TX 77042-4900
(713) 784-7444
Fax: (713) 784-5049
Email: albrecht@albrecht-assoc.com
Web: www.albrecht-assoc.com

Description: We specialize in energy, including all areas of electric power and the legal area in oil and gas, as well as pharmaceutical, and biotechnology. Our database includes virtually every company in these industries, and we have an extensive network of clients and professionals in these organizations.

Key Contact:
Ms. Franke M. Albrecht, President

Salary minimum: $60,000

Functions: Generalist

Industries: Energy, Utilities, Drugs Mfg., Pharm Svcs., Legal, Biotech

Professional Associations: AAMI, ACCP, ACRP, AMCP, ASHP, DIA, MMA, NAHQ, PDA, RAPS, UMA

MRI of LBJ Park/Dallas
6311 N O'Connor Blvd Ste 214
Dallas Communications Complex
Irving, TX 75039
(972) 488-1133 x101
Fax: (972) 488-1099
Email: rvlasek@mridfw.com
Web: www.mridfw.com

Description: My background includes 18 years' experience in electronics companies based in personnel management and training.

Key Contact - Specialty:
Mr. Ray Vlasek, President - *Technical*

Salary minimum: $40,000

Functions: Generalist

Industries: Mfg., Chemicals, Metal Products, Machine, Appliance, Computer Equip., Test, Measure Equip., Misc. Mfg., Retail, Telecoms, Aerospace

Professional Associations: IEEE

Networks: IMSA

MRI of Houston-Northeast

(also known as LinGate Corporation Inc)
1412-A Stonehollow Dr
Kingwood, TX 77339
(281) 359-7940
(800) 234-9316
Fax: (281) 359-7947
Email: lindak@mrihouston.com
Web: www.mrihouston.com

Description: Our specialty divisions partner with all the leading companies in those industries to provide talented employees in technical, managerial, and executive positions. Our specialties include: lumber, and building products, accounting/finance, architectural services, logistics, and real estate. Our reputation in those industries is impeccable. We conduct retained and contingency searches for our client companies.

Key Contact - Specialty:
Ms. Linda Copeland, President - *Client development*
Mr. Gates Copeland, Vice President - *Forest products*
Mr. Jeff Flowers, Account Executive - *Forest products*
Ms. Susan Crusham, Account Executive - *Logistics, supply chain management*
Mr. Christopher Rowland, Account Executive - *Architectural services*
Ms. Amy Salsman, Account Executive - *Real estate*
Mr. Maria Wojciechowski, Account Executive - *Real estate, hospitality*
Mr. Vernon Massey, Account Executive - *Building products*

Salary minimum: $40,000

Functions: Generalist, Directors, Senior Mgmt., Middle Mgmt., Finance, Architects

Industries: Generalist, Agri., Forestry, Mining, Construction, Lumber, Furniture, Paper, Medical Devices, Motor Vehicles, Wholesale, Retail, Finance, Banking, Invest. Banking, Accounting, HR Services, Insurance, Real Estate, Accounting SW, Development SW, Non-classifiable

Professional Associations: CPA, SFPA, SHRM

MRI of Lewisville

1660 S Stemmons Ste 460
Brookhollow N
Lewisville, TX 75067
(972) 434-9612
Fax: (972) 221-0268
Email: mrlrec@swbell.net
Web: www.mrlewisville.com

Key Contact - Specialty:
Ms. Desni C. Kramer, General Manager - *Auto ID, data collection, software*

Salary minimum: $50,000

Functions: Materials, Sales & Mktg., IT

Industries: Generalist

Professional Associations: TAPPI

MRI of Round Rock

301 Hesters Xing Ste 110
Round Rock, TX 78681
(512) 310-1918
Fax: (512) 310-8318
Email: jomanly@msn.com
Web: www.mrroundrock.com

Description: We are a highly focused professional recruitment team specializing in the permanent placement of professionals who work with OEMs of special machinery, automation, and robotics. We also specialize in the transportation, logistics, and warehouse distribution industry. We pride ourselves on minimizing relocation whenever possible.

Key Contact - Specialty:
Ms. Jodi Hohlstein, Account Executive - *Electrical, electro-mechanical controls, automation & robotics*
Mr. Jeff Hohlstein, Account Executive - *Electrical, electro-mechanical controls, automation & robotics*
Ms. Jo Manly, Account Executive - *Electrical, electro-mechanical controls, automation & robotics*
Ms. Ramona Thompson, Account Executive - *Electrical, electro-mechanical controls, automation & robotics*
Ms. Sara Smith, Account Executive - *Warehouse distribution, transportation, logistics*
Mr. Bill Turner, Account Executive - *Warehouse distribution, transportation & logistics*

Functions: Generalist, Middle Mgmt., Automation, Engineering

Industries: Generalist, Food, Bev., Tobacco, Machine, Appliance, Misc. Mfg., Transportation, Retail

MRI of San Antonio

8700 Crownhill Ste 701
San Antonio, TX 78209
(210) 829-8666
Fax: (210) 822-2218
Email: manager@mrisanantonio.com
Web: www.mrisanantonio.com

Description: Additional client services include reduced rate moves, reduced rate mortgages, refinancing and closing costs, video conference network for interviewing (all financial services available to clients and candidates placed by us).

Key Contact - Specialty:
Mr. James L. Cornfoot, Co-Manager - *Food and beverage industry, senior level management, Engineering*
Ms. Denise Carrigan, Co-Manager - *Food and beverage industry, senior management, marketing, operations*

Salary minimum: $70,000

Functions: General Mgmt., Middle Mgmt., Mfg., Production, Plant Mgmt., Purchasing, Packaging, Finance, R&D

Industries: Food, Bev., Tobacco, Finance

MRI of San Marcos

101 Uhland Rd Ste 203
San Marcos, TX 78666
(512) 392-3838
Fax: (512) 392-3133
Email: cberry@mrsanmarcos.com

Description: Our firm offers over 40 years of experience to assist with opportunities and growth. Our office specializes in all aspects of agriculture, banking, consumer products, sales, and marketing.

Key Contact - Specialty:
Dr. Charles D. Berry, President - *Agricultural, chemical seed, biotechnology, research & development, sales & marketing*
Ms. Jennifer Justus, Office Manager
Ms. Judy Aswell, Account Executive - *Consumer products, licensing, design, sales & marketing, merchandising*
Ms. Liz Elliott, Project Coordinator - *Consumer products, sales & marketing*
Ms. Rhonda Galloway, Account Executive - *Banking*

Salary minimum: $35,000

Functions: Generalist, Senior Mgmt., Middle Mgmt., Sales & Mktg., Sales Mgmt., R&D

Industries: Generalist, Agri., Forestry, Mining, Banking, Telecoms, Biotech

Professional Associations: ASA, ASTA, SHOPA

MRI of Sugar Land

12919 SW Fwy 100
Stafford, TX 77477-4001
(281) 240-0220
Fax: (281) 240-0880
Email: shayna@mylinuxisp.com

Description: We are an executive search firm, more specifically 80% contingency and 20% retainer. We work mainly in the following areas: lumber/plywood and manufacturing wood products; pulp, paper, and packaging; oil and gas; and engineering; and accounting and finance. All of our recruiting is done nationwide.

Key Contact - Specialty:
Mr. John R. Gandee, President - *Lumber, plywood, millwork, oil and gas*
Ms. Joan C. Gandee, Vice President - *Lumber, plywood, millworks, oil and gas*
Mr. Don Hayes, Senior Search Consultant - *Pulp, paper, packaging*
Mr. Jason Ford, Senior Search Consultant - *Accounting, finance*
Mr. Brad Gandee, Research Associate - *Covers entire office*
Ms. Shayna Gandee, Project Coordination - *Lumber, plywood, millwork, oil and gas*

Salary minimum: $30,000

Functions: Generalist, General Mgmt., Mfg., Sales & Mktg., HR Mgmt., Engineering

Industries: Energy, Utilities, Lumber, Furniture, Paper, Finance, Accounting, Packaging

Professional Associations: NHLA, SLMA

MRI of Ogden

533 26th St Ste 203 B
Ogden, UT 84401
(801) 621-1777
Fax: (801) 621-1788
Email: recruiter@mrogden.com
Web: www.mrogden.com

Description: Permanent and contract placement of technical and manufacturing individuals on a nationwide basis. Emphasis in HVAC, electric heat, appliance, trucks and tractors, power tools, wireless communication design, installation and sales, biotechnology, wood cabinetry.

Key Contact:
Mr. Jerry Manning, Owner/Manager - *General manufacturing, technical, quality*
Mr. Ray Baker, Account Executive - *Wireless communication, engineering*
Mrs. Rebecca DeHart, Account Executive - *Wood cabinetry*
Mr. Scott Dwire, Account Executive - *RF/microwave components*
Mr. Rich Horwitz, Account Executive - *Biotechnology*
Mr. Darrel Stage, Administrative Assistant

Salary minimum: $40,000

Functions: Generalist

Industries: Mfg., Lumber, Furniture, Machine, Appliance, Test, Measure Equip., Misc. Mfg., Electronic, Elec. Components, Biotech

MRI of Provo

1933 N 1120 W
Provo, UT 84604-1044
(801) 375-0777
Fax: (801) 375-5757
Email: info@jobsforpros.com
Web: www.jobsforpros.com

Description: We are a national search and recruiting firm specializing in telecommunications and DataCom, fiber optics, microelectronics, RF engineering, software, and test and measurement. Our clients include start-ups, pre-IPO firms, midsize and Fortune 100 high-technology companies. Our recruiting focus is on technical/engineering personnel, sales/marketing professionals, and managerial/executive positions.

Key Contact:
Mr. Larry Massung, BSME, President

Salary minimum: $60,000

Functions: Senior Mgmt., Middle Mgmt., Mfg., Packaging, Sales & Mktg., IT, R&D, Engineering

Industries: Test, Measure Equip., Electronic, Elec. Components, Telecoms, Telephony, Digital, Wireless, Fiber Optic, Network Infrastructure, Packaging, Database SW, Development SW, Networking, Comm. SW, System SW

MRI of Loudoun County S
PO Box 220685
Chantilly, VA 20153-6685
(703) 430-3700
Fax: (703) 378-9762
Email: mri@cox.rr.com
Web: www.mriloudoun.com

Description: Complete human resources services provider: permanent and interim placement; outplacement assistance; management consulting; financial, travel and relocation services offered to client companies.

Key Contact - Specialty:
Mr. Jerry Gilmore, President - *Chemical process industry, engineering disciplines*
Ms. Pamela Nix Gilmore, Vice President/General Manager - *Chemical process industry, manufacturing, engineering disciplines*

Salary minimum: $50,000

Functions: Middle Mgmt., Production, Automation, Plant Mgmt., Quality, Engineering, Minorities

Industries: Generalist, Chemicals, Drugs Mfg., Plastics, Rubber, Paints, Petro. Products, Consumer Elect., Electronic, Elec. Components, IT Implementation

Professional Associations: AICHE

MRI of Lynchburg
2511 Memorial Ave Ste 202
Memorial Professional Bldg
Lynchburg, VA 24501
(804) 528-1611
Fax: (804) 528-1617
Email: mrlynchburg@lynchburg.net

Description: The firm specializes primarily in the fields of finance and accounting and the technical aspects of manufacturing. The scope is nationwide.

Key Contact:
Mr. C. David Blue, Manager

Functions: Mfg.

Industries: Generalist, Mfg., Plastics, Rubber, Metal Products, Motor Vehicles, Test, Measure Equip., Misc. Mfg.

MRI of Manassas
7520 Diplomat Dr Ste B
Manassas, VA 20109
(703) 392-7580
Fax: (703) 392-7570
Email: jobs@mrimanassas.com
Web: www.mrimanassas.com

Description: Our firm has specialists in the following: IT with in insurance, financial, biotech, and other industries; telecommunications; insurance/financial; and aviation. We pride ourselves on getting to know our clients and candidates to make the right fit!

Key Contact - Specialty:
Mr. Anthony Kioussis, President - *Aviation*
Ms. Chris Sherwood, Recruiting Manager - *IT, aviation*

Salary minimum: $60,000

MRI of McLean
6849 Old Dominion Dr Ste 225
McLean, VA 22101
(703) 442-4842
Fax: (703) 356-8251
Email: mri@mrmclean.com
Web: www.mrmclean.com

Description: Our firm is a member of the nation's number one contingency search organization with access to its 1000 offices. We work with administrative, financial, information technology, market research, and sales people.

Key Contact - Specialty:
Mr. Howard H. Reitkopp, President - *Hospital information systems*
Ms. Ellen L. Reitkopp, Secretary/Treasurer - *Geographic information systems*
Mr. Albert Visco, Vice President - *Computer sales*

Salary minimum: $30,000

Functions: Generalist, General Mgmt., Sales & Mktg., Finance, IT, MIS Mgmt.

Industries: Generalist, Finance, Pharm Svcs., New Media, Software, Biotech

MRI of Oakton
2944 Hunter Mill Rd Ste 204
Oakton, VA 22124-1761
(703) 319-0206
Fax: (703) 319-0213
Email: manager@mroakton.com
Web: www.mroakton.com

Description: Senior executives (director and above), IS/IT sales, marketing IS/IT technical professionals

Key Contact:
Mr. Paul Rogers, President - *Senior executives, IS/IT, sales & marketing*
Ms. Suzanne Rogers, VP- General Counsel

Functions: Senior Mgmt., Sales & Mktg., IT

Industries: New Media, Software

MRI of Piedmont
Rte 7 Box 7327
Palmyra, VA 22963
(434) 591-1028
(800) 976-1972
Fax: (434) 591-1139
Email: rxsales@cstone.net
Web: www.pharmarecruiting.com

Description: We provide domestic and international recruitment services within the pharmaceutical and industrial industries in three key areas: permanent placement, flexible staffing and ancillary staffing services.

Key Contact - Specialty:
Ms. Rebecca Leinen, President - *Pharmaceutical, sales & marketing*

Functions: Generalist, Advertising, Mkt. Research, Mktg. Mgmt., Sales Mgmt., Customer Svc.

Industries: Generalist, Drugs Mfg., Medical Devices, Pharm Svcs., Healthcare

Professional Associations: SHRM

MRI of Roanoke
1950 Electric Rd Ste B
Roanoke, VA 24018
(540) 989-1676
Fax: (540) 989-7556
Email: info@mriroanoke.com

Description: We specialize in manufacturing, management, finance and accounting, paint and coatings and have 25 years of industry experience.

Key Contact - Specialty:
Mr. Paul S. Sharp, President - *Chemical industry, sales, technical, accounting, manufacturing*

Functions: Generalist, Senior Mgmt., Middle Mgmt., Mfg., Sales Mgmt., Finance, R&D

Industries: Generalist, Textiles, Apparel, Lumber, Furniture, Chemicals, Paints, Petro. Products, Retail

MRI of Loudoun County North
2 Pidgeon Hill Dr 430
Sterling, VA 20165
(703) 450-9001
Fax: (703) 450-9010
Email: bbutler@unidial.com
Web: www.mrihitechrecruiters.com

Description: We are a 21st century professional search and recruiting firm. We specialize in finding the top talent in the communications services and technology sector, for example: e-Business/e-Commerce, enterprise software, software solutions, the Internet, and telecommunications.

Key Contact - Specialty:
Mr. Bobby Butler, Owner - *E-business, e-commerce, enterprise software solutions, senior sales (internet, telecom), management (executive, sales)*

Salary minimum: $85,000

Functions: Senior Mgmt., Sales & Mktg., Sales Mgmt., IT, Minorities

Industries: Generalist, Venture Cap., E-commerce, IT Implementation, PSA/ASP, Communications, Telecoms, Telephony, Digital, Network Infrastructure, Database SW, ERP SW

MRI of Lakewood-Tacoma
9315 Gravelly Lake Dr SW Ste 306
Lakewood, WA 98499-1581
(253) 582-8488
Email: adminnw@careers-nw.com
Web: www.careers-nw.com

Description: We are a national executive search consulting firm focused in the following specialties: medical device and medical supply manufacturers and distribution, healthcare information systems, biotechnology, and telecommunications.

Key Contact:
Mr. Len Holmes, Managing Director - *Medical device, medical information systems*
Mr. Doug Roberts, General Manager - *Medical device, biotechnology*
Miss Laurie Cebula, Account Executive
Mr. John Wishart, Account Executive
Ms. Claudia O'Connor, Account executive

Salary minimum: $60,000

Functions: Generalist

Industries: Medical Devices, Pharm Svcs., Telecoms, Biotech

MRI of Lynnwood
19105 36th Ave W Ste 211
Alderwood Business Ctr
Lynnwood, WA 98036-5767
(425) 778-1212
Fax: (425) 778-7840
Email: budnaff@mri-lynnwood.com
Web: www.mri-lynnwood.com

Description: Contingency search firm specializing in the recruitment and placement of professionals in the environmental consulting, engineering, construction and chemical industries.

Key Contact - Specialty:
Mr. Robert Naff, Owner - *Environmental, civil engineering, construction*

Salary minimum: $30,000

Functions: Generalist, Directors, Senior Mgmt., Middle Mgmt., Health Admin., Engineering, Environmentalists

Industries: Generalist, Construction, Environmental Svcs., Haz. Waste

MRI of Mercer Island
9725 SE 36th St Ste 312
Globe Bldg
Mercer Island, WA 98040-3896
(206) 232-0204
Fax: (206) 232-6172
Email: jim@mrmi.com
Web: www.mrmi.com

Description: We specialize in connectors, footwear, apparel, actuary, nutrition, vitamin supplements, nutriceticals, Internet advertising, interactive advertising, and energy power generation.

Key Contact:
Mr. James J. Dykeman, Manager/Owner - *Nutrition, actuary*
Mr. Vince Holt

Salary minimum: $50,000

Functions: Generalist

Industries: Food, Bev., Tobacco, Textiles, Apparel, Chemicals, Drugs Mfg., Consumer Elect., Insurance, Biotech

MRI of Seattle
2510 Fairview Ave E
Seattle, WA 98120
(206) 328-0936
(800) 237-6562
Fax: (206) 328-3256
Email: jobs@mriseattle.com
Web: www.mriseattle.com

Description: We have 11 professionals who specialize in high-tech, electronics, software, health and managed care, engineering, food, beverage, industrial, consumer products, marketing, and retail.

Key Contact:
Mr. Dan Jilka, General Manager - *Engineering*
Ms. Ronda Clark, President - *Engineering*
Mr. Howard Hegwer, Managing Partner

Functions: Generalist, Senior Mgmt., Product Dev., Plant Mgmt., Health Admin., Mktg. Mgmt., R&D, Engineering

Industries: Generalist, Food, Bev., Tobacco, Medical Devices, Aerospace, Software, Biotech, Healthcare

Professional Associations: DPMA, IEEE, SAMPE, WSA

MRI of Spokane
316 W Boone Ave Ste 370
Spokane, WA 99201
(509) 324-3333
Fax: (509) 324-3334
Email: usajobs@mrspokane.com
Web: www.mrspokane.com

Description: We provide executive search specializing in the medical, call center, sales, information systems, food, e-Commerce, biotechnology, packaging, and telecommunications industries.

Key Contact - Specialty:
Mr. Dale Gilliam, President - *Executive, sales, large projects*
Mrs. Toni Gilliam, Vice President - *Call center, insurance, packaging*

Salary minimum: $40,000

Functions: Generalist, General Mgmt., Mfg., Healthcare, Sales & Mktg., Finance, IT, R&D

Industries: Generalist, Mfg., Finance, Services, Restaurants, Communications, Packaging, Insurance, Software, Biotech, Healthcare

MRI of Vancouver
703 Broadway St Ste 695
Vancouver, WA 98660
(360) 695-4688
Fax: (360) 695-4384
Email: jpoloni@mrvancouver.com
Web: www.mrvancouver.com

Description: Our firm specializes in the following industries: biotechnology, pharmaceutical, energy, fiber optics, and heavy equipment. We work a vertical market. We have the ability to mobilize project teams to fulfill our clients' needs for multiple positions within time sensitive constraints. We work both retainer and contingency assignments.

Key Contact - Specialty:
Mr. James A. Poloni, Principal - *Biotech, RX*
Ms. Jennifer Poloni, Principal - *Biotech, RX*

Salary minimum: $65,000

Functions: General Mgmt., Directors, Senior Mgmt., Middle Mgmt., Product Dev., Quality, Sales & Mktg., R&D

Industries: Energy, Utilities, Chemicals, Drugs Mfg., Medical Devices, Misc. Mfg., Pharm Svcs., IT Implementation, Fiber Optic, Biotech, Healthcare

Professional Associations: AESC

Networks: Global Search Partners

MRI of Kanawha Valley
3772 Teays Valley Rd Ste 3
Hurricane, WV 25526
(304) 757-4399
Fax: (304) 757-4398
Email: info@mrikv.com
Web: www.mrikv.com

Description: We specialize in the recruitment of engineering and sales professionals in the energy services, HVAC, and automated building controls industries. The positions that we place are in sales, engineering, and management.

Key Contact:
Mr. Harry Ray, Jr., Managing Partner - *Energy services, HVAC, building controls, mechanical contractors*
Ms. Stephanie Glandon, Recruiter - *Energy services, HVAC, building controls, mechanical contractors*
Miss Lisa Ronk, Executive Administrative Assistant

Functions: Generalist, Directors, Middle Mgmt., Mfg., Mkt. Research, Sales Mgmt., Engineering

Industries: Generalist, Energy, Utilities, Misc. Mfg.

MRI of Morgantown
1714 Mileground Ste 200
Morgantown, WV 26505
(304) 284-8500
Fax: (304) 284-8985
Email: mrivicki@westco.net
Web: www.mrmorgantown.com

Description: We currently specialize in recruiting for healthcare management positions.

Key Contact - Specialty:
Ms. Vickie Adams, Owner / Manager - *Healthcare management*
Ms. Betsey Schmidt, Executive Recruiter - *Healthcare management*

Functions: General Mgmt., Directors, Middle Mgmt., Admin. Svcs.

Industries: Healthcare

MRI of Appleton
(also known as CompuSearch)
911 N Lynndale Dr
Appleton, WI 54914
(920) 731-5221
Fax: (920) 731-9427
Email: mriappleton@mrappleton.com
Web: www.mrappleton.com

Description: Offer the full range of placement services. Senior executive through all levels of technical, administrative, sales search. Search specialties include engineering and construction, film and packaging, printing, pulp and paper, general manufacturing, plastics, MIS, finance and accounting, telecommunications, medical devices

Key Contact:
Mr. Russell V. Hanson, President

Salary minimum: $45,000

Functions: Generalist

Industries: Energy, Utilities, Construction, Food, Bev., Tobacco, Paper, Metal Products, Machine, Appliance, Electronic, Elec. Components, Accounting, IT Implementation, Telecoms

MRI of Madison
119 S Main St
Cottage Grove, WI 53527
(608) 839-9000
Fax: (608) 839-9744
Email: pac@mriofmadison.com
Web: www.mriofmadison.com

Description: Executive recruiters for engineering and manufacturing in the outdoor sports and recreational vehicle industry and sales in the telecommunications industry and sales and marketing for OEMs that market to the semiconductor industry in the US and worldwide.

Key Contact - Specialty:
Ms. Patricia A. Capanna, President - *Manufacturing, engineering, engineering management, outdoor sports and recreation industry, telecommunications sales*

Salary minimum: $40,000

Functions: Generalist, Middle Mgmt., Plant Mgmt., Quality, Materials Plng., Sales Mgmt., Engineering

Industries: Generalist, Mfg., Metal Products, Machine, Appliance, Motor Vehicles, Misc. Mfg., Electronic, Elec. Components, Transportation, Wholesale, Communications, Telecoms, Call Centers, Telephony, Digital, Wireless, Fiber Optic, Network Infrastructure, Aerospace, Industry Specific SW, Mfg. SW

Professional Associations: SHRM, WMC

Networks: Top Echelon Network

MRI of Milwaukee-West
13000 W Bluemound Rd Ste 310
Elm Grove, WI 53122
(262) 797-7500
(800) 463-0298
Fax: (262) 797-7515
Email: mrmilw@ameritech.net
Web: www.mrmilw.com

Description: Nationwide management recruiting affiliation, specializing in middle management and professional people. Most industries and services.

Key Contact - Specialty:
Mr. Frank Hocker, Vice President - *Pharmaceutical*
Mr. Peder Medtlie, President - *Information technology*

Salary minimum: $35,000

Functions: Generalist, Senior Mgmt., Middle Mgmt., Quality, IT, MIS Mgmt., Systems Implem., Engineering

Industries: Generalist, Drugs Mfg., Accounting, Software

MRI of Germantown

W175 N11163 Stonewood Dr Ste 105
Germantown, WI 53022
(262) 532-0400
Fax: (262) 532-0402
Email: mail@mricareerlink.com
Web: www.mricareerlink.com

Description: We specialize in employee benefits, including: persons who sell, administrate, convert, manage client relationships, etc. for defined benefit, defined contribution, health, and welfare plans.

Key Contact:
Mrs. Diana Popp, Managing Partner

MRI of Janesville

20 E Milwaukee St Ste 304
Janesville, WI 53545
(608) 752-2125
Fax: (608) 752-2903
Email: cvsmri@inwave.com

Description: We have strong recruiting experience in automotive and general manufacturing. We place in the areas of ISO/QS 9000 and executive management. Our value added services include outplacement, video conferencing, and contract executive placement. Established divisions in manufacturing management, food and sales and marketing, stampings, machining, rubber and plastics are strengths, as well as all assembly and fabrication companies.

Key Contact - Specialty:
Mr. Carroll V. Smith, General Manager - *General manufacturing*

Functions: Generalist

Industries: Food, Bev., Tobacco, Lumber, Furniture, Paper, Plastics, Rubber, Metal Products, Machine, Appliance, Motor Vehicles, Transportation, Services, Aerospace

MRI of Lake Wisconsin

609A N Main St
Lodi, WI 53555-1232
(608) 592-2151
Fax: (608) 592-2133
Email: mrlakewi@chorus.net

Description: We are an executive search firm, focusing on technical and professional permanent placements. We focus on the development of client companies in the manufacturing and industrial automation sectors, for whom we recruit and place highly qualified candidates to support their aggressive growth plans and significantly enhance the careers of those candidates.

Key Contact:
Mr. Merle Morack, Manager

Functions: Production, Automation, Finance, CFO's, Budgeting, MIS Mgmt., Systems Analysis, Systems Dev., Network Admin., Engineering

Industries: Mfg.

MRI of Milwaukee-North

1333 W Towne Square Rd
Mequon, WI 53092
(262) 241-1600
Fax: (262) 241-1640
Email: mrsc@mri-execsearch.com
Web: www.recruiters-jobs.com

Description: Recruitment of professionals, managers and executives. Office is in top 5% of MR/SC offices nationwide - President's Platinum Club Award. 84% of our business is repeat business. This office in business since 1976.

Key Contact - Specialty:
Mr. Timothy M. Lawler, III, President - *International, manufacturing*
Ms. Amy Palmer, Account Executive - *Information technology, e-business, biotechnology*
Mr. Jim Schwiner, Account Executive - *Manufacturing, metal products, machine, appliance, food, dairy industry*
Mr. David Lopez, Account Executive - *Manufacturing, plastics, rubber, motor vehicles*
Mr. Gavin McNeil, Account Executive - *Engineering, materials, purchasing, procurement, executive management*
Mr. Bill Stoner, Account Executive - *Engineering, HVAC engineering, operations*
Ms. Linda Graebner-Smith, Account Executive - *Project management, operations, project coordination, key account management, sales management*
Mr. John Loebl, Account Executive - *Chemicals, drug manufacturing, accounting, human resources*
Ms. Alice Bronstad, Account Executive - *IT, telecom, CRM, e-business, competitive intelligence, knowledge management*
Mr. Mark Jungers, Account Executive - *Attorneys (partners, associates, in-house counsel)*

Functions: Generalist

Industries: Generalist

Professional Associations: APICS, ASQ, CLM, SMEI

MRI of Stevens Point

1117 County Rd DB W
DuBay Professional Centre
Mosinee, WI 54455
(715) 341-4900
Fax: (715) 341-4992
Email: mri@coredcs.com

Description: Our firm concentrates on working with quality insurance organizations and accepts only those candidates who have a validated career record of progression and excel from those who are average. The criteria applied in selecting the companies we would like to develop as clients are two-fold. One, the company has made the same commitment to excellence in the staff they hire as our company has in the professionals we recruit; and two, that they possess a very positive reputation in the industry.

Key Contact - Specialty:
Mr. Bradford L. Barick, President - *Commercial insurance, safety*
Ms. Jennifer A. Swoboda, Account Executive - *Commercial insurance*

Salary minimum: $50,000

Functions: Generalist

Industries: Insurance

Professional Associations: AIHA, ASSE

MRI of Oconomowoc

110 S Main St
Oconomowoc, WI 53066
(262) 569-0800
Fax: (262) 569-0804
Email: kristie.c@mrijc.com
Web: www.mrijc.com

Description: We are an executive search firm specializing in the chemical, plastic and adhesive industries.

Key Contact - Specialty:
Mr. Dave Trepton, President - *Chemicals*

Functions: Generalist

Industries: Food, Bev., Tobacco, Chemicals, Soap, Perf., Cosmtcs., Plastics, Rubber, Paints, Petro. Products, HR Services

MRI of Racine

8411 Corporate Dr Ste 100
Racine, WI 53406
(262) 886-8000
Fax: (262) 886-7260
Email: info@mrracine.com
Web: www.mrracine.com

Description: Our company is part of the world's largest recruiting firm, with over 700 offices and 3000 recruiters in North America, as well as 50 associate offices and an additional 100 recruiters throughout the world. With nearly 100 years of combined recruiting experience, we know where talent is located, and possess a thorough understanding of the job market.

Key Contact:
Mr. John J. Henkel, Owner/Manager
Ms. Ellen L. Jante, CSAM, Manager

Salary minimum: $50,000

Functions: Mfg., Engineering

Industries: Generalist, Mfg., Plastics, Rubber

MRI of Wausau

3309 Terrace Ct
Wausau, WI 54401-3952
(715) 842-1750
Fax: (715) 842-1741
Email: mriwausau@mriwausau.com
Web: www.mriwausau.com

Description: We are the #1 search firm in the US. We have a nationwide database of employers who have positions available and recruit candidates for these positions. We have received the "Best of Class" designation based on customer satisfaction for our clients.

Key Contact - Specialty:
Ms. Laurie Prochnow, President/Account Executive - *MIS managers, programmers, project leaders, LAN managers*
Mr. Ross McCullion, Internet Researcher
Ms. Kay Babicky, Account Executive - *Programmers, analysts, operators*
Ms. Barbara Roland, Account Executive - *MIS managers, programmers, project leaders, LAN managers*
Mr. Mark Salzer, Account Executive - *MIS managers, programmers, project leaders, LAN managers*
Mr. Dave Dohe, Account Executive - *Banking*
Ms. Patsy Baltus, Project Coordinator - *MIS managers, programmers, project leaders, LAN managers*
Mr. Brian A. Wojchik, Account Executive - *MIS managers, programmers, project leaders, LAN managers*
Mr. Jim Finucan, Account Executive - *Banking*
Ms. Laura Jakubek, Project Coordinator - *Banking*
Ms. Shelley Osborne, Project Coordinator - *Banking*
Mr. Clint Ruesch, Account Executive - *Information technology*
Ms. Lorrie Stahl, Account Executive - *Banking*
Ms. Jennifer Zinser, Account Executive - *Banking*

Functions: Generalist, MIS Mgmt., Systems Analysis, Systems Dev., Systems Implem., Systems Support, DB Admin.

Industries: Generalist, Finance, Banking, New Media, Network Infrastructure, Software

Professional Associations: AITP, SHRM

MRI of Milwaukee-Mayfair

11611 W North Ave Ste 201
Wauwatosa, WI 53226-2129
(414) 607-3677
Fax: (414) 607-3660
Email: mri-milw@execpc.com
Web: www.mrindustrial.com

Description: Recruit nationwide for middle and top management professionals to grow construction, agricultural, outdoor power and motorized recreation equipment manufacturers.

Key Contact - Specialty:
Mr. Greg Lee, President - *Mobile equipment, motorized recreational vehicles*

Salary minimum: $50,000

Functions: Generalist

Industries: Agri., Forestry, Mining, Construction, Mfg., Motor Vehicles, Mgmt. Consulting, HR Services

MRI of Cheyenne
1008 E 21st St
Cheyenne, WY 82001
(307) 635-8731
Fax: (307) 635-6653
Web: www.mrwy@mrwy.net

Description: We provide contingency search with four people working coast to coast in manufacturing and healthcare.

Key Contact:
Mr. Verle Meister, President - *Manufacturing, software engineering*
Ms. Connie Meister

Functions: Generalist

Industries: Metal Products, Machine, Appliance, Motor Vehicles, Consumer Elect., Healthcare

MRI of Mexico
Av Domingo Diez 1589 Ste 121
Cuernavaca, MOR 62250
Mexico
52 73 114045
Fax: 52 73 114046
Email: mrimex@mrimex.com
Web: www.mrimex.com

Description: Executive staffing consultants specializing in international corporations with activity in Mexico and Latin America.

Key Contact - Specialty:
Mr. Carlos Kingwergs, Country Manager - *Generalist, latin american market*
Mr. Jens Hagedorn, Country Manager - *Generalist, latin american market*

Functions: General Mgmt., Senior Mgmt., Mfg., Sales & Mktg., Finance, CFO's, IT, Int'l.

Industries: Generalist

Management Recruiting Group
21318 Via Colombard
Sonoma, CA 95476
(707) 935-7777
Fax: (707) 939-1848
Email: john@hernandez-talentbank.com

Description: Contingency recruiting firm focusing on the Commercial Banking industry in Northern California.

Key Contact - Specialty:
Mr. John Hernandez, OWNER - *Banking*

Salary minimum: $40,000

Functions: Generalist

Industries: Finance, Banking, Invest. Banking, Brokers, Venture Cap., Misc. Financial

Management Resource Associates Inc
9044 Pine Springs Dr
Boca Raton, FL 33428
(561) 852-5650
Fax: (561) 852-5656
Email: mraboca@ix.netcom.com
Web: www.netcom.com/~mraboca/search.html

Description: A dynamic middle to upper-management, management search firm, specializing in the high-tech industry and multi-nationals, with access to local, national and international resources, with twenty-five years of corporate management and executive search experience.

Key Contact - Specialty:
Mr. Gerald Schneiderman, President - *Finance & accounting, MIS, international*
Ms. Sheila Schneiderman, Secretary/Treasurer - *Human resources*

Salary minimum: $70,000

Functions: HR Mgmt., Finance, MIS Mgmt., Int'l.

Industries: Generalist

Professional Associations: FEI, NAER

Management Resource Group Inc
77 Bleecker St Ste 124
New York, NY 10012
(212) 475-5327
Fax: (413) 487-0538

Description: All positions for sports entertainment and banking except system/DP. Human resources/personnel/training and development - all industries.

Key Contact - Specialty:
Mr. Matthew J. DeLuca, President - *Sports entertainment, television, live events, merchandise/licensing, publishing*

Salary minimum: $40,000

Functions: Generalist, Mktg. Mgmt., Systems Support, Graphic Artists

Industries: Generalist, HR Services, Hospitality, Publishing, New Media

Professional Associations: NYPMA, SHRM

Management Resources
(also known as James W Heineman & Assoc Inc)
131 W Church St Ste 100
Weatherford, TX 76086
(817) 599-3249
Fax: (817) 599-3260
Email: jim@managementresources.com
Web: www.managementresources.com

Description: We were founded on the premise that lasting business relationships are built through mutual trust and respect. We are committed to a philosophy of maintaining a true partnership with our clients.

Key Contact - Specialty:
Mr. James W. Heineman, President - *Managed care*

Salary minimum: $75,000

Functions: Senior Mgmt., Health Admin.

Industries: Healthcare

Management Search Associates
PO Box 460086
Aurora, CO 80046-0086
(303) 699-7501
Fax: (303) 693-9467
Email: mgtsearcha@aol.com

Description: We are an executive search based in the Denver area serving national and international clients. Our core business is for technical, medical equipment, power generation equipment and manufacturing firms. We place presidents, VP in sales and quality, directors of engineering and finance, controllers, and cost accounting managers.

Key Contact:
Mr. Richard Crow, President
Mrs. Veronika F. Crow, Vice President

Networks: Top Echelon Network

Management Search
750 Lake Cook Rd
Buffalo Grove, IL 60089
(847) 537-5660
Fax: (847) 537-1007
Email: frankwol@core.com

Description: National firm specializing in all areas of accounting, finance and financial systems development and implementation. Scope includes audit, cost, tax, reporting and analysis, treasury, general, etc. Staff level to upper-management.

Key Contact - Specialty:
Mr. Frank Wolowicz, President - *Accounting & finance*

Salary minimum: $50,000

Functions: Finance

Industries: Generalist

Networks: Top Echelon Network

Management Search Associates Inc
6303 Deerings Hollow
Norcross, GA 30092
(770) 300-0775
Fax: (770) 300-9965

Description: Total of 10 years of production in healthcare field. Specializing in hospital administrative management, nursing management, home health nurses, clinical nurse specialists and nurse practitioners.

Key Contact - Specialty:
Ms. Jean W. Hyman, President - *RN's, management level nurses, financial, administrative management, hospitals*

Salary minimum: $35,000

Functions: Directors, Middle Mgmt., Nurses, Health Admin.

Industries: Healthcare

Management Search Inc
117 S Cook St Ste 201
Barrington, IL 60010
(847) 304-1775
Fax: (847) 304-8948
Email: steflink@ix.netcom.com

Description: Fast, effective recruitment services. Strategic networking to provide Internet and communications companies with targeted executives, capital, strategic-alliance and merger/acquisition opportunities.

Key Contact - Specialty:
Mr. Stefan Levy, President - *Insurance, venture capital, internet*

Salary minimum: $70,000

Functions: M&A, IT

Industries: Venture Cap., Insurance

Professional Associations: ACG

Management Search Inc
3013 NW 59th St Ste A-1
Oklahoma City, OK 73112
(405) 842-3173
Fax: (405) 842-8360
Email: dorwig@juno.com
Web: www.mgmtsearch.com

Description: Agriculture research and technical service positions, both agronomic and livestock. Agriculture sales and sales management positions.

Key Contact - Specialty:
Mr. David L. Orwig, President - *Agriculture*

Salary minimum: $25,000

Functions: Generalist, Middle Mgmt., Mkt. Research, Sales Mgmt., R&D

Industries: Generalist, Agri., Forestry, Mining, Biotech

Management Services Group Inc
PO Box 974
Bayport, NY 11705
(631) 738-9710
Email: info@taxhunt.com
Web: www.taxhunt.com

Description: Nationwide retained and contingency recruitment in taxation.

Key Contact - Specialty:
Mr. Michael Gordon, President - *Taxation*

Salary minimum: $50,000

Functions: Finance

Industries: Generalist

Management Solutions Inc
970 W 190th St Ste 600
Torrance, CA 90502-1000
(310) 225-2900
Fax: (310) 225-2901
Web: www.mgmtsolutions.com

Description: We recommend professionals who thrive on challenge and keep their expertise current. These are achievers, dedicated to the industry and excellence. We represent the cream of the crop.

Key Contact:
Mr. Richard Williams, President

Salary minimum: $30,000

Functions: Generalist, CFO's, Cash Mgmt., MIS Mgmt., Systems Analysis, Systems Dev., Systems Implem., Systems Support

Industries: Generalist, Invest. Banking, Brokers, Venture Cap., Misc. Financial, Software

Professional Associations: NAWBO, SHRM, WIM

Mancini Technical Recruiting
PO Box 4829
Alexandria, VA 22303
(703) 768-3880
Fax: (703) 765-8111
Email: debbie@m-t-r.com
Web: www.m-t-r.com

Description: We are a technical recruiting firm that assists companies nationwide in their staffing efforts. Our recent searches have included web developer, database administrator, network engineer, Internet project manager, software engineer, web architect, technical manager, versant developer, etc.

Key Contact - Specialty:
Ms. Deborah Mancini, Owner - *High technology, software*

Salary minimum: $35,000

Functions: IT, MIS Mgmt., Systems Dev., Systems Support, Network Admin., DB Admin.

Industries: Generalist, Services, HR Services, Publishing, New Media, Telecoms, Insurance, Software, Non-classifiable

Professional Associations: AWC, DCWW, WIT

Mangieri/Solutions LLC
1 Riverside Rd
Sandy Hook, CT 06482
(203) 270-4800
Fax: (203) 270-4815
Email: cmangieri@mangierisolutions.com
Web: www.mangierisolutions.com

Description: We produce top caliber people that ideally match your job descriptions and your company culture. Our specialty is the direct

marketing industry, including call center operations, along with finance and accounting.

Key Contact - Specialty:
Mr. Chris Mangieri - *Direct marketing*

Salary minimum: $50,000

Functions: Generalist, Advertising, Mkt. Research, Mktg. Mgmt., Direct Mktg., Customer Svc., Training, MIS Mgmt.

Industries: Generalist, Software, Healthcare

Mankuta Gallagher & Associates Inc
8333 W McNab Rd Ste 231
Ft. Lauderdale, FL 33321
(954) 720-9645
Fax: (954) 720-5813
Email: emankuta@mankutagallagher.com
Web: www.mankutagallagher.com

Description: We are a client driven firm specializing in biotechnology, engineering, hospitality, restaurants, and law. We have over 30 years of combined experience and strive to do excellent work on a consistent basis. We offer a total quality guarantee.

Key Contact - Specialty:
Dr. Michael Gallagher, Managing Partner - *Pharmaceutical, biotechnology, information systems*
Mr. Eric Mankuta, Managing Partner - *Pharmaceutical, biotechnology*

Salary minimum: $60,000

Functions: General Mgmt., Healthcare, IT, R&D, Engineering

Industries: Mfg., Drugs Mfg., Retail, Hospitality, Biotech, Healthcare

Networks: National Personnel Assoc (NPA)

Manning Associates
99 High St Ste 23
Boston, MA 02110
(617) 523-8866
Fax: (617) 988-0818
Web: www.manningassociates.com

Description: We are a recruiting practice specializing in accounting, finance, systems, and consulting. We work with a large number of multi-national, middle-market, and e-Commerce/Internet start-ups. We are recruiting qualified candidates from entry level accountant to chief financial officer.

Key Contact - Specialty:
Mr. Jack Manning, President - *Accounting, finance, systems, consulting*
Mr. Mike Manning, Manager - *Healthcare, high tech*
Mr. Brian O'Leary, Manager - *Internet, e-commerce*
Ms. Helane Childs, Manager - *Financial services, manufacturing*
Mr. Robert Barash, Manager - *Public accounting, systems, retail*

Salary minimum: $30,000

Functions: Finance, CFO's, Budgeting, Cash Mgmt., Credit, Taxes, M&A, Risk Mgmt., IT

Industries: Generalist

Professional Associations: AICPA, MSCPA, NAPS

Branches:
4 Faneuil Hall Marketplace Fl 4
S Market
Boston, MA 02109
(617) 227-5115
Email: mmanning@manningassociates.com
Key Contact - Specialty:
Mr. Mike Manning, Manager - *Healthcare, high tech*

Manning Lloyd Associates Ltd
53 N Park Ave Ste 50
Rockville Centre, NY 11570
(516) 678-9700
Fax: (516) 678-9763

Description: Boutique specializing in search for compensation and benefits professionals for domestic and international positions; both corporate and consulting.

Key Contact - Specialty:
Ms. Dianne Manning, President - *Compensation & benefit professionals*

Salary minimum: $50,000

Functions: Benefits

Industries: HR Services

Professional Associations: SHRM, WAW, WEB

Manufacturing Resource Group Ltd
1204 Main St Ste 209
Branford, CT 06405
(203) 483-4672
Fax: (203) 481-7634
Email: mfgresource@cs.com

Description: National firm whose partners are former COO/CEOs for technology driven manufacturing and research organizations. Firm specializes in placement of high skilled technical, managerial, engineering and research professionals in manufacturing, medical research and technical environment.

Key Contact - Specialty:
Mr. Richard A. Gallentine, President - *Manufacturing technologies, human resources, manufacturing*
Ms. Martha Roush, Vice President - *Medical*

Salary minimum: $75,000

Functions: Senior Mgmt.

Industries: Mfg., Medical Devices, Plastics, Rubber, Metal Products, Pharm Svcs., Mgmt. Consulting

Professional Associations: WAI

Manulogic Inc
2091 Kinridge Trl
Marietta, GA 30062
(770) 509-7494
(800) 993-8973
Fax: (770) 565-9613
Email: manulogic@aol.com
Web: www.manulogic.com

Description: We search nationwide for high tech candidates that specialize in sales, pre-sales, post-sales, product management, solution selling and marketing for software companies. We specialize in the following: process and discrete MRP, SCM, APS, B2B, ERP, WMS, CRM, EDI, business intelligence, e-Commerce, data warehousing, HR/payroll, EPM, financials, transportation, logistics, energy, etc.

Key Contact - Specialty:
Ms. Marilyn Campbell, President - *Executive recruiter*

Salary minimum: $80,000

The Marathon Group
4456 Karls Gate Dr
Marietta, GA 30068
(770) 971-7198
Fax: (770) 971-9186
Email: dchamp50@aol.com

Description: We provide sales and engineering search in the industries of electrical/electronics, process control/automation, packaging, graphics, and chemicals.

Key Contact - Specialty:
Mr. Dale Champion, VP-Packaging Division - *Sales & marketing, process controls & packaging*

Salary minimum: $40,000

Functions: General Mgmt., Automation, Packaging, Sales & Mktg., Sales Mgmt., Engineering

Industries: Generalist, Energy, Utilities, Mfg., Paper, Printing, Chemicals, Test, Measure Equip., Electronic, Elec. Components, Packaging, Insurance

Professional Associations: TAPPI

Branches:
2320 S 3rd St Ste 8
Jacksonville Beach, FL 32250
(904) 270-2121
Fax: (904) 270-2120
Email: jobs@pslabels.com
Web: www.pslabels.com
Key Contact - Specialty:
Mr. Michael Moore, Vice President - *Sales & marketing, labels & graphics*

MARBL Consultants Inc
350 Bishop's Way Ste 200
Brookfield, WI 53005
(262) 796-6960
Fax: (262) 796-6970
Email: marblcons@aero.net

Description: Client-driven organization committed to successfully completing a project in a timely manner. We are dedicated to excellence in five major areas: manufacturing, engineering, materials/purchasing/logistics, information technology/MIS and human resources.

Key Contact - Specialty:
Mr. Allan G. Adzima, President/Consultant - *Engineering, manufacturing, materials, purchasing, logistics*
Mr. Dennis J. Pradarelli, Admin/IT Sr. Recruiting Manager - *Information technology, MIS, finance, accounting, administrative management*
Ms. Diane Pruitt, Recruiter/Customer Service Manager - *Generalist*

Salary minimum: $45,000

Functions: General Mgmt., Mfg., Materials, HR Mgmt., Finance, IT, R&D, Engineering, Minorities, Int'l.

Industries: Generalist, Mfg., Plastics, Rubber, Machine, Appliance, Motor Vehicles, Consumer Elect., Transportation, Retail, Finance, Accounting, Mgmt. Consulting, HR Services, Aerospace, Packaging, Software

Professional Associations: ASQ, MAPM, NAPM, NAPS, SHRM, WAPS

Networks: National Personnel Assoc (NPA)

Branches:
45 Kelleys Trail Ste 100
E Lake Woodlands
Oldsmar, FL 34677-1919
(727) 789-5627
Fax: (727) 772-1222
Email: aamarbl@aol.com
Key Contact:
Mr. Allan Adzima, President/Consultant

Marc-Allen Associates Inc
7770 W Oakland Park Blvd Ste 280
Ft. Lauderdale, FL 33351
(954) 572-3771
Fax: (954) 748-6583
Email: mike@marc-allen.com
Web: www.marc-allen.com

Description: We are a nationwide executive search firm specializing in the placement of management talent in all divisions of the following industries: retail, technology, consumer products,

manufacturing, and wholesale. We have the talent and experience to provide trusted creative solutions to the ongoing challenges of management recruitment and placement.

Key Contact - Specialty:
Mr. Mike Powell, President/CEO - *Retail, general management, accounting, finance, logistics*

Salary minimum: $40,000

Functions: Generalist, General Mgmt., Senior Mgmt., Middle Mgmt., Advertising, HR Mgmt., Finance

Industries: Mfg., Consumer Elect., Wholesale, Retail, Finance

Professional Associations: ABWA, NAPS, NRF, SHRM

Branches:
1459 W Fullerton
Chicago, IL 60614
(773) 525-6926
Fax: (773) 525-6937
Email: sarah@marc-allen.com
Key Contact - Specialty:
Ms. Sarah Hatfield, Managing Director - *Retail*

8314 Pineville - Matthews Rd Ste 291
Charlotte, NC 28226
(866) 723-3416
Fax: (704) 969-2727
Email: dean@marc-allen.com
Key Contact - Specialty:
Mr. Dean Emmans, Branch President - *Retail, wholesale, manufacturing, consumer products*

Marconi Search Consultants Inc
3168 Masters Dr
Clearwater, FL 34615.
(727) 772-0555
Fax: (727) 723-3990
Email: mmarc10252@aol.com

Description: Executive recruiting to the insurance industry.

Key Contact - Specialty:
Mr. Mark Marconi - *Insurance, PEO*

Salary minimum: $50,000

Functions: General Mgmt., Sales & Mktg., Benefits, Finance, CFO's, M&A, Risk Mgmt., MIS Mgmt.

Industries: Insurance

Branches:
PO Box 6016
Atlanta, GA 31107-0016
(404) 584-1333
Email: marconisearch@aol.com
Key Contact - Specialty:
Ms. Libby Marconi - *Advertising*

Marcus & Associates
358 Saw Mill River Rd
Millwood Business Ctr
Millwood, NY 10546
(914) 941-7100
Fax: (914) 941-8629
Email: info@marcusassoc.com
Web: www.marcusassoc.com

Description: We are a general firm with special expertise in searches for research and development, clinical and regulatory affairs, marketing and corporate staff personnel in the pharmaceutical, biotechnology, and consumer healthcare industries.

Key Contact - Specialty:
Mr. Alvin B. Marcus, President - *Senior management*
Ms. Catherine McKenna, VP/ General Manager - *Human resources, finance, legal*
Ms. Denise Clements, VP Search Operations - *Clinical research, medical affairs*

Mr. Brian Harrington, Search Consultant - *Research & development*
Mr. Peter Tomassi, Search Consultant - *Biostatistics, clinical data management*
Mr. Greg Flanagan, Search Consultant - *Pharmaceutical marketing, managed care*
Ms. Debbie Yablonsky, Search Consultant - *Regulatory affairs, quality assurance*
Mr. T Gordon, Senior Consultant - *Consumer marketing, business development*

Salary minimum: $60,000

Functions: Generalist

Industries: Drugs Mfg., Medical Devices, Consumer Elect., Pharm Svcs., Biotech, Healthcare

Professional Associations: NAER

Marentz & Company
PO Box 926101
Houston, TX 77292
(713) 290-9172
Fax: (713) 856-9188
Email: frankmar@marentzco.com
Web: www.marentzco.com

Description: The ability to generate viable candidates from selected databases, industry networks and referrals allow our search consultants to provide the type of service demanded by the client. The firm offers flexible financial options for our search services and can be tailored to the needs of the client.

Key Contact - Specialty:
Mr. Frank Marentez, Vice President/GM - *Accounting, financial, real estate, sales, energy*
Mr. Richard Ramirez, Vice President - *Accounting, financial, real estate, manufacturing*
Ms. Lily Campos, Associate - *Healthcare*
Mr. Jim Rand, Vice President - *Engineering, sales, industrial sales, process, energy*

Salary minimum: $60,000

Functions: Generalist, Sales Mgmt., CFO's, Budgeting, Cash Mgmt., Taxes, Network Admin., Engineering

Industries: Generalist, Energy, Utilities, Finance, Accounting, Hospitality, Insurance, Real Estate, Healthcare

Maresca & Associates
PO Box 235498
Honolulu, HI 96823
(808) 545-7991
Email: smaresca@att.net

Description: Our firm has served the Pacific Basin with a focus on the Hawaiian Islands by recruiting managers, executives, administrators, financial controllers, and operational expertise for a variety of industries. We now have expanded to the mainland, US, and will be serving clients on both the east and west coast.

Key Contact - Specialty:
Ms. Shannon Maresca, Owner/Manager - *Generalist*

Salary minimum: $50,000

Functions: Generalist

Industries: Generalist

Professional Associations: HSCP, SHRM

Margolin Consultants Inc
350 5th Ave Ste 2819
Empire State Bldg
New York, NY 10118
(212) 268-1940
Fax: (212) 268-2695

Description: Executive search, product development, market research, mergers and acquisitions, venture capital and joint venture.

Key Contact - Specialty:
Mr. Efraim Margolin, President - *Management*

Salary minimum: $50,000

Functions: Generalist, Middle Mgmt., Product Dev., Production, Automation, Plant Mgmt., Sales Mgmt., Engineering

Industries: Generalist, Lumber, Furniture, Plastics, Rubber, Metal Products, Machine, Appliance, Telecoms, Packaging

---

Mark III Personnel Inc
5140 Morrowick Rd
Charlotte, NC 28226
(704) 542-0553
Email: lamarkiii@aol.com

Description: All professional and managerial positions. Focus areas are engineers, chemists for process industries, manufacturing, materials/logistics management, environmental. Contingency and retained; minimum salary $40K.

Key Contact - Specialty:
Mr. Lindsay Allen, Jr. - *Engineering (all disciplines), research & development, chemists, technical specialties, environmental*

Salary minimum: $40,000

Functions: Mfg., Materials, Healthcare, R&D, Engineering, Environmentalists

Industries: Textiles, Apparel, Chemicals, Medical Devices, Pharm Svcs., Environmental Svcs.

Professional Associations: AICHE, NCASP

Markent Personnel Inc
121 E Conant St
PO Box 423
Portage, WI 53901
(608) 742-7300
Fax: (608) 742-7737
Email: contactus@markentpersonnel.com
Web: www.markentpersonnel.com

Description: One hundred mailings a week to alumni of Wisconsin engineering schools. Permanent recruiting of engineering and manufacturing/process management, food and medical equipment specialists.

Key Contact - Specialty:
Mr. Thomas L. Udulutch, President - *Engineering*
Mr. Mark Udulutch, JD, Vice President - *Engineering*

Salary minimum: $40,000

Functions: Generalist

Industries: Food, Bev., Tobacco, Medical Devices, Metal Products, Machine, Appliance, Motor Vehicles, Misc. Mfg., Biotech

Professional Associations: NAPS

Networks: Top Echelon Network

Branches:
W 6407 20th St
Necedah, WI 54646
(608) 565-2101
Fax: (608) 565-6920
Key Contact - Specialty:
Mr. Dave Arnold - *Engineering*

PO Box 242
Oxford, WI 53952
(608) 586-6147
Fax: (608) 586-5216
Email: wally@markentpersonnel.com
Key Contact:
Mr. Wally Huntley

Market Niche Consulting
10224 E Minnesota Ave
Sun Lakes, AZ 85248
(480) 802-9529
Email: sampson@topechelon.com

Description: IT specialists with emphasis on bankcard/credit card field. Software development, credit scoring, artificial intelligence, higher order neuro networks, systems within risk management and marketing research technologies.

Key Contact - Specialty:
Mr. Ron Sampson, Principal - *Information systems technology, management*

Salary minimum: $50,000

Functions: IT, MIS Mgmt., Systems Analysis, Systems Dev., Systems Implem., Systems Support, Network Admin., DB Admin., R&D

Industries: Generalist, Retail, Finance, Banking, Misc. Financial, Software, Healthcare

Professional Associations: ATRA

Networks: Top Echelon Network

Marketing & Sales Resources Inc
14000 Military Trl
Delray Beach, FL 33484
(561) 637-7711
Fax: (561) 637-7555
Email: msresources@mindspring.com

Description: Uniquely specialized in the recruitment of mid- and senior-level marketing and sales management executives within the consumer, industrial, chemicals, plastics and service industries.

Key Contact - Specialty:
Mr. Alan H. Gross, Vice President - *Marketing & sales management*
Mr. Robert C. Kleinman, Vice President - *Marketing & sales management*

Salary minimum: $60,000

Functions: Sales & Mktg., Mkt. Research, Mktg. Mgmt., Sales Mgmt.

Industries: Generalist, Mfg., Chemicals, Plastics, Rubber, Metal Products, Machine, Appliance, Consumer Elect., Test, Measure Equip.

Marketing Consultants
3015 N Shepard Ave
Milwaukee, WI 53211-3437
(414) 962-6611
Fax: (414) 962-6623
Email: carole@marketingrecruiters.com
Web: www.marketingrecruiters.com

Description: Specializing in the search and placement of candidates in the fields of consumer marketing management, advertising, sales promotion and market research.

Key Contact - Specialty:
Ms. Carole E. Smolizer, President - *Marketing*

Salary minimum: $50,000

Functions: Generalist, Advertising, Mkt. Research, Mktg. Mgmt., Minorities, Int'l.

Industries: Generalist, Food, Bev., Tobacco, Paper, Soap, Perf., Cosmtcs.

Professional Associations: WAPS, WWE

Marketing Recruiters Inc
PO Box 4098
Asheboro, NC 27204
(336) 626-4009
Fax: (336) 626-5116

Description: We specialize in finding and placing sales and marketing professionals. Our area of expertise lies within the medical industry.

Key Contact - Specialty:
Mr. Rass Bagley, President - *Medical sales*

Salary minimum: $50,000

Functions: Sales Mgmt.

Industries: Medical Devices

Marketing Resources
18 North Rd
PO Box 463
Chelmsford, MA 01824
(978) 256-8001
Fax: (978) 250-4336
Email: resomark@medjobs.com
Web: www.medjobs.com

Description: Executive search and placement services for marketing managers or specialists with focus on medical technologies. Segments are medical-surgical, clinical chemistry, patient monitoring, cardiovascular, medical computer and medical device companies.

Key Contact - Specialty:
Mr. Joseph D. Sheedy, President - *Medical products, medical services*

Salary minimum: $90,000

Functions: Middle Mgmt., Sales & Mktg.

Industries: Drugs Mfg., Medical Devices, Computer Equip., Misc. Mfg., Electronic, Elec. Components, Software, Industry Specific SW, Mfg. SW, Marketing SW, Networking, Comm. SW, Biotech, Healthcare

---

Marketing/Public Relations Research Recruiting
8 Norwalk Ave
Westport, CT 06880
(203) 226-6738
Email: benluden@earthlink.net

Description: Succeeding over 10 years' diversified marketing, public relations, and research work at General Electric, A.C. Nielsen, Opinion Research and Yankelovich, I offer clients an active, successful, competitively priced recruiting service in marketing and P.R. research.

Key Contact - Specialty:
Mr. Ben V. Luden, Owner/Principal - *Marketing, public relations research*

Salary minimum: $50,000

Functions: Directors, Senior Mgmt., Middle Mgmt., Admin. Svcs., Mfg., Plant Mgmt., Mkt. Research, Mktg. Mgmt., Sales Mgmt., PR

Industries: Generalist

MarketPro Inc
235 Peachtree St Ste 1750
Atlanta, GA 30303
(404) 222-9992
(866) 284-9992
Fax: (404) 222-9099
Email: mktpro@marketproinc.com
Web: www.marketproinc.com

Description: Our firm specializes in placing mid to senior level marketing and sales executives in permanent and contract opportunities. Our unique model allows us to provide the best talent in the shortest possible period of time, nationally.

Key Contact:
Ms. Melissa Van Rossum, CEO - *Marketing*
Mr. Bob Van Rossum, President

Salary minimum: $60,000

Functions: Generalist, Directors, Middle Mgmt., Advertising, Mkt. Research, Mktg. Mgmt., Sales Mgmt., Direct Mktg., PR, Minorities

Industries: Generalist, Marketing SW

Professional Associations: AMA, TAG

MarketWise Inc
60 E Chestnut St Ste 388
Chicago, IL 60611
(312) 786-1700
Email: jprice@mwpro.com

Description: We specialize in the financial industry and information technology placement in Chicago.

Key Contact:
Mr. John Price, President

Functions: IT

Industries: Finance

Professional Associations: IAPS

Marksmen Consultants
805 W Shepherds Ln
Santa Claus, IN 47579
(812) 544-5200
(812) 544-5201
Fax: (812) 544-5202
Email: dvsearch@psci.net

Description: We are on target with your staffing needs. This office has over 25 years of experience servicing the aluminum extrusion industry providing managers, supervisors, engineers, and technical specialists throughout North America.

Key Contact - Specialty:
Mr. Don Vogel, President - *Aluminum*

Salary minimum: $30,000

Functions: Generalist, Mfg., Materials, Sales & Mktg., HR Mgmt., Engineering

Industries: Generalist, Metal Products

Networks: Top Echelon Network

Marley Group Ltd
275 Madison Ave Fl 36
New York, NY 10016
(212) 883-6850
Email: general@marleygroup.com
Web: www.marleylaw.com

Description: Attorney placement: associates, partners, in-house counsel, groups & mergers, retainer and contingency.

Key Contact:
Ms. Hazel S. Kandall, Chairwoman - *Generalist*
Mr. John H. Parker, President - *Generalist*
Mr. Roy Kessler, Vice President - *Intellectual property*
Mr. Richard Kirschner, Senior Vice President
Ms. Esther Koslow, Executive Director

Salary minimum: $80,000

Functions: Generalist, Attorneys

Industries: Generalist

Marquis Management
35 Corporate Dr Ste 400
Burlington, MA 01803
(781) 685-4940
Email: info@marquismanagement.com
Web: www.marquismanagement.com

Description: We are the preeminent executive search firm serving the software/technology industry. We provide retained and contingency search services for sales, marketing, and general management positions within the software and technology sectors.

Key Contact - Specialty:
Mr. Tom Robinson, Managing Partner - *Software & technology*

Salary minimum: $80,000

Functions: Generalist

Industries: Mgmt. Consulting, IT Implementation, Software, Database SW, ERP SW, Marketing SW, Networking, Comm. SW, System SW, Training SW

The Marr Roy Group
8 Stavebank Rd N Ste 402
Mississauga, ON L5G 2T4
Canada
(905) 271-2710
(866) 222-2710
Fax: (905) 271-2783
Email: info@webmrg.com
Web: www.webmrg.com

Description: We are executive recruiters specializing in information technology, e-Commerce, and m-Commerce.

Key Contact:
Ms. Laurie Marr
Mr. Steve Roy

Salary minimum: $50,000

Functions: Generalist

Industries: Banking, Venture Cap., Mgmt. Consulting, E-commerce, New Media, Telecoms, Digital, Wireless, Network Infrastructure, Networking, Comm. SW

Professional Associations: ACSESS

Marsar & Company Inc
1831 N Belcher Rd Unit G-1
Clearwater, FL 33765-1417
(727) 726-3766
Fax: (727) 726-3767
Email: marsar@marsearch.com
Web: www.marsearch.com

Description: Ten plus years' recruiting experience in West Central Florida covering all of Florida. Mature, high integrity, honest service to clients and candidates (=future clients), efficient, serious and competent.

Key Contact - Specialty:
Mr. Kevin P. Marsar, CEO/President - *Accounting, finance, treasury, human resources, information technology*

Salary minimum: $60,000

Functions: HR Mgmt., Finance, IT

Industries: Generalist

Professional Associations: FAPS, NAPS

Karen Marshall Associates
7896 Ashley View Dr
Cincinnati, OH 45227
(513) 561-4102

Description: Recruiter, search and placement of MIS professionals and executives since 1983.

Key Contact:
Ms. Karen Marshall, President - *MIS*
Mr. Dennis Marshall, Vice President

Salary minimum: $30,000

Functions: Distribution, IT, MIS Mgmt., Systems Analysis, Systems Dev., Systems Implem., Systems Support, Network Admin., DB Admin.

Industries: Generalist, Transportation

Professional Associations: DPMA

Marshall Career Service Inc
6500 W Fwy Ste 200
Ft. Worth, TX 76116
(817) 737-2645
Email: hmorrison@marshallcareerservice.com
Web: www.marshallcareerservice.com

Description: We provide mid-management to executive-level search and placements in

accounting, financial, engineering, and operational positions. Our clients are primarily manufacturing and service related companies. We exclusively serve Dallas/Ft Worth Metroplex.

Key Contact:
Mr. Jim Ashworth, CPC, Vice President - *Upper-level management, accounting/finance*
Mr. Rick Marshall, President

Salary minimum: $45,000

Functions: Senior Mgmt., Middle Mgmt., Production, Plant Mgmt., Materials, Purchasing, Finance, CFO's, Budgeting, Engineering

Industries: Generalist

Professional Associations: APICS, IMA, NAPS, TAPC

Marshall Resource Group
1537 4th St Ste 169
San Rafael, CA 94901
(415) 456-4882
(415) 258-0721
Fax: (415) 456-0558
Email: marshallresourcegroup@home.com

Description: Our firm is a global executive recruiting firm based in the San Francisco Bay Area that specializes in the telecommunications industry. Our search services are focused on sales and marketing, operations, and engineering from middle management to executive level personnel.

Key Contact - Specialty:
Mr. Toni Marshall, Principal
Ms. Virginia Lotridge, Partner - *Telecommunications sales*

Salary minimum: $50,000

Networks: Top Echelon Network

Marshall-Alan Associates Inc
5 W 37th St Fl 8
New York, NY 10018
(212) 382-2440
Fax: (212) 764-5411
Email: alanm@marshallalan.com

Description: Executive search organization specializing in the hospitality industry.

Key Contact - Specialty:
Mr. Alan Massarsky, President - *Hospitality*
Ms. Joan Steinberg, Vice President - *Hospitality*

Salary minimum: $50,000

Functions: Generalist, Senior Mgmt., Middle Mgmt., Purchasing, Sales Mgmt., Training, CFO's, MIS Mgmt.

Industries: Hospitality, Hotels, Resorts, Clubs, Restaurants

Professional Associations: HS&MA

Marsteller Wilcox Associates
799 Roosevelt Rd Bldg 3 Ste 108
Glen Ellyn, IL 60137
(630) 790-4300
(630) 790-4394
Fax: (630) 790-4495
Email: mark@mwaltd.com
Web: www.mwaltd.com

Description: We offer non-traditional search programs to meet clients' changing needs. Call to discuss performance retained search, target research project or contingency programs. We are dedicated to quality and excellence.

Key Contact - Specialty:
Mr. Mark Wilcox, Partner - *Engineering, operations management*
Ms. Linda Marsteller, Partner - *Paper & pulp*
Ms. Carol Ranberg - *Printing, inks*

Ms. Surette Joseph - *Engineering, operations management*

Mr. John Lange - *Information systems*

Mr. Chris Augustine - *Information systems, operations*

Salary minimum: $50,000

Functions: Generalist, General Mgmt., Mfg., Materials, Sales & Mktg., Finance, R&D, Engineering

Industries: Generalist, Paper, Printing, Chemicals, Paints, Petro. Products, Motor Vehicles, HR Services, Software

Professional Associations: TAPPI

Networks: Top Echelon Network

Lloyd Martin & Associates

15 Lake Side Dr Ste A
Lake St. Louis, MO 63367
(636) 561-6750
Fax: (888) 438-2114
Email: fred@careersincomputers.com
Web: www.careersincomputers.com

Description: We are an information systems search firm specializing in client server and web based development, network design/infrastructure, database, and technical support positions within the Saint Louis marketplace.

Key Contact:
Mr. Fred Lloyd, Owner

Functions: IT

Industries: Generalist

Professional Associations: MAPS

Networks: Top Echelon Network

The Martin Group

8866 Gulf Fwy Ste 215
Houston, TX 77017
(713) 910-0900
Fax: (713) 947-1031
Email: asearch@martingroupusa.com
Web: www.martingroupusa.com

Description: We specialize in accounting/finance and information technology staffing. We serve clients ranging from entrepreneurial, venture capital financed start-ups to Fortune 500 companies. The principals of the firm personally conduct all search assignments.

Key Contact - Specialty:
Mr. Bruce Martin, CPA, President - *Accounting/finance*
Mr. John Hall, Executive Recruiter - *Information technology*
Ms. Susy Pardillo, CPA, Executive Recruiter - *Accounting/finance*

Salary minimum: $50,000

Functions: Finance, IT

Industries: Generalist

Mitchell Martin Inc

80 Wall St Ste 1215
New York, NY 10005
(212) 943-1404
Fax: (212) 328-0964
Email: rd@mitchellmartin.com
Web: www.itmmi.com

Description: We are a full-service information technology organization servicing the contract and permanent staffing needs of our clients throughout the tri-state area. We also provide various healthcare providers with nurses, PTs, OTs and SLps on a contract and permanent basis.

Key Contact - Specialty:
Mr. Gene Holtzman, President - *Information technology*

Mr. Joseph Schimpf, Chief Operating Officer - *Finance, information technology, HR*

Salary minimum: $40,000

Functions: Healthcare, Nurses, IT, MIS Mgmt., Systems Analysis, Systems Dev., Systems Support, Network Admin., DB Admin., Graphic Artists

Industries: Generalist, Physical Therapy, Occupational Therapy

Professional Associations: NACCB

Networks: National Personnel Assoc (NPA)

Martrex Resources

(formerly known as MB Inc)
9 E 40th St
New York, NY 10016
(212) 661-4937
Fax: (212) 949-9782
Email: martrexresources@msn.com
Web: www.martrexresources.com

Description: Our firm is a national executive staffing resource for marketing, sales, and general management disciplines, serving corporate clients in the high-tech, consumer, and consumer package goods industries

Key Contact - Specialty:
Mr. Steven C. Wisch, President - *Marketing, sales, general management*

Salary minimum: $75,000

Functions: Sales & Mktg.

Industries: Generalist, Food, Bev., Tobacco, Soap, Perf., Cosmtcs., Drugs Mfg., Computer Equip., Consumer Elect., Mgmt. Consulting, E-commerce, Media, Software

Marvel Consultants Inc

28601 Chagrin Blvd Ste 470
Cleveland, OH 44122
(216) 292-2855
Fax: (216) 292-7207
Email: recruiters@marvelconsultants.com
Web: www.marvelconsultants.com

Description: Each of our 25 recruiters is a niche market specialist with tenures ranging up to 27 years, recruiting on a vertical market basis. Specialties: information technology, rubber, plastics, hydraulics, manufacturing, pumps, linear motion, sales, accounting, legal, medical, chemical, engineering.

Key Contact - Specialty:
Mr. John Sowers, CPC, President - *Information technology*
Mr. Lester Tavens, CPC, Vice President - *Medical, sales & marketing*

Functions: Generalist

Industries: Generalist

Networks: National Personnel Assoc (NPA)

Massachusetts Medical Bureau

PO Box 122 1
Falmouth, MA 02556
(508) 457-1447
Fax: (508) 457-5226
Email: gllwng@aol.com

Description: As a result of our extremely intensive recruiting campaigns and contacts through the USA, we are able to attract a large number of applicants who might never contact you otherwise.

Key Contact - Specialty:
Mr. Bill Cass - *Healthcare*
Ms. Alison Stewart - *Healthcare*

Salary minimum: $25,000

Functions: Generalist, Physicians, Nurses, Allied Health, Health Admin.

Industries: Generalist, Healthcare

Master Consultants Association Agency Inc

851 Burlway Rd Ste 618
Burlingame, CA 94010
(650) 340-0416
Fax: (650) 340-7156
Email: jantonis@everdream.com

Description: We specialize in all types of sales positions. We have been at the same location for 19 years.

Key Contact:
Mr. Steven Anderson, President - *Sales & marketing*
Mr. James Antonis, Vice President
Mr. Sonny Park, Sales Executive - *Sales*
Ms. June Hartley, Account Executive

Salary minimum: $25,000

Functions: Generalist, Sales & Mktg., Advertising, Mktg. Mgmt., Sales Mgmt.

Industries: Generalist, Construction, Mfg., Transportation, Communications, Software, Biotech, Healthcare

MasterTeam 2 Inc

1155 S Telshor Ste 302 A
Las Cruces, NM 88011
(877) 633-0202
Fax: (877) 659-0303
Email: meg@masterteam2.com
Web: www.masterteam2.com

Description: Software, hardware, semiconductor engineering and marketing jobs at the best networking and communications startups in Silicon Valley, Massachusetts, and beyond. Our firm also places high-tech sales, high-tech executives, and all areas of the medical profession.

Key Contact - Specialty:
Ms. Meg Murray, President - *Network hardware, software engineers*

Salary minimum: $70,000

Functions: Generalist, Healthcare, Physicians, Nurses, Health Admin., Sales & Mktg., Engineering

Industries: Generalist, Mfg., Plastics, Rubber, Metal Products, HR Services, Software, Healthcare

Mata & Associates

180 Harbor Dr Ste 208
Sausalito, CA 94965
(415) 332-2893
(415) 637-8840
Fax: (415) 332-3916
Email: dickmata@ix.netcom.com

Description: Specialize in recruitment of information technology professionals in the San Francisco Bay area. Placements range from help desk to senior technology management.

Key Contact:
Mr. Dick Mata, Owner

Salary minimum: $50,000

Functions: IT

Industries: Generalist

Match Point Associates Inc

35 N Central Ave Ste 406
St. Louis, MO 63105-3871
(314) 727-0400
Fax: (314) 727-1245
Email: jsexton727@aol.com
Web: www.adagencypositions.com

Description: We specialize in search assignments for agencies engaged advertising, public relations and sales promotion. If you have experience in these fields, these opportunities will advance your career.

Key Contact - Specialty:
Ms. Maryann Sexton, Owner - *Account management*
Mr. Jerry Saxton, President - *Account management, media, PR, sales promotion*

Salary minimum: $40,000

Functions: Advertising, PR

Industries: Advertising

Matchstix Consulting

970 Queen St E
PO Box 98052
Toronto, ON M4M 1J0
Canada
(416) 778-0793
(416) 716-7822
Email: matchstix@sympatico.ca

Key Contact:
Ms. Rhonda Belous, Executive Consultant

Salary minimum: $30,000

Functions: Generalist, General Mgmt., Mfg., Materials, Sales & Mktg., HR Mgmt., Benefits, Budgeting, IT, Engineering

Industries: Generalist, Food, Bev., Tobacco, Textiles, Apparel, Transportation, Retail, Advertising

Richard L Mather & Associates

PO Box 1183
Glastonbury, CT 06033
(860) 633-8130
Fax: (860) 657-8660
Email: dickmather@aol.com

Description: Specializing in manufacturing, engineering and corporation/division management recruiting for computer, energy, water, environmental, utility, information systems and other technical industries.

Key Contact:
Mr. Richard L. Mather, President

Salary minimum: $40,000

Functions: Generalist

Industries: Energy, Utilities, Mfg., Computer Equip., HR Services, Telecoms, Haz. Waste, Aerospace, Software, Biotech, Healthcare

Mathey Services

15170 Bethany Rd
Sycamore, IL 60178
(815) 895-3846
Fax: (815) 895-1046
Email: jam151@aol.com
Web: www.matheyservices.com

Description: Executive recruiting, searching, screening and placement services provided to clients in the Plastics, Packaging and Chemical industries. Specializing in the fields of sales and marketing, research and development and management and manufacturing, nationwide.

Key Contact - Specialty:
Ms. Joyce Mathey, President - *Plastics*

Salary minimum: $30,000

Functions: Generalist

Industries: Chemicals, Plastics, Rubber

Professional Associations: ISPE, SPI

Matrix Consultants Inc

PO Box 986
Wrightsville Beach, NC 28480
(910) 256-8080
Fax: (910) 256-9500
Email: ojwomble@worldnet.att.net
Web: www.ojwomble.com

Description: Specialize in recruiting and conducting searches in the food ingredient industry. Positions in research, sales and marketing to vice president and presidents for the largest companies in the industry.

Key Contact - Specialty:
Mr. O. J. Womble, Vice President-Marketing - *Food ingredients, nutraceuticals*
Mr. Joe Marion, Director of Marketing - *Chemicals, allied products*
Mr. Bill Jordan, Executive Recruiter - *Chemicals, allied products*
Ms. Rebecca Charles, Executive Recruiter - *Food ingredients, food service, nutraceuticals*

Salary minimum: $65,000

Functions: Generalist, Directors, Senior Mgmt., Middle Mgmt., Product Dev., Mktg. Mgmt., Sales Mgmt.

Industries: Generalist, Food, Bev., Tobacco, Chemicals, Biotech

Professional Associations: IFT, RON

MATRIX Resources Inc

115 Perimeter Ctr Pl NE Ste 250
Atlanta, GA 30346
(770) 677-2400
Fax: (770) 668-0384
Email: bill_hetherington@matrixresources.com
Web: www.matrixresources.com

Description: Our firm is a premier IT staffing provider for both permanent placement and contract consulting positions in the Atlanta, Birmingham, Dallas New Jersey, Phoenix, and Research Triangle Park markets. MATRIX currently has over 1,500 contract consultants on staff and in 2000 made 1,593 contract and 1,378 permanent placements, with total revenues of $221 million.

Key Contact:
Mr. Shannon Brandon, President, Field Operations
Mr. Jim Huling, President, Corporate Services
Mr. Bill Hetherington, Director of Marketing

Salary minimum: $25,000

Functions: Training, IT, MIS Mgmt., Systems Analysis, Systems Dev., Systems Implem., Systems Support, Network Admin., DB Admin.

Industries: Generalist

Professional Associations: NACCB, NAPS

Matrix Search Network

558 Leff St
San Luis Obispo, CA 93401
(805) 541-1182
Fax: (805) 541-1355
Email: info@matrixsearch.net
Web: www.matrixsearch.net

Description: We specialize solely in the software industry. We excel in the tough searches, the ones that everyone else has given up on. We are quick, ethical and discreet.

Key Contact - Specialty:
Mr. James F. Parker, Managing Director - *Software*
Ms. Nicole Miller, Senior Consultant - *Software*

Salary minimum: $75,000

Functions: Generalist, Senior Mgmt., Middle Mgmt., Mkt. Research, Mktg. Mgmt., Engineering

Industries: Generalist, Software

Matteson Management Inc

1200 Bay St Ste 405
Toronto, ON M5R 2A5
Canada
(416) 960-8600
Fax: (416) 960-8602
Email: sm@mattesonmanagement.com
Web: www.mattesonmanagement.com

Description: We are a competency-based retained executive search practice specializing in mid- to senior-level roles, with an emphasis on the greater Toronto area and Paris, France. Please send resumes in Word or RTF format only.

Key Contact - Specialty:
Ms. Sandra Matteson, Principal (Owner) - *Public relations (agency, corporate)*
Ms. Deborah Magidson, Senior Consultant - *Sales & marketing, communications, human resources*
Mr. Peter Laurence, Senior Consultant - *Retail*
Mr. Patrick Bruneteau, Senior Consultant - *High technology, industry, electronics, professional services, luxury goods*

Salary minimum: $50,000

Functions: Directors, Senior Mgmt., Middle Mgmt., Mktg. Mgmt., Sales Mgmt., PR

Industries: Generalist

Matthews & Stephens Associates Inc

1344 Silas Deane Hwy Ste 303
Rocky Hill, CT 06067
(860) 258-1995
Fax: (860) 258-1998
Email: sab@msaventurepartners.com
Web: www.matthews-stephens.com

Description: We have a national practice with unique customized approach and alternatives. We have an extremely personalized seasoned staff that listens to you, and then develops a search plan. We specialize in healthcare administration, insurance, financial accounting, engineering, and call centers.

Key Contact - Specialty:
Mr. Stephen A. Baskowski, CPC, Executive Recruiter - *Accounting, information technology, marketing*
Mr. Stephen W. Harvey, CPC, Executive Recruiter - *Healthcare*

Salary minimum: $50,000

Functions: Generalist, Health Admin., Finance, CFO's, IT, Engineering

Industries: Generalist, Insurance, Healthcare

Professional Associations: CAPS, NAPS

Networks: National Personnel Assoc (NPA)

The Matthews Group Inc

440 West St Ste 7N
Ft. Lee, NJ 07024
(201) 585-2211
Fax: (201) 585-2214
Email: thematgrp@aol.com

Description: We place sales, marketing and category management professionals to the consumer products industry, nationwide and at all levels of expertise.

Key Contact - Specialty:
Ms. Alyce Matthews, President - *Sales, marketing, consumer products*

Functions: Generalist, Senior Mgmt., Middle Mgmt., Mkt. Research, Mktg. Mgmt., Sales Mgmt., Systems Implem.

Industries: Generalist, Food, Bev., Tobacco, Hospitality

Matthews Management

33 Arnold Crescent
Richmond Hill, ON L4C 3R6
Canada
(905) 884-6970
Fax: (905) 884-6716
Email: mattman1@sympatico.ca

Description: Recruitment for automotive manufacturing of program managers, project, product, design, manufacturing and quality engineers. Processes include moulding, finishing, plating, stamping, extruding, rollforming and assembly. If it's automotive, it's us.

Key Contact:
Ms. Angela K. Matthews, President/Owner

Salary minimum: $50,000

Functions: Mfg.

Industries: Generalist, Mfg., Plastics, Rubber, Motor Vehicles, Mfg. SW

G P Mattocks & Associates Inc

5015 Country Club Dr N
Wilson, NC 27896-9123
(252) 399-0589
(800) 754-8129
Fax: (252) 291-8467
Email: paul@gpmrecruiters.com
Web: www.gpmrecruiters.com

Description: We are a privately owned and operated search firm working with our affiliates throughout the nation to search and recruit top candidates in the rubber, plastics, metals and automotive industry for our clients. We search for technical and management personnel.

Key Contact - Specialty:
Mr. Paul Mattocks, Owner/Recruiter - *Rubber, plastics, metal, technical, management*
Mr. Robert Krieger, Owner/Recruiter - *Rubber, plastics, automotive*
Ms. Trina McCormick, Recruiter - *Rubber, plastics, automotive*
Mrs. Brenda Mattocks, Research/Data Input - *Office management*

Salary minimum: $30,000

Functions: Mfg., Product Dev., Plant Mgmt., Quality, HR Mgmt.

Industries: Mfg., Chemicals, Medical Devices, Plastics, Rubber, Metal Products, Machine, Appliance, Motor Vehicles, Computer Equip., Misc. Mfg.

Professional Associations: NCASP, RON

Networks: Top Echelon Network

Maximum Management Corp

230 Park Ave Ste 635
New York, NY 10169
(212) 867-4646
Fax: (212) 682-4882
Email: mmc@maxmanhr.com
Web: www.maxmanhr.com

Description: We are dedicated exclusively to human resource placement in the New York tri-state area. We place permanent, interim and entry level human resource professionals in all human resource disciplines.

Key Contact - Specialty:
Ms. Melissa Brophy, President - *Human resources*
Ms. Nancy Shield, Vice President - *Human resources*

Functions: Generalist, Benefits, Personnel, Training

Industries: Generalist

Professional Associations: IACPR, ASTD, MAAP, SHRM

Mayhall Search Group Inc

4410 Executive Blvd Ste 1A
Ft. Wayne, IN 46808
(219) 484-7770
Fax: (219) 482-9397
Email: sheryl@mayhall.com
Web: www.mayhall.com

Description: We place positions with salaries from $50,000 to $200,000 in all major disciplines. We have done business with the majority of the Fortune 500 companies.

Key Contact - Specialty:
Mr. Dale Mayhall - *Engineering, sales*
Ms. Sheryl Mayhall, President - *Manufacturing, engineering, quality all materials*
Mr. Matt Niezer, Recruiter - *Accounting and finance*
Mr. Wade Walker, Recruiter - *IT, logistics, materials, supply*

Salary minimum: $40,000

Functions: Generalist

Industries: Mfg., Plastics, Rubber, Metal Products, Consumer Elect., Finance, Software

Networks: National Personnel Assoc (NPA)

MB Fisher Int'l

17950 Preston Rd Ste 912
Dallas, TX 75252
(888) 969-6904
(972) 239-6904
Fax: (972) 239-6905
Email: brian@mbfisher.com
Web: www.mbfisher.com

Description: We are committed to providing quality service both to our clients and candidates by matching elite professionals with Fortune level organizations.

Key Contact:
Mr. Brian Fisher, President
Mr. Lance Van Winkle, CPA, VP- Financial Services

Salary minimum: $50,000

Functions: Finance, CFO's

Industries: Generalist

MBA Management Inc

14900 Conference Center Dr Ste 300
Chantilly, VA 20151
(703) 273-0028
Fax: (703) 961-7950
Web: www.mbamgmt.com

Description: We are a leading executive search firm providing our clients with top talent. We offer our clients services in the following specialties: architecture, engineering, construction, finance, accounting, human resources, information technology, and telecommunications. Additionally, we offer specialized services in interim executives, contract staffing, and mergers & acquisitions in all of the listed specialties.

Key Contact - Specialty:
Mr. James Mugnolo, President & CEO - *General management*
Mr. Philip Hamilton, Executive Vice President - *General management*
Mr. John Zanelotti, Chief Operating Officer
Mr. Carl Mugnolo, Vice President of Information Technology
Mr. Richard Gardella, Vice President Marketing
Ms. Susan Yoder, VP- Engineering - *Architects, engineering, construction*
Ms. Brenda Gary, VP- Finance & Accounting - *Accounting, CFOs, finance*
Mr. Mark Antalosky, VP- Special Projects
Ms. Laura Breslin, VP- Contract Services - *Interim executives, contract staffing*

Salary minimum: $50,000

Functions: Sales & Mktg., HR Mgmt., Finance, CFO's, IT, MIS Mgmt., Engineering, Environmentalists, Architects

Industries: Generalist, Energy, Utilities, Construction, Communications, Government, Haz. Waste, Aerospace, Real Estate, Industry Specific SW, Security SW, System SW

Professional Associations: ASCE, ASHE, ASIS, AUSA, HFMA, NABA, NCHEA, NMS, NVTC, ROA, SAME, SHRM, SMPS

McCarthy Associates

(also known as National BancSearch LLC)
2727 Prytania St Ste 6
(At The Rink)
New Orleans, LA 70130
(504) 897-6688
Fax: (504) 891-0102
Email: info@nationalbanksearch.com
Web: www.nationalbanksearch.com

Description: With integrity, credibility, utmost confidentiality, we identify, profile, present only top notch candidates matched to the needs of client companies and serve as invaluable liaison during the sensitive hiring process.

Key Contact - Specialty:
Mr. Richard McCarthy, Owner/Manager - *Bank marketing, retail, commercial*
Mr. Bud Creech, Recruiter - *Bank, commercial lending, accounting, finance*
Ms. Stacy Komendera, Partner - *Investment banking, banking, IT*
Ms. Stone Davis, Executive Recruiter - *IT, banking*

Functions: Generalist, Finance, Cash Mgmt., M&A, IT

Industries: Generalist, Finance, Banking, Invest. Banking, Brokers, Venture Cap., Misc. Financial, Accounting, Mgmt. Consulting, PSA/ASP, Advertising, Call Centers, Real Estate, Marketing SW

Networks: National Banking Network (NBN)

McCord Consulting Group Inc

4533 Pine View Dr NE
PO Box 11024
Cedar Rapids, IA 52410
(319) 378-0077
Fax: (319) 378-1577
Email: smmccord@home.com
Web: www.mccordgroup.com

Description: We provide executive and engineering searches. We specialize in the plastics industry. We represent companies ranging from small privately owned to Fortune 500.

Key Contact - Specialty:
Mr. Sam McCord, President/CEO
Mrs. Mary McCord, Vice President - *Finance*

Salary minimum: $40,000

Functions: Senior Mgmt., Engineering

Industries: Plastics, Rubber, Mfg. SW

Professional Associations: SPE

Networks: Top Echelon Network

Branches:
210 Reid Ln
PO Box 744
South St. Paul, MN 55075
(651) 552-1877
Fax: (651) 552-1877
Email: wegmann@quixnet.net
Key Contact:
Ms. Ann Wegmann, Manager Marketing and Research

McCoy Ltd
3705 Beacon Ave Ste 200
Fremont, CA 94538-1413
(510) 745-7700
Fax: (510) 745-8663
Email: john@mccoyltd.com
Web: www.mccoyltd.com

Description: We are a full-service executive search firm specializing in all facets of hardware, software and MIS for the high-tech industry.

Key Contact - Specialty:
Mr. Bob Walker, Director - *Hardware, software*
Mr. John R. McNally, President - *Software, hardware*
Mr. Eric Baxley - *Software*
Mr. Benjamin Dicicco - *Telecommunications*

Salary minimum: $35,000

Functions: Generalist, General Mgmt., Mfg., Quality, Sales & Mktg., IT, Systems Dev., Engineering

Industries: Generalist, Computer Equip., Software

Branches:
22916 Lyons Ave Ste 1C
Newhall, CA 91321
(805) 287-9262
Fax: (805) 287-4412
Email: james@mccoyltd.com
Key Contact - Specialty:
Mr. James Brandle, Director - *Hardware, software*

616 Stevens Ave Ste B
Solana Beach, CA 92075
(619) 350-1117
Fax: (619) 350-1158
Email: daniel@mccoyltd.com
Key Contact - Specialty:
Mr. Daniel P. Loftus, Director - *Hardware, software*

McCrea & Company Worldwide
8626 Hollis RD
One Deer Run Compound
Brecksville, OH 44141
(440) 526-1672
Email: mccreaco2@aol.com

Description: We specialize in placing storage architects, system engineers, hardware/software sales executives, pre-sales engineers, and sales engineers.

Key Contact:
Mr. James McCrea, President - *Information technology, hardware, software*
Mr. John Manocchio, General Manager

Salary minimum: $75,000

Functions: Generalist, IT, Systems Analysis, Systems Dev., Systems Implem., Systems Support, Network Admin., DB Admin.

Industries: Generalist, Test, Measure Equip., Telecoms, Telephony, Digital, Wireless, Fiber Optic, Network Infrastructure, Software

The Paul McDaniel Company
PO Box 381672
Memphis, TN 38183
(901) 757-9220
Fax: (901) 758-1111
Email: info@paulmcdaniel.com
Web: www.paulmcdaniel.com

Description: Over 20 years' successfully recruiting for companies in categories previously listed. Excellent industry reputation.

Key Contact - Specialty:
Mr. Paul McDaniel, Owner - *Supermarket, wholesale grocery distributors, food service distributors*

Functions: Middle Mgmt.

Industries: Generalist, Wholesale, Retail

Earl L McDermid & Associates
PO Box 6202
Buffalo Grove, IL 60089
(847) 541-9066
Fax: (847) 537-5381
Email: earlmcdermid@aol.com

Description: A specialized executive search firm working in the business and industry, vending, healthcare, schools, colleges, food/equipment manufacturers and distributors segments of the hospitality industry.

Key Contact - Specialty:
Mr. Earl McDermid, President - *Food service*
Mr. W. John McGinnis, Vice President - *Food service*

Salary minimum: $25,000

Functions: Generalist

Industries: Generalist, Food, Bev., Tobacco, Hospitality

Professional Associations: SFM

McDermott-Sears Associates LLC
711 Hwy 10 Ste 205
Randolph, NJ 07869
(973) 537-6450
(973) 285-0258
Fax: (973) 989-6907
Email: dlsears@iteamtalent.com
Web: www.iteamtalent.com

Description: We provide retained executive search, talent strategy, and related talent services focused on technology intensive businesses.

Key Contact:
Mr. David L. Sears, Principal - *Technology, general management, senior information technology, sales & marketing, product management*
Mr. Donald McDermott, Principal
Ms. Michelle Geary, Client Services Manager

Salary minimum: $90,000

Functions: Generalist

Industries: Electronic, Elec. Components, Misc. Financial, Mgmt. Consulting, HR Services, IT Implementation, Publishing, New Media, Communications, Software

Professional Associations: EMA, NJTC, SHRM, WAW

McDowell & Company
11300 N Central Expy Ste 610
Dallas, TX 75243
(214) 373-0045
Fax: (214) 343-5192
Email: jmc21@flash.net
Web: www.mcdowell-co.com

Description: We strive to provide our clients a quality not quantity approach in todays fast paced business environment. Time is the most valuable asset that we offer.

Key Contact - Specialty:
Mr. John McDowell, Principal - *Data communications, telecommunications, networking, information technology, computer software*

Functions: Generalist, Sales Mgmt., MIS Mgmt., Systems Implem., Systems Support, Network Admin., DB Admin., Engineering

Industries: Generalist, Hospitality, Telecoms, Software

Professional Associations: RON

McDuffy-Edwards
3117 Medina Dr
Garland, TX 75041
(972) 864-1174
Fax: (972) 864-8559
Email: tomedwards@earthlink.net

Description: Nationwide recruiting for sales, marketing and sales support professionals in the information technology world.

Key Contact - Specialty:
Mr. Tom Edwards, Owner - *Information technology, sales & marketing*

Salary minimum: $60,000

Functions: Senior Mgmt., Mktg. Mgmt., Sales Mgmt., Customer Svc., Benefits

Industries: Computer Equip., Mgmt. Consulting, Telecoms, Software

McGinnis & Associates
112 W Adams St Ste 902
Jacksonville, FL 32202
(904) 356-7337
Fax: (904) 356-7335
Email: recruite@aol.com
Web: www.aafa.com

Description: We place candidates in middle and senior management accounting, tax, and financial positions.

Key Contact:
Mr. Fred McGinnis

Salary minimum: $50,000

Functions: Finance

Industries: Generalist

Professional Associations: AAFA

McGowan Associates Inc
PO Box 693
Kimberton, PA 19442
(610) 917-9094
Fax: (610) 917-0308
Email: bamcgowan@worldnet.att.net
Web: www.mcgowanassociates.com

Description: As a food service recruitment company, we discover management, culinary and executive talent for the hospitality and healthcare industries. We focus on the candidates' professional skills and competencies, as well as their sociability and service quotients.

Key Contact - Specialty:
Mr. Brian A. McGowan, President - *Food service, hospitality, healthcare*

Salary minimum: $30,000

Functions: Generalist, General Mgmt., Middle Mgmt.

Industries: Hospitality

McHale & Associates
(a division of Personnel Opportunities LLC)
5064 Roswell Rd Ste D-301
Atlanta, GA 30342
(404) 252-9020
(800) 253-2429
Fax: (404) 843-3588
Email: mbillings@persopps.com
Web: www.persopps.com

Description: We are a full service firm in business in Atlanta, Ga. Maria Billings Schneider, CPC, deals in general office permanent placement, accounting, finance, auditing, some IT, as well as customer service, marketing, and sales for Southeast US. An alternate fax number that we have available is as follows: 770-434-5468.

Key Contact - Specialty:
Mrs. Maria Billings Schneider, CPC, CPC, Senior Account recruiter - *Accounting, finance,audit,general office,sales*

Salary minimum: $40,000

Functions: Admin. Svcs., Mfg., Sales & Mktg., Customer Svc., Finance

Industries: Agri., Forestry, Mining, Food, Bev., Tobacco, Motor Vehicles, Legal, Accounting, HR Services, Accounting SW, Mfg. SW

Professional Associations: GAPS

McInturff & Associates Inc
209G W Central St
Natick, MA 01760
(781) 237-0220
Fax: (508) 653-1418
Email: bob@mcinturff.com

Description: Over twenty years as specialists in supply chain and manufacturing management. Our firm staffed by professionals who bring in-depth knowledge to your unique requirements.

Key Contact - Specialty:
Mr. Robert E. McInturff, President - *Materials, manufacturing, logistics*

Salary minimum: $90,000

Functions: Mfg., Materials

Industries: Medical Devices, Plastics, Rubber, Metal Products, Computer Equip.

Professional Associations: APICS, APICS, MPPC

McIntyre Management Resources
1030 Upper James St Ste 301
Hamilton, ON L9C 6X6
Canada
(905) 574-6765
Email: jobs@mcintyrejobs.com
Web: www.mcintyrejobs.com

Description: Best known for partnering with clients, establishing in-depth, long-term relationships. Relationships may be by industry specialty or position/equipment specialty.

Key Contact - Specialty:
Ms. Marlene McIntyre, President - *Information technology, executives all markets*

Salary minimum: $40,000

Functions: Generalist

Industries: Generalist

Professional Associations: ACSESS

Networks: National Personnel Assoc (NPA)

McKavis Associates
3724 Clove Way
Oceanside, CA 92057-8338
(760) 966-1292
(800) 800-0046
Fax: (760) 966-1292

Description: Executive recruiting in the field of occupational medicine and managed care. Working with corporations, clinics and hospitals placing physicians, physician assistants, nurse practitioners and COHNs within the field of occupational medicine.

Key Contact - Specialty:
Ms. Adel McKavis, President - *Occupational medicine, managed care*

Functions: Generalist, Physicians, Nurses, Health Admin.

Industries: Generalist, Healthcare

McKinnon Management Group Inc
5160 Yonge St Ste 700
Toronto, ON M2N 6L9
Canada
(416) 250-6763
Fax: (416) 250-6916
Email: info@mckinnon.com
Web: www.mckinnon.com

Description: Executive search firm focusing on leading edge business enterprise placing sales, marketing and healthcare professionals throughout North America.

Key Contact - Specialty:
Mr. Greg McKinnon, President - *Sales & marketing*
Mr. Chris Bradshaw, Vice President - *High technology*

Functions: Generalist

Industries: Misc. Financial, Pharm Svcs., E-commerce, IT Implementation, Advertising

The McKnight Group
1465 Post Rd E
Westport, CT 06880
(203) 256-3570
Fax: (203) 256-3574
Email: mcknightgroup@mail.com

Description: We are executive search consultants with expertise in finance, accounting, tax, banking, insurance, human resources, marketing, public relations, and office support.

Key Contact:
Mr. Richard F. McKnight, Managing Partner
Ms. Maureen Ekberg, Executive Recruiter

Functions: Generalist, Mktg. Mgmt., Sales Mgmt., Benefits, Taxes, M&A, Network Admin., DB Admin.

Industries: Generalist, Energy, Utilities, Machine, Appliance, Banking, Hospitality, Telecoms, Insurance

William K McLaughlin Associates Inc
PO Box 10308
Rochester, NY 14610-0308
(800) 728-1964
Fax: (716) 442-8587
Email: information@wkmclaughlin.com
Web: www.wkmclaughlin.com

Description: For over 35 years, we have assisted patent attorneys in finding positions with the leading law firms and corporations throughout the United States. Visit our web site for over 180 pages of detailed job descriptions.

Key Contact - Specialty:
Mr. William K. McLaughlin, President - *Attorney (patent)*
Mr. John F. McLaughlin, Vice President - *Attorney (patent)*

Salary minimum: $60,000

Functions: Legal, Attorneys

Industries: Generalist, Legal

Branches:
626 Summerlea St
Pittsburgh, PA 15232
(800) 618-0715
Fax: (800) 342-7486
Email: information@wkmclaughlin.com
Key Contact - Specialty:
Ms. Patricia M. Cheshire, Vice President - *Patent attorney*

Dan P McLean Associates Inc
RR 4
Tottenham, ON L0G 1W0
Canada
(905) 880-4724
Fax: (905) 880-2651
Email: dmclean284@aol.com

Description: Formed to provide professional services including executive search, lease-a-professional and sales/management consulting to high-technology companies - programmer analysts to presidents.

Key Contact - Specialty:
Mr. Dan P. McLean, President - *High technology (programmer analysts to presidents)*
Ms. Luella McLean, Vice President - *High technology (programmer analysts to presidents)*
Mrs. Paula Dermott, Consultant - *High technology (programmer analysts to presidents)*

Salary minimum: $40,000

Functions: General Mgmt., Senior Mgmt., Sales & Mktg.

Industries: IT Implementation, Software

Professional Associations: APEO

Networks: National Personnel Assoc (NPA)

McPherson Square Associates Inc
1025 Connecticut Ave NW Ste 1012
Washington, DC 20036
(202) 737-8777
Fax: (202) 364-0066

Description: Specializing in placement of partners and groups with law firms and law firm mergers. Corporate legal placement.

Key Contact - Specialty:
Mr. Ronald G. Russell, President - *Attorney placement*

Salary minimum: $140,000

Functions: Legal

Industries: Generalist

Professional Associations: NALSC

McRoberts & Associates
36437 S Reserve Cir
Avon, OH 44011
(440) 934-4742
Fax: (440) 934-4742

Description: Generalists with emphasis on technical searches. We have proven to our clients that we can fill those difficult assignments.

Key Contact - Specialty:
Mr. C. F. McRoberts - *Engineering*

Salary minimum: $40,000

Functions: Generalist

Industries: Generalist

Joseph J McTaggart
5710 Arapaho Dr
San Jose, CA 95123-3202
(408) 226-3203
Email: mct@sirius.com

Description: Solo practitioner. 100% search. No time limit guarantee. Candidate is guaranteed to earn you a profit or I replace. Specialty: general manager and supporting high-level staff. Serving a potpourri of industries throughout the USA.

Key Contact - Specialty:
Mr. Joseph J. McTaggart, Owner - *Management (upper)*

Salary minimum: $100,000

Functions: General Mgmt.

Industries: Generalist

MDR & Associates
11 Ontur Ln
Hot Springs Village, AR 71909
(501) 915-0244
(800) 264-9701
Fax: (501) 915-0240
Email: info@mdr-associates.com
Web: www.mdrandassociates.com

Description: We specialize in placing executives in the casino industry. We are very client oriented. We try to walk the extra mile to find the exact person described by the client. By doing this, we have developed a very good client list. Companies call us when they have a search. We treat both clients and candidates with equal respect.

Key Contact - Specialty:
Mr. Mel Robinson, D., President - *Casino industry (executives)*

Salary minimum: $45,000

Functions: Generalist

Industries: Hospitality

Med-Ex Services
5000 Rockside Rd Ste 100
Independence, OH 44131
(216) 573-1130
Fax: (216) 573-0727
Email: med-ex@stratos.net
Web: www.med-exservices.com

Description: Permanent and temporary medical/healthcare staffing with hospitals, clinics, doctors, dentists, labs, MCOs, PPOs, HMOs and more. If it's healthcare-related, we will fill the position.

Key Contact - Specialty:
Ms. Karin E. Deffler, CPC, President - *Medical (clerical, clinical)*

Functions: Generalist, Healthcare, Physicians, Nurses, Allied Health, Health Admin., Mkt. Research, Sales Mgmt.

Industries: Generalist, Healthcare

Professional Associations: ICTS, NATSS, NAWBO, OSSA

Branches:
445 Griswold Rd C
Elyria, OH 44035
(440) 324-6000
Fax: (440) 324-6003
Key Contact - Specialty:
Ms. Karin E. Deffler, CPC - *Healthcare*

MED-PRO
12220 Yorkshire
PO Box 207
Richland, MI 49083
(616) 629-2203
Fax: (616) 629-2205
Email: medpro@net-link.net

Description: We have over 25 years in healthcare recruiting. Radiology recruiting by radiology professionals = specialty. Permanent placement of physicians, physician assistants, nurse practitioners and administration.

Key Contact - Specialty:
Ms. Sharon Wiley, President/CEO - *Physicians, nurse practitioners, physician assistants*

Salary minimum: $35,000

Functions: Healthcare, Physicians, Nurses, Allied Health, Health Admin.

Industries: Healthcare

Professional Associations: ARRT, ASRT

Med-Search Recruiting Network Inc
15933 Clayton Rd
St. Louis, MO 63011
(877) 897-5627
Fax: (623) 230-9483
Email: info@medrecruiters.com
Web: www.medrecruiters.com

Description: Our firm, the gateway to career success, is a dynamic search firm specializing in the recruitment of sales, sales management, executive management, and marketing professionals in the healthcare, medical pharmaceutical, IT, and telecommunication industry. Med-Search recruits on a nationwide basis and does so on all levels vertically from entry-level sales to VPs of sales and marketing.

Key Contact:
Mr. Tim Charow, President

Functions: Senior Mgmt., Sales & Mktg.

Industries: Healthcare

Media Recruiting Group Inc
1 Bridge St Ste P2
Irvington, NY 10533
(914) 591-5511
Fax: (914) 591-8911
Email: steve@mediarecruitinggroup.com
Web: www.mediarecruitinggroup.com

Description: Our firm is a leading executive search firm specializing in the publishing, direct marketing, and new media industries. Our clients include both large and small consumer and business-to-business companies. The firm has thrived on its reputation as being exceptional in delivering quality service to clients and candidates

Key Contact - Specialty:
Mrs. Risa Goldberg, President - *Magazine publishing, ad sales & marketing, promotion*
Mr. Steve Goldberg, Executive VP, Managing Partner - *Magazine publishing, circulation, consumer marketing, new media, marketing*

Salary minimum: $30,000

Functions: Sales & Mktg., Advertising, Mktg. Mgmt., Sales Mgmt., Direct Mktg.

Industries: Advertising, Publishing, New Media

Professional Associations: AWNY, DMA, DMCNY, FMA, NYNMA

Medical Executive Recruiters
1198 Melody Ln Ste 109
Roseville, CA 95678
(916) 786-8615
Fax: (916) 786-8609
Email: medexec@pacbell.net

Description: Our firm specializes in recruiting qualified sales, marketing and management candidates for the medical and technology industries nationwide.

Key Contact - Specialty:
Mr. John Cunningham, Owner/President - *Medical, software*
Ms. Kandi Williams, Senior Recruiter - *Medical, biotechnology, biopharmaceutical*

Salary minimum: $50,000

Functions: Generalist, Mkt. Research, Mktg. Mgmt., Sales Mgmt.

Industries: Generalist, Medical Devices, Software, Biotech, Healthcare

Medical Executive Recruiters
21751 W Nine Mile Rd Ste 202
Southfield, MI 48075-3280
(248) 357-5373
Fax: (248) 357-5379

Key Contact - Specialty:
Mr. Charles Greening - *Medical, consumer, electrical, mechanical, manufacturing*

Functions: Middle Mgmt., Mfg., Materials, Physicians, Sales & Mktg., Benefits, Personnel, MIS Mgmt., Systems Dev.

Industries: Generalist

Medical Executive Search Associates Inc
1823 E 10th St
Tucson, AZ 85719-5920
(888) 884-2550
(520) 885-2252
Fax: (520) 885-2542
Email: wlp@mesaworldwide.com
Web: www.mesaworldwide.com

Description: We have had nineteen years of recruitment experience in the medical device, biotech, orthopedic, and pharmaceutical industries worldwide.

Key Contact:
Mr. William L. Piatkiewicz, President/General Manager - *Medical devices, biotech, pharmaceuticals, orthopedics*
Mrs. Mary Lou Piatkiewicz, Vice President/CFO - *Medical devices, biotech, pharmaceuticals, orthopedics*
Mr. David Brokaw, Director/Development & Recruitment

Salary minimum: $50,000

Functions: Generalist

Industries: Mfg., Drugs Mfg., Medical Devices, Computer Equip., Packaging, Software, Biotech, Healthcare

The Medical Industry Search Group
637 Wycoff Ave Ste 231
Wyckoff, NJ 07481
(201) 891-8015
Fax: (201) 891-8025
Email: misgroup@prodigy.net

Description: We realize that in any company, people are the most important asset, and we strive to provide individuals that have the capability of providing the highest level of performance and business results.

Key Contact - Specialty:
Mr. Edward E. Chanod, President - *Medical products, pharmaceutical, biotech, medical devices, diagnostics*

Salary minimum: $55,000

Functions: General Mgmt., Mfg., Materials, Sales & Mktg., HR Mgmt., Finance, R&D, Engineering

Industries: Drugs Mfg., Medical Devices, Biotech

Professional Associations: AACC, ACS, ASQ, ISPE, RAPS

Medical Innovations
605 Village Ln
PO Box 224
Orient, NY 11957
(631) 323-3899
(631) 477-0338
Fax: (631) 477-0337
Email: medinnov@aol.com
Web: www.medicalinnovations.cc

Description: Our specialty is placement in reputable healthcare manufacturers whose products are considered cutting edge technology. This is achieved only in an ethical, professional and compassionate process.

Key Contact - Specialty:
Ms. Carol Martin, President - *Medical sales, management, marketing, product development*

Salary minimum: $60,000

Functions: Sales & Mktg.

Industries: Drugs Mfg., Medical Devices, Healthcare

Medical Recruiters Inc
12400 Olive Blvd Ste 555
St. Louis, MO 63141
(314) 275-4466
Fax: (314) 523-4566
Email: hnd@medrecinc.com

Description: Specialists in medical sales and sales management placement.

Key Contact - Specialty:
Ms. Heidi Oberman, Recruitment Specialist - *Medical sales, sales management, RNs, clinical, consumer sales*
Ms. Denise Wottowa, Recruitment Specialist - *Medical sales, sales management, RNs, clinical, consumer sales*

Functions: Healthcare, Nurses, Sales Mgmt.

Industries: Drugs Mfg., Medical Devices, Pharm Svcs.

Networks: First Interview Network (FIN)

Medical Search Group
790 Turnpike St Ste 202
North Andover, MA 01845
(978) 683-9800
Fax: (978) 683-8600
Email: resumes@medicalsearchgroup.com
Web: www.medicalsearchgroup.com

Description: National recruiters specializing in medical and pharmaceutical sales with over 20 years of experience in the industry.

Key Contact:
Jean H. Khoury, CPC

Salary minimum: $40,000

Functions: Sales & Mktg.

Industries: Drugs Mfg., Medical Devices, Services, Pharm Svcs., Equip Svcs., Software, Biotech, Healthcare

Professional Associations: MAPS

Networks: US Recruiters.com

Medical Search of America Inc
3500 McClure Bridge Rd Ste 114
PO Box 1716
Duluth, GA 30096
(800) 523-1351
(770) 232-0530
Fax: (770) 232-0610
Email: chassearch@earthlink.net

Description: We are a multi-faceted national health care search firm specializing in the location and placement of medical professionals - physician, executive administrative, nursing, technical and allied health personnel.

Key Contact - Specialty:
Mr. Charles Sikes, President - *Medical placement*

Salary minimum: $45,000

Functions: Generalist

Industries: Healthcare

Medicorp Inc
330 Jungermann Rd
St. Peters, MO 63376
(636) 447-7500
(877) 295-7778
Fax: (636) 447-7577
Email: jack@medicorpinc.com
Web: www.medicorpinc.com

Description: We are an established and reputable, professional, physician placement firm with a diverse national clientele offering full time placement. All of our consultants are specialists in their field.

Key Contact - Specialty:
Mr. Jack Johnson, President/CEO - *Physicians*
Ms. Madison Grace, Vice President - *Physicians*

Salary minimum: $90,000

Functions: Physicians, Direct Mktg., DB Admin.

Industries: Healthcare

Professional Associations: AMA

The Medley Group
3540 Wilshire Blvd Ste PH 8
Los Angeles, CA 90010
(213) 616-0225
(800) 535-7757
Fax: (213) 616-0226
Email: jerry@medleyrecruits.com
Web: www.medleyrecruits.com

Description: We are one of the premier West Coast based executive search firms in the US. The principal partners have extensive experience in executive search and recruitment, working with senior-level management, elected officials and community groups.

Key Contact - Specialty:
Mr. Jerry Medley, President - *Diversity, sales & marketing, finance & accounting*

Salary minimum: $80,000

Functions: Generalist, Senior Mgmt.

Industries: Generalist, Leather, Stone, Glass, Finance, Services, Accounting, IT Implementation, Hospitality, Hotels, Resorts, Clubs, Advertising, Communications, Network Infrastructure, Defense, Aerospace, Entertainment SW, System SW

MedPro Personnel Inc
1955 Cliff Valley Way Ste 116
Atlanta, GA 30329
(404) 633-8280
(800) 737-3101
Email: med.pro@mindspring.com
Web: www.medpropersonnel.com

Description: We place medical personnel in hospitals, clinics and physician practices. We work with clerical and clinical staff in permanent, temp to hire and temporary positions.

Key Contact - Specialty:
Ms. Marilyn Feingold, President/CEO - *Medical*

Functions: Generalist, Nurses, Health Admin.

Industries: Generalist, Healthcare

Professional Associations: NATSS

MedQuest Associates
9250 E Costilla Ave Ste 600
Englewood, CO 80112
(303) 790-2009
Fax: (303) 790-2021
Email: judystiles@aol.com

Description: Recruitment of sales, sales management, product management, engineering/research and development, marketing management. General management in medical product industries.

Key Contact - Specialty:
Ms. Judy Stiles, Director - *Medical devices*

Salary minimum: $45,000

Functions: Generalist, Mkt. Research, Mktg. Mgmt., Sales Mgmt., Customer Svc.

Industries: Generalist, Drugs Mfg., Medical Devices, Pharm Svcs., Biotech

Medserve & Associates Inc
3801 Canterbury Rd Ste 716
Baltimore, MD 21218
(888) 782-3337
(410) 366-5570
Fax: (410) 366-4420
Email: info@medserve.net
Web: www.medserve.net

Description: We are a nationwide search and recruitment firm specializing in physician placements.

Key Contact - Specialty:
Mr. Sal Eren, Director of Placement - *Physicians, allied health*

Functions: Physicians, Nurses, Allied Health

Industries: Generalist

MedXec USA Inc
1701 W Hillsboro Blvd Ste 102
Deerfield Beach, FL 33442
(954) 360-9980
Fax: (954) 425-0975
Email: medxecusa@mindspring.com
Web: www.medxecusa.com

Description: Full-service contingent recruiting firm exclusively serving the home healthcare and ambulatory industries.

Key Contact - Specialty:
Mr. Richard L. Myers, President/CEO - *Home healthcare senior executives*
Ms. Dana L. Lihan, Vice President - *Home healthcare, clinical, QA executives*

Salary minimum: $30,000

Functions: Generalist, General Mgmt., Healthcare, Sales & Mktg., HR Mgmt., Finance, IT

Industries: Healthcare

Professional Associations: NATSS

Branches:
102 F Commonwealth Ct
Cary, NC 27511
(919) 481-2333
Fax: (919) 481-1103
Email: midatlantic@tempxecusa.com
Key Contact:
Mr. Gregory L. Greenland, COO
Mr. Harry Clew, General Manager
Ms. Beth Salyers, Executive Recruiter
Mr. Jim Stella, Executive Recruiter

1428 Tiki Lane Rd
Lancaster, OH 43130
(740) 681-9920
Fax: (740) 681-9935
Email: greatlakes@tempxecusa.com
Web: www.tempxecusa.com
Key Contact:
Mr. Gregory L. Greenland, President/COO

Mehta Consulting
4 Bryant Ln
PO Box 547
Dover, MA 02030-0547
(508) 785-2055
Fax: (508) 785-2994
Email: nkmehta@aol.com
Web: www.mehtaconsulting.com

Description: We are managed by a seasoned professional in the credit industry. We specialize in collections, call center management, credit risk management, and sales positions in the credit industry.

Key Contact - Specialty:
Mr. Narinder K. Mehta, President - *Credit risk management, collection operations, sales*

Salary minimum: $50,000

Functions: Generalist

Industries: Finance, Banking

MEI Int'l Search Consultants

(also known as Sales Consultants of Keene)
272 Main St
Keene, NH 03431
(603) 357-5000
Email: bob@meisearch.net
Web: www.meisearch.net

Description: We are an MRI affiliate dedicated principally to meeting the growing needs of internationally oriented businesses. Our work represents a balance of retained and contingency searches for US-based international business talent. Through our membership with MRI, we are able to use over 200 overseas offices and foreign search partners. We actively participate in searches in Latin America, Europe, and Asia.

Key Contact - Specialty:
Mr. Bob Meissner, Jr., President/General Manager - *International search and selection*
Ms. Ana Saavedra, Search Consultant - *International search and selection*
Ms. Frances Provencher-Kambour, APR, Search Consultant - *International search and selection*
Mr. Phil Tanguay, Search Consultant - *International search and selection*
Ms. Pamela Hathaway, Project Coordinator - *International search and selection*

Salary minimum: $50,000

Functions: Generalist, Int'l.

Industries: Generalist, Energy, Utilities, Mfg., Printing, Medical Devices, Transportation, Advertising, Biotech

Professional Associations: WTCA

Juan Menefee & Associates

503 S Oak Park Ave Ste 206
Oak Park, IL 60304
(708) 848-7722
Fax: (708) 848-6008
Email: jmenefee@jmarecruiter.com
Web: www.jmarecruiter.com

Description: We are a minority owned and operated, full-service search firm. We specialize in the recruitment of minority professionals.

Key Contact:
Mr. Juan F. Menefee, President

Salary minimum: $35,000

Functions: Generalist, Directors, Advertising, Sales Mgmt., Personnel, Engineering, Minorities

Industries: Generalist, Energy, Utilities, Food, Bev., Tobacco, Finance, Media, Healthcare

Networks: First Interview Network (FIN)

J M Meredith & Associates Inc

11111 E Pantano Trl
Tucson, AZ 85730
(520) 522-5855
Fax: (520) 722-9161
Email: ira@jmmeredith.com
Web: www.jmmeredith.com

Description: Twenty year old firm. Executive search in semi-conductor instrumentation and capital equipment. We will be happy to supply a list of references.

Key Contact - Specialty:
Mr. Ira Alan Marks, President/CEO - *High technology, semiconductor, capital equipment, electron beam*

Salary minimum: $100,000

Functions: Generalist

Industries: Mfg., Test, Measure Equip., Mgmt. Consulting, Software

Professional Associations: IEEE, OSA, SPIE

Meridian Executive Partners

201 Sutton Cir
Danville, CA 94506-1147
(925) 648-4448
(415) 860-3063
Fax: (925) 648-4669
Email: sandyddf@ccnet.com
Web: www.meridianep.com

Description: We are an entrepreneurial search group representing our clients to potential candidates, partners, and funding sources. We work exclusively with early stage company on senior management and company development. We offer the following services as an integrated or individual basis: executive search, funding, interim management, strategic development, and technology introductions.

Key Contact - Specialty:
Mr. Sandy Sanderson, President - *Early stage company development*
Mr. Steve Shank, Senior Partner - *Strategic development*
Mr. Charlie Dunn, Chief Financial Officer - *Financial business planning*

Salary minimum: $125,000

Functions: Senior Mgmt.

Industries: Computer Equip., Test, Measure Equip., Non-profits, Telecoms, Telephony, Digital, Wireless, Security SW

Meridian Executive Search

24 Perimeter Ctr E Ste 2416
Atlanta, GA 30346
(770) 351-0200
(800) 540-9666
Fax: (770) 351-0400
Email:
mary.wynkoop@meridianexecutivesearch.com
Web: www.meridianexecutivesearch.com

Description: Providing comprehensive search services at all management levels. Focused in healthcare, information technology and consulting, as well as entrepreneurial and early growth stage companies. Work nationally with a strong base in the Southeast. Dedicated to serving our clients and candidates with integrity.

Key Contact - Specialty:
Ms. Mary Wynkoop, Senior Vice President - *Healthcare, technology*
Ms. Teresa Unser, Vice President - *Healthcare, technology, early stage companies*

Salary minimum: $45,000

Functions: Generalist, Senior Mgmt., Middle Mgmt., Product Dev., Sales Mgmt.

Industries: Software, Healthcare

Professional Associations: ACHE, CHIM, WIT

Meridian Legal Search/Legal Temps

25 W 43rd St Ste 700
New York, NY 10036
(212) 354-9300
Fax: (212) 921-1127
Email: jberger@meridianlegal.com
Web: www.meridianlegal.com

Description: Attorney staffing, permanent & contract, organization (founded 1936)/corporate law firm, not-for-profit clients. Discreet representation of clients on a contingent or retainer basis. Computerized research and targeted recruiting of credentialed and high achieving attorney candidates at all levels resulting in an extremely high-level of client satisfaction.

Key Contact - Specialty:
Mr. Joel Berger, Esq., President - *Attorneys (permanent, temporary)*

Salary minimum: $50,000

Functions: Legal

Industries: Mfg., Finance, Services, Hospitality, Media, Packaging, Insurance, Software, Biotech, Healthcare

Professional Associations: APCNY, NALSC

Meridian Resources

1415 E Dublin-Granville Rd 208
Columbus, OH 43229
(614) 846-3124
Fax: (614) 846-3197
Email: meridianres@aol.com

Description: We are an executive search firm founded to provide services to the healthcare industry. This includes physician groups, physician practice management companies, MSOs, IPAs, integrated delivery systems, and hospitals.

Key Contact - Specialty:
Mr. Bradley McLaughlin, Executive Recruiter - *Healthcare*

Salary minimum: $60,000

Functions: Healthcare

Industries: Generalist, Healthcare

Professional Associations: MGMA

Meridian Search Inc

PO Box 1201
Parker, CO 80138
(303) 840-0312
Fax: (303) 840-7280
Email: merisearch@aol.com

Description: We specializes in the plastic packaging industry. We are national in scope and provide recruitment of sales/marketing, sales management, and manufacturing personnel.

Key Contact:
Mr. Terry McManus, CRM

Salary minimum: $25,000

Functions: Senior Mgmt., Plant Mgmt., Sales & Mktg., Sales Mgmt.

Industries: Soap, Perf., Cosmtcs., Drugs Mfg., Medical Devices, Plastics, Rubber, Motor Vehicles, Computer Equip., Consumer Elect., Misc. Mfg., Packaging

Networks: US Recruiters.com

Merit Professional Search Inc

PO Box 10
Ardmore, TN 38449
(931) 425-0100
Fax: (931) 425-0485
Email: jsmerit@bellsouth.net

Description: We work with all the major companies in the meat/poultry and food related industries. Place people in management, operations, accounting, safety, personnel, R&D, quality control, sanitation, marketing, sales, engineering and maintenance.

Key Contact - Specialty:
Mr. Jim Smitherman, President/Consultant - *Meat, poultry, food (further processed)*
Mr. Ronald Daffala, Consultant - *Meat, poultry, food (further processed)*

Salary minimum: $20,000

Functions: Generalist, Senior Mgmt., Middle Mgmt., Production, Plant Mgmt., Quality, Purchasing, Packaging

Industries: Generalist, Food, Bev., Tobacco

Merit Resource Group Inc
7950 Dublin Blvd Ste 205
Dublin, CA 94568
(925) 828-4700
Fax: (925) 828-4796
Email: info@merithr.com
Web: www.merithr.com

Description: Our focus is delivering human resource management services, this includes regular full time and contract staffing of human resources professionals. We also deliver a full spectrum of human resource consulting services.

Key Contact:
Mr. J. M. Burke, President
Ms. Cindy Kirkman, Client Service Manager
Ms. Patricia Maloney, Client Service Manager
Ms. Linda Tatum, Client Service Manager

Salary minimum: $75,000

Functions: HR Mgmt., Benefits, Personnel, Training

Industries: Generalist

Professional Associations: NCHRA, SHRM

Branches:
1290 Oakmead Pkwy Ste 105
Sunnyvale, CA 94085
(408) 732-4300
Fax: (408) 732-4388
Key Contact:
Ms. Anne Hausler, Client Service Manager
Ms. Tish Wallace, Client Service Manager

Merlin Int'l Inc
PO Box 313
Ramsey, NJ 07446
(201) 825-7220
Fax: (201) 825-1043
Email: merlin4u@verizon.net
Web: www.merlin4u.com

Description: Highly specialized firm. Devoted exclusively to all pharmaceutical and biotechnology, research and development. Clinical research physicians and staff. Pharmaceutical marketing and advertising services, domestic and international.

Key Contact - Specialty:
Mr. V. James Cinquina, Jr., President - *Physicians*
Mr. Alan Fitzpatrick, Secretary - *Medical advertising, marketing, business development*

Salary minimum: $50,000

Functions: Generalist, Physicians, Advertising, Mkt. Research, Direct Mktg., R&D

Industries: Generalist, Drugs Mfg., Pharm Svcs., Advertising, Healthcare

Professional Associations: NAER

Merraine Group Inc
254 S Main St Fl 3
New City, NY 10956
(845) 639-4900
(845) 362-4260
Fax: (845) 639-1996
Email: info@sensationaltalent.com
Web: www.sensationaltalent.com

Description: Our firm is an international executive search firm specializing in a variety of industries. In addition to recruiting, The Merraine Group has a consulting division for businesses and non-profit institutions, a training division and an on-site legal services group. We are a female owned business located approximately 45 minutes from Manhattan.

Key Contact:
Ms. Meredith J. Gantshar, President and CEO
Mr. David J. Gantshar, Managing Director
Ms. Barbara Ratner, Senior Consultant

Salary minimum: $35,000

Functions: Generalist, General Mgmt., Sales & Mktg., IT, Engineering, Non-profits

Industries: Generalist, Paper, Printing, Drugs Mfg., Medical Devices, Pharm Svcs., Publishing, Biotech, Healthcare, Hospitals, Long-term Care

Jeffrey Meryl Associates Inc
18 Fenimore Dr
Scotch Plains, NJ 07076
(908) 889-6459
Email: headhunterr@home.com

Description: We specialize in the recruitment and placement of information technology professionals in New Jersey and NYC.

Key Contact - Specialty:
Mr. David Rien, President - *Information systems*

Functions: Generalist, IT, Systems Analysis, Systems Dev., Systems Implem., Systems Support, Network Admin., DB Admin.

Industries: Generalist, Drugs Mfg., Computer Equip., Banking, Invest. Banking, Brokers, Advertising

MES Search Company
4526 Chelton Ct SE
Smyrna, GA 30080-6901
(770) 437-8222
Fax: (770) 805-0679
Email: info@messearch.com
Web: www.messearch.com

Description: Search services for manufacturing, industrial services, construction, and high-technology. Positions filled include upper and middle-level management, staff and individual level producers in engineering and sales and other significant level achievers.

Key Contact - Specialty:
Mr. James O. Cox, Managing Director - *Manufacturing, industrial services, high technology*

Salary minimum: $40,000

Functions: General Mgmt., Mfg., Materials, Sales & Mktg., HR Mgmt., Specialized Svcs., Mgmt. Consultants, Environmentalists

Industries: Construction, Mfg., Test, Measure Equip., Services, Equip Svcs., Mgmt. Consulting, New Media, Telecoms, Environmental Svcs., Haz. Waste, Non-classifiable

MetaSearch Inc
112 Spaulding Ste A
PO Box 129
San Anselmo, CA 94960
(415) 256-2900
Fax: (415) 256-2979
Email: resumes@metasearchinc.com
Web: www.metasearchinc.com

Description: We are one of the country's leading recruiting firms representing emerging growth companies in technology. We focus on one major strategic difficulty: locating the best talent to build dynamic teams.

Key Contact - Specialty:
Ms. Cathey Cotten, Managing Principal - *Database, knowledge management*
Mr. Owen Lampe, Principal - *Information technology*

Functions: Generalist, Directors, Senior Mgmt., MIS Mgmt., Systems Analysis, Systems Dev., Systems Implem., DB Admin.

Industries: Generalist, Invest. Banking, Software

MetroVantage
30101 Town Center Dr Ste 140
Laguna Niguel, CA 92677
(949) 249-8885
(800) 900-METRO
Fax: (949) 249-8886
Email: info@metrovantage.com
Web: www.metrovantage.com

Description: Our firm is a leading supplier of interim and direct staffing within the fiber optics, radio frequency, microwave, and wireless communications markets. The candidates we represent are technical, managerial, and sales.

Key Contact - Specialty:
Mr. Benson D. Garfinkle, CEO - *Technical, technical management, sales*
Ms. Gayle Garren, Vice President - *Temp, contract*
Mr. Bryan Roberts, Principal RF Staffing Consultant - *Technical*
Mr. Daniel Lozano, Director of Operations - *RF staffing*

Salary minimum: $35,000

Functions: Generalist, Middle Mgmt., Product Dev., Production, Automation, Quality, Sales Mgmt., DB Admin.

Industries: Generalist, Software

Professional Associations: CSP

Networks: Top Echelon Network

Bert M Mezo & Associates Inc
1235 Bay St Ste 1000
Toronto, ON M5R 3K4
Canada
(416) 944-0396

Description: Prompt, reliable service. Very well connected in certain markets we specialize in. Most clients have been with us for over 10 years.

Key Contact - Specialty:
Mr. Bert Mezo, President - *Sales & marketing*

Salary minimum: $50,000

Functions: Generalist, Automation, Distribution, Mkt. Research, Mktg. Mgmt., Sales Mgmt., Systems Analysis, Systems Implem.

Industries: Generalist, Medical Devices, Computer Equip., Consumer Elect., Test, Measure Equip., Telecoms

MGA Executive Search
3000 Gulf To Bay Blvd Ste 503
Clearwater, FL 33759
(727) 791-7890
(800) MGA-GRAY
Fax: (727) 724-8039
Email: clearwater@mgatechnologies.com
Web: www.mgatechnologies.com

Description: Our mission is to provide timely, high quality and cost effective contingency search services when undertaking nationwide MIS technical and managerial recruiting assignments for our clients.

Key Contact - Specialty:
Ms. Peggy Kivler, Director/MIS Placement - *Information technology*

Salary minimum: $55,000

Functions: Generalist, MIS Mgmt., Systems Analysis, Systems Dev., Systems Implem., Systems Support

Industries: Generalist, Energy, Utilities, Misc. Mfg., Finance, Aerospace, Insurance, Healthcare

MGRM Associates Ltd
32 W Burlington Ave Ste 1B
Westmont, IL 60559
(630) 724-9458
Fax: (630) 852-1309
Email: logrecruiter@earthlink.net

Description: We specialize in all areas of logistics including senior management, international, business development, supply chain, third party, for hire carriers, rail, distribution, and project management.

Key Contact - Specialty:
Mr. Terrence R. McDorman, President - *Logistics, transportation, for hire carriers*

Salary minimum: $65,000

Functions: Generalist, Distribution

Industries: Generalist, Transportation

Professional Associations: CLM

MH Executive Search Group
35246 US Hwy 19 N 108
Palm Harbor, FL 34684-1931
(727) 442-2011
(727) 641-7120
Email: pkgjobs@mhgroup.com
Web: www.mhgroup.com

Description: We recruit qualified individuals in the packaging and flexographic industries in sales, marketing, plant and management personnel. Recently relocated to the Tampa area from the Dallas area, our firm has company researchers in Palm Harbor, Dallas, St. Louis, and Cincinnati. We have been recruiting nationally since 1978.

Key Contact - Specialty:
Mr. Mike Hochwalt, Senior Vice President - *Packaging, flexographics-sales & marketing managers*
Mr. Lee Walt, Recruiter - *BSME's, marketing, ISO 9000, quality managers, industrial marketplace*

Salary minimum: $60,000

Functions: Generalist, General Mgmt., Senior Mgmt., Plant Mgmt., Packaging, Sales & Mktg.

Industries: Generalist, Paper, Printing, Plastics, Rubber, Packaging

Professional Associations: IOPP, SERC

John Michael Personnel Group Inc
PO Box 4437
Chattanooga, TN 37405
(423) 756-6544
Fax: (423) 266-5334
Email: johnmichael@mindspring.com
Web: www.johnmichaelpersonnel.com

Description: We are a national executive search firm strictly specializing in the placement of purchasing, materials management, and logistics professionals.

Key Contact:
Mr. John J. Zoboro, Founder

Functions: Materials, Purchasing

Industries: Mfg.

Michael Thomas Inc
(also known as MTIsearch)
3360 Tremont Rd
Upper Arlington, OH 43221
(614) 273-0926
Email: mtisearch@aol.com
Web: www.mtisearch.com

Description: Central Ohio's oldest and largest specialist in information technology recruiting.

Key Contact - Specialty:
Mr. Thomas Joswick, President - *Information technology*

Salary minimum: $50,000

Functions: Generalist, MIS Mgmt., Systems Analysis, Systems Dev., Systems Implem., Systems Support, Network Admin., DB Admin.

Industries: Generalist, Energy, Utilities, Banking, Misc. Financial, Insurance, Software

Michael Wayne Recruiters
59 St Mary's Ln
Lindenhurst, IL 60046
(847) 245-7100
Fax: (847) 245-7199
Email: mwrecruit@aol.com
Web: www.michaelwaynerecruiters.com

Description: Full range of services; preferred client status; national contacts in retail, food service, manufacturing and wholesale food segments.

Key Contact - Specialty:
Mr. Irwin Goldman, President - *Wholesale (food companies), retail (food companies)*

Salary minimum: $35,000

Functions: Generalist

Industries: Food, Bev., Tobacco, Wholesale, Retail

Michael/Merrill
PO Box 7509
Shawnee Mission, KS 66207
(877) 341-6072
Fax: (913) 383-2962

Description: A full-service search firm.

Key Contact - Specialty:
Mr. Wilson M. Liggett - *Generalist*

Salary minimum: $25,000

Functions: Generalist

Industries: Mfg., Transportation, Finance, Services, Packaging, Software

Robert Michaels & Associates Inc
8417 Raintree Ln
Charlotte, NC 28277
(704) 544-2822
Fax: (704) 541-8088
Email: peter.lass@rmichaels.com

Description: Executive search and recruiting consultants within the continental United States. Special emphasis areas include healthcare, financial and retail executive management.

Key Contact:
Mr. Peter Lass, President & Managing Partner

Salary minimum: $50,000

Functions: Generalist, General Mgmt.

Industries: Generalist, Consumer Elect., Retail, Finance, Mgmt. Consulting, Advertising, Healthcare

Michaels & Moere
PO Box 728
Roscoe, IL 61073
(815) 623-6888
Fax: (815) 623-3848
Email: search@michaels-moere.com
Web: www.michaels-moere.com

Description: We work most disciplines (general management, operations, materials, sales/marketing, engineering) within consumer durable goods companies (housewares, hardware, appliances, etc) in the USA.

Key Contact - Specialty:
Mr. Michael R. Smith, Principal - *Operations, manufacturing, engineering, materials*
Ms. Linda A. Moere, Principal - *Sales, marketing*

Salary minimum: $50,000

Functions: Generalist

Industries: Plastics, Rubber, Machine, Appliance, Consumer Elect.

Networks: Top Echelon Network

Lou Michaels Associates Inc
1230 E Columbia Ave
Battle Creek, MI 49014
(616) 965-1486
Fax: (616) 965-2232
Email: lma@lmasearch.com
Web: www.lmasearch.com

Description: Engineering and industrial management personnel/manufacturing industries, automotive, plastics, foundry, die cast, metal working, aerospace, electronics, machining, metal fabrication, stamping, primary metals, medical plastics and automotive plastics.

Key Contact - Specialty:
Mr. Lou Michaels, President - *Machining, foundry, diecast, metal stamping*
Mr. Bill Roth, Industrial Recruiter - *Plastics, rubber, metal stampings, foundry, food-bev*
Mr. John Craig, Recruiter - *Manufacturing position automotive,*

Salary minimum: $35,000

Functions: General Mgmt., Mfg., Materials, Sales & Mktg., HR Mgmt., Finance

Industries: Plastics, Rubber, Metal Products, Machine, Appliance, Motor Vehicles, Misc. Mfg., Aerospace, Packaging

Professional Associations: AFS, MAPS, NFIB

Networks: Top Echelon Network

Joseph Michaels Inc
582 Market St 910
San Francisco, CA 94104
(415) 732-6142
(800) 786-1099
Fax: (415) 434-1165
Email: jpelayo@josephmichaels.com
Web: www.josephmichaels.com

Description: We are the name to know in accounting. We perform temporary and permanent accounting placement from accounting manager to CFO nationwide

Key Contact - Specialty:
Mr. Joe Pelayo, CPC, President - *Accounting, finance*
Mr. Dennis Billingsley, CPC, Vice President-Recruiting - *Accounting, finance*

Salary minimum: $30,000

Functions: Generalist, CFO's, Budgeting, Cash Mgmt., Credit, Taxes, M&A, Risk Mgmt.

Industries: Generalist, Misc. Mfg., Misc. Financial, Accounting, Real Estate, Software, Biotech

Professional Associations: IMA, NAER, NAPS

E J Michaels Ltd
2 Madison Ave Ste 201
Larchmont, NY 10538
(914) 833-1700
(800) 333-2999
Email: ejmsearch@aol.com
Web: www.ejmichaels.com

Description: Physician recruiting for hospitals, HMOs, general practices, corporate needs, pharmaceutical firms, individual practices.

Recruiting for domestic and int'l pharmaceutical firms.

Key Contact - Specialty:
Mr. Phillip E. Jacobs, Ph.D., President - *Physicians, healthcare*

Functions: Generalist, Physicians, Nurses, Health Admin., MIS Mgmt., Systems Analysis, Mgmt. Consultants

Industries: Generalist, Mgmt. Consulting, Healthcare

Professional Associations: NAPR

Micro Staff Solutions Inc
3201 Pinehurst Dr
Plano, TX 75075-1760
(972) 612-0075
Fax: (972) 612-0025
Email: mbenum@mstaff.com
Web: www.mstaff.com

Description: An executive search firm that specializes in the placement of high-tech professionals in a variety of industries. We place in both permanent and contract positions. We place both technical, sales and sales support personnel.

Key Contact - Specialty:
Ms. Michele S. Benum, CPC, CEO/President - *Data processing, telecommunications, sales, information technology*
Ms. Gina Lawrence, EVP/General Manager - *Data processing, telecommunications, information technology*

Salary minimum: $30,000

Functions: Middle Mgmt., Sales & Mktg., Sales Mgmt., MIS Mgmt., Systems Analysis, Systems Implem., Systems Support, Mgmt. Consultants

Industries: Mgmt. Consulting, Software

Professional Associations: AITP, DPMA

Mid-America Placement Service Inc
1941 S 42nd St Ste 520
Omaha, NE 68105-2945
(402) 341-3338
Fax: (402) 341-6266
Email: jobs@nejobs.net
Web: www.nejobs.net

Description: We specialize in nationwide recruitment, screening and placement of experienced professionals. We pride ourselves in our professional approach and service both applicants and companies. Our reputation has been impeccable in the industry.

Key Contact - Specialty:
Mr. Ron Distransky, President - *Sales, sales management*
Mr. John Glantz, Recruiter Consultant - *Technical sales, industrial sales*

Salary minimum: $18,000

Functions: Generalist, Sales & Mktg., Sales Mgmt., HR Mgmt., Finance, IT, Engineering

Industries: Generalist, Computer Equip., Retail, Finance, Services, Media, Insurance

Midas Management Inc
508 Westport Ave
Norwalk, CT 06851
(203) 750-8243
(203) 750-8240
Fax: (203) 750-8241
Email: mmsearch@midasmgt.com
Web: www.midasmgt.com

Description: We have always specialized in the placement of all levels of sales, sales support and executives in the computer software and hardware industry.

Key Contact - Specialty:
Mr. Joel Berger, Consultant - *Computer software & hardware sales management, sales representatives, information technology professionals*

Salary minimum: $70,000

Functions: Sales Mgmt., IT

Industries: Software

Midland Consultants
(a division of Century Business Services)
4401 Rockside Rd Ste 214
Independence, OH 44131
(216) 447-1557
Fax: (216) 447-6035
Email: midland@midlandconsultants.com
Web: www.midlandconsultants.com

Description: Servicing the entire rubber, plastic, adhesive and packaging industries from sales through technical staffing. Specialties also include information systems and metal chip cutting.

Key Contact - Specialty:
Mr. Ron Eliason, Vice President - *Rubber, plastics, adhesives*

Functions: Generalist, General Mgmt., Mfg., Materials, Sales & Mktg., IT, R&D, Engineering

Industries: Generalist, Printing, Chemicals, Plastics, Rubber, Paints, Petro. Products, Metal Products, Packaging

Networks: National Personnel Assoc (NPA)

Midwest Recruiters Inc
1600 W 40 Hwy Ste 206
Blue Springs, MO 64015
(816) 224-3070
Email: admin@foodheadhunters.com
Web: www.foodheadhunters.com

Key Contact - Specialty:
Mr. Bob Leckbee, President - *Manufacturing*

Salary minimum: $40,000

Functions: Directors

Industries: Mfg.

Networks: Top Echelon Network

J Miles Personnel Services
3029 E Sunshine Ste A
Springfield, MO 65804
(417) 882-5585
Fax: (417) 882-0656
Email: jmiles@jmiles.com
Web: www.jmiles.com

Description: We are an independently owned and highly selective recruiting and placement firm specializing in the nationwide search, recruitment and placement of professionals in engineering, technical and manufacturing management positions within the food manufacturing and consumer products industries.

Key Contact:
Ms. Jean Miles, Owner
Ms. Julie Alexander, Recruiter/Manager

Functions: Generalist

Industries: Mfg., Food, Bev., Tobacco, Chemicals, Soap, Perf., Cosmtcs., Drugs Mfg., Medical Devices, Wholesale, Retail

Professional Associations: IFT, MAPS

Networks: Inter-City Personnel Assoc (IPA)

Military Transition Group
PO Box 2310
Alpharetta, GA 30023-2310
(770) 740-2393
Fax: (770) 740-8693

Email: info@careercommandpost.com
Web: www.careercommandpost.com

Description: Our firm helps employers recruit transitioning military personnel and armed forces veterans that possess special experience, skills, and training of value in the civilian workplace. The occupations served include engineering, information technology, manufacturing, defense contracting, and skilled trades.

Key Contact - Specialty:
Mr. Bill Thomas, Senior Partner - *Engineering, IT, manufacturing, trades*

Functions: Generalist, Middle Mgmt.

Industries: Energy, Utilities, Construction, Mfg., Finance, Services, Hospitality, Communications, Software, Biotech, Healthcare

The Millenia Group Inc
6 Venture Ste 100
Irvine, CA 92618
(949) 851-0000
Fax: (949) 851-0001
Email: rh@themilleniagroup.com
Web: www.themilleniagroup.com

Description: We are a retained, boutique firm specializing in senior-level and mid-management finance and human resources placement with expertise in the high technology sector, for example: broadband, semiconductors, network access, wireless communications, etc.

Key Contact - Specialty:
Mr. Martin Foxman, Principal - *CFO, controller, VP, human resources*
Ms. Rhonda Hamade, Consultant - *Controller, senior level (treasury, tax, finance)*

Salary minimum: $75,000

Professional Associations: SHRM

Millennial Group
925 Executive Park Dr D
Salt Lake City, UT 84117
(801) 265-8055
Email: admin@millennialgroup.com
Web: www.millennialgroup.com

Description: High Tech Search Firm specializing in the Optics, Electro-optics, Photonic, Electronic and Telecommunications Industry

Key Contact - Specialty:
Ms. Diana Cropper, CPC, President/CEO - *Optics*

Functions: Generalist

Industries: Medical Devices, Electronic, Elec. Components, Digital, Fiber Optic, Government, Defense, Aerospace, Packaging, Industry Specific SW, Biotech

Professional Associations: NAPS

Millennium Technology Solutions
5825 Glenridge Dr Ste 101
Bldg 3
Atlanta, GA 30328
(404) 250-6514
Fax: (404) 843-9344
Email: careers@milltechsolution.com
Web: www.milltechsolution.com

Description: Our firm specializes in the permanent placement of all aspects of IT, pharmaceutical, and biotechnical professionals. We are a small organization offering personal attention, with the capacity to source outstanding professionals locally, across the nation, and internationally. The majority of recruiters in the company have been in the industry for several years in most aspects of technical and pharmaceutical recruitment.

Key Contact:
Mr. Arty Antoniades

Functions: Generalist

Industries: Chemicals, Drugs Mfg., Medical Devices, Electronic, Elec. Components, Pharm Svcs., E-commerce, Communications, Environmental Svcs., Software, Biotech

Professional Associations: GAPS

Miller & Associates
201 E Kennedy Blvd Ste 950
Tampa, FL 33602
(813) 224-9658
Fax: (813) 221-7491

Description: We specialize exclusively in legal search, assisting law firms and corporations in associate, partner and in-house corporate placements.

Key Contact - Specialty:
Ms. Dixie Miller, Owner - *Attorneys*

Functions: Legal

Industries: Legal

Miller & Associates Inc
9036 NW 37th St
Polk City, IA 50226
(888) 965-2727
(515) 965-5727
Email: millagsrch@aol.com
Web: www.ag-careers.com

Description: We recruit quality candidates and list employment opportunities in the agriculture industry. We assist job placement in a variety of areas including agronomy, seed, feed, petroleum, animal health, grain, and agricultural accounting.

Key Contact - Specialty:
Mr. Roger Miller, President - *Agriculture*

Berry Miller Inc
144 N 44th St Ste 200
Lincoln, NE 68503
(402) 434-0460
Fax: (402) 434-0462
Email: mail@berrysrp.com
Web: www.berrysrp.com

Description: We recruit nationally only in administration, management and advanced practice nurses in maternal/child and women's ambulatory service arena.

Key Contact - Specialty:
Ms. Debra Berry Miller, President - *Administration, maternal & child service, nursing*
Mr. Mike Miller, Vice President - *Administration, maternal & child service, nursing*
Mr. Lyle Working, Assistant Vice President - *Administrative, maternal/child service, nursing*
Mr. John Fritts, Assistant Vice President - *Administrative, maternal/child service, nursing*
Mrs. Wilma Malcom, Recruiter - *Administrative, maternal/child service, nursing*
Ms. Kathy Schultz, Office Manager - *Administrative, maternal/child services, nursing*

Salary minimum: $50,000

Functions: Generalist, Health Admin.

Industries: Healthcare, Hospitals, Women's

Professional Associations: AONE, AWHONN, NANN, NAWH

Miller Jones Inc
13101 Preston Rd Ste 300
Dallas, TX 75240
(972) 239-5322
Fax: (972) 239-7060
Email: jjm@aepnet.com

Description: Miller Jones is the #1 direct recruiter in the world. The firm does in excess of 100

placements annually, nationally and internationally. High-level,(president, etc.) retained director-level and below are fee contingent. The firm is six years old and has an excellent reputation and references.

Key Contact:
Mr. John Moffett
Mr. Mike Nunally

Salary minimum: $80,000

Functions: Directors, Senior Mgmt., Sales & Mktg., Mkt. Research, Mktg. Mgmt., Sales Mgmt., Direct Mktg., HR Mgmt., Systems Implem., Network Admin.

Industries: Generalist, Software

Miller Personnel Consultants Inc
931 E 86th St Ste 103
Indianapolis, IN 46240
(317) 251-5938
Fax: (317) 251-5762
Email: markmiller@netdirect.net
Web: www.millerpersonnel.com

Description: We provide confidential search/placement within automotive and other metals related industry. We offer direct, hands-on experience in many areas of engineering and manufacturing management. I am a BSIE from GMI. We recruit primarily BSME, EE, IE, and technology degrees. We belong to a national and overseas network affiliates. We charge no fees to candidates. We primarily work with salaries in the $55,000 to $75,000 range.

Key Contact - Specialty:
Mr. Mark Miller, President - *Engineering, manufacturing management*

Functions: Engineering

Industries: Motor Vehicles, Consumer Elect., Test, Measure Equip.

Professional Associations: IAPS

Networks: National Personnel Assoc (NPA)

Miller-Collins Associates Inc
4507 Furling Ln Ste 206
Destin, FL 32541
(850) 650-4704
Fax: (850) 650-4706
Email: tmearhart@seii.net

Description: National financial and banking executive recruiters. Specializing in commercial finance.

Key Contact - Specialty:
Mrs. Sherry Miller-Collins, President
Ms. Teresa Earhart, MBA, Professional Recruiter - *Banking, financial services*

Salary minimum: $40,000

Functions: Finance

Industries: Finance, Banking, Accounting

Miller.Miller LLC
PO Box 3088
Kirkland, WA 98083
(425) 822-3145
(800) 820-1055
Fax: (425) 827-9194
Email: info@millermiller.com
Web: www.millermiller.com

Description: We represent biotechnology, medical device and pharmaceutical companies ranging from start-ups to major international corporations. We place individuals in senior management, marketing, research, product development, quality assurance, regulatory and clinical affairs, and manufacturing positions.

Key Contact - Specialty:
Ms. Shirley M. Miller, President - *Biotechnology, medical products*

Functions: Generalist, Senior Mgmt., Middle Mgmt., Product Dev., Quality, Mkt. Research, Mktg. Mgmt., R&D

Industries: Generalist, Biotech

Miller/Davis & Associates Inc
60 E 42nd St Ste 1440
New York, NY 10165
(212) 682-8144
Fax: (212) 682-8218
Email: millerdavis@msn.com
Web: www.millerdavisny.com

Description: Specialists in corporate banking/finance positions, analyst/associate to senior management; credit/lending in structured finance, asset securitization/mortgaged-backed finance, project/public finance, international, Fortune 500, middle market, etc., in the New York metropolitan area.

Key Contact - Specialty:
Ms. Suzanne M. Johnson, President - *Corporate banking, corporate finance*

Salary minimum: $50,000

Functions: Finance, M&A

Industries: Finance, Banking, Invest. Banking

Danette Milne Corporate Search Inc
4981 Hwy 7 E Unit 12A Ste 205
Markham, ON L3R 1N1
Canada
(905) 410-1814
Fax: (905) 426-2552
Email: dmcs@sprint.ca

Key Contact:
Ms. Danette Milne, Owner - *Human resources, finance, information technology, marketing*
Ms. Carole Milne, Associate - *Administration, engineering*
Ms. Evette Milne, Associate - *Support, sales*
Ms. Monique Peebles, Associate

Salary minimum: $30,000

Functions: Generalist, Production, Materials Plng., Sales Mgmt., Personnel, Budgeting, Systems Analysis

Industries: Generalist

Minority Executive Search Inc
2490 Lee Blvd Ste 301
PO Box 18063
Cleveland, OH 44118
(216) 932-2022
Fax: (216) 932-7988
Email: info@minorityexecsearch.com
Web: www.minorityexecsearch.com

Description: Specializing in female and minority job placements nationwide in the following fields information systems, engineering (chem, EE, ME, civil, etc.), sales/marketing, human resources, finance/accounting, purchasing, operations & legal.

Key Contact:
Mr. Eral Burks, President

Salary minimum: $50,000

Functions: Minorities

Industries: Generalist

Professional Associations: BDPA, NABA, NBMBAA, NSBA, NSHMBA

Networks: Top Echelon Network

MIS Computer Professionals Inc
5104 Foxridge Dr Ste 1A
Mission, KS 66202
(913) 384-3056
Fax: (913) 384-9516
Email: ncapps@cpnotes.com
Web: www.cpnotes.com

Description: We specialize in IT placements and contracting nationally and internationally. We place emphasis on software developers, package implementers, database administrators, software implementers, programmers/analysts, CIOs, and system programmers. The skill areas that we work with are B2B, B2C, Ariba, CommerceOne, Java, EJB, WML, WAP, XML, i2, SAP, Oracle, telephony, and PeopleSoft.

Key Contact - Specialty:
Mr. Norm Capps, President - *Client/server, computer (software)*

Salary minimum: $60,000

Functions: Generalist, MIS Mgmt., Systems Analysis, Systems Dev., Systems Implem., Systems Support, Network Admin., DB Admin.

Industries: Generalist, Misc. Financial, Mgmt. Consulting, Telecoms, Software

Networks: National Personnel Assoc (NPA)

MIS Technical Staffing Inc
8951 Eastman Dr
Tampa, FL 33626
(813) 926-7651
Fax: (813) 926-7671
Email: mdavidson@mistechstaff.com
Web: www.mistechstaff.com

Description: Our firm is primarily targeted at recruiting technical professionals for permanent positions in Central Florida.

Key Contact:
Mr. Michael Davidson, President

Salary minimum: $30,000

Functions: IT

Industries: Generalist

Professional Associations: ASA

Paul Misarti Inc
327 Kilburn Rd S
Garden City, NY 11530-5311
(516) 486-1497
Email: pmisarti@pmcareers.com
Web: www.pmcareers.com

Description: Over 240 search assignments have been completed in the field of information technology. These positions have been in executive management, project management, product management, applications development, systems engineering, technical support, sales, marketing, and consulting.

Key Contact - Specialty:
Mr. Paul R. Misarti, President/CEO - *Banking, securities, information technology managers, business applications solutions providers*

Salary minimum: $75,000

Functions: Senior Mgmt., Middle Mgmt., Sales Mgmt., MIS Mgmt., Systems Analysis, Systems Dev., Systems Implem., Systems Support, Network Admin., DB Admin.

Industries: Computer Equip., Finance, Banking, Invest. Banking, Brokers, Misc. Financial, Services, Mgmt. Consulting, E-commerce, IT Implementation, Media, New Media, Communications, Call Centers, Digital, Network Infrastructure, Insurance, Software, Database SW, Development SW, Doc. Mgmt., Production SW, Security SW, System SW

The Mitchell Group
4 Woodhaven Dr
New City, NY 10956
(845) 638-2700
Fax: (845) 708-6035
Email: information@kennethmitchell.com
Web: www.kennethmitchell.com

Description: We have 21 years of experience in recruiting actuaries and consultants, within the life insurance, health insurance, employee benefit retirement, health and welfare, and compensation and benefit communication fields.

Key Contact:
Mr. Ken Mitchell, President

Functions: Generalist, General Mgmt., Senior Mgmt., Middle Mgmt., Sales Mgmt., Benefits, Specialized Svcs., Mgmt. Consultants

Industries: Energy, Utilities, Finance, Misc. Financial, HR Services, Insurance, Healthcare

MJF Associates
49 Northford Rd
PO Box 132
Wallingford, CT 06492
(203) 284-9878
Fax: (203) 284-9871
Email: mjf@mail.imcinternet.net
Web: www.imcinternet.net/mjf

Description: Professional and technical search and placement firm. Clients are nationwide. Accent is industrial, hi-tech, electronic, computer, mechanical, electrical, with sales, marketing, management, engineering and executive search disciplines.

Key Contact - Specialty:
Mr. Matt Furman, President - *Sales & marketing, engineering, professional/technical requirement, executive search, management*

Salary minimum: $30,000

Functions: Generalist

Industries: Generalist

Professional Associations: CAPS

MLA Resources Inc
PO Box 35115
Tulsa, OK 74153-0115
(918) 877-3202
Fax: (918) 877-3203
Email: mikeayling@mlaresources.com
Web: www.mlaresources.com

Description: Executive and technical recruitment worldwide for the upstream oil and gas industry.

Key Contact - Specialty:
Mr. Michael L. Ayling, President - *Upstream oil & gas*

Functions: Generalist, General Mgmt., Directors, Senior Mgmt., Middle Mgmt., Production, Technicians

Industries: Energy, Utilities

MLB Associates
110 Main St Ste 301
Lake Placid, NY 12946
(518) 523-2371
Fax: (518) 523-9011
Email: info@mlbassociates.com
Web: www.mlbassociates.com

Description: Our firm provides executive search services to corporations and organizations that value customer information as a strategic marketing resource. We pride ourselves on our understanding of this dynamic force in interactive marketing and build long-term relationships by thoroughly understanding our client's business and the qualifications for senior staff positions.

Key Contact - Specialty:
Ms. Robin Anthony, Director of Client Services - *Direct marketing, integrated marketing*
Ms. MaryLou Brown, President - *Relationship marketing*

Salary minimum: $65,000

Functions: Direct Mktg.

Industries: Generalist

Professional Associations: AIM, AMA, CIMA, DMA, NYNMA, RON

MMW Intl
PO Box 1116
Danville, CA 94526
(925) 838-9163
Fax: (925) 215-2429
Email: marie@mmwi.com
Web: www.mmwi.com

Description: Our firm is an executive search and technical recruiting firm. MMW has been set up to provide a highly specialized and tailored recruitment service to the information technology industry. Our business is based on solid IT industry knowledge and experience, combined with business and recruitment skills.

Key Contact:
Ms. Marie Minder, President

Salary minimum: $75,000

Functions: MIS Mgmt.

Industries: Generalist

Professional Associations: IEEE, SHRM, WIT

Modicom
1072 S De Anza Blvd Ste 339
San Jose, CA 95129
(408) 873-7100
Fax: (408) 873-7101
Email: tony@modicom.com
Web: www.modicom.com

Description: Our firm is an executive search firm specializing in the placement of software engineers and developers in the Silicon Valley/Northern California.

Key Contact - Specialty:
Mr. Tony Zammikiel, Manager - *Software developer*
Mr. Blair Gibbs, Sr Technical Recruiter - *Software developer*

Functions: IT

Industries: Software, Database SW, Development SW, HR SW, Marketing SW, Networking, Comm. SW, System SW

Diedre Moire Corp Inc
510 Horizon Ctr
Robbinsville, NJ 08691
(609) 584-9000
Fax: (609) 584-9575
Email: smr@diedremoire.com
Web: www.diedremoire.com

Description: Retainer quality search without the retainer. We have successfully concluded over 2000 searches nationwide. We love searching for those highly technical professionals which others shy away from.

Key Contact:
Mr. Stephen M. Reuning, CPC, President
Ms. Cynthia Angelini, Assistant to President
Ms. Nicole Bakos, Information Services Engineer
Mr. Laurence Chiaravallo, Group Leader - *Biomedical, biopharmaceutical*
Mr. Scott Shanes, Consultant - *Biotechnology*
Ms. Megan McCullough, Data Warehousing Group Leader - *IT, data warehousing*

Mr. Stephen Casano, Group Leader - *Neuroscience, biotech*

Mr. Bryan Grossman, Consultant - *Molecular biology*

Ms. Cynthia Alznauer, Consultant - *Automation, new pharmaceuticals*

Mr. David Eide, Group Leader - *Information technology*

Mr. Gregory Foss, Group Leader - *Insurance*

Mr. Winston Reuning, Information Coordinator

Functions: Generalist

Industries: Mfg., Medical Devices, Test, Measure Equip., Venture Cap., Pharm Svcs., New Media, Telecoms, Insurance, Software, Biotech

Professional Associations: AAAS, ATLA, AWRA, CAS, ISPE, MAAPC, NAER, NSWMA, NWWA, PDA, RAPS, SHRM, WEO, YEO

The Moisson Group Inc
701 W Pipeline Rd Ste 5
Hurst, TX 76053
(817) 268-0747
Fax: (817) 268-0776
Email: corcas1@aol.com

Description: The firm specializes in recruiting executives working in the investment management arena. This includes sales and marketing executives, consultants, and portfolio managers. Our clients include firms providing asset management services to corporations, endowments, foundations, pension funds, and individuals.

Key Contact - Specialty:
Mr. Casey M. Corrie, President - *Qualified retirement plans, asset management*

Salary minimum: $75,000

Functions: Sales Mgmt.

Industries: Banking, Invest. Banking, Marketing SW

Molecular Solutions Inc
412 Carolina Blvd
Isle of Palms, SC 29451-2113
(843) 886-8775
Email: mambos@molsol.com
Web: www.molsol.com

Description: With over twenty years' experience in pharmaceutical research, we are the only executive search firm which can leverage technical expertise and industry contacts to effectively locate qualified computational scientists.

Key Contact - Specialty:
Mr. Allen Richon, President - *R&D scientists*
Ms. Merry Ambos, Vice President - *R&D scientists*

Salary minimum: $80,000

Functions: Generalist, Directors, Senior Mgmt., Middle Mgmt., MIS Mgmt., Systems Dev., DB Admin., R&D

Industries: Generalist, Pharm Svcs., Biotech

Professional Associations: AAAS

Monarch Technology Management LLC
9030 Troon Way
Colorado Springs, CO 80920
(719) 533-0920
(800) 779-6338
Fax: (719) 533-0970
Email: monarch@monarchtech.com
Web: www.monarchtech.com

Description: We focus on technical and sales positions in software and technology companies and IBM mainframe specialty positions.

Key Contact - Specialty:
Mr. Richard P. Nashleanas - *Data processing*

Salary minimum: $45,000

Functions: Sales Mgmt., IT

Industries: Generalist, Software

The Montgomery Group Inc
PO Box 30791
Knoxville, TN 37930-0791
(865) 693-0325
Fax: (865) 691-1900
Email: tmg@tmgincknox.com
Web: www.tmgincknox.com

Description: We serve as consultants to agri-business and the food industry on a worldwide basis. Emphasis on recruiting the right person for the position. We have industry experience.

Key Contact - Specialty:
Mr. Larry. Suchomski, Executive Vice President/COO - *Agribusiness, food industry management, sales, operations*

Salary minimum: $35,000

Functions: Generalist, Senior Mgmt., Plant Mgmt., Distribution, Mktg. Mgmt., Personnel, CFO's, R&D

Industries: Generalist, Agri., Forestry, Mining, Food, Bev., Tobacco

Montgomery Resources Inc
555 Montgomery St Ste 1650
San Francisco, CA 94111
(415) 956-4242
Email: montres@montres.com
Web: www.montres.com

Description: Recruitment of finance and accounting professionals for middle-management positions.

Key Contact:
Mr. Roger A. Lee, Partner
Mr. Thomas K. McAteer, Partner

Salary minimum: $45,000

Functions: Finance

Industries: Generalist, Mfg., Retail, Finance, Services, Communications, Real Estate, Software

Professional Associations: AAFA

Montgomery, Thomason & Associates
53 Village Ctr Pl Ste 203
Mississauga, ON L4Z 1V9
Canada
(905) 896-7103
Fax: (905) 566-0177
Email: thomason@compuserve.com

Description: We recruit technical people who enjoy working in sales, marketing, research engineering and production.

Key Contact - Specialty:
Mr. Ronald Thomason, Partner - *Technical, production, research, engineering*
Ms. Nancy Thomason, Partner - *Technical, sales & marketing*

Salary minimum: $50,000

Functions: Generalist

Industries: Chemicals, Plastics, Rubber, Paints, Petro. Products, Metal Products, Misc. Mfg., Environmental Svcs.

The Monticello Group
(also known as MRI of Charlottesville)
675 Peter Jefferson Pkwy Ste 290
Charlottesville, VA 22911
(434) 817-5300
Fax: (434) 817-5310
Email: banda@mr-monticello.com
Web: www.mr-monticello.com

Key Contact:
Mr. Bill Anda
Ms. Stevia Anda

C A Moore & Associates Inc
15500 Wayzata Blvd Ste 803C
800 Twelve Oaks Ctr
Wayzata, MN 55391
(952) 473-0990
Fax: (952) 473-7080
Email: camoore@qwest.net
Web: www.camoore.net

Description: Principal has been in search business since 1967; our firm has experience that few others have. Strong network of contacts. We take the time to do the job well - even when working on a contingent search.

Key Contact - Specialty:
Ms. Connie Moore, CPC, President - *Insurance, risk management, financial services, generalist, direct marketing*

Salary minimum: $50,000

Functions: Generalist

Industries: Finance, Banking, Invest. Banking, Brokers, Misc. Financial, Services, HR Services, Law Enforcement, Insurance

Professional Associations: INS, NIRA

Larry Moore & Associates
11474 Sandpiper Way
Penn Valley, CA 95946
(530) 432-8490
Fax: (781) 623-5550
Email: larrymoore@thegrid.net

Description: I have been recruiting information system professionals since 1979 with emphasis in Northern California.

Key Contact - Specialty:
Mr. Larry W. Moore, President - *Information systems*

Functions: Generalist, IT, Systems Analysis, Systems Dev., Systems Implem., Systems Support, Network Admin., DB Admin.

Industries: Generalist, Software

Networks: Top Echelon Network

James Moore & Associates
90 New Montgomery St Ste 412
San Francisco, CA 94105
(415) 392-3933
Fax: (415) 896-0931
Email: info@jamesmoore.com
Web: www.jamesmoore.com

Description: Our search firm has thirteen years of experience in delivering well qualified computer professionals to a diverse mix of Bay area client companies.

Key Contact - Specialty:
Mr. Leslie Fenyves, Director - *Software engineering, information technology*

Salary minimum: $45,000

Functions: Generalist, MIS Mgmt., Systems Analysis, Systems Dev., Systems Implem., Systems Support, Network Admin., DB Admin.

Industries: Generalist, Computer Equip., Finance, Software, Biotech, Healthcare

Moran & Associates
1 Edgell Rd Ste 9
1 Framingham Ctr
Framingham, MA 01701
(508) 875-6025
Email: jobs@moranassoc.com
Web: www.moranassoc.com

Description: We specialize in the recruitment and placement of tax, accounting and financial professionals. Our target placements have a base salary ranging from $40,000 to $125,000+, plus incentives; within industries ranging from Fortune 100 to small venture backed start-ups; in companies located in New Hampshire, Massachusetts and Rhode Island.

Key Contact - Specialty:
Mr. Dennis Moran, Managing Director - *Accounting*

Salary minimum: $85,000

Functions: Finance, Taxes

Industries: Generalist

Mordue, Allen, Roberts, Bonney Ltd
PO Box 450
Gig Harbor, WA 98335
(253) 851-5355
Fax: (253) 851-7969
Email: mordue@marbl.com

Description: Recruiting and placement for engineers, managers, directors, vice presidents specializing in the software, electronic and other high-tech industries. Nationwide services with special recognition to Rockies and Pacific Northwest.

Key Contact - Specialty:
Mr. Michael J. Mordue, President - *Software, high technology*
Ms. Sheila A. Schultz, Vice President - *Software (engineers, managers)*

Salary minimum: $60,000

Functions: MIS Mgmt., Systems Analysis, Systems Dev., R&D, Engineering

Industries: Medical Devices, Computer Equip., Test, Measure Equip., Software

Networks: National Personnel Assoc (NPA)

More Personnel Services Inc
3016 Spring Hill Pkwy Ste D
Smyrna, GA 30080-4712
(770) 803-9332
Fax: (770) 801-0541
Email: morepersonnel@aol.com
Web: www.job-morepersonnel.com

Description: We specialize in placing experienced college graduates in sales, marketing, and management training positions within Fortune 500 companies. We prefer that resumes be sent to us by fax along with a detailed cover letter.

Key Contact:
Ms. Linda K. Moore

Functions: General Mgmt., Sales & Mktg.

Industries: Generalist

Professional Associations: GAPS, WBOA

Morency Associates
301 Newbury St 242
Danvers, MA 01923
(978) 750-4460
Fax: (978) 750-4465
Email: mmorency@aol.com

Description: Providing very personal search and recruitment services to national and international companies.

Key Contact - Specialty:
Ms. Marcia Morency, President - *Sales & marketing management*

Salary minimum: $30,000

Functions: Middle Mgmt., Sales & Mktg.

Industries: Generalist, Media, Advertising, Publishing, New Media, Telecoms, Software

MoreTech Consulting
412 Delaware Ave
Wilmington, DE 19803
(302) 478-6595
Email: bill@moretechconsulting.com
Web: www.moretechconsulting.com

Description: We believe in having adequate recruiting bandwidth in place when the attention focuses on hiring is essential to a corporation's success. MoreTech Consulting has developed a tried and proven methodology to help our clients achieve their hiring goals. Through our relationship-based approach, we learn the drivers behind our client's hiring needs and the selling features of our client's employment opportunity. This allows us to bring the most suitable candidates to the table in a timely manner.

Key Contact:
Mr. Willard Ashmore, President
Mr. Eric Rupert, Vice President - *Business development*
Mr. Richard Collins, Principal Technical Recruiter

Salary minimum: $50,000

Functions: Directors, IT, MIS Mgmt., Systems Analysis

Industries: Generalist, Finance, Media, Communications, Telecoms, Call Centers, Telephony, Digital, Wireless, Fiber Optic, Network Infrastructure, Software, Security SW, System SW, Biotech, Healthcare

Morgan & Associates
PO Box 379
Granby, MA 01033
(413) 467-9156
Fax: (413) 467-3003
Email: employment@morgan-jobs.com
Web: www.morgan-jobs.com

Description: We were founded in 1981 and have specialized in the manufacturing automation field including both mechanical and electronic automation companies.

Key Contact - Specialty:
Ms. Diane R. Morgan, Owner - *Automation*
Mr. Arthur Klebba, Consultant - *Engineers (electrical, software), automation*

Salary minimum: $35,000

Functions: Mfg.

Industries: Mfg., Misc. Mfg., Electronic, Elec. Components, Digital, Fiber Optic, Defense, Aerospace, Software

Networks: Top Echelon Network

Morgan Executive Search
2307 Parham Rd N Ste 100
Richmond, VA 23229
(804) 422-7800
Fax: (804) 422-7813
Email: search@mesearch.com
Web: www.mesearch.com

Description: We conduct a timely, professional search assignment with a personal approach. We find the right fit for clients, as well as candidates.

Key Contact - Specialty:
Mr. Kenneth M. Morgan, President - *Banking, financial*
Mr. Jim McRady, Director- Technology Group - *E-commerce, on-line services*

Salary minimum: $75,000

Functions: General Mgmt., Senior Mgmt., Sales & Mktg., Direct Mktg., HR Mgmt., Finance, CFO's, IT, Engineering

Industries: Generalist, Construction, Finance, Banking

Networks: National Banking Network (NBN)

The Morgan Group
PO Box 121153
Nashville, TN 37212-1153
(615) 297-5272

Description: MBA, accounting referrals from national and local CPA firms. Work with multi-national, publicity-held, and private companies.

Key Contact - Specialty:
Mr. Allen E. Morgan, Managing Partner, Ivy league - *Accounting & finance*

Salary minimum: $50,000

Functions: Finance, CFO's, Budgeting, Cash Mgmt., Taxes, M&A

Industries: Generalist

Professional Associations: FEI

Landon Morgan
3350 Merrittville Hwy Ste 12
Thorold, ON L2V 4Y6
Canada
(905) 641-2476
Fax: (905) 641-2735
Email: team@landonmorgan.com
Web: www.landonmorgan.com

Description: Primary experience in outreach recruiting. We don't work with our clients' competition. Our success rate is 95%. We are considered an extension of our clients.

Key Contact - Specialty:
Mr. Don Hetherington, President - *Engineering, plant management, technical*
Ms. Traci Polak, Assistant Manager - *Information technology, administration*

Functions: Generalist, Production, Plant Mgmt., Customer Svc., Personnel, MIS Mgmt., Engineering

Industries: Generalist, Mfg., Plastics, Rubber, Misc. Mfg.

Professional Associations: HRPAO

Morgan, Palmer, Morgan & Hill
(a division of The Fleetwood Group Inc)
PO Box 13353
Burton, WA 98013
(206) 463-5721
Email: mpmh@mpmhthefirm.com

Description: We are headquartered in the northwest. We perform searches nationally for both foreign and domestic financial institutions. Our primary focus is the transaction side of the corporate finance arena. We represent investment banks, venture capital/private equity firms and their portfolio companies, turnaround and restructuring practices, and commercial banking/finance companies.

Key Contact:
Mr. Warren Lee Hill, Jr., Senior Managing Partner

Salary minimum: $125,000

Functions: Finance, M&A

Industries: Finance, Banking, Invest. Banking

The Morgan/Geoffries Group
21755 Ventura Blvd Ste 305
Woodland Hills, CA 91364
(818) 704-1100
Email: geoffries@aol.com

Description: Multi-functional executive search focusing upon the factory automation and independent power production industries since 1977, offering a milestone-based fee disbursal system which ties remuneration to performance.

Key Contact - Specialty:
Mr. J. Lawrence Pepin, Senior Partner - *Automation systems*

Salary minimum: $60,000

Functions: Generalist, Directors, Senior Mgmt., Middle Mgmt., Automation, Plant Mgmt., Mktg. Mgmt., Sales Mgmt.

Industries: Generalist, Energy, Utilities, Metal Products, Machine, Appliance, Motor Vehicles, Computer Equip., Test, Measure Equip., Misc. Mfg.

Morgenstern Int'l Inc
3700 Airport Rd Ste 307
Boca Raton, FL 33431
(561) 620-8450
Fax: (801) 720-3719
Email: morgenstern@attorney-search.com
Web: www.attorney-search.com

Description: We pride ourselves in having a national reputation for helping our clients recruit attorneys with superb reputations and practice experience. Our clients include many of the most profitable law firms identified in The AM Law 100 and various prominent corporations and financial institutions. For law firm clients, we conduct strategic searches for partners and practice groups with significant portable practices. We also advise law firm clients on merger and acquisition matters.

Key Contact - Specialty:
Mr. Richard L. Morgenstern, Esq., President - *Attorney (partner level)*
Herrick A. Zeefe, Esq. - *Attorney (partner level)*

Salary minimum: $200,000

Functions: Legal

Industries: Generalist

The Morley Group
6201 Corporate Dr
Indianapolis, IN 46278
(317) 879-4770
(317) 616-1720
Fax: (317) 879-4787
Email: smorley@themorleygroup.com
Web: www.themorleygroup.com

Description: Over 20 years' experience. Recruiting, temp-direct and contract for engineering, accounting/finance/banking, healthcare, information technology, administration/secretarial services. Other services include outplacement, human resource surrogacy, quality audit and certification, vendor management, resume preparation and competency testing.

Key Contact:
Mr. Michael A. Morley, CPC, President
Ms. Sharon M. Morley, CPC, Vice President
Mr. Roger Brummett, CPC, Vice President/General Manager

Salary minimum: $16,500

Functions: Admin. Svcs., Mfg., Quality, Allied Health, Finance, IT, Systems Dev., Systems Implem., Systems Support, DB Admin.

Industries: Energy, Utilities, Construction, Mfg., Metal Products, Machine, Appliance, Motor Vehicles, Computer Equip., Transportation, Finance, Banking, Invest. Banking, Misc. Financial, Services, Equip Svcs., Mgmt. Consulting, Media, Telecoms, Software, Biotech, Healthcare

Professional Associations: NAPC

The Morris Group
PO Box 188
Bryn Mawr, PA 19010
(610) 520-0100
Email: morris@dplus.net

Description: Broad national contacts-especially strong in H/R, manufacturing, sales and marketing.

Three recruiters specialize in corporate human resources.

Key Contact - Specialty:
Mr. Paul T. Morris, President/Director - *Human resource*

Salary minimum: $40,000

Functions: Sales & Mktg., HR Mgmt.

Industries: Generalist

Professional Associations: SHRM

Mortgage & Financial Personnel Services
23564 Calabasas Rd Ste 104
Calabasas, CA 91302
(818) 591-8367
(800) 443-5627
Fax: (818) 591-7509
Email: mf-jobs@pacbell.net
Web: www.mortgageandfinancial.com

Description: Since 1984, we have been providing the highest caliber of mortgage and lending professionals into financial firms. Many interim employees have been converted into full-time workers with promising careers. All experienced loan originators and servicing experts are invited to apply.

Key Contact - Specialty:
Mr. Robert Sherman, President - *Mortgage, banking*
Mr. John Gordon, Contract Services Manager - *Legal (due diligence-fraud detection-underwriting)*
Ms. Denise Arthur, Office Manager - *Mortgage, banking*
Ms. Patty Easton, Account Manager - *Mortgage, banking*
Ms. Susan Sherman, Vice President - *Mortgage, banking*

Salary minimum: $50,000

Functions: Generalist

Industries: Finance, Banking, Real Estate

Professional Associations: CMBA

The Morton Group
5151 N 16th St Ste 234
Phoenix, AZ 85016
(602) 279-5662
Fax: (602) 279-6215
Email: legaljobs@mortongrp.com
Web: www.mortongrp.com

Description: We are the leading legal placement agency specializing in direct hire, temporary contract, and temp-to-hire recruitment of attorneys, paralegals, legal secretaries, support staff, and administrative assistants. Human resource support is provided to clients and career counseling to candidates.

Key Contact:
Ms. Susan B. Morton, President

Functions: Admin. Svcs., Legal, Personnel, Attorneys, Paralegals

Industries: Generalist, Legal

Professional Associations: AALS, AAPS, APA, ASPA, NAWBO

Motion Medical Solutions Inc
7750 Zionsville Rd Ste 850
Indianapolis, IN 46268
(317) 704-3311
Fax: (317) 704-3303
Email: info@betterjobs.com
Web: www.betterjobs.com

Description: Small firm specializing in healthcare related professions. High quality perm and temp

placements. We also provide consulting services for in-house recruiting departments. Owner has over 10 years' professional recruiting experience.

Key Contact:
Mr. John T. O'Conner, CPC

Functions: Physicians, Nurses, Allied Health, Health Admin.

Industries: Healthcare

MRD Group
441 NE Hillwood Dr
Hillsboro, OR 91724-3442
(877) 693-7666
Fax: (503) 648-7222
Email: edoran@mrdgroup.com
Web: www.mrdgroup.com

Description: Our firm specializes in recruiting for the IT/IS, data center infrastructure, LAN/WAN, NAS/SAN, and the computer and Internet telephony marketplace within North America, Europe, and Asia. IT/IS, sales, marketing, engineering/R&D, and support are the five components necessary to drive the engine of a hi-tech company. MRD has been recruiting the sales, sales management, product marketing/marketing management, and engineering talent that companies require since 1985.

Key Contact - Specialty:
Mr. Edward Doran, Director of National Accounts - *IT/IS, sales/marketing, systems engineering*

Salary minimum: $75,000

Functions: IT

Industries: Computer Equip.

Professional Associations: RON

Networks: Top Echelon Network

MRF Enterprises Inc
24165 IH-10 West Ste 217
PMB 303
San Antonio, TX 78257
(800) 645-4516
(210) 755-2347
Fax: (830) 755-2374

Description: Seventeen years of success based on personalized service that is responsive to the individual needs of client companies.

Key Contact - Specialty:
Ms. Jane M. Rupp, Executive Recruiter - *Information technology*

Functions: Generalist, IT, MIS Mgmt., Systems Analysis, Systems Dev., Systems Implem., Systems Support

Industries: Generalist, Software

MRI The Washington Group
(also known as The Washington Group)
12520 Prosperity Dr Ste 220
Silver Spring, MD 20904
(301) 625-5100
Fax: (301) 625-3001
Email: info@mriwashington.com
Web: www.mriwashington.com

Description: Specialize in the industries of marketing, managed care and healthcare, pharmaceuticals, accounting and finance, marketing research, and information technology.

Key Contact - Specialty:
Mr. Frank S. Black, Jr., President - *Marketing, marketing research*
Ms. Marilyn Staley, General Manager
Ms. Barbara Silver, Senior Account Manager - *Managed care*
Mr. Stuart Meyers, Account Manager - *Managed care (behavioral)*
Ms. Deborah Bandzerewicz, Senior Account Manager - *Tax accounting*

Functions: Generalist, Healthcare, Health Admin., Mkt. Research, Taxes, IT

Industries: Generalist, Pharm Svcs., Accounting, Mgmt. Consulting, Healthcare

MSI Int'l

245 Peachtree Center Ave Ste 2500
Marquis One Twr
Atlanta, GA 30303
(404) 659-5050
Fax: (404) 659-7139
Email: info@msi-intl.com
Web: www.msi-intl.com

Description: Recruitment in the fields including physicians, manufacturing, sales, marketing, locum tenens, banking, investment banking, accounting, contract and permanent information technology, healthcare, construction, and biomedical.

Key Contact - Specialty:
Mr. Eric J. Lindberg, President - *CEOs, banking, healthcare, investment banking, information technology (permanent, contract)*
Mr. Larry Cooper, General Manager - *Sales, marketing*
Mr. David McAnally, General Manager - *IT contracting*
Mr. Doug Dershimer, General Manager - *Allied health*

Salary minimum: $30,000

Functions: Generalist, Senior Mgmt., Physicians, Nurses, Allied Health, IT, R&D, Int'l.

Industries: Generalist, Construction, Mfg., Banking, Invest. Banking, Biotech, Healthcare

Professional Associations: GAPS, NAPR, NAPS, NTSA, PMA

Branches:
4275 Executive Sq Dr Ste 510
La Jolla, CA 92037
(858) 552-6888
Fax: (858) 552-6891
Email: mca@n2.net
Key Contact - Specialty:
Mr. George Colberg, General Manager - *Biomedical, pharmacy*

1050 Crown Pointe Pkwy Ste 100
Atlanta, GA 30338
(770) 394-2494
Fax: (770) 394-2251
Email: msimsp@mindspring.com
Key Contact - Specialty:
Mr. Jim Watson, CPC, Vice President - *Banking, healthcare, construction, manufacturing, accounting*

6151 Powers Ferry Rd Ste 540
Atlanta, GA 30339
(770) 850-6465
Fax: (770) 850-6468
Email: keith.colson@msi-intl.com
Key Contact - Specialty:
Mr. Keith Colson, General Manager - *Information technology*

1900 N 18th St Ste 306
Premier Plz
Monroe, LA 71201
(318) 324-0406
Fax: (318) 329-8188
Email: medical1@msi-monroe.com
Key Contact - Specialty:
Ms. Laurelle Williams, Vice President - *Healthcare, physicians*

701 Poydras St Ste 3880
1 Shell Sq
New Orleans, LA 70139
(504) 522-6700
Fax: (504) 522-1998
Email: david.dietz@mindspring.com

Key Contact - Specialty:
Mr. David Dietz, CPC, Vice President - *Physicians, banking, healthcare*

5215 N O'Connor Blvd
1875 Williams Sq Central Twr
Irving, TX 75039
(972) 869-3939
Fax: (972) 869-0085
Email: msi_mda@mindspring.com
Key Contact - Specialty:
Mr. Larry Klos, Vice President - *Healthcare, banking*

3401 Custer Rd Ste 113
Plano, TX 75023
(972) 758-0938
Fax: (972) 612-7444
Key Contact - Specialty:
Mr. Chris Wheeler, Manager - *Information technology*

MSK Manufacturing Solutions

3487 Center Rd Unit 1-B
Brunswick, OH 44212
(330) 273-0122
Fax: (330) 273-2651
Email: msk@mskjobs.com
Web: www.mskjobs.com

Description: We are a nationwide search firm that specializes in the automatic machining field, such as screw machines, Swiss CNC, and CNC machinery. We work nationwide and work with engineers, managers, and programmers within this industry. We have been recruiting in this industry for 17 years.

Key Contact - Specialty:
Mr. Lance Solak, Partner - *Automatic machine industry*
Mr. TOM Medvec, Parner - *Automatic machine industry*

Salary minimum: $50,000

Mulcahy Company

535 High Bluff Dr
Grafton, WI 53024
(262) 375-2356
Fax: (262) 375-3031
Email: pat@mulcahycompany.com
Web: www.mulcahycompany.com

Description: We specialize in working closely with our client companies to conduct in-depth searches in order to identify and recruit highly qualified talent in the information technology and software engineering.

Key Contact - Specialty:
Mr. Patrick Mulcahy, Owner - *Information technology, software, engineering*

Salary minimum: $40,000

Functions: IT, MIS Mgmt., Systems Analysis, Systems Dev., Systems Implem., Systems Support, Network Admin., DB Admin.

Industries: Generalist, Motor Vehicles, Computer Equip., Consumer Elect., Misc. Mfg., Electronic, Elec. Components, Banking, Brokers, Misc. Financial

Networks: National Personnel Assoc (NPA)

Mullin Company

3100 W End Ave Ste 900
Nashville, TN 37203
(615) 312-5070
Fax: (615) 312-5101
Email: mullinco@isdn.net
Web: www.construction-job.com

Description: We are a recruiting firm that specializes in construction professionals for the construction industry.

Key Contact - Specialty:
Mr. Dale H. Mullin, President - *Construction professionals*

Salary minimum: $65,000

Functions: Generalist, Senior Mgmt., Middle Mgmt., Admin. Svcs., Engineering, Architects

Industries: Generalist, Construction, Accounting, Hotels, Resorts, Clubs, Hospitals

Professional Associations: AAA, NAHB

The Mullings Group

(also known as MRI of Delray Beach)
220 Congress Park Dr Ste 245
Delray Beach, FL 33445
(800) 754-5440
Fax: (561) 243-1622
Email: joe@mullingsgroup.com
Web: www.mullingsgroup.com

Description: We are a retainer search firm with practices in the medical device, healthcare, pharmaceutical, and automation and systems integration industry.

Key Contact - Specialty:
Mr. Joseph S. Mullings, President - *Medical device, pharmaceutical, aerospace*
Mrs. Holly Scott, Vice President
Mr. James Hall, Vice President
Ms. Patricia Sheehan, Managing Partner - *Healthcare*
Mr. Lorne Yaffe, Vice President - *Medical device*

Salary minimum: $60,000

Functions: Healthcare, Engineering

Industries: Energy, Utilities, Drugs Mfg., Medical Devices, Computer Equip., Consumer Elect., Aerospace, Packaging, Biotech, Healthcare

Professional Associations: ASME, ASQ, RAPS, SAE

Branches:
34 Goodsell Hill Rd
Redding, CT 06896
(800) 754-5440
Email: joe@mullingsgroup.com
Key Contact:
Mr. Joseph Mullings, President

The Multicultural Advantage

600 W Harvey St Ste A416
Philadelphia, PA 19144
(215) 849-0946
Fax: (603) 806-7986
Email: tminor@tmaonline.net
Web: www.tmaonline.net

Description: We offer a number of highly effective and innovative diversity staffing and development services including placement, recruitment training, Internet campaigns, recruitment program development, recruitment event coordination and multicultural communications tools.

Key Contact - Specialty:
Ms. Tracey L. Minor, President - *Diversity, information systems, sales, engineering, marketing*

Functions: Generalist, Quality, Sales Mgmt., Personnel, Budgeting, Systems Analysis, Engineering, Minorities

Industries: Generalist, Food, Bev., Tobacco, Chemicals, Soap, Perf., Cosmtcs., Drugs Mfg., Medical Devices, Software

Professional Associations: BHRN, SHRM

Multisearch Recruiters

PO Box 309
Ballico, CA 95303
(209) 634-5814
Fax: (209) 634-2648

Description: Executive and technical search firm emphasizing the plastics, building materials and fenestration manufacturing industries, nationwide. Growing niche in confidential replacements and world class manufacturing.

Key Contact - Specialty:
Mr. Dennis Gallagher, Owner - *Manufacturing (executive, technical)*

Salary minimum: $50,000

Functions: General Mgmt., Directors, Senior Mgmt., Middle Mgmt., Production, Plant Mgmt., Quality, Sales & Mktg., Engineering

Industries: Mfg., Lumber, Furniture, Plastics, Rubber, Leather, Stone, Glass, Misc. Mfg.

Professional Associations: AAMA

Murdock & Associates
PO Box 172551
Arlington, TX 76003
(817) 784-2789
Fax: (817) 557-6147
Email: kmurdock15@home.com

Description: We specialize in sales, accounting, and operations professionals for manufacturing industries.

Key Contact:
Mr. Ken Murdock, Owner/President

Functions: Generalist

Industries: Mfg., Accounting, Mgmt. Consulting, Packaging, Accounting SW, Industry Specific SW, Mfg. SW

Professional Associations: SERC

Kenneth Murphy & Associates
5112 Prince St
Halifax, NS B3J 1L3
Canada
(902) 425-4495
Fax: (902) 425-6691
Email: jobs@kma.ns.ca
Web: www.kma.ns.ca

Description: We specialize in recruitment of information technology professionals and executive search.

Key Contact - Specialty:
Mr. Ken Murphy, President - *Information technology professionals*
Ms. Karin Dobson, Recruiter - *Executive search*

Salary minimum: $40,000

Functions: General Mgmt., Sales & Mktg., HR Mgmt., Finance, IT, Engineering

Industries: Generalist

Professional Associations: CMCAC, ITANS

The Murphy Group
630 N Washington
Naperville, IL 60563
(630) 753-8890
Fax: (630) 357-2636
Email: info@murphygroup.com
Web: www.murphygroup.com

Description: Serving the placement of full time and temp employees for 40 years plus.

Key Contact - Specialty:
Mr. William Murphy, II, CPC, CIPC, President - *Sales, IT, professional*
Ms. Suzy Packard, CPC, Director - *Administrative, office support, IT*

Salary minimum: $25,000

Functions: Generalist, Admin. Svcs., Health Admin., Sales Mgmt., Customer Svc., Benefits, MIS Mgmt., Network Admin.

Industries: Generalist, Mfg., Retail, Finance, Services, Media, Software

Professional Associations: IAPS, NAPS, NATSS

Murray & Tatro
2458 Creston Way
Los Angeles, CA 90068-2212
(323) 467-3553
Fax: (323) 467-3878
Email: murraytatro@cs.com

Description: Copywriters, art directors, creative directors at all levels for advertising agencies throughout the United States and Canada.

Key Contact - Specialty:
Ms. Marcia Murray, Owner - *Advertising copywriters, art directors*
Mr. Richard Tatro, Partner - *Advertising copywriters, art directors*

Functions: Advertising

Industries: Advertising

The Murray Group
23-75 Brittany Ct
Lake Carroll, IL 61046
(815) 493-8770
Fax: (815) 493-8772
Email: murrayfeld@aol.com

Description: Seasoned business/recruitment professionals recognized for quality, integrity and confidentiality. Industry-focused with blow molded plastics and food divisions; most functions, most levels, nationwide. Full/customized service.

Key Contact - Specialty:
Mr. Patrick Murray, President - *Blow molding, injection molding, plastics*
Ms. Jeanette M. Murray, President - *Food*

Salary minimum: $30,000

Functions: Generalist

Industries: Plastics, Rubber, Packaging

Professional Associations: SPE

Musick & Associates
4831 CR 222
Durango, CO 81303
(970) 259-8647
Fax: (970) 259-8659
Email: stevem@professionalplacement.com
Web: www.professionalplacement.com

Description: Contingency and retained firm specializing in accounting, finance, information technology, IT consulting, e-commerce/Internet solutions, operations, business process re-engineering, supply chain consulting, marketing and general management.

Key Contact - Specialty:
Mr. Stephen Musick, Principal - *Accounting, finance, tax, audit, marketing*
Mrs. Diana Musick, Principal - *Accounting, finance, tax, audit, operations*

Salary minimum: $25,000

Functions: Generalist

Industries: Construction, Mfg., Wholesale, Retail, Finance, Hospitality, Media, Communications, Insurance, Software

Networks: Top Echelon Network

The MVP Group
150 Broadway Ste 2101
New York, NY 10038
(212) 571-1833
Fax: (212) 393-1048
Email: jvalenti@mvpgroup.net
Web: www.mvpgroup.net

Description: Our approach is to know our clients, most of whom have worked with the firm for years. The key to a successful search is to identify the specifications and understand the company culture in conjunction with managing the candidate process.

Key Contact:
Mr. Joseph Valenti, CEO
Mr. Stephen C. Brown, Managing Director

Functions: Generalist, Benefits, Training, CFO's, Credit, Systems Analysis, Systems Implem., Minorities

Industries: Generalist, Finance, Banking, Invest. Banking, Brokers

Professional Associations: FWA, NYPMA, SHRM

N2 Technologies
3790 El Camino Real # 400
El Camino Real
Palo Alto, CA 94306
(650) 493-1500
Fax: (650) 493-9263
Email: john@n2tech.com
Web: www.n2tech.com

Description: We are an executive search firm specializing in the placement of software engineers and developers in Silicon Valley/Northern California.

Key Contact - Specialty:
Mr. John D. Owen, Director - *Software developer*
Ms. Jennifer Siemens, Manager - *Software developer*

Nachman BioMedical
50 Church St
Cambridge, MA 02138
(617) 492-8911
Email: phil@nachmanbiomedical.com
Web: www.nachmanbiomedical.com

Description: Medical industry specialists: medical device, medical electronics, instrumentation, biotechnology, pharmaceuticals. VPs through industry experienced individual contributors skilled in R&D, scale-up, manufacturing, marketing, regulatory affairs, quality assurance.

Key Contact - Specialty:
Mr. Philip S. Nachman, President - *Medical products*

Salary minimum: $60,000

Functions: General Mgmt., Senior Mgmt., Middle Mgmt., Product Dev., Production, Quality, Mktg. Mgmt., R&D, Engineering, Specialized Svcs.

Industries: Drugs Mfg., Medical Devices, Biotech

Professional Associations: MPPC

Nagle & Associates Inc
104 W Spring St
Fremont, IN 46737
(219) 495-9610
Fax: (219) 495-7113
Email: j.jnagle@gte.net
Web:
www.geocities.com/executivesearch2001/classic_tan.html

Description: We are an executive search firm that has been in the asset lending recruiting industry for over 30 years. We work with corporations all over the world conducting searches for these positions: auditors, calling officers, portfolio managers, credit analysts, etc. All of these positions having asset based lending experience in their backgrounds.

Key Contact - Specialty:
Ms. Jan Nagle, President/CEO - *Asset based lending for banks & corporations*

Functions: Senior Mgmt., Mktg. Mgmt., Sales Mgmt., Finance, CFO's, Cash Mgmt., Credit, Risk Mgmt.

Industries: Finance, Banking

Nail & Associates

1401 Johnson Ferry Rd Ste 328
PMB-D13
Marietta, GA 30062-6436
(770) 565-2445
Email: nailassoc@aol.com

Description: We are highly skilled in identifying and matching the culture with the candidate profile in an exceptionally timely manner. The net results are long-term placements on a consistent basis that offers a win-win solution for both the candidate and the employer.

Key Contact - Specialty:
Mr. Peter A. Nail, President - *Research & development, quality assurance, engineering, production manager*

Salary minimum: $35,000

Functions: Admin. Svcs.

Industries: Food, Bev., Tobacco, Drugs Mfg.

NAP Executive Services Inc (Canada)

3101 Bathurst St Ste 300
Toronto, ON M6A 2A6
Canada
(416) 949-8896
Email: toronto@fashion-career.com
Web: www.fashion-career.com

Description: We specialize in recruiting at all levels within the apparel and textiles industries both at wholesale and retail (mostly Canada). Our recruiters all have industry experience.

Key Contact - Specialty:
Mr. Steve Rothstein, President - *Apparel, textiles, retail*

Salary minimum: $40,000

Functions: Generalist

Industries: Generalist, Textiles, Apparel, Retail

Professional Associations: ACSESS, AMIQ, CAF

Branches:
1230 Docteur Penfield Ste 904
Montreal, QC H3G IB5
Canada
(514) 592-8896
Email: montreal@fashion-career.com
Key Contact:
Mr. Steve Rothstein, President - *Apparel, textiles, retail*
Ms. Janet Presser

Napolitano & Wulster LLC

311 S Main St
Cheshire, CT 06410
(203) 272-2820
Fax: (203) 250-7207
Email: napwul@aol.com

Description: We specialize in pharmaceutical, biotech, and contract research organizations.

Key Contact:
Mr. Anthony M. Napolitano

Functions: Healthcare

Industries: Pharm Svcs.

Nason & Nason

501 Brickell Key Dr Ste 202
Miami, FL 33131
(305) 379-9400
Fax: (305) 372-9959
Email: nason@bellsouth.net
Web: www.nason-nason.com

Description: We are a professional search and recruiting firm including CFO and like positions. We have separate division that addresses marketing administrative, HR, and international positions. We specialize in banking, brokerage, and other financial services. We also have a separate division, which addresses Internet companies.

Key Contact - Specialty:
Mr. Dennis H. Nason, Senior Partner - *Banking, finance*
Ms. Alexandra Nason-Aymerich, Partner - *Banking, finance*
Mr. John M. Porges, Partner - *Banking*

Salary minimum: $50,000

Functions: Generalist, Senior Mgmt., Middle Mgmt., Mktg. Mgmt., HR Mgmt., Finance, CFO's, Risk Mgmt., Attorneys

Industries: Generalist, Finance, Banking, Invest. Banking, Brokers, Legal, Accounting

Branches:
251 Royal Palm Way Ste 301 C
Palm Beach, FL 33480
(561) 653-9996
Fax: (561) 653-9926
Email: dpinto18@aol.com
Key Contact - Specialty:
Mr. David Pinto, Partner - *Finance*

NaTek Corp

27 Summerfield Ln
Saratoga Springs, NY 12866
(518) 583-0456
Fax: (518) 583-0558
Email: m.dillon@natek.com
Web: www.natek.com

Description: We are a national technical search firm specializing in the recruitment of technical professionals. We specialize in mid-to upper-level search assignments with Fortune 1000 companies. Our firm covers all engineering, sales, and management disciplines.

Key Contact - Specialty:
Mr. Mark Dillon, President - *Energy, power, D/G, sales, engineering, management, construction*
Mr. Ed Hoffman, Senior Recruiter - *Pulp paper, manufacturing*
Mr. John Roche, Senior Recruiter - *Energy, power, sales, engineering, management*
Mr. Brian Britt, Senior Recruiter - *Energy, power, DG, sales, engineering*

Salary minimum: $40,000

Functions: Mfg., Materials, Sales Mgmt., HR Mgmt., Engineering

Industries: Energy, Utilities, Construction, Mfg., Consumer Elect., Test, Measure Equip., Services, Pharm Svcs., Equip Svcs., Mgmt. Consulting, HR Services, Government, Defense, Packaging, Healthcare

Professional Associations: AEE, ASHRAE, TAPPI

National Affirmative Action Career Network Inc

4255 S Buckley Rd Ste 299
Aurora, CO 80013
(303) 699-8599
Fax: (303) 699-8525
Email: calvinbook@aol.com

Description: Specialize in recruiting minority and women degreed professionals.

Key Contact - Specialty:
Mr. Calvin Booker, President - *Accounting, communications, sales & marketing*

Salary minimum: $25,000

Functions: General Mgmt.

Industries: Generalist

Professional Associations: CHRA

Branches:
7109 Staples Mill Rd
PO Box 411
Richmond, VA 23228
(804) 346-2290
Fax: (804) 346-2271
Email: calvinbook@aol.com
Key Contact:
Mr. Calvin Booker, President

National Bank & Finance Executive Search

(also known as NBF Executive Search, Inc.)
550 W Vista Way Ste 107
Vista, CA 92083
(760) 630-3400
Fax: (760) 630-2001
Email: wayne@nbfsearch.com
Web: www.nbfsearch.com

Description: We are banking and finance executive recruiters, mid- to executive level positions on a nationwide basis. We are commercial finance and banking recruiters in all skill sets, including, but not limited to; asset-based, leasing, and e-Commerce.

Key Contact - Specialty:
Mr. Wayne Wedderien, CEO - *Banking, finance*
Ms. Bobbie Back, President - *Banking, finance*

Salary minimum: $40,000

Functions: Sales & Mktg., HR Mgmt., Finance, IT, MIS Mgmt., Systems Dev., Attorneys

Industries: Wholesale, Retail, Finance, Banking, Invest. Banking, Venture Cap., Misc. Financial, Accounting, Real Estate

Professional Associations: CBC, CFA, CFCC, ELA

Networks: National Banking Network (NBN)

National Career Connection

206 Wyndmere Dr
Pittsburgh, PA 16066
(724) 772-1149
Email: donalyn@recruitshop.com
Web: www.recruitshop.com

Description: Contingency recruiter working nationwide to aide companies and candidates in the areas of sales and marketing, information systems, and information technology.

Key Contact - Specialty:
Ms. Donalyn Spisak, President - *Sales, information systems, information technology*

Functions: Sales & Mktg.

Industries: Generalist

Professional Associations: RON

Networks: Inter-City Personnel Assoc (IPA)

National Career Search

7898 E Acoma Dr Ste 208
Scottsdale, AZ 85260
(480) 905-0755
Fax: (480) 905-0751
Email: ncs@ionet.net
Web: www.nationalcareersearch.com

Description: We specifically specialize in home healthcare, home infusion, home medical equipment, home respiratory therapy, hospice, long-term care, medical products, medical supply and medical device industries. We work on clinical, operational, sales and financial positions.

Key Contact - Specialty:
Mr. Ben Krawetz, President - *Healthcare*

Functions: Generalist, Senior Mgmt., Middle Mgmt., Nurses, Health Admin., Sales & Mktg., Sales Mgmt., Finance

Industries: Generalist, Healthcare

National Computerized Employment Service Inc
2014 W 8th St
Erie, PA 16505
(814) 454-3874
Fax: (208) 330-7866
Email: nces@erie.net

Description: Twenty-five years of distinguished personnel recruitment/assessment experience. References available. Plastics industry our specialty.

Key Contact - Specialty:
Mr. Joseph W. Beck, President - *Plastics*

Functions: Generalist, Mfg., Product Dev., Production, Plant Mgmt., Quality

Industries: Plastics, Rubber, Metal Products, Motor Vehicles, Consumer Elect., Electronic, Elec. Components

Professional Associations: SPE

Networks: Inter-City Personnel Assoc (IPA)

National Corporate Consultants Inc
409 E Cook Rd Ste 200
Ft. Wayne, IN 46825
(219) 489-0900
Fax: (219) 489-2699
Email: jcorya@hr-edge.com
Web: www.hr-edge.com

Description: We are industry experienced search consultants dedicated to assisting client organizations in identifying, qualifying, and attracting managerial, technical, and professional talent.

Key Contact - Specialty:
Mr. James E. Corya, President
Mr. John Hursh, Manager - *Technical & plant managers*
Mr. Patrick Haar, Manager - *Transportation, logistics, warehousing, distribution*
Mr. Lance Diffendarfer, Manager - *Robotics, factory automation*

Salary minimum: $40,000

Functions: Generalist, Plant Mgmt., Quality, Materials, Purchasing, Distribution, Sales Mgmt., Engineering

Industries: Mfg., Food, Bev., Tobacco, Plastics, Rubber, Metal Products, Motor Vehicles, Electronic, Elec. Components, Services

National Engineering Search
158 NE Greenwood Ave Ste 4
Bend, OR 97701
(541) 317-4150
(800) 248-7020
Email: careers@nesnet.com
Web: www.empnet.com/nes

Description: We are a full-service engineering recruiting firm with a significant client base throughout the United States. Primary disciplines include geotechnical, structural, civil, transportation, wastewater, mining and environmental engineering.

Key Contact - Specialty:
Mr. Garry W. Todd, President - *Geotechnical, structural, civil, transportation, wastewater*

Salary minimum: $40,000

Functions: Generalist, Engineering

Industries: Generalist, Energy, Utilities, Construction, Transportation

National Executive
3200 Dufferin St Ste 305
Toronto, ON M6A 3B2
Canada
(416) 256-0300
Fax: (416) 256-0035
Email: resume@national-executive.com
Web: www.national-executive.com

Description: Can offer a current salary survey at our website.

Key Contact - Specialty:
Mr. Don Cormier, Partner - *Electronic, software engineering*
Mr. Peter Ferrante, Partner - *Information technology*

Salary minimum: $35,000

Functions: Generalist, IT

Industries: Mfg., Computer Equip., Transportation, Retail, Finance, Services, Media, Communications, Telecoms, Aerospace, Insurance, Software, Biotech, Healthcare

Professional Associations: ACSESS

National Executive Resources Inc
8361 S Sangre De Cristo Rd Ste 150
Littleton, CO 80127
(303) 721-7672
(800) 886-7672
Fax: (303) 721-0608
Email: careers@nerisearch.com

Description: Recruiting and search for manufacturing including the metals, minerals, chemicals, food and pharmaceuticals industries.

Key Contact - Specialty:
Mr. Alan Pike, President - *Key management positions*

Functions: General Mgmt., Mfg.

Industries: Energy, Utilities, Construction, Mfg., Transportation

Professional Associations: AICHE, AIME, NSA, TMS

National Field Service Corp
162 Orange Ave
Nat'l Bldg
Suffern, NY 10901
(845) 368-1600
(800) 368-1602
Fax: (845) 368-1989
Email: nfsco@aol.com
Web: www.nfsco.com

Description: Our firm is a full service company meets the technical needs of its client corporations. NFSCO has placed qualified individuals in the telecommunications, information technologies and site acquisition industries, and has developed a specialization in telecommunications requirements for both wire line as well as wireless companies.

Key Contact - Specialty:
Mr. Richard W. Avazian, President - *Communications technicians, right of way, information technology*
Mr. Floyd Cole, Vice President - *Energy*
Ms. Margaret M. Forman, Vice President - *Communications technicians, administration, data processing*
Mr. Robert M. Hayward, Human Resources Director - *Gas inspectors, communications technicians, right of way*
Ms. Mary Ann Avazian, Recruiter - *Administration, clerical*
Ms. Lisa Saunders, Recruiter - *MIS, programmers, systems analysts, IT*

Functions: MIS Mgmt., Systems Analysis, Systems Dev., Systems Implem., Systems Support,

Network Admin., DB Admin., Engineering, Mgmt. Consultants

Industries: Computer Equip., Mgmt. Consulting, HR Services, Telecoms, Software

Professional Associations: NYATSS

National Human Resource Group Inc (NHRG Inc)
PO Box 340940
Austin, TX 78734
(512) 328-4448
Fax: (512) 328-1696
Email: nhrg@nhrg.com
Web: www.nhrg.com

Description: A full-service consulting company with extensive experience in the personnel industry. Our technical services division specializes in the placement of software and hardware engineering professionals.

Key Contact - Specialty:
Mr. Thomas Volick, Senior Vice President - *Information technology, software, hardware*

Salary minimum: $60,000

Functions: Generalist, MIS Mgmt., Systems Analysis, Systems Dev., Systems Implem., Systems Support, Network Admin., DB Admin., Specialized Svcs.

Industries: Generalist, Computer Equip., Communications, Telecoms, Software

National Medical Recruiting & Consulting Inc
9445 SW 192nd Court Rd
Dunnellon, FL 34432-4234
(800) 755-6954
(800) 868-6488
Fax: (352) 465-5081
Email: nmrcinc@aol.com
Web: www.nmrinc.com

Description: We specialize in physician/staff placements: anesthesiology, cardiology, dermatology, hem/oncology, gastroentrology, neurology, orthopedics, pulmonology, rhumatology along with sales of medical practices.

Key Contact - Specialty:
Ms. Jackie S. Griffin, BBA, CEO, Medical Recruiter - *Recruitment, physicians*
Mr. Joseph A. Masino, BBS, Practice Broker/ Medical Recruiter - *Medical practice brokerage*
Ms. Judy Udall, Healthcare Recruiter - *Physician, RN*

Salary minimum: $100,000

Functions: Healthcare, Physicians, Nurses

Industries: Brokers, Non-profits, Mgmt. Consulting, HR Services, Healthcare

Professional Associations: ACPE, FAR

Networks: Recruiters Professional Network (RPN)

National Metal Services Corp
PO Box 39
Dyer, IN 46311-0039
(219) 322-4664
Fax: (219) 322-2957
Email: ntnlmtl@concentric.net
Web: www.concentric.net/~ntnlmtl

Description: Thirty six years of recruiting experience for the fully integrated steels companies, mini-mills, foundries, die casters, forging companies, mining, equipment manufacturers, steel service centers, engineering firms, automotive and farm equipment manufacturers.

Key Contact - Specialty:
Mr. John V. Penrod, President - *Metals*
Mr. William A. McGinnis, Senior Consultant - *Engineering, process control*

Ms. Eleanor Woods, Office Manager - *Secretarial, administrative*

Salary minimum: $50,000

Functions: General Mgmt., Product Dev., Production, Plant Mgmt., Quality, Productivity, Materials, Purchasing, Mkt. Research, Sales Mgmt.

Industries: Metal Products

Professional Associations: AIME, AISE, ISS, NFIB

Networks: Top Echelon Network

National Recruiters
720 N Commerce Ste 345
Ardmore, OK 73401
(800) 776-6285
Fax: (580) 561-6600
Email: national@natrec.com
Web: www.natrec.com

Description: Nationwide search firm for executive, managerial, engineering and professional services in wireless/telecommunications, HRMS software and consulting.

Key Contact - Specialty:
Ms. Lynn Tackett, Recruiting Manager - *Software*

Salary minimum: $50,000

Functions: HR Mgmt.

Industries: Mgmt. Consulting, HR Services, Telecoms, Software

Professional Associations: APA, SHRM

Networks: Top Echelon Network

Branches:
513A 65th St
Waianae, HI 96792
(808) 668-4199
Email: natl@natrec.com
Key Contact:
Ms. Laura Moore

National Recruiting Service
1832 Hart St
PO Box 218
Dyer, IN 46311-0218
(219) 865-2373
Fax: (219) 865-2375
Email: stanhen@jorsm.com

Description: Exclusive search and contingency recruiters for the steel tubular products and basic metals industries. Specializing in management, technical and sales positions on a national basis.

Key Contact - Specialty:
Mr. Stanley M. Hendricks, II, Owner - *Tubular products, metals, management, technical, sales*

Salary minimum: $50,000

Functions: Generalist

Industries: Mfg., Metal Products, Machine, Appliance

Networks: Inter-City Personnel Assoc (IPA)

National Register Columbus Inc
2700 E Dublin Granville Rd Ste 555
Columbus, OH 43231
(614) 890-1200
Fax: (614) 890-1259
Web: www.nrcols.com

Description: We provide broad market sales search in the following areas: telecommunications, more specifically GAM, NAM, MAR, and Executive; IT software/hardware/services; medical/pharmaceutical; industrial; office products; publishing; and banking.

Key Contact - Specialty:
Mr. David Molnar, President - *Sales, sales management*

Functions: Generalist, Sales & Mktg., Sales Mgmt.

Industries: Construction, Mfg., Retail, Services, IT Implementation, Publishing, Communications, Telecoms, Government, Packaging, Software, Biotech, Healthcare

Professional Associations: NAPS, OSSA

National Resources Inc
23901 Calabasas Rd Ste 2009
Calabasas, CA 91302
(818) 703-1994
Fax: (818) 703-1915
Email: gene@nationalrecruiting.com
Web: www.nationalrecruiting.com

Description: Southern California's largest search specializing in all disciplines in the Information Systems area. Placement of both permanent and contract professionals.

Key Contact:
Mr. Gene Jenkins

Salary minimum: $60,000

Functions: IT

Industries: Generalist, Agri., Forestry, Mining

National Resources Inc
2119 B Vermont Rd
Vail, CO 81657
(970) 476-0901
Fax: (970) 476-0839
Email: maxine@drjob.com
Web: www.drjob.com

Description: Since 1984, we have specialized in nationwide physician recruitment, physician placement and physician relocation. Completely database and web oriented, we assist in finding physicians jobs and positions. Our clients pay all fees and travel expenses. We enjoy understanding our candidates needs and professionally presenting them in the areas they choose to live and practice.

Key Contact:
Dr. Warren Graboyes

Functions: Physicians

Industries: Healthcare

National Search Associates
2035 Corte del Nogal Ste 100
Carlsbad, CA 92009
(760) 431-1115
Fax: (760) 431-0660
Email: philp@nsasearch.com
Web: www.nsasearch.com

Description: Executive search for pharmaceutical, biotech, biomedical, software development and telecommunications industries. Clients range from start-up companies to Fortune 500 corporations. Exceptional references provided.

Key Contact - Specialty:
Mr. Philip Peluso, President - *Pharmaceutical, biotechnology*
Mr. Richard Cimicata, Vice President - *Pharmaceutical, biotechnology*

Salary minimum: $70,000

Functions: Generalist

Industries: Medical Devices, Software, Biotech

Professional Associations: NYAS, RAPS

National Search Committee Inc
4190 Belfort Rd Ste 200
Enterprise Park
Jacksonville, FL 32216
(904) 448-2000
Fax: (904) 448-2004
Email: nsc@mediaone.net
Web: www.natlsearchcommittee.com

Description: Retained and contingency search in the fields of finance, accounting, administration and technologies.

Key Contact - Specialty:
Mr. Daniel B. Miller, CPA, President - *Finance & accounting, information technology*

Salary minimum: $40,000

Functions: Finance, IT

Industries: Generalist

Professional Associations: AICPA, FICPA

National Search Inc®
2902 University Dr
The Walk at University
Coral Springs, FL 33065
(800) 935-4355
Fax: (954) 755-7913
Email: natlsrch@aol.com
Web: www.nationalsearch.com

Description: Established nationwide recruiting organization specializing in the healthcare and insurance industries, providing cost-effective, location-specific, retained search performance, on a contingency basis.

Key Contact - Specialty:
Mr. Ivan Schere, President - *Insurance*
Ms. Nanci Gould, Vice President - *Healthcare*

Salary minimum: $35,000

Functions: Generalist, General Mgmt., Mfg., Healthcare, Sales & Mktg., HR Mgmt., CFO's, Risk Mgmt., Minorities, Attorneys

Industries: Generalist, Brokers, Insurance, Healthcare

National Staffing by Noelle & Associates
13701 Riverside Dr Ste 707
Sherman Oaks, CA 91423
(818) 907-8660
Fax: (818) 905-1889
Email: hedhntress@aol.com
Web: www.natlstaffing.com

Description: We specialize in placing medical and dental professionals, for example physicians, physician assistants, nurse practitioners, dentist, hygienists, RDAs, and DAs.

Key Contact - Specialty:
Ms. Noelle Lea King, Owner - *Medical, dental, MD's, PA's, NP's*

Functions: Generalist, Healthcare, Physicians, Nurses, Allied Health, Health Admin.

Industries: Generalist, Healthcare, Hospitals, Dental, Occupational Therapy

Professional Associations: NAPR

National Staffing Group Ltd
6200 Som Center Rd Ste B-20
PO Box 39361
Solon, OH 44139
(440) 248-7261
Fax: (440) 248-1832
Email: kim@nsgl.com
Web: www.nsgl.com

Description: Retained and contingency search services specializing in the automotive, power transmission, polymer and plastics industries.

Key Contact - Specialty:
Ms. Kim Barnett, President - *Automotive*

Salary minimum: $50,000

Functions: Senior Mgmt., Middle Mgmt., Product
Dev., Production, Plant Mgmt., Quality, Materials
Plng., Sales & Mktg., Engineering, Int'l.

Industries: Plastics, Rubber, Metal Products,
Machine, Appliance, Motor Vehicles

Nations Executive Recruiters
(a division of Nations Group Inc)
PO Box 5697
Glen Allen, VA 23058-5697
(804) 965-0084
Fax: (804) 965-2092
Email: dpk@nationsgroupinc.com
Web: www.nationsgroupinc.com

Key Contact - Specialty:
Mr. Don Kirkpatrick, Officer/Senior Consultant -
*knowledge management, sales (web based),
business development, online services*

Salary minimum: $50,000

Nations Executive Search Group Inc
152 Overlook Ave
Queenstown, MD 21658-1260
(410) 827-0180
Fax: (410) 827-0181
Email: info@nesgroup.net

Description: Our firm features national search and
recruitment services for the competitive
intelligence, market research/advisory, and Internet
content-related marketplaces. We specialize in sales,
marketing, and business development executive
talent.

Key Contact - Specialty:
Mr. Robert B. Milner, Managing Partner - *Sales,
marketing, business development executive talent*

Salary minimum: $50,000

Functions: Directors, Senior Mgmt., Middle
Mgmt., Mktg. Mgmt., Sales Mgmt.

Industries: Misc. Financial, Publishing, New
Media, Software, Database SW, Doc. Mgmt.,
Production SW

Professional Associations: RON

Nationwide Personnel Group
474 Elmwood Ave
PO Box 26
Buffalo, NY 14222
(716) 881-2144
Fax: (716) 881-0711
Email: gademsky@localnet.com
Web: www.nationwidepersonnel.com

Description: Since 1973, We have been recruiting
and placing computer and engineering personnel
with companies coast-to-coast. Our corporate clients
range from Fortune-50, to small, closely held, and
entrepreneurial. We are often quoted in national
publications as an authority on the technical job
market, and frequently invited to speak on career
opportunities, interviewing and resume preparation.

Key Contact:
Mr. Mark Gademsky, CPC, President

Salary minimum: $40,000

Functions: Generalist, Product Dev., Automation,
IT, R&D, Engineering, Mgmt. Consultants

Industries: Generalist, Non-classifiable

Networks: Top Echelon Network

Nationwide Personnel Placement Inc
PO Box 206
Loveland, OH 45140
(513) 677-1998
Fax: (513) 683-9163
Email: moose-kopko@msn.com
Web: www.angelfire.com/biz/personnel/index.html

Description: Over 30 years of industrial experience
in nine different firms, including three Fortune 500
firms and over eight years in the recruiting business,
therefore I know both sides of the recruiting and
placement business.

Key Contact - Specialty:
Mr. K. Michael Gowetski, President - *Technical*

Salary minimum: $20,000

Functions: Generalist

Industries: Generalist

Nationwide Personnel Recruiting & Consulting Inc
20834 SW Martinazzi Ave
Tualatin, OR 97062
(503) 692-4925
Fax: (503) 692-6764
Email: barbarab@barbara-nprc.com
Web: www.barbara-nprc.com

Description: We are executive search specialists
serving the industrial marketplace in process control
sales, chemical, environmental, automation, MMI,
quality, sales, and mid- to upper-level management.

Key Contact:
Ms. Barbara Bodle, President - *High technology,
instrumentation, measurement, controls*
Mr. Darryl Bodle, CFO

Salary minimum: $60,000

Functions: Generalist, Directors, Senior Mgmt.,
Middle Mgmt., Production, Quality, Sales Mgmt.,
Engineering

Industries: Generalist, Chemicals, Test, Measure
Equip., Misc. Mfg.

Professional Associations: IEEE, TAPPI

NatStaff
PO Box 8624
New Orleans, LA 70182
(504) 523-5117
Email: nsjobsrl@bellsouth.net

Description: Our areas of concentration are
petrochemical and oil & gas. However, we will
work in all areas of engineering, computer
professionals and manufacturing should one of my
clients request my assistance. I regularly help clients
find high level managers and most professional as
their needs dictate. Always on the lookout for good
partners to work with.

Key Contact:
Mr. Ron Leonard, Technical Recruiter/Manager

Functions: Senior Mgmt.

Industries: Mfg., Textiles, Apparel, Chemicals,
Drugs Mfg., Medical Devices, Plastics, Rubber,
Paints, Petro. Products, Motor Vehicles,
Computer Equip., Consumer Elect., Test, Measure
Equip., Electronic, Elec. Components,
Government, Defense, Environmental Svcs.,
Software, HR SW, Mfg. SW

Networks: Top Echelon Network

Mason Naudin & Associates Inc
28562 Oso Pkwy Ste D-123
Las Flores, CA 92688
(949) 589-9944
Fax: (949) 589-4496
Email: mason-naudin@home.com
Web: www.mason-naudin.com

Description: We were founded in 1998. Our
expertise is that we all come from "hiring" manager
sections and have a clearer understanding of how to
hire "quality" candidate in the sales and marketing
area. We are 80% telecommunications.

Key Contact - Specialty:
Ms. Cheri Mason Naudin, President - *Sales,
marketing, telecommunications*

Functions: Sales & Mktg., Advertising, Mkt.
Research, Mktg. Mgmt., Sales Mgmt., Direct
Mktg., PR

Industries: Computer Equip., Telecoms

Navigator Resources
64 E Uwchlan Ave Ste 236
Exton, PA 19341
(610) 321-9800
Fax: (610) 321-9803
Email: rsrolis@navigatorresources.com
Web: www.navigatorresources.com

Description: Our firm provides executive search
and related services to customers across a wide
variety of industries. We distinguish ourselves
through extraordinary responsiveness to our
customers' needs, through our energy and focus, and
through the half-century of combined experience
that we bring to each assignment. Please allow us to
demonstrate what this difference can mean to you.

Key Contact - Specialty:
Mr. Robert B. Srolis, Managing Partner - *Financial
services, managed care, healthcare*
Mr. Gary R. Sigman, Vice President, Operations -
Pharmaceutical, biotechnology, contract services

Functions: Generalist

Industries: Drugs Mfg., Finance, Services, Pharm
Svcs., Mgmt. Consulting, Insurance, Biotech,
Healthcare

Navin Group
80 Washington St Ste 27-28D
Norwell, MA 02061
(781) 871-6770
Fax: (781) 878-8703
Email: search@navingroup.com
Web: www.navingroup.com

Description: Healthcare recruiting in the provider,
software vendor and information technology
consulting marketplace.

Key Contact - Specialty:
Mr. James L. Navin, President - *Healthcare, MIS,
operations, hospitals, consulting*
Mr. Douglas McLean, Vice President - *Healthcare,
directors, nursing, operations, hospitals*

Functions: Generalist, Physicians, Nurses, Allied
Health, Health Admin., Sales Mgmt., MIS Mgmt.,
Systems Implem.

Industries: Generalist, Mgmt. Consulting, Software,
Healthcare

Professional Associations: HIMSS, NAPS

Branches:
PO Box 11527
Clayton, MO 63105
(314) 721-4355
Fax: (314) 721-1249
Email: mercer@navingroup.com
Key Contact - Specialty:
Mr. Mercer O. Van Den Burg, Vice President -
*Healthcare, software vendors, sales management,
field management*

NCC Executive Search Consultants
1300 B Santa Barbara St Ste B
Santa Barbara, CA 93101
(800) 622-0431
Fax: (805) 966-9857
Email: gkravetz@nccx.com

Description: Full placement service in administrative and technical disciplines with emphasis on senior technical & executive search. Specializing in upper and mid-management in high-tech, software, Internet, biotechnology, pharmaceutical, medical devices, engineering, sales and finance.

Key Contact - Specialty:
Mr. Gary Kravetz, CEO
Ms. Mickie Diamont, Admin./Mgmt. Recruiting - *Financial, sales, administrative, banking*
Mr. Bill Vincent, Healthcare, insurance, biotech recruiter - *Benefits consultants, healthcare actuaries, biotech, healthcare, pharmacuetical*
Ms. Elizabeth Packard, Administrative/Sales Recruiter - *CFO, controller, sales VP, engineering VP, senior staffing, healthcare*
Ms. Jennifer Veblen, Director, Technical Recruiting - *High technology, software, engineering, software management, wireless*
Mrs. Joann Cracknell, Director Biotech & Pharma Recruiting - *SR managers, scientists, biotech & pharma (officers, directors)*
Mr. Bruce Hopper, Senior Recruiter; IT and Contract - *Engineering, IT (contract, direct placement)*

Salary minimum: $50,000

Functions: Generalist

Industries: Generalist

Networks: National Personnel Assoc (NPA)

Branches:
4601 Telephone Rd Ste 111
Ventura, CA 93003
(805) 639-2022
Fax: (805) 639-2015
Email: vs@nccx.com
Web: www.venturajobs.com
Key Contact - Specialty:
Ms. Katherine Carlton, Executive & Technical Recruiter - *Engineering, software, sales, IT*
Ms. Lisa Chapman, Office/Administrative Recruiter - *Sales, administration, accounting, technical, finance, human resources*

3075 E Thousand Oaks Blvd
Westlake, CA 91361
(805) 370-8236
Web: www.venturajobs.com
Key Contact - Specialty:
Ms. Lindy Sternlight, Regional Manager - *HR, executives, managers, technical*

NDB Associates Inc
RR 2 Box 2276 @ Great Oak Dr
Village of the Eagles
East Stroudsburg, PA 18301-9642
(570) 476-6650
(570) 476-6686
Fax: (570) 476-6691
Email: ndb1@ndbassociates.com

Description: Our focus is cross-disciplinary, integrated communications management within the advertising and marketing sectors. Our agency and individual service is grounded in professionalism, integrity, and discretion. The director, who has 20 years of agency account management and corporate product marketing experience, personally manages our firm.

Key Contact - Specialty:
Ms. Nancy Dolan-Brady, Director - *Advertising, marketing*

Salary minimum: $40,000

Functions: Generalist, Advertising, Mkt. Research, Mktg. Mgmt., Direct Mktg., PR, Graphic Artists

Industries: Generalist, Media, Advertising, Publishing, New Media

NDS Associates Ltd
8 John Walsh Blvd 302
Peekskill, NY 10566
(914) 736-3666
Fax: (914) 736-0902
Email: nelson@ndsassoc.com
Web: www.ndsassoc.com

Description: Global recruitment for the printed circuit board manufacturing industry and related supplier companies since 1982 - general management, sales mgt/sales, marketing, product mgt. quality control mgt., and engineering.

Key Contact - Specialty:
Mr. Nelson Silverstein, President - *Printed circuit boards*
Ms. Sue Kornfeld, Director of Recruitment - *Printed circuit board manufacturing*

Salary minimum: $75,000

Functions: General Mgmt., Middle Mgmt., Product Dev., Production, Quality, Sales & Mktg., Sales Mgmt., Engineering, Int'l.

Industries: Electronic, Elec. Components

Don Neal & Associates
404 W Main
Stroud, OK 74079
(918) 968-2568
(800) 359-3990
Fax: (918) 968-2121
Email: dneal@brightok.net
Web: www.donneal.com

Description: National and international search in the areas of commercial bank, loan review, risk analysis, underwriting, and managed assets.

Key Contact - Specialty:
Mr. Don Neal, President - *Loan administration, credit & compliance, commercial underwriting, risk analysis, managed assets*
Ms. Martha Gaches, Administrative Assistant - *Loan administration, credit & compliance, commercial underwriting, risk analysis, managed assets*

Salary minimum: $45,000

Functions: Generalist

Industries: Banking

Neal Management Inc
152 Madison Ave Ste 605
New York, NY 10016
(212) 686-1686
Fax: (212) 686-1590
Email: info@nealmanagement.com
Web: www.nealmanagement.com

Description: We are a unique recruiting firm specializing in the placement of high caliber accounting and financial professionals geared towards the financial service industry. We are a market leader in permanent, long term consulting, and temporary staffing!

Key Contact - Specialty:
Mr. Peter Tannenbaum, President - *Accounting, financial support*

Salary minimum: $50,000

Functions: Finance, Budgeting, Cash Mgmt.

Industries: Generalist, Accounting

Professional Associations: APCNY

Needham Consultants Inc
2277 Hall Rd
Hartford, WI 53027
(262) 670-6795
Fax: (262) 670-6794
Email: mike@needhamconsultants.com

Description: We specialize in power generation and energy industry.

Key Contact - Specialty:
Mr. Mike Needham, President - *Manufacturing environment*
Ms. Bobbie Needham, Vice President - *Manufacturing*

Functions: General Mgmt., Mfg., Sales & Mktg., Engineering

Industries: Generalist

The Neely Group
(also known as Sales Consultants of Alpharetta)
314 Maxwell Rd Ste 600
Alpharetta, GA 30004
(770) 569-9511
Fax: (770) 569-0477
Email: meely@mindspring.com
Web: www.mrinet.com

Description: We specialize in the placement of valued sales, manufacturing, and management personnel in the plastics, packaging, and specialty chemical industries.

Key Contact - Specialty:
Mr. Bob E. Neely, Manager
Mr. Bill Lide, Account Executive - *Specialty chemicals*
Mrs. Geri Gray, Account Executive/ Project Manager - *Plastics, packaging*

Salary minimum: $50,000

Functions: Sales & Mktg.

Industries: Agri., Forestry, Mining, Food, Bev., Tobacco, Paper, Chemicals, Plastics, Rubber, Paints, Petro. Products, Metal Products, Machine, Appliance, Haz. Waste, Packaging

Networks: Recruiters Professional Network (RPN)

Beverly Nelson & Associates Inc
11770 Bernardo Plz Ct Ste 212
San Diego, CA 92128
(858) 613-1000
Fax: (858) 613-1001
Email: nelsnassoc@aol.com

Description: Executive search firm specializing in the placement of management and technical personnel in the property/casualty insurance area.

Key Contact - Specialty:
Ms. Beverly M. Nelson, Owner - *Insurance (property, casualty)*

Salary minimum: $25,000

Functions: Generalist

Industries: Insurance

Professional Associations: NIRA

Len Nelson & Associates Inc
PO Box 690570
San Antonio, TX 78269-0570
(210) 690-9191
(210) 828-8750
Fax: (210) 690-3020
Email: lennelson@lensjobs.com
Web: www.lensjobs.com

Description: Work with other affiliates across the United States. Can market people in any location they prefer.

Key Contact - Specialty:
Mr. Len Nelson, President - *Manufacturing (all types), hardware, software, electronics, telecommunications*

Salary minimum: $30,000

Functions: Mfg., Product Dev., Production, Automation, Quality, Productivity, Materials, Materials Plng., Engineering, Minorities

Industries: Medical Devices, Plastics, Rubber, Metal Products, Machine, Appliance, Motor Vehicles, Computer Equip., Telecoms, Defense, Aerospace, Packaging, Software

NESCO Search
1655 Brittian Rd
Akron, OH 44310
(330) 630-2556
Fax: (330) 630-2536
Email: akron@nescoservice.com
Web: www.nescoservice.com

Description: Our forte is technical search. 60% of our business is in the engineering field and 40% is in the information technology industry. 70% of our clients are in the Midwest.

Key Contact:
Ms. Karen Schmitt, Administrator

Salary minimum: $40,000

Functions: Generalist, Middle Mgmt., Product Dev., Production, Automation, Plant Mgmt., IT, Engineering

Industries: Generalist, Plastics, Rubber, Metal Products, Machine, Appliance, Motor Vehicles, Consumer Elect., Misc. Mfg., Packaging

Netsoft
2727 Walsh Ave Ste 101
Santa Clara, CA 95051
(408) 562-2080 x68
Fax: (408) 562-2070
Email: eric@netsofts.com
Web: www.netsofts.com

Description: We service California-based network infrastructure startups. We have worked with Riverstone, Redback, Extreme Networks, Grand Junction, and Netscape, which are all prepublic. We specialize in engineering, marketing and sales, and individual contributor to VP. We place no entry-level positions. We place California positions only.

Key Contact:
Mr. Eric Thoreson, Founder
Mr. Randy Prout, Co-Founder

Salary minimum: $60,000

Functions: Middle Mgmt., Product Dev., Mkt. Research, Mktg. Mgmt., Sales Mgmt., Customer Svc., Engineering

Industries: Communications, Telecoms, Telephony, Digital, Wireless, Fiber Optic, Network Infrastructure, Database SW, Development SW, Doc. Mgmt., Production SW, Networking, Comm. SW, Security SW, System SW

Branches:
4660 La Jolla Village Dr Ste 500
San Diego, CA 92122
(858) 625-4608
Fax: (858) 625-4603
Email: rick@netsofts.com
Key Contact - Specialty:
Mr. Rick Raimondi, Managing Director - *Network infrastructure engineering*
Mr. Marc "Rogie" Robinson, Managing Director - *Wireless engineering*

The Network Corporate Search Personnel Inc
500 - 4th Ave SW Altius Ctr Ste 510
Calgary, AB T2P 2V6
Canada
(403) 262-6630
Fax: (403) 262-5150
Email: info@networksearch.net
Web: www.networksearch.net

Description: A talented group of dynamic recruiters committed to servicing the marketplace in a professional manner.

Key Contact - Specialty:
Ms. Pat Riddell, President - *Information technology*
Ms. Kim McKay, Vice President - *Insurance*

Salary minimum: $40,000

Functions: IT

Industries: Insurance, Software

Network Dynamics Enterprise Inc
200 W 57th St Ste 1104
New York, NY 10019
(212) 258-2600
(800) 677-5634
Fax: (212) 258-2236
Email: walter@networkdynamics.com
Web: www.networkdynamics.com

Description: We are a permanent placement search firm specialized in placing experienced sales and technical sales candidates servicing the software industry on a national level.

Key Contact:
Mr. Mark O'Brien, Owner, Founder
Mr. Walter Zem, Managing Partner

Salary minimum: $75,000

Functions: Sales Mgmt.

Industries: Software

Network Search Inc
1651 Yarmouth Ave
Boulder, CO 80304
(303) 444-1714
Fax: (303) 440-3408
Email: russ@networksearchinc.com
Web: www.networksearchinc.com

Description: Specialize in high-tech start-ups, research and development, engineers in the Silicon Valley and Colorado.

Key Contact - Specialty:
Mr. Russell Agee, President - *High technology research & development, hardware & software engineering*

Salary minimum: $65,000

Functions: Generalist, Directors, Middle Mgmt., Systems Analysis, Systems Dev., Systems Implem., Network Admin., Engineering

Industries: Generalist, Aerospace, Software

Networking Unlimited of NH Inc
67 W Surry Rd
PO Box 802
Keene, NH 03431
(603) 357-1918
Fax: (603) 352-2627
Email: denis@monad.net

Description: We are an executive search firm specializing in the placement of healthcare and information services professionals on a permanent, temporary and locum tenen basis.

Key Contact - Specialty:
Mr. Denis R. Dubois, President - *Medical, information systems*

Salary minimum: $50,000

Functions: Generalist, Admin. Svcs., IT, MIS Mgmt., Systems Analysis, Systems Implem.

Industries: Generalist, Pharm Svcs., Software, Healthcare

Professional Associations: NHAPS

New Dimensions in Technology Inc
74 Atlantic Ave Ste 101
Seaside Office Bldg
Marblehead, MA 01945
(781) 639-0866
Fax: (781) 639-0863

Email: bk@ndt.com
Web: www.ndt.com

Description: Our firm services early-stage start-ups, mid-size, and Fortune 500 companies in need of technology and techno-business professionals. We specialize in the "global" placement of junior through senior/executive-level professionals in the areas of: software/hardware, information technology, marketing/business development; and consulting/professional services.

Key Contact - Specialty:
Ms. Beverly A. Kahn, President/CEO - *Software, e-commerce, internet, intranet, consulting*
Mr. Laurence S. Kahn, Vice President-Sales - *Technology (business)*

Salary minimum: $60,000

Functions: Generalist

Industries: Computer Equip., Mgmt. Consulting, IT Implementation, Telephony, Wireless, Defense, Software, Database SW, Development SW, Networking, Comm. SW

Professional Associations: HRC, TCI, WIT, WPO

New Venture Development Inc
596 Canyon Vista Dr
The Du Ket Bldg
Thousand Oaks, CA 91320
(805) 498-8506
(805) 480-1892
Fax: (805) 498-2735
Email: duketnvd@gte.net
Web: www.home1.gte.net/dukenvd/

Description: We are known (by industry leaders) for our quite-low-key searches that install confidence and invite candor in the candidates. Our high degree of integrity assures that each individual candidate will have positive feelings about your company after the search has concluded.

Key Contact - Specialty:
Mr. David R. Du Ket, President - *Telecommunications, sales & marketing engineers, product engineers-memory/processor test engineers*
Mrs. Holly V. Du Ket, CFO - *RF microwave amplifier development engineers, VSAT modem*
Mr. Eric S. Pommer, Corporate Executive Vice President - *RF microwave design engineers, test, produce, applications engineers, OA reliability engineers*
Mr. Tim Aspell, Executive VP, Engineering - *ATE sales, marketing, applications, test & product engineers, systems engineers*

Salary minimum: $70,000

Functions: Product Dev., Production, Productivity, Sales & Mktg., Sales Mgmt., Systems Dev., R&D, Engineering

Industries: Mfg., Computer Equip., Consumer Elect., Test, Measure Equip., Misc. Mfg., Equip Svcs., Mgmt. Consulting, HR Services, Media, Telecoms, Defense, Aerospace, Packaging, Software

Professional Associations: NCMA

Newcomb-Desmond & Associates Inc
PO Box 201
Milford, OH 45150-0201
(513) 831-9522
Fax: (513) 831-9557
Email: nda1@earthlink.net
Web: www.newcombdesmond.com

Description: Aggressive national recruiting firm, broad client base, all resumes welcome. Specialists in information systems (hardware & software), sales and marketing, human resources, engineering.

Key Contact - Specialty:
Mr. Mike Desmond, COO - *MIS, technology*

Salary minimum: $45,000

Functions: General Mgmt.

Industries: Plastics, Rubber, Paints, Petro. Products, Metal Products, Machine, Appliance, Motor Vehicles, Computer Equip., Aerospace, Insurance, Software

Professional Associations: OSSA

The Newell Group
(also known as MRI of Greer)
3921 S Hwy 14 Ste C
Greenville, SC 29615
(864) 288-0011
Fax: (413) 653-4778
Email: recruiters@mgmttalent.com

Description: We are an executive recruiting firm specializing in the retail industry.

Key Contact:
Mr. Daniel Newell

Functions: Generalist

Industries: Wholesale, Retail, Finance, Hospitality

Newlon Services Inc
10535 E Washington St Ste 318
PO Box 29157
Indianapolis, IN 46229
(317) 891-9330
Fax: (775) 640-7994
Email: dthomas@newlonservices.com
Web: www.newlonservices.com

Description: We offer career opportunities for professionals in ERP, consulting, software/hardware, engineering manufacturing, and other high-tech fields.

Key Contact:
Mr. Donald Thomas, Partner

Functions: IT

Industries: E-commerce, IT Implementation, Telecoms, Call Centers, Telephony, Digital, Wireless, Fiber Optic, Network Infrastructure, ERP SW

Networks: Top Echelon Network

Newman Hawkins Legal Search
31017 Westwood
Farmington Hills, MI 48331
(248) 661-8900
Fax: (248) 661-9018
Email: lawjobhunt@aol.com
Web: www.michiganrecruiter.com

Description: Firm specializes in attorney placement in Michigan. Nancy Newman is a 1986 graduate of Wayne State University Law School and practiced litigation at a prestigious Michigan law firm. We work with corporations and law firms to satisfy all attorney hiring needs.

Key Contact - Specialty:
Ms. Nancy L. Newman, JD, President - *Attorney placement*

Functions: Legal

Industries: Generalist

Professional Associations: NALSC

Newman-Johnson-King Inc
PO Box 0729
Rockport, TX 78381
(361) 790-5959
Fax: (361) 790-5391
Email: jking@pyramid3.net

Description: A 40-year history of ethical, professional, effective service to nationwide firms and candidates. A portion of current 10,000 searches may be seen at web site.

Key Contact - Specialty:
Mr. Jack King, President - *Engineering, sales, information technologists, manufacturing*

Salary minimum: $40,000

Functions: Mfg., Sales Mgmt., IT, R&D, Engineering

Industries: Generalist

Networks: National Personnel Assoc (NPA)

Newport Management
100 E Hartsdale Ave
Hartsdale, NY 10530
(914) 725-5244
Email: newport@.att.net

Description: Specialize in sales, sales management, marketing and technical support in computer hardware, software and networking.

Key Contact - Specialty:
Mr. Kenneth Zeif, President - *Computer software sales, computer hardware sales, computer networking sales*

Salary minimum: $50,000

Functions: Senior Mgmt., Sales Mgmt.

Industries: Software

Newport Strategic Search LLC
3088 Pio Pico Dr Ste 203
Carlsbad, CA 92008
(760) 434-9940
Fax: (760) 434-9896
Email: nsearch@sprynet.com
Web: www.newportsearch.com

Description: We have five distinct areas in which we specialize: telecommunications, including carriers and equipment providers; information technology; digital entertainment; biotechnology/pharmaceutical; and accounting/finance.

Key Contact - Specialty:
Mr. John Fitzpatrick, President - *Telecommunications*

Salary minimum: $60,000

Functions: Generalist, Senior Mgmt., Middle Mgmt., Sales Mgmt., Systems Implem., Network Admin., Engineering, Technicians

Industries: Generalist, Mgmt. Consulting, Telecoms, Biotech

Branches:
23141 Verdugo Dr Ste 204
Laguna Hills, CA 92653
(949) 465-9960
Key Contact:
Mr. John C. Fitzpatrick

Newtown Consulting Group Inc
(also known as Sales Consultants of Newtown)
301 S State St
Newtown, PA 18940-1997
(215) 579-2450
Fax: (215) 579-2458
Email: jplappert@mrinewtown.com
Web: www.mrinewtown.com

Description: We are specialists in two areas. The first is sales, sales management, underwriting, claims, and general management recruiting in the group life, disability, health, managed care, and pension/retirement insurance industry. Secondly in computer security, more specifically: software, hardware, engineering, and architecture and system network administration

Key Contact:
Mr. James Plappert, President

Salary minimum: $35,000

Functions: General Mgmt., Senior Mgmt., Middle Mgmt., Sales & Mktg., Mktg. Mgmt., Sales Mgmt., Systems Dev., Systems Implem., Network Admin., DB Admin.

Industries: Computer Equip., Insurance, Database SW, Development SW, Security SW, System SW

Nex Canada Inc
55 University Ave Ste 305
Toronto, ON M5J 2H7
Canada
(416) 867-1162
Fax: (416) 867-1369
Web: www.pasona.co.jp

Description: We specialize in placing individuals into Japan-related organizations. We provide bilingual and unilingual staff from entry level to senior management to such firms.

Key Contact - Specialty:
Ms. Joy Haywood, Vice President - *Japanese & english bilingual (senior & junior)*
Ms. Fumie Wada, Branch Manager - *Japanese & english bilingual (senior & junior)*

Functions: Generalist

Industries: Motor Vehicles, Consumer Elect., Misc. Mfg., Finance, Banking, Invest. Banking, Services, Accounting, HR Services

Networks: Pasona Group Global Network

Next Step Recruiting
3130 La Selva Dr Ste 105
San Mateo, CA 94403
(650) 577-8000
Fax: (650) 577-9000
Email: info@4nextstep.com
Web: www.4nextstep.com

Description: Close proximity to San Francisco airport. Onsite interview facilities. Consistently ranked as one of the top 10 search firms in Silicon Valley and San Francisco every year.

Key Contact - Specialty:
Mr. Glenn S. Davis, President - *Software, consulting, outsourcing (sales & sales management)*
Mr. Jeffrey Spangler, Partner - *Business services, contract furniture*

Salary minimum: $75,000

Functions: General Mgmt., Directors, Sales & Mktg., Sales Mgmt., HR Mgmt., Training, IT, MIS Mgmt., Systems Implem., Systems Support

Industries: Services, Mgmt. Consulting, HR Services, E-commerce, IT Implementation, Wireless, Software, ERP SW, Marketing SW, Training SW, Biotech

Professional Associations: CLM

NHA Plastics Recruiters
211 S Lakeshore Blvd
Howey in the Hills, FL 34737
(888) 365-9708
Fax: (888) 365-9707
Email: greg@bittner.net
Web: www.nha-recruiters.com

Description: Specializing in sales, operating, design and maintenance personnel in primarily injection, extrusion and blowmolding machinery manufacturers. Extensive contacts at the highest levels of the industry.

Key Contact - Specialty:
Ms. Susan E. Bittner, President - *Plastics machinery*
Mr. Greg Bittner, Vice President - *Plastics processing, plastics machinery*

Functions: Generalist, Senior Mgmt., Product Dev., Production, Sales Mgmt., Systems Analysis, Engineering, Technicians

Industries: Generalist, Plastics, Rubber

Networks: Top Echelon Network

Marc Nichols Associates Inc
205 Lexington Ave Fl 9
New York, NY 10016
(212) 725-1750
Fax: (212) 725-1790
Email: bmoore@mna.com
Web: www.mna.com

Description: Our firm includes fifteen specialists, two generalists, and a large research staff. Our departments include: banking, brokerage, investments, capital, emerging markets, MIS, accounting, EDP audit, marketing, sales, HR, compliance, telecommunications, and tax.

Key Contact - Specialty:
Mr. Marc Nichols, Senior Partner - *Generalist*
Mr. Bill Moore, Senior Partner - *Generalist*

Functions: General Mgmt., Senior Mgmt., Middle Mgmt., Sales & Mktg., HR Mgmt., Finance, Taxes, Risk Mgmt., Mgmt. Consultants, Int'l.

Industries: Generalist, Finance, Banking, Invest. Banking, Brokers, Venture Cap., Misc. Financial, Services, IT Implementation, Telephony, Insurance, Accounting SW, HR SW, Marketing SW, Networking, Comm. SW

P J Nicholson & Associates
1301 W 22nd St Ste 604
Oak Brook, IL 60521
(630) 574-0555
Fax: (630) 574-0559

Description: We are a custom firm that specializes in financial, operations and general management.

Key Contact - Specialty:
Mr. Philip J. Nicholson, Principal - *Finance, operations, general management*

Salary minimum: $70,000

Functions: Generalist, Senior Mgmt., Product Dev., Mktg. Mgmt., CFO's, M&A, Minorities

Industries: Generalist, Chemicals, Medical Devices, Metal Products, Misc. Mfg., Aerospace

Nied-Newman & Associates
6040 Verde Trail S Unit 302
La Provence
Boca Raton, FL 33433
(561) 218-1544
Fax: (561) 218-0801

Description: My clients pay me the fee. Fee being 20%-30% of candidates first year salary and some clients include the bonus for the year.

Key Contact - Specialty:
Ms. Georgette J. Newman, President/Owner - *Actuaries, lawyers, environmental, engineers, telecommunications*

Salary minimum: $100,000

Functions: General Mgmt., Legal, Automation, Healthcare, Benefits, Finance, CFO's, IT, Engineering, Environmentalists

Industries: Generalist

Ira Z Nitzberg
60
Granite Springs, NY 10527
(914) 245-9070
Fax: (914) 245-3743
Email: execrecruiter@bigfoot.com

Description: Recruitment of data processing, healthcare and medical professionals in

management, development and implementation in both the user and vendor environments. In the vendor environment we also place sales, marketing and support personnel.

Key Contact - Specialty:
Mr. Ira Z. Nitzberg, CDP, Owner - *Information technology, executive management*
Ms. Shelly Heller, Senior Consultant - *Information technology, medical*

Functions: Generalist, Middle Mgmt., Physicians, Mktg. Mgmt., MIS Mgmt., Systems Analysis, Systems Dev., Mgmt. Consultants

Industries: Generalist, Drugs Mfg., Computer Equip., Pharm Svcs., Mgmt. Consulting, Telecoms, Network Infrastructure, Software, Database SW, Development SW, Marketing SW, Networking, Comm. SW, Security SW, System SW, Biotech, Healthcare, Hospitals

J L Nixon Consulting
3846 County Rd 1147
Celeste, TX 75423
(903) 568-4111
Fax: (903) 568-4114
Email: recruiters@jlnixon.com
Web: www.jlnixon.com

Description: We are a full-service personnel consulting and executive search firm dedicated to the search and recruitment of professionals in the insurance and managed care industry. As industry specialists in property/casualty, life, accident and health insurance and managed care, our organization provides one of the most comprehensive array of services in the search business.

Key Contact - Specialty:
Mr. Jeffrey L. Nixon, CPC, President - *Insurance, managed care*

Salary minimum: $45,000

Functions: Generalist

Industries: Insurance

Professional Associations: INS, NIRA, RON

NJ Solutions Inc
1127 Victoria Ln
Spring Branch, TX 78070
(830) 885-6755
Fax: (830) 885-6757
Email: njsolutn@gvtc.com

Description: Principal is a degreed chemist with 20+ years' experience in the petroleum industry with a background in research & development, sales and operations. The executive search and placement business has been active for eight years with related industries.

Key Contact - Specialty:
Mr. Gail Johnston, CAC, Owner - *Chemical sales, oil refining, chemists, environmental*

Salary minimum: $35,000

Functions: Generalist, Sales Mgmt., R&D, Engineering

Industries: Generalist, Chemicals, Paints, Petro. Products

NL Associates Inc
701 Westchester Ave Ste 308W
White Plains, NY 10604
(914) 684-2600
Fax: (914) 684-2605
Email: neil@nlassociates.com
Web: www.nlassociates.com

Description: Sales and marketing on a national basis.

Key Contact - Specialty:
Mr. Neil Liguori, President - *Sales & marketing*

Functions: Directors, Middle Mgmt., Sales & Mktg., Mktg. Mgmt., Sales Mgmt.

Industries: Generalist

Networks: US Recruiters.com

Branches:
25 Sunswept Dr
New Fairfield, CT 06812
(203) 746-6060
Fax: (203) 746-5433
Key Contact:
Mr. Erik Liguori
Ms. Susan Liguori

Noble & Associates Inc
420 Madison Ave Ste 803
New York, NY 10017
(212) 838-7020
Fax: (212) 838-7344
Email: nobleinc@inch.com

Description: Marketing, advertising and corporate communications to include direct marketing, product management, sports marketing research, advertising account management, sales promotion, creative, new business, media database marketing, general administration of marketing oriented company, international.

Key Contact:
Mr. Donald Noble, Principal

Salary minimum: $50,000

Functions: Generalist

Industries: Media, Advertising, New Media

Noble/Sander Search
535 16th St Ste 620
Denver, CO 80202
(303) 825-3646
Fax: (303) 629-6056
Email: resumes@noblesandersearch.com

Description: We specialize in positions in the advertising, marketing, public relations, and communications fields. We also work on behalf of non-profit organizations to help them find new leadership. We were founded by veteran recruiter Don Noble and advertising executive Steve Sander. Our offices are located in New York City and Denver, CO.

Key Contact:
Mr. Don Noble, Principal - *Advertising, marketing, corporate communications, product management, market research*
Mr. Steve Sander, Principal - *Advertising, marketing, corporate communications, marketing, sports marketing*
Ms. Megan Lemieux, Senior Consultant - *Advertising, marketing*
Mrs. Raleigh Decker, Senior Consultant

Salary minimum: $50,000

Functions: Sales & Mktg., Advertising, Mktg. Mgmt., PR, Non-profits, Graphic Artists

Industries: Generalist, Non-profits, Advertising, Publishing, New Media, Broadcast, Film, Telecoms, Software

Professional Associations: AMA, PRSA

L S Noel Consulting Ltd
162 Mill Pond Ct
Richmond Hill, ON L4C 4W5
Canada
(905) 770-1517
Fax: (905) 884-9433
Email: head-hunter@bigfoot.com
Web: www.lesnoel.com

Description: We specialize in software, consulting and Internet/intranet search, assisting the recruiting efforts of vendors and consulting firms in Canada and the United States. While our focus is on full-time placements, we also handle contract positions. Applications and systems software are our main focus areas, with emphasis on sales and sales support, at all levels within the corporate infrastructure.

Key Contact:
Mr. Les Noel, President

Salary minimum: $60,000

Functions: Generalist

Industries: Computer Equip., Software

NOJ Executive USA
1994 N Kolb Rd
Tucson, AZ 85715
(520) 290-8880
Fax: (520) 290-8888
Email: nojusa@classic.msn.com

Description: We recruit management executives and specialists nationally and internationally. The search process is custom tailored for each individual assignment to ensure that the correct candidate is found in every case.

Key Contact - Specialty:
Mr. Peter Siragna, Managing Partner - *Banking, financial, forfeiting*
Ms. Terry Young-Delgado, Recruiter - *Sales & marketing, medical*

Salary minimum: $50,000

Functions: Generalist, Senior Mgmt., Production, Health Admin., Mkt. Research, CFO's, Systems Analysis, Engineering

Industries: Generalist, Banking, Invest. Banking, Venture Cap., Misc. Financial, Pharm Svcs., Accounting

Networks: National Personnel Assoc (NPA)

The Nolan Group Inc
16415-A Northcross Dr
Huntersville, NC 28078
(704) 944-7700
Fax: (704) 944-7744
Email: info@nolangroupusa.com
Web: www.nolangroupusa.com

Description: We have multiple practices including attorney search, software industry sales and marketing, implementation, and development, wireless technology from executive level to contracting, and miscellaneous general practices of varied function and industry.

Key Contact:
Mr. John Nolan, CEO/President

Functions: Generalist

Industries: Construction, Mfg., Transportation, Wholesale, Retail, Finance, Services, Communications, Software, Biotech

Networks: Top Echelon Network

The Nolan Group
100 Pringle Ave Ste 250
Walnut Creek, CA 94596
(925) 938-6700
Fax: (925) 938-7740
Web: www.thenolangroup.com

Description: Executive search and consulting for accounting and finance professionals. Concentration at the controller, CFO, VP level.

Key Contact - Specialty:
Ms. Nancy C. Nolan, President - *Finance & accounting*
Ms. Lynn Scott, Vice President - *Finance & accounting*

Salary minimum: $60,000

Functions: Generalist, Senior Mgmt., Middle Mgmt., CFO's, Budgeting, Cash Mgmt., M&A

Industries: Generalist, Energy, Utilities, Computer Equip., Legal, Accounting, Real Estate, Software

Noll Human Resource Services
(also known as J Douglas Scott & Assoc)
12905 W Dodge Rd
Omaha, NE 68154
(402) 334-9200
(800) 798-7736
Fax: (402) 334-7333
Email: nollinc@aol.com
Web: www.noll-inc.com

Description: Experienced high integrity recruiters who get the job done in virtually every area of executive search.

Key Contact - Specialty:
Mr. William T. Noll, CPC, President - *Generalist, information systems, logistics, sales, accounting, retail*

Functions: Generalist

Industries: Mfg., Accounting, Mgmt. Consulting, Telecoms, Packaging, Software, Healthcare

Branches:
1515 W 22nd St Ste 850
Oak Brook Twrs
Oak Brook, IL 60523
(630) 928-0800
(888) 536-7600
Fax: (630) 928-0900
Email: nollchi@enteract.com
Key Contact - Specialty:
Mr. Michael Anton - *Information systems, sales, telecom, quality engineers, management*

55 Westport Plz Ste 575
St. Louis, MO 63146
(314) 542-9200
(888) 509-0800
Fax: (314) 542-0400
Email: slnoll@inlink.com
Key Contact - Specialty:
Mr. William Mueller - *IS, manufacturing, engineering & operations, sales & marketing, insurance*

5720 LBJ Fwy Ste 610
Bankers Commercial Life Bldg
Dallas, TX 75240
(972) 392-2900
(800) 536-7600
Fax: (972) 934-3600
Email: nolldallas@aol.com
Key Contact - Specialty:
Mr. Perry Smith, Manager - *Information systems, logistics, environmental, healthcare*

Norgate Technology Inc
170 Old Country Rd Ste 311
Mineola, NY 11501
(516) 248-0444
Fax: (516) 248-0488
Email: info@norgate.com
Web: www.norgate.com

Description: Technical search and recruiting of programmers and systems administrators specializing in Internet and client/server technologies. Java, UNIX/Solaris/HP-UX/AIX, Windows NT, object oriented technology, C++, Oracle, SQL Server, Sybase and DB2.

Key Contact - Specialty:
Mr. Lawrence J. Cohen, President - *Client/server technologies, internet, web, systems administration*

Salary minimum: $35,000

Functions: Generalist, IT, MIS Mgmt., Systems Analysis, Systems Dev., Systems Implem., Systems Support, Network Admin., DB Admin.

Industries: Generalist, Finance, Software, Database SW, Development SW, Networking, Comm. SW

The Normyle/Erstling Health Search Group
350 W Passaic St
Rochelle Park, NJ 07662
(201) 843-6009
Fax: (201) 843-2060
Email: jobs@medpharmsales.com
Web: www.medpharmsales.com

Description: Our firm was founded by two former vice presidents and long time sales managers for the pharmaceutical and medical device industries. We specialize in sales, sales management, marketing, and operations. We are professional, confidential, and connected.

Key Contact - Specialty:
Mr. Charles D. Kreps, Managing Partner - *Medical, healthcare, pharmaceutical*

Salary minimum: $50,000

Functions: Healthcare, Nurses, Sales & Mktg., Mkt. Research, Mktg. Mgmt., Sales Mgmt.

Industries: Medical Devices, Pharm Svcs., Biotech, Healthcare

Networks: First Interview Network (FIN)

John B Norris & Associates Inc
PO Box 2068
Westminster, MD 21158
(410) 876-5550
Fax: (410) 876-5551
Email: jbninc@infi.net

Description: A commitment to provide an acceptable candidate within four-six working days after placing a job order.

Key Contact - Specialty:
Mr. John B. Norris, President - *Food (all management levels), beverage, dairy*

Salary minimum: $30,000

Functions: Generalist, General Mgmt., Mfg., Sales & Mktg., HR Mgmt., Finance, R&D, Engineering, Int'l.

Industries: Generalist, Food, Bev., Tobacco

Professional Associations: MAPRC

Ronald Norris & Associates
8457 E Prairie Rd
Skokie, IL 60076
(847) 679-6074

Description: Over 30 years of concentration in equipment finance/leasing and asset base lending and bank commercial lending.

Key Contact - Specialty:
Mr. Ronald Norris, Owner - *Commercial finance, leasing*

Salary minimum: $25,000

Functions: Generalist, Middle Mgmt., Sales Mgmt., Credit

Industries: Generalist, Banking, Equip Svcs.

Norris Agency
6112 Oakcrest Rd
Dallas, TX 75248
(972) 701-0110
(888) 327-6971
Fax: (972) 701-0613
Email: headhunt@norrisagency.com

Description: Certified personnel consultant working nationwide. Executive searches within the food and beverage industry.

Key Contact - Specialty:
Ms. Cathy A. Norris, CPC, Owner - *Food, beverage industry*

Salary minimum: $40,000

Functions: Directors, Senior Mgmt., Middle Mgmt., Product Dev., Quality, R&D

Industries: Food, Bev., Tobacco, Soap, Perf., Cosmtcs.

Professional Associations: AACC, AACT, AChemS, ADSA, AICHE, AOCS, ASAS, ASTM, FASEB, IFT, IOPP, IRG, NAPS, SFA

NorTech Resources
321 Delaware Ave
Delmar, NY 12054
(518) 475-9700
Email: info@nortechresources.com
Web: www.nortechresources.com

Description: Serving suppliers to the adhesives, coatings, radiation curing fine chemicals and thermoset polymer industries via contingency and retained searches for chemists, technical managers, technical service and technically trained marketing people.

Key Contact - Specialty:
Mr. Michael T. Fahey, General Manager - *Chemical industry*

Salary minimum: $60,000

Functions: Product Dev., Sales & Mktg.

Industries: Printing, Chemicals, Soap, Perf., Cosmtcs., Drugs Mfg., Plastics, Rubber, Paints, Petro. Products, Biotech

Professional Associations: RI

North Coast Meridian Inc
PO Box 640
Pine Bush, NY 12566
(845) 744-3061
Fax: (845) 744-3961
Email: nrcoastm@frontiernet.net
Web: www.ncmrecruiters.com

Description: Nationwide technical recruiters specializing in manufacturing, industrial, process engineering, related disciplines. Operations and plant management, materials and logistics management, quality assurance, related. Contingency and retained search.

Key Contact - Specialty:
Mr. Charles F. Thomaschek - *Engineering, manufacturing, supply chain, quality, operations*

Salary minimum: $40,000

Functions: Mfg., Materials, IT, Engineering, Technicians

Industries: Energy, Utilities, Mfg., Equip Svcs., Aerospace, Packaging, Software

Professional Associations: APICS, ASQ, NAPS, SME, SMTA

Networks: Inter-City Personnel Assoc (IPA)

The North Peak Group
16208 Madison Ave
Lakewood, OH 44107
(216) 221-8300
Email: mbruns6108@aol.com

Description: We are a national search firm concentrating in, but not limited to, information technology, data processing, environmental, and engineering industries. We are affiliated with Top Echelon, a group of the best search professionals nationwide. We have helped over 300 clients and candidates find their "perfect" match!

Key Contact - Specialty:
Mr. Matthew Bruns, President - *MIS, environmental*

Salary minimum: $50,000

Functions: Senior Mgmt., MIS Mgmt., Systems Analysis, Systems Dev., Network Admin., DB Admin., Engineering

Industries: Generalist

Professional Associations: SHRM

Networks: Top Echelon Network

Northland Employment Services Inc
400 S Hwy 169 Ste 450
St. Louis Park, MN 55426
(952) 541-1060
Fax: (952) 595-9878
Email: northland@iso.net
Web: www.jobsmn.com

Description: Specialist in information systems, programming and systems analysts. Multidisciplined engineering placement in a broad range of technical fields. Financial executive search and interim placement.

Key Contact - Specialty:
Mr. David R. Gavin, President - *Technical, engineering, data processing*
Mr. Mike Grahek, MS, Vice President - *Information technology*
Mr. Skip Black, CPC, Vice President Engineering Recruitment - *Engineering*

Functions: Generalist

Industries: Generalist

Northstar Int'l Insurance Recruiters Inc
10 James Thomas Rd
Malvern, PA 19355
(610) 889-4800
Fax: (610) 889-4802
Email: nstar@northstarjobs.com
Web: www.northstarjobs.com

Description: We exclusively work in the property and casualty insurance industry. Our two specialties/areas of concentration are actuarial, in which we have twenty years of experience, and underwriting and claims for commercial lines and reinsurance.

Key Contact:
Mr. Michael C. Crawford, President - *Actuarial (property, casualty)*
Mr. John G. Carew, Vice President
Mr. William D Jones, Vice President - *Actuarial (property, casualty)*
Mr. Ron Robert, Vice President

Functions: Generalist

Industries: Insurance

NorthStar Technologies Inc
132 Nassau St Ste 309
New York, NY 10038-2400
(212) 267-4100
Fax: (212) 267-4468
Email: info@northstar.com
Web: www.northstar.com

Description: We are a technology company, not just a recruiting firm. Besides our first-class recruiting practice, we also specialize in re-engineering, world wide web/Internet development, mission-critical application development, management consulting and systems integration.

Key Contact:
Mr. Khurshed F. Birdie, President - *Information technology*
Mr. Imran Anwar

Salary minimum: $100,000

Functions: Generalist, MIS Mgmt., Systems Analysis, Systems Dev., Systems Implem., DB Admin., Mgmt. Consultants, Graphic Artists

Industries: Generalist, Banking, Invest. Banking, Brokers, Mgmt. Consulting, New Media, Software

Norton & Associates
7 Michigan Ave
Dundee, IL 60118
(847) 428-9255
Email: gnorton2@msn.com

Description: Specialists in advanced technologies and microelectronics.

Key Contact - Specialty:
Mr. Greg Norton, Principal - *Microelectronics*

Salary minimum: $40,000

Functions: Generalist, Directors, Senior Mgmt., Product Dev., Automation, Productivity, Systems Dev., Engineering

Industries: Generalist, Chemicals, Computer Equip., Consumer Elect., Test, Measure Equip., Aerospace, Software

Novation Legal Services
111 Elm St Ste 390
San Diego, CA 92101
(619) 233-5151
Fax: (619) 233-4321
Email: fs@novationlegal.com
Web: www.novationlegal.com

Description: We place attorneys all over the world, including partners, general counsel, associates, paralegals, and legal secretaries. We accept only two to three clients per city. Our clients receive exclusivity of our candidates. We have filled searches other search firms were unsuccessful at completing. Our specjalties include: intellectual property, bankruptcy, corporate, litigation, health, labor, tax, ERISA, and international.

Key Contact - Specialty:
Mr. Frederick L. Shelton, CPC, President - *Attorneys*
Mr. Rachele Rickert, Esq. - *Attorneys*
Mr. Phil Prodehl - *Attorneys*

Functions: Attorneys

Industries: Generalist

Professional Associations: NALSC

NPC Staffing Inc
1897 Palm Beach Lakes Blvd Ste 208
West Palm Beach, FL 33409
(561) 688-2999
(800) 245-8227
Email: npcs12345@aol.com
Web: www.npcstaffing.com

Description: Our firm was established as a specialized placement firm for managed care, with a service concentration in quality management, utilization management and case management nursing positions, including non patient care nursing services, nationwide.

Key Contact - Specialty:
Mr. Victor Pecaro, BS, Owner/Administrator - *Non patient care nursing, services*

Salary minimum: $40,000

Functions: Generalist, Nurses, Allied Health, Health Admin.

Industries: Healthcare

NR Search Inc
505 Sheridan Rd Ste 2-W
Evanston, IL 60202
(847) 475-3100
Fax: (847) 475-3131
Email: nancy@nrsearch.com
Web: www.nrsearch.com

Description: We've taken the retail search process to a new level from merchandise planning, allocation, and replenishment to buying, design, and product development. Our clients are sent the right candidates the first time and not a bundle of resumes. Our global executive search and recruitment services allow you to meet tomorrow's challenges today.

Key Contact:
Ms. Nancy Shikoff

Salary minimum: $70,000

Functions: Generalist, Senior Mgmt., Product Dev., Purchasing, Distribution, Mktg. Mgmt., CFO's

Industries: Retail, Non-profits

NRI Staffing Resources

1899 L St NW Ste 300
Washington, DC 20036
(202) 466-2160
Fax: (202) 466-6593
Email: nri@nri-staffing.com
Web: www.nri-staffing.com

Description: With 35 recruiters in 12 offices, we operate in five disciplines in the Washington, D.C. Metropolitan area. Our disciplines include accounting and finance, legal office services, general office support and administrative, healthcare, and technical. We also provide temporary staffing services in all five disciplines.

Key Contact - Specialty:
Mr. Robert M. McClimans, Executive Vice President
Mr. Robert D. Mulberger, President
Mr. Eric Malloy, General Manager - *Office support*

Salary minimum: $25,000

Functions: Generalist

Industries: Banking, Misc. Financial, Non-profits, Legal, Accounting, Mgmt. Consulting, Call Centers, Software, Accounting SW, Healthcare

Professional Associations: ASA, BOT, GWSAE, NAPS

Networks: National Personnel Assoc (NPA)

Branches:
734 15th St NW Ste 200
Washington, DC 20005
(202) 628-3060
Fax: (202) 628-2838
Email: nri-legal-dc@nri-staffing.com
Key Contact - Specialty:
Ms. Dori Konopka, General Manager - *Accounting, legal*

1302 Concourse Dr Ste 203
Linthicum, MD 21090
(410) 850-0730
Fax: (410) 850-5263
Email: nri-baltimore@nri-staffing.com
Key Contact:
Ms. Meredith Millet, General Manager - *Legal, administrative, healthcare*
Ms. Wanda Smith Watt

11400 Rockville Pike Ste 820
Rockville, MD 20852
(301) 230-0440
Fax: (301) 230-0451
Email: nri-staffing-md@nri-staffing.com
Key Contact:
Mr. John Giannone, General Manager - *Accounting, office support, healthcare*
Ms. Sonia Benson
Mr. John O'Connell

7611 Little River Tpke Ste 402 W
Annandale, VA 22003
(703) 658-1705
Fax: (703) 658-1493
Email: nri-annandale@nri-staffing.com

Key Contact - Specialty:
Ms. Fran Whatley, General Manager - *Office support, healthcare*
Ms. Mary Covell - *Office support, healthcare*

10780/90 Parkridge Blvd Ste 140
Reston, VA 22091
(703) 391-8000
Fax: (703) 391-9091
Email: nri-reston@nri-staffing.com
Key Contact - Specialty:
Ms. Marianne Earley, General Manager - *Office support, technical*
Ms. Dawn Stauffer - *Office support, technical*

Nstar

5412 Courseview Dr Ste 430
Mason, OH 45040
(513) 459-0384
Fax: (513) 459-1325
Email: lhirnikel@nstarsearch.com
Web: www.nstarsearch.com

Description: We are specializing in recruiting engineers, information technology, and manufacturing.

Key Contact:
Mr. L. J. Hirnikel, President

Salary minimum: $65,000

Functions: Mfg., IT, Engineering

Industries: Generalist, Electronic, Elec. Components, Pharm Svcs., Digital, Wireless, Environmental Svcs., Software, Database SW, Networking, Comm. SW, Biotech

Professional Associations: NAPS

Nuance Personnel Search Inc

103 Woodstream Rd
Mooresville, NC 28117
(704) 663-5831
Fax: (704) 663-5869
Email: recruiter@nc.prestige.net
Web: www.nirassn.com

Description: Eighteen years of contingency search experience. Specializing in: commercial property and casualty insurance. Technical to mid-management. National networking offers unlimited resources for candidates and career opportunities nationwide.

Key Contact - Specialty:
Ms. Lynn Green, CPC, President - *Insurance (property, casualty)*

Salary minimum: $40,000

Functions: Generalist

Industries: Insurance

Professional Associations: NIRA

Nunnelee & Associates Inc

628 Old Hickory Rd
Grenada, MS 38901
(662) 229-0144
Fax: (662) 229-9794
Email: enunle@watervalley.net

Description: We provide staffing solutions for manufacturing companies. We offer 17 years of professional experience in recruiting for leading manufacturing companies.

Key Contact - Specialty:
Ms. Edith Nunnelee, Owner/Manager
Mr. Wayne Nunnelee, Vice-President - *Manufacturing*

Functions: General Mgmt.

Industries: Misc. Mfg., Mfg. SW

Networks: Top Echelon Network

Nyborg•Dow Associates Inc

12781 Woodlake Rd
Grass Valley, CA 95949
(530) 477-7817
Fax: (530) 477-0745
Email: marilyn@nydow.com

Description: Specializing in hardware and software design engineers and management. Working with a variety of start-ups and larger companies in Silicon Valley. Networking, optical, routers, multimedia and a variety of new technologies.

Key Contact:
Ms. Marilyn Nyborg, Co-Owner
Ms. Georgia Dow, Co-Owner
Mr. Steven Russell, Recruiter

Salary minimum: $80,000

Functions: Engineering

Industries: Software

NYCOR Search Inc

4930 W 77th St Ste 300
Minneapolis, MN 55435
(952) 831-6444
(800) 675-6527
Fax: (952) 835-2883
Email: info@nycor.com
Web: www.nycor.com

Description: We are a national engineering, IS, and IT search firm. Nycor offers technical, management, and executive level search and contract services. We have been an industry leader. We provide direct access to our clients who range from emerging growth and dynamic technology companies to Fortune 500s.

Key Contact - Specialty:
Mr. John Nymark, President - *Technical, engineering, IS, IT*

Salary minimum: $40,000

Functions: Generalist, Senior Mgmt., Product Dev., IT, MIS Mgmt., Systems Dev., Network Admin., DB Admin., R&D, Engineering

Industries: Generalist, Medical Devices, Misc. Mfg., E-commerce, IT Implementation, Telecoms, Digital, Wireless, Software, Database SW, Biotech

Professional Associations: MAPS, NAPS, SAM

O'Brien and Roof

6812 Caine Rd
Columbus, OH 43235-4233
(614) 766-8500
Fax: (614) 766-8505
Email: inforeq@obrienroof.com
Web: www.obrienroof.com

Description: Generalist firm whose principals offer 25+ years of recruiting experience. Searches conducted on either a contingency or retainer basis. Over 75% of search assignments comes from satisfied clients.

Key Contact - Specialty:
Ms. Lindy O'Brien, President - *Generalist*
Mr. Howard Roof, CEO - *Generalist*

Salary minimum: $40,000

Functions: Generalist, General Mgmt., Sales & Mktg., HR Mgmt., Finance

Industries: Generalist, Construction, Mfg., Retail, Hospitality, Advertising, Real Estate

Professional Associations: ICSC, SHRM

O'Connell Group Inc

475 Danbury Rd
Wilton, CT 06897
(203) 834-2900
Fax: (203) 834-2728

Email: search@oconnellgroup.com
Web: www.oconnellgroup.com

Description: We are experts in marketing and marketing research disciplines in the consumer packaged goods industries only. This the stuff you'd purchase in a grocery store and/or repeat purchases. Please see our website.

Key Contact - Specialty:
Mr. Brian M. O'Connell, CPC, President - *Marketing, marketing research*

Salary minimum: $70,000

Functions: Mkt. Research, Mktg. Mgmt.

Industries: Food, Bev., Tobacco, Paper, Soap, Perf., Cosmtcs., Drugs Mfg.

Professional Associations: AMA, AMA, NAPS, SHRM

Branches:
9666 Olive Blvd Ste 796
Olive Corporate Ctr
St. Louis, MO 63132
(314) 997-3441
Fax: (314) 997-3931
Email: search@oconnellgroup.com
Key Contact:
Ms. Kris S. Holmes, CPC, Vice President
Mr. Dixon A. Smith, Vice President
Ms. Joanne K. Abernathy, Vice President

1959 N Peace Haven Rd
PO Box 328
Winston-Salem, NC 27106
(336) 794-9075
Fax: (336) 794-9076
Email: search@oconnellgroup.com
Key Contact:
Ms. Robin D. Graves, Vice President

O'Connor Resources

806 N 48th Ave Ste D
Omaha, NE 68132-2477
(402) 551-1001
Email: oconnor01@home.com

Description: Nationally respected in managed care development, marketing, operations, MIS; joint ventures with providers, vendors, insurers, corporations. Expert in reorganization, mergers, downsizing and management succession.

Key Contact:
Mr. Rod O'Connor, President

Salary minimum: $80,000

Functions: Generalist, Senior Mgmt., Middle Mgmt., Health Admin., Mktg. Mgmt., Sales Mgmt., MIS Mgmt., Systems Implem.

Industries: Generalist, Drugs Mfg., Venture Cap., Mgmt. Consulting, New Media, Telecoms, Insurance, Healthcare

O'Hare Search Group

(also known as MRI of O'Hare)
1400 E Touhy Ave Ste 160
Des Plaines, IL 60018-3374
(800) 940-7532
Fax: (847) 297-6744
Email: jobs@mr-ohare.com
Web: www.mr-ohare.com

Description: We have had twenty-six years of experience in the following specialties: IT, accounting/finance, manufacturing, and telecommunications.

Key Contact:
Mr. Richard A. Kurz, President - *Finance & accounting*
Mr. Ward Larkin

Salary minimum: $60,000

Functions: Production, Plant Mgmt., Materials Plng., Mkt. Research, Budgeting, Taxes, Systems Implem.

Industries: Generalist

O'Keefe & Associates

PO Box 90608
Austin, TX 78709-0608
(888) 446-2137
Fax: (240) 332-8085
Email: resumes@okeefeasearch.com
Web: www.okeefeassociates.com

Description: Austin's high-tech headhunters. We specialize in advanced technologies; OOP, Windows, NT, Multiplatform UNIX, Java, Oracle and Powerbuilder. We strive to keep on the cutting edge of new technologies.

Key Contact - Specialty:
Mr. John P. O'Keefe, CPC, Partner - *High technology management, software development, data processing, hardware engineering*

Functions: Generalist, MIS Mgmt., Systems Analysis, Systems Dev., Systems Implem., Systems Support, Network Admin., DB Admin.

Industries: Generalist, Telecoms, Software

Professional Associations: CCAPS, DPMA, NAPS, PINNACLE, TAPS

Branches:
HC 70 Box 225
Jasper, AR 72641
(870) 446-2137
Fax: (870) 446-2129
Email: resumes@okeefesearch.com
Web: www.okeefesearch.com
Key Contact - Specialty:
Mr. Ian O'Keefe - *Software, hardware, engineers, MIS professionals*

O'Neill Group

PO Box 614
Lake Hopatcong, NJ 07849
(973) 663-6634
(973) 663-5753
Fax: (973) 663-5301
Email: sheilas1@mindspring.com
Web: www.oneillgrp.com

Description: We are an international executive search firm specializing in placement of senior management and supporting staff functions. We are also involved with contracts and handling payrolls.

Key Contact - Specialty:
Ms. Sheila Manning, Executive Director - *Executive level management, human resources*

Salary minimum: $70,000

Functions: Generalist, Middle Mgmt., HR Mgmt., CFO's, Systems Analysis, Mgmt. Consultants, Minorities, Int'l.

Industries: Generalist, Drugs Mfg., Consumer Elect., Pharm Svcs., Telecoms

Professional Associations: SHRM

O'Sullivan Search Inc

2300 Yonge St Ste 401
PO Box 2427
Toronto, ON M4P 1E4
Canada
(416) 481-2992
Fax: (416) 481-3424
Email: resumes@osullivansearch.com
Web: www.osullivansearch.com

Description: Our mission statement: to put the right person in the right place at the right time.

Key Contact - Specialty:
Ms. Kathleen O'Sullivan, President - *Insurance*

Salary minimum: $22,000

Functions: Generalist, Admin. Svcs., Customer Svc., Personnel, Budgeting, Credit, Engineering

Industries: Generalist, Invest. Banking, Misc. Financial, Accounting, Insurance

Oberg & Associates

5495 Beltline Rd Ste 240
Dallas, TX 75254
(972) 239-3315
Fax: (972) 239-2988
Email: roy_oberg@obergassociates.com
Web: www.obergassociates.com

Description: We have a systems-driven recruiting process that provides predictable results to our clients and candidates. We service the North American corrugated packaging industry.

Key Contact:
Mr. Roy Oberg, Company Leader

Salary minimum: $40,000

Functions: Generalist, Senior Mgmt., Middle Mgmt., Production, Plant Mgmt., Quality, Packaging, Sales Mgmt.

Industries: Generalist, Paper, Packaging

Professional Associations: MAPS, NAPS, TAPS

Odell & Associates Inc

1901 N. Central 200
Richardson, TX 75080
(972) 458-7900
Fax: (972) 233-1215
Email: odell@odellrecruits.com
Web: www.odellrecruits.com

Description: We are a twenty-eight year old multi-specialty firm. We are consistently highly rated in Dallas Morning News and Dallas/Fort Worth Business Journal. Our recruiting consultants are awarded top honors at personnel awards programs. We specialize in information technology, accounting, physicians, attorneys, and healthcare technology.

Key Contact:
Mr. Steve N. Odell, CPC, President

Salary minimum: $30,000

Functions: Legal, Physicians, Finance, Cash Mgmt., Taxes, IT, Systems Implem., Systems Support, Network Admin., Attorneys

Industries: Generalist

Professional Associations: MAPS, TAPC

OEI Inc

PO Box 22
Basking Ridge, NJ 07920
(908) 647-4774
Fax: (908) 647-4774
Email: njoei@aol.com

Description: The firm services clients in the architectural, engineering, planning environmental and construction fields. We focus in the placement of personnel in all major disciplines involved with the planning, design, engineering and construction of private and public facilities.

Key Contact:
Mr. Eugene F. Kenny, President
Ms. Mary R. Kenny, Vice President/Treasurer
Mr. Michael Helmer, Vice President/Secretary

Salary minimum: $55,000

Functions: Generalist, Sales Mgmt., Engineering, Environmentalists, Architects

Industries: Generalist, Energy, Utilities, Transportation, Environmental Svcs., Haz. Waste

Professional Associations: AAAE, AICHE, ANS, ASCE, ASTM, IEEE, SAME

Pam Older & Associates

8 Larchmont Ave
Larchmont, NY 10538
(914) 834-8744
Email: pamolder@pamolder.com
Web: www.pamolder.com

Description: Pam Older & Associates offers a wide range of consulting & staffing services for publishing, new media, graphic arts and advertising companies. We specialize in: executive search, production & technology operations, new business launches, and interim management

Key Contact:
Mr. Pamela Older, CEO

Salary minimum: $70,000

Functions: Generalist, General Mgmt., Materials, Sales & Mktg., Mkt. Research, Direct Mktg., Finance, IT, Systems Implem., Graphic Artists

Industries: Generalist, Printing, E-commerce, Media, Advertising, Publishing, New Media, Software

Professional Associations: WIP

Olesky Associates Inc

310 Washington St Ste 201
Wellesley, MA 02481
(781) 235-4330
(800) 486-4330
Fax: (781) 239-1454
Email: laurinda@olesky.com
Web: www.olesky.com

Description: We offer over 3,100 physician jobs nationwide in all specialties at no fee to the physician. Permanent/locum positions, confidentiality insured.

Key Contact - Specialty:
Mr. Roy Olesky, President - *Physician, primary care*

Functions: Generalist, Physicians, Health Admin.

Industries: Generalist, HR Services, Healthcare

Professional Associations: AHA, NAPR, NRHA

Omega Executive Search

2033 Monroe Dr NE
Atlanta, GA 30324
(404) 873-2000
Fax: (404) 873-2006
Email: omega1@bellsouth.net
Web: www.hospitalitypros.com

Description: We specialize in searches for the hospitality and related industries.

Key Contact - Specialty:
Mr. Dave Dorries, President - *Hospitality*
Mr. David Zakin, Principal - *Hospitality*

Salary minimum: $50,000

Functions: Generalist

Industries: Hospitality, Hotels, Resorts, Clubs, Restaurants, Entertainment, Recreation

Omega Search Inc

4425 Randolph Rd Ste 319
Charlotte, NC 28211
(704) 364-8875
Fax: (704) 364-9290
Email: omegaemail@aol.com

Description: With over 20 years' executive recruitment experience, we are dedicated to being thorough and accomplishment-oriented as well as providing outstanding customer service throughout North America.

Key Contact - Specialty:
Mr. Jeffrey M. Turk, President - *Generalist*

Salary minimum: $40,000

Functions: Senior Mgmt., Legal, Mktg. Mgmt., HR Mgmt., Finance, MIS Mgmt., R&D, Engineering, Architects, Attorneys

Industries: Generalist

Omega Systems LLC

921 First Colonial Rd Ste 1703
Virginia Beach, VA 23454
(757) 437-1800
Fax: (757) 437-7737
Email: omegajobs@aol.com
Web: www.topechelon.com/omegasystems

Description: Identify highest quality sales, marketing, engineering and service candidates for technical and high-tech markets by capitalizing on in-depth industry knowledge and practical experience as former senior executive. Specialize in the semiconductor, instrumentation, industrial gas, chemical, vacuum, ultra-high vacuum, mechanical, welding, precision manufacturing, and other hi-tech industries.

Key Contact - Specialty:
Mr. Daniel Lear, President - *Sales, marketing, service, engineering, high technology*

Salary minimum: $40,000

Functions: General Mgmt., Senior Mgmt., Middle Mgmt., Automation, Sales Mgmt., Engineering, Minorities, Technicians

Industries: Generalist, Energy, Utilities, Mfg., Chemicals, Plastics, Rubber, Paints, Petro. Products, Metal Products, Non-classifiable

Professional Associations: AVS, NWSA

Networks: Top Echelon Network

OMNI Personnel Services

1313 Golf Course Cir
Lexington, KY 40517
(859) 271-9701
Fax: (859) 271-9703
Email: opersserv@aol.com

Description: Specialize in executive search and human resources consulting serving the mining industry, coal and hardrock, and manufacturing. We handle professional, technical and administrative, mid-level management to CEO level.

Key Contact - Specialty:
Mr. Norman L. Cornett, President - *Coal & hard rock mining, automotive manufacturing, professional, technical, administrative*

Salary minimum: $50,000

Functions: Generalist

Industries: Chemicals, Plastics, Rubber, Motor Vehicles

Networks: National Personnel Assoc (NPA)

Omni Search Inc

5743 Corsa Ave Ste 123
Westlake Village, CA 91362
(818) 707-4500
(800) 511-0587
Fax: (818) 707-4528
Email: loryg@earthlink.net
Web: www.omnisearchinc.com

Description: We are a nationwide recruiting firm specializing in "long-term care," administrators, directors of nursing, nurse consultants, and upper-level management personnel. We recognize your most urgent and consistent needs for quality staffing.

Key Contact:
Mr. Lory Goldstein, President

Functions: Generalist, Nurses, Health Admin.

Industries: Generalist, Healthcare

Omnisearch Associates

1260 N Dutton Ave Ste 205
Santa Rosa, CA 95401
(707) 566-8100
Email: searchxprt@aol.com

Description: Particularly qualified to recruit for product sales, pre/post-sales applications engineers, field service, technical support, training, systems administration, hardware and software development engineers, also accounting and finance professionals.

Key Contact - Specialty:
Mr. David Scardifield, Owner - *High technology, engineering, support, sales*

Salary minimum: $40,000

Functions: Generalist, Sales Mgmt., HR Mgmt., CFO's, Cash Mgmt., Systems Support, DB Admin., Technicians

Industries: Generalist, Accounting, Software

OmniSearch Inc

3442 Eastlake Rd Ste 308
Palm Harbor, FL 34685
(727) 789-4442
Fax: (727) 787-7743
Email: omni@the-salesnet.com
Web: www.the-salesnet.com

Description: We have excellent, documented experience in pharmaceutical sales force expansion projects and pharmaceutical marketing experience from product and brand manager to marketing director.

Key Contact - Specialty:
Mr. Samuel Moyer, Vice President - *Sales & marketing*
Ms. Laurene F. Moyer, President - *Sales & marketing*

Salary minimum: $40,000

Functions: Sales & Mktg.

Industries: Drugs Mfg., Medical Devices, Pharm Svcs., Biotech

Networks: First Interview Network (FIN)

On Target Recruiting

316 Lookout Dr
Richardson, TX 75080
(972) 671-0816
Email: timgaffney@worldnet.att.net
Web: www.ontargetrecruiting.com

Description: A nationwide professional search firm, we specialize in the placement of sales and marketing professionals in the consumer products arena. We place brand, category and channel managers as well as field sales positions including directors and vp level spots.

Key Contact - Specialty:
Mr. Tim Gaffney, President - *Sales & marketing, consumer packaged goods*

Salary minimum: $50,000

Functions: Product Dev., Sales & Mktg., Sales Mgmt.

Industries: Food, Bev., Tobacco, Drugs Mfg., Consumer Elect., Advertising, Telephony, Wireless

The Onesi Group Inc

34841 Mound Rd Ste 116
Sterling Heights, MI 48310
(810) 759-4044
Fax: (810) 759-4042
Email: search@onesigroup.com

Description: We specialize in the true surgical recruitment of sales and marketing professionals, from executive level (presidents), to entry level.

Key Contact:
Mr. Don Onesi, President

Professional Associations: MASS, NAPS

Networks: Top Echelon Network

OneSource Management Group Inc
2501 Riverside Dr Ste A305
Coral Springs, FL 33065
(954) 340-0311
Fax: (954) 340-7702
Email: aweinstein@onesourcemg.com
Web: www.onesourcemg.com

Description: We offer executive search specializing in the staffing industry, sales management, and medical placements, including registered nurses/nursing management.

Key Contact:
Mr. Adam Weinstein, Managing Director/Senior Partner

Salary minimum: $45,000

Functions: Sales Mgmt.

Industries: Mgmt. Consulting, Hospitals, Long-term Care

Networks: Recruiters Professional Network (RPN)

Open Concepts
PO Box 4554
San Clemente, CA 92674-4554
(949) 369-7231
Fax: (949) 369-5631
Email: opencoencep@aol.com

Description: We are a professional search and recruiting firm focused on manufacturing industries. We accept cross functional assignments for management and selected technical positions.

Key Contact - Specialty:
Ms. Linda McClosky, President - *Manufacturing (cross functional)*
Mr. John McClosky, Vice President - *Manufacturing (cross functional)*
Mr. Evan McClosky, Vice President - *Manufacturing (cross functional)*

Salary minimum: $70,000

Functions: General Mgmt., Mfg., Materials, Sales & Mktg., Finance, Engineering

Industries: Mfg., Wholesale, Media

Open Systems Technologies Inc
225 W 34th St Ste 1715
New York, NY 10122
(212) 643-3100
Fax: (212) 643-4412
Email: esultzer@opensystemstech.com
Web: www.opensystemstech.com

Description: We are a highly specialized technical recruiting firm with a reputation for exceptional services to the Boston and New York financial services and software industries.

Key Contact:
Mr. Harold Herling, Principal
Mr. Steven Young, Principal
Mr. Eric Sultzer, Managing Director - *Financial technology*
Mr. Max Cohen, Managing Director

Salary minimum: $55,000

Functions: Generalist, MIS Mgmt., Systems Analysis, Systems Dev., Systems Implem., Systems Support, Network Admin., DB Admin.

Industries: Generalist, Banking, Invest. Banking, Brokers, Misc. Financial, New Media, Software

Branches:
585 Stewart Ave Ste 536
Garden City, NY 11570
(516) 357-9777
Fax: (516) 357-9676
Email: esultzer@opensystemstech.com
Key Contact:
Mr. Eric Sultzer, Managing Director

The Options Group
121 E 18th St
New York, NY 10003
(212) 982-0900
(212) 982-2800
Fax: (212) 982-5577
Email: info@optionsgroup.com
Web: www.optionsgroup.com

Description: We are the foremost boutique recruitment firm in global derivative sales, trading, research and technology, with coverage for every exchange-traded product in every major international market.

Key Contact - Specialty:
Mr. Praveen Bhutani, CEO
Mr. Michael Karp, Managing Partner - *Financial services*
Mr. Bob Reed, Managing Partner - *Financial services*

Salary minimum: $100,000

Functions: Generalist, Cash Mgmt., MIS Mgmt., Systems Analysis, Systems Implem., Systems Support, Attorneys, Int'l.

Industries: Generalist, Finance, Banking, Invest. Banking, Brokers, Misc. Financial, Legal

OPUS Int'l Inc
1191 E Newport Center Dr Ph-E
Deerfield Beach, FL 33442
(954) 428-3888
(800) 488-2611
Fax: (954) 428-5470
Email: opusintl@foodscience.com
Web: www.foodscience.com

Description: Our firm is both a contingency and retained search firm specializing in placing technical people in the food industry. Primarily we place research scientists with major food and food ingredients manufacturers in their R&D departments. The level of positions vary from senior scientists up to director and vp level.

Key Contact:
Ms. Moira McGrath, President

Salary minimum: $45,000

Functions: Directors, Middle Mgmt., Quality, R&D

Industries: Food, Bev., Tobacco

Professional Associations: AACC, IFT, IFTPS

Opus Marketing
23151 Moulton Pkwy
Laguna Hills, CA 92653
(949) 581-0962
Fax: (949) 581-1497
Email: resumes@opusmarketing.com
Web: www.opusmarketing.com

Description: We offer fully integrated staffing services - including search plans, hiring models and thorough screening of candidates - our clients have cut turnover and improved new hire retention rates significantly.

Key Contact - Specialty:
Mr. Robert S. Kreisberg, President - *High technology sales, sales management, pre sales, technical support, professional services*

Salary minimum: $40,000

Functions: Generalist, Sales Mgmt., Systems Analysis, Systems Dev., Systems Implem., Systems Support, Network Admin., DB Admin.

Industries: Generalist, Computer Equip., Telecoms, Software

Branches:
10180 Bluff Rd
Eden Prairie, MN 55347
(612) 828-9642
Fax: (612) 828-9553
Email: shughes@opusmarketing.com
Key Contact - Specialty:
Ms. Susan F. Hughes, Senior Consultant - *High technology sales, technical support*

The Origin Group LLC
124 N York Rd
PMB 215
Elmhurst, IL 60126
(630) 782-0900 x12
(630) 782-0990
Email: recruiters@theorigingroup.com
Web: www.theorigingroup.com

Description: Our firm specializes in permanent placement for professionals in the actuarial, employee benefit, human resource, and HR technology fields. We work nationally, but do have access to a global market.

Key Contact - Specialty:
Mrs. Christine Sahlas, Principal - *Insurance, benefits, HR consulting*

Functions: Senior Mgmt., HR Mgmt., Benefits

Industries: Misc. Financial, Accounting, Mgmt. Consulting, HR Services

Networks: National Personnel Assoc (NPA)

Orion Corporate Resources
1 Embarcadero Ctr Ste 711
San Francisco, CA 94111
(415) 981-2100

Description: Our top candidates come from the following areas: banking and investment firms, high-technology with an emphasis in facilities and human resources.

Key Contact:
Mr. Joseph Forde, Principal

Salary minimum: $50,000

Functions: Generalist, Senior Mgmt., Middle Mgmt., Personnel, Budgeting, Cash Mgmt., M&A, IT

Industries: Generalist, Invest. Banking, Brokers, Accounting, HR Services, Real Estate, Software

Orion Int'l
5511 Capital Ctr Ste 216
Raleigh, NC 27606
(919) 851-3309
(919) 851-8366
Fax: (919) 851-7268
Email: ral@orioninternational.com
Web: www.orioninternational.com

Description: Former military service members specializing in identifying the best talent leaving the services for career opportunities with leading companies.

Key Contact - Specialty:
Mr. Jim Tully, CEO/Co-Founder - *Generalist, transition (military to civilian)*
Mr. Bill Laughlin, Co-Founder - *Generalist, transition (military to civilian)*
Mr. Randy Nelson, CFO/Co-Founder - *Generalist, transition (military to civilian)*

Salary minimum: $30,000

Functions: Generalist, Production, Materials Plng., Sales Mgmt., Personnel, CFO's, MIS Mgmt., Technicians

Industries: Generalist, Construction, Drugs Mfg., Plastics, Rubber, Misc. Mfg., Misc. Financial, Aerospace, Healthcare

Professional Associations: NFIB, RSS, SHRM, YEO

Branches:
9665 Chesapeake Dr Ste 450
San Diego, CA 92123
(858) 715-1501
(888) 756-7466
Fax: (858) 715-1510
Email: sd@orioninternational.com
Key Contact:
Mr. Brian Henry, Operations Manager

10151 Deerwood Park Blvd Bldg 300 Ste 105
Jacksonville, FL 32256
(904) 998-2211
(888) 767-4660
Fax: (904) 998-4009
Email: jac@orioninternational.com
Key Contact:
Mr. Dave Catalano, Operation Manager

98-211 Pali Momi Rd Ste 504
Aiea, HI 96701
(808) 486-4700
(877) 451-4700
Fax: (808) 486-4710
Email: hawaii@orioninternational.com
Key Contact:
Mr. Wayne Dewees, Recruiter

441 S Salina St Ste 280
Syracuse, NY 13202
(315) 423-9960
(800) 896-0024
Fax: (315) 423-9954
Email: syr@orioninternational.com
Key Contact:
Mr. Joe Brownell, Operation Manager

5412 Courseview Dr Ste 220
Mason, OH 45040
(513) 459-8311
(800) 298-0432
Fax: (513) 459-9087
Email: cin@orioninternational.com
Key Contact - Specialty:
Mr. Tony Santora, Operations Manager - *Technicians, (permanent non-exempt)*

501 Corporate Center Dr Ste 360
Franklin, TN 37606
(615) 771-0099
(800) 667-4667
Fax: (615) 771-0063
Email: nas@orioninternational.com
Key Contact:
Mr. Dan Sproul, Strategic Account Manager
Mr. Dan Weick, Operations Manager

1250 Capital of Texas Hwy Bldg 1 Ste 270
Austin, TX 78746
(512) 327-9696
(800) 336-7466
Fax: (512) 327-4286
Email: aus@orioninternational.com
Key Contact:
Mr. Bill Key, Operation Manager

5800 Lake Wright Dr Ste 101
Norfolk, VA 23452
(757) 455-6931
(800) 544-3787
Fax: (757) 455-6943
Email: vb@orioninternational.com
Key Contact:
Mr. David Wilson, Operation Manager

4411 Point Fosdick Dr NW Ste 303
Gig Harbor, WA 98335
(253) 853-6925
(888) 674-6693
Fax: (253) 853-6926

Email: sea@orioninternational.com
Key Contact:
Mr. David Derr, Strategic Account Manager
Mr. Jim Perdue, Operations Manager

Orion Resources
1411 4th Ave Ste 1410
Seattle, WA 98101
(206) 382-8400
Email: lisam@orionresources.com
Web: www.orionresources.com
Key Contact:
Ms. Jennifer Girard, Owner
Functions: Finance
Industries: Software
Professional Associations: WSA

Orion Search Group Inc
12908 SW Doug Dr
Lake Suzy, FL 34266
(800) 777-2902
(941) 624-0088
Email: orionsearchgroup@home.com

Description: We specialize in the property and casualty insurance industry. We place candidates in legal, claims, loss control & premium audit positions.

Key Contact - Specialty:
Mr. Ronald B. Myron, President - *Attorneys, senior claims examiners, managers, loss control engineers*
Ms. Mona George Myron, Vice President - *Audit*
Mr. Lowell Gannon, Vice President - *Underwriting, loss control, inland marine U/W*
Mr. Michael Moss, Assistant Vice President - *Claims*

Functions: Middle Mgmt., Legal, Engineering, Attorneys

Industries: Generalist, Construction, Legal, Insurance

Professional Associations: NAER, NAPC

Networks: National Personnel Assoc (NPA)

Ortman Recruiting Int'l
1101 Sylvan Ave Ste B-20
Modesto, CA 95350
(209) 529-5051
Fax: (209) 529-5054
Email: ortmanrec@msn.com
Web: www.waterjobs.com

Description: Number one recruiting agency in the world for high purity water/waste water systems and related components.

Key Contact - Specialty:
Mr. Jim Ortman, Owner - *Biotechnology, pharmaceutical, high purity water, waste water, pumps*

Salary minimum: $30,000

Functions: Generalist

Industries: Construction, Mfg., Environmental Svcs.

Osborn & Associates Inc
337 E Wakefield Blvd
Winsted, CT 06098
(860) 738-4129
Fax: (860) 738-0622
Email: recruit@esslink.com

Description: Ten years of happy clients and successful candidates in the Fortune 500. Candidates say "yes" to offer - 94%. For professional growth for you or your company call us first. Partners have combined 30 years experience with plastics professionals.

Key Contact - Specialty:
Mr. Fred Hoban, Partner - *Plastics generalist*
Ms. Mary Osborn, Owner - *Plastics generalist*

Salary minimum: $45,000

Functions: Generalist

Industries: Chemicals, Plastics, Rubber

Professional Associations: SAMPE, SPE

OSI
PO Box 81092
Conyers, GA 30013
(770) 760-7661
Fax: (770) 760-7729
Email: tim@osijobs.com
Web: www.osijobs.com

Description: Specialize in search and recruitment in the food industry. Retained and contingency search.

Key Contact - Specialty:
Mr. Tim Oliver, President - *Food*

Functions: Mfg.

Industries: Food, Bev., Tobacco

Professional Associations: GAPS, IFT, NAPS

Branches:
1028 Washington St
Raleigh, NC 27605
(919) 834-2110
Fax: (919) 834-2922
Email: dave@osijobs.com
Key Contact - Specialty:
Mr. David Buergler - *Food*

OTEC Inc
24 W 40th St Fl 11
New York, NY 10018
(212) 840-8600
Fax: (212) 768-8309
Email: jobs@otec.com
Web: www.otec.com

Description: We are the elite, one-stop provider of top technical talent. We place key technologists as employees, consultants, and executives in "destined to win" Fortune 500, mature start-up, and new venture clients.

Key Contact - Specialty:
Mr. Bennett Carroccio, President - *Financial industry, information technology*

Functions: Generalist, MIS Mgmt., Systems Analysis, Systems Dev., Systems Implem., Systems Support, Graphic Artists

Industries: Generalist, Textiles, Apparel, Machine, Appliance, Finance, Hospitality, Media, Software

Branches:
580 Market St Fl 4
San Francisco, CA 94104-5411
(415) 362-6362
Fax: (415) 362-6366
Email: jobs-sf@otec.com
Key Contact - Specialty:
Mr. Bill Beer, Vice President - *Technology, software, internet*

Outbay Inc
100 E Whitestone 200
Cedar Park, TX 78613
(512) 260-7200
(888) 7OUTBAY
Email: dustin.little@outbay.com
Web: www.outbay.com

Description: Executive search specializing in the semiconductor and related industries. Disciplines include: design, sales/marketing, product/test, management, and operations. Our geographic focus are the developing hubs of semiconductor activity... Austin TX, Boston MA, Boulder CO, San Diego CA, Portland OR, etc.

Key Contact - Specialty:
Mr. Dustin Little, CPC, President/CEO - *Semiconductor*
Mrs. Rosanne Bonnet, CPC, Senior Technical Recruiter - *Semiconductor*
Ms. Tracy Menzel, MBA, CFO - *Semiconductor*

Salary minimum: $55,000

Functions: Engineering

Industries: Venture Cap., Telecoms

Professional Associations: TAPC

Networks: National Personnel Assoc (NPA)

Outsource Professionals
110 Barnard Pl
Atlanta, GA 30328
(678) 297-0196
Fax: (678) 297-0197
Email: lisa.ramsey@outsource-professionals.com
Web: www.outsource-professionals.com

Description: Specialization on emerging growth software companies, with emphasis on management, sales, technical, pre- and post-sales positions.

Key Contact - Specialty:
Ms. Lisa Ramsey, Partner - *Software management, sales, technical*
Mrs. Karen Moss, PHR, Partner - *Hi-Tech, software*

Salary minimum: $50,000

Functions: Sales & Mktg., HR Mgmt., IT, Systems Dev., Systems Implem.

Industries: Services, Software

The Oxbridge Group Ltd
1735 Market St Fl 43
Philadelphia, PA 19103
(215) 567-8800
Fax: (215) 567-8815
Email: info@oxbridgegroup.com

Description: We target investment banks, venture capital and private equity firms where we place people from the analyst to managing director both domestically and internationally.

Key Contact - Specialty:
Ms. Nina E. Swift, President - *Investment banking, financial services, merchant banking*
Ms. Marty Brady, Consultant - *Investment banking, financial services, merchant banking*

Salary minimum: $50,000

Functions: Generalist, M&A

Industries: Generalist, Invest. Banking, Venture Cap., Misc. Financial

Branches:
21 Custom House St
Boston, MA 02110
(617) 946-9600
Fax: (617) 946-9605
Key Contact:
Ms. Martha Chayet, Consultant
Ms. Samantha Goodman, Principal
Ms. Pamela Palmer, Principal

150 E 52nd St Fl 23
New York, NY 10022
(212) 980-0800
Fax: (212) 888-6062
Email: info@oxbridgegroup.com
Key Contact:
Ms. Ann Kraftson, Consultant - *Investment banking, merchant banking*
Ms. Carlyn Henry, Consultant

The P & L Group
366 N Broadway Ste 312
Jericho, NY 11753
(516) 938-7337
Fax: (516) 939-2490
Email: p-l-group@att.net

Description: Most placements in manufacturing, supply chain management (including materials management, purchasing and logistics) quality assurance, information technology, marketing, finance and human resources. Considerable success in start-ups and venture-capital funded operations.

Key Contact - Specialty:
Mr. Hyman Livingston, President - *General management, manufacturing, materials management, marketing, quality assurance*

Salary minimum: $80,000

Functions: Generalist, General Mgmt., Mfg., Plant Mgmt., Materials, Purchasing, Distribution, Sales & Mktg., MIS Mgmt., Engineering

Industries: Generalist, Mfg., Electronic, Elec. Components, Services, Non-classifiable

Professional Associations: AME, APICS, APICS, ASQ, NAPM

P R Management Consultants Inc
601 Ewing St
Princeton, NJ 08540
(609) 921-6565
Fax: (609) 924-7911
Email: findem6565@aol.com

Description: Specialists in targeted executive search - plastics, biomedical, chemical, paper and all related industries. Typical recent searches: division president; CFO; director/VP R&D; V.P. marketing; European country managers, and many others from plant management to engineering, environmental, and clinical and regulatory management.

Key Contact - Specialty:
Mr. Jerrold Koenig, President - *General technical, marketing management (many industries)*

Salary minimum: $50,000

Functions: Generalist

Industries: Mfg., Paper, Chemicals, Soap, Perf., Cosmtcs., Drugs Mfg., Medical Devices, Plastics, Rubber, Misc. Mfg.

P.R.Y. Resources Inc
20 Carlton St Ste123
Toronto, ON M5B 2H5
Canada
(416) 599-0929
Fax: (416) 599-4708
Email: pryresource@idirect.com

Description: Recruitment and placement of permanent, contract and temporary office support and information technology personnel including software engineers from entry to management levels.

Key Contact - Specialty:
Ms. Ann Ragwen, Partner - *Office support, information technology*
Mr. Harry Yong, Partner - *Office support, information technology*

Functions: Generalist, Mfg., Sales & Mktg., HR Mgmt., Finance, IT, Engineering

Industries: Generalist, Mfg., Finance, Services, Media, Insurance, Software

P1 Results
4015 Brahma St
Powell, OH 43065
(614) 275-2000
Fax: (614) 275-2077
Email: p1result@columbus.rr.com

Description: Contract recruiting, contingency search, HR and hiring process consulting - largely focusing on the IT/IS arena.

Key Contact:
Mr. Randall Stevens, Principal

Salary minimum: $40,000

Functions: Generalist, IT

Industries: Generalist

Pacific Advisory Service Inc
200 W Madison St Ste 630
Chicago, IL 60606
(312) 407-6771
Fax: (312) 407-6773
Email: pasinc@paschgo.com

Description: Specialize in recruiting (1) Asian professionals for U.S. multinational corporations and (2) American executives and professionals for Japanese banks and corporations in the Midwest.

Key Contact:
Mr. Hideki Terada, President

Salary minimum: $30,000

Functions: Generalist, Senior Mgmt., Middle Mgmt., Product Dev., Production, Plant Mgmt., Purchasing, Sales Mgmt.

Industries: Generalist, Medical Devices, Plastics, Rubber, Machine, Appliance, Motor Vehicles, Misc. Mfg., Accounting, Healthcare

Professional Associations: JAS

Pacific Bridge Inc
1155 Connecticut Ave NW Ste 850
Washington, DC 20036
(202) 467-5020
Fax: (202) 833-2279
Email: info@pacificbridge.com
Web: www.pacificbridge.com

Description: We are a recruiting company that specializes in placing bilingual candidates in the U.S. and Asia.

Key Contact:
Mr. Ames Gross, President

Functions: Int'l.

Industries: Generalist

Pacific Coast Recruiting
1579 Farmers Ln Ste 342
Santa Rosa, CA 95405
(707) 541-7070
Fax: (707) 541-0230
Email: pacificcoastrecruiting@msn.com
Web: www.pacificcoastrecruiting.com

Description: We are "supply chain specialists." We specialize in the intermediate, senior, management, and director level positions in all areas of the supply chain. Please don't let our name confuse you. We have clients in 38 states. Our excellent reputation in the industry is evidenced by a loyal client base located nationwide. This firm attracts and keeps as clients some of the most prestigious corporations in the country.

Key Contact - Specialty:
Mr. Robert Abbott, Senior Partner - *Supply chain recruiting*
Ms. Barbara Rahmn, Managing Partner - *Client Relations*

Salary minimum: $55,000

Functions: Materials, Purchasing, Materials Plng., Distribution

Industries: Generalist

Pacific Coast Recruiters (PCR)

65 W-1 Division Ave
PMB 144
Eugene, OR 97404
(541) 345-6866
Fax: (541) 345-0547
Email: pcr1@attglobal.net
Web: www.pacificcoastrecruiters.com

Description: Our firm is an executive search firm that specializes in all aspects of the insurance industry with an emphasis on property/casualty and worker's compensation. Our specialty market is the West Coast, Pacific Northwest, and nationwide.

Key Contact - Specialty:
Mr. David L. B. Watson, Director - *Insurance (property, casualty, worker's compensation, claims), risk management, underwriting, sales & marketing*

Salary minimum: $30,000

Functions: Generalist, Senior Mgmt., Middle Mgmt., Mktg. Mgmt., Sales Mgmt., Finance, CFO's, Risk Mgmt.

Industries: Insurance

Professional Associations: NIRA

Pacific Executive Search Group

18500 Von Karman Ave Ste 800
Irvine, CA 92612
(949) 864-9525
Fax: (949) 864-9511
Email: jobs@pacificexecutivesearch.com
Web: www.pacificexecutivesearch.com

Description: We consist of recruiters who specialize in placing accounting and finance professionals. All partners were previous Big 6 CPAs or controllers. Our geographic focus is Southern California.

Key Contact - Specialty:
Mr. Kevin Herbert, President - *Accounting, finance*
Mr. George Merrick, Partner - *Accounting, finance*
Mr. John Dyer, Partner - *Accounting, finance*
Mr. Ken Dewitt, Manager of Recruiting - *Accounting, finance*

Salary minimum: $30,000

Functions: Generalist, Finance, Budgeting, Taxes

Industries: Generalist, Construction, Mfg., Services, Real Estate, Software, Healthcare

Professional Associations: CSP

The Pacific Group

8117 W Manchester Ave Ste 558
Playa del Rey, CA 90293
(310) 521-4061
Email: losangeles@pacific-lighthouse.com
Web: www.pacific-lighthouse.com

Description: The Pacific Group specializes in meeting the very unique needs of your company at these early stages of development. The services range from "Complete Recruitment & Human Resources Outsourcing" to "Simple Contingency Search." Our goal is to take the burden of recruitment and human resources off your hands so that you can focus on making your business the next Microsoft, Yahoo, or Amazon.com. Please contact our firm to find out more about how we can help you get your company to next step.

Key Contact - Specialty:
Mr. John Bavaro, Managing Director
Ms. Pamela Shahin, Director of Recruiting - *Finance, administration, human resources*
Mr. Jim Hazboun, Advisor - *Start ups, Pre-IPO practice*

Salary minimum: $50,000

Pacific Recruiting

32395 Clinton Keith Rd Ste B7-196
Wildomar, CA 92595
(909) 696-7000
Fax: (909) 696-7052
Email: hdorland@ez2.net

Description: Twenty years' experience exclusively recruiting in the insurance industry. Membership in NIRA gives us access to openings and candidates on a nationwide basis.

Key Contact - Specialty:
Mr. Harvey Dorland, President - *Insurance*

Functions: Generalist

Industries: Insurance

Professional Associations: NIRA

Pacific Resource Solutions Inc

PO Box 1393
Healdsburg, CA 95448
(707) 473-0130
Fax: (707) 473-0110
Email: rose@pacificrecruiters.com
Web: www.pacificrecruiters.com

Description: Full service contingency firm specializing in the search and recruitment of candidates for construction, architecture, and engineering industries.

Key Contact - Specialty:
Ms. Rosanne Polidora, President - *Construction, engineering, architecture*
Ms. Marie Butler, Sr Account Executive - *Construction, engineering, architecture*

Salary minimum: $35,000

Functions: General Mgmt., Sales & Mktg., Finance, Engineering, Architects

Industries: Construction

Pacific Search Consultants

2377 S El Camino Real Ste 201
San Clemente, CA 92672
(949) 366-9000
Fax: (949) 366-9200
Email: arnold@pacific.com
Web: www.pacific.com

Description: Our firm focuses on research and development. We place in all levels of management, business development, marketing, and product management in addressing the professional staffing needs of start-up ventures through Fortune 100 companies. Our emphasis over the past 22 years in recruiting has been in: speech technology, computer telephony, performance engineering, data storage management systems, software engineering development, SQA/test, compilers, distributed systems, operating systems internals, and networking/multi-modal communications.

Key Contact:
Mr. Arnold L. Garlick, III, President

Salary minimum: $60,000

Functions: Directors, Systems Dev., R&D

Industries: Computer Equip., Communications, Software, Development SW, Networking, Comm. SW, Security SW, System SW

Professional Associations: ACM, CMG, HFES

Pacific Search Consultants Inc

PO Box 1369
Snohomish, WA 98291-1369
(360) 568-5568
Fax: (360) 568-8187
Email: info@pacificsearch.com
Web: www.pacsearch.com

Description: Our firm is an ethical and successful consulting firm providing permanent placement

services, contract engineering services, and human resource consulting work within the wireless communications industry.

Key Contact:
Ms. Paula Smith, President
Mr. David Bouthot, Executive Vice President

Functions: Generalist

Industries: Telecoms, Telephony, Digital, Wireless, Fiber Optic, Network Infrastructure

Pacific Search Group Inc

1801 Century Park E Ste 1801
Los Angeles, CA 90067-2320
(310) 286-6921
(310) 712-0770
Fax: (310) 712-0777
Email: nickerpsg@aol.com

Description: Specialists in recruiting executives, consultants, CPAs and other financial and MIS personnel for industry.

Key Contact - Specialty:
Mr. Nick Roberts, President - *Accounting & financial personnel, COOs, CEOs, MIS*

Salary minimum: $75,000

Functions: Generalist, Senior Mgmt., Finance, CFO's, Taxes, M&A, MIS Mgmt., Systems Analysis

Industries: Generalist, Wholesale, Retail, Services, Hospitality, Media, Healthcare

Professional Associations: AICPA, CSCPA

Packaging Personnel Company Ltd

1485 Avondale Dr
PO Box 12495
Green Bay, WI 54307-2495
(920) 498-8657
Fax: (920) 499-9512
Email: dtaylor@ppcltd.com
Web: www.ppcltd.com

Description: We recruit exclusively for the packaging machinery industry, a narrow focus that allows us to help our client companies correctly identify and hire the best professionals for the job. With a 17-year history in this unique specialty, we know "who's who" in the industry. We cover all disciplines: sales, marketing, engineering, manufacturing, and technical services at all levels from entry to top management. We do retained searched for senior management positions.

Key Contact - Specialty:
Mr. Dick Taylor, President - *Packaging machinery*
Ms. Robin Huettl, Vice President - *Packaging machinery*

Salary minimum: $40,000

Functions: Packaging

Industries: Machine, Appliance, Equip Svcs.

Professional Associations: IOPP, WAPS

Branches:
W 1405 Beach Ct
Oostburg, WI 53070-1620
(920) 564-6361
Fax: (920) 564-6362
Email: walt@packstaff.com
Key Contact - Specialty:
Mr. Walter Ellis, President - *Packaged goods*

Packaging Resources

3317 Partipilo St
Mount Home, AR 72653
(870) 425-8807
Fax: (870) 425-7949
Email: pcarveth@northarkansas.net
Web: www.packaging-resources.com

Description: A search firm owned and operated by one individual, Peter Carveth, who has been a packaging engineer or packaging manager for over 35 years. Searches are conducted on a contingency basis for large consumer, food, pharmaceutical, or medical companies for packaging professionals in R&D, operations, sales/marketing.

Key Contact - Specialty:
Mr. Peter Carveth, Business Owner - *Recruiting, packaging professional*

Salary minimum: $35,000

Functions: Packaging, Engineering

Industries: Food, Bev., Tobacco, Drugs Mfg., Medical Devices, Plastics, Rubber, Paints, Petro. Products, Pharm Svcs., Packaging, Biotech, Healthcare

Professional Associations: IOPP

T Page & Associates
2905 FM 620 N
Austin, TX 78734
(512) 263-5377
Fax: (512) 263-5783
Email: theresa@pageandassociates.net
Web: www.pageandassociates.net

Key Contact - Specialty:
Ms. Theresa Page, President - *Distribution, logistics, supply chain consulting*
Ms. Yvonne Jones, Associate - *Manufacturing engineering*
Ms. Janet Rodriguez - *Distribution operations*

Salary minimum: $50,000

Functions: Generalist, Production, Purchasing, Materials Plng., Distribution, Systems Implem., Engineering

Industries: Generalist, Food, Bev., Tobacco, Paper, Drugs Mfg., Computer Equip., Consumer Elect., Misc. Mfg., Retail

Professional Associations: CLM

Page Staffing & Training
(also known as PAGE Consulting LLC)
289 Rte 33 E Ste 6 Bldg A
Manalapan, NJ 07726
(732) 786-8210
Fax: (732) 786-8110
Email: abrown@turntothepage.com
Web: www.turntothepage.com

Description: We specialize in accounting and financial recruitment. We are industry specialist in construction, and real estate, although we recruit for clients in various industries. We recruit in NY, NJ, and PA.

Key Contact - Specialty:
Mr. Alan V. Brown, President - *Finance & accounting, sales, sales management, MIS management, environmental services*

Salary minimum: $30,000

Functions: Admin. Svcs., HR Mgmt., Finance

Industries: Generalist, Construction, Real Estate

Professional Associations: ASTD, MAAPC, SHRM

Janou Pakter Inc
5 W 19th St Ste 6
New York, NY 10011
(212) 989-1288
Fax: (212) 989-9079
Email: info@jpakter.com
Web: www.janoupakter.com

Description: We offer global, retainer and contingency executive recruiting, and consulting for the design, fashion, publishing, corporate, and advertising industries on an international basis, for example: art direction, creative direction, graphic design, interactive new media, copy, marketing, account management, and marketing.

Key Contact - Specialty:
Ms. Janou Pakter, President
Mr. Jerry Tavin, Vice President
Ms. Vicki Martin - *Business development*

Salary minimum: $40,000

Functions: Generalist, Senior Mgmt., Advertising, Mkt. Research, PR, Architects, Graphic Artists, Int'l.

Industries: Generalist, Advertising, Publishing, New Media, Broadcast, Film

Professional Associations: ADC, AIGA, NYNMA, TDC

Wade Palmer & Associates Inc
3830 Pioneer Rd
Rogersville, MO 65742
(417) 889-3434
Fax: (417) 889-3636
Email: wep@job-recruiters.com
Web: www.job-recruiters.com

Description: We offer nationwide executive search in the food and beverage industries. We specialize in engineering, production, QC, maintenance, research and development, logistics, packaging, human resources, and accounting. We have had twenty-six years experience as headhunters. We work in contingency only.

Key Contact - Specialty:
Mr. Wade Palmer, Owner - *Food & beverage manufacturing*
Mrs. Phyllis Palmer, Recruiter - *Dairy manufacturing*

Salary minimum: $40,000

Functions: Generalist, Plant Mgmt., Productivity, Purchasing, Distribution, HR Mgmt., Budgeting, Engineering

Industries: Generalist, Agri., Forestry, Mining, Mfg., Food, Bev., Tobacco, Soap, Perf., Cosmtcs., Drugs Mfg., Packaging

Lynne Palmer Inc
342 Madison Ave Ste 1430
New York, NY 10173
(212) 883-0203
Fax: (212) 883-0149
Email: careers@lynnepalmerinc.com
Web: www.lpalmer.com

Description: We handle entry to senior-level positions in the publishing, new media, corporate communications, and public relations industry. Our nationwide client base includes magazine, book, public relations and multimedia companies.

Key Contact:
Ms. Susan Gordon, President

Functions: Generalist, General Mgmt., Sales & Mktg., HR Mgmt., Finance, IT

Industries: Generalist, HR Services, Media, Advertising, Publishing, New Media

Professional Associations: APCNY, WIP, WNBA

Pan American Search Inc
600 Sunland Park Dr 2-200
El Paso, TX 79912
(915) 833-9991
Fax: (915) 833-9476
Email: resume@panamsearch.com

Description: We are an executive search firm specializing in manufacturing off shore professional/management positions up and down the US/Mexico border and the Mexican interior. We specialize in the placement of US and foreign nationals.

Key Contact - Specialty:
Ms. Stephanie Caviness, President - *Executive level manufacturing, offshore professionals*

Functions: Generalist

Industries: Mfg., Transportation, Finance

Professional Associations: TAPC

Networks: Top Echelon Network

Arthur Pann Associates Inc
701 Westchester Ave Ste 3A1
White Plains, NY 10604
(914) 686-0700
Fax: (914) 686-0788
Email: apann@arthurpann.com
Web: www.arthurpann.com

Description: We are a boutique executive search firm specializing in accounting/ finance, information technology and human resources. We are committed to confidentially identifying only the most qualified individuals for our clients' needs in the Tri-State area.

Key Contact - Specialty:
Mr. Arthur J. Pann, CPC, President - *Finance & accounting, tax, information technology, sales, human resources*

Salary minimum: $50,000

Functions: HR Mgmt., Finance, CFO's, IT

Industries: Generalist, Mfg., Food, Bev., Tobacco, Textiles, Apparel, Paper, Soap, Perf., Cosmtcs., Drugs Mfg., Services, Hospitality, Media, Publishing, New Media, Broadcast, Film, Software

Professional Associations: ACSS, APCNY, IIA, IMA, NAA, NAPS, PF

Networks: National Personnel Assoc (NPA)

Florence Pape Legal Search Inc
1208 Washington St
Hoboken, NJ 07030
(201) 798-0200
(800) 762-0096
Fax: (201) 798-9088
Email: fpape@fpls.com

Description: Placement of attorneys nationally in law firms or corporations.

Key Contact - Specialty:
Ms. Florence Pape - *Legal*

Salary minimum: $60,000

Functions: Attorneys

Industries: Legal

Paper Industry Recruitment (PIR)
36 Main St
Gorham, ME 04038
(207) 839-2633
Fax: (207) 839-2634
Email: mc@pirecruitment.com
Web: www.pirecruitment.com

Description: We do senior-level searches for low up-front fee. We have twenty-three years of experience in the paper industry recruiting. We have a new division being launched, PIRFinancial, for 100K to 300K top-level financial executives in the paper industry only.

Key Contact - Specialty:
Mr. Maynard G. Charron, Owner - *Pulp, paper, recycling*

Salary minimum: $65,000

Functions: Generalist, Senior Mgmt., Product Dev., Plant Mgmt., Quality, Purchasing, Materials Plng., CFO's, Engineering

Industries: Paper

Professional Associations: NNEAPS, PIMA, TAPPI

Paradigm HR Solutions LLC

502 Montana Blvd #801
Terry, MT 59349
(406) 635-4170
Fax: (406) 635-4171
Email: paradigmhr@hotmail.com

Description: Paradigm HR Solutions, LLC is a national executive search firm focused primarily on the service industry. The firm concentrates on Engineering, Financial, IT, and Human Resources fields at the mid-management and top levels.

Key Contact - Specialty:
Mr. Michael Cohan, President - *Engineering, financial, IT, human resources*

Salary minimum: $50,000

Functions: General Mgmt., Directors, Senior Mgmt., Middle Mgmt., Production

Industries: Energy, Utilities, Mfg., Chemicals, Medical Devices, Plastics, Rubber, Computer Equip., Test, Measure Equip., Electronic, Elec. Components, Finance, Banking, Invest. Banking, Brokers, Venture Cap., Services, Legal, Accounting, Mgmt. Consulting, HR Services, E-commerce, IT Implementation, PSA/ASP, Hospitality, Hotels, Resorts, Clubs, Media, Advertising, Publishing, New Media, Communications, Telecoms, Telephony, Digital, Wireless, Fiber Optic, Network Infrastructure, Government, Defense, Aerospace, Insurance, Software, Accounting SW, Database SW, Development SW, HR SW, Networking, Comm. SW, System SW, Training SW, Biotech, Healthcare, Hospitals, Long-term Care, Dental, Physical Therapy, Occupational Therapy

Professional Associations: SHRM

Networks: Top Echelon Network

Paradigm Management Solutions Inc

21 St. Claire Ave E Penthouse Ste
Toronto, ON M4T 1L9
Canada
(416) 515-2904
Email: paradigm@pathcom.com
Web: www.pathcom.com/~paradigm

Description: As a management consulting organization, we assist you, our corporate clients, to accomplish your strategic goals. Blending retainer and contingent search, selection and placement services within the Canadian market, we deliver 21st Century thinkers-the people who make businesses successful.

Key Contact:
Ms. Coralee Sheridan, President

Salary minimum: $30,000

Functions: Middle Mgmt., Finance, CFO's, Budgeting, Cash Mgmt., Taxes, M&A, Int'l.

Industries: Generalist

Paragon Recruiting

17 W 10th St Ste 120
Holland, MI 49423
(616) 494-0001
Fax: (616) 494-0002
Email: foundit@paragonusa.com
Web: www.paragonusa.com

Description: We are a recruiting firm specializing in the direct and contract placement of computer and engineering professionals.

Key Contact - Specialty:
Ms. Elizabeth Nielsen DeWilde, Principal - *Information systems, engineering*

Salary minimum: $20,000

Functions: Generalist, MIS Mgmt., Systems Analysis, Systems Dev., Systems Implem., Systems Support, Network Admin., DB Admin.

Industries: Generalist, Plastics, Rubber, Machine, Appliance, Motor Vehicles, Computer Equip., Misc. Mfg., Software

---

Paragon Recruiting Officials Inc

2000 W Henderson Rd Ste 220
Columbus, OH 43220
(614) 442-8900
Fax: (614) 457-1211
Email: kris@paragonrecruiting.net
Web: www.paragonrecruiting.net

Description: We specialize in information technology candidates with at least three years of experience, especially systems architects, project managers and ERP consultants looking to better themselves by examining options in other permanent positions.

Key Contact - Specialty:
Mr. Vince Procopio, President - *Senior level tech positions*

Salary minimum: $60,000

Functions: MIS Mgmt., Systems Analysis, Systems Dev., Systems Implem., Systems Support, Network Admin., DB Admin.

Industries: Generalist

The Park Group & Associates Inc

2 Evergreen Rd
Severna Park, MD 21146
(410) 384-9120
Fax: (410) 384-9923
Email: info@tpgassociates.com
Web: www.tpgassociates.com

Description: Specialize in healthcare, insurance, banking and technology. Services include executive search and management consulting in the healthcare and banking industry.

Key Contact - Specialty:
Ms. Lise Perunovich, Principal - *Healthcare, financial services*
Ms. Katherine Ryan - *Healthcare*
Ms. Michele Sheiko - *Technology*
Mr. Robert P. Pratz - *Financial services*
Mr. R. J. "Kip" Conville - *Healthcare*
Ms. Frances Kirkland - *Financial services*

Salary minimum: $60,000

Functions: Generalist, General Mgmt., Healthcare, Sales & Mktg., HR Mgmt., Finance, IT, Specialized Svcs.

Industries: Generalist, Finance, Services, Insurance, Software, Healthcare

---

Carol Park

819 Walnut Ste 412
Kansas City, MO 64106
(816) 421-1326
Fax: (816) 421-8226
Email: carol.park@att.net
Web: www.nbn-jobs.com/mbrpages/prkwebpg.cfm

Description: I have been a bank recruiter since 1979. I work only in the area of banking.

Key Contact - Specialty:
Ms. Carol Park, Owner - *Banking*

Salary minimum: $45,000

Functions: Finance

Industries: Banking

Networks: National Banking Network (NBN)

Parker & Lynch

(a division of Accounting Principals Inc)
260 California St Ste 400
San Francisco, CA 94111
(415) 956-6700
Fax: (415) 956-5642
Email: chantelle.morrier@parkerlynch.com
Web: www.parkerlynch.com

Description: We place finance and accounting professionals with clients throughout the San Francisco Bay area. Clients range in size from start-ups to Fortune 50 organizations and cover all industries. The firm's geographic and functional specialization provides our clients and candidates with an unparalleled network of resources.

Key Contact - Specialty:
Mr. Montie Parker, Director - *Accounting & finance*
Ms. Chantelle Morrier, Managing Director - *Accounting & finance*

Functions: Finance

Industries: Generalist

Branches:
2880 Lakeside Dr Ste 135
Santa Clara, CA 95054
(408) 298-6700
Fax: (408) 298-5642
Email: jennifer.rhodes@parkerlynch.com
Key Contact - Specialty:
Ms. Jennifer Rhodes, Managing Director - *Finance, accounting*

Parker Page Group

12555 Biscayne Blvd Ste 745
Miami, FL 33181
(305) 892-2822
Fax: (305) 892-2880

Description: Seventeen years in business/upper-level management; resorts and country clubs, hotels, restaurants, specialty, gaming and entertainment, also medical, banking, finance, engineering, environmental services and human resource directors. Also, interim executive placements.

Key Contact - Specialty:
Mr. Harry Harfenist, President - *Hospitality, medical, banking, finance, engineering*

Salary minimum: $40,000

Functions: Generalist, Directors, Senior Mgmt., Health Admin., Personnel, CFO's, MIS Mgmt., Engineering

Industries: Generalist, Banking, Mgmt. Consulting, HR Services, Hospitality, Healthcare

Professional Associations: NCA

Parker, McFadden & Associates

1581 Phoenix Blvd Ste 3
Atlanta, GA 30349
(770) 991-0873
Fax: (770) 996-2455
Email: pma.info@parker-mcfadden.com
Web: www.parker-mcfadden.com

Description: We recruit at the middle and senior management levels in all disciplines in metal working manufacturing industries.

Key Contact:
Mr. Kenneth Parker, Principal
Mr. James McFadden, Principal

Salary minimum: $40,000

Functions: Generalist, General Mgmt., Mfg., Production, Plant Mgmt., Materials, Purchasing, Engineering

Industries: Generalist, Metal Products, Machine, Appliance, Motor Vehicles, Misc. Mfg., Aerospace

Parker-Worthington Inc
1915 Rebecca Creek Rd
Canyon Lake, TX 78133
(830) 885-5535
(210) 601-7700
Fax: (210) 479-9911
Email: susanp@parkerworthington.com
Web: www.parkerworthington.com

Description: Female-owned, efficient performance company committed to business practices and ethics that create value for our clients and our candidates. We represent many positions that include company equity.

Key Contact - Specialty:
Ms. Susan Parker, CEO - *Software sales*

Functions: Generalist, Mktg. Mgmt., Sales Mgmt.

Industries: Generalist, New Media, Software

Professional Associations: WAW

Largent Parks & Partners
12770 Coit Rd Ste 900
Dallas, TX 75251
(972) 991-7713
Email: awilson1@aol.com

Description: We conduct retained search and contingency recruiting nationwide.

Key Contact - Specialty:
Mr. Akira Wilson, General Manager - *International marketing, freight-forwarding*
Ms. Cynthia LaBarge-Wilson, Vice President - *Telecommunications, credit*
Ms. Jane Mangiafico, Vice President - *Mortgage, credit*
Mr. Bill Stynetski, Vice President - *Construction, engineering*
Ms. Beth Wolchansky, Vice President - *Insurance*

Salary minimum: $30,000

Functions: Generalist, Purchasing, Nurses, Direct Mktg., Credit, MIS Mgmt., Engineering, Mgmt. Consultants

Industries: Generalist, Transportation, Finance, Mgmt. Consulting, Telecoms, Insurance

Parsons, Anderson & Gee Inc
44 Georgetown Ln
Fairport, NY 14450
(716) 223-3770
(716) 223-3770
Fax: (716) 223-8536
Email: info@parandge.com
Web: www.parandge.com

Description: Principal has worked for Fortune 25 company as well as for small organization and has been responsible for internal recruitment. Additionally, principal is experienced in competency based interviewing. Principal has 15 years in recruiting.

Key Contact:
Mr. Arthur J. Fandel, President/Owner - *Generalist*
Ms. Carole Fandel, VP - *Administration*

Salary minimum: $35,000

Functions: Generalist

Industries: Energy, Utilities, Mfg., Misc. Financial, Services, Media, Haz. Waste, Insurance, Software, Biotech

Professional Associations: SHRM

Networks: Inter-City Personnel Assoc (IPA)

Partners in Recruiting
6260 E Riverside Blvd Ste 325
Rockford, IL 61111
(815) 885-2028
Fax: (815) 885-2048
Email: partnersir@att.net

Description: As a business partner, we work with your agenda and strive to complete assignments in the shortest possible time. We identify, recruit, screen, interview and qualify interested candidates from your industry that can do the job and are ready to make a career move. These candidates will begin contributing to your organization immediately, thus saving you time and money, and overall, improve your bottom line.

Key Contact - Specialty:
Ms. Diann Helnore, President/Technical Recruiting Manager - *Engineering, management, manufacturing, sales & marketing, mechanical*
Mr. Kim Helnore, Quality Assurance Account Manager - *Quality (assurance, control), materials management, production and inventory control, logistics, final parts inspection*
Mr. Douglas Helnore, Manager - *Accounting, banking, finance services, food, beverage*
Ms. Dawn Wenzel, Account Manager /HR Mgmt /Training - *Education, human resources, training*
Ms. Linda Mack, Mgr. Marketing/ Sales/Telemarketing/Data - *Project management, database management, direct marketing, computer (related help desk functions)*
Mr. Lowell Clapp, Director - Executive Mgmt Search . - *Executive management (retained and contingency), industrial manufacturing, capital equipment, technical products*
Mr. Austin Davis, Executive Safety Director - *Safety professionals and safety management*

Salary minimum: $50,000

Functions: Generalist

Industries: Generalist

Professional Associations: ASSE, BCSP, DMA, NIIA

Networks: Inter-City Personnel Assoc (IPA)

Rick Pascal & Associates Inc
PO Box 543 Dept K
Fair Lawn, NJ 07410
(201) 791-9541
Fax: (201) 791-1861
Email: info@packagecareers.com
Web: www.packagecareers.com

Description: In the area of packaging, we work only with engineers, developers, designers, and closely related technical positions.

Key Contact - Specialty:
Mr. Rick Pascal, CPC, President - *Packaging industry*

Salary minimum: $60,000

Functions: Directors, Senior Mgmt., Middle Mgmt., Product Dev., Packaging, Engineering, Graphic Artists

Industries: Packaging

Professional Associations: IOPP, NJPEC, SHRM

Pascale & LaMorte LLC
391 Meadow St
Fairfield, CT 06430
(203) 337-8155
Fax: (203) 337-8136
Email: pascale@pascale-lamorte.com
Web: www.pascale-lamorte.com

Description: Financial, Accounting and Information Technology recruitment for middle managers through executive management.

Key Contact - Specialty:
Mr. Ron Pascale, Principal - *Information technology*
Mr. Brian A. LaMorte, Principal - *Accounting, finance, tax*

Salary minimum: $75,000

Functions: Finance, CFO's, Budgeting, Cash Mgmt., Taxes, IT, MIS Mgmt., Systems Analysis, Systems Implem., Systems Support

Industries: Generalist

Professional Associations: AICPA

Paster & Associates
5556 Dayna Ct
New Orleans, LA 70124
(504) 486-7080
Fax: (504) 486-4555
Email: sdpaster@aol.com

Description: We do medical sales, pharmaceutical sales, sales management, marketing. We do business in primarily Southern California and New Orleans, Louisiana.

Key Contact - Specialty:
Mr. Steve Paster, President - *Sales, medical, surgical, pharmaceutical, biotech*

Functions: Generalist, Mkt. Research, Mktg. Mgmt., Sales Mgmt.

Industries: Generalist, Pharm Svcs., Biotech

Networks: First Interview Network (FIN)

Patch & Associates Inc
2435 Polk St Ste 21
San Francisco, CA 94109
(415) 353-0272
Fax: (415) 353-0274
Email: info@patchassociates.com
Web: www.patchassociates.com

Description: We are a full service search firm that specializes in placing public relations, marketing, product marketing, sales, and investor-relations professionals in high technology, Internet, software, new media, and agencies focused in those industries. We are a small agency with a large appetite for success.

Key Contact - Specialty:
Ms. Tracy Patch, Principal - *High tech public relations, marketing communications, product marketing*

Functions: Generalist, Directors, Senior Mgmt., Middle Mgmt., Advertising, Mkt. Research, Mktg. Mgmt., PR

Industries: Generalist, Media, Advertising, Publishing, New Media, Telecoms, Software

Professional Associations: CSP, IABC, PRSA

Pathfinders Health Search
5554 Reseda Blvd Ste 202
Tarzana, CA 91356
(818) 758-8383
Fax: (818) 758-8382
Email: ormanagers@aol.com

Description: Number 1 in placement of surgery nurse managers.

Key Contact - Specialty:
Mr. Adam Silbar, General Manager - *Surgery management*

Salary minimum: $50,000

Functions: Nurses, Health Admin.

Industries: Generalist

Pathway Executive Search Inc
60 E 42nd St Ste 405
Lincoln Bldg
New York, NY 10165
(212) 557-2650
Fax: (212) 682-1743
Email: jberger@pesearch.com
Web: www.pesearch.com

Description: Specialized, trained professionals that work with clients in identifying and securing the highest caliber of information technology, new media, emerging technology and business professionals. We also have an affiliate company, The Vantage Group, a retained search firm that specializes in building management teams in the high-growth and emerging industries.

Key Contact:
Mr. Jay Berger, President - *Systems & technology (computer related)*
Ms. Barbara Grossman, Principal

Functions: Generalist, Directors, Senior Mgmt., MIS Mgmt., Systems Analysis, Systems Dev., Systems Implem., Systems Support

Industries: Generalist, Food, Bev., Tobacco, Drugs Mfg., Brokers, Mgmt. Consulting, Publishing, New Media

Professional Associations: APCNY

Patriot Associates
125 Strafford Ave Ste 300
Wayne, PA 19087
(610) 687-7770
(610) 975-4589
Fax: (610) 975-4512
Email: tompatriot@aol.com

Description: Firm specializes in pharmaceutical/healthcare. Principal was a recruitment manager for a major pharmaceutical firm. Has strong contacts throughout the industry. Knows and understands the lingo.

Key Contact - Specialty:
Mr. Thomas Meltser, Executive Director - *Pharmaceutical, healthcare*

Salary minimum: $40,000

Functions: Product Dev., Healthcare, Sales & Mktg., Mkt. Research, Mktg. Mgmt., Sales Mgmt., HR Mgmt., Personnel, Training, Int'l.

Industries: Drugs Mfg., Pharm Svcs., Biotech, Healthcare

Professional Associations: AAAS, DIA

Networks: Medical Search Consortium (MSC)

Joel H Paul & Associates Inc
352 7th Ave Ste 810
New York, NY 10001-5012
(212) 564-6500
Fax: (212) 868-2671
Email: jhpaul@earthlink.net

Description: Executive search firm specializing in identifying executives, fundraisers, directors, educators, etc. For non-profit organizations nationally.

Key Contact - Specialty:
Mr. Joel H. Paul, President - *Non-profit executives, education, culture, healthcare, philanthropy*
Ms. Lillian Amcis, Senior Partner - *Non-profit executives, education, culture, healthcare, philanthropy*
Ms. Myra Mogilner, Vice President - *Non-profit executives, education, culture, healthcare, philanthropy*
Ms. Judy Magen, Vice President - *Non-profit executives, education, culture, healthcare, philanthropy*

Salary minimum: $50,000

Functions: Directors, Senior Mgmt., Middle Mgmt., Health Admin., HR Mgmt., CFO's, Non-profits

Industries: Non-profits

Payton & Associates
210 Meidinger Twr
Louisville, KY 40202
(502) 583-1530
Fax: (502) 587-6960

Description: Committed to conducting high quality national searches for organizations based in Kentucky, Indiana, Tennessee, West Virginia and Southern Ohio. Senior positions in law, finance, HR, sales and marketing.

Key Contact - Specialty:
Mr. Andrew J. Payton, President - *Generalist*

Salary minimum: $60,000

Functions: Generalist, General Mgmt., Sales Mgmt., HR Mgmt., Finance, Non-profits, Attorneys

Industries: Generalist, Energy, Utilities, Food, Bev., Tobacco, Transportation, Finance, Services

PC Associates
2682 S Holman St
Lakewood, CO 80228
(303) 986-4111
Fax: (303) 986-8996

Description: Focus on high-technology industries for executive and technical recruiting, specialist in engineering, sales and marketing.

Key Contact - Specialty:
Mr. Paul T. Cochlan, President - *Engineering*

Salary minimum: $35,000

Functions: Generalist, General Mgmt., Packaging, Engineering, Environmentalists

Industries: Agri., Forestry, Mining, Mfg., Medical Devices, Environmental Svcs.

Peachtree Peopleware Inc
1 Meca Way
Norcross, GA 30093
(770) 564-5585
Fax: (770) 564-5584
Email: chyder@ppwi.com
Web: www.ppwi.com

Description: We use retained recruiting techniques on a contingency fee basis to provide technical recruiting services for high-tech clients nationwide. We place permanent and contract professionals in software and hardware engineering and technical marketing and sales positions. Our focus is on the cable TV, energy, and telecommunications industries.

Key Contact - Specialty:
Mr. Chuck Hyder, President - *Technical marketing, sales*
Mr. Burke Sisco, Vice President - *Software, firmware, hardware engineering*

Salary minimum: $45,000

Functions: IT

Industries: Telecoms, Software

Professional Associations: AEA, GAPS

Peachtree Search Group
1117 Perimeter Ctr W Ste 510E
Atlanta, GA 30338
(770) 394-5585
Email: peachtreesg@mindspring.com

Description: We are a contingency search firm conducting national search and placement with a focus on sales, marketing, management, and clinical positions in the healthcare software, medical device, and biotechnology markets.

Key Contact - Specialty:
Mr. Christopher McDearman, President - *Healthcare information technology, medical devices, biotechnology*

Salary minimum: $45,000

Functions: Senior Mgmt., Middle Mgmt., Product Dev., Sales & Mktg.

Industries: Medical Devices, Software, Biotech, Healthcare

Professional Associations: HIMSS

Peachtree Staffing LLC
100 Colony Sq Ste 1820
Atlanta, GA 30361
(404) 875-1696
Fax: (404) 875-1992
Email: main@peachtreestaffing.com
Web: www.peachtreestaffing.com

Description: We have a recruiting staff comprised of individuals who specialize in software, information system recruiting, engineering, CAD specialists, finance and accounting, human resource outsourcing and high capability administrative staffing.

Key Contact - Specialty:
Mr. Chris Miles, Vice President-Operations - *Engineering, information technology, accounting & finance*

Functions: Generalist, Middle Mgmt., Plant Mgmt., Health Admin., Sales Mgmt., Personnel, Cash Mgmt., Systems Dev.

Industries: Generalist, Energy, Utilities, Drugs Mfg., Transportation, HR Services, Biotech

Professional Associations: GAPS, SHRM

Branches:
515 Seabreeze Blvd Ste 227
Ft. Lauderdale, FL 33316
(954) 713-8155
Fax: (954) 713-8174
Email: rlewis@peachtreestaffing.com
Web: www.peachtree.com

Peak Associates
170 University Ave Ste 901
Toronto, ON M5H 3B3
Canada
(416) 979-7303
Fax: (416) 979-7457
Email: resumes@peakassociates.com
Web: www.peakassociates.com

Description: Our consultants apply industry experience to the searches in their area of specialty.

Key Contact - Specialty:
Mr. Robert Baron, Partner - *Real estate, construction, insurance, accounting, financial services*

Salary minimum: $50,000

Functions: Generalist, General Mgmt., Sales & Mktg., Finance, IT, Architects

Industries: Generalist, Construction, Finance, Services, Insurance, Real Estate, Software

Professional Associations: ACSESS, APPAC

Networks: National Personnel Assoc (NPA)

Pearce & Associates
9116 Cypress Green Dr Ste 202
Jacksonville, FL 32256
(904) 739-1736
Fax: (904) 739-1746
Email: fpearce@leading.net

Description: We provide search and placement consultants recruiting sales professionals in B2B, IT-related products and services, e-Business, telecommunications, and executive search.

Key Contact:
Mr. Frank Pearce, Owner - *Management*
Ms. Lois Pearce, Owner - *Sales & marketing*
Mrs. Faye Delaney, Admin. Assistant

Salary minimum: $35,000

Functions: Sales & Mktg., Sales Mgmt.

Industries: Mgmt. Consulting, HR Services, Telecoms

Professional Associations: FASS, NAPS

Peden & Associates
2000 Broadway
Redwood City, CA 94063
(650) 367-1181
Fax: (650) 367-7525
Email: apeden@pedenassoc.com
Web: www.pedenassoc.com

Description: We specialize in building software development and technical marketing teams for newly funded software and start-up companies, whose corporate headquarter is located in the Silicon Valley, from San Francisco to the South Bay.

Key Contact - Specialty:
Ms. Ann Peden, Principal - *High technology, software development & marketing, start-ups*

Salary minimum: $60,000

Functions: Generalist, Mktg. Mgmt., Customer Svc., Systems Dev., R&D, Engineering

Industries: Generalist, Software

M A Pelle Associates Inc
PO Box 476
Huntington, NY 11743
(631) 385-8925
Fax: (631) 385-5636
Email: mapelleinc@aol.com
Web: www.mapellestaffing.com

Description: Executive search, technical high-technology staffing, human resource management consulting - HRM audits, legal compliance issues, compensation, training and development and workplace issues. On-Site recruitment assignments.

Key Contact - Specialty:
Mr. Michael A. Pelle, President - *Technical staffing*

Salary minimum: $50,000

Functions: Generalist, Directors, Middle Mgmt.

Industries: Generalist, Mfg., Computer Equip., Test, Measure Equip., Accounting, Mgmt. Consulting, HR Services, IT Implementation, Communications, Telecoms, Defense, Aerospace, Software

Professional Associations: SHRM

Pemberton & Associates
75 Market St
Portland, ME 04101
(207) 775-1772
Fax: (207) 775-1983
Email: tpemberton@oldporthr.com
Web: www.oldporthr.com

Description: This company operates in executive search and retention-based human resource consulting services in the New England area. Our search focus is in banking/finance, IT, and executive management, for example CEO, COO, CFO, HR, and marketing.

Key Contact - Specialty:
Mr. Theodore Pemberton, President - *Banking, executive management*

Salary minimum: $40,000

Functions: Generalist, Senior Mgmt.

Industries: Generalist, Finance, Services, Legal, HR Services, E-commerce, IT Implementation, Advertising, Telecoms, Call Centers, Network Infrastructure, Software, Accounting SW, Database SW

Networks: National Banking Network (NBN)

Pennington Consulting Group
65 S Main St Bldg B
Pennington, NJ 08534
(609) 737-8500
Fax: (609) 737-8576
Email: rbw5725@aol.com
Web: www.penningtonconsulting.com

Description: Executive search and consulting firm specializing in wireless communications services.

Key Contact:
Mr. Robert B. White, President
Ms. Elizabeth Ludlow, Vice President
Ms. Trish Ambrosio, Office Manager
Ms. Karen Britt, Account Executive

Functions: Generalist, HR Mgmt., Personnel

Industries: Generalist, Mgmt. Consulting, HR Services, Telecoms

The Pennmor Group
25 Chestnut St Ste 107
Haddonfield, NJ 08033
(856) 354-1414
Fax: (856) 354-7660
Email: info@pennmor.com
Web: www.pennmor.com

Description: Experts in discreet one-on-one recruiting process. Specialty areas include all functions in human resources, finance, operations, accounting and senior management. Known for our professional approach to clients and candidates and our long-term client relationships.

Key Contact - Specialty:
Mr. Anthony Trasatti, President - *Finance, accounting, human resources, operations management, marketing*
Ms. Jennifer Bartolomeo, Research Manager - *Finance, accounting, human resources, operations management, marketing*

Salary minimum: $75,000

Functions: General Mgmt., Sales & Mktg., HR Mgmt., Finance

Industries: Mfg., Finance, Services, Insurance

Professional Associations: MAAPC, NHRA, SHRM, WAW

People Consultants LLC
5555 Glenridge Connector Ste 200
Atlanta, GA 30342
(770) 394-1670
Fax: (404) 459-6031
Email: fshackelford@peopleconsultants.net
Web: www.peopleconsultants.net

Description: Our firm recruits for senior level positions in customer care or customer service and call center management nationwide. We work on two search models, contingency search and engaged search. Our send-out-to-hire rate is at a remarkable 55%. All of our searches are guaranteed for 90 days. Our average search takes three weeks to complete.

Key Contact - Specialty:
Mr. Fletcher Shackelford, Partner - *Customer care, contact center management*
Mr. Michael Prozer, Business Development Manager - *Customer care, contact center management*

Functions: Directors, Senior Mgmt., Middle Mgmt., Direct Mktg., Customer Svc.

Industries: Generalist

Networks: Top Echelon Network
Branches:
9481 Highland Oak Dr Ste 1402
Tampa, FL 33647
(813) 994-0721
Fax: (404) 459-6031
Email: tampa@peopleconsultants.com
Key Contact - Specialty:
Mr. Michael Prozer, Business Manager - *Customer care, contact center management*

People Options LLC
44 Hickory Hill Rd
Wilton, CT 06897
(203) 761-1201
Email: alan@peopleoptions.com
Web: www.peopleoptions.com

Description: Our primary focus is recruiting the management team for emerging ventures. General management, marketing, business development, sales, finance, human resources, and information technology are our functional strengths.

Key Contact:
Mr. Alan Nierenberg, CMC, Principal

Salary minimum: $100,000

Functions: Generalist

Industries: Generalist

People Pipeline LLC
518 Gregory Ave Ste C209
Weehawken, NJ 07087
(201) 348-8888
Fax: (201) 348-8886
Email: aluchangco@ppline.com
Web: www.ppline.com

Description: We are a New Jersey based information technology search firm specializing in the placement of mid to senior level professionals, including project managers, directors, AVPs, and VPs seeking full-time/permanent positions. Our charter provides the focus in achieving two purposes: providing the company with the most suitable candidate to fulfill company objectives by implementing a thorough screening process and providing the best opportunity for success for the job seeker. We provide services to regional and US based clients.

Key Contact:
Ms. Ana Luchangco, Director

Salary minimum: $50,000

Functions: IT

Industries: Drugs Mfg., Finance, Services, Non-profits, Pharm Svcs., Broadcast, Film

Professional Associations: NAFE, NAWBO, NYNJMPC

Peopleclick
9009 Corporate Lakes Dr Ste 125
Tampa, FL 33634
(813) 584-0883
Fax: (813) 496-8873
Email: tracey.friend@peopleclick.com
Web: www.peopleclick.com

Description: Our firm is the market leader of web-native HR process management software and services, providing enterprises with the ability to attain, train, and retain their most valuable asset, which is people. We are headquartered in the Research Triangle area of North Carolina, Peopleclick products currently serve more than 10 million employees at over 3000 enterprise clients including: 52 Fortune 100 companies, 3 big 5 consulting firms, and 13 of the nations largest financial

Key Contact - Specialty:
Ms. Tracey Friend, Vice President - *Strategic HR*

Functions: Generalist, Senior Mgmt.

Industries: Generalist

Networks: EMA Partners Int'l

PeopleSource Solutions
(also known as MRI of Smyrna)
2840 Johnson Ferry Rd NE Ste 150
Marietta, GA 30062
(770) 643-9990
Fax: (770) 643-0818
Email: manager@peoplesourcesolutions.com
Web: www.peoplesourcesolutions.com

Key Contact - Specialty:
Mr. David Borel, Partner - *Healthcare technologies*
Mr. Doug Malcolm, Partner - *Information technology, consulting*
Mrs. Shannon Wolfe, Vice President - *Pharmaceuticals, bio-tech*
Ms. Debbie Davis, Partner - *Database marketing*
Mr. Chris Dean, Vice President - *Supply chain, logistics*
Mr. Rick Arritola, Director - *Logistics, global trade*
Mr. Derek Busch, Director - *Distribution, warehousing, logistics*
Mr. Andy Granger, Director - *Audio, video, digital design*
Mr. Richard Dumont, Recruiter - *HVAC, mechanical, construction*
Mr. Helgi Legi, Recruiter - *Supply chain, logistics*
Mr. Tom Pritchard, Recruiter - *Telecommunication technologies*
Mr. Chris Slover, Recruiter - *Engineering, supply chain*
Ms. Kathleen Stutzman, Recruiter - *Healthcare management*

Salary minimum: $45,000

Functions: Directors, Senior Mgmt., Production, Plant Mgmt., Materials, Purchasing, Distribution, Engineering, Mgmt. Consultants

Industries: Generalist, Mfg., Soap, Perf., Cosmtcs., Drugs Mfg., Medical Devices, Wholesale, Retail, Pharm Svcs., Mgmt. Consulting, New Media, Haz. Waste, Aerospace, Packaging, Software, Biotech, Healthcare

Professional Associations: AMA, APICS, ATA, CLM, EIA, IARW, IIE, MHIA, NAPM, SCL, WERC

PERC Ltd
PO Box 15327
Phoenix, AZ 85060-5327
(800) 874-7246
(602) 553-9896
Fax: (602) 553-9897
Email: gordonstoa@qwest.net

Description: Change is constant. We offer strategic partnership in your search for qualified and competent candidates.

Key Contact - Specialty:
Mr. Gordon Stoa, Manager - *Food, agriculture, manufacturing*
Ms. Jackie Stoa, Vice President/Administration - *Administration, office management*

Salary minimum: $35,000

Functions: Generalist

Industries: Energy, Utilities, Construction, Mfg., Food, Bev., Tobacco, Chemicals, Misc. Mfg., Pharm Svcs., Mgmt. Consulting, Biotech, Non-classifiable

Professional Associations: AOM

Peregrine Staffing
2245 Eagles Nest Dr
Lafayette, CO 80026
(303) 926-8875
Fax: (303) 350-9349

Email: hunters@peregrinestaffing.com
Web: www.peregrinestaffing.com

Description: We are an elite firm focusing on IT professionals experienced in the EAI and B2B integration areas.

Key Contact:
Ms. Elisa Wells, Partner

Salary minimum: $85,000

Functions: Generalist

Industries: Mgmt. Consulting, E-commerce, IT Implementation, Software, ERP SW, Mfg. SW

Perfect Search Inc
7800 Congress Ave Ste 204
Boca Raton, FL 33487
(561) 995-7533
Fax: (561) 995-7477
Email: psiadmin@perfectsearch.org
Web: www.perfectsearch.org

Description: We work on behalf of client companies to recruit sales, sales management and marketing talent for medical, pharmaceutical and biotech manufacturers. We also place executive and director-level individuals within healthcare providers and consulting firms.

Key Contact - Specialty:
Ms. Robin D. Callicott, President - *Healthcare sales, management, marketing*

Salary minimum: $40,000

Functions: Generalist

Industries: Drugs Mfg., Medical Devices, Pharm Svcs., Telecoms, Biotech, Healthcare

Networks: First Interview Network (FIN)

The Performance Group Inc
(also known as Sales Consultants of Stamford-Darien)
111 Prospect St Ste 410
Stamford, CT 06901-1208
(203) 327-3270
Fax: (203) 327-6578
Email: scstamford@aol.com

Description: We have twenty years' experience in sales executive and general manager in the training and HR consulting industry. We also have outstanding knowledge of the market and functions.

Key Contact - Specialty:
Mr. James M. Burt, Managing Director - *Training, human resource consulting industry*

Salary minimum: $70,000

Functions: Sales & Mktg., Training, Mgmt. Consultants

Industries: Generalist, Mgmt. Consulting, HR Services, Software

Professional Associations: ASTD, ASTD, NSPI, SHRM

Performance Resources Inc
235 Promenade St Ste 417
Providence, RI 02908
(401) 854-2410
Fax: (401) 854-2305
Email: perres1@aol.com
Web: www.performance-resources.com

Description: We handle a full range of industries/disciplines; our specialty is the search process. Specialty practice includes mid-senior operations and finance for consumer packaged goods companies. High potential opportunities for high potential talent.

Key Contact - Specialty:
Mr. Kevin R. O'Neill, President - *Generalist, senior management, plant operations*

Mr. Richard Wolf, Senior Vice President - *Operations general, IT manufacturing, beverage*
Mr. Mark Kennedy, Administrator/Manager - *General*

Salary minimum: $50,000

The Perimeter Group
(also known as MRI of Atlanta-Sandy Springs)
500 Sugar Mill Rd Ste 170-A
Atlanta, GA 30350
(770) 642-7676
(888) 738-6665
Fax: (770) 642-7685
Email: info@tpg-jobs.com
Web: www.tpg-jobs.com

Description: We offer executive search and consulting firm specializing in the placement of sales, marketing, and management talent, worldwide.

Key Contact - Specialty:
Mr. John Mason, President - *Consumer products*

Salary minimum: $50,000

Functions: General Mgmt., Sales & Mktg.

Industries: Energy, Utilities, Construction, Mfg., Wholesale, Retail, Finance, Communications, Packaging, Insurance, Software, Healthcare

Permanent Solutions Inc
201 City Center Dr Ste 608
Mississauga, ON L5B 2T4
Canada
(905) 566-5950
Fax: (905) 566-5991
Email: resumes@permanentsolutions.com
Web: www.permanentsolutions.com

Description: We provide expert recruitment services to all levels of organizations through our executive, permanent, contract, and temporary divisions. We are experienced in administration, finance, sales, marketing, logistics, customer service, and human resources. Each division is able to focus on the level of skills needed.

Key Contact:
Ms. Heather Eaton, Vice President/Operations

Salary minimum: $30,000

Functions: General Mgmt., Directors, Senior Mgmt., Middle Mgmt., Admin. Svcs.

Industries: Generalist, Construction, Mfg., Wholesale, Finance, Misc. Financial, Pharm Svcs., Accounting, HR Services, Media, Advertising, New Media, Telecoms, Packaging, Insurance, Healthcare, Non-classifiable

Perry • Newton Associates
PO Box 1158
Rockville, MD 20849-1158
(301) 340-3360
Fax: (301) 340-3080
Email: executive_recruiter@perrynewton.com
Web: www.perrynewton.com

Description: We provide retail search and placement, exclusively. We identify, recruit, and place mid/upper level retailers nationwide. Positions that we work on include: director/VP of stores, district/regional management, human resource executives, financial officers, and merchants.

Key Contact - Specialty:
Mr. Dick Perry, President - *Retailing*
Ms. Marje Newton, Senior Vice President - *Retailing*

Salary minimum: $40,000

Functions: Generalist

Industries: Retail

Professional Associations: MAPRC

David Perry Associates

525 Rte 73 S Ste 201
Marlton, NJ 08053
(856) 596-9400
Fax: (856) 596-9125
Email: davperas@att.net
Web: www.davidperryassociates.com

Description: Mainly recruit and place candidates in the consumer packaged goods industry. In sales-anyone from key account manager to VP of sales. In marketing - brand managers to general managers.

Key Contact - Specialty:
Mr. Raymond Spadaro, President - *Sales, marketing, general management*

Salary minimum: $55,000

Functions: Generalist, Middle Mgmt., Sales & Mktg., Mkt. Research, Mktg. Mgmt., Sales Mgmt.

Industries: Food, Bev., Tobacco, Textiles, Apparel, Soap, Perf., Cosmtcs., Drugs Mfg., Media, Communications

Professional Associations: MAAPC

Networks: First Interview Network (FIN)

Fred Perry Associates

PO Box 680487
Houston, TX 77268
(281) 350-2809
Fax: (281) 350-2894
Email: fred@fperry.com
Web: www.fperry.com

Description: Fifteen years' experience recruiting nationally for the nation's leading consulting engineering firms specializing in environmental and infrastructure.

Key Contact - Specialty:
Mr. Fred Perry, Executive Recruiter - *Engineering, consulting*

Functions: Generalist

Industries: Environmental Svcs., Haz. Waste

Professional Associations: AWWA, WEF

Perry Search Associates

1443 Main St Ste 120-C
Napa, CA 94559
(707) 257-8215
Fax: (707) 259-4852
Email: perrysearch@aol.com

Description: A professional search firm with particular expertise in the datacommunications, telecommunications, computer networking industries. Specializing in sales, sales support, product marketing, hardware and software engineering personnel.

Key Contact:
Mr. Marcus Perry, President

Salary minimum: $40,000

Functions: Generalist, Mkt. Research, Sales Mgmt., Systems Analysis, Systems Dev., Systems Implem., Systems Support, Engineering

Industries: Generalist, Computer Equip., New Media, Telecoms, Software

Professional Associations: RON

Networks: Top Echelon Network

The Persichetti Group

5758 Havensport Rd NW
Carroll, OH 43112
(740) 756-1301
Email: pgroup5758@aol.com
Web: www.pgroup.net

Description: Quality focused generalist professional & executive-level search for a select national

clientbase. Name generation and research services available on hourly basis.

Key Contact:
Ms. Kelly Persichetti, President

Salary minimum: $50,000

Functions: General Mgmt., Directors, Middle Mgmt., Plant Mgmt., Sales & Mktg., IT

Industries: Generalist, Mfg., Food, Bev., Tobacco, Metal Products, Consumer Elect., Misc. Mfg., HR Services, Telecoms, Packaging

Personalized Management Associates Inc

1950 Spectrum Cir Ste B-310
Marietta, GA 30067-6059
(800) 466-7822
(770) 916-1668
Fax: (770) 916-1429
Email: jobs@pmasearch.com
Web: www.pmasearch.com/

Description: We are a national executive search chain specializing in management in all industries, including, but not limited to, human resources, management, marketing, manufacturing, retail, restaurant, real estate, and franchising. We are retained and contingency.

Key Contact - Specialty:
Mr. David Hottle, CPC, Executive Vice President - *Executive search, franchise training*
Mr. Bill Lins, CPC, Director, Operations - *Management*

Salary minimum: $30,000

Functions: Generalist

Industries: Mfg., Retail, HR Services, E-commerce, Hospitality, Call Centers

Professional Associations: GAPS, NAPS

Personnel Assistance Corp

1242 Homestead Trl
Long Lake, MN 55356
(612) 476-0674
Fax: (612) 476-0675

Description: Specialize in metal, machining, sheet metal stampings, supervision, manufacturing engineering, tooling, IE, QA/QC, management and support functions and general industry.

Key Contact - Specialty:
Mr. Don Pearson, Owner - *Manufacturing*

Functions: Middle Mgmt., Mfg., Product Dev., Production, Automation, Plant Mgmt., Quality, Engineering

Industries: Generalist, Plastics, Rubber, Metal Products

Personnel Associates

23 Maracay
San Clemente, CA 92672-6050
(949) 492-0030

Description: Searches conducted in most areas of publishing: specialize in acquisitions editorial and in sales/marketing for medical, college and professional and reference publishing. Work with some electronic publishing houses.

Key Contact - Specialty:
Ms. Marjorie Crawford, Recruiter - *Publishing*
Mr. Edward Wells, General Manager - *Publishing*

Salary minimum: $35,000

Functions: Middle Mgmt.

Industries: Publishing

Personnel Associates Inc

120 E Washington St Ste 928
Syracuse, NY 13202
(315) 422-0070
Fax: (315) 474-7293
Email: pbaskin@concentric.net

Description: Nationwide recruiting of property/casualty and life/health professionals. We specialize in branch level management positions. Over 100 affiliated offices.

Key Contact - Specialty:
Mr. Peter J. Baskin, CPC, President - *Insurance*

Salary minimum: $45,000

Functions: Generalist

Industries: Insurance

Professional Associations: INS, NAPS, NIRA, SHRM

Personnel Associates

140 McIntyre Rd
Cherryville, NC 28021
(704) 480-7603
Fax: (704) 445-0081
Email: perassoc@shelby.net

Description: Executive search firm with expertise in minority recruitment serving the business professional through our nationwide network. Our Charlotte office has 30 years' experience in supporting operations, manufacturing, engineering and quality professionals.

Key Contact - Specialty:
Mr. Cliff Neighbors, President - *Generalist*
Ms. Betty Neighbors - *Generalist*
Ms. Chasity Tindall - *Generalist*

Salary minimum: $40,000

Functions: Generalist, General Mgmt., Mfg., Materials, Sales & Mktg., HR Mgmt., IT, Engineering

Industries: Generalist, Mfg., Finance, Media, Environmental Svcs., Packaging

Networks: Inter-City Personnel Assoc (IPA)

Personnel Consultants

14042 NE 8th Ste 201B
na
Bellevue, WA 98007
(425) 641-0657
Fax: (425) 641-0657
Email: buzy73a@aol.com

Description: Twenty-five years' experience insurance only. Education: MBA and J.D. Geographic specialty Washington, Oregon, Idaho and Alaska.

Key Contact - Specialty:
Mr. Larry L. Dykes, President - *Insurance*

Salary minimum: $35,000

Functions: Generalist

Industries: Generalist, Insurance

Professional Associations: NIRA

The Personnel Consulting Group

(formerly known as Accounting & Engineering Personnel Conslts)
210 Baronne St Ste 922
New Orleans, LA 70112
(800) 783-7533
(504) 581-7800
Fax: (504) 568-1222
Email: personnel@personnel-group.com
Web: www.personnel-group.com

Description: We have thirty-two years of specialization experience in direct and contract placement of accounting and financial executives, information technology professionals, human resources, attorneys, sales, office support, and administrative personnel.

Key Contact - Specialty:
Mr. Frank Loria,, CPC, President
Mr. Norman "Chip" Kerth, CPC, Manager - *Accounting & finance*

Functions: Generalist

Industries: Generalist

Professional Associations: AAFA, LSA, NAPS

Networks: Inter-City Personnel Assoc (IPA)

Personnel Consulting Associates
7600 Jericho Tpke Ste 304
Woodbury, NY 11797
(516) 364-1460
(800) 741-7199
Fax: (516) 364-2520
Email: pcasearch@earthlink.net
Web: www.pcasearch.com

Description: We are an executive search firm serving the financial services industry. We've successfully completed searches for senior management and staff in commercial, retail, and private banking, capital markets, risk, marketing, human resources, and accounting. Our consultants have industry expertise, a broad base of contacts, and strong assessment skills.

Key Contact:
Mr. Joseph Slater, Principal
Mr. Adam Andrews, Associate
Mr. Howard Barnowitz, Associate
Ms. Kerri Gordon, Office Manager

Salary minimum: $50,000

Functions: Generalist

Industries: Finance, Banking, Invest. Banking, Misc. Financial, Mgmt. Consulting, HR Services, Advertising, Publishing

Personnel Inc
PO Box 1413
Huntsville, AL 35807
(256) 536-4431
Fax: (256) 539-0583
Email: projobs1@bellsouth.net

Description: Presently work with 34 agencies 50/50 who met through networks. Engineering and manufacturing firms in the South are the appeal.

Key Contact - Specialty:
Mr. Bill Breen, President/Manager - *Executive, management, engineering*

Salary minimum: $50,000

Functions: Generalist, Middle Mgmt., Production, Materials, HR Mgmt., IT, Engineering

Industries: Generalist, Mfg., Computer Equip., Misc. Mfg., Telecoms, Aerospace, Software

Personnel Inc
604 Locust St Ste 516
Des Moines, IA 50309-3720
(515) 243-7687
Fax: (515) 243-3350
Email: pincjt@ix.netcom.com
Web: www.iajobs.com

Description: Full-service personnel consulting firm. We have expertise in the areas of executive search, placements, psychological testing, outplacements, management consulting and have been in business over 37 years. Resumes will not be processed unless salary requirements are included.

Key Contact - Specialty:
Mr. Jack T. Textor, President - *Generalist*

Functions: Generalist

Industries: Generalist

Professional Associations: SHRM

Personnel Management Resources
PO Box 1522
Manhattan, KS 66505
(785) 776-6000
Fax: (785) 776-3178
Email: clay@pmrjobs.com
Web: www.pmrjobs.com

Description: PMR is a health care search firm specializing in physicians, nurse managers and pharmacists.

Key Contact - Specialty:
Mr. Clay Zapletal, President - *Healthcare*

Networks: Top Echelon Network

Personnel Management Group
209 Notre Dame Ave Ste 300
Winnipeg, MB R3B 1M9
Canada
(204) 982-1100
Fax: (204) 943-9535
Email: yvonne@pmg.mb.ca
Web: www.pmg.mb.ca

Description: We have over 24 years experience in technical, engineering, management, manufacturing, and transportation/logistics recruiting. We have intimate knowledge of the Manitoba market in systems, engineering, accounting, manufacturing, transportation, and logistics. We cooperate with other Canadian recruiters, particularly in Western Canada. We have a high profile in Winnipeg in the area of systems, engineering, and logistics.

Key Contact - Specialty:
Ms. Yvonne Baert, Director/Owner - *Systems, engineering, accounting, manufacturing*
Mr. Robert A. Baert, Director/Owner - *Special projects, construction (large scale hires, call centers)*
Ms. Cynthia Wharton, Recruiter - *Transportation, logistics, distribution*
Ms. Danielle Baert, P.Eng., Recruiter - *Engineering, manufacturing*

Salary minimum: $40,000

Functions: Generalist, Mfg., Quality, Materials Plng., Distribution, HR Mgmt., CFO's, IT, Engineering

Industries: Generalist, Construction, Mfg., Food, Bev., Tobacco, Textiles, Apparel, Motor Vehicles, Transportation, Wholesale, Accounting, Communications, Software

The Personnel Network Inc
1246 Lake Murray Blvd
PO Box 1426
Irmo, SC 29063
(803) 781-2087
(803) 749-9355
Fax: (803) 732-7986
Email: chuckirmo@aol.com

Description: Management and professional staff recruited confidentially in all areas of: manufacturing, public administration, marketing, hospitality, engineering, industrial, healthcare and environmental. Fax service on resumes for instant results.

Key Contact - Specialty:
Mr. Charles L. Larsen, Managing Director/CEO - *Environmental, public administration, industrial, hospitality*
Mr. C. Lars Larsen, President - *Engineering, generalist*
Mr. James K. Larsen, Executive Vice President - *Industrial*
Ms. Sarah K. Hochstetter, Associate Director - *Government, public administration, hospitality*

Salary minimum: $25,000

Functions: Generalist, Senior Mgmt., Middle Mgmt., Production, Allied Health, Engineering, Environmentalists

Industries: Generalist, Textiles, Apparel, HR Services, Hospitality, Government, Environmental Svcs., Healthcare

Professional Associations: SCAPS

Personnel Solutions
PO Box 32963
Phoenix, AZ 85064
(480) 946-0999
Fax: (480) 990-2045
Email: rick@personnelsols.com
Web: www.personnelsols

Description: Recruit sales and sales management nationally and in the Southwest; specializing in the medical, pharmaceutical, biotech, disposable and device markets.

Key Contact - Specialty:
Mr. Rick Spargo, Principal - *Medical sales, pharmaceutical sales*

Functions: Sales Mgmt.

Industries: Medical Devices, Pharm Svcs., Biotech, Healthcare

Networks: First Interview Network (FIN)

Personnel Unlimited/Executive Search
25 W Nora
Spokane, WA 99205
(509) 326-8880
Fax: (509) 326-0112
Email: gary@puinc.net

Description: We are a local firm with national exposure in all areas of employment. We have been serving Spokane and the entire US for over 23 years, and we have many very satisfied national client companies.

Key Contact - Specialty:
Mr. Gary P. Desgrosellier, President - *Management (all levels of upper disciplines)*

Salary minimum: $60,000

Functions: Generalist

Industries: Generalist

Networks: First Interview Network (FIN)

Perspective Inc
91 Roslyn Dr
New Britain, CT 06052
(860) 832-9499
(860) 225-6650
Email: steve-miglizzi@home.com
Web: www.perspectiveinc.com

Description: Our firm is solely dedicated to serving software and hardware engineering and accounting and finance professionals who have proven abilities and experience. We are able to identify excellent permanent career opportunities through our extensive client base and highly automated network association. We work to place individuals on a national basis in a broad spectrum of industries.

Key Contact - Specialty:
Mr. Joe Miglizzi, CPC, Principal - *Accounting, finance*
Mr. Steve Miglizzi, Recruiter - *Engineering (software, hardware)*

Salary minimum: $60,000

Functions: Finance, Systems Analysis, Systems Dev., Engineering

Industries: Generalist

Networks: National Personnel Assoc (NPA)

J R Peterman Associates Inc
PO Box 3083
Stowe, VT 05672
(802) 253-6304
Fax: (802) 253-6314
Email: peterman@jrpeterman.com
Web: www.jrpeterman.com

Description: We specialize in life and health
insurance, especially group and pension. We
provide both contingency and retained search
service on a national basis. Our specialties include
executives, underwriters, actuaries, sales, contract
analysts, marketers, and administrators.

Key Contact - Specialty:
Mr. James R. Peterman, President - *Insurance (life,
health), pensions*

Salary minimum: $50,000

Functions: Generalist

Industries: Insurance

Professional Associations: INS

Petro Staff Int'l
444 - 5th Ave SW Ste 1250
Calgary, AB T2P 2T8
Canada
(403) 266-8988
Fax: (403) 262-1310
Email: resumes@petro-staff.com
Web: www.petro-staff.com

Description: We specialize in recruitment of
professionals for international oil and gas
companies as well as petroleum specialists. We also
recruit IS and IT professionals, as well as medical
personnel.

Key Contact:
Mr. Iqbal E. Ali, Managing Director

Functions: Generalist, General Mgmt., Healthcare,
HR Mgmt., Finance, IT, Engineering, Int'l.

Industries: Generalist, Energy, Utilities, Misc.
Mfg., Aerospace, Software, Healthcare

Petruzzi Associates
PO Box 141
Scotch Plains, NJ 07076
(908) 928-9083
Fax: (908) 928-9084
Email: vjp@home.com

Description: In search of excellence of hard to find
individuals in the areas of manufacturing,
packaging, engineering, clinical data and marketing.
Primarily in the medical device, pharmaceutical,
chemical and plastics industry.

Key Contact - Specialty:
Mr. Vincent J. Petruzzi, President - *Manufacturing,
engineering, scientific*

Salary minimum: $40,000

Functions: Generalist, General Mgmt., Mfg.,
Materials, Mktg. Mgmt., Sales Mgmt., R&D,
Engineering

Industries: Generalist, Chemicals, Soap, Perf.,
Cosmtcs., Drugs Mfg., Medical Devices, Plastics,
Rubber, Paints, Petro. Products, Packaging

Robert E Pfaendler & Associates Inc
15405 SW 116th Ste 101
PO Box 23025
Tigard, OR 97281-3025
(503) 968-7777
Fax: (503) 620-8881
Email: bpfaendler@aol.com

Description: Only the highest code of professional
and ethical standards.

Key Contact - Specialty:
Mr. Robert E. Pfaendler, President - *Banking*

Salary minimum: $85,000

Functions: Finance

Industries: Banking, Misc. Financial

Professional Associations: OBA

Pharmaceutical Search Professionals Inc
311 N Sumneytown Pike Ste 1A
North Wales, PA 19454
(215) 699-1900
Fax: (215) 699-9189
Email: pspi@pharmaceutical-search.com
Web: www.pharmaceutical-search.com

Description: We have earned an unprecedented
reputation for placing M.D., Ph.D. and MBA level
executives. Our clientele consists of the top
pharmaceutical, biotech and medical device
companies.

Key Contact - Specialty:
Mr. Tony M. Fischetti, President & CEO - *Senior
level executives*
Mr. John D. Wuko, Corporate Vice President -
MDs, PhDs, directors, CEOs, vice presidents
Mr. David Graham, Corporate Vice President -
*MDs, PhDs, associate directors, CEOs, clinical
research*

Functions: Generalist

Industries: Pharm Svcs., Biotech

PHD Conseil en Ressources Humaines Inc
1 Pl Ville-Marie Ste 2821
Montreal, QC H3B 4R4
Canada
(514) 861-7100
Fax: (514) 879-3281
Email: phdelisle@videotron.ca

Description: Selection and recruitment of
executives and seasoned professionals in
information technology and information technology
sales.

Key Contact - Specialty:
Mr. Pierre H. Delisle, President - *Information
technology*

Salary minimum: $70,000

Functions: Mktg. Mgmt., Sales Mgmt., MIS
Mgmt., Systems Analysis, Systems Implem.,
Network Admin., DB Admin.

Industries: Generalist, Agri., Forestry, Mining,
Computer Equip., Consumer Elect., Equip Svcs.,
Mgmt. Consulting, New Media, Telecoms,
Software

Professional Associations: CIPS, FIQ, OCRIQ

Phelps Personnel Associates
(also known as Strategic Recruiters Inc)
PO Box 26442K
Greenville, SC 29616
(864) 232-6212
Fax: (864) 271-1426
Email: info@phelpspersonnel.com
Web: www.phelpspersonnel.com

Description: We have over twenty-five years of
experience in recruiting for southeastern,
manufacturing clients. Our services are always
company fee-paid. We place permanent,
engineering, technical, human resources, and other
manufacturing support positions. Our client
companies include automotive and consumer
products, film, plastics, electro-mechanical, and
various metal working processes.

Key Contact - Specialty:
Mr. Ronald A. Phelps, CPC, Founder -
Engineering, quality, purchasing

Mr. Dwight H. Smith, Jr., President - *Engineering,
technical, human resources*

Salary minimum: $40,000

Functions: Generalist

Industries: Mfg., Packaging

Professional Associations: SCAPS

Networks: Inter-City Personnel Assoc (IPA)

Phillips Associates
PO Box 83-2020
Delray Beach, FL 33483
(561) 272-2120

Description: We are a national executive search
firm with a specialty in finance and
telecommunications and in all related fields.

Key Contact - Specialty:
Ms. Veronica Phillips, President -
Telecommunications

Salary minimum: $30,000

Functions: Generalist, Credit, IT, MIS Mgmt.,
Systems Implem., Network Admin., DB Admin.,
Mgmt. Consultants

Industries: Generalist, Banking, Advertising,
Broadcast, Film, Telecoms

Phillips Int'l Inc
PO Box 6613
Greenville, SC 29606
(864) 297-0000
Fax: (864) 297-0114
Email: search@phillipsintl.com
Web: www.phillipsintl.com

Description: We provide executive search services
for client companies ranging from presidents
through sales and manufacturing to engineers in the
apparel/textile industries and in industrial
automation, the packaging industry, and related
manufacturing, as well as provide people for the
MIS/IT field and telecommunications.

Key Contact - Specialty:
Mr. Walter Phillips, CPC, President - *Apparel,
textile, information technology, automation,
packaging*

Salary minimum: $40,000

Functions: Generalist

Industries: Textiles, Apparel, IT Implementation,
Telecoms, Packaging

Professional Associations: NAPS, SCAPS

Phillips Personnel/Search
1675 Broadway Ste 2410
Denver, CO 80202
(303) 893-1850
Fax: (303) 893-0639
Email: phil@phillipspersonnel.com

Description: Contingency and retained search -
finance and accounting, sales and marketing,
information technology and information systems,
engineering, production, administration, general and
executive management.

Key Contact - Specialty:
Mr. Phil Heinschel, CPC, President -
*Telecommunications, distribution, financial
services, managers to CEOs of small to medium
size companies*

Salary minimum: $45,000

Functions: Middle Mgmt., Admin. Svcs.,
Distribution, Sales & Mktg., HR Mgmt., Finance,
IT

Industries: Generalist, Finance, Misc. Financial,
Non-profits, Accounting, HR Services, Telecoms,
Software

Networks: National Personnel Assoc (NPA)

Phillips Resource Group

PO Box 5664
Greenville, SC 29615
(864) 271-6350
Fax: (864) 271-8499
Email: info@sbphillips.com
Web: www.sbphillips.com

Description: Industry specialists, former officer level managers offer a high degree of client consciousness and business understanding supporting organization planning as well as executive search for all management and staff levels.

Key Contact - Specialty:
Mr. Sam B. Phillips, Jr. - *Textile industries, executive level*
Mr. Albert M. Hicks, Executive Recruiter - *Technical industries*
Ms. Jane Green, Executive Recruiter - *Information technology*
Ms. Jane Ko, Executive Recruiter - *Information technology*
Mr. Crawford Chavous, Executive Recruiter - *Textile industries, manufacturing*
Ms. Suzanne Malo, Executive Recruiter - *Accounting & finance*
Mr. Pete Foley, Executive Recruiter - *Engineering, manufacturing*
Ms. Bobby Kidd, Executive Recruiter - *Information technology*

Salary minimum: $50,000

Functions: Generalist, General Mgmt., Mfg., Sales & Mktg., Finance, IT, R&D, Engineering

Industries: Generalist, Textiles, Apparel, Paper, Chemicals, Plastics, Rubber, Machine, Appliance, Misc. Mfg., Banking

Professional Associations: NAPS, SCAPS

Networks: Top Echelon Network

Branches:
1338 AA Hundred Oaks Blvd
Charlotte, NC 28217
(704) 527-3838
Fax: (704) 527-5571
Email: info@sbphillips.com
Key Contact - Specialty:
Mr. Mike Plunkett, Executive Recruiter - *Textiles, manufacturing*
Mr. Pierce Sawyer, Executive Recruiter - *Manufacturing*
Mr. Buddy Collins, Executive Recruiter - *HR, accounting & finance*
Mr. Cam Donovan, Executive Recruiter - *Healthcare*

3402 H W Wendover Ave Wendover Office Park
Greensboro, NC 27407
(336) 292-1414
(336) 292-9787
Fax: (336) 292-1445
Key Contact - Specialty:
Ms. Nancy Brown, Executive Recruiter - *Staffing industry*
Ms. Robin Clark, Executive Recruiter - *Information technology (all levels)*
Ms. Debbie Gill, Executive Recruiter - *Information technology (all levels)*

The Phoenix Health Search Group

PO Box 453
Ramsey, NJ 07446-0453
(201) 818-7355
Fax: (201) 818-7365
Email: phoenix@nis.net
Web: www.managedcarecareer.com

Description: We provide professional executive-level search and recruitment of healthcare personnel, in the managed healthcare, medical

devices, sub-acute healthcare services, and pharmaceutical fields.

Key Contact - Specialty:
Mr. Gregory J. Erstling, Principal - *Sales, management, marketing, administration*

Salary minimum: $40,000

Functions: General Mgmt., Healthcare, Sales & Mktg., IT

Industries: Generalist

Phoenix Partners Inc

2451 Cumberland Pkwy Ste 3417
Atlanta, GA 30339
(404) 250-1133
Email: bobm@phoenixpartners.com
Web: www.phoenixpartners.com

Description: We are a retain/contingency search firm specializing in corporate contracted searches for individuals who have focused their careers in the direct sales and support of computer software products and services. Our firm is involved in searches for software sales managers, sales representatives, accounts executives, pre and post sales engineers, systems architects, and software consultants. Our clients are corporations providing software products and services to Fortune 1000 companies.

Key Contact - Specialty:
Mr. Robert A. Martin, Managing Director - *Computer hardware, software, service sales*

Salary minimum: $150,000

Functions: Sales & Mktg.

Industries: Computer Equip., Software

Professional Associations: RON, SHRM

Networks: Top Echelon Network

Phoenix Technical Services Inc

5495 Fox Rdg
West Bloomfield, MI 48322-2014
(248) 788-7671
Fax: (248) 788-7669
Email: resumes@ptscareers.com
Web: www.ptscareers.com

Description: We specialize in engineering, technical, and executive recruiting for the automotive, aerospace, and durable consumer goods industries. We provide contingent and retained searches.

Key Contact:
Mr. Nimish Desai, President - *Automotive*
Mr. Louis Wassel, Vice President

Salary minimum: $50,000

Functions: Middle Mgmt., Mfg., Materials, R&D, Engineering

Industries: Mfg., Metal Products, Motor Vehicles, Transportation, Aerospace

Physician Recruiting Services Inc

1001 Craig Rd Ste 330
St. Louis, MO 63146
(800) 872-2106
(314) 872-2181
Fax: (314) 569-9874
Email: cmcprs1@aol.com

Description: Our contingency firm provides a virtually risk free service to physicians, hospitals, medical groups, etc. assisting in matching physician staffing needs with appropriate candidates, sourced on a nationwide basis.

Key Contact - Specialty:
Mr. Chuck McMillan, Principal - *Physicians*

Functions: Generalist, Physicians

Industries: Generalist, Healthcare

Professional Associations: MGMA

Physician Search Consultants (PSC)

1111 Cumberland St
St. Paul, MN 55117
(800) 345-9350
(651) 488-6005
Fax: (888) 345-9350
Email: jonr@locumdoctor.com
Web: www.locumdoctor.com

Description: Work exclusively with Medical Doctors M.D.or D.O. only; Locum Tenens and Permanent Placement, with a special emphasis in Family Practice.

Key Contact:
Mr. Jon Richard, President
Mrs. Elizabeth Richard, Secretary

Physicians Search® Inc

5521 E Stetson Ct
Anaheim, CA 92807-4650
(714) 685-1047
(800) 748-6320
Fax: (714) 685-1143
Email: info@physicianssearch.com
Web: www.physicianssearch.com

Description: Established, reputable physician search and practice brokerage firm serving clients in the healthcare industry. As professionals we are licensed in both fields.

Key Contact:
Mr. Clifford W. Rauch, President
Ms. Janet Rauch, Vice President

Salary minimum: $50,000

Functions: Senior Mgmt., Physicians, Nurses, Allied Health, Health Admin., M&A

Industries: HR Services, Real Estate, Healthcare

Professional Associations: IBA, IBBA, NAPR

Piedmont Group Inc

1316 W Chester Pike
PMB 179
West Chester, PA 19382
(610) 436-6556
Fax: (610) 436-6545
Email: bob@piedmontgroup.net
Web: www.piedmontgroup.net

Description: Specializing in the chemical and petro chemical industry. Staffing solutions in the areas of management, engineering, research, environmental, safety, sales and marketing. Nation wide service through our network of affiliates.

Key Contact - Specialty:
Mr. Robert Meitz, President - *Chemical industry*

Salary minimum: $50,000

Functions: Generalist

Industries: Printing, Chemicals, Soap, Perf., Cosmtcs., Drugs Mfg., Plastics, Rubber, Paints, Petro. Products

Professional Associations: AICHE

Pine Lake Executive Search

55 Ingleside Dr
Hudson, OH 44236
(330) 528-3644
Email: jverlinde@pinelakesearch.com
Web: www.pinelakesearch.com

Description: Our team of search consultants partnered with respected Northeast Ohio organizations to assist them in isolating high-performance information technology professionals for direct-hire employment.

Key Contact - Specialty:
Mr. James Verlinde, President - *Information technology*

Salary minimum: $50,000

Functions: IT

Industries: Generalist

Pinnacle Group
6 Greenleaf Woods Ste 201
Portsmouth, NH 03801
(603) 427-1700
Fax: (603) 427-0526
Email: info@pinnaclejobs.com
Web: www.pinnaclejobs.com

Description: We are specialists in actuarial search for annuity, life, health, property-casualty, and pension companies. Our client list includes the nation's largest insurance, reinsurance, and consulting firms.

Key Contact:
Mr. Thomas Miller, Principal
Ms. Kathryn Davis, Principal

Salary minimum: $40,000

Functions: Finance, Risk Mgmt.

Industries: Services, Insurance

Pinnacle Group Int'l
PO Box 5690
Carefree, AZ 85377
(480) 575-6636
(888) 208-8714
Fax: (480) 575-9679
Email: info@pinngrpintl.com
Web: www.pinngrpintl.com

Description: Our executive recruitment firm specializes in investment banking and private equity/venture capital at the analyst, associate and vice president levels.

Key Contact - Specialty:
Mr. Stephen F. Flynn - *Investment banking*
Ms. Joanne T. Flynn - *Investment banking*

Salary minimum: $50,000

Functions: Generalist, M&A

Industries: Generalist, Invest. Banking, Venture Cap.

The Pinnacle Group
1902 Winding View
San Antonio, TX 78258
(830) 980-4671
Fax: (830) 980-5806
Email: veronica@thepinnacle-group.com
Web: www.thepinnacle-group.com

Description: We are a minority owned permanent recruiting agency with dedicated divisions trained to serve select industries, such as: medical, finance, IT, telecommunications, energy, consulting, and call centers. We have extensive experience with complete build-outs and confidential executive searches. All of our executive search consultants have over ten years of industry/recruiting experience.

Key Contact:
Ms. Veronica Edwards, President

Salary minimum: $40,000

Functions: Generalist

Industries: Energy, Utilities, Finance, Services, Mgmt. Consulting, Communications, Software, HR SW, Healthcare

Networks: Top Echelon Network

Pinnacle Search & Recruit
PO Box 25141
Scottsdale, AZ 85255
(800) 745-9309
Fax: (480) 585-8469
Email: pinnaclesearch@bigfoot.com

Description: Specializing in the telecommunications field nationwide. Sales, sales management, tech personnel.

Key Contact - Specialty:
Mr. William J. Marcoux, Director - *Telecommunications*

Salary minimum: $35,000

Functions: General Mgmt., Sales & Mktg., Training, CFO's, Risk Mgmt., IT, Systems Dev., Systems Implem., Engineering, Technicians

Industries: Telecoms

Professional Associations: RON

The Pinnacle Source Inc
4600 S Ulster St Ste 975
Denver, CO 80237
(303) 796-9900
Fax: (303) 796-9901
Email: pinnacle@rmi.net
Web: www.pinnaclesource.com

Description: Our unique approach to executive recruitment is supported by thirty-five years of successful executive search and placement experience. Our client companies are high-technology industry leaders, as well as Colorado owned and operated start-up firms in the software/Internet arena.

Key Contact - Specialty:
Mr. Jordan A. Greenberg, President - *Information systems, sales & marketing, management*

Salary minimum: $75,000

Functions: Generalist, Mkt. Research, Mktg. Mgmt., Sales Mgmt., Direct Mktg., MIS Mgmt., Systems Implem., Systems Support

Industries: Generalist, Computer Equip., Mgmt. Consulting, New Media, Broadcast, Film, Software

Pioneer Executive Consultants
904 E Mall 201
Toronto, ON M9B 6K2
Canada
(416) 620-5563
(416) 620-5373
Fax: (416) 620-5648
Email: pioneer.executive@sympatico.ca

Description: Full recruitment services to the chemical, paint, adhesives and ink industries in positions from general management, plant management, R&D, quality, engineering, sales and services.

Key Contact - Specialty:
Mr. Ed Gres, President - *Chemical, paint, adhesives*
Mr. Paul Sinclair, Senior Consultant - *Chemical, paint, adhesives*

Salary minimum: $40,000

Functions: Generalist

Industries: Agri., Forestry, Mining, Mfg., HR Services, Environmental Svcs., Haz. Waste, Packaging, Biotech

Pioneer Placement Inc
PO Box 434
Westfield, MA 01086
(413) 568-2442
Fax: (413) 568-2444
Email: nate@pioneerplacement.com
Web: www.pioneerplacement.com

Description: Client companies receive the experience of a seasoned recruiter with national exposure; yet the personal touch of the individual.

Key Contact - Specialty:
Mr. Nathan Rosenthal, CPC, President - *Insurance*

Functions: Generalist, Legal, Benefits, Finance, Risk Mgmt.

Industries: Generalist, Insurance

Professional Associations: NIRA

Pitcher & Crow
135 W 27th St Fl 10
New York, NY 10001
(212) 352-2255
Fax: (212) 352-2304
Email: mail@pitcher-crow.com
Web: www.pitcher-crow.com

Description: Our firm has over 25 years of experience in human resources, operations, and sales in large corporate, as well as small business environments. Whether you are considering starting, augmenting, or outsourcing your human resources function, or just focusing on improving your company's people management skills. Pitcher & Crow can tailor fees and service packages to suit your specific needs.

Key Contact - Specialty:
Ms. Janine Walter, Managing Director - *Advertising, human resources*
Mr. Kevin Bergin, Managing Director - *Marketing, human resources*

Salary minimum: $75,000

Functions: Generalist

Industries: Mfg., Finance, Hospitality, Media, Telecoms, Insurance, Real Estate, Software, Healthcare

Professional Associations: ABA, ICF, SHRM

Pittleman & Associates
336 E 43rd St
New York, NY 10017
(212) 370-9600
Fax: (212) 370-9608
Email: attysearch@pittlemanassociates.com
Web: www.pittlemanassociates.com

Description: We specialize in placing attorneys at investment banks and corporations.

Key Contact - Specialty:
Mr. Steven Pittleman, Esq., President - *Law firms, management consulting*
Ms. Linda Pittleman, Esq., Chairman - *Corporations, investment banks, commercial banks*

Salary minimum: $75,000

Functions: Legal, Personnel, Paralegals

Industries: Generalist, Legal

Professional Associations: NALSC

PLA Inc
4425 Kensington Park Rd
Lake Worth, FL 33467
(561) 966-4688
Fax: (561) 966-3583
Email: kaarla@pla-inc.com
Web: www.pla-inc.com

Description: We are a national executive search and recruiting firm specializing in the placement of advertising and marketing executives.

Key Contact:
Ms. Pat Lipton
Ms. Kaarla McKenzie

Functions: Advertising, Mkt. Research, Mktg. Mgmt.

Industries: Generalist

Branches:
9713 Little Pond Way
Tampa, FL 33647
(813) 991-9467
Fax: (813) 991-9526
Email: kaarla@pla-inc.com
Key Contact:
Ms. Kaarla McKenzie

Placemart Personnel Service
5 Elm Row
New Brunswick, NJ 08901
(732) 247-8844
(800) 394-7522
Fax: (732) 247-8973
Email: info@placemart.com
Web: www.placemart.com

Description: Recruiting for technical and administrative positions in clinical research: including data management, statistics, medical writing, regulatory affairs, clinical research scientists and operations for medical product research and development.

Key Contact - Specialty:
Mr. William R. Kuhl, President - *Biostatistics, drug information, clinical research & development*

Salary minimum: $40,000

Functions: Healthcare, Physicians, R&D

Industries: Drugs Mfg., Medical Devices, Pharm Svcs., Biotech, Healthcare

Professional Associations: AMWA, ASA, DIA, NJSA, PHARMASUG, SCDM

Placement Group
(formerly known as Executrade Personnel)
100 736 6th Ave SW
Calgary, AB T2P 3T7
Canada
(403) 777-9000
Fax: (403) 777-9007
Email: executrade@ddgstaff.com
Web: www.ddgstaff.com

Description: We are a full-service recruitment agency. We provide temporary, permanent and contract staff in the areas of administration, accounting, data entry, management and marketing.

Key Contact - Specialty:
Ms. Lisa Gandossi, Account Manager - *Business development, corporate*
Ms. Judy Tidlund, Account Manager - *Business development, light industrial*

Functions: Generalist, Admin. Svcs., Plant Mgmt., Distribution, Customer Svc., Credit, Systems Support, Engineering

Industries: Generalist, Construction, Misc. Mfg., Transportation, Banking, Accounting, HR Services

Professional Associations: ACSESS, HRAC

Placement Solutions
W270 S3979 Heather Dr
Waukesha, WI 53189
(262) 542-2250
Email: msshort@financerecruiting.com
Web: www.financerecruiting.com

Description: Executive, managerial, professional accounting, and information systems audit are specialties. All industries/businesses. Our levels range from CFO down to $50K in salary. Other key positions that we place are are VPs, general counsel, CEO, etc.

Key Contact - Specialty:
Ms. Mary Sue Short, Owner - *Executive, accounting, finance*

Functions: General Mgmt., Directors, Senior Mgmt., Finance

Industries: Energy, Utilities, Mfg., Wholesale, Finance, Services, Hospitality, Media, Telecoms, Environmental Svcs., Aerospace, Packaging, Insurance, Biotech

Professional Associations: IIA, ISACA

Placements by Jesse Reid Associates Inc
152 1/2 E 63rd St
New York, NY 10021
(212) 355-1300
Fax: (212) 355-1648

Description: A boutique firm offering timely, discreet, personal service to media clients using an extensive, comprehensive database, on-going research and face-to-face interviews.

Key Contact - Specialty:
Ms. Georgia M. Petry, President - *Advertising, sales, management, marketing management*

Functions: Generalist, Sales & Mktg., Advertising, Mktg. Mgmt., Sales Mgmt., Direct Mktg.

Industries: Generalist, Media, Publishing

PLC Associates
7004 Blvd E Ste 3-31G
Guttenberg, NJ 07093
(201) 854-4004
Fax: (201) 869-8611
Email: plcassoc@aol.com

Description: Our primary service is executive search, diversity staffing and executive search research.

Key Contact - Specialty:
Ms. Peggy L. Cave, President - *R & D, IT, marketing, finance, minorities, diversity*
Ms. Lillian Cave, Principal - *Higher education, human resource management*

Functions: Generalist, Materials, Sales & Mktg., HR Mgmt., Finance, IT, R&D, Minorities

Industries: Generalist, Food, Bev., Tobacco, Drugs Mfg., Transportation, Banking, Higher Ed., Media, Healthcare

Professional Associations: DIA, IFT, NBMBAA

PMB Executive Recruiters Inc
210 Interstate N Pkwy Ste 700
Atlanta, GA 30339
(770) 618-0877
Fax: (770) 618-0855
Email: patrickb@pmber.com
Web: www.pmber.com

Description: Based on our experience and continuos research, we provide an in-depth knowledge of the targeted discipline, industry and career opportunity. We fulfill our ethical and professional commitment to our clients both candidates and companies.

Key Contact - Specialty:
Mr. Patrick M. Bradshaw, PHR, Executive Placement Coordinator - *Finance & accounting, human resources*
Mr. Edward L. Bailey, Senior Recruitment Specialist - *Sales & marketing, telecommunications, mortgage banking*
Ms. Heather Johnson, Senior Recruitment Specialist - *Banking*
Ms. Paula Stewart, Recruitment Specialist - *Executive assistants*

Salary minimum: $45,000

Functions: Directors, Senior Mgmt., Middle Mgmt., Admin. Svcs., Sales & Mktg., HR Mgmt., Finance

Industries: Generalist, Services, Pharm Svcs., Accounting, Mgmt. Consulting, HR Services, Hospitality

Professional Associations: AHRA, SHRM

PMJ & Associates
15 Toronto Str Ste 602
Toronto, ON M5C 2E3
Canada
(416) 364-9997
Fax: (416) 364-8735
Email: resumes@pmjpersonnel.com
Web: www.pmjpersonnel.com

Description: Twenty years' experience and specializing in one geographic area along with our expertise in accounting/finance, insurance and bilingualism enables us to have proper understanding of today's market.

Key Contact - Specialty:
Mr. Allen Fink, Manager - *Accounting, finance, investments, taxation*
Ms. Miriam Frankel, Senior Consultant - *Bilingual, insurance, credit*
Mr. Jeffrey Gillespie, Consultant - *Accounting, finance, taxation*

Functions: Generalist, Middle Mgmt., Budgeting, Cash Mgmt., Credit, Taxes, M&A, Systems Analysis

Industries: Generalist, Mfg., Food, Bev., Tobacco, Finance, Packaging, Insurance

PMK Management Consultants Inc
11250 Roger Bacon Dr Ste 17
Reston, VA 20191
(800) 768-0743
Email: pmk@patriot.net

Description: We offer 23 years and experience in most industries. Though our principle business is staffing and recruiting, we have become well known for our expertise in training, human resource management, benefits, compensation analysis and EEO.

Key Contact - Specialty:
Mr. Pat Kuzniewski, Human Resource Manager - *High technology*
Mr. Peter Borman, Staffing Manager - *Construction, call centers*
Ms. Tracy Houde, Staffing Manager - *Food service*

Functions: Generalist, General Mgmt., Mfg., Sales & Mktg., HR Mgmt., Finance, IT, Engineering

Industries: Generalist, Mfg., Services, Media, Aerospace, Software

PMR Search Consultants Inc
428B Osceola Ave
Jacksonville Beach, FL 32250
(904) 270-0505
Fax: (904) 270-0520
Email: peterpmr@bellsouth.net

Description: We place attorneys in the state of Florida in all disciplines of law and specialize in health law, government contracting, antitrust, telecommunications and high-technology in the Washington DC area. Health law searches conducted nationally for both candidates and clients.

Key Contact - Specialty:
Mr. Mark Rosenblum, Vice President - *Attorneys*
Mr. Peter Gurtenstein, President - *Attorneys*

Functions: Legal, Healthcare

Industries: Generalist, Drugs Mfg., Medical Devices, Pharm Svcs., Legal, Healthcare

Pam Pohly Associates
2707 Woodrow Ct Ste 100
Hays, KS 67601
(785) 625-9790
Email: pam@pohly.com
Web: www.pohly.com

Description: National healthcare firm provides executive search, interim management and consulting services. Recruit CEOs, CFOs, COOs and upper-management candidates for permanent employment in medical centers and specialty hospitals. Interim management service provides CEO, CFO and service line leaders on temporary basis. Consulting to hospitals for business planning, turnaround and start-up.

Key Contact:
Ms. Pam Pohly

Functions: General Mgmt., Senior Mgmt., Admin. Svcs., Health Admin., Mktg. Mgmt., CFO's, Mgmt. Consultants

Industries: Healthcare

The Polen Group
1445 Washington Rd
Washington, PA 15301
(724) 225-9500
Fax: (724) 225-8907
Email: jpolen@polengroup.com
Web: www.polengroup.com

Description: We have been in the recruiting business since 1961. All assignments, either retained or contingency are directed by a project manager. All Project Managers have at least ten (10) years' experience with our firm.

Key Contact:
Mr. Jerry B. Polen, President

Functions: Generalist, General Mgmt., Mfg., Materials, Sales & Mktg., IT, R&D, Engineering

Industries: Generalist, Mfg., Chemicals, Plastics, Rubber, Aerospace, Packaging, Software

Networks: National Personnel Assoc (NPA)

Bob Poline Associates Inc
12625 High Bluff Dr Ste 114
San Diego, CA 92130-2053
(858) 481-3700
(858) 481-1202
Fax: (858) 481-5187
Email: bobpoline@pacbell.net
Web: www.bobpoline.com

Description: We make a total commitment to excellence in the executive search process. We treasure our reputation and recognition for professional service, performance and client satisfaction. We've stayed consistent since 1979.

Key Contact - Specialty:
Mr. Bob Poline, President - *Shopping centers*

Salary minimum: $50,000

Functions: Senior Mgmt., CFO's, Architects, Attorneys

Industries: Construction, Retail, Real Estate

Professional Associations: ICSC

Rich Poline Associates Inc
7 Ascot Manor
Atlanta, GA 30327
(770) 955-9306
Email: rpoline@mindspring.com
Web: www.bobpoline.com

Description: We are nationwide specialists in recruitment for the shopping center industry. We provide leasing, property/asset management, operations, marketing, development, tenant coordination, construction, design, legal/lease

administration, accounting and finance. We do extensive work in retail real estate, construction, architecture/design, and store planning.

Key Contact - Specialty:
Mr. Rich Poline, President - *Shopping centers*

Functions: Senior Mgmt., Architects, Attorneys

Industries: Construction, Retail, Real Estate

Professional Associations: ICSC

The Pollack Group
176 Bronson Ave
Pollack Pl
Ottawa, ON K1R 6H4
Canada
(613) 238-2233
Fax: (613) 238-4407
Email: tpg@pollackgroup.com
Web: www.pollackgroup.com

Description: Being in the center of high-technology in Canada (Ottawa), the nation's capital, we have been supplying top prospects to Canada's best high-technology companies and all federal government departments.

Key Contact - Specialty:
Mr. Paul Pollack, President/CEO - *Executive sales*
Mr. Charles Durning, Director, Professional Services - *High technology*
Mr. Brian McKenna, Senior Recruiter - *Information technology (contract, permanent)*
Ms. Colette Purchase, Senior Recruiter - *Technology*

Salary minimum: $40,000

Functions: Generalist, Mktg. Mgmt., Sales Mgmt., Systems Analysis, Systems Dev., Systems Implem., Systems Support, Engineering

Industries: Generalist, HR Services, Aerospace, Software, Healthcare

Professional Associations: NAPS

Polymer Network Inc
1922 Clyde Rd
Madison, OH 44057
(440) 428-7747
Fax: (440) 428-4831
Email: greg@polymernetwork.net
Web: www.polymernetwork.net

Description: We are recruiters for the plastics and rubber industry focusing on engineering, design, managerial, and technical positions.

Key Contact:
Mr. Greg Weber, President - *Molding, plastic, rubber injection*
Ms. Karen Weber, Owner

Salary minimum: $35,000

Functions: Mfg.

Industries: Plastics, Rubber

Professional Associations: SPE

Polytechnical Consultants Inc
7328 W Lunt Ave
Chicago, IL 60631
(773) 467-7777

Description: Search, recruiting and placement firm. Activity includes all technical/engineering markets, at all professional levels.

Key Contact - Specialty:
Mr. Walt Zimmer, Manager - *Engineering*

Salary minimum: $25,000

Functions: Generalist, Product Dev., Production, Automation, Plant Mgmt., Quality, Engineering

Industries: Generalist, Medical Devices, Plastics, Rubber, Metal Products, Machine, Appliance,

Consumer Elect., Test, Measure Equip., Misc. Mfg.

Al Ponaman Company Inc
10041-5 Larwin Ave
Chatsworth, CA 91311-7406
(818) 993-9100
Fax: (818) 993-9412
Email: info@banking-careers.com
Web: www.banking-careers.com

Description: Over two decades of confidential searches for major and independent banks and credit unions. We are a member of the largest network of banks and professional bankers and credit union professionals. Resumes are always welcome and confidentiality is always maintained.

Key Contact - Specialty:
Mr. Albert L. Ponaman, President - *Banking, credit unions*
Ms. Bernice Ponaman, CFO - *Controller*

Salary minimum: $25,000

Functions: Generalist

Industries: Banking

Professional Associations: MAC

Don V Poole & Associates Inc
7700 S Glencoe Way
Littleton, CO 80122
(303) 721-6644
Fax: (303) 721-7724
Email: dvpoole@attglobal.net

Description: We are specialists in the semiconductor equipment industries placing executives and middle management sales and marketing professionals.

Key Contact - Specialty:
Mr. Don V. Poole, President - *Semiconductor equipment, telecommunications, sales, product management, marketing management*

Salary minimum: $80,000

Functions: Generalist, Senior Mgmt., Admin. Svcs., Product Dev., Mkt. Research, Sales Mgmt., CFO's, Int'l.

Industries: Generalist, Computer Equip., Test, Measure Equip., Misc. Mfg., Telecoms

Porter & Associates Inc
PO Box 1585
Santa Rosa Beach, FL 32459
(850) 622-1896
Fax: (850) 622-1906
Email: pranan@gnt.net

Description: Nationwide retail & e-commerce search and recruitment for corporate and field executives. Expertise includes merchandising, advertising, product development, planning and distribution, human resources, finance, MIS, operations and field management positions.

Key Contact - Specialty:
Ms. Nancy Porter, President - *Retail*

Salary minimum: $75,000

Functions: Generalist

Industries: Retail

Professional Associations: NRF

Jack Porter Associates Inc
24119 SE 18th Pl
Sammamish, WA 98075-1808
(425) 392-9252
Fax: (425) 391-9107
Email: jackporterassocs@msn.com
Web: www.international-employment.net

Description: Placement of engineers, scientists, manufacturing and sales professionals on a national and international basis at all levels in all industries. Also have opportunities for VP, GM, CFO, MIS, SW, DP and administrative professionals, and foreign national professionals with international experience and native foreign language capability.

Key Contact - Specialty:
Mr. Jack Porter, President - *Generalist*

Salary minimum: $30,000

Functions: Production, Plant Mgmt., Quality, Productivity, IT, R&D, Engineering, Mgmt. Consultants, Minorities, Int'l.

Industries: Generalist, Telecoms

Networks: Inter-City Personnel Assoc (IPA)

The Porter Hamel Group Inc
565 Congress St Ste 203
Portland, ME 04101
(207) 828-1134
Fax: (207) 828-1540
Email: phg@porterhamel.com
Web: www.porterhamel.com

Description: Operations and technical recruiting from entry level to CEO for food manufacturing companies.

Key Contact - Specialty:
Mr. Jeffrey C. Porter, President - *Operations, technical, food manufacturing*
Mr. Richard Hazelton, Director - *Operations, technical, food manufacturing*

Functions: Generalist, Directors, Mfg., Materials, HR Mgmt., R&D, Engineering

Industries: Generalist, Mfg., Food, Bev., Tobacco, Soap, Perf., Cosmtcs., Drugs Mfg., Services, HR Services

Branches:
211 Pinecrest Ln Ste 100
Lansdale, PA 19446
(215) 362-1414
Fax: (215) 362-1266
Email: don@proterhamel.com
Key Contact - Specialty:
Mr. Don Rietscha - *Baking industry*

Positions Inc
1 Faneuil Hall Marketplace
S Market Fl 5
Boston, MA 02109
(617) 367-9200
Fax: (617) 367-4906
Email: positionsinc@worldnet.att.net
Web: www.positionsinc.com

Description: Our firm has been one of the most successful executive recruiting firms in New England for 32 years. Our success has resulted from our concern for our clients. We approach every client with the goal of a long-term relationship and repeat business based on high quality service and results.

Functions: Admin. Svcs., Nurses, HR Mgmt., Finance, Engineering

Industries: Generalist, Biotech

Firm declined to update.

Edward J Pospesil & Company
44 Long Hill Rd
Guilford, CT 06437-1870
(203) 458-6566
Fax: (203) 458-6564
Email: ed@ejp.com
Web: www.ejp.com

Description: Provide contingency and retained search in IT, technology marketing and competitive intelligence. Clients range from Fortune 500

through mid-tier and entrepreneurial, across a wide variety of industries.

Key Contact:
Mr. Edward J. Pospesil, Owner/Principal

Salary minimum: $60,000

Functions: Mkt. Research, IT

Industries: Generalist, Wireless, Network Infrastructure, Software

---

Post & Company
845 Pleasant St Ste 3
Oak Park, IL 60302
(708) 383-5844
Fax: (708) 383-6817
Email: postsearch@aol.com

Description: We specialize in focused searches seeking skilled candidates for the food industry. Our placement categories include sales, marketing, research, engineering, technical service, and purchasing.

Key Contact:
Ms. Ann J. Post

Salary minimum: $45,000

Functions: Middle Mgmt., Product Dev., Purchasing, Sales & Mktg., R&D

Industries: Mfg., Food, Bev., Tobacco, Chemicals, Restaurants

Professional Associations: IFT, NAPS

Power Recruiting Group
4833 Twin Valley Dr
Austin, TX 78731
(512) 420-0767
(888) 386-8672
Fax: (512) 420-8032
Email: medwards@powerrecruiting.com
Web: www.powerrecruiting.com

Description: Our president has more than ten years of energy industry experience. Our firm is exclusively focused on the energy industry..

Key Contact - Specialty:
Mr. J. Michael Edwards, President - *Energy & utilities*
Ms. Bonny Block, Vice President - *Energy & utilities*

Functions: Generalist, General Mgmt., Sales & Mktg., Finance, Int'l.

Industries: Generalist, Energy, Utilities

Professional Associations: AEE, AESP

Power Search
512 Willow Spring Dr
Heath, TX 75032
(972) 772-5577
Fax: (972) 772-0051
Email: moon@mypowersearch.com
Web: www.mypowersearch.com

Description: Executive retained search. Recruiting for high-tech software - sales and executive management.

Key Contact - Specialty:
Mr. Thomas A. Moon, President - *High technology software*

Salary minimum: $65,000

Functions: Generalist, Mktg. Mgmt., Sales Mgmt.

Industries: Generalist, Software

Power Technology Associates Inc
1200 Providence Hwy
Sharon, MA 02067
(781) 784-4200
Fax: (781) 784-4302

Email: info@powercareers.com
Web: www.powercareers.com

Description: We specialize in the areas of power electronics, motion control, energy storage, lighting, RF, microwave and analog electronics.

Key Contact - Specialty:
Mr. Richard Cardafella, President - *Power electronics*
Mr. Matt McGuill, Recruiter - *Power electronics*
Mr. Bob Chambers, Recruiter - *Power electronics*
Mr. Andy Kilgour, Recruiter - *Power electronics*
Ms. Holly Henderson, Recruiter - *Power electronics*
Ms. Kathy Kelley, Recruiter - *Sales & marketing*
Mr. Andy Mulcahy, Contract Recruiter - *Contract engineering*
Mr. Rick Millikan, Recruiter - *Radio frequency, microwave engineering*
Mr. Mark Larochelle, Recruiter - *IC's*

Functions: Engineering

Industries: Mfg., Telecoms, Defense, Aerospace, Packaging, Software

---

PowerBrokers LLC
(also known as MRI of Cass County)
12635 S Izard St
Omaha, NE 68154
(402) 498-8981
Fax: (402) 445-9736
Email: efisher@tconl.com
Web: www.powerbrokersllc.com

Description: Ph.D. level account executives with 20 years of technical and management experience. Focus on all areas of the electric utility and natural gas industries emphasizing wholesale and retail sales and marketing, energy traders, risk management and individuals in asset acquisition and development.

Key Contact - Specialty:
Mr. Earl Fisher - *Energy, electric, power, natural gas*

Salary minimum: $75,000

Functions: Generalist, Legal, Mkt. Research, Mktg. Mgmt., Sales Mgmt., Risk Mgmt., Engineering

Industries: Generalist, Energy, Utilities, Misc. Financial, Legal

Professional Associations: PMA, UMA

Branches:
10836 W Beloit Pl
Lakewood, CO 80227
(303) 716-2987
Fax: (303) 716-3426
Email: kszablya@powerbrokersllc.com
Key Contact:
Ms. Kate Szablya, Principal

PO Box 263
Newark, DE 19715-0263
(302) 293-3500
Fax: (302) 369-3999
Email: rfodge@powerbrokersllc.com
Key Contact:
Mr. Robert Fodge, Principal

Powers & Associates
4286 Redwood Hwy Ste 308
San Rafael, CA 94903
(415) 492-1122
Email: larry@executive-jobs.com
Web: www.executive-jobs.com

Description: Our firm recruits and places experienced sales and marketing oriented high technology professionals. These professionals have titles such as president, CEO, COO, vice president, director, in-house counsel, account executive, and manager. Larry Powers personally conducts all recruiting activities and does not use assistants.

Key Contact:
Mr. Larry Powers

Salary minimum: $50,000

Functions: Senior Mgmt., Sales & Mktg.

Industries: Computer Equip., Electronic, Elec. Components, Equip Svcs., E-commerce, IT Implementation, PSA/ASP, Communications, Software

Robert Powers & Associates
PO Box 1085
Placentia, CA 92870
(714) 524-7279
Fax: (714) 524-8410

Description: Specialists in the restaurant, hospitality and specialty retail industries. Cover line, staff and executive management positions.

Key Contact - Specialty:
Mr. Robert Powers, CPC, President - *Restaurant, specialty retail, hospitality*
Ms. Susan Powers, Vice President - *Restaurant, specialty retail, hospitality*

Salary minimum: $25,000

Functions: Generalist, Senior Mgmt., Purchasing, Mkt. Research, Mktg. Mgmt., HR Mgmt., Finance, Risk Mgmt., R&D, Minorities

Industries: Food, Bev., Tobacco, Retail, Hospitality, Restaurants

Professional Associations: CRA, CSP, NAPS, NRA

Norman Powers Associates Inc
PO Box 3221
Framingham, MA 01705-3221
(508) 877-2025
Fax: (508) 877-0541
Email: normpowers@aol.com
Web: www.npa.qpg.com

Description: Electronics, hi-tech and computer industry-military, commercial and industrial professional placement since 1964. Disciplines include: technical, BSEE, BSME, computer science; manufacturing-technical, management, material control, technical sales/marketing.

Key Contact - Specialty:
Mr. Norman S. Powers, President - *Electronics, hardware, software, manufacturing, marketing*

Salary minimum: $25,000

Functions: Generalist

Industries: Computer Equip., Software

Professional Associations: MPPC

PPS Information Systems Staffing
1420 E Joppa Rd
Towson, MD 21286
(410) 823-5630
Fax: (410) 821-9423
Email: headhunter@ppsinfo.com
Web: www.ppsinfo.com

Description: We are a technical recruitment firm which specializes in all areas of information technology, telecommunications and sales.

Key Contact - Specialty:
Mr. Neal Fisher, President - *Network engineering, telecommunications*

Salary minimum: $20,000

Functions: IT

Industries: Generalist

Professional Associations: AITP, NATSS

Practice Dynamics Inc
11222 Richmond Ste 125
Houston, TX 77082
(281) 531-0911
Fax: (281) 531-9014
Email: pdi@practice-dynamics.com

Description: All physician specialties in the South, Southeast, Mid-Atlantic, Southwest and Midwest. National expertise in ORS, ONC, URO, RHU. Over 10 years' experience in medical practice appraisals.

Key Contact - Specialty:
Ms. Karen M. Lovett, President - *Physicians*
Mr. John S. Harrison, Vice President - *Physicians*

Functions: Generalist, Physicians

Industries: Generalist, Healthcare

Professional Associations: NAPR

P G Prager Search Associates Ltd
1461 Franklin Ave
Garden City, NY 11530
(516) 294-4400
Fax: (516) 294-4443
Email: pgprager@att.net
Web: www.pgprager.com

Description: One of Long Island's top recruitment firms specializing in legal, financial, insurance and general management, personalized service, no candidate referred without a personal interview. Substantial guarantee.

Key Contact:
Mr. Michael B. Prager, President

Functions: Generalist, Senior Mgmt., Admin. Svcs., Legal, Sales & Mktg., Mktg. Mgmt., Sales Mgmt., Taxes, Attorneys, Paralegals

Industries: Generalist, Legal

Professional Associations: APCNY, NALSC

The Prairie Group
1 Westbrook Corp Ctr Ste 300
Westchester, IL 60154
(708) 449-7710
Email: resumes@theprairiegroup.net

Description: Top candidates for blue chip clients in all areas of HR, corporate finance and consulting. Emphasis on candidates that have demonstrated the ability to add immediate value and grow quickly. Frequently selected to recruit outstanding diversity candidates due to our extensive network in minority communities.

Key Contact - Specialty:
Mr. James Kick, Principal - *Finance, marketing, consulting*
Mr. Romero Manzo, Principal - *Human resources*
Mr. Mark Scott, Principal - *Human resources*

Salary minimum: $60,000

Functions: HR Mgmt., Finance

Industries: Generalist, Mfg., Food, Bev., Tobacco, Chemicals, Machine, Appliance, Motor Vehicles, Finance, Accounting, Mgmt. Consulting

Precision Search Group Inc
PO Box 131988
The Woodlands, TX 77393
(936) 321-9122
Fax: (936) 321-9280
Email: psg@electrotex.com
Web: www.psg2000.com

Description: Executive search exclusively for the information technology marketplace throughout North America. Positions include: sales, technical, marketing, managers, tech support, VP sales, branch/regional managers, project managers, network system engineers, etc.

Key Contact:
Mr. Ken Lucas

Salary minimum: $40,000

Functions: Generalist

Industries: Software

Precision Solutions Inc
7307 E Indian Plz Ste 111
Scottsdale, AZ 85251
(480) 874-1001
Email: michelle@hotrecruits.com
Web: www.hotrecruits.com

Description: We are a nationwide boutique search firm. We specialize exclusively in the fast paced and dynamic Information Technology marketplace, which includes software, electronic commerce, hardware & consulting.

Key Contact:
Ms. Michelle Floriano, President - *High technology*
Mr. Michael Floriano, Vice President - *High technology*
Mr. Lincoln Aul, Vice President - *Pulp and paper*
Ms. Roxanne Becker, Recruiter - *Storage*
Ms. Brenda Depas, Recruiter - *High technology*
Ms. Gigi Melchiorre, Business Manager

Functions: General Mgmt., Senior Mgmt., Middle Mgmt., Sales & Mktg., CFO's, IT, MIS Mgmt., Engineering, Mgmt. Consultants, Int'l.

Industries: Agri., Forestry, Mining, Energy, Utilities, Mfg., Lumber, Furniture, Paper, Venture Cap., Services, E-commerce, Media, Communications, Telecoms, Call Centers, Telephony, Digital, Wireless, Fiber Optic, Network Infrastructure, Software, Accounting SW, Database SW, Development SW, Doc. Mgmt., Production SW, Entertainment SW, ERP SW, HR SW, Industry Specific SW, Mfg. SW, Marketing SW, Networking, Comm. SW, Security SW, System SW, Training SW

Networks: Top Echelon Network

Preferred Personnel
731 W Wadley Ave Bldg O Ste 130
Midland, TX 79705
(915) 684-5900
Fax: (915) 683-5336
Email: resumes@preferred-personnel.com
Web: www.preferred-personnel.com

Description: We provide executive recruiting worldwide in a broad range of industries, specializing in the oil & gas industry.

Key Contact:
Mr. Larry Bledsoe, President
Mr. Paula Bledsoe, Vice President

Functions: Generalist, General Mgmt., Mfg., Sales & Mktg., HR Mgmt., Finance, IT, Engineering

Industries: Generalist, Energy, Utilities, Construction, Mfg., Finance, Media, Telecoms, Insurance, Accounting SW

Professional Associations: NAPC, TAPC

Networks: National Personnel Assoc (NPA)

Preferred Professional Recruiters
PO Box 8747
Maumee, OH 43537
(419) 865-2406
Fax: (419) 865-2409
Email: neilgreebe@aol.com
Web: www.preferred-recruiters.com

Description: We specialize in accounting, computer/data processing, engineering, management personnel, sales and marketing, executives, technical and production supervisors in manufacturing.

Key Contact - Specialty:
Mr. Neil Greebe, CPC, Partner - *Manufacturing, generalist*

Salary minimum: $40,000

Functions: Generalist, General Mgmt., Mfg., Materials, HR Mgmt., Finance, IT, Engineering

Industries: Generalist, Mfg., Chemicals, Plastics, Rubber, Metal Products, Machine, Appliance, Motor Vehicles, Computer Equip.

Professional Associations: OSSA, RON

Networks: Inter-City Personnel Assoc (IPA)

Preferred Professional Recruiters

(a subsidiary of Zingaro & Company)
21936 Briarcliff Dr
Briarcliff, TX 78669-2012
(512) 327-7275
Fax: (512) 327-1774
Email: search@pprecruiters.com
Web: www.pprecruiters.com

Description: An executive search firm specializing in the search and selection of healthcare professionals for industry areas including - but not limited to - pharmaceutical, pharmaceutical services, medical device, diagnostics, and biotechnology.

Key Contact:
Dr. Ronald J. Zingaro, Ph.D., President
Ms. Mary H. Johnson, Vice President

Functions: General Mgmt., Mfg., Healthcare, Sales & Mktg., Finance, IT, R&D, Engineering, Specialized Svcs., Int'l.

Industries: Drugs Mfg., Medical Devices, Pharm Svcs., Biotech, Healthcare

Professional Associations: AAAS, ACRP, DIA, RAPS

Premier Business Advisors Inc

2537 Crestline Dr
Lansdale, PA 19446
(215) 544-7030
(866) 722-3627
Fax: (610) 544-6166
Email: jpacini@pbadvisors.com
Web: www.pbadvisors.com

Description: The industries that we serve are pharmaceutical and biotechnology. Our focus is physician-scientists and executives.

Key Contact - Specialty:
Mr. Joseph Pacini, President - *Pharmaceutical, biotechnology*

Salary minimum: $100,000

Functions: Generalist, Physicians, R&D

Industries: Generalist, Drugs Mfg., Pharm Svcs., Biotech, Healthcare

Premier Careers Inc

1345 S Missouri Ave Ste 120
Clearwater, FL 33756
(727) 467-0220
Fax: (727) 467-0222
Email: jroark@premiercareers.com
Web: www.premiercareers.com

Description: We offer specialized service in selected fields, including the property and casualty, life insurance industries, accounting, and sales organizations. Our success is achieved by establishing strong client relationships and through well thought out, comprehensive candidate searches. Internet marketing and a large database of professionals add to our effectiveness.

Key Contact - Specialty:
Mr. James P. Roark, President - *Insurance (P&C and Life), sales, accounting*

Mr. Ryan P. Roark, Account Executive - *Insurance (property, casualty)*
Mr. Marc V. Perreault, Executive Recruiter - *Property and casualty insurance*
Mr. John J. Havel, Executive Recruiter - *Financial services*

Salary minimum: $40,000

Functions: Generalist, Finance

Industries: Accounting, Insurance

Premier Consulting

8400 E Prentice Ave Ste 1380
Greenwood Village, CO 80111
(303) 779-1006
Fax: (303) 773-2191
Email: jan@premiersearch.com
Web: www.premiersearch.com

Key Contact:
Ms. Jan Hanbery, President
Ms. Mary Ross, Search consultant

Premier Healthcare Recruiters Inc

5 Woodbury Ln Ste B
Dearborn, MI 48120
(313) 441-6450
Fax: (313) 441-6460
Email: premierhealthcare@ameritech.net

Description: We provide professional recruiting of physicians for both clinical and administrative positions on a contingency basis.

Key Contact - Specialty:
Ms. Diana L. Watson, CPC, President - *Physicians, physicians assistants, nurse practitioners, administrative physicians, physical therapists*

Salary minimum: $100,000

Functions: Generalist, Physicians

Industries: Generalist, Healthcare

Professional Associations: NAPR

Premier Placement Inc

PO Box 3436
Allentown, PA 18106
(610) 395-9123
Email: premierpal@mindspring.com
Web: www.premierplacement.com

Description: Specialize in Engineering, Manufacturing and Materials Management - including Sales, Marketing, Finance, Accounting, HR and IT positions. Member of Lehigh Valley Chamber of Commerce since 1986, Inter-City Personnel Association since 1988, serving as Congress Rep

Key Contact - Specialty:
Ms. Laura Schmieder, Recruiter - *Engineering, manufacturing, materials management*

Functions: Mfg., Materials, Sales & Mktg., HR Mgmt., Engineering

Industries: Mfg., Packaging, Software, Biotech

Professional Associations: ASME, SHRM

Networks: Inter-City Personnel Assoc (IPA)

Premier Recruiting Group Inc

1719 S Burdick St Ste A
Kalamazoo, MI 49001
(616) 344-7370
Fax: (616) 344-7476
Email: PremierRec@aol.com

Description: We specialize in the permanent, full-time placement of professionals in the financial services, human resources, and information technology fields. The employers pay all fees; therefore, our candidates pay nothing.

Key Contact:
Mr. William Jaques, Co-Owner
Ms. Laura Van Popering, Co-owner
Mr. Greg McLogan, Senior Account Executive

Salary minimum: $40,000

Functions: General Mgmt.

Industries: Generalist

Premier Recruiting Group

(a division of Michigan Consulting Group)
3037 Benjamin
Royal Oak, MI 48073
(248) 549-7178
Fax: (248) 549-7178
Email: mcg@provide.net

Description: We are general practice recruiting consultants. We utilize our extensive networking and database resources providing recruiting and management consulting services for our Fortune 500, metal forming, stamping, plastics, electronics, medical devices, general manufacturing, and automotive clients.

Key Contact - Specialty:
Mr. David Southworth, President - *Senior & general management*
Mr. Rich Krezo, Managing Director - *Technical automotive, engineering, manufacturing*
Mr. Doug Kramer, Director - *Automotive, metal forming, stamping, manufacturing, sales & account managers*
Mr. Pedro Salinas Gasga, Director - *Senior management, manufacturing management (Mexico, Central America, South America)*
Mr. Edward Southworth, Vice President - *Pharmaceuticals, medical devices, senior, management, general & middle management*
Mr. Gary Bussa, Director - *CFO, finance & accounting, information technology, human resources management*
Ms. Kathy Palazzolo, Director - *Senior, general & middle management, manufacturing, engineers*
Mr. Steven Gust, Director - *Information technology, MIS management, software development, systems analysis & design, network administration*

Salary minimum: $65,000

Functions: General Mgmt., Senior Mgmt., Mfg., Quality, Sales & Mktg., HR Mgmt., Finance, CFO's, IT, Engineering

Industries: Generalist, Mfg., Chemicals, Drugs Mfg., Medical Devices, Plastics, Rubber, Leather, Stone, Glass, Metal Products, Machine, Appliance, Motor Vehicles, Computer Equip., Misc. Mfg.

Professional Associations: ACG, AMA, FMA, SAE, SPI

The Premier Staffing Group

611 Quimby Ave
Wooster, OH 44691
(330) 263-1300
Fax: (330) 263-9258
Email: kelly@premierstaff.com
Web: www.premierstaff.com

Description: Professional search in management, engineering, finance and operations for manufacturing companies making parts for automotive or metal parts manufacturing. Also executive and hourly contract staffing for factory and clerical engineering.

Key Contact:
Mr. James A. Babcock, President - *General management, engineering, operations, contract staffing*
Ms. Kelly Williams, Manager

Salary minimum: $40,000

Functions: Generalist, Product Dev., Production, Plant Mgmt., Quality, CFO's, Engineering

Industries: Generalist, Lumber, Furniture, Plastics, Rubber, Metal Products, Machine, Appliance, Motor Vehicles, Finance

Branches:
4932 Everhard Rd NW
Canton, OH 44718
(330) 499-8677
Fax: (330) 499-8779
Email: cheryl@premierstaff.com
Key Contact:
Ms. Cheryl Watkins, Manager

2021 Park Ave Ste 101
Mansfield, OH 44906
(419) 522-2789
Fax: (419) 522-5849
Email: bonnie@premierstaff.com
Key Contact:
Ms. Bonnie Thomas, Manager

115 Broad St
Wadsworth, OH 44282
(330) 334-4911
Fax: (330) 334-4456
Email: amy@premierstaff.com
Key Contact:
Ms. Amy Wilson, Manager

Premiere Resources

2018 - 156th Ave NE Ste 100
Bellevue, WA 98008
(425) 748-5018
Fax: (425) 644-2185
Email: info@pr-hr.com
Web: www.pr-hr.com

Description: We are your total HR Solution! We are pioneering a new age in "digital HR," by transitioning companies from filing cabinet to virtual systems. We handle placement of top level executives with our client companies in the technology industry.

Key Contact:
Ms. Amber O'Brien, SPHR, President and CEO
Ms. Jayna Westmoreland, Executive Vice President

Salary minimum: $100,000

Functions: Senior Mgmt.

Industries: Finance, Mgmt. Consulting, HR Services, IT Implementation, Communications, Software

Professional Associations: SHRM, SHRMCF

PreQuest Inc

1933 S Wright Blvd
Schaumburg, IL 60193
(847) 352-0700
Fax: (847) 352-0800
Email: prequest@prequest.com
Web: www.prequest.com

Description: Our firm is a professional recruitment research firm with state of the art technology, an extensive database, proven best practices, and a structured research methodology. We provide our clients strategic research services from targeted companies. We proactively target, identify, and profile the candidates, who are passively job seeking, that you want to hire.

Key Contact:
Mr. J. Randy Severinsen, CPC, Principal
Mr. William R. Lange, CPC, Principal

Salary minimum: $50,000

Functions: Generalist, Middle Mgmt., MIS Mgmt., Systems Analysis, Systems Dev., Systems Implem., Network Admin., Mgmt. Consultants

Industries: Generalist, Misc. Financial, Mgmt. Consulting, HR Services, Telecoms, Software

Professional Associations: IAPS, NAPS

Networks: National Personnel Assoc (NPA)

Lloyd Prescott Associates Inc

4803 George Rd Ste 360
President's Plz Ctr
Tampa, FL 33634
(813) 881-1110
(800) 486-3463
Fax: (813) 889-8458
Email: headhunt7@lloydprescott.net
Web: www.lloydprescott.com

Description: Generalist firm providing nationwide executive and professional search. Specializing in senior management, healthcare, legal, insurance, high-tech, sales/marketing, finance/banking, manufacturing, consultants, food industry. Offering our clients the best and the brightest candidates in their field.

Key Contact - Specialty:
Mr. Sheldon M. Ginsberg, Managing Partner - *Senior management*
Mr. Manuel F. Gordon, Business Affairs Partner - *Senior management*

Salary minimum: $70,000

Functions: Generalist, Senior Mgmt., Middle Mgmt., Legal, Health Admin., Sales Mgmt., MIS Mgmt., Engineering

Industries: Generalist, Food, Bev., Tobacco, Drugs Mfg., Computer Equip., Legal, Advertising, Healthcare

The Prescott Group

2305 Monticello Cir
Plano, TX 75075
(972) 758-0779

Description: We specialize in advertising and marketing personnel.

Key Contact:
Mr. David Poole, President

Salary minimum: $50,000

Functions: Senior Mgmt., Advertising, Mkt. Research, Mktg. Mgmt., Sales Mgmt.

Industries: Advertising, Publishing, New Media

Prescott Legal Search Inc

3900 Essex Ln Ste 1110
Houston, TX 77027
(713) 439-0911
Fax: (713) 439-1317
Web: www.prescottlegal.com

Description: We are the largest legal recruiting firm in Texas with offices in Houston, Dallas, and Austin. Our staff includes 13 former practicing attorneys, and we have a proprietary database containing confidential information on over 20,000 lawyers.

Key Contact - Specialty:
Mr. Larry W. Prescott, JD - *Lawyers*
Ms. Lauren Eaton Prescott, JD - *Lawyers*
Mr. Stephen Mims, JD - *Lawyers*
Ms. Susan Pye, JD - *Temporary lawyers*
Ms. Laura B. Eastman, JD - *Lawyers*
Ms. Delia Johnson, JD - *Lawyers*
Ms. Tonda Hyde, CLA - *Paralegals*
Ms. Linda Carrette, CLA - *Paralegals*

Functions: Attorneys, Paralegals

Industries: Generalist

Professional Associations: NALSC, TBA

Branches:
1717 W 6th St Ste 240
Austin, TX 78703
(512) 482-9442
Fax: (512) 482-9160
Key Contact - Specialty:
Ms. M. Tish Honojosa, JD - *Lawyers*

Ms. Jane Fields Pollard, JD - *Lawyers*
Ms. Courtney B. Legg, JD - *Temporary attorneys*
Ms. Mary Alice Naiser - *Paralegals*
Ms. Holly E. Coe - *Paralegals*

3102 Oak Lawn Ave Ste 700
Dallas, TX 75219
(972) 210-2930
Fax: (214) 210-2989
Key Contact - Specialty:
Ms. Anita S. Worth, JD - *Lawyers*
Ms. Henny Wright, JD - *Lawyers*
Ms. Holly Sherman Pena, JD - *Lawyers*
Ms. Electra Harelson - *Contract lawyers, paralegals*

Presley Consultants Inc

812 3rd St
Norco, CA 91760
(909) 734-2237
Fax: (909) 734-1775
Email: presleyinc@aol.com
Web: www.presleyconsultants.com

Description: Executive search, recruitment specifically in the hospitality and healthcare (administration) industries; exclusively client retained and primarily contingency; will conduct and have conducted retained search assignments.

Key Contact - Specialty:
Mr. Philip E. Presley, President/COO-Hospitality Div - *General Management, operations, sales, finance, food*
Mr. Jason T. Presley, VP- Operations, Hospitality Division - *Food & beverage, operations, sales*
Ms. Linda C. Presley, Senior Vice President - *Finance*

Salary minimum: $75,000

Functions: Generalist

Industries: Services, Mgmt. Consulting, HR Services, Hospitality

Professional Associations: HSMAI

Lloyd Pressel & Company Inc

Box AA
Bisbee, AZ 85603
(520) 432-5361
Fax: (520) 432-7005
Email: pressel@topechelon.com

Description: Specialists in employeee placement since 1962. We recruit management nationwide of all industries and functions. We specialize in electro-optics, fiberoptics, telecommunications, photonics, engineering, sales R&D, construction, construction engineers and sales. Preferred member of 650-Member Recruiting Agency (World'd Largest), 3500 recruiters total. Database of 3 million resumes.

Key Contact - Specialty:
Dr. Lloyd Pressel, President - *Electro-optic, fiberoptic, telecommunications, photonics, construction, general management, engineering, sales*
Ms. Lexie Hartmann, President, Bay Search - *Electro-optic, fiberoptic, telecommunications, photonics, construction, general management, engineering, sales*

Functions: Generalist, Senior Mgmt., Mfg., Product Dev., Production, Plant Mgmt., Sales & Mktg., MIS Mgmt., R&D, Engineering

Industries: Construction, Mfg., Electronic, Elec. Components, Telecoms, Digital, Wireless, Fiber Optic, Network Infrastructure, Networking, Comm. SW

Networks: Top Echelon Network

Branches:
350 Firethorn Dr
Rohnert Park, CA 94928
(707) 584-9037
Fax: (707) 584-9038
Key Contact - Specialty:
Ms. Lexie Hartmann, Regional President - *Fiber optics, telecom, photonics, high tech, thin film coatings*

Prestige Inc
PO Box 421
Reedsburg, WI 53959
(608) 524-4032
Fax: (608) 524-8577

Description: Industry specialization affords us the opportunity to know the language, methods and personnel before we begin a search, eliminating many of the risks involved in the hiring process.

Key Contact - Specialty:
Mr. James A. Sammons, Managing Director - *Consumer products (all positions)*

Salary minimum: $50,000

Functions: General Mgmt., Product Dev., Plant Mgmt., Quality, Materials, Healthcare, Sales & Mktg., CFO's, Graphic Artists, Int'l.

Industries: Mfg., Transportation, Wholesale, Retail, Services, Media, Packaging, Healthcare

Branches:
PO Box 105
LaValle, WI 53941
(608) 985-8410
Fax: (608) 524-8577
Key Contact - Specialty:
Mr. Marc Douglas, Director - *Retail*

Price & Associates Inc
760 Lynnhaven Pkwy Ste 108
Virginia Beach, VA 23452
(757) 306-4777
Fax: (757) 306-8943
Email: vprice@earthlink.net
Web: www.worldrecruiting.com

Description: An accomplished recruitment/consulting firm that work closely with our client companies to meet their hiring demands. Areas of expertise include: telecommunications, wireless communications, cable, Internet and e-commerce with special emphasis in executive recruitment, sales/sales management, human resources, marketing, finance, engineering, technicians, and all aspects of computer programming (hardware and software).

Key Contact - Specialty:
Ms. Velinda Hodge Price, President - *Sales, sales management, engineering, executive level, technicians*

Salary minimum: $40,000

Functions: Generalist

Industries: Retail, Finance, Venture Cap., Broadcast, Film, Telecoms

Professional Associations: NAFE

Prime Management Group Inc
365 Queens Ave
London, ON N6B 1X5
Canada
(519) 672-7710
Fax: (519) 672-5155
Email: jobs@pmg.on.ca
Web: www.pmg.on.ca

Description: We are an executive search and recruitment firm specializing in the recruitment of professionals for both management and non-management positions. Servicing London,

Southwestern Ontario, Canada, US and overseas, we encompass multiple areas of search and recruitment.

Key Contact:
Ms. Kimberley Chesney, President

Functions: General Mgmt., Directors, Senior Mgmt., Mfg., Sales & Mktg., HR Mgmt., Finance, IT, R&D, Int'l.

Industries: Generalist

Professional Associations: ACSESS

Networks: National Personnel Assoc (NPA)

Branches:
260 Holiday Inn Dr
Cambridge, ON N3C 4E8
Canada
(519) 220-0310
Fax: (519) 220-0327
Email: jobs2@pmg.on.ca
Key Contact:
Ms. Colleen Young, Sr Recruitment Specialist/Operations Mgr

Prime Resource Associates Inc
PO Box 490
Brookfield, WI 53008-0490
(262) 860-1260
Fax: (262) 860-1264
Email: prime@powercom.net

Description: We excel at identifying the clients' needs as to technical requirements and target market, then identify and qualify all candidates for technical match and personal interest prior to submittal.

Key Contact - Specialty:
Mr. Paul J. Schneider, President - *Engineering, technical, manufacturing*

Salary minimum: $40,000

Functions: Generalist

Industries: Generalist, Energy, Utilities, Mfg., Packaging, Software, Biotech

Primus Search
22 Trundy Rd
Cape Elizabeth, ME 04107-2819
(207) 741-9058
Fax: (207) 741-2817
Email: pmoson1@maine.rr.com

Description: We are a recruiting agency that provides job placement to companies that provide products, such as medical imaging, medical devices, healthcare software, medical equipment, medical supplies, etc. to the healthcare market, for example hospitals, long term care facilities, HMO's, home care, medical offices, etc.

Key Contact - Specialty:
Mr. Paul F. Moson, President - *Generalist*
Mrs. Anne-Lise Moson, Vice President - *Sales & marketing*

Salary minimum: $70,000

Functions: Generalist

Industries: Medical Devices, Software, Biotech, Healthcare

Princetec Inc
4365 Rte 1
Princeton, NJ 08540
(609) 720-9800
Fax: (609) 720-9899
Email: info@princetec.com
Web: www.princetec.com

Description: We are a leading staffing and IT consulting firm that provides strategic and creative technical resource solutions for some of the world's most successful future-focused businesses. We provide highly qualified software engineers,

internet/client-server developers/programmers, database experts, telecom engineers, embedded systems engineers, and network engineers.

Key Contact - Specialty:
Mr. Raj Sajankila, Co-Founder - *Engineers, programmers, project managers, computers, electronics*

Salary minimum: $40,000

Functions: IT, Systems Dev., Systems Implem., Network Admin., DB Admin., Engineering

Industries: Generalist, Telecoms

Professional Associations: NJSA, RON

Networks: Top Echelon Network

Princeton Corp Consultants
420 W Baseline Rd C
Claremont, CA 91711
(909) 625-3007
Fax: (909) 621-0315
Email: sadams7727@aol.com
Web: www.princetonconsultants.com

Description: EXECUTIVE SEARCH--MEDICAL DEVICE AND PHARMACEUTICAL DRUG COMPANIES

Key Contact - Specialty:
Mr. Steve Adams, Sr Vice President - *Medical device, biotechnology*

Salary minimum: $60,000

Functions: General Mgmt., Product Dev.

Industries: Mfg., Drugs Mfg., Medical Devices, Plastics, Rubber, Pharm Svcs., IT Implementation, Packaging, Mfg. SW, Biotech, Healthcare

Networks: Medical Search Consortium (MSC)

Princeton Entrepreneurial Resources Inc
PO Box 2051
Princeton, NJ 08543-2051
(609) 921-7400
Fax: (609) 921-6334
Email: results@per-inc.com
Web: www.per-inc.com

Description: We support organizations in forming strategy-based working relationships and provide leaders of change, critical projects, strategic initiatives and new ventures.

Key Contact - Specialty:
Ms. Kristen H. Callahan, President - *Senior level executives*

Salary minimum: $100,000

Functions: Generalist, General Mgmt., Mfg., Sales & Mktg., HR Mgmt., Finance, IT

Industries: Generalist, Paints, Petro. Products, Machine, Appliance, Computer Equip., Pharm Svcs., HR Services, Biotech

Princeton Executive Search
PO Box 7373
Princeton, NJ 08543-7373
(609) 584-1100
Fax: (609) 584-1141
Email: dick@bonifield.com
Web: www.bonifield.com/pes

Description: Executive search and placement. Management level and supporting staff. High specialty in accounting, finance, banking, human resources, engineering and information systems.

Key Contact - Specialty:
Mr. Richard Tyson, President - *Accounting*

Salary minimum: $25,000

Functions: Finance

Industries: Generalist

Professional Associations: IMA, MAAPC

Princeton Legal Staffing Group LLC
116 Village Blvd Ste 200
Princeton Forrestal Village
Princeton, NJ 08540-5799
(609) 730-8240
Fax: (609) 730-8363
Email: dgarber@princetonlegal.com
Web: www.princetonlegal.com

Description: Owned and operated by former law firm partner David S. Garber, Esq., we specialize in the permanent placement of exceptionally qualified attorneys in all practice areas with law firms and corporate legal departments.

Key Contact - Specialty:
Mr. David S. Garber, Esq., President - *Attorneys*

Functions: Attorneys

Industries: Generalist

Priority Employment
6501 N Himes 302
Tampa, FL 33614
(888) 345-4080
Fax: (413) 473-4848
Email: danc@priorityemployment.com
Web: www.priorityemployment.com

Description: We have been recruiting quality candidates for quality companies for over 20 years. HR, engineering, automotive, manufacturing, quality and aerospace engineers.

Key Contact - Specialty:
Mr. Dan Carpenter, CEO - *Human resources, engineering, quality, automotive, manufacturing*
Ms. Juanita Carpenter, President - *Banking, financial*

Functions: Generalist, General Mgmt., Directors, Mfg., Plant Mgmt., Quality, HR Mgmt., Engineering

Industries: Generalist, Mfg., Medical Devices, Metal Products, Machine, Appliance, Motor Vehicles, HR Services, Aerospace

Professional Associations: GAPS

Priority Executive Search
14317 Ravenwood Ln
Tampa, FL 33618
(813) 961-8074
Fax: (813) 962-6027
Email: prioriti@ix.netcom.com

Description: Healthcare (administration, nursing, therapy, pharmacy; insurance risk management, benefits, compensation, actuarial), HMOs, PPOs, TPLs, managed care. Pharmaceutical $ medical sales.

Key Contact - Specialty:
Mr. Rolf H. Kausch, President - *Medical, healthcare*
Ms. Beatriz J. Oliveira, Executive Vice President - *General management, insurance*

Salary minimum: $20,000

Functions: Generalist, Directors, Healthcare

Industries: Generalist, Mgmt. Consulting, Insurance, Software, Healthcare, Hospitals, Non-classifiable

Networks: Top Echelon Network

Pro Search National Recruiting Services
216 W Pacific Ave Ste 104
Spokane, WA 99201
(509) 363-1986
Fax: (509) 363-1987

Email: pat@prosearchnational.com

Description: I am a recruiter with 11 years of experience, who specializes in sale and sales management placement on a national basis.

Key Contact - Specialty:
Mr. Patrick Bopray, Owner - *Sales & sales management*

Functions: Sales Mgmt.

Industries: Construction, Mfg., Food, Bev., Tobacco, Textiles, Apparel, Lumber, Furniture, Printing, Paints, Petro. Products, Computer Equip., Consumer Elect., Misc. Mfg., Media, Publishing, Telecoms, Packaging, Software

Pro Tec Global Staffing
8500 Leslie St Ste 600
Thornhill, ON L3T 7M8
Canada
(905) 707-2300
Fax: (905) 707-0332
Email: protec@protecstaff.com
Web: www.protecstaff.com

Description: A staffing service with an extensive database of qualified professionals in engineering, information technology, manufacturing, human resources and finance. Experienced in international work assignments.

Key Contact - Specialty:
Mr. John J. Chrobak, President - *Engineering, senior management*
Mr. Reg Baraniuk, Senior Associate - *Engineering, professional*
Mr. Glen Collard, Senior Associate - *Manufacturing, finance*
Mr. Mike Slimkowich, Senior Associate - *Manufacturing, information technology*
Mr. Dave Clark, Senior Associate - *Information technology*
Mr. Bill Johnson, Senior Associate - *Engineering*
Mr. J. P. Belanger, Senior Associate - *Human resources*
Mr. Iain Purves, Senior Associate - *Information technology*

Functions: Generalist

Industries: Energy, Utilities, Construction, Mfg., Transportation, Banking, HR Services, Media, Broadcast, Film, Telecoms, Software

Pro-Tech Search Inc
400 Chatham Rd Ste 201
Springfield, IL 62704
(217) 793-2790
Fax: (217) 793-2791
Email: kmccoy@pro-techsearch.com
Web: www.pro-techsearch.com

Description: Contractual and permanent placement of healthcare and computer professionals in the Midwest with a specialty area of Central Illinois.

Key Contact - Specialty:
Mr. Karl McCoy, President - *Information technology, healthcare*
Ms. Janet Bascom, Recruiter - *Information technology*
Ms. Rita Brummett, Vice President-Operations - *Information technology*

Salary minimum: $40,000

Functions: General Mgmt., IT, MIS Mgmt., Systems Analysis, Systems Dev., Systems Implem., Network Admin., DB Admin.

Industries: Generalist, Healthcare

Professional Associations: NAPS

Probe Technology
PO Box 60521
King of Prussia, PA 19406
(610) 337-8544
Fax: (610) 337-8068
Email: probetfb@aol.com
Web: www.busdir.com/probetech/

Description: Individualized service specializing in engineering, manufacturing and manufacturing support and sales/marketing. Many services offered with unique fee arrangements and creative approaches to recruiting.

Key Contact - Specialty:
Mr. Thomas F. Belletieri, Principal - *Generalist*
Ms. Nancy Belletieri, Principal - *Generalist*

Salary minimum: $40,000

Functions: Generalist, General Mgmt., Mfg., Materials, Sales & Mktg., Engineering

Industries: Generalist, Chemicals, Medical Devices, Metal Products, Machine, Appliance, Computer Equip., Test, Measure Equip.

Probus Executive Search
4962 El Camino Real Ste 126
Los Altos, CA 94022
(650) 960-3751
(650) 960-3756
Fax: (650) 960-0331
Email: meetus@probus-exec.com
Web: www.probus-exec.com

Description: Finance and accounting professionals for technology companies located in the San Francisco Bay Area.

Key Contact - Specialty:
Mr. Jack McNeal, Partner - *Accounting & finance*
Ms. Paulette Clements, Partner - *Accounting & finance*

Salary minimum: $40,000

Functions: Generalist, CFO's, Budgeting, Cash Mgmt., Credit, M&A, Risk Mgmt.

Industries: Generalist, New Media, Telecoms, Software

Procom
2323 Yonge St Ste 605
Toronto, ON M4P 2C9
Canada
(416) 483-0766
(800) 461-4878
Fax: (416) 483-8102
Email: frankk@procom.ca
Web: www.procom.ca

Description: We are one of the leading providers of full time and contract computer personnel in North America with over 100 clients in industries such as banking, automotive and software manufacturing, telecommunications, retail, insurance, transportation and oil refining.

Key Contact:
Mr. Frank McCrea, President - *IT*
Ms. Angela Campbell
Mr. Pierre Cho
Mr. John Csatari
Ms. Christina De Palo
Mr. Eric Descoteaux
Ms. Lisa Elliot
Mr. Michael Elliot
Mr. Mark Galloway
Ms. Stacey Glass
Ms. Shelly Hogan
Mr. Kevin Jaques
Mr. Jeff Kobryn
Ms. Jen Lacka
Ms. Salma Ladak
Mr. Michael Low
Mr. Alex Mackenzie
Mr. Dave Mahood

Ms. Frances Markicevic
Ms. Sheri McLean
Ms. Patty Niles
Mr. Jeff Nugent
Mr. Kevin O'Connell
Ms. Diane Pap
Ms. Deborah Potts
Ms. Frances Rotstein
Ms. Lisa Satin
Mr. Eti Sepia
Mr. Imad Sidahmed
Ms. Judith Stephenson
Mr. Tom Fetherston
Ms. Vi Trinh
Ms. Katie Turner
Ms. Monica Volpintesta

Salary minimum: $45,000

Functions: Generalist, MIS Mgmt., Systems Analysis, Systems Dev., Systems Implem., Systems Support, Network Admin., DB Admin.

Industries: Generalist, Transportation, Banking, Mgmt. Consulting, Insurance, Software

Branches:
275 Battery St Ste 950
San Francisco, CA 94111-3050
(415) 773-1873
(800) 231-1616
Fax: (415) 773-1833
Web: www.procomservices.com
Key Contact:
Ms. Roberta D'Alois - *Managing director*
Ms. Sylvia Herczku
Mr. Jeremy Kmet - *Information technology*
Ms. Annie Yee

3000 RDU Center Dr Ste 114
Morrisville, NC 27560
(919) 840-0606
Fax: (919) 840-0777
Email: richardk@procomservices.com
Web: www.procomservices.com
Key Contact:
Mr. Rich Kviring, Managing Director
Ms. Rosemarie S. Brady
Mr. Dan Colby
Ms. Michelle Harrelson
Mr. Jon Michalec
Ms. Donna Rose
Ms. Donna Stainback
Ms. Stacey Young
Mr. Joe Zuchlewski

801 E Campbell Rd Ste 375
Richardson, TX 75081-1890
(972) 234-6055
Fax: (972) 234-5661
Email: neilb@procomtexas.com
Web: www.procomservices.com
Key Contact:
Mr. Neil Brooks, Managing Director
Ms. Amy Askins
Mr. Ivor Bon
Mr. Scott Bucholz
Mr. Ron Hunt
Mr. Casey Judkins
Ms. April Oliver
Jeet Sikdar
Mr. Gregg Wright

250 - 6th Ave SW Ste 1200
Bow Valley Sq IV
Calgary, AB T2P 3H7
Canada
(403) 571-7241
Fax: (403) 571-7195
Email: sallyd@procom.ca
Key Contact:
Ms. Sally Drysdale, Managing Director
Ms. Karen Jefferson
Ms. Jennifer MacGregor
Ms. Wendy Mah
Ms. Lynn Wilsack

300 March Rd Ste 600
Kanata, ON K2K 2E2
Canada
(613) 270-9339
Fax: (613) 270-9449
Email: keithc@procom.ca
Key Contact:
Mr. Keith Carter, Managing Director
Ms. Maggie Alves
Mr. Paul Brown
Moodie Cheikh
Ms. Lesley Collins
Mr. Joe Kerub
Ms. Shawn Mountain
Mr. Derek Weber

405 King St N Ste 106
Waterloo, ON N2J 2Z4
Canada
(519) 885-4331
Fax: (519) 885-5308
Email: lukem@procom.ca
Key Contact:
Mr. Luke Morrison

1260 Crescent Ste 210
Montreal, QC H3G 2A9
Canada
(514) 731-7224
Fax: (514) 731-7244
Email: andrec@procom.ca
Key Contact:
Mr. André Couillard
Mr. Joe Kerub
Mr. Cristopher Paget

Procurement Resources
1500 Delaware Ct
Finksburg, MD 21048
(410) 840-3692
Fax: (410) 840-3692
Email: procres@aol.com
Web: members.aol.com/procres/index.html

Description: Specializing in the recruitment of purchasing, logistics, materials and supply chain professionals capable of meeting today's challenges in supply chain management, global sourcing and quality criteria.

Key Contact - Specialty:
Mr. John L. Cousins, Principal - *Purchasing, materials management, logistics, distribution*

Salary minimum: $40,000

Functions: Generalist, Middle Mgmt., Production, Materials, Purchasing, Materials Plng., Distribution

Industries: Generalist, Drugs Mfg., Motor Vehicles, Computer Equip., Misc. Mfg., Telecoms, Biotech

Professional Associations: APICS, NAPM, NCMA, RON

Product Management Resources
44 E Parkwood Dr
Dayton, OH 45405
(937) 277-1212
Fax: (208) 988-6947
Email: mary_pmr@topechelon.com

Description: We are a preferred member of Top Echelon, (OHAH), the world's largest network of independent recruiters. We specialize in the permanent and contract placement of marketing, product management, and product marketing professionals

Key Contact:
Ms. Mary Nurrenbrock, Owner

Salary minimum: $75,000

Functions: Senior Mgmt., Middle Mgmt., Mkt. Research, Mktg. Mgmt., Direct Mktg.

Industries: Software

Networks: Top Echelon Network

Professional Career Service
PO Box 3472
Omaha, NE 68103-3472
(402) 633-2070
Email: bbarritt@pcscareer.com
Web: www.pcscareer.com

Key Contact - Specialty:
Mr. Barry Barritt, Vice President - *Sales*

Salary minimum: $40,000

Functions: Generalist

Industries: Finance, Banking, Invest. Banking, Brokers, Venture Cap.

Professional Careers Inc
1310 Raeford Rd Ste 2
PO Box 53629
Fayetteville, NC 28305
(910) 323-3987
Fax: (910) 323-1819
Email: vicki@procareer.com
Web: www.procareer.com

Description: We specialize in information systems and technology positions in the US. We handle opportunities in IT management, applications software development, client server, and network (LAN/WAN/MAN) management. We target the development of clients for long-term business relationships. We guarantee the professionals that we place.

Key Contact - Specialty:
Ms. Vicki Hayes Sturgill, Owner/MIS Recruiter - *Information systems*

Salary minimum: $40,000

Functions: IT, MIS Mgmt., Systems Analysis, Systems Dev., Systems Implem., Network Admin., DB Admin.

Industries: Generalist, IT Implementation

Networks: National Personnel Assoc (NPA)

Professional Computer Resources Inc (PCR)
328 Rensselaer Ave
Charlotte, NC 28203
(704) 335-1312
(888) 727-2458
Fax: (704) 335-8763
Email: resumes@pcr.net
Web: www.pcr.net

Description: Our eight recruiters place IT professionals within the Internet/intranet (Java or VB/ASP), client server, networking, and mainframe areas on a full-time and contract basis in Charlotte, NC and USA clients.

Key Contact - Specialty:
Ms. Dianne C. Gold, President - *DBAs, java project managers*
Mr. Christian Militello, VP- Sales & Marketing - *MIS management, VP, CIO, senior management*
Mr. Paul Keating, Recruiter - *Networking, PC support, LAN/WAN*
Mr. Richard Troy, Recruiter - *Cobol (mainframe), CICS, DB2, IMS, database*
Mr. Bryant Hinnant, Recruiter - *Database (oracle, sybase, sql server, watcom)*

Salary minimum: $50,000

Functions: Generalist, IT, MIS Mgmt., Systems Analysis, Systems Dev., Systems Implem., Systems Support, Network Admin., DB Admin.

Industries: Generalist, Banking, Invest. Banking, Brokers, Misc. Financial, Software, Development SW

Professional Consulting Network Inc

595 Market St 1400
San Francisco, CA 94105
(415) 777-4321
Fax: (415) 777-8632
Email: info@pcninc.com
Web: www.pcninc.com

Description: Recruit for full time contract positions. Employ consultants or represent independent contractor for temporary consulting assignments in data processing/software engineering assignments.

Key Contact:
Mr. Heinz Bartesch, Director-Search/Recruiting -
MIS, software engineering
Mr. Peter Jozwik, President
Mr. Jim Schneider, Vice President

Salary minimum: $45,000

Functions: MIS Mgmt., Systems Analysis, Systems Dev., Systems Implem., Systems Support

Industries: Generalist

Professional Corporate Search Inc

99 Park Ave Ste 455A
New York, NY 10016
(212) 213-3434
Fax: (212) 213-3433
Email: info@procorpsearch.com
Web: www.procorpsearch.com

Description: We are an executive search firm specializing in the placement of sales professionals. We recruit for Fortune 100, 500 and 1,000 Corporations, as well as entrepreneurial growth companies involved in the expansion and development of top quality sales forces.

Key Contact - Specialty:
Mr. Errol Tucker, President - *Sales & marketing*

Salary minimum: $40,000

Functions: Sales Mgmt.

Industries: Energy, Utilities, Mfg., Services, Hospitality, Telecoms, Software, Non-classifiable

Branches:
207 E Redwood St Ste 510
Baltimore, MD 21202
(410) 347-4848
Fax: (410) 347-1389
Email: info_md@procorpsearch.com
Key Contact:
Mr. Errol Tucker, President

Professional Corporate Solutions

6300 I-40 W Ste 200
Amarillo, TX 79106
(806) 359-9001
Fax: (866) 271-8618
Email: billie@pcsglobal.net
Web: www.pcsglobal.net

Description: We are a full service permanent and contract staffing firm, focusing on resource development solutions. Our services include permanent/contractor staffing, HR consulting, assessments, and benchmarking.

Key Contact - Specialty:
Mr. Ted Cave, President - *Generalist, IT*
Ms. Billie Horning, Business Associate -
Generalist

Salary minimum: $60,000

Functions: Generalist

Industries: Generalist

Professional Associations: SHRMCF

Professional Edge Consulting Ltd

PO Box 393
Princeton, IL 61356
(815) 437-2727
Fax: (815) 437-2227
Email: nancy@proedgejobs.com
Web: www.proedgejobs.com

Description: We offer national search and recruitment of information technology, management consultant, and accounting professionals. We have 900 affiliate offices. We specialize in the top 10% of talent. We serve a variety of business types and sizes. Our mission is true customer service with honest interaction and personalized attention.

Key Contact - Specialty:
Ms. Nancy J. Faso, Managing Partner -
Management consultants, information technology, accounting

Salary minimum: $40,000

Functions: Finance, IT, Mgmt. Consultants

Industries: Generalist, Mfg., Computer Equip., Finance, Banking, Legal, Accounting, Mgmt. Consulting, E-commerce, IT Implementation, Hospitality, Media, Communications, Call Centers, Telephony, Network Infrastructure, Insurance, Software

Professional Engineering Technical Personnel Consultants

8504 Ragan Rd
Apex, NC 27502
(919) 387-0070
Email: ick_uffman@netzero.net

Description: Retained and contingency search provided for all disciplines and levels within the power electronics, industrial, motion, sensor and electronic industries.

Key Contact - Specialty:
Mr. Richard B. Huffman, President - *Electronics (power, industrial)*

Salary minimum: $35,000

Functions: Generalist

Industries: Mfg., Equip Svcs., Communications, Software, Development SW, Mfg. SW, Marketing SW

Professional Executive Recruiters Inc (PERI)

1700 Alma Dr Ste 242
Plano, TX 75075-6988
(972) 509-5000
Fax: (972) 509-5001
Email: peri@pericorp.com
Web: www.pericorp.com

Description: Over 25 years in recruiting mid- to executive-level personnel in the construction industry nationally and internationally.

Key Contact:
Mr. Ken Roberts, President

Functions: Generalist, General Mgmt., Senior Mgmt., Middle Mgmt., CFO's, Attorneys, Int'l.

Industries: Construction

Professional Outlook Inc

825 N Cass Ave Ste 109
Westmont, IL 60559
(630) 887-1444
Email: dmandolesi@professionaloutlook.com
Web: www.professionaloutlook.com

Description: Professional search firm focusing on engineers and operations management for the chemical process industries, environmental, health and safety professionals and human resource professionals.

Key Contact - Specialty:
Ms. Bethany Brevard-Harned, President -
Environmental, health and safety, human resources
Mr. Dan Mandolesi, Vice President - *Chemical process industry, engineering*

Salary minimum: $30,000

Functions: Directors, Middle Mgmt., Mfg., Packaging, HR Mgmt., Benefits, Engineering, Environmentalists

Industries: Generalist, Energy, Utilities, Mfg., Food, Bev., Tobacco, Chemicals, Soap, Perf., Cosmtcs., Drugs Mfg., Medical Devices, Plastics, Rubber, Paints, Petro. Products, Environmental Svcs., Haz. Waste, HR SW, Biotech

Networks: Inter-City Personnel Assoc (IPA)

Branches:
381 Garden Ave
Holland, MI 49424
(616) 396-9600
Email: bharned@professionaloutlook.com
Key Contact - Specialty:
Ms. Bethany Brevard-Harned, President -
Environmental, health and safety, human resources

Professional Personnel Consultants Inc

28200 Orchard Lake Rd Ste 100
Farmington Hills, MI 48334
(248) 737-5860
Fax: (248) 737-5886
Email: dmistura@ppcinconline.com
Web: www.personnelconsultants.com

Description: We specialize in recruiting, technical, professional and management in accounting, marketing, engineering, technical, manufacturing, information technology, transportation & logistics.

Key Contact - Specialty:
Mr. Dan Mistura, President - *Generalist*

Functions: Mfg., HR Mgmt., IT

Industries: Construction, Mfg., Plastics, Rubber, Misc. Mfg., Transportation, Finance, Services, HR Services, IT Implementation, Packaging, Software, Mfg. SW, Marketing SW

Professional Associations: MAPS, NAPS

Networks: National Personnel Assoc (NPA)

Professional Placement Associates Inc

287 Bowman Ave Ste 309
Purchase, NY 10577
(914) 251-1000
Fax: (914) 251-1055
Email: lschachter@ppasearch.com

Description: We are a high-quality firm in operation since 1974, with a focused expertise in the healthcare field. We render a highly personalized, intensive cost effective service.

Key Contact - Specialty:
Ms. Laura J. Schachter, President - *Healthcare, medical*

Salary minimum: $50,000

Functions: Generalist, Physicians, Nurses, Health Admin., MIS Mgmt., Systems Implem., Network Admin., DB Admin.

Industries: Generalist, Healthcare

Professional Associations: NAPR

Professional Recruiting Offices Inc (PRO)

2558 Roosevelt St Ste 200
Carlsbad, CA 92008
(760) 400-0123
Fax: (760) 400-0100
Email: info@proinc.com
Web: www.proinc.com

Description: We are nationwide executive search specialists. We have over 100 years of combined executive search experience concentrating in the managed care, employee benefits, legal, national IT banking, and gaming applications.

Key Contact:
Mr. Mark J. Schneekluth, President

Salary minimum: $40,000

Functions: Benefits, IT, Systems Dev., Attorneys

Industries: Generalist, Banking, Brokers, Mgmt. Consulting, Software

Networks: Top Echelon Network

Professional Recruiting Consultants

(also known as PRC)
6167 Bristol Pkwy Ste 300
Culver City, CA 90230
(310) 642-7373
Fax: (310) 642-7377
Email: prorecruit@earthlink.net
Web: www.professionalrecruitingconsultants.com

Description: We are an executive recruiting firm that provides management, technical, financial, and administrative pre-screened and reference-checked candidates for our clients. PRC utilizes the latest e-Recruitment strategies and skills to source high quality candidates beyond the "Internet job boards." We maintain confidentiality for clients and candidates alike.

Key Contact:
Ms. Karen Smith, Manager

Salary minimum: $50,000

Functions: Generalist

Industries: Generalist

Professional Recruiting Consultants Inc

3617-A Silverside Rd
Wilmington, DE 19810
(302) 479-9550
Fax: (302) 479-9560
Email: roger@prcstaffing.com
Web: www.prcstaffing.com

Description: We are engaged in the business of identifying and recruiting qualified personnel for a variety of technical and non-technical disciplines at both the management and staff levels.

Key Contact - Specialty:
Mr. Roger Malatesta, President - *Engineering, information technology, management, HR, purchasing*

Functions: Generalist, General Mgmt., Directors, Senior Mgmt., Middle Mgmt., Mfg., Sales & Mktg., IT

Industries: Generalist, Energy, Utilities, Mfg., Chemicals, Drugs Mfg., Medical Devices, Telecoms, Software

Professional Associations: AICHE, ETC, IEEE, ISA, MAAPC, NAPS

Networks: Top Echelon Network

Professional Recruiters Inc

17641 Kettering Trail Ste 100
Lakeville, MN 55044
(952) 892-3700
(800) 594-8414
Fax: (952) 892-3711
Email: bob@professionalrecruiters.com
Web: www.professionalrecruiters.com

Description: Very strong track record of success recruiting technically oriented sales, marketing and sales/marketing management talent primarily for the industrial electrical, electronic, hi-tech equipment markets. Recruiting since 1984. National market.

Key Contact - Specialty:
Mr. Robert Reinitz, President - *Electrical, electronic, high technology, sales & marketing, sales & marketing management*

Salary minimum: $60,000

Functions: Automation, Sales & Mktg., Advertising, Mkt. Research, Mktg. Mgmt., Sales Mgmt.

Industries: Computer Equip., Test, Measure Equip.

Professional Associations: MAPS

Networks: The Acumen Society

Professional Recruiters Inc

PO Box 4
Bala Cynwyd, PA 19004
(610) 667-9355
Fax: (610) 667-5333

Description: We perform national searches for sales, sales management, management, and consulting positions for companies involved in healthcare and high-tech to include healthcare information systems, healthcare, the Internet, dot.com healthcare companies, etc.

Key Contact - Specialty:
Ms. Joan Kool, Senior Consultant - *Healthcare, management, sales & marketing, consulting*
Mr. Stephen Lenobel, Senior Consultant - *Healthcare, management, sales & marketing, consulting*

Functions: Senior Mgmt., Middle Mgmt., Mktg. Mgmt., Sales Mgmt.

Industries: Software, Healthcare

Professional Associations: MAAPC

Professional Recruiters

220 E 3900 Ste 9
Salt Lake City, UT 84107
(801) 268-9940
Fax: (801) 268-9825
Email: brooke@icw.com
Web: www.recruitersslc.com

Description: We are dedicated to addressing the need for quality placement services. As professionals, we concentrate on the placement requirements of businesses and refer only those individuals who are specifically qualified.

Key Contact - Specialty:
Ms. Lora Lea Mock, President - *Technology*
Ms. Clair Simpson, Recruiter - *Medical*
Ms. Franci Eisenborg, Recruiter - *Technology*
Ms. Lynda Moore, Recruiter - *Technology*
Mr. Brad Brian, Recruiter - *Technology*

Salary minimum: $50,000

Functions: Generalist, Middle Mgmt., Mktg. Mgmt., Sales Mgmt., MIS Mgmt., Systems Analysis, Systems Dev., Systems Implem.

Industries: Generalist, Medical Devices, Computer Equip., Consumer Elect., Misc. Mfg., E-commerce, Telecoms, Telephony, Digital, Wireless, Software

Professional Associations: ITAA, SHRM, UEDC

Networks: National Personnel Assoc (NPA)

Professional Resources

(also known as Executive Tax Recruiter)
PO Box 1038
Ponte Vedra Beach, FL 32004-1038
(904) 280-5246
Fax: (904) 280-5263
Email: john@taxjobs.com
Web: www.taxjobs.com

Description: We are an nationally-focused executive search firm specializing in the placement of tax professionals.

Key Contact - Specialty:
Mr. John W. Cowling, Owner - *Taxation*

Functions: Generalist, Taxes

Industries: Generalist, Energy, Utilities, Mfg., Wholesale, Retail, Finance, Services

Professional Associations: OAPS, RON

Professional Resource Group Inc

PO Box 1007
Muncie, IN 47308
(765) 281-1000
Fax: (765) 281-1001
Email: prg@nursequest.com
Web: www.nursequest.com

Description: Our firm specializes in national search and placement of nursing management and advanced practice nurses.

Key Contact - Specialty:
Ms. Jeanna Bozell, RN, President - *Nursing management, nurse executives, advanced practice nurses*

Salary minimum: $50,000

Functions: Nurses

Industries: Healthcare

Professional Associations: IAPS, NAPS

Professional Resources

31 Beaumont Dr
New City, NY 10956
(845) 638-4296
Fax: (845) 638-4323
Email: irwin@mail.creativeonline.com
Web: www.proresourcesystems.com/executivesearch.html

Description: We are retail specialists, who are involved in department stores, discount stores, jewelry, and specialty retailing. We are covering all areas of merchandising operations and corporate staff functions. We are specializing in emerging new retail concepts, such as fashion apparel manufacturing, focusing on marketing, production design, and administration.

Key Contact - Specialty:
Mr. Irwin J. Feigenbaum, President - *Retailing, apparel manufacturing*

Salary minimum: $40,000

Functions: Generalist

Industries: Mfg., Consumer Elect., Wholesale, Retail, Finance

The Professional Sales Search Company Inc

PO Box 1858
Pleasanton, CA 94566
(925) 398-0100
Fax: (925) 398-0105
Email: execadmin@psscinc.com
Web: www.psscinc.com

Description: We provide quality, national sales personnel staffing, executive search and sales management consulting services for corporate America.

Key Contact - Specialty:
Mr. Douglas R. Letts, Managing Partner - *Sales, sales management, senior sales management*

Salary minimum: $75,000

Functions: Sales & Mktg.

Industries: Mfg., Transportation, Services, Communications, Software, Biotech, Healthcare, Hospitals

Networks: First Interview Network (FIN)

Professional Search Inc
PO Box 19908
San Diego, CA 92159
(619) 697-2138
Fax: (619) 303-6578
Email: jobs@psiwest.com
Web: www.psiwest.com

Description: Specializing exclusively in the placement of engineering, manufacturing, and software professionals in San Diego County.

Key Contact:
Mr. Vernon Kleist, President

Salary minimum: $50,000

Functions: Product Dev., Automation, Quality, Productivity, Packaging, Systems Dev., R&D, Engineering

Industries: Generalist

Professional Search Inc
7909 S Monaco Ct
Centennial, CO 80112
(303) 694-1210

Description: A professional approach and expert applicant selection for positions resulting in quality placements, thus eliminating costly interviewing for employers.

Key Contact - Specialty:
Mr. Lawrence M. Jock, President - *Generalist*

Salary minimum: $30,000

Functions: Generalist, General Mgmt., Mfg., Sales & Mktg., Finance, IT, Engineering

Industries: Generalist, Finance, Hospitality, Media, Environmental Svcs., Software

Professional Search Centre Ltd
1450 E American Ln 1875
Schaumburg, IL 60173
(847) 330-3250
Fax: (847) 330-3255
Email: jerryh@psc-usa.com
Web: www.psc-usa.com

Description: Direct placement in information technology. We take time to understand your corporate culture and learn a candidate's goals/needs, assuring an excellent fit and fulfilling your hiring needs by providing experienced quality professionals.

Key Contact - Specialty:
Mr. Jerry S. Hirschel, CPC, President - *Information technology*

Salary minimum: $40,000

Functions: IT

Industries: Generalist

Professional Associations: IAPS, NAPS

Professional Search Consultants (PSC)
5151 San Felipe Ste 420
Houston, TX 77056
(713) 960-9215
Fax: (713) 960-1172
Email: recruit@psctech.com

Description: Use direct approach, knowledgeable industry sources and contacts. Early successful completing, providing services worldwide, 23 years' experience. Formal executive searches on a non-retained basis.

Key Contact - Specialty:
Mr. L. Malek - *Engineering, information technology, accounting, finance*

Salary minimum: $75,000

Functions: Generalist

Industries: Generalist

Professional Support Inc
1 Towne Ctr
West Amherst, NY 14228
(716) 688-0235
Fax: (716) 688-0239
Email: buffalo@psi4jobs.com
Web: www.psi4jobs.com

Description: Executive recruiting (retainer search), in accounting and data processing (IT), disciplines; contract and rent-to-own programs, temporary clerical & DP operational services; contract data processing (project) services, individual and group outplacement services, training programs, facilities planning and disaster recovery services.

Key Contact - Specialty:
Mr. Paul H. Eastmer, President - *IS, accounting*
Mr. Gregory Eastmer, Director-Recruiting/Placement - *IS, SAP*

Salary minimum: $30,000

Functions: Generalist, Senior Mgmt., Personnel, Budgeting, M&A, Systems Dev., Systems Implem., Mgmt. Consultants

Industries: Generalist, Metal Products, Mgmt. Consulting, Software

Networks: Top Echelon Network

Branches:
500 Helendale Rd Ste 190
Rochester, NY 14609
(716) 654-7800
Fax: (716) 654-9265
Key Contact - Specialty:
Mr. Edward Sandusky, Director Account Management - *DP, IS*

8221 Brecksville Rd 3-107
Brecksville, OH 44141
(440) 526-7650
Fax: (216) 526-6612
Key Contact - Specialty:
Mr. Richard Beldon, Senior Recruiter - *DP, IS*

Professional Team Search Inc
PO Box 30185
Phoenix, AZ 85046-0185
(602) 482-3600
Fax: (602) 788-0710
Email: pts@ww-web.com

Description: Our company focus is to work with individual company management teams on a one-to-one basis. Our search efforts are targeted toward computer and engineering to executive-level professionals.

Key Contact - Specialty:
Ms. Denise M. Chaffin, President - *Computer engineering, electrical engineering, wireless telecommunications*

Salary minimum: $55,000

Functions: Generalist, Senior Mgmt., MIS Mgmt., Systems Analysis, Systems Dev., Systems Implem., Systems Support, Engineering

Industries: Generalist, Computer Equip., Consumer Elect., Telecoms, Aerospace, Software, Biotech

Professional Technical Search Inc
PO Box 440351
Houston, TX 77244-0351
(936) 321-7000
Fax: (832) 358-1307
Email: resume@pts-us.net
Web: www.pts-us.net

Description: We are a diverse recruiting firm, providing you with experience, expertise and service. We specialize in recruiting candidates of all levels in the technical areas of information systems.

Key Contact - Specialty:
Mr. Michael Geier, President - *Information technology*
Ms. Kathleen Geier, Vice President - *Information technology*

Functions: IT, MIS Mgmt., Systems Analysis, Systems Dev., Systems Implem., Systems Support, Network Admin., DB Admin.

Industries: Generalist, Computer Equip., IT Implementation

Professionals in Recruiting Company
1028 Cresthaven Rd Ste 202
Memphis, TN 38119
(901) 685-2042
Fax: (901) 685-2729

Description: Any accepted search is handled in a confidential, ethical and professional manner with a vigorous and knowledgeable effort that promotes the client company and a mutually beneficial union with a candidate. We are strong in searches for executives, especially medical directors.

Key Contact - Specialty:
Mr. James O. Murrell, Co-Owner - *Managed healthcare, healthcare, insurance*
Ms. Maxine W. Murrell, Co-Owner - *Medical directors*

Salary minimum: $40,000

Functions: Physicians, Nurses, Health Admin., Sales Mgmt., CFO's, MIS Mgmt., Attorneys

Industries: Insurance, Healthcare

Professions Inc
3600 Park 42 Dr Ste 125A
Cincinnati, OH 45241
(513) 530-0909
Fax: (513) 530-0916
Email: recruiters@professionsinc.com
Web: www.professionsinc.com

Description: Twenty-five-year-old search and recruiting firm based in Cincinnati, Ohio. Our strength is our intensity and commitment to increase our clients' competitive advantage by recruiting the highest caliber professionals.

Key Contact - Specialty:
Ms. Kim Valmore, Vice President - *Sales, paper, packaging*
Mr. Carl Coco, Jr., Chairman of the Board - *Sales, paper, packaging*

Salary minimum: $40,000

Functions: Sales & Mktg.

Industries: Paper, Telecoms, Packaging

Networks: National Personnel Assoc (NPA)

Profile Int'l USA Inc
156 W 56th St Fl 12
New York, NY 10019
(212) 957-1404
(212) 957-1407
Fax: (212) 957-1446
Email: newyork@pmsr.com
Web: www.pmsr.com

Description: We are specialist in management recruitment for the upscale hospitality industry worldwide. Units, as well as corporate positions are handled. We also have offices in London and Paris.

Key Contact - Specialty:
Mr. Christopher Mumford, Vice President - *Executive management, deluxe hotels, restaurants*

Salary minimum: $60,000

Functions: Generalist

Industries: Hospitality, Hotels, Resorts, Clubs, Restaurants

Professional Associations: BABA, HANYC, HSMAI

Profiler Digital Media Recruiters
10474 Santa Monica Blvd Ste 305
Los Angeles, CA 90025
(310) 446-8343
Fax: (310) 446-8242
Email: bibs@profilerusa.com
Web: www.profilerusa.com

Description: Profiler specializes in the placement of sales, marketing, technical and creative talent for companies in the Internet technology space. Located in LA, we have extensive contacts in the LA, SF, NYC and Chicago marketplaces.

Key Contact - Specialty:
Ms. Bib Scott, Partner - *Marketing, sales*
Ms. Kim Scott, Partner - *Sales, marketing*
Ms. Julie Scott, Senior Associate - *Technical, creative talent*

Salary minimum: $60,000

Functions: Middle Mgmt., Sales & Mktg., Advertising, IT, MIS Mgmt., Systems Dev., DB Admin., Graphic Artists

Industries: Hospitality, Advertising, Publishing, New Media, Broadcast, Film, Telecoms, Software

Profiles Inc
801 W Big Beaver Ste 670
Troy, MI 48084
(248) 244-9444
Fax: (248) 244-9447
Email: jobs@career1.com
Web: www.career1.com

Description: We are recruiters of sales, management, technical, and medical professionals.

Key Contact:
Mr. Michael Wilson, President

Salary minimum: $50,000

Functions: General Mgmt., Healthcare, Sales & Mktg.

Industries: Generalist

Networks: First Interview Network (FIN)

ProFinders Inc
PO Box 124
Orlando, FL 32802-0124
(407) 894-0840
(407) 425-8660
Fax: (407) 894-5818
Email: sheri@profinders.com
Web: www.profinders.com

Description: Specializing in the recruitment of sales, marketing and operations in central Florida.

Key Contact - Specialty:
Ms. Sheri Mitchell, President - *Sales, marketing, operations*
Ms. Lisa Sconyers, Recruiting Manager - *Sales, marketing, operations*

Salary minimum: $30,000

Functions: Sales & Mktg.

Industries: Generalist

Profit Pros Inc
23945 Calabasas Rd 203
Calabasas, CA 91302
(818) 801-9330
Email: profitpros@msn.com

Description: Twenty-five years of executive search experience at senior and middle management levels in both retained and contingency divisions committed to quality performance and results.

Key Contact:
Mr. David L. Gaffney, President

Salary minimum: $40,000

Functions: Generalist

Industries: Paints, Petro. Products, Transportation, Wholesale, Retail, Finance, Services, Environmental Svcs., Insurance, Real Estate

Professional Associations: SHRM

Progressive Resources
1608 Calle Corte
Santa Barbara, CA 93101
(805) 682-7884
Fax: (520) 752-8256
Email: progressiveresources@home.com
Web: www.sbjobs.com

Description: Executive and technical recruiting services serving Santa Barbara, San Luis Obispo, and Ventura counties.

Key Contact - Specialty:
Ms. Jill R. t'Sas, Executive Recruiter - *Technical, executive*

Functions: Generalist, General Mgmt., Production, IT, R&D, Engineering

Industries: Generalist, Medical Devices, Computer Equip.

ProNet Inc
3200 Glen Royal Rd Ste 100
Raleigh, NC 27612
(919) 782-2760
Email: dicks@pronetnc.com

Description: Recruiting in the data processing and data communication industry nationwide since 1980, providing qualified candidates in a timely manner. Principals have held national sales and marketing positions with Fortune 500 companies.

Key Contact - Specialty:
Mr. Dick Starling, President - *Computer hardware, software vendors, communications vendors*

Salary minimum: $35,000

Functions: Generalist, Mkt. Research, Mktg. Mgmt., Sales Mgmt., CFO's, MIS Mgmt., Systems Analysis, Systems Dev.

Industries: Generalist, Computer Equip., Telecoms, Software

Proquest Inc
1200 Woodruff Rd A-3
Greenville, SC 29607
(864) 239-0289
Fax: (864) 239-0293
Email: proquest@mindspring.com
Web: www.proquest-hr.com

Description: We are specialists in pharmaceutical, biotechnology, and medical devices/equipment segments of the healthcare products industry. Our emphasis is on regulatory affairs, QA/QC, engineering, medical/clinical affairs, R&D and manufacturing. We also offer contract and permanent employment services.

Key Contact - Specialty:
Mr. Donald Powell, MS, R.Ph, Managing Director - *Medical products manufacturing*

Salary minimum: $60,000

Functions: Generalist, Healthcare

Industries: Drugs Mfg., Medical Devices, Test, Measure Equip., Misc. Mfg., HR Services, Software, Biotech

Professional Associations: ACRP, ASQ, RAPS, RON

Networks: Top Echelon Network

Prosearch Associates
5004 Natkarni Cres
Mississauga, ON L5V 1L2
Canada
(905) 567-6497
Fax: (905) 567-8068
Email: careers@prosearch.ca
Web: www.prosearch.ca

Key Contact:
Mr. Daniel Duquette, Principal Consultant

Salary minimum: $40,000

Functions: Generalist

Industries: Construction, Mfg., Plastics, Rubber, Paints, Petro. Products, Metal Products, Machine, Appliance, Motor Vehicles, Misc. Mfg., HR Services

ProSearch Group Inc
39255 Country Club Dr Ste B 38
Farmington Hills, MI 48331
(248) 488-3330
(800) 848-4978
Fax: (248) 488-2156

Description: We offer retained and contingency placement of accounting, finance and banking professionals. Clients serviced are both corporations and public accounting firms.

Key Contact - Specialty:
Mr. Robert Eberline, Vice President - *Finance*

Functions: Generalist, Finance, IT, Mgmt. Consultants

Industries: Generalist, Construction, Mfg., Finance, Services

Professional Associations: AICPA, MACPA

ProSearch Inc
70 Center St Fl 3
Portland, ME 04112
(207) 775-7600
Email: emckersie@psicareers.com
Web: www.psicareers.com

Description: Small, high quality firm dedicated to high ethics and confidentiality. Owner has over ten years in the search and staffing industry. We strive to develop strong relationships with client companies in an effort to match company culture and management styles.

Key Contact - Specialty:
Mr. Edward S. McKersie, CPC, President/Owner - *Sales, marketing, accounting, finance, information technology*

Salary minimum: $25,000

Functions: Generalist, Mktg. Mgmt., Sales Mgmt., Direct Mktg., HR Mgmt., Finance, IT, Engineering

Industries: Generalist, Insurance

Networks: First Interview Network (FIN)

Branches:
4 Courthouse Ln Ste12
Chelmsford, MA 01824
(978) 454-1100
Email: fkearney@psirecruiters.com
Key Contact:
Mr. Frank Kearney, Senior Partner

ProSearch Inc
29017 Chardon Rd Ste 220
Willoughby Hills, OH 44092
(440) 585-9099
Fax: (440) 585-8030
Email: cwayne@prosearchrecruiters.com
Web: www.prosearchrecruiters.com

Description: Specialists in accounting & finance, engineering & manufacturing, sales & marketing, data processing & MIS, operations management, general management, corporate and firm attorneys.

Key Contact - Specialty:
Mr. Cary S. Wayne, President - *Accounting, tax*

Salary minimum: $40,000

Functions: Generalist

Industries: Generalist

ProSearch Inc
3555 Welsh Rd
Willow Grove, PA 19090
(215) 659-9005
Fax: (215) 659-8474
Email: info@prosearch.com
Web: www.prosearch.com

Description: Specialize in placing information systems professionals for Fortune 500's in Mid Atlantic area. Known for professionally interviewing/screening all candidates and arranging interviews only where appropriate for your requirements. Positions: DBAs, programmers, system architects, data modelers, business analysts, CIOs. Member of Pinnacle- honorary of Nation's Top 50 recruiters.

Key Contact - Specialty:
Ms. Suzanne F. Fairlie, CPC, President - *MIS, client/server, data warehousing, system architect, application directors*

Salary minimum: $45,000

Functions: Generalist

Industries: Generalist

Professional Associations: MAAPC, NAWBO, PAPS

ProSearch Recruiting
2503 Sandy Creek Dr
Westlake Village, CA 91361
(818) 597-0300
Email: prosearchcareers@aol.com

Description: We specialize in media, including Internet, print publishing, events and research companies, broadcast, and film. We attract experienced and successful professionals in sales and sales management, marketing, content, operations, and top management. Our extensive network and over 25 years of publishing and recruiting experience combine to give you the support you need!

Key Contact - Specialty:
Ms. Susan J. Curtis, President/Owner - *Publishing, internet, events, advertising sales management, top management*
Ms. Suzanne Baird, Vice President-Research - *Publishing, internet marketing, circulation, editorial*

Salary minimum: $60,000

Functions: General Mgmt., Senior Mgmt., Middle Mgmt., Mktg. Mgmt., Sales Mgmt.

Industries: Venture Cap., Non-profits, Higher Ed., Mgmt. Consulting, HR Services, Media, Advertising, Publishing, New Media, Broadcast, Film, Wireless

Networks: Top Echelon Network

Prospective Personnel Service Inc
PO Box 4727
Tulsa, OK 74159-4727
(918) 584-5000
Fax: (918) 584-5002
Email: bankrcrtr@aol.com

Description: CPC with 20+ years' experience, specialization in professional level banking positions primarily in Oklahoma and surrounding states. Permanent positions.

Key Contact:
Ms. Linda Kinney, CPC, Owner

Functions: Generalist

Industries: Banking

Professional Associations: NAPS, TAHRA

ProStar Systems Inc
PO Box 1216
Chatham, VA 24531
(804) 432-8038
Fax: (804) 432-8037
Email: prostarsys@earthlink.net

Description: Our owner has over 30 years experience in the computer industry. Most of these years were spent in software sales and management. Our firm primarily places sales and technical support positions in North America and Canada.

Key Contact:
Mr. Ronald G. Shepherd, President

Functions: Sales Mgmt., Systems Dev., Systems Implem., Systems Support, Mgmt. Consultants

Industries: Generalist, E-commerce, PSA/ASP, Telecoms, Call Centers, Digital, Wireless, Network Infrastructure, Software, Database SW, Development SW, Doc. Mgmt., Production SW, ERP SW, Marketing SW, Networking, Comm. SW, Security SW, System SW, Training SW

Networks: Top Echelon Network

Protech@onlinehires.com
271 Madison Ave Ste 1407
New York, NY 10016
(212) 685-1400
Fax: (212) 685-4340
Email: protech@onlinehires.com
Web: www.onlinehires.com

Description: Our firm specializes in servicing manufacturers in FDA regulated, manufacturing, and other chemical process industries nationwide, including: pharmaceutical, biotech, health and beauty aids, food and beverage, purchasing, material management, and more.

Key Contact - Specialty:
Mr. H. R. Brakel, President/Owner - *Technical, manufacturing, engineering, scientists, FDA/GMP/EPA regulated industries*

Salary minimum: $40,000

Functions: Generalist, Production, Automation, Plant Mgmt., Purchasing, Materials Plng., Packaging, R&D

Industries: Generalist, Food, Bev., Tobacco, Chemicals, Soap, Perf., Cosmtcs., Drugs Mfg., Medical Devices, Packaging, Biotech

Protis Executive Innovations
(also known as MRI of Avon (W Indianapolis))
99 S Dan Jones Rd Ste 200
Avon, IN 46123-9771
(317) 272-5454
Fax: (317) 272-5440
Email: protisei@protisei.com
Web: www.protisei.com

Description: We use a blend of technology, expertise and insight as a leading executive search firm that adds measurable value with each search and each point of contact. We provides total human capital solutions geared around traditional search, e-search and organizational development. Our clients are form the fortune 100 to e-business and emerging technology start-ups.

Key Contact:
Mr. Bert Miller, President - *Consumer sales*
Mr. Michael Bitar, Vice President - *Consumer sales*
Ms. Laura Gonzalez-Miller, VP- Marketing

Salary minimum: $35,000

Functions: Generalist

Industries: Mfg., Food, Bev., Tobacco, Soap, Perf., Cosmtcs., Medical Devices, Plastics, Rubber, Machine, Appliance, Venture Cap., Mgmt. Consulting, Software, Security SW

Protocol Agency Inc
300 N Lake Ave Ste 208
Pasadena, CA 91101
(626) 449-2214
(323) 681-3900
Fax: (626) 577-0484
Email: pas@protocolagency.com
Web: www.protocolagency.com

Description: Search and selection firm specializing in contingency and retained placement of accounting, financial, mid-range programmers, medical, human resources, middle and upper-level management professionals.

Key Contact - Specialty:
Mr. Robert W. Sparks, President - *Executive management*
Ms. Kelly J. Lucas, Vice President - *Accountants, managers*

Salary minimum: $30,000

Functions: Generalist, Senior Mgmt., Allied Health, Customer Svc., Training, CFO's, Network Admin., DB Admin.

Industries: Generalist, Mfg., Finance, Accounting, Haz. Waste, Real Estate, Healthcare

Branches:
2659 Townsgate Rd Ste 203
Westlake Village, CA 91361-2774
(805) 371-0069
(818) 706-1571
Fax: (805) 371-0048
Email: wlv@protocolagency.com
Key Contact - Specialty:
Mr. Chris Salcido, Branch Manager - *Programmers, AS400, client servers, network specialists*

7300 S 13th St Ste 204
Oak Creek, WI 53154
(414) 570-1600
Key Contact:
Mr. John Cox, Vice President/Branch Manager

Proven Edge
32409 San Marco Dr
Temecula, CA 92592
(909) 303-2221
Fax: (909) 303-2221
Email: theprovenedge@yahoo.com

Description: A recruiting firm dedicated to adhering to the highest level of ethics, respecting the confidentiality of the client and the candidate while searching the corporate maze for either one.

Key Contact - Specialty:
Mr. Walter Gold, Executive Officer - *Middle management, professional, technical, senior management*

Salary minimum: $60,000

Functions: Generalist, Senior Mgmt., Middle Mgmt., Product Dev., Production, Mktg. Mgmt., Sales Mgmt., R&D

Industries: Generalist, Printing, Chemicals, Drugs Mfg., Plastics, Rubber, Paints, Petro. Products, Publishing, Biotech

Providence Personnel Consultants
2404 4th St Ste 1
Cuyahoga Falls, OH 44221
(330) 929-6431
Fax: (330) 929-4335
Email: ppcconsult@aol.com
Web: www.providence-personnel.com

Description: We are dedicated to assisting organizations in all phases of recruiting and staffing. Our local and regional contacts give us the ability to attract quality candidates and our national resources provide us the ability to recruit for the most specialized positions. Our expertise has been developed through recruiting in fields such as: manufacturing/engineering, information technology, accounting/finance/banking/insurance, administrative/clerical, sales/marketing/advertising, and human resources.

Key Contact:
Ms. Donna Early, CPC, President

Functions: General Mgmt., Mfg., Materials, Healthcare, Sales & Mktg., HR Mgmt., Finance, IT, Engineering, Specialized Svcs.

Industries: Generalist

Provident Services
125 Valley Glen Ct
Greer, SC 29650
(800) 507-2286
(864) 801-1440
Fax: (864) 801-1441
Email: jobs@provserv.com
Web: www.provserv.com

Description: South Carolina licensed, nationwide recruiting agency. We recruit physicians, surgeons, psychiatrists, physician assistants, nurse practitioners, nurse managers, and more.

Key Contact:
Ms. Laurie Radcliffe, President

Functions: Healthcare, Physicians, Nurses

Industries: Healthcare, Hospitals

Pryor & Associates
90 New Montgomery St Ste 401
San Francisco, CA 94105
(415) 908-1388
Fax: (415) 908-1383
Email: insurancejob@pryorsearch.com
Web: www.pryorsearch.com

Description: Provides specialized search and recruitment services for the insurance industry - management, administrative, finance, systems, underwriting, loss control, marketing/sales, claims, risk management, producers, account servicers and technical/clerical.

Key Contact - Specialty:
Ms. Jo-Ann Pryor, Managing Partner - *Insurance (all areas)*

Salary minimum: $40,000

Functions: Generalist, Senior Mgmt., Middle Mgmt., Admin. Svcs., Product Dev., Sales & Mktg., HR Mgmt., Finance, IT

Industries: Insurance

Professional Associations: CSP, NAFE

Pryor Knowledge Recruiting Inc
PO Box 2773
La Crosse, WI 54602
(608) 784-6278
(800) 218-1902
Fax: (608) 784-6389
Email: lpryor@charter.net

Description: We recruit for positions in sales, sales management, pre-sales engineering, and product marketing. Midwestern, as well as nation-wide searches are conducted in software, hardware, telecommunications, services, pharmaceutical, medical, and consumer areas.

Key Contact:
Ms. Laura Pryor, President

Functions: Sales Mgmt.

Industries: Drugs Mfg., Medical Devices, Computer Equip., E-commerce, IT Implementation, Telecoms, Call Centers, Telephony, Wireless, Fiber Optic, Network Infrastructure, Database SW, Doc. Mgmt., Production SW, ERP SW, Industry Specific SW, Mfg. SW, Marketing SW, Networking, Comm. SW

Professional Associations: MNAPS

Networks: First Interview Network (FIN)

Pryor Personnel Agency Inc
147 Old Country Rd
Hicksville, NY 11801
(516) 935-0100
Fax: (516) 931-7842
Email: ppryor1578@aol.com
Web: www.ppryor.com

Description: We have thirty years of successful experience in local, national, and international placements in the insurance, actuarial, and pension industry.

Key Contact - Specialty:
Ms. Patricia Pryor Bonica, President - *Marketing administration*
Mr. Gerald O'Gorman, Secretary/Treasurer - *Property, casualty claims, risk management, loss control, auditing*
Ms. Pauline Reimer, ASA, Account Executive - *Pension, actuary*
Ms. Maureen Boehm - *Insurance (property, casualty), agency, brokerage specialist*
Ms. Cathy Pryor, Senior Account Executive - *Insurance (life, health, medical), human resources, insurance sales*
Mr. Richard J. Pokorny, Account Executive - *Insurance (property, casualty), brokerage, company underwriting, account executives*
Mr. Paul LaVacca - *Claims (property, casualty)*

Functions: Generalist, Middle Mgmt., Nurses, Customer Svc., Benefits, Credit, Systems Analysis, Systems Dev.

Industries: Generalist, Insurance

Professional Associations: APCNY, IIAA, INS

PSD Group Inc
595 Market St Ste 2430
San Francisco, CA 94105
(415) 882-0220
Fax: (415) 882-0559
Email: general@psdsf.com
Web: www.psdgroup.com

Description: Our firm's six hundred specialist consultants provide world-class executive search

and selection recruitment services from 11 offices and research and conference facilities in Europe, Asia Pacific, and the US.

Key Contact - Specialty:
Mr. Robert Graham-Bryce, Regional Director - *Software*
Ms. Susan Peto, Managing Consultant - *Software*
Mr. Edmund Alvey, Executive Consultant - *Communications*
Mr. David Lau, Senior Consultant - *Software*
Dr. Maziar Soltani-Farshi, Senior Consultant - *Electronics*
Ms. Victoria Ivanova, Consultant - *Communications*
Ms. Jamie Souza, Consultant - *Software*
Ms. Tamina Vahidy, Consultant - *Software*
Ms. Heidi Murphy, Consultant - *Software*

Salary minimum: $80,000

Functions: Generalist, Directors, Senior Mgmt., Product Dev., Sales Mgmt., Customer Svc., CFO's, Systems Dev., R&D, Int'l.

Industries: Electronic, Elec. Components, Telecoms, Fiber Optic, Software

PSP Agency
188 Montague St
Brooklyn, NY 11201
(718) 596-3786
Fax: (718) 596-9157
Email: pspagency@aol.com

Description: Targeting engineering, telecommunications, sales and marketing.

Key Contact - Specialty:
Ms. Angela D. Harvey, President - *Engineering, sales & marketing*
Mr. Arnold D. Harvey, Account Executive - *Telecommunications*
Mr. James McFadden, Account Executive - *Engineers, sales (computer software & hardware)*

Salary minimum: $40,000

Functions: General Mgmt., Product Dev., Quality, Materials, Sales & Mktg., Systems Implem., Network Admin., DB Admin., Engineering, Technicians

Industries: Mfg., Drugs Mfg., Metal Products, Computer Equip., Test, Measure Equip., Pharm Svcs., Equip Svcs., Mgmt. Consulting, Telecoms, Software

PsychPros Executive Search
2404 Auburn Ave
Cincinnati, OH 45219
(513) 651-9500
(888) 651-8367
Fax: (513) 651-9558
Email: lori@psychpros.com
Web: www.psychpros.com

Description: We are the nation's only search firm dedicated exclusively to the behavioral health industry. We place upper-level professionals such as CEOs, CFOs, medical directors, clinical supervisors, psychiatrists, and quality improvement directors into challenging positions across the US. Our customers include community mental health agencies, managed behavioral healthcare companies, hospitals, private practices, and other mental health and chemical dependency organizations.

Key Contact - Specialty:
Ms. Holly Dorna, MA, LPCC, President/CEO - *Mental health, chemical dependency industry*

Salary minimum: $65,000

Functions: Healthcare, Physicians, Nurses, Allied Health, Health Admin., Mgmt. Consultants

Industries: Healthcare, Hospitals, Long-term Care

Branches:
1300 W Belmont Ave Ste 310
Chicago, IL 60657
(773) 880-8832
Fax: (773) 883-5361
Email: jim@psychtemps.com
Key Contact:
Mr. Jim Hudson, Director

43173 Woodward Ave 254
Bloomfield Hills, MI 48302
(248) 593-3071
Fax: (248) 593-3280
Email: sue@psychtemps.com
Key Contact:
Ms. Sue Owen, Director

212 W 123 St Ste 5
New York, NY 10027
(917) 493-1743
Fax: (917) 493-1771
Email: brett@psychtemps.com
Key Contact:
Dr. Brett Kennedy, Director

4287 Beltline Rd 119
Addison, TX 75001
(972) 733-3660
Fax: (972) 733-3664
Email: jennifer@psychtemps.com
Key Contact:
Ms. Jennifer Hall, Director

PTC Financial Staffing Inc
1600 Steeles Ave W Ste 300
Concord, ON L4K 4M2
Canada
(905) 660-9550
(877) 303-9550
Fax: (416) 946-1089
Email: resume@ptcstaffing.com
Web: www.ptcstaffing.com

Description: Our firm is your source for financial professionals. We are a leader in the recruitment and placement of financial professionals on a contract basis. We provide fast turnaround. We identify quality candidates, conduct in-depth interviews, undertake skills assessment, check references, verify designations, and ensure that you get the right person, on time, and at reasonable prices. We are based in Ontario, Canada. We service Greater Toronto, Barrie, Hamilton, Kitchener, London, Mississauga, Niagara, Oshawa, and surrounding areas.

Key Contact - Specialty:
Mr. Bruce Singer, CA, Owner - *Client services*

Functions: Finance

Industries: Generalist

Professional Associations: ACSESS, ASA

Pulp & Paper Int'l Inc
PO Box 540929
Orlando, FL 32854
(407) 444-9960
(407) 444-9964
Email: pulppaper@hotmail.com
Web: www.ppicareersearch.com

Key Contact - Specialty:
Mr. Phil Riesling, President - *Pulp & paper, producers, converters, suppliers*

Salary minimum: $30,000

Functions: Generalist

Industries: Paper

Professional Associations: PIMA, TAPPI

Branches:
2480 Hastings E St
PO Box 57114
Vancouver, BC V5K 5G6
Canada
(888) 222-9960
(866) 408-8181
Email: bob@ppicareersearch.com
Key Contact:
Ms. Cathy Thomson, Principal

Quality Search
1496 Pope Ct
Chesterton, IN 46304
(219) 926-8202
Fax: (219) 926-3834
Email: info@qsjobs.com
Web: www.qsjobs.com

Description: We place/recruit technical/engineering personnel for most manufacturing related firms. Our specialization is packaging engineers, quality control and manufacturing management.

Key Contact:
Mr. James L. Jeselnick, President

Salary minimum: $40,000

Functions: Generalist, Senior Mgmt., Production, Plant Mgmt., Productivity, Packaging, Engineering

Industries: Generalist, Food, Bev., Tobacco, Chemicals, Soap, Perf., Cosmtcs., Drugs Mfg., Medical Devices, Paints, Petro. Products, Consumer Elect.

Professional Associations: ASQ, IOPP

Networks: Top Echelon Network

Quality Search Inc
PO Box 752294
Dayton, OH 45475-2294
(937) 439-0744
Fax: (937) 439-0766
Email: bjohnson@qualitysearch.com
Web: www.qualitysearch.com

Description: Sharply focused in serving individuals with technical backgrounds: i.e. engineers, scientists, computer specialists, finance, chemists and sales; in automotive, telecommunications, information technology, automation, aerospace, hydraulics, pneumatics, rubber & plastics, seals & gasketing, filtration.

Key Contact - Specialty:
Mr. Robert J. Johnson, President - *Technical careers, engineering, sales, management*
Mr. Kevin Johnson, Technical Recruiter - *Hydraulics, pneumatics, seals & gasketing*

Salary minimum: $30,000

Functions: Product Dev., Automation, Quality, Sales Mgmt., Budgeting, Systems Analysis, Engineering

Industries: Medical Devices, Plastics, Rubber, Computer Equip., Telecoms, Aerospace, Software

Networks: Top Echelon Network

Branches:
PO Box 360711
Cleveland, OH 44136
(440) 572-3336
Email: kjohnson@qualitysearch.com
Key Contact - Specialty:
Mr. Kevin S. Johnson, Principal Recruiter - *Hydraulics, pneumatics, seals & gasketing, filtration, motion control*

Quality Search Unlimited
PO Box 1786
Big Bear City, CA 92314-1786
(909) 584-8400
Fax: (909) 584-8420

Email: Lindalee@QualitySearch.cc
Web: www.QualitySearch.cc

Description: We are an executive search firm that specializes in the commercial lines property, casualty, and worker's compensation insurance industry. We place executives and support staff throughout the US, but our focus is mainly in California and more specifically, Southern California. Please send your word.doc resume and salary history for consideration to my email address or fax it to the number indicated. Best wishes in your career search!

Key Contact - Specialty:
Ms. Lindalee Green, CAC, COO - *Commercial lines insurance*
Mr. Dennis Wilkinson, CFO - *Finance & accounting*

Salary minimum: $45,000

Functions: Generalist, General Mgmt., Legal, Sales & Mktg., HR Mgmt., Finance, IT, Engineering, Environmentalists, Int'l.

Industries: Insurance

Professional Associations: CSP

Quantum Advantage Inc
16054 Sawyer Ranch Rd
Austin, TX 78737
(512) 894-3695
Fax: (512) 894-4432
Email: qai@austin.rr.com

Description: We specialize in recruiting and placement of degreed engineers into technical and management positions of chemical and allied companies in North America.

Key Contact:
Mr. Giles J. Andrews, Executive Recruiter - *Petrochemicals, refining, engineers, managers*
Mrs. Antoinette Andrews, Marketing Director

Salary minimum: $50,000

Functions: General Mgmt., Engineering

Industries: Paper, Chemicals, Drugs Mfg., Plastics, Rubber, Paints, Petro. Products

Professional Associations: AICHE, ASME, IEEE

The Quantum Group
10102 Hidden Pl
Miami, FL 33156
(305) 663-9274
Fax: (305) 663-8174
Email: resumes@quantum-group.com
Web: www.quantum-group.com

Description: We are a professional recruiting organization specializing in telecommunications sales, sales management and support employment opportunities. We only work with experienced telecommunications professionals.

Key Contact - Specialty:
Ms. Dawn Schlesinger, President - *Telecommunications, utilities (sales, management, support)*
Mr. Michael Schlesinger, Officer
Mrs. Susanna McKeon, Associate - *Telecommunications, utilities (sales, network, equipment)*

Salary minimum: $40,000

Functions: Generalist, Directors, Senior Mgmt., Middle Mgmt., Sales & Mktg., Sales Mgmt., Technicians

Industries: Generalist, Energy, Utilities, New Media, Telecoms, Telephony, Wireless, Fiber Optic

Branches:
513 Lesher Ln
Hatboro, PA 19040
(215) 957-5963

Key Contact - Specialty:
Mrs. Suzanna McKeon, Associate -
Telecommunications, utilities

The Quantum Group
317 Clarkson Rd Ste 203
St. Louis, MO 63011
(800) 216-1330
(636) 207-7887
Fax: (636) 207-7444
Email: quantmgrp@aol.com
Web: www.thequantumgrp.com

Description: Specialization in placing salaried
personnel in manufacturing operations.

Key Contact - Specialty:
Mr. James G. Fitzgerald, President - *Manufacturing*

Salary minimum: $30,000

Functions: Generalist, Mfg., Production, Plant
Mgmt., Quality, HR Mgmt., CFO's, Engineering

Industries: Generalist, Mfg., Lumber, Furniture,
Plastics, Rubber, Metal Products, Machine,
Appliance, HR Services, Environmental Svcs.

Professional Associations: AFS, SME

Quantum Technology Recruiting Inc
2000 Ave McGill College Bureau 1800
Montreal, QC H3A 3H3
Canada
(514) 842-5555
Fax: (514) 849-8846
Web: www.quantum-qtr.com

Description: We are a recruitment firm specializing
in the placement of IT and technology professionals.
We are Canada's largest, privately held recruiting
firm.

Key Contact - Specialty:
Mr. Louis Camus, General Manager North America
- *Information technology*

Functions: Personnel

Industries: Finance, Banking, Mgmt. Consulting,
New Media, Telecoms, Software

Branches:
420 Lexington Ave Ste 2221
New York, NY 10170
(212) 972-1313
Fax: (212) 983-7087
Key Contact:
Mr. Michael Higgins

8601 Six Forks Rd Ste 400
Raleigh, NC 27615
(919) 676-5311
Fax: (919) 676-5313
Key Contact:
Mr. Louis Camus

45 O'Connor St Ste 1860
Ottawa, ON K1P IA4
Canada
(613) 237-8888
Fax: (613) 565-7329
Key Contact:
Mr. Terry Scullion, Group Manager

55 University Ave Ste 301
Toronto, ON M5J 2H7
Canada
(416) 366-3660
Fax: (416) 777-5817
Key Contact:
Mr. John Baglieri, Recruitment Manager

Quest Consultants
2323 Yonge St Ste 302
Toronto, ON M4P 2C9
Canada
(416) 489-6411
Email: questcon@netcom.ca
Web: www.questqpc.com

Description: We are a boutique personnel agency
dedicated to excellence. We provide a range of
services, from resume counseling to permanent and
temporary placement, including the upper middle
management range. We pride ourselves in putting
the person back into personnel.

Key Contact:
Ms. Nicky Perry, President

Salary minimum: $30,000

Functions: Middle Mgmt., Admin. Svcs., HR
Mgmt., Finance

Industries: Generalist

Quest Enterprises Ltd
112 W Liberty Dr
Wheaton, IL 60187-5124
(630) 588-8400
Fax: (630) 588-0675
Email: admin@questent.com
Web: www.questent.com

Description: Due to the industry experience of our
entire staff and strong client relationships, we
successfully fill over 80 percent of our available
positions with a 98 percent retention ratio.

Key Contact - Specialty:
Mr. Richard W. Honquest, President - *Information
technology*

Functions: Generalist, MIS Mgmt., Systems
Analysis, Systems Dev., Systems Implem.,
Systems Support, Network Admin., DB Admin.

Industries: Generalist, Software

The Quest Organization
11 Pennsylvania Plz Ste 935
New York, NY 10001
(212) 971-0033
Fax: (212) 967-3332
Email: mrosenbl@questorg.com
Web: www.questorg.com

Description: We function as an extension of our
client management. We have CPAs with CFO
experience in public companies on our staff and we
provide personalized high quality business
consulting along with every search assignment.

Key Contact - Specialty:
Mr. Michael F. Rosenblatt, President - *Finance,
accounting, tax, human resources, operations*

Salary minimum: $100,000

Functions: Finance

Industries: Construction, Mfg., Retail, Finance,
Services, Hospitality, Insurance, Real Estate,
Software, Biotech

Professional Associations: APCNY, NYSSCPA

Questar Partners Inc
100 Winners Cir Ste 160
Brentwood, TN 37027
(615) 371-8800
Fax: (615) 371-8804
Email: rwharton@questarstaffing.com
Web: www.questarstaffing.com

Description: We are a generalist firm working in
the areas of health care, manufacturing, engineering,
finance, and information technology on both a
retained and a contingency basis..

Key Contact:
Mr. J. Russell Wharton, Division President

Functions: Generalist

Industries: Construction, Mfg., Finance, Higher
Ed., Legal, Mgmt. Consulting, IT
Implementation, Media, Environmental Svcs.,
Healthcare

Questor Consultants Inc
2515 N Broad St
Colmar, PA 18915
(215) 997-9262
Fax: (215) 997-9226
Email: sbevivino@questorconsultants.com
Web: www.questorconsultants.com

Description: P/C insurance industry specialists.
Heavily specializing in claims and underwriting on
a national basis.

Key Contact - Specialty:
Mr. Sal Bevivino, President - *Insurance (property,
casualty) claims, bond underwriting*

Salary minimum: $35,000

Functions: Risk Mgmt.

Industries: Insurance

Professional Associations: MAAPC, NIRA

QuestPro Consultants
17300 Preston Rd Ste 120
Dallas, TX 75252
(972) 960-1305
Fax: (972) 960-1357
Email: jobs@questpro.com
Web: www.questpro.com

Description: Our firm is a full-service recruiting
and consulting firm focusing strictly on the
insurance industry. We service all levels of the
insurance industry from large international carriers
to small regional agencies. QuestPro offers its
services primarily on the retainer level with
additional services involved in consulting, direct-
hire and contract staffing when needed.

Key Contact - Specialty:
Ms. Lauren Levinson, President - *Executive and
managerial search, property and casualty
insurance*
Mr. Trey Hugley, Vice President - *Executive and
managerial search, property and casualty
insurance*

Salary minimum: $30,000

Functions: Generalist, Directors, Senior Mgmt.,
Middle Mgmt., Admin. Svcs., Mktg. Mgmt., Risk
Mgmt., Int'l.

Industries: Generalist, Government, Insurance

Professional Associations: ASA, INS, IRG, MAPS,
NAPS, RON, SERC

Martin Quinn Group Ltd
2211 W Ohio St
Chicago, IL 60612
(312) 666-9960
Fax: (312) 666-9960
Email: recruit@chicagotechjobs.com
Web: www.chicagotechjobs.com

Description: We are Chicago area executive
recruiters in high-technology and information
technology. We serve all Chicagoland and only
information technology.

Key Contact - Specialty:
Mr. Quinn Dolan, President
Ms. Betsy Smith, Executive Recruiter - *Information
technology*

Salary minimum: $50,000

Functions: IT

Industries: Generalist

Quintal & Associates

133 rue de la Commune Ouest
Bureau 301
Montreal, QC H2Y 2C7
Canada
(514) 284-7444
(800) 284-7444
Fax: (514) 284-9290
Email: quintal@total.net
Web: www.quintal.ca

Description: We are a human resources organization specialized in the healthcare industry. Our clients, such as a pharmaceutical company, consult us for their recruitment, organizational development and training needs.

Key Contact - Specialty:
Mr. Yves Quintal, President - *Medical, pharmaceutical, biotechnology, healthcare*
Ms. Elise St. Jean, Vice President Operation & Sr Consultant - *Medical, pharmaceutical*
Mr. Marcel Lahaie, Senior Consultant - *Medical, pharmaceutical*

Salary minimum: $50,000

Functions: Directors, Senior Mgmt., Middle Mgmt., Product Dev., Production, Healthcare, Mktg. Mgmt., Sales Mgmt., HR Mgmt., R&D

Industries: Chemicals, Soap, Perf., Cosmtcs., Drugs Mfg., Medical Devices, Pharm Svcs., Biotech, Healthcare

Quiring Associates Inc

7267 C Jessman Rd W Dr
Indianapolis, IN 46256
(317) 841-7575
Fax: (317) 577-8240
Email: quiring@iquest.net
Web: www.iquest.net/quiring

Description: Our firm is a member of the Indianapolis Chamber of Commerce, Better Business Bureau. We are debt-free and have an extremely favorable credit history. We also have strategic alliances in split fee situations. Our firm specializes in permanent, full-time search.

Key Contact - Specialty:
Ms. Patti L. Quiring, CPC, President - *Data processing, human resources, medical*

Functions: Mfg., Healthcare, Physicians, HR Mgmt., Benefits, Personnel, Finance/IT, Engineering

Industries: Generalist

Professional Associations: IAPS

Quirk-Corporon & Associates Inc

1229 N Jackson Ste 205
Milwaukee, WI 53202-2651
(414) 224-9399
(414) 271-8711
Fax: (414) 224-9472
Email: quirkcorpco@aol.com

Description: Recruit at executive-level for major insurance companies and national brokers. Principals have more than 25 years of experience in the insurance business and twenty years in placement.

Key Contact - Specialty:
Mr. Charles E. Corporon, President - *Insurance, financial*
Ms. Therese M. Quirk, Vice President - *Insurance, financial*

Salary minimum: $30,000

Functions: Generalist

Industries: Finance, Banking, Insurance

Professional Associations: INS, NIRA

R & K Associates Inc

1296 W Stacey Ln
Tempe, AZ 85284-5102
(480) 961-2983
Fax: (480) 940-5190
Email: icrecruiter@mindspring.com
Web: www.icrecruiter.com

Description: Specializing in high-technology, the firm offers a cost effective alternative and short cycle times for searches. Experience handling large ramp ups is a key ingredient of experience and expertise.

Key Contact - Specialty:
Mr. Karl J. Reichardt, Principal/Owner - *Semiconductors, personal computers, miscellaneous high technology*

Salary minimum: $45,000

Functions: Mfg., Product Dev., Production, Automation

Industries: Computer Equip.

R C Services

200 W 34th Ave Ste 825
Anchorage, AK 99503
(907) 351-5201
Fax: (907) 258-1843
Email: gordonlcol@aol.com

Description: Work exclusively in the construction and engineering areas associated with chemical, petrochemical, refinery and cogeneration.

Key Contact - Specialty:
Mr. Gordon L. Collier, General Manager - *Engineering, construction with heavy emphasis for oil, gas, mining, petrochemical*

Salary minimum: $40,000

Functions: Senior Mgmt., Materials, Purchasing, Engineering

Industries: Energy, Utilities, Construction, Paper, Chemicals

Professional Associations: AACE, ASSE

R E P & Associates Inc

PO Box 55
Washington, NC 27889
(252) 946-6643
Fax: (252) 974-0668
Email: aa_rep@computerplacement.com

Description: Over 20 years' information technology combined with over 30 years' recruiting experience. Knowledge of the Southeast information technology market.

Key Contact - Specialty:
Mr. Richard Phelan, President - *Information technology, mainframe system programmers, database specialists*
Ms. Betty Powers, Secretary/Treasurer - *Applications developers*
Ms. Sharon Sawyer, Senior Recruiter - *AS/400, client-server*

Functions: Generalist, MIS Mgmt., Systems Analysis, Systems Dev., Systems Implem., Systems Support, Network Admin., DB Admin.

Industries: Generalist, Leather, Stone, Glass, Retail, Finance, Banking, Insurance, Software

Networks: National Personnel Assoc (NPA)

R J Associates

30 Glenn St
White Plains, NY 10603
(914) 946-0278
Fax: (914) 946-2019
Email: info@rjsearch.com
Web: www.rjsearch.com

Description: Complete staffing service for major corporate clients with consultants specializing by discipline.

Key Contact - Specialty:
Mr. Richard Birnbaum, Managing Director - *Senior management, human resources, finance, operations, general management*

Salary minimum: $75,000

Functions: Generalist, Senior Mgmt., Mfg., Materials, Mktg. Mgmt., HR Mgmt., Finance, IT

Industries: Generalist, Food, Bev., Tobacco, Soap, Perf., Cosmtcs., Medical Devices, Hospitality, Publishing, Telecoms

R&D Consulting Services

4736 Pleasant Garden Rd
PO Box 831
Pleasant Garden, NC 27313
(336) 676-9300
Fax: (336) 676-9397
Email: rdconsultnc@aol.com

Description: We offer expertise for recruitment in world class manufacturing environments for the areas of operations, materials and engineering. In addition, we now offer all areas of IT and Is recruiting services.

Key Contact:
Mr. Ronald R. Roach, President - *Plant management, operations*
Ms. Janet L. Roach, Director-Research

Salary minimum: $60,000

Functions: Generalist

Industries: Medical Devices, Plastics, Rubber, Metal Products, Machine, Appliance, Motor Vehicles, Computer Equip., Equip Svcs., Mgmt. Consulting, HR Services, Telecoms

Professional Associations: APICS, ASQ

R&M Associates

2610 Sunset Dr SE
Lacey, WA 98503
(360) 413-7605
Fax: (360) 413-7191
Email: ronkrenz@csi.com
Web: www.rmacareers.com

Key Contact - Specialty:
Mr. Ron Krenz, General Manager - *Packaging*
Ms. Meri Masters, Director of IT Services - *High tech, information technology*

Functions: Generalist

Industries: Paper, Printing, Computer Equip., IT Implementation, Packaging, Software, Industry Specific SW

Networks: Recruiters Professional Network (RPN)

R2 Services LLC

2300 N Barrington Rd Ste 315
Hoffman Estates, IL 60195
(847) 854-1000
Fax: (847) 490-1050
Email: info@r2services.com
Web: www.r2services.com

Description: We specialize in development, sales and management positions associated with real-time embedded systems software development. Additionally, we have significant expertise with client-server object-oriented software development. Our staff is comprised of engineers with real-world experience.

Key Contact - Specialty:
Mr. Randall E. Smith, Senior Partner - *Software engineering, sales, management*
Mr. Rory J. Patchin, Senior Partner - *Software engineering, sales, management*

Salary minimum: $80,000

Functions: Sales Mgmt., IT, Systems Analysis, Systems Dev., Engineering

Industries: Motor Vehicles, Computer Equip., Consumer Elect., Software

Branches:
6716 Alexander Bell Dr Ste 120
Columbia, MD 21046
(443) 656-9100
Fax: (443) 506-6801
Email: info@r2services.com
Key Contact:
Mr. Randall E. Smith, Senior Partner

25 Burlington Mall Rd Ste 300
Burlington, MA 01803
(781) 608-1000

The Rachman Group
(also known as MRI of Huntington)
202 E Main St Ste 301
Huntington, NY 11743-2993
(631) 547-5464
Fax: (631) 547-5465
Email: scott@mrhuntington.com
Web: www.mrhuntington.com

Description: We specialize in senior sales positions throughout the US. Our desk focus is outsourcing, software,legal technologies, ASP,consulting companies and document management positions. We were recently awarded for one of the fastest growing recruitment firms in the US within MRI.

Key Contact:
Mr. Scott Rachman, Managing Partner

Salary minimum: $60,000

Functions: Sales Mgmt.

Industries: Printing, Services, Legal, Equip Svcs., Mgmt. Consulting, HR Services, Software, Non-classifiable

RACTech
PO Box 5712
Cary, NC 27512
(919) 467-4636
Fax: (919) 467-4636
Email: ractech@nc.rr.com

Description: Our firm specializes in technical bio-pharma, bio-informatics, medical devices, IT systems, and telecommunication personnel from entry level to senior executive. We do in permanent, contract, retained, or contingency searches. We are also minority recruiters.

Key Contact:
Mr. Ron Capell, Owner
Ms. Ellen Mosher, Chief Recruiter, Site Director
Mr. Rich Burns, Electronics/IT Recruiter

Functions: General Mgmt.

Industries: Mfg., Drugs Mfg., Medical Devices, Electronic, Elec. Components, IT Implementation, Telecoms, Software, Database SW, Development SW, Doc. Mgmt., Production SW, Mfg. SW, Biotech

Networks: Top Echelon Network

Raging Mouse
220 Sansome St Ste 800
San Francisco, CA 94104
(415) 956-6400
Fax: (415) 956-6450
Email: resume@ragingmouse.com
Web: www.ragingmouse.com

Description: We specialize in staffing early stage technology companies in both the US, Europe and Australia.

Key Contact - Specialty:
Mr. Roger M. King, CEO - *Senior level management, CEO, CTO, VP of engineering*

Salary minimum: $50,000

Functions: Generalist, Senior Mgmt., Middle Mgmt., MIS Mgmt., Systems Dev., Systems Implem., Network Admin., Int'l.

Industries: Generalist, Computer Equip., Consumer Elect., Telecoms, Software

Professional Associations: NCHRC

Branches:
915 L St Ste 1235
Sacramento, CA 95814
(916) 325-1200
(888) 812-1200
Fax: (916) 325-1208

4655 Old Ironside Dr Ste 270
Santa Clara, CA 95054
(408) 982-0733
(877) 506-6873
Fax: (408) 982-0733

8080 E Central Ste 300
Wichita, KS 67206
(316) 219-2829
(877) 506-6873
Fax: (316) 219-2841

Railey & Associates
5102 Westerham Pl
Houston, TX 77069
(281) 444-4346

Description: Established in 1978. Legal only. Nationwide--all industries and law firms. All practice levels especially mid- and upper echelons: associates, partners, legal administrators, attorneys, general counsel. Law firm mergers.

Key Contact - Specialty:
Mr. J. Larry Railey, President - *Legal*

Salary minimum: $100,000

Functions: Generalist, Attorneys

Industries: Generalist, Energy, Utilities, Construction, Misc. Mfg., Transportation, Services

Raley & Associates Inc
7901 Grenezay Rd
Wilmington, NC 28411
(800) 350-7881
(910) 686-6034
Fax: (910) 686-6046
Email: fraley3804@aol.com
Web: www.smart-office.net/4820

Description: We specialize in recruiting technical and professional personnel in the manufacturing, fabrication, design, and production of plastic, rubber and metal components and assemblies that possess the specific skills and experiences requested by our clients. We are an independent firm, networked with thousands of other recruiters nationwide for fast and effective service.

Key Contact - Specialty:
Mr. Frank Raley, CPC, Owner/President - *Engineers, managers, manufacturing, metal, plastics*

Salary minimum: $30,000

Functions: Mfg.

Industries: Plastics, Rubber, Metal Products, Motor Vehicles, Computer Equip.

Professional Associations: NCASP, RON, SPE

Networks: Recruiters Professional Network (RPN)

Ramer Search Consultants Inc
24 Colony Dr E
West Orange, NJ 07052
(973) 324-0240
Fax: (973) 324-0016
Email: mramer@ramergroup.com
Web: www.ramergroup.com

Description: Specializing in services and technology based industries including communications, information and financial services. Executive search in finance/accounting and marketing/sales. Packages from $75K to $250K+.

Key Contact:
Mr. Michael Ramer, Principal

Salary minimum: $75,000

Functions: Sales & Mktg., Finance, Int'l.

Industries: Finance, Banking, Invest. Banking, Misc. Financial, Communications, Telecoms, Call Centers, Digital, Wireless, Fiber Optic, Insurance, Real Estate, Software, Accounting SW, Database SW

Professional Associations: ASA, NAPS, NJSA

Ramming & Associates
3 Thackery Ln
Cherry Hill, NJ 08003-1925
(856) 428-7172
Fax: (856) 428-7173
Email: ghr21@home.com
Web:
www.members.tripod.com/~ramming/index.html

Description: Most industries served. Extensive executive search and Internet recruiting experience. Firm established in 1978.

Key Contact:
Mr. George Ramming, Principal

Salary minimum: $50,000

Functions: Generalist

Industries: Generalist

Bruce L Ramstad
PO Box 290518
Port Orange, FL 32129
(904) 322-0348
Fax: (386) 322-0023
Email: bruce@ramstad.com
Web: www.ramstad.com

Description: Totally candidate oriented. Provide engineering and manufacturing professionals for other recruiters in their disciplines.

Key Contact - Specialty:
Mr. Bruce L. Ramstad, Owner - *Engineering, manufacturing*

Salary minimum: $40,000

Functions: Middle Mgmt., Mfg., Product Dev., Production, Automation, Plant Mgmt., Quality

Industries: Mfg.

Networks: National Personnel Assoc (NPA)

Rand-Curtis Resources
10611 N Indian Wells Dr
Fountain Hills, AZ 85268
(480) 837-2100
Fax: (480) 837-9415
Email: randcurtis@msn.com

Description: Twenty plus years' experience in recruiting mid- to upper-level management for major restaurant companies, quick service and full-service. We offer integrity, experience and industry knowledge. We recruit for all functions within the industry.

Key Contact - Specialty:
Ms. Judy Kopulos, Owner - *Restaurants*

Salary minimum: $65,000

Functions: Generalist, Directors, Senior Mgmt., Middle Mgmt., Personnel

Industries: Generalist, Retail, Services, Hospitality

Lea Randolph & Associates Inc
10100 N Central Expwy Ste 620
Dallas, TX 75231
(214) 987-4415
(800) 388-2407
Fax: (214) 369-9548
Email: troyrandolph@hotmail.com
Web: www.lra-recruiting.com

Description: We are professional recruiters specializing in mid-level, upper level, and senior level management positions in clinical and administrative healthcare, finance/accounting in all industries, general business at all levels, sales in mid-level and above and IT, more specifically developers, middle and senior executives.

Key Contact - Specialty:
Ms. Lea Randolph, President - *General business, healthcare*
Mr. Troy Randolph, Recruiter - *Accounting, finance, general business*

Functions: Senior Mgmt., Middle Mgmt., Healthcare, Physicians, Nurses, Sales & Mktg., HR Mgmt., Finance, CFO's, IT

Industries: Generalist

Professional Associations: HICD, IRG

J E Ranta Associates
112 Washington St
Marblehead, MA 01945
(781) 639-0788
Fax: (781) 631-9828
Email: eranta@erols.com
Web: www.southpawcorp.com/ranta

Description: Contingency firm serving the information technology needs of clients throughout New England. Primary emphasis on software engineering opportunities at all levels especially in the web, e-commerce and networking areas. Extensive activity in the consulting and product development and support areas. Success of the firm has been built upon industry knowledge and relationships with key management level personnel.

Key Contact - Specialty:
Mr. Ed Ranta - *Computer software, call center management, telecommunications*

Salary minimum: $60,000

Functions: IT, MIS Mgmt., Systems Analysis, Systems Dev., Systems Implem., Systems Support, Network Admin., DB Admin.

Industries: Generalist

Harold L Rapp Associates
80 Hemlock Dr
Roslyn, NY 11576-2303
(516) 625-4341
Fax: (516) 625-4517
Email: hlrassoc@aol.com
Web: www.jewelryheadhunter.com

Description: Recruitment of executives for the jewelry industry. Searches performed for wholesalers, importers and manufacturers of jewelry and watches.

Key Contact - Specialty:
Mr. Harold L. Rapp, President - *Jewelry executives*

Salary minimum: $40,000

Functions: Generalist, Senior Mgmt., Middle Mgmt., Product Dev., Plant Mgmt., Mktg. Mgmt., Sales Mgmt., Customer Svc.

Industries: Generalist, Mgmt. Consulting, Non-classifiable

Rasch & Associates Ltd
2124 Broadway-Ste 128
New York, NY 10023
(212) 799-7134
Fax: (212) 799-7126
Email: raschjf@aol.com

Description: We are a contingency and retained search firm specializing as a generalist and placing candidates within the financial services industry nationwide in the functional areas of credit, finance, marketing, sales, operations, and human resources.

Key Contact - Specialty:
Ms. Judith Fredericks, President - *Finance, marketing, human resources, credit*

Salary minimum: $65,000

Functions: Generalist, Sales & Mktg., Mkt. Research, Direct Mktg., Customer Svc., Finance, Budgeting, Cash Mgmt., Credit, Risk Mgmt.

Industries: Finance, Banking

Vera L Rast Partners Inc (VLRPI)
1 S Wacker Dr Ste 3890
Chicago, IL 60606
(312) 629-0339
Fax: (312) 629-0347
Email: vlrpi@vlrpilegalsearch.com
Web: www.vlrpilegalsearch.com

Description: Chicago-based legal search organization focused on lateral placement of attorneys for client law firms and corporations. VLRPI concentrates its activities in the Midwest with national coverage through its affiliates.

Key Contact - Specialty:
Ms. Vera L. Rast, President - *Legal*
Mr. Alex Trent, Consultant - *Legal*
Ms. Suzanne English Jones, Consultant - *Legal*

Functions: Legal

Industries: Generalist

Joanne E Ratner Search
10 E 39th St Ste 514
New York, NY 10016
(212) 683-1975
Fax: (212) 683-4682
Email: jobs@jrsearch.com
Web: www.jrsearch.com

Description: Minority (female) owned boutique firm specializing in finance, accounting and marketing positions.

Key Contact - Specialty:
Ms. Joanne E. Ratner, President - *Finance, marketing, accounting*

Salary minimum: $60,000

Functions: Generalist, Senior Mgmt., Finance

Industries: Generalist, Consumer Elect., Finance, Banking, Invest. Banking, Non-profits, Hospitality, Advertising, Publishing, New Media, Broadcast, Film

Professional Associations: NYNMA, SHRM

Razzino-Claymore Associates
277 Fairfield Rd Ste 332
Fairfield, NJ 07004
(973) 882-3388
Fax: (973) 882-2764
Email: janelle@razzino-claymore.com

Description: A boutique search firm offering the foremost in executive recruiting with a personal touch.

Key Contact - Specialty:
Ms. Janelle Razzino, Principal - *Information technology, telecommunications, accounting & finance*
Mr. Robert Casillo, Principal - *Accounting, finance, audit*

Salary minimum: $75,000

Functions: Finance, IT

Industries: Mfg., Retail, Finance, Services, Mgmt. Consulting, Hospitality, Media, Telecoms, Insurance, Biotech, Healthcare

Professional Associations: EDPAA, NAFE

RBW Associates
30352 Lassen Ln
Junction City, OR 97448
(541) 688-9212
Fax: (541) 688-9312
Email: ray@rbwassoc.com
Web: www.rbwassoc.com

Description: We are an executive search firm specializing in the pulp and paper industry, offering expedient and confidential service based on the highest professional ethics. Professional recruiting for industries top 10% talent - management, technical, engineering/maintenance, administrative and sales.

Key Contact - Specialty:
Mr. Ray B. Wheeler, President - *Pulp & paper industry professionals*

Salary minimum: $40,000

Functions: Generalist, Senior Mgmt., Middle Mgmt., Mfg., Production, Plant Mgmt., Packaging, MIS Mgmt., Engineering

Industries: Agri., Forestry, Mining, Energy, Utilities, Construction, Lumber, Furniture, Paper, Printing, Chemicals, Packaging, Industry Specific SW

Professional Associations: PIMA, TAPPI

Networks: Inter-City Personnel Assoc (IPA)

Branches:
204 San Mateo Dr
Hot Springs Village, AR 71913'
(501) 525-3579
Fax: (501) 525-3579
Email: ecorder@ipa.net
Key Contact - Specialty:
Ms. Eutha Corder, Owner - *Lumber, wood, furniture & fixtures, paper & allied industry, high technology*

RCM Technologies Inc
1156 Ave of the Americas Fl 4
New York, NY 10036
(212) 221-1544
Fax: (212) 221-4392
Email: it.ny@rcmt.com
Web: www.rcmt.com

Description: We provide executive search and consulting services to the data processing, bank/finance and health services communities on retainer, contingency, or consulting/contract.

Key Contact - Specialty:
Ms. Mary Beth Leggett, Manager - *Finance*

Functions: Generalist, Nurses, Allied Health, Systems Analysis, Systems Dev., Systems Implem., Network Admin., DB Admin.

Industries: Generalist, Banking, Invest. Banking, Brokers, Pharm Svcs., Mgmt. Consulting, Software, Healthcare

Branches:
2500 McClellan Ave
Pennsauken, NJ 08109
(856) 486-1777

Key Contact:
Mr. Leon Kopyt, CEO

Re-Mark Associates Inc
PO Box 215
Aberdeen, NJ 07747-0215
(732) 619-5100
Fax: (732) 536-7119
Email: futrgar8@worldnet.att.net
Web: www.exchange7.com

Description: Retained search, contingency search and enhanced candidate searches limited to staffing senior management, marketing, sales, engineering and purchasing personnel for the semiconductor, electronics, optical, fiber optics and chemical industries.

Key Contact - Specialty:
Mr. Gary Leffer - *High technology*
Mr. Philip Kase, Vice President - *High technology, medical*

Salary minimum: $40,000

Functions: Generalist, General Mgmt., Mfg., Healthcare, Sales & Mktg., IT, R&D, Engineering

Industries: Generalist, Mfg., Media, Aerospace, Biotech

Professional Associations: AICHE, IEEE, OSA, SPIE

Roberta Rea & Co Inc
4510 Executive Dr Plz 4
San Diego, CA 92121-3021
(858) 457-3566
Fax: (858) 457-4409
Email: roberta@robertareaco.com
Web: www.robertareaco.com

Description: National executive search firm specializing in the shopping center industry; real estate and retail. Job placements are in the areas of management, marketing, leasing and development. On the retail side, we specialize in e-commerce, district and regional managers, human resource generalists and executives, buyers and divisional merchandise managers, as well as vice presidents and directors.

Key Contact - Specialty:
Ms. Roberta Rea, President - *Shopping center industry, leasing, management, development, marketing*
Ms. Shelle Orlansky, Executive Recruiter - *Retail, internet, buyers, divisional, managers*
Mr. John McAuliffe, Executive Recruiter - *Real estate executive, leasing, site selection, construction, development*

Salary minimum: $50,000

Functions: General Mgmt., HR Mgmt.

Industries: Construction, Retail, HR Services

Professional Associations: ICSC

Reach Consulting Group Inc
401 E Colfax Ave Ste 207
South Bend, IN 46617
(219) 232-1818
Fax: (219) 288-3838
Email: don@execsearchplus.com
Web: www.execsearchplus.com

Description: We provide executive search, outplacement, and contract services in engineering, management, telecommunication, manufacturing, data processing, banking, accounting, and financial areas.

Key Contact - Specialty:
Mr. Donald G. Walker, President - *Manufacturing, engineering, information technology, quality, materials*

Salary minimum: $40,000

Functions: Senior Mgmt., Production, Plant Mgmt., Quality, Purchasing, Materials Plng., Personnel, CFO's, Cash Mgmt., IT

Industries: Mfg., Plastics, Rubber, Metal Products, Machine, Appliance, Motor Vehicles, Consumer Elect., Misc. Mfg., Banking, Invest. Banking

Professional Associations: IIE

Networks: Top Echelon Network

Reaction Search Inc
5017 Muir Way
Tampa Bay Area
Lithia, FL 33547
(813) 571-2919
Email: robert@reactionsearch.com
Web: www.reactionsearch.com

Description: Our client's success is our primary mission. We are devoted to reacting to our client's needs, while enhancing each diverse corporate culture. Executive search is the cornerstone of Reaction Search International's (RSI) services. The managing partners of our firm have been involved with placing CEOs to staffing national sales force's.

Key Contact - Specialty:
Mr. Robert Boroff, CSAM, Managing Partner - *Executive search*
Mr. Jason Damaschino, Managing Partner - *Executive search*

Salary minimum: $75,000

Functions: Generalist

Industries: Mfg., Finance, Services, Media, Communications, Aerospace, Packaging, Software, Biotech

Real Estate Executive Search Inc
PO Box 387
San Francisco, CA 94104-0387
(415) 398-4116
(213) 625-7337
Fax: (415) 543-7392
Email: jhavrees@aol.com

Description: Twenty seven years of service to the real estate and finance community.

Key Contact - Specialty:
Mr. J. A. Havens, President - *Management*

Salary minimum: $40,000

Functions: General Mgmt.

Industries: Real Estate

Reality Group
PO Box 2675
Broken Arrow, OK 74013-2675
(918) 451-4057
Fax: (918) 451-4743
Email: lsims@webzone.net

Description: The intricacies of hiring top talent requires a highly trained, competent and certified staff. Our staff is headed by an internationally renowned speaker and trainer who in the last 15 years has trained literally thousands of recruiters worldwide.

Key Contact - Specialty:
Mr. Larry Sims, President - *Safety, health, environmental*

Salary minimum: $25,000

Functions: Generalist, Middle Mgmt., Engineering, Environmentalists

Industries: Generalist, Paper, Chemicals, Plastics, Rubber, Environmental Svcs., Haz. Waste

Professional Associations: ASSE

Networks: Top Echelon Network

Recruiter Consultants
8957 SW Terwilliger Blvd
Portland, OR 97219
(503) 244-2411
Fax: (503) 244-8655
Email: ariel.klein@home.com

Description: We specialize in the national recruitment of advertising and marketing professionals in the areas of account services, creative, media, interactive and account planning.

Key Contact - Specialty:
Ms. Ariel Klein, Principal - *Advertising*

Salary minimum: $25,000

Functions: Generalist, Advertising, Mkt. Research, Mktg. Mgmt., Direct Mktg., PR

Industries: Generalist, Advertising, New Media

Recruiter Solutions Int'l
8200-A Tyler Blvd
Mentor, OH 44060
(800) 992-3875
(440) 255-7457
Fax: (800) 992-3874
Email: diane@rsirecruiters.com
Web: www.rsirecruiters.com

Description: For over 23 years, we have provided search and recruiting services in a wide variety of industries at all professional levels, including: sales, production supervision and management, engineering, financial, and senior corporate executives. Our specific areas of specialization include: forest products, building products, packaging, plastics and polymers, and finance and accounting.

Key Contact - Specialty:
Mr. Robert Gandee, President
Mr. Jon Olson, Vice President - *Forest & building products*
Ms. Julie Freeman, Vice President - *Packaging*
Mr. Daniel Regovich, Vice President - *Finance & accounting*
Mr. Scott Neuhofs, Vice President - *Plastics*
Mr. Tim Gandee, Vice President - *Plastics*

Functions: Generalist, General Mgmt., Senior Mgmt., Mfg., Production, Plant Mgmt., Sales & Mktg., HR Mgmt., Finance, Engineering

Industries: Agri., Forestry, Mining, Lumber, Furniture, Paper, Plastics, Rubber, Misc. Financial, Accounting, Packaging, Accounting SW

Networks: US Recruiters.com

Recruiters Advantage Inc
6800 Paragon Pl Ste 501
Richmond, VA 23230
(804) 282-1044
Fax: (804) 282-2652
Email: recruiters@recruitingadvantage.com
Web: www.recruitingadvantage.com

Description: We are specialist in recruiting accounting, financial, IT, legal, and general management professionals.

Key Contact - Specialty:
Mr. Steve Barley, CPA, CDP, President/Owner - *Accounting/finance*

Salary minimum: $50,000

Functions: Senior Mgmt., Legal, Finance, M&A, MIS Mgmt., Attorneys, Paralegals

Industries: Generalist

Recruiters Professional Network - Fairview
28435 Quince Rd
Fairview, MO 64842
(417) 632-4395
Fax: (417) 632-4413
Email: vickie@mo-net.com

Key Contact - Specialty:
Mrs. Vickie Dent - *Medical*

Salary minimum: $50,000

Functions: Generalist, Physicians, Nurses, Allied Health, Health Admin.

Industries: Generalist, Healthcare, Hospitals, Long-term Care, Dental, Physical Therapy, Occupational Therapy, Women's

Recruiting & Consulting Professionals (RCP)
PO Box 30987
Phoenix, AZ 85046
(602) 996-9953
(877) 996-9953
Fax: (602) 493-8867
Email: excitingcareers@rcpintl.com
Web: www.rcpintl.com

Description: We are an experienced search firm placing accounting and finance professionals nationwide. We specialize in hi-tech, manufacturing, telecommunications and consumer products industries. Our mission is the continuation of a successful alliance with our company and Fortune 500 organizations as well as emerging industry leaders that are well-respected by both their employees and competitors.

Key Contact:
Ms. Lisa Martin, Executive Recruiter

Salary minimum: $50,000

Functions: Finance

Industries: Mfg., Retail, Finance, Services, Software, Biotech

Networks: Top Echelon Network

Recruiting Associates of Amarillo
PO Box 8473
Amarillo, TX 79114
(806) 353-9548
Fax: (806) 353-9540
Email: info@recruitingassociates.com
Web: www.recruitingassociates.com

Description: Professional recruiting and staffing service, both permanent and contract nationwide affiliations, reasonable fees.

Key Contact:
Mr. Michael Rokey, CPC, Owner/Manager

Functions: Generalist, Systems Analysis, Systems Dev., Systems Implem., Systems Support, Network Admin., DB Admin., Engineering

Industries: Generalist, Metal Products, Machine, Appliance, Misc. Mfg., Software

Networks: Top Echelon Network

The Recruiting Group
(formerly known as Accounting Personnel of Minnesota)
5354 Parkdale Dr Ste 104
Minneapolis, MN 55416
(952) 544-1005
Fax: (952) 546-2806
Email: recruiter@recruitinggroup.com
Web: www.recruitinggroup.com

Description: Custom search and placement for all levels of professionals in a variety of specialties.

Key Contact - Specialty:
Ms. Julie Valine, President - *Generalist*

Functions: General Mgmt., Materials, Sales Mgmt., HR Mgmt., Finance, IT, Engineering

Industries: Generalist

Recruiting Options Inc
1375 Northview Ave NE
Atlanta, GA 30306
(404) 874-1003
Fax: (404) 249-9108
Email: martha@recruitingoptions.com
Web: www.recruitingoptions.com

Description: We offer national caliber service without the high cost of a national retained search firm. Unbundling the components means a program can be tailored to meet your hiring goals, time frame and budget. We offer career management coaching working with mid and upper level executives to manage their career to a promotion, a new opportunity, an exit strategy, or a new career.

Key Contact - Specialty:
Ms. Martha Eskew, President - *Advertising, public relations, marketing communications, account service, media*

Salary minimum: $75,000

Functions: Sales & Mktg., Advertising, Mkt. Research, Mktg. Mgmt., PR, Graphic Artists

Industries: Generalist, Media, Advertising, New Media

Recruiting Resources
PO Box 53134
Lubbock, TX 79453
(806) 796-0621
Email: letham@nts-online.net
Web: www.onlinemedicaljobs.com

Description: Recruit and placement of all healthcare professionals on national basis.

Key Contact - Specialty:
Ms. Letha Miller - *Health care*

Salary minimum: $20,000

Functions: General Mgmt., Quality, Healthcare, Physicians, Nurses, Allied Health, Health Admin., CFO's, MIS Mgmt., Minorities

Industries: Generalist, Pharm Svcs., Healthcare

Recruiting Resources Inc
13813 Village Mill Dr
Midlothian, VA 23113
(804) 794-1813
Fax: (804) 379-5421
Email: recres@alcnet.com

Description: Working closely with management and your personnel department, we can customize our services to ensure that the most qualified candidates are presented for your consideration.

Key Contact - Specialty:
Mr. Richard Baltimore, President - *Engineering, manufacturing*
Ms. Sandy Lemaire, Recruiter - *Information systems*
Ms. Ruth Catlin, CPC, Recruiter - *Middle management, senior level management, general managers, CEO, CFO*
Mrs. Karen Waterfield, Technical Recruiter - *IT*
Mr. Bernie Furman, Recruiter - *Health care*

Functions: Generalist, General Mgmt., Mfg., Materials, HR Mgmt., Finance, IT, Engineering

Industries: Generalist, Mfg.

Recruiting Services Group Inc
3533 Ridge Meadows Pkwy
Memphis, TN 38115
(901) 367-0778
Fax: (901) 367-0868

Email: resumes@rsghunt.com
Web: www.rsghunt.com

Description: We are an executive search firm specializing in providing quality talent nationwide. The industries that we serve are manufacturing, supply chain, logistics, technology, and retail corporate operations. We focus on finding the best possible career match for both client and individual. RSG is a certified WBE and can be found on Pronet.

Key Contact - Specialty:
Ms. Whitney Hodges, President - *Distribution, operations, manufacturing management, IT, software sales*

Salary minimum: $50,000

Functions: Generalist, Directors, Senior Mgmt., Mfg., Materials, Distribution, Sales Mgmt., HR Mgmt., IT

Industries: Energy, Utilities, Mfg., Transportation, HR Services, E-commerce, Aerospace, Software

Recruiting Specialists
75 McNeil Way Ste 211
PO Box 572
Dedham, MA 02027
(781) 329-5850
Fax: (781) 329-5840
Email: recruitsp@aol.com
Web: www.recruitingspecialists.com

Description: We attribute our success to our ability to develop a feel for the style of a company and the unique needs of the specific position. We find not only qualified candidates-but the best candidates! We work with you through the interview process and continue after the hire is made until you are fully satisfied.

Key Contact - Specialty:
Ms. Cindy Laughlin, President - *Retail, specialty hardlines, softlines, off-price, hospitality*
Mr. Wayne Penwell, Consultant - *Retail, mass merchandising, hardlines*
Ms. Tracy Wolcott, Consultant - *Retail, food, hospitality*
Mr. Rob Bowerman, Consultant - *Retail, specialty, luxury goods, value retail*
Mrs. Rhonda Dresner, Recruiter - *Food, hospitality, retail*
Mr. Bill DiSandro, Jr., Consultant - *Food, hospitality*
Mrs. Barbara Fundora, Recruiter - *Retail, food, hospitality*
Ms. Joyce Clinton, Recruiter - *Retail*

Salary minimum: $25,000

Functions: Generalist, Directors, Senior Mgmt., Middle Mgmt.

Industries: Generalist, Retail, Hospitality

Professional Associations: MAPS, NAFE

Recruiting/Solutions
5655 Lindero Canyon Rd Ste 521
Westlake Village, CA 91362
(818) 597-8310
Fax: (818) 597-8323
Email: joelrice@datastreet.net

Description: We are known for our ability to perform quickly for our clients. We will recruit and screen three to five qualified and interested candidates within seven working days!

Key Contact - Specialty:
Mr. Joel Rice, Senior Vice President - *Consumer (products, services)*

Salary minimum: $50,000

Functions: Generalist, General Mgmt., Directors, Senior Mgmt., Sales & Mktg., Mktg. Mgmt., Sales Mgmt.

Industries: Generalist, Food, Bev., Tobacco, Lumber, Furniture, Paper, Soap, Perf., Cosmtcs.,

Machine, Appliance, Computer Equip., Consumer Elect., Equip Svcs., Mgmt. Consulting

The Recruitment Company
17 State St Fl 41
New York, NY 10004
(212) 943-2023
Fax: (212) 943-8504
Email: gking@trcny.com
Web: www.trcny.com

Description: We are a global provider of executive search and selection services specializing in the banking, finance, sales and marketing, and information technology sectors. Our offices are located in New York, London, Hong Kong and Sydney.

Key Contact:
Mr. Graham King, Managing Director

Salary minimum: $50,000

Functions: General Mgmt., Sales & Mktg., Finance, IT

Industries: Finance, Banking, Invest. Banking, Brokers, Venture Cap., Misc. Financial, Services, Legal, Accounting, Media, Advertising, Publishing, New Media, Broadcast, Film, Communications, Telecoms, Digital, Software

Recruitment Int'l Group Ltd
298 5th Ave Fl 4
New York, NY 10001
(212) 971-0262
Fax: (212) 971-0228
Web: www.employment-search.org

Description: Full-service executive search firm specializing in management, finance and information systems.

Key Contact:
Mr. Ted Zupa, Director

Salary minimum: $50,000

Functions: Generalist, General Mgmt., Mfg., Healthcare, Sales & Mktg., Finance, IT

Industries: Generalist, Mfg., Finance, Media, Software, Healthcare

Recruitment Resources Inc
1 City Blvd W Ste 820
Orange, CA 92868
(714) 978-7383
Fax: (714) 978-7386
Email: pharmsearch@msn.com

Description: We are an executive search firm that specializes in the placement of medical, pharmaceutical sales reps and sales managers.

Key Contact - Specialty:
Ms. Ruthie M. Ross, President - *Pharmaceutical, medical sales*

Salary minimum: $40,000

Functions: Sales & Mktg.

Industries: Medical Devices, Pharm Svcs.

Professional Associations: CSP

Networks: First Interview Network (FIN)

Recruitment Specialists Inc
1412 E Joppa Rd
Towson, MD 21286
(410) 825-6186
Email: recruit1@erols.com
Web: www.healthcareheadhunter.com

Description: A nurse owned and operated firm with 15+ years of experience recruiting mid-level and senior executives for national healthcare organizations. Specialties: managed care

organizations, healthcare systems, home health and sales management.

Key Contact - Specialty:
Ms. Roxanne Giannerini, President - *Healthcare*

Salary minimum: $45,000

Functions: Nurses

Industries: Healthcare

Mary Rector & Associates Inc
40 S Prospect Ste 200
Roselle, IL 60172
(630) 894-5060
Fax: (630) 894-5607
Web: www.mrector.com

Description: Our firm specializes in placement of mid and senior level management professionals in sales, marketing, education, operations, and general management for the professional beauty industry, for example: haircare, skincare, and nailcare manufacturers, distributors and national chain accounts.

Key Contact:
Ms. Debra Cherdron, President

Salary minimum: $50,000

Functions: Generalist, Directors, Senior Mgmt., Mkt. Research, Mktg. Mgmt., Sales Mgmt., PR, Training

Industries: Generalist, Food, Bev., Tobacco, Textiles, Apparel, Soap, Perf., Cosmtcs., Drugs Mfg., Retail, Media, Advertising

Professional Associations: BBSI

P J Reda & Associates Inc
1150 Lake Hearn Dr NE Ste 200
Atlanta, GA 30342-1506
(404) 250-3216
Fax: (404) 250-3218
Email: predainc@mindspring.com
Web: www.pjredainc.com

Description: Executive search firm specializing in middle- to executive-level of restaurant and hotel operations management including corporate salaried management positions; anywhere in the U.S.

Key Contact - Specialty:
Ms. Pat Reda, President - *Restaurant, hospitality, hotels, country clubs*

Salary minimum: $45,000

Functions: Generalist

Industries: HR Services, Hospitality

Professional Associations: GAPS, NAPS, SHRM

Redell Search Inc
6101 N Sheridan Rd E Ste 31A
Chicago, IL 60660
(773) 764-6100
Fax: (773) 764-6111
Email: redell@ix.netcom.com
Web: www.pw1.netcom.com/~redell/search.html

Description: We specialize in doing recruitment for major IT consulting firms, software developers, Big 5 Consulting firms and hardware vendors.

Key Contact - Specialty:
Mr. John Redell, Principal - *Information systems*

Functions: IT

Industries: Generalist

Cedric L Reese Inc
PO Box 8573
Fresno, CA 93747-8573
(559) 261-9566
Email: creeseqs@ix.netcom.com

Description: Central California recruiters specializing in accounting, engineering and computer programming. We seek to establish a long-term, high-quality strategic relationship with our clients.

Key Contact:
Mr. Cedric Reese, Manager

Functions: Generalist, Senior Mgmt., Middle Mgmt., Mfg., Distribution, Finance, IT, Engineering

Industries: Generalist, Agri., Forestry, Mining, Construction, Mfg., Services, Software

Reeve & Associates
700 Canal St
Stamford, CT 06902
(203) 328-3726
Fax: (208) 293-7403
Email: phil@reevejobs.com
Web: www.reevejobs.com

Description: We are an innovative recruiting services provider specializing in identifying and qualifying passive and active market research candidates, so we can bring our clients and candidates together for a mutually successful working relationship. We have full time and contract positions.

Key Contact - Specialty:
Mr. Philip Reeve, President - *Marketing*

Salary minimum: $35,000

Functions: Sales & Mktg., Mkt. Research

Industries: Generalist, Mfg., Retail, Finance, Services, Media, Communications, Packaging, Software

Professional Associations: AMA

The Regency Group Ltd
256 N 115th St Ste 1
Omaha, NE 68154-2521
(402) 334-7255
Fax: (402) 334-7148
Email: info@regencygroup.com
Web: www.regencygroup.com

Description: Information systems and telecommunications specialists. Performance oriented search and recruiting firm. Capable of providing companies in a variety of industries with the latest technologies via performance driven business people with strong IS/telecom backgrounds. Contracting services available.

Key Contact - Specialty:
Mr. Dan J. Barrow, CPC, General Manager - *Information systems, telecommunications*

Salary minimum: $30,000

Functions: IT, MIS Mgmt., Systems Analysis, Systems Dev., Systems Implem., Network Admin., DB Admin.

Industries: Generalist, Computer Equip., Software

David H Reid & Associates LLC
1 E Camelback Rd Ste 550
Phoenix, AZ 85012
(602) 234-2010
Fax: (602) 234-2030
Email: dreidassoc@aol.com

Description: We offer financial and banking industry executive and professional recruiting in the Southwest market.

Key Contact - Specialty:
Mr. David H. Reid, President - *Banking, finance*

Salary minimum: $50,000

Functions: Generalist

Industries: Finance, Banking, Invest. Banking

Professional Associations: NBN

Networks: National Banking Network (NBN)

Reinecke & Associates
PO Box 1141
Secaucus, NJ 07094
(201) 865-5935
Fax: (201) 865-6081
Email: reinecke.schumann@home.com

Description: Specializing in the search of transportation managers and executives.

Key Contact - Specialty:
Mr. Robert Schumann, President - *Transportation, logistics executives*
Mr. G. Reinecke, Chairman - *General management*

Salary minimum: $35,000

Functions: Generalist, Middle Mgmt., Distribution, Sales Mgmt., CFO's, Credit, M&A, Int'l.

Industries: Generalist, Transportation, Accounting, Mgmt. Consulting

Branches:
7947 Redondo Ln
Orland Park, IL 60462
(708) 349-9992
Fax: (708) 349-9993
Email: allencons@aol.com
Key Contact - Specialty:
Ms. Cynthia Y. Allen, Associate - *Transportation*

RemTech Business Solutions Inc
23097 Farmington Rd
Farmington, MI 48336
(248) 426-6212
Fax: (248) 426-6216
Email: lcattermole@remtech-solutions.com
Web: www.remtech-solutions.com

Description: Our firm offers clients the option of information technology consultants, direct hire employees, or outsourcing their projects to us. Our careful technical screening and personality analysis ensures high quality employees to match client specifications.

Key Contact - Specialty:
Mrs. Laura Cattermole, CPC, President/CEO - *Information technology*

Salary minimum: $45,000

Functions: IT

Industries: Generalist, Services, Mgmt. Consulting

Professional Associations: AITP, NAPS, NAWBO, SBAM

The Renaissance Network
2 Oliver St Fl 8
Boston, MA 02109
(617) 946-2222
Fax: (617) 946-2220
Email: recruiting@ren-network.com
Web: www.ren-network.com

Description: We realize the importance of talented/skilled personnel to the success of an organization. We work closely with clients to develop focused job descriptions and carefully select and prescreen candidates before submitting them for consideration.

Key Contact - Specialty:
Ms. Lisa Sacchetti, President - *Information technology, software engineering, IT consulting*

Functions: Generalist, MIS Mgmt., Systems Analysis, Systems Dev., Systems Implem., Systems Support, DB Admin., Engineering

Industries: Generalist, Telecoms, Software

Research Recruiters
6349 N 78th St Ste 108
Scottsdale, AZ 85250
(480) 315-0190
(800) 275-3552
Fax: (480) 315-1039
Email: lb@researchrecruiters.com
Web: www.researchrecruiters.com

Description: We are an executive search firm focusing on the placement of equity research professionals. Our clients include investment and merchant banks, brokerage firms, and niche boutiques. The majority of our business is on the sell-side, although Research Recruiters does accept limited assignments within asset management. Our specialization is placing equity research analysts and associates at all levels, supervisory analysts & editors, product managers, research strategists, portfolio/asset managers and directors of research.

Key Contact:
Ms. Lorraine Barnicoat

Salary minimum: $80,000

Functions: Finance

Industries: Invest. Banking

Resource Development Company Inc
925 Harvest Dr Ste 190
Blue Bell, PA 19422-1956
(215) 628-2293
Fax: (215) 628-2780
Email: rdc@rdcinc.com
Web: www.rdcinc.com

Description: We provide services, which help companies build progressive, high performance organizations that attract and retain talented individuals, acknowledge individual greatness, and reward their contributions.

Key Contact:
Mr. Christopher Bilotta, President

Salary minimum: $75,000

Functions: General Mgmt.

Industries: Generalist, Agri., Forestry, Mining

Professional Associations: EMA, SHRM

Networks: Top Echelon Network

Branches:
343 W Bagley Rd Ste 402
Berea, OH 44017
(440) 234-2205
Fax: (440) 243-7082
Email: rdc@rdcinc.com
Key Contact:
Mr. Craig B. Toedtman, SPHR, Chairman

Resource Management Group
177 Broad St Fl 11
Stamford, CT 06901
(203) 961-7000
Fax: (203) 961-7001
Email: dl@rmginc.net
Web: www.rmginc.net

Description: Our firm specializes in the recruitment of finance and accounting professionals. We have attracted numerous Fortune 500 companies, financial service organizations, public and privately held businesses and emerging entrepreneurial organizations. Our network of clients provides us with growing opportunities.

Key Contact - Specialty:
Mr. Denis LaPolice, President - *Finance*

Salary minimum: $50,000

Functions: Generalist, Finance, CFO's, Budgeting, Cash Mgmt., Credit, Taxes, M&A, Risk Mgmt.

Industries: Generalist, Mfg., Finance, Services, Media, Real Estate

Professional Associations: NABA, NBMBAA, NSHMBA

Resource Recruiting
547 Amherst St Fl 4
Nashua, NH 03063
(603) 595-2822
Fax: (603) 886-1822
Email: info@resourcerecruiting.com
Web: www.resourcerecruiting.com

Description: We are staffed with individuals experienced not only in recruiting, but with substantial experience in the disciplines they service. Our consultants conduct searches from staff-level to senior management.

Key Contact - Specialty:
Mr. Alan C. Etlinger, President - *Accounting, finance, MIS, operations management*
Mr. Robert C. Harrington, Executive Vice President - *Accounting, finance, MIS*
Mr. Steven R. Etlingen, Vice President - *Sales and marketing*

Functions: Mfg., Purchasing, Distribution, Sales & Mktg., Mkt. Research, Mktg. Mgmt., Sales Mgmt., Direct Mktg., PR, HR Mgmt.

Industries: Generalist

Resource Services Inc
20 Crossways Park N
Woodbury, NY 11797
(516) 496-4100
Fax: (516) 496-4110
Email: jt@resourceservices.com
Web: www.resourceservices.com

Description: Executive search firm with nationwide affiliations specializing in the placement of information technology and communication professionals.

Key Contact:
Mr. Joseph Trainor, Director
Ms. Mary Ann Trainor, President

Salary minimum: $50,000

Functions: IT, MIS Mgmt., Systems Analysis, Systems Dev., Systems Implem., Systems Support, Network Admin., DB Admin.

Industries: Generalist

Networks: National Personnel Assoc (NPA)

Resource360
3081 Holcomb Bridge Rd Ste A-1
Norcross, GA 30071
(770) 734-9943
Fax: (770) 734-0443
Email: rrice@r360.net
Web: www.r360.net

Description: We specialize in placing both full-time and contracting professionals in information technology, finance/accounting, and human resource positions.

Key Contact - Specialty:
Mr. Rick Rice, President/CEO - *Information technology*
Mr. Martin Drucker, Vice President - *Information technology*
Mr. Michael Woodworth, Vice President - *Information technology*

Salary minimum: $30,000

Functions: Directors, Senior Mgmt., Product Dev., HR Mgmt., Finance, IT, MIS Mgmt.

Industries: Generalist, Accounting SW, Database SW, Doc. Mgmt., Production SW

ResourceOptions Inc
31 Fremont St
Needham, MA 02494
(781) 455-0224
Fax: (781) 455-7132
Email: info@resourceoptions.com
Web: www.resourceoptions.com

Description: Our firm is Boston's largest locally owned staffing firm specializing in the environmental, laboratory, and engineering industries. We provide both permanent and contract services to a broad range of clients. The cornerstone of our business is forming lasting and mutually successful relationships between employers and employees.

Key Contact:
Mr. Matthew Carlin, President

Salary minimum: $30,000

Functions: Generalist

Industries: Transportation, HR Services, Environmental Svcs.

Results Group Int'l Inc
172 W 79th St Ste16A
New York, NY 10024
(212) 873-6291
Fax: (212) 873-6291
Email: resultsg@aol.com

Description: Recruitment for advertising agency account management and corporate communications, as well as media management, sales promotion, public relations, direct marketing and integrated marketing. Domestic and international.

Key Contact - Specialty:
Mr. James Brink, Principal - *Advertising, marketing communications*

Salary minimum: $40,000

Functions: Advertising, Mkt. Research, Direct Mktg., PR, HR Mgmt.

Industries: Generalist, Media, Advertising, Publishing, New Media, Broadcast, Film

Results Search Group
1728 N Dayton St Ste B
Chicago, IL 60614
(312) 587-9898
Email: resultssearch@aol.com

Description: Firm specializes in placement of proven sales professionals in direct marketing, database marketing, software related industries, print related to direct mail. Account executive to sales management placement.

Key Contact - Specialty:
Mr. David Heaton, President - *Sales, direct marketing, database marketing, crm software sales, e-commerce*

Salary minimum: $60,000

Functions: Directors, Sales & Mktg., Advertising, Sales Mgmt., Direct Mktg.

Industries: Printing, Software

Professional Associations: CADM, DMAW, LADMA, RMDMA

Retail Connection Inc
271 Rte 46 W Ste D 105
Fairfield, NJ 07004
(973) 882-6662
Fax: (973) 575-5858
Email: retailconn@aol.com
Web: www.retailconnectioninc.com

Description: We are specializing in the recruitment and placement of retail executives. We place store

and field management, as well as, corporate merchandising and operations positions.

Key Contact - Specialty:
Ms. Carole Thaller, President - *Retail*

Salary minimum: $30,000

Functions: Middle Mgmt.

Industries: Retail

Professional Associations: NJAPS

Retail Executive Search
4620 N State Rd 7 Ste 212
Ft. Lauderdale, FL 33319
(954) 731-2300
(800) 771-7130
Fax: (954) 733-0642
Email: res@retsearch.com
Web: www.retsearch.com

Description: In the search field since 1980, all consultants are former retail professionals. Strong ethics oriented professional organization. Same management since inception of business. Searches conducted nationally for middle- & senior-level retail executives in merchandising, operations & support positions.

Key Contact - Specialty:
Mr. Manuel Kaye, President - *Retail*
Mr. Edward Kaye, Executive Vice President - *Retail executive placement*

Salary minimum: $50,000

Functions: Generalist

Industries: Retail

Professional Associations: FAPS

The Retail Network
161 Forbes Rd Ste 104
Braintree, MA 02184
(781) 380-8830
Fax: (781) 380-7656
Email: retail@retailnetwork.com
Web: www.retailnetwork.com

Description: Executive search firm specializing in search and placement for retail and retail related industries.

Key Contact - Specialty:
Mr. Luke Roberts, President - *Buyers, assistant buyers, planners, store managers (regional, district)*
Mr. Gary Belastock, Vice President - *Buyers, assistant buyers, planners, merchandisers, store managers (regional, district)*

Salary minimum: $30,000

Functions: Generalist, Directors, Senior Mgmt., Middle Mgmt., Purchasing, Distribution, Direct Mktg., Benefits, Training, CFO's

Industries: Generalist, Retail

Retail Recruiters
2189 Silas Deane Hwy
Rocky Hill, CT 06067
(860) 721-9550
Fax: (860) 257-8813
Email: retailcareers@aol.com
Web: www.retailrecruitersusa.com

Description: We specialize in the placement of retail personnel for the specialty, department and discount store industry.

Key Contact - Specialty:
Mr. Nathan Friedman, President - *Retail management*

Functions: General Mgmt.

Industries: Retail

Retail Recruiters/Spectrum Consultants Inc
111 Presidential Blvd Ste 105
Bala Pointe
Bala Cynwyd, PA 19004
(610) 667-6565
Fax: (610) 667-5323

Description: Consultants are specialists in areas of retail, manufacturing. Well-known for our effectiveness in the search process.

Key Contact - Specialty:
Ms. Shirlee J. Berman, President - *Retail, healthcare, medical*

Functions: Generalist, Mfg., Materials, Distribution, Sales & Mktg., HR Mgmt., Finance, MIS Mgmt., DB Admin., Graphic Artists

Industries: Generalist, Mfg., Retail

Retail Search Group
(also known as MRI of Grass Valley)
11364 Pleasant Valley Rd
Penn Valley, CA 95946
(530) 432-1966
Fax: (530) 432-3606
Email: recruiter@retailsearchgroup.com
Web: www.retailsearchgroup.com

Description: We specialize in the placement of retail & e-commerce professionals in all areas including field operations, merchandising/buying and executive positions.

Key Contact - Specialty:
Mr. Ridge Eagan, Managing Partner - *Retail*
Ms. Karen Eagan, Managing Partner - *Retail*

Salary minimum: $40,000

Functions: Generalist, General Mgmt., Senior Mgmt., Middle Mgmt., Purchasing, Distribution, HR Mgmt., Finance, MIS Mgmt.

Industries: Retail

Retis Associates Inc
1550 N Lake Shore Dr Ste 11A
Chicago, IL 60610
(312) 337-3077
Fax: (312) 337-3177
Email: retis123@aol.com

Description: Professional, effective recruitment services for healthcare executives and physicians. Successful nationwide placement at reasonable fees to clients.

Key Contact - Specialty:
Ms. Lillian Retis, President - *Healthcare*

Functions: Generalist, Physicians, Nurses, Allied Health, Health Admin., MIS Mgmt.

Industries: Generalist, Healthcare

R S Reynolds Technical Recruiting
4740 E Euclid Ave
Phoenix, AZ 85044
(602) 426-8924
Fax: (602) 426-8923
Email: scott@rsreynolds.com
Web: www.rsreynolds.com

Description: Founded in 1980 Reynolds Technical Recruiting specializes in recruiting and placement of Data Processing professionals. Thru our affiliation with The Top Echelon Network of recruiters we can offer the added service of national and international placement. We do contract placement as well as permanent placement.

Key Contact - Specialty:
Mr. Scott Reynolds, Owner/Recruiter
Ms. Debra Reynolds, Research Assistant - *IT disciplines (all)*

Functions: IT

Industries: Generalist

Networks: Top Echelon Network

RGA Associates Inc
465 California St
San Francisco, CA 94104
(415) 397-4646
Fax: (415) 951-7979
Email: rga@rgatech.com
Web: www.rgatech.com

Description: For 20 years, we have provided the highest calibre of engineering talent in the most cost and time efficient manner.

Key Contact - Specialty:
Mr. Richard Engelhardt, President - *High tech engineering, hardware, software*
Ms. Marguerite Bruchez, Vice President - *High tech engineering, hardware, software*

Functions: Generalist, Systems Dev., R&D, Engineering

Industries: Generalist, Computer Equip., New Media, Broadcast, Film, Telecoms, Software

RGE
2106-D Gallows Rd
Vienna, VA 22182
(703) 917-0573
Fax: (703) 917-0668
Email: repstein@rgeconsulting.com
Web: www.rgeconsulting.com

Description: Permanent placement, temporary and consulting placement, retained search, executive recruiting in information technology, accounting and finance, telecommunications and financial service specialty.

Key Contact - Specialty:
Mr. Robert G. Epstein, President - *Information technology, accounting & finance, telecommunications*

Salary minimum: $30,000

Functions: Finance, CFO's, Taxes, MIS Mgmt., Systems Analysis, Systems Dev., Systems Implem., Systems Support

Industries: Generalist

Professional Associations: NATSS

RGT Associates Inc
2 Greenleaf Woods Dr Elmwood Bldg Ste 101
PO Box 1032
Portsmouth, NH 03801
(603) 431-9500
Fax: (603) 431-6984
Email: recruitrgt@aol.com

Description: We provide confidential, professional search and placement services for management positions throughout New England. The specialized services offered are most effective with small and medium-sized organizations and middle- and senior-level management positions.

Key Contact - Specialty:
Mr. Bob Thiboutot, CPC, President - *Manufacturing management*

Salary minimum: $35,000

Functions: Generalist, Mfg.

Industries: Generalist, Mfg.

Professional Associations: IPSA, NAPS, NNEAPS

RHAssoc Inc
10103 Switzer St Ste 101
Overland Park, KS 66212-5439
(913) 438-8433
Email: rhassociates@rha-staffing.com
Web: www.rha-staffing.com

Description: Information technology staff search firm based in the Kansas City region servicing regional and U.S. based clients. Firm specializes in retainer, container, contingency, contract, and employer of record placements.

Key Contact - Specialty:
Mr. Russell Hacker, President - *IT*

Salary minimum: $70,000

Functions: IT

Industries: Generalist, Mfg., Transportation, Finance, Government, Aerospace, Insurance, Software, Healthcare

Professional Associations: NAPS

Networks: National Personnel Assoc (NPA)

Riccione & Associates Inc
17300 Dallas Pkwy 2080
Dallas, TX 75248-1156
(972) 380-6432
Fax: (972) 407-0659
Email: nick@riccione.com
Web: www.riccione.com

Description: We specialize in executive search and placement of quality employees for software and hardware engineering positions, both full-time and contract.

Key Contact - Specialty:
Mr. Nicholas Riccione, President - *Software engineers, hardware engineers*

Salary minimum: $50,000

Functions: Generalist, Engineering

Industries: Generalist, Software

Professional Associations: IRG, RON

Networks: National Personnel Assoc (NPA)

Jeff Rich Associates
67 Walnut Ave Ste 303
Clark, NJ 07066
(732) 574-3888
Fax: (732) 574-1424
Email: jefrichassoc@aol.com
Web: www.clarknj.com/jeffrich

Description: We develop a long lasting relationship with our clients which enables us to better understand the culture of each company and the personality of the management involved in the selection process for new employees.

Key Contact - Specialty:
Mr. Richard A. Thunberg, President - *Accounting, finance, tax, audit*

Salary minimum: $40,000

Functions: Generalist, Finance, CFO's, Budgeting, Cash Mgmt., Credit, Taxes, M&A, Risk Mgmt.

Industries: Generalist

Don Richard Associates of Tidewater
4701 Columbus St Ste 102
Virginia Beach, VA 23462-6725
(757) 518-8600
Fax: (757) 518-9436
Email: donrich@dravb.com
Web: www.dravb.com

Description: We have built a reputation for outstanding professionalism and quality service. The key to our long-term success is founded in the caliber of our counselors and support staff. We are focused on the needs of our clients, as well as the desires of our candidates. As a result, our reputation for recruitment is unparalleled.

Key Contact:
Mr. Ed Greene, CPA, President

Salary minimum: $25,000

Functions: Generalist

Industries: Accounting

Richard, Wayne & Roberts
24 Greenway Plz Ste 1304
Houston, TX 77046
(713) 629-6681
(800) 364-7979
Fax: (713) 623-2740
Web: www.rwr.com

Description: We approach each recruiting assignment with a minimum three member team, designating one recruiter as the principal contact for the client. Our mission is to be recognized as the leading recruiting firm in the industries and disciplines we serve.

Key Contact - Specialty:
Mr. Dick Weiss, CPC, Principal, Managing partner
Mr. Neal Hirsch, Partner - *Accounting*
Ms. Alexis Cannon, CPC, Associate Partner - *Accounting, legal, IT*
Mr. Mark Dremely, CPC, Associate Partner - *Real estate, construction, project manager*
Ms. Ruth Schlanger, CPC, Associate Partner - *Legal*
Ms. Amy Adams, CPC, Associate Partner - *Healthcare, accounting, human resources*
Mr. Bobby Doyle, CPC, Associate Partner - *Technical engineering*

Salary minimum: $40,000

Functions: Generalist, Mfg., Healthcare, HR Mgmt., Finance, IT, Engineering, Attorneys

Industries: Generalist, Construction, Chemicals, Finance, Telecoms, Software

Professional Associations: HAAPC

Branches:
4625 S Wendler Dr Ste 111
Tempe, AZ 85282
(602) 438-1496
(800) 364-7979
Fax: (602) 431-0322
Key Contact - Specialty:
Mr. Mike Coltrane, Executive Recruiter - *Telecommunications*

2999 David Ave
San Jose, CA 95128
(800) 291-2949
(408) 866-1887
Fax: (408) 866-1399
Email: annam@rwr.com
Key Contact - Specialty:
Ms. Anna Colosimo, Executive Recruiter - *Accounting*

26 Maroon Dr
Aspen, CO 81611
(877) 416-6352
(970) 544-0702
Fax: (970) 544-0706
Email: abbyg@rwr.com
Key Contact - Specialty:
Ms. Abby Gold, Senior Executive Recruiter - *Real estate, construction project manager*

1110 Fidler Ln Ste 310
Silver Spring, MD 20910
(301) 585-4287
(800) 364-7979
Fax: (301) 585-4289
Key Contact - Specialty:
Mr. Randy Gooch, Executive recruiter - *Healthcare, accounting*

121 SW Salmon Fl 11
Portland, OR 97204
(888) 808-6701
(503) 471-1335
Fax: (503) 471-1401
Email: dhilton@rwr.com

Key Contact - Specialty:
Ms. Diane Hilton, Executive Recruiter - *Engineering, oil & gas*

147 Finch Pl SW Ste 1
Bainbridge Island, WA 98110
(800) 232-6943
(206) 855-9736
Fax: (206) 855-9746
Key Contact - Specialty:
Mr. Paul McEwan, CPC, Executive Recruiter - *Sales, technical sales, marketing*

Terry Richards
36 Public Sq
Willoughby, OH 44094
(440) 918-1800
Fax: (440) 975-1499
Email: trcpcrec@apk.net

Description: We are an independent recruiting firm specializing in management positions and above for manufacturing and distribution companies.

Key Contact - Specialty:
Mr. Terry Richards, CPC, President - *Generalist, manufacturing, distribution*

Salary minimum: $75,000

Functions: Generalist, Senior Mgmt., Middle Mgmt., Plant Mgmt., Quality, Purchasing, Materials Plng., Distribution, Sales Mgmt.

Industries: Generalist, Mfg., Metal Products, Machine, Appliance, Motor Vehicles, Computer Equip., Consumer Elect., Misc. Mfg., Wholesale

Professional Associations: ASQ, SHRM

Jack Richman & Associates
PO Box 25412
Ft. Lauderdale, FL 33320
(305) 940-0721
(954) 389-9563
Fax: (954) 389-9572
Email: jrafl@bellsouth.net
Web: www.floridatechjobs.com

Description: Our firm specializes exclusively in the information technology industry. Geographic market is South Florida and nationwide. Multinational experience, as well as spanish is preferred.

Key Contact - Specialty:
Mr. Jack Richman, President - *Information systems technology, telecommunications, client/server*
Ms. Gloria Newman, Senior Consultant - *Information systems technology, mid-range, client/server*

Salary minimum: $50,000

Functions: IT

Industries: Generalist, Computer Equip., Invest. Banking, Mgmt. Consulting, Software

Richmond Associates
9 Pioneer St
Cooperstown, NY 13326
(607) 547-9236
(607) 544-1031
Fax: (607) 547-7456
Email: jhulse@msn.com

Description: We specialize in searching for and placing sales professionals and technical sales support professionals in software and hardware sales positions nationwide.

Key Contact - Specialty:
Ms. Jeanne Hulse, Management Consultant - *Information systems professionals (sales & pre-sales)*
Mr. Rick Hulse, Management Consultant - *Information systems*

Salary minimum: $65,000

Functions: Sales & Mktg.

Industries: New Media, Telecoms, Software

Ridgefield Search Int'l
224 Barlow Mountain Rd
Ridgefield, CT 06877-1937
(203) 438-8000

Description: Twenty one years' search and recruitment international management talent for Fortune 1500 manufacturer clients. Emphasis: country managers, marketing sales, finance, plant and MIS directors. Geography: Latin America, Asia, Middle East and Eastern Europe. Jobs USA based or overseas.

Key Contact - Specialty:
Mr. Ralph Bailey, Owner/General Manager - *International managers (middle, upper-level)*

Salary minimum: $75,000

Functions: Int'l.

Industries: Generalist

Ridgewood Intermediaries
51 S Broad St
Ridgewood, NJ 07450
(201) 251-8111
Fax: (201) 652-8996
Email: hdhunter03@aol.com

Description: Full-service recruitment firm specializing in the medical and healthcare field placing sales, sales management and marketing personnel.

Key Contact - Specialty:
Mr. George Learn, President - *Medical, surgical, cardiovascular*

Functions: Sales & Mktg., Mkt. Research, Mktg. Mgmt., Sales Mgmt.

Industries: Generalist, Healthcare

RightSource Inc
217 Riverbend Rd
Ormond Beach, FL 32174
(386) 672-7282
Fax: (386) 672-0114
Email: rsi1@bellsouth.net
Web: www.rsi1.com

Description: Executive search specialists for the food industry exclusively, nationally & internationally.

Key Contact:
Mr. Ronald Bynum, President - *Food ingredients industry*
Mrs. Susan Milovanovic, Search Consultant

Salary minimum: $50,000

Functions: Generalist

Industries: Food, Bev., Tobacco

Professional Associations: IFT, RCA

Branches:
2811 N 161st Ave
Omaha, NE 68116
(402) 431-8633
Fax: (402) 431-8633
Email: susanmilovanovic@aol.com
Key Contact - Specialty:
Mrs. Susan Milovanovic, Search Consultant - *Food industry*

Riley Cole
PO Box 10635
Oakland, CA 94610
(510) 336-2333
Fax: (510) 336-2777
Email: riled@pacbell.net

Description: Over 35 years of successful, in-depth recruiting experience. Competitive knowledge, organizational design understanding, as well as proven integrity and discretion allow us to individualize each search assignment.

Key Contact - Specialty:
Mr. Jim Riley, Partner - *Retail, consumer packaged goods, sales & marketing*
Mr. Don Cole, Partner - *Manufacturing management, engineering, quality assurance, research & development*

Salary minimum: $40,000

Functions: Generalist

Industries: Mfg., Food, Bev., Tobacco, Soap, Perf., Cosmtcs., Wholesale, Retail

Ritt-Ritt & Associates
5105 Tollview Dr Ste 110
Rolling Meadows, IL 60008
(847) 483-9330
Fax: (847) 483-9331
Email: ritt1@hotmail.com

Description: We are one of the oldest and most respected placement firms in the country specializing solely in the foodservice and hospitality industry.

Key Contact - Specialty:
Mr. William Morris, President
Mr. Joseph D'Alessandro, Senior Recruiter - *Foodservice, hospitality*

Salary minimum: $30,000

Functions: Generalist

Industries: Hospitality

Professional Associations: ACF, CHRIE, IFSEA, MPI, SFM, SHRM

Ritta Professional Search Inc
6 Automation Ln
Albany, NY 12205
(518) 458-7340
Fax: (518) 458-7017

Description: Specialize in metallurgical, mechanical and electrical engineering for R&D. Also, environmental/safety engineering and technical cellular telephone requirements. Strong gas/steam turbine client base. National coverage.

Key Contact - Specialty:
Mr. Arthur E. Hansen, President - *Engineering (research & development)*
Mr. James P. Salfi, Vice President - *Telecommunications (cellular)*
Dr. Joe Palko - *Materials, ceramic, engineering*

Salary minimum: $50,000

Functions: Product Dev., Production, MIS Mgmt., Systems Analysis, Systems Implem., Systems Support, Network Admin., DB Admin., R&D, Engineering

Industries: Generalist, Mfg.

Rittenhouse Executive Search Inc
1700 Benjamin Franklin Pkwy
The Windsor, Penthouse Ste
Philadelphia, PA 19103
(215) 564-6007
(215) 564-6057
Fax: (215) 564-6051
Email: recruiter@ritsearch.com
Web: www.ritsearch.com

Description: Rittenhouse executive search specializes in the recruitment and permanent placement of accountants, financial professionals and attorneys. Clients include accounting firms, law firms and corporations.

Key Contact:
Ms. Susan VanCola, CPA

Functions: Legal

Industries: Legal, Accounting

Professional Associations: MAAPC

River Glen Associates

75 Glen Rd Ste 100
Rocky Glen Mill
Sandy Hook, CT 06482-1161
(203) 270-3400
Fax: (203) 270-3405
Email: davids@riverglen.net
Web: www.riverglen.net

Description: Our firm is chartered with the singular mission of delivering competitively superior talent who create real value for our clients. Our goal is to be a critical resource needed to build world-class organizations. We specialize in sales, marketing, business development, and general management candidates.

Key Contact - Specialty:
Mr. David Sigovich, Managing Director - *Senior management (sales, marketing, bisdev)*
Mr. Craig Sigovich, Vice President - *Internet security, e-commerce, sales/marketing*
Mr. Michael Sigovich, Director - *Sales, marketing, business development*

Salary minimum: $60,000

Functions: Generalist

Industries: Generalist

River Region Personnel Inc

1537 Metairie Rd Ste D
Metairie, LA 70005
(504) 831-4746
Fax: (504) 831-9916
Email: czamjahn@aol.com

Description: Thirty years of experience in serving national process industry employers. Previous chemical industry HR positions with Monsanto Co. and American Cyanamid. Specialists in expanded foam packaging, polymers, plastics, and chemicals.

Key Contact - Specialty:
Mr. Charles J. Zamjahn, President - *Chemical, refining, plastics, manufacturing, expanded foam packaging*

Salary minimum: $50,000

Functions: Generalist

Industries: Generalist

Professional Associations: LSA, SHRM

Networks: National Personnel Assoc (NPA)

River West Consultants Ltd

200 W Madison Ste 2650
Chicago, IL 60606
(312) 332-8300
Fax: (312) 332-8303
Email: rwcltd@aol.com

Description: Legal search and consulting firm providing services in these areas to law firms and corporations. We place experienced attorneys, both at law firms and in-house and the merger of practice groups and firms.

Key Contact - Specialty:
Mr. Jeffrey M. Simon, Esq., Principal - *Legal*
Ms. Pamela J. Simon, Principal - *Legal*

Functions: Legal, Attorneys

Industries: Generalist

Professional Associations: NALSC

Rivera Legal Search Inc

PO Box 63343
Los Angeles, CA 90063
(323) 780-0000
Fax: (323) 780-0388
Email: jdhuntr@pacbell.net

Description: We recruit and places attorneys at all levels of experience. Clients include major law firms and corporations worldwide.

Key Contact - Specialty:
Mr. Al Rivera, President - *Legal*

Salary minimum: $70,000

Functions: Generalist, Legal, Attorneys

Industries: Generalist, Legal

Professional Associations: NALSC

The Riverbend Group

36 Four Seasons Ctr Ste 343
St. Louis, MO 63017
(314) 579-9729
Fax: (888) 735-4436
Email: resume@dbajobs.com
Web: www.dbajobs.com

Description: We specialize in solving your relational database hiring problems! Our candidates are career-minded professionals with relational database development, tools and techniques expertise.

Key Contact:
Mr. John Sroka, Partner - *Information systems professionals*
Ms. Sue Thieme, Partner - *Information systems professionals*
Ms. Kathy Fish
Ms. Cynthia Pruski

Salary minimum: $50,000

Functions: Generalist, DB Admin.

Industries: Generalist, Database SW

Professional Associations: MAPS

Networks: Top Echelon Network

Riverwood Consulting

N611 County Rd Z
Eau Galle, WI 54737-9557
(715) 283-4922
Fax: (715) 283-4926
Email: tomm@wwt.net

Description: Specializing in the upper Midwest states, primarily in manufacturing industries. Very knowledgeable in the Minneapolis, St. Paul area and 200 mile radius. Current assignments include numerous high-technology electronics manufacturing companies. Positions range from senior technical level to upper-management positions.

Key Contact - Specialty:
Mr. Tom Martin, President - *Middle management, upper management, technical, manufacturing*

Salary minimum: $50,000

Functions: Generalist, Senior Mgmt., Middle Mgmt., Mfg., Materials, Mktg. Mgmt., Sales Mgmt., Engineering

Industries: Generalist, Plastics, Rubber, Metal Products, Machine, Appliance, Motor Vehicles, Test, Measure Equip., Misc. Mfg.

Professional Associations: RON

RJ Associates

23730 Canzonet St
Woodland Hills, CA 91367
(818) 715-7121
Fax: (818) 715-9438
Email: rja@socal.rr.com

Description: Providing highly personalized professional search services within a wide array of industries for positions from CEO to financial analyst, from CIO to controller. Because we engage in a limited number of searches, we focus our full attention on each assignment. We are the names on the front door.

Key Contact - Specialty:
Ms. Judith Fischer, President - *Accounting, finance, information technology, middle & upper management*
Mr. Ronald Fischer, Executive Vice President - *Accounting, finance, information technology, middle & upper management*

Salary minimum: $85,000

Functions: Finance, CFO's, Budgeting, Cash Mgmt., Taxes, M&A, IT, MIS Mgmt.

Industries: Generalist

RJK & Associates

7270 Woodbine Ave Ste 200
Markham, ON L3R 4B9
Canada
(905) 947-8454
(877) 353-0330
Fax: (905) 947-8439
Email: robert.kahler@home.com

Description: We have enjoyed over 20 years of successful experience in the identification, recruitment and referral of quality candidates, particularly in the areas of sales, engineering and manufacturing.

Key Contact - Specialty:
Mr. Robert Kahler, President - *Generalist*

Salary minimum: $50,000

Functions: Generalist, Plant Mgmt., Purchasing, Sales Mgmt., Customer Svc., HR Mgmt., Budgeting

Industries: Generalist, Drugs Mfg., Plastics, Rubber, Motor Vehicles, Test, Measure Equip., Electronic, Elec. Components, Packaging

RJL Staffing Inc

PO Box 948
Island Lake, IL 60042
(847) 526-9520
Fax: (847) 526-9522
Email: kmosier@rjlstaffing.com
Web: www.rjlstaffing.com

Description: RJL Staffing, Inc. is a Chicago based executive search firm that specializes exclusively in the placement of Sales professionals.

Key Contact:
Ms. Kathryn Mosier

Salary minimum: $25,000

Functions: Sales Mgmt.

Industries: Generalist

Professional Associations: NAPS

RJS Associates Inc

10 Columbus Blvd
Hartford, CT 06106
(860) 278-5840
Fax: (860) 522-8313
Email: rjs@rjsassoc.com
Web: www.rjsassoc.com

Description: We are a search firm specializing in technical positions in the engineering, scientific, information systems, finance, environmental, software, retail/grocery, and distribution fields.

Key Contact:
Mr. Richard Stewart, CPC, President - *Insurance, finance, administration*

Mr. Brian Greer, CPC, Vice President - *Engineering*
Mr. John Reever, CPC, Manager - *Information systems, software engineering, finance*
Mr. Rich Dunn, CPC, Manager - *Information systems, finance*
Mr. Steve Dewey, CPC, Manager - *Food, retail, logistics*
Mr. Paul Smith, CPC, Manager - *Information systems, software engineering*
Mr. Brad Earnest, CPC, Manager - *Engineering*
Ms. Amy Sternberg, Office Manager
Mr. Alan Gravelle, MCSE, Network Manager/Webmaster

Salary minimum: $24,000

Functions: Generalist

Industries: Generalist

Professional Associations: ACS, AICHE, AIPG, APICS, ASQ, AWMA, AWMA, BWUA, CAPS, CBIA, CGA, CIA, CPA, EAR, EPOC, FES, HOUNY, HRACC, IFT, IHOUA, IIA, IIE, IOPP, ISACA, LSPA, MAEP, MHOLUA, NAPS, NEHOU, NGWA, NHOU, NRF, SAE, SME, SMTA, SPE, SWS, WAHLU

RKP Group Executive Search

(also known as MRI of Clarksville)
10451 Twin Rivers Rd Ste 244
Columbia, MD 21044
(410) 992-3400
Fax: (410) 992-7767
Email: rkprandy@mindspring.com
Web: www.rpkgroup.com

Description: We provide executive and senior level placements within the technology/entertainment industry. Our search assignments are at the CEO, COO, sales VP, marketing VP, technical management, and field level senior. We take on retained and contingency assignments depending upon requirements.

Key Contact - Specialty:
Mr. Randall Pinato
Ms. Karla Gattozzi, GM - *Entertainment industry*

Functions: Senior Mgmt., Middle Mgmt.

Industries: Entertainment, Media, Wireless, Software, Entertainment SW

RLR Resources

56 Calle Conejo
Corrales, NM 87048
(505) 897-1201
Fax: (505) 897-1246
Email: rlrr@rlrresources.com
Web: www.rlrresources.com

Description: We utilize a proactive approach to identify candidates who will best fit your company's job requirements. By developing the job specifications, we will focus in on the key talent in the energy industry.

Key Contact - Specialty:
Ms. Rita Longino, President - *Experienced personnel for unregulated energy companies*
Mr. Roy Soto, Vice President - *Experienced personnel for unregulated energy companies*

Salary minimum: $40,000

Functions: Personnel

Industries: Energy, Utilities

RML Associates

1215 Granada Ct
Lady Lake, FL 32159
(352) 750-1399
Fax: (352) 750-6135
Email: boblr@lcia.com
Web: www.members.lcia.com/larson

Description: We are a consulting and recruiting firm with over 50 years' combined experience. We offer companies unique solutions to their needs.

Key Contact:
Mr. Robert L. Larson, PE, President

Salary minimum: $20,000

Functions: Generalist, Middle Mgmt., Mfg., Materials, Engineering

Industries: Generalist, Lumber, Furniture, Plastics, Rubber, Metal Products, Machine, Appliance, Motor Vehicles, Misc. Mfg.

Professional Associations: IIE, RON

Roadrunner Personnel

4015 Carlisle Blvd NE Ste C
Albuquerque, NM 87107
(505) 881-1994
Fax: (505) 881-8749
Email: mail@exec-recuiter.com
Web: www.exec-recuiter.com

Description: Major telecommunications, computer industry, pharmaceutical and medical device industries. Sales, marketing and management recruiting only. USA, US/Mexico border area, international.

Key Contact:
Mr. Doug Elliott, Owner - *Medical, pharmaceutical, sales, sales management*
Mr. Greg Trost, President

Salary minimum: $50,000

Functions: Generalist, Senior Mgmt., Middle Mgmt., Mkt. Research, Mktg. Mgmt., Sales Mgmt., MIS Mgmt.

Industries: Generalist, Drugs Mfg., Medical Devices, Computer Equip., Pharm Svcs., Biotech

Networks: First Interview Network (FIN)

Roberson & Company

10752 N 89th Pl Ste 202
Scottsdale, AZ 85260
(480) 391-3200
Fax: (602) 296-0165
Email: roberson@recruiterpro.com
Web: www.recruiterpro.com

Description: Founded in 1967, we are a full-service firm affiliates with over a 400 member network, computer linked nationally and internationally. Capable of the most specialized kinds of searches.

Key Contact - Specialty:
Mr. Stephen D. Silvas, President - *Generalist*

Salary minimum: $50,000

Functions: Generalist

Industries: Generalist, Mfg., Transportation, Services, Telecoms, Fiber Optic, Packaging, Software, Mfg. SW, Healthcare

Networks: National Personnel Assoc (NPA)

Bart Roberson & Company

1445 N Loop W Ste 800
Houston, TX 77008
(713) 863-1445
Fax: (713) 863-1616
Email: info@bartroberson.com
Web: www.bartroberson.com

Description: Specializing in finance and accounting, technical, staffing, information technology, sales and marketing, contingency, retainer, contract, international.

Key Contact:
Mr. Barthell Roberson, Chairman - *Accounting, financial*
Mr. Boyd H. Rowland, President & CEO - *Power, co-generation, utility*
Mr. Brett Bauman, General Manager

Mr. Michael Hayes, Manager of National Staffing
Mr. Felix Romero, Manager of Financial & Accounting Div

Functions: Generalist, Senior Mgmt., Mktg. Mgmt., CFO's, M&A, MIS Mgmt., Engineering, Int'l.

Industries: Generalist, Energy, Utilities, Construction, Mfg., Finance, Accounting

Eric Robert Associates Inc

363 7th Ave Fl 6
New York, NY 10001
(212) 695-5900
Email: eric@ericrobert.com
Web: www.ericrobert.com

Description: We are a large established IT staffing company representing established financial institutions, e-Commerce, advertising, insurance, banking, and brokerage companies. We are an involved at all levels from programmer thru project manager to chief technology officer.

Key Contact - Specialty:
Mr. Eric Silverman, Managing Partner - *Information technology*
Mr. Robert Midoneck, Managing Partner - *Information technology*

Salary minimum: $65,000

Functions: IT

Industries: Wholesale, Retail, Finance, Services, Hospitality, Media, Insurance, Real Estate, Software

Networks: Recruiters Professional Network (RPN)

Robert William James & Associates

(also known as Express Professional Services)
6300 NW Expy
Oklahoma City, OK 73132
(405) 840-5000
Fax: (405) 720-9390
Web: www.rwj.com

Description: Personnel search firm providing comprehensive human resource consulting services to emerging growth Northwest companies.

Key Contact:
Ms. Shirley Webb

Functions: Generalist, General Mgmt., Mfg., Materials, Sales & Mktg., IT

Industries: Generalist, Mfg., Wholesale, Services, Media, Software

Professional Associations: SAO

Branches:
4925 University Dr Ste 166
Huntsville, AL 35816-1849
(866) 721-5627
Fax: (256) 830-5102
Email:
mklambert@huntsvilleal.expresspersonnel.com
Key Contact:
Ms. Reba Sulava

9029 Soquel Ave Ste D
Santa Cruz, CA 95062-2085
(831) 462-4115
(831) 462-4979
Fax: (831) 462-0557
Email: santacruz@rwj.com
Key Contact:
Ms. Lauren Anderson, Manager

2006 N Federal Hwy
Boca Raton, FL 33431
(561) 362-5550
Fax: (561) 362-7854
Email: jean.goetz@expresspersonnel.com
Key Contact:
Mr. Carl Goetz

6807 W Commercial Blvd
Ft. Lauderdale, FL 33319-2116
(954) 721-2429
Fax: (954) 721-2542
Email: jean.goetz@expresspersonnel.com
Key Contact:
Ms. Jean Goetz

4047 Okeechobee Blvd
Habitat Ctr 209
West Palm Beach, FL 33409
(561) 471-8285
Fax: (561) 471-5927
Email: lee.fossett@expresspersonnel.com
Key Contact:
Mr. Lee Fossett

712 W Taylor St
Griffin, GA 30223-2720
(877) 588-8218
Fax: (770) 227-1139
Email: phillip.purser@expresspersonnel.com
Key Contact:
Mr. Phillip Purser

9539 Hwy 92 Ste 140
Woodstock, GA 30188-6423
(770) 928-8786
Fax: (770) 928-8386
Email:
rerobinson@woodstockga.expresspersonnel.com
Key Contact:
Mr. Robert Robinson

1714 G St
Lewiston, ID 83501-2021
(208) 743-6507
(208) 883-4855
Fax: (208) 743-6508
Email: tedi.roach@expresspersonnel.com
Key Contact:
Mr. Tedi Roach, CTS, CPC

608 Eastgate Dr
Carbondale, IL 62901-3304
(618) 549-4404
Fax: (618) 549-8471
Email: sue.endres@expresspersonnel.com
Key Contact:
Ms. Sue Endres

563 N York Rd
Elmhurst, IL 60126-1902
(630) 834-6900
Fax: (630) 834-6950
Email: dan.sepe@expresspersonnel.com
Key Contact:
Mr. Dan Sepe

3000 Professional Dr
Springfield, IL 62703-5912
(217) 528-3000
Fax: (217) 528-3400
Email: kayla.edwards@expresspersonnel.com
Key Contact:
Ms. Kayla Edwards, CPC

977 Lakeview Pkwy Ste 190
Vernon Hills, IL 60061-1429
(847) 816-8422
Email: dan.vantassel@expresspersonnel.com
Key Contact:
Mr. Dan VanTassel

2229 S 3rd St
Terre Haute, IN 47802-3046
(812) 232-9090
Fax: (812) 232-9098
Email: anita.crane@expresspersonnel.com
Key Contact:
Ms. Anita Crane

15707 Hall Rd
Malcolm Township, MI 48044
(810) 566-8400
Fax: (810) 566-7433
Email: joann.wiegand@expresspersonnel.com
Key Contact:
Ms. JoAnn Wiegand

1707 W Big Beaver Rd Ste100
Troy, MI 48084-3510
(248) 643-8900
Fax: (248) 205-7267
Email: troy@rwj.com
Key Contact:
Mr. Marty Rosenau

7101 France Ave S
Edina, MN 55435-4221
(952) 915-2003
Fax: (952) 920-9527
Email: rasannerud@rwj.com
Key Contact:
Mr. Robert Sannerud

812 S Elm St
Owatonna, MN 55060-4061
(507) 451-9396
Fax: (507) 455-0271
Email: rroberts@rwj.com
Key Contact:
Mr. Rick Roberts, Manager

2518 N Broadway
Rochester, MN 55906
(507) 285-9270
Fax: (507) 529-9419
Email: stasler@rwj.com
Key Contact:
Ms. Sheryl Tasler, Manager

1425 Lakeland Dr Ste 250
Jackson, MS 39216-4725
(601) 944-1673
Fax: (601) 353-5014
Email: steve.scully@expresspersonnel.com
Key Contact:
Ms. Jessica Kinard
Mr. Steve Scully

709 Robert E Lee Dr
Tupelo, MS 38801
(662) 842-5500
Fax: (662) 842-5971
Email: jean.parker@expresspersonnel.com
Key Contact:
Jean Parker

601 Business Loop 70 W Ste 128
Parkade Ctr
Columbia, MO 65203
(573) 443-1800
Fax: (573) 499-4473
Email:
msfinnegan.colombiamo@expresspersonnel.com
Key Contact:
Ms. Melinda Finnegan

2569 Rte 10 Galleria 10
Morris Plains, NJ 07950
(973) 898-1001
Fax: (973) 898-1005
Email:
mjkemp@morrisplainsnj.expresspersonnel.com
Key Contact:
Ms. Marianne Kemp

4766 Cornell Rd
Cincinnati, OH 45241-2414
(513) 489-7787
Fax: (513) 489-3069
Email: cdharris@cintioh.expresspersonnel.com
Key Contact:
Mr. Chuck Harris

3453 Great Western Blvd
Columbus, OH 43204-1235
(614) 278-7707
Fax: (614) 278-9965
Email: lori.edwards@expresspersonnel.com
Key Contact:
Ms. Lori Edwards

2741 Miamisburg-Centerville Rd Ste 217
Dayton, OH 45414-3729
(937) 438-4932
Fax: (937) 435-8931
Email: dkortjohn@rwj.com

Key Contact:
Mr. Dick Kortjohn, Manager

2200 N Limestone St Ste 116
Springfield, OH 45503-2692
(937) 399-5323
Fax: (937) 399-2961
Email: lori.edwards@expresspersonnel.com
Key Contact:
Ms. Kristina Dowling
Ms. Lori Edwards

4200 E Skelly Dr Ste 970
Tulsa, OK 74135-3251
(918) 499-5900
Fax: (918) 499-2293
Email: scott.davis@expresspersonnel.com
Key Contact:
Ms. Tracy McCoy
Mr. Scott Davis

901 NW Carlon Ave Ste 3
Bend, OR 97701-2636
(541) 330-1585
Fax: (541) 330-5037
Email: bend@rwj.com
Key Contact:
Ms. Rebecca Kooy
Ms. Connie Worrell-Druliner

977 Garfield Ste 6
Eugene, OR 97402-2750
(541) 988-1138
Fax: (541) 686-0004
Email: pat.murphy@expresspersonnel.com
Key Contact:
Mr. Pat Murphy

10011 SE Division Ste 101
Portland, OR 97266-1351
(503) 253-1200
Fax: (503) 254-1567
Email: richard.yoerk@expresspersonnel.com
Key Contact:
Mr. Richard Yoerk

7401 SW Washo Ct Ste 200
Tualatin, OR 97062
(503) 612-1414
Fax: (503) 612-1410
Email: johns@express-rwj.com
Key Contact:
Mr. John Sullivan

2601 H Elm Hill Pike
Nashville, TN 37214
(615) 391-0966
Fax: (615) 872-0932
Email: rochelle.kelley@expresspersonnel.com
Key Contact:
Mr. Elwin Roe
Ms. Rochelle Kelley

7940 Shoal Creek Ste 210
Austin, TX 78757-7571
(512) 380-0311
Fax: (512) 452-8539
Email: austin@rwj.com
Key Contact:
Mr. Jason Paez
Terry Golden

1405 W Adams
Temple, TX 76504-2449
(254) 771-5595
Fax: (254) 773-5611
Email:
smgromacki@templetx.expresspersonnel.com
Key Contact:
Mr. Frances Zuck
Mr. George Gromacki

6681-I Backlick Rd
Springfield, VA 22150-3009
(703) 866-9675
Fax: (703) 569-6271
Email: art.wenk@expressprofessional.com
Key Contact:
Mr. Art Wenk

8230 Boone Blvd Ste 160
Vienna, VA 22182-2621
(703) 288-0311
Fax: (703) 288-0799
Email: nshewitt@viennava.expresspersonnel.com
Key Contact:
Ms. Natalie Hewitt

1126 S Gold Ste 102
Centralia, WA 98531-3768
(360) 330-9050
Fax: (360) 330-9060
Email: david.gibson@expresspersonnel.com
Key Contact:
Mr. David Gibson

19125 33rd Ave W Ste D
Lynnwood, WA 98036-4735
(425) 775-4903
Fax: (425) 778-3090
Email: donna.knutsen@expresspersonnel.com
Key Contact:
Ms. Donna Knutsen

525 E College Way Ste F
Mt. Vernon, WA 98273
(360) 336-1980
Fax: (360) 336-1540
Email: tara.panek-bringle@expresspersonnel.com
Key Contact:
Ms. Tara Panek-Bringle

1175 Johnson St Ste 208
Coquitlam, BC V3B 7K1
Canada
(604) 944-8530
Fax: (604) 944-0897
Email: brad.braekevelt@expressprofessional.com
Key Contact:
Mr. Brad Braekevelt

50 Queen St N Ste 704
The Commerce House
Kitchener, ON N2H 6P4
Canada
(519) 578-9030
Fax: (519) 578-1121
Email: cmarttini@rwj.com
Key Contact:
Ms. Carol Marttini

2825 Lauzon Pkwy Unit 213
Windsor, ON N8T 3H5
Canada
(519) 988-1115
Fax: (519) 251-1118
Email: cgaudette@rwj.com
Key Contact:
Ms. Colleen Gaudette

Thomas Roberts & Company

PO Box 25733
Cleveland, OH 44125
(216) 883-1245
Fax: (216) 883-0963
Email: trl@thomasroberts.com
Web: www.thomasroberts.com

Description: By the diversity of our associates
backgrounds (human resources, sales, finance and
manufacturing), we are able to work with clients
and candidates on a more in depth level.

Key Contact - Specialty:
Mr. Tom Longano, CPC, President - *Mid-level
management, executive level sales*
Ms. Kathy Kosakowski, Partner - *Mid-level
management, executive level sales*

Salary minimum: $50,000

Functions: Generalist, Sales & Mktg.

Industries: Mfg., Test, Measure Equip., Electronic,
Elec. Components, Wholesale, Pharm Svcs.,
Equip Svcs., E-commerce, Publishing, New
Media, Telecoms, Packaging, Software, Database
SW

Professional Associations: SHRM, SME

Jean Roberts Associates

30 Montgomery St Ste 1255
Jersey City, NJ 07302
(201) 432-4100
(877) 564-5563
Email: pparis@jra2001.com
Web: www.jra2001.org

Description: We are career placement and
outplacement specialists in finance and banking,
from mid level to CEOs. We specialize in the
placement of corporate stock option plan
professionals nationwide.

Key Contact - Specialty:
Mr. Paul Paris, President - *Financial services*
Ms. Sandra Quasarano, Sr Vice President -
Finance, corporate stock plan

Salary minimum: $50,000

Functions: Generalist

Industries: Finance, Banking, Invest. Banking,
Brokers, Misc. Financial, Accounting, HR
Services, Publishing, Broadcast, Film, Call
Centers

Professional Associations: CIA, NASPP, NCEO,
SHRM

Robertson & Associates

300 W Adams St Ste 330
Chicago, IL 60606
(312) 364-9484
Fax: (312) 364-9487

Description: Dedicated to the selection of
professional executives for industry and commerce.
Our 23rd year of serving clients nationwide from
Mid-America.

Key Contact - Specialty:
Mr. Peter C. Chappell, Principal - *Finance, treasury*

Salary minimum: $70,000

Functions: Generalist, Directors, Senior Mgmt.,
Middle Mgmt., Mktg. Mgmt., Finance

Industries: Generalist, Finance, Accounting, Equip
Svcs., Insurance

V Robinson & Company Inc

1125 Grand Blvd Ste 915
Kansas City, MO 64106
(816) 421-4944
Fax: (816) 421-3559
Email: vrinc@aol.com

Description: We contract with organizations to help
fill middle to senior management positions with
highly qualified professionals. Additionally, we
provide counseling and advice during the
interviewing and hiring process.

Key Contact - Specialty:
Mr. H. Jordan White, Manager, Executive Search -
*Information systems, information technology,
engineering, sales & marketing*
Ms. Verneda Robinson, President/CEO -
*Manufacturing, engineering, general
management, sales/marketing*

Salary minimum: $50,000

Functions: Generalist, General Mgmt., Mfg., Sales
& Mktg., HR Mgmt., IT, Engineering

Industries: Generalist, Energy, Utilities

Branches:
726 Armstrong Ave Ste 200
Kansas City, KS 66101
(913) 371-1192
Fax: (913) 371-1179
Email: vrinc@aol.com
Key Contact - Specialty:
Ms. Verneda Robinson - *Utilities, sales &
marketing, management*

The Robinson Group DA Ltd

3 Hawthorn Pkwy Ste 190
Vernon Hills, IL 60061
(847) 327-0700
Email: robgrp@aol.com

Description: Big 5 public accounting/tax &
consulting in state & local, international & hi
wealth.

Key Contact - Specialty:
Mr. Donald Alan Robinson, President - *Public
accounting (Big 6 focus)*

Salary minimum: $55,000

Functions: Finance

Industries: Generalist

Rockwood Associates

PO Box 637
Spring Lake, NJ 07762
(732) 681-2811
Email: rocksearch@aol.com

Description: Functions: sales, trading, finance,
investment analytics and operations. Industries:
natural gas marketers, refiners, utilities, bank/broker
capital markets groups and commodity firms.
Products: oil, gas, electricity, commodities, financial
futures and derivatives.

Key Contact:
Mr. Charles R. Bamford, Partner

Salary minimum: $50,000

Functions: Generalist

Industries: Energy, Utilities, Banking

Rocky Mountain Recruiters Inc

2000 S Colorado Blvd Ste 200
The Annex Bldg
Denver, CO 80222
(303) 296-2000
Fax: (303) 296-2223
Email: miket@rmrecruiters.com
Web: www.rmrecruiters.com

Description: We are Colorado's oldest specialty
recruiting firm. We are specializing in placing
accounting and financial professionals and
executive search.

Key Contact - Specialty:
Mr. Michael Turner, President - *Accounting &
finance*

Salary minimum: $40,000

Functions: General Mgmt., Finance

Industries: Generalist

Professional Associations: AAFA

J P Roddy Consultants

258 S 3rd St Ste 101
Philadelphia, PA 19106
(215) 923-6770
Fax: (215) 923-6773
Email: jproddy@aol.com

Description: Positions at corporate technical centers
and corporate headquarters of automotive divisions
of Fortune 500 companies. Also, key positions at
plant facilities such as general manager, plant
manager, quality manager, materials, manufacturing
and industrial engineering.

Key Contact - Specialty:
Mr. Jack P. Roddy, President/Owner - *Automotive,
plastics*

Salary minimum: $40,000

Functions: Generalist, Middle Mgmt., Production,
Automation, Quality, Materials Plng., R&D,
Engineering

Industries: Generalist, Chemicals, Plastics, Rubber, Metal Products, Machine, Appliance, Motor Vehicles, Mgmt. Consulting, HR Services

Professional Associations: MAAPC

Networks: Inter-City Personnel Assoc (IPA)

J Rodgers & Associates
608 S Washington St Ste 101
Naperville, IL 60540
(630) 961-9143
Fax: (630) 961-3545
Email: j_rodgers@ameritech.net
Web: www.jrodgers.com

Description: We are a small cohesive, results-oriented contingency firm, serving the high-tech and packaging industries for sales, sales, management, and marketing placements.

Key Contact - Specialty:
Mr. Roger Bakken, President - *Office products, high technology, computer hardware & software, sales & marketing*
Ms. Sandy Wasilauski, Recruiter - *Computer industry*

Salary minimum: $30,000

Functions: Sales & Mktg.

Industries: Paper, Printing, Equip Svcs., IT Implementation, Packaging, Software

Professional Associations: BTA, RON

Networks: First Interview Network (FIN)

Rodgers, Ramsey Inc
3401 Louisiana Ste 240
Houston, TX 77002
(713) 529-7010
Fax: (713) 529-2209
Email: gayle@rodgers-ramsey.com
Web: www.rodgers-ramsey.com

Description: We specialize in employee benefits. Pension/retirement and health and welfare professionals are our bread and butter. We work nationwide. This is our 21st year in business. We are well known for discretion and results.

Key Contact - Specialty:
Ms. Gayle Rodgers - *Employee benefits*

Salary minimum: $58,000

Functions: Senior Mgmt., Mktg. Mgmt., Sales Mgmt., Direct Mktg., Benefits, Training

Industries: Generalist, HR Services, Healthcare

Professional Associations: INS

R A Rodriguez and Associates Inc
1326 Henry Brennan Dr
El Paso, TX 79936
(915) 858-1676
Fax: (915) 858-3766
Email: rarjobs@jobcareers.com
Web: www.jobcareers.com

Description: We are a manufacturing executive search firm specializing in the search and recruitment of qualified individuals for the Maquiladora/Twin Plant, international, and US manufacturing industries. Confidentiality is absolutely guaranteed when required.

Key Contact - Specialty:
Mr. Fred W. Smithson, CPC, Executive Vice President - *Manufacturing, international*
Ms. Raquel Rodriguez Smithson, President - *Manufacturing, international*

Salary minimum: $40,000

Functions: General Mgmt., Mfg., Materials, HR Mgmt., Finance, IT, Int'l.

Industries: Mfg., Packaging

Professional Associations: APICS, ASQ, NAPS, SHRM

Networks: Top Echelon Network

Craig Roe & Associates LLC
3711 Ashley Way Ste A
Owings Mills, MD 21117
(410) 654-6636
Fax: (410) 654-6630
Email: sylvia@craigroeassocs.com
Web: www.craigroeassocs.com

Description: We assist clients in locating the best sales talent in the marketplace. We match a candidate's experience, ability and work ethic to the requirements and culture of our client companies.

Key Contact - Specialty:
Ms. Sylvia A. Roe, Vice President - *Sales & marketing, healthcare, medical, biotechnology, pharmaceutical*
Mr. Craig T. Roe, President - *Sales & marketing*

Salary minimum: $45,000

Functions: Middle Mgmt., Mktg. Mgmt., Sales Mgmt.

Industries: Drugs Mfg., Medical Devices, Pharm Svcs., Biotech, Healthcare

Professional Associations: AACC, ASM, BMA, CLMA, NAFE

Roevin Technical People Ltd
2500 Meadowpine Blvd Ste 201
Mississauga, ON L5N 6C4
Canada
(905) 826-4155
Fax: (905) 826-5336
Email: resumes@roevin.ca
Web: www.roevin.ca

Description: Specialists in temporary hire and placement of all levels and disciplines of technical and engineering personnel.

Key Contact - Specialty:
Mr. Ian Wright, President - *Technical, engineering*

Functions: Generalist, Product Dev., Production, Automation, Plant Mgmt., Quality, Productivity, Engineering

Industries: Generalist, Agri., Forestry, Mining, Energy, Utilities, Construction, Mfg., Chemicals, Drugs Mfg., Plastics, Rubber

Roevin Technical People
265 N Front St Ste 411
Sarnia, ON N7T 7X1
Canada
(519) 383-6630
Fax: (519) 383-6631
Email: sthomson@roevin.ca
Web: www.roevin.ca

Description: We specialize in engineering personnel for petrochemical, refineries, manufacturing, industrial, automotive, nuclear power and aerospace. We place CEOs, project managers, project engineers, engineers, designers, draftsmen, cad operators, technicians, technologists, tradesmen, construction, safety, industrial, warehouse, clerical, and support staff.

Key Contact:
Mr. Steve Thomson, President
Ms. Melanie Thomson, Vice President

Functions: Generalist, Mfg., Physicians, Nurses, IT, R&D, Engineering, Int'l.

Industries: Generalist, Construction, Mfg., Aerospace, Healthcare

Gene Rogers Associates Inc
13211 SW 32nd Ct
Davie, FL 33330-4604
(954) 476-0221
Fax: (954) 476-8437
Email: grogers190@aol.com
Web: www.generogers.com

Description: We are specialists in banking, both domestic and international; trust; investments; and mortgages. Our professionals are eminently qualified to assist you in identifying key individuals needed for your organization, or to assist those who are seeking a new career opportunity. Please see our secondary website: www.trustofficers.com.

Key Contact - Specialty:
Ms. Rosa Rogers, Vice President - *International*
Ms. Adrianne Austin, Secretary - *Banking*

Salary minimum: $25,000

Functions: Senior Mgmt., Mktg. Mgmt., HR Mgmt., Finance, Cash Mgmt., Int'l.

Industries: Banking

Networks: National Banking Network (NBN)

Branches:
444 Brickell Ave Ste 51367
Miami, FL 33131
(305) 476-0221
Fax: (954) 476-8437
Email: grogers190@aol.com
Key Contact:
Mr. Gene Rogers

ROI Associates Inc
PO Box 136
Massapequa Park, NY 11762
(516) 541-3800
Fax: (516) 795-2300
Email: info@roisch.com
Web: www.roisch.com

Description: Executive search consultants specializing in manufacturing, quality, materials management, purchasing, systems and manufacturing consulting professionals. Principal is a nationally known speaker on career planning.

Key Contact - Specialty:
Mr. Peter M. Portanova, Partner - *Manufacturing, materials management, purchasing*
Mr. Adele Peters, Research Assistant - *Supply chain*

Salary minimum: $70,000

Functions: General Mgmt., Plant Mgmt., Materials, Distribution

Industries: Mfg., Chemicals, Drugs Mfg., Medical Devices, Metal Products, Banking

Professional Associations: APICS, CLM

Networks: Inter-City Personnel Assoc (IPA)

Roll Int'l
7171 Helsem BND
LB 22
Dallas, TX 75230
(972) 239-3800
Email: mroll@rollintl.com
Web: www.rollintl.com

Description: We are international specialist in mid-to upper-level executive ERP, supply chain management, customer relationship management, enterprise commerce management, private trading exchange, knowledge management, and recruitment encompassing leadership in operations, consulting, sales, marketing, implementation, software development, pre-/post-IPO, and board of director assignments.

Key Contact - Specialty:
Mr. M. A. Roll, President - *IS executives, IS management, IPO, directors, international*

Salary minimum: $80,000

Functions: Directors, Senior Mgmt., Middle Mgmt., Materials Plng., Sales Mgmt., Customer Svc., IT, Systems Analysis, Systems Implem., Mgmt. Consultants

Industries: Generalist, Venture Cap., Mgmt. Consulting, E-commerce, IT Implementation, PSA/ASP, Call Centers, Software, ERP SW

Professional Associations: AAFA, IGAS

Branches:
Lic Arturo Monjaras Soto
Benjamin Franklin No 47
Mexico City, DF 06140
Mexico
Key Contact:
Ms. Cindy Calhoun, Executive Recruiter

Rollins & Associates
4010 Watson Plz Dr Ste 105
Lakewood, CA 90712
(562) 421-6649
Fax: (562) 421-8918
Email: info@rollins-associates.com
Web: www.rollins-associates.com

Description: Import and/or export searches including international sales/marketing, logistics management and support staff, bilingual employees. Also service customs brokerages, freight forwarders and carriers. Searches conducted in North America and Far East.

Key Contact - Specialty:
Ms. Joan E. Rollins, President - *International trade & transportation*

Salary minimum: $30,000

Functions: Senior Mgmt., Middle Mgmt., Admin. Svcs., Purchasing, Distribution, Sales Mgmt., Customer Svc.

Industries: Mfg., Food, Bev., Tobacco, Textiles, Apparel, Soap, Perf., Cosmtcs., Drugs Mfg., Computer Equip., Consumer Elect., Transportation, Wholesale

Romano McAvoy Associates Inc
872 Jericho Tpke
St. James, NY 11780
(631) 265-7878
Fax: (631) 265-1252
Email: ed@mcazoysearch.com
Web: www.mcavoysearch.com

Description: Networked with other quality and responsive recruiting firms with extensive job listing database. Service national firms, as well as Long Island key firms.

Key Contact - Specialty:
Mr. Edward P. McAvoy, Vice President - *Technical software, programming*
Mr. Joseph C. Romano, President - *Human resources, sales & marketing, finance, public relations*

Salary minimum: $40,000

Functions: Generalist, Production, Quality, Purchasing, Advertising, PR, Benefits, Systems Dev.

Industries: Generalist, Computer Equip., Consumer Elect., Aerospace, Software

Networks: National Personnel Assoc (NPA)

Romeo Consulting
309 Fellowship Rd Ste 210
E Gate Ctr
Mt. Laurel, NJ 08054
(856) 642-4054
Fax: (856) 486-0387
Email: promeo@msn.com
Web: www.paulromeo.tripod.com

Description: We provide executive search for the pharmaceutical and biotechnology industries covering disciplines in drug research and development

Key Contact - Specialty:
Mr. Paul C. Romeo, President - *Pharmaceutical, biotechnology, medical devices, physicians, research & development*

Salary minimum: $70,000

Functions: Middle Mgmt., Product Dev., Quality, Physicians, Mktg. Mgmt., Sales Mgmt., R&D

Industries: Drugs Mfg., Biotech

Professional Associations: ACS, ASA, DIA, PDA, RAPS

Rooney Personnel Company
149 Pierce St
Birmingham, MI 48009
(248) 258-5533
(800) 755-5888
Fax: (248) 258-5671
Email: mrooney@careers-hri.com
Web: www.careers-hri.com

Description: The technology to locate managers in any industry fast and affordably. National firm with 20 year history recruiting successful candidates and retaining clients in the hopitality and retail industries.

Key Contact - Specialty:
Mr. Michael Rooney, President - *Hospitality, retail*
Mr. John Rooney - *Hospitality, retail*

Salary minimum: $25,000

Functions: Generalist, Middle Mgmt., Mktg. Mgmt.

Industries: Generalist, Retail, Hospitality, Hotels, Resorts, Clubs, Restaurants

Professional Associations: ACF, MRHRA

Emery A Rose & Associates
5916 Armour Loop SE
Olympia, WA 98513
(360) 413-9300
Fax: (360) 413-9400

Description: Executive recruiting and marketing consulting in aerospace-defense, electronics and telecommunications industries specializing in marketing-sales, engineering, executive and technical professionals.

Key Contact - Specialty:
Mr. Emery Rose, President - *Generalist*

Functions: Generalist

Industries: Generalist

Professional Associations: AFA, AFCEA, NL

The Rose Search Group Inc
7810 Ballantyne Commons Pkwy Ste 300
Charlotte, NC 28277-3408
(704) 543-3150
Fax: (815) 371-2943
Email: info@rosesearch.com
Web: www.rosesearch.com

Description: Clinical and support management positions throughout the healthcare industry including physician placement management, managed care, PHO/MSO, long-term care and hospitals.

Key Contact - Specialty:
Mr. Jim Rosenberger, President - *Healthcare*

Salary minimum: $50,000

Functions: Generalist

Industries: Medical Devices, Pharm Svcs., Healthcare, Hospitals, Long-term Care, Dental,

Physical Therapy, Occupational Therapy, Women's

Networks: National Personnel Assoc (NPA)

Keith Ross & Associates Inc
45 S Park Blvd Ste 250
Glen Ellyn, IL 60137-6203
(630) 858-1000
Fax: (630) 858-9307
Email: lawyers@keithross.com
Web: www.keithross.com

Description: We focus on recruitment and placement of attorneys who specialize in intellectual property, patent, trademark, and copyright law including litigation.

Key Contact - Specialty:
Mr. Keith Ross, President - *Legal*
Mr. Christian Vaughn, Vice President - *Patent attorneys, intellectual property attorneys*
Mr. Mark Vincent, Vice President - *General attorneys*

Functions: Attorneys

Industries: Generalist

Professional Associations: NALSC

Ross Consulting Int'l
630 Freedom Business Ctr Ste 314
King of Prussia, PA 19406
(610) 768-7735
Email: rossconsultingintl@erols.com
Web: www.rcisearch.com

Description: We are a leading insurance and financial services executive search firm with clients throughout the US, Canada and other global markets. Our insurance clients include group, individual, retirement and other businesses and our recruiting concentration extends across all business areas. We represent Fortune, consulting firms and other corporate clients.

Key Contact - Specialty:
Mr. Adam Ross, Managing Partner- *Global Recruiting - Insurance, financial services industries*
Mr. Michael Blumberg, Manager, Candidate Research/Development - *Insurance, financial services industries*

Salary minimum: $40,000

Functions: Generalist

Industries: Finance, Banking, Invest. Banking, Brokers, Venture Cap., Misc. Financial, Services, Mgmt. Consulting, Insurance

Ross Personnel Consultants Inc
161 East Ave Ste 105
Norwalk, CT 06851
(203) 866-2033
Email: rossconsult@snet.net
Web: www.rossconsult.adpebs.com

Description: An executive search and recruiting firm specializing in sales, marketing, systems, training, field engineering and general management in the computer, telecommunications and copier industries.

Key Contact - Specialty:
Mr. Anthony J. Barca, President - *Sales & marketing, office automation*
Mrs. Tracy A. Franzen, Associate - *Sales & marketing, copier, PC's, peripheral, network*
Ms. Dana Tarzia, Research Specialist - *Sales & marketing, copier, PC's, peripheral, network*

Salary minimum: $40,000

Functions: Generalist, Mkt. Research, Mktg. Mgmt., Sales Mgmt., Systems Analysis, Systems Dev., Systems Implem., Systems Support

Industries: Generalist, Computer Equip., Consumer Elect., Equip Svcs., Telecoms, Software

Professional Associations: BTA, CBIA, NAPS

Rossi & Associates Inc
1500 W Georgia St Ste 1400
Vancouver, BC V6G 2Z6
Canada
(604) 683-3755
Fax: (604) 683-3721
Email: donna@rossipeople.com
Web: www.rossipeople.com

Description: Specialists in the recruitment of business-to-business sales executives to a cross section of industries, including telecommunications, information technology. Positions are from president to general business to business teams.

Key Contact - Specialty:
Ms. Donna Rossi, President - *Sales & marketing, business-to-business*
Mr. Bruce Spence, Associate - *Sales recruiter*

Salary minimum: $30,000

Functions: Senior Mgmt., Sales & Mktg., Sales Mgmt.

Industries: Computer Equip., Media, Telecoms, Software

The Rossi Search Group
608 Northlawn Dr
Lancaster, PA 17603
(717) 396-9111
Fax: (717) 396-9786
Email: rosco123@earthlink.net

Description: Focus is on engineering, scientific software, computer hardware and manufacturing professionals, with concentration in polymers, plastics and packaging.

Key Contact - Specialty:
Mr. Alfred F. Rossi, President - *Technology managers, directors, vice presidents, chemical professionals*
Ms. Doris Reitz, Communications Assistant - *Engineers*
Ms. Jeanne Cleary, Research Assistant - *MIS, software, computer hardware professionals*
Ms. Laurie Warner, Senior Consultant - *Chemicals, plastics*

Salary minimum: $50,000

Functions: Generalist, Senior Mgmt., Middle Mgmt., Product Dev., Plant Mgmt., IT, R&D, Engineering

Industries: Generalist, Paper, Chemicals, Plastics, Rubber, Machine, Appliance, Computer Equip., Misc. Mfg., Packaging

---

Roster Technologies Inc
6209 Constitution Dr
Ft. Wayne, IN 46804
(219) 436-6330
Fax: (219) 432-7126
Email: roster1@rosternetwork.com
Web: www.rosternetwork.com

Description: We are extremely automated and research driven. To assure constant quality, we use and teach the Position Matrix (TM), which is a tool described in the book identifying, placing, and evaluating employees.

Key Contact:
Mr. Steve Trimarchi, Operations Manager
Mr. John King, President
Mr. Dennis Payne, Vice President
Mr. Glenn W. Johnson, Vice President

Functions: Generalist, General Mgmt., Mfg., HR Mgmt., Finance

Industries: Generalist

Professional Associations: IACPR

Patricia Roth Int'l
2682 NE 135th St
North Miami, FL 33181
(305) 940-9130
Fax: (305) 940-8572
Email: rothint2@aol.com
Web: www.rothinternational.com

Description: Our twenty-four years of experience in providing highly qualified personnel for the manufacturers and dealers throughout the world enables our client to place the responsibility of locating their new employee in our hands.

Key Contact - Specialty:
Ms. Patricia Roth, President - *Construction equipment, mining equipment, engines*

Functions: Senior Mgmt., Middle Mgmt., Mktg. Mgmt., Sales Mgmt., CFO's, Engineering, Int'l.

Industries: Generalist

Professional Associations: AED, AED

Roth Young of Jacksonville
PO Box 8299
Amelia Island, FL 32035-8299
(904) 321-0606
Email: rothyoungjax@net-magic.net
Web: www.rothyoung.com

Description: National search firm in accounting, finance, food manufacturing, hospitality and retail.

Key Contact - Specialty:
Mr. Anthony Capece, CEO - *Food manufacturing, hospitality, retail, accounting, finance*

Functions: Senior Mgmt., Middle Mgmt., Mfg., Mkt. Research, Customer Svc., Finance

Industries: Construction, Mfg., Wholesale, Retail, Finance, Banking, Pharm Svcs., Accounting, HR Services, Hospitality

---

Roth Young of Tampa Bay Inc
14914 Winding Creek Ct Ste 103B
Tampa, FL 33613
(813) 269-9889
Fax: (813) 269-9919
Email: pbarry97@tampabay.rr.com
Web: www.rothyoungoftampabay.com

Description: Currently the only Roth Young office in the Southeast, offering national Roth Young interchange service.

Key Contact - Specialty:
Mr. P. Barry Cushing, President - *Supermarkets, food (sales, manufacturing), food service, hospitality, wholesale food*
Mr. Dennis Pimm - *Hospitality*

Salary minimum: $20,000

Functions: Generalist, Middle Mgmt., Productivity, Physicians, Allied Health, Sales Mgmt., Training, MIS Mgmt.

Industries: Generalist, Food, Bev., Tobacco, Hospitality

Roth Young of Chicago
1100 W Northwest Hwy Ste 106
Mt. Prospect, IL 60056-2271
(847) 797-9211
Fax: (847) 797-9303
Email: rothyoungchi@aol.com

Description: We are specialists to the food and industrial manufacturing companies. We place in the functions of sales/marketing, operations, engineering, research and development, and quality.

Key Contact:
Ms. Mary Jo Garvey - *Food manufacturing, primary market research*

Mr. Timothy McNally

Salary minimum: $40,000

Functions: Generalist

Industries: Mfg., Food, Bev., Tobacco, Plastics, Rubber, Metal Products, Misc. Mfg., Transportation

Professional Associations: AMA, CLM, IFT, SHRM

Roth Young of Detroit
31275 Northwestern Hwy Ste 116
Farmington Hills, MI 48334
(248) 626-6033
Fax: (248) 626-7079
Email: rydetroit@worldnet.att.net

Description: Executive recruitment specializing in the food, drug, medical and retail industries.

Key Contact - Specialty:
Mr. Samuel Skeegan, President - *Food, drug, medical, retail, pharmaceutical, marketing industries*
Ms. Rebecca Tate, Recruiter - *Hospitality*

Salary minimum: $60,000

Functions: Mktg. Mgmt.

Industries: Mfg., Chemicals, Drugs Mfg., Medical Devices, Packaging, Software, Biotech

---

Roth Young of Minneapolis
6212 Vernon Ct
Minneapolis, MN 55436
(952) 831-6655
Fax: (952) 831-7413
Email: info@rymn.com
Web: www.rymn.com

Description: We are a nationwide recruiting service with offices coast to coast, placing mid- to upper-management positions in all facets of the hospitality, food and retail industries; food, pharmaceutical and consumer sales.

Key Contact - Specialty:
Mr. Donald B. Spahr, President - *Professional and executive position (retail, supermarkets, food wholesales)*

Salary minimum: $40,000

Functions: Generalist, General Mgmt., Senior Mgmt., Middle Mgmt., HR Mgmt.

Industries: Generalist, Food, Bev., Tobacco, Wholesale, Retail, Pharm Svcs., Hospitality

---

Roth Young of Philadelphia
188 Liberty Way
Deptford, NJ 08096
(856) 384-4774
Fax: (856) 384-8074
Email: rothyoungphl@mindspring.com
Web: www.rothyoung.com

Description: We are an executive recruiting firm specializing in all aspects of the food, hospitality, and consumer packaged goods industry.

Key Contact:
Mr. Paul Sundstrom, President - *Food sales, food marketing, food service distribution, hospitality, food service operations*
Mr. Andy Sundstrom, Account Executive

Salary minimum: $40,000

Functions: Generalist, General Mgmt., Mfg., Materials, Sales & Mktg., HR Mgmt., Finance, IT, Engineering

Industries: Food, Bev., Tobacco, Hospitality, Hotels, Resorts, Clubs, Restaurants

---

Roth Young of Long Island
PO Box 7365
Hicksville, NY 11802-7365
(516) 822-6000
Fax: (516) 822-6018
Email: careers@rothyoung-li.com
Web: www.rothyoung-li.com

Description: Specialists in accounting, banking, food industry, healthcare, hospitality, human resources, marketing, operations, retail, sales, technology.

Key Contact - Specialty:
Mr. George T. Jung, President - *Accounting, banking, food industry, healthcare, hospitality*

Roth Young of Pittsburgh
3087 Carson St
Murrysville, PA 15668
(724) 733-5900
Fax: (724) 733-0183
Email: rothyoungpit@cs.com
Web: www.rothyoung-pittsburgh.com

Description: Specialists in healthcare, supermarket and hospitality industries. Healthcare placements: physicians.

Key Contact - Specialty:
Mr. Len Di Naples, President - *Healthcare, food industry, hospitality*

Salary minimum: $25,000

Functions: General Mgmt., Senior Mgmt., Middle Mgmt.

Industries: Food, Bev., Tobacco, Wholesale, Retail, Hospitality

Roth Young of Houston
11999 Katy Fwy Ste 490
Houston, TX 77079
(281) 368-8550
Fax: (281) 368-8560
Email: ryhouston@aol.com
Web: www.rothyounghouston.com

Description: With over 30 years in operation, we have grown to a staff of eight recruiters and three recruiter assistants with operations in restaurant & hospitality, grocery wholesale & retail, retail (non-food) and food & beverage processing.

Key Contact - Specialty:
Mr. Robert Gladstone, President
Mr. Ray Schorejs, Vice President - *Supermarkets, retail, wholesale consumer products*
Mr. Bob O'Dell, Vice President - *Retail*
Mr. Jim Hillier, Division Manager - *Restaurant, hospitality*
Mr. Brian Pearson, Account Executive - *Food (manufacturing, processing)*
Ms. Joy Matheson, Account Executive - *Retail (operations, merchandising)*
Mr. Ron Higgins, Account Executive - *Grocery (operations, merchandising)*
Ms. Teresa McKee, Account Executive - *Beverage processing*
Mr. James Skaggs, Account Executive - *Sales & marketing*
Ms. Sherry Wilson, Account Executive - *Retail*

Salary minimum: $50,000

Functions: Generalist

Industries: Food, Bev., Tobacco, Textiles, Apparel, Consumer Elect., Wholesale, Retail, Accounting, Hospitality, Advertising, Packaging

Roth Young of Seattle
305 111th Ave NE
PO Box 3307
Bellevue, WA 98009
(425) 455-2141
Fax: (425) 455-0067

Email: rothyoung@wolfenet.com
Web: www.rothyoungseattle.com

Description: Our commitment to excellence, understanding our clients business and staff requirements, and creating a sphere of mutual respect, has enabled us to develop many longstanding relationships with companies who appreciate the value of using recruiters for their top management positions.

Key Contact - Specialty:
Mr. David Salzberg, President - *Sales, manufacturing, hospitality, food*

Salary minimum: $40,000

Functions: General Mgmt., Senior Mgmt., Middle Mgmt., Plant Mgmt.

Industries: Generalist, Mfg., Food, Bev., Tobacco, Lumber, Furniture

Professional Associations: NRA, NWFPA, SHRM, WPA

Roth Young of Portland
24 S A St Ste A
Washougal, WA 98671
(360) 835-3136
Email: rothyoungpdx@earthlink.net
Web: www.rothyoung-li.com

Description: We recruit supermarket executives only.

Key Contact - Specialty:
Mr. Bob Mann - *Wholesale, mass merchandiser*

Roth Young of Milwaukee
5215 N Ironwood Rd Ste 201
Milwaukee, WI 53217
(414) 962-7684
Fax: (414) 962-6261
Email: rothyong@execpc.com
Web: www.rothyoungmilwaukee.com

Description: We are an executive search firm specializing in the selection and placement of executive, managerial, and technical professionals with salaries between $50,000 and $200,000 within food related industries to include food ingredients and technology, food manufacturing, and food sales and marketing for over 35 years.

Key Contact - Specialty:
Mr. Thomas E. Brenneman, President/CEO - *General management, manufacturing, technologies*
Ms. Kay S. Boxer, Vice President - *Food (manufacturing, sales & marketing)*

Salary minimum: $50,000

Functions: Generalist, General Mgmt., Mfg., Materials, Sales & Mktg., HR Mgmt., R&D, Engineering

Industries: Generalist, Food, Bev., Tobacco, Non-classifiable

Professional Associations: AMI, APICS, IFT

Rothrock Associates Inc (RAI)
PO Box 698
Cary, NC 27512-0698
(919) 460-0070
Fax: (919) 460-6472
Email: rainc@raijobs.com
Web: www.raijobs.com

Description: We conduct nationwide searches for purchasing, materials, manufacturing and quality engineers, electronics, RF/voice/data communications, computer software programmers/engineers, hardware engineers, computers, networking, electromechanical, and metals industries. We place human resources professionals.

Key Contact:
Mr. T. Hardy Rothrock, Jr., President

Salary minimum: $45,000

Functions: Mfg., Product Dev., HR Mgmt., Engineering

Industries: Mfg., Metal Products, Computer Equip., Consumer Elect., Test, Measure Equip.

Professional Associations: RON

Networks: Top Echelon Network

Rowland Mountain & Associates
2600 Century Pky Ste 120
Atlanta, GA 30345
(404) 325-2189
Fax: (404) 321-1842
Email: shari_combs@rmasales.com
Web: www.rmasales.com

Key Contact:
Mr. Russell D. Mountain, President

Functions: Generalist, Middle Mgmt., Sales & Mktg., Mktg. Mgmt., Sales Mgmt., Mgmt. Consultants

Industries: Generalist, Chemicals, Medical Devices, Plastics, Rubber, Misc. Mfg., Telecoms, Software

Professional Associations: GAPS

Rowlette Executive Search
6025 Frantz Rd
Dublin, OH 43017
(614) 799-2311
Fax: (614) 799-0219
Email: psrowlette@aol.com

Description: We are a retained search firm specializing in the securities industry, with a major emphasis in recruiting investment brokers.

Key Contact - Specialty:
Ms. Patti S. Rowlette, President - *Securities brokerage*

Functions: Generalist

Industries: Brokers

Royal Associates
14011 Ventura Blvd Ste 214-W
Sherman Oaks, CA 91423
(818) 981-1080
Fax: (818) 981-1338
Email: consultants@royalstaff.com
Web: www.royalstaff.com

Description: We have the capability, resources and experienced staff to successfully fill requirements for quality personnel. A state-of-the-art industry-specific search and retrieval system allows access to all employers stored in the database.

Key Contact - Specialty:
Ms. Gail Sullivan, Recruiter - *Management, human resources, administrative*

Salary minimum: $45,000

Functions: General Mgmt., Mfg., Product Dev., Production, Materials, Purchasing, Health Admin., Sales & Mktg., HR Mgmt., Finance

Industries: Generalist

Branches:
3625 Thousand Oaks Blvd
Westlake Village, CA 91362
(805) 373-9909
(818) 889-8689
Fax: (805) 494-4365
Email: trudy@royalstaff.com
Key Contact - Specialty:
Ms. Trudy Shields, Executive Recruiter - *Administrative, human resources, management, insurance, legal*

Royce Ashland Group Inc

1 Rossmoor Dr
Monroe Township, NJ 08831
(609) 409-3601
Fax: (609) 409-3606
Email: royce@myexcel.com
Web: www.royceashland.com

Description: We place sales/marketing professionals, systems people, and information technology professionals.

Key Contact - Specialty:
Mr. Ronald Cali, CPC, President - *Computer, information technology, printing, graphics*

Salary minimum: $65,000

Functions: Sales & Mktg., IT

Industries: Printing, Computer Equip., Equip Svcs., Telecoms, Software

Professional Associations: NJASP

Networks: National Personnel Assoc (NPA)

RTX Inc

(a subsidiary of Veco Corp)
10184 W Belleview Ave Ste 130
Littleton, CO 80127
(877) 904-1600
Fax: (303) 904-1700
Email: rtx-inc@rtx-inc.com
Web: www.rtx-inc.com

Description: Quality-driven recruiting for our parent company. A worldwide consulting engineering firm. We place key talent within the fields of petrochemical, pharmaceutical, biotechnical, O and M, instrumentation. Permanent/contract.

Key Contact - Specialty:
Ms. Paige Robertson, Manager - *Engineering*
Mr. John Evans, Recruiter - *Instrumentation, controls, PLC/DCS programming*

Salary minimum: $40,000

Functions: Generalist, Production, Plant Mgmt., Quality, Purchasing, Engineering, Architects, Int'l.

Industries: Generalist, Construction, Food, Bev., Tobacco, Drugs Mfg., Test, Measure Equip., Biotech

Professional Associations: ISA

The Rubicon Group

7553 E Santa Catalina
Scottsdale, AZ 85255
(602) 515-9225
Fax: (602) 515-9213
Email: rubicongroup@aol.com

Description: Confidential search for life and health actuaries, pension actuaries and casualty actuaries. National and international search.

Key Contact - Specialty:
Mr. Martin Jacobs - *Administrative*
Ms. Judith Jacobs - *General management*

Salary minimum: $40,000

Functions: Generalist, Middle Mgmt., Health Admin., Mktg. Mgmt., HR Mgmt., Cash Mgmt., Mgmt. Consultants

Industries: Generalist, Misc. Financial, Insurance, Healthcare

Ruderfer & Company Inc

908 Pompton Ave Ste A-2
Cedar Grove, NJ 07009
(973) 857-2400
Fax: (973) 857-4343
Email: search@ruderfer.com

Key Contact - Specialty:
Mr. Irwin A. Ruderfer, CPC, President - *Regulatory affairs*
Ms. Nan Kanoff, Director-Physician/Biopharm
Mr. Richard Levy, Director-Financial/MIS
Ms. Alice Osur - *Marketing*
Ms. Alice Osur, Manager of Marketing
Ms. Bonnie Roseman, Director-Marketing
Mr. Harold Tapler - *Technical, R&D, quality*
Dr. Louise Greenberg - *Clinical research-pharmacy*

Salary minimum: $50,000

Functions: Generalist, Mfg., Healthcare, Sales & Mktg., HR Mgmt., Finance, MIS Mgmt., R&D

Industries: Generalist, Chemicals, Drugs Mfg., Medical Devices, Accounting, HR Services, Advertising, Biotech

Professional Associations: AAAS, DIA, RAPS

Susan Rudich

20 E 9th St
New York, NY 10003
(212) 228-8126
(212) 989-7891

Description: Over 35 years' experience, lecturer, advisor art schools and associations. Former New York state sole textile placement specialist.

Key Contact - Specialty:
Ms. Susan Rudich, President - *Creative textiles, design, development*

Salary minimum: $25,000

Functions: Graphic Artists

Industries: Textiles, Apparel

Louis Rudzinsky Associates Inc

PO Box 640
Lexington, MA 02420
(781) 862-6727
Fax: (781) 862-6868
Email: lra@lra.com
Web: www.lra.com

Description: Established in 1968, serving technology companies in optics, electronics, electro-optics, fiber optics, software, systems, solid state devices and instrumentation. Covering engineering, R&D, marketing, sales and general management, nationwide.

Key Contact - Specialty:
Mr. Howard Rudzinsky, Senior Vice President - *Photonics, optics, imaging, solid state, semiconductor*
Mr. Jeff Rudzinsky, Senior Vice President - *Hardware, software, systems, test engineers (commercial, DOD)*
Mr. Mark Joyce, Consultant - *Hardware, software, mechanical, electrical*

Salary minimum: $40,000

Functions: Generalist, Product Dev., Production, Systems Analysis, Systems Dev., Systems Implem., R&D, Engineering

Industries: Generalist, Printing, Medical Devices, Computer Equip., Test, Measure Equip., Aerospace, Software

Professional Associations: EMA, MPPC

Networks: National Personnel Assoc (NPA)

Rush Personnel Service

PO Box 2542
East Peoria, IL 61611-0542
(309) 699-4184
Fax: (877) 699-4186
Email: randall@rushpersonnel.com
Web: www.rushpersonnel.com

Description: A generalist supplying qualified, pre-screened candidates to select client companies to satisfy their management and technical needs.

Key Contact - Specialty:
Mr. Randall Rush, CPC, Owner - *Generalist*

Salary minimum: $25,000

Functions: Generalist

Industries: Generalist

Networks: Top Echelon Network

Russillo/Gardner

60 State St Ste 700
Boston, MA 02109
(617) 350-8600
(617) 345-0700
Fax: (617) 973-5745
Email: tom@russillogardner.com
Web: www.russillogardner.com

Description: Twenty one years' serving insurance/risk management/risk financing/employee benefits and information technology/software engineering industries for executive-level management and senior-level technical specialists. All the firm's consultants have substantial experience in the fields they represent.

Key Contact - Specialty:
Mr. Thomas P Russillo, Partner - *Insurance, reinsurance, risk management, risk financing*
Mr. Richard E Gardner, Partner - *Information technology, financial, software engineering*

Salary minimum: $100,000

Functions: General Mgmt., Mktg. Mgmt., Sales Mgmt., Benefits, Finance, CFO's, Risk Mgmt., IT, Mgmt. Consultants, Environmentalists

Industries: Generalist, Insurance, Software

K Russo Associates Inc

151 Railroad Ave Fl 1
Greenwich, CT 06830
(203) 552-0100
Fax: (203) 552-0865
Email: solutions@krussoassociates.com
Web: www.krussoassociates.com

Description: We are a specialist firm focusing on executive search for the human resource and public relations arena. The firm also offers human resource consulting including competency modeling and organizational analysis.

Key Contact - Specialty:
Ms. Karen Russo, Principal - *Human resources, public relations*
Ms. Toni Mahr, Senior Consultant - *Human resources, public relations*
Ms. Nancy Morgan, Consultant - *Human resources*

Salary minimum: $40,000

Functions: Generalist, PR, HR Mgmt., Benefits, Personnel, Training

Industries: Generalist, Mfg., Food, Bev., Tobacco, Finance, HR Services, Hospitality, Media, Advertising

Professional Associations: CAPS, PINNACLE, PRSA, SHRM, WIM, WPO

RWK & Associates

PO Box 917523
Longwood, FL 32791
(407) 774-9004
Fax: (407) 774-0966
Email: rwkassociates@mindspring.com
Web: www.rkwassociates.com

Description: Experienced executive recruiter and researcher specializing in executive senior positions.

Key Contact - Specialty:
Ms. Rona Kaplan - *Generalist*

Salary minimum: $50,000

Functions: Generalist

Industries: Construction, Chemicals, Drugs Mfg., Misc. Financial, Pharm Svcs., Accounting, HR Services, Insurance, Biotech, Healthcare

J Ryan & Associates Inc
1119 Huntington Ln
Safety Harbor, FL 34695
(727) 791-8002
Fax: (727) 791-8971
Email: jryan@tampabay.rr.com

Description: Specializing in all areas of manufacturing, to include, but not limited to: accounting and finance, administration, human resources, traffic and distribution, engineering, production, global sourcing, product management, product development, purchasing, contract management, quality control and assurance, design, merchandising, marketing, brand and category, research and strategy, sales, and sales management. Consumer goods, consumer packaged goods, apparel, textiles, automotive, plastics, and rubber. Services such as telecommunications, insurance, banking.

Key Contact - Specialty:
Ms. Nancy Kahn, President - *Apparel manufacturing, telecommunications, consumer goods*

Salary minimum: $35,000

Functions: Production, Plant Mgmt., Quality, Purchasing, Sales & Mktg., HR Mgmt., Finance, Engineering

Industries: Food, Bev., Tobacco, Textiles, Apparel, Chemicals, Soap, Perf., Cosmtcs., Medical Devices, Electronic, Elec. Components, Pharm Svcs., Telecoms, Biotech

Professional Associations: SHRM

John Ryan Associates LLC
450 7th Ave Ste 2906A
New York, NY 10123
(212) 279-5151
Fax: (212) 279-3377
Email: john@john-ryan.com

Description: Over 15 years' experience as a resource provider to the major banks, brokerage and Fortune 500 companies. Providing local and foreign resources at highly competitive rates quickly and efficiently, in addition to full-time placement of IT professionals.

Key Contact - Specialty:
Mr. John Mark Arceri, Director - *Data processing, client/server, brokerage, banking, fortune 100*
Mr. Ryan Richter, Director - *Data processing, client/server, brokerage, banking, fortune 100*

Salary minimum: $60,000

Functions: Generalist, Directors, MIS Mgmt., Systems Analysis, Systems Dev., Systems Implem., Systems Support, Mgmt. Consultants

Industries: Generalist, Banking, Invest. Banking, Brokers, Mgmt. Consulting, HR Services

Networks: National Consulting Network (NCN)

The Ryan Charles Group Inc
2151 W Hillsboro Blvd Ste 203
Deerfield Beach, FL 33442
(954) 421-9112
Fax: (954) 428-4940
Email: contact@rcgfl.com
Web: www.ryancharlesgroup.com

Description: A creative nationwide recruiting firm that provides personalized, results-oriented service to a select group of client companies. Committed to excellence and cost effective results.

Key Contact - Specialty:
Mr. Norman D. St. Jean, President - *Generalist*
Ms. Joan Harris, Search Consultant - *Generalist*

Salary minimum: $40,000

Functions: General Mgmt., Mfg., Materials, Sales & Mktg., HR Mgmt., Finance, Int'l.

Industries: Mfg.

Networks: Inter-City Personnel Assoc (IPA)

Branches:
2021 Midwest Rd Ste 200
Oak Brook, IL 60523
(773) 233-9111
Email: contact@rcgfl.com
Key Contact:
Mr. N. St. Jean, President

Ryan Executive Search & Outplacement
P H 1615
Mercantil Plz
San Juan, PR 00918
(787) 766-1666
Fax: (787) 766-1467
Email: ryan@isla.net
Web: www.ryanrecruiters.com

Description: Full service recruiting firm of Certified personnel Consultants; executive search, headhunters, recruiters, consultants, bilingual executives, outplacement, employment, occupation, jobs, work, service, positions, English/Spanish professionals, careers, candidates, hire, global experience, career change, benchmarking, personnel,outsourcing.

Key Contact - Specialty:
Ms. Evelyn Ryan, CPC, CEO - *Management (upper-level)*
Mr. Terence L. Ryan, President - *Sales & marketing*
Ms. Jennifer Ryan, CPC, Vice President/Public Affairs - *New business*
Ms. Elisa Favale, CPC, Partner/Senior Finance Consultant - *Finance*
Ms. Madeline Figueroa, MA, Partner/Senior Human Resources - *Human resources, outplacement*

Salary minimum: $20,000

Functions: Generalist

Industries: Generalist

Professional Associations: AMA, NAPS, PRMA, SHRM, SME

Networks: Career Partners Int'l

Ryan, Miller & Associates
4601 Wilshire Blvd Ste 225
Los Angeles, CA 90010
(323) 938-4768
Fax: (323) 857-7009
Email: lee@ryanmiller.com
Web: www.ryanmiller.com

Description: An executive search firm specializing in the recruitment of accounting, banking and financial professionals; national and international level.

Key Contact - Specialty:
Mr. Lee Ryan, President - *Generalist, CPAs, MBAs*
Mr. Michael O'Connell, Treasurer - *Generalist, CPAs, MBAs*

Salary minimum: $50,000

Functions: Finance, CFO's, Budgeting, Cash Mgmt., Taxes, M&A

Industries: Generalist

Professional Associations: AAFA, AAHCPA

Branches:
790 E Colorado Blvd 506
Pasadena, CA 91101
(626) 568-3100
Fax: (626) 568-3772
Web: www.aafa.com
Key Contact - Specialty:
Mr. Roger Miller, President - *Banking, corporate finance, investment banking*

Ryan-Allen & Associates
732 Devon Ct
San Diego, CA 92109
(858) 576-0737
Fax: (858) 488-2621
Email: rya@myexcel.com

Description: Specialize in the recruitment of professionals in accounting, banking, finance and human resources.

Key Contact - Specialty:
Ms. Sheila R. Hawley, CPC, President - *Executive search consultant*

Functions: Generalist, HR Mgmt., Finance, CFO's

Industries: Generalist, Finance, Banking, Accounting, HR SW

Professional Associations: AAFA, SHRM

Networks: National Banking Network (NBN)

Ryman, Bell, Green & Michaels Inc
PO Box 741
Fulshear, TX 77441-0741
(281) 232-2311
Fax: (281) 232-2427
Email: rbgm@nstci.com

Description: National and international search firm representing Fortune 5000 and law firms of all sizes.

Key Contact - Specialty:
Mr. Phil Forman, President
Mr. David Broadway, Chair-Legal Division
Ms. Roseanne Ellis, Chair-Hi-Tech - *Senior high-tech*

Salary minimum: $150,000

Functions: Generalist

Industries: Finance, Invest. Banking, Brokers, Services, Legal

S C Int'l Ltd
1315 Butterfield Rd Ste 224
Downers Grove, IL 60515
(630) 963-3033
Fax: (630) 963-3170
Email: search@scinternational.com
Web: www.scinternational.com

Description: Specialists in insurance and employee benefits recruitment: actuaries, claims, underwriting, benefits consultants. Additionally healthcare professionals.

Key Contact - Specialty:
Mr. Scott Rollins, President - *Actuaries*

Salary minimum: $40,000

Functions: Generalist, HR Mgmt.

Industries: Generalist, HR Services, Insurance, Healthcare

Professional Associations: IABC

S P Associates Inc
(formerly known as Amcell Assoc)
5970 Fairview Rd Ste 512
Charlotte, NC 28210
(704) 643-7250
Fax: (704) 643-1249
Email: spassociates@mindspring.com
Web: www.spassociates.com

Description: All functions only in following industries: textile and fibers, non-woven, pulp and paper mills, packaging, high exotic metals, pharmaceutical, data processing and plastics.

Key Contact - Specialty:
Mr. A. J. Edahl
Mr. Gabe C. Hill, III - *Textiles, non-wovens*

Salary minimum: $30,000

Functions: General Mgmt.

Industries: Mfg., Textiles, Apparel, Paper, Printing, Chemicals, Drugs Mfg., Medical Devices, Plastics, Rubber, Packaging

Networks: National Personnel Assoc (NPA)

S R & Associates
5001 Birch St
Newport Beach, CA 92660
(949) 756-3271
Fax: (949) 756-6565
Email: sraross@srassociatesinc.com
Web: www.srassociatesinc.com

Description: We are a HR corporation focused on recruiting for the high-technology "vendors" only. We place in all sales' fields and related categories, up to and including VP of sales. We place additional focus in professional services management including implementation and practice managers and consultants.

Key Contact - Specialty:
Mr. Steve Ross, President/Founder - *Sales management, account executives, vendors only*

Salary minimum: $75,000

Functions: Sales & Mktg., Sales Mgmt.

Industries: Mfg., Computer Equip., Services, Mgmt. Consulting, Communications, Software, Biotech

The Saddlebrook Group LLC
420 NW 11th Ave Ste 1101
Portland, OR 97209
(971) 544-0952
Email: jobs@saddlebrookgroup.com
Web: www.saddlebrookgroup.com

Description: We are an executive search firm focused on the medical device, pharmaceutical, and biotech industries, with an emphasis on searches for sales and marketing executives, information systems managers, financial managers, and general managers.

Key Contact:
Mr. Michael Stringer, Principal

Salary minimum: $75,000

Functions: Generalist

Industries: Pharm Svcs., Biotech, Healthcare

R S Sadow Associates
24 Heather Dr
Somerset, NJ 08873
(732) 545-4550
Fax: (732) 545-0797
Email: rssadow@aol.com

Description: Operates as a contingency search office. Unsolicited resumes accepted. Appointment required.

Key Contact - Specialty:
Mr. Raymond Sadow, President - *Accounting, information technology*

Salary minimum: $30,000

Functions: Mfg., Finance, IT, Systems Analysis, Systems Dev., Systems Support, Network Admin., DB Admin., R&D, Engineering

Industries: Generalist, Mfg.

Sage Employment Recruiters
127 E Windsor Ave
Elkhart, IN 46514
(219) 264-1126
Fax: (219) 264-1128

Description: Industries with wheels, manufactured housing, marine, recreation vehicles, van conversion, truck/trailer body and the supply companies for these industries. Effective, discreet approach gets assignment accomplished in weeks not months. Recognized for confidentiality.

Key Contact:
Mr. Frank Alvey, Partner - *Industries with wheels, marine, supplier companies*
Mr. John Dwire, President
Mr. John McGuire, Partner - *Recreational vehicle, van conversions*
Mr. Bill Hudson, Partner - *Manufactured housing & related suppliers*
Ms. Ella Schaeffer, Office Manager
Mr. Jean Messner, Partner

Salary minimum: $40,000

Functions: Generalist, Mfg., Materials, Sales Mgmt., Finance, IT, Mgmt. Consultants

Industries: Generalist, Metal Products, Motor Vehicles

Saito & Associates
620 Newport Center Dr Ste 1100
Newport Beach, CA 92660
(949) 721-6655
Fax: (949) 721-6656
Email: scott@saitoassociates.com

Description: Specialists in executive search assisting real estate organizations identify, attract and retain top candidates for middle and senior-level management opportunities.

Key Contact - Specialty:
Mr. Scott T. Saito, Owner - *Commercial, industrial, land, retail, residential*

Salary minimum: $50,000

Functions: Generalist, Directors, Senior Mgmt., Middle Mgmt., Finance, CFO's, M&A

Industries: Generalist, Construction, Accounting, Real Estate

Sales & Marketing Search
100 Cummings Ctr Ste 453H
Beverly, MA 01915
(978) 921-8282
Fax: (978) 921-8283
Email: sms@smsearch.com
Web: www.smsearch.com

Description: We recruit exclusively in the sales and marketing arenas for high-technology companies.

Key Contact:
Ms. Betsy Harper, Managing Partner/CEO
Mr. Donald Harper, Senior Consultant - *International*
Ms. Michelle Theriault, Senior Recruiter

Salary minimum: $100,000

Functions: Sales & Mktg.

Industries: Software, Database SW, Networking, Comm. SW, System SW

Professional Associations: MAPS, MITEF, MPPC, SBANE

Sales & Search Associates Inc
3 Cashie Dr
Hertford, NC 27944
(252) 426-2300
Fax: (252) 426-2305
Email: eschlueter@inteliport.com

Description: We place professional sales in software, Internet, DataCom, and e-Commerce all over the US. We work with the Fortune 500.

Key Contact - Specialty:
Ms. Elaine Schlueter, President - *Software, data communications, sales, technical support, sales management*
Ms. Kathryn Tenenholz, Vice President - *Software, hardware, sales, sales support*
Mr. David Lund, Vice President - *Internet, intranet, sales, sales support*

Salary minimum: $80,000

Functions: Generalist, Sales Mgmt.

Industries: Generalist, Computer Equip., Software

Sales Advantage
2101 W Commercial Blvd Ste 3000
Ft. Lauderdale, FL 33309
(954) 351-9461
Fax: (954) 776-5855
Email: mkaufman@salesadvantage.com
Web: www.salesadvantage.com

Description: We target professionals in the top 20% of their respective fields to ensure that your company hires the candidate with the most positive impact on your bottom line.

Key Contact - Specialty:
Mr. Matt Kaufman, Vice President - *Sales & marketing*

Salary minimum: $50,000

Functions: Sales & Mktg.

Industries: Food, Bev., Tobacco, Soap, Perf., Cosmtcs., Medical Devices, Computer Equip., Services, Mgmt. Consulting, E-commerce, IT Implementation, Media, Software

Networks: First Interview Network (FIN)

Sales Consultants Int'l
200 Public Sq Fl 31
Cleveland, OH 44114-2301
(216) 696-1122
Fax: (216) 696-3221
Email: abs@mrinet.com
Web: www.brilliantpeople.com

Description: Search and recruitment - mid- to senior management and professional. Also provides interim staffing, assessment programs, and international capability and videoconferencing services. Full range of staffing services.

Key Contact:
Mr. Allen Salikof, President/CEO
Mr. William E. Aglinsky, Senior Vice President/CFO
Mr. Robert A. Angell, VP-Franchise Sales
Mr. Donald L. Goldman, VP-General Counsel/Assistant Secretary
Mr. Jerry R. Hill, VP-Training
Mr. Gary P. Williams, SVP-Franchise Development
Mr. Micahel DeMuch, Vice President-Marketing
Mr. Neil Fox, Vice President/CIO
Mr. George Bojalad, VP-Human Resources
Mr. David Campeas, VP-Company Office Operations
Mr. Michael Rode, VP/Associate Counsel

Salary minimum: $45,000

Functions: Generalist

Industries: Generalist

Professional Associations: IFA

Branches:
PO Box 13144
Huntsville, AL 35802
(256) 882-5011
Fax: (256) 882-5015
Email: rdavidson@midsouthconsultant.com

Key Contact:
Mr. Bob Davidson

6343-B Airport Blvd Ste 3
Mobile, AL 36608-3163
(334) 342-8811
Fax: (334) 342-8817
Email: geraldg@sc-mobile.com
Key Contact:
Mr. Gerald Grovenstein, Manager

4300 N Miller Rd Ste 214
Scottsdale, AZ 85251
(602) 424-7958
Fax: (602) 424-3960
Email: johara@scscottsdalemetro.com
Web: www.scscottsdalemetro.com
Key Contact:
Mr. Jim O'Hara, Co-Manager
Mr. Bob Lasker, Co-Manager

7950 E Redfield Rd Ste 179
Scottsdale, AZ 85260
Key Contact:
Mr. Louis Bunz
Ms. Esther Bunz

8283 N Hayden Rd Ste 190
Scottsdale, AZ 85253
(480) 443-3343
Fax: (480) 443-0526
Email: betty@fcaserta.com
Key Contact:
Mr. Andrew Caserta
Mr. Frank Caserta

40 W Baseline Rd Ste 104
Tempe, AZ 85283-1259
(480) 897-4747
Fax: (480) 897-4272
Key Contact:
Mr. Tim Kocsis, Co-Manager
Mr. Ken Martinez, Co-Manager

2131 Palomar Airport Rd 300
Alliance Business Ctr
Carlsbad, CA 92009
(760) 431-5163
Fax: (760) 431-5164
Email: scretail@aol.com
Key Contact:
Mr. Jim A. Yager, General Manager
Mr. Jerry Harris, Manager

100 Corporate Pointe Ste 380
Culver City, CA 90230
(310) 670-3040
Fax: (310) 670-2981
Email: info@mrila.com
Key Contact:
Mr. Mike Bryant, CSAM, Manager

5715 N West Ave Ste 101
Fresno, CA 93711
(559) 432-3700
Fax: (559) 432-9937
Email: ron@mri-fresno.com
Key Contact:
Mr. Ron L. Johnson, Manager

2081 Business Center Dr Ste 290
Irvine, CA 92612-1117
(949) 474-9222
Fax: (949) 474-8222
Email: info@scirvine.com
Key Contact:
Mr. Mark Tabbert, Manager

1055 Torrey Pines Rd Ste 203-205
La Jolla, CA 92037
(858) 456-1412
Fax: (858) 456-7271
Web: www.axisexecutivesearch.com
Key Contact:
Mr. Ulf Schaefer

PO Box 337
Los Olivos, CA 93441
(805) 693-8027
Fax: (805) 693-8428

Key Contact:
Mr. Gary Earle

103 Providence Mine Rd Ste 201
Nevada City, CA 95959
(530) 478-9300
Fax: (530) 478-9313
Email: confidential@mrihightech.com
Web: www.mrihightech.com
Key Contact:
Mr. Cameron Hawley

74 W Neal St Ste 200
Pleasanton, CA 94566-6632
(925) 461-6980
Fax: (925) 461-6986
Email: scpleas!manager@mrinet.com
Key Contact:
Mr. David G. Gaulden, Manager

3550 Camino Del Rio N Ste 104
San Diego, CA 92108
(760) 720-9666
Fax: (760) 720-9966
Email: sccarlsbad@earthlink.net
Web: www.sccarlsbad.com
Key Contact:
Ms. Carmine Malanga

6540 Lusk Blvd Ste C 254
San Diego, CA 92121-2782
(858) 450-6006
Fax: (858) 450-6007
Key Contact:
Mr. Marty Pierce, Managing Director

126 W 25th St Ste 200
San Mateo, CA 94403
(650) 548-4800
Fax: (650) 548-4805
Email: admin@mrica.com
Web: www.mrica.cm
Key Contact:
Ms. Crystal Z. S. Parsons
Mr. Michael Shaffer

2425 Cleveland Ave Ste 175
Santa Rosa, CA 95403-2910
(707) 575-3699
Fax: (707) 575-3644
Email: info@scsantarosa.com
Web: www.scsantarosa.com
Key Contact:
Mr. Russ Maney, Manager

300 Union Blvd Ste 370
Lakewood, CO 80228
(303) 988-1011
Fax: (303) 988-1699
Email: mmcnamara@telecomrecruiter.com
Key Contact:
Mr. Michael McNamara, Manager

326 W Main St Ste 202
Milford, CT 06460
(203) 876-4949
Fax: (203) 876-4959
Email: lewismri@aol.com
Web: www.htinfo.com/mriscnh.htm
Key Contact:
Ms. Sarah S. Fink, Co-Manager
Mr. Ronald L. Fink, Co-Manager

2139 Silas Deane Hwy Ste 206A
Rocky Hill, CT 06067-2336
(860) 563-5171
Fax: (860) 563-2305
Email: resume@schartford.com
Key Contact:
Mr. Frederick O. Raley, Manager

196 Danbury Rd
Wilton, CT 06897-4029
(203) 761-1288
Fax: (203) 761-1258
Email: apratt@scwilton.com
Key Contact:
Mr. Andy E. Pratt, Manager

375 Douglas Ste 2009
Altamonte Springs, FL 32714-3315
(407) 786-1650
Fax: (407) 786-1710
Email: mri@activecom.net
Web: www.salesconsultantsfl.20m.com
Key Contact:
Mr. Michael Bernstein

9900 W Sample Rd Ste 407
Coral Springs, FL 33065-4436
(954) 340-8000
Fax: (954) 340-8300
Email: scijobs@bellsouth.net
Key Contact:
Mr. Frank Braile, Jr., Manager

16430 Millstone Cir Ste 201
Ft. Myers, FL 33908
(941) 437-6395
Fax: (941) 437-6399
Email: scnaples@aol.com
Key Contact:
Mr. Virgil L. Metcalf, Manager

2600 Maitland Center Pkwy Ste 295
Maitland, FL 32751-7227
(407) 660-0089
Fax: (407) 660-2066
Email: tgoodman@prioritysearch.com
Web: www.prioritysearch.com
Key Contact:
Ms. Arlene Brown, Co-Manager
Mr. Thomas Brown, Co-Manager

150 S Pine Island Rd Ste 240
Plantation, FL 33324
(954) 475-2525
Fax: (954) 475-9383
Email: info@scplantation.com
Key Contact:
Mr. Cliff Bass

500 N Westshore Blvd Ste 530
Tampa, FL 33609
(813) 289-9355
(888) 289-3555
Fax: (813) 282-3449
Email: dsmith@mritampa.com
Web: www.mritampa.com
Key Contact:
Mr. Dan Smith, Manager

3440 Preston Ridge Rd Ste 450
Alpharetta, GA 30005
(678) 879-1005
Fax: (678) 879-1030
Email: mriatlanta@earthlink.net
Key Contact:
Mr. Phillip Sciro

1303 Hightower Trl Ste 150
Atlanta, GA 30350
(770) 668-0000
Fax: (770) 668-0999
Email: bsillins@scnorthridge.com
Web: www.financialrecruiters.com
Key Contact - Specialty:
Mr. Benjamin Sillins, Managing Director -
Financial services

8800 Roswell Rd Ste 248
Atlanta, GA 30350
(770) 992-9200
Fax: (770) 992-1501
Email: office@mrigeorgia.com
Key Contact:
Mr. Nate Schemo, Manager

3250 Peachtree Industrial Blvd Ste 105
Duluth, GA 30096
(770) 813-3320
Fax: (770) 813-8776
Email: gb@mriexecsearch.com
Web: www.mriexecsearch.com
Key Contact:
Mr. Lee Williamson
Mr. George Bradbury

45 W Crossville Rd Ste 514
Roswell, GA 30075
(770) 650-0835
Fax: (770) 650-0836
Email: mderby@scroswell.com
Web: www.scroswell.com
Key Contact:
Ms. Cheryl Derby
Mr. Michael Derby

345 Bobwhite Ct Ste 215
Boise, ID 83706
(208) 336-6770
Fax: (208) 336-2499
Email: mriboise@mriboise.com
Web: www.mriboise.com
Key Contact:
Mr. Craig Alexander, CSAM, Manager

707 N East St Ste 4
Bloomington, IL 61701
(309) 829-6000
Fax: (309) 827-3023
Email: scbloom@scbloomington.com
Key Contact:
Ms. Lyn M. Edwards, Co-Owner/Manager
Mr. Jack O. Edwards, Co-Owner/Manager

130 N Lagrange Rd Ste 315
La Grange, IL 60525
(708) 354-2023
Fax: (708) 354-2866
Email: shereck@aol.com
Key Contact:
Mr. Mike Shereck

300 W Broadway Ste 36
Omni Ctr
Council Bluffs, IA 51503-9030
(712) 325-6884
Fax: (712) 325-6691
Email: receivable@scriverside.com
Web: www.scriverside.com
Key Contact:
Mr. Jim Finocchiaro, Manager

1365 N Ctr Point Rd Ste B
Hiawatha, IA 52233
(319) 743-9830
Fax: (319) 294-8882
Key Contact:
Mr. Justin Saylor

9401 Indian Creek Pkwy Ste 920
Corporate Woods Bldg 40
Overland Park, KS 66210-2098
(913) 661-9200
Fax: (913) 661-9030
Email: mriopks@aol.com
Key Contact:
Mr. Danny Buda, General Manager
Mr. Bob Belcher, CSAM, Manager

100 N Broadway Ste 405
Wichita, KS 67202
(316) 265-2520
Fax: (316) 265-9105
Key Contact:
Mr. Marvin Reimer, Manager

2237 S Acadian Thruway Ste 707
Baton Rouge, LA 70808
(225) 928-2212
Fax: (225) 928-1109
Email: info@pharmacyjobs.com
Web: www.pharmacyjobs.com
Key Contact:
Mr. Gregory L. Fell, Manager

3527 Ridgelake Dr
PO Box 6605
Metairie, LA 70009
(504) 831-7333
Fax: (504) 838-9009
Email: pmlno1@aol.com
Key Contact:
Mr. Edward N. Ameen, General Manager
Mr. Paul M. Luce, CSAM, Manager

575 S Charles St Ste 401
Baltimore, MD 21201
(410) 727-5750
Fax: (410) 727-1253
Email: mms@salesconsultants.org
Web: www.salesconsultants.org
Key Contact:
Mr. Steven R. Braun, Manager

10320 Little Patuxent Pkwy Ste 511
Columbia, MD 21044-3346
(410) 992-4900
Fax: (410) 992-4905
Email: sccolmd@earthlink.net
Key Contact:
Mr. David S. Rubin, Manager

508 Beaumont Rd
Silver Spring, MD 20904
(301) 731-4201
Fax: (301) 731-4200
Email: thummel@erols.com
Key Contact:
Mr. Thomas F. Hummel, Manager

300 Brickstone Sq Fl 9
Andover, MA 01810
(978) 475-5500
Fax: (978) 475-9116
Email: rstockard@scboston.com
Key Contact:
Mr. Robert G. Stockard, General Manager
Ms. Maria Massaro, Manager

314 Gifford St Unit 4
Falmouth, MA 02540
(508) 540-2145
Fax: (508) 540-1541
Key Contact:
Ms. Pamela Alden
Mr. Thomas Fitzpatrick

31 Schoosett St Rte 139 Ste 305
Pembroke, MA 02359
(781) 826-0098
Fax: (781) 826-9193
Key Contact:
Mr. Edward Kacik

180 State Rd Ste 5-L
PO Box 420
Sagamore Beach, MA 02562-0420
(508) 888-8704
Fax: (508) 888-9265
Email: sciofcc@aol.com
Key Contact:
Mr. Edward T. Cahan, Manager

2860 Carpenter Rd Ste 300
Sparrow Wood Office Ctr
Ann Arbor, MI 48108-1193
(734) 971-4900
Fax: (734) 971-5332
Email: sc.watson@prodigy.net
Web: www.scannarbor.com
Key Contact:
Ms. Barbara A. Watson, Manager

W 4111 Andover Ste 120
Bloomfield Hills, MI 48302-1911
(248) 594-0880
Fax: (248) 594-5993
Email: bloomfld!smk@mrinet.com
Key Contact:
Mr. Gerry Anger, Co-Manager
Mr. Tom Kilkenney, Co-Manager

11460 Highland Rd
Hartland, MI 48353-2710
(810) 632-6587
Fax: (810) 632-6591
Email: hartland!manager@mrinet.com
Key Contact:
Mr. John Ragnoli, Manager

912 Centennial Way Ste 340
Lansing, MI 48917
(517) 323-4404
Fax: (517) 323-8083
Email: jeffyeager@voyager.net

Key Contact:
Mr. Jeffrey A. Yeager, CSAM, Manager

124 N Division St Ste D-3
Traverse City, MI 49684-2263
(616) 935-4000
Fax: (616) 935-4505
Email: sctc@traverse.com
Key Contact:
Mr. E. J. Eckert, III, Manager

4700 W 77th St Ste 110
Minneapolis, MN 55435
(952) 830-1420
Fax: (952) 893-9254
Email: scminna!manager@mrinet.com
Web: www.scmrminneapolis.com
Key Contact - Specialty:
Mr. Richard Fox - *Hospitality management, retail*

2200 2nd St SW Ste 122
Rochester, MN 55902
(507) 536-4510
Fax: (507) 536-4511
Web: www.woodhunter.com
Key Contact:
Mr. Randy Dennis

100 S Fuller St Ste 240
Shakopee, MN 55379-1319
(952) 496-3030
Fax: (952) 496-1425
Email: mike@scchaska.com
Web: www.scchaska.com
Key Contact:
Mr. Michael Smith, Manager

955 Executive Pkwy Ste 221
Creve Coeur, MO 63141
(314) 878-0121
Fax: (314) 878-0128
Email: scadmin@swbell.net
Web: www.sccrevecoeur
Key Contact:
Mr. Jeff Rehr

2388 Scheutz Rd C-90
St. Louis, MO 63146
(314) 872-3600
Fax: (314) 872-3623
Email: msc@hunterconsultants.com
Web: www.hunterconsultants.com
Key Contact:
Mr. Brian Baynes
Mr. Matthew Castle

3301 Rider Trl S Ste 100
St. Louis, MO 63045-1309
(314) 344-0900
Fax: (314) 298-7706
Email: phoen@mricorp.mrinet.com
Key Contact:
Mr. Patrick Hoene, Manager

1106 Hooksett Rd
Hooksett, NH 03106
(603) 626-8400
Fax: (603) 626-1288
Key Contact:
Mr. John J. Cote, Manager

33 Main St Fl 2
Clinton, NJ 08809
(908) 735-0250
Fax: (908) 735-6322
Key Contact:
Mr. Michael Fuchs
Mr. Robert Balseiro

1 Bethany Rd & Rte 35 Ste 20
Bldg 1
Hazlet, NJ 07730-1659
(732) 739-4334
Fax: (732) 739-2990
Email: heg@midltwn.mrinet.com
Key Contact - Specialty:
Mr. Eric Gonzalez, Manager - *Consumer packaged goods (food, beverage)*

2 Hudson Pl Fl 3
Baker Bldg
Hoboken, NJ 07030-5515
(201) 659-5205
Fax: (201) 659-5009
Email: manager@davalyncorp.com
Web: www.davalyncorp.com
Key Contact:
Mr. Richard K. Sinay, President

2516 Hwy 35
Manasquan, NJ 08736
(732) 223-0300
Fax: (732) 223-0450
Email: scocean@bellatlantic.net
Key Contact:
Mr. Mark R. Daly, Manager

67 Main St Ste 200
Ogdensburg, NJ 07439
(973) 209-1957
Fax: (973) 209-0720
Email: les@myrecruiter.com
Web: www.myrecruiter.tv
Key Contact:
Mr. Leslie Agius, Manager

376 Rte 15 Ste 200
Sparta, NJ 07871
(973) 579-5555
Fax: (973) 579-2220
Email: stascom@stascomtech.com
Web: www.stascomtech.com
Key Contact:
Mr. Harvey C. Bass, Manager

86 Summit Ave
Summit, NJ 07901
(908) 522-0700
Fax: (908) 522-0785
Email: klimaski@bellatlantic.net
Key Contact:
Mr. Remus J. Klimaski, CSAM, Manager

11005 Spain NE Ste 3
Albuquerque, NM 87111
(505) 323-7300
Fax: (505) 323-7337
Email: jt@mrisales.com
Key Contact:
Ms. Judith Terry, Manager

8555 Main St Ste 308
Baptist Life Bldg
Buffalo, NY 14221-7456
(716) 631-3100
Fax: (716) 631-3140
Email: scbuffalo@scfuffalo.com
Key Contact:
Mr. Robert E. Artis, Manager

200 Parkway Dr S Ste 200
Hauppauge Ion, NY 11788
(631) 864-2650
Fax: (631) 864-3838
Email: scsc@networker-search.com
Web: www.networker-search.com
Key Contact:
Mr. Bob Levitt, Manager

145 Pinelawn Rd Ste 345N
Melville, NY 11747
(631) 777-2710
Fax: (516) 777-2714
Email: info@securitysearch.com
Web: www.securitysearch.com
Key Contact:
Mr. Harris Cohen, Manager

60 Madison Ave Ste 1020 Ste 911-A
New York, NY 10010
(212) 251-0100
Fax: (212) 251-0768
Email: arthur@recruiter.com
Web: www.scnyc.com
Key Contact:
Ms. Marcia Clarke, Manager - *Enterprise
computing*
Mr. Arthur Young

5955 Carnegie Blvd Ste 300
Charlotte, NC 28209
(704) 944-9800
Fax: (704) 944-8098
Email: admin@mricharlotte.com
Key Contact:
Mr. Thomas Near, General Manager
Mr. Dave Camp
Mr. Earl Baer
Mr. Mark Hastings

2554 Lewisville-Clemmons Rd Ste 302
First Citizens Bank Bldg
Clemmons, NC 27012-8749
(336) 766-4750 x204
(800) 585-5368 x204
Fax: (336) 766-4751
Email: wes@mrisc.com
Web: www.mrisc.com
Key Contact:
Mr. Wes McCracken, Manager

3925 N Duke St Ste 124
Durham, NC 27704
(919) 620-8220
Fax: (919) 620-8222
Email: slr@scdurham.com
Web: www.scdurham.com
Key Contact:
Ms. Sharon Reed
Mr. Mike Reed

218-2 Swing Rd
Greensboro, NC 27409
(336) 854-3931
Fax: (336) 854-3932
Email: bpbames@bellsouth.net
Key Contact:
Mr. Bruce P. Barnes, Manager

2411 Penny Rd Ste 101
High Point, NC 27265
(336) 883-4433
Fax: (336) 884-4433
Email: scihp@hpe.infi.net
Key Contact:
Mr. Tom Bunton, III, Co-Manager
Mr. James Pervis Greene, Co-Manager

16419 N Cross Dr Ste D
Huntersville, NC 28078
(704) 895-5525
Fax: (704) 895-5526
Email: mrisales@earthlink.net
Key Contact:
Mr. Hardy McConnell

322 E Center Ave
Mooresville, NC 28115
(704) 664-4997
Fax: (704) 664-0841
Email: hsykesnet@aol.com
Key Contact:
Mr. Hugh Sykes, Manager

636 Northland Blvd Ste 210
Cincinnati, OH 45240
(513) 742-9424
Fax: (513) 742-5742
Email: info@mri-sc.net
Web: www.mri-sc.net
Key Contact:
Mr. Lou Breyley

851 Ohio Pike Ste A
Cincinnati, OH 45245
(513) 947-0922
Fax: (513) 947-0959
Email: janet@bcgpharma.com
Web: www.bcgpharma.com
Key Contact:
Mr. Janet Murphy

20600 Chagrin Blvd Ste 703 Twr E
Cleveland, OH 44122
(216) 561-6776
Fax: (216) 561-2393
Email: manager@clevecent.mrinet.com
Web: www.careers-recruiters.com

Key Contact:
Mr. Bob Gandee, Manager
Ms. Mary Hardy

7530 Lucerne Dr Ste 303
Islander Park Two
Cleveland, OH 44130
(440) 243-5151
Fax: (440) 243-4868
Email: manager@cleveair.mrinet.com
Web: www.mricleveland.com
Key Contact:
Mr. Jeff Dipaolo, Manager

1041 Dublin Rd Ste 101
Columbus, OH 43215
(614) 481-0000
Fax: (208) 474-0919
Key Contact:
Mr. Rick Simmonds

555 S Front St Ste 100
Columbus, OH 43215
(614) 252-6200
Fax: (614) 252-4744
Email: geh@mricols.com
Web: www.mricolumbusdt.com
Key Contact:
Mr. Gerry E. Harris, CSAM, Manager
Mr. Todd Williams, CSAM, Co-Manager
Mr. John Zambito, CSAM, Co-Manager

9930 Johnnycake Ridge Rd Ste 3F
Concord, OH 44060
(440) 352-7599
Fax: (440) 352-7564
Email: jan@oh.verio.com
Key Contact:
Mr. William Downing

34100 Ctr Ridge Rd Ste 110
Liberty Ctr
North Ridgeville, OH 44039-3220
(440) 327-2800
Fax: (440) 327-6991
Email: poejo@ix.netcom.com
Key Contact:
Mr. James P. Spellacy, Manager

5600 Monroe St Ste 206 B
Sylvania, OH 43560-2731
(419) 882-5088
Fax: (419) 882-4119
Email: sctoledo@earthlink.net
Key Contact:
Mr. Dick Hite, Co-Manager
Ms. Lynn Hite, Co-Manager

7364 Kingsgate Way
West Chester, OH 45069
(513) 755-6060
Fax: (513) 755-6161
Email: jon@barcodejobs.com
Web: www.barcodejobs.com
Key Contact:
Mr. Jonathan Bartos, Owner/Manager

8090 Market St Ste 5
Youngstown, OH 44512
(330) 726-3333
Fax: (330) 726-4115
Email: martym@jobsdimension.com
Web: www.jobsdimension.com
Key Contact:
Mr. Martin Milush

563 SW 13th St Ste 100
Bend, OR 97702
(541) 382-9779
Fax: (541) 382-9772
Email: robert@pangaeatek.com
Web: www.pangaeatek.com
Key Contact:
Mr. Rob Schluter, Manager

2020 Lloyd Ctr
Portland, OR 97232-1376
(503) 287-8701
Fax: (503) 282-4380
Email: manager@mri.pdx.com

Key Contact:
Mr. Larry Engelgau, Co-Manager
Ms. Elvita Engelgau, Co-Manager

1104 Fernwood Ave Ste 402
Camp Hill, PA 17011
(717) 737-7500
Fax: (717) 737-7400
Email: doug@hotsalesjobs.com
Web: www.hotsalesjobs.com
Key Contact:
Mr. Doug Miller

PO Box 866
Fogelsville, PA 18051-0866
(610) 336-4599
Fax: (610) 336-4447
Email: marc@mriscallentown.com
Key Contact:
Mr. Marc Sablow

2 Chatham Ctr Ste 1400
112 Washington Pl
Pittsburgh, PA 15219-3427
Email: ic@mrpitt.com
Key Contact:
Ms. Laura Connelly

747 Aquidneck Ave
Middletown, RI 02874
(401) 845-5000
Fax: (401) 847-5843
Email: rcalvano@scnewport.com
Key Contact:
Mr. Bob Calvano

116 High St Ste 212
Westerly, RI 02891
(401) 596-8600
Fax: (401) 596-8900
Key Contact:
Mr. Grant MacSwain

1203 Two Island Ct Ste 103
Mt. Pleasant, SC 29466
(843) 849-8080
Fax: (843) 849-7070
Email: recruiter@salesconsultantsinc.com
Web: www.salesconsultantsinc.com
Key Contact:
Mr. Joe D. Rigter, Co-Manager
Ms. Kay H. Rigter, Co-Manager

750 Miller Dr Ste B2
Leesburg, VA 20175
(703) 777-0790
Fax: (703) 777-0791
Email: lparrotte@scnova.com
Key Contact - Specialty:
Mr. Larry Parrotte, President - *Aviation, aerospace, transportation, outsourcing, security*
Mr. Bob Hill, Account Executive - *IT, telecom*
Mr. Mason Preddy, Account Executive - *Aviation*
Ms. Terrie Bonfiglio, Account Executive - *Pharmaceutical and medical devices*

7229 Forest Ave Ste 210
Highland II
Richmond, VA 23226
(804) 285-2071
Fax: (804) 282-4990
Email: info@richgroupusa.com
Web: www.richgroupusa.com
Key Contact:
Mr. Jay S. Schwartz, Manager

2840-G Hershberger Rd
Roanoke, VA 24017
(540) 563-1688
Fax: (540) 563-1687
Email: mkennedy@executivetalentsearch.com
Web: www.executivetalentsearch.com
Key Contact:
Mr. Mark Kennedy, Owner

4560 South Blvd Ste 250
Virginia Beach, VA 23452-1160
(757) 490-0331
Fax: (757) 490-0129
Email: murphey@series2000.com

Key Contact:
Mr. James F. Murphey, Manager

8195 166th Ave NE Ste 201
Redmond, WA 98052
(425) 883-1313
Fax: (425) 883-8103
Key Contact:
Mr. Bill Zbitnoff

101 W Edison Ave Ste 224
Appleton, WI 54915
(920) 830-8080
Fax: (920) 830-8090
Key Contact:
Mr. Jay Rhodes

5576 Hwy 50 Unit F
Delavan, WI 53115
(262) 740-9000
Fax: (262) 740-9100
Email: info@mri-salesconsultants.com
Web: www.mri-salesconsultants.com
Key Contact:
Mr. Joseph Almburg, Jr.
Ms. Lori Almburg

375 AMS Ct
Green Bay, WI 54313
(920) 434-8770
Fax: (920) 434-9155
Email: sc@mrijobs.com
Web: www.mrijobs.com
Key Contact:
Mr. Garland E. Ross, Manager

8411 Corporate Dr Ste 100
Racine, WI 53406
(262) 886-8000
Fax: (262) 886-7260
Email: info@mrracine.com
Web: www.mrracine.com
Key Contact:
Ms. Ellen Jante
Mr. Thomas Hurt

Sales Consultants of Birmingham

(also known as MRI of Birmingham)
100 Carnoustie N
PO Box 381626
Birmingham, AL 35238-1626
(205) 408-0855
Fax: (205) 991-9086
Email: cpark@mri-bham.com
Web: www.brilliantpeople.com

Description: Our objective is to satisfy the critical demand for people, the resource that ultimately determines an organization's profitability.

Key Contact - Specialty:
Mr. Cleve A. Park, President - *Engineering*

Salary minimum: $40,000

Functions: Production, Sales & Mktg.

Industries: Mfg., Lumber, Furniture, Chemicals, Drugs Mfg., Medical Devices, Consumer Elect., Venture Cap., Pharm Svcs., Accounting, Healthcare, Non-classifiable

Sales Consultants of Eastern Shore/Mobile Bay

184 Fairway Dr
PO Box 2784
Daphne, AL 36526
(334) 625-0200
Fax: (334) 625-0203
Email: jan@industrial-sales.com
Web: www.industrial-sales.com

Description: We are a franchise location of MRI's, specializing in recruiting and placing sales, marketing and management talent in the industrial arena with an emphasis on the valve, bearings, and power transmission fields for the OEM and distribution markets. We also specialize in recruiting for banking and finance in the executive management, and lending areas.

Key Contact - Specialty:
Mrs. Janet Luckey, Co-Manager
Mr. Horace Luckey, Co-Manager - *Industrial sales*

Functions: Sales & Mktg., Finance

Industries: Generalist, Mfg., Finance, Banking

Sales Consultants of Huntsville

(also known as MRI)
190 Lime Quarry Rd Ste 220
Madison, AL 35758
(256) 464-9570
Fax: (256) 464-5684
Email: billmay@hiwaay.net

Description: National retained and contingency executive search firm specializing in the paper, plastic and packaging industries.

Key Contact - Specialty:
Mr. William May, President - *Paper, plastics, packaging*

Salary minimum: $40,000

Functions: Generalist, Packaging

Industries: Generalist, Paper, Printing, Plastics, Rubber, Packaging

Professional Associations: TAPPI

Sales Consultants of Scottsdale

12005 N Panorama Dr Ste 103
Fountain Hills, AZ 85268
(480) 816-4526
Fax: (480) 816-4973
Email: scscottsdale@extremezone.com

Description: We are part of MRI, a nationwide recruiting organization. Our clients are Fortune 100-500 companies. We place from sales reps up to executive VPs and CEOs.

Key Contact - Specialty:
Mr. Gary Jewett, President - *Sales & marketing, sales management*

Salary minimum: $40,000

Functions: Directors, Mktg. Mgmt., Sales Mgmt.

Industries: Generalist, Food, Bev., Tobacco, Printing, Chemicals, Transportation, Biotech

Sales Consultants of Goodyear Inc

250 N Litchfield Rd Ste 230
Goodyear Financial Ctr
Goodyear, AZ 85338
(623) 536-7136
Fax: (623) 536-7138
Email: rjb@princeton.mrinet.com

Description: Professional management consulting firm specializing in executive search - organized by divisions to address specific client needs. Management consulting services available to compliment the client's executive search needs. Specialize in interpreting strategic and tactical plans into HR requirements, both quantitative and qualitative.

Key Contact:
Mr. Robert J. Bodnar, President - *Energy, utilities*
Ms. Beverly H. Bodnar, Vice President

Salary minimum: $60,000

Functions: Generalist, Senior Mgmt., Sales Mgmt., CFO's, Cash Mgmt., MIS Mgmt., Mgmt. Consultants, Int'l.

Industries: Generalist, Energy, Utilities, Finance, Banking, Invest. Banking, Mgmt. Consulting, Environmental Svcs., Biotech

Sales Consultants of Phoenix Camelback Corridor

(also known as The De Angelis Group)
2201 E Camelback Rd Ste 506B
Phoenix, AZ 85016
(602) 468-6000
Fax: (602) 954-1506
Email: info@biotech-recruiter.com
Web: www.biotech-recruiter.com

Description: Our firm's team of recruiters is a dynamic group of very successful people some with prior experience as a recruiter and others who were recruited directly out of the medical device arena to join the team. The common denominator is that they all have relevant experience that is germane to the industry, commitment to integrity, and excellence.

Key Contact:
Mr. Drue De Angelis

Functions: Generalist

Industries: Medical Devices, Biotech

Sales Consultants of Northwest Arkansas

1 W Mountain Executive Sq
Fayetteville, AR 72701
(501) 521-9700
Fax: (501) 521-9770
Email: denver@leasingcareers.com
Web: www.leasingcareers.com

Description: Our firm targets, recruits, and delivers high-impact talent for the equipment leasing industry.

Key Contact - Specialty:
Mr. Denver Wilson, President - *Equipment leasing*

Functions: Sales Mgmt.

Industries: Services

Professional Associations: ELA

Sales Consultants of Oceanside/San Diego

31499 Lake Vista Cir
Bonsall, CA 92003
(760) 631-8020
Fax: (760) 631-0513
Email: bob@careermatching.com
Web: www.careermatching.com

Description: We specialize in the placement of top sales & management professionals in the high-tech software & dot-com arenas. Part of MRI, the worlds largest search and recruitment organization.

Key Contact:
Mr. Bob Enright, Manager

Salary minimum: $90,000

Sales Consultants of Chico

55 Independence Cir Ste 108
Chico, CA 95973
(530) 892-8880
Fax: (530) 896-5480
Email: kl@medicaljobs.net
Web: www.medicaljobs.net

Description: We specialize in placing and recruiting sales and marketing people in the medical arena for Northern California, the West Coast and national.

Key Contact - Specialty:
Mr. K. L. Johnson, Co-Owner - *Medical sales & marketing, research & development*
Ms. Carol Johnson, Co-Owner - *Medical sales*

Functions: Sales & Mktg., Sales Mgmt.

Industries: Drugs Mfg., Medical Devices, Biotech

Sales Consultants of Palo Alto

2680 Bayshore Pkwy Ste 304
Mountain View, CA 94043
(650) 237-9097
Fax: (650) 237-9086
Email: dwhite@scpaloalto.com
Web: www.scpaloalto.com

Description: We are a successful executive search firm specializing in high performance sales and marketing professionals in the software and communications industries.

Key Contact - Specialty:
Mr. David White, President - *High-tech executives*

Functions: Sales & Mktg.

Industries: E-commerce, IT Implementation, Telecoms, Telephony, Digital, Wireless, Fiber Optic, Network Infrastructure

Sales Consultants of Newport Beach

4120 Birch St Ste 106
Newport Beach, CA 92660
(949) 622-0232
Fax: (949) 622-0240
Email: scnbeach@earthlink.net
Web: www.mrinet.com

Description: As part of MRI, the largest recruiting firm in the world, our firm specializes in the recruitment of qualified personnel in the software, legal, financial services, and professional services industries. We work with clients on a nation-wide basis to attract qualified individuals for their staffing needs.

Key Contact:
Mr. Ray Stockstill

Functions: Generalist

Industries: Finance, Services, E-commerce, IT Implementation, Telecoms, Telephony, Digital, Wireless, Network Infrastructure, Software

Sales Consultants of Oakland

480 Roland Way Ste 103
Oakland, CA 94621-2065
(510) 635-7901
Fax: (510) 562-7237
Email: mrsc@dnai.com
Web: www.scsanfran.com

Description: We work all markets in sales, sales management, marketing, food, medical and computers, chemical, biotech, agriculture, auto, consumer, electronic, environmental, health, home care, industrial and telecommunications.

Key Contact - Specialty:
Mr. Tom Thrower, General Manager - *Medical*

Salary minimum: $50,000

Functions: Generalist, Senior Mgmt., Product Dev., Purchasing, Healthcare, Sales & Mktg., IT, Engineering

Industries: Generalist, Communications, Packaging, Software, Biotech, Healthcare

Sales Consultants of Orange

1 City Blvd W Ste 300
Orange, CA 92868
(714) 978-0500
Web: www.brilliantpeople.com

Description: Fifty million dollar corporate group-owned field office specializing in e-business, high-technology, industrial and building products sales, sales marketing and sales management positions.

Key Contact - Specialty:
Mr. David Pahl, General Manager - *E-business*
Mr. Ray Stayer, CSAM, Senior Account Manager - *Building products*
Mr. Bob Ward, Search Consultant - *Industrial specialist*

Mr. Scott Besso, Search Consultant - *IT, software*
Ms. Erin Favilla, Search Consultant - *Information technology*
Ms. Katie Archer, Search Consultant - *Healthcare*
Mr. Ken King, Search Consultant - *Healthcare, biotech*
Mr. Richard DiGioia, Search Consultant - *Insurance, financial*

Functions: Generalist, General Mgmt., Mfg., Healthcare, Sales & Mktg., HR Mgmt., IT, Specialized Svcs.

Industries: Generalist, Construction, Mfg., Wholesale, Services, Packaging, Software

Sales Consultants of Sacramento

2267 Lava Ridge Ct Ste 220
Roseville, CA 95661
(916) 677-7700
Fax: (916) 677-7710
Email: resumes@scsacramento.com
Web: www.scsacramento.com

Description: We are a franchise of MRI, the country's largest recruiter of sales and sales management personnel with more than 160 offices serving every business market. Using this network of recruiters, we can locate the most highly trained candidate.

Key Contact - Specialty:
Mr. Ron Whitney, Owner/Manager - *Industrial, building products, computers, agriculture*

Salary minimum: $30,000

Functions: Generalist, Sales Mgmt.

Industries: Generalist, Agri., Forestry, Mining, Machine, Appliance, Test, Measure Equip., Publishing, Packaging, Healthcare

Sales Consultants of San Diego

9455 Ridgehaven Ct Ste 100
San Diego, CA 92123-1647
(858) 565-6600
Fax: (858) 565-4937
Email: contact@mrisandiego.com
Web: www.mrisandiego.com

Description: We are a company that specializes in the recruiting of technical and industrial sales representatives on a national basis.

Key Contact:
Mr. Harvey J. Baron, President

Functions: Sales Mgmt.

Industries: Food, Bev., Tobacco, Drugs Mfg., Medical Devices, Paints, Petro. Products, Metal Products, Consumer Elect., Pharm Svcs., Publishing, Haz. Waste, Packaging

Sales Consultants of Boulder

6325 Gunpark Dr Ste 202
Boulder, CO 80301-3390
(303) 527-1440
Fax: (303) 527-1449
Email: bgils@bouldervalleypartners.con
Web: www.scboulder.com

Description: Our firm focuses on the placement of high-powered sales, support, marketing and management professionals for computer telephony integration, telecommunications and call center industries.

Key Contact - Specialty:
Mr. Robert D. Gills, Jr., President - *Computer telephony integration (CTI), call center executives*

Salary minimum: $40,000

Functions: Generalist, Senior Mgmt., Mktg. Mgmt., Sales Mgmt., Direct Mktg., Customer Svc., Systems Dev., Systems Implem.

Industries: Generalist, Computer Equip., Telecoms, Software

Sales Consultants of Denver

6312 S Fiddlers Green Cir Ste 250N
Englewood, CO 80111
(303) 706-0123
Fax: (303) 706-0204
Email: gzoch@scdenver.com
Web: www.scdenver.com

Description: Our firm, a corporately owned and operated branch, has been serving the needs of local and national clients. We specialize in locating top talent in a variety of disciplines and industries. Our offices are located in the Denver Technology Center in the MCI Plaza building.

Key Contact:
Mr. Greg Zoch

Functions: Generalist, Product Dev., Sales Mgmt., MIS Mgmt., Systems Analysis, Systems Implem., Engineering

Industries: Generalist, Construction, Media, Insurance, Software, Healthcare

Sales Consultants of Westminster

8774 Yates Dr Ste 325
Westminster, CO 80030
(303) 542-0500
(877) 551-0570
Fax: (720) 542-0600
Email: info@scwestminster.com
Web: www.scwestminster.com

Key Contact:
Mr. Thomas Verzuh

Sales Consultants of Danbury

10 Clearview Dr
Sandy Hook, CT 06482
(203) 270-0700
Fax: (203) 270-6288
Email: mri.scdanbury@snet.net
Web: www.mri.scdanbury.com

Description: We specialize in telecommunications, sales, engineering, marketing and operations professionals.

Key Contact - Specialty:
Mr. Bob Smith, Manager - *Telecommunications*

Salary minimum: $50,000

Functions: Generalist, Senior Mgmt., Middle Mgmt., Mktg. Mgmt., Sales Mgmt., Systems Implem., Network Admin., Engineering

Industries: Generalist, Computer Equip., New Media, Telecoms, Software

Sales Consultants of Boca Raton

(a Boca Group company)
4800 N Federal Hwy Ste 104 Bldg D
Boca Raton, FL 33431
(561) 393-9998
Fax: (561) 393-9984
Email: scboca1@evcom.net
Web: www.scboca.com

Description: Award winning staff of executive recruiters dedicated to professional service and providing staffing solutions.

Key Contact - Specialty:
Mr. Juergen E. Buller, Managing Partner - *Generalist*
Ms. Cynthia K. Buller, Partner - *Generalist*

Salary minimum: $60,000

Functions: Generalist

Industries: Drugs Mfg., Medical Devices, Computer Equip., Pharm Svcs., Software

Sales Consultants of Manatee County

710 60th St Court E
Bradenton, FL 34208
(941) 756-7765
Fax: (941) 756-7313
Email: jpitz@gte.net
Web: www.scmanatee.com

Description: We specialize in recruitment and placement of top-notch sales and marketing talent with data communications companies, particularly start-up firms.

Key Contact - Specialty:
Ms. Judy A. Pitz - *Data communications, sales & marketing*

Salary minimum: $50,000

Functions: Generalist, Mkt. Research, Mktg. Mgmt., Sales Mgmt.

Industries: Generalist, Computer Equip.

Sales Consultants of Bradenton

(also known as The Denson Group)
1111 3rd Ave W Ste 130
Bradenton, FL 34205-7834
(941) 708-3838
Fax: (941) 708-3939
Email: jsd@global-careers.com
Web: www.densongroup.com

Description: We specialize in marketing, sales management, engineering, QA, QC, and regulatory affairs in the medical device industry.

Key Contact - Specialty:
Mr. Steve Denson, General Manager
Mrs. Kip Denson, Vice President - *Medical device*

Salary minimum: $50,000

Functions: Generalist

Industries: Medical Devices

Sales Consultants of Clearwater

(also known as Galileo Group LLC)
611 Druid Rd Ste 304
Clearwater, FL 33756-3919
(727) 447-8610
Fax: (727) 447-8620
Email: resume@scgalileo.com
Web: www.scgalileo.com

Description: We are specialists who recruit in retained and contingency searches in recreational consumer products industry including marine, lawn and garden, aviation, recreational vehicles and sporting goods for sales, marketing, finance, manufacturing, engineering, and production.

Key Contact - Specialty:
Mr. Ken Candela, Executive Director - *Executive management, sales and marketing*
Ms. Sandy Candela, Executive Director - *Production, manufacturing, engineering, finance*

Salary minimum: $55,000

Functions: General Mgmt., Senior Mgmt., Mfg., Sales & Mktg., Finance, Engineering

Industries: Motor Vehicles, Misc. Mfg., Transportation, Recreation, Aerospace, Entertainment SW, Mfg. SW, Marketing SW

Sales Consultants of Ft. Lauderdale

100 W Cypress Creek Rd Ste 880
Ft. Lauderdale, FL 33309
(954) 772-5100
Fax: (954) 772-0777
Email: resume@mri-sc-usa.com
Web: www.mri-sc-usa.com

Description: We specialize in sales, sales management, marketing and executive placement throughout the southeast region. We also specialize in the medical, data processing, corporate financial,

services, automotive and spirits, packaging-corrugated, and folding carton industries.

Key Contact - Specialty:
Mr. Jeffrey A. Taylor, Vice President/General Manager - *Medical, sales, sales management, executive*
Mr. Greg Peterson, Vice President - *Food & beverage, data processing, sales management, executive*

Salary minimum: $30,000

Functions: Generalist, Senior Mgmt., Middle Mgmt., Plant Mgmt., Packaging, Mkt. Research, Sales Mgmt.

Industries: Generalist, Food, Bev., Tobacco, Medical Devices, Motor Vehicles, Computer Equip., Wholesale, Services, Media, Packaging, Mfg. SW, Biotech, Healthcare

Professional Associations: FAPS, PERC

Sales Consultants of Lee County

16521 San Carlos Blvd Ste 103C
Ft. Myers, FL 33908-5245
(877) 560-4997
(941) 278-4997
Fax: (941) 278-1380
Email: mpasquale@telcosales.com

Description: We specialize in recruiting top talent for excellent career opportunities in the telecom, data, and Internet industry. Positions we place for include sales, management, technical and customer service in major markets nationwide.

Key Contact - Specialty:
Mr. Ted Lyke, President - *Telecommunications, data, internet*

Salary minimum: $30,000

Functions: Sales Mgmt.

Industries: Telecoms, Fiber Optic, Network Infrastructure

Sales Consultants of Jacksonville

(also known as The Duval Group)
9471 Baymeadows Rd Ste 204
Jacksonville, FL 32256
(904) 737-5770
Fax: (904) 737-7927
Email: scott@duvalgroup.com
Web: www.duvalgroup.com

Description: We active in the permanent placement of consulting engineers within transportation and traffic design (not logistics) disciplines. We are also very active in placing professionals in the design, manufacture, marketing and sales of industrial machinery.

Key Contact - Specialty:
Mr. Scott Sheridan, CSAM, President - *Industrial Machinery*

Salary minimum: $45,000

Functions: Generalist

Industries: Energy, Utilities, Mfg., Metal Products, Machine, Appliance, Equip Svcs.

Sales Consultants of The Emerald Coast

4400 Hwy 20 E Ste 407
Niceville, FL 32578
(850) 897-2800
Fax: (850) 897-3055
Email: sales@sc-emeraldcoast.com
Web: www.sc-emeraldcoast.com

Key Contact - Specialty:
Mr. Tim Stapleton, General Manager - *Consumer packaged goods, food*

Sales Consultants of North Palm Beach

(also known as The DeSantis Group)
760 US Hwy 1 Ste 306
North Palm Beach, FL 33408
(561) 694-0011
Fax: (561) 694-8910
Email: desantisvictor@hotmail.com
Web: www.mrinet.com

Description: Our office specializes in the aerospace, automotive, steel, transportations, telecommunications, and information technology industries.

Key Contact:
Mr. Victor Desantis, President - *Aerospace, automotive, steel, transportation*
Mr. Nick DeSantis, Account Executive - *Telecommunications, information technology*
Mr. Dima Smidovich, Account Executive - *Telecommunications, information technology*
Ms. Ramona DeSantis, Office Manager
Mrs. Lindy DeSantis, Vice President

Salary minimum: $18,000

Functions: Generalist

Industries: Mfg., Transportation, E-commerce, IT Implementation, Hospitality, Telecoms, Environmental Svcs., Aerospace, Packaging, Mfg. SW

Sales Consultants of Sarasota East

5540 Bee Ridge Rd Ste F3
Sarasota, FL 34233-1505
(941) 371-9622
Fax: (941) 371-9623
Email: resumes@techpeoplesearch.com
Web: www.techpeoplesearch.com

Key Contact:
Mr. Walter Colgan

Functions: Sales Mgmt.

Industries: Software, Accounting SW, Database SW, Development SW, Doc. Mgmt., Production SW

Sales Consultants of Sarasota

1343 Main St Ste 600
Sarasota, FL 34236
(941) 365-5151
Fax: (941) 365-1869
Email: office@scsarasota.com
Web: www.scsarasota.com

Description: Our firm recruits mid to senior level manufacturing, engineering, sales, and marketing executives in commercial, industrial, and consumer products.

Key Contact:
Ms. Rose Castellano, Managing Partner
Mr. Donald A. Mattran, General Manager

Sales Consultants of Sunrise

10001 NW 50th St Ste 202
Sunrise, FL 33351-8093
(954) 747-4340
Fax: (954) 747-4342
Email: nbooth@scsunrise.com
Web: www.scsunrise.com

Description: We are executive recruiters placing sales, technical and marketing personnel into the paints, pigments, coatings, resins, plastics, adhesives, sealants, specialty chemical, and IT industries.

Key Contact:
Mr. Juacane Reynolds, Manager/Owner

Functions: Sales & Mktg.

Industries: Chemicals, Plastics, Rubber, Paints, Petro. Products

Sales Consultants of Tampa North

4012 Gunn Hwy Ste 140
Tampa, FL 33624-4724
(813) 264-7165
Fax: (813) 968-6450
Email: mrtn@mrtampanorth.com
Web: www.mrtampanorth.com

Description: We specialize in the executive placement of sales and marketing professionals. Specific industries include telecommunications, high-technology positions, hardware and software sales, food and beverage sales.

Key Contact - Specialty:
Mr. Gary King, President - *Telecommunications*
Mr. Stephen Fox, Sales Manager - *Food, beverage*

Salary minimum: $40,000

Functions: Generalist

Industries: Food, Bev., Tobacco, Drugs Mfg., Consumer Elect., Brokers, Media, Telecoms

Sales Consultants of St. Petersburg

275 - 104th Ave Unit A
Treasure Island, FL 33706
(727) 367-8787
Email: scstpete1g@netscape.net
Web: www.mrinet.com

Description: We deal with Abbot Laboratories, Johnson & Johnson, Hillrom, Striker, Zimmer, GE, Siemens, Agilent, Smith & Nephew, Owens & Minor, Aesculap, 3M, Acuson, Marconi, Allegience Healthcare, Philips Medical, and McKessing (General Medical).

Key Contact - Specialty:
Mr. Hank Mays, Manager - *Medical sales, medical marketing, IT, sales management, senior level medical management*

Salary minimum: $50,000

Functions: Healthcare, Physicians, Health Admin., Sales & Mktg., Mktg. Mgmt., Sales Mgmt., HR Mgmt., R&D

Industries: Chemicals, Drugs Mfg., Medical Devices, Pharm Svcs., Advertising, Training SW, Biotech, Healthcare, Hospitals

Sales Consultants of Richmond Hill

PO Box 1746
Richmond Hill, GA 31324-1746
(912) 756-5060
Fax: (912) 756-5070
Email: dapper@g-net.net
Web: www.mrinet.com

Description: We work with companies in the life science research industry. The positions that we place range from entry level sales to senior sales and marketing management. We also fill technical support and applications positions that support sales teams.

Key Contact:
Mr. David A. Pearl, Manager

Salary minimum: $50,000

Functions: Sales & Mktg., R&D

Industries: Biotech

Sales Consultants of Honolulu

(also known as MRI of Honolulu)
1001 Bishop St Ste 720
Pacific Tower
Honolulu, HI 96813
(808) 533-3282
(800) 879-0448
Fax: (808) 599-4760
Email: schon@lava.net
Web: www.mrihonolulu.com

Description: We place sales, sales support marketing and sales management for United States and the Pacific Rim. We are also very strong in the Hawaiian marketplace. We place people in high-tech positions in Hawaii.

Key Contact:
Mr. James A. Morse
Mr. Don Bishop

Salary minimum: $30,000

Functions: Generalist

Industries: Mfg., Wholesale, Finance, Services, Hospitality, Media, Packaging, Software, Biotech, Healthcare

Networks: First Interview Network (FIN)

Sales Consultants of Arlington Heights

3415 N Arlington Heights Rd
Arlington Heights, IL 60004
(847) 590-8880
Fax: (847) 590-0847
Email: mri@jobwish.com
Web: www.jobwish.com

Description: Placing Sales, Sales Management, Product Management nad Marketing Management talent with Manufacturing companies worldwide

Key Contact:
Mr. Steve Briody, General Manager

Functions: Sales & Mktg.

Industries: Mfg., Packaging, Marketing SW

Sales Consultants of Aurora

1245 Corporate Blvd Ste 101
Aurora, IL 60504
(630) 236-6610
Fax: (630) 236-6615
Email: steve@mrisearchteam.com
Web: www.mrisearchteam.com

Description: Our firm is an affiliate of Management Recruiters International, and specializes in recruiting and placing top performing sales and marketing professionals in the payment services and information technology industries. In payment services, our focus is on credit cards, debit cards, stored value cards, and electronic bill presentment and payment. Our information technology recruiting includes ERP, CRM, e-Business and document management software across a wide range of vertical markets.

Key Contact:
Mr. Steve Wade
Sandy Wade

Salary minimum: $60,000

Functions: Sales Mgmt.

Industries: Banking, Misc. Financial, Mgmt. Consulting, E-commerce, IT Implementation, Software

Sales Consultants of Fox Valley

495 N Commons Dr Ste 105
Aurora, IL 60504
(630) 692-7970
Fax: (630) 692-7975
Email: marlin@foxpartners.com
Web: www.foxpartners.com

Description: We are an executive search firm with a mission statement that includes providing the best possible service to our employers and employees. This includes multiple searches with the use of MRI International, as well as individual executive searches for management personnel. Our industries include the IT market, as well as the industrial automation industry.

Key Contact:
Mr. Marlin Walgrave

Nik Veerachat

Salary minimum: $70,000

Functions: Generalist

Industries: Energy, Utilities, Computer Equip., Consumer Elect., Test, Measure Equip., Electronic, Elec. Components, E-commerce, IT Implementation, Doc. Mgmt., Production SW, ERP SW, Networking, Comm. SW

Sales Consultants of Barrington
18-4 E Dundee Rd Ste 202
Barrington, IL 60010
(847) 277-1150
Email: cb@cleartalent.com
Web: www.cleartalent.com

Description: We place pre-sales, sales, post-sales, and marketing talent with technology companies at all levels and on a national basis. The industries that we serve include software, computer hardware, telecommunications, and the Internet. We also place information technology professionals in technical and managerial positions.

Key Contact - Specialty:
Mr. Curtis L. Baer, President - *Software, sales & pre-sales, post-sales, marketing*

Salary minimum: $50,000

Functions: IT

Industries: Generalist, Computer Equip., Services, Mgmt. Consulting, Software

Sales Consultants of Chicago-Downtown
815 W Van Buren Ste 309
Chicago, IL 60607
(312) 733-4700
Fax: (312) 733-9769
Email: jack@sc-chicago.com
Web: www.sc-chicago.com

Description: We specialize in the recruitment of telecommunications and data communications sales and sales support professionals. It is our philosophy that it takes world class talent to run world class organizations.

Key Contact - Specialty:
Mr. Jack W. Downing, Managing Partner - *Telecommunications, data communications*

Salary minimum: $75,000

Functions: Directors, Senior Mgmt., Middle Mgmt., Sales Mgmt., Systems Support

Industries: Energy, Utilities, Brokers, Telecoms, Call Centers, Telephony, Wireless, Fiber Optic, Network Infrastructure, Networking, Comm. SW, Biotech

Sales Consultants of Mount Prospect
500 Central Rd Ste 210
Mt. Prospect, IL 60056
(847) 222-1433
Fax: (847) 222-1437
Email: kbower@core.com

Description: We offer retained and contingency recruiting services in the electronics, chemical, IT, healthcare, security, and financial industries. We recruit from middle management to executive levels. We specialize in generalists, engineers, plant managers, sales/marketing managers, customer service, and financial managers.

Key Contact:
Mr. Kenneth Bower, Managing Director

Salary minimum: $40,000

Sales Consultants of Oak Brook
(also known as MRI of Oak Brook)
1415 W 22nd St Ste 725
Oak Brook Regency Twrs
Oak Brook, IL 60523
(630) 990-8233
Fax: (630) 990-2973
Email: glm@scoakbrook.com
Web: www.scoakbrook.com

Description: We are one of the leading franchises of MRI. We are a generation of successful search and staffing work in the professional and managerial ranks. The industries that we have served include all major sectors with heavy emphasis on Chicago area firms.

Key Contact:
Mr. Gary L. Miller, General Manager

Salary minimum: $60,000

Functions: Generalist

Industries: Generalist

Sales Consultants of Buffalo Grove
1540 E Dundee Rd Ste 245
Palatine, IL 60074-8321
(847) 202-0202
Fax: (847) 202-0200
Email: broberts@insnet.com
Web: www.mriscdata-tele.com

Description: We specialize in the pharmaceutical, medical, and data communication industries. We assist candidates in sales, senior sales, major account sales, national account sales, primary care, hospital representatives, institutional representatives, sales managers, district managers, and regional managers.

Key Contact - Specialty:
Mr. Brian Roberts, Owner/President - *Telecommunications*

Functions: Senior Mgmt., Healthcare, Sales & Mktg., Sales Mgmt., Engineering

Industries: Drugs Mfg., Medical Devices, Communications, Telecoms, Call Centers, Telephony, Digital, Wireless, Fiber Optic, Network Infrastructure, Biotech, Healthcare, Hospitals, Long-term Care, Dental, Physical Therapy, Occupational Therapy, Women's

Sales Consultants of Chicago South
6420 W 127th St Ste 209
Palos Heights, IL 60463
(708) 371-9677
Fax: (708) 371-9678
Email: frontdesk@card-recruiter.com
Web: www.card-recruiter.com

Description: We specialize in the credit card and consumer finance industries, sales, sales management, marketing, operations, risk, payment processing, e-commerce and legal.

Key Contact - Specialty:
Ms. Judy Collins, Manager - *Credit cards, consumer finance*

Salary minimum: $30,000

Functions: Generalist

Industries: Finance, Banking, Services

Professional Associations: ICA

Sales Consultants of Western McHenry County
6601 Main St
PO Box 425
Union, IL 60180
(815) 923-2500
Fax: (815) 923-2587
Email: sci@scwmc.com
Web: www.scwmc.com

Description: We provide nationwide search and recruitment for the software vendor industry. Our principals possess over 60 years' experience within this industry in senior management capacities prior to creating this executive search practice.

Key Contact - Specialty:
Mr. Daniel M. Grant, President - *Software, senior management, sales & marketing*
Mr. Jeffrey M. Wilson, Vice President - *Healthcare software vendors, senior management, sales & marketing, installation, support*
Mr. Greg Ammirati, Vice President - *Software vendors, senior management, sales & marketing*

Functions: Generalist, Senior Mgmt., Mktg. Mgmt., Sales Mgmt., CFO's, MIS Mgmt., Systems Implem.

Industries: Generalist, Software, Healthcare

Sales Consultants of Indianapolis-North
11611 N Meridian St Ste 220
Carmel, IN 46032
(317) 582-0202
Fax: (317) 582-0303
Email: mrindy@mrindianapolis.com
Web: www.mrindianapolis.com

Description: Thirty years of outstanding success in identifying top talent and meeting corporate America's total staffing needs. This outstanding firm is lead by Mr. George Ceryak, 30 years with MRI and winner of the prestigious Office of the Decade award for the 80s.

Key Contact:
Mr. George V. Ceryak, Co-Owner - *Executive sales*
Mr. David J. Oberting, Co-Owner

Salary minimum: $20,000

Functions: Generalist, Senior Mgmt., Mfg., Sales & Mktg., Mkt. Research, Finance, IT, R&D

Industries: Generalist, Construction, Mfg., Retail, Finance, Media, Communications, Real Estate, Software, Biotech, Healthcare

Networks: Recruiters Professional Network (RPN)

Sales Consultants of Ft. Wayne
126 W Columbia St Ste 208
Ft. Wayne, IN 46802-1719
(219) 426-2805
Email: nharris@scfortwayne.com
Web: www.dentalheadhunter.com

Description: We specialize in finding and placing sales and marketing talent in the dental industry; from the individual contributor to the director or VP level.

Key Contact:
Mr. Nick Harris, VP/General Manager

Functions: Sales & Mktg.

Industries: Medical Devices, Biotech, Healthcare

Sales Consultants of Indianapolis-Central
8200 Haverstick Rd Ste 240
Indianapolis, IN 46240-2472
(317) 257-5411
Fax: (317) 259-6886
Email: search@mriindy.com
Web: www.mriindy.com

Description: Our office has served hundreds of client companies. Collectively possessing several years of recruiting experience, our team of 55 recruiters filled over 800 positions last year alone.

Key Contact:
Mr. William A. Kuntz, General Manager - *Sales, sales management, marketing*
Mr. Mark Haering, MBA, Director of Operations

Salary minimum: $40,000

Functions: Generalist, General Mgmt., Production, Materials, Distribution, Sales & Mktg., HR Mgmt., Finance, IT, Engineering

Industries: Generalist, Energy, Utilities, Construction, Mfg., Transportation, Wholesale, Finance, Services, Pharm Svcs., Communications, Aerospace, Packaging, Insurance, Software, Biotech, Healthcare

Professional Associations: SHRM

Sales Consultants of Lawrence
5030 W 15th St Ste B
Lawrence, KS 66049
(785) 331-2233
Fax: (785) 331-2266
Email: c224@earthlink.net
Web: www.mrinet.com

Description: Sales and Marketing Executives in the Medical,Dental and Optical field. Also animal health and Consumables.

Key Contact:
Mr. Bill Eckles, Manager

Salary minimum: $24,000

Functions: Sales & Mktg.

Industries: Medical Devices, Hospitality

Sales Consultants of Lenexa
8325 Lenexa Dr Ste 105
Lenexa, KS 66214
(913) 894-4400
Fax: (913) 894-4410
Email: joakley@sclenexa.com
Web: www.sclenexa.com

Key Contact:
Mr. Jeff Miller
Mr. Jimmy Oakley

Sales Consultants of The Bluegrass
3138 Custer Dr Ste 220
Lexington, KY 40517-4064
(606) 245-8228
Fax: (606) 245-9590
Email: manager@bluegrass.mrinet.com

Description: We specialize in permanent placement of sales and marketing professionals in the following industries: general manufacturing, corrugated packaging, printing, and business services.

Key Contact - Specialty:
Mr. Darrell B. Barber, President - *Sales & marketing, general manufacturing, packaging, prining, business services*

Functions: Generalist, Senior Mgmt., Middle Mgmt., Sales & Mktg., Mktg. Mgmt., Sales Mgmt.

Industries: Generalist, Mfg., Printing, Wholesale, Services, Accounting, Equip Svcs., Media, Publishing, Packaging

Sales Consultants of Alexandria
201 Johnston St Ste 206
Alexandria, LA 71301
(318) 561-2882
Fax: (318) 561-2883
Email: salesconsultants@aol.com

Key Contact - Specialty:
Ms. Markay Dunn, President - *Office products, office supplies, furniture, office equipment, printing*

Functions: Generalist, Directors, Senior Mgmt., Middle Mgmt., Sales & Mktg., Mkt. Research, Mktg. Mgmt., Sales Mgmt.

Industries: Generalist, Mfg., Lumber, Furniture, Paper, Printing, Plastics, Rubber, Metal Products,

Consumer Elect., Misc. Mfg., Wholesale, Pharm Svcs., Packaging, Insurance, Healthcare

Sales Consultants of Portland
2145 Post Rd Ste 4
Business Ctr at Litchfield Sq
Wells, ME 04090
(207) 646-9200
Fax: (207) 646-9300
Email: psmith@scportland.com
Web: www.scportland.com

Description: We are one of the fastest growing executive search firms in the country. We only focus on sales, sales management & marketing professionals in the information technology sector. We work closely with clients in the e-commerce, Internet, data storage, application software, data warehousing, supply chain, ERP, CRM, enterprise software, CAD, e-learning, portal, hardware, networks, telecommunications, professional services and e-business sectors.

Key Contact:
Mr. Pete Smith, Manager

Salary minimum: $75,000

Sales Consultants of Rockville, MD
51 Monroe St Ste 1405
Rockville, MD 20850
(301) 610-7300
Fax: (301) 610-0100
Email: brian@scisuccess.com
Web: www.scisuccess.com

Description: Through the Sales Consultants franchise, we have access to one thousand offices and 600 videoconferencing centers worldwide. We are the world's largest e-Search and recruiting firms.

Key Contact - Specialty:
Mr. Brian Hoffman, General Manager - *Telecommunications, data communications*

Salary minimum: $80,000

Functions: Generalist, Senior Mgmt., Middle Mgmt., Mktg. Mgmt., Sales Mgmt., MIS Mgmt., Systems Implem.

Industries: Generalist, Computer Equip., Equip Svcs., Mgmt. Consulting, Telecoms, Software

Networks: Associated Consultants in Executive Search Int'l

Sales Consultants of Baltimore
9515 Deereco Rd Ste 900
Timonium, MD 21093
(410) 252-6616
Fax: (410) 252-7076
Email: info@mribaltimore.com
Web: www.mribaltimore.com

Description: We are the world's largest professional search organization specializing in managerial, sales and professional talent. As part of a national organization, we serve firms of all types and sizes through the expertise and efforts of over 750 affiliated offices. We are recognized as a leader in executive search. 1999 recipient of MRI's elite Diamond Club, we are experts at identifying, qualifying and attracting top talent.

Key Contact:
Ms. Linda A. Burton, President
Mr. Glen Davis

Functions: Generalist, Production, Plant Mgmt., Mktg. Mgmt., Sales Mgmt., MIS Mgmt., Systems Dev., Engineering

Industries: Generalist, Food, Bev., Tobacco, Drugs Mfg., Medical Devices, Plastics, Rubber, Test, Measure Equip., Packaging

Professional Associations: MAPRC

Sales Consultants of Brockton
567 Pleasant St Ste 8
Brockton, MA 02301
(508) 587-2030
Fax: (508) 587-9261
Email: mfeinsonsc@aol.com

Description: Largest company in United States specializing in sales and marketing with 150 offices nationally.

Key Contact - Specialty:
Mr. Milton M. Feinson, President - *Generalist*

Functions: Sales & Mktg., Mktg. Mgmt., Sales Mgmt.

Industries: Generalist

Sales Consultants of Needham
329 Chestnut St
Needham, MA 02492
(781) 449-3838
Fax: (781) 449-7866
Email: jrichards.scneedham@verizon.net
Web: www.scneedhamma.com

Description: We specialize in the recruitment of professionals in the areas of top down/bottoms up assortment inventory planners for national retail chains. We also specialize in the recruitment of buyers for the national apparel specialty and department store chains.

Key Contact - Specialty:
Mr. James Richards, Jr.
Mr. James Richards, President - *Retail*
Mr. Murray Lee, Account Executive - *Retail*

Functions: Specialized Svcs.

Industries: Retail

Sales Consultants of Southborough Inc
54 Central St
Southborough, MA 01745
(508) 480-8889
Fax: (508) 480-0020
Email: info@sales-consultants.com
Web: www.sales-consultants.com

Description: Specializing in recruiting software, Internet and other IT sales and marketing personnel.

Key Contact - Specialty:
Mr. Dave Railsback, General Manager - *Computer software, internet sales & marketing*
Ms. Mary Sharkey, General Manager - *Computer software, internet, sales & marketing*

Functions: Sales & Mktg.

Industries: Computer Equip., Software

Sales Consultants of Wellesley
888 Worcester St Ste 95
Wellesley, MA 02482-3717
(781) 235-7700
Fax: (781) 237-7207
Email: scwellesley@scwellesley.com
Web: www.scwellesley.com

Description: We are committed to offering honest and confidential recruiting services. We take pride in our ability to understand our assignment, conduct a successful confidential search, and evaluate candidates in a competent and professional manner.

Key Contact:
Mrs. Susan Durante, President

Functions: Sales & Mktg., Mktg. Mgmt.

Industries: Generalist

Professional Associations: MAPS

Sales Consultants of Auburn Hills

2701 Cambridge Ct Ste 205
Auburn Hills, MI 48326-2565
(248) 373-7177
(800) 699-7446
Fax: (248) 373-7759
Email: scah@scauburnhills.com
Web: www.scauburnhills.com

Description: We are located in the heart of automotive manufacturing and development. We specialize in sales, sales management and engineering positions to the automotive industry. We are also extremely strong on local Southeastern Michigan searches for exceptional sales talent in the areas of: pharmaceutical, medical, consumer products, IT, e-commerce, building products and general industrial sales professionals.

Key Contact - Specialty:
Mr. Boe E. Embrey, President - *Sales & marketing*

Functions: Generalist, General Mgmt.

Industries: Generalist

Sales Consultants of Birmingham

30700 Telegraph Rd Ste 3650
Bingham Farms, MI 48025-4527
(248) 647-7766
Fax: (248) 647-9722
Email: bbinke@recruiters-mri.com
Web: www.recruiters-mri.com

Description: We bring the finest talent in the nation to our clients.

Key Contact:
Mr. Brian Binke, President - *Information technology*
Ms. Ellen McCowan-Binke

Salary minimum: $40,000

Functions: Generalist, Senior Mgmt., Middle Mgmt., Mfg., Sales & Mktg., Sales Mgmt., IT, MIS Mgmt., Network Admin.

Industries: Generalist, Construction, Mfg., Motor Vehicles, Media, New Media, Telecoms, Telephony, Wireless, Fiber Optic, Network Infrastructure, Insurance, Software, Mfg. SW

Sales Consultants of Farmington Hills

30445 Northwestern Hwy Ste 360
Farmington Hills, MI 48334-3102
(248) 626-6600
Fax: (248) 626-7542
Email: salcon@scfarmington.com
Web: www.scfarmington.com

Description: Leading contingency and retained recruiting organization for executives, marketing, sales representatives and sales management specializing in communications and telecommunications.

Key Contact - Specialty:
Mr. Harvey Gersin, President - *Controls, instrumentation, machinery*

Functions: Sales & Mktg.

Industries: Advertising

Sales Consultants of Grand Rapids

900 E Paris Ave SE Ste 301
Grand Rapids, MI 49546
(616) 940-3900
Fax: (616) 940-3041
Email: scgr@sales-consult.com
Web: www.sales-consult.com

Description: A division of MRI, recognized as the world's premier sales search firm and the largest, most progressive firm devoted solely to the placement of sales, marketing and management professionals.

Key Contact - Specialty:
Mr. David L. Underwood, President - *Furniture*

Functions: General Mgmt., Sales & Mktg.

Industries: Lumber, Furniture, Drugs Mfg., Plastics, Rubber, Computer Equip., Consumer Elect., Pharm Svcs., Telecoms, Packaging, Biotech

Sales Consultants of Kalamazoo

5320 Holiday Ter
Kalamazoo, MI 49009-2122
(616) 372-8007
Fax: (616) 372-8388
Email: sckalamazoo@kalamazoo.net
Web: www.sckazoo.com

Description: We specialize in sales talent for the automotive, software, automation, instrumentation, and fluid power industries

Key Contact - Specialty:
Mr. Mark Bielecki, President - *Fluid power, electronics*

Functions: Sales Mgmt.

Industries: Metal Products, Machine, Appliance, Motor Vehicles, Computer Equip., Test, Measure Equip., Electronic, Elec. Components, Software

Sales Consultants of Laurel Park

17177 N Laurel Park Dr Ste 256
Livonia, MI 48152-2659
(734) 542-9099
(734) 542-1454
Fax: (734) 542-9098
Email: carnold@pacesettercareers.com

Description: We offer client firms in-depth working knowledge of these industries: food processing, equipment & supply manufacturing, plastic, rubber, material handling, and industrial manufacturing for the following functions: sales, marketing, food science/technology, engineering, plant management, and quality control.

Key Contact - Specialty:
Mr. Chris Arnold, President & CEO - *Sales & marketing management*

Salary minimum: $60,000

Functions: Senior Mgmt., Product Dev., Mktg. Mgmt., Sales Mgmt.

Industries: Generalist, Mfg., Food, Bev., Tobacco, Textiles, Apparel, Paper, Chemicals, Plastics, Rubber, Machine, Appliance, Wholesale, Retail, Mfg. SW, Marketing SW

Professional Associations: IFMA, IFT, NAFEM, NRA

Sales Consultants of Novi

27780 Novi Rd Ste 240
Novi, MI 48377-3427
(248) 305-9727
Fax: (248) 305-9767
Email: jgscnovi@earthlink.net

Description: We are part of Management Recruiters International, the world's largest executive search firm. Our office specializes in industrial sales, placing candidates in both sales and sales management positions.

Key Contact - Specialty:
Mr. James Guerrera, President - *Industrial sales*
Mr. Scott Henderson, Account Executive - *Industrial sales*

Sales Consultants of Detroit

29777 Telegraph Rd Ste 2260
Southfield, MI 48034
(248) 352-9200
Fax: (248) 352-9374

Email: info@scjob.com
Web: www.scjob.com

Description: We provide sales, marketing and technical support professionals for growing corporations. From top executives to new college graduates, we promise quick turn around on qualified candidates, which lowers the cost per hire.

Key Contact - Specialty:
Mr. Thomas J. Hoy, General Manager - *Chemical, automotive, industrial, IT, capital equipment*

Functions: Senior Mgmt., Middle Mgmt., Automation, Sales & Mktg., Mktg. Mgmt., Sales Mgmt., Technicians

Industries: Generalist, Food, Bev., Tobacco, Paper, Chemicals, Medical Devices, Plastics, Rubber, Paints, Petro. Products, Metal Products, Machine, Appliance, Telecoms

Sales Consultants of Chesterfield

1415 El Bridge Payne Rd Ste 105
Chesterfield, MO 63017
(636) 537-5295
Fax: (636) 537-9201
Email: manager@scstlouis.com
Web: www.scstlouis.com

Description: We specialize in the placement of top sales, sales management, and marketing talent. Our industry specialties include automotive, building products, consumer products, consumer hardware, house-ware, educational, publishing, and all areas of marketing, such as product management and marketing services.

Key Contact - Specialty:
Mr. Don Borgschulte, General Manager
Ms. Cindy Krus, Director of Recruiting - *Hardware, house ware, automotive*

Salary minimum: $40,000

Functions: Product Dev., Sales & Mktg., Sales Mgmt.

Industries: Food, Bev., Tobacco, Textiles, Apparel, Lumber, Furniture, Plastics, Rubber, Leather, Stone, Glass, Motor Vehicles, Computer Equip., Consumer Elect., Higher Ed., Publishing

Sales Consultants of Omaha

409 N 130th St
Omaha, NE 68154
(402) 342-7300
Fax: (402) 342-7100
Email: ask@scomaha.com
Web: www.scomaha.com

Key Contact:
Mr. Jeffrey Miller
Mr. Randall Jackson

Functions: Generalist, Senior Mgmt., Sales Mgmt., Mgmt. Consultants, Environmentalists, Technicians, Graphic Artists

Industries: Generalist, Printing, Medical Devices, Plastics, Rubber, Computer Equip., Banking, Telecoms

Sales Consultants of Las Vegas Inc

1771 E Flamingo Ste B125
Las Vegas, NV 89119
(702) 735-9300
Fax: (702) 735-9310
Email: frontdesk@sclasvagas.com
Web: www.mrinet.com

Description: We provide the highest quality executive search solutions through our commitment to integrity, efficiency, and innovation by working closely with our clients and candidates.

Key Contact:
Mr. Jeff Miller, Owner

Salary minimum: $60,000

Sales Consultants of Nashua-Manchester

Greeley St & Rte 3 6 Medallion Ctr
Merrimack, NH 03054
(603) 424-3282
Fax: (603) 424-3286
Email: salesconsultants-nash-man@att.net

Description: We specialize in recruiting and placing sales, sales management, marketing, computers, banking and insurance people in permanent and temporary positions. Our staff is expertly trained and each is well versed in the industries they represent, enabling them to talk your language and understand your needs.

Key Contact - Specialty:
Mr. Sheldon S. Baron, Manager - *Sales, banking, employee benefits, insurance, computers*

Salary minimum: $15,000

Functions: Generalist, Middle Mgmt., Advertising, Mkt. Research, Mktg. Mgmt., Sales Mgmt., Direct Mktg., Customer Svc.

Industries: Generalist, Mfg., Computer Equip., Banking, Misc. Financial, Insurance, Software

Professional Associations: NNEAPS

Sales Consultants of Bridgewater

1011 Rte 22 - W Ste 301 Fl 3
Bridgewater, NJ 08807
(908) 725-2595
Fax: (908) 725-0439
Email: mr@mrbridgewater.com
Web: www.mrbridgewater.com

Description: Part of a network of over 900 offices in the United States and Canada, we offer executive recruitment and interim executive placement using cutting edge technology.

Key Contact:
Mr. Barry S. Smith, President - *Banking*
Mr. Mark Egner
Ms. Joanne Orazecz

Functions: Sales Mgmt.

Industries: Drugs Mfg., Medical Devices, Banking

Sales Consultants of Cherry Hill

800 N Kings Hwy Ste 402
Cherry Hill, NJ 08034-1511
(856) 779-9100
Fax: (856) 779-9193
Email: sccherryhill@aol.com
Web: www.mriphiladelphia.com

Description: Our office places sales and marketing professionals in all industries nationally and internationally and has a network with over 800 other MRI and SC offices worldwide.

Key Contact - Specialty:
Mr. Jere Chambers, General Manager - *Consumer products, industrial sales*
Mr. Gene Grim, Certified Senior Account Manager - *Technical services, business services, business equipment*
Ms. Nadine DeAngelis - *Medical sales*
Ms. Kathy Genuardi - *Intangibles, printing*

Salary minimum: $30,000

Functions: Generalist, Senior Mgmt., Middle Mgmt., Sales & Mktg., Mkt. Research, Mktg. Mgmt., Sales Mgmt., Customer Svc.

Industries: Generalist, Mfg., Transportation, Misc. Financial, Services, Media, Insurance

Sales Consultants of Trenton

(also known as DJV Assoc)
1230 Pkwy Ave Ste 102
Ewing, NJ 08628
(609) 882-1944
Fax: (609) 882-4862

Email: dvlad@djvassociates.com

Description: We are an executive search focused on attracting and retaining middle and senior level management, sales professionals, management consultants and legal professionals. Our areas of specialization include CRM, call centers/customer care, management consulting, and law.

Key Contact - Specialty:
Mr. Derrick Vlad, President
Ms. Chris Miller, Account Executive - *Information technology*
Ms. Jill Arnstein, J.D., Account Executive - *Legal*

Salary minimum: $70,000

Functions: General Mgmt., Legal, Sales & Mktg., Customer Svc., Mgmt. Consultants, Int'l.

Industries: Generalist, Mfg., Computer Equip., Transportation, Finance, Services, Mgmt. Consulting, Media, Communications, Telecoms, Call Centers, Insurance, Software, Healthcare

Sales Consultants of Essex County

30 2 Bridges Rd Ste 270
Fairfield, NJ 07004
(973) 227-8292
Fax: (973) 575-4901
Email: sci@sci-intl.com
Web: www.sci-intl.com

Description: We are top-level information technology executive consulting and software/solutions sales search specialists.

Key Contact:
Ms. Debbie Seminerio, Co-Manager
Mr. Charles Seminerio, Co-Manager

Sales Consultants of Livingston

355 Eisenhower Pkwy Ste 212
Livingston, NJ 07039-1017
(973) 597-1870
Fax: (973) 597-1871
Email: manager@livngstn.mrinet.com

Description: We recruit information technology sales, recruiters and all levels of technical people.

Key Contact - Specialty:
Mr. Sheldon Wohl, President - *Information technology*

Functions: Sales Mgmt.

Industries: Generalist

Sales Consultants of Northern Jersey

11 E Oak St
Oakland, NJ 07436
(201) 651-9200
Fax: (201) 651-1320
Email: whs@scnorthjersey.com
Web: www.scnorthjersey.com

Description: We specialize in finding sales, sales management and marketing professionals with proven track records of success.

Key Contact - Specialty:
Mr. William Soodsma, President - *Sales & marketing*

Functions: Generalist, Senior Mgmt., Advertising, Mkt. Research, Mktg. Mgmt., Sales Mgmt.

Industries: Generalist

Sales Consultants of Morris County

364 Parsippany Rd Ste 8B
Parsippany, NJ 07054-5109
(973) 887-3838
Fax: (973) 887-2304
Email: webresumes@marketing-sales.com
Web: www.mrinet.com/sales

Description: We specialize in sales and sales management and secondarily in marketing. We also

specialize in market areas related to business services, chemicals, process equipment and healthcare related products and services. Staff tenure includes consultants with 24 years' experience.

Key Contact - Specialty:
Mr. Ernest Bivona, Manager - *Sales & marketing*

Salary minimum: $30,000

Functions: Sales & Mktg., Mkt. Research, Sales Mgmt.

Industries: Construction, Mfg., Drugs Mfg., Misc. Financial, Services, Packaging, Insurance, Software, Biotech, Healthcare

Professional Associations: NJASP

Sales Consultants of Middlesex County

242 Old New Brunswick Rd Ste 340
Piscataway, NJ 08854-3754
(732) 981-8008
Fax: (732) 981-1187
Email: scmidlsx@bellatlantic.net
Web: www.scmiddlesex.com

Description: Our office specializes in the packaging industry; mainly the corrugated box sector. We concentrate in sales, sales management, marketing, production, operations, general management and corporate level positions in the industry.

Key Contact - Specialty:
Mr. James K. Malloy, President - *Packaging*

Salary minimum: $50,000

Functions: Generalist

Industries: Paper, Packaging

Sales Consultants of Red Bank

1800 Bloomsbury Ave
Wanamassa, NJ 07712
(732) 918-6006
Fax: (732) 918-7311
Email: w.maurer3@verizon.net
Web: www.mrinet.com

Key Contact:
Mr. Walter Maurer

Functions: Generalist

Industries: Food, Bev., Tobacco

Sales Consultants of Gloucester County

6 N Broad St Ste 311
Woodbury, NJ 08096
(856) 686-9818
Fax: (856) 686-9828
Email: mlindsay@mri-sales.com
Web: www.mrinet.com

Description: We provide executive search and placement services for the banking, accounting and finance industry; the industrial and manufacturing industries, and the architectural/engineering, procurement, and construction industries.

Key Contact - Specialty:
Mr. Michael Lindsay, MIKE, President - *Architect, engineering*
Mr. John Fynes, Vice President & Market Manager - *Banking, accounting, finance*
Mr. Tony Gala, Account Executive - *Industrial, manufacturing*

Functions: Generalist

Industries: Generalist

Sales Consultants of Syracuse
212 Highbridge St Ste B
Fayetteville, NY 13066
(315) 637-0619
Fax: (315) 637-0621
Email: dwelker@accucom.net

Description: Our firm is an executive recruiter that specializes in sales and sales management.

Key Contact - Specialty:
Mr. Douglas L. Welker, Manager - *Sales, sales management*

Functions: Sales & Mktg., Sales Mgmt.

Industries: Generalist, Medical Devices, Pharm Svcs., Database SW

Sales Consultants of Nassau
363 Hempstead Ave
Malverne, NY 11565-1297
(516) 599-5824
Fax: (516) 599-2066
Email: jjacobs@mriscn.com

Description: We specialize in all aspects of the insurance, agricultural, specialty chemicals, and electrical industries.

Key Contact:
Mr. James F. Jacobs, Managing Director
Salary minimum: $75,000

Sales Consultants of Rochester
16 Main St W Ste 225
Powers Bldg
Rochester, NY 14614-1601
(716) 454-6650
Fax: (716) 454-4092
Email: rocmri@yahoo.com

Description: Recruit salespersons in the pharmaceutical, medical, software and technology fields.

Key Contact:
Mr. Jerry Annesi, Manager

Functions: Sales & Mktg.

Industries: Medical Devices, Pharm Svcs.

Sales Consultants of Asheville
204 Charlotte Hwy Ste H
Asheville, NC 28803-8681
(828) 296-1986
Fax: (828) 296-1987
Email: info@searchexecs.com
Web: www.searchexecs.com

Description: We specialize in helping companies in the publishing and printing industries locate qualified personnel to meet their staffing needs, both in the sales/sales management and editorial/management areas.

Key Contact - Specialty:
Mr. Walter Dinteman, President - *College publishing*
Mr. Michael Gibson, Account Executive - *Newspapers, printing*

Functions: Generalist

Industries: Printing, Publishing, New Media

Sales Consultants of Raleigh-Durham-RTP
107 Edinburgh S Ste 213
Cary, NC 27511
(919) 460-9595
Fax: (919) 460-0642
Email: dcb@mrirecruiter.net
Web: www.mrirecruiter.net

Description: Office specialties: medical/pharmaceutical, packaging industry, industrial, instrumentation, insurance and advertising-nationally, and all technical sales.

Key Contact - Specialty:
Mr. David C. Bunce, President - *Information technology*

Salary minimum: $70,000

Functions: Generalist, General Mgmt., Senior Mgmt., Sales Mgmt.

Industries: Mfg., Computer Equip., Test, Measure Equip., Services, Pharm Svcs., Equip Svcs., Mgmt. Consulting, HR Services, Media, Advertising, Telecoms, Software, Biotech

Sales Consultants of Concord
254 Church St NE
Concord, NC 28025-4737
(704) 786-0700
Fax: (704) 782-1356
Email: alp@scconcord.com
Web: www.scconcord.com

Description: Full service search and recruiting for companies that are re-engineering or preparing for IPOs as well as specialty searches for sales and marketing management professionals in high-tech industries.

Key Contact:
Mr. A. B. Pearson, Co-Manager
Ms. Anna Lee Pearson, Co-Manager

Functions: Sales & Mktg.

Industries: E-commerce, IT Implementation, Software, ERP SW, Networking, Comm. SW

Sales Consultants of High Point West
175 Northpoint Ave Ste 106
High Point, NC 27262-7724
(336) 869-8700
Fax: (336) 869-8719
Email: schpw@northstate.net
Web: www.schighpoint.com

Description: We are part of the franchise Management Recruiters International (MRI) system with teams specializing in technical and technical sales for the specialty and fine chemical industry.

Key Contact - Specialty:
Dr. Jim Stowers, Managing Director - *Chemical*

Salary minimum: $50,000

Functions: Generalist

Industries: Chemicals, Soap, Perf., Cosmtcs., Drugs Mfg.

Sales Consultants of Wrightsville Beach
7741 Market St Unit C
Wilmington, NC 28411
(910) 686-2848
Fax: (910) 686-2818
Email: scottharriman@earthlink.net

Description: Our firm is a diverse recruiting organization with over 100 years experience in the general manufacturing, lighting, power protection, and pharmaceutical industries. We are also one of the only recruiting organizations with an industrial psychologist on staff to assist our clients with their candidate assessment needs.

Key Contact:
Mr. Scott Harriman

Functions: Generalist

Industries: Mfg., Plastics, Rubber, Metal Products, Misc. Mfg., Electronic, Elec. Components, HR SW, Mfg. SW, Biotech, Healthcare

Sales Consultants of Franklin County
64 Wheaton Ave
Youngsville, NC 27596
(919) 562-1800
Fax: (919) 562-1801
Email: info@werecruit4u.com
Web: www.werecruit4u.com

Description: Our firm specializes in recruiting for technology industries. We have senior account executives that bring a wealth of real world and recruiting experience to bear on your staffing requirements. Blair Bost, our owner/manager, has over 21 years of technology industry experience ranging from IBM systems engineer, to vice president of sales, to launching a new product in the US. Other specialties in the office include industries such as software, biotech, bioinformatics, CAD, CAI, and utilities.

Key Contact - Specialty:
Mr. Blair Bost, General Manager - *IT sales, sales management*
Mr. Buddy Ferguson, BSMT, MPA, Senior Account Executive - *Biotechnology, bioinformatics*
Mr. Joe Reiner, Senior Account Executive - *Utility industry software*
Mr. Carl Norgarrd, Senior Account Executive - *CAD, CAI, industry automation software*

Functions: Sales & Mktg.

Industries: Energy, Utilities, IT Implementation, Software, Biotech

Sales Consultants of Broadview Heights
3505 Royalton Rd Ste 170
Broadview Heights, OH 44147
(440) 546-9154
Email: bdoherty@scbroadviewheights.com
Web: www.mrinet.com

Key Contact:
Mr. Brian Doherty, CSAM, Manager

Functions: Sales Mgmt.

Industries: Finance

Sales Consultants of Blue Ash
(also known as Quinlan and Associates Inc)
4410 Carver Woods Dr Ste 205
Cincinnati, OH 45242
(513) 985-9000
Fax: (513) 985-0975
Email: mail@qnasearch.com
Web: www.qnasearch.com

Description: Our firm is part of the Management Recruiters International (MRI) network. MRI is the world's largest executive search organization. We provide a full range of employment services, from single searches for a key manager to major projects involving hundreds of assignments for a single-source client.

Key Contact - Specialty:
Mr. Bill Quinlan, President - *Food industry*
Ms. Jennifer Quinlan, Account Executive - *Food industry*

Functions: Generalist

Industries: Food, Bev., Tobacco

Sales Consultants of Cincinnati
9435 Waterstone Blvd Ste 290
Cincinnati, OH 45249
(513) 677-6800
Fax: (513) 677-6816
Email: rrp@scjobsearch.com
Web: www.scjobsearch.com

Description: We are a total human resource service organization providing staffing solutions to companies throughout the world. We serve all industries placing sales, marketing, management, and technical professionals with our client companies with special emphasis on the pharmaceutical, medical, IT, telecommunication, industrial, plastics, legal, retail, food and beverage, and insurance industries.

Key Contact:
Mr. Rick Phillips, General Manager
Mr. Joe Doyle, Operations Manager

Salary minimum: $25,000

Functions: Middle Mgmt., Legal, Sales & Mktg., Sales Mgmt., HR Mgmt., Finance, IT, Systems Dev., Engineering, Attorneys

Industries: Generalist, Food, Bev., Tobacco, Drugs Mfg., Medical Devices, Plastics, Rubber, Retail, Finance, Services, Restaurants, Communications, Insurance, Software

Professional Associations: ITA, ITAA, PHARMASUG, SPE

Sales Consultants of Dublin
6805 Perimeter Dr
PO Box 3307
Dublin, OH 43016-0141
(614) 799-8801
Fax: (614) 799-8802

Description: Our areas of specialization include the: energy, sales, marketing, banking, and finance industries.

Key Contact - Specialty:
Mr. Gary VonFischer, Managing Director - *Energy industry*

Functions: General Mgmt.

Industries: Finance, Banking

Sales Consultants of Shaker Heights
16800 Chagrin Blvd
Shaker Heights, OH 44120
(216) 283-3401
Fax: (216) 283-3419
Email: tj@staffingsearch.com
Web: www.staffingsearch.com

Description: Executive and contingent search firm that functions as a source for marketing, sales, operations and technical management personnel for the outsourcing staffing industries.

Key Contact - Specialty:
Mr. Thomas K. Johnston, Manager - *PEO industry, retained search, temporary staffing*
Ms. Jennifer Snyder, Vice President - *Temporary staffing, contingency search*
Mr. Scott Chmielowicz, Vice President - *Temporary staffing, retained search*

Salary minimum: $40,000

Functions: Generalist, Directors, Senior Mgmt., Sales & Mktg., Sales Mgmt., CFO's, Risk Mgmt., MIS Mgmt.

Industries: Generalist, HR Services

Professional Associations: NAPEO, NATSS, OSSA

Sales Consultants of Oklahoma City
5909 NW Xwy Ste 135 Signator Pl 135
Oklahoma City, OK 73132
(405) 721-6400
Fax: (405) 728-6716
Email: admin@scokc.com
Web: www.scokc.com

Key Contact:
Ms. Darla Salisbury, Owner

Functions: Sales & Mktg.

Industries: Energy, Utilities, Drugs Mfg., Medical Devices, Pharm Svcs., Software, Development SW, Hospitals

Networks: Associated Consultants in Executive Search Int'l

Sales Consultants of Tulsa
5801 E 41st St Ste 440
Tulsa, OK 74135-5614
(918) 663-6744
Fax: (918) 663-1783
Email: mritulsa@mritulsa.com

Description: Our firm is part of the largest and most respected staffing company in the world. Our goal is to find the best talent for our client companies. We have held claim to the title #1 Office of the Year, received a quality excellence award, and ranked consistently in the top 10% in competition with over 800 offices nationwide.

Key Contact:
Mr. Tony A. Wolters, Manager
Mr. Mark Wolters

Functions: General Mgmt.

Industries: Generalist

Sales Consultants of Lake Oswego
1 Centerpointe Dr Ste 535
Lake Oswego, OR 97035
(503) 443-6008
Fax: (503) 443-6028
Email: jheim@financialplacements.com
Web: www.financialplacements.com

Description: Our firm is a team of inspired recruiting specialists. We believe remarkable employees are the secret to successful companies. We work with clients in the equipment leasing and banking markets to provide them with the best candidates the industry offers.

Key Contact - Specialty:
Mr. Tim Mulvaney, Manager - *Banking, equipment leasing*

Salary minimum: $30,000

Functions: Generalist

Industries: Finance, Banking

Professional Associations: ABA, ELA

Sales Consultants of Harrisburg
225 S 19th St
Camp Hill, PA 17011-7423
(717) 731-8550
Fax: (717) 731-8729
Email: tom@salesconsultants.net
Web: www.salesconsultants.net

Description: We specialize in voice/data/video technologies in the executive, sales or marketing job titles.

Key Contact - Specialty:
Mr. Thomas M. Waite, President - *Emerging communications technologies*

Functions: General Mgmt., Sales & Mktg., IT

Industries: Generalist

Sales Consultants of Chester County, PA
5 Frame Ave Ste 101
Frame Ave Business Complex
Malvern, PA 19355
(610) 695-8420
Fax: (610) 695-8442
Email: springco@erols.com

Description: We specialize in sales and marketing with a primary emphasis on the healthcare industry including: pharmaceutical, medical devices, biotechnology and oncology.

Key Contact - Specialty:
Mr. Mark W. Hetzel, Vice President/Manager - *Pharmaceutical, medical, technology*

Ms. Terrie Hetzel, President - *Generalist*

Functions: Generalist

Industries: Drugs Mfg., Medical Devices, Pharm Svcs., Biotech, Healthcare

Sales Consultants of The Poconos
544 Rte 6 & 209 Ste 2A
Milford, PA 18337
(570) 409-1088
Fax: (570) 409-1188
Email: mrisc@careersearches.com
Web: www.careersearches.com

Description: We are a leading search firm in the communications industry. Our search consultants are continually among the top performers in the industry. We work in all facets of the communication field. We fill positions at all levels of management, sales, marketing and technical areas.

Key Contact - Specialty:
Mr. Geoffrey J Pitcher, Partner - *Fiber optics (passive and active components, equipment)*
Ms. Nancy J Pitcher, Partner - *SONET, DWDM, transmission, optical networks*

Salary minimum: $50,000

Functions: General Mgmt., Directors, Senior Mgmt., Middle Mgmt., Sales & Mktg., Mktg. Mgmt., Sales Mgmt., Engineering

Industries: Telecoms

Sales Consultants of Wexford
2591 Wexford Bayne Rd Ste 205
Sewickley, PA 15143
(724) 935-1774
Fax: (724) 935-1744
Email: pj@scwexford.com
Web: www.scwexford.com

Description: Our firm places sales and sales management candidates with Fortune 2000 companies. We specialize in IT, logistics, and business-to-business services, for example leasing, credit card, and information services.

Key Contact - Specialty:
P. J. Jones, CSAM, General Manager, Vice President - *Business services*
Mr. Richard Geicek, NAM, National Account Manager - *IT*
Ms. Syd Sheehy, NAM, National Account Manager - *Logistics*

Functions: Sales Mgmt.

Industries: Generalist

Sales Consultants of Southampton
80 Second St Pk Ste 10
Southampton, PA 18966
(215) 364-7559
Fax: (215) 364-7579
Email: georgem@mriscs.com
Web: www.mriscs.com

Description: Based in Philadelphia, PA suburb, our firm specializes in contingency search assignments in the high and emerging technology areas, outsourcing industry and specialized areas of telecommunications. MRISCS actively recruits in all of North America in sales and various management positions.

Key Contact:
Mr. George McCafferty, Managing Partner - *Sales & management*
Ms. Dee McCafferty, Managing Partner, Operations

Salary minimum: $50,000

Functions: General Mgmt.

Industries: Services, Communications, Software, Security SW, System SW

Sales Consultants of Rhode Island

2348 Post Rd Ste 101
Airport Professional Pk
Warwick, RI 02886-2271
(401) 737-3200
Fax: (401) 737-4322
Email: bestsalestalent@mrisales.net
Web: www.mrisales.net

Description: Sales, sales management and marketing search and recruitment. InterExec (temporary professionals); ConferView videoconferencing services; Career Pathways (outplacement programs); Sales Staffers (temporary sales placement and outsourcing). Local, regional, national.

Key Contact - Specialty:
Mr. Peter C. Cotton, President - *Sales, sales management, marketing*

Salary minimum: $25,000

Functions: Sales & Mktg.

Industries: Generalist

Sales Consultants of Greenville

330 Pelham Rd Ste 109-B
Greenville, SC 29615
(864) 370-1341
Email: tommy@scgreenville.com

Description: We are specialists in finding and placing sales, sales management, marketing, construction, manufacturing, and engineering professionals.

Key Contact:
Mr. Thomas Blackmon, President

Salary minimum: $50,000

Functions: Sales Mgmt., Engineering

Industries: Construction, Mfg., Lumber, Furniture, Paper, Chemicals, Plastics, Rubber, Metal Products, Machine, Appliance, Misc. Mfg.

Sales Consultants of Orangeburg

145 Centre St
PO Box 1578
Orangeburg, SC 29116-1578
(803) 536-4601
Fax: (803) 536-4401
Email: scoburg@msn.com

Description: Specialists in sales, sales management and marketing professionals. Industry concentrations: electronics, electrical, industrial controls, instrumentation, industrial supplies. Additional services: outplacement, executive temporary placement, relocation, video teleconferencing.

Key Contact - Specialty:
Mr. Richard Jackson, President - *Industrial sales & marketing*
Ms. Carolyn Jackson, Vice President - *Industrial sales & marketing*

Salary minimum: $25,000

Functions: Generalist, Senior Mgmt., Middle Mgmt., Product Dev., Automation, Sales Mgmt., Systems Implem., Engineering

Industries: Generalist, Metal Products, Machine, Appliance, Computer Equip., Test, Measure Equip., Misc. Mfg.

Sales Consultants of Chattanooga-Brainerd

7010 Lee Hwy Ste 216
Chattanooga, TN 37421
(423) 894-5500
Fax: (423) 894-1177
Email: mrichatt@cdc.net
Web: www.mrichattanooga.com

Description: An integral part of MRI Cleveland, OH, the world's largest contingency search and placement firm. Over 1000 offices worldwide. Specializing in pharmaceutical sales/marketing, IT/IS and engineering and technical management.

Key Contact - Specialty:
Mr. Bill Cooper, President - *Medical, pharmaceutical*
Mr. David Adams, Senior Account Manager - *Medical, diagnostic, sales & marketing*
Mr. David Stephens, Senior Account Manager - *Pharmaceutical, sales & marketing*
Mr. Thomas Clark, Senior Account Manager - *Pharmaceutical sales*

Salary minimum: $30,000

Functions: Generalist

Industries: Generalist

Sales Consultants of Austin

2301 S Capital of TX Hwy Bldg J-101
Austin, TX 78746
(512) 328-9955
Fax: (512) 328-8659
Email: scaustin@scaustin.com
Web: www.scaustin.com

Description: We specialize in airport architectural and design both national and international. Staff features over thirty years' combine total recruiting experience. We get the job done!

Key Contact - Specialty:
Mr. C. Jay Middlebrook, President
Ms. Linda Middlebrook, Co-Manager - *Medical device*

Functions: Generalist, Nurses, Mkt. Research, Sales Mgmt., IT, MIS Mgmt., Mgmt. Consultants, Architects

Industries: Generalist, Food, Bev., Tobacco, Medical Devices, Mgmt. Consulting, Telecoms, Biotech

Sales Consultants of Dallas

3010 LBJ Fwy Ste 1470
Dallas, TX 75234
(972) 488-9191
Fax: (972) 488-9090
Email: scdallas@scdallas.com
Web: www.scdallas.com

Description: We have had thirty-four years of experience in professional sales and sales management staffing.

Key Contact:
Mr. Mark B. Rednick, President

Functions: Sales & Mktg.

Industries: Mfg., Banking, Venture Cap., Pharm Svcs., Call Centers, Packaging, Software, Biotech

Sales Consultants of Houston

5075 Westheimer Ste 790W
Financial Twrs/ Galleria II
Houston, TX 77056
(713) 627-0880
Fax: (713) 622-7285
Email: jdefor3261@aol.com
Web: www.schouston.com

Description: Single source human resource services which include: custom search projects, permanent placement, interim executives, sales blitz management, videoconferencing, outplacement and relocation assistance/management.

Key Contact:
Mr. Jim DeForest, Executive Vice President/General Manager
Mr. Mark Rednick, President

Salary minimum: $30,000

Functions: Generalist, Senior Mgmt., Mfg., Sales & Mktg., Benefits, Training, IT, Int'l.

Industries: Generalist, Mfg., Chemicals, Pharm Svcs., Law Enforcement, Publishing, Telecoms, Packaging

Sales Consultants of San Antonio

8626 Tesoro Dr Ste 515
San Antonio, TX 78217
(210) 805-0900
Fax: (210) 805-0904
Email: careers@scsanantonio.com
Web: www.scsanantonio.com

Key Contact:
Mr. Chuck Wright

Functions: General Mgmt., Sales & Mktg.

Industries: Food, Bev., Tobacco, Fiber Optic

Sales Consultants of Salt Lake City

428 E Winchester St Ste 210
Salt Lake City, UT 84107
(801) 263-2400
Email: rhawks@scslc.com
Web: www.scslc.com

Description: We are specialists in placing sales, sales management, pre-sales and marketing talent with application software companies. We have a strong track record of success in major metro areas in the US with particular success in the Western United States.

Key Contact:
Mr. Robert L. Hawks, Manager

Salary minimum: $50,000

Functions: Mktg. Mgmt., Sales Mgmt.

Industries: Computer Equip., Software

Sales Consultants of Madison

515 Junction Rd Ste 2500
Madison, WI 53717
(608) 836-5566
(800) 887-4969
Fax: (608) 836-1906
Email: schultzy@mriscmadison.com
Web: www.mriscmadison.com

Description: Specialize in territory sales, sales management and general management recruitment for growth corporations.

Key Contact - Specialty:
Mr. William A. Schultz, President - *Software, insurance, services, natural foods*

Salary minimum: $50,000

Functions: Senior Mgmt., Middle Mgmt., Mktg. Mgmt., Sales Mgmt., Risk Mgmt., Mgmt. Consultants

Industries: Food, Bev., Tobacco, Drugs Mfg., Restaurants, New Media, Environmental Svcs., Haz. Waste, Insurance, Software

Professional Associations: PLUS, SHRM, SMEI

Sales Consultants of Milwaukee

1333 W Towne Square Rd
Mequon, WI 53092-5047
(262) 241-1600
Fax: (262) 241-1640
Email: mr-sc@mri-execsearch.com
Web: www.recruiters-jobs.com

Description: Recruitment of sales and marketing professionals, managers and executives and project-based sales staffing. Our office is in top 5% of MRI offices nationwide. President's Platinum Club Award. 1996 Office of the Year.

Key Contact - Specialty:
Mr. Jim Luzar, President/Partner - *Manufacturing, paper, chemicals, plastics, metal products*

Mr. Tim Lawler, Partner - *International, manufacturing*

Ms. Beth Culbertson, Account Executive - *Power transmission motors, industrial, metal products, machine, appliance*

Ms. Beth Seurer, Account Executive - *Printing, computer equipment, advertising, telecommunications, software*

Ms. Joyce Bongard, Account Executive - *Sales and marketing, automotive, industrial*

Functions: General Mgmt., Sales & Mktg., Advertising, Mkt. Research, Mktg. Mgmt., Sales Mgmt., Direct Mktg., Customer Svc., PR

Industries: Generalist, Mfg., Wholesale, Advertising, Telecoms, Software, Healthcare

Professional Associations: SMEI

Sales Development Inc

2700 Delk Rd Ste 125
Marietta, GA 30067
(770) 712-9700
Fax: (770) 612-9191
Email: sdijobs@mindspring.com
Web: www.sdijobs.com

Description: We are one of the nation's premier software sales recruiting companies. We specialize in the placement of software sales, pre-sales and sales management professionals.

Key Contact - Specialty:
Mr. David Sheehan, President - *Software sales, software sales management*
Mr. John Drohan, Vice President - *Software sales, software sales management*

Salary minimum: $50,000

Functions: Sales & Mktg., Sales Mgmt.

Industries: Software

Sales Executives Inc

755 W Big Beaver Rd Ste 2107
Top of Troy Bldg
Troy, MI 48084
(248) 362-1900
Fax: (248) 362-0253
Email: info@salesexecutives.com
Web: www.salesexecutives.com

Description: We specialize in sales, marketing and sales management.

Key Contact - Specialty:
Mr. Dale E. Statson, President - *Medical*
Mr. William Rabe - *Graphics*

Salary minimum: $40,000

Functions: Generalist, Sales Mgmt.

Industries: Generalist, Food, Bev., Tobacco, Medical Devices, Computer Equip., Telecoms, Software

Sales Executives Inc

9005 Overlook Blvd
Brentwood, TN 37027
(615) 236-1110
Fax: (615) 236-1240
Email: chouston@salesexecutivesinc.com
Web: www.salesexecutivesinc.com

Description: We specialize in business-to-business sales and sales management professionals. Sales Executives partners with companies from all industries from small local companies to Fortune 500 companies nationwide. The industries that we specialize in include medical/pharmaceutical, transportation, industrial, consumer goods, IT, telecommunications, etc. We work on a contingency basis with our clients. There is no fee to the candidates.

Key Contact:
Ms. Cindy Houston Hazen, Co-owner

Ms. Janet Meek, Co-owner

Salary minimum: $24,000

Functions: Sales & Mktg.

Industries: Generalist

Networks: First Interview Network (FIN)

Sales Hunters Inc

(also known as MicroPhotonic Recruiters)
58 Penncroft Dr
Holtwood, PA 17532
(717) 284-5828
Fax: (717) 284-5920
Email: slshunters@aol.com

Description: We are specialists in presenting senior sales and marketing business development talent. Our highly targeted resources are applied to locating the "Gazelles" within the sales community. Our Tier II focus is applied to all executive level positions, including: CEO, CTO, CIO, CFO, COO, etc. Our target industries include high technology, fiber optics, industrial automation, and experimental research and development.

Key Contact:
Mr. James A. Collura, Director of Strategic Alliances
Ms. Lisa A. Collura, Strategic Alliance Coordinator

Salary minimum: $100,000

Functions: Sales & Mktg.

Industries: Mfg., Misc. Mfg., Electronic, Elec. Components, Telecoms, Fiber Optic, Biotech

Networks: Inter-City Personnel Assoc (IPA)

Sales Management Resources Inc

24040 Camino Del Avion Ste A177
Monarch Beach, CA 92629-4014
(949) 248-9429
Fax: (949) 248-8567
Email: smr@smrcareer.com
Web: www.smrcareer.com

Description: Southern California-based executive search firm which provides retained and contingency recruiting and consulting services to the United States corporate consumer products industry clients. We specialize in mid-senior-level sales and marketing management positions.

Key Contact - Specialty:
Mr. Clancy Salway, President - *Sales & marketing, consumer products company clients*

Salary minimum: $50,000

Functions: Sales & Mktg., Advertising, Mkt. Research, Mktg. Mgmt., Sales Mgmt., Direct Mktg.

Industries: Food, Bev., Tobacco, Textiles, Apparel, Soap, Perf., Cosmtcs., Drugs Mfg.

Networks: First Interview Network (FIN)

Sales Professionals Personnel Services

595 Market St Ste 2500
San Francisco, CA 94105
(415) 543-2828
Fax: (415) 543-3047
Email: sysadmin@salesprof.com
Web: www.salesprof.com

Description: Placement of sales, sales management and marketing management personnel.

Key Contact - Specialty:
Mrs. Linda Glover, Vice President - *Generalist*

Salary minimum: $30,000

Functions: General Mgmt., Distribution, Sales & Mktg., Sales Mgmt.

Industries: Generalist

Sales Recruiters

340 N Sam Houston Pkwy E Ste 263
Houston, TX 77060
(281) 447-0309
Email: sales@saleshire.com
Web: www.saleshire.com

Key Contact:
Mr. Sam Stitt, Executive Recruiter

Sales Recruiters Inc

85 Stiles Rd Ste 104
Salem, NH 03079
(603) 894-0007
Fax: (603) 894-6666
Email: info@salesrecruiters.com
Web: www.salesrecruiters.com

Description: We are a job placement agency that recruits, screens and presents qualified sales professionals to different types of organizations. While other recruiting firms are often impersonal resume factories, we offer a more comprehensive, personal approach to recruiting.

Key Contact - Specialty:
Mr. Henry Glickel, CPC, President - *Sales*

Salary minimum: $20,000

Functions: Sales & Mktg.

Industries: Generalist

Professional Associations: NNEAPS

Networks: First Interview Network (FIN)

Sales Recruiters Int'l Ltd

660 White Plains Rd # 19
Tarrytown, NY 10591
(914) 631-0090
Fax: (914) 631-1089
Email: info@salesrecruiters.net
Web: www.salesrecruiters.net

Description: We have identified, recruited and placed top sales, sales management and marketing professionals nationally for quality companies, where they are recognized, developed and rewarded for over 22 years.

Key Contact - Specialty:
Mr. Richard Harris, CPC, President - *Sales, sales management, marketing*

Functions: Sales & Mktg.

Industries: Mfg., Services, Hospitality, Media, Telecoms, Software

Networks: First Interview Network (FIN)

Sales Recruiters of Oklahoma City

6803 S Western Ave Ste 305
Oklahoma City, OK 73139
(405) 848-1536
Fax: (405) 636-1561
Email: salesrec@telepath.com
Web: www.telepath.com/salesrec/

Description: We are a search firm specializing in outside sales.

Key Contact - Specialty:
Mr. J. R. Rimele, President - *Medical, industrial, pharmaceutical, sales*
Mr. Glen Johnson, Marketing Manager - *Sales, medical*
Mr. Greg Johnson - *Sales, medical*

Functions: Healthcare, Sales & Mktg.

Industries: Food, Bev., Tobacco, Paper, Pharm Svcs., Accounting, Equip Svcs., Hospitality, Publishing, Packaging, Biotech, Healthcare, Hospitals, Long-term Care, Dental

Sales Recruiting Network
344 Mason Rd
Tarentum, PA 15084
(724) 226-9900
Fax: (724) 226-2299
Email: cain@salesrecruitingnetwork.com
Web: www.salesrecruitingnetwork.com

Description: Our primary recruiting areais outside sales and sales management positions in consumer, food service, medical, pharmaceutical and industrial areas. Our recruiting network covers outside sales opportunities in the US and Canada.

Key Contact - Specialty:
Mr. Douglas Cain, President - *Sales, consumer, industrial, food service, medical*

Salary minimum: $35,000

Functions: Sales Mgmt.

Industries: Generalist

Networks: First Interview Network (FIN)

Sales Resource Group Inc
1000 Winter St Ste 4550
Waltham, MA 02451
(781) 290-5700
Email: chris@salesresourcegroup.com
Web: www.salesresourcegroup.com

Description: We are a boutique firm specializing in placing sales professionals in the Internet and telecommunications infrastructure industry, for example service providers, networking hardware and software. The founder has 12 years of experience working directly in the industry, enabling us to provide our clients with insight and contacts to efficiently address their search requirements in this market.

Key Contact:
Ms. Christine Lauzon

Salary minimum: $100,000

Functions: Sales & Mktg.

Industries: Telecoms, Wireless, Fiber Optic, Network Infrastructure

Networks: National Personnel Assoc (NPA)

Sales Search
17 Goodwill Ave
Toronto, ON M3H 1V5
Canada
(416) 636-3660
Fax: (416) 638-9997
Email: ssearch@ionsys.com
Web: www.salessearch-toronto.com

Description: With over 25 years of specialized expertise, we are known for saving valuable time and effort in providing only qualified candidates for sales, sales management, and marketing positions.

Key Contact - Specialty:
Mr. Bob Glassberg, General Manager - *Sales, marketing & related management*

Functions: Middle Mgmt., Sales & Mktg., Sales Mgmt.

Industries: Energy, Utilities, Construction, Mfg., Wholesale, Services, Equip Svcs., Media, Communications, Aerospace, Packaging, Software, Biotech

Professional Associations: ACSESS

Sales Search Associates Inc
16 S Bothwell
Palatine, IL 60067
(847) 358-7865
Fax: (847) 358-7862
Email: salessearch@ameritech.net
Web: wwww.salesearchassociates.com

Description: We are specializing in search of sales, marketing, and management professionals in the packaging industry on a national basis. Our clients include manufacturers of materials and equipment, converters, and manufacturers in related industries.

Key Contact:
Ms. Dianna Rudd

Salary minimum: $50,000

Functions: General Mgmt., Packaging, Sales & Mktg., Sales Mgmt.

Industries: Generalist, Mfg., Paper, Printing, Plastics, Rubber, Machine, Appliance, Packaging

Professional Associations: IOPP

Sales Search Specialist
2408 Happy Hollow Rd
Glenview, IL 60025-1115
(847) 564-1595
Fax: (847) 564-1597

Description: We only work on sales and marketing middle management. We pride ourselves on quality people. We work fast and smart.

Key Contact - Specialty:
Ms. Darlene Fidlow, President
Mr. Elliott Fidlow, Senior Recruiter - *Consumer products (sales & marketing)*

Functions: Directors, Middle Mgmt., Sales Mgmt.

Industries: Mfg., Food, Bev., Tobacco, Soap, Perf., Cosmtcs., Drugs Mfg., Wholesale, Pharm Svcs., HR Services

Sales Solutions
PO Box 3557
Walnut Creek, CA 94598
(925) 932-8900
Fax: (925) 935-3530
Email: salessol@ccnet.com
Web: www.salessol.com

Description: We specialize in the placement of professionals in sales and marketing, nationwide. Our primary focus is in chemical and plastics industries. We pay specific attention to industrial and specialty gases.

Key Contact - Specialty:
Mr. Bill Schmeh, President - *Sales & marketing*

Salary minimum: $50,000

Functions: General Mgmt., Sales & Mktg.

Industries: Chemicals, Plastics, Rubber

Professional Associations: CSP

Sales Source
331 Ushers Rd
Ballston Lake, NY 12019
(518) 877-6706
(800) 229-3093
Fax: (518) 877-8161
Email: home@salessource.net
Web: www.salessource.net

Description: We are one of the oldest medical sales search firms in upstate NY. We do national searches and can fill positions anywhere in the United States. Winner of nine Award of Excellence from First Interview.

Key Contact - Specialty:
Mr. Clay Ward, Vice President - *Medical products sales*
Mr. Bill Ward, Treasurer - *Medical sales, pharmaceutical sales*

Salary minimum: $40,000

Functions: Sales Mgmt.

Industries: Drugs Mfg., Medical Devices, Computer Equip., Pharm Svcs., Telecoms, Software, Biotech

Networks: First Interview Network (FIN)
Branches:
5144 Sheridan Dr
Williamsville, NY 14221
(716) 626-5520
(800) 201-8203
Fax: (716) 626-0042
Email: home@salessource.net
Key Contact - Specialty:
Mr. Paul Briand, Office Manager - *Medical sales, pharmaceutical sales*

Sales Talent Inc
2320 130th Ave NE 104
Bellevue, WA 98005
(425) 497-2805
Fax: (425) 376-1078
Email: yaffa@salestalentinc.com
Web: www.salestalentinc.com

Description: We are a national search firm that specializes in the placement of sales professionals with companies that range from the hottest startups to the most respected Blue Chips. The searches range from entry level to experienced sales positions including sales management.

Key Contact:
Mr. Yaffa Carlson, VP of Sales

Salesforce
3294 Woodrow Way
Atlanta, GA 30319
(404) 252-8566
Fax: (404) 257-9312
Email: fred@shankweiler.com
Web: www.shankweiler.com

Description: We are an executive recruiting firm specializing in recruitment of personnel for: sales, sales management, mortgage management and staff, software, and financial industry related.

Key Contact - Specialty:
Mr. Fred Shankweiler, President
Mr. Marilyn Shankweiler, Y., Co-owner - *Mortgage, software, financial related positions*

Functions: Sales Mgmt.

Industries: Finance, E-commerce, Software

SalesHunter Inc
(also known as Sales Consultants of Memphis)
PO Box 38328
Memphis, TN 38183-0328
(901) 751-1995
Email: info@saleshunter.com
Web: www.saleshunter.com

Description: Finding and placing sales talent is our only business.

Key Contact:
Mr. Wayne Williams, President

Functions: Sales & Mktg.

Industries: Generalist

A N Salloway Executive Search & Consulting LLC
176 Federal St Fl 5
Boston, MA 02110-2214
(617) 428-0703
Fax: (617) 428-0707
Email: sallowayexecsrch@aol.com

Description: My practice is completely dedicated to the financial services industry, with an emphasis toward mutual fund/brokerage companies. I place people in positions that concentrate on mutual fund transfer-agency/operations management, project/conversions management, business systems analysts/management, client service/relationship management, retirement plan record keeping, wholesalers/management, and marketing/management. Occasionally, we assist with resume revision and updating.

Key Contact - Specialty:
Mr. Andrew N. Salloway, President - *Mutual fund operations, sales & marketing, client relations, communications*

Salary minimum: $45,000

Functions: General Mgmt., Directors, Senior Mgmt., Middle Mgmt., Sales & Mktg., Sales Mgmt., Customer Svc., Training, Systems Analysis, Systems Implem.

Industries: Finance, Banking, Invest. Banking, Brokers, Misc. Financial, Accounting, Mgmt. Consulting, Telecoms, Call Centers, Telephony, Insurance, Accounting SW, HR SW

Professional Associations: ICI, NICSA, SIA

Sampson Associates
4109 Redwood Rd 359
Oakland, CA 94619
(510) 531-4237
(650) 756-7575
Fax: (510) 531-2920
Email: jsampson@sampsonassociates.com
Web: www.sampsonassociates.com

Description: Founded in 1990 as a National Recruiting sales, technical and managerial search firm, our greatest asset and notable advantage is our network of nation wide contacts. We have assisted hundreds of companies to locate technical and sales professionals, management and executive men and women at all income levels from virtually all fields.

Key Contact - Specialty:
Mr. James S. Sampson, President/Managing Director
Mr. Brian Sampson, Vice President Product Services - *Management*

Salary minimum: $75,000

Functions: General Mgmt., Directors, Middle Mgmt., Sales & Mktg., Mkt. Research, Mktg. Mgmt., Systems Dev., Systems Implem., DB Admin., Architects

Industries: Computer Equip., Equip Svcs., Software, Biotech, Healthcare

Networks: Computer Search

George D Sandel Associates
PO Box 588
Waltham, MA 02454
(781) 558-7770
Fax: (781) 558-7771
Email: irsxgdsa@erols.com

Description: Since 1958, we place technical professionals and mid- to upper-management in the computer, electronics, UI, HF, web design, defense and medical industries.

Key Contact - Specialty:
Mr. Ivan R. Samuels, President - *High technology*

Functions: Middle Mgmt.

Industries: Metal Products, Computer Equip., Consumer Elect., Test, Measure Equip., Aerospace, Software

Professional Associations: HFES, MPPC

Sanderson Employment Service
500 Chama NE
Albuquerque, NM 87108
(505) 265-8827
Fax: (505) 268-5536
Email: sandersonq@aol.com
Web: www.sandersonemployment.com

Description: We recruit and place candidates in technical and professional sales, computer software

and hardware specialists and accounting professionals.

Key Contact - Specialty:
Mr. Bill Sanderson, Recruiter - *Information technology, administrative/professional, management*
Ms. Angela Romo, Recruiter/ Office Manager - *Office support, customer service*

Salary minimum: $40,000

Functions: General Mgmt., Admin. Svcs., Mfg., Sales Mgmt., Customer Svc., Systems Analysis, Systems Dev., Engineering, Environmentalists, Technicians

Industries: Generalist, Lumber, Furniture, Plastics, Rubber, Metal Products, Machine, Appliance, Motor Vehicles, Computer Equip., Consumer Elect., Test, Measure Equip., Misc. Mfg., Electronic, Elec. Components, Wholesale, Retail, Misc. Financial, Non-profits, Legal, Accounting, Mgmt. Consulting, HR Services, Call Centers, Digital, Haz. Waste, Software, Database SW, Development SW, Doc. Mgmt., Production SW, Networking, Comm. SW, System SW

SRA Int'l
3737 Embassy Pkwy Ste 200
Akron, OH 44333-8369
(330) 670-9797
(800) 731-7724
Fax: (330) 670-9798
Email: hq@sanfordrose.com
Web: www.sanfordrose.com

Description: We represent companies and institutions around the world in finding high-quality executives, managers and professionals for important position openings through our proprietary Dimensional Search ® process.

Key Contact:
Mr. George R. Snider, Jr., President/CEO
Mr. Douglas R. Rogers, Vice President-Operations

Salary minimum: $40,000

Functions: Generalist, General Mgmt., Materials, Sales & Mktg., IT, R&D, Engineering

Industries: Generalist

Professional Associations: CFA, IFA, NAPS

Branches:
210 Bradford St
Gainesville, GA 30501
(770) 297-9696
Fax: (770) 297-9151
Email: langmand@msn.com
Key Contact:
Mr. Douglas H. Langman

PO Box 2577
Orland Park, IL 60462
(708) 403-9933
Key Contact:
Mr. J. Michael Kane

75 Cavalier Blvd
Florence, KY 41042
(859) 647-6472
Fax: (859) 647-6942
Email: srankentucky@sanfordrose.com
Key Contact:
Mr. Richard J. Premec, Jr.

1627 Blue Grouse Cir
Lexington, KY 40511
(847) 328-6770
Email: bbass@sanfordrose.com
Key Contact:
Mr. Bill Bass

806 Stone Creek Pkwy Ste 10
Louisville, KY 40223
(502) 426-4900
Key Contact:
Mr. George S. Griffiths

101 Log Canoe Cir Ste H
Stevensville, MD 21666
(410) 604-3370
Key Contact:
Mr. Peter A. Norton

150 JFK Pkwy Ste 100
Short Hills, NJ 07078
(973) 847-5938
Fax: (973) 847-5994
Key Contact:
Mr. Dennis L. Stevens

3532 Irwin-Simpson Rd Ste 50
Mason, OH 45040
(513) 229-0350
Fax: (513) 229-0353
Email: mdduffy@sanfordrose.com
Key Contact:
Mr. Meahal Duffy

8904 Old #6 Hwy
Santee, SC 29142
(803) 854-0003
Fax: (803) 854-0044
Email: santeesc@sanfordrose.com
Key Contact:
Mr. John P. Malloy

Sanford Rose Associates - Fairhope
22873 U S Hwy 98 Bldg I
Fairhope, AL 36532
(334) 928-7072
Fax: (334) 928-7738
Email: sraprint@aol.com
Web: www.sanfordrose.com

Description: Our firm specializes in the recruitment of senior-level executives and managers for the printing industry. Over 65 years' total industry experience gives us a working knowledge of our clients products, services and needs before a search even begins. Our numerous contacts throughout the industry round out our capability.

Key Contact - Specialty:
Mr. Paul Marquez, President - *Commercial printing (business forms, direct mail, labels)*

Salary minimum: $50,000

Functions: General Mgmt., Senior Mgmt., Legal, Mfg., Plant Mgmt., Sales & Mktg., Sales Mgmt., Direct Mktg., Customer Svc., CFO's

Industries: Printing, Packaging

Professional Associations: NAPS

Sanford Rose Associates - Bentonville
810-D NW 3rd St Ste 1
Bentonville, AR 72712
(501) 271-9288
Fax: (501) 271-9260
Email: rgeguzys@arkansasusa.com
Web: www.sanfordrose.com

Description: We specialize in senior level executives and engineers in machining, industrial lighting, and contract manufacturing.

Key Contact:
Mr. Ronald P. Geguzys

Salary minimum: $75,000

Functions: Generalist

Industries: Consumer Elect., Misc. Mfg., Electronic, Elec. Components, Mgmt. Consulting, ERP SW, Mfg. SW

Sanford Rose Associates - San Diego
613 W Valley Pkwy Ste 103
Escondido, CA 92025
(760) 480-9010
Fax: (760) 480-9020
Email: srasdc@sanfordrose.com
Web: www.sanfordrose.com

Description: We specialize in the following industries: food, beverage, pharmaceutical, medical devices, IT, telecommunications, multimedia, and construction.

Key Contact - Specialty:
Mr. David Miller, CEO - *Food/beverage, telecommunications*
Mr. David Felker, Co-Owner - *Pharmaceuticals, medical devices*
Mrs. Edith Felker, President - *Food, neutraceuticals*

Functions: Generalist

Industries: Construction, Mfg., Transportation, Misc. Financial, Services, Restaurants, Communications, Packaging, Software, Biotech

Networks: National Personnel Assoc (NPA)

Sanford Rose Associates - Laguna Beach
9 St. Francis Ct Ste D
Monarch Beach, CA 92629
(949) 487-9055
Fax: (949) 487-9214
Email: bdudley@sralaguna.com
Web: www.sralaguna.com

Description: We offer specialized custom recruiting of senior information technology and biotechnology professionals nationwide.e.

Key Contact:
Mr. Robert R. Dudley, CPC, President

Salary minimum: $50,000

Functions: General Mgmt., Sales & Mktg., IT

Industries: Generalist, Software, Biotech

Professional Associations: CSP, NAPS

Networks: Top Echelon Network

Sanford Rose Associates - Santa Ana
2030 E 4th St Ste 140
Santa Ana, CA 92705-3922
(714) 558-1622
(888) 817-5396
Fax: (714) 558-3739
Email: srasna@aol.com
Web: www.sra92705.com/

Description: We specialize in all disciplines for the semiconductor component industry.

Key Contact:
Mr. Charles S. McCarthy, Director

Salary minimum: $60,000

Functions: Generalist

Industries: Mfg., Software

Professional Associations: NAPS

Sanford Rose Associates - Santa Barbara
748 Dos Hermanos Rd
Santa Barbara, CA 93111
(805) 967-1846
Fax: (805) 967-1846
Email: jmyatt@silcom.com
Web: www.sanfordrose.com

Description: A management professional with extensive background in corporate management of high-technology industries, both aerospace and commercial.

Key Contact - Specialty:
Mr. James S. Myatt, Jr., Director - *Technical and management personnel, electronic industries*
Mr. Francis Crusit, Research Associate - *MIS, information services*

Salary minimum: $75,000

Functions: Generalist, Senior Mgmt., Middle Mgmt., Automation, Mktg. Mgmt., Sales Mgmt., R&D, Engineering

Industries: Generalist, Medical Devices, Computer Equip., Consumer Elect., Test, Measure Equip., Telecoms, Aerospace

Sanford Rose Associates - San Francisco East Bay
1415 Oakland Blvd Ste 215
Walnut Creek, CA 94596-4349
(925) 974-1760
Fax: (925) 974-1763
Email: rjc@srasf.com
Web: www.srasf.com

Description: We are an executive/key employee search firm specializing in the medical diagnostics/device, biotechnology, and pharmaceuticals industries. Our clients span a wide range of companies from start-ups to international conglomerate corporations. Its placements range from the senior scientist to chief executive/general management levels.

Key Contact:
Mr. Rich Carter, President

Functions: Generalist

Industries: Biotech

Professional Associations: NAPS

Sanford Rose Associates - Clearwater
2623 McCormick Dr Ste 104
Clearwater, FL 33759-1046
(727) 796-2201
Fax: (727) 669-2942
Email: search104@aol.com
Web: www.sanfordrose.com

Description: Firm offers retained and contingency search assignment services. With our Dimensional Search ® process, computer database, industry network and the resources of other SRA offices, we can move quickly to find qualified candidates.

Key Contact - Specialty:
Mr. Kenneth R. Monroe, Jr., Managing Director - *Pharmaceuticals, medical equipment, medical devices, nutritional*

Salary minimum: $100,000

Functions: Senior Mgmt., Mfg., Sales & Mktg., HR Mgmt.

Industries: Drugs Mfg., Medical Devices, Pharm Svcs.

Professional Associations: NAPS

Sanford Rose Associates - Orlando
1310 W Colonial Dr Ste 8
Orlando, FL 32804
(407) 245-8999
Fax: (407) 245-8922
Email: sra-orl@sanfordrose.com
Web: www.sanfordrose.com

Description: We specialize in filling marketing, sales, and engineering management positions for telecommunications, power quality, and power protection companies.

Key Contact:
Mr. James A. Roach

Salary minimum: $100,000

Functions: General Mgmt., Sales & Mktg., Engineering

Industries: Electronic, Elec. Components, Telecoms

Sanford Rose Associates - Fort Lauderdale
9000 Sheridan St Ste 158
Pembroke Pines, FL 33024-8801
(954) 437-6750
Fax: (954) 437-6766
Email: fortlauderdale@sanfordrose.com
Web: www.sanfordrose.com/fortlauderdale

Description: We are part of SRA-International. The Fort Lauderdale office is an international executive search firm that specializes in the consumer products industry. We pride ourselves on finding the right people to make a difference through providing custom searches for our clients.

Key Contact - Specialty:
Mrs. Sonseenahray Hambrick, President - *General management*
Mr. LeRoy Hambrick, Vice President and COO - *General management*

Salary minimum: $80,000

Functions: General Mgmt., Sales & Mktg., HR Mgmt., Finance, IT, Engineering, Specialized Svcs.

Industries: Mfg., Wholesale, Retail, Finance, Services, Communications

Professional Associations: NAPS

Networks: National Personnel Assoc (NPA)

Sanford Rose Associates - Norcross
9650 Ventana Way Ste 204
1 Medlock Crossing
Alpharetta, GA 30022
(770) 232-9900
Fax: (770) 232-1933
Email: sra@searchforsuccess.com
Web: www.searchforsuccess.com

Description: We perform ethical search services with an emphasis on custom recruiting in the telecommunications marketplace, with a focus on wireless. Mid-to-staff level technical, information technology, sales/marketing, and general/senior management positions are our specialty.

Key Contact - Specialty:
Mr. Donald R. Patrick, CPC, President - *General, sales & marketing management, staff positions, telecommunications focus*
Ms. Janet L. Patrick, Vice President - *Research*
Mr. David Kouse, CPC, Vice President
Mr. Stephen Samdperil, Recruiter
Ms. Aimee Griffin, Research Assistant - *Research*

Salary minimum: $75,000

Functions: Generalist

Industries: Telecoms, Call Centers, Telephony, Digital, Wireless, Fiber Optic, Network Infrastructure

Professional Associations: GAPS, NAPS

Sanford Rose Associates - Athens
2500 W Broad St Ste 106
Athens, GA 30606
(706) 548-3942
Fax: (706) 548-3786
Email: sraathens@aol.com
Web: www.sanfordrose.com

Description: Custom recruiting for key manufacturing plant positions and division/staff management, QA, accounting, materials and engineers including, plant/IE/design/mfg/project/product.

Key Contact - Specialty:
Mr. Art Weiner, President - *Engineering, technical, operations management*
Ms. Arlene Weiner - *Accounting, materials, technical management*

Mr. Ken Weiner, CPC, Executive Search Consultant - *Engineering, operations (key & management people)*

Salary minimum: $40,000

Functions: General Mgmt., Senior Mgmt., Mfg., Product Dev., Plant Mgmt., Quality, Materials, HR Mgmt., Finance, Engineering

Industries: Mfg., Medical Devices, Plastics, Rubber, Metal Products, Machine, Appliance

Professional Associations: GAPS, NAPS

Sanford Rose Associates - Chicago
233 E Erie St Ste 410
Chicago, IL 60611-5936
(312) 787-7171
Email: sra@wiltshiregroup.com
Web: www.sanfordrose.com

Description: We specialize in placing mid- to upper-level executives in the medical device and products industry. Over 50 percent of our work is in marketing.

Key Contact:
Mr. R. Vic Robertson, CPC, President - *Medical device*
Mr. Mike Griffin, Director of Research
Mrs. Sandra Robertson, Secretary

Salary minimum: $70,000

Functions: Directors, Senior Mgmt., Middle Mgmt., Mfg., Product Dev., Sales & Mktg., Mktg. Mgmt., MIS Mgmt., R&D, Engineering

Industries: Medical Devices

Professional Associations: NAPS

Sanford Rose Associates - Crystal Lake
44 N Virginia St Ste 2A
Crystal Lake, IL 60014
(815) 444-8382
Fax: (815) 444-8390
Email: info@careerfasttrack.com
Web: www.careerfasttrack.com

Description: Our company finds people who make a difference in specialty chemicals and food industries. We serve the specialty chemicals industry with 15 years of experience and the food industry with 30 years of experience. Our thorough, detailed, and quality focused Dimension/Search® process yields results for both the client and candidate.

Key Contact - Specialty:
Mr. Steven J. Burks, CEO - *Specialty chemicals*
Mr. Edward Bergmann, Search Consultant - *Food industry*
Ms. Scottie Godar, Executive Recruiter - *Specialty chemicals*
Ms. Julie A. Dunn, Executive Recruiter - *Food industry*

Salary minimum: $70,000

Functions: Generalist, General Mgmt., Middle Mgmt., Product Dev., Production, Quality, Sales & Mktg., Finance, R&D, Engineering

Industries: Food, Bev., Tobacco, Chemicals, Soap, Perf., Cosmtcs., Plastics, Rubber, Paints, Petro. Products, Biotech

Professional Associations: ACS, ASQ, FSCT, IFT, NAPS, SMTA, SSPC

Sanford Rose Associates - Dieterich
7932 N 2200th St
PO Box 33
Dieterich, IL 62424
(217) 925-5928
Fax: (217) 925-5755
Email: sradieterich@sanfordrose.com
Web: www.sanfordrose.com

Key Contact - Specialty:
Mr. William "Bill" Teichmiller, President - *RF communications*

Salary minimum: $75,000

Functions: Generalist

Industries: Digital, Wireless, Fiber Optic, Network Infrastructure

Professional Associations: NAPS

Sanford Rose Associates - Effingham
444 S Willow Ste 11
Effingham, IL 62401
(217) 342-3928
Fax: (217) 347-7111
Email: sraeff@hotmail.com

Description: Experience and in-depth knowledge about printing 35 years' and recruiting 13 years' and active participation with printing related organizations like R&E council & PIA. Therefore efficient searches are conducted resulting in timely placements.

Key Contact - Specialty:
Mr. Robert A. St. Denis, Owner/Director - *Printing*
Ms. Sherry St. Denis, A., Consultant - *Printing*
Mr. Albert Hemenway, Office Manager - *Printing*

Salary minimum: $30,000

Functions: Generalist, Directors, Senior Mgmt., Middle Mgmt., Admin. Svcs., Plant Mgmt., Distribution, Sales Mgmt.

Industries: Generalist, Printing

Sanford Rose Associates - Orland Park
9405 W Bormet Dr Ste 1
Mokena, IL 60448
(708) 403-9933
(708) 479-4954
Fax: (708) 479-4750
Email: sraop1@aol.com
Web: www.sanfordrose.com

Description: Executive search and professional recruiting for mid- to upper-level positions.

Key Contact - Specialty:
Mr. J. Michael Kane, President - *Materials management (all industries)*

Salary minimum: $75,000

Functions: Generalist, General Mgmt., Mfg., Materials, Sales & Mktg., HR Mgmt., IT

Industries: Generalist, Mfg., Transportation, Wholesale, Retail, Services, Packaging

Professional Associations: CLM

Sanford Rose Associates - Rockford
PO Box 4573
Rockford, IL 61110-4573
(815) 636-0848
Email: sra-rockford@home.com
Web: www.sanfordrose.com

Description: Our specializes are tooling engineers for stamping, plastic and metal cutting industries. Clients are manufacturers utilizing highspeed equipment, automation, robotics, automated or semiautomated welding processes and high speed CNC machining. Recent efforts have also included industrial sales positions.

Key Contact - Specialty:
Mr. Dennis M. Wallace - *Tooling engineers*

Salary minimum: $50,000

Functions: Generalist, Production, Automation, Quality, Productivity, Packaging, Sales Mgmt., Engineering

Industries: Generalist, Soap, Perf., Cosmtcs., Plastics, Rubber, Metal Products, Machine, Appliance, Motor Vehicles, Misc. Mfg.

Sanford Rose Associates - Carmel
11405 N Pennsylvania St Ste 104
Carmel, IN 46033
(317) 848-9987
(800) 201-2463
Fax: (317) 848-9979
Email: sracarmel@aol.com
Web: www.sanfordrose.com/carmel

Description: Recruiting services for critical executive, managerial and professional position openings in the insurance industry.

Key Contact - Specialty:
Mr. Michael A. Nichipor - *Insurance*

Salary minimum: $35,000

Functions: Generalist, General Mgmt., Senior Mgmt., Benefits, CFO's, Risk Mgmt., MIS Mgmt., Attorneys

Industries: Generalist, Accounting, HR Services, Insurance

Sanford Rose Associates - Evansville
PO Box 1106
Newburgh, IN 47629-1106
(812) 853-9325
Fax: (812) 853-1953
Email: kforbes@aol.com
Web: www.sraevansville.com

Description: We provide executive search and professional staffing in a broad range of industries with special emphasis in advertising and advertising agencies and marketing disciplines.

Key Contact - Specialty:
Mr. Kenneth P. Forbes, President - *Advertising, advertising agencies, graphic arts,*
Ms. Kay Koob Forbes, Vice President - *Advertising, advertising agencies, media, market research*

Salary minimum: $30,000

Functions: Generalist

Industries: Printing, Advertising, Publishing, New Media

Professional Associations: NAPS

Sanford Rose Associates - Cedar Rapids
3343 Southgate Ct Ste 205
Cedar Rapids, IA 52404
(319) 286-2969
Fax: (319) 286-2971
Email: scr12@aol.com
Web: www.sanfordrose.com

Description: We have a strong track record in selecting quality candidates in sales and marketing management, finance, human resources, operations, and engineering.

Key Contact - Specialty:
Mr. Michael Fleming, Owner - *Industrial products, all disciplines*

Salary minimum: $60,000

Functions: Generalist

Industries: Mfg., HR Services

Professional Associations: NAPS

Sanford Rose Associates - Nauset Bay
19A Cove Rd Ste 1
Orleans, MA 02653-2444
(508) 240-5655
Fax: (508) 240-5495

Email: sranb@c4.net
Web: www.sanfordrose.com

Description: Our 27 years' previous industrial experience in R&D, engineering management and manufacturing in the medical device and chemical fields ensures that client's needs are understood and met.

Key Contact - Specialty:
Mr. Howard I. Gostin, President - *Medical device, biotechnology, pharmaceutical (executive, managerial & technical)*

Salary minimum: $50,000

Functions: General Mgmt., Mfg., Product Dev., Quality, R&D, Engineering

Industries: Chemicals, Drugs Mfg., Medical Devices, Plastics, Rubber, Pharm Svcs., Biotech, Healthcare

Professional Associations: AAAS, ACRP, AICHE, DIA, NAPS

Sanford Rose Associates - Rochester
2657 Stoodeigh Dr
Rochester, MI 48309
(248) 375-2501
Fax: (248) 375-2502
Email: srarmi@customnet.net
Web: www.sanfordrose.com

Description: Executive search and professional recruiting for mid- to upper-level executives.

Key Contact:
Mr. William J. Gongloff, Jr., President

Functions: Generalist, Directors, Middle Mgmt., Production, Plant Mgmt., Quality, Purchasing, MIS Mgmt.

Industries: Generalist, Printing, Drugs Mfg., Medical Devices, Motor Vehicles, Pharm Svcs., HR Services, Biotech

Professional Associations: NAPS, SHRM

Sanford Rose Associates - Traverse City
416 St. Joseph St
PO Box 156
Suttons Bay, MI 49682
(231) 271-6100
Fax: (231) 271-6106
Email: tsheidler@aol.com
Web: www.sanfordrose.com

Description: We are facility management recruiters.

Key Contact:
Mr. Thomas R. Sheidler

Functions: General Mgmt., Production, Engineering

Industries: Generalist

Professional Associations: AFE, IFMA

Sanford Rose Associates - Amherst NY
5500 Main St Ste 340
Williamsville, NY 14221
(716) 626-2265
(716) 626-4118
Fax: (716) 626-4997
Email: sraamh@localnet.com
Web: www.sanfordrose.com

Description: We provide contingency and retainer searches for the automotive OEMs and their Tier I & II suppliers. We also conduct searches for the healthcare and information technology companies. Customized searches for executive and managerial staff are conducted globally.

Key Contact - Specialty:
Mr. Dinesh V. Parekh, CPC, President - *Automotive, IT, healthcare executives*

Salary minimum: $75,000

Functions: Senior Mgmt., Middle Mgmt., Mfg., Production, Plant Mgmt., Purchasing, Mktg. Mgmt., Sales Mgmt., CFO's, Int'l.

Industries: Mfg., Motor Vehicles, Transportation, Biotech, Healthcare

Professional Associations: ASME, ASQ, NAPR, SAE

Sanford Rose Associates - Charlotte
338 S Sharon Amity Rd 374
Charlotte, NC 28211-2806
(704) 366-0730
Fax: (704) 365-0620
Email: jdownssra@aol.com
Web: www.sra-charlotte.com

Description: Industry experience by all consultants in information services gives us a unique ability to meet the needs of our clients.

Key Contact:
Mr. James L. Downs, CPC, President - *Information technology*
Mr. Eugene Dominy, Consultant - *Information technology*
Mr. Steve Kane, Principal - *Pharmaceutical, medical devices*
Mr. Martin Vann, International Principal
Ms. Michelle Fowler, Consultant - *Information technology*
Mr. Dick Jordan, Consultant - *Information technology*
Mr. Warren Francois, Consultant - *Information technology*
Mr. James Hungate, Consultant - *Information technology*
Mr. James J. Clegg, Principal - *Information technology*
Ms. Diann C. Downs, Director-Administration
Mr. Bob Bruton, Principal - *Information technology*
Mr. Joe Utley, Consultant

Salary minimum: $50,000

Functions: IT

Industries: Generalist

Professional Associations: NACCB, NCASP, RON, SHRM

Networks: Top Echelon Network

Sanford Rose Associates - Akron
265 S Main St
Akron, OH 44308
(330) 762-6211
(888) 333-3828
Fax: (330) 762-6161
Email: sra4oc@aol.com
Web: www.sanfordrose.com

Description: Our firm devotes its practice to serving the aerospace, aircraft, avionics, defense electronics, and power utility industries. We are committed to providing recruiting services of the highest caliber. Our relationships with our client companies have been forged over 40 years of excellence.

Key Contact - Specialty:
Mr. Sanford Rose, President
Mr. David Ally, Vice President
Mrs. Martha Harris, Sr Technical Recruiter - *Aerospace, avionics, defense electronics*
Mr. Odell McLeod, Sr Technical Recruiter - *Power utilities*
Mrs. Sharon Schank, Sr Technical Recruiter - *Aircraft, defense electronics*
Mr. Ben Hottinger, Sr Technical Recruiter - *Aircraft, aerospace*
Mr. Kris Palinchak, Sr Technical Recruiter - *IT, IT Sales*

Salary minimum: $60,000

Sanford Rose Associates - Youngstown
545 N Broad St Ste 2
Canfield, OH 44406-9204
(330) 533-9270
Fax: (330) 533-9272
Email: ellisor@aol.com
Web: www.sanfordrose.com

Description: We are information systems recruiters.

Key Contact - Specialty:
Mr. Richard H. Ellison, CPC, CSP, President - *Information technology*

Salary minimum: $40,000

Functions: IT, MIS Mgmt., Systems Analysis, Systems Dev., Systems Implem., Systems Support, Network Admin., DB Admin.

Industries: Generalist

Professional Associations: NAPS

Sanford Rose Associates - Canton
4450 Belden Village St NW Ste 209
Canton, OH 44718
(330) 649-9100
Fax: (330) 649-9101
Email: cantonoh@sanfordrose.com
Web: www.sanfordrose.com

Description: Custom recruiting for middle- and upper-level positions in management and engineering. We focus on manufacturing industries, primarily automotive OEM and aftermarket.

Key Contact - Specialty:
Mr. William Kuehnling, President - *Managerial, engineering, manufacturing*

Salary minimum: $50,000

Functions: General Mgmt., Senior Mgmt., Middle Mgmt., Product Dev., Production, Automation, Plant Mgmt., Quality, Materials, Engineering

Industries: Motor Vehicles

Professional Associations: NAPS

Sanford Rose Associates - Cincinnati South
4355 Ferguson Dr Ste 210
Cincinnati, OH 45245
(513) 752-5100
Fax: (513) 752-5490
Email: dlittleton@sanfordrose.com
Web: www.sanfordrose.com

Description: Specialists in executive placement in all functions of manufacturing enterprise. Our staff has former Senior Executive as well as research and recruiting support. Client base is diverse in size and type. Clients involved in growth as well as turnarounds.

Key Contact - Specialty:
Mr. Darryl Littleton, President - *Manufacturing*

Salary minimum: $80,000

Sanford Rose Associates - Cincinnati East
431 Ohio Pike Ste 214
Cincinnati, OH 45255
(513) 528-3400
Email: fniolet@sraceo.com
Web: www.sraceo.com

Description: We pride ourselves on finding better candidates faster and moving people in the right direction in the life sciences, including pharmaceutical and healthcare, telecommunications, IT, and DCOM industries.

Key Contact - Specialty:
Mr. Frank Niolet, President - *Life sciences, high technology*

Functions: Generalist

Industries: Generalist, Services, Communications, Government, Aerospace, Software, Biotech, Healthcare

Professional Associations: NAPS

Sanford Rose Associates - Fairlawn
3040 W Market St
Fairlawn, OH 44333
(330) 865-4545
Fax: (330) 865-4544
Email: dlcreeger@aol.com
Web: www.sanfordrose.com

Description: We specialize in chemicals, plastics, rubber, and allied industries such as adhesives, plastic additives, personal care, for marketing, sales, general management technical, and engineering functions. We have had over 30 years experience in the chemical/plastic industry.

Key Contact - Specialty:
Mr. David Creeger, Director - *Chemicals, plastics, rubber*

Salary minimum: $75,000

Functions: General Mgmt., Middle Mgmt., Product Dev., Sales & Mktg., Mkt. Research, Mktg. Mgmt., Sales Mgmt., Engineering

Industries: Chemicals, Soap, Perf., Cosmtcs., Plastics, Rubber, Paints, Petro. Products

Professional Associations: NAPS

Sanford Rose Associates - New Albany
428 Beecher Rd Ste A
Gahanna, OH 43230
(614) 939-1309
Fax: (614) 939-1308
Email: inquire@sranewalbany.com
Web: www.sranewalbany.com

Description: Our firm handles a broad range of property casualty insurance and reinsurance positions including: accounting, actuarial, claims, general management, marketing, product management, sales management, and underwriting. Because we understand the insurance industry, we are also well positioned to handle professional liability, specialty commercial, excess and surplus, and other specialty or niche-type positions.

Key Contact - Specialty:
Ms. Jodelle K. "Jodi" Corrier, President/CEO - *Insurance executives*

Salary minimum: $60,000

Functions: Generalist

Industries: Insurance

Professional Associations: NAPS

Sanford Rose Associates - Hudson
70 W Streetsboro St Ste 109
Hudson, OH 44236
(330) 653-3325
Fax: (330) 650-4801
Email: srahudson@alltel.net
Web: www.sanfordrose.com

Description: We specialize in filling senior-level positions within the chemical and specialty materials industries. We are called upon by our clients to find the best possible candidates in the shortest possible time. We stake our ability to do so on our considerable technical expertise, state-of-the-art technology, commitment to our clients and use of Sanford Rose Associates' proprietary Dimensional Search® process. Not only do we identify job candidates with the right skills and experience, we also match their individual style to the employer's corporate culture.

Key Contact - Specialty:
Mr. Allen Wass, President - *Chemicals, specialty materials*

Salary minimum: $75,000

Functions: General Mgmt.

Industries: Chemicals

Professional Associations: AICHE, NAPS, TMS

Sanford Rose Associates - Cleveland West
26777 Lorain Rd Ste 304
North Olmsted, OH 44070
(440) 716-8855
(440) 716-8854
Email: sracw@sanfordrose.com
Web: www.sanfordrose.com

Description: We are a small, highly focused firm professionally serving only a few select clients on a repeat basis. Clients include private developers, REITs and other corporate owners and managers of income properties. We know our industry very well.

Key Contact - Specialty:
Mr. Earl L. Martin, Jr., Managing Director - *Real estate, CEOs, COOs, managers*
Mr. Jacob Wotsch, Recruiting Consultant - *Real estate*

Salary minimum: $65,000

Functions: Generalist

Industries: Real Estate

Professional Associations: ICSC, NAPS, NAREIT

Sanford Rose Associates - Euclid
PO Box 21615
South Euclid, OH 44121
(216) 731-0005
Email: sraeuclid@aol.com
Web: www.sanfordrose.com

Description: Concentration in information systems and information technology across all industries.

Key Contact - Specialty:
Mr. Ralph Orkin, Director - *Information systems*

Salary minimum: $30,000

Functions: IT, Systems Analysis, Systems Dev., Systems Implem., Systems Support, Network Admin., DB Admin.

Industries: Generalist

Sanford Rose Associates - Columbus North
130 Wetherby Ln Ste 101
Westerville, OH 43081
(614) 523-1663
(800) 560-4984
Fax: (614) 523-1689
Email: bill@sracolumbus.com
Web: www.sracolumbus.com

Description: We work on national as well as local openings. Specializes in the areas of: MIS/EDP; computer hardware and software; software engineering. Appointment requested; unsolicited resumes accepted.

Key Contact - Specialty:
Mr. Bill Earhart, President - *Information systems technology*
Mr. Marko Ensminger, Recruiting Consultant - *Information systems technology*

Functions: Generalist, MIS Mgmt., Systems Analysis, Systems Dev., Systems Implem., Systems Support, Network Admin., DB Admin.

Industries: Generalist

Professional Associations: DPMA, NAPS, OSSA

Networks: National Personnel Assoc (NPA)

Sanford Rose Associates - Portland
15280 NW Central Dr Ste 202-2
Portland, OR 97229
(503) 614-1861
Fax: (503) 614-0636
Email: srapdx@aol.com

Description: We serve the following industries: food/beverage processing and consumer packaging.

Key Contact - Specialty:
Mr. Jack D. Stiles, Director - *Food processing*
Mr. Timothy W. Stiles, Director - *Food processing*

Salary minimum: $50,000

Functions: Generalist, Product Dev., Production, Plant Mgmt., Quality, Materials, Distribution, Packaging, Sales Mgmt., R&D

Industries: Generalist, Food, Bev., Tobacco, Chemicals, Soap, Perf., Cosmtcs., Drugs Mfg., Packaging

Professional Associations: IFT, NAPS, NFIB

Sanford Rose Associates - Greenville
211 Century Dr Ste 106D
Greenville, SC 29607
(864) 233-6100
Email: greenvillesc@sanfordrose.com
Web: www.sanfordrose.com

Description: We have twenty-five years of management experience helping world-class companies problem solve. We specialize in mid to upper level management in all functions of a manufacturing environment, including precision machining, machinery, and automation.

Key Contact - Specialty:
Mr. Richard Witowski, CPC, President - *Manufacturing management (all functions)*

Salary minimum: $50,000

Functions: Generalist

Industries: Mfg., Misc. Mfg.

Networks: National Personnel Assoc (NPA)

Sanford Rose Associates - Nashville
9000 Church St E Ste 100
Brentwood, TN 37027
(615) 346-3000
Fax: (615) 346-3003
Email: nashville@sanfordrose.com

Description: Senior and middle management searches in the printing and graphic arts industries. Specialize in general management, sales and marketing management, plant management and financial management positions.

Key Contact - Specialty:
Mr. Terry Tringle, Managing Director - *Printing, graphic arts*

Salary minimum: $60,000

Functions: Generalist

Industries: Printing

Sanford Rose Associates - Austin
2222 Western Trails Blvd Ste 203
Austin, TX 78745
(512) 448-9555
Fax: (512) 448-9567
Email: sraaustin@aol.com
Web: www.sanfordrose.com

Description: We have significant field experience in the designated industry sector, and we fill key positions that focus on: electronics; avionics; medical devices including implants, industrial and commercial engines, motors, pumps, and hydraulics; and building products.

Key Contact:
Mr. Stephen M. Sackmary, President - *Manufacturing operations, executive, managerial, technical*
Ms. Marcia T. Sackmary, Research Director

Salary minimum: $60,000

Functions: Senior Mgmt., Middle Mgmt., Plant Mgmt., Quality, Materials, Distribution, Engineering

Industries: Mfg., Medical Devices, Metal Products, Machine, Appliance, Motor Vehicles, Computer Equip., Consumer Elect., Test, Measure Equip., Misc. Mfg., Electronic, Elec. Components, Defense, Aerospace

Professional Associations: ASQ, IEEE, IMPS, NAPS, SAE, SME, SMTA

Sanford Rose Associates - Salt Lake City
3112 S 950 E
Bountiful, UT 84010
(435) 640-2134
Fax: (801) 299-9384
Email: srautah@sprynet.com
Web: www.sanfordrose.com

Description: We provide professional custom recruiting services for consumer product firms with a special focus in the sporting goods, recreational products, toys, and other consumer products industries. We specialize in placing executive, marketing, sales, manufacturing, and engineering disciplines. We also specialize in IT particularly for object oriented data base total management solution firms

Key Contact - Specialty:
Mr. Rodger A. Lee, President - *Sporting goods, consumer goods, toys, recreational products*

Salary minimum: $50,000

Functions: Generalist, Senior Mgmt., Middle Mgmt., Mfg., Advertising, Mkt. Research, Finance, IT

Industries: Generalist, Food, Bev., Tobacco, Soap, Perf., Cosmtcs., Drugs Mfg., Plastics, Rubber, Computer Equip., Consumer Elect.

Sanford Rose Associates - Vienna
510 29th St
Vienna, WV 26105
(304) 295-7080
(304) 295-7098
Fax: (304) 295-7099
Email: sravwv@aol.com
Web: www.sanfordrose.com

Description: Office run by former manufacturing executive. Specializes in director-level and their staffs. Process and labor intensive industries.

Key Contact - Specialty:
Mr. Sidney J. Mitchell, President - *Manufacturing*

Functions: Mfg.

Industries: Lumber, Furniture, Paper, Chemicals, Soap, Perf., Cosmtcs., Plastics, Rubber, Paints, Petro. Products, Metal Products, Misc. Mfg., HR Services

Professional Associations: NAPS

Sanford Rose Associates - Janesville
103 S Jackson St Ste 02
Janesville, WI 53545
(608) 757-8060
Fax: (608) 757-8061
Email: srajanesville@aol.com
Web: www.sanfordrose.com

Description: We provide executive, managerial, and professional searches for the aerospace and defense and electronics industries.

Key Contact:
Mr. William E. Dowell

Salary minimum: $75,000

Functions: Senior Mgmt., Middle Mgmt., Mfg., Engineering

Industries: Electronic, Elec. Components, Defense, Aerospace

Santa Fe Services Inc
142 Lincoln Ave Ste 205
Santa Fe, NM 87501
(505) 984-8511
Fax: (505) 986-8122
Email: sfservices@cnsp.com
Web: www.santafeservices.net

Description: We are a regional generalist in the employment field. Our main clients base is mid-size private sector employers, who need management and administrative personnel.

Key Contact - Specialty:
Mr. Don Wooden, Owner/President - *Generalist*
Ms. Kathy Kegel, Operations Manager - *Generalist*

Salary minimum: $12,000

Functions: Generalist, Admin. Svcs., Health Admin., Sales Mgmt., DB Admin., Graphic Artists, Paralegals

Industries: Generalist, Banking, Misc. Financial, Legal, Hospitality, Real Estate, Healthcare

Professional Associations: NNMHRA, SHRM

Santangelo Consultants Inc
60 E 42nd St Ste 1333
New York, NY 10165
(212) 867-6664
(201) 868-4380
Email: sciinc@bellatlantic.net
Web: www.santangeloconsultants.com

Description: Exclusive placement of management consultants. Emphasis on information systems, process redesign, operations improvement, healthcare, banking, brokerage, insurance, finance, customer service, management accounting, strategic planning, supply chain, inventory planning and control systems.

Key Contact - Specialty:
Mr. Richard Santangelo, President - *Management consulting*

Salary minimum: $70,000

Functions: Mfg., Productivity, Sales Mgmt., Customer Svc., Finance, IT, Systems Analysis, Systems Dev., Systems Implem., Mgmt. Consultants

Industries: Banking, Invest. Banking, Pharm Svcs., Mgmt. Consulting, Call Centers, Insurance, Software, Database SW, Development SW, ERP SW, Healthcare

Branches:
7000 Blvd E Ste 35D
Guttenberg, NJ 07093
(201) 868-4380
Email: sciinc@bellatlantic.net
Key Contact - Specialty:
Mr. Richard Santangelo, President - *Management consulting*

Sarver & Carruth Associates
3927 N 1st St
Durant, OK 74701
(580) 931-0472
Fax: (580) 931-0473
Email: cjsarver@simplynet.net

Description: We are an executive and technical recruitment firm dedicated to providing excellent service both to client companies and candidates.

Key Contact - Specialty:
Ms. Catherine J. Sarver, President - *Engineering*

Salary minimum: $50,000

Functions: Generalist, Senior Mgmt., Middle Mgmt., Product Dev., Systems Implem., R&D, Engineering

Industries: Generalist, Computer Equip., Telecoms

Professional Associations: ABWA, NAFE, NAWBO, SHRM

Savalli & Associates Inc
1747 Van Buren St Ste 925
Hollywood, Fl 33020
(954) 923-2324
Fax: (253) 369-9081
Email: savallicom@aol.com

Description: We are an executive recruiting firm specializing in the placement of individuals in brand management, market research, promotions management within consumer packaged goods companies.

Key Contact - Specialty:
Mr. Frank Savalli, President - *Brand management, marketing research, consumer promotions*
Mrs. Barbara Tata, Market Researcher - *Internet recruiting*

Salary minimum: $50,000

Functions: Plant Mgmt., Mkt. Research, Mktg. Mgmt.

Industries: Food, Bev., Tobacco, Paper, Soap, Perf., Cosmtcs., Drugs Mfg., Mgmt. Consulting, Packaging

Branches:
24 Hiawatha Dr Ste B
Battle Creek, MI 49015
(616) 968-5100
Fax: (253) 369-9081
Email: savallicom@aol.com
Key Contact:
Mr. Michael Savalli, Principal

Saviar Inc
4110 N Scottsdale Rd Ste 380
Scottsdale, AZ 85251
(480) 946-9933
Email: info@saviar.com
Web: www.saviar.com

Description: Our firm specializes in the recruitment and placement of senior management, sales, and information technology professionals in the high-tech industry, with a direct focus on Internet and telecommunication disciplines.

Key Contact:
Mr. Dominick M. Nardone, II, President/CEO

Salary minimum: $75,000

Functions: Senior Mgmt., Sales Mgmt., Systems Dev., Mgmt. Consultants

Industries: Mgmt. Consulting, E-commerce

Networks: Computer Search

SC Search Consultants
424 Beecher Rd A
Columbus, OH 43230
(614) 939-4240
Fax: (614) 939-4250
Email: info@scsearchconsultants.com
Web: www.scsearchconsultants.com

Description: We are an executive search firm committed to actively communicating with our clients and understanding their organizational culture to enable us to successfully identify qualified individuals who will impact our clients' business performance and enhance their competitive advantage in the marketplace. Experience reaffirms that a company is as good as the people they hire.

Key Contact:
Ms. Cindy Hilsheimer, Partner
Ms. Suzy Swanson, Partner

Functions: General Mgmt., Sales & Mktg., Advertising, PR, Finance, IT, Non-profits, Architects, Graphic Artists

Industries: Generalist

Professional Associations: HRACO, MOAESP

Scepter Enterprises LLC
1 Dock St
Stamford, CT 06902
(203) 969-7535
Fax: (203) 969-7536
Email: info@sceptercareers.com
Web: www.sceptercareers.com

Description: We are the premier executive placement firm in the technology business today. Our corporate mission statement is to be the premier placement firm in the telecommunications industry placing top talent in top opportunities.

Key Contact - Specialty:
Mr. Jeff Rockwell, Managing Director - *Telecommunications*
Mr. David Gordon, Managing Director - *Telecommunications*

Functions: Generalist, Directors, Senior Mgmt., Middle Mgmt., Sales Mgmt., Customer Svc., CFO's, Engineering

Industries: Generalist, New Media, Telecoms, Software

Professional Associations: CAPS

Networks: Top Echelon Network

The Schatz Company
13610 Barrett Office Dr Ste 101 G
St. Louis, MO 63021
(314) 966-8699
Fax: (314) 966-5499
Email: schatzco@yahoo.com

Description: One hundred percent concentration of the search and placement of middle- to senior-level executives in manufacturing operations. Majority of positions are with companies that manufacture new, fabricate, assemble, or process. We specialize in the manufacturing industry.

Key Contact:
Mr. William G. Schatz, Jr., President - *Operations, manufacturing, general management*
Ms. Kathleen Schatz, Vice President/General Partner

Salary minimum: $70,000

Functions: General Mgmt., Mfg., Materials

Industries: Mfg., Lumber, Furniture, Metal Products, Machine, Appliance, Motor Vehicles, Test, Measure Equip., Misc. Mfg.

Professional Associations: NAER

Schenck & Associates SC
PO Box 1739
Appleton, WI 54913
(920) 731-8111
Fax: (920) 731-8037
Email: eganp@schenckcpa.com
Web: www.schenckcpa.com

Description: Management search consultants providing professionalism, ethical and long lasting relationships, confidentiality, thoroughness and commitment to success through service.

Key Contact:
Mr. Patrick J. Egan, Principal

Salary minimum: $35,000

Functions: Generalist, Senior Mgmt., Plant Mgmt., Purchasing, Materials Plng., CFO's, Budgeting, Engineering

Industries: Generalist, Paper, Metal Products, Banking, Accounting, Packaging, Healthcare

Schick Professional Search Inc
11440 Market St
PO Box 326
North Lima, OH 44452
(330) 549-3961
Fax: (330) 549-3963
Email: rschicksps@aol.com

Description: We specialize in recruiting engineers for motors, electromechanical, electronic, consumer and automotive positions in design, manufacturing and sales and marketing.

Key Contact - Specialty:
Mr. Rex Schick, CPC, President - *Technical (motors & motor control), hardware & software engineers*
Mr. Jon Schick - *Technical (consumer, automotive products)*

Salary minimum: $45,000

Functions: Product Dev., Automation, Mktg. Mgmt., Engineering

Industries: Plastics, Rubber, Motor Vehicles, Computer Equip., Consumer Elect., Test, Measure Equip., Electronic, Elec. Components, Transportation, Aerospace, Development SW, System SW

A D Schiff & Associates Ltd
869 Creek Bend Dr
Vernon Hills, IL 60061
(847) 821-9220
Fax: (847) 821-9298
Email: adschiff@theramp.net

Description: We specialize in the healthcare industry. We have over 20 years' experience in the medical profession. We are search and recruitment consultants in all areas of healthcare; sales, e-commerce, marketing, executive, physician, management. We also have a division, which specializes in e-commerce opportunities.

Key Contact - Specialty:
Ms. Arlene D. Schiff, President - *Medical sales, medical management, medical marketing*
Mr. Kim Feeny, Vice President - *Medical*

Functions: Generalist

Industries: Drugs Mfg., Medical Devices, Pharm Svcs., Equip Svcs., Hospitality, Advertising, Software, Biotech, Healthcare

Networks: First Interview Network (FIN)

Schlatter & Associates
388 Market St Ste 400
San Francisco, CA 94111
(415) 296-2582
Fax: (415) 296-2592

Description: We specialize in CFO, controller, financial and accounting management positions.

Key Contact - Specialty:
Mr. Craig Schlatter, Managing Partner - *Finance, accounting, systems*

Salary minimum: $75,000

Functions: Generalist, Middle Mgmt., CFO's, Budgeting, Cash Mgmt., M&A, MIS Mgmt.

Industries: Generalist, Mfg., Finance, Services, Real Estate, Software, Biotech

Schoales & Associates Inc
145 King St W Ste 1000
Toronto, ON M5H 1J8
Canada
(416) 863-9978
Fax: (416) 491-1223
Email: mikeschoales@hotmail.com

Description: We specialize in recruiting sales and marketing and administrative individuals primarily in the stock brokerage industry other assignments have been successfully completed in similar disciplines.

Key Contact - Specialty:
Mr. Michael Schoales, President - *Financial services, brokerage senior*
Ms. Gloria Schoales, Vice President - *Senior administrative*

Functions: Sales Mgmt., M&A

Industries: Generalist

Don W Schooler & Associates Inc
4810 E Farm Rd 132 Chestnut Expwy
Springfield, MO 65802
(417) 831-0004
Fax: (417) 831-5101
Email: don@donschooler.com
Web: www.donschooler.com

Description: Executive recruiting for banking, trust institutions and farm credit only. We fill all officer positions. Candidates must have experience in one of the above institutions.

Key Contact - Specialty:
Mr. Don W. Schooler, Owner - *Banking officers, trust officers, farm credit officers*

Salary minimum: $40,000

Functions: Generalist, CFO's

Industries: Generalist, Banking, Misc. Financial

Schrenzel Technical Staffing
16526 161st Ave SE
Renton, WA 98058
(425) 271-4700
Fax: (425) 271-4722
Email: ben@schrenzel.com
Web: www.schrenzel.com

Description: Our firm conducts a recruiting practice for clients who need to hire hard-to-find technical, sales, or executive employees. We work on either on a committed/retained or contingent basis. We have extensive references.

Key Contact:
Mr. Ben Schrenzel, President - *High-tech, sales, executives*
Mrs. Christine Schrenzel, Business Manager

Salary minimum: $70,000

Schuetter & Associates
11754 Brookshire Dr
Orland Park, IL 60467
(708) 479-4870
Fax: (708) 479-4870
Email: bschuetter@aol.com

Description: Placement of experienced healthcare professionals into management-level positions, both clinical and non-clinical in nature. No physician recruiting.

Key Contact - Specialty:
Mr. Bill Schuetter, President - *Healthcare, management, professional, technical*

Functions: General Mgmt., Quality, Materials, Healthcare, Nurses, Allied Health, HR Mgmt., Finance, IT

Industries: Misc. Financial, Non-profits, Pharm Svcs., Accounting, HR Services, Hospitality, Advertising, Biotech, Healthcare

Schulenburg & Associates
3232 Cobb Pkwy Ste 183
Atlanta, GA 30339
(770) 745-4206
(888) 248-2116
Fax: (208) 275-1822
Email: neil@schulenburg-assoc.com
Web: www.schulenburg-assoc.com

Description: Professional search services for information technology professionals.

Key Contact - Specialty:
Mr. Neil P. Schulenburg, Principal/Founder - *Information systems*
Mrs. Kathryn Schulenburg, Principal/Owner/Operator - *Information technology recruiting*

Functions: IT

Industries: Generalist

Networks: Top Echelon Network

G L Schwartz & Associates Inc
9040 Martin Rd
Roswell, GA 30076
(770) 552-3140
Fax: (770) 552-3145
Email: glsainc@aol.com

Description: We specialize in the management, operations and administration side of healthcare. Our primary focus is in the e-healthcare business, particulary on the B2B side as opposed to consumer inormation.

Key Contact - Specialty:
Mr. Gary L. Schwartz, President - *Medical, healthcare*
Ms. Beth O. Schwartz, Secretary/Treasurer - *Medical, healthcare*

Functions: Middle Mgmt., Admin. Svcs., Healthcare, Sales & Mktg., Mktg. Mgmt., Sales Mgmt., Customer Svc.

Industries: Software, Healthcare

Networks: First Interview Network (FIN)

SCI & Associates Inc
1163 E Ogden Ave Ste 705
PMB 347
Naperville, IL 60563
(630) 778-9644
Fax: (630) 778-0268
Email: plabine@worldnet.att.net
Web: www.search-consultants-inc.com

Description: We recruit sales engineers, sales managers, marketing managers, technical experts and executives with technical degrees.

Key Contact - Specialty:
Mr. Paul Labine, President - *Sales, technical, executive, specialty chemical*

Salary minimum: $50,000

Functions: Generalist

Industries: Chemicals, Drugs Mfg., Medical Devices, Biotech

Professional Associations: NAER

Scientific Placement Inc
800 Tully Rd Ste 200
Houston, TX 77079
(281) 496-6100
Email: das@scientific.com
Web: www.scientific.com

Description: We are a high-technology recruitment firm. No geographical bias. We have 75 employees

and offices nationwide. We emphasis on quality service, professionalism, and ethics. Our client base covers the entire spectrum of the computer & software industries, from start-ups to industry giants. We place junior engineers to VPs of engineering at major corporations.

Key Contact:
Mr. Dan A. Redwine, Vice President
Mr. David A. Small, President

Salary minimum: $40,000

Functions: Product Dev., Systems Dev., R&D, Engineering, Graphic Artists

Industries: Computer Equip., Test, Measure Equip., Telecoms, Software

Networks: National Personnel Assoc (NPA)

Branches:
PO Box 7842
Berkeley, CA 94707-0842
(510) 548-4171
Fax: (510) 548-4857
Email: agray@scientific.com

PO Box 248
Merrimack, NH 03054-0248
(603) 424-3875
Fax: (603) 424-9671
Email: gel@scientific.com

PO Box 202676
Austin, TX 78720-2676
(512) 331-1828
Fax: (512) 331-0302
Email: tml@scientific.com

Scientific Search Inc
560 Fellowship Rd Ste 309
Plz Office Ctr
Mt. Laurel, NJ 08054
(856) 866-0200
Fax: (856) 722-5307
Email: rigreenberg@hotmail.com

Description: Solid knowledge of available information technology candidates in the Delaware valley from developers through CIOs.

Key Contact - Specialty:
Mr. Robert I. Greenberg, President - *Information technology*
Mr. Frank Ross, Vice President - *Information technology*
Ms. Marlyn Bennett, Vice President - *Medical, healthcare*

Salary minimum: $40,000

Functions: Generalist, Health Admin., MIS Mgmt., Systems Analysis, Systems Dev., Systems Implem., Systems Support, Network Admin.

Industries: Generalist, Software, Healthcare

Professional Associations: MAAPC

J R Scott & Associates Ltd
(a division of Esquire Personnel Services Inc)
1 S Wacker Dr Ste 1616
Chicago, IL 60606-4616
(312) 795-4300
(312) 795-4400
Fax: (312) 795-4329
Email: jolene@esquirestaffing.com
Web: www.esquirestaffing.com

Description: We are the executive search division of The Esquire Companies. Our consultants have a history of locating and motivating some of the most prestigious professionals in the financial services arena both on LaSalle Street and across the country including complete office staffings.

Key Contact - Specialty:
Mr. Sherwin J. Fischer, CEO - *Retail brokerage, financial, securities, banking*

Functions: Generalist, Directors, Senior Mgmt., Mkt. Research, Sales Mgmt., Cash Mgmt., M&A, Risk Mgmt.

Industries: Generalist, Finance, Banking, Invest. Banking, Brokers, Venture Cap., Misc. Financial

Professional Associations: NAPS

C Scott & Associates
70 York St Ste 1510
Toronto, ON M5J 1S9
Canada
(416) 214-9822
Fax: (416) 214-9820
Email: info@cscottinc.com
Web: www.cscottinc.com

Description: Information Technology recruiting for the financial services industry.

Key Contact:
C. Scott

Devin Scott Associates
2125 Center Ave Ste 402
Ft. Lee, NJ 07024
(201) 346-0331
Fax: (201) 346-0338
Email: searchdsa@aol.com
Web: www.devinscottassociates.com

Description: Strongest nationwide contacts for operational management and all staff support departments for the hospitality industry.

Key Contact - Specialty:
Mr. Rocco M. Fedele, President - *Hospitality (restaurants only), restaurants*

Salary minimum: $70,000

Functions: Generalist, Directors, Senior Mgmt., Advertising, Mkt. Research, Personnel

Industries: Generalist, Hospitality

Professional Associations: NAER

Robert Scott Associates
PO Box 486
Rancocas, NJ 08073-0486
(609) 835-2224
Fax: (609) 835-1933
Email: robert_scott@mindspring.com

Description: Helping companies recruit the finest technically trained professionals in research, engineering, operations and maintenance for over 25 years.

Key Contact - Specialty:
Mr. Bob Scott, President - *Operations, engineering, manufacturing management, research & development management, environmental health & safety, human resources, strategic consulting*

Salary minimum: $50,000

Functions: Mfg.

Industries: Mfg., Chemicals, Environmental Svcs., Packaging, Software

Scott-Marlow Agency
206 N Signal St Ste E
Ojai, CA 93023
(805) 646-5609
Fax: (805) 646-5230
Email: dank@scott-marlow.com
Web: www.scott-marlow.com

Description: We are an executive and middle management search firm dedicated solely to the placement of financial and accounting personnel. We offer our clients and candidates conscientious, high level service. We provide complete, objective information, and a superior ability to understand the unique personalities of our client companies and applicants and match them accordingly. We get the job done, and we are not interested in encouraging anyone to choose a job or situation that isn't exactly right for them.

Key Contact - Specialty:
Mr. Daniel Komaiko, Owner - *Accounting, finance*

Salary minimum: $30,000

Functions: Finance

Industries: Generalist, Finance, Accounting

Networks: Top Echelon Network

Scott-Thaler Associates Agency Inc
110 E 9th St Ste C277
Los Angeles, CA 90079-5277
(800) 968-1562
(213) 312-9312
Fax: (213) 312-9324
Email: careers@scott-thaler.com

Description: We specialize in the apparel, textile, retail, e-commerce, transportation and distribution industries. We offer extensive, specialized industry experience, as our recruiters have anywhere from 15-30 years' experience in these areas. We offer a distinctively personalized approach to recruiting, in order to meet the immediate needs of the client and to establish a productive long-term relationship.

Key Contact:
Mr. Brian D. Thaler, CPC, President - *Apparel, textile, distribution services, logistics, retail*
Ms. Mary Oliva, CAC, General Manager

Salary minimum: $30,000

Functions: Generalist, Materials, Sales & Mktg., HR Mgmt., M&A, Technicians, Graphic Artists

Industries: Generalist, Mfg., Textiles, Apparel, Lumber, Furniture, Soap, Perf., Cosmtcs., Misc. Mfg., Electronic, Elec. Components, Transportation, Wholesale, Retail, Venture Cap., Mgmt. Consulting, HR Services

Professional Associations: CSP

Scott-Wayne Associates Inc
(a division of Personnel Group of America)
425 Boylston St Fl 4
Boston, MA 02116
(617) 587-3000
Fax: (617) 587-3030
Email: swa@gte.net

Description: Specialists in the search and placement of accounting, financial and temporary personnel for over twenty-five years.

Key Contact - Specialty:
Mr. R. Steven Dow, Executive Vice President - *Accounting & finance*

Salary minimum: $50,000

Functions: Finance

Industries: Generalist

SCS & Associates
PO Box 2294
Chapel Hill, NC 27515
(800) 733-3387
Fax: (919) 932-6900
Email: steve@scs-associates.com

Description: We have a background of over 25 years in graphic arts, and are in our 15th year of successfully recruiting executives in the printing industry. We also have an office in New York.

Key Contact - Specialty:
Mr. Steve Soltan, President - *Printing*

Salary minimum: $40,000

Functions: Middle Mgmt., Plant Mgmt., Sales Mgmt., Direct Mktg., Customer Svc., IT

Industries: Generalist, Printing

Branches:
65-38 Laurel Hill Blvd
Woodside, NY 11377
(718) 651-6645
(718) 505-1888
Fax: (718) 651-6645
Email: brian@scs-associates.com
Key Contact - Specialty:
Mr. Brian Barsher, Manager - *Information technology*

Sea Bright Enterprises Inc
665 S Skinker
St. Louis, MO 63105
(314) 862-7972
(760) 729-2892
Fax: (314) 862-2178
Email: seabright@seabrightenterprises.com
Web: www.seabrightenterprises.com

Description: Full-service management consulting firm with offices in St. Louis, MO and Carlsbad, CA.

Key Contact:
Mr. Gerald Linehan, CEO
Mr. John Eugene Linehan, President

Functions: Generalist

Industries: Generalist, Banking, Invest. Banking, Brokers, Aerospace, Biotech, Healthcare

Seaport Recruiting Group
3438 Don Lorenzo Dr
Carlsbad, CA 92008-3925
(760) 431-8595
Email: rfullerton@att.net

Description: Recruiting of actuaries at all levels of experience and exams throughout the USA, Bermuda, Mexico and Western Europe. Employers include insurance companies, consulting and risk management firms, ISO, NCCI and AIPSO. 100% fee paid by employers: contingency or retained search.

Key Contact:
Mr. Ralph Fullerton

Search & Placement Int'l
5825 W Judy Ct
Visalia, CA 93277
(559) 635-0500
Fax: (559) 635-0233
Email: sphillips377@earthlink.net

Description: We can offer professional, honest, competent and discreet recruiting services for professional positions. Seven years of experience in the industry and the contacts engendered by professional associations will insure success at serving our clients.

Key Contact - Specialty:
Mr. Steve Phillips, CPC, Managing Director - *Insurance underwriters, compliance, group sales*

Salary minimum: $30,000

Functions: Generalist, Finance

Industries: Insurance

Professional Associations: NAPS

Search & Recruit Int'l
4455 South Blvd
Virginia Beach, VA 23452
(757) 490-3151
Fax: (757) 497-6503
Email: britt@searchandrecruit.com
Web: www.searchandrecruit.com

Description: We recruit at all levels of high-technology, skilled technicians, engineers and professional management people. We specialtize in engineers, techs, environmental, manufacturing,

nuclear and software. Financial (all types), medical device manufacturing and heavy industrial sales.

Key Contact - Specialty:
Mr. R. P. Brittingham, General Manager - *Technical*

Salary minimum: $25,000

Functions: Mfg., Product Dev., Automation, Plant Mgmt., Packaging, Engineering, Technicians

Industries: Generalist, Energy, Utilities, Mfg., Pharm Svcs., Telecoms, Defense, Haz. Waste, Aerospace, Packaging, Biotech, Healthcare

Professional Associations: EMA, NAER, NAPS, VAPS

Search America Inc
105 Webster St Ste 6
Hanover, MA 02339
(781) 871-9798
Email: careervalet@search-america.com
Web: www.search-america.com

Description: We offer retained and contingency recruitment for management consultants and business development professionals, at mid to senior levels - for software companies, consulting organizations, and select innovative e-Commerce companies.

Key Contact:
Mr. Steve Lombardo, President
Mrs. Jacqui Buckley, Director

Salary minimum: $100,000

Functions: Generalist, Senior Mgmt., Sales & Mktg., Mgmt. Consultants

Industries: Energy, Utilities, Mfg., Wholesale, Retail, Finance, Services, Mgmt. Consulting, Media, Publishing, Software, ERP SW, Industry Specific SW, Mfg. SW, Marketing SW

Search America Inc
678 Burmont Rd Ste 600-K
Drexel Hill, PA 19026
(610) 259-2800
Fax: (610) 259-6110
Email: resumes@searchamericainc.com
Web: www.searchamericainc.com

Description: Our recruiters have extensive training in the behavioral aspects, sensitivity and art of recruiting. Our goal is to partner with our clients by increasing trust, loyalty and continued mutual success.

Key Contact - Specialty:
Mr. Thomas V. Giacoponello, President/Executive Recruiter - *Market research, management consulting*

Salary minimum: $60,000

Functions: Generalist, Mkt. Research, Mktg. Mgmt., Mgmt. Consultants

Industries: Generalist, Misc. Financial, Pharm Svcs., Mgmt. Consulting, Healthcare

Professional Associations: PAPS

Search Associates
PO Box 131 R
Eastwood, KY 40018-0131
(502) 245-2928
Fax: (502) 245-2923
Email: search@metaljobs.net
Web: www.metaljobs.net

Description: We specialize in all aspects of steel, aluminum, copper and other primary metal industries including engineers, plant management, QA staff, metallurgists; and all types of processes: casting, melting, rolling, extrusion, etc.

Key Contact - Specialty:
Mr. Bill Johnstone, Executive Recruiter - *Primary metals*
Ms. Glenda Dixon, Executive Recruiter - *Primary metals*

Functions: Middle Mgmt., Production, Plant Mgmt., Quality, Productivity, Engineering

Industries: Metal Products

Networks: Top Echelon Network

Search Associates Inc

5900 Sepulveda Blvd Ste 104
Sherman Oaks, CA 91411
(818) 988-5600
Fax: (818) 787-0110
Email: mail@swjobs.com
Web: www.swjobs.com

Description: We have a major emphasis in IT, direct marketing, real estate and development, electronics, semiconductor, multimedia, telecommunications, pharmacists, and software. We also place professionals on a contract and temporary basis.

Key Contact - Specialty:
Mr. Lee Woodward, Co-President - *Programming, software*
Mr. Bernard Sharf, Co-President - *Multimedia*

Salary minimum: $40,000

Functions: Generalist, Mfg., Healthcare, Sales & Mktg., IT, Systems Analysis, Systems Dev., Engineering

Industries: Generalist, Mfg., Computer Equip., Broadcast, Film, Telecoms, Software, Healthcare

Professional Associations: NACCB

Search Bureau Int'l

PO Box 377608
Chicago, IL 60637
(708) 210-1834
Fax: (708) 210-1834
Email: bhu5450778@aol.com

Description: We are a group of professionals who specialize in the areas of accounting, finance, engineering, insurance, human resource management, data processing, and marketing. We also provide outplacement service to Fortune 500 companies.

Key Contact - Specialty:
Mr. Reginald M. Hudson, President - *Accounting & finance*

Salary minimum: $50,000

Functions: Senior Mgmt., Sales & Mktg., Mkt. Research, Mktg. Mgmt., Direct Mktg., HR Mgmt., Finance, IT

Industries: Generalist

The Search Center Inc

1155 Dairy Ashford Ste 404
Houston, TX 77079-3011
(281) 589-8303
Fax: (281) 589-8425
Web: www.thesearchcenter.com

Description: We specialize in oil, natural gas power, petroleum products, petrochemical, chemical, and plastics industries. We focus on professional sales, trading, and senior executive management positions, with a strong emphasis in energy derivatives and trade finance.

Key Contact - Specialty:
Ms. Susan M. Magnani, President - *Energy (market, trades)*

Salary minimum: $100,000

Functions: Senior Mgmt., Sales & Mktg.

Industries: Energy, Utilities, Chemicals, Plastics, Rubber, Banking, Invest. Banking, Brokers, Misc. Financial

The Search Committee

8 Westbury Rd
Lutherville, MD 21093
(888) 732-6752
(410) 825-7811
Fax: (410) 825-9035
Email: search@home.com
Web: www.erols.com/secor

Description: Having spent my adult life working in the medical industry, I can assure you that I will supply you with a tailored fit, not a generic solution.

Key Contact - Specialty:
Mr. David B. Secor, President - *Medical (managed care), healthcare, payers, providers, pharmaceuticals*

Salary minimum: $65,000

Functions: Generalist, Directors, Senior Mgmt., Physicians, Health Admin., Sales Mgmt., CFO's, MIS Mgmt.

Industries: Generalist, Drugs Mfg., Insurance, Healthcare

Networks: Medical Search Consortium (MSC)

Search Connection LLC

10490 Little Patuxent Pkwy Ste 500
Columbia, MD 21044
(410) 715-0900
Fax: (410) 715-1137
Email: contact@searchconnection.com
Web: www.searchconnection.com

Description: One of the largest executive search firms in the DC metro area, we specialize in senior information systems, accounting and finance positions.

Key Contact - Specialty:
Mr. Chad Houck - *Accounting, finance, healthcare*
Mr. Dave Hall - *Information technology*
Mr. Mike Bogdan - *Information technology*

Functions: Generalist, Senior Mgmt., Health Admin., Finance, IT

Industries: Generalist, Mfg., Finance, Services, Media, Software, Healthcare

Professional Associations: IACPR, AITP, SHRM

Branches:
1430 Spring Hill Rd
McLean, VA 22102
(703) 288-0900
Fax: (703) 288-0500
Email: searchva@searchconnection.com
Key Contact - Specialty:
Mr. Mark Horning - *IT*

Search Consultants Inc

1 E Ridgewood Ave
Paramus, NJ 07652
(201) 444-1770

Description: Looking for guaranteed satisfaction in hiring a HR executive? For the record: 30 years of success in the NJ/NY/CT region; a very efficient and timely hiring process; virtually no relo costs.

Key Contact - Specialty:
Mr. Walter Perog, President - *Human resources*

Salary minimum: $65,000

Functions: Generalist, HR Mgmt., Benefits, Personnel, Training

Industries: Generalist

Professional Associations: ASTD, HRPS

Search Consultants Int'l Inc

4545 Post Oak Pl Ste 208
Houston, TX 77027
(713) 622-9188
Fax: (713) 622-9186
Email: info@searchconsultants.com
Web: www.searchconsultants.com

Description: Extensive experience in mid- and senior management executive search, with technical expertise in power marketing and trading, environmental health and safety, the energy industry (natural gas and electricity), oil & gas technology for exploration / production, manufacturing (petrochem/refining & cement), and independent power/cogeneration (IPP).

Key Contact:
Mr. S. Joseph Baker, CPC, President - *Energy, traders (gas, electric), marketers, power (marketing managers, executives), purchasing & supply chain management*
Mr. Michael Brentari, Vice President - *Energy industry, gas & electric traders, marketer operation & maintenance managers & executive partners*
Mr. Richard Fiore, Vice President - *Environmental engineers, safety & industrial (hygiene professionals), scientists (environmental engineering)*
Mr. Steve McAleavy, Director-Energy Division - *Energy industry, gas & electric traders, marketers, power (marketing managers, executives), senior consultants*
Mr. Lon McAllister, Senior Consultant - *Environmental engineering (contract), geophysical professionals (oil & gas exploration & production)*
Ms. Judith M. Baker, VP/Controller & Finance

Salary minimum: $75,000

Functions: General Mgmt., Senior Mgmt., Middle Mgmt., Mfg., Plant Mgmt., Purchasing, Risk Mgmt., Engineering, Environmentalists

Industries: Energy, Utilities, Mfg., Services, Mgmt. Consulting, Environmental Svcs.

Professional Associations: AWMA, HAAPC, PMA, TAPS

Search Enterprises Inc

12358 Wiles Rd
Coral Springs, FL 33076
(954) 755-3121
Fax: (954) 755-1094
Email: sesi@searchenterprises.com
Web: www.searchenterprises.com

Description: Specialists in the recruitment of engineering, manufacturing management and maintenance professionals. We serve mainly the chemical process, food, pharmaceutical, plastics and paper industries.

Key Contact - Specialty:
Mr. Frank Polacek, President - *Engineers*

Salary minimum: $40,000

Functions: Generalist, Automation, Plant Mgmt., Engineering

Industries: Generalist, Food, Bev., Tobacco, Chemicals, Soap, Perf., Cosmtcs., Drugs Mfg., Paints, Petro. Products, Biotech

The Search Firm LLC

94 Portland Ave
Dover, NH 03820
(603) 742-4950
Fax: (603) 749-4540
Email: bballaro@aol.com
Web: www.thesearchfirmllc.com

Description: We are employment specialists for contract and permanent/placement in all technical disciplines, for example: all engineering disciplines, controls, sheet metal fabrication, manufacturing, all IT, and software. If it's technical, we work it.

Key Contact - Specialty:
Mr. William Ballaro, Principal - *High level*
Mrs. Paula Ballaro, CFO - *Accounting, finance*

Functions: IT

Industries: Metal Products, Misc. Mfg., Electronic, Elec. Components, Telecoms, Software, Biotech

Search Force Inc
626 N Park Ave
Indianapolis, IN 46204
(800) 837-9902
Email: hotjobs@searchforceinc.com
Web: www.searchforceinc.com

Description: We are a full service contingency and retained search firm specializing in information systems.

Key Contact - Specialty:
Mr. Shawn Miller, CSAM, President - *Client server, web development*
Mrs. Tammy Miller, Vice President - *As 400, Unix based systems*
Mr. Don Pottenger, CDP, Senior Consultant - *Legacy systems, IT management*

Salary minimum: $45,000

Functions: IT, MIS Mgmt., Systems Analysis, Systems Dev., Systems Implem., Network Admin., DB Admin.

Industries: Generalist

Networks: Top Echelon Network

The J B Search Group Inc
5738 Meadows Del Mar
San Diego, CA 91230
(714) 672-9278
(440) 423-0470
Fax: (714) 672-9279
Email: no.limits@gateway.net
Web: www.jbsearch.com

Description: Our firm specializes in the nationwide placement of sales management, sales support, product development, product management, marketing, and marketing management talent for consumer products. We help our clients find professionals that make an immediate impact.

Key Contact - Specialty:
Mr. J. Michael DeClouet, President - *Sales, marketing, middle management, directors*

Salary minimum: $40,000

Functions: Generalist, Senior Mgmt., Middle Mgmt., Purchasing, Mkt. Research, Mktg. Mgmt., Sales Mgmt.

Industries: Generalist, Food, Bev., Tobacco, Textiles, Apparel, Soap, Perf., Cosmtcs., Plastics, Rubber, Paints, Petro. Products, Consumer Elect., Packaging, Mfg. SW, Marketing SW

Branches:
PO Box 247
Gates Mills, OH 44040
(440) 423-0470
Fax: (440) 423-0877
Email: skeefe@neuco.com
Key Contact - Specialty:
Mr. Steve Keefe, President, Steve Keefe & Assoc - *Sales & marketing*

The Search Group
9405 Hickory Limb
Columbia, MD 21045
(410) 381-3940
(800) 296-8256
Fax: (410) 381-5264
Email: hruska@thesearchgroup.net
Web: www.thesearchgroup.net

Description: We are a search practice working exclusively with the property and casualty insurance industry. During the past thirty years, we have completed assignments for some of the top companies and brokers in the country.

Key Contact - Specialty:
Mr. Thomas Hruska, CPC, Managing Director - *Insurance (property, casualty)*

Functions: Generalist

Industries: Insurance

Professional Associations: MAPRC, RON

Search Masters USA
4598 Hamlets Grv
Sarasota, FL 34235
(941) 351-7307
Fax: (941) 351-5416
Email: searchmastersusa@yahoo.com

Description: We are a medical search and recruiting firm. We specialize in sales and marketing talent in the medical diagnostics, microbiology, biotechnology, hospital equipment, lab equipment, doctor office clinics, and commercial and research labs. We also focus on sales, marketing, and management.

Key Contact - Specialty:
Mr. Alex Stevenson, President - *Sales, sales management, marketing, medical, biomedical*

Salary minimum: $50,000

Functions: Senior Mgmt., Middle Mgmt., Healthcare, Sales & Mktg., Mktg. Mgmt., Sales Mgmt.

Industries: Food, Bev., Tobacco, Chemicals, Drugs Mfg., Medical Devices, Pharm Svcs., Mfg. SW, Marketing SW, Biotech, Healthcare, Hospitals, Dental, Physical Therapy, Occupational Therapy

Networks: First Interview Network (FIN)

Search Net
14 CR 225
Glen, MS 38846
(662) 427-9000
Fax: (662) 427-9080
Email: jshullco@aol.com
Web: www.printingjobs.com

Description: We are a premier search firm for the graphic arts and printing industries. We are targeting talent at all levels. We place CEO, sales, plant management, and skilled craft persons. No search is too big or too small. We offer retained, modified retainer, and contingency programs for your project(s).

Key Contact - Specialty:
Mr. John Shull, Owner and Recruiter - *Printing, graphic arts*

Functions: Generalist

Industries: Paper, Printing, Publishing, HR SW, Industry Specific SW, Mfg. SW

The Search Network
5755 Oberlin Dr Ste 312
San Diego, CA 92121
(858) 535-0015
Fax: (858) 535-0152
Email: resume@searchnetworkinc.com
Web: www.searchnetworkinc.com

Description: By placing excellent technical professionals, we have built strong lasting relationships with top hi-tech firms in San Diego. We find the best position to suit your needs. Confidentiality guaranteed.

Key Contact - Specialty:
Ms. Kaaren Liz Henderson, President - *High technology*

Salary minimum: $30,000

Functions: Generalist, Middle Mgmt., Product Dev., Production, Quality, Engineering

Industries: Generalist, Medical Devices, Computer Equip., Consumer Elect., New Media, Telecoms, Software

Professional Associations: ASQ, SWE, SWE

Search North America Inc
PO Box 3577
Sunriver, OR 97707
(503) 222-6461
(541) 593-2777
Fax: (503) 227-2804
Email: carlj@searchna.com
Web: www.searchna.com

Description: To improve the future performance of our client companies in the forest products, pulp and paper, and power generation industries, we locate and place results-oriented candidates.

Key Contact - Specialty:
Mr. Carl Jansen, President - *Forest products, pulp & paper & related industries*

Salary minimum: $45,000

Functions: Senior Mgmt., Mfg., Sales & Mktg., CFO's, R&D, Engineering, Int'l.

Industries: Energy, Utilities, Lumber, Furniture, Paper

Professional Associations: AIIE, AMA, ASME, ASSE, FPS, IEEE, NABE, PIMA, SFPA, TAPPI

Search Plus Int'l
25882 Orchard Lake Rd Ste 207
Farmington Hills, MI 48336
(248) 471-6110
Fax: (248) 471-6572
Email: searchintl@aol.com
Web: www.searchplusintl.com

Description: Our firm has over 10 years' experience in automotive, aerospace, plastics and other manufacturing areas; specializing in executives, engineers, quality, human resources, purchasing, sales and other administrative areas.

Key Contact:
Ms. Christine Greeneisen - *Industrial, manufacturing, sales & marketing, engineering, executives*
Mr. Gary Morris

Salary minimum: $50,000

Functions: Generalist, Senior Mgmt., Mfg., Materials, Sales & Mktg., HR Mgmt., Finance, IT

Industries: Generalist, Plastics, Rubber, Motor Vehicles, Misc. Mfg., Finance

Search Point LLC
750 W Lake Cook Rd Ste 165
Buffalo Grove, IL 60089
(847) 520-0400
Fax: (847) 520-9063
Email: mark@searchpointusa.com

Description: With over 19 years of experience, we are a national executive search firm dedicated to helping exceptional organizations identify and attract top sales and marketing talent.

Key Contact - Specialty:
Mr. Steve Fried, Manager - *Sales, service industries*
Mr. Mark Rafferty, Manager - *Sales & marketing, electrical, mechanical, electronics*

Functions: Sales & Mktg., Sales Mgmt.

Industries: Energy, Utilities, Mfg., Computer Equip., Test, Measure Equip., Misc. Mfg., Electronic, Elec. Components, Transportation, Law Enforcement, Telecoms, Fiber Optic,

Software, Mfg. SW, Marketing SW, Non-classifiable

Networks: US Recruiters.com

Search Pro Inc
280 Clinton Pl
Hackensack, NJ 07601
(201) 489-0908
Fax: (201) 342-3229
Email: searchpro@aol.com
Web: www.search-pro.com

Description: Hospitality experienced executives with a broad scope of knowledge of your industry ready to serve you.

Key Contact - Specialty:
Ms. Pat Romero, President - *Middle management, executives*
Ms. Vicky Farhi, Manager - *Restaurant management, culinary*

Salary minimum: $25,000

Functions: Generalist, General Mgmt., Senior Mgmt., Middle Mgmt., Mkt. Research, HR Mgmt., CFO's

Industries: Generalist, Hospitality

Professional Associations: ACF, NRA

Branches:
20173 Canyon View Dr
Canyon Country, CA 91351
(661) 298-7008
Fax: (661) 298-7026
Email: searchpro@aol.com
Key Contact - Specialty:
Mr. Michael Anthonoy - *Restaurant management, culinary*

Search Professionals Inc
36 Rte 6A
Sandwich, MA 02563
(508) 833-6161
Fax: (508) 833-6106
Email: searchpros@searchprosinc.com
Web: www.searchprosinc.com

Description: We specialize in mass merchants, specialty stores, discount, home centers, e-commerce, catalog, direct marketing, supply chain management, food retailing and telemarketing.

Key Contact - Specialty:
Mr. Richard Barzelay, President - *Retail, e-commerce, distribution*
Mr. Frank Tonini, Vice President - *Retail, direct marketing*

Functions: Generalist, Senior Mgmt., Middle Mgmt., Purchasing, Distribution, Direct Mktg.

Industries: Generalist, Transportation, Wholesale, Retail, Non-profits, Hospitality

Branches:
PO Box 16675
Surfside Beach, SC 29587
(843) 215-2638
Fax: (843) 215-2642
Email: pmulln@aol.com
Key Contact - Specialty:
Mr. Paul Mullen - *Retail, home centers*

Search Solutions Inc
7200 Redwood Blvd Ste 401
Novato, CA 94945
(415) 898-1800
Fax: (415) 898-2439
Email: searchsi@searchsolutions.com
Web: www.searchsolutions.com

Description: My search firm specializes in the full-time placement of software implementation consultants and managers who work with and implement Oracle, SAP, Peoplesoft, and JD

Edwards software. We also place software sales and sales managing professionals.

Key Contact - Specialty:
Mr. Mark Robbins, President/Owner - *Programmers, oracle, SAP, peoplesoft, software implementation (consultants, managers)*

Salary minimum: $60,000

Functions: General Mgmt.

Industries: Mgmt. Consulting, Software

Search South Inc
1000 Quintard Ave Ste 409
PO Box 2224
Anniston, AL 36202
(256) 237-1868
Fax: (256) 237-1850
Email: arthuryoung@searchsouth.com
Web: www.searchsouth.com

Description: We provide professional, technical, and management recruitment in the South and nationwide. We recruit primarily in accounting, engineering, and manufacturing to include metal processing and fabrication, automotive parts/assembly, energy, packaging, consumer products, electric motors, composite material, CD/DVD, consulting engineering (structural and civil), mobile equipment, distribution, and environmental.

Key Contact - Specialty:
Mr. Arthur L. Young, President/Owner - *Accounting, manufacturing, distribution, multimedia*
Ms. Lynn Higdon, Search Consultant - *Manufacturing, healthcare, distribution, accounting*
Mr. Bill Simril, Search Consultant - *Consulting engineering*
Ms. Jamie Holland, Research/Sourcing Coordinator - *Generalist*

Salary minimum: $40,000

Functions: Generalist, Senior Mgmt., Middle Mgmt., Admin. Svcs., Mfg., Plant Mgmt., Quality, Distribution, CFO's, Engineering

Industries: Generalist, Energy, Utilities, Mfg., Paper, Chemicals, Metal Products, Machine, Appliance, Motor Vehicles, Misc. Mfg., Electronic, Elec. Components, Transportation, Finance, Higher Ed., Accounting, Packaging

Networks: National Personnel Assoc (NPA)

Search West Inc
2049 Century Park E Ste 650
Los Angeles, CA 90067-3101
(310) 203-9797
Fax: (310) 282-8590
Email: bob.cowan@searchwest.com
Web: www.searchwest.com

Description: Thirty-four years in California, 60 industry specialists recruiting executives and professionals in sales, marketing, finance, administration, engineering, manufacturing, information technologies, direct mail, retailing, insurance, health, real estate, high-tech and financial services.

Key Contact:
Mr. Robert A. Cowan, President
Mr. Lawrence G. Cowan, CEO
Mr. Michael Schulman, COO
Ms. Angela Barfield, General Manager
Ms. Ashton Rice, Manager of Corporate Services

Salary minimum: $50,000

Functions: General Mgmt., Mfg., Materials, Nurses, Health Admin., Sales & Mktg., HR Mgmt., Finance, IT

Industries: Generalist, Construction, Mfg., Venture Cap., Services, Packaging, Insurance, Real Estate, Software, Biotech, Healthcare

Networks: First Interview Network (FIN)

Branches:
2049 Century Park E Ste 650
Los Angeles, CA 90067-3101
(310) 284-8888
Fax: (310) 284-3409
Email: swlosangeles@searchwest.com
Key Contact:
Ms. Angela Barfield, General Manager

2151 Convention Center Way Ste 121 E
Ontario, CA 91764-5421
(909) 937-0100
Fax: (909) 937-0101
Email: ontariosw@searchwest.com
Key Contact:
Ms. Rosalie Russell, General Manager

750 The City Dr S Ste 100
Orange, CA 92868-4940
(714) 748-0400
Fax: (714) 748-8973
Email: orangeco@searchwest.com
Key Contact:
Ms. Merrilyn Spicer, General Manager

100 Pine St Ste 2860
San Francisco, CA 94111-5203
(415) 788-1770
Fax: (415) 989-7706
Email: sanfran@searchwest.com
Key Contact:
Ms. Ellen Williams, General Manager/Vice President

340 N Westlake Blvd Ste 200
Westlake Village, CA 91362-3761
(805) 496-6811
Fax: (805) 496-9431
Email: westvil@searchwest.com
Key Contact:
Mr. Vince Della Monica, General Manager

Search wide
324 S Main St Ste 260
Stillwater, MN 55082
(651) 275-1370
(888) 386-6390
Email: info@searchwide.com
Web: www.searchwide.com

Description: We specialize in recruiting executives for the hospitality industry, convention, and visitors bureaus, along with associations and not-for-profit organizations around the country. With offices in Washington DC, Philadelphia, Dallas, San Francisco, Minneapolis, and Traverse City, MI, SearchWide offers its clients personalized service within the client's time frame and budget.

Key Contact:
Mr. Mike Gamble, President/CEO
Mr. Jim Carra, Executive Vice President

Salary minimum: $50,000

Search Wizards Inc
5100 Gamble Dr Ste 392
St. Louis Park, MN 55416
(952) 593-9676
Fax: (952) 593-9764
Email: rtv@searchwizards.com
Web: www.searchwizards.com

Description: We specialize in working with engineering professionals in Minneapolis/St Paul, MN. Our mission is to match our clients' needs with our candidates' aspirations and to ensure our recruiters success through ongoing training and development, all while maintaining the highest ethical standards.

Key Contact - Specialty:
Mr. R. Terry Vaught, President/Owner - *Engineering (EE), Information technology*

Functions: Generalist, Engineering

Industries: Generalist, Computer Equip., Consumer Elect., Test, Measure Equip., Misc. Mfg., Electronic, Elec. Components, Communications, Software

SearchAmerica Inc
2 Robbins Ln Ste 210
Jericho, NY 11753
(516) 939-9099
Fax: (516) 939-3335
Email: messer@jsmsearch.com

Description: We are specialists in the securities, brokerage, banking, investment banking, marketing, financial services industries, and law. We deliver efficient and lasting professional manpower, talent, and growth in the areas of: management, sales, marketing, attorneys, compliance, information technology, plus data mining and warehousing, communications technology, and all back office operations functions.

Key Contact - Specialty:
Mr. Jonathan S. Messer, President - *Sales, marketing, stockbrokers, surveillance & compliance, management*

Functions: Generalist, Middle Mgmt., Admin. Svcs., Sales & Mktg., Sales Mgmt., HR Mgmt., Specialized Svcs., Int'l.

Industries: Finance, Banking, Invest. Banking, Brokers, Venture Cap., Misc. Financial, Legal, Accounting, Media, Advertising, Publishing, New Media

SearchCorp
1000 Brickell Ave Ste 450
Miami, FL 33131
(305) 358-1575
Fax: (305) 358-1530
Email: jobs@searchcorp.com
Web: www.e-mailjobs.com

Description: The Job Communication Company – leading provider of web technologies and executive recruiting solutions. SearchCorp now with offices in Miami, Boca Raton, and Puerto Rico – for more information visit www.SearchCorp.com

Key Contact - Specialty:
Mr. Rafael E. Hernandez, Executive Vice President - *General management, finance, sales & marketing, human resources, international*
Mr. Mario Alonso, Executive Vice President - *General management, finance, sales & marketing, human resources, international*

Salary minimum: $35,000

Functions: Generalist, General Mgmt., Sales & Mktg., HR Mgmt., Finance, IT, Int'l.

Industries: Generalist, Food, Bev., Tobacco, Retail, Finance, Services, Media, Software

SearchCorp Int'l
(a division of Baldwin Staffing Group Ltd)
550 - 17th Ave SW
Calgary, AB T2S 0B1
Canada
(403) 228-1999
Fax: (403) 228-5533

Description: More than a decade in business, we have a reputation for quick, efficient service of a confidential nature. Niche markets in Canada, U.S. and abroad include information technology professionals, lawyers, CAs, sales management and engineers.

Key Contact - Specialty:
Mr. Stephen Baldwin, President - *Financial, management, engineering, information technology*

Salary minimum: $30,000

Functions: Generalist, Sales Mgmt., Finance, MIS Mgmt., Systems Dev., Systems Implem., Engineering, Attorneys

Industries: Generalist, Finance, Legal, Accounting, Software

The SearchLogix Group
(also known as Sales Consultants of Cherokee)
275 Pkwy 575 Ste 203
Woodstock, GA 30188
(770) 517-2660
Email: resumes@searchlogixgroup.com
Web: www.searchlogixgroup.com

Description: We are a full-service executive search and consulting firm. We specialize in logistics, supply chain, software, retail, and sales.

Key Contact - Specialty:
Mr. Brett M. Stevens, President - *Software, consulting*
Ms. Gina O'Leary, General Manager - *Logistics, supply chain, software sales, HR*

Salary minimum: $40,000

Functions: Generalist

Industries: Generalist, Retail, Software, ERP SW, Marketing SW

Professional Associations: APICS, CLM, SHRM, WERC

SearchNet
3527 Fortuna Ranch Rd
Encinitas, CA 92024
(858) 756-1631
Fax: (858) 756-0431
Email: careers@searchnet.net
Web: www.searchnet.net

Description: Our firm specializes in IT and software development related technical recruitment for San Diego companies. Paul and Danna Korn offer a refreshing, quality-oriented approach that puts the candidate's needs and requirements first to ensure good, long-lasting career matches.

Key Contact:
Mr. Paul Korn, President
Mr. Danna Korn, Vice President

Functions: IT, DB Admin.

Industries: Medical Devices, Computer Equip., Pharm Svcs., Mgmt. Consulting, HR Services, E-commerce, IT Implementation, Entertainment, Communications, Call Centers, Network Infrastructure, Software

SearchOne Inc
11300 Rodney Parham Ste 320
PO Box 17407
Little Rock, AR 72212
(501) 224-8800
Fax: (501) 224-8806
Email: john@searchoneinc.com
Web: www.officerecruiters.com

Description: We specialize in manufacturing and other technical service industries; most specific to information systems, materials, distribution, food industry and engineering.

Key Contact:
Ms. Vickie H. Siebenmorgen, CPC, President
Mr. John Siebenmorgen, VP-Finance

Salary minimum: $40,000

Functions: Generalist, General Mgmt., Mfg., Materials, Finance, IT, Engineering

Industries: Generalist, Mfg., Transportation, Packaging

Professional Associations: NAPS, SME

Networks: National Personnel Assoc (NPA)

SearchPro Group Medical Services
3500 DePauw Blvd Ste 2050
Indianapolis, IN 46268-1155
(317) 879-4795
Fax: (317) 879-1233
Email: mail@searchprogroup.com
Web: www.hmoexecsearch.com

Description: Established in 1985, we are a nationwide recruiting firm specializing in executive personnel placement with health maintenance organizations and other alternative delivery healthcare systems.

Key Contact:
Mr. Timothy P Dugger, Owner - *Managed care*
Mr. John Thompson, General Manager

Salary minimum: $60,000

Functions: Healthcare

Industries: Generalist

Networks: National Personnel Assoc (NPA)

SearchPro Inc
8206-1200 Providence Rd Ste 400
Charlotte, NC 28277
(704) 849-9092
Fax: (704) 849-9095
Email: info@searchpro.com
Web: www.searchpro.com

Description: Since 1990, we have been providing quality banking searches nationwide. As a National Banking Network affiliate, our search firm partners with over 50 banking specialty recruiters to offer a current enhanced database of premier talent. Our mission is to deliver exceptional confidential service. Our team goes the distance!

Key Contact - Specialty:
Ms. Mary J. Mallett, CPC, Owner/President - *Banking, HIO*

Salary minimum: $50,000

Functions: Generalist, Finance

Industries: Generalist, Finance, Banking, Invest. Banking, Brokers, Venture Cap., Misc. Financial

Professional Associations: ICBA, NAPS, NCASP, NCBA

Networks: National Banking Network (NBN)

SearchWorks Inc
PO Box 8033
Coral Springs, FL 33075
(954) 340-1000
Fax: (954) 340-1002
Email: searchworks@msn.com

Description: We have an outstanding reputation for our expertise in the healthcare and insurance industries. Our reputation has been built upon service, perseverance and above all performance. Research intensive.

Key Contact - Specialty:
Ms. Kim Schindel, Principal - *Healthcare, insurance (life & health, property & casualty, medical), pharmaceutical, software, information technology*

Salary minimum: $50,000

Functions: Generalist

Industries: Generalist

Sears & Associates

7491 N Federal Hwy Ste C-5
Boca Raton, FL 33487-1658
(561) 673-7000
(561) 638-4750
Fax: (561) 637-6585
Email: jerrysears@aol.com
Web: www.jdcotter.com

Description: We recruit senior attorneys for both law firms and in-house (corporate) positions.

Key Contact - Specialty:
Mr. Jerry Sears, Principal - *Attorneys*

Salary minimum: $80,000

Functions: Attorneys

Industries: Generalist

Professional Associations: CLA, CSP, LES, NALSC, ODN

Doug Sears & Associates (DS&A)

320 Corporate Way Ste 100
Jacksonville, FL 32073
(904) 215-1103
(800) 557-1104
Fax: (904) 215-9970
Email: dsa@rainmakerlawyers.com
Web: www.rainmakerlawyers.com

Description: We are an executive legal search firm. For more information, please go to our website.

Key Contact - Specialty:
Mr. J. Douglas Sears, CEO - *Legal*

Salary minimum: $70,000

Functions: General Mgmt., Legal, Sales Mgmt., M&A, MIS Mgmt., Mgmt. Consultants, Attorneys, Int'l.

Industries: Generalist, Legal

Professional Associations: ASTD, SHRM

SEC Services LLC

(also known as South Eastern Careers)
1889 General George Patton Dr Ste 200A
Franklin, TN 37067
(615) 846-2200
Fax: (615) 846-2201
Email: recruiter@secjobs.com
Web: www.secjobs.com

Description: We provide consulting and full time placement of IT professionals.

Key Contact - Specialty:
Mr. Rick Bellar, President - *Information technology*
Mr. John Kepley, Director, Consulting Services - *Information systems*
Mr. James Barry, Director, Business Development - *Information technology*

Functions: Mfg., Healthcare, IT

Industries: Generalist

Networks: Top Echelon Network

Seco & Zetto Associates Inc

PO Box 225
Harrington Park, NJ 07640
(201) 784-0674
(845) 353-0662
Fax: (845) 348-0410
Email: szsearch@aol.com

Description: We are specialists in keeping abreast of sudden or sensitive changes in the information technology, and Internet/telecommunications industries, while exhibiting an exceptionally rapid response time.

Key Contact - Specialty:
Mr. William M. Seco, President - *Management*
Ms. Kathryn Zetto, Executive Vice President - *Management*

Salary minimum: $85,000

Functions: General Mgmt., Sales & Mktg., Sales Mgmt., IT, Systems Implem.

Industries: Mgmt. Consulting, PSA/ASP, Network Infrastructure, Software, Networking, Comm. SW

Security Management Resources Inc

19170 Springs Rd #113
Jeffersonton, VA 22724
(540) 428-2020
Fax: (703) 995-4343
Email: services@smrgroup.org
Web: www.smrgroup.org

Description: International executive search firm with global, niche market expertise, focused exclusively on professional and executive level security positions. Our services also include recruiting assistance, temporary executive staffing, and consulting. SMR principals and associates all have significant senior level experience managing corporate security programs for the world's leading organizations.

Key Contact - Specialty:
Mr. Jerry Brennan, Managing Director
Mr. Paul Geaneas, JD, Vice President - *Security & loss prevention*

Salary minimum: $75,000

Functions: Generalist, General Mgmt., Middle Mgmt., Admin. Svcs., HR Mgmt., Specialized Svcs., Int'l.

Industries: Generalist, Law Enforcement, Security SW

Select Medical Solutions

16303 Autumn View Ter
St. Louis, MO 63011
(636) 405-0333
Fax: (636) 458-4657
Email: steve@selectmedicalsolutions.com

Description: We are recruitment specialists for sales and sales management in medical device/products and pharmaceutical industries. Our strong ethics and personalized service have resulted in solid relationships with both clients and candidates.

Key Contact - Specialty:
Mr. Steve Huffman - *Medical sales, pharmaceutical sales, sales management, clinical*
Ms. Amy Hood - *Medical sales, pharmaceutical sales, sales management, clinical*

Salary minimum: $30,000

Functions: Sales Mgmt.

Industries: Drugs Mfg., Medical Devices, Computer Equip., Pharm Svcs., Biotech, Healthcare

Select Search

3411 N Arlington Heights Rd
Arlington Heights, IL 60004
(847) 368-8900
Fax: (847) 368-8999
Email: dept-it@selectsearch.com

Description: We specialize in high-tech computer personnel. There are seven full-time account executives with a combined experience of 50 years to help you.

Key Contact - Specialty:
Mr. Richard Nasatir, President - *MIS, computers, information technology*

Salary minimum: $35,000

Functions: MIS Mgmt., Systems Analysis, Systems Dev., Systems Implem., Systems Support, Network Admin., DB Admin.

Industries: Generalist

Select Services

37 W 222 Rte 64 Ste 130
St. Charles, IL 60175
(630) 587-1050
Fax: (630) 587-1060
Email: selectteam@aol.com

Description: Our objective is to partner with respective clients to lower their overall search costs.

Key Contact - Specialty:
Mr. Joseph Mills, President - *Manufacturing management*

Salary minimum: $50,000

Functions: Generalist, General Mgmt., Mfg., Materials, Sales Mgmt., HR Mgmt., Finance, Engineering

Industries: Generalist, Plastics, Rubber, Metal Products, Machine, Appliance, Motor Vehicles, Consumer Elect., Misc. Mfg., HR Services

Selected Executives Inc

76 Winn St
Woburn, MA 01801
(781) 933-1500
Fax: (781) 933-4145
Email: seilrs@aol.com

Description: More than 30 years' experience, we specialize in diversity professionals and demonstrating that, with just a little extra effort, qualified diversity candidates can be identified for every key position.

Key Contact:
Mr. Lee R. Sanborn, Jr., President
Mr. Jackson A. Brookins, Manager
Ms. K. Jane Lewis, Systems Manager
Ms. Suzanne S. Martin, Senior Counselor
Mr. Kenneth T. Dinklage, Vice President

Salary minimum: $50,000

Functions: Generalist

Industries: Generalist

Selectis Corp

3125 N Wilke Rd Ste D
Arlington Heights, IL 60004
(847) 454-1100
Fax: (847) 454-1109
Email: selectis@selectis.com
Web: www.selectis.com/selectis

Description: We provide high quality recruitment services for growing organizations with specialized, time critical job openings. Extensive research, recruiter expertise and urgency involved in each search.

Key Contact - Specialty:
Mr. Frank Lutostanski, President - *Senior management, information technology*

Salary minimum: $60,000

Functions: Production, Sales Mgmt., IT, DB Admin., Engineering

Industries: Insurance, Software

Selective Management Services Inc

PO Box 17008
Sarasota, FL 34276-0008
(941) 923-7114
Fax: (941) 923-0247
Email: mdssms2000@aol.com
Web: www.packagingonline.com

Description: Recruiters, executive search and management consultants specializing in packaging and allied industries: corrugated, folding cartons, paper, pharmaceuticals, plastics, and printing.

Key Contact - Specialty:
Mr. Alan M. Schwartz, President - *Packaging, paper, corrugated box industry, folding carton, printing*
Mr. Mark D. Steel, Senior Consultant - *Packaging, paper, corrugated box industry, folding carton, printing*

Salary minimum: $35,000

Functions: Senior Mgmt., Plant Mgmt., Mktg. Mgmt., Sales Mgmt., CFO's, MIS Mgmt.

Industries: Packaging

Professional Associations: AICC, IOPP, TAPPI

Selective Recruiting Associates Inc
3290 W N Territorial Rd
Ann Arbor, MI 48105-9224
(734) 994-5632
Fax: (734) 996-8181
Email: recruiter@selectiverecruiting.com
Web: www.selectiverecruiting.com

Description: Serving the automotive industry in the Great Lakes Region, we specialize in management positions in engineering and manufacturing.

Key Contact - Specialty:
Mr. Dave Calhoun, CEO - *Engineering management*
Ms. Gilda Bone, President - *Engineering*

Salary minimum: $40,000

Functions: Mfg., Sales Mgmt., Engineering

Industries: Motor Vehicles

Professional Associations: MAPS

Networks: National Personnel Assoc (NPA)

Selective Search Associates
1206 N Main St Ste 112
North Canton, OH 44720
(330) 494-5584
Email: ssa@jobman.com
Web: www.jobman.com

Description: Primary area of specialization is the recruitment and placement of information systems/information technology and software engineering personnel.

Key Contact - Specialty:
Mr. Michael E. Ziarko, President - *Information technology, electronic commerce, software*
Mr. Michael P. Ziarko, Executive Recruiter - *Information technology, engineering*

Salary minimum: $35,000

Functions: Generalist, Systems Analysis, Systems Dev., Systems Implem., Network Admin., DB Admin.

Industries: Generalist, Energy, Utilities, Plastics, Rubber, Metal Products, Machine, Appliance, Computer Equip., Software

Networks: National Personnel Assoc (NPA)

Selective Staffing
4905 N West Ave Ste 115
Fresno, CA 93705
(559) 227-9159
(559) 227-9100
Fax: (559) 227-2950
Email: selectivestaffing_2000@yahoo.com

Description: Founded in 1987, we have 15 years experience in recruiting. We specialize in insurance.

Key Contact:
Ms. Jane Small

Salary minimum: $25,000

Functions: Generalist, Mfg., Healthcare, Sales & Mktg., Sales Mgmt., HR Mgmt., Finance, Attorneys

Industries: Generalist, Insurance, Software, Healthcare

Selectquest
(also known as MRI of Alpharetta)
1031 Cambridge Sq Ste G
Alpharetta, GA 30004
(770) 619-0060
Fax: (770) 619-0061
Email: nick@selectquest.com
Web: www.selectquest.com

Description: We specialize in information technology and software development professionals in all industries nationwide. We find the best individuals in development, IT management, networking, sales, support and related disciplines.

Key Contact - Specialty:
Mr. Nick Barillas, President - *Information technology*
Ms. Mary Morris, Principal - *Data warehousing*

Salary minimum: $70,000

Functions: Generalist

Industries: IT Implementation, Wireless, Network Infrastructure, Software, Database SW, Networking, Comm. SW, Biotech

---

Selig Executive Search
PO Box 160
Laconia, NH 03247-0160
(603) 527-0111
Fax: (603) 527-2597
Email: shoe@together.net

Description: As former CEOs who have restructured footwear marketing and manufacturing companies, we provide the insights needed to help structure the management team. Then, we identify, recruit, and reference strong groups of viable candidates. We help to prepare an offer, which we, then, negotiate for our clients.

Key Contact - Specialty:
Mr. Robert J. Selig, Chairman - *Footwear, apparel (all disciplines), manufacturing, finance, distribution*

Salary minimum: $50,000

Functions: General Mgmt.

Industries: Textiles, Apparel, Leather, Stone, Glass, Industry Specific SW

Seligman & Herrod
2690 Crooks Rd Ste 109
Troy, MI 48084
(248) 269-7131
Email: vh@seligmanherrod.com
Web: www.seligmanherrod.com

Description: High quality, individualized service to both clients and executives in a broad range of industry and disciplines.

Key Contact:
Ms. Vicki Herrod, President

Salary minimum: $60,000

Functions: Generalist

Industries: Mfg., Transportation, Retail, Services, Media, Telecoms, Packaging, Biotech, Healthcare, Non-classifiable

Professional Associations: AICPA, SHRM, WAW

Branches:
2609 E Main St
PO Box 230
Plainfield, IN 46168-2710
(317) 837-5104
Email: ng@seligmanherrod.com
Key Contact:
Ms. Nancy Gethers, Practice Director

Sell & Associates Inc
27 E Russell St Ste 300
Columbus, OH 43215
(614) 221-8199
Fax: (614) 221-0201
Email: msell@sellandassociates.com
Web: www.sellandassociates.com

Description: We are an executive recruiting firm specializing in accounting, finance, banking and MIS. Our recruiters have significant experience in their respective fields and all are CPAs. Our services are available on a retainer basis.

Key Contact - Specialty:
Mr. Mark Sell
Mr. James Bliss, Principal - *Accounting, finance*

Seltzer Fontaine Beckwith
2999 Overland Ave Ste 120
Los Angeles, CA 90064
(310) 839-6000
Fax: (310) 839-4408
Email: info@sfbsearch.com
Web: www.sfbsearch.com

Description: Our principals each have over 15 years' search experience and four of the five are former practicing attorneys. We place individuals and groups of attorneys of all specialties with local, regional, national and international law firms and corporations.

Key Contact - Specialty:
Ms. Valerie A. Fontaine, Partner - *Law*
Ms. Madeleine E. Seltzer, Partner - *Law*
Ms. Randy Beckwith, Partner - *Law*
Ms. Roberta Kass, Recruiter - *Law*
Ms. K. C. Victor, Recruiter - *Law*

Salary minimum: $80,000

Functions: Attorneys

Industries: Legal

Professional Associations: NALSC, NAWBO, SBC, WLALA

The Sequel Group LLC
(also known as MRI of Denver Tech Center)
385 Inverness Dr S Ste 280
Englewood, CO 80112
(303) 267-0600
Fax: (303) 267-9400
Email: sequelgroup@sequelgroup.com
Web: www.hightech-jobs.com

Description: We provide services individualized to our clients (hardware, software, systems integration, telecommunications companies). These services include executive search and related project consulting and on-site service.

Key Contact - Specialty:
Mr. Robert Heisser, Managing Partner - *Software, hardware, system integration, upper-level management, individual contributor*

Functions: Generalist, Directors, Senior Mgmt., Middle Mgmt., Sales Mgmt., MIS Mgmt., Mgmt. Consultants

Industries: Generalist, Software

Sequoia Partners
920 Saratoga Ave Ste 106
San Jose, CA 95129
(408) 244-2999
Fax: (408) 244-1431
Email: don@sequoia-partners.com
Web: www.sequoia-partners.com

Description: Sequoia Partners is dedicated to finding the best people for your current employment needs. We are neither resume printers or buzz word head hunters. Our experience allows us to help develop and work to very exacting and well defined job specifications. Consequently, our client companies see only very hirable candidates. We are dedicated to high quality search services specializing in the high tech industry. It is our intention to provide services to a select number of companies so that we can concentrate on our clients needs. It is our belief that we can do an outstanding job for a few companies rather than an ordinary job for a large number of companies.

Key Contact - Specialty:
Mr. Donald Fernandez, Managing Partner - *Software*
Mr. Scott Fernandez, Recruiter - *Professional services*

Functions: General Mgmt., Sales & Mktg., IT, R&D

Industries: Software, Database SW, Development SW, Doc. Mgmt., Production SW, ERP SW, Marketing SW, Networking, Comm. SW, Security SW, System SW

Setla Consulting

1357 Ballena Blvd C
Alameda, CA 94501
(510) 769-7900
(510) 823-8088
Fax: (240) 282-4045
Email: ted@setlaconsulting.com
Web: www.setlaconsulting.com

Description: Our firm specializes in contingency, retained, or contract recruiting, and organizational and staffing development of professionals for corporations large and small with specific attention to medical, telecommunications, software, and HVAC industries. We follow up the recruiting efforts with team building adventures to remember. Please visit our website www.corporateascent.com.

Key Contact:
Mr. Thaddeus Setla, Principal/Owner

Salary minimum: $65,000

Functions: Generalist

Industries: Generalist

Professional Associations: SHRM

SFB Legal Search

150 E 58th St Fl 39
New York, NY 10155
(212) 688-1128
Fax: (212) 688-1169
Email: stacylegal@aol.com

Description: We specialize in attorney placements within corporations throughout the US and abroad, with substantial success in diversity legal hiring needs. Our principals have 33 combined years of experience, plus two part-time recruiters.

Key Contact - Specialty:
Ms. Stacia Foster Blake, President - *Attorney placements within corporations*

Salary minimum: $75,000

Functions: Attorneys

Industries: Generalist

Branches:
670 White Plains Rd Ste 118
Scarsdale, NY 10583
(914) 472-2700
Fax: (914) 472-2585
Email: stacylegal@aol.com
Key Contact - Specialty:
Ms. Joan Blum Simon, Vice President - *Legal placements within corporations*

Sharrow & Associates Inc

24735 Van Dyke
Center Line, MI 48015
(810) 759-6910
(219) 665-1261
Fax: (810) 759-6914
Email: lorraine@sharrowgroup.com
Web: www.sharrowgroup.com

Description: Our group has been a leader in the executive search and recruiting industry since 1968. Our center line specializes in the placement of intellectual property attorneys, engineers and chemists in the automotive industry and information technology professionals in a variety of industries. Our Angola Indiana division specializes in the recruitment of upper-level executives in the residential construction industry.

Key Contact:
Mrs. Beth Sharrow, CEO

Salary minimum: $60,000

Functions: Generalist, Senior Mgmt., Legal, Sales & Mktg., IT

Industries: Generalist, Construction, Mfg., Chemicals, Drugs Mfg., Plastics, Rubber

Professional Associations: MAPS, NAPS

Branches:
207 Hoosier Dr Ste 3
Angola, IN 46703
(219) 665-1261
(800) 823-1001
Fax: (219) 665-1343
Email: sharrow@fwi.com
Key Contact:
Mrs. Beth Sharrow, President

John Shell Associates Inc

115 Atrium Way Ste 122
PO Box 23291
Columbia, SC 29224
(803) 788-6619
Fax: (803) 788-1758
Email: mail@shellaccounting.com
Web: www.shellaccounting.com

Description: South Carolina's specialists in accounting and financial placement.

Key Contact - Specialty:
Mr. John C. Shell, III, President - *Accounting, finance*
Ms. Kay H. Mayes, Executive Dir-Shell Acct Temps - *Accounting, finance, bookkeeping*

Salary minimum: $30,000

Functions: Finance

Industries: Generalist

Professional Associations: AAFA

Sherbrooke Associates Inc

727 Raritan Rd Ste 202B
Clark, NJ 07066
(732) 382-5505
Fax: (732) 382-0052
Email: sajobsq@aol.com

Description: Recruiting generalists with a Northeast customer base; strengths in both cosmetic, food and pharmaceutical and in high-technology firms.

Key Contact - Specialty:
Mr. William M. Levy, Vice President - *Engineering, operations, sales & marketing*
Mr. James D. Scanlon, President - *Human resources, engineering, operations*

Salary minimum: $60,000

Functions: Generalist

Industries: Drugs Mfg., Medical Devices, Paints, Petro. Products, Metal Products

Sherriff & Associates

4200 Somerset Ste 256
Prairie Village, KS 66208
(913) 341-7117
Email: bsherriff@sherriff.com

Description: We have provided nearly 20 years of quality, ethical physician search, physician executive placement, sourcing, and pre-credentialing services. Our firm has been the past-president of the National Association of Physician Recruiters (NAPR) and the past-chair of the NAPR Ethics Committee.

Key Contact - Specialty:
Mr. William W. Sherriff, Vice President - *Physicians, executive healthcare, allied healthcare*
Ms. Julie A. Sherriff, President - *Physicians, executive healthcare*
Ms. Stephanie Cassandras, Vice President-Retained Search - *Physicians*

Functions: Physicians

Industries: Generalist

Professional Associations: NAPR

Networks: First Choice (FC)

Shey-Harding Associates Inc

PO Box 67
Seal Beach, CA 90740-6153
(562) 799-8854
Fax: (562) 799-6174
Email: hq@shey-harding.com
Web: www.shey-harding.com

Description: We specialize in recruiting for the transportation/logistics industries. We have an extensive database of expert, professional candidates and will conduct worldwide confidential searches to supply the best and brightest.

Key Contact - Specialty:
Ms. Deborah Shey-Harding, Vice President - *Transportation, logistics*
Mr. Michael W. Harding, President - *Transportation, logistics*

Functions: General Mgmt., Materials, Purchasing, Distribution, Sales & Mktg., HR Mgmt., Finance, Credit, IT

Industries: Mfg., Transportation, Wholesale

Professional Associations: CLM, FTA, PC, SHRM

Robert Shields & Associates

(also known as Technology Transfer Inc)
1560 W Bay Area Blvd Ste 200
Friendswood, TX 77546
(281) 488-7961
(281) 679-1500
Fax: (281) 486-1496
Email: george@itjobstoday.com
Web: www.itjobstoday.com

Description: Specialists in data processing and software engineering positions nationally and overseas. Extensive contacts with established and start-up software vendors including Internet ASPs.

Key Contact - Specialty:
Mr. George F. Black, President - *Information technology*
Mr. Richard Gross, Vice President - *Information technology*
Ms. Jani Clemons, Vice President - *Midrange technology*

Salary minimum: $40,000

Functions: IT

Industries: Generalist

Professional Associations: HAAPC, NACCB, NAPS, TAPC

Networks: National Personnel Assoc (NPA)

Branches:
2470 Gray Falls Ste 260
Houston, TX 77077
(281) 679-1500
Fax: (281) 679-1508
Email: dave@itjobstoday.com
Key Contact - Specialty:
Mr. David Schwee, Senior Counselor/Principal -
Information technology

Shiell Personnel
2040 N Causeway Blvd
Mandeville, LA 70471
(504) 674-1616
Fax: (504) 674-1611

Description: We specialize in medical and
pharmaceutical sales.

Key Contact - Specialty:
Mr. Donald M. Shiell, Owner - *Medical equipment,
pharmaceutical sales*

Salary minimum: $30,000

Functions: Generalist, Middle Mgmt., Sales Mgmt.,
Minorities, Int'l.

Industries: Generalist, Pharm Svcs., Healthcare

Networks: First Interview Network (FIN)

Shifrin-Fischer Group Inc
409 N Ave E
Cranford, NJ 07016-2437
(908) 931-1000
Fax: (908) 931-1009
Email: brad@shifrinfischer.com
Web: www.shifrinfischer.com

Description: We specialize in the recruitment of
sales and marketing individuals with a
specialization in pharmaceutical, biotechnology,
high technology, telecommunications, and computer
software.

Key Contact:
Mr. Brad Shifrin, President - *Sales & marketing*
Mr. Michael L. Fischer, Director
Ms. Lori E. Winter, Director of Biotechnology

Salary minimum: $50,000

Functions: Sales & Mktg.

Industries: Drugs Mfg., Computer Equip.,
Consumer Elect., Invest. Banking, Services,
Advertising, Telecoms, Packaging, Software,
Biotech

Networks: First Interview Network (FIN)

Shiloh Careers Int'l Inc
7105 Peach Ct Ste 102
PO Box 831
Brentwood, TN 37024-0831
(615) 373-3090
Email: maryann@shilohcareers.com
Web: www.shilohcareers.com

Description: We have been successfully recruiting
in the property and casualty insurance industry.

Key Contact - Specialty:
Ms. Mary Ann Webber, President - *Insurance
(property, casualty)*

Functions: Generalist, Middle Mgmt.

Industries: Insurance

Professional Associations: ASSE, NIRA, TAPS

Shoreline Digital
809 B Cuesta Dr Ste 180
Mountain View, CA 94040
(650) 564-9400
Fax: (650) 564-9401
Email: martha@shoredg.com
Web: www.shoredg.com

Description: We are an executive search firm
specializing in the placement of software engineers
and developers in Silicon Valley/Northern
California.

Key Contact - Specialty:
Ms. Martha J. Lewis, Director - *Software developer*
Mr. Sean Fitzgerald, Manager - *Software developer*

Functions: Engineering

Industries: Software, Database SW, Development
SW, HR SW, Marketing SW, Networking,
Comm. SW, System SW

The Shoreline Group
2644 Henry Ct
Belvidere, IL 61008
(815) 547-4173
Fax: (815) 547-8263
Email: larry@shorelinegroup.net
Web: www.shorelinegroup.net

Description: We are a service oriented, national
recruiting firm specializing in sales and
management for manufacturing, sales, and service
companies. Our searches are performed on a
contingent or retained basis.

Key Contact:
Mr. Larry Cunningham

Functions: General Mgmt., Directors, Senior
Mgmt., Middle Mgmt., Packaging, Sales Mgmt.

Industries: Mfg., Equip Svcs., Packaging

SHS Inc
205 W Wacker Dr Ste 600
Chicago, IL 60606
(312) 419-0370
Fax: (312) 419-8953
Email: info@shsinc.com
Web: www.shsinc.com

Description: Our firm is a dynamic and progressive
recruitment firm capable of handling either
contingency or retainer search assignments. Our
focus is in the biotechnology, pharmaceutical
development, pharmaceutical advertising,
continuing medical education, and healthcare
communications industries. Our consultants
specialize in one or more of these industries. The
firm is based in Chicago and serves clients in all
major US cities and internationally.

Key Contact:
Mr. Timothy Jadwin, CPC, President

Salary minimum: $35,000

Functions: Generalist

Industries: Pharm Svcs., Advertising, Publishing,
New Media, Biotech, Healthcare

Professional Associations: IAPS, NAPS

SHS of Allentown
4327 Rte 309
Schnecksville, PA 18078-2513
(610) 799-2131
Fax: (610) 799-2141
Email: shsofatn@ptd.net
Web: www.shsofallentown.com

Description: Nationwide coverage of the minerals,
explosives, crushed stone, construction materials,
battery and chemical industries.

Key Contact:
Mr. David Mostow, President

Salary minimum: $45,000

Functions: Generalist

Industries: Food, Bev., Tobacco, Chemicals

Branches:
PO Box 6868
Louisville, KY 40206-0868
(502) 897-7666
Fax: (502) 897-7668
Email: shsofatn@ptd.net
Key Contact:
Mr. Donald R. Beltz, Account Executive

SHS of Cherry Hill
929 N Kings Hwy
Cherry Hill, NJ 08034
(856) 779-9030
Fax: (856) 779-0898
Web: www.shsofcherryhill.com

Description: Our firm provides recruiting services
on a contingency basis. Our specialization is
engineering/technical and manufacturing. Our
clients are mid-sized organizations. Our firm utilizes
a database candidate system. We were established
over 20 years ago.

Key Contact - Specialty:
Mr. Louis Kennedy - *Technical*

Salary minimum: $30,000

Functions: Mfg., Plant Mgmt., Engineering

Industries: Mfg., Food, Bev., Tobacco, Chemicals,
Drugs Mfg., Medical Devices, Metal Products,
Machine, Appliance, Motor Vehicles, Misc. Mfg.

Professional Associations: NAPS

SHS TechStaffing
1124 Rte 315
Wilkes-Barre, PA 18702
(570) 825-3411
Fax: (570) 825-7790
Email: info@shstechstaffing.com
Web: www.shstechstaffing.com

Description: Offering professional recruiting
services for direct hire and contract professionals.
Emphasis on information technology, accounting
and engineering.

Key Contact:
Mr. Charles Davenport, Professional Recruiter -
Information technology, accounting, engineering
Mr. Nicholas J. Michalisin, Jr., Professional
Recruiter - *Information technology, engineering*
Mr. John McGraw, Professional Recruiter

Salary minimum: $35,000

Functions: Mfg., Materials, Finance, IT

Industries: Generalist, Mfg., Printing, Chemicals,
Plastics, Rubber, Metal Products, Computer
Equip., Test, Measure Equip.

Branches:
3220-D Corporate Ct
Ellicott City, MD 21042
(410) 461-7300
Fax: (410) 461-5595
Email: paxelrod@ix.netcom.com
Key Contact - Specialty:
Mr. Peter Axelrod, Professional Recruiter -
*Manufacturing, information technology, human
resources*

Shupack & Michaels Inc
27 Monmouth Dr Ste 277
East Northport, NY 11731-1332
(631) 757-4559
Fax: (631) 757-3880
Email: jshupack@aol.com
Web: www.shupackandmichaels.com

Description: Contingency and retainer recruitment
and placement of engineers at all levels for
consulting, and A/E firms-mechanical/hvac,
electrical, civil, structural, architects, etc. Domestic
and international.

Key Contact - Specialty:
Mr. Joseph Shupack, President - *Consulting, architectural engineering firms*
Ms. Ellen Michaels, Vice President - *Consulting, architectural engineering firms*

Functions: Senior Mgmt., Middle Mgmt., Engineering, Architects

Industries: Generalist, Energy, Utilities, Construction, Transportation

Networks: Inter-City Personnel Assoc (IPA)

Scott Sibley Associates
24 Bent Oak Trl
Fairport, NY 14450
(716) 425-1300
Fax: (716) 325-5923

Description: Understanding our client's business and dedication to their success is our strength. We provide highly motivated, qualified career oriented candidates in whom we take a personal interest.

Key Contact - Specialty:
Mr. Scott S. McElhearn, Owner/President - *Medical*

Salary minimum: $25,000

Functions: Generalist, Directors, Physicians, Nurses, Allied Health, Health Admin., Sales & Mktg., Mktg. Mgmt., Sales Mgmt., Engineering

Industries: Generalist, Misc. Mfg., Banking, Higher Ed., HR Services, Software, Healthcare

Professional Associations: SHRM

Branches:
215 Alexander St
Rochester, NY 14607
(716) 232-2020
Fax: (716) 325-5923
Key Contact - Specialty:
Mr. Scott S. McElhearn, Owner/President - *Medical*

Peter Siegel & Company
PO Box 920218
Needham, MA 02492-0003
(781) 455-9057
Fax: (781) 455-6246
Email: psiegco@aol.com

Description: A candor, a personality and an expertise that sources prospective employees to complement the diverse corporate cultures of clients represented.

Key Contact - Specialty:
Mr. Peter A. Siegel, President - *Retail executives, direct marketing executives*

Salary minimum: $40,000

Functions: Generalist

Industries: Retail

Sierra Int'l Group Inc
(also known as MRI of Roseville)
3001 Douglas Blvd Ste 203
Roseville, CA 95661-4523
(916) 781-8110
Fax: (916) 781-6719
Email: recruit@sierrasearch.com
Web: www.sierrasearch.com

Description: Our team of professionals is your single source for worldwide high technology recruiting of executive, technical, sales, and marketing talent. We specialize in the Enterprise software, IT, and telecommunications industries.

Key Contact - Specialty:
Mr. David Sanders, President - *Information technology, telecommunications*
Ms. Lorena Stanley, Vice President - *Enterprise software*

Salary minimum: $80,000

Functions: General Mgmt., Senior Mgmt., Mktg. Mgmt., Sales Mgmt., CFO's, IT

Industries: Generalist, Communications, Telecoms, Wireless, Network Infrastructure, Software, ERP SW, Networking, Comm. SW, Security SW

Professional Associations: AEA

Siger & Associates LLC
966 Westover Rd
Stamford, CT 06902
(203) 348-0976
Fax: (203) 348-0698

Description: Specialists in executive recruitment for the financial services industry. Areas include: portfolio management, mergers & acquisitions, capital markets, derivative products, sales, trading, research, structured and project finance and emerging markets.

Key Contact - Specialty:
Mr. J. Raymond Milo, President - *Financial services*

Salary minimum: $75,000

Functions: Finance

Industries: Brokers, Venture Cap., Services, Accounting

SignatureSoft Inc
7353 Melodia Ter
Carlsbad, CA 92009
(760) 431-8866
(800) 999-8829
Email: bob@signaturesoft.com
Web: www.signaturesoft.com

Description: We are a full-service professional search firm, specializing in the high-tech, communications and networking industries in California. Software and hardware engineering is our main focus.

Key Contact - Specialty:
Mr. Bob DeGrasse, President - *Engineering (softwarem, hardware), communications, networking*

Salary minimum: $50,000

Functions: Engineering

Industries: Media, Telecoms, Software

Silcott & Associates Inc
5477 Glen Lakes Dr Ste 204
Dallas, TX 75231
(972) 369-7802
(800) 969-7802
Fax: (214) 369-7875
Email: mlsilcott@aol.com

Description: We specialize in attorneys, all areas of practice, including intellectual properties, corporate and private practice, law firm mergers, and the placement of large or small groups.

Key Contact:
Mr. Michael Silcott, President - *Legal*
Mr. William W. Robertson, Vice President - *Legal*
Ms. Marilyn Elliott, Executive Recruiter

Salary minimum: $60,000

Functions: Generalist, General Mgmt., HR Mgmt., Attorneys

Industries: Generalist, Finance, Services

Silicon Executive Search Inc
4214 Dundas St W Ste 203
Toronto, ON M8X 1Y6
Canada
(416) 232-0600
Fax: (416) 232-0410
Email: josie_erent@yahoo.com

Description: Mid-level to senior management level specializing in hi-tech IT vendor market - software, professional services, telecom, Internet etc. Specializing in mid-level and senior-level sales professional positions including management. Also specializing in mid-level to senior-level IT human resources management positions.

Key Contact - Specialty:
Ms. Josie Erent, President - *Software, professional services, telecom*

Salary minimum: $90,000

Functions: Generalist, General Mgmt., Sales & Mktg., Sales Mgmt., HR Mgmt.

Industries: Computer Equip., Mgmt. Consulting, New Media, Telecoms, Software

Professional Associations: HRPAO, SLF, SMEI

The Silicon Network
40 King St W Ste 4900
Scotia Plz
Toronto, ON M5H 4A2
Canada
(416) 777-6746
Fax: (416) 777-6748
Email: silicon@passport.ca
Web: www.silicon-network.com

Description: We are a professional recruitment firm specializing in full-time and contract placement of individuals in the data, telecommunications industry. Professionalism and confidentiality are the cornerstone of our business philosophy.

Key Contact - Specialty:
Mr. Michael Fernandez, President - *Engineering, data communications*
Mr. Rolph Laresen, Recruiter - *Engineering, data communications, telecommunications*
Mr. Walter Wimmer, Recruiter - *Engineering, data communications, telecommunications*
Mr. Kevin McGinty, Recruiter - *Engineering, data communications, telecommunications*

Functions: Generalist, Systems Analysis, Systems Dev., Systems Implem., Systems Support, Network Admin., Engineering, Technicians

Industries: Generalist, Computer Equip., Software

Silicon Talent Corp
(formerly known as Bozich & Cruz Inc)
2540 N First St Ste 309
San Jose, CA 95131
(408) 955-9800
Fax: (408) 955-9868
Email: response@silicontalent.com
Web: www.silicontalent.com

Description: Formerly known as Bozich & Cruz, Inc., we are a high-technology recruiting firm focusing on the engineering and marketing functions within the software industry.

Key Contact - Specialty:
Ms. Linda Bozich, Executive Vice President - *Engineering*
Mr. Joe Maxwell, President
Mr. Master Burnett, Director of Marketing - *Internet, new media executives*

Functions: Generalist

Industries: New Media, Telecoms, Software

Sill Technical Associates Inc
PO Box 898
Mechanicsburg, PA 17055
(717) 691-6730
Fax: (717) 691-6873
Email: dsill1@aol.com

Description: I am a graduate engineer (BSME) with 15 years of recruiting/placement experience I practiced engineering for 15 years before opening this employment service.

Key Contact - Specialty:
Mr. Darrell E. Sill, BSME, Manager - *Engineering*

Functions: Mfg., Product Dev.

Industries: Generalist

Networks: Top Echelon Network

Silver Associates
11925 Wilshire Blvd Ste 317
Los Angeles, CA 90025
(310) 312-4820
Fax: (310) 312-1294
Email: susan@silverassociates.com

Description: We provide executive search in finance, strategic planning, accounting, tax, audit, MIS, sales/marketing, EDP audit, consulting, human resources, entertainment, Internet/new media, distribution, etc. Our principals have over 36 years of combined search industry experience.

Key Contact - Specialty:
Ms. Susan Silver - *Entertainment, finance, accounting, internet, new media*

Salary minimum: $35,000

Functions: Generalist, General Mgmt., Sales & Mktg., HR Mgmt., Finance, IT, Mgmt. Consultants, Graphic Artists

Industries: Generalist, Mfg., Finance, Services, Media, Communications, Software

---

The Silver Scott Group LLC
550 N Maple Ave
Ridgewood, NJ 07450
(201) 493-1500
Fax: (201) 493-1502
Email: ssg@silverscott.com
Web: www.silverscott.com

Description: We are a full-service recruiting firm with a solution-oriented approach to information technology needs. Our experience and dedication provides our clients with the highest level of service and integrity.

Key Contact:
Mr. Scott Boyarsky, President

Salary minimum: $50,000

Functions: IT, MIS Mgmt., Systems Dev., Systems Implem., Network Admin., DB Admin., Mgmt. Consultants

Industries: Mfg., Drugs Mfg., Finance, Brokers, Mgmt. Consulting, Media, Insurance, Software, Healthcare

---

Silverman & Associates
2640 Caminito Carino
La Jolla, CA 92037
(858) 456-8589
Fax: (858) 456-8591
Email: beth@silvermanandassociates.com
Web: www.silvermanandassociates.com

Description: We serve shopping center developers and retailers nationwide. Specializing in retail real estate, leasing, development, legal, construction, financial and asset management. Principals bring over 40 years of collective experience in the industry.

Key Contact - Specialty:
Ms. Beth Silverman, Partner - *Real estate*

Salary minimum: $50,000

Functions: Specialized Svcs.

Industries: Retail, Real Estate

SilverSands Int'l
759 Bear Creek Cir
Winter Springs, FL 32708
(407) 365-8854

Email: jmulvey@cfl.rr.com

Description: Executive search services to computer software companies who market their products to high-technology companies. Executive-levels from middle management and higher, including CEO and president positions.

Key Contact - Specialty:
Mr. James E. Mulvey - *Software (sales & marketing, technical support, project management, imp cons)*

Salary minimum: $50,000

Functions: Generalist, Middle Mgmt., Mktg. Mgmt., Sales Mgmt., Systems Implem., Systems Support

Industries: Software

Professional Associations: APICS

D W Simpson & Company
1800 W Larchmont Ave
Chicago, IL 60613
(312) 867-2300
Fax: (312) 951-8386
Email: actuaries@dwsimpson.com
Web: www.dwsimpson.com

Description: Serving the actuarial profession nationwide and at all levels from student to fellow. We use a straight forward approach to meet the objectives of client companies and candidates.

Key Contact - Specialty:
Ms. Patricia Jacobsen, Principal - *Actuarial*
Ms. Sally Ezra, Senior Manager - *Actuarial*
Mr. Bob Morand, Senior Manager - *Actuarial*
Mr. David Simpson, Managing Principal - *Actuarial*

Functions: Generalist

Industries: Insurance

Professional Associations: CAS, NACE, SHRM

Simpson Associates
106 Central Park S Ste 3B
Trump Parc
New York, NY 10019
(212) 767-0006
Fax: (212) 767-0660
Email: simpsonassociates@msn.com
Web: www.simpsonassociates.com

Description: We specialize in middle/senior executives for retail, apparel manufacturing and direct mail industry.

Key Contact:
Ms. Terre Simpson, President - *Retailing, catalogues, wholesale manufacturing (softlines, hardlines)*
Ms. Susan Haubenstock, Vice President

Salary minimum: $80,000

Functions: Generalist, Product Dev., Advertising, Mkt. Research, Sales Mgmt., Direct Mktg., Finance, IT

Industries: Generalist, Textiles, Apparel, Wholesale, Retail, New Media

Professional Associations: DMA, IFG, NAFE, NRF

Sinclair-Smith & Associates
3607 Elie Auclair
Ste. Polycarpe, QC J0P 1X0
Canada
(450) 265-3539
(450) 845-4208
Fax: (450) 265-4018
Email: sinclair@rocler.qc.ca
Web: www.sinclair-smithassoc.com

Description: Since 1968, we have been recruiting all levels of engineers in all industries and all

functions. We work in Canada, America and other locations around the world. We specialize in multi-lingual engineers for overseas locations.

Key Contact:
Mr. Michael Sinclair-Smith

Salary minimum: $60,000

Functions: Middle Mgmt., Mfg., Product Dev., Production

Industries: Agri., Forestry, Mining, Energy, Utilities, Construction, Mfg.

Marina Sirras & Associates LLC
420 Lexington Ave Ste 2545
New York, NY 10170
(212) 490-0333
(800) 440-5490
Fax: (212) 490-2074
Email: info@lawseek.com
Web: www.lawseek.com

Description: We specialize in placement of attorneys in law firms and corporations. Presently, along with conducting searches in NYC and other cities in the US, we are actively recruiting candidates who are interested in working overseas. Our firm is an active member of the National Association of Legal Search Consultants and Marina Sirras is a member of its board of directors.

Key Contact:
Ms. Marina Sirras, Principal/Member
Ms. Jennifer Sirras, Member

Functions: Attorneys

Industries: Generalist

Professional Associations: NALSC

Sissom & Associates
4204 Westgate Dr
Knoxville, TN 37921
(865) 546-0645
Fax: (865) 546-0541
Email: csissom@nxs.net

Description: We focus exclusively in human resources and related areas including compensation, benefits, training, and organizational development in all regions of the US.

Key Contact - Specialty:
Mr. Chuck Sissom, Owner - *Human resources*

Salary minimum: $45,000

Functions: Generalist, Mfg., HR Mgmt., Benefits, Personnel, Training

Industries: Generalist, Mfg.

Networks: Inter-City Personnel Assoc (IPA)

Patricia Sklar & Associates Ltd
205 N Michigan Ave 3306
Chicago, IL 60601
(312) 467-4600
Fax: (312) 467-4664
Email: patricia@sklarsearch.com

Description: We are dedicated exclusively to the communications industry. Our goal is to provide media organizations with knowledge and contacts. We recruit sales people, media buyers and media planning professionals.

Key Contact - Specialty:
Ms. Patricia Sklar, President - *Advertising, communications*

Functions: Advertising

Industries: Generalist

Slack & Associates Professional Placement

151 S Whittier
Wichita, KS 67207
(316) 681-4441
Fax: (316) 681-4449
Email: jobs@getajob-wichita.com
Web: www.getajob-wichita.com

Description: We offer a full-time permanent placement service specializing office, clerical, administrative, accounting, sales, and management positions. Most of our jobs are in Wichita, Kansas. There is no fee to the applicant.

Key Contact:
Mr. Kelly W. Slack, President
Ms. Marilyn Joyce, Office Administrator
Mr. John Joyce, Administrative Support
Ms. Karla Fulk, Receptionist

Functions: Generalist

Industries: Generalist

Tom Sloan & Associates Inc

1530 Utah St
PO Box 50
Watertown, WI 53094
(920) 261-8890
Fax: (920) 261-6357
Email: sloan@gdinet.com

Description: Food industry specialization, R&D, production management, engineering, sales/marketing. Industries: meat, dairy, canning/freezing, milling, baking candy, fat/oils, beverage, food ingredient, snack foods, animal feed and supplements.

Key Contact - Specialty:
Mr. Tom Sloan, President - *Food manufacturing, engineering*
Ms. Terri Sherman, Vice President - *Food ingredients, research & development, technical support, sales*

Salary minimum: $25,000

Functions: Generalist, General Mgmt., Product Dev., Materials, Sales & Mktg., HR Mgmt., R&D, Engineering

Industries: Generalist, Food, Bev., Tobacco

Professional Associations: IFT, SFA

Sloan & Associates PC

1769 Jamestown Rd
Williamsburg, VA 23185-2324
(757) 220-1111
Fax: (757) 220-1694
Email: sloansearch@erols.com
Web: www.sloansearch.com

Description: Our firm specializes in the consumer packaged goods industry. Our emphasis is on sales and marketing, and mid- and upper-level management positions. Our sub- specialization by geography allows ultimate market penetration. Employment law, testing and assessment, and compensation services are also available.

Key Contact:
Mr. Mike Sloan, President - *Consumer packaged goods*
Ms. Shelly Wren, Executive Assistant to President - *Consumer packaged goods*
Mr. John Holland, Western Area Director - *Consumer packaged goods*
Mr. Tom Coffey, Southern Area Director
Mr. Russell Murphy, Northeast Area Director
Mr. Craig Minton, Marketing Director
Mr. Mark Bernecker, Director of Customer Marketing

Salary minimum: $50,000

Functions: Sales & Mktg.

Industries: Food, Bev., Tobacco

Sloane & Associates Inc

(also known as MRI of Brookfield)
13160 W Burleigh Rd Ste 204
Brookfield, WI 53005-7712
(262) 790-8820
Fax: (262) 790-8830
Email: rsloane@sloaneassociates.com

Description: We are nationwide search consultants to the design and construction industry. We know the industry; our candidates are all proven performers. Because of our established reputation and industry experience, we are widely recognized by both clients and candidates, and are often the first stop for professionals in the design, construction, program management, real estate and corporate facilities markets. We provide retained and contingency search.

Key Contact - Specialty:
Mr. Ronald Sloane, CPA, President - *Architecture, construction, real estate, program management*

Salary minimum: $75,000

Functions: Senior Mgmt., Sales Mgmt., Architects

Industries: Generalist, Construction, Real Estate

Professional Associations: CFMA, SME

Martha Sloane Professional Placements Inc

500 5th Ave Ste 1130
New York, NY 10110
(212) 269-7789
Fax: (212) 269-7793
Email: msloane@ucs.net

Description: Recruits senior-level editorial and compliance professionals for investment banking industry.

Key Contact:
Ms. Martha E. Sloane

Salary minimum: $85,000

Functions: Finance

Industries: Invest. Banking, Media, New Media

Slone & Associates

2862 28th St NW Ste 200
Washington, DC 20008
(202) 234-5999
Fax: (202) 318-4302
Email: aslone@sloneandassociates.com
Web: www.sloneandassociates.com

Description: We are a leading executive search firm that specializes in working with communications and sales professionals/organizations within the healthcare, pharmaceutical, and biotechnology industries.

Key Contact:
Mr. Adam Slone, President
Mr. Michael Mosunic, Senior Associate

Functions: Healthcare, Sales & Mktg.

Industries: Non-profits, Pharm Svcs., Media, Advertising, Biotech, Healthcare

Professional Associations: BIO

J L Small Associates

312 N Burbank Dr
Birmingham, AL 35226
(205) 823-4545

Description: We are generalist specializing in engineering, accounting, manufacturing, and human resources. Pulp and paper is our main specialty

Key Contact - Specialty:
Mr. Jim Small, Owner - *Engineers, accountants, manufacturing, generalist*

Industries: Food, Bev., Tobacco

Salary minimum: $35,000

Functions: Generalist, Mfg., Materials, HR Mgmt., Finance, CFO's, IT

Industries: Generalist, Construction, Mfg., Paper, Chemicals, Metal Products

Smartsource Inc

500 Ygnacio Valley Rd Ste 390
Walnut Creek, CA 94596
(925) 935-4200
Fax: (925) 935-0645
Email: sf-resume@smartsourceinc.com
Web: www.smartsourceinc.com

Description: We place technical professionals in personal computing/local and wide area networking in all platforms and methodologies, telecommunications, project managers, MIS directors, Lotus Notes, 2nd and 3rd level help desk support, web development, etc.

Key Contact - Specialty:
Ms. Dee Dee Melmet, President - *Technical, PC LAN/WAN, telecommunication, help desk*

Functions: MIS Mgmt., Systems Analysis, Systems Dev., Systems Implem., Systems Support, Network Admin., DB Admin.

Industries: Generalist

Branches:
2377 Gold Meadow Way Ste 120
Gold River, CA 95670
(916) 631-1999
Fax: (916) 631-1994
Email: sac-resume@smartsourceinc.com
Key Contact - Specialty:
Ms. Patty Taylor, Senior Vice President - *Technical, PC LAN/WAN, telecommunication, help desk*

5201 Great America Pkwy Ste 320
Santa Clara, CA 95054
(408) 982-2121
Email: sac-resume@smartsourceinc.com
Key Contact:
Ms. Stacee Nelson

Smith & Associates

3826 Monteith Dr Ste 300
Los Angeles, CA 90043-1747
(323) 295-8198
Fax: (323) 293-9825
Email: darrell@searchsmith.com
Web: www.searchsmith.com

Description: Our practice is established primarily along functional lines with special emphasis on mid- and senior management to executive-level positions in sales, marketing, supply chain, finance, human resources, and general management.

Key Contact:
Mr. Darrell G. Smith, President

Salary minimum: $50,000

Functions: Generalist, Materials, Healthcare, Sales & Mktg., Advertising, Mktg. Mgmt., Sales Mgmt., Finance, Minorities

Industries: Generalist, Food, Bev., Tobacco, Soap, Perf., Cosmtcs., Computer Equip., Retail, Finance, Services, Hospitals, Physical Therapy, Occupational Therapy

Networks: National Personnel Assoc (NPA)

Smith & Associates

5513 Woodland Dr
Savannah, GA 31406-2143
(800) 611-4043
(912) 354-7884
Fax: (801) 697-0593
Email: raysmith@technojobs.com
Web: www.technojobs.com

Description: Recruitment and placement of Computer Information Systems Professionals including Programmers, Analysts, Developers, Administrators and Engineers. Particular emphasis on AS/400, Web and Client Server experts. Primarily permanent placement, but increasing number of contract positions.

Key Contact:
Mr. Ray E. Smith

Salary minimum: $40,000

Functions: IT

Industries: Construction, Mfg., Transportation, Pharm Svcs., Telecoms, Aerospace, Packaging, Software

Sylvia Smith & Associates

PO Box 829
Brandon, FL 33509
(813) 689-2611
Fax: (813) 651-5446
Email: personel@gte.net
Web: home1.gte.net/personel/index.htm

Description: Nationwide placements of all areas of manufacturing, engineering, aerospace, environmental, chemical, quality, power generation, buyers, data processing, and metals & plastics industries, etc.

Key Contact - Specialty:
Ms. Sylvia Smith, Owner - *Manufacturing, aerospace*

Functions: Generalist

Industries: Energy, Utilities, Mfg., Finance, Accounting, Telecoms, Environmental Svcs., Haz. Waste, Aerospace, Software

Networks: Top Echelon Network

James F Smith & Associates

4651 Roswell Rd NE Ste B102
Atlanta, GA 30342
(404) 256-6408

Description: Consulting psychologists who provide executive search/recruiting services to their corporate clients.

Key Contact:
Dr. James F. Smith

Salary minimum: $50,000

Functions: Generalist, Senior Mgmt., Middle Mgmt., Plant Mgmt., Sales Mgmt., Mgmt. Consultants, Int'l.

Industries: Generalist, Metal Products, Misc. Mfg., Retail, Mgmt. Consulting, Hospitality, Defense

Professional Associations: APA

Ralph Smith & Associates

540 Frontage Rd Ste 3335
Northfield, IL 60093
(847) 441-0900
Fax: (847) 441-0902

Description: General search practice, all functional areas, most industries including manufacturing, services firms, packaged goods, consumer products, advertising and public relations. Specialize in Chicago area clients and candidates.

Key Contact - Specialty:
Mr. Ralph E. Smith, President - *Generalist*

Salary minimum: $50,000

Functions: Generalist, Middle Mgmt., Plant Mgmt., Advertising, Mktg. Mgmt., Sales Mgmt., Cash Mgmt.

Industries: Generalist, Food, Bev., Tobacco, Soap, Perf., Cosmtcs., Machine, Appliance, Advertising, Packaging

Peter A Smith & Associates

2390 Cal Young Rd
Eugene, OR 97401
(541) 302-8100
Fax: (541) 302-6570
Email: psmithsearch@aol.com

Description: Corporate and property level hospitality management and sales executives. Twenty-five years' industry experience in sales & marketing, and operations. Emphasis on GM and sales positions, nationally. Major hotel companies as clients.

Key Contact - Specialty:
Mr. Peter A. Smith, Principal - *Hospitality*

Salary minimum: $50,000

Functions: General Mgmt., Sales & Mktg., Finance

Industries: Hospitality

J Harrington Smith Associates

PO Box 90065
Indianapolis, IN 46290
(317) 251-0678
Fax: (317) 251-1138

Description: Human resource consultant to management.

Key Contact - Specialty:
Mr. James H. Smith, Principal - *Mining*

Salary minimum: $60,000

Functions: Generalist, General Mgmt., Senior Mgmt., Middle Mgmt., Production, Materials, Engineering, Mgmt. Consultants, Environmentalists

Industries: Agri., Forestry, Mining, Paper, HR Services

Smith Bridges and Associates Inc

555 S Old Woodward Ave Ste 603
Birmingham, MI 48009
(248) 540-2448
Fax: (248) 540-2801
Email: resumes@smithbridges.com
Web: www.smithbridges.com

Description: The areas that we cover include: corporate finance, printing and graphic arts, electronic document management, sales and sales management, senior level management, and nonprofit organizations.

Key Contact - Specialty:
Mr. Mike Smith - *Printing, electronic document management, nonprofit organizations, management consulting*
Mr. Peter Bridges - *Corporate finance, management consulting*

Salary minimum: $40,000

Functions: General Mgmt., Mfg., Sales & Mktg., Finance, Specialized Svcs.

Industries: Printing, Invest. Banking, Venture Cap., Non-profits, Doc. Mgmt., Production SW, HR SW

Networks: First Interview Network (FIN)

Smith Executive Search

PO Box 922392
Norcross, GA 30010
(770) 416-1341
Fax: (503) 210-1150
Email: tysmith@earthlink.net
Web: www.smithexecutivesearch.com

Description: We are a tax executive search firm. We specialize in the recruitment of tax professionals up to VP/partner level.

Key Contact:
Mr. Ty Smith, Managing Partner

Functions: Taxes

Industries: Generalist

Smith Hanley Associates Inc

99 Park Ave Fl 9
New York, NY 10016
(212) 687-9696
(800) 989-5627
Fax: (212) 818-9067
Email: thanley@smithhanley.com
Web: www.smithhanley.com

Description: Retained and contingency recruitment concentrating on work in investment research, market research, fixed income analysis, corporate finance, technical services for financial service, consumer product, consulting firms, advertising agencies, insurance and risk management.

Key Contact:
Mr. Thomas A. Hanley, Jr., CEO

Salary minimum: $50,000

Functions: Generalist, Distribution, Mkt. Research, Direct Mktg., Cash Mgmt., M&A, Risk Mgmt., Mgmt. Consultants

Industries: Generalist, Drugs Mfg., Finance, Pharm Svcs., Accounting, Mgmt. Consulting, Advertising, Insurance

Professional Associations: ORSA, TIMS

Branches:
107 John St
Southport, CT 06490
(203) 319-4300
(888) 221-2900
Fax: (203) 319-4320
Key Contact - Specialty:
Mr. Andrew Davis - *Risk management, insurance*
Ms. Jacqueline Paige - *Marketing services*

1025 Greenwood Blvd Ste 231
Lake Mary, FL 32746
(407) 805-3010
(800) 684-9921
Fax: (407) 805-3020
Key Contact:
Mr. Keith Shelly, Managing Partner

200 W Madison Ste 2110
Chicago, IL 60606
(312) 629-2400
Fax: (312) 629-0615
Key Contact - Specialty:
Ms. Linda Burtch - *Marketing services*

15915 Katy Fwy 210
Houston, TX 77094
(281) 829-1110
Fax: (281) 829-1515
Key Contact:
Ms. Shelley Muhs, Office Administrator

Smith Professional Search

600 S Adams Rd 210
Birmingham, MI 48009-6863
(248) 540-8580
Fax: (248) 540-2136
Email: susan@spshr.com
Web: www.spshr.com

Description: We represent companies in Michigan and specialize in the placement of human resources professionals. Our emphasis is on quality service and the highest level of professionalism in the recruiting business. Our goal is to make the search process efficient, timely and to provide superior service.

Key Contact - Specialty:
Ms. Susan P. Smith, SPHR, Principal - *Human resources, professionals*

Salary minimum: $45,000

Functions: HR Mgmt.

Industries: Energy, Utilities, Mfg., Finance, Services, Media, Communications, Aerospace, Software, Biotech, Healthcare

Professional Associations: EMA, HRAD, SHRM

Smith Scott & Associates
PO Box 38475
Colorado Springs, CO 80937
(719) 538-4404
Fax: (719) 538-0147
Email: gary.smith@smithscott.com
Web: www.smithscott.com

Description: We are an executive search firm focused on recruiting in the areas of human resources, information technology and management consulting.

Key Contact - Specialty:
Mr. Gary J. Smith, Managing Partner - *Human resources, information technology, management consulting*

Salary minimum: $60,000

Functions: Senior Mgmt., Mktg. Mgmt., HR Mgmt., IT, Mgmt. Consultants

Industries: Generalist

Professional Associations: CCA, WAW

Smith's Fifth Avenue
230 Park Ave
New York, NY 10169
(212) 808-3003
Fax: (914) 472-6207

Description: Executive recruitment in consumer market research, strategic, account planning, syndicated research, qualitative and quantitative research, competitive intelligence.

Key Contact - Specialty:
Mr. Arthur Teicher, Chairman - *Marketing research*
Ms. Vivian Werner, President - *Marketing research*

Salary minimum: $40,000

Functions: Advertising, Mkt. Research

Industries: Generalist

Professional Associations: AMA, APCNY

Smith, Brown & Jones
7415 W 130th St Ste 100
Overland Park, KS 66213
(913) 814-7770
Fax: (913) 814-8440
Email: dlsmith@smithbrownjones.com
Web: www.smithbrownjones.com

Description: The only food and agri-business recruiter in United States that is in the Pinnacle Organization,the top 60 billing recruiters in the United States.

Key Contact - Specialty:
Mr. Donald L. Smith, President - *Food, agribusiness*
Mr. Bob Brown, Vice President - *Financial*
Ms. Sally Smith, Treasurer - *Engineers*

Functions: Generalist, Production, Physicians, Mktg. Mgmt., CFO's, R&D, Int'l.

Industries: Generalist, Mfg., Finance, Legal, Environmental Svcs., Packaging, Biotech

Branches:
4100 Bel Air Ln
Naples, FL 34103
(941) 263-2548
Fax: (941) 263-4323
Key Contact - Specialty:
Mr. Don Smith, II - *Retail, real estate*

SmithAvery & Associates
112 N 5th St
PO Box 828
Columbus, MS 39703-0828
(662) 328-1463
(662) 328-1042
Fax: (662) 329-1017
Email: davery@smithavery.com
Web: www.smithavery.com

Description: We develop recruiting and retention solutions for companies located in the Deep South. Our focus is on engineering, management, and information technology, primarily within the manufacturing sector. We also have clients within telecommunications and finance.

Key Contact - Specialty:
Mr. Danny Avery, SPHR, Managing Partner - *Executive management, quality, accounting*
Mr. Mark Smith, President - *Marketing, management*

Salary minimum: $25,000

Functions: Generalist

Industries: Mfg., Banking, Accounting, HR Services, Telecoms, Network Infrastructure, Aerospace, Software, HR SW

Professional Associations: ASQ, SHRM

Networks: Top Echelon Network

Smythe Masterson & Judd Inc
551 Madison Ave Ste 1700
New York, NY 10022
(212) 286-0003
Fax: (212) 421-9665
Email: smj@smythemasterson.com

Description: We are one of the nation's oldest, most established legal search firms. We engage in partner and associate placements, firm mergers and practice group acquisitions. We also represents major companies and financial institutions.

Key Contact:
Mr. Mark D. J. Henley, Mgr. Director-Law Firm Merger

Salary minimum: $90,000

Functions: Generalist, Attorneys

Industries: Generalist, Finance, Legal, Hospitality, Media

Ron Snead Associates
15720 John J Delaney Dr Ste 300
Charlotte, NC 28277
(704) 541-8844
Fax: (704) 542-5912
Email: ronsnead@aol.com
Web: www.yp.bellsouth.com/ronsnead

Description: We were founded by a retired Army Lt. Col., who has extensive civilian and military recruiting experience.

Key Contact - Specialty:
Mr. Ronald B. Snead, Owner - *Industrial sales & marketing*

Salary minimum: $40,000

Functions: Generalist, General Mgmt., Senior Mgmt., Middle Mgmt., Sales & Mktg., Mktg. Mgmt., Sales Mgmt.

Industries: Generalist, Paper, Chemicals, Plastics, Rubber, Paints, Petro. Products, Machine, Appliance, Test, Measure Equip., Misc. Mfg.

Professional Associations: NCASP

Networks: First Interview Network (FIN)

Snelling & Snelling Inc
6555 NW 9th Ave Ste 203
Ft. Lauderdale, FL 33309
(954) 771-0090
(800) 393-0090
Fax: (954) 771-8583
Email: sneling@bellsouth.net
Web: www.snelling.com/ftlauderdale

Description: We are a professional recruitment service with recruiting specialists in construction management placement. We specialize in operations, superintendents, controller project managers, estimators, office management, executive administration contracts, administration, and job site secretaries. We also have a division that specializes in placing dental professionals.

Key Contact:
Mr. K. Jerry Phillips, Manager - *Generalist*
Ms. Suzanne Upham, Recruiter Manager - *Construction management*
Ms. Vicki Hutchinson, Recruiter - *Personnel manager (dental division)*
Ms. Robyn Weiss, Recruiter Assistant - *Construction management*
Ms. Heidi Casey, Administrative Manager

Functions: Generalist, General Mgmt., Healthcare, Sales & Mktg., Sales Mgmt., Engineering

Industries: Generalist, Construction, Mfg., Services, Media, Software

Professional Associations: ASPE, NAWIC

Snelling Personnel
5151 Belt Line Rd Ste 365
Dallas, TX 75240-7545
(972) 934-9030
Fax: (972) 934-3639
Email: snelling@winstarmail.com
Web: www.snelling.com/northdallas

Description: Our office specializes in placing sales professionals on a nationwide basis. Our particular focus in on sales engineers within the chemical and water treatment industries. Our office has been one of the most successful within the Snelling system for over 35 years, and our recruiters have over 100 years of combined experience.

Key Contact:
Mr. Sam Bingham, CPC, Owner

Functions: Admin. Svcs., Sales & Mktg., Sales Mgmt., Engineering

Industries: Generalist, Energy, Utilities, Mfg., Paper, Chemicals, Plastics, Rubber, Paints, Petro. Products, Metal Products, Environmental Svcs., Industry Specific SW

Snelling Personnel of Summit NJ
47 River Rd
Summit, NJ 07901
(908) 273-6500
Email: garyf@snellingsummit.com
Web: www.snelling.com

Description: I actively share your concerns, expectations, and career goals. I will work with you to develop a profile of your ideal environment. I also conduct in-depth "interviews" with my corporate clients' hiring manager to get the real story, to help ensure the long-term success of your new relationship. I only work with corporations within which I have established personal relationships with individual recruiters or managers who accept me as a peer. This ensures your expedited consideration with the companies we submit your resume! So, please contact me ASAP.

Key Contact - Specialty:
Mr. Gary Frischman, Vice President - *Information technology*

Salary minimum: $50,000

Functions: IT

Industries: Misc. Financial, IT Implementation, New Media, Telecoms, Telephony, Wireless, Fiber Optic, Network Infrastructure, Software, Biotech

Professional Associations: NAPS

Snelling Personnel Services
12801 N Central Expy Ste 600
Dallas, TX 75243
(972) 701-8080
Email: dallascoit@snelling.com
Web: www.snelling.com

Key Contact:
Mr. Robert O. Snelling

Branches:
400 Vestavia Pkwy Ste 221
I-65 & Hwy 31
Birmingham, AL 35216
(205) 822-7878
Fax: (205) 979-7663

400 E 14th St
Decatur, AL 35601
(256) 355-5424
Fax: (256) 355-2298
Email: jorgeval@mindspring.com

1102 Bradshaw Dr
Florence, AL 35630
(256) 760-8033
Fax: (256) 760-5909
Email: flosnell@hiwaay.net

1900 28th Ave S Ste 1
Homewood, AL 35209
(205) 879-9950
Fax: (205) 879-9150
Email: davidh@snelling-search.com

3100 Cottage Hill Rd Ste 501
Mobile, AL 36606
(334) 473-1001
Fax: (334) 473-1006
Email: info@snellingmobile.com

3001 Zelda Rd Ste 100
Montgomery, AL 36106
(334) 270-0100
Fax: (334) 270-8096
Email: lawson@mnw.net

2815 S Alma School Rd Ste 125
Regal Sq
Mesa, AZ 85210
(480) 777-8037
Fax: (480) 777-8194
Email: snellingmesa@uswest.net

1661 E Camelback Ave Ste 186
Phoenix, AZ 85016
(602) 277-8181
Fax: (602) 277-4946
Email: phxsnelling@aol.com

900 S Craycroft
Tucson, AZ 85711
(520) 790-2733
Fax: (520) 790-3901
Email: snelling@uswest.net

2850 Prince St Ste 39
Conway, AR 72032
(501) 513-2800
Fax: (501) 513-0619
Email: jobsconway@snellingar.com

3901 Rogers Ave Ste B
Ft. Smith, AR 72903
(501) 782-4911
Fax: (501) 782-4916
Email: snel1@ipa.net

3901 McCain Park Dr Ste 101
Little Rock, AR 72116
(501) 758-3200
Fax: (501) 758-6285
Email: jobsnlr@snellingar.com

650 S Shackleford
One Financial Ctr Ste 312
Little Rock, AR 72211
(501) 223-2069
Fax: (501) 223-9427
Email: jobslr@snellingar.com

601 E 8th Ave
Pine Bluff, AR 71601
(870) 535-5500
Fax: (870) 535-5502

1320 Harbor Bay Pkwy Ste 225
Alameda, CA 94502
(510) 769-4400
Fax: (510) 769-4404
Email: snelling27@aol.com

7070 Schirra Ct Ste 201 Bldg 2
PO Box 10055
Bakersfield, CA 93313
(661) 665-1349
Fax: (661) 665-9402

950 S Coast Dr Ste 280
Costa Mesa, CA 92626
(714) 557-7767
Fax: (714) 557-9675
Email: costamesa@snelling.com

1290B St Ste 101
Hayward, CA 94541
(510) 887-8210
Fax: (510) 887-8533
Email: haysnell@tdl.com

265 S Anita Dr Ste 202
Orange, CA 92868
(714) 939-1625
Fax: (714) 939-1366
Email: kellieschnabel@aol.com

3825 Hopyard Rd Ste 101
Pleasanton, CA 94588-8528
(925) 469-8150
Fax: (925) 469-8154
Email: rods@ca02.snelling.com
Key Contact:
Mr. Stan Medved, President

3825 Hopyard Rd Ste 101B
Pleasanton, CA 94588
(925) 469-8160
Fax: (925) 469-8157
Email: pleasanton@snelling.com

490 C W Arrow Hwy
San Dimas, CA 91773
(909) 592-3199
Fax: (909) 592-0792
Email: snelling@tstonramp.com

1900 State St Ste B
Santa Barbara, CA 93101
(805) 563-0994
Fax: (805) 563-0830
Email: jo@snellinsb.com

21600 Oxnard
Main Plaza Lvl
Woodland Hills, CA 91367
(818) 676-8080
Fax: (818) 676-8862
Email: kelli.hansen@healthnet.com

2460 W 26th Ave Ste 360C
Denver, CO 80211
(303) 964-8200
Fax: (303) 964-9312
Email: fdgsnelling@msn.com

655 Broadway Ste 825
Denver, CO 80203
(303) 534-3581
Fax: (303) 534-0101
Email: snellingdenver@uswest.net

2900 S College Ave Ste 3C
Ft. Collins, CO 80525
(970) 225-9292
Fax: (970) 225-0830
Email: snelling@srii.com

7730 E Belleview Ste AG4
Greenwood Village, CO 80111
(303) 779-3060
Fax: (303) 741-4992
Email: snellingdtc@uswest.net

1279 W Littleton Blvd
Littleton, CO 80120
(303) 794-4331
Fax: (303) 797-0164
Email: snelling13@aol.com

One Hartfield Blvd
East Windsor, CT 06088
(860) 292-5330
Fax: (860) 292-5322
Email: jobs@snellingctma.com

1000 16th St NW Ste 805
Washington, DC 20006
(202) 223-3540
Fax: (202) 872-1967
Email: jobs@snellingdc.com

818 Connecticut Ave Ste 325
Washington, DC 20006
(202) 833-6100
Fax: (202) 833-6105
Email: parker@snellingmetro.com

222 S Westmonte Dr Ste 202
Altamonte Springs, FL 32714
(407) 788-7300
Fax: (407) 788-7309
Email: jkirby@snellingorlando.com

1700 N Dixie Hwy Ste 100
Boca Raton, FL 33432
(561) 338-8707
Fax: (561) 338-8702
Email: dan@snellingbocaraton.com

2963 Gulf To Bay Blvd Ste 110
Clearwater, FL 33759
(727) 799-1170
Fax: (727) 799-9522
Email: careers@snelling-clearwater.com

1620 S Clyde Morris Blvd Ste 210
Daytona Beach, FL 32119
(904) 322-3533
Fax: (904) 322-8130
Email: snellingdb@jobs-orlando.com

145 E Rich Ave Ste F
Deland, FL 32724
(904) 822-4700
Fax: (904) 322-8130
Email: snellingdb@jobs-orlando.com

1919 Courtney Dr Ste 3
Ft. Myers, FL 33901
(941) 936-2440
Fax: (941) 936-0509
Email: snellingfm@tntonline.com

10199 Southside Blvd Ste 100
Jacksonville, FL 32256
(904) 464-0233
Fax: (904) 464-0324
Email: snelling_jacksonville@compuserve.com

4741 Atlantic Blvd Parkpoint Ste A2
Jacksonville, FL 32207
(904) 858-7004
Fax: (904) 858-7090
Email: meury_snelling@email.msn.com

1310 N Main St Ste 102
Kissimmee, FL 34741
(407) 847-8700
Fax: (407) 847-8781
Email: snellingksm@jobs-orlando.com

3575 W Lake Mary Blvd Ste 107
Lake Mary, FL 32746
(407) 324-0001
Fax: (407) 324-5061
Email: snellinglm@jobs-orlando.com

913 E North Blvd Ste H
Leesburg, FL 34748
(352) 314-2911
Fax: (352) 314-9271
Email: snellinglee@jobs-orlando.com

1103 Hibiscus Blvd Ste 301
Melbourne, FL 32901
(321) 725-4100
Fax: (321) 724-5348
Email: ewglum@mindspring.com

8685 NW 53rd Ter Ste 103
Miami, FL 33166
(305) 591-8835
Fax: (305) 593-9689
Email: snepersv@bellsouth.net

201 8th St S Ste 208
Naples, FL 34102
(941) 262-3974
Fax: (941) 262-5738
Email: snellingnaples@naplesnews.net

3655 Maguire Blvd Ste 180
Orlando, FL 32803
(407) 898-1890
Fax: (407) 898-7960
Email: jkirby@snellingorlando.com

7616 Southland Blvd Ste 200
Orlando, FL 32809
(407) 812-9524
Fax: (407) 812-5516
Email: snellingorl@jobs-orlando.com

1613 St. Andrews Blvd
Panama City, FL 32405
(850) 769-1441
Fax: (850) 785-1770
Email: finder@digita;exp.com

4300 Bayou Blvd Ste 33
Pensacola, FL 32503
(850) 474-9495
Fax: (850) 479-9447

3380 Tamiami Trl Ste A2
Port Charlotte, FL 33952
(941) 624-5570
Fax: (941) 764-6629
Email: neumba@peganet.com

1217 S Tamiami Trl
Midtown Plz
Sarasota, FL 34239
(941) 953-6999
Fax: (941) 953-6454
Email: snellingmp@aol.com

4200 W Cypress St Ste 480
Tampa, FL 33607
(813) 877-4300
Fax: (813) 877-5854
Email: resume@snellingtampa.com

2161 Palm Beach Lakes Blvd Ste 412
West Palm Beach, FL 33409
(561) 689-5400
Fax: (561) 689-5055
Email:
snelling_westpalmbeach02@compuserve.com

1220 W Colonial Dr Ste 300C
Winter Garden, FL 34787
(352) 861-7220
Fax: (352) 861-7222
Email: snellingocl@hitter.net

6578 University Blvd
Winter Park, FL 32792
(407) 679-0055
Fax: (407) 679-7934
Email: snellingwp@jobs-orlando.com

3366 Cypress Mill Rd
Brunswick, GA 31520
(912) 262-6882
Fax: (912) 280-0884
Email: snelldot@gate.net

3555 Koger Blvd Ste 330
Duluth, GA 30096
(770) 381-2838
Fax: (770) 381-0631
Email: jkirby@snellingorlando.com
Key Contact:
Jaime Jones, CPC, CTS

3333 Northside Dr Ste A
Macon, GA 31210
(912) 477-7747
Fax: (912) 477-2909
Email: snellingga@aol.com

5902 Hwy 41 N
PO Box 190
Ringgold, GA 30736
(706) 965-9850
Fax: (706) 965-6514
Email: blang4515@aol.com

7601 H Waters Ave
Savannah, GA 31406
(912) 356-6900
Fax: (912) 356-6920
Email: pamc@snelling-search.com

106 B Savannah Ave
Statesboro, GA 30458
(912) 764-8800
Fax: (912) 764-8805
Email: pamc@snelling-search.com

748E N Houston Rd
Warner Robbins, GA 31093
(912) 922-4455
Fax: (912) 922-6110

733 Bishop St Ste 1570
Honolulu, HI 96813
(808) 524-0100
Fax: (808) 528-4570
Email: snelling@lava.net

1101 W River St Ste 120
Boise, ID 83702
(208) 342-3470
Fax: (208) 426-8368

308 N 15th St
Boise, ID 83702
(208) 426-8367
Fax: (208) 426-8368

415 E Main St
Belleville, IL 62220
(618) 277-1141
Fax: (618) 277-3218

6512 W Cermak
Berwyn, IL 60402
(708) 484-9359
Fax: (708) 484-9884
Email: arnoldg199@msn.com

290 Springfield Dr Ste 225
Bloomingdale, IL 60108
(630) 671-2200
Fax: (630) 671-2204
Email: findacareer@yahoo.com

2401 E Washington St Ste 1B
Bloomington, IL 61704
(309) 663-0482
Fax: (309) 663-6686
Email: jobs@careergaines.com

409 S Prospect
Bloomington, IL 61704
(309) 663-5627
Fax: (309) 663-4877
Email: snellingbl@aol.com

134 Briarcliff Ave E
Bolingbrook, IL 60440
(630) 783-9178
Fax: (630) 783-9378
Email: snelling@megsinet.net

206 N Randolf Ste 1
Champaign, IL 61820
(217) 352-0074
Fax: (217) 352-4523

Email: geich30105@aol.com

100 N LaSalle St Ste 2005
Chicago, IL 60602
(312) 419-6100
Fax: (312) 419-6646
Email: snellingmw@aol.com

6222 NW Hwy
Crystal Lake, IL 60014
(815) 477-2200
Fax: (815) 477-1959
Email: crystallake@snelling.com

999 E Touhy Ave Ste 135
Des Plaines, IL 60018
(847) 296-1026
Fax: (847) 299-3681
Email: desplains@snelling.com

999 E Touhy Ave Ste 167
Des Plaines, IL 60018
(847) 391-4172
Fax: (847) 391-4176
Email: desplains@snelling.com

4239 Commercial Way
Dearlove Office Ctr
Glenview, IL 60025
(847) 699-9660
Fax: (847) 699-9899
Email: arnoldg199@msn.com

2200 W Higgins Rd Ste 125
Hoffman Estates, IL 60195
(847) 839-4649
Fax: (847) 839-4654
Email: findacareer@yahoo.com

2029 Ogden Ave
Lisle, IL 60532
(630) 515-9088
Fax: (630) 515-9616
Email: snelling@megsinet.net

14929 Archer Ave
Lockport, IL 60441
(815) 834-4104
Fax: (815) 834-4107
Email: snelling@megsinet.net

1979 N Mill St Ste 200
Naperville, IL 60563
(630) 637-6050
Fax: (630) 637-6055
Email: findacareer@yahoo.com

18 W 100 22nd St Ste 128
Oak Brook Terrace, IL 60181
(630) 620-2580
Fax: (630) 620-2586
Email: oakbrook@snelling.com

331 Fulton Ste 322
River Valley Plz
Peoria, IL 61602
(309) 676-5581
Fax: (309) 676-5591
Email: snelling@flink.com

236 N 5th St
Quincy, IL 62301
(217) 222-7721
Fax: (217) 222-7995
Email: snelling@adams.net

3995 Algonquin Rd
Snelling Plz
Rolling Meadows, IL 60008
(847) 303-1115
Fax: (847) 303-6869
Email: rollingmeadows@snelling.com

3100 Montvale Dr
Springfield, IL 62704
(217) 689-4969
Fax: (217) 698-9496
Email: tbonansing@earthlink.net

8263 James Ave
Woodridge, IL 60517
(630) 427-1861
Fax: (630) 424-9135

Email: snelling@megsinet.net

26 W 7th ST
Anderson, IN 46016
(765) 649-0126
Fax: (765) 641-2359
Email: snelland@netusa1.net

3417 E State Blvd
Ft. Wayne, IN 46805
(219) 482-1511
Fax: (219) 483-1095
Email: careers@snellingfw.com

5610 Crawfordsville Rd Ste 2302
Indianapolis, IN 46224
(317) 244-5544
Fax: (317) 244-5695
Email: snellingwest@msn.com

6801 Lake Plaza Dr Ste D403
Indianapolis, IN 46220
(317) 845-2929
Fax: (317) 845-8400
Email: indyjobs@msn.com

9700 Lakeshore Dr E
Indianapolis, IN 46280
(317) 566-1000
Fax: (317) 566-1011
Email: snelling@snellingcareers.com

1305 Cass St Ste 132
Wabash Shopping Ctr Mall
Wabash, IN 46992
(219) 563-2933
Fax: (219) 569-9097
Email: snelling@ctlnet.com

2435 Kimberly Rd Ste 110 N
Bettendorf, IA 52722-3505
(319) 355-4411
Fax: (319) 355-3635
Email: bbureau@netexpress.com

1409 Broadway
Council Bluffs, IA 51501
(712) 322-2315
Fax: (712) 322-6517

2423 Ingersoll Ave
Des Moines, IA 50312
(515) 244-9999
Fax: (515) 244-9915
Email: cdrake@snellingdm.com
Key Contact:
Mr. Charles Drake

1000 C Broadway
Red Oak, IA 51566
(712) 623-2335
Fax: (712) 623-6063

7123 W 95th St
Overland Park, KS 66212
(913) 385-5100
Fax: (913) 385-5111
Email: overlandpark@snelling.com

216 N Waco Ste A
Wichita, KS 67202
(316) 265-5100
Fax: (316) 265-9713
Email: berniebeckman@snellingwichita.net

301 E Main Ste 930
Lexington, KY 40507
(859) 233-0583
Fax: (859) 255-7641
Email: snell.lex@gte.net

3200 Commerce Ctr Pl
Louisville, KY 40211
(502) 778-6008
Fax: (502) 778-4443
Email: snellinglo@win.net

332 W Broadway Ste 110 & 404
Louisville, KY 40202
(502) 625-1930
Fax: (502) 625-1939
Email: snelling@snellingoflouisville.com

4010 Dupont Cir Ste 124
Louisville, KY 40207
(502) 895-9494
Fax: (502) 893-1631
Email: snellinglo@win.net

7742 Office Park Blvd Ste C1
Baton Rouge, LA 70809
(225) 927-0550
Fax: (225) 928-5193
Email: spsbr@spsbr.com

203 Carondelet St Ste 530
New Orleans, LA 70130-3014
(504) 529-5781
Fax: (504) 592-8288
Email: juliek@snellingneworleans.net
Key Contact:
Ms. Julie Kent, Franchisee

636 E Kings Hwy
Shreveport, LA 71102
(318) 865-2696
Fax: (318) 868-3102
Email: dhendricks@snelling-arklatex.com

9881 Broken Land Pkwy Ste 101
Columbia, MD 21046
(410) 312-7850
Fax: (410) 312-7860
Email: columbia@jobs4u.com

545 Boylston St
Boston, MA 02116
(617) 262-5151
Fax: (617) 267-9789
Email: snelltime@aol.com

3 Courthouse Ln Ste 2
Courthouse Sq Office Park
Chelmsford, MA 01824
(978) 970-3434
Fax: (978) 970-3637
Email: bernice@snelling-ma.com

425 Union St
West Springfield, MA 01089
(413) 747-2516
Fax: (413) 747-2914
Email: jobs@snellingctma.com

65 James St Plz Ste 12
Worcester, MA 01603
(508) 792-4545
Fax: (508) 752-8240
Email: lpalazzi@pop.net

2759 University Dr
Auburn Hills, MI 48326
(248) 373-7500
Fax: (248) 373-7359
Email: tblome@snellingjobs.com

30100 Telegraph Rd Ste 474
Bingham Farms, MI 48025
(248) 644-4600
Fax: (248) 644-4739
Email: jaroinc@aol.com

2990 W Grand Blvd Ste 300
Detroit, MI 48202
(313) 871-2700
Fax: (313) 871-2152
Email: info@snellingmetrodetroit.com

2100 Raybrook SE Ste 109
Grand Rapids, MI 49546-0616
(616) 957-1616
Fax: (616) 957-4447
Email: employ@snellinggr.com

4485 Plainfield Ave
Grand Rapids, MI 49525
(616) 361-5500
Fax: (616) 361-1647
Email: employ@snellinggr.com

950 28th St SE Bldg B
Brookfield Office Plz
Grand Rapids, MI 49508
(616) 452-2154
Fax: (616) 452-1685

Email: shellmark@netzero.net

2845 Wilson Ave
Grandville, MI 49418
(616) 249-9495
Fax: (616) 249-9699
Email: employ@snellinggr.com

3711 S Westnedge Ave
Kalamazoo, MI 49008
(616) 343-8282
Fax: (616) 343-0836
Email: kalamazoo@snelling.com

36167 Plymouth Rd
Livonia, MI 48150
(734) 266-8600
Fax: (734) 266-5104
Email: lstover@snellingjobs.com

150 Twelve Mile Rd
Madison Heights, MI 48071
(248) 547-1100
Fax: (248) 547-7175
Email: mdelegato@snellingjobs.com

18600 Florence St Ste C6
Roseville, MI 48066
(810) 772-6760
(810) 447-9690
Fax: (810) 772-6788
Email: ron-d@snelling-jobs.com

25600 S Woodward Ave Ste 108
Royal Oak, MI 48067
(248) 399-3450
Fax: (248) 399-3539
Email: spsroyaloak@aol.com

3216 Christy Way Ste 1
Saginaw, MI 48602
(517) 790-3000
Fax: (517) 790-3005
Email: employ@snellinggr.com

29777 Telegraph Rd Ste 1311
Southfield, MI 48034
(248) 352-1300
Fax: (248) 352-0124
Email: kfelker@snellingjobs.com

22647 N Line Rd
Taylor, MI 48180
(734) 287-2221
Fax: (734) 287-4579
Email: dlecroy@snellingjobs.com

2265 Livernois Ste 200
Troy, MI 48083
(248) 362-5090
Fax: (248) 362-4540
Email: info@snellingmetrodetroit.com

2009 Hardy St Ste 2B
Hattiesburg, MS 39401
(601) 544-0821
Fax: (601) 544-0823
Email: snelling@c-gate.net

112 Hwy 15 S
New Albany, MS 38652
(662) 538-3335
Fax: (662) 538-3355

499 Gloster St Ste D4S
Tupelo, MS 38801
(662) 842-1045
Fax: (662) 842-3677
Email: snelltup@dixie-net.com

2749 Thomas Rd
PO Box 633
Cape Girardeau, MO 63702-0633
(573) 334-0665
Fax: (573) 335-7898
Email: capesnelling@hotmail.com

16052 Swingley Ridge Rd
Chesterfield, MO 63017
(314) 537-2717
Key Contact:
Mr. A. H. Harter, Jr., President

7777 Bonhomme Ste 1720
Clayton, MO 63105
(314) 726-2717

1722 QQ S Glenstone
Springfield, MO 65804
(417) 887-2700
Fax: (417) 887-2709
Email: jobs@snellingandsnelling.com

1034 S Brentwood Blvd Ste 778
St. Louis, MO 63117
(314) 862-2727
Fax: (314) 862-2319
Email: dlangsam@swbell.net

111 Westport Plz Ste 506
St. Louis, MO 63146
(314) 469-2799

11719 Old Ballas Rd Ste D
St. Louis, MO 63141
(314) 993-7800
Fax: (314) 995-3700
Email: snellingcc@aol.com

1610 Des Peres Rd Ste 350
St. Louis, MO 63131
(314) 822-2208
Fax: (314) 822-5158

4193 Crescent
St. Louis, MO 63129
(314) 487-9675
Fax: (314) 416-4329
Email: snellingcc@aol.com

9717 Landmark Pkwy
St. Louis, MO 63129
(314) 537-8481

307 Mid Rivers Mall Rd
St. Peters, MO 63376
(314) 970-2137

2118 Grand Ave
Billings, MT 59102
(406) 652-5267
Fax: (406) 652-6058
Email: snelling1@uswest.net

25 5th St N
Western Federal Savings Bank
Great Falls, MT 59401
(406) 727-2414
Fax: (406) 727-9958
Email: snellinggf@montana.com

135 Lakewood Dr
Lincoln, NE 68510
(402) 489-2501
Fax: (402) 489-2586
Email: snellnk@aol.com

13304 W Center Rd Ste 109
Old Orchard W
Omaha, NE 68144
(402) 330-0100
Fax: (402) 333-5289
Email: omahasnell@aol.com

4735 S 24th St
Omaha, NE 68107
(402) 731-2737
Fax: (402) 731-0904
Email: snelling_omaha29@compuserve.com

616 N 114th St
Omaha, NE 68154
(402) 493-3366
Fax: (402) 493-0222
Email: snelling_omaha27@compuserve.com

1900 E Flamingo Rd Ste 272
Las Vegas, NV 89119
(702) 369-0087
Fax: (702) 737-0831
Email: lasvegas@snelling.com
Key Contact:
Ms. Gloria E. Grisham

4 Cornwall Dr Ste 105
East Brunswick, NJ 08816
(732) 390-9700
Fax: (732) 390-4242
Email: admin@snellingnj.com

142 Hwy 35 Ste 202A
Eatontown, NJ 07724
(732) 389-0300
Fax: (732) 542-2509
Email: admin@snellingnj.com

363 Rte 46W
Fairfield, NJ 07004
(973) 276-0166
Fax: (973) 276-0173
Email: info@snellingsearchnj.com

305 Main St Ste A
Lakewood, NJ 08701
(732) 364-2011
Fax: (732) 942-1845
Email: admin@snellingnj.com

354-356 George St
New Brunswick, NJ 08901
(732) 729-7777
Fax: (732) 729-7788
Email: newbrunswick@snellingnj.com

Gateway I Fl 5
Newark, NJ 07102
(973) 623-2400
Fax: (973) 623-2404

1915 New Rd
Northfield, NJ 08225
(609) 646-6470
Fax: (609) 383-0410
Email: snellingac@aol.com

5425 Rte 70
Pennsauken, NJ 08109
(856) 662-5424
Fax: (856) 662-0146
Email: cdeggler@aol.com

350 Alexander Rd
Princeton, NJ 08540
(609) 683-4040
Fax: (609) 683-5621
Email: princeton@snellingeast.com

72 W End Ave
Somerville, NJ 08876
(908) 707-8778
Fax: (908) 707-0339
Email: snellingsom@aol.com

1 Woodbridge Ctr Ste 205
Woodbridge, NJ 07095
(732) 596-9770
Fax: (732) 596-1971
Email: woodbridge@snellingeast.com

2601 Wyoming St NE Ste 106
Albuquerque, NM 87112
(505) 293-7800
Fax: (505) 298-7408
Email: snelling@sandia.net

5981 Jefferson NE Ste C
Albuquerque, NM 87109
(505) 345-3334
Fax: (505) 343-0790
Email: jpmwww@aol.com

1717 Central Ave
Albany, NY 12205
(518) 869-9575
Fax: (518) 869-9256
Email: kristi@snellingpersonnel.com

4 Computer Dr W
Albany, NY 12205
(518) 437-9095
Fax: (518) 437-9098
Email: wrichards@snelling.com

528 Liberty Bldg
Buffalo, NY 14202-3699
(716) 842-2242
Fax: (716) 842-0593

42 W Market St
Corning, NY 14830
(607) 962-1245
Fax: (607) 962-1247

122 E 42nd St Ste 2609
The Chanin Bldg
New York, NY 10168
(212) 331-9325
Fax: (646) 227-0436
Email: midtown@snelling.com

150 Broadway Ste 902
New York, NY 10038
(212) 374-1980
Fax: (212) 227-9803
Email: manhattan@snelling.com

1234 Upper Lennox Ave
Oneida, NY 13421
(315) 361-1100
Fax: (315) 361-1101

53 N Park Ave
Rockville Centre, NY 11570
(516) 764-0700
Fax: (516) 763-6596
Email: jobzone@aol.com

5815 Rome Taberg Rd
Rome, NY 13440
(315) 336-2000
Fax: (315) 337-1299
Email: snellingpersonnel@juno.com

301 Bleecker St
Utica, NY 13501
(315) 793-1900
Fax: (315) 793-1966
Email: snellingpersonnel@juno.com

180 E Post Rd
White Plains, NY 10601
(914) 761-1120
Fax: (914) 997-8319
Email: whiteplains@snelling.com

34 S Broadway Fl 6
White Plains, NY 10601
(914) 949-0550
Fax: (914) 949-0628
Email: snellingsearch@aol.com

325 Essjay Rd Ste 108
Williamsville, NY 14221
(716) 631-8282
Fax: (716) 631-8964
Email: williamsville@snelling.com

3 Walden Ridge Dr Ste 400
PO Box 5879
Asheville, NC 28813-5879
(828) 654-0310
Fax: (828) 654-9738
Email: snelling-jobs@home.com

5970 Fairview Rd Ste 220
Charlotte, NC 28210
(704) 553-0050
Fax: (704) 553-9578
Email: snelling_charlotte@compuserve.com

1911 Hillandale Rd Ste 1210
Durham, NC 27705
(919) 383-2575
Fax: (919) 383-5706
Email: snelling_durham@compuserve.com

609 1/2 1st Ave N Ste 200
Fargo, ND 58102
(701) 237-0600
Fax: (701) 241-9998
Email: snelling@fargocity.com

3250 W Market St Ste 102
Akron, OH 44333
(330) 836-9901
Fax: (330) 836-9910
Email: georgegotschall@hotmail.com

839 E Market St
Akron, OH 44305
(330) 315-5555
Fax: (330) 458-0003

24700 Chagrin Blvd Ste 105
Beachwood, OH 44122
(216) 831-0320
Fax: (216) 831-0779
Email: snellingbeachwood@prodigy.net

1901 Fulton Rd
Canton, OH 44709
(330) 458-1030
Fax: (330) 458-0003
Email: snellingofcanton@neo.rr.com

130 Tri-County Pkwy Ste 105
Cincinnati, OH 45246
(513) 771-5999
Fax: (513) 782-4263
Email: snellingcincinnati@msn.com

4763 Glendale-Milford Rd
Cincinnati, OH 45242
(513) 469-2020
Fax: (513) 247-8443
Email: davico@one.net

2008 Needmore Rd
Dayton, OH 45414
(937) 279-1000
Fax: (937) 279-1100
Email: anita.wales@snellingofdayton.com

3460 S Dixie Ste 200
Dayton, OH 45439
(937) 297-2300
Fax: (937) 297-2305
Email: doug.wales@snellingofdayton.com

8401 Claude Thomas Rd Ste 8
Franklin, OH 45005
(513) 743-1000
Fax: (513) 743-1011
Email: doug.wales@snellingofdayton.com

355 Park Ave W
Mansfield, OH 44906
(419) 522-8112
Fax: (419) 524-7929
Email: snellingmansfield@neo.rr.com

6072 Youngstown Rd
Niles, OH 44446
(330) 505-1715
Fax: (330) 505-1724
Email: snelling@ztrain.com

1664 N Main St
North Canton, OH 44720
(330) 499-9956
·*Fax:* (330) 499-9957
Email: snellingcanton@hotmail.com

3550 Secor Rd Ste 201
Toledo, OH 43606
(419) 534-5627
Fax: (419) 534-5649
Email: snellingtoledo@msn.com

243 E Liberty St
Wooster, OH 44691
(330) 262-4114
Fax: (330) 263-1640
Email: snelling@sssnet.com

4845 Market St Ste 6
Youngstown, OH 44512
(330) 788-1580
Fax: (330) 782-3680
Email: snelling@ztrain.com

111 Presidential Blvd Ste 233
Bala Cynwyd, PA 19004
(610) 667-4222
Fax: (215) 628-4886

18 N Main St Ste 100
Doylestown, PA 18901
(215) 348-0110
Fax: (215) 348-0114
Email: doylestown@snellingeast.com

600 W Dekalb St Ste 305
King of Prussia, PA 19406
(610) 491-9300
Fax: (610) 491-9520
Email: kingofprussia@snellingeast.com

160 N Pointe Blvd Ste 101
Lancaster, PA 17601
(717) 560-1110
Fax: (717) 560-2828
Email: snellinglancas@aol.com

1617 JFK Blvd Ste 1040
Philadelphia, PA 19103
(215) 568-1414
Fax: (215) 568-1655
Email: philadelphia@snellingeast.com

1704 Ponce de Leon Ave Pda 24 1/2
Santurce, PR 00909
(787) 726-6868
Fax: (787) 726-6890
Email: snelling@tld.net

2090 Executive Hall Rd
Charleston, SC 29407
(843) 277-6900
Fax: (843) 277-6906
Email: suzanneg@snelling-search.com

2026 Assembly St Ste 104
Columbia, SC 29202-8839
(803) 252-8888
Fax: (803) 256-9242
Email: snellingofcolumbia@worldnet.att.net

2704 E North St
Greenville, SC 29615
(864) 268-9300
Fax: (864) 268-7676
Email: snellinggville@aol.com

114 Haygood Ave
Lexington, SC 29072
(803) 359-7644
Fax: (803) 359-3008
Email: lexsnelling@yahoo.com

4925 LaCross Rd Ste 209
North Charleston, SC 29406
(843) 744-4100
Fax: (843) 744-4144
Email: catherinet@snelling-search.com

1002 S Pine St
Spartanburg, SC 29302
(864) 583-7201
Fax: (864) 583-1244
Email: sps@upstate.net

1508 Mt. View Rd Ste 101
Rapid City, SD 57702
(605) 341-4111
Fax: (605) 341-0641
Email: pmdsnelling@rushmore.com

2720 W 12th Ste 200
Sioux Falls, SD 57104
(605) 334-1434
Fax: (605) 334-3276
Email: snelling@dakota.net

2175 Hwy 75 Ste 7
Blountville, TN 37617
(423) 279-5920
Fax: (423) 323-5958
Email: snelling_blountville@compuserve.com

214 Centerville Dr Ste 190
Shiloh Bldg
Brentwood, TN 37027
(615) 661-0330
Fax: (615) 661-0360
Email: snellingoftn@mindspring.com

10805 Kingston Pike Ste 110
Farragut, TN 37922
(865) 777-2150
Fax: (865) 777-2158
Email: snellwe2@aol.com

5049 Bobby Hicks Hwy Ste 101
PO Box 8098
Gray, TN 37615
(423) 477-4277
Fax: (423) 477-7071
Email: pthornton@snelling.net

2290 E Andrew Johnson Hwy Ste 101
Greenville, TN 37745
(423) 639-7123
Fax: (423) 639-2418
Email: pthornton@snelling.net

112 E Myrtle St Ste 505
Professional Bldg
Johnson City, TN 37601
(423) 928-6461
Fax: (423) 928-9659
Email: snelling@preferred.com

6060 Poplar Ave Ste 251
Memphis, TN 38119
(901) 767-5835
Fax: (901) 761-4116
Email: snelling_memphis@compuserve.com

1808 W End Ave Ste 1217
Nashville, TN 37203
(615) 329-0223
Fax: (615) 321-4551
Email: snellwe@aol.com

204 N Greenville Ste 130
Allen, TX 75002
(972) 747-7144
Fax: (972) 747-8089
Email: allen@snelling.com

1521 N Cooper Ste 214 218
Arlington, TX 76011
(817) 608-0432
Fax: (817) 652-9822
Email: seelysr@aol.com

1701 E Lamar Blvd Ste 155
Arlington, TX 76006
(817) 261-2484
Fax: (817) 261-7447
Email: arlington@snelling.com

2225 E Randol Mill Rd Ste 323
Arlington, TX 76011
(817) 608-0877
Fax: (817) 608-0436
Email: info@snellingtexas.com

5415 S Cooper Ste 121
Arlington, TX 76017
(817) 467-6911
Fax: (817) 467-3909
Email: stevejenkins@snellingtexas.com

896 Ridgewood Ste C
Brownsville, TX 78520
(956) 550-8454
Fax: (956) 550-8950
Email: snellingmcallen@yahoo.com

1925 Beltline Rd Ste 403
Carrollton, TX 75006
(972) 417-1704
Fax: (972) 417-0931
Email: joniw@snellingcarrollton.com

1121 Hurst St Ste 6
Center, TX 75935
(936) 591-9111
Fax: (936) 591-9001
Email: dhendricks@snelling-arklatex.com

5350 S Staples St Ste 220
Corpus Christi, TX 78411
(361) 992-4809
Fax: (361) 991-2232
Email: snellingcc2@interconnect.net

5350 S Staples St Ste 220
Corpus Christi, TX 78411
(361) 906-1213
Fax: (361) 906-1264
Email: snellingcc@interconnect.net

17101 Preston Rd Ste 165
Dallas, TX 75248-1331
(972) 248-1444
Fax: (972) 248-4811
Email: snellingtx@prodigy.net

625 Dallas Dr Ste 150
Denton, TX 76205
(940) 891-3755
Fax: (940) 891-4314
Email: snellingsearch@snellingdenton.com

2501 Parkview Dr Ste 314
Ft. Worth, TX 76102
(817) 877-4466
Fax: (817) 877-4467
Email: snelling.fortworth@att.net

1518 E Northwest Hwy Ste G
Garland, TX 75041
(972) 613-1311
Fax: (972) 613-1315
Email: garland@snelling.com

1000 Main St Ste 290
Grapevine, TX 76051
(817) 424-3760
Fax: (817) 424-5823
Email: snellinggrapevine@snellingdenton.com

11811 N Fwy
Houston, TX 77060
(281) 847-1700
Fax: (281) 847-2700
Email: bt@snellinghouston.com

9990 Richmond Ste 120
Houston, TX 77042
(713) 783-6900
Fax: (713) 783-7755
Email: houston@snelling.com

1845 Precinct Line Rd Ste 110
Hurst, TX 76054
(817) 529-5627
Fax: (817) 577-2416
Email: jobs@snelling.com

3559 N Beltline Rd
Irving, TX 75062
(972) 258-5973
Fax: (972) 258-1092
Email: irving@snelling.com

902 A S Jackson
Jacksonville, TX 75766
(903) 589-9992
Fax: (903) 589-6973
Email: dhendricks@snelling-arklatex.com

1800 W Loop 281 Ste 205
Longview, TX 75604
(903) 297-2223
Fax: (903) 297-2270
Email: snellinglv@hotmail.com

2222 Indiana Ave
Lubbock, TX 79410
(806) 797-3281
Fax: (806) 797-7125
Email: snelling@cleanweb.net

4100 S Medford Ste 208
Lufkin, TX 75901
(409) 632-8888
Fax: (409) 632-8920
Email: dhendricks@snelling-arklatex.com

2805 North St Ste A
Nacogdoches, TX 75961
(936) 552-7888
Fax: (936) 559-8088
Email: dhendricks@snelling-arklatex.com

1169 E 42nd St Ste 3
Odessa, TX 79762
(915) 367-7066
Fax: (915) 550-7066
Email: snelling@apex2000.net

299 W Campbell Rd
Richardson, TX 75080
(972) 470-9696
Fax: (972) 470-0827
Email: richardson@snelling.com

6800 Park Ten Blvd Ste 190 W
San Antonio, TX 78213
(210) 734-6288
Fax: (210) 734-6118
Email: jobs@snellingsa.com

8626 Tesoro Dr Ste 130
San Antonio, TX 78217
(210) 822-8224
Fax: (210) 822-0351
Email: jobs@snellingsa.com

2004 Loy Lake Rd
Sherman, TX 76090
(903) 813-1004
Email: dhendricks@snelling-arklatex.com

5201 S Broadway Ste 200
Tyler, TX 75703
(903) 561-1181
Fax: (903) 534-8004
Email: snelling@tyler.net

801 Sam Houston Dr
Vicotoria, TX 77901
(361) 578-3671
Fax: (361) 578-0919
Email: snelling@tisd.net

1227 N Valley Mills Dr Ste 229
Waco, TX 76710
(254) 751-0090
Fax: (254) 751-1003
Email: jaimet@snellingwaco.com

6420 Denton Hwy
Watauga, TX 76148
(817) 427-3434
Fax: (817) 427-3939
Email: snellingnorthftworth@snellingdenton.com

395 E 60 S
American Fork, UT 85062
(801) 492-0134
Fax: (801) 492-3500

102 W 500 S Ste 610
Salt Lake City, UT 84101
(801) 521-9263
Fax: (801) 521-9272
Email: pat@snellingslc.com

1030 W Atherton Dr Ste 202
Atherton Plz
Salt Lake City, UT 84123
(801) 268-8444
Fax: (801) 268-8796
Email: don@snellingutah.com

1417 Battlefield Blvd Ste 150
Chesapeake, VA 23320
(757) 548-1187
Fax: (757) 548-9966
Email: sps01@pinn.net

8614 Westwood Ctr Dr Ste 640
Vienna, VA 22182
(703) 448-0050
Fax: (703) 448-3770
Email: psuk@snellingva.com

154 Newtown Rd Ste B5
Virginia Beach, VA 23462
(757) 497-7500
Fax: (757) 497-9215
Email: spsvb3@infi.net

45 W Boscawen St
Winchester, VA 22601-4790
(540) 667-1911
Fax: (540) 667-1984
Email: snelling@visuallink.com

15 S Grady Way Evergreen Bldg Ste 246
Renton, WA 98055
(425) 228-6500
Fax: (425) 228-8661

Email: userindex@msn.com

2101 4th Ave Ste 1330
Seattle, WA 98121
(206) 441-8895
Fax: (206) 448-5373
Email: snelling@serv.net

403 N Chelan Ave
Wenatchee, WA 98801
(509) 663-1619
Fax: (509) 664-9546
Email: seemanss@cs.com

3677 US Rte 60 E
Barboursville, WV 25504
(304) 736-7483
Fax: (304) 736-7486

3624 MacCorkle Ave SE Lower Lvl
PO Box 4522
Charleston, WV 25304
(304) 925-1818
Fax: (304) 925-1877

125 N Executive Dr Ste 364
Brookfield, WI 53005
(262) 796-0722
Fax: (262) 796-0734
Email: driley@snelling.com

9700 W Blue Mound Rd
Milwaukee, WI 53226
(414) 771-3456
Fax: (414) 771-5105
Email: snelling@jadetech.com

Snelling Personnel Services
2224 25th Ave
Gulfport, MS 39501
(228) 822-2225
Fax: (228) 822-0604
Email: lauralea_snelling@yahoo.com
Web: www.snelling.com

Description: Our principal has a B.S. in accounting, M.Ed. and CPC. And is experienced in governmental and public accounting.

Key Contact:
Ms. Laura Lea Reese, Temporary Division Manager

Functions: Generalist, Senior Mgmt., Middle Mgmt., Health Admin., Sales & Mktg., Sales Mgmt., HR Mgmt., Finance

Industries: Generalist, Construction, Mfg., Retail, Finance, Services, Healthcare

---

Snelling Personnel Service
7719 Wood Hollow Dr Ste 211
Austin, TX 78731
(512) 345-4775
(512) 721-1993
Fax: (512) 345-5719
Email: search@snellingaustin.com
Web: www.snelling.com/austin

Description: Our firm is a full-service staffing organization specializing in two general areas of employment. The first is the skilled office worker: primarily serving Austin-based companies, this includes general clerks to administrative office management, customer service, technical communications, and accounting. Secondly, executive search: specializing in accounting, sales, engineering and general management professionals in high-tech manufacturing, telecommunication, and information technology.

Key Contact - Specialty:
Ms. Judy Crowell, General Manager-Administrative
Mr. Richard Crowell, Director - Search Division - *Semiconductor, IT, sales, engineering*
Mr. Brett Anderson, Branch Manager - *Software sales*

Salary minimum: $50,000

Functions: Generalist

Industries: Generalist, Mfg., Computer Equip., Telecoms, Software

Professional Associations: ASA, NAPS

Snelling Search

1813 University Dr Ste 201
Huntsville, AL 35801
(800) 239-1410
(256) 382-3000
Fax: (888) 562-6683
Email: resumes@snellinghsv.com
Web: www.snelling.com/huntsville

Description: We are regarded as one of the premier recruiting firms in the Southeastern United States. In business for over 25 years doing national searches and recruiting.

Key Contact - Specialty:
Mr. George Barnes, General Manager - *Technical, sales, engineering*
Mr. Dave Deerwester, Executive Recruiter - *Healthcare, medical*
Mr. Richard Hudson, Executive Recruiter - *Sales*
Ms. Nancy Mallard, Executive Recruiter - *IT, engineering*
Ms. Kelly Newman, Executive Recruiter - *IT, engineering*
Ms. Sydne Hudson, Executive Recruiter - *Sales*

Salary minimum: $30,000

Functions: Generalist, Senior Mgmt., Automation, Healthcare, Advertising, CFO's, MIS Mgmt., Engineering

Industries: Generalist, Mfg., Food, Bev., Tobacco, Wholesale, Retail, Software, Healthcare

Professional Associations: ASA, NAPS

Snelling Search

1003 SE 28th St
PO Box 1627
Bentonville, AR 72712
(501) 271-0505
Fax: (501) 271-0707
Email: tbailey@snellingtrans.com
Web: www.snellingtrans.com

Description: We are a professionally trained staff with executive-level experience in the transportation industry. We know the trucking and transportation industry. Our process makes the difference.

Key Contact - Specialty:
Mr. Howard Harlson, Owner - *Transportation*
Mr. Tom Bailey, CPC, Manager - *Transportation*

Salary minimum: $45,000

Functions: Generalist

Industries: Transportation

Networks: National Personnel Assoc (NPA)

Snelling Search

2201 5th Ave Ste 5
Moline, IL 61265
(309) 797-1101
Fax: (309) 797-7099
Web: www.snellingmoline.com

Description: We are an established, award winning office, specializing in engineering, manufacturing, purchasing, IT, and accounting. With over thirty years in the recruiting business, we can meet your hiring and employment needs.

Key Contact:
Mr. James V. Roeder, CPC, Vice President

Salary minimum: $30,000

Functions: Generalist, Mfg., Materials, Sales & Mktg., IT

Industries: Generalist

Professional Associations: NAPS, RON

Snelling Search

(a division of Willstaff Inc)
1500 Louisville Ave Ste 102
Monroe, LA 71201
(318) 387-0099
Fax: (318) 361-0386
Email: monroe@willstaff.net
Web: www.willstaff.net

Description: We are the largest Will Staff office worldwide. Will Staff has 40 branches, 60 recruiters, and nationwide clients. We are specialist in assisting and have been in business for thirty-one years.

Key Contact - Specialty:
Mr. David Duffey, Manager - *Senior level management*

Salary minimum: $50,000

Functions: Plant Mgmt., Quality, Healthcare, Physicians, Personnel, CFO's, Systems Analysis, Systems Dev., Engineering

Industries: Generalist, Medical Devices, Healthcare

Professional Associations: AGC, NAPS, NATSS

Snelling Search Recruiters

5838 Faringdon Pl Ste 1
Raleigh, NC 27609
(919) 876-0660
Fax: (919) 876-0355
Email: recruit2@mindspring.com
Web: www.recruit-search.com

Description: We are successful, professional, and experienced recruiters assisting qualified companies location matched candidates that will contribute to their bottom line. We only work sales disciplines.

Key Contact - Specialty:
Mr. Robert J. Helfenbein, Sr., CPC, President
Ms. Cheryl Liles, CPC, Senior Recruiter - *Sales, marketing*

Salary minimum: $30,000

Functions: Sales & Mktg.

Industries: Generalist

SnellingSearch

80 Scenic Dr Ste 1
Freehold, NJ 07728
(732) 431-2600
Fax: (732) 431-2811
Email: frankd@jobs-recruiters.com
Web: www.snelling.com

Description: We are an IT search firm specializing in the recruitment and placement of computer/networking professionals with companies in the New Jersey/New Your regional area.

Key Contact - Specialty:
Mr. Frank Dalotto, General Manager - *Information technology*

Functions: IT

Industries: E-commerce, IT Implementation, Marketing SW, Networking, Comm. SW

C Snow & Associates

1 Yonge St Ste 1801
Toronto, ON M4L 3K4
Canada
(416) 465-8735
Fax: (416) 369-0515

Description: With over 20 years' experience in the recruitment industry, we provide service of the highest integrity to professionals.

Key Contact - Specialty:
Ms. Christine Snow, President - *Financial accounting, marketing, telecommunications*

Salary minimum: $50,000

Functions: Generalist, Middle Mgmt., Mkt. Research, Mktg. Mgmt., Finance

Industries: Generalist, Food, Bev., Tobacco, Computer Equip., Misc. Financial, Telecoms, Software

Professional Associations: HRPAO

Networks: National Personnel Assoc (NPA)

Snyder Executive Search Inc

8840 Southampton Dr
Miramar, FL 33025
(954) 436-2803
Fax: (954) 436-3465
Email: snyder@aaahawk.com
Web: www.asnyder.com

Description: We are executive recruiters specializing in the computer industry. We place computer high level executives, marketing, sales reps, system engineers, business developers, and software developers, nationwide.

Key Contact - Specialty:
Ms. Phyllis Snyder, President
Mr. Alfred Snyder, Vice President - *Computer industry*

Functions: Senior Mgmt., Sales & Mktg., Mktg. Mgmt., Systems Analysis, Systems Dev., DB Admin.

Industries: Computer Equip., E-commerce, IT Implementation, PSA/ASP, Communications, Telecoms, Call Centers, Software, Database SW, Development SW, Doc. Mgmt., Production SW, ERP SW, Mfg. SW, Marketing SW, Networking, Comm. SW, System SW

Andrea Sobel & Associates Inc

8087 Willow Glen Rd
Los Angeles, CA 90046
(323) 650-2996
Fax: (323) 654-3486
Email: andrea8087@aol.com

Description: We have twenty years of experience matching data processing professionals, including client/server, PC support, networking, and mainframe to a variety of clients, including entertainment, new media, healthcare, and banking.

Key Contact - Specialty:
Ms. Andrea Sobel, President - *Information services*

Functions: Generalist, Systems Analysis, Systems Dev., Systems Implem., Systems Support

Industries: Generalist, Banking, Hospitality, Network Infrastructure, Software, Database SW, Entertainment SW, ERP SW, Healthcare

SoftSearch Inc

PO Box 8416
Turnersville, NJ 08012
(856) 218-1000
(888) 703-5400
Fax: (856) 218-9600
Email: info@jobpros.com
Web: www.jobpros.com

Description: Our firm is an executive search firm specializing in information systems, accounting/finance, and sales/marketing personnel. Our sister company Interhunt LLC, specializes in the placement of senior level management personnel in all industries. You can visit their web site at www.interhunt.com. We build long lasting relationships with our clients and candidates, which sets us apart from other firms.

Key Contact - Specialty:
Mr. Joseph Chelston, President - *Information systems, finance*

Functions: Senior Mgmt., Finance, IT, MIS Mgmt., Systems Analysis, Systems Dev., Systems Support, Network Admin., DB Admin., Technicians

Industries: Generalist

Professional Associations: MAAPC

Softstream Corp
1331 Kendall Dr Ste 2-120
San Bernardino, CA 92407
(760) 875-7138
Fax: (909) 880-0095
Email: hr@softstream.net
Web: www.softstream.net

Description: Specialize in full-time and contract placement of information technology professionals in all industries. Provide services in sectors such as software development, e-commerce, networks, database, communications and ERP solutions.

Key Contact - Specialty:
Ms. Pam Lanka, Manager - *Information technology*
Ms. Dixie Ybarra, Marketing Coordinator - *Information technology*

Salary minimum: $35,000

Functions: Generalist, IT, Mgmt. Consultants, Minorities

Industries: Generalist

Branches:
5001 LBJ Fwy Ste 875
Dallas, TX 75244
(972) 387-5278
Fax: (972) 387-5227
Email: info@softstream.net
Web: www.softstream.net/hr
Key Contact - Specialty:
Mr. Kevin Oluoha - *Information technology*

Software Engineering Staffing
950 N Rengstorff Ave
Mountain View, CA 94043
(650) 964-1381
Fax: (650) 964-1347
Email: staff@sestaff.com
Web: www.sestaff.com

Description: We provide high quality consulting, project management, contract staffing and placement services in Silicon Valley. Specialties include networking, network management, UNIX system administration, systems engineer, device driver developers and technical writers.

Key Contact:
Mr. Brad Albom, President

Functions: Generalist, MIS Mgmt., Systems Analysis, Systems Dev., Systems Support, Network Admin., DB Admin., Engineering

Industries: Generalist, Computer Equip., Misc. Financial, Software

Software Resource Consultants
PO Box 38118
Memphis, TN 38183
(901) 759-7225
Fax: (901) 759-1721
Email: pinakini@onlinesrc.com
Web: www.onlinesrc.com

Description: Specialized recruiting for IT, telecommunication industry and wireless technology. Middle to senior management, programmers, analysts, engineers, development managers, business managers. Nationwide search. Work closely with hiring organization to develop recruiting plan.

Key Contact - Specialty:
Ms. Pinakini Sheth, President - *Wireless communications, telecommunications*

Salary minimum: $50,000

Functions: IT, R&D, Engineering, Specialized Svcs., Mgmt. Consultants

Industries: Mgmt. Consulting, Software

Professional Associations: AMA, IEEE

Phyllis Solomon Executive Search Inc
120 Sylvan Ave
Englewood Cliffs, NJ 07632
(201) 947-8600
Fax: (201) 947-9894
Email: mail@solomonsearch.com
Web: www.solomonsearch.com

Description: Expertise with pharmaceuticals, we gear ourselves to isolate the top talent in the industry. We pride ourselves on an unparalleled record of customer satisfaction.

Key Contact - Specialty:
Ms. Phyllis Solomon, President - *Pharmaceutical, marketing, advertising, account management, medical education*

Salary minimum: $90,000

Functions: Physicians, Advertising, Mkt. Research, Mktg. Mgmt., Direct Mktg., PR

Industries: Generalist

Professional Associations: NJSA

Solutions
7301 Blue Heron Cv
Leander, TX 78641
(512) 219-0224
(512) 258-1236
Fax: (512) 918-2805
Email: kbeall@austin.rr.com

Description: I am an independent search consultant specializing in healthcare and well-being. I offer highly personalized services within a wide variety of disciplines and settings. Particular focus of mine is on personal, professional, and organizational development.

Key Contact - Specialty:
Ms. Karen Beall, Owner - *Healthcare*

Functions: Directors, Senior Mgmt., Admin. Svcs., Physicians, Nurses, Allied Health, Health Admin., Mktg. Mgmt., CFO's, Mgmt. Consultants

Industries: Generalist, Services, Non-profits, Pharm Svcs., Accounting, Mgmt. Consulting, HR Services, HR SW, Marketing SW, Healthcare, Hospitals, Long-term Care, Dental, Physical Therapy, Occupational Therapy

Solutions ClickonJob.com
6850 Sherbrooke Est Ste 300
Montreal, QC H1N 1E1
Canada
(514) 256-8000
Fax: (514) 256-8007
Email: client@clickonjob.com
Web: www.clickonjob.com

Description: Provider of choice of IT specialists in key business markets across Canada and the United States.

Key Contact - Specialty:
Mr. Claude Daigneault, President - *Information systems technology*

Salary minimum: $30,000

Functions: Generalist, Admin. Svcs., Direct Mktg., Personnel, MIS Mgmt., Systems Analysis, Systems Dev., Systems Implem.

Industries: Generalist, Services, Accounting, HR Services

Professional Associations: APRHQ, FIQ

Solutns Recruiting Services
3407 N Nebraska Ct
Chandler, AZ 85225
(480) 813-0796
Web: www.solutns.com

Description: Our firm specializes in healthcare, sales, and IT positions. We are a network of experienced recruiters and can fill any position, anywhere in the country. Our fees are very reasonable and reflect the efficiencies of modern recruiting methods and techniques.

Key Contact - Specialty:
Mr. John Power, National Accounts Manager - *Sales, healthcare, IT*

Salary minimum: $50,000

Functions: Generalist

Industries: Computer Equip., Electronic, Elec. Components, HR Services, Telecoms, HR SW, Healthcare, Hospitals, Long-term Care

Somerset Group Inc
39 Sherman Ct
Fairfield, CT 06430
(203) 255-3232
Fax: (203) 255-5143
Email: resumes@somersetgroup.com
Web: www.somersetgroup.com

Description: Specialize in custom and syndicated marketing research. Clients consist of corporations, research suppliers and consulting firms. Industries include consumer packaged goods, pharmaceuticals, telecommunications, financial services, high-tech, business-to-business and healthcare.

Key Contact - Specialty:
Mr. Richard Brenner, President - *Marketing research*
Mr. Gregory King, Executive Vice President - *Marketing research*

Salary minimum: $50,000

Functions: Mkt. Research

Industries: Generalist

Sondra Search
PO Box 101
Roswell, GA 30077-0101
(770) 552-1910
Fax: (770) 552-7340
Email: sondrasearch@earthlink.net

Description: We are a nationwide executive placement agent specializing in recruiting professional sales and sales management in all industries, including: medical, information technology, industrial, business products, and consumer. All of our fees are paid by the employer.

Key Contact - Specialty:
Ms. Sondra Katnik, Vice President - *Sales, sales management*

Functions: Senior Mgmt., Middle Mgmt., Healthcare, Sales Mgmt., IT

Industries: Mfg., Medical Devices, Services, Pharm Svcs., Equip Svcs., Communications, Wireless, Software, Networking, Comm. SW, Biotech, Healthcare, Hospitals, Long-term Care, Dental, Non-classifiable

Hilmon Sorey Associates
(also known as MRI of Monticello)
1140 Renae Way
Tallahassee, FL 32312
(850) 422-3200
Fax: (850) 385-5950
Email: hilmon@mrievanston.com
Web: www.mrievanston.com

Description: We specialize in healthcare (management, clinical and technical) and education staffing solutions.

Key Contact:
Mr. Hilmon Sorey, Jr., Principal

Salary minimum: $40,000

Functions: Healthcare

Industries: Non-profits, Higher Ed., Accounting, HR Services, Healthcare

Professional Associations: ACHE

SOS Financial Staffing

6700 France Ave S Ste 150
Edina, MN 55435
(952) 926-9554
Fax: (952) 926-9188
Email: info@sosfinancial.com

Description: Benefit from our expertise in the areas of mortgage banking, banking, administrative, title insurance, property management and accounting placements.

Key Contact - Specialty:
Ms. Tiffany Clark, Executive Search Consultant - *Mortgage, banking, title*

Salary minimum: $30,000

Functions: Middle Mgmt., Admin. Svcs., Customer Svc., Finance

Industries: Retail, Finance, Banking, Misc. Financial, Accounting, Insurance, Real Estate

Professional Associations: MAPS

Soundview Business Solutions Inc

40 Soundview Dr
Northport, NY 11768
(631) 757-2936
Fax: (631) 262-8958
Email: mail@soundviewsearch.com

Description: We provide both retained and contingency search specializing in sales, marketing, and management.

Key Contact:
Mr. Jack Signorelli

Functions: Sales Mgmt.

Industries: Printing, Computer Equip., Equip Svcs., Mgmt. Consulting, E-commerce, Digital, Software

SourceWynds Executive Search

833 Chelsea Park Dr
Marietta, GA 30068
(770) 973-2520
Fax: (770) 973-4795
Email: wynr1@aol.com
Web: www.sourcewynds.com

Description: We specialize in the recruitment of professional sales talent and executive candidates to vendor organizations serving the power, chemical, petrochemical, process, pulp and paper, mining, and biotech industries.

Key Contact - Specialty:
Mr. Wyn Robinson, President - *Power, process, chemical*
Mr. Kent Hudson, Vice President - *Power, process, pulp & paper*
Mr. Richard LaBarba, Director - *Power, biotech*

Salary minimum: $75,000

Functions: Generalist, General Mgmt., Senior Mgmt., Sales & Mktg., Engineering, Int'l.

Industries: Energy, Utilities, Chemicals, Test, Measure Equip., Biotech

Professional Associations: ABMA, TAPPI

Southern Chemical & Plastics Search

759 Omaha Dr Ste 100
Norcross, GA 30093-4921
(770) 921-7693
Fax: (770) 923-6873
Email: chemrecrut@aol.com
Web: www.hometown.aol.com/chemrecrut/myhomepage/index.html

Description: We specialize in sales, sales management, and marketing in the raw materials chemical and plastics industries. Our thorough and confidential searches within an industry enable us to process qualified individuals who meet the specific needs of the client.

Key Contact - Specialty:
Mr. Allan Hytowitz, Director - *Chemical intermediates*
Mr. Jim Allen, Director - *Plastic resins*
Mr. Robert Christian, Director - *Packaging*

Salary minimum: $30,000

Functions: Generalist, Mfg., Sales & Mktg., Mktg. Mgmt., Sales Mgmt.

Industries: Chemicals, Soap, Perf., Cosmtcs., Drugs Mfg., Plastics, Rubber, Paints, Petro. Products

Professional Associations: SPE, TAPPI

Networks: The Acumen Society

Southern Medical Recruiters

121 Del Mar Blvd
Corpus Christi, TX 78404
(361) 883-4469
Fax: (361) 883-4425
Email: recruiter@southernmed.com
Web: www.southernmed.com

Description: We have had twenty plus years experience in healthcare recruitment nationwide. Ewe charge employer paid fees only. We specialize in CEO, CFO, CNO/CNE, nursing directors, business office directors, pharmacy, lab, radiology, ancillary, M.D./D.O.s, CRNA, nuclear, ultrasound, MRI, dietary, pediatrics, maternal child, LTC/skilled, rehab, Psychiatric, staff RNs, nurses, critical care directors/emergency room, OB, dosimetry, radiation therapist, cardiovascular, and cath lab.

Key Contact - Specialty:
Ms. Adela Guerrero-Dryden, President - *Healthcare*

Salary minimum: $200,000

Functions: Generalist, Senior Mgmt., Healthcare, Physicians, Nurses, Allied Health, Health Admin.

Industries: Generalist, Medical Devices, Healthcare, Hospitals, Long-term Care, Physical Therapy, Occupational Therapy, Women's

Southern Recruiters & Consultants Inc

PO Box 2745
Aiken, SC 29802
(803) 648-7834
Email: recruiters@southernrecruiters.com
Web: www.southernrecruiters.com

Description: We are in an award winning firm dedicated to professional, ethical and long-term service for our candidates and client companies. We handle all disciplines in manufacturing - one stop shopping for client companies.

Key Contact - Specialty:
Mr. Ray Fehrenbach, CPC, President - *Human resources*
Mr. Bill Irwin, CPC, Recruiter - *Pharmaceutical, technical, operations, chemicals, plant engineering*
Ms. Amy Snyder, CPC, Recruiter - *Metalworking & finishing, technical, operations*

Mr. Chris Bethmann, CPC, Recruiter - *Plastics, materials management, logistics, accounting & finance*
Ms. Monika Dailey, CPC, Recruiter - *Information technology, hardware engineers, software engineers*
Mrs. Tonya Strickland, CPC, Recruiter - *Technology, telecommunications, consumer products, retail*
Ms. Michelle Nelms, CPC, Recruiter - *Design engineers other than electric & electronics, ceramic engineers, operations (ceramics)*
Mrs. Kathy Burress, CPC, Recruiter - *Electrical, I&C engineers, electronics engineers, manufacturing management, electronic*
Mr. David Eubanks, Recruiter - *Plastics, medical devices, HVAC industries*

Salary minimum: $35,000

Functions: Generalist

Industries: Mfg., Finance, Accounting, Equip Svcs., Environmental Svcs., Haz. Waste, Aerospace, Packaging, Software, Biotech

Professional Associations: SCAPS

Networks: Inter-City Personnel Assoc (IPA)

Southern Technical Recruiters

2640 Willard Dairy Rd Ste 100
High Point, NC 27265
(336) 841-7999
Fax: (336) 841-8001
Email: recruiters@southerntechnical.com
Web: www.southerntechnical.com

Description: We have over 25 years of recruiting experience with particular emphasis in the engineering and technical fields. We specialize in engineering, manufacturing/operations, sales/marketing and international positions.

Key Contact - Specialty:
Mr. Bill Roberts, Owner / Technical Recruiter - *Manufacturing operations*
Ms. Michele Wille, Technical Recruiter - *Design, manufacturing engineers, six sigma*
Mr. Jim Heath, Technical Recruiter - *Technical sales & marketing, defense, aerospace*
Mrs. Catherine Hinson, Technical Recruiter - *IT division*

Salary minimum: $45,000

Functions: Generalist, Mfg., Purchasing, Mktg. Mgmt., Sales Mgmt., Engineering

Industries: Generalist, Construction, Mfg.

Southwest Search & Consulting Inc

4500 S Lakeshore Dr Ste 520
Tempe, AZ 85282
(480) 838-0333
Fax: (480) 838-0368
Email: azjobs@azjobs.com
Web: www.azjobs.com

Description: We are the largest recruiting firm in the Phoenix area that specializes exclusively in information technology. All of our recruiters are tenured, with at least ten years' experience each. Our client base includes top fifty companies in Arizona.

Key Contact - Specialty:
Ms. Marilyn McDannel, President - *Information technology*

Salary minimum: $40,000

Functions: MIS Mgmt., Systems Analysis, Systems Dev., Systems Implem., Systems Support, Network Admin., DB Admin.

Industries: Generalist

Southwest Selective Search Inc
1600 Airport Fwy Ste 328
Bedford, TX 76022
(817) 540-6195
Fax: (817) 267-2240
Email: swsearch@flash.net
Web: www.flash.net/~swsearch

Description: Our staff comes from the industries we serve. We take the time to fully understand your company and personnel needs to serve you better.

Key Contact - Specialty:
Mr. Paul Neir, President - *Insurance (property, casualty)*
Ms. Karla Neir, Vice President - *Insurance (property, casualty)*

Salary minimum: $25,000

Functions: Generalist

Industries: Services, Insurance, Accounting SW

Professional Associations: INS

Southwestern Business Resources
2451 Atrium Way
Nashville, TN 37214
(615) 391-2617
Fax: (615) 231-4000
Email: info@thinkingahead.com
Web: www.thinkingahead.com

Description: We recruit executive, middle management and contract labor for Fortune 100 companies and small private firms, nationally and internationally. The contract labor is for technical personnel.

Key Contact - Specialty:
Dr. Carl R. Roberts, Ph.D., Vice President - *Sales & marketing*
Mr. Greg Boucher, Associate Vice President - *Sales & marketing*
Mr. Tom Truitt, Vice President - *Management consultants*

Functions: Generalist, Sales Mgmt., CFO's, Budgeting, Systems Dev., Systems Support, Engineering, Mgmt. Consultants

Industries: Generalist, Mfg., Accounting, Equip Svcs., IT Implementation, Telecoms, Aerospace, Insurance, Software, Accounting SW, Healthcare

Professional Associations: NAPS, NTSA

Networks: First Interview Network (FIN)

Branches:
2005 Concord Pike Fl 2
Wilmington, DE 19803
(302) 425-0272
Fax: (302) 425-0277
Key Contact - Specialty:
Mr. Bill Hutchison, Business Unit Manager - *Information technology*

1600 Parkwood Cir Ste 611
Atlanta, GA 30339
(770) 635-1120
Fax: (770) 635-1110
Key Contact - Specialty:
Mr. Jeff Young, Manager - *Information technology*

1111 Military Cutoff Rd Ste 171
Wilmington, NC 28405
(910) 509-3831
Fax: (910) 509-3832
Key Contact - Specialty:
Ms. Cathy Moll, Manager - *Regulatory affairs, quality assurance, healthcare*

10925 Reed Hartman Hwy Ste 311
Cincinnati, OH 45242
(877) 740-7977
Key Contact:
Ms. Theresa Oldfield, Manager

2828 Trinity Mills Ste 106
Carrollton, TX 75006
(214) 390-8616
Fax: (214) 390-8046
Key Contact - Specialty:
Mr. James Hutchins, Manager - *Military officers (former), technical enlistees into civilian jobs*

1604 Hilltop Executive Ctr Ste 308
Virginia Beach, VA 23451
(757) 428-2660
Fax: (757) 428-0394
Key Contact - Specialty:
Mr. Bill Knipp, Manager - *Placement of former military officers & technical enlistees into civilian jobs*

Sparks, McDonough & Associates Inc
1001 Craig Rd Ste 330
St. Louis, MO 63146
(314) 872-2166
Fax: (314) 872-2167
Email: smsearch@aol.com

Description: A leading Mid-western executive search firm, we specialize in Internet, software, networking and wireless communications for high-level sales, management and technical sales positions.

Key Contact - Specialty:
Mr. Tom Sparks, President - *High technology, telecommunications*

Salary minimum: $90,000

Functions: General Mgmt., Senior Mgmt., Sales Mgmt.

Industries: New Media, Telecoms, Software

SPC Symcox Personnel Consultants
16607 Blanco Rd Ste 707
The Park on Blanco
San Antonio, TX 78232
(210) 479-5991
Fax: (210) 479-5994
Email: spc@symcox.com
Web: www.symcox.com

Description: We provide a full range of professional search, recruiting and placement services with consultants specializing in exclusive concentrations of various disciplines and industries.

Key Contact - Specialty:
Mr. Jim Symcox, President - *Information technology, finance & accounting, materials management, human resources, sales*

Salary minimum: $40,000

Functions: Senior Mgmt., Middle Mgmt., Production, Materials, Materials Plng., Mkt. Research, Mktg. Mgmt., HR Mgmt., Finance, Technicians

Industries: Generalist, Mfg., Food, Bev., Tobacco, Printing, Consumer Elect., Transportation, Retail, Finance, Services, Accounting, HR Services, Media, Telecoms, Aerospace, Insurance, Software, Biotech

Networks: National Personnel Assoc (NPA)

Spear-Izzo Associates LLC
(a division of SIA Group)
651 Holiday Dr Foster Plz Bldg 5 Ste 300
Pittsburgh, PA 15220-2740
(412) 928-3290
Fax: (724) 940-1959
Email: info@siasearch.com
Web: www.siasearch.com

Description: We specialize in serving the recruiting needs of the management consulting profession. We provide both permanent and contract candidates to over 95 domestic and international consulting firms. Our clients include those in operations

improvement, the Big 5, strategy, change management, IT, engineering and process change.

Key Contact - Specialty:
Mr. Kenneth T. Spear, Partner - *Generalist*
Mr. Donald Wesley, Principal - *Generalist*

Salary minimum: $30,000

Functions: Mfg., Productivity, Materials, Sales & Mktg., Training, Finance, IT, Engineering, Mgmt. Consultants, Int'l.

Industries: Mgmt. Consulting

Professional Associations: AMOD, NAPS, PTC

Networks: Top Echelon Network

Branches:
35 Technology Pkwy S Ste 170
Norcross, GA 30092
(770) 613-5312
Fax: (770) 279-9110
Email: consultant@siasearch.com
Key Contact - Specialty:
Mr. Thomas M. Izzo, Partner - *Generalist*
Mr. John Snellen, Principal - *Generalist*

D P Specialists Inc
2141 Rosecrans Ste 5100
El Segundo, CA 90245
(310) 416-9846
Fax: (310) 416-9003
Email: dps@dpsla.com
Web: www.dpsla.com

Description: As a full-service firm recruit all levels of data processing professionals from vice presidents to programmers. Also provide consulting services to all levels specializing in new technologies.

Key Contact - Specialty:
Mr. Ed Myers, President - *Information technology*

Salary minimum: $40,000

Functions: Generalist, MIS Mgmt., Systems Analysis, Systems Dev., Systems Implem., Systems Support

Industries: Generalist, Energy, Utilities, Finance, Misc. Financial, Broadcast, Film, Insurance

Specialized Search Associates
15200 Jog Rd Ste 201
Delray Beach, FL 33446
(561) 499-3711
Fax: (561) 499-3770
Email: lm7524@aol.com

Description: We specialize in the executive recruiting of engineers for the construction industry. We place in the areas of marketing, operations, and sales. We provide services within the following areas of engineering: civil, structural, mechanical, electrical, process, environmental, bridges, roads and highways, airports, infrastructure, transit, etc.

Key Contact - Specialty:
Mr. Leonard Morris, President - *Engineering (construction industry)*

Salary minimum: $75,000

Functions: Generalist, Middle Mgmt.

Industries: Construction

Professional Associations: AGC, ASCE, ASHE, ISPE, ITE, SAME, SMPS

Specialized Search Company
15203 NW Troon Dr
Portland, OR 97229
(503) 617-9484
Fax: (503) 629-0984
Email: wieber3@home.com
Web: www.specializedsearchco.com

Description: We work primarily in the chemical field with an emphasis on materials associated with paint coatings and adhesives. Sales, technical and management positions are all part of our involvement. We work nationwide.

Key Contact - Specialty:
Mr. William Wieber, Owner - *Chemical, paint, coatings*

Functions: Generalist

Industries: Chemicals, Paints, Petro. Products

Networks: US Recruiters.com

Specialty Employment Services Inc
PO Box 567054
Atlanta, GA 31156
(800) 297-5401
Email: michael@sesijobs.com
Web: www.sesijobs.com

Description: We provide the employment solutions to better your organization. We evaluate your needs and develop a specific search assignment marketing plan and present only pre-screened candidates that meet your objectives.

Key Contact - Specialty:
Mr. Michael Siegel, President - *Sales, marketing, technical, chemical*
Ms. Karen Cheng - *Engineering, research & development, chemical*
Mr. Tony Blixt, Principal - *Telecommunications, equipment sales & marketing*

Salary minimum: $40,000

Functions: Sales & Mktg.

Industries: Generalist

Professional Associations: FSCT, GAPS, IEEE, IFT, PIMA, TAPPI

SpectraWest
37053 Cherry St Ste 117
Newark, CA 94560
(510) 791-1700
Fax: (510) 791-8900
Email: fred@spectrawest.com
Web: www.spectrawest.com

Description: We recruit engineering directors, managers, and senior project engineers who specialize in computer network systems development, hardware design, connectivity software development, graphics software development, and operating systems development. We seek a minimum of four years of technical development experience plus an electrical engineering, computer engineering, or computer science degree.

Key Contact - Specialty:
Mr. Fred Arredondo, Director - *Computer hardware, software engineers*

Salary minimum: $85,000

Functions: Product Dev., Systems Dev., Engineering

Industries: Computer Equip., Telecoms, Software

Professional Associations: IEEE

The Spectrum Group
2620 Enterprise Rd E Ste 22
Clearwater, FL 33759
(727) 791-3200
Fax: (727) 791-3800
Email: spectrum@usafoodjobs.com
Web: www.usafoodjobs.com

Description: Offering an extensive database of clients to the meat processing and food manufacturing industry, we are experienced.

Key Contact - Specialty:
Mr. Arnie Holder, President - *Meat processing, food & beverage manufacturing*

Salary minimum: $40,000

Functions: Senior Mgmt., Middle Mgmt., Mfg., Product Dev., Production, Plant Mgmt., Quality, Packaging, Engineering

Industries: Generalist, Food, Bev., Tobacco

Spectrum Scientific Recruiters
666 Plainsboro Rd Ste 220
Plainsboro, NJ 08536
(609) 936-8850
Fax: (609) 936-9344
Email: info@spectrumscientific.com
Web: www.spectrumscientific.com

Description: We are recruiters of pharmaceutical industry and clinical research professionals who support the IND-NDA and post marketed process. We provide retained and contingency search, as well as contract staffing.

Key Contact:
Mr. Scott Nagrod, President

Salary minimum: $65,000

Professional Associations: ACRP, AMWA, ARMA, DIA, RAPS

Spectrum Search Agency Inc
60 E Highland Ave
Sierra Madre, CA 91024
(323) 256-4564
Email: joe79@pacbell.net

Description: Specializing in telephony sales and sales support.

Key Contact - Specialty:
Mr. Joe Florence, Owner - *Telephony sales*

Salary minimum: $50,000

Functions: Generalist, Sales & Mktg.

Industries: Generalist, Telecoms

Spherion Legal Group
2050 Spectrum Blvd
Ft. Lauderdale, FL 33309
(954) 351-3825
Fax: (954) 489-6370
Email: gregmazares@spherion.com
Web: www.spherion.com

Description: We provide the broadest range of human resources and other legal support services to corporate law departments and law firms including staffing services, managed service, recruiting and search services, consulting and administrative staffing and deposition services.

Key Contact - Specialty:
Mr. Greg Mazares, President - Interim Legal Services - *Attorneys, paralegals, office, administrative, management*
Ms. Merle Isgett, Senior Director of Operations - *Attorney, paralegal, legal secretary, professional development, deposition services*

Salary minimum: $35,000

Functions: Legal

Industries: Legal

Professional Associations: ACCA, ALA, ALP, LAMA, NFPA

Branches:
700 S Flower Ste 1050
Los Angeles, CA 90017
(213) 688-8770
Fax: (213) 688-8366
Email: spherionlegalla@spherion.com
Key Contact - Specialty:
Mr. Greg Mazares, Esq., Branch Manager - *Attorney, paralegal, legal secretary, professional development*

27281 Las Ramblas Ste 169
Mission Viejo, CA 92691
(714) 582-2503
Fax: (714) 582-8569
Email: stanleyweinberg@spherion.com
Key Contact - Specialty:
Mr. Stan Weinberg - *Deposition services*

501 W Broadway Plz 2
The Koll Center
San Diego, CA 92101
(619) 696-3800
Fax: (619) 696-3808
Email: sandiegolegal@spherion.com.com
Key Contact - Specialty:
Mr. Allen Etling, Licensee - *Attorneys, paralegal*

550 West "C" St
San Diego, CA 92101
(619) 235-2400
Fax: (619) 235-0718
Email: barbarabretherton@spherion.com
Key Contact - Specialty:
Ms. Barbara Bretherton - *Deposition services*

475 Sansome St Ste 720
San Francisco, CA 94111
(415) 362-6666
Fax: (415) 362-0907
Email: sfcourtreporting@spherion.com
Key Contact:
Marimart Paulbitski

475 Sansome St Ste 760
San Francisco, CA 94111
(415) 397-9354
Fax: (415) 397-9454
Email: marimartpaulbitski@spherion.com
Key Contact - Specialty:
Marimart Paulbitski, Esq., Branch Director - *Attorneys, paralegals, legal secretary, professional development, deposition services*

4500 Cherry Creek S Dr Ste 1050
Denver, CO 80246
(303) 729-0187
Fax: (303) 446-0136
Email: spherionlegalden@spherion.com
Key Contact:
Ms. Naomi Campbell

1120 G St NW Ste 1000
Washington, DC 20005
(202) 737-9333
Fax: (202) 223-8186
Email: trishalatorre-ridings@spherion.com
Key Contact - Specialty:
Ms. Trish Alatorre-Ridings, Branch Director - *Attorney, paralegal, legal secretary, professional development, deposition services*

4901 NW 17th Way Ste 504
Ft. Lauderdale, FL 33309
(954) 229-3480
Fax: (954) 229-3489
Email: marisadelinks@spherion.com
Key Contact - Specialty:
Ms. Marissa Delinks, JD, Branch Manager - *Attorney, paralegal, legal secretary, professional development, deposition services*

1639 Hendry St
Ft. Myers, FL 33901
(941) 334-7766
Fax: (941) 334-7136
Key Contact:
Mr. Bernie Goldstein

2500 Airport Rd Ste 310
Naples, FL 34112
(941) 774-2141
Fax: (941) 774-9562
Key Contact:
Mr. Bernie Goldstein

1400 Centrepark Blvd Ste 960
West Palm Beach, FL 33401
(561) 478-0401
Fax: (561) 478-6570

Key Contact:
Mr. Bernie Goldstein

2931 Piedmont Rd Ste A
Atlanta, GA 30305
(404) 875-0400
Fax: (404) 875-2979
Key Contact:
Mr. Steve Huseby

459 EE Butler Pkwy SE
Gainesville, GA 30501
(770) 536-7028
Fax: (770) 532-7453
Key Contact:
Mr. Scott Huseby

1387 Butterfield Rd
Aurora, IL 60504
(630) 851-8030
Fax: (630) 851-0600
Email: elizabetheastwood@spherion.com
Key Contact:
Ms. Liz Eastwood

11 S La Salle St Ste 2140
Chicago, IL 60603
(312) 553-0733
Fax: (312) 553-0735
Email: elizabetheastwood@spherion.com
Key Contact:
Ms. Elisabeth Ori

11 S LaSalle Ste 1150
Chicago, IL 60603
(312) 917-1515
Fax: (312) 917-1590
Email: elisabethori@spherion.com
Key Contact - Specialty:
Ms. Elisabeth Ori, Branch Manager - *Attorney,
paralegal, legal secretary, professional
development, deposition services*

2700 River Rd Ste 118
Des Plaines, IL 60018
(847) 635-0828
Fax: (847) 635-0854
Email: elizabetheastwood@spherion.com
Key Contact:
Mr. Steve Arnstein

80 S 8th St Ste 3918
IDS Ctr
Minneapolis, MN 55402
(612) 339-7663
Fax: (612) 339-9274
Email: jasonobler@spherion.com
Key Contact - Specialty:
Ms. Karen Whitman - *Attorney, paralegal*
Mr. Brett Arnold, Esq., JD, Legal Recruiter -
Attorney

704 W High St
Jefferson City, MO 65109
(573) 636-7551
Fax: (573) 636-9065
Key Contact:
Ms. Debbie Weaver

4435 Main St Ste 845
Kansas City, MO 64111
(816) 753-4644
Fax: (816) 753-0540
Email: danryan@spherion.com
Key Contact - Specialty:
Ms. Mary Shuster - *Attorney, paralegal*
Mr. Dan Ryan, JD, Legal Recruiter - *Attorney,
paralegal, legal secretary, professional
development*

1014 Lami
St. Louis, MO 63104
(314) 644-2191
Fax: (314) 644-1334
Email: kellywillis@spherion.com
Key Contact:
Ms. Debbie Weaver

8860 Ladue Rd Ste 120
St. Louis, MO 63124
(314) 862-1922
Fax: (314) 862-7087
Email: spherionlegalstl@spherion.com
Key Contact - Specialty:
Ms. Lynn Ann Whaley, JD, Branch Manager -
*Attorney, paralegal, legal secretary, professional
development, deposition services*

200 Old Country Rd Ste 620
Mineola, NY 11501
(516) 747-9393
Fax: (516) 742-1288
Key Contact:
Ms. Florence Seff

545 5th Ave Ste 715
New York, NY 10017
(212) 953-0050
Fax: (212) 953-3691
Email: lorenmustion@spherion.com
Key Contact - Specialty:
Ms. Loren Mustion, JD, Branch Manager -
*Attorney, paralegal, legal secretary, professional
development, deposition services*

545 5th Ave Ste 900
New York, NY 10017
(212) 490-3430
Fax: (212) 490-3534
Email: spheriondepony@spherion.com
Key Contact:
Ms. Loren Mustion

One W Pack Sq Ste 1402 BB&T Bldg
Asheville, NC 28801
(828) 253-7033
Fax: (828) 372-4593
Key Contact:
Mr. Scott Huseby

301 S McDowell St Ste 1000
Charlotte, NC 28204
(704) 333-9889
Fax: (704) 372-4593
Email: spheriondeponc@spherion.com
Key Contact:
Mr. Scott Huseby

7031 Albert Pick Rd Ste 100
Greensboro, NC 27409
(336) 373-0985
Fax: (336) 574-2665
Key Contact:
Mr. Scott Huseby

150 Fayetteville St Mall Fl 17
Raleigh, NC 27601
(919) 831-8877
Fax: (800) 442-2082
Key Contact:
Mr. Scott Huseby

2990 Bethesda Pl Ste 603
Winston-Salem, NC 27103
(336) 774-1822
Fax: (800) 442-2082
Key Contact:
Mr. Scott Huseby

250 E Fifth St 1121 Chicuita Ctr
Cincinnati, OH 45202
(513) 621-1701
Fax: (513) 621-1702
Email: garretneisonger@spherion.com
Key Contact - Specialty:
Mr. Garret Neiswonger, Legal Practice Director -
*Attorney, paralegal, legal secretary, professional
development, deposition services*
Ms. Beth Brown, Branch Manager - *Attorney,
paralegal, legal secretary, professional
development*

5151 Pfeiffer Rd Ste 120
Cincinnati, OH 45242
(513) 621-1701
Fax: (513) 792-6655
Email: garretneisonger@spherion.com

Key Contact:
Mr. Garret Neiswonger

1617 JFK Blvd Ste 1020
Philadelphia, PA 19103
(215) 568-5899
Fax: (215) 568-5810
Email: meronhewis@spherion.com
Key Contact - Specialty:
Ms. Stacey Beck, JD, Branch Manager - *Attorney,
paralegal, legal secretary, professional
development, deposition services*

400 Market St Fl 11
Philadelphia, PA 19106
(215) 928-9300
Fax: (215) 627-0555
Email: kcacohen@aol.com
Key Contact:
Ms. Stacey Beck

500 Thurmond Mall Fl 3
The Pavillion Office Center
Columbia, SC 29204
(803) 779-8787
Fax: (800) 442-2083
Key Contact:
Ms. Joy Huseby

181 E Evans St
B&T Center 011
Florence, SC 29506
(843) 664-2896
Fax: (800) 442-2082
Key Contact:
Ms. Joy Huseby

1200 Woodruff Rd Bldg A-3
Merovan Executive Ste
Greenville, SC 29607
(864) 297-9776
Fax: (800) 442-2082
Key Contact:
Ms. Joy Huseby

707 Georgia Ave Ste 404
Chattanooga, TN 37402
(423) 267-0989
Fax: (423) 267-0980
Key Contact:
Mr. Scott Huseby

5000 Quorum Dr Ste 550
Dallas, TX 75240
(972) 661-1485
Fax: (972) 385-1006
Email: hbloom@legaljobsdfw.com
Key Contact - Specialty:
Mr. Howard Bloom, Owner - *Attorney, paralegal,
legal secretary*

1360 Post Oak Blvd Ste 1780
Houston, TX 77056
(713) 993-9733
Fax: (713) 993-9847
Email: spherionlegalhouston@spherion.com
Key Contact:
Ms. Karen Schoeve

1801 Columbia
Houston, TX 77002
(713) 650-3500
Fax: (713) 650-3545
Email: shellydann@spherion.com
Key Contact:
Mr. Shelly Dan

400 E Wisconsin Ave Ste 102
Milwaukee, WI 53202
(414) 271-0566
Fax: (414) 271-8230
Email: elizabetheastwood@spherion.com
Key Contact:
Ms. Elizabeth Eastwood

Spherion Professional Recruiting Group

7900 Glades Rd Ste 520
Boca Raton, FL 33434
(561) 477-6061
Fax: (561) 483-4604
Email: yoshiannwilson@spherion.com
Web: www.spherion.com/professionalrecruiting

Description: Our goal is to be your strategic partner, providing a consultative approach, impacting your growth and profitability. Our solutions are delivered through search-direct hire, and contract and project staffing. Our dedicated practice areas of expertise include: finance and accounting, human resources, technology, engineering and manufacturing, legal, sales and marketing, and interim executives.

Key Contact:
Mr. Eric Archer, President

Salary minimum: $30,000

Functions: Generalist, CFO's, Budgeting, Cash Mgmt., Credit, Taxes, M&A, Risk Mgmt.

Industries: Generalist, Food, Bev., Tobacco, Computer Equip., Finance, Environmental Svcs., Biotech

Professional Associations: NAPS, NATSS

Branches:
18500 Von Karman Ave Ste 510
Irvine, CA 92612
(949) 756-1028
Fax: (949) 756-1225
Email: clintpyatt@spherion.com
Key Contact - Specialty:
Mr. Clint Pyatt, Branch Director - *Finance, accounting, banking, engineering & manufacturing, sales & marketing*

4660 LaJolla Village Dr Ste 910
San Diego, CA 92122
(858) 458-9200
Fax: (858) 458-1830
Email: robburden@spherion.com
Key Contact - Specialty:
Mr. Rob Burden, Branch Director - *Finance, accounting, banking, mortgage banking, human resource*

475 Sansome St Ste 770
San Francisco, CA 94111
(415) 391-0200
Fax: (415) 391-0280
Email: warrencohn@spherion.com
Key Contact - Specialty:
Mr. Warren S. Cohn, Branch Director - *Finance, accounting, banking, mortgage banking, human resource*

2150 N First St Ste 230
San Jose, CA 95131
(408) 452-4745
Fax: (408) 383-0413
Email: markvoege@spherion.com
Key Contact - Specialty:
Mr. Mark Voege, Branch Director - *Finance, accounting, banking, mortgage banking, human resource*

200 Pringle Ave Ste 325
Walnut Creek, CA 94596
(925) 934-7092
Fax: (925) 934-2011
Email: kerryquinn@spherion.com
Key Contact - Specialty:
Ms. Kerry Quinn, Branch Director - *Finance, accounting, banking, mortgage banking, human resource*

4500 Cherry Creek S Dr Ste 1050
Denver, CO 80246
(303) 729-0187
Fax: (303) 729-1153
Email: naomiwarchol@spherion.com

Key Contact - Specialty:
Ms. Naomi Warchol, Branch Director - *Finance, accounting, banking, mortgage banking, human resource*

1120 G St NW Ste 1000
Washington, DC 20005
(202) 737-0075
Fax: (202) 296-7387
Email: trishalatorre-ridings@spherion.com
Key Contact - Specialty:
Mr. Mike Bettick, Area Director - *Finance, accounting, banking, mortgage banking, human resource*

2600 Douglas Rd
Penthouse 4
Coral Gables, FL 33134
(305) 444-9900
Fax: (305) 444-9160
Email: mattshore@spherion.com
Key Contact - Specialty:
Mr. Matt Shore, Area Director - *Finance, accounting, banking, mortgage banking, human resource*

1 Financial Plz Ste 1514
Ft. Lauderdale, FL 33394
(954) 462-6979
Fax: (954) 462-6885
Email: danayaver@spherion.com
Key Contact - Specialty:
Ms. Dana Yaver, Branch Director - *Finance, accounting, banking engineering & manufacturing, sales & marketing, legal*

668 N Orlando Ave Ste 1009
Maitland, FL 32751
(407) 647-8117
Fax: (407) 647-5449
Email: jeannejewett@spherion.com
Web: www.spherion.com
Key Contact - Specialty:
Ms. Jeanne Jewett, Branch Director - *Finance, accounting, banking, mortgage banking, human resource*

6710 Main St Ste 234
Miami Lakes, FL 33014
(305) 558-1700
Fax: (305) 558-5772
Email: chrisgarbow@spherion.com
Key Contact - Specialty:
Mr. Matt Shore, Area Director - *Finance, accounting, banking, mortgage banking, human resource*

3111 W Martin Luther King Blvd Ste 350
Tampa, FL 33607
(813) 864-1111
Fax: (813) 864-1121
Email: leechaffin@spherion.com
Key Contact - Specialty:
Mr. Lee Chaffin, Branch Director - *Finance, accounting, banking, mortgage banking, human resource*

1601 Forum Pl Ste 600
West Palm Beach, FL 33401
(561) 686-9101
Fax: (561) 686-9404
Email: randystefano@spherion.com
Key Contact - Specialty:
Mr. Randy Stefano, Branch Director - *Finance, accounting, banking, mortgage banking, human resource*

3333 Peachtree Rd NE
310 Atlanta Financial Ctr N
Atlanta, GA 30326
(404) 364-4660
Fax: (404) 364-4650
Email: jezabelcher@spherion.com
Key Contact - Specialty:
Mr. Mike Loftus, Branch Director - *Finance, accounting, banking, mortgage banking, human resource*

10 S Riverside Plz Ste 1570
Chicago, IL 60606
(312) 474-9140
Fax: (312) 474-9160
Email: billheafey@spherion.com
Key Contact - Specialty:
Ms. Tammy Mancl, Branch Director - *Finance, accounting, banking, mortgage banking, human resource*

450 E 96th St Ste 175
Indianapolis, IN 46240
(317) 815-6320
Fax: (317) 815-6344
Email: steveskillern@spherion.com
Key Contact - Specialty:
Mr. Steve Skillern, Branch Director - *Finance, accounting, banking, mortgage banking, human resource*

151 W St Ste 201
Annapolis, MD 21401
(410) 269-1092
Fax: (410) 269-1072
Email: johnruffini@spherion.com
Key Contact - Specialty:
Mr. John Ruffini, Branch Director - *Finance, accounting, banking, mortgage banking, human resource*

120 E Baltimore St Ste 2220
Baltimore, MD 21202
(410) 752-5244
Fax: (410) 752-5924
Email: trishspencer@interim.com
Web: www.spherion.com
Key Contact:
Mr. Carl A. J. Wright, Sr Vice President
Mr. Brendan Courtney, Area Director
Mr. Mitch Halbrich, Area Director - *Executive project consulting*
Mr. Craig Walker, Area Director
Mr. Mike Bettick, Area Director

4550 Montgomery Ave Ste 325 N
Bethesda, MD 20814
(301) 654-0082
Fax: (301) 653-1455
Email: rdhelt@spherion.com
Web: www.spherion.com
Key Contact - Specialty:
Mr. Michael Bettick, Area Director - *Finance, accounting, banking, mortgage banking, human resource*

9891 Broken Land Pkwy Ste 401
Woodmere 2
Columbia, MD 21046
(410) 290-5755
Fax: (410) 309-6029
Email: tomsabia@spherion.com
Key Contact - Specialty:
Mr. Thomas Sabia, Branch Director - *Finance, accounting, banking, mortgage banking, human resource*

100 E Big Beaver Rd Ste 330
Troy, MI 48083
(248) 689-5055
Fax: (248) 689-1730
Email: dougscott@spherion.com
Key Contact - Specialty:
Mr. Doug Scott, Branch Director - *Finance, accounting, banking, mortgage banking, human resource*

80 S Eighth St Ste 3939
IDS Ctr
Minneapolis, MN 55402
(612) 313-7997
Fax: (612) 313-7999
Email: davidbell@spherion.com
Key Contact - Specialty:
Mr. David Bell, Branch Director - *Finance, accounting, banking, mortgage banking, human resource*

12655 Olive Blvd Ste 390
Creve Coeur, MO 63141
(314) 205-8373
Fax: (314) 205-0167
Email: jeffreyklein@spherion.com
Key Contact - Specialty:
Mr. Jeff Klein, Branch Director - *Finance, accounting, banking, mortgage banking, human resource*

4 Century Dr Fl 1
Parsippany, NJ 07054
(973) 290-7881
Fax: (973) 290-0162
Email: faithpucci@spherion.com
Key Contact - Specialty:
Ms. Faith Pucci, Branch Director - *Finance, accounting, banking, mortgage banking, human resource*

6000 Fairview Rd Ste 550
Charlotte, NC 28210
(704) 643-7822
Fax: (704) 643-7078
Email: brianjohnson@spherion.com
Key Contact - Specialty:
Mr. Brian Johnson, Branch Director - *Finance, accounting, banking, mortgage banking, human resource*

4825 Creekstone Dr Ste 100
Overlook Bldg at Creekstone Park
Durham, NC 27703
(919) 474-8003
Fax: (919) 941-0073
Email: jeffscolnick@spherion.com
Key Contact - Specialty:
Mr. Jeff Scolnick, Branch Director - *Finance, accounting, banking, mortgage banking, human resource*

5151 Pfeiffer Rd Ste 120
Cincinnati, OH 45242
(513) 791-8600
Fax: (513) 792-6655
Email: larryhoelscher@spherion.com
Key Contact - Specialty:
Mr. Larry Hoelscher, Area Director - *Finance, accounting, banking, mortgage banking, human resource*

6120 Parkland Blvd
Cleveland, OH 44124
(440) 460-3200
Fax: (440) 460-3202
Email: cathyczaplicki@spherion.com
Key Contact - Specialty:
Mr. Mark Melfi, Branch Director - *Finance, accounting, banking, mortgage banking, human resource*

1070 Polaris Pkwy Ste 100
Columbus, OH 43240
(614) 888-0008
Fax: (614) 888-6172
Email: patriciadinunzio@spherion.com
Key Contact - Specialty:
Ms. Pat DiNunzio, Area Director - *Finance, accounting, banking, mortgage banking, human resource*

7887 Washington Village Dr Ste 200
Dayton, OH 45459
(937) 439-5501
Fax: (937) 439-5520
Email: yvonneproffitt@spherion.com
Web: www.spherion.com
Key Contact - Specialty:
Mr. Eric Sedwick, Branch Director - *Finance, accounting, banking, mortgage banking, human resource*

1760 Manley Rd
Maumee, OH 43537
(419) 893-2400
Fax: (419) 893-2491
Email: marygrappin@spherion.com

Key Contact - Specialty:
Mr. Scott Gearig, Branch Director - *Finance, accounting, banking, mortgage banking, human resource*

24950 Country Club Blvd Ste 370
North Olmsted, OH 44070
(440) 716-8905
Fax: (440) 716-8903
Email: stevetschan@spherion.com
Key Contact - Specialty:
Mr. Steve Tschan, Vice President - *Finance, accounting, banking, mortgage banking, human resource*

1150 1st Ave Ste 725
King of Prussia, PA 19406
(610) 337-0923
Fax: (610) 337-1147
Email: donitacalef@spherion.com
Key Contact - Specialty:
Ms. Donita Calef - *Finance, accounting, banking, mortgage banking, human resource*

155 Westminster St Ste 1250
Providence, RI 02903
(401) 272-1200
Fax: (401) 272-1201
Email: prgprovidence@spherion.com
Web: www.spherion.com
Key Contact - Specialty:
Ms. Michelle Antunes, Branch Director - *Finance, accounting, banking, mortgage banking, human resource*

110 W North St
Greenville, SC 29601
(864) 241-8000
Fax: (864) 241-8024
Email: markcrist@spherion.com
Key Contact - Specialty:
Mr. Mark Crist, Branch Director - *Finance, accounting, banking, mortgage banking, human resource*

5400 LBJ Fwy Ste 1520
One Lincoln Center
Dallas, TX 75240
(214) 691-9471
Fax: (214) 691-8976
Email: jmitchell@new.rr.com
Key Contact - Specialty:
Mr. Jack Mitchell, Vice President - *Finance, accounting, banking, mortgage banking, human resource*

2501 Parkview Dr Ste 520
Ft. Worth, TX 76102
(817) 332-8891
Fax: (817) 332-9721
Email: jmitchell@new.rr.com
Key Contact - Specialty:
Mr. Jack Mitchell, Vice President - *Finance, accounting, banking, mortgage banking, human resource*

5177 Richmond Ste 1070
Houston, TX 77056
(713) 965-9191
Fax: (713) 355-3549
Email: greghammond@spherion.com
Key Contact - Specialty:
Mr. Greg Hammond, Branch Director - *Finance, accounting, banking, engineering, manufacturing, sales & marketing*

1750 Tysons Blvd Ste 260
McLean, VA 22102
(703) 790-1100
Fax: (703) 790-1123
Email: ronsall@spherion.com
Key Contact - Specialty:
Mr. Ron Sall, Area Director - *Finance, accounting, banking, mortgage banking, human resource*

9020 Stoney Point Pkwy Ste 175
Stony Point II
Richmond, VA 23235
(804) 320-0500
Fax: (804) 327-7409

Email: richreinecke@spherion.com
Key Contact - Specialty:
Mr. Rich Reinecke, Branch Director - *Finance, accounting, banking, mortgage banking, human resource*

Kenn Spinrad Inc
3925 Perkiomen Ave
Reading, PA 19606
(610) 779-0944
Fax: (610) 779-8338
Email: kspinrad@ptd.net
Web: www.elecsp.com/kspin/kspin.htm

Description: We are a highly specialized contingency firm handling production/manufacturing only positions in the sewn products and textile industry, as well as the engineering and computer fields.

Key Contact - Specialty:
Ms. Sharon Spinrad, Vice President - *Apparel manufacturing, textile manufacturing*
Mr. Kenn Spinrad, President - *Home fashions manufacturing, mattress manufacturing*
Mr. James Thorpe, Executive Consultant - *Data processing, engineering*

Functions: Generalist, Senior Mgmt., Middle Mgmt., Production, Plant Mgmt., Purchasing, Materials Plng., MIS Mgmt.

Industries: Generalist, Textiles, Apparel, Metal Products, Machine, Appliance, HR Services, Software

Professional Associations: PAPS, RON

Networks: Top Echelon Network

Toby Spitz Associates Inc
110 E 59th St Fl 29
New York, NY 10022
(212) 319-0990
Fax: (212) 319-1555
Email: tobyspitz@jdsearch.com
Web: www.jdsearch.com

Description: Successor to Corporate Counsel Search, Inc., we place the following practice: corporate, regulatory, intellectual property, international, litigation, labor and employment, real estate, tax and benefits. Our clients are corporations and law firms.

Key Contact - Specialty:
Ms. Toby Spitz, President - *Legal*

Functions: Generalist, Attorneys

Industries: Generalist, Mfg., Finance, Legal, Biotech, Healthcare

Professional Associations: NALSC

Sprout/Standish Inc
82 Palomino Ln Ste 503
Bedford, NH 03110
(603) 622-0700
Fax: (603) 622-4172
Email: ssi@printquest.com
Web: www.printquest.com

Description: We are a highly specialized firm dedicated to serving the printing, publishing, packaging, and multimedia industry-only. Vertically and horizontally integrated, so as to allow complete coverage including senior executives, mid-management and top spots in the GAM top 100.

Key Contact - Specialty:
Mr. David A. Clark, Chairman/President - *Printing, pre-press, multimedia communication, sales, manufacturing*

Salary minimum: $60,000

Functions: Generalist

Industries: Mfg., Printing, Advertising, Publishing, New Media, Packaging

Squires Resources Inc

301 Bryne Dr Unit 6
Barrie, ON L4N 8V4
Canada
(705) 725-7660
(877) 435-0921
Fax: (705) 725-7665
Email: info@squiresresources.com
Web: www.squiresresources.com

Description: We offer a unique insight into career opportunities available for IT and financial/accounting professionals particularly in Bermuda, secondaries in Cayman, Bahamas, and Canada.

Key Contact:
Mr. Frank Squires, President - *Information systems, accounting*
Mr. David White, Consultant - *Information systems*
Ms. Jocelyn Squires, Consultant
Ms. Rebekah d'Amboise, Consultant
Mr. David Squires, Consultant

Salary minimum: $40,000

Functions: Generalist, Sales Mgmt., Systems Analysis, Systems Dev., Systems Implem., Systems Support, Network Admin., DB Admin.

Industries: Generalist, Computer Equip., Accounting, E-commerce, IT Implementation, New Media, Telecoms, Wireless, Fiber Optic, Network Infrastructure, Software

Networks: National Personnel Assoc (NPA)

Staff Extension Int'l

13612 Midway Ste 103
Dallas, TX 75244
(972) 991-4737
Fax: (972) 991-5325
Email: dallas@staffext.com
Web: www.staffext.com

Description: We are experienced in providing corporations with customized executive search services, professional and executive contract placements, human resources and executive staffing.

Key Contact - Specialty:
Mr. Jack R. Williams, President/CEO - *Executive, human resources*
Mr. Wes Gross, Senior Vice President - *Sales & marketing, human resources, executive*

Salary minimum: $30,000

Functions: General Mgmt., Healthcare, Sales & Mktg., HR Mgmt., Training, Finance, IT, Engineering

Industries: Generalist

Professional Associations: IPA, RON, SHRM

Networks: Top Echelon Network

Branches:
3300 S Gessner Ste 252
Houston, TX 77063
(713) 784-8696
Fax: (713) 784-5131
Email: houston@staffext.com
Key Contact - Specialty:
Mr. Bob Tann, Managing Principal - *Executive, human resources, organizational development, training*

Staff Resources Inc

130 E Main St
PO Box 4557
Rock Hill, SC 29732-6557
(803) 366-0500
Fax: (803) 366-1021
Email: sri@srijobs.com
Web: www.srijobs.com

Description: We specialize in manufacturing and all functions that support a manufacturing facility. Most all of our clients are Fortune 500 firms and are located all over the world. Many of our clients are located in the Southeast and have excellent benefits and relocation packages. We are members of NPA, an international network of over 1500 recruiters from around the world.

Key Contact - Specialty:
Mr. Dick Jordan, Senior Partner - *Manufacturing, human resources, quality, finance, materials*
Mr. Jeff Jordan, Director Business Development - *Sales & marketing, finance, information systems, operations, human resources*
Mr. Casey Hamilton, Senior Recruiter - *Engineering, purchasing, materials, operations management, quality*
Ms. Sandy Hamilton, Senior Recruiter - *Human resources, manufacturing, engineering, purchasing, materials*
Ms. Carol Dodd, Research Assistant - *Manufacturing, engineering, IS/IT, human resources, purchasing*
Mr. Richard Pitt, Sr Recruiter - *Materials, purchasing, manufacturing*

Salary minimum: $25,000

Functions: Generalist

Industries: Mfg., Transportation, Finance, Accounting, Equip Svcs., Mgmt. Consulting, HR Services, Hospitality, Telecoms, Packaging

Professional Associations: APICS, NAPM, SCAPS, SHRM

Networks: National Personnel Assoc (NPA)

Staffcity.com Inc

700 Canal St
Stamford, CT 06902
(203) 328-3027
Fax: (203) 328-3028
Email: dardrey@staffcity.com
Web: www.staffcity.com

Description: We are an executive recruiting and contract staffing firm specializing in accounting and financial professionals. We offer permanent placement and contract assignments.

Key Contact - Specialty:
Mr. Douglas Ardrey, President - *Accounting & finance*

Salary minimum: $50,000

Functions: Finance

Industries: Generalist

Staffing Advantage Inc

3020 Westchester Ave Ste 309
Purchase, NY 10577
(914) 251-0688
Fax: (914) 251-0699
Email: jobs@staffing-advantage.com
Web: www.staffing-advantage.com

Description: A full-service staffing agency, we provide a full range of temporary and permanent placement services. Our areas of specialization include administrative/secretarial, accounting, customer service, human resources, marketing, sales and many more. We represent Fortune 500 corporations in Westchester, Connecticut and NY City.

Key Contact:
Ms. Lynda Greenbaum, President
Mr. Robert Greenbaum, Vice President

Professional Associations: ASA, NYATSS

Staffing Now Inc

4600 W Town Pkwy Ste 113
Regency West 6
West Des Moines, IA 50266
(515) 222-6350
Fax: (515) 222-6360
Email: corporate@staffingnow.com
Web: www.staffingnow.com

Description: We are a premier employment firm, specializing in the placement of permanent and temporary accounting, office clerical, information technology, and legal professionals within organizations. We are directed by professionals with years of experience in the management of multi-state temporary and permanent placement companies. This experience and professionalism have made our company such a success.

Key Contact:
Mr. Mark Schaul, CFO
Mr. Ron Smith, CEO

Functions: General Mgmt., Legal, Materials, Sales & Mktg., HR Mgmt., Finance, IT, Attorneys, Paralegals

Industries: Generalist

Professional Associations: ASA

Branches:
98 Mill Plain Rd
Danbury, CT 06811
(203) 744-6020
Fax: (203) 744-6270
Email: dantemps@cssit.com
Key Contact:
Mr. Jeff Schneider, Regional Manager

1077 Bridgeport Ave
Shelton, CT 06484
(203) 929-5771
Fax: (203) 929-5515
Email: shelton@cssit.com
Key Contact:
Mr. Jeff Schneider, Regional Manager

1062 Barnes Rd Ste 105
Wallingford, CT 06492
(203) 265-1946
Fax: (203) 294-6334
Email: info@cssit.com
Key Contact:
Mr. Jeff Schneider, Regional Manager

433 S Main St Ste 108
West Hartford, CT 06110
(860) 561-1952
Fax: (860) 561-9755
Email: whtemps@cssit.com
Key Contact:
Mr. Jeff Schneider, Regional Manager

1101 Connecticut Ave NW Ste 1250
Washington, DC 20036
(202) 429-2244
Fax: (202) 429-8717
Email: dc@friendsandcompany.com
Key Contact:
Mr. Mark Roush, Regional Manager

7000 W Palmetto Park Rd Ste 110
Boca Raton, FL 33433-3430
(561) 392-0202
Fax: (561) 362-6448
Email: boca@staffingnow.com
Key Contact:
Mr. Harland Medford, Regional Manager

1901 S Congress Ave Ste 118
Boynton Beach, FL 33426
(561) 742-3776
Fax: (561) 742-9470
Email: boynton@staffingnow.com
Key Contact:
Mr. Harlan Medford, Regional Manager

25400 US 19 N Ste 203
Clearwater, FL 33763-2144
(727) 797-5859
Fax: (727) 669-6107
Email: clearwater@staffingnow.com
Key Contact:
Mr. Harlan Medford, Regional Manager

1 Financial Plz Ste 2512
Ft. Lauderdale, FL 33396
(954) 524-7780
Fax: (954) 524-3067
Email: ftlauderdale@staffingnow.com
Key Contact:
Mr. Harlan Medford, Regional Manager

4786 W Commercial Blvd
Ft. Lauderdale, FL 33319-2878
(954) 735-5392
Fax: (954) 735-5418
Email: ftlauderdale@staffingnow.com
Key Contact:
Mr. Harlan Medford, Regional Manager

800 Corporate Dr Ste 206
Ft. Lauderdale, FL 33334
(954) 772-7177
Fax: (954) 772-4452
Email: ftlauderdale@staffingnow.com
Key Contact:
Mr. Harlan Medford, Regional Manager

12515 N Kendall Dr Ste 216
Miami, FL 33186-1830
(305) 270-1338
Fax: (305) 270-3212
Email: kendall@staffingnow.com
Key Contact:
Mr. Harlan Medford, Regional Manager

1390 Brickell Ave Ste 104
Miami, FL 33131-3320
(305) 358-1333
Fax: (305) 358-8884
Email: miami@staffingnow.com
Key Contact:
Mr. Harlan Medford, Regional Manager

3900 NW 79th Ave Ste 222
Miami, FL 33166
(305) 471-7737
Fax: (305) 471-9733
Email: doral@staffingnow.com
Key Contact:
Mr. Harlan Medford, Regional Manager

3300 PGA Blvd Ste 625
Palm Beach Gardens, FL 33410-2821
(561) 691-0202
Fax: (561) 691-0492
Email: westpalm@staffingnow.com
Key Contact:
Mr. Harlan Medford, Regional Manager

9050 Pines Blvd Ste 190
Pembroke Pines, FL 33024-6415
(954) 437-0094
Fax: (954) 437-1385
Email: pembrokepines@staffingnow.com
Key Contact:
Mr. Harlan Medford, Regional Manager

300 S Pine Island Rd Ste 3032
Plantation, FL 33324-2621
(954) 370-4700
Fax: (954) 370-3507
Email: plantation@staffingnow.com
Key Contact:
Mr. Harlan Medford, Regional Manager

9887 4th St N Ste 228
St. Petersburg, FL 33702
(727) 577-4294
Fax: (727) 577-6040
Email: stpete@staffingnow.com
Key Contact:
Mr. Harlan Medford, Regional Manager

2002 N Lois Ave Ste 110
Tampa, FL 33607-2366
(813) 870-3801
Fax: (813) 870-3959
Email: tampa@staffingnow.com
Key Contact:
Mr. Harlan Medford, Regional Manager

2090 Palm Beach Lakes Blvd Ste 502
West Palm Beach, FL 33409-6507
(561) 686-9306
Fax: (561) 640-0656
Email: westpalm@staffingnow.com
Key Contact:
Mr. Harlan Medford, Regional Manager

750 W Lake Cook Rd Ste 160
Buffalo Grove, IL 60089
(847) 325-2980
Fax: (847) 325-2984
Email: buffalogrove@staffingnow.com
Key Contact:
Ms. Bonny Koffler, Regional Manager

125 S Wacker Dr Ste 305
Chicago, IL 60606
(312) 214-7135
Fax: (312) 214-7136
Email: acctg83@staffingnow.com
Key Contact:
Ms. Bonny Koffler, Regional Manager

5440 N Cumberland Ste A-135
Chicago, IL 60656
(773) 693-8510
Fax: (773) 693-8515
Email: ohare@staffingnow.com
Key Contact:
Ms. Bonny Koffler, Regional Manager

1827 Walden Office Sq Ste 325
Schaumburg, IL 60173
(847) 925-8210
Fax: (847) 925-8215
Email: schaumburg@staffingnow.com
Key Contact:
Ms. Bonny Koffler, Regional Manager

20251 Century Blvd Fl 4
Germantown, MD 20874
(301) 428-3789
Fax: (301) 428-3166
Email: grm@friendsandcompany.com
Key Contact:
Mr. Mark Roush, Regional Manager

194 Cabot St
Beverly, MA 01915
(978) 927-4194
Fax: (978) 927-6907
Email: beverly@staffingnow.com
Key Contact:
Mr. Jon Samuels, Regional Manager

126-G Northampton St
Easthampton, MA 01027
(413) 529-7100
Fax: (413) 529-2209
Email: ehtemps@cssit.com
Key Contact:
Mr. Jon Samuels, Regional Manager

100 Erdman Way Ste 202
Leominster, MA 01453
(978) 534-2422
Fax: (978) 534-2424
Email: leominster@staffingnow.com
Key Contact:
Mr. Jon Samuels, Regional Manager

1226 Merrimack St
Methuen, MA 01844
(978) 688-9003
Fax: (978) 688-2098
Email: methuen@staffingnow.com
Key Contact:
Mr. Jon Samuels, Regional Manager

19 Cummings Park
Woburn, MA 01801
(781) 938-8247
Fax: (781) 932-8622
Email: woburn@staffingnow.com
Key Contact:
Mr. Jon Samuels, Regional Manager

125 Village Blvd Ste 330
Princeton, NJ 08540
(609) 452-0287
Fax: (609) 452-0289
Email: njtemps@staffingnow.com
Key Contact:
Ms. Laurie Knafo, Regional Manager

11150 Sunset Hills Rd Ste 140
Reston, VA 20190
(703) 796-0333
Fax: (703) 796-0688
Email: res@friendsandcompany.com
Key Contact:
Mr. Mark Roush, Regional Manager

6564 Loisdale Rd Ste 1020
Springfield, VA 22150
(703) 313-0121
Fax: (703) 313-7161
Email: spf@friendsandcompany.com
Key Contact:
Mr. Mark Roush, Regional Manager

Staffing Solutions USA Inc

370 Lexington Ave Ste 2110
New York, NY 10017
(212) 972-5100
Fax: (212) 972-1377
Email: cisusa@aol.com
Web: www.staffingsolutionsusa.com

Description: Specializing in all levels of
information technology. From CIO/Director level to
computer operations. Permanent placement and
consulting.

Key Contact:
Mr. Cliff Shaw, President

Salary minimum: $35,000

Functions: IT, MIS Mgmt., Systems Dev., Systems
Implem., Systems Support, Network Admin., DB
Admin.

Industries: Generalist

Staffing USA

PO Box 310863
Birmingham, AL 35231
(205) 648-2300
(800) 648-2301
Fax: (205) 648-4400
Email: careers@staffingusa.net
Web: www.staffingusa.net

Description: National Firm that specializes in
Information Technology, Engineering, and
Accountants.

Key Contact - Specialty:
Mrs. Mary Nell Blackburn, Owner - *Information
technology, engineering, accounting*

Networks: Top Echelon Network

Staffingit Inc

4880 Lower Roswell Rd Ste 40 Rm 230
Marietta, GA 30068-4375
(770) 645-6665
Email: paul@staffingit.com
Web: www.staffingit.com

Description: We are staffing technical and sales
professionals throughout the US.

Key Contact:
Mr. Paul Lipman, CPC

Salary minimum: $50,000

Functions: Product Dev., Sales & Mktg., Systems
Analysis, Systems Dev.

Industries: E-commerce, IT Implementation,
Communications, Telecoms, Call Centers,
Telephony, Wireless, Software, Database SW,
Development SW, Doc. Mgmt., Production SW,
ERP SW

Professional Associations: GAPS

Staffopolis Inc

(formerly known as eCommerce Staffing Inc)
7251 W Lake Mead Blvd Ste 300
Las Vegas, NV 89128
(702) 947-4720
Email: bh@staffopolis.com
Web: www.staffopolis.com

Description: Our firm is the central place for all of your permanent or contract sales, IT, e-Commerce, executive, and software and hardware engineer staffing needs. Staffopolis makes extensive use of human touch and multimedia technology, such as SeeMyJob for job seekers and SeeMyInterview services for clients to reduce your cost of hire. Our clients can hear or see the applicant initial screening interview responses using our multimedia services. Our services are high quality to win your repeat business. Our firm is proud of its zero fall-off performance record. We cover the US and Canada.

Key Contact:
Mr. Bruce Hiatt, CEO
Mr. Simon Chen, CFO
Mrs. Sandi Borba, Manager of Recruiting Services

Salary minimum: $65,000

Functions: Generalist

Industries: Generalist

Professional Associations: IBAII, IHRIM, NDA, SHRM, TVG

Networks: National Personnel Assoc (NPA)

C J Stafford & Associates

2323 Yonge St Ste 501
Toronto, ON M4P 2C9
Canada
(416) 484-1960
Fax: (416) 484-0626
Email: cjstaff@cjstafford.com
Web: www.cjstafford.com

Description: We are industry-focused specialists in search and selection for international mining/metals and construction/engineering companies and those service industries associated with them.

Key Contact - Specialty:
Mr. Chris Stafford, President - *Mining, metals, heavy industrial, engineering, construction*
Mr. Vince Keenan, Senior Recruiting Consultant - *Building, construction*
Mr. Keith Labbett, Senior Recruiter
Ms. Tara Wooller, Senior Researcher - *Mining, metals*
Mr. Nat Scott, Senior Consultant - *Open pit mining, underground mining*
Mr. Rhys Goodall, Senior Recruiter - *Metallurgical, mineral processing, maintenance, mechanical, human resources*
Mr. Charles Sharpe - *Construction, building, utilities, civil engineering*

Salary minimum: $50,000

Functions: Generalist, Directors, Senior Mgmt., IT, Engineering, Environmentalists, Int'l.

Industries: Generalist, Agri., Forestry, Mining, Energy, Utilities, Construction, Brokers, Hospitality

Professional Associations: CIMM, NPA, PDAC

StaffWriters Plus

2150 Joshua's Path Ste 102
Hauppauge, NY 11788
(631) 582-9000
Fax: (631) 582-8828
Email: info@staffwriters.com
Web: www.staffwriters.com

Description: We offer access to the country's best writers and editors in more than 200 highly specialized areas. We offer temporary and permanent placement and a free job board on our web site. We also supply publishers in all industries with content, especially special sections for newspapers.

Key Contact:
Mr. George Giokas, President/CEO - *Writers, editors*
Mr. Andrew Sherman, Vice President

Functions: Admin. Svcs., Healthcare, Sales & Mktg., Mkt. Research, Direct Mktg., PR, Training, IT, Specialized Svcs., Graphic Artists

Industries: Generalist, Media, Advertising, Publishing, New Media, Broadcast, Film, Hospitals

Professional Associations: LISTNET, NYATSS, SHRM

Stamm Personnel Agency Inc

27 Whitehall St Ste 500
New York, NY 10004
(212) 509-6600
Fax: (212) 509-3773
Email: pstamm@stammagency.com
Web: www.stammagency.findhere.com

Description: We have been in the employment business for more than 30 years. Our recruiting expertise is recognized throughout the financial community with special emphasis on Wall Street assignments. We have maintained meaningful relationships with both broker/dealers and institutions, from the very large to the specialist or boutique firms.

Key Contact:
Mr. Peter W. Stamm, President
Mr. Arthur J. Barbato, Vice President

Salary minimum: $20,000

Functions: Finance

Industries: Wholesale, Retail, Finance, Services, Telecoms, Software, Biotech, Healthcare, Non-classifiable

Morgan Stampfl Inc

2 Penn Plz Ste 1500
New York, NY 10121
(212) 292-5098
Fax: (212) 292-5097
Web: www.morganstampfl.com

Description: An executive search firm specializing in middle and senior-level assignments in investment and commercial banking.

Key Contact - Specialty:
Mr. David G. Morgan - *Capital markets, corporate finance*
Mr. Eric Stampfl - *Capital markets, corporate finance*

Salary minimum: $50,000

Functions: Generalist

Industries: Banking, Invest. Banking

Stanewick, Hart & Associates Inc

7829 Briarcreek Rd
Tallahassee, FL 32312-3661
(850) 893-7849

Description: In-depth recruiting and search in technical development for the logistics and telecommunications industry. Technical programmers through management. Management mostly by search and Southeast U.S. preferably.

Key Contact - Specialty:
Mr. David Hunter, Vice President - *Data processing, big 6 (accounting, consulting firms)*
Mr. B. David Stanewick, President - *Data processing, logistics industry, power generation utility companies*

Salary minimum: $30,000

Functions: Generalist, Directors, Systems Analysis, Systems Implem., Network Admin., DB Admin., Mgmt. Consultants

Industries: Generalist, Mgmt. Consulting, Software, Non-classifiable

Professional Associations: DPMA

The Stanton Group Inc

374 E Marseilles St
Vernon Hills, IL 60061
(847) 955-0540
Fax: (847) 955-0541
Email: keister@stantongp.com
Web: www.stantongp.com

Description: Our small-size enables us to offer excellent personal service to both clients and candidates. We are proud that our clients are among the leaders in software technologies.

Key Contact - Specialty:
Mr. John Keister, Partner - *Software engineering*
Ms. Beth Keister, Partner - *Software quality*

Salary minimum: $60,000

Functions: Generalist, IT, MIS Mgmt., Systems Dev., Systems Implem., Systems Support, R&D, Engineering

Industries: Generalist, Motor Vehicles, Computer Equip., Consumer Elect., Telecoms, Software

Professional Associations: ASQ, SAE

Star Search Consultants

211 Consumers Rd Ste 204
Toronto, ON M2J 4G8
Canada
(416) 491-4440
Fax: (416) 491-4451
Email: star@searchstar.com
Web: www.searchstar.com

Description: We are the one-stop recruitment center for all your personnel requirements. We recruit on a contingency and executive search basis for positions in accounting/finance, administration/management, engineering/technical, insurance, MIS/IT, sales/marketing, and transportation/logistics

Key Contact:
Mr. John Weiss, CPC

Functions: Generalist, General Mgmt., Mfg., Materials, Sales & Mktg., Finance, Engineering

Industries: Generalist, Mfg., Transportation, Aerospace, Packaging, Insurance

Networks: National Personnel Assoc (NPA)

Starbridge Group Inc

(also known as Sales Consultants of Fairfax)
10801 Main St Ste 500
Fairfax, VA 22030-4744
(703) 691-3900
Fax: (703) 691-3999
Email: web@starbridgegroup.com
Web: www.starbridgegroup.com

Description: Industry segmented specialization in order to provide added value and expertise to our clients. We aggressively deliver on our commitments to our clients with high integrity and professionalism. We specialize in permanent and project based placement at mid-level to senior-level professionals.

Key Contact - Specialty:
Mr. David S. Kurke, President - *Training, consulting, multimedia*

Functions: Generalist, Senior Mgmt., Sales & Mktg., Sales Mgmt., Training, Mgmt. Consultants

Industries: Generalist, Services, Non-profits, Higher Ed., Pharm Svcs., Mgmt. Consulting, HR

Services, E-commerce, IT Implementation, PSA/ASP, New Media, HR SW, Training SW

Professional Associations: ASQ, ASTD

StarDot PRG Inc

633 - 6 Ave SW Ste 2020
Calgary, AB T2P 2Y5
Canada
(403) 264-3897
Fax: (403) 264-3901
Email: jobs@stardotprg.com
Web: www.stardotprg.com

Description: From our thousands of pre-screened information technology professionals, we provide a short list of qualified people for your permanent or contract position.

Key Contact - Specialty:
Mr. Don Van Mierlo, President - *Information technology*
Ms. Alice Matthews, Vice President-Recruiting/Administration - *information technology*

Functions: Generalist, IT

Industries: Generalist

Stargate Group

(also known as MRI & Sales Consultants of Goodyear)
250 N Litchfield Rd Ste 230
Goodyear Financial Ctr
Goodyear, AZ 85338
(623) 536-7136
Fax: (623) 536-7138
Email: rjb@princeton.mrinet.com

Description: Provides professional consultative services at senior executive-levels regarding strategic and tactical planning interpretation into quantitative and qualitative human resource requirements to achieve goals as part of the executive search services.

Key Contact:
Mr. Robert J. Bodnar, President - *Energy, management consulting*
Ms. Beverly H. Bodnar, Co-Manager

Salary minimum: $70,000

Functions: Generalist, Senior Mgmt., Middle Mgmt., Sales & Mktg., Finance, IT, Engineering, Mgmt. Consultants

Industries: Generalist, Energy, Utilities, Finance, Banking, Invest. Banking, Mgmt. Consulting, Biotech

Starpoint Solutions

115 Broadway Fl 20
New York, NY 10006
(212) 962-1550
Fax: (212) 962-7175
Email: info@starpoint.com
Web: www.starpoint.com

Description: For more than a decade, we have been finding experienced IT talent for contract and permanent positions for major corporations like Chase, Citigroup, Ernst & Young, Merrill Lynch, and Gillette. We have recruiters nationwide with extensive training to find you the talented technology professionals you need. Rely on us.

Key Contact - Specialty:
Mr. Bob Gold, CEO - *Technology professionals*
Mr. Jeffrey Najarian, Chairman - *Technology professionals*

Functions: Generalist, MIS Mgmt., Systems Analysis, Systems Dev., Systems Implem., Systems Support

Industries: Generalist, Finance, E-commerce, IT Implementation, Media, Communications, Software

Professional Associations: ETC, NJTC

Marjorie Starr & Associates

PO Box 41024
Mesa, AZ 85274-1059
(480) 730-6050
Fax: (480) 730-6292
Email: mstarr273@aol.com

Description: We are proud to say that we have assisted thousands of candidates and hundreds of clients over the last twenty years. Our mission is to bring higher quality and a personal level of professional service to both our clients and candidates.

Key Contact - Specialty:
Ms. Marjorie Starr, CPC, Certified Personnel Consultant - *Sales, technical*

Functions: Sales & Mktg., Sales Mgmt.

Industries: Generalist, Pharm Svcs., HR Services, Communications, Telecoms, Telephony, Wireless, Software, HR SW, Marketing SW

Professional Associations: CPC

Fern G Stasiuk Executive Search Inc

880 S Lake Blvd Putnam Professional Park
Mahopac, NY 10541
(845) 621-2966
Fax: (845) 621-7067
Email: fernfgs@bestweb.net
Web: www.bestweb.net/~fernfgs

Description: Executive search specialists with over 16 years in the telecommunications and emerging technologies industries. We offer expertise in the identification and screening of sales, marketing and general management talent nationwide.

Key Contact - Specialty:
Ms. Fern Stasiuk, President - *Telecommunications, data communications, emerging technologies*

Salary minimum: $90,000

Functions: Generalist

Industries: Telecoms

STAT Search

7 Colby Ct 4
PMB 204
Bedford, NH 03110
(603) 666-5500
(877) 623-5321
Fax: (603) 623-5322
Email: hunter@statsearch.com
Web: www.statsearch.com

Description: We conduct nationwide searches and have satisfied clients across the country. We specialize in e-health, healthcare and call center search. We listen to your needs and provide well screened candidates in an efficient and timely manner. These candidates are not only able to do your job, but want to do it and will enjoy your corporate culture.

Key Contact - Specialty:
Ms. Dale Poklemba, MS, Principal/Founder - *Healthcare, e health, pharmaceutical staffing*
Ms. Jill Mooney, MBA, Principal - *Healthcare, call centers*
Ms. Kimberly Caron, Principal - *Medical software, e-commerce*
Ms. Mary Comerford, Principal - *Healthcare*
Ms. Victoria Travis, Principal - *Healthcare*

Salary minimum: $50,000

Functions: General Mgmt., Directors, Senior Mgmt., Middle Mgmt., Healthcare, Nurses, Allied Health, Health Admin., Mktg. Mgmt., CFO's

Industries: Generalist, Healthcare

Professional Associations: CMSA, NNEAPS

Branches:
3140 S Peoria
PMB 293
Aurora, CO 80014-3155
(720) 535-6433
Email: victoria@statsearch.com
Key Contact:
Ms. Victoria Travis, Principal

356 Rea St
North Andover, MA 01845
(603) 666-5500
Email: kimberly@statsearch.com
Key Contact:
Ms. Kimberly Caron, Principal

31 Daniel Webster Hwy Ste 322
Nashua, NH 03062
(603) 897-0770
Email: jill@statsearch.com
Key Contact:
Ms. Jill Mooney, Principal

95 Windermere Ave
PO Box 1808
Greenwood Lake, NY 10925
(845) 477-0400
Email: mary@statsearch.com
Key Contact:
Ms. Mary Comerford, Principal

Stebbins & Associates

520 N Lincoln Way Ste 2
Galt, CA 95632
(209) 744-2003
Fax: (209) 744-1718
Email: resumes@greengrads.com
Web: www.greengrads.com

Description: We are an executive search firm serving clients in agri-business, horticulture and turf industries.

Key Contact - Specialty:
Mr. Steve Stebbins, President - *Sales & marketing*

Salary minimum: $50,000

Functions: General Mgmt., Materials, Sales & Mktg., CFO's

Industries: Agri., Forestry, Mining

Steele & Associates

4347 W Northwest Hwy Ste 120-115
Dallas, TX 75220
(214) 351-6363
Fax: (214) 351-4688
Email: ncarey@steeleassoc.com
Web: www.steeleassoc.com

Description: We conduct professional and thorough searches for attorneys and legal assistants to meet the needs of its clients, and to present quality employment opportunities to attorneys and legal assistants. We have more than 12 years of experience in the legal search business.

Key Contact:
Ms. Nancy Steele Carey, President

Functions: Legal

Industries: Generalist

Steinbach & Company

6 Dana Rd
Maynard, MA 01754
(978) 857-8661
(978) 897-8661
Fax: (978) 897-8661
Email: hrconsult@usa.net
Web: www.hrdotcom.com

Description: We provide architect and implement staffing and retention solutions in advanced high-technology environments. We have over twenty years of recruiting and search experience. We place source software and hardware technologists, consultants, and management, who are experienced in e-Business, ASIC, XML, ASP, OOP, multimedia, RT, Internet/www, DB, OPSYS, Windows, MIS/IT, MPP, investment, insurance, and financial.

Key Contact - Specialty:
Mr. David M. Steinbach, CPC, Owner - *MIS, scientific software, hardware technologists, managers, information technology*

Salary minimum: $75,000

Functions: Generalist

Industries: Computer Equip., Test, Measure Equip., Mgmt. Consulting, HR Services, Media, New Media, Digital, Wireless, Government, Software

Professional Associations: ACM, AIRS, IEEE, NAPS

Steinfield & Associates
2626 Cole Ave Ste 400
Dallas, TX 75204
(214) 220-0535
Fax: (214) 665-9535
Email: steinfield@airmail.net

Description: We are an executive search firm specializing in the placement of finance, accounting, consulting, audit, tax, and human resources professionals.

Key Contact - Specialty:
Mr. David Steinfield, President - *Finance, accounting, consulting, audit, human resources*

Salary minimum: $70,000

Functions: HR Mgmt., Benefits, Personnel, Finance, CFO's, Budgeting, Cash Mgmt., Taxes, M&A, Mgmt. Consultants

Industries: Generalist

The Stelton Group Inc
904 Oak Tree Rd Ste A
South Plainfield, NJ 07080
(908) 757-9888
Fax: (908) 757-3179
Email: steltongroup@msn.com
Web: www.steltongroup.com

Description: Industry specific recruiting of professional and executive candidates for all industries.

Key Contact - Specialty:
Mr. Al Lewis, President - *Engineering, plastic, medical devices*
Ms. Alexia Sulish, Account Executive - *Human resources, finance, marketing & sales*
Ms. Cindy L. Slusser, Account Executive - *Scientific, information technology*

Functions: Generalist

Industries: Generalist

Professional Associations: MAAPC, NJASP

Networks: Top Echelon Network

A Stephens & Associates
PO Box 14154
Springfield, MO 65814-0154
(417) 886-4114
Fax: (417) 886-5962
Email: info@stephensrecruiters.com
Web: www.stephensrecruiters.com

Description: Our firm is a nationwide executive search firm in the pharmaceutical, biotech and medical device industries. We develop effective recruitment strategies tailored to meet our client's specific needs.

Key Contact:
Ms. Angela Stephens, President

Functions: Generalist, Directors, Senior Mgmt., Middle Mgmt., Quality, Mkt. Research, Mktg. Mgmt., Sales Mgmt.

Industries: Generalist, Drugs Mfg., Medical Devices, Pharm Svcs., Advertising, Healthcare

Professional Associations: RON

Stephens Int'l Recruiting Inc
171 Helton Rd
Lakeview, AR 72642
(870) 431-5485
Fax: (870) 431-5489
Email: dstephens@bmets-usa.com
Web: www.bmets-usa.com

Description: Located in Lakeview, Arkansas, we are a health care technical recruiting firm of executive-level consultants with diverse experience and background in health care support services. We became a well-known resource for finding quality technicians, as well as providing individual counseling/consultation for career development in the biomedical equipment field for technicians and managers.

Key Contact - Specialty:
Ms. Cindy Stephens, Chief Executive Officer - *Clinical engineering*

Salary minimum: $50,000

Networks: National Personnel Assoc (NPA)

Sterling Int'l Business Partners Inc
PO Box 18201
Greensboro, NC 27410
(336) 218-0339
Fax: (336) 218-5116

Description: Achieving excellence through quality people we provide a full candidate consolidated file to the hiring company prior to on-site interviewing.

Key Contact - Specialty:
Ms. Joanna Williams Campbell, President - *Generalist*
Ms. K. J. Campbell, Vice President - *Generalist*

Salary minimum: $60,000

Functions: Generalist

Industries: Mfg., Mgmt. Consulting, Media, Packaging

Sterling Systems Inc
2525 Greentech Dr Ste D
State College, PA 16801
(814) 234-1747
Fax: (814) 234-1749
Email: jteeter@sterlingsys.com
Web: www.sterlingsys.com

Description: Business strategy, information systems technology, process engineering, re-engineering and change management.

Key Contact:
Mr. John Evans, President

Functions: Generalist, General Mgmt., Mfg., Sales & Mktg., IT, Mgmt. Consultants

Industries: Generalist, Energy, Utilities, Mfg., Wholesale, Retail, Finance, Services, Media

Daniel Stern & Associates
228 Isabella St
The Osterling Bldg
Pittsburgh, PA 15212
(412) 323-3636
(800) 438-2476
Fax: (800) 892-2781
Email: sternd@danielstern.com
Web: www.danielstern.com

Description: Twenty-five years of specialized physician recruiting, healthcare administration and consulting services including practice set-up and enhancement, maximizing revenues, practice sales

and acquisitions, contract development, negotiations and billing services.

Key Contact - Specialty:
Mr. Daniel Stern, Chairman - *Physician specialties (all), hospital administration, nursing administration, healthcare technical (MIS)*

Salary minimum: $75,000

Functions: Physicians

Industries: Healthcare

Professional Associations: ACHE, HFMA

Stern Professional Search
680 N Lake Shore Dr Ste 607
Lake Twr
Chicago, IL 60611
(312) 587-7777
Fax: (312) 587-8907
Email: jg@sternprosearch.com
Web: www.sternprosearch.com

Description: Furniture and interior design industry, contract furniture, office furniture, hospitality, health care, residential furniture, lighting, signage, textiles, carpeting, wallcovering, flooring. Positions include vice presidents, national accounts, sales, marketing, administrative, customer service, engineers, interior designers, architects, project managers and facility managers. Clients: architectural firms, interior design firms, manufacturers and dealerships.

Key Contact - Specialty:
Ms. Janet Grodsky, President - *Furniture, design*

Salary minimum: $50,000

Functions: Generalist, Senior Mgmt., Middle Mgmt., Plant Mgmt., Sales & Mktg., Sales Mgmt., Architects, Graphic Artists

Industries: Generalist, Mfg., Textiles, Apparel, Lumber, Furniture, Leather, Stone, Glass, Misc. Mfg.

Ron Stevens & Associates Inc
4501 Galloway Blvd
Bradenton, FL 34210-2949
(800) 458-1611
Fax: (800) 458-1611
Email: rsa-inc@worldnet.att.net

Description: We are a contingency search firm concentrating in the recruitment and placement of middle- and senior-level management executives for the chemical, retail, utilities/energy, and management consulting business.

Key Contact - Specialty:
Mr. Ron Stevens, President - *Technical (sales, service)*

Salary minimum: $65,000

Functions: General Mgmt., Middle Mgmt., Sales & Mktg., Mktg. Mgmt.

Industries: Generalist, Energy, Utilities, Mfg., Chemicals, Drugs Mfg., Plastics, Rubber, Paints, Petro. Products, Metal Products, Consumer Elect., Retail, Mgmt. Consulting, Mfg. SW, Marketing SW

Professional Associations: TAPPI

Stevens Associates
65 Forest St Ste 3
Marshfield, MA 02050-2818
(781) 834-0800
Fax: (781) 837-8044
Email: wjstevens@fastdial.net

Description: Our firm is a software, network, computer, and allied high-tech industry specialist. We primarily focus on senior-levels of marketing, business development, sales, executive management and technical support personnel.

Key Contact - Specialty:
Mr. Wayne J. Stevens, Principal - *High technology, marketing & sales*

Salary minimum: $60,000

Functions: Generalist, Advertising, Mkt. Research, Mktg. Mgmt., Sales Mgmt., Direct Mktg., PR, Systems Support

Industries: Generalist, Computer Equip., Test, Measure Equip., New Media, Telecoms, Software

Networks: Top Echelon Network

The Stevens Grp
Warner Ctr Plz
PO Box 367
Woodland Hills, CA 91365
(818) 712-0242
Fax: (818) 712-0325
Email: stevensgroup@earthlink.net

Description: We are a boutique executive search practice committed to excellence and results. We are proud of our long-standing client and candidate relationships based on a high degree of integrity and personal involvement. All of our new alliances are a result of client referrals. Our clients appreciate our reputation for integrity, honesty, and high completion ratio on engagements.

Key Contact:
Ms. Martha Stevens, President

Salary minimum: $50,000

Functions: Generalist

Industries: Mfg., Wholesale, Retail, Finance, Accounting, Mgmt. Consulting, Hospitality, Packaging, Software, Biotech

Professional Associations: IMA

Stewart Associates
181 Windover Turn
Lancaster, PA 17601
(717) 299-9242
Fax: (717) 299-4879
Email: waltp@redrose.net

Description: Broad range of recruiting services for the high-tech, commercial and defense sectors of the economy. Specializing in engineering and manufacturing management.

Key Contact - Specialty:
Mr. Walter S. Poyck, President - *Manufacturing*

Salary minimum: $35,000

Functions: General Mgmt., Mfg., Materials, HR Mgmt., Finance, M&A, Risk Mgmt., MIS Mgmt., R&D, Engineering

Industries: Food, Bev., Tobacco, Chemicals, Metal Products, Motor Vehicles, Consumer Elect., Transportation

Networks: Inter-City Personnel Assoc (IPA)

The Stewart Group
201 ATP Tour Blvd Ste 130
PO Box 2588
Ponte Vedra Beach, FL 32004-2588
(904) 285-6622
Fax: (904) 285-0076
Email: corp@stewartgroup.net
Web: www.stewartgroup.net

Description: Pharmaceutical and medical in all departments. Mid- to senior-level searches in most industries. Hospital and physician practice and executive. MIS and related areas, engineering and telecommunications.

Key Contact - Specialty:
Mr. James H. Stewart, President/Managing Director - *Pharmaceutical (sales & marketing), clinical, medical, regulatory*

Mr. James Helms, Executive Search Consultant - *E-Commerce, IT, IS (sales & marketing), legal, big 5 consultants*
Mr. Brian Stewart, Executive Search Consultant - *Sales, marketing, senior management*
Ms. Cathi Stewart, Recruiter - *Sales, managed care, financial, communications*

Salary minimum: $80,000

Functions: Generalist

Industries: Mfg., Finance, Services, Media, Communications, Aerospace, Software, Biotech, Healthcare

Professional Associations: AAPS, ACCP, ACG, ACP, ASCO, DIA, MGMA, ONS, RAPS

Networks: First Interview Network (FIN)

Stewart Search Advisors LLC
10 Vaughan Ste 6
Worth Plz
Portsmouth, NH 03801
(603) 430-2122
Fax: (603) 430-7339
Email: info@stewartsearch.com
Web: www.stewartsearch.com

Description: We are dedicated to the placement of actuaries in life, annuity, disability, investment and health careers. Our clients include the nation's leading insurance, reinsurance, consulting, investment and health companies.

Key Contact - Specialty:
Mr. William M. Stewart, Manager/Search Advisor - *Insurance, actuarial science*
Ms. Susan Pearson Spaulding, Manager/Search Advisor - *Insurance, actuarial science*

Functions: Generalist

Industries: Insurance

Stoakley-Dudley Consultants Ltd
6547A Mississauga Rd
Mississauga, ON L5N 1A6
Canada
(905) 821-3455
Fax: (905) 821-3467
Email: stoakley@stoakley.com
Web: www.stoakley.com

Description: International high-technology search firm specializing in sales and marketing, engineering, hardware, software development, electronics, senior management and finance.

Key Contact - Specialty:
Mr. Ernie Stoakley, President - *Telecommunications engineering, marketing*
Mr. Reg Shortt, Consultant - *Information technology*
Mr. Patrick Laforet, Consultant - *Manufacturing*
Ms. Deborah Milo, Consultant - *Automotive*
Mr. Don Christensen, Consultant - *Information technology, finance*
Mr. Steve Watts, Consultant - *IT finance insurance*

Functions: Generalist

Industries: Generalist

Professional Associations: ACSESS

Networks: National Personnel Assoc (NPA)

Stone & Youngblood
304 Newbury St Ste 210
Boston, MA 02115
(781) 647-0070
Fax: (781) 647-0460
Email: information@stoneandyoungblood.com
Web: www.stoneandyoungblood.com

Description: Consultants best known for executive searches conducted for clients in media, communications, advertising, public relations, sales and marketing. Affiliated with offices coast to coast.

Key Contact:
Mr. Stephen Sarkis, General Manager

Functions: Generalist, General Mgmt., Advertising, Mktg. Mgmt., Sales Mgmt., Direct Mktg., PR, HR Mgmt.

Industries: Generalist, Services, Advertising, Publishing, New Media, Broadcast, Film, Telecoms, Software

Stone Enterprises Ltd
645 N Michigan Ave Ste 800
Chicago, IL 60611
(773) 404-9300
(312) 836-0470
Fax: (773) 404-9388
Email: info@stoneenterprisesltd.com

Description: We are a successful boutique recruitment firm catering to Big 5, Fortune 2000, hardware, software, distribution, and manufacturing firms. Our company is affiliated with a network of over 600 recruiters nationwide.

Key Contact - Specialty:
Ms. Susan L. Stone, President - *Accounting, software, hardware, telecommunications, manufacturing*

Salary minimum: $45,000

Functions: Generalist

Industries: Mfg., Transportation, Mgmt. Consulting, E-commerce, IT Implementation, Telecoms, Software, Accounting SW, ERP SW, Networking, Comm. SW

Professional Associations: RON

Networks: Top Echelon Network

Branches:
2000 N Racine Ste 2210
Chicago, IL 60614
(773) 404-9300
Fax: (773) 404-9388
Email: chicagolandjobs@aol.com
Key Contact:
Ms. Susan L. Stone, Owner

Stone Legal Resources Group
50 Milk St Fl 5
Boston, MA 02109
(617) 482-4100
Fax: (617) 482-9601
Email: stone.legal@stonelegal.com
Web: www.stonelegal.com

Description: We are a leading East Coast firm devoted to the highest levels of placement for attorneys and paralegals and administrative support staff.

Key Contact - Specialty:
Mr. Alan R. Stone, Esq. - *Attorney, paralegal*
Mr. Mike Baley
Mr. Peter P. Twining, Esq. - *Attorneys, paralegals*

Functions: Senior Mgmt., Legal, Attorneys, Paralegals

Industries: Generalist, Construction, Retail, Legal

Professional Associations: ALA, LAMA, MBA, WBA

DM Stone Recruitment Solutions
100 Bush St Ste 650
San Francisco, CA 94104
(415) 391-5151
Fax: (415) 391-5536
Email: mailbox@dmstone.com
Web: www.dmstone.com

Description: We are a financial services specialist, serving clients in banking, brokerage, insurance, investment banking, asset management, accounting and information technology. Providing temporary, temp-to-hire and direct hire placement, from entry-level to executive management.

Key Contact:
Mr. Dave M. Stone, President - *Financial services, investment banking, stockbrokerage, trust, investment management*
Mr. Stephen Gallen, Managing Director

Salary minimum: $40,000

Functions: Admin. Svcs., Legal, Sales Mgmt., Customer Svc., Finance, CFO's, Budgeting, Cash Mgmt., Credit, Taxes

Industries: Generalist, Finance, Banking, Invest. Banking, Brokers, Venture Cap., Misc. Financial

Professional Associations: AICPA, CSP

Branches:
11808 Rancho Bernardo Rd Ste 123-483
San Diego, CA 92128
(858) 521-0164
Fax: (858) 521-0165
Email: traci@dmstone.com
Key Contact:
Ms. Traci Weitzenfeld

Stoneburner Associates Inc
10000 W 75th St Ste 102
King's Cove
Shawnee Mission, KS 66204
(913) 432-0055
Fax: (913) 432-0056
Email: sacareers@aol.com

Description: We provide executive search or contingency placement in a wide variety of industries. Our emphasis is on high-tech firms and professionals. We have had nationwide recruiting activity. We offer a ninety-day pro-rated guarantee.

Key Contact - Specialty:
Mr. Dwight T. Stoneburner, Owner - *Technical*

Salary minimum: $45,000

Functions: Generalist

Industries: Food, Bev., Tobacco, Drugs Mfg., Plastics, Rubber, Metal Products, Electronic, Elec. Components, IT Implementation, Fiber Optic, Software, Mfg. SW, Biotech

Networks: Inter-City Personnel Assoc (IPA)

Stonington Associates
800 Summer St
Franklin, MA 02038
(508) 541-8505
Fax: (508) 541-8303
Email: resumes@stoningtonassoc.com
Web: www.stoningtonassoc.com

Description: We support the professional staffing needs of commercial and community banks throughout the Northeast. We provide contingency and retained search services for our clients.

Key Contact - Specialty:
Mr. Philip A. Morton, President - *Banking*

Salary minimum: $30,000

Functions: Generalist, Senior Mgmt., Middle Mgmt., Mktg. Mgmt., Personnel, CFO's, Cash Mgmt., Risk Mgmt.

Industries: Generalist, Banking, Venture Cap., Misc. Financial

---

Storevik Financial Search & Associates Inc
2640 Del Mar Heights Rd Ste 213
Del Mar, CA 92014
(858) 792-0433
Fax: (858) 792-0455
Email: tstorev1@san.rr.com

Description: We specialize in placement of professionals into major CPA and consulting firms.

Preferred experience in tax, litigation services, insolvency, turnarounds, forensic, valuations, financial or information systems.

Key Contact - Specialty:
Mr. Terry R. Storevik, CPA, President - *Consulting professionals for major consulting firms*

Salary minimum: $50,000

Functions: Legal, Finance

Industries: Generalist, Services, Legal, Accounting, HR Services, Law Enforcement

Professional Associations: AICPA, IMA

Networks: National Consulting Network (NCN)

Storey & Associates
67 Yonge St Ste 700
Toronto, ON M5E 1J8
Canada
(416) 366-1212
Fax: (416) 366-4100
Email: mail@storey.ca
Web: www.storey.ca

Description: We are an executive search company specializing in middle and senior management positions in marketing and sales, consumer packaged goods, financial services & brokerage, finance, telecommunications, advertising, direct response, database, graphic design and public relations.

Key Contact - Specialty:
Mr. Roy Storey, President - *Senior positions*
Ms. Cathy Storey, President - *Marketing*
Mr. Rajula Gupta, Senior Consultant - *Sales & marketing*
Mr. Don Fry, Senior Consultant - *Sales*
Mr. Deepak Pershad, Senior Consultant - *Finance*

Salary minimum: $50,000

Functions: Generalist, Directors, Senior Mgmt., Middle Mgmt., Advertising, Mkt. Research, Mktg. Mgmt., Sales Mgmt.

Industries: Generalist, Banking, Pharm Svcs., Hospitality, Advertising, New Media, Aerospace, Insurance

---

Suzanne Strange Enterprises Inc
PO Box 4889
Greenville, SC 29608
(864) 246-1200
Fax: (864) 246-3492
Email: info@ceramics-personnel.com
Web: www.ceramics-personnel.com

Description: We are a technical recruiting firm serving the ceramic industry. We specialize in placing the best ceramic engineers, materials engineers, and other professionals with the finest companies nationwide.

Key Contact - Specialty:
Mrs. Suzanne Strange, President/Recruiter - *Engineers (ceramic, materials)*

Professional Associations: ACerS

Strategic Executive Search Solutions
PO Box 85
Dexter, ME 04930
(877) 871-3800
(207) 924-3800
Fax: (877) 780-4777
Email: j.parker@strategicexecsearch.com
Web: www.strategicexecsearch.com

Description: A professional retained executive search firm that specializes in the placement and recruitment of sales and sales management personnel and middle- to senior-level management executives.

Key Contact - Specialty:
Mr. Jack A. Parker, Owner/Senior Executive Consultant - *Sales, sales management*
Mrs. Tammy A. Parker, Co-Owner - *Sales, sales management*
Mr. Allan E. Bishop, Executive Recruiter - *Sales, sales management*

Functions: Sales & Mktg., Sales Mgmt.

Industries: Generalist

Professional Associations: AMA

Strategic Resources Biotechnology & Medical Group
6210 146th Pl SE
Bellevue, WA 98006-4337
(425) 688-9807
Fax: (425) 747-4274
Email: info@srbmg.com
Web: www.srbmg.com

Description: Nationwide executive search firm specializing in recruiting for biotechnology, medical, pharmaceutical industries. Typical candidates have three to five years of relevant industry experience. Sales, product managers, director to vice president level.

Key Contact:
Ms. Rena Roberts Bouchard, President - *Pharmaceuticals, biotechnology, medical devices*
Mr. Marc J. Bouchard, Executive Vice President

Salary minimum: $80,000

Functions: Directors, Senior Mgmt., Middle Mgmt., Product Dev., Sales & Mktg., Mkt. Research, Mktg. Mgmt., Sales Mgmt.

Industries: Drugs Mfg., Medical Devices, Biotech

Strategic Resources
14645 Bel-Red Rd Ste 201
Bellevue, WA 98007
(425) 688-1151
Fax: (425) 688-1272
Email: info@strategicresources.com
Web: www.strategicresources.com

Description: We are a principals only executive search firm specializing in advertising/public relations, apparel and home furnishings, biotechnology and life sciences, casino management, ethnic marketing, new media content and production (B2B, B2C, and interactive), high-technology (telecommunications, wireless, cable, and satellite) sales and marketing, operations, engineering, and senior management, software sales, and marketing.

Key Contact - Specialty:
Mr. Philip Kagan, President - *Casino management*
Mr. Ted Warren, President - *Advertising, public relations*
Mr. Allen Brady, Sr Principal - *Telecomm sales, marketing, operations*
Ms. Joan Cascio, Director, Business Development
Mr. Art Dreeben, Principal - *Apparel, home furnishings*
Mr. Gary Leatham, Ph.D., Principal - *Biotechnology, life sciences*
Ms. Carolyn Lindsley, Principal - *Computer hardware*
Ms. Barbara Stellman, Principal - *Corporate communications, public relations*
Mr. Bernd Schumann, Principal - *Software (sales and marketing)*

Salary minimum: $125,000

Functions: Generalist

Industries: Textiles, Apparel, Drugs Mfg., Medical Devices, Mgmt. Consulting, Hotels, Resorts, Clubs, Media, Advertising, Communications, Biotech, Healthcare

Professional Associations: AFTRA, IFT, PRSA

Strategic Search & Staffing Inc (TeamS3)

7720 El Camino Real Ste B106
La Costa, CA 92009
(760) 510-1797
Fax: (760) 510-1798
Email: info@teams3.com
Web: www.teams3.com

Description: Our firm is a full service executive level human resources company offering premium services on a local, regional, and national level. Our clients range from the smallest start-up companies to Big 5 consulting firms and Fortune 500 companies. Team S3 provides high quality personnel staffing, human resources consulting, and employee development training services tailored for your company.

Key Contact:
Mr. Paul Cevolani, President/CEO - *Information technology, human resources, sales, marketing*
Mr. Michael Danler, COO - *Information technology*
Ms. Alison Gross, Marketing Director

Functions: Generalist, Directors, Senior Mgmt., Middle Mgmt., Quality, Health Admin., HR Mgmt., Training

Industries: Services, Mgmt. Consulting, HR Services, E-commerce, IT Implementation, Communications, Government, Software, HR SW

Professional Associations: CSP, SDSIC, SHRM

Networks: PRO/NET

Strategic Search Consultants

3450 W Central Ave Ste 232
Toledo, OH 43606
(419) 324-2424
Email: ssc-admin@ssc-online.com
Web: www.ssc-online.com

Description: We provide elite companies access to information technology's premiere talent in the electronic document/direct marketing and e-commerce/bill presentment/Internet content arenas.

Key Contact - Specialty:
Mr. Ken Leslie, President - *Electronic document, direct marketing, internet content, e-commerce*

Functions: Generalist, Direct Mktg., MIS Mgmt., Systems Analysis, Systems Dev., Systems Implem., Systems Support, Mgmt. Consultants

Industries: Generalist, Printing, Computer Equip., Mgmt. Consulting, Software

Professional Associations: DMA, XPLOR

Strategic Search Partners

303 Bandera Ct
PO Box 93132
Southlake, TX 76092
(817) 424-1277
Fax: (817) 488-4497
Email: info@searchssp.com
Web: www.searchssp.com

Description: We offer high quality executive search work performed in the following specialty areas: consumer products industry, for all functions. We also place heavy emphasis on supply chain, purchasing, logistics, sales/marketing, and human resources.

Key Contact:
Mr. Frank J. Laux, President

Salary minimum: $100,000

Functions: Generalist, Directors

Industries: Food, Bev., Tobacco, Soap, Perf., Cosmtcs., Drugs Mfg., HR Services, ERP SW, HR SW, Mfg. SW, Marketing SW

Networks: First Interview Network (FIN)

Strategic Technologies Inc

2183 Buckingham Rd Ste 232
Richardson, TX 75081
(972) 490-9192
Fax: (972) 490-9193
Email: sandi1@airmail.net

Description: We offer professional recruiting. We specialize in the plastics and composites industries, more specifically: materials manufacturers, molders, processors, and fabricators. We have vertically integrated to serve our clients, from the Fortune 500 to smaller companies. We offer professional recruiting of management, sales, marketing, manufacturing, R&D, and applications/product development. Our clients are resin producers, compounders, glass and carbon fiber manufacturers, molders, other plastics and composites processors and manufacturers, downstream through to the OEMs.

Key Contact - Specialty:
Ms. Sandi M. Taylor, Owner/Manager - *Management (executive, general), sales, marketing, business, product*

Salary minimum: $60,000

Functions: Generalist, General Mgmt., Mfg., Sales & Mktg., HR Mgmt., R&D, Engineering, Int'l.

Industries: Generalist, Medical Devices, Plastics, Rubber, Computer Equip., Consumer Elect., Misc. Mfg., Aerospace

Professional Associations: APICS, SAMPE, SPE, SPI

Strategic Technology Resource

PO Box 3183
Dublin, OH 43016
(614) 873-4648
Fax: (614) 873-0222
Email: info@hrgameplan.com
Web: www.hrgameplan.com

Description: We are an executive search firm specializing in the placement of information technology and telecommunications professionals. With the successful completion of each search, founder and president, Angela Walters grew more convinced that in addition to helping companies find the brightest and best candidates, there was also a need to help organizations retain and develop those new recruits. The HR technology consulting practice was unleashed in January of 2000.

Key Contact:
Mrs. Angela Walters, Principal

Functions: Production, HR Mgmt., IT, Engineering

Industries: Generalist, Construction, Biotech

Stratin Associates

242 Old New Brunswick Rd Ste 100
Piscataway, NJ 08854
(732) 562-9337
Fax: (732) 562-9448
Email: lgold@sai-hr.com

Description: A full-service human resource consulting firm specializing in the placement of mid- and lower-level management positions.

Key Contact - Specialty:
Mr. Andrew Borkin, President
Ms. Lisa Gold, Vice President - *Banking, financial services*

Salary minimum: $40,000

Functions: Generalist

Industries: Drugs Mfg., Metal Products, Computer Equip., Finance, Accounting, Mgmt. Consulting, HR Services, Insurance, Software, Biotech

Professional Associations: SHRM

Sullivan & Company

111 Presidential Blvd Ste 173
Bala Cynwyd, PA 19004
(610) 664-9000
Fax: (610) 664-8675
Email: dave@sullivancompany.com
Web: www.sullivancompany.com

Description: We are a Mid-Atlantic banking and financial specialist firm with a 12 year track record of mid- to senior-level recruitment. If you are looking for (or to fill)a banking or financial job in this region, this may be the firm for you.

Key Contact:
Mr. David Sullivan

Salary minimum: $60,000

Functions: Middle Mgmt.

Industries: Banking, Invest. Banking, Venture Cap., Mgmt. Consulting, Real Estate

Summerfield Associates Inc

6555 Quince Rd Ste 311
Memphis, TN 38119
(901) 753-7068
Fax: (901) 755-3001
Email: dsummerfield@summerfield.net
Web: www.summerfield.net

Description: Our principals bring to our firm over 40 years of combined experience in recruiting and consulting services. We consistently establish solid rapport with client companies by meeting their business goals and objectives. We are a recognized top producer in field.

Key Contact - Specialty:
Ms. Dotty Giusti, CPC, President - *Human resources, information systems, corporate attorneys*
Mrs. Janice Lee, Operations Manager, Consultant - *Logistics, distribution, human resources*
Ms. Lorraine Steinberg, CPC, Senior Consultant - *Marketing, finance, human resources*

Salary minimum: $35,000

Functions: Generalist

Industries: Mfg., Legal, HR Services, Media, Telecoms

Professional Associations: NAPS, SHRM, TAPS

Networks: National Personnel Assoc (NPA)

Summit Group Consultants Inc

64 Lambert Dr
Sparta, NJ 07871
(973) 726-0800
Fax: (973) 726-9188
Email: garyp@nac.net

Description: With 29 years of placement experience, we can assist with resumes, marketing techniques, interviewing preparation and salary issues, as well as career planning strategies, all at no cost to the candidate.

Key Contact - Specialty:
Mr. Gary W. Pezzuti, Senior Partner - *Materials management, manufacturing management*

Salary minimum: $50,000

Functions: Mfg., Production, Plant Mgmt., Materials, Purchasing, Materials Plng., Distribution, Packaging

Industries: Mfg., Food, Bev., Tobacco, Chemicals, Soap, Perf., Cosmtcs., Drugs Mfg., Medical Devices, Plastics, Rubber, Metal Products, Test, Measure Equip., Electronic, Elec. Components, Packaging

Professional Associations: APICS, APICS, NAPM

The Summit Group

275 E Hillcrest Dr Ste 165
Thousand Oaks, CA 91360
(805) 449-1323
Fax: (805) 449-1326
Email: sumgroup@earthlink.net

Description: Executive search/information technology recruiting, specializing in software engineering, programmers and information services/MIS placement, software quality assurance and technical marketing.

Key Contact - Specialty:
Mr. Larry Ross, Principal - *Software engineering, software quality assurance, programming, telecommunications, information technology marketing*

Salary minimum: $30,000

Functions: Generalist, Directors, Senior Mgmt., MIS Mgmt., Systems Dev., Systems Implem., Network Admin., DB Admin.

Industries: Generalist, Mgmt. Consulting, Telecoms, Software

Networks: Top Echelon Network

Summit Recruiting Corp

1097 W Hawthorn Dr
Itasca, IL 60143
(800) 391-4355
Fax: (847) 259-0828
Email: dignacek@srjobs.com
Web: www.srjobs.com

Description: Our firm provides its national and international clients both contract and permanent placement services. Below are some of the areas in which our professionals specialize: consulting practice managers/principals, business developers, engagement managers, architects, project executives, applications developers, PKI, privacy, wireless, knowledge management., CRM, ERP, and industry specialists.

Key Contact - Specialty:
Mr. John De Ano, President - *CRM*
Mr. Steve Fugatt, Director of Recruiting - *Security*
Mr. Dennis Ignacek, Director of Operations - *Business development*

Salary minimum: $35,000

Functions: Senior Mgmt., Quality, Healthcare, Sales & Mktg., Risk Mgmt., IT, DB Admin., Mgmt. Consultants, Architects, Technicians

Industries: Generalist, Energy, Utilities, Mfg., Transportation, Finance, Services, Mgmt. Consulting, E-commerce, IT Implementation, Communications, Telecoms, Call Centers, Telephony, Digital, Wireless, Fiber Optic, Network Infrastructure, Aerospace, Software, Database SW, Networking, Comm. SW, Security SW, Biotech, Healthcare

Sun Information Systems Inc

18139 W Catawba Ave
Cornelius, NC 28031
(704) 655-9000
Fax: (704) 655-9900
Email: jobs@suninfosys.com
Web: www.suninfosys.com

Description: International provider of information technology executive recruitment and supplemental, contract services.

Key Contact:
Mr. Tony Termini, Executive Vice President

Functions: Generalist, IT, Systems Analysis, Systems Dev., Systems Implem., Systems Support, Network Admin., DB Admin.

Industries: Generalist, Mgmt. Consulting, HR Services, IT Implementation

Sun Valley Search

10th St Industrial Park Ste 8-A
PO Box 599
Ketchum, ID 83340-0599
(208) 725-5055
Fax: (208) 726-7591
Email: tom@svsearch.com
Web: www.sunvalleysearch.com

Description: We are industry specific recruiting only in the rotating equipment industries, pumps, compressors, turbines, seals and mixers with four recruiters doing all positions within the industries.

Key Contact - Specialty:
Mr. Tom Lampl, Owner - *Equipment (rotating)*

Salary minimum: $40,000

Functions: Generalist, General Mgmt.

Industries: Machine, Appliance, Misc. Mfg.

Ron Sunshine & Associates

2800 W Parker Rd Ste 104
Plano, TX 75075
(972) 599-2482
Fax: (972) 599-9583
Email: ron@ronsunshineassociates.com
Web: www.ronsunshineassociates.com

Description: Placement of middle and upper-management in all fields of manufacturing and engineering-metals, plastics and consumer goods.

Key Contact - Specialty:
Mr. Ron Sunshine, President - *Manufacturing, engineering*
Ms. Barbara Blake - *Food, executive temp*
Ms. Stacy Moscowitz, Vice President - *Human resources*

Salary minimum: $50,000

Functions: Mfg.

Industries: Mfg., Medical Devices, Plastics, Rubber, Metal Products, Machine, Appliance, Motor Vehicles, Computer Equip., Consumer Elect., Misc. Mfg.

Survival Systems Staffing Inc

2149 Portola Rd
Ventura, CA 93003
(805) 650-8888
Email: email@survivalsystems.com
Web: www.survivalsystems.com

Description: We are a national leading, award winning, high technology electronics search firm with skills ranging from engineers and managers of engineering, operations, manufacturing, quality, sales and marketing, CFOs, and CEOs. Our areas of expertise include power conversion, motors, drives, semiconductors, electric vehicle, magnetics, photonics, lighting, batteries, fuel cell, information control technology, utility, and telecommunications.

Key Contact - Specialty:
Mr. Dennis Nickerson, President - *Engineers, CEOs (high level technology searches)*
Ms. Sandy Schreiber - *Electronic power conversion - retained only*

Salary minimum: $50,000

Functions: Generalist, Senior Mgmt., Product Dev., Quality, Mktg. Mgmt., Sales Mgmt., Systems Analysis, Engineering

Industries: Generalist, Energy, Utilities, Computer Equip., Test, Measure Equip., Electronic, Elec. Components, Broadcast, Film, Telecoms, Digital, Wireless, Fiber Optic, Aerospace

Professional Associations: IACPR, CSP, NAPS

Svenneby & Associates Inc

7307 S Waco St
Foxfield, CO 80016-1650
(303) 617-4481
Fax: (303) 617-4482
Email: peter@svenneby.com
Web: www.svenneby.com

Description: We are a national search firm specializing in the placement of mid to senior level sales, marketing and management professionals. Our specialty is the enterprise/corporate software industries including: ERP, SCM, e-Business, CAD, PDM, etc.

Key Contact - Specialty:
Mr. Peter Svenneby, Principal - *CAD/CAM, ERP/MRP/ASP, sales & marketing*

Salary minimum: $60,000

Functions: General Mgmt., Sales & Mktg.

Industries: Computer Equip., Software

The Swan Group

PO Box 620
Buckingham, PA 18912
(215) 230-9612
Email: barbara@swangroup.net
Web: www.swangroup.net

Description: Search firm specializing in the IT area. Have completed assignments for major pharmaceutical firms, .com companies, technical firms looking for high level IT professionals. We perform and have very happy customers.

Key Contact - Specialty:
Ms. Barbara Swan, CPA, Owner - *IT*

Salary minimum: $100,000

Functions: Directors, IT, MIS Mgmt., Mgmt. Consultants, Int'l.

Industries: Mfg., Chemicals, Drugs Mfg., Computer Equip., Pharm Svcs., Equip Svcs., Mgmt. Consulting, Software, Biotech, Healthcare

Branches:
35 W High St
Somerville, NJ 08876
(908) 526-5440
Email: Steve@swangroup.com
Key Contact - Specialty:
Mr. Steve Swan, Associate - *SAP Positions*

Swift & Associates

65 W Commercial St
Portland, ME 04101
(207) 773-0330
Fax: (207) 773-7445
Email: cswift@swiftassociates.com
Web: www.swiftassociates.com

Description: We are an executive recruitment firm that offers highly targeted and customized search services for our clients, all located in Northern New England, including Maine, New Hampshire, and Vermont. Catherine Swift has twenty years of experience successfully directing and implementing executive search strategies in the legal, investment, manufacturing, and retail professions. She was formerly president of Maine's first legal

Key Contact:
Ms. Catherine Swift, President
Ms. Lisa Hutchison, Vice President

Salary minimum: $40,000

Functions: Generalist

Industries: Mfg., Wholesale, Finance, Legal, HR Services, E-commerce, Media, Communications, Software, Biotech

Sylvestro Associates
5586 Post Rd Ste 208
East Greenwich, RI 02818
(401) 885-0855
Fax: (401) 885-0896
Email: sylvestroassoc@aol.com

Description: Placement of engineers and related technical personnel within manufacturing companies.

Key Contact - Specialty:
Mr. Gary Sylvestro, Owner - *Manufacturing engineers*

Salary minimum: $50,000

Functions: Generalist, Mfg., Materials, Engineering

Industries: Generalist, Mfg.

Synagent Inc
5412 Torbolton Ridge Rd
Woodlawn, ON K0A 3M0
Canada
(613) 832-1122
(877) 287-8997
Fax: (613) 832-1227
Email: johnb@synagent.com
Web: www.synagent.com

Description: Recruit sales and credit personnel for financial services companies specialized in inventory finance and equipment leasing in North America.

Key Contact - Specialty:
Mr. John Bickerstaff, President - *Inventory finance, equipment leasing, vehicle leasing*

Salary minimum: $50,000

Functions: Generalist, Directors

Industries: Generalist, Wholesale, Retail, Finance, Banking, Misc. Financial, Equip Svcs.

Synergistech Communications
1824 Byron Ave
San Mateo, CA 94401-3404
(650) 344-2141
Fax: (650) 344-5664
Email: pubpros@synergistech.com
Web: www.synergistech.com

Description: We recruit staff and contract technical writers, editors, trainers, web content creators, and desktop publishers for San Francisco Bay area software companies. We charge low commissions and offer the highest rates.

Key Contact - Specialty:
Mr. Andrew Davis, President - *Technical writing, software development*

Salary minimum: $45,000

Functions: Generalist, Training, Graphic Artists

Industries: Generalist, Publishing, New Media, Communications, Telecoms, Software, Database SW, Development SW, Doc. Mgmt., Production SW, Networking, Comm. SW, Biotech

Professional Associations: IABC, STC

Synergy 2000
1825 I St NW Ste 400
Washington, DC 20006
(202) 452-1227
(703) 527-3270
Fax: (703) 527-3921
Email: densyn2000@aol.com
Web: www.synergy2000search.com

Description: We specialize in recruiting senior-level professionals/executives for technology companies, consulting firms including the Big 5, and Fortune 1000 companies. Our specialty areas include e-Commerce, e-CRM, Enterprise Application Integration (EAI), data warehousing, compensation and benefits consultants/managers, tax managers, human capital managers, strategy consultants, retirement consultants, assurance and business advisory managers, and corporate finance managers. The industries that we serve include high technology, financial services, health care, utilities/energy, telecommunications, and state/local governments.

Key Contact - Specialty:
Mr. Denman Hamilton, Sr Partner-Global Technology Practice - *E-technology executives, e-CRM managers, EAI managers*
Mr. Sherman Hamilton, Senior Partner - *Tax managers, marketing communication managers, finance*

Salary minimum: $75,000

Functions: Directors, Senior Mgmt., Benefits, Finance, IT, MIS Mgmt., Systems Implem., Mgmt. Consultants, Minorities

Industries: Energy, Utilities, Mgmt. Consulting, Telecoms, Government, Insurance, Software

Professional Associations: SHRM, WARN

Synergy Search Ltd
3914 Miami Rd Ste 101
Cincinnati, OH 45227
(513) 272-1000
Fax: (513) 272-1004
Email: synergysearch@email.com

Description: A professional contingency search firm specializing in sales, manufacturing and operations positions within the packaging industry.

Key Contact - Specialty:
Mr. John W. Petru, Partner - *Packaging, sales, management*
Mr. Garrett Levy, Partner - *Packaging, manufacturing, management*

Functions: Generalist, Senior Mgmt., Production, Plant Mgmt., Quality, Sales Mgmt., Customer Svc., Graphic Artists

Industries: Generalist, Paper, Printing, Packaging

Synergy Solutions Ltd
PO Box 28328
Bellingham, WA 98228-0328
(360) 988-2066
Email: synergy@becksolutions.com
Web: www.becksolutions.com

Description: We specialize in assisting organizations fill positions in the areas of IT, high-tech, EDA, medical, health care, aerospace, semi-conductor, and other industries at all levels and in all geographic regions

Key Contact - Specialty
Mr. Larry Beck, President - *Executive, information technology, supply chain, six sigma, EDA engineers*
Ms. Margaret Tlustos, Recruiter - *Entry to mid-level*

Salary minimum: $40,000

Functions: Generalist, Purchasing, Healthcare, Allied Health, Systems Analysis, Systems Dev., Systems Implem., Network Admin., DB Admin., Engineering

Industries: Generalist, Motor Vehicles, Test, Measure Equip., Misc. Mfg., Electronic, Elec. Components, Pharm Svcs., Mgmt. Consulting, Communications, Telecoms, Telephony, Defense, Aerospace, Software, Database SW, Development SW, Hospitals

Synergy Systems
264 Queens Key W Ste 803
Toronto, ON M5J 1B5
Canada
(416) 597-2686

Email: synsys@interlog.com

Description: Senior recruiters who know the computer vendor environment in eastern Canada both permanent and contract. Quick, discreet, professional service is our credo.

Key Contact - Specialty:
Mr. John Hall, Consultant - *Computer vendor, market*

Salary minimum: $65,000

Functions: Generalist, Senior Mgmt., Middle Mgmt., Mktg. Mgmt., Sales Mgmt., Systems Dev., Systems Implem., Systems Support

Industries: Generalist, Software

System 1 Search
3021 Citrus Cir Ste 230
Walnut Creek, CA 94598
(510) 925-8801
Fax: (925) 932-3651
Email: system1@ccnet.com
Web: www.system1search.com

Description: Technical recruiting for engineers, production, maintenance, quality, R&D, primarily for the chemical and pharma operations in N.CA. We also work for other mfg. operations. Client driven so we will do whatever is needed.

Key Contact - Specialty:
Mr. David Doyle, President - *Technical, engineers, production, quality*

Salary minimum: $40,000

Functions: Mfg., Production

Industries: Chemicals, Drugs Mfg.

Networks: National Personnel Assoc (NPA)

System Two Inc
24W500 Maple Ave Ste 219
Naperville, IL 60540
(630) 717-2713
(630) 717-6500
Fax: (630) 717-6569
Email: twrona@systemtwo.com
Web: www.systemtwo.com

Description: We specialize in IT recruitment in the Chicago Area. Additionally, we are members of a nationwide association of independent recruitment firms.

Key Contact - Specialty:
Ms. Vicki Starr, Vice President - *Information technology*
Mr. Thomas Wrona, President - *Information technology*

Salary minimum: $15,000

Functions: Sales Mgmt., IT, MIS Mgmt., Systems Analysis, Systems Dev., Systems Implem., Systems Support, Network Admin., DB Admin., Mgmt. Consultants

Industries: Generalist, Mgmt. Consulting, E-commerce, IT Implementation, Software, Database SW, Development SW

Networks: Top Echelon Network

Systems Careers
211 Sutter St Ste 607
San Francisco, CA 94108
(415) 434-4770
Fax: (415) 434-1529
Email: wayne_sarchett@msn.com

Description: We provide a broad range of executive placement services in the computing industry in the areas of systems development, product development, software engineering, technical marketing, customer support, QA management, consulting, and hardware and software vendor professionals.

Key Contact - Specialty:
Mr. A. Wayne Sarchett, Principal - *Software, consulting*

Salary minimum: $90,000

Functions: Senior Mgmt., Middle Mgmt., Product Dev., Mkt. Research, Mktg. Mgmt., DB Admin., R&D, Engineering, Mgmt. Consultants, Architects

Industries: Software

Systems One LLC
1700 E Golf Rd Ste 1101
Schaumburg, IL 60173
(847) 619-9300
Fax: (847) 619-0071
Email: info@systems-one.com
Web: www.systems-one.com

Description: We offer effective information technology and human resources recruiting services to our corporate clients in the Chicagoland area.

Key Contact - Specialty:
Mr. Edward V. Hildy, CPC, General Manager - *Information technology, human resources*

Salary minimum: $60,000

Functions: Generalist, HR Mgmt., MIS Mgmt., Systems Analysis, Systems Dev., Systems Implem., Systems Support

Industries: Generalist, HR Services, Software

Professional Associations: HRMAC, IAPS, NAPS

Branches:
111 W Washington St Ste 841
Chicago, IL 60602
(312) 214-4343
Fax: (312) 214-4344
Key Contact:
Ms. Diana Eagen, Branch Manager

Systems Personnel Inc
9688 Union Rd Ste 3
West Seneca, NY 14224
(716) 677-2667
Fax: (716) 677-0658
Email: compro@pce.net
Web: www.systemspersonnel.com

Description: Is a firm that provides computer staffing on a direct or temporary basis. We strive to differentiate ourselves by providing value added computer services and by thoroughly understanding our client's needs.

Key Contact - Specialty:
Mr. Jim Cipriani, Jr., President - *Computer*
Mr. Jim Cipriani, Sr., Vice President - *Computer*

Functions: IT

Industries: Generalist

Professional Associations: RON

Systems Personnel Inc
115 W State St
Media, PA 19063
(610) 565-8880
Fax: (610) 565-1482
Email: info@systemspersonnelinc.com
Web: www.systemspersonnelinc.com

Description: Information technology and management assignments across all industry segments and all technology.

Key Contact - Specialty:
Mr. James Doherty, Partner - *Information technology management, leadership*

Salary minimum: $75,000

Functions: IT, MIS Mgmt., Systems Analysis, Systems Dev., Systems Implem., Systems Support, DB Admin.

Industries: Generalist

Systems Research Group
617 Saxony Pl Ste 104
Encinitas, CA 92024
(760) 436-1575
Fax: (760) 634-3614
Email: jobs@systemsresearchgroup.com
Web: www.systemsresearchgroup.com

Description: Specializes in placing executives, sales, and marketing with vertical market application software manufacturers and systems including B2B, Internet, ASP, scientific, engineering, computer graphics, ERP, visualization, and CRM. We place executive staff, sales, marketing, application engineering and customer support professionals throughout North America and the Asia Pacific region.

Key Contact - Specialty:
Mr. Stephen Gebler, President - *High tech executives, sales & marketing, computer industry, CAD/CAM/CAE simulation, animation*

Salary minimum: $75,000

Functions: Generalist

Industries: Software

Systems Research Group
231 W 4th St Ste 607A
Cincinnati, OH 45202
(513) 381-2222
Fax: (513) 381-2204
Email: srg@fuse.net
Web: www.srgroup.com

Description: We recruit top talent in the US, Latin America, Europe, and the Pacific Rim. Our clients include the top architecture, engineering, and construction firms in the world today.

Key Contact - Specialty:
Mr. James Cole, President - *Architecture, consulting engineering, competitive intelligence, construction*

Functions: Engineering, Architects

Industries: Generalist

Professional Associations: ACEC, AIA, DBIA, PSMA

Systems Research Inc (SRI)
1250 E Bank Dr
Schaumburg, IL 60173
(847) 330-1222
Fax: (847) 330-1411
Email: sriinc1@aol.com
Web: www.systemsresearchinc.com

Description: For over 30 years, our firm has been recognized and respected as a leader in providing industry with the HR resources to solve needs for executive, management and staff level positions in the areas of engineering, IT, finance, and technical/manufacturing. We have succeeded in this venture due to SRI's core philosophy of providing our clients with 100% satisfaction.

Key Contact - Specialty:
Mr. Dan Kuesis, President - *Technical, engineering, manufacturing, materials*
Mr. Frank Agnello, Senior Account Manager - *Technical, engineering, manufacturing, materials*
Mr. Art Hurley, Senior Account Manager - *Technical, engineering, manufacturing, materials*

Salary minimum: $40,000

Functions: Generalist, Mfg., Materials, Finance, IT, Engineering, Architects, Technicians

Industries: Generalist, Mfg., Finance, Aerospace, Packaging, Software

Professional Associations: EMA, SHRM

Industries: Generalist

Systems Search
2366 Bradshire Ct
Arlington Heights, IL 60004-4367
(847) 577-0595
Fax: (847) 632-0224
Email: ed@sysearch.com
Web: www.sysearch.com

Description: Concentrate on client satisfaction which has developed our reputation for excellence in IT recruiting. We screen, interview and evaluate candidates and clients, to make sure you're getting the service and results you expect.

Key Contact - Specialty:
Mr. Edward Nathan, Principal - *Information technology*

Salary minimum: $30,000

Functions: Generalist

Industries: E-commerce, IT Implementation, Software, Accounting SW, Database SW, Development SW, Doc. Mgmt., Production SW

Networks: Top Echelon Network

Systems Search Consultants (SSC)
130 S State Rd Ste 102
Springfield, PA 19064
(610) 544-8690
Fax: (610) 544-8694
Email: thinkssc@sscsearch.com
Web: www.sscsearch.com

Description: We offer vendor organizations ten years' experience recruiting exclusively in the data communications industry. Recruiting sales, systems engineers, marketing, training and management of frame relay, ATM, LAN/WAN, fiber optics, WDM, XDSL, and SONET professionals.

Key Contact - Specialty:
Mr. John Grant, Senior Partner - *Data communications, vendor organizations*
Ms. Bernadette McCall, Partner - *Data communications, vendor organizations*

Salary minimum: $90,000

Functions: Generalist, Directors, Mktg. Mgmt., Sales Mgmt., Training, Systems Implem., Systems Support, Network Admin.

Industries: Generalist, Telecoms

Networks: First Interview Network (FIN)

Systems Search Group
8213 Village Harbor Dr
Cornelius, NC 28031
(704) 895-8440
Fax: (704) 895-8441
Email: recruiter@ssgnc.com
Web: www.ssgnc.com

Description: Information systems search and placement of operational, analysts/programmers, systems programmers, administrators and management professionals in the Southeast region of the US, predominantly in North Carolina, targeting industry leading, Fortune 500 companies.

Key Contact - Specialty:
Ms. Eileen Brady, CPC, President - *Information technology*

Functions: IT

Industries: Generalist

Professional Associations: NCASP

T E M Associates
1114 Trailwood Dr
PO Box 5243
De Pere, WI 54115
(920) 339-8055
Fax: (920) 339-6177
Email: cmtm@execpc.com

Description: We specialize in the paper and forest products areas, as well as related industries and consumer products. Nationwide focus with special attention to Midwest region.

Key Contact - Specialty:
Ms. Terri McCracken, President/Owner - *Pulp, paper, converting industry, consumer products*

Salary minimum: $50,000

Functions: Generalist, Production, Plant Mgmt., Materials, Sales & Mktg., HR Mgmt., Engineering

Industries: Generalist, Paper, Chemicals, Soap, Perf., Cosmtcs., Machine, Appliance, Packaging, Mfg. SW

Professional Associations: PIMA, SHRM, TAPPI

Networks: Inter-City Personnel Assoc (IPA)

T H Hunter Inc
815 Nicollet Mall Ste 210
Minneapolis, MN 55402
(612) 339-0530
Fax: (612) 339-1937
Email: mwright@thhunter.com
Web: www.thhunter.com

Description: A downtown Minneapolis generalist firm with a national practice specializing in client oriented custom tailored searches, focusing on active recruiting of the best possible candidates.

Key Contact - Specialty:
Mr. Milton Wright, Associate Director - *Generalist*
Mr. Robert Beller, Executive Director - *Generalist*

Salary minimum: $50,000

Functions: Generalist, General Mgmt., Sales & Mktg., HR Mgmt., Finance, Credit, IT

Industries: Generalist, Finance, Accounting, Telecoms, Software, Healthcare

T/A : Sales Management
10040 Cairn Mountain Way
Bristow, VA 20136
(703) 478-0720
(800) 376-1095
Fax: (703) 551-3232
Email: jim@smgmt.com
Web: www.smgmt.com

Description: We specialize in the recruitment of professional sales and marketing personnel in the Virginia, District of Columbia and Maryland area. We have been affiliated more than 10 years with First Interview Company, the Atlanta based international network of sales and marketing recruiters.

Key Contact:
Mr. Jim Wheatley, President

Functions: Generalist

Industries: Healthcare

Networks: First Interview Network (FIN)

TAD Telecom Canada
60 Queen St Ste 200
Ottawa, ON K1P 5Y7
Canada
(613) 232-4744
Web: www.tadcanada.com

Description: We are one of the fastest growing providers of professional staffing resources and managed services to clients that develop or depend on technology for their success.

Key Contact:
Mr. Garry Logue, Regional Vice President

Salary minimum: $75,000

Functions: Generalist, Directors, Senior Mgmt., Training, IT, Systems Analysis, Systems Dev., R&D, Engineering, Specialized Svcs.

Industries: Telecoms

Professional Associations: CTN, TEMIC

Branches:
212-7710, 5th St SE
Calgary, AB T2H 2L9
Canada
(403) 215-1280
Email: calgary@tadcanada.com
Key Contact:
Mr. Ken Kyswaty, Branch Manager

1600 Bedford Hwy 100-134
Bedford, NS B4A 1E8
Canada
(902) 484-3901
Email: halifax@tadcanada.com
Key Contact:
Mr. Peter Landry, Branch Manager

50 Burnhamthorpe Rd W Ste 704
Mississauga, ON L5B 3C2
Canada
(905) 848-0087
Email: toronto@tadcanada.com
Key Contact:
Mr. Andy Greeny, Area Manager

100-4025 Industriel Blvd
Laval, QC H7L 4S3
Canada
(450) 628-6677
Email: montreal@tadcanada.com
Key Contact:
Mr. Benoît Chalifoux, Area Manager

Talent Scouts Inc
115 S 18th St Ste 210
Parsons, KS 67357
(620) 423-3500
(888) 423-2292
Email: paul@tscouts.com
Web: www.tscouts.com

Description: Our firm is headquartered in the Midwest with satellite offices on the East and West Coasts. We offer the "best fit" solution. We bring together qualified, highly motivated candidates with client companies offering challenge, opportunity, and recognition in the area of information and network security.

Key Contact:
Mr. Paul Constans, Account Executive & Partner
Mr. Sherman Walker, Account Executive & Partner
Mr. Terry Hunter, CFO

Functions: Generalist

Industries: Finance, Misc. Financial, Services, E-commerce, IT Implementation, Communications, Software

Branches:
8 Mayfair Ct
Ipswich, MA 01938
(978) 312-1181
Email: evagenas@mediaone.net
Key Contact:
Ms. Liz Vagenas, Senior Executive

Talentude Search & Consulting
5328 Strawflower Dr Ste B
North Syracuse, NY 13212
(315) 458-8382
Fax: (315) 458-2927
Email: talentude@hotmail.com

Description: We specialize in sales, marketing and purchasing at all levels of management. Our client base is composed of corporations and small businesses from a variety of industries.

Key Contact - Specialty:
Mr. Charles K. Bartlett, Principal/Owner - *Sales & marketing*

Salary minimum: $40,000

Functions: Senior Mgmt., Mfg., Sales & Mktg., Mktg. Mgmt., Sales Mgmt.

Industries: Generalist

Networks: Top Echelon Network

The Talley Group
600 Lee Hwy
Verona, VA 24482
(540) 248-7009
Fax: (540) 248-7046
Email: talley@cfw.com
Web: www.talley-group.com

Description: We conduct searches for growth oriented companies, strong emphasis on mid-senior-level positions. For the past 15 years we have specialized in human resources and, more recently, information systems, finance, marketing and engineering recruiting.

Key Contact - Specialty:
Mr. J. L. Burkhill, President - *Marketing, engineering, human resources*
Mr. T. C. Jorgensen, Vice President - *Finance & accounting, engineering*
Ms. Carolyn Szabad, Recruiter - *Human resources, accounting*
Ms. Donna May, Technical Recruiter - *IT*
Ms. Brenda Marshall, Recruiter - *Food industry*

Salary minimum: $30,000

Functions: Generalist, IT

Industries: Mfg., Food, Bev., Tobacco, Chemicals, Drugs Mfg., Medical Devices, Electronic, Elec. Components, Transportation, Wholesale, Retail, Finance, Media, Government, ERP SW, Mfg. SW, Biotech

Professional Associations: ASTD, SHRM

Networks: Inter-City Personnel Assoc (IPA)

Roy Talman & Associates Inc
150 S Wacker Dr Ste 2250
Chicago, IL 60606
(312) 425-1300
Fax: (312) 425-0100
Email: resume@roytalman.com
Web: www.roytalman.com

Description: Contingency technology search firm. We specialize in software and related information technology. All positions are for Chicago area employers.

Key Contact - Specialty:
Mr. Ilya Talman, President - *Information technology, software*

Salary minimum: $45,000

Functions: IT

Industries: Generalist

Tamarac Executive Search LLC
7600 E Eastman Ave Ste 408
Tamarac Plz III
Denver, CO 80231
(303) 751-4141
(303) 751-4455
Fax: (303) 751-6600
Email: info@tamaracsearch.com
Web: www.tamaracsearch.com

Description: We are focusing on front range mid to senior level management and professional staff in finance, accounting, sales, marketing, HR, training, and operations. We full service, including psychometric profiling and 360 degree reference checking.

Key Contact:
Mr. Steve McBride, CMC, Founder

Salary minimum: $60,000

Functions: General Mgmt., Senior Mgmt., Sales Mgmt., HR Mgmt., Training, Finance, CFO's, Mgmt. Consultants

Industries: Generalist, Mgmt. Consulting, HR Services

Professional Associations: FFI, IMC

TAMB Associates Inc
1000 Johnson Ferry Rd Ste E-150
Marietta, GA 30068
(770) 565-8074
(888) 318-8531
Fax: (770) 565-3238
Email: Sara@tamb.com
Web: www.tamb.com

Description: TAMB Associates specialize in placing experienced candidates nationally and internationally in senior level executive positions, consulting, information services, human resources, engineering, sales and marketing.

Key Contact - Specialty:
Mr. Ted Daywalt, President
Ms. Sara Lykins, General Manager - *IT, Sales*
Ms. Karen Vereb, Manager - *Sales, engineering, IT*

Salary minimum: $75,000

Functions: General Mgmt.

Industries: Mfg., Transportation, Finance, Communications, Aerospace

Professional Associations: GAPS, NAPS, RON, SHRM

Tangent Associates
PO Box 3054
Thousand Oaks, CA 91359-0054
(805) 496-2555
Email: tangentweb@aol.com

Description: We are a successful, ethical, nationwide search work in all aspects of commercial banking by an experienced recruiting team of former bank executive officers. Assignment driven, we are matchmakers committed to developing long-term relationships.

Key Contact:
Mr. Terry White

Salary minimum: $50,000

Functions: Generalist

Industries: Banking

Networks: National Banking Network (NBN)

S Tanner & Associates Inc
710 Dorval Dr Ste 115
Oakville, ON L6K 3V7
Canada
(905) 339-2233
(905) 403-8496
Fax: (905) 339-2230
Email: resume@tannerinc.net
Web: www.tannerinc.net

Description: We specialize in engineering, operations management, and logistics search. Our goal is quality searches, because quality is never an accident. It is always the result of high intentions, sincere effort, intelligent direction, and skillful execution. It represents the wise choice of many alternatives.

Key Contact - Specialty:
Mr. Steve Tanner, President - *Engineering, operations management, logistics*
Ms. Joanne Tanner, Vice President - *Engineering, operations management, logistics*

Salary minimum: $35,000

Functions: Middle Mgmt., Production, Plant Mgmt., Quality, Materials, Purchasing, Materials Plng., Distribution, Packaging, Engineering

Industries: Mfg., Food, Bev., Tobacco, Soap, Perf., Cosmtcs., Drugs Mfg., Misc. Mfg., Transportation, Wholesale

Tantivy Group
1280 Bison Ste B9-480
Newport Beach, CA 92660
(714) 535-5558
Email: tantivysearch@aol.com

Description: Confidential searches are our specialty. Nationwide, prestigious clients.

Key Contact:
Ms. Mary Ann Schuessler, President

Salary minimum: $60,000

Functions: Middle Mgmt., Legal, Sales Mgmt., Finance, Cash Mgmt.

Industries: Finance, Legal, Accounting, Mgmt. Consulting, Entertainment, Broadcast, Film, Wireless

Tarbex
4545 Connecticut Ave NW Ste 326
Washington, DC 20008-6009
(202) 244-9258
Email: seniorrecruiter@tarbex.com
Web: www.tarbex.com

Description: We conduct highly selective searches in a timely and cost effective manner for e-commerce, startups, telecom, major national, international, regional and boutique consulting firms using personalized and customized partnership approach.

Key Contact - Specialty:
Ms. Parul Bhandari, Senior Recruiter - *Generalist, information technology, consulting*

Salary minimum: $40,000

Functions: Generalist, General Mgmt., Healthcare, Sales & Mktg., Finance, IT, Systems Implem., Mgmt. Consultants

Industries: Generalist, Finance, Mgmt. Consulting, Media, Telecoms, Software, Healthcare

Target Pros Inc
80 Main St
West Orange, NJ 07052-3034
(973) 324-0900
Fax: (973) 324-0901
Email: info@targetpros.com
Web: www.targetpros.com

Description: We specialize in the recruitment of sales and marketing professionals in the pharmaceutical, medical, biotechnology, healthcare, and consumer products industries.

Key Contact - Specialty:
Mr. David Marshall, President - *Sales & marketing, healthcare*

Salary minimum: $50,000

Functions: Generalist, Sales & Mktg., Mkt. Research, Mktg. Mgmt., Sales Mgmt., Specialized Svcs., Minorities

Industries: Generalist, Pharm Svcs., Biotech, Healthcare

Target Search Inc
PO Box 3379
Maple Glen, PA 19002
(215) 542-1110
Fax: (215) 542-1145
Email: target@target-search.com

Description: Our firm is a client driven, innovative, flexible service with 20 years of industry experience

in related field management experience. We have thirteen years of successful recruiting experience in food, contract management, and restaurants.

Key Contact:
Mr. Paul S. Berry, Principal/CPC

Salary minimum: $45,000

Functions: General Mgmt., Senior Mgmt., Middle Mgmt.

Industries: Hospitality

Professional Associations: RCA, SFM

Networks: Recruiters Professional Network (RPN)

Tarquinio Recruiting Group/Workforce Development Inc
(also known as Sales Consultants of Butler County)
1 Williamsburg Pl Ste 110
Warrendale, PA 15086
(724) 772-2000
Fax: (724) 772-2088
Email: job4you@nauticom.net
Web: www.tarquiniorecruiting.com

Description: We are a provider of permanent placement within the communications industry including voice, video, data, local access sectors and the information technology industry including hardware and software companies.

Key Contact:
Ms. Leslie Tarquinio, Managing Partner
Mr. Alfred Tarquinio, Managing Partner

Functions: Generalist

Industries: Telecoms

Tarris Associates Inc
511 Escambia St
Indian Habor Beach, FL 32937
(888) 217-8842
Fax: (888) 217-8842
Email: resume@tarrisassociates.com
Web: www.tarrisassociates.com

Description: We specialize in telecommunication and datacommunication industry search and recruiting. Marketing, sales, engineering and management.

Key Contact - Specialty:
Mr. Trebor Tarris, President - *Telecommunications, data communications, internet services*

Salary minimum: $50,000

Functions: Mktg. Mgmt., Sales Mgmt., Engineering

Industries: Computer Equip., New Media, Telecoms

M L Tawney & Associates
PO Box 179
Seabrook, TX 77586
(281) 326-0208
Email: meltaw@msn.com

Description: We specialize in executive search in technical and information technology industries and applications.

Key Contact - Specialty:
Mr. Mel Tawney, Chairman/President - *ERP package based solutions, information technology*

Salary minimum: $60,000

Functions: Generalist, General Mgmt., Sales & Mktg., IT, Engineering, Mgmt. Consultants

Industries: Generalist, Energy, Utilities, Construction, Chemicals, Computer Equip., Mgmt. Consulting, Software

Networks: Computer Search

Tax Advantage Personnel

PO Box 92422
Nashville, TN 37209
(866) 279-3687
(866) 279-2386
Email: advantage@taxprofessionals4hire.com
Web: www.taxprofessionals4hire.com

Description: Our firm specializes in identifying and attracting talented tax professionals for corporations and public accounting firms throughout the Southeast. We make the right fit for the long term. Our job is to understand each candidate's present position and their career goals to achieve a good fit.

Key Contact:
Mr. Larry Barlow

Salary minimum: $35,000

Functions: Taxes, M&A, Attorneys

Industries: Generalist

Professional Associations: NAPS

Tax Network Resources Inc

7 Lee Pl Ste 241
Hicksville, NY 11804-1452
(516) 777-7167
Fax: (516) 752-8553
Email: taxcareers@aol.com

Description: We specialize in tax, accounting, audit and consulting in NYC metro, Philadelphia and Hartford areas. President has hands-on experience after working for CPA firms in audit/tax/accounting departments.

Key Contact - Specialty:
Mr. Mike Marino, President - *Public accounting (all areas), audit & tax, internal audit, corporate tax*

Salary minimum: $25,000

Functions: Taxes

Industries: Generalist

Professional Associations: AICPA, NJSCPA, NYSCPA

Branches:
60 E 42nd St Ste 746
New York, NY 10165
(516) 777-7167
Key Contact:
Mr. Mike Marino, President

Tax Recruitment Services

208 E 51st St No 104
New York, NY 10022
(212) 753-2737
Email: taxrecruit@lanline.com
Web: www.taxrecruitonline.com

Description: We are one of the leading tax recruiting firms in the NY Metro area. Our niche is serving CPA firms and Fortune 500 corporations by placing tax accountants and tax attorneys at all levels and fuctions.

Key Contact:
Mr. Matt Sanders, Recruiter/Principal

Salary minimum: $35,000

Functions: Taxes

Industries: Generalist

Terry Taylor & Associates

459 Bechman St
Springdale, PA 15144-1170
(724) 274-5627
Fax: (724) 274-5627
Email: tdtassoc@bellatlantic.net

Description: Our firm is a nationally recognized executive search consulting firm with twenty years in financial, litigation support, performance improvement, and management information systems recruitment. We specialize in recruitment and placement of experienced professionals in the consulting firm industry.

Key Contact:
Mr. Terry Taylor, Vice President

Salary minimum: $100,000

Peter R Taylor Associates Inc

43 Orchard Dr
East Williston, NY 11596
(516) 742-9292
Fax: (516) 742-9296
Email: peterrtaylor@aol.com

Description: We specialize in corporate real estate executive search, retail chains, financial institutions, developers, industrial corporations.

Key Contact - Specialty:
Mr. Peter R. Taylor, President - *Retail real estate*

Salary minimum: $50,000

Functions: Generalist

Industries: Real Estate

Professional Associations: ICSC, NACORE

TCM Enterprises

57 W Timonium Rd Ste 310
Timonium, MD 21093
(410) 561-5244
Fax: (410) 561-5248
Email: tmcpoyle@erols.com

Description: Our clients include defense electronics, material scientists, meteorologists, shock physicists, chemical and environmental specialties, intelligent vehicle highway systems and experts in marketing and accounting/finance.

Key Contact - Specialty:
Mr. Thomas C. McPoyle, Jr., Director - *Engineers, scientists*

Functions: Generalist, General Mgmt., Materials, Sales & Mktg., Finance, IT, R&D, Engineering

Industries: Generalist, Mfg., Transportation, Defense, Environmental Svcs., Aerospace, Software

Networks: Inter-City Personnel Assoc (IPA)

TDM & Associates

101 W Tomaras Ave Ste 2
Savoy, IL 61874
(217) 352-3844
Fax: (217) 352-3855
Email: tim@tdm-assoc.com
Web: www.tdm-assoc.com

Description: We are a boutique search firm with an excellent track record of recruiting and placing professional, technical and executive-level candidates.

Key Contact - Specialty:
Mr. Tim Maupin, President - *Generalist*

Salary minimum: $40,000

Functions: Generalist, Middle Mgmt., Materials, HR Mgmt., Finance, IT, Engineering

Industries: Generalist, Mfg., Food, Bev., Tobacco, Printing, Chemicals, Plastics, Rubber, Paints, Petro. Products, Metal Products, Misc. Mfg., Transportation

Professional Associations: APICS, ASQC, SHRM

Networks: Inter-City Personnel Assoc (IPA)

TE Inc

PO BOX 9034
Oak Brook, IL 60522
(630) 325-8627
(630) 325-8384
Fax: (630) 325-8630
Email: erics@teinc.com
Web: www.teinc.com

Description: We have the philosophy of catering to the client needs and to determine the most effective candidate for the position. Our management consulting group caters to the middle tier of management. We work in the areas of MIS, software and the Internet. We have new start-up division.

Key Contact - Specialty:
Mr. Eric K. Schuller, President - *Generalist*
Ms. Bonita Mae, Vice President-Consulting - *Generalist*

Salary minimum: $35,000

Functions: Generalist, Production, Mkt. Research, MIS Mgmt., Systems Analysis, Systems Dev., Systems Implem., Systems Support

Industries: Generalist

Team Place

1010 Wayne Ave Ste 355
Silver Spring, MD 20910
(301) 495-1008
Fax: (301) 565-3915
Email: rkaminski@bio-search.com
Web: www.teamplace.com

Description: We are an executive search firm specializing in the recruitment of healthcare and pharmaceutical administrators, executives and physicians.

Key Contact:
Ms. Elisabeth Peebles, President - *Research*
Mr. Rob Kaminski, Vice President of Bio-Research Division

Functions: Generalist, Senior Mgmt., Physicians, Health Admin., Sales Mgmt., CFO's

Industries: Generalist, Drugs Mfg., Medical Devices, Pharm Svcs., Mgmt. Consulting

Professional Associations: AHHRA, HRN, NATSS, NCHEA, RAPS

Team-Stat Statistical Services

3208 Dupont Ave S
Minneapolis, MN 55408
(612) 825-0332
Email: tmelander@team-stat.com
Web: www.team-stat.com

Description: We are a statistical warehouse providing statistical consulting, recruiting, and other data analysis services. We have successfully placed statisticians in the fields of health care, biotech, research and development, and marketing.

Key Contact - Specialty:
Mr. Todd E. Melander, President - *Statistical consulting*

Professional Associations: ASA

TeamBuilders

3081 Holcomb Bridge Rd Ste A1
Norcross, GA 30071
(770) 416-0996
Fax: (770) 416-0894
Email: teambldr@mindspring.com
Web: www.teambuilder.com

Description: We serve employers by understanding technology as it relates to business. We locate people who demonstrate, by their attitude and experience, their commitment to an integrity-based work ethic.

Key Contact - Specialty:
Mr. Buz Mayo, President - *Information systems management, systems networking, programming, web applications*

Functions: General Mgmt., Senior Mgmt., IT, Network Admin.

Industries: Generalist, Computer Equip., Mgmt. Consulting, Hospitality, Software

Professional Associations: GAPS

Teamsearch Inc
27600 Farmington Rd Ste 108
Farmington Hills, MI 48334
(248) 553-9881
Fax: (248) 553-9883
Email: passons@bignet.net

Description: We are a nationwide network of service to the assembly and automation equipment and metal working machine and equipment industries.

Key Contact - Specialty:
Mr. Steven A. Passon, President - *Automation machinery, machine tool, special machinery*

Salary minimum: $35,000

Functions: Mfg., Product Dev., Production, Automation, Plant Mgmt., Sales Mgmt., IT, Systems Analysis, Systems Dev., Engineering

Industries: Metal Products, Machine, Appliance, Motor Vehicles, Test, Measure Equip.

Tech Connect Corp
5540 Fairmount Ste 115
Downers Grove, IL 60516
(630) 963-8489
Fax: (630) 963-8479
Email: efalco@tech-connection.com
Web: www.tech-connection.com

Description: We partner with our clients evaluating their IT staffing needs from their point of view with our recruiting expertise, staffing flexibility and responsive service.

Key Contact - Specialty:
Ms. Elena S. Falco, CPC, President - *Information technology*

Functions: Generalist, MIS Mgmt., Systems Analysis, Systems Dev., Systems Implem., Systems Support, Network Admin., DB Admin.

Industries: Generalist, Software

Professional Associations: IACPR, IAPS

Tech Consulting
50 S Belcher Rd Ste 113
Clearwater, FL 33765
(727) 443-5335
Email: hdhunter99@aol.com

Description: We recruit for Fortune 500 companies and startups in the areas of telecommunications only, more specifically wireless and wire line, equipment and Semiconductors. We also place in the areas of engineering and product management.

Key Contact - Specialty:
Mr. Mark Bavli, Manager - *Telecommunications, engineering*

Salary minimum: $70,000

Functions: R&D, Engineering

Industries: Telecoms, Digital, Wireless, Fiber Optic, Network Infrastructure

Networks: Top Echelon Network

Tech Int'l
PO Box 18
Hopkinton, RI 02833
(401) 539-2191
Fax: (401) 539-0185
Email: sean@jobgalileo.com
Web: www.jobgalileo.com

Description: We specialize in sales/marketing/management/field service and high level executive positions for the analytical instrumentation and biotech industries.

Key Contact - Specialty:
Ms. Helen M. Brophy, CEO - *Analytical instrumentation, biotech*
Mr. Sean K. Smith, VP- of Marketing - *Science, engineering*
Mr. Howard A. Smith, Vice President - *Optics*

Salary minimum: $50,000

Functions: Generalist, Senior Mgmt., Sales & Mktg., Sales Mgmt., Engineering

Industries: Chemicals, Drugs Mfg., Medical Devices, Computer Equip., Test, Measure Equip., Pharm Svcs., Mgmt. Consulting, Advertising, Aerospace, Biotech

Professional Associations: OSA, SPIE

Tech-Center
(an affilliate of Sanford Rose Opportunity Center)
265 S Main St Ste 200
Akron, OH 44308
(330) 762-6212
Fax: (330) 762-2035
Email: mail@techcenterinc.com
Web: www.techcenterinc.com

Description: We are a personnel services firm providing contract engineering, professional services, temporary personnel, and direct placement.

Key Contact - Specialty:
Mr. Douglas Eilertson, President - *Engineering (general, regional), computer technology (general, regional)*

Functions: General Mgmt.

Industries: Generalist

Tech/Data Recruiters Inc
5851 Southwest Fwy Ste 503
Houston, TX 77057
(713) 592-8989
Fax: (713) 668-4488
Email: info@techdatarecruiters.com
Web: www.techdatarecruiters.com

Description: Our firm is an established, highly awarded, fast growing, and challenging recruiting firm. In 1999 and 2000, TECH/data Recruiters, Inc. was ranked in The Houston 100®, an award spotlighting Houston's top 100, fastest growing, privately held companies. Our clients receive real time market information, which allows them to stay ahead of the competition. We dedicate ourselves to providing the best service in the industry. Our firm specializes in placing candidates in the engineering and information technology fields.

Key Contact - Specialty:
Mr. Demond Kenebrew, Account Manager - *Computer, IT industry, engineering industry*

Salary minimum: $40,000

Functions: Generalist, IT

Industries: Generalist, Energy, Utilities, Mfg., Electronic, Elec. Components, Venture Cap., E-commerce, IT Implementation, Communications, Software, Networking, Comm. SW

Techaid Inc
5165 Queen Mary Rd Ste 401
Montreal, QC H3W 1X7
Canada
(514) 482-6790
(800) 341-6790
Fax: (514) 482-0324
Email: info@techaid.ca
Web: www.techaid.ca

Description: We recruit and provide experienced technical staff on a temporary or permanent basis. We are the longest established technical personnel agency in Quebec with over 1500 customers in 37 years.

Key Contact - Specialty:
Mr. William F. Allen, President - *Engineering, information technology, manufacturing*

Salary minimum: $30,000

Functions: Mfg., Materials, IT, R&D, Engineering, Int'l.

Industries: Generalist

Professional Associations: ACSESS, NAPS

TechFind Inc
PO Box 626
Natick, MA 01760
(508) 647-0111
Fax: (508) 647-0110
Email: amy@techfind.com
Web: www.techfind.com

Description: We are a retained search firm specializing in the placement of highly trained scientists, business development, technical sales and medical professionals. Our recruiters are trained scientists in the life science area. We have all worked in a chemical, biotech or pharmaceutical company and have experience in placing scientists.

Key Contact - Specialty:
Ms. Amy B. Lurier, President - *Pharmaceuticals, biotechnology*

Salary minimum: $80,000

Functions: Healthcare, Sales & Mktg., IT, R&D

Industries: Pharm Svcs., Biotech

Professional Associations: AAAS, ACP, ACS, RAPS

TechHi Consultants Ltd
22 Frederick St Ste 200
Kitchener, ON N2H 6M6
Canada
(519) 749-1020
Fax: (519) 749-1070
Web: www.techhi.com

Description: We specialize in high-technology and automotive industries.

Key Contact:
Mr. Jack Hougasian, General Manager

Functions: Generalist, General Mgmt., Mfg., Materials, Sales & Mktg., IT, R&D, Engineering

Industries: Generalist, Motor Vehicles, Computer Equip., Media, Aerospace, Software, Biotech

TECHNET Staffing Services Inc
2280 W Tyler Ste 204
Fairfield, IA 52556
(641) 472-5529
Fax: (641) 472-9009
Email: resumes@technet-inc.com
Web: www.technet-inc.com

Description: We work with the top technical companies to help them meet their demand for highly skilled technical talent. We have openings nationally for both contract and permanent positions.

Key Contact:
Mr. Tim Mahaney, President

Functions: Mfg., IT, MIS Mgmt., Systems Analysis, Systems Dev., Network Admin., DB Admin., Engineering

Industries: Generalist

Technical Connections Inc
11400 Olympic Blvd Ste 700
Los Angeles, CA 90064
(310) 479-8830
Fax: (310) 445-8726
Email: info@technicalconnections.com
Web: www.technicalconnections.com

Description: We are the largest Southern California firm specializing strictly in computer systems professionals including IT, software development and consulting. Staffed by computer professionals, we conduct face-to-face interviews with all candidates.

Key Contact:
Ms. Helen MacKinnon, President - *Computer science, information technology*
Mr. Peter MacKinnon, Chief Executive Officer

Salary minimum: $35,000

Functions: Generalist, MIS Mgmt., Systems Analysis, Systems Dev., Systems Implem., Systems Support, Network Admin., DB Admin.

Industries: Generalist, Non-classifiable

Professional Associations: NAWBO, WIB, WPO

Technical Management Resources Inc
110 Dunlop St E Ste 304
Barrie, ON L4M 1A5
Canada
(800) 811-1456
(705) 727-7678
Fax: (705) 727-7989
Email: info@tmr.ca
Web: www.tmr.ca

Description: We specialize in the permanent placement of highly qualified technical, engineering and managerial professionals. We are professional and honest, with a commitment to service. We build success by placing people first.

Key Contact - Specialty:
Mr. Robert N. Rice, President - *Manufacturing, engineering, consulting engineering, financial, construction*

Salary minimum: $50,000

Functions: General Mgmt., Mfg., Materials, Sales & Mktg., HR Mgmt., Finance, R&D, Engineering

Industries: Generalist, Agri., Forestry, Mining, Construction, Mfg., Transportation, Aerospace, Packaging

Technical Recruiting Consultants Inc
1100 W Northwest Hwy Ste 208
Mt. Prospect, IL 60056
(847) 394-1101

Description: We are specialists in information systems, engineering and manufacturing positions.

Key Contact - Specialty:
Mr. Dick Latimer, President - *MIS, engineering, manufacturing*

Functions: MIS Mgmt., Systems Analysis, Systems Dev., Systems Implem., Systems Support

Industries: Generalist

Technical Search Associates
20325 Center Ridge Rd Ste 622
Rocky River, OH 44116
(440) 356-0880

Description: We specialize in electrical, mechanical and manufacturing engineers in the electronics, automotive and aerospace industries. Also perform specialized searches per client requirements.

Key Contact - Specialty:
Mr. John M. Brunschwig - *Engineering*

Salary minimum: $40,000

Functions: Product Dev., Engineering

Industries: Mfg., Motor Vehicles, Computer Equip., Consumer Elect., Electronic, Elec. Components, Defense, Aerospace, Software

Professional Associations: SAE

Networks: National Personnel Assoc (NPA)

Technical Service Consultants of Manitoba Ltd
125 Garry St Ste 890
Winnipeg, MB R3C 3P2
Canada
(204) 987-8080
Fax: (204) 987-8086
Email: tsc@escape.ca

Description: We specialize in executive search, recruitment and outplacement services for the manufacturing and engineering sectors. Local, national, and international search; with associate offices in Vancouver, Calgary, Edmonton, and Toronto.

Key Contact:
Mr. Brian Hayes, General Manager
Mr. Rick Tetreault, Associate

Salary minimum: $40,000

Functions: Generalist

Industries: Agri., Forestry, Mining, Mfg., Lumber, Furniture, Plastics, Rubber, Paints, Petro. Products, Metal Products, Motor Vehicles, Transportation, Aerospace, Mfg. SW

Technical Staffing Professionals LLC
7 W State St Ste 307
Sharon, PA 16146
(724) 982-4175
Fax: (724) 982-4185
Email: techjobs@techstaffingpros.com
Web: www.techstaffingpros.com

Description: We are an independent recruiting firm providing direct hire, contract, and contract-to-perm employment options. We focus on engineering and technical positions within manufacturing companies, primarily in sales, engineering, and operations. Our experienced account executives find and present quality candidates, and assist companies throughout the hiring and interviewing process.

Key Contact:
Mr. Bruce Bille, President

Salary minimum: $50,000

Functions: General Mgmt., Mfg., Engineering

Industries: Mfg., Communications, Telecoms, Digital, Wireless, Fiber Optic, Network Infrastructure

Technical Staffing Solutions
16775 Addison Rd Ste 240
Addison, TX 75001
(972) 248-0700
Fax: (972) 248-1175
Email: don@technicalstaffing.com
Web: www.technicalstaffing.com

Description: We recruit process, project, production, environmental engineers for the chemical, petrochemical and petroleum refining industries on a regular employment or contractual employment basis. We also recruit and place information technology professionals.

Key Contact - Specialty:
Mr. Don J. Fink, CPC, President - *Information technology*

Salary minimum: $40,000

Functions: Generalist, Systems Analysis, Systems Dev., Systems Implem., Network Admin., DB Admin., Engineering

Industries: Generalist, Chemicals

Technifind Int'l
5959 Gateway W Ste 601
El Paso, TX 79925
(915) 775-1176
Fax: (915) 778-9314
Email: info@technifind.com
Web: www.technifind.com

Description: We are an extensive network established throughout North, South and Central America. We are very familiar with demographics in various markets and industries. Most clients in Fortune 1000 list.

Key Contact:
Mr. Tim Vida, President
Mr. Bruce Steiner, Vice President

Salary minimum: $50,000

Functions: Generalist, General Mgmt., Mfg., Materials, Sales & Mktg., Finance, Engineering, Int'l.

Industries: Generalist, Energy, Utilities, Mfg., Environmental Svcs., Packaging, Software

Professional Associations: APICS, APICS, ASQ, FTA

TechniQuest
PO Box 548
San Jose, CA 95106-0548
(408) 293-1122
Fax: (408)
Email: claudia@techniquest.com
Web: www.techniquest.com

Description: We focus on candidates/searches from the individual, technical, or engineering contributor to CTOs.

Key Contact - Specialty:
Ms. Claudia Lindquist, General Manager - *Technologies*

Salary minimum: $50,000

Functions: Generalist, Directors, Senior Mgmt., Middle Mgmt., Product Dev., Automation, Systems Dev., Engineering

Industries: Generalist, Medical Devices, Software, Biotech

TechniSearch
5105-C Monroe Rd
Charlotte, NC 28205
(704) 536-8776
Fax: (704) 536-1797
Email: jopfl@mindspring.com
Web: www.rcrtr.com

Description: We have specialized in recruiting technical and management personnel in powder metallurgy, technical ceramics, and carbides since 1982.

Key Contact - Specialty:
Mr. John Pflug, Owner - *Powder metallurgy, technical ceramics, carbides*

Salary minimum: $30,000

Functions: Generalist, Product Dev., Automation, Plant Mgmt., Quality, Sales & Mktg., Engineering

Industries: Generalist, Mfg., Plastics, Rubber, Metal Products, Machine, Appliance, Misc. Mfg.

Professional Associations: ACerS, APMI

Networks: Top Echelon Network

TechNix Inc

100 Esgore Dr
Toronto, ON M5M 3S2
Canada
(416) 250-9195
Fax: (416) 485-7964
Email: tnixon@technix.ca
Web: www.technix.ca

Description: We are specialists in recruiting sales, marketing, pre and post-sales, senior architects, CTOs, and executive management for technology vendors and IT consultancies.

Key Contact - Specialty:
Mr. Ted Nixon, President - *High tech vendors (software, hardware, consulting, internet)*

Salary minimum: $60,000

Functions: Generalist, General Mgmt., Sales & Mktg., HR Mgmt., IT, MIS Mgmt., Systems Analysis, Systems Dev., Systems Implem.

Industries: Mgmt. Consulting, Media, Advertising, New Media, Software

Techno-Trac Systems Inc

251 Central Park W
New York, NY 10024
(212) 769-8722
Fax: (212) 873-1596
Email: technomt@bigfoot.com

Description: We are a NY/metropolitan based information technology search firm. Our president's over twenty years of experience in the field yields broad client base, especially in the areas of brokerage, banking, and financial. We have a supportive candidate relationship. We have a full range of IT programming, systems, business analysis, support and Internet positions, from over one-year juniors through senior executives.

Key Contact - Specialty:
Mr. Mort Trachtenberg, President - *Information technology professionals*

Salary minimum: $25,000

Functions: Generalist, MIS Mgmt., Systems Analysis, Systems Dev., Systems Implem., Systems Support, Network Admin., DB Admin.

Industries: Generalist, Finance, Banking, Invest. Banking, Brokers, Software

Technoforce LLC

4 Knollwood Ter Ste 210
Randolph, NJ 07869
(973) 328-1047
Email: robin@technoforce.com
Web: www.technoforce.com

Description: We specialize in permanent placement for e-commerce and high-technology companies. We place junior and senior programmers, web developers/designers, technical managers, e-commerce directors and strategic marketing managers.

Key Contact - Specialty:
Ms. Robin Berg Tabakin, Managing Director - *Information technology*

Salary minimum: $25,000

Functions: Generalist, General Mgmt., Mktg. Mgmt., IT, MIS Mgmt., Systems Dev., R&D, Engineering, Graphic Artists

Industries: Generalist, Pharm Svcs., IT Implementation, New Media, Telecoms, Aerospace

Professional Associations: VANJ

Technology Consultants Int'l

7720 El Camino Real Ste 2P
Carlsbad, CA 92009
(760) 436-8400
Fax: (760) 436-8900
Email: tom@techconsultants.com
Web: www.techconsultants.com

Description: We serve the high end computer hardware and software vendor community whose applications consist of scientific, engineering, manufacturing, intranet and enterprise wide business applications. The positions we place are in the areas of executive management, sales, marketing and sales support.

Key Contact:
Mr. Thomas Conway, Senior Partner

Salary minimum: $80,000

Functions: Generalist, Product Dev., Automation, Purchasing, Materials Plng., Sales Mgmt., Systems Implem., Engineering

Industries: Generalist, Software

Branches:
9134 Union Cemetery Rd Ste 212
Cincinnati, OH 45249
(513) 489-2327
Fax: (513) 489-3038
Key Contact:
Mr. Ed Neenan, Senior Partner

Technology Resources Inc

2424 Madrid Ave
PO Box 103
Safety Harbor, FL 34695
(727) 799-2100
Fax: (727) 724-1323
Email: bill@erpjobcenter.net
Web: www.erpjobcenter.com

Description: We are an executive recruiting firm working with the major "Big 5" and second tier Fortune companies to provide top level IT professionals with career opportunities on a permanent basis. We work with the professionals to find the "right" career opportunity on a proactive basis rather than fit them into a specific slot!

Key Contact - Specialty:
Mr. William S. Lee, President - *IT recruiting (All areas)*
Mrs. Emily J. Lee, Vice President - *Big 5 recruiting*

Salary minimum: $100,000

Functions: IT

Industries: Generalist

Networks: Top Echelon Network

Technology Search Int'l

1737 N 1st St Ste 600
San Jose, CA 95112-4524
(408) 437-9500
Fax: (408) 437-1033
Email: info@tsearch.com
Web: www.tsearch.com

Description: We specialize in software development, in particular hands-on developers in the operating systems, client/server, distributed systems, database and Internet/Extranet/WWW spaces.

Key Contact - Specialty:
Mr. Steve Dyson, Vice President - *Client/server, www, distributed systems, database*
Mr. Alan Shapiro, President - *Operating systems, management*
Mr. Chris Dangerfield, Technical Recruiting Manager - *Consulting, operating systems, client/server*
Mr. Don Sirey, Vice President - *Database, operating systems, marketing*

Functions: Systems Dev.

Industries: Software

Professional Associations: ACM, IEEE

TechScreen

76 Northeastern Blvd Ste 34B
Nashua, NH 03062
(603) 674-2041
Email: contact@techscreen.com
Web: www.techscreen.com

Description: We are a technical executive (and contingency) recruiting firm made up of experienced, technical professionals.

Key Contact - Specialty:
Mr. Bob Misita, Managing Partner - *Technology, computer software, networking*

Salary minimum: $50,000

Functions: Generalist, Directors, Senior Mgmt., Middle Mgmt., IT, MIS Mgmt., R&D, Engineering

Industries: Generalist, Mfg., Finance, Services, Media, Insurance, Software

Techsearch Services Inc

46 Wickford Pl
Madison, CT 06443
(203) 318-1100
Fax: (203) 318-8800
Email: dtaft@snet.net
Web: www.techsearchservices.com

Description: We are an executive recruiter of information/financial service professionals and traders for major investment companies/commercial banks. Emphasis on financial services community. We have particular expertise in the more analytical systems and business analysis. Fixed income, equities and derivatives.

Key Contact:
Mr. David G. Taft, President

Salary minimum: $50,000

Functions: Risk Mgmt., IT, Systems Dev.

Industries: Finance, Banking, Invest. Banking, Brokers

Professional Associations: NAER

Techstaff Inc

11270 W Park Pl Ste 460
Milwaukee, WI 53224
(414) 359-4444
Fax: (414) 359-4949
Email: recruiter@techstaff.com
Web: www.techstaff.com

Description: We specialize in the recruitment and placement of engineering and technical personnel.

Key Contact - Specialty:
Mr. Thomas Montgomery, Director of Placement - *Generalist, technical*
Ms. Susan Metzger, Recruiting Coordinator - *Generalist, technical*

Salary minimum: $35,000

Functions: Generalist, Mfg., Materials, HR Mgmt., Finance, IT, Engineering, Specialized Svcs.

Industries: Generalist, Medical Devices, Plastics, Rubber, Metal Products, Machine, Appliance, Consumer Elect., Misc. Mfg.

Professional Associations: NAPS, NATSS

Branches:
3900 E Camelback Rd Ste 108
Phoenix, AZ 85018
(602) 955-6464
Fax: (602) 955-8784
Email: recruiter@techstaffaz.com
Key Contact:
Ms. Cindy Robidoux, Branch Manager

500 Esplanade Dr Ste 1200
Oxnard, CA 93030
(805) 485-7456
Fax: (805) 485-0070
Key Contact:
Ms. Jenifer Peterson, Branch Manager

2880 Sunrise Blvd Ste 120
Rancho Cordova, CA 95670
(916) 852-6222
Fax: (916) 852-6242
Email: recruiter1@techstaffca.com
Key Contact:
Mr. Dennis Jones

1200 W Hillcrest Dr Ste 201
Thousand Oaks, CA 91320
(805) 376-2250
Fax: (805) 376-2551
Email: mike@techstaffca.com
Key Contact:
Mr. Mike Moran, Manager

1100 N Florida Ave
PO Box 172126
Tampa, FL 33602
(813) 221-1222
Fax: (813) 221-6658
Email: recruiter@techstafftb.com
Key Contact:
Mr. Adam Mainzer, Owner

9801 W Higgins Rd Ste 580
Rosemont, IL 60018
(847) 692-3090
(800) 652-8324
Fax: (847) 692-2294
Email: recruiter@techstaffil.com
Key Contact:
Mr. Steve Bauer

5115 Utica Ridge Rd
Davenport, IA 52807
(319) 355-4400
Fax: (319) 355-0694
Email: scott@techstaffia.com
Key Contact:
Mr. Steve Nord

28104 Orchard Lake Rd Ste 150
Farmington Hills, MI 48334
(248) 932-3290
Fax: (248) 932-3143
Email: terry@techstaffmi.com
Key Contact:
Mr. Bill Gansser, Owner

4829 E Beltline Ave NE
Grand Rapids, MI 49525
(616) 361-0033
Fax: (616) 361-1630
Email: julie@techstaffmi.com
Key Contact:
Mr. Bill Gansser, Owner

2670 S Ashland Ave Ste 206
Ashland Ctr
Green Bay, WI 54304
(920) 498-9870
Fax: (920) 498-0673
Email: recruiter@techstaffgb.com
Key Contact:
Mr. Chris Kahn, Owner

techVenture Inc
167 Hamilton Ave Fl 2
Palo Alto, CA 94301
(650) 321-6970
(877) 832-4836
Fax: (650) 321-6961
Email: fadi@techVenture.com
Web: www.techVenture.com

Description: Our firm is a specialized high stake
hire retained search firm that places executive,
managerial, and technical staff with early growth
software companies. Our mission is to provide a
relationship-based recruiting service, one that meets
the needs of both pre-public new technology

companies and the top-notch talent that powers
them.
Key Contact:
Mr. Fadi Bishara, President
Salary minimum: $120,000

Tecmark Associates Inc
PO Box 545
Port Washington, NY 11050
(516) 883-6336
(212) 947-6027
Fax: (516) 883-6388
Email: info@tecmark.com
Web: www.tecmark.com

Description: We specialize in electronic industry
worldwide executive, managerial and professional
searches for all technology/market sensitive
positions from president/CEO on through R&D,
development, hard & software design engineering,
manufacturing, sales, marketing, support for
semiconductors, computers, instrumentation, EDA,
ATE, CIM, etc.

Key Contact - Specialty:
Mr. Donald U. Valentine, President - *Electronic
high technology industry*
Mr. Bradford M. Kennedy, Vice President -
Electronic high technology industry

Salary minimum: $40,000

Functions: Generalist, General Mgmt., Mfg., Sales
& Mktg., IT, R&D, Engineering, Technicians

Industries: Generalist, Medical Devices, Machine,
Appliance, Computer Equip., Consumer Elect.,
Test, Measure Equip.

Branches:
10675 S DeAnza Blvd Ste 4
Cupertino, CA 95014-4449
(408) 446-4672
Email: cw@tecmark.com
Key Contact - Specialty:
Mr. Charles R. Wilkenson, Director - *Electronic
industry technical, professional & management*

Tecnix LLC
PO Box 240
Alpharetta, GA 30009
(770) 751-7759
Fax: (208) 988-4047
Email: jobs@tecnix.net
Web: www.tecnix.net

Description: Our firm provides recruiting and
knowledge management consulting services, to the
medical device, diagnostic, pharmaceutical,
biotechnology, and related industries. In addition to
recruiting and staffing, Tecnix can source and
deliver the intellectual property, competitive
intelligence, technology, financing, or initiate the
strategic contact you may need to successfully bring
your product to market or project to completion.

Key Contact - Specialty:
Mr. Mario Martinez, CSIIIE, Managing Partner -
Medical device, diagnostic industry

Functions: Generalist, Senior Mgmt., Product Dev.,
Engineering

Industries: Mfg., Drugs Mfg., Medical Devices,
Invest. Banking, Venture Cap., Pharm Svcs.,
Defense, Packaging, Software, ERP SW, Mfg.
SW, Biotech, Dental, Non-classifiable

Teeman, Perley, Gilmartin Inc
230 Park Ave Ste 2425
New York, NY 10169
(212) 972-5544
Web: www.tpgsearch.com

Description: We are a worldwide full-service
executive search firm specializing in the
international financial community. Our expertise

spans the breadth of Wall Street products including
sales, trading, research and capital markets in both
the equity and fixed income areas, domestically and
internationally.

Key Contact:
Ms. Susan S. Teeman, President
Ms. Ellen Perley, Partner
Ms. Marybeth Gilmartin, Partner

Functions: Generalist

Industries: Finance

Teknon Employment Resources Inc
17 S St. Clair St Ste 300
Dayton, OH 45402-2137
(937) 222-5300
Fax: (937) 222-6311
Email: teknon@teknongroup.com
Web: www.teknongroup.com

Description: Our team provides targeted
contingency search within the telecommunications
and engineering disciplines while providing access
to top talent in all disciplines through network
affiliations with search firms throughout the US.
Our specialties include: electronics, fiber optics,
optical networking, OEM, VP, CEO, sales,
marketing, ASIC, telecommunications, DataComm,
networks, B2B, e-Commerce, and engineering.

Key Contact:
Mr. Raymond B. Gooch, CPC, President/CEO
Mr. Joseph S. Murawski, CPC, Executive Search
Consultant - *Electronic manufacturing, (contract
service providers)*
Mr. Stephen R. White, CPC, Executive Search
Consultant - *Retail, online, logistics, distribution*
Mr. Clark L. Miller, PHR, Executive Search
Consultant - *Telecommunications contract
manufacturing management*
Mr. Michael W. Little, Executive Search
Consultant - *MIS (engineering, management)*
Mr. Pattie Johnson, Research Manager

Salary minimum: $50,000

Functions: General Mgmt., Directors, Senior
Mgmt., Mfg., Production, Plant Mgmt., Quality

Industries: Mfg., Plastics, Rubber, Motor Vehicles,
Computer Equip., Consumer Elect., Test, Measure
Equip., Misc. Mfg., Electronic, Elec.
Components, Digital, Wireless, Fiber Optic,
Network Infrastructure, Mfg. SW, Marketing SW,
Networking, Comm. SW

Professional Associations: NAPS, OSSA

Networks: Top Echelon Network

Tele-Media Int'l Inc
336 King of Prussia Rd Ste 101
Radnor, PA 19087
(610) 225-0500
Fax: (610) 225-2655
Email: wrd@tmistaffing.com
Web: www.tmistaffing.com

Description: Our firm is a national search firm
specializing in biotech, telecommunications, and the
related fields of information technology, data
storage, and e-Commerce. TMI identifies mutually
beneficial permanent and retained employment
opportunities for both candidates and clients using
our extensive experience, as well as our recruiting
and placement skills.

Key Contact - Specialty:
Mr. William R. DePhillipo, President -
Telecommunications, information technology

Salary minimum: $45,000

Functions: Senior Mgmt., Middle Mgmt., Sales
Mgmt., Direct Mktg., Customer Svc., IT, R&D,
Technicians

Industries: Generalist, Communications, Telecoms, Telephony, Wireless, Fiber Optic, Network Infrastructure, Biotech, Healthcare

Professional Associations: ASA

Branches:
619 Main St Ste 10B
Frisco, CO 80443
(970) 668-0808
Fax: (970) 668-0909
Email: cmd@tmistaffing.com
Key Contact:
Mr. Christopher DePhillipo

Tele-Solutions of Arizona Inc
8655 E Via De Ventura Ste F-127
Scottsdale, AZ 85258
(480) 483-1300
Fax: (480) 483-7221
Email: carole@telesolutionsearch.com
Web: www.telesolutionsearch.com

Description: We are a hi-tech national search firm. We specialize in optical networking, optics, ATM, SONET, telephony and datacom. We search for hardware, software, system developers, product marketing, business development, network planners, technology managers, directors, vice presidents up to the executive-level.

Key Contact - Specialty:
Ms. Carole Wichansky, Owner/Manager - *Software, telecommunications, engineering*
Ms. Janice Robertson, Senior Recruiter - *Hardware, telecommunications, engineering*
Ms. Christine Hoppler - *Telecommunications, engineering, hardware, software*
Ms. Sandy Neundorfer - *Sales & marketing*

Salary minimum: $60,000

Functions: Generalist, Systems Analysis, Systems Dev., Systems Implem., Systems Support, Network Admin., DB Admin., Engineering

Industries: Generalist, Media, Software

Professional Associations: ASA

Telecom Connections Inc
602 Golf Crest Ln Ste 200
Austin, TX 78734
(512) 261-3290
Fax: (512) 261-3278
Email: gorr@telecomconnections.com
Web: www.telecomconnections.com

Description: We specialize in placement of middle management through executive-level candidates primarily in wireless telecommunications companies, for example: PCS, cellular, LMDS, and messaging. This also includes sales and marketing, operations, telecommunications engineers, and technical personnel. Our clients consist of wireless system operators, as well as suppliers to the industry, primarily domestic.

Key Contact - Specialty:
Mr. George H. Orr, President - *Wireless telecommunications*

Salary minimum: $50,000

Functions: Generalist

Industries: Telecoms

Professional Associations: EMA, SHRM, TAPS

Telecom Recruiters Int'l Inc
2101 W Commercial Blvd Ste 3000
Ft. Lauderdale, FL 33309
(954) 343-2659
Fax: (954) 776-5855
Email: ehorowitz@telecomrecruitersintl.com
Web: www.telecomrecruitersintl.com

Description: Our firm is a telecommunications executive search specialist.

Key Contact - Specialty:
Mr. Eric Horowitz, President - *Telecommunications*

Salary minimum: $50,000

Functions: General Mgmt., Sales & Mktg.

Industries: Telecoms, Telephony, Digital, Wireless, Fiber Optic, Network Infrastructure

---

Telecom Recruiters Inc
12531 Lieutenant Nichols Rd
Fairfax, VA 22033
(703) 620-4096
Fax: (703) 620-2973
Email: tom@telecom-recruiters.com
Web: www.telecom-recruiters.com

Description: We specialize in providing telecommunications professionals to service providers for landline, wireless and call centers. In addition we conduct searches for telecommunication's manufacturers covering both hardware and software.

Key Contact - Specialty:
Mr. Thomas L. Fitzgerald, President - *Telecommunications, technical*
Mr. Matthew A. Fitzgerald, Director - *Telecommunications, marketing & sales*

Salary minimum: $40,000

Functions: Generalist

Industries: Telecoms

Professional Associations: RON

Networks: Top Echelon Network

The Telecom Search Group
PO Box 326
Bella Vista, CA 96008
(530) 549-5331
Email: randy@telecomsg.com
Web: www.telecomsg.com

Description: We are a contingency search firm who specializes in the placement of contract and perm senior engineers and executive managers whose occupations are in the wireless, optical transport and CLEC telecommunications industries.

Key Contact - Specialty:
Mr. Randall Chambers, Owner - *Telecommunications*

Salary minimum: $75,000

Functions: General Mgmt., Directors, Senior Mgmt., Sales & Mktg., Training, CFO's, MIS Mgmt., Systems Implem., R&D, Engineering

Industries: Telecoms

Networks: Top Echelon Network

Telem Adhesive Search Corp
PO Box 656
Owings Mills, MD 21117
(410) 356-6200
Fax: (410) 356-5189
Email: telemadhesive@home.com
Web: www.adhesivesearch.com

Description: We are widely recognized as one of the nation's preeminent search firms, satisfying the personnel needs of the adhesives, coatings and converting industries since 1984.

Key Contact - Specialty:
Mr. Peter B. Telem, President - *Adhesives, polymers, coatings, medical devices, film converting*

Salary minimum: $50,000

Functions: Generalist

Industries: Mfg., Paper, Printing, Chemicals, Drugs Mfg., Medical Devices, Plastics, Rubber, Paints, Petro. Products, Packaging

---

Professional Associations: ACS, FSCT, MAPRC, TAPPI

Networks: Inter-City Personnel Assoc (IPA)

TeleManagement Search
114 E 32nd St Ste 931
New York, NY 10016
(212) 684-3500
(312) 527-1166
Fax: (212) 696-1287
Email: telemgnt@pipeline.com
Web: www.tmrecruiters.com

Description: We are a national executive search firm dedicated to recruiting professional managerial inbound, outbound and customer service personnel. Recruit at all management levels including presidents, vice presidents, directors and managers.

Key Contact - Specialty:
Ms. Connie Caroli, President - *Call center, customer service professionals, telemarketing management professionals*

Salary minimum: $40,000

Functions: Direct Mktg., Customer Svc.

Industries: Generalist

Professional Associations: ATSA

Telequest Communications Inc
PO Box 94
Mahwah, NJ 07430
(845) 357-2212
Fax: (845) 369-8724
Email: mail@telequestcom.com
Web: www.telequestcom.com

Description: We are a telecommunications search firm specializing in all areas of telecommunications including voice, data and local and wide area networks. We place temporary, permanent, sales and technical candidates at all levels.

Key Contact - Specialty:
Mr. Thomas Bartchak, President - *Telecommunications*
Ms. Ellen Dansky, Vice President - *Telecommunications*

Salary minimum: $40,000

Functions: General Mgmt.

Industries: Generalist

Professional Associations: NJASP

Tell/Com Recruiters
6990 Lake Elenor Dr Ste 106b
Orlando, FL 32809
(407) 251-2051
Fax: (407) 251-2091
Email: nikiking@ctirecruiters.com
Web: www.tellcom.com

Description: We specialize in placements within the telecommunications industry in sales, engineering and management within voice processing, ACD, CDR, long distance, predictive dialing and video conferencing, CTI, and voice over IP, as well as with leading interconnects and manufacturers of PBX and KEY systems.

Key Contact:
Mr. Dennis F. Young, President - *Telecommunications*
Mr. Bob Bradford, Director of Sales

Salary minimum: $50,000

Functions: Generalist, Mkt. Research, Mktg. Mgmt., Sales Mgmt.

Industries: Generalist, Telecoms, Software

Networks: First Interview Network (FIN)

Templeton & Associates

15 S 5th St Ste 1000
Minneapolis, MN 55402
(612) 334-8900
Fax: (612) 334-8905
Email: dtempleton@templetonandassociates.com

Description: We provide a full range of legal staff on both a temporary and direct hire basis to top law firms and corporate legal departments throughout the country.

Key Contact - Specialty:
Ms. Denise Templeton, President - *Legal*
Mr. Thomas J. Nolan, Jr., Vice President - *Legal staffing*

Functions: Legal, Attorneys, Paralegals

Industries: Legal, HR Services

Professional Associations: ASA

Branches:
535 16th St Mall Ste 810
Denver, CO 80202
(303) 571-0311
Fax: (303) 571-0809
Key Contact - Specialty:
Ms. Cathy Robertus, Vice President - *Legal staffing*

1 E Wacker Dr Ste 3130
Chicago, IL 60601
(312) 644-8400
Fax: (312) 644-8700
Key Contact - Specialty:
Ms. Shirley Campos, Vice President - *Legal staffing*

Terik Company

83 Baybridge Park
PO Box 1146
Gulf Breeze, FL 32562
(850) 932-4474
Fax: (850) 932-4635

Description: Our firm specialties include the store fixture industry, both metal and wood. We work with the metal-working industry and finished products. We place mid to upper-level management.

Key Contact - Specialty:
Mr. Tom Williams, President - *Metal fabricated products, wood stone fixtures, metal stone fixtures*

Salary minimum: $50,000

Functions: Generalist, General Mgmt., Mfg., Materials, Purchasing, Sales & Mktg., Sales Mgmt., HR Mgmt., Finance, Engineering

Industries: Mfg., Lumber, Furniture, Metal Products, Machine, Appliance, Motor Vehicles, Misc. Mfg.

Terran Systems

3567 Benton St Ste 400
Santa Clara, CA 95051
(408) 727-9000
Fax: (408) 727-9018
Email: terran@terransys.com
Web: www.terransys.com

Description: We are an executive search firm specializing in the placement of software engineers and developers in Silicon Valley/Northern California.

Key Contact:
Mr. Patrick Ross, Director - *Software developers*
Mr. Eric Lawrence, Manager - *Software developers*
Mr. Nelson Smith, Senior Technical Recruiter

Functions: Systems Dev., Network Admin., DB Admin., Engineering

Industries: Generalist

Branches:
16633 Ventura Blvd 815
Encino, CA 91436
(818) 995-9330
Fax: (818) 995-9326
Email: terran@terransys.com
Key Contact - Specialty:
Ms. Monica Greenwood - *Software engineers*

Lee Terry & Associates

PO Box 5427
San Mateo, CA 94402
(650) 570-7913
Fax: (650) 572-1600
Email: leeterry@lterryrecruiter.com
Web: www.lterryrecruiter.com

Description: We are specialists in executive search for homebuilders and land developers within the Western US. Member of various building industry groups in California and Nevada. Our firm is an active member of National Association of Home Builders.

Key Contact - Specialty:
Ms. Lee Terry, President - *Homebuilding, land development*

Functions: Generalist

Industries: Construction, Real Estate

Professional Associations: CSP, NAHB

The Teton Group

70 S Winooski Ave 125
Burlington, VT 05401
(888) 721-9700 x1
Email: info@thetetongroup.com
Web: www.thetetongroup.com

Description: We are a contingency search firm specializing in the placement of sales people and sales engineers in the business intelligence software industry.

Key Contact - Specialty:
Mr. David Robinson, President - *Business intelligence, software sales*

Salary minimum: $70,000

Functions: Sales Mgmt.

Industries: Generalist

The TGA Company

PO Box 331121
Ft. Worth, TX 76163
(817) 370-0865
Fax: (817) 292-6451
Email: trgreen@swbell.net

Description: We handle contingency and retained searches for financial executives - all industries.

Key Contact - Specialty:
Mr. Thomas R. Green, President - *Finance*
Ms. Carolyn M. Byrne, Senior Associate - *Finance, MIS*
Mr. Thomas C. Green, Senior Associate - *Finance, sales, marketing*

Salary minimum: $30,000

Functions: Taxes, M&A, Risk Mgmt., Systems Analysis, Systems Implem., Systems Support, Network Admin., DB Admin., Engineering

Industries: Generalist

Networks: National Personnel Assoc (NPA)

Thinkpath

55 University Ave Ste 500
Toronto, ON M5J 2H7
Canada
(416) 364-8800
Fax: (364) 364-2424
Email: csukhabut@thinkpath.com
Web: www.thinkpath.com

Description: Our firm is an IT and engineering services company offering a blended suite of outsourcing, recruiting, training, and technology to enhance the resource performance of large and high-growth corporations.

Key Contact:
Mr. Declan French, Chairman & CEO
Ms. Laurie Bradley, President
Ms. Kelly Hankinson, CFO
Mr. Tony French, Executive Vice President
Mr. Mike Reid, CIO

Salary minimum: $45,000

Functions: General Mgmt., IT

Industries: Generalist, Banking, Invest. Banking, Misc. Financial, Telecoms, Call Centers, Telephony, Digital, Wireless, Fiber Optic, Network Infrastructure, Government

Networks: Canadian Personnel Services Inc (CPSI)

Branches:
1211 N Westshore Blvd Ste 410
Tampa, FL 33607
(813) 636-8227
Fax: (813) 636-9059
Email: tampa@cadcaminc.com
Key Contact:
Mr. Ed Godwin, Branch Manager

6160 Peachtree-Dunwoody Rd Ste B100
Atlanta, GA 30328
(770) 350-9323
Fax: (770) 350-0039
Email: atlanta@cadcaminc.com
Key Contact:
Mr. Tim Long, Branch Manager

2505 Taylor Rd
Columbus, IN 47203
(812) 376-8519
Fax: (812) 376-7530
Email: columbus@thinkpath.com
Key Contact:
Mr. Jeff Anderson, Branch Manager

8455 Keystone Crossing Ste 201
Indianapolis, IN 46240
(317) 253-2204
Fax: (317) 253-2294
Email: indianapolis@thinkpath.com
Key Contact:
Mr. Mike Tribul, Branch Manager

375 Totten Pond Rd Ste 200
Waltham, MA 02451
(781) 890-6444
Fax: (781) 890-3355
Email: boston@thinkpath.com
Key Contact:
Mr. Denise Dunne, Branch Manager

25840 Sherwood
Warren, MI 48901
(810) 754-2700
Fax: (810) 754-2700
Email: detroit@thinkpath.com
Key Contact:
Mr. Rick Simon, Branch Manager

1 World Trade Ctr Ste 7847
New York, NY 10048
(212) 912-1169
Email: newyork@thinkpath.com
Key Contact:
Ms. Grace Piscopo

110 Boggs Ln Ste 365
Cincinnati, OH 45246
(513) 326-4760
Fax: (513) 326-4765
Email: cincinnati@thinkpath.com
Key Contact:
Mr. Dave Hoffmann, Branch Manager

2800 E River Rd Fl 4
Dayton, OH 45439
(937) 643-4100
Fax: (973) 643-4100
Email: dayton@thinkpath.com
Key Contact:
Mr. Rob Liput, Branch Manager

1941 Savage Rd Ste 400C
Charleston, SC 29047
(843) 556-2511
Fax: (843) 556-1920
Email: charleston@thinkpath.com
Key Contact:
Mr. Jeff Sheidow, Branch Manager

38 Auriga Dr Ste 245
Ottawa, ON K2E 8A5
Canada
(613) 226-9292
Fax: (613) 226-7907
Email: ottowa@thinkpath.com
Key Contact:
Mr. Tony French, Branch Manager

Thomas & Associates
75817 Via Allegre
Indian Wells, CA 92210-8490
(760) 773-0717
Fax: (760) 862-9207
Email: thomas.associates@prodigy.net
Web: www.pages.prodigy.net/d.c.thomas/

Description: We are a national executive staffing resource for the telecommunications, information technology, high-technology and pharmaceutical industries for engineering, sales and marketing, financial and general management disciplines.

Key Contact - Specialty:
Mr. Donald C. Thomas, Chairman - *High technology, senior management*

Salary minimum: $80,000

Functions: Generalist, General Mgmt., Directors

Industries: Food, Bev., Tobacco, Textiles, Apparel, Medical Devices, Computer Equip., Consumer Elect., Pharm Svcs., Mgmt. Consulting, HR Services, Hospitality, Telecoms, Real Estate, Software, Biotech, Healthcare

Raymond Thomas & Associates
407 Wekiva Springs Rd Ste 221
Longwood, FL 32779
(407) 774-8300
Fax: (407) 339-8591

Description: Our firm has 40 years of experience in metal working industries along with 25 years of experience in executive recruiting specializing, worldwide with machine tool and related factory automation OEMs, as well as users. We have an extensive network in mid-upper- to upper-levels of management.

Key Contact - Specialty:
Mr. Ray Huegel, Owner - *Factory automation, machine tools*
Mr. Mike Garland, Principal - *Factory automation, machine tools*

Salary minimum: $60,000

Functions: Generalist

Industries: Metal Products, Machine, Appliance, Misc. Mfg.

Thomas & Associates of Michigan
16283 Red Arrow Hwy
PO Box 366
Union Pier, MI 49129
(616) 469-5760
Fax: (616) 469-5774
Email: tzonka@triton.net
Web: www.career-change.com

Description: We are a computerized nationwide affiliation with over 680 recruiting firms. Permanent - contract - outplacement.

Key Contact - Specialty:
Mr. Thomas J. Zonka, President - *Executive, engineering, manufacturing, MIS, sales & marketing*

Salary minimum: $50,000

Functions: General Mgmt., Mfg., Materials, Sales & Mktg., Sales Mgmt., HR Mgmt., Finance, CFO's, IT, Engineering

Industries: Generalist, Mfg.

Networks: Top Echelon Network

Thomas, Whelan Associates, Inc
PO Box 40237
Washington, DC 20016-2523
(202) 966-3960
Fax: (202) 966-3970
Email: twahunt1@earthlink.net
Web: www.twahunt.com

Description: We specialize in the recruitment and placement of mid-management and senior-level accounting, finance and systems professionals in the Baltimore/Washington/Virginia area.

Key Contact - Specialty:
Ms. Cheryl Molliver Ross, President - *Finance, accounting, systems, mid-management, senior level*

Functions: Generalist, CFO's, Budgeting, Cash Mgmt., Taxes, M&A, Risk Mgmt., Mgmt. Consultants

Industries: Generalist, Finance, Services, Hospitality, Media, Telecoms, Real Estate, Biotech

Professional Associations: NBN

Judy Thompson & Associates
5080 Shoreham Pl Ste 204
San Diego, CA 92122
(858) 452-1200
Fax: (858) 623-5910
Email: judy@jtaa.net
Web: www.jtaa.net

Description: We specialize in recruiting experienced degreed accounting/financial professionals for all industries in San Diego (excluding lending and operations for financial institutions and financial sales).

Key Contact - Specialty:
Ms. Judy Thompson, President - *Accounting & finance*

Salary minimum: $50,000

Functions: Finance, CFO's, Budgeting, Cash Mgmt., Credit, Taxes, M&A

Industries: Generalist

Professional Associations: ACG, CDF, CDF, CFC, IMA

Rand Thompson Executive Search Consultants
261 Madison Ave
New York, NY 10016
(212) 972-0090
Fax: (212) 370-0047
Email: rtconsultg@worldnet.att.net

Description: We have grown and maintained relationships with many firms rated #1 in their respective industries. Currently 75% of search assignments are completed with individuals referred by satisfied applicants.

Key Contact - Specialty:
Mr. John Kelly, President - *Accounting, finance, wall street, generalist*

Mr. Harold Kost, Executive Vice President - *Generalist*

Salary minimum: $75,000

Functions: General Mgmt., Senior Mgmt., Middle Mgmt., Legal, Mfg., Materials, Sales & Mktg., HR Mgmt., Finance, IT

Industries: Generalist

Thomson, Sponar & Adams Inc
10116 36th Ave Ct SW Ste 200
Lakewood, WA 98499
(253) 588-1216
Fax: (253) 588-2528
Email: tsa@tsacareers.com
Web: www.tsacareers.com

Description: We collectively represent over 400 years of experience. We specialize in helping firms find quality people and we help quality people find exceptional opportunities.

Key Contact - Specialty:
Mr. Frank S. Adams, President - *High energy physics, applied superconductivity, electronics, instrumentation, optics*

Salary minimum: $50,000

Functions: Generalist, Middle Mgmt., Production, Quality, Materials, Mkt. Research, Mktg. Mgmt., R&D, Engineering

Industries: Generalist, Energy, Utilities, Chemicals, Medical Devices, Metal Products, Computer Equip., Test, Measure Equip., Electronic, Elec. Components, Communications, Digital, Fiber Optic, Defense, Aerospace

Professional Associations: AUSA, CSA, MRS, SPIE

Thorne Consulting Inc
4067 Riverlook Pkwy
Marietta, GA 30067
(770) 951-8075
Fax: (770) 951-1823
Email: thorcon@mindspring.com
Web: www.thorneconsulting.com

Description: We are a retained executive search firm specializing in placement solutions within the healthcare and related industries. We serve nationwide leadership placement needs.

Key Contact - Specialty:
Mr. Richard Thorne, President - *Healthcare and related industries*

Salary minimum: $65,000

Functions: Middle Mgmt., Healthcare, Health Admin.

Industries: Generalist, Non-profits, Mgmt. Consulting, Healthcare, Hospitals, Long-term Care, Women's

Thorsen Associates Inc
2020 Grand Ave
Baldwin, NY 11510
(516) 868-6500
Fax: (516) 868-7842
Email: info@thorsenassociates.com
Web: www.thorsenassociates.com

Description: We are a contingency search firm specializing within the manufacturing market for management and engineering. Strong contacts and twenty years of experience in the local Metro NYC and the LI/NJ/CT market.

Key Contact - Specialty:
Mr. Peter Thorsen, President - *Manufacturing management, engineering*

Salary minimum: $35,000

Functions: Generalist

Industries: Mfg.

Professional Associations: LIFT

The Tidewater Group
115 Main St
Crescent Vlg
Monroe, CT 06468
(203) 459-2500
Fax: (203) 459-8373
Email: info@tidewater.org
Web: www.tidewater.org

Description: We are recruiters working nationally for a diversified clientele. We have 30 years' recruiting nationally.

Key Contact:
Mr. John Kalas, President

Salary minimum: $50,000

Functions: Generalist

Industries: Generalist

TMP Worldwide
(formerly known as System One Technical)
9119 Corporate Lakes Dr Ste 200
Tampa, FL 33634
(813) 249-1757
Fax: (813) 880-9145
Email: inquiry@tmp.com
Web: www.na.eresourcing.tmp.com

Description: Our firm is the world's leading supplier of human capital solutions. We provide temporary, contract, and permanent technical, professional, and managerial talent in information technology, telecommunications, accounting and finance, legal, human resources, sales and marketing, consumer products, retail, engineering and scientific systems, and other specialist areas.

Key Contact:
Ms. Denise Malivuk

Salary minimum: $40,000

Functions: Generalist

Industries: HR Services

TMP Worldwide
1809 7th Ave Ste 408
Seattle, WA 98101
(206) 344-6222
Fax: (206) 344-8108
Email: sabrina.harris@tmp.com
Web: www.tmpw.com

Description: Practice consists of middle/senior-level management recruitment. Serve manufacturing, high-technology, public accounting and industrial clients. Recruit accounting/financial and human resource professionals. In addition, we serve the information technology and engineering marketplace.

Key Contact:
Ms. Sabrina Harris, Branch Manager

Salary minimum: $50,000

Functions: Generalist, Sales & Mktg., HR Mgmt., Finance, IT, Engineering

Industries: Generalist, Mfg., Finance, Services, Aerospace, Software, Biotech

Professional Associations: AAFA

TNGGLOBAL
4115 Sherbrooke St W Ste 320
Westmount, QC H3Z 1K9
Canada
(514) 931-8542
Fax: (514) 931-8310
Email: inquiries@tngglobal.com
Web: www.tngglobal.com

Description: We specialize in recruiting enterprise resource planning (ERP), customer relationship

management (CRM), and e-Commerce professionals.

Key Contact - Specialty:
Mr. Norman Gold, President - *Information technology*
Ms. Nancy Gold, VP- Sales - *Information technology*

Salary minimum: $55,000

Functions: Generalist, MIS Mgmt., Systems Analysis, Systems Dev., Systems Implem., Systems Support, Network Admin., DB Admin.

Industries: Generalist, Energy, Utilities, Mfg., Finance, Services, Media, Software

Professional Associations: ACSESS

The Toberson Group
884 Woods Mill Rd Ste 101
Ballwin, MO 63011-3656
(636) 891-9774
(800) 726-0990
Fax: (636) 891-9784
Email: mpranger@toberson.com

Description: We are a contingency search firm, that has been serving clients since 1980. Our main areas of specialty include: retail executives, all levels and warehousing, transportation and distribution executives.

Key Contact:
Mr. Michael Pranger, Vice President

Salary minimum: $35,000

Functions: Generalist, General Mgmt., Directors, Senior Mgmt., Distribution

Industries: Transportation, Wholesale, Retail

Tolfrey Group
PO Box 1982
El Cerrito, CA 94530
(510) 234-0090
Fax: (419) 818-1219
Email: resumes@tolfrey.com
Web: www.tolfrey.com

Description: We specialize in world class search in ERP, CRM and e-Business. Our firm focuses on technology. The primary software that we work with is PeopleSoft, Siebel, Oracle, Java, etc.

Key Contact - Specialty:
Mr. Grant Du Plooy, Managing Partner - *ERP, CRM, B2B, data warehouse*

Functions: Generalist, Systems Implem.

Industries: HR Services, E-commerce, IT Implementation, Development SW, ERP SW, HR SW

Tomass Executive Group Ltd
330 N Main St
New City, NY 10956
(845) 639-9000
Fax: (845) 639-9043
Email: teg@rcknet.com
Web: www.rcknet.com/teg

Description: We specialize in placing capital markets professionals predominantly in the NY Metro area. With some select clients up and down the East Coast.

Key Contact - Specialty:
Mr. Frank Tomass, President - *Wall street, finance, accounting, operations*
Ms. Joanne Finochio, Executive Vice President - *Finance, accounting, operations, technology*

Functions: Generalist, Middle Mgmt., Budgeting, M&A, Risk Mgmt., Systems Analysis, Systems Support, DB Admin.

Industries: Generalist, Chemicals, Drugs Mfg., Brokers, Pharm Svcs., Mgmt. Consulting, Software

Tomlinson Associates Inc
401 N Michigan Ave Ste 1200
Chicago, IL 60611
(312) 840-8250
Fax: (312) 840-8251
Email: tomlinsonassociates@msn.com

Description: We are a boutique retainer firm offering highly personalized service for reasonable fees. We specialize in market research. Clients include Fortune 100 manufacturers and smaller privately held firms in market research, advertising and management consulting.

Key Contact - Specialty:
Ms. Betsy Tomlinson, President - *Market research, marketing consulting*

Salary minimum: $60,000

Functions: Generalist, Mkt. Research, Personnel

Industries: Generalist, Services

Tomlinson-Miller Inc
301 S Adams St Ste 103
Marion, IN 46952
(765) 668-3213
Fax: (765) 651-6616
Email: tmi@tmi-careers.com
Web: www.tmi-careers.com

Description: We recruit and place all types of engineers and professionals with manufacturing companies in the Midwest. This includes all professional positions in engineering, manufacturing, production, quality, and materials.

Key Contact - Specialty:
Mr. Dan L. Tomlinson, President - *Manufacturing*
Ms. Teresa R. Miller, Vice President - *Manufacturing*

Salary minimum: $50,000

Functions: Mfg., Product Dev., Production, Automation, Plant Mgmt., Quality, Productivity, Materials, Purchasing, Materials Plng.

Industries: Generalist

Networks: Top Echelon Network

Tondorf & Associates Inc
720 Washington St Standish Executive Ctr
Hanover, MA 02339
(781) 826-1440
Fax: (781) 826-2827
Email: tondorfasc@aol.com
Web: www.tondorfandassociates.com

Description: We are an executive search and recruiting firm which specializes in the consumer products and healthcare industry. Specializes in category management and trade marketing positions, leading to future sales management positions.

Key Contact:
Mr. Paul Tondorf, Jr., Principal

Salary minimum: $60,000

Functions: Healthcare, Sales & Mktg., Sales Mgmt.

Industries: Food, Bev., Tobacco, Drugs Mfg., Medical Devices

Professional Associations: NACDS

Top of the World
6107 Webb Bridge Ct
Alpharetta, GA 30004
(678) 366-3430
Fax: (770) 740-0544
Email: topoftheworld@mindspring.com

Description: We are a full-service professional search firm specializing in hospitality executives and information technology. We listen to your needs and provide candidates in a timely manner. We will provide only the "top" candidates to your organization, thus avoiding the cycles of hiring, firing, and laying off employees who don't quite fit into your organization.

Key Contact:
Mr. Glenn Topps, CEO/Founder
Mr. Edward Falls, Vice President

Salary minimum: $35,000

Functions: General Mgmt.

Industries: Food, Bev., Tobacco, Hospitality

Topaz Attorney Search
383 Northfield Ave 104
West Orange, NJ 07052
(973) 669-7300
Fax: (973) 669-9811
Email: info@topattorneys.com
Web: www.topattorneys.com

Description: We provide premier attorney search for law firms and corporate legal departments in all disciplines and levels. We also assist in all phases of the search and recruitment process. Our clients range from large firms, boutiques and small corporations to the top international and Fortune 100 companies. Our specialties include: establishing/expanding branch offices of national firms, law firm mergers, and legal consulting services.

Key Contact - Specialty:
Ms. Ronni L. Gaines, Principal - *Attorneys*
Mr. Stewart Michaels, Principal - *Consulting, mergers & acquisitions, attorneys*
Ms. Pamela S. Cohen, Esq., Vice President-General Counsel - *Attorneys*

Salary minimum: $70,000

Functions: Legal

Industries: Generalist

Professional Associations: ABA, ACCA, ACCA, ACG, NALSC, NATSS

Lisa Torres & Associates Inc
PO BOX 227085
Miami, FL 33122-7085
(305) 669-8600
Fax: (801) 730-0156
Email: torres@letusrecruit.com
Web: www.letusrecruit.com

Description: We specialize in the executive recruitment and placement of middle and senior-level executives. Our focus is in the areas of accounting/finance, sales/marketing, human resources, and general management. The firm assists regional and multinational corporations with their staffing needs. As executive recruitment specialists, we are able to provide customized services.

Key Contact:
Ms. Lisa Torres, President

Salary minimum: $50,000

Functions: General Mgmt., Sales & Mktg., HR Mgmt., Finance, Int'l.

Industries: Generalist

Professional Associations: NAWBO, NSHMBA, SHRM

The Touchstone Group
340 Main St Ste 814
Worcester, MA 01608
(877) 795-0707
(508) 795-0769
Fax: (508) 798-0671

Email: info@touchstonegroup.com
Web: www.touchstonegroup.com

Description: We are dedicated to assisting emerging high-technology firms in finding talented sales and marketing professionals at a reasonable cost.

Key Contact - Specialty:
Mr. James P. Vozekas, General Manager - *Sales, marketing*
Ms. Connie Palmer, Consultant - *Sales support, marketing communication*
Mr. Roger Moslow, Consultant - *Healthcare*

Salary minimum: $50,000

Functions: Sales & Mktg.

Industries: Software

Professional Associations: RON

Networks: First Interview Network (FIN)

Townsend Resources
PO Box 923
Camp Hill, PA 17001
(717) 763-9866
Fax: (717) 763-9873
Email: townsend.resources@paonline.com
Web: www.salesrecruit.com

Description: A sales search firm covering greater central Pennsylvania in depth for all areas of sales. Industrial sales specialists. We perform nationwide custom searches for industrial clients.

Key Contact - Specialty:
Mr. Bill Molin, Owner - *Sales & marketing*

Salary minimum: $30,000

Functions: Sales & Mktg.

Industries: Construction, Mfg., Government, Environmental Svcs., Aerospace, Packaging, Software, Biotech, Healthcare, Non-classifiable

Networks: First Interview Network (FIN)

Toy Jobs
26 Park St Ste 2001
Montclair, NJ 07042
(973) 744-0818
Fax: (973) 744-0775
Email: tom@toyjobs.com
Web: www.toyjobs.com

Description: Discreet and personal handling of worldwide recruitment of all disciplines within the toy, gift and juvenile products industries.

Key Contact - Specialty:
Mr. Thomas Keoughan, President - *Toy, gift, juvenile products*

Functions: Generalist, Senior Mgmt., Product Dev., Purchasing, Mkt. Research, Sales Mgmt., Engineering, Graphic Artists

Industries: Generalist, Plastics, Rubber, Hospitality

Professional Associations: IDSA, SPE

TPG & Associates
10619 Burgoyne Rd
Houston, TX 77042
(713) 781-2010
Email: porter@staffing.net

Description: We specialize in oil and gas exploration, production, refining and marketing, power generation, environmental, chemical, aerospace, and biotech. We also specialize in R&D, administrative, and computer staff related to the above industries. We place some contractors.

Key Contact - Specialty:
Ms. Mary C. Porter, Principal - *Oil & gas, biotechnology, aerospace*

Salary minimum: $60,000

Functions: Generalist

Industries: Energy, Utilities, Chemicals, Defense, Haz. Waste, Aerospace, Biotech

Professional Associations: AAPG

Networks: Top Echelon Network

TPS Staffing Solutions
6284 Rucker Rd Ste M
Indianapolis, IN 46220
(317) 257-6220
(317) 257-7757
Email: justaskhr@aol.com
Web: www.tpsstaffingsolutions.com

Description: We specialize in a full range of long-term, short-term, temporary and permanent placement in addition to human resources consulting.

Key Contact - Specialty:
Mr. Dean A. Black, Managing Partner - *Executive management, human resources*

Functions: Generalist, Senior Mgmt., Plant Mgmt., Purchasing, Mktg. Mgmt., Personnel, Cash Mgmt.

Industries: Generalist, Mfg., Finance, Services, Media, Insurance

Professional Associations: HRACI, IAPS, SHRM

Trace Executive Search
(a division of Trace Marketing Inc)
5550 Bee Ridge Rd Ste E-3
Sarasota, FL 34233
(941) 925-0313
Web: www.tracemarketing.com

Description: We are dedicated to conducting thorough searches for clients seeking top-level candidates for executive positions in the retirement and long-term care industries. We specialize in the senior housing industry including nursing homes, assisted living facilities, retirement communities, and active adult communities.

Key Contact - Specialty:
Ms. Andrea Coblentz, Director of Executive Search - *Healthcare, marketing, retirement*
Ms. Tracy Lux, President - *Marketing, healthcare administration*

Salary minimum: $35,000

Functions: Directors, Senior Mgmt., Middle Mgmt., Admin. Svcs., Sales & Mktg.

Industries: Long-term Care

Professional Associations: ALFA

Jay Tracey Associates Inc
19A Central Str
Woodstock, VT 05091
(802) 457-4200
Fax: (802) 457-4114
Email: info@jaytracey.com
Web: www.jaytracey.com

Description: We work with sales, engineering, marketing, service technicians for the drives, process control (DCS), PLC, industrial controls, factory automation and converting industry. Also work with all disciplines in the plastic extrusion and blow molding industry.

Key Contact - Specialty:
Mr. Jay E. Tracey - *Plastics, automation, PLC, SCADA, drives*
Mr. Mark H. Auriema - *Industrial controls, automation, PLC, SCADA, drives*

Salary minimum: $75,000

Functions: Generalist, Senior Mgmt., Middle Mgmt., Automation, Mkt. Research, Mktg. Mgmt., Sales Mgmt., Engineering, Technicians

Industries: Generalist, Paper, Printing, Plastics, Rubber, Metal Products, Machine, Appliance, Computer Equip., Software

Trademark Recruiting Inc
101 E Kennedy Blvd Ste 1425
Tampa, FL 33602
(813) 472-7200
Fax: (813) 472-7210
Web: www.trademark1.net

Description: With over 25 years of recruiting experience, we provide in-depth knowledge of our functional areas, personal interaction, an extensive network of qualified candidates, and expertise in candidate evaluation and negotiation.

Key Contact - Specialty:
Ms. Christina D. Roy, Partner - *Information technology, human resources*
Mr. Michael C. Carideo, Partner - *Information technology, human resources*
Mr. Timothy W. Barnett, Partner - *Finance & accounting, human resources*
Mr. A. James Tagg, Partner - *Finance & accounting, human resources*

Salary minimum: $40,000

Functions: HR Mgmt., Finance, IT

Industries: Generalist

Trambley the Recruiter
5353 Wyoming Blvd NE Ste 8
Albuquerque, NM 87109-3132
(505) 821-5440
Fax: (505) 821-8509

Description: We are specialists in design and development personnel for the off road equipment industries including hydraulics, mechanical, structural and electronic controls engineers and engineering managers.

Key Contact - Specialty:
Mr. J. Brian Trambley, CPC - *Engineering, manufacturing*

Functions: Middle Mgmt., Product Dev., Production, Automation, Plant Mgmt., Materials, Engineering

Industries: Agri., Forestry, Mining, Metal Products, Machine, Appliance, Motor Vehicles, Test, Measure Equip., Misc. Mfg.

Professional Associations: NAPS, NMAPS

Networks: Inter-City Personnel Assoc (IPA)

Trans-United Consultants Ltd
3228 S Service Rd Ste 110
Burlington, ON L7N 3H8
Canada
(905) 632-7176
Fax: (905) 632-5777
Email: tuc@trans-united.net
Web: www.trans-united.net

Description: We specialize in the placement of contract and permanent engineering, design drafting/Cad, technical support and information technology personnel.

Key Contact - Specialty:
Mr. Brian L. de Lottinville, Partner - *Engineering*
Mr. John L. Train, Partner - *Engineering*

Functions: Generalist, Product Dev., Production, Automation, Purchasing, Engineering

Industries: Generalist, Mfg., Environmental Svcs., Aerospace, Packaging

Transportation Recruiting Services Inc
5719 Hwy 25 Ste 204 (Box 5)
PO Box 4040
Brandon, MS 39047
(601) 992-7900
Fax: (601) 992-7999
Web: www.autoheadhunter.com

Description: We are transportation manufacturers' and major component suppliers' search specialists for management, engineering and manufacturing professionals. National/international, retained and contingency recruiting services.

Key Contact - Specialty:
Mr. Dave Bradshaw, President
Mr. Pat Stephens, Vice President - *General manufacturing*

Salary minimum: $35,000

Functions: Generalist, General Mgmt., Mfg., Product Dev., Materials, Sales & Mktg., HR Mgmt., Engineering

Industries: Generalist, Motor Vehicles

Professional Associations: SAE, SME

Travel Executive Search
(a division of Workstyles Inc)
5 Rose Ave
Great Neck, NY 11021
(516) 829-8829
Email: tesintl@aol.com

Description: We are executive recruitment specialists for the travel industry: airlines, car rentals, motorcoach, tours, corporate travel, hotel and resorts, retail, incentives, conventions and meetings, cruise companies and tourist offices; import and export; international; sports and entertainment; Internet and e-commerce.

Key Contact - Specialty:
Ms. Karen Rubin, President - *Travel, tourism, hospitality, transportation, e-commerce*

Salary minimum: $30,000

Functions: Generalist, General Mgmt., Product Dev., Sales & Mktg., HR Mgmt., Finance, IT, Int'l.

Industries: Transportation, Finance, Hospitality, Media

Travel Personnel
1189 Beargrass Way
Maineville, OH 45039
(513) 899-3388
Email: omalley01@msn.com

Description: We are a travel industry search firm serving staffing needs of tour operators, airlines, cruise lines, travel agencies, travel management firms, CVB's, adventure travel, guides and expedition leaders.

Key Contact - Specialty:
Mr. Chris O'Malley, President - *Travel, tourism*

Salary minimum: $20,000

Functions: Generalist, Senior Mgmt., Middle Mgmt., Mktg. Mgmt., Sales Mgmt.

Industries: Generalist, Transportation, Non-profits, Hospitality, Advertising

Tri-Star Group
PO Box 482
DeKalb, IL 60115
(815) 758-6903
Fax: (815) 758-7087
Email: tristargrp@aol.com

Description: We recruit exclusively for Human Resource professionals on a nationwide basis. All specialties under the Human Resources umbrella.

Key Contact - Specialty:
Mr. Tom Roff, General Partner - *Human resources*
Mr. Tom Burke, General Partner - *Human resources*

Salary minimum: $30,000

Functions: HR Mgmt., Benefits, Personnel, Training

Industries: Generalist

Professional Associations: ASTD, ODN, SHRM

Tri-Tech Associates Inc
40 Baldwin Rd
Parsippany, NJ 07054
(973) 299-0055
Fax: (973) 299-0549
Email: tta@tritechnj.com
Web: www.tritechnj.com

Description: We specialize in staffing in technical areas in manufacturing, pharmaceuticals and electronics. We focus on product development, design, plant maintenance, QA/QC, materials management, production and tech support. We also have an IT division in addition to contract assignments and payroll division.

Key Contact - Specialty:
Ms. Marlene Levitt, President - *Engineering, chemists, scientist, manufacturing, pharmaceuticals*

Salary minimum: $40,000

Functions: Middle Mgmt., Mfg., Plant Mgmt., Quality, Materials, IT, Systems Dev., R&D, Engineering, Technicians

Industries: Mfg., Chemicals, Drugs Mfg., Medical Devices, Metal Products, Consumer Elect., Test, Measure Equip., Packaging, Software, Biotech

Professional Associations: NJSA

Triad Consultants Inc
PO Box 717
West Caldwell, NJ 07007-0717
(973) 890-1655
Fax: (973) 890-9201

Description: We are focused solely on benefits and compensation positions to $200K, we offer corporations and consulting firms the thoroughness and attention of retained search without advanced payment.

Key Contact - Specialty:
Mr. Jack Daudt, CPC, President - *Benefits, compensation*

Salary minimum: $50,000

Functions: Generalist, Benefits, Mgmt. Consultants, Non-profits

Industries: Generalist, Banking, HR Services, Insurance

Professional Associations: WAW

Triad Technology Group
10260 SW Greenburg Rd Ste 560
Portland, OR 97223
(503) 293-9547
(503) 293-9545
Fax: (503) 293-9546
Email: triadjob@triadtechnology.com
Web: www.triadtechnology.com

Description: We are a Pacific northwest based information technology recruiting and contracting firm founded to provide a wide range of systems development and software engineering services including programming, relational database management system design, development and implementation and system integration.

Key Contact - Specialty:
Mr. Bruno C. Amicci, CEO - *Information technology*

Salary minimum: $45,000

Functions: Generalist, IT, MIS Mgmt., Systems Analysis, Systems Dev., Systems Implem., Systems Support, DB Admin.

Industries: Generalist, Software

Professional Associations: RON

Networks: National Personnel Assoc (NPA)

Triangle Associates

PO Box 506
Warrington, PA 18976
(215) 343-3702
Fax: (215) 343-3703
Email: triangle42@aol.com

Description: We are recruiters of engineering and
technical management talent for the process and
manufacturing industries. Specialties - chemical
engineers, manufacturing/industrial engineers,
engineering management.

Key Contact - Specialty:
Mr. Stephen R. Ostroff, President - *Engineers,
management*

Salary minimum: $45,000

Functions: Mfg., Engineering

Industries: Energy, Utilities, Chemicals, Drugs
Mfg., Plastics, Rubber, Paints, Petro. Products

Triangle Consulting Group

PO Box 13236
Durham, NC 27709
(919) 419-0445
Email: tricongr@aol.com

Description: We are a full-service technical
consulting firm specializing in the contract and
permanent placement of engineering, information
technology, and technical sales/marketing
professionals. We service a broad spectrum of
industries and disciplines. We are a certified
woman-owned business enterprise.

Key Contact - Specialty:
Ms. Gina Roper, Resource Manager - *IT,
Engineering, Technical Sales*

Salary minimum: $50,000

Functions: Generalist, IT, MIS Mgmt., Systems
Analysis, Systems Dev., Systems Implem.,
Network Admin., DB Admin.

Industries: Generalist, Energy, Utilities, Mfg., IT
Implementation, Communications, Telecoms, Call
Centers, Telephony, Digital, Wireless, Fiber
Optic, Network Infrastructure, Insurance,
Software, Biotech, Healthcare

Triangle Technology

10713 RR 620 N 512
Austin, TX 78726
(512) 498-9090
Fax: (512) 498-9206
Email: info@triangletechnology.com
Web: www.triangletechnology.com

Description: We are agents for the top technical
talent. Our unique personal approach to technical
staffing is focused on one goal...your goal.

Key Contact:
Mr. Ray Schwitters, President
Mrs. Tiffany Howard, Principal
Mr. Jon Howard, Principal

Salary minimum: $50,000

Trillium Staffing Solutions

2323 Gull Rd Ste A
Kalamazoo, MI 49001
(616) 345-4400
(616) 345-0150
Fax: (616) 345-0913
Email: kalamazoo@trilliumstaffing.com
Web: www.trilliumstaffing.com

Description: Our expanding executive recruiting
division offers clients a broad recruiting network
due to the support by our two technical contract
companies and our 28 branch offices.

Key Contact - Specialty:
Mr. Mark Ciosek, Professional Placement
Specialist - *Information technology, information
systems*
Ms. Ruth Bergsma, Professional Placement
Specialist - *Generalist*
Ms. Carol Cosgiff, Professional Placement -
Generalist

Functions: Generalist, General Mgmt., Mfg., Sales
& Mktg., Finance, IT, Engineering

Industries: Generalist, Mfg., Transportation

Branches:
750 Almar Pkwy Ste 202
Bourbonnais, IL 60914
(815) 937-5300
Fax: (815) 937-5594

3401 16th St
Moline, IL 61265
(888) 695-4239
(309) 762-0045
Fax: (309) 762-0084

125 Webster St
Montgomery, IL 60538
(630) 844-5500

100 S Main St
Morton, IL 61550
(309) 263-2277
Email: morton@allstaffinc.com
Key Contact:
Ms. Kathy Volmer

209 W Maumee
Adrian, MI 49221
(517) 263-6600
Fax: (517) 263-1091
Email: adrian@trilliumstaffing.com
Key Contact:
Ms. Carol Cosgriff

225 E Superior Ste E
Alma, MI 48801-1818
(989) 463-5933
Email: alma@trilliumstaffing.com
Key Contact:
Ms. Barbara Dutcher, Recruiter

2393 Pontiac Rd
Auburn Hills, MI 48326
(248) 377-4342
Fax: (248) 377-4180
Email: auburnhills@trilliumstaffing.com
Key Contact:
Ms. Loretta Ferguson, Branch Manager
Mr. Darryl Sullivan, Staffing Consultant

249 E Huron Ave Ste 1
Bad Axe, MI 48413
(989) 269-6923
Fax: (989) 269-8392
Email: badaxe@trilliumstaffing.com
Key Contact:
Ms. Yvette Serrato, Area Manager
Ms. Joan Zemer, Account Representative

4055 W Dickman Rd Ste A
Battle Creek, MI 49015
(616) 964-2225
Fax: (616) 964-9710
Email: battlecreek@trilliumstaffing.com
Key Contact:
Ms. Cindi Liezert

10524 E Grand River Ste 109
Brighton, MI 48116
(810) 229-2033
Email: brighton@trilliumstaffing.com
Key Contact:
Ms. Stephanie Pahl, Branch Manager
Ms. Kerie Dwyer, Staffing Consultant
Ms. Kristin Long, Staffing Consultant

114 W Harris Ste B
Charlotte, MI 48813
(989) 543-2023
Fax: (989) 543-5992
Email: charlotte@trilliumstaffing.com

Key Contact:
Ms. Ginny Chase

397 W Chicago Dr
Coldwater, MI 49036
(517) 278-2935
Fax: (517) 278-2057
Email: coldwater@trilliumstaffing.com
Key Contact:
Ms. Kathy O'Whene

836 E Bay St
East Tawas, MI 48730
(989) 362-3452
Fax: (989) 362-6444
Email: etawas@trilliumstaffing.com
Key Contact:
Ms. Carole Adams, Staffing Consultant

2222 S Linden Rd
Flint, MI 48532
(810) 733-7180
Fax: (810) 733-2560
Email: flint@trilliumstaffing.com
Key Contact:
Ms. Anne Magalski, Area Manager
Ms. Nicole Bixby, Staffing Consultant
Ms. Linda Niedecken, Staffing Consultant
Ms. Lisa Kolander, Staffing Consultant

255 28th St SE
Grand Rapids, MI 49548
(616) 245-3300
Fax: (616) 245-3353
Key Contact:
Mr. Mark Coisck

950 W Monroe St Ste G200
Jackson, MI 49202
(517) 782-3921
Fax: (517) 782-9341

950 W Monroe Ste G-200
Jackson, MI 49202
(517) 782-8231
Fax: (517) 782-9341
Email: jackson@trilliumstaffing.com
Key Contact:
Ms. Judy Romanowski, Branch Manager

588 Olds St
Jonesville, MI 49250
(616) 849-0062
Fax: (516) 849-0067
Email: jonesville@trilliumstaffing.com
Key Contact:
Ms. Kathy O'Whene

558 Main St Ste 3
Lapeer, MI 48446
(810) 664-6688
Fax: (810) 664-1773
Email: lapeer@trilliumstaffing.com
Key Contact:
Ms. Sherry Hemingway, Branch Manager
Ms. Lisa LeMieux, Account Representative
Ms. Jamie Swett, Staffing Consultant

422 E Michigan Ave
Marshall, MI 49068
(616) 781-9727
Fax: (616) 781-7080
Email: marshall@trilliumstaffing.com
Key Contact:
Ms. Cindy Fidler

901 E Indian St
Midland, MI 48640
(517) 631-7851
Fax: (517) 631-5770
Email: midland@trilliumstaffing.com
Key Contact:
Mr. Todd Johnroe, Branch Manager
Ms. Lisa Maxwell, Staffing Consultant
Ms. Melody Liverett, Staffing Consultant

1956 S 11th St
Bell Plz Shopping Ctr
Niles, MI 49120-4059
(616) 684-6141
Fax: (616) 684-1677

Email: niles@trilliumstaffing.com
Key Contact:
Ms. Cathie McIntyre

576 Romence Rd Ste 227
Portage, MI 49024
(616) 324-9700
Fax: (616) 784-6255

4800 Fashion Sq Blvd Plz N Ste 120
Saginaw, MI 48604
(989) 799-5960
Fax: (989) 799-8570
Email: saginaw@trilliumstaffing.com
Key Contact:
Ms. Karen Gentle, Account Representative
Ms. Karen Musial, Staffing Consultant
Ms. Janie Thayer, Staffing Consultant

912 W Chicago Rd
Sturgis, MI 49091
(616) 651-9902
Fax: (616) 659-4886
Email: sturgis@trilliumstaffing.com
Key Contact:
Ms. Lisa Stewart

1100 N Main St Ste 7
Three Rivers, MI 49093
(616) 273-2692
Fax: (616) 278-7301
Email: threerivers@trilliumstaffing.com
Key Contact:
Ms. Lisa Stewart

844 Willard Dr
Green Bay, WI 54307
(920) 498-9090
Fax: (920) 498-9095
Email: greenbay@trilliumstaffing.com
Key Contact:
Mr. Tom Valeko

3949 Calumet Ave Ste 5
Manitowoc, WI 54220
(920) 682-3808
Fax: (920) 682-8226
Email: manitowoc@trilliumstaffing.com
Key Contact:
Mr. Tom Valeko

Trillium Talent Resource Group
150 Consumers Rd Ste 210
Toronto, ON M2J 1P9
Canada
(416) 497-2624
(877) 722-8522
Fax: (416) 497-8491
Email: ttr@trilliumhr.com
Web: www.trilliumhr.com

Description: We provide recruitment solutions to the healthcare and supply chain (including manufacturing, distribution, retail and transportation) sectors. We recruit management and professional talent for our clients from the domestic and international markets.

Key Contact - Specialty:
Ms. Poonam Kathuria, President - *International business*
Mr. Mark Byles, MBA, Vice President - *Marketing corporate development, project management*
Ms. Sabina DiNinio, BA, General Manager-Healthcare Recruiting - *Healthcare*
Mr. Robert Masters, Vice President - *Supply chain management*
Mr. Jaime Williston, Recruitment Consultant - *Agency business, international recruiting*
Mr. David Hong, Recruitment Consultant - *Healthcare*
Ms. Julia Fletcher, Recruitment Consultant - *Healthcare*

Functions: General Mgmt., Mfg., Distribution, Healthcare, Nurses, Allied Health, Advertising, Direct Mktg., Benefits, Personnel

Industries: Generalist, Mfg., Food, Bev., Tobacco, Textiles, Apparel, Paper, Printing, Drugs Mfg., Medical Devices, Plastics, Rubber, Leather, Stone, Glass, Metal Products, Machine, Appliance, Misc. Mfg., Transportation, Wholesale, Retail, Pharm Svcs., Mgmt. Consulting, HR Services, Packaging, Biotech, Healthcare, Hospitals, Long-term Care, Dental, Physical Therapy, Occupational Therapy

Branches:
99 Main St Ste 204
Cambridge, ON N1R 1W1
Canada
(519) 620-9683
(800) 335-9668
Fax: (519) 620-9681
Email: thr@trilliumhr.com

TriQuest
6237 Guadalupe Mines Rd
San Jose, CA 95120
(408) 388-2966
Fax: (408) 927-8777
Email: mredburn@tri-quest.com
Web: www.tri-quest.com

Description: We are a Silicon Valley based professional, technical, and executive-level search firm with over ten years experience as an established leader in the recruiting industry nationwide.

Key Contact - Specialty:
Mr. Mark C. Redburn, President - *Technical engineering, executive professionals*
Ms. Kathy D. McLemore, Director of Operations - *Technical engineering, executive professionals*
Ms. Hayley B. Redburn, Staffing Manager - *Sales & marketing executive professionals*

Salary minimum: $65,000

Functions: Generalist, General Mgmt., Sales & Mktg., HR Mgmt., Finance, IT, R&D, Engineering

Industries: Generalist, Computer Equip., Consumer Elect., Test, Measure Equip., Electronic, Elec. Components, Accounting, HR Services, E-commerce, IT Implementation, Media, Communications, Telecoms, Aerospace, Software

Professional Associations: SHRM

TriStaff Group
4350 Executive Dr Ste 100
San Diego, CA 92121
(858) 453-1331
Fax: (858) 453-6022
Email: tristaff@tristaff.com
Web: www.tristaff.com

Description: We utilize resources that are untapped by conventional recruiting methods. We focus our efforts on top performers who may not be actively seeking a new position or answering employment ads.

Key Contact - Specialty:
Mr. Gary van Eik, CEO - *Managed healthcare*
Mr. Richard Papike, President - *Newspaper, publishing, media*
Ms. Amy Moser, Vice President - *Software engineering, information technology*

Functions: Generalist, Senior Mgmt., Physicians, Health Admin., CFO's, Systems Analysis, Systems Dev., Engineering

Industries: Generalist, Computer Equip., Accounting, Mgmt. Consulting, Publishing, Broadcast, Film, Healthcare

Professional Associations: CSP

Branches:
3730 S Susan St Ste 100
Santa Ana, CA 92705
(714) 513-9414
Fax: (714) 513-9417
Email: orangecounty@tristaff.com
Key Contact - Specialty:
Mr. Jason van Eik, Manager - *Software consultants*

TRS Associates
9769 Chaucer Ct
Pickerington, OH 43147
(614) 837-6556
Email: nicklang@trsassociates.com
Web: www.trsassociates.com

Description: We are a professional firm with 24 years of industry experience placing sales, marketing, senior-level management and technical personnel with companies in the metals and materials industries. We offer permanent and contract placement.

Key Contact - Specialty:
Mr. Nick Lang, President - *Metals, materials*

Salary minimum: $35,000

Functions: Generalist

Industries: Metal Products, Misc. Mfg.

Professional Associations: APMI, ASM

The Truman Agency
13200 Crossroads Parkway N Ste 470
City of Industry, CA 91746
(562) 908-1233
Fax: (562) 908-1238
Email: bob@trumanagency.com
Web: www.trumanagency.com

Description: We offer confidential management recruiting serving the manufacturing and distribution industry sectors. Strengths in administration, sales, accounting, plant/production management, engineering, IT. Full-service agency can also provide administrative support staff. Permanent placement, contract/temp services.

Key Contact - Specialty:
Mr. Robert P. Truman, Vice President - *Manufacturing*

Functions: General Mgmt., Mfg., Materials, Sales & Mktg., HR Mgmt., Finance, IT

Industries: Generalist

Trust Bankers
(also known as Dunhill Professional Search of Richmond)
8100 Three Chopt Rd Ste 133
Richmond, VA 23229-4833
(804) 282-2216
Email: dpsricva@email.msn.com
Web: www.dunhillsearch.com

Description: In business for over 25 years. Part of a large franchise network.

Key Contact - Specialty:
Mr. P. Frank Lassiter, President - *Trust officers (administration, investments)*

Salary minimum: $40,000

Functions: Middle Mgmt.

Industries: Banking

TSC Group
6 Lansing Sq Ste 226
North York, ON M2J 1T5
Canada
(416) 494-6868
Fax: (416) 494-6171
Email: tscgroup@sprint.ca
Web: www.tscgroupcanada.com

Description: We specialize in the placement of technical and engineering related positions for numerous types of organizations: manufacturing, consulting engineering, government, construction, automotive, etc.

Key Contact:
Mr. Lesley Wieser

Salary minimum: $30,000

Functions: Mfg., Product Dev., Production, Plant Mgmt., Quality, Purchasing, Sales & Mktg., R&D, Engineering, Architects

Industries: Generalist

TSC Management Services Group Inc
112 Wool St
Barrington, IL 60010
(847) 381-0167
Fax: (847) 381-2169
Email: tscapply@tscsearch.com
Web: www.tscsearch.com

Description: We are well known specialists in engineering-manufacturing-materials management. Our practice is predominantly Midwestern and both contingency, as well as retained. Our subspecialty is video gaming, more specifically: coin-operated, home systems, internet, and wagering in all areas/professions, worldwide.

Key Contact - Specialty:
Mr. Robert G. Stanton, Sr., President - *Executive and management level searches*
Mr. Grant Stanton, Vice President - *Gaming (casino, consumer video, internet)*

Salary minimum: $35,000

Functions: Generalist, Senior Mgmt.

Industries: Mfg., Computer Equip., Consumer Elect., Electronic, Elec. Components, Entertainment, Media, New Media, Digital, Wireless, Fiber Optic, Software

Professional Associations: AMOA, IGDA, NAPS

TSI Group
(also known as TSI Staffing Services)
2630 Skymark Ave Ste 301
Mississauga, ON L4W 5A4
Canada
(905) 629-3701
Fax: (905) 629-0799
Email: tsi@tsigroup.com
Web: www.tsigroup.com

Description: We are a recruitment firm specializing in providing human resource solutions in supply chain management. We have the proven expertise and extensive network to source logistics and transportation professionals.

Key Contact:
Ms. Pamela Ruebusch, Senior Partner
Ms. Stacy Agnos, Senior Partner

Salary minimum: $30,000

Functions: Production, Distribution

Industries: Mfg., Transportation, Wholesale, Aerospace, Packaging, Software, ERP SW

Professional Associations: CLM, SCL, TCT

TSS Consulting Ltd
2525 E Camelback Rd Ste 560
Phoenix, AZ 85016
(602) 955-7000
Fax: (602) 957-3948
Email: resume@tss-consulting.com
Web: www.tss-consulting.com

Description: We are a high-technology/executive recruitment firm with concentration in CAD/CAE, system software, semiconductor, government

electronics, artificial intelligence and associated executive functions.

Key Contact - Specialty:
Mr. John R. McDonald, President - *High technology, electronics*

Salary minimum: $70,000

Functions: Generalist, Systems Dev., R&D, Engineering

Industries: Generalist, Computer Equip., Test, Measure Equip., Aerospace

Professional Associations: IEEE

Networks: National Personnel Assoc (NPA)

TSS Resources
8191 Glencree Pl
Dublin, OH 43016
(614) 799-9300
Fax: (614) 799-1012
Email: tss@tssresources.com
Web: www.tssresources.com

Description: We specialize in identifying and recruiting internetworking and telecommunications professionals. Our industry-experienced staff provides an unusually high-level of technical and interpersonal pre-qualification, so our clients see only the best candidates.

Key Contact - Specialty:
Ms. Ginny Berke, President - *Internetworking, telecommunications*

Salary minimum: $50,000

Functions: General Mgmt., Sales & Mktg., IT, Engineering, Technicians

Industries: Generalist, Computer Equip., Equip Svcs., E-commerce, IT Implementation, PSA/ASP, New Media, Communications, Database SW, ERP SW, Networking, Comm. SW, Security SW

Professional Associations: IEEE, MOAESP

Networks: Top Echelon Network

Turnage Employment Service Group
1225 Breckenridge Dr Ste 206
Little Rock, AR 772205
(501) 224-6870
Fax: (501) 224-5709
Email: lindad@turnage-employment.com
Web: www.turnage-employment.com

Key Contact:
Ms. Linda Dicus

Networks: Inter-City Personnel Assoc (IPA)

J Q Turner & Associates Inc
200 S Wilcox St Ste 217
Castle Rock, CO 80104-1913
(303) 688-0188
Email: jqt@jqt.com
Web: www.jqt.com

Description: We specialize placing people with a B.S., M.S., Ph.D., EE, ME, or a physical/life science degree, or technical professionals. We place in the following: R&D, process, manufacturing, quality, test, project, plant, for electronics (ASICs), semiconductor, telecom, biomedical, mass storage, energetic materials, instrumentation, etc.

Key Contact:
Mr. Jim Turner, President

Salary minimum: $50,000

Functions: Generalist

Industries: Mfg., Medical Devices, Plastics, Rubber, Machine, Appliance, Computer Equip., Consumer Elect., Test, Measure Equip., Telecoms, Software, Biotech

The Twin Oaks Team Inc
3604 Penhurst Pl
Raleigh, NC 27613
(919) 870-5737
Fax: (919) 870-9464
Email: morse@mindspring.com

Description: We recruit experienced sales, management and manufacturing candidates for sheet-fed and web offset, flexo and gravure printers. Emergency consulting to solve problems that cause crisis for printing companies.

Key Contact - Specialty:
Mr. Stan Morse, Owner - *Printed arts, graphic arts*

Salary minimum: $30,000

Functions: Senior Mgmt., Middle Mgmt., Plant Mgmt., Purchasing, Packaging, Sales & Mktg., HR Mgmt., CFO's, Engineering, Graphic Artists

Industries: Paper, Printing, Packaging

Professional Associations: GATF, IAPHC, NAPL, PICA

Tyler Search Consultants
42 W 38th St
New York, NY 10018
(212) 719-2200
Fax: (212) 719-2898
Email: careers@tylersearch.com
Web: www.tylersearch.com

Description: We are dedicated to the logistics, supply chain management, and transportation community. All of our recruiters are former logistics professionals with a thorough understanding of our marketplace.

Key Contact - Specialty:
Mr. William Conroy, Executive Director - *Logistics*
Mr. Roy Tapia, Managing Director - *Transportation*
Mr. Sean Moore, Managing Director - *Supply chain, logistics*

Salary minimum: $50,000

Functions: Directors, Senior Mgmt., Production, Plant Mgmt., Materials, Purchasing, Distribution, Customer Svc.

Industries: Generalist, Mfg., Transportation, E-commerce, IT Implementation, Packaging, Software, Doc. Mgmt., Production SW, ERP SW, Industry Specific SW, Mfg. SW

Professional Associations: APICS, CLM, CONECT, LIIEA, WIIT

Branches:
511 Stonecrest Dr
Birmingham, AL 35242
(205) 408-9493
Fax: (205) 408-9469
Email: careers@tylersearch.com
Key Contact - Specialty:
Mr. Coren Allen, Manager - *Logistics, distribution, transportation*

332 Victory Rd Marina Bay
Quincy, MA 02171
(617) 689-0500
Fax: (617) 689-0517
Email: careers@tylersearch.com
Key Contact - Specialty:
Mr. Sean Moore, Managing Director - *Logistics, supply chain, transportation*

UNI Accounting Services
PO Box 11454
Shawnee Mission, KS 66207-1454
(913) 498-3900
(816) 880-9797
Fax: (913) 498-0707
Email: generalinfo@cmc-uni.com
Web: www.uniaccountingservices.com

Description: We are human capital experts that know that people are companies' most valuable assets. Our mission is to provide companies with accounting and finance professionals who will add value to their organization and to provide our candidates with the best career opportunities so that they can achieve their goals.

Key Contact - Specialty:
Mr. Bruce C. Kaplan, Managing Partner - *Accounting, finance*
Mr. John A. Thomas, CTS, Principal - *Accounting, finance, management consulting*

Salary minimum: $40,000

Functions: Generalist, Personnel, Training, Finance, Mgmt. Consultants

Industries: Generalist, Mfg., Packaging, Software

Professional Associations: ASA, NAPS

UniQuest Int'l Inc

4350 W Cypress St Ste 450
Tampa, FL 33607
(813) 387-1000
Fax: (813) 387-3000
Email: info@uniquest.com
Web: www.uniquest.com

Description: Our consultants specialize by industry and function, staying abreast of the latest developments and trends. They focus on locating and tracking the top performers within their specialty.

Key Contact - Specialty:
Mr. Anthony F. Valone, President - *Healthcare, legal*
Mr. Michael Valone, Vice President - *Healthcare, decision support, IS, legal*
Mr. John Horton, Senior Consultant - *Healthcare*
Mr. Mike Pond, Sr Consultant - *Healthcare, HR, finance*
Ms. Judi Valone, Senior Consultant - *Healthcare*
Mr. Tim Harris, Consultant - *Healthcare*

Salary minimum: $50,000

Functions: Generalist

Industries: Generalist, Finance, Pharm Svcs., Legal, Accounting, Mgmt. Consulting, HR Services, Healthcare

Professional Associations: HFMA

Unisearch Search & Recruiting Inc

790 The City Dr S Ste 150
Orange, CA 92868
(714) 748-0700
Email: unisearchorange@juno.com

Description: Executive and high-tech search in the following: healthcare, finance, plastics, electronics, banking, legal, construction, food technology. An account executive specializes in a particular field.

Key Contact - Specialty:
Mr. James L. Rose, President - *Electronics*
Ms. Patricia Ergas, Vice President - *Accounting, finance*

Functions: Generalist, Legal, Mfg., Healthcare, Finance, IT, Engineering, Attorneys

Industries: Generalist, Construction, Mfg., Plastics, Rubber, Computer Equip., Banking, Healthcare

Branches:
PO Box 810
Lake Havasu City, AZ 86405-0810
(520) 680-6077
Fax: (520) 680-6037
Key Contact - Specialty:
Mr. Jim Enrico - *Plastics*

United Search

34 Market St
PO Box 21
Onancock, VA 23417
(757) 787-2332
Fax: (757) 787-2448
Email: usearch@intercom.net
Web: www.unitedsearch1.com

Key Contact:
Mr. Ed Oswald

Salary minimum: $50,000

Functions: Mfg., Purchasing, Sales & Mktg., Engineering

Industries: Mfg., Food, Bev., Tobacco, Chemicals, Drugs Mfg., Medical Devices, Plastics, Rubber, Paints, Petro. Products, Metal Products, Misc. Mfg., Biotech, Healthcare

Networks: Inter-City Personnel Assoc (IPA)

United Search Associates

(dba Health Network USA)
3201 Chimneyrock Dr
Plano, TX 75023
(972) 519-0863
Fax: (972) 964-8696
Email: info@unitedsearch.com
Web: www.unitedsearch.com

Description: Placement of healthcare professionals across the USA. Clients include hospitals, clinics and other providers.

Key Contact - Specialty:
Mr. David J. Elliott, President - *Healthcare*
Ms. C. J. Elliott, Vice President - *Healthcare*

Salary minimum: $40,000

Functions: Healthcare

Industries: Generalist

Professional Associations: ACHE

Unlimited Staffing Solutions Inc

22 W Huron St
Pontiac, MI 48342
(248) 253-1505
(248) 258-5111
Fax: (248) 253-1512
Email: recruiter@unlimitedstaffing.com
Web: www.unlimitedstaffing.com

Description: Temporary/contract staffing, employee leasing

Key Contact:
Ms. Caleene Jones Newman, President - *Technical*
Mr. Jason Midds, Vice President, General Manager

Functions: Generalist, Mfg., Materials, HR Mgmt., Finance, IT, Engineering

Industries: Generalist, Mfg., Transportation, Finance, Services

Professional Associations: NTSA

Uptheladder

290 Riverside Dr Ste 11A
New York, NY 10025
(212) 222-6543
Fax: (212) 865-2008
Email: uptheladder@earthlink.net

Description: Our firm is an executive search agency specializing in recruiting sales, marketing, and technical candidates for high-tech companies, including Internet, dot-com, telecommunications, etc. Uptheladder focuses on providing custom-tailored services for a limited number of corporate clients each year. Our candidates include high-level sales executives, all levels of management and key corporate personnel. Our philosophy is to develop a strong understanding of our clients needs and exceed their recruiting expectations.

Key Contact - Specialty:
Ms. Lucy Lasky, CEO - *Sales/marketing/technical for high tech companies (internet, telecommunications, dot-com)*

Salary minimum: $45,000

Functions: Generalist

Industries: Misc. Mfg., Banking, Invest. Banking, Misc. Financial, New Media, Broadcast, Film, Communications

The Urban Placement Service

PO Box 8040
Houston, TX 77288
(713) 880-2211
Fax: (713) 880-5577
Email: urbanplacement@msn.com
Web: www.urbanplacement.com

Description: Professional search: minority recruitment; accounting/finance, engineering, marketing/sales, production/logistics and human resources.

Key Contact - Specialty:
Mr. Willie S. Bright, Owner - *Diversity generalist*
Mr. Develous A. Bright, Employment Consultant - *Diversity generalist*

Salary minimum: $35,000

Functions: Generalist, Mfg., Materials, Sales & Mktg., HR Mgmt., Finance, Engineering, Minorities

Industries: Generalist, Mfg., Food, Bev., Tobacco, Drugs Mfg., Finance, Services, Telecoms, Aerospace, Healthcare

Professional Associations: MHRA, NBMBAA, NSBE, NSHMBA, NUL

Urpan Technologies Inc

6426 Devonshire Dr
San Jose, CA 95129
(408) 973-1529
(408) 887-5566
Fax: (408) 973-1529
Email: urpantech@yahoo.com
Web: www.premurpan.org

Description: Our firm is into technical permanent staff augmentation and management consulting for market entry services.

Key Contact - Specialty:
Mr. Pad N. Swami, VP
Mrs. Usha Padmanabhan, CEO - *Customer relationships*

Salary minimum: $50,000

Functions: Generalist

Industries: Energy, Utilities, Construction, Mfg., Retail, Finance, Services, Mgmt. Consulting, E-commerce, IT Implementation, PSA/ASP, Hospitality, Hotels, Resorts, Clubs, Communications, Fiber Optic, Software, Database SW, Development SW, ERP SW, Non-classifiable

Networks: US Recruiters.com

US Gas/Search

5215 E 71St St Ste 1500
Tulsa, OK 74136
(918) 492-6668
Fax: (918) 492-6674
Email: keithl@ionet.net

Description: We possess one of the finest networks of contacts, knowledge and ability of matching needs and talents in the gas industry today. This enables us to attract the very finest talent available and allows us to excel in gathering data important to your continued success.

Key Contact - Specialty:
Mr. Keith Louderback, Owner - *Natural gas, gas liquids, marketing, trading*

Salary minimum: $70,000

Functions: Generalist, Senior Mgmt., Middle Mgmt., Mktg. Mgmt., Engineering

Industries: Generalist, Energy, Utilities

US Search LLC
712 W Broad St Ste 3
Falls Church, VA 22046
(703) 448-1900
(800) 784-0099
Fax: (703) 448-1907
Email: ahsearch@aol.com
Web: www.ussearchllc.com

Description: We provide industry specialized recruitment and are a search firm with more than 19 years experience of timely, discrete service. We provide effective service to our clients in all phases of the plastics and specialty materials industries. We have always believed that "our clients are our best references."

Key Contact - Specialty:
Mr. Arnie Hiller, President - *Plastics, ceramics, composite materials, plastics processing, plastics equipment*

Salary minimum: $50,000

Functions: Senior Mgmt., Mfg., Product Dev., Purchasing, Mktg. Mgmt., Sales Mgmt., R&D, Engineering

Industries: Mfg., Chemicals, Plastics, Rubber, Paints, Petro. Products, Leather, Stone, Glass, Machine, Appliance, Packaging

Professional Associations: SAE, SPE, SPI

US-Recruiters.com
11325 172nd St
Lakeville, MN 55044-9325
(952) 898-1352
Fax: (509) 351-9797
Email: admin@us-recruiters.com
Web: www.us-recruiters.com

Description: The nation's leading recruiters are members of our firm. We invite you to check out our posted jobs and submit your resume to our candidate database.

Key Contact:
Ms. Sally A. Rystrom, President - *Computer hardware, software, data communication, computer services*
Mr. Robert Rystrom, CEO

Salary minimum: $60,000

Functions: Generalist, Middle Mgmt., Mkt. Research, Mktg. Mgmt.

Industries: Generalist, Computer Equip., Test, Measure Equip., Mgmt. Consulting, Software

Networks: The Acumen Society

USA Medical Placement Inc
3604 Date Palm
McAllen, TX 78501
(956) 631-3540
Fax: (956) 686-3540
Email: usamedpt@aol.com

Description: We are a medical search firm specializing in administration, nursing, and physicians. We treat each hospital or candidate with individual consideration. The degree of abilities, whether client or candidate, is a factor in our searches.

Key Contact - Specialty:
Ms. Patricia Tracy, President - *Medical healthcare*

Salary minimum: $50,000

Functions: Senior Mgmt., Physicians, Nurses, Health Admin.

Industries: Generalist, Hospitals

Valacon Inc
466 E Foothill Blvd Ste 206
La Canada, CA 91011
(818) 949-7911
(626) 296-2751
Fax: (626) 296-2760
Email: info@valacon.com
Web: www.valacon.com

Description: All recruiters have relevant industry experience. We only present candidate approved resumes to clients. Our website features our background, ethical philosophy, candidates and clients bill of rights.

Key Contact - Specialty:
Mr. Sandy Geffner, President - *Information systems audit, information systems*
Mr. Stuart Fried, Vice President - *Information systems audit, internal audit*
Ms. Helen Kang, Director - *Accounting, finance, audit, tax*

Salary minimum: $30,000

Functions: Finance, Risk Mgmt., IT, Systems Analysis, Systems Implem., Mgmt. Consultants

Industries: Generalist

Professional Associations: CSP, IIA, ISACA

Valmar Technical Staffing
1174 Whitfield Dr
Grand Blanc, MI 48439
(810) 694-5236
(810) 694-5236
Fax: (810) 694-0686
Email: valmartec@aol.com

Description: We are a recruiting company that targets and delivers high quality professionals to our client companies. We specialize in engineering and information technology.

Key Contact - Specialty:
Mr. L. Keith Johnson, Co-Owner - *Engineering, information technology*
Ms. Valda Greenhill, Co-Owner - *Engineering, information technology, office administration*

Salary minimum: $40,000

Functions: Generalist

Industries: Mfg., Motor Vehicles, Computer Equip., Finance, Accounting, Telecoms

Van Curan & Associates
9 Standley St
PO Box 148
Prides Crossing, MA 01965-0148
(978) 922-4460
Fax: (603) 754-9500
Email: cdvc@mediaone.net

Description: We do retained and contingent executive and professional searches focused on the financial services industries, especially insurance and banking. We publish an insurance compensation survey annually.

Key Contact - Specialty:
Mr. Christopher D. Van Curan, Principal - *Financial services, insurance*
Mr. Chester Larner, Senior Consultant - *Insurance*
Mr. Frank Hoskin, Jr., CPCU, Senior Consultant - *Insurance*

Salary minimum: $75,000

Functions: Generalist

Industries: Finance, Banking, Invest. Banking, Brokers, Venture Cap., Misc. Financial, Insurance, Healthcare

Professional Associations: FEI, NEERC

Van Houten & Rogers Inc
339 East Ave Ste 450
Rochester, NY 14604
(716) 787-0219
Fax: (716) 797-0832
Email: rtomlin@frontiernet.net

Description: Our principal possesses an MBA and fortune corporate experience in addition to twelve years of recruiting. She is an expert at identifying exceptional candidates.

Key Contact - Specialty:
Ms. Rita M. Tomlinson, President - *Marketing, supply chain, finance, human resources, general management*

Salary minimum: $50,000

Functions: Middle Mgmt., Product Dev., Sales & Mktg., HR Mgmt., Finance, Minorities

Industries: Textiles, Apparel, Drugs Mfg., Medical Devices, Plastics, Rubber, Computer Equip., Consumer Elect., Advertising, Telecoms, Software, Healthcare

Dick Van Vliet & Associates
2401 Fountainview Ste 322
Houston, TX 77057
(713) 952-0371
Email: dick@dickvanvliet.com
Web: www.dickvanvliet.com

Description: We have numerous long-term client relationships with Fortune 500 companies, Big 5, and national and local CPA firms. We also serve growth industry and service companies. We recruit accounting/financial professionals for positions primarily in the Houston area. We meticulously over-screen candidates to insure a good match for our clients and candidates.

Key Contact - Specialty:
Mr. Dick Van Vliet, President - *Accounting, financial*

Salary minimum: $35,000

Functions: Middle Mgmt., Finance

Industries: Generalist

Van Zant Inc
9712 E Pershing Ave
Scottsdale, AZ 85260
(480) 314-5750
Fax: (480) 314-1963
Email: infotech@primenet.com

Description: Our firm specializes in information technology, sales and marketing, and high-level management positions. We are a "Preferred Member" of Top Echelon Network, Inc., the largest and most prestigious network of independent executive and technical firms. We offer clients and candidates the widest range of staffing services available anywhere in search, recruiting, or employment agent business.

Key Contact:
Mr. Mike Van Zant, Owner

Functions: Directors, Senior Mgmt., Sales & Mktg., IT, MIS Mgmt., Systems Dev., Network Admin., DB Admin.

Industries: Generalist, Energy, Utilities, Transportation, Banking, Legal, Mgmt. Consulting, E-commerce, IT Implementation, PSA/ASP, Communications, Aerospace, Software, Healthcare

Professional Associations: ASPA

Networks: Top Echelon Network

Van Zeeland Associates Inc

1750 Freedom Rd
PO Box 188
Little Chute, WI 54140
(920) 788-5222
Fax: (920) 788-5281
Email: gvze@gvze.com
Web: www.gvze.com

Description: We are a direct placement staffing agency specializing in the placement of highly qualified sales/marketing professionals, engineers, upper-level management, and executives within the electrical and mechanical industries.

Key Contact:
Mr. Gary Van Zeeland, Founder
Ms. Kelly Koch, Placement Specialist
Ms. Penny Grissman, Placement Specialist

Functions: Generalist

Industries: Electronic, Elec. Components

Professional Associations: WAPS

Vaughan & Company Executive Search Inc

9 Executive Cir Ste 240
Irvine, CA 92614
(949) 623-3300
Fax: (949) 623-3333
Email: recruiters@vaughanandcompany.com
Web: www.vaughanandcompany.com

Description: We offer search and placement services for professionals in the aviation, aerospace, bio-tech/life sciences, industrial, broadband communications, semiconductor, overhaul/repair, electronics, and other high-technology industries. Our service is provided nationally and internationally, and we offer both contingency and retained services.

Key Contact - Specialty:
Mr. David B. Vaughan, President - *Industrial, aviation, sales & marketing, engineering*
Ms. Julie Raab, Director of Major Accounts - *Aviation, high technology, industrial, manufacturing, engineering*

Salary minimum: $75,000

Functions: Generalist, Senior Mgmt., Production, Sales Mgmt., Engineering

Industries: Mfg., Chemicals, Plastics, Rubber, Metal Products, Machine, Appliance, Misc. Mfg., Electronic, Elec. Components, Communications, Aerospace, Biotech

Professional Associations: CSP

Venator Partners

1025 Monarch St Ste A201
Lexington, KY 40513
(859) 296-2823
Email: recruiter@venatorpartners.com
Web: www.venatorpartners.com

Description: We are an international executive search firm specializing in serving telecom, datacom and Internet technology companies; The communications industry. We handle searches for sales, marketing, general management and engineering positions worldwide.

Key Contact - Specialty:
Mr. Randall L. Bogue, President - *Telecommunications, fiber optics, opt electronics, internet, software, sales & marketing, general management*
Mr. Stan Settle, Director of Research - *Telecommunications, fiber optics, opt electronics, internet, software*
Mr. Phill Gunning, Executive Recruiter - *Telecommunications, fiber optics, opt electronics, internet, software*

Mr. Doug Combs, Executive Recruiter - *Telecommunications, fiber optics, opt electronics, internet, software*

Salary minimum: $100,000

Functions: General Mgmt., Sales & Mktg., Engineering

Industries: Electronic, Elec. Components, Telecoms, Telephony, Digital, Wireless, Fiber Optic, Network Infrastructure

Venpro Consulting Inc

37 Rainbow Creekway
North York, ON M2K 2T9
Canada
(416) 223-3341
Email: venpro@sympatico.ca

Description: We have worked exclusively with Canada's computer vendors for over a decade, and our mission is to recruit quality professionals in the following job functions: sales, pre-sales support, telesales, telemarketing, consulting, and sales/marketing management.

Key Contact - Specialty:
Mr. Brian H. Campbell, President - *Sales, sales support, consultants, marketing for vendors in computer hardware, integration (software, systems)*

Salary minimum: $50,000

Functions: Generalist, Sales & Mktg., Mktg. Mgmt., Sales Mgmt., Direct Mktg.

Industries: Generalist, Computer Equip., Telecoms, Software

Vento Associates

11130 Kingston Pike Ste 1-405
Knoxville, TN 37922
(865) 777-3900
Fax: (865) 777-3904
Email: jvento@tcmm.net
Web: www.vento.com

Description: We specialize in technical applications, with an emphasis on CEO, president, vice president, general management, sales management, marketing, sales, application engineering, pre- and post-sales, consulting and implementation positions for the application software & service markets.

Key Contact - Specialty:
Mr. Joseph P. Vento, President - *High technology, software applications*

Salary minimum: $65,000

Functions: Generalist, Automation, Mktg. Mgmt., Sales Mgmt., Systems Dev., Systems Implem.

Industries: Generalist, Medical Devices, Computer Equip., Test, Measure Equip., E-commerce, IT Implementation, PSA/ASP, Software, ERP SW

Vermillion Group

(also known as MRI & Sales Consultants of Des Moines)
1801 25th St
West Des Moines, IA 50266
(515) 224-9142
Fax: (515) 224-7187
Email: mri@vermilliongroup.com
Web: www.vermilliongroup.com

Description: We are the largest executive search firm in the Midwest focusing exclusively on telecommunications, information technologies and financial services.

Key Contact - Specialty:
Mr. Michael Vermillion, President - *Telecommunications*
Mr. Russ Tessman, Vice President - *Information technology*

Ms. Janette Weber, Vice President - *Telecommunications*
Mr. Ken Dickerson, Vice President - *Information technology*
Mr. Jim Roth, Vice President - *Insurance, financial services*

Salary minimum: $50,000

Functions: Generalist

Industries: Finance, Media, Telecoms, Insurance, Software

Vermont Business Ventures Inc

60 Brickyard Rd Ste 26
Essex Junction, VT 05452
(802) 872-7746
Email: vbv@together.net
Web: www.vbvjobs.com

Description: Our company is dedicated to providing industry-leading services in the field of professional placement. High-quality placement services are offered to meet the needs of employers requiring assistance in locating qualified candidates as well as to individual candidates desiring relocation, professional advancement or change of career.

Key Contact:
Ms. Cheryl L. Moomey, President/CEO

Functions: Generalist

Industries: Generalist

Victor White Int'l (VWI)

23072 Lake Center Dr Ste 210
PO Box 3318
Lake Forest, CA 92630
(949) 380-4800
Fax: (949) 380-7477
Email: vic@victorwhite.com
Web: www.victorwhite.com

Description: Our firm is a retained medical research recruitment firm. VWI is also in a niche area, assisting established medical firms seeking technology or specialist in specific technologies. Our expertise in medical early stage technology/startup companies, with our 16 years of experience is a perfect match. A recent spin off MEDCareerNET (www.medcareernet.com) is a special retained and contingent firm in the medical markets. As we continue, "MCN" will engage in the recruitment function assisting firms to build their infrastructure for success.

Key Contact - Specialty:
Mr. Victor Chapa, Managing Partner - *Medical, technologies (early stage)*
Ms. Kate Maurina, VP- Technical Recruitment - *Clinical, marketing, R/A, Q/A, software*
Mr. Stephen Izabal, Director, Recruitment/Technology - *Software, engineering, R&D*
Ms. Donna Figlioli, Director of Administration
Mr. Sam Mandegar, Operations Manager, Web Development - *Biotechnical, genetics, bioscientific, pharmaceuticals, software*

Salary minimum: $90,000

Functions: General Mgmt., Directors, Senior Mgmt., Middle Mgmt., Automation, Healthcare

Industries: Mfg., Drugs Mfg., Medical Devices, Plastics, Rubber, Computer Equip., Electronic, Elec. Components, Invest. Banking, Venture Cap., Pharm Svcs., Mgmt. Consulting, HR Services, Telecoms, Government, Insurance, Software, Biotech, Healthcare

ViLinks

210 Susannah Pl
Costa Mesa, CA 92627
(949) 252-1772
Email: info@vilinks.com
Web: www.vilinks.com

Description: We offer professional services, such as consulting, software, Internet/www, and systems development and support. Our major geographical focus is in California, as well as national. Our specialties are consultants, PSO, software engineering, marketing, technical support.

Key Contact - Specialty:
Mr. Richard Nelson, Principal - *High technology, software, engineering, MIS, consulting*

Salary minimum: $36,000

Functions: Engineering

Industries: Software

Villasenor & Associates
6546 San Vicente Blvd
Los Angeles, CA 90048
(323) 936-4880
Fax: (323) 936-8066
Email: clickonlaw@aol.com

Description: We specialize exclusively in placement of attorneys in law firms and corporations; ability to successfully match job description with qualified high caliber candidates.

Key Contact:
Mr. Hector Villasenor, Principal
Ms. Carole Howard, Principal

Salary minimum: $75,000

Functions: Attorneys

Industries: Legal

C J Vincent Associates LLC
2669 Legends Way
Ellicott City, MD 21042
(410) 461-2600
Fax: (410) 461-7304
Email: cucuzzella@home.com

Description: We conduct professional recruitment for sales and marketing in the computer industry based on prior sales management experience in the computer system field.

Key Contact - Specialty:
Mr. Vincent J. Cucuzzella, Principal - *Computer system, software sales & marketing*

Salary minimum: $50,000

Functions: Mktg. Mgmt., Sales Mgmt.

Industries: Computer Equip., Software

Professional Associations: MAPRC

Vines & Associates Inc
6294 Beaver Creek Rd
New Hill, NC 27562
(919) 303-1249
Email: brian@vines-associates.com
Web: www.vines-associates.com

Description: We specialize in recruiting for the telecommunications and networking industries. We recruit nationally for hardware and software design, development, test, operations, QA, systems, and sales/marketing positions at the VP, director, manager, project lead, and individual contributor levels for exciting leading edge companies.

Key Contact:
Mr. Brian Vines, President

Functions: Generalist

Industries: Mfg., E-commerce, IT Implementation, Communications, Database SW, Mfg. SW, Networking, Comm. SW

Vintage Resources Inc
11 E 44th St Ste 708
New York, NY 10017
(212) 867-1001
Fax: (212) 490-9277

Email: careers@vintageresourcesinc.com

Description: Clients seeking a cost efficient, personalized approach from a select staff of recruitment professionals serving the advertising/direct marketing industries are encouraged to call us.

Key Contact:
Mr. Perry Fishman, Vice President
Ms. Judy Fishman, Vice President

Salary minimum: $40,000

Functions: Sales & Mktg., Advertising, Mkt. Research, Mktg. Mgmt., Direct Mktg.

Industries: Media, Advertising, Publishing, New Media, Broadcast, Film, Telecoms

VIP Resources Inc
2 Bartlett Rd Ste 2000
Monsey, NY 10952
(845) 356-8000
Email: jgross@vipresource.com

Description: We are a specialized firm that provides professional, confidential search and recruitment services in compensation and employee benefits. Areas of specialty include group and retirement benefits, health, and managed care, communication and all aspects of compensation including web communications.

Key Contact - Specialty:
Mr. Joe Gross, Vice President - *Employee benefits*

Salary minimum: $40,000

Functions: Generalist, Benefits

Industries: Generalist, HR Services, Healthcare

Professional Associations: IABC, WAW

Virtual Search Inc
10693 Wiles Rd
Coral Springs, FL 33076
(800) 779-3334
Fax: (800) 779-3369
Email: marc@vsearch.com
Web: www.vsearch.com

Description: Staffed by ex-game developers, we focus on the Interactive multimedia video games industry. We have offices in San Francisco, Austin and Ft. Lauderdale.

Key Contact - Specialty:
Mr. Marc Mencher, President - *Video game industry*

Functions: Generalist

Industries: Hospitality, Software

Professional Associations: IGDA

Visions Personnel
33 Main St Ste 400
Nashua, NH 03064
(603) 883-5897
Fax: (603) 889-9534
Email: careers@visionspersonnel.com
Web: www.visionspersonnel.com

Description: We are a major force in placing qualified candidates in restaurant careers across the United States. We place staff in every sector of the restaurant industry from entry level management to senior corporate executives. We represent clients in all styles of restaurants; from quick serve, to casual theme, and fine dining; our clients range from local independents to major national chains.

Key Contact:
Mr. Steve Varrieur, President
Mr. Pete Greene, President
Ms. Maude Laurence, Vice President
Ms. Lynn Burtsell, Office Manager
Mr. John Roemer, Vice President
Ms. Charlene Lambert, Vice President

Mr. Dan Dadoun, Staffing Manager

Functions: Generalist

Industries: Restaurants

Vista Associates
214 Hwy 18
East Brunswick, NJ 08816
(732) 937-6788
Fax: (732) 937-6130
Email: bob@vistaassoc.com

Description: We have over 20 successful years in the placement of executive, management and technical professionals in many functions and geographical areas.

Key Contact - Specialty:
Mr. Bob Jones, CPC, President - *Engineering, manufacturing, logistics, packaging, human resources*

Salary minimum: $40,000

Functions: Generalist, Directors

Industries: Mfg., Food, Bev., Tobacco, Drugs Mfg., Medical Devices, Wholesale, Pharm Svcs., Mgmt. Consulting, Hospitality, Haz. Waste, Packaging, HR SW, Mfg. SW, Healthcare

Professional Associations: IIE, ISPE, MHMS, NJSA, PI

Vista Technology
800 Turnpike St Ste 300
North Andover, MA 01845
(978) 686-2200
Fax: (978) 686-1313
Email: rich@vista-technology.com
Web: www.vista-technology.com

Description: We are a contingency search firm specializing the biotechnology/biopharmaceutical industry. Our client companies include start-ups to well established companies. Our client candidates include research associates/scientists, clinical and medical affairs, informatics, quality and manufacturing scientists. Browse our web site to review some of the positions we have successfully filled or to look at some of our open positions!

Key Contact - Specialty:
Mr. Richard Connors, Principal - *Biopharmaceutical, biotechnology*

Salary minimum: $40,000

Functions: Generalist

Industries: Biotech

Professional Associations: MAPS

Vogel Associates
PO Box 269R
Huntingdon Valley, PA 19006-0269
(215) 938-1700
Fax: (215) 938-1789
Email: resumes@vogelassociates.com
Web: www.vogelassociates.com

Description: We are a professional recruiting and search specializing exclusively in all areas of human resources: employment, training, MD/OD, compensation, benefits, labor and employee relations, EEO/AA, HRIS, etc. Client and candidate bases are national.

Key Contact - Specialty:
Mr. Michael S. Vogel, President - *Human resources*

Salary minimum: $50,000

Functions: HR Mgmt.

Industries: Generalist

Professional Associations: ASTD, CPC, EMA, IAPW, NAPS, ODN, SHRM, TPS, WAW

Networks: National Personnel Assoc (NPA)

Beverly von Winckler & Associates

123 W Madison Ste 205
1018 Lee
Evanston, IL 60202
(312) 332-6262
Fax: (312) 332-6284
Email: vonwinckler@earthlink.net

Description: Our specialties include communications, marketing, hitech, consulting for agencies, corporations, suppliers. Concentration in Chicago and Midwest. Form career long associations with both clients and candidates. Provide six month guarantee on placements.

Key Contact - Specialty:
Ms. Beverly von Winckler, President - *Communications*

Functions: Product Dev., Healthcare, Sales & Mktg., Advertising, Mkt. Research, Mktg. Mgmt., Direct Mktg., PR, DB Admin., Graphic Artists

Industries: Generalist, Misc. Mfg., Media, Advertising, Publishing

The Vortech Group Inc

12221 Bentwood Ct
Pickerington, OH 43147
(614) 755-2222
Email: glen@7552222.com
Web: www.7552222.com

Description: Our firm seeks to place top technical talent in a company that is a fit both technically and culturally. We treat you with respect, listen to what you want and need, and will find your next career stepping-stone in a timely fashion. We are dedicated to being honest and forthright in our placements, for the company's happiness and yours.

Key Contact:
Mr. Glen Gardner, President
Ms. Karin Warner
Ms. Bea Gardner

Salary minimum: $50,000

Functions: Directors

Industries: Computer Equip., Mgmt. Consulting, Software, Database SW, Doc. Mgmt., Production SW, System SW

VZ Int'l Inc

7411 E 6th Ave Ste 205
Scottsdale, AZ 85251
(480) 946-1907
Fax: (480) 946-3005
Email: vzintl1@ix.netcom.com

Description: We service the semiconductor market, conducting executive searches on an international basis for process engineers, general management, sales, marketing, engineering and field service personnel.

Key Contact - Specialty:
Mr. William Van Zanten, Partner - *Semiconductor executives, technical, sales & marketing*
Mr. Jerry Farro, Partner - *Semiconductor executives, technical, sales & marketing*

Salary minimum: $60,000

Functions: Senior Mgmt., Middle Mgmt., Mfg., Sales & Mktg., IT, Int'l.

Industries: Computer Equip., Test, Measure Equip., Software

W P Associates

(formerly known as Solutions HCl)
4020 Jones Ave Ste 108
Riverside, CA 92505
(909) 687-1927
Fax: (909) 687-1927
Email: medquests@lycos.com

Description: Principal has 20 years of experience working in medical device and pharmaceutical companies and 12 years working as a recruiter (contingency and retained) and placing regulatory, quality engineering, sales and marketing, and executives at all levels.

Key Contact - Specialty:
Mr. William D. Piper, President - *Medical device, pharmaceutical*

Salary minimum: $50,000

Functions: Generalist, Senior Mgmt., Middle Mgmt., Production, Quality, Mktg. Mgmt., Sales Mgmt., Engineering

Industries: Generalist, Soap, Perf., Cosmtcs., Drugs Mfg., Medical Devices, Plastics, Rubber, Pharm Svcs., Biotech

Wachendorfer & Associates

13047 Chandler Dr Ste 100
Dallas, TX 75243
(972) 783-0999
Fax: (972) 783-0995
Email: n.wachendorfer@att.net
Web: www.wachendorfer.com

Description: We specialize in placements for the food and food ingredient industries. We work closely with both the candidate and company to insure a good match. All recruiters are CPCs.

Key Contact - Specialty:
Ms. Nancy Wachendorfer, President - *Research & development, engineers, QC, food industry*
Mr. Tom Wachendorfer, Vice President - *Sales & marketing, production management, food industry*
Ms. Lauren Mitchell, Recruiter - *Plant management, QC, food industry*
Ms. Adrienne McKinney, Recruiter - *Plant management, engineers, food industry*

Salary minimum: $40,000

Functions: Generalist, Directors, Senior Mgmt., Product Dev., Plant Mgmt., Quality, Sales Mgmt., Engineering

Industries: Generalist, Food, Bev., Tobacco

Professional Associations: IRG, MAPS, NAPS, TAPS

Wagner & Associates

360 rue St Francois Xavier Bureau 200
Montreal, QC H2Y 2S8
Canada
(514) 842-5494
Fax: (514) 842-4529

Description: Our recruitment specialty is IT, computing, and MIS professionals at all levels, including: technical, more specifically SW developers, database, networks, architects, Q.A., and technical support; and management, more specifically projects, product, directors, and VP. We prefer to place our applicants in the Montreal area.

Key Contact - Specialty:
Ms. Gabriel Wagner, President - *IT*

Salary minimum: $35,000

Functions: Directors, Senior Mgmt., Middle Mgmt., Admin. Svcs., Product Dev.

Industries: Computer Equip., Software

Donald C Wagner Associates Inc

2411 Crofton Ln Ste 16A
Crofton, MD 21114
(410) 451-4401
Fax: (410) 451-8288
Email: searchdcw@erols.com

Description: We specialize in pharmaceutical, biotechnology, medical devices and related healthcare industries. We conduct searches in all functional areas within these industries.

Key Contact:
Mr. Donald Wagner
Ms. Mary Cramer

Salary minimum: $50,000

Functions: Generalist

Industries: Mfg., Drugs Mfg., Biotech, Healthcare

Professional Associations: HTCM, SHRM

Gordon Wahls Executive Search

450 Parkway Blvd
PO Box 386
Broomall, PA 19008-0386
(610) 359-8800
(800) 523-7112
Fax: (610) 359-8803
Email: search@gwahls.com
Web: www.gwahls.com

Description: We specialize in commercial printing, newspaper publishing, flexible packaging, graphic arts, labels, folding carton, and corrugated paper industries. Most of our searches are in the $50,000 to $150,000 range. Our professional staff includes twenty consultants..

Key Contact - Specialty:
Mr. Thomas F. Glancey, Jr., President - *Printing, publishing, packaging*

Salary minimum: $30,000

Functions: Generalist

Industries: Paper, Printing, Publishing, Packaging

Professional Associations: MAAPC, PIA

Networks: National Personnel Assoc (NPA)

Wakefield Executive Search Group

(also known as Sales Consultants of Muskegon)
340 Terrace Plz
Muskegon, MI 49440
(231) 728-1500
Fax: (231) 728-0500
Email: wesg@wakefieldsearchgroup.com
Web: www.wakefieldsearchgroup.com

Description: Our firm is a Sales Consultants' network affiliate that specializes in the automotive, transportation, healthcare, and general manufacturing industries. Our recruiting efforts are focused on mid-level to senior executive level positions.

Key Contact - Specialty:
Mr. William Wakefield, President - *Automotive, transportation, general manufacturing*

Waldon Associates

1715 N Westshore Blvd Ste 460
Westshore Ctr
Tampa, FL 33607
(813) 289-0051
Fax: (813) 289-6004
Email: waldonas@winstarmail.com
Web: www.waldonassociates.com

Description: Our knowledge of accounting, marketing, sales, human resources enables us to test, screen and qualify only the best candidates available. We offer the most professional service and follow through in our industry.

Key Contact:
Mr. Jeffrey Waldon, President - *Management*
Ms. Maita Waldon, Vice President

Functions: Generalist, CFO's, Budgeting, Cash Mgmt., Credit, Taxes, M&A

Industries: Generalist, Finance, Misc. Financial, Accounting, Insurance, Real Estate, Healthcare

Professional Associations: IMA

Waldorf Associates Inc

11400 W Olympic Blvd Fl 2
Los Angeles, CA 90064-1507
(310) 445-8886
(310) 445-8881
Fax: (310) 445-8810
Email: info@waldorfsearch.com
Web: www.waldorfsearch.com

Description: We specialize in attorney search and placement, California and nationally for lawyers, law firms, corporations and businesses. Partners, associates, law firm mergers, legal specialty practice groups, branch office development; in-house and corporate law department attorney staffing.

Key Contact - Specialty:
Mr. Michael Waldorf, Esq., President - *Law, partners, associates, law firm practice groups, mergers*
Mr. Michael Waldorf, JD, President - *Partners, practice groups, mergers, senior counsel*

Functions: Legal, Attorneys

Industries: Generalist, Services, Legal

Professional Associations: ABA, ACCA, ACCA, BHBA, CCBA, LACBA, NALSC, SBC

Walker & Associates

PO Box 526
Claysville, PA 15323
(724) 663-3634
Fax: (724) 663-3635
Email: del@walkerbio.com
Web: www.bio-jobs.com

Description: We provide contingent recruiting services to the biotechnology industry, as well as assist industry professionals in finding career opportunities. We offer an online career search website sponsored by our company.

Key Contact - Specialty:
Mr. Del Walker, President
Ms. Lauren Hathaway, BA, Recruiter - *Biotechnology*
Ms. Lori Wilkerson, BA, Manager, Bio-Jobs.com - *Internet job postings*

Salary minimum: $20,000

Functions: Generalist

Industries: Biotech

Kelly Walker Associates

949 Forest Grove Dr
Dallas, TX 75218
(214) 320-3006
Fax: (214) 324-5105
Email: kellywalker@kellywalker.com
Web: www.kellywalker.com

Description: Manufacturers and distributors of construction and mining equipment and fleets which use heavy equipment utilize our specialized knowledge of this industry to recruit world class managers.

Key Contact - Specialty:
Mr. Kelly Walker, President - *Construction, mining, industrial, governmental, public utility (manufacturers, dealers, equipment fleets)*
Mr. Jack Mears, Associate - *Construction, mining, trucking (manufacturers, dealers, equipment fleets)*

Salary minimum: $40,000

Functions: General Mgmt., Senior Mgmt., Distribution, Sales & Mktg., Training

Industries: Agri., Forestry, Mining, Energy, Utilities, Construction, Wholesale, Equip Svcs.

Professional Associations: AED, AGC, EMC

Walker Forest

(also known as Sales Consultants of King of Prussia)
992 Old Eagle School Rd Ste 913
Wayne, PA 19087-1803
(610) 989-8500
Fax: (610) 989-8501
Email: pdl@walkerforest.com
Web: www.walkerforest.com

Description: Our mission is to improve the quality of your life. Our primary focus is on sales and marketing professionals in emerging and leading edge technology related companies.

Key Contact - Specialty:
Mr. Peter David Levitt, Partner - *Banking, technology*

Salary minimum: $75,000

Functions: Generalist

Industries: Computer Equip., Banking, Mgmt. Consulting, E-commerce, Call Centers, Telephony, Fiber Optic, Doc. Mgmt., Production SW, ERP SW, Marketing SW

Jarvis Walker Group

30 Vreeland Rd
Florham Park, NJ 07932
(973) 966-0900
Fax: (973) 966-6925
Email: resumes@jwnj.com
Web: www.jarviswalker.com

Description: Our firm, a division of Human Resource Management Inc., has specializes in the recruitment of information technology professionals. For three decades, we have worked closely with client companies to identify and recruit the highest caliber candidates for challenging and rewarding career opportunities.

Key Contact - Specialty:
Mr. Dan Jarvis, President
Mr. Jerry West, Senior Vice President - *Information technology*

Salary minimum: $90,000

Functions: IT, MIS Mgmt., Systems Analysis

Industries: Mfg., Food, Bev., Tobacco, Drugs Mfg., Consumer Elect., Finance, Invest. Banking, Pharm Svcs., E-commerce, IT Implementation, Publishing, Communications, Software, Biotech, Healthcare

Professional Associations: SIM

Walker Personnel Inc

3000 26th St Ste A
Metairie, LA 70002
(504) 831-4767
Fax: (504) 831-2979

Description: We specialize in property/casualty insurance placement. Fee paid only. National contacts.

Key Contact - Specialty:
Ms. Linda G. Walker, CPC, President - *Insurance (property, casualty)*

Functions: Generalist

Industries: Insurance

Professional Associations: CSANO, PIA

K K Walker Professional Recruitment

PO Box 552
Placerville, CA 95667
(530) 642-2211
Fax: (530) 642-2211
Email: kkwjobs@pacbell.net
Web: www.geocities.com/kkwalker/

Description: Specialize in all areas of healthcare-clinical, administrative-hospital and non-hospital.

Special attention to laboratory, nursing, home health, medical records.

Key Contact - Specialty:
Ms. Karen K. Walker, Owner - *Healthcare*

Functions: Generalist

Industries: Healthcare

B D Wallace & Associates

217 Georgetown Rd
Annapolis, MD 21403
(410) 268-2024
Fax: (410) 267-8374
Email: dick@bdwallace.com
Web: www.bdwallace.com

Description: We are an executive search firm specializing in information technology. We focus our strengths on searching, recruiting and placing of top- notch sales, sales management, hardware/software engineers and management professionals. Our commitment is to provide the best qualified candidate to match our client's requirements in a professional, ethical and timely manner.

Key Contact - Specialty:
Mr. Dick Duval, President - *Sales, sales management, technical, systems integration*
Ms. Barbara Heacock, Managing Partner - *IT systems development, analysis, design, programming integration, wireless telecommunications*

Functions: Generalist

Industries: Computer Equip., Electronic, Elec. Components, Communications, Software, Database SW, Development SW, Doc. Mgmt., Production SW, Networking, Comm. SW

Networks: Top Echelon Network

Wallace Associates

49 Leavenworth St Ste 200
PO Box 11294
Waterbury, CT 06703
(203) 879-2011
Fax: (203) 879-2407
Email: walstaff@pcsinternet.net
Web: www.pcsinternet.net/walstaff

Description: Personal consulting expertise to clients throughout the U.S. with concentration in engineering and manufacturing support disciplines, up to and including the executive-level.

Key Contact - Specialty:
Mr. Gregory Gordon, Principal - *Engineering*

Salary minimum: $40,000

Functions: Generalist

Industries: Mfg., Soap, Perf., Cosmtcs., Medical Devices, Motor Vehicles, Computer Equip., Electronic, Elec. Components, Aerospace, Packaging, Software, Biotech

Professional Associations: APICS, ASM, ASQ, IEEE, SME, SPE

Denis P Walsh & Associates Inc

5402 Bent Bough Ln Ste 100
Houston, TX 77088-5501
(281) 931-9121
Fax: (281) 820-4285
Email: denwalsh@swbell.net

Description: We cover most functions, especially the oil and gas strategy consulting. We serve the heavy engineering and construction industries, refining, petrochemical, pulp, paper, and power industries. We also serve the GIS industry and are actively recruiting sales and marketing personnel.

Key Contact - Specialty:
Mr. Denis P. Walsh, Jr., President - *Refining, petrochemical engineering, construction*

Salary minimum: $40,000

Functions: Engineering

Industries: Energy, Utilities, Construction, Mgmt. Consulting

Gerald Walsh Recruitment Services Inc

1801 Hollis St Ste 220
Halifax, NS B3J 3N4
Canada
(902) 421-1676
Fax: (902) 491-1300
Email: info@geraldwalsh.com
Web: www.geraldwalsh.com

Description: We specialize in the recruitment of middle to senior-level managers and professionals.

Key Contact:
Mr. Gerald Walsh, President
Mrs. Rose Marie Pangman, Manager Contract Staffing
Ms. Jane Skiffington, Consultant
Mr. Scott Lainge, Managing Director of eCompass
Ms. Debbie Murphy, Research Assistant

Functions: Generalist, General Mgmt., Mfg., Sales & Mktg., HR Mgmt., Finance, IT, Engineering

Industries: Generalist

Walter & Associates Inc

PO Box 3358
15730 W 150th St
Olathe, KS 66063-3358
(913) 764-4930
(800) 236-4930
Fax: (913) 764-9381
Email: jpwalter@topechelon.com
Web: www.ltopps.com

Description: Our firm is a professional search group, specializing in the successful placement of information technology/system professionals and reliability engineers. We pride ourselves in our continuing ability to locate individuals of outstanding character and qualifications for placement in positions with clients on a nationwide basis. Whether you are a job seeker looking for a new career or a hiring manager seeking to fill employment opportunities, we will assist you in all aspects of your personal or staffing needs. After all, we are the one-stop, multi-service recruiting firm.

Key Contact:
Mr. Jerry P. Walter, President

Functions: IT

Industries: Generalist

Networks: National Consulting Network (NCN)

Linda Walter & Associates

291 Montee Sagala
Ile Perrot, QC J7V 3C8
Canada
(514) 425-7000
Fax: (514) 425-6170

Description: We have more than 20 years of experience. Our selective screening is customized to your company's needs.

Key Contact:
Ms. Linda Walter, President

Functions: Generalist, General Mgmt.

Industries: Generalist

Robert Walters Associates Inc

1500 Broadway Ste 1801
New York, NY 10036
(212) 704-9900
Fax: (212) 704-4312

Email: kurt.kraeger@robertwalters.com
Web: www.robertwalters.com

Description: We are a financial recruitment firm specializing in all areas of finance.

Key Contact - Specialty:
Mr. Kurt H. Kraeger, President - *Finance, energy*

Salary minimum: $50,000

Functions: General Mgmt., Directors, Senior Mgmt., Middle Mgmt., Finance, CFO's, Credit, M&A, Systems Implem., Mgmt. Consultants

Industries: Generalist, Mfg., Banking, Invest. Banking, Brokers, Mgmt. Consulting, Media, Real Estate

R Walters Resources

PO Box 51214
Kalamazoo, MI 49005
(616) 381-5463
Fax: (616) 381-1141
Email: jrwawa@jrwalters.com
Web: www.jrwalters.com

Description: We are specialists in the placement of professionals in the architectural and engineering industry.

Key Contact:
Ms. Joan R. Walters, CPC

Functions: Engineering, Environmentalists, Architects

Industries: Construction, Services

Professional Associations: AIA, ASHRAE, MSPE

Networks: Top Echelon Network

Walters, Rhodes & Associates LLC

67 S Bedford St Ste 400W
Burlington, MA 01803
(781) 229-5852
(617) 513-2410
Fax: (781) 229-5853
Email: jkrhodes@tiac.net
Web: www.staffing-search.com

Description: We specialize in placing recruiters, and management professionals exclusively in the staffing and consulting industry. We specialize in branch, area and regional level searches for national as well as local firms.

Key Contact - Specialty:
Mr. James Rhodes, Partner - *Staffing, consulting industries*
Mr. Roy Walters, Partner - *Staffing, consulting industries*

Salary minimum: $30,000

Functions: Middle Mgmt.

Industries: Mgmt. Consulting, HR Services

J P Walton & Associates

9601 Dorothy Ave
Cleveland, OH 44125
(216) 883-4141
Fax: (216) 883-5117
Email: boxjobs@aol.com

Description: We are a firm that recruits exclusively for the corrugated container and folding cartons industries. We make placements from superintendent to plant general manager and corporate staffing of all levels.

Key Contact - Specialty:
Mr. Jack Walton, Owner - *Corrugated boxes, folding cartons*
Mr. Patrick Walton, Owner - *Corrugated boxes, folding cartons*

Salary minimum: $50,000

Functions: Generalist, General Mgmt., Production, Plant Mgmt., Quality, Packaging, Mktg. Mgmt., Sales Mgmt.

Industries: Generalist, Mfg., Paper, Printing, Packaging

Ward & Associates

800 W 5th Ave
Naperville, IL 60563
(630) 717-6111
Email: bmw@robertward.com
Web: www.robertward.com

Description: We are a boutique search firm serving a broad variety of clients. Our primary focus is middle management positions in finance, accounting and operations.

Key Contact - Specialty:
Mr. Robert M. Ward, Principal - *Finance, accounting, tax*

Salary minimum: $100,000

Functions: HR Mgmt., Finance

Industries: Generalist

MacInnis Ward & Associates Inc

551 5th Ave Ste 3300
New York, NY 10176
(212) 808-8080
Fax: (212) 808-8088
Email: info@macinnisward.com
Web: www.macinnisward.com

Description: We provide a uniquely responsive, highly personalized approach to servicing the needs of our clients and candidates. Our clients include some of the most prestigious owners/developers, REITS, pension fund advisors, management companies, and opportunity funds in the New York Tri-State Area.

Key Contact:
Ms. Mary A. Ward, President

Functions: General Mgmt.

Industries: Accounting, Real Estate

Professional Associations: BOMA, NACORE

Ward & Ward Int'l Recruiters & Consultants

9301 E Crystal Dr
Sun Lakes, AZ 85248
(800) 800-6181
(480) 502-9900
Fax: (480) 802-7800
Email: allward@netvalue.net
Web: www.allward.com

Description: International recruiting specializing in mining, construction, food processing, high-tech and medical.

Key Contact - Specialty:
Mr. Al L. Ward, President - *Construction, engineering*
Ms. Gayle E. Ward, Vice President - *Medical, food processing*

Salary minimum: $50,000

Functions: Generalist, General Mgmt.

Industries: Energy, Utilities, Construction, Mfg., Accounting, Mgmt. Consulting, Telecoms, Fiber Optic, Haz. Waste

Martha Ward Executive Search Inc

4 Laurel Hill Ln
PO Box 2759
Amagansett, NY 11930-2759
(631) 267-3730
Fax: (631) 267-6335
Email: marketing@marthaward.com
Web: www.marthaward.com

Description: Our firm has thirty-four years worth of experience and specializes in national and global consumer products marketing and advertising.

Key Contact:
Ms. Martha Ward, President - *Marketing, marketing services, market research, sales promotion*
Mr. Paul Poutouves, Vice President - *Advertising, sales*
Mr. Eric Lane, Senior Executive Consultant

Salary minimum: $70,000

Functions: Generalist, Directors, Senior Mgmt., Middle Mgmt., Mkt. Research, Mktg. Mgmt., Sales Mgmt., Direct Mktg.

Industries: Generalist, Food, Bev., Tobacco, Textiles, Apparel, Soap, Perf., Cosmtcs., Drugs Mfg., Advertising, Telecoms

Wardrup Associates
2508 Springpark Ln Ste 300
Richardson, TX 75082
(972) 437-9333
Fax: (972) 437-1208
Email: dwardrup@wardrup.com
Web: www.wardrup.com

Description: Our firm offers retained/contingency search nationally for qualified, experienced mid to senior management professionals to the nation's most business-aggressive established and emerging high technology companies. We specialize in computer hardware/software, telecommunications, and IT/ professional services with a focus on customer service, sales/marketing, operations, and consulting.

Key Contact:
Ms. Diane Wardrup, Principal
Mr. Jim Wardrup, Principal

Functions: Generalist

Industries: Medical Devices, Computer Equip., Test, Measure Equip., Equip Svcs., Mgmt. Consulting, Telecoms, Software

Networks: Recruiters Professional Network (RPN)

Warner & Associates Inc
101 E College Ave
Westerville, OH 43081
(614) 891-9003
Fax: (614) 890-8405
Email: warnerassoc@netzero.net

Description: We are a well established, owner managed firm offering customized and personal response to the needs of our clients. Specialist within most functional areas of manufacturing management. Guaranteed success in recruitment and search.

Key Contact - Specialty:
Mr. Thomas P. Warner, President - *Manufacturing, industrial clients*

Salary minimum: $40,000

Functions: Generalist

Industries: Mfg., Plastics, Rubber, Leather, Stone, Glass, Metal Products, Machine, Appliance, Motor Vehicles, Computer Equip.

Professional Associations: COAPS

Networks: Top Echelon Network

C D Warner & Associates
12 Davenport Dr
Downingtown, PA 19335
(610) 458-8335
Email: doug@cdwarner.com
Web: www.cdwarner.com

Description: We are an international executive search firm specializing in information technology and high-tech computing and focusing on

management, more specifically CEOs, CIOs, CTOs, COOs, VPs, and directors; marketing; sales; and technical professionals. Our services cover North America, Europe, Asia, Middle East, and the Pacific Rim.

Key Contact - Specialty:
Mr. C. Douglas Warner, President - *Information technology, executive management*
Mr. Chris Duffey, VP & GM International Division - *International searches*
Ms. Susan C Warner, Vice President-Finance & Operations - *Executive financial managers*
Mr. William D Adams, Managing Partner - *Information technology, executive management*
Mr. Don Hunter, Managing Partner - *Information technology, sales, management*
Mr. Dick Duval, Chief Technical Officer - *Technical searches*
Ms. Lisa Maynard, North East Partner - *IT, finance & accounting*

Functions: Generalist, Senior Mgmt., Automation, Sales Mgmt., CFO's, IT, MIS Mgmt., Int'l.

Industries: Generalist, E-commerce, IT Implementation, Communications, Telecoms, Call Centers, Telephony, Digital, Wireless, Fiber Optic, Network Infrastructure, Software

Professional Associations: MAAPC, RON

Warren Executive Services
437 Parker Branch Rd
Barnesville, GA 30204
(770) 358-3595
Fax: (770) 358-3595
Email: wesco@mindspring.net
Web: www.mindspring.com/~wesco/

Description: We are recruiters for manufacturing industries, with emphasis on manufacturing support, personnel, automation, plant engineering and logistical support.

Key Contact - Specialty:
Mr. Robert L. Warren, Owner - *Engineering, manufacturing, manufacturing support*
Ms. Wanda Chappelle, Associate - *Human resources, materials, purchasing, manufacturing support*

Salary minimum: $25,000

Functions: Generalist, Product Dev., Production, Purchasing, Materials Plng., Benefits, MIS Mgmt., Engineering

Industries: Generalist, Medical Devices, Plastics, Rubber, Motor Vehicles, Consumer Elect., Aerospace, Software

Professional Associations: ASQ

Networks: Top Echelon Network

Wasserman Associates Inc
604 Sunspot Rd
Reisterstown, MD 21136
(410) 517-0060
Fax: (410) 517-0080
Email: swass@home.com
Web: www.wassermanassociates.com

Description: We have over 29 years of experience specializing in consumer product sales and marketing. Our emphasis is on food, drug, beverage, health and beauty aids, OTC, personal care products, and general merchandise/non-food areas. We place first level managers to VP-sales, and marketing. We also place trade marketing managers, category managers, and sales planning managers.

Key Contact - Specialty:
Mr. Stan Wasserman - *Consumer (product sales & category), management, trade marketing*

Salary minimum: $50,000

Functions: Sales & Mktg.

Industries: Food, Bev., Tobacco, Paper, Soap, Perf., Cosmtcs., Drugs Mfg., Consumer Elect.

Networks: First Interview Network (FIN)

Waterford Executive Group Ltd
1 N 141 County Farm Rd Ste 220 D
Winfield, IL 60190
(630) 690-0055
Fax: (630) 690-5533
Email: info@waterfordgroup.com
Web: www.waterfordgroup.com

Description: Our firm will fulfill our clients' needs via retainer or contingency arrangements with a highly personalized and focused approach, mainly in compensation and benefits consulting industry, as well as corporate HR.

Key Contact - Specialty:
Mr. Patrick J. Atkinson, President - *Compensation, human resources*
Mr. Ted Tomei, Principal - *Organizational effectiveness, organizational development, change management, health & welfare*
Ms. Joan Krings, Principal - *Benefits (consultants, actuaries)*

Salary minimum: $40,000

Functions: HR Mgmt., Benefits, IT, Mgmt. Consultants

Industries: Generalist, Mgmt. Consulting, HR Services

Professional Associations: ASHHRA, IABC, SA, SHRM, WAW

Watring & Associates Inc
402 E Roosevelt Rd Ste 210
Wheaton, IL 60187
(630) 690-2707
Fax: (630) 690-2243
Email: bawatring@aol.com

Description: We conduct placement of all medical pharmaceutical and biotech sales marketing, management, engineering, including R&D, quality control; also dealer sales forces and clinical applications specialists, for U.S. and international.

Key Contact - Specialty:
Ms. Bernie Watring, President - *Medical sales, medical marketing management, medical corporation CEO's, clinical specialists, RN's*
Ms. Janet Blue, Associate - *Pharmaceutical, biotech, sales & marketing*

Functions: Physicians, Nurses, Sales & Mktg., Sales Mgmt., Training, Int'l.

Industries: Generalist

Networks: First Interview Network (FIN)

Wayne Associates Inc
2628 Barrett St
Virginia Beach, VA 23452
(757) 340-0555
Fax: (757) 340-0826
Email: info@wayneassociates.com
Web: www.wayneassociates.com

Description: We have over 23 years of experience working with top chemical companies filling sales, marketing, and research and development positions.

Key Contact:
Mr. Michael C. Cozzens, Managing Partner

Salary minimum: $50,000

Functions: Generalist, Mkt. Research, Mktg. Mgmt., Sales Mgmt., R&D

Industries: Generalist, Paper, Chemicals, Soap, Perf., Cosmtcs., Drugs Mfg., Pharm Svcs., Biotech

Professional Associations: RON

Networks: First Interview Network (FIN)

Wegner & Associates

11270 W Park Pl Ste 310
1 Park Plz
Milwaukee, WI 53224
(414) 359-2333
Fax: (414) 359-2325
Email: wegner33@execpc.com

Description: We specialize in upper and middle management recruiting with particular emphasis in financial, accounting and the MIS areas. Also do extensive staff level recruiting in the accounting and MIS areas.

Key Contact - Specialty:
Mr. Carl Wegner, President - *Financial, general management*
Mr. Bob Schultz, Vice President - *MIS, information systems*

Salary minimum: $30,000

Functions: Middle Mgmt., Finance, IT

Industries: Generalist

Professional Associations: AICPA, DPMA, EDPAA

David Weinfeld Group

6512 Six Forks Rd Ste 603B
Raleigh, NC 27615
(919) 676-7828
Fax: (919) 676-7399
Email: email@weinfeldgroup.com
Web: www.weinfeldgroup.com

Description: We specialize in customized recruitment of key executives in sales, marketing, engineering and management consultants in the telecommunications, data com, cable TV, broadcasting, networking and other related applications including consulting functions and software applications.

Key Contact:
Mr. David C. Weinfeld, President - *Telecommunications, computers, software, data communications, CATV*
Mr. Drew Karkow, Executive Recruiter - *Telecommunications, computers, software, data communications, CATV*
Mr. Lauren Dunne, Research Assistant
Ms. Beth Massey, Research Assistant
Mr. Steve Ashcraft, Executive Recruiter
Ms. Karen Cousin, Executive Recruiter

Salary minimum: $60,000

Functions: Generalist

Industries: Telecoms

Professional Associations: IEEE, NCASP, RON

Weinman & Associates

7110 E McDonald Dr Ste B-6
Scottsdale, AZ 85253
(480) 483-2132
Fax: (480) 922-9248
Email: mweinman@primenet.com
Web: www.weinmanassociates.com

Description: We are a full-service executive search firm.

Key Contact - Specialty:
Ms. Mary Weinman, President - *Hospitality*
Ms. Robin Duncan, Vice President - *Hospitality*

Salary minimum: $50,000

Functions: Generalist, General Mgmt., HR Mgmt., IT, MIS Mgmt., Specialized Svcs., Attorneys, Paralegals

Industries: Generalist, Construction, Services, Hospitality

Professional Associations: NAWIC

Weinpel Search Inc

Hamburg Tpke
PO Box 248
Riverdale, NJ 07457
(973) 628-0858
Fax: (973) 694-7319
Email: weinpel@juno.com

Description: We have over 35 years worth of technology staffing "savvy." We specialize in engineering and most other functions with a technology content. Our staff members and most of our vendors are trained in technology that helps to assure professionalism with industry and candidates.

Key Contact - Specialty:
Mr. Charles J. Weinpel - *Engineering, science, software (all levels)*

Salary minimum: $75,000

Functions: Generalist, Middle Mgmt., Production, Plant Mgmt., Mktg. Mgmt., Systems Analysis, R&D, Engineering

Industries: Generalist, Consumer Elect., Defense, Aerospace, Software

Weisberg Associates

2477 Church Ln Willowood Business Campus
Kintnersville, PA 18930
(610) 847-5999
Fax: (610) 847-8071
Email: allo@epix.net

Description: We are specialists in difficult-to-fill technical, engineering, and executive management positions in industries engaged in design, manufacturing, sales, and distribution. Alan places an emphasis on the automotive OEM components industry. Jeff is focused on heavy construction including the processing of stone, sand, aggregate, concrete, and asphalt products. The firm also services a variety of top ranking clients in the architectural and consumer products marketplace.

Key Contact - Specialty:
Mr. Alan M. Weisberg, Principal - *Automotive, technical, engineering, facility management, executive management*
Mr. Jeffrey A. Weisberg, Search Consultant - *Construction, excavation, paving operations, precast concrete manufacturing*

Salary minimum: $40,000

Functions: Generalist

Industries: Generalist, Construction, Mfg., Motor Vehicles, Consumer Elect., Misc. Mfg., Transportation, Call Centers

Professional Associations: SAE, SPE

Networks: Inter-City Personnel Assoc (IPA)

Weiss & Associates Legal Search Inc

PO Box 915656
Longwood, FL 32791-5656
(407) 774-1212
Fax: (407) 880-9933
Email: lawhunter@aol.com

Description: We are a legal search firm that specializes with experienced partners and associates for major law firms. In addition to this, we specialize in tax attorneys and "key" tax professionals throughout the US and Europe. We have earned a reputation for identifying and attracting outstanding candidates for our clients. Our clients consist of major multi-national corporations and prominent law firms in their respective cities.

Key Contact - Specialty:
Mr. Terry M. Weiss, Esq., President - *Law, tax professionals*

Salary minimum: $100,000

Functions: Generalist, Directors, Senior Mgmt., Legal, Taxes, M&A, Attorneys

Industries: Generalist, Mfg., Legal, Real Estate, Accounting SW, Biotech, Healthcare

Professional Associations: CBA, NALSC

C Weiss Associates Inc

60 W 57th St
New York, NY 10019
(212) 581-4040
Email: cweissinc@aol.com

Description: We specialize in recruiting for consumer financial services. Our excellent research department is capable of handling unique assignments. Principal has a personal background in marketing, with an impressive career with a money center bank, national exposure.

Key Contact - Specialty:
Ms. Cathy Weiss, President - *Consumer marketing, direct marketing, database management, product management*

Salary minimum: $40,000

Functions: Direct Mktg.

Industries: Banking, Invest. Banking, Misc. Financial, Services, Advertising, New Media

Professional Associations: APCNY

Networks: National Personnel Assoc (NPA)

Weitz & Associates

20914 Pacific Coast Hwy
Malibu, CA 90265
(310) 456-5455
(310) 456-1856
Fax: (310) 456-1028
Email: laweitz@earthlink.net

Description: We represent a select few companies within a given industry. This allows us to recruit from a broader base of candidates for you! Our service is to represent top firms and to present top talent.

Key Contact - Specialty:
Mr. Larry A. Weitz, Principal - *Consumer products, food & beverage, sales & marketing, executive & senior level management, entertainment*
Ms. Laurie R. Weitz, Principal - *Consumer products, senior & executive level, sales & marketing, human resource & finance*

Salary minimum: $75,000

Functions: Senior Mgmt., Middle Mgmt., Product Dev., Sales & Mktg., HR Mgmt., Benefits, Training, Finance, Mgmt. Consultants, Minorities

Industries: Generalist, Food, Bev., Tobacco, Soap, Perf., Cosmtcs., Drugs Mfg., Mgmt. Consulting, HR Services, Entertainment, Advertising, Mfg. SW, Marketing SW

Welivers

92 Fletcher Pl
Mount Home, AR 72653
(877) 935-4837
Fax: (734) 913-0079
Email: bwelivers@netscape.net

Description: We have consultants who specialize in systems mainframe, midrange and PC in Southeast Michigan, Arkansas and Massachusetts. Ranging from entry to CIO in all environments. We work in all peripheral areas; i.e. finance, sales, training and engineers. We interface in the total US.

Key Contact:
Mr. Edward A. Weliver, Owner - *Information technology, human resources, engineers*
Ms. Billie S. Weliver, President

Functions: Generalist, Personnel, MIS Mgmt., Systems Analysis, Systems Dev., Systems Implem., Systems Support, Network Admin.

Industries: Generalist, Computer Equip., Consumer Elect., New Media, Software

Professional Associations: HRA, NAPS, NATSS

Branches:
19 Bean Hill Rd
Bolton, MA 01740
(978) 779-5196
Key Contact:
Mr. David Weliver

PO Box 15-135
Ann Arbor, MI 48105
(734) 913-0070
Key Contact:
R. S. Weliver

Henry Welker & Associates
PO Box 530846
Livonia, MI 48153-0846
(734) 953-4900
Fax: (734) 953-5918
Email: welkerh@aol.com

Description: We specialize in management, information technology, information systems, resources, engineering, and sales engineering.

Key Contact - Specialty:
Mr. Henry A. Welker, President - *Information technology, engineering, sales (technical)*

Salary minimum: $40,000

Functions: General Mgmt., Mfg., Materials, Sales Mgmt., IT, R&D, Engineering, Mgmt. Consultants

Industries: Generalist, Mfg., Motor Vehicles

Wellington Thomas Ltd
5040 White Pine Cir NE
St. Petersburg, FL 33703
(800) 779-1233
Fax: (888) 363-7704
Email: wellthom@earthlink.net

Description: We are a premier national search firm serving the healthcare marketplace. Our reputation for integrity and work ethic is our bond. Our emphasis is in clinical, operational, business development and administrative positions from staff to vice president level.

Key Contact - Specialty:
Ms. Jean M. De Mange, Senior Consultant - *Healthcare, medical, nursing, regulatory, healthcare (clinical, managed)*

Salary minimum: $40,000

Functions: Generalist, Admin. Svcs., Healthcare, Physicians, Nurses, Allied Health

Industries: Healthcare

R A Wells Company
107 N Lakeside Dr
Kennesaw, GA 30144
(770) 424-8493
Fax: (770) 424-8545
Email: rawco@mindspring.com

Description: Our firm specializes in conducting search activity for clients in the telecommunications and plastic packaging industry throughout the world market.

Key Contact - Specialty:
Mr. Robert A. Wells, Owner - *Plastics*

Salary minimum: $45,000

Functions: General Mgmt., Mfg., Sales & Mktg., HR Mgmt., Benefits, IT, R&D, Engineering, Attorneys, Int'l.

Industries: Chemicals, Plastics, Rubber, Media, New Media, Communications, Telecoms, Call Centers, Telephony, Digital, Wireless, Fiber

---

Optic, Network Infrastructure, Packaging, Software, Development SW

Wells, Bradley & Associates Inc
520 Lake Elmo Ave N
Lake Elmo, MN 55042-9711
(651) 731-9202
Fax: (651) 436-3827
Email: kennedyinfo@wellsbradley.com
Web: www.wellsbradley.com

Description: Our company specializes in the banking & credit card industry. Includes: alternative delivery, analytical positions, B2B, B2C, commercial banking, consumer finance, credit cards, credit management, decision technology, e-banking, e-commerce, executive management, payment systems, lending, private banking, retail banking, risk management, sales/marketing, statistics, treasury management, trust & investments, training & development

Key Contact - Specialty:
Ms. Gillis Lindberg, CEO - *Banking, credit card*

Salary minimum: $50,000

Functions: Directors, Senior Mgmt., Middle Mgmt., Product Dev., Quality, Mktg. Mgmt., Direct Mktg., Finance, CFO's, IT

Industries: Finance, Banking

Professional Associations: FWI, NBN

Networks: National Banking Network (NBN)

Welzig, Lowe & Associates
761 W Birch Ct
Louisville, CO 80027
(303) 666-4195
Email: frank_welzig@headhuntersecrets.com
Web: www.headhuntersecrets.com

Description: We specialize in management and senior engineers for fast-growth companies in all industries.

Key Contact - Specialty:
Mr. Frank E. Welzig, President - *Generalist, high technology*

Salary minimum: $60,000

Functions: Generalist

Industries: Computer Equip., Mgmt. Consulting, New Media, Aerospace, Software

Wenglar & Associates Inc
1861 Brown Blvd Ste 731
Arlington, TX 76006
(817) 649-2999
Fax: (817) 649-2742

Description: We are a nationwide search firm in the long-term healthcare and retirement home industry.

Key Contact:
Ms. Nancy Wenglar, President
Mr. Roger Scott, Executive Vice President

Functions: Generalist

Industries: Healthcare

Werbin Associates Executive Search Inc
140 Riverside Dr Ste 10N
New York, NY 10024-2605
(212) 799-6111
Email: swerb@bellatlantic.net

Description: We are oriented towards assisting the computer, research, finance and management science professionals, technical management-all levels.

Key Contact - Specialty:
Ms. Susan Werbin, President - *Information technology, operations, market research, finance*

Functions: General Mgmt., Product Dev., Production, Sales & Mktg., Mkt. Research, HR Mgmt., Personnel, IT, R&D

Industries: Generalist, Energy, Utilities, Mfg., Computer Equip., Transportation, Finance, Banking, Invest. Banking, Services, Mgmt. Consulting, HR Services, Advertising, New Media, Communications, Telecoms, Insurance, Software, Database SW, Marketing SW, System SW

Professional Associations: CDG, DAMAI, INFORMS

Wert & Company Inc
222 5th Ave Fl 5
New York, NY 10001
(212) 684-2796
Fax: (212) 685-4859
Email: info@wertco.com
Web: www.wertco.com

Description: We are an executive recruitment firm specializing in search within the creative community. We represent a portfolio of innovative companies within design, interactive media, communications, entertainment, retail and fashion, publishing, technology and broadcast media - treating each assignment as a unique undertaking, encouraging excellence and cultivating enduring relationships.

Key Contact - Specialty:
Ms. Judy Wert, President - *Design, interactive media, content development, marketing, strategic services*

Salary minimum: $50,000

Functions: Generalist

Industries: Publishing, New Media, Broadcast, Film

AT Wertheimer Inc
70 Suffern Ln Ste 111A
Thiells, NY 10984
(845) 947-1120
Fax: (845) 947-8253
Email: executivesearch@atwertheimer.com
Web: www.atwertheimer.com

Description: We are an executive search firm, which provides recruitment services for banking and financial professionals. Our specialized areas of recruitment include: human resources; sales, trading and research (equity); information technology (MIS and CIOs), and public speaking.

Key Contact - Specialty:
Ms. Amy S. Toneatti, Executive Recruiter - *Banking & finance, human resources, equity research, sales & trading, public speakers*

Salary minimum: $60,000

Functions: HR Mgmt., Finance, IT

Industries: Finance

WESearch Executive Recruiting
110 Pacific Ave 133
San Francisco, CA 94111
(415) 531-8551
Fax: (415) 464-9687
Email: wes@wesearch.net
Web: www.wesearch.net

Description: We specialize in placing sales and marketing professionals in the software industry. We only work on contingency and retained searches in the Bay area.

Key Contact - Specialty:
Mr. Wes Strausbaugh, Owner - *Marketing & sales, high technology*
Ms. Michelle Piper, Account Executive - *Marketing & sales*

Ms. Victoria Harrison, Account Executive - *Marketing & sales*

Salary minimum: $50,000

Functions: Generalist, Directors, Senior Mgmt., Middle Mgmt., Mktg. Mgmt., Sales Mgmt., CFO's

Industries: Generalist, Software

West Coast Recruiting Inc
290 E Verdugo Ave Ste 204
Burbank, CA 91502
(818) 556-6056
Fax: (818) 556-6102
Email: lprec@aol.com
Web: www.westcoastrecruiting.com

Description: We are the preferred executive search organization in loss prevention and security for the nations' Fortune 500 companies. We have developed long lasting partnerships with the foremost loss prevention and security professionals within the retail and manufacturing industries of North America.

Key Contact - Specialty:
Ms. Tracy A. Nini, President - *Loss prevention, security*
Mr. Steven B. Nini, Vice President/General Manager - *Loss prevention, security*

Salary minimum: $40,000

Functions: Generalist

Industries: Mfg., Food, Bev., Tobacco, Computer Equip., Retail

Professional Associations: ASIS, IMRA, NRF

Western HR Consulting Ltd
5920 MacLeod Trl SW Ste 610
Calgary, AB T2H 0K2
Canada
(403) 215-2150
Fax: (403) 215-2151
Email: careers@westernhr.com
Web: www.westernhr.com

Description: We service the food and beverage industry.

Key Contact:
Mr. Don Murchie, Vice President
Mr. Steve Morrison, President

Functions: Generalist

Industries: Agri., Forestry, Mining, Mfg., Food, Bev., Tobacco, Finance, Services, Media, Packaging

Professional Associations: AAMS

Western Int'l Recruiters Inc
7580 E Gray Rd Ste 103
Scottsdale, AZ 85260
(800) 486-1757
Fax: (480) 596-6888
Email: recruiters@westerninternational.com
Web: www.westerninternational.com

Description: We are an insurance staffing firm providing full service staffing solutions to insurance carriers, TPA'S risk management firms, brokers and self-insureds worldwide. Our services are client fee paid and include direct hire positions, contract and temporary assignments, as well as special projects.

Key Contact:
Ms. Dayne Hayes, President

Functions: Generalist

Industries: Insurance, Industry Specific SW

Professional Associations: ASA

Western Technical Resources
2033 Gateway Pl Ste 600
San Jose, CA 95110
(408) 358-8533
(800) 600-5351
Fax: (408) 358-8535
Email: wtr@wtrusa.com
Web: www.wtrusa.com

Description: We are a worldwide contingent and temporary placement firm limited to the engineering and computer disciplines.

Key Contact - Specialty:
Mr. Bruce Weinstein, Principal - *High technology engineering, information sciences*

Salary minimum: $45,000

Functions: Generalist, Automation, Systems Dev., Systems Implem., R&D, Engineering

Industries: Generalist, New Media, Telecoms, Aerospace, Software, Biotech

The Westfield Group
1010 Washington Blvd
Stamford, CT 06901
(203) 406-2300
Fax: (203) 406-2315
Email: jfiala@westfieldhr.com
Web: www.westfieldgroup.com

Description: We are a contingency and retained search firm specializing in human resources, accounting and finance. We have a Fortune 500 and a national client base. The salaries range from $80,000 to $200,000 and up.

Key Contact - Specialty:
Ms. Joanne C. Fiala, President - *Human resources, accounting, finance*

Salary minimum: $80,000

Functions: Generalist, Benefits, Personnel, Training, Budgeting, Cash Mgmt., Mgmt. Consultants

Industries: Generalist

Professional Associations: ACA, ASTD, IMA, SHRM, SIOP

Westfields Int'l Inc
508 Lakeview Ave
Jamestown, NY 14701
(716) 484-0303
Fax: (716) 484-0354
Email: westflds@cecomet.net

Description: We are a full-service executive search firm offering over a decade of experience in medium to high-level searches. Highly experienced in handling quick turnaround situations with professionalism.

Key Contact - Specialty:
Mr. Bruce A. Boje, President - *Pharmaceutical, biotech, information systems, engineering, management*

Functions: General Mgmt., Mkt. Research, HR Mgmt., Finance, IT, R&D, Minorities, Int'l.

Industries: Drugs Mfg., Medical Devices, Pharm Svcs.

Networks: Top Echelon Network

Westover & Associates Inc
71 Walnut Ave
Atherton, CA 94027
(650) 323-2607
Fax: (650) 323-2739
Email: info@westoverinc.com
Web: www.westoverinc.com

Description: We specialize in thorough industry-wide searches for high-level sales, sales

management, design, sourcing, and product development positions in the home fashion industry.

Key Contact - Specialty:
Ms. Catherine Westover, CPC, President - *Sales executives*

Salary minimum: $75,000

Functions: Generalist

Industries: Textiles, Apparel

Professional Associations: NAPS

Weterrings & Agnew Inc
132 Allens Creek Rd
Rochester, NY 14618
(716) 241-9040
Fax: (716) 241-9044
Email: info@weterrings.com
Web: www.weterrings.com

Description: We provide professional recruitment services in all functional areas and across virtually all industry lines contingent and retained search.

Key Contact - Specialty:
Ms. Elaine McKenna, Partner - *Finance, administration, human resources, banking, general management*
Mr. Richard F. Corey, Partner - *Engineering, manufacturing, software development, MIS*
Mr. Thomas H. Quinn, Partner - *Sales, sales management, marketing*

Salary minimum: $30,000

Functions: Generalist, Product Dev., Mkt. Research, Benefits, CFO's, MIS Mgmt., R&D, Engineering

Industries: Generalist

Networks: First Interview Network (FIN)

Kevin White & Associates
3740 Wembley Ln Ste 201
Lexington, KY 40515
(859) 245-8000
Email: kwasc@home.com
Web: www.kwasearch.com

Description: We recruit services for the manufacturing industry, specializing in metal working, machining, and assembly for automotive and glass manufacturing facilities. Manufacturing, engineering, quality, materials, safety.

Key Contact - Specialty:
Mr. Kevin White, Executive Recruiter - *Manufacturing*

Salary minimum: $40,000

Functions: General Mgmt., Middle Mgmt., Mfg., Production, Plant Mgmt., Quality, Materials Plng., HR Mgmt., Engineering

Industries: Mfg., Metal Products, Machine, Appliance, Motor Vehicles, Computer Equip., Misc. Mfg.

Networks: Top Echelon Network

White Associates
10000 W 75th St Ste 118
Shawnee Mission, KS 66204
(913) 831-1821
Fax: (913) 831-1834
Email: temtech@gvi.net

Description: We are an executive search firm specializing in engineering, manufacturing and top management. We work both nationwide and international.

Key Contact - Specialty:
Ms. Carlene White, President - *Engineering, manufacturing, management*

Salary minimum: $50,000

Functions: Generalist

Industries: Agri., Forestry, Mining, Construction, Mfg., Transportation, Media

Professional Associations: AFE, SME, SPE

Networks: Top Echelon Network

Whitehead & Associates Inc
49 Egret Trl
Palm Coast, FL 32164
(386) 437-2318
Fax: (386) 437-2319
Email: white330@pcfl.net

Description: We specialize in machine design, mechanical, electro-mechanical, and electronic for the manufacturing industry. We cover all engineering disciplines, including automotive engineering for Big 3, Tier I and Tier II; automotive design, brakes, fuel systems, etc. We also specialize in motorcycle design and systems.

Key Contact - Specialty:
Mr. Robert S. Whitehead, Personnel Consultant - *Software engineers, hardware engineers, manufacturing, engineering*
Ms. Elizabeth S. Whitehead, President/Owner - *MIS management, systems analysis & design, software development*

Functions: Generalist, Mfg., Product Dev., Quality

Industries: Plastics, Rubber, Metal Products, Motor Vehicles

Professional Associations: SAE

Robert Whitfield Associates
155 N Michigan Ave Ste 523
Chicago, IL 60601
(312) 938-9120
Fax: (312) 938-9172
Email: info@robertwhitfieldassoc.com
Web: www.robertwhitfieldassoc.com

Description: We were founded in order to provide the legal profession with a full range of consulting services including retainer search, associate placement, management planning and marketing.

Key Contact - Specialty:
Mr. Robert Whitfield, Esq., President - *Legal*
Ms. Kay Whitfield, Vice President - *Legal*

Functions: Generalist, Legal, Attorneys

Industries: Generalist, Legal

Whitney Group
3605 Sandy Plains Rd Ste 240-163
Marietta, GA 30066
(770) 592-1840
Fax: (770) 592-2012
Email: jewgenie@aol.com

Description: We have been a recruiter for the past 25 years, specializing in all areas of industrial sales, sales, management and marketing.

Key Contact - Specialty:
Mr. Paul Komorner, President - *Sales, sales management, marketing management*

Salary minimum: $40,000

Functions: Sales & Mktg., Mktg. Mgmt., Sales Mgmt.

Industries: Plastics, Rubber, Metal Products, Machine, Appliance, Test, Measure Equip., Misc. Mfg., Packaging

Networks: US Recruiters.com

The Whitney Smith Company Inc
301 Commerce St Ste 1950
Ft. Worth, TX 76102
(817) 877-4120
(817) 877-4314
Fax: (817) 877-3846

Email: dfarmer@whitneysmithco.com
Web: www.whitneysmithco.com

Description: The firm specializes in recruiting and placement of executive and professionals in banking, financial services, human resources, engineering, transportation, governmental, education, non-profits, and sales/marketing.

Key Contact - Specialty:
Mr. David W. Farmer, Director of Recruiting - *Banking, financial services, general management, accounting, human resources*
Mrs. Donna R. Parker, Executive Search Consultant - *Transportation, engineering, education, non-profit, government*

Salary minimum: $30,000

Functions: General Mgmt., Senior Mgmt., Mfg., Healthcare, Sales & Mktg., HR Mgmt., Finance, Engineering, Non-profits, Architects

Industries: Generalist, Transportation, Banking, Higher Ed., Government

Professional Associations: SERC

Whittaker & Associates Inc
2675 Cumberland Pkwy Ste 263
Atlanta, GA 30339
(770) 434-3779
Fax: (770) 431-0213
Email: jobs@whittakersearch.com
Web: www.whittakersearch.com

Description: We specialize in the search and placement of managerial, supervisory and executive-level positions within the food industry nationwide with emphasis on dairy, meat, poultry, bakery ingredient and related products.

Key Contact - Specialty:
Ms. Millie A. Boatman, Vice President
Mr. Arnold G. Whittaker, Chairman of the Board - *Ingredients, pet food*
Mr. Brad Winkler, CPC, President - *Bakery, snack foods*

Salary minimum: $30,000

Functions: Senior Mgmt., Middle Mgmt., Production, Plant Mgmt., Quality, Distribution, Sales Mgmt., R&D, Engineering

Industries: Food, Bev., Tobacco

Professional Associations: GAPS

Networks: Inter-City Personnel Assoc (IPA)

The Whittaker Group Inc
1000 S Woodward Ave Ste 105
Birmingham, MI 48009
(248) 489-3900
Fax: (248) 489-1419
Email: mwhittaker@wgsearch.com
Web: www.wgsearch.com

Description: We provide national recruiting, executive search and consulting services exclusively to the healthcare, managed care, physician organization/ambulatory management and employer benefit specialities.

Key Contact - Specialty:
Ms. Michelle A. Whittaker-McCracken, CPC, SPHR, Principal - *Healthcare*
Ms. Irene Yasenetskaya, CPC, Director - *Healthcare*

Salary minimum: $60,000

Functions: Generalist, Physicians, Nurses, Health Admin., Training, CFO's, Budgeting, Cash Mgmt.

Industries: Generalist, Pharm Svcs., Healthcare

Professional Associations: MGMA

Wilcox, Miller & Nelson
(a member of Career Partners Int'l)
100 Howe Ave Ste 155N
Sacramento, CA 95825
(916) 977-3700
Fax: (916) 977-3733
Email: wilcoxcareer@wilcoxcareer.com
Web: www.wilcoxcareer.com

Description: We are an executive search firm specializing in middle and upper executives, financial managers, financial healthcare professionals, bankers, IT, human resources, associate management resources and outplacement consulting.

Key Contact - Specialty:
Mr. Fred T. Wilcox, Founder - *Healthcare, financial, operational management (senior), financial management*
Ms. Diane Miller, President - *Association management, senior management*
Mr. Raymond Nelson, Vice President - *Healthcare*

Salary minimum: $60,000

Functions: Generalist, Senior Mgmt., Middle Mgmt., Plant Mgmt., Health Admin., CFO's, Budgeting, Systems Analysis

Industries: Generalist, Banking, Misc. Financial, Accounting, Mgmt. Consulting, Software, Healthcare

Professional Associations: CBA, HFMA, HIMSS, NACD

Networks: Career Partners Int'l

Joel H Wilensky Associates Inc
PO Box 155
Sudbury, MA 01776
(978) 443-5176
Fax: (978) 443-3009
Email: jhwassoc@joelhwilensky.com
Web: www.joelhwilensky.com

Description: We are a one person contingency recruiting firm specializing in retail chain placement. Specific emphasis on corporate or home office placement i.e. finance, information systems, etc.

Key Contact - Specialty:
Mr. Joel H. Wilensky, Executive Recruiter - *Retail chains*

Salary minimum: $70,000

Functions: Generalist, Finance, CFO's, Taxes, IT, MIS Mgmt., Systems Dev.

Industries: Retail

Networks: National Personnel Assoc (NPA)

Wilkinson SoftSearch Inc
10613 Moore St Ste 210
Fairfax, VA 22030-3911
(703) 352-1795
Fax: (703) 352-1797
Email: info@softsearch.net
Web: www.softsearch.net

Description: As a trusted recruiting resource in the information technology field, we represent premier management consulting firms and leading edge software vendors and start-ups throughout the U.S.

Key Contact - Specialty:
Mr. Kurt A. Wilkinson, President - *Information technology*
Ms. Ann Trego Wilkinson, Vice President - *Information technology*

Salary minimum: $70,000

Functions: Generalist, MIS Mgmt., Systems Analysis, Systems Dev., Systems Implem., DB Admin., Mgmt. Consultants

Industries: Generalist, Mgmt. Consulting, New Media, Software

Professional Associations: IEEE, RON

The Willard Group
3575 Autumnleaf Crescent
Mississauga, ON L5L 1K6
Canada
(905) 607-5777
Fax: (905) 607-5007
Email: jwillard@thewillardgroup.com

Description: We specialize in the recruitment and placement of Canadian professionals and executives within the private sector. Integrity and confidentiality are our hallmarks.

Key Contact - Specialty:
Ms. Julie Willard, President - *Generalist, sales, engineering management*

Salary minimum: $50,000

Functions: General Mgmt., Mfg., Materials, Sales & Mktg., HR Mgmt., Engineering, Graphic Artists

Industries: Construction, Mfg., Lumber, Furniture, Printing, Plastics, Rubber, Metal Products, Motor Vehicles, Transportation, Advertising, Packaging

William-Johns Company Inc
31 Rancho
Tustin, CA 92780
(714) 547-7012
Fax: (714) 543-7300

Description: We consist of four full-time recruiters with an accumulated history of 100 years of experience in the hospitality industry who have spent 50 of those 100 years in the search industry.

Key Contact - Specialty:
Mr. William J. Kresich, President - *Hospitality*
Mr. William Thomas, III, Vice President - *Hospitality*
Ms. Renate Mettler, Director - *Hospitality*
Ms. Carmen Anne Collier, Director - *Hospitality*

Salary minimum: $75,000

Functions: Generalist, Directors, Senior Mgmt., Healthcare, Sales & Mktg., Advertising, Personnel, Training

Industries: Generalist, Construction, Retail, Finance, Venture Cap., Services, Hospitality, Media, Communications, Software, Healthcare

Dick Williams & Associates
5776 Stoneridge Mall Rd Ste 295
Pleasanton, CA 94588
(925) 468-0304
Fax: (925) 468-0306
Email: david@dwasearch.com
Web: www.dwasearch.com

Description: We are a dynamic, responsive, effective recruitment firm specializing in high quality semiconductor capitol equipment, chemical, and related technology companies. These positions include CEO, sales, marketing executives, process engineers and managers, ME, EE, SW design engineers and managers, operations, and service.

Key Contact - Specialty:
Mr. Dick Williams, President - *Semiconductor, process equipment, sales, engineers*
Mr. Kenn Giles - *Semiconductor, process equipment, sales*

Salary minimum: $60,000

Functions: Senior Mgmt., Middle Mgmt., Automation, Sales & Mktg., Sales Mgmt., CFO's, Engineering

Industries: Chemicals, Plastics, Rubber, Metal Products, Computer Equip., Test, Measure Equip.,

Electronic, Elec. Components, Mfg. SW, Marketing SW

John R Williams & Associates Inc
338 N Elm St Rm 213
Greensboro, NC 27401
(336) 279-8800

Description: We specialize in confidential executive searches and placement services in manufacturing industries with particular emphasis on textiles, furniture, chemicals and related supporting companies. Corporate, division and plant levels.

Key Contact - Specialty:
Mr. John R. Williams, President - *Manufacturing management executives*

Salary minimum: $50,000

Functions: Generalist, Middle Mgmt., Production, Plant Mgmt., Purchasing, HR Mgmt., Finance

Industries: Generalist, Textiles, Apparel, Lumber, Furniture, Chemicals, Drugs Mfg., Plastics, Rubber, Misc. Mfg., Environmental Svcs.

John Williams & Associates
401 W Pecan St Ste 2A
Pflugerville, TX 78660
(512) 990-9750
Fax: (512) 990-7807
Email: jwilliams401@aol.com

Description: We are a full-service executive recruiting firm specializing in manufacturing operations, engineering, quality assurance and distribution/logistics disciplines, within the consumer food and beverage industries(both retained and exclusive contingency searches.)

Key Contact - Specialty:
Mr. John G. Williams, President - *Manufacturing, engineering, food industry*
Ms. Victoria Deyeaux, Senior Associate - *Quality assurance*

Salary minimum: $40,000

Functions: Generalist, Middle Mgmt., Plant Mgmt., Quality, Distribution, Engineering, Mgmt. Consultants, Minorities

Industries: Generalist, Food, Bev., Tobacco, Soap, Perf., Cosmtcs., Drugs Mfg.

Williams & Delmore Inc
1800 Violet Hill Ln Ste 210
Raleigh, NC 27610
(919) 217-4600
Fax: (612) 632-4085
Email: hilles@wdinc.net
Web: www.wdinc.net

Description: We conduct confidential and ethical placement of engineering and sales professionals in the network and wireless telecommunications industry. Our primary focus is in infrastructure and component product development.

Key Contact - Specialty:
Mr. Jeffrey W. Hilles, Vice President - *Networks, wireless*

Salary minimum: $60,000

Functions: Generalist

Industries: Telecoms, Defense, Software

Networks: Top Echelon Network

The Williams Company
8080 N Central Expwy Ste 400
Dallas, TX 75206
(214) 891-8530
Fax: (214) 891-8531
Email: ssw26@aol.com

Description: Our founder is a former federated department store executive and has been a retail

search consultant for 18 years, as well as owned firm for 9 years. We specialize in middle to upper-level retail management positions.

Key Contact - Specialty:
Ms. Sandra Williams, President/Owner - *Retail*

Salary minimum: $50,000

Functions: Product Dev., Distribution, Advertising, Mkt. Research, Mktg. Mgmt., PR, HR Mgmt., Finance, CFO's, MIS Mgmt.

Industries: Retail

Williams Recruiting
16336 NE 81st St
Redmond, WA 98052-3811
(425) 869-7775
Fax: (425) 869-1849
Email: info@williamsrecruiting.com
Web: www.williamsrecruiting.com

Description: We work with pharmaceutical and biotechnology companies. Four functions within pharmaceutical and biotech are R&D, manufacturing, and process development, regulatory and clinical, quality, engineering, marketing, and business development.

Key Contact:
Ms. Gail Williams, President
Mr. David Kloppman

Functions: R&D

Industries: Drugs Mfg., Pharm Svcs., Biotech

Williamsburg Group
PO Box 212
Dayton, NJ 08810
(732) 329-3344
Fax: (732) 329-1620
Email: wgeileen@home.com

Description: Our reputation for success is built on pride, ethics, integrity and quality of service to our clients. Save valuable time and money by speaking to only our best candidates. We are a service, providing company information and candidate information nationwide.

Key Contact - Specialty:
Ms. Eileen Levine, President - *Technical, manufacturing*

Functions: Generalist, Product Dev., Production, Plant Mgmt., Quality, Purchasing, Packaging, R&D

Industries: Generalist, Chemicals, Soap, Perf., Cosmtcs., Drugs Mfg., Medical Devices, Plastics, Rubber, Metal Products, Misc. Mfg.

Willmott & Associates
922 Waltham St Ste 103
Lexington, MA 02173
(781) 863-5400
Fax: (781) 863-8000
Email: willmott@willmott.com
Web: www.willmott.com

Description: We are a human resource consulting firm specializing in the search and placement of human resource professionals both permanent and temporary. We also provide fully customizable talent acquisition solutions to organizations that need to implement new or complement existing research/recruiting efforts.

Key Contact - Specialty:
Mr. D. Clark Willmott, President - *Human resources*

Salary minimum: $40,000

Functions: Generalist, HR Mgmt., Benefits, Personnel, Training

Industries: Generalist

Professional Associations: BHRA, NEHRA, SHRM

Branches:
PO Box 602
West Kennebunk, ME 04094
(207) 499-0099
Fax: (207) 499-7842
Key Contact:
Ms. Barbara A. Thornton

1 Boston Pl
Boston, MA 02108
(617) 728-0990
Fax: (617) 728-0991
Key Contact:
Ms. Joanne A. Lynch, Vice President-Contract Services

501 Islington St Fl 3 Ste 25
Portsmouth, NH 03801
(603) 334-6663
(603) 334-6664
Fax: (603) 334-6688
Key Contact:
Ms. Joyce Baldassare

95 Sockanosset Rd Unit 107
Cranston, RI 02920
(401) 943-5556
Fax: (401) 943-5575
Email: wilmtri@tiac.net
Key Contact:
Mr. David Zito, President

7799 Leesburg Pike Ste 900 N
Falls Church, VA 22043
(703) 847-6784
Fax: (703) 847-9396
Key Contact:
Ms. Betsy Friedlander

N Willner & Company Inc

PO Box 746
Matawan, NJ 07747
(732) 566-8882
Fax: (732) 566-2001
Email: info@nwillner.com
Web: www.nwillner.com

Description: We specialize in all areas of consumer marketing from the manager level thru VP/GM. Our strengths are in marketing management, sales promotion, marketing research and sales management.

Key Contact - Specialty:
Mr. Nathaniel Willner, President - *Consumer (marketing & sales)*

Salary minimum: $70,000

Functions: Sales & Mktg., Advertising, Mktg. Mgmt.

Industries: Food, Bev., Tobacco, Soap, Perf., Cosmtcs., Drugs Mfg., Consumer Elect., Misc. Mfg., Advertising

The Wilmington Group

(also known as MRI of Wilmington-North)
1318 Airlie Rd
Wilmington, NC 28403
(910) 256-1056
Fax: (910) 256-1057
Email: mri@wilmingtongroup.com
Web: www.wilmingtongroup.com

Description: Our mission is to be a high integrity executive search and recruiting organization, national in scope, who specializes in placing top level professionals for world class pharmaceutical, information & telecommunication technology, e-commerce, and manufacturing organizations.

Key Contact - Specialty:
Mr. Kirk P. Sears, Managing Director - *Engineering, technical sales, information technology, international placements*

Mr. Richard G. Sears, Managing Director - *General manufacturing, automotive, venture capitalist*

Salary minimum: $60,000

Functions: Senior Mgmt., Middle Mgmt., Mfg., Healthcare, Sales Mgmt., IT, Engineering, Int'l.

Industries: Generalist, Mfg., Textiles, Apparel, Chemicals, Drugs Mfg., Medical Devices, Metal Products, Machine, Appliance, Motor Vehicles, Pharm Svcs., Telecoms, Packaging, Software, Biotech, Healthcare

Professional Associations: AMWA, ASME, DIA, SAE, STC, TAPPI

Wilson & Associates Int'l Inc

PO Box 4220
Clearwater, FL 33758
(727) 796-4955
Fax: (727) 796-4014
Email: ww@wilsonandassociates.com
Web: www.wilsonandassociates.com

Description: We are a search firm that specializes in the apparel, home furnishings, and textile industry. Our consultants specialize in all levels of management, engineering, quality control, IT, design, product development, production and sourcing.

Key Contact - Specialty:
Mr. Wayne Wilson, President - *Apparel, textile industry (executives)*
Ms. Lucie Campisi, Secretary/Treasurer
Ms. Cheri Boudreau, Vice President - *Information technology*
Mr. Paul Correll, Jr., Vice President - *Manufacturing, executives*
Mr. Paul Friedlander, Executive Consultant - *Manufacturing, sales, information technology*
Ms. Norma Brady, Administrative Assistant
Ms. Lorraine Costanza, Executive Consultant - *Merchandisers, manufacturing*

Functions: Generalist, Senior Mgmt., Middle Mgmt., Mfg., Materials, Mktg. Mgmt., Sales Mgmt., IT, R&D, Engineering

Industries: Generalist, Textiles, Apparel, Retail

Professional Associations: AAFA, AAPN, NKSA, SPAI

S R Wilson Inc

520 Mendocino Ave Ste 263
Santa Rosa, CA 95401
(707) 571-5993
Fax: (707) 571-1755
Email: stoney@sonic.net

Description: We are historically strong in legal search and telecommunication equipment and components. We are focused about 80% in telecommunications vs. 20 % legal today and have worked in both. Our business is national and is 75% contingency vs. 25% retainer search. In photonics, we place management at all levels engineers, scientists, and lawyers.

Key Contact:
Mr. Stoney Wilson, President
Ms. Pamela J. Wilson, Vice President

Salary minimum: $45,000

Functions: Generalist, General Mgmt., Engineering, Attorneys

Industries: Generalist, Energy, Utilities, Mfg., Consumer Elect., Test, Measure Equip., Electronic, Elec. Components, Transportation, Legal, Media, Communications, Environmental Svcs., Mfg. SW, Marketing SW

Wilson Personnel Inc

134 Montford Ave
Asheville, NC 28801-2130
(828) 258-3900
Fax: (828) 258-3902
Email: wilsonpersonnel@ioa.com

Description: We have been in business for thirty years in the recruitment and placement of engineers, technical and manufacturing management professionals. Nationwide. We have specialists in serving the manufacturing industries.

Key Contact - Specialty:
Mr. Charles K. Wilson, President
Mr. Kenneth Schapira, Executive Vice President - *Engineering, technical management*

Salary minimum: $35,000

Functions: Generalist, Middle Mgmt., Mfg., Materials, HR Mgmt., Engineering

Industries: Generalist, Mfg., Packaging, Non-classifiable

Wilson-Douglas-Jordan

1755 Park St Ste 200
Naperville, IL 60563
(312) 782-0286
(630) 778-3838
Fax: (312) 214-3424
Email: wdjinc@aol.com

Description: We provide executive and professional searches for the information technology industry. Particular specialization is given to CRM, ERP, client/server and object-oriented technologies. Target market: Fortune 200 and management consulting firms.

Key Contact - Specialty:
Mr. John T. Wilson, President - *Management consulting, information technology*

Salary minimum: $60,000

Functions: Senior Mgmt., IT, Systems Dev., Systems Implem.

Industries: Retail, Finance, Mgmt. Consulting, E-commerce, IT Implementation, Call Centers, Wireless, Insurance, Software, Accounting SW, Database SW, Development SW, ERP SW, System SW

Windsor Consultants Inc

13201 NW Fwy Ste 704
Houston, TX 77040-6025
(713) 460-0586
(212) 563-4275
Fax: (713) 460-0945
Email: windsor@pdq.net
Web: www.smart-office.net/2689

Description: We are a top team of 12 recruiters. We are highly successful in all areas of healthcare including front office, nursing and middle management, legal both nationwide and worldwide, sales, especially of technology-related products and services and hospitality. Flexible rates. Both contingent fee and retained. All fees company paid.

Key Contact - Specialty:
Mr. Daniel Narsh, CEO - *Legal, intellectual property*
Mr. Carlton Porter, CPC, Manager - *Healthcare*
Mr. Bruce Litvin, CPC, Manager - *Legal, general practice*
Mr. William Fraser, Manager - *Outside sales, computer, general*
Ms. Amy Schneider, Manager - *Software, IT recruiting*

Salary minimum: $35,000

Networks: National Personnel Assoc (NPA)

Windsor Partners Inc
70 W Madison St Ste 1400
3 First National Plaza
Chicago, IL 60602
(312) 214-3760
Email: alan.freemond@windsorpartners.com

Description: We recruit and place financial professionals for a diverse client base. Our search engagements cross all financial functions. Our typical candidate has a post graduate degree and usually started their career with a large CPA firm.

Key Contact:
Mr. Alan S. Freemond, Jr., Principal
Mr. Frank J. Weisz, Principal

Salary minimum: $70,000

Functions: Finance

Industries: Generalist

Windward Executive Search Inc
1121 Hershey Dr
Marietta, GA 30062
(770) 579-3877
Fax: (775) 306-4344
Email: tarnette@mindspring.com

Description: We see every assignment as our opportunity to help you build a stronger organization.

Key Contact:
Mr. Tom Arnette, Vice President

Salary minimum: $80,000

Functions: Generalist, Mfg.

Industries: Paper, Packaging

Professional Associations: IOPP, TAPPI

Winfield Associates Inc
53 Winter St
Weymouth, MA 02188
(781) 337-1010
Fax: (781) 335-0089
Email: winfieldassociates@yahoo.com

Description: We provide recruiting services for personnel in sales, marketing, general management, technical disciplines and regulatory affairs. The industries served are limited to manufacturers of medical and biotechnical products.

Key Contact - Specialty:
Mr. Carl W. Siegel, Owner - *Medical product manufacturers*

Salary minimum: $40,000

Functions: Middle Mgmt., Product Dev., Production, Quality, Materials, Packaging, Mkt. Research, Mktg. Mgmt., Sales Mgmt.

Industries: Medical Devices

Professional Associations: RAPS

Networks: Inter-City Personnel Assoc (IPA)

Winfield Scott Associates
1020 Park Ave
Cranston, RI 02910
(401) 943-1254
(877) 767-0326
Fax: (401) 946-8141
Email: mscott@scottjobs.com

Description: We specialize in experienced sales and marketing positions in the high end graphic and "value added" brown box marketplaces.

Key Contact - Specialty:
Mr. Michael Scott, President - *POP/POS packaging displays, graphic packaging, blister cards*

Functions: General Mgmt., Directors, Senior Mgmt., Middle Mgmt., Sales & Mktg., Advertising, Mktg. Mgmt., Sales Mgmt.

Industries: Packaging

Wing Tips & Pumps Inc
PO Box 99580
Troy, MI 48099
(248) 641-0980
(248) 641-0896
Fax: (248) 641-0895
Email: wingtipsandpumps@home.com

Description: We are a minority-owned executive search corporation emphasizing world class service to corporate America.

Key Contact - Specialty:
Mr. Verba Lee Edwards, President/CEO - *Engineering, manufacturing, data processing, finance, sales*

Salary minimum: $20,000

Functions: Generalist, Mfg., Plant Mgmt., Quality, Purchasing, Sales Mgmt., Benefits, Cash Mgmt., Systems Dev., Engineering

Industries: Generalist, Plastics, Rubber, Motor Vehicles, Banking, Environmental Svcs., Packaging, Software

Professional Associations: NBMBAA

Networks: Medical Search Consortium (MSC)

The Winn Group Inc
501 Lawrence Ave
Lawrence, KS 66049-4211
(785) 842-7111
(800) 844-9466
Fax: (785) 842-6333
Email: jim@thewinngroup.com
Web: www.thewinngroup.com

Description: We are a sharply focused and selective recruiting practice limited exclusively to property and casualty actuaries, U.S. and U.K. trained, for domestic and international positions.

Key Contact - Specialty:
Mr. James G. Winn, President - *Actuaries (property, casualty)*
Mrs. Pamela A. Heath, Vice President - *Actuaries (property, casualty)*
Mr. Thomas A. Heath, Vice President - *Actuaries (property, casualty)*

Salary minimum: $50,000

Functions: Generalist

Industries: Insurance

Branches:
4205 Harvard Rd
Lawrence, KS 66049-3583
(800) 337-5054
Fax: (785) 843-6008
Email: pam@thewinngroup.com
Key Contact - Specialty:
Ms. Pamela A. Heath, Vice President - *Actuaries (property, casualty)*

The Winsor Group
2000 S Colorado Blvd Ste 620 Twr 2
Denver, CO 80222
(303) 785-7600
Fax: (303) 785-7601
Email: kassidy@winsorgroup.com

Description: Our firm places executives and sales and marketing professionals within the financial services arena. Our team of search consultants is dedicated to the highest level of quality service. We provide a top of the market search of highly qualified financial services professionals in a variety of disciplines. Our clients and candidates are acquired as result of referral with efforts to maintain

confidentiality. We place exceptional people, with exception results.

Key Contact - Specialty:
Ms. Kassidy Hall, Executive Vice President - *Insurance, banking, agency development*
Ms. Kathleen Winsor-Games, Executive Vice President - *Managed money, wholesale distribution*

Salary minimum: $50,000

Functions: General Mgmt., Product Dev., Sales & Mktg., Sales Mgmt., Cash Mgmt.

Industries: Wholesale, Finance, Banking, Invest. Banking, Brokers, Misc. Financial, Mgmt. Consulting, Insurance, Marketing SW

Networks: National Consulting Network (NCN)

Winston & Green
225 W Washington 525
Chicago, IL 60606
(312) 201-9777
Fax: (312) 201-9781
Email: lawlag@aol.com

Description: We specialize in general counsel, senior corporate counsel and staff attorneys for corporations and law firms of all sizes. Law firm mergers and acquisitions. We also conduct marketing and research studies for law firms.

Key Contact - Specialty:
Mr. Larry A. Green, Vice President - *Attorneys (in house & small to medium law firms), minorities*

Salary minimum: $50,000

Functions: Legal

Industries: Generalist

Professional Associations: NALSC

Winter, Wyman & Company
950 Winter St Ste 3100
Waltham, MA 02451
(781) 890-7000
Fax: (781) 890-3266
Email: global@winterwyman.com
Web: www.winterwyman.com

Description: Our firm is staffed by consultants whom are experienced in their specialty fields.

Key Contact:
Mr. Kevin Steele, President
Mr. David J. Melville, Founder

Salary minimum: $35,000

Functions: Generalist, Sales & Mktg., Mktg. Mgmt., Sales Mgmt., Personnel, CFO's, Budgeting, MIS Mgmt., Systems Analysis

Industries: Generalist, Banking, Invest. Banking, Brokers, Misc. Financial, Accounting, E-commerce, IT Implementation, HR SW, Marketing SW

Branches:
2 Ravinia Dr Ste 950
Atlanta, GA 30346
(770) 698-0500
Fax: (770) 698-0531
Email: atlanta@winterwyman.com

1 Washington Mall Fl 3
Boston, MA 02108
(617) 217-7000
Email: boston@winterwyman.com
Key Contact - Specialty:
Mr. Brad Williams - *Technology*

75 Federal St Ste 720
Boston, MA 02110
(617) 880-3000
Email: boston@winterwyman.com
Key Contact - Specialty:
Ms. Lisa Fenandez - *Human resources*
Mr. Ken Martin - *Accounting & finance*

200 Ames Pond Dr
Tewksbury, MA 01876
(978) 328-3000
Email: tewksbury@winterwyman.com

400-1 Totten Pond Rd
Waltham, MA 02451
(781) 530-3300
Email: smjobs@winterwyman.com
Key Contact - Specialty:
Mr. Tony Maglione - *Technology, sales & marketing*

405 Lexington Ave Fl 26
Chrysler Bldg
New York, NY 10174
(888) 529-9300
Fax: (888) 321-5782
Email: newyork@winterwyman.com
Key Contact - Specialty:
Mr. Ian Ide - *Technology*

405 Lexington Ave FL 26
Chrysler Bldg
New York, NY 10174
(866) 624-3900
Email: nyaf@winterwyman.com
Key Contact - Specialty:
Mr. Jon Mazzocchi - *Accounting & finance*

11921 Freedom Dr Ste 550
PMB 5517
Reston, VA 20190
(888) 986-6800
Email: dc@winterwyman.com
Key Contact - Specialty:
Mr. Mike Fitzgerald - *Technology*

Wisconsin Executive Search Group Ltd
PO Box 45826
Madison, WI 53744-5826
(608) 231-5280
(608) 233-1759
Fax: (608) 231-5299
Email: jhr@wisexec.com
Web: www.wisexec.com

Description: We provide national service area specializing in banking, finance, engineering, manufacturing, utilities, e-Business, business-to-business, insurance, healthcare, IT, retail, and marketing.

Key Contact - Specialty:
Mr. John Richert, Ph.D., President
Mr. George Evers, Executive Recruiter - *Banking, finance*
Mr. Stan Fox, Executive Recruiter - *Engineering, manufacturing, marketing, IT*
Ms. Constance Fox, Executive Rescruiter - *Banking, finance, accounting, IT*
Mr. Michael Eisele, Vice President - *Insurance, healthcare, e-commerce, business to business, marketing*

Salary minimum: $50,000

Networks: Top Echelon Network

Wise Men Consultants
1500 S Dairy Ashford Ste 477
Houston, TX 77077
(281) 497-5302
(281) 497-1174
Email: recruiter@wisemen.net
Web: www.wisemen.net

Description: Wise Men Consultants specializes in full time and contract placement of Software professionals with the best companies in the industry.

Key Contact:
Mrs. Juhi Ahuja, President - *Recruiting of project managers, CIO*
Mr. Randy Lorah, Recruiting Manager
Ms. Priti Mody, Recruiter

Ms. Sonja Rabie, Administrative Manager
Salary minimum: $36,000
Functions: MIS Mgmt., Systems Dev., Systems Implem., Network Admin., DB Admin., Mgmt. Consultants

Industries: Generalist, Mgmt. Consulting

The Witt Group
PO Box 521281
Longwood, FL 32752-1281
(407) 324-4137
Fax: (407) 322-5172

Description: We specialize in technical placements in the chemical industry. Over 25 years' experience, results-oriented. Excellent ratio of offers to interviews. Guaranteed satisfaction.

Key Contact - Specialty:
Mr. Gerald E. Witt, President - *Chemical industry, technical, sales & marketing*

Salary minimum: $50,000

Functions: Generalist, Mfg., Product Dev., Plant Mgmt., Quality, Sales & Mktg., R&D, Engineering

Industries: Generalist, Chemicals, Soap, Perf., Cosmtcs., Drugs Mfg., Plastics, Rubber, Paints, Petro. Products, Biotech

Professional Associations: ACS, AICHE

WMD Inc
PO Box 321
Pittstown, NJ 08867
(908) 735-2471
Fax: (908) 735-4556

Description: We are a worldwide recruiter with 30 years of experience within the areas of search. We understand both sides, from the company's viewpoint and the candidate's viewpoint.

Key Contact - Specialty:
Mr. Wayne Donelon, Senior Partner - *Power, main drivers (turbines, diesels, boilers), air quality*

Salary minimum: $50,000

Functions: General Mgmt., Directors, Senior Mgmt., Middle Mgmt., Mfg., Materials, Purchasing, Sales & Mktg., Engineering, Int'l.

Industries: Energy, Utilities

L Wolf & Associates
3 Oriole Rd
New City, NY 10956
(845) 634-1800
Fax: (845) 634-8105
Email: larrywolf@mindspring.com

Description: We are an executive search firm specializing in accounting and finance. We have over thirty years of experience in the placement profession.

Key Contact:
Mr. Lawrence Wolf, President

Salary minimum: $50,000

Functions: Finance

Industries: Generalist, Finance, Banking, Invest. Banking, Accounting, Accounting SW

Wolikow Associates
155 N Main St
New City, NY 10956
(800) 298-6136
(845) 708-6000
Fax: (845) 634-8726
Email: info@wolikow.com
Web: www.wolikow.com

Description: Our firm helps companies hire technology professionals, working with both large and small firms. Our smaller clients, many of, which are "start ups," use our recruiting services to establish their technology teams while others, such as large financial institutions, use us to identify top professionals with transaction-based technology experience. We've also done quite a bit of work in the sales arena; about a third of our practice focuses on sales. We pride ourselves on being easy to do business with and on finding candidates who our clients won't see from anyone else.

Key Contact:
Mr. Michael Loewenberg, President
Mr. Lee Deutsch, Senior Vice President

Salary minimum: $65,000

Functions: IT, MIS Mgmt., Systems Analysis, Systems Dev., Network Admin., DB Admin.

Industries: Generalist

Wonderling Recruiting
PO Box 67
Clymer, NY 14724
(716) 355-4100
Fax: (716) 355-4206
Email: slw@alltel.net
Web: www.wonderling.com

Description: We conduct searches in engineering and manufacturing. Specialty areas include: mechanical, metallurgical, automotive, quality, machines and machining, managers and engineers, tool & die, tooling, tool design, general manufacturing.

Key Contact - Specialty:
Ms. Susan Wonderling, Owner - *Manufacturing, engineering*

Salary minimum: $22,000

Functions: Middle Mgmt., Product Dev., Production, Automation, Quality, Productivity, Engineering

Industries: Medical Devices, Metal Products, Machine, Appliance, Motor Vehicles

Professional Associations: RON

Networks: Inter-City Personnel Assoc (IPA)

Wood & Associates
17 Escalle Ln
Larkspur, CA 94939
(415) 927-3112
Fax: (415) 927-3117
Email: mwood51319@aol.com

Description: We specialize in the placement of civil, structural, environmental, and geo-technical engineering professionals.

Key Contact - Specialty:
Mr. Milo Wood, Owner - *Civil, structural, environmental, geotech*

Salary minimum: $50,000

Functions: Engineering

Industries: Energy, Utilities, Construction, Transportation, Environmental Svcs., Haz. Waste

Professional Associations: ASCE

Wood Search & Consulting Inc
PO Box 92985
Southlake, TX 76092
(817) 424-9162
Fax: (817) 251-9408
Email: woodconsulting@aol.com
Web: www.smart-office.net/?member_id=18797

Description: We are a search firm and human resource services provider that is based upon professional knowledge, responsiveness, integrity, and guaranteed results. We specialize in accounting, administration, construction, engineering, hospitality, and sales. Wood Search and Consulting will bring together highly qualified candidates to their clients in a timely manner.

Key Contact - Specialty:
Ms. Dorothy Wood, President - *Management (executive and mid-level)*

Functions: Generalist

Industries: Generalist, Pharm Svcs., Legal, Accounting, Healthcare

Wood West & Partners Inc
700 - 1281 West Georgia St
Vancouver, BC V6E 3J7
Canada
(604) 682-3141
Fax: (604) 688-5749
Email: search@wood-west.com
Web: www.wood-west.com

Description: We conduct executive search and recruitment for managers and specialists in information technology, engineering, telecommunications, accounting, finance and banking, marketing and sales, insurance, manufacturing, and construction.

Key Contact - Specialty:
Mr. Ron Wood, BA, Principal - *Information technology, marketing & sales, finance*
Mr. Fred West, PEng., Principal - *Engineering, telecommunications, manufacturing, construction*

Salary minimum: $35,000

Functions: Senior Mgmt., Middle Mgmt.

Industries: Generalist

Professional Associations: ACSESS

Networks: National Personnel Assoc (NPA)

Woodbury Personnel Consultants LLC
244 Gray St
Manchester, NH 03103-2809
(603) 665-9700
Fax: (603) 665-9800
Email: woodburypc@sprynet.com
Web: www.woodburypc.com

Description: We are a generalist direct hire search firm servicing a wide range of industries and candidates at the executive, management, and professional/technical levels. Our primary service area includes New Hampshire, Maine, Vermont, and Northern Massachusetts.

Key Contact:
Ms. Frances Routhier, Owner
Mr. Guy Routhier, Consultant

Salary minimum: $45,000

Functions: Generalist

Industries: Generalist

Professional Associations: MAHRA, NNEAPS, RON, SHRM

Networks: National Personnel Assoc (NPA)

Woodmoor Group Inc
PO Box 1383
Monument, CO 80132
(719) 488-8589
Fax: (719) 488-9043
Email: woodmoor@woodmoor.com
Web: www.woodmoor.com

Description: Experienced, energetic and tenacious, we conduct comprehensive searches with professionalism, always mindful that we are an extension of your company. We consider it a point of honor to complete every search assigned to us.

Key Contact - Specialty:
Mr. Ray N. Bedingfield, President - *Manufacturing*

Mr. Brian McQuiddy, Vice President - *Manufacturing*
Ms. Lara Brennan, Group Vice President - *Logistics, e-commerce*
Mr. Joe Brennan, Group Vice President - *Contract electronics, manufacturing*
Mr. Jeffrey Mitten, Senior Associate - *Transportation, logistics*

Salary minimum: $60,000

Functions: Generalist

Industries: Generalist

Professional Associations: AAAS, AAPG, ACS, AICHE, AMA, APICS, FMA, IOPP, ISPE, SCIP, SHRM

Woodruff Associates
2450 6th Ave S
PO Box 25036
Seattle, WA 98125
(206) 622-9634
Fax: (206) 622-4149
Email: rick@rickwoodruff.com
Web: www.rickwoodruff.com

Description: We are a supermarket/wholesale, grocery/food service recruiting firm for middle management and senior management. We have had over 30 years of recruiting experience with an outstanding track record.

Key Contact - Specialty:
Mr. Rick Woodruff, President - *Food industry, supermarkets, wholesalers*

Salary minimum: $50,000

Functions: Generalist

Industries: Food, Bev., Tobacco, Soap, Perf., Cosmtcs., Consumer Elect., Wholesale, Retail, Pharm Svcs.

Professional Associations: SRS

Jim Woodson & Associates Inc
1080 River Oaks Dr Ste B-102
Jackson, MS 39208
(601) 936-4037
Fax: (601) 936-4041
Email: jwood0335@aol.com

Description: Established in 1979. We recruit heavily in engineering/manufacturing to include metal fab, high volume assembly, machined products, consumer appliances, consumer electronics, automotive, electric motors and environmental. Also actively recruit accounting/financial people.

Key Contact - Specialty:
Mr. Jim Woodson, President - *Generalist*

Salary minimum: $40,000

Functions: Generalist

Industries: Drugs Mfg., Medical Devices, Plastics, Rubber, Metal Products, Machine, Appliance, Motor Vehicles, Computer Equip., Consumer Elect., Electronic, Elec. Components, Accounting

Networks: National Personnel Assoc (NPA)

Chris Woolsey & Associates LLC
1949 E Sunshine St Ste 2-106
Springfield, MO 65804
(417) 887-1229
Fax: (417) 888-2452
Email: cow@cwoolsey.com
Web: www.cwoolsey.com

Description: We specialize in the placement of degreed professionals in the food and beverage manufacturing industry nationwide. Focusing on operations, engineering, maintenance, quality assurance, supply chain, human resources, logistics, distribution, purchasing, etc.

Key Contact - Specialty:
Mr. Chris O. Woolsey, Principal - *Operations, engineering, maintenance*
Ms. Jackie Woolsey, Principal - *Quality assurance, human resources, supply chain management*

Salary minimum: $38,000

Functions: Mfg.

Industries: Food, Bev., Tobacco, Paper, Soap, Perf., Cosmtcs., Drugs Mfg.

Networks: Inter-City Personnel Assoc (IPA)

The Works
197 Eighth St
Charlestown Navy Yard
Boston, MA 02129
(617) 241-0647
Fax: (617) 241-4904
Email: resume@theworksnet.com
Web: www.theworksnet.com

Description: We offer clients marketing, public relations and creative talent on a freelance, contract, or permanent basis. We have expertise in contingency, retained, temporary, and project based consulting and search services.

Key Contact - Specialty:
Mr. Peter Eleftherio, Principal - *Marketing*
Ms. Alicia Recupero, Principal - *Marketing*
Ms. Melanie Lewis, Principal - *Marketing*

Functions: Senior Mgmt., Middle Mgmt., Product Dev., Advertising, Mkt. Research, Mktg. Mgmt., Direct Mktg., PR

Industries: Generalist, Drugs Mfg., Medical Devices, Consumer Elect., Finance, Venture Cap., Services, Mgmt. Consulting, Advertising, New Media, Communications, Telecoms, Software, Marketing SW

Professional Associations: AMA, BIG, MAPS, MIMC, PRSA

Worlco Computer Resources Inc
997 Old Eagle School Rd Ste 219
Wayne, PA 19087-1706
(610) 293-9070
Fax: (610) 293-1027
Email: parisi@worlco.com
Web: www.worlco.com

Description: We provide full range of recruiting, executive search and personnel consulting services relating to computer professionals and executives in Philadelphia area marketplace; the leading organization of its kind. Also places consultants and undertakes project professional service assignments.

Key Contact - Specialty:
Mr. Frank Parisi, Managing Partner - *Computer, communications (data)*

Salary minimum: $25,000

Functions: Generalist, Mktg. Mgmt., Sales Mgmt., IT, MIS Mgmt., Systems Analysis, Systems Implem., Systems Support

Industries: Generalist, Software

Professional Associations: MAAPC

Branches:
901 Rte 38
Cherry Hill, NJ 08002
(856) 665-4700
Fax: (856) 665-8142
Email: hughes@worlco.com
Key Contact:
Mr. Robert J. Hughes, Managing Partner

World Search
4130 Linden Ave Ste 125
Dayton, OH 45432
(937) 254-9071
Fax: (937) 254-0229

Email: world@erinet.com

Description: We conduct contingency and retained search, with emphasis in the engineering, production management.

Key Contact - Specialty:
Mr. Robert Bannister, Co-Owner
Ms. Sherry Bannister, Co-Owner
Mr. Thomas A. Baehl, Director of Search - *Engineering, production management, HVAC*

Salary minimum: $40,000

Functions: Generalist, Product Dev., Automation, Productivity, Sales Mgmt., Systems Analysis, Systems Implem., Engineering

Industries: Generalist, Plastics, Rubber, Metal Products, Computer Equip., Transportation, Aerospace

Networks: Top Echelon Network

WorldSearch Consultants LLC
PO Box 7928
Mesa, AZ 85216
(480) 354-1350
(800) 959-1666
Email: mail@worldsearchconsultants.com
Web: www.worldsearchconsultants.com

Description: Our firm provides executive search recruitment for wireless telecommunications focusing on emerging technologies. We specialize in upper level management and software engineer/developer jobs. More specifically, we focus on 3G, WAP, m-Commerce, SMS, Bluetooth, and wireless Internet.

Key Contact:
Mr. Kirk Krein, President / Recruiter

Functions: Generalist

Industries: Telecoms

Worldwide Executive Search
620 Newport Center Dr Ste 1100
Newport Beach, CA 92660
(949) 721-6685
(949) 721-6603
Fax: (949) 640-1044
Email: jim_ginther@hotmail.com
Web: www.worldwideexecsearch.com

Description: We are a global, multi-industry search firm that produces leaders with an impressive record of success. We are both a contingency and retain search firm specializing in hospitality, retail, accounting and finance, and sales and marketing.

Key Contact:
Mr. Jim Ginther, Managing Director

Salary minimum: $70,000

Functions: General Mgmt., Senior Mgmt., Middle Mgmt., Sales & Mktg., Sales Mgmt., CFO's

Industries: Generalist, Food, Bev., Tobacco, Retail, Finance, Accounting, Hospitality, Telecoms, Real Estate, Software

Professional Associations: CSP

Networks: National Personnel Assoc (NPA)

Worldwide Medical Services
619 S State St
Ukiah, CA 95482
(707) 462-9420
Fax: (707) 462-5208
Email: locumnet@wwmedical.com
Web: www.wwmedical.com

Description: We are worldwide medical recruiters and place physicians all medical, surgical, radiology and anesthesia specialties, nurse anesthetists, medical and nursing administrators and executives both permanent and temporary.

Key Contact:
Mr. John Paju, President

Functions: Generalist, Directors, Admin. Svcs., Healthcare, Direct Mktg., HR Mgmt., Int'l.

Industries: Services, HR Services, Government, Healthcare

Professional Associations: NAPR

Worldwide Recruiters
7 N Main St
PO Box 11
Rushville, NY 14544
(716) 554-5185
Fax: (716) 554-5192
Email: jim@wwrec.com
Web: www.wwrec.com

Key Contact - Specialty:
Mr. James Grant, Partner
Mrs. Liz Grant, Partner - *Engineers*
Ms. Stacey White, CPC, Executive Recruiter - *High Tech*

Salary minimum: $50,000

Functions: Engineering

Industries: Mfg., Communications, Defense, Aerospace, Software

Networks: Top Echelon Network

The Worth Group
50 Technology Pkwy S
Norcross, GA 30092
(678) 221-2050
Fax: (678) 221-2051
Email: bbuckwald@theworthgroup.com
Web: www.theworthgroup.com

Description: Our firm is a retained and contingency search firm focusing in the communications and call center industries nationally. Our clients range from start-ups to Fortune 500 companies. Our applications include CTI, CRM, ERP, sales force automation, workforce management, e-Commerce, Internet, LAN/WAN, and much more. We place in executive level management, sales, sales support, and technical support. Our successful performance has led to confidence, and credibility among our clients. Our clients represent the majority of our business. We screen our client companies and candidates.

Key Contact:
Mr. Brett Buckwald, President - *Telecommunications*
Mr. Alan Rosenblum, Vice President

Salary minimum: $75,000

Functions: Generalist

Industries: Media, Telecoms, Software

Branches:
129 Broadway
Lynbrook, NY 11563
(516) 887-8555
Fax: (516) 596-4987
Key Contact - Specialty:
Mr. Al Rosenblum - *Telecommunications*

Jay Wren & Associates
6355 Riverside Blvd Ste P
Sacramento, CA 95831
(916) 394-2920
Fax: (916) 424-8192
Email: jay_wren@msn.com

Description: We have placed sales managers, sales support managers, product and brand managers with over 50 major consumer package goods companies and package goods promotional, service and information companies.

Key Contact:
Mr. Jay Wren, Owner - *Consumer packaged goods region sales*
Ms. Carol Chase, Recruiter

Salary minimum: $50,000

Functions: Sales & Mktg., Mkt. Research, Direct Mktg.

Industries: Food, Bev., Tobacco, Soap, Perf., Cosmtcs.

Professional Associations: FMI, NFBA

Arthur Wright & Associates Inc
50 Crestwood Executive Ctr Ste 500
St. Louis, MO 63126
(314) 729-7373
Fax: (314) 842-4962
Email: awasearch@inlink.com

Description: Recruiting specialists for the manufacturing industry. We cover all salary positions inside the manufacturing facility.

Key Contact:
Mr. Craig S. Nowotny, President

Salary minimum: $25,000

Functions: Generalist, Middle Mgmt., Production, Automation, Plant Mgmt., Materials Plng., Advertising, Training

Industries: Generalist, Food, Bev., Tobacco, Lumber, Furniture, Printing, Soap, Perf., Cosmtcs., Medical Devices, Paints, Petro. Products, Metal Products, Motor Vehicles

Professional Associations: MAPS, NAPS

Wright Associates
PO Box 3047
South Attleboro, MA 02703
(508) 761-6354
Fax: (508) 761-9587
Email: garywright@prodigy.net
Web: www.wrightassociates.org

Description: We are a privately owned recruiting and executive search firm specializing in the high-technology industry. Management consulting services are also available. Specialized in customer service.

Key Contact:
Mr. Gary Wright, President

Functions: Generalist

Industries: Computer Equip., Equip Svcs., Mgmt. Consulting, Telecoms, Software

The Wright Group
5706 Preston Fairways
Dallas, TX 75252
(214) 351-1115
(972) 447-0996
Fax: (972) 447-9206
Email: jayj6@airmail.net
Web: www.nationjob.com

Description: We are a nationwide executive search firm specializing in the placement of marketing research professionals, marketing science, database and targeting marketing professionals.

Key Contact - Specialty:
Ms. Jay J. Wright, President - *Marketing research, target base, marketing science executives*

Salary minimum: $30,000

Functions: Directors, Senior Mgmt., Middle Mgmt., Mkt. Research, Direct Mktg., DB Admin.

Industries: Generalist

Professional Associations: AMA, IRG

Bob Wright Recruiting Inc
56 DeForest Rd
Wilton, CT 06897-1907
(203) 762-9046
Fax: (203) 762-5807
Email: bwri@optonline.net

Description: Our principal has worked in direct
marketing, sales promotion, and business
information industries. We specialize in placing new
business development sales, sales management, and
marketing talent.

Key Contact - Specialty:
Mr. J. Robert Wright, President - *Sales, marketing,
general management*

Salary minimum: $40,000

Functions: General Mgmt., Senior Mgmt., Middle
Mgmt., Sales & Mktg., Advertising, Mkt.
Research, Mktg. Mgmt., Sales Mgmt., Direct
Mktg., Customer Svc.

Industries: Advertising, New Media, Database SW,
Development SW, Marketing SW

WSA Associates Restaurant Management Recruiting
2361 Hyde Park Blvd 101
Lake Havasu City, AZ 86404
(928) 764-2200
Fax: (928) 764-3709
Email: lhcstone@interworldnet.net

Description: We offer placement services in all
areas to the restaurant industry including operations,
human resources, finance, training, construction,
site selection, real estate and others.

Key Contact - Specialty:
Mr. Jeff Stone, Managing Partner - *Restaurant
management*

Salary minimum: $30,000

Functions: Generalist

Industries: Restaurants

John Wylie Associates Inc
1727 E 71st St
Tulsa, OK 74136
(918) 496-2100
Email: jlwylie@inetmail.att.net

Description: We are a professional, technical and
managerial recruitment firm in the Southwest,
principally for the petroleum/chemical processing
and manufacturing industries. We have over 26
years of corporate recruiting experience.

Key Contact - Specialty:
Mr. John L. Wylie, President - *Manufacturing
managerial, technical, chemical processing
(managers, engineers)*

Salary minimum: $25,000

Functions: Generalist, General Mgmt., Mfg.,
Materials, HR Mgmt., IT, R&D, Engineering

Industries: Generalist, Energy, Utilities, Mfg.,
Environmental Svcs., Software

Networks: Inter-City Personnel Assoc (IPA)

Dennis Wynn Associates Inc
PO Box 7100
St. Petersburg, FL 33734-7100
(727) 823-2042
Email: denniswynn@msn.com

Description: We are an Information systems
recruitment specialist.

Key Contact:
Mr. Dennis N. Wynn, President
Ms. Jean Wynn, Treasurer

Salary minimum: $35,000

Functions: Generalist, MIS Mgmt., Systems
Analysis, Systems Dev., Systems Implem.,
Systems Support, Network Admin., DB Admin.

Industries: Generalist, Software

XiTech Staffing Solutions
766 Shrewsbury Ave
Tinton Falls, NJ 07024
(732) 450-9600
Fax: (732) 450-9680
Email: recruiters@xitechstaffing.com
Web: www.xitechstaffing.com

Key Contact:
Mr. Nicholas Ciccone, President

Functions: Generalist

Industries: Energy, Utilities, Mfg., Food, Bev.,
Tobacco, Chemicals, Drugs Mfg., Medical
Devices, Plastics, Rubber, Metal Products,
Machine, Appliance, Biotech

Xycorp Inc
365 Bloor St E Ste 2001
Toronto, ON M4W 3L4
Canada
(416) 923-4344
Fax: (416) 923-0120
Email: david@xycorp.com
Web: www.xycorp.com

Description: We specialize in the placement of
information technology professionals, both contract
and permanent into both the vendor community and
end users of information techology.

Key Contact - Specialty:
Mr. David Smith, VP-Professional Services -
Information technology, senior level
Mr. Chris Cullen, Customer Relationship Manager
- *Contractors*
Mr. Roy Cope, Sales Manager - *Oracle, AS-400*
Mr. Frank Switt, Vice President-Sales -
Information technology, mid level

Salary minimum: $30,000

Functions: Generalist, IT

Industries: Generalist, IT Implementation

Professional Associations: ACSESS

Xyon Business Solutions Inc
5995 Crow Ct
San Diego, CA 92120
(619) 501-4567
Fax: (619) 501-4568
Email: kevinloomis@xyonglobal.com
Web: www.xyonglobal.com

Description: We specialize in the placement of IT
professionals throughout the US and world. We
offer consultants and permanent personnel. Our
specialty is within the JD Edwards environment.

Key Contact:
Mr. Kevin Loomis, President

Functions: IT

Industries: Generalist

The Yaiser Group
PO Box 222
Brielle, NJ 08730-1635
(732) 528-0443
Fax: (732) 528-4824
Email: dickyaiser@att.net

Description: We are ethical, on target and waste
neither our time nor yours in our efforts to identify
proper candidates based upon your specifications.

Key Contact - Specialty:
Mr. Richard A. Yaiser, President - *Pharmaceutical*
Mr. Tom Coghan, Executive Consultant -
Pharmaceutical

Salary minimum: $40,000

Functions: Generalist, Mfg., Product Dev., Quality,
Engineering, Specialized Svcs.

Industries: Drugs Mfg.

Professional Associations: AAPS

Yankee Hospitality Search LLC
406 Farmington Ave
Farmington, CT 06032
(860) 738-4972
Fax: (860) 738-4972
Email: info@yankeehospitality.com
Web: www.yankeehospitality.com

Description: High quality executive and middle
management recruitment for the hospitality
industry.

Key Contact:
Mr. Dan Tolman, President
Mr. Joseph Cresci, Recruiter
Mr. Allen Bellview, Recruiter

Salary minimum: $35,000

Functions: Generalist

Industries: Mgmt. Consulting, Hospitality

Yes! Executive Solutions
508 Highland Park Dr
Irving, TX 75061
(972) 399-0009
Fax: (972) 986-0324
Email: mjsyessolutions@cs.com

Description: We are an Executive and Professional
search firm which matches an elite group of
"Difference Makers" with companies who will only
consider the best of the best. Our company clientele
range from Fortune 100, to emerging, and start-ups,
throughout the U.S.

Key Contact - Specialty:
Mr. Marcus Strother, Executive Director -
Executives and professionals

Salary minimum: $75,000

Functions: Directors

Industries: Computer Equip., Misc. Mfg.,
Electronic, Elec. Components, Telecoms,
Telephony, Digital, Wireless, Fiber Optic,
Aerospace, Mfg. SW

York & Associates
1019 9th St
Greeley, CO 80631
(970) 352-3086
Fax: (970) 352-3087
Email: teriyork@hotmail.com

Description: Focus is on mid-size construction
companies, including commercial, industrial and
public works companies. We provide the most
thorough screening in the search industry. Clients
interview only the perfect match candidates.

Key Contact - Specialty:
Ms. Teri F. York, President - *Construction*

Functions: Generalist

Industries: Construction

York Group
(also known as MRI of York County)
121 Stone Village Dr
Ft. Mill, SC 29708
(803) 802-0400
Fax: (803) 802-0510
Email: info@mryork.com
Web: www.mryork.com

Description: We are specialists in
telecommunications, international placements, and
information technology.

Key Contact:
Mr. Richard Reichmann
Ms. Valerie Reichmann

Salary minimum: $45,000

Functions: Generalist

Industries: Mgmt. Consulting, E-commerce, IT Implementation, Communications, Industry Specific SW, Mfg. SW, Marketing SW

Professional Associations: SCTE, USTA

The York Group
3958 Rambla Orienta
Malibu, CA 90265
(310) 317-8568
Fax: (310) 317-8570
Email: yorkgrp@gte.net
Web: www.yorkgroup.com

Description: Serving the healthcare industry and their marketing/communications needs.

Key Contact - Specialty:
Ms. Karen York, Principal Consultant - *Healthcare marketing, healthcare advertising*
Ms. Leslie Betts, Senior Associate - *Healthcare technologies, internet*

Salary minimum: $75,000

Functions: Healthcare

Industries: Medical Devices, Pharm Svcs., Advertising, New Media, Marketing SW, Biotech, Healthcare, Hospitals, Long-term Care, Dental

Professional Associations: AAAA, AHSM, HMC, MMA

Yormak & Associates
3780 Kilroy Airport Way Ste 200
Long Beach, CA 90806
(562) 988-6555
Fax: (562) 988-6566
Email: syormak@aol.com

Description: Southern California based recruitment firm serving the public accounting industry - including the Big 5, local and regional CPA firms, as well as private industry companies. We focus on placing highly qualified accounting and finance professionals in full-time regular positions.

Key Contact - Specialty:
Mr. Stuart I. Yormak, President - *Accounting & finance*

Salary minimum: $30,000

Functions: Generalist, CFO's, Budgeting, Cash Mgmt., Credit, Taxes

Industries: Generalist, Finance, Hospitality, Broadcast, Film, Real Estate, Software, Healthcare

Professional Associations: AICPA

Bill Young & Associates Inc
273 Oak Dale Ln
Stuarts Draft, VA 24477
(804) 361-1883
Email: byoung@billyoung.com
Web: www.billyoung.com

Description: Retained and contingency permanent searches for sales, information systems, telecommunications professionals. Placements are Washington, DC metro area to include Virginia, Maryland and West Virginia. Principals have over 25 years' corporate high-tech search recruiting.

Key Contact - Specialty:
Mr. William H. Young, President - *Information systems, telecommunications*

Salary minimum: $40,000

Functions: Senior Mgmt., Sales & Mktg., IT

Industries: Generalist, Software

Professional Associations: NAPS

Youngblood Associates
131 4th Ave W Ste 212
Hendersonville, NC 28792
(800) 545-9123
Fax: (828) 698-3272
Email: youngbloodas@ioa.com

Description: Our president is a recognized leader in recruiting for the investment management industry. For over 13 years, he has been successfully placing analysts, portfolio managers, marketers, client servicing people, consultants, and traders throughout the US.

Key Contact - Specialty:
Mr. Robert S. Youngblood, President - *Investment management, banking*

Salary minimum: $50,000

Functions: Senior Mgmt., Middle Mgmt., Sales Mgmt., Customer Svc., Cash Mgmt., Mgmt. Consultants

Industries: Finance, Banking, Misc. Financial

Professional Associations: NYSSA

Youngman & Associates Inc
6304 Northwood Unit 2
St. Louis, MO 63105
(314) 878-0228
Email: youngmanassoc@nbn-jobs.com

Description: Our firm is an executive search firm entering its 17th year of service to the banking industry. We have enjoyed an excellent reputation for locating, recruiting, and evaluating top industry talent for our clients, having conducted hundreds of successful searches for middle and upper level executives on a local, regional, and national basis. As a result, we have established long-term partnerships with many of our clients, primarily located in the Upper and Lower Midwest.

Key Contact - Specialty:
Mr. Grant Youngman - *Banking, mid-level management*

Salary minimum: $40,000

Functions: Finance, Credit

Industries: Finance, Banking, Invest. Banking

Networks: National Banking Network (NBN)

Your Advantage Staffing Consultants Inc
426 Queen St W
Cambridge, ON N3C 1H1
Canada
(519) 651-2120
(888) 213-3375
Fax: (519) 651-2780
Email: info@yasci.com
Web: www.yasci.com

Description: We offer significant expertise in the recruitment and selection of staff for the ground transportation industry.

Key Contact - Specialty:
Ms. Lori Van Opstal, President - *Transportation*

Functions: Generalist

Industries: Transportation

Professional Associations: ACSESS

YourNet Int'l
7516 Rowland Rd
Edmonton, AB T6A 3W1
Canada
(780) 440-2300
Fax: (780) 490-6200

Email: brent@yournet.ca
Web: www.yournet.ca

Description: Our firm is a multi-faceted telecommunications and technology consulting and staffing company, providing services to high-tech companies worldwide. YourNet's mandate is to help its clients become 'Top Dogs' in their respective industries. Our specialty is emerging technologies and markets, and we pride ourselves in providing quality, professional service. Our clients know that they will receive pragmatic, timely, and creative solutions that are integral to their unique business or workforce management needs.

Key Contact:
Mr. Brent Baim, President

Functions: Int'l.

Industries: Energy, Utilities, Electronic, Elec. Components, E-commerce, IT Implementation, Communications

Networks: Top Echelon Network

Yours In Travel Personnel Agency Inc
12 W 37 St Fl 5
New York, NY 10018
(212) 697-7855
Email: info@yoursintravel.com
Web: www.yoursintravel.com

Description: Largest recruitment firm specializing solely in the travel industry. Retained & contingency searches; worldwide; fully automated. Our specialty. CEO, COO, CFO, CIO, CMO, Presidents, EVP, SVP. Free analysis and first consultation.

Key Contact - Specialty:
Mr. P. Jason King, President - *Travel industry*

Salary minimum: $70,000

Functions: Generalist, General Mgmt., Directors, Senior Mgmt., Middle Mgmt., Mktg. Mgmt., HR Mgmt., CFO's, MIS Mgmt.

Industries: Generalist, Hospitality, Hotels, Resorts, Clubs, Restaurants, Entertainment, Recreation

Professional Associations: ACTE, AGTE, AHMA, ATME, COPE, CTO, HSMAI, MPI, NBTA, PATA, TIAA, USTOA, WEXITA

Zackrison Associates Inc
PO Box 1843
Venice, FL 34284
(941) 493-8211
Web: www.zackrison.com

Description: We are an executive recruiting firm which specializes in pharmaceutical and biotech search in clinical and medical affairs, research and development, and executive officers.

Key Contact - Specialty:
Mr. Walter Zackrison, President - *Pharmaceutical, biotechnological*

Salary minimum: $60,000

Functions: Physicians, HR Mgmt., R&D

Industries: Generalist, Drugs Mfg., Pharm Svcs.

Professional Associations: ACRP, DIA, RAPS

R L Zapin Associates Inc
420 Lexington Ave Ste 300
New York, NY 10170
(212) 297-6244
Email: resumes@rlzapinassociates.com
Web: www.rlzapinassociates.com

Description: We are direct and database marketing specialists including marketing research, credit risk/policy, product/program marketing, loyalty/retention/acquisition/CRM, list management, database analysis, SAS, statistics, and quantitative analysis.

Key Contact:
Ms. Roni Zapin, President

Salary minimum: $50,000

Functions: Middle Mgmt., Mkt. Research, Direct Mktg., Risk Mgmt., MIS Mgmt., DB Admin.

Industries: Banking, E-commerce, Entertainment, Advertising, Publishing, New Media, Insurance

Professional Associations: DMA

Rosalind Zarlin Associates
10 E 39th St Ste 514
New York, NY 10016
(212) 683-1951
Fax: (212) 683-4682
Email: rzarlin@aol.com

Description: Staff totaling 25 years of recruiting experience with top research staff specializing in accounting and finance.

Key Contact - Specialty:
Ms. Rosalind Zarlin, President - *Accounting, finance*

Functions: Generalist, CFO's, Budgeting, Cash Mgmt., Credit, Taxes, M&A, Risk Mgmt.

Industries: Generalist, Banking, Invest. Banking, Mgmt. Consulting, Advertising, Publishing, Telecoms, Real Estate

Zeiger Associates LLC
4766 Park Granada Blvd Ste 211
Calabasas, CA 91302
(818) 222-0052
Fax: (818) 222-0232
Email: sazeiger@pacbell.net

Description: We specialize in design, project, program, and engineering, including A&D, test, software, hardware, computer hard disk development, IC and ASIC design and development, SCSI engineering, and management. We are specialists in disk drive and semiconductor executives, and executive technical management, for example: president, CEO, COO, etc.

Key Contact - Specialty:
Mr. Stephen A. Zeiger, President - *Hard disk drive executives, engineers, VP, directors, ASIC*
Mr. David Barkin Zeiger, Vice President - *ASIC, hard disk drive, semiconductor*

Salary minimum: $45,000

Functions: Generalist, Directors, Senior Mgmt., Middle Mgmt., MIS Mgmt., R&D, Engineering

Industries: Generalist, Computer Equip., Consumer Elect., Telecoms, Software

Networks: Top Echelon Network

Zen Zen Int'l Inc
385 St. Mary Ave
Winnipeg, MB R3C 0N1
Canada
(204) 837-7943
Fax: (204) 837-4646
Email: zenzenmy@mb.sympatico.ca
Web: www.zenzen.ca

Description: Specialists in recruitment and placement of information technology professionals. Secondary specialties include: accountants, engineers, sales & marketing, merchandisers, human resource management. Expertise in apparel manufacturing/distribution/retail industry.

Key Contact - Specialty:
Mr. Michael Yakimishyn, President - *Information technology, engineering, accounting, sales & marketing, human resources*

Salary minimum: $25,000

Functions: General Mgmt., Mfg., Healthcare, Sales & Mktg., Finance, IT

Industries: Generalist, Mfg., Textiles, Apparel, Lumber, Furniture, Wholesale, Retail, Accounting, Telecoms, Aerospace, Software, Healthcare

Professional Associations: HRMAM

Zenner Consulting Group LLC
400 N Michigan Ave Ste 1220
Chicago, IL 60611
(312) 645-0400
Fax: (312) 645-0200
Email: info@lawposition.com
Web: www.lawposition.com

Description: We are comprised of six attorneys who practiced law at premier national firms. Our recruiters graduated from the following law schools: Northwestern, the University of Chicago, Boalt Hall School of Law (Berkeley), the University of Wisconsin, and Loyola University.

Key Contact - Specialty:
Teri E. Zenner, Esq., President - *Lawyers*

Functions: Generalist

Industries: Legal

Helen Ziegler & Associates Inc
180 Dundas St W Ste 2403
Toronto, ON M5G 1Z8
Canada
(416) 977-6941
(800) 387-4616
Fax: (416) 977-6128
Email: hza@hziegler.com
Web: www.hziegler.com

Description: We specialize in identifying hard-to-get candidates for challenging assignments and assessing their suitability for the given assignment.

Key Contact - Specialty:
Ms. Helen Ziegler, President - *Doctors, administrators*

Salary minimum: $36,000

Functions: Generalist, Senior Mgmt., Healthcare, Personnel, Int'l.

Industries: Generalist, Healthcare

Professional Associations: APPAC

P D Zier Associates
14 Ascolese Rd
Trumbull, CT 06611
(203) 452-0078
Email: pdzier@aol.com

Description: Professional, experienced, knowlegeable and successful high-technology recruiters.

Key Contact - Specialty:
Ms. Patricia D. Zier - *High technology, information systems*

Salary minimum: $45,000

Functions: IT

Industries: Generalist

Professional Associations: BIC, CBIA, DPMA, NAFE

Zillifro & Associates
PO Box 1238
Manteo, NC 27954-1238
(252) 473-2021
Fax: (252) 473-5581
Email: zanda@zillifro.com
Web: www.zillifro.com

Description: We have nearly 20 years of highly specialized experience and contacts. The hallmark on both sides of the equation is strong, personal relationships. Our focus is on understanding and filling needs. We are experts in recruiting for chemical suppliers, particularly those moving product into the pulp and paper industry. Our ethics reputation is second to none.

Key Contact - Specialty:
Mr. W. Keith Zillifro, President - *Paper chemicals, paint & coating additives, food additives, chemical products*

Salary minimum: $50,000

Functions: General Mgmt., Materials, Sales & Mktg., HR Mgmt., Finance, IT, Engineering, Technicians, Attorneys, Int'l.

Industries: Chemicals

Professional Associations: TAPPI

Networks: US Recruiters.com

Chuck Zimering Advertising Recruitment (CZAR)
170 W End Ave Ste 11G
New York, NY 10023
(212) 724-7904
Fax: (212) 724-7163
Email: czar4@msn.com

Description: I specialize in recruiting for general, direct, and interactive advertising agencies most in the New York City area. My area of expertise is media and account services.

Key Contact - Specialty:
Mr. Chuck Zimering, Director - *Media, account (interactive to general & direct advertising agencies)*

Salary minimum: $30,000

Functions: Advertising

Industries: Advertising, New Media

Zion Technologies Inc
PO Box 180584
Casselberry, FL 32718
(407) 699-8080
Fax: (407) 699-8005
Email: services@ziontec.net
Web: www.ziontec.net

Description: Zion Technologies, Inc. is a human resources support firm that provides employment services for professionals in Construction Project Management, Computer Programming, Engineering, and Technical Sales throughout the United States.

Key Contact:
Mr. Jim Stephanopoulos

Salary minimum: $40,000

Functions: General Mgmt.

Industries: Food, Bev., Tobacco, Hospitality, Restaurants, Communications, Telecoms, Environmental Svcs., Software, Database SW, Development SW, Doc. Mgmt., Production SW, Mfg. SW, Marketing SW, Healthcare, Hospitals, Physical Therapy

Ziptekk
19672 Stevens Creek Blvd #100
Cupertino, CA 95014
(408) 376-3990
Fax: (408) 376-3995
Email: sal@ziptekk.com
Web: www.ziptekk.com

Description: We are an executive search firm specializing in the placement of software/hardware engineers and developers in Silicon Valley/Northern California.

Key Contact - Specialty:
Mr. Sal Pena, Director - *Software developers*

Functions: Generalist

Industries: E-commerce, Digital, Wireless, Fiber Optic, Network Infrastructure, Software, Database SW, Networking, Comm. SW

ZSA Legal Recruitment

20 Richmond St E Ste 315
Toronto, ON M5C 2R9
Canada
(416) 368-2051
Fax: (416) 368-5699
Email: csweeney@zsa.ca
Web: www.zsa.ca

Description: We are Canada's legal recruitment firm. We introduced high-end recruitment techniques into the Canadian legal marketplace and have experienced unparalleled success. We now have offices across the country staffed by former practicing lawyers, law clerks, and human relations specialists, all focused on their particular area of expertise. We offer the only national database of lawyers, law clerks, and legal support staff in existence. We assist law firms, large and small, as well as corporations.

Key Contact - Specialty:
Mr. Christopher Sweeney, President - *Legal*
Mr. Warren Bongard, Vice President - *Legal*
Ms. Susan Ann Kennedy, Senior Consultant - *Legal*
Ms. Nancie Lataille, Consultant - *Legal*
Ms. Sheila Hepworth, Consultant - *Legal*

Salary minimum: $50,000

Functions: Generalist, Legal, M&A, Attorneys, Paralegals

Industries: Generalist, Invest. Banking, Legal, New Media

Branches:
250 6th Ave SW Ste 1200
Calgary, AB T2P 3H7
Canada
(403) 205-3444
Fax: (403) 205-3428
Email: caroline@zsa.ca
Key Contact - Specialty:
Ms. Caroline Carnerie, Manager - *Legal*
Ms. Shannon Quinney, Consultant - *Legal support*

1055 W Hastings St Ste 300
Vancouver, BC V6E 2E9
Canada
(604) 681-0706
Fax: (604) 681-0566
Email: cshaw@zsa.ca
Key Contact - Specialty:
Ms. Catherine Shaw, Managing Consultant - *Legal*
Ms. Stephanie Hacksel, Consultant - *Legal*

1200 McGill College Ave Ste 1100
Montreal, QC H3B 4G7
Canada
(514) 390-2300
Fax: (514) 390-2320
Email: chaney@zsa.ca
Key Contact - Specialty:
Ms. Caroline Haney, Managing Consultant - *Legal*
Ms. Lucie Cote, Consultant - *Legal*

Zymac Inc

46B Nashua Rd Ste 8B
Londonderry, NH 03053
(603) 537-0400
Fax: (603) 537-0114
Email: cdavidson@zymac.com
Web: www.zymac.com

Description: We are a nationwide technical and executive search firm, specializing in the telecommunications, datacommunications, semiconductor and system design industries and technologies.

Key Contact - Specialty:
Mr. Bob MacLeod, President - *Data communication, telecommunication, semiconductor, electronic design automation*

Salary minimum: $80,000

Functions: Generalist, Senior Mgmt., Middle Mgmt., Mktg. Mgmt., Sales Mgmt., CFO's, Engineering

Industries: Generalist, Computer Equip., Telecoms, Software

Index by Functions

Firms with (R) are from the Retainer Section.
Firms with (C) are from the Contingency Section.

Basis of Functions Classification

This proprietary classification system was developed by Kennedy Information.

00.0	**GENERALIST**
01.0	**GENERAL MANAGEMENT**
01.1	Directors
01.2	Senior management (*e.g. CEO, COO, President, General Manager*)
01.3	Middle management
01.4	Administrative services
01.5	Legal
02.0	**MANUFACTURING**
02.1	Product development
02.2	Production engineering, planning, scheduling & control
02.3	Automation, robotics
02.4	Plant management
02.5	Quality
02.6	Productivity
03.0	**MATERIALS MANAGEMENT**
03.1	Purchasing, inventory management
03.2	Materials & requirement planning
03.3	Physical distribution, traffic & transportation, logistics
03.4	Packaging
04.0	**MEDICAL/HEALTHCARE**
04.1	Physicians
04.2	Nurses
04.3	Allied health (*e.g. chiropractors, therapists, psychologists*)
04.4	Administration
05.0	**SALES & MARKETING**
05.1	Advertising, sales promotion
05.2	Marketing & product research
05.3	Marketing management
05.4	Sales & sales management
05.5	Direct mail, marketing, telemarketing
05.6	Customer service
05.7	Public relations

06.0	**HUMAN RESOURCE MANAGEMENT**
06.1	Benefits, compensation planning
06.2	Personnel selection, placement & records
06.3	Training
07.0	**FINANCE & ACCOUNTING**
07.1	CFO's
07.2	Budgeting, cost controls
07.3	Cash management, financing & management of funds, portfolios
07.4	Credit & collection
07.5	Taxes
07.6	Mergers & acquisitions
07.7	Risk management
08.0	**INFORMATION TECHNOLOGY**
08.1	MIS management (*e.g. CIO, VP-MIS*)
08.2	Systems analysis & design
08.3	Systems development / programming
08.4	Systems integration / implementation
08.5	Systems support
08.6	Network administration
08.7	Database administration
09.0	**RESEARCH & DEVELOPMENT/SCIENTISTS**
10.0	**ENGINEERING**
11.0	**SPECIALIZED SERVICES**
11.1	Management consultants
11.2	Minorities
11.3	Fund-raisers & other non-profit services
11.4	Environmentalists
11.5	Architects
11.6	Technicians
11.7	Attorneys
11.8	Graphic artists, designers
11.9	Paralegals
12.0	**INTERNATIONAL**

00.0 GENERALIST

(R) = Retainer; (C) = Contingency

FUNCTIONS

(R) = Retainer; (C) = Contingency

FUNCTIONS

FUNCTIONS

(R) = Retainer; (C) = Contingency

FUNCTIONS

(R) = Retainer; (C) = Contingency

FUNCTIONS

FUNCTIONS

(R) = Retainer; (C) = Contingency

01.0 GENERAL MANAGEMENT

FUNCTIONS

(R) = Retainer; (C) = Contingency

FUNCTIONS

(R) = Retainer; (C) = Contingency

01.1 Directors

(R) = Retainer; (C) = Contingency

01.2 Senior management (e.g. CEO, COO, President)

FUNCTIONS

FUNCTIONS

FUNCTIONS

01.3 Middle management

(R) = Retainer; (C) = Contingency

FUNCTIONS

FUNCTIONS

(R) = Retainer; (C) = Contingency

FUNCTIONS

01.4 Administrative services

01.5 Legal

02.0 MANUFACTURING

FUNCTIONS

FUNCTIONS

(R) = Retainer; (C) = Contingency

FUNCTIONS

02.1 Product development

02.2 Production engineering, planning, scheduling & control

FUNCTIONS

02.3 Automation, robotics

FUNCTIONS

02.5 Quality

FUNCTIONS

(R) = Retainer; (C) = Contingency

02.6 Productivity

03.0 MATERIALS MANAGEMENT

FUNCTIONS

(R) = Retainer; (C) = Contingency

03.1 Purchasing, inventory management

FUNCTIONS

03.2 Materials & requirement planning

03.3 Physical distribution, traffic & transportation, logistics

03.4 Packaging

04.1 Physicians

04.4 Administration

05.0 SALES & MARKETING

FUNCTIONS

FUNCTIONS

(R) = Retainer; (C) = Contingency

FUNCTIONS

(R) = Retainer; (C) = Contingency

05.1 Advertising, sales promotion

05.2 Marketing & product research

FUNCTIONS

05.3 Marketing management

(R) = Retainer; (C) = Contingency

FUNCTIONS

FUNCTIONS

(R) = Retainer; (C) = Contingency

05.4 Sales & sales management

FUNCTIONS

(R) = Retainer; (C) = Contingency

FUNCTIONS

(R) = Retainer; (C) = Contingency

05.5 Direct mail, marketing, telemarketing

05.6 Customer service

05.7 Public relations

FUNCTIONS

06.0 HUMAN RESOURCE MANAGEMENT

FUNCTIONS

(R) = Retainer; (C) = Contingency

FUNCTIONS

06.1 Benefits, compensation planning

06.2 Personnel selection, placement & records

06.3 Training

FUNCTIONS

07.0 FINANCE & ACCOUNTING

(R) = Retainer; (C) = Contingency

FUNCTIONS

(R) = Retainer; (C) = Contingency

07.1 CFO's

FUNCTIONS

(R) = Retainer; (C) = Contingency

07.2 Budgeting, cost controls

07.3 Cash management, financing & management of funds, portfolios

07.4 Credit & collection

FUNCTIONS

07.5 Taxes

07.6 Mergers & acquisitions

07.7 Risk management

08.0 INFORMATION TECHNOLOGY

FUNCTIONS

FUNCTIONS

FUNCTIONS

08.1 MIS management (e.g. CIO, VP-MIS)

FUNCTIONS

(R) = Retainer; (C) = Contingency

08.2 Systems analysis & design

FUNCTIONS

08.3 Systems development / programming

FUNCTIONS

(R) = Retainer; (C) = Contingency

08.4 Systems integration / implementation

FUNCTIONS

(R) = Retainer; (C) = Contingency

08.5 Systems support

08.6 Network administration

FUNCTIONS

08.7 Database administration

FUNCTIONS

09.0 RESEARCH & DEVELOPMENT/SCIENTISTS

FUNCTIONS

10.0 ENGINEERING

FUNCTIONS

(R) = Retainer; (C) = Contingency

FUNCTIONS

(R) = Retainer; (C) = Contingency

11.0 SPECIALIZED SERVICES

FUNCTIONS

11.1 Management consultants

11.2 Minorities

11.3 Fund-raisers & other non-profit services

11.4 Environmentalists

FUNCTIONS

11.8 Graphic artists, designers

11.9 Paralegals

12.0 INTERNATIONAL

FUNCTIONS

Firms with (R) are from the Retainer Section.
Firms with (C) are from the Contingency Section.

Basis of Industries Classification

This proprietary classification system was developed by Kennedy Information.

0.00	**Generalist**	H.13	Venture Cap	N.00	**Environmental Svcs**	
		H.14	Misc Financial	N.10	Haz Waste	
A.00	**Agri, Forestry, Mining**					
		I.00	**Services**	P.00	**Aerospace**	
B.00	**Energy, Utilities**	I.10	Non-profits			
		I.11	Higher Ed	Q.00	**Packaging**	
C.00	**Construction**	I.12	Pharm Svcs			
		I.13	Legal	R.00	**Insurance**	
D.00	**Manufacturing**	I.14	Accounting			
D.10	Food, Bev, Tobacco	I.15	Equip Svcs	S.00	**Real Estate**	
D.11	Textiles, Apparel	I.16	Mgmt Consulting			
D.12	Lumber, Furniture	I.17	HR Services	T.00	**Software**	
D.13	Paper	I.18	Law Enforcement	T.10	Accounting	
D.14	Printing	I.19	E-commerce	T.11	Database	
D.15	Chemicals	I.20	IT Implementation	T.12	Development	
D.16	Soap, Perf, Cosmtcs	I.21	PSA/ASP	T.13	Document Mgmt, Production	
D.17	Drugs Mfg			T.14	Entertainment	
D.18	Medical Devices	J.00	**Hospitality**	T.15	ERP	
D.19	Plastics, Rubber	J.10	Hotels, Resorts, Clubs	T.16	Human Resource	
D.20	Paints, Petro Products	J.11	Restaurants	T.17	Industry specific	
D.21	Leather, Stone, Glass	J.12	Entertainment	T.18	Manufacturing	
D.22	Metal Products	J.13	Recreation	T.19	Marketing	
D.23	Machine, Appliance			T.20	Networking, Communications	
D.24	Motor Vehicles	K.00	**Media**	T.21	Security	
D.25	Computer Equip	K.10	Advertising	T.22	System	
D.26	Consumer Elect	K.11	Publishing	T.23	Training	
D.27	Test, Measure Equip	K.12	New Media			
D.28	Misc Mfg	K.13	Broadcast, Film	U.00	**Biotech**	
D.29	Electronic, Electrical					
	Components	L.00	**Communications**	V.00	**Healthcare**	
		L.10	Telecoms	V.10	Hospitals	
E.00	**Transportation**	L.11	Call centers	V.11	Long-term Care	
		L.12	Telephony	V.12	Dental	
F.00	**Wholesale**	L.13	Digital	V.13	Physical Therapy	
		L.14	Wireless	V.14	Occupational Therapy	
G.00	**Retail**	L.15	Fiber Optic	V.15	Women's	
		L.16	Network Infrastructure			
H.00	**Finance**			W.00	**Non-classifiable**	
H.10	Banking	M.00	**Government**			
H.11	Invest Banking	M.10	Defense			
H.12	Brokers					

0.00 GENERALIST

INDUSTRIES

INDUSTRIES

INDUSTRIES

(R) = Retainer; (C) = Contingency

INDUSTRIES

(R) = Retainer; (C) = Contingency

INDUSTRIES

(R) = Retainer; (C) = Contingency

INDUSTRIES

INDUSTRIES

A.00 AGRICULTURE, FORESTRY, FISHING, MINING

B.00 ENERGY/UTILITIES

INDUSTRIES

C.00 CONSTRUCTION

INDUSTRIES

D.00 MANUFACTURING

INDUSTRIES

INDUSTRIES

INDUSTRIES

D.10 Food, beverage, tobacco & kindred products

D.11 Textile, apparel, related products

INDUSTRIES

D.12 Lumber, wood, furniture, fixtures

D.13 Paper & allied products

D.14 Printing & allied industry

D.15 Chemicals & allied products

INDUSTRIES

(R) = Retainer; (C) = Contingency

D.16 Soap, perfume, cosmetics

INDUSTRIES

D.17 Drugs, pharmaceuticals

INDUSTRIES

(R) = Retainer; (C) = Contingency

D.18 Medical devices & instruments

INDUSTRIES

D.19 Plastics, rubber products

INDUSTRIES

D.20 Paints, allied products, petroleum products

INDUSTRIES

D.21 Leather, stone, glass, concrete, clay products

D.22 Primary & fabricated metal products

(R) = Retainer; (C) = Contingency

D.23 Industrial machinery & consumer appliances

D.24 Transportation equipment (e.g. automobiles)

INDUSTRIES

D.25 Computer equipment & components

(R) = Retainer; (C) = Contingency

INDUSTRIES

D.26 Consumer electronics

INDUSTRIES

D.27 Test & measurement equipment

(R) = Retainer; (C) = Contingency

INDUSTRIES

D.28 Miscellaneous manufacturing industries

INDUSTRIES

(R) = Retainer; (C) = Contingency

D.29 Electronic/electrical components

E.00 TRANSPORTATION

INDUSTRIES

F.00 WHOLESALE TRADE

INDUSTRIES

(R) = Retainer; (C) = Contingency

INDUSTRIES

H.00 FINANCE

INDUSTRIES

(R) = Retainer; (C) = Contingency

(R) = Retainer; (C) = Contingency

INDUSTRIES

H.10 Commercial banking

INDUSTRIES

(R) = Retainer; (C) = Contingency

H.11 Investment banking

INDUSTRIES

(R) = Retainer; (C) = Contingency

H.12 Securities & commodities brokers

H.13 Venture capital

INDUSTRIES

H.14 Other financial services

INDUSTRIES

INDUSTRIES

(R) = Retainer; (C) = Contingency

I.10 Non-profits, museums, galleries, music/arts, libraries, information services, membership

I.11 Higher education

INDUSTRIES

I.12 Pharmaceutical (other than manufacturing)

I.13 Legal

I.14 Accounting, miscellaneous business services

INDUSTRIES

I.15 Equipment services (including leasing)

I.16 Management consulting

INDUSTRIES

(R) = Retainer; (C) = Contingency

INDUSTRIES

I.17 Human resource services

INDUSTRIES

(R) = Retainer; (C) = Contingency

I.18 Law enforcement, security

I.19 E-commerce

INDUSTRIES

I.20 IT implementation

I.21 Professional services automation/application services providers

J.00 HOSPITALITY

INDUSTRIES

J.10 Hotels, resorts, clubs

J.11 Restaurants, food & beverage services

J.12 Entertainment, leisure, amusement

J.13 Recreation, sports, travel

K.00 MEDIA

INDUSTRIES

(R) = Retainer; (C) = Contingency

K.10 Advertising, public relations

INDUSTRIES

K.12 New media (e.g. Internet, multimedia)

INDUSTRIES

K.13 TV, cable, motion pictures, video, radio

L.00 COMMUNICATIONS

INDUSTRIES

(R) = Retainer; (C) = Contingency

L.10 Telephone, telecommunications

INDUSTRIES

INDUSTRIES

(R) = Retainer; (C) = Contingency

L.11 Call centers

L.12 Telephony

L.13 Digital

INDUSTRIES

(R) = Retainer; (C) = Contingency

L.14 Wireless

L.15 Fiber optic

INDUSTRIES

M.00 PUBLIC ADMINISTRATION, GOVERNMENT

M.10 Defense

INDUSTRIES

P.00 AEROSPACE

INDUSTRIES

Q.00 PACKAGING

INDUSTRIES

R.00 INSURANCE

INDUSTRIES

S.00 REAL ESTATE

INDUSTRIES

T.00 SOFTWARE

INDUSTRIES

(R) = Retainer; (C) = Contingency

INDUSTRIES

(R) = Retainer; (C) = Contingency

INDUSTRIES

T.10 Accounting

T.11 Database

INDUSTRIES

T.12 Development

T.13 Document management, production

T.14 Entertainment

T.15 Enterprise resource planning

T.16 Human resource

T.17 Industry specific

T.18 Manufacturing

INDUSTRIES

T.19 Marketing

T.20 Networking, communications

T.21 Security

INDUSTRIES

T.22 System

T.23 Training

U.00 BIOTECH & GENETIC ENGINEERING

INDUSTRIES

INDUSTRIES

V.00 HEALTHCARE

INDUSTRIES

INDUSTRIES

(R) = Retainer; (C) = Contingency

V.10 Hospitals

V.11 Long-term care

V.12 Dental

V.13 Physical therapy

V.14 Occupational therapy

V.15 Women's

W.00 NON-CLASSIFIABLE INDUSTRIES

INDUSTRIES

Recruiter Specialties Index

Firms with (R) are from the Retainer Section.
Firms with (C) are from the Contingency Section.

This is a relatively new index allowing individuals to pinpoint their particular area of specialization in addition or in conjunction with what their firms have selected. It is a particularly helpful tool both for identifying individuals within the larger firms and when your need is very specific.

The categories were created by the recruiters themselves, without the constraints of established (but limited) indexes such as the Standard Industrial Classification. While this enabled us to collect deep and detailed data, it proved an ambitious task to corral into a logical index. We present it largely as it was collected; hence broad headings with several hundred entries appearing next to unique, detailed ones with but a single entry.

To maximize the usefulness of this indexing approach, we encourage you to scan the master list with as many words as you can associate with your need. For example, Hospitality would produce a long list, but searches on bakery, food, beverage, casinos, clubs, food service, hotels, restaurants and tourism might get you closer to a specific breakout of hospitality.

In the index you will find the recruiter's name, his/her firm, whether firm operates on R (retainer) or C (contingency) basis, office location by state, and page number. Please note minor categories are listed alphabetically under their major headings (for example: computer networking is listed under networking within computers).

Building products
Business development
Business to Business
Cabinetry
Cable
Call centers
Capital
    Markets
Capital goods
Carbides
Cardiovascular
Casinos
CATV
Cellular
Cement/concrete
CEOs
Ceramics
CFOs
Change management
Chemical
CIOs
Circulation management
Civil
Clerical
Client/server
Clinical
Closely-held business
Club
Coatings
Communications
Compensation
Compliance
Components
Composites
Compounds
Computer
    Hardware
Computers
    Automation
    Engineering
    Executives
    Manufacturing
    Marketing
    Networking
    Sales
    Science
    Services
    Support
Confectionery
Conference centers
Construction
Consulting

Consumer
    Durables
    General
    Goods
    Marketing
    Packaged goods
    Products
    Promotions
Controllers
Convenience stores
Convention centers
Convergence
Converting
COOs
Copiers
Corporate communication
Cosmetics
Creative
Credit
Credit cards
CRM
Cruise management
CTOs
Culinary
Customer Retention
Customer services
Dairy
Database
    Administration
    Analysts
Defense
Dental
Derivatives
Design
Diagnostics
Dialysis
Diecast
Digital
Direct marketing
Dirt
Distribution
Diversity
Domestic
Doors
E-Business
Economic development
Economics
EDP
Education
    Higher
Electrical
Electromechanical
Electron beam
electronic
Electronic commerce
Electronics
Energy
Engineering

Entertainment
Environmental
Equipment
Equity
Ergonomics
ERP
Escrow
Estates
Estimators
Euro-Conversion
Event planning
Executives
Experts
Exploration
Extrusion
Fabrication
Facilities engineering
Facility
Factories
    Automation
Family business
Fashion
Females
Fiber-optics
Film
Filtration
Finance
Financial
    Management
Financial services
Fire protection
Firmware
Fixtures
Flat panel display
Flexographic printing
Floriculture
Fluid handling
Food
    Flavors
Food service
Footwear
Forest industry
Forest products
Fortune plus
Foundries
Fragrances
Franchises
Franchising
Fraternal groups
Freight
Fundraising
Furniture
Fuzzy logic
Galleries
Gaming
Gas
Gay/lesbian
General management

Genetics
Genomics
Geology
Geotechnical
Gifts
Giftware
Glass
Golf
Government
GPS
Graphics
Groceries
Hardlines
Hardware
Health
    Insurance
    Safety
Healthcare
    Administration
Heavy industry
High energy physics
High purity water
High technology
Highways
Hispanic
HMOs
Home
    Fashion
Home and building controls
Home health
Horticulture
Hospital
    Administration
Hospitality
Hotels
Housewares
Human resources
HVAC
Imaging
Industrial
    Services
    Technology
Information
Information service
Ink
Instrumentation
Insurance
    Casualty
    Claims
    Life
Intellectual property
Interactive
Interim
Interior design
International
Internet
Internetworking
Intranet

Investment
Investment management
Investor relations
IPP
IS
ISO 9000
IT
Jewelry
Juvenile products
Labor
Laboratory
Landscaping
Leasing
Legal
    Attorneys
    Lawyers
    Right of way
Leisure
Lending
Libraries
Licensing
Life science
Linux
Loans
Locum Tenen
Logistics
Long term care
    Control
    Prevention
Lotus Notes
Lubricants
Lumber
Luxury goods
Machine tools
Machinery
Machining
Magazine
Main drivers
Maintenance
Managed care
Management
Management consulting
Manufacturing
    General
    Management
Marine
Market research
Marketing
    Database
Materials
    Handling
    Management
Mathematics
MBAs
Meat
Mechanical
Media

Medical
    Devices
    Sales
Medical technology
Medicine
Merchandising
Mergers & acquisitions
Metals
Micro brew
Microwave
Middle management
Military
Millwork
Mineral processing
Mining
Minorities
MIS
Mobile equipment
Molding
    Blown
    Injection
Multimedia
Museums
Mutual funds
Natural resources
Networking
Neural networks
Neuroscience
New media
Noise control
Non-profit
Nuclear power
Nursing
Nursing   Practitioners
Nutraceuticals
Nutrition
Occupational therapy
Off shore
Office
    Administration
    Products
    Services
    Support
Oil
On-line
Operations
    Management
Optics
Oracle
Organizational development
Orthopedics
OTC
Packaging
    Food
Paint
Paper
PeopleSoft
Peripherals

Pet food
Petrochemical
Pharmaceutical
PHDs
Philanthropy
Photonics
Physical therapy
Physicians
    Administration
    Assistants
    Executives
Physicists
Pipe & tube
Plant
Plant
    Management
Plastics
Plumbing
Plywood
Polymers
Polyurethane
Portfolio management
Poultry
Power
Presidents
Printing
Private equity
Process
    Equipment
Process control
Procurement
Produce
Product development
Product management
Production
Professional services
Programming
    C
    Object oriented
Property management
Prosthetic devices
Psychology
Public affairs
Public relations
Public sector
Publishing
Pulp
Pumps
Purchasing
Quality
Quantitative methods
Radio
Radiology
Railroad
Real estate

Recreational vehicles
Recreations
Recruiters
Recycling
Refineries
Refining
Refrigeration
Regulated Industries
Regulatory
Rehabilitation
Research
Research & development
Resins
Resorts
Respiratory therapy
Restaurants
Retail
Retirement housing
Risk management
Robotics
Rubber
Safety
Sales
Sales
    Management
Sales & marketing
SAP
Satellites
Sawmill
SCADA
Science
Security
Semiconductors
Senior management
Service industry
Shopping centers
Softline
Software
Solid waste
Sonet
Speech
Sports
Staffing
Stairs
Stamping
Start-Up companies
Statisticians
Steel
Stockbrokers
Strategic Planning
Superconductivity
Supermarkets
Suppliers
Supply
Surety

Surgery
Surgical
Sybase
Systems
    Analysts
    Integration
Tax
Technology
Telecommunications
Telemarketing
Telephony
Television
Temperature control
Temporary
Test
Textiles
Thermoforming
Tooling
Tourism
Toxicology
Toys
Trading
Traffic
Training
Transportation
Travel
Treasury
Trust
Tubular products
Ultrasound
Underwriting
Unix
Utilities
Valves
Van conversion
Venture capital
Vice president
Video conferencing
Video games
Virtual reality
Vision
VSAT
Wall Street
WANs
Watches
Water
Wholesale
Window
Wireless
Women
Wood
Worldwide
Worldwide web

SPECIALTIES

Big 5

Bookkeeping

Public

Accounting & finance

SPECIALTIES

Advertising

SPECIALTIES

Aerospace

Agribusiness/agriculture

Aluminum

Amusement Parks

Analysts

Anesthesia

Animation

Annuities

Apparel

Appliances

SPECIALTIES

Automation

Automotive

Aviation

SPECIALTIES

SPECIALTIES

Beverages

Bilingual

Biology

Biomedical

Biometrics

Biostatistics

Biotechnology

Board search

SPECIALTIES

Bond underwriting

Brand management

Bridges

Broadband

Broadcasting

Brokerage

BSME

Building products

Business development

Business to Business

Cabinetry

Cable

Call centers

Capital

Markets

Capital goods

Carbides

Cardiovascular

Casinos

CATV

Cellular

Cement/concrete

CEOs

SPECIALTIES

Ceramics

CFOs

Change management

Chemical

CIOs

Circulation management

Civil

Clerical

Client/server

SPECIALTIES

Clinical

Closely-held business

Club

Coatings

Communications

Pencarski, Robert, Computer Technology
Staffing LLC (C) 292
Perlman, Willa, The Cheyenne Group (R) 34
Petty, Scott, Spencer Stuart (R) 182
Piché, Jérôme, Spencer Stuart (R) 182
Podolsky, Samuel, Spencer Stuart (R) 182
Price, Terry W., Spencer Stuart (R) 182
Pryor, Carrie, Spencer Stuart (R) 182
Reed, Charlene, Spencer Stuart (R) 181
Reynolds, Smooch S., The Repovich-Reynolds
Group (TRRG Inc) (R) 161
Robin, Stephen, Grant Cooper & Associates
Inc (R) 79
Robinson, Conchita, Spencer Stuart (R) 182
Rosenthal, Susan, S H Jacobs & Associates Inc
(C) 409
Rudy, Sharon, Spencer Stuart (R) 182
Sabio, Kathy, The Brentwood Group Inc (R) 24
Salloway, Andrew N., A N Salloway Executive
Search & Consulting LLC (C) 586
Scanlan, Tom, Spencer Stuart (R) 182
Schwartz, Stephen D., MRI of Gramercy (C) 466
Seclow, Tom, Spencer Stuart (R) 181
Sheth, Pinakini, Software Resource
Consultants (C) 615
Sheweloff, William J., McCray, Shriver,
Eckdahl & Associates Inc (R) 128
Shulman, Fran, Asset Resource Inc (C) 244
Sklar, Patricia, Patricia Sklar & Associates Ltd
(C) 604
Smith, Rick, Spencer Stuart (R) 182
Spero, Esq., Joseph B., DPSI Medical (C) 317
Spring, Dennis, Spring Associates Inc (R) 183
Starling, Dick, ProNet Inc (C) 544
Stevens, Martin, Martin Stevens Tamaren &
Associates Inc (R) 190
Stewart, Cathi, The Stewart Group (C) 627
Sweet, Robert J., Atlanta Executive Partners
Inc (R) 10
Tarzian, Wendy, Tarzian Search Consultants
Inc (R) 191
Thompson, Tony, Spencer Stuart (R) 182
Vennat, Manon, Spencer Stuart (R) 182
Virgili, Franca, The Cheyenne Group (R) 34
von Ranson, Joel, Spencer Stuart (R) 182
von Winckler, Beverly, Beverly von Winckler
& Associates (C) 653
Wallace, Kate, Whittlesey & Associates Inc
(R) 204
Ward, James M., The Ward Group (R) 200
Ware, John, Spencer Stuart (R) 181
Wasp, Jr., Warren T., WTW Associates Inc (R) . 209
Webster, Larry, Technology Management
Partners (R) 192
White, Jonathan O., Spencer Stuart (R) 181
Wild, Lois, S H Jacobs & Associates Inc (C) 409
Wills, James C., Wills Consulting Associates
Inc (R) 205
Wood, John, Spencer Stuart (R) 182
Wyatt, James R., Wyatt & Jaffe (R) 209
Wyman, Sue, Jivaro Group (C) 411
Young, Rich, Chaloner Associates Inc (R) 34

Compensation

Atkinson, Patrick J., Waterford Executive
Group Ltd (C) 656
Boscacci, Gene, IR Search (R) 100
Daudt, Jack, Triad Consultants Inc (C) 645
Hughes, R. Kevin, Handy Associates Corp (R) 83
Manning, Dianne, Manning Lloyd Associates
Ltd (C) 482
Rivera-Lopez, Elba, Kenexa (R) 106

Rodebaugh, Jr., Thomas L., MRI of Lancaster
(C) 472

Compliance

Bezold, Joe, MRI of The Baltimore
Washington Corridor (C) 461
Bunker, Ralph, MRI of San Luis Obispo (C) 449
Dawson, Mary, Allard Associates Inc (C) 230
Gaches, Martha, Don Neal & Associates (C) 508
Holohan, Jr., Barth A., Holohan Group Ltd (R) ... 92
Kaufmann, Esq., Anita D., A-K-A (Anita
Kaufmann Associates) (C) 216
Langley, Dianna, MRI of High Point-North (C) .. 468
Messer, Jonathan S., SearchAmerica Inc (C) 598
Neal, Don, Don Neal & Associates (C) 508
Phillips, Steve, Search & Placement Int'l (C) 594

Components

Bentley, Mark A., Kraemer, Bentley, Wong &
Sermone (R) 111
Kraemer, Katherine R., Kraemer, Bentley,
Wong & Sermone (R) 111
Sermone, Ed E., Kraemer, Bentley, Wong &
Sermone (R) 111
Wong, Walter W., Kraemer, Bentley, Wong &
Sermone (R) 111

Composites

Curci, Ronald L., ARI Int'l (R) 8
Hiller, Arnie, US Search LLC (C) 650

Compounds

Palyo, Alex, AP Associates (APA) (C) 239
Richards, R. Glenn, Executive Directions (R) 64

Computer

Hardware

Arredondo, Fred, SpectraWest (C) 618
Bakken, Roger, J Rodgers & Associates (C) 563
Berger, Joel, Midas Management Inc (C) 496
Campbell, Brian H., Venpro Consulting Inc (C) .. 651
Cleary, Jeanne, The Rossi Search Group (C) 565
Lewis, Marc, Christian & Timbers (R) 35
Lindsley, Carolyn, Strategic Resources (C) 628
Martin, Robert A., Phoenix Partners Inc (R) 530
McFadden, James, PSP Agency (C) 546
Rystrom, Sally A., US-Recruiters.com (C) 650
Shue, Colleen, Bennett Search & Consulting
Company Inc (R) 16
Starling, Dick, ProNet Inc (C) 544
Travis, Michael J., Travis & Company Inc (R) 195
Zeif, Kenneth, Newport Management (C) 510
Zeiger, David Barkin, Zeiger Associates LLC
(C) 669
Zeiger, Stephen A., Zeiger Associates LLC (C) .. 669

Computers

Alexander, Gary, Mark Christian & Associates
Inc (C) 284
Alexander, Myra, Mark Christian & Associates
Inc (C) 284
Bach, Donald, Future Employment Service Inc
(C) 364
Barkan, Stacey, Current Resource Group Inc
(C) 304
Baron, Sheldon S., Sales Consultants of
Nashua-Manchester (C) 580
Berger, Jay, Pathway Executive Search Inc (C) .. 524
Bradley, Mark, The Landstone Group (R) 113

Byrne, Colm, Aran Rock (C) 241
Cadmus, Stephen T., Cadmus Int'l (R) 27
Caldwell, Kate, Caldwell Legal Recruiting
Consultants (C) 271
Cali, Ronald, Royce Ashland Group Inc (C) 567
Cipriani, Jr., Jim, Systems Personnel Inc (C) 632
Cipriani, Sr., Jim, Systems Personnel Inc (C) 632
Clarke, Marcia, Sales Consultants of New York
City (C) 572
Clinton, Omari, Clinton, Charles, Wise &
Company (C) 287
Collins, Philip M., Collins & Associates (C) 289
Credidio, Thomas J., The DataFinders Group
Inc (C) 308
Doherty, Leonard J., L J Doherty & Associates
(R) 55
Drohan, Robert, American Heritage Group Inc
(C) 234
Fernow, Charles S., Fernow Associates (C) 346
Fisher, Mel V., Fisher Group (R) 68
Franzen, Tracy A., Ross Personnel Consultants
Inc (C) 564
Fraser, William, Windsor Consultants Inc (C) 662
Frazer, Mel, Mel Frazer Consultant (C) 363
Fredrick, Amanda, Chaves & Associates (C) 283
Frishman, Robert, Greenwich Search Partners
LLC (C) 373
Galka, John, Huntley Associates Inc (C) 399
Gebler, Stephen, Systems Research Group (C) ... 632
Gurney, Darrell W., A Permanent Success Nat'l
Career/Search Partners (C) 216
Hall, John, Synergy Systems (C) 631
Hall, Scott, Advancement Inc (C) 226
Halstead, Joseph, Kuhn Med-Tech Inc (C) 425
Hills, Glen, G H Enterprises (C) 365
Holliday, John, American Heritage Group Inc
(C) 234
Israel, Jake, Chaves & Associates (C) 283
Jackson, Jennifer, Jackson Resources (R) 100
Johnson, Jennifer, JenKim Int'l Ltd Inc (C) 410
Jones, M. Susan, Greenwich Search Partners
LLC (C) 373
Kahn, Gale, FPC of Boulder (C) 354
Karkow, Drew, David Weinfeld Group (C) 657
Kenebrew, Demond, Tech/Data Recruiters Inc
(C) 636
Kishun, Randy, Merrill Lynch & Company (R) 132
Leofsky, Peter J., Dapexs Consultants Inc (C) ... 307
Lipsky, Marla J., Lipsky Group Inc (R) 119
Mack, Linda, Partners in Recruiting (C) 523
Martin, Judy R., J Martin & Associates (R) 126
Mellos, James S., Ki Technologies Inc
Executive Search Div (C) 422
Mitchell, Mike, Chaves & Associates (C) 283
Nasatir, Richard, Select Search (C) 599
Norton, Robert W., JenKim Int'l Ltd Inc (C) 410
Parisi, Frank, Worlco Computer Resources Inc
(C) 665
Park, Tammy, Robert Larned Associates Inc
(C) 428
Prok, Daniel, Dunhill Professional Search of
Los Angeles (C) 320
Reichardt, Karl J., R & K Associates Inc (C) 549
Richards, David P., Insight Personnel Group
Inc (C) 402
Richer, Joyce Eidenberg, W F Richer
Associates Inc (R) 164
Richer, William F., W F Richer Associates Inc
(R) 164
Riley, Gil, Irvine Search Partners (C) 406
Rogers, Roc, Dynamic Computer Consultants
Inc (C) 325
Sajankila, Raj, Princetec Inc (C) 538
Salottolo, Al, Tactical Alternatives (R) 190

SPECIALTIES

Consulting

SPECIALTIES

Consumer

Durables

General

Goods

Marketing

Packaged goods

Products

Promotions

Controllers

SPECIALTIES

Huntley, David E., Huntley Associates Inc (C)... *399*
Lombard, Carole, MRI of The Baltimore
    Washington Corridor (C)................................ *461*
Marks, Dan, MRI of Moreland Hills (C)............. *470*
Sennett, Lynn, 1 to1 Executive Search (R) *1*
Swami, Pad N., Fortuna Technologies Inc (C)..... *352*
Tuttle, Tyler, Raycor Search (R)........................ *159*
Vairo, Len, Christian & Timbers (R) *36*
Voghel, Karen, 1 to1 Executive Search (R) *1*

Cruise management

Rutherford, Frank H., Gaming Consultants Inc
    (R).. *74*
Stafford, Susan P., Hospitality Int'l (C)............... *394*

CTOs

Dent, Amy, Cornell Group Int'l Consulting Inc
    (R) *43*
Heffelfinger, Thomas V., Heffelfinger
    Associates Inc (R) *86*
King, Roger M., Raging Mouse (C)...................... *550*
McCarthy, Maureen, MRI of Fresno (C) *450*
Weidner, John, Cornell Group Int'l Consulting
    Inc (R) *43*

Culinary

Anthonoy, Michael, Search Pro Inc (C) *597*
Eagar, Brian, Search Int'l (R) *172*
Farhi, Vicky, Search Pro Inc (C)......................... *597*
Gasnier, Jack, Search Int'l (R) *173*
Reich, Joshua, The Alfus Group Inc (C) *230*
Stanley, John, Search Int'l (R) *172*

Customer services

Bates, Nina, Allard Associates Inc (C) *230*
Bencin, Richard L., Richard L Bencin &
    Associates (C) *254*
Brockett, Gail, Dunhill Professional Search of
    Rockport (C) *324*
Buggy, Linda, Bonnell Associates Ltd (R) *20*
Caroli, Connie, TeleManagement Search (C) *640*
Knox, Dave, APA Employment Agency Inc
    (C).. *239*
Martin, Rose, HeadhunterUSA.com (C) *383*
Romo, Angela, Sanderson Employment
    Service (C) *586*

Dairy

McLafferty, Tim, Focus Executive Search (C) ... *351*
Norris, John B., John B Norris & Associates
    Inc (C)... *512*
Schwiner, Jim, MRI of Milwaukee-North (C) *480*

Database

Bliss, Barbara P., Lamay Associates (R)............. *113*
Cotten, Cathey, MetaSearch Inc (C) *494*
Daugherty, Sue, Allard Associates Inc (C) *230*
Davis, Jeff, DataPro Personnel Consultants (C).. *308*
Dixon, Cynthia R., A la Carte Int'l Inc (R).............. *1*
Du Plooy, Grant, Tolfrey Group (C) *643*
Dyson, Steve, Technology Search Int'l (C) *638*
Fairlie, Suzanne F., ProSearch Inc (C)............... *545*
Giacalone, Lou, Allard Associates Inc (C) *230*
Lubin, Paul, Edelman & Associates (C).............. *328*
Mack, Linda, Partners in Recruiting (C) *523*
McCullough, Megan, Diedre Moire Corp Inc
    (C).. *498*
Miller, Harry, Equate Executive Search Inc (C).. *333*
Morris, Mary, Selectquest (C) *600*
Phelan, Richard, R E P & Associates Inc (C)...... *549*

Sennett, Lynn, 1 to1 Executive Search (R)............... *1*
Shindler, Stanley L., Franklin Int'l Search Inc
    (C).. *363*
Sirey, Don, Technology Search Int'l (C).............. *638*
Troy, Richard, Professional Computer
    Resources Inc (PCR) (C)................................ *540*
Walsh, Bob, Global Data Services Inc (R) *77*
Weiss, Cathy, C Weiss Associates Inc (C) *657*

Administration

Ciaramitaro, Paul, Corporate Search
    Consultants Inc (C) *298*
Gold, Dianne C., Professional Computer
    Resources Inc (PCR) (C)................................ *540*
Harrison, Harold M., InfoTech Search (C) *402*
Kapaun, Kevin, Emerging Technology
    Services Inc (C)... *331*
Milano, Denise, Joseph Associates Inc (C).......... *413*
Swami, Pad N., Fortuna Technologies Inc (C) *352*

Analysts

Kapaun, Kevin, Emerging Technology
    Services Inc (C)... *331*
Peragine, Ralph P., The Resource Group (R) *162*

Defense

Hansen, Ty E., Blake/Hansen Ltd (R) *19*
Heath, Jim, Southern Technical Recruiters (C)... *616*
Lockleer, Julia, Everett Career Management
    Consultants Inc (C) *335*
Waltz, Bruce, Ki Technologies Inc Executive
    Search Div (C) *422*

Dental

Berger, Jerry, ACC Consultants Inc (C) *217*
Chavez, Gloria, ACC Consultants Inc (C)............ *217*
DuBois, Jr., Joseph W., Horizon Medical
    Search of NH (C)... *394*
Esparza, Lisa, ACC Consultants Inc (C).............. *217*
Henry, Bruce, Bruce Henry Associates Inc (R) *88*
Hutchinson, Vicki, Snelling & Snelling Inc (C) .. *607*
King, Noelle Lea, National Staffing by Noelle
    & Associates (C).. *506*
Martino, LeeAnne, Barrett & Company Inc (C) .. *250*
Seebinger, Larry, ACC Consultants Inc (C) *217*
Seebinger, Virginia, ACC Consultants Inc (C).... *217*

Derivatives

Rountree, John, Lexington Software Inc (C) *431*

Design

Anderson, Gregory D., Anderson Industrial
    Associates Inc (C)... *237*
Aswell, Judy, MRI of San Marcos (C) *477*
Brockman, Trowby, Dan B Brockman (C).......... *266*
Buckley, Michael, High Tech Opportunities
    Inc (C) *390*
Burns-Noble, Cheryl, Design Profiles (C) *311*
Byrne, Mary Beth, M B Partners (R)................... *122*
Conroy, Daniel J., Michael Latas & Associates
    Inc (R) *115*
Cooper, Ron, High Tech Opportunities Inc (C) ... *390*
Cooper, Ross, High Tech Opportunities Inc (C).. *390*
Cooperson, Doug, Rice Cohen Int'l (R)............... *163*
Corazolla, Susan, Archer Resource Solutions
    Inc (C) *241*
Espinoza, Brisa, General Engineering
    Tectonics (C) *367*
Foster, Kathie, Michael Latas & Associates Inc
    (R).. *115*

Fry, Don, Dunhill Professional Search of
    Corpus Christi (C) *324*
Gregory, Ronald J., Michael Latas &
    Associates Inc (R) *115*
Grodsky, Janet, Stern Professional Search (C) *626*
Heacock, Barbara, B D Wallace & Associates
    (C).. *654*
Holland, Lee, Carnegie Resources Inc (C) *277*
Hosey, Debra, Pailin Group Professional
    Search Consultants (R) *145*
Hudson, Judy K., The Hudson Group (C) *396*
Huntley, David E., Huntley Associates Inc (C) ... *399*
Jesberg, Gary H., Michael Latas & Associates
    Inc (R) *115*
Kelly, Jack, Jack Kelly & Partners LLC (C) *417*
Klatch, Michael B., Michael Latas &
    Associates Inc (R) *115*
Leonard, William C., Michael Latas &
    Associates Inc (R) *115*
Munger, Donald, Berkshire Search Associates
    (C).. *256*
Murphy, Donald, Stevens, Valentine &
    McKeever (C) *185*
Natowitz, Robert, DeMatteo Associates (C) *311*
Palyo, Alex, AP Associates (APA) (C) *239*
Prutow, Jerry, The Barton Group Inc (C) *251*
Putiri, Vincent, Asheville Search & Consulting
    (C).. *243*
Rice, Gene, Rice Cohen Int'l (R)........................ *163*
Roda, Janet, Jack Kelly & Partners LLC (C)....... *417*
Rudich, Susan, Susan Rudich (C) *567*
Siegel, RitaSue, RitaSue Siegel Resources Inc
    (R) *176*
Vance, Donna, Ki Technologies Inc Executive
    Search Div (C).. *422*
Verwegan, Christine, ATS Reliance Technical
    Group (C) *246*
Wert, Judy, Wert & Company Inc (C).................. *658*
Wille, Michele, Southern Technical Recruiters
    (C).. *616*

Diagnostics

Adams, David, Sales Consultants of
    Chattanooga-Brainerd (C) *583*
Allison, Ken, The Chase Group Inc (R) *34*
Besen, Douglas, Besen Associates Inc (C).......... *256*
Bowman, Mary, Bowman & Associates Inc (R) ... *21*
Chanod, Edward E., The Medical Industry
    Search Group (C) *491*
Fong, Ping, The Cassie Group (R) *32*
Hauck, Fred P., The Cassie Group (R)................. *32*
Hebel, Robert W., R W Hebel Associates (R)....... *86*
Heiser, Charles, The Cassie Group (R) *32*
Jagielo, Thomas A., Martin Partners LLC (R)..... *126*
Johnson, Mary H, Zingaro & Company (R) *211*
Kazan, J. Neil, Kazan Int'l Inc (R) *105*
Lareau, Belle, The Hampton Group (C) *379*
Leathers, Karen, The Chase Group Inc (R) *34*
Len, Ronald D., HealthCare Recruiters Int'l •
    NY/NJ (C) *386*
Martinez, Mario, Tecnix LLC (C)....................... *639*
Moore, Richard, HealthCare Recruiters Int'l •
    Rockies (C)... *385*
Robbins, Melvyn, HealthCare Recruiters Int'l •
    New England (C)... *386*
Sawhill, Louise, Bowman & Associates Inc (R) ... *21*
Stratman, Sandra L., MRI of Milford (C)............ *452*
Westmore, Diane, Bowman & Associates Inc
    (R) *21*
Wimberly, Jim, Healthcare Recruiters Int'l •
    Dallas (C) *384*
Zingaro, Ronald J, Zingaro & Company (R) *211*

SPECIALTIES

Dialysis

Maurizio, Michael, The Fortus Group (C) 361

Diecast

Adams, Kevin, Anthony Davis & Associates
(C)... 308
Michaels, Lou, Lou Michaels Associates Inc
(C)... 495
Poucher, Brian, The Mackenzie Group (C)........ 436

Digital

Baldwin, Jenny, Sunny Bates Associates (R)...... 14
Bates, Sunny, Sunny Bates Associates (R) 14
Byrd, Marilyn, Sunny Bates Associates (R)......... 14
Granger, Andy, PeopleSource Solutions (C)...... 526
Happillon, Jennifer, cFour Partners (R) 33
Hudson, Judy K., The Hudson Group (C)........... 396
Hudson, Paul E., The Hudson Group (C)............ 396
Kramer, Edward C., WTW Associates Inc (R) 209
Vance, Donna, Ki Technologies Inc Executive
Search Div (C) 422

Direct marketing

Anthony, Robin, MLB Associates (C) 498
Badanes, Anne, Satterfield & Associates Inc
(R)... 170
Banach-Osenni, Doris, The Brentwood Group
Inc (R).. 24
Bernhart, Jerry, Bernhart Associates (C)........... 256
Bliss, Barbara P., Lamay Associates (R)............ 113
Boren, Susan, Spencer Stuart (R)....................... 182
Brolin, Lawrence E., DLB Associates (R) 55
Buffkin, Craig, Buffkin & Associates LLC (R) 26
Candiotti, Lee, Bristol Associates Inc (C).......... 265
Carey, Peter N., Peter N Carey & Associates
Inc (C) 277
Carpenter, Elsie, Carpenter & Associates (C) 278
Carpenter, Judi, Carpenter Associates Inc (R) 31
Cyr, Maury N., Cyr Associates Inc (C)............... 305
Daugherty, Judy, MRI of Dallas-Northwest (C) . 447
Dowd, Patricia, Patricia Dowd Inc (C) 316
Erickson, Elaine, Kenzer Corp (R) 107
Fabian, Jeanne, Fabian Associates Inc (C)......... 344
Fitzgibbon, Michael T., Fitzgibbon &
Associates (R)... 69
Ford, Eileen F., Ford & Ford (C) 351
Fulgham-MacCarthy, Ann, Columbia
Consulting Group (R)...................................... 39
Gagliardi, Peter W., The Atticus Graham
Group (C) 379
Glover, Peg, MRI of Moreland Hills (C) 470
Glynn, Mary Anne, E A Hughes & Company
Inc (R).. 95
Goodman-Brolin, Dorothy, DLB Associates
(R)... 55
Hall, Sharon, Spencer Stuart (R)....................... 182
Hamilton, Lisa J., Hamilton & Company (C)...... 379
Hammond, Terry, TERHAM Management
Consultants Ltd (R) 192
Harberth, Janet M., The Atticus Graham Group
(C) 379
Hart, Laurie, Chad Management Group (C)........ 282
Havas, Judy, Spencer Stuart (R) 181
Heaton, David, Results Search Group (C)........... 556
Hoyda, Brad W., Aegis Consulting (R) 3
Hughes, Cathy N., The Ogdon Partnership (R) ... 143
Hughes, Elaine A., E A Hughes & Company
Inc (R).. 94
Ingala, Thomas A., Direct Marketing Solutions
(C).. 314

James, Victoria, Victoria James Executive
Search Inc (C)... 409
Kenzer, Robert D., Kenzer Corp (R) 107
Lapham, Craig L., The Lapham Group Inc (R) ...114
Lapham, Lawrence L., The Lapham Group Inc
(R).. 114
Leslie, Ken, Strategic Search Consultants (C)....629
Levine, Alan C., Alan Levine Associates (R)......117
Levy, Eve, hallevy.com (C)............................... 378
Levy, Hal, hallevy.com (C)................................ 378
Lord, Marvin, E A Hughes & Company Inc (R)....95
Macan, Sandi, The Beam Group (R) 15
Mack, Linda, Partners in Recruiting (C)............523
Mangieri, Chris, Mangieri/Solutions LLC (C)....482
Marks, Dan, MRI of Moreland Hills (C) 470
Marquez, Paul, Sanford Rose Associates -
Fairhope (C)... 586
McBryde, Marnie, Spencer Stuart (R) 182
McGrath Faller, Laura, Redden & McGrath
Associates Inc (R)... 160
McHugh, David T., The Atticus Graham Group
(C).. 379
Moore, Connie, C A Moore & Associates Inc
(C).. 499
Nadherny, Christopher C., Spencer Stuart (R).....181
Peragine, Ralph P., The Resource Group (R) 162
Richards, Sharon, Richards Associates Inc (R)...163
Richardson, J. Rick, Spencer Stuart (R)............. 182
Ridenour, Suzanne S., Ridenour & Associates
(R) 164
Schroeder, John W., Spencer Stuart (R) 182
Sennett, Lynn, 1 to1 Executive Search (R)............. 1
Siegel, Peter A., Peter Siegel & Company (C)....603
Smolen, Dan, Victoria James Executive Search
Inc (C) 410
Sprowls, Linda, Allard Associates Inc (C)..........230
Sullivan, Dan, Direct Marketing Resources Inc
(C).. 314
Tonini, Frank, Search Professionals Inc (C) 597
Troyanos, Dennis, Gundersen Partners LLC
(R) 81
Van Remmen, Roger, Brown, Bernardy, Van
Remmen Inc (C).. 267
Voghel, Karen, 1 to1 Executive Search (R)............. 1
Walsh, Martin, Cook Associates® Inc (R) 42
Weiss, Cathy, C Weiss Associates Inc (C) 657
Wood, John, Spencer Stuart (R) 182
Zwiff, Jeffrey, Aegis Consulting (R) 3

Dirt

Kainady, John J., Michael Latas & Associates
Inc (R) 115
Robinson, Rodney, Michael Latas &
Associates Inc (R) 115
Sippel, Rick L., Michael Latas & Associates
Inc (R) 115
Stepanek, Gary, Michael Latas & Associates
Inc (R) 115

Distribution

Abbene, John, FPC of Fairfax (C) 361
Airheart, Jerry, MRI of Pasadena (R) 124
Allen, Coren, Tyler Search Consultants (C) 648
Anderson, Jim, Howard Clark Associates (C) 286
Anderson, Richard L., Grant Cooper &
Associates (R)... 79
Anderson, Wayne F., Anderson Network
Group (C)..237
Bailey, David C., MRI of Lake Tahoe, NV (C)....464
Barzelay, Richard, Search Professionals Inc
(C)...597
Besner, Elliott J., Besner EJ Consultant Inc (C) ..256

Buntrock, George, MRI of Dallas North (C)....... 476
Busch, Derek, PeopleSource Solutions (C) 526
Campbell, Dan, Campbell/Carlson LLC (R) 29
Carey, Harvey, Carion Resource Group Inc (C)..277
Cousins, John L., Procurement Resources (C) 540
D'Aoust, Pierre, Yves Elkas Inc (R).................... 60
Daugherty, Hal, MRI of Dallas-Northwest (C)... 447
Farra, David D., MRI of Marietta (C) 456
Ford, Eileen F., Ford & Ford (C) 351
Foster, William A., Bridgecreek Personnel
Agency (C) 265
Goldsmith, Fred J., Fred J Goldsmith
Associates (R) 78
Griffiths, Bob, Griffiths & Associates (C)........... 374
Haar, Patrick, National Corporate Consultants
Inc (C) 505
Heinschel, Phil, Phillips Personnel/Search (C)....529
Herring, Bill, The Herring Group (C).................. 389
Higdon, Lynn, Search South Inc (C) 597
Hindman, Jeffrey J., The Hindman Group Inc
(C).. 391
Hodges, Whitney, Recruiting Services Group
Inc (C) 553
Hood, Fred L., Fred Hood & Associates (C)....... 393
Horne, Tony, The Herring Group (C)................. 389
Jacobson, Donald, Hunt Ltd (C)........................ 398
Johnson, Scott, Johnson Associates Inc (C) 412
Krumel, Richard, The Perkins Group (R)............ 149
Lee, Janice, Summerfield Associates Inc (C) 629
Matté, Norman E., Matté & Company Inc (R) 127
Melanson, Peter, Besner EJ Consultant Inc (C)...256
Metz, Alex, Hunt Ltd (C).................................. 398
Moore, Robert, MRI of Rockville (C).................. 461
Nunziata, Fred A., Eden & Associates Inc (C) 328
Okonski, Bill, FPC of Huntsville (C) 353
Orlich, Joseph, Hughes & Wilden Associates
(C).. 397
Page, Theresa, T Page & Associates (C) 521
Pelisson, Charles J., Marra Peters & Partners
(R) 126
Perkins, R. Patrick, The Perkins Group (R)......... 149
Raeburn, Alan, ARC Staffing Inc (C) 241
Remillard, Brad M., CJA-The Adler Group Inc
(R) 36
Richards, Terry, Terry Richards (C).................... 558
Rodriguez, Janet, T Page & Associates (C).........521
Selig, Robert J., Selig Executive Search (C) 600
Smith, Sara, MRI of Round Rock (C) 477
Spilman, Mary P., Spilman & Associates (R) 183
Sulkowski, Roger, Hughes & Wilden
Associates (C) 397
Sundstrom, Paul, Roth Young of Philadelphia
(C).. 565
Thaler, Brian D., Scott-Thaler Associates
Agency Inc (C) 594
Tommarello, Tony, Lucas Group (C)................... 435
Turner, Bill, MRI of Round Rock (C) 477
Wharton, Cynthia, Personnel Management
Group (C) 528
White, Stephen R., Teknon Employment
Resources Inc (C) 639
Wickline, Jason L., Judge Inc (C) 414
Winsor-Games, Kathleen, The Winsor Group
(C).. 663
Wise, David E., MRI of Hunt Valley (C)............. 461
Young, Arthur L., Search South Inc (C).............. 597
Zarkin, Norman, The Zarkin Group Inc (R) 210
Zaslav, Debra M., Telford, Adams &
Alexander (R) 192

Diversity

Arroyo Roldan, Kenneth, Wesley, Brown &
Bartle Company Inc (R)................................. 202

Domestic

Doors

E-Business

Economic development

Economics

EDP

SPECIALTIES

(R) = Retainer; (C) = Contingency

Stasiuk, Fern, Fern G Stasiuk Executive Search
    Inc (C) 625
Stensars, Jo, MRI of Boise (C) 457
Stepler, Paul, Gallin Associates Inc (C) 366
Tarris, Trebor, Tarris Associates Inc (C) 634
Thorpe, James, Kenn Spinrad Inc (C) 621
Vandegrift, Tom, Kiley, Owen & McGovern
    Inc (R) 107
Waltz, Bruce, Ki Technologies Inc Executive
    Search Div (C) 422
Weinfeld, David C., David Weinfeld Group
    (C)... 657
Wimmer, Walter, The Silicon Network (C) 603
Wood, Thomas C., Trac One (R) 195
Young, Susan M., MRI of Morris County, NJ
    (C)... 465
Zabor, Richard, Leader Institute Inc (C) 429

Education

Abruzzo, James, StratfordGroup (R) 188
Amcis, Lillian, Joel H Paul & Associates Inc
    (C)... 524
Antoniak, Peggy, The Executive Tree Research
    Consultants (R) 66
Archer-Martin, Nancy, Witt/Kieffer, Ford,
    Hadelman & Lloyd (R) 206
Attea, William, Hazard, Young, Attea &
    Associates Ltd (C).................................... 383
Baird-Counter, Michele, StratfordGroup (R) 188
Berger, Emanuel, Witt/Kieffer, Ford,
    Hadelman & Lloyd (R) 206
Biggers, Maureen S., Jon McRae & Associates
    Inc (R) 130
Carabelli, Paula, Witt/Kieffer, Ford, Hadelman
    & Lloyd (R) 206
Casey, Carol, Joy Reed Belt Search
    Consultants Inc (R) 16
Decker, Robert, Ray & Associates Inc (R) 158
Dingman, Bruce, Robert W Dingman
    Company Inc (R) 53
Dingman, Robert W., Robert W Dingman
    Company Inc (R) 53
Eldredge, L. Lincoln, Brigham Hill
    Consultancy (R) 25
Funk, Bill, Korn/Ferry Int'l (R) 110
Himmelfarb, Susan, The Himmelfarb Group
    (R)... 90
Hockett, Bill, Hockett Associates Inc (R) 91
Hughes, Don, ProLinks Inc (R) 156
Hurley, Elizabeth, Davies Park (R) 48
Kelly, Mary K., Kelly Associates (R) 106
Kelly, Ronald, Kelly Associates (R) 106
Kelly, William W., Jon McRae & Associates
    Inc (R) 130
Lantz, Delores, A C Personnel Services Inc (C) . 215
Lyttle, Jordene, PricewaterhouseCoopers
    Executive Search (R) 154
Magee, Dylan, MRI of Dallas (C).................... 476
Magen, Judy, Joel H Paul & Associates Inc (C).. 524
Matthews, Tim, MRI of Dallas (C)................... 476
McLean, B. Keith, PricewaterhouseCoopers
    Executive Search (R) 154
McRae, O. Jon, Jon McRae & Associates Inc
    (R)... 130
Meehling, Catherine E., Management
    Associates (C) 438
Mogilner, Myra, Joel H Paul & Associates Inc
    (C)... 524
Murray, Colette, Paschal•Murray Executive
    Search (R) 147
Orr, Kenneth B., Jon McRae & Associates Inc
    (R)... 130
Park, K. Darwin, Davies Park (R)..................... 48

Parker, Donna R., The Whitney Smith
    Company Inc (C) 660
Paul, Joel H., Joel H Paul & Associates Inc (C) ..524
Posner, Gary J., Witt/Kieffer, Ford, Hadelman
    & Lloyd (R) 206
Presser, Janice, Gabriel Worldwide Inc (C).......... 365
Ray, Gary L., Ray & Associates Inc (R)............. 158
Solomon, Phyllis, Phyllis Solomon Executive
    Search Inc (C).. 615
Victor, Johnathon, The Executive Tree
    Research Consultants (R)............................. 66
Wenzel, Dawn, Partners in Recruiting (C)........... 523
Wheel, Eric, MRI of Northern California (C)....... 450

Higher

Auerbach, Judith A., Auerbach Associates Inc
    (R)... 10
Bachhuber, Thomas, The Diversity
    Advantage (R)... 54
Berger, Emanuel D., Educational Management
    Network (R) 58
Berger, Emmanuel, Educational Management
    Network (R) 58
Burton, Catherine C., Innovative Partnerships
    Executive Search (R) 98
Carabelli, Paula, Educational Management
    Network (R) 58
Cattie, Jr., Gerard F., Diversified Search Inc
    (R)... 54
Cave, Lillian, PLC Associates (C)..................... 532
Dinteman, Walter, Sales Consultants of
    Asheville (C) 581
Donnelly, Patrick, Christopher-Westmont &
    Associates Inc (R) 36
Dowdall, Jean, A T Kearney Executive Search
    (R)... 105
Ginley, Michael, The Lear Group Inc (R)........... 116
Godfrey, Robert G., Robert G Godfrey
    Associates Ltd (R) 78
Gossage, Wayne, Gossage Sager Associates
    LLC (R) 78
Hall, Nancy M., The Hollins Group Inc (R) 92
Hard, Sally-Ann, Educational Management
    Network (R) 59
Justus McGinty, Julia, Berkhemer Clayton Inc
    (R)... 17
Koenig, Allen E., R H Perry & Associates Inc
    (R)... 149
Kolacia, V., Murphy Partners Int'l (R)................. 138
Leske, Lucy, Educational Management
    Network (R) 58
MacNaughton, Sperry, MacNaughton
    Associates (R) 122
Martin, Nancy, Educational Management
    Network (R) 58
Meehling, Catherine E., First Advisory
    Services Int'l Inc (R) 68
Molloy, Thomas, Molloy Partners (R)................. 135
Morrisson, Kim, Diversified Search Inc (R)......... 54
Neff, Ph.D., Charles B., Development Search
    Specialists (R) 50
Noeske, Nancy R., Overton Consulting (R)......... 144
Pamenter, Fred, Pamenter, Pamenter, Brezer &
    Deganis Ltd (R) 145
Perry, R. H., R H Perry & Associates Inc (R).... 149
Posner, Gary J., Educational Management
    Network (R) 59
Posner, Gary, Educational Management
    Network (R) 58
Regan, Muriel, Gossage Sager Associates LLC
    (R)... 79
Rehner, Leonard, R & L Associates Ltd (R)........ 157
Sager, Donald J., Gossage Sager Associates
    LLC (R) 79

Smith, Craig V., Diversified Search Inc (R)......... 54
Smith, Herbert E., The Enfield Company (R) 61
Taylor, Mary Elizabeth, Educational
    Management Network (R) 59

Electrical

Archie, Jr., Otis, Kuhn Med-Tech Inc (C)........... 425
Baker, S. Joseph, Search Consultants Int'l Inc
    (C) 595
Botto, Joe, Electric Systems Personnel (ESP)
    (C) 329
Bowers, Bob, CBI Group Inc (C)...................... 280
Brentari, Michael, Search Consultants Int'l Inc
    (C) 595
Burress, Kathy, Southern Recruiters &
    Consultants Inc (C) 616
Ceresi, Carole, MRI of Bay Head (C) 464
Ceresi, Robert P., MRI of Bay Head (C)............. 464
Chapman, John, Johnson Brown Associates Inc
    (C) 267
Culbertson, Beth, Sales Consultants of
    Milwaukee (C)... 584
Dorko, George A., The Clertech Group Inc (C) .. 286
Fisher, Earl, PowerBrokers LLC (C)................... 534
Gardiner, Gary, MRI of Chagrin Falls, OH (C)... 470
Gray, Lynette, Electric Systems Personnel
    (ESP) (C)... 329
Greening, Charles, Medical Executive
    Recruiters (C) 491
Hohlstein, Jeff, MRI of Round Rock (C) 477
Hohlstein, Jodi, MRI of Round Rock (C)............. 477
Joyce, Mark, Louis Rudzinsky Associates Inc
    (C) 567
Klebba, Arthur, Morgan & Associates (C)........... 500
Lopez, David, MRI of Milwaukee-North (C)....... 480
Lowery, Gene, MRI of Harrison County (C)........ 464
Manly, Jo, MRI of Round Rock (C)................... 477
McAleavy, Steve, Search Consultants Int'l Inc
    (C) 595
Munger, Donald, Berkshire Search Associates
    (C) 256
Nickels, Edward L., Michael Latas &
    Associates Inc (R) 115
O'Brien, Brent, Executive Search Consultants
    Corp (C) 341
Rafferty, Mark, Search Point LLC (C)................ 596
Ragan, William, Michael Latas & Associates
    Inc (R) 115
Reinitz, Robert, Professional Recruiters Inc (C).. 542
Scarboro, M. D., MRI of Greenville (C) 474
Schick, Rex, Schick Professional Search Inc
    (C) 592
Sharkey, Jeffrey, The Barton Group Inc (C) 251
Snider, Jr., L. Bryan, Bryan & Louis Research
    (C) 267
Snider, Les, Bryan & Louis Research (C) 267
Thomp, Prudence, MRI of Mundelein (C) 458
Thompson, Ramona, MRI of Round Rock (C)...... 477
Williams, Bill, Executive Search Consultants
    Corp (C) 341

Electromechanical

Bertram, John J., Jack Bertram Executive
    Recruiting (C).. 256
Hall, James E., The Duncan-O'Dell Group Inc
    (C) 318
Hohlstein, Jeff, MRI of Round Rock (C) 477
Hohlstein, Jodi, MRI of Round Rock (C)............. 477
Johnson, Kevin S., Quality Search Inc (C).......... 547
Lineal, Lisa, Lineal Recruiting Services (C) 432
Manly, Jo, MRI of Round Rock (C)................... 477
Reed, Dave, MRI of Flint (C) 462

SPECIALTIES

Energy

Engineering

SPECIALTIES

SPECIALTIES

Entertainment

Environmental

Equipment

Equity

SPECIALTIES

Experts

Exploration

Extrusion

Fabrication

SPECIALTIES

SPECIALTIES

(R) = Retainer; (C) = Contingency

Financial

Raemer-Rodriguez, Susan, FERS Business Services Inc (R)........ 67
Ragazzo, Elaine, Ratliff, Taylor & Lekan Inc (R)........ 158
Ramirez, Richard, Marentz & Company (C)........ 483
Rascher, Linda, Bert Davis Publishing Placement Consultants (C)........ 309
Rice, Robert N., Technical Management Resources Inc (C)........ 637
Rivera-Lopez, Elba, Kenexa (R)........ 106
Roberson, Barthell, Bart Roberson & Company (C)........ 560
Rotella, Marshall W., The Corporate Connection Ltd (C)........ 295
Sadaka, Steve, Steven Douglas Associates (C)... 316
Sadovnick, Mark, Steven Douglas Associates (C)........ 316
Sarch, Daniel, Leitner Sarch Consultants (C)...... 430
Scaturro, Leonard, Boone-Scaturro Associates Inc (C)........ 260
Schwartz, Alan, Advice Personnel Inc (C)........ 227
Shankweiler, Y., Marilyn, Salesforce (C)........ 585
Siragna, Peter, NOJ Executive USA (C)........ 512
Smith, Craig V., Diversified Search Inc (R)........ 54
Spiek, Martin, Averon (C)........ 247
Sponseller, Vern, Richard Kader & Associates (C)........ 415
Staton, Tim, The Executive Consulting Group (C)........ 337
Stephens, Ken, Leader Resources Group (C)...... 429
Stewart, Cathi, The Stewart Group (C)........ 627
Sultzer, Eric, Open Systems Technologies Inc (C)........ 517
Tannenbaum, Peter, Neal Management Inc (C).. 508
Taylor, F. E. (Rick), Ratliff, Taylor & Lekan Inc (R)........ 158
Tedla, Solomon, Creative HR Solutions (C)........ 302
Van Vliet, Dick, Dick Van Vliet & Associates (C)........ 650
Vangel, Peter V., Access/Resources Inc (C)........ 218
Vitanza, Jocelyne, DARE Human Resources Corp (C)........ 307
Wegner, Carl, Wegner & Associates (C)........ 657
Weiner, Chuck, Rice Cohen Int'l (R)........ 163
Weinstock, Michael A., Advisors' Search Group Inc (C)........ 227
Werlin, Paul A., Human Capital Resources Inc (C)........ 397
Wieder, Thomas, MRI of Nassau Inc (R)........ 124
Wilcox, Fred T., Wilcox, Miller & Nelson (C)... 660
Wilkerson, Jr., Robert P., Andrews & Associates (C)........ 238

Management

Ambroso, Joseph, Lucerne Partners LLC (R)..... 120
Beecher, Arthur P., J Nicholas Arthur (R)........ 9
Bogard, Nicholas C., J Nicholas Arthur (R)........ 9
Dickens, Marcia, R Gaines Baty Associates Inc (R)........ 14
Glover, Russell, Shore Paralax Inc (R)........ 176
Guilford, David J., DLG Associates Inc (R)........ 55
Johnson, Lowell D., Lowell Johnson Associates LLC (R)........ 120
Lindell, James T., The Cooke Group (R)........ 43
Mazziota, Daniel R., Ruth Sklar Associates Inc (RSA Executive Search) (R)........ 177
McCracken, Gary W., Metzler & Company (R). 132
McGowan, Malcolm, Holloway, Schulz & Partners (C)........ 393
O'Neill, Stephen, O'Neill & Company (R)........ 142
Ohman, Gregory L., Graystone Partners LLC (R)........ 80
Pierce, Matthew J., Pierce & Associates (R)....... 151
Sarch, Daniel, Leitner Sarch Consultants (C)...... 430
Schiavone, Mary Rose, Conboy, Sur & Associates Inc (R)........ 40
Sedlar, Jeri L., Sedlar & Miners (R)........ 174
Semel, Betty, Shore Paralax Inc (R)........ 176
Shipley, Alison, DARE Human Resources Corp (C)........ 307
Walker, Gordon, Rushmore · Judge Inc (R)........ 168
Warner, Susan C, C D Warner & Associates (C)........ 656
Weis, Robert, CFOs2GO (C)........ 281
Wilcox, Fred T., Wilcox, Miller & Nelson (C).... 660
Wilensky, Ivy S., Anderson & Schwab Inc (R)....... 7
Williams, Walter, Clarity Partners LLC (R)........ 37

Financial services

Abert, Janice, TMP Worldwide Executive Search (R)........ 193
Adams, Len, KPA Associates Inc (C)........ 424
Ahrensdorf, Lee, Ahrensdorf & Associates (R)....... 4
Aldrich, Michael R., Martin Partners LLC (R).... 126
Allard, Susan, Allard Associates Inc (C)........ 230
Allman, Steven L., Allman & Company Inc (C).. 232
Andersen, Phil, Blackhawk Executive Search Inc (C)........ 258
Anderson, Michael, Spencer Stuart (R)........ 182
André, Jacques P., Ray & Berndtson (R)........ 159
Armato, Nick, Corporate Search America Inc (C)........ 297
Armitage, John D., Armitage Associates Ltd (R)........ 8
Armstrong, Robert, Kenzer Corp (R)........ 107
Aronow, Lawrence E., Aronow Associates Inc (C)........ 242
Aruza, Al, Cornell Group Int'l Consulting Inc (R)........ 43
Bacher, Judith, Spencer Stuart (R)........ 182
Baker, G. Craig, GCB Executive Search (C)........ 367
Banach-Osenni, Doris, The Brentwood Group Inc (R)........ 24
Barnum, Toni, Stone Murphy (R)........ 186
Baron, Robert, Peak Associates (C)........ 524
Bell, Jeff, Spencer Stuart (R)........ 182
Bishop, Sandra K., FPC of Boise (C)........ 355
Blumberg, Michael, Ross Consulting Int'l (C)..... 564
Boghos, Jacqueline, Corporate Search America Inc (C)........ 297
Boghos, James G., Corporate Search America Inc (C)........ 297
Bonnell, William R., Bonnell Associates Ltd (R)........ 20
Bovich, Maryann, Higdon Group Inc (R)........ 90
Brady, Marty, The Oxbridge Group Ltd (C)........ 519
Bridgeman, John, TTG Search (R)........ 196
Brown, Franklin Key, Horton Int'l LLC (R)........ 93
Bruce, Michael C., Spencer Stuart (R)........ 181
Buggy, Linda, Garthwaite Partners Int'l (R)........ 75
Burton, Catherine C., Innovative Partnerships Executive Search (R)........ 98
Bush, William C., Cook & Company (R)........ 42
Butler, Donald W., The Lane Group (C)........ 427
Butler, T. Christopher, Spencer Stuart (R)........ 181
Cain, David, The Pacific Firm (R)........ 145
Cantor, Paul, Russell Reynolds Associates Inc (R)........ 163
Castine, Michael, TMP Worldwide Executive Search (R)........ 194
Castriota, Dominic, Rhodes Associates (R)........ 163
Chadick, Susan L., Gould, McCoy & Chadick Inc (R)........ 79
Cherney, Lynn K., Ray & Berndtson (R)........ 159
Childs, Helane, Manning Associates (C)........ 482
Christensen, Garn, FPC of Boise (C)........ 355
Clark, Donald B., Ray & Berndtson (R)........ 159
Clarke, Virginia, Spencer Stuart (R)........ 181
Claude, Jr., Abram, Ray & Berndtson (R)........ 159
Clemens, William, Spencer Stuart (R)........ 182
Coffina, Richard, The Beam Group (R)........ 15
Colasanto, Frank M., W R Rosato & Associates Inc (R)........ 166
Coleman, John A., Boardroom Consultants (R).... 20
Collins, Steve, Johnson Enterprises Inc (C)........ 412
Colton, W. Hoyt, The Colton Partnership Inc (R)........ 39
Connelly, Kevin M., Spencer Stuart (R)........ 181
Cook, Patricia S., Cook & Company (R)........ 42
Coppola, Anna, The Flagship Group (R)........ 69
Costa, Karen, The Kinlin Company Inc (R)........ 108
Crath, Paul F., PricewaterhouseCoopers Executive Search (R)........ 154
Crooks, Thomas, Brentwood Int'l (R)........ 24
Daratany, Ron, DMR Global Inc (R)........ 55
Daum, Julie H., Spencer Stuart (R)........ 182
de Cholnoky, Andrea, Spencer Stuart (R)........ 182
de Rham, Amy, Spencer Stuart (R)........ 181
deBerry, Marian Alexander, Boulware & Associates Inc (R)........ 21
DeVre', Art, Hreshko Consulting Group (C)........ 396
Donnelly, Patrick, Christopher-Westmont & Associates Inc (R)........ 36
Donovan, John, Human Capital Resources Inc (C)........ 397
Doyle, John P., Ray & Berndtson (R)........ 159
Ducruet, Linda K., The Directorship Search Group Inc (R)........ 53
Dunn, Mary Hellen, Ray & Berndtson (R)........ 159
Earhart, Teresa, Miller-Collins Associates Inc (C)........ 497
Edington, Patti D., Drinkwater & Associates (R)........ 57
Egan, John, Jones & Egan Inc (R)........ 102
Egan, John, Peters, Dalton & Graham Inc (R)..... 150
Egan, Kate, Fisource.com (C)........ 349
Elam, Kimarra, MRI of Lincoln (R)........ 124
Ellsworth, Peter, Jay Gaines & Company Inc (R)........ 73
Fagan, III, Charles A., Fagan & Company (R)...... 66
Farmer, David W., The Whitney Smith Company Inc (C)........ 660
Federman, Jack, W R Rosato & Associates Inc (R)........ 166
Fee, J. Curtis, Spencer Stuart (R)........ 181
Fell, III, John R., Howe & Associates (R)........ 93
Ferrari, S. Jay, Ferrari Search Group (R)........ 67
Fiess, Kathy, Picard Int'l Ltd (R)........ 151
Finn, Eileen, Eileen Finn & Associates Inc (R)..... 67
Fisher, Richard, Richard A Eisner & Company LLP (R)........ 59
Fitzpatrick, Peter, Gundersen Partners LLC (R).... 81
Follrath, Noel A., Ray & Berndtson (R)........ 159
Fox, Amanda, Spencer Stuart (R)........ 181
Franklin, Michael, Hreshko Consulting Group (C)........ 396
Furr, C. Franklin, C F Furr & Company (R)........ 72
Gagan, Kevin, Spencer Stuart (R)........ 181
Gaines, Jay, Jay Gaines & Company Inc (R)........ 73
Galante, Suzanne M., Vlcek & Company Inc (R)........ 199
Gardiner, E. Nicholas P., Gardiner, Townsend & Associates (R)........ 74
Gardner, Nina-Marie, Higdon Group Inc (R)........ 90
Garthwaite, Candace, Garthwaite Partners Int'l (R)........ 75
Gasperini, Peter, Peter Gasperini & Associates Inc (R)........ 75
Geister, Barry, Anderson Young Associates (C)........ 237
Genel, George, Genel Associates (C)........ 367

SPECIALTIES

Fire protection

Firmware

Fixtures

Flat panel display

Flexographic printing

Floriculture

SPECIALTIES

SPECIALTIES

SPECIALTIES

Health

Insurance

Safety

Healthcare

SPECIALTIES

Administration

Heavy industry

High energy physics

High purity water

High technology

Highways

Hispanic

HMOs

Home

Fashion

Home and building controls

Home health

Horticulture

Hospital

SPECIALTIES

SPECIALTIES

SPECIALTIES

(R) = Retainer; (C) = Contingency

HVAC

Imaging

Industrial

Services

Technology

Information

SPECIALTIES

(R) = Retainer; (C) = Contingency

SPECIALTIES

Information service

Ink

SPECIALTIES

(R) = Retainer; (C) = Contingency

Mullen, James J., Mullen Associates Inc (R) 137
Ranberg, Carol, Marsteller Wilcox Associates
(C).. 485

Instrumentation

Adams, Frank S., Thomson, Sponar & Adams
Inc (C).. 642
Bassler, Mitchell, RSMR Global Resources (R) . 167
Bawza, Leo F., Chelsea Resources Inc (C) 283
Bodle, Barbara, Nationwide Personnel
Recruiting & Consulting Inc (C) 507
Brophy, Helen M., Tech Int'l (C) 636
Campbell, Sandra, MRI of Milford (C).............. 452
Cuomo, Frank, Frank Cuomo & Associates Inc
(C).. 304
Evans, John, RTX Inc (C)................................... 567
Frazer, Mel, Mel Frazer Consultant (C)............. 363
Frazier, Shane, MRI of Brownsburg (C)............. 458
Gersin, Harvey, Sales Consultants of
Farmington Hills (C)....................................... 579
Kunkel, Thomas J., Bayland Associates (C) 252
Patronella, Larry, W Robert Eissler &
Associates Inc (C) 329
Soo Hoo, Patrick J., Chelsea Resources Inc (C).. 283
Southworth, Edward, Michigan Consulting
Group (R).. 133

Insurance

Albright, Carol, HRQuest (C) 396
Amato, Bobbi, Amato & Associates Insurance
Recruiters (C).. 233
Amato, Joseph D., Amato & Associates Inc (C) . 233
Anderson, Michael, Spencer Stuart (R)............... 182
Antoniak, Peggy, The Executive Tree Research
Consultants (R) 66
Baker, Bill, Kaye/Bassman Int'l Corp (R)........... 104
Barick, Bradford L., MRI of Stevens Point (C)... 480
Barker, Steve, Insurance Recruiting Specialists
(C)... 403
Baron, Robert, Peak Associates (C) 524
Baron, Sheldon S., Sales Consultants of
Nashua-Manchester (C)................................... 580
Baskin, Peter J., Personnel Associates Inc (C) 527
Bass, Nate, Jacobson Associates (C).................... 409
Bass, Nate, Jacobson Executive Search (R) 100
Beaudine, Robert E., Eastman & Beaudine Inc
(R).....;... 58
Benkwitt, Barbara, The Brentwood Group Inc
(R).. 24
Blumberg, Michael, Ross Consulting Int'l (C) 564
Blythe, Thomas J., Halo Insurance Service (C) .. 378
Bradley, Ken, Bradley & Associates (C) 263
Bredeson, Nancy, Artemis HRC (C) 242
Buchanan, Christine, MRI of Bordentown (C).... 465
Bull, Lisa, Lechner & Associates Inc (C) 429
Burkholder, John, Burkholder Group Inc (R)........ 26
Butler, Jr., Kirby B., The Butlers Company
Insurance Recruiters (C)................................. 269
Butler, Martha, The Butlers Company
Insurance Recruiters (C)................................. 269
Butz, Richard R., Providyn LLP (R)................... 156
Cahill, Maureen E., William K Long
Associates Inc (C) 434
Carter, Jeffrey M., CE Insurance Services (C) 280
Cavallo, Vincent L., Behavioral Science
Associates Inc (R) 15
Connelly, Kevin M., Spencer Stuart (R)............. 181
Corey, Mike, TMP Worldwide Executive
Search (R) 194
Corey, Patrick, TMP Worldwide Executive
Search (R) 194

Corporon, Charles E., Quirk-Corporon &
Associates Inc (C)... 549
Corrier, Jodelle K. "Jodi", Sanford Rose
Associates - New Albany (C)........................... 590
Darter, Steven, People Management Northeast
Inc (R) 148
Davis, Andrew, Smith Hanley Associates Inc
(C) 606
Davis, Barry, Martin Grant Associates Inc (C)....372
Davis, Carolyn, Carolyn Davis Associates Inc
(C) 308
Dawson, Todd, MRI of Omaha (C) 464
De Funiak, William S., De Funiak & Edwards
(R).. 49
Descheneaux, Pat, Descheneaux Recruitment
Services Ltd (C).. 311
Dietsch, Roger A., Dietsch & Associates (C) 312
DiGioia, Richard, MRI of Orange (C)................. 451
DiGioia, Richard, Sales Consultants of Orange
(C) 574
Dionne, Bert, Insurance Search (C) 403
Dorland, Harvey, Pacific Recruiting (C)............. 520
Dougherty, Juanita, R Dann & Associates LLC
(C) 307
Dykes, Larry L., Personnel Consultants (C) 527
Edwards, Randolph J., De Funiak & Edwards
(R).. 49
Eisele, Michael, Wisconsin Executive Search
Group Ltd (C) 664
Elizondo, Jennifer, MRI of Fresno (C) 450
Elwess, Dana, Dana Elwess Placements Inc (C)...331
Esposito, Mark, Christian & Timbers (R)............. 35
Evan-Cook, James W., IPS Search Inc (R)........... 99
Evan-Cook, James, IPS Search Inc (R) 99
Fiore, Richard, R C Fiore (C) 348
Flanders, Beverly, IOS-Information
Connection Inc (C)... 406
Flynn, Jack, Executive Search Consultants
Corp (C) 341
Foss, Gregory, Diedre Moire Corp Inc (C).........499
Fox, Amanda, Spencer Stuart (R)....................... 181
Frankel, Miriam, PMJ & Associates (C)............. 532
Friedman, Ken, The Primary Group Inc (R)........154
Garrison, Cory, The Garrison Organization (R)....75
Gazzolo, Diana, Martin Grant Associates Inc
(C) 372
Gelpi, Gerry, Gelpi & Associates (C)................. 367
Gilliam, Toni, MRI of Spokane (C)..................... 479
Godfrey, James R., Godfrey Personnel Inc (C)....370
Gold, Barry M., Barry M Gold & Company (C)..371
Gold, Lisa, Strategic Advancement Inc (R) 187
Goode, Thomas F., The Insurance Staffing
Group (C) 403
Graham, Shane, MRI of Athens (C) 455
Green, Lindalee, Quality Search Unlimited (C)...547
Hall, Kassidy, The Winsor Group (C) 663
Hanson, Paul David, TMP Worldwide
Executive Search (R) 194
Hanson, Paul L., TMP Worldwide Executive
Search (R) 194
Hanson, Ron, Ronald B Hanson Associates (R)....84
Haugen, Audrey D., Dietsch & Associates (C)....312
Heller, Steven A., Martin H Bauman
Associates LLC (C) 14
Higgins, Bruce W., B W Higgins Inc (C) 390
Hochman, Judith L., Hochman & Associates
Inc (C) 392
Hodges, Wanda, Insurance Search (C) 403
Hoskin, Jr., Frank, Van Curan & Associates
(C) 650
Howard, Brian E., The Howard Group Inc (C)....395
Howard, Ted, American Human Resource
Associates Ltd (AHRA) (R)................................ 7
Hraur, Alex, McGrath & Associates Inc (R)........129

Hudson, George A., Hudson Associates Inc (C).. 396
Hunter, Sherri, Career Image Inc (C) 275
Illsley, Hugh, TMP Worldwide Executive
Search (R) 195
Jacobson, David, Jacobson Associates (C).......... 409
Jacobson, Greg, Jacobson Associates (C)............ 409
Jacobson, Gregory P., Jacobson Executive
Search (R) 100
Jacobson, Gregory, Jacobson Associates (C) 409
Jacobson, Gregory, Jacobson Executive Search
(R)... 100
Jacobson, Rick, The Windham Group (R)........... 205
Jenkins, Jeffrey, Jacobson Associates (C) 409
Kennedy, Michael, The Danbrook Group Inc
(C) 306
Kinderis, Paul, Kinderis & Loercher Group (C).. 422
Kiner, Linda, Insurance Career Center Inc (C).... 403
King, Robert E., Behavioral Science Associates
Inc (R) 15
King, Steven, Ashway Ltd Agency (C) 243
Knowles, Scott, MRI of Georgetown (C) 474
Koestenblatt, Erik, Allen, Austin, Lowe &
Powers (R)... 5
Kolacia, V., Murphy Partners Int'l (R) 138
Kostmayer, John B., Kostmayer Associates Inc
(R)... 111
Krantz, Deborah, BenchMark Resources LLC
(C) 254
Krisniski, Cheryl, Artemis HRC (C) 242
LaMorte, Michelle, LaMorte Search Associates
Inc (C) 427
LaMorte, William, LaMorte Search Associates
Inc (C) 427
Larner, Chester, Van Curan & Associates (C).... 650
Lawrence, Liam, TMP Worldwide Executive
Search (R) 194
Leeds, Gerald I., Leeds and Leeds (C) 430
Leslie, C. C., TMP Worldwide Executive
Search (R) 193
Levy, Stefan, Management Search Inc (C) 481
Lichty, Brett P., Chicago Consulting Partners
Ltd (R).. 34
Magic, Michael F., Scott Douglas Inc (C)........... 316
Mann, Douglas, TMP Worldwide Executive
Search (R) 193
Marconi, Mark, Marconi Search Consultants
Inc (C) 483
Marsh, Norman R., California Management
Search (C) 271
Marsteller, Franklin D., Spencer Stuart (R)......... 182
Martin, Jason, MRI of Cordova (C) 475
Marver-Ilhan, Nancy, Executive Directions Inc
(C) 337
Marx, Gary, New World Healthcare Solutions
Inc (R) 139
McCarthy, Maureen, MRI of Fresno (C) 450
McDonough, Mike, General Search and
Recruitment (C).. 367
McGinty, Michelle, Dunhill Professional
Search of Wilkes-Barre/Scranton (C) 323
McKay, Kim, The Network Corporate Search
Personnel Inc (C).. 509
Milkint, Margaret Resce, Jacobson Executive
Search (R) 100
Miller, Kenneth, Computer Network Resources
Inc (C) 291
Miller, Roxxanne, Pailin Group Professional
Search Consultants (R) 145
Moore, Connie, C A Moore & Associates Inc
(C) 499
Moran, Tom, TMP Worldwide Executive
Search (R) 194
Mueller, William, Noll Human Resource
Services (C)... 512

SPECIALTIES

SPECIALTIES

SPECIALTIES

Palinchak, Kris, Sanford Rose Associates - Akron (C) 589
Parekh, Dinesh V., Sanford Rose Associates - Amherst NY (C) 589
Perkins, Barbara, Harcourt & Associates (C) 380
Petersen, Brian, MRI of Flagstaff (C) 449
Polson, Christopher C., Polson & Company Inc (R) 152
Pottenger, Don, Search Force Inc (C) 596
Power, John, Solutns Recruiting Services (C) 615
Reynolds, Carol, Exclusive Search Consultants (C) 335
Reynolds, Debra, R S Reynolds Technical Recruiting (C) 556
Rimmele, Michael, Executive Directions Inc (C) 337
Rochés, Roberto, ExSearch Latinoamérica (R) 66
Roper, Gina, Triangle Consulting Group (C) 646
Rubin, Larry, IT Services (C) 407
Sacchetti, Lisa, The Renaissance Network (C) ... 555
Saunders, Lisa, National Field Service Corp (C) 505
Schneider, Amy, Windsor Consultants Inc (C) ... 662
Schwarz, Meredith Barnes, Barnes & Associates Executive Search (C) 250
Shellhammer, James, Executive Search Int'l (ESI) Inc (C) 342
Sherwood, Chris, MRI of Manassas (C) 478
Smith, Craig, Inteliant (C) 405
Spencer, David, Computer Careers (C) 291
Sprotte, Erik, Carnegie Partners Inc (R) 31
Staton, Leana, Russ Hadick & Associates Inc (C) 376
Strohbeen, Doug, MRI of Siouxland (C) 459
Sullivan, Russell M., Accelerated Data Decision Inc (C) 217
Surovick, Rudy, Exclusive Search Consultants (C) 335
Swan, Barbara, The Swan Group (C) 630
Tatar, Steven M., Magellan Int'l LP (C) 437
Teague, Shanda, Cowan Search Group (C) 300
Thomas, Bill, Military Transition Group (C) 496
Treshnell, Lisa, Herrerias & Associates (R) 89
Ulrich, Mary Ann, D S Allen Associates (C) 231
Unger, Paul, Christian & Timbers (R) 36
Vereb, Karen, TAMB Associates Inc (C) 634
Vollmer, George, Kenexa (R) 106
Wagner, Gabriel, Wagner & Associates (C) 653
Walker, Wade, Mayhall Search Group Inc (C) ... 488
Waterfield, Karen, Recruiting Resources Inc (C) 553
Watts, Steve, Stoakley-Dudley Consultants Ltd (C) 627
Wheat, Donnie, Huntley Associates Inc (C) 399
Williams, Aurora, Joe L Giles & Associates (C) 369
Wiltgen, Richard, Chicago Financial Search (C) 284
Wolf, Richard, Performance Resources Inc (C) .. 526
Yoksh, Larry, AmiTech Group (R) 7
Zambito, John R., MRI of Columbus-Downtown (C) 471

Jewelry

Brown, Polly M., Polly Brown Associates (C) 267
Durino, Pat, Polly Brown Associates (C) 267
Feldman, Abe, A E Feldman Associates Inc (C) 346
Fulgham-MacCarthy, Ann, Columbia Consulting Group (R) 39
Lemire, Edward A., Executive's Silent Partner Ltd (C) 343

Juvenile products

Keoughan, Thomas, Toy Jobs (C) 644

Labor

Edelman, Diane, Stephen M Haas Legal Placement (C) 375
Goich, S. George, Fernow Associates (C) 346

Laboratory

Clark, Jim, CPS Inc (C) 300
Len, Ronald D., HealthCare Recruiters Int'l • NY/NJ (C) 386
Waller, Victoria, Health Search Inc (C) 384

Landscaping

Day, Jr., M. Rice, MRI of Chapel Hill (C) 467
Dummer, Charles F., Charles & Associates Inc (C) 283
Sharpe, Howard, Brooke Chase Associates Inc (R) 25

Leasing

Bickerstaff, John, Synagent Inc (C) 631
McAuliffe, John, Roberta Rea & Co Inc (C) 552
Norris, Ronald, Ronald Norris & Associates (C) 512
Rea, Roberta, Roberta Rea & Co Inc (C) 552
Ward, Madeleine, L T S Associates (C) 425

Legal

Abelson, Cathy B., Cathy Abelson Legal Search (C) 217
Alatorre-Ridings, Trish, Spherion Legal Group (C) 618
Arnstein, Jill, Sales Consultants of Trenton (C) ... 580
Ash, Esq., Patricia A., H Hertner Associates Inc (C) 389
Ash, Howard, CorpLegal Services (C) 295
Ashleigh, Karah H., H Hertner Associates Inc (C) 389
Bavly, Ted, John Kurosky & Associates (R) 113
Beck, Stacey, Spherion Legal Group (C) 619
Becker, Laurie, E P Dine Inc (C) 313
Beckman, Susan R., Beckman & Associates Legal Search (C) 253
Beckwith, Randy, Seltzer Fontaine Beckwith (C) 600
Belt, Joy Reed, Joy Reed Belt Search Consultants Inc (R) 16
Bilodeau, Michael, Charter Resources Int'l LC (C) 283
Blake, Sharon, Baldwin & Associates (C) 248
Block, Esq., David J., H Hertner Associates Inc (C) 389
Bloom, Howard, Spherion Legal Group (C) 619
Bongard, Warren, ZSA Legal Recruitment (C) ... 670
Boreham, Judy, Diversified Search Inc (R) 54
Bowser, Esq., Danielle G., H Hertner Associates Inc (C) 389
Bredeson, Esq., D. A., Bredeson Executive Recruitment LLC (R) 24
Bredeson, Sheri, Bredeson Executive Recruitment LLC (R) 24
Brogan, Pat, Human Resource Bureau (C) 397
Brown, Beth, Spherion Legal Group (C) 619
Buckner, Carol, Mruk & Partners (R) 137
Campos, Shirley, Templeton & Associates (C) ... 641
Cannon, Alexis, Richard, Wayne & Roberts (C) 557
Carnerie, Caroline, ZSA Legal Recruitment (C) .. 670

Carrette, Linda, Prescott Legal Search Inc (C) 537
Casey, William B., Hughes & Company (R) 94
Coe, Holly E., Prescott Legal Search Inc (C) 537
Coleman, Michael M., Coleman Legal Staffing (C) 288
Comeford, Esq., Patricia A., The Esquire Group (C) 334
Cote, Lucie, ZSA Legal Recruitment (C) 670
Cottington, Kaye, Bennett Search & Consulting Company Inc (R) 16
Cottington, Michael, Bennett Search & Consulting Company Inc (R) 16
D'Alessio, Esq., Gary A., Chicago Legal Search Ltd (C) 284
DeCaster, Paul, DeCaster Associates (C) 309
Delinks, Marissa, Spherion Legal Group (C) 618
Demetrovich, Tom, Kforce (C) 419
Dine, Elaine, E P Dine Inc (C) 313
Edelman, Diane, Stephen M Haas Legal Placement (C) 375
Elfus, Brian, Jeffrey Allan Company Inc (C) 230
English Jones, Suzanne, Vera L Rast Partners Inc (VLRPI) (C) 551
Etling, Allen, Spherion Legal Group (C) 618
Fergus, Colin, Fergus Partnership Consulting Inc (C) 346
Fergus, Jean M. H., Fergus Partnership Consulting Inc (C) 346
Fontaine, Valerie A., Seltzer Fontaine Beckwith (C) 600
Foster, Dennis J., Major Legal Services LLC (C) 437
Frey, Florence, Frey & Sher Associates Inc (C) .. 364
Gallopo, Charles P., H Hertner Associates Inc (C) 389
Genel, George, Genel Associates (C) 367
Gillard, Cheryl A., Gillard Associates Legal Search (C) 369
Ginley, Michael, The Lear Group Inc (R) 116
Greene, Karin L., Greene-Levin-Snyder LLC (C) 373
Gury, Chris, The Goodkind Group Inc (C) 372
Haberman, Meyer, Interquest Inc (R) 99
Hacksel, Stephanie, ZSA Legal Recruitment (C) 670
Haney, Caroline, ZSA Legal Recruitment (C) 670
Harelson, Electra, Prescott Legal Search Inc (C) 537
Harris, Victoria, Houser Martin Morris (C) 394
Hebert, Kristin, TMP Worldwide Executive Search (R) 194
Helms, James, The Stewart Group (C) 627
Hepworth, Sheila, ZSA Legal Recruitment (C) ... 670
Herd, Jim, Herd Freed Hartz (R) 89
Hertner, Herbert H., H Hertner Associates Inc (C) 389
Hertner, Pamela R., H Hertner Associates Inc (C) 389
Hoetger, Craig M., Esq., Chicago Legal Search Ltd (C) 284
Hopkins, Scott, Kforce (C) 419
Huck, Donna H., H Hertner Associates Inc (C) ... 389
Hyde, Tonda, Prescott Legal Search Inc (C) 537
Isgett, Merle, Spherion Legal Group (C) 618
Johnson, Cindy, CareerTrac Employment Services Inc (C) 277
Kaiser, Elaine, Dunhill Professional Search of New Haven (C) 321
Kalyna, Adrianne, Martin Partners LLC (R) 126
Kass, Roberta, Seltzer Fontaine Beckwith (C) 600
Kaufman, Stuart, MRI of Great Neck (C) 466
Kellett, Jr., Samuel B., eAttorneys (C) 327
Kennedy, Susan Ann, ZSA Legal Recruitment (C) 670

Attorneys

Lawyers

Right of way

Leisure

SPECIALTIES

RECRUITER SPECIALTIES INDEX / MANAGEMENT / 1015

Ballaro, William, The Search Firm LLC (C)....... 596
Balunas, David A., Executive Resource Group Inc (R)........ 64
Barbachano, Berenice, Barbachano Int'l Inc (C). 249
Barnett, Megan, HRCG Inc Executive Search Management Consulting (R) 94
Barnhart, David, Lechner & Associates Inc (C).. 429
Barraclough, Roy, Paul Bodner & Associates Inc (R)........ 20
Bauman, Ina, The Bauman Group (R) 14
Beeson, William B., Lawrence-Leiter & Company (R)........ 115
Belastock, Gary, The Retail Network (C) 556
Benton, Kevin, Benton & Associates (C)........ 255
Bergeris, Jim, Bergeris & Company Inc (R) 17
Bezold, Joe, MRI of The Baltimore Washington Corridor (C)........ 461
Bigger, Brian B., ARG Associates (C)........ 241
Bising, Shawn, Bising Group (C) 257
Blaushild, Eric, AutoPeople (C) 247
Boje, Bruce A., Westfields Int'l Inc (C) 659
Bond, Ann F., Ann Bond Associates Inc (C) 260
Bond, Paul, SeBA Int'l LLC (R) 173
Bond, Robert S., Ann Bond Associates Inc (C) .. 260
Boyle, Michael, Boyle Ogata Bregman (R) 22
Boyle, Paul R., Boyle & Associates Retained Search Corp (R) 22
Bradbury, Jr., Paul W., The Bradbury Management Group Inc (R)........ 23
Bradford, Carl, Bradford Consulting Companies (C) 263
Brady, Karen, Management Principals (C) 439
Bredeson, Nancy, Artemis HRC (C)........ 242
Breen, Bill, Personnel Inc (C)........ 528
Bridgman, Michael, Executive Recruiters (C) 339
Brogan, Pat, Human Resource Bureau (C)........ 397
Bronstad, Alice, MRI of Milwaukee-North (C) .. 480
Brown Oude Kotte, Elisabeth, AutoPeople (C)... 247
Brown, Donald V., The Corim Group (R) 43
Brown-Alcala, Sheila, Michael J Hall & Company (R)........ 83
Bufkin, E. Ralph, BFW Inc (C) 257
Buggy, Linda, Garthwaite Partners Int'l (R)........ 75
Bullis, Kate, SeBA Int'l LLC (R)........ 173
Bulmer, Robert E., Alaska Executive Search Inc (C)........ 229
Butler, Jr., Kirby B., The Butlers Company Insurance Recruiters (C)........ 269
Byles, Mark, Trillium Talent Resource Group (C)........ 647
Cagan, Randy A., FPC of Raleigh (C) 359
Callicott, Robin D., Perfect Search Inc (C) 526
Capo, John, Carter McKenzie Inc (C)........ 278
Caraway, Suzanne, Austin Group Int'l (R)........ 10
Carey, Harvey, Carion Resource Group Inc (C).. 277
Carson, Sandra, Carson-Thomas & Associates (C)........ 278
Cinco, Lawrence K., MRI of Melbourne (C) 453
Clancey, Mark, Broadband Media Communications Inc (C) 266
Clutter, David E., David E Clutter (C) 287
Cole, Leslie C., MRI of Middlesex (C)........ 452
Cooke, Jeffrey R., The Cooke Group (R)........ 43
Corazolla, Susan, Archer Resource Solutions Inc (C)........ 241
Cotten, Cathey, MetaSearch Inc (C) 494
Courtright, Robert J., Courtright & Associates Inc (R)........ 44
Cowall, Frank A., Altec/HRC (C)........ 233
Cracknell, Joann, NCC Executive Search Consultants (C) 508
Cremeans, Cynthia, Gail Darling & Associates (C)........ 307
Crutchfield, Bob, Crutchfield Associates Inc (C) 304
Curtis, Susan J., ProSearch Recruiting (C) 545
Daugherty, Sue, Allard Associates Inc (C) 230
DeRario, Donna, FPC of San Diego (C)........ 353
DeRiso, J., Ash & Associates Executive Search (C) 242
DeRose, Rick, DigitalHire (C) 313
Desgrosellier, Gary P., Personnel Unlimited/Executive Search (C) 528
DesLandes, Lynda, Engineering Solutions Int'l (C) 332
Di Veto, Daina, Card Resource Group Inc (C) 273
Dillon, Mark, NaTek Corp (C) 504
Dishaw, Raymond J., R J Dishaw & Associates (R) 53
Dixon, Sayre, Employ® (C) 332
Downs, Greg, Executive Recruiters Agency Inc (C) 338
Dremely, Mark, Richard, Wayne & Roberts (C) 557
Dusome, Terry, Holloway, Schulz & Partners (C) 393
Elzweig, Mark, Mark Elzweig Company Ltd (R) 60
Empey, David, MRI of Franktown (C) 452
Erspamer, Roy C., Erspamer Associates (C) 333
Erstling, Gregory J., The Phoenix Health Search Group (C) 530
Eskra, Michael D., The Michael David Group (C) 308
Fisch, Bob, J S Robertson - Retained Search (R) 165
Fischer, Judith, RJ Associates (C) 559
Fischer, Ronald, RJ Associates (C) 559
Fitzgerald, Geoffrey, Fitzgerald Associates (R)..... 69
Fitzpatrick, James, Fitzpatrick & Associates (C) 349
Foster, Jennifer, Lexington Software Inc (C)...... 431
Foster, Sande, Major Consultants Inc (C)........ 437
Fox, Caryn, Equate Executive Search Inc (C) 333
Fremon, Michael W., The Revere Associates Inc (R) 162
Froehlich, Peter, Peter Froehlich & Company (C) 364
Furman, Matt, MJF Associates (C)........ 498
Gaches, Martha, Don Neal & Associates (C)...... 508
Gallin, Lawrence, Gallin Associates Inc (C)........ 365
Garfinkle, Benson D., MetroVantage (C) 494
Garrison, Randall, The Garrison Organization (R) 75
Gauger, Dianne, Dianne Gauger & Associates (C) 367
Gerald, C. Richard, C R Gerald & Associates (R) 76
Gibson, Bruce, Gibson & Company Inc (R) 76
Gideon, Mark, Eagle Search Associates (C) 326
Gilmore, Cynthia K., Whitehouse & Pimms (R) 204
Glassberg, Bob, Sales Search (C) 585
Glosser, Elizabeth B., The Executive Exchange Corp (C)........ 337
Glou, Alan, Glou Int'l Inc (R)........ 77
Goehring, Hal, H L Goehring & Associates Inc (C) 370
Golding, Michael S., Michael Associates (R)...... 133
Graebner-Smith, Linda, MRI of Milwaukee-North (C) 480
Greenberg, Jordan A., The Pinnacle Source Inc (C) 531
Greist, Robin, Management Principals (C) 439
Gricius, Suzanne, AddStaff Executive Search (C) 225
Guarino, Alan, Cornell Group Int'l Consulting Inc (R) 43
Guarino, Kathleen, Cornell Group Int'l Consulting Inc (R) 43
Guzzetta, Mr. Christy, GES Services Inc (R) 76
Hadick, Russ, Russ Hadick & Associates Inc (C) 376
Hahn, Kevin, Career Forum Inc (C) 275
Hamblin, Donna S., Hamblin & Associates (C) .. 378
Hamill, Robert W., Robert Howe & Associates (R) 93
Hamilton, Denman, Synergy 2000 (C) 631
Hamilton, Dianne, The Barton Group Inc (C) 251
Hansen, David G., Ott & Hansen Inc (R) 144
Harcourt, Peter, Harcourt & Associates (C) 380
Harris, David L., FPC of Decatur (C)........ 353
Havener, Robert W., Robert W Havener Associates Inc (C) 382
Havens, J. A., Real Estate Executive Search Inc (C) 552
Hawthorne, Christine, Search Int'l (R) 172
Hay, Elaine, Campbell, Edgar Inc (C)........ 272
Heisser, Robert, The Sequel Group LLC (C) 600
Helnore, Diann, Partners in Recruiting (C) 523
Hendricks, II, Stanley M., National Recruiting Service (C) 506
Hershman, Robert, AutoPeople (C)........ 247
Hidde, Robert, Hidde & Associates (C) 389
Hoff, Sarah, HTSS Executive Search (C)........ 396
Hogg, Jr., James G., Whittlesey & Associates Inc (R) 204
Hopkins, Mark, Shore Paralax Inc (R) 176
Howells, Pat, HTSS Executive Search (C)........ 396
Howett, Nancy, Executive Recruiters (C) 339
Hunter, Don, C D Warner & Associates (C) 656
Iannacone, Paul, Dumont & Associates Retail Recruitment (C)........ 318
Iommazzo, Robert, SeBA Int'l LLC (R)........ 173
Johnson, Cheri, Johnson & Associates Inc (R).... 101
Johnson, Frank Y., HealthCare Recruiters Int'l • Alabama (C)........ 385
Johnson, Robert J., Quality Search Inc (C)........ 547
Kalinowski, Bob, FMK Staffing Services LLC (C)........ 350
Kane, John F., HRCG Inc Executive Search Management Consulting (R)........ 94
Karp, Linda S., Karp & Associates (C) 416
Kashinsky, Richard J., MRI of Monterey (C)...... 450
Kennedy, James G., HRCG Inc Executive Search Management Consulting (R) 94
Kern, Kathleen G., ADOW Professionals (C) 225
Kershaw, Blair, Blair Kershaw Associates Inc (C)........ 418
Kilbreath, Troy, Management Principals (C) 439
Kirkpatrick, Don, Nations Executive Recruiters (C)........ 507
Klinger, Michael, Major Consultants Inc (C) 437
Knox, Dave, APA Employment Agency Inc (C)........ 239
Koenig, Jerrold, P R Management Consultants Inc (C) 519
Komorner, Paul, Whitney Group (C) 660
Kool, Joan, Professional Recruiters Inc (C) 542
Korkuch, Sandy, The Addison Consulting Group (C) 224
Kosakowski, Kathy, Thomas Roberts & Company (C)........ 562
Koski, Sherry, Adams & Ryan Inc (C)........ 224
Krieger, Dennis F., Seiden Krieger Associates Inc (R) 112
Krisniski, Cheryl, Artemis HRC (C) 242
Kuehnling, William, Sanford Rose Associates - Canton (C)........ 589

SPECIALTIES

(R) = Retainer; (C) = Contingency

Management consulting

Manufacturing

SPECIALTIES

SPECIALTIES

1020 / MANUFACTURING / THE DIRECTORY OF EXECUTIVE RECRUITERS

Mattison, Frank, W G Baird & Associates (C).... 248
Mayhall, Sheryl, Mayhall Search Group Inc (C)........ 488
Maynard, Dave, ATS Reliance Technical Group (C)........ 245
McAnney, Michael, Renaissance Resources (R)........ 161
McCain, Morgan, Allen, Austin, Lowe & Powers (R)........ 5
McClosky, Evan, Open Concepts (C)........ 517
McClosky, John, Open Concepts (C)........ 517
McClosky, Linda, Open Concepts (C)........ 517
McDougall, Philip, ATS Reliance Technical Group (C)........ 245
McFarland, Neal, ADOW Professionals (C)....... 225
McGill, Ed, MRI of Columbia (C)........ 461
McInturff, Robert E., McInturff & Associates Inc (C)........ 490
McLane, Thomas L., The Directorship Search Group Inc (R)........ 53
McMillin, Robert, PricewaterhouseCoopers Executive Search (R)........ 154
McNamara, Lynda Hook, McNamara Search Associates Inc (R)........ 129
McQuiddy, Brian, Woodmoor Group Inc (C)..... 665
Mears, Jack, Kelly Walker Associates (C)........ 654
Meister, Verle, MRI of Cheyenne (C)........ 481
Mellinger, Cathy, Continental Design & Engineering (C)........ 294
Melotti, Rita, MRI of Traverse City (C)........ 463
Mendez-Tucker, Barbara, Wesley, Brown & Bartle Company Inc (R)........ 202
Menefee, Shawn, Corporate Plus Ltd (C)........ 297
Metz, Nancy, Dominguez-Metz & Associates (R)........ 56
Meyer, Rick M., Meyer Associates Inc (R)........ 132
Miller, Edward R., Ratliff, Taylor & Lekan Inc (R)........ 158
Miller, James G., Crowe Chizek & Company LLP (C)........ 303
Miller, Teresa R., Tomlinson-Miller Inc (C)....... 643
Millius, Paul, Paul Millius Associates (R)........ 134
Mirsky, Al, The Barton Group Inc (C)........ 251
Mitchell, Sidney J., Sanford Rose Associates - Vienna (C)........ 591
Mojek, Chuck, American Resources Corp (C).... 235
Molina, Dominique, Winthrop Partners Inc (R).. 206
Monchamp, Cathy, Allen Personnel Services Ltd (C)........ 231
Moore, Sandee, Moore Research Associates (R)........ 135
Morales, Carmen, Williger & Associates (R)...... 205
Morones, Juan-Carlos, Confisa Int'l Group (C)... 292
Morris, Harry G., Dunhill Professional Search of Mansfield (C)........ 324
Morris, Lana K., Dunhill Professional Search of Mansfield (C)........ 324
Morris, Ted, Cleveland Business Consultants (C)........ 286
Morrison, Julie A., Agri-Business Services Inc (C)........ 228
Morrison, Michael J., Agri-Business Services Inc (C)........ 228
Morrow, Michael, RSMR Global Resources (R)........ 167
Mueller, William, Noll Human Resource Services (C)........ 512
Mullane, Gerry, Executive Resources (C)........ 340
Mulvaney, Ronald F., R F Mulvaney & Associates Inc (R)........ 137
Munro, Jennifer, Jennifer Munro & Partners Inc (R)........ 138
Murawski, Joseph S., Teknon Employment Resources Inc (C)........ 639
Nagler, Leon G., Nagler, Robins & Poe Inc (R)..139
Natowitz, Robert, DeMatteo Associates (C)........311
Needham, Bobbie, Needham Consultants Inc (C)........508
Needham, Mike, Needham Consultants Inc (C)...508
Nelson, David G., The Personnel Group Inc (R)........149
Nelson, Len, Len Nelson & Associates Inc (C)....508
Nephew, Robert, Christian & Timbers (R)........36
Newman, Ellen, MRI of Rochester (C)........463
Nix Gilmore, Pamela, MRI of Loudoun County S (C)........478
Nocifora, David, Christian & Timbers (R)........35
Nomer, Gary, American Recruiters Consolidated Inc (C)........235
Noorani, Firoz, MRI of Edison (C)........465
Noorani, Frank, MRI of Edison (C)........465
Nunnelee, Wayne, Nunnelee & Associates Inc (C)........514
O'Brien, Timothy M., O'Brien & Company Inc (R)........141
O'Daniel, Beverly W., The Elsworth Group (C)..331
O'Steen, Ray, American Professional Search Inc (C)........235
Oglesbee, Shawn M., Christian & Timbers (R).....35
Ortiz, Martha, R A Briones & Company (C).......265
Owens, Jesse W., Merle W Owens & Associates (R)........144
Owens, Merle W., Merle W Owens & Associates (R)........144
Owens, Reggie, Gabriel Worldwide Inc (C)........365
Pailin, Cheryl, Pailin Group Professional Search Consultants (R)........145
Palazzolo, Kathy, Premier Recruiting Group (C)........536
Pallotto, Victoria, Bohan & Bradstreet Inc (C)....259
Palmer, Phyllis, Wade Palmer & Associates Inc (C)........521
Palmer, Wade, Wade Palmer & Associates Inc (C)........521
Pantelas, Jim, Artemis HRC (C)........242
Park, Cleve A., MRI of Birmingham (C)........448
Parr, Thomas A., Holland & Associates Inc (R)....91
Pearson, Brian, Roth Young of Houston (C).......566
Pearson, Don, Personnel Assistance Corp (C).....527
Pedelty, Lori K., Capstone Consulting Inc (R)......30
Penley, Jeffrey M., Highlander Search (C)........390
Pepple, Bob, FPC of Jacksonville (C)........354
Perkins, R. Patrick, The Perkins Group (R)........149
Petruzzi, Vincent J., Petruzzi Associates (C).......529
Pezim, Howard J., The Bedford Consulting Group Inc (R)........15
Picarella, Greg, Gregory, Kyle & Associates Inc (C)........374
Pines, Howard, The Beam Group (R)........15
Pitt, Richard, Staff Resources Inc (C)........622
Plunkett, Mike, Phillips Resource Group (C)......530
Podway, Hope, Executive BioSearch (C)........336
Polson, Christopher C., Polson & Company Inc (R)........152
Popham, Harold C., Emerson & Company (C)....331
Portanova, Peter M., ROI Associates Inc (C)......563
Porter, Jeffrey C., The Porter Hamel Group Inc (C)........534
Powell, Donald, Proquest Inc (C)........544
Powell, Marie, Kenzer Corp (R)........107
Powers, Norman S., Norman Powers Associates Inc (C)........535
Poyck, Walter S., Stewart Associates (C)........627
Preger, George, Lamon + Stuart + Michaels Inc (R)........113
Premister, Sal, M T Donaldson Associates Inc (C)........315
Presley-Cannon, Judy, Corporate Image Group (C)........296
Priftis, Tony, Evie Kreisler & Associates Inc (C)........424
Pritchett, Philip H., FPC of North Dallas (C)......361
Provda, Peter, FPC of Menlo Park (C)........358
Purkerson, David A., Sanford Rose Associates - Pensacola (R)........169
Putiri, Vincent, Asheville Search & Consulting (C)........243
Pyatt, Clint, Spherion Professional Recruiting Group (C)........620
Raab, Julie, Vaughan & Company Executive Search Inc (C)........651
Rackley, Collette M., McDonald-Rackley Consulting Group (R)........129
Raeburn, Alan, ARC Staffing Inc (C)........241
Raley, Frank, Raley & Associates Inc (C)........550
Ramirez, Richard, Marentz & Company (C)......483
Ramstad, Bruce L., Bruce L Ramstad (C)........550
Rardin, Ed, Brentwood Int'l (R)........24
Reid, Tom, Compton & Associates (C)........290
Rice, Robert N., Technical Management Resources Inc (C)........637
Richards, Terry, Terry Richards (C)........558
Riddle, James E., Riddle & McGrath LLC (R).... 164
Roberts, Bill, Southern Technical Recruiters (C)........616
Robinson, Verneda, V Robinson & Company Inc (C)........562
Rockwell, Sr., Richard B., Applied Search Associates Inc (C)........240
Rodriguez Smithson, Raquel, R A Rodriguez and Associates Inc (C)........563
Roethlein, John, MRI of Tucson-Foothills (C)....449
Roethlein, Lorian E., MRI of Tucson-Foothills (C)........449
Rogers, George W., Dunhill Executive Search of Brown County (C)........322
Rogers, S. L., Dunhill Executive Search of Brown County (C)........322
Rolland, Guy, Rolland Ressources Humaines Inc (R)........166
Roodvoets, Jan, J E Lessner Associates Inc (R)..117
Rose, John M., The Curtiss Group Int'l (R)........46
Rosenow, Richard, Heath/Norton Associates Inc (R)........86
Ross, Eric W., Flowers & Associates (C)........350
Ross, William J., Flowers & Associates (C)........350
Rotondo, Michael, Samson Findings (R)........169
Roy, Candace L., Northeast Consulting Group (R)........140
Roy, Jr., G. Charles, Northeast Consulting Group (R)........140
Rubin, Stephanie, Amherst Human Resource Group Ltd (C)........236
Sackmary, Stephen M., Sanford Rose Associates - Austin (C)........591
Salzberg, David, Roth Young of Seattle (C).......566
Sargis, Scott R., Strategic Search Corp (R)........187
Sarna, Edmund, Flannery, Sarna & Associates (R)........69
Sawyer, Pierce, Phillips Resource Group (C)......530
Schatz, Jr., William G., The Schatz Company (C)........592
Schmidt, Gregory, Cleveland Business Consultants (C)........286
Schmidt, III, William "Kip" C., Christian & Timbers (R)........35
Schmieder, Laura, Premier Placement Inc (C)....536
Schneider, Margo, Geller Braun & White Inc (C)........367
Schneider, Paul J., Prime Resource Associates Inc (C)........538

General

management

SPECIALTIES

SPECIALTIES

Database

Materials

handling

SPECIALTIES

SPECIALTIES

SPECIALTIES

Brolin, Lawrence E., DLB Associates (R) 55

New media

Bentley, David, Nordeman Grimm Inc (R) 140
Brolin, Lawrence E., DLB Associates (R) 55
Burnett, Master, Silicon Talent Corp (C) 603
Campbell, Robert S., Wellington Management Group (R) 202
Daily, John, Christian & Timbers (R) 36
Farrell, Frank J., Nordeman Grimm Inc (R) 140
Fippinger, Steve, Fipp Associates Inc (C) 348
Flannery, Michael, Redwood Partners Ltd (R) 160
Fulgham-MacCarthy, Ann, Columbia Consulting Group (R) 39
Goldberg, Steve, Media Recruiting Group Inc (C) 491
Goodman-Brolin, Dorothy, DLB Associates (R) 55
Goodwin, Catherine, Richards Associates Inc (R) 163
Greger, Kenneth R., Greger/Peterson Associates Inc (R) 80
Hamilton, Lisa J., Hamilton & Company (C) 379
Houchins, William C. Buster, Christian & Timbers (R) 36
Kanuit, Cathie, Brown, Bernardy, Van Remmen Inc (C) 267
Kelch, Anna McCormick, The Cheyenne Group (R) 34
Klein, Robert, Allen Evans Klein Int'l (R) 5
Koch, Gail Kleinberg, CAS Comsearch Inc (C) 279
Koller, Jr., Edward R., The Howard-Sloan-Koller Group (R) 93
Kuklinski, John, Satterfield & Associates Inc (R) 170
Liota, C., Murphy Partners Int'l (R) 138
Lucarelli, Joan, Diversified Search Inc (R) 54
Macalister, Kim, The Cheyenne Group (R) 34
Mastandrea, Pat, The Cheyenne Group (R) 34
Mattes, Jr., Edward C., The Ogdon Partnership (R) 143
Maurer, James, Berardi & Associates (R) 17
Metschke, Rebecca S., Convergence Executive Search (C) 294
Myer, Rusty, Diversified Search Inc (R) 54
Perlman, Willa, The Cheyenne Group (R) 34
Quarin, Randy, Partners Executive Search Consultants Inc (R) 146
Ridenour, Suzanne S., Ridenour & Associates (R) 164
Rosen, Betsi, The Cutting Edge Group Inc (C) 305
Ross, Elsa, Gardner-Ross Associates Inc (R) 74
Schloss, Dee, Joseph Associates Inc (C) 413
Schoenfeld, Randy, Redwood Partners Ltd (R) 160
Seibel, Paula, Christian & Timbers (R) 36
Silver, Susan, Silver Associates (C) 604
Stone, Michael, Kaye-Stone Partners (C) 417
Thompson, Kelvin, Norman Broadbent Int'l Inc (R) 140
Van Remmen, Roger, Brown, Bernardy, Van Remmen Inc (C) 267
Venable, William, Thorndike Deland Associates LLC (R) 50
Virgili, Franca, The Cheyenne Group (R) 34
Wayne, Vici, Christian & Timbers (R) 35
Webster, Larry, Technology Management Partners (R) 192
Zwiff, Jeffrey G., Thorndike Deland Associates LLC (R) 50

Noise control

Fetridge, Guild, Guild Fetridge Acoustical Search Inc (C) 346

Non-profit

Abruzzo, James, StratfordGroup (R) 188
Amcis, Lillian, Joel H Paul & Associates Inc (C) 524
Andrews, James G., Rusher, Loscavio & LoPresto (R) 168
Ast, Steven T., AST/BRYANT (R) 9
Auerbach, Judith A., Auerbach Associates Inc (R) 10
Badger, Carole, Tuft & Associates Inc (R) 197
Baird-Counter, Michele, StratfordGroup (R) 188
Barnes, Roanne L., Barnes Development Group LLC (R) 13
Beezat, Robert A., The PAR Group (R) 146
Berger, Emanuel, Witt/Kieffer, Ford, Hadelman & Lloyd (R) 206
Berger, Jay V., Morris & Berger (R) 136
Bernard, G. Stevens, The PAR Group (R) 146
Biggers, Maureen S., Jon McRae & Associates Inc (R) 130
Boulware, Christine, Boulware & Associates Inc (R) 21
Brimeyer, James, The Brimeyer Group Inc (R) 25
Bronder, Stephanie L., Fagan & Company (R) 66
Bryant, Christopher P., AST/BRYANT (R) 9
Butler, Carol, Leonard Corwen Corporate Recruiting Services (C) 299
Caldwell, Clarke, Carnegie Partners Inc (R) 31
Callaghan, Meg, Diversified Search Inc (R) 54
Carabelli, Paula, Witt/Kieffer, Ford, Hadelman & Lloyd (R) 206
Casey, Carol, Joy Reed Belt Search Consultants Inc (R) 16
Cattie, Jr., Gerard F., Diversified Search Inc (R) 54
Dingman, Bruce, Robert W Dingman Company Inc (R) 53
Dingman, Robert W., Robert W Dingman Company Inc (R) 53
Dougherty, Juanita, R Dann & Associates LLC (C) 307
Douglas, Cal, Boyden (R) 22
Dowdy, Jennifer Owens, Merle W Owens & Associates (R) 144
Ducharme, Lynda, Ducharme Group Inc (R) 57
Eldredge, L. Lincoln, Brigham Hill Consultancy (R) 25
Erickson, Elaine, Kenzer Corp (R) 107
Erickson-Pearson, David, Boulware & Associates Inc (R) 21
French, Peter N., P N French Associates Inc (R) 72
Funk, Bill, Korn/Ferry Int'l (R) 110
Gahan, Carolyn M., Gahan Associates (R) 73
Gibbs, Beth, Arthur Diamond Associates Inc (R) 52
Hagman, Gerald E., The PAR Group (R) 146
Henry, Bruce, Bruce Henry Associates Inc (R) 88
Justus McGinty, Julia, Berkhemer Clayton Inc (R) 17
Kelly, William W., Jon McRae & Associates Inc (R) 130
Kenzer, Robert D., Kenzer Corp (R) 107
Kile, Robert W., Rusher, Loscavio & LoPresto (R) 168
Kuhn, Gregory T., The PAR Group (R) 146
Kulper, Keith D., Kulper & Company LLC (R) 112
Lindauer, Lois L., Lois L Lindauer Searches (R) 118
Loscavio, J. Michael, Rusher, Loscavio & LoPresto (R) 168
Lyttle, Jordene, PricewaterhouseCoopers Executive Search (R) 154
Machlowitz, Marilyn, Machlowitz Consultants Inc (R) 122
Magen, Judy, Joel H Paul & Associates Inc (C) 524
Malkewicz, Lisa M., Crowe Chizek & Company LLP (C) 303
Marcello, Joe, Executive Search Consultants Corp (C) 341
Matthews, James Mickey, Stanton Chase Int'l (R) 184
May, Lori E., The Harris Consulting Corp (R) 84
McCormack, Joseph A., McCormack & Associates (R) 128
McLean, B. Keith, PricewaterhouseCoopers Executive Search (R) 154
McMillen, Kristina, Brigham Hill Consultancy (R) 25
McRae, O. Jon, Jon McRae & Associates Inc (R) 130
Mindlin, Freda, Opportunity Resources Inc (R) 143
Mogilner, Myra, Joel H Paul & Associates Inc (C) 524
Morris, Kristine A., Morris & Berger (R) 136
Morrisson, Kim, Diversified Search Inc (R) 54
Murray, Colette, Paschal•Murray Executive Search (R) 147
Nixon, Barbara, PricewaterhouseCoopers Executive Search (R) 154
Noeske, Nancy R., Overton Consulting (R) 144
Orr, Kenneth B., Jon McRae & Associates Inc (R) 130
Parker, Donna R., The Whitney Smith Company Inc (C) 660
Paul, Joel H., Joel H Paul & Associates Inc (C) 524
Pelton, Margaret, PricewaterhouseCoopers Executive Search (R) 154
Pettway, Samuel H., Spencer Stuart (R) 182
Pickering, Dorothy C., Livingston, Robert & Company (R) 119
Piper, Jr., James R., Stanton Chase Int'l (R) 184
Posner, Gary J., Witt/Kieffer, Ford, Hadelman & Lloyd (R) 206
Reaume, Paul A., The PAR Group (R) 146
Ross, Donal, The Lear Group Inc (R) 116
Ross, Martin, StratfordGroup (R) 188
Sedlar, Jeri L., Sedlar & Miners (R) 174
Segal, Eric B., Kenzer Corp (R) 107
Segil, Annette R., Executive Careers Ltd (R) 63
Sellery, Jr., Robert A., Robert Sellery Associates Ltd (R) 174
Sharman, Andy, TMP Worldwide Executive Search (R) 194
Sierra, Rafael, TMP Worldwide Executive Search (R) 194
Smith, Craig V., Diversified Search Inc (R) 54
Smith, Mike, Smith Bridges and Associates Inc (C) 606
Smith, Toni S., Spencer Stuart (R) 181
Sykes, Arnold, Arnold Sykes & Associates (R) 189
Tandy, Charles W., Tandy, Morrison & LaTour LLC (R) 190
Tucker, Michael, MTA Partners (R) 137
Tunnell, Deborah, Brigham Hill Consultancy (R) 25
Van Dyke, Roger, Van Dyke Associates (R) 197
Vennat, Manon, Spencer Stuart (R) 182
Whitney, William A., Larsen, Whitney, Blecksmith & Zilliacus Inc (R) 114
Wilke, William, Management Resource Group Ltd (R) 124
Wooller, Edmund A. M., Riddle & McGrath LLC (R) 164

SPECIALTIES

management

Optics

Oracle

Organizational development

Orthopedics

Piatkiewicz, Mary Lou, Medical Executive
  Search Associates Inc (C)............................... 491
Piatkiewicz, William L., Medical Executive
  Search Associates Inc (C)............................... 491

OTC

Besen, Douglas, Besen Associates Inc (C).......... 256
Musso, Connie, Consumer Search Inc (C).......... 294

Packaging

Austin, Larry, Lucas Group (C).......................... 435
Bahr, Frank, Focus Executive Search (C)........... 351
Banks, Paul C., Paul C Banks Associates (C)...... 249
Barber, Darrell B., Sales Consultants of The
  Bluegrass (C) 578
Bason, Maurice L., Bason Associates (R)............. 13
Bauman, Bobbi, BJB Associates (C) 258
Brann, Rudy, Executive Search Group Inc (C) 341
Briody, Steve, MRI of Arlington Heights (C)..... 457
Brown, C. C. "Jay", FPC of Raleigh (C)............. 359
Burke, Kaye, J Burke & Associates Inc (C)........ 268
Burke, Stoney, J Burke & Associates Inc (C) 268
Caprio, Jerry, Caprio & Associates Inc (R).......... 30
Carlin, James, Graphic Arts Employment
  Services Inc (C)... 372
Carveth, Peter, Packaging Resources (C)............. 521
Christian, Robert, Southern Chemical &
  Plastics Search (C) 616
Coco, Jr., Carl, Professions Inc (C)..................... 543
Daugherty, Judy, MRI of Dallas-Northwest (C) . 447
Ellis, Walter, Packaging Personnel Company
  Ltd (C) 520
Filippelli, Frank J., The Glenwood Group (C) ... 369
Flamer, Michael, The Dorfman Group (C) 315
Freeman, Julie, Recruiter Solutions Int'l (C)...... 552
Gardner, Marvin, Gardner-Ross Associates Inc
  (R)... 74
Gilliam, Toni, MRI of Spokane (C) 479
Glancey, Jr., Thomas F., Gordon Wahls
  Executive Search (C)..................................... 653
Gray, Geri, The Neely Group (C) 508
Griffin, Al, Gardner-Ross Associates Inc (R) 74
Hammock, Robert E., Robert W Havener
  Associates Inc (C).. 382
Havener, Robert W., Robert W Havener
  Associates Inc (C).. 382
Hayes, Don, MRI of Sugar Land (C) 477
Hill, Rodney, MRI of Atlanta West (C) 456
Hochwalt, Mike, MH Executive Search Group
  (C).. 495
Huettl, Robin, Packaging Personnel Company
  Ltd (C) 520
Jones, Bob, Vista Associates (C) 652
Kirchgessner, Ken, MRI of Pensacola (C).......... 454
Klavins, Larissa, Briant Associates Inc (R).......... 24
Krenz, Ron, R&M Associates (C) 549
Kuehling, Mark, FPC of Cincinnati (C)............. 359
Kunkle, Denise, D Kunkle & Associates (C)...... 425
Lee, Robert, MRI of Jacksonville (C) 453
Levy, Garrett, Synergy Search Ltd (C) 631
Lovegrove, Geoff, Morgan Executive Search
  Group Ltd (R) 135
Malloy, James K., Sales Consultants of
  Middlesex County (C).................................... 580
Marshall, John C., JM & Company (R) 101
May, William, Sales Consultants of Huntsville
  (C).. 573
O'Reilly, William E., MRI of Cincinnati-
  Sharonville (C) 470
Pascal, Rick, Rick Pascal & Associates Inc (C) .. 523
Petru, John W., Synergy Search Ltd (C) 631

Pettengill, Maurice A., Associated Recruiters
  (C)... 244
Phillips, Walter, Phillips Int'l Inc (C) 529
Pilcher, James, FPC of Cincinnati (C)................ 359
Post, Dick, MRI of Michigan Ave (C)................ 457
Reyes, Renee, MRI of Columbia (C).................. 461
Richards, R. Glenn, Executive Directions (R)....... 64
Rossen, Michael, Direct Recruiters Inc (C) 314
Rusnov, Samuel, Michael Latas & Associates
  Inc (R) 115
Schinke, Brenda, HCI Corp (C)......................... 383
Schwartz, Alan M., Selective Management
  Services Inc (C) 600
Scott, Michael, Winfield Scott Associates (C)..... 663
Smith, Gayle, J Burke & Associates Inc (C)....... 268
Steel, Mark D., Selective Management
  Services Inc (C) 600
Steinberg, Paul D., IMA Search Inc (R) 97
Storfer, Herbert F., The Dartmouth Group (R) ...48
Taylor, Dick, Packaging Personnel Company
  Ltd (C) 520
Tuttle, Tim, MRI of North Pinellas County (C)...455
Vague, Mark, FPC of Portland (C) 359
Valmore, Kim, Professions Inc (C) 543
Walton, Jack, J P Walton & Associates (C)........ 655
Walton, Patrick, J P Walton & Associates (C)..... 655
Wynn, John, Cook Associates® Inc (R) 42
Zamjahn, Charles J., River Region Personnel
  Inc (C) 559

Food

Harvey, John K., Harvco Consulting (C)............. 382

Paint

Asquith, Peter, Leigh Hunt & Associates Inc
  (C).. 398
Fisher, Lawrence C., Mullen Associates Inc
  (R) 137
Gres, Ed, Pioneer Executive Consultants (C) 531
Hunt, Leigh, Leigh Hunt & Associates Inc (C)... 398
Jentlie, Paul, Career Search Consultants llc (C)...275
Mullen, James J., Mullen Associates Inc (R)...... 137
Sinclair, Paul, Pioneer Executive Consultants
  (C).. 531
Wieber, William, Specialized Search Company
  (C).. 618
Zillifro, W. Keith, Zillifro & Associates (C)........ 669

Paper

Ambruster, David L., Renaissance Resources
  (R)... 161
Angell, Tryg R., Tryg R Angell Ltd (C) 238
Argenio, Paul J., Tierney Associates Inc (R)...... 193
Asquith, Peter, Leigh Hunt & Associates Inc
  (C).. 398
Aul, Lincoln, Precision Solutions Inc (C)........... 535
Baiko, Leisa, FPC of Bangor (C)....................... 356
Bjong, Mary, The Lawson Group Inc (C)........... 429
Brown, C. C. "Jay", FPC of Raleigh (C)............. 359
Brown, Caren, FPC of Bangor (C) 356
Charron, Maynard G., Paper Industry
  Recruitment (PIR) (C) 521
Coco, Jr., Carl, Professions Inc (C) 543
Corder, Eutha, RBW Associates (C) 551
Draper, Gary, Heritage Pacific Corp (C) 388
Fremon, Michael W., The Revere Associates
  Inc (R) 162
Froelich, K., Murphy Partners Int'l (R)............... 138
Gaw, F. William, Brandywine Management
  Group (R) 23
Gehle, Frederick P., Dunhill Professional
  Search of Augusta (C)................................... 322

Haugen, Bill, Pearson & Associates Inc (R)........ 147
Hayes, Don, MRI of Sugar Land (C).................. 477
Hitchcock, Gilly, FPC of Bangor (C) 356
Hoffman, Ed, NaTek Corp (C)........................... 504
Hudson, Kent, SourceWynds Executive Search
  (C)... 616
Hughes, Tim, Hughes & Associates Int'l Inc
  (C)... 396
Jansen, Carl, Search North America Inc (C) 596
Lasini, Dennis, Genesis Research (C) 368
Lawson, James W., The Lawson Group Inc (C).. 429
Leo, Brian, MRI of Atlanta Perimeter Center
  (C)... 455
Lovegrove, Geoff, Morgan Executive Search
  Group Ltd (R)... 135
Luzar, Jim, Sales Consultants of Milwaukee
  (C)... 583
Marsteller, Linda, Marsteller Wilcox
  Associates (C)... 485
May, William, Sales Consultants of Huntsville
  (C)... 573
McCracken, Terri, T E M Associates (C)............ 633
McFall, Ian, Forest People Int'l Search Ltd (C) ... 352
Morse, Jeffrey A., Brandywine Management
  Group (R) 23
O'Reilly, William E., MRI of Cincinnati-
  Sharonville (C).. 470
Oster, R. Rush, MRI of Anna Maria Island (C)... 453
Parker, Murray B., The Borton Wallace
  Company (R) 21
Pezim, Steven, The Bedford Consulting Group
  Inc (R) 15
Riesling, Phil, Pulp & Paper Int'l Inc (C) 547
Schwartz, Alan M., Selective Management
  Services Inc (C)... 600
Shearer, Gary F., MRI of Bonita Springs (C)...... 453
Siegrist, Jeffrey, Diversified Search Inc (R)......... 54
Smith, Heather, Whittlesey & Associates Inc
  (R)... 204
Steel, Mark D., Selective Management
  Services Inc (C)... 600
Thompson, Russ, FPC of Boise (C) 355
Vague, Mark, FPC of Portland (C)..................... 359
Valmore, Kim, Professions Inc (C) 543
Wheeler, Ray B., RBW Associates (C) 551
Wynn, John, Cook Associates® Inc (R)............... 42
Young, Paula G., Career Counseling Inc (CCI)
  (C)... 274

PeopleSoft

De Carolis, Mario, MRI of Traverse City (C) 463
Gerlach, Mary, Empire Consulting Group (C) 332
Mesina, Roman, The Consulting Group of
  North America Inc (C)................................... 293
Plavin, Avery, The Consulting Group of North
  America Inc (C)... 293
Robbins, Mark, Search Solutions Inc (C)............ 597
Shelton, Jim, MRI of North Canton (C) 471
Swami, Pad N., Fortuna Technologies Inc (C) ... 352
Zabor, Richard, Leader Institute Inc (C) 429

Peripherals

Franzen, Tracy A., Ross Personnel Consultants
  Inc (C)... 564
Kahn, Gale, FPC of Boulder (C) 354
Tarzia, Dana, Ross Personnel Consultants Inc
  (C)... 564

Pet food

Whittaker, Arnold G., Whittaker & Associates
  Inc (C)... 660

SPECIALTIES

Petrochemical

Pharmaceutical

PHDs

Philanthropy

Photonics

SPECIALTIES

Plastics

Adams, Kevin, Anthony Davis & Associates (C).................. 308
Allen, Jim, Southern Chemical & Plastics Search (C)................ 616
Anderson, Lea, Cypress Research Consultants Inc (C)................ 305
Banks, Paul C., Paul C Banks Associates (C).... 249
Bason, Maurice L., Bason Associates (R)............. 13
Bauzenberger, III, E. H., The Currier-Winn Company Inc (C)............ 305
Beck, Joseph W., National Computerized Employment Service Inc (C)............ 505
Bethmann, Chris, Southern Recruiters & Consultants Inc (C)............ 616
Bittner, Greg, NHA Plastics Recruiters (C)........ 510
Braxton, Jody, MRI of Pensacola (C)............ 454
Brown, James D., Northern Consultants Inc (R).. 141
Butler, Kevin, MRI of Akron (C)............ 470
Cahn, Juliette Lang, Juliette Lang Cahn Executive Search (C)............ 271
Creeger, David, Sanford Rose Associates - Fairlawn (C)............ 590
David, Dave, Executive Resource Associates (C)............ 339
DiDuca, Nancy, MRI of Prospect Heights (C)... 442
Dixson, Robert, MRI of Akron (C)............ 470
Dragomire, Jake, MRI of Akron (C)............ 470
Dugan, John H., J H Dugan & Associates Inc (R)............ 57
Eliason, Ron, Midland Consultants (C)............ 496
Enrico, Jim, Unisearch Search & Recruiting Inc (C)............ 649
Eubanks, David, Southern Recruiters & Consultants Inc (C)............ 616
Ford, Travis, Ford & Associates Inc (C)............ 351
Fountas, N. G., JLI-Boston (R)............ 101
Freese, Hal, Dunhill Professional Search of Greenwood (C)............ 324
Fremon, Michael W., The Revere Associates Inc (R)............ 162
Fruchtman, Gary, The Kent Group Inc (C)........ 418
Gandee, Tim, Recruiter Solutions Int'l (C)........ 552
Gentile, Craig, Cypress Research Consultants Inc (C)............ 305
Gentile, Wendy, Cypress Research Consultants Inc (C)............ 305
Gerst, Mike, MRI of Akron (C)............ 470
Gerst, Tom, MRI of Akron (C)............ 470
Gray, Geri, The Neely Group (C)............ 508
Gros, Dennis, Gros Plastics Recruiters (C)........ 374
Hanson, Hugh, FPC of Huntsville (C)............ 353
Hildebrand, John D., JM & Company (R)......... 101
Hiller, Arnie, US Search LLC (C)............ 650
Hoban, Fred, Osborn & Associates Inc (C)........ 518
Holloway, Roger M., MRI of Lake County Inc (C)............ 454
Just, Debra, Just Management Services Inc (C).. 414
Just, Susan, Just Management Services Inc (C).. 414
Kane, Len, MRI of Aiken (C)............ 473
Kerr, Jr., John B., Kerr Executive Recruiting (C)............ 418
Kirchgessner, Ken, MRI of Pensacola (C)........ 454
Krieger, Robert, G P Mattocks & Associates Inc (C)............ 488
Lawry, William R., W R Lawry Inc (R)............ 116
Lewis, Al, The Stelton Group Inc (C)............ 626
Linstead, Rick, Carnegie Resources Inc (C)....... 277
Lopez, David, MRI of Milwaukee-North (C)..... 480
Ludlow, Randy, The Icard Group Inc (C)............ 400
Luzar, Jim, Sales Consultants of Milwaukee (C)............ 583
Lybrook, David, Lybrook Associates Inc (C)..... 435

Lyons, Olin, Lyons Pruitt Int'l (R)............ 121
Machi, Michael T., MRI of Pleasanton (C)......... 451
Mathey, Joyce, Mathey Services (C)............ 487
Mattocks, Paul, G P Mattocks & Associates Inc (C)............ 488
May, William, Sales Consultants of Huntsville (C)............ 573
McCormick, Trina, G P Mattocks & Associates Inc (C)............ 488
McElhaney, Jr., Ron, MRI of Savannah (C)........ 456
McElhaney, Ron, MRI of Savannah (C)............ 456
Messervy, Mike, FPC of Huntsville (C)............ 353
Murray, Patrick, The Murray Group (C)............ 503
Neuhofs, Scott, Recruiter Solutions Int'l (C)..... 552
O'Reilly, William E., MRI of Cincinnati-Sharonville (C)............ 470
Olvera, Catherine, MRI of Fresno (C)............ 450
Osborn, Mary, Osborn & Associates Inc (C)...... 518
Pajak, Michael A., The Danielson Group Inc (C)............ 306
Petralia, Joe, FPC of Huntsville (C)............ 353
Pike, Dick, MRI of Burlington (C)............ 467
Post, Dick, MRI of Michigan Ave (C)............ 457
Raley, Frank, Raley & Associates Inc (C)............ 550
Rappaport, Richard, Business Answers Int'l (C)..269
Reed, Dave, MRI of Flint (C)............ 462
Roddy, Jack P., J P Roddy Consultants (C)......... 562
Roth, Bill, Lou Michaels Associates Inc (C)....... 495
Sawyer, Lynn, Cypress Research Consultants Inc (C)............ 305
Schnieder, Walter, Business Answers Int'l (C)...269
Siegrist, Jeffrey, Diversified Search Inc (R)........ 54
Slate, James E., FPC of Topsfield (C)............ 356
Snider, Jr., L. Bryan, Bryan & Louis Research (C)............ 267
Snider, Les, Bryan & Louis Research (C)............ 267
Teater, Sr., William G., Executive Resources Int'l, Inc (C)............ 340
Telleri, Frank C., The Eliot & Carr, Curry Telleri Group (R)............ 60
Tierney, Launa, Hans Becker Associates (C)...... 252
Tracey, Jay E., Jay Tracey Associates Inc (C).....644
Vague, Mark, FPC of Portland (C)............ 359
Warner, Laurie, The Rossi Search Group (C)...... 565
Weber, Greg, Polymer Network Inc (C)............ 533
Wells, Robert A., R A Wells Company (C)........658
White, David, W Robert Eissler & Associates Inc (C)............ 329
Willhoit, Davey, MRI of Pensacola (C)............ 454
Wynn, John, Cook Associates® Inc (R)............ 42
Young, Paula G., Career Counseling Inc (CCI) (C)............ 274
Zamjahn, Charles J., River Region Personnel Inc (C)............ 559

Plumbing

Creasy, Nancy, Michael Latas & Associates Inc (R)............ 115
Hoose, Dan Van, Michael Latas & Associates Inc (R)............ 115
Sharpe, Howard, Brooke Chase Associates Inc (R)............ 25

Plywood

Gandee, Joan C., MRI of Sugar Land (C)............ 477
Gandee, John R., MRI of Sugar Land (C)............ 477
Gandee, Shayna, MRI of Sugar Land (C)............ 477

Polymers

Telem, Peter B., Telem Adhesive Search Corp (C)............ 640

Polyurethane

Hunt, Leigh, Leigh Hunt & Associates Inc (C) ... 398

Portfolio management

Baccarini, Daniel J., The B & B Group Inc (C)... 247
Bufkin, E. Ralph, BFW Inc (C)............ 257
Elzweig, Mark, Mark Elzweig Company Ltd (R)............ 60
Miller, Nancy, Mark Elzweig Company Ltd (R)............ 60
Muskopf, Aaron, The B & B Group Inc (C)...... 248
Olschwanger, Paul F., Olschwanger Partners LLC (R)............ 143
Smith, Dickson, The Kinlin Company Inc (R).... 108
Wysocki, Robert, Cornell Group Int'l Consulting Inc (R)............ 43

Poultry

Daffala, Ronald, Merit Professional Search Inc (C)............ 493
Haggard, Luke, First Search America Inc (C)..... 348
Johnson, Ray, First Search America Inc (C)....... 348
Smitherman, Jim, Merit Professional Search Inc (C)............ 493

Power

Ambruster, David L., Renaissance Resources (R)............ 161
Bielecki, Mark, Sales Consultants of Kalamazoo (C)............ 579
Britt, Brian, NaTek Corp (C)............ 504
Clark, Jennifer, IDC Executive Search Inc (C)...400
Cutler, Robert, Cutler/Krenzke LLC (C)............ 47
Devaney, Marie, W Robert Eissler & Associates Inc (C)............ 329
Dillon, Mark, NaTek Corp (C)............ 504
Donelon, Wayne, WMD Inc (C)............ 664
Fisher, Earl, PowerBrokers LLC (C)............ 534
Gergen, Michael, Allen, Austin, Lowe & Powers (R)............ 6
Granet, Marc, IDC Executive Search Inc (C)..... 400
Howe, Timothy L., The Resource Group (R)....... 162
Hudson, Kent, SourceWynds Executive Search (C)............ 616
Kane, Michael, Kane & Associates (C)............ 416
LaBarba, Richard, SourceWynds Executive Search (C)............ 616
Nickels, Edward L., Michael Latas & Associates Inc (R)............ 115
Ragan, William, Michael Latas & Associates Inc (R)............ 115
Robinson, Wyn, SourceWynds Executive Search (C)............ 616
Roche, John, NaTek Corp (C)............ 504
Rotter, Stephen, RSMR Global Resources (R).... 167
Rowland, Boyd H., Bart Roberson & Company (C)............ 560
Weir, David G., Intercontinental Executive Group (C)............ 406
White, King, Allen, Austin, Lowe & Powers (R)............ 5

Presidents

Berger, Emanuel D., Educational Management Network (R)............ 58
Berger, Emmanuel, Educational Management Network (R)............ 58
Besen, Douglas, Besen Associates Inc (C)............ 256
Biggers, Maureen S., Jon McRae & Associates Inc (R)............ 130

SPECIALTIES

Carabelli, Paula, Educational Management
Network (R) 58
Deckelbaum, Rick, FPC of Raleigh (C) 359
Edwards, S. Bruce, Bruce Edwards &
Associates Inc (R) 59
Fischer, Howard, Howard Fischer Associates
Int'l Inc (R) 68
Gaffney, William, Gaffney Management
Consultants Inc (R) 73
Hard, Sally-Ann, Educational Management
Network (R) 59
Jerome, Gerald E., Jerome & Co (C) 411
Kelly, William W., Jon McRae & Associates
Inc (R) 130
Kohn, Steven, Affinity Executive Search (C) 227
Leske, Lucy, Educational Management
Network (R) 58
Love, Scott T., The Leadership Group (R) 116
Martin, Nancy, Educational Management
Network (R) 58
McClain, Duane, Construction Search
Specialists Inc (C) 293
McCray, Harold C., McCray, Shriver, Eckdahl
& Associates Inc (R) 128
McFeely, Clarence E., Clarence E McFeely Inc
(R)... 129
McRae, O. Jon, Jon McRae & Associates Inc
(R)... 130
Mellos, James S., Ki Technologies Inc
Executive Search Div (C) 422
Orr, Kenneth B., Jon McRae & Associates Inc
(R)... 130
Posner, Gary J., Educational Management
Network (R) 59
Silivanch, Garry, Global Data Services Inc (R) 77
Taylor, Mary Elizabeth, Educational
Management Network (R)............................. 59
Tierney, George F., Tierney Associates Inc (R).. 193

Printing

Bozza, Gary L., MRI of Chicago-Northwest
(C)... 458
Cali, Ronald, Royce Ashland Group Inc (C)....... 567
Caprio, Jerry, Caprio & Associates Inc (R)........ 30
Clark, David A., Sprout/Standish Inc (C) 621
Crosthwait, Bruce, MRI of Bellaire (C).............. 476
Daugherty, Judy, MRI of Dallas-Northwest (C) . 447
Dunn, Markay, Sales Consultants of
Alexandria (C) 578
Genuardi, Kathy, Sales Consultants of Cherry
Hill (C).. 580
Gibson, Michael, Sales Consultants of
Asheville (C)... 581
Glancey, Jr., Thomas F., Gordon Wahls
Executive Search (C)................................. 653
Griffin, Al, Gardner-Ross Associates Inc (R) 74
Hammock, Robert E., Robert W Havener
Associates Inc (C)................................... 382
Havener, Robert W., Robert W Havener
Associates Inc (C).................................... 382
Hemenway, Albert, Sanford Rose Associates -
Effingham (C) 588
Hobbs, Robert, Hobbs & Towne Inc (R)............. 91
Huff, David, Kutt Inc (C) 425
Link, Wayne, The Magenta Group (C) 437
Maiola, Diana E., Maiola & Company (C) 437
Marriott, Gloria A., MRI of Franklin (C).......... 475
Marriott, Roger H., MRI of Franklin (C) 475
Neighbors, Greg, Kutt Inc (C) 425
O'Reilly, William E., MRI of Cincinnati-
Sharonville (C).. 470
Petrello-Pray, Gina, Direct Recruiters Inc (C) 314
Phelps, Grace, Hardage Group (C) 380

Pilcher, James, FPC of Cincinnati (C) 359
Pulito, Carol M., Maiola & Company (C) 437
Ranberg, Carol, Marsteller Wilcox Associates
(C) 485
Robison, Margaret H., Robison Humphreys &
Associates Inc (R) 165
Schwartz, Alan M., Selective Management
Services Inc (C) 600
Seurer, Beth, Sales Consultants of Milwaukee
(C) 584
Shull, John, Search Net (C) 596
Smith, Mike, Smith Bridges and Associates Inc
(C) 606
Sneathen, Diane, The Magenta Group (C).......... 437
Soltan, Steve, SCS & Associates (C)................. 594
St. Denis, A., Sherry, Sanford Rose Associates
- Effingham (C) 588
St. Denis, Robert A., Sanford Rose Associates
- Effingham (C) 588
Steel, Mark D., Selective Management
Services Inc (C) 600
Tringle, Terry, Sanford Rose Associates -
Nashville (C) 590

Private equity

Bochner, Stephen, TMP Worldwide Executive
Search (R)... 194
Bovich, Maryann, Higdon Group Inc (R) 90
Choi, Julie A., Choi & Burns LLC (R) 35
Fitzpatrick, Susan, Martin Partners LLC (R) 126
Gardner, Nina-Marie, Higdon Group Inc (R) 90
Goldfarb, Abbe, TMP Worldwide Executive
Search (R)... 193
Gordon, Elliot, Korn/Ferry Int'l (R)................... 110
Healey, Joseph, TMP Worldwide Executive
Search (R)... 193
Higdon, Henry G., Higdon Group Inc (R) 90
Hynson, Tamara, Executive Search Int'l (ESI)
Inc (C) 342
Klein, Sloan, TMP Worldwide Executive
Search (R)... 194
Kreuzberger, Neil L., Kreuzberger &
Associates (C)... 424
Maslan, Neal, TMP Worldwide Executive
Search (R)... 194
Meyers, Leslie R., Higdon Group Inc (R)............. 90
Miles, D. Scott, Executive Search Int'l (ESI)
Inc (C) 342
Norris, Melissa, TMP Worldwide Executive
Search (R)... 193
Poster, Lawrence D., Catalyx Group (R).............. 33
Rothschild, John, TMP Worldwide Executive
Search (R)... 194
Russo, Amy, Baines Gwinner NA Inc (R)............. 11
Scherck, Terry, TMP Worldwide Executive
Search (R)... 193
Schibli, Peter, Twin Oaks Partners LLC (R)........ 197
Shea, Diane, Cross Hill Partners LLC (R)............ 45
Smith, Mark L., Korn/Ferry Int'l (R) 110
Stevens, Glenn, TMP Worldwide Executive
Search (R)... 193
Strickland, Cynthia S., Higdon Group Inc (R)....... 90
Waldman, Noah, TMP Worldwide Executive
Search (R)... 194
Webster, Judi, TMP Worldwide Executive
Search (R)... 194
Welles, Christopher, Twin Oaks Partners LLC
(R) 197
Whitman, Nicholas, Twin Oaks Partners LLC
(R) 197

Process

Equipment

Eissler, W. Robert, W Robert Eissler &
Associates Inc (C) 329
Giles, Kenn, Dick Williams & Associates (C) 661
McDermott, Tom, Corporate Environment Ltd
(R) 43
Williams, Dick, Dick Williams & Associates
(C) 661

Process control

Champion, Dale, The Marathon Group (C)......... 483
Daum, Alan N., Alan N Daum & Associates
Inc (C) 308
Gehle, Frederick P., Dunhill Professional
Search of Augusta (C) 322
McGinnis, William A., National Metal
Services Corp (C) 505

Procurement

Beaudin, Elizabeth C., Callan Associates Ltd
(R).. 28
McNeil, Gavin, MRI of Milwaukee-North (C).... 480
Pleva, Will, Leslie Kavanagh Associates Inc
(C) 417
Podway, Hope, Executive BioSearch (C)........... 336

Produce

Allison, Tom, Tom Allison Associates (C) 232
Pollack, Eric S., Ambiance Personnel Inc (C) 234
Pommer, Eric S., New Venture Development
Inc (C) 509
Schultz, Tim, Focus Executive Search (C) 351

Product development

Colantoni, John, JWC Associates Inc (C) 414
Domann,, Jr., William A., The Domann
Organization Inc (R) 55
Foster, Barton T., The Barton Group Inc (C) 251
Grubb, Peg Iversen, Executive Search
Consultants (C)....................................... 341
Holland, Lee, Carnegie Resources Inc (C) 277
Kunkle, Denise, D Kunkle & Associates (C) 425
Larsen, Ken, FPC of San Antonio (C)................ 361
Martin, Carol, Medical Innovations (C) 491
Mellinger, Cathy, Continental Design &
Engineering (C) 294
Reed, Rick, MRI of Flint (C) 462
Reyes, Randolph, MRI of Columbia (C) 461
Wikle, Patty, Continental Design &
Engineering (C) 294

Product management

Adams, Clarke, HeadhunterUSA.com (C)........... 383
Aggado, Adrien, Consumer Connection Inc (C).. 293
Anderson, Jim, Howard Clark Associates (C)..... 286
Bailey, Nair H., Bailey Professional Search (C).. 248
Berg, Charlie, MRI of Lake Forest, IL (C).......... 458
Cutcher, Ralph, Rojek Marketing Group Inc
(R) 166
Fox, Caryn, Equate Executive Search Inc (C) 333
Gorberg, Richard D., FPC of Raleigh (C) 359
Koch, Candice L., Ernest, Evans & Koch (R) 62
Noble, Don, Noble/Sander Search (C) 511
Ocon, Olga, Busch Int'l (R).............................. 27
Osborn, Susan, Emerging Medical
Technologies Inc (R) 61

SPECIALTIES

Quality

Quantitative methods

Radio

Radiology

Railroad

Real estate

SPECIALTIES

Recreational vehicles

Recreations

Recruiters

Recycling

Refineries

Refining

SPECIALTIES

Retirement housing

Risk management

Robotics

SPECIALTIES

Rubber

Creeger, David, Sanford Rose Associates -
Fairlawn (C)... 590
Dragomire, Jake, MRI of Akron (C)................... 470
Eliason, Ron, Midland Consultants (C) 496
Kerr, Jr., John B., Kerr Executive Recruiting
(C)... 418
Krieger, Robert, G P Mattocks & Associates
Inc (C) 488
Lopez, David, MRI of Milwaukee-North (C)...... 480
Mattocks, Paul, G P Mattocks & Associates Inc
(C) 488
McCormick, Trina, G P Mattocks & Associates
Inc (C) 488
Pajak, Michael A., The Danielson Group Inc
(C) 306
Roth, Bill, Lou Michaels Associates Inc (C)....... 495
Smucker, Art, MRI of Akron (C)...................... 470
Weber, Greg, Polymer Network Inc (C) 533

Safety

Barick, Bradford L., MRI of Stevens Point (C)... 480
Butler, Jr., Kirby B., The Butlers Company
Insurance Recruiters (C)............................. 269
Davis, Austin, Partners in Recruiting (C)........... 523
Garrison, Liz, Garrison Resources (C)............... 366
Hunkins, Deborah J., Career Images (C)............ 275
Nicastro, Kelley P., A la Carte Int'l Inc (R)............ 1
Pilcher, Chris, FPC of Cincinnati (C) 359
Reasons, Patsy, Hardage Group (C)................... 380
Sims, Larry, Reality Group (C)........................ 552
Williams, Randy L., Environmental, Health &
Safety Search Associates Inc (EH&S) (C)...... 333

Sales

Abrams, Burton J., B J Abrams & Associates
Inc (C) 217
Adams, Bill, Adams & Associates (C)................ 224
Adler, David, Don Allan Associates Inc (C) 230
Adolfson, Edwin, Adolfson & Associates (C) 225
Adzema, Marlene, Career Forum Inc (C)............ 275
Alexander, Gary, Mark Christian & Associates
Inc (C) 284
Alexander, Myra, Mark Christian & Associates
Inc (C) 284
Andersen, Phil, Blackhawk Executive Search
Inc (C) 258
Anderson, Brett, Snelling Personnel Service
(C)... 613
Anton, Michael, Noll Human Resource
Services (C)... 512
Aquavella, Charles P., Charles P Aquavella &
Associates (C) 241
Arbas, Karen, Campbell, Edgar Inc (C)............. 272
Archibald, David Eldridge, The Eldridge
Group Ltd (C) 329
Archie, Jr., Otis, Kuhn Med-Tech Inc (C).......... 425
Aspell, Tim, New Venture Development Inc
(C) 509
Baccarini, Daniel J., The B & B Group Inc (C) .. 247
Bach, Donald, Future Employment Service Inc
(C).. 364
Baer, Curtis L., Sales Consultants of
Barrington (C) 577
Baker, Susan F., Diversified Consulting
Services Inc (C).. 314
Balakonis, Charles L., Lawrence-Balakonis &
Associates Inc (C) 429
Baracani, Bill, Harbeck Associates Inc (C)......... 379
Barlow, Geoffrey L., Fast Switch Ltd (C).......... 345
Barnes, Gary, Executive Solutions Inc (R) 65
Barnes, George, Snelling Search (C) 614

Baron, Sheldon S., Sales Consultants of
Nashua-Manchester (C) 580
Barritt, Barry, Professional Career Service (C)....540
Batisto, Phil, Mark Christian & Associates Inc
(C)..284
Beaudin, Elizabeth C., Callan Associates Ltd
(R)..28
Becker, B. Hans, Hans Becker Associates (C).....252
Becker, John, BPR Associates (C).....................262
Beebe, Eric, MRI of Gaithersburg (C)................461
Bender, Alan, Bender Executive Search
Management Consulting (R) 16
Bennett, Marilyn, Brentwood Int'l (R) 24
Benum, Michele S., Micro Staff Solutions Inc
(C) 496
Benum, Michele S., The Alternatives Group
Inc (C) 233
Berger, Joel, Midas Management Inc (C) 496
Beruldsen, Arne, Hemingway Personnel Inc
(C) 388
Bijoux, R., Executive Solutions Inc (R)................65
Billings Schneider, CPC, Maria, McHale &
Associates (C)..490
Bishop, Allan E., Strategic Executive Search
Solutions (C)...628
Blake, Sharon, Baldwin & Associates (C)...........248
Bolen, Dan, Dan Bolen & Associates LLC (C) ...260
Bongard, Joyce, Sales Consultants of
Milwaukee (C)...584
Bornholdt, Elizabeth, Bornholdt Shivas &
Friends Executive Recruiters (C) 261
Bornholdt, John, Bornholdt Shivas & Friends
Executive Recruiters (C)...............................261
Bosch, Eric E., Bosch & Associates LLC (R)........21
Boyle, Lori, JDC Associates (C) 410
Brady, Jack, J T Brady & Associates (R) 23
Brandon, John W. C., MRI of Columbia (C).......474
Brauninger, John C., AmeriPro Search Inc (C)....236
Bredeson, Nancy, Artemis HRC (C) 242
Brewster, Barbara, Hospitality Int'l (C)...............394
Bridgman, Michael, Executive Recruiters (C).....339
Britt, Brian, NaTek Corp (C)............................504
Brooks, Debbie, DBC Recruiting Network (C) ...309
Brown, Alan V., Page Staffing & Training (C) 521
Bryant, Ed, Kiley, Owen & McGovern Inc (R) 107
Bryer, Bob, High Technology Recruiters Inc
(C)..390
Buckeridge, John, FPC of Cedar Rapids (C) 356
Burgess, III, William H., The Burgess Group-
Corporate Recruiters Int'l Inc (R) 26
Burns, Patrick J., Career Alternatives
Executive Search (C) 274
Cain, Douglas, Sales Recruiting Network (C) 585
Campbell, Brian H., Venpro Consulting Inc (C)..651
Candela, Ken, Sales Consultants of Clearwater
(C)..575
Carlson, Cynthia, Campbell/Carlson LLC (R)........29
Carlton, Katherine, NCC Executive Search
Consultants (C)..508
Case, Andria, Card Resource Group Inc (C)........273
Casey-Moll, Carolyn, Executive Resources
LLC (C)...340
Cevolani, Paul, Strategic Search & Staffing Inc
(TeamS3) (C)...629
Chaitin, Dick, Chaitin & Associates Inc (C)........282
Chapman, Lisa, NCC Executive Search
Consultants (C)..508
Chatwin, Gary, Consumer Connection Inc (C) 293
Chavoen, James E., Mannard & Associates Inc
(R) 125
Chiulli, Joseph, Lucerne Partners LLC (R)..........120
Christine, Rich, R Christine Associates (C).........284
Ciaramitaro, Anthony, Corporate Search
Consultants Inc (C) 298

Clark, David A., Sprout/Standish Inc (C)............ 621
Clark, Larry A., The Clark Group (C)................. 286
Clarke, Brian G., Kensington Int'l Inc (R)........... 107
Coco, Jr., Carl, Professions Inc (C)................... 543
Contractor, Shakir, MRI of The Baltimore
Washington Corridor (C)............................. 461
Cooper, Larry, MSI Int'l (C)............................ 502
Corbin, Earl, Corbin Packaging Professionals
(C).. 295
Cotton, Peter C., Sales Consultants of Rhode
Island (C) 583
Craig, Susan E., Fast Switch Ltd (C)................. 345
Credidio, Thomas J., The DataFinders Group
Inc (C) 308
Crothers, Steve, Burton & Grove Inc (C) 269
Crowell, Richard, Snelling Personnel Service
(C).. 613
Curlett, Charles N., Access Associates Inc (C).... 217
Curtis, Howard, Tony Curtis & Associates (C).... 305
Curtis, Tony, Tony Curtis & Associates (C) 305
Daggett, Dave, Mark Christian & Associates
Inc (C) 284
Damon, Richard E., Damon & Associates Inc
(C) 306
Dato, Thomas, L T S Associates (C)................. 425
Deakmann, Richard, Management Decision
Systems Inc (MDSI) (C).............................. 439
DeClouet, J. Michael, The J B Search Group
Inc (C) 596
Delray, Victor, Management Decision Systems
Inc (MDSI) (C).. 439
DeRose, Rick, DigitalHire (C) 313
Despres, Raoul, Despres & Associates Inc (C).... 311
Devlin, Jack, The Devlin Search Group Inc
(DSG) (C) 312
Devoto, Andrea, Devoto & Associates Inc (C).... 312
Devoto, Jeffrey, Devoto & Associates Inc (C) 312
Diamont, Mickie, NCC Executive Search
Consultants (C) 508
Dietsch, B. E., Dietsch & Associates (C) 312
Dillon, Mark, NaTek Corp (C) 504
Distransky, Ron, Mid-America Placement
Service Inc (C) 496
Donnelly, Dan, The Donnelly Group-Sales
Recruiters Inc (C) 315
Doran, Edward, MRD Group (C)...................... 501
Doro, Chip, Career Marketing Associates Inc
(C).. 275
Dreyfus, Bruce, Dialogue Consulting Group
(C).. 312
Driscoll, Donald L., MRI of Boone (C).............. 469
Drohan, John, Sales Development Inc (C) 584
Drum, Harry, Drum Associates Inc (C)............... 317
Dunlap, Thomas, Charles Dahl Group Inc (C) 306
Durr, Lamar, C A I Personnel Search Group
(C).. 270
Dusome, Terry, Holloway, Schulz & Partners
(C).. 393
Dussick, Vince, Dussick Management
Associates (C) 325
Dutra, Gerard A., Holohan Group Ltd (R) 92
Duval, Dick, B D Wallace & Associates (C)....... 654
Eastern, Susan, Consumer Connection Inc (C).... 293
Ebeling, Brandon, American Incite (C)............... 234
Edelberg, Frank, Management One Consultants
(C).. 439
Edwards, Greg, Eden & Associates Inc (C)........ 328
Edwards, Lisa, Edwards & Associates (C).......... 328
Edwards, Verba Lee, Wing Tips & Pumps Inc
(C).. 663
Elliott, Doug, Roadrunner Personnel (C) 560
Erdrich, John, Executive Search Management
Inc (C) 342

SPECIALTIES

SPECIALTIES

Sales & marketing

SPECIALTIES

SAP

Satellites

Sawmill

SCADA

Science

Security

Semiconductors

Senior management

SPECIALTIES

SPECIALTIES

Shopping centers

Softline

Software

(R) = Retainer; (C) = Contingency

SPECIALTIES

Systems

Baert, Yvonne, Personnel Management Group
(C) 528
Barash, Ray, Manning Associates (C) 482
Barbosa, Franklin, Skott/Edwards Consultants
(R) 178
Behrens, Rick, Behrens & Company (C) 253
Bentley, Mark A., Kraemer, Bentley, Wong &
Sermone (R) 111
Bland, Carmen, Camacho Group Inc (C) 272
Brody, Steve, Executive Resource Systems (C).. 340
Campbell, Brian H., Venpro Consulting Inc (C). 651
Cohen, Lawrence J., Norgate Technology Inc
(C) 512
Cucuzzella, Vincent J., C J Vincent Associates
LLC (C) 652
Dangerfield, Chris, Technology Search Int'l (C). 638
DeAngelo, Tom, LAS Management Consulting
Group Inc (C) 428
Di Veto, Daina, Card Resource Group Inc (C).... 273
Dickson, Lisa, Excel Human Resources Inc (C). 335
Douglas, Bob, Chase Hunter Group Inc (R)......... 34
Dyson, Steve, Technology Search Int'l (C) 638
Erickson, Elvin, Erickson & Associates Inc (C). 333
George, CPC, Delores F., DFG Executive
Search (C) 312
Hebert, Robert, Austin Michaels Ltd Inc (C) 246
Kraemer, Katherine R., Kraemer, Bentley,
Wong & Sermone (R) 111
Manning, Jack, Manning Associates (C)............. 482
Mayo, Buz, TeamBuilders (C)............................. 636
Miller, Tammy, Search Force Inc (C) 596
Morshedi, Tony, Advanced Technology
Consultants Inc (ATC) (C) 226
Nephew, Robert, Christian & Timbers (R) 36
Patronella, Larry, W Robert Eissler &
Associates Inc (C) 329
Pottenger, Don, Search Force Inc (C) 596
Ross, Cheryl Molliver, Thomas, Whelan
Associates, Inc (C) 642
Rudzinsky, Jeff, Louis Rudzinsky Associates
Inc (C).. 567
Schlatter, Craig, Schlatter & Associates (C) 592
Schneider, Jim, Chase Hunter Group Inc (R)........ 34
Sermone, Ed E., Kraemer, Bentley, Wong &
Sermone (R) 111
Shapiro, Alan, Technology Search Int'l (C) 638
Sirey, Don, Technology Search Int'l (C) 638
Wong, Walter W., Kraemer, Bentley, Wong &
Sermone (R) 111
Young, Susan M., MRI of Morris County, NJ
(C)... 465
Zabor, Richard, Leader Institute Inc (C) 429

Analysts

Gust, Steven, Premier Recruiting Group (C)....... 536
Saunders, Lisa, National Field Service Corp
(C)... 505
Whitehead, Elizabeth S., Whitehead &
Associates Inc (C)................................... 660

Integration

Daily, John, Christian & Timbers (R) 36
Duval, Dick, B D Wallace & Associates (C) 654
Heisser, Robert, The Sequel Group LLC (C) 600
Herlihy, Jack, J J Herlihy & Associates Inc (C).. 389
Myeroff, Sheldon, Direct Recruiters Inc (C)....... 314
Nephew, Robert, Christian & Timbers (R) 36
Raeburn, Adam, ARC Staffing Inc (C) 241
Talarico, Joseph, Hreshko Consulting Group
(C)... 396

Tax

Abkin, Stephen J., Millennium Search Group
Inc (R) 134
Adams, Ray, Ray Adams & Associates
Executive Search Consultants (C).................... 224
Bynum, Sam, TaxSearch Inc (R)......................... 191
Chorba, Dale C., Action Management Services
(C) 223
Cowling, John W., Professional Resources (C)...542
Davis, Guy, Kane & Associates (C) 416
Dickey, Douglas H., The Ransford Group (R).....158
Ferrara, David M., Millennium Search Group
Inc (R) 133
Fink, Allen, PMJ & Associates (C) 532
Gandin, David L., Gandin & Associates Inc (C)..366
Gandin, David L., The Executive Consulting
Group (C) 337
Gillespie, Jeffrey, PMJ & Associates (C) 532
Glaser, David, ECG Resources Inc (C) 327
Gordon, Michael, Management Services Group
Inc (C) 482
Grue, Douglas Harrison, Harrison Consulting
Group Inc (C) 381
Hamilton, Sherman, Synergy 2000 (C)................ 631
Heino, Jay J., Jay Heino Company LLC (C)........ 388
Henderson, Laurie M., Lowell Johnson
Associates LLC (R) 120
Hermann, George A., Hermann & Westmore
(R) 89
Hunter, Steven, Diamond Tax Recruiting (C)......312
Jennings, Kathleen, ET Search Inc (R)................. 62
Kang, Helen, Valacon Inc (C) 650
Krueger, Todd L., Todd L Krueger &
Associates (C).. 424
Kutcher, Howard, Kutcher Tax Careers Inc (C) ..425
LaMorte, Brian A., Pascale & LaMorte LLC
(C) 523
Langella, Gina, Dunhill Professional Search of
New Haven (C)... 321
Lee, Joseph J., Larsen & Lee Inc (R)................... 114
Leff, Lisa A, Berger & Leff (C) 255
Lo Grasso, Stephen C., Lowell Johnson
Associates LLC (R) 120
Marino, Mike, Tax Network Resources Inc (C)...635
Miramontes, Dawn, ET Search Inc (R) 62
Musick, Diana, Musick & Associates (C)............503
Musick, Stephen, Musick & Associates (C) 503
Ormond, Mark R., Capstone Consulting Inc
(R) 30
Pann, Arthur J., Arthur Pann Associates Inc (C)..521
Pedelty, Lori K., Capstone Consulting Inc (R) 30
Posadas, Elizabeth, ET Search Inc (R) 62
Rosenblatt, Michael F., The Quest
Organization (C)...................................... 548
Santiago, Anthony, TaxSearch Inc (R) 191
Santiago, Tony, TaxSearch Inc (R) 191
Smith, Thomas W., The Ransford Group (R).......158
Staton, Tim, The Executive Consulting Group
(C) 337
Stewart, Diane, ET Search Inc (R) 62
Thunberg, Richard A., Jeff Rich Associates (C)..557
Toynbee, Brad J., John Michael Associates (R)...133
Ullstein, Ashley B., Drinkwater & Associates
(R) 57
Ward, Robert M., Callan Associates Ltd (R)..........28
Ward, Robert M., Ward & Associates (C)...........655
Wayne, Cary S., ProSearch Inc (C) 545
Weiss, Esq., Terry M., Weiss & Associates
Legal Search Inc (C)................................ 657
Westmore, Robert J., Hermann & Westmore
(R) 89

Technology

Aavik, Karl, Spencer Stuart (R) 181
Aldrich, Michael R., Martin Partners LLC (R)... 126
Allred, Michael, TMP Worldwide Executive
Search (R) 194
Anderson, Gregory D., Anderson Industrial
Associates Inc (C) 237
Anderson, Kristine, TMP Worldwide
Executive Search (R) 194
Anderson, Mark, TMP Worldwide Executive
Search (R) 194
Andrews, Pamela, TMP Worldwide Executive
Search (R) 194
Ayers, Jr., William L., The Ayers Group Inc
(R) 11
Bagby, Linda, Norman Broadbent Int'l Inc (R) ... 140
Baker Arrington, Renee, Ray & Berndtson (R)... 159
Baker, Walter U., Meridian Partners (R)............. 131
Balkin, Linda, Martin Partners LLC (R) 126
Ballach, Allen, Allen Ballach Associates Inc
(R) 12
Bass, Mary, Spencer Stuart (R) 182
Baty, R. Gaines, R Gaines Baty Associates Inc
(R) 14
Beer, Bill, OTEC Inc (C) 518
Bellano, Robert W., cFour Partners (R) 33
Bender, Tilman, TMP Worldwide Executive
Search (R) 194
Bernard, Gary D., Byron Leonard Int'l Inc (R)...... 27
Beuerlein, David, Spencer Stuart (R) 182
Bidlake, Mark, The Carter Group LLC (R) 32
Birarda, Richard W., JSG Group Management
Consultants (R).. 103
Borchers, Christina, Williams Executive
Search Inc (R) 205
Bosell, Keith, Dunhill Professional Search of
Indianapolis (C)....................................... 322
Boykin, Steven H., Whitehouse & Pimms (R) 204
Brandenburger, Gary H., Holohan Group Ltd
(R) 92
Brenneman, Thomas E., Roth Young of
Milwaukee (C).. 566
Brian, Brad, Professional Recruiters (C) 542
Bridgeman, John, TTG Search (R)....................... 196
Brockman, Trowby, Dan B Brockman (C)...........266
Buckley, James, Spencer Stuart (R) 181
Buffkin, Craig, Buffkin & Associates LLC (R).....26
Butterfield, N. Blair, Butterfield & Company
Int'l Inc (C)... 270
Callaghan, Meg, Diversified Search Inc (R)......... 54
Campbell, Dan, Campbell/Carlson LLC (R) 29
Carey, Dennis C., Spencer Stuart (R) 182
Carlson, Cynthia, Campbell/Carlson LLC (R) 29
Castine, Michael, TMP Worldwide Executive
Search (R) 194
Chong, Peggy V., Berkhemer Clayton Inc (R) 17
Citrin, James M., Spencer Stuart (R) 182
Clarkson, Roger, Spencer Stuart (R) 182
Clemons, Jani, Robert Shields & Associates
(C)... 601
Collins, Clarke, Ray & Berndtson (R).................. 159
Cruse, O. D. Dan, Spencer Stuart (R) 182
Currie, Robert, Spencer Stuart (R) 181
Custer, Dwight, The Custer Group Inc (R)............ 47
Czermak, Dan, Rein & Company Inc (R) 161
Dahl, Tamara, Allen Personnel Services Ltd
(C)... 231
Daly, Dan, Daly & Company Inc (R).................... 47
Davis, Stephanie, Spencer Stuart (R) 181
Deissig, Robert, The Ayers Group Inc (R) 11
Delhougne, Patrick A., Ray & Berndtson (R) 159
Desautels, Noel, Spencer Stuart (R) 182

SPECIALTIES

Robinson, Conchita, Spencer Stuart (R) 182
Robinson, Tom, Marquis Management (C)......... 485
Rogers, Anne, Epsen, Fuller & Associates LLC (R)........ 61
Rogge, Chrys, GreyLee Professionals Inc (C) 374
Rollo, Robert, TMP Worldwide Executive Search (R) 194
Rosenfeld, Jay, TMP Worldwide Executive Search (R) 194
Rossi, Alfred F., The Rossi Search Group (C) 565
Rothschild, John, TMP Worldwide Executive Search (R) 194
Rovner, Bettyann, Rovner & Associates Inc (R)........ 167
Rowe, Mark, Dunhill Professional Search of Indianapolis (C) 322
Rudy, Sharon, Spencer Stuart (R)........ 182
Ruggiero, Richard, Epsen, Fuller & Associates LLC (R) 61
Sanders, Robert, Alphanumeric Group Inc (R) 6
Saracen, Bob, Bishop Partners (R)........ 18
Sargent, Robert A., JM & Company (R)........ 101
Saxe, Eugene, Livingston, Robert & Company (R)........ 119
Scanlan, Tom, Spencer Stuart (R)........ 182
Schmidt, Lisa, MRI of Rockville (C)........ 461
Schultz, Helen, DillonGray (R) 53
Schweiger, Michael, Search Int'l (R) 172
Sears, David L., McDermott-Sears Associates LLC (C) 489
Seclow, Tom, Spencer Stuart (R)........ 181
Sheiko, Michele, The Park Group & Associates Inc (C)........ 522
Simon, Robert, New Media Staffing LLC (R) 139
Simpson, Tom, Brentwood Int'l (R)........ 24
Smith, Craig V., Diversified Search Inc (R) 54
Smith, Rick, Spencer Stuart (R)........ 182
Sowerby, David K., Meridian Partners (R) 131
Spence, Gene, Spence Associates Int'l Inc (R).... 181
Spilman, Mary P., Spilman & Associates (R) 183
Stebbings, Dave, Heywood Associates LLC (C)........ 389
Stirn, Bradley, TMP Worldwide Executive Search (R) 194
Stow, Ralph P., Whitehouse & Pimms (R) 203
Strickland, Tonya, Southern Recruiters & Consultants Inc (C) 616
Sullivan, Mike, TMP Worldwide Executive Search (R) 193
Swann, Al, The Beam Group (R)........ 15
Swartz, William K., Swartz & Associates Inc (R)........ 189
Sweet, Robert J., Atlanta Executive Partners Inc (R)........ 10
Tazzia, Ed, Gundersen Partners LLC (R)........ 81
Testani, Bernadette, TMP Worldwide Executive Search (R)........ 195
Thomas, Carrie, Taylor Winfield (R)........ 192
Thompson, Kelvin, Norman Broadbent Int'l Inc (R)........ 140
Tobin-McCarthy, Denise, TMP Worldwide Executive Search (R)........ 195
Toland, Brian, Studley/Toland Executive Search (R) 189
Toynbee, Brad J., John Michael Associates (R).. 133
Ullstein, Ashley B., Drinkwater & Associates (R)........ 57
Unser, Teresa, Meridian Executive Search (C) ... 493
Velez, Hector, HireStrategy (C)........ 391
Venable, William, Thorndike Deland Associates LLC (R)........ 50
Vennat, Manon, Spencer Stuart (R) 182
von Ranson, Joel, Spencer Stuart (R)........ 182
Wagner, Kristen, Corporate Search Partners (C) 298
Wallace, John, TMP Worldwide Executive Search (R)........ 195
Walsh, Denis, Find (C)........ 347
Watkins, Robert J., R J Watkins & Company Ltd (R) 201
Wein, Michael S., Media Management Resources Inc (R) 131
Wein, William, Media Management Resources Inc (R) 131
White, Jonathan O., Spencer Stuart (R)........ 181
Williams, Brad, Winter, Wyman & Company (C) 663
Winston, Peggy, Brentwood Int'l (R)........ 24
Wolf, Stephen M., Byron Leonard Int'l Inc (R) 27
Wood, Marty, TMP Worldwide Executive Search (R)........ 194
Wynkoop, Mary, Meridian Executive Search (C) 493
York, Bill, TMP Worldwide Executive Search (R) 194
Young, Susan M., MRI of Morris County, NJ (C) 465
Young, Wayne, MRI of Morris County, NJ (C) ..465
Zinn, Michael D., Michael D Zinn & Associates Inc (R)........ 211

Telecommunications

Ames, George C., Ames-O'Neill Associates Inc (C) 236
Anczarki, Chris, Adams & Ryan Inc (C)........ 224
Andrews, Aris, AllStaff (C)........ 232
Anton, Michael, Noll Human Resource Services (C) 512
Antoniak, Peggy, The Executive Tree Research Consultants (R) 66
Ashton, Barbara L., Ashton Computer Professionals Inc (C)........ 243
Austin, Cami, Cami Austin & Associates (C)......246
Badanes, Anne, Satterfield & Associates Inc (R) 170
Bailey, Edward L., PMB Executive Recruiters Inc (C) 532
Bailey, Jerald W., Dunhill Professional Search of Greater New Orleans (C) 322
Baker, Charles D., Corporate Staffing Group Inc (C)........ 299
Baker, Chet, Diversified Consulting Services Inc (C) 314
Baker, Lynette, Carlyn Int'l Inc (R) 31
Barish, Lonnie, ACHIEVE Technical Services (C) 222
Barlow, Geoffrey L., Fast Switch Ltd (C) 345
Barrow, Dan J., The Regency Group Ltd (C) 554
Bartchak, Thomas, Telequest Communications Inc (C)........ 640
Bavli, Mark, Tech Consulting (C) 636
Bellano, Robert W., cFour Partners (R)........ 33
Belvedere, Tina, Wesley, Brown & Bartle Company Inc (R) 202
Bennett, Hal, Kirkbride Associates Inc (C) 423
Benum, Michele S., Micro Staff Solutions Inc (C) 496
Benum, Michele S., The Alternatives Group Inc (C) 233
Berke, Ginny, TSS Resources (C) 648
Bishop, Susan, Bishop Partners (R)........ 18
Blixt, Tony, Specialty Employment Services Inc (C) 618
Boate, Mike, Tanner & Associates Inc (R) 191
Bogue, Randall L., Venator Partners (C) 651
Boguski, Ronald T., The Hamilton Group (R)....... 83
Born, Al, Electronic Search Inc (C) 329
Bornholdt, John, Bornholdt Shivas & Friends Executive Recruiters (C)........ 261
Boyle, Michael, Boyle Ogata Bregman (R)........ 22
Brady, Allen, Strategic Resources (C)........ 628
Bratland, A. J., Bratland & Associates (C) 264
Breitfeller, Daniel, MRI of Palm Beach (R) 124
Bronstad, Alice, MRI of Milwaukee-North (C)... 480
Brown, Andrew, MRI of Palm Beach (R) 124
Brown, David F., ETI Search Int'l (R)........ 62
Brown, Erika, eBconnects Inc (R)........ 58
Buckwald, Brett, The Worth Group (C) 666
Burton, Catherine C., Innovative Partnerships Executive Search (R) 98
Butler, Bobby, MRI of Loudoun County North (C)........ 478
Cadmus, Stephen T., Cadmus Int'l (R) 27
Cain, David, The Pacific Firm (R) 145
Campbell, Robert S., Wellington Management Group (R) 202
Capanna, Patricia A., MRI of Madison (C) 479
Carey, Laurie B., Corporate Staffing Group Inc (C)........ 299
Chaffin, Denise M., Professional Team Search Inc (C) 543
Chambers, Randall, The Telecom Search Group (C) 640
Christ, Celeste, Amber Systems Group LLC (C)........ 233
Christian, Jeffrey E., Christian & Timbers (R)...... 35
Cimino, Ron, Paul-Tittle Associates Inc (R) 147
Coe, Karen, TMP Worldwide Executive Search (R)........ 194
Cohen, Margie, MRI of Franktown (C)........ 452
Coltrane, Mike, Richard, Wayne & Roberts (C).. 557
Combs, Doug, Venator Partners (C)........ 651
Connelly, Laura, MRI of Pittsburgh (C)........ 472
Cosgrave, John, Abraxas Technologies Inc (C)... 217
Cotton, Rob, MRI of Traverse City (C)........ 463
Craig, Susan E., Fast Switch Ltd (C)........ 345
Cremeans, Cynthia, Gail Darling & Associates (C)........ 307
Crigler, James, MRI of Winona (C) 463
Crosthwait, Bruce, MRI of Bellaire (C) 476
Crowley, David G., DSR-Search & Recruitment (C)........ 318
Cunningham, Shelly, AllStaff (C)........ 232
Dansky, Ellen, Telequest Communications Inc (C)........ 640
DePhillipo, William R., Tele-Media Int'l Inc (C)........ 639
Dermady, Tim, Executivefit (C)........ 343
DeSantis, Nick, Sales Consultants of North Palm Beach (C) 576
DesLandes, Lynda, Engineering Solutions Int'l (C)........ 332
Dicicco, Benjamin, McCoy Ltd (C) 489
Dick, Andy, Emerson Personnel Group (C) 331
Dietrich, Sandra, FPC of Hilton Head (C)........ 360
DiLorenzo, Matthew B., The Inside Track (C).... 402
Dixon, Renee, American Recruiters Int'l (C)....... 235
Dorst, Martin, Dorst Information Services Inc (C)........ 315
Dowd, Charlie, Dowd Group Inc (C) 316
Downing, Jack W., Sales Consultants of Chicago-Downtown (C)........ 577
Dreier, John S., Dreier Consulting Staff (C)........ 317
Du Ket, David R., New Venture Development Inc (C) 509
Dursi, Carolyn, Thorndike Deland Associates LLC (R)........ 50
Eldredge, Peter W., Boardroom Consultants (R) 20

SPECIALTIES

(R) = Retainer; (C) = Contingency

Telemarketing

Telephony

Television

Temperature control

Temporary

Test

Textiles

SPECIALTIES

Tubular products

Hendricks, II, Stanley M., National Recruiting
Service (C)... *506*

Ultrasound

DuBois, Anthony G., Horizon Medical Search
of NH (C).. *394*

Underwriting

Buchanan, Christine, MRI of Bordentown (C).... *465*
Gaches, Martha, Don Neal & Associates (C)...... *508*
Gannon, Lowell, Orion Search Group Inc (C) *518*
Gordon, John, Mortgage & Financial Personnel
Services (C)... *501*
Haugen, Audrey D., Dietsch & Associates (C) ... *312*
Kyle, Michael, Lear & Associates Inc (C) *429*
Lear, Roger R., Lear & Associates Inc (C) *429*
Moore, Keneth, A W Forrester Company (C)..... *352*
Neal, Don, Don Neal & Associates (C) *508*
Pendergast, William, Corporate Technologies
Executive Search (R)................................... *44*
Phillips, Steve, Search & Placement Int'l (C)...... *594*
Pilgrim, Ron, Lear & Associates Inc (C) *429*
Pokorny, Richard J., Pryor Personnel Agency
Inc (C).. *546*
Rowls, Gene, E J Ashton & Associates Ltd (C).. *243*
Svetic, Mark, Lear & Associates Inc (C) *429*
Watson, David L. B., Pacific Coast Recruiters
(PCR) (C) *520*

Unix

Gardiner, Earl, Austin Park Management
Group Inc (C) *246*
Nair, Sanjay, Fortuna Technologies Inc (C)........ *352*
Prince, Howard, Austin Park Management
Group Inc (C) *246*

Utilities

Bailey, Jerald W., Dunhill Professional Search
of Greater New Orleans (C) *322*
Block, Bonny, Power Recruiting Group (C) *534*
Bodnar, Robert J., Sales Consultants of
Goodyear Inc (C) *573*
Bostick, Tim, Ray & Berndtson (R).................... *159*
Botto, Joe, Electric Systems Personnel (ESP)
(C).. *329*
Cooke, Gerald W., STM Associates (R) *186*
Crystal, Jonathan A., Spencer Stuart (R)............ *182*
Cutler, Robert, Cutler/Krenzke LLC (R)............. *47*
Dickin, Noranne, Conroy Partners Ltd (R) *41*
Doupe, S. Scott, Conroy Partners Ltd (R) *41*
Edwards, J. Michael, Power Recruiting Group
(C).. *534*
Gray, Lynette, Electric Systems Personnel
(ESP) (C) *329*
Hobart, John N., Ray & Berndtson (R)................ *159*
Hopkins, Mark, Conroy Partners Ltd (R)............ *41*
Humphreys, Scott W., Robison Humphreys &
Associates Inc (R) *165*
Kainady, John J., Michael Latas & Associates
Inc (R) *115*
Kelso, Richard, Search Advisors Int'l Corp (R) .. *172*
Kirkman, Mike, Korn/Ferry Int'l (R)................... *110*
Kohn, Adam, Christian & Timbers (R)................ *35*
Langley, Carol M., Langley & Associates Inc
(R).. *113*
Little, Bradley, cFour Partners (R)...................... *34*
Lowry, Randy, Ray & Berndtson (R) *159*
McKeon, Suzanna, The Quantum Group (C)...... *548*

McLeod, Odell, Sanford Rose Associates -
Akron (C) *589*
Morgan, Richard J., Morgan Samuels
Company (R) *169*
Nickels, Edward L., Michael Latas &
Associates Inc (R)....................................... *115*
Poindexter, Clay, Wyndham Mills Int'l Inc (R) ... *209*
Preng, David E., Preng & Associates Inc (R) *153*
Ragan, William, Michael Latas & Associates
Inc (R) *115*
Ray, Breck, Ray & Berndtson (R) *159*
Reiner, Joe, Sales Consultants of Franklin
County (C)... *581*
Reynolds, John H., BMF Reynolds Inc (R) *20*
Rickus, George M., Preng & Associates Inc (R)..*153*
Robinson, Rodney, Michael Latas &
Associates Inc (R)....................................... *115*
Robinson, Verneda, V Robinson & Company
Inc (C) *562*
Rowland, Boyd H., Bart Roberson & Company
(C).. *560*
Roylance, Robert L., STM Associates (R)........... *186*
Ruggiero, Richard, Epsen, Fuller & Associates
LLC (R)... *61*
Ruschak, Randy R., MRI of Bordentown (C)......*465*
Samuels, Lewis J., Morgan Samuels Company
(R).. *169*
Schlect, Nancy J., Morgan Samuels Company
(R).. *169*
Sharpe, Charles, C J Stafford & Associates (C)...*624*
Shields, Robert G., Spencer Stuart (R) *181*
Sippel, Rick L., Michael Latas & Associates
Inc (R) *115*
Stanewick, B. David, Stanewick, Hart &
Associates Inc (C)....................................... *624*
Stepanek, Gary, Michael Latas & Associates
Inc (R) *115*
Swan, Christopher, RSMR Global Resources
(R).. *167*
Wright, Mark A., Wyndham Mills Int'l Inc (R) ...*209*

Valves

Eissler, W. Robert, W Robert Eissler &
Associates Inc (C)....................................... *329*

Van conversion

McGuire, John, Sage Employment Recruiters
(C).. *569*

Venture capital

Aylward, Colleen, Devon James Associates Inc
(C).. *409*
Bartholdi, Sr., Theodore G., Bartholdi &
Company Inc (R) *13*
Bauman, Martin H., Martin H Bauman
Associates LLC (R)..................................... *14*
Bellano, Robert W., cFour Partners (R)............... *33*
Brown, Jerry, Brown Venture Associates Inc
(R).. *25*
Burfield, Elaine, Diversified Search Inc (R)......... *54*
Burns, Bethany E., Choi & Burns LLC (R) *35*
Chiulli, Joseph, Lucerne Partners LLC (R)..........*120*
Choi, Julie A., Choi & Burns LLC (R) *35*
Gardner, Marvin, Gardner-Ross Associates Inc
(R).. *74*
Goode, Jr., Richard W., Kiradjieff & Goode
Inc (R) *108*
Goode, Laura K., Kiradjieff & Goode Inc (R).....*108*
Hockett, Bill, Hockett Associates Inc (R)............. *91*
Holodnak, William A., J Robert Scott (R)...........*172*
Kaplan, Alan J., Kaplan & Associates Inc (R).....*104*
Kinley, David, Christian & Timbers (R)...............*36*

Kohn, Adam, Christian & Timbers (R) *35*
Kreuzberger, Neil L., Kreuzberger &
Associates (C) *424*
Lambert, Robert J., Christian & Timbers (R) *35*
Levy, Stefan, Management Search Inc (C)........... *481*
MacLean, Jr., B. A., Diversified Search Inc (R).... *54*
Malouf, Terry, Bartholdi & Company Inc (R)....... *13*
Petroff, David, Kreuzberger & Associates (C) *424*
Poster, Lawrence D., Catalyx Group (R).............. *33*
Raisman, Ronald H., BDK Global Search Inc
(R).. *15*
Reis, Brenda G., Kaplan & Associates Inc (R).... *104*
Sears, Richard G., The Wilmington Group (C) ...*662*
Segal, Eric B., Kenzer Corp (R)......................... *107*

Vice president

Allen, David, Century Associates Inc (C) *281*
Berger, Emanuel D., Educational Management
Network (R).. *58*
Berger, Emmanuel, Educational Management
Network (R).. *58*
Besen, Douglas, Besen Associates Inc (C) *256*
Blaney, John A., Blaney Executive Search (R) *19*
Carabelli, Paula, Educational Management
Network (R).. *58*
Comstock, Cheri, Focus Tech (C) *351*
Deckelbaum, Rick, FPC of Raleigh (C) *359*
Dressler, Carol F., Dressler Associates (R) *56*
Edwards, S. Bruce, Bruce Edwards &
Associates Inc (R) *59*
Fairbrother, Scott, A W Forrester Company (C) . *352*
Fischer, Howard, Howard Fischer Associates
Int'l Inc (R) *68*
Foxman, Martin, The Millenia Group Inc (C) *496*
Gaffney, Keith, Gaffney Management
Consultants Inc (R)..................................... *73*
Gaffney, William, Gaffney Management
Consultants Inc (R)..................................... *73*
Gates, Tom, TheLinkPartners (R) *119*
Graham, Robert W., Robert Graham Associates
(R).. *79*
Grantham, John D., Grantham, Griffin & Buck
Inc (R) *80*
Hard, Sally-Ann, Educational Management
Network (R).. *59*
Hickey, Tom, Integrity Network Inc (R) *99*
Jerome, Gerald E., Jerome & Co (C).................. *411*
Johnston, J. Reid, Hughes & Company (R).......... *94*
Kennelley, Judy, Integrity Network Inc (R) *99*
King, Roger M., Raging Mouse (C) *550*
Laguzza, John, Laguzza Associates Ltd (R)........ *113*
Larsen, Michael G., Barnes & Associates
Executive Search (C) *250*
Larson, Jackie, Focus Tech (C) *351*
Leske, Lucy, Educational Management
Network (R).. *58*
Levin, Phillip, Executive Search Team (C) *342*
Martin, Donovan, Donovan Martin &
Associates (R) *126*
Martin, Nancy, Educational Management
Network (R).. *58*
Mehta, Mike, Future Executive Personnel Ltd
(C).. *364*
Mellos, James S., Ki Technologies Inc
Executive Search Div (C) *422*
Militello, Christian, Professional Computer
Resources Inc (PCR) (C) *540*
Packard, Elizabeth, NCC Executive Search
Consultants (C).. *508*
Posner, Gary J., Educational Management
Network (R).. *59*
Posner, Gary, Educational Management
Network (R).. *58*

SPECIALTIES

Geographical Index

Firms with (R) are from the Retainer Section.
Firms with (C) are from the Contingency Section.

United States

Alabama

Anniston
Search South Inc (C) 597

Birmingham
Blanton & Company (C)................................. 258
Dunhill Professional Search of South
  Birmingham (C) 320
HealthCare Recruiters Int'l • Alabama (C) 385
Human Resource Management Inc (R) 95
Paul Johnson & Associates Inc (C)..................... 412
The Langford Search Inc (C) 427
MRI of Birmingham (C) 448
Sales Consultants of Birmingham (C)................ 573
J L Small Associates (C).................................. 605
Snelling Personnel Services (C)........................ 608
Solutions Group - Birmingham (R)..................... 180
Staffing USA (C).. 623
Tyler Search Consultants (C)............................. 648

Daphne
Sales Consultants of Eastern Shore/Mobile Bay
  (C).. 573

Decatur
First Search America Inc (C)............................. 348
FPC of Decatur (C)....................................... 353
Snelling Personnel Services (C)........................ 608

Fairhope
MRI of Mobile Company (C) 448
Sanford Rose Associates - Fairhope (C) 586

Florence
Snelling Personnel Services (C).......................... 608

Homewood
Snelling Personnel Services (C)........................ 608

Huntsville
FPC of Huntsville (C)..................................... 353
Management Recruiters Int'l Inc (MRI) (C)......... 439
Personnel Inc (C)... 528
Robert William James & Associates (C)............. 560
Sales Consultants Int'l (C) 569
Snelling Search (C).. 614

Madison
Sales Consultants of Huntsville (C) 573

Mobile
Clark Personnel Service Inc (C)........................ 286
Halo Insurance Service (C)............................... 378
Hughes & Associates Int'l Inc (C)..................... 396
Sales Consultants Int'l (C) 570
Snelling Personnel Services (C)........................ 608

Montgomery
Locke & Associates (R).................................. 119
Snelling Personnel Services (C)......................... 608

Alaska

Anchorage
Alaska Executive Search Inc (C) 229
R C Services (C)... 549

Kenai
Management Recruiters Int'l Inc (MRI) (C).........439

Arizona

Bisbee
Lloyd Pressel & Company Inc (C) 537

Buckeye
G H Enterprises (C)...................................... 365

Carefree
Pinnacle Group Int'l (C) 531

Cave Creek
Hospitality Career Services (C) 394

Chandler
Career Search Consultants llc (C)...................... 275
Solutns Recruiting Services (C)....................... 615

Flagstaff
MRI of Flagstaff (C) 449

Fountain Hills
Henson Enterprises Inc (C) 388
Rand-Curtis Resources (C)............................. 550
Sales Consultants of Scottsdale (C).................... 573

Glendale
BSC Inc (C) 268

Goodyear
Sales Consultants of Goodyear Inc (C)................ 573
Stargate Group (C)....................................... 625

Green Valley
Gaudette & Company (R).................................. 75

Lake Havasu City
Unisearch Search & Recruiting Inc (C) 649
WSA Associates Restaurant Management
  Recruiting (C)... 667

Mesa
Accountants On Call (C)................................. 218
Accounting & Finance Personnel Inc (C) 222
Behavioral Science Associates Inc (R) 15
Pat Brown & Associates (C)............................. 266
Hall Kinion & Associates (C)............................ 377
Snelling Personnel Services (C) 608
Marjorie Starr & Associates (C)....................... 625
WorldSearch Consultants LLC (C)..................... 666

Nutrioso
Calver Associates Inc (C) 272

Phoenix
Accountants On Call (C).................................. 218
Accounting & Finance Personnel Inc (C) 222
Boyden (R)... 22
Catalina Medical Recruiters Inc (C) 279
Cizek Associates Inc (R) 36
Commercial Programming Systems Inc (C) 289
Crosby Associates (C).................................... 303
DHR Int'l (R) 51
Executive Search Network (C) 342
Fishel HR Associates Inc (C) 349
Phyllis Hawkins & Associates Inc (C)................. 382

HealthCare Recruiters Int'l • Phoenix (C)............ 385
Healthsearch USA Inc (C) 387
Hyland Bay Executive Search LLC (C) 399
James & Company (C)..................................... 409
Kforce (C)... 419
Lucas Group (C)... 435
The Morton Group (C)..................................... 501
DDJ Myers Ltd (R)....................................... 138
Nativesun Inc (R)... 139
PERC Ltd (C) 526
Personnel Solutions (C) 528
Professional Team Search Inc (C)...................... 543
Recruiting & Consulting Professionals (RCP)
  (C) 553
David H Reid & Associates LLC (C).................... 554
R S Reynolds Technical Recruiting (C)................ 556
Sales Consultants of Phoenix Camelback
  Corridor (C).. 574
Snelling Personnel Services (C)........................ 608
SSA Executive Search Int'l (R) 183
Techstaff Inc (C)... 638
TSS Consulting Ltd (C) 648
Witt/Kieffer, Ford, Hadelman & Lloyd (R)......... 206

Scottsdale
Ancilla Resource Corp (C) 237
ARC Partners Inc (C) 241
Austin Michaels Ltd Inc (C) 246
Bartholdi & Company Inc (R).............................. 13
Dan Bolen & Associates LLC (C) 260
BSA Hospitality (C).. 268
The Chapman Group Inc (C).............................. 282
Mark Christian & Associates Inc (C) 284
Computech Corp (C)....................................... 290
Corporate Dynamix (C) 296
DiBari & Associates (C) 312
The Dorfman Group (C) 315
Dynamic Computer Consultants Inc (C) 325
EFL Int'l (R) 59
Executive Management Resources (C).................. 337
J K Executive Search (C) 343
LCC Companies (C) 429
The Leadership Group (R) 116
Reynolds Lebus Associates (C).......................... 429
Management Consultants Corporate Recruiters
  (C) 438
Management Recruiters Int'l Inc (MRI) (C) 439
Moss & Company (R)..................................... 136
National Career Search (C) 504
Pearson & Associates Inc (R)............................ 147
Pinnacle Search & Recruit (C)........................... 531
Precision Solutions Inc (C) 535
Research Recruiters (C) 555
Roberson & Company (C) 560
The Rubicon Group (C) 567
Sales Consultants Int'l (C) 570
Saviar Inc (C)... 591
StratfordGroup (R)... 188
Swartz & Associates Inc (R) 189
Tele-Solutions of Arizona Inc (C) 640
Peter Van Leer & Associates (R) 198
Van Zant Inc (C)... 650
VZ Int'l Inc (C) 653
Weinman & Associates (C)............................... 657
Western Int'l Recruiters Inc (C) 659

Sedona
Austin Group Int'l (R)....................................... 10
The Bren Group (C)....................................... 264
Erickson & Associates Inc (C)........................... 333

Sun Lakes
Market Niche Consulting (C).............................. 484

GEOGRAPHIC

GEOGRAPHIC

GEOGRAPHIC

(R) = Retainer; (C) = Contingency

GEOGRAPHIC

GEOGRAPHIC

Snelling Personnel Services (C)........................... 608

Highlands Ranch
Langley & Associates Inc (R)............................ 113

Lafayette
Peregrine Staffing (C)...................................... 526

Lakewood
Advanced Recruiting Inc (C)............................ 226
Executives by Sterling Inc (C)........................... 344
FPC of Golden (C) 354
HRCG Inc Executive Search Management
   Consulting (R).. 94
i j & associates inc (C).................................... 400
MRI of Denver-Golden Hill (C) 452
PC Associates (C)... 524
PowerBrokers LLC (C)..................................... 534
Sales Consultants Int'l (C) 570

Littleton
Tom Bogle & Associates (C)............................. 259
Boulware & Associates Inc (R) 21
David E Clutter (C) 287
DRZ Medical Recruiters (C)............................. 318
Forager (R) 70
FPC of Denver (C) 354
Heritage Search Group Inc (C) 389
National Executive Resources (C) 505
Don V Poole & Associates Inc (C) 533
The Poole Group (R) 152
RTX Inc (C) 567
Snelling Personnel Services (C)........................... 608

Louisville
Welzig, Lowe & Associates (C) 658

Manitou Springs
Health Care Dimensions (C)................................ 384

Monument
Allenetics Executive Search (C) 231
Woodmoor Group Inc (C) 665

Morrison
Career Staffing Int'l Inc (C) 276
Executive Resources LLC (C) 340

Niwot
DiMarchi Partners Inc (R) 53
Dunhill Professional Search of Boulder (C)........ 321

Parker
Management Executive Services Associates
   Inc (MESA) (R) 123
Meridian Search Inc (C) 493

Pine
Fox Interlink Partners (C)................................. 362

Silverthorne
Robert Hess & Associates Inc (C) 389

Steamboat Springs
Ethan Andrews Associates (C) 238
Automotive Management Search Inc (C)............ 247

Vail
National Resources Inc (C)................................ 506

Westminster
Management Recruiters Int'l Inc (MRI) (C).........440
Sales Consultants of Westminster (C) 575

Woodland Park
Management Recruiters Int'l Inc (MRI) (C).........440

Yellow Jacket
Career Consulting Services Inc (CCS) (C) 274

Connecticut

Avon
ESearch Group (R)..62
K C Hale Inc (R) 82
Horton Int'l LLC (R) 93
People Management Northeast Inc (R)...............148
Snyder & Company (R)....................................179

Bethel
Heritage Recruiting Group LLC (R)......................89

Branford
Ryan Abbott Search Associates Inc (C)...............216
Allen, Austin, Lowe & Powers (R).........................6
Bohan & Bradstreet Inc (C) 259
Manufacturing Resource Group Ltd (C).............482

Cheshire
Development Systems Inc (DSI) (C) 311
Hobson Associates (C)....................................392
Napolitano & Wulster LLC (C)..........................504

Colchester
Executive Search Group Inc (C).........................341

Cos Cob
Flexible Resources Inc (C) 350

Cromwell
MRI of Middlesex (C)......................................452

Danbury
Abraham & London Ltd (C) 217
Argus National Inc (R) 8
E O Technical (C) 326
Executive Register Inc (C) 339
Staffing Now Inc (C)......................................622

Darien
Koll-Fairfield LLC (C).....................................423
Lindsey & Company Inc (R) 118
W D Nolte & Company (R)...............................140
Spence Associates Int'l Inc (R)..........................181

East Hartford
Dunhill Staffing Systems Inc (C) 318
Kforce (C)..420

East Windsor
Snelling Personnel Services (C) 608

Fairfield
Blackshaw, Olmstead, Lynch & Koenig (R)..........19
The Cantor Concern Inc (R) 29
Impex Services Inc (C)....................................400
Pascale & LaMorte LLC (C) 523
Somerset Group Inc (C) 615

Farmington
Thomas Byrne Associates (C).............................270
Executive Network & Research Associates (C) ..338
The Kilman Advisory Group (R) 107
McIntyre Associates (R) 129
Yankee Hospitality Search LLC (C) 667

Glastonbury
Executive Partners Inc (R) 64
R C Handel Associates Inc (R) 83
The Hudson Consulting Group LLC (R) 94
Infonet Resources LLC (C) 401
Kinkead Partners (R) 108
Richard L Mather & Associates (C)...................487

Greens Farms
Bosch & Associates LLC (R)...............................21

Greenwich
Americas Project Management Services (C)........235
The Directorship Search Group Inc (R)................53
Earley Kielty LLC (R) 57
Erlanger Associates (R) 62
Greenwich Search Partners LLC (C)...................373
Heidrick & Struggles Int'l Inc (R) 87
K2 Resources LP (C) 415
Kostmayer Associates Inc (R) 111
Livingston, Robert & Company (R)....................119
Matté & Company Inc (R) 127
K Russo Associates Inc (C) 567
William Willis Worldwide Inc (R)......................205
Wills Consulting Associates Inc (R) 205

Guilford
JFW Associates LLC (C) 411
Edward J Pospesil & Company (C)....................534
The Resource Group (R) 161

Hamden
Cheney Associates (C).....................................283

Hartford
Executive Directions Inc (R)...............................63
Kelly Law Registry (C)....................................418
RJS Associates Inc (C).....................................559
Howard W Smith Associates (R) 178

Hawleyville
Biomedical Search Consultants (R)......................18

Madison
Bankers Search LLC (C)....................................249
Tom Bogle & Associates (C) 259
J David Associates Inc (R) 48
Dussick Management Associates (C)..................325
ESA (R) 62
Techsearch Services Inc (C)..............................638

Manchester
Lutz Associates (C)..435

Marlborough
S W Delano & Company (C) 310

Meriden
New Media Staffing LLC (R) 139

Middletown
The Millard Group (R)......................................133

(R) = Retainer; (C) = Contingency

GEOGRAPHIC

(R) = Retainer; (C) = Contingency

GEOGRAPHIC

Lutz
Business Partners Inc (C) 269
Management Recruiters Int'l Inc (MRI) (C) 441

Maitland
Dunhill Professional Search of Orlando (C) 321
Management Recruiters Int'l Inc (MRI) (C) 441
Sales Consultants Int'l (C) 570
Spherion Professional Recruiting Group (C)...... 620

Marathon
MRI of Florida Keys (C) 454

Margate
Born & Bicknell Inc (C) 261

Melbourne
Snelling Personnel Services (C).......................... 609

Melbourne Beach
Computer Placement Services (C) 291

Miami
Accountants On Call (C) 219
Ambiance Personnel Inc (C)............................... 233
American Medical Consultants Inc (C)............... 234
American Recruiters Consolidated Inc (C) 235
American Recruiters Int'l (C)............................ 235
Boyden (R) 22
Capital Markets Search Int'l (R) 29
Careerxchange (C).. 277
Corporate Advisors Inc (C)............................... 295
Dunhill Professional Search of Miami (C) 321
Hastings & Hastings Inc (C) 382
Healthcare Recruiters Int'l • Dallas (C)............. 384
Heidrick & Struggles Int'l Inc (R) 87
H Hertner Associates Inc (C) 389
A T Kearney Executive Search (R)...................... 105
Korn/Ferry Int'l (R) 110
MRI of Miami-North (C).................................. 454
Maxecon Executive Search Consultants (R) 127
MDR Associates Inc (R)................................... 130
Messett Associates Inc (R) 132
Nason & Nason (C) 504
Parker Page Group (C) 522
Peyser Associates Inc (R) 150
The Quantum Group (C).................................. 547
Gene Rogers Associates Inc (C) 563
SearchCorp (C)... 598
Snelling Personnel Services (C)......................... 609
Staffing Now Inc (C) 623
Summit Executive Search Consultants Inc (R) ... 189
Ned Tannebaum & Partners (R)......................... 191
Lisa Torres & Associates Inc (C)....................... 644
Egon Zehnder Int'l Inc (R) 210

Miami Lakes
Creative Financial Staffing (C) 301
Kforce (C) 420
Spherion Professional Recruiting Group (C)....... 620

Milton
MRI of Santa Rosa (C) 454
Ropella & Associates (R) 166

Miramar
Snyder Executive Search Inc (C) 614

Mt. Dora
MRI of Lake County Inc (C) 454

Naples
Bennett Search & Consulting Company Inc (R)....16
Carlson Research Group (R) 31
DHR Int'l (R) 51
Gallin Associates Inc (C) 366
Hanley & Associates (R) 84
Management Recruiters Int'l Inc (MRI) (C)........441
Smith, Brown & Jones (C) 607
Snelling Personnel Services (C) 609
Spherion Legal Group (C)................................. 618

Niceville
Sales Consultants of The Emerald Coast (C).......575

North Miami
Patricia Roth Int'l (C) 565

North Miami Beach
Affinity Executive Search (C) 227

North Palm Beach
Erlanger Associates (R)..................................... 62
FPC of Palm Beach (C)..................................... 355
Sales Consultants of North Palm Beach (C) 576

Ocala
MRI of Chicago West and Ocala, FL (C) 454

Oldsmar
Helffrich Int'l (R) 88
MARBL Consultants Inc (C)............................ 483

Orange Park
The Caradyne Group (C)................................... 273
MRI of Orange Park (C)................................... 454

Orlando
APOGEE Inc (C) 240
Corporate Search Consultants Inc (C) 297
Executive Search Int'l (ESI) (C) 341
Int'l Recruiting Service (C)............................... 404
Kforce (C).. 420
Machine Tool Staffing (C) 436
Petrie Partners Inc (R)..................................... 150
ProFinders Inc (C)... 544
Pulp & Paper Int'l Inc (C)................................ 547
Sanford Rose Associates - Orlando (C) 587
Snelling Personnel Services (C) 609
Tell/Com Recruiters (C)................................... 640

Ormond Beach
R C Fiore (C) 348
RightSource Inc (C) 558

Osprey
Fortune Personnel Consultants (FPC) (C) 352

Oviendo
Abraxas Technologies Inc (C)............................ 217

Palm Beach
Creative Search Affiliates (C) 302
Nason & Nason (C)... 504

Palm Beach Gardens
The Andre Group Inc (R) 8
Business Answers Int'l (C) 269
ChaseAmerica Inc (R)...................................... 34
MRI of Northern Palm Beaches (C) 454
Staffing Now Inc (C).. 623

Palm Coast
Whitehead & Associates Inc (C)......................... 660

Palm Harbor
Career Images (C) 275
Chase-Gardner Executive Search Associates
   Inc (C) 283
Environmental, Health & Safety Search
   Associates Inc (EH&S) (C).............................. 333
Impact Source Inc (C)...................................... 400
Kay Concepts Inc (C)....................................... 417
MH Executive Search Group (C) 495
OmniSearch Inc (C)... 516

Palmetto
FPC of Manatee County (C) 355

Panama City
Dunhill Staffing Systems Inc (C) 319
Snelling Personnel Services (C).......................... 609

Panama City Beach
JCL & Associates (C) 410
MRI of Panama City Beach (C) 454

Parkland
FMK Staffing Services LLC (C)......................... 350

Pembroke Pines
Careerxchange (C)... 277
MRI of The Everglades (C)............................... 454
Sanford Rose Associates - Fort Lauderdale (C)... 587
Staffing Now Inc (C) 623

Pensacola
Engineering Profiles (C) 332
MRI of Pensacola (C)....................................... 454
Sanford Rose Associates - Pensacola (R) 169
Snelling Personnel Services (C) 609

Plantation
FPC of Ft Lauderdale (C)................................... 355
MRI of Plantation (C) 455
Sales Consultants Int'l (C)................................ 570
Staffing Now Inc (C) 623

Pompano
American Recruiters Consolidated Inc (C)..........235

Pompano Beach
Ash & Associates Executive Search (C) 242
Auguston and Associates Inc (R) 10
Resolve Associates Int'l (R) 161
Allan Stolee Inc (R) 186

Ponte Vedra Beach
ASSET Associates Inc (C) 243
BKG Inc (C) 258
Professional Resources (C) 542
The Stewart Group (C)...................................... 627

Port Charlotte
Snelling Personnel Services (C)........................... 609

Port Orange
Bruce L Ramstad (C) 550

Port St. Lucie
Heritage Search Group Inc (C)........................... 388
MRI of St. Lucie County (C) 455

(R) = Retainer; (C) = Contingency

GEOGRAPHIC

GEOGRAPHIC

(R) = Retainer; (C) = Contingency

GEOGRAPHIC

Hoffman Estates

Homewood

Inverness

Island Lake

Itasca

Joliet

Kenilworth

La Grange

Lake Barrington

Lake Bluff

Lake Carroll

Lake Forest

Lake Villa

Lake Zurich

Lemont

Libertyville

Lincoln

Lincolnshire

Lindenhurst

Lisle

Lockport

Mattoon

McHenry

Mokena

Moline

Montgomery

Morton

Mt. Prospect

Mundelein

Naperville

Normal

North Barrington

Northbrook

Northfield

Oak Brook

Oak Brook Terrace

Oak Park

Oregon

Orland Park

(R) = Retainer; (C) = Contingency

GEOGRAPHIC

Fremont
Nagle & Associates Inc (C) 503

Ft. Wayne
Bone Personnel Inc (C)................................. 260
Corporate Management Solutions Inc (C).......... 296
Crowe Chizek & Company LLP (C)................... 303
Dunhill Professional Search of Fort Wayne (C).. 322
FPC of Ft Wayne (C).................................. 356
Gemini Executive Search Inc (C) 367
Hope Resource Partners Inc (C)..................... 393
The Mallard Group (C)................................ 438
Management Recruiters Int'l Inc (MRI) (C)........ 442
Mayhall Search Group Inc (C)........................ 488
National Corporate Consultants Inc (C)............ 505
Roster Technologies Inc (C).......................... 565
Sales Consultants of Ft. Wayne (C) 577
Snelling Personnel Services (C)....................... 610

Greenwood
Dunhill Staffing Systems Inc (C)..................... 319

Indianapolis
Accountants On Call (C) 219
The Bennett Group Inc (R) 16
Johnson Brown Associates Inc (C) 266
CMS Management Services Company (C) 287
Covenant Staffing Inc (C).............................. 299
Creative Financial Staffing (C) 301
Crowe Chizek & Company LLP (C) 303
Dunhill Professional Search of Indianapolis (C). 322
First Call Professional Services (C) 348
B W Higgins Inc (C).................................... 390
Kforce (C) 420
MRI of Indianapolis-Central (C)...................... 459
Miller Personnel Consultants Inc (C)................ 497
The Morley Group (C).................................. 501
Motion Medical Solutions Inc (C) 501
Newlon Services Inc (C)................................ 510
Pergal and Company (R) 148
Providyn LLP (R)....................................... 156
Quiring Associates Inc (C) 549
Sales Consultants of Indianapolis-Central (C) 577
Search Force Inc (C)................................... 596
SearchPro Group Medical Services (C) 598
Secura Burnett Company LLC (R) 174
J Harrington Smith Associates (C).................... 606
Snelling Personnel Services (C)....................... 610
Spherion Professional Recruiting Group (C)....... 620
Thinkpath (C) 641
TPS Staffing Solutions (C) 644

Kokomo
FPC of Kokomo (C) 356

Lafayette
Allhands Placement Consultants (C) 231

Long Beach
De Funiak & Edwards (R) 49

Marion
Tomlinson-Miller Inc (C) 643

Merrillville
Creative Financial Staffing (C) 301
Crowe Chizek & Company LLP (C)................... 303

Mt. Vernon
FPC of Mt Vernon (C).................................. 356
FPC of SW Indiana (C) 356

Muncie
Professional Resource Group Inc (C) 542

Nashville
Dunhill Executive Search of Brown County (C)..322

Newburgh
MRI of Newburgh (C)................................... 459
Sanford Rose Associates - Evansville (C) 588

Noblesville
Career Concepts (C)................................... 274
MRI of Noblesville Inc (C) 459

Peru
Agra Placements Ltd (C) 227

Plainfield
Management Recruiters Int'l Inc (MRI) (C)......... 442
Seligman & Herrod (C) 600

Porter
Williger & Associates (R) 205

Richmond
Financial Recruiters (C) 347
Management Recruiters Int'l Inc (MRI) (C)......... 442

Santa Claus
Marksmen Consultants (C)............................. 485

South Bend
AmeriSearch Group Inc (C) 236
CMS Management Services Company (C) 287
Creative Financial Staffing (C)........................ 301
Crowe Chizek & Company LLP (C) 303
FPC of South Bend (C) 356
MRI of South Bend (C)................................. 459
mfg/Search Inc (R)..................................... 132
Reach Consulting Group Inc (C) 552

Terre Haute
Corporate Search Consultants (C) 298
Robert William James & Associates (C) 561

Wabash
Lange & Associates Inc (C) 427
Snelling Personnel Services (C) 610

Warsaw
The Lake City Group (C) 426

Zionsville
Management Recruiters Int'l Inc (MRI) (C)......... 442

Iowa

Arnolds Park
MRI of Spencer (C)..................................... 459

Bettendorf
AGRI- Associates (C) 228
Bryant Bureau Sales Recruiters (C).................. 267
MRI of Quad Cities (C)................................. 459
Snelling Personnel Services (C) 610
Triumph Consulting Inc (R) 196

Cedar Falls
Future Employment Service Inc (C)................... 364

Cedar Rapids
FPC of Cedar Rapids (C)............................... 356
Future Employment Service Inc (C)................... 364
Kaas Employment Services (C) 415
Management Recruiters Int'l Inc (MRI) (C) 442
McCord Consulting Group Inc (C)..................... 488
Ray & Associates Inc (R)............................... 158
Sanford Rose Associates - Cedar Rapids (C) 588

Clive
The Alliance Search Group Inc (C)..................... 232
Career Search Associates (C)........................... 275

Council Bluffs
Sales Consultants Int'l (C) 571
Snelling Personnel Services (C) 610

Davenport
Management Resource Group Ltd (R) 124
Techstaff Inc (C).. 639

Des Moines
Creative Financial Staffing (C) 301
Executive Resources (C)................................ 340
Eyler Associates Inc (R) 66
Personnel Inc (C) 528
RSM McGladrey Search Group (R) 167
Snelling Personnel Services (C) 610

Dubuque
Future Employment Service Inc (C)................... 364

Fairfield
ASAP Search & Placement (C).......................... 242
MRI of Fairfield (C) 459
J R Seehusen Associates Inc (R) 174
TECHNET Staffing Services Inc (C) 636

Hiawatha
Sales Consultants Int'l (C)............................. 571

Iowa City
Dunhill Staffing Systems Inc (C) 319

Maquoketa
Future Employment Service Inc (C)................... 364

Marshalltown
Andersen & Associates (C).............................. 237

Mason City
Action Recruiters (C)................................... 223
Management Recruiters Int'l Inc (MRI) (C) 442

Polk City
Miller & Associates Inc (C) 497

Red Oak
Snelling Personnel Services (C) 610

Sioux City
MRI of Siouxland (C)................................... 459

Waukee
The Garrison Organization (R) 75

West Des Moines
Agra Placements Ltd (C)................................ 227
Carlson & Czeswik (R).................................. 31

(R) = Retainer; (C) = Contingency

(R) = Retainer; (C) = Contingency

GEOGRAPHIC

R2 Services LLC (C) *550*
Walters, Rhodes & Associates LLC (C) *655*
Witt/Kieffer, Ford, Hadelman & Lloyd (R) *206*

Cambridge
California Search Consultants Corp (CSC) (C)... *271*
Executive Search Associates (C) *341*
Nachman BioMedical (C) *503*

Canton
Breitner Clark & Hall Inc (R) *24*
Laboratory Resource Group (C) *426*
Alan Levine Associates (R) *117*
Stephen M Sonis Associates (R) *180*
The Zarkin Group Inc (R) *210*

Carlisle
P N French Associates Inc (R) *72*

Charlestown
The Elliott Company (R) *60*

Chelmsford
Timothy D Crowe Jr (R) *45*
Marketing Resources (C) *484*
ProSearch Inc (C) *545*
Snelling Personnel Services (C) *610*

Concord
Blaney Executive Search (R) *19*
DHR Int'l (R) *51*
Ford Webb Associates Inc (R) *70*
K Jaeger & Associates (C) *409*

Danvers
Architechs (C) *241*
HM Associates (C) *391*
Morency Associates (C) *500*

Dedham
Gillard Associates Legal Search (C) *369*
JNB Associates Inc (C) *411*
S D Kelly & Associates Inc (R) *106*
Recruiting Specialists (C) *553*

Dover
Mehta Consulting (C) *492*

Duxbury
M Campbell Associates (C) *272*
S B Webster & Associates (R) *201*

East Longmeadow
Fortune Personnel Consultants (FPC) (C) *352*

East Sandwich
Hunt For Executives (C) *398*

Easthampton
Staffing Now Inc (C) *623*

Essex
Essex Consulting Group Inc (R) *62*

Falmouth
Massachusetts Medical Bureau (C) *486*
Sales Consultants Int'l (C) *571*

Foxboro
Executive Directions Inc (R) *63*

Framingham
Accountants On Call (C) *219*
Franklin Int'l Search Inc (C) *363*
Moran & Associates (C) *499*
Norman Powers Associates Inc (C) *535*
L A Silver Associates Inc (R) *177*

Franklin
Franklin Key Associates (C) *419*
Stonington Associates (C) *628*

Gloucester
Hamilton-Chase & Associates Inc (R) *83*

Granby
Morgan & Associates (C) *500*

Hamilton
Kirk Palmer & Associates Inc (R) *145*

Hanover
Boston Executive Search (C) *261*
Search America Inc (C) *594*
Tondorf & Associates Inc (C) *643*

Hingham
AKS Associates Ltd (R) *4*
The Longfellow Group (R) *120*
Phillips & Associates Inc (R) *150*
Springbrook Partners Inc (R) *183*
Sullivan Associates (R) *189*

Hubbardston
Kimball Personnel Sales Recruiters (C) *422*

Ipswich
Talent Scouts Inc (C) *633*

Lakeville
Edelman & Associates (C) *328*

Leeds
The Spelman & Johnson Group (R) *181*

Leominster
Staffing Now Inc (C) *623*

Lexington
The Corporate Source Group Inc (R) *44*
Fitzgerald Associates (R) *69*
Hamilton-Chase & Associates Inc (R) *83*
IT Resources (C) *407*
Lynx Inc (C) *436*
Louis Rudzinsky Associates Inc (C) *567*
Willmott & Associates (C) *661*

Lynnfield
The Insurance Staffing Group (C) *403*

Marblehead
Richard D Holbrook Associates (R) *91*
New Dimensions in Technology Inc (C) *509*
J E Ranta Associates (C) *551*

Marion
The Jeremiah Group Inc (R) *101*

Marshfield
Stevens Associates (C) *626*

Marshfield Hills
Resource Inc (R) *162*

Martha's Vineyard
DHR Int'l (R) *51*

Maynard
Steinbach & Company (C) *625*

Medfield
Gatti & Associates (C) *366*
J S Lord & Company Inc (R) *120*
Prestonwood Associates (R) *153*

Mendon
Derek Associates Inc (C) *311*

Methuen
Staffing Now Inc (C) *623*

Milton
The Bray Group (R) *23*

Nantucket
Educational Management Network (R) *58*
Witt/Kieffer, Ford, Hadelman & Lloyd (R)......... *206*

Natick
McInturff & Associates Inc (C) *490*
TechFind Inc (C) *636*
Weinstein & Company (R) *201*
The Yorkshire Group Ltd (R) *209*
ZweigWhite (sm) (R) *211*

Needham
Ford & Ford (C) *351*
Glou Int'l Inc (R) *77*
ResourceOptions Inc (C) *556*
Sales Consultants of Needham (C) *578*
Peter Siegel & Company (C) *603*
Trowbridge & Company Inc (R) *196*

Newburyport
Search Int'l (R) *172*

Newton
E M Heath & Company (C) *387*
Kforce (C) *420*
The Spiegel Group Inc (R) *183*

Newton Lower Falls
Gustin Partners Ltd (R) *82*

Newton Upper Falls
Flexible Resources Inc (C) *350*

North Andover
The Devlin Search Group Inc (DSG) (C) *312*
Financial Search Group Inc (R) *67*
HRCG Inc Executive Search Management
   Consulting (R) *94*
Medical Search Group (C) *492*
STAT Search (C) *625*
Straube Associates (R) *188*
Vista Technology (C) *652*

North Eaton
Xavier Associates Inc (R) *209*

GEOGRAPHIC

Bad Axe
Trillium Staffing Solutions (C) 646

Battle Creek
Management Recruiters Int'l Inc (MRI) (C) 443
Lou Michaels Associates Inc (C) 495
Savalli & Associates Inc (C) 591
Trillium Staffing Solutions (C) 646

Bingham Farms
Executive Search Team (C) 342
MRI of Birmingham (C) 462
Sales Consultants of Birmingham (C) 579
Snelling Personnel Services (C) 610

Birmingham
Compass Group Ltd (R) 40
Continental Search Associates Inc (C) 294
Rooney Personnel Company (C) 564
Smith Bridges and Associates Inc (C) 606
Smith Professional Search (C) 606
Sullivan & Associates (R) 189
The Whittaker Group Inc (C) 660

Blissfield
MRI of Southeastern Michigan (C) 462

Bloomfield Hills
Altec/HRC (C) 233
Boyden (R) 22
Crowder & Company (R) 45
FPC of Bloomfield Inc (C) 357
Joseph Goldring & Associates Inc (C) 371
Gundersen Partners LLC (R) 81
The Hunter Group Inc (C) 398
Kuttnauer Search Group Inc (C) 425
mfg/Search Inc (R) 132
PsychPros Executive Search (C) 547
Sales Consultants Int'l (C) 571
TMP Worldwide Executive Search (R) 194

Brighton
Artemis HRC (C) 242
HealthCare Recruiters Int'l • Michigan (C) 386
Trillium Staffing Solutions (C) 646

Brownstown
American Resources Corp (C) 235

Center Line
Sharrow & Associates Inc (C) 601

Charlotte
Trillium Staffing Solutions (C) 646

Chelsea
Holland & Associates Inc (R) 91

Clinton Township
Dunhill Staffing Systems Inc (C) 319

Coldwater
Trillium Staffing Solutions (C) 646

Dearborn
Gene Ellefson & Associates Inc (C) 330
MRI of Dearborn (C) 462
Premier Healthcare Recruiters Inc (C) 536

Detroit
Accountants On Call (C) 220
Edwards-Polk & Associates (C) 328
Joe L Giles & Associates (C) 368
Snelling Personnel Services (C) 610

East Lansing
The Mercer Group Inc (R) 131
The Stark Wilton Group (R) 184

East Tawas
Trillium Staffing Solutions (C) 646

Farmington
RemTech Business Solutions Inc (C) 555

Farmington Hills
Creative Financial Staffing (C) 301
Elwell & Associates Inc (R) 60
FPC of Farmington Hills (C) 357
Harper Associates (C) 380
MRI of E Detroit/Farmington Hills (C) 462
Newman Hawkins Legal Search (C) 510
Professional Personnel Consultants Inc (C) 541
ProSearch Group Inc (C) 544
Roth Young of Detroit (C) 565
Sales Consultants of Farmington Hills (C) 579
Search Plus Int'l (C) 596
Teamsearch Inc (C) 636
Techstaff Inc (C) 639

Flint
Action Management Corp (C) 223
Trillium Staffing Solutions (C) 646

Gladstone
Automotive Recruiters Int'l Inc (R) 10

Grand Blanc
MRI of Flint (C) 462
Valmar Technical Staffing (C) 650

Grand Haven
Associates (C) 244
Management Recruiters Int'l Inc (MRI) (C) 443

Grand Rapids
Account Ability Now (C) 218
Accountants On Call (C) 220
The Adams Consulting Group Inc (C) 224
Advanced Executive Resources (R) 3
Collins & Associates (C) 289
CompHealth (C) 290
Creative Financial Staffing (C) 301
Crowe Chizek & Company LLP (C) 303
Dunlap & Sullivan Associates (R) 57
ExecuQuest Inc (R) 63
Kforce (C) 420
Leadership Capital Group LLC (R) 116
Management Recruiters Int'l Inc (MRI) (C) 443
Sales Consultants of Grand Rapids (C) 579
Snelling Personnel Services (C) 610
Techstaff Inc (C) 639
Trillium Staffing Solutions (C) 646

Grandville
Snelling Personnel Services (C) 610

Grosse Pointe Farms
Daudlin, De Beaupre & Company Inc (R) 48

Grosse Pointe Park
Lowell Johnson Associates LLC (R) 120

Harbor Springs
Career Alternatives Executive Search (C) 273
The Clark Group (C) 286

Hartland
Sales Consultants Int'l (C) 571

Holland
G L Dykstra Associates Inc (C) 325
Management Recruiters Int'l Inc (MRI) (C) 443
Paragon Recruiting (C) 522
Professional Outlook Inc (C) 541

Holt
Management Recruiters Int'l Inc (MRI) (C) 443

Houghton Lake
Management Recruiters Int'l Inc (MRI) (C) 443

Jackson
Management Recruiters Int'l Inc (MRI) (C) 443
Trillium Staffing Solutions (C) 646

Jonesville
Trillium Staffing Solutions (C) 646

Kalamazoo
Circlewood Search Group Inc (C) 285
Collins & Associates (C) 288
Hallman Group Inc (C) 378
Management Recruiters Int'l Inc (MRI) (C) 443
Premier Recruiting Group Inc (C) 536
Sales Consultants of Kalamazoo (C) 579
Snelling Personnel Services (C) 610
Trillium Staffing Solutions (C) 646
R Walters Resources (C) 655

Lambertville
Graphic Arts Marketing Associates Inc (C) 372

Lansing
Advance Employment Inc (C) 226
DHR Int'l (R) 51
Sales Consultants Int'l (C) 571

Lapeer
J E Lessner Associates Inc (R) 117
Trillium Staffing Solutions (C) 646

Livonia
Access/Resources Inc (C) 218
The Barton Group Inc (C) 251
MRI of Livonia (C) 462
Sales Consultants of Laurel Park (C) 579
Snelling Personnel Services (C) 610
Henry Welker & Associates (C) 658

Madison Heights
American Heritage Group Inc (C) 234
Snelling Personnel Services (C) 610

Malcolm Township
Robert William James & Associates (C) 561

Marine City
Management Recruiters Int'l Inc (MRI) (C) 443

GEOGRAPHIC

GEOGRAPHIC

GEOGRAPHIC

(R) = Retainer; (C) = Contingency

Lakewood
Jack Stuart Fisher Associates (C)....................... 349
Rein & Company Inc (R).................................. 161
Snelling Personnel Services (C)......................... 611

Lawrenceville
Alexander Associates (R) 4
Carnegie Executive Search Inc (C)..................... 277
Ken Clark Int'l (R).. 37
Kenexa (R) 106
McGrath & Associates Inc (R) 129
Moore Research Associates (R).......................... 135

Lincroft
Freeman Enterprises (C) 363

Little Silver
Allen Thomas Associates Inc (C) 231

Livingston
Accountants On Call (C) 220
Sales Consultants of Livingston (C) 580

Long Valley
Bonner/Menard Int'l (R) 20

Lyndhurst
Fox-Morris Associates Inc (C)........................... 362
Hunt Ltd (C)... 398

Madison
Joseph R Burns & Associates Inc (R).................... 27
The Goodkind Group Inc (C)............................. 372
Karras Personnel Inc (C) 416

Mahwah
Butterfass, Pepe & MacCallan Inc (R).................. 27
Executive Dynamics Inc (EDI) (C)..................... 337
Telequest Communications Inc (C) 640

Manalapan
The Howard Group Ltd (C) 395
JWC Associates Inc (C)................................... 414
Page Staffing & Training (C)............................. 521

Manasquan
R W Apple & Associates (C)............................. 240
The Executive Exchange Corp (C) 337
The Mulshine Company Inc (R) 137
Sales Consultants Int'l (C) 572

Manasquan Township
Management Recruiters Int'l Inc (MRI) (C)........ 444

Maplewood
FPC of New Brunswick (C)............................... 357

Marlton
Accountants On Call (C) 220
Bonifield Associates (C)................................... 260
DigitalHire (C) 313
Dorothy W Farnath & Associates Inc (C) 345
HealthCare Recruiters Int'l • Philadelphia (C)..... 386
David Perry Associates (C)............................... 527

Matawan
N Willner & Company Inc (C) 662

Maywood
The DataFinders Group Inc (C) 308

Medford
The Addison Consulting Group (C).................... 224
MRI of Medford, NJ (C) 465
Munroe, Curry & Bond Associates (R) 138

Mendham
Kazan Int'l Inc (R)... 105

Metuchen
Clinical Staffing Associates LLC (CSA) (C)....... 286
Dunhill Professional Search of Middlesex (C) 322
FPC of Menlo Park (C) 358
MRI of Edison (C) 465

Milford
ALS Group (C)... 233

Millburn
MRI of Short Hills (C) 465
Marra Peters & Partners (R).............................. 126

Milltown
Harrison Group (C).. 381

Monmouth Beach
Graham & Company (R) 79

Monroe
Coughlin & Associates (C)................................ 299

Monroe Township
Royce Ashland Group Inc (C) 567

Montclair
Epsen, Fuller & Associates LLC (R) 61
Flexible Resources Inc (C) 350
Toy Jobs (C)... 644

Moorestown
Lawrence Glaser Associates Inc (C)................... 369

Morganville
Judd Associates (R).. 103
LAS Management Consulting Group Inc (C) 428

Morris Plains
Access Systems (C).. 218
Engineering Resource Group Inc (C) 332
Robert William James & Associates (C) 561

Morristown
Ballos & Company Inc (R).................................. 12
Foley Proctor Yoskowitz (R)............................. 70
Kulper & Company LLC (R) 112
Skott/Edwards Consultants (R) 178

Mountain Lakes
Besen Associates Inc (C)................................. 256
Brandywine Management Group (R)..................... 23
Orion Consulting Inc (R).................................. 144

Mountainside
MRI of Union County (C) 465

Mt. Freedom
Paul Falcone Associates (R)............................... 66

Mt. Laurel
MRI of Bordentown (C).................................... 465

Romeo Consulting (C) 564
Scientific Search Inc (C) 593

Murray Hill
Michael E Marion & Associates Inc (R) 125

Neshanic Station
AP Associates (APA) (C) 239

New Brunswick
Management Recruiters Int'l Inc (MRI) (C) 444
Placemart Personnel Service (C)........................ 532
Snelling Personnel Services (C)......................... 611

New Monmouth
J R Fox Recruiters (C) 362

New Providence
MRI of New Providence (C) 465

Newark
L J Gonzer Associates (C) 371
Snelling Personnel Services (C)......................... 611

Newton
American Recruiters Consolidated Inc (C).......... 235

North Bergen
KL Consultants (R) 108

North Brunswick
Hreshko Consulting Group (C) 396
Key Employment (C)....................................... 419

Northfield
Golden Opportunities Employment (C)................ 371
Snelling Personnel Services (C)......................... 611

Nutley
Headhunters Executive Search Inc (C)................ 383

Oakland
Dunhill Professional Search of Ramsey (C) 322
Sales Consultants of Northern Jersey (C)............ 580

Ocean Grove
Electronic Search Inc (C).................................. 330

Ogdensburg
Sales Consultants Int'l (C)................................ 572

Oradell
Management Decision Systems Inc (MDSI)
  (C).. 439

Paramus
Accountants On Call (C)................................... 220
AES Search (C) 227
David Anthony Personnel Associates Inc (C) 239
Berman, Larson, Kane (C) 256
Kforce (C)... 420
Search Consultants Inc (C)............................... 595

Parsippany
Accountants On Call (C)................................... 220
Baker, Scott & Company (C) 248
Bosland Gray Assoc (R) 21
Polly Brown Associates (C)............................... 267
Chester Hill MedEd (C) 284
The Garret Group (R).. 74

(R) = Retainer; (C) = Contingency

GEOGRAPHIC

GEOGRAPHIC

(R) = Retainer; (C) = Contingency

(R) = Retainer; (C) = Contingency

GEOGRAPHIC

GEOGRAPHIC

(R) = Retainer; (C) = Contingency

Pennsylvania

(R) = Retainer; (C) = Contingency

GEOGRAPHIC

W G Tucker & Associates Inc (R) *196*

Plymouth Meeting
Concord Search Group (C) 292
Evan Scott Group Int'l (R) *171*

Pottsville
Management Recruiters Int'l Inc (MRI) (C) 446

Quakertown
Barr Associates (C).. 250

Radnor
Howe & Associates (R) *93*
Soltis Management Services (R) *180*
Tele-Media Int'l Inc (C)...................................... *639*

Reading
America at Work (C) 234
Kenn Spinrad Inc (C).. 621

Schnecksville
SHS of Allentown (C) *602*

Selinsgrove
Fortune Personnel Consultants (FPC) (C) *353*

Sewickley
MRI of Pittsburgh-North (C) *473*
Sales Consultants of Wexford (C) *582*

Sharon
Technical Staffing Professionals LLC (C) *637*

Sinking Spring
American Logistics Consultants Inc (C) 234

Skippack
Management Recruiters Int'l Inc (MRI) (C) 446

Southampton
M A Churchill & Associates Inc (R)..................... *36*
Sales Consultants of Southampton (C)............... *582*

Spring City
Ogilvie-Smartt Associates LLC (R).................... *143*

Spring House
Management Recruiters Int'l Inc (MRI) (C) 446

Springdale
Terry Taylor & Associates (C) 635

Springfield
Integrity Search Inc (R) *99*
Systems Search Consultants (SSC) (C).............. *632*

St. Davids
Ahrensdorf & Associates (R)................................ *4*

St. Peters
The Mayes Group Ltd (R) *127*

State College
J N Adams & Associates Inc (C) 224
Sterling Systems Inc (C)..................................... 626

Tarentum
Sales Recruiting Network (C)............................. *585*

Trevose
Jacobson Associates (C)......................................*409*
Jacobson Executive Search (R) *100*

Upper Black Edox
T J Koellhoffer & Associates (R) *109*

Upper St. Clair
E W Dean & Associates Inc (C)............................*309*

Valley Forge
Hobbs & Towne Inc (R)..*91*

Warminster
FPC of Abington (C)...*359*
Intercontinental Executive Group (C)...................*406*
MRI of Bucks County (C).....................................*473*

Warrendale
Tarquinio Recruiting Group/Workforce
   Development Inc (C)..*634*

Warrington
Triangle Associates (C)..*646*

Washington
The Polen Group (C)...*533*

Waverly
Computer Career Services (C)...............................*290*

Wayne
ACSYS Resources Inc (C) *223*
Caliber Associates (R)..*28*
Criterion Search Group Inc (R) *45*
The Ford Group Inc (R) *70*
FPC of Wayne PA (C)..*359*
JM & Company (R)...*101*
Kenexa (R)..*106*
Kforce (C)...*421*
Patriot Associates (C)...*524*
Salveson Stetson Group Inc (R) *169*
Samson Findings (R)..*169*
Walker Forest (C)..*654*
Worlco Computer Resources Inc (C)....................*665*

West Chester
Jack Bertram Executive Recruiting (C) *256*
William J Christopher Associates Inc (R)..............*36*
Dunhill Staffing Systems Inc (C) ....:............*319*
Nursing Technomics (R) *141*
Piedmont Group Inc (C).......................................*530*
Search Innovations Inc (R) *172*
Whittlesey & Associates Inc (R) *204*

Wexford
J T Brady & Associates (R)....................................*23*
Helbling & Associates Inc (R)...............................*88*

Whitehall
Management Recruiters Int'l Inc (MRI) (C).........446

Wilkes-Barre
Dunhill Professional Search of Wilkes-
   Barre/Scranton (C)...*323*
Parente Search LLC (R) *146*
SHS TechStaffing (C) *602*

Willow Grove
Management Recruiters Int'l Inc (MRI) (C).........446

ProSearch Inc (C) *545*

Wynnewood
Amato & Associates Insurance Recruiters (C) 233
Kaplan & Associates Inc (R)................................ *104*

Wyomissing
MRI of Reading (C).. *473*

Yardley
Dunhill Professional Search of Yardley (C) 324
The Hennessy Group (R) *88*
Rice Cohen Int'l (R) *163*

York
ESC2000 (C) 334
Leader Network (C) 429

Puerto Rico

Hato Rey
Careers Inc (C)... *276*
Creative Financial Staffing (C) *301*

San Juan
MRI of Puerto Rico (C) *473*
Palacios & Associates Inc (R)............................. *145*
Ryan Executive Search & Outplacement (C) *568*

Santurce
Snelling Personnel Services (C) *612*

Rhode Island

Charlestown
Alper Associates Inc (R) *6*

Cranston
Willmott & Associates (C).................................. *662*
Winfield Scott Associates (C) *663*

East Greenwich
DHR Int'l (R) *52*
Sylvestro Associates (C) *631*

Hope Valley
Carter, Lavoie Associates (C) *278*

Hopkinton
Tech Int'l (C).. *636*

Lincoln
Computer Technology Staffing LLC (C) 292

Little Compton
The Bedford Group (R)... *15*

Middletown
Sales Consultants Int'l (C)................................... *573*

Narragansett
Search Partners (R)... *173*

Newport
Lybrook Associates Inc (C) *435*

North Kingstown
The Schattle Group (R) *171*

GEOGRAPHIC

GEOGRAPHIC

GEOGRAPHIC

(R) = Retainer; (C) = Contingency

Stowe
J R Peterman Associates Inc (C).........................529

Warren
Dunhill Professional Search of Vermont (C) 324

West Townshend
Daniel F Reilly & Associates Inc (R).................160

White River Junction
J Ryder Search (C) 408

Woodstock
Alexander, Wollman & Stark (R) 5
Eckler Personnel Network (C)............................327
Jay Tracey Associates Inc (C)..............................644

Virginia

Alexandria
Association Strategies (R) 9
The Brannon Group Inc (C) 264
Flores Financial Services (C)...............................350
Hughes & Company (R) 94
A T Kearney Executive Search (R)......................105
Mancini Technical Recruiting (C) 482
ProLinks Inc (R)..156

Annandale
Financial Connections Company (C)...................346
NRI Staffing Resources (C)..................................514

Arlington
Action Management Corp (C) 223
Frey & Sher Associates Inc (C) 363
Management Recruiters Int'l Inc (MRI) (C).........447
Adam Smith Executive Search Consulting (R) ...178

Berryville
FPC of Fairfax (C)...361

Bridgewater
Souder & Associates (R) 180

Bristow
T/A : Sales Management (C) 633

Burke
HR Advantage Inc (C)..395

Chantilly
GateSource Partners (C) 366
Harbor Consultants Int'l Inc (C).........................379
Larson, Katz & Young Inc (C) 428
MRI of Loudoun County S (C).............................478
MBA Management Inc (C) 488

Charlottesville
CountryHouse Hotels Executive Search (C) 299
Management Recruiters Int'l Inc (MRI) (C) 448
The Monticello Group (C) 499

Chatham
ProStar Systems Inc (C) 545

Chesapeake
Snelling Personnel Services (C)...........................613

Fairfax
Halbrecht & Company (C) 376
Kforce (C) 421
Starbridge Group Inc (C).....................................624
Telecom Recruiters Inc (C) 640
Wilkinson SoftSearch Inc (C)..............................660

Falls Church
US Search LLC (C)...650
Willmott & Associates (C) 662

Glen Allen
Nations Executive Recruiters (C) 507

Hampton
Carol Maden Group (C) 436

Herndon
Accountants On Call (C) 221
Lucas Group (C)...435
Management Recruiters Int'l Inc (MRI) (C).........448
MDR Associates Inc (R) 130
Pro2Serve Recruiting Solutions (R) 155
StrategicHire (R)..187

Jeffersonton
Security Management Resources Inc (C)..............599

Leesburg
Brault & Associates Ltd (R) 23
Dahl-Morrow Int'l (R) 47
Sales Consultants Int'l (C)...................................573

Lightfoot
Executive Career Search (C) 336

Lynchburg
MRI of Lynchburg (C) 478

Manassas
Management Recruiters Int'l Inc (MRI) (C).........448
MRI of Manassas (C) 478

Martinsville
Management Recruiters Int'l Inc (MRI) (C).........448

McLean
Cabot Consultants (R) 27
Christian & Timbers (R)...36
The Consulting Group of North America Inc
   (C) 293
Dinte Resources Inc (R) 53
F Gloss Int'l (R)...77
Government Contract Solutions Inc (C) 372
Hall Kinion & Associates (C)...............................378
Heidrick & Struggles Int'l Inc (R) 87
Korn/Ferry Int'l (R)..110
MRI of McLean (C) 478
Paul-Tittle Associates Inc (R)..............................147
Search Connection LLC (C).................................595
Spherion Professional Recruiting Group (C) 621
StratfordGroup (R) 188

Mechanicsville
Charter Resources Int'l LC (C) 283

Middleburg
Fortune Personnel Consultants (FPC) (C) 353

Midlothian
Recruiting Resources Inc (C) 553

Millboro
FPC of The Virginia Highland (C)........................361

Norfolk
Orion Int'l (C) 518

Oakton
MRI of Oakton (C) 478

Onancock
United Search (C) 649

Palmyra
MRI of Piedmont (C)..478

Portsmouth
JLM Consulting Inc (R) 101

Pulaski
Management Recruiters Int'l Inc (MRI) (C) 448

Reston
Bartholdi & Company Inc (R)................................13
Creative Financial Staffing (C) 302
Doleman Enterprises (R).......................................55
HireStrategy (C)...391
IndustrySalesPros.com (C)...................................401
NRI Staffing Resources (C) 514
PMK Management Consultants Inc (C) 532
Rowan & Ruggles LLC (R) 167
Staffing Now Inc (C) 623
Winter, Wyman & Company (C) 664

Richmond
Accountants On Call (C).....................................221
Lee Calhoon & Company Inc (R) 28
The Corporate Connection Ltd (C)......................295
Dunhill Staffing Systems Inc (C) 320
Executive Sales Search Inc (C) 340
Management Recruiters Int'l Inc (MRI) (C) 448
Morgan Executive Search (C).............................500
National Affirmative Action Career Network
   Inc (C) 504
Pro Forma Search (R) 155
Recruiters Advantage Inc (C)..............................552
Renaissance Resources (R) 161
Sales Consultants Int'l (C)...................................573
Spherion Professional Recruiting Group (C).......621
Trust Bankers (C) 647

Roanoke
Hartman Personnel (R) 85
MRI of Roanoke (C)...478
Sales Consultants Int'l (C)...................................573

Springfield
Robert William James & Associates (C).............561
Staffing Now Inc (C) 623

Stafford
Victoria James Executive Search Inc (C)............410

Staunton
Recruiting Options (R)..160

Sterling
MRI of Loudoun County North (C) 478

GEOGRAPHIC

Snohomish
Pacific Search Consultants Inc (C) 520

Spokane
MRI of Spokane (C) 479
Personnel Unlimited/Executive Search (C)......... 528
Pro Search National Recruiting Services (C) 539

Tacoma
Accountants On Call (C) 221
Management Recruiters Int'l Inc (MRI) (C)........ 448

Vancouver
APA Employment Agency Inc (C) 239
MRI of Vancouver (C) 479

Vashon
Luna Tech Inc (C) 435
Moss & Company (R).. 136

Washougal
Roth Young of Portland (C)............................... 566

Wenatchee
Snelling Personnel Services (C)......................... 613

West Virginia

Barboursville
Snelling Personnel Services (C)......................... 613

Charleston
Management Recruiters Int'l Inc (MRI) (C) 448
Snelling Personnel Services (C)......................... 613

Hurricane
MRI of Kanawha Valley (C) 479

Morgantown
Management Recruiters Int'l Inc (MRI) (C)........ 448
MRI of Morgantown (C) 479

New Haven
Locus Inc (C)... 433

Vienna
Sanford Rose Associates - Vienna (C)................. 591

Wisconsin

Appleton
Creative Financial Staffing (C)........................... 302
Eagle Technology Group Inc (C)........................ 326
MRI of Appleton (C) 479
Sales Consultants Int'l (C) 573
Schenck & Associates SC (C)............................. 592
Signature Search (R)... 176

Brookfield
Boettcher Associates (R) 20
Cutler/Krenzke LLC (R)....................................... 47
Fortune Personnel Consultants (FPC) (C).......... 353
Gibson & Company Inc (R)................................... 76
KGA Inc (C).. 421
MARBL Consultants Inc (C).............................. 483
Prime Resource Associates Inc (C)..................... 538
Sloane & Associates Inc (C) 605
Snelling Personnel Services (C)......................... 613

Jude M Werra & Associates LLC (R)...................202

Cottage Grove
MRI of Madison (C)..479

De Pere
T E M Associates (C)...632

Delavan
Robert Ham & Associates Inc (C) 378
Management Recruiters Int'l Inc (MRI) (C)..........448
Sales Consultants Int'l (C) 573

Dodgeville
The Corim Group (R)...43

Eau Galle
Riverwood Consulting (C)...................................559

Elkhart Lake
Hunter, Rowan & Crowe (R)................................96

Elm Grove
Koehler & Company (R) 109
Maglio & Company Inc (R) 123
MRI of Milwaukee-West (C) 479

Fond du Lac
Amber Systems Group LLC (C)...........................233
Empire Consulting Group (C) 331

Germantown
MRI of Germantown (C)......................................480

Grafton
Management Recruiters Int'l Inc (MRI) (C)..........448
Mulcahy Company (C)..502

Green Bay
DeCaster Associates (C)......................................309
Dunhill Staffing Systems Inc (C) 320
The H S Group Inc (C)..375
Management Recruiters Int'l Inc (MRI) (C)..........448
Packaging Personnel Company Ltd (C)................520
Sales Consultants Int'l (C) 573
Techstaff Inc (C)...639
Trillium Staffing Solutions (C)...........................647

Hales Corners
Management Recruiters Int'l Inc (MRI) (C)..........448

Hartford
Needham Consultants Inc (C)..............................508

Hartland
Executive Resource Inc (C).................................340

Hudson
DHR Int'l (R) 52

Janesville
MRI of Janesville (C)..480
Sanford Rose Associates - Janesville (C) 591

La Crosse
Construction Search Specialists Inc (C)...............293
Pryor Knowledge Recruiting Inc (C)...................546

Lake Geneva
Fred Anthony Associates (C).............................. 239
Flores Financial Services (C) 350
Management Recruiters Int'l Inc (MRI) (C) 448
The Rankin Group Ltd (R)................................. 158

LaValle
Prestige Inc (C).. 538

Little Chute
Van Zeeland Associates Inc (C)........................... 651

Lodi
MRI of Lake Wisconsin (C)................................ 480

Madison
Creative Financial Staffing (C) 302
Future Employment Service Inc (C).................... 364
HR Management Services (C).............................. 396
Cathy L Hurless Executive Recruiting (C).......... 399
innovativestaffsearch (C)................................... 402
Kelly Associates (R)... 106
Sales Consultants of Madison (C)...................... 583
Wisconsin Executive Search Group Ltd (C)........ 664

Manitowoc
Trillium Staffing Solutions (C) 647

Mequon
Barnes Development Group LLC (R) 13
The Cooke Group (R) 42
J M Eagle Partners Ltd (C)................................. 326
Healthcare Recruiters Int'l • Dallas (C) 384
MRI of Milwaukee-North (C)............................. 480
Overton Consulting (R)..................................... 144
Sales Consultants of Milwaukee (C)................... 583
Strelcheck & Associates Inc (R) 188

Merrillan
Ronald B Hanson Associates (R) 84

Middleton
Joseph Chris Partners (C)................................... 284

Milwaukee
Accountants On Call (C).................................... 221
American Resources Corp (C) 235
Associated Recruiters (C) 244
CareerTrac Employment Services Inc (C)............ 277
Consultant Recruiters (C)................................... 293
Creative Financial Staffing (C) 302
Eagle Technology Group Inc (C)......................... 326
Fogec Consultants Inc (R).................................... 70
Jonas, Walters & Associates Inc (R) 102
Kforce (C)... 421
Kordus Consulting Group (C)............................. 423
The Lane Group (C)... 427
Management Recruiters Int'l Inc (MRI) (C) 448
Marketing Consultants (C)................................. 484
P J Murphy & Associates Inc (R)....................... 138
Pappas DeLaney LLC (R).................................. 145
Quirk-Corporon & Associates Inc (C)................. 549
Roth Young of Milwaukee (C)............................ 566
Snelling Personnel Services (C)......................... 613
Spherion Legal Group (C).................................. 619
Techstaff Inc (C).. 638
Wegner & Associates (C) 657

Mosinee
MRI of Stevens Point (C).................................... 480

(R) = Retainer; (C) = Contingency

GEOGRAPHIC

GEOGRAPHIC

(R) = Retainer; (C) = Contingency

ZSA Legal Recruitment (C)................................ 670

Quebec
PricewaterhouseCoopers Executive Search (R) .. 154

Ste. Polycarpe
Sinclair-Smith & Associates (C)......................... 604

Westmount
Denell-Archer Int'l Executive Search (R) 50
Executive Resources Int'l (C) 340
Rolland Consulting Group Inc (R)...................... 166
TNGGLOBAL (C) 643

Saskatchewan

Regina
The Executive Source (R).................................. 65

Saskatoon
The Executive Source (R).................................. 65
Lock & Associates (C) 433
Western Management Consultants (R) 202

Mexico

Distrito Federal

Mexico City
CMB Conasa Consulting SC (R) 38
ExSearch Latinoamérica (R)............................... 66
Frank P Hill (R)... 90
Hornberger Management Company (R)............... 92
Intelcap de Mexico SC (R) 99
Korn/Ferry Int'l (R) 110
Korn/Ferry Int'l SA de CV (R)........................... 110
Phoenix Search (R).. 150
Ray & Berndtson (R)....................................... 159
Russell Reynolds Associates Inc (R) 163
Roll Int'l (C) 564
Shore Asociados Ejecutivos S A de CV (R) 175
Smith Search SC (R) 179
Spencer Stuart (R) 182
Stanton Chase Int'l (R)..................................... 184
Stoopen Asociados SC (R) 186
Egon Zehnder Int'l Inc (R)................................ 211

Jalisco

Guadalajara
Fresquez & Associates (C) 363
Gomez Fregoso y Asociados (C) 371
Shore Asociados Ejecutivos S A de CV (R) 175

Mexico

Mexico City
Creative Financial Staffing (C).......................... 302
Heidrick & Struggles Int'l Inc (R)....................... 87
A T Kearney Executive Search (R)..................... 105
Leaders-Trust Int'l (R) 116

Morelos

Cuernavaca
MRI of Mexico (C)... 481

Nuevo Leon

Garza García
Heidrick & Struggles Int'l Inc (R) 88
Intelcap de Mexico SC (R).................................. 99
Shore Asociados Ejecutivos S A de CV (R) 176

Monterrey
Korn/Ferry Int'l (R) 110

Queretaro

Queretaro
Confisa Int'l Group (C)...................................... 292

Sonora

Hermosillo
JDG y Asociados SA de CV (R)......................... 100

Firms Index

Firms with (R) are from the Retainer Section.
Firms with (C) are from the Contingency Section.

FIRMS

(R) = Retainer; (C) = Contingency

FIRMS

FIRMS

(R) = Retainer; (C) = Contingency

FIRMS

FIRMS

(R) = Retainer; (C) = Contingency

(R) = Retainer; (C) = Contingency

(R) = Retainer; (C) = Contingency

FIRMS

(R) = Retainer; (C) = Contingency

FIRMS

FIRMS

(R) = Retainer; (C) = Contingency

FIRMS

(R) = Retainer; (C) = Contingency

(R) = Retainer; (C) = Contingency

FIRMS

(R) = Retainer; (C) = Contingency

(R) = Retainer; (C) = Contingency

FIRMS

NOTES

NOTES

NOTES

NOTES

NOTES

NOTES

How many of these can you answer "Yes"?

- You are or should be earning over $100,000
- You are seeking new challenges in your career
- You are a busy middle or senior manager
- You have an MBA or equivalent advanced degree
- You have worked with, or plan to work with executive recruiters (aka headhunters)

If you answered two or more "yes" you definitely need the practical help you'll get with *Executive Resumes: Marketing Yourself at $100,000+*

Table of Contents:

Aiming for the top? ExecutiveAgent.com can take you there!

When your resume is ready for prime time, check out ExecutiveAgent.com – the only place on the web where you can personally select from 7,000 recruiting professionals by Industry, Function, Salary Level, Geographical Location and more. Mail your resume and cover letter to them right from your PC. *Get ExecutiveAgent.com working for you today!*

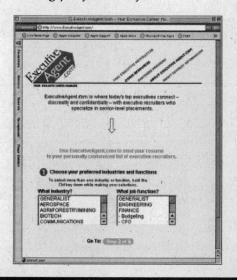

Other Useful Recruiter Resources

THE DIRECTORY OF EXECUTIVE RECRUITERS: CORPORATE EDITION (2 volume set)

Deluxe hardcover version designed for corporate executives and other users of executive search services. Over 1,600 pages, including expanded information on each firm.

KENNEDY'S INTERNATIONAL DIRECTORY OF EXECUTIVE RECRUITERS

This directory is arranged by country and indexed by functions, industries, firm names and key principals. Includes 3,702 individual recruiters in 67 countries. Introductory articles are written by industry leaders.

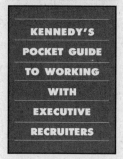

KENNEDY'S POCKET GUIDE TO WORKING WITH EXECUTIVE RECRUITERS

Highly recommended as a companion to *The Directory of Executive Recruiters*, *Kennedy's Pocket Guide to Working with Executive Recruiters* contains 30 chapters written by the experts themselves. Contains all the information you need to know when working with an executive recruiter.

Venture Capital

THE GOLD BOOK OF VENTURE CAPITAL FIRMS

The venture capital market is red hot. Venture capital firms invested over $12.5 billion in more than 1,800 companies in 1998 alone. Secrets to tapping this booming financial resource include a compelling idea...a strong business plan...a skilled management team and...*targeting the right venture capital firms - "the firms that invest in your industry, geography, and stage of development."*

KENNEDY INFORMATION
800-531-0007   603-585-6544   FAX:603-585-9555   bookstore@kennedyinfo.com   www.kennedyinfo.com

Monthly Intelligence

EXECUTIVE RECRUITER NEWS

This monthly newsletter presents search firm rankings, eye-opening profiles of interesting firms, exclusive interviews with recruiters and clients, trends, valuable statistics on the changing size and shape of the executive search profession, and updates on management techniques for staff development, compensation, marketing and client relationships.

RECRUITING TRENDS

The monthly newsletter that provides strategies and tactics for creating and maintaining a competitive workforce. Practical guidance on college recruiting, finding 'in demand' talent, interviewing, diversity, legal issues, reference checking, managing cost-per-hire expenses and much more.

Executive Temporary Placement

THE DIRECTORY OF TEMPORARY PLACEMENT FIRMS, FOR EXECUTIVES MANAGERS AND PROFESSIONALS

This directory combines an analysis of the burgeoning exec temp market with the most comprehensive listings of executive, managerial and professional-level specialists available.

Fax Back Order Form   603-585-9555

❏ **THE DIRECTORY OF EXECUTIVE RECRUITERS:**
PAPERBACK EDITION $47.95 +$4.95 p&h

❏ **THE DIRECTORY OF EXECUTIVE RECRUITERS:**
CORPORATE EDITION (2 volume set) $179.95 +$10.95 p&h

❏ **KENNEDY'S INTERNATIONAL DIRECTORY**
OF EXECUTIVE RECRUITERS $149.95 +$10.95 p&h

❏ **KENNEDY'S POCKET GUIDE TO WORKING WITH**
EXECUTIVE RECRUITERS $9.95 +$4.95 p&h

❏ **EXECUTIVE RECRUITER NEWS** $197.00/year, 12 monthly issues

❏ **RECRUITING TRENDS** $179.00/year, 12 monthly issues

❏ **THE DIRECTORY OF TEMPORARY PLACEMENT FIRMS FOR EXECUTIVES**
MANAGERS AND PROFESSIONALS $39.95 +$4.95 p&h

❏ **THE GOLD BOOK OF VENTURE CAPITAL FIRMS** $37.95 +$4.95 p&h

❏ **SEARCHSELECT® FOR WINDOWS SINGLE COPY** $245.00

❏ **SEARCHSELECT® FOR WINDOWS ANNUAL SUBSCRIPTION**
(includes 4 updates) $595.00

Or, let us create a customized list just for you on PC discs or mailing labels:
Please phone for counts & costs.

Name: _____

Company: _____

Address: _____

City, State, Zip: _____

Phone: _____

Orders must be pre-paid by check, money order or credit card. Orders are shipped within 24 hours.

Amount of order $ _____   Charge my: ❏ VISA ❏ MasterCard ❏ 　 ❏ Check enclosed

Card # _____ Exp. _____ Signature: _____

Commercial use specifically prohibited.

KENNEDY INFORMATION
800-531-0007   603-585-6544   FAX:603-585-9555   bookstore@kennedyinfo.com   www.kennedyinfo.com

LABELS, REPORTS, PC DISKS, AND MAILING SERVICE
Let us help you with your mailing!

❑ **Executive Recruiting Firm Labels**

Our convenient, self-stick labels list key contact person, company name and full address. A contact sheet listing names and phone numbers is included with label orders. See selection sorting options below. *Cost: $75 processing fee plus 25¢ per label.*

❑ **Executive Recruiting Firm Reports**

Designed as job seekers' tools for contacting search firms, our reports list the key contact person, company name, full address, phone number, fax number, e-mail address and function/industry specialties. See selection sorting options below. *Cost: $75 processing fee plus 25¢ per name.*

❑ **Executive Recruiting Firm Disks**

Use our Directory Selections disks with your word processor to personalize your cover letters to recruiters. The key contact person, firm name, full address, telephone number and fax number are available on 3.5" HD disks. Choose from WordPerfect, Microsoft Word, Lotus Ami-Pro or ascii comma delimited files. See selection sorting options below. *Cost: $75 processing fee plus 25¢ per name.*

❑ **Custom Mailing Service**

Simply send us your resume and cover letter by fax, E-mail or on disk and we will do your complete mailing. We hand sign and stamp each letter on the highest quality, genuine Strathmore paper. *Call for pricing.*

Selection Sorting Options: You may choose from the following options for your labels, report, PC disk or mailing service:

- Firm type: Retainer, Contingency or both
- Branch offices: Include U.S. only, worldwide, or do not include
- Functions and/or Industries: Choose up to 25 of each
- Salary: Choose a salary range
- Geography: choose from cities, states, area codes, regions, zip codes or countries
- Leading and/or Largest Retained Recruiters can be added
  Label/report/disk/mailing service orders are shipped within one week

KENNEDY INFORMATION 800-531-0007 FAX 603-585-9555 E-MAIL: bookstore@kennedyinfo.com

HIGHLY RECOMMENDED AS A COMPANION TO THIS DIRECTORY

The Insider's Guide to Executive Recruiting

Strategies for working with executive recruiters.

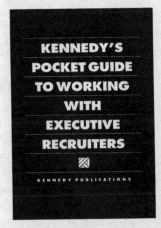

KENNEDY'S POCKET GUIDE TO WORKING WITH EXECUTIVE RECRUITERS

KENNEDY PUBLICATIONS

30 chapters by the experts, including Robert Half, Richard Bolles, Dick Wedemeyer, Tony Lee, Bill Wilkinson, John Sibbald and others . . .

Topics include:

- *How to Enlist the Support of an Executive Recruiter*
- *How Recruiters Do — and Do Not — Fit into Your Job Search*
- *Pros and Cons of Contacting Executive Search Firms*
- *13 Tips on Responding to Executive Recruiters*
- *What to Do when Headhunters Call . . . and How to Cultivate Long-Term Relationships with Them*

Plus! *A glossary of recruiting buzzwords and more!*

Use the CD-Rom included free with The Directory of Executive Recruiters to read five articles excerpted from the Pocket Guide.

Kennedy's Pocket Guide, $9.95. Check with your local bookstore or order direct from:

 KENNEDY INFORMATION 800-531-0007 FAX 603-585-9555 E-MAIL: bookstore@kennedyinfo.com